THE RIVERSIDE
ANTHOLOGY
OF LITERATURE

THE RIVERSIDE
ANTHOLOGY
OF LITERATURE

DOUGLAS HUNT

University of Missouri

HOUGHTON MIFFLIN COMPANY

BOSTON

DALLAS   GENEVA, ILLINOIS   PALO ALTO   PRINCETON, NEW JERSEY

Cover woodcut by Michael McCurdy

Library of Congress Catalog Card Number: 87-081368

ISBN: 0-395-43264-2
ABCDEFGHIJ-DOC-9543210-8987

PHOTO CREDITS
Greek Theatre, Epidaurus: Ned Haines/Photo Researcher
Medea set: Angus McBean Photograph/Harvard Theatre Collection
Medea: Jack Buxbaum ©/J.F. Kennedy Center
Hamlet: Boyd Hagen/The Guthrie Theatre
Measure for Measure: Angus McBean Photograph/Harvard Theatre Collection (full stage);
   Jay Thompson
Twelfth Night: Angus McBean Photograph/Harvard Theatre Collection
Hedda Gabler: Jay Thompson
Crimes of the Heart: Gerry Goodstein
Painting Churches: Martha Swope
Fool for Love: Tom Bloom/Trinity Repertory Company
Master Harold: Gerry Goodstein
Three Sisters: C.G. Wolfson/Williamstown Theatre Festival

ACKNOWLEDGMENTS

SHORT FICTION
   Chinua Achebe. "Civil Peace" copyright © 1973 by Chinua Achebe. From *Girls at War and Other Stories* by Chinua Achebe. Reprinted by permission of Doubleday & Company. Extract from *Chants of Saints: A Gathering of Afro-American Literature, Art and Scholarship,* Harper & Steptoe, Eds., reprinted by permission of Chinua Achebe.
   Alice Adams. From *Return Trips,* by Alice Adams. Copyright © 1984 by Alice Adams. Reprinted by permission of Alfred A. Knopf, Inc.
   Margaret Atwood. Extract from *Second Words* by Margaret Atwood. Copyright © 1982 by O.W. Toad Ltd. First published in 1984 by Beacon Press. Reprinted by permission of Beacon

(Acknowledgments continue on p. 2139)

CONTENTS

POETRY ANTHOLOGY

To Shape Our Perceptions of the World:
The Art of Poetry   668

DRAMA ANTHOLOGY

"To Hold the Mirror Up to Nature:"
The Art of Drama   1210

PREFACE

Anthologies can be built on a number of principles: they can be designed as collections of great works that have withstood the test of time, reflections of the anthologist's tastes, explorations of a theme, or overviews of literary history. *The Riverside Anthology* is all of these things to some degree, but principally it aims to be a book that gives students the tools to develop independent judgments, tastes, and enthusiasms about literature. In short, this is a textbook that aims to make students less dependent on textbooks.

We cannot ask students to develop independent judgments with an anthology that raises no eyebrows and challenges no assumptions. Therefore, *The Riverside Anthology* contains a very broad selection of works: the Anglo-American tradition is well represented, but there is also a healthy representation of writers from Europe, Latin America, and Africa; the great authors of the past are well represented, but there is also a generous representation of authors so contemporary that no one can know whether they will have a place in literary history.

If students are to form their own judgments about literature, they should not have the textbook writer's judgments thrust on them at every turn. One of my favorite stories about the way literature ought ideally to be presented involves Sir Joshua Reynolds, the eighteenth-century painter, who, having nothing to do one evening, picked up a book by an author unknown to him and leaned against a mantlepiece to leaf through it. The book, Samuel Johnson's *Life of Savage,* "seized his attention so strongly that, not being able to lay down the book till he had finished it, when he attempted to move, he found his arm totally benumbed." I doubt that Reynolds could have had this experience if the *Life of Savage* had appeared in a textbook as an illustration of a textbook writer's generalizations about the use of setting as an aid to characterization. The important discoveries about literature come to us as surprises.

The apparatus in *The Riverside Anthology* aims to prepare the reader to be surprised. The elements of literature are discussed (often in lesson-length essays) in the Handbook of Literature and in the introductions to the three genres; but this apparatus is separated from the works themselves, so that the story, poem, or play is not dulled by explication. The form of the book makes it clear that one learns about literature primarily by reading it and only secondarily by reading what a textbook has to say about it. A good deal of the commentary about literature is made by the authors themselves, in the "counterpoints" that follow the works. These counterpoints sometimes give one writer's view of another, sometimes a writer's comment on the underpinnings of his or her own work. Collectively, they provide an interesting and varied picture of how writers view their art, a picture that raises provocative questions.

Because writing about literature is so crucial a way of learning about it, the chapter on this subject shows one interpreter's struggle to come to grips with a prose poem, first in an informal journal entry, then in a draft and revision of a short essay, then in a research paper. The instructor's *Guide to The Riverside Anthology* offers over 350 questions appropriate for journal writing, short essays, or class discussion. Each question is "answered" with an essay of 200 to 500 words, intended to show where the question is likely to lead a student who pursues it.

Listed after each work is the earliest date of publication we could confirm; works published posthumously, however, are followed by the generally recognized date of composition. For translated works we have given the date of the first publication in the original language, followed by the date of the English translation we are printing. In glossing the works themselves, we have aimed to give only the information needed to make them accessible: words easily findable in the dictionary are not glossed, nor is every potentially unfamiliar reference.

For their remarkable work on the *Guide,* I thank and salute Melody Daily and W. Raymond Smith of the University of Missouri. For excellent help in research, in drafting portions of the handbook, and in writing most of the biographical sketches of the authors, I owe a great deal to Carolyn Perry, also of the University of Missouri. Marcia Sankey was tenacious in searching out dates of publication; Glenn Hopp (Howard Payne University) found useful material on dramatists; Mary Weaks (University of Missouri) helped pinpoint difficult references in several contemporary poems. For useful reviews of the work in progress, I want to thank Michael Allen, The College of Wooster; Ray Anschel, Normandale Community College; Peter Baker, Southern Connecticut State University; Patricia Bizzell, College of The Holy Cross; Irene Brenalvirez, Nassau Community College; Barbara T. Christian, University of California, Berkeley; James V. Catano, Tulane University; Robert Coleman, Palomar College; John A. R. Dick, University of Texas at El Paso; Mary Fonseca, Santa Monica College; C. J. Gianakaris, Western Michigan University; Robert D. Habich, Ball State University; Kevin J. Harty, La Salle University; Kathleen Hickok, Iowa State University; David Himber, St. Petersburg Junior College; Bert G. Hornback, The University of Michigan; Jill Levenson, Trinity College of Canada; Marjorie Lewis, Texas Christian University; Shirley Lim, Westchester Community College; Paul Mariani, University of Massachusetts, Amherst; Michelle A. Massé, Louisiana State University, Baton Rouge; Paul A. Parrish, Texas A&M University; Compton Rees, The University of Connecticut; Kate Ronald, University of Nebraska-Lincoln; Carol J. Singley, Swarthmore College; Cheryl Walker, Scripps College.

Houghton Mifflin, if it will not blush at being praised in its own print, should be thanked for sparing no effort to bring outstanding contemporary writers into *The Riverside Anthology*. Finally, I remain grateful to my editors for their great discernment, intelligence, and perseverance.

DOUG HUNT

THE RIVERSIDE
ANTHOLOGY
OF LITERATURE

SHORT
FICTION

ANTH

To Challenge Our Assumptions About Life: The Art of Fiction

The fifty stories in the following pages are collected under the name of fiction, but having a name in common does not mean that they are alike in every important respect. The horse, the whale, and the bat are all called mammals, but that fact does not make us declare the whale a disappointment because it does not run like a horse or fly like a bat. Yet we very often fail to take a story on its own terms. If we have learned that great fiction must be realistic, we may dismiss Nathaniel Hawthorne's story "Rappaccini's Daughter," with its poison gardens and impossible characters, as a "mere fairy tale." If we conclude too hastily that stories should be filled with beauty and romance, we may read Guy de Maupassant's "The String" and wonder why we should care about its realistic details: the men who walk with their left shoulders raised and their torsos twisted from the pull of the horse-drawn plough, their blue smocks "starched, shining as if varnished." Yet both stories are extraordinary, and it is a pity that we should blind ourselves to the virtues of either one.

The principle that draws these fifty stories together is, frankly, diversity. They represent a wide range of literary techniques, themes, and periods. But beneath the diversity are some common characteristics. All the stories create a separate world that stands beside this everyday one and becomes a commentary on it. All

challenge our complacent and sometimes unexamined assumptions about life. Perhaps most significantly, all explore a region opened up by the oldest recorded stories, the region of our deep hopes and fears.

THE EXPRESSION OF DEEP HOPES AND FEARS: THE STORY AND THE TALE

Biography, psychology, and history attempt to explain our lives by referring to objective reality. They are built on the solid rock of what we now call "the data." Traditional tales, myths, and fables are built on another rock: the psyche—the wishes, hopes, and fears of humankind, which have remained remarkably constant over the centuries. In fact, the story, like the dream, can be a machine that allows these wishes, hopes, and fears to take on a form and substance. In the ancient fable, King Midas wishes to have unlimited wealth, wishes that everything he touches would turn to gold. Everything he touches does—branch, stone, sod, apple, bread, wine—and he is therefore doomed to starve unless the gods release him from his greedy wish. In one version he reaches out to touch his daughter and is horrified when she turns into a gold statue. The story has the logic of a dream or nightmare. So, too, does the story of Cinderella. Cinderella experiences the things we have feared since childhood: our mother's death, being thrown into the power of pitiless strangers (the stepmother and the half-sisters), being poor and ugly and unwanted. She also experiences things we only wish for: communicating with animals, having our true worth discovered, and (in the unexpurgated version of the brothers Grimm) taking a gruesome revenge. One of the half-sisters, in order to get the tiny slipper on, cuts off her big toe, and the other cuts off her heel. Lamed for life by their own efforts, they then have their eyes pecked out by the pigeons who are Cinderella's allies. Deep wishes and fears are not always morally acceptable.

The stories of King Midas and Cinderella have come down to us in such diluted form that they lose some of their emotional impact, but other ancient stories have fared much better. The story of Faust, who sells his soul to the devil for knowledge, wealth, and power, never seems to go out of date, though it is now at least four hundred years old. It lies just beneath the surface of innumerable science fiction plots about mad scientists, including (though not everyone will like to call it science fiction) "Rappaccini's Daughter." The daughter, too, is part of an old story about a woman whose kisses are poison. Hawthorne took it from the *Gesta Romanorum* (circa 1300) but it can probably be traced back with slight changes at least as far as the biblical story of Eve. Even the Midas story may make an indirect appearance in "Rappaccini's Daughter": the megalomaniac scientist turns his world to poison just as Midas turns his world to gold. The point here is not that Hawthorne is a plagiarist, but that his story, like many others, takes its basic elements from something other than daily life or personal experience: something other and far older, a cauldron of stories that has been simmering on the back burner of human consciousness so long that it has become practically a part of the back burner—what the psychologist Carl Jung calls "the collective subconscious." Hawthorne, writing before the days of modern psychology, used a far simpler term. His purpose as a writer, he said, was not to reproduce the surface appearance of life, but to reach beneath that surface to reveal "the truth of the human heart."

Not all stories of deep wishes and fears are based on ancient originals and not all are sinister, but they *seem* old and to have a great deal of emotional weight. Take, for example, a one-paragraph story from Henry David Thoreau's *Walden*.

> There was an artist in the city of Kouroo who was disposed to strive after perfection. One day it came into his mind to make a staff. Having considered that in an imperfect work time is an ingredient, but into a perfect work time does not enter, he said to himself, It shall be perfect in all respects, though I should do nothing else in my life. He proceeded instantly to the forest for wood, being resolved that it should not be made of unsuitable material; and as he searched for and rejected stick after stick, his friends gradually deserted him, for they grew old in their works and died, but he grew not older by a moment. His singleness of purpose and resolution, and his elevated piety, endowed him,

without his knowledge, with perennial youth. As he made no compromise with Time, Time kept out of his way, and only sighed at a distance because he could not overcome him. Before he had found a stock in all respects suitable the city of Kouroo was a hoary ruin, and he sat on one of its mounds to peel the stick. Before he had given it the proper shape the dynasty of the Candahars was at an end, and with the point of the stick he wrote the name of the last of that race in the sand, and then resumed his work. By the time he had smoothed and polished the staff Kalpa was no longer the pole-star; and ere he had put on the ferule and the head adorned with precious stones, Brahma had awoke and slumbered many times. But why do I stay to mention these things? When the finishing stroke was put to his work, it suddenly expanded before the eyes of the astonished artist into the fairest of all the creations of Brahma. He had made a new system in making the staff, a world of full and fair proportions; in which, though the old cities and dynasties had passed away, fairer and more glorious ones had taken their places. And now he saw by the heap of shavings still fresh at his feet, that, for him and his work, the former lapse of time had been an illusion, and that no more time had elapsed than is required for a single scintillation from the brain of Brahma to fall on and inflame the tinder of a mortal brain. The material was pure, and his art was pure; how could the result be other than wonderful.

Scholars tell us that this story, despite its Buddhist trimmings, was invented by Thoreau himself. It is perhaps more accurate to say that he discovered it —not by looking into the old religious texts, but by looking into his own spirit and finding there the impulse that moves men who "will not be shipwrecked on a reality." Almost a hundred years later, Marguerite Yourcenar discovered a parallel story told by the Taoists of ancient China and developed it into "How Wang-Fo Was Saved." That Yourcenar and Thoreau should reach such similar destinations by such different paths is an indication that their theme is universal: the escape through purity of heart into a realm free from the tyranny of time, death, and pain. Sin, death, love, salvation, repentance, retribution, forgiveness—these large themes weave through our fiction just as they do through our religions. It seems that if we go far enough beneath the surface of our individual identities, we find ourselves caught up in these great hopes and fears. It is not surprising, then, to find them at the core of most of our significant fiction.

THE SCRUTINY OF EVERYDAY LIFE: FICTION AND REALISM

The expression of deep wishes and fears is one impulse behind fiction, but equally strong is an impulse that seems at first opposed to it: the impulse to explore the whole life around us, the surface as well as the depth, the ordinary as well as the magical. We live our lives in the world as well as in the psyche; we *are*, like it or not, "shipwrecked on a reality." We are naturally curious about what the world *is*, not merely what we wish or fear it to be.

Guy de Maupassant was one of the earliest proponents of the short story as a serious study of ordinary life, "the revelation of the real, contemporary man." For Maupassant, the story does not begin in traditions about princesses, goblins, and glass mountains, nor in emotions that the writer wishes to express. It begins in close observation of the daily routines and habits of real people, the sort of observation we might expect of a first-rate journalist or biographer. Maupassant learned to write under the instruction of Gustave Flaubert, who used to pose him exercises in precision:

> "When you pass," he would say, "a grocer seated at his shop door, a janitor smoking a pipe, a stand of hackney coaches, show me that grocer and that janitor, their whole physical appearance, including also a description of their whole moral nature, so that I cannot confound them with any other grocer or janitor; make me see, in one word, that a certain cab horse does not resemble the fifty others that follow or precede it."

This sort of skill at capturing the external world is essential to Maupassant's art, but it is not an end in itself. At the core of his stories is still the push toward the large themes, the deep wishes and fears. His goal was not to produce merely "realistic" stories; this would be a technical trick serving no purpose. Perhaps the best statement of the true aims of realism was made by the idealist Thoreau: ". . . to front only the essential facts of life, to drive life into the corner and reduce it to its lowest terms, and if it proved to be mean, then to publish its meaness to the world." Outside the story, as Maupassant points out, life is incoherent: "full of inexplicable, illogical, and contradictory catastrophes which ought to be classed under the heading 'Various Events.'" Inside the story, purged of "accidents and trivialities," life should make itself clear. We should be able to see when it is dominated by love, hate, or indifference, when it is forgiving, or cruel.

As we first begin to read writers like Maupassant we see only the realistic details, but eventually we recognize the mind of the maker behind the illusion of reality. The realist finds the raw materials of his art in the external world but he discards much and reassembles the rest into something that Maupassant frankly calls a "personal vision of life." Consider, for example, the opening paragraph of "The String."

> Along all the roads around Goderville the peasants and their wives were coming towards the little town, for it was market-day. The men walked with plodding steps, their bodies bent forward at each thrust of their long bowed legs. They were deformed by hard work, by the pull of the heavy plough which raises the left shoulder

and twists the torso, by the reaping of the wheat which forces the knees apart to get a firm stand, by all the slow and strenuous labors of life on the farm. Their blue smocks, starched, shining as if varnished, ornamented with a little design in white at the neck and wrists, puffed about their bony bodies, seemed like balloons ready to carry them off. From each smock a head, two arms, and two feet protruded.

This paragraph, which we might be inclined to rush through on our way to the "real story," is constructed from details any observer might have seen in a French market town in the 1870's; it creates, however, a miniature of Maupassant's fictional world. In this world people are completely shaped (or deformed) by their environment. Their hard lives unsuit them for great joy, leaving them small and somewhat pitiable pleasures: the shining blue smocks with the little designs in white seem misplaced on their bony, plodding bodies. In one sense we are very far from the city of Kouroo or the garden of Dr. Rappaccini: life in Goderville is squeezed down into a narrow emotional range, incapable of producing ecstasy or tragedy. In another sense, Goderville has a distinct place in the geography of our imagination. It is a hell on earth. Or to put the case as a realist might, it is a statement that earth is hell, unredeemed and unredeemable. Goderville is a miniature world painted in such a way that we recognize it as being simultaneously true to external reality and true to the writer's somber vision of life. Into this world, four paragraphs later, Maupassant introduces his protagonist.

Maitre Hauchecorne, of Breaute, had just arrived at Goderville. He was directing his steps toward the square, when he perceived upon the ground a little piece of string. Maitre Hauchecorne, economical like a true Norman, thought that everything useful ought to be picked up, and he stooped painfully, for he suffered from rheumatism. He took up the bit of string from the ground and was beginning to roll it carefully when he noticed Maitre Malandain, the harness-maker on the threshold of his door, looking at him. They had once had a quarrel on the subject of a halter, and they had remained on bad terms, being both good haters. Maitre Hauchecorne was seized with a sort of shame to be seen thus by his enemy, picking a bit of string out of the dirt. He hid his find quickly under his smock, and slipped it into his trouser pocket; then he pretended to be still looking on the ground for something which he did not find, and he went towards the market, his head thrust forward, bent double by his pain.

Here again is a paragraph that we might pass over carelessly on our way to the plot, but we should stop to relish it. It is a brilliant piece of characterization: we learn more about a man in these 150 words than we will ever learn about most of our neighbors. We see his miserliness, his physical pain, his capacity for hatred, and above all his pride—the pride of a man who has nothing else to comfort him. Maupassant learned Flaubert's lessons in realism admirably, but what he saw around him was rarely admirable: deformed bodies and spirits in a world that offers little room for joy.

"Too bleak" we may say, and many readers of Maupassant's own time did say so, preferring stories that would amuse them or uplift them. Maupassant's response was to say that he was a realistic artist and that he had no choice but to consider the life around him and present his findings about it: "Let us rise to the heights of poetry when we criticize an idealist, and show him that his dream is commonplace, vulgar, not mad enough or magnificent enough. But if we criticise a naturalist, let us show him wherein the truth of life differs from the truth in his book." When I said some paragraphs ago that fiction is challenging, I meant that in the most literal way. Most of the stories in this book throw down the gauntlet, insist on a vision of life that some readers, perhaps most, will find at first (and perhaps at last) uncomfortable, foreign, even shocking. As Maupassant noted, the good reader of fiction ought to be able to approach a story two ways. As a critic, he or she ought to be able to see it as a work of art, well or ill constructed, compelling or not compelling. At this level, the reader should be able to "commend the very books which, as a man, he does not like. . . ." But this critical reading needs to be accompanied by a human reading in which we accept the writer's challenge "to think, and to understand the deep, hidden meanings of events." In some fiction the question at this human level will be whether we share the writer's deep fears and hopes; in others it will be whether we accept the writer's conclusions about how justified these fears and hopes are.

THE SCRUTINY OF CHARACTER: FICTION "FREED FROM THE HEAVY BURDEN OF PLOT"

Maupassant's realism, so revolutionary in some respects, left one cornerstone of traditional fiction untouched. A story was still a story. It had a clearly defined plot: rising action, a climax, and a denouement. We have a feeling at the conclusion of "The String" that an action has been completed and that Maitre Hauchecorne has been taken from one phase of his life to another. In much twentieth-century fiction (especially in the United States), plot has ceased to be the cornerstone and character has emerged to take its place. Possibly this change can be explained historically: in a prosperous and politically stable society, the external conflicts between people and their environment become less and less important. The conflicts that consume us become increasingly internal and harder to capture in a neat plot line. Our hopes and fears have less to do with whether a particular action will succeed or fail than with whether we and our friends are living in a state of grace: spiritually, emotionally, psychologically, existentially.

Eventually these concerns produced a new type of short story which was "freed from the heavy burden of plot."[1]

An excellent example of such a story is Elizabeth Tallent's "No One's a Mystery," selected by the international writers' organization P.E.N. as a syndicated fiction project in 1985. I will break this very short story into three parts so that we can examine it closely, but please begin by reading the story straight through, ignoring the comments sandwiched between parts.

> For my eighteenth birthday Jack gave me a five-year diary with a latch and a little key, light as a dime. I was sitting beside him scratching at the lock, which didn't seem to want to work, when he thought he saw his wife's Cadillac in the distance, coming toward us. He pushed me down onto the dirty floor of the pickup and kept one hand on my head while I inhaled the musk of his cigarettes in the dashboard ashtray and sang along with Rosanne Cash on the tape deck. We'd been drinking tequila and the bottle was between his legs, resting up against his crotch, where the seam of his Levi's was bleached linen-white, though the Levi's were nearly new. I don't know why his Levi's always bleached like that, along the seams and at the knees. In a curve of cloth his zipper glinted, gold.

Tallent begins her story in the middle of the action, without any opening exposition, and immerses herself immediately in the point of view of her protagonist. She maintains this perspective throughout, never making her own presence felt. This use of a strictly limited point of view denies the reader the comfort of relying on the author's judgment. Compare Doris Lessing's opening sentence in "To Room Nineteen": "This is a story, I suppose, about a failure in intelligence: the Rawlings' marriage was grounded in intelligence."[2] Tallent is mum; if we want to know what this story is about, we will have to figure it out for ourselves. The point of view also allows her to make every sentence serve a dual purpose, both enlightening us about the "objective" situation the girl is in and giving us an insight into the workings of the character's mind. It turns out to be a very interesting mind, as we will see later.

The point of view does, however, create a technical problem: how can Tallent tell the reader what the relationship between Jack and the unnamed protagonist is? It would hardly be credible to have the girl think as she slips to the floor of the truck, "I'm barely eighteen, and here I am running around with a man named Jack, who is married. He has enough money to be a respectable, solid-citizen sort, but he isn't at all interested in

---

1. The phrase was coined by Katharine Sergeant White (1893–1977), the first fiction editor for *The New Yorker*.
2. Lessing's sentence, by the way, reveals less than it seems. In the final analysis, the reader must decide whose intelligence has failed, and how.

being a pillar of the community, though his wife goes in for social status. Jack is wild, and really sexy, and sometimes he treats me like a little kid." Tallent manages to get this information across by the ingenious use of detail and incident: the diary, the tequila bottle, and the accidental encounter with the wife.

> "It's her," he said. "She keeps the lights on in the day-time. I can't think of a single habit in a woman that irritates me more than that." When he saw that I was going to stay still he took his hand from my head and ran it through his own dark hair.
> "Why does she?" I said.
> "She thinks it's safer. Why does she need to be safer? She's driving exactly fifty-five miles an hour. She believes in those signs: 'Speed Monitored by Aircraft.' It doesn't matter that you can look up and see that the sky is empty."
> "She'll see your lips move, Jack. She'll know you're talking to someone."
> "She'll think I'm singing along with the radio."
> He didn't lift his hand, just raised the fingers in salute while the pressure of his palm steadied the wheel, and I heard the Cadillac honk twice, musically; he was driving easily eighty miles an hour. I studied his boots. The elk heads stitched into the leather were bearded with frayed thread, the toes were scuffed, and there was a compact wedge of muddy manure between the heel and the sole—the same boots he'd been wearing for the two years I'd known him. On the tape deck Rosanne Cash sang, "Nobody's into me, no one's a mystery."
> "Do you think she's getting famous because of who her daddy is or for herself?" Jack said.
> "There are about a hundred pop tops on the floor, did you know that? Some little kid could cut a bare foot on one of these, Jack."
> "No little kids get into this truck except for you."
> "How come you let it get so dirty?"
> " 'How come,' " he mocked. "You even sound like a kid. You can get back into the seat now, if you want. She's not going to look over her shoulder and see you."
> "How do you know?"
> "I just know," he said. "Like I know I'm going to get meat loaf for supper. It's in the air. Like I know what you'll be writing in that diary."

The wife, whom we never see because we are down on the floor of the truck, looking at the world from the girl's perspective, becomes a point of reference within the universe the story creates. She plays it safe: lights on in the daytime, driving fifty-five. The talk about speed limits opens playfully a serious theme—abiding by the rules. The wife does: she believes that the speed limit is enforced by airborne police who peer down like a retributive God seeking out sinners. Jack does not: he sees an empty sky. He drives eighty, drinking tequila in broad daylight with a girl so young (until today) that his romance could get him thrown into jail. He cringes at the idea of playing it safe (he can't "think of a single habit in a woman that irritates" him more than driving with lights on in the daytime!), hates routine (". . . meatloaf for supper. It's in the air."), and doesn't trouble to clean the manure off his boots. This man is not every parent's picture of an ideal date, and when we learn that the relationship has been going on since the girl was fifteen or sixteen, alarm bells are going off in our minds. Better meatloaf and fifty-five than a world in which self-indulgent cowboys seduce girls barely out of junior high.

"What will I be writing?" I knelt on my side of the seat and craned around to look at the butterfly of dust printed on my jeans. Outside the window Wyoming was dazzling in the heat. The wheat was fawn and yellow and parted smoothly by the thin dirt road. I could smell the water in the irrigation ditches hidden in the wheat.

"Tonight you'll write, 'I love Jack. This is my birthday present from him. I can't imagine anybody loving anybody more than I love Jack.' "

"I can't."

"In a year you'll write, 'I wonder what I ever really saw in Jack. I wonder why I spent so many days just riding around in his pickup. It's true he taught me something about sex. It's true there wasn't ever much else to do in Cheyenne.' "

"I won't write that."

"In two years you'll write, 'I wonder what that old guy's name was, the one with the curly hair and the filthy dirty pickup truck and time on his hands.' "

"I won't write that."

"No?"

"Tonight I'll write, 'I love Jack. This is my birthday present from him. I can't imagine anybody loving anybody more than I love Jack.' "

"No, you can't," he said. "You can't imagine it."

"In a year I'll write, 'Jack should be home any minute now. The table's set—my grandmother's linen and her old silver and the yellow candles left over from the wedding—but I don't know if I can wait until after the trout à la Navarra to make love to him.' "

"It must have been a fast divorce."

"In two years I'll write, 'Jack should be home by now. Little Jack is hungry for his supper. He said his first word today besides "Mama" and "Papa." He said "kaka." ' "

Jack laughed. "He was probably trying to finger-paint with kaka on the bathroom wall when you heard him say it."

"In three years I'll write, 'My nipples are a little sore from nursing Eliza Rosamund.' "

"Rosamund. Every little girl should have a middle name she hates."

"'Her breath smells like vanilla and her eyes are just Jack's color of blue.' "

"That's nice." Jack said.

"So, which one do you like?"

"I like yours," he said. "But I believe mine."

"It doesn't matter. I believe mine."

"Not in your heart of hearts, you don't."

"You're wrong."

"I'm not wrong," he said. "And her breath would smell like your milk, and it's kind of a bittersweet smell, if you want to know the truth."

What an unexpected turn the story takes at last! The girl sees and smells the freshness of the open country and suddenly she and Jack are telling each other stories about what the future will be like. Jack's vision is darker, and there is a trace in it of the hardness we had feared, but finally it is merely a sad story, where the deep fear is loss, disillusionment, separation. We read it and realize that Jack has a heart after all. The girl offers a brighter story, a fairy-tale ending complete with grandmother's old linen and a daughter with a name straight from a romance: Rosamund, whose "breath smells like vanilla and her eyes are just Jack's color of blue." From this point the bantering dialogue gains surprising weight.

Since Tallent has limited herself to the girl's point of view and given us no clear signal about her values and opinions, we are left to interpret this dialogue ourselves, just as the characters, alone in the pickup truck under an empty sky, are left to interpret life themselves. Throughout the story we have been watching two people who are living outside the rules that are supposed to keep us safe from harm. Gradually (if anything can be gradual in so short a story) we have come to care about these people, to fear that they will be crushed, to hope that they will be happy. Now, after the girl has given a vision of life's coming right—despite everything—because of love, they have to face the question of whether her story is true. Everything is at stake. Jack likes her story, but he believes his, believes that the dream and the reality can never meet. She is unshaken: "It doesn't matter. I believe mine." Jack might let it rest there, but he doesn't: "Not in your heart of hearts, you don't." This is a fine moment. Jack is giving a birthday present to a woman coming of age: the right to get beyond the starry-eyed dreams of girlhood. But (if I read the story right) she does not need the gift, she has matured enough to stand by her dream as steadily as Jack stands by his realism: "You're wrong." Jack does not cease to be Jack: "I'm not wrong," he begins, but now, for the first time, he follows her lead, joins in her story:

> And her breath would smell like your milk, and it's kind of a bittersweet smell, if you want to know the truth.

Some readers of Elizabeth Tallent's stories find them inconclusive, but something has happened here, or something has been revealed. We have seen a girl show surprising force of character, a somewhat sinister man express a faith in life, and the two together create a bittersweet vision of the future that joins hope and realism. That vision is a story, and Tallent's story is partly about how much all of us depend upon such stories to give our lives order and meaning.

Perhaps you will not believe that the story the girl and Jack concoct tells the truth about the world. Perhaps in your version Jack turns out to be a monster and the girl a damsel in distress. That is a different story, and you will find a version of it in Joyce Carol Oates' "Where Are You Going, Where Have You Been?" Perhaps you believe they will have years of suffering ahead before they begin to understand what their lives mean, in which case you will favor Anton Chekhov's "The Lady with the Pet Dog." Each of these three stories, and each story in this anthology, holds up a world for our examination. Part of our job as readers is to understand the skill with which these worlds are made, another part is to judge how they correspond to the world we know.

JACOB GRIMM

(1785–1863)

WILHELM GRIMM

(1786–1859)

THE JUNIPER TREE

translated from the German by Margaret Hunt and James Stern

It is now long ago, quite two thousand years, since there was a rich man who had a beautiful and pious wife, and they loved each other dearly. They had, however, no children, though they wished for them very much, and the woman prayed for them day and night, but still they had none. Now there was a court-yard in front of their house in which was a juniper tree, and one day in winter the woman was standing beneath it, paring herself an apple, and while she was paring herself the apple she cut her finger, and the blood fell on the snow. "Ah," said the woman, and sighed right heavily, and looked at the blood before her, and was most unhappy, "ah, if I had but a child as red as blood and as white as snow!" And while she thus spoke, she became quite happy in her mind, and felt just as if that were going to happen. Then she went into the house, and a month went by and the snow was gone, and two months, and then everything was green, and three months, and then all the flowers came out of the earth, and four months, and then all the trees in the wood grew thicker, and the green branches were all closely entwined, and the birds sang until the wood resounded and the blossoms fell from the trees, then the fifth month passed away and she stood under the juniper tree, which smelt so sweetly that her heart leapt, and she fell on her knees and was beside herself with joy, and when the sixth month was over the fruit was large and fine, and then she was quite still, and the seventh month she snatched at the juniper-berries and ate them greedily, then she grew sick and sorrowful, then the eighth month passed, and she called her husband to her, and wept and said: "If I die, then bury me beneath the juniper tree." Then she was quite comforted and happy until the next month was over, and then she had a child as white as snow and as red as blood, and when she beheld it she was so delighted that she died.

Then her husband buried her beneath the juniper tree, and he began to weep sore; after some time he was more at ease, and though he still wept he could bear it, and after some time longer he took another wife.

By the second wife he had a daughter, but the first wife's child was a little son, and he was as red as blood and as white as snow. When the woman looked at her daughter she loved her very much, but then she looked at the little boy and it seemed to cut her to the heart, for the thought came into her mind that he would always stand in her way, and she was for ever thinking how she could get all the fortune for her daughter, and the Evil One filled her mind with this till she was quite wroth with the little boy and she pushed him from one corner to the other and slapped him here and cuffed him there, until the poor child was in continual terror, for when he came out of school he had no peace in any place.

One day the woman had gone upstairs to her room, and her little daughter went up too, and said: "Mother, give me an apple." "Yes, my child," said the woman, and gave her a fine apple out of the chest, but the chest had a great heavy lid with a great sharp iron lock. "Mother," said the little daughter, "is brother not to have one too?" This made the woman angry, but she said: "Yes, when he comes out of school." And when she saw from the window that he was coming, it was just as if the Devil entered into her, and she snatched at the apple and took it away again from her daughter, and said: "You shall not have one before your brother." Then she threw the apple into the chest, and shut it. Then the little boy came in at the door, and the Devil made her say to him kindly: "My son, will you have an apple?" and she looked wickedly at him. "Mother," said the little boy, "how dreadful you look! Yes, give me an apple." Then it seemed to her as if she were forced to say to him: "Come with me," and she opened the lid of the chest and said: "Take out an apple for yourself," and while the little boy was stooping inside, the Devil prompted her, and crash! she shut the lid down, and his head flew off and fell among the red apples. Then she was overwhelmed with terror, and thought: "If I could but make them think that it was not done by me!" So she went upstairs to her room to her chest of drawers, and took a white handkerchief out of the top drawer, and set the head on the neck again, and folded the handkerchief so that nothing could be seen, and she set him on a chair in front of the door, and put the apple in his hand.

After this Marlinchen came into the kitchen to her mother, who was standing by the fire with a pan of hot water before her which she was constantly stirring round. "Mother," said Marlinchen, "brother is sitting at the door, and he looks quite white, and has an apple in his hand. I asked him to give me the apple, but he did not answer me, and I was quite frightened." "Go back to him," said her mother, "and if he will not answer you, give him a box on the ear." So Marlinchen went to him and said: "Brother, give me the apple." But he was silent, and she gave him a box on the ear, whereupon his head fell off. Marlinchen was terrified, and began crying and screaming, and ran to her mother, and said: "Alas, mother, I have knocked my brother's head off!" and she wept and wept and could not be comforted. "Marlinchen," said the mother, "what have you done? but be quiet and let no one know it; it cannot be helped now, we will make him into black-puddings." Then the mother took the little boy and chopped him in pieces, put him into the pan and made him into black-puddings; but Marlinchen stood by weeping and weeping, and all her tears fell into the pan and there was no need of any salt.

Then the father came home, and sat down to dinner and said: "But where is my son?" And the mother served up a great dish of black-puddings, and Marlinchen wept and could not leave off. Then the father again said: "But where is my son?" "Ah," said the mother, "he has gone across the country to his mother's great uncle; he will stay there awhile." "And what is he going to do there? He did not even say good-bye to me."

"Oh, he wanted to go, and asked me if he might stay six weeks, he is well taken care of there." "Ah," said the man, "I feel so unhappy lest all should not be right. He ought to have said good-bye to me." With that he began to eat and said: "Marlinchen, why are you crying? Your brother will certainly come back." Then he said: "Ah, wife, how delicious this food is, give me some more." And the more he ate the more he wanted to have, and he said: "Give me some more, you shall have none of it. It seems to me as if it were all mine." And he ate and ate and threw all the bones under the table, until he had finished the whole. But Marlinchen went away to her chest of drawers, and took her best silk handkerchief out of the bottom drawer, and got all the bones from beneath the table, and tied them up in her silk handkerchief, and carried them outside the door, weeping tears of blood. Then she lay down under the juniper tree on the green grass, and after she had lain down there, she suddenly felt light-hearted and did not cry any more. Then the juniper tree began to stir itself, and the branches parted asunder, and moved together again, just as if someone were rejoicing and clapping his hands. At the same time a mist seemed to arise from the tree, and in the center of this mist it burned like a fire, and a beautiful bird flew out of the fire singing magnificently, and he flew high up in the air, and when he was gone, the juniper tree was just as it had been before, and the handkerchief with the bones was no longer there. Marlinchen, however, was as gay and happy as if her brother were still alive. And she went merrily into the house, and sat down to dinner and ate.

But the bird flew away and lighted on a goldsmith's house, and began to sing:

> "My mother she killed me,
> My father he ate me,
> My sister, little Marlinchen,
> Gathered together all my bones,
> Tied them in a silken handkerchief,
> Laid them beneath the juniper tree,
> Kywitt, kywitt, what a beautiful bird am I!"

The goldsmith was sitting in his workshop making a golden chain, when he heard the bird which was sitting singing on his roof, and very beautiful the song seemed to him. He stood up, but as he crossed the threshold he lost one of his slippers. But he went away right up the middle of the street with one shoe on and one sock; he had his apron on, and in one hand he had the golden chain and in the other the pincers, and the sun was shining brightly on the street. Then he went right on and stood still, and said to the bird: "Bird," said he then, "how beautifully you can sing! Sing me that piece again." "No," said the bird, "I'll not sing it twice for nothing! Give me the golden chain, and then I will sing it again for you." "There," said the goldsmith, "there is the golden chain for you, now sing me that song again." Then the bird came and took the golden chain in his right claw, and went and sat in front of the goldsmith, and sang:

"My mother she killed me,
My father he ate me,
My sister, little Marlinchen,
Gathered together all my bones,
Tied them in a silken handkerchief,
Laid them beneath the juniper tree,
Kywitt, kywitt, what a beautiful bird am I!"

Then the bird flew away to a shoemaker, and lighted on his roof and sang:

"My mother she killed me,
My father he ate me,
My sister, little Marlinchen,
Gathered together all my bones,
Tied them in a silken handkerchief,
Laid them beneath the juniper tree,
Kywitt, kywitt, what a beautiful bird am I!"

The shoemaker heard that and ran out of doors in his shirt sleeves, and looked up at his roof, and was forced to hold his hand before his eyes lest the sun should blind him. "Bird," said he, "how beautifully you can sing!" Then he called in at his door: "Wife, just come outside, there is a bird, look at that bird, he certainly can sing." Then he called his daughter and children, and apprentices, boys and girls, and they all came up the street and looked at the bird and saw how beautiful he was, and what fine red and green feathers he had, and how like real gold his neck was, and how the eyes in his head shone like stars. "Bird," said the shoemaker, "now sing me that song again." "Nay," said the bird, "I do not sing twice for nothing; you must give me something." "Wife," said the man, "go to the garret, upon the top shelf there stands a pair of red shoes, bring them down." Then the wife went and brought the shoes. "There, bird," said the man, "now sing me that piece again." Then the bird came and took the shoes in his left claw, and flew back on the roof, and sang:

"My mother she killed me,
My father he ate me,
My sister, little Marlinchen,
Gathered together all my bones,
Tied them in a silken handkerchief,

> *Laid them beneath the juniper tree,*
> *Kywitt, kywitt, what a beautiful bird am I!"*

And when he had finished his song he flew away. In his right claw he had the chain and in his left the shoes, and he flew far away to a mill, and the mill went "klipp klapp, klipp klapp, klipp klapp," and in the mill sat twenty miller's men hewing a stone, and cutting, hick hack, hick hack, hick hack, and the mill went klipp klapp, klipp klapp, klipp klapp. Then the bird went and sat on a lime-tree which stood in front of the mill, and sang:

> *"My mother she killed me,"*

Then one of them stopped working,

> *"My father he ate me,"*

Then two more stopped working and listened to that,

> *"My sister, little Marlinchen,"*

Then four more stopped,

> *"Gathered together all my bones,*
> *Tied them in a silken handkerchief,"*

Now eight only were hewing,

> *"Laid them beneath"*

Now only five,

> *"The juniper tree,"*

And now only one,

> *"Kywitt, kywitt, what a beautiful bird am I!"*

Then the last stopped also, and heard the last words. "Bird," said he, "how beautifully you sing! Let me, too, hear that. Sing that once more for me."

"Nay," said the bird, "I will not sing twice for nothing. Give me the millstone, and then I will sing it again."

"Yes," said he, "if it belonged to me only, you should have it."

"Yes," said the others, "if he sings again he shall have it." Then the bird came down, and the twenty millers all set to work with a beam and raised the stone up. And the bird stuck his neck through the hole, and put the stone on as if it were a collar, and flew on to the tree again, and sang:

> "My mother she killed me,
>   My father he ate me,
>   My sister, little Marlinchen,
>   Gathered together all my bones,
>   Tied them in a silken handkerchief,
>   Laid them beneath the juniper tree,
>   Kywitt, kywitt, what a beautiful bird am I!"

And when he had done singing, he spread his wings, and in his right claw he had the chain, and in his left the shoes, and round his neck the millstone, and he flew far away to his father's house.

In the room sat the father, the mother, and Marlinchen at dinner, and the father said: "How light-hearted I feel, how happy I am!" "Nay," said the mother, "I feel so uneasy, just as if a heavy storm were coming." Marlinchen, however, sat weeping and weeping, and then came the bird flying, and as it seated itself on the roof the father said: "Ah, I feel so truly happy, and the sun is shining so beautifully outside, I feel just as if I were about to see some old friend again." "Nay," said the woman, "I feel so anxious, my teeth chatter, and I seem to have fire in my veins." And she tore her stays open, but Marlinchen sat in a corner crying, and held her plate before her eyes and cried till it was quite wet. Then the bird sat on the juniper tree, and sang:

> "My mother she killed me,"

Then the mother stopped her ears, and shut her eyes, and would not see or hear, but there was a roaring in her ears like the most violent storm, and her eyes burnt and flashed like lightning:

> "My father he ate me,"

"Ah, mother," says the man, "that is a beautiful bird! He sings so splendidly, and the sun shines so warm, and there is a smell just like cinnamon."

> "My sister, little Marlinchen,"

Then Marlinchen laid her head on her knees and wept without ceasing, but the man said: "I am going out, I must see the bird quite close." "Oh, don't go," said the woman, "I feel as if the whole house were shaking and on fire." But the man went out and looked at the bird:

> "Gathered together all my bones,
>   Tied them in a silken handkerchief,

Laid them beneath the juniper tree,
Kywitt, kywitt, what a beautiful bird am I!"

On this the bird let the golden chain fall, and it fell exactly round the man's neck, and so exactly round it that it fitted beautifully. Then he went in and said: "Just look what a fine bird that is, and what a handsome golden chain he has given me, and how pretty he is!" But the woman was terrified, and fell down on the floor in the room, and her cap fell off her head. Then sang the bird once more:

"My mother she killed me,"

"Would that I were a thousand feet beneath the earth so as not to hear that!"

"My father he ate me,"

Then the woman fell down again as if dead.

"My sister, little Marlinchen,"

"Ah," said Marlinchen, "I too will go out and see if the bird will give me anything," and she went out.

"Gathered together all my bones,
Tied them in a silken handkerchief,"

Then he threw down the shoes to her.

"Laid them beneath the juniper tree,
Kywitt, kywitt, what a beautiful bird am I!"

Then she was light-hearted and joyous, and she put on the new red shoes, and danced and leaped into the house. "Ah," said she, "I was so sad when I went out and now I am so light-hearted; that is a splendid bird, he has given me a pair of red shoes!" "Well," said the woman, and sprang to her feet and her hair stood up like flames of fire, "I feel as if the world were coming to an end! I, too, will go out and see if my heart feels lighter." And as she went out at the door, crash! the bird threw down the millstone on her head, and she was entirely crushed by it. The father and Marlinchen heard what had happened and went out, and smoke, flames and fire were rising from the place, and when that was over, there stood the little brother, and he took his father and Marlinchen by the hand, and all three were right glad, and they went into the house to dinner, and ate.

1812

The German "fairy tales" collected by the Grimm brothers rarely have fairies in them, and they are not stories primarily for children. They are folk tales, dictated to the two German scholars by people who had first heard them told in cottages lacking even kerosene lamps to keep the darkness back. The tales developed under these circumstances paid less heed to what Randall Jarrell calls "the learned principle of reality" than to a more "primary" psychological truth.

"The root of all stories is in Grimm": Randall Jarrell

A story, then, tells the truth or a lie—is a wish, or a truth, or a wish modified by a truth. Children ask first of all: "Is it a *true* story?" They ask this of the storyteller, but they ask of the story what they ask of a dream: that it satisfy their wishes. The Muses are the daughters of hope and the stepdaughters of memory. The wish is the first truth about us, since it represents not that learned principle of reality which half-governs our workaday hours, but the primary principle of pleasure which governs infancy, sleep, daydreams— and, certainly, many stories. Reading stories, we cannot help remembering Groddeck's "We have to reckon with what exists, and dreams, daydreams too, are also facts; if anyone really wants to investigate realities, he cannot do better than to start with such as these. If he neglects them, he will learn little or nothing of the world of life." If wishes were stories, beggars would read; if stories were true, our saviors would speak to us in parables. Much of our knowledge of, our compensation for, "the world of life" comes from stories; and the stories themselves are part of "the world of life." Shakespeare wrote:

> *This is an art*
> *Which does mend nature, change it rather, but*
> *The art itself is nature . . .*

and Goethe, agreeing, said: "A work of art is just as much a work of nature as a mountain."

In showing that dreams sometimes both satisfy our wishes and punish us for them, Freud compares the dreamer to the husband and wife in the fairy tale of The Three Wishes: the wife wishes for a pudding, the husband wishes it on the end of her nose, and the wife wishes it away again. A contradictory family! But it is this family—wife, husband, and pudding—which the story must satisfy: the writer is, and is writing for, a doubly- or triply-natured creature, whose needs, understandings, and ideals—whether they are called id, ego, and superego, or body, mind, and soul—contradict one another.

The truths that he systematized, Freud said, had already been discovered by the poets; the tears of things, the truth of things, are there in their fictions. And yet, as he knew, the root of all stories is in Grimm, not in La Rochefoucauld; in dreams, not in cameras and tape recorders. . . .

Freud was right, profoundly right, when he showed "that the dream is a compromise between the expression of and the defence against the unconscious emotions; that in it the unconscious wish is represented as being fulfilled; . . . and that myth and poetical productions come into being in the same way and have the same meaning."

NATHANIEL HAWTHORNE

(1804–1864)

RAPPACCINI'S DAUGHTER

A young man, named Giovanni Guasconti, came, very long ago, from the more southern region of Italy, to pursue his studies at the University of Padua.[1] Giovanni, who had but a scanty supply of gold ducats in his pocket, took lodgings in a high and gloomy chamber of an old edifice which looked not unworthy to have been the palace of a Paduan noble, and which, in fact, exhibited over its entrance the armorial bearings of a family long since extinct. The young stranger, who was not unstudied in the great poem of his country, recollected that one of the ancestors of this family, and perhaps an occupant of this very mansion, had been pictured by Dante as a partaker of the immortal agonies of his Inferno. These reminiscences and associations, together with the tendency to heartbreak natural to a young man for the first time out of his native sphere, caused Giovanni to sigh heavily as he looked around the desolate and ill-furnished apartment.

"Holy Virgin, signor!" cried old Dame Lisabetta, who, won by the youth's remarkable beauty of person, was kindly endeavoring to give the chamber a habitable air, "what a sigh was that to come out of a young man's heart! Do you find this old mansion gloomy? For the love of Heaven, then, put your head out of the window, and you will see as bright sunshine as you have left in Naples."

Guasconti mechanically did as the old woman advised, but could not quite agree with her that the Paduan sunshine was as cheerful as that of southern Italy. Such as it was, however, it fell upon a garden beneath the

---

1. A city in northeastern Italy, west of Venice.

window and expended its fostering influences on a variety of plants, which seemed to have been cultivated with exceeding care.

"Does this garden belong to the house?" asked Giovanni.

"Heaven forbid, signor, unless it were fruitful of better pot herbs than any that grow there now," answered old Lisabetta. "No; that garden is cultivated by the own hands of Signor Giacomo Rappaccini, the famous doctor, who, I warrant him, has been heard of as far as Naples. It is said that he distils these plants into medicines that are as potent as a charm. Oftentimes you may see the signor doctor at work, and perchance the signora, his daughter, too, gathering the strange flowers that grow in the garden."

The old woman had now done what she could for the aspect of the chamber; and, commending the young man to the protection of the saints, took her departure.

Giovanni still found no better occupation than to look down into the garden beneath his window. From its appearance, he judged it to be one of those botanic gardens which were of earlier date in Padua than elsewhere in Italy or in the world. Or, not improbably, it might once have been the pleasure-place of an opulent family; for there was the ruin of a marble fountain, in the centre, sculptured with rare art, but so wofully shattered that it was impossible to trace the original design from the chaos of remaining fragments. The water, however, continued to gush and sparkle into the sunbeams as cheerfully as ever. A little gurgling sound ascended to the young man's window, and made him feel as if the fountain were an immortal spirit that sung its song unceasingly and without heeding the vicissitudes around it, while one century imbodied it in marble and another scattered the perishable garniture on the soil. All about the pool into which the water subsided grew various plants, that seemed to require a plentiful supply of moisture for the nourishment of gigantic leaves, and, in some instances, flowers gorgeously magnificent. There was one shrub in particular, set in a marble vase in the midst of the pool, that bore a profusion of purple blossoms, each of which had the lustre and richness of a gem; and the whole together made a show so resplendent that it seemed enough to illuminate the garden, even had there been no sunshine. Every portion of the soil was peopled with plants and herbs, which, if less beautiful, still bore tokens of assiduous care, as if all had their individual virtues, known to the scientific mind that fostered them. Some were placed in urns, rich with old carving, and others in common garden pots; some crept serpent-like along the ground or climbed on high, using whatever means of ascent was offered them. One plant had wreathed itself round a statue of Vertumnus, which was thus quite veiled and shrouded in a drapery of hanging foliage, so happily arranged that it might have served a sculptor for a study.

While Giovanni stood at the window he heard a rustling behind a screen of leaves, and became aware that a person was at work in the garden. His figure soon emerged into view, and showed itself to be that of no common laborer, but a tall, emaciated, sallow, and sickly-looking man, dressed in a scholar's garb of black. He was beyond the middle term of life, with gray hair, a thin, gray beard, and a face singularly marked with intellect and cultivation, but which could never, even in his more youthful days, have expressed much warmth of heart.

Nothing could exceed the intentness with which this scientific gardener examined every shrub which grew in his path: it seemed as if he was looking into their inmost nature, making observations in regard to their creative essence, and discovering why one leaf grew in this shape and another in that, and wherefore such and such flowers differed among themselves in hue and perfume. Nevertheless, in spite of this deep intelligence on his part, there was no approach to intimacy between himself and these vegetable existences. On the contrary, he avoided their actual touch or the direct inhaling of their odors with a caution that impressed Giovanni most disagreeably; for the man's demeanor was that of one walking among malignant influences, such as savage beasts, or deadly snakes, or evil spirits, which, should he allow them one moment of license, would wreak upon him some terrible fatality. It was strangely frightful to the young man's imagination to see this air of insecurity in a person cultivating a garden, that most simple and innocent of human toils, and which had been alike the joy and labor of the unfallen parents of the race. Was this garden, then, the Eden of the present world? And this man, with such a perception of harm in what his own hands caused to grow,—was he the Adam?

The distrustful gardener, while plucking away the dead leaves or pruning the too luxuriant growth of the shrubs, defended his hands with a pair of thick gloves. Nor were these his only armor. When, in his walk through the garden, he came to the magnificent plant that hung its purple gems beside the marble fountain, he placed a kind of mask over his mouth and nostrils, as if all this beauty did but conceal a deadlier malice; but, finding his task still too dangerous, he drew back, removed the mask, and called loudly, but in the infirm voice of a person affected with inward disease,—

"Beatrice! Beatrice!"

"Here am I, my father. What would you?" cried a rich and youthful voice from the window of the opposite house—a voice as rich as a tropical sunset, and which made Giovanni, though he knew not why, think of deep hues of purple or crimson and of perfumes heavily delectable. "Are you in the garden?"

"Yes, Beatrice," answered the gardener, "and I need your help."

Soon there emerged from under a sculptured portal the figure of a young girl, arrayed with as much richness of taste as the most splendid of the flowers, beautiful as the day, and with a bloom so deep and vivid that one shade more would have been too much. She looked redundant with life, health, and energy; all of which attributes were bound down and compressed, as it were, and girdled tensely, in their luxuriance, by her virgin zone. Yet Giovanni's fancy must have grown morbid while he looked down into the garden: for the impression which the fair stranger made upon him was as if here were another flower, the human sister of those vegetable ones, as beautiful as they, more beautiful than the richest of them, but still to be touched only with a glove, nor to be approached without a mask. As Beatrice came down the garden path, it was observable that she handled and inhaled the odor of several of the plants which her father had most sedulously avoided.

"Here, Beatrice," said the latter, "see how many needful offices require to be done to our chief treasure. Yet, shattered as I am, my life might pay the penalty of approaching it so closely as circumstances demand. Henceforth, I fear, this plant must be consigned to your sole charge."

"And gladly will I undertake it," cried again the rich tones of the young lady, as she bent towards the magnificent plant and opened her arms as if to embrace it. "Yes, my sister, my splendor, it shall be Beatrice's task to nurse and serve thee; and thou shalt reward her with thy kisses and perfumed breath, which to her is as the breath of life."

Then, with all the tenderness in her manner that was so strikingly expressed in her words, she busied herself with such attentions as the plant seemed to require; and Giovanni, at his lofty window, rubbed his eyes and almost doubted whether it were a girl tending her favorite flower, or one sister performing the duties of affection to another. The scene soon terminated. Whether Dr. Rappaccini had finished his labors in the garden, or that his watchful eye had caught the stranger's face, he now took his daughter's arm and retired. Night was already closing in; oppressive exhalations seemed to proceed from the plants and steal upward past the open window; and Giovanni, closing the lattice, went to his couch and dreamed of a rich flower and beautiful girl. Flower and maiden were different, and yet the same, and fraught with some strange peril in either shape.

But there is an influence in the light of morning that tends to rectify whatever errors of fancy, or even of judgment, we may have incurred during the sun's decline, or among the shadows of the night, or in the less wholesome glow of moonshine. Giovanni's first movement, on starting from sleep, was to throw open the window and gaze down into the garden which his dreams had made so fertile of mysteries. He was surprised and a little ashamed to find how real and matter-of-fact an affair it proved to be, in the first rays of the sun which gilded the dew-drops that hung upon leaf and blossom, and, while giving a brighter beauty to each rare flower, brought everything within the limits of ordinary experience. The young man rejoiced that, in the heart of the barren city, he had the privilege of overlooking this spot of lovely and luxuriant vegetation. It would serve, he said to himself, as a symbolic language to keep him in communion with Nature. Neither the sickly and thoughtworn Dr. Giocomo Rappaccini, it is true, nor his brilliant daughter, were now visible; so that Giovanni could not determine how much of the singularity which he attributed to both was due to their own qualities and how much to his wonder-working fancy; but he was inclined to take a most rational view of the whole matter.

In the course of the day he paid his respects to Signor Pietro

Baglioni, professor of medicine in the university, a physician of eminent repute, to whom Giovanni had brought a letter of introduction. The professor was an elderly personage, apparently of genial nature, and habits that might almost be called jovial. He kept the young man to dinner, and made himself very agreeable by the freedom and liveliness of his conversation, especially when warmed by a flask or two of Tuscan wine. Giovanni, conceiving that men of science, inhabitants of the same city, must needs be on familiar terms with one another, took an opportunity to mention the name of Dr. Rappaccini. But the professor did not respond with so much cordiality as he had anticipated.

"Ill would it become a teacher of the divine art of medicine," said Professor Pietro Baglioni, in answer to a question of Giovanni, "to withhold due and well-considered praise of a physician so eminently skilled as Rappaccini; but, on the other hand, I should answer it but scantily to my conscience were I to permit a worthy youth like yourself, Signor Giovanni, the son of an ancient friend, to imbibe erroneous ideas respecting a man who might hereafter chance to hold your life and death in his hands. The truth is, our worshipful Dr. Rappaccini has as much science as any member of the faculty—with perhaps one single exception—in Padua, or all Italy; but there are certain grave objections to his professional character."

"And what are they?" asked the young man.

"Has my friend Giovanni any disease of body or heart, that he is so inquisitive about physicians?" said the professor, with a smile. "But as for Rappaccini, it is said of him—and I, who know the man well, can answer for its truth—that he cares infinitely more for science than for mankind. His patients are interesting to him only as subjects for some new experiment. He would sacrifice human life, his own among the rest, or whatever else was dearest to him, for the sake of adding so much as a grain of mustard seed to the great heap of his accumulated knowledge."

"Methinks he is an awful man indeed," remarked Guasconti, mentally recalling the cold and purely intellectual aspect of Rappaccini. "And yet; worshipful professor, is it not a noble spirit? Are there many men capable of so spiritual a love of science?"

"God forbid," answered the professor, somewhat testily: "at least, unless they take sounder views of the healing art than those adopted by Rappaccini. It is his theory that all medicinal virtues are comprised within those substances which we term vegetable poisons. These he cultivates with his own hands, and is said even to have produced new varieties of poison, more horribly deleterious than Nature, without the assistance of this learned person, would ever have plagued the world withal. That the signor doctor does less mischief than might be expected with such dangerous substances is undeniable. Now and then, it must be owned, he has effected, or seemed to effect, a marvellous cure; but, to tell you my private mind, Signor Giovanni, he should receive little credit for such instances of success,—they being probably the work of chance,—but should be held strictly accountable for his failures, which may justly be considered his own work."

The youth might have taken Baglioni's opinions with many grains of allowance had he known that there was a professional warfare of long continuance between him and Dr. Rappaccini, in which the latter was generally thought to have gained the advantage. If the reader be inclined to judge for himself, we refer him to certain black-letter tracts on both sides, preserved in the medical department of the University of Padua.

"I know not, most learned professor," returned Giovanni, after musing on what had been said of Rappaccini's exclusive zeal for science,— "I know not how dearly this physician may love his art; but surely there is one object more dear to him. He has a daughter."

"Aha!" cried the professor, with a laugh. "So now our friend Giovanni's secret is out. You have heard of this daughter, whom all the young men in Padua are wild about, though not half a dozen have ever had the good hap to see her face. I know little of the Signora Beatrice save that Rappaccini is said to have instructed her deeply in his science, and that, young and beautiful as fame reports her, she is already qualified to fill a professor's chair. Perchance her father destines her for mine! Other absurd rumors there be, not worth talking about or listening to. So now, Signor Giovanni, drink off your glass of lachryma."

Guasconti returned to his lodgings somewhat heated with the wine he had quaffed, and which caused his brain to swim with strange fantasies in reference to Dr. Rappaccini and the beautiful Beatrice. On his way, happening to pass by a florist's, he bought a fresh bouquet of flowers.

Ascending to his chamber, he seated himself near the window, but within the shadow thrown by the depth of the wall, so that he could look down into the garden with little risk of being discovered. All beneath his eye was a solitude. The strange plants were basking in the sunshine, and now and then nodding gently to one another, as if in acknowledgment of sympathy and kindred. In the midst, by the shattered fountain, grew the magnificent shrub, with its purple gems clustering all over it; they glowed in the air, and gleamed back again out of the depths of the pool, which thus seemed to overflow with colored radiance from the rich reflection that was steeped in it. At first, as we have said, the garden was a solitude. Soon, however,—as Giovanni had half hoped, half feared, would be the case,—a figure appeared beneath the antique sculptured portal, and came down between the rows of plants, inhaling their various perfumes as if she were one of those beings of old classic fable that lived upon sweet odors. On again beholding Beatrice, the young man was even startled to perceive how much her beauty exceeded his recollection of it; so brilliant, so vivid, was its character, that she glowed amid the sunlight, and, as Giovanni whispered to himself, positively illuminated the more shadowy intervals of the garden path. Her face being now more revealed than on the former occasion, he was struck by its expression of simplicity and sweetness,—qualities that had not entered into his idea of her character, and which made him ask anew what manner of mortal she might be. Nor did he fail again to observe, or imagine, an analogy between the beautiful girl and the gorgeous shrub that hung its gemlike flowers over the fountain,—a resemblance which Beatrice seemed to have indulged a fantastic humor in heightening, both by the arrangement of her dress and the selection of its hues.

Approaching the shrub, she threw open her arms, as with a passionate ardor, and drew its branches into an intimate embrace—so intimate that her features were hidden in its leafy bosom and her glistening ringlets all intermingled with the flowers.

"Give me thy breath, my sister," exclaimed Beatrice; "for I am faint with common air. And give me this flower of thine, which I separate with gentlest fingers from the stem and place it close beside my heart."

With these words the beautiful daughter of Rappaccini plucked one of the richest blossoms of the shrub, and was about to fasten it in her bosom. But now, unless Giovanni's draughts of wine had bewildered his senses, a singular incident occurred. A small orange-colored reptile, of the lizard or chameleon species, chanced to be creeping along the path, just at the feet of Beatrice. It appeared to Giovanni,—but, at the distance from which he gazed, he could scarcely have seen anything so minute,—it appeared to him, however, that a drop or two of moisture from the broken stem of the flower descended upon the lizard's head. For an instant the reptile contorted itself violently, and then lay motionless in the sunshine. Beatrice observed this remarkable phenomenon, and crossed herself, sadly, but without surprise; nor did she therefore hesitate to arrange the fatal flower in her bosom. There it blushed, and almost glimmered with the dazzling effect of a precious stone, adding to her dress and aspect the one appropriate charm which nothing else in the world could have supplied. But Giovanni, out of the shadow of his window, bent forward and shrank back, and murmured and trembled.

"Am I awake? Have I my senses?" said he to himself. "What is this being? Beautiful shall I call her, or inexpressibly terrible?"

Beatrice now strayed carelessly through the garden, approaching closer beneath Giovanni's window, so that he was compelled to thrust his head quite out of its concealment in order to gratify the intense and painful curiosity which she excited. At this moment there came a beautiful insect over the garden wall; it had, perhaps, wandered through the city, and found no flowers or verdure among those antique haunts of men until the heavy perfumes of Dr. Rappaccini's shrubs had lured it from afar. Without alighting on the flowers, this winged brightness seemed to be attracted by Beatrice, and lingered in the air and fluttered about her head. Now, here it could not be but that Giovanni Guasconti's eyes deceived him. Be that as it might, he fancied that, while Beatrice was gazing at the insect with childish delight, it grew faint and fell at her feet; its bright wings shivered; it was dead—from no cause that he could discern, unless it were the atmosphere of her breath. Again Beatrice crossed herself and sighed heavily as she bent over the dead insect.

An impulsive movement of Giovanni drew her eyes to the window. There she beheld the beautiful head of the young man—rather a Grecian than an Italian head, with fair, regular features, and a glistening of gold among his ringlets—gazing down upon her like a being that hovered in mid air. Scarcely knowing what he did, Giovanni threw down the bouquet which he had hitherto held in his hand.

"Signora," said he, "there are pure and healthful flowers. Wear them for the sake of Giovanni Guasconti."

"Thanks, signor," replied Beatrice, with her rich voice, that came forth as it were like a gush of music, and with a mirthful expression half childish and half woman-like. "I accept your gift, and would fain recompense it with this precious purple flower; but if I toss it into the air it will not reach you. So Signor Guasconti must even content himself with my thanks."

She lifted the bouquet from the ground, and then, as if inwardly ashamed at having stepped aside from her maidenly reserve to respond to a stranger's greeting, passed swiftly homeward through the garden. But few as the moments were, it seemed to Giovanni, when she was on the point of vanishing beneath the sculptured portal, that his beautiful bouquet was already beginning to wither in her grasp. It was an idle thought; there could be no possibility of distinguishing a faded flower from a fresh one at so great a distance.

For many days after this incident the young man avoided the window that looked into Dr. Rappaccini's garden, as if something ugly and monstrous would have blasted his eyesight had he been betrayed into a glance. He felt conscious of having put himself, to a certain extent, within the influence of an unintelligible power by the communication which he had opened with Beatrice. The wisest course would have been, if his heart were in any real danger, to quit his lodgings and Padua itself at once; the next wiser, to have accustomed himself, as far as possible, to the familiar and daylight view of Beatrice—thus bringing her rigidly and systematically within the limits of ordinary experience. Least of all, while avoiding her sight, ought Giovanni to have remained so near this extraordinary being that the proximity and possibility even of intercourse should give a kind of substance and reality to the wild vagaries which his imagination ran riot continually in producing. Guasconti had not a deep heart—or, at all events, its depths were not sounded now; but he had a quick fancy, and an ardent southern temperament, which rose every instant to a higher fever pitch. Whether or no Beatrice possessed those terrible attributes, that fatal breath, the affinity with those so beautiful and deadly flowers which were indicated by what Giovanni had witnessed, she had at least instilled a fierce and subtle poison into his system. It was not love, although her rich beauty was a madness to him; nor horror, even while he fancied her spirit to be imbued with the same baneful essence that seemed to pervade her physical frame; but a wild offspring of both love and horror that had each parent in it, and burned like one and shivered like the other. Giovanni knew not what to dread; still less did he know what to hope; yet hope and dread kept a continual warfare in his breast, alternately vanquishing one another and starting up afresh to renew the contest. Blessed are all simple emotions, be they dark or bright! It is the lurid intermixture of the two that produces the illuminating blaze of the infernal regions.

Sometimes he endeavored to assuage the fever of his spirit by a rapid walk through the streets of Padua or beyond its gates: his footsteps kept time with the throbbings of his brain, so that the walk was apt to accelerate itself to a race. One day he found himself arrested; his arm was seized by a portly personage, who had turned back on recognizing the young man and expended much breath in overtaking him.

"Signor Giovanni! Stay, my young friend!" cried he. "Have you forgotten me? That might well be the case if I were as much altered as yourself."

It was Baglioni, whom Giovanni had avoided ever since their first meeting, from a doubt that the professor's sagacity would look too deeply into his secrets. Endeavoring to recover himself, he stared forth wildly from his inner world into the outer one and spoke like a man in a dream.

"Yes; I am Giovanni Guasconti. You are Professor Pietro Baglioni. Now let me pass!"

"Not yet, not yet, Signor Giovanni Guasconti," said the professor, smiling, but at the same time scrutinizing the youth with an earnest glance. "What! did I grow up side by side with your father? and shall his son pass me like a stranger in these old streets of Padua? Stand still, Signor Giovanni; for we must have a word or two before we part."

"Speedily, then, most worshipful professor, speedily," said Giovanni, with feverish impatience. "Does not your worship see that I am in haste?"

Now, while he was speaking there came a man in black along the street, stooping and moving feebly like a person in inferior health. His face was all overspread with a most sickly and sallow hue, but yet so pervaded with an expression of piercing and active intellect that an observer might easily have overlooked the merely physical attributes and have seen only this wonderful energy. As he passed, this person exchanged a cold and distant salutation with Baglioni, but fixed his eyes upon Giovanni with an intentness that seemed to bring out whatever was within him worthy of notice. Nevertheless, there was a peculiar quietness in the look, as if taking merely a speculative, not a human, interest in the young man.

"It is Dr. Rappaccini!" whispered the professor when the stranger had passed. "Has he ever seen your face before?"

"Not that I know," answered Giovanni, starting at the name.

"He *has* seen you! he must have seen you!" said Baglioni, hastily. "For some purpose or other, this man of science is making a study of you. I know that look of his! It is the same that coldly illuminates his face as he bends over a bird, a mouse, or a butterfly, which, in pursuance of some experiment, he has killed by the perfume of a flower; a look as deep as Nature itself, but without Nature's warmth of love. Signor Giovanni, I will stake my life upon it, you are the subject of one of Rappaccini's experiments!"

"Will you make a fool of me?" cried Giovanni, passionately. "*That*, signor professor, were an untoward experiment."

"Patience! Patience!" replied the imperturbable professor. "I tell thee, my poor Giovanni, that Rappaccini has a scientific interest in thee. Thou hast fallen into fearful hands! And the Signora Beatrice,—what part does she act in this mystery?"

But Guasconti, finding Baglioni's pertinacity intolerable, here broke away, and was gone before the professor could again seize his arm. He looked after the young man intently and shook his head.

"This must not be," said Baglioni to himself. "The youth is the son of my old friend, and shall not come to any harm from which the arcana of medical science can preserve him. Besides, it is too insufferable an impertinence in Rappaccini, thus to snatch the lad out of my own hands, as I may say, and make use of him for his infernal experiments. This daughter of his! It shall be looked to. Perchance, most learned Rappaccini, I may foil you where you little dream of it!"

Meanwhile Giovanni had pursued a circuitous route, and at length found himself at the door of his lodgings. As he crossed the threshold he was met by old Lisabetta, who smirked and smiled, and was evidently desirous to attract his attention; vainly, however, as the ebullition of his feelings had momentarily subsided into a cold and dull vacuity. He turned his eyes full upon the withered face that was puckering itself into a smile, but seemed to behold it not. The old dame, therefore, laid her grasp upon his cloak.

"Signor! signor!" whispered she, still with a smile over the whole breadth of her visage, so that it looked not unlike a grotesque carving in wood, darkened by centuries. "Listen, signor! There is a private entrance into the garden!"

"What do you say?" exclaimed Giovanni, turning quickly about, as if an inanimate thing should start into feverish life. "A private entrance into Dr. Rappaccini's garden?"

"Hush! hush! not so loud!" whispered Lisabetta, putting her hand over his mouth. "Yes; into the worshipful doctor's garden, where you may see all his fine shrubbery. Many a young man in Padua would give gold to be admitted among those flowers."

Giovanni put a piece of gold into her hand.

"Show me the way," said he.

A surmise, probably excited by his conversation with Baglioni, crossed his mind, that this interposition of old Lisabetta might perchance be connected with the intrigue, whatever were its nature, in which the professor seemed to suppose that Dr. Rappaccini was involving him. But such a suspicion, though it disturbed Giovanni, was inadequate to restrain him. The instant that he was aware of the possibility of approaching Beatrice, it seemed an absolute necessity of his existence to do so. It mattered not whether she were angel or demon; he was irrevocably within her sphere, and must obey the law that whirled him onward, in ever-lessening circles, towards a result which he did not attempt to foreshadow; and yet, strange to say, there came across him a sudden doubt whether this intense interest on his part were not delusory; whether it were really of so deep and positive a nature as to justify him in now thrusting himself into an incalculable position; whether it were not merely the fantasy of a young man's brain, only slightly or not at all connected with his heart.

He paused, hesitated, turned half about, but again went on. His withered guide led him along several obscure passages, and finally undid a door, through which, as it was opened, there came the sight and sound of rustling leaves, with the broken sunshine glimmering among them. Giovanni stepped forth, and, forcing himself through the entanglement of a shrub that wreathed its tendrils over the hidden entrance, stood beneath his own window in the open area of Dr. Rappaccini's garden.

How often is it the case that, when impossibilities have come to pass and dreams have condensed their misty substance into tangible realities, we find ourselves calm, and even coldly self-possessed, amid circumstances which it would have been a delirium or joy or agony to anticipate! Fate delights to thwart us thus. Passion will choose his own time to rush upon the scene, and lingers sluggishly behind when an appropriate adjustment of events would seem to summon his appearance. So was it now with Giovanni. Day after day his pulses had throbbed with feverish blood at the improbable idea of an interview with Beatrice, and of standing with her, face to face, in this very garden, basking in the Oriental sunshine of her beauty, and snatching from her full gaze the mystery which he deemed the riddle of his own existence. But now there was a singular and untimely equanimity within his breast. He threw a glance around the garden to discover if Beatrice or her father were present, and perceiving that he was alone, began a critical observation of the plants.

The aspect of one and all of them dissatisfied him; their gorgeousness seemed fierce, passionate, and even unnatural. There was hardly an individual shrub which a wanderer, straying by himself through a forest, would not have been startled to find growing wild, as if an unearthly face had glared at him out of the thicket. Several also would have shocked a delicate instinct by an appearance of artificialness indicating that there had been such commixture, and, as it were, adultery, of various vegetable species, that the production was no longer of God's making, but the monstrous offspring of man's depraved fancy, glowing with only an evil mockery of beauty. They were probably the result of experiment, which in one or two cases had succeeded in mingling plants individually lovely into a compound possessing the questionable and ominous character that distinguished the whole growth of the garden. In fine, Giovanni recognized but two or three plants in the collection, and those of a kind that he well knew to be poisonous. While busy with these contemplations he heard the rustling of a silken garment, and, turning, beheld Beatrice emerging from beneath the sculptured portal.

Giovanni had not considered with himself what should be his deportment; whether he should apologize for his intrusion into the garden, or assume that he was there with the privity at least, if not by the desire, of Dr. Rappaccini or his daughter; but Beatrice's manner placed him at his ease, though leaving him still in doubt by what agency he had gained admittance. She came lightly along the path and met him near the broken fountain. There was surprise in her face, but brightened by a simple and kind expression of pleasure.

"You are a connoisseur in flowers, signor," said Beatrice, with a smile, alluding to the bouquet, which he had flung her from the window. "It is no marvel, therefore, if the sight of my father's rare collection has tempted you to take a nearer view. If he were here, he could tell you many strange and interesting facts as to the nature and habits of these shrubs; for he has spent a lifetime in such studies, and this garden is his world."

"And yourself, lady," observed Giovanni, "if fame says true,—you likewise are deeply skilled in the virtues indicated by these rich blossoms and these spicy perfumes. Would you deign to be my instructress, I should prove an apter scholar than if taught by Signor Rappaccini himself."

"Are there such idle rumors?" asked Beatrice, with the music of a pleasant laugh. "Do people say that I am skilled in my father's science of plants? What a jest is there! No; though I have grown up among these flowers, I know no more of them than their hues and perfume; and sometimes methinks I would fain rid myself of even that small knowledge. There are many flowers here, and those not the least brilliant, that shock and offend me when they meet my eye. But pray, signor, do not believe these stories about my science. Believe nothing of me save what you see with your own eyes."

"And must I believe all that I have seen with my own eyes?" asked Giovanni, pointedly, while the recollection of former scenes made him shrink. "No, signora; you demand too little of me. Bid me believe nothing save what comes from your own lips."

It would appear that Beatrice understood him. There came a deep flush to her cheek; but she looked full into Giovanni's eyes, and responded to his gaze of uneasy suspicion with a queenlike haughtiness.

"I do so bid you, signor," she replied. "Forget whatever you may have fancied in regard to me. If true to the outward senses, still it may be false in its essence; but the words of Beatrice Rappaccini's lips are true from the depths of the heart outward. Those you may believe."

A fervor glowed in her whole aspect and beamed upon Giovanni's consciousness like the light of truth itself; but while she spoke there was a fragrance in the atmosphere around her, rich and delightful, though evanescent, yet which the young man, from an indefinable reluctance, scarcely dared to draw into his lungs. It might be the odor of the flowers. Could it be Beatrice's breath which thus embalmed her words with a strange richness, as if by steeping them in her heart? A faintness passed like a shadow over Giovanni and flitted away; he seemed to gaze through the beautiful girl's eyes into her transparent soul, and felt no more doubt or fear.

The tinge of passion that had colored Beatrice's manner vanished; she became gay, and appeared to derive a pure delight from her communion with the youth not unlike what the maiden of a lonely island might have felt conversing with a voyager from the civilized world. Evidently her experience of life had been confined within the limits of that garden. She talked now about matters as simple as the daylight or summer clouds, and now asked questions in reference to the city, or Giovanni's distant home, his friends, his mother, and his sisters—questions indicating such seclusion, and such lack of familiarity with modes and forms, that Giovanni responded as if to an infant. Her spirit gushed out before him like a fresh rill that was just catching its first glimpse of the sunlight and wondering at the reflections of earth and sky which were flung into its bosom. There came thoughts, too, from a deep source, and fantasies of a gemlike brilliancy, as if diamonds and rubies sparkled upward among the bubbles of the fountain. Ever and anon there gleamed across the young man's mind a sense of wonder that he should be walking side by side with the being who had so wrought upon his imagination, whom he had idealized in such hues of terror, in whom he had positively witnessed such manifestations of dreadful attributes,—that he should be conversing with Beatrice like a brother, and should find her so human and so maidenlike. But such reflections were only momentary; the effect of her character was too real not to make itself familiar at once.

In this free intercourse they had strayed through the garden, and now, after many turns among its avenues, were come to the shattered fountain, beside which grew the magnificent shrub, with its treasury of glowing blossoms. A fragrance was diffused from it which Giovanni recognized as identical with that which he had attributed to Beatrice's breath, but incomparably more powerful. As her eyes fell upon it, Giovanni beheld her press her hand to her bosom as if her heart were throbbing suddenly and painfully.

"For the first time in my life," murmured she, addressing the shrub, "I have forgotten thee."

"I remember, signora," said Giovanni, "that you once promised to reward me with one of these living gems for the bouquet which I had the happy boldness to fling to your feet. Permit me now to pluck it as a memorial of this interview."

He made a step towards the shrub with extended hand; but Beatrice darted forward, uttering a shriek that went through his heart like a dagger. She caught his hand and drew it back with the whole force of her slender figure. Giovanni felt her touch thrilling through his fibres.

"Touch it not!" exclaimed she, in a voice of agony. "Not for thy life! It is fatal!"

Then, hiding her face, she fled from him and vanished beneath the sculptured portal. As Giovanni followed her with his eyes, he beheld the emaciated figure and pale intelligence of Dr. Rappaccini, who had been watching the scene, he knew not how long, within the shadow of the entrance.

No sooner was Guasconti alone in his chamber than the image of Beatrice came back to his passionate musings, invested with all the witchery that had been gathering around it ever since his first glimpse of her, and now likewise imbued with a tender warmth of girlish womanhood. She was human; her nature was endowed with all gentle and feminine qualities; she was worthiest to be worshipped; she was capable, surely, on her part, of the height and heroism of love. Those tokens which he had hitherto considered as proofs of a frightful peculiarity in her physical and moral system were now either forgotten, or, by the subtle sophistry of passion transmitted into a golden crown of enchantment, rendering Beatrice the more admirable by so much as she was the more unique. Whatever had looked ugly was now beautiful; or, if incapable of such a change, it stole away and hid itself among those shapeless half ideas which throng the dim region beyond the daylight of our perfect consciousness. Thus did he spend the night, nor fell asleep until the dawn had begun to awake the slumbering flowers in Dr. Rappaccini's garden, whither Giovanni's dreams doubtless led him. Up rose the sun in his due season, and, flinging his beams upon the young man's eyelids, awoke him to a sense of pain. When thoroughly aroused, he became sensible of a burning and tingling agony in his hand—in his right hand—the very hand which Beatrice had grasped in her own when he was on the point of plucking one of the gemlike flowers. On the back of that hand there was now a purple print like that of four small fingers, and the likeness of a slender thumb upon his wrist.

Oh, how stubbornly does love,—or even that cunning semblance of love which flourishes in the imagination, but strikes no depth of root into the heart,—how stubbornly does it hold its faith until the moment comes when it is doomed to vanish into thin mist! Giovanni wrapped a handkerchief about his hand and wondered what evil thing had stung him, and soon forgot his pain in a reverie of Beatrice.

After the first interview, a second was in the inevitable course of what we call fate. A third; a fourth; and a meeting with Beatrice in the garden was no longer an incident in Giovanni's daily life, but the whole space in which he might be said to live; for the anticipation and memory of that ecstatic hour made up the remainder. Nor was it otherwise with the daughter of Rappaccini. She watched for the youth's appearance, and flew to his side with confidence as unreserved as if they had been playmates from early infancy—as if they were such playmates still. If, by any unwonted chance, he failed to come at the appointed moment, she stood beneath the window and sent up the rich sweetness of her tones to float around him in his chamber and echo and reverberate throughout his heart: "Giovanni! Giovanni! Why tarriest thou! Come down!" And down he hastened into that Eden of poisonous flowers.

But, with all this intimate familiarity, there was still a reserve in Beatrice's demeanor, so rigidly and invariably sustained that the idea of infringing it scarcely occurred to his imagination. By all appreciable signs, they loved; they had looked love with eyes that conveyed the holy secret from the depths of one soul into the depths of the other, as if it were too sacred to be whispered by the way; they had even spoken love in those gushes of passion when their spirits darted forth in articulated breath like tongues of long-hidden flame; and yet there had been no seal of lips, no clasp of hands, nor any slightest caress such as love claims and hallows. He had never touched one of the gleaming ringlets of her hair; her garment— so marked was the physical barrier between them—had never been waved against him by a breeze. On the few occasions when Giovanni had seemed tempted to overstep the limit, Beatrice grew so sad, so stern, and withal wore such a look of desolate separation, shuddering at itself, that not a spoken word was requisite to repel him. At such times he was startled at the horrible suspicions that rose, monster-like, out of the caverns of his heart and stared him in the face; his love grew thin and faint as the morning mist, his doubts alone had substance. But, when Beatrice's face brightened again after the momentary shadow, she was transformed at once from the mysterious, questionable being whom he had watched with so much awe and horror; she was now the beautiful and unsophisticated girl whom he felt his spirit knew with a certainty beyond all other knowledge.

A considerable time had now passed since Giovanni's last meeting with Baglioni. One morning, however, he was disagreeably surprised by a visit from the professor, whom he had scarcely thought of for whole weeks, and would willingly have forgotten still longer. Given up as he had long been to a pervading excitement, he could tolerate no companions except upon condition of their perfect sympathy with his present state of feeling. Such sympathy was not to be expected from Professor Baglioni.

The visitor chatted carelessly for a few moments about the gossip of the city and the university, and then took up another topic.

"I have been reading an old classic author lately," said he, "and met with a story that strangely interested me. Possibly you may remember it. It is of an Indian prince, who sent a beautiful woman as a present to Alexander the Great. She was as lovely as the dawn and gorgeous as the sunset; but what especially distinguished her was a certain rich perfume in her breath—richer than a garden of Persian roses. Alexander, as was natural to a youthful conqueror, fell in love at first sight with this magnificent stranger; but a certain sage physician, happening to be present, discovered a terrible secret in regard to her."

"And what was that?" asked Giovanni, turning his eyes downward to avoid those of the professor.

"That this lovely woman," continued Baglioni, with emphasis, "had been nourished with poisons from her birth upward, until her whole nature was so imbued with them that she herself had become the deadliest poison in existence. Poison was her element of life. With that rich perfume of her breath she blasted the very air. Her love would have been poison—her embrace death. Is not this a marvellous tale?"

"A childish fable," answered Giovanni, nervously starting from his chair. "I marvel how your worship finds time to read such nonsense among your graver studies."

"By and by," said the professor, looking uneasily about him, "what singular fragrance is this in your apartment? Is it the perfume of your gloves? It is faint, but delicious; and yet, after all, by no means agreeable. Were I to breathe it long, methinks it would make me ill. It is like the breath of a flower; but I see no flowers in the chamber."

"Nor are there any," replied Giovanni, who had turned pale as the professor spoke; "nor, I think, is there any fragrance except in your worship's imagination. Odors, being a sort of element combined of the sensual and the spiritual, are apt to deceive us in this manner. The recollection of a perfume, the bare idea of it, may easily be mistaken for a present reality."

"Ay; but my sober imagination does not often play such tricks," said Baglioni; "and, were I to fancy any kind of odor, it would be that of some vile apothecary drug, wherewith my fingers are likely enough to be imbued. Our worshipful friend Rappaccini, as I have heard, tinctures his medicaments with odors richer than those of Araby. Doubtless, likewise, the fair and learned Signora Beatrice would minister to her patients with draughts as sweet as a maiden's breath; but woe to him that sips them!"

Giovanni's face evinced many contending emotions. The tone in which the professor alluded to the pure and lovely daughter of Rappaccini was a torture to his soul; and yet the intimation of a view of her character, opposite to his own, gave instantaneous distinctness to a thousand dim suspicions, which now grinned at him like so many demons. But he strove hard to quell them and to respond to Baglioni with a true lover's perfect faith.

"Signor professor," said he, "you were my father's friend; perchance, too, it is your purpose to act a friendly part toward his son. I would fain feel nothing towards you save respect and deference; but I pray you to observe, signor, that there is one subject on which we must not speak. You know not the Signora Beatrice. You cannot, therefore, estimate the wrong —the blasphemy, I may even say—that is offered to her character by a light or injurious word."

"Giovanni! my poor Giovanni!" answered the professor, with a calm expression of pity. "I know this wretched girl far better than yourself. You shall hear the truth in respect to the poisoner Rappaccini and his poisonous daughter; yes, poisonous as she is beautiful. Listen; for, even should you do violence to my gray hairs, it shall not silence me. That old fable of the Indian woman has become a truth by the deep and deadly science of Rappaccini and in the person of the lovely Beatrice."

Giovanni groaned and hid his face.

"Her father," continued Baglioni, "was not restrained by natural affection from offering up his child in this horrible manner as the victim of his insane zeal for science; for, let us do him justice, he is as true a man of science as ever distilled his own heart in an alembic. What, then, will be your fate? Beyond a doubt you are selected as the material of some new experiment. Perhaps the result is to be death; perhaps a fate more awful still. Rappaccini, with what he calls the interest of science before his eyes, will hesitate at nothing."

"It is a dream," muttered Giovanni to himself; "surely it is a dream."

"But," resumed the professor, "be of good cheer, son of my friend. It is not yet too late for the rescue. Possibly we may even succeed in bringing back this miserable child within the limits of ordinary nature, from which her father's madness has estranged her. Behold this little silver vase! It was wrought by the hands of the renowned Benvenuto Cellini, and is well worthy to be a love gift to the fairest dame in Italy. But its contents are invaluable. One little sip of this antidote would have rendered the most virulent poisons of the Borgias[2] innocuous. Doubt not that it will be as efficacious against those of Rappaccini. Bestow the vase, and the precious liquid within it, on your Beatrice, and hopefully await the result."

Baglioni laid a small, exquisitely wrought silver vial on the table and withdrew, leaving what he had said to produce its effect upon the young man's mind.

"We will thwart Rappaccini yet," thought he, chuckling to himself, as he descended the stairs; "but, let us confess the truth of him, he is a wonderful man—a wonderful man indeed; a vile empiric, however, in his practice, and therefore not to be tolerated by those who respect the good old rules of the medical profession."

Throughout Giovanni's whole acquaintance with Beatrice, he had occasionally, as we have said, been haunted by dark surmises as to her character; yet so thoroughly had she made herself felt by him as a simple, natural, most affectionate, and guileless creature, that the image now held up by Professor Baglioni looked as strange and incredible as if it were not in accordance with his own original conception. True, there were ugly recollections connected with his first glimpses of the beautiful girl; he could not quite forget the bouquet that withered in her grasp, and the insect that perished amid the sunny air, by no ostensible agency save the fragrance of her breath. These incidents, however, dissolving in the pure light of her character, had no longer the efficacy of facts, but were acknowledged as mistaken fantasies, by whatever testimony of the senses they might appear to be substantiated. There is something truer and more real than what we can see with the eyes and touch with the finger. On such better evidence had Giovanni founded his confidence in Beatrice, though rather by the necessary

---

2. An influential Italian family in the twelfth and thirteenth centuries, famed for their treachery and knowledge of poisons.

force of her high attributes than by any deep and generous faith on his part. But now his spirit was incapable of sustaining itself at the height to which the early enthusiasm of passion had exalted it; he fell down, grovelling among earthly doubts, and defiled therewith the pure whiteness of Beatrice's image. Not that he gave her up; he did but distrust. He resolved to institute some decisive test that should satisfy him, once for all, whether there were those dreadful peculiarities in her physical nature which could not be supposed to exist without some corresponding monstrosity of soul. His eyes, gazing down afar, might have deceived him as to the lizard, the insect, and the flowers; but if he could witness, at the distance of a few paces, the sudden blight of one fresh and healthful flower in Beatrice's hand, there would be room for no further question. With this idea he hastened to the florist's and purchased a bouquet that was still gemmed with the morning dew-drops.

It was now the customary hour of his daily interview with Beatrice. Before descending into the garden, Giovanni failed not to look at his figure in the mirror,—a vanity to be expected in a beautiful young man, yet, as displaying itself at that troubled and feverish moment, the token of a certain shallowness of feeling and insincerity of character. He did gaze, however, and said to himself that his features had never before possessed so rich a grace, nor his eyes such vivacity, nor his cheeks so warm a hue of superabundant life.

"At least," thought he, "her poison has not yet insinuated itself into my system. I am no flower to perish in her grasp."

With that thought he turned his eyes on the bouquet, which he had never once laid aside from his hand. A thrill of indefinable horror shot through his frame on perceiving that those dewy flowers were already beginning to droop; they wore the aspect of things that had been fresh and lovely yesterday. Giovanni grew white as marble, and stood motionless before the mirror, staring at his own reflection there as at the likeness of something frightful. He remembered Baglioni's remark about the fragrance that seemed to pervade the chamber. It must have been the poison in his breath! Then he shuddered—shuddered at himself. Recovering from his stupor, he began to watch with curious eye a spider that was busily at work hanging its web from the antique cornice of the apartment, crossing and recrossing the artful system of interwoven lines—as vigorous and active a spider as ever dangled from an old ceiling. Giovanni bent towards the insect, and emitted a deep, long breath. The spider suddenly ceased its toil; the web vibrated with a tremor originating in the body of the small artisan. Again Giovanni sent forth a breath, deeper, longer, and imbued with a venomous feeling out of his heart: he knew not whether he were wicked, or only desperate. The spider made a convulsive gripe with his limbs and hung dead across the window.

"Accursed! accursed!" muttered Giovanni, addressing himself. "Hast thou grown so poisonous that this deadly insect perishes by thy breath?"

At that moment a rich, sweet voice came floating up from the garden.

"Giovanni! Giovanni! It is past the hour! Why tarriest thou? Come down!"

"Yes," muttered Giovanni again. "She is the only being whom my breath may not slay! Would that it might!"

He rushed down, and in an instant was standing before the bright and loving eyes of Beatrice. A moment ago his wrath and despair had been so fierce that he could have desired nothing so much as to wither her by a glance; but with her actual presence there came influences which had too real an existence to be at once shaken off: recollections of the delicate and benign power of her feminine nature, which had so often enveloped him in a religious calm; recollections of many a holy and passionate outgush of her heart, when the pure fountain had been unsealed from its depths and made visible in its transparency to his mental eye; recollections which, had Giovanni known how to estimate them, would have assured him that all this ugly mystery was but an earthly illusion, and that, whatever mist of evil might seem to have gathered over her, the real Beatrice was a heavenly angel. Incapable as he was of such high faith, still her presence had not utterly lost its magic. Giovanni's rage was quelled into an aspect of sullen insensibility. Beatrice, with a quick spiritual sense, immediately felt that there was a gulf of blackness between them which neither he nor she could pass. They walked on together, sad and silent, and came thus to the marble fountain and to its pool of water on the ground, in the midst of which grew the shrub that bore gem-like blossoms. Giovanni was affrighted at the eager enjoyment—the appetite, as it were—with which he found himself inhaling the fragrance of the flowers.

"Beatrice," asked he, abruptly, "whence came this shrub?"

"My father created it," answered she, with simplicity.

"Created it! created it!" repeated Giovanni. "What mean you, Beatrice?"

"He is a man fearfully acquainted with the secrets of Nature," replied Beatrice; "and, at the hour when I first drew breath, this plant sprang from the soil, the offspring of his science, of his intellect, while I was but his earthly child. Approach it not!" continued she, observing with terror that Giovanni was drawing nearer to the shrub. "It has qualities that you little dream of. But I, dearest Giovanni,—I grew up and blossomed with the plant and was nourished with its breath. It was my sister, and I loved it with a human affection; for, alas!—hast thou not suspected it?—there was an awful doom."

Here Giovanni frowned so darkly upon her that Beatrice paused and trembled. But her faith in his tenderness reassured her, and made her blush that she had doubted for an instant.

"There was an awful doom," she continued, "the effect of my father's fatal love of science, which estranged me from all society of my kind. Until Heaven sent thee, dearest Giovanni, oh, how lonely was thy poor Beatrice!"

"Was it a hard doom?" asked Giovanni, fixing his eyes upon her.

"Only of late have I known how hard it was," answered she, tenderly. "Oh, yes; but my heart was torpid, and therefore quiet."

Giovanni's rage broke forth from his sullen gloom like a lightning flash out of a dark cloud.

"Accursed one!" cried he, with venomous scorn and anger. "And, finding thy solitude wearisome, thou hast severed me likewise from all the warmth of life and enticed me into thy region of unspeakable horror!"

"Giovanni!" exclaimed Beatrice, turning her large bright eyes upon his face. The force of his words had not found its way into her mind; she was merely thunderstruck.

"Yes, poisonous thing!" repeated Giovanni, beside himself with passion. "Thou hast done it! Thou hast blasted me! Thou hast filled my veins with poison! Thou hast made me as hateful, as ugly, as loathsome and deadly a creature as thyself—a world's wonder of hideous monstrosity! Now, if our breath be happily as fatal to ourselves as to all others, let us join our lips in one kiss of unutterable hatred, and so die!"

"What has befallen me?" murmured Beatrice, with a low moan out of her heart. "Holy Virgin, pity me, a poor heartbroken child!"

"Thou,—dost thou pray?" cried Giovanni, still with the same fiendish scorn. "Thy very prayers, as they come from thy lips, taint the atmosphere with death. Yes, yes; let us pray! Let us to church and dip our fingers in the holy water at the portal! They that come after us will perish as by a pestilence! Let us sign crosses in the air! It will be scattering curses abroad in the likeness of holy symbols!"

"Giovanni," said Beatrice, calmly, for her grief was beyond passion, "why dost thou join thyself with me thus in those terrible words? I, it is true, am the horrible thing thou namest me. But thou,—what hast thou to do, save with one other shudder at my hideous misery to go forth out of the garden and mingle with thy race, and forget that there ever crawled on earth such a monster as poor Beatrice?"

"Dost thou pretend ignorance?" asked Giovanni, scowling upon her. "Behold! this power have I gained from the pure daughter of Rappaccini."

There was a swarm of summer insects flitting through the air in search of the food promised by the flower odors of the fatal garden. They circled round Giovanni's head, and were evidently attracted towards him by the same influence which had drawn them for an instant within the sphere of several of the shrubs. He sent forth a breath among them, and smiled bitterly at Beatrice as at least a score of the insects fell dead upon the ground.

"I see it! I see it!" shrieked Beatrice. "It is my father's fatal science! No, no, Giovanni; it was not I! Never! never! I dreamed only to love thee and be with thee a little time, and so to let thee pass away, leaving but thine image in mine heart; for, Giovanni, believe it, though my body be nourished with poison, my spirit is God's creature, and craves love as its daily food. But my father,—he has united us in this fearful sympathy. Yes; spurn me, tread upon me, kill me! Oh, what is death after such words as thine? But it was not I. Not for a world of bliss would I have done it."

Giovanni's passion had exhausted itself in its outburst from his lips. There now came across him a sense, mournful, and not without tenderness, of the intimate and peculiar relationship between Beatrice and himself. They stood, as it were, in an utter solitude, which would be made none the less solitary by the densest throng of human life. Ought not, then, the desert of humanity around them to press this insulated pair closer together? If they should be cruel to one another, who was there to be kind to them? Besides, thought Giovanni, might there not still be a hope of his returning within the limits of ordinary nature, and leading Beatrice, the redeemed Beatrice, by the hand? O, weak, and selfish, and unworthy spirit, that could dream of an earthly union and earthly happiness as possible, after such deep love had been so bitterly wronged as was Beatrice's love by Giovanni's blighting words! No, no; there could be no such hope. She must pass heavily, with that broken heart, across the borders of Time—she must bathe her hurts in some fount of paradise, and forget her grief in the light of immortality, and *there* be well.

But Giovanni did not know it.

"Dear Beatrice," said he, approaching her, while she shrank away as always at his approach, but now with different impulse, "dearest Beatrice, our fate is not yet so desperate. Behold! there is a medicine, potent, as a wise physician has assured me, and almost divine in its efficacy. It is composed of ingredients the most opposite to those by which thy awful father has brought this calamity upon thee and me. It is distilled of blessed herbs. Shall we not quaff it together, and thus be purified from evil?"

"Give it me!" said Beatrice, extending her hand to receive the little silver vial which Giovanni took from his bosom. She added, with a peculiar emphasis, "I will drink; but do thou await the result."

She put Baglioni's antidote to her lips; and, at the same moment, the figure of Rappaccini emerged from the portal and came slowly towards the marble fountain. As he drew near, the pale man of science seemed to gaze with a triumphant expression at the beautiful youth and maiden, as might an artist who should spend his life in achieving a picture or a group of statuary and finally be satisfied with his success. He paused; his bent form grew erect with conscious power; he spread out his hands over them in the attitude of a father imploring a blessing upon his children; but those were the same hands that had thrown poison into the stream of their lives. Giovanni trembled. Beatrice shuddered nervously, and pressed her hand upon her heart.

"My daughter," said Rappaccini, "thou art no longer lonely in the world. Pluck one of those precious gems from thy sister shrub and bid they bridegroom wear it in his bosom. It will not harm him now. My science and the sympathy between thee and him have so wrought within his system that he now stands from common men, as thou dost, daughter of my pride and triumph, from ordinary women. Pass on, then, through the world, most dear to one another and dreadful to all besides!"

"My father," said Beatrice, feebly,—and still as she spoke she kept her hand upon her heart,—"wherefore didst thou inflict this miserable doom upon thy child?"

"Miserable!" exclaimed Rappaccini. "What mean you, foolish girl? Dost thou deem it misery to be endowed with marvellous gifts against which no power nor strength could avail an enemy—misery, to be able to quell the mightiest with a breath—misery, to be as terrible as thou art beautiful? Wouldst thou, then, have preferred the condition of a weak woman, exposed to all evil and capable of none?"

"I would fain have been loved, not feared," murmured Beatrice, sinking down upon the ground. "But now it matters not. I am going, father, where the evil which thou hast striven to mingle with my being will pass away like a dream—like the fragrance of these poisonous flowers, which will no longer taint my breath among the flowers of Eden. Farewell, Giovanni! Thy words of hatred are like lead within my heart; but they, too, will fall away as I ascend. Oh, was there not, from the first, more poison in thy nature than in mine?"

To Beatrice,—so radically had her earthly part been wrought upon by Rappaccini's skill,—as poison had been life, so the powerful antidote was death; and thus the poor victim of man's ingenuity and of thwarted nature, and of the fatality that attends all such efforts of perverted wisdom, perished there, at the feet of her father and Giovanni. Just at that moment Professor Pietro Baglioni looked forth from the window, and called loudly, in a tone of triumph mixed with horror, to the thunderstricken man of science,—

"Rappaccini! Rappaccini! and is *this* the upshot of your experiment!"

1844

Nathaniel Hawthorne, though very conscious of the realistic tradition of fiction, concentrated his attention on "romances" that present "the truth of the human heart." As his contemporary Herman Melville points out, this truth had for Hawthorne an "uneven balance."

"His bright gildings but fringe and play upon the edges of thunder-clouds": Herman Melville

For spite of all the Indian-summer sunlight on the hither side of Hawthorne's soul, the other side—like the dark half of the physical sphere—is shrouded in a blackness, ten times black. But this darkness but gives more effect to the ever-moving dawn, that for ever advances through it, and circumnavigates his world. Whether Hawthorne has simply availed himself of this mystical blackness as a means to the wondrous effects he makes it to produce in his lights and shades; or whether there really lurks in him, perhaps unknown to himself, a touch of Puritanic gloom,—this, I cannot altogether tell. Certain it is, however, that this great power of blackness in him derives its force from its appeals to that Calvinistic sense of Innate Depravity and Original Sin, from whose visitations, in some shape or other, no deeply thinking mind is always and wholly free. For, in certain moods, no man can weigh this world without throwing in something, somehow like Original Sin, to strike the uneven balance. At all events, perhaps no writer has ever wielded this terrific thought with greater terror than this same harmless Hawthorne. Still more: this black conceit pervades him through and through. You may be witched by his sunlight,—transported by the bright gildings in the skies he builds over you; but there is the blackness of darkness beyond; and even his bright gildings but fringe and play upon the edges of thunder-clouds. In one word, the world is mistaken in this Nathaniel Hawthorne. He himself must often have smiled at its absurd misconception of him. He is immeasurably deeper than the plummet of the mere critic. For it is not the brain that can test such a man; it is only the heart. Yet cannot come to know greatness by inspecting it; there is no glimpse to be caught of it, except by intuition; you need not ring it, you but touch it, and you find it is gold.

Now, it is that blackness in Hawthorne, of which I have spoken, that so fixes and fascinates me. . . .

EDGAR ALLAN POE

(1809–1849)

THE FALL OF THE HOUSE OF USHER

During the whole of a dull, dark, and soundless day in the autumn of the year, when the clouds hung oppressively low in the heavens, I had been passing alone, on horseback, through a singularly dreary tract of country;

and at length found myself, as the shades of the evening drew on, within view of the melancholy House of Usher. I know not how it was—but, with the first glimpse of the building, a sense of insufferable gloom pervaded my spirit. I say insufferable; for the feeling was unrelieved by any of that half-pleasurable, because poetic, sentiment, with which the mind usually receives even the sternest natural images of the desolate or terrible. I looked upon the scene before me—upon the mere house, and the simple landscape features of the domain, upon the bleak walls, upon the vacant eye-like windows, upon a few rank sedges, and upon a few white trunks of decayed trees—with an utter depression of soul which I can compare to no earthly sensation more properly than to the after-dream of the reveller upon opium: the bitter lapse into everyday life, the hideous dropping off of the veil. There was an iciness, a sinking, a sickening of the heart, an unre-deemed dreariness of thought which no goading of the imagination could torture into aught of the sublime. What was it—I paused to think—what was it that so unnerved me in the contemplation of the House of Usher? It was a mystery all insoluble; nor could I grapple with the shadowy fancies that crowded upon me as I pondered. I was forced to fall back upon the unsatisfactory conclusion, that while, beyond doubt, there *are* combinations of very simple natural objects which have the power of thus affecting us, still the analysis of this power lies among considerations beyond our depth. It was possible, I reflected, that a mere different arrangement of the particu-lars of the scene, of the details of the picture, would be sufficient to modify, or perhaps to annihilate its capacity for sorrowful impression; and, acting upon this idea, I reined my horse to the precipitous brink of a black and lurid tarn[1] that lay in unruffled lustre by the dwelling, and gazed down— but with a shudder even more thrilling than before—upon the remodelled and inverted images of the gray sedge, and the ghastly tree-stems, and the vacant and eye-like windows.

Nevertheless, in this mansion of gloom I now proposed to myself a sojourn of some weeks. Its proprietor, Roderick Usher, had been one of my boon companions in boyhood; but many years had elapsed since our last meeting. A letter, however, had lately reached me in a distant part of the country—a letter from him—which, in its wildly importunate nature, had admitted of no other than a personal reply. The MS. gave evidence of ner-vous agitation. The writer spoke of acute bodily illness, of a mental dis-order which oppressed him, and of an earnest desire to see me, as his best, and indeed his only personal friend, with a view of attempting, by the cheer-fulness of my society, some alleviation of his malady. It was the manner in which all this, and much more, was said—it was the apparent *heart* that went with his request—which allowed me no room for hesitation; and I accord-ingly obeyed forthwith what I still considered a very singular summons.

Although, as boys, we had been even intimate associates, yet I really

---

1. A small mountain lake.

knew little of my friend. His reserve had been always excessive and habitual. I was aware, however, that his very ancient family had been noted, time out of mind, for a peculiar sensibility of temperament, displaying itself, through long ages, in many works of exalted art, and manifested, of late, in repeated deeds of munificent yet unobtrusive charity, as well as in a passionate devotion to the intricacies, perhaps even more than to the orthodox and easily recognizable beauties, of musical science. I had learned, too, the very remarkable fact, that the stem of the Usher race, all time-honored as it was, had put forth, at no period, any enduring branch; in other words, that the entire family lay in the direct line of descent, and had always, with very trifling and very temporary variation, so lain. It was this deficiency, I considered, while running over in thought the perfect keeping of the character of the premises with the accredited character of the people, and while speculating upon the possible influence which the one, in the long lapse of centuries, might have exercised upon the other—it was this deficiency, perhaps, of collateral issue, and the consequent undeviating transmission, from sire to son, of the patrimony with the name, which had, at length, so identified the two as to merge the original title of the estate in the quaint and equivocal appellation of the "House of Usher"—an appellation which seemed to include, in the minds of the peasantry who used it, both the family and the family mansion.

I have said that the sole effect of my somewhat childish experiment, that of looking down within the tarn, had been to deepen the first singular impression. There can be no doubt that the consciousness of the rapid increase of my superstition—for why should I not so term it?—served mainly to accelerate the increase itself. Such, I have long known, is the paradoxical law of all sentiments having terror as a basis. And it might have been for this reason only, that, when I again uplifted my eyes to the house itself, from its image in the pool, there grew in my mind a strange fancy—a fancy so ridiculous, indeed, that I but mention it to show the vivid force of the sensations which oppressed me. I had so worked upon my imagination as really to believe that about the whole mansion and domain there hung an atmosphere peculiar to themselves and their immediate vicinity: an atmosphere which had no affinity with the air of heaven, but which had reeked up from the decayed trees, and the gray wall, and the silent tarn: a pestilent and mystic vapor, dull, sluggish, faintly discernible, and leaden-hued.

Shaking off from my spirit what *must* have been a dream, I scanned more narrowly the real aspect of the building. Its principal feature seemed to be that of an excessive antiquity. The discoloration of ages had been great. Minute fungi overspread the whole exterior, hanging in a fine tangled webwork from the eaves. Yet all this was apart from any extraordinary dilapidation. No portion of the masonry had fallen; and there appeared to be a wild inconsistency between its still perfect adaptation of parts and the crumbling condition of the individual stones. In this there was much that reminded me of the specious totality of old wood-work which has rotted for long years in some neglected vault, with no disturbance from the breath of the external air. Beyond this indication of extensive decay, however, the fabric gave little token of instability. Perhaps the eye of a scrutinizing observer might have discovered a barely perceptible fissure, which, extending from the roof of the building in front, made its way down the wall in a zigzag direction, until it became lost in the sullen waters of the tarn.

Noticing these things, I rode over a short causeway to the house. A servant in waiting took my horse, and I entered the Gothic archway of the hall. A valet, of stealthy step, thence conducted me, in silence, through many dark and intricate passages in my progress to the *studio* of his master. Much that I encountered on the way contributed, I know not how, to heighten the vague sentiments of which I have already spoken. While the objects around me—while the carvings of the ceilings, the sombre tapestries of the walls, the ebon blackness of the floors, and the phantasmagoric armorial trophies which rattled as I strode, were but matters to which, or to such as which, I had been accustomed from my infancy—while I hesitated not to acknowledge how familiar was all this—I still wondered to find how unfamiliar were the fancies which ordinary images were stirring up. On one of the staircases, I met the physician of the family. His countenance, I thought, wore a mingled expression of low cunning and perplexity. He accosted me with trepidation and passed on. The valet now threw open a door and ushered me into the presence of his master.

The room in which I found myself was very large and lofty. The windows were long, narrow, and pointed, and at so vast a distance from the black oaken floor as to be altogether inaccessible from within. Feeble gleams of encrimsoned light made their way through the trellised panes, and served to render sufficiently distinct the more prominent objects around; the eye, however, struggled in vain to reach the remoter angles of the chamber, or the recesses of the vaulted and fretted ceiling. Dark draperies hung upon the walls. The general furniture was profuse, comfortless, antique, and tattered. Many books and musical instruments lay scattered about, but failed to give any vitality to the scene. I felt that I breathed an atmosphere of sorrow. An air of stern, deep, and irredeemable gloom hung over and pervaded all.

Upon my entrance, Usher arose from a sofa on which he had been lying at full length, and greeted me with a vivacious warmth which had much in it, I at first thought, of an overdone cordiality—of the constrained effort of the *ennuyé*[2] man of the world. A glance, however, at his countenance, convinced me of his perfect sincerity. We sat down; and for some moments, while he spoke not, I gazed upon him with a feeling half of pity, half of awe. Surely, man had never before so terribly altered, in so brief a period, as had Roderick Usher! It was with difficulty that I could bring myself to admit the identity of the wan being before me with the companion of my early boyhood. Yet the character of his face had been at all times remarkable. A

---

2. Bored.

cadaverousness of complexion; an eye large, liquid, and luminous beyond comparison, lips somewhat thin and very pallid, but of a surpassingly beautiful curve; a nose of a delicate Hebrew model, but with a breadth of nostril unusual in similar formations; a finely moulded chin, speaking, in its want of prominence, of a want of moral energy; hair of a more than web-like softness and tenuity; these features, with an inordinate expansion above the regions of the temple, made up altogether a countenance not easily to be forgotten. And now in the mere exaggeration of the prevailing character of these features, and of the expression they were wont to convey, lay so much of change that I doubted to whom I spoke. The now ghastly pallor of the skin, and the now miraculous lustre of the eye, above all things startled and even awed me. The silken hair, too, had been suffered to grow all unheeded, and as, in its wild gossamer texture, it floated rather than fell about the face, I could not, even with effort, connect its Arabesque expression with any idea of simple humanity.

In the manner of my friend I was at once struck with an incoherence, an inconsistency; and I soon found this to arise from a series of feeble and futile struggles to overcome an habitual trepidancy, an excessive nervous agitation. For something of this nature I had indeed been prepared, no less by his letter, than by reminiscences of certain boyish traits, and by conclusions deduced from his peculiar physical conformation and temperament. His action was alternately vivacious and sullen. His voice varied rapidly from a tremulous indecision (when the animal spirits seemed utterly in abeyance) to that species of energetic concision—that abrupt, weighty, unhurried, and hollow-sounding enunciation—that leaden, self-balanced and perfectly modulated guttural utterance, which may be observed in the lost drunkard, or the irreclaimable eater of opium, during the periods of his most intense excitement.

It was thus that he spoke of the object of my visit, of his earnest desire to see me, and of the solace he expected me to afford him. He entered, at some length, into what he conceived to be the nature of his malady. It was, he said, a constitutional and a family evil, and one for which he despaired to find a remedy—a mere nervous affection, he immediately added, which would undoubtedly soon pass off. It displayed itself in a host of unnatural sensations. Some of these, as he detailed them, interested and bewildered me; although, perhaps, the terms, and the general manner of the narration had their weight. He suffered much from a morbid acuteness of the senses; the most insipid food was alone endurable; he could wear only garments of certain texture; the odors of all flowers were oppressive; his eyes were tortured by even a faint light; and there were but peculiar sounds, and these from stringed instruments, which did not inspire him with horror.

To an anomolous species of terror I found him a bounden slave. 'I shall perish,' said he, 'I *must* perish in this deplorable folly. Thus, thus, and not otherwise, shall I be lost. I dread the events of the future, not in themselves, but in their results. I shudder at the thought of any, even the most trivial, incident, which may operate upon this intolerable agitation of soul.

I have, indeed, no abhorrence of danger, except in its absolute effect—in terror. In this unnerved—in this pitiable condition, I feel that the period will sooner or later arrive when I must abandon life and reason together, in some struggle with the grim phantasm, FEAR.'

I learned, moreover, at intervals, and through broken and equivocal hints, another singular feature of his mental condition. He was enchained by certain superstitious impressions in regard to the dwelling which he tenanted, and whence, for many years, he had never ventured forth—in regard to an influence whose suppositious force was conveyed in terms too shadowy here to be re-stated—an influence which some peculiarities in the mere form and substance of his family mansion, had, by dint of long sufferance, he said, obtained over his spirit—an effect which the *physique* of the gray walls and turrets, and of the dim tarn into which they all looked down, had, at length, brought about upon the *morale* of his existence.

He admitted, however, although with hesitation, that much of the peculiar gloom which thus afflicted him could be traced to a more natural and far more palpable origin—to the severe and long-continued illness, indeed to the evidently approaching dissolution, of a tenderly beloved sister—his sole companion for long years, his last and only relative on earth. 'Her decease,' he said, with a bitterness which I can never forget, 'would leave him (him the hopeless and the frail) the last of the ancient race of the Ushers.' While he spoke, the lady Madeline (for so was she called) passed slowly through a remote portion of the apartment, and, without having noticed my presence, disappeared. I regarded her with an utter astonishment not unmingled with dread, and yet I found it impossible to account for such feelings. A sensation of stupor oppressed me, as my eyes followed her retreating steps. When a door, at length, closed upon her, my glance sought instinctively and eagerly the countenace of the brother; but he had buried his face in his hands, and I could only perceive that a far more than ordinary wanness had overspread the emaciated fingers through which trickled many passionate tears.

The disease of the lady Madeline had long baffled the skill of her physicians. A settled apathy, a gradual wasting away of the person, and frequent although transient affections of a partially cataleptical character, were the unusual diagnosis. Hitherto she had steadily borne up against the pressure of her malady, and had not betaken herself finally to bed; but, on the closing in of the evening of my arrival at the house, she succumbed (as her brother told me at night with inexpressible agitation) to the prostrating power of the destroyer; and I learned that the glimpse I had obtained of her person would thus probably be the last I should obtain—that the lady, at least while living, would be seen by me no more.

For several days ensuing, her name was unmentioned by either Usher or myself: and during this period I was busied in earnest endeavors to alleviate the melancholy of my friend. We painted and read together; or I listened, as if in a dream, to the wild improvisations of his speaking guitar. And thus, as a closer and still closer intimacy admitted me more unreservedly into the recesses of his spirit, the more bitterly did I perceive the futility of all attempt at cheering a mind from which darkness, as if an inherent positive quality, poured forth upon all objects of the moral and physical universe, in one unceasing radiation of gloom.

I shall ever bear about me a memory of the many solemn hours I thus spent alone with the master of the House of Usher. Yet I should fail in any attempt to convey an idea of the exact character of the studies, or of the occupations, in which he involved me, or led me the way. An excited and highly distempered ideality threw a sulphureous lustre over all. His long improvised dirges will ring forever in my ears. Among other things, I hold painfully in mind a certain singular perversion and amplification of the wild air of the last waltz of Von Weber. From the paintings over which his elaborate fancy brooded, and which grew, touch by touch, into vaguenesses at which I shuddered the more thrillingly, because I shuddered knowing not why;—from these paintings (vivid as their images now are before me) I would in vain endeavor to educe more than a small portion which should lie within the compass of merely written words. By the utter simplicity, by the nakedness of his designs, he arrested and overawed attention. If ever mortal painted an idea, that mortal was Roderick Usher. For me at least, in the circumstances then surrounding me, there arose out of the pure abstractions which the hypochondriac contrived to throw upon his canvas, an intensity of intolerable awe, no shadow of which felt I ever yet in the contemplation of the certainly glowing yet too concrete reveries of Fuseli.

One of the phantasmagoric conceptions of my friend, partaking not so rigidly of the spirit of abstraction, may be shadowed forth, although feebly, in words. A small picture presented the interior of an immensely long and rectangular vault or tunnel, with low walls, smooth, white, and without interruption or device. Certain accessory points of the design served well to convey the idea that this excavation lay at an exceeding depth below the surface of the earth. No outlet was observed in any portion of its vast extent, and no torch, or other artificial source of light was discernible; yet a flood of intense rays rolled throughout, and bathed the whole in a ghastly and inappropriate splendor.

I have just spoken of that morbid condition of the auditory nerve which rendered all music intolerable to the sufferer, with the exception of certain effects of stringed instruments. It was, perhaps, the narrow limits to which he thus confined himself upon the guitar, which gave birth, in great measure, to the fantastic character of his performances. But the fervid *facility* of his *impromptus* could not be so accounted for. They must have been, and were, in the notes, as well as in the words of his wild fantasias (for he not unfrequently accompanied himself with rhymed verbal improvisations), the result of that intense mental collectedness and concentration to which I have previously alluded as observable only in particular moments of the highest artificial excitement. The words of one of these rhapsodies I have easily remembered. I was, perhaps, the more forcibly impressed with it, as he gave it, because, in the under or mystic current of its meaning, I fancied that I perceived, and for the first time, a full consciousness on the part of Usher, of the tottering of his lofty reason upon her throne. The verses, which were entitled 'The Haunted Palace,' ran very nearly, if not accurately, thus:

> In the greenest of our valleys
>   By good angels tenanted,
> Once a fair and stately palace—
>   Radiant palace—reared its head.
> In the monarch Thought's dominion,
>   It stood there!
> Never seraph spread a pinion
>   Over fabric half so fair!
>
> Banners yellow, glorious, golden,
>   On its roof did float and flow
> (This—all this—was in the olden
>   Time long ago)
> And every gentle air that dallied,
>   In that sweet day,
> Along the ramparts plumed and pallid,
> A wingèd odor went away.
>
> Wanderers in that happy valley,
>   Through two luminous windows, saw
> Spirits moving musically
>   To a lute's well-tunèd law,
> Round about a throne where, sitting,
>   Porphyrogene!
> In state his glory well befitting,
>   The ruler of the realm was seen.
>
> And all with pearl and ruby glowing
>   Was the fair palace door,
> Through which came flowing, flowing, flowing,
>   And sparkling evermore,
> A troop of Echoes, whose sweet duty
>   Was but to sing,
> In voices of surpassing beauty,
>   The wit and wisdom of their king.
>
> But evil things, in robes of sorrow,
>   Assailed the monarch's high estate;
> (Ah, let us mourn!—for never morrow
>   Shall dawn upon him, desolate!)
> And round about his home the glory

> That blushed and bloomed
> Is but a dim-remembered story
> Of the old time entombed.
>
> And travellers, now, within that valley,
> Through the red-litten windows see
> Vast forms that move fantastically
> To a discordant melody;
> While, like a ghastly rapid river,
> Through the pale door
> A hideous throng rush out forever,
> And laugh—but smile no more.

I well remember that suggestions arising from this ballad led us into a train of thought wherein there became manifest an opinion of Usher's which I mention not so much on account of its novelty, (for other men have thought thus), as on account of the pertinacity with which he maintained it. This opinion, in its general form, was that of the sentience of all vegetable things. But, in his disordered fancy, the idea had assumed a more daring character, and trespassed, under certain conditions, upon the kingdom of inorganization. I lack words to express the full extent, or the earnest *abandon* of his persuasion. The belief, however, was connected (as I have previously hinted) with the gray stones of the home of his forefathers. The conditions of the sentience had been here, he imagined, fulfilled in the method of collocation of these stones—in the order of their arrangement, as well as in that of the many *fungi* which overspread them, and of the decayed trees which stood around—above all, in the long undisturbed endurance of this arrangement, and in its reduplication in the still waters of the tarn. Its evidence—the evidence of the sentience—was to be seen, he said, (and I here started as he spoke), in the gradual yet certain condensation of an atmosphere of their own about the waters and the walls. The result was discoverable, he added, in that silent, yet importunate and terrible influence which for centuries had moulded the destinies of his family, and which made *him* what I now saw him—what he was. Such opinions need no comment, and I will make none.

Our books—the books which, for years, had formed no small portion of the mental existence of the invalid—were, as might be supposed, in strict keeping with this character of phantasm. We pored together over such works as the *Ververt et Chartreuse* of Gresset; the *Belphegor* of Machiavelli; the *Heaven and Hell* of Swedenborg; the *Subterranean Voyage of Nicholas Klimm* by Holberg; the *Chiromancy* of Robert Flud, of Jean D'Indaginé, and of De la Chambre; the *Journey into the Blue Distance* of Tieck; and the *City of the Sun* of Campanella. One favorite volume was a small octavo edition of the *Directorium Inquisitorum*, by the Dominican Eymeric de Gironne; and there were passages in Pomponius Mela, about the old African Satyrs and Aegipans, over which Usher would sit dreaming for hours. His chief delight, however, was found in the perusal of an exceedingly rare and curious book in quarto Gothic—the manual of a forgotten church—the *Vigilæ Mortuorum Secundum Chorum Ecclesiæ Maguntinæn.*[3]

I could not help thinking of the wild ritual of this work, and of its probable influence upon the hypochondriac, when, one evening, having informed me abruptly that the lady Madeline was no more, he stated his intention of preserving her corpse for a fortnight, (previously to its final interment), in one of the numerous vaults within the main walls of the building. The worldly reason, however, assigned for this singular proceeding, was one which I did not feel at liberty to dispute. The brother had been led to his resolution (so he told me) by consideration of the unusual character of the malady of the deceased, of certain obtrusive and eager inquiries on the part of her medical men, and of the remote and exposed situation of the burial-ground of the family, I will not deny that when I called to mind the sinister countenance of the person whom I met upon the staircase, on the day of my arrival at the house, I had no desire to oppose what I regarded as at best but a harmless, and by no means an unnatural, precaution.

At the request of Usher, I personally aided him in the arrangements for the temporary entombment. The body having been en-coffined, we two alone bore it to its rest. The vault in which we placed it (and which had been so long unopened that our torches, half smothered in its oppressive atmosphere, gave us little opportunity for investigation) was small, damp, and entirely without means of admission for light; lying, at great depth, immediately beneath that portion of the building in which was my own sleeping apartment. It had been used, apparently, in remote feudal times, for the worst purposes of a donjon-keep, and, in later days, as a place of deposit for powder, or some other highly combustible substance, as a portion of its floor, and the whole interior of a long archway through which we reached it, were carefully sheathed with copper. The door, of massive iron, had been, also, similarly protected. Its immense weight caused an unusually sharp grating sound, as it moved upon its hinges.

Having deposited our mournful burden upon tressels within this region of horror, we partially turned aside the yet unscrewed lid of the coffin, and looked upon the face of the tenant. A striking similitude between the brother and sister now first arrested my attention; and Usher, divining, perhaps, my thoughts, murmured out some few words from which I learned that the deceased and himself had been twins, and that sympathies of a scarcely intelligible nature had always existed between them. Our glances, however, rested not long upon the dead—for we could not regard her unawed. The disease which had thus entombed the lady in the maturity of youth, had left, as usual in all maladies of a strictly cataleptical character, the mockery of a faint blush upon the bosom and the face, and that suspiciously lingering smile upon the lip which is so terrible in death. We

---

3. Vigils of the Dead According to the Chorus of the Church of Minz.

replaced and screwed down the lid, and, having secured the door of iron, made our way, with toil, into the scarcely less gloomy apartments of the upper portion of the house.

And now, some days of bitter grief having elapsed, an observable change came over the features of the mental disorder of my friend. His ordinary manner had vanished. His ordinary occupations were neglected or forgotten. He roamed from chamber to chamber with hurried, unequal, and objectless step. The pallor of his countenance had assumed, if possible, a more ghastly hue—but the luminousness of his eye had utterly gone out. The once occasional huskiness of his tone was heard no more; and a tremulous quaver, as if of extreme terror, habitually characterized his utterance. There were times, indeed, when I thought his unceasingly agitated mind was laboring with some oppressive secret, to divulge which he struggled for the necessary courage. At times, again, I was obliged to resolve all into the mere inexplicable vagaries of madness, for I beheld him gazing upon vacancy for long hours, in an attitude of the profoundest attention, as if listening to some imaginary sound. It was no wonder that his condition terrified—that it infected me. I felt creeping upon me, by slow yet certain degrees, the wild influences of his own fantastic yet impressive superstitions.

It was, especially, upon retiring to bed late in the night of the seventh or eighth day after the placing of the lady Madeline within the donjon, that I experienced the full power of such feelings. Sleep came not near my couch, while the hours waned and waned away. I struggled to reason off the nervousness which had dominion over me. I endeavored to believe that much, if not all of what I felt, was due to the bewildering influence of the gloomy furniture of the room—of the dark and tattered draperies, which, tortured into motion by the breath of a rising tempest, swayed fitfully to and fro upon the walls, and rustled uneasily about the decorations of the bed. But my efforts were fruitless. An irrepressible tremor gradually pervaded my frame; and, at length, there sat upon my very heart an incubus[4] of utterly causeless alarm. Shaking this off with a gasp and a struggle, I uplifted myself upon the pillows, and, peering earnestly within the intense darkness of the chamber, hearkened—I know not why, except that an instinctive spirit prompted me—to certain low and indefinite sounds which came, through the pauses of the storm, at long intervals I knew not whence. Overpowered by an intense sentiment of horror, unaccountable yet unendurable, I threw on my clothes with haste (for I felt that I should sleep no more during the night), and endeavored to arouse myself from the pitiable condition into which I had fallen, by pacing rapidly to and fro through the apartment.

I had taken but few turns in this manner, when a light step on an adjoining staircase arrested my attention. I presently recognized it as that

———
4. Something that is nightmarishly oppressive; a nightmare.

of Usher. In an instant afterward he rapped, with a gentle touch, at my door, and entered, bearing a lamp. His countenance was, as usual, cadaverously wan—but, moreover, there was a species of mad hilarity in his eyes—an evidently restrained *hysteria* in his whole demeanor. His air appalled me—but anything was preferable to the solitude which I had so long endured, and I even welcomed his presence as a relief.

'And you have not seen it?' he said abruptly, after having stared about him for some moments in silence—'you have not then seen it?—but, stay! you shall.' Thus speaking, and having carefully shaded his lamp, he hurried to one of the casements and threw it freely open to the storm.

The impetuous fury of the entering gust nearly lifted us from our feet. It was, indeed, a tempestuous yet sternly beautiful night, and one wildly singular in its terror and its beauty. A whirlwind had apparently collected its force in our vicinity; for there were frequent and violent alterations in the direction of the wind; and the exceeding density of the clouds (which hung so low as to press upon the turrets of the house) did not prevent our perceiving the life-like velocity with which they flew careering from all points against each other, without passing away into the distance. I say that even their exceeding density did not prevent our perceiving this; yet we had no glimpse of the moon or stars, nor was there any flashing forth of the lightning. But the under surfaces of the huge masses of agitated vapor, as well as all terrestrial objects immediately around us, were glowing in the unnatural light of a faintly luminous and distinctly visible gaseous exhalation which hung about and enshrouded the mansion.

'You must not—you shall not behold this!' said I, shudderingly, to Usher, as I led him, with a gentle violence, from the window to a seat. 'These appearances, which bewilder you, are merely electrical phenomena not uncommon—or it may be that they have their ghastly origin in the rank miasma of the tarn. Let us close this casement; the air is chilling and dangerous to your frame. Here is one of your favorite romances. I will read, and you shall listen;—and so we will pass away this terrible night together.'

The antique volume which I had taken up was the *Mad Trist* of Sir Launcelot Canning; but I had called it a favorite of Usher's more in sad jest than in earnest; for, in truth, there is little in its uncouth and unimaginative prolixity which could have had interest for the lofty and spiritual ideality of my friend. It was, however, the only book immediately at hand; and I indulged a vague hope that the excitement which now agitated the hypochondriac might find relief (for the history of mental disorder is full of similar anomalies) even in the extremeness of the folly which I should read. Could I have judged, indeed, by the wild overstrained air of vivacity with which he hearkened, or apparently hearkened, to the words of the tale, I might well have congratulated myself upon the success of my design.

I had arrived at that well-known portion of the story where Ethelred, the hero of the *Trist*, having sought in vain for peaceable admission into the dwelling of the hermit, proceeds to make good an entrance by force. Here, it will be remembered, the words of the narrative run thus:

And Ethelred, who was by nature of a doughty heart, and who was now mighty withal, on account of the powerfulness of the wine which he had drunken, waited no longer to hold parley with the hermit, who, in sooth, was of an obstinate and maliceful turn, but, feeling the rain upon his shoulders, and fearing the rising of the tempest, uplifted his mace outright, and, with blows, made quickly room in the plankings of the door for his gauntleted hand; and now pulling therewith sturdily, he so cracked, and ripped, and tore all asunder, that the noise of the dry and hollow-sounding wood alarumed and reverberated throughout the forest.

At the termination of this sentence I started, and for a moment, paused; for it appeared to me (although I at once concluded that my excited fancy had deceived me)—it appeared to me that, from some very remote portion of the mansion, there came, indistinctly, to my ears, what might have been, in its exact similarity of character, the echo (but a stifled and dull one certainly) of the very cracking and ripping sound which Sir Launcelot had so particularly described. It was, beyond doubt, the coincidence alone which had arrested my attention; for, amid the rattling of the sashes of the casements, and the ordinary commingled noises of the still increasing storm, the sound, in itself, had nothing, surely, which should have interested or disturbed me. I continued the story:

But the good champion Ethelred, now entering within the door, was sore enraged and amazed to perceive no signal of the maliceful hermit; but, in the stead thereof, a dragon of a scaly and prodigious demeanor, and of a fiery tongue, which sate in guard before a palace of gold, with a floor of silver; and upon the wall there hung a shield of shining brass with this legend enwritten—

Who entereth herein, a conqueror hath bin;
Who slayeth the dragon, the shield he shall win;

And Ethelred uplifted his mace, and struck upon the head of the dragon, which fell before him, and gave up his pesty breath, with a shriek so horrid and harsh, and withal so piercing, that Ethelred had fain to close his ears with his hands against the dreadful noise of it, the like whereof was never before heard.

Here again I paused abruptly, and now with a feeling of wild amazement—for there could be no doubt whatever that, in this instance, I did actually hear (although from what direction it proceeded I found it impossible to say) a low and apparently distant, but harsh, protracted, and most unusual screaming or grating sound—the exact counterpart of what my fancy had already conjured up for the dragon's unnatural shriek as described by the romancer.

Oppressed, as I certainly was, upon the occurrence of the second and most extraordinary coincidence, by a thousand conflicting sensations, in which wonder and extreme terror were predominant, I still retained sufficient presence of mind to avoid exciting, by any observation, the sensitive nervousness of my companion. I was by no means certain that he had noticed the sounds in question; although, assuredly, a strange alteration had, during the last few minutes, taken place in his demeanor. From a position fronting my own, he had gradually brought round his chair, so as to sit with his face to the door of the chamber; and thus I could but partially perceive his features, although I saw that his lips trembled as if he were murmuring inaudibly. His head had dropped upon his breast—yet I knew that he was not asleep, from the wide and rigid opening of the eye as I caught a glance of it in profile. The motion of his body, too, was at variance with this idea—for he rocked from side to side with a gentle yet constant and uniform sway. Having rapidly taken notice of all this, I resumed the narrative of Sir Launcelot, which thus proceeded:

> And now, the champion, having escaped from the terrible fury of the dragon, bethinking himself of the brazen shield, and of the breaking up of the enchantment which was upon it, removed the carcass from out of the way before him, and approached valorously over the silver pavement of the castle to where the shield was upon the wall; which in sooth tarried not for his full coming, but fell down at his feet upon the silver floor, with a mighty great and terrible ringing sound.

No sooner had these syllables passed my lips, than—as if a shield of brass had indeed, at the moment, fallen heavily upon a floor of silver—I became aware of a distinct, hollow, metallic and clangorous yet apparently muffled reverberation. Completely unnerved, I leaped to my feet; but the measured rocking movement of Usher was undisturbed. I rushed to the chair in which he sat. His eyes were bent fixedly before him, and throughout his whole countenance there reigned a stony rigidity. But as I placed my hand upon his shoulder, there came a strong shudder over his whole person; a sickly smile quivered about his lips; and I saw that he spoke in a low, hurried, and gibbering murmur, as if unconscious of my presence. Bending closely over him. I at length drank in the hideous import of his words.

'Not hear it?—yes, I hear it, and *have* heard it. Long—long—long —many minutes, many hours, many days, have I heard it—yet I dared not —oh, pity me, miserable wretch that I am!—I dared not—I *dared* not speak! *We have put her living in the tomb!* Said I not that my senses were acute? I *now* tell you that I heard her first feeble movements in the hollow coffin. I heard them—many, many days ago—yet I dared not—*I dared not speak!* And now—to-night—Ethelred—ha! ha!—the breaking of the hermit's door, and the death-cry of the dragon, and the clangor of the shield! —say, rather, the rending of her coffin, and the grating of the iron hinges of her prison, and her struggles within the coppered archway of the vault! Oh whither shall I fly? Will she not be here anon? Is she not hurrying to upbraid me for my haste? Have I not heard her footstep on the stair? Do I not distinguish that heavy and horrible beating of her heart? MADMAN!' here he sprang furiously to his feet, and shrieked out his syllables, as if in the effort he were giving up his soul—'*Madman! I tell you that she now stands without the door!*'

As if in the superhuman energy of his utterance there had been found the potency of a spell, the huge antique panels to which the speaker pointed, threw slowly back, upon the instant, their ponderous and ebony jaws. It was the work of the rushing gust—but then without those doors there DID stand the lofty and enshrouded figure of the lady Madeline of Usher. There was blood upon her white robes, and the evidence of some bitter struggle upon every portion of her emaciated frame. For a moment she remained trembling and reeling to and fro upon the threshold—then, with a low moaning cry, fell heavily inward upon the person of her brother, and in her violent and now final death-agonies, bore him to the floor a corpse, and a victim to the terrors he had anticipated.

From that chamber, and from that mansion, I fled aghast. The storm was still abroad in all its wrath as I found myself crossing the old causeway. Suddenly there shot along the path a wild light, and I turned to see whence a gleam so unusual could have issued; for the vast house and its shadows were alone behind me. The radiance was that of the full, setting, and blood-red moon which now shone vividly through that once barely-discernible fissure of which I have before spoken as extending from the roof of the building, in a zigzag direction, to the base. While I gazed, this fissure rapidly widened—there came a fierce breath of the whirlwind—the entire orb of the satellite burst at once upon my sight—my brain reeled as I saw the mighty walls rushing asunder—there was a long tumultuous shouting sound like the voice of a thousand waters—and the deep and dank tarn at my feet closed sullenly and silently over the fragments of the HOUSE OF USHER.

1840

Many of Edgar Allan Poe's stories, like Grimm fairy tales, owe less allegiance to the external realities of life than to the internal realities of the psyche: dreams, nightmares, wishes, and fears. As Poe noted in a review of Nathaniel Hawthorne's stories, this allegiance to internal reality requires the story to cast something like a spell over the reader.

"A certain unique or single effect to be wrought out": Edgar Allan Poe

The ordinary novel is objectionable, from its length, for reasons already stated in substance. As it cannot be read at one sitting, it deprives itself, of course, of the immense force derivable from *totality*. Worldly interests intervening during the pauses of perusal, modify, annul, or counteract, in a greater or less degree, the impressions of the book. But simple cessation in reading would, of itself, be sufficient to destroy the true unity. In the brief tale, however, the author is enabled to carry out the fulness of his intention, be it what it may. During the hour of perusal the soul of the reader is at the writer's control. There are no external or extrinsic influences—resulting from weariness or interruption.

A skillful literary artist has constructed a tale. If wise, he has not fashioned his thoughts to accommodate his incidents; but having conceived, with deliberate care, a certain unique or single *effect* to be wrought out, he then invents such incidents—he then combines such events as may best aid him in establishing this preconceived effect. If his very initial sentence tend not to the outbringing of this effect, then he has failed in his first step. In the whole composition there should be no word written, of which the tendency, direct or indirect, is not to the one pre-established design. And by such means, with such care and skill, a picture is at length painted which leaves in the mind of him who contemplates it with a kindred art, a sense of the fullest satisfaction. The idea of the tale has been presented unblemished, because undisturbed; and this is an end unattainable by the novel.

HERMAN MELVILLE

(1819–1891)

BARTLEBY THE SCRIVENER

A STORY OF WALL STREET

I am a rather elderly man. The nature of my avocations for the last thirty years has brought me into more than ordinary contact with what would seem an interesting and somewhat singular set of men, of whom as yet nothing that I know of has ever been written:—I mean the law-copyists or scriveners. I have known very many of them, professionally and privately, and if I pleased, could relate divers histories, at which good-natured gentlemen might smile, and sentimental souls might weep. But I waive the biographies of all other scriveners for a few passages in the life of Bartleby, who was a scrivener and strangest I ever saw or heard of. While of other law-copyists I might write the complete life, of Bartleby nothing of that sort can be done. I believe that no materials exist for a full and satisfactory biography of this man. It is an irreparable loss to literature. Bartleby was one of those beings of whom nothing is ascertainable, except from the original sources, and in his case those are very small. What my own astonished eyes saw of Bartleby, *that* is all I know of him, except, indeed, one vague report which will appear in the sequel.

Ere introducing the scrivener, as he first appeared to me, it is fit I make some mention of myself, my *employés,* my business, my chambers, and general surroundings; because some such description is indispensable to an adequate understanding of the chief character about to be presented.

Imprimis.[1] I am a man who, from his youth upward, has been filled with a profound conviction that the easiest way of life is the best. Hence, though I belong to a profession proverbially energetic and nervous, even to turbulence, at times, yet nothing of that sort have I ever suffered to invade my peace. I am one of those unambitious lawyers who never addresses a jury, or in any way draws down public applause; but in the cool tranquillity of a snug retreat, do a snug business among rich men's bonds and mort-gages and title-deeds. All who know me, consider me an eminently *safe* man. The late John Jacob Astor, a personage little given to poetic enthusi-asm, had no hesitation in pronouncing my first grand point to be prudence; my next, method. I do not speak it in vanity, but simply record the fact, that I was not unemployed in my profession by the late John Jacob Astor; a name which, I admit, I love to repeat, for it hath a rounded and orbicular sound to it, and rings like unto bullion. I will freely add, that I was not insensible to the late John Jacob Astor's good opinion.

Some time prior to the period at which this little history begins, my avocations had been largely increased. The good old office, now extinct in the State of New York, of a Master in Chancery, had been conferred upon me. It was not a very arduous office, but very pleasantly remunerative. I seldom lose my temper; much more seldom indulge in dangerous indigna-tion at wrongs and outrages; but I must be permitted to be rash here and declare, that I consider the sudden and violent abrogation of the office of Master in Chancery, by the new Constitution, as a——premature act; inas-much as I had counted upon a life-lease of the profits, whereas I only received those of a few short years. But this is by the way.

My chambers were upstairs at No.——Wall Street. At one end they looked upon the white wall of the interior of a spacious skylight shaft, pene-trating the building from top to bottom. This view might have been consid-ered rather tame than otherwise, deficient in what landscape painters call

---

1. In the first place.

"life." But if so, the view from the other end of my chambers offered, at least, a contrast, if nothing more. In that direction my windows commanded an unobstructed view of a lofty brick wall, black by age and everlasting shade; which wall required no spy-glass to bring out its lurking beauties, but for the benefit of all near-sighted spectators, was pushed up to within ten feet of my window panes. Owing to the great height of the surrounding buildings, and my chambers being on the second floor, the interval between this wall and mine not a little resembled a huge square cistern.

At the period just preceding the advent of Bartleby, I had two persons as copyists in my employment, and a promising lad as an office-boy. First, Turkey; second, Nippers; third, Ginger Nut. These may seem names, the like of which are not usually found in the Directory. In truth they were nicknames, mutually conferred upon each other by my three clerks, and were deemed expressive of their respective persons or characters. Turkey was a short, pursy Englishman of about my own age, that is, somewhere not far from sixty. In the morning, one might say, his face was of a fine florid hue, but after twelve o'clock, meridian—his dinner hour—it blazed like a grate full of Christmas coals; and continued blazing—but, as it were, with a gradual wane—till 6 o'clock P.M. or thereabouts, after which I saw no more of the proprietor of the face, which, gaining its meridian with the sun, seemed to set with it, to rise, culminate, and decline the following day, with the like regularity and undiminished glory. There are many singular coincidences I have known in the course of my life, not the least among which was the fact, that exactly when Turkey displayed his fullest beams from his red and radiant countenance, just then, too, at that critical moment, began the daily period when I considered his business capacities as seriously disturbed for the remainder of the twenty-four hours. Not that he was absolutely idle, or averse to business then; far from it. The difficulty was, he was apt to be altogether too energetic. There was a strange, inflamed, flurried, flighty recklessness of activity about him. He would be incautious in dipping his pen into his inkstand. All his blots upon my documents, were dropped there after twelve o'clock, meridian. Indeed, not only would he be reckless and sadly given to making blots in the afternoon, but some days he went further, and was rather noisy. At such times, too, his face flamed with augmented blazonry, as if cannel coal had been heaped on anthracite. He made an unpleasant racket with his chair; spilled his sand-box; in mending his pens, impatiently split them all to pieces, and threw them on the floor in a sudden passion; stood up and leaned over his table, boxing his papers about in a most indecorous manner, very sad to behold in an elderly man like him. Nevertheless, as he was in many ways a most valuable person to me, and all the time before twelve o'clock, meridian, was the quickest, steadiest creature, too, accomplishing a great deal of work in a style not easy to be matched—for these reasons, I was willing to overlook his eccentricities, though indeed, occasionally, I remonstrated with him. I did this very gently, however, because, though the civilest, nay, the blandest and most reverential of men in the morning, yet in the afternoon he was disposed, upon provocation, to be slightly rash with his tongue, in fact, insolent. Now, valuing his morning services as I did, and resolving not to lose them—yet, at the same time, made uncomfortable by his inflamed ways after twelve o'clock; and being a man of peace, unwilling by my admonitions to call forth unseemly retorts from him—I took upon me, one Saturday noon (he was always worse on Saturdays), to hint to him, very kindly, that perhaps now that he was growing old, it might be well to abridge his labours; in short, he need not come to my chambers after twelve o'clock, but, dinner over, had best go home to his lodgings and rest himself till tea-time. But no; he insisted upon his afternoon devotions. His countenance became intolerably fervid, as he oratorically assured me—gesticulating, with a long ruler, at the other side of the room—that if his services in the morning were useful, how indispensable, then, in the afternoon?

"With submission, sir," said Turkey on this occasion, "I consider myself your right-hand man. In the morning I but marshal and deploy my columns; but in the afternoon I put myself at their head, and gallantly charge the foe, thus!"—and he made a violent thrust with the ruler.

"But the blots, Turkey," intimated I.

"True,—but, with submission, sir, behold these hairs! I am getting old. Surely, sir, a blot or two of a warm afternoon is not to be severely urged against grey hairs. Old age—even if it blot the page—is honourable. With submission, sir, we *both* are getting old."

This appeal to my fellow-feeling was hardly to be resisted. At all events, I saw that go he would not. So I made up my mind to let him stay, resolving, nevertheless, to see to it, that during the afternoon he had to do with my less important papers.

Nippers, the second on my list, was a whiskered, sallow, and, upon the whole, rather piratical-looking young man of about five and twenty. I always deemed him the victim of two evil powers—ambition and indigestion. The ambition was evinced by a certain impatience of the duties of a mere copyist—an unwarrantable usurpation of strictly professional affairs, such as the original drawing up of legal documents. The indigestion seemed betokened in an occasional nervous testiness and grinning irritability, causing the teeth to audibly grind together over mistakes committed in copying; unnecessary maledictions, hissed, rather than spoken, in the heat of business; and especially by a continual discontent with the height of the table where he worked. Though of a very ingenious mechanical turn, Nippers could never get this table to suit him. He put chips under it, blocks of various sorts, bits of pasteboard, and at last went so far as to attempt an exquisite adjustment by final pieces of folded blotting-paper. But no invention would answer. If, for the sake of easing his back, he brought the table lid at a sharp angle well up toward his chin, and wrote there like a man using the steep roof of a Dutch house for his desk—then he declared that it stopped the circulation in his arms. If now he lowered the table to his waistbands, and stooped over it in writing, then there was a sore aching in his back. In short, the truth of the matter was, Nippers knew not what he wanted. Or, if he wanted anything, it was to be rid of a scrivener's table altogether. Among the manifestations of his diseased ambition was a fondness he had for receiving visits from certain ambiguous-looking fellows in seedy coats, whom he called his clients. Indeed I was aware that not only was he, at times, considerable of a ward-politician, but he occasionally did a little business at the Justices' courts, and was not unknown on the steps of the Tombs. I have good reason to believe, however, that one individual who called upon him at my chambers, and who, with a grand air, he insisted was his client, was no other than a dun, and the alleged title-deed, a bill. But with all his failings, and the annoyances he caused me, Nippers, like his compatriot Turkey, was a very useful man to me; wrote a neat, swift hand; and, when he chose, was not deficient in a gentlemanly sort of deportment. Added to this, he always dressed in a gentlemanly sort of way; and so, incidentally, reflected credit upon my chambers. Whereas with respect to Turkey, I had much ado to keep him from being a reproach to me. His clothes were apt to look oily and smell of eating-houses. He wore his pantaloons very loose and baggy in summer. His coats were execrable; his hat not to be handled. But while the hat was a thing of indifference to me, inasmuch as his natural civility and deference, as a dependent Englishman, always led him to doff it the moment he entered the room, yet his coat was another matter. Concerning his coats, I reasoned with him; but with no effect. The truth was, I suppose, that a man with so small an income, could not afford to sport such a lustrous face and a lustrous coat at one and the same time. As Nippers once observed, Turkey's money went chiefly for red ink. One winter day I presented Turkey with a highly-respectable looking coat of my own, a padded grey coat, of a most comfortable warmth, and which buttoned straight up from the knee to the neck. I thought Turkey would appreciate the favour, and abate his rashness and obstreperousness of afternoons. But no. I verily believe that buttoning himself up in so downy and blanketlike a coat had a pernicious effect upon him; upon the same principle that too much oats are bad for horses. In fact, precisely as a rash, restive horse is said to feel his oats, so Turkey felt his coat. It made him insolent. He was a man whom prosperity harmed.

Though concerning the self-indulgent habits of Turkey I had my own private surmises, yet touching Nippers I was well persuaded that whatever might be his faults in other respects, he was, at least, a temperate young man. But, indeed, nature herself seemed to have been his vintner, and at his birth charged him so thoroughly with an irritable, brandy-like disposition, that all subsequent potations were needless. When I consider how, amid the stillness of my chambers, Nippers would sometimes impatiently rise from his seat, and stooping over his table, spread his arms wide apart, seize the whole desk, and move it, and jerk it, with a grim, grinding motion on the floor, as if the table were a perverse voluntary agent, intent on thwarting and vexing him; I plainly perceive that for Nippers, brandy and water were altogether superfluous.

It was fortunate for me that, owing to its peculiar cause—

indigestion—the irritability and consequent nervousness of Nippers, were mainly observable in the morning, while in the afternoon he was comparatively mild. So that Turkey's paroxysms only coming on about twelve o'clock, I never had to do with their eccentricities at one time. Their fits relieved each other like guards. When Nipper's was on, Turkey's was off; and *vice versa.* This was a good natural arrangement under the circumstances.

Ginger Nut, the third on my list, was a lad some twelve years old. His father was a carman, ambitious of seeing his son on the bench instead of a cart, before he died. So he sent him to my office as student at law, errand boy, and cleaner and sweeper, at the rate of one dollar a week. He had a little desk to himself, but he did not use it much. Upon inspection, the drawer exhibited a great array of the shells of various sorts of nuts. Indeed, to this quick-witted youth the whole noble science of the law was contained in a nut-shell. Not the least among the employments of Ginger Nut, as well as one which he discharged with the most alacrity, was his duty as cake and apple purveyor for Turkey and Nippers. Copying law papers being proverbially a dry, husky sort of business, my two scriveners were fain to moisten their mouths very often with Spitzenbergs to be had at the numerous stalls nigh the Custom House and Post Office. Also, they sent Ginger Nut very frequently for that peculiar cake—small, flat, round, and very spicy—after which he had been named by them. Of a cold morning, when business was but dull, Turkey would gobble up scores of these cakes, as if they were mere wafers—indeed they sell them at the rate of six or eight for a penny—the scrape of his pen blending with the crunching of the crisp particles in his mouth. Of all the fiery afternoon blunders and flurried rashness of Turkey, was his once moistening a ginger-cake between his lips, and clapping it on to a mortgage for a seal. I came within an ace of dismissing him then. But he mollified me by making an oriental bow and saying—"With submission, sir, it was generous of me to find you in stationery on my own account."

Now my original business—that of a conveyancer and title hunter, and drawer-up of recondite documents of all sorts—was considerably increased by receiving the master's office. There was now great work for scriveners. Not only must I push the clerks already with me, but I must have additional help. In answer to my advertisement, a motionless young man one morning stood upon my office threshold, the door being open, for it was summer. I can see that figure now—pallidly neat, pitiably respectable, incurably forlorn! It was Bartleby.

After a few words touching his qualifications, I engaged him, glad to have among my corps of copyists a man of so singularly sedate an aspect, which I thought might operate beneficially upon the flighty temper of Turkey, and the fiery one of Nippers.

I should have stated before that ground glass folding-doors divided my premises into two parts, one of which was occupied by my scriveners, the other by myself. According to my humour I threw open these doors, or closed them. I resolved to assign Bartleby a corner by the folding-doors, but on my side of them, so as to have this quiet man within easy call, in case any trifling thing was to be done. I placed his desk close up to a small side-window in that part of the room, a window which originally had afforded a lateral view of certain grimy back-yards and bricks, but which, owing to subsequent erections, commanded at present no view at all, though it gave some light. Within three feet of the panes was a wall, and the light came down from far above, between two lofty buildings, as from a very small opening in a dome. Still further to a satisfactory arrangement, I procured a high green folding screen, which might entirely isolate Bartleby from my sight, though not remove him from my voice. And thus, in a manner, privacy and society were conjoined.

At first Bartleby did an extraordinary quantity of writing. As if long famishing for something to copy, he seemed to gorge himself on my documents. There was no pause for digestion. He ran a day and night line, copying by sun-light and by candle-light. I should have been quite delighted with his application, had he been cheerfully industrious. But he wrote on silently, palely, mechanically.

It is, of course, an indispensable part of a scrivener's business to verify the accuracy of his copy, word by word. Where there are two or more scriveners in an office, they assist each other in this examination, one reading from the copy, the other holding the original. It is a very dull, wearisome, and lethargic affair. I can readily imagine that to some sanguine temperaments it would be altogether intolerable. For example, I cannot credit that the mettlesome poet Byron would have contentedly sat down with Bartleby to examine a law document of, say five hundred pages, closely written in a crimpy hand.

Now and then, in the haste of business, it had been my habit to assist in comparing some brief document myself, calling Turkey or Nippers for this purpose. One object I had in placing Bartleby so handy to me behind the screen, was to avail myself of his services on such trivial occasions. It was on the third day, I think, of his being with me, and before any necessity had arisen for having his own writing examined, that, being much hurried to complete a small affair I had in hand, I abruptly called to Bartleby. In my haste and natural expectancy of instant compliance, I sat with my head bent over the original on my desk, and my right hand sideways, and somewhat nervously extended with the copy, so that immediately upon emerging from his retreat, Bartleby might snatch it and proceed to business without the least delay.

In this very attitude did I sit when I called to him, rapidly stating what it was I wanted him to do—namely, to examine a small paper with me. Imagine my surprise, nay, my consternation, when without moving from his privacy, Bartleby in a singularly mild, firm voice, replied, "I would prefer not to."

I sat awhile in perfect silence, rallying my stunned faculties. Immediately it occurred to me that my ears had deceived me, or Bartleby had entirely misunderstood my meaning. I repeated my request in the clearest tone I could assume. But in quite as clear a one came the previous reply, "I would prefer not to."

"Prefer not to," echoed I, rising in high excitement, and crossing the room with a stride. "What do you mean? Are you moonstruck? I want you to help me compare this sheet here—take it," and I thrust it toward him.

"I would prefer not to," said he.

"I looked at him steadfastly. His face was leanly composed; his grey eye dimly calm. Not a wrinkle of agitation rippled him. Had there been the least uneasiness, anger, impatience or impertinence in his manner; in other words, had there been anything ordinarily human about him, doubtless I should have violently dismissed him from the premises. But as it was, I should have as soon thought of turning my pale plaster-of-paris bust of Cicero out of doors. I stood gazing at him awhile, as he went on with his own writing, and then reseated myself at my desk. This is very strange, thought I. What had one best do? But my business hurried me. I concluded to forget the matter for the present, reserving it for my future leisure. So calling Nippers from the other room, the paper was speedily examined.

A few days after this, Bartleby concluded four lengthy documents, being quadruplicates of a week's testimony taken before me in my High Court of Chancery. It became necessary to examine them. It was an important suit, and great accuracy was imperative. Having all things arranged, I called Turkey, Nippers and Ginger Nut from the next room, meaning to place the four copies in the hands of my four clerks, while I should read from the original. Accordingly Turkey, Nippers and Ginger Nut had taken their seats in a row, each with his document in hand, when I called to Bartleby to join this interesting group.

"Bartleby! quick, I am waiting."

I heard a slow scrape of his chair legs on the uncarpeted floor, and soon he appeared standing at the entrance of his hermitage.

"What is wanted?" said he mildly.

"The copies, the copies," said I hurriedly. "We are going to examine them. There"—and I held toward him the fourth quadruplicate.

"I would prefer not to," he said, and gently disappeared behind the screen.

For a few moments I was turned into a pillar of salt, standing at the head of my seated column of clerks. Recovering myself, I advanced toward the screen, and demanded the reason for such extraordinary conduct.

"*Why* do you refuse?"

"I would prefer not to."

With any other man I should have flown outright into a dreadful passion, scorned all further words, and thrust him ignominiously from my presence. But there was something about Bartleby that not only strangely disarmed me, but in a wonderful manner touched and disconcerted me. I began to reason with him.

"These are your own copies we are about to examine. It is labour saving to you, because one examination will answer for your four papers. It is common usage. Every copyist is bound to help examine his copy. Is it not so? Will you not speak? Answer!"

"I prefer not to," he replied in a flute-like tone. It seemed to me that while I had been addressing him, he carefully revolved every statement that I made; fully comprehended the meaning; could not gainsay the irresistible conclusion; but, at the same time, some paramount consideration prevailed with him to reply as he did.

"You are decided, then, not to comply with my request—a request made according to common usage and common sense?"

He briefly gave me to understand that on that point my judgment was sound. Yes: his decision was irreversible.

It is not seldom the case that when a man is browbeaten in some unprecedented and violently unreasonable way, he begins to stagger in his own plainest faith. He begins, as it were, vaguely to surmise that, wonderful as it may be, all the justice and all the reason are on the other side. Accordingly, if any disinterested persons are present, he turns to them for some reinforcement for his own faltering mind.

"Turkey," said I, "what do you think of this? Am I not right?"

"With submission, sir," said Turkey, with his blandest tone, "I think that you are."

"Nippers," said I, "what do *you* think of it?"

"I think I should kick him out of the office."

(The reader of nice perceptions will here perceive that, it being morning, Turkey's answer is couched in polite and tranquil terms but Nippers's reply in ill-tempered ones. Or, to repeat a previous sentence, Nippers's ugly mood was on duty, and Turkey's off.)

"Ginger Nut," said I, willing to enlist the smallest suffrage in my behalf, "what do *you* think of it?"

"I think, sir, he's a little *luny*," replied Ginger Nut, with a grin.

"You hear what they say," said I, turning towards the screen, "come forth and do your duty."

But he vouchsafed no reply. I pondered a moment in sore perplexity. But once more business hurried me. I determined again to postpone the consideration of this dilemma to my future leisure. With a little trouble we made out to examine the papers without Bartleby, though at every page or two, Turkey deferentially dropped his opinion that this proceeding was quite out of the common; while Nippers, twitching in his chair with a dyspeptic nervousness, ground out between his set teeth occasional hissing maledictions against the stubborn oaf behind the screen. And for his (Nippers's) part, this was the first and the last time he would do another man's business without pay.

Meanwhile Bartleby sat in his hermitage, oblivious to everything but his own peculiar business there.

Some days passed, the scrivener being employed upon another lengthy work. His late remarkable conduct led me to regard his ways narrowly. I observed that he never went to dinner; indeed that he never went any where. As yet I had never of my personal knowledge known him to be outside of my office. He was a perpetual sentry in the corner. At about eleven o'clock though, in the morning, I noticed that Ginger Nut would advance towards the opening in Bartleby's screen, as if silently beckoned thither by a gesture invisible to me where I sat. The boy would then leave the office jingling a few pence, and reappear with a handful of ginger-nuts which he delivered in the hermitage, receiving two of the cakes for his trouble.

He lives, then, on ginger-nuts, thought I; never eats a dinner, properly speaking; he must be a vegetarian then; but no; he never eats even vegetables, he eats nothing but ginger-nuts. My mind then ran on in reveries concerning the probable effects upon the human constitution of living entirely on ginger-nuts. Ginger-nuts are so called because they contain ginger as one of their peculiar constituents, and the final flavouring one. Now what was ginger? A hot, spicy thing. Was Bartleby hot and spicy? Not at all. Ginger, then, had no effect upon Bartleby. Probably he preferred it should have none.

Nothing so aggravates an earnest person as a passive resistance. If the individual so resisted be of a not inhumane temper, and the resisting one perfectly harmless in his passivity; then, in the better moods of the former, he will endeavour charitably to construe to his imagination what proves impossible to be solved by his judgment. Even so, for the most part, I regarded Bartleby and his ways. Poor fellow! thought I, he means no mischief; it is plain he intends no insolence; his aspect sufficiently evinces that his eccentricities are involuntary. He is useful to me. I can get along with him. If I turn him away, the chances are he will fall in with some less indulgent employer, and then he will be rudely treated, and perhaps driven forth miserably to starve. Yes. Here I can cheaply purchase a delicious self-approval. To befriend Bartleby; to humour him in his strange wilfulness, will cost me little or nothing, while I lay up in my soul what will eventually prove a sweet morsel for my conscience. But this mood was not invariable with me. The passiveness of Bartleby sometimes irritated me. I felt strangely goaded on to encounter him in new opposition, to elicit some angry spark from him answerable to my own. But indeed I might as well have essayed to strike fire with my knuckles against a bit of Windsor soap. But one afternoon the evil impulse in me mastered me, and the following little scene ensued:

"Bartleby," said I, "when those papers are all copied, I will compare them with you."

"I would prefer not to."

"How? Surely you do not mean to persist in that mulish vagary?"
No answer.

I threw open the folding-doors near by, and turning upon Turkey and Nippers, exclaimed in an excited manner:

"He says, a second time, he won't examine his papers. What do you think of it, Turkey?"

It was afternoon, be it remembered. Turkey sat glowing like a brass boiler, his bald head steaming, his hands reeling among his blotted papers.

"Think of it?" roared Turkey; "I think I'll just step behind his screen, and black his eyes for him!"

So saying, Turkey rose to his feet and threw his arms into a pugilistic position. He was hurrying away to make good his promise, when I detained him, alarmed at the effect of incautiously rousing Turkey's combativeness after dinner.

"Sit down, Turkey," said I, "and hear what Nippers has to say. What do you think of it, Nippers? Would I not be justified in immediately dismissing Bartleby?"

"Excuse me, that is for you to decide, sir. I think his conduct quite unusual, and indeed unjust, as regards Turkey and myself. But it may only be a passing whim."

"Ah," exclaimed I, "You have strangely changed your mind then— you speak very gently of him now."

"All beer," cried Turkey; "gentleness is effects of beer—Nippers and I dined together to-day. You see how gentle *I* am, sir. Shall I go and black his eyes?"

"You refer to Bartleby, I suppose. No, not to-day, Turkey," I replied; "pray, put up your fists."

I closed the doors, and again advanced towards Bartleby. I felt additional incentives tempting me to my fate. I burned to be rebelled against again. I remembered that Bartleby never left the office.

"Bartleby," said I, "Ginger Nut is away; just step round to the Post Office, won't you? (it was but a three minutes' walk), and see if there is anything for me."

"I would prefer not to."

"You *will* not?"

"I *prefer* not."

I staggered to my desk, and sat there in a deep study. My blind inveteracy returned. Was there any other thing in which I could procure myself to be ignominiously repulsed by this lean, penniless wight?—my hired clerk? What added thing is there, perfectly reasonable, that he will be sure to refuse to do?

"Bartleby!"
No answer.

"Bartleby," in a louder tone.
No answer.

"Bartleby," I roared.

Like a very ghost, agreeably to the laws of magical invocation, at the third summons, he appeared at the entrance of his hermitage.

"Go to the next room, and tell Nippers to come to me."

"I prefer not to," he respectfully and slowly said, and mildly disappeared.

"Very good, Bartleby," said I, in a quiet sort of serenely severe self-possessed tone, intimating the unalterable purpose of some terrible retribution very close at hand. At the moment I half intended something of the kind. But upon the whole, as it was drawing towards my dinner-hour, I thought it best to put on my hat and walk home for the day, suffering much from perplexity and distress of mind.

Shall I acknowledge it? The conclusion of this whole business was, that it soon became a fixed fact of my chambers, that a pale young scrivener, by the name of Bartleby, had a desk there; that he copied for me at the usual rate of four cents a folio (one hundred words); but he was permanently exempt from examining the work done by him, that duty being transferred to Turkey and Nippers, out of compliment doubtless to their superior acuteness; moreover, said Bartleby was never on any account to be despatched on the most trivial errand of any sort; and that even if entreated to take upon him such a matter, it was generally understood that he would prefer not to—in other words, that he would refuse point-blank.

As days passed on, I became considerably reconciled to Bartleby. His steadiness, his freedom from all dissipation, his incessant industry (except when he chose to throw himself into a standing revery behind his screen), his great stillness, his unalterableness of demeanour under all circumstances, made him a valuable acquisition. One prime thing was this,— *he was always there*;—first in the morning, continually through the day, and the last at night. I had a singular confidence in his honesty. I felt my most precious papers perfectly safe in his hands. Sometimes to be sure I could not, for the very soul of me, avoid falling into sudden spasmodic passions with him. For it was exceeding difficult to bear in mind all the time those strange peculiarities, privileges, and unheard of exemptions, forming the tacit stipulations on Bartleby's part under which he remained in my office. Now and then, in the eagerness of despatching pressing business, I would inadvertently summon Bartleby, in a short, rapid tone, to put his finger, say, on the incipient tie of a bit of red tape with which I was about compressing some papers. Of course, from behind the screen the usual answer, "I prefer not to," was sure to come; and then, how could a human creature with the common infirmities of our nature, refrain from bitterly exclaiming upon such perverseness—such unreasonableness. However, every added repulse of this sort which I received only tended to lessen the probability of my repeating the inadvertence.

Here it must be said, that according to the custom of most legal gentlemen occupying chambers in densely-populated law buildings, there were several keys to my door. One was kept by a woman residing in the attic, which person weekly scrubbed and daily swept and dusted my apartments. Another was kept by Turkey for convenience sake. The third I sometimes carried in my own pocket. The fourth I knew not who had.

Now, one Sunday morning I happened to go to Trinity Church, to hear a celebrated preacher, and finding myself rather early on the ground, I thought I would walk round to my chambers for awhile. Luckily I had my key with me; but upon applying it to the lock, I found it resisted by something inserted from the inside. Quite surprised, I called out; when to my consternation a key was turned from within; and thrusting his lean visage at me, and holding the door ajar, the apparition of Bartleby appeared, in his shirt sleeves, and otherwise in a strangely tattered dishabille, saying quietly that he was sorry, but he was deeply engaged just then, and—preferred not admitting me at present. In a brief word or two, he moreover added, that perhaps I had better walk round the block two or three times, and by that time he would probably have concluded his affairs.

Now, the utterly unsurmised appearance of Bartleby, tenanting my law-chambers of a Sunday-morning, with his cadaverously gentlemanly *nonchalance,* yet withal firm and self-possessed, had such a strange effect upon me, that incontinently I slunk away from my own door, and did as desired. But not without sundry twinges of impotent rebellion against the mild effrontery of this unaccountable scrivener. Indeed, it was his wonderful mildness chiefly, which not only disarmed me, but unmanned me, as it were. For I consider that one, for the time, is in a way unmanned when he tranquilly permits his hired clerk to dictate to him, and order him away from his own premises. Furthermore, I was full of uneasiness as to what Bartleby could possibly be doing in my office in his shirt sleeves, and in an otherwise dismantled condition of a Sunday morning. Was anything amiss going on? Nay, that was out of the question. It was not to be thought of for a moment that Bartleby was an immoral person. But what could he be doing there— copying? Nay again, whatever might be his eccentricities, Bartleby was an eminently decorous person. He would be the last man to sit down to his desk in any state approaching to nudity. Besides, it was Sunday; and there was something about Bartleby that forbade the supposition that he would by any secular occupation violate the proprieties of the day.

Nevertheless, my mind was not pacified; and full of a restless curiosity, at last I returned to the door. Without hindrance I inserted my key, opened it, and entered. Bartleby was not to be seen. I looked around anxiously, peeped behind his screen; but it was very plain that he was gone. Upon more closely examining the place, I surmised that for an indefinite period Bartleby must have ate, dressed, and slept in my office, and that too without plate, mirror, or bed. The cushioned seat of a ricketty old sofa in one corner bore the faint impress of a lean, reclining form. Rolled away under his desk, I found a blanket; under the empty grate, a blacking box and brush; on a chair, a tin basin, with soap and a ragged towel; in a newspaper a few crumbs of ginger-nuts and a morsel of cheese. Yes, thought I, it is evident enough that Bartleby has been making his home here, keeping bachelor's hall all by himself. Immediately then the thought came sweeping across me, What miserable friendlessness and loneliness are here revealed! His poverty is great; but his solitude, how horrible! Think of it. Of a Sunday, Wall street is deserted as Petra; and every night of every day it is an emptiness. This building too, which of week-days hums with industry and life, at nightfall echoes with sheer vacancy, and all through Sunday is forlorn. And here Bartleby makes his home; sole spectator of a solitude which he has seen all populous—a sort of innocent and transformed Marius[2] brooding among the ruins of Carthage![3]

For the first time in my life a feeling of overpowering stinging melancholy seized me. Before, I had never experienced aught but a not-unpleasing sadness. The bond of a common humanity now drew me irresistibly to gloom. A fraternal melancholy! For both I and Bartleby were sons of Adam. I remembered the bright silks and sparkling faces I had seen that day, in gala trim, swan-like sailing down the Mississippi of Broadway; and I contrasted them with the pallid copyist, and thought to myself, Ah, happiness courts the light, so we deem the world is gay; but misery hides aloof, so we deem that misery there is none. These sad fancyings—chimeras, doubtless, of a sick and silly brain—led on to other and more special thoughts, concerning the eccentricities of Bartleby. Presentiments of strange discoveries hovered round me. The scrivener's pale form appeared to me laid out, among uncaring strangers, in its shivering winding sheet.

Suddenly I was attracted by Bartleby's closed desk, the key in open sight left in the lock.

I mean no mischief, seek the gratification of no heartless curiosity, thought I; besides, the desk is mine, and its contents, too, so I will make bold to look within. Everything was methodically arranged, the papers smoothly placed. The pigeon holes were deep, and, removing the files of documents, I groped into their recesses. Presently I felt something there, and dragged it out. It was an old bandana handkerchief, heavy and knotted. I opened it, and saw it was a savings' bank.

I now recalled all the quiet mysteries which I had noted in the man. I remembered that he never spoke but to answer; that though at intervals he had considerable time to himself, yet I had never seen him reading—no, not even a newspaper; that for long periods he would stand looking out, at his pale window behind the screen, upon the dead brick wall; I was quite sure he never visited any refectory or eating-house; while his pale face clearly indicated that he never drank beer like Turkey, or tea and coffee even, like other men; that he never went anywhere in particular that I could learn; never went out for a walk, unless indeed that was the case at present; that he had declined telling who he was, or whence he came, or whether he had any relatives in the world; that though so thin and pale, he never com-

---

2. Gaius Marius, a powerful Roman general, alive between 155 (?) B.C.–86 B.C.
3. Ancient city and state on the northern coast of Africa, in the Bay of Tunis; northeast of the modern Tunis.

plained of ill health. And more than all, I remembered a certain unconscious air of pallid—how shall I call it?—of pallid haughtiness, say, or
rather an austere reserve about him, which had positively awed me into my
tame compliance with his eccentricities, when I had feared to ask him to do
the slightest incidental thing for me, even though I might know, from his
long-continued motionlessness, that behind his screen he must be standing
in one of those dead-wall reveries of his.

Revolving all these things, and coupling them with the recently discovered fact that he made my office his constant abiding place and home,
and not forgetful of his morbid moodiness; revolving all these things, a pru-
dential feeling began to steal over me. My first emotions had been those of
pure melancholy and sincerest pity; but just in proportion as the forlorn-
ness of Bartleby grew and grew to my imagination, did that same melancholy merge into fear, that pity into repulsion. So true it is, and so terrible,
too, that up to a certain point the thought or sight of misery enlists our best
affections; but, in certain special cases, beyond that point it does not. They
err who would assert that invariably this is owing to the inherent selfishness
of the human heart. It rather proceeds from a certain hopelessness of rem-
edying excessive and organic ill. To a sensitive being, pity is not seldom
pain. And when at last it is perceived that such pity cannot lead to effectual
succour, common sense bids the soul be rid of it. What I saw that morning
persuaded me that the scrivener was the victim of innate and incurable disorder. I might give alms to his body; but his body did not pain him; it was his
soul that suffered, and his soul I could not reach.

I did not accomplish the purpose of going to Trinity Church that
morning. Somehow, the things I had seen disqualified me for the time from
church-going. I walked homeward, thinking what I would do with Bartleby. Finally, I resolved upon this:—I would put certain calm questions to
him the next morning, touching his history, &c., and if he declined to
answer them openly and unreservedly (and I supposed he would prefer
not), then to give him a twenty dollar bill over and above whatever I might
owe him, and tell him his services were no longer required; but that if in any
other way I could assist him, I would be happy to do so, especially if he
desired to return to his native place, wherever that might be, I would willingly help to defray the expenses. Moreover, if, after reaching home, he
found himself at any time in want of aid, a letter from him would be sure of
a reply.

The next morning came.

"Bartleby," said I, gently calling to him behind his screen.

No reply.

"Bartleby," said I, in a still gentler tone, "come here; I am not
going to ask you to do anything you would prefer not to do—I simply wish
to speak to you."

Upon this he noiselessly slid into view.

"Will you tell me, Bartleby, where you were born?"

"I would prefer not to."

"Will you tell me *anything* about yourself?"

"I would prefer not to."

"But what reasonable objection can you have to speak to me? I feel friendly towards you."

He did not look at me while I spoke, but kept his glance fixed upon my bust of Cicero, which, as I then sat, was directly behind me, some six inches above my head.

"What is your answer, Bartleby?" said I, after waiting a considerable time for a reply, during which his countenance remained immovable, only there was the faintest conceivable tremor of the white attenuated mouth.

"At present I prefer to give no answer," he said, and retired into his hermitage.

It was rather weak in me I confess, but his manner on this occasion nettled me. Not only did there seem to lurk in it a certain calm disdain, but his perverseness seemed ungrateful, considering the undeniable good usage and indulgence he had received from me.

Again I sat ruminating what I should do. Mortified as I was at his behaviour, and resolved as I had been to dismiss him when I entered my office, nevertheless I strangely felt something superstitious knocking at my heart, and forbidding me to carry out my purpose, and denouncing me for a villain if I dared to breathe one bitter word against this forlornest of mankind. At last, familiarly drawing my chair behind his screen, I sat down and said: "Bartleby, never mind then about revealing your history; but let me entreat you, as a friend, to comply as far as may be with the usages of this office. Say now you will help to examine papers to-morrow or next day: in short, say now that in a day or two you will begin to be a little reasonable:— say so, Bartleby."

"At present I would prefer not to be a little reasonable," was his mildly cadaverous reply.

Just then the folding-doors opened, and Nippers approached. He seemed suffering from an unusually bad night's rest, induced by severer indigestion than common. He overheard those final words of Bartleby.

"*Prefer not*, eh?" gritted Nippers—"I'd *prefer* him, if I were you, sir," addressing me—"I'd *prefer* him; I'd give him preferences, the stubborn mule! What is it, sir, pray, that he *prefers* not to do now?"

Bartleby moved not a limb.

"Mr. Nippers," said I, "I'd prefer that you would withdraw for the present."

Somehow, of late I had got into the way of involuntarily using this word "prefer" upon all sorts of not exactly suitable occasions. And I trembled to think that my contact with the scrivener had already and seriously affected me in a mental way. And what further and deeper aberration might it not yet produce? This apprehension had not been without efficacy in determining me to summary means.

As Nippers, looking very sour and sulky, was departing, Turkey blandly and deferentially approached.

"With submission, sir," said he, "yesterday I was thinking about Bartleby here, and I think that if he would but prefer to take a quart of good ale every day, it would do much towards mending him, and enabling him to assist in examining his papers."

"So you have got the word, too," said I, slightly excited.

"With submission, what word, sir," asked Turkey, respectfully crowding himself into the contracted space behind the screen, and by so doing, making me jostle the scrivener. "What word, sir?"

"I would prefer to be left alone here," said Bartleby, as if offended at being mobbed in his privacy.

"*That's* the word, Turkey," said I—"*that's* it."

"Oh, *prefer*? oh, yes—queer word. I never used it myself. But, sir as I was saying, if he would but prefer—"

"Turkey," interrupted I, "you will please withdraw."

"Oh certainly, sir, if you prefer that I should."

As he opened the folding-door to retire, Nippers at his desk caught a glimpse of me, and asked whether I would prefer to have a certain paper copied on blue paper or white. He did not in the least roguishly accent the word prefer. It was plain that it involuntarily rolled from his tongue. I thought to myself, surely I must get rid of a demented man, who already has in some degree turned the tongues, if not the heads, of myself and clerks. But I thought it prudent not to break the dismission at once.

The next day I noticed that Bartleby did nothing but stand at his window in his dead-wall revery. Upon asking him why he did not write, he said that he had decided upon doing no more writing.

"Why, how now? what next?" exclaimed I, "do no more writing?"

"No more."

"And what is the reason?"

"Do you not see the reason for yourself?" he indifferently replied.

I looked steadfastly at him, and perceived that his eyes looked dull and glazed. Instantly it occurred to me, that his unexampled diligence in copying by his dim window for the first few weeks of his stay with me might have temporarily impaired his vision.

I was touched. I said something in condolence with him. I hinted that, of course, he did wisely in abstaining from writing for a while, and urged him to embrace that opportunity of taking wholesome exercise in the open air. This, however, he did not do. A few days after this, my other clerks being absent, and being in a great hurry to despatch certain letters by the mail, I thought that, having nothing else earthly to do, Bartleby would surely be less inflexible than usual, and carry these letters to the Post Office. But he blankly declined. So, much to my inconvenience, I went myself.

Still added days went by. Whether Bartleby's eyes improved or not,

I could not say. To all appearance, I thought they did. But when I asked him if they did, he vouchsafed no answer. At all events, he would do no copying. At last, in reply to my urgings, he informed me that he had permanently given up copying.

"What!" exclaimed I; "suppose your eyes should get entirely well —better than ever before—would you not copy then?"

"I have given up copying," he answered and slid aside.

He remained, as ever, a fixture in my chamber. Nay—if that were possible—he became still more of a fixture than before. What was to be done? He would do nothing in the office: why should he stay there? In plain fact, he had now become a millstone to me, not only useless as a necklace, but afflictive to bear. Yet I was sorry for him. I speak less than truth when I say that, on his own account, he occasioned me uneasiness. If he would but have named a single relative or friend, I would instantly have written, and urged their taking the poor fellow away to some convenient retreat. But he seemed alone, absolutely alone in the universe. A bit of wreckage in the mid-Atlantic. At length, necessities connected with my business tyrannized over all other considerations. Decently as I could, I told Bartleby that in six days' time he must unconditionally leave the office. I warned him to take measures, in the interval, for procuring some other abode. I offered to assist him in this endeavour, if he himself would but take the first step towards a removal. "And when you finally quit me, Bartleby," added I. "I shall see that you go away not entirely unprovided. Six days from this hour, remember."

At the expiration of that period, I peeped behind the screen, and lo! Bartleby was there.

I buttoned up my coat, balanced myself; advanced slowly towards him, touched his shoulder, and said, "The time has come; you must quit this place; I am sorry for you; here is money; but you must go."

"I would prefer not," he replied, with his back still towards me.

"You *must*."

He remained silent.

Now I had an unbounded confidence in this man's common honesty. He had frequently restored to me sixpences and shillings carelessly dropped upon the floor, for I am apt to be very reckless in such shirt-button affairs. The proceeding then which followed will not be deemed extraordinary.

"Bartleby," said I, "I owe you twelve dollars on account; here are thirty-two; the odd twenty are yours.—Will you take it?" and I handed the bills towards him.

But he made no motion.

"I will leave them here then," putting them under a weight on the table. Then taking my hat and cane and going to the door, I tranquilly turned and added—"After you have removed your things from these offices, Bartleby, you will of course lock the door—since every one is now gone for the day but you—and if you please, slip your key underneath the mat, so that I may have it in the morning. I shall not see you again; so good-bye to you. If hereafter in your new place of abode I can be of any service to you, do not fail to advise me by letter. Good-bye, Bartleby, and fare you well."

But he answered not a word; like the last column of some ruined temple, he remained standing mute and solitary in the middle of the otherwise deserted room.

As I walked home in a pensive mood, my vanity got the better of my pity. I could not but highly plume myself on my masterly management in getting rid of Bartleby. Masterly I call it, and such it must appear to any dispassionate thinker. The beauty of my procedure seemed to consist in its perfect quietness. There was no vulgar bullying, no bravado of any sort, no choleric hectoring, no striding to and fro across the apartment, jerking out vehement commands for Bartleby to bundle himself off with his beggarly traps. Nothing of the kind. Without loudly bidding Bartleby depart—as an inferior genius might have done—I *assumed* the ground that depart he must; and upon that assumption built all I had to say. The more I thought over my procedure, the more I was charmed with it. Nevertheless, next morning, upon awakening, I had my doubts,—I had somehow slept off the fumes of vanity. One of the coolest and wisest hours a man has, is just after he awakes in the morning. My procedure seemed as sagacious as ever,—but only in theory. How it would prove in practice—there was the rub. It was truly a beautiful thought to have assumed Bartleby's departure; but, after all, that assumption was simply my own, and none of Bartleby's. The great point was, not whether I had assumed that he would quit me, but whether he would prefer so to do. He was more a man of preferences than assumptions.

After breakfast, I walked down town, arguing the probabilities *pro* and *con*. One moment I thought it would prove a miserable failure, and Bartleby would be found all alive at my office as usual; the next moment it seemed certain that I should see his chair empty. And so I kept veering about. At the corner of Broadway and Canal Street, I saw quite an excited group of people standing in earnest conversation.

"I'll take odds he doesn't," said a voice as I passed.

"Doesn't go?—done!" said I, "put up your money."

I was instinctively putting my hand in my pocket to produce my own, when I remembered that this was an election day. The words I had overheard bore no reference to Bartleby, but to the success or non-success of some candidate for the mayoralty. In my intent frame of mind, I had, as it were, imagined that all Broadway shared in my excitement, and were debating the same question with me. I passed on, very thankful that the uproar of the street screened my momentary absent-mindedness.

As I had intended, I was earlier than usual at my office door. I stood listening for a moment. All was still. He must be gone. I tried the knob. The door was locked. Yes, my procedure had worked to a charm; he indeed must be vanished. Yet a certain melancholy mixed with this: I was almost sorry for my brilliant success. I was fumbling under the door mat for the key, which Bartleby was to have left there for me, when accidentally my knee knocked against a panel, producing a summoning sound, and in response a voice came to me from within—"Not yet; I am occupied."

It was Bartleby.

I was thunderstruck. For an instant I stood like the man who, pipe in mouth, was killed one cloudless afternoon long ago in Virginia, by summer lightning; at his own warm open window he was killed, and remained leaning out there upon the dreamy afternoon, till some one touched him, and he fell.

"Not gone!" I murmured at last. But again obeying that wondrous ascendency which the inscrutable scrivener had over me—and from which ascendency, for all my chafing, I could not completely escape—I slowly went down stairs and out into the street, and while walking round the block, considered what I should next do in this unheard-of perplexity. Turn the man out by an actual thrusting I could not; to drive him away by calling him hard names would not do; calling in the police was an unpleasant idea; and yet, permit him to enjoy his cadaverous triumph over me,—this too I could not think of. What was to be done? or, if nothing could be done, was there anything further that I could *assume* in the matter? Yes, as before I had prospectively assumed that Bartleby would depart, so now I might retrospectively assume that departed he was. In the legitimate carrying out of this assumption, I might enter my office in a great hurry, and pretending not to see Bartleby at all, walk straight against him as if he were air. Such a proceeding would in a singular degree have the appearance of a home-thrust. It was hardly possible that Bartleby could withstand such an application of the doctrine of assumptions. But, upon second thought, the success of the plan seemed rather dubious. I resolved to argue the matter over with him again.

"Bartleby," said I, entering the office, with a quietly severe expression, "I am seriously displeased. I am pained, Bartleby. I had thought better of you. I had imagined you of such a gentlemanly organization, that in any delicate dilemma a slight hint would suffice—in short, an assumption; but it appears I am deceived. Why," I added, unaffectedly starting, "you have not even touched that money yet," pointing to it, just where I had left it the evening previous.

He answered nothing.

"Will you, or will you not, quit me?" I now demanded in a sudden passion, advancing close to him.

"I would prefer *not* to quit you," he replied, gently emphasizing the *not*.

"What earthly right have you to stay here? Do you pay any rent? Do you pay my taxes? Or is this property yours?"

He answered nothing.

"Are you ready to go on and write now? Are your eyes recovered?

Could you copy a small paper for me this morning? or help examine a few lines? or step round to the Post Office? In a word, will you do any thing at all, to give a colouring to your refusal to depart the premises?"

He silently retired into his hermitage.

I was now in such a state of nervous resentment that I thought it but prudent to check myself, at present, from further demonstrations. Bartleby and I were alone. I remembered the tragedy of the unfortunate Adams and the still more unfortunate Colt in the solitary office of the latter; and how poor Colt, being dreadfully incensed by Adams, and imprudently permitting himself to get wildly excited, was at unawares hurried into his fatal act—an act which certainly no man could possibly deplore more than the actor himself. Often it had occurred to me in my ponderings upon the subject, that had that altercation taken place in the public street, or at a private residence, it would not have terminated as it did. It was the circumstance of being alone in a solitary office, upstairs, of a building entirely unhallowed by humanizing domestic associations—an uncarpeted office, doubtless, of a dusty, haggard sort of appearance;—this it must have been, which greatly helped to enhance the irritable desperation of the hapless Colt.

But when this old Adam of resentment rose in me and tempted me concerning Bartleby, I grappled him and threw him. How? Why, simply by recalling the divine injunction: "A new commandment give I unto you, that ye love one another." Yes, this it was that saved me. Aside from higher considerations, charity often operates as a vastly wise and prudent principle—a great safeguard to its possessor. Men have committed murder for jealousy's sake, and anger's sake, and hatred's sake, and selfishness' sake, and spiritual pride's sake; but no man that ever I heard of, ever committed a diabolical murder for sweet charity's sake. Mere self-interest, then, if no better motive can be enlisted, should, especially with high-tempered men, prompt all beings to charity and philanthropy. At any rate, upon the occasion in question, I strove to drown my exasperated feelings toward the scrivener by benevolently construing his conduct. Poor fellow, poor fellow! thought I, he doesn't mean any thing; and besides, he has seen hard times, and ought to be indulged.

I endeavoured also immediately to occupy myself, and at the same time to comfort my despondency. I tried to fancy that in the course of the morning, at such time as might prove agreeable to him, Bartleby, of his own free accord, would emerge from his hermitage, and take up some decided line of march in the direction of the door. But no. Half-past twelve o'clock came; Turkey began to glow in the face, overturn his inkstand, and become generally obstreperous; Nippers abated down into quietude and courtesy; Ginger Nut munched his noon apple; and Bartleby remained standing at his window in one of his profoundest dead-wall reveries. Will it be credited? Ought I to acknowledge it? That afternoon I left the office without saying one further word to him.

Some days now passed, during which at leisure intervals I looked a little into "Edwards on the Will," and "Priestley on Necessity." Under the circumstances, those books induced a salutary feeling. Gradually I slid into the persuasion that these troubles of mine, touching the scrivener, had been all predestinated from eternity, and Bartleby was billeted upon me for some mysterious purpose of an all-wise Providence, which it was not for a mere mortal like me to fathom. Yes, Bartleby, stay there behind your screen, thought I; I shall persecute you no more; you are harmless and noiseless as any of these old chairs; in short, I never feel so private as when I know you are here. At least I see it, I feel it; I penetrate to the predestinated purpose of my life. I am content. Others may have loftier parts to enact; but my mission in this world, Bartleby, is to furnish you with office room for such period as you may see fit to remain.

I believe that this wise and blessed frame of mind would have continued with me had it not been for the unsolicited and uncharitable remarks obtruded upon me by my professional friends who visited the rooms. But thus it often is, that the constant friction of illiberal minds wears out at last the best resolves of the more generous. Though to be sure, when I reflected upon it, it was not strange that people entering my office should be struck by the peculiar aspect of the unaccountable Bartleby, and so be tempted to throw out some sinister observations concerning him. Sometimes an attorney having business with me, and calling at my office, and finding no one but the scrivener there, would undertake to obtain some sort of precise information from him touching my whereabouts; but without heeding his idle talk, Bartleby would remain standing immovable in the middle of the room. So, after contemplating him in that position for a time, the attorney would depart, no wiser than he came.

Also, when a Reference was going on, and the room full of lawyers and witnesses and business was driving fast, some deeply occupied legal gentleman present, seeing Bartleby wholly unemployed, would request him to run round to his (the legal gentleman's) office and fetch some papers for him. Thereupon, Bartleby would tranquilly decline, and yet remain idle as before. Then the lawyer would give a great stare, and turn to me. And what could I say? At last I was made aware that all through the circle of my professional acquaintance, a whisper of wonder was running round, having reference to the strange creature I kept at my office. This worried me very much. And as the idea came upon me of his possibly turning out a long-lived man, and keep occupying my chambers, and denying my authority; and perplexing my visitors; and scandalizing my professional reputation; and casting a general gloom over the premises; keeping soul and body together to the last upon his savings (for doubtless he spent but half a dime a day), and in the end perhaps outlive me, and claim possession of my office by right of his perpetual occupancy: as all these dark anticipations crowded upon me more and more, and my friends continually intruded their relentless remarks upon the apparition in my room, a great change was wrought in me. I resolved to gather all my faculties together, and for ever rid me of this intolerable incubus.[4]

Ere resolving any complicated project, however, adapted to this end, I first simply suggested to Bartleby the propriety of his permanent departure. In a calm and serious tone, I commended the idea to his careful and mature consideration. But having taken three days to meditate upon it, he apprised me that his original determination remained the same; in short, that he still preferred to abide with me.

What shall I do? I now said to myself, buttoning up my coat to the last button. What shall I do? what ought I to do? what does conscience say I *should* do with this man, or rather ghost? Rid myself of him, I must; go, he shall. But how? You will not thrust him, the poor, pale, passive mortal,— you will not thrust such a helpless creature out of your door? you will not dishonour yourself by such cruelty? No, I will not, I cannot do that. Rather would I let him live and die here, and then mason up his remains in the wall. What then will you do? For all your coaxing, he will not budge. Bribes he leaves under your own paper-weight on your table; in short, it is quite plain that he prefers to cling to you.

Then something severe, something unusual must be done. What! surely you will not have him collared by a constable, and commit his inno-cent pallor to the common jail? And upon what ground could you procure such a thing to be done?—a vagrant, is he? What! he a vagrant, a wan-derer, who refuses to budge? It is because he will *not* be a vagrant, then, that you seek to count him *as* a vagrant. That is too absurd. No visible means of support: there I have him. Wrong again: for indubitably he *does* support himself, and that is the only unanswerable proof that any man can show of his possessing the means so to do. No more then. Since he will not quit me, I must quit him. I will change my offices; I will move elsewhere; and give him fair notice, that if I find him on my new premises I will then proceed against him as a common trespasser.

Acting accordingly, next day I thus addressed him: "I find these chambers too far from the City Hall; the air is unwholesome. In a word, I propose to remove my offices next week, and shall no longer require your services. I tell you this now, in order that you may seek another place."

He made no reply, and nothing more was said.

On the appointed day I engaged carts and men, proceeded to my chambers, and having but little furniture, everything was removed in a few hours. Throughout all, the scrivener remained standing behind the screen, which I directed to be removed the last thing. It was withdrawn; and being folded up like a huge folio, left him the motionless occupant of a naked room. I stood in the entry watching him a moment, while something from within me upbraided me.

---

4. Something that is nightmarishly oppressive; a nightmare.

I re-entered, with my hand in my pocket—and—and my heart in my mouth.

"Good-bye, Bartleby; I am going—good-bye, and God some way bless you; and take that," slipping something in his hand. But it dropped upon the floor and then—strange to say—I tore myself from him whom I had so longed to be rid of.

Established in my new quarters, for a day or two I kept the door locked, and started at every football in the passages. When I returned to my rooms after any little absence, I would pause at the threshold for an instant, and attentively listen, ere applying my key. But these fears were needless. Bartleby never came nigh me.

I thought all was going well, when a perturbed looking stranger visited me, inquiring whether I was the person who had recently occupied rooms at No.——Wall street.

Full of forebodings, I replied that I was.

"Then sir," said the stranger, who proved a lawyer, "you are responsible for the man you left there. He refuses to do any copying, he refuses to do anything; and he says he prefers not to; and he refuses to quit the premises."

"I am very sorry, sir," said I, with assumed tranquillity, but an inward tremor, "but, really, the man you allude to is nothing to me—he is no relation or apprentice of mine, that you should hold me responsible for him."

"In mercy's name, who is he?"

"I certainly cannot inform you. I know nothing about him. Formerly I employed him as a copyist; but he has done nothing for me now for some time past."

"I shall settle him then,—good morning, sir."

Several days passed, and I heard nothing more; and though I often felt a charitable prompting to call at the place and see poor Bartleby, yet a certain squeamishness of I know not what withheld me.

All is over with him, by this time, thought I at last, when through another week no further intelligence reached me. But coming to my room the day after, I found several persons waiting at my door in a high state of nervous excitement.

"That's the man—here he comes," cried the foremost one, whom I recognized as the lawyer who had previously called upon me alone.

"You must take him away, sir, at once," cried a portly person among them, advancing upon me, and whom I knew to be the landlord of No.——Wall street. "These gentlemen, my tenants, cannot stand it any longer; Mr. B——," pointing to the lawyer, "has turned him out of his room, and he now persists in haunting the building generally, sitting upon the banisters of the stairs by day, and sleeping in the entry by night. Everybody here is concerned; clients are leaving the offices; some fears are entertained of a mob; something you must do, and that without delay."

Aghast at this torrent, I fell back before it, and would fain have locked myself in my new quarters. In vain I persisted that Bartleby was nothing to me—no more than to any one else there. In vain:—I was the last person known to have anything to do with him, and they held me to the terrible account. Fearful then of being exposed in the papers (as one person present obscurely threatened) I considered the matter, and at length said, that if the lawyer would give me a confidential interview with the scrivener, in his (the lawyer's) own room, I would that afternoon strive my best to rid them of the nuisance they complained of.

Going up stairs to my old haunt, there was Bartleby silently sitting upon the banister at the landing.

"What are you doing here, Bartleby?" said I.

"Sitting upon the banister," he mildly replied.

I motioned him into the lawyer's room, who then left us.

"Bartleby," said I, "are you aware that you are the cause of great tribulation to me, by persisting in occupying the entry after being dismissed from the office?"

No answer.

"Now one of two things must take place. Either you must do something, or something must be done to you. Now what sort of business would you like to engage in? Would you like to re-engage in copying for some one?"

"No; I would prefer not to make any change."

"Would you like a clerkship in a dry-goods store?"

"There is too much confinement about that. No, I would not like a clerkship; but I am not particular."

"Too much confinement," I cried, "why you keep yourself confined all the time!"

"I would prefer not to take a clerkship," he rejoined, as if to settle that little item at once.

"How would a bartender's business suit you? There is no trying of the eyesight in that."

"I would not like it at all; though, as I said before, I am not particular."

His unwonted wordiness inspirited me. I returned to the charge.

"Well then, would you like to travel through the country collecting bills for the merchants? That would improve your health."

"No, I would prefer to be doing something else."

"How then would going as a companion to Europe to entertain some young gentleman with your conversation,—how would that suit you?"

"Not at all. It does not strike me that there is anything definite about that. I like to be stationary. But I am not particular."

"Stationary you shall be then," I cried, now losing all patience, and for the first time in all my exasperating connection with him fairly flying into a passion. "If you do not go away from these premises before night, I shall feel bound—indeed I *am* bound—to—to—to quit the premises myself!" I rather absurdly concluded, knowing not with what possible threat to try to frighten his immobility into compliance. Despairing of all further efforts, I was precipitately leaving him, when a final thought occurred to me—one which had not been wholly unindulged before.

"Bartleby," said I, in the kindest tone I could assume under such exciting circumstances, "will you go home with me now—not to my office, but my dwelling—and remain there till we can conclude upon some convenient arrangement for you at our leisure? Come, let us start now, right away."

"No: at present I would prefer not to make any change at all."

I answered nothing; but effectually dodging every one by the suddenness and rapidity of my flight, rushed from the building, ran up Wall street toward Broadway, and then jumping into the first omnibus was soon removed from pursuit. As soon as tranquillity returned I distinctly perceived that I had now done all that I possibly could, both in respect to the demands of the landlord and his tenants, and with regard to my own desire and sense of duty, to benefit Bartleby, and shield him from rude persecution. I now strove to be entirely care-free and quiescent; and my conscience justified me in the attempt; though indeed it was not so successful as I could have wished. So fearful was I of being again hunted out by the incensed landlord and his exasperated tenants, that, surrendering my business to Nippers, for a few days I drove about the upper part of the town and through the suburbs, in my rockaway;[5] crossed over to Jersey City and Hoboken, and paid fugitive visits to Manhattanville and Astoria. In fact I almost lived in my rockaway for the time.

When again I entered my office, lo, a note from the landlord lay upon the desk. I opened it with trembling hands. It informed me that the writer had sent to the police, and had Bartleby removed to the Tombs as a vagrant. Moreover, since I knew more about him than any one else, he wished me to appear at that place, and make a suitable statement of the facts. These tidings had a conflicting effect upon me. At first I was indignant; but at last almost approved. The landlord's energetic, summary disposition had led him to adopt a procedure which I do not think I would have decided upon myself; and yet as a last resort, under such peculiar circumstances, it seemed the only plan.

As I afterwards learned, the poor scrivener, when told that he must be conducted to the Tombs, offered not the slightest obstacle, but in his own pale, unmoving way silently acquiesced.

Some of the compassionate and curious bystanders joined the party; and headed by one of the constables, arm-in-arm with Bartleby the silent procession filed its way through all the noise, and heat, and joy of the roaring thoroughfares at noon.

The same day I received the note I went to the Tombs, or, to speak more properly, the Halls of Justice. Seeking the right officer, I stated the

----
5. A four-wheeled carriage with two seats and a standing top.

purpose of my call, and was informed that the individual I described was indeed within. I then assured the functionary that Bartleby was a perfectly honest man, and greatly to be a compassionated (however unaccountable) eccentric. I narrated all I knew, and closed by suggesting the idea of letting him remain in as indulgent confinement as possible till something less harsh might be done—though indeed I hardly knew what. At all events if nothing else could be decided upon, the alms-house must receive him. I then begged to have an interview.

Being under no disgraceful charge, and quite serene and harmless in all his ways, they had permitted him freely to wander about the prison, and especially in the inclosed grass-platted yards thereof. And so I found him there, standing all alone in the quietest of the yards, his face toward a high wall—while all around, from the narrow slits of the jail windows, I thought I saw peering out upon him the eyes of murderers and thieves.

"Bartleby!"

"I know you," he said, without looking around,—"and I want nothing to say to you."

"It was not I that brought you here, Bartleby," said I, keenly pained at his implied suspicion. "And to you, this should not be so vile a place. Nothing reproachful attaches to you by being here. And see, it is not so sad a place as one might think. Look, there is the sky and here is the grass."

"I know where I am," he replied, but would say nothing more, and so I left him.

As I entered the corridor again a broad, meat-like man in an apron accosted me, and jerking his thumb over his shoulder said—"Is that your friend?"

"Yes."

"Does he want to starve? If he does, let him live on the prison fare, that's all."

"Who are you?" asked I, not knowing what to make of such an unofficially speaking person in such a place.

"I am the grub-man. Such gentlemen as have friends here, hire me to provide them with something good to eat."

"Is this so?" said I, turning to the turnkey.

He said it was.

"Well then," said I, slipping some silver into the grub-man's hands (for so they called him), "I want you to give particular attention to my friend there: let him have the best dinner you can get. And you must be as polite to him as possible."

"Introduce me, will you?" said the grub-man, looking at me with an expression which seemed to say he was all impatience for an opportunity to give a specimen of his breeding.

Thinking it would prove of benefit to the scrivener, I acquiesced; and asking the grub-man his name, went up with him to Bartleby.

"Bartleby, this is Mr. Cutlets; you will find him very useful to you."

"Your sarvant, sir, your sarvant," said the grub-man, making a low salutation behind his apron. "Hope you find it pleasant here, sir;—spacious grounds—cool apartments, sir—hope you'll stay with us some time—try to make it agreeable. May Mrs. Cutlets and I have the pleasure of your company to dinner, sir, in Mrs. Cutlets' private room?"

"I prefer not to dine to-day," said Bartleby, turning away. "It would disagree with me; I am unused to dinners." So saying, he slowly moved to the other side of the inclosure and took up a position fronting the dead-wall.

"How's this?" said the grub-man, addressing me with a stare of astonishment. "He's odd, ain't he?"

"I think he is a little deranged," said I, sadly.

"Deranged? deranged is it? Well now, upon my word, I thought that friend of yourn was a gentleman forger; they are always pale and genteel-like, them forgers. I can't help pity 'em—can't help it, sir. Did you know Monroe Edwards?" he added touchingly, and paused. Then, laying his hand pityingly on my shoulder, sighed, "he died of the consumption at Sing-Sing.[6] So you weren't acquainted with Monroe?"

"No, I was never socially acquainted with any forgers. But I cannot stop longer. Look to my friend yonder. You will not lose by it. I will see you again."

Some few days after this, I again obtained admission to the Tombs, and went through the corridors in quest of Bartleby; but without finding him.

"I saw him coming from his cell not long ago," said a turnkey, "maybe he's gone to loiter in the yards."

So I went in that direction.

"Are you looking for the silent man?" said another turnkey passing me. "Yonder he lies—sleeping in the yard there. 'Tis not twenty minutes since I saw him lie down."

The yard was entirely quiet. It was not accessible to the common prisoners. The surrounding walls, of amazing thickness, kept off all sounds behind them. The Egyptian character of the masonry weighed upon me with its gloom. But a soft imprisoned turf grew under foot. The heart of the eternal pyramids, it seemed, wherein by some strange magic, through the clefts grass-seed, dropped by birds, had sprung.

Strangely huddled at the base of the wall—his knees drawn up, and lying on his side, his head touching the cold stones—I saw the wasted Bartleby. But nothing stirred. I paused; then went close up to him; stooped over, and saw that his dim eyes were open; otherwise he seemed profoundly sleeping. Something prompted me to touch him. I felt his hand, when a tingling shiver ran up my arm and down my spine to my feet.

---

6. Founded in 1825, Sing-Sing is a state prison for men that became infamous for its harsh measures.

The round face of the grub-man peered upon me now. "His dinner is ready. Won't he dine to-day, either? Or does he live without dining?"

"Lives without dining," said I, and closed the eyes.

"Eh!—He's asleep, ain't he?"

"With kings and counsellors," murmured I.

There would seem little need for proceeding further in this history. Imagination will readily supply the meagre recital of poor Bartleby's interment. But ere parting with the reader, let me say, that if this little narrative has sufficiently interested him, to awaken curiosity as to who Bartleby was, and what manner of life he led prior to the present narrator's making his acquaintance, I can only reply, that in such curiosity I fully share—but am wholly unable to gratify it. Yet here I hardly know whether I should divulge one little item of rumour, which came to my ear a few months after the scrivener's decease. Upon what basis it rested, I could never ascertain; and hence, how true it is I cannot now tell. But inasmuch as this vague report has not been without a certain strange suggestive interest to me, however sad, it may prove the same with some others; and so I will briefly mention it. The report was this: that Bartleby had been a subordinate clerk in the Dead Letter Office at Washington, from which he had been suddenly removed by a change in the administration. When I think over this rumour I cannot adequately express the emotions which seize me. Dead letters! Does it not sound like dead men? Conceive a man by nature and misfortune prone to a pallid hopelessness: can any business seem more fitted to heighten it than that of continually handling these dead letters, and assorting them for the flames? For by the cartload they are annually burned. Sometimes from out the folded paper the pale clerk takes a ring:—the finger it was meant for, perhaps, moulders in the grave; a bank-note sent in swiftest charity:—he whom it would relieve, nor eats nor hungers any more; pardon for those who died despairing; hope for those who died unhoping; good tidings for those who died stifled by unrelieved calamities. On errands of life, these letters speed to death.

Ah Bartleby! Ah humanity!

1853

Herman Melville's fiction sometimes combines the realism of the typical nineteenth-century novel with a surrealism that reaches back toward the folk tale or forward toward such twentieth-century writers as Franz Kafka. Argentinian writer Jorge Luis Borges, himself no stranger to such a melding of styles, notes that "Bartleby" mixes these elements in a surprising way.

"The universe teems with confirmation of this fear": Jorge Luis Borges

Moby Dick is written in a romantic dialect of English, an impassioned dialect that alternates or combines rhetorical schemes of Shakespeare and Thomas De Quincey, of Browne and Carlyle; "Bartleby" is written in a calm, even droll diction whose deliberate application to an infamous subject matter seems to prefigure Kafka. Nevertheless, between both fictions, there is a secret, central affinity. In the former, Ahab's monomania disturbs and finally destroys all the men on the boat; in the latter, Bartleby's frank nihilism contaminates his companions and even the stolid man who tells Bartleby's story, the man who pays him for his imaginary labors. It is as if Melville had written: "It is enough that one man is irrational for others to be irrational and for the universe to be irrational." The history of the universe teems with confirmations of this fear.

"Bartleby" belongs to the volume entitled *The Piazza Tales* (New York and London, 1856). About another narrative in that book, John Freeman observes that it could not be fully understood until Joseph Conrad published certain analogous works, almost half a century later. I would observe that the work of Kafka projects a curious, hind light on "Bartleby." "Bartleby" already defines a genre that Kafka would re-invent and quarry around 1919: the genre of fantasies of conduct and feeling or, as it is unfortunately termed today, the psychological. Beyond that, the opening pages of "Bartleby" do not foreshadow Kafka; rather, they allude to or repeat Dickens. . . . In 1849, Melville had published *Mardi,* an entangled and even unreadable novel, but one whose basic argument anticipates the obsessions and the mechanism of *The Castle, The Trial* and *Amerika*: it presents an infinite persecution across an infinite sea.

GUSTAVE FLAUBERT

(1821–1880)

THE LEGEND OF SAINT JULIAN THE HOSPITALLER

translated from the French by Michele Grimaud

1

Julian's father and mother dwelt in a castle built on the slope of a hill, in the heart of the woods.

The towers at its four corners had pointed roofs covered with leaden tiles, and the foundation rested upon solid rocks, which descended abruptly to the bottom of the moat.

In the courtyard, the stone flagging was as immaculate as the floor of a church. Long rain-spouts, representing dragons with yawning jaws, directed the water towards the cistern, and on each window-sill of the castle a basil or a heliotrope bush bloomed, in painted flower-pots.

A second enclosure, surrounded by a fence, comprised a fruit-orchard, a garden decorated with figures wrought in bright-hued flowers, an arbour with several bowers, and a mall for the diversion of the pages. On the other side were the kennel, the stables, the bakery, the wine-press and the barns. Around these spread a pasture, also enclosed by a strong hedge.

Peace had reigned so long that the portcullis was never lowered; the moats were filled with water; swallows built their nests in the cracks of the battlements, and as soon as the sun shone too strongly, the archer who all day long paced to and fro on the curtain, withdrew to the watch-tower and slept soundly.

Inside the castle, the locks on the doors shone brightly; costly tapestries hung in the apartments to keep out the cold; the closets over-flowed with linen, the cellar was filled with casks of wine, and the oak chests fairly groaned under the weight of money-bags.

In the armoury could be seen, between banners and the heads of wild beasts, weapons of all nations and of all ages, from the slings of the Amalekites and the javelins of the Garamantes, to the broad-swords of the Saracens and the coats of mail of the Normans.

The largest spit in the kitchen could hold an ox; the chapel was as gorgeous as a king's oratory. There was even a Roman bath in a secluded part of the castle, though the good lord of the manor refrained from using it, as he deemed it a heathenish practice.

Wrapped always in a cape made of fox-skins, he wandered about the castle, rendered justice among his vassals and settled his neighbours' quarrels. In the winter, he gazed dreamily at the falling snow, or had stories read aloud to him. But as soon as the fine weather returned, he would mount his mule and sally forth into the country roads, edged with ripening wheat, to talk with the peasants, to whom he distributed advice. After a number of adventures he took unto himself a wife of high lineage.

She was pale and serious, and a trifle haughty. The horns of her head-dress touched the top of the doors and the hem of her gown trailed far behind her. She conducted her household like a cloister. Every morning she distributed work to the maids, supervised the making of preserves and unguents, and afterwards passed her time in spinning, or in embroidering altar-cloths. In response to her fervent prayers, God granted her a son!

Then there was great rejoicing; and they gave a feast which lasted three days and four nights, with illuminations and soft music. Chickens as large as sheep, and the rarest spices were served; for the entertainment of the guests, a dwarf crept out of a pie; and when the bowls were too few, for the crowd swelled continuously, the wine was drunk from helmets and hunting-horns.

The young mother did not appear at the feast. She was quietly resting in bed. One night she awoke, and beheld in a moonbeam that crept through the window something that looked like a moving shadow. It was an old man clad in sackcloth, who resembled a hermit. A rosary dangled at his side and he carried a beggar's sack on his shoulder. He approached the foot of the bed, and without opening his lips said: "Rejoice, O mother! Thy son shall be a saint."

She would have cried out, but the old man, gliding along the moonbeam, rose through the air and disappeared. The songs of the banqueters grew louder. She could hear angels' voices, and her head sank back on the pillow, which was surmounted by the bone of a martyr, framed in precious stones.

The following day, the servants, upon being questioned, declared, to a man, that they had seen no hermit. Then, whether dream or fact, this must certainly have been a communication from heaven; but she took care not to speak of it, lest she should be accused of presumption.

The guests departed at daybreak, and Julian's father stood at the castle gate, where he had just bidden farewell to the last one, when a beggar suddenly emerged from the mist and confronted him. He was a gipsy—for he had a braided beard and wore silver bracelets on each arm. His eyes burned and, in an inspired way, he muttered some disconnected words: "Ah! Ah! thy son!—great bloodshed—great glory—happy always—an emperor's family."

Then he stooped to pick up the alms thrown to him, and disappeared in the tall grass.

The lord of the manor looked up and down the road and called as loudly as he could. But no one answered him! The wind only howled and the morning mists were fast dissolving.

He attributed his vision to a dullness of the brain resulting from too much sleep. "If I should speak of it," quoth he, "people would laugh at me." Still, the glory that was to be his son's dazzled him, albeit the meaning of the prophecy was not clear to him, and he even doubted that he had heard it.

The parents kept their secret from each other. But both cherished the child with equal devotion, and as they considered him marked by God, they had great regard for his person. His cradle was lined with the softest feathers, and a lamp representing a dove burned continually over it; three nurses rocked him night and day, and with his pink cheeks and blue eyes, brocaded cloak and embroidered cap, he looked like a little Jesus. He cut all his teeth without even a whimper.

When he was seven years old his mother taught him to sing, and his father lifted him upon a tall horse, to inspire him with courage. The child smiled with delight, and soon became familiar with everything pertaining to chargers. An old and very learned monk taught him the Gospel, the Arabic numerals, the Latin letters, and the art of painting delicate designs on vellum. They worked in the top of a tower, away from all noise and disturbance.

When the lesson was over, they would go down into the garden and study the flowers.

Sometimes a herd of cattle passed through the valley below, in charge of a man in Oriental dress. The lord of the manor, recognising him as a merchant, would despatch a servant after him. The stranger, becoming confident, would stop on his way and after being ushered into the castle-hall, would display pieces of velvet and silk, trinkets and strange objects whose use was unknown in those parts. Then, in due time, he would take leave, without having been molested and with a handsome profit.

At other times, a band of pilgrims would knock at the door. Their wet garments would be hung in front of the hearth and after they had been refreshed by food they would relate their travels, and discuss the uncertainty of vessels on the high seas, their long journeys across burning sands, the ferocity of the infidels, the caves of Syria, the Manger and the Holy Sepulchre. They made presents to the young heir of beautiful shells, which they carried in their cloaks.

The lord of the manor very often feasted his brothers-at-arms, and over the wine the old warriors would talk of battles and attacks, of war-machines and of the frightful wounds they had received, so that Julian, who was a listener, would scream with excitement; then his father felt convinced that some day he would be a conqueror. But in the evening, after the Angelus, when he passed through the crowd of beggars who clustered about the church-door, he distributed his alms with so much modesty and nobility that his mother fully expected to see him become an archbishop in time.

His seat in the chapel was next to his parents, and no matter how long the services lasted, he remained kneeling on his *prie-dieu,* with folded hands and his velvet cap lying close beside him on the floor.

One day, during mass, he raised his head and beheld a little white mouse crawling out of a hole in the wall. It scrambled to the first altar-step and then, after a few gambols, ran back in the same direction. On the following Sunday, the idea of seeing the mouse again worried him. It returned; and every Sunday after that he watched for it; and it annoyed him so much that he grew to hate it and resolved to do away with it.

So, having closed the door and strewn some crumbs on the steps of the altar, he placed himself in front of the hole with a stick. After a long while a pink snout appeared, and then the whole mouse crept out. He struck it lightly with his stick and stood stunned at the sight of the little, lifeless body. A drop of blood stained the floor. He wiped it away hastily with his sleeve, and picking up the mouse, threw it away, without saying a word about it to anyone.

All sorts of birds pecked at the seeds in the garden. He put some peas in a hollow reed, and when he heard birds chirping in a tree, he would approach cautiously, lift the tube and swell his cheeks; then, when the little creatures dropped about him in multitudes, he could not refrain from laughing and being delighted with his own cleverness.

One morning, as he was returning by way of the curtain, he beheld a fat pigeon sunning itself on the top of the wall. He paused to gaze at it; where he stood the rampart was cracked and a piece of stone was near at hand; he gave his arm a jerk and the well-aimed missile struck the bird squarely, sending it straight into the moat below.

He sprang after it, unmindful of the brambles, and ferreted around the bushes with the litheness of a young dog.

The pigeon hung with broken wings in the branches of a privet hedge.

The persistence of its life irritated the boy. He began to strangle it, and its convulsions made his heart beat quicker, and filled him with a wild, tumultuous voluptuousness, the last throb of its heart making him feel like fainting.

At supper that night, his father declared that at his age a boy should begin to hunt; and he arose and brought forth an old writing-book which contained, in questions and answers, everything pertaining to the pastime. In it, a master showed a supposed pupil how to train dogs and falcons, lay traps, recognise a stag by its fumets, and a fox or a wolf by footprints. He also taught the best way of discovering their tracks, how to start them, where their refuges are usually to be found, what winds are the most favourable, and further enumerated the various cries, and the rules of the quarry.

When Julian was able to recite all these things by heart, his father made up a pack of hounds for him. There were twenty-four greyhounds of Barbary, speedier than gazelles, but liable to get out of temper; seventeen couples of Breton dogs, great barkers, with broad chests and russet coats flecked with white. For wild-boar hunting and perilous doublings, there were forty boarhounds as hairy as bears.

The red mastiffs of Tartary, almost as large as donkeys, with broad backs and straight legs, were destined for the pursuit of the wild bull. The black coats of the spaniels shone like satin; the barking of the setters equalled that of the beagles. In a special enclosure were eight growling bloodhounds that tugged at their chains and rolled their eyes, and these dogs leaped at men's throats and were not afraid even of lions.

All ate wheat bread, drank from marble troughs, and had high-sounding names.

Perhaps the falconry surpassed the pack; for the master of the castle, by paying great sums of money, had secured Caucasian hawks, Babylonian sakers, German gerfalcons, and pilgrim falcons captured on the cliffs edging the cold seas, in distant lands. They were housed in a thatched shed and were chained to the perch in the order of size. In front of them was a little grass-plot where, from time to time, they were allowed to disport themselves.

Bag-nets, baits, traps and all sorts of snares were manufactured.

Often they would take out pointers who would set almost immediately; then the whippers-in, advancing step by step, would cautiously spread a huge net over their motionless bodies. At the command, the dogs would bark and arouse the quails; and the ladies of the neighbourhood, with their husbands, children and hand-maids, would fall upon them and capture them with ease.

At other times they used a drum to start hares; and frequently foxes fell into the ditches prepared for them, while wolves caught their paws in the traps.

But Julian scorned these convenient contrivances; he preferred to hunt away from the crowd, alone with his steed and his falcon. It was almost always a large, snow-white, Scythian bird. His leather hood was ornamented with a plume, and on his blue feet were bells; and he perched firmly on his master's arm while they galloped across the plains. Then Julian would suddenly untie his tether and let him fly, and the bold bird would dart through the air like an arrow. One might perceive two spots circle around, unite, and then disappear in the blue heights. Presently the falcon would return with a mutilated bird, and perch again on his master's gauntlet with trembling wings.

Julian loved to sound his trumpet and follow his dogs over hills and streams, into the woods; and when the stag began to moan under their teeth, he would kill it deftly, and delight in the fury of the brutes, which would devour the pieces spread out on the warm hide.

On foggy days, he would hide in the marshes to watch for wild geese, otters and wild ducks.

At daybreak, three equerries waited for him at the foot of the steps; and though the old monk leaned out of the dormer-window and made signs to him to return, Julian would not look around.

He heeded neither the broiling sun, the rain nor the storm; he drank spring water and ate wild berries, and when he was tired, he lay down under a tree; and he would come home at night covered with earth and blood, with thistles in his hair and smelling of wild beasts. He grew to be like them. And when his mother kissed him, he responded coldly to her caress and seemed to be thinking of deep and serious things.

He killed bears with a knife, bulls with a hatchet, and wild boars with a spear; and once, with nothing but a stick, he defended himself against some wolves, which were gnawing corpses at the foot of a gibbet.

One winter morning he set out before daybreak, with a bow slung across his shoulder and a quiver of arrows attached to the pummel of his saddle. The hoofs of his steed beat the ground with regularity and his two beagles trotted close behind. The wind was blowing hard and icicles clung to his cloak. A part of the horizon cleared, and he beheld some rabbits playing around their burrows. In an instant, the two dogs were upon them, and seizing as many as they could, they broke their backs in the twinkling of an eye.

Soon he came to a forest. A woodcock, paralysed by the cold, perched on a branch, with its head hidden under its wing. Julian, with a lunge of his sword, cut off its feet, and without stopping to pick it up, rode away.

Three hours later he found himself on the top of a mountain so high that the sky seemed almost black. In front of him, a long, flat rock hung over a precipice, and at the end, two wild goats stood gazing down into the abyss. As he had no arrows (for he had left his steed behind), he thought he would climb down to where they stood; and with bare feet and bent back he at last reached the first goat and thrust his dagger below its ribs. But the second animal, in its terror, leaped into the precipice. Julian threw himself forward to strike it, but his right foot slipped, and he fell, face downward and with outstretched arms, over the body of the first goat.

After he returned to the plains, he followed a stream bordered by willows. From time to time, some cranes, flying low, passed over his head. He killed them with his whip, never missing a bird. He beheld in the distance the gleam of a lake which appeared to be of lead, and in the middle of it was an animal he had never seen before, a beaver with a black muzzle. Notwithstanding the distance that separated them, an arrow ended its life and Julian only regretted that he was not able to carry the skin home with him.

Then he entered an avenue of tall trees, the tops of which formed a triumphal arch to the entrance of a forest. A deer sprang out of the thicket and a badger crawled out of its hole, a stag appeared in the road, and a peacock spread its fan-shaped tail on the grass—and after he had slain them all, other deer, other stags, other badgers, other peacocks, and jays, blackbirds, foxes, porcupines, polecats, and lynxes, appeared; in fact, a host of beasts that grew more and more numerous with every step he took. Trembling, and with a look of appeal in their eyes, they gathered around Julian, but he did not stop slaying them; and so intent was he on stretching his bow, drawing his sword and whipping out his knife, that he had little thought for aught else. He knew that he was hunting in some country since an indefinite time, through the very fact of his existence, as everything seemed to occur with the ease one experiences in dreams. But presently an extraordinary sight made him pause.

He beheld a valley shaped like a circus and filled with stags which, huddled together, were warming one another with the vapour of their breaths that mingled with the early mist.

For a few minutes, he almost choked with pleasure at the prospect of so great a carnage. Then he sprang from his horse, rolled up his sleeves, and began to aim.

When the first arrow whizzed through the air, the stags turned their heads simultaneously. They huddled closer, uttered plaintive cries, and a great agitation seized the whole herd. The edge of the valley was too high to admit of flight; and the animals ran around the enclosure in their efforts to escape. Julian aimed, stretched his bow and his arrows fell as fast and thick as raindrops in a shower.

Maddened with terror, the stags fought and reared and climbed on top of one another; their antlers and bodies formed a moving mountain which tumbled to pieces whenever it displaced itself.

Finally the last one expired. Their bodies lay stretched out on the sand with foam gushing from the nostrils and the bowels protruding. The heaving of their bellies grew less and less noticeable, and presently all was still.

Night came, and behind the trees, through the branches, the sky appeared like a sheet of blood.

Julian leaned against a tree and gazed with dilated eyes at the enormous slaughter. He was now unable to comprehend how he had accomplished it.

On the opposite side of the valley, he suddenly beheld a large stag, with a doe and their fawn. The buck was black and of enormous size; he had a white beard and carried sixteen antlers. His mate was the color of dead leaves, and she browsed upon the grass, while the fawn, clinging to her udder, followed her step by step.

Again the bow was stretched, and instantly the fawn dropped dead, and seeing this, its mother raised her head and uttered a poignant, almost human wail of agony. Exasperated, Julian thrust his knife into her chest, and felled her to the ground.

The great stag had watched everything and suddenly he sprang forward. Julian aimed his last arrow at the beast. It struck him between his antlers and stuck there.

The stag did not appear to notice it; leaping over the bodies, he was coming nearer and nearer with the intention, Julian thought, of charging at him and ripping him open, and he recoiled with inexpressible horror. But presently the huge animal halted, and, with eyes aflame and the solemn air of a patriarch and a judge, repeated thrice, while a bell tolled in the distance:

"Accursed! Accursed! Accursed! some day, ferocious soul, thou wilt murder thy father and thy mother!"

Then he sank on his knees, gently closed his lids and expired.

At first Julian was stunned, and then a sudden lassitude and an immense sadness came over him. Holding his head between his hands, he wept for a long time.

His steed had wandered away; his dogs had forsaken him; the solitude seemed to threaten him with unknown perils. Impelled by a sense of sickening terror, he ran across the fields, and choosing a path at random, found himself almost immediately at the gates of the castle.

That night he could not rest, for, by the flickering light of the hanging lamp, he beheld again the huge black stag. He fought against the obsession of the prediction and kept repeating: "No! No! No! I cannot slay them!" and then he thought: "Still, supposing I desired to?—" and he feared that the devil might inspire him with this desire.

During three months, his distracted mother prayed at his bedside, and his father paced the halls of the castle in anguish. He consulted the most celebrated physicians, who prescribed quantities of medicine. Julian's illness, they declared, was due to some injurious wind or to amorous desire. But in reply to their questions, the young man only shook his head. After a time, his strength returned, and he was able to take a walk in the courtyard, supported by his father and the old monk.

But after he had completely recovered, he refused to hunt.

His father, hoping to please him, presented him with a large Saracen sabre.

It was placed on a panoply that hung on a pillar, and a ladder was required to reach it. Julian climbed up to it one day, but the heavy weapon slipped from his grasp, and in falling grazed his father and tore his cloak. Julian, believing he had killed him, fell in a swoon.

After that, he carefully avoided weapons. The sight of a naked sword made him grow pale, and this weakness caused great distress to his family.

In the end, the old monk ordered him in the name of God, and of his forefathers, once more to indulge in the sports of a nobleman.

The equerries diverted themselves every day with javelins and Julian soon excelled in the practice.

He was able to send a javelin into bottles, to break the teeth of the weather-cocks on the castle and to strike door-nails at a distance of one hundred feet.

One summer evening, at the hour when dusk renders objects indistinct, he was in the arbour in the garden, and thought he saw two white wings in the background hovering around the espalier. Not for a moment did he doubt that it was a stork, and so he threw his javelin at it.

A heart-rending scream pierced the air.

He had struck his mother, whose cap and long streamers remained nailed to the wall.

Julian fled from home and never returned.

2

He joined a horde of adventurers who were passing through the place.

He learned what it was to suffer hunger, thirst, sickness and filth. He grew accustomed to the din of battles and to the sight of dying men. The wind tanned his skin. His limbs became hardened through contact with armour, and as he was very strong and brave, temperate and of good counsel, he easily obtained command of a company.

At the outset of a battle, he would electrify his soldiers by a motion of his sword. He would climb the walls of a citadel with a knotted rope, at night, rocked by the storm, while sparks of fire clung to his cuirass, and molten lead and boiling tar poured from the battlements.

Often a stone would break his shield. Bridges crowded with men gave way under him. Once, by turning his mace, he rid himself of fourteen horsemen. He defeated all those who came forward to fight him on the field of honour, and more than a score of times it was believed that he had been killed.

However, thanks to Divine protection, he always escaped, for he shielded orphans, widows, and aged men. When he caught sight of one of the latter walking ahead of him, he would call to him to show his face, as if he feared that he might kill him by mistake.

All sorts of intrepid men gathered under his leadership, fugitive slaves, peasant rebels, and penniless bastards; he then organized an army which increased so much that he became famous and was in great demand.

He succoured in turn the Dauphin of France, the King of England, the Templars of Jerusalem, the General of the Parths, the Negus of Abyssinia and the Emperor of Calicut. He fought against Scandinavians covered with fish-scales, against negroes mounted on red asses and armed with shields made of hippopotamus hide, against gold-coloured Indians who wielded great, shining swords above their heads. He conquered the Troglodytes and the cannibals. He travelled through regions so torrid that the heat of the sun would set fire to the hair on one's head; he journeyed through countries so glacial that one's arms would fall from the body; and he passed through places where the fogs were so dense that it seemed like being surrounded by phantoms.

Republics in trouble consulted him; when he conferred with ambassadors, he always obtained unexpected concessions. Also, if a monarch behaved badly, he would arrive on the scene and rebuke him. He freed nations. He rescued queens sequestered in towers. It was he and no other that killed the serpent of Milan and the dragon of Oberbirbach.

Now, the Emperor of Occitania, having triumphed over the Spanish Mussulmans, had taken the sister of the Caliph of Cordova as a concubine, and had had one daughter by her, whom he brought up in the teachings of Christ. But the Caliph, feigning that he wished to become converted, made him a visit, and brought with him a numerous escort. He slaughtered the entire garrison and threw the Emperor into a dungeon, and treated him with great cruelty in order to obtain possession of his treasures.

Julian went to his assistance, destroyed the army of infidels, laid siege to the city, slew the Caliph, chopped off his head and threw it over the fortifications like a cannon-ball.

As a reward for so great a service, the Emperor presented him with a large sum of money in baskets; but Julian declined it. Then the Emperor, thinking that the amount was not sufficiently large, offered him three quarters of his fortune, and on meeting a second refusal, proposed to share his kingdom with his benefactor. But Julian only thanked him for it, and the Emperor felt like weeping with vexation at not being able to show his gratitude, when he suddenly tapped his forehead and whispered a few words in the ear of one of his courtiers; the tapestry curtains parted and a young girl appeared.

Her large black eyes shone like two soft lights. A charming smile parted her lips. Her curls were caught in the jewels of her half-opened bodice, and the grace of her youthful body could be divined under the transparency of her tunic.

She was small and quite plump, but her waist was slender.

Julian was absolutely dazzled, all the more since he had always led a chaste life.

So he married the Emperor's daughter, and received at the same time a castle she had inherited from her mother; and when the rejoicings were over, he departed with his bride, after many courtesies had been exchanged on both sides.

The castle was of Moorish design, in white marble, erected on a promontory and surrounded by orange-trees.

Terraces of flowers extended to the shell-strewn shores of a beautiful bay. Behind the castle spread a fan-shaped forest. The sky was always blue, and the trees were swayed in turn by the ocean-breeze and by the winds that blew from the mountains that closed the horizon.

Light entered the apartments through the incrustations of the walls. High, reed-like columns supported the ceiling of the cupolas, decorated in imitation of stalactites.

Fountains played in the spacious halls; the courts were inlaid with mosaic; there were festooned partitions and a great profusion of architectural fancies; and everywhere reigned a silence so deep that the swish of a sash or the echo of a sigh could be distinctly heard.

Julian now had renounced war. Surrounded by a peaceful people, he remained idle, receiving every day a throng of subjects who came and knelt before him and kissed his hand in Oriental fashion.

Clad in sumptuous garments, he would gaze out of the window and think of his past exploits; and wish that he might again run in the desert in pursuit of ostriches and gazelles, hide among the bamboos to watch for leopards, ride through forests filled with rhinoceroses, climb the most inaccessible peaks in order to have a better aim at the eagles, and fight the polar bears on the icebergs of the northern sea.

Sometimes, in his dreams, he fancied himself like Adam in the midst of Paradise, surrounded by all the beasts; by merely extending his arm, he was able to kill them; or else they filed past him, in pairs, by order of size, from the lions and the elephants to the ermines and the ducks, as on the day they entered Noah's Ark.

Hidden in the shadow of a cave, he aimed unerring arrows at them; then came others and still others, until he awoke, wild-eyed.

Princes, friends of his, invited him to their meets, but he always refused their invitations, because he thought that by this kind of penance he might possibly avert the threatened misfortune; it seemed to him that the fate of his parents depended on his refusal to slaughter animals. But he suffered because he could not see them, and his other desire was growing well-nigh unbearable.

In order to divert his mind, his wife had dancers and jugglers come to the castle.

She went abroad with him in an open litter; at other times, stretched out on the edge of a boat, they watched for hours the fish disport themselves in the water, which was as clear as the sky. Often she playfully threw flowers at him or nestling at his feet she played melodies on an old mandolin; then, clasping her hands on his shoulder, she would inquire tremulously: "What troubles thee, my dear lord?"

He would not reply, or else he would burst into tears; but at last, one day, he confessed his fearful dread.

His wife scorned the idea and reasoned wisely with him: probably his father and mother were dead; and even if he should ever see them again, through what chance, to what end, would he arrive at this abomination? Therefore, his fears were groundless, and he should hunt again.

Julian listened to her and smiled, but he could not bring himself to yield to his desire.

One August evening when they were in their bedchamber, she having just retired and he being about to kneel in prayer, he heard the yelping of a fox and light footsteps under the window; and he thought he saw things in the dark that looked like animals. The temptation was too strong. He seized his quiver.

His wife appeared astonished.

"I am obeying you," quoth he, "and I shall be back at sunrise."

However, she feared that some calamity would happen. But he reassured her and departed, surprised at her illogical moods.

A short time afterwards, a page came to announce that two strangers desired, in the absence of the lord of the castle, to see its mistress at once.

Soon a stooping old man and an aged woman entered the room; their coarse garments were covered with dust and each leaned on a stick.

They grew bold enough to say that they brought Julian news of his parents. She leaned out of the bed to listen to them. But after glancing at each other, the old people asked her whether he ever referred to them and if he still loved them.

"Oh! yes!" she said.

Then they exclaimed:

"We are his parents!" and they sat themselves down, for they were very tired.

But there was nothing to show the young wife that her husband was their son.

They proved it by describing to her the birthmarks he had on his body. Then she jumped out of bed, called a page, and ordered that a repast be served to them.

But although they were very hungry, they could scarcely eat, and she observed surreptitiously how their lean fingers trembled whenever they lifted their cups.

They asked a hundred questions about their son, and she answered each one of them, but she was careful not to refer to the terrible idea that concerned them.

When he failed to return, they had left their château; and had wandered for several years, following vague indications but without losing hope.

So much money had been spent at the tolls of the rivers and in inns, to satisfy the rights of princes and the demands of highwaymen, that now their purse was quite empty and they were obliged to beg. But what did it matter, since they were about to clasp again their son in their arms? They lauded his happiness in having such a beautiful wife, and did not tire of looking at her and kissing her.

The luxuriousness of the apartment astonished them; and the old man, after examining the walls, inquired why they bore the coat-of-arms of the Emperor of Occitania.

"He is my father," she replied.

And he marvelled and remembered the prediction of the gipsy, while his wife meditated upon the words the hermit had spoken to her. The glory of their son was undoubtedly only the dawn of eternal splendours, and the old people remained awed while the light from the candelabra on the table fell on them.

In the heyday of youth, both had been extremely handsome. The mother had not lost her hair, and bands of snowy whiteness framed her cheeks; and the father, with his stalwart figure and long beard, looked like a carved image.

Julian's wife prevailed upon them not to wait for him. She put them in her bed and closed the curtains; and they both fell asleep. The day broke and outdoors the little birds began to chirp.

Meanwhile, Julian had left the castle grounds and walked nervously through the forest, enjoying the velvety softness of the grass and the balminess of the air.

The shadow of the trees fell on the earth. Here and there, the moonlight flecked the glades and Julian feared to advance, because he mistook the silvery light for water and the tranquil surface of the pools for grass. A great stillness reigned everywhere, and he failed to see any of the beasts that only a moment ago were prowling around the castle. As he walked on, the woods grew thicker, and the darkness more impenetrable. Warm winds, filled with enervating perfumes, caressed him; he sank into masses of dead leaves, and after a while he leaned against an oak-tree to rest and catch his breath.

Suddenly a body blacker than the surrounding darkness sprang from behind the tree. It was a wild boar. Julian did not have time to stretch his bow, and he bewailed the fact as if it were some great misfortune. Presently, having left the woods, he beheld a wolf slinking along a hedge.

He aimed an arrow at him. The wolf paused, turned his head and quietly continued on his way. He trotted along, always keeping at the same distance, pausing now and then to look around and resuming his flight as soon as an arrow was aimed in his direction.

In this way Julian traversed an apparently endless plain, then sand-hills, and at last found himself on a plateau that dominated a great stretch of land. Large flat stones were interspersed among crumbling vaults; bones and skeletons covered the ground, and here and there some mouldy crosses stood desolate. But presently, shapes moved in the darkness of the tombs, and from them came panting, wild-eyed hyenas. They approached him and smelled him, grinning hideously and disclosing their gums. He whipped out his sword, but they scattered in every direction and continuing their swift, limping gallop, disappeared in a cloud of dust.

Some time afterwards, in a ravine, he encountered a wild bull, with threatening horns, pawing the sand with his hoofs. Julian thrust his lance between his dewlaps. But his weapon snapped as if the beast were made of bronze; then he closed his eyes in anticipation of his death. When he opened them again, the bull had vanished.

Then his soul collapsed with shame. Some supernatural power destroyed his strength, and he set out for home through the forest. The woods were a tangle of creeping plants that he had to cut with his sword, and while he was thus engaged, a weasel slid between his feet, a panther jumped over his shoulder, and a serpent wound itself around an ash-tree.

Among its leaves was a monstrous jackdaw that watched Julian intently, and here and there, between the branches, appeared great, fiery sparks as if the sky were raining all its stars upon the forest. But the sparks were the eyes of wild-cats, owls, squirrels, monkeys and parrots.

Julian aimed his arrows at them, but the feathered weapons lighted on the leaves of the trees and looked like white butterflies. He threw stones at them; but the missiles did not strike, and fell to the ground. Then he cursed himself, and howled imprecations, and in his rage he could have struck himself.

Then all the beasts he had pursued appeared, and formed a narrow circle around him. Some sat on their hind-quarters, while others stood at full height. And Julian remained among them, transfixed with terror and absolutely unable to move. By a supreme effort of his will-power, he took a step forward; those that perched in the trees opened their wings, those that trod the earth moved their limbs, and all accompanied him.

The hyenas strode in front of him, the wolf and the wild boar brought up the rear. On his right, the bull swung its head and on his left the serpent crawled through the grass; while the panther, arching its back, advanced with velvety footfalls and long strides. Julian walked as slowly as possible, so as not to irritate them, while in the depth of the bushes he could distinguish porcupines, foxes, vipers, jackals, and bears.

He began to run; the brutes followed him. The serpent hissed, the malodorous beasts frothed at the mouth, the wild boar rubbed his tusks against his heels, and the wolf scratched the palms of his hands with the hairs of his snout. The monkeys pinched him and made faces, the weasel rolled over his feet. A bear knocked his cap off with its huge paw, and the panther disdainfully dropped an arrow it was about to put in its mouth.

Irony seemed to incite their sly actions. As they watched him out of the corners of their eyes, they seemed to meditate a plan of revenge, and Julian, who was deafened by the buzzing of the insects, bruised by the wings and tails of the birds, choked by the stench of animal breaths, walked with outstretched arms and closed lids, like a blind man, without even the strength to beg for mercy.

The crowing of a cock vibrated in the air. Other cocks responded; it was day; and Julian recognised the top of his palace rising above the orange-trees.

Then, on the edge of a field, he beheld some red partridges fluttering around a stubble-field. He unfastened his cloak and threw it over them like a net. When he lifted it, he found only a bird that had been dead a long time and was decaying.

This disappointment irritated him more than all the others. The thirst for carnage stirred afresh within him; animals failing him, he desired to slaughter men.

He climbed the three terraces and opened the door with a blow of his fist; but at the foot of the staircase, the memory of his beloved wife softened his heart. No doubt she was asleep, and he would go up and surprise her. Having removed his sandals, he unlocked the door softly and entered.

The stained windows dimmed the pale light of dawn. Julian stumbled over some garments lying on the floor and a little further on, he knocked against a table covered with dishes. "She must have eaten," he thought; so he advanced cautiously towards the bed which was concealed by the darkness in the back of the room. When he reached the edge, he leaned over the pillow where the two heads were resting close together and stooped to kiss his wife. His mouth encountered a man's beard.

He fell back, thinking he had become crazed; then he approached the bed again and his searching fingers discovered some hair which seemed to be very long. In order to convince himself that he was mistaken, he once more passed his hand slowly over the pillow. But this time he was sure that it was a beard and that a man was there! a man lying beside his wife!

Flying into an ungovernable passion, he sprang upon them with his drawn dagger, foaming, stamping and howling like a wild beast. After a while he stopped.

The corpses, pierced through the heart, had not even moved. He listened attentively to the two death-rattles, they were almost alike, and as they grew fainter, another voice, coming from far away, seemed to continue them. Uncertain at first, this plaintive voice came nearer and nearer, grew louder and louder and presently he recognised, with a feeling of abject terror, the bellowing of the great black stag.

And as he turned around, he thought he saw the spectre of his wife standing at the threshold with a light in her hand.

The sound of the murder had aroused her. In one glance she understood what had happened and fled in horror, letting the candle drop from her hand. Julian picked it up.

His father and mother lay before him, stretched on their backs, with gaping wounds in their breasts; and their faces, the expression of which was full of tender dignity, seemed to hide what might be an eternal secret.

Splashes and blotches of blood were on their white skin, on the bed-clothes, on the floor, and on an ivory Christ which hung in the alcove. The scarlet reflection of the stained window, which just then was struck by the sun, lighted up the bloody spots and appeared to scatter them around the whole room. Julian walked toward the corpses, repeating to himself and trying to believe that he was mistaken, that it was not possible, that there are often inexplicable likenesses.

At last he bent over to look closely at the old man and he saw, between the half-closed lids, a dead pupil that scorched him like fire. Then he went over to the other side of the bed, where the other corpse lay, but the face was partly hidden by bands of white hair. Julian slipped his finger beneath them and raised the head, holding it at arm's length to study its features, while, with his other hand he lifted the torch. Drops of blood oozed from the mattress and fell one by one upon the floor.

At the close of the day, he appeared before his wife, and in a changed voice commanded her first not to answer him, not to approach him, not even to look at him, and to obey, under the penalty of eternal damnation, every one of his orders, which were irrevocable.

The funeral was to be held in accordance with the written instructions he had left on a chair in the death-chamber.

He left her his castle, his vassals, all his worldly goods, without keeping even his clothes or his sandals, which would be found at the top of the stairs.

She had obeyed the will of God in bringing about his crime, and accordingly she must pray for his soul, since henceforth he should cease to exist.

The dead were buried sumptuously in the chapel of a monastery which it took three days to reach from the castle. A monk wearing a hood that covered his head followed the procession alone, for nobody dared to speak to him. And during the mass, he lay flat on the floor with his face downward and his arms stretched out at his sides.

After the burial, he was seen to take the road leading into the mountains. He looked back several times, and finally passed out of sight.

3

He left the country and begged his daily bread on his way.

He stretched out his hand to the horsemen he met in the roads, and humbly approached the harvesters in the fields; or else remained motionless in front of the gates of castles; and his face was so sad that he was never turned away.

Obeying a spirit of humility, he related his history to all men, and they would flee from him and cross themselves. In villages through which he had passed before, the good people bolted the doors, threatened him, and threw stones at him as soon as they recognised him. The more charitable ones placed a bowl on the window-sill and closed the shutters in order to avoid seeing him.

Repelled and shunned by everyone, he avoided his fellow-men and nourished himself with roots and plants, stray fruits and shells which he gathered along the shores.

Often, at the bend of a hill, he could perceive a mass of crowded roofs, stone spires, bridges, towers and narrow streets, from which arose a continual murmur of activity.

The desire to mingle with men impelled him to enter the city. But the gross and beastly expression of their faces, the noise of their industries and the indifference of their remarks, chilled his very heart. On holidays, when the cathedral bells rang out at daybreak and filled the people's hearts with gladness, he watched the inhabitants coming out of their dwellings, the dancers in the public squares, the fountains of ale, the damask hangings spread before the houses of princes; and then, when night came, he would peer through the windows at the long tables where families gathered and where grandparents held little children on their knees; then sobs would rise in his throat and he would turn away and go back to his haunts.

He gazed with yearning at the colts in the pastures, the birds in their nests, the insects on the flowers; but they all fled from him at his approach and hid or flew away. So he sought solitude. But the wind brought to his ears sounds resembling death-rattles; the tears of the dew reminded him of heavier drops, and every evening, the sun would spread blood in the sky, and every night, in his dreams, he lived over his parricide.

He made himself a hair-cloth lined with iron spikes. On his knees, he ascended every hill that was crowned with a chapel. But the unrelenting thought spoiled the splendour of the tabernacles and tortured him in the midst of his penances.

He did not rebel against God, who had inflicted his action, but he despaired at the thought that he had committed it.

He had such a horror of himself that he took all sorts of risks. He rescued paralytics from fire and children from the waves. But the ocean scorned him and the flames spared him. Time did not allay his torment, which became so intolerable that he resolved to die.

One day, while he was stooping over a fountain to judge of its depth, an old man appeared on the other side. He wore a white beard and his appearance was so lamentable that Julian could not keep back his tears. The old man also was weeping. Without recognising him, Julian remembered confusedly a face that resembled his. He uttered a cry; for it was his father who stood before him; and he gave up all thought of taking his own life.

Thus weighted down by his recollections, he travelled through many countries and arrived at a river which was dangerous, because of its violence and the slime that covered its shores. Since a long time nobody had ventured to cross it.

The bow of an old boat, whose stern was buried in the mud, showed among the reeds. Julian, on examining it closely, found a pair of oars and hit upon the idea of devoting his life to the service of his fellow-men.

He began by establishing on the bank of the river a sort of road which would enable people to approach the edge of the stream; he broke his nails in his efforts to lift enormous stones which he pressed against the pit of his stomach in order to transport them from one point to another; he slipped in the mud, he sank into it, and several times was on the very brink of death.

Then he took to repairing the boat with debris of vessels, and afterwards built himself a hut with putty and trunks of trees.

When it became known that a ferry had been established, passengers flocked to it. They hailed him from the opposite side by waving flags, and Julian would jump into the boat and row over. The craft was very heavy, and the people loaded it with all sorts of baggage, and beasts of burden, who reared with fright, thereby adding greatly to the confusion. He asked nothing for his trouble; some gave him left-over victuals which they took from their sacks or worn-out garments which they could no longer use.

The brutal ones hurled curses at him, and when he rebuked them gently they replied with insults, and he was content to bless them.

A little table, a stool, a bed made of dead leaves and three earthen bowls were all he possessed. Two holes in the wall served as windows. On one side, as far as the eye could see, stretched barren wastes studded here and there with pools of water; and in front of him flowed the greenish waters of the wide river. In the spring, a putrid odour arose from the damp sod. Then fierce gales lifted clouds of dust that blew everywhere, even settling in the water and in one's mouth. A little later swarms of mosquitoes appeared, whose buzzing and stinging continued night and day. After that, came frightful frosts which communicated a stone-like rigidity to everything and inspired one with an insane desire for meat. Months passed when Julian never saw a human being. He often closed his lids and endeavoured to recall his youth;—he beheld the courtyard of a castle, with greyhounds stretched out on a terrace, an armoury filled with valets, and under a bower of vines a youth with blond curls, sitting between an old man wrapped in furs and a lady with a high cap; presently the corpses rose before him, and then he would throw himself face downward on his cot and sob:

"Oh! poor father! poor mother! poor mother!" and would drop into a fitful slumber in which the terrible visions recurred.

One night he thought that some one was calling to him in his sleep. He listened intently, but could hear nothing save the roaring of the waters.

But the same voice repeated: "Julian!"

It proceeded from the opposite shore, a fact which appeared extraordinary to him, considering the breadth of the river.

The voice called a third time: "Julian!"

And the high-pitched tones sounded like the ringing of a church-bell.

Having lighted his lantern, he stepped out of his cabin. A frightful storm raged. The darkness was complete and was illuminated here and there only by the white waves leaping and tumbling.

After a moment's hesitation, he untied the rope. The water presently grew smooth and the boat glided easily to the opposite shore, where a man was waiting.

He was wrapped in a torn piece of linen; his face was like a chalk mask, and his eyes were redder than glowing coals. When Julian held up his lantern he noticed that the stranger was covered with hideous sores; but notwithstanding this, there was in his attitude something like the majesty of a king.

As soon as he stepped into the boat, it sank deep into the water, borne downward by his weight; then it rose again and Julian began to row.

With each stroke of the oars, the force of the waves raised the bow of the boat. The water, which was blacker than ink, ran furiously along the sides. It formed abysses and then mountains, over which the boat glided, then it fell into yawning depths where, buffeted by the wind, it whirled around and around.

Julian leaned far forward and, bracing himself with his feet, bent backwards so as to bring his whole strength into play. Hail-stones cut his hands, the rain ran down his back, the velocity of the wind suffocated him. He stopped rowing and let the boat drift with the tide. But realising that an important matter was at stake, a command which could not be disregarded, he picked up the oars again; and the rattling of the tholes mingled with the clamourings of the storm.

The little lantern burned in front of him. Sometimes birds fluttered past it and obscured the light. But he could distinguish the eyes of the leper who stood at the stern, as motionless as a column.

And the trip lasted a long, long time.

When they reached the hut, Julian closed the door and saw the man sit down on the stool. The species of shroud that was wrapped around him had fallen below his loins, and his shoulders and chest and lean arms were hidden under blotches of scaly pustules. Enormous wrinkles crossed his forehead. Like a skeleton, he had a hole instead of a nose, and from his bluish lips came breath which was fetid and as thick as mist.

"I am hungry," he said.

Julian set before him what he had, a piece of pork and some crusts of coarse bread.

After he had devoured them, the table, the bowl, and the handle of the knife bore the same scales that covered his body.

Then he said: "I thirst!"

Julian fetched his jug of water and when he lifted it, he smelled an aroma that dilated his nostrils and filled his heart with gladness. It was wine; what a boon! but the leper stretched out his arm and emptied the jug at one draught.

Then he said: "I am cold!"

Julian ignited a bundle of ferns that lay in the middle of the hut. The leper approached the fire and, resting on his heels, began to warm himself; his whole frame shook and he was failing visibly; his eyes grew dull, his sores began to break, and in a faint voice he whispered:

"Thy bed!"

Julian helped him gently to it, and even laid the sail of his boat over him to keep him warm.

The leper tossed and moaned. The corners of his mouth were drawn up over his teeth; an accelerated death-rattle shook his chest and with each one of his aspirations, his stomach touched his spine. At last, he closed his eyes.

"I feel as if ice were in my bones! Lay thyself beside me!" he commanded. Julian took off his garments; and then, as naked as on the day he was born, he got into the bed; against his thigh he could feel the skin of the leper, and it was colder than a serpent and as rough as a file.

He tried to encourage the leper, but he only whispered:

"Oh! I am about to die! Come closer to me and warm me! Not with thy hands! No! with thy whole body."

So Julian stretched himself out upon the leper, lay on him, lips to lips, chest to chest.

Then the leper clasped him close and presently his eyes shone like stars; his hair lengthened into sunbeams; the breath of his nostrils had the scent of roses; a cloud of incense rose from the hearth, and the waters began to murmur harmoniously; an abundance of bliss, a superhuman joy, filled the soul of the swooning Julian, while he who clasped him to his breast grew and grew until his head and his feet touched the opposite walls of the cabin. The roof flew up in the air, disclosing the heavens, and Julian ascended into infinity face to face with our Lord Jesus Christ, who bore him straight to heaven.

And this is the story of Saint Julian the Hospitaller, as it is given on the stained-glass window of a church in my birthplace.

1877

Gustave Flaubert is one of the founders of literary realism, but we can see from a story like "The Legend of Saint Julian" that his realism did not

always express itself in expected ways. Flannery O'Connor's comment on a sentence from Flaubert's novel Madame Bovary shows her admiration for his ability to construct a credible setting for a story. A fair question is whether this same sort of credibility comes into play when Flaubert writes a "saint's life," a literary form that for centuries had emphasized the miraculous and avoided references to the unpleasant or mundane details of daily life.

"Flaubert had to create a believable village": Flannery O'Connor

All the sentences in *Madame Bovary* could be examined with wonder, but there is one in particular that always stops me in admiration. Flaubert has just shown us Emma at the piano with Charles watching her. He says, "She struck the notes with aplomb and ran from top to bottom of the keyboard without a break. Thus shaken up, the old instrument, whose strings buzzed, could be heard at the other end of the village when the window was open, and often the bailiff's clerk, passing along the highroad, bareheaded and in list slippers, stopped to listen, his sheet of paper in his hand."

The more you look at a sentence like that, the more you can learn from it. At one end of it, we are with Emma and this very solid instrument "whose strings buzzed," and at the other end of it we are across the village with this very concrete clerk in his list slippers. With regard to what happens to Emma in the rest of the novel, we may think that it makes no difference that the instrument has buzzing strings or that the clerk wears list slippers and has a piece of paper in his hand, but Flaubert had to create a believable village to put Emma in. It's always necessary to remember that the fiction writer is much less *immediately* concerned with grand ideas and bristling emotions than he is with putting list slippers on clerks.

HENRY JAMES

(1843–1916)

THE REAL THING

1

When the porter's wife, who used to answer the house-bell, announced "A gentleman and a lady, sir" I had, as I often had in those days—the wish being father to the thought—an immediate vision of sitters. Sitters my visitors in this case proved to be; but not in the sense I should have preferred.

There was nothing at first however to indicate that they mightn't have come for a portrait. The gentleman, a man of fifty, very high and very straight, with a moustache slightly grizzled and a dark grey walking-coat admirably fitted, both of which I noted professionally—I don't mean as a barber or yet as a tailor—would have struck me as a celebrity if celebrities often were striking. It was a truth of which I had for some time been conscious that a figure with a good deal of frontage was, as one might say, almost never a public institution. A glance at the lady helped to remind me of this para-doxical law: she also looked too distinguished to be a "personality." More-over one would scarcely come across two variations together.

Neither of the pair immediately spoke—they only prolonged the preliminary gaze suggesting that each wished to give the other a chance. They were visibly shy; they stood there letting me take them in—which, as I afterwards perceived, was the most practical thing they could have done. In this way their embarrassment served their cause. I had seen people pain-fully reluctant to mention that they desired anything so gross as to be repre-sented on canvas; but the scruples of my new friends appeared almost insurmountable. Yet the gentleman might have said "I should like a por-trait of my wife," and the lady might have said "I should like a portrait of my husband." Perhaps they weren't husband and wife—this naturally would make the matter more delicate. Perhaps they wished to be done together—in which case they ought to have brought a third person to break the news.

"We come from Mr. Rivet," the lady finally said with a dim smile that had the effect of a moist sponge passed over a "sunk" piece of painting, as well as of a vague allusion to vanished beauty. She was as tall and straight, in her degree, as her companion, and with ten years less to carry. She looked as sad as a woman could look whose face was not charged with expression; that is her tinted oval mask showed waste as an exposed surface shows friction. The hand of time had played over her freely, but to an effect of elimination. She was slim and stiff, and so well-dressed, in dark blue cloth, with lappets and pockets and buttons, that it was clear she employed the same tailor as her husband. The couple had an indefinable air of pros-perous thrift—they evidently got a good deal of luxury for their money. If I was to be one of their luxuries it would behoove me to consider my terms.

"Ah Claude Rivet recommended me?" I echoed; and I added that it was very kind of him, though I could reflect that, as he only painted land-scape, this wasn't a sacrifice.

The lady looked very hard at the gentleman, and the gentleman looked round the room. Then staring at the floor a moment and stroking his moustache, he rested his pleasant eyes on me with the remark: "He said you were the right one."

"I try to be, when people want to sit."

"Yes, we should like to," said the lady anxiously.

"Do you mean together?"

My visitors exchanged a glance. "If you could do anything with *me* I suppose it would be double," the gentleman stammered.

"Oh yes, there's naturally a higher charge for two figures than for one."

"We should like to make it pay," the husband confessed.

"That's very good of you," I returned, appreciating so unwonted a sympathy—for I supposed he meant pay the artist.

A sense of strangeness seemed to dawn on the lady.

"We mean for the illustrations—Mr. Rivet said you might put one in."

"Put in—an illustration?" I was equally confused.

"Sketch her off, you know," said the gentleman, colouring.

It was only then that I understood the service Claude Rivet had rendered me; he had told them how I worked in black-and-white, for magazines, for storybooks, for sketches of contemporary life, and consequently had copious employment for models. These things were true, but it was not less true—I may confess it now; whether because the aspiration was to lead to everything or to nothing I leave the reader to guess—that I couldn't get the honours, to say nothing of the emoluments, of a great painter of portraits out of my head. My "illustrations" were my pot-boilers; I looked to a different branch of art—far and away the most interesting it had always seemed to me—to perpetuate my fame. There was no shame in looking to it also to make my fortune; but that fortune was by so much further from being made from the moment my visitors wished to be "done" for nothing. I was disappointed; for in the pictorial sense I had immediately *seen* them. I had seized their type—I had already settled what I would do with it. Something that wouldn't absolutely have pleased them, I afterwards reflected.

"Ah you're—you're—a—?" I began as soon as I had mastered my surprise. I couldn't bring out the dingy word "models": it seemed so little to fit the case.

"We haven't had much practice," said the lady.

"We've got to *do* something, and we've thought that an artist in your line might perhaps make something of us," her husband threw off. He further mentioned that they didn't know many artists and that they had gone first, on the off-chance—he painted views of course, but sometimes put in figures; perhaps I remembered—to Mr. Rivet, whom they had met a few years before at a place in Norfolk where he was sketching.

"We used to sketch a little ourselves," the lady hinted.

"It's very awkward, but we absolutely *must* do something," her husband went on.

"Of course we're not so *very* young," she admitted with a wan smile.

With the remark that I might as well know something more about them the husband had handed me a card extracted from a neat new pocketbook—their appurtenances were all of the freshest—and inscribed with the words "Major Monarch." Impressive as these words were they didn't carry my knowledge much further; but my visitor presently added: "I've left the army and we've had the misfortune to lose our money. In fact our means are dreadfully small."

"It's awfully trying—a regular strain," said Mrs. Monarch.

They evidently wished to be discreet—to take care not to swagger because they were gentlefolk. I felt them willing to recognize this as something of a drawback, at the same time that I guessed at an underlying sense —their consolation in adversity—that they *had* their points. They certainly had; but these advantages struck me as preponderantly social; such for instance as would help to make a drawing-room look well. However, a drawing-room was always, or ought to be, a picture.

In consequence of his wife's allusion to their age Major Monarch observed: "Naturally it's more for the figure that we thought of going in. We can still hold ourselves up." On the instant I saw that the figure was indeed their strong point. His "naturally" didn't sound vain, but it lighted up the question. "*She* has the best one," he continued, nodding at his wife with a pleasant after-dinner absence of circumlocution. I could only reply, as if we were in fact sitting over our wine, that this didn't prevent his own from being very good; which led him in turn to make answer: "We thought that if you ever had to do people like us we might be something like it. *She* particularly—for a lady in a book, you know."

I was so amused by them that, to get more of it, I did my best to take their point of view; and though it was an embarrassment to find myself appraising physically, as if they were animals on hire or useful blacks, a pair whom I should have expected to meet only in one of the relations in which criticism is tacit, I looked at Mrs. Monarch judicially enough to be able to exclaim after a moment with conviction: "Oh yes, a lady in a book!" She was singularly like a bad illustration.

"We'll stand up, if you like," said the Major; and he raised himself before me with a really grand air.

I could take his measure at a glance—he was six feet two and a perfect gentleman. It would have paid any club in process of formation and in want of a stamp to engage him at a salary to stand in the principal window. What struck me at once was that in coming to me they had rather missed their vocation; they could surely have been turned to better account for advertising purposes. I couldn't of course see the thing in detail, but I could see them make somebody's fortune—I don't mean their own. There was something in them for a waistcoat-maker, an hotel-keeper or a soap-vendor. I could imagine "We always use it" pinned on their bosoms with the greatest effect; I had a vision of the brilliancy with which they would launch a table d'hôte.

Mrs. Monarch sat still, not from pride but from shyness, and presently her husband said to her: "Get up, my dear, and show how smart you are." She obeyed, but she had no need to get up to show it. She walked to the end of the studio and then came back blushing, her fluttered eyes on the partner of her appeal. I was reminded of an incident I had accidentally had a glimpse of in Paris being with a friend there, a dramatist about to produce a play, when an actress came to him to ask to be entrusted with a part. She went through her paces before him, walked up and down as Mrs. Monarch was doing. Mrs. Monarch did it quite as well, but I abstained from applauding. It was very odd to see such people apply for such poor pay. She looked as if she had ten thousand a year. Her husband had used the word that described her: she was in the London current jargon essentially and typically "smart." Her figure was, in the same order of ideas, conspicuously and irreproachably "good." For a woman of her age her waist was surprisingly small; her elbow moreover had the orthodox crook. She held her head at the conventional angle, but why did she come to *me*? She ought to have tried on jackets at a big shop. I feared my visitors were not only destitute but "artistic"—which would be a great complication. When she sat down again I thanked her, observing that what a draughtsman most valued in his model was the faculty of keeping quiet.

"Oh *she* can keep quiet," said Major Monarch. Then he added jocosely: "I've always kept her quiet."

"I'm not a nasty fidget, am I?" It was going to wring tears from me, I felt, the way she hid her head, ostrich-like, in the other broad bosom.

The owner of this expanse addressed his answer to me. "Perhaps it isn't out of place to mention—because we ought to be quite business-like, oughtn't we?—that when I married her she was known as the Beautiful Statue."

"Oh dear!" said Mrs. Monarch ruefully.

"Of course I should want a certain amount of expression," I rejoined.

"Of *course*!"—and I had never heard such unanimity.

"And then I suppose you know that you'll get awfully tired."

"Oh we *never* get tired!" they eagerly cried.

"Have you had any kind of practice?"

They hesitated—they looked at each other. "We've been photographed—*immensely*," said Mrs. Monarch.

"She means the fellows have asked us themselves," added the Major.

"I see—because you're so good-looking."

"I don't know what they thought, but they were always after us."

"We always got our photographs for nothing," smiled Mrs. Monarch.

"We might have brought some, my dear," her husband remarked.

"I'm not sure we have any left. We've given quantities away," she explained to me.

"With our autographs and that sort of thing," said the Major.

"Are they to be got in the shops?" I enquired as a harmless pleasantry.

"Oh yes, *hers*—they used to be."

"Not now," said Mrs. Monarch with her eyes on the floor.

2

I could fancy the "sort of thing" they put on the presentation copies of their photographs, and I was sure they wrote a beautiful hand. It was odd how quickly I was sure of everything that concerned them. If they were now so poor as to have to earn shillings and pence they could never have had much of a margin. Their good looks had been their capital, and they had good-humouredly made the most of the career that this resource marked out for them. It was in their faces, the blankness, the deep intellectual repose of the twenty years of country-house visiting that had given them pleasant intonations. I could see the sunny drawing-rooms, sprinkled with periodicals she didn't read, in which Mrs. Monarch had continuously sat; I could see the wet shrubberies in which she had walked, equipped to admiration for either exercise. I could see the rich covers the Major had helped to shoot and the wonderful garments in which, late at night, he repaired to the smoking-room to talk about them. I could imagine their leggings and waterproofs, their knowing tweeds and rugs, their rolls of sticks and cases of tackle and neat umbrellas; and I could evoke the exact appearance of their servants and the compact variety of their luggage on the platforms of country stations.

They gave small tips, but they were liked; they didn't do anything themselves, but they were welcome. They looked so well everywhere; they gratified the general relish for stature, complexion and "form." They knew it without fatuity or vulgarity, and they respected themselves in consequence. They weren't superficial; they were thorough and kept themselves up—it had been their line. People with such a taste for activity had to have some line. I could feel how even in a dull house they could have been counted on for the joy of life. At present something had happened—it didn't matter what, their little income had grown less, it had grown least— and they had to do something for pocket-money. Their friends could like them, I made out, without liking to support them. There was something about them that represented credit—their clothes, their manners, their type; but if credit is a large empty pocket in which an occasional chink reverberates, the chink at least must be audible. What they wanted of me was to help to make it so. Fortunately they had no children—I soon divined that. They would also perhaps wish our relations to be kept secret: this was why it was "for the figure"—the reproduction of the face would betray them.

I liked them—I felt, quite as their friends must have done—they were so simple; and I had no objection to them if they would suit. But somehow with all their perfections I didn't easily believe in them. After all they were amateurs, and the ruling passion of my life was the detestation of the amateur. Combined with this was another perversity—an innate preference for the represented subject over the real one: the defect of the real one was so apt to be a lack of representation. I like things that appeared; then one was sure. Whether they *were* or not was a subordinate and almost always a profitless question. There were other considerations, the first of which was that I already had two or three recruits in use, notably a young person with big feet, in alpaca, from Kilburn, who for a couple of years had come to me regularly for my illustrations and with whom I was still—perhaps ignobly—satisfied. I frankly explained to my visitors how the case stood, but they had taken more precautions than I supposed. They had reasoned out their opportunity, for Claude Rivet had told them of the projected *édition de luxe* of one of the writers of our day—the rarest of the novelists—who, long neglected by the multitudinous vulgar and dearly prized by the attentive (need I mention Philip Vincent?) had had the happy fortune of seeing, late in life, the dawn and then the full light of a higher criticism; an estimate in which on the part of the public there was something really of expiation. The edition preparing, planned by a publisher of taste, was practically an act of high reparation; the wood-cuts with which it was to be enriched were the homage of English art to one of the most independent representatives of English letters. Major and Mrs. Monarch confessed to me they had hoped I might be able to work *them* into my branch of the enterprise. They knew I was to do the first of the books, "Rutland Ramsay," but I had to make clear to them that my participation in the rest of the affair—this first book was to be a test—must depend on the satisfaction I should give. If this should be limited my employers would drop me with scarce common forms. It was therefore a crisis for me, and naturally I was making special preparations, looking about for new people, should they be necessary, and securing the best types. I admitted however that I should like to settle down to two or three good models who would do for everything.

"Should we have often to—a—put on special clothes?" Mrs. Monarch timidly demanded.

"Dear yes—that's half the business."

"And should we be expected to supply our own costumes?"

"Oh no; I've got a lot of things. A painter's models put on—or put off—anything he likes."

"And you mean—a—the same?"

"The same?"

Mrs. Monarch looked at her husband again.

"Oh she was just wondering," he explained, "if the costumes are in *general* use." I had to confess that they were, and I mentioned further that some of them—I had a lot of genuine greasy last-century things—had served their time, a hundred years ago, on living world-stained men and women; on figures not perhaps so far removed, in that vanished world, from *their* type, the Monarchs', *quoi!*[1] of a breeched and bewigged age. "We'll put on anything that *fits*," said the Major.

"Oh I arrange that—they fit in the pictures."

"I'm afraid I should do better for the modern books. I'd come as you like," said Mrs. Monarch.

"She has got a lot of clothes at home: they might do for contemporary life," her husband continued.

---

1. What!

"Oh I can fancy scenes in which you'd be quite natural." And indeed I could see the slipshod rearrangements of stale properties—the stories I tried to produce pictures for without the exasperation of reading them—whose sandy tracts the good lady might help to people. But I had to return to the fact that for this sort of work—the daily mechanical grind—I was already equipped: the people I was working with were fully adequate.

"We only thought we might be more like *some* characters," said Mrs. Monarch mildly, getting up.

Her husband also rose; he stood looking at me with a dim wistfulness that was touching in so fine a man.

"Wouldn't it be rather a pull sometimes to have—a—to have—?" He hung fire; he wanted me to help him by phrasing what he meant. But I couldn't—I didn't know. So he brought it out awkwardly: "The *real* thing; a gentleman, you know, or a lady." I was quite ready to give a general assent—I admitted that there was a great deal in that. This encouraged Major Monarch to say, following up his appeal with an unacted gulp: "It's awfully hard—we've tried everything." The gulp was communicative; it proved too much for his wife. Before I knew it Mrs. Monarch had dropped again upon a divan and burst into tears. Her husband sat down beside her, holding one of her hands; whereupon she quickly dried her eyes with the other, while I felt embarrassed as she looked up at me. "There isn't a confounded job I haven't applied for—waited for—prayed for. You can fancy we'd be pretty bad first. Secretaryships and that sort of thing? You might as well ask for a peerage. I'd be *anything*—I'm strong; a messenger or a coalheaver. I'd put on a gold-laced cap and open carriage-doors in front of the haberdasher's; I'd hang about a station to carry portmanteaux; I'd be a postman. But they won't *look* at you; there are thousands as good as yourself already on the ground. *Gentlemen*, poor beggars, who've drunk their wine, who've kept their hunters!"

I was as reassuring as I knew how to be, and my visitors were presently on their feet again while, for the experiment, we agreed on an hour. We were discussing it when the door opened and Miss Churm came in with a wet umbrella. Miss Churm had to take the omnibus to Maida Vale and then walk half a mile. She looked a trifle blowsy and slightly splashed. I scarcely ever saw her come in without thinking fresh how odd it was that, being so little in herself, she should yet be so much in others. She was a meagre little Miss Churm, but was such an ample heroine of romance. She was only a freckled cockney, but she could represent everything, from a fine lady to a shepherdess; she had the faculty as she might have had a fine voice or long hair. She couldn't spell and she loved beer, but she had two or three "points," and practice, and a knack, and mother-wit, and a whimsical sensibility, and a love of the theatre, and seven sisters, and not an ounce of respect, especially for the *h*. The first thing my visitors saw was that her umbrella was wet, and in their spotless perfection they visibly winced at it. The rain had come on since their arrival.

"I'm all in a soak; there *was* a mess of people in the 'bus. I wish you lived near a stytion," said Miss Churm. I requested her to get ready as quickly as possible, and she passed into the room in which she always changed her dress. But before going out she asked me what she was to get into this time.

"It's the Russian princess, don't you know?" I answered; "The one with the 'golden eyes,' in black velvet, for the long thing in the *Cheapside*."

"Golden eyes? I *say*!" cried Miss Churm, while my companions watched her with intensity as she withdrew. She always arranged herself, when she was late, before I could turn around; and I kept my visitors a little on purpose, so that they might get an idea, from seeing her, what would be expected of themselves. I mentioned that she was quite my notion of an excellent model—she was really very clever.

"Do you think she looks like a Russian princess?" Major Monarch asked with lurking alarm.

"When I make her, yes."

"Oh if you have to *make* her—!" he reasoned, not without point.

"That's the most you can ask. There are so many who are not makeable."

"Well now, *here's* a lady"—and with a persuasive smile he passed his arm into his wife's—"who's already made!"

"Oh I'm not a Russian princess," Mrs. Monarch protested a little coldly. I could see she had known some and didn't like them. There at once was a complication of a kind I never had to fear with Miss Churm.

This young lady came back in black velvet—the gown was rather rusty and very low on her lean shoulders—and with a Japanese fan in her red hands. I reminded her that in the scene I was doing she had to look over some one's head. "I forget whose it is; but it doesn't matter. Just look over a head."

"I'd rather look over a stove," said Miss Churm; and she took her station near the fire. She fell into position, settled herself into a tall attitude, gave a certain backward inclination to her head and a certain forward droop to her fan, and looked, at least to my prejudiced sense, distinguished and charming, foreign and dangerous. We left her looking so while I went downstairs with Major and Mrs. Monarch.

"I believe I could come about as near it as that," said Mrs. Monarch.

"Oh, you think she's shabby, but you must allow for the alchemy of art."

However, they went off with an evident increase of comfort founded on their demonstrable advantage in being the real thing. I could fancy them shuddering over Miss Churm. She was very droll about them when I went back, for I told her what they wanted.

"Well, if *she* can sit I'll tyke to bookkeeping," said my model.

"She's very ladylike," I replied as an innocent form of aggravation.

"So much the worse for *you*. That means she can't turn round."

"She'll do for the fashionable novels."

"Oh yes, she'll *do* for them!" my model humorously declared.

"Ain't they bad enough without her?" I had often sociably denounced them to Miss Churm.

3

It was for the elucidation of a mystery in one of these works that I first tried Mrs. Monarch. Her husband came with her, to be useful if necessary—it was sufficiently clear that as a general thing he would prefer to come with her. At first I wondered if this were for "propriety's" sake—if he were going to be jealous and meddling. The idea was too tiresome, and if it had been confirmed it would speedily have brought our acquaintance to a close. But I soon saw there was nothing in it and that if he accompanied Mrs. Monarch it was—in addition to the chance of being wanted—simply because he had nothing else to do. When they were separate his occupation was gone and they never *had* been separate. I judged rightly that in their awkward situation their close union was their main comfort and that this union had no weak spot. It was a real marriage, an encouragement to the hesitating, a nut for pessimists to crack. Their address was humble—I remember afterwards thinking it had been the only thing about them that was really professional—and I could fancy the lamentable lodgings in which the Major would have been left alone. He could sit there more or less grimly with his wife—he couldn't sit there anyhow without her.

He had too much tact to try and make himself agreeable when he couldn't be useful; so when I was too absorbed in my work to talk he simply sat and waited. But I liked to hear him talk—it made my work, when not interrupting it, less mechanical, less special. To listen to him was to combine the excitement of going out with the economy of staying at home. There was only one hindrance—that I seemed not to know any of the people this brilliant couple had known. I think he wondered extremely, during the term of our intercourse, whom the deuce I *did* know. He hadn't a stray sixpence of an idea to fumble for, so we didn't spin it very fine; we confined ourselves to questions of leather and even of liquor—saddlers and breeches-makers and how to get excellent claret cheap—and matters like "good trains" and the habits of small game. His lore on these last subjects was astonishing—he managed to interweave the station-master with the ornithologist. When he couldn't talk about greater things he could talk cheerfully about smaller, and since I couldn't accompany him into reminiscences of the fashionable world he could lower the conversation without a visible effort to my level.

So earnest a desire to please was touching in a man who could so easily have knocked one down. He looked after the fire and had an opinion on the draught of the stove without my asking him, and I could see that he thought many of my arrangements not half knowing. I remember telling him that if I were only rich I'd offer him a salary to come and teach me how to live. Sometimes he gave a random sigh of which the essence might have been: "Give me even such a bare old barrack as *this*, and I'd do something with it!" When I wanted to use him he came alone; which was an illustration of the superior courage of women. His wife could bear her solitary second floor, and she was in general more discreet; showing by various small reserves that she was alive to the propriety of keeping our relations markedly professional—not letting them slide into sociability. She wished it to remain clear that she and the Major were employed, not cultivated, and if she approved of me as a superior, who could be kept in his place, she never thought me quite good enough for an equal.

She sat with great intensity, giving the whole of her mind to it, and was capable of remaining for an hour almost as motionless as before a photographer's lens. I could see she had been photographed often, but somehow the very habit that made her good for that purpose unfitted her for mine. At first I was extremely pleased with her ladylike air, and it was a satisfaction, on coming to follow her lines, to see how good they were and how far they could lead the pencil. But after a little skirmishing I began to find her too insurmountably stiff; do what I would with it my drawing looked like a photograph or a copy of a photograph. Her figure had no variety of expression—she herself had no sense of variety. You may say that this was my business and was only a question of placing her. Yet I placed her in every conceivable position and she managed to obliterate their differences. She was always a lady certainly, and into the bargain was always the same lady. She was the real thing, but always the same thing. There were moments when I rather writhed under the serenity of her confidence that she *was* the real thing. All her dealings with me and all her husband's were an implication that this was lucky for *me*. Meanwhile I found myself trying to invent types that approached her own, instead of making her own transform itself—in the clever way that was not impossible for instance to poor Miss Churm. Arrange as I would and take the precautions I would, she always came out, in my pictures, too tall—landing me in the dilemma of having represented a fascinating woman as seven feet high, which (out of respect perhaps to my own very much scantier inches) was far from my idea of such personage.

The case was worse with the Major—nothing I could do would keep *him* down, so that he became useful only for the representation of brawny giants. I adored variety and range, I cherished human accidents, the illustrative note; I wanted to characterise closely, and the thing in the world I most hated was the danger of being ridden by a type. I had quarrelled with some of my friends about it; I had parted company with them for maintaining that one *had* to be, and that if the type was beautiful—witness Raphael and Leonardo—the servitude was only a gain. I was neither Leonardo nor Raphael—I might only be a presumptuous young modern searcher; but I held that everything was to be sacrificed sooner than character. When they claimed that the obsessional form could easily *be* character I retorted, perhaps superficially, "Whose?" It couldn't be everybody's—it might end in being nobody's.

After I had drawn Mrs. Monarch a dozen times I felt surer even than before that the value of such a model as Miss Churm resided precisely in the fact that she had no positive stamp, combined of course with the other fact that what she did have was a curious and inexplicable talent for imitation. Her usual appearance was like a curtain which she could draw up at request for a capital performance. This performance was simply suggestive; but it was a word to the wise—it was vivid and pretty. Sometimes even I thought it, though she was plain herself, too insipidly pretty; I made it a reproach to her that the figures drawn from her were monotonously (*bêtement*,[2] as we used to say) graceful. Nothing made her more angry: it was so much her pride to feel she could sit for characters that had nothing in common with each other. She would accuse me at such moments of taking away her "reputytion."

It suffered a certain shrinkage, this queer quantity, from the repeated visits of my new friends. Miss Churm was greatly in demand, never in want of employment, so I had no scruple in putting her off occasionally, to try them more at my ease. It was certainly amusing at first to do the real thing—it was amusing to do Major Monarch's trousers. They *were* the real thing, even if he did come out colossal. It was amusing to do his wife's back hair—it was so mathematically neat—and the particular "smart" tension of her tight stays. She lent herself especially to positions in which the face was somewhat averted or blurred; she abounded in ladylike back views and *profils perdus*.[3] When she stood erect she took naturally one of the attitudes in which court-painters represent queens and princesses; so that I found myself wondering whether, to draw out this accomplishment, I couldn't get the editor of the *Cheapside* to publish a really royal romance, "A Tale of Buckingham Palace." Sometimes however the real thing and the make-believe came into contact; by which I mean that Miss Churm, keeping an appointment or coming to make one on days when I had much work in hand, encountered her invidious rivals. The encounter was not on their part, for they noticed her no more than if she had been the housemaid; not from intentional loftiness, but simply because as yet, professionally, they didn't know how to fraternise, as I could imagine they would have liked—or at least that the Major would. They couldn't talk about the omnibus—they always walked; and they didn't know what else to try—she wasn't interested in good trains or cheap claret. Besides, they must have felt—in the air— that she was amused at them, secretly derisive of their ever knowing how. She wasn't a person to conceal the limits of her faith if she had had a chance to show them. On the other hand Mrs. Monarch didn't think her tidy; for why else did she take pains to say to me—it was going out of the way, for Mrs. Monarch—that she didn't like dirty women?

One day when my young lady happened to be present with my

---

2. Beastishly, stupidly, foolishly.
3. Lost profiles (French); poses in which the model's head is viewed over the shoulder.

other sitters—she even dropped in, when it was convenient, for a chat—I asked her to be so good as to lend a hand in getting tea, a service with which she was familiar and which was one of a class that, living as I did in a small way, with slender domestic resources, I often appealed to my models to render. They liked to lay hands on my property, to break the sitting, and sometimes the china—it made them feel Bohemian. The next time I saw Miss Churm after this incident she surprised me greatly by making a scene about it—she accused me of having wished to humiliate her. She hadn't resented the outrage at the time, but had seemed obliging and amused, enjoying the comedy of asking Mrs. Monarch, who sat vague and silent, whether she would have cream and sugar, and putting an exaggerated simper into the question. She had tried intonations—as if she too wished to pass for the real thing—till I was afraid my other visitors would take offence.

Oh they were determined not to do this, and their touching patience was the measure of their great need. They would sit by the hour, uncomplaining, till I was ready to use them; they would come back on the chance of being wanted and would walk away cheerfully if it failed. I used to go to the door with them to see in what magnificent order they retreated. I tried to find other employment for them—I introduced them to several artists. But they didn't "take," for reasons I could appreciate, and I became rather anxiously aware that after such disappointments they fell back upon me with a heavier weight. They did me the honor to think me most *their* form. They weren't romantic enough for the painters, and in those days there were few serious workers in black-and-white. Besides, they had an eye to the great job I had mentioned to them—they had secretly set their hearts on supplying the right essence for my pictorial vindication of our fine novelist. They knew that for this undertaking I should want no costume-effects, none of the trippery of past ages—that it was a case in which everything would be contemporary and satirical and presumably genteel. If I could work them into it their future would be assured, for the labour would of course be long and the occupation steady.

One day Mrs. Monarch came without her husband—she explained his absence by his having had to go to the City. While she sat there in her usual relaxed majesty there came at the door a knock which I immediately recognised as the subdued appeal of a model out of work. It was followed by the entrance of a young man whom I at once saw to be a foreigner and who proved in fact an Italian acquainted with no English word but my name, which he uttered in a way that made it seem to include all others. I hadn't then visited his country, nor was I proficient in his tongue; but as he was not so meanly constituted—what Italian is?—as to depend only on that member for expression he conveyed to me, in familiar but graceful mimicry, that he was in search of exactly the employment in which the lady before me was engaged. I was not struck with him at first, and while I continued to draw I dropped few signs of interest or encouragement. He stood his ground however—not importunately, but with a dumb dog-like fidelity in his eyes that amounted to innocent impudence, the manner of a devoted servant—he might have been in the house for years—unjustly suspected. Suddenly it struck me that this very attitude and expression made a picture; whereupon I told him to sit down and wait till I should be free. There was another picture in the way he obeyed me, and I observed as I worked that there were others still in the way he looked wonderingly, with his head thrown back, about the high studio. He might have been crossing himself in Saint Peter's. Before I finished I said to myself "The fellow's a bankrupt orange-monger, but a treasure."

When Mrs. Monarch withdrew he passed across the room like a flash to open the door for her, standing there with the rapt pure gaze of the young Dante spell-bound by the young Beatrice. As I never insisted, in such situations, on the blankness of the British domestic, I reflected that he had the making of a servant—and I needed one, but couldn't pay him to be only that—as well as of a model; in short I resolved to adopt my bright adventurer if he would agree to officiate in the double capacity. He jumped at my offer, and in the event my rashness—for I had really known nothing about him—wasn't brought home to me. He proved a sympathetic though a desultory ministrant, and had in a wonderful degree the *sentiment de la pose.*[4] It was uncultivated, instinctive, a part of the happy instinct that had guided him to my door and helped him to spell out my name on the card nailed to it. He had had no other introduction to me than a guess, from the shape of my high north window, seen outside, that my place was a studio and that as a studio it would contain an artist. He had wandered to England in search of fortune, like other itinerants, and had embarked, with a partner and a small green hand-cart, on the sale of penny ices. The ices had melted away and the partner had dissolved in their train. My young man wore tight yellow trousers with reddish stripes and his name was Oronte. He was sallow but fair, and when I put him into some old clothes of my own he looked like an Englishman. He was as good as Miss Churm, who could look, when requested, like an Italian.

4

I thought Mrs. Monarch's face slightly convulsed when, on her coming back with her husband, she found Oronte installed. It was strange to have to recognise in a scrap of a lazzarone a competitor to her magnificent Major. It was she who scented danger first, for the Major was anecdotically unconscious. But Oronte gave us tea, with a hundred eager confusions—he had never been concerned in so queer a process—and I think she thought better of me for having at last an "establishment." They saw a couple of drawings that I had made of the establishment, and Mrs. Monarch hinted that it never would have struck her he had sat for them. "Now the drawings you make from *us*, they look exactly like us," she

4. A sense of the correct pose.

reminded me, smiling in triumph; and I recognized that this was indeed just their defect. When I drew the Monarchs I couldn't anyhow get away from them—get into the character I wanted to represent; and I hadn't the least desire my model should be discoverable in my picture. Miss Churm never was, and Mrs. Monarch thought I hid her, very properly, because she was vulgar; whereas if she was lost it was only as the dead who go to heaven are lost—in the gain of an angel the more.

By this time I had got a certain start with "Rutland Ramsay," the first novel in the great projected series; that is I had produced a dozen drawings, several with the help of the Major and his wife, and I had sent them in for approval. My understanding with the publishers, as I have already hinted, had been that I was to be left to do my work, in this particular case, as I liked, with the whole book committed to me; but my connexion with the rest of the series was only contingent. There were moments when, frankly, it *was* a comfort to have the real thing under one's hand; for there were characters in "Rutland Ramsay" that were very much like it. There were people presumably as erect as the Major and women of as good a fashion as Mrs. Monarch. There was a great deal of country-house life— treated, it is true, in a fine fanciful ironical generalised way—and there was a considerable implication of knickerbockers and kilts. There were certain things I had to settle at the outset; such things for instance as the exact appearance of the hero and the particular bloom and figure of the heroine. The author of course gave me a lead, but there was a margin for interpretation. I took the Monarchs into my confidence, I told them frankly what I was about, I mentioned my embarrassments and alternatives. "Oh take *him*!" Mrs. Monarch murmured sweetly, looking at her husband; and "What could you want better than my wife?" the Major enquired with the comfortable candour that now prevailed between us.

I wasn't obliged to answer these remarks—I was only obliged to place my sitters. I wasn't easy in mind, and I postponed a little timidly perhaps the solving of my question. The book was a large canvas, the other figures were numerous, and I worked off at first some of the episodes in which the hero and the heroine were not concerned. When once I had set *them* up I should have to stick to them—I couldn't make my young man seven feet high in one place and five feet nine in another. I inclined on the whole to the latter measurement, though the Major more than once reminded me that *he* looked about as young as any one. It was indeed quite possible to arrange him, for the figure, so that it would have been difficult to detect his age. After the spontaneous Oronte had been with me a month, and after I had given him to understand several times over that his native exuberance would presently constitute an insurmountable barrier to our further intercourse, I waked to a sense of his heroic capacity. He was only five feet seven, but the remaining inches were latent. I tried him almost secretly at first for I was really rather afraid of the judgment my other models would pass on such a choice. If they regarded Miss Churm as little better than a snare what would they think of the representation by a person so little the real thing as an Italian street-vendor of a protagonist formed by a public school?

If I went a little in fear of them it wasn't because they bullied me, because they had got an oppressive foothold, but because in their really pathetic decorum and mysteriously permanent newness they counted on me so intensely. I was therefore very glad when Jack Hawley came home: he was always of such good counsel. He painted badly himself, but there was no one like him for putting his finger on the place. He had been absent from England for a year; he had been somewhere—I don't remember where—to get a fresh eye. I was in a good deal of dread of any such organ, but we were old friends; he had been away for months and a sense of emptiness was creeping into my life. I hadn't dodged a missile for a year.

He came back with a fresh eye, but with the same old black velvet blouse, and the first evening he spent in my studio we smoked cigarettes till the small hours. He had done no work himself, he had only got the eye; so the field was clear for the production of my little things. He wanted to see what I had produced for the *Cheapside*, but he was disappointed in the exhibition. That at least seemed the meaning of two or three comprehensive groans which, as he lounged on my big divan, his leg folded under him, looking at my latest drawings, issued from his lips with the smoke of the cigarette.

"What's the matter with you?" I asked.

"What's the matter with *you*?"

"Nothing save that I'm mystified."

"You are indeed. You're quite off the hinge. What's the meaning of this new fad?" And he tossed me, with visible irreverence, a drawing in which I happened to have depicted both my elegant models. I asked if he didn't think it good, and he replied that it struck him as execrable, given the sort of thing I had always represented myself to him as wishing to arrive at; but I let that pass—I was so anxious to see exactly what he meant. The two figures in the picture looked colossal, but I supposed this was *not* what he meant, inasmuch as, for aught he knew to the contrary, I might have been trying for some such effect. I maintained that I was working exactly in the same way as when he last had done me the honour to tell me I might do something some day. "Well, there's a screw loose somewhere," he answered; "wait a bit and I'll discover it." I depended upon him to do so: where else was the fresh eye? But he produced at last nothing more luminous than "I don't know—I don't like your types." This was lame for a critic who had never consented to discuss with me anything but the question of execution, the direction of strokes and the mystery of values.

"In the drawings you've been looking at I think my types are very handsome."

"Oh they won't do!"

"I've been working with new models."

"I see you have. *They* won't do."

"Are you very sure of that?"

"Absolutely—they're stupid."

"You mean *I* am—for I ought to get round that."

"You *can't*—with such people. Who are they?"

I told him, so far as was necessary, and he concluded heartlessly:

"Ce sont des gens qu'il faut mettre à la porte."

"You've never seen them; they're awfully good"—I flew to their defence.

"Not seen them? Why all this recent work of yours drops to pieces with them. It's all I want to see of them."

"No one else has said anything against it—the *Cheapside* people are pleased."

"Every one else is an ass, and the *Cheapside* people the biggest asses of all. Come, don't pretend at this time of day to have pretty illusions about the public, especially about publishers and editors. It's not for *such* animals you work—it's for those who know, *coloro che sanno*;[5] so keep straight for *me* if you can't keep straight for yourself. There was a certain sort of thing you used to try for—and a very good thing it was. But this twaddle isn't *in* it." When I talked with Hawley later about "Rutland Ramsay" and its possible successors he declared that I must get back into my boat again or I should go to the bottom. His voice in short was the voice of warning.

I noted the warning, but I didn't turn my friends out of doors. They bored me a good deal; but the very fact that they bored me admonished me not to sacrifice them—if there was anything to be done with them —simply to irritation. As I look back at this phase they seem to me to have pervaded my life not a little. I have a vision of them as most of the time in my studio, seated against the wall on an old velvet bench to be out of the way, and resembling the while a pair of patient courtiers in a royal antechamber. I'm convinced that during the coldest weeks of the winter they held their ground because it saved them fire. Their newness was losing its gloss, and it was impossible not to feel them objects of charity. Whenever Miss Churm arrived they went away, and after I was fairly launched in "Rutland Ramsay" Miss Churm arrived pretty often. They managed to express to me tacitly that they supposed I wanted her for the low life of the book, and I let them suppose it, since they had attempted to study the work—it was lying about the studio—without discovering that it dealt only with the highest circles. They had dipped into the most brilliant of our novelists without deciphering many passages. I still took an hour from them, now and again, in spite of Jack Hawley's warning: it would be time enough to dismiss them, if dismissal should be necessary, when the rigour of the season was over. Hawley had made their acquaintance—he had met them at my fireside—and thought them a ridiculous pair. Learning that he was a painter they tried to approach him, to show him too that they were the real thing; but he looked at them, across the big room, as if they were miles away:

---

5. Those who know.

they were a compendium of everything he most objected to in the social system of his country. Such people as that, all convention and patent-leather, with ejaculations that stopped conversation, had no business in a studio. A studio was a place to learn to see, and how could you see through a pair of feather-beds?

The main inconvenience I suffered at their hands was that at first I was shy of letting it break upon them that my artful little servant had begun to sit to me for "Rutland Ramsay." They knew I had been odd enough—they were prepared by this time to allow oddity to artists—to pick a foreign vagabond out of the streets when I might have had a person with whiskers and credentials; but it was some time before they learned how high I rated his accomplishments. They found him in an attitude more than once, but they never doubted I was doing him as an organ-grinder. There were several things they never guessed, and one of them was that for a striking scene in the novel, in which a footman briefly figured, it occurred to me to make use of Major Monarch as the menial. I kept putting this off, I didn't like to ask him to don the livery—besides the difficulty of finding a livery to fit him. At last, one day late in the winter, when I was at work on the despised Oronte, who caught one's idea on the wing, and was in the glow of feeling myself go very straight, they came in, the Major and his wife, with their society laugh about nothing (there was less and less to laugh at); came on like country-callers—they always reminded me of that—who have walked across the park after church and are presently persuaded to stay to luncheon. Luncheon was over, but they could stay to tea—I knew they wanted it. The fit was on me, however, and I couldn't let my ardour cool and my work wait, with the fading daylight, while my model prepared it. So I asked Mrs. Monarch if she would mind laying it out—a request which for an instant brought all the blood to her face. Her eyes were on her husband's for a second, and some mute telegraphy passed between them. Their folly was over the next instant; his cheerful shrewdness put an end of it. So far from pitying their wounded pride, I must add, I was moved to give it as complete a lesson as I could. They bustled about together and got out the cups and saucers and made the kettle boil. I know they felt as if they were waiting on my servant, and when the tea was prepared I said: "He'll have a cup, please—he's tired." Mrs. Monarch brought him one where he stood, and he took it from her, as if he had been a gentleman at a party squeezing a crush-hat with an elbow.

Then it came over me that she had made a great effort for me—made it with a kind of nobleness—and that I owed her a compensation. Each time I saw her after this I wondered what the compensation could be. I couldn't go on doing the wrong thing to oblige them. Oh it *was* the wrong thing, the stamp of the work for which they sat—Hawley was not the only person to say it now. I sent in a large number of the drawings I had made for "Rutland Ramsay," and I received a warning that was more to the point than Hawley's. The artistic adviser of the house for which I was working was of opinion that many of my illustrations were not what had been looked for. Most of these illustrations were the subjects in which the Monarchs had figured. Without going into the question of what *had* been looked for, I had to face the fact that at this rate I shouldn't get the other books to do. I hurled myself in despair on Miss Churm—I put her through all her paces. I not only adopted Oronte publicly as my hero, but one morning when the Major looked in to see if I didn't require him to finish a *Cheapside* figure for which he had begun to sit the week before, I told him I had changed my mind—I'd do the drawing from my man. At this my visitor turned pale and stood looking at me. "Is *he* your idea of an English gentleman?" he asked.

I was disappointed, I was nervous, I wanted to get on with my work; so I replied with irritation: "Oh my dear Major—I can't be ruined for *you*!"

It was a horrid speech, but he stood another moment—after which, without a word, he quitted the studio. I drew a long breath, for I said to myself that I shouldn't see him again. I hadn't told him definitely that I was in danger of having my work rejected, but I was vexed at his not having felt the catastrophe in the air, read with me the moral of our fruitless collaboration, the lesson that in the deceptive atmosphere of art even the highest respectability may fail of being plastic.

I didn't owe my friends money, but I did see them again. They reappeared together three days later, and, given all the other facts, there was something tragic in that one. It was a clear proof they could find nothing else in life to do. They had threshed the matter out in a dismal conference—they had digested the bad news that they were not in for the series. If they weren't useful to me even for the *Cheapside* their function seemed difficult to determine, and I could only judge at first that they had come, forgivingly, decorously, to take a last leave. This made me rejoice in secret that I had little leisure for a scene; for I had placed both my other models in position together and I was pegging away at a drawing from which I hoped to derive glory. It had been suggested by the passage in which Rutland Ramsay, drawing up a chair to Artemisia's piano-stool, says extraordinary things to her while she ostensibly fingers out a difficult piece of music. I had done Miss Churm at the piano before—it was an attitude in which she knew how to take on an absolutely poetic grace. I wished the two figures to "compose" together with intensity, and my little Italian had entered perfectly into my conception. The pair were vividly before me, the piano had been pulled out; it was a charming show of blended youth and murmured love, which I had only to catch and keep. My visitors stood and looked at it, and I was friendly to them over my shoulder.

They made no response, but I was used to silent company and went on with my work, only a little disconcerted—even though exhilarated by the sense that *this* was at least the ideal thing—at not having got rid of them after all. Presently I heard Mrs. Monarch's sweet voice beside or rather above me: "I wish her hair were a little better done." I looked up and she was staring with a strange fixedness at Miss Churm, whose back was turned to her. "Do you mind my just touching it?" she went on—a question which made me spring up for an instant as with the instinctive fear that she might do the young lady a harm. But she quieted me with a glance I shall never forget—I confess I should like to have been able to paint *that*—and went for a moment to my model. She spoke to her softly, laying a hand on her shoulder and bending over her; and as the girl, understanding, gratefully assented, she disposed her rough curls, with a few quick passes, in such a way as to make Miss Churm's head twice as charming. It was one of the most heroic personal services I've ever seen rendered. Then Mrs. Monarch turned away with a low sigh and, looking about her as if for something to do, stooped to the floor with a noble humility and picked up a dirty rag that had dropped out of my paint-box.

The Major meanwhile had also been looking for something to do, and, wandering to the other end of the studio, saw before him my breakfast-things neglected, unremoved. "I say, can't I be useful *here*?" he called out to me with an irrepressible quaver. I assented with a laugh that I fear was awkward, and for the next ten minutes, while I worked, I heard the light clatter of china and the tinkle of spoons and glass. Mrs. Monarch assisted her husband—they washed up my crockery, they put it away. They wandered off into my little scullery, and I afterwards found that they had cleaned my knives and that my slender stock of plate had an unprecedented surface. When it came over me, the latent eloquence of what they were doing, I confess that my drawing was blurred for a moment—the picture swam. They had accepted their failure, but they couldn't accept their fate. They had bowed their heads in bewilderment to the perverse and cruel law in virtue of which the real thing could be so much less precious than the unreal; but they didn't want to starve. If my servants were my models; then my models might be my servants. They would reverse the parts—the others would sit for the ladies and gentlemen and *they* would do the work. They would still be in the studio—it was an intense dumb appeal to me not to turn them out. "Take us on," they wanted to say—"we'll do *anything*."

My pencil dropped from my hand; my sitting was spoiled and I got rid of my sitters, who were also evidently rather mystified and awestruck. Then, alone with the Major and his wife I had a most uncomfortable moment. He put their prayer into a single sentence: "I say, you know—just let *us* do for you, can't you?" I couldn't—it was dreadful to see them emptying my slops; but I pretended I could, to oblige them, for about a week. Then I gave them a sum of money to go away, and I never saw them again. I obtained the remaining books, but my friend Hawley repeats that Major and Mrs. Monarch did me a permanent harm, got me into false ways. If it be true I'm content to have paid the price—for the memory.

1892

In writers like Flaubert and de Maupassant we find a strain of realism that keeps us firmly grounded in the external world. In Henry James we find a

strain devoted to realistically delineating the consciousness of characters. Such psychological realism presents the writer with the special problem of creating a consciousness interesting enough to bear examination. As James points out in the preface to his novel The Princess Casamassima, *one requirement is that the character be perceptive; but this is not enough.*

"If we were never bewildered there would never be a story": Henry James

I recognise at the same time, and in planning "The Princess Casamassima" felt it highly important to recognise, the danger of filling too full any supposed and above all any obviously limited vessel of consciousness. If persons either tragically or comically embroiled with life allow us the comic or tragic value of their embroilment in proportion as their struggle is a measured and directed one, it is strangely true, none the less, that beyond a certain point they are spoiled for us by this carrying of a due light. They may carry too much of it for our credence, for our compassion, for our derision. They may be shown as knowing too much and feeling too much—not certainly for their remaining remarkable, but for their remaining "natural" and typical, for their having the needful communities with our own precious liability to fall into traps and be bewildered. It seems probable that if we were never bewildered there would never be a story to tell about us; we should partake of the superior nature of the all-knowing immortals whose annals are dreadfully dull so long as flurried humans are not, for the positive relief of bored Olympians, mixed up with them. Therefore it is that the wary reader for the most part warns the novelist against making his characters too *interpretative* of the muddle of fate, or in other words too divinely, too priggishly clever. "Give us plenty of bewilderment," this monitor seems to say, "so long as there is plenty of slashing out in the bewilderment too. But don't, we beseech you, give us too much intelligence; for intelligence— well, *endangers;* endangers not perhaps the slasher himself, but the very slashing, the subject-matter of any self-respecting story. It opens up too many considerations, possibilities, issues; it *may* lead the slasher into dreary realms where slashing somehow fails and falls to the ground."

GUY DE MAUPASSANT

(1850–1893)

THE STRING

translated from the French by Ernest Boyd

Along all the roads around Goderville the peasants and their wives were coming towards the little town, for it was market-day. The men walked with plodding steps, their bodies bent forward at each thrust of their long bowed legs. They were deformed by hard work, by the pull of the heavy plough which raises the left shoulder and twists the torso, by the reaping of the wheat which forces the knees apart to get a firm stand, by all the slow and strenuous labors of life on the farm. Their blue smocks, starched, shining as if varnished, ornamented with a little design in white at the neck and wrists, puffed about their bony bodies, seemed like balloons ready to carry them off. From each smock a head, two arms, and two feet protruded.

Some led a cow or a calf at the end of a rope, and their wives, walking behind the animal, whipped its haunches with a leafy branch to hasten its progress. They carried on their arms large wicker-baskets, out of which here a chicken and there a duck thrust forth its head. The women walked with a quicker, livelier step than their husbands. Their spare, straight figures were wrapped in a scanty little shawl, pinned over their flat bosoms, and their heads were enveloped in a piece of white linen tightly pressed on the hair and surmounted by a cap.

Then a wagon passed, its nag's jerky trot shaking up and down two men seated side by side and a woman in the bottom of the vehicle, the latter holding on to the sides to lessen the stiff jolts.

The square of Goderville was filled with a milling throng of human beings and animals. The horns of the cattle, the rough-napped top-hats of the rich peasants, and the headgear of the peasant women stood out in the crowd. And the clamorous, shrill, shouting voices made a continuous and savage din dominated now and again by the robust lungs of some countryman's laugh, or the long lowing of a cow tied to the wall of a house.

The scene smacked of the stable, the dairy and the dung-heap, of hay and sweat, and gave forth that sharp, unpleasant odor, human and animal, peculiar to the people of the fields.

Maître Hauchecorne, of Bréauté, had just arrived at Goderville. He was directing his steps toward the square, when he perceived upon the ground a little piece of string. Maître Hauchecorne, economical like a true Norman, thought that everything useful ought to be picked up, and he stooped painfully, for he suffered from rheumatism. He took up the bit of string from the ground and was beginning to roll it carefully when he noticed Maître Malandain, the harness-maker, on the threshold of his door, looking at him. They had once had a quarrel on the subject of a halter, and they had remained on bad terms, being both good haters. Maître Hauchecorne was seized with a sort of shame to be seen thus by his enemy, picking a bit of string out of the dirt. He hid his find quickly under his smock, and slipped it into his trouser pocket; then he pretended to be still looking on the ground for something which he did not find, and he went towards the market, his head thrust forward, bent double by his pain.

He was soon lost in the noisy and slowly moving crowd, which was busy with interminable bargainings. The peasants looked at cows, went away, came back, perplexed, always in fear of being cheated, not daring to decide, watching the vendor's eye, ever trying to find the trick in the man and the flaw in the beast.

The women, having placed their great baskets at their feet, had taken out the poultry, which lay upon the ground, tied together by the feet, with terrified eyes and scarlet crests.

They listened to offers, stated their prices with a dry air and impassive face, or perhaps, suddenly deciding on some proposed reduction, shouted to the customer who was slowly going away: "All right, Maître Anthime, I'll let you have it for that."

Then little by little the square was deserted, the church bell rang out the hour of noon, and those who lived too far away went to the different inns.

At Jourdain's the great room was full of people eating, and the big yard was full of vehicles of all kinds, gigs, wagons, nondescript carts, yellow with dirt, mended and patched, some with their shafts rising to the sky like two arms, others with their shafts on the ground and their backs in the air.

Behind the diners seated at table, the immense fireplace, filled with bright flames, cast a lively heat on the backs of the row on the right. Three spits were turning on which were chickens, pigeons, and legs of mutton; and an appetizing odor of roast meat and gravy dripping over the nicely browned skin rose from the fireplace, lightening all hearts and making the mouth water.

All the aristocracy of the plough ate there, at Maître Jourdain's, tavern keeper and horse dealer, a clever fellow and well off.

The dishes were passed and emptied, as were the jugs of yellow cider. Everyone told his affairs, his purchases, and sales. They discussed the crops. The weather was favorable for the greens but rather damp for the wheat.

Suddenly the drum began to beat in the yard, before the house. Everybody rose, except a few indifferent persons, and ran to the door, or to the windows, their mouths still full, their napkins in their hands.

After the public crier had stopped beating his drum, he called out in a jerky voice, speaking his phrases irregularly:

"It is hereby made known to the inhabitants of Goderville, and in general to all persons present at the market, that there was lost this morning, on the road to Benzeville, between nine and ten o'clock, a black leather pocketbook containing five hundred francs and some business papers. The finder is requested to return same to the Mayor's office or to Maître Fortuné Houlbrèque of Manneville. There will be twenty francs' reward."

Then the man went away. The heavy roll of the drum and the crier's voice were again heard at a distance.

Then they began to talk of this event discussing the chances that Maître Houlbrèque had of finding or not finding his pocketbook.

And the meal concluded. They were finishing their coffee when the chief of the gendarmes appeared upon the threshold.

He inquired:

"Is Maître Hauchecorne, of Bréauté, here?"

Maître Hauchecorne, seated at the other end of the table, replied: "Here I am."

And the officer resumed:

"Maître Hauchecorne, will you have the goodness to accompany me to the Mayor's office? The Mayor would like to talk to you."

The peasant, surprised and disturbed, swallowed at a draught his tiny glass of brandy, rose, even more bent than in the morning, for the first steps after each rest were specially difficult, and set out, repeating: "Here I am, here I am."

The Mayor was waiting for him, seated in an armchair. He was the local lawyer, a stout, solemn man, fond of pompous phrases.

"Maître Hauchecorne," said he, "you were seen this morning picking up, on the road to Benzeville, the pocketbook lost by Maître Houlbrèque, of Manneville."

The countryman looked at the Mayor in astonishment, already terrified by this suspicion resting on him without his knowing why.

"Me? Me? I picked up the pocketbook?"

"Yes, you, yourself."

"On my word of honor, I never heard of it."

"But you were seen."

"I was seen, me? Who says he saw me?"

"Monsieur Malandain, the harness-maker."

The old man remembered, understood, and flushed with anger.

"Ah, he saw me, the clodhopper, he saw me pick up this string, here, Mayor." And rummaging in his pocket he drew out the little piece of string.

But the Mayor, incredulous, shook his head.

"You will not make me believe, Maître Hauchecorne, that Monsieur Malandain, who is a man we can believe, mistook this string for a pocketbook."

The peasant, furious, lifted his hand, spat at one side to attest his honor, repeating:

"It is nevertheless God's own truth, the sacred truth. I repeat it on my soul and my salvation."

The Mayor resumed:

"After picking up the object, you went on staring, looking a long while in the mud to see if any piece of money had fallen out."

The old fellow choked with indignation and fear.

"How anyone can tell—how anyone can tell—such lies to take away an honest man's reputation! How can anyone——"

There was no use in his protesting, nobody believed him. He was confronted with Monsieur Malandain, who repeated and maintained his affirmation. They abused each other for an hour. At his own request, Maître Hauchecorne was searched. Nothing was found on him.

Finally the Mayor, very much perplexed, discharged him with the warning that he would consult the Public Prosecutor and ask for further orders.

The news had spread. As he left the Mayor's office, the old man was surrounded and questioned with a serious or bantering curiosity, in which there was no indignation. He began to tell the story of the string. No one believed him. They laughed at him.

He went along, stopping his friends, beginning endlessly his statement and his protestations, showing his pockets turned inside out, to prove that he had nothing.

They said:

"Ah, you old rascal!"

And he grew angry, becoming exasperated, hot and distressed at not being believed, not knowing what to do and endlessly repeating himself.

Night came. He had to leave. He started on his way with three neighbors to whom he pointed out the place where he had picked up the bit of string; and all along the road he spoke of his adventure.

In the evening he took a turn in the village of Bréauté, in order to tell it to everybody. He only met with incredulity.

It made him ill all night.

The next day about one o'clock in the afternoon, Marius Paumelle, a hired man in the employ of Maître Breton, husbandman at Ymauville, returned the pocketbook and its contents to Maître Houlbrèque of Manneville.

This man claimed to have found the object in the road; but not knowing how to read, he had carried it to the house and given it to his employer.

The news spread through the neighborhood. Maître Hauchecorne was informed of it. He immediately went the circuit and began to recount his story completed by the happy climax. He triumphed.

"What grieved me so much was not the thing itself, as the lying. There is nothing so shameful as to be placed under a cloud on account of a lie."

He talked of his adventure all day long, he told it on the highway to people who were passing by, in the inn to people who were drinking there, and to persons coming out of church the following Sunday. He stopped strangers to tell them about it. He was calm now, and yet something disturbed him without his knowing exactly what it was. People seemed to wink at him while they listened. They did not seem convinced. He had the feeling that remarks were being made behind his back.

On Tuesday of the next week he went to the market at Goderville, urged solely by the necessity he felt of discussing the case.

Malandain, standing at his door, began to laugh on seeing him pass. Why?

He approached a farmer from Criquetot, who did not let him finish, and giving him a poke in the stomach said to his face:

"You clever rogue."

Then he turned his back on him.

Maître Hauchecorne was confused, why was he called a clever rogue?

When he was seated at the table, in Jourdain's tavern he commenced to explain "the affair."

A horse-dealer from Monvilliers called to him:

"Come, come, old sharper, that's an old trick; I know all about your piece of string!"

Hauchecorne stammered:

"But the pocketbook was found."

But the other man replied:

"That'll do to tell, pop. One man finds a thing, and another man brings it back. No one is any the wiser, so you get out of it."

The peasant stood choking. He understood. They accused him of having had the pocketbook returned by a confederate, by an accomplice.

He tried to protest. All the table began to laugh.

He could not finish his dinner and went away in the midst of jeers.

He went home ashamed and indignant, choking with anger and confusion, the more dejected for the fact that he with his Norman cunning was capable of doing what they had accused him of, and even of boasting of it as a good trick. His innocence seemed to him, in a confused way, impossible to prove, for his sharpness was well known. And he was stricken to the heart by the injustice of the suspicion.

Then he began to recount the adventure again, enlarging his story every day, adding each time new reasons, more energetic protestations, more solemn oaths which he formulated and prepared in his hours of solitude, his whole mind given up to the story of the string. The more complicated his defense and the more subtle his argument, the less he was believed.

"Those are lying excuses," people said behind his back.

He felt it, ate his heart out over it, and wore himself out with useless efforts. He was visibly wasting away.

The wags now made him tell about the string to amuse them, as they make a soldier who has been on a campaign tell about his battles. His mind, seriously affected, began to weaken.

Towards the end of December he took to his bed.

He died early in January, and in the delirium of his death struggles he continued to protest his innocence, and to repeat his story:

"A piece of string, a piece of string—look—here it is."

1884

Guy de Maupassant was one of the first masters of the short story and one of the earliest of the self-conscious "realists." He was also a penetrating literary theorist. His discussion of the delicate balance between realism and artistic form in the preface to his novel Pierre *and* Jean *is a particularly useful counterpoint to "The String."*

"More cogent than reality itself": Guy de Maupassant

But even when we place ourselves at the same point of view as these realistic artists, we may discuss and dispute their theory, which seems to be comprehensively stated in these words: "The whole Truth and nothing but the Truth." Since the end they have in view is to bring out the philosophy of certain constant and current facts, they must often correct events in favor of probability and to the detriment of truth; for

"Le vrai peut quelquefois, n'être pas le vraisemblable." (Truth may sometimes not seem probable.)

The realist, if he is an artist, will endeavor not to show us a commonplace photograph of life, but to give us a presentment of it which shall be more complete, more striking, more cogent than reality itself. To tell everything is out of the question; it would require at least a volume for each day to enumerate the endless, insignificant incidents which crowd our existence. A choice must be made—and this is the first blow to the theory of "the whole truth."

Life, moreover, is composed of the most dissimilar things, the most unforeseen, the most contradictory, the most incongruous; it is merciless, without sequence or connection, full of inexplicable, illogical, and contradictory catastrophes, such as can only be classed as miscellaneous facts. This is why the artist, having chosen his subject, can only select such characteristic details as are of use to it, from this life overladen with chances and trifles, and reject everything else, everything by the way. . . .

Again, in life there is no difference of foreground and distance, and events are sometimes hurried on, sometimes left to linger indefinitely. Art, on the contrary, consists in the employment of foresight, and elaboration in arranging skillful and ingenious transitions, in setting essential events in a strong light, simply by the craft of composition, and giving all else the degree of relief, in proportion to their importance, requisite to produce a convincing sense of the special truth to be conveyed.

"Truth" in such work consists in producing a complete illusion by following the common logic of facts and not by transcribing them pell-mell, as they succeed each other.

Whence I conclude that the higher order of Realists should rather call themselves Illusionists.

ARTHUR CONAN DOYLE

(1859–1930)

THE ADVENTURE OF THE SPECKLED BAND

On glancing over my notes of the seventy odd cases in which I have during the last eight years studied the methods of my friend Sherlock Holmes, I find many tragic, some comic, a large number merely strange, but none commonplace; for, working as he did rather for the love of his art than for the acquirement of wealth, he refused to associate himself with any investigation which did not tend towards the unusual, and even the fantastic. Of all these varied cases, however, I cannot recall any which presented more singular features than that which was associated with the well-known Surrey family of the Roylotts of Stoke Moran. The events in question occurred in the early days of my association with Holmes, when we were sharing rooms as bachelors in Baker Street. It is possible that I might have placed them upon record before, but a promise of secrecy was made at the time, from which I have only been freed during the last month by the untimely death of the lady to whom the pledge was given. It is perhaps as well that the facts should now come to light, for I have reasons to know that there are widespread rumors as to the death of Dr. Grimesby Roylott which tend to make the matter even more terrible than the truth.

It was early in April in the year '83 that I woke one morning to find Sherlock Holmes standing, fully dressed, by the side of my bed. He was a late riser as a rule, and as the clock on the mantel-piece showed me that it was only a quarter past seven, I blinked up at him in some surprise, and perhaps just a little resentment, for I was myself regular in my habits.

"Very sorry to knock you up, Watson," said he, "but it's the common lot this morning. Mrs. Hudson has been knocked up, she retorted upon me, and I on you."

"What is it, then—a fire?"

"No; a client. It seems that a young lady has arrived in a considerable state of excitement, who insists upon seeing me. She is waiting now in the sitting-room. Now, when young ladies wander about the metropolis at this hour of the morning, and knock sleepy people up out of their beds, I presume that it is something very pressing which they have to communicate. Should it prove to be an interesting case, you would, I am sure, wish to follow it from the outset. I thought, at any rate, that I should call you and give you the chance."

"My dear fellow, I would not miss it for anything."

I had no keener pleasure than in following Holmes in his professional investigations, and in admiring the rapid deductions, as swift as intuitions, and yet always founded on a logical basis, with which he unravelled the problems which were submitted to him. I rapidly threw on my clothes, and was ready in a few minutes to accompany my friend down to the sitting-room. A lady dressed in black and heavily veiled, who had been sitting in the window, rose as we entered.

"Good-morning, madam," said Holmes, cheerily. "My name is Sherlock Holmes. This is my intimate friend and associate, Dr. Watson, before whom you can speak as freely as before myself. Ha! I am glad to see that Mrs. Hudson has had the good sense to light the fire. Pray draw up to it, and I shall order you a cup of hot coffee, for I observe that you are shivering."

"It is not cold which makes me shiver," said the woman, in a low voice, changing her seat as requested.

"What, then?"

"It is fear, Mr. Holmes. It is terror." She raised her veil as she spoke, and we could see that she was indeed in a pitiable state of agitation, her face all drawn and gray, with restless, frightened eyes, like those of some hunted animal. Her features and figure were those of a woman of thirty, but her hair was shot with premature gray, and her expression was weary and haggard. Sherlock Holmes ran her over with one of his quick, all-comprehensive glances.

"You must not fear," said he, soothingly, bending forward and patting her forearm. "We shall soon set matters right, I have no doubt. You have come in by train this morning, I see."

"You know me, then?"

"No, but I observe the second half of a return ticket in the palm of your left glove. You must have started early, and yet you had a good drive in a dog-cart, along heavy roads, before you reached the station."

The lady gave a violent start, and stared in bewilderment at my companion.

"There is no mystery, my dear madam," said he, smiling. "The left arm of your jacket is spattered with mud in no less than seven places. The marks are perfectly fresh. There is no vehicle save a dog-cart which throws up mud in that way, and then only when you sit on the left-hand side of the driver."

"Whatever your reasons may be, you are perfectly correct," said she. "I started from home before six, reached Leatherhead at twenty past, and came in by the first train to Waterloo. Sir, I can stand this strain no longer; I shall go mad if it continues. I have no one to turn to—none, save only one, who cares for me, and he, poor fellow, can be of little aid. I have heard of you, Mr. Holmes; I have heard of you from Mrs. Farintosh, whom you helped in the hour of her sore need. It was from her that I had your address. Oh, sir, do you not think that you could help me, too, and at least throw a little light through the dense darkness which surrounds me? At present it is out of my power to reward you for your services, but in a month or six weeks I shall be married, with the control of my own income, and then at least you shall not find me ungrateful."

Holmes turned to his desk, and unlocking it, drew out a small case-book, which he consulted.

"Farintosh," said he. "Ah yes, I recall the case; it was concerned with an opal tiara. I think it was before your time, Watson. I can only say, madam, that I shall be happy to devote the same care to your case as I did to that of your friend. As to reward, my profession is its own reward; but you are at liberty to defray whatever expenses I may be put to, at the time which suits you best. And now I beg that you will lay before us everything that may help us in forming an opinion upon the matter."

"Alas!" replied our visitor, "the very horror of my situation lies in the fact that my fears are so vague, and my suspicions depend so entirely upon small points, which might seem trivial to another, that even he to whom of all others I have a right to look for help and advice looks upon all that I tell him about it as the fancies of a nervous woman. He does not say so, but I can read it from his soothing answers and averted eyes. But I have heard, Mr. Holmes, that you can see deeply into the manifold wickedness of the human heart. You may advise me how to walk amid the dangers which encompass me."

"I am all attention, madam."

"My name is Helen Stoner, and I am living with my stepfather, who is the last survivor of one of the oldest Saxon families in England, the Roylotts of Stoke Moran, on the western border of Surrey."

Holmes nodded his head. "The name is familiar to me," said he.

"The family was at one time among the richest in England, and the estates extended over the borders into Berkshire in the north, and Hampshire in the west. In the last century, however, four successive heirs were of a dissolute and wasteful disposition, and the family ruin was eventually completed by a gambler in the days of the Regency. Nothing was left save a few acres of ground, and the two-hundred-year-old house, which is itself crushed under a heavy mortgage. The last squire dragged out his existence there, living the horrible life of an aristocratic pauper; but his only son, my stepfather, seeing that he must adapt himself to the new conditions, obtained an advance from a relative, which enabled him to take a medical degree, and went out to Calcutta, where, by his professional skill and his force of character, he established a large practice. In a fit of anger, however, caused by some robberies which had been perpetrated in the house, he beat his native butler to death, and narrowly escaped a capital sentence. As it was, he suffered a long term of imprisonment, and afterwards returned to England a morose and disappointed man.

"When Dr. Roylott was in India he married my mother, Mrs. Stoner, the young widow of Major-general Stoner, of the Bengal Artillery. My sister Julia and I were twins, and we were only two years old at the time of my mother's remarriage. She had a considerable sum of money—not less than £1000 a year—and this she bequeathed to Dr. Roylott entirely while we resided with him, with a provision that a certain annual sum should be allowed to each of us in the event of our marriage. Shortly after our return to England my mother died—she was killed eight years ago in a railway accident near Crewe. Dr. Roylott then abandoned his attempts to establish himself in practice in London, and took us to live with him in the old ancestral house at Stoke Moran. The money which my mother had left was enough for all our wants, and there seemed to be no obstacle to our happiness.

"But a terrible change came over our step-father about this time. Instead of making friends and exchanging visits with our neighbors, who had at first been overjoyed to see a Roylott of Stoke Moran back in the old family seat, he shut himself up in his house, and seldom came out save to indulge in ferocious quarrels with whoever might cross his path. Violence of temper approaching to mania has been hereditary in the men of the family, and in my step-father's case it had, I believe, been intensified by his long residence in the tropics. A series of disgraceful brawls took place, two of which ended in the police-court, until at last he became the terror of the village, and the folks would fly at his approach, for he is a man of immense strength, and absolutely uncontrollable in his anger.

"Last week he hurled the local blacksmith over a parapet into a stream, and it was only by paying over all the money which I could gather together that I was able to avert another public exposure. He had no friends at all save the wandering gypsies, and he would give these vagabonds leave to encamp upon the few acres of bramble-covered land which represent the family estate, and would accept in return the hospitality of their tents, wandering away with them sometimes for weeks on end. He has a passion also for Indian animals, which are sent over to him by a correspondent, and he has at this moment a cheetah and a baboon, which wander freely over his grounds, and are feared by the villagers almost as much as their master.

"You can imagine from what I say that my poor sister Julia and I had no great pleasure in our lives. No servant would stay with us, and for a long time we did all the work of the house. She was but thirty at the time of her death, and yet her hair had already begun to whiten, even as mine has."

"Your sister is dead, then?"

"She died just two years ago, and it is of her death that I wish to speak to you. You can understand that, living the life which I have described, we were little likely to see any one of our own age and position.

We had, however, an aunt, my mother's maiden sister, Miss Honoria West-phail, who lives near Harrow, and we were occasionally allowed to pay short visits at this lady's house. Julia went there at Christmas two years ago, and met there a half-pay major of marines, to whom she became engaged. My step-father learned of the engagement when my sister returned, and offered no objection to the marriage; but within a fortnight of the day which had been fixed for the wedding, the terrible event occurred which has deprived me of my only companion."

Sherlock Holmes had been leaning back in his chair with his eyes closed and his head sunk in a cushion, but he half opened his lids now and glanced across at his visitor.

"Pray be precise as to details," said he.

"It is easy for me to be so, for every event of that dreadful time is seared into my memory. The manor-house is, as I have already said, very old, and only one wing is now inhabited. The bedrooms in this wing are on the ground floor, the sitting-rooms being in the central block of the buildings. Of these bedrooms the first is Dr. Roylott's, the second my sister's, and the third my own. There is no communication between them, but they all open out into the same corridor. Do I make myself plain?"

"Perfectly so."

"The windows of the three rooms open out upon the lawn. That fatal night Dr. Roylott had gone to his room early, though we knew that he had not retired to rest, for my sister was troubled by the smell of the strong Indian cigars which it was his custom to smoke. She left her room, therefore, and came into mine, where she sat for some time, chatting about her approaching wedding. At eleven o'clock she rose to leave me but she paused at the door and looked back.

" 'Tell me, Helen,' said she, 'have you ever heard any one whistle in the dead of the night?'

" 'Never,' said I.

" 'I suppose that you could not possibly whistle, yourself, in your sleep?'

" 'Certainly not. But why?'

" 'Because during the last few nights I have always, about three in the morning, heard a low, clear whistle. I am a light sleeper, and it has awakened me. I cannot tell where it came from—perhaps from the next room, perhaps from the lawn. I thought that I would just ask you whether you had heard it.'

" 'No, I have not. It must be those wretched gypsies in the plantation.'

" 'Very likely. And yet if it were on the lawn, I wonder that you did not hear it also.'

" 'Ah, but I sleep more heavily than you.'

" 'Well, it is of no great consequence, at any rate.' She smiled back at me, closed my door, and a few moments later I heard her key turn in the lock."

"Indeed," said Holmes. "Was it your custom always to lock your-selves in at night?"

"Always."

"And why?"

"I think that I mentioned to you that the doctor kept a cheetah and a baboon. We had no feeling of security unless our doors were locked."

"Quite so. Pray proceed with your statement."

"I could not sleep that night. A vague feeling of impending mis-fortune impressed me. My sister and I, you will recollect, were twins, and you know how subtle are the links which bind two souls which are so closely allied. It was a wild night. The wind was howling outside, and the rain was beating and splashing against the windows. Suddenly, amid all the hubbub of the gale, there burst forth the wild scream of a terrified woman. I knew that it was my sister's voice. I sprang from my bed, wrapped a shawl round me, and rushed into the corridor. As I opened my door I seemed to hear a low whistle, such as my sister described, and a few moments later a clanging sound, as if a mass of metal had fallen. As I ran down the passage, my sis-ter's door was unlocked, and revolved slowly upon its hinges. I stared at it horror-stricken, not knowing what was about to issue from it. By the light of the corridor-lamp I saw my sister appear at the opening, her face blanched with terror, her hands groping for help, her whole figure swaying to and fro like that of a drunkard. I ran to her and threw my arms round her, but at that moment her knees seemed to give way and she fell to the ground. She writhed as one who is in terrible pain, and her limbs were dreadfully convulsed. At first I thought that she had not recognized me, but as I bent over her she suddenly shrieked out in a voice which I shall never forget, 'Oh, my God! Helen! It was the band! The speckled band!' There was something else which she would fain have said, and she stabbed with her finger into the air in the direction of the doctor's room, but a fresh convulsion seized her and choked her words. I rushed out, calling loudly for my step-father, and I met him hastening from his room in his dressing-gown. When he reached my sister's side she was unconscious, and though he poured brandy down her throat and sent for medical aid from the vil-lage, all efforts were in vain, for she slowly sank and died without having recovered her consciousness. Such was the dreadful end of my beloved sister."

"One moment," said Holmes; "are you sure about this whistle and metallic sound? Could you swear to it?"

"That was what the county coroner asked me at the inquiry. It is my strong impression that I heard it, and yet, among the crash of the gale and the creaking of an old house, I may possibly have been deceived."

"Was your sister dressed?"

"No, she was in her night-dress. In her right hand was found the charred stump of a match, and in her left a matchbox."

"Showing that she had struck a light and looked about her when the alarm took place. That is important. And what conclusions did the coroner come to?"

"He investigated the case with great care, for Dr. Roylott's conduct had long been notorious in the county, but he was unable to find any satisfactory cause of death. My evidence showed that the door had been fastened upon the inner side, and the windows were blocked by old-fashioned shutters with broad iron bars, which were secured every night. The walls were carefully sounded, and were shown to be quite solid all round, and the flooring was also thoroughly examined, with the same result. The chimney is wide, but is barred up by four large staples. It is certain, therefore, that my sister was quite alone when she met her end. Besides, there were no marks of any violence upon her."

"How about poison?"

"The doctors examined her for it, but without success."

"What do you think that this unfortunate lady died of, then?"

"It is my belief that she died of pure fear and nervous shock, though what it was that frightened her I cannot imagine."

"Were there gypsies in the plantation at the time?"

"Yes, there are nearly always some there."

"Ah, and what did you gather from this allusion to a band—a speckled band?"

"Sometimes I have thought that it was merely the wild talk of delirium, sometimes that it may have referred to some band of people, perhaps to these very gypsies in the plantation. I do not know whether the spotted handkerchiefs which so many of them wear over their heads might have suggested the strange adjective which she used."

Holmes shook his head like a man who is far from being satisfied.

"These are very deep waters," said he; "pray go on with your narrative."

"Two years have passed since then, and my life has been until lately lonelier than ever. A month ago, however, a dear friend, whom I have known for many years, has done me the honor to ask my hand in marriage. His name is Armitage—Percy Armitage—the second son of Mr. Armitage, of Crane Water, near Reading. My step-father has offered no opposition to the match, and we are to be married in the course of the spring. Two days ago some repairs were started in the west wing of the building, and my bed-room wall has been pierced, so that I have had to move into the chamber in which my sister died, and to sleep in the very bed in which she slept. Imagine, then, my thrill of terror when last night, as I lay awake, thinking over her terrible fate, I suddenly heard in the silence of the night the low whistle which had been the herald of her own death. I sprang up and lit the lamp, but nothing was to be seen in the room. I was too shaken to go to bed again, however, so I dressed, and as soon as it was daylight I slipped down, got a dog-cart at the 'Crown Inn,' which is opposite, and drove to Leatherhead, from whence I have come on this morning with the one object of seeing you and asking your advice."

"You have done wisely," said my friend. "But have you told me all?"

"Yes, all."

"Miss Roylott, you have not. You are screening your stepfather."

"Why, what do you mean?"

For answer Holmes pushed back the frill of black lace which fringed the hand that lay upon our visitor's knee. Five little livid spots, the marks of four fingers and a thumb, were printed upon the white wrist.

"You have been cruelly used," said Holmes.

The lady colored deeply and covered over her injured wrist. "He is a hard man," she said, "and perhaps he hardly knows his own strength."

There was a long silence, during which Holmes leaned his chin upon his hands and stared into the crackling fire.

"This is a very deep business," he said, at last. "There are a thousand details which I should desire to know before I decide upon our course of action. Yet we have not a moment to lose. If we were to come to Stoke Moran to-day, would it be possible for us to see over these rooms without the knowledge of your step-father?"

"As it happens, he spoke of coming into town to-day upon some most important business. It is probable that he will be away all day, and that there would be nothing to disturb you. We have a house-keeper now, but she is old and foolish, and I could easily get her out of the way."

"Excellent. You are not averse to this trip, Watson?"

"By no means."

"Then we shall both come. What are you going to do yourself?"

"I have one or two things which I would wish to do now that I am in town. But I shall return by the twelve o'clock train, so as to be there in time for your coming."

"And you may expect us early in the afternoon. I have myself some small business matters to attend to. Will you not wait and breakfast?"

"No, I must go. My heart is lightened already since I have confided my trouble to you. I shall look forward to seeing you again this afternoon." She dropped her thick black veil over her face and glided from the room.

"And what do you think of it all, Watson?" asked Sherlock Holmes, leaning back in his chair.

"It seems to me to be a most dark and sinister business."

"Dark enough and sinister enough."

"Yet if the lady is correct in saying that the flooring and walls are sound, and that the door, window, and chimney are impassable, then her sister must have been undoubtedly alone when she met her mysterious end."

"What becomes, then, of these nocturnal whistles, and what of the very peculiar words of the dying woman?"

"I cannot think."

"When you combine the ideas of whistles at night, the presence of a band of gypsies who are on intimate terms with this old doctor, the fact that we have every reason to believe that the doctor has an interest in preventing his step-daughter's marriage, the dying allusion to a band, and, finally, the fact that Miss Helen Stoner heard a metallic clang, which might have been caused by one of those metal bars which secured the shutters falling back into their place, I think that there is good ground to think that the mystery may be cleared along those lines."

"But what, then, did the gypsies do?"

"I cannot imagine."

"I see many objections to any such theory."

"And so do I. It is precisely for that reason that we are going to Stoke Moran this day. I want to see whether the objections are fatal, or if they may be explained away. But what in the name of the devil!"

The ejaculation had been drawn from my companion by the fact that our door had been suddenly dashed open, and that a huge man had framed himself in the aperture. His costume was a peculiar mixture of the professional and of the agricultural, having a black top-hat, a long frock-coat, and a pair of high gaiters, with a hunting-crop swinging in his hand. So tall was he that his hat actually brushed the cross bar of the doorway, and his breadth seemed to span it across from side to side. A large face, seared with a thousand wrinkles, burned yellow with the sun, and marked with every evil passion, was turned from one to the other of us, while his deep-set, bile-shot eyes, and his high, thin, fleshless nose, gave him somewhat the resemblance to a fierce old bird of prey.

"Which of you is Holmes?" asked this apparition.

"My name, sir; but you have the advantage of me," said my companion, quietly.

"I am Dr. Grimesby Roylott, of Stoke Moran."

"Indeed, doctor," said Holmes, blandly. "Pray take a seat."

"I will do nothing of the kind. My step-daughter has been here. I have traced her. What has she been saying to you?"

"It is a little cold for the time of the year," said Holmes.

"What has she been saying to you?" screamed the old man, furiously.

"But I have heard that the crocuses promise well," continued my companion, impertubably.

"Ha! You put me off, do you?" said our new visitor, taking a step forward and shaking his hunting-crop. "I know you, you scoundrel! I have heard of you before. You are Holmes, the meddler."

My friend smiled.

"Holmes, the busybody!"

His smile broadened.

"Holmes, the Scotland-yard Jack-in-office!"

Holmes chuckled heartily. "Your conversation is most entertaining," said he. "When you go out close the door, for there is a decided draught."

"I will go when I have said my say. Don't you dare to meddle with my affairs. I know that Miss Stoner has been here. I traced her! I am a dangerous man to fall foul of! See here." He stepped swiftly forward, seized the poker, and bent it into a curve with his huge brown hands.

"See that you keep yourself out of my grip," he snarled, and hurling the twisted poker into the fireplace, he strode out of the room.

"He seems a very amiable person," said Holmes, laughing. "I am not quite so bulky, but if he had remained I might have shown him that my grip was not much more feeble than his own." As he spoke he picked up the steel poker, and with a sudden effort straightened it out again.

"Fancy his having the insolence to confound me with the official detective force! This incident gives zest to our investigation, however, and I only trust that our little friend will not suffer from her imprudence in allowing this brute to trace her. And now, Watson, we shall order breakfast, and afterwards I shall walk down to Doctors' Commons, where I hope to get some data which may help us in this matter."

It was nearly one o'clock when Sherlock Holmes returned from his excursion. He held in his hand a sheet of blue paper, scrawled over with notes and figures.

"I have seen the will of the deceased wife," said he. "To determine its exact meaning I have been obliged to work out the present prices of the investments with which it is concerned. The total income, which at the time of the wife's death was little short of £1100, is now, through the fall in agricultural prices, not more than £750. Each daughter can claim an income of £250, in case of marriage. It is evident, therefore, that if both girls had married, this beauty would have had a mere pittance, while even one of them would cripple him to a very serious extent. My morning's work has not been wasted, since it has proved that he has the very strongest motives for standing in the way of anything of the sort. And now, Watson, this is too serious for dawdling, especially as the old man is aware that we are interesting ourselves in his affairs; so if you are ready, we shall call a cab and drive to Waterloo. I should be very much obliged if you would slip your revolver into your pocket. An Eley's No. 2 is an excellent argument with gentlemen who can twist steel pokers into knots. That and a tooth-brush are, I think, all that we need."

At Waterloo we were fortunate in catching a train for Leatherhead, where we hired a trap at the station inn, and drove for four or five miles through the lovely Surrey lanes. It was a perfect day, with a bright sun and a few fleecy clouds in the heavens. The trees and way-side hedges were just throwing out their first green shoots, and the air was full of the pleasant smell of the moist earth. To me at least there was a strange contrast between the sweet promise of the spring and this sinister quest upon which we were engaged. My companion sat in the front of the trap, his arms folded, his hat pulled down over his eyes, and his chin sunk upon his breast, buried in the deepest thought. Suddenly, however, he tapped me on the shoulder, and pointed over the meadows.

"Look there!" said he.

A heavily timbered park stretched up in a gentle slope, thickening into a grove at the highest point. From amidst the branches there jutted out the gray gables and high roof-tree of a very old mansion.

"Stoke Moran?" said he.

"Yes, sir, that be the house of Dr. Grimesby Roylott," remarked the driver.

"There is some building going on there," said Holmes; "that is where we are going."

"There's the village," said the driver, pointing to a cluster of roofs some distance to the left; "but if you want to get to the house, you'll find it shorter to go over this stile, and so by the footpath over the fields. There it is, where the lady is walking."

"And the lady, I fancy, is Miss Stoner," observed Holmes, shading his eyes. "Yes, I think we had better do as you suggest."

We got off, paid our fare, and the trap rattled back on its way to Leatherhead.

"I thought it as well," said Holmes, as we climbed the stile, "that this fellow should think we had come here as architects, or on some definite business. It may stop his gossip. Good afternoon, Miss Stoner. You see that we have been as good as our word."

Our client of the morning had hurried forward to meet us with a face which spoke her joy. "I have been waiting so eagerly for you," she cried, shaking hands with us warmly. "All has turned out splendidly. Dr. Roylott has gone to town, and it is unlikely that he will be back before evening."

"We have had the pleasure of making the Doctor's acquaintance," said Holmes, and in a few words he sketched out what had occurred. Miss Stoner turned white to the lips as she listened.

"Good heavens!" she cried, "he has followed me, then."

"So it appears."

"He is so cunning that I never know when I am safe from him. What will he say when he returns?"

"He must guard himself, for he may find that there is some one more cunning than himself upon his track. You must lock yourself up from him to-night. If he is violent, we shall take you away to your aunt's at Harrow. Now, we must make the best use of our time, so kindly take us at once to the rooms which we are to examine."

The building was of gray, lichen-blotched stone, with a high central portion, and two curving wings, like the claws of a crab, thrown out on each side. In one of these wings the windows were broken, and blocked with wooden boards, while the roof was partly caved in, a picture of ruin. The central portion was in little better repair, but the right-hand block was comparatively modern, and the blinds in the windows, with the blue smoke curling up from the chimneys, showed that this was where the family resided. Some scaffolding had been erected against the end wall, and the stone-work had been broken into, but there were no signs of any workmen at the moment of our visit. Holmes walked slowly up and down the ill-trimmed lawn, and examined with deep attention the outsides of the windows.

"This, I take it, belongs to the room in which you used to sleep, the centre one to your sister's, and the one next to the main building to Dr. Roylott's chamber?"

"Exactly so. But I am now sleeping in the middle one."

"Pending the alterations, as I understand. By-the-way, there does not seem to be any very pressing need for repairs at that end wall."

"There were none. I believe that it was an excuse to move me from my room."

"Ah! that is suggestive. Now, on the other side of this narrow wing runs the corridor from which these three rooms open. There are windows in it, of course?"

"Yes, but very small ones. Too narrow for any one to pass through."

"As you both locked your doors at night, your rooms were unapproachable from that side. Now, would you have the kindness to go into your room and bar your shutters."

Miss Stoner did so, and Holmes, after a careful examination through the open window, endeavored in every way to force the shutter open, but without success. There was no slit through which a knife could be passed to raise the bar. Then with his lens he tested the hinges, but they were of solid iron, built firmly into the massive masonry. "Hum!" said he, scratching his chin in some perplexity; "my theory certainly presents some difficulties. No one could pass these shutters if they were bolted. Well, we shall see if the inside throws any light upon the matter."

A small side door led into the whitewashed corridor from which the three bedrooms opened. Holmes refused to examine the third chamber, so we passed at once to the second, that in which Miss Stoner was now sleeping, and in which her sister had met with her fate. It was a homely little room, with a low ceiling and a gaping fireplace, after the fashion of old country-houses. A brown chest of drawers stood in one corner, a narrow white-counterpaned bed in another, and a dressing-table on the left-hand side of the window. These articles, with two small wicker-work chairs, made up all the furniture in the room, save for a square of Wilton carpet in the centre. The boards round and the panelling of the walls were of brown, worm-eaten oak, so old and discolored that it may have dated from the original building of the house. Holmes drew one of the chairs into a corner and sat silent, while his eyes travelled round and round and up and down, taking in every detail of the apartment.

"Where does that bell communicate with?" he asked, at last, pointing to a thick bell-rope which hung down beside the bed, the tassel actually lying upon the pillow.

"It goes to the house-keeper's room."

"It looks newer than the other things?"

"Yes, it was only put there a couple of years ago."

"Your sister asked for it, I suppose?"

"No, I never heard of her using it. We used always to get what we wanted for ourselves."

"Indeed, it seemed unnecessary to put so nice a bell-pull there. You will excuse me for a few minutes while I satisfy myself as to this floor." He threw himself down upon his face with his lens in his hand, and crawled swiftly backward and forward, examining minutely the cracks between the boards. Then he did the same with the wood-work with which the chamber was panelled. Finally he walked over to the bed, and spent some time in staring at it, and in running his eye up and down the wall. Finally he took the bell-rope in his hand and gave it a brisk tug.

"Why, it's a dummy," said he.

"Won't it ring?"

"No, it is not even attached to a wire. This is very interesting. You can see now that it is fastened to a hook just above where the little opening for the ventilator is."

"How very absurd! I never noticed that before."

"Very strange!" muttered Holmes, pulling at the rope. "There are one or two very singular points about this room. For example, what a fool a builder must be to open a ventilator into another room, when, with the same trouble, he might have communicated with the outside air!"

"That is also quite modern," said the lady.

"Done about the same time as the bell-rope?" remarked Holmes.

"Yes, there were several little changes carried out about that time."

"They seem to have been of a most interesting character—dummy bell-ropes, and ventilators which do not ventilate. With your permission, Miss Stoner, we shall now carry our researches into the inner apartment."

Dr. Grimesby Roylott's chamber was larger than that of his step-daughter, but was as plainly furnished. A camp-bed, a small wooden shelf full of books, mostly of a technical character, an arm-chair beside the bed, a plain wooden chair against the wall, a round table, and a large iron safe were the principal things which met the eye. Holmes walked slowly round and examined each and all of them with the keenest interest.

"What's in here?" he asked, tapping the safe.

"My step-father's business papers."

"Oh! you have seen inside, then?"

"Only once, some years ago. I remember that it was full of papers."

"There isn't a cat in it, for example?"

"No. What a strange idea!"

"Well, look at this!" He took up a small saucer of milk which stood on the top of it.

"No; we don't keep a cat. But there is a cheetah and a baboon."

"Ah, yes, of course! Well, a cheetah is just a big cat, and yet a saucer of milk does not go very far in satisfying its wants, I dare say. There is one point which I should wish to determine." He squatted down in front of the wooden chair, and examined the seat of it with the greatest attention.

"Thank you. That is quite settled," said he, rising and putting his lens in his pocket. "Hello! Here is something interesting!"

The object which had caught his eye was a small dog-lash hung on one corner of the bed. The lash, however, was curled upon itself, and tied so as to make a loop of whipcord.

"What do you make of that, Watson?"

"It's a common enough lash. But I don't know why it should be tied."

"That is not quite so common, is it? Ah, me! it's a wicked world, and when a clever man turns his brains to crime it is the worst of all. I think that I have seen enough now, Miss Stoner, and with your permission we shall walk out upon the lawn."

I had never seen my friend's face so grim or his brow so dark as it was when we turned from the scene of this investigation. We had walked several times up and down the lawn, neither Miss Stoner nor myself liking to break in upon his thoughts before he roused himself from his reverie.

"It is very essential, Miss Stoner," said he, "that you should absolutely follow my advice in every respect."

"I shall most certainly do so."

"The matter is too serious for any hesitation. Your life may depend upon your compliance."

"I assure you that I am in your hands."

"In the first place, both my friend and I must spend the night in your room."

Both Miss Stoner and I gazed at him in astonishment.

"Yes, it must be so. Let me explain. I believe that that is the village inn over there?"

"Yes, that is the 'Crown.' "

"Very good. Your windows would be visible from there?"

"Certainly."

"You must confine yourself to your room, on pretence of a headache, when your step-father comes back. Then when you hear him retire for the night, you must open the shutters of your window, undo the hasp, put your lamp there as a signal to us, and then withdraw quietly with everything which you are likely to want into the room which you used to occupy. I have no doubt that, in spite of the repairs, you could manage there for one night."

"Oh yes, easily."

"The rest you will leave in our hands."

"But what will you do?"

"We shall spend the night in your room, and we shall investigate the cause of this noise which has disturbed you."

"I believe, Mr. Holmes, that you have already made up your mind," said Miss Stoner, laying her hand upon my companion's sleeve.

"Perhaps I have."

"Then for pity's sake tell me what was the cause of my sister's death."

"I should prefer to have clearer proofs before I speak."

"You can at least tell me whether my own thought is correct, and if she died from some sudden fright."

"No, I do not think so. I think that there was probably some more tangible cause. And now, Miss Stoner, we must leave you, for if Dr. Roylott returned and saw us, our journey would be in vain. Good-bye, and be brave, for if you will do what I have told you, you may rest assured that we shall soon drive away the dangers that threaten you."

Sherlock Holmes and I had no difficulty in engaging a bedroom and sitting-room at the "Crown Inn." They were on the upper floor, and from our window we could command a view of the avenue gate, and of the inhabited wing of Stoke Moran Manor House. At dusk we saw Dr. Grimesby Roylott drive past, his huge form looming up beside the little figure of the lad who drove him. The boy had some slight difficulty in undoing the heavy iron gates, and we heard the hoarse roar of the doctor's voice, and saw the fury with which he shook his clinched fists at him. The trap drove on, and a few minutes later we saw a sudden light spring up among the trees as the lamp was lit in one of the sitting-rooms.

"Do you know, Watson," said Holmes, as we sat together in the gathering darkness, "I have really some scruples as to taking you to-night. There is a distinct element of danger."

"Can I be of assistance?"

"Your presence might be invaluable."

"Then I shall certainly come."

"It is very kind of you."

"You speak of danger. You have evidently seen more in these rooms than was visible to me."

"No, but I fancy that I may have deduced a little more. I imagine that you saw all that I did."

"I saw nothing remarkable save the bell-rope, and what purpose that could answer I confess is more than I can imagine."

"You saw the ventilator, too?"

"Yes, but I do not think it is such a very unusual thing to have a small opening between two rooms. It was so small that a rat could hardly pass through."

"I knew that we should find a ventilator before ever we came to Stoke Moran."

"My dear Holmes!"

"Oh yes, I did. You remember in her statement she said that her sister could smell Dr. Roylott's cigar. Now, of course that suggested at once that there must be a communication between the two rooms. It could only be a small one, or it would have been remarked upon at the coroner's inquiry. I deduced a ventilator."

"But what harm can there be in that?"

"Well, there is at least a curious coincidence of dates. A ventilator is made, a cord is hung, and a lady who sleeps in the bed dies. Does not that strike you?"

"I cannot as yet see any connection."

"Did you observe anything very peculiar about that bed?"

"No."

"It was clamped to the floor. Did you ever see a bed fastened like that before?"

"I cannot say that I have."

"The lady could not move her bed. It must always be in the same relative position to the ventilator and to the rope—for so we may call it, since it was clearly never meant for a bell-pull."

"Holmes," I cried, "I seem to see dimly what you are hinting at. We are only just in time to prevent some subtle and horrible crime."

"Subtle enough and horrible enough. When a doctor does go wrong, he is the first of criminals. He has nerve and he has knowledge. Palmer and Pritchard were among the heads of their profession. This man strikes even deeper, but I think, Watson, that we shall be able to strike deeper still. But we shall have horrors enough before the night is over; for goodness' sake let us have a quiet pipe, and turn our minds for a few hours to something more cheerful."

About nine o'clock the light among the trees was extinguished, and all was dark in the direction of the Manor House. Two hours passed slowly away, and then, suddenly, just at the stroke of eleven, a single bright light shone out right in front of us.

"That is our signal," said Holmes, springing to his feet; "it comes from the middle window."

As we passed out he exchanged a few words with the landlord, explaining that we were going on a late visit to an acquaintance, and that it was possible that we might spend the night there. A moment later we were out on the dark road, a chill wind blowing in our faces, and one yellow light twinkling in front of us through the gloom to guide us on our sombre errand.

There was little difficulty in entering the grounds, for unrepaired breaches gaped in the old park wall. Making our way among the trees, we reached the lawn, crossed it, and were about to enter through the window, when out from a clump of laurel bushes there darted what seemed to be a hideous and distorted child, who threw itself upon the grass with writhing limbs, and then ran swiftly across the lawn into the darkness.

"My God!" I whispered; "did you see it?"

Holmes was for the moment as startled as I. His hand closed like a vice upon my wrist in his agitation. Then he broke into a low laugh, and put his lips to my ear.

"It is a nice household," he murmured. "That is the baboon."

I had forgotten the strange pets which the doctor affected. There was a cheetah, too; perhaps we might find it upon our shoulders at any moment. I confess that I felt easier in my mind when, after following Holmes's example and slipping off my shoes, I found myself inside the bed-room. My companion noiselessly closed the shutters, moved the lamp onto the table, and cast his eyes round the room. All was as we had seen it in the daytime. Then creeping up to me and making a trumpet of his hand, he whispered into my ear again so gently that it was all that I could do to distinguish the words:

"The least sound would be fatal to our plans."

I nodded to show that I had heard.

"We must sit without light. He would see it through the ventilator."

I nodded again.

"Do not go asleep; your very life may depend upon it. Have your pistol ready in case we should need it. I will sit on the side of the bed, and you in that chair."

I took out my revolver and laid it on the corner of the table.

Holmes had brought up a long thin cane, and this he placed upon the bed beside him. By it he laid the box of matches and the stump of a candle. Then he turned down the lamp, and we were left in darkness.

How shall I ever forget that dreadful vigil? I could not hear a sound, not even the drawing of a breath, and yet I knew that my companion sat open-eyed, within a few feet of me, in the same state of nervous tension in which I was myself. The shutters cut off the least ray of light, and we waited in absolute darkness. From outside came the occasional cry of a night-bird, and once at our very window a long drawn cat-like whine, which told us that the cheetah was indeed at liberty. Far away we could hear the deep tones of the parish clock, which boomed out every quarter of an hour. How long they seemed, those quarters! Twelve struck, and one and two and three, and still we sat waiting silently for whatever might befall.

Suddenly there was the momentary gleam of a light up in the direction of the ventilator, which vanished immediately, but was succeeded by a strong smell of burning oil and heated metal. Some one in the next room had lit a dark-lantern. I heard a gentle sound of movement, and then all was silent once more, though the smell grew stronger. For half an hour I sat with straining ears. Then suddenly another sound became audible—a very gentle, soothing sound, like that of a small jet of steam escaping continually from a kettle. The instant that we heard it, Holmes sprang from the bed, struck a match, and lashed furiously with his cane at the bell-pull.

"You see it, Watson?" he yelled. "You see it?"

But I saw nothing. At the moment when Holmes struck the light I heard a low, clear whistle, but the sudden glare flashing into my weary eyes made it impossible for me to tell what it was at which my friend lashed so savagely. I could, however, see that his face was deadly pale, and filled with horror and loathing.

He had ceased to strike, and was gazing up at the ventilator, when suddenly there broke from the silence of the night the most horrible cry to which I have ever listened. It swelled up louder and louder, a hoarse yell of pain and fear and anger all mingled in the one dreadful shriek. They say that away down in the village, and even in the distant parsonage, that cry raised the sleepers from their beds. It struck cold to our hearts, and I stood gazing at Holmes, and he at me, until the last echoes of it had died away into the silence from which it rose.

"What can it mean?" I gasped.

"It means that it is all over," Holmes answered. "And perhaps, after all, it is for the best. Take your pistol, and we will enter Dr. Roylott's room."

With a grave face he lit the lamp and led the way down the corridor. Twice he struck at the chamber door without any reply from within. Then he turned the handle and entered, I at his heels, with the cocked pistol in my hand.

It was a singular sight which met our eyes. On the table stood a dark-lantern with the shutter half open, throwing a brilliant beam of light upon the iron safe, the door of which was ajar. Beside this table, on the wooden chair, sat Dr. Grimesby Roylott, clad in a long gray dressing-gown, his bare ankles protruding beneath, and his feet thrust into red heelless Turkish slippers. Across his lap lay the short stock with the long lash which we had noticed during the day. His chin was cocked upward and his eyes were fixed in a dreadful, rigid stare at the corner of the ceiling. Round his brow he had a peculiar yellow band, with brownish speckles, which seemed to be bound tightly round his head. As we entered he made neither sound nor motion.

"The band! the speckled band!" whispered Holmes.

I took a step forward. In an instant his strange head-gear began to move, and there reared itself from among his hair the squat diamond-shaped head and puffed neck of a loathsome serpent.

"It is a swamp adder!" cried Holmes; "the deadliest snake in India. He has died within ten seconds of being bitten. Violence does, in truth, recoil upon the violent, and the schemer falls into the pit which he digs for another. Let us thrust this creature back into its den, and we can then remove Miss Stoner to some place of shelter, and let the county police know what has happened."

As he spoke he drew the dog-whip swiftly from the dead man's lap, and throwing the noose round the reptile's neck, he drew it from its horrid perch, and carrying it at arm's length, threw it into the iron safe, which he closed upon it.

Such are the true facts of the death of Dr. Grimesby Roylott, of Stoke Moran. It is not necessary that I should prolong a narrative which has already run to too great a length, by telling how we broke the sad news to the terrified girl, how we conveyed her by the morning train to the care of her good aunt at Harrow, of how the slow process of official inquiry came to the conclusion that the doctor met his fate while indiscreetly playing with a dangerous pet. The little which I had yet to learn of the case was told me by Sherlock Holmes as we travelled back next day.

"I had," said he, "come to an entirely erroneous conclusion which shows, my dear Watson, how dangerous it always is to reason from insufficient data. The presence of the gypsies, and the use of the word 'band,' which was used by the poor girl, no doubt to explain the appearance which she had caught a hurried glimpse of by the light of her match, were sufficient to put me upon an entirely wrong scent. I can only claim the merit that I instantly reconsidered my position when, however, it became clear to me that whatever danger threatened an occupant of the room could not come either from the window or the door. My attention was speedily drawn, as I have already remarked to you, to this ventilator, and to the bell-rope which hung down to the bed. The discovery that this was a dummy, and that the bed was clamped to the floor, instantly gave rise to the suspicion that the rope was there as a bridge for something passing through the hole, and coming to the bed. The idea of a snake instantly occurred to me, and when I coupled it with my knowledge that the doctor was furnished with a supply of creatures from India, I felt that I was probably on the right track. The idea of using a form of poison which could not possibly be discovered by any chemical test was just such a one as would occur to a clever and ruthless man who had had an Eastern training. The rapidity with which such a poison would take effect would also, from his point of view, be an advantage. It would be a sharp-eyed coroner, indeed, who could distinguish the two little dark punctures which would show where the poison fangs had done their work. Then I thought of the whistle. Of course he must recall the snake before the morning light revealed it to the victim. He had trained it, probably by the use of the milk which we saw, to return to him when summoned. He would put it through this ventilator at the hour that he thought best, with the certainty that it would crawl down the rope and land on the bed. It might or might not bite the occupant, perhaps she might escape every night for a week, but sooner or later she must fall a victim.

"I had come to these conclusions before ever I had entered his room. An inspection of his chair showed me that he had been in the habit of standing on it, which of course would be necessary in order that he should reach the ventilator. The sight of the safe, the saucer of milk, and the loop of whipcord were enough to finally dispel any doubts which may have remained. The metallic clang heard by Miss Stoner was obviously caused by her step-father hastily closing the door of his safe upon its terrible occupant. Having once made up my mind, you know the steps which I took in order to put the matter to the proof. I heard the creature hiss, as I have no doubt that you did also, and I instantly lit the light and attacked it."

"With the result of driving it through the ventilator."

"And also with the result of causing it to turn upon its master at the other side. Some of the blows of my cane came home, and roused its snakish temper, so that it flew upon the first person it saw. In this way I am no doubt indirectly responsible for Dr. Grimesby Roylott's death, and I cannot say that it is likely to weigh very heavily upon my conscience."

1892

Anyone who knows detective stories from books, television, or film will recognize that they are built on a fairly predictable formula, one that Arthur Conan Doyle helped popularize. As W. H. Auden points out, this formula is surprisingly similar to that of Greek tragedy.

"The job of the detective is to restore the state of grace": W. H. Auden

As in the Aristotelian description of tragedy, there is Concealment (the innocent seem guilty and the guilty seem innocent) and Manifestation (the real guilt is brought to consciousness). There is also peripeteia, in this case not a reversal of fortune but a double reversal from apparent guilt to innocence and from apparent innocence to guilt. The formula may be diagrammed as follows:

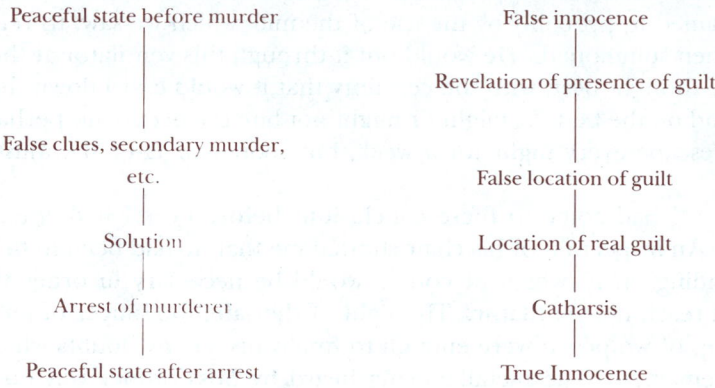

Peaceful state before murder   False innocence

Revelation of presence of guilt

False clues, secondary murder, etc.

False location of guilt

Solution   Location of real guilt

Arrest of murderer   Catharsis

Peaceful state after arrest   True Innocence

In Greek tragedy the audience knows the truth; the actors do not, but discover or bring to pass the inevitable. In modern, e.g., Elizabethan, tragedy the audience knows neither less nor more than the most knowing of the actors. In the detective story the audience does not know the truth at all; one of the actors—the murderer—does; and the detective, of his own free will, discovers and reveals what the murderer, of his own free will, tries to conceal. . . .

The characters in a detective story should . . . be eccentric (aesthetically interesting individuals) and good (instinctively ethical)—good, that is, either in appearance, later shown to be false, or in reality, first concealed by an appearance of bad. . . .

The job of the detective is to restore the state of grace in which the aesthetic and the ethical are as one. Since the murderer who caused their disjunction is the aesthetically defiant individual, his opponent, the detective, must be either the official representative of the ethical or the exceptional individual who is himself in a state of grace. If he is the former, he is a professional; if he is the latter, he is an amateur. In either case, the detective must be the total stranger who cannot possibly be involved in the crime; this excludes the local police and should, I think, exclude the detective who is a friend of one of the suspects. The professional detective has the advantage that, since he is not an individual but a representative of the ethical, he does not need a motive for investigating the crime; but for the same reason he has the disadvantage of being unable to overlook the minor ethical violations of the suspects, and therefore it is harder for him to gain their confidence.

Most amateur detectives, on the other hand, are unsatisfactory either because they are priggish supermen, like Lord Peter Wimsey and Philo Vance, who have no motive for being detectives except caprice, or because, like the detectives of the hard-boiled school, they are motivated by avarice or ambition and might just as well be murderers.

The amateur detective genius may have weaknesses to give him aesthetic interest, but they must not be of a kind which outrage ethics. The most satisfactory weaknesses are the solitary oral vices of eating and drinking or childish boasting. In his sexual life, the detective must be either celibate or happily married.

ANTON CHEKHOV

(1860–1904)

THE LADY WITH THE PET DOG

translated from the Russian by Avrahm Yarmolinsky

1

A new person, it was said, had appeared on the esplanade: a lady with a pet dog. Dmitry Dmitrich Gurov, who had spent a fortnight at Yalta and had got used to the place, had also begun to take an interest in new arrivals. As he sat in Vernet's confectionery shop, he saw, walking on the esplanade, a fair-haired young woman of medium height, wearing a beret; a white Pomeranian was trotting behind her.

And afterwards he met her in the public garden and in the square several times a day. She walked alone, always wearing the same beret and always with the white dog; no one knew who she was and everyone called her simply "the lady with the pet dog."

"If she is here alone without husband or friends," Gurov reflected, "it wouldn't be a bad thing to make her acquaintance."

He was under forty, but he already had a daughter twelve years old, and two sons at school. They had found a wife for him when he was very young, a student in his second year, and by now she seemed half as old again as he. She was a tall, erect woman with dark eyebrows, stately and dignified and, as she said of herself, intellectual. She read a great deal, used simplified spelling in her letters, called her husband, not Dmitry, but Dimitry, while he privately considered her of limited intelligence, narrow-minded, dowdy, was afraid of her, and did not like to be at home. He had begun being unfaithful to her long ago—had been unfaithful to her often and, probably for that reason, almost always spoke ill of women, and when they were talked of in his presence used to call them "the inferior race."

It seemed to him that he had been sufficiently tutored by bitter experience to call them what he pleased, and yet he could not have lived without "the inferior race" for two days together. In the company of men he was bored and ill at ease, he was chilly and uncommunicative with them; but when he was among women he felt free, and knew what to speak to them about and how to comport himself; and even to be silent with them was no strain on him. In his appearance, in his character, in his whole make-up there was something attractive and elusive that disposed women in his favor and allured them. He knew that, and some force seemed to draw him to them, too.

Oft-repeated and really bitter experience had taught him long ago that with decent people—particularly Moscow people—who are irresolute and slow to move, every affair which at first seems a light and charming adventure inevitably grows into a whole problem of extreme complexity, and in the end a painful situation is created. But at every new meeting with an interesting woman this lesson of experience seemed to slip from his memory, and he was eager for life, and everything seemed so simple and diverting.

One evening while he was dining in the public garden the lady in the beret walked up without haste to take the next table. Her expression, her gait, her dress, and the way she did her hair told him that she belonged to the upper class, that she was married, that she was in Yalta for the first time and alone, and that she was bored there. The stories told of the immorality in Yalta are to a great extent untrue; he despised them, and knew that such stories were made up for the most part by persons who would have been glad to sin themselves if they had had the chance; but when the lady sat down at the next table three paces from him, he recalled these stories of easy conquests, of trips to the mountains, and the tempting thought of a swift, fleeting liaison, a romance with an unknown woman of whose very name he was ignorant suddenly took hold of him.

He beckoned invitingly to the Pomeranian, and when the dog approached him, shook his finger at it. The Pomeranian growled; Gurov threatened it again.

The lady glanced at him and at once dropped her eyes.

"He doesn't bite," she said and blushed.

"May I give him a bone?" he asked; and when she nodded he inquired affably, "Have you been in Yalta long?"

"About five days."

"And I am dragging out the second week here."

There was a short silence.

"Time passes quickly, and yet it is so dull here!" she said, not looking at him.

"It's only the fashion to say it's dull here. A provincial will live in Belyov or Zhizdra and not be bored, but when he comes here it's 'Oh, the dullness! Oh, the dust!' One would think he came from Granada."

She laughed. Then both continued eating in silence, like strangers, but after dinner they walked together and there sprang up between them the light banter of people who are free and contented, to whom it does not matter where they go or what they talk about. They walked and talked of the strange light on the sea: the water was a soft, warm, lilac color, and there was a golden band of moonlight upon it. They talked of how sultry it was after a hot day. Gurov told her that he was a native of Moscow, that he had studied languages and literature at the university, but had a post in a bank; that at one time he had trained to become an opera singer but had given it up, that he owned two houses in Moscow. And he learned from her that she had grown up in Petersburg, but had lived in S—— since her marriage two years previously, that she was going to stay in Yalta for about another month, and that her husband, who needed a rest, too, might perhaps come to fetch her. She was not certain whether her husband was a member of a Government Board or served on a Zemstvo Council, and this amused her. And Gurov learned too that her name was Anna Sergeyevna.

Afterwards in his room at the hotel he thought about her—and was certain that he would meet her the next day. It was bound to happen. Getting into bed he recalled that she had been a schoolgirl only recently, doing lessons like his own daughter; he thought how much timidity and angularity there was still in her laugh and her manner of talking with a stranger. It must have been the first time in her life that she was alone in a setting in which she was followed, looked at, and spoken to for one secret purpose alone, which she could hardly fail to guess. He thought of her slim, delicate throat, her lovely gray eyes.

"There's something pathetic about her, though," he thought, and dropped off.

2

A week had passed since they had struck up an acquaintance. It was a holiday. It was close indoors, while in the street the wind whirled the dust about and blew people's hats off. One was thirsty all day, and Gurov often went into the restaurant and offered Anna Sergeyevna a soft drink or ice cream. One did not know what to do with oneself.

In the evening when the wind had abated they went out on the pier to watch the steamer come in. There were a great many people walking about the dock; they had come to welcome someone and they were carrying bunches of flowers. And two peculiarities of a festive Yalta crowd stood out: the elderly ladies were dressed like young ones and there were many generals.

Owing to the choppy sea, the steamer arrived late, after sunset, and it was a long time tacking about before it put in at the pier. Anna Sergeyevna peered at the steamer and the passengers through her lorgnette as though looking for acquaintances, and whenever she turned to Gurov her eyes were shining. She talked a great deal and asked questions jerkily, forgetting the next moment what she had asked; then she lost her lorgnette in the crush.

The festive crowd began to disperse; it was now too dark to see people's faces; there was no wind any more, but Gurov and Anna Sergeyevna still stood as though waiting to see someone else come off the steamer. Anna Sergeyevna was silent now, and sniffed her flowers without looking at Gurov.

"The weather has improved this evening," he said. "Where shall we go now? Shall we drive somewhere?"

She did not reply.

Then he looked at her intently, and suddenly embraced her and kissed her on the lips, and the moist fragrance of her flowers enveloped him; and at once he looked round him anxiously, wondering if anyone had seen them.

"Let us go to your place," he said softly. And they walked off together rapidly.

The air in her room was close and there was the smell of the perfume she had bought at the Japanese shop. Looking at her, Gurov thought: "What encounters life offers!" From the past he preserved the memory of carefree, good-natured women whom love made gay and who were grateful to him for the happiness he gave them, however brief it might be; and of women like his wife who loved without sincerity, with too many words, affectedly, hysterically, with an expression that it was not love or passion that engaged them but something more significant; and of two or three others, very beautiful, frigid women, across whose faces would suddenly flit a rapacious expression—an obstinate desire to take from life more than it could give, and these were women no longer young, capricious, unreflecting, domineering, unintelligent, and when Gurov grew cold to them their beauty aroused his hatred, and the lace on their lingerie seemed to him to resemble scales.

But here there was the timidity, the angularity of inexperienced youth, a feeling of awkwardness; and there was a sense of embarrassment, as though someone had suddenly knocked at the door. Anna Sergeyevna, "the lady with the pet dog," treated what had happened in a peculiar way, very seriously, as though it were her fall—so it seemed, and this was odd and inappropriate. Her features drooped and faded, and her long hair hung down sadly on either side of her face; she grew pensive and her dejected pose was that of a Magdalene in a picture by an old master.

"It's not right," she said. "You don't respect me now, you first of all."

There was a watermelon on the table. Gurov cut himself a slice and began eating it without haste. They were silent for at least half an hour.

There was something touching about Anna Sergeyevna; she had the purity of a well-bred, naive woman who has seen little of life. The single candle burning on the table barely illuminated her face, yet it was clear that she was unhappy.

"Why should I stop respecting you, darling?" asked Gurov. "You don't know what you're saying."

"God forgive me," she said, and her eyes filled with tears. "It's terrible."

"It's as though you were trying to exonerate yourself."

"How can I exonerate myself? No. I am a bad, low woman; I despise myself and I have no thought of exonerating myself. It's not my husband but myself I have deceived. And not only just now; I have been deceiving myself for a long time. My husband may be a good, honest man, but he is a flunkey! I don't know what he does, what his work is, but I know he is a flunkey! I was twenty when I married him. I was tormented by curiosity; I wanted something better. 'There must be a different sort of life,' I said to myself. I wanted to live! To live, to live! Curiosity kept eating at me —you don't understand it, but I swear to God I could no longer control myself; something was going on in me; I could not be held back. I told my husband I was ill, and came here. And here I have been walking about as though in a daze, as though I were mad; and now I have become a vulgar, vile woman whom anyone may despise."

Gurov was already bored with her; he was irritated by her naive tone, by her repentance, so unexpected and so out of place, but for the tears in her eyes he might have thought she was joking or play-acting.

"I don't understand, my dear," he said softly. "What do you want?"

She hid her face on his breast and pressed close to him.

"Believe me, believe me, I beg you," she said, "I love honesty and purity, and sin is loathsome to me; I don't know what I'm doing. Simple people say, 'The Evil One has led me astray.' And I may say of myself now that the Evil One has led me astray."

"Quiet, quiet," he murmured.

He looked into her fixed, frightened eyes, kissed her, spoke to her softly and affectionately, and by degrees she calmed down, and her gaiety returned; both began laughing.

Afterwards when they went out there was not a soul on the esplanade. The town with its cypresses looked quite dead, but the sea was still sounding as it broke upon the beach; a single launch was rocking on the waves and on it a lantern was blinking sleepily.

They found a cab and drove to Oreanda.

"I found out your surname in the hall just now: it was written on the board—von Dideritz," said Gurov. "Is your husband German?"

"No; I believe his grandfather was German, but he is Greek Orthodox himself."

At Oreanda they sat on a bench not far from the church, looked down at the sea, and were silent. Yalta was barely visible through the morning mist; white clouds rested motionlessly on the mountaintops. The leaves did not stir on the trees, cicadas twanged, and the monotonous muffled sound of the sea that rose from below spoke of the peace, the eternal sleep awaiting us. So it rumbled below when there was no Yalta, no Oreanda here; so it rumbles now, and it will rumble as indifferently and as hollowly when we are no more. And in this constancy, in this complete indifference to the life and death of each of us, there lies, perhaps, a pledge of our eternal salvation, of the unceasing advance of life upon earth, of unceasing movement towards perfection. Sitting beside a young woman who in the dawn seemed so lovely, Gurov, soothed and spellbound by these magical surroundings—the sea, the mountains, the clouds, the wide sky—thought how everything is really beautiful in this world when one reflects: everything except what we think or do ourselves when we forget the higher aims of life and our own human dignity.

A man strolled up to them—probably a guard—looked at them and walked away. And this detail, too, seemed so mysterious and beautiful. They saw a steamer arrive from Feodosia, its lights extinguished in the glow of dawn.

"There is dew on the grass," said Anna Sergeyevna, after a silence.

"Yes, it's time to go home."

They returned to the city.

Then they met every day at twelve o'clock on the esplanade, lunched and dined together, took walks, admired the sea. She complained that she slept badly, that she had palpitations, asked the same questions, troubled now by jealousy and now by the fear that he did not respect her sufficiently. And often in the square or the public garden, when there was no one near them, he suddenly drew her to him and kissed her passionately. Complete idleness, these kisses in broad daylight exchanged furtively in dread of someone's seeing them, the heat, the smell of the sea, and the continual flitting before his eyes of idle, well-dressed, well-fed people, worked a complete change in him; he kept telling Anna Sergeyevna how beautiful she was, how seductive, was urgently passionate; he would not move a step away from her, while she was often pensive and continually pressed him to confess that he did not respect her, did not love her in the least, and saw in her nothing but a common woman. Almost every evening rather late they drove somewhere out of town, to Oreanda or to the waterfall; and the excursion was always a success, the scenery invariably impressed them as beautiful and magnificent.

They were expecting her husband, but a letter came from him saying that he had eye-trouble, and begging his wife to return home as soon as possible. Anna Sergeyevna made haste to go.

"It's a good thing I am leaving," she said to Gurov. "It's the hand of Fate!"

She took a carriage to the railway station, and he went with her. They were driving the whole day. When she had taken her place in the express, and when the second bell had rung, she said, "Let me look at you once more—let me look at you again. Like this."

She was not crying but was so sad that she seemed ill and her face was quivering.

"I shall be thinking of you—remembering you," she said. "God bless you; be happy. Don't remember evil against me. We are parting for-ever—it has to be, for we ought never to have met. Well, God bless you."

The train moved off rapidly, its lights soon vanished, and a minute later there was no sound of it, as though everything had conspired to end as quickly as possible that sweet trance, that madness. Left alone on the plat-form, and gazing into the dark distance, Gurov listened to the twang of the grasshoppers and the hum of the telegraph wires, feeling as though he had just waked up. And he reflected, musing, that there had now been another episode or adventure in his life, and it, too, was at an end, and nothing was left of it but a memory. He was moved, sad, and slightly remorseful: this young woman whom he would never meet again had not been happy with him; he had been warm and affectionate with her, but yet in his manner, his tone, and his caresses there had been a shade of light irony, the slightly coarse arrogance of a happy male who was, besides, almost twice her age. She had constantly called him kind, exceptional, high-minded; obviously he had seemed to her different from what he really was, so he had involuntarily deceived her.

Here at the station there was already a scent of autumn in the air; it was a chilly evening.

"It is time for me to go north, too," thought Gurov as he left the platform. "High time!"

3

At home in Moscow the winter routine was already established; the stoves were heated, and in the morning it was still dark when the children were having breakfast and getting ready for school, and the nurse would light the lamp for a short time. There were frosts already. When the first snow falls, on the first day the sleighs are out, it is pleasant to see the white earth, the white roofs; one draws easy, delicious breaths, and the season brings back the days of one's youth. The old limes and birches, white with hoar-frost, have a good-natured look; they are closer to one's heart than cypresses and palms, and near them one no longer wants to think of moun-tains and the sea.

Gurov, a native of Moscow, arrived there on a fine frosty day, and when he put on his fur coat and warm gloves and took a walk along Petrovka, and when on Saturday night he heard the bells ringing, his recent trip and the places he had visited lost all charm for him. Little by little he became immersed in Moscow life, greedily read three newspapers a day, and declared that he did not read the Moscow papers on principle. He already felt a longing for restaurants, clubs, formal dinners, anniversary celebrations, and it flattered him to entertain distinguished lawyers and actors, and to play cards with a professor at the physicians' club. He could eat a whole portion of meat stewed with pickled cabbage and served in a pan, Moscow style.

A month or so would pass and the image of Anna Sergeyevna, it seemed to him, would become misty in his memory, and only from time to time he would dream of her with her touching smile as he dreamed of others. But more than a month went by, winter came into its own, and everything was still clear in his memory as though he had parted from Anna Sergeyevna only yesterday. And his memories glowed more and more vividly. When in the evening stillness the voices of his children preparing their lessons reached his study, or when he listened to a song or to an organ playing in a restaurant, or when the storm howled in the chimney, suddenly everything would rise up in his memory; what had happened on the pier and the early morning with the mist on the mountains, and the steamer coming from Feodosia, and the kisses. He would pace about his room a long time, remembering and smiling; then his memories passed into reveries, and in his imagination the past would mingle with what was to come. He did not dream of Anna Sergeyevna, but she followed him about everywhere and watched him. When he shut his eyes he saw her before him as though she were there in the flesh, and she seemed to him lovelier, younger, tenderer than she had been, and he imagined himself a finer man than he had been in Yalta. Of evenings she peered out at him from the bookcase, from the fireplace, from the corner—he heard her breathing, the caressing rustle of her clothes. In the street he followed the women with his eyes, looking for someone who resembled her.

Already he was tormented by a strong desire to share his memories with someone. But in his home it was impossible to talk of his love, and he had no one to talk to outside; certainly he could not confide in his tenants or in anyone at the bank. And what was there to talk about? He hadn't loved her then, had he? Had there been anything beautiful, poetical, edifying, or simply interesting in his relations with Anna Sergeyevna? And he was forced to talk vaguely of love, of women, and no one guessed what he meant; only his wife would twitch her black eyebrows and say, "The part of a philanderer does not suit you at all, Dimitry."

One evening, coming out of the physicians' club with an official with whom he had been playing cards, he could not resist saying:

"If you only knew what a fascinating woman I became acquainted with at Yalta!"

The official got into his sledge and was driving away, but turned suddenly and shouted:

"Dmitry Dmitrich!"

"What is it?"

"You were right this evening: the sturgeon was a bit high."

These words, so commonplace, for some reason moved Gurov to indignation, and struck him as degrading and unclean. What savage manners, what mugs! What stupid nights, what dull, humdrum days! Frenzied gambling, gluttony, drunkenness, continual talk always about the same thing! Futile pursuits and conversations always about the same topics take up the better part of one's time, the better part of one's strength, and in the end there is left a life clipped and wingless, an absurd mess, and there is no escaping or getting away from it—just as though one were in a madhouse or a prison.

Gurov, boiling with indignation, did not sleep all night. And he had a headache all the next day. And the following nights too he slept badly; he sat up in bed, thinking, or paced up and down his room. He was fed up with his children, fed up with the bank; he had no desire to go anywhere or to talk of anything.

In December during the holidays he prepared to take a trip and told his wife he was going to Petersburg to do what he could for a young friend—and he set off for S——. What for? He did not know, himself. He wanted to see Anna Sergeyevna and talk with her, to arrange a rendezvous if possible.

He arrived at S—— in the morning, and at the hotel took the best room, in which the floor was covered with gray army cloth, and on the table there was an inkstand, gray with dust and topped by a figure on horseback; its hat in its raised hand and its head broken off. The porter gave him the necessary information: von Dideritz lived in a house of his own on Staro-Goncharnaya Street, not far from the hotel: he was rich and lived well and kept his own horses; everyone in the town knew him. The porter pronounced the name: "Dridiritz."

Without haste Gurov made his way to Staro-Goncharnaya Street and found the house. Directly opposite the house stretched a long gray fence studded with nails.

"A fence like that would make one run away," thought Gurov, looking now at the fence, now at the windows of the house.

He reflected: this was a holiday, and the husband was apt to be at home. And in any case, it would be tactless to go into the house and disturb her. If he were to send her a note, it might fall into her husband's hands, and that might spoil everything. The best thing was to rely on chance. And he kept walking up and down the street and along the fence, waiting for the chance. He saw a beggar go in at the gate and heard the dogs attack him; then an hour later he heard a piano, and the sound came to him faintly and indistinctly. Probably it was Anna Sergeyevna playing. The front door opened suddenly, and an old woman came out, followed by the familiar white Pomeranian. Gurov was on the point of calling to the dog, but his heart began beating violently, and in his excitement he could not remember the Pomeranian's name.

He kept walking up and down, and hated the gray fence more and more, and by now he thought irritably that Anna Sergeyevna had forgotten him, and was perhaps already diverting herself with another man, and that that was very natural in a young woman who from morning till night had to look at that damn fence. He went back to his hotel room and sat on the couch for a long while, not knowing what to do, then he had dinner and a long nap.

"How stupid and annoying all this is!" he thought when he woke and looked at the dark windows: it was already evening. "Here I've had a good sleep for some reason. What am I going to do at night?"

He sat on the bed, which was covered with a cheap gray blanket of the kind seen in hospitals, and he twitted himself in his vexation:

"So there's your lady with the pet dog. There's your adventure. A nice place to cool your heels in."

That morning at the station a playbill in large letters had caught his eye. *The Geisha* was to be given for the first time. He thought of this and drove to the theater.

"It's quite possible that she goes to first nights," he thought.

The theater was full. As in all provincial theaters, there was a haze above the chandelier, the gallery was noisy and restless; in the front row, before the beginning of the performance the local dandies were standing with their hands clasped behind their backs; in the Governor's box the Governor's daughter, wearing a boa, occupied the front seat, while the Governor himself hid modestly behind the portiere and only his hands were visible; the curtain swayed; the orchestra was a long time tuning up. While the audience was coming in and taking their seats, Gurov scanned the faces eagerly.

Anna Sergeyevna, too, came in. She sat down in the third row, and when Gurov looked at her his heart contracted, and he understood clearly that in the whole world there was no human being so near, so precious, and so important to him; she, this little, undistinguished woman, lost in a provincial crowd, with a vulgar lorgnette in her hand, filled his whole life now, was his sorrow and his joy, the only happiness that he now desired for himself, and to the sounds of the bad orchestra, of the miserable local violins, he thought how lovely she was. He thought and dreamed.

A young man with small side-whiskers, very tall and stooped, came in with Anna Sergeyevna and sat down beside her; he nodded his head at every step and seemed to be bowing continually. Probably this was the husband whom at Yalta, in an access of bitter feeling, she had called a flunkey. And there really was in his lanky figure, his side-whiskers, his small bald patch, something of a flunkey's retiring manner; his smile was mawkish, and in his buttonhole there was an academic badge like a waiter's number.

During the first intermission the husband went out to have a smoke; she remained in her seat. Gurov, who was also sitting in the orchestra, went up to her and said in a shaky voice, with a forced smile:

"Good evening!"

She glanced at him and turned pale, then looked at him again in horror, unable to believe her eyes, and gripped the fan and the lorgnette tightly together in her hands, evidently trying to keep herself from fainting. Both were silent. She was sitting, he was standing, frightened by her distress and not daring to take a seat beside her. The violins and the flute that were being tuned up sang out. He suddenly felt frightened: it seemed as if all the people in the boxes were looking at them. She got up and went hurriedly to the exit; he followed her, and both of them walked blindly along the corridors and up and down stairs, and figures in the uniforms prescribed for magistrates, teachers, and officials of the Department of Crown Lands, all wearing badges, flitted before their eyes, as did also ladies, and fur coats on hangers; they were conscious of drafts and the smell of stale tobacco. And Gurov, whose heart was beating violently, thought:

"Oh, Lord! Why are these people here and this orchestra!"

And at that instant he suddenly recalled how when he had seen Anna Sergeyevna off at the station he had said to himself that all was over between them and that they would never meet again. But how distant the end still was!

On the narrow, gloomy staircase over which it said "To the Amphitheatre," she stopped.

"How you frightened me!" she said, breathing hard, still pale and stunned. "Oh, how you frightened me! I am barely alive. Why did you come? Why?"

"But do understand, Anna, do understand—" he said hurriedly, under his breath. "I implore you, do understand—"

She looked at him with fear, with entreaty, with love; she looked at him intently, to keep his features more distinctly in her memory.

"I suffer so," she went on, not listening to him. "All this time I have been thinking of nothing but you; I live only by the thought of you. And I wanted to forget, to forget; but why, oh, why have you come?"

On the landing above them two high school boys were looking down and smoking, but it was all the same to Gurov; he drew Anna Sergeyevna to him and began kissing her face and hands.

"What are you doing, what are you doing!" she was saying in horror, pushing him away. "We have lost our senses. Go away today; go away at once—I conjure you by all that is sacred, I implore you—People are coming this way!"

Someone was walking up the stairs.

"You must leave," Anna Sergeyevna went on in a whisper. "Do you hear, Dmitry Dmitrich? I will come and see you in Moscow. I have never been happy; I am unhappy now, and I never, never shall be happy, never! So don't make me suffer still more! I swear I'll come to Moscow. But now let us part. My dear, good, precious one, let us part!"

She pressed his hand and walked rapidly downstairs, turning to look round at him, and from her eyes he could see that she really was unhappy. Gurov stood for a while, listening, then when all grew quiet, he found his coat and left the theater.

4

And Anna Sergeyevna began coming to see him in Moscow. Once every two or three months she left S—— telling her husband that she was going to consult a doctor about a woman's ailment from which she was suffering—and her husband did and did not believe her. When she arrived in Moscow she would stop at the Slavyansky Bazar Hotel, and at once send a man in a red cap to Gurov. Gurov came to see her, and no one in Moscow knew of it.

Once he was going to see her in this way on a winter morning (the messenger had come the evening before and not found him in). With him walked his daughter, whom he wanted to take to school; it was on the way. Snow was coming down in big wet flakes.

"It's three degrees above zero, and yet it's snowing," Gurov was saying to his daughter. "But this temperature prevails only on the surface of the earth; in the upper layers of the atmosphere there is quite a different temperature."

"And why doesn't it thunder in winter, papa?"

He explained that, too. He talked, thinking all the while that he was on his way to a rendezvous, and no living soul knew of it, and probably no one would ever know. He had two lives, an open one, seen and known by all who needed to know it, full of conventional truth and conventional falsehood, exactly like the lives of his friends and acquaintances; and another life that went on in secret. And through some strange, perhaps accidental, combination of circumstances, everything that was of interest and importance to him, everything that was essential to him, everything about which he felt sincerely and did not deceive himself, everything that constituted the core of his life, was going on concealed from others; while all that was false, the shell in which he hid to cover the truth—his work at the bank, for instance, his discussions at the club, his references to the "inferior race," his appearances at anniversary celebrations with his wife—all that went on in the open. Judging others by himself, he did not believe what he saw, and always fancied that every man led his real, most interesting life under cover of secrecy as under cover of night. The personal life of every individual is based on secrecy, and perhaps it is partly for that reason that civilized man is so nervously anxious that personal privacy should be respected.

Having taken his daughter to school, Gurov went on to the Slavyansky Bazar Hotel. He took off his fur coat in the lobby, went upstairs, and knocked gently at the door. Anna Sergeyevna, wearing his favorite gray dress, exhausted by the journey and by waiting, had been expecting him since the previous evening. She was pale, and looked at him without a smile, and he had hardly entered when she flung herself on his breast. That kiss was a long, lingering one, as though they had not seen one another for two years.

"Well, darling, how are you getting on there?" he asked. "What news?"

"Wait; I'll tell you in a moment—I can't speak."

She could not speak; she was crying. She turned away from him, and pressed her handkerchief to her eyes.

"Let her have her cry; meanwhile I'll sit down," he thought, and he seated himself in an armchair.

Then he rang and ordered tea, and while he was having his tea she remained standing at the window with her back to him. She was crying out of sheer agitation, in the sorrowful consciousness that their life was so sad; that they could only see each other in secret and had to hide from people like thieves! Was it not a broken life?

"Come, stop now, dear!" he said.

It was plain to him that this love of theirs would not be over soon, that the end of it was not in sight. Anna Sergeyevna was growing more and more attached to him. She adored him, and it was unthinkable to tell her that their love was bound to come to an end some day; besides, she would not have believed it!

He went up to her and took her by the shoulders, to fondle her and say something diverting, and at that moment he caught sight of himself in the mirror.

His hair was already beginning to turn gray. And it seemed odd to him that he had grown so much older in the last few years, and lost his looks. The shoulders on which his hands rested were warm and heaving. He felt compassion for this life, still so warm and lovely, but probably already about to begin to fade and wither like his own. Why did she love him so much? He always seemed to women different from what he was, and they loved in him not himself, but the man whom their imagination created and whom they had been eagerly seeking all their lives; and afterwards, when they saw their mistake, they loved him nevertheless. And not one of them had been happy with him. In the past he had met women, come together with them, parted from them, but he had never once loved; it was anything you please, but not love. And only now when his head was gray he had fallen in love, really, truly—for the first time in his life.

Anna Sergeyevna and he loved each other as people do who are very close and intimate, like man and wife, like tender friends; it seemed to them that Fate itself had meant them for one another, and they could not understand why he had a wife and she a husband; and it was as though they were a pair of migratory birds, male and female, caught and forced to live in different cages. They forgave each other what they were ashamed of in their past, they forgave everything in the present, and felt that this love of theirs had altered them both.

Formerly in moments of sadness he had soothed himself with whatever logical arguments came into his head, but now he no longer cared for logic; he felt profound compassion, he wanted to be sincere and tender.

"Give it up now, my darling," he said. "You've had your cry; that's enough. Let us have a talk now, we'll think up something."

Then they spent a long time taking counsel together, they talked of how to avoid the necessity for secrecy, for deception, for living in different cities, and not seeing one another for long stretches of time. How could they free themselves from these intolerable fetters?

"How? How?" he asked, clutching his head. "How?"

And it seemed as though in a little while the solution would be found, and then a new and glorious life would begin; and it was clear to both of them that the end was still far off, and that what was to be most complicated and difficult for them was only just beginning.

1899

Anton Chekhov's fidelity to the details of external reality seems to put his fiction at a pole opposite that of writers of tales and fantasies that express an inward reality. As Virginia Woolf observes, however, Chekhov's stories reveal his soul, a soul she admires but cannot be entirely sympathetic with.

"The emphasis is laid upon such unexpected places": Virginia Woolf

The emphasis is laid upon such unexpected places that at first it seems as if there were no emphasis at all; and then, as the eyes accustom themselves to twilight and discern the shapes of things in a room we see how complete the story is, how profound, and how truly in obedience to his vision Tchekov has chosen this, that, and the other, and placed them together to compose something new. But it is impossible to say 'this is comic', or 'that is tragic', nor are we certain, since short stories, we have been taught, should be brief and conclusive, whether this, which is vague and inconclusive, should be called a short story at all. . . . In every great Russian writer we seem to discern the features of a saint, if sympathy for the sufferings of others, love towards them, endeavour to reach some goal worthy of the most exacting demands of the spirit constitute saintliness. It is the saint in them which confounds us with a feeling of our own irreligious triviality, and turns so many of our famous novels to tinsel and trickery. The conclusions of the Russian mind, thus comprehensive and compassionate, are inevitably, perhaps, of the utmost sadness. More accurately indeed we might speak of the inconclusiveness of the Russian mind. It is the sense that there is no answer, that if honestly examined life presents question after question which must be left to sound on and on after the story is over in hopeless interrogation that fills us with a deep, and finally it may be with a resentful, despair. They are right perhaps; unquestionably they see further than we do and without our gross impediments of vision. But perhaps we see something that escapes them, or why should this voice of protest mix itself with our gloom? The voice of protest is the voice of another and an ancient civilization which seems to have bred in us the instinct to enjoy and fight rather than to suffer and understand.

CHARLOTTE PERKINS GILMAN

(1860–1935)

THE YELLOW WALLPAPER

It is very seldom that mere ordinary people like John and myself secure ancestral halls for the summer.

A colonial mansion, a hereditary estate, I would say a haunted house and reach the height of romantic felicity—but that would be asking too much of fate!

Still I will proudly declare that there is something queer about it.

Else, why should it be let so cheaply? And why have stood so long untenanted?

John laughs at me, of course, but one expects that.

John is practical in the extreme. He has no patience with faith, an intense horror of superstition, and he scoffs openly at any talk of things not to be felt and seen and put down in figures.

John is a physician, and *perhaps*—(I would not say it to a living soul, of course, but this is dead paper and a great relief to my mind)—*perhaps* that is one reason I do not get well faster.

You see, he does not believe I am sick! And what can one do?

If a physician of high standing, and one's own husband, assures friends and relatives that there is really nothing the matter with one but temporary nervous depression—a slight hysterical tendency—what is one to do?

My brother is also a physician, and also of high standing, and he says the same thing.

So I take phosphates or phosphites—whichever it is—and tonics, and air and exercise, and journeys, and am absolutely forbidden to "work" until I am well again.

Personally, I disagree with their ideas.

Personally, I believe that congenial work, with excitement and change, would do me good.

But what is one to do?

I did write for a while in spite of them; but it *does* exhaust me a good deal—having to be so sly about it, or else meet with heavy opposition.

I sometimes fancy that in my condition, if I had less opposition and more society and stimulus—but John says the very worst thing I can do is to think about my condition, and I confess it always makes me feel bad.

So I will let it alone and talk about the house.

The most beautiful place! It is quite alone, standing well back from the road, quite three miles from the village. It makes me think of English places that you read about, for there are hedges and walls and gates that lock, and lots of separate little houses for the gardeners and people.

There is a *delicious* garden! I never saw such a garden—large and shady, full of box-bordered paths, and lined with long grape-covered arbors with seats under them.

There were greenhouses, but they are all broken now.

There was some legal trouble, I believe, something about the heirs and co-heirs; anyhow, the place has been empty for years.

That spoils my ghostliness, I am afraid, but I don't care—there is something strange about the house—I can feel it.

I even said so to John one moonlight evening, but he said what I felt was a draught, and shut the window.

I get unreasonably angry with John sometimes. I'm sure I never used to be so sensitive. I think it is due to this nervous condition.

But John says if I feel so I shall neglect proper self-control; so I take pains to control myself—before him, at least, and that makes me very tired.

I don't like our room a bit. I wanted one downstairs that opened onto the piazza and had roses all over the window, and such pretty old-fashioned chintz hangings! But John would not hear of it.

He said there was only one window and not room for two beds, and no near room for him if he took another.

He is very careful and loving, and hardly lets me stir without special direction.

I have a schedule prescription for each hour in the day; he takes all care from me, and so I feel basely ungrateful not to value it more.

He said he came here solely on my account, that I was to have perfect rest and all the air I could get. "Your exercise depends on your strength, my dear," said he, "and your food somewhat on your appetite; but air you can absorb all the time." So we took the nursery at the top of the house.

It is a big, airy room, the whole floor nearly, with windows that look all ways, and air and sunshine galore. It was nursery first, and then playroom and gymnasium, I should judge, for the windows are barred for little children, and there are rings and things in the walls.

The paint and paper look as if a boys' school had used it. It is stripped off—the paper—in great patches all around the head of my bed, about as far as I can reach, and in a great place on the other side of the room low down. I never saw a worse paper in my life. One of those sprawling, flamboyant patterns committing every artistic sin.

It is dull enough to confuse the eye in following, pronounced enough constantly to irritate and provoke study, and when you follow the lame uncertain curves for a little distance they suddenly commit suicide —plunge off at outrageous angles, destroy themselves in unheard-of contradictions.

The color is repellent, almost revolting: a smouldering unclean yellow, strangely faded by the slow-turning sunlight. It is a dull yet lurid orange in some places, a sickly sulphur tint in others.

No wonder the children hated it! I should hate it myself if I had to live in this room long.

There comes John, and I must put this away—he hates to have me write a word.

We have been here two weeks, and I haven't felt like writing before, since that first day.

I am sitting by the window now, up in this atrocious nursery, and there is nothing to hinder my writing as much as I please, save lack of strength.

John is away all day, and even some nights when his cases are serious.

I am glad my case is not serious!

But these nervous troubles are dreadfully depressing.

John does not know how much I really suffer. He knows there is no reason to suffer, and that satisfies him.

Of course it is only nervousness. It does weigh on me so not to do my duty in any way!

I meant to be such a help to John, such a real rest and comfort, and here I am a comparative burden already!

Nobody would believe what an effort it is to do what little I am able —to dress and entertain, and order things.

It is fortunate Mary is so good with the baby. Such a dear baby!

And yet I *cannot* be with him, it makes me so nervous.

I suppose John never was nervous in his life. He laughs at me so about this wallpaper!

At first he meant to repaper the room, but afterward he said that I was letting it get the better of me, and that nothing was worse for a nervous patient than to give way to such fancies.

He said that after the wallpaper was changed it would be the heavy bedstead, and then the barred windows, and then that gate at the head of the stairs, and so on.

"You know the place is doing you good," he said, "and really, dear, I don't care to renovate the house just for a three months' rental."

"Then do let us go downstairs," I said. "There are such pretty rooms there."

Then he took me in his arms and called me a blessed little goose, and said he would go down cellar, if I wished, and have it whitewashed into the bargain.

But he is right enough about the beds and windows and things.

It is as airy and comfortable a room as anyone need wish, and, of course, I would not be so silly as to make him uncomfortable just for a whim.

I'm really getting fond of the big room, all but that horrid paper.

Out of one window I can see the garden—those mysterious deep-shaded arbors, the riotous old-fashioned flowers, and bushes and gnarly trees.

Out of another I get a lovely view of the bay and a little private wharf belonging to the estate. There is a beautiful shaded lane that runs down there from the house. I always fancy I see people walking in these numerous paths and arbors, but John has cautioned me not to give way to fancy in the least. He says that with my imaginative power and habit of story-making, a nervous weakness like mine is sure to lead to all manner of excited fancies, and that I ought to use my will and good sense to check the tendency. So I try.

I think sometimes that if I were only well enough to write a little it would relieve the press of ideas and rest me.

But I find I get pretty tired when I try.

It is so discouraging not to have any advice and companionship about my work. When I get really well, John says we will ask Cousin Henry and Julia down for a long visit; but he says he would as soon put fireworks in my pillow-case as to let me have those stimulating people about now.

I wish I could get well faster.

But I must not think about that. This paper looks to me as if it *knew* what a vicious influence it had!

There is a recurrent spot where the pattern lolls like a broken neck and two bulbous eyes stare at you upside down.

I get positively angry with the impertinence of it and the everlastingness. Up and down and sideways they crawl, and those absurd unblinking eyes are everywhere. There is one place where two breadths didn't match, and the eyes go all up and down the line, one a little higher than the other.

I never saw so much expression in an inanimate thing before, and we all know how much expression they have! I used to lie awake as a child and get more entertainment and terror out of blank walls and plain furniture than most children could find in a toy-store.

I remember what a kindly wink the knobs of our big old bureau used to have, and there was one chair that always seemed like a strong friend.

I used to feel that if any of the other things looked too fierce I could always hop into that chair and be safe.

The furniture in this room is no worse than inharmonious, however, for we had to bring it all from downstairs. I suppose when this was used as a playroom they had to take the nursery things out, and no wonder! I never saw such ravages as the children have made here.

The wallpaper, as I said before, is torn off in spots, and it sticketh closer than a brother—they must have had perseverance as well as hatred.

Then the floor is scratched and gouged and splintered, the plaster itself is dug out here and there, and this great heavy bed, which is all we found in the room, looks as if it had been through the wars.

But I don't mind it a bit—only the paper.

There comes John's sister. Such a dear girl as she is, and so careful of me! I must not let her find me writing.

She is a perfect and enthusiastic housekeeper, and hopes for no better profession. I verily believe she thinks it is the writing which made me sick!

But I can write when she is out, and see her a long way off from these windows.

There is one that commands the road, a lovely shaded winding road, and one that just looks off over the country. A lovely country, too, full of great elms and velvet meadows.

This wallpaper has a kind of sub-pattern in a different shade, a particularly irritating one, for you can only see it in certain lights, and not clearly then.

But in the places where it isn't faded and where the sun is just so—I can see a strange, provoking, formless sort of figure that seems to skulk about behind that silly and conspicuous front design.

There's sister on the stairs!

Well, the Fourth of July is over! The people are all gone, and I am tired out. John thought it might do me good to see a little company, so we just had Mother and Nellie and the children down for a week.

Of course I didn't do a thing. Jennie sees to everything now.

But it tired me all the same.

John says if I don't pick up faster he shall send me to Weir Mitchell in the fall.

But I don't want to go there at all. I had a friend who was in his hands once, and she says he is just like John and my brother, only more so!

Besides, it is such an undertaking to go so far.

I don't feel as if it was worthwhile to turn my hand over for anything, and I'm getting dreadfully fretful and querulous.

I cry at nothing, and cry most of the time.

Of course I don't when John is here, or anybody else, but when I am alone.

And I am alone a good deal just now. John is kept in town very often by serious cases, and Jennie is good and lets me alone when I want her to.

So I walk a little in the garden or down that lovely lane, sit on the porch under the roses, and lie down up here a good deal.

I'm getting really fond of the room in spite of the wallpaper. Perhaps *because* of the wallpaper.

It dwells in my mind so!

I lie here on this great immovable bed—it is nailed down, I believe —and follow that pattern about by the hour. It is as good as gymnastics, I assure you. I start, we'll say, at the bottom, down in the corner over there where it has not been touched, and I determine for the thousandth time that I *will* follow that pointless pattern to some sort of a conclusion.

I know a little of the principle of design, and I know this thing was not arranged on any laws of radiation, or alternation, or repetition, or symmetry, or anything else that I ever heard of.

It is repeated, of course, by the breadths, but not otherwise.

Looked at in one way, each breadth stands alone; the bloated curves and flourishes—a kind of "debased Romanesque" with delirium tremens go waddling up and down in isolated columns of fatuity.

But, on the other hand, they connect diagonally, and the sprawling outlines run off in great slanting waves of optic horror, like a lot of wallowing sea-weeds in full chase.

The whole thing goes horizontally, too, at least it seems so, and I exhaust myself trying to distinguish the order of its going in that direction.

They have used a horizontal breadth for a frieze, and that adds wonderfully to the confusion.

There is one end of the room where it is almost intact, and there, when the crosslights fade and the low sun shines directly upon it, I can almost fancy radiation after all—the interminable grotesque seems to form around a common center and rush off in headlong plunges of equal distraction.

It makes me tired to follow it. I will take a nap, I guess.

I don't know why I should write this.

I don't want to.

I don't feel able.

And I know John would think it absurd. But I *must* say what I feel and think in some way—it is such a relief!

But the effort is getting to be greater than the relief.

Half the time now I am awfully lazy, and lie down ever so much. John says I mustn't lose my strength, and has me take cod liver oil and lots of tonics and things, to say nothing of ale and wine and rare meat.

Dear John! He loves me very dearly, and hates to have me sick. I tried to have a real earnest reasonable talk with him the other day, and tell him how I wish he would let me go and make a visit to Cousin Henry and Julia.

But he said I wasn't able to go, nor able to stand it after I got there; and I did not make out a very good case for myself, for I was crying before I had finished.

It is getting to be a great effort for me to think straight. Just this nervous weakness, I suppose.

And dear John gathered me up in his arms, and just carried me upstairs and laid me on the bed, and sat by me and read to me till it tired my head.

He said I was his darling and his comfort and all he had, and that I must take care of myself for his sake, and keep well.

He says no one but myself can help me out of it, that I must use my will and self-control and not let any silly fancies run away with me.

There's one comfort—the baby is well and happy, and does not have to occupy this nursery with the horrid wallpaper.

If we had not used it, that blessed child would have! What a fortunate escape! Why, I wouldn't have a child of mine, an impressionable little thing, live in such a room for worlds.

I never thought of it before, but it is lucky that John kept me here after all; I can stand it so much easier than a baby, you see.

Of course I never mention it to them any more—I am too wise—but I keep watch for it all the same.

There are things in that wallpaper that nobody knows about but me, or ever will.

Behind that outside pattern the dim shapes get clearer every day.

It is always the same shape, only very numerous.

And it is like a woman stooping down and creeping about behind that pattern. I don't like it a bit. I wonder—I begin to think—I wish John would take me away from here!

It is so hard to talk with John about my case, because he is so wise, and because he loves me so.

But I tried it last night.

It was moonlight. The moon shines in all around just as the sun does.

I hate to see it sometimes, it creeps so slowly, and always comes in by one window or another.

John was asleep and I hated to waken him, so I kept still and watched the moonlight on that undulating wallpaper till I felt creepy.

The faint figure behind seemed to shake the pattern, just as if she wanted to get out.

I got up softly and went to feel and see if the paper *did* move, and when I came back John was awake.

"What is it, little girl?" he said. "Don't go walking about like that —you'll get cold."

I thought it was a good time to talk, so I told him that I really was not gaining here, and that I wished he would take me away.

"Why, darling!" said he. "Our lease will be up in three weeks, and I can't see how to leave before.

"The repairs are not done at home, and I cannot possibly leave town just now. Of course, if you were in any danger, I could and would, but you really are better, dear, whether you can see it or not. I am a doctor, dear, and I know. You are gaining flesh and color, your appetite is better, I feel really much easier about you."

"I don't weigh a bit more," said I, "nor as much; and my appetite may be better in the evening when you are here but it is worse in the morning when you are away!"

"Bless her little heart!" said he with a big hug. "She shall be as sick as she pleases! But now let's improve the shining hours by going to sleep, and talk about it in the morning!"

"And you won't go away?" I asked gloomily.

"Why, how can I, dear? It is only three weeks more and then we will take a nice little trip of a few days while Jennie is getting the house ready. Really, dear, you are better!"

"Better in body perhaps—" I began, and stopped short, for he sat up straight and looked at me with such a stern, reproachful look that I could not say another word.

"My darling," said he, "I beg of you, for my sake and for our child's sake, as well as for your own, that you will never for one instant let that idea enter your mind! There is nothing so dangerous, so fascinating, to a temperament like yours. It is a false and foolish fancy. Can you not trust me as a physician when I tell you so?"

So of course I said no more on that score, and we went to sleep before long. He thought I was asleep first, but I wasn't, and lay there for hours trying to decide whether that front pattern and the back pattern really did move together or separately.

On a pattern like this, by daylight, there is a lack of sequence, a defiance of law, that is a constant irritant to a normal mind.

The color is hideous enough, and unreliable enough, and infuriating enough, but the pattern is torturing.

You think you have mastered it, but just as you get well under way in following, it turns a back-somersault and there you are. It slaps you in the face, knocks you down, and tramples upon you. It is like a bad dream.

The outside pattern is a florid arabesque, reminding one of a fungus. If you can imagine a toadstool in joints, an interminable string of toadstools, budding and sprouting in endless convolutions—why, that is something like it.

That is, sometimes!

There is one marked peculiarity about this paper, a thing nobody seems to notice but myself, and that is that it changes as the light changes.

When the sun shoots in through the east window—I always watch for that first long, straight ray—it changes so quickly that I never can quite believe it.

That is why I watch it always.

By moonlight—the moon shines in all night when there is a moon —I wouldn't know it was the same paper.

At night in any kind of light, in twilight, candlelight, lamplight, and worst of all by moonlight, it becomes bars! The outside pattern, I mean, and the woman behind it is as plain as can be.

I didn't realize for a long time what the thing was that showed behind, that dim sub-pattern, but now I am quite sure it is a woman.

By daylight she is subdued, quiet. I fancy it is the pattern that keeps her so still. It is so puzzling. It keeps me quiet by the hour.

I lie down ever so much now. John says it is good for me, and to sleep all I can.

Indeed he started the habit by making me lie down for an hour after each meal.

It is a very bad habit, I am convinced, for you see, I don't sleep.

And that cultivates deceit, for I don't tell them I'm awake—oh, no!

The fact is I am getting a little afraid of John.

He seems very queer sometimes, and even Jennie has an inexplicable look.

It strikes me occasionally, just as a scientific hypothesis, that perhaps it is the paper!

I have watched John when he did not know I was looking, and come into the room suddenly on the most innocent excuses, and I've caught him several times *looking at the paper*! And Jennie too. I caught Jennie with her hand on it once.

She didn't know I was in the room, and when I asked her in a quiet, a very quiet voice, with the most restrained manner possible, what she was doing with the paper, she turned around as if she had been caught stealing, and looked quite angry—asked me why I should frighten her so!

Then she said that the paper stained everything it touched, that she had found yellow smooches on all my clothes and John's and she wished we would be more careful!

Did not that sound innocent? But I know she was studying that pattern, and I am determined that nobody shall find it out but myself!

Life is very much more exciting now than it used to be. You see, I have something more to expect, to look forward to, to watch. I really do eat better, and am more quiet than I was.

John is so pleased to see me improve! He laughed a little the other day, and said I seemed to be flourishing in spite of my wallpaper.

I turned it off with a laugh. I had no intention of telling him it was *because* of the wallpaper—he would make fun of me. He might even want to take me away.

I don't want to leave now until I have found it out. There is a week more, and I think that will be enough.

I'm feeling so much better!

I don't sleep much at night, for it is so interesting to watch developments; but I sleep a good deal during the daytime.

In the daytime it is tiresome and perplexing.

Charlotte Perkins Gilman   *179*

There are always new shoots on the fungus, and new shades of yellow all over it. I cannot keep count of them, though I have tried conscientiously.

It is the strangest yellow, that wallpaper! It makes me think of all the yellow things I ever saw—not beautiful ones like buttercups, but old, foul, bad yellow things.

But there is something else about that paper—the smell! I noticed it the moment we came into the room, but with so much air and sun it was not bad. Now we have had a week of fog and rain, and whether the windows are open or not, the smell is here.

It creeps all over the house.

I find it hovering in the dining-room, skulking in the parlor, hiding in the hall, lying in wait for me on the stairs.

It gets into my hair.

Even when I go to ride, if I turn my head suddenly and surprise it —there is that smell!

Such a peculiar odor, too! I have spent hours in trying to analyze it, to find what it smelled like.

It is not bad—at first—and very gentle, but quite the subtlest, most enduring odor I ever met.

In this damp weather it is awful. I wake up in the night and find it hanging over me.

It used to disturb me at first. I thought seriously of burning the house—to reach the smell.

But now I am used to it. The only thing I can think of that it is like is the *color* of the paper! A yellow smell.

There is a very funny mark on this wall, low down, near the mop-board. A streak that runs round the room. It goes behind every piece of furniture, except the bed, a long, straight, even *smooch,* as if it had been rubbed over and over.

I wonder how it was done and who did it, and what they did it for. Round and round and round—round and round and round—it makes me dizzy!

I really have discovered something at last.

Through watching so much at night, when it changes so, I have finally found out.

The front pattern *does* move—and no wonder! The woman behind shakes it!

Sometimes I think there are a great many women behind, and sometimes only one, and she crawls around fast, and her crawling shakes it all over.

Then in the very bright spots she keeps still, and in the very shady spots she just takes hold of the bars and shakes them hard.

And she is all the time trying to climb through. But nobody could climb through that pattern—it strangles so; I think that is why it has so many heads.

They get through and then the pattern strangles them off and turns them upside down, and makes their eyes white!

If those heads were covered or taken off it would not be half so bad.

I think that woman gets out in the daytime!

And I'll tell you why—privately—I've seen her!

I can see her out of every one of my windows!

It is the same woman, I know, for she is always creeping, and most women do not creep by daylight.

I see her in that long shaded lane, creeping up and down. I see her in those dark grape arbors, creeping all around the garden.

I see her on that long road under the trees, creeping along, and when a carriage comes she hides under the blackberry vines.

I don't blame her a bit. It must be very humiliating to be caught creeping by daylight!

I always lock the door when I creep by daylight. I can't do it at night, for I know John would suspect something at once.

And John is so queer now that I don't want to irritate him. I wish he would take another room! Besides, I don't want anybody to get that woman out at night but myself.

I often wonder if I could see her out of all the windows at once.

But, turn as fast as I can, I can only see out of one at one time.

And though I always see her, she *may* be able to creep faster than I can turn! I have watched her sometimes away off in the open country, creeping as fast as a cloud shadow in a wind.

If only that top pattern could be gotten off from the under one! I mean to try it, little by little.

I have found out another funny thing, but I shan't tell it this time! It does not do to trust people too much.

There are only two more days to get this paper off, and I believe John is beginning to notice. I don't like the look in his eyes.

And I heard him ask Jennie a lot of professional questions about me. She had a very good report to give.

She said I slept a good deal in the daytime.

John knows I don't sleep very well at night, for all I'm so quiet!

He asked me all sorts of questions, too, and pretended to be very loving and kind.

As if I couldn't see through him!

Still, I don't wonder he acts so, sleeping under this paper for three months.

It only interests me, but I feel sure John and Jennie are affected by it.

Hurrah! This is the last day, but it is enough. John is to stay in town over night, and won't be out until this evening.

Jennie wanted to sleep with me—the sly thing; but I told her I should undoubtedly rest better for a night all alone.

Charlotte Perkins Gilman   **181**

That was clever, for really I wasn't alone a bit! As soon as it was moonlight and that poor thing began to crawl and shake the pattern, I got up and ran to help her.

I pulled and she shook. I shook and she pulled, and before morning we had peeled off yards of that paper.

A strip about as high as my head and half around the room.

And then when the sun came and that awful pattern began to laugh at me, I declared I would finish it today!

We go away tomorrow, and they are moving all my furniture down again to leave things as they were before.

Jennie looked at the wall in amazement, but I told her merrily that I did it out of pure spite at the vicious thing.

She laughed and said she wouldn't mind doing it herself, but I must not get tired.

How she betrayed herself that time!

But I am here, and no person touches this paper but Me—not *alive*!

She tried to get me out of the room—it was too patent! But I said it was so quiet and empty and clean now that I believed I would lie down again and sleep all I could, and not to wake me even for dinner—I would call when I woke.

So now she is gone, and the servants are gone, and the things are gone, and there is nothing left but that great bedstead nailed down, with the canvas mattress we found on it.

We shall sleep downstairs tonight, and take the boat home tomorrow.

I quite enjoy the room, now it is bare again.

How those children did tear about here!

This bedstead is fairly gnawed!

But I must get to work.

I have locked the door and thrown the key down into the front path.

I don't want to go out, and I don't want to have anybody come in, till John comes.

I want to astonish him.

I've got a rope up here that even Jennie did not find. If that woman does get out, and tries to get away, I can tie her!

But I forgot I could not reach far without anything to stand on!

This bed will *not* move!

I tried to lift and push it until I was lame, and then I got so angry I bit off a little piece at one corner—but it hurt my teeth.

Then I peeled off all the paper I could reach standing on the floor. It sticks horribly and the pattern just enjoys it! All those strangled heads and bulbous eyes and waddling fungus growths just shriek with derision!

I am getting angry enough to do something desperate. To jump out of the window would be admirable exercise, but the bars are too strong even to try.

Besides I wouldn't do it. Of course not. I know well enough that a step like that is improper and might be misconstrued.

I don't like to *look* out of the windows even—there are so many of those creeping women, and they creep so fast.

I wonder if they all come out of that wallpaper as I did?

But I am securely fastened now by my well-hidden rope—you don't get *me* out in the road there!

I suppose I shall have to get back behind the pattern when it comes night, and that is hard!

It is so pleasant to be out in this great room and creep around as I please!

I don't want to go outside. I won't, even if Jennie asks me to.

For outside you have to creep on the ground, and everything is green instead of yellow.

But here I can creep smoothly on the floor, and my shoulder just fits in that long smooch around the wall, so I cannot lose my way.

Why, there's John at the door!

It is no use, young man, you can't open it!

How he does call and pound!

Now he's crying to Jennie for an axe.

It would be a shame to break down that beautiful door!

"John, dear!" said I in the gentlest voice. "The key is down by the front steps, under a plantain leaf!"

That silenced him for a few moments.

Then he said, very quietly indeed, "Open the door, my darling!"

"I can't," said I. "The key is down by the front door under a plantain leaf!" And then I said it again, several times, very gently and slowly, and said it so often that he had to go and see, and he got it of course, and came in. He stopped short by the door.

"What is the matter?" he cried. "For God's sake, what are you doing!"

I kept on creeping just the same, but I looked at him over my shoulder.

"I've got out at last," said I, "in spite of you and Jane. And I've pulled off most of the paper, so you can't put me back!"

Now why should that man have fainted? But he did, and right across my path by the wall, so that I had to creep over him every time!

1892

"The Yellow Wallpaper" can be seen as a story of obsession, related therefore to Edgar Allan Poe's "The Fall of the House of Usher." But the psychological state of Charlotte Perkins Gilman is of more than literary interest. Gil-

man herself was a double victim of what we now would call depression: a victim once from the disease, and once again from the failure of others to understand the disease. In her autobiography Gilman records the "nervous prostration" she experienced in 1886.

"I lay all day on the lounge and cried": Charlotte Perkins Gilman

---

Presently we moved to a better house, on Humboldt Avenue near by, and a German servant girl of unparalleled virtues was installed. Here was a charming home; a loving and devoted husband; an exquisite baby, healthy, intelligent and good; a highly competent mother to run things; a wholly satisfactory servant—and I lay all day on the lounge and cried. . . .

In those days a new disease had dawned on the medical horizon. It was called "nervous prostration." No one knew much about it, and there were many who openly scoffed, saying it was only a new name for laziness. To be recognizably ill one must be confined to one's bed, and preferably in pain.

That a heretofore markedly vigorous young woman, with every comfort about her, should collapse in this lamentable manner was inexplicable. "You should use your will," said earnest friends. I had used it, hard and long, perhaps too hard and too long; at any rate it wouldn't work now.

"Force some happiness into your life," said one sympathizer. "Take an agreeable book to bed with you, occupy your mind with pleasant things." She did not realize that I was unable to read, and that my mind was exclusively occupied with unpleasant things. This disorder involved a growing melancholia, and that, as those know who have tasted it, consists of every painful mental sensation, shame, fear, remorse, a blind oppressive confusion, utter weakness, a steady brainache that fills the conscious mind with crowding images of distress. . . .

"If you would get up and do something you would feel better," said my mother. I rose drearily, and essayed to brush up the floor a little, with a dustpan and small whiskbroom, but soon dropped those implements exhausted, and wept again in helpless shame.

EDITH WHARTON

(1862–1937)

ROMAN FEVER

1

From the table at which they had been lunching two American ladies of ripe but well-cared-for middle age moved across the lofty terrace of the Roman restaurant and, leaning on its parapet, looked first at each other, and then down on the outspread glories of the Palatine and the Forum, with the same expression of vague but benevolent approval.

As they leaned there a girlish voice echoed up gaily from the stairs leading to the court below. "Well, come along, then," it cried, not to them but to an invisible companion, "and let's leave the young things to their knitting"; and a voice as fresh laughed back: "Oh, look here, Babs, not actually *knitting*—" "Well, I mean figuratively," rejoined the first. "After all, we haven't left our poor parents much else to do. . . ." and at that point the turn of the stairs engulfed the dialogue.

The two ladies looked at each other again, this time with a tingle of smiling embarrassment, and the smaller and paler one shook her head and colored slightly.

"Barbara!" she murmured, sending an unheard rebuke after the mocking voice in the stairway.

The other lady, who was fuller, and higher in color, with a small determined nose supported by vigorous black eyebrows, gave a good-humored laugh. "That's what our daughters think of us!"

Her companion replied by a deprecating gesture. "Not of us individually. We must remember that. It's just the collective modern idea of Mothers. And you see—" Half-guiltily she drew from her handsomely mounted black handbag a twist of crimson silk run through by two fine knitting needles. "One never knows," she murmured. "The new system has certainly given us a good deal of time to kill; and sometimes I get tired just looking—even at this." Her gesture was now addressed to the stupendous scene at their feet.

The dark lady laughed again, and they both relapsed upon the view, contemplating it in silence, with a sort of diffused serenity which might have been borrowed from the spring effulgence of the Roman skies. The luncheon hour was long past, and the two had their end of the vast terrace to themselves. At its opposite extremity a few groups, detained by a lingering look at the outspread city, were gathering up guidebooks and fumbling for tips. The last of them scattered, and the two ladies were alone on the air-washed height.

"Well, I don't see why we shouldn't just stay here," said Mrs. Slade, the lady of the high color and energetic brows. Two derelict basket chairs stood near, and she pushed them into the angle of the parapet, and settled herself in one, her gaze upon the Palatine. "After all, it's still the most beautiful view in the world."

"It always will be, to me," assented her friend Mrs. Ansley, with so slight a stress on the "me" that Mrs. Slade, though she noticed it, wondered if it were not merely accidental, like the random underlinings of old-fashioned letter writers.

"Grace Ansley was always old-fashioned," she thought; and added aloud, with a retrospective smile: "It's a view we've both been familiar with for a good many years. When we first met here we were younger than our girls are now. You remember?"

"Oh, yes, I remember," murmured Mrs. Ansley, with the same undefinable stress. "There's that headwaiter wondering," she interpolated. She was evidently far less sure than her companion of herself and of her rights in the world.

"I'll cure him of wondering," said Mrs. Slade, stretching her hand toward a bag as discreetly opulent-looking as Mrs. Ansley's. Signing to the headwaiter, she explained that she and her friend were old lovers of Rome, and would like to spend the end of the afternoon looking down on the view —that is, if it did not disturb the service? The headwaiter, bowing over her gratuity, assured her that the ladies were most welcome, and would be still more so if they would condescend to remain for dinner. A full-moon night, they would remember. . . .

Mrs. Slade's black brows drew together, as though references to the moon were out of place and even unwelcome. But she smiled away her frown as the headwaiter retreated. "Well, why not? We might do worse. There's no knowing, I suppose, when the girls will be back. Do you even know back from *where*? I don't!"

Mrs. Ansley again colored slightly. "I think those young Italian aviators we met at the Embassy invited them to fly to Tarquinia for tea. I suppose they'll want to wait and fly back by moonlight."

"Moonlight—moonlight! What a part it still plays. Do you suppose they're as sentimental as we were?"

"I've come to the conclusion that I don't in the least know what they are," said Mrs. Ansley. "And perhaps we didn't know much more about each other."

"No; perhaps we didn't."

Her friend gave her a shy glance. "I never should have supposed you were sentimental, Alida."

"Well, perhaps I wasn't." Mrs. Slade drew her lids together in retrospect; and for a few moments the two ladies, who had been intimate since childhood, reflected how little they knew each other. Each one, of course, had a label ready to attach to the other's name; Mrs. Delphin Slade, for instance, would have told herself, or anyone who asked her, that Mrs. Horace Ansley, twenty-five years ago, had been exquisitely lovely—no, you wouldn't believe it, would you? . . . though, of course, still charming, distinguished. . . . Well, as a girl she had been exquisite; far more beautiful than her daughter Barbara, though certainly Babs, according to the new standards at any rate, was more effective—had more *edge,* as they say. Funny where she got it, with those two nullities as parents. Yes; Horace Ansley was—well, just the duplicate of his wife. Museum specimens of old New York. Good-looking, irreproachable, exemplary. Mrs. Slade and Mrs. Ansley had lived opposite each other—actually as well as figuratively—for years. When the drawing-room curtains in No. 20 East 73rd Street were renewed, No. 23, across the way, was always aware of it. And of all the movings, buyings, travels, anniversaries, illnesses—the tame chronicle of an estimable pair. Little of it escaped Mrs. Slade. But she had grown bored with it by the time her husband made his big *coup* in Wall Street, and when they bought in upper Park Avenue had already begun to think: "I'd rather live opposite a speakeasy for a change; at least one might see it raided." The idea of seeing Grace raided was so amusing that (before the move) she launched it at a woman's lunch. It made a hit, and went the rounds—she sometimes wondered if it had crossed the street, and reached Mrs. Ansley. She hoped not, but didn't much mind. Those were the days when respectability was at a discount, and it did the irreproachable no harm to laugh at them a little.

A few years later, and not many months apart, both ladies lost their husbands. There was an appropriate exchange of wreaths and condolences, and a brief renewal of intimacy in the half-shadow of their mourning; and now, after another interval, they had run across each other in Rome, at the same hotel, each of them the modest appendage of a salient daughter. The similarity of their lot had again drawn them together, lending itself to mild jokes, and the mutual confession that, if in old days it must have been tiring to "keep up" with daughters, it was now, at times, a little dull not to.

No doubt, Mrs. Slade reflected, she felt her unemployment more than poor Grace ever would. It was a big drop from being the wife of Delphin Slade to being his widow. She had always regarded herself (with a certain conjugal pride) as his equal in social gifts, as contributing her full share to the making of the exceptional couple they were: but the difference after his death was irremediable. As the wife of the famous corporation lawyer, always with an international case or two on hand, every day brought its exciting and unexpected obligation: the impromptu entertaining of eminent colleagues from abroad, the hurried dashes on legal business to London, Paris or Rome, where the entertaining was so handsomely reciprocated; the amusement of hearing in her wake: "What, that handsome woman with the good clothes and the eyes is Mrs. Slade—*the* Slade's wife? Really? Generally the wives of celebrities are such frumps."

Yes; being *the* Slade's widow was a dullish business after that. In living up to such a husband all her faculties had been engaged; now she had only her daughter to live up to, for the son who seemed to have inherited his father's gifts had died suddenly in boyhood. She had fought through that agony because her husband was there, to be helped and to help; now, after the father's death, the thought of the boy had become unbearable. There was nothing left but to mother her daughter; and dear Jenny was such a perfect daughter that she needed no excessive mothering. "Now with Babs Ansley I don't know that I *should* be so quiet," Mrs. Slade sometimes half-enviously reflected; but Jenny, who was younger than her brilliant friend, was that rare accident, an extremely pretty girl who somehow made youth and prettiness seem as safe as their absence. It was all perplexing—and to Mrs. Slade a little boring. She wished that Jenny would fall in love—with the wrong man, even; that she might have to be watched, out-maneuvered, rescued. And instead, it was Jenny who watched her mother, kept her out of drafts, made sure that she had taken her tonic. . . .

Mrs. Ansley was much less articulate than her friend, and her mental portrait of Mrs. Slade was slighter, and drawn with fainter touches. "Alida Slade's awfully brilliant; but not as brilliant as she thinks," would have summed it up; though she would have added, for the enlightenment of strangers, that Mrs. Slade had been an extremely dashing girl; much more so than her daughter, who was pretty, of course, and clever in a way, but had none of her mother's—well, "vividness," someone had once called it. Mrs. Ansley would take up current words like this, and cite them in quotation marks, as unheard-of audacities. No; Jenny was not like her mother. Sometimes Mrs. Ansley thought Alida Slade was disappointed; on the whole she had had a sad life. Full of failures and mistakes; Mrs. Ansley had always been rather sorry for her. . . .

So these two ladies visualized each other, each through the wrong end of her little telescope.

2

For a long time they continued to sit side by side without speaking. It seemed as though, to both, there was a relief in laying down their somewhat futile activities in the presence of the vast Memento Mori[1] which faced them. Mrs. Slade sat quite still, her eyes fixed on the golden slope of the Palace of the Caesars, and after a while Mrs. Ansley ceased to fidget with her bag, and she too sank into meditation. Like many intimate friends, the two ladies had never before had occasion to be silent together, and Mrs. Ansley was slightly embarrassed by what seemed, after so many years, a new stage in their intimacy, and one with which she did not yet know how to deal.

Suddenly the air was full of that deep clangor of bells which periodically covers Rome with a roof of silver. Mrs. Slade glanced at her wristwatch. "Five o'clock already," she said, as though surprised.

Mrs. Ansley suggested interrogatively: "There's bridge at the Embassy at five." For a long time Mrs. Slade did not answer. She appeared to be lost in contemplation, and Mrs. Ansley thought the remark had

---

1. Reminder, memory of death.

escaped her. But after a while she said, as if speaking out of a dream: "Bridge, did you say? Not unless you want to. . . . But I don't think I will, you know."

"Oh, no," Mrs. Ansley hastened to assure her. "I don't care to at all. It's so lovely here; and so full of old memories, as you say." She settled herself in her chair, and almost furtively drew forth her knitting. Mrs. Slade took sideway note of this activity, but her own beautifully cared-for hands remained motionless on her knee.

"I was just thinking," she said slowly, "what different things Rome stands for to each generation of travelers. To our grandmothers, Roman fever; to our mothers, sentimental dangers—how we used to be guarded! —to our daughters, no more dangers than the middle of Main Street. They don't know it—but how much they're missing!"

The long golden light was beginning to pale, and Mrs. Ansley lifted her knitting a little closer to her eyes. "Yes; how we were guarded!"

"I always used to think," Mrs. Slade continued, "that our mothers had a much more difficult job than our grandmothers. When Roman fever stalked the streets it must have been comparatively easy to gather in the girls at the danger hour; but when you and I were young, with such beauty calling us, and the spice of disobedience thrown in, and no worse risk than catching cold during the cool hour after sunset, the mothers used to be put to it to keep us in—didn't they?"

She turned again toward Mrs. Ansley, but the latter had reached a delicate point in her knitting. "One, two, three—slip two; yes, they must have been," she assented, without looking up.

Mrs. Slade's eyes rested on her with a deepened attention. "She can knit—in the face of *this!* How like her. . . ."

Mrs. Slade leaned back, brooding, her eyes ranging from the ruins which faced her to the long green hollow of the Forum, the fading glow of the church fronts beyond it, and the outlying immensity of the Colosseum. Suddenly she thought: "It's all very well to say that our girls have done away with sentiment and moonlight. But if Babs Ansley isn't out to catch that young aviator—the one who's a Marchese—then I don't know anything. And Jenny has no chance beside her. I know that too. I wonder if that's why Grace Ansley likes the two girls to go everywhere together? My poor Jenny as a foil—!" Mrs. Slade gave a hardly audible laugh, and at the sound Mrs. Ansley dropped her knitting.

"Yes—?"

"I—oh, nothing. I was only thinking how your Babs carries everything before her. That Campolieri boy is one of the best matches in Rome. Don't look so innocent, my dear—you know he is. And I was wondering, ever so respectfully, you understand . . . wondering how two such exemplary characters as you and Horace had managed to produce anything quite so dynamic." Mrs. Slade laughed again, with a touch of asperity.

Mrs. Ansley's hands lay inert across her needles. She looked straight out at the great accumulated wreckage of passion and splendor at her feet. But her small profile was almost expressionless. At length she said: "I think you overrate Babs, my dear."

Mrs. Slade's tone grew easier. "No; I don't. I appreciate her. And perhaps envy you. Oh, my girl's perfect; if I were a chronic invalid I'd— well, I think I'd rather be in Jenny's hands. There must be times . . . but there! I always wanted a brilliant daughter . . . and never quite understood why I got an angel instead."

Mrs. Ansley echoed her laugh in a faint murmur. "Babs is an angel too."

"Of course—of course! But she's got rainbow wings. Well, they're wandering by the sea with their young men; and here we sit . . . and it all brings back the past a little too acutely."

Mrs. Ansley had resumed her knitting. One might almost have imagined (if one had known her less well, Mrs. Slade reflected) that, for her also, too many memories rose from the lengthening shadows of those august ruins. But no; she was simply absorbed in her work. What was there for her to worry about? She knew that Babs would almost certainly come back engaged to the extremely eligible Campolieri. "And she'll sell the New York house, and settle down near them in Rome, and never be in their way . . . she's much too tactful. But she'll have an excellent cook, and just the right people in for bridge and cocktails . . . and a perfectly peaceful old age among her grandchildren."

Mrs. Slade broke off this prophetic flight with a recoil of self-disgust. There was no one of whom she had less right to think unkindly than of Grace Ansley. Would she never cure herself of envying her? Perhaps she had begun too long ago.

She stood up and leaned against the parapet, filling her troubled eyes with the tranquilizing magic of the hour. But instead of tranquilizing her the sight seemed to increase her exasperation. Her gaze turned toward the Colosseum. Already its golden flank was drowned in purple shadow, and above it the sky curved crystal clear, without light or color. It was the moment when afternoon and evening hang balanced in mid-heaven.

Mrs. Slade turned back and laid her hand on her friend's arm. The gesture was so abrupt that Mrs. Ansley looked up, startled.

"The sun's set. You're not afraid, my dear?"

"Afraid—?"

"Of Roman fever or pneumonia? I remember how ill you were that winter. As a girl you had a very delicate throat, hadn't you?"

"Oh, we're all right up here. Down below, in the Forum, it does get deathly cold, all of a sudden . . . but not here."

"Ah, of course you know because you had to be so careful." Mrs. Slade turned back to the parapet. She thought: "I must make one more effort not to hate her." Aloud she said: "Whenever I look at the Forum from up here, I remember that story about a great-aunt of yours, wasn't she? A dreadfully wicked great-aunt?"

"Oh, yes; great-aunt Harriet. The one who was supposed to have sent her young sister out to the Forum after sunset to gather a night-blooming flower for her album. All our great-aunts and grandmothers used to have albums of dried flowers."

Mrs. Slade nodded. "But she really sent her because they were in love with the same man—"

"Well, that was the family tradition. They said Aunt Harriet confessed it years afterward. At any rate, the poor little sister caught the fever and died. Mother used to frighten us with the story when we were children."

"And you frightened *me* with it, that winter when you and I were here as girls. The winter I was engaged to Delphin."

Mrs. Ansley gave a faint laugh. "Oh, did I? Really frighten you? I don't believe you're easily frightened."

"Not often; but I was then. I was easily frightened because I was too happy. I wonder if you know what that means?"

"I—yes . . . ." Mrs. Ansley faltered.

"Well, I suppose that was why the story of your wicked aunt made such an impression on me. And I thought: "There's no more Roman fever, but the Forum is deathly cold after sunset—especially after a hot day. And the Colosseum's even colder and damper."

"The Colosseum—?"

"Yes. It wasn't easy to get in, after the gates were locked for the night. Far from easy. Still, in those days it could be managed; it *was* managed, often. Lovers met there who couldn't meet elsewhere. You knew that?"

"I—I dare say. I don't remember."

"You don't remember? You don't remember going to visit some ruins or other one evening, just after dark, and catching a bad chill? You were supposed to have gone to see the moon rise. People always said that expedition was what caused your illness."

There was a moment's silence; then Mrs. Ansley rejoined: "Did they? It was all so long ago."

"Yes. And you got well again—so it didn't matter. But I suppose it struck your friends—the reason given for your illness, I mean—because everybody knew you were so prudent on account of your throat, and your mother took such care of you. . . . You *had* been out late sight-seeing, hadn't you, that night?"

"Perhaps I had. The most prudent girls aren't always prudent. What made you think of it now?"

Mrs. Slade seemed to have no answer ready. But after a moment she broke out: "Because I simply can't bear it any longer—!"

Mrs. Ansley lifted her head quickly. Her eyes were wide and very pale. "Can't bear what?"

"Why—your not knowing that I've always known why you went."

"Why I went——?"

"Yes. You think I'm bluffing, don't you? Well, you went to meet the man I was engaged to—and I can repeat every word of the letter that took you there."

While Mrs. Slade spoke Mrs. Ansley had risen unsteadily to her feet. Her bag, her knitting and gloves, slid in a panic-stricken heap to the ground. She looked at Mrs. Slade as though she were looking at a ghost.

"No, no—don't," she faltered out.

"Why not? Listen, if you don't believe me. 'My one darling, things can't go on like this. I must see you alone. Come to the Colosseum immediately after dark tomorrow. There will be somebody to let you in. No one whom you need fear will suspect'—but perhaps you've forgotten what the letter said?"

Mrs. Ansley met the challenge with an unexpected composure. Steadying herself against the chair she looked at her friend, and replied: "No; I know it by heart too."

"And the signature? 'Only *your* D.S.' Was that it? I'm right, am I? That was the letter that took you out that evening after dark?"

Mrs. Ansley was still looking at her. It seemed to Mrs. Slade that a slow struggle was going on behind the voluntarily controlled mask of her small quiet face. "I shouldn't have thought she had herself so well in hand," Mrs. Slade reflected, almost resentfully. But at this moment Mrs. Ansley spoke. "I don't know how you knew. I burnt that letter at once."

"Yes; you would, naturally—you're so prudent!" The sneer was open now. "And if you burnt the letter you're wondering how on earth I know what was in it. That's it, isn't it?"

Mrs. Slade waited, but Mrs. Ansley did not speak.

"Well, my dear, I know what was in that letter because I wrote it!"

"You wrote it?"

"Yes."

The two women stood for a minute staring at each other in the last golden light. Then Mrs. Ansley dropped back into her chair. "Oh," she murmured, and covered her face with her hands.

Mrs. Slade waited nervously for another word or movement. None came, and at length she broke out: "I horrify you."

Mrs. Ansley's hands dropped to her knee. The face they uncovered was streaked with tears. "I wasn't thinking of you. I was thinking—it was the only letter I ever had from him!"

"And I wrote it. Yes; I wrote it! But I was the girl he was engaged to. Did you happen to remember that?"

Mrs. Ansley's head drooped again. "I'm not trying to excuse myself . . . I remembered. . . ."

"And still you went?"

"Still I went."

Mrs. Slade stood looking down on the small bowed figure at her side. The flame of her wrath had already sunk, and she wondered why she had ever thought there would be any satisfaction in inflicting so purposeless a wound on her friend. But she had to justify herself.

"You do understand? I'd found out—and I hated you, hated you. I knew you were in love with Delphin—and I was afraid; afraid of you, of your quiet ways, your sweetness . . . your . . . well, I wanted you out of the way, that's all. Just for a few weeks; just till I was sure of him. So in a blind fury I wrote that letter . . . I don't know why I'm telling you now."

"I suppose," said Mrs. Ansley slowly, "it's because you've always gone on hating me."

"Perhaps. Or because I wanted to get the whole thing off my mind." She paused. "I'm glad you destroyed the letter. Of course I never thought you'd die."

Mrs. Ansley relapsed into silence, and Mrs. Slade, leaning above her, was conscious of a strange sense of isolation, of being cut off from the warm current of human communion. "You think me a monster!"

"I don't know. . . . It was the only letter I had, and you say he didn't write it?"

"Ah, how you care for him still!"

"I cared for that memory," said Mrs. Ansley.

Mrs. Slade continued to look down at her. She seemed physically reduced by the blow—as if, when she got up, the wind might scatter her like a puff of dust. Mrs. Slade's jealousy suddenly leapt up again at the sight. All these years the woman had been living on that letter. How she must have loved him, to treasure the mere memory of its ashes! The letter of the man her friend was engaged to. Wasn't it she who was the monster?

"You tried your best to get him away from me, didn't you? But you failed; and I kept him. That's all."

"Yes. That's all."

"I wish now I hadn't told you. I'd no idea you'd feel about it as you do; I thought you'd be amused. It all happened so long ago, as you say; and you must do me the justice to remember that I had no reason to think you'd ever taken it seriously. How could I, when you were married to Horace Ansley two months afterward? As soon as you could get out of bed your mother rushed you off to Florence and married you. People were rather surprised—they wondered at its being done so quickly; but I thought I knew. I had an idea you did it out of *pique*—to be able to say you'd got ahead of Delphin and me. Girls have such silly reasons for doing the most serious things. And your marrying so soon convinced me that you'd never really cared."

"Yes. I suppose it would," Mrs. Ansley assented.

The clear heaven overhead was emptied of all its gold. Dusk spread over it, abruptly darkening the Seven Hills. Here and there lights began to twinkle through the foliage at their feet. Steps were coming and going on the deserted terrace—waiters looking out of the doorway at the head of the stairs, then reappearing with trays and napkins and flasks of wine. Tables were moved, chairs straightened. A feeble string of electric lights flickered out. Some vases of faded flowers were carried away, and brought back replenished. A stout lady in a dust coat suddenly appeared, asking in broken Italian if anyone had seen the elastic band which held together her tattered Baedeker.[2] She poked with her stick under the table at which she had lunched, the waiters assisting.

The corner where Mrs. Slade and Mrs. Ansley sat was still shadowy and deserted. For a long time neither of them spoke. At length Mrs. Slade began again: "I suppose I did it as a sort of joke—"

"A joke?"

"Well, girls are ferocious sometimes, you know. Girls in love especially. And I remember laughing to myself all that evening at the idea that you were waiting around there in the dark, dodging out of sight, listening for every sound, trying to get in—Of course I was upset when I heard you were so ill afterward."

Mrs. Ansley had not moved for a long time. But now she turned slowly toward her companion. "But I didn't wait. He'd arranged everything. He was there. We were let in at once," she said.

Mrs. Slade sprang up from her leaning position. "Delphin there? They let you in?—Ah, now you're lying!" she burst out with violence.

Mrs. Ansley's voice grew clearer, and full of surprise. "But of course he was there. Naturally he came—"

"Came? How did he know he'd find you there? You must be raving!"

Mrs. Ansley hesitated, as though reflecting. "But I answered the letter. I told him I'd be there. So he came."

Mrs. Slade flung her hands up to her face. "Oh, God—you answered! I never thought of your answering. . . ."

"It's odd you never thought of it, if you wrote the letter."

"Yes. I was blind with rage."

Mrs. Ansley rose, and drew her fur scarf about her. "It is cold here. We'd better go. . . . I'm sorry for you," she said, as she clasped the fur about her throat.

The unexpected words sent a pang through Mrs. Slade. "Yes; we'd better go." She gathered up her bag and cloak. "I don't know why you should be sorry for me," she muttered.

Mrs. Ansley stood looking away from her toward the dusky secret mass of the Colosseum. "Well—because I didn't have to wait that night."

Mrs. Slade gave an unquiet laugh. "Yes; I was beaten there. But I oughtn't to begrudge it to you, I suppose. At the end of all these years. After all, I had everything; I had him for twenty-five years. And you had nothing but that one letter that he didn't write."

2. A guidebook named after Karl Baedeker (1801–1859), a publisher of guidebooks to Europe.

Mrs. Ansley was again silent. At length she turned toward the door of the terrace. She took a step, and turned back, facing her companion.

"I had Barbara," she said, and began to move ahead of Mrs. Slade toward the stairway.

1936

For practical reasons, few short stories involve a span of years as long as that Edith Wharton covers in "Roman Fever," and few undertake as much development of the principal characters. The story appears to press the limits of what can be done in short fiction, and it is thus worthwhile to see Wharton's own assessment of what those limits are.

"The incident . . . which a single retrospective flash sufficiently lights up": Edith Wharton

There are at least two reasons why a subject should find expression in novel-form rather than as a tale; but neither is based on the number of what may be conveniently called incidents, or external happenings, which the narrative contains. There are novels of action which might be condensed into short stories without the loss of their distinguishing qualities. The marks of the subject requiring a longer development are, first, the gradual unfolding of the inner life of its characters, and secondly the need of producing in the reader's mind the sense of the lapse of time. Outward events of the most varied and exciting nature may without loss of probability be crowded into a few hours, but moral dramas usually have their roots deep in the soul, their rise far back in time; and the suddenest-seeming clash in which they culminate should be led up to step by step if it is to explain and justify itself.

There are cases, indeed, when the short story may make use of the moral drama at its culmination. If the incident dealt with be one which a single retrospective flash sufficiently lights up, it is qualified for use as a short story; but if the subject be so complex, and its successive phases so interesting, as to justify elaboration, the lapse of time must necessarily be suggested, and the novel-form becomes appropriate.

E. M. FORSTER

(1879–1970)

THE ETERNAL MOMENT

1

Do you see that mountain just behind Elizabeth's toque? A young man fell in love with me there so nicely twenty years ago. Bob your head a minute, would you, Elizabeth, kindly."

"Yes'm," said Elizabeth, falling forward on the box like an unstiffened doll. Colonel Leyland put on his pince-nez, and looked at the mountain where the young man had fallen in love.

"Was he a nice young man?" he asked, smiling, though he lowered his voice a little on account of the maid.

"I never knew. But it is a very gratifying incident to remember at my age. Thank you, Elizabeth."

"May one ask who he was?"

"A porter," answered Miss Raby in her usual tones. "Not even a certificated guide. A male person who was hired to carry the luggage, which he dropped."

"Well! well! What did you do?"

"What a young lady should. Screamed and thanked him not to insult me. Ran, which was quite unnecessary, fell, sprained my ankle, screamed again; and he had to carry me half a mile, so penitent that I thought he would fling me over a precipice. In that state we reached a certain Mrs. Harbottle, at sight of whom I burst into tears. But she was so much stupider than I was, that I recovered quickly."

"Of course you said it was all your own fault?"

"I trust I did," she said more seriously. "Mrs. Harbottle, who, like most people, was always right, had warned me against him; we had had him for expeditions before."

"Ah! I see."

"I doubt whether you do. Hitherto he had known his place. But he was too cheap: he gave us more than our money's worth. That, as you know, is an ominous sign in a low-born person."

"But how was this your fault?"

"I encouraged him: I greatly preferred him to Mrs. Harbottle. He was handsome and what I call agreeable; and he wore beautiful clothes. We lagged behind, and he picked me flowers. I held out my hand for them— instead of which he seized it and delivered a love oration which he had prepared out of *I Promessi Sposi*."

"Ah! an Italian."

They were crossing the frontier at that moment. On a little bridge amid fir trees were two poles, one painted red, white and green, and the other black and yellow.

"He lived in Italia Irredenta," said Miss Raby. "But we were to fly to the Kingdom. I wonder what would have happened if we had."

"Good Lord!" said Colonel Leyland, in sudden disgust. On the box Elizabeth trembled.

"But it might have been a most successful match."

She was in the habit of talking in this mildly unconventional way. Colonel Leyland, who made allowances for her brilliancy, managed to exclaim: "Rather! yes, rather!"

She turned on him with: "Do you think I'm laughing at him?"

He looked a little bewildered, smiled, and did not reply. Their carriage was now crawling round the base of the notorious mountain. The road was built over the debris which had fallen and which still fell from its sides; and it had scarred the pine woods with devastating rivers of white stone. But farther up, Miss Raby remembered, on its gentler eastern slope, it possessed tranquil hollows, and flower-clad rocks, and a most tremendous view. She had not been quite as facetious as her companion supposed. The incident, certainly, had been ludicrous. But she was somehow able to laugh at it without laughing much at the actors or the stage.

"I had rather he made me a fool than that I thought he was one," she said, after a long pause.

"Here is the Custom House," said Colonel Leyland, changing the subject.

They had come to the land of *Ach* and *Ja*. Miss Raby sighed; for she loved the Latins, as every one must who is not pressed for time. But Colonel Leyland, a military man, respected Teutonia.

"They still talk Italian for seven miles," she said, comforting herself like a child.

"German is the coming language," answered Colonel Leyland. "All the important books on any subject are written in it."

"But all the books on any important subject are written in Italian. Elizabeth—tell me an important subject."

"Human Nature, ma'am," said the maid, half shy, half impertinent.

"Elizabeth is a novelist, like her mistress," said Colonel Leyland. He turned away to look at the scenery, for he did not like being entangled in a mixed conversation. He noted that the farms were more prosperous, that begging had stopped, that the women were uglier and the men more rotund, that more nourishing food was being eaten outside the wayside inns.

"Colonel Leyland, shall we go to the *Grand Hôtel des Alpes,* to the *Hôtel de Londres,* to the *Pension Liebig,* to the *Pension Atherley-Simon,* to the *Pension Belle Vue,* to the *Pension Old-England,* or to the *Albergo Biscione?*"

"I suppose you would prefer the *Biscione.*"

"I really shouldn't mind the *Grand Hôtel des Alpes.* The *Biscione* people own both, I hear. They have become quite rich."

"You should have a splendid reception—if such people know what gratitude is."

For Miss Raby's novel, "The Eternal Moment," which had made her reputation, had also made the reputation of Vorta.

"Oh, I was properly thanked. Signor Cantù wrote to me about three years after I had published. The letter struck me as a little pathetic, though it was very prosperous: I don't like transfiguring people's lives. I wonder whether they live in their old house or in the new one."

Colonel Leyland had come to Vorta to be with Miss Raby; but he was very willing that they should be in different hotels. She, indifferent to such subtleties, saw no reason why they should not stop under the same roof, just as she could not see why they should not travel in the same carriage. On the other hand, she hated anything smart. He had decided on the *Grand Hôtel des Alpes,* and she was drifting towards the *Biscione,* when the tiresome Elizabeth said: "My friend's lady is staying at the *Alpes.*"

"Oh! if Elizabeth's friend is there that settles it: we'll all go."

"Very well'm," said Elizabeth, studiously avoiding even the appearance of gratitude. Colonel Leyland's face grew severe over the want of discipline.

"You spoil her," he murmured, when they had all descended to walk up a hill.

"There speaks the military man."

"Certainly I have had too much to do with Tommies to enter into what you call 'human relations.' A little sentimentality, and the whole army would go to pieces."

"I know; but the whole world isn't an army. So why should I pretend I'm an officer. You remind me of my Anglo-Indian friends, who were so shocked when I would be pleasant to some natives. They proved, quite conclusively, that it would never do for them, and have never seen that the proof didn't apply. The unlucky people here are always trying to lead the lucky; and it must be stopped. You've been unlucky: all your life you've had to command men, and exact prompt obedience and other unprofitable virtues. I'm lucky: I needn't do the same—and I won't."

"Don't then," he said, smiling. "But take care that the world isn't an army after all. And take care, besides, that you aren't being unjust to the unlucky people: we're fairly kind to your beloved lower orders, for instance."

"Of course," she said dreamily, as if he had made her no concession. "It's becoming usual. But they see through it. They, like ourselves, know that only one thing in the world is worth having."

"Ah! yes," he sighed. "It's a commercial age."

"No!" exclaimed Miss Raby, so irritably that Elizabeth looked back to see what was wrong. "You are stupid. Kindness and money are both quite easy to part with. The only thing worth giving away is yourself. Did you ever give yourself away?"

"Frequently."

"I mean, did you ever, intentionally, make a fool of yourself before your inferiors?"

"Intentionally, never." He saw at last what she was driving at. It was her pleasure to pretend that such self-exposure was the only possible basis of true intercourse, the only gate in the spiritual barrier that divided class from class. One of her books had dealt with the subject; and very agreeable reading it made. "What about you?" he added playfully.

"I've never done it properly. Hitherto I've never felt a really big fool; but when I do, I hope I shall show it plainly."

"May I be there!"

"You might not like it," she replied. "I may feel it at any moment and in mixed company. Anything might set me off."

"Behold Vorta!" cried the driver, cutting short the sprightly conversation. He and Elizabeth and the carriage had reached the top of the hill. The black woods ceased; and they emerged into a valley whose sides were emerald lawns, rippling and doubling and merging each into each, yet always with an upward trend, so that it was 2000 feet to where the rock burst out of the grass and made great mountains, whose pinnacles were delicate in the purity of evening.

The driver, who had the gift of repetition, said: "Vorta! Vorta!"

Far up the valley was a large white village, tossing on undulating meadows like a ship in the sea, and at its prow, breasting a sharp incline, stood a majestic tower of new gray stone. As they looked at the tower it became vocal and spoke magnificently to the mountains, who replied.

They were again informed that this was Vorta, and that that was the new campanile—like the campanile of Venice, only finer—and that the sound was the sound of the campanile's new bell.

"Thank you; exactly," said Colonel Leyland, while Miss Raby rejoiced that the village had made such use of its prosperity. She had feared to return to the place she had once loved so well, lest she should find something new. It had never occurred to her that the new thing might be beautiful. The architect had indeed gone south for his inspiration, and the tower which stood among the mountains was akin to the tower which had once stood beside the lagoons. But the birthplace of the bell it was impossible to determine, for there is no nationality in sound.

They drove forward into the lovely scene, pleased and silent. Approving tourists took them for a well-matched couple. There was indeed nothing offensively literary in Miss Raby's kind angular face; and Colonel Leyland's profession had made him neat rather than aggressive. They did very well for a cultured and refined husband and wife, who had spent their lives admiring the beautiful things with which the world is filled.

As they approached, other churches, hitherto unnoticed, replied —tiny churches, ugly churches, churches painted pink with towers like pumpkins, churches painted white with shingle spires, churches hidden altogether in the glades of a wood or the folds of a meadow—till the evening air was full of little voices, with the great voice singing in their midst.

Only the English church, lately built in the Early English style, kept chaste silence.

The bells ceased, and all the little churches receded into darkness. Instead, there was a sound of dressing-gongs, and a vision of tired tourists hurrying back for dinner. A landau, with *Pension Atherley-Simon* upon it, was trotting to meet the diligence, which was just due. A lady was talking to her mother about an evening dress. Young men with rackets were talking to young men with alpenstocks. Then, across the darkness, a fiery finger wrote *Grand Hôtel des Alpes.*

"Behold the electric light!" said the driver, hearing his passengers exclaim.

Pension Belle Vue started out against a pinewood, and from the brink of the river the *Hôtel de Londres* replied. *Pensions Liebig* and *Lorelei* were announced in green and amber respectively. The *Old-England* appeared in scarlet. The illuminations covered a large area, for the best hotels stood outside the village, in elevated or romantic situations. This display took place every evening in the season, but only while the diligence arrived. As soon as the last tourist was suited, the lights went out, and the hotel-keepers, cursing or rejoicing, retired to their cigars.

"Horrible!" said Miss Raby.

"Horrible people!" said Colonel Leyland.

The *Hôtel des Alpes* was an enormous building, which, being made of wood, suggested a distended chalet. But this impression was corrected by a costly and magnificent view terrace, the squared stones of which were visible for miles, and from which, as from some great reservoir, asphalt paths trickled over the adjacent country. Their carriage, having ascended a private drive, drew up under a vaulted portico of pitch-pine, which opened on to this terrace on one side, and into the covered lounge on the other. There was a whirl of officials—men with gold braid, smarter men with more gold braid, men smarter still with no gold braid. Elizabeth assumed an arrogant air, and carried a small straw basket with difficulty. Colonel Leyland became every inch a soldier. Miss Raby, whom, in spite of long experience, a large hotel always flustered, was hurried into an expensive bedroom, and advised to dress herself immediately if she wished to partake of table d'hôte.

As she came up the staircase, she had seen the dining-room filling with English and Americans and with rich, hungry Germans. She liked company, but to-night she was curiously depressed. She seemed to be confronted with an unpleasing vision, the outlines of which were still obscure.

"I will eat in my room," she told Elizabeth. "Go to your dinner: I'll do the unpacking."

She wandered round, looking at the list of rules, the list of prices, the list of excursions, the red plush sofa, the jugs and basins on which was lithographed a view of the mountains. Where amid such splendour was there a place for Signor Cantù with his china-bowled pipe, and for Signora Cantù with her snuff-coloured shawl?

When the waiter at last brought up her dinner, she asked after host and hostess.

He replied, in cosmopolitan English, that they were both well.

"Do they live here, or at the *Biscione?*"

"Here, why yes. Only poor tourists go to the *Biscione.*"

"Who lives there, then?"

"The mother of Signor Cantù. She is unconnected," he continued, like one who has learnt a lesson, "she is unconnected absolutely with us. Fifteen years back, yes. But now, where is the *Biscione?* I beg you contradict if we are spoken about together."

Miss Raby said quietly: "I have made a mistake. Would you kindly give notice that I shall not want my room, and say that the luggage is to be taken, immediately, to the *Biscione.*"

"Certainly! certainly!" said the waiter, who was well trained. He added with a vicious snort, "You will have to pay."

"Undoubtedly," said Miss Raby.

The elaborate machinery which had so recently sucked her in began to disgorge her. The trunks were carried down, the vehicle in which she had arrived was recalled. Elizabeth, white with indignation, appeared in the hall. She paid for beds in which they had not slept, and for food which they had never eaten. Amidst the whirl of gold-laced officials, who hoped even in that space of time to have established a claim to be tipped, she moved towards the door. The guests in the lounge observed her with amusement, concluding that she had found the hotel too dear.

"What is it? Whatever is it? Are you not comfortable?" Colonel Leyland in his evening dress ran after her.

"Not that; I've made a mistake. This hotel belongs to the son; I must go to the *Biscione.* He's quarrelled with the old people: I think the father's dead."

"But really—if you are comfortable here——"

"I must find out to-night whether it is true. And I must also"—her voice quivered—"find out whether it is my fault."

"How in the name of goodness——"

"I shall bear it if it is," she continued gently. "I am too old to be a tragedy queen as well as an evil genius."

"What does she mean? Whatever does she mean?" he murmured, as he watched the carriage lights descending the hill. "What harm has she done? What harm is there for that matter? Hotel-keepers always quarrel: it's no business of ours." He ate a good dinner in silence. Then his thoughts were turned by the arrival of his letters from the post office.

"DEAREST EDWIN,—It is with the greatest diffidence that I write to you, and I know you will believe me when I say that I do not write from curiosity. I only require an answer to one plain question. Are you engaged to Miss Raby or no? Fashions have altered even since my young days. But, for all that an engagement is still an engagement, and should be announced at once, to save all parties discomfort. Though your health has broken down and you have abandoned your profession, you can still protect the family honour."

"Drivel!" exclaimed Colonel Leyland. Acquaintance with Miss Raby had made his sight keener. He recognized in this part of his sister's letter nothing but an automatic conventionality. He was no more moved by its perusal than she had been by its composition.

"As for the maid whom the Bannons mentioned to me, she is not a chaperone—nothing but a sop to throw in the eyes of the world. I am not saying a word against Miss Raby, whose books we always read. Literary people are always unpractical, and we are confident that she does not know. Perhaps I do not think her the wife for you; but that is another matter.

"My babes, who all send love (so does Lionel), are at present an unmitigated joy. One's only anxiety is for the future, when the crushing expenses of good education will have to be taken into account."

"Your loving NELLY."

How could he explain the peculiar charm of the relations between himself and Miss Raby? There had never been a word of marriage, and would probably never be a word of love. If, instead of seeing each other frequently, they should come to see each other always it would be as sage companions, familiar with life, not as egoistic lovers, craving for infinities of passion which they had no right to demand and no power to supply. Neither professed to be a virgin soul, or to be ignorant of the other's limitations and inconsistencies. They scarcely even made allowances for each other. Toleration implies reserve; and the greatest safeguard of unruffled intercourse is knowledge. Colonel Leyland had courage of no mean order: he cared little for the opinion of people whom he understood. Nelly and Lionel and their babes were welcome to be shocked or displeased. Miss Raby was an authoress, a kind of radical; he a soldier, a kind of aristocrat. But the time for their activities was passing; he was ceasing to fight, she to write. They could pleasantly spend together their autumn. Nor might they prove the worst companions for a winter.

He was too delicate to admit, even to himself, the desirability of marrying two thousand a year. But it lent an unacknowledged perfume to his thoughts. He tore Nelly's letter into little pieces, and dropped them into the darkness out of the bedroom window.

"Funny lady!" he murmured, as he looked towards Vorta, trying to detect the campanile in the growing light of the moon. "Why have you gone to be uncomfortable? Why will you interfere in the quarrels of people who can't understand you, and whom you don't understand. How silly you are to think you've caused them. You think you've written a book which has spoilt the place and made the inhabitants corrupt and sordid. I know just how you think. So you will make yourself unhappy, and go about trying to put right what never was right. Funny lady!"

Close below him he could now see the white fragments of his sister's letter. In the valley the campanile appeared, rising out of wisps of silvery vapour.

"Dear lady!" he whispered, making towards the village a little movement with his hands.

2

Miss Raby's first novel, "The Eternal Moment," was written round the idea that man does not live by time alone, that an evening gone may become like a thousand ages in the courts of heaven—the idea that was afterwards expounded more philosophically by Maeterlinck. She herself now declared that it was a tiresome, affected book, and that the title suggested the dentist's chair. But she had written it when she was feeling young and happy; and that, rather than maturity, is the hour in which to formulate a creed. As years pass, the conception may become more solid, but the desire and the power to impart it to others are alike weakened. It did not altogether displease her that her earliest work had been her most ambitious.

By a strange fate, the book made a great sensation, especially in unimaginative circles. Idle people interpreted it to mean that there was no harm in wasting time, vulgar people that there was no harm in being fickle, pious people interpreted it as an attack upon morality. The authoress became well known in society, where her enthusiasm for the lower classes only lent her an additional charm. That very year Lady Anstey, Mrs. Heriot, the Marquis of Bamburgh, and many others, penetrated to Vorta, where the scene of the book was laid. They returned enthusiastic. Lady Anstey exhibited her water-colour drawings; Mrs. Heriot, who photographed, wrote an article in *The Strand;* while *The Nineteenth Century* published a long description of the place by the Marquis of Bamburgh, entitled "The Modern Peasant, and his Relations with Roman Catholicism."

Thanks to these efforts, Vorta became a rising place, and people who liked being off the beaten track went there, and pointed out the way to others. Miss Raby, by a series of trivial accidents, had never returned to the village whose rise was so intimately connected with her own. She had heard from time to time of its progress. It had also been whispered that an inferior class of tourist was finding it out, and, fearing to find something spoilt, she had at last a certain diffidence in returning to scenes which once had given her so much pleasure. Colonel Leyland persuaded her; he wanted a cool healthy spot for the summer, where he could read and talk and find walks suitable for an athletic invalid. Their friends laughed; their acquaintances gossiped; their relatives were furious. But he was courageous and she was indifferent. They had accomplished the expedition under the scanty ægis of Elizabeth.

Her arrival was saddening. It displeased her to see the great hotels in a great circle, standing away from the village where all life should have centred. Their illuminated titles, branded on the tranquil evening slopes, still danced in her eyes. And the monstrous *Hôtel des Alpes* haunted her like a nightmare. In her dreams she recalled the portico, the ostentatious lounge, the polished walnut bureau, the vast rack for the bedroom keys; the panoramic bedroom crockery, the uniforms of the officials, and the smell of smart people—which is to some nostrils quite as depressing as the smell of poor ones. She was not enthusiastic over the progress of civilization, knowing by Eastern experiences that civilization rarely puts her best foot foremost, and is apt to make the barbarians immoral and vicious before her compensating qualities arrive. And here there was no question of progress: the world had more to learn from the village than the village from the world.

At the *Biscione*, indeed, she had found little change—only the pathos of a survival. The old landlord had died, and the old landlady was ill in bed, but the antique spirit had not yet departed. On the timbered front was still painted the dragon swallowing the child—the arms of the Milanese Visconti, from whom the Cantus might well be descended. For there was something about the little hotel which compelled a sympathetic guest to believe, for the time at all events, in aristocracy. The great manner, only to be obtained without effort, ruled throughout. In each bedroom were three or four beautiful things—a little piece of silk tapestry, a fragment of rococo carving, some blue tiles, framed and hung upon the whitewashed wall. There were pictures in the sitting-rooms and on the stairs—eighteenth-century pictures in the style of Carlo Dolce and the Caracci—a blue-robed Mater Dolorosa, a fluttering saint, a magnanimous Alexander with a receding chin. A debased style—so the superior person and the textbooks say. Yet, at times, it may have more freshness and significance than a newly-purchased Fra Angelico. Miss Raby, who had visited dukes in their residences without a perceptible tremor, felt herself blatant and modern when she entered the *Albergo Biscione*. The most trivial things—the sofa cushions, the table cloths, the cases for the pillows—though they might be made of poor materials and be æsthetically incorrect, inspired her with reverence and humility. Through this cleanly, gracious dwelling there had once moved Signor Cantù with his china-bowled pipe, Signora Cantù in her snuff-coloured shawl, and Bartolommeo Canù, now proprietor of the *Grand Hôtel des Alpes*.

She sat down to breakfast next morning in a mood which she tried to attribute to her bad night and her increasing age. Never, she thought, had she seen people more unattractive and more unworthy than her fellow-guests. A black-browed woman was holding forth on patriotism and the duty of English tourists to present an undivided front to foreign nations. Another woman kept up a feeble lament, like a dribbling tap which never gathers flow yet never quite ceases, complaining of the food, the charges, the noise, the clouds, the dust. She liked coming here herself, she said; but she hardly liked to recommend it to her friends: it was the kind of hotel one felt like that about. Males were rare, and in great demand; a young one was describing, amid fits of laughter, the steps he had taken to astonish the natives.

Miss Raby was sitting opposite the famous fresco, which formed the only decoration of the room. It had been discovered during some repairs; and, though the surface had been injured in places, the colours were still bright. Signora Cantù attributed it now to Titian, now to Giotto, and declared that no one could interpret its meaning; professors and artists had puzzled themselves in vain. This she said because it pleased her to say it; the meaning was perfectly clear, and had been frequently explained to her. Those four figures were sibyls, holding prophecies of the Nativity. It was uncertain for what original reason they had been painted high up in the mountains, at the extreme boundary of Italian art. Now, at all events, they were an invaluable source of conversation; and many an acquaintance had been opened, and argument averted, by their timely presence on the wall.

"Aren't those saints cunning!" said an American lady, following Miss Raby's glance.

The lady's father muttered something about superstition. They were a lugubrious couple, lately returned from the Holy Land, where they had been cheated shamefully, and their attitude towards religion had suffered in consequence.

Miss Raby said, rather sharply, that the saints were sibyls.

"But I don't recall sibyls," said the lady, "either in the N.T. or the O."

"Inventions of the priests to deceive the peasantry," said the father sadly. "Same as their churches; tinsel pretending to be gold, cotton pretending to be silk, stucco pretending to be marble; same as their processions, same as their—(he swore)—campaniles."

"My father," said the lady, bending forward, "he does suffer so from insomnia. Fancy a bell every morning at six!"

"Yes, ma'am; you profit. We've stopped it."

"Stopped the early bell ringing?" cried Miss Raby.

People looked up to see who she was. Some one whispered that she wrote.

He replied that he had come up all these feet for rest, and that if he did not get it he would move on to another centre. The English and American visitors had co-operated, and forced the hotel-keepers to take action. Now the priests rang a dinner bell, which was endurable. He believed that "corperation" would do anything: it had been the same with the peasants.

"How did the tourists interfere with the peasants?" asked Miss Raby, getting very hot, and trembling all over.

"We said the same; we had come for rest, and we would have it. Every week they got drunk and sang till two. Is that a proper way to go on, anyhow?"

"I remember," said Miss Raby, "that some of them did get drunk. But I also remember how they sang."

"Quite so. Till two," he retorted.

They parted in mutual irritation. She left him holding forth on the necessity of a new universal religion of the open air. Over his head stood the four sibyls, gracious for all their clumsiness and crudity, each proffering a tablet inscribed with concise promise of redemption. If the old religions had indeed become insufficient for humanity, it did not seem probable that an adequate substitute would be produced in America.

It was too early to pay her promised visit to Signora Cantù. Nor was Elizabeth, who had been rude overnight and was now tiresomely penitent, a possible companion. There were a few tables outside the inn, at which some women sat, drinking beer. Pollarded chestnuts shaded them; and a low wooden balustrade fenced them off from the village street. On this balustrade Miss Raby perched, for it gave her a view of the campanile. A critical eye could discover plenty of faults in its architecture. But she looked at it all with increasing pleasure, in which was mingled a certain gratitude.

The German waitress came out and suggested very civilly that she should find a more comfortable seat. This was the place where the lower classes ate; would she not go to the drawing-room?

"Thank you, no; for how many years have you classified your guests according to their birth?"

"For many years. It was necessary," replied the admirable woman. She returned to the house full of meat and common sense, one of the many signs that the Teuton was gaining on the Latin in this debatable valley.

A gray-haired lady came out next, shading her eyes from the sun, and cracking *The Morning Post*. She glanced at Miss Raby pleasantly, blew her nose, apologized for speaking, and spoke as follows:

"This evening, I wonder if you know, there is a concert in aid of the stained-glass window for the English Church. Might I persuade you to take tickets? As has been said, it is so important that English people should have a rallying point, is it not?"

"Most important," said Miss Raby; "but I wish the rallying point could be in England."

The gray-haired lady smiled. Then she looked puzzled. Then she realized that she had been insulted, and, crackling *The Morning Post*, departed.

"I have been rude," thought Miss Raby dejectedly. "Rude to a lady as silly and as gray-haired as myself. This is not a day on which I ought to talk to people."

Her life had been successful, and on the whole happy. She was unaccustomed to that mood, which is termed depressed, but which certainly gives visions of wider, if grayer, horizons. That morning her outlook altered. She walked through the village, scarcely noticing the mountains by which it was still surrounded, or the unaltered radiance of its sun. But she was fully conscious of something new; of the indefinable corruption which is produced by the passage of a large number of people.

Even at that time the air was heavy with meat and drink, to which were added dust and tobacco smoke and the smell of tired horses. Carriages were huddled against the church, and underneath the campanile a woman was guarding a stack of bicycles. The season had been bad for climbing; and groups of young men in smart Norfolk suits were idling up and down, waiting to be hired as guides. Two large inexpensive hotels stood opposite the post office; and in front of them innumerable little tables surged out into the street. Here, from an early hour in the morning, eating had gone on, and would continue till a late hour at night. The customers, chiefly German, refreshed themselves with cries and with laughter, passing their arms round the waists of their wives. Then, rising heavily, they departed in single file towards some view-point, whereon a red flag indicated the possibility of another meal. The whole population was employed, even down to the little girls, who worried the guests to buy picture postcards and edelweiss. Vorta had taken to the tourist trade.

A village must have some trade; and this village had always been full of virility and power. Obscure and happy, its splendid energies had found employment in wresting a livelihood out of the earth, whence had come a certain dignity, and kindliness, and love for other men. Civilization did not relax these energies, but it had diverted them; and all the precious qualities, which might have helped to heal the world, had been destroyed. The family affection, the affection for the commune, the sane pastoral virtues—all had perished while the campanile which was to embody them was being built. No villain had done this thing: it was the work of ladies and gentlemen who were good and rich and often clever—who, if they thought about the matter at all, thought that they were conferring a benefit, moral as well as commercial, on any place in which they chose to stop.

Never before had Miss Raby been conscious of such universal misdoing. She returned to the *Biscione* shattered and exhausted, remembering that terrible text in which there is much semblance of justice: "But woe to him through whom the offence cometh."

Signora Cantù, somewhat over-excited, was lying in a dark room on the ground floor. The walls were bare; for all the beautiful things were in the rooms of her guests whom she loved as a good queen might love her subjects—and the walls were dirty also, for this was Signora Cantù's own room. But no palace had so fair a ceiling; for from the wooden beams were suspended a whole dowry of copper vessels—pails, cauldrons, water pots, of every colour from lustrous black to the palest pink. It pleased the old lady to look up at these tokens of prosperity. An American lady had lately departed without them, more puzzled than angry.

The two women had little in common; for Signora Cantù was an inflexible aristocrat. Had she been a great lady of the great century, she would have gone speedily to the guillotine, and Miss Raby would have howled approval. Now, with her scanty hair in curl-papers, and the snuff-coloured shawl spread over her, she entertained the distinguished authoress with accounts of other distinguished people who had stopped, and might again stop, at the *Biscione*. At first her tone was dignified. But before long she proceeded to village news, and a certain bitterness began to show itself. She chronicled deaths with a kind of melancholy pride. Being old herself, she liked to meditate on the fairness of Fate, which had not spared her contemporaries, and often had not spared her juniors. Miss Raby was unaccustomed to extract such consolation. She too was growing old, but it would have pleased her better if others could have remained young. She remembered few of these people well, but deaths were symbolical, just as the death of a flower may symbolize the passing of all the spring.

Signora Cantù then went on to her own misfortunes, beginning with an account of a landslip, which had destroyed her little farm. A landslip, in that valley, never hurried. Under the green coat of turf water would collect, just as an abscess is formed under the skin. There would be a lump on the sloping meadow, then the lump would break and discharge a slowly-moving stream of mud and stones. Then the whole area seemed to be corrupted; on every side the grass cracked and doubled into fantastic creases, the trees grew awry, the barns and cottages collapsed, all the beauty turned gradually to indistinguishable pulp, which slid downwards till it was washed away by some stream.

From the farm they proceeded to other grievances, over which Miss Raby became almost too depressed to sympathize. It was a bad season; the guests did not understand the ways of the hotel; the servants did not understand the guests; she was told she ought to have a concierge. But what was the good of a concierge?

"I have no idea," said Miss Raby, feeling that no concierge would ever restore the fortunes of the *Biscione*.

"They say he would meet the diligence and entrap the new arrivals. What pleasure should I have from guests I entrapped?"

"The other hotels do it," said Miss Raby, sadly.

"Exactly. Every day a man comes down from the *Alpes*."

There was an awkward silence. Hitherto they had avoided mentioning that name.

"He takes them all," she continued, in a burst of passion. "My son takes all my guests. He has taken all the English nobility, and the best Americans, and all my old Milanese friends. He slanders me up and down the valley, saying that the drains are bad. The hotel-keepers will not recommend me; they send on their guests to him, because he pays them five per cent. for every one they send. He pays the drivers, he pays the porters, he pays the guides. He pays the band, so that it hardly ever plays down in the village. He even pays the little children to say my drains are bad. He and his wife and his concierge, they mean to ruin me, they would like to see me die."

"Don't—don't say these things, Signora Cantù." Miss Raby began to walk about the room, speaking, as was her habit, what was true rather than what was intelligible. "Try not to be so angry with your son. You don't know what he had to contend with. You don't know who led him into it. Some one else may be to blame. And whoever it may be—you will remember them in your prayers."

"Of course I am a Christian!" exclaimed the angry old lady. "But he will not ruin me. I seem poor, but he has borrowed—too much. That hotel will fail!"

"And perhaps," continued Miss Raby, "there is not much wickedness in the world. Most of the evil we see is the result of little faults—of stupidity or vanity."

"And I even know who led him into it—his wife, and the man who is now his concierge."

"This habit of talking, of self-expression—it seems so pleasant and necessary—yet it does harm——"

They were both interrupted by an uproar in the street. Miss Raby opened the window; and a cloud of dust, heavy with petrol, entered. A passing motor car had twitched over a table. Much beer had been spilt, and a little blood.

Signora Cantù sighed peevishly at the noise. Her ill-temper had exhausted her, and she lay motionless, with closed eyes. Over her head two copper vases clinked gently in the sudden gust of wind. Miss Raby had been on the point of a great dramatic confession, of a touching appeal for forgiveness. Her words were ready; her words always were ready. But she looked at those closed eyes, that suffering enfeebled frame, and she knew that she had no right to claim the luxury of pardon.

It seemed to her that with this interview her life had ended. She had done all that was possible. She had done much evil. It only remained for her to fold her hands and to wait, till her ugliness and her incompetence went the way of beauty and strength. Before her eyes there arose the pleasant face of Colonel Leyland, with whom she might harmlessly conclude her days. He would not be stimulating, but it did not seem desirable that she should be stimulated. It would be better if her faculties did close, if the senseless activity of her brain and her tongue were gradually numbed. For the first time in her life, she was tempted to become old.

Signora Cantù was still speaking of her son's wife and concierge; of the vulgarity of the former and the ingratitude of the latter, whom she had been kind to long ago, when he first wandered up from Italy, an obscure boy. Now he had sided against her. Such was the reward of charity.

"And what is his name?" asked Miss Raby absently.

"Feo Ginori," she replied. "You would not remember him. He used to carry——"

From the new campanile there burst a flood of sound to which the copper vessels vibrated responsively. Miss Raby lifted her hands, not to her ears but to her eyes. In her enfeebled state, the throbbing note of the bell had the curious effect of blood returning into frozen veins.

"I remember that man perfectly," she said at last; "and I shall see him this afternoon."

3

Miss Raby and Elizabeth were seated together in the lounge of the *Hôtel des Alpes*. They had walked up from the *Biscione* to see Colonel Leyland. But he, apparently, had walked down there to see them, and the only thing to do was to wait, and to justify the wait by ordering some refreshment. So Miss Raby had afternoon tea, while Elizabeth behaved like a perfect lady over an ice, occasionally turning the spoon upside down in the mouth when she saw that no one was looking. The under-waiters were clearing cups and glasses off the marble-topped tables, and the gold-laced officials were rearranging the wicker chairs into seductive groups of three and two. Here and there the visitors lingered among their crumbs, and the Russian Prince had fallen asleep in a prominent and ungraceful position. But most people had started for a little walk before dinner, or had gone to play tennis, or had taken a book under a tree. The weather was delightful, and the sun had so far declined that its light had become spiritualized, suggesting new substance as well as new colour in everything on which it fell. From her seat Miss Raby could see the great precipices under which they had passed the day before; and beyond those precipices she could see Italy —the Val d'Aprile, the Val Senese and the mountains she had named "The Beasts of the South." All day those mountains were insignificant—distant chips of white or gray stone. But the evening sun transfigured them, and they would sit up like purple bears against the southern sky.

"It is a sin you should not be out, Elizabeth. Find your friend if you can, and make her go with you. If you see Colonel Leyland, tell him I am here."

"Is that all, ma'am?" Elizabeth was fond of her eccentric mistress, and her heart had been softened by the ice. She saw that Miss Raby did not look well. Possibly the course of love was running roughly. And indeed gentlemen must be treated with tact, especially when both parties are getting on.

"Don't give pennies to the children: that is the only other thing."

The guests had disappeared, and the number of officials visibly diminished. From the hall behind came the genteel sniggers of those two most vile creatures, a young lady behind the bureau and a young man in a frock coat who shows new arrivals to their rooms. Some of the porters joined them, standing at a suitable distance. At last only Miss Raby, the Russian Prince, and the concierge were left in the lounge.

The concierge was a competent European of forty or so, who spoke all languages fluently, and some well. He was still active, and had evidently once been muscular. But either his life or his time of life had been unkind to his figure: in a few years he would certainly be fat. His face was less easy to decipher. He was engaged in the unquestioning performance of his duty, and that is not a moment for self-revelation. He opened the windows, he filled the match-boxes, he flicked the little tables with a duster, always keeping an eye on the door in case any one arrived without luggage, or left without paying. He touched an electric bell, and a waiter flew up and cleared away Miss Raby's tea things. He touched another bell, and sent an underling to tidy up some fragments of paper which had fallen out of a bedroom window. Then "Excuse me, madam!" and he had picked up Miss Raby's handkerchief with a slight bow. He seemed to bear her no grudge for her abrupt departure of the preceding evening. Perhaps it was into his hand that she had dropped a tip. Perhaps he did not remember she had been there.

The gesture with which he returned the handkerchief troubled her with vague memories. Before she could thank him he was back in the door-way, standing sideways, so that the slight curve of his stomach was outlined against the view. He was speaking to a youth of athletic but melancholy appearance, who was fidgeting in the portico without. "I told you the per-centage," she heard. "If you had agreed to it, I would have recommended you. Now it is too late. I have enough guides."

Our generosity benefits more people than we suppose. We tip the cabman, and something goes to the man who whistled for him. We tip the man who lights up the stalactite grotto with magnesium wire, and some-thing goes to the boatman who brought us there. We tip the waiter in the restaurant, and something goes off the waiter's wages. A vast machinery, whose existence we seldom realize, promotes the distribution of our wealth. When the concierge returned, Miss Raby asked: "And what is the percentage?"

She asked with the definite intention of disconcerting him, not because she was unkind, but because she wished to discover what qualities, if any, lurked beneath that civil, efficient exterior. And the spirit of her inquiry was sentimental rather than scientific.

With an educated man she would have succeeded. In attempting to reply to her question, he would have revealed something. But the con-cierge had no reason to pay even lip service to logic. He replied: "Yes, madam! this is perfect weather, both for our visitors and for the hay," and hurried to help a bishop, who was selecting a picture postcard.

Miss Raby, instead of moralizing on the inferior resources of the lower classes, acknowledged a defeat. She watched the man spreading out the postcards, helpful yet not obtrusive, alert yet deferential. She watched him make the bishop buy more than he wanted. This was the man who had talked of love to her upon the mountain. But hitherto he had only revealed his identity by chance gestures bequeathed to him at birth. Intercourse with the gentle classes had required new qualities—civility, omniscience, imperturbability. It was the old answer: the gentle classes were responsible for him. It is inevitable, as well as desirable, that we should bear each other's burdens.

It was absurd to blame Feo for his worldliness—for his essential vulgarity. He had not made himself. It was even absurd to regret his trans-formation from an athlete: his greasy stoutness, his big black kiss-curl, his waxed moustache, his chin which was dividing and propagating itself like some primitive form of life. In England, nearly twenty years before, she had altered his figure as well as his character. He was one of the products of "The Eternal Moment."

A great tenderness overcame her—the sadness of an unskilful demiurge, who makes a world and beholds that it is bad. She desired to ask pardon of her creatures, even though they were too poorly formed to grant it. The longing to confess, which she had suppressed that morning beside the bed of Signora Cantù, broke out again with the violence of a physical desire. When the bishop had gone she renewed the conversation, though on different lines, saying: "Yes, it is beautiful weather. I have just been enjoying a walk up from the *Biscione*. I am stopping there!"

He saw that she was willing to talk, and replied pleasantly: "The *Biscione* must be a very nice hotel: many people speak well of it. The fresco is very beautiful." He was too shrewd to object to a little charity.

"What lots of new hotels there are!" She lowered her voice in order not to rouse the Prince, whose presence weighed on her curiously.

"Oh, madam! I should indeed think so. When I was a lad—Excuse me one moment."

An American girl, who was new to the country, came up with her hand full of coins, and asked him hopelessly "whatever they were worth." He explained, and gave her change: Miss Raby was not sure that he gave her right change.

"When I was a lad——" He was again interrupted, to speed two parting guests. One of them tipped him; he said, "Thank you." The other did not tip him; he said, "Thank you," all the same but not in the same way. Obviously he had as yet no recollections of Miss Raby.

"When I was a lad, Vorta was a poor little place."

"But a pleasant place?"

"Very pleasant, madam."

"Kouf!" said the Russian Prince, suddenly waking up and startling them both. He clapped on a felt hat, and departed at full speed for a constitutional. Miss Raby and Feo were left together.

It was then that she ceased to hesitate, and determined to remind him that they had met before. All day she had sought for a spark of life, and it might be summoned by pointing to that other fire which she discerned, far back in the travelled distance, high up in the mountains of youth. What he would do, if he also discerned it, she did not know; but she hoped that he would become alive, that he at all events would escape the general doom which she had prepared for the place and the people. And what she would do, during their joint contemplation, she did not even consider.

She would hardly have ventured if the sufferings of the day had not hardened her. After much pain, respectability becomes ludicrous. And she had only to overcome the difficulty of Feo's being a man, not the difficulty of his being a concierge. She had never observed that spiritual reticence towards social inferiors which is usual at the present day.

"This is my second visit," she said boldly. "I stayed at the *Biscione* twenty years ago."

He showed the first sign of emotion: *that* reference to the *Biscione* annoyed him.

"I was told I should find you up here," continued Miss Raby. "I remember you very well. You used to take us over the passes."

She watched his face intently. She did not expect it to relax into an expansive smile. "Ah!" he said, taking off his peaked cap, "I remember you perfectly, madam. What a pleasure, if I may say so, to meet you again!"

"I am pleased, too," said the lady, looking at him doubtfully.

"You and another lady, madam, was it not? Miss——"

"Mrs. Harbottle."

"To be sure; I carried your luggage. I often remember your kindness."

She looked up. He was standing near an open window, and the whole of fairyland stretched behind him. Her sanity forsook her, and she said gently: "Will you misunderstand me, if I say that I have never forgotten your kindness either?"

He replied: "The kindness was yours, madam; I only did my duty."

"Duty?" she cried; "what about duty?"

"You and Miss Harbottle were such generous ladies. I well remember how grateful I was: you always paid me above the tariff fare——"

Then she realized that he had forgotten everything; forgotten her, forgotten what had happened, even forgotten what he was like when he was young.

"Stop being polite," she said coldly. "You were not polite when I saw you last."

"I am very sorry," he exclaimed, suddenly alarmed.

"Turn round. Look at the mountains."

"Yes, yes." His fishy eyes blinked nervously. He fiddled with his watch chain which lay in a furrow of his waistcoat. He ran away to warn some poorly dressed children off the view-terrace. When he returned she still insisted.

"I must tell you," she said, in calm, businesslike tones. "Look at that great mountain, round which the road goes south. Look halfway up, on its eastern side—where the flowers are. It was there that you once gave yourself away."

He gaped at her in horror. He remembered. He was inexpressibly shocked.

It was at that moment that Colonel Leyland returned.

She walked up to him, saying, "This is the man I spoke of yesterday."

"Good afternoon; what man?" said Colonel Leyland fussily. He saw that she was flushed, and concluded that some one had been rude to her. Since their relations were somewhat anomalous, he was all the more particular that she should be treated with respect.

"The man who fell in love with me when I was young."

"It is untrue!" cried the wretched Feo, seeing at once the trap that had been laid for him. "The lady imagined it. I swear, sir—I meant nothing. I was a lad. It was before I learnt behaviour. I had even forgotten it. She reminded me. She has disturbed me."

"Good Lord!" said Colonel Leyland. "Good Lord!"

"I shall lose my place, sir; and I have a wife and children. I shall be ruined."

"Sufficient!" cried Colonel Leyland. "Whatever Miss Raby's intentions may be, she does not intend to ruin you."

"You have misunderstood me, Feo," said Miss Raby gently.

"How unlucky we have been missing each other," said Colonel Leyland, in trembling tones that were meant to be nonchalant. "Shall we go for a little walk before dinner? I hope that you are stopping."

She did not attend. She was watching Feo. His alarm had subsided; and he revealed a new emotion, even less agreeable to her. His shoulders straightened, he developed an irresistible smile, and, when he saw that she was looking and that Colonel Leyland was not, he winked at her.

It was a ghastly sight, perhaps the most hopelessly depressing of all the things she had seen at Vorta. But its effect on her was memorable. It evoked a complete vision of that same man as he had been twenty years before. She could see him to the smallest detail of his clothes or his hair, the flowers in his hand, the graze on his wrist, the heavy bundle that he had loosed from his back, so that he might speak as a freeman. She could hear his voice, neither insolent nor diffident, never threatening, never apologizing, urging her first in the studied phrases he had learnt from books, then, as his passion grew, becoming incoherent, crying that she must believe him, that she must love him in return, that she must fly with him to Italy, where they would live for ever, always happy, always young. She had cried out then, as a young lady should, and had thanked him not to insult her. And now, in her middle age, she cried out again, because the sudden shock and the contrast had worked a revelation. "Don't think I'm in love with you now!" she cried.

For she realized that only now was she not in love with him: that the incident upon the mountain had been one of the great moments of her life —perhaps the greatest, certainly the most enduring: that she had drawn unacknowledged power and inspiration from it, just as trees draw vigour from a subterranean spring. Never again could she think of it as a half-humorous episode in her development. There was more reality in it than in all the years of success and varied achievement which had followed, and which it had rendered possible. For all her correct behaviour and lady-like display, she had been in love with Feo, and she had never loved so greatly again. A presumptuous boy had taken her to the gates of heaven; and, though she would not enter with him, the eternal remembrance of the vision had made life seem endurable and good.

Colonel Leyland, by her side, babbled respectabilities, trying to pass the situation off as normal. He was saving her, for he liked her very much, and it pained him when she was foolish. But her last remark to Feo had frightened him; and he began to feel that he must save himself. They were no longer alone. The bureau lady and the young gentleman were listening breathlessly, and the porters were tittering at the discomfiture of their superior. A French lady had spread amongst the guests the agreeable news that an Englishman had surprised his wife making love to the concierge. On the terrace outside, a mother waved away her daughters. The bishop was preparing, very leisurely, for a walk.

But Miss Raby was oblivious. "How little I know!" she said. "I never knew till now that I had loved him and that it was a mere chance—a little catch, a kink—that I never told him so."

It was her habit to speak out; and there was no present passion to disturb or prevent her. She was still detached, looking back at a fire upon the mountains, marvelling at its increased radiance, but too far off to feel its heat. And by speaking out she believed, pathetically enough, that she was making herself intelligible. Her remark seemed inexpressibly coarse to Colonel Leyland.

"But these beautiful thoughts are a poor business, are they not?" she continued, addressing Feo, who was losing his gallant air, and becoming bewildered. "They're hardly enough to grow old on. I think I would give all my imagination, all my skill with words, if I could recapture one crude fact, if I could replace one single person whom I have broken."

"Quite so, madam," he responded, with downcast eyes.

"If only I could find some one here who would understand me, to whom I could confess, I think I should be happier. I have done so much harm in Vorta, dear Feo——"

Feo raised his eyes. Colonel Leyland struck his stick on the parquetry floor.

"—and at last I thought I would speak to you, in case you understood me. I remembered that you had once been very gracious to me—yes, gracious: there is no other word. But I have harmed you also: how could you understand?"

"Madam, I understand perfectly," said the concierge, who had recovered a little, and was determined to end the distressing scene, in which his reputation was endangered, and his vanity aroused only to be rebuffed. "It is you who are mistaken. You have done me no harm at all. You have benefited me."

"Precisely," said Colonel Leyland. "That is the conclusion of the whole matter. Miss Raby has been the making of Vorta."

"Exactly, sir. After the lady's book, foreigners come, hotels are built, we all grow richer. When I first came here, I was a common ignorant porter who carried luggage over the passes; I worked, I found opportunities, I was pleasing to the visitors—and now!" He checked himself suddenly. "Of course I am still but a poor man. My wife and children——"

"Children!" cried Miss Raby, suddenly seeing a path of salvation. "What children have you?"

"Three dear little boys," he replied, without enthusiasm.

"How old is the youngest?"

"Madam, five."

"Let me have that child," she said impressively, "and I will bring him up. He shall live among rich people. He shall see that they are not the vile creatures he supposes, always clamouring for respect and deference and trying to buy them with money. Rich people are good: they are capable of sympathy and love: they are fond of the truth; and when they are with each other they are clever. Your boy shall learn this, and he shall try to teach it to you. And when he grows up, if God is good to him he shall teach the rich: he shall teach them not to be stupid to the poor. I have tried myself, and people buy my books and say that they are good, and smile and lay them down. But I know this: so long as the stupidity exists, not only our charities and missions and schools, but the whole of our civilization, is vain.''

It was painful for Colonel Leyland to listen to such phrases. He made one more effort to rescue Miss Raby. "Je vous prie de ne pas——"[1] he began gruffly, and then stopped, for he remembered that the concierge must know French. But Feo was not attending, nor, of course, had he attended to the lady's prophecies. He was wondering if he could persuade his wife to give up the little boy, and, if he did, how much they dare ask from Miss Raby without repulsing her.

"That will be my pardon," she continued, "if out of the place where I have done so much evil I bring some good. I am tired of memories, though they have been very beautiful. Now, Feo, I want you to give me something else: a living boy. I shall always puzzle you; and I cannot help it. I have changed so much since we met, and I have changed you also. We are both new people. Remember that; for I want to ask you one question before we part, and I cannot see why you shouldn't answer it. Feo! I want you to attend."

"I beg your pardon, madam," said the concierge, rousing himself from his calculations. "Is there anything I can do for you?"

"Answer 'yes' or 'no'; that day when you said you were in love with me—was it true?"

It was doubtful whether he could have answered, whether he had now any opinion about that day at all. But he did not make the attempt. He saw again that he was menaced by an ugly, withered, elderly woman, who was trying to destroy his reputation and his domestic peace. He shrank towards Colonel Leyland, and faltered: "Madam, you must excuse me, but I had rather you did not see my wife; she is so sharp. You are most kind about my little boy; but, madam, no, she would never permit it."

"You have insulted a lady!" shouted the colonel, and made a chivalrous movement of attack. From the hall behind came exclamations of horror and expectancy. Some one ran for the manager.

Miss Raby interposed, saying, "He will never think me respectable." She looked at the dishevelled Feo, fat, perspiring, and unattractive, and smiled sadly at her own stupidity, not at his. It was useless to speak to

---

1. "I beg of you not to . . ."

him again; her talk had scared away his competence and his civility, and scarcely anything was left. He was hardly more human than a frightened rabbit. "Poor man," she murmured, "I have only vexed him. But I wish he would have given me the boy. And I wish he would have answered my question, if only out of pity. He does not know the sort of thing that keeps me alive." She was looking at Colonel Leyland, and so discovered that he too was discomposed. It was her peculiarity that she could only attend to the person she was speaking with, and forgot the personality of the listeners. "I have been vexing you as well: I am very silly."

"It is a little late to think about me," said Colonel Leyland grimly.

She remembered their conversation of yesterday, and understood him at once. But for him she had no careful explanation, no tender pity. Here was a man who was well born and well educated, who had all those things called advantages, who imagined himself full of insight and cultivation and knowledge of mankind. And he had proved himself to be at the exact spiritual level of the man who had no advantages, who was poor and had been made vulgar, whose early virtue had been destroyed by circumstances, whose manliness and simplicity had perished in serving the rich. If Colonel Leyland also believed that she was now in love with Feo, she would not exert herself to undeceive him. Nor indeed would she have found it possible.

From the darkening valley there rose up the first strong singing note of the campanile, and she turned from the men towards it with a motion of love. But that day was not to close without the frustration of every hope. The sound inspired Feo to make conversation and, as the mountains reverberated, he said: "Is it not unfortunate, sir? A gentleman went to see our fine new tower this morning and he believes that the land is slipping from underneath, and that it will fall. Of course it will not harm us up here."

His speech was successful. The stormy scene came to an abrupt and placid conclusion. Before they had realized it, she had taken up her Baedeker and left them, with no tragic gesture. In that moment of final failure, there had been vouchsafed to her a vision of herself, and she saw that she had lived worthily. She was conscious of a triumph over experience and earthly facts, a triumph magnificent, cold, hardly human, whose existence no one but herself would ever surmise. From the view-terrace she looked down on the perishing and perishable beauty of the valley, and, though she loved it no less, it seemed to be infinitely distant, like a valley in a star. At that moment, if kind voices had called her from the hotel, she would not have returned. "I suppose this is old age," she thought. "It's not so very dreadful."

No one did call her. Colonel Leyland would have liked to do so; for he knew she must be unhappy. But she had hurt him too much; she had exposed her thoughts and desires to a man of another class. Not only she, but he himself and all their equals, were degraded by it. She had discovered their nakedness to the alien.

People came in to dress for dinner and for the concert. From the hall there pressed out a stream of excited servants, filling the lounge as an operatic chorus fills the stage, and announcing the approach of the manager. It was impossible to pretend that nothing had happened. The scandal would be immense, and must be diminished as it best might.

Much as Colonel Leyland disliked touching people he took Feo by the arm, and then quickly raised his finger to his forehead.

"Exactly, sir," whispered the concierge. "Of course we understand——Oh, thank you, sir, thank you very much: thank you very much indeed!"

1928

Like many of E. M. Forster's stories and novels, "The Eternal Moment" studies characters who are definitely English in their outlook but have an opportunity to develop a side of their character sometimes limited by English reserve. In "Notes on the English Character," Forster describes the relation between the English in life and the English in literature.

"Beauty and emotion exist in the salt, inhospitable sea": E.M. Forster

The trouble is that the English nature is not at all easy to understand. It has a great air of simplicity, it advertises itself as simple, but the more we consider it, the greater the problems we shall encounter. People talk of the mysterious East, but the West also is mysterious. It has depths that do not reveal themselves at the first gaze. We know what the sea looks like from a distance: it is of one colour, and level, and obviously cannot contain such creatures as fish. But if we look into the sea over the edge of a boat, we see a dozen colours, and depth below depth, and fish swimming in them. That sea is the English character—apparently imperturbable and even. The depths and the colours are the English romanticism and the English sensitiveness—we do not expect to find such things, but they exist. And—to continue my metaphor—the fish are the English emotions, which are always trying to get up to the surface, but don't quite know how. For the most part we see them moving far below, distorted and obscure. Now and then they succeed and we exclaim, "Why, the Englishman has emotions! He actually can feel!" And occasionally we see that beautiful creature the flying fish, which rises out of the water altogether into the air and the sunlight. English literature is a flying fish. It is a sample of the life that goes on day after day beneath the surface; it is a proof that beauty and emotion exist in the salt, inhospitable sea.

JAMES JOYCE

(1882–1941)

ARABY

North Richmond Street, being blind, was a quiet street except at the hour when the Christian Brothers' School set the boys free. An uninhabited house of two storeys stood at the blind end, detached from its neighbours in a square ground. The other houses of the street, conscious of decent lives within them, gazed at one another with brown imperturbable faces.

The former tenant of our house, a priest, had died in the back drawing-room. Air, musty from having been long enclosed, hung in all the rooms, and the waste room behind the kitchen was littered with old useless papers. Among these I found a few paper-covered books, the pages of which were curled and damp: *The Abbot,* by Walter Scott, *The Devout Communicant* and *The Memoirs of Vidocq.* I liked the last best because its leaves were yellow. The wild garden behind the house contained a central apple-tree and a few straggling bushes under one of which I found the late tenant's rusty bicycle-pump. He had been a very charitable priest; in his will he had left all his money to institutions and the furniture of his house to his sister.

When the short days of winter came dusk fell before we had well eaten our dinners. When we met in the street the houses had grown sombre. The space of sky above us was the colour of ever-changing violet and towards it the lamps of the street lifted their feeble lanterns. The cold air stung us and we played till our bodies glowed. Our shouts echoed in the silent street. The career of our play brought us through the dark muddy lanes behind the houses where we ran the gauntlet of the rough tribes from the cottages, to the back doors of the dark dripping gardens where odours arose from the ashpits, to the dark odorous stables where a coachman smoothed and combed the horse or shook music from the buckled harness. When we returned to the street, light from the kitchen windows had filled the areas. If my uncle was seen turning the corner we hid in the shadow until we had seen him safely housed. Or if Mangan's sister came out on the doorstep to call her brother in to his tea we watched her from our shadow peer up and down the street. We waited to see whether she would remain or go in and, if she remained, we left our shadow and walked up to Mangan's steps resignedly. She was waiting for us, her figure defined by the light from the half-opened door. Her brother always teased her before he obeyed and I stood by the railings looking at her. Her dress swung as she moved her body and the soft rope of her hair tossed from side to side.

Every morning I lay on the floor in the front parlour watching her door. The blind was pulled down to within an inch of the sash so that I could not be seen. When she came out on the doorstep my heart leaped. I ran to the hall, seized my books and followed her. I kept her brown figure always in my eye and, when we came near the point at which our ways diverged, I quickened my pace and passed her. This happened morning after morning. I had never spoken to her, except for a few casual words, and yet her name was like a summons to all my foolish blood.

Her image accompanied me even in places the most hostile to romance. On Saturday evenings when my aunt went marketing I had to go to carry some of the parcels. We walked through the flaring streets, jostled by drunken men and bargaining women, amid the curses of labourers, the shrill litanies of shop-boys who stood on guard by the barrels of pigs' cheeks, the nasal chanting of street-singers, who sang a *come-all-you* about O'Donovan Rossa, or a ballad about the troubles in our native land. The noises converged in a single sensation of life for me: I imagined that I bore my chalice[1] safely through a throng of foes. Her name sprang to my lips at moments in strange prayers and praises which I myself did not understand. My eyes were often full of tears (I could not tell why) and at times a flood from my heart seemed to pour itself out into my bosom. I thought little of the future. I did not know whether I would ever speak to her or not or, if I spoke to her, how I could tell her of my confused adoration. But my body was like a harp and her words and gestures were like fingers running upon the wires.

One evening I went into the back drawing-room in which the priest had died. It was a dark rainy evening and there was no sound in the house. Through one of the broken panes I heard the rain impinge upon the earth, the fine incessant needles of water playing in the sodden beds. Some distant lamp or lighted window gleamed below me. I was thankful that I could see so little. All my senses seemed to desire to veil themselves and, feeling that I was about to slip from them, I pressed the palms of my hands together until they trembled, murmuring: "*O love! O love!*" many times.

At last she spoke to me. When she addressed the first words to me I was so confused that I did not know what to answer. She asked me was I going to *Araby*. I forgot whether I answered yes or no. It would be a splendid bazaar, she said she would love to go.

"And why can't you?" I asked.

While she spoke she turned a silver bracelet round and round her wrist. She could not go, she said, because there would be a retreat that week in her convent. Her brother and two other boys were fighting for

---

1. A cup or goblet, especially one used to contain the consecrated wine of the Eucharist.

their caps and I was alone at the railings. She held one of the spikes, bowing her head towards me. The light from the lamp opposite our door caught the white curve of her neck, lit up her hair that rested there and, falling, lit up the hand upon the railing. It fell over one side of her dress and caught the white border of a petticoat, just visible as she stood at ease.

"It's well for you," she said.

"If I go," I said, "I will bring you something."

What innumerable follies laid waste my waking and sleeping thoughts after that evening! I wished to annihilate the tedious intervening days. I chafed against the work of school. At night in my bedroom and by day in the classroom her image came between me and the page I strove to read. The syllables of the word *Araby* were called to me through the silence in which my soul luxuriated and cast an Eastern enchantment over me. I asked for leave to go to the bazaar on Saturday night. My aunt was surprised and hoped it was not some Freemason affair. I answered few questions in class. I watched my master's face pass from amiability to sternness; he hoped I was not beginning to idle. I could not call my wandering thoughts together. I had hardly any patience with the serious work of life which, now that it stood between me and my desire, seemed to me child's play, ugly monotonous child's play.

On Saturday morning I reminded my uncle that I wished to go to the bazaar in the evening. He was fussing at the hallstand, looking for the hat-brush, and answered me curtly:

"Yes, boy, I know."

As he was in the hall I could not go into the front parlour and lie at the window. I left the house in bad humour and walked slowly toward the school. The air was pitilessly raw and already my heart misgave me.

When I came home to dinner my uncle had not yet been home. Still it was early. I sat staring at the clock for some time and, when its ticking began to irritate me, I left the room. I mounted the staircase and gained the upper part of the house. The high cold empty gloomy rooms liberated me and I went from room to room singing. From the front window I saw my companions playing below in the street. Their cries reached me weakened and indistinct and, leaning my forehead against the cool glass, I looked over at the dark house where she lived. I may have stood there for an hour, seeing nothing but the brown-clad figure cast by my imagination, touched discreetly by the lamplight at the curved neck, at the hand upon the railings and at the border below the dress.

When I came downstairs again I found Mrs. Mercer sitting at the fire. She was an old garrulous woman, a pawnbroker's widow, who collected used stamps for some pious purpose. I had to endure the gossip of the tea-table. The meal was prolonged beyond an hour and still my uncle did not come. Mrs. Mercer stood up to go: she was sorry she couldn't wait any longer, but it was after eight o'clock and she did not like to be out late, as the night air was bad for her. When she had gone I began to walk up and down the room, clenching my fists. My aunt said:

"I'm afraid you may put off your bazaar for this night of Our Lord."

At nine o'clock I heard my uncle's latchkey in the halldoor. I heard him talking to himself and heard the hallstand rocking when it had received the weight of his overcoat. I could interpret these signs. When he was midway through his dinner I asked him to give me the money to go to the bazaar. He had forgotten.

"The people are in bed and after their first sleep now," he said.

I did not smile. My aunt said to him energetically:

"Can't you give him the money and let him go? You've kept him late enough as it is."

My uncle said he was very sorry he had forgotten. He said he believed in the old saying: "All work and no play makes Jack a dull boy." He asked me where I was going and, when I had told him a second time he asked me did I know *The Arab's Farewell to his Steed*. When I left the kitchen he was about to recite the opening lines of the piece to my aunt.

I held a florin tightly in my hand as I strode down Buckingham Street towards the station. The sight of the streets thronged with buyers and glaring with gas recalled to me the purpose of my journey. I took my seat in a third-class carriage of a deserted train. After an intolerable delay the train moved out of the station slowly. It crept onward among ruinous houses and over the twinkling river. At Westland Row Station a crowd of people pressed to the carriage doors; but the porters moved them back, saying that it was a special train for the bazaar. I remained alone in the bare carriage. In a few minutes the train drew up beside an improvised wooden platform. I passed out on to the road and saw by the lighted dial of a clock that it was ten minutes to ten. In front of me was a large building which displayed the magical name.

I could not find any sixpenny entrance and, fearing that the bazaar would be closed, I passed in quickly through a turnstile, handing a shilling to a weary-looking man. I found myself in a big hall girdled at half its height by a gallery. Nearly all the stalls were closed and the greater part of the hall was in darkness. I recognised a silence like that which pervades a church after a service. I walked into the centre of the bazaar timidly. A few people were gathered about the stalls which were still open. Before a curtain, over which the words *Café Chantant* were written in coloured lamps, two men were counting money on a salver. I listened to the fall of the coins.

Remembering with difficulty why I had come I went over to one of the stalls and examined porcelain vases and flowered tea-sets. At the door of the stall a young lady was talking and laughing with two young gentlemen. I remarked their English accents and listened vaguely to their conversation.

"O, I never said such a thing!"

"O, but you did!"

"O, but I didn't!"

"Didn't she say that?"

"Yes. I heard her."

"O, there's a . . . fib!"

Observing me the young lady came over and asked me did I wish to buy anything. The tone of her voice was not encouraging; she seemed to have spoken to me out of a sense of duty. I looked humbly at the great jars that stood like eastern guards at either side of the dark entrance to the stall and murmured:

"No, thank you."

The young lady changed the position of one of the vases and went back to the two young men. They began to talk of the same subject. Once or twice the young lady glanced at me over her shoulder.

I lingered before her stall, though I knew my stay was useless, to make my interest in her wares seem the more real. Then I turned away slowly and walked down the middle of the bazaar. I allowed the two pennies to fall against the sixpence in my pocket. I heard a voice call from one end of the gallery that the light was out. The upper part of the hall was now completely dark.

Gazing up into the darkness I saw myself as a creature driven and derided by vanity; and my eyes burned with anguish and anger.

1914

James Joyce's fiction often presents moments of sudden insight, when ordinary things are suddenly seen freshly and take on new significance. In Joyce's novel A Portrait of the Artist as a Young Man, *the protagonist Stephen Dedalus attempts to define philosophical terms from St. Thomas Aquinas by referring to such moments. His definitions shed some light on the consciousness of the protagonist in "Araby."*

"Beauty being a light from some other world": James Joyce

The connotation of the word—Stephen said—is rather vague. Aquinas uses a term which seems to be inexact. It baffled me for a long time. It would lead you to believe that he had in mind symbolism or idealism, the supreme quality of beauty being a light from some other world, the idea of which the matter was but the shadow, the reality of which it was but the symbol. I thought he might mean that *claritas* was the artistic discovery and representation of the divine purpose in anything or a force of generalization which would make the esthetic image a universal one, make it outshine its proper conditions. But that is literary talk. I understand it so. When you have apprehended that basket as one thing and have then analysed it according to its form and apprehended it as a thing you make the only synthesis which is logically and esthetically permissible. You see that it is that thing which it is and no other thing. The radiance of which he speaks in the scholastic *quidditas,* the *whatness* of a thing. This supreme quality is felt by the artist when the esthetic image is first conceived in his imagination. The mind in that mysterious instant Shelley likened beautifully to a fading coal. The instant wherein that supreme quality of beauty, the clear radiance of the esthetic image, is apprehended luminously by the mind which has been arrested by its wholeness and fascinated by its harmony is the luminous silent stasis of esthetic pleasure, a spiritual state very like to that cardiac condition which the Italian physiologist Luigi Galvani, using a phrase almost as beautiful as Shelley's, called the enchantment of the heart.—

VIRGINIA WOOLF

(1882–1941)

SOLID OBJECTS

The only thing that moved upon the vast semicircle of the beach was one small black spot. As it came nearer to the ribs and spine of the stranded pilchard boat, it became apparent from a certain tenuity in its blackness that this spot possessed four legs; and moment by moment it became more unmistakable that it was composed of the persons of two young men. Even thus in outline against the sand there was an unmistakable vitality in them; an indescribable vigour in the approach and withdrawal of the bodies, slight though it was, which proclaimed some violent argument issuing from the tiny mouths of the little round heads. This was corroborated on closer view by the repeated lunging of a walking-stick on the right-hand side. 'You mean to tell me. . . You actually believe . . .' thus the walking-stick on the right-hand side next the waves seemed to be asserting as it cut long straight stripes on the sand.

'Politics be damned!' issued clearly from the body on the left-hand side, and, as these words were uttered, the mouths, noses, chins, little moustaches, tweed caps, rough boots, shooting coats, and check stockings of the two speakers became clearer and clearer; the smoke of their pipes went up into the air; nothing was so solid, so living, so hard, red, hirsute and virile as these two bodies for miles and miles of sea and sandhill.

They flung themselves down by the six ribs and spine of the black pilchard boat. You know how the body seems to shake itself free from an argument, and to apologise for a mood of exaltation; flinging itself down and expressing in the looseness of its attitude a readiness to take up with something new—whatever it may be that comes next to hand. So Charles, whose stick had been slashing the beach for half a mile or so, began skimming flat pieces of slate over the water; and John, who had exclaimed 'Politics be damned!' began burrowing his fingers down, down, into the sand. As his hand went further and further beyond the wrist, so that he had to hitch his sleeve a little higher, his eyes lost their intensity, or rather the background of thought and experience which gives an inscrutable depth to the eyes of grown people disappeared, leaving only the clear transparent surface, expressing nothing but wonder, which the eyes of young children display. No doubt the act of burrowing in the sand had something to do with it. He remembered that, after digging for a little, the water oozes round your finger-tips; the hole then becomes a moat; a well; a spring; a secret channel to the sea. As he was choosing which of these things to make it, still working his fingers in the water, they curled round something hard —a full drop of solid matter—and gradually dislodged a large irregular lump, and brought it to the surface. When the sand coating was wiped off, a green tint appeared. It was a lump of glass, so thick as to be almost opaque; the smoothing of the sea had completely worn off any edge or shape, so that it was impossible to say whether it had been bottle, tumbler or window-pane; it was nothing but glass; it was almost a precious stone. You had only to enclose it in a rim of gold, or pierce it with a wire, and it became a jewel; part of a necklace, or a dull, green light upon a finger. Perhaps after all it was really a gem; something worn by a dark Princess trailing her finger in the water as she sat in the stern of the boat and listened to the slaves singing as they rowed her across the Bay. Or the oak sides of a sunk Elizabethan treasure-chest had split apart, and, rolled over and over, over and over, its emeralds had come at last to shore. John turned it in his hands; he held it to the light; he held it so that its irregular mass blotted out the body and extended right arm of his friend. The green thinned and thickened slightly as it was held against the sky or against the body. It pleased him; it puzzled him; it was so hard, so concentrated, so definite an object compared with the vague sea and the hazy shore.

Now a sigh disturbed him—profound, final, making him aware that his friend Charles had thrown all the flat stones within reach, or had come to the conclusion that it was not worth while to throw them. They ate their sandwiches side by side. When they had done, and were shaking themselves and rising to their feet, John took the lump of glass and looked at it in silence. Charles looked at it too. But he saw immediately that it was not flat, and filling his pipe he said with the energy that dismisses a foolish strain of thought,

'To return to what I was saying—'

He did not see, or if he had seen would hardly have noticed, that John after looking at the lump for a moment, as if in hesitation, slipped it inside his pocket. That impulse, too, may have been the impulse which leads a child to pick up one pebble on a path strewn with them, promising it a life of warmth and security upon the nursery mantelpiece, delighting in the sense of power and benignity which such an action confers, and believing that the heart of the stone leaps with joy when it sees itself chosen from a million like it, to enjoy this bliss instead of a life of cold and wet upon the high road. 'It might so easily have been any other of the millions of stones, but it was I, I, I!'

Whether this thought or not was in John's mind, the lump of glass had its place upon the mantelpiece, where it stood heavy upon a little pile of bills and letters, and served not only as an excellent paperweight, but also as a natural stopping place for the young man's eyes when they wandered from his book. Looked at again and again half consciously by a mind thinking of something else, any object mixes itself so profoundly with the stuff of thought that it loses its actual form and recomposes itself a little differently in an ideal shape which haunts the brain when we least expect it. So John found himself attracted to the windows of curiosity shops when he was out walking, merely because he saw something which reminded him of the lump of glass. Anything, so long as it was an object of some kind, more or less round, perhaps with a dying flame deep sunk in its mass, anything—china, glass, amber, rock, marble—even the smooth oval egg of a prehistoric bird would do. He took, also, to keeping his eyes upon the ground, especially in the neighbourhood of waste land where the household refuse is thrown away. Such objects often occurred there—thrown away, of no use to anybody, shapeless, discarded. In a few months he had collected four or five specimens that took their place upon the mantelpiece. They were useful, too, for a man who is standing for Parliament upon the brink of a brilliant career has any number of papers to keep in order—addresses to constituents, declarations of policy, appeals for subscriptions, invitations to dinner, and so on.

One day, starting from his rooms in the Temple to catch a train in order to address his constituents, his eyes rested upon a remarkable object lying half-hidden in one of those little borders of grass which edge the bases of vast legal buildings. He could only touch it with the point of his stick through the railings; but he could see that it was a piece of china of the most remarkable shape, as nearly resembling a starfish as anything—shaped, or broken accidentally, into five irregular but unmistakable points. The colouring was mainly blue, but green stripes or spots of some kind overlaid the blue, and lines of crimson gave it a richness and lustre of the most attractive kind. John was determined to possess it; but the more he pushed, the further it receded. At length he was forced to go back to his rooms and improvise a wire ring attached to the end of a stick, with which, by dint of great care and skill, he finally drew the piece of china within reach of his hands. As he seized hold of it he exclaimed in triumph. At that moment the clock struck. It was out of the question that he should keep his appointment. The meeting was held without him. But how had the piece of china been broken into this remarkable shape? A careful examination put it beyond doubt that the star shape was accidental, which made it all the more strange, and it seemed unlikely that there should be another such in existence. Set at the opposite end of the mantelpiece from the lump of glass that had been dug from the sand, it looked like a creature from another world—freakish and fantastic as a harlequin. It seemed to be pirouetting through space, winking light like a fitful star. The contrast between the china so vivid and alert, and the glass so mute and contemplative, fascinated him, and wondering and amazed he asked himself how the two came to exist in the same world, let alone to stand upon the same narrow strip of marble in the same room. The question remained unanswered.

He now began to haunt the places which are most prolific of broken china, such as pieces of waste land between railway lines, sites of demolished houses, and commons in the neighbourhood of London. But china is seldom thrown from a great height; it is one of the rarest of human actions. You have to find in conjunction a very high house, and a woman of such reckless impulse and passionate prejudice that she flings her jar or pot straight from the window without thought of who is below. Broken china was to be found in plenty, but broken in some trifling domestic accident, without purpose or character. Nevertheless, he was often astonished, as he came to go into the question more deeply, by the immense variety of shapes to be found in London alone, and there was still more cause for wonder and speculation in the differences of qualities and designs. The finest specimens he would bring home and place upon his mantelpiece, where, however, their duty was more and more of an ornamental nature, since papers needing a weight to keep them down became scarcer and scarcer.

He neglected his duties, perhaps, or discharged them absentmindedly, or his constitutents when they visited him were unfavourably impressed by the appearance of his mantelpiece. At any rate he was not elected to represent them in Parliament, and his friend Charles, taking it much to heart and hurrying to condole with him, found him so little cast down by the disaster that he could only suppose that it was too serious a matter for him to realise all at once.

In truth, John had been that day to Barnes Common, and there under a furze bush had found a very remarkable piece of iron. It was almost identical with the glass in shape, massy and globular, but so cold and heavy, so black and metallic, that it was evidently alien to the earth and had its origin in one of the dead stars or was itself the cinder of a moon. It weighed his pocket down; it weighed the mantelpiece down; it radiated cold. And yet the meteorite stood upon the same ledge with the lump of glass and the star-shaped china.

As his eyes passed from one to another, the determination to possess objects that even surpassed these tormented the young man. He devoted himself more and more resolutely to the search. It he had not been consumed by ambition and convinced that one day some newly-discovered rubbish heap would reward him, the disappointments he had suffered, let alone the fatigue and derision, would have made him give up the pursuit. Provided with a bag and a long stick fitted with an adaptable hook, he ransacked all deposits of earth; raked beneath matted tangles of scrub; searched all alleys and spaces between walls where he had learned to expect to find objects of this kind thrown away. As his standard became higher and his taste more severe the disappointments were innumerable, but always some gleam of hope, some piece of china or glass curiously marked or broken, lured him on. Day after day passed. He was no longer young. His career—that is his political career—was a thing of the past. People gave up visiting him. He was too silent to be worth asking to dinner. He never talked to anyone about his serious ambitions; their lack of understanding was apparent in their behaviour.

He leaned back in his chair now and watched Charles lift the stones on the mantelpiece a dozen times and put them down emphatically to mark what he was saying about the conduct of the Government, without once noticing their existence.

'What was the truth of it, John?' asked Charles suddenly, turning and facing him. 'What made you give it up like that all in a second?'

'I've not given it up,' John replied.

'But you've not a ghost of a chance now,' said Charles roughly.

'I don't agree with you there,' said John with conviction. Charles looked at him and was profoundly uneasy; the most extraordinary doubts possessed him; he had a queer sense that they were talking about different things. He looked round to find some relief for his horrible depression, but the disorderly appearance of the room depressed him still further. What was that stick, and the old carpet bag hanging against the wall? And then those stones? Looking at John, something fixed and distant in his expression alarmed him. He knew only too well that his mere appearance upon the platform was out of the question.

'Pretty stones,' he said as cheerfully as he could; and saying that he had an appointment to keep, he left John—for ever.

Like the impressionist painters whom she admired, Virginia Woolf was impatient with the conventions of realism, which she felt could distort reality rather than convey it accurately. Her rebellion against these conventions is manifest in both her fiction and such critical writings as her essay "Modern Fiction," from which the following passage is taken.

"Life is not a series of gig-lamps symmetrically arranged": Virginia Woolf

So much of the enormous labour of providing the solidity, the likeness to life, of the story is not merely labour thrown away but labour misplaced to the extent of obscuring and blotting out the light of the conception. The writer seems constrained, not by his own free will but by some powerful and unscrupulous tyrant who has him in thrall, to provide a plot, to provide comedy, tragedy, love interest, and an air of probability embalming the whole so impeccable that if all his figures were to come to life they would find themselves dressed down to the last button of their coats in the fashion of the hour. The tyrant is obeyed; the novel is done to a turn. But sometimes, more and more often as time goes by, we suspect a momentary doubt, a spasm of rebellion, as the pages fill themselves in the customary way. Is life like this? Must novels be like this?

Look within and life, it seems, is very far from being 'like this'. Examine for a moment an ordinary mind on an ordinary day. The mind receives a myriad impressions—trivial, fantastic, evanescent, or engraved with the sharpness of steel. From all sides they come, an incessant shower of innumerable atoms; and as they fall, as they shape themselves into the life of Monday or Tuesday, the accent falls differently from of old; the moment of importance came not here but there; so that, if a writer were a free man and not a slave, if he could write what he chose, not what he must, if he could base his work upon his own feeling and not upon convention, there would be no plot, no comedy, no tragedy, no love interest or catastrophe in the accepted style, and perhaps not a single button sewn on as the Bond Street tailors would have it. Life is not a series of gig-lamps symmetrically arranged; life is a luminous halo, a semi-transparent envelope surrounding us from the beginning of consciousness to the end. Is it not the task of the novelist to convey this varying, this unknown and uncircumscribed spirit, whatever aberration or complexity it may display, with as little mixture of the alien and external as possible? We are not pleading merely for courage and sincerity; we are suggesting that the proper stuff of fiction is a little other than custom would have us believe it.

FRANZ KAFKA

(1883–1924)

THE METAMORPHOSIS

translated from the German by Edwin and Willa Muir

1

As Gregor Samsa awoke one morning from uneasy dreams he found himself transformed in his bed into a gigantic insect. He was lying on his hard, as it were armor-plated, back and when he lifted his head a little he could see his dome-like brown belly divided into stiff arched segments on top of which the bed quilt could hardly keep in position and was about to slide off completely. His numerous legs, which were pitifully thin compared to the rest of his bulk, waved helplessly before his eyes.

What has happened to me? he thought. It was no dream. His room, a regular human bedroom, only rather too small, lay quiet between the four familiar walls. Above the table on which a collection of cloth samples was unpacked and spread out—Samsa was a commercial traveler—hung the picture which he had recently cut out of an illustrated magazine and put into a pretty gilt frame. It showed a lady, with a fur cap on and a fur stole, sitting upright and holding out to the spectator a huge fur muff into which the whole of her forearm had vanished!

Gregor's eyes turned next to the window, and the overcast sky—one could hear rain drops beating on the window gutter—made him quite melancholy. What about sleeping a little longer and forgetting all this nonsense, he thought, but it could not be done, for he was accustomed to sleep on his right side and in his present condition he could not turn himself over. However violently he forced himself towards his right side he always rolled on to his back again. He tried it at least a hundred times, shutting his eyes to keep from seeing his struggling legs, and only desisted when he began to feel in his side a faint dull ache he had never experienced before.

Oh God, he thought, what an exhausting job I've picked on! Traveling about day in, day out. It's much more irritating work than doing the actual business in the office, and on top of that there's the trouble of constant traveling, of worrying about train connections, the bed and irregular meals, casual acquaintances that are always new and never become intimate friends. The devil take it all! He felt a slight itching up on his belly; slowly pushed himself on his back nearer to the top of the bed so that he could lift his head more easily; identified the itching place which was surrounded by many small white spots the nature of which he could not understand and made to touch it with a leg, but drew the leg back immediately, for the contact made a cold shiver run through him.

He slid down again into his former position. This getting up early, he thought, makes one quite stupid. A man needs his sleep. Other commercials live like harem women. For instance, when I come back to the hotel of a morning to write up the orders I've got, these others are only sitting down to breakfast. Let me just try that with my chief; I'd be sacked on the spot. Anyhow, that might be quite a good thing for me, who can tell? If I didn't have to hold my hand because of my parents I'd have given notice long ago, I'd have gone to the chief and told him exactly what I think of him. That would knock him endways from his desk! It's a queer way of doing, too, this sitting on high at a desk and talking down to employees, especially when they have to come quite near because the chief is hard of hearing. Well, there's still hope; once I've saved enough money to pay back my parents' debts to him—that should take another five or six years—I'll do it without fail. I'll cut myself completely loose then. For the moment, though, I'd better get up, since my train goes at five.

He looked at the alarm clock ticking on the chest. Heavenly Father! he thought. It was half-past six o'clock and the hands were quietly moving on, it was even past the half-hour, it was getting on toward a quarter to seven. Had the alarm clock not gone off? From the bed one could see that it had been properly set for four o'clock; of course it must have gone off. Yes, but was it possible to sleep quietly through that ear-splitting noise? Well, he had not slept quietly, yet apparently all the more soundly for that. But what was he to do now? The next train went at seven o'clock; to catch that he would need to hurry like mad and his samples weren't even packed up, and he himself wasn't feeling particularly fresh and active. And even if he did catch the train he wouldn't avoid a row with the chief, since the firm's porter would have been waiting for the five o'clock train and would have long since reported his failure to turn up. The porter was a creature of the chief's, spineless and stupid. Well, supposing he were to say he was sick? But that would be most unpleasant and would look suspicious, since during his five years' employment he had not been ill once. The chief himself would be sure to come with the sick-insurance doctor, would reproach his parents with their son's laziness and would cut all excuses short by referring to the insurance doctor, who of course regarded all mankind as perfectly healthy malingerers. And would he be so far wrong on this occasion? Gregor really felt quite well, apart from a drowsiness that was utterly superfluous after such a long sleep, and he was even unusually hungry.

As all this was running through his mind at top speed without his being able to decide to leave his bed—the alarm clock had just struck a quarter to seven—there came a cautious tap at the door behind the head of his bed. "Gregor," said a voice—it was his mother's—"it's a quarter to seven. Hadn't you a train to catch?" That gentle voice! Gregor had a shock as he heard his own voice answering hers, unmistakably his own voice, it was true, but with a persistent horrible twittering squeak behind it like an undertone, that left the words in their clear shape only for the first moment and then rose up reverberating round them to destroy their sense, so that one could not be sure one had heard them rightly. Gregor wanted to answer at length and explain everything, but in the circumstances he confined himself to saying: "Yes, yes, thank you, Mother, I'm getting up now." The wooden door between them must have kept the change in his voice from being noticeable outside, for his mother contented herself with this statement and shuffled away. Yet this brief exchange of words had made the other members of the family aware that Gregor was still in the house, as they had not expected, and at one of the side doors his father was already knocking, gently, yet with his fist. "Gregor, Gregor," he called, "what's the matter with you?" And after a little while he called again in a deeper voice: "Gregor! Gregor!" At the other side door his sister was saying in a low, plaintive tone: "Gregor? Aren't you well? Are you needing anything?" He answered them both at once: "I'm just ready," and did his best to make his voice sound as normal as possible by enunciating the words very clearly and leaving long pauses between them. So his father went back to his breakfast, but his sister whispered: "Gregor, open the door, do." However, he was not thinking of opening the door, and felt thankful for the prudent habit he had acquired in traveling of locking all doors during the night, even at home.

His immediate intention was to get up quietly without being disturbed, to put on his clothes and above all eat his breakfast, and only then to consider what else was to be done, since in bed, he was well aware, his meditations would come to no sensible conclusion. He remembered that often enough in bed he had felt small aches and pains, probably caused by awkward postures, which had proved purely imaginary once he got up, and he looked forward eagerly to seeing this morning's delusions gradually fall away. That the change in his voice was nothing but the precursor of a severe chill, a standing ailment of commercial travelers, he had not the least possible doubt.

To get rid of the quilt was quite easy; he had only to inflate himself a little and it fell off by itself. But the next move was difficult, especially because he was so uncommonly broad. He would have needed arms and hands to hoist himself up; instead he had only the numerous little legs which never stopped waving in all directions and which he could not control in the least. When he tried to bend one of them it was the first to stretch itself straight; and did he succeed at last in making it do what he wanted, all the other legs meanwhile waved the more wildly in a high degree of unpleasant agitation. "But what's the use of lying idle in bed," said Gregor to himself.

He thought that he might get out of bed with the lower part of his body first, but this lower part, which he had not yet seen and of which he could form no clear conception, proved too difficult to move; it shifted so slowly; and when finally, almost wild with annoyance, he gathered his forces together and thrust out recklessly, he had miscalculated the direction and bumped heavily against the lower end of the bed, and the stinging pain he felt informed him that precisely this lower part of his body was at the moment probably the most sensitive.

So he tried to get the top part of himself out first, and cautiously moved his head towards the edge of the bed. That proved easy enough, and despite its breadth and mass the bulk of his body at last slowly followed the movement of his head. Still, when he finally got his head free over the edge of the bed he felt too scared to go on advancing, for after all if he let himself fall in this way it would take a miracle to keep his head from being injured. And at all costs he must not lose consciousness now, precisely now; he would rather stay in bed.

But when after a repetition of the same efforts he lay in his former position again, sighing, and watched his little legs struggling against each other more wildly than ever, if that were possible, and saw no way of bringing any order into this arbitrary confusion, he told himself again that it was impossible to stay in bed and that the most sensible course was to risk everything for the smallest hope of getting away from it. At the same time he did not forget meanwhile to remind himself that cool reflection, the coolest possible, was much better than desperate resolves. In such moments he focused his eyes as sharply as possible on the window, but, unfortunately, the prospect of the morning fog, which muffled even the other side of the narrow street, brought him little encouragement and comfort. "Seven o'clock already," he said to himself when the alarm clock chimed again, "seven o'clock already and still such a thick fog." And for a little while he lay quiet, breathing lightly, as if perhaps expecting such complete repose to restore all things to their real and normal condition.

But then he said to himself: "Before it strikes a quarter past seven I must be quite out of this bed, without fail. Anyhow, by that time someone will have come from the office to ask for me, since it opens before seven." And he set himself to rocking his whole body at once in a regular rhythm, with the idea of swinging it out of the bed. If he tipped himself out in that way he could keep his head from injury by lifting it at an acute angle when he fell. His back seemed to be hard and was not likely to suffer from a fall on the carpet. His biggest worry was the loud crash he would not be able to help making, which would probably cause anxiety, if not terror, behind all the doors. Still, he must take the risk.

When he was already half out of the bed—the new method was more a game than an effort, for he needed only to hitch himself across by rocking to and fro—it struck him how simple it would be if he could get help. Two strong people—he thought of his father and the servant girl—would be amply sufficient; they would only have to thrust their arms under his convex back, lever him out of the bed, bend down with their burden and then be patient enough to let him turn himself right over on to the floor, where it was to be hoped his legs would then find their proper function. Well, ignoring the fact that the doors were all locked, ought he really to call for help? In spite of his misery he could not suppress a smile at the very idea of it.

He had got so far that he could barely keep his equilibrium when he rocked himself strongly, and he would have to nerve himself very soon for the final decision since in five minutes' time it would be a quarter past seven—when the front door bell rang. "That's someone from the office," he said to himself, and grew almost rigid, while his little legs only jigged about all the faster. For a moment everything stayed quiet. "They're not going to open the door," said Gregor to himself, catching at some kind of irrational hope. But then of course the servant girl went as usual to the door with her heavy tread and opened it. Gregor needed only to hear the first good morning of the visitor to know immediately who it was—the chief clerk himself. What a fate, to be condemned to work for a firm where the smallest omission at once gave rise to the gravest suspicion! Were all employees in a body nothing but scoundrels, was there not among them one single loyal devoted man who, had he wasted only an hour or so of the firm's time in a morning, was so tormented by conscience as to be driven out of his mind and actually incapable of leaving his bed? Wouldn't it really have been sufficient to send an apprentice to inquire—if any inquiry were necessary at all—did the chief clerk himself have to come and thus indicate to the entire family, an innocent family, that this suspicious circumstance could be investigated by no one less versed in affairs than himself? And more through the agitation caused by these reflections than through any act of will Gregor swung himself out of bed with all his strength. There was a loud thump, but it was not really a crash. His fall was broken to some extent by the carpet, his back, too, was less stiff than he thought, and so there was merely a dull thud, not so very startling. Only he had not lifted his head carefully enough and had hit it; he turned it and rubbed it on the carpet in pain and irritation.

"That was something falling down in there," said the chief clerk in the next room to the left. Gregor tried to suppose to himself that something like what had happened to him today might some day happen to the chief clerk; one really could not deny that it was possible. But as if in brusque reply to this supposition the chief clerk took a couple of firm steps in the next-door room and his patent leather boots creaked. From the right-hand room his sister was whispering to inform him of the situation: "Gregor, the chief clerk's here." "I know," muttered Gregor to himself; but he didn't dare to make his voice loud enough for his sister to hear it.

"Gregor," said his father now from the left-hand room, "the chief clerk has come and wants to know why you didn't catch the early train. We don't know what to say to him. Besides, he wants to talk to you in person. So open the door, please. He will be good enough to excuse the untidiness of your room." "Good morning, Mr. Samsa," the chief clerk was calling amiably meanwhile. "He's not well," said his mother to the visitor, while his father was still speaking through the door, "he's not well, sir, believe me. What else would make him miss a train! The boy thinks about nothing but his work. It makes me almost cross the way he never goes out in the evenings; he's been here the last eight days and has stayed at home every single evening. He just sits there quietly at the table reading a newspaper or looking through railway timetables. The only amusement he gets is doing fretwork. For instance, he spent two or three evenings cutting out a little picture frame; you would be surprised to see how pretty it is; it's hanging in his room; you'll see it in a minute when Gregor opens the door. I must say I'm glad you've come, sir; we should never have got him to unlock the door by ourselves; he's so obstinate; and I'm sure he's unwell, though he wouldn't have it to be so this morning." "I'm just coming," said Gregor slowly and carefully, not moving an inch for fear of losing one word of the conversation. "I can't think of any other explanation, madam," said the chief clerk. "I hope it's nothing serious. Although on the other hand I must say that we men of business—fortunately or unfortunately—very often simply have to ignore any slight indisposition, since business must be attended to." "Well, can the chief clerk come in now?" asked Gregor's father impatiently, again knocking on the door. "No," said Gregor. In the left-hand room a painful silence followed this refusal, in the right-hand room his sister began to sob.

Why didn't his sister join the others? She was probably newly out of bed and hadn't even begun to put on her clothes yet. Well, why was she crying? Because he wouldn't get up and let the chief clerk in, because he was in danger of losing his job, and because the chief would begin dunning his parents again for the old debts? Surely these were things one didn't need to worry about for the present. Gregor was still at home and not in the least thinking of deserting the family. At the moment, true, he was lying on the carpet and no one who knew the condition he was in could seriously expect him to admit the chief clerk. But for such a small discourtesy, which could plausibly be explained away somehow later on, Gregor could hardly be dismissed on the spot. And it seemed to Gregor that it would be much more sensible to leave him in peace for the present than to trouble him with tears and entreaties. Still, of course, their uncertainty bewildered them all and excused their behavior.

"Mr. Samsa," the chief clerk called now in a louder voice, "what's the matter with you? Here you are, barricading yourself in your room, giving only 'yes' and 'no' for answers, causing your parents a lot of unnecessary trouble and neglecting—I mention this only in passing—neglecting your business duties in an incredible fashion. I am speaking here in the name of your parents and of your chief, and I beg you quite seriously to give me an immediate and precise explanation. You amaze me, you amaze me. I thought you were a quiet, dependable person, and now all at once you seem bent on making a disgraceful exhibition of yourself. The chief did hint to me early this morning a possible explanation for your disappearance—with reference to the cash payments that were entrusted to you recently—but I almost pledged my solemn word of honor that this could not be so. But now that I see how incredibly obstinate you are, I no longer have the slightest desire to take your part at all. And your position in the firm is not so unassailable. I came with the intention of telling you all this in private, but since you are wasting my time so needlessly I don't see why your parents shouldn't hear it too. For some time past your work has been most unsatisfactory; this is not the season of the year for a business boom, of course, we admit that, but a season of the year for doing no business at all, that does not exist, Mr. Samsa, must not exist."

"But, sir," cried Gregor, beside himself and in his agitation forgetting everything else, "I'm just going to open the door this very minute. A slight illness, an attack of giddiness, has kept me from getting up. I'm still lying in bed. But I feel all right again. I'm getting out of bed now. Just give me a moment or two longer! I'm not quite so well as I thought. But I'm all right, really. How a thing like that can suddenly strike one down! Only last night I was quite well, my parents can tell you, or rather I did have a slight presentiment. I must have showed some sign of it. Why didn't I report it at the office! But one always thinks that an indisposition can be got over without staying in the house. Oh sir, do spare my parents! All that you're reproaching me with now has no foundation; no one has ever said a word to me about it. Perhaps you haven't looked at the last orders I sent in. Anyhow, I can still catch the eight o'clock train, I'm much the better for my few hours' rest. Don't let me detain you here, sir; I'll be attending to business very soon, and do be good enough to tell the chief so and to make my excuses to him!"

And while all this was tumbling out pell-mell and Gregor hardly knew what he was saying, he had reached the chest quite easily, perhaps because of the practice he had had in bed, and was now trying to lever himself upright by means of it. He meant actually to open the door, actually to show himself and speak to the chief clerk; he was eager to find out what the others, after all their insistence, would say at the sight of him. If they were horrified then the responsibility was no longer his and he could stay quiet. But if they took it calmly, then he had no reason either to be upset, and could really get to the station for the eight o'clock train if he hurried. At first he slipped down a few times from the polished surface of the chest, but at length with a last heave he stood upright; he paid no more attention to the pains in the lower part of his body, however they smarted. Then he let himself fall against the back of a near-by chair, and clung with his little legs to the edges of it. That brought him into control of himself again and he stopped speaking, for now he could listen to what the chief clerk was saying.

"Did you understand a word of it?" the chief clerk was asking; "surely he can't be trying to make fools of us?" "Oh dear," cried his mother, in tears, "perhaps he's terribly ill and we're tormenting him. Grete! Grete!" she called out then. "Yes Mother?" called his sister from the other side. They were calling to each other across Gregor's room. "You must go this minute for the doctor. Gregor is ill. Go for the doctor, quick. Did you hear how he was speaking?" "That was no human voice," said the chief clerk in a voice noticeably low beside the shrillness of the mother's. "Anna! Anna!" his father was calling through the hall to the kitchen, clapping his hands, "get a locksmith at once!" And the two girls were already running through the hall with a swish of skirts—how could his sister have got dressed so quickly?—and were tearing the front door open. There was no sound of its closing again; they had evidently left it open, as one does in houses where some great misfortune has happened.

But Gregor was now much calmer. The words he uttered were no longer understandable, apparently, although they seemed clear enough to him, even clearer than before, perhaps because his ear had grown accustomed to the sound of them. Yet at any rate people now believed that something was wrong with him, and were ready to help him. The positive certainty with which these first measures had been taken comforted him. He felt himself drawn once more into the human circle and hoped for great and remarkable results from both the doctor and the locksmith, without really distinguishing precisely between them. To make his voice as clear as possible for the decisive conversation that was now imminent he coughed a little, as quietly as he could, of course, since this noise too might not sound like a human cough for all he was able to judge. In the next room meanwhile there was complete silence. Perhaps his parents were sitting at the table with the chief clerk, whispering, perhaps they were all leaning against the door and listening.

Slowly Gregor pushed the chair towards the door, then let go of it, caught hold of the door for support—the soles at the end of his little legs were somewhat sticky—and rested against it for a moment after his efforts. Then he set himself to turning the key in the lock with his mouth. It seemed, unhappily, that he hadn't really any teeth—what could he grip the key with?—but on the other hand his jaws were certainly very strong; with their help he did manage to set the key in motion, heedless of the fact that he was undoubtedly damaging them somewhere, since a brown fluid issued from his mouth, flowed over the key and dripped on the floor. "Just listen to that," said the chief clerk next door; "he's turning the key." That was a great encouragement to Gregor; but they should all have shouted encouragement to him, his father and mother too: "Go on, Gregor," they should have called out, "keep going, hold on to that key!" And in the belief that they were all following his efforts intently, he clenched his jaws recklessly on the key with all the force at his command. As the turning of the key progressed he circled round the lock, holding on now only with his mouth, pushing on the key, as required, or pulling it down again with all the weight of his body. The louder click of the finally yielding lock literally quickened Gregor. With a deep breath of relief he said to himself: "So I didn't need the locksmith," and laid his head on the handle to open the door wide.

Since he had to pull the door towards him, he was still invisible when it was really wide open. He had to edge himself slowly round the near half of the double door, and to do it very carefully if he was not to fall plump upon his back just on the threshold. He was still carrying out this difficult manoeuvre, with no time to observe anything else, when he heard the chief clerk utter a loud "Oh!"—it sounded like a gust of wind—and now he could see the man, standing as he was nearest to the door, clapping one hand before his open mouth and slowly backing away as if driven by some invisible steady pressure. His mother—in spite of the chief clerk's being there her hair was still undone and sticking up in all directions—first clasped her hands and looked at his father, then took two steps towards Gregor and fell on the floor among her outspread skirts, her face quite hidden on her breast. His father knotted his fist with a fierce expression on his face as if he meant to knock Gregor back into his room, then looked uncertainly round the living room, covered his eyes with his hands and wept till his great chest heaved.

Gregor did not go now into the living room, but leaned against the inside of the firmly shut wing of the door, so that only half his body was visible and his head above it bending sideways to look at the others. The light had meanwhile strengthened; on the other side of the street one could see clearly a section of the endlessly long, dark gray building opposite—it was a hospital—abruptly punctuated by its row of regular windows; the rain was still falling, but only in large singly discernible and literally singly splashing drops. The breakfast dishes were set out on the table lavishly, for breakfast was the most important meal of the day to Gregor's father, who lingered it out for hours over various newspapers. Right opposite Gregor on the wall hung a photograph of himself on military service, as a lieutenant, hand on sword, a carefree smile on his face, inviting one to respect his uniform and military bearing. The door leading to the hall was open, and one could see that the front door stood open too, showing the landing beyond and the beginning of the stairs going down.

"Well," said Gregor, knowing perfectly that he was the only one who had retained any composure, "I'll put my clothes on at once, pack up my samples and start off. Will you only let me go? You see, sir, I'm not obstinate, and I'm willing to work; traveling is a hard life, but I couldn't live without it. Where are you going, sir? To the office? Yes? Will you give a true account of all this? One can be temporarily incapacitated, but that's just the moment for remembering former services and bearing in mind that later on, when the incapacity has been got over, one will certainly work with all the more industry and concentration. I'm loyally bound to serve the chief, you know that very well. Besides, I have to provide for my parents and my sister. I'm in great difficulties, but I'll get out of them again. Don't make things any worse for me than they are. Stand up for me in the firm. Travelers are not popular there, I know. People think they earn sacks of money and just have a good time. A prejudice there's no particular reason for revising. But you, sir, have a more comprehensive view of affairs than the rest of the staff, yes, let me tell you in confidence, a more comprehensive view than the chief himself, who, being the owner, lets his judgment easily be swayed against one of his employees. And you know very well that the traveler, who is never seen in the office almost the whole year round, can so easily fall a victim to gossip and ill luck and unfounded complaints, which he mostly knows nothing about, except when he comes back exhausted from his rounds, and only then suffers in person from their evil consequences, which he can no longer trace back to the original causes. Sir, sir, don't go away without a word to me to show that you think me in the right at least to some extent!"

But at Gregor's very first words the chief clerk had already backed away and only stared at him with parted lips over one twitching shoulder. And while Gregor was speaking he did not stand still one moment but stole away towards the door, without taking his eyes off Gregor, yet only an inch at a time, as if obeying some secret injunction to leave the room. He was already at the hall, and the suddenness with which he took his last step out of the living room would have made one believe he had burned the sole of his foot. Once in the hall he stretched his right arm before him towards the staircase, as if some supernatural power were waiting there to deliver him.

Gregor perceived that the chief clerk must on no account be allowed to go away in this frame of mind if his position in the firm were not to be endangered to the utmost. His parents did not understand this so well; they had convinced themselves in the course of years that Gregor was settled for life in this firm, and besides they were so occupied with their immediate troubles that all foresight had forsaken them. Yet Gregor had this foresight. The chief clerk must be detained, soothed, persuaded and finally won over; the whole future of Gregor and his family depended on it! If only his sister had been there! She was intelligent; she had begun to cry while Gregor was still lying quietly on his back. And no doubt the chief clerk, so partial to ladies, would have been guided by her; she would have shut the door of the flat and in the hall talked him out of his horror. But she was not there, and Gregor would have to handle the situation himself. And without remembering that he was still unaware what powers of movement he possessed, without even remembering that his words in all possibility, indeed in all likelihood, would again be unintelligible, he let go the wing of the door, pushed himself through the opening, started to walk towards the chief clerk, who was already ridiculously clinging with both hands to the railing on the landing; but immediately, as he was feeling for a support, he fell down with a little cry upon all his numerous legs. Hardly was he down when he experienced for the first time this morning a sense of physical comfort; his legs had firm ground under them; they were completely obedient, as he noted with joy; they even strove to carry him forward in whatever direction he chose; and he was inclined to believe that a final relief from all his sufferings was at hand. But in the same moment as he found himself on the floor, rocking with suppressed eagerness to move, not far from his mother, indeed just in front of her, she, who had seemed so completely crushed, sprang all at once to her feet, her arms and fingers outspread, cried: "Help, for God's sake, help!" bent her head down as if to see Gregor better, yet on the contrary kept backing senselessly away; had quite forgotten that the laden table stood behind her; sat upon it hastily, as if in absence of mind, when she bumped into it; and seemed altogether unaware that the big coffee pot beside her was upset and pouring coffee in a flood over the carpet.

"Mother, Mother," said Gregor in a low voice, and looked up at her. The chief clerk, for the moment, had quite slipped from his mind; instead, he could not resist snapping his jaws together at the sight of the streaming coffee. That made his mother scream again, she fled from the table and fell into the arms of his father, who hastened to catch her. But Gregor had now no time to spare for his parents; the chief clerk was already on the stairs; with his chin on the banisters he was taking one last backward look. Gregor made a spring, to be as sure as possible of overtaking him; the chief clerk must have divined his intention, for he leaped down several steps and vanished; he was still yelling "Ugh!" and it echoed through the whole staircase.

Unfortunately, the flight of the chief clerk seemed completely to upset Gregor's father, who had remained relatively calm until now, for instead of running after the man himself, or at least not hindering Gregor in his pursuit, he seized in his right hand the walking stick which the chief clerk had left behind on a chair, together with a hat and greatcoat, snatched in his left hand a large newspaper from the table and began stamping his feet and flourishing the stick and the newspaper to drive Gregor back into his room. No entreaty of Gregor's availed, indeed no entreaty was even understood, however humbly he bent his head his father only stamped on the floor the more loudly. Behind his father his mother had torn open a window, despite the cold weather, and was leaning far out of it with her face in her hands. A strong draught set in from the street to the staircase, the window curtains blew in, the newspapers on the table fluttered, stray pages whisked over the floor. Pitilessly Gregor's father drove him back, hissing and crying "Shoo!" like a savage. But Gregor was quite unpracticed in walking backwards, it really was a slow business. If he only had a chance to turn round he could get back to his room at once, but he was afraid of exasperating his father by the slowness of such a rotation and at any moment the stick in his father's hand might hit him a fatal blow on the back or on the head. In the end, however, nothing else was left for him to do since to his horror he observed that in moving backwards he could not even control the direction he took; and so, keeping an anxious eye on his father all the time over his shoulder, he began to turn round as quickly as he could, which was in reality very slowly. Perhaps his father noted his good intentions, for he did not interfere except every now and then to help him in the manoeuvre from a distance with the point of the stick. If only he would have stopped making that unbearable hissing noise! It made Gregor quite lose his head. He had turned almost completely round when the hissing noise so distracted him that he even turned a little the wrong way again. But when at last his head was fortunately right in front of the doorway, it appeared that his body was too broad simply to get through the opening. His father, of course, in his present mood was far from thinking of such a thing as opening the other half of the door, to let Gregor have enough space. He had merely the fixed idea of driving Gregor back into his room as quickly as possible. He would never have suffered Gregor to make the circumstantial preparations for standing up on end and perhaps slipping his way through the door. Maybe he was now making more noise than ever to urge Gregor forward, as if no obstacle impeded him; to Gregor, anyhow, the noise in his rear sounded no longer like the voice of one single father; this was really no joke, and Gregor thrust himself—come what might—into the doorway. One side of his body rose up, he was tilted at an angle in the doorway, his flank was quite bruised, horrid blotches stained the white door, soon he was stuck fast and, left to himself, could not have moved at all, his legs on one side fluttered trembling to the air, those on the other were crushed painfully to the floor—when from behind his father gave him a strong push which was literally a deliverance and he flew far into the room, bleeding freely. The door was slammed behind him with the stick, and then at last there was silence.

2

Not until it was twilight did Gregor awake out of a deep sleep, more like a swoon than a sleep. He would certainly have waked up of his own accord not much later, for he felt himself sufficiently rested and well-slept, but it seemed to him as if a fleeting step and a cautious shutting of the door leading into the hall had aroused him. The electric lights in the street cast a pale sheen here and there on the ceiling and the upper surfaces of the furniture, but down below, where he lay, it was dark. Slowly, awkwardly trying out his feelers, which he now first learned to appreciate, he pushed his way to the door to see what had been happening there. His left side felt like one single long, unpleasantly tense scar, and he had actually to limp on his two rows of legs. One little leg, moreover, had been severely damaged in the course of that morning's events—it was almost a miracle that only one had been damaged—and trailed uselessly behind him.

He had reached the door before he discovered what had really drawn him to it: the smell of food. For there stood a basin filled with fresh milk in which floated little sops of white bread. He could almost have laughed with joy, since he was now still hungrier than in the morning, and he dipped his head almost over the eyes straight into the milk. But soon in disappointment he withdrew it again; not only did he find it difficult to feed because of his tender left side—and he could only feed with the palpitating collaboration of his whole body—he did not like the milk either, although milk had been his favorite drink and that was certainly why his sister had set it there for him, indeed it was almost with repulsion that he turned away from the basin and crawled back to the middle of the room.

He could see through the crack of the door that the gas was turned on in the living room, but while usually at this time his father made a habit of reading the afternoon newspaper in a loud voice to his mother and occasionally to his sister as well, not a sound was now to be heard. Well, perhaps his father had recently given up this habit of reading aloud, which his sister had mentioned so often in conversation and in her letters. But there was the same silence all around, although the flat was certainly not empty of occupants. "What a quiet life our family has been leading," said Gregor to himself, and as he sat there motionless staring into the darkness he felt great pride in the fact that he had been able to provide such a life for his parents and sister in such a fine flat. But what if all the quiet, the comfort, the contentment were now to end in horror? To keep himself from being lost in such thoughts Gregor took refuge in movement and crawled up and down the room.

Once during the long evening one of the side doors was opened a little and quickly shut again, later the other side door too; someone had apparently wanted to come in and then thought better of it. Gregor now stationed himself immediately before the living room door, determined to persuade any hesitating visitor to come in or at least to discover who it might be; but the door was not opened again and he waited in vain. In the early morning, when the doors were locked, they had all wanted to come in, now that he had opened one door and the other had apparently been opened during the day, no one came in and even the keys were on the other side of the doors.

It was late at night before the gas went out in the living room, and Gregor could easily tell that his parents and his sister had all stayed awake until then, for he could clearly hear the three of them stealing away on tiptoe. No one was likely to visit him, not until the morning, that was certain; so he had plenty of time to meditate at his leisure on how he was to arrange his life afresh. But the lofty, empty room in which he had to lie flat on the floor filled him with an apprehension he could not account for, since it had been his very own room for the past five years—and with a half-unconscious action, not without a slight feeling of shame, he scuttled under the sofa, where he felt comfortable at once, although his back was a little cramped and he could not lift his head up, and his only regret was that his body was too broad to get the whole of it under the sofa.

He stayed there all night, spending the time partly in a light slumber, from which his hunger kept waking him up with a start, and partly in worrying and sketching vague hopes, which all led to the same conclusion, that he must lie low for the present and, by exercising patience and the utmost consideration, help the family to bear the inconvenience he was bound to cause them in his present condition.

Very early in the morning, it was still almost night, Gregor had the chance to test the strength of his new resolutions, for his sister, nearly fully dressed, opened the door from the hall and peered in. She did not see him at once, yet when she caught sight of him under the sofa—well, he had to be somewhere, he couldn't have flown away, could he?—she was so startled that without being able to help it she slammed the door shut again. But as if regretting her behavior she opened the door again immediately and came in on tiptoe, as if she were visiting an invalid or even a stranger. Gregor had pushed his head forward to the very edge of the sofa and watched her. Would she notice that he had left the milk standing, and not for lack of hunger, and would she bring in some other kind of food more to his taste? If she did not do it of her own accord, he would rather starve than draw her attention to the fact, although he felt a wild impulse to dart out from under the sofa, throw himself at her feet and beg her for something to eat. But his sister at once noticed, with surprise, that the basin was still full, except for a little milk that had been spilt all around it, she lifted it immediately, not with her bare hands, true, but with a cloth and carried it away. Gregor was wildly curious to know what she would bring instead, and made various speculations about it. Yet what she actually did next, in the goodness of her heart, he could never have guessed at. To find out what he liked she brought him a whole selection of food, all set out on an old newspaper. There were old, half-decayed vegetables, bones from last night's supper covered with a white sauce that had thickened; some raisins and almonds; a piece of cheese that Gregor would have called uneatable two days ago; a dry roll of bread, a buttered roll, and a roll both buttered and salted. Besides all that, she set down again the same basin, into which she had poured some water, and which was apparently to be reserved for his exclusive use. And with fine tact, knowing that Gregor would not eat in her presence, she withdrew quickly and even turned the key, to let him understand that he could take his ease as much as he liked. Gregor's legs all whizzed towards the food. His wounds must have healed completely, moreover, for he felt no disability, which amazed him and made him reflect how more than a month ago he had cut one finger a little with a knife and had still suffered pain from the wound only the day before yesterday. Am I less sensitive now? he thought, and sucked greedily at the cheese, which above all the other edibles attracted him at once and strongly. One after another and with tears of satisfaction in his eyes he quickly devoured the cheese, the vegetables and the sauce; the fresh food, on the other hand, had no charms for him, he could not even stand the smell of it and actually dragged away to some little distance the things he could eat. He had long finished his meal and was only lying lazily on the same spot when his sister turned the key slowly as a sign for him to retreat. That roused him at once, although he was nearly asleep, and he hurried under the sofa again. But it took considerable self-control for him to stay under the sofa, even for the short time his sister was in the room, since the large meal had swollen his body somewhat and he was so cramped he could hardly breathe. Slight attacks of breathlessness afflicted him and his eyes were starting a little out of his head as he watched his unsuspecting sister sweeping together with a broom not only the remains of what he had eaten but even the things he had not touched, as if these were now of no use to anyone, and hastily shoveling it all into a bucket, which she covered with a wooden lid and carried away. Hardly had she turned her back when Gregor came from under the sofa and stretched and puffed himself out.

In this manner Gregor was fed, once in the early morning while his parents and the servant girl were still asleep, and a second time after they had all had their midday dinner, for then his parents took a short nap and the servant girl could be sent out on some errand or other by his sister. Not that they would have wanted him to starve, of course, but perhaps they could not have borne to know more about his feeding than from hearsay, perhaps too his sister wanted to spare them such little anxieties wherever possible, since they had quite enough to bear as it was.

Under what pretext the doctor and the locksmith had been got rid of on that first morning Gregor could not discover, for since what he said was not understood by the others it never struck any of them, not even his sister, that he could understand what they said, and so whenever his sister came into his room he had to content himself with hearing her utter only a sigh now and then and an occasional appeal to the saints. Later on, when she had got a little used to the situation—of course she could never get completely used to it—she sometimes threw out a remark which was kindly meant or could be so interpreted. "Well, he liked his dinner today," she would say when Gregor had made a good clearance of his food; and when he had not eaten, which gradually happened more and more often, she would say almost sadly: "Everything's been left standing again."

But although Gregor could get no news directly, he overheard a lot from the neighboring rooms, and as soon as voices were audible, he would run to the door of the room concerned and press his whole body against it. In the first few days especially there was no conversation that did not refer to him somehow, even if only indirectly. For two whole days there were family consultations at every mealtime about what should be done; but also between meals the same subject was discussed, for there were always at least two members of the family at home, since no one wanted to be alone in the flat and to leave it quite empty was unthinkable. And on the very first of these days the household cook—it was not quite clear what and how much she knew of the situation—went down on her knees to his mother and begged leave to go, and when she departed, a quarter of an hour later, gave thanks for her dismissal with tears in her eyes as if for the greatest benefit that could have been conferred on her, and without any prompting swore a solemn oath that she would never say a single word to anyone about what had happened.

Now Gregor's sister had to cook too, helping her mother; true, the cooking did not amount to much, for they ate scarcely anything. Gregor was always hearing one of the family vainly urging another to eat and getting no answer but: "Thanks, I've had all I want," or something similar. Perhaps they drank nothing either. Time and again his sister kept asking his father if he wouldn't like some beer and offered kindly to go and fetch it herself, and when he made no answer suggested that she could ask the concierge[1] to fetch it, so that he need feel no sense of obligation, but then a round "No" came from his father and no more was said about it.

In the course of that very first day Gregor's father explained the family's financial position and prospects to both his mother and his sister. Now and then he rose from the table to get some voucher or memorandum out of the small safe he had rescued from the collapse of his business five years earlier. One could hear him opening the complicated lock and rustling papers out and shutting it again. This statement made by his father was the first cheerful information Gregor had heard since his imprisonment. He had been of the opinion that nothing at all was left over from his father's business, at least his father had never said anything to the contrary, and of course he had not asked him directly. At that time Gregor's sole desire was to do his utmost to help the family to forget as soon as possible the catastrophe which had overwhelmed the business and thrown them all into a state of complete despair. And so he had set to work with unusual ardor and almost overnight had become a commercial traveler instead of a little clerk, with of course much greater chances of earning money, and his success was immediately translated into good round coin which he could lay on the table for his amazed and happy family. These had been fine times, and they had never recurred, at least not with the same sense of glory, although later on Gregor had earned so much money that he was able to

---

1. The person who is caretaker of a building or a hotel.

meet the expenses of the whole household and did so. They had simply got used to it, both the family and Gregor; the money was gratefully accepted and gladly given, but there was no special uprush of warm feeling. With his sister alone had he remained intimate, and it was a secret plan of his that she, who loved music, unlike himself, and could play movingly on the violin, should be sent next year to study at the Conservatorium, despite the great expense that would entail, which must be made up in some other way. During his brief visits home the Conservatorium was often mentioned in the talks he had with his sister, but always merely as a beautiful dream which could never come true, and his parents discouraged even these innocent references to it; yet Gregor had made up his mind firmly about it and meant to announce the fact with due solemnity on Christmas Day.

Such were the thoughts, completely futile in his present condition, that went through his head as he stood clinging upright to the door and listening. Sometimes out of sheer weariness he had to give up listening and let his head fall negligently against the door, but he always had to pull himself together again at once, for even the slight sound his head made was audible next door and brought all conversation to a stop. "What can he be doing now?" his father would say after a while, obviously turning towards the door, and only then would the interrupted conversation gradually be set going again.

Gregor was now informed as amply as he could wish—for his father tended to repeat himself in his explanations, partly because it was a long time since he had handled such matters and partly because his mother could not always grasp things at once—that a certain amount of investments, a very small amount it was true, had survived the wreck of their fortunes and had even increased a little because the dividends had not been touched meanwhile. And besides that, the money Gregor brought home every month—he had kept only a few dollars for himself—had never been quite used up and now amounted to a small capital sum. Behind the door Gregor nodded his head eagerly, rejoiced at this evidence of unexpected thrift and foresight. True, he could really have paid off some more of his father's debts to the chief with his extra money, and so brought much nearer the day on which he could quit his job, but doubtless it was better the way his father had arranged it.

Yet this capital was by no means sufficient to let the family live on the interest of it; for one year, perhaps, or at the most two, they could live on the principal, that was all. It was simply a sum that ought not to be touched and should be kept for a rainy day; money for living expenses would have to be earned. Now his father was still hale enough but an old man, and he had done no work for the past five years and could not be expected to do much; during these five years, the first years of leisure in his laborious though unsuccessful life, he had grown rather fat and become sluggish. And Gregor's old mother, how was she to earn a living with her asthma, which troubled her even when she walked through the flat and kept her lying on a sofa every other day panting for breath beside an open window? And was his sister to earn her bread, she who was still a child of seventeen and whose life hitherto had been so pleasant, consisting as it did in dressing herself nicely, sleeping long, helping in the housekeeping, going out to a few modest entertainments and above all playing the violin? At first whenever the need for earning money was mentioned Gregor let go his hold on the door and threw himself down on the cool leather sofa beside it, he felt so hot with shame and grief.

Often he just lay there the long nights through without sleeping at all, scrabbling for hours on the leather. Or he nerved himself to the great effort of pushing an armchair to the window, then crawled up over the window sill and, braced against the chair, leaned against the window panes, obviously in some recollection of the sense of freedom that looking out of a window always used to give him. For in reality day by day things that were even a little way off were growing dimmer to his sight; the hospital across the street, which he used to execrate for being all too often before his eyes, was now quite beyond his range of vision, and if he had not known that he lived in Charlotte Street, a quiet street but still a city street, he might have believed that his window gave on a desert waste where gray sky and gray land blended indistinguishably into each other. His quick-witted sister only needed to observe twice that the armchair stood by the window; after that whenever she had tidied the room she always pushed the chair back to the same place at the window and even left the inner casements open.

If he could have spoken to her and thanked her for all she had to do for him, he could have borne her ministrations better; as it was, they oppressed him. She certainly tried to make as light as possible of whatever was disagreeable in her task, and as time went on she succeeded, of course, more and more, but time brought more enlightenment to Gregor too. The very way she came in distressed him. Hardly was she in the room when she rushed to the window, without even taking time to shut the door, careful as she was usually to shield the sight of Gregor's room from the others, and as if she were almost suffocating tore the casements open with hasty fingers, standing then in the open draught for a while even in the bitterest cold and drawing deep breaths. This noisy scurry of hers upset Gregor twice a day; he would crouch trembling under the sofa all the time, knowing quite well that she would certainly have spared him such a disturbance had she found it at all possible to stay in his presence without opening a window.

On one occasion, about a month after Gregor's metamorphosis, when there was surely no reason for her to be still startled at his appearance, she came a little earlier than usual and found him gazing out of the window, quite motionless, and thus well placed to look like a bogey. Gregor would not have been surprised had she not come in at all, for she could not immediately open the window while he was there, but not only did she retreat, she jumped back as if in alarm and banged the door shut; a stranger might well have thought that he had been lying in wait for her there meaning to bite her. Of course he hid himself under the sofa at once, but he had to wait until midday before she came again, and she seemed more ill at ease than usual. This made him realize how repulsive the sight of him still was to her, and that it was bound to go on being repulsive, and what an effort it must cost her not to run away even from the sight of the small portion of his body that stuck out from under the sofa. In order to spare her that, therefore, one day he carried a sheet on his back to the sofa—it cost him four hours' labor—and arranged it there in such a way as to hide him completely, so that even if she were to bend down she could not see him. Had she considered the sheet unnecessary, she would certainly have stripped it off the sofa again, for it was clear enough that this curtaining and confining of himself was not likely to conduce Gregor's comfort, but she left it where it was, and Gregor even fancied that he caught a thankful glance from her eye when he lifted the sheet carefully a very little with his head to see how she was taking the new arrangement.

For the first fortnight his parents could not bring themselves to the point of entering his room, and he often heard them expressing their appreciation of his sister's activities, whereas formerly they had frequently scolded her for being as they thought a somewhat useless daughter. But now, both of them often waited outside the door, his father and his mother, while his sister tidied his room, and as soon as she came out she had to tell them exactly how things were in the room, what Gregor had eaten, how he had conducted himself this time and whether there was not perhaps some slight improvement in his condition. His mother, moreover, began relatively soon to want to visit him, but his father and sister dissuaded her at first with arguments which Gregor listened to very attentively and altogether approved. Later, however, she had to be held back by main force, and when she cried out: "Do let me in to Gregor, he is my unfortunate son! Can't you understand that I must go to him?" Gregor thought that it might be well to have her come in, not every day, of course, but perhaps once a week; she understood things, after all, much better than his sister, who was only a child despite the efforts she was making and had perhaps taken on so difficult a task merely out of childish thoughtlessness.

Gregor's desire to see his mother was soon fulfilled. During the daytime he did not want to show himself at the window, out of consideration for his parents, but he could not crawl very far around the few square yards of floor space he had, nor could he bear lying quietly at rest all during the night, while he was fast losing any interest he had ever taken in food, so that for mere recreation he had formed the habit of crawling crisscross over the walls and ceiling. He especially enjoyed hanging suspended from the ceiling; it was much better than lying on the floor; one could breathe more freely; one's body swung and rocked lightly; and in the almost blissful absorption induced by this suspension it could happen to his own surprise that he let go and fell plump on the floor. Yet he now had his body much better under control than formerly, and even such a big fall did him no harm. His sister at once remarked the new distraction Gregor had found for himself—he left traces behind him of the sticky stuff on his soles wherever he crawled—and she got the idea in her head of giving him as wide a field as possible to crawl in and of removing the pieces of furniture that hindered him, above all the chest of drawers and the writing desk. But that was more than she could manage all by herself; she did not dare ask her father to help her; and as for the servant girl, a young creature of sixteen who had had the courage to stay on after the cook's departure, she could not be asked to help, for she had begged as an especial favor that she might keep the kitchen door locked and open it only on a definite summons; so there was nothing left but to apply to her mother at an hour when her father was out. And the old lady did come, with exclamations of joyful eagerness, which, however, died away at the door of Gregor's room. Gregor's sister, of course, went in first, to see that everything was in order before letting his mother enter. In great haste Gregor pulled the sheet lower and rucked it more in folds so that it really looked as if it had been thrown accidentally over the sofa. And this time he did not peer out from under it; he renounced the pleasure of seeing his mother on this occasion and was only glad that she had come at all. "Come in, he's out of sight," said his sister, obviously leading her mother in by the hand. Gregor could now hear the two women struggling to shift the heavy old chest from its place, and his sister claiming the greater part of the labor for herself, without listening to the admonitions of her mother who feared she might overstrain herself. It took a long time. After at least a quarter of an hour's tugging his mother objected that the chest had better be left where it was, for in the first place it was too heavy and could never be got out before his father came home, and standing in the middle of the room like that it would only hamper Gregor's movements, while in the second place it was not at all certain that removing the furniture would be doing a service to Gregor. She was inclined to think to the contrary; the sight of the naked walls made her own heart heavy, and why shouldn't Gregor have the same feeling, considering that he had been used to his furniture for so long and might feel forlorn without it. "And doesn't it look," she concluded in a low voice—in fact she had been almost whispering all the time as if to avoid letting Gregor, whose exact whereabouts she did not know, hear even the tones of her voice, for she was convinced that he could not understand her words—"doesn't it look as if we were showing him, by taking away his furniture, that we have given up hope of his ever getting better and are just leaving him coldly to himself? I think it would be best to keep his room exactly as it has always been, so that when he comes back to us he will find everything unchanged and be able all the more easily to forget what has happened in between."

On hearing these words from his mother Gregor realized that the lack of all direct human speech for the past two months together with the monotony of family life must have confused his mind, otherwise he could not account for the fact that he had quite earnestly looked forward to having his room emptied of furnishing. Did he really want his warm room, so comfortably fitted with old family furniture, to be turned into a naked den in which he would certainly be able to crawl unhampered in all directions but at the price of shedding simultaneously all recollection of his human background? He had indeed been so near the brink of forgetfulness that only the voice of his mother, which he had not heard for so long, had drawn him back from it. Nothing should be taken out of his room; everything must stay as it was; he could not dispense with the good influence of the furniture on his state of mind; and even if the furniture did hamper him in his senseless crawling round and round, that was no drawback but a great advantage.

Unfortunately his sister was of the contrary opinion; she had grown accustomed, and not without reason, to consider herself an expert in Gregor's affairs as against her parents, and so her mother's advice was now enough to make her determined on the removal not only of the chest and the writing desk, which had been her first intention, but of all the furniture except the indispensable sofa. This determination was not, of course, merely the outcome of childish recalcitrance and of the self-confidence she had recently developed so unexpectedly and at such cost; she had in fact perceived that Gregor needed a lot of space to crawl about in, while on the other hand he never used the furniture at all, so far as could be seen. Another factor might have been also the enthusiastic temperament of an adolescent girl, which seeks to indulge itself on every opportunity and which now tempted Grete to exaggerate the horror of her brother's circumstances in order that she might do all the more for him. In a room where Gregor lorded it all alone over empty walls no one save herself was likely ever to set foot.

And so she was not to be moved from her resolve by her mother who seemed moreover to be ill at ease in Gregor's room and therefore unsure of herself, was soon reduced to silence and helped her daughter as best she could to push the chest outside. Now, Gregor could do without the chest, if need be, but the writing desk he must retain. As soon as the two women had got the chest out of his room, groaning as they pushed it, Gregor stuck his head out from under the sofa to see how he might intervene as kindly and cautiously as possible. But as bad luck would have it, his mother was the first to return, leaving Grete clasping the chest in the room next door where she was trying to shift it all by herself, without of course moving it from the spot. His mother however was not accustomed to the sight of him, it might sicken her and so in alarm Gregor backed quickly to the other end of the sofa, yet could not prevent the sheet from swaying a little in front. That was enough to put her on the alert. She paused, stood still for a moment and then went back to Grete.

Although Gregor kept reassuring himself that nothing out of the way was happening, but only a few bits of furniture were being changed round, he soon had to admit that all this trotting to and fro of the two women, their little ejaculations and the scraping of furniture along the floor affected him like a vast disturbance coming from all sides at once, and however much he tucked in his head and legs and cowered to the very floor he was bound to confess that he would not be able to stand it for long. They were clearing his room out; taking away everything he loved; the chest in which he kept his fret saw and other tools was already dragged off; they were now loosening the writing desk which had almost sunk into the floor, the desk at which he had done all his homework when he was at the commercial academy, at the grammar school before that, and, yes, even at the primary school—he had no more time to waste in weighing the good intentions of the two women, whose existence he had by now almost forgotten, for they were so exhausted that they were laboring in silence and nothing could be heard but the heavy scuffling of their feet.

And so he rushed out—the women were just leaning against the writing desk in the next room to give themselves a breather—and four times changed his direction, since he really did not know what to rescue first, then on the wall opposite, which was already otherwise cleared, he was struck by the picture of the lady muffled in so much fur and quickly crawled up to it and pressed himself to the glass, which was a good surface to hold on to and comforted his hot belly. This picture at least, which was entirely hidden beneath him, was going to be removed by nobody. He turned his head towards the door of the living room so as to observe the women when they came back.

They had not allowed themselves much of a rest and were already coming; Grete had twined her arm round her mother and was almost supporting her. "Well, what shall we take now?" said Grete, looking round. Her eyes met Gregor's from the wall. She kept her composure, presumably because of her mother, bent her head down to her mother, to keep her from looking up, and said, although in a fluttering, unpremeditated voice: "Come, hadn't we better go back to the living room for a moment?" Her intentions were clear enough to Gregor, she wanted to bestow her mother in safety and then chase him down from the wall. Well, just let her try it! He clung to his picture and would not give it up. He would rather fly in Grete's face.

But Grete's words had succeeded in disquieting her mother, who took a step to one side, caught sight of the huge brown mass on the flowered wallpaper, and before she was really conscious that what she saw was Gregor screamed in a loud, hoarse voice: "Oh God, oh God!" fell with outspread arms over the sofa as if giving up and did not move. "Gregor!" cried his sister, shaking her fist and glaring at him. This was the first time she had directly addressed him since his metamorphosis. She ran into the next room for some aromatic essence with which to rouse her mother from her fainting fit. Gregor wanted to help too—there was still time to rescue the picture—but he was stuck fast to the glass and had to tear himself loose; he then ran after his sister into the next room as if he could advise her, as he used to do; but then had to stand helplessly behind her; she meanwhile searched among various small bottles and when she turned round started in alarm at the sight of him; one bottle fell on the floor and broke; a splinter of glass cut Gregor's face and some kind of corrosive medicine splashed him; without pausing a moment longer Grete gathered up all the bottles she could carry and ran to her mother with them; she banged the door shut with her foot. Gregor was now cut off from his mother, who was perhaps nearly dying because of him; he dared not open the door for fear of frightening away his sister, who had to stay with her mother; there was nothing he could do but wait; and harassed by self-reproach and worry he began now to crawl to and fro, over everything, walls, furniture and ceiling, and finally in his despair, when the whole room seemed to be reeling round him, fell down on to the middle of the big table.

A little while elapsed, Gregor was still lying there feebly and all around was quiet, perhaps that was a good omen. Then the doorbell rang. The servant girl was of course locked in her kitchen, and Grete would have to open the door. It was his father. "What's been happening?" were his first words; Grete's face must have told him everything. Grete answered in a muffled voice, apparently hiding her head on his breast: "Mother has been fainting, but she's better now. Gregor's broken loose." "Just what I expected," said his father, "just what I've been telling you, but you women would never listen." It was clear to Gregor that his father had taken the worst interpretation of Grete's all too brief statement and was assuming that Gregor had been guilty of some violent act. Therefore Gregor must now try to propitiate his father, since he had neither time nor means for an explanation. And so he fled to the door of his own room and crouched against it, to let his father see as soon as he came in from the hall that his son had the good intention of getting back into his room immediately and that it was not necessary to drive him there, but that if only the door were opened he would disappear at once.

Yet his father was not in the mood to perceive such fine distinctions. "Ah!" he cried as soon as he appeared, in a tone which sounded at once angry and exultant. Gregor drew his head back from the door and lifted it to look at his father. Truly, this was not the father he had imagined to himself; admittedly he had been too absorbed of late in his new recreation of crawling over the ceiling to take the same interest as before in what was happening elsewhere in the flat, and he ought really to be prepared for some changes. And yet, and yet, could that be his father? The man who used to lie wearily sunk in bed whenever Gregor set out on a business journey; who welcomed him back of an evening lying in a long chair in a dressing gown; who could not really rise to his feet but only lifted his arms in greeting, and on the rare occasions when he did go out with his family, on one or two Sundays a year and on high holidays, walked between Gregor and his mother, who were slow walkers anyhow, even more slowly than they did, muffled in his old great-coat, shuffling laboriously forward with the help of his crook-handled stick which he set down most cautiously at every step and, whenever he wanted to say anything, nearly always came to a full stop and gathered his escort around him? Now he was standing there in fine shape; dressed in a smart blue uniform with gold buttons, such as bank messengers wear; his strong double chin bulged over the stiff high collar of his jacket;

from under his bushy eyebrows his black eyes darted fresh and penetrating glances; his onetime tangled white hair had been combed flat on either side of a shining and carefully exact parting. He pitched his cap, which bore a gold monogram, probably the badge of some bank, in a wide sweep across the whole room on to a sofa and with the tail-ends of his jacket thrown back, his hands in his trouser pockets, advanced with a grim visage towards Gregor. Likely enough he did not himself know what he meant to do; at any rate he lifted his feet uncommonly high, and Gregor was dumbfounded at the enormous size of his shoe soles. But Gregor could not risk standing up to him, aware as he had been from the very first day of his new life that his father believed only the severest measures suitable for dealing with him. And so he ran before his father, stopping when he stopped and scuttling forward again when his father made any kind of move. In this way they circled the room several times without anything decisive happening; indeed the whole operation did not even look like a pursuit because it was carried out so slowly. And so Gregor did not leave the floor, for he feared that his father might take as a piece of peculiar wickedness any excursion of his over the walls or the ceiling. All the same, he could not stay this course much longer, for while his father took one step he had to carry out a whole series of movements. He was already beginning to feel breathless, just as in his former life his lungs had not been very dependable. As he was staggering along, trying to concentrate his energy on running, hardly keeping his eyes open; in his dazed state never even thinking of any other escape than simply going forward; and having almost forgotten that the walls were free to him, which in this room were well provided with finely carved pieces of furniture full of knobs and crevices—suddenly something lightly flung landed close behind him and rolled before him. It was an apple; a second apple followed immediately; Gregor came to a stop in alarm; there was no point in running on, for his father was determined to bombard him. He had filled his pockets with fruit from the dish on the sideboard and was now shying apple after apple, without taking particularly good aim for the moment. The small red apples rolled about the floor as if magnetized and cannoned into each other. An apple thrown without much force grazed Gregor's back and glanced off harmlessly. But another following immediately landed right on his back and sank in; Gregor wanted to drag himself forward, as if this startling, incredible pain could be left behind him: but he felt as if nailed to the spot and flattened himself out in a complete derangement of all his senses. With his last conscious look he saw the door of his room being torn open and his mother rushing out ahead of his screaming sister, in her underbodice, for her daughter had loosened her clothing to let her breathe more freely and recover from her swoon, he saw his mother rushing towards his father, leaving one after another behind her on the floor her loosened petticoats, stumbling over her petticoats straight to his father and embracing him, in complete union with him—but here Gregor's sight began to fail—with her hands clasped round his father's neck as she begged for her son's life.

3

The serious injury done to Gregor, which disabled him for more than a month—the apple went on sticking in his body as a visible reminder, since no one ventured to remove it—seemed to have made even his father recollect that Gregor was a member of the family, despite his present unfortunate and repulsive shape, and ought not to be treated as an enemy, that, on the contrary, family duty required the suppression of disgust and the exercise of patience, nothing but patience.

And although his injury had impaired, probably for ever, his power of movement, and for the time being it took him long, long minutes to creep across his room like an old invalid—there was no question now of crawling up the wall—yet in his own opinion he was sufficiently compensated for this worsening of his condition by the fact that towards evening the living-room door, which he used to watch intently for an hour or two beforehand, was always thrown open, so that lying in the darkness of his room, invisible to the family, he could see them all at the lamp-lit table and listen to their talk, by general consent as it were, very different from his earlier eavesdropping.

True, their intercourse lacked the lively character of former times, which he had always called to mind with a certain wistfulness in the small hotel bedrooms where he had been wont to throw himself down, tired out, on damp bedding. They were now mostly very silent. Soon after supper his father would fall asleep in his armchair; his mother and sister would admonish each other to be silent; his mother, bending low over the lamp, stitched at fine sewing for an underwear firm; his sister, who had taken a job as a salesgirl, was learning shorthand and French in the evenings on the chance of bettering herself. Sometimes his father woke up, and as if quite unaware that he had been sleeping said to his mother: "What a lot of sewing you're doing today!" and at once fell asleep again, while the two women exchanged a tired smile.

With a kind of mulishness his father persisted in keeping his uniform on even in the house; his dressing gown hung uselessly on its peg and he slept fully dressed where he sat, as if he were ready for service at any moment and even here only at the beck and call of his superior. As a result, his uniform, which was not brand-new to start with, began to look dirty, despite all the loving care of the mother and sister to keep it clean, and Gregor often spent whole evenings gazing at the many greasy spots on the garment, gleaming with gold buttons always in a high state of polish, in which the old man sat sleeping in extreme discomfort and yet quite peacefully.

As soon as the clock struck ten his mother tried to rouse his father with gentle words and to persuade him after that to get into bed, for sitting there he could not have a proper sleep and that was what he needed most, since he had to go to duty at six. But with the mulishness that had obsessed him since he became a bank messenger he always insisted on staying longer at the table, although he regularly fell asleep again and in the end only with the greatest trouble could be got out of his armchair and into his bed. How-

Franz Kafka   253

ever insistently Gregor's mother and sister kept urging him with gentle reminders, he would go on slowly shaking his head for a quarter of an hour, keeping his eyes shut, and refuse to get to his feet. The mother plucked at his sleeve, whispering endearments in his ear, the sister left her lessons to come to her mother's help, but Gregor's father was not to be caught. He would only sink down deeper in his chair. Not until the two women hoisted him up by the armpits did he open his eyes and look at them both, one after the other, usually with the remark: "This is a life. This is the peace and quiet of my old age." And leaning on the two of them he would heave himself up, with difficulty, as if he were a great burden to himself, suffer them to lead him as far as the door and then wave them off and go on alone, while the mother abandoned her needlework and the sister her pen in order to run after him and help him farther.

Who could find time, in this overworked and tired-out family, to bother about Gregor more than was absolutely needful? The household was reduced more and more; the servant girl was turned off; a gigantic bony charwoman with white hair flying round her head came in morning and evening to do the rough work; everything else was done by Gregor's mother, as well as great piles of sewing. Even various family ornaments, which his mother and sister used to wear with pride at parties and celebrations, had to be sold, as Gregor discovered of an evening from hearing them all discuss the prices obtained. But what they lamented most was the fact that they could not leave the flat which was much too big for their present circumstances, because they could not think of any way to shift Gregor. Yet Gregor saw well enough that consideration for him was not the main difficulty preventing the removal, for they could have easily shifted him in some suitable box with a few air holes in it; what really kept them from moving into another flat was rather their own complete hopelessness and the belief that they had been singled out for a misfortune such as had never happened to any of their relations or acquaintances. They fulfilled to the uttermost all that the world demands of poor people, the father fetched breakfast for the small clerks in the bank, the mother devoted her energy to making underwear for strangers, the sister trotted to and fro behind the counter at the behest of customers, but more than this they had not the strength to do. And the wound in Gregor's back began to nag at him afresh when his mother and sister, after getting his father into bed, came back again, left their work lying, drew close to each other and sat cheek by cheek; when his mother, pointing towards his room, said: "Shut that door now, Grete," and he was left again in darkness, while next door the women mingled their tears or perhaps sat dry-eyed staring at the table.

Gregor hardly slept at all by night or by day. He was often haunted by the idea that next time the door opened he would take the family's affairs in hand again just as he used to do; once more, after this long interval, there appeared in his thoughts the figures of the chief and the chief clerk, the commercial travelers and the apprentices, the porter who was so dull-witted, two or three friends in other firms, a chambermaid in one of the rural hotels, a sweet and fleeting memory, a cashier in a milliner's shop, whom he had wooed earnestly but too slowly—they all appeared, together with strangers or people he had quite forgotten, but instead of helping him and his family they were one and all unapproachable and he was glad when they vanished. At other times he would not be in the mood to bother about his family, he was only filled with rage at the way they were neglecting him, and although he had no clear idea of what he might care to eat he would make plans for getting into the larder to take the food that was after all his due, even if he were not hungry. His sister no longer took thought to bring him what might especially please him, but in the morning and at noon before she went to business hurriedly pushed into his room with her foot any food that was available, and in the evening cleared it out again with one sweep of the broom, heedless of whether it had been merely tasted, or—as most frequently happened—left untouched. The cleaning of his room, which she now did always in the evenings, could not have been more hastily done. Streaks of dirt stretched along the walls, here and there lay balls of dust and filth. At first Gregor used to station himself in some particularly filthy corner when his sister arrived, in order to reproach her with it, so to speak. But he could have sat there for weeks without getting her to make any improvements; she could see the dirt as well as he did, but she had simply made up her mind to leave it alone. And yet, with a touchiness that was new to her, which seemed anyhow to have infected the whole family, she jealously guarded her claim to be the sole caretaker of Gregor's room. His mother once subjected his room to a thorough cleaning, which was achieved only by means of several buckets of water—all this dampness of course upset Gregor too and he lay widespread, sulky and motionless on the sofa—but she was well punished for it. Hardly had his sister noticed the changed aspect of his room that evening than she rushed in high dudgeon into the living room and, despite the imploringly raised hands of her mother, burst into a storm of weeping, while her parents—her father had of course been startled out of his chair—looked on at first in helpless amazement; then they too began to go into action; the father reproached the mother on his right for not having left the cleaning of Gregor's room to his sister; shrieked at the sister on his left that never again was she to be allowed to clean Gregor's room; while the mother tried to pull the father into his bedroom, since he was beyond himself with agitation; the sister, shaken with sobs, then beat upon the table with her small fists; and Gregor hissed loudly with rage because not one of them thought of shutting the door to spare him such a spectacle and so much noise.

Still, even if the sister, exhausted by her daily work, had grown tired of looking after Gregor as she did formerly, there was no need for his mother's intervention or for Gregor's being neglected at all. The charwoman was there. This old widow, whose strong bony frame had enabled her to survive the worst a long life could offer, by no means recoiled from Gregor. Without being in the least curious she had once by chance opened the door of his room and at the sight of Gregor, who, taken by surprise, began to rush to and fro although no one was chasing him, merely stood there with her arms folded. From that time she never failed to open his door a little for a moment, morning and evening, to have a look at him. At first she even used to call him to her, with words which apparently she took to be friendly, such as: "Come along, then, you old dung beetle!" or "Look at the old dung beetle, then!" To such allocutions Gregor made no answer, but stayed motionless where he was, as if the door had never been opened. Instead of being allowed to disturb him so senselessly whenever the whim took her, she should rather have been ordered to clean out his room daily, that charwoman! Once, early in the morning—heavy rain was lashing on the windowpanes, perhaps a sign that spring was on the way—Gregor was so exasperated when she began addressing him again that he ran at her, as if to attack her, although slowly and feebly enough. But the charwoman instead of showing fright merely lifted high a chair that happened to be beside the door, and as she stood there with her mouth wide open it was clear that she meant to shut it only when she brought the chair down on Gregor's back. "So you're not coming any nearer?" she asked, as Gregor turned away again, and quietly put the chair back into the corner.

Gregor was now eating hardly anything. Only when he happened to pass the food laid out for him did he take a bit of something in his mouth as a pastime, kept it there for an hour at a time and usually spat it out again. At first he thought it was chagrin over the state of his room that prevented him from eating, yet he soon got used to the various changes in his room. It had become a habit in the family to push into his room things there was no room for elsewhere, and there were plenty of these now, since one of the rooms had been let to three lodgers. These serious gentlemen—all three of them with full beards, as Gregor once observed through a crack in the door —had a passion for order, not only in their own room but, since they were now members of the household, in all its arrangements, especially in the kitchen. Superfluous, not to say dirty, objects they could not bear. Besides, they had brought with them most of the furnishings they needed. For this reason many things could be dispensed with that it was no use trying to sell but that should not be thrown away either. All of them found their way into Gregor's room. The ash can likewise and the kitchen garbage can. Anything that was not needed for the moment was simply flung into Gregor's room by the charwoman, who did everything in a hurry; fortunately Gregor usually saw only the object, whatever it was, and the hand that held it. Perhaps she intended to take the things away again as time and opportunity offered, or to collect them until she could throw them all out in a heap, but in fact they just lay wherever she happened to throw them, except when Gregor pushed his way through the junk heap and shifted it somewhat, at first out of necessity, because he had not room enough to crawl, but later with increasing enjoyment, although after such excursions, being sad and weary to death, he would lie motionless for hours. And since the lodgers often ate their supper at home in the common living room, the living-room door stayed shut many an evening, yet Gregor reconciled himself quite easily to the shutting of the door, for often enough on evenings when it was opened he had disregarded it entirely and lain in the darkest corner of his room, quite unnoticed by the family. But on one occasion the charwoman left the door open a little and it stayed ajar even when the lodgers came in for supper and the lamp was lit. They set themselves at the top end of the table where formerly Gregor and his father and mother had eaten their meals, unfolded their napkins and took knife and fork in hand. At once his mother appeared in the other doorway with a dish of meat and close behind her his sister with a dish of potatoes piled high. The food steamed with a thick vapor. The lodgers bent over the food set before them as if to scrutinize it before eating, in fact the man in the middle, who seemed to pass for an authority with the other two, cut a piece of meat as it lay on the dish, obviously to discover if it were tender or should be sent back to the kitchen. He showed satisfaction, and Gregor's mother and sister, who had been watching anxiously, breathed freely and began to smile.

The family itself took its meals in the kitchen. Nonetheless, Gregor's father came into the living room before going into the kitchen and with one prolonged bow, cap in hand, made a round of the table. The lodgers all stood up and murmured something in their beards. When they were alone again they ate their food in almost complete silence. It seemed remarkable to Gregor that among the various noises coming from the table he could always distinguish the sound of their masticating teeth, as if this were a sign to Gregor that one needed teeth in order to eat, and that with toothless jaws even of the finest make one could do nothing. "I'm hungry enough," said Gregor sadly to himself, "But not for that kind of food. How these lodgers are stuffing themselves, and here am I dying of starvation!"

On that very evening—during the whole of his time there Gregor could not remember ever having heard the violin—the sound of violin-playing came from the kitchen. The lodgers had already finished their supper, the one in the middle had brought out a newspaper and given the other two a page apiece, and now they were leaning back at ease reading and smoking. When the violin began to play they pricked up their ears, got to their feet, and went on tiptoe to the hall door where they stood huddled together. Their movements must have been heard in the kitchen, for Gregor's father called out: "Is the violin-playing disturbing you, gentlemen? It can be stopped at once." "On the contrary," said the middle lodger, "could not Fräulein Samsa come and play in this room, beside us, where it is much more convenient and comfortable?" "Oh certainly," cried Gregor's father, as if he were the violin-player. The lodgers came back into the living room and waited. Presently Gregor's father arrived with the music stand, his mother carrying the music and his sister with the violin. His sister quietly made everything ready to start playing; his parents, who had never let rooms before and so had an exaggerated idea of the courtesy due to lodgers, did not venture to sit down on their own chairs; his father leaned against the door, the right hand thrust between two buttons of his livery coat, which was formally buttoned up; but his mother was offered a chair by one of the lodgers and, since she left the chair just where he had happened to put it, sat down in a corner to one side.

Gregor's sister began to play; the father and mother, from either side, intently watched the movements of her hands. Gregor, attracted by the playing, ventured to move forward a little until his head was actually inside the living room. He felt hardly any surprise at his growing lack of consideration for the others; there had been a time when he prided himself on being considerate. And yet just on this occasion he had more reason than ever to hide himself, since owing to the amount of dust which lay thick in his room and rose into the air at the slightest movement, he too was covered with dust; fluff and hair and remnants of food trailed with him, caught on his back and along his sides; his indifference to everything was much too great for him to turn on his back and scrape himself clean on the carpet, as once he had done several times a day. And in spite of his condition, no shame deterred him from advancing a little over the spotless floor of the living room.

To be sure, no one was aware of him. The family was entirely absorbed in the violin-playing; the lodgers, however, who first of all had stationed themselves, hands in pockets, much too close behind the music stand so that they could all have read the music, which must have bothered his sister, had soon retreated to the window, half-whispering with downbent heads, and stayed there while his father turned an anxious eye on them. Indeed, they were making it more than obvious that they had been disappointed in their expectation of hearing good or enjoyable violin-playing, that they had had more than enough of the performance and only out of courtesy suffered a continued disturbance of their peace. From the way they all kept blowing the smoke of their cigars high in the air through nose and mouth one could divine their irritation. And yet Gregor's sister was playing so beautifully. Her face leaned sideways, intently and sadly her eyes followed the notes of music. Gregor crawled a little farther forward and lowered his head to the ground so that it might be possible for his eyes to meet hers. Was he an animal, that music had such an effect upon him? He felt as if the way were opening before him to the unknown nourishment he craved. He was determined to push forward till he reached his sister, to pull at her skirt and so let her know that she was to come into his room with her violin, for no one here appreciated her playing as he would appreciate it. He would never let her out of his room, at least, not so long as he lived; his frightful appearance would become, for the first time, useful to him; he would watch all the doors of his room at once and spit at intruders; but his sister should need no constraint, she should stay with him of her own free will; she should sit beside him on the sofa, bend down her ear to him and hear him confide that he had had the firm intention of sending her to the Conservatorium, and that, but for his mishap, last Christmas—surely Christmas was long past?—he would have announced it to everybody without allowing a single objection. After this confession his sister would be so touched that she would burst into tears, and Gregor would then raise himself to her shoulder and kiss her on the neck, which, now that she went to business, she kept free of any ribbon or collar.

"Mr. Samsa!" cried the middle lodger, to Gregor's father, and pointed, without wasting any more words, at Gregor, now working himself slowly forwards. The violin fell silent, the middle lodger first smiled to his friends with a shake of the head and then looked at Gregor again. Instead of driving Gregor out, his father seemed to think it more needful to begin by soothing down the lodgers, although they were not at all agitated and apparently found Gregor more entertaining than the violin-playing. He hurried toward them and, spreading out his arms, tried to urge them back into their own room and at the same time to block their view of Gregor. They now began to be really a little angry, one could not tell whether because of the old man's behavior or because it had just dawned on them that all unwittingly they had such a neighbor as Gregor next door. They demanded explanations of his father, they waved their arms like him, tugged uneasily at their beards, and only with reluctance backed towards their room. Meanwhile Gregor's sister, who stood there as if lost when her playing was so abruptly broken off, came to life again, pulled herself together all at once after standing for a while holding violin and bow in nervelessly hanging hands and staring at her music, pushed her violin into the lap of her mother, who was still sitting in her chair fighting asthmatically for breath, and ran into the lodgers' room to which they were now being shepherded by her father rather more quickly than before. One could see the pillows and blankets on the beds flying under her accustomed fingers and being laid in order. Before the lodgers had actually reached their room she had finished making the beds and slipped out.

The old man seemed once more to be so possessed by his mulish self-assertiveness that he was forgetting all the respect he should show to his lodgers. He kept driving them on and driving them on until in the very door of the bedroom the middle lodger stamped his foot loudly on the floor and so brought him to a halt. "I beg to announce," said the lodger, lifting one hand and looking also at Gregor's mother and sister, "that because of the disgusting conditions prevailing in this household and family"—here he spat on the floor with emphatic brevity—"I give you notice on the spot. Naturally I won't pay you a penny for the days I have lived here, on the contrary I shall consider bringing an action for damages against you, based on claims—believe me—that will be easily susceptible of proof." He ceased and stared straight in front of him, as if he expected something. In fact his two friends at once rushed into the breach with these words: "And we too give notice on the spot." On that he seized the door-handle and shut the door with a slam.

Gregor's father, groping with his hands, staggered forward and fell into his chair; it looked as if he were stretching himself there for his ordinary evening nap, but the marked jerkings of his head, which was as if uncontrollable, showed that he was far from asleep. Gregor had simply stayed quietly all the time on the spot where the lodgers had espied him.

Disappointment at the failure of his plan, perhaps also the weakness arising from extreme hunger, made it impossible for him to move. He feared, with a fair degree of certainty, that at any moment the general tension would discharge itself in a combined attack upon him, and he lay waiting. He did not react even to the noise made by the violin as it fell off his mother's lap from under her trembling fingers and gave out a resonant note.

"My dear parents," said his sister, slapping her hand on the table by way of introduction, "things can't go on like this. Perhaps you don't realize that, but I do. I won't utter my brother's name in the presence of this creature, and so all I say is: we must try to get rid of it. We've tried to look after it and to put up with it as far as is humanly possible, and I don't think anyone could reproach us in the slightest."

"She is more than right," said Gregor's father to himself. His mother, who was still choking for lack of breath, began to cough hollowly into her hand with a wild look in her eyes.

His sister rushed over to her and held her forehead. His father's thoughts seemed to have lost their vagueness at Grete's words, he sat more upright, fingering his service cap that lay among the plates still lying on the table from the lodgers' supper, and from time to time looked at the still form of Gregor.

"We must try to get rid of it," his sister now said explicitly to her father, since her mother was coughing too much to hear a word, "it will be the death of both of you, I can see that coming. When one has to work as hard as we do, all of us, one can't stand this continual torment at home on top of it. At least I can't stand it any longer." And she burst into such a passion of sobbing that her tears dropped on her mother's face, where she wiped them off mechanically.

"My dear," said the old man sympathetically, and with evident understanding, "but what can we do?"

Gregor's sister merely shrugged her shoulders to indicate the feeling of helplessness that had now overmastered her during her weeping fit, in contrast to her former confidence.

"If he could understand us," said her father, half questioningly; Grete, still sobbing, vehemently waved a hand to show how unthinkable that was.

"If he could understand us," repeated the old man, shutting his eyes to consider his daughter's conviction that understanding was impossible, "then perhaps we might come to some agreement with him. But as it is—"

"He must go," cried Gregor's sister, "That's the only solution, Father. You must just try to get rid of the idea that this is Gregor. The fact that we've believed it for so long is the root of all our trouble. But how can it be Gregor? If this were Gregor, he would have realized long ago that human beings can't live with such a creature, and he'd have gone away on his own accord. Then we wouldn't have any brother, but we'd be able to go on living and keep his memory in honor. As it is, this creature persecutes us, drives away our lodgers, obviously wants the whole apartment to himself and would have us all sleep in the gutter. Just look, Father," she shrieked all at once, "he's at it again!" And in an access of panic that was quite incomprehensible to Gregor she even quitted her mother, literally thrusting the chair from her as if she would rather sacrifice her mother than stay so near to Gregor, and rushed behind her father, who also rose up, being simply upset by her agitation, and half-spread his arms out as if to protect her.

Yet Gregor had not the slightest intention of frightening anyone, far less his sister. He had only begun to turn round in order to crawl back to his room, but it was certainly a startling operation to watch, since because of his disabled condition he could not execute the difficult turning movements except by lifting his head and then bracing it against the floor over and over again. He paused and looked round. His good intentions seemed to have been recognized; the alarm had only been momentary. Now they were all watching him in melancholy silence. His mother lay in her chair, her legs stiffly outstretched and pressed together, her eyes almost closing for sheer weariness; his father and his sister were sitting beside each other, his sister's arm around the old man's neck.

Perhaps I can go on turning round now, thought Gregor, and began his labors again. He could not stop himself from panting with the effort, and had to pause now and then to take breath. Nor did anyone harass him, he was left entirely to himself. When he had completed the turn-round he began at once to crawl straight back. He was amazed at the distance separating him from his room and could not understand how in his weak state he had managed to accomplish the same journey so recently, almost without remarking it. Intent on crawling as fast as possible, he barely noticed that not a single word, not an ejaculation from his family, interfered with his progress. Only when he was already in the doorway did he turn his head round, not completely, for his neck muscles were getting stiff, but enough to see that nothing had changed behind him except that his sister had risen to her feet. His last glance fell on his mother, who was not quite overcome by sleep.

Hardly was he well inside his room when the door was hastily pushed shut, bolted and locked. The sudden noise in his rear startled him so much that his little legs gave beneath him. It was his sister who had shown such haste. She had been standing ready waiting and had made a light spring forward, Gregor had not even heard her coming, and she cried "At last!" to her parents as she turned the key in the lock.

"And what now?" said Gregor to himself, looking round in the darkness. Soon he made the discovery that he was now unable to stir a limb. This did not surprise him, rather it seemed unnatural that he should ever actually have been able to move on these feeble little legs. Otherwise he felt relatively comfortable. True, his whole body was aching, but it seemed that the pain was gradually growing less and would finally pass away. The rotting apple in his back and the inflamed area around it, all covered with soft dust, already hardly troubled him. He thought of his family with tenderness and love. The decision that he must disappear was one that he held to even more strongly than his sister, if that were possible. In this state of vacant and peaceful meditation he remained until the tower clock struck three in the morning. The first broadening of light in the world outside the window entered his consciousness once more. Then his head sank to the floor of its own accord and from his nostrils came the last faint flicker of his breath.

When the charwoman arrived early in the morning—what between her strength and her impatience she slammed all the doors so loudly, never mind how often she had been begged not to do so, that no one in the whole apartment could enjoy any quiet sleep after her arrival—she noticed nothing unusual as she took her customary peep into Gregor's room. She thought he was lying motionless on purpose, pretending to be in the sulks; she credited him with every kind of intelligence. Since she happened to have the long-handled broom in her hand she tried to tickle him up with it from the doorway. When that too produced no reaction she felt provoked and poked at him a little harder, and only when she had pushed him along the floor without meeting any resistance was her attention aroused. It did not take her long to establish the truth of the matter, and her eyes widened, she let out a whistle, yet did not waste much time over it but tore open the door of the Samsas' bedroom and yelled into the darkness at the top of her voice: "Just look at this, it's dead; it's lying here dead and done for!"

Mr. and Mrs. Samsa started up in their double bed and before they realized the nature of the charwoman's announcement had some difficulty in overcoming the shock of it. But then they got out of bed quickly, one on either side, Mr. Samsa throwing a blanket over his shoulders, Mrs. Samsa in nothing but her nightgown; in this array they entered Gregor's room. Meanwhile the door of the living room opened, too, where Grete had been sleeping since the advent of the lodgers; she was completely dressed as if she had not been to bed, which seemed to be confirmed also by the paleness of her face. "Dead?" said Mrs. Samsa, looking questioningly at the charwoman, although she could have investigated for herself, and the fact was obvious enough without investigation. "I should say so," said the charwoman, proving her words by pushing Gregor's corpse a long way to one side with her broomstick. Mrs. Samsa made a movement as if to stop her, but checked it. "Well," said Mr. Samsa, "now thanks be to God." He crossed himself, and the three women followed his example. Grete, whose eyes never left the corpse, said: "Just see how thin he was. It's such a long time since he's eaten anything. The food came out again just as it went in." Indeed, Gregor's body was completely flat and dry, as could only now be seen when it was no longer supported by the legs and nothing prevented one from looking closely at it.

"Come in beside us, Grete, for a little while," said Mrs. Samsa with a tremulous smile, and Grete, not without looking back at the corpse, followed her parents into their bedroom. The charwoman shut the door and opened the window wide. Although it was so early in the morning a certain softness was perceptible in the fresh air. After all, it was already the end of March.

The three lodgers emerged from their room and were surprised to see no breakfast; they had been forgotten. "Where's our breakfast?" said the middle lodger peevishly to the charwoman. But she put her finger to her lips and hastily, without a word, indicated by gestures that they should go into Gregor's room. They did so and stood, their hands in the pockets of their somewhat shabby coats, around Gregor's corpse in the room where it was now fully light.

At that the door of the Samsas' bedroom opened and Mr. Samsa appeared in his uniform, his wife on one arm, his daughter on the other. They all looked a little as if they had been crying; from time to time Grete hid her face on her father's arm.

"Leave my house at once!" said Mr. Samsa, and pointed to the door without disengaging himself from the women. "What do you mean by that?" said the middle lodger, taken somewhat aback, with a feeble smile. The two others put their hands behind them and kept rubbing them together, as if in gleeful expectation of a fine set-to in which they were bound to come off the winners. "I mean just what I say," answered Mr. Samsa, and advanced in a straight line with his two companions towards the lodger. He stood his ground at first quietly, looking at the floor as if his thoughts were taking a new pattern in his head. "Then let us go, by all means," he said, and looked up at Mr. Samsa as if in a sudden access of humility he were expecting some renewed sanction for this decision. Mr. Samsa merely nodded briefly once or twice with meaning eyes. Upon that the lodger really did go with long strides into the hall, his two friends had been listening and had quite stopped rubbing their hands for some moments and now went scuttling after him as if afraid that Mr. Samsa might get into the hall before them and cut them off from their leader. In the hall they all three took their hats from the rack, their sticks from the umbrella stand, bowed in silence and quitted the apartment. With a suspiciousness which proved quite unfounded Mr. Samsa and the two women followed them out to the landing; leaning over the banister they watched the three figures slowly but surely going down the long stairs, vanishing from sight at a certain turn of the staircase on every floor and coming into view again after a moment or so; the more they dwindled, the more the Samsa family's interest in them dwindled, and when a butcher's boy met them and passed them on the stairs coming up proudly with a tray on his head, Mr. Samsa and the two women soon left the landing and as if a burden had been lifted from them went back into their apartment.

They decided to spend this day in resting and going for a stroll; they had not only deserved such a respite from work, but absolutely needed it. And so they sat down at the table and wrote three notes of excuse, Mr. Samsa to his board of management, Mrs. Samsa to her employer and Grete to the head of her firm. While they were writing, the charwoman came in to say that she was going now, since her morning's work was finished. At first they only nodded without looking up, but as she kept hovering there they eyed her irritably. "Well?" said Mr. Samsa. The charwoman stood grinning in the doorway as if she had good news to impart to the family but meant not to say a word unless properly questioned. The small ostrich feather standing upright on her hat, which had annoyed Mr. Samsa ever since she was engaged, was waving gaily in all directions. "Well, what is it then?" asked Mrs. Samsa, who obtained more respect from the charwoman than the others. "Oh," said the charwoman, giggling so amiably that she could not at once continue, "just this, you don't need to bother about how to get rid of the thing next door. It's been seen to already." Mrs. Samsa and Grete bent over their letters again, as if preoccupied; Mr. Samsa, who perceived that she was eager to begin describing it all in detail, stopped her with a decisive hand. But since she was not allowed to tell her story, she remembered the great hurry she was in, being obviously deeply huffed: "Bye, everybody," she said, whirling off violently, and departed with a frightful slamming of doors.

"She'll be given notice tonight," said Mr. Samsa, but neither from his wife nor his daughter did he get any answer, for the charwoman seemed to have shattered again the composure they had barely achieved. They rose, went to the window and stayed there, clasping each other tight. Mr. Samsa turned to his chair to look at them and quietly observed them for a little. Then he called out: "Come along, now, do. Let bygones be bygones. And you might have some consideration for me." The two of them complied at once, hastened to him, caressed him and quickly finished their letters.

Then they all three left the apartment together, which was more than they had done for months, and went by tram into the open country outside the town. The tram, in which they were the only passengers, was filled with warm sunshine. Leaning comfortably back in their seats they canvassed their prospects for the future, and it appeared on closer inspection that these were not at all bad, for the jobs they had got, which so far they had never really discussed with each other, were all three admirable and likely to lead to better things later on. The greatest immediate improvement in their condition would of course arise from moving to another house; they wanted to take a smaller and cheaper but also better situated and more easily run apartment than the one they had, which Gregor had selected. While they were thus conversing, it struck both Mr. and Mrs. Samsa, almost at the same moment, as they became aware of their daughter's increasing vivacity, that in spite of all the sorrow of recent times, which had made her cheeks pale, she had bloomed into a pretty girl with a good figure. They grew quieter and half unconsciously exchanged glances of complete agreement, having come to the conclusion that it would soon be time to find a good husband for her. And it was like a confirmation of their new dreams and excellent intentions that at the end of their journey their daughter sprang to her feet first and stretched her young body.

1915

Franz Kafka's stories are extreme instances of the dual nature of fiction, its attempt to deal simultaneously with the concrete details of the external world and the writer's impressions of an internal life. Flannery O'Connor, whose "grotesque" fiction is in some ways like Kafka's, often used Kafka as a point of reference when she attempted to teach others how fiction works.

"A thing is fantastic because it is so real": Flannery O'Connor

Fiction is an art that calls for the strictest attention to the real—whether the writer is writing a naturalistic story or a fantasy. I mean that we always begin with what is or with what has an eminent possibility of truth about it. Even when one writes a fantasy, reality is the proper basis of it. A thing is fantastic because it is so real, so real that it is fantastic. Graham Greene has said that he can't write, "I stood over a bottomless pit," because that couldn't be true, or "Running down the stairs I jumped into a taxi," because that couldn't be true either. But Elizabeth Bowen can write about one of her characters that "she snatched at her hair as if she heard something in it," because that is eminently possible.

I would even go so far as to say that the person writing a fantasy has to be even more strictly attentive to the concrete detail than someone writing in a naturalistic vein—because the greater the story's strain on the credulity, the more convincing the properties in it have to be.

A good example of this is a story called "The Metamorphosis" by Franz Kafka. This is a story about a man who wakes up one morning to find that he has turned into a cockroach overnight, while not discarding his human nature. The rest of the story concerns his life and feelings and eventual death as an insect with human nature, and this situation is accepted by the reader because the concrete detail of the story is absolutely convincing. The fact is that this story describes the dual nature of man in such a realistic fashion that it is almost unbearable. The truth is not distorted here, but rather, a certain distortion is used to get at the truth.

WILLIAM CARLOS WILLIAMS

(1883–1963)

JEAN BEICKE

During a time like this, they kid a lot among the doctors and nurses on the obstetrical floor because of the rushing business in new babies that's pretty nearly always going on up there. It's the Depression, they say, nobody has any money so they stay home nights. But one bad result of this is that in the children's ward, another floor up, you see a lot of unwanted children.

The parents get them into the place under all sorts of pretexts. For instance, we have two premature brats, Navarro and Cryschka, one a boy and one a girl; the mother died when Cryschka was born, I think. We got them within a few days of each other, one weighing four pounds and one a few ounces more. They dropped down below four pounds before we got them going but there they are; we had a lot of fun betting on their daily gains in weight but we still have them. They're in pretty good shape though now. Most of the kids that are left that way get along swell. The nurses grow attached to them and get a real thrill when they begin to pick up. It's great to see. And the parents sometimes don't even come to visit them, afraid we'll grab them and make them take the kids out, I suppose.

A funny one is a little Hungarian Gypsy girl that's been up there for the past month. She was about eight weeks old maybe when they brought her in with something on her lower lip that looked like a chancre. Everyone was interested but the Wassermann was negative. It turned out finally to be nothing but a peculiarly situated birthmark. But that kid is still there too. Nobody can find the parents. Maybe they'll turn up some day.

Even when we do get rid of them, they often come back in a week or so—sometimes in terrible condition, full of impetigo, down in weight—everything we'd done for them to do over again. I think it's deliberate neglect in most cases. That's what happened to this little Gypsy. The nurse was funny after the mother had left the second time. I couldn't speak to her, she said. I just couldn't say a word I was so mad. I wanted to slap her.

We had a couple of Irish girls a while back named Cowley. One was a red head with beautiful wavy hair and the other a straight haired blonde. They really were good looking and not infants at all. I should say they must have been two and three years old approximately. I can't imagine how the parents could have abandoned them. But they did. I think they were habitual drunkards and may have had to beat it besides on short notice. No fault of theirs maybe.

But all these are, after all, not the kind of kids I have in mind. The ones I mean are those they bring in stinking dirty, and I mean stinking. The poor brats are almost dead sometimes, just living skeletons, almost, wrapped in rags, their heads caked with dirt, their eyes stuck together with pus and their legs all excoriated from the dirty diapers no one has had the interest to take off them regularly. One poor little tot we have now with a thin purplish skin and big veins standing out all over its head had a big sore place in the fold of its neck under the chin. The nurse told me that when she started to undress it it had on a shirt with a neckband that rubbed right into that place. Just dirt. The mother gave a story of having had it in some sort of home in Paterson. We couldn't get it straight. We never try. What the hell? We take 'em and try to make something out of them.

Sometimes, you'd be surprised, some doctor has given the parents a ride before they bring the child to the clinic. You wouldn't believe it. They clean 'em out, maybe for twenty-five dollars—they maybe had to borrow—and then tell 'em to move on. It happens. Men we all know too. Pretty bad. But what can you do?

And sometimes the kids are not only dirty and neglected but sick, ready to die. You ought to see those nurses work. You'd think it was the brat of their best friend. They handle those kids as if they were worth a million dollars. Not that some nurses aren't better than others but in general they break their hearts over those kids, many times, when I, for one, wish they'd never get well.

I often kid the girls. Why not? I look at some miserable specimens they've dolled up for me when I make the rounds in the morning and I tell them: Give it an enema, maybe it will get well and grow up into a cheap prostitute or something. The country needs you, brat. I once proposed that we have a mock wedding between a born garbage hustler we'd saved and a little female with a fresh mug on her that would make anybody smile.

Poor kids! You really wonder sometimes if medicine isn't all wrong to try to do anything for them at all. You actually want to see them pass out, especially when they're deformed or—they're awful sometimes. Every one has rickets in an advanced form, scurvy too, flat chests, spindly arms and legs. They come in with pneumonia, a temperature of a hundred and six, maybe, and before you can do a thing, they're dead.

This little Jean Beicke was like that. She was about the worst you'd expect to find anywhere. Eleven months old. Lying on the examining table with a blanket half way up her body, stripped, lying there, you'd think it a five months baby, just about that long. But when the nurse took the blanket away, her legs kept on going for a good eight inches longer. I couldn't get used to it. I covered her up and asked two of the men to guess how long she was. Both guessed at least half a foot too short. One thing that helped the illusion besides her small face was her arms. They came about to her hips. I don't know what made that. They should come down to her thighs, you know.

She was just skin and bones but her eyes were good and she looked straight at you. Only if you touched her anywhere, she started to whine and then cry with a shrieking, distressing sort of cry that no one wanted to hear. We handled her as gently as we knew how but she had to cry just the same.

She was one of the damnedest looking kids I've ever seen. Her head was all up in front and flat behind, I suppose from lying on the back of her head so long the weight of it and the softness of the bones from the rickets had just flattened it out and pushed it up forward. And her legs and arms seemed loose on her like the arms and legs of some cheap dolls. You could bend her feet up on her shins absolutely flat—but there was no real deformity, just all loosened up. Nobody was with her when I saw her though her mother had brought her in.

It was about ten in the evening, the interne had asked me to see her because she had a stiff neck, and how! and there was some thought of meningitis—perhaps infantile paralysis. Anyhow, they didn't want her to go through the night without at least a lumbar puncture if she needed it. She had a fierce cough and a fairly high fever. I made it out to be a case of broncho-pneumonia with meningismus but no true involvement of the central nervous system. Besides she had inflamed ear drums.

I wanted to incise the drums, especially the left, and would have done it only the night superintendent came along just then and made me call the ear man on service. You know. She also looked to see if we had an operative release from the parents. There was. So I went home, the ear man came in a while later and opened the ears—a little bloody serum from both sides and that was that.

Next day we did a lumbar puncture, tapped the spine that is, and found clear fluid with a few lymphocytes in it, nothing diagnostic. The X-ray of the chest clinched the diagnosis of broncho-pneumonia, there was an extensive involvement. She was pretty sick. We all expected her to die from exhaustion before she'd gone very far.

I had to laugh every time I looked at the brat after that, she was such a funny looking one but one thing that kept her from being a total loss was that she did eat. Boy! how that kid could eat! As sick as she was she took her grub right on time every three hours, a big eight ounce bottle of whole milk and digested it perfectly. In this depression you got to be such a hungry baby, I heard the nurse say to her once. It's a sign of intelligence, I told her. But anyway, we all got to be crazy about Jean. She'd just lie there and eat and sleep. Or she'd lie and look straight in front of her by the hour. Her eyes were blue, a pale sort of blue. But if you went to touch her, she'd begin to scream. We just didn't, that's all, unless we absolutely had to. And she began to gain in weight. Can you imagine that? I suppose she had been so terribly run down that food, real food, was an entirely new experience to her. Anyway she took her food and gained on it though her temperature continued to run steadily around between a hundred and three and a hundred and four for the first eight or ten days. We were surprised.

When we were expecting her to begin to show improvement, however, she didn't. We did another lumbar puncture and found fewer cells. That was fine and the second X-ray of the chest showed it somewhat improved also. That wasn't so good though, because the temperature still kept up and we had no way to account for it. I looked at the ears again and thought they ought to be opened once more. The ear man disagreed but I kept after him and next day he did it to please me. He didn't get anything but a drop of serum on either side.

Well, Jean didn't get well. We did everything we knew how to do except the right thing. She carried on for another two—no I think it was three—weeks longer. A couple of times her temperature shot up to a hundred and eight. Of course we knew then it was the end. We went over her six or eight times, three or four of us, one after the other, and nobody thought to take an X-ray of the mastoid regions. It was dumb, if you want to say it, but there wasn't a sign of anything but the history of the case to point to it. The ears had been opened early, they had been watched carefully, there was no discharge to speak of at any time and from the external examination, the mastoid processes showed no change from the normal. But that's what she died of, acute purulent mastoiditis of the left side, going on to involvement of the left lateral sinus and finally the meninges. We might, however, have taken a culture of the pus when the ear was first opened and I shall always, after this, in suspicious cases. I have been told since that if you get a virulent bug like the streptococcus mucosus capsulatus it's wise at least to go in behind the ear for drainage if the temperature keeps up. Anyhow she died.

I went in when she was just lying there gasping. Somehow or other, I hated to see that kid go. Everybody felt rotten. She was such a scrawny, misshapen, worthless piece of humanity that I had said many times that somebody ought to chuck her in the garbage chute—but after a month watching her suck up her milk and thrive on it—and to see those alert blue eyes in that face—well, it wasn't pleasant. Her mother was sitting by the bed crying quietly when I came in, the morning of the last day. She was a young woman, didn't look more than a girl, she just sat there looking at the child and crying without a sound.

I expected her to begin to ask me questions with that look on her face all doctors hate—but she didn't. I put my hand on her shoulder and told her we had done everything we knew how to do for Jean but that we really didn't know what, finally, was killing her. The woman didn't make any sign of hearing me. Just sat there looking in between the bars of the crib. So after a moment watching the poor kid beside her, I turned to the infant in the next crib to go on with my rounds. There was an older woman there looking in at that baby also—no better off than Jean, surely. I spoke to her, thinking she was the mother of this one, but she wasn't.

Before I could say anything, she told me she was the older sister of Jean's mother and that she knew that Jean was dying and that it was a good thing. That gave me an idea—I hated to talk to Jean's mother herself—so I beckoned the woman to come out into the hall with me.

I'm glad she's going to die, she said. She's got two others home, older, and her husband has run off with another woman. It's better off dead—never was any good anyway. You know her husband came down from Canada about a year and a half ago. She seen him and asked him to come back and live with her and the children. He come back just long enough to get her pregnant with this one then he left her again and went back to the other woman. And I suppose knowing she was pregnant, and suffering, and having no money and nowhere to get it, she was worrying and this one never was formed right. I seen it as soon as it was born. I guess the condition she was in was the cause. She's got enough to worry about now without this one. The husband's gone to Canada again and we can't get a thing out of him. I been keeping them, but we can't do much more. She'd work if she could find anything but what can you do with three kids in times like this? She's got a boy nine years old but her mother-in-law sneaked it away from her and now he's with his father in Canada. She worries about him too, but that don't do no good.

Listen, I said, I want to ask you something. Do you think she'd let us do an autopsy on Jean if she dies? I hate to speak to her of such a thing now but to tell you the truth, we've worked hard on that poor child and we don't exactly know what is the trouble. We know that she's had pneumonia but that's been getting well. Would you take it up with her for me, if—of course—she dies.

Oh, she's gonna die all right, said the woman. Sure, I will. If you can learn anything, it's only right. I'll see that you get the chance. She won't make any kick, I'll tell her.

Thanks, I said.

The infant died about five in the afternoon. The pathologist was dog-tired from a lot of extra work he'd had to do due to the absence of his assistant on her vacation so he put off the autopsy till next morning. They packed the body in ice in one of the service hoppers. It worked perfectly.

Next morning they did the postmortem. I couldn't get the nurse to go down to it. I may be a sap, she said, but I can't do it, that's all. I can't. Not when I've taken care of them. I feel as if they're my own.

I was amazed to see how completely the lungs had cleared up. They were almost normal except for a very small patch of residual pneumonia here and there which really amounted to nothing. Chest and abdomen were in excellent shape, otherwise, throughout—not a thing aside from the negligible pneumonia. Then he opened the head.

It seemed to me the poor kid's convolutions were unusually well developed. I kept thinking it's incredible that that complicated mechanism of the brain has come into being just for this. I never can quite get used to an autopsy.

The first evidence of the real trouble—for there had been no gross evidence of meningitis—was when the pathologist took the brain in his hand and made the long steady cut which opened up the left lateral ventricle. There was just a faint color of pus on the bulb of the choroid plexus there. Then the diagnosis all cleared up quickly. The left lateral sinus was completely thrombosed and on going into the left temporal bone from the inside the mastoid process was all broken down.

I called up the ear man and he came down at once. A clear miss, he said. I think if we'd gone in there earlier, we'd have saved her.

For what? said I. Vote the straight Communist ticket.
Would it make us any dumber? said the ear man.

1938

Like Anton Chekhov, William Carlos Williams was a physician as well as a writer. Unlike Chekhov, Williams devoted himself unstintingly to his medical career, doing a good deal of his writing on a typewriter hidden in his office for use in the odd five or ten minutes that could be snatched between patients. In his autobiography, Williams discusses the relation between treating the patient's ailments and viewing the patient "as material for a work of art."

"Entrance to these secret gardens of the self": William Carlos Williams

The cured man, I want to say, is no different from any other. It is a trivial business unless you add the zest, whatever that is, to the picture. That's how I came to find writing such a necessity, to relieve me from such a dilemma. I found by practice, by trial and error, that to treat a man as something to which surgery, drugs and hoodoo applied was an indifferent matter; to treat him as material for a work of art made him somehow come alive to me.

What I wanted to do with him (or her, or it) fascinated me. And it didn't make any difference, apparently, that he was in himself distinguished or otherwise. It wasn't that I wanted to save him because he was a good and useful member of society. Death had no respect for him for that reason, neither does the artist, neither did I. As far as I can tell that kind of "use" doesn't enter into it; I am myself curious as to what I do find. The attraction is bizarre. . . . And my "medicine" was the thing which gained me entrance to these secret gardens of the self. It lay there, another world, in the self. I was permitted by my medical badge to follow the poor, defeated body into those gulfs and grottos. And the astonishing thing is that at such times and in such places—foul as they may be with the stinking ischio, rectal abscesses of our comings and goings—just there, the thing, in all its greatest beauty, may for a moment be freed to fly for a moment guiltily about the room. In illness, in the permission I as a physician have had to be present at deaths and births, at the tormented battles between daughter and diabolic mother, shattered by a gone brain—just there—for a split second—from one side or the other, it has fluttered before me for a moment, a phrase which I quickly write down on anything at hand, any piece of paper I can grab.

It is an identifiable thing, and its characteristic, its chief character is that it is sure, all of a piece and, as I have said, instant and perfect: it comes, it is there, and it vanishes. But I have seen it, clearly. I have seen it. I know it because there it is.

KATHERINE ANNE PORTER

(1890–1980)

THE JILTING OF GRANNY WEATHERALL

She flicked her wrist neatly out of Doctor Harry's pudgy careful fingers and pulled the sheet up to her chin. The brat ought to be in knee breeches. Doctoring around the country with spectacles on his nose! "Get along now, take your schoolbooks and go. There's nothing wrong with me."

Doctor Harry spread a warm paw like a cushion on her forehead where the forked green vein danced and made her eyelids twitch. "Now, now, be a good girl, and we'll have you up in no time."

"That's no way to speak to a woman nearly eighty years old just because she's down. I'd have you respect your elders, young man."

"Well, Missy, excuse me." Doctor Harry patted her cheek. "But I've got to warn you, haven't I? You're a marvel, but you must be careful or you're going to be good and sorry."

"Don't tell me what I'm going to be. I'm on my feet now, morally speaking. It's Cornelia. I had to go to bed to get rid of her."

Her bones felt loose, and floated around in her skin, and Doctor Harry floated like a balloon around the foot of the bed. He floated and pulled down his waistcoat and swung his glasses on a cord. "Well, stay where you are, it certainly can't hurt you."

"Get along and doctor your sick," said Granny Weatherall. "Leave a well woman alone. I'll call for you when I want you. . . . Where were you forty years ago when I pulled through milk-leg[1] and double pneumonia? You weren't even born. Don't let Cornelia lead you on," she shouted, because Doctor Harry appeared to float up to the ceiling and out. "I pay my own bills, and I don't throw my money away on nonsense!"

She meant to wave good-by, but it was too much trouble. Her eyes

---

1. A painful condition in women after childbirth, which causes great swelling of the leg because of clotting and inflammation of the femoral veins.

closed of themselves, it was like a dark curtain drawn around the bed. The pillow rose and floated under her, pleasant as a hammock in a light wind. She listened to the leaves rustling outside the window. No, somebody was swishing newspapers: no, Cornelia and Doctor Harry were whispering together. She leaped broad awake, thinking they whispered in her ear.

"She was never like this, *never* like this!" "Well, what can we expect?" "Yes, eighty years old. . . ."

Well, and what if she was? She still had ears. It was like Cornelia to whisper around doors. She always kept things secret in such a public way. She was always being tactful and kind. Cornelia was dutiful; that was the trouble with her. Dutiful and good: "So good and dutiful," said Granny, "that I'd like to spank her." She saw herself spanking Cornelia and making a fine job of it.

"What'd you say, Mother?"

Granny felt her face tying up in hard knots.

"Can't a body think, I'd like to know?"

"I thought you might want something."

"I do. I want a lot of things. First off, go away and don't whisper."

She lay and drowsed, hoping in her sleep that the children would keep out and let her rest a minute. It had been a long day. Not that she was tired. It was always pleasant to snatch a minute now and then. There was always so much to be done, let me see: tomorrow.

Tomorrow was far away and there was nothing to trouble about. Things were finished somehow when the time came; thank God there was always a little margin over for peace: then a person could spread out the plan of life and tuck in the edges orderly. It was good to have everything clean and folded away, with the hair brushes and tonic bottles sitting straight on the white embroidered linen: the day started without fuss and the pantry shelves laid out with rows of jelly glasses and brown jugs and white stone-china jars with blue whirligigs and words painted on them: coffee, tea, sugar, ginger, cinnamon, allspice: and the bronze clock with the lion on top nicely dusted off. The dust that lion could collect in twenty-four hours! The box in the attic with all those letters tied up, well, she'd have to go through that tomorrow. All those letters—George's letters and John's letters and her letters to them both—lying around for the children to find afterwards made her uneasy. Yes, that would be tomorrow's business. No use to let them know how silly she had been once.

While she was rummaging around she found death in her mind and it felt clammy and unfamiliar. She had spent so much time preparing for death there was no need for bringing it up again. Let it take care of itself now. When she was sixty she had felt very old, finished, and went around making farewell trips to see her children and grandchildren, with a secret in her mind: This is the very last of your mother, children! Then she made her will and came down with a long fever. That was all just a notion like a lot of other things, but it was lucky too, for she had once for all got over the idea of dying for a long time. Now she couldn't be worried. She hoped she had better sense now. Her father had lived to be one hundred and two years old and had drunk a noggin of strong hot toddy on his last birthday. He told the reporters it was his daily habit, and he owed his long life to that. He had made quite a scandal and was very pleased about it. She believed she'd just plague Cornelia a little.

"Cornelia! Cornelia!" No footsteps, but a sudden hand on her cheek. "Bless you, where have you been?"

"Here, Mother."

"Well, Cornelia, I want a noggin of hot toddy."

"Are you cold, darling?"

"I'm chilly, Cornelia. Lying in bed stops the circulation. I must have told you that a thousand times."

Well, she could just hear Cornelia telling her husband that Mother was getting a little childish and they'd have to humor her. The thing that most annoyed her was that Cornelia thought she was deaf, dumb, and blind. Little hasty glances and tiny gestures tossed around her and over her head saying, "Don't cross her, let her have her way, she's eighty years old," and she sitting there as if she lived in a thin glass cage. Sometimes Granny almost made up her mind to pack up and move back to her own house where nobody could remind her every minute that she was old. Wait, wait, Cornelia, till your own children whisper behind your back!

In her day she had kept a better house and had got more work done. She wasn't too old yet for Lydia to be driving eighty miles for advice when one of the children jumped the track, and Jimmy still dropped in and talked things over: "Now, Mammy, you've a good business head, I want to know what you think of this?. . ." Old. Cornelia couldn't change the furniture around without asking. Little things, little things! They had been so sweet when they were little. Granny wished the old days were back again with the children young and everything to be done over. It had been a hard pull, but not too much for her. When she thought of all the food she had cooked, and all the clothes she had cut and sewed, and all the gardens she had made—well, the children showed it. There they were, made out of her, and they couldn't get away from that. Sometimes she wanted to see John again and point to them and say, Well, I didn't do so badly, did I? But that would have to wait. That was for tomorrow. She used to think of him as a man, but now all the children were older than their father, and he would be a child beside her if she saw him now. It seemed strange and there was something wrong in the idea. Why, he couldn't possibly recognize her. She had fenced in a hundred acres once, digging the post holes herself and clamping the wires with just a negro boy to help. That changed a woman. John would be looking for a young woman with the peaked Spanish comb in her hair and the painted fan. Digging post holes changed a woman. Riding country roads in the winter when women had their babies was another thing: sitting up nights with sick horses and sick negroes and sick children and hardly ever losing one. John, I hardly ever lost one of them! John would see that in a minute, that would be something he could understand, she wouldn't have to explain anything!

It made her feel like rolling up her sleeves and putting the whole place to rights again. No matter if Cornelia was determined to be everywhere at once, there were a great many things left undone on this place. She would start tomorrow and do them. It was good to be strong enough for everything, even if all you made melted and changed and slipped under your hands, so that by the time you finished you almost forgot what you were working for. What was it I set out to do? she asked herself intently, but she could not remember. A fog rose over the valley, she saw it marching across the creek swallowing the trees and moving up the hill like an army of ghosts. Soon it would be at the near edge of the orchard, and then it was time to go in and light the lamps. Come in, children, don't stay out in the night air.

Lighting the lamps had been beautiful. The children huddled up to her and breathed like little calves waiting at the bars in the twilight. Their eyes followed the match and watched the flame rise and settle in a blue curve, then they moved away from her. The lamp was lit, they didn't have to be scared and hang on to Mother any more. Never, never never more. God, for all my life I thank Thee. Without Thee, my God, I could never have done it. Hail, Mary, full of grace.

I want you to pick all the fruit this year and see that nothing is wasted. There's always someone who can use it. Don't let good things rot for want of using. You waste life when you waste good food. Don't let things get lost. It's bitter to lose things. Now, don't let me get to thinking, not when I am tired and taking a little nap before supper. . . .

The pillow rose about her shoulders and pressed against her heart and the memory was being squeezed out of it: oh, push down the pillow, somebody; it would smother her if she tried to hold it. Such a fresh breeze blowing and such a green day with no threats in it. But he had not come, just the same. What does a woman do when she has put on the white veil and set out the white cake for a man and he doesn't come? She tried to remember. No, I swear he never harmed me but in that. He never harmed me but in that . . . and what if he did? There was the day, the day, but a whirl of dark smoke rose and covered it, crept up and over into the bright field where everything was planted so carefully in orderly rows. That was hell, she knew hell when she saw it. For sixty years she had prayed against remembering him and against losing her soul in the deep pit of hell, and now the two things were mingled in one and the thought of him was a smoky cloud from hell that moved and crept in her head when she had just got rid of Doctor Harry and was trying to rest a minute. Wounded vanity, Ellen, said a sharp voice in the top of her mind. Don't let your wounded vanity get the upper hand of you. Plenty of girls get jilted. You were jilted, weren't you? Then stand up to it. Her eyelids wavered and let in streamers of blue-gray light like tissue paper over her eyes. She must get up and pull the shades down or she'd never sleep. She was in bed again and the shades were not down. How could that happen? Better turn over, hide from the light, sleeping in the light gave you nightmares. "Mother, how do you feel now?" and a stinging wetness on her forehead. But I don't like having my face washed in cold water!

Hapsy? George? Lydia? Jimmy? No, Cornelia, and her features were swollen and full of little puddles. "They're coming, darling, they'll all be here soon." Go wash your face, child, you look funny.

Instead of obeying, Cornelia knelt down and put her head on the pillow. She seemed to be talking but there was no sound. "Well, are you tongue-tied? Whose birthday is it? Are you going to give a party?"

Cornelia's mouth moved urgently in strange shapes. "Don't do that, you bother me, daughter."

"Oh, no, Mother. Oh, no. . . ."

Nonsense. It was strange about children. They disputed your every word. "No what, Cornelia?"

"Here's Doctor Harry."

"I won't see that boy again. He just left five minutes ago."

"That was this morning, Mother. It's night now. Here's the nurse."

"This is Doctor Harry, Mrs. Weatherall. I never saw you look so young and happy!"

"Ah, I'll never be young again—but I'd be happy if they'd let me lie in peace and get rested."

She thought she spoke up loudly, but no one answered. A warm weight on her forehead, a warm bracelet on her wrist, and a breeze went on whispering, trying to tell her something. A shuffle of leaves in the everlasting hand of God, He blew on them and they danced and rattled. "Mother, don't mind, we're going to give you a little hypodermic." "Look here, daughter, how do ants get in this bed? I saw sugar ants yesterday." Did you send for Hapsy too?

It was Hapsy she really wanted. She had to go a long way back through a great many rooms to find Hapsy standing with a baby on her arm. She seemed to herself to be Hapsy also, and the baby on Hapsy's arm was Hapsy and himself and herself, all at once, and there was no surprise in the meeting. Then Hapsy melted from within and turned flimsy as gray gauze and the baby was a gauzy shadow, and Hapsy came up close and said, "I thought you'd never come," and looked at her very searchingly and said, "You haven't changed a bit!" They leaned forward to kiss, when Cornelia began whispering from a long way off, "Oh, is there anything you want to tell me? Is there anything I can do for you?"

Yes, she had changed her mind after sixty years and she would like to see George. I want you to find George. Find him and be sure to tell him I forgot him. I want him to know I had my husband just the same and my children and my house like any other woman. A good house too and a good husband that I loved and fine children out of him. Better than I hoped for even. Tell him I was given back everything he took away and more. Oh, no, oh, God, no, there was something else besides the house and the man and the children. Oh, surely they were not all? What was it? Something not given back. . . . Her breath crowded down under her ribs and grew into a monstrous frightening shape with cutting edges; it bored up into her head, and the agony was unbelievable: Yes, John, get the Doctor now, no more talk, my time has come.

When this one was born it should be the last. The last. It should have been born first, for it was the one she had truly wanted. Everything came in good time. Nothing left out, left over. She was strong, in three days she would be as well as ever. Better. A woman needed milk in her to have her full health.

"Mother, do you hear me?"

"I've been telling you—"

"Mother, Father Connolly's here."

"I went to Holy Communion only last week. Tell him I'm not so sinful as all that."

"Father just wants to speak to you."

He could speak as much as he pleased. It was like him to drop in and inquire about her soul as if it were a teething baby, and then stay on for a cup of tea and a round of cards and gossip. He always had a funny story of some sort, usually about an Irishman who made his little mistakes and confessed them, and the point lay in some absurd thing he would blurt out in the confessional showing his struggles between native piety and original sin. Granny felt easy about her soul. Cornelia, where are your manners? Give Father Connolly a chair. She had her secret comfortable understanding with a few favorite saints who cleared a straight road to God for her. All as surely signed and sealed as the papers for the new Forty Acres. Forever . . . heirs and assigns forever. Since the day the wedding cake was not cut, but thrown out and wasted. The whole bottom dropped out of the world, and there she was blind and sweating with nothing under her feet and the walls falling away. His hand had caught her under the breast, she had not fallen, there was the freshly polished floor with the green rug on it, just as before. He had cursed like a sailor's parrot and said, "I'll kill him for you." Don't lay a hand on him, for my sake leave something to God. "Now, Ellen, you must believe what I tell you. . . ."

So there was nothing, nothing to worry about any more, except sometimes in the night one of the children screamed in a nightmare, and they both hustled out shaking and hunting for the matches and calling, "There, wait a minute, here we are!" John, get the doctor now, Hapsy's time has come. But there was Hapsy standing by the bed in a white cap. "Cornelia, tell Hapsy to take off her cap. I can't see her plain."

Her eyes opened very wide and the room stood out like a picture she had seen somewhere. Dark colors with the shadows rising towards the ceiling in long angles. The tall black dresser gleamed with nothing on it but John's picture, enlarged from a little one, with John's eyes very black when they should have been blue. You never saw him, so how do you know how he looked? But the man insisted the copy was perfect, it was very rich and handsome. For a picture, yes, but it's not my husband. The table by the bed had a linen cover and a candle and a crucifix. The light was blue from Cornelia's silk lampshades. No sort of light at all, just frippery. You had to live forty years with kerosene lamps to appreciate honest electricity. She felt very strong and she saw Doctor Harry with a rosy nimbus around him.

"You look like a saint, Doctor Harry, and I vow that's as near as you'll ever come to it."

"She's saying something."

"I heard you, Cornelia. What's all this carrying-on?"

"Father Connolly's saying—"

Cornelia's voice staggered and bumped like a cart in a bad road. It rounded corners and turned back again and arrived nowhere. Granny stepped up in the cart very lightly and reached for the reins, but a man sat beside her and she knew him by his hands, driving the cart. She did not look in his face, for she knew without seeing, but looked instead down the road where the trees leaned over and bowed to each other and a thousand birds were singing a Mass. She felt like singing too, but she put her hand in the bosom of her dress and pulled out a rosary, and Father Connolly murmured Latin in a very solemn voice and tickled her feet. My God, will you stop that nonsense? I'm a married woman. What if he did run away and leave me to face the priest by myself? I found another a whole world better. I wouldn't have exchanged my husband for anybody except St. Michael himself, and you may tell him that for me with a thank you in the bargain.

Light flashed on her closed eyelids, and a deep roaring shook her. Cornelia, is that lightning? I hear thunder. There's going to be a storm. Close all the windows. Call the children in. . . . "Mother, here we are, all of us." "Is that you, Hapsy?" "Oh, no, I'm Lydia. We drove as fast as we could." Their faces drifted above her, drifted away. The rosary fell out of her hands and Lydia put it back. Jimmy tried to help, their hands fumbled together, and Granny closed two fingers around Jimmy's thumb. Beads wouldn't do, it must be something alive. She was so amazed her thoughts ran round and round. So, my dear Lord, this is my death and I wasn't even thinking about it. My children have come to see me die. But I can't, it's not time. Oh, I always hated surprises. I wanted to give Cornelia the amethyst set—Cornelia, you're to have the amethyst set, but Hapsy's to wear it when she wants, and, Doctor Harry, do shut up. Nobody sent for you. Oh, my dear Lord, do wait a minute. I meant to do something about the Forty Acres, Jimmy doesn't need it and Lydia will later on, with that worthless husband of hers. I meant to finish the altar cloth and send six bottles of wine to Sister Borgia for her dyspepsia. I want to send six bottles of wine to Sister Borgia, Father Connolly, now don't let me forget.

Cornelia's voice made short turns and tilted over and crashed. "Oh, Mother, oh, Mother, oh, Mother. . . ."

"I'm not going. Cornelia. I'm taken by surprise. I can't go."

You'll see Hapsy again. What about her? "I thought you'd never come." Granny made a long journey outward, looking for Hapsy. What if I don't find her? What then? Her heart sank down and down, there was no bottom to death, she couldn't come to the end of it. The blue light from Cornelia's lampshade drew into a tiny point in the center of her brain, it flickered and winked like an eye, quietly it fluttered and dwindled. Granny lay curled down within herself, amazed and watchful, staring at the point of light that was herself; her body was now only a deeper mass of shadow in an endless darkness and this darkness would curl around the light and swallow it up. God, give a sign!

For the second time there was no sign. Again no bridegroom and the priest in the house. She could not remember any other sorrow because this grief wiped them all away. Oh, no, there's nothing more cruel than this —I'll never forgive it. She stretched herself with a deep breath and blew out the light.

1929

"The Jilting of Granny Weatherall" reveals Katherine Anne Porter's ability to give us the world from the perspective of a particular character. Part of her ability to produce such a convincing perspective comes from her awareness (shown in the journal entry below) or her own mental processes, particularly the coexistence in her mind of the past and the present. As Eudora Welty points out, the result is narration that seems to look "through the gauze of the passing scene, not distracted by the immediate or the transitory."

"Only the past is 'real' ": Katherine Anne Porter

Perhaps in time I shall learn to live more deeply and consistently in that undistracted center of being where the will does not intrude, and the sense of time passing is lost, or has no power over the imagination. Of the three dimensions of time, only the past is "real" in the absolute sense that it has occurred, the future is only a concept, and the present is that fateful split second in which all action takes place. One of the most disturbing habits of the human mind is its willful and destructive forgetting of whatever in its past does not flatter or confirm its present point of view. I must very often refer far back in time to seek the meaning or explanation of today's smallest event, and I have long since lost the power to be astonished at what I find there. This constant exercise of memory seems to be the chief occupation of my mind, and all my experience seems to be simply memory, with continuity, marginal notes, constant revision and comparison of one thing with another. Now and again thousands of memories converge, harmonize, arrange themselves around a central idea in a coherent form, and I write a story.

"Looking through the gauze at the passing scene": Eudora Welty

Most good stories are about the interior of our lives, but Katherine Anne Porter's stories take place there; they show surface only at her choosing. Her use of the physical world is enough to meet her needs and no more; she is not wasteful with anything. This artist, writing her stories with a power that stamps them to their last detail on the memory, does so to an extraordinary degree without sensory imagery.

I have the most common type of mind, the visual, and when first I began to read her stories it stood in the way of my trust in my own certainty of what was there that, for all my being bowled over by them, I couldn't see them happening. This was a very good thing for me. As her work has done in many other respects, it has shown me a thing or two about the eye of fiction, about fiction's visibility and invisibility, about its clarity, its radiance. . . .

Katherine Anne Porter shows us that we do not have to see a story happen to know what is taking place. For all we are to know, she is not looking at it happen herself when she writes it; for her eyes are always looking through the gauze of the passing scene, not distracted by the immediate and transitory; her vision is reflective.

Her imagery is as likely as not to belong to a time other than the story's present, and beyond that it always differs from it in nature; it is *memory* imagery, coming into the story from memory's remove. It is a distilled, a re-formed imagery, for it is part of a language made to speak directly of premonition, warning, surmise, anger, despair.

DOROTHY PARKER

(1893–1967)

HERE WE ARE

The young man in the new blue suit finished arranging the glistening luggage in tight corners of the Pullman compartment. The train had leaped at curves and bounced along straightaways, rendering balance a praiseworthy achievement and a sporadic one; and the young man had pushed and hoisted and tucked and shifted the bags with concentrated care.

Nevertheless, eight minutes for the settling of two suitcases and a hat-box is a long time.

He sat down, leaning back against bristled green plush, in the seat opposite the girl in beige. She looked as new as a peeled egg. Her hat, her fur, her frock, her gloves were glossy and stiff with novelty. On the arc of the thin, slippery sole of one beige shoe was gummed a tiny oblong of white paper, printed with the price set and paid for that slipper and its fellow, and the name of the shop that had dispensed them.

She had been staring raptly out of the window, drinking in the big weathered signboards that extolled the phenomena of codfish without bones and screens no rust could corrupt. As the young man sat down, she turned politely from the pane, met his eyes, started a smile and got it about half done, and rested her gaze just above his right shoulder.

'Well!' the young man said.

'Well!' she said.

'Well, here we are,' he said.

'Here we are,' she said. 'Aren't we?'

'I should say we were,' he said. 'Eeyop. Here we are.'

'Well!' she said.

'Well!' he said. 'Well. How does it feel to be an old married lady?'

'Oh, it's too soon to ask me that,' she said. 'At least—I mean. Well, I mean, goodness, we've only been married about three hours, haven't we?'

The young man studied his wrist-watch as if he were just acquiring the knack of reading time.

'We have been married,' he said, 'exactly two hours and twenty-six minutes.'

'My,' she said. 'It seems like longer.'

'No,' he said. 'It isn't hardly half-past six yet.'

'It seems like later,' she said. 'I guess it's because it starts getting dark so early.'

'It does, at that,' he said. 'The nights are going to be pretty long from now on. I mean. I mean—well, it starts getting dark early.'

'I didn't have any idea what time it was,' she said. 'Everything was so mixed up, I sort of don't know where I am, or what it's all about. Getting back from the church, and then all those people, and then changing all my

Dorothy Parker   281

clothes, and then everybody throwing things, and all. Goodness, I don't see how people do it every day.'

'Do what?' he said.

'Get married,' she said. 'When you think of all the people, all over the world, getting married just as if it was nothing. Chinese people and everybody. Just as if it wasn't anything.'

'Well, let's not worry about people all over the world,' he said. 'Let's don't think about a lot of Chinese. We've got something better to think about. I mean. I mean—well, what do we care about them?'

'I know,' she said. 'But I just sort of got to thinking of them, all of them, all over everywhere, doing it all the time. At least, I mean—getting married, you know. And it's—well, it's sort of such a big thing to do, it makes you feel queer. You think of them, all of them, all doing it just like it wasn't anything. And how does anybody know what's going to happen next?'

'Let them worry,' he said. 'We don't have to. We know darn well what's going to happen next. I mean. I mean—well, we know it's going to be great. Well, we know we're going to be happy. Don't we?'

'Oh, of course,' she said. 'Only you think of all the people, and you have to sort of keep thinking. It makes you feel funny. An awful lot of people that get married, it doesn't turn out so well. And I guess they all must have thought it was going to be great.'

'Come on, now,' he said. 'This is no way to start a honeymoon, with all this thinking going on. Look at us—all married and everything done. I mean. The wedding all done and all.'

'Ah, it was nice, wasn't it?' she said. 'Did you really like my veil?'

'You looked great,' he said. 'Just great.'

'Oh, I'm terribly glad,' she said. 'Ellie and Louise looked lovely, didn't they? I'm terribly glad they did finally decide on pink. They looked perfectly lovely.'

'Listen,' he said. 'I want to tell you something. When I was standing up there in that old church waiting for you to come up, and I saw those two bridesmaids, I thought to myself, I thought, "Well, I never knew Louise could look like that!" Why, she'd have knocked anybody's eye out.'

'Oh, really?' she said. 'Funny. Of course, everybody thought her dress and hat were lovely, but a lot of people seemed to think she looked sort of tired. People have been saying that a lot, lately. I tell them I think it's awfully mean of them to go around saying that about her. I tell them they've got to remember that Louise isn't so terribly young any more, and they've got to expect her to look like that. Louise can say she's twenty-three all she wants to, but she's a good deal nearer twenty-seven.'

'Well, she was certainly a knock-out at the wedding,' he said. 'Boy!'

'I'm terribly glad you thought so,' she said. 'I'm glad someone did. How did you think Ellie looked?'

'Why, I honestly didn't get a look at her,' he said.

'Oh, really?' she said. 'Well, I certainly think that's too bad. I don't suppose I ought to say it about my own sister, but I never saw anybody look as beautiful as Ellie looked today. And always so sweet and unselfish, too. And you didn't even notice her. But you never pay attention to Ellie, anyway. Don't think I haven't noticed it. It makes me feel just terrible. It makes me feel just awful, that you don't like my own sister.'

'I do like her!' he said. 'I'm crazy for Ellie. I think she's a great kid.'

'Don't think it makes any difference to Ellie!' she said. 'Ellie's got enough people crazy about her. It isn't anything to her whether you like her or not. Don't flatter yourself she cares! Only, the only thing is, it makes it awfully hard for me you don't like her, that's the only thing. I keep thinking, when we come back and get in that apartment and everything, it's going to be awfully hard for me that you won't want my own sister to come and see me. It's going to make it awfully hard for me that you won't ever want my family around. I know how you feel about my family. Don't think I haven't seen it. Only, if you don't ever want to see them, that's your loss. Not theirs. Don't flatter yourself!'

'Oh, now, come on!' he said. 'What's all this talk about not wanting your family around? Why, you know how I feel about your family. I think your old lady—I think your mother's swell. And Ellie. And your father. What's all this talk?'

'Well, I've seen it,' she said. 'Don't think I haven't. Lots of people they get married, and they think it's going to be great and everything, and then it all goes to pieces because people don't like people's families, or something like that. Don't tell me! I've seen it happen.'

'Honey,' he said, 'what is all this? What are you getting all angry about? Hey, look, this is our honeymoon. What are you trying to start a fight for? Ah, I guess you're just feeling sort of nervous.'

'Me?' she said. 'What have I got to be nervous about? I mean. I mean, goodness, I'm not nervous.'

'You know, lots of times,' he said, 'they say that girls get kind of nervous and yippy on account of thinking about—I mean. I mean—well, it's like you said, things are all so sort of mixed up and everything, right now. But afterwards, it'll be all right. I mean. I mean—well, look, honey, you don't look any too comfortable. Don't you want to take your hat off? And let's don't ever fight, ever. Will we?'

'Ah, I'm sorry I was cross,' she said. 'I guess I did feel a little bit funny. All mixed up, and then thinking of all those people all over everywhere, and then being sort of 'way off here, all alone with you. It's so sort of different. It's sort of such a big thing. You can't blame a person for thinking, can you? Yes, don't let's ever, ever fight. We won't be like a whole lot of them. We won't fight or be nasty or anything. Will we?'

'You bet your life we won't,' he said.

'I guess I will take this darned old hat off,' she said. 'It kind of presses. Just put it up on the rack, will you, dear? Do you like it, sweetheart?'

'Looks good on you,' he said.

'No, but I mean,' she said, 'do you really like it?'

'Well, I'll tell you,' he said. 'I know this is the new style and every-thing like that, and it's probably great. I don't know anything about things like that. Only I like the kind of a hat like that blue hat you had. Gee, I liked that hat.'

'Oh, really?' she said. 'Well, that's nice. That's lovely. The first thing you say to me, as soon as you get me off on a train away from my family and everything, is that you don't like my hat. The first thing you say to your wife is you think she has terrible taste in hats. That's nice, isn't it?'

'Now, honey,' he said, 'I never said anything like that. I only said—'

'What you don't seem to realize,' she said, 'is this hat cost twenty-two dollars. Twenty-two dollars. And that horrible old blue thing you think you're so crazy about, that cost three ninety-five.'

'I don't give a darn what they cost,' he said. 'I only said—I said I liked that blue hat. I don't know anything about hats. I'll be crazy about this one as soon as I get used to it. Only it's kind of not like your other hats. I don't know about the new styles. What do I know about women's hats?'

'It's too bad,' she said, 'you didn't marry somebody that would get the kind of hats you'd like. Hats that cost three ninety-five. Why didn't you marry Louise? You always think she looks so beautiful. You'd love her taste in hats. Why didn't you marry her?'

'Ah, now, honey,' he said. 'For heaven's sakes!'

'Why didn't you marry her?' she said. 'All you've done, ever since we got on this train, is talk about her. Here I've sat and sat, and just listened to you saying how wonderful Louise is. I suppose that's nice, getting me all off here alone with you, and then raving about Louise right in front of my face. Why didn't you ask her to marry you? I'm sure she would have jumped at the chance. There aren't so many people asking her to marry them. It's too bad you didn't marry her. I'm sure you'd have been much happier.'

'Listen, baby,' he said, 'while you're talking about things like that, why didn't you marry Joe Brooks? I suppose he could have given you all the twenty-two-dollar hats you wanted, I suppose!'

'Well, I'm not so sure I'm not sorry I didn't,' she said. 'There! Joe Brooks wouldn't have waited until he got me all off alone and then sneered at my taste in clothes. Joe Brooks wouldn't ever hurt my feelings. Joe Brooks has always been fond of me. There!'

'Yeah,' he said. 'He's fond of you. He was so fond of you he didn't even send a wedding present. That's how fond of you he was.'

'I happen to know for a fact,' she said, 'that he was away on busi-ness, and as soon as he comes back he's going to give me anything I want, for the apartment.'

'Listen,' he said. 'I don't want anything he gives you in our apart-ment. Anything he gives you, I'll throw right out the window. That's what I think of your friend Joe Brooks. And how do you know where he is and what he's going to do, anyway? Has he been writing to you?'

'I suppose my friends can correspond with me,' she said. 'I didn't hear there was any law against that.'

'Well, I suppose they can't!' he said. 'And what do you think of that? I'm not going to have my wife getting a lot of letters from cheap travelling salesmen!'

'Joe Brooks is not a cheap travelling salesman!' she said. 'He is not! He gets a wonderful salary.'

'Oh yeah?' he said. 'Where did you hear that?'

'He told me so himself,' she said.

'Oh, he told you so himself,' he said. 'I see. He told you so himself.'

'You've got a lot of right to talk about Joe Brooks,' she said. 'You and your friend Louise. All you ever talk about is Louise.'

'Oh, for heaven's sakes!' he said. 'What do I care about Louise? I just thought she was a friend of yours, that's all. That's why I ever even noticed her.'

'Well, you certainly took an awful lot of notice of her today,' she said. 'On our wedding day! You said yourself when you were standing there in the church you just kept thinking of her. Right up at the altar. Oh, right in the presence of God! And all you thought about was Louise.'

'Listen, honey,' he said, 'I never should have said that. How does anybody know what kind of crazy things come into their heads when they're standing there waiting to get married? I was just telling you that because it was so kind of crazy. I thought it would make you laugh.'

'I know,' she said. 'I've been all sort of mixed up today, too. I told you that. Everything so strange and everything. And me all the time thinking about all those people all over the world, and now us here all alone, and everything. I know you get all mixed up. Only I did think, when you kept talking about how beautiful Louise looked, you did it with malice and forethought.'

'I never did anything with malice and forethought!' he said. 'I just told you that about Louise because I thought it would make you laugh.'

'Well, it didn't,' she said.

'No, I know it didn't,' he said. 'It certainly did not. Ah, baby, and we ought to be laughing, too. Hell, honey lamb, this is our honeymoon. What's the matter?'

'I don't know,' she said. 'We used to squabble a lot when we were going together and then engaged and everything, but I thought everything would be so different as soon as you were married. And now I feel so sort of strange and everything. I feel so sort of alone.'

'Well, you see, sweetheart,' he said, 'we're not really married yet. I mean. I mean—well, things will be different afterwards. Oh, hell. I mean, we haven't been married very long.'

'No,' she said.

'Well, we haven't got much longer to wait now,' he said. 'I mean—well, we'll be in New York in about twenty minutes. Then we can have dinner, and sort of see what we feel like doing. Or I mean. Is there anything special you want to do tonight?'

'What?' she said.

'What I mean to say,' he said, 'would you like to go to a show or something?'

'Why, whatever you like,' she said. 'I sort of didn't think people went to theatres and things on their—I mean, I've got a couple of letters I simply must write. Don't let me forget.'

'Oh,' he said. 'You're going to write letters tonight?'

'Well, you see,' she said. 'I've been perfectly terrible. What with all the excitement and everything. I never did thank poor old Mrs Sprague for her berry spoon, and I never did a thing about those book ends the McMasters sent. It's just too awful to me. I've got to write them this very night.'

'And when you've finished writing your letters,' he said, 'maybe I could get you a magazine or a bag of peanuts.'

'What?' she said.

'I mean,' he said, 'I wouldn't want you to be bored.'

'As if I could be bored with you!' she said. 'Silly! Aren't we married? Bored!'

'What I thought,' he said, 'I thought when we got in, we could go right up to the Biltmore and anyway leave our bags, and maybe have a little dinner in the room, kind of quiet, and then do whatever we wanted. I mean. I mean—well, let's go right up there from the station.'

'Oh, yes, let's,' she said. 'I'm so glad we're going to the Biltmore. I just love it. The twice I've stayed in New York we've always stayed there, Papa and Mamma and Ellie and I, and I was crazy about it. I always sleep so well there. I go right off to sleep the minute I put my head on the pillow.'

'Oh, you do?' he said.

'At least, I mean,' she said. 'Way up high it's so quiet.'

'We might go to some show or other tomorrow night instead of tonight,' he said. 'Don't you think that would be better?'

'Yes, I think it might,' she said.

He rose, balanced a moment, crossed over and sat down beside her.

'Do you really have to write those letters tonight?' he said.

'Well,' she said, 'I don't suppose they'd get there any quicker than if I wrote them tomorrow.'

There was a silence with things going on in it.

'And we won't ever fight any more, will we?' he said.

'Oh, no,' she said. 'Not ever! I don't know what made me do like that. It all got so sort of funny, sort of like a nightmare, the way I got thinking of all those people getting married all the time; and so many of them, everything spoils on account of fighting and everything. I got all mixed up thinking about them. Oh, I don't want to be like them. But we won't be, will we?'

'Sure we won't,' he said.

'We won't go all to pieces,' she said. 'We won't fight. It'll all be different, now we're married. It'll all be lovely. Reach me down my hat, will you, sweetheart? It's time I was putting it on. Thanks. Ah, I'm so sorry you don't like it.'

'I do so like it!' he said.

'You said you didn't,' she said. 'You said you thought it was perfectly terrible.'

'I never said any such thing,' he said. 'You're crazy.'

'All right, I may be crazy,' she said. 'Thank you very much. But that's what you said. Not that it matters—it's just a little thing. But it makes you feel pretty funny to think you've gone and married somebody that says you have perfectly terrible taste in hats. And then goes and says you're crazy, beside.'

'Now, listen here,' he said. 'Nobody said any such thing. Why, I love that hat. The more I look at it the better I like it. I think it's great.'

'That isn't what you said before,' she said.

'Honey,' he said. 'Stop it, will you? What do you want to start all this for? I love the damned hat. I mean, I love your hat. I love anything you wear. What more do you want me to say?'

'Well, I don't want you to say it like that,' she said.

'I said I think it's great,' he said. 'That's all I said.'

'Do you really?' she said. 'Do you honestly? Ah, I'm so glad. I'd hate you not to like my hat. It would be—I don't know, it would be sort of such a bad start.'

'Well, I'm crazy for it,' he said. 'Now we've got that settled, for heaven's sakes. Ah, baby. Baby lamb. We're not going to have any bad starts. Look at us—we're on our honeymoon. Pretty soon we'll be regular old married people. I mean. I mean, in a few minutes we'll be getting in to New York, and then we'll be going to the hotel, and then everything will be all right. I mean—well, look at us! Here we are married! Here we are!'

'Yes, here we are,' she said. 'Aren't we?'

1939

Interviewed in 1956 for the Paris Review, *Dorothy Parker seemed to classify herself as a wit: someone operating, by her standards, above the level of humorists and below the level of satirists. Both the interview and "One Perfect Rose" reflect the tone of Parker's wit and so cast an indirect light on such stories as "Here We Are."*

"I don't want to be classed as a humorist.": Dorothy Parker

Interviewer: You have an extensive reputation as a wit. Has this interfered, do you think, with your acceptance as a serious writer?

Parker: I don't want to be classed as a humorist. It makes me feel guilty. I've never read a good tough quotable female humorist, and I never was one myself. I couldn't do it. A "smart-cracker" they called me, and that makes me sick and unhappy. There's a hell of a distance between wisecracking and wit. Wit has truth in it; wisecracking is simply calisthenics with words. I didn't mind so much when they were good, but for a long time anything that was called a crack was attributed to me—and then they got the shaggy dogs.

Interviewer: How about satire?

Parker: Ah, satire. That's another matter. They're the big boys. If I'd been called a satirist there'd be no living with me. But by satirist I mean those boys in the other centuries. The people we call satirists now are those who make cracks at topical topics and consider themselves satirists—creatures like George S. Kaufman and such who don't even know what satire is. Lord knows, a writer should show his times, but not show them in wisecracks. Their stuff is not satire; it's as dull as yesterday's newspaper. Successful satire has got to be pretty good the day after tomorrow.

Interviewer: And how about contemporary humorists? Do you feel about them as you do about satirists?

Parker: You get to a certain age and only the tried writers are funny. I read my verses now and I ain't funny. I haven't been funny for twenty years.

One Perfect Rose

A single flow'r he sent me, since we met,
    All tenderly his messenger he chose;
Deep-hearted, pure, with scented dew still wet—
    One perfect rose.

I knew the language of the floweret;   5
    "My fragile leaves," it said, "his heart enclose."

Love long has taken for his amulet
  One perfect rose.

Why is it no one ever sent me yet
  One perfect limousine, do you suppose?   10
Ah no, it's always just my luck to get
  One perfect rose.

DASHIELL HAMMETT

(1894–1961)

FLY PAPER

It was a wandering daughter job.

The Hambletons had been for several generations a wealthy and decently prominent New York family. There was nothing in the Hambleton history to account for Sue, the youngest member of the clan. She grew out of childhood with a kink that made her dislike the polished side of life, like the rough. By the time she was twenty-one, in 1926, she definitely preferred Tenth Avenue to Fifth, grifters to bankers, and Hymie the Riveter to the Honorable Cecil Windown, who had asked her to marry him.

The Hambletons tried to make Sue behave, but it was too late for that. She was legally of age. When she finally told them to go to hell and walked out on them there wasn't much they could do about it. Her father, Major Waldo Hambleton, had given up all the hopes he ever had of salvaging her, but he didn't want her to run into any grief that could be avoided. So he came into the Continental Detective Agency's New York office and asked to have an eye kept on her.

Hymie the Riveter was a Philadelphia racketeer who had moved north to the big city, carrying a Thompson submachine gun wrapped in blue-checkered oil cloth, after a disagreement with his partners. New York wasn't so good a field as Philadelphia for machine gun work. The Thompson lay idle for a year or so while Hymie made expenses with an automatic, preying on small-time crap games in Harlem.

Three or four months after Sue went to live with Hymie he made what looked like a promising connection with the first of the crew that came into New York from Chicago to organize the city on the western scale. But the boys from Chi didn't want Hymie; they wanted the Thompson. When he showed it to them, as the big item in his application for employment, they shot holes in the top of Hymie's head and went away with the gun.

Sue Hambleton buried Hymie, had a couple of lonely weeks in which she hocked a ring to eat, and then got a job as hostess in a speakeasy run by a Greek named Vassos.

One of Vassos' customers was Babe McCloor, two hundred and fifty pounds of hard Scotch-Irish-Indian bone and muscle, a black-haired, blue-eyed, swarthy giant who was resting up after doing a fifteen-year hitch in Leavenworth for ruining most of the smaller post offices between New Orleans and Omaha. Babe was keeping himself in drinking money while he rested by playing with pedestrians in dark streets.

Babe liked Sue. Vassos liked Sue. Sue liked Babe. Vassos didn't like that. Jealousy spoiled the Greek's judgment. He kept the speakeasy door locked one night when Babe wanted to come in. Babe came in, bringing pieces of the door with him. Vassos got his gun out, but couldn't shake Sue off his arm. He stopped trying when Babe hit him with the part of the door that had the brass knob on it. Babe and Sue went away from Vassos' together.

Up to that time the New York office had managed to keep in touch with Sue. She hadn't been kept under constant surveillance. Her father hadn't wanted that. It was simply a matter of sending a man around every week or so to see that she was still alive, to pick up whatever information he could from her friends and neighbors, without, of course, letting her know she was being tabbed. All that had been easy enough, but when she and Babe went away after wrecking the gin mill, they dropped completely out of sight.

After turning the city upside-down, the New York office sent a journal on the job to the other Continental branches throughout the country, giving the information above and enclosing photographs and descriptions of Sue and her new playmate. That was late in 1927.

We had enough copies of the photographs to go around, and for the next month or so whoever had a little idle time on his hands spent it looking through San Francisco and Oakland for the missing pair. We didn't find them. Operatives in other cities, doing the same thing, had the same luck.

Then, nearly a year later, a telegram came to us from the New York office. Decoded, it read:

> Major Hambleton today received telegram from daughter in San Francisco quote Please wire me thousand dollars care apartment two hundred six number six hundred one Eddis Street stop I will come home if you will let me stop Please tell me if I can come but please please wire money anyway unquote Hambleton authorizes payment of money to her immediately stop Detail competent operative to call on her with money and to arrange for her return home stop If possible have man and woman operative accompany her here stop Hambleton wiring her stop Report immediately by wire.

The Old Man gave me the telegram and a check, saying, "You know the situation. You'll know how to handle it."

I pretended I agreed with him, went down to the bank, swapped the check for a bundle of bills of several sizes, caught a streetcar, and went up to 601 Eddis Street, a fairly large apartment building on the corner of Larkin.

The name on Apartment 206's vestibule mail box was J. M. Wales.

I pushed 206's button. When the locked door buzzed off I went into the building, past the elevator to the stairs, and up a flight. 206 was just around the corner from the stairs.

The apartment door was opened by a tall, slim man of thirty-something in neat dark clothes. He had narrow dark eyes set in a long pale face. There was some gray in the dark hair brushed flat to his scalp.

"Miss Hambleton," I said.

"Uh—what about her?" His voice was smooth, but not too smooth to be agreeable.

"I'd like to see her."

His upper eyelids came down a little and the brows over them came a little closer together. He asked, "Is it—?" and stopped, watching me steadily.

I didn't say anything. Presently he finished his question, "Something to do with a telegram?"

"Yeah."

His long face brightened immediately. He asked, "You're from her father?"

"Yeah."

He stepped back and swung the door wide open, saying, "Come in. Major Hambleton's wire came to her only a few minutes ago. He said someone would call."

We went through a small passageway into a sunny living room that was cheaply furnished, but neat and clean enough.

"Sit down," the man said, pointing at a brown rocking chair.

I sat down. He sat on the burlap-covered sofa facing me. I looked around the room. I didn't see anything to show that a woman was living there.

He rubbed the long bridge of his nose with a longer forefinger and asked slowly, "You brought the money?"

I said I'd feel more like talking with her there.

He looked at the finger with which he had been rubbing his nose, and then up at me, saying softly, "But I'm her friend."

I said, "Yeah?" to that.

"Yes," he repeated. He frowned slightly, drawing back the corners of his thin-lipped mouth. "I've only asked whether you've brought the money."

I didn't say anything.

"The point is," he said quite reasonably, "that if you brought the money she doesn't expect you to hand it over to anybody except her. If you didn't bring it she doesn't want to see you. I don't think her mind can be changed about that. That's why I asked if you had brought it."

"I brought it."

He looked doubtfully at me. I showed him the money I had got from the bank. He jumped up briskly from the sofa.

"I'll have her here in a minute or two," he said over his shoulder as his long legs moved him toward the door. At the door he stopped to ask, "Do you know her? Or shall I have her bring means of identifying herself?"

"That would be best," I told him.

He went out, leaving the corridor door open.

In five minutes he was back with a slender blonde girl of twenty-three in pale green silk. The looseness of her small mouth and the puffiness around her blue eyes weren't yet pronounced enough to spoil her prettiness.

I stood up.

"This is Miss Hambleton," he said.

She gave me a swift glance and then lowered her eyes again, nervously playing with the strap of a handbag she held.

"You can identify yourself?" I asked.

"Sure," the man said. "Show them to him, Sue."

She opened the bag, brought out some papers and things, and held them up for me to take.

"Sit down, sit down," the man said as I took them.

They sat on the sofa. I sat in the rocking chair again and examined the things she had given me. There were two letters addressed to Sue Hambleton here, her father's telegram welcoming her home, a couple of receipted department store bills, an automobile driver's license, and a savings account pass book that showed a balance of less than ten dollars.

By the time I had finished my examination the girl's embarrassment was gone. She looked levelly at me, as did the man beside her. I felt in my pocket, found my copy of the photograph New York had sent us at the beginning of the hunt, and looked from it to her.

"Your mouth could have shrunk, maybe," I said, "but how could your nose have got that much longer?"

"If you don't like my nose," she said, "how'd you like to go to hell?" Her face had turned red.

"That's not the point. It's a swell nose, but it's not Sue's." I held the photograph out to her. "See for yourself."

She glared at the photograph and then at the man.

"What a smart guy you are," she told him.

He was watching me with dark eyes that had a brittle shine to them between narrow-drawn eyelids. He kept on watching me while he spoke to her out of the side of his mouth, crisply. "Pipe down."

She piped down. He sat and watched me. I sat and watched him. A clock ticked seconds away behind me. His eyes began shifting their focus from one of my eyes to the other. The girl sighed.

He said in a low voice, "Well?"

I said, "You're in a hole."

"What can you make out of it?" he asked casually.

"Conspiracy to defraud."

The girl jumped up and hit one of his shoulders angrily with the back of a hand, crying, "What a smart guy you are, to get me in a jam like this. It was going to be duck soup—yeh! Eggs in the coffee—yeh! Now look at you. You haven't even got guts enough to tell this guy to go chase himself." She spun around to face me, pushing her red face down at me—I was still sitting in the rocker—snarling, "Well, what are you waiting for? Waiting to be kissed goodbye? We don't owe you anything, do we? We didn't get any of your lousy money, did we? Outside, then. Take the air. Dangle."

"Stop it, sister," I growled. "You'll bust something."

The man said, "For God's sake stop that bawling, Peggy, and give somebody else a chance." He addressed me, "Well, what do you want?"

"How'd you get into this?" I asked.

He spoke quickly, eagerly, "A fellow named Kenny gave me that stuff and told me about this Sue Hambleton, and her old man having plenty. I thought I'd give it a whirl. I figured the old man would either wire the dough right off the reel or wouldn't send it at all. I didn't figure on this send-a-man stuff. Then when his wire came, saying he was sending a man to see her, I ought to have dropped it.

"But hell! Here was a man coming with a grand in cash. That was too good to let go of without a try. It looked like there still might be a chance of copping, so I got Peggy to do Sue for me. If the man was coming today, it was a cinch he belonged out here on the Coast, and it was an even bet he wouldn't know Sue, would only have a description of her. From what Kenny had told me about her, I knew Peggy would come pretty close to fitting her description. I still don't see how you got that photograph. I only wired the old man yesterday. I mailed a couple of letters to Sue, here, yesterday, so we'd have them with the other identification stuff to get the money from the telegraph company on."

"Kenny gave you the old man's address?"

"Sure he did."

"Did he give you Sue's?"

"No."

"How'd Kenny get hold of the stuff?"

"He didn't say."

"Where's Kenny now?"

"I don't know. He was on his way east, with something else on the fire, and couldn't fool with this. That's why he passed it on to me."

"Big-hearted Kenny," I said. "You know Sue Hambleton?"

"No," emphatically. "I'd never even heard of her till Kenny told me."

"I don't like this Kenny," I said, "though without him your story's got some good points. Could you tell it leaving him out?"

He shook his head slowly from side to side, saying, "It wouldn't be the way it happened."

"That's too bad. Conspiracies to defraud don't mean as much to me as finding Sue. I might have made a deal with you."

He shook his head again, but his eyes were thoughtful, and his lower lip moved up to overlap the upper a little.

The girl had stepped back so she could see both of us as we talked, turning her face, which showed she didn't like us, from one to the other as we spoke our pieces. Now she fastened her gaze on the man, and her eyes were growing angry again.

I got up on my feet, telling him, "Suit yourself. But if you want to play it that way I'll have to take you both in."

He smiled with indrawn lips and stood up.

The girl thrust herself in between us, facing him.

"This is a swell time to be dummying up," she spit at him. "Pop off, you lightweight, or I will. You're crazy if you think I'm going to take the fall with you."

"Shut up," he said in his throat.

"Shut me up," she cried.

He tried to, with both hands. I reached over her shoulders and caught one of his wrists, knocked the other hand up.

She slid out from between us and ran around behind me, screaming, "Joe does know her. He got the things from her. She's at the St. Martin on O'Farrell Street—her and Babe McCloor."

While I listened to this I had to pull my head aside to let Joe's right hook miss me, had got his left arm twisted behind him, had turned my hip to catch his knee, and had got the palm of my left hand under his chin. I was ready to give his chin the Japanese tilt when he stopped wrestling and grunted, "Let me tell it."

"Hop to it," I consented, taking my hands away from him and stepping back.

He rubbed the wrist I had wrenched, scowling past me at the girl. He called her four unlovely names, the mildest of which was "a dumb twist," and told her, "He was bluffing about throwing us in the can. You don't think old man Hambleton's hunting for newspaper space, do you?" That wasn't a bad guess.

He sat on the sofa again, still rubbing his wrist. The girl stayed on the other side of the room, laughing at him through her teeth.

I said, "All right, roll it out, one of you."

"You've got it all," he muttered. "I glaumed that stuff last week when I was visiting Babe, knowing the story and hating to see a promising layout like that go to waste."

"What's Babe doing now?" I asked.

"I don't know."

"Is he still puffing them?"

"I don't know."

"Like hell you don't."

"I don't," he insisted. "If you know Babe you know you can't get anything out of him about what he's doing."

"How long have he and Sue been here?"

"About six months that I know of."

"Who's he mobbed up with?"

"I don't know. Any time Babe works with a mob he picks them up on the road and leaves them on the road."

"How's he fixed?"

"I don't know. There's always enough grub and liquor in the joint."

Half an hour of this convinced me that I wasn't going to get much information about my people here.

I went to the phone in the passageway and called the Agency. The boy on the switchboard told me MacMan was in the operative's room. I asked to have him sent up to me, and went back to the living room. Joe and Peggy took their heads apart when I came in.

MacMan arrived in less than ten minutes. I let him in and told him, "This fellow says his name's Joe Wales, and the girl's supposed to be Peggy Carroll who lives upstairs in 421. We've got them cold for conspiracy to defraud, but I've made a deal with them. I'm going out to look at it now. Stay here with them, in this room. Nobody goes in or out, and nobody but you gets to the phone. There's a fire escape in front of the window. The window's locked now. I'd keep it that way. If the deal turns out O.K. we'll let them go, but if they cut up on you while I'm gone there's no reason why you can't knock them around as much as you want."

MacMan nodded his hard round head and pulled a chair out between them and the door. I picked up my hat.

Joe Wales called, "Hey, you're not going to uncover me to Babe, are you? That's got to be part of the deal."

"Not unless I have to."

"I'd just as leave stand the rap," he said. "I'd be safer in jail."

"I'll give you the best break I can," I promised, "but you'll have to take what's dealt you."

Walking over to the St. Martin—only half a dozen blocks from Wales's place—I decided to go up against McCloor and the girl as a Continental op who suspected Babe of being in on a branch bank stick-up in Alameda the previous week. He hadn't been in on it—if the bank people had described half-correctly the men who had robbed them—so it wasn't likely my supposed suspicions would frighten him much. Clearing himself, he might give me some information I could use. The chief thing I wanted, of course, was a look at the girl, so I could report to her father that I had seen her. There was no reason for supposing that she and Babe knew her father was trying to keep an eye on her. Babe had a record. It was natural enough for sleuths to drop in now and then and try to hang something on him.

The St. Martin was a small three-story apartment house of red brick between two taller hotels. The vestibule register showed R. K. McCloor, 313, as Wales and Peggy had told me.

I pushed the bell button. Nothing happened. Nothing happened any of the four times I pushed it. I pushed the button labeled *Manager*.

The door clicked open. I went indoors. A beefy woman in a pink-striped cotton dress that needed pressing stood in an apartment doorway just inside the street door.

"Some people named McCloor live here?" I asked.

"Three-thirteen," she said.

"Been living here long?"

She pursed her fat mouth, looked intently at me, hesitated, but finally said, "Since last June."

"What do you know about them?"

She balked at that, raising her chin and her eyebrows.

I gave her my card. That was safe enough; it fit in with the pretext I intended using upstairs.

Her face, when she raised it from reading the card, was oily with curiosity.

"Come in here," she said in a husky whisper, backing through the doorway.

I followed her into her apartment. We sat on a chesterfield and she whispered, "What is it?"

"Maybe nothing." I kept my voice low, playing up to her theatricals. "He's done time for safe burglary. I'm trying to get a line on him now, on the off chance that he might have been tied up in a recent job. I don't know that he was. He may be going straight for all I know." I took his photograph—front and profile, taken at Leavenworth—out of my pocket. "This him?"

She seized it eagerly, nodded, said, "Yes, that's him, all right," turned it over to read the description on the back, and repeated, "Yes, that's him, all right."

"His wife is here with him?" I asked.

She nodded vigorously.

"I don't know her," I said. "What sort of looking girl is she?"

She described a girl who could have been Sue Hambleton. I couldn't show Sue's picture; that would have uncovered me if she and Babe heard about it.

I asked the woman what she knew about the McCloors. What she knew wasn't a great deal: paid their rent on time, kept irregular hours, had occasional drinking parties, quarreled a lot.

"Think they're in now?" I asked. "I got no answer on the bell."

"I don't know," she whispered. "I haven't seen either of them since night before last, when they had a fight."

"Much of a fight?"

"Not much worse than usual."

"Could you find out if they're in?" I asked.

She looked at me out of the ends of her eyes.

"I'm not going to make any trouble for you," I assured her. "But if they've blown I'd like to know it, and I reckon you would too."

"All right, I'll find out." She got up, patting a pocket in which keys jingled. "You wait here."

"I'll go as far as the third floor with you," I said, "and wait out of sight there."

"All right," she said reluctantly.

On the third floor, I remained by the elevator. She disappeared around a corner of the dim corridor, and presently a muffled electric bell rang. It rang three times. I heard her keys jingle and one of them grate in a lock. The lock clicked. I heard the doorknob rattle as she turned it.

Then a long moment of silence was ended by a scream that filled the corridor from wall to wall.

I jumped for the corner, swung around it, saw an open door ahead, went through it, and slammed the door shut behind me.

The scream stopped.

I was in a small dark vestibule with three doors beside the one I had come through. One door was shut. One opened into a bathroom. I went to the other.

The fat manager stood just inside it, her round back to me. I pushed past her and saw what she was looking at.

Sue Hambleton, in pale yellow pajamas trimmed with black lace, was lying across the bed. She lay on her back. Her arms were stretched out over her head. One leg was bent under her, one stretched out so that its bare foot rested on the floor. That bare foot was whiter than a live foot could be. Her face was white as her foot, except for a mottled swollen area from the right eyebrow to the right cheek-bone and dark bruises on her throat.

"Phone the police," I told the woman, and began poking into corners, closets and drawers.

It was late afternoon when I returned to the Agency. I asked the file clerk to see if we had anything on Joe Wales and Peggy Carroll, and then went into the Old Man's office.

He put down some reports he had been reading, gave me a nodded invitation to sit down, and asked, "You've seen her?"

"Yeah. She's dead."

The Old Man said, "Indeed," as if I had said it was raining, and smiled with polite attentiveness while I told him about it—from the time I had rung Wales's bell until I had joined the fat manager in the dead girl's apartment.

"She had been knocked around some, was bruised on the face and neck," I wound up. "But that didn't kill her."

"You think she was murdered?" he asked, still smiling gently.

"I don't know. Doc Jordan says he thinks it could have been arsenic. He's hunting for it in her now. We found a funny thing in the joint. Some thick sheets of dark gray paper were stuck in a book—*The Count of Monte Cristo*—wrapped in a month-old newspaper and wedged into a dark corner between the stove and the kitchen wall."

"Ah, arsenical fly paper," the Old Man murmured. "The Maybrick-Seddons trick. Mashed in water, four to six grains of arsenic can be soaked out of a sheet—enough to kill two people."

I nodded, saying, "I worked on one in Louisville in 1916. The mulatto janitor saw McCloor leaving at half-past nine yesterday morning. She was probably dead before that. Nobody's seen him since. Earlier in the morning the people in the next apartment had heard them talking, her groaning. But they had too many fights for the neighbors to pay much attention to that. The landlady told me they had a fight the night before that. The police are hunting for him."

"Did you tell the police who she was?"

"No. What do we do on that angle? We can't tell them about Wales without telling them all."

"I dare say the whole thing will have to come out," he said thoughtfully. "I'll wire New York."

I went out of his office. The file clerk gave me a couple of newspaper clippings. The first told me that fifteen months ago Joseph Wales, alias Holy Joe, had been arrested on the complaint of a farmer named Toomey that he had been taken for twenty-five hundred dollars on a phony "business opportunity" by Wales and three other men. The second clipping said the case had been dropped when Toomey failed to appear against Wales in court—bought off in the customary manner by the return of part or all of his money. That was all our files held on Wales, and they had nothing on Peggy Carroll.

MacMan opened the door for me when I returned to Wales's apartment.

"Anything doing?" I asked him.

"Nothing—except they've been belly-aching a lot." Wales came forward, asking eagerly, "Satisfied now?"

The girl stood by the window, looking at me with anxious eyes.

I didn't say anything.

"Did you find her?" Wales asked, frowning. "She was where I told you?"

"Yeah," I said.

"Well, then." Part of his frown went away. "That lets Peggy and me out, doesn't—" He broke off, ran his tongue over his lower lip, put a hand to his chin, asked sharply, "You didn't give them the tip-off on me, did you?"

I shook my head, no.

He took his hand from his chin and asked irritably, "What's the matter with you, then? What are you looking like that for?"

Behind him the girl spoke bitterly. "I knew damned well it would be like this," she said. "I knew damned well we weren't going to get out of it. Oh, what a smart guy you are!"

"Take Peggy into the kitchen, and shut both doors," I told Mac-Man. "Holy Joe and I are going to have a real heart-to-heart talk."

The girl went out willingly, but when MacMan was closing the door she put her head in again to tell Wales, "I hope he busts you in the nose if you try to hold out on him."

MacMan shut the door.

"Your playmate seems to think you know something," I said.

Wales scowled at the door and grumbled, "She's more help to me than a broken leg." He turned his face to me, trying to make it look frank and friendly. "What do you want? I came clean with you before. What's the matter now?"

"What do you guess?"

He pulled his lips in between his teeth. "What do you want to make me guess for?" he demanded. "I'm willing to play ball with you. But what can I do if you won't tell me what you want? I can't see inside your head."

"You'd get a kick out of it if you could."

He shook his head wearily and walked back to the sofa, sitting down bent forward, his hands together between his knees. "All right," he sighed. "Take your time about asking me. I'll wait for you."

I went over and stood in front of him. I took his chin between my left thumb and fingers, raising his head and bending my own down until our noses were almost touching. I said, "Where you stumbled, Joe, was in sending the telegram right after the murder."

"He's dead?" It popped out before his eyes had even had time to grow round and wide.

The question threw me off balance. I had to wrestle with my forehead to keep it from wrinkling, and I put too much calmness in my voice when I asked, "Is who dead?"

"Who? How do I know? Who do you mean?"

"Who did you think I meant?" I insisted.

"How do I know? Oh, all right! Old man Hambleton, Sue's father."

"That's right," I said, and took my hand away from his chin.

"And he was murdered, you say?" He hadn't moved his face an inch from the position into which I had lifted it. "How?"

"Arsenic fly paper."

"Arsenic fly paper." He looked thoughtful. "That's a funny one."

"Yeah, very funny. Where'd you go about buying some if you wanted it?"

"Buying it? I don't know. I haven't seen any since I was a kid. Nobody uses fly paper here in San Francisco anyway. There aren't enough flies."

"Somebody used some here," I said, "on Sue."

"Sue?" He jumped so that the sofa squeaked under him.

"Yeah. Murdered yesterday morning—arsenical fly paper."

"Both of them?" he asked incredulously.

"Both of who?"

"Her and her father."

"Yeah."

He put his chin far down on his chest and rubbed the back of one hand with the palm of the other. "Then I am in a hole," he said slowly.

"That's what," I cheerfully agreed. "Want to try talking yourself out of it?"

"Let me think."

I let him think, listening to the tick of the clock while he thought. Thinking brought drops of sweat out on his gray-white face. Presently he sat up straight, wiping his face with a fancily colored handkerchief. "I'll talk," he said. "I've got to talk now. Sue was getting ready to ditch Babe. She and I were going away. She—Here, I'll show you."

He put his hand in his pocket and held out a folded sheet of thick note paper to me. I took it and read:

Dear Joe:—

I can't stand this much longer—we've simply got to go soon. Babe beat me again tonight. Please, if you really love me, let's make it soon.

Sue

The handwriting was a nervous woman's, tall, angular, and piled up.

"That's why I made the play for Hambleton's grand," he said. "I've been shatting on my uppers for a couple of months, and when that letter came yesterday I just had to raise dough somehow to get her away. She wouldn't have stood for tapping her father though, so I tried to swing it without her knowing."

"When did you see her last?"

"Day before yesterday, the day she mailed that letter. Only I saw her in the afternoon—she was here—and she wrote it that night."

"Babe suspect what you were up to?"

"We didn't think he did. I don't know. He was jealous as hell all the time, whether he had any reason to be or not."

"How much reason did he have?"

Wales looked me straight in the eye and said, "Sue was a good kid."

I said, "Well, she's been murdered."

He didn't say anything.

Day was darkening into evening. I went to the door and pressed the light button. I didn't lose sight of Holy Joe Wales while I was doing it.

As I took my finger away from the button, something clicked at the window. The click was loud and sharp.

I looked at the window.

A man crouched there on the fire escape, looking in through the glass and lace curtain. He was a thick-featured dark man whose size identified him as Babe McCloor. The muzzle of a big black automatic was touching the glass in front of him. He had tapped the glass with it to catch our attention.

He had our attention.

There wasn't anything for me to do just then. I stood there and looked at him. I couldn't tell whether he was looking at me or at Wales. I could see him clearly enough, but the lace curtain spoiled my view of details like that. I imagined he wasn't neglecting either of us, and I didn't imagine the lace curtain hid much from him. He was closer to the curtain than we, and I had turned on the room's lights.

Wales, sitting dead-still on the sofa, was looking at McCloor. Wales's face wore a peculiar, stiffly sullen expression. His eyes were sullen. He wasn't breathing.

McCloor flicked the nose of his pistol against the pane, and a triangular piece of glass fell out, tinkling apart on the floor. It didn't, I was afraid, make enough noise to alarm MacMan in the kitchen. There were two closed doors between here and there.

Wales looked at the broken pane and closed his eyes. He closed them slowly, little by little, exactly as if he were falling asleep. He kept his stiffly sullen blank face turned straight to the window.

McCloor shot him three times.

The bullets knocked Wales down on the sofa, back against the wall. Wales's eyes popped open, bulging. His lips crawled back over his teeth, leaving them naked to the gums. His tongue came out. Then his head fell down and he didn't move any more.

When McCloor jumped away from the window I jumped to it. While I was pushing the curtain aside, unlocking the window and raising it, I heard his feet land on the cement paving below.

MacMan flung the door open and came in, the girl at his heels.

"Take care of this," I ordered as I scrambled over the sill. "McCloor shot him."

Wales's apartment was on the second floor. The fire escape ended there with a counter-weighted iron ladder that a man's weight would swing down into a cement-paved court.

I went down as Babe McCloor had gone, swinging down on the ladder till within dropping distance of the court, and then letting go.

There was only one street exit to the court. I took it.

A startled looking, smallish man was standing in the middle of the sidewalk close to the court, gaping at me as I dashed out.

I caught his arm, shook it. "A big guy running." Maybe I yelled. "Where?"

He tried to say something, couldn't, and waved his arm at billboards standing across the front of a vacant lot on the other side of the street.

I forgot to say, "Thank you," in my hurry to get over there.

I got behind the billboards by crawling under them instead of going to either end, where there were openings. The lot was large enough and weedy enough to give cover to anybody who wanted to lie down and bush-whack a pursuer—even anybody as large as Babe McCloor.

While I considered that, I heard a dog barking at one corner of the lot. He could have been barking at a man who had run by. I ran to that corner of the lot. The dog was in a board-fenced backyard, at the corner of a narrow alley that ran from the lot to a street.

I chinned myself on the board fence, saw a wire-haired terrier alone in the yard, and ran down the alley while he was charging my part of the fence.

I put my gun back in my pocket before I left the alley for the street.

A small touring car was parked at the curb in front of a cigar store some fifteen feet from the alley. A policeman was talking to a slim dark-faced man in the cigar store doorway.

"The big fellow that come out of the alley a minute ago," I said. "Which way did he go?"

The policeman looked dumb. The slim man nodded his head down the street, said, "Down that way," and went on with his conversation.

I said, "Thanks," and went on down the corner. There was a taxi phone there and two idle taxis. A block and a half below, a streetcar was going away. "Did the big fellow who came down here a minute ago take a taxi or the streetcar?" I asked the two taxi chauffeurs who were leaning against one of the taxis.

The rattier-looking one said, "He didn't take a taxi."

I said, "I'll take one. Catch that streetcar for me."

The streetcar was three blocks away before we got going. The street wasn't clear enough for me to see who got on and off it. We caught it when it stopped at Market Street.

"Follow along," I told the driver as I jumped out.

On the rear platform of the streetcar I looked through the glass. There were only eight or ten people aboard.

"There was a great big fellow got on at Hyde Street," I said to the conductor. "Where'd he get off?"

The conductor looked at the silver dollar I was turning over in my fingers and remembered that the big man got off at Taylor Street. That won the silver dollar.

I dropped off as the streetcar turned into Market Street. The taxi, close behind, slowed down, and its door swung open. "Sixth and Mission," I said as I hopped in.

McCloor could have gone in any direction from Taylor Street. I had to guess. The best guess seemed to be that he would make for the other side of Market Street.

It was fairly dark by now. We had to go down to Fifth Street to get off Market, then over to Mission, and back up to Sixth. We got to Sixth

Street without seeing McCloor. I couldn't see him on Sixth Street—either way from the crossing.

"On up to Ninth," I ordered, and while we rode told the driver what kind of man I was looking for.

We arrived at Ninth Street. No McCloor. I cursed and pushed my brains around.

The big man was a yegg. San Francisco was on fire for him. The yegg instinct would be to use a rattler to get away from trouble. The freight yards were in this end of town. Maybe he would be shifty enough to lie low instead of trying to powder. In that case, he probably hadn't crossed Market Street at all. If he stuck, there would still be a chance of picking him up tomorrow. If he was high-tailing, it was catch him now or not at all.

"Down to Harrison," I told the driver.

We went down to Harrison Street, and down Harrison to Third, up Bryant to Eighth, down Brannan to Third again, and over to Townsend— and we didn't see Babe McCloor.

"That's tough, that is," the driver sympathized as we stopped across the street from the Southern Pacific passenger station.

"I'm going over and look around in the station," I said. "Keep your eyes open while I'm gone."

When I told the copper in the station my trouble he introduced me to a couple of plain-clothes men who had been planted there to watch for McCloor. That had been done after Sue Hambleton's body was found. The shooting of Holy Joe Wales was news to them.

I went outside again and found my taxi in front of the door, its horn working overtime, but too asthmatically to be heard indoors. The ratty driver was excited.

"A guy like you said come up out of King Street just now and swung on a Number 16 car as it pulled away," he said.

"Going which way?"

"Thataway," pointing southeast.

"Catch him," I said, jumping in.

The streetcar was out of sight around a bend in Third Street two blocks below. When we rounded the bend, the streetcar was slowing up, four blocks ahead. It hadn't slowed up very much when a man leaned far out and stepped off. He was a tall man, but didn't look tall on account of his shoulder spread. He didn't check his momentum, but used it to carry him across the sidewalk and out of sight.

We stopped where the man had left the car.

I gave the driver too much money and told him, "Go back to Townsend Street and tell the copper in the station that I've chased Babe McCloor into the S. P. yards."

I thought I was moving silently down between two strings of box cars, but I had gone less than twenty feet when a light flashed in my face and a sharp voice ordered, "Stand still, you."

I stood still. Men came from between cars. One of them spoke my name, adding, "What are you doing here? Lost?" It was Harry Pebble, a police detective.

I stopped holding my breath and said, "Hello, Harry. Looking for Babe?"

"Yes. We've been going over the rattlers."

"He's here. I just tailed him in from the street."

Pebble swore and snapped the light off.

"Watch, Harry," I advised. "Don't play with him. He's packing plenty of gun and he's cut down one boy tonight."

"I'll play with him," Pebble promised, and told one of the men with him to go over and warn those on the other side of the yard that McCloor was in, and then to ring for reinforcements.

"We'll just sit on the edge and hold him in till they come," he said.

That seemed a sensible way to play it. We spread out and waited. Once Pebble and I turned back a lanky bum who tried to slip into the yard between us, and one of the men below us picked up a shivering kid who was trying to slip out. Otherwise nothing happened until Lieutenant Duff arrived with a couple of carloads of coppers.

Most of our force went into a cordon around the yard. The rest of us went through the yard in small groups, working it over car by car. We picked up a few hoboes that Pebble and his men had missed earlier, but we didn't find McCloor.

We didn't find any trace of him until somebody stumbled over a railroad bum huddled in the shadow of a gondola. It took a couple of minutes to bring him to, and he couldn't talk then. His jaw was broken. But when we asked if McCloor had slugged him, he nodded, and when we asked in which direction McCloor had been headed, he moved a feeble hand to the east.

We went over and searched the Santa Fe yards.

We didn't find McCloor.

I rode up to the Hall of Justice with Duff. MacMan was in the captain of detectives' office with three or four police sleuths.

"Wales die?" I asked.

"Yep."

"Say anything before he went?"

"He was gone before you were through the window."

"You held on to the girl?"

"She's here."

"She say anything?"

"We were waiting for you before we tapped her," detective-sergeant O'Gar said, "not knowing the angle on her."

"Let's have her in. I haven't had any dinner yet. How about the autopsy on Sue Hambleton?"

"Chronic arsenic poisoning."

"Chronic? That means it was fed to her little by little, and not in a lump?"

"Un-huh. From what he found in her kidneys, intestines, liver, stomach and blood, Jordan figures there was less than a grain of it in her. That wouldn't be enough to knock her off. But he says he found arsenic in the tips of her hair, and she'd have to be given some at least a month ago for it to have worked out that far."

"Any chance that it wasn't arsenic that killed her?"

"Not unless Jordan's a bum doctor."

A policewoman came in with Peggy Carroll.

The blonde girl was tired. Her eyelids, mouth corners and body drooped, and when I pushed a chair out toward her she sagged down in it.

O'Gar ducked his grizzled bullet head at me.

"Now, Peggy," I said, "tell us where you fit into this mess."

"I don't fit into it." She didn't look up. Her voice was tired. "Joe dragged me into it. He told you."

"You his girl?"

"If you want to call it that," she admitted.

"You jealous?"

"What," she asked, looking up at me, her face puzzled, "has that got to do with it?"

"Sue Hambleton was getting ready to go away with him when she was murdered."

The girl sat up straight in the chair and said deliberately, "I swear to God I didn't know she was murdered."

"But you did know she was dead," I said positively.

"I didn't," she replied just as positively.

I nudged O'Gar with my elbow. He pushed his undershot jaw at her and barked, "What are you trying to give us? You knew she was dead. How could you kill her without knowing it?"

While she looked at him I waved the others in. They crowded close around her and took up the chorus of the sergeant's song. She was barked, roared, and snarled at plenty in the next few minutes.

The instant she stopped trying to talk back to them I cut in again. "Wait," I said, very earnestly. "Maybe she didn't kill her."

"The hell she didn't," O'Gar stormed, holding the center of the stage so the others could move away from the girl without their retreat seeming too artificial. "Do you mean to tell me this baby—"

"I didn't say she didn't," I remonstrated. "I said maybe she didn't."

"Then who did?"

I passed the question to the girl. "Who did?"

"Babe," she said immediately.

O'Gar snorted to make her think he didn't believe her.

I asked, as if I were honestly perplexed, "How do you know that if you didn't know she was dead?"

"It stands to reason he did," she said. "Anybody can see that. He found out she was going away with Joe, so he killed her and then came to Joe's and killed him. That's just exactly what Babe would do when he found it out."

"Yeah? How long have *you* known they were going away together?"

"Since they decided to. Joe told me a month or two ago."

"And you didn't mind?"

"You've got this all wrong," she said. "Of course I didn't mind. I was being cut in on it. You know her father had the bees. That's what Joe was after. She didn't mean anything to him but an in to the old man's pockets. And I was to get my dib. And you needn't think I was crazy enough about Joe or anybody else to step off in the air for them. Babe got next and fixed the pair of them. That's a cinch."

"Yeah? How do you figure Babe would kill her?"

"That guy? You don't think he'd—"

"I mean how would he go about killing her?"

"Oh!" She shrugged. "With his hands, likely as not."

"Once he'd made up his mind to do it, he'd do it quick and violent?" I suggested.

"That would be Babe," she agreed.

"But you can't see him slow-poisoning her—spreading it out over a month?"

Worry came into the girl's blue eyes. She put her lower lip between her teeth, then said slowly, "No, I can't see him doing it that way. Not Babe."

"Who can you see doing it that way?"

She opened her eyes wide, asking, "You mean Joe?"

I didn't say anything.

"Joe might have," she said persuasively. "God only knows what he'd want to do it for, why he'd want to get rid of the kind of meal ticket she was going to be. But you couldn't always guess what he was getting at. He pulled plenty of dumb ones. He was too slick without being smart. If he was going to kill her, though, that would be about the way he'd go about it."

"Were he and Babe friendly?"

"No."

"Did he go to Babe's much?"

"Not at all that I know about. He was too leery of Babe to take a chance on being caught there. That's why I moved upstairs, so Sue could come over to our place to see him."

"Then how could Joe have hidden the fly paper he poisoned her with in her apartment?"

"Fly paper!" Her bewilderment seemed honest enough.

"Show it to her," I told O'Gar.

He got a sheet from the desk and held it close to the girl's face.

She stared at it for a moment and then jumped up and grabbed my arm with both hands.

"I didn't know what it was," she said excitedly. "Joe had some a couple of months ago. He was looking at it when I came in. I asked him what it was for, and he smiled that wisenheimer smile of his and said, 'You make angles out of it,' and wrapped it up again and put it in his pocket. I didn't pay much attention to him; he was always fooling with some kind of tricks that were supposed to make him wealthy, but never did."

"Ever see it again?"

"No."

"Did you know Sue very well?"

"I didn't know her at all. I never even saw her. I used to keep out of the way so I wouldn't gum Joe's play with her."

"But you know Babe?"

"Yes, I've been on a couple of parties where he was. That's all I know him."

"Who killed Sue?"

"Joe," she said. "Didn't he have that paper you say she was killed with?"

"Why did he kill her?"

"I don't know. He pulled some awful dumb tricks sometimes."

"You didn't kill her?"

"No, no, no!"

I jerked the corner of my mouth at O'Gar.

"You're a liar," he bawled, shaking the fly paper in her face. "You killed her." The rest of the team closed in, throwing accusations at her. They kept it up until she was groggy and the policewoman beginning to look worried.

Then I said angrily, "All right. Throw her in a cell and let her think it over." To her, "You know what you told Joe this afternoon: this is no time to dummy up. Do a lot of thinking tonight."

"Honest to God I didn't kill her," she said.

I turned my back to her. The policewoman took her away.

"Ho-hum," O'Gar yawned. "We gave her a pretty good ride at that, for a short one."

"Not bad," I agreed. "If anybody else looked likely, I'd say she didn't kill Sue. But if she's telling the truth, then Holy Joe did it. And why should he poison the goose that was going to lay nice yellow eggs for him? And how and why did he cache the poison in their apartment? Babe had the motive, but damned if he looks like a slow-poisoner to me. You can't tell, though; he and Holy Joe could even have been working together on it."

"Could," Duff said. "But it takes a lot of imagination to get that one down. Anyway you twist it, Peggy's our best bet so far. Go up against her again, hard, in the morning?"

"Yeah," I said. "And we've got to find Babe."

The others had had dinner. MacMan and I went out and got ours. When we returned to the detective bureau an hour later it was practically deserted of the regular operatives.

"All gone to Pier 42 on a tip that McCloor's there," Steve Ward told us.

"How long ago?"

"Ten minutes."

MacMan and I got a taxi and set out for Pier 42. We didn't get to Pier 42.

On First Street, half a block from the Embarcadero, the taxi suddenly shrieked and slid to a halt.

"What—?" I began, and saw a man standing in front of the machine. He was a big man with a big gun. "Babe," I grunted, and put my hand on MacMan's arm to keep him from getting his gun out.

"Take me to—" McCloor was saying to the frightened driver when he saw us. He came around to my side and pulled the door open, holding the gun on us.

He had no hat. His hair was wet, plastered to his head. Little streams of water trickled down from it. His clothes were dripping wet.

He looked surprised at us and ordered, "Get out."

As we got out he growled at the driver, "What the hell you got your flag up for if you had fares?"

The driver wasn't there. He had hopped out the other side and was scooting away down the street. McCloor cursed him and poked his gun at me, growling, "Go on, beat it."

Apparently he hadn't recognized me. The light here wasn't good, and I had a hat on now. He had seen me for only a few seconds in Wales's room.

I stepped aside. MacMan moved to the other side.

McCloor took a backward step to keep us from getting him between us and started an angry word.

MacMan threw himself on McCloor's gun arm.

I socked McCloor's jaw with my fist. I might just as well have hit somebody else for all it seemed to bother him.

He swept me out of his way and pasted MacMan in the mouth. MacMan fell back till the taxi stopped him, spit out a tooth, and came back for more.

I was trying to climb up McCloor's left side.

MacMan came in on his right, failed to dodge a chop of the gun, caught it square on the top of the noodle, and went down hard. He stayed down.

I kicked McCloor's ankle, but couldn't get his foot from under him. I rammed my right fist into the small of his back and got a left-handful of his wet hair, swinging on it. He shook his head, dragging me off my feet.

He punched me in the side and I could feel my ribs and guts flattening together like leaves in a book.

I swung my fist against the back of his neck. That bothered him. He made a rumbling noise down in his chest, crunched my shoulder in his left hand, and chopped at me with the gun in his right.

I kicked him somewhere and punched his neck again.

Down the street, at the Embarcadero, a police whistle was blowing. Men were running up First Street toward us.

McCloor snorted like a locomotive and threw me away from him. I didn't want to go. I tried to hang on. He threw me away from him and ran up the street.

I scrambled up and ran after him, dragging my gun out.

At the first corner he stopped to squirt metal at me—three shots. I squirted one at him. None of the four connected.

He disappeared around the corner. I swung wide around it, to make him miss if he were flattened to the wall waiting for me. He wasn't. He was a hundred feet ahead, going into a space between two warehouses. I went in after him, and out after him at the other end, making better time with my hundred and ninety pounds than he was making with his two-fifty.

He crossed a street, turning up, away from the waterfront. There was a light on the corner. When I came into its glare he wheeled and leveled his gun at me. I didn't hear it click, but I knew it had when he threw it at me. The gun went past with a couple of feet to spare and raised hell against a door behind me.

McCloor turned and ran up the street. I ran up the street after him.

I put a bullet past him to let the others know where we were. At the next corner he started to turn to the left, changed his mind, and went straight on.

I sprinted, cutting the distance between us to forty or fifty feet, and yelped, "Stop or I'll drop you."

He jumped sidewise into a narrow alley.

I passed it on the jump, saw he wasn't waiting for me, and went in. Enough light came in from the street to let us see each other and our surroundings. The alley was blind—walled on each side and at the other end by tall concrete buildings with steel-shuttered windows and doors.

McCloor faced me, less than twenty feet away. His jaw stuck out. His arms curved down free of his sides. His shoulders were bunched.

"Put them up," I ordered, holding my gun level.

"Get out of my way, little man," he grumbled, taking a stiff-legged step toward me. "I'll eat you up."

"Keep coming," I said, "and I'll put you down."

"Try it." He took another step, crouching a little. "I can still get to you *with* slugs in me."

"Not where I'll put them." I was wordy, trying to talk him into waiting till the others came up. I didn't want to have to kill him. We could have done that from the taxi. "I'm no Annie Oakley, but if I can't pop your kneecaps with two shots at this distance, you're welcome to me. And if you think smashed kneecaps are a lot of fun, give it a whirl."

"Hell with that," he said and charged.

I shot his right knee.

He lurched toward me.

I shot his left knee.

He tumbled down.

"You would have it," I complained.

He twisted around, and with his arms pushed himself into a sitting position facing me.

"I didn't think you had sense enough to do it," he said through his teeth.

I talked to McCloor in the hospital. He lay on his back in bed with a couple of pillows slanting his head up. The skin was pale and tight around his mouth and eyes, but there was nothing else to show he was in pain.

"You sure devastated me, bo," he said when I came in.

"Sorry," I said, "but—"

"I ain't beefing. I asked for it."

"Why'd you kill Holy Joe?" I asked, off-hand, as I pulled a chair up beside the bed.

"Uh-uh—you're tooting the wrong ringer."

I laughed and told him I was the man in the room with Joe when it happened.

McCloor grinned and said, "I thought I'd seen you somewheres before. So that's where it was. I didn't pay no attention to your mug, just so your hands didn't move."

"Why'd you kill him?"

He pursed his lips, screwed up his eyes at me, thought something over, and said, "He killed a broad I knew."

"He killed Sue Hambleton?" I asked.

He studied my face a while before he replied, "Yep."

"How do you figure that out?"

"Hell," he said, "I don't have to. Sue told me. Give me a butt."

I gave him a cigarette, held a lighter under it, and objected. "That doesn't exactly fit in with other things I know. Just what happened and what did she say? You might start back with the night you gave her the goog."

He looked thoughtful, letting smoke sneak slowly out of his nose, then said, "I hadn't ought to hit her in the eye, that's a fact. But, see, she had been out all afternoon and wouldn't tell me where she'd been, and we had a row about it. What's this—Thursday morning? That was Monday, then. After the row I went out and spent the night in a dump over on Army Street. I got home about seven the next morning. Sue was sick as hell, but she wouldn't let me get a croaker for her. That was kind of funny, because she was scared stiff."

McCloor scratched his head meditatively and suddenly drew in a great lungful of smoke, practically eating up the rest of the cigarette. He let the smoke leak out of mouth and nose together, looking dully through the cloud at me. Then he said brusquely, "Well, she went under. But before she went she told me she'd been poisoned by Holy Joe."

"She say how he'd given it to her?"

McCloor shook his head.

"I'd been asking her what was the matter, and not getting anything out of her. Then she starts whining that she's poisoned. 'I'm poisoned, Babe,' she whines. 'Arsenic. That damned Holy Joe,' she says. Then she won't say anything else, and it's not a hell of a while after that that she kicks off."

"Yeah? Then what'd you do?"

"I went gunning for Holy Joe. I knew him but didn't know where he jungled up, and didn't find out till yesterday. You was there when I came. You know about that. I had picked up a boiler and parked it over on Turk Street, for the getaway. When I got back to it, there was a copper standing close to it. I figured he might have spotted it as a hot one and was waiting to see who came for it, so I let it alone, and caught a streetcar instead, and cut for the yards. Down there I ran into a whole flock of hammer and saws and had to go overboard in China Basin, swimming up to a pier, being ranked again by a watchman there, swimming off to another, and finally getting through the line only to run into another bad break. I wouldn't of flagged that taxi if the *For Hire* flag hadn't been up."

"You knew Sue was planning to take a run-out on you with Joe?"

"I don't know it yet," he said. "I knew damned well she was cheating on me, but I didn't know who with."

"What would you have done if you had known that?" I asked.

"Me?" He grinned wolfishly. "Just what I did."

"Killed the pair of them," I said.

He rubbed his lower lip with a thumb and asked calmly, "You think I killed Sue?"

"You did."

"Serves me right," he said. "I must be getting simple in my old age. What the hell am I doing barbering with a lousy dick? That never got nobody nothing but grief. Well, you might just as well take it on the heel and toe now, my lad. I'm through spitting."

And he was. I couldn't get another word out of him.

The Old Man sat listening to me, tapping his desk lightly with the point of a long yellow pencil, staring past me with mild blue rimless-spectacled eyes. When I had brought my story up to date, he asked pleasantly, "How is MacMan?"

"He lost two teeth, but his skull wasn't cracked. He'll be out in a couple of days."

The Old Man nodded and asked, "What remains to be done?"

"Nothing. We can put Peggy Carroll on the mat again, but it's not likely we'll squeeze much more out of her. Outside of that, the returns are pretty well all in."

"And what do you make of it?"

I squirmed in my chair and said, "Suicide."

The Old Man smiled at me, politely but skeptically.

"I don't like it either," I grumbled. "And I'm not ready to write in a report yet. But that's the only total that what we've got will add up to. That fly paper was hidden behind the kitchen stove. Nobody would be crazy enough to try to hide something from a woman in her own kitchen like that. But the woman might hide it there.

"According to Peggy, Holy Joe had the fly paper. If Sue hid it, she got it from him. For what? They were planning to go away together, and were only waiting till Joe, who was on the nut, raised enough dough. Maybe they were afraid of Babe, and had the poison there to slip him if he tumbled to their plan before they went. Maybe they meant to slip it to him before they went anyway.

"When I started talking to Holy Joe about murder, he thought Babe was the one who had been bumped off. He was surprised, maybe, but as if he was surprised that it had happened so soon. He was more surprised when he heard that Sue had died too, but even then he wasn't so surprised as when he saw McCloor alive at the window.

"She died cursing Holy Joe, and she knew she was poisoned, and she wouldn't let McCloor get a doctor. Can't that mean that she had turned against Joe, and had taken the poison herself instead of feeding it to Babe? The poison was hidden from Babe. But even if he found it, I can't figure him as a poisoner. He's too rough. Unless he caught her trying to poison him and made her swallow the stuff. But that doesn't account for the month-old arsenic in her hair."

"Does your suicide hypothesis take care of that?" the Old Man asked.

"It could," I said. "Don't be kicking holes in my theory. It's got enough as it stands. But, if she committed suicide this time, there's no reason why she couldn't have tried it once before—say after a quarrel with Joe a month ago—and failed to bring it off. That would have put the arsenic in her. There's no real proof that she took any between a month ago and day before yesterday."

"No real proof," the Old Man protested mildly, "except the autopsy's finding—chronic poisoning."

I was never one to let experts' guesses stand in my way. I said, "They base that on the small amount of arsenic they found in her remains —less than a fatal dose. And the amount they find in your stomach after you're dead depends on how much you vomit before you die."

The Old Man smiled benevolently at me and asked, "But you're not, you say, ready to write this theory into a report? Meanwhile, what do you propose doing?"

"If there's nothing else on tap, I'm going home, fumigate my brains with Fatimas, and try to get this thing straightened out in my head. I think I'll get a copy of *The Count of Monte Cristo* and run through it. I haven't read it since I was a kid. It looks like the book was wrapped up with the fly paper to make a bundle large enough to wedge tightly between the wall and stove, so it wouldn't fall down. But there might be something in the book. I'll see anyway."

"I did that last night," the Old Man murmured.

I asked, "And?"

He took a book from his desk drawer, opened it where a slip of paper marked a place, and held it out to me, one pink finger marking a paragraph.

"Suppose you were to take a milligramme of this poison the first day, two milligrammes the second day, and so on. Well, at the end of ten days you would have taken a centigramme: at the end of twenty days increasing another milligramme, you would have taken three hundred centigrammes; that is to say, a dose you would support without inconvenience, and which would be very dangerous for any other person who had not taken the same precautions as yourself. Well, then, at the end of the month, when drinking water from the same carafe, you would kill the person who had drunk this water, without your perceiving otherwise than from slight inconvenience that there was any poisonous substance mingled with the water."

"That does it," I said. "That does it. They were afraid to go away without killing Babe, too certain he'd come after them. She tried to make herself immune from arsenic poisoning by getting her body accustomed to it, taking steadily increasing doses, so when she slipped the big shot in Babe's food she could eat it with him without danger. She'd be taken sick, but wouldn't die, and the police couldn't hang his death on her because she too had eaten the poisoned food.

"That clicks. After the row Monday night, when she wrote Joe the note urging him to make the getaway soon, she tried to hurry up her immunity, and increased her preparatory doses too quickly, took too large a shot. That's why she cursed Joe at the end; it was his plan."

"Possibly she overdosed herself in an attempt to speed it along," the Old Man agreed, "but not necessarily. There are people who can cultivate an ability to take large doses of arsenic without trouble, but it seems to be a sort of natural gift with them, a matter of some constitutional peculiarity. Ordinarily, anyone who tried it would do what Sue Hambleton did— slowly poison themselves until the cumulative effect was strong enough to cause death."

Babe McCloor was hanged, for killing Holy Joe Wales, six months later.

1929

The English tradition in detective writing has long operated within the formula W. H. Auden describes in "The Guilty Vicarage" (see excerpt, p. 156). American detective fiction, however, has tended to be more "hardboiled" and realistic, largely because of the influence of Dashiell Hammett and Raymond Chandler. Chandler, who admired Hammett greatly,

doubted that he "had any artistic aims whatever," but approved of the way he removed the crime story from the artificial English tradition: "Hammett took murder out of the Venetian vase and dropped it into the alley. . . . Hammett gave murder back to the kind of people that commit it for reasons, not just to provide a corpse; and with the means at hand, not hand-wrought dueling pistols, curare, and tropical fish." This sort of realism, however, can imply a statement about social values. When Chilean poet Pablo Neruda was asked by an interviewer about the detective novel, he was very quick to locate the statement he thought Hammett and other "hard-boiled" detective writers were making.

"He . . . changed the genre . . . and gave it a strong backbone": Pablo Neruda

Of course, whenever the detective story is spoken of, I think of Dashiell Hammett. He is the one who changed the genre from a subliterary phantasm and gave it a strong backbone. He is the great creator, and after him there are hundreds of others, John MacDonald among the most brilliant. All of them are prolific writers and they work extraordinarily hard. And almost all of the North American novelists of this school—the detective novel—are perhaps the most severe critics of the crumbling North American capitalist society. There is no greater denunciation than that which turns up in those detective novels about the fatigue and corruption of the politicians and the police, the influence of money in the big cities, the corruption which pops up in all parts of the North American system, in "the American way of life." It is, possibly, the most dramatic testimony to an epoch, and yet it is considered the flimsiest accusation, since detective stories are not taken into account by literary critics.

WILLIAM FAULKNER

(1897–1962)

BARN BURNING

The store in which the Justice of the Peace's court was sitting smelled of cheese. The boy, crouched on his nail keg at the back of the crowded room, knew he smelled cheese, and more: from where he sat he could see the ranked shelves close-packed with the solid, squat, dynamic shapes of tin cans whose labels his stomach read, not from the lettering which meant nothing to his mind but from the scarlet devils and the silver curve of fish—

314   *Short Fiction*

this, the cheese which he knew he smelled and the hermetic meat which his intestines believed he smelled coming in intermittent gusts momentary and brief between the other constant one, the smell and sense just a little of fear because mostly of despair and grief, the old fierce pull of blood. He could not see the table where the Justice sat and before which his father and his father's enemy (*our enemy* he thought in that despair; *ourn! mine and hisn both! He's my father!*) stood, but he could hear them, the two of them that is, because his father had said no word yet:

"But what proof have you, Mr. Harris?"

"I told you. The hog got into my corn. I caught it up and sent it back to him. He had no fence that would hold it. I told him so, warned him. The next time I put the hog in my pen. When he came to get it I gave him enough wire to patch up his pen. The next time I put the hog up and kept it. I rode down to his house and saw the wire I gave him still rolled on to the spool in his yard. I told him he could have the hog when he paid me a dollar pound fee. That evening a nigger came with the dollar and got the hog. He was a strange nigger. He said, 'He say to tell you wood and hay kin burn.' I said, 'What?' 'That whut he say to tell you,' the nigger said. 'Wood and hay kin burn.' That night my barn burned. I got the stock out but I lost the barn."

"Where is the nigger? Have you got him?"

"He was a strange nigger, I tell you. I don't know what became of him."

"But that's not proof. Don't you see that's not proof?"

"Get that boy up here. He knows." For a moment the boy thought too that the man meant his older brother until Harris said, "Not him. The little one. The boy," and, crouching, small for his age, small and wiry like his father, in patched and faded jeans even too small for him, with straight, uncombed, brown hair and eyes gray and wild as storm scud, he saw the men between himself and the table part and become a lane of grim faces, at the end of which he saw the Justice, a shabby, collarless, graying man in spectacles, beckoning him. He felt no floor under his bare feet; he seemed to walk beneath the palpable weight of the grim turning faces. His father, stiff in his black Sunday coat donned not for the trial but for the moving, did not even look at him. *He aims for me to lie,* he thought, again with that frantic grief and despair. *And I will have to do hit.*

"What's your name, boy?" the Justice said.

"Colonel Sartoris Snopes," the boy whispered.

"Hey?" the Justice said. "Talk louder. Colonel Sartoris? I reckon anybody named for Colonel Sartoris in this country can't help but tell the truth, can they?" The boy said nothing. *Enemy! Enemy!* he thought; for a moment he could not even see, could not see that the Justice's face was kindly nor discern that his voice was troubled when he spoke to the man named Harris: "Do you want me to question this boy?" But he could hear, and during those subsequent long seconds while there was absolutely no sound in the crowded little room save that of quiet and intent breathing it was as if he had swung outward at the end of a grape vine, over a ravine, and at the top of the swing had been caught in a prolonged instant of mesmerized gravity, weightless in time.

"No!" Harris said violently, explosively. "Damnation! Send him out of here!" Now time, the fluid world, rushed beneath him again, the voices coming to him again through the smell of cheese and sealed meat, the fear and despair and the old grief of blood:

"This case is closed. I can't find against you, Snopes, but I can give you advice. Leave this country and don't come back to it."

His father spoke for the first time, his voice cold and harsh, level, without emphasis: "I aim to. I don't figure to stay in a country among people who . . ." he said something unprintable and vile, addressed to no one.

"That'll do," the Justice said. "Take your wagon and get out of this country before dark. Case dismissed."

His father turned, and he followed the stiff black coat, the wiry figure walking a little stiffly from where a Confederate provost's man's[1] musket ball had taken him in the heel on a stolen horse thirty years ago, followed the two backs now, since his older brother had appeared from somewhere in the crowd, no taller than the father but thicker, chewing tobacco steadily, between the two lines of grim-faced men and out of the store and across the worn gallery and down the sagging steps and among the dogs and half-grown boys in the mild May dust where as he passed a voice hissed:

"Barn burner!"

Again he could not see, whirling; there was a face in a red haze, moonlike, bigger than the full moon, the owner of it half again his size, he leaping in the red haze toward the face, feeling no blow, feeling no shock when his head struck the earth, scrabbling up and leaping again, feeling no blow this time either and tasting no blood, scrabbling up to see the other boy in full flight and himself already leaping into pursuit as his father's hand jerked him back, the harsh, cold voice speaking above him: "Go get in the wagon."

It stood in a grove of locusts and mulberries across the road. His two hulking sisters in their Sunday dresses and his mother and her sister in calico and sunbonnets were already in it, sitting on and among the sorry residue of the dozen and more movings which even the boy could remember —the battered stove, the broken beds and chairs, the clock inlaid with mother-of-pearl, which would not run, stopped at some fourteen minutes past two o'clock of a dead and forgotten day and time, which had been his mother's dowry. She was crying, though when she saw him she drew her sleeve across her face and began to descend from the wagon. "Get back," the father said.

"He's hurt. I got to get some water and wash his . . ."

"Get back in the wagon," his father said. He got in too, over the

---

1. provost's man: a military policeman.

tail-gate. His father mounted to the seat where the older brother already sat and struck the gaunt mules two savage blows with the peeled willow, but without heat. It was not even sadistic; it was exactly that same quality which in later years would cause his descendants to overrun the engine before putting a motor car into motion, striking and reining back in the same movement. The wagon went on, the store with its quiet crowd of grimly watching men dropped behind; a curve in the road hid it. *Forever* he thought. *Maybe he's done satisfied now, now that he has* . . . stopping himself, not to say it aloud even to himself. His mother's hand touched his shoulder.

"Does hit hurt?" she said.

"Naw," he said. "Hit don't hurt. Lemme be."

"Can't you wipe some of the blood off before hit dries?"

"I'll wash to-night," he said. "Lemme be, I tell you."

The wagon went on. He did not know where they were going. None of them ever did or ever asked, because it was always somewhere, always a house of sorts waiting for them a day or two days or even three days away. Likely his father had already arranged to make a crop on another farm before he . . . Again he had to stop himself. He (the father) always did. There was something about his wolf-like independence and even courage when the advantage was at least neutral which impressed strangers, as if they got from his latent ravening ferocity not so much a sense of dependability as a feeling that his ferocious conviction in the rightness of his own actions would be of advantage to all whose interest lay with his.

That night they camped, in a grove of oaks and beeches where a spring ran. The nights were still cool and they had a fire against it, of a rail lifted from a nearby fence and cut into lengths—a small fire, neat, niggard almost, a shrewd fire; such fires were his father's habit and custom always, even in freezing weather. Older, the boy might have remarked this and wondered why not a big one; why should not a man who had not only seen the waste and extravagance of war, but who had in his blood an inherent voracious prodigality with material not his own, have burned everything in sight? Then he might have gone a step farther and thought that that was the reason: that niggard blaze was the living fruit of nights passed during those four years in the woods hiding from all men, blue or gray, with his strings of horses (captured horses, he called them). And older still, he might have divined the true reason: that the element of fire spoke to some deep mainspring of his father's being, as the element of steel or of powder spoke to other men, as the one weapon for the preservation of integrity, else breath were not worth the breathing, and hence to be regarded with respect and used with discretion.

But he did not think this now and he had seen those same niggard blazes all his life. He merely ate his supper beside it and was already half asleep over his iron plate when his father called him, and once more he followed the stiff back, the stiff and ruthless limp, up the slope and on to the starlit road where, turning, he could see his father against the stars but without face or depth—a shape black, flat, and bloodless as though cut from tin in the iron folds of the frockcoat which had not been made for him, the voice harsh like tin and without heat like tin:

"You were fixing to tell them. You would have told him." He didn't answer. His father struck him with the flat of his hand on the side of the head, hard but without heat, exactly as he had struck the two mules at the store, exactly as he would strike either of them with any stick in order to kill a horse fly, his voice still without fear or anger: "You're getting to be a man. You got to learn. You got to learn to stick to your own blood or you ain't going to have any blood to stick to you. Do you think either of them, any man there this morning, would? Don't you know all they wanted was a chance to get at me because they knew I had them beat? Eh?" Later, twenty years later, he was to tell himself, "If I had said they wanted only truth, justice, he would have hit me again." But now he said nothing. He was not crying. He just stood there. "Answer me," his father said.

"Yes," he whispered. His father turned.

"Get on to bed. We'll be there tomorrow."

Tomorrow they were there. In the early afternoon the wagon stopped before a paintless two-room house identical almost with the dozen others it had stopped before even in the boy's ten years, and again, as on the other dozen occasions, his mother and aunt got down and began to unload the wagon, although his two sisters and his father and brother had not moved.

"Likely hit ain't fitten for hawgs," one of the sisters said.

"Nevertheless, fit it will and you'll hog it and like it," his father said. "Get out of them chairs and help your Ma unload."

The two sisters got down, big, bovine, in a flutter of cheap ribbons; one of them drew from the jumbled wagon bed a battered lantern, the other a worn broom. His father handed the reins to the older son and began to climb stiffly over the wheel. "When they get unloaded, take the team to the barn and feed them." Then he said, and at first the boy thought he was still speaking to his brother: "Come with me."

"Me?" he said.

"Yes," his father said. "You."

"Abner," his mother said. His father paused and looked back— the harsh level stare beneath the shaggy, graying, irascible brows.

"I reckon I'll have a word with the man that aims to begin tomorrow owning me body and soul for the next eight months."

They went back up the road. A week ago—or before last night, that is—he would have asked where they were going, but not now. His father had struck him before last night but never before had he paused afterward to explain why; it was as if the blow and the following calm, outrageous voice still rang, repercussed, divulging nothing to him save the terrible handicap of being young, the light weight of his few years, just heavy enough to prevent his soaring free of the world as it seemed to be ordered but not heavy enough to keep him footed solid in it, to resist it and try to change the course of its events.

Presently he could see the grove of oaks and cedars and the other flowering trees and shrubs, where the house would be, though not the house yet. They walked beside a fence massed with honeysuckle and Cherokee roses and came to a gate swinging open between two brick pillars, and now, beyond a sweep of drive, he saw the house for the first time and at that instant he forgot his father and the terror and despair both, and even when he remembered his father again (who had not stopped) the terror and despair did not return. Because, for all the twelve movings, they had sojourned until now in a poor country, a land of small farms and fields and houses, and he had never seen a house like this before. *Hit's big as a courthouse* he thought quietly, with a surge of peace and joy whose reason he could not have thought into words, being too young for that: *They are safe from him. People whose lives are a part of this peace and dignity are beyond his touch, he no more to them than a buzzing wasp: capable of stinging for a little moment but that's all; the spell of this peace and dignity rendering even the barns and stable and cribs which belong to it impervious to the puny flames he might contrive . . .* this, the peace and joy, ebbing for an instant as he looked again at the stiff black back, the stiff and implacable limp of the figure which was not dwarfed by the house, for the reason that it had never looked big anywhere and which now, against the serene columned backdrop, had more than ever that impervious quality of something cut ruthlessly from tin, depthless, as though, sidewise to the sun, it would cast no shadow. Watching him, the boy remarked the absolutely undeviating course which his father held and saw the stiff foot come squarely down in a pile of fresh droppings where a horse had stood in the drive and which his father could have avoided by a simple change of stride. But it ebbed only for a moment, though he could not have thought this into words either, walking on in the spell of the house, which he could even want but without envy, without sorrow, certainly never with that ravening and jealous rage which unknown to him walked in the ironlike black coat before him: *Maybe he will feel it too. Maybe it will even change him now from what maybe he couldn't help but be.*

They crossed the portico. Now he could hear his father's stiff foot as it came down on the boards with clocklike finality, a sound out of all proportion to the displacement of the body it bore and which was not dwarfed either by the white door before it, as though it had attained to a sort of vicious and ravening minimum not to be dwarfed by anything—the flat, wide, black hat, the formal coat of broadcloth which had once been black but which had now that friction-glazed greenish cast of the bodies of old house flies, the lifted sleeve which was too large, the lifted hand like a curled claw. The door opened so promptly that the boy knew the Negro must have been watching them all the time, an old man with neat grizzled hair, in a linen jacket, who stood barring the door with his body, saying, "Wipe yo foots, white man, fo you come in here. Major ain't home nohow."

"Get out of my way, nigger," his father said, without heat too, flinging the door back and the Negro also and entering, his hat still on his head. And now the boy saw the prints of the stiff foot on the doorjamb and saw them appear on the pale rug behind the machinelike deliberation of the foot which seemed to bear (or transmit) twice the weight which the body compassed. The Negro was shouting "Miss Lula! Miss Lula!" somewhere behind them, then the boy, deluged as though by a warm wave by a suave turn of carpeted stair and a pendant glitter of chandeliers and a mute gleam of gold frames, heard the swift feet and saw her too, a lady—perhaps he had never seen her like before either—in a gray, smooth gown with lace at the throat and an apron tied at the waist and the sleeves turned back, wiping cake or biscuit dough from her hands with a towel as she came up the hall, looking not at his father at all but at the tracks on the blond rug with an expression of incredulous amazement.

"I tried," the Negro cried. "I tole him to . . ."

"Will you please go away?" she said in a shaking voice. "Major de Spain is not at home. Will you please go away?"

His father had not spoken again. He did not speak again. He did not even look at her. He just stood stiff in the center of the rug, in his hat, the shaggy iron-gray brows twitching slightly above the pebble-colored eyes as he appeared to examine the house with brief deliberation. Then with the same deliberation he turned; the boy watched him pivot on the good leg and saw the stiff foot drag round the arc of the turning, leaving a final long and fading smear. His father never looked at it, he never once looked down at the rug. The Negro held the door. It closed behind them, upon the hysteric and indistinguishable woman-wail. His father stopped at the top of the steps and scraped his boot clean on the edge of it. At the gate he stopped again. He stood for a moment, planted stiffly on the stiff foot, looking back at the house. "Pretty and white, ain't it?" he said. "That's sweat. Nigger sweat. Maybe it ain't white enough yet to suit him. Maybe he wants to mix some white sweat with it."

Two hours later the boy was chopping wood behind the house within which his mother and aunt and the two sisters (the mother and aunt, not the two girls, he knew that; even at this distance and muffled by walls the flat loud voices of the two girls emanated an incorrigible idle inertia) were setting up the stove to prepare a meal, when he heard the hooves and saw the linen-clad man on a fine sorrel mare, whom he recognized even before he saw the rolled rug in front of the Negro youth following on a fat bay carriage horse—a suffused, angry face vanishing, still at full gallop, beyond the corner of the house where his father and brother were sitting in the two tilted chairs; and a moment later, almost before he could have put the axe down, he heard the hooves again and watched the sorrel mare go back out of the yard, already galloping again. Then his father began to shout one of the sisters' names, who presently emerged backward from the kitchen door dragging the rolled rug along the ground by one end while the other sister walked behind it.

"If you ain't going to tote, go on and set up the wash pot," the first said.

"You, Sarty!" the second shouted. "Set up the wash pot!" His father appeared at the door, framed against that shabbiness, as he had been against that other bland perfection, impervious to either, the mother's anxious face at his shoulder.

"Go on," the father said. "Pick it up." The two sisters stooped, broad, lethargic; stooping, they presented an incredible expanse of pale cloth and a flutter of tawdry ribbons.

"If I thought enough of a rug to have to git hit all the way from France I wouldn't keep hit where folks coming in would have to tromp on hit," the first said. They raised the rug.

"Abner," the mother said. "Let me do it."

"You go back and git dinner," his father said. "I'll tend to this."

From the woodpile through the rest of the afternoon the boy watched them, the rug spread flat in the dust beside the bubbling wash-pot, the two sisters stooping over it with that profound and lethargic reluctance, while the father stood over them in turn, implacable and grim, driving them though never raising his voice again. He could smell the harsh homemade lye they were using; he saw his mother come to the door once and look toward them with an expression not anxious now but very like despair; he saw his father turn, and he fell to with the axe and saw from the corner of his eye his father raise from the ground a flattish fragment of field stone and examine it and return to the pot, and this time his mother actually spoke: "Abner. Abner. Please don't. Please, Abner."

Then he was done too. It was dusk; the whippoorwills had already begun. He could smell coffee from the room where they would presently eat the cold food remaining from the mid-afternoon meal, though when he entered the house he realized they were having coffee again probably because there was a fire on the hearth, before which the rug now lay spread over the backs of the two chairs. The tracks of his father's foot were gone. Where they had been were now long, water-cloudy scoriations resembling the sporadic course of a Lilliputian mowing machine.

It still hung there while they ate the cold food and then went to bed, scattered without order or claim up and down the two rooms, his mother in one bed, where his father would later lie, the older brother in the other, himself, the aunt, and the two sisters on pallets on the floor. But his father was not in bed yet. The last thing the boy remembered was the depthless, harsh silhouette of the hat and coat bending over the rug and it seemed to him that he had not even closed his eyes when the silhouette was standing over him, the fire almost dead behind it, the stiff foot prodding him awake. "Catch up the mule," his father said.

When he returned with the mule his father was standing in the black door, the rolled rug over his shoulder. "Ain't you going to ride?" he said.

"No. Give me your foot."

He bent his knee into his father's hand, the wiry, surprising power flowed smoothly, rising, he rising with it, on to the mule's bare back (they had owned a saddle once; the boy could remember it though not when or where) and with the same effortlessness his father swung the rug up in front of him. Now in the starlight they retraced the afternoon's path, up the dusty road rife with honeysuckle, through the gate and up the black tunnel to the drive to the lightless house, where he sat on the mule and felt the rough warp of the rug drag across his thighs and vanish.

"Don't you want me to help?" he whispered. His father did not answer and now he heard again that stiff foot striking the hollow portico with that wooden and clocklike deliberation, that outrageous overstatement of the weight it carried. The rug, hunched, not flung (the boy could tell that even in the darkness) from his father's shoulder struck the angle of wall and floor with a sound unbelievably loud, thunderous, then the foot again, unhurried and enormous; a light came on in the house and the boy sat, tense, breathing steadily and quietly and just a little fast, though the foot itself did not increase its beat at all, descending the steps now; now the boy could see him.

"Don't you want to ride now?" he whispered. "We kin both ride now," the light within the house altering now, flaring up and sinking. *He's coming down the stairs now,* he thought. He had already ridden the mule up beside the horse block; presently his father was up behind him and he doubled the reins over and slashed the mule across the neck, but before the animal could begin to trot the hard, thin arm came round him, the hard, knotted hand jerking the mule back to a walk.

In the first red rays of the sun they were in the lot, putting plow gear on the mules. This time the sorrel mare was in the lot before he heard it at all, the rider collarless and even bareheaded, trembling, speaking in a shaking voice as the woman in the house had done, his father merely looking up once before stooping again to the hame he was buckling, so that the man on the mare spoke to his stooping back:

"You must realize you have ruined that rug. Wasn't there anybody here, any of your women . . ." he ceased, shaking, the boy watching him, the older brother leaning now in the stable door, chewing, blinking slowly and steadily at nothing apparently. "It cost a hundred dollars. But you never had a hundred dollars. You never will. So I'm going to charge you twenty bushels of corn against your crop. I'll add it in your contract and when you come to the commissary you can sign it. That won't keep Mrs. de Spain quiet but maybe it will teach you to wipe your feet off before you enter her house again."

Then he was gone. The boy looked at his father, who still had not spoken or even looked up again, who was now adjusting the logger-head in the hame.

"Pap," he said. His father looked at him—the inscrutable face, the shaggy brows beneath which the gray eyes glinted coldly. Suddenly the boy went toward him, fast, stopping as suddenly. "You done the best you could!" he cried. "If he wanted hit done different why didn't he wait and tell you how? He won't git no twenty bushels! He won't git none! We'll gether hit and hide hit! I kin watch . . ."

"Did you put the cutter back in that straight stock like I told you?"

"No, sir," he said.

"Then go do it."

That was Wednesday. During the rest of that week he worked steadily, at what was within his scope and some which was beyond it, with an industry that did not need to be driven nor even commanded twice; he had this from his mother, with the difference that some at least of what he did he liked to do, such as splitting wood with the half-size axe which his mother and aunt had earned, or saved money somehow, to present him with at Christmas. In company with the two older women (and on one afternoon, even one of the sisters), he built pens for the shoat and the cow which were a part of his father's contract with the landlord, and one afternoon, his father being absent, gone somewhere on one of the mules, he went to the field.

They were running a middle buster now, his brother holding the plow straight while he handled the reins, and walking beside the straining mule, the rich black soil shearing cool and damp against his bare ankles, he thought *Maybe this is the end of it. Maybe even that twenty bushels that seems hard to have to pay for just a rug will be a cheap price for him to stop forever and always from being what he used to be;* thinking, dreaming now, so that his brother had to speak sharply to him to mind the mule: *Maybe he even won't collect the twenty bushels. Maybe it will all add up and balance and vanish—corn, rug, fire; the terror and grief, the being pulled two ways like between two teams of horses— gone, done with for ever and ever.*

Then it was Saturday; he looked up from beneath the mule he was harnessing and saw his father in the black coat and hat. "Not that," his father said. "The wagon gear." And then, two hours later, sitting in the wagon bed behind his father and brother on the seat, the wagon accomplished a final curve, and he saw the weathered paintless store with its tattered tobacco- and patent-medicine posters and the tethered wagons and saddle animals below the gallery. He mounted the gnawed steps behind his father and brother, and there again was the lane of quiet, watching faces for the three of them to walk through. He saw the man in spectacles sitting at the plank table and he did not need to be told this was a Justice of the Peace; he sent one glare of fierce, exultant, partisan defiance at the man in collar and cravat now, whom he had seen but twice before in his life, and that on a galloping horse, who now wore on his face an expression not of rage but of amazed unbelief which the boy could not have known was at the incredible circumstance of being sued by one of his own tenants, and came and stood against his father and cried at the Justice: "He ain't done it! He ain't burnt . . ."

"Go back to the wagon," his father said.

"Burnt?" the Justice said. "Do I understand this rug was burned too?"

"Does anybody here claim it was?" his father said. "Go back to the wagon." But he did not, he merely retreated to the rear of the room, crowded as that other had been, but not to sit down this time, instead, to stand pressing among the motionless bodies, listening to the voices:

"And you claim twenty bushels of corn is too high for the damage you did to the rug?"

"He brought the rug to me and said he wanted the tracks washed out of it. I washed the tracks out and took the rug back to him."

"But you didn't carry the rug back to him in the same condition it was in before you made the tracks on it."

His father did not answer, and now for perhaps half a minute there was no sound at all save that of breathing, the faint, steady suspiration of complete and intent listening.

"You decline to answer that, Mr. Snopes?" Again his father did not answer. "I'm going to find against you, Mr. Snopes. I'm going to find that you were responsible for the injury to Major de Spain's rug and hold you liable for it. But twenty bushels of corn seems a little high for a man in your circumstances to have to pay. Major de Spain claims it cost a hundred dollars. October corn will be worth about fifty cents. I figure that if Major de Spain can stand a ninety-five dollar loss on something he paid cash for, you can stand a five-dollar loss you haven't earned yet. I hold you in damages to Major de Spain to the amount of ten bushels of corn over and above your contract with him, to be paid to him out of your crop at gathering time. Court adjourned."

It had taken no time hardly, the morning was but half begun. He thought they would return home and perhaps back to the field, since they were late, far behind all other farmers. But instead his father passed on behind the wagon, merely indicating with his hand for the older brother to follow with it, and crossed the road toward the blacksmith shop opposite, pressing on after his father, overtaking him, speaking, whispering up at the harsh, calm face beneath the weathered hat: "He won't git no ten bushels neither. He won't git one. We'll . . ." until his father glanced for an instant down at him, the face absolutely calm, the grizzled eyebrows tangled above the cold eyes, the voice almost pleasant, almost gentle:

"You think so? Well, we'll wait till October anyway."

The matter of the wagon—the setting of a spoke or two and the tightening of the tires—did not take long either, the business of the tires accomplished by driving the wagon into the spring branch behind the shop and letting it stand there, the mules nuzzling into the water from time to time, and the boy on the seat with the idle reins, looking up the slope and through the sooty tunnel of the shed where the slow hammer rang and where his father sat on an upended cypress bolt, easily, either talking or listening, still sitting there when the boy brought the dripping wagon up out of the branch and halted it before the door.

"Take them on to the shade and hitch," his father said. He did so and returned. His father and the smith and a third man squatting on his heels inside the door were talking, about crops and animals; the boy, squatting too in the ammoniac dust and hoof-parings and scales of rust, heard his father tell a long and unhurried story out of the time before the birth of the older brother even when he had been a professional horsetrader. And then his father came up beside him where he stood before a tattered last year's circus poster on the other side of the store, gazing rapt and quiet at the scarlet horses, the incredible poisings and convolutions of tulle and tights and the painted leers of comedians, and said, "It's time to eat."

But not at home. Squatting beside his brother against the front wall, he watched his father emerge from the store and produce from a paper sack a segment of cheese and divide it carefully and deliberately into three with his pocket knife and produce crackers from the same sack. They all three squatted on the gallery and ate, slowly, without talking; then in the store again, they drank from a tin dipper tepid water smelling of the cedar bucket and of living beech trees. And still they did not go home. It was a horse lot this time, a tall rail fence upon and along which men stood and sat and out of which one by one horses were led, to be walked and trotted and then cantered back and forth along the road while the slow swapping and buying went on and the sun began to slant westward, they—the three of them—watching and listening, the older brother with his muddy eyes and his steady, inevitable tobacco, the father commenting now and then on certain of the animals, to no one in particular.

It was after sundown when they reached home. They ate supper by lamplight, then, sitting on the doorstep, the boy watched the night fully accomplish, listening to the whippoorwills and the frogs, when he heard his mother's voice: "Abner! No! No! Oh, God. Oh, God. Abner!" and he rose, whirled, and saw the altered light through the door where a candle stub now burned in a bottle neck on the table and his father, still in the hat and coat, at once formal and burlesque as though dressed carefully for some shabby and ceremonial violence, emptying the reservoir of the lamp back into the five-gallon kerosene can from which it had been filled, while the mother tugged at his arm until he shifted the lamp to the other hand and flung her back, not savagely or viciously, just hard, into the wall, her hands flung out against the wall for balance, her mouth open and in her face the same quality of hopeless despair as had been in her voice. Then his father saw him standing in the door.

"Go to the barn and get that can of oil we were oiling the wagon with," he said. The boy did not move. Then he could speak.

"What . . ." he cried. "What are you . . ."

"Go get that oil," his father said. "Go."

Then he was moving, running, outside the house, toward the stable: this the old habit, the old blood which he had not been permitted to choose for himself, which had been bequeathed him willy nilly and which had run for so long (and who knew where, battening on what of outrage and savagery and lust) before it came to him. *I could keep on,* he thought. *I could run on and on and never look back, never need to see his face again. Only I can't. I can't,* the rusted can in his hand now, the liquid sploshing in it as he ran back to the house and into it, into the sound of his mother's weeping in the next room, and handed the can to his father.

"Ain't you going to even send a nigger?" he cried. "At least you sent a nigger before!"

This time his father didn't strike him. The hand came even faster than the blow had, the same hand which had set the can on the table with almost excruciating care flashing from the can toward him too quick for him to follow it, gripping him by the back of his shirt and on to tiptoe before he had seen it quit the can, the face stooping at him in breathless and frozen ferocity, the cold, dead voice speaking over him to the older brother who leaned against the table, chewing with that steady, curious, sidewise motion of cows:

"Empty the can into the big one and go on. I'll catch up with you."

"Better tie him up to the bedpost," the brother said.

"Do like I told you," the father said. Then the boy was moving, his bunched shirt and the hard, bony hand between his shoulder-blades, his toes just touching the floor, across the room and into the other one, past the sisters sitting with spread heavy thighs in the two chairs over the cold hearth, and to where his mother and aunt sat side by side on the bed, the aunt's arms about his mother's shoulders.

"Hold him," the father said. The aunt made a startled movement. "Not you," the father said. "Lennie. Take hold of him. I want to see you do it." His mother took him by the wrist. "You'll hold him better than that. If he gets loose don't you know what he is going to do? He will go up yonder." He jerked his head toward the road. "Maybe I'd better tie him."

"I'll hold him," his mother whispered.

"See you do then." Then his father was gone, the stiff foot heavy and measured upon the boards, ceasing at last.

Then he began to struggle. His mother caught him in both arms, he jerking and wrenching at them. He would be stronger in the end, he knew that. But he had no time to wait for it. "Lemme go!" he cried. "I don't want to have to hit you!"

"Let him go!" the aunt said. "If he don't go, before God, I am going up there myself!"

"Don't you see I can't?" his mother cried. "Sarty! Sarty! No! No! Help me, Lizzie!"

Then he was free. His aunt grasped at him but it was too late. He whirled, running, his mother stumbled forward on to her knees behind him, crying to the nearer sister: "Catch him, Net! Catch him!" But that was too late too, the sister (the sisters were twins, born at the same time, yet either of them now gave the impression of being, encompassing as much living meat and volume and weight as any other two of the family) not yet having begun to rise from the chair, her head, face, alone merely turned, presenting to him in the flying instant an astonishing expanse of young female features untroubled by any surprise even, wearing only an expression of bovine interest. Then he was out of the room, out of the house, in the mild dust of the starlit road and the heavy rifeness of honeysuckle, the pale ribbon unspooling with terrific slowness under his running feet, reaching the gate at last and turning in, running, his heart and lungs drumming, on up the drive toward the lighted house, the lighted door. He did not knock, he burst in, sobbing for breath, incapable for the moment of speech; he saw the astonished face of the Negro in the linen jacket without knowing when the Negro had appeared.

"De Spain!" he cried, panted. "Where's . . ." then he saw the white man too emerging from a white door down the hall. "Barn!" he cried. "Barn!"

"What?" the white man said. "Barn?"

"Yes!" the boy cried. "Barn!"

"Catch him!" the white man shouted.

But it was too late this time too. The Negro grasped his shirt, but the entire sleeve, rotten with washing, carried away, and he was out that door too and in the drive again, and had actually never ceased to run even while he was screaming into the white man's face.

Behind him the white man was shouting, "My horse! Fetch my horse!" and he thought for an instant of cutting across the park and climbing the fence into the road, but he did not know the park nor how high the vine-massed fence might be and he dared not risk it. So he ran on down the drive, blood and breath roaring; presently he was in the road again though he could not see it. He could not hear either: the galloping mare was almost upon him before he heard her, and even then he held his course, as if the very urgency of his wild grief and need must in a moment more find him wings, waiting until the ultimate instant to hurl himself aside and into the weed-choked roadside ditch as the horse thundered past and on, for an instant in furious silhouette against the stars, the tranquil early summer night sky which, even before the shape of the horse and rider vanished, stained abruptly and violently upward: a long, swirling roar incredible and soundless, blotting the stars, and he springing up and into the road again, running again, knowing it was too late yet still running even after he heard the shot and, an instant later, two shots, pausing now without knowing he had ceased to run, crying "Pap! Pap!", running again before he knew he had begun to run, stumbling, tripping over something and scrabbling up again without ceasing to run, looking backward over his shoulder at the glare as he got up, running on among the invisible trees, panting, sobbing, "Father! Father!"

At midnight he was sitting on the crest of a hill. He did not know it was midnight and he did not know how far he had come. But there was no glare behind him now and he sat now, his back toward what he had called home for four days anyhow, his face toward the dark woods which he would enter when breath was strong again, small, shaking steadily in the chill darkness, hugging himself into the remainder of his thin, rotten shirt, the grief and despair now no longer terror and fear but just grief and despair. *Father. My father*, he thought. "He was brave!" he cried suddenly, aloud but not loud, no more than a whisper: "He was! He was in the war! He was in Colonel Sartoris' cav'ry!" not knowing that his father had gone to that war a private in the fine old European sense, wearing no uniform, admitting the authority of and giving fidelity to no man or army or flag, going to war as Malbrouck himself did: for booty—it meant nothing and less than nothing to him if it were enemy booty or his own.

The slow constellations wheeled on. It would be dawn and then sun-up after a while and he would be hungry. But that would be tomorrow and now he was only cold, and walking would cure that. His breathing was easier now and he decided to get up and go on, and then he found that he had been asleep because he knew it was almost dawn, the night almost over. He could tell that from the whippoorwills. They were everywhere now among the dark trees below him, constant and inflectioned and ceaseless, so that, as the instant for giving over to the day birds drew nearer and nearer, there was no interval at all between them. He got up. He was a little stiff, but walking would cure that too as it would the cold, and soon there would be the sun. He went on down the hill, toward the dark woods within which the liquid silver voices of the birds called unceasing—the rapid and urgent beating of the urgent and quiring heart of the late spring night. He did not look back.

1939

Ab Snopes, the protagonist in "Barn Burning," is the founder of a clan of ne'er-do-wells who appear repeatedly in William Faulkner's fiction. Colonel Sartoris is the father of a clan that produces many of Faulkner's more high-minded characters. Faulkner's comments on the Father of Evil may illuminate aspects of both characters.

"The splendid, dark incorrigible one": William Faulkner

During all this time, the angels (with one exception; God had probably had trouble with this one before) merely looked on and watched—the serene and blameless seraphim. . . . Because they were white, immaculate, negative, without past, without thought or grief or regrets or hopes, except that one—the splendid dark incorrigible one, who possessed the arrogance and pride to demand with, and the temerity to object with, and the ambition to substitute with—not only to decline to accept a condition just because it was a fact, but to want to substitute another condition in its place.

But this one's opinion of man was even worse than that of the negative and shining ones. This one not only believed that man was incapable of anything but baseness, this one believed that baseness had been inculcated in man to be used for base personal aggrandizement by them of a higher and more ruthless baseness. So God used the dark spirit too. He did not merely cast it shrieking out of the universe, as He could have done. Instead, He used it. He already presaw the long roster of the ambition's ruthless avatars—Genghis and Caesar and William and Hitler and Barca and Stalin and Bonaparte and Huey Long. But He used more—not only the ambition and the ruthlessness and the arrogance to show man what to revolt against, but also the temerity to revolt and the will to change what one does not like. Because He presaw the long roster of the other avatars of that rebellious and uncompromising pride also, the long roster of names longer and more enduring than those of the tyrants and oppressors.

ERNEST HEMINGWAY

(1899–1961)

A CLEAN, WELL-LIGHTED PLACE

It was late and every one had left the café except an old man who sat in the shadow the leaves of the tree made against the electric light. In the day time the street was dusty, but at night the dew settled the dust and the old man liked to sit late because he was deaf and now at night it was quiet and he felt the difference. The two waiters inside the café knew that the old man was a little drunk, and while he was a good client they knew that if he became too drunk he would leave without paying, so they kept watch on him.

"Last week he tried to commit suicide," one waiter said.

"Why?"

"He was in despair."

"What about?"

"Nothing."

"How do you know it was nothing?"

"He has plenty of money."

They sat together at a table that was close against the wall near the door of the café and looked at the terrace where the tables were all empty except where the old man sat in the shadow of the leaves of the tree that moved slightly in the wind. A girl and a soldier went by in the street. The street light shone on the brass number on his collar. The girl wore no head covering and hurried beside him.

"The guard will pick him up," one waiter said.

"What does it matter if he gets what he's after?"

"He had better get off the street now. The guard will get him. They went by five minutes ago."

The old man sitting in the shadow rapped on his saucer with his glass. The younger waiter went over to him.

"What do you want?"

The old man looked at him. "Another brandy," he said.

"You'll be drunk," the waiter said. The old man looked at him. The waiter went away.

"He'll stay all night," he said to his colleague. "I'm sleepy now. I never get into bed before three o'clock. He should have killed himself last week."

The waiter took the brandy bottle and another saucer from the counter inside the café and marched out to the old man's table. He put down the saucer and poured the glass full of brandy.

"You should have killed yourself last week," he said to the deaf man. The old man motioned with his finger. "A little more," he said. The waiter poured on into the glass so that the brandy slopped over and ran down the stem into the top saucer of the pile. "Thank you," the old man said. The waiter took the bottle back inside the café. He sat down at the table with his colleague again.

"He's drunk now," he said.

"He's drunk every night."

"What did he want to kill himself for?"

"How should I know."

"How did he do it?"

"He hung himself with a rope."

"Who cut him down?"

"His niece."

"Why did they do it?"

"Fear for his soul."

"How much money has he got?"

"He's got plenty."

"He must be eighty years old."

"Anyway I should say he was eighty."

"I wish he would go home. I never get to bed before three o'clock. What kind of hour is that to go to bed?"

"He stays up because he likes it."

"He's lonely. I'm not lonely. I have a wife waiting in bed for me."

"He had a wife once too."

"A wife would be no good to him now."

"You can't tell. He might be better with a wife."

"His niece looks after him. You said she cut him down."

"I know."

"I wouldn't want to be that old. An old man is a nasty thing."

"Not always. This old man is clean. He drinks without spilling. Even now, drunk. Look at him."

"I don't want to look at him. I wish he would go home. He has no regard for those who must work."

The old man looked from his glass across the square, then over at the waiters.

"Another brandy," he said, pointing to his glass. The waiter who was in a hurry came over.

"Finished," he said, speaking with that omission of syntax stupid people employ when talking to drunken people or foreigners. "No more tonight. Close now."

"Another," said the old man.

"No. Finished." The waiter wiped the edge of the table with a towel and shook his head.

The old man stood up, slowly counted the saucers, took a leather coin purse from his pocket and paid for the drinks, leaving half a peseta tip.

The waiter watched him go down the street, a very old man walking unsteadily but with dignity.

"Why didn't you let him stay and drink?" the unhurried waiter asked. They were putting up the shutters. "It is not half-past two."

"I want to go home to bed."

"What is an hour?"

"More to me than to him."

"An hour is the same."

"You talk like an old man yourself. He can buy a bottle and drink at home."

"It's not the same."

"No, it is not," agreed the waiter with a wife. He did not wish to be unjust. He was only in a hurry.

"And you? You have no fear of going home before your usual hour?"

"Are you trying to insult me?"

"No, hombre, only to make a joke."

"No," the waiter who was in a hurry said, rising from pulling down the metal shutters. "I have confidence. I am all confidence."

"You have youth, confidence, and a job," the older waiter said. "You have everything."

"And what do you lack?"

"Everything but work."

"You have everything I have."

"No. I have never had confidence and I am not young."

"Come on. Stop talking nonsense and lock up."

"I am of those who like to stay late at the café," the older waiter said. "With all those who do not want to go to bed. With all those who need a light for the night."

"I want to go home and into bed."

"We are of two different kinds," the older waiter said. He was now dressed to go home. "It is not only a question of youth and confidence although those things are very beautiful. Each night I am reluctant to close up because there may be some one who needs the café."

"Hombre, there are bodegas open all night long."

"You do not understand. This is a clean and pleasant café. It is well lighted. The light is very good and also, now, there are shadows of the leaves."

"Good night," said the younger waiter.

"Good night," the other said. Turning off the electric light he continued the conversation with himself. It is the light of course but it is necessary that the place be clean and pleasant. You do not want music. Certainly you do not want music. Nor can you stand before a bar with dignity although that is all that is provided for these hours. What did he fear? It was not fear or dread. It was a nothing that he knew too well. It was all a nothing and a man was nothing too. It was only that and light was all it needed and a certain cleanness and order. Some lived in it and never felt it but he knew it all was nada y pues nada y nada y pues nada.[1] Our nada who art in nada, nada be thy name thy kingdom nada thy will be nada in nada as it is in nada. Give us this nada our daily nada and nada us our nada as we nada our nadas and nada us not into nada but deliver us from nada; pues nada. Hail nothing full of nothing, nothing is with thee. He smiled and stood before a bar with a shining steam pressure coffee machine.

"What's yours?" asked the barman.

"Nada."

"Otro loco mas,[2]" said the barman and turned away.

"A little cup," said the waiter.

The barman poured it for him.

"The light is very bright and pleasant but the bar is unpolished," the waiter said.

The barman looked at him but did not answer. It was too late at night for conversation.

"You want another copita?" the barman asked.

"No, thank you," said the waiter and went out. He disliked bars and bodegas. A clean, well-lighted café was a very different thing. Now, without thinking further, he would go home to his room. He would lie in the bed and finally, with daylight, he would go to sleep. After all, he said to himself, it is probably only insomnia. Many must have it.

1933

In many of Ernest Hemingway's stories the point of view is largely objective and the dialogue is only occasionally supported by glimpses into the unspoken thoughts of the characters. Hemingway enthusiasts like Eudora Welty

---

1. . . . nothing and so nothing and nothing and so nothing.
2. another mad one

applaud Hemingway's reluctance to comment directly on the story or use the omniscient point of view. Others, like Virginia Woolf, are less enthusiastic.

"Not radiant from the front; but from the side": Eudora Welty

Part of Hemingway's power comes straight out of this conditioning he imposes on his stories. In San Francisco there's a painting by Goya, who himself used light, action, and morality dramatically, of course. The bull ring and the great tossing wall of spectators are cut in diagonal half by a great shadow of afternoon. There lies the wonder of the painting—the opaque paired with the clear, golden sun; half of the action, with dense, clotting shade. It's like this in Hemingway's plots.

In the same way, one power of Hemingway's famous use of conversation derives from the fact that it's often in translated or broken sentences —a shadow inserted between the direct speakers. It is an obscuring and at the same time a magical touch; it illuminates from the side. It makes us aware of the fact that communication is going on.

As we now picture Hemingways' story, isn't it something like this— not transparent, not radiant from the front; but from the side, from without his story, from a moral source, comes its beam of light; and his story is not radiant, but spotlighted.

"Please please please stop talking": Virginia Woolf

For some reason the book of short stories does not seem to us to go as deep or to promise as much as the novel. Perhaps it is the excessive use of dialogue, for Mr. Hemingway's use of it is surely excessive. A writer will always be chary of dialogue because dialogue puts the most violent pressure upon the reader's attention. He has to hear, to see, to supply the right tone, and to fill in the background from what the characters say without any help from the author. Therefore, when fictitious people are allowed to speak it must be because they have something so important to say that it stimulates the reader to do rather more than his share of the work of creation. But, although Mr. Hemingway keeps us under the fire of dialogue constantly, his people, half the time, are saying what the author could say much more economically for them. At last we are inclined to cry out with the little girl in 'Hills Like White Elephants': 'Would you please please please please please please stop talking?'

JORGE LUIS BORGES

(1899–1986)

THE ALEPH

translated from the Spanish by Anthony Kerrigan

O God, I could be bounded in a nutshell and count myself a King of infinite space.

Hamlet, II, 2.

But they will teach us that Eternity is the Standing still of the Present Time, a *Nunc-stans* (as the Schools call it); which neither they, nor any else understand, no more than they would a *Hic-stans* for an Infinite greatness of Place.

Leviathan, IV, 46.

On the incandescent February morning Beatriz Viterbo died, after a death agony so imperious it did not for a moment descend into sentimentalism or fear, I noticed that the iron billboards in the Plaza Constitución[1] bore new advertisements for some brand or other of Virginia tobacco; I was saddened by this fact, for it made me realize that the incessant and vast universe was already moving away from her and that this change was the first in an infinite series. The universe would change but I would not, I thought with melancholy vanity; I knew that sometimes my vain devotion had exasperated her; now that she was dead, I could consecrate myself to her memory, without hope but also without humiliation. I thought of how the thirtieth of April was her birthday; to visit her house in Calle Garay on that day and pay my respects to her father and Carlos Argentino Daneri, her first cousin, would be an act of courtesy, irreproachable and perhaps even unavoidable. I would wait, once again, in the twilight of the overladen entrance hall, I would study, one more time, the particulars of her numerous portraits: Beatriz Viterbo in profile, in color; Beatriz wearing a mask, during the Carnival of 1921; Beatriz at her First Communion; Beatriz on the day of her wedding to Roberto Alessandri; Beatriz a little while after the divorce, at a dinner in the Club Hípico; Beatriz with Delia San Marco Porcel and Carlos Argentino; Beatriz with the Pekingese which had been a present from Villegas Haedo; Beatriz from the front and in a three-quarter view, smiling, her hand under her chin. . . . I would not be obliged, as on other occasions, to justify my presence with moderate-priced offerings of books, with books whose pages, finally, I learned to cut beforehand, so as to avoid finding, months later, that they were still uncut.

---

1. Constitution Square, the main plaza in Mexico City.

Beatriz Viterbo died in 1929. From that time on, I never let a thirtieth of April go by without a visit to her house. I used to arrive there around seven-fifteen and stay about twenty-five minutes. Every year I came a little later and stayed a little longer. In 1933 a torrential rain worked to my advantage: they were forced to invite me to dine. I did not fail to avail myself of this advantageous precedent. In 1934, I appeared, just after eight, with a honey nutcake from Santa Fe. With the greatest naturalness, I remained for supper. And thus, on these melancholy and vainly erotic anniversaries, Carlos Argentino Daneri began gradually to confide in me.

Beatriz was tall, fragile, lightly leaning forward: there was in her walk (if the oxymoron is acceptable) a kind of gracious torpor, the beginnings of an ecstasy. Carlos Argentino is rosy, important, gray-haired, fine-featured. He holds some subordinate position or other in an illegible library in the south side suburbs. He is authoritarian, but also ineffective. Until very recently, he took advantage of nights and holidays to avoid going out of his house. At a remove of two generations, the Italian s and the copious gesticulation of the Italians survive in him. His mental activity is continuous, impassioned, versatile, and altogether insignificant. He abounds in useless analogies and fruitless scruples. He possesses (as did Beatriz) long, lovely, tapering hands. For several months he was obsessed with Paul Fort, less with his ballads than with the idea of irreproachable glory. "He is the Prince of the poets of France," he would repeat fatuously. "You will set yourself against him in vain; no, not even your most poisoned barb will reach him."

The thirtieth of April, 1941, I allowed myself to add to the gift of honey nutcake a bottle of Argentine cognac. Carlos Argentino tasted it, judged it "interesting," and, after a few glasses, launched on a vindication of modern man.

"I evoke him," he said with rather inexplicable animation, "in his studio-laboratory, in the city's watchtowers, so to say, supplied with telephones, telegraphs, phonographs, radiotelephone apparatus, cinematographic equipment, magic lanterns, glossaries, timetables, compendiums, bulletins. . . ."

He remarked that for a man of such faculties the act of travel was useless. Our twentieth century had transformed the fable of Mohammed and the mountain: the mountains, now, converged upon the modern Mohammed.

His ideas seemed so inept to me, their exposition so pompous and so vast, that I immediately related them to literature: I asked him why he did not write them down. Foreseeably he replied that he had already done so: these concepts, and others no less novel, figured in the Augural Canto, or more simply, the Prologue Canto, of a poem on which he had been working for many years, without publicity, without any deafening to-do, putting his entire reliance on those two props known as work and solitude. First, he opened the floodgates of the imagination; then he made use of a sharp file. The poem was titled *The Earth;* it consisted of a description of the planet, wherein, naturally, there was no lack of picturesque digression and elegant apostrophe.

I begged him to read me a passage, even though brief. He opened a drawer in his desk, took out a tall bundle of pages from a pad, each sheet stamped with the letterhead of the Juan Crisóstomo Lafinur Library, and, with sonorous satisfaction, read out:

> *I have seen, like the Greek, the cities of men and their fame,*
> *Their labor, days of various light, hunger's shame;*
> *I correct no event, falsify no name,*
> *But the voyage I narrate is . . .* autour de ma chambre.

"By all lights an interesting strophe," he opined. "The first line wins the applause of the professor, the academician, the Hellenist, if not of superficial pedants, who form, these last, a considerable sector of public opinion. The second passes from Homer to Hesiod (the entire verse an implicit homage, writ on the façade of the resplendent building, to the father of didactic poetry), not without rejuvenating a procedure whose lineage goes back to Scripture, that of enumeration, congeries or conglomeration. The third line—Baroquism? Decadentism? Purified and fanatical cult of form?—is composed of two twin hemistichs. The fourth, frankly bilingual, assures me the unconditional support of every spirit sensitive to the gay lure of graceful play. I say nothing of the rare rhyme, nor of the learning which permits me—without any pedantry!—to accumulate, in four lines, three erudite allusions encompassing thirty centuries of compressed literature: first to the *Odyssey*, second to *Works and Days,* third to the immortal bagatelle proffered us through the idling of the Savoyard's pen. . . . Once more I have understood that modern art requires the balsam of laughter, the *scherzo.* Decidedly, Goldoni has the floor!"

He read me many another stanza, each of which obtained his approbation and profuse commentary, too. There was nothing memorable in any of them. I did not even judge them very much worse than the first one. There had been a collaboration, in his writing, between application, resignation, and chance; the virtues which Daneri attributed to them were posterior. I realized that the poet's labor lay not with the poetry, but with the invention of reasons to make the poetry admirable; naturally, this ulterior and subsequent labor modified the work for him, but not for others. Daneri's oral style was extravagant; his metric heaviness hindered his transmitting that extravagance, except in a very few instances, to the poem.*

Only once in my life have I had occasion to examine the fifteen

---

* Among my memories are also some lines of a satire in which he lashed out unsparingly at bad poets. After accusing them of dressing their poems in the warlike armor of erudition, and of flapping in vain their unavailing wings, he concluded with this verse: "But they forget, alas, one foremost fact—BEAUTY!"
    Only the fear of creating an army of implacable and powerful enemies dissuaded him (he told me) from fearlessly publishing this poem. [author's note]

thousand dodecasyllabic verses of the *Poly-Olbion,* that topographic epic poem in which Michael Drayton recorded the flora, fauna, hydrography, orography, military and monastic history of England; I am sure that this considerable, but limited, production is less tedious than the vast congeneric enterprise of Carlos Argentino. The latter proposed to put into verse the entire face of the planet; in 1941, he had already dispatched several hectares of the State of Queensland, in addition to one kilometer of the course of the River Ob, a gasometer north of Veracruz, the main business houses in the parish of La Concepción, the villa owned by Mariana Cambaceres de Alvear on Eleventh of September street, in Belgrano, and an establishment devoted to Turkish baths not far from the famous Brighton Aquarium. He read me from his poem certain laborious passages concerning the Australian zone; these large and formless alexandrines lacked the relative agitation of the Preface. I copy one stanza:

> *Know ye. To the right hand of the routinary post*
> *(Coming, of course, from the North-northwest)*
> *One wearies out a skeleton—Color? White-celeste—*
> *Which gives the sheep run an ossuary cast.*

"Two audacious strokes," he cried out in exultation, "redeemed, I can hear you muttering, by success! I admit it, I admit it. One, the epithet *routinary,* which accurately proclaims, *en passant,*[2] the inevitable tedium inherent in pastoral and farming chores, a tedium which neither georgic poetry nor our already laureled *Don Segundo* ever ventured to denounce in this way, in red-hot heat. The other, the energetic prosaicism of *one wearies out a skeleton,* a phrase which the prudish will want to excommunicate in horror, but which the critic with virile taste will appreciate more than his life. For the rest, the entire line is of high carat, the highest. The second hemistich engages the reader in the most animated converse; it anticipates his lively curiosity, places a question in his mouth and answers it . . . instantly. And what do you tell me of that find of mine: *white-celeste?* This picturesque neologism insinuates the sky, which is a very important factor in the Australian landscape. Without this evocation, the colors of the sketch would be much too somber, and the reader would find himself compelled to close the book, wounded in the innermost part of his soul by a black and incurable melancholy."

Toward midnight, I took my leave.

Two Sundays later, Daneri called me on the telephone, for the first time in his life, I believe. He proposed that we meet at four o'clock, "to drink a glass of milk together, in the salon-bar next door, which the progressivism of Zunino and of Zungri—the proprietors of my house, you will recall—is causing to be inaugurated on the corner. Truly, a confectionery

---

2. in passing

shop you will be interested in knowing about." I accepted, with more resignation than enthusiasm. There was no difficulty in finding a table; the "salon-bar," inexorably modern, was just slightly less atrocious than what I had foreseen; at the neighboring tables an excited public mentioned the sums which Zunino and Zungri had invested without batting an eye. Carlos Argentino feigned astonishment over some wonder or other in the lighting installations (which he doubtless already knew about), and he said to me, with a certain severity:

"You'll have to admit, no matter how grudgingly, that these premises vie successfully with the most renowned of Flores."

Then, he reread me four or five pages of his poem. He had made corrections in accordance with a depraved principle of verbal ostentation: where he had formerly written *azurish*,[3] he now put *azuritic, azuritish,* and even *azury*. The word *lacteous* proved not ugly enough for him; in the course of an impetuous description of a wool washer, he preferred *lactary, lactinous, lactescent, lactiferous.*[4]. . . He bitterly reviled the critics; later, in a more benign spirit, he compared them to persons "who dispose of no precious metals, nor steam presses, nor rolling presses, nor sulphuric acids for minting treasures, but who can *indicate* to *others* the *site* of a treasure." Next he censured *prologomania*[5] "which the Prince of Talents,[6] in the graceful prefacing of his *Don Quixote,* already ridiculed." He nevertheless admitted to me now that by way of frontispiece to the new work a showy prologue, an accolade signed by the feather pen of a bird of prey, of a man of weight, would be most convenient. He added that he planned to bring out the initial cantos of his poems. I understood, then, the singular telephonic invitation; the man was going to ask me to preface his pedantic farrago.[7] My fears proved unfounded: Carlos Argentino observed, with rancorous admiration, that he did not misuse the epithet in denominating as *solid* the prestige achieved in all circles by Álvaro Melián Lafinur, man of letters, who would, if I insisted on it, delightfully prologue the poem. So as to avoid the most unpardonable of failures, I was to make myself spokesman for two undeniable merits: formal perfection and scientific rigor, "inasmuch as this vast garden of tropes, figures of speech, and elegance, allows no single detail which does not confirm the severe truth." He added that Beatriz had always enjoyed herself with Álvaro.

I assented, assented profusely. For greater conviction, I promised to speak to Álvaro on Thursday, rather than wait until the following Monday: we could meet at the small supper that usually climaxes every reunion of the Writers' Club. (There are no such suppers, but it is an irrefutable fact that the reunions do take place on Thursdays, a point which Carlos

---

3. A light purplish blue.
4. Producing and/or secreting milk.
5. Daneri's opinion of overkill on the part of the author in explaining his text.
6. Miguel de Cervantes (1547–1616), Spanish author of *Don Quixote*
7. A medley or an arrangement.

Argentino Daneri would find confirmed in the daily newspapers, and which lent a certain reality to the phrase.) Adopting an air halfway between divinatory and sagacious, I told him that before taking up the question of a prologue, I would delineate the curious plan of the book. We took our leave of each other. As I turned the corner into Calle Bernardo de Irigoyen, I impartially considered the alternatives before me: a) I could talk to Álvaro and tell him how that cousin of Beatriz' (this explicatory euphemism would allow me to say her name) had elaborated a poem which seemed to dilate to infinity the possibilities of cacophony and chaos; b) I could fail to speak to Álvaro altogether. I foresaw, lucidly, that my indolence would choose b.

From early Friday morning the telephone began to disquiet me. It made me indignant to think that this instrument, which in other days had produced the irrecoverable voice of Beatriz, could lower itself to being a receptacle for the useless and perhaps even choleric complaints of that deceived man Carlos Argentino Daneri. Luckily, nothing awful occurred —except the inevitable animosity inspired by that man, who had imposed on me a delicate mission and would later forget me altogether.

The telephone lost its terrors; but then toward the end of October, Carlos Argentino called me again. He was terribly agitated; at first I could not identify the voice. Sadly and yet wrathfully he stammered that the now uncurbed Zunino and Zungri, under the pretext of enlarging their outrageous confectionery, were going to demolish his house.

"The house of my fathers! My house, the inveterate house of the Calle Garay!" he went on repeating, perhaps forgetting his grief in the melody.

It was not difficult for me to share his grief. Once past forty, every change is a detestable symbol of the passage of time. Besides, at stake was a house that, for me, infinitely alluded to Beatriz. I wanted to bring out this most delicate point; my interlocutor did not hear me. He said that if Zunino and Zungri persisted in their absurd proposal, Doctor Zunni, his lawyer, would enter an action *ipso facto*[8] for damages and would oblige them to pay one hundred thousand *pesos nacionales*[9] in compensation.

I was impressed to hear the name of Zunni: his practice, out of his office at the corner of Caseros and Tacuarí, was of a proverbial and solemn reliability. I asked if Zunni had already taken charge of the matter. Daneri said he would speak to him that very afternoon. He hesitated, and then, in that level, impersonal voice to which we all have recourse for confiding something very intimate, he told me that in order to finish the poem the house was indispensable to him, for in one of the cellar corners there was an Aleph. He indicated that an Aleph is one of the points in space containing all points.

"It's in the dining-room cellar," he explained, his diction grown

---

8. by that very fact
9. national coins; in other words, in domestic currency.

hasty from anxiety. "It's mine, it's mine; I discovered it in childhood, before I was of school age. The cellar stair is steep, and my aunt and uncle had forbidden me to go down it. But someone said that there was a world in the cellar. They were referring, I found out later, to a trunk, but I understood there was a world there. I descended secretly, went rolling down the forbidden stairs, fell off. When I opened my eyes I saw the Aleph."

"The Aleph?" I echoed.

"Yes, the place where, without any possible confusion, all the places in the world are found, seen from every angle. I revealed my discovery to no one, and I returned there. The child could not understand that this privilege was proffered him so that the man might chisel out the poem! Zunino and Zungri will not dislodge me, no, a thousand times no. With the code of laws in hand, Doctor Zunni will prove that my Aleph is *inalienable.*"

I attempted to reason with him.

"But, isn't the cellar very dark?"

"Really, truth does not penetrate a rebellious understanding. If all the places on earth are in the Aleph, the Aleph must also contain all the illuminations, all the lights, all the sources of light."

"I will go and see it at once."

I hung up, before he could issue a prohibition. The knowledge of one fact is enough to allow one to perceive at once a whole series of confirming traits, previously unsuspected. I was astonished not to have understood until that moment that Carlos Argentino was a madman. All the Viterbos, for that matter . . . Beatriz (I often say so myself) was a woman, a girl, of an almost implacable clairvoyance, but there was about her a negligence, a distraction, a disdain, a real cruelty, which perhaps called for a pathological explanation. The madness of Carlos Argentino filled me with malicious felicity; in our innermost beings, we had always detested each other.

In Calle Garay, the serving woman asked me if I would be kind enough to wait. The child was, as always, in the cellar, developing photographs. Next to the flower vase without a single flower in it, atop the useless piano, there smiled (more timeless than anachronic) the great portrait of Beatriz, in dull colors. No one could see us; in an access of tender despair I went up close and told her:

"Beatriz, Beatriz Elena, Beatriz Elena Viterbo, beloved Beatriz, Beatriz lost forever, it's me, Borges."

A little later Carlos came in. He spoke with a certain dryness. I understood that he was incapable of thinking of anything but the loss of the Aleph.

"A glass of the pseudo-cognac," he ordered, "and then you can duck into the cellar. As you already know, the dorsal decubitus is imperative. And so are darkness, immobility, and a certain ocular accommodation. You lie down on the tile floor and fix your eyes on the nineteenth step of the pertinent stairs. I leave, lower the trap door, and you're alone.

Quite likely—it should be easy!—some rodent will scare you! In a few minutes you will see the Aleph. The microcosm of alchemists and cabalists, our proverbial concrete friend, the *multum in parvo!*"[10]

Once we were in the dining room he added:

"Of course if you don't see it, your incapacity in no way invalidates my testimony. . . . Now, down with you. Very shortly you will be able to engage in a dialogue with *all* of the images of Beatriz."

I rapidly descended, tired of his insubstantial words. The cellar, barely wider than the stairs, had much of a well about it. I gazed about in search of the trunk of which Carlos Argentino had spoken. Some cases with bottles in them and some canvas bags cluttered one corner. Carlos picked up one of the bags, folded it in half and placed it exactly in a precise spot.

"A humble pillow," he explained, "but if I raise it one centimeter, you won't see a thing, and you'll be left abashed and ashamed. Stretch your bulk out on the floor and count off nineteen steps."

I complied with his ridiculous requisites; and at last he went away. Carefully he closed the trap door; the darkness, despite a crevice which I discovered later, seemed total. And suddenly I realized the danger I ran: I had allowed myself to be buried by a madman, after having drunk some poison! Behind the transparent bravado of Carlos was the intimate terror that I would not see the prodigy; to defend his delirium, to avoid knowing that he was mad, Carlos *had to kill me.* A confused malaise swept over me; I attempted to attribute it to my rigid posture rather than to the operation of a narcotic. I closed my eyes; opened them. Then I saw the Aleph.

I arrive, now, at the ineffable center of my story. And here begins my despair as a writer. All language is an alphabet of symbols whose use presupposes a past shared by all the other interlocutors. How, then, transmit to others the infinite Aleph, which my fearful mind scarcely encompasses? The mystics, in similar situations, are lavish with emblems: to signify the divinity, a Persian speaks of a bird that in some way is all birds; Alanus de Insulis speaks of a sphere whose center is everywhere and whose circumference is nowhere; Ezekiel,[11] of an angel with four faces who looks simultaneously to the Orient and the Occident, to the North and the South. (Not vainly do I recall these inconceivable analogies; they bear some relation to the Aleph.) Perhaps the gods would not be against my finding an equivalent image, but then this report would be contaminated with literature, with falsehood. For the rest, the central problem is unsolvable: the enumeration, even if only partial, of an infinite complex. In that gigantic instant I saw millions of delightful and atrocious acts; none astonished me more than the fact that all of them together occupied the same point, without superposition and without transparency. What my eyes saw was simultaneous:

---

10. A great deal in a small space.
11. One of the major Hebrew prophets; see Ezekiel 1:5–6

what I shall transcribe is successive, because language is successive. Nevertheless, I shall cull something of it all.

In the lower part of the step, toward the right, I saw a small iridescent sphere, of almost intolerable brilliance. At first I thought it rotary; then I understood that this movement was an illusion produced by the vertiginous sights it enclosed. The Aleph's diameter must have been about two or three centimeters, but Cosmic Space was in it, without diminution of size. Each object (the mirror's glass, for instance) was infinite objects, for I clearly saw it from all points in the universe. I saw the heavy-laden sea; I saw the dawn and the dusk; I saw the multitudes of America; I saw a silver-plated cobweb at the center of a black pyramid; I saw a tattered labyrinth (it was London); I saw interminable eyes nearby looking at me as if in a mirror; I saw all the mirrors in the planet and none reflected me; in an inner patio in the Calle Soler I saw the same paving tile I had seen thirty years before in the entranceway to a house in the town of Fray Bentos; I saw clusters of grapes, snow, tobacco, veins of metal, steam; I saw convex equatorial deserts and every grain of sand in them; I saw a woman at Inverness whom I shall not forget: I saw her violent switch of hair, her proud body, the cancer in her breast; I saw a circle of dry land on a sidewalk where formerly there had been a tree; I saw a villa in Adrogué; I saw a copy of the first English version of Pliny, by Philemon Holland, and saw simultaneously every letter on every page (as a boy I used to marvel that the letters in a closed book did not get mixed up and lost in the course of a night); I saw night and day contemporaneously; I saw a sunset in Querétaro which seemed to reflect the color of a rose in Bengal; I saw my bedroom with nobody in it; I saw in a study in Alkmaar a terraqueous[12] globe between two mirrors which multiplied it without end; I saw horses with swirling manes on a beach by the Caspian Sea at dawn; I saw the delicate bone structure of a hand; I saw the survivors of a battle sending out post cards; I saw a deck of Spanish playing cards in a shopwindow in Mirzapur; I saw the oblique shadows of some ferns on the floor of a hothouse; I saw tigers, emboli, bison, ground swells, and armies; I saw all the ants on earth; I saw a Persian astrolabe; in a desk drawer I saw (the writing made me tremble) obscene, incredible, precise letters, which Beatriz had written Carlos Argentino; I saw an adored monument in La Chacarita cemetery; I saw the atrocious relic of what deliciously had been Beatriz Viterbo; I saw the circulation of my obscure blood; I saw the gearing of love and the modifications of death; I saw the Aleph from all points; I saw the earth in the Aleph and in the earth the Aleph once more and the earth in the Aleph; I saw my face and my viscera; I saw your face and felt vertigo and cried because my eyes had seen that conjectural and secret object whose name men usurp but which no man has gazed on: the inconceivable universe.

---

12. Consisting of land and water.

I felt infinite veneration, infinite compassion.

"You must be good and dizzy from peering into things that don't concern you," cried a hateful, jovial voice. "Even if you rack your brains, you won't be able to pay me back in a century for this revelation. What a formidable observatory, eh, Borges!"

Carlos Argentino's feet occupied the highest step. In the half-light I managed to get up and to stammer:

"Formidable, yes, formidable."

The indifference in the sound of my voice surprised me. Anxiously Carlos Argentino insisted:

"You saw it all, in colors?"

It was at that instant that I conceived my revenge. Benevolently, with obvious pity, nervous, evasive, I thanked Carlos Argentino for the hospitality of his cellar and urged him to take advantage of the demolition of his house to get far away from the pernicious capital, which is easy on no one, believe me, on no one! I refused, with suave energy, to discuss the Aleph; I embraced him on leaving, and repeated that the country and its quiet are two grand doctors.

In the street, on the Constitución stairs, in the subway, all the faces struck me as familiar. I feared that not a single thing was left to cause me surprise; I was afraid I would never be quit of the impression that I had "returned." Happily, at the end of a few nights of insomnia, forgetfulness worked in me again.

P.S. March 1, 1943

Six months after the demolition of the building in Calle Garay, Procusto Publishers did not take fright at the length of Argentino's considerable poem and launched upon the reading public a selection of "Argentino Extracts." It is almost needless to repeat what happened: Carlos Argentino Daneri received Second Prize, of the National Prizes for Literature.* First Prize was awarded to Doctor Aita; Third, to Doctor Mario Bonfanti; incredibly, my book *The Cards of the Cardsharp* did not get a single vote. Once again incomprehension and envy won the day! For a long time now I have not been able to see Daneri; the daily press says he will soon give us another volume. His fortunate pen (no longer benumbed by the Aleph) has been consecrated to versifying the epitomes of Doctor Acevedo Díaz.

I would like to add two further observations: one, on the nature of the Aleph; the other, on its name. As is well known, the latter is the name of the first letter of the alphabet of the sacred language. Its application to the cycle of my story does not appear mere chance. For the cabala, this letter

----

* "I received your pained congratulations," he wrote me. "You rage, my poor friend, with envy, but you must confess—even if it chokes you!—that this time I have crowned my cap with the reddest of feathers; my turban with the most *caliph* of rubies." [author's note]

signifies the En-Sof, the limitless and pure divinity; it has also been said that it has the form of a man who points out heaven and earth, to indicate that the inferior world is the mirror and map of the superior; for the *Mengenlehre*, it is the symbol of transfinite numbers, in which the whole is no greater than any of its parts. I wanted to know: Had Carlos Argentino chosen this name, or had he read it, *applied to another point where all points converge,* in some one of the innumerable texts revealed to him by the Aleph in his house? Incredible as it may seem, I believe there is (or was) another Aleph, I believe that the Aleph in the Calle Garay was a false Aleph.

Here are my reasons. Toward 1867, Captain Burton held the office of British Consul in Brazil. In July, 1942, Pedro Henríquez Ureña discovered, in a library at Santos, a manuscript by Burton dealing with the mirror which the Orient attributes to Iskandar Zu al-Karnayn, or Alexander Bicornis of Macedonia. In its glass the entire world was reflected. Burton mentions other artifices of like kind: the septuple goblet of Kai Josru; the mirror which Tarik Benzeyad found in a tower (*The Thousand and One Nights,* 272); the mirror which Lucian of Samosata was able to examine on the moon (*True History,* I, 26); the diaphanous spear which the first book of Capella's *Satyricon* attributes to Jupiter; the universal mirror of Merlin, "round and hollow . . . and seemed a world of glass" (*The Faerie Queene,* III, 2, 19). And he adds these curious words: "But the former (besides the defect of not existing) are mere instruments of optics. The Faithful who attend the Mosque of Amr, in Cairo, know very well that the universe is in the interior of one of the stone columns surrounding the central courtyard. . . . No one, of course, can see it, but those who put their ears to the surface claim to hear, within a short time, its workaday rumor. . . . The mosque dates from the seventh century; the columns come from other, pre-Islamic, temples, for as ibn-Khaldûn has written: '*In republics founded by nomads, the assistance of foreigners is indispensable in all that concerns masonry.*' "

Does that Aleph exist in the innermost recess of a stone? Did I see it when I saw all things, and have I forgotten it? Our minds are porous with forgetfulness; I myself am falsifying and losing, through the tragic erosion of the years, the features of Beatriz.

trans. 1970

The fiction of Jorge Luis Borges, like that of several other contemporary Latin American writers, is built on lines very different from those that characterize the realistic fiction of his North American contemporaries Hemingway and Steinbeck. We can get some sense of the tone and method of Borges' work from comments he made during an interview with L. S. Dembo.

"I wonder why a dream . . . should be less real than this table": Jorge Luis Borges

Q. One of your chief themes seems to be the ability of the mind to influence or recreate reality. Are you in fact a philosophic idealist or do you simply delight in paradoxes made possible by idealistic reasoning, or both?

A. Well, my father—I seem to be referring to him all the time; I greatly loved him, and I think of him as living—my father was a professor of psychology, and I remember—I was quite a small boy—when he began trying to teach me something of the puzzles that constitute the idealistic philosophy. And I remember once he explained to me, or he tried to explain to me, with a chessboard, the paradoxes of Xeno, Achilles and the Tortoise, and so on. I also remember that he held an orange in his hand and asked me, "Would you think of the taste of the orange as belonging to it?" And I said, "Well, I hardly know that. I suppose I'd have to taste the orange. I don't think the orange is tasting itself all the time." He replied, "That's quite a good answer," and then he went on to the color of the orange and asked, "Well, if you close your eyes, and if I put out the light, what color is the orange?" He didn't say a word about Berkeley or Hume, but he was really teaching me the philosophy of idealism, although, of course, he never used those words, because he thought they might scare me away. But he was teaching me a good many things, and he taught them as if they were of no importance at all. He was teaching me philosophy and psychology—that was his province—and he used William James as his textbook. He was teaching me all those things, and yet not allowing me to suspect that he was teaching me something.

Q. But you would say that you more or less were brought up on idealism?

A. Yes, and now when people tell me that they're down-to-earth and they tell me that I should be down-to-earth and think of reality, I wonder why a dream or an idea should be less real than this table for example, or why Macbeth should be less real than today's newspaper. I cannot quite understand this. I suppose if I had to define myself, I would define myself as an idealist, philosophically speaking. But I'm not sure I have to define myself. I'd rather go on wondering and puzzling about things, for I find that very enjoyable.

JOHN STEINBECK

(1902–1968)

THE CHRYSANTHEMUMS

The high grey-flannel fog of winter closed off the Salinas Valley from the sky and from all the rest of the world. On every side it sat like a lid on the mountains and made of the great valley a closed pot. On the broad, level land floor the gang plows bit deep and left the black earth shining like metal where the shares had cut. On the foothill ranches across the Salinas River, the yellow stubble fields seemed to be bathed in pale cold sunshine, but there was no sunshine in the valley now in December. The thick willow scrub along the river flamed with sharp and positive yellow leaves.

It was a time of quiet and of waiting. The air was cold and tender. A light wind blew up from the southwest so that the farmers were mildly hopeful of a good rain before long; but fog and rain do not go together.

Across the river, on Henry Allen's foothill ranch there was little work to be done, for the hay was cut and stored and the orchards were plowed up to receive the rain deeply when it should come. The cattle on the higher slopes were becoming shaggy and rough-coated.

Elisa Allen, working in her flower garden, looked down across the yard and saw Henry, her husband, talking to two men in business suits. The three of them stood by the tractor shed, each man with one foot on the side of the little Fordson. They smoked cigarettes and studied the machine as they talked.

Elisa watched them for a moment and then went back to her work. She was thirty-five. Her face was lean and strong and her eyes were as clear as water. Her figure looked blocked and heavy in her gardening costume, a man's black hat pulled low down over her eyes, clodhopper shoes, a figured print dress almost completely covered by a big corduroy apron with four big pockets to hold the snips, the trowel and scratcher, the seeds and the knife she worked with. She wore heavy leather gloves to protect her hands while she worked.

She was cutting down the old year's chrysanthemum stalks with a pair of short and powerful scissors. She looked down toward the men by the tractor shed now and then. Her face was eager and mature and handsome; even her work with the scissors was over-eager, over-powerful. The chrysanthemum stems seemed too small and easy for her energy.

She brushed a cloud of hair out of her eyes with the back of her glove, and left a smudge of earth on the cheek in doing it. Behind her stood the neat white farm house with red geraniums close-banked around it as high as the windows. It was a hard-swept looking little house, with hard-polished windows, and a clean mud-mat on the front steps.

Elisa cast another glance toward the tractor shed. The strangers were getting into their Ford coupe. She took off a glove and put her strong fingers down into the forest of new green chrysanthemum sprouts that were growing around the old roots. She spread the leaves and looked down among the close-growing stems. No aphids were there, no sowbugs or snails or cutworms. Her terrier fingers destroyed such pests before they could get started.

Elisa started at the sound of her husband's voice. He had come near quietly, and he leaned over the wire fence that protected her flower garden from cattle and dogs and chickens.

"At it again," he said. "You've got a strong new crop coming."

Elisa straightened her back and pulled on the gardening glove again. "Yes. They'll be strong this coming year." In her tone and on her face there was a little smugness.

"You've got a gift with things," Henry observed. "Some of those yellow chrysanthemums you had this year were ten inches across. I wish you'd work out in the orchard and raise some apples that big."

Her eyes sharpened. "Maybe I could do it, too. I've a gift with things, all right. My mother had it. She could stick anything in the ground and make it grow. She said it was having planters' hands that knew how to do it."

"Well, it sure works with flowers," he said.

"Henry, who were those men you were talking to?"

"Why, sure, that's what I came to tell you. They were from the Western Meat Company. I sold those thirty head of three-year-old steers. Got nearly my own price, too."

"Good," she said. "Good for you."

"And I thought," he continued, "I thought how it's Saturday afternoon, and we might go into Salinas for dinner at a restaurant, and then to a picture show—to celebrate, you see."

"Good," she repeated. "Oh, yes. That will be good."

Henry put on his joking tone. "There's fights tonight. How'd you like to go to the fights?"

"Oh, no," she said breathlessly. "No, I wouldn't like fights."

"Just fooling, Elisa. We'll go to a movie. Let's see. It's two now. I'm going to take Scotty and bring down those steers from the hill. It'll take us maybe two hours. We'll go in town about five and have dinner at the Cominos Hotel. Like that?"

"Of course I'll like it. It's good to eat away from home."

"All right, then. I'll go get up a couple of horses."

She said, "I'll have plenty of time to transplant some of these sets, I guess."

She heard her husband calling Scotty down by the barn. And a little later she saw the two men ride up the pale yellow hillside in search of the steers.

There was a little square sandy bed kept for rooting the chrysanthemums. With her trowel she turned the soil over and over, and smoothed it and patted it firm. Then she dug ten parallel trenches to receive the sets. Back at the chrysanthemum bed she pulled out the little crisp shoots, trimmed off the leaves of each one with her scissors and laid it on a small orderly pile.

A squeak of wheels and plod of hoofs came from the road. Elisa looked up. The country road ran along the dense bank of willows and cottonwoods that bordered the river, and up this road came a curious vehicle, curiously drawn. It was an old spring-wagon, with a round canvas top on it like the cover of a prairie schooner. It was drawn by an old bay horse and a little grey-and-white burro. A big stubble-bearded man sat between the cover flaps and drove the crawling team. Underneath the wagon, between the hind wheels, a lean and rangy mongrel dog walked sedately. Words were painted on the canvas in clumsy, crooked letters. "Pots, pans, knives, sisors, lawn mores. Fixed." Two rows of articles and the triumphantly definitive "Fixed" below. The black paint had run down in little sharp points beneath each letter.

Elisa, squatting on the ground, watched to see the crazy, loose-jointed wagon pass by. But it didn't pass. It turned into the farm road in front of her house, crooked old wheels skirling and squeaking. The rangy dog darted from between the wheels and ran ahead. Instantly the two ranch shepherds flew out at him. Then all three stopped, and with stiff and quivering tails, with taut straight legs, with ambassadorial dignity, they slowly circled, sniffing daintily. The caravan pulled up to Elisa's wire fence and stopped. Now the newcomer dog, feeling outnumbered, lowered his tail and retired under the wagon with raised hackles and bared teeth.

The man on the wagon seat called out. "That's a bad dog in a fight when he gets started."

Elisa laughed. "I see he is. How soon does he generally get started?"

The man caught up her laughter and echoed it heartily. "Sometimes not for weeks and weeks," he said. He climbed stiffly down, over the wheel. The horse and the donkey drooped like unwatered flowers.

Elisa saw that he was a very big man. Although his hair and beard were greying, he did not look old. His worn black suit was wrinkled and spotted with grease. The laughter had disappeared from his face and eyes the moment his laughing voice ceased. His eyes were dark, and they were full of the brooding that gets in the eyes of teamsters and of sailors. The calloused hands he rested on the wire fence were cracked, and every crack was a black line. He took off his battered hat.

"I'm off my general road, ma'am," he said. "Does this dirt road cut over across the river to the Los Angeles highway?"

Elisa stood up and shoved the thick scissors in her apron pocket. "Well, yes, it does, but it winds around and then fords the river. I don't think your team could pull through the sand."

He replied with some asperity. "It might surprise you what them beasts can pull through."

"When they get started?" she asked.

He smiled for a second. "Yes. When they get started."

"Well," said Elisa, "I think you'll save time if you go back to the Salinas road and pick up the highway there."

He drew a big finger down the chicken wire and made it sing. "I ain't in any hurry, ma'am. I go from Seattle to San Diego and back every year. Takes all my time. About six months each way. I aim to follow nice weather."

Elisa took off her gloves and stuffed them in the apron pocket with the scissors. She touched the under edge of her man's hat, searching for fugitive hairs. "That sounds like a nice kind of a way to live," she said.

He leaned confidentially over the fence. "Maybe you noticed the writing on my wagon. I mend pots and sharpen knives and scissors. You got any of them things to do?"

"Oh, no," she said quickly. "Nothing like that." Her eyes hardened with resistance.

"Scissors is the worst thing," he explained. "Most people just ruin scissors trying to sharpen 'em but I know how. I got a special tool. It's a little bobbit kind of thing, and patented. But it sure does the trick."

"No. My scissors are all sharp."

"All right, then. Take a pot," he continued earnestly, "a bent pot, or a pot with a hole. I can make it like new so you don't have to buy no new ones. That's a saving for you."

"No," she said shortly. "I tell you I have nothing like that for you to do."

His face fell to an exaggerated sadness. His voice took on a whining undertone. "I ain't had a thing to do today. Maybe I won't have no supper tonight. You see I'm off my regular road. I know folks on the highway clear from Seattle to San Diego. They save their things for me to sharpen up because they know I do it so good and save them money."

"I'm sorry," Elisa said irritably. "I haven't anything for you to do."

His eyes left her face and fell to searching the ground. They roamed about until they came to the chrysanthemum bed where she had been working. "What's them plants, ma'am?"

The irritation and resistance melted from Elisa's face. "Oh, those are chrysanthemums, giant whites and yellows. I raise them every year, bigger than anybody around here."

"Kind of a long-stemmed flower? Looks like a quick puff of colored smoke?" he asked.

"That's it. What a nice way to describe them."

"They smell kind of nasty till you get used to them," he said.

"It's a good bitter smell," she retorted, "not nasty at all."

He changed his tone quickly. "I like the smell myself."

"I had ten-inch blooms this year," she said.

The man leaned farther over the fence. "Look. I know a lady down the road a piece, has got the nicest garden you ever seen. Got nearly every kind of flower but no chrysanthemums. Last time I was mending a copper-bottom washtub for her (that's a hard job but I do it good), she said to me, 'If you ever run acrost some nice chrysanthemums I wish you'd try to get me a few seeds.' That's what she told me."

Elisa's eyes grew alert and eager. "She couldn't have known much about chrysanthemums. You can raise them from seed, but it's much easier to root the little sprouts you see there."

"Oh," he said. "I s'pose I can't take none to her, then."

"Why yes you can," Elisa cried. "I can put some in damp sand, and you can carry them right along with you. They'll take root in the pot if you keep them damp. And then she can transplant them."

"She'd sure like to have some, ma'am. You say they're nice ones?"

"Beautiful," she said. "Oh, beautiful." Her eyes shone. She tore off the battered hat and shook out her dark pretty hair. "I'll put them in a flower pot, and you can take them right with you. Come into the yard."

While the man came through the picket gate Elisa ran excitedly along the geranium-bordered path to the back of the house. And she returned carrying a big red flower pot. The gloves were forgotten now. She kneeled on the ground by the starting bed and dug up the sandy soil with her fingers and scooped it into the bright new flower pot. Then she picked up the little pile of shoots she had prepared. With her strong fingers she pressed them into the sand and tamped around them with her knuckles. The man stood over her. "I'll tell you what to do," she said. "You remember so you can tell the lady."

"Yes, I'll try to remember."

"Well, look. These will take root in about a month. Then she must set them out, about a foot apart in good rich earth like this, see?" She lifted a handful of dark soil for him to look at. "They'll grow fast and tall. Now remember this. In July tell her to cut them down, about eight inches from the ground."

"Before they bloom?" he asked.

"Yes, before they bloom." Her face was tight with eagerness. "They'll come right up again. About the last of September the buds will start."

She stopped and seemed perplexed. "It's the budding that takes the most care," she said hesitantly. "I don't know how to tell you." She looked deep into his eyes, searchingly. Her mouth opened a little, and she seemed to be listening. "I'll try to tell you," she said. "Did you ever hear of planting hands?"

"Can't say I have, ma'am."

"Well, I can only tell you what it feels like. It's when you're picking off the buds you don't want. Everything goes right down into your finger-tips. You watch your fingers work. They do it themselves. You can feel how it is. They pick and pick the buds. They never make a mistake. They're with the plant. Do you see? Your fingers and the plant. You can feel that, right up your arm. They know. They never make a mistake. You can feel it.

When you're like that you can't do anything wrong. Do you see that? Can you understand that?"

She was kneeling on the ground looking up at him. Her breast swelled passionately.

The man's eyes narrowed. He looked away, self-consciously. "Maybe I know," he said. "Sometimes in the night in the wagon there—"

Elisa's voice grew husky. She broke in on him. "I've never lived as you do, but I know what you mean. When the night is dark—why, the stars are sharp-pointed, and there's quiet. Why, you rise up and up! Every pointed star gets driven into your body. It's like that. Hot and sharp and—lovely."

Kneeling there, her hand went out toward his legs in the greasy black trousers. Her hesitant fingers almost touched the cloth. Then her hand dropped to the ground. She crouched low like a fawning dog.

He said, "It's nice, just like you say. Only when you don't have no dinner, it ain't."

She stood up then, very straight, and her face was ashamed. She held the flower pot out to him and placed it gently in his arms. "Here. Put it in your wagon, on the seat, where you can watch it. Maybe I can find something for you to do."

At the back of the house she dug in the can pile and found two old and battered aluminum saucepans. She carried them back and gave them to him. "Here, maybe you can fix these."

His manner changed. He became professional. "Good as new I can fix them." At the back of his wagon he set a little anvil, and out of an oily tool box dug a small machine hammer. Elisa came through the gate to watch him while he pounded out the dents in the kettles. His mouth grew sure and knowing. At a difficult part of the work he sucked his under-lip.

"You sleep right in the wagon?" Elisa asked.

"Right in the wagon, ma'am. Rain or shine I'm dry as a cow in there."

"It must be nice," she said. "It must be very nice. I wish women could do such things."

"It ain't the right kind of a life for a woman."

Her upper lip raised a little, showing her teeth. "How do you know? How can you tell?" she said.

"I don't know, ma'am," he protested. "Of course I don't know. Now here's your kettles, done. You don't have to buy no new ones."

"How much?"

"Oh, fifty cents'll do. I keep my prices down and my work good. That's why I have all them satisfied customers up and down the highway."

Elisa brought him a fifty-cent piece from the house and dropped it in his hand. "You might be surprised to have a rival some time. I can sharpen scissors, too. And I can beat the dents out of little pots. I could show you what a woman might do."

He put his hammer back in the oily box and shoved the little anvil out of sight. "It would be a lonely life for a woman, ma'am, and a scarey life, too, with animals creeping under the wagon all night." He climbed over the singletree, steadying himself with a hand on the burro's white rump. He settled himself in the seat, picked up the lines. "Thank you kindly, ma'am," he said. "I'll do like you told me; I'll go back and catch the Salinas road."

"Mind," she called, "if you're long in getting there, keep the sand damp."

"Sand, ma'am? . . . Sand? Oh, sure. You mean round the chrysanthemums. Sure I will." He clucked his tongue. The beasts leaned luxuriously into their collars. The mongrel dog took his place between the back wheels. The wagon turned and crawled out the entrance road and back the way it had come, along the river.

Elisa stood in front of her wire fence watching the slow progress of the caravan. Her shoulders were straight, her head thrown back, her eyes half-closed, so that the scene came vaguely into them. Her lips moved silently, forming the words "Good-bye—goodbye." Then she whispered. "That's a bright direction. There's a glowing there." The sound of her whisper startled her. She shook herself free and looked about to see whether anyone had been listening. Only the dogs had heard. They lifted their heads toward her from their sleeping in the dust, and then stretched out their chins and settled asleep again. Elisa turned and ran hurriedly into the house.

In the kitchen she reached behind the stove and felt the water tank. It was full of hot water from the noonday cooking. In the bathroom she tore off her soiled clothes and flung them into the corner. And then she scrubbed herself with a little block of pumice, legs and thighs, loins and chest and arms, until her skin was scratched and red. When she had dried herself she stood in front of a mirror in her bedroom and looked at her body. She tightened her stomach and threw out her chest. She turned and looked over her shoulder at her back.

After a while she began to dress, slowly. She put on her newest underclothing and her nicest stockings and the dress which was the symbol of her prettiness. She worked carefully on her hair, pencilled her eyebrows and rouged her lips.

Before she was finished she heard the little thunder of hoofs and the shouts of Henry and his helper as they drove the red steers into the corral. She heard the gate bang shut and set herself for Henry's arrival.

His step sounded on the porch. He entered the house calling "Elisa, where are you?"

"In my room, dressing. I'm not ready. There's hot water for your bath. Hurry up. It's getting late."

When she heard him splashing in the tub, Elisa laid his dark suit on the bed, and shirt and socks and tie beside it. She stood his polished shoes on the floor beside the bed. Then she went to the porch and sat primly and stiffly down. She looked toward the river road where the willow-line was still yellow with frosted leaves so that under the high grey fog they seemed a thin band of sunshine. This was the only color in the grey afternoon. She sat unmoving for a long time. Her eyes blinked rarely.

Henry came banging out of the door, shoving his tie inside his vest as he came. Elisa stiffened and her face grew tight. Henry stopped short and looked at her. "Why—why, Elisa. You look so nice!"

"Nice? You think I look nice? What do you mean by 'nice'?"

Henry blundered on. "I don't know. I mean you look different, strong and happy."

"I am strong? Yes, strong. What do you mean 'strong'?"

He looked bewildered. "You're playing some kind of a game," he said helplessly. "It's a kind of a play. You look strong enough to break a calf over your knee, happy enough to eat it like a watermelon."

For a second she lost her rigidity. "Henry! Don't talk like that. You didn't know what you said." She grew complete again. "I'm strong," she boasted. "I never knew before how strong."

Henry looked down toward the tractor shed, and when he brought his eyes back to her, they were his own again. "I'll get out the car. You can put on your coat while I'm starting."

Elisa went into the house. She heard him drive to the gate and idle down his motor, and then she took a long time to put on her hat. She pulled it here and pressed it there. When Henry turned the motor off she slipped into her coat and went out.

The little roadster bounced along on the dirt road by the river, raising the birds and driving the rabbits into the brush. Two cranes flapped heavily over the willow-line and dropped into the riverbed.

Far ahead on the road Elisa saw a dark speck. She knew. She tried not to look as they passed it, but her eyes would not obey. She whispered to herself sadly, "He might have thrown them off the road. That wouldn't have been much trouble, not very much. But he kept the pot," she explained. "He had to keep the pot. That's why he couldn't get them off the road."

The roadster turned a bend and she saw the caravan ahead. She swung full around toward her husband so she could not see the little covered wagon and the mismatched team as the car passed them.

In a moment they had left behind them the man who had not known or needed to know what she said, the bargainer. She did not look back.

To Henry, she said loudly, to be heard above the motor, "It will be good, tonight, a good dinner."

"Now you're changed again," Henry complained. He took one hand from the wheel and patted her knee. "I ought to take you in to dinner oftener. It would be good for both of us. We get so heavy out on the ranch."

"Henry," she asked, "could we have wine at dinner?"

"Sure. Say! That will be fine."

She was silent for a while; then she said, "Henry, at those prize fights do the men hurt each other very much?"

"Sometimes a little, not often. Why?"

"Well, I've read how they break noses, and blood runs down their chests. I've read how the fighting gloves get heavy and soggy with blood."

He looked round at her. "What's the matter, Elisa? I didn't know you read things like that." He brought the car to a stop, then turned to the right over the Salinas River bridge.

"Do any women ever go to the fights?" she asked.

"Oh, sure, some. What's the matter, Elisa? Do you want to go? I don't think you'd like it, but I'll take you if you really want to go."

She relaxed limply in the seat. "Oh, no. I don't want to go. I'm sure I don't." Her face was turned away from him. "It will be enough if we can have wine. It will be plenty." She turned up her coat collar so he could not see that she was crying weakly—like an old woman.

1938

Like many writers who lived through the Great Depression of the 1930s, John Steinbeck directly observed the suffering caused by economic and social injustice, and much of his best work has an element of protest about it. His readers sometimes disagree about whether the protest note or the note of optimism (sounded below in an interview with Paris Review) *is dominant.*

"It is the duty of the writer to lift up, to extend, to encourage.": John Steinbeck

It is the fashion now in writing to have every man defeated and destroyed. And I do not believe all men are destroyed. I can name a dozen who were not and they are the ones the world lives by. It is true of the spirit as it is of battles—the defeated are forgotten, only the winners come themselves into the race. The writers of today, even I, have a tendency to celebrate the destruction of the spirit and god knows it is destroyed often enough. But the beacon thing is that sometimes it is not. And I think I can take time right now to say that. There will be great sneers from the neurosis belt of the south, from the hard-boiled writers, but I believe that the great ones, Plato, Lao Tze, Buddha, Christ, Paul, and the great Hebrew prophets are not remembered for negation or denial. Not that it is necessary to be remembered but there is one purpose in writing that I can see, beyond simply doing it interestingly. It is the duty of the writer to lift up, to extend, to encourage. If the written word has contributed anything at all to our developing species and our half developed culture, it is this: Great writing has been a staff to lean on, a mother to consult, a wisdom to pick up stumbling folly, a strength in weakness and a courage to support sick cowardice. And how any negative or despairing approach can pretend to be literature I do not know. It is true that we are weak and sick and ugly and quarrelsome but if that is all we ever were, we would millenniums ago have disappeared from the face of the earth, and a few remnants of fossilized jaw bones, a few teeth in strata of limestone would be the only mark our species would have left on the earth.

It is too bad we have not more humor about this. After all it is only a book and no worlds are made or destroyed by it.

ZORA NEALE HURSTON

(1903–1960)

SPUNK

1

A giant of a brown-skinned man sauntered up the one street of the village and out into the palmetto thickets with a small pretty woman clinging lovingly to his arm.

"Looka theah, folkses!" cried Elijah Mosley, slapping his leg gleefully. "Theah they go, big as life an' brassy as tacks."

All the loungers in the store tried to walk to the door with an air of nonchalance but with small success.

"Now pee-eople!" Walter Thomas gasped. "Will you look at 'em!"

"But that's one thing Ah likes about Spunk Banks—he ain't skeered of nothin' on God's green footstool—*nothin'!* He rides that log down at saw-mill jus' like he struts 'round wid another man's wife—jus' don't give a kitty. When Tes' Miller got cut to giblets on that circle-saw, Spunk steps right up and starts ridin'. The rest of us was skeered to go near it."

A round-shouldered figure in overalls much too large came nervously in the door and the talking ceased. The men looked at each other and winked.

"Gimme some soda-water. Sass'prilla Ah reckon," the newcomer ordered, and stood far down the counter near the open pickled pig-feet tub to drink it.

Elijah nudged Walter and turned with mock gravity to the new-comer.

"Say, Joe, how's everything up yo' way? How's yo' wife?"

Joe started and all but dropped the bottle he was holding. He swallowed several times painfully and his lips trembled.

"Aw 'Lige, you oughtn't to do nothin' like that," Walter grumbled. Elijah ignored him.

"She jus' passed heah a few minutes ago goin' thata way," with a wave of his hand in the direction of the woods.

Now Joe knew his wife had passed that way. He knew that the men lounging in the general store had seen her, moreover, he knew that the men knew *he* knew. He stood there silent for a long moment staring blankly, with his Adam's apple twitching nervously up and down his throat. One could actually *see* the pain he was suffering, his eyes, his face, his hands, and even the dejected slump of his shoulders. He set the bottle down upon the counter. He didn't bang it, just eased it out of his hand silently and fiddled with his suspender buckle.

"Well, Ah'm goin' after her to-day. Ah'm goin' an' fetch her back. Spunk's done gone too fur."

He reached deep down into his trouser pocket and drew out a hollow ground razor, large and shiny, and passed his moistened thumb back and forth over the edge.

"Talkin' like a man, Joe. 'Course that's *yo'* fambly affairs, but Ah like to see grit in anybody."

Joe Kanty laid down a nickel and stumbled out into the street.

Dusk crept in from the woods. Ike Clarke lit the swinging oil lamp that was almost immediately surrounded by candle-flies. The men laughed boisterously behind Joe's back as they watched him shamble woodward.

"You oughtn't to said whut you said to him, 'Lige—look how it worked him up," Walter chided.

"And Ah hope it did work him up. Tain't even decent for a man to take and take like he do."

"Spunk will sho' kill him."

"Aw, Ah doan know. You never kin tell. He might turn him up an' spank him fur gettin' in the way, but Spunk wouldn't shoot no unarmed man. Dat razor he carried outa heah ain't gonna run Spunk down an' cut him, an' Joe ain't got the nerve to go to Spunk with it knowing he totes that Army .45. He makes that break outa heah to bluff us. He's gonna hide that razor behind the first palmetto root an' sneak back home to bed. Don't tell me nothin' 'bout that rabbit-foot colored man. Didn't he meet Spunk an' Lena face to face one day las' week an' mumble sumthin' to Spunk 'bout lettin' his wife alone?"

"What did Spunk say?" Walter broke in. "Ah like him fine but tain't right the way he carries on wid Lena Kanty, jus' 'cause Joe's timid 'bout fightin'."

"You wrong theah, Walter. Tain't 'cause Joe's timid at all, it's 'cause Spunk wants Lena. If Joe was a passle of wile cats Spunk would tackle the job just the same. He'd go after *anything* he wanted the same way. As Ah wuz sayin' a minute ago, he tole Joe right to his face that Lena was his. 'Call her and see if she'll come. A woman knows her boss an' she answers when he calls.' 'Lena, ain't I yo' husband?' Joe sorter whines out. Lena looked at him real disgusted but she don't answer and she don't move outa her tracks. Then Spunk reaches out an' takes hold of her arm an' says:

'Lena, youse mine. From now on Ah works for you an' fights for you an' Ah never wants you to look to nobody for a crumb of bread, a stitch of close or a shingle to go over yo' head, but *me* long as Ah live. Ah'll git the lumber foh owah house to-morrow. Go home an' git yo' things together!'

" 'Thass mah house,' Lena speaks up. 'Papa gimme that.'

" 'Well,' says Spunk, 'doan give up whut's yours, but when youse inside doan forgit youse mine, an' let no other man git outa his place wid you!'

"Lena looked up at him with her eyes so full of love that they wuz runnin' over, an' Spunk seen it an' Joe seen it too, and his lip started to tremblin' and his Adam's apple was galloping up and down his neck like a race horse. Ah bet he's wore out half a dozen Adam's apples since Spunk's been on the job with Lena. That's all he'll do. He'll be back heah after while swallowin' an' workin' his lips like he wants to say somethin' an' can't."

"But didn't he do *nothin'* to stop 'em?"

"Nope, not a frazzlin' thing—jus' stood there. Spunk took Lena's arm and walked off jus' like nothin' ain't happened and he stood there gazin' after them till they was outa sight. Now you know a woman don't want no man like that. I'm jus' waitin' to see whut he's goin' to say when he gits back."

2

But Joe Kanty never came back, never. The men in the store heard the sharp report of a pistol somewhere distant in the palmetto thicket and soon Spunk came walking leisurely, with his big black Stetson set at the same rakish angle and Lena clinging to his arm, came walking right into the general store. Lena wept in a frightened manner.

"Well," Spunk announced calmly, "Joe came out there wid a meat axe an' made me kill him."

He sent Lena home and led the men back to Joe—crumpled and limp with his right hand still clutching his razor.

"See mah back? Mah close cut clear through. He sneaked up an' tried to kill me from the back, but Ah got him, an' got him good, first shot," Spunk said.

The men glared at Elijah, accusingly.

"Take him up an' plant him in Stony Lonesome," Spunk said in a careless voice. "Ah didn't wanna shoot him but he made me do it. He's a dirty coward, jumpin' on a man from behind."

Spunk turned on his heel and sauntered away to where he knew his love wept in fear for him and no man stopped him. At the general store later on, they all talked of locking him up until the sheriff should come from Orlando, but no one did anything but talk.

A clear case of self-defense, the trial was a short one, and Spunk walked out of the court house to freedom again. He could work again, ride the dangerous log-carriage that fed the singing, snarling, biting circle-saw;

he could stroll the soft dark lanes with his guitar. He was free to roam the woods again; he was free to return to Lena. He did all these things.

3

"Whut you reckon, Walt?" Elijah asked one night later. "Spunk's gittin' ready to marry Lena!"

"Naw! Why, Joe ain't had time to git cold yit. Nohow Ah didn't figger Spunk was the marryin' kind."

"Well, he is," rejoined Elijah. "He done moved most of Lena's things—and her along wid 'em—over to the Bradley house. He's buying it. Jus' like Ah told yo' all right in heah the night Joe was kilt. Spunk's crazy 'bout Lena. He don't want folks to keep on talkin' 'bout her—thass reason he's rushin' so. Funny thing 'bout that bob-cat, wan't it?"

"What bob-cat, 'Lige? Ah ain't heered 'bout none."

"Ain't cher? Well, night befo' las' as they was goin' to bed, a big black bob-cat, black all over, you hear me, *black,* walked round and round that house and howled like forty, an' when Spunk got his gun an' went to the winder to shoot it, he says it stood right still an' looked him in the eye, an' howled right at him. The thing got Spunk so nervoused up he couldn't shoot. But Spunk says twan't no bob-cat nohow. He says it was Joe done sneaked back from Hell!"

"Humph!" sniffed Walter, "he oughter be nervous after what he done. Ah reckon Joe come back to dare him to marry Lena, or to come out an' fight. Ah bet he'll be back time and again, too. Know what Ah think? Joe wuz a braver man than Spunk."

There was a general shout of derision from the group.

"Thass a fact," went on Walter. "Lookit whut he done; took a razor an' went out to fight a man he knowed toted a gun an' wuz a crack shot, too; 'nother thing Joe wuz skeered of Spunk, skeered plumb stiff! But he went jes' the same. It took him a long time to get his nerve up. Tain't nothin' for Spunk to fight when he ain't skeered of nothin'. Now, Joe's done come back to have it out wid the man that's got all he ever had. Y'all know Joe ain't never had nothin' nor wanted nothin' besides Lena. It musta been a h'ant cause ain't nobody never seen no black bob-cat."

"'Nother thing," cut in one of the men, "Spunk was cussin' a blue streak to-day 'cause he 'lowed dat saw wuz wobblin'—almos' got 'im once. The machinist come, looked it over an' said it wuz alright. Spunk musta been leanin' t'wards it some. Den he claimed somebody pushed 'im but twan't nobody close to 'im. Ah wuz glad when knockin' off time came. I'm skeered of dat man when he gits hot. He'd beat you full of button holes as quick as he'd look atcher."

4

The men gathered the next evening in a different mood, no laughter. No badinage this time.

"Look, 'Lige, you goin' to set up wid Spunk?"

"Naw, Ah reckon not, Walter. Tell yuh the truth, Ah'm a li'l bit skittish. Spunk died too wicket—died cussin' he did. You know he thought he was done outa life."

"Good Lawd, who'd he think done it?"

"Joe."

"Joe Kanty? How come?"

"Walter, Ah b'leeve Ah will walk up thata way an' set. Lena would like it Ah reckon."

"But whut did he say, 'Lige?"

Elijah did not answer until they had left the lighted store and were strolling down the dark street.

"Ah wuz loadin' a wagon wid scantlin' right near the saw when Spunk fell on the carriage but 'fore Ah could git to him the saw got him in the body—awful sight. Me an' Skint Miller got him off but it was too late. Anybody could see that. The fust thing he said wuz: 'He pushed me, 'Lige —the dirty hound pushed me in the back!'—he was spittin' blood at ev'ry breath. We laid him on the sawdust pile with his face to the East so's he could die easy. He helt mah han' till the last, Walter, and said: 'It was Joe, 'Lige . . . the dirty sneak shoved me . . . he didn't dare come to mah face . . . but Ah'll git the son-of-a-wood louse soon's Ah get there an' make hell too hot for him . . . Ah felt him shove me . . .!' Thass how he died."

"If spirits kin fight, there's a powerful tussle goin' on somewhere ovah Jordan 'cause Ah b'leeve Joe's ready for Spunk an' ain't skeered any more—yas, Ah b'leeve Joe pushed 'im mahself."

They had arrived at the house. Lena's lamentations were deep and loud. She had filled the room with magnolia blossoms that gave off a heavy sweet odor. The keepers of the wake tipped about whispering in frightened tones. Everyone in the village was there, even old Jeff Kanty, Joe's father, who a few hours before would have been afraid to come within ten feet of him, stood leering triumphantly down upon the fallen giant as if his fingers had been the teeth of steel that laid him low.

The cooling board consisted of three sixteen-inch boards on saw horses, a dingy sheet was his shroud.

The women ate heartily of the funeral baked meats and wondered who would be Lena's next. The men whispered coarse conjectures between guzzles of whiskey.

1927

Alice Walker, one of Zora Neale Hurston's admirers, points out that in a period when many black writers were struggling to define themselves (see

*comments by Langston Hughes and Countee Cullen, pp. 1025 and 1026)
Hurston was absolutely at ease and self-confident. Some of her confidence
and generosity shows in the closing paragraphs of her autobiography.*

"You lose nothing by not looking just like me":
Zora Neale Hurston

When I get old, and my joints and bones tell me about it, I can sit around
and write for myself, if for nobody else, and read slowly and carefully the
mysticism of the East, and re-read Spinoza with love and care. All the while
my days can be a succession of coffee cups. Then when the sleeplessness of
old age attacks me, I can have a likker bottle snug in my pantry and sip away
and sleep. Get mellow and think kindly of the world. I think I can be like
that because I have known the joy and pain of deep friendship. I have
served and been served. I have made some good enemies for which I am
not a bit sorry. I have loved unselfishly, and I have fondled hatred with the
red-hot tongs of Hell. That's living.

I have no race prejudice of any kind. My kinfolks, and my "skin-
folks" are dearly loved. My own circumference of everyday life is there.
But I see their same virtues and vices everywhere I look. So I give you all my
right hand of fellowship and love, and hope for the same from you. In
my eyesight, you lose nothing by not looking just like me. I will remember
you all in my good thoughts, and I ask you kindly to do the same for me.
Not only just me. You, who play the zig-zag lightning of power over the
world, and the grumbling thunder in your wake, think kindly of those who
walk in the dust. And you who walk in humble places, think kindly too, of
others. There has been no proof in the world so far that you would be less
arrogant if you held the lever of power in your hands. Let us all be kissing-
friends. Consider that with tolerance and patience, we godly demons may
breed a noble world in a few hundred generations or so. Maybe all of us
who do not have the good fortune to meet, or meet again, in this world, will
meet at a barbecue.

ISAAC BASHEVIS SINGER

(b. 1904)

GIMPEL THE FOOL

translated from the Yiddish by Saul Bellow

1

I am Gimpel the fool. I don't think myself a fool. On the contrary. But that's what folks call me. They give me the name while I was still in school. I had seven names in all: imbecile, donkey, flax-head, dope, glump, ninny, and fool. The last name stuck. What did my foolishness consist of? I was easy to take in. They said, "Gimpel, you know the rabbi's wife has been brought to childbed?" So I skipped school. Well, it turned out to be a lie. How was I supposed to know? She hadn't had a big belly. But I never looked at her belly. Was that really so foolish? The gang laughed and hee-hawed, stomped and danced and chanted a good-night prayer. And instead of the raisins they give when a woman's lying in, they stuffed my hand full of goat turds. I was no weakling. If I slapped someone he'd see all the way to Cracow. But I'm really not a slugger by nature. I think to myself: Let it pass. So they take advantage of me.

I was coming home from school and heard a dog barking. I'm not afraid of dogs, but of course I never want to start up with them. One of them may be mad, and if he bites there's not a Tartar in the world who can help you. So I made tracks. Then I looked around and saw the whole market place wild with laughter. It was no dog at all but Wolf-Leib the Thief. How was I supposed to know it was he? It sounded like a howling bitch.

When the pranksters and leg-pullers found that I was easy to fool, every one of them tried his luck with me. "Gimpel, the Czar is coming to Frampol; Gimpel, the moon fell down in Turbeen; Gimpel, little Hodel Fur-piece found a treasure behind the bathhouse." And I like a golem[1] believed everyone. In the first place, everything is possible, as it is written in the Wisdom of the Fathers, I've forgotten just how. Second, I had to believe when the whole town came down on me! If I ever dared to say, "Ah, you're kidding!" there was trouble. People got angry. "What do you mean! You want to call everyone a liar?" What was I to do? I believed them, and I hope at least that did them some good.

I was an orphan. My grandfather who brought me up was already bent toward the grave. So they turned me over to a baker, and what a time they gave me there! Every woman or girl who came to bake a batch of noo-

---

1. According to Jewish folklore, an artificially created human being, an automaton; here, a clumsy person.

dles had to fool me at least once. "Gimpel, there's a fair in heaven; Gimpel, the rabbi gave birth to a calf in the seventh month; Gimpel, a cow flew over the roof and laid brass eggs." A student from the yeshiva[2] came once to buy a roll, and he said, "You, Gimpel, while you stand here scraping with your baker's shovel the Messiah has come. The dead have arisen." "What do you mean?" I said. "I heard no one blowing the ram's horn!" He said, "Are you deaf?" And all began to cry, "We heard it, we heard!" Then in came Rietze the Candle-dipper and called out in her hoarse voice, "Gimpel, your father and mother have stood up from the grave. They're looking for you."

To tell the truth, I knew very well that nothing of the sort had happened, but all the same, as folks were talking, I threw on my wool vest and went out. Maybe something had happened. What did I stand to lose by looking? Well, what a cat music went up! And then I took a vow to believe nothing more. But that was no go either. They confused me so that I didn't know the big end from the small.

I went to the rabbi to get some advice. He said, "It is written, better to be a fool all your days than for one hour to be evil. You are not a fool. They are the fools. For he who causes his neighbor to feel shame loses Paradise himself." Nevertheless the rabbi's daughter took me in. As I left the rabbinical court she said, "Have you kissed the wall yet?" I said, "No; what for?" She answered, "It's the law; you've got to do it after every visit." Well, there didn't seem to be any harm in it. And she burst out laughing. It was a fine trick. She put one over on me, all right.

I wanted to go off to another town, but then everyone got busy matchmaking, and they were after me so they nearly tore my coat tails off. They talked at me and talked until I got water on the ear. She was no chaste maiden, but they told me she was virgin pure. She had a limp, and they said it was deliberate, from coyness. She had a bastard, and they told me the child was her little brother. I cried, "You're wasting your time. I'll never marry that whore." But they said indignantly, "What a way to talk! Aren't you ashamed of yourself? We can take you to the rabbi and have you fined for giving her a bad name." I saw then that I wouldn't escape them so easily and I thought: They're set on making me their butt. But when you're married the husband's the master, and if that's all right with her it's agreeable to me too. Besides, you can't pass through life unscathed, nor expect to.

I went to her clay house, which was built on the sand, and the whole gang hollering and chorusing, came after me. They acted like bear-baiters. When we came to the well they stopped all the same. They were afraid to start anything with Elka. Her mouth would open as if it were on a hinge, and she had a fierce tongue. I entered the house. Lines were strung from wall to wall and clothes were drying. Barefoot she stood by the tub, doing the wash. She was dressed in a worn hand-me-down gown of plush. She

---

2. A Jewish institute where students study the word of God, the Talmud.

had her hair put up in braids and pinned across her head. It took my breath away, almost, the reek of it all.

Evidently she knew who I was. She took a look at me and said, "Look who's here! He's come, the drip. Grab a seat."

I told her all; I denied nothing. "Tell me the truth," I said, "are you really a virgin; and is that mischievous Yechiel actually your little brother? Don't be deceitful with me, for I'm an orphan."

"I'm an orphan myself," she answered, "and whoever tries to twist you up, may the end of his nose take a twist. But don't let them think they can take advantage of me. I want a dowry of fifty guilders, and let them take up a collection besides. Otherwise they can kiss my you-know-what." She was very plainspoken. I said, "It's the bride and not the groom who gives a dowry." Then she said, "Don't bargain with me. Either a flat 'yes' or a flat 'no'—Go back where you came from."

I thought: No bread will ever be baked from *this* dough. But ours is not a poor town. They consented to everything and proceeded with the wedding. It so happened that there was a dysentery epidemic at the time. The ceremony was held at the cemetery gates, near the little corpse-washing hut. The fellows got drunk. While the marriage contract was being drawn up I heard the most pious high rabbi ask, "Is the bride a widow or a divorced woman?" And the sexton's wife answered for her, "Both a widow and divorced." It was a black moment for me. But what was I to do, run away from under the marriage canopy?

There was singing and dancing. An old granny danced opposite me, hugging a braided white *chalah*.[3] The master of revels made a "God 'a mercy" in memory of the bride's parents. The schoolboys threw burrs, as on Tishe b'Av fast day.[4] There were a lot of gifts after the sermon: a noodle board, a kneading trough, a bucket, brooms, ladles, household articles galore. Then I took a look and saw two strapping young men carrying a crib. "What do we need this for?" I asked. So they said, "Don't rack your brains about it. It's all right, it'll come in handy." I realized I was going to be rooked. Take it another way though, what did I stand to lose? I reflected: I'll see what comes of it. A whole town can't go altogether crazy.

2

At night I came where my wife lay, but she wouldn't let me in. "Say, look here, is this what they married us for?" I said. And she said, "My monthly has come." "But yesterday they took you to the ritual bath, and that's afterward, isn't it supposed to be?" "Today isn't yesterday," said she, "and yesterday's not today. You can beat it if you don't like it." In short, I waited.

---

3. A loaf of braided yeast-leavened white, egg bread. It is traditional fare at Jewish holidays, the Sabbath, and ceremonial occasions.
4. A Jewish day of fast to commemorate the Roman sacking of the Temple of Jerusalem, first in 586 B.C. and then in 70 B.C.

Not four months later she was in childbed. The townsfolk hid their laughter with their knuckles. But what could I do? She suffered intolerable pains and clawed at the walls. "Gimpel," she cried, "I'm going. Forgive me!" The house filled with women. They were boiling pans of water. The screams rose to the welkin.

The thing to do was to go to the House of Prayer to repeat Psalms, and that was what I did.

The townsfolk liked that, all right. I stood in a corner saying Psalms and prayers, and they shook their heads at me. "Pray, pray!" they told me. "Prayer never made any woman pregnant." One of the congregation put a straw to my mouth and said, "Hay for the cows." There was something to that too, by God!

She gave birth to a boy. Friday at the synagogue the sexton stood up before the Ark, pounded on the reading table, and announced, "The wealthy Reb Gimpel invites the congregation to a feast in honor of the birth of a son." The whole House of Prayer rang with laughter. My face was flaming. But there was nothing I could do. After all, I *was* the one responsible for the circumcision honors and rituals.

Half the town came running. You couldn't wedge another soul in. Women brought peppered chick-peas, and there was a keg of beer from the tavern. I ate and drank as much as anyone, and they all congratulated me. Then there was a circumcision, and I named the boy after my father, may he rest in peace. When all were gone and I was left with my wife alone, she thrust her head through the bed-curtain and called me to her.

"Gimpel," said she, "why are you silent? Has your ship gone and sunk?"

"What shall I say?" I answered. "A fine thing you've done to me! If my mother had known of it she'd have died a second time."

She said, "Are you crazy, or what?"

"How can you make such a fool," I said, "of one who should be the lord and master?"

"What's the matter with you?" she said. "What have you taken it into your head to imagine?"

I saw that I must speak bluntly and openly. "Do you think this is the way to use an orphan?" I said. "You have borne a bastard."

She answered, "Drive this foolishness out of your head. The child is yours."

"How can he be mine?" I argued. "He was born seventeen weeks after the wedding."

She told me then that he was premature. I said, "Isn't he a little too premature?" She said, she had had a grandmother who carried just as short a time and she resembled this grandmother of hers as one drop of water does another. She swore to it with such oaths that you would have believed a peasant at the fair if he had used them. To tell the plain truth, I didn't believe her; but when I talked it over next day with the schoolmaster he told me that the very same thing had happened to Adam and Eve. Two they went up to bed, and four they descended.

"There isn't a woman in the world who is not the granddaughter of Eve," he said.

That was how it was; they argued me dumb. But then, who really knows how such things are?

I began to forget my sorrow. I loved the child madly, and he loved me too. As soon as he saw me he'd wave his little hands and want me to pick him up, and when he was colicky I was the only one who could pacify him. I bought him a little bone teething ring and a little gilded cap. He was forever catching the evil eye from someone, and then I had to run to get one of those abracadabras for him that would get him out of it. I worked like an ox. You know how expenses go up when there's an infant in the house. I don't want to lie about it; I didn't dislike Elka either, for that matter. She swore at me and cursed, and I couldn't get enough of her. What strength she had! One of her looks could rob you of the power of speech. And her orations! Pitch and sulphur, that's what they were full of, and yet somehow also full of charm. I adored her every word. She gave me bloody wounds though.

In the evening I brought her a white loaf as well as a dark one, and also poppyseed rolls I baked myself. I thieved because of her and swiped everything I could lay hands on: macaroons, raisins, almonds, cakes. I hope I may be forgiven for stealing from the Saturday pots the women left to warm in the baker's oven. I would take out scraps of meat, a chunk of pudding, a chicken leg or head, a piece of tripe, whatever I could nip quickly. She ate and became fat and handsome.

I had to sleep away from home all during the week, at the bakery. On Friday nights when I got home she always made an excuse of some sort. Either she had heartburn, or a stitch in the side, or hiccups, or headaches. You know what women's excuses are. I had a bitter time of it. It was rough. To add to it, this little brother of hers, the bastard, was growing bigger. He'd put lumps on me, and when I wanted to hit back she'd open her mouth and curse so powerfully I saw a green haze floating before my eyes. Ten times a day she threatened to divorce me. Another man in my place would have taken French leave and disappeared. But I'm the type that bears it and says nothing. What's one to do? Shoulders are from God, and burdens too.

One night there was a calamity in the bakery; the oven burst, and we almost had a fire. There was nothing to do but go home, so I went home. Let me, I thought, also taste the joy of sleeping in bed in mid-week. I didn't want to wake the sleeping mite and tiptoed into the house. Coming in, it seemed to me that I heard not the snoring of one but, as it were, a double snore, one a thin enough snore and the other like the snoring of a slaughtered ox. Oh, I didn't like that! I didn't like it at all. I went up to the bed, and things suddenly turned black. Next to Elka lay a man's form.

Another in my place would have made an uproar, and enough noise to rouse the whole town, but the thought occurred to me that I might wake the child. A little thing like that—why frighten a little swallow, I thought. All right then, I went back to the bakery and stretched out on a sack of flour and till morning I never shut an eye. I shivered as if I had had malaria. "Enough of being a donkey," I said to myself. "Gimpel isn't going to be a sucker all his life. There's a limit even to the foolishness of a fool like Gimpel."

In the morning I went to the rabbi to get advice, and it made a great commotion in the town. They sent the beadle for Elka right away. She came, carrying the child. And what do you think she did? She denied it, denied everything, bone and stone! "He's out of his head," she said. "I know nothing of dreams or divinations." They yelled at her, warned her, hammered on the table, but she stuck to her guns: it was a false accusation, she said.

The butchers and the horse-traders took her part. One of the lads from the slaughterhouse came by and said to me, "We've got our eye on you, you're a marked man." Meanwhile the child started to bear down and soiled itself. In the rabbinical court there was an Ark of the Covenant, and they couldn't allow that, so they sent Elka away.

I said to the rabbi, "What shall I do?"

"You must divorce her at once," said he.

"And what if she refuses?" I asked.

He said, "You must serve the divorce. That's all you'll have to do."

I said, "Well, all right, Rabbi. Let me think about it."

"There's nothing to think about," said he. "You mustn't remain under the same roof with her."

"And if I want to see the child?" I asked.

"Let her go, the harlot," said he, "and her brood of bastards with her."

The verdict he gave was that I mustn't even cross her threshold—never again, as long as I should live.

During the day it didn't bother me so much. I thought: It was bound to happen, the abscess had to burst. But at night when I stretched out upon the sacks I felt it all very bitterly. A longing took me, for her and for the child. I wanted to be angry, but that's my misfortune exactly, I don't have it in me to be really angry. In the first place—this was how my thoughts went—there's bound to be a slip sometimes. You can't live without errors. Probably that lad who was with her led her on and gave her presents and what not, and women are often long on hair and short on sense, and so he got around her. And then since she denies it so, maybe I was only seeing things? Hallucinations do happen. You see a figure or a mannikin or something, but when you come up closer it's nothing, there's not a thing there. And if that's so, I'm doing her an injustice. And when I got so far in my thoughts I started to weep. I sobbed so that I wet the flour where I lay. In the morning I went to the rabbi and told him that I had made a mistake. The rabbi wrote on with his quill, and he said that if that were so he would have to reconsider the whole case. Until he had finished I wasn't to go near my wife, but I might send her bread and money by messenger.

3

Nine months passed before all the rabbis could come to an agreement. Letters went back and forth. I hadn't realized that there could be so much erudition about a matter like this.

Meanwhile Elka gave birth to still another child, a girl this time. On the Sabbath I went to the synagogue and invoked a blessing on her. They called me up to the Torah, and I named the child for my mother-in-law—may she rest in peace. The louts and loudmouths of the town who came into the bakery gave me a going over. All Frampol refreshed its spirits because of my trouble and grief. However, I resolved that I would always believe what I was told. What's the good of *not* believing? Today it's your wife you don't believe; tomorrow it's God Himself you won't take stock in.

By an apprentice who was her neighbor I sent her daily a corn or a wheat loaf, or a piece of pastry, rolls or bagels, or, when I got the chance, a slab of pudding, a slice of honeycake, or wedding strudel—whatever came my way. The apprentice was a goodhearted lad, and more than once he added something on his own. He had formerly annoyed me a lot, plucking my nose and digging me in the ribs, but when he started to be a visitor to my house he became kind and friendly. "Hey, you, Gimpel," he said to me, "you have a very decent little wife and two fine kids. You don't deserve them."

"But the things people say about her," I said.

"Well, they have long tongues," he said, "and nothing to do with them but babble. Ignore it as you ignore the cold of last winter."

One day the rabbi sent for me and said, "Are you certain, Gimpel, that you were wrong about your wife?"

I said, "I'm certain."

"Why, but look here! You yourself saw it."

"It must have been a shadow," I said.

"The shadow of what?"

"Just one of the beams, I think."

"You can go home then. You owe thanks to the Yanover rabbi. He found an obscure reference in Maimonides[5] that favored you."

I seized the rabbi's hand and kissed it.

I wanted to run home immediately. It's no small thing to be separated for so long a time from wife and child. Then I reflected: I'd better go

---

5. A Jewish philosopher and physician (1135–1204) and a great interpreter of the Torah.

back to work now, and go home in the evening. I said nothing to anyone, although as far as my heart was concerned it was like one of the Holy Days. The women teased and twitted me as they did every day, but my thought was: Go on, with your loose talk. The truth is out, like the oil upon the water. Maimonides says it's right, and therefore it is right!

At night, when I had covered the dough to let it rise, I took my share of bread and a little sack of flour and started homeward. The moon was full and the stars were glistening, something to terrify the soul. I hurried onward, and before me darted a long shadow. It was winter, and a fresh snow had fallen. I had a mind to sing, but it was growing late and I didn't want to wake the householders. Then I felt like whistling, but I remembered that you don't whistle at night because it brings the demons out. So I was silent and walked as fast as I could.

Dogs in the Christian yards barked at me when I passed, but I thought: Bark your teeth out! What are you but mere dogs? Whereas I am a man, the husband of a fine wife, the father of promising children.

As I approached the house my heart started to pound as though it were the heart of a criminal. I felt no fear, but my heart went thump! thump! Well, no drawing back. I quietly lifted the latch and went in. Elka was asleep. I looked at the infant's cradle. The shutter was closed, but the moon forced its way through the cracks. I saw the newborn child's face and loved it as soon as I saw it—immediately—each tiny bone.

Then I came nearer to the bed. And what did I see but the apprentice lying there beside Elka. The moon went out all at once. It was utterly black, and I trembled. My teeth chattered. The bread fell from my hands, and my wife waked and said, "Who is that, ah?"

I muttered, "It's me."

"Gimpel?" she asked. "How come you're here? I thought it was forbidden."

"The rabbi said," I answered and shook as with a fever.

"Listen to me, Gimpel," she said, "go out to the shed and see if the goat's all right. It seems she's been sick." I have forgotten to say that we had a goat. When I heard she was unwell I went into the yard. The nanny goat was a good little creature. I had a nearly human feeling for her.

With hesitant steps I went up to the shed and opened the door. The goat stood there on her four feet. I felt her everywhere, drew her by the horns, examined her udders, and found nothing wrong. She had probably eaten too much bark. "Good night, little goat," I said. "Keep well." And the little beast answered with a "Maa" as though to thank me for the good will.

I went back. The apprentice had vanished.

"Where," I asked, "is the lad?"

"What lad?" my wife answered.

"What do you mean?" I said. "The apprentice. You were sleeping with him."

"The things I have dreamed this night and the night before," she said, "may they come true and lay you low, body and soul! An evil spirit has taken root in you and dazzles your sight." She screamed out, "You hateful creature! You moon calf! You spook! You uncouth man! Get out, or I'll scream all Frampol out of bed!"

Before I could move, her brother sprang out from behind the oven and struck me a blow on the back of the head. I thought he had broken my neck. I felt that something about me was deeply wrong, and I said, "Don't make a scandal. All that's needed now is that people should accuse me of raising spooks and *dybbuks*."[6] For that was what she had meant. "No one will touch bread of my baking."

In short, I somehow calmed her.

"Well," she said, "that's enough. Lie down, and be shattered by wheels."

Next morning I called the apprentice aside. "Listen here, brother!" I said. And so on and so forth. "What do you say?" He stared at me as though I had dropped from the roof or something.

"I swear," he said, "you'd better go to an herb doctor or some healer. I'm afraid you have a screw loose, but I'll hush it up for you." And that's how the thing stood.

To make a long story short, I lived twenty years with my wife. She bore me six children, four daughters and two sons. All kinds of things happened, but I neither saw nor heard. I believed, and that's all. The rabbi recently said to me, "Belief in itself is beneficial. It is written that a good man lives by his faith."

Suddenly my wife took sick. It began with a trifle, a little growth upon the breast. But she evidently was not destined to live long; she had no years. I spent a fortune on her. I have forgotten to say that by this time I had a bakery of my own and in Frampol was considered to be something of a rich man. Daily the healer came, and every witch doctor in the neighborhood was brought. They decided to use leeches, and after that to try cupping. They even called a doctor from Lublin, but it was too late. Before she died she called me to her bed and said, "Forgive me, Gimpel."

I said, "What is there to forgive? You have been a good and faithful wife."

"Woe, Gimpel!" she said. "It was ugly how I deceived you all these years. I want to go clean to my Maker, and so I have to tell you that the children are not yours."

If I had been clouted on the head with a piece of wood it couldn't have bewildered me more.

"Whose are they?" I asked.

"I don't know," she said. "There were a lot . . . but they're not yours." And as she spoke she tossed her head to the side, her eyes turned

---

6. Evil spirits; usually the soul of a dead person who enters a living person on whom the dead one had some claim.

glassy, and it was all up with Elka. On her whitened lips there remained a smile.

I imagined that, dead as she was, she was saying, "I deceived Gimpel. That was the meaning of my brief life."

<h1 style="text-align:center">4</h1>

One night, when the period of mourning was done, as I lay dreaming on the flour sacks, there came the Spirit of Evil himself and said to me, "Gimpel, why do you sleep?"

I said, "What should I be doing? Eating *kreplach?*"[7]

"The whole world deceives you," he said, "and you ought to deceive the world in your turn."

"How can I deceive the world?" I asked him.

He answered, "You might accumulate a bucket of urine every day and at night pour it into the dough. Let the sages of Frampol eat filth."

"What about the judgment in the world to come?" I said.

"There is no world to come," he said. "They've sold you a bill of goods and talked you into believing you carried a cat in your belly. What nonsense!"

"Well then," I said, "and is there a God?"

He answered, "There is no God either."

"What," I said, "*is* there, then?"

"A thick mire."

He stood before my eyes with a goatish beard and horn, long-toothed, and with a tail. Hearing such words, I wanted to snatch him by the tail, but I tumbled for the flour sacks and nearly broke a rib. Then it happened that I had to answer the call of nature, and, passing, I saw the risen dough, which seemed to say to me, "Do it!" In brief, I let myself be persuaded.

At dawn the apprentice came. We kneaded the bread, scattered caraway seeds on it, and set it to bake. Then the apprentice went away, and I was left sitting in the little trench by the oven, on a pile of rags. Well, Gimpel, I thought, you've revenged yourself on them for all the shame they've put on you. Outside the frost glittered, but it was warm beside the oven. The flames heated my face. I bent my head and fell into a doze.

I saw in a dream, at once, Elka in her shroud. She called to me, "What have you done, Gimpel?"

I said to her, "It's all your fault," and started to cry.

"You fool!" she said. "You fool! Because I was false is everything false too? I never deceived anyone but myself. I'm paying for it all, Gimpel. They spare you nothing here."

---

7. A triangular or square dumpling (like Italian ravioli) that contains meat or cheese, etc. Kreplach traditionally is eaten on Purim and Rosh Hoshanah and the day before Yom Kippur.

I looked at her face. It was black; I was startled and waked, and remained sitting dumb. I sensed that everything hung in the balance. A false step now and I'd lose Eternal Life. But God gave me His help. I seized the long shovel and took out the loaves, carried them into the yard, and started to dig a hole in the frozen earth.

My apprentice came back as I was doing it. "What are you doing, boss?" he said, and grew pale as a corpse.

"I know what I'm doing," I said, and I buried it all before his very eyes.

Then I went home, took my hoard from its hiding place, and divided it among the children. "I saw your mother tonight," I said. "She's turning black, poor thing."

They were so astounded they couldn't speak a word.

"Be well," I said, "and forget that such a one as Gimpel ever existed." I put on my short coat, a pair of boots, took the bag that held my prayer shawl in one hand, my stock in the other, and kissed the *mezzuzah*.[8] When people saw me in the street they were greatly surprised.

"Where are you going?" they said.

I answered, "Into the world." And so I departed from Frampol.

I wandered over the land, and good people did not neglect me. After many years I became old and white; I heard a great deal, many lies and falsehoods, but the longer I lived the more I understood that there were really no lies. Whatever doesn't really happen is dreamed at night. It happens to one if it doesn't happen to another, tomorrow if not today, or a century hence if not next year. What difference can it make? Often I heard tales of which I said, "Now this is a thing that cannot happen." But before a year had elapsed I heard that it actually had come to pass somewhere.

Going from place to place, eating at strange tables, it often happens that I spin yarns—improbable things that could never have happened—about devils, magicians, windmills, and the like. The children run after me, calling, "Grandfather, tell us a story." Sometimes they ask for particular stories, and I try to please them. A fat young boy once said to me, "Grandfather, it's the same story you told us before." The little rogue, he was right.

So it is with dreams too. It is many years since I left Frampol, but as soon as I shut my eyes I am there again. And whom do you think I see? Elka. She is standing by the washtub, as at our first encounter, but her face is shining and her eyes are as radiant as the eyes of a saint, and she speaks outlandish words to me, strange things. When I wake I have forgotten it all. But while the dream lasts I am comforted. She answers all my queries, and what comes out is that all is right. I weep and implore, "Let me be with you." And she consoles me and tells me to be patient. The time is nearer

---

8. A little oblong container with a tiny rolled-up paper or parchment inside. The verses from Deuteronomy 6:4–9 and 11:13–21 are printed on the parchment. The first sentence is Israel's great watchword: "Hear, O Isreal, the Lord our God is One." The mezzuzah is usually inserted to the right of the front door-jamb of the home.

than it is far. Sometimes she strokes and kisses me and weeps upon my face. When I awaken I feel her lips and taste the salt of her tears.

No doubt the world is entirely an imaginary world, but it is only once removed from the true world. At the door of the hovel where I lie, there stands the plank on which the dead are taken away. The gravedigger Jew has his spade ready. The grave waits and the worms are hungry; the shrouds are prepared—I carry them in my beggar's sack. Another *shnorrer*[9] is waiting to inherit my bed of straw. When the time comes I will go joyfully. Whatever may be there, it will be real, without complication, without ridicule, without deception. God be praised: there even Gimpel cannot be deceived.

1953

Isaac Bashevis Singer, son of an orthodox rabbi and himself deeply interested in the writings of the Jewish mystics, is often praised for his ability to meld the mystical and the realistic in a story. In an interview with Cyrena Pondrom, he discussed how these different planes of experience can be brought together.

"A miracle must be invented amid realism": Isaac Bashevis Singer

Q. What have you read in particular? Have you gone back to the Cabala at all?

A. Oh, yes. I studied the Cabala when I was still young, and once in a while I will go back to it. I have even written a speech which I call "Cabala and Modern Man." I read Hasidic books, and a lot of books about the occult, about psychic research, like *The Phantoms of the Living,* and many others. I also read a lot of magazines, and I'm especially interested in the letters which readers write to these magazines, because these naive letters sometimes discover to me whole worlds. Not discover, the give *hints* of hidden things. To me a writer must be interested in the mystery of life. A writer who says to me that he's a complete realist, to me he's not a writer anymore.

---

9. A beggar, a professional moocher.

Q. And yet your own work often uses extremely detailed. . . .

A. Yes, realism—because the so-called real world itself is a great secret, a great mystery. Also, I don't like writers who write about great miracles and mysteries without even describing the background. In other words, a miracle must be invented amid realism because, if it's one miracle after the other and there's no realism, the miracle itself becomes nothing.

Q. All great literature begins in realism then?

A. I think, yes. Once a man brought me a story which began with a cut-off head which spoke. And I said to the man, "Isn't it miracle enough that a head which is not chopped off can talk?" . . .

Q. Have you read any Kafka? Do you like Kafka?

A. Yes, I like him, but one Kafka in a century is enough. It's not good to have whole armies, whole multitudes, of Kafkas. He's not the kind of writer whom one should imitate or even emulate. There could have been only one Kafka, like one Joyce and one Proust. While there could have been another Tolstoy—it couldn't do any damage if you would have a hundred Tolstoys; but a hundred Kafkas wouldn't be good. He's a unique case.

Q. Why wouldn't it be good?

A. It wouldn't be good because it's description of dreams, *completely* so. Kafka is not enough embedded in life—his miracles are too arbitrary to create the kind of literature that could last forever. The reader gets very tired if life is distorted, or too much invented, completely defying the order of things. In other words, the real mystic should describe life as it is, and then bring out the other side. But when you begin immediately with symbolism or with distortions, you create a kind of literature which even if it is unique, you cannot have too much of it. Like with food, you can eat a lot of bread, a lot of potatoes, a lot of vegetables, you cannot eat a lot of mustard. You can only have a little bit of it. And this is true even about spiritual things.

RICHARD WRIGHT

(1908–1960)

THE LIBRARY CARD

One morning I arrived early at work and went into the bank lobby where the Negro porter was mopping. I stood at a counter and picked up the Memphis *Commercial Appeal* and began my free reading of the press. I came finally to the editorial page and saw an article dealing with one H. L. Mencken. I knew by hearsay that he was the editor of the *American Mercury*, but aside from that I knew nothing about him. The article was a furious denunciation of Mencken, concluding with one, hot, short sentence: Mencken is a fool.

I wondered what on earth this Mencken had done to call down upon him the scorn of the South. The only people I had ever heard denounced in the South were Negroes, and this man was not a Negro. Then what ideas did Mencken hold that made a newspaper like the *Commercial Appeal* castigate him publicly? Undoubtedly he must be advocating ideas that the South did not like. Were there, then, people other than Negroes who criticized the South? I knew that during the Civil War the South had hated northern whites, but I had not encountered such hate during my life. Knowing no more of Mencken than I did at that moment, I felt a vague sympathy for him. Had not the South, which had assigned me the role of a non-man, cast at him its hardest words?

Now, how could I find out about this Mencken? There was a huge library near the riverfront, but I knew that Negroes were not allowed to patronize its shelves any more than they were the parks and playgrounds of the city. I had gone into the library several times to get books for the white men on the job. Which of them would now help me to get books? And how could I read them without causing concern to the white men with whom I worked? I had so far been successful in hiding my thoughts and feelings from them, but I knew that I would create hostility if I went about the business of reading in a clumsy way.

I weighed the personalities of the men on the job. There was Don, a Jew; but I distrusted him. His position was not much better than mine and I knew that he was uneasy and insecure; he had always treated me in an off-hand, bantering way that barely concealed his contempt. I was afraid to ask him to help me get books; his frantic desire to demonstrate a racial solidarity with the whites against Negroes might make him betray me.

Then how about the boss? No, he was a Baptist and I had the suspicion that he would not be quite able to comprehend why a black boy would want to read Mencken. There were other white men on the job whose attitudes showed clearly that they were Kluxers or sympathizers, and they were out of the question.

There remained only one man whose attitude did not fit into an anti-Negro category, for I had heard the white men refer to him as a "Pope lover." He was an Irish Catholic and was hated by the white Southerners. I knew that he read books, because I had got him volumes from the library several times. Since he, too, was an object of hatred, I felt that he might refuse me but would hardly betray me. I hesitated, weighing and balancing the imponderable realities.

One morning I paused before the Catholic fellow's desk.

"I want to ask you a favor," I whispered to him.

"What is it?"

"I want to read. I can't get books from the library. I wonder if you'd let me use your card?"

He looked at me suspiciously.

"My card is full most of the time," he said.

"I see," I said and waited, posing my question silently.

"You're not trying to get me into trouble, are you, boy?" He asked, staring at me.

"Oh, no sir."

"What book do you want?"

"A book by H. L. Mencken."

"Which one?"

"I don't know. Has he written more than one?"

"He has written several."

"I didn't know that."

"What makes you want to read Mencken?"

"Oh, I just saw his name in the newspaper," I said.

"It's good of you to want to read," he said. "But you ought to read the right things."

I said nothing. Would he want to supervise my reading?

"Let me think," he said. "I'll figure out something."

I turned from him and he called me back. He stared at me quizzically.

"Richard, don't mention this to the other white men," he said.

"I understand," I said. "I won't say a word."

A few days later he called me to him.

"I've got a card in my wife's name," he said. "Here's mine."

"Thank you, sir."

"Do you think you can manage it?"

"I'll manage fine," I said.

"If they suspect you, you'll get in trouble," he said.

"I'll write the same kind of notes to the library that you wrote when you sent me for books," I told him. "I'll sign your name."

He laughed.

"Go ahead. Let me see what you get," he said.

That afternoon I addressed myself to forging a note. Now, what were the names of books written by H. L. Mencken? I did not know any of them. I finally wrote what I thought would be a foolproof note: *Dear Madam: Will you please let this nigger boy*—I used the word "nigger" to make the librarian feel that I could not possibly be the author of the note—*have some books by H. L. Mencken?* I forged the white man's name.

I entered the library as I had always done when on errands for whites, but I felt that I would somehow slip up and betray myself. I doffed my hat, stood a respectful distance from the desk, looked as unbookish as possible, and waited for the white patrons to be taken care of. When the desk was clear of people, I still waited. The white librarian looked at me.

"What do you want, boy?"

As thought I did not possess the power of speech, I stepped forward and simply handed her the forged note, not parting my lips.

"What books by Mencken does he want?" she asked.

"I don't know, ma'am," I said, avoiding her eyes.

"Who gave you this card?"

"Mr. Falk," I said.

"Where is he?"

"He's at work, at the M——Optical Company," I said. "I've been in here for him before."

"I remember," the woman said. "But he never wrote notes like this."

Oh, God, she's suspicious. Perhaps she would not let me have the books? If she had turned her back at that moment, I would have ducked out the door and never gone back. Then I thought of a bold idea.

"You can call him up, ma'am," I said, my heart pounding.

"You're not using these books, are you?" she asked pointedly.

"Oh, no, ma'am. I can't read."

"I don't know what he wants by Mencken," she said under her breath.

I knew now that I had won; she was thinking of other things and the race question had gone out of her mind. She went to the shelves. Once or twice she looked over her shoulder at me, as though she was still doubtful. Finally she came foreward with two books in her hand.

"I'm sending him two books," she said. "But tell Mr. Falk to come in next time, or send me the names of the books he wants. I don't know what he wants to read."

I said nothing. She stamped the card and handed me the books. Not daring to glance at them, I went out of the library, fearing that the woman would call me back for further questioning. A block away from the library I opened one of the books and read a title: *A Book of Prefaces.* I was nearing my nineteenth birthday and I did not know how to pronounce the word "preface." I thumbed the pages and saw strange words and strange names. I shook my head, disappointed. I looked at the other book; it was called *Prejudices.* I knew what that word meant; I had heard it all my life. And right off I was on guard against Mencken's books. Why would a man want to call a book *Prejudices?* The word was so stained with all my memories of racial hate that I could not conceive of anybody using it for a title. Perhaps I had made a mistake about Mencken? A man who had prejudices must be wrong.

When I showed the books to Mr. Falk, he looked at me and frowned.

"That librarian might telephone you," I warned him.

"That's all right," he said. "But when you're through reading those books, I want you to tell me what you get out of them."

That night in my rented room, while letting the hot water run over my can of pork and beans in the sink, I opened *A Book of Prefaces* and began to read. I was jarred and shocked by the style, the clear, clean, sweeping sentences. Why did he write like that? And how did one write like that? I pictured the man as a raging demon, slashing with his pen, consumed with hate, denouncing everything American, extolling everything European or German, laughing at the weaknesses of people, mocking God, authority. What was this? I stood up, trying to realize what reality lay behind the meaning of the words . . . Yes, this man was fighting, fighting with words. He was using words as a weapon, using them as one would use a club. Could words be weapons? Well, yes, for here they were. Then, maybe, perhaps, I could use them as a weapon? No. It frightened me. I read on and what amazed me was not what he said, but how on earth anybody had the courage to say it.

Occasionally I glanced up to reassure myself that I was alone in the room. Who were these men about whom Mencken was talking so passionately? Who was Anatole France? Joseph Conrad? Sinclair Lewis, Sherwood Anderson, Dostoevski, George Moore, Gustave Flaubert, Maupassant, Tolstoy, Frank Harris, Mark Twain, Thomas Hardy, Arnold Bennett, Stephen Crane, Zola, Norris, Gorky, Bergson, Ibsen, Balzac, Bernard Shaw, Dumas, Poe, Thomas Mann, O. Henry, Dreiser, H. G. Wells, Gogol, T. S. Eliot, Gide, Baudelaire, Edgar Lee Masters, Stendhal, Turgenev, Huneker, Nietzsche, and scores of others? Were these men real? Did they exist or had they existed? And how did one pronounce their names?

I ran across many words whose meanings I did not know, and I either looked them up in a dictionary or, before I had a chance to do that, encountered the word in a context that made its meaning clear. But what strange world was this? I concluded the book with the conviction that I had somehow overlooked something terribly important in life. I had once tried to write, had once reveled in feeling, had let my crude imagination roam, but the impulse to dream had been slowly beaten out of me by experience. Now it surged up again and I hungered for books, new ways of looking and seeing. It was not a matter of believing or disbelieving what I read, but of feeling something new, of being affected by something that made the look of the world different.

As dawn broke I ate my pork and beans, feeling dopey, sleepy. I went to work, but the mood of the book would not die; it lingered, coloring everything I saw, heard, did. I now felt that I knew what the white men were feeling. Merely because I had read a book that had spoken of how they lived and thought, I identified myself with that book. I felt vaguely guilty. Would I, filled with bookish notions, act in a manner that would make the whites dislike me?

I forged more notes and my trips to the library became frequent. Reading grew into a passion. My first serious novel was Sinclair Lewis's *Main Street*. It made me see my boss, Mr. Gerald, and identify him as an American type. I would smile when I saw him lugging his golf bags into the office. I had always felt a vast distance separating me from the boss, and now I felt closer to him, though still distant. I felt now that I knew him, that I could feel the very limits of his narrow life. And this had happened because I had read a novel about a mythical man called George F. Babbitt.

The plots and stories in the novels did not interest me so much as the point of view revealed. I gave myself over to each novel without reserve, without trying to criticize it; it was enough for me to see and feel something different. And for me, everything was something different. Reading was like a drug, a dope. The novels created moods in which I lived for days. But I could not conquer my sense of guilt, my feeling that the white men around me knew that I was changing, that I had begun to regard them differently.

Whenever I brought a book to the job, I wrapped it in newspaper —a habit that was to persist for years in other cities and under other circumstances. But some of the white men pried into my packages when I was absent and they questioned me.

"Boy, what are you reading those books for?"

"Oh, I don't know, sir."

"That's deep stuff you're reading, boy."

"I'm just killing time, sir."

"You'll addle your brains if you don't watch out."

I read Dreiser's *Jennie Gerhardt* and *Sister Carrie* and they revived in me a vivid sense of my mother's suffering; I was overwhelmed. I grew silent, wondering about the life around me. It would have been impossible for me to have told anyone what I derived from these novels, for it was nothing less than a sense of life itself. All my life had shaped me for the realism, the naturalism of the modern novel, and I could not read enough of them.

Steeped in new moods and ideas, I bought a ream of paper and tried to write; but nothing would come, or what did come was flat beyond telling. I discovered that more than desire and feeling were necessary to write and I dropped the idea. Yet I still wondered how it was possible to know people sufficiently to write about them? Could I ever learn about life and people? To me, with my vast ignorance, my Jim Crow station in life, it seemed a task impossible of achievement. I now knew what being a Negro meant. I could endure the hunger I had learned to live with hate. But to feel that there were feelings denied me, that the very breath of life itself was beyond my reach, that more than anything else hurt, wounded me. I had a new hunger.

In buoying me up, reading also cast me down, made me see what was possible, what I had missed. My tension returned, new, terrible, bitter, surging, almost too great to be contained. I no longer *felt* that the world about me was hostile, killing; I *knew* it. A million times I asked myself what I could do to save myself, and there were no answers. I seemed forever condemned, ringed by walls.

I did not discuss my reading with Mr. Falk, who had lent me his library card; it would have meant talking about myself and that would have been too painful. I smiled each day, fighting desperately to maintain my old behavior, to keep my disposition seemingly sunny. But some of the white men discerned that I had begun to brood.

"Wake up there, boy!" Mr. Olin said one day.

"Sir!" I answered for the lack of a better word.

"You act like you've stolen something," he said.

I laughed in the way I knew he expected me to laugh, but I resolved to be more conscious of myself, to watch my every act, to guard and hide the new knowledge that was dawning within me.

If I went north, would it be possible for me to build a new life then? But how could a man build a life upon vague, unformed yearnings? I wanted to write and I did not even know the English language. I bought English grammars and found them dull. I felt that I was getting a better sense of the language from novels than from grammars. I read hard, discarding a writer as soon as I felt that I had grasped his point of view. At night the printed page stood before my eyes in sleep.

Mrs. Moss, my landlady, asked me one Sunday morning:

"Son, what is this you keep on reading?"

"Oh, nothing. Just novels."

"What you get out of 'em?"

"I'm just killing time," I said.

"I hope you know your own mind," she said in a tone which implied that she doubted if I had a mind.

I knew of no Negroes who read the books I liked and I wondered if any Negroes ever thought of them. I knew that there were Negro doctors, lawyers, newspapermen, but I never saw any of them. When I read a Negro newspaper I never caught the faintest echo of my pre-occupation in its pages. I felt trapped and occasionally, for a few days, I would stop reading. But a vague hunger would come over me for books, books that opened up new avenues of feeling and seeing, and again I would forge another note to the white librarian. Again I would read and wonder as only the naïve and unlettered can read and wonder, feeling that I carried a secret, criminal burden about with me each day.

That winter my mother and brother came and we set up housekeep-

ing, buying furniture on the installment plan, being cheated and yet knowing no way to avoid it. I began to eat warm food and to my surprise found
that regular meals enabled me to read faster. I may have lived through
many illnesses and survived them, never suspecting that I was ill. My
brother obtained a job and we began to save toward the trip north, plotting
our time, setting tentative dates for departure. I told none of the white
men on the job that I was planning to go north; I knew that the moment
they felt I was thinking of the North they would change toward me. It
would have made them feel that I did not like the life I was living, and
because my life was completely conditioned by what they said or did, it
would have been tantamount to challenging them.

I could calculate my chances for life in the South as a Negro fairly
clearly now.

I could fight the southern whites by organizing with other Negroes,
as my grandfather had done. But I knew that I could never win that way;
there were many whites and there were but few blacks. They were strong
and we were weak. Outright black rebellion could never win. If I fought
openly I would die and I did not want to die. News of lynchings were
frequent.

I could submit and live the life of a genial slave, but that was impossible. All of my life had shaped me to live by my own feelings, and
thoughts. I could make up to Bess and marry her and inherit the house.
But that, too, would be the life of a slave; if I did that, I would crush to death
something within me, and I would hate myself as much as I knew the whites
already hated those who had submitted. Neither could I ever willingly
present myself to be kicked, as Shorty had done. I would rather have died
than do that.

I could drain off my restlessness by fighting with Shorty and Harrison. I had seen many Negroes solve the problem of being black by transfer-
ring their hatred of themselves to others with a black skin and fighting
them. I would have to be cold to do that, and I was not cold and I could
never be.

I could, of course, forget what I had read, thrust the whites out of
my mind, forget them; and find release from anxiety and longing in sex and
alcohol. But the memory of how my father had conducted himself made
that course repugnant. If I did not want others to violate my life, how could
I voluntarily violate it myself?

I had no hope whatever of being a professional man. Not only had
I been so conditioned that I did not desire it, but the fulfillment of such an
ambition was beyond my capabilities. Well-to-do Negroes lived in a world
that was almost as alien to me as the world inhabited by whites.

What, then, was there? I held my life in my mind, in my consciousness each day, feeling at times that I would stumble and drop it, spill it forever. My reading had created a vast sense of distance between me and the
world in which I lived and tried to make a living, and that sense of distance
was increasing each day. My days and nights were one long, quiet, contin-

uously contained dream of terror, tension, and anxiety. I wondered how long I could bear it.

1937

Even more than John Steinbeck, Richard Wright has a writer whose political commitments show clearly in his stories. Whether such direct expressions of conviction are aesthetically damaging is one of the recurring questions in literature. In the interview excerpted below, Ralph Ellison, who knew Wright well, discusses this question of his art and ideology.

"I felt that Wright was overcommitted to ideology": Ralph Ellison

Stern: At that time were you dissatisfied with the sort of work Wright was doing?

Ellison: Dissatisfied? I was too amazed with watching the process of creation. I didn't understand quite what was going on, but by this time I had talked with Wright a lot and he was very conscious of technique. He talked about it not in terms of mystification but as writing know-how. "You must read so-and-so," he'd say. "You have to go about learning to write *consciously*. People have talked about such and such a problem and have written about it. You must learn how Conrad, Joyce, Dostoievsky get their effects . . ." He guided me to Henry James and to Conrad's prefaces, that type of thing. Of course, I knew that my own feelings about the world, about life, were different, but this was not even a matter to question. Wright knew what he was about, what he wanted to do, while I hadn't even discovered myself. I knew only that what I would want to express would not be an imitation of his kind of a thing.

Stern: So what sort of thing did you feel Wright was not doing that you wanted to do?

Ellison: Well, I don't suppose I judged. I am certain I did not judge in quite so conscious a way, but I think I felt more complexity in life, and my background made me aware of a larger area of possibility. Knowing Wright himself and something of what he was doing increased that sense of the possible. Also, I think I was less interested in an ideological interpretation of Negro experience. For all my interest in music, I had been in love with literature for years and years—if a writer may make such a confession. I read everything. I must have read fairy tales until I was thirteen, and I was always taken with the magical quality of writing, with the poetry of it. When I came to discover a little more about what I wanted to express I felt that Wright was overcommitted to ideology—even though I, too, wanted many of the same things for our people. You might say that I was much less a social determinist. But I suppose that basically it comes down to a difference in our concepts of the individual. I, for instance, found it disturbing that Bigger Thomas had none of the finer qualities of Richard Wright, none of the imagination, none of the sense of poetry, none of the gaiety. And I preferred Richard Wright to Bigger Thomas. Do you see? Which gets you in on the—directs you back to the difference between what Wright was himself and how he conceived of the individual; back to his conception of the quality of Negro humanity.

EUDORA WELTY

(b. 1909)

LIVVIE

Solomon carried Livvie twenty-one miles away from her home when he married her. He carried her away up on the Old Natchez Trace into the deep country to live in his house. She was sixteen—an only girl, then. Once people said he thought nobody would ever come along there. He told her himself that it had been a long time, and a day she did not know about, since that road was a traveled road with *people* coming and going. He was good to her, but he kept her in the house. She had not thought that she could not get back. Where she came from, people said an old man did not want anybody in the world to ever find his wife, for fear they would steal her back from him. Solomon asked her before he took her, "Would she be happy?"—very dignified, for he was a colored man that owned his land and had it written down in the courthouse; and she said, "Yes, sir," since he was an old man and she was young and just listened and answered. He asked her, if she was choosing winter, would she pine for spring, and she said, "No indeed." Whatever she said, always, was because he was an old man . . . while nine years went by. All the time, he got old, and he got so old he gave out. At last he slept the whole day in bed, and she was young still.

It was a nice house, inside and outside both. In the first place, it had three rooms. The front room was papered in holly paper, with green palmettos from the swamp spaced at careful intervals over the walls. There was fresh newspaper cut with fancy borders on the mantel-shelf, on which were propped photographs of old or very young men printed in faint yellow —Solomon's people. Solomon had a houseful of furniture. There was a double settee, a tall scrolled rocker and an organ in the front room, all around a three-legged table with a pink marble top, on which was set a lamp with three gold feet, besides a jelly glass with pretty hen feathers in it. Behind the front room, the other room had the bright iron bed with the polished knobs like a throne, in which Solomon slept all day. There were snow-white curtains of wiry lace at the window, and a lace bed-spread belonged on the bed. But what old Solomon slept so sound under was a big feather-stitched piece-quilt in the pattern "Trip Around the World," which had twenty-one different colors, four hundred and forty pieces, and a thousand yards of thread, and that was what Solomon's mother made in her life and old age. There was a table holding the Bible, and a trunk with a key. On the wall were two calendars, and a diploma from somewhere in Solomon's family, and under that Livvie's one possession was nailed, a picture of the little white baby of the family she worked for, back in Natchez before she was married. Going through that room and on to the kitchen, there was a big wood stove and a big round table always with a wet top and with the knives and forks in one jelly glass and the spoons in another, and a cut-glass vinegar bottle between, and going out from those, many shallow dishes of pickled peaches, fig preserves, watermelon pickles and blackberry jam always sitting there. The churn sat in the sun, the doors of the safe were always both shut, and there were four baited mouse-traps in the kitchen, one in every corner.

The outside of Solomon's house looked nice. It was not painted, but across the porch was an even balance. On each side there was one easy chair with high springs, looking out, and a fern basket hanging over it from the ceiling, and a dishpan of zinnia seedlings growing at its foot on the floor. By the door was a plow-wheel, just a pretty iron circle, nailed up on one wall and a square mirror on the other, a turquoise-blue comb stuck up in the frame, with the wash stand beneath it. On the door was a wooden knob with a pearl in the end, and Solomon's black hat hung on that, if he was in the house.

Out front was a clean dirt yard with every vestige of grass patiently uprooted and the ground scarred in deep whorls from the strike of Livvie's broom. Rose bushes with tiny blood-red roses blooming every month grew in threes on either side of the steps. On one side was a peach tree, on the other a pomegranate. Then coming around up the path from the deep cut of the Natchez Trace below was a line of bare crape-myrtle trees with every branch of them ending in a colored bottle, green or blue. There was no word that fell from Solomon's lips to say what they were for, but Livvie knew that there could be a spell put in trees, and she was familiar from the time she was born with the way bottle trees kept evil spirits from coming into the house—by luring them inside the colored bottles, where they cannot get out again. Solomon had made the bottle trees with his own hands over the nine years, in labor amounting to about a tree a year, and without a sign that he had any uneasiness in his heart, for he took as much pride in his precautions against spirits coming in the house as he took in the house, and sometimes in the sun the bottle trees looked prettier than the house did.

It was a nice house. It was in a place where the days would go by and surprise anyone that they were over. The lamplight and the firelight would shine out the door after dark, over the still and breathing country, lighting the roses and the bottle trees, and all was quiet there.

But there was nobody, nobody at all, not even a white person. And if there had been anybody, Solomon would not have let Livvie look at them, just as he would not let her look at a field hand, or a field hand look at her. There was no house near, except for the cabins of the tenants that were forbidden to her, and there was no house as far as she had been, stealing away down the still, deep Trace. She felt as if she waded a river when she went, for the dead leaves on the ground reached as high as her knees, and when she was all scratched and bleeding she said it was not like a road that went anywhere. One day, climbing up the high bank, she had found a graveyard without a church, with ribbon-grass growing about the foot of an angel (she had climbed up because she thought she saw angel wings), and in the sun, trees shining like burning flames through the great caterpillar nets which enclosed them. Scarey thistles stood looking like the prophets in the Bible in Solomon's house. Indian paint brushes grew over her head, and the mourning dove made the only sound in the world. Oh for a stirring of the leaves, and a breaking of the nets! But not by a ghost, prayed Livvie, jumping down the bank. After Solomon took to his bed, she never went out, except one more time.

Livvie knew she made a nice girl to wait on anybody. She fixed things to eat on a tray like a surprise. She could keep from singing when she ironed, and to sit by a bed and fan away the flies, she could be so still she could not hear herself breathe. She could clean up the house and never drop a thing, and wash the dishes without a sound, and she would step outside to churn, for churning sounded too sad to her, like sobbing, and if it made her home-sick and not Solomon, she did not think of that.

But Solomon scarcely opened his eyes to see her, and scarcely tasted his food. He was not sick or paralyzed or in any pain that he mentioned, but he was surely wearing out in the body, and no matter what nice hot thing Livvie would bring him to taste, he would only look at it now, as if he were past seeing how he could add anything more to himself. Before she could beg him, he would go fast asleep. She could not surprise him any more, if he would not taste, and she was afraid that he was never in the world going to taste another thing she brought him—and so how could he last?

But one morning it was breakfast time and she cooked his eggs and grits, carried them in on a tray, and called his name. He was sound asleep.

He lay in a dignified way with his watch beside him, on his back in the middle of the bed. One hand drew the quilt up high, though it was the first day of spring. Through the white lace curtains a little puffy wind was blowing as if it came from round cheeks. All night the frogs had sung out in the swamp, like a commotion in the room, and he had not stirred, though she lay wide awake and saying "Shh, frogs!" for fear he would mind them.

He looked as if he would like to sleep a little longer, and so she put back the tray and waited a little. When she tiptoed and stayed so quiet, she surrounded herself with a little reverie, and sometimes it seemed to her when she was so stealthy that the quiet she kept was for a sleeping baby, and that she had a baby and was its mother. When she stood at Solomon's bed and looked down at him, she would be thinking, "He sleeps so well," and she would hate to wake him up. And in some other way, too, she was afraid to wake him up because even in his sleep he seemed to be such a strict man.

Of course, nailed to the wall over the bed—only she would forget who it was—there was a picture of him when he was young. Then he had a fan of hair over his forehead like a king's crown. Now his hair lay down on his head, the spring had gone out of it. Solomon had a lightish face, with eyebrows scattered but rugged, the way privet grows, strong eyes, with second sight, a strict mouth, and a little gold smile. This was the way he looked in his clothes, but in bed in the daytime he looked like a different and smaller man, even when he was wide awake, and holding the Bible. He looked like somebody kin to himself. And then sometimes when he lay in sleep and she stood fanning the flies away, and the light came in, his face was like new, so smooth and clear that it was like a glass of jelly held to the window, and she could almost look through his forehead and see what he thought.

She fanned him and at length he opened his eyes and spoke her name, but he would not taste the nice eggs she had kept warm under a pan.

Back in the kitchen she ate heartily, his breakfast and hers, and looked out the open door at what went on. The whole day, and the whole night before, she had felt the stir of spring close to her. It was as present in the house as a young man would be. The moon was in the last quarter and outside they were turning the sod and planting peas and beans. Up and down the red fields, over which smoke from the brush-burning hung showing like a little skirt of sky, a white horse and a white mule pulled the plow. At intervals hoarse shouts came through the air and roused her as if she dozed neglectfully in the shade, and they were telling her, "Jump up!" She could see how over each ribbon of field were moving men and girls, on foot and mounted on mules, with hats set on their heads and bright with tall hoes and forks as if they carried streamers on them and were going to some place on a journey—and how as if at a signal now and then they would all start at once shouting, hollering, cajoling, calling and answering back, running, being leaped on and breaking away, flinging to earth with a shout and lying motionless in the trance of twelve o'clock. The old women came out of the cabins and brought them the food they had ready for them, and then all

worked together, spread evenly out. The little children came too, like a
bouncing stream overflowing the fields, and set upon the men, the women,
the dogs, the rushing birds, and the wave-like rows of earth, their little
voices almost too high to be heard. In the middle distance like some white
and gold towers were the haystacks, with black cows coming around to eat
their edges. High above everything, the wheel of fields, house, and cabins,
and the deep road surrounding like a moat to keep them in, was the turning
sky, blue with long, far-flung white mare's-tail clouds, serene and still as
high flames. And sound asleep while all this went around him that was his,
Solomon was like a little still spot in the middle.

Even in the house the earth was sweet to breathe. Solomon had
never let Livvie go any farther than the chicken house and the well. But
what if she would walk now into the heart of the fields and take a hoe and
work until she fell stretched out and drenched with her efforts, like other
girls, and laid her cheek against the laid-open earth, and shamed the old
man with her humbleness and delight? To shame him! A cruel wish could
come in uninvited and so fast while she looked out the back door. She
washed the dishes and scrubbed the table. She could hear the cries of the
little lambs. Her mother, that she had not seen since her wedding day, had
said one time, "I rather a man be anything, than a woman be mean."

So all morning she kept tasting the chicken broth on the stove, and
when it was right she poured off a nice cupful. She carried it in to Solomon,
and there he lay having a dream. Now what did he dream about? For she
saw him sigh gently as if not to disturb some whole thing he held round in
his mind, like a fresh egg. So even an old man dreamed about something
pretty. Did he dream of her, while his eyes were shut and sunken, and his
small hand with the wedding ring curled close in sleep around the quilt? He
might be dreaming of what time it was, for even through his sleep he kept
track of it like a clock, and knew how much of it went by, and waked up
knowing where the hands were even before he consulted the silver watch
that he never let go. He would sleep with the watch in his palm, and even
holding it to his cheek like a child that loves a plaything. Or he might dream
of journeys and travels on a steamboat to Natchez. Yet she thought he
dreamed of her; but even while she scrutinized him, the rods of the foot of
the bed seemed to rise up like a rail fence between them, and she could see
that people never could be sure of anything as long as one of them was
asleep and the other awake. To look at him dreaming of her when he might
be going to die frightened her a little, as if he might carry her with him that
way, and she wanted to run out of the room. She took hold of the bed and
held on, and Solomon opened his eyes and called her name, but he did not
want anything. He would not taste the good broth.

Just a little after that, as she was taking up the ashes in the front
room for the last time in the year, she heard a sound. It was somebody
coming. She pulled the curtains together and looked through the slit.

Coming up the path under the bottle trees was a white lady. At first she looked young, but then she looked old. Marvelous to see, a little car stood steaming like a kettle out in the field-track—it had come without a road.

Livvie stood listening to the long, repeated knockings at the door, and after a while she opened it just a little. The lady came in through the crack, though she was more than middle-sized and wore a big hat.

"My name is Miss Baby Marie," she said.

Livvie gazed respectfully at the lady and at the little suitcase she was holding close to her by the handle until the proper moment. The lady's eyes were running over the room, from palmetto to palmetto, but she was saying, "I live at home . . . out from Natchez . . . and get out and show these pretty cosmetic things to the white people and the colored people both . . . all around . . . years and years. . . . Both shades of powder and rouge. . . . It's the kind of work a girl can do and not go clear 'way from home . . ." And the harder she looked, the more she talked. Suddenly she turned up her nose and said, "It is not Christian or sanitary to put feathers in a vase," and then she took a gold key out of the front of her dress and began unlocking the locks on her suitcase. Her face drew the light, the way it was covered with intense white and red, with a little patty-cake of white between the wrinkles by her upper lip. Little red tassels of hair bobbed under the rusty wires of her picture-hat, as with an air of triumph and secrecy she now drew open her little suitcase and brought out bottle after bottle and jar after jar, which she put down on the table, the mantel-piece, the settee, and the organ.

"Did you ever see so many cosmetics in your life?" cried Miss Baby Marie.

"No'm," Livvie tried to say, but the cat had her tongue.

"Have you ever applied cosmetics?" asked Miss Baby Marie next.

"No'm," Livvie tried to say.

"Then look!" she said, and pulling out the last thing of all, "Try this!" she said. And in her hand was unclenched a golden lipstick which popped open like magic. A fragrance came out of it like incense, and Livvie cried out suddenly, "Chinaberry flowers!"

Her hand took the lipstick, and in an instant she was carried away in the air through the spring, and looking down with a half-drowsy smile from a purple cloud she saw from above a chinaberry tree, dark and smooth and neatly leaved, neat as a guinea hen in the dooryard, and there was her home that she had left. On one side of the tree was her mama holding up her heavy apron, and she could see it was loaded with ripe figs, and on the other side was her papa holding a fish-pole over the pond, and she could see it transparently, the little clear fishes swimming up to the brim.

"Oh, no, not chinaberry flowers—secret ingredients," said Miss Baby Marie. "My cosmetics have secret ingredients—not chinaberry flowers."

"It's purple," Livvie breathed, and Miss Baby Marie said, "Use it freely. Rub it on."

Livvie tiptoed out to the wash stand on the front porch and before the mirror put the paint on her mouth. In the wavery surface her face danced before her like a flame. Miss Baby Marie followed her out, took a look at what she had done, and said, "That's it."

Livvie tried to say "Thank you" without moving her parted lips where the paint lay so new.

By now Miss Baby Marie stood behind Livvie and looked in the mirror over her shoulder, twisting up the tassels of her hair. "The lipstick I can let you have for only two dollars," she said, close to her neck.

"Lady, but I don't have no money, never did have," said Livvie.

"Oh, but you don't pay the first time. I make another trip, that's the way I do. I come back again—later."

"Oh," said Livvie, pretending she understood everything so as to please the lady.

"But if you don't take it now, this may be the last time I'll call at your house," said Miss Baby Marie sharply. "It's far away from anywhere, I'll tell you that. You don't live close to anywhere."

"Yes'm. My husband, he keep the *money*," said Livvie, trembling. "He is strict as he can be. He don't know *you* walk in here—Miss Baby Marie!"

"Where is he?"

"Right now, he in yonder sound asleep, an old man. I wouldn't ever ask him for anything."

Miss Baby Marie took back the lipstick and packed it up. She gathered up the jars for both black and white and got them all inside the suitcase, with the same little fuss of triumph with which she had brought them out. She started away.

"Goodbye," she said, making herself look grand from the back, but at the last minute she turned around in the door. Her old hat wobbled as she whispered, "Let me see your husband."

Livvie obediently went on tiptoe and opened the door to the other room. Miss Baby Marie came behind her and rose on her toes and looked in.

"My, what a little tiny old, old man!" she whispered, clasping her hands and shaking her head over them. "What a beautiful quilt! What a tiny old, old man!"

"He can sleep like that all day," whispered Livvie proudly.

They looked at him awhile so fast asleep, and then all at once they looked at each other. Somehow that was as if they had a secret, for he had never stirred. Livvie then politely, but all at once, closed the door.

"Well! I'd certainly like to leave you with a lipstick!" said Miss Baby Marie vivaciously. She smiled in the door.

"Lady, but I told you I don't have no money, and never did have."

"And never will?" In the air and all around, like a bright halo around the white lady's nodding head, it was a true spring day.

"Would you take eggs, lady?" asked Livvie softly.

"No, I have plenty of eggs—plenty," said Miss Baby Marie.

"I still don't have no money," said Livvie, and Miss Baby Marie took her suitcase and went on somewhere else.

Livvie stood watching her go, and all the time she felt her heart beating in her left side. She touched the place with her hand. It seemed as if her heart beat and her whole face flamed from the pulsing color of her lips. She went to sit by Solomon and when he opened his eyes he could not see a change in her. "He's fixin' to die," she said inside. That was the secret. That was when she went out of the house for a little breath of air.

She went down the path and down the Natchez Trace a way, and she did not know how far she had gone, but it was not far, when she saw a sight. It was a man, looking like a vision—she standing on one side of the Old Natchez Trace and he standing on the other.

As soon as this man caught sight of her, he began to look himself over. Starting at the bottom with his pointed shoes, he began to look up, lifting his peg-top pants the higher to see fully his bright socks. His coat long and wide and leaf-green he opened like doors to see his high-up tawny pants and his pants he smoothed downward from the points of his collar, and he wore a luminous baby-pink satin shirt. At the end, he reached gently above his wide platter-shaped round hat, the color of a plum, and one finger touched at the feather, emerald green, blowing in the spring winds.

No matter how she looked, she could never look so fine as he did, and she was not sorry for that, she was pleased.

He took three jumps, one down and two up, and was by her side.

"My name is Cash," he said.

He had a guinea pig in his pocket. They began to walk along. She stared on and on at him, as if he were doing some daring spectacular thing, instead of just walking beside her. It was not simply the city way he was dressed that made her look at him and see hope in its insolence looking back. It was not only the way he moved along kicking the flowers as if he could break through everything in the way and destroy anything in the world, that made her eyes grow bright. It might be, if he had not appeared the way he did appear that day she would never have looked so closely at him, but the time people come makes a difference.

They walked through the still leaves of the Natchez Trace, the light and the shade falling through trees about them, the white irises shining like candles on the banks and the new ferns shining like green stars up in the oak branches. They came out at Solomon's house, bottle trees and all. Livvie stopped and hung her head.

Cash began whistling a little tune. She did not know what it was, but she had heard it before from a distance, and she had a revelation. Cash was a field hand. He was a transformed field hand. Cash belonged to Solomon. But he had stepped out of his overalls into this. There in front of Solomon's house he laughed. He had a round head, a round face, all of him was young, and he flung his head up, rolled it against the mare's-tail sky in his round hat, and he could laugh just to see Solomon's house sitting there.

Livvie looked at it, and there was Solomon's black hat hanging on the peg on the front door, the blackest thing in the world.

"I been to Natchez," Cash said, wagging his head around against the sky. "*I* taken a trip, *I* ready for Easter!"

How was it possible to look so fine before the harvest? Cash must have stolen the money, stolen it from Solomon. He stood in the path and lifted his spread hand high and brought it down again and again in his laughter. He kicked up his heels. A little chill went through her. It was as if Cash was bringing that strong hand down to beat a drum or to rain blows upon a man, such an abandon and menace were in his laugh. Frowning, she went closer to him and his swinging arm drew her in at once and the fright was crushed from her body, as a little match-flame might be smothered out by what it lighted. She gathered the folds of his coat behind him and fastened her red lips to his mouth, and she was dazzled by herself then, the way he had been dazzled at himself to begin with.

In that instant she felt something that could not be told—that Solomon's death was at hand, that he was the same to her as if he were dead now. She cried out, and uttering little cries turned and ran for the house.

At once Cash was coming, following after, he was running behind her. He came close, and halfway up the path he laughed and passed her. He even picked up a stone and sailed it into the bottle trees. She put her hands over her head, and sounds clattered through the bottle trees like cries of outrage. Cash stamped and plunged zigzag up the front steps and in at the door.

When she got there, he had stuck his hands in his pockets and was turning slowly about in the front room. The little guinea pig peeped out. Around Cash, the pinned-up palmettos looked as if a lazy green monkey had walked up and down and around the walls leaving green prints of his hands and feet.

She got through the room and his hands were still in his pockets, and she fell upon the closed door to the other room and pushed it open. She ran to Solomon's bed, calling "Solomon! Solomon!" The little shape of the old man never moved at all, wrapped under the quilt as if it were winter still.

"Solomon!" She pulled the quilt away, but there was another one under that, and she fell on her knees beside him. He made no sound except a sigh, and then she could hear in the silence the light springy steps of Cash walking and walking in the front room, and the ticking of Solomon's silver watch, which came from the bed. Old Solomon was far away in his sleep, his face looked small, relentless, and devout, as if he were walking somewhere where she could imagine the snow falling.

Then there was a noise like a hoof pawing the floor, and the door gave a creak, and Cash appeared beside her. When she looked up, Cash's face was so black it was bright, and so bright and bare of pity that it looked sweet to her. She stood up and held up her head. Cash was so powerful that his presence gave her strength even when she did not need any.

Under their eyes Solomon slept. People's faces tell of things and places not known to the one who looks at them while they sleep, and while Solomon slept under the eyes of Livvie and Cash his face told them like a mythical story that all his life he had built, little scrap by little scrap, respect. A beetle could not have been more laborious or more ingenious in the task of its destiny. When Solomon was young, as he was in his picture overhead, it was the infinite thing with him, and he could see no end to the respect he would contrive and keep in a house. He had built a lonely house, the way he would make a cage, but it grew to be the same with him as a great monumental pyramid and sometimes in his absorption of getting it erected he was like the builder-slaves of Egypt who forgot or never knew the origin and meaning of the thing to which they gave all the strength of their bodies and used up all their days. Livvie and Cash could see that as a man might rest from a life-labor he lay in his bed, and they could hear how, wrapped in his quilt, he sighed to himself comfortably in sleep, while in his dreams he might have been an ant, a beetle, a bird, an Egyptian, assembling and carrying on his back and building with his hands, or he might have been an old man of India or a swaddled baby, about to smile and brush all away.

Then without warning old Solomon's eyes flew wide open under the hedge-like brows. He was wide awake.

And instantly Cash raised his quick arm. A radiant sweat stood on his temples. But he did not bring his arm down—it stayed in the air, as if something might have taken hold.

It was not Livvie—she did not move. As if something said "Wait," she stood waiting. Even while her eyes burned under motionless lids, her lips parted in a stiff grimace, and with her arms stiff at her sides she stood above the prone old man and the panting young one, erect and apart.

Movement when it came came in Solomon's face. It was an old and strict face, a frail face, but behind it, like a covered light, came an animation that could play hide and seek, that would dart and escape, had always escaped. The mystery flickered in him, and invited from his eyes. It was that very mystery that Cash with his quick arm would have to strike, and that Livvie could not weep for. But Cash only stood holding his arm in the air, when the gentlest flick of his great strength, almost a puff of his breath, would have been enough, if he had known how to give it, to send the old man over the obstruction that kept him away from death.

If it could not be that the tiny illumination in the fragile and ancient face caused a crisis, a mystery in the room that would not permit a blow to fall, at least it was certain that Cash, throbbing in his Easter clothes, felt a pang of shame that the vigor of a man would come to such an end that he could not be struck without warning. He took down his hand and stepped back behind Livvie, like a round-eyed schoolboy on whose unsuspecting head the dunce cap has been set.

"Young ones can't wait," said Solomon.

Livvie shuddered violently, and then in a gush of tears she stooped for a glass of water and handed it to him, but he did not see her.

"So here come the young man Livvie wait for. Was no prevention. No prevention. Now I lay eyes on young man and it come to be somebody I know all the time, and been knowing since he were born in a cotton patch, and watched grow up year to year, Cash McCord, growed to size, growed up to come in my house in the end—ragged and barefoot."

Solomon gave a cough of distaste. Then he shut his eyes vigorously, and his lips began to move like a chanter's.

"When Livvie married, her husband were already somebody. He had paid great cost for his land. He spread sycamore leaves over the ground from wagon to door, day he brought her home, so her foot would not have to touch ground. He carried her through his door. Then he growed old and could not lift her, and she were still young."

Livvie's sobs followed his words like a soft melody repeating each thing as he stated it. His lips moved for a little without sound, or she cried too fervently, and unheard he might have been telling his whole life, and then he said, "God forgive Solomon for sins great and small. God forgive Solomon for carrying away too young girl for wife and keeping her away from her people and from all the young people would clamor for her back."

Then he lifted up his right hand toward Livvie where she stood by the bed and offered her his silver watch. He dangled it before her eyes, and she hushed crying; her tears stopped. For a moment the watch could be heard ticking as it always did, precisely in his proud hand. She lifted it away. Then he took hold of the quilt; then he was dead.

Livvie left Solomon dead and went out of the room. Stealthily, nearly without noise, Cash went beside her. He was like a shadow, but his shiny shoes moved over the floor in spangles, and the green downy feather shone like a light in his hat. As they reached the front room, he seized her deftly as a long black cat and dragged her hanging by the waist round and round him, while he turned in a circle, his face bent down to hers. The first moment, she kept one arm and its hand stiff and still, the one that held Solomon's watch. Then the fingers softly let go, all of her was limp, and the watch fell somewhere on the floor. It ticked away in the still room, and all at once there began outside the full song of a bird.

They moved around and around the room and into the brightness of the open door, then he stopped and shook her once. She rested in silence in his trembling arms, unprotesting as a bird on a nest. Outside the redbirds were flying and criss-crossing, the sun was in all the bottles on the prisoned trees, and the young peach was shining in the middle of them with the bursting light of spring.

1943

The atmosphere of a story by Eudora Welty is often more important than its plot or characters. Her own comments on writing fiction emphasize the need to achieve an effect that goes beyond the more mechanical aspects of storytelling.

"Experience is the worst kind of emptiness.": Eudora Welty

How can I express outside fiction what I think this reality of fiction is?

As a child I was led, an unwilling sightseer, into Mammoth Cave in Kentucky, and after our party had been halted in the blackest hole yet and our guide had let us wait guessing in cold dark what would happen to us, suddenly a light was struck. And we stood in a prism. The chamber was bathed in color, and there was nothing else, we and our guide alike were blotted out by radiance. As I remember, nobody said boo. Gradually we could make out that there was a river in the floor, black as night, which appeared to come out of a closet in the wall; and then, on it, a common rowboat, with ordinary countrified people like ourselves sitting in it, mute, wearing hats, came floating out and on by, and exited into the closet in the opposite wall. I suppose they were simply a party taking the more expensive tour. As we tourists mutually and silently stared, our guide treated us to a recitation on bats, how they lived in uncounted numbers down here and reached light by shooting up winding mile-high chimneys through rock, never touching by so much as the crook of a wing. He had memorized the speech, and we didn't see a bat. Then the light was put out—just as it is after you've had your two cents' worth in the Baptistry of Florence, where of course more happens: the thing I'm trying here to leave out. As again we stood damp and cold and not able to see our feet, while we each now had something of our own out of it, presumably, what I for one remember is how right I had been in telling my parents it would be a bore. For I was too ignorant to know there might be more, or even less, in there than I could see unaided. . . .

Without the act of human understanding—and it is a double act through which we make sense to each other—experience is the worst kind of emptiness; it is obliteration, black or prismatic, as meaningless as was indeed that loveless cave. Before there is meaning, there has to occur some personal act of vision. And it is this that is continuously projected as the novelist writes, and again as we, each to ourselves, read.

If this makes fiction sound full of mystery, I think it's fuller than I know how to say. Plot, characters, setting, and so forth, are not what I'm referring to now; we all deal with those as best we can. The mystery lies in the use of language to express human life.

In writing, do we try to solve this mystery? No, I think we take hold of the other end of the stick. In very practical ways, we rediscover the mystery. We even, I might say, take advantage of it.

MARGUERITE YOURCENAR

(b. 1913)

HOW WANG-FO WAS SAVED

translated from the French by Alberto Manguel and Marguerite Yourcenar

The old painter Wang-Fo and his disciple Ling were wandering along the roads of the Kingdom of Han.

They made slow progress because Wang-Fo would stop at night to watch the stars and during the day to observe the dragonflies. They carried hardly any luggage, because Wang-Fo loved the image of things and not the things themselves, and no object in the world seemed to him worth buying, except brushes, pots of lacquer and China ink, and rolls of silk and rice paper. They were poor, because Wang-Fo would exchange his paintings for a ration of boiled millet, and paid no attention to pieces of silver. Ling, his disciple, bent beneath the weight of a sack full of sketches, bowed his back with respect as if he were carrying the heavens' vault, because for Ling the sack was full of snow-covered mountains, torrents in spring, and the face of the summer moon.

Ling had not been born to trot down the roads, following an old man who seized the dawn and captured the dusk. His father had been a banker who dealt in gold, his mother the only child of a jade merchant who had left her all his worldly possessions, cursing her for not being a son. Ling had grown up in a house where wealth made him shy: he was afraid of insects, of thunder and the face of the dead. When Ling was fifteen, his father chose a bride for him, a very beautiful one because the thought of the happiness he was giving his son consoled him for having reached the age in which the night is meant for sleep. Ling's wife was as frail as a reed, childish as milk, sweet as saliva, salty as tears. After the wedding, Ling's parents became discreet to the point of dying, and their son was left alone in a house painted vermilion, in the company of his young wife who never stopped smiling and a plum tree that blossomed every spring with pale-pink flowers. Ling loved this woman of a crystal-clear heart as one loves a mirror that will never tarnish, or a talisman that will protect one forever. He visited the tea-houses to follow the dictates of fashion, and only moderately favored acrobats and dancers.

One night, in the tavern, Wang-Fo shared Ling's table. The old man had been drinking in order to better paint a drunkard, and he cocked his head to one side as if trying to measure the distance between his hand and his bowl. The rice wine undid the tongue of the taciturn craftsman, and that night Wang spoke as if silence were a wall and words the colors with which to cover it. Thanks to him, Ling got to know the beauty of the drunkards' faces blurred by the vapors of hot drink, the brown splendor of the roasts unevenly brushed by tongues of fire, and the exquisite blush of wine stains strewn on the tablecloths like withered petals. A gust of wind broke the window: the downpour entered the room. Wang-Fo leaned out to make Ling admire the livid zebra stripes of lightning, and Ling, spellbound, stopped being afraid of storms.

Ling paid the old painter's bill, and as Wang-Fo was both without money and without lodging, he humbly offered him a resting place. They walked away together; Ling held a lamp whose light projected unexpected fires in the puddles. That evening, Ling discovered with surprise that the walls of his house were not red, as he had always thought, but the color of an almost rotten orange. In the courtyard, Wang-Fo noticed the delicate shape of a bush to which no one had paid any attention until then, and compared it to a young woman letting down her hair to dry. In the passageway, he followed with delight the hesitant trail of an ant along the cracks in the wall, and Ling's horror of these creatures vanished into thin air. Realizing that Wang-Fo had just presented him with the gift of a new soul and a new vision of the world, Ling respectfully offered the old man the room in which his father and mother had died.

For many years now, Wang-Fo had dreamed of painting the portrait of a princess of olden days playing the lute under a willow. No woman was sufficiently unreal to be his model, but Ling would do because he was not a woman. Then Wang-Fo spoke of painting a young prince shooting an arrow at the foot of a large cedar tree. No young man of the present was sufficiently unreal to serve as his model, but Ling got his own wife to pose under the plum tree in the garden. Later on, Wang-Fo painted her in a fairy costume against the clouds of twilight, and the young woman wept because it was an omen of death. As Ling came to prefer the portraits painted by Wang-Fo to the young woman herself, her face began to fade, like a flower exposed to warm winds and summer rains. One morning, they found her hanging from the branches of the pink plum tree: the ends of the scarf that was strangling her floated in the wind, entangled with her hair. She looked even more delicate than usual, and as pure as the beauties celebrated by the poets of days gone by. Wang-Fo painted her one last time, because he loved the green hue that suffuses the face of the dead. His disciple Ling mixed the colors and the task needed such concentration that he forgot to shed tears.

One after the other, Ling sold his slaves, his jades, and the fish in his pond to buy his master pots of purple ink that came from the West. When the house was emptied, they left it, and Ling closed the door of his past behind him. Wang-Fo felt weary of a city where the faces could no longer teach him secrets of ugliness or beauty, and the master and his disciple walked away together down the roads of the Kingdom of Han.

Their reputation preceded them into the villages, to the gateway of fortresses, and into the atrium of temples where restless pilgrims halt at dusk. It was murmured that Wang-Fo had the power to bring his paintings to life by adding a last touch of color to their eyes. Farmers would come and beg him to paint a watchdog, and the lords would ask him for portraits of their best warriors. The priests honored Wang-Fo as a sage; the people feared him as a sorcerer. Wang enjoyed these differences of opinion which gave him the chance to study expressions of gratitude, fear, and veneration.

Ling begged for food, watched over his master's rest, and took advantage of the old man's raptures to massage his feet. With the first rays of the sun, when the old man was still asleep, Ling went in pursuit of timid landscapes hidden behind bunches of reeds. In the evening, when the master, disheartened, threw down his brushes, he would carefully pick them up. When Wang became sad and spoke of his old age, Ling would smile and show him the solid trunk of an old oak; when Wang felt happy and made jokes, Ling would humbly pretend to listen.

One day, at sunset, they reached the outskirts of the Imperial City and Ling sought out and found an inn in which Wang-Fo could spend the night. The old man wrapped himself up in rags, and Ling lay down next to him to keep him warm because spring had only just begun and the floor of beaten earth was still frozen. At dawn, heavy steps echoed in the corridors of the inn; they heard the frightened whispers of the innkeeper and orders shouted in a foreign, barbaric tongue. Ling trembled, remembering that the night before, he had stolen a rice cake for his master's supper. Certain that they would come to take him to prison, he asked himself who would help Wang-Fo ford the next river on the following day.

The soldiers entered carrying lanterns. The flames gleaming through the motley paper cast red and blue lights on their leather helmets. The string of a bow quivered over their shoulders, and the fiercest among them suddenly let out a roar for no reason at all. A heavy hand fell on Wang-Fo's neck, and the painter could not help noticing that the soldiers' sleeves did not match the color of their coats.

Helped by his disciple, Wang-Fo followed the soldiers, stumbling along uneven roads. The passing crowds made fun of these two criminals who were certainly going to be beheaded. The soldiers answered Wang's questions with savage scowls. His bound hands hurt him, and Ling in despair looked smiling at his master, which for him was a gentler way of crying.

They reached the threshold of the Imperial Palace, whose purple walls rose in broad daylight like a sweep of sunset. The soldiers led Wang-Fo through countless square and circular rooms whose shapes symbolized the seasons, the cardinal points, the male and the female, longevity, and the prerogatives of power. The doors swung on their hinges with a musical note, and were placed in such a manner that one followed the entire scale when crossing the palace from east to west. Everything combined to give an impression of superhuman power and subtlety, and one could feel that here the simplest orders were as final and as terrible as the wisdom of the ancients. At last, the air became thin and the silence so deep that not even a man under torture would have dared to scream. A eunuch lifted a tapestry; the soldiers began to tremble like women, and the small troop entered the chamber in which the Son of Heaven sat on a high throne.

It was a room without walls, held up by thick columns of blue stone. A garden spread out on the far side of the marble shafts, and each and every flower blooming in the greenery belonged to a rare species brought here from across the oceans. But none of them had any perfume, so that the Celestial Dragon's meditations would not be troubled by fine smells. Out of respect for the silence in which his thoughts evolved, no bird had been allowed within the enclosure, and even the bees had been driven away. An enormous wall separated the garden from the rest of the world, so that the wind that sweeps over dead dogs and corpses on the battlefield would not dare brush the Emperor's sleeve.

The Celestial Master sat on a throne of jade, and his hands were wrinkled like those of an old man, though he had scarcely reached the age of twenty. His robe was blue to symbolize winter, and green to remind one of spring. His face was beautiful but blank, like a looking glass placed too high, reflecting nothing except the stars and the immutable heavens. To his right stood his Minister of Perfect Pleasures, and to his left his Counselor of Just Torments. Because his courtiers, lined along the base of the columns, always lent a keen ear to the slightest sound from his lips, he had adopted the habit of speaking in a low voice.

"Celestial Dragon," said Wang-Fo, bowing low, "I am old, I am poor, I am weak. You are like summer; I am like winter. You have Ten Thousand Lives; I have but one, and it is near its close. What have I done to you? My hands have been tied, these hands that never harmed you."

"You ask what you have done to me, old Wang-Fo?" said the Emperor.

His voice was so melodious that it made one want to cry. He raised his right hand, to which the reflections from the jade pavement gave a pale sea-green hue like that of an underwater plant, and Wang-Fo marveled at the length of those thin fingers, and hunted among his memories to discover whether he had not at some time painted a mediocre portrait of either the Emperor or one of his ancestors that would now merit a sentence of death. But it seemed unlikely because Wang-Fo had not been an assiduous visitor at the Imperial Court. He preferred the farmers' huts or, in the cities, the courtesans' quarters and the taverns along the harbor where the dockers liked to quarrel.

"You ask me what it is you have done, old Wang-Fo?" repeated the

Emperor, inclining his slender neck toward the old man waiting attentively. "I will tell you. But, as another man's poison cannot enter our veins except through our nine openings, in order to show you your offenses I must take you with me down the corridors of my memory and tell you the story of my life. My father had assembled a collection of your work and hidden it in the most secret chamber in the palace, because he judged that the people in your paintings should be concealed from the world since they cannot lower their eyes in the presence of profane viewers. It was in those same rooms that I was brought up, old Wang-Fo, surrounded by solitude. To prevent my innocence from being sullied by other human souls, the restless crowd of my future subjects had been driven away from me, and no one was allowed to pass my threshold, for fear that his or her shadow would stretch out and touch me. The few aged servants that were placed in my service showed themselves as little as possible; the hours turned in circles; the colors of your paintings bloomed in the first hours of the morning and grew pale at dusk. At night, when I was unable to sleep, I gazed at them, and for nearly ten years I gazed at them every night. During the day, sitting on a carpet whose design I knew by heart, I dreamed of the joys the future had in store for me. I imagined the world, with the Kingdom of Han at the center, to be like the flat palm of my hand crossed by the fatal lines of the Five Rivers. Around it lay the sea in which monsters are born, and farther away the mountains that hold up the heavens. And to help me visualize these things I used your paintings. You made me believe that the sea looked like the vast sheet of water spread across your scrolls, so blue that if a stone were to fall into it, it would become a sapphire; that women opened and closed like flowers, like the creatures that come forward, pushed by the wind, along the paths of your painted gardens; and that the young, slim-waisted warriors who mount guard in the fortresses along the frontier were themselves like arrows that could pierce my heart. At sixteen I saw the doors that separated me from the world open once again; I climbed onto the balcony of my palace to look at the clouds, but they were far less beautiful than those in your sunsets. I ordered my litter; bounced along roads on which I had not foreseen either mud or stones, I traveled across the provinces of the Empire without ever finding your gardens full of women like fireflies, or a woman whose body was in itself a garden. The pebbles on the beach spoiled my taste for oceans; the blood of the tortured is less red than the pomegranates in your paintings; the village vermin prevented me from seeing the beauty of the rice fields; the flesh of mortal women disgusted me like the dead meat hanging from the butcher's hook, and the coarse laughter of my soldiers made me sick. You lied, Wang-Fo, you old impostor. The world is nothing but a mass of muddled colors thrown into the void by an insane painter, and smudged by our tears. The Kingdom of Han is not the most beautiful of kingdoms, and I am not the Emperor. The only empire which is worth reigning over is that which you alone can enter, old Wang, by the road of One Thousand Curves and Ten Thousand Colors. You alone reign peacefully over mountains covered in snow that cannot melt, and over fields of daffodils that cannot die. And that is why, Wang-Fo, I have conceived a punishment for you, for you whose enchantment has filled me with disgust at everything I own, and with desire for everything I shall never possess. And in order to lock you up in the only cell from which there is no escape, I have decided to have your eyes burned out, because your eyes, Wang-Fo, are the two magic gates that open onto your kingdom. And as your hands are the two roads of ten forking paths that lead to the heart of your kingdom, I have decided to have your hands cut off. Have you understood, old Wang-Fo?"

Hearing the sentence, Ling, the disciple, tore from his belt an old knife and leaped toward the Emperor. Two guards immediately seized him. The Son of Heaven smiled and added, with a sigh: "And I also hate you, old Wang-Fo, because you have known how to make yourself beloved. Kill that dog."

Ling jumped to one side so that his blood would not stain his master's robe. One of the soldiers lifted his sword and Ling's head fell from his neck like a cut flower. The servants carried away the remains, and Wang-Fo, in despair, admired the beautiful scarlet stain that his disciple's blood made on the green stone floor.

The Emperor made a sign and two eunuchs wiped Wang's eyes.

"Listen, old Wang-Fo," said the Emperor, "and dry your tears, because this is not the time to weep. Your eyes must be clear so that the little light that is left to them is not clouded by your weeping. Because it is not only the grudge I bear you that makes me desire your death; it is not only the cruelty in my heart that makes me want to see you suffer. I have other plans, old Wang-Fo. I possess among your works a remarkable painting in which the mountains, the river estuary, and the sea reflect each other, on a very small scale certainly, but with a clarity that surpasses the real landscapes themselves, like objects reflected on the walls of a metal sphere. But that painting is unfinished, Wang-Fo; your masterpiece is but a sketch. No doubt, when you began your work, sitting in a solitary valley, you noticed a passing bird, or a child running after the bird. And the bird's beak or the child's cheeks made you forget the blue eyelids of the sea. You never finished the frills of the water's cloak, or the seaweed hair of the rocks. Wang-Fo, I want you to use the few hours of light that are left to you to finish this painting, which will thus contain the final secrets amassed during your long life. I know that your hands, about to fall, will not tremble on the silken cloth, and infinity will enter your work through those unhappy cuts. I know that your eyes, about to be put out, will discover bearings far beyond all human senses. This is my plan, old Wang-Fo, and I can force you to fulfill it. If you refuse, before blinding you, I will have all your paintings burned, and you will be like a father whose children are slaughtered and all hopes of posterity extinguished. However, believe, if you wish, that this last order stems from nothing but my kindness, because I know that the silken scroll is the only mistress you ever deigned to touch. And to offer you brushes, paints, and inks to occupy your last hours is like offering the favors of a harlot to a man condemned to death."

Upon a sign from the Emperor's little finger, two eunuchs respectfully brought forward the unfinished scroll on which Wang-Fo had outlined the image of the sea and the sky. Wang-Fo dried his tears and smiled, because that small sketch reminded him of his youth. Everything in it spoke of a fresh new spirit which Wang-Fo could no longer claim as his, and yet something was missing from it, because when Wang had painted it he had not yet looked long enough at the mountains or at the rocks bathing their naked flanks in the sea, and he had not yet penetrated deep enough into the sadness of the evening twilight. Wang-Fo selected one of the brushes which a slave held ready for him and began spreading wide strokes of blue onto the unfinished sea. A eunuch crouched by his feet, mixing the colors; he carried out his task with little skill, and more than ever Wang-Fo lamented the loss of his disciple Ling.

Wang began by adding a touch of pink to the tip of the wing of a cloud perched on a mountain. Then he painted onto the surface of the sea a few small lines that deepened the perfect feeling of calm. The jade floor became increasingly damp, but Wang-Fo, absorbed as he was in his painting, did not seem to notice that he was working with his feet in water.

The fragile rowboat grew under the strokes of the painter's brush and now occupied the entire foreground of the silken scroll. The rhythmic sound of the oars rose suddenly in the distance, quick and eager like the beating of wings. The sound came nearer, gently filling the whole room, then ceased, and a few trembling drops appeared on the boatman's oars. The red iron intended for Wang's eyes lay extinguished on the executioner's coals. The courtiers, motionless as etiquette required, stood in water up to their shoulders, trying to lift themselves onto the tips of their toes. The water finally reached the level of the imperial heart. The silence was so deep one could have heard a tear drop.

It was Ling. He wore his everyday robe, and his right sleeve still had a hole that he had not had time to mend that morning before the soldiers' arrival. But around his neck was tied a strange red scarf.

Wang-Fo said to him softly, while he continued painting, "I thought you were dead."

"You being alive," said Ling respectfully, "how could I have died?"

And he helped his master into the boat. The jade ceiling reflected itself in the water, so that Ling seemed to be inside a cave. The pigtails of submerged courtiers rippled up toward the surface like snakes, and the pale head of the Emperor floated like a lotus.

"Look at them," said Wang-Fo sadly. "These wretches will die, if they are not dead already. I never thought there was enough water in the sea to drown an Emperor. What are we to do?"

"Master, have no fear," murmured the disciple. "They will soon be dry again and will not even remember that their sleeves were ever wet. Only the Emperor will keep in his heart a little of the bitterness of the sea. These people are not the kind to lose themselves inside a painting."

And he added: "The sea is calm, the wind high, the seabirds fly to their nests. Let us leave, Master, and sail to the land beyond the waves."

"Let us leave," said the old painter.

Wang-Fo took hold of the helm, and Ling bent over the oars. The sound of rowing filled the room again, strong and steady like the beating of a heart. The level of the water dropped unnoticed around the large vertical rocks that became columns once more. Soon only a few puddles glistened in the hollows of the jade floor. The courtiers' robes were dry, but a few wisps of foam still clung to the hem of the Emperor's cloak.

The painting finished by Wang-Fo was leaning against a tapestry. A rowboat occupied the entire foreground. It drifted away little by little, leaving behind it a thin wake that smoothed out into the quiet sea. One could no longer make out the faces of the two men sitting in the boat, but one could still see Ling's red scarf and Wang-Fo's beard waving in the breeze.

The beating of the oars grew fainter, then ceased, blotted out by the distance. The Emperor, leaning forward, a hand above his eyes, watched Wang's boat sail away till it was nothing but an imperceptible dot in the paleness of the twilight. A golden mist rose and spread over the water. Finally the boat veered around a rock that stood at the gateway to the ocean; the shadow of a cliff fell across it; its wake disappeared from the deserted surface, and the painter Wang-Fo and his disciple Ling vanished forever on the jade-blue sea that Wang-Fo had just created.

1938, trans. 1984

"How Wang-Fo Was Saved" is a Taoist fable from ancient China transcribed and, Marguerite Yourcenar says, "freely developed." It is one indication of the breadth and depth of Yourcenar's religious interests, which she discussed in a series of interviews with Matthieu Galey.

"True religion counts on fervor and love": Marguerite Yourcenar

Matthieu Galey: To take what you say literally would be to ask men to be saints.

Marguerite Yourcenar: I will answer you by citing one of the most beautiful sentences in all of French literature. Hold on to your hat; it's from Léon Bloy: "The only calamity is that we are not saints." The word "saint" frightens people, but they're wrong to be frightened. Let me, if I may, remind you of the story of the three schoolchildren in fourteenth-century Flanders who went to see Ruysbroeck the Admirable and said to him, "We would like to be saints, but we don't know how to go about it." Ruysbroeck, who was not especially eloquent, reflected a while and no doubt scratched his head before answering, "You are saints as much as you want to be." *(Vos estis tam sancti sicut vultis.)* It is in our power to be more saintly, which is to say, better than we now are, just as it is to some extent in our power to make ourselves more beautiful or intelligent.

G. Have you achieved this form of sainthood?

Y. I wish I had, because I believe that perfecting oneself is life's principal purpose. But my attention flags; willfulness or sloth gets the better of me; or I succumb to the stupidity that afflicts all of us at times. I am not at every moment what I ought to be. I do my best, when very often I might do better than my best.

G. What you're describing is an asceticism that is not without certain dangers. For it may confer power that is subject to possible abuse.

Y. Indeed it may, and that's why both Buddhist and Christian wisdom warn against this power, which is frequently an early, if secondary and quite negligible, product of ascetic practices. Therein lies the whole, vast difference between religion in the broadest possible sense of the word and magic. Magic wants to *coerce;* true religion counts on fervor and love. Ancient alchemists issued similar warnings against the abuse of power, though alchemy frequently verged on magic. You surely remember the three stages of the alchemical process: the black, which is renunciation and destruction; the white, which is utility and service; and the red, which is the appearance of supreme powers in the operator. "Beware of allowing the red to appear too quickly," the alchemists constantly reiterate.

RALPH ELLISON

(b. 1914)

DID YOU EVER DREAM LUCKY?

After the hurried good-bys the door had closed and they sat at the table with the tragic wreck of the Thanksgiving turkey before them, their heads turned regretfully toward the young folks' laughter in the hall. Then they could hear the elevator open and shut and the gay voices sinking swiftly beneath the floor and they were left facing one another in a room suddenly quiet with disappointment. Each of them, Mary, Mrs. Garfield, and Portwood, missed the young roomers, but in his disappointment Portwood had said something about young folks being green and now Mary was challenging him.

"Green," she said, "shucks, you don't know nothing about green!"

"Just wait a minute now," Portwood said, pushing back from the table, "Who don't? Who you talking about?"

"I'm talking about you," Mary said. "Them chillun is gone off to the dance, so *I must* be talking 'bout you. And like I *shoulda* said, you don't even know green when you see it."

"Let me get on out of here," Portwood said, getting up. "Mrs. Garfield, she's just tuning up to lie. I can't understand why we live here with an ole lying woman like her anyway. And contentious with it too. Talking 'bout *I* don't know nothing 'bout green. Why, I been meeting green folks right at the dam' station for over twenty-five years. . . ."

"Sit down, man. Just sit on back down," said Mary, placing her hand upon the heavy cut-glass decanter. "You got nowhere in this whole wide world to go—probably cause you make so much noise with your mouth . . ."

Mrs. Garfield smiled with gentle amusement. She'd been through it all before. A retired cook whose husband was dead, she had roomed with Mary almost as long as Portwood and knew that just as this was his way of provoking Mary into telling a story, it was Mary's way of introducing the story she would tell. She watched Mary cut her eyes from Portwood's frowning face to look through the window to where, far beyond the roofs of Harlem, mist-shrouded buildings pierced the sky. It was raining.

"It's gon' be cold out there on the streets this winter," Mary said. "I guess you know all about that."

"Don't be signifying at me," Portwood said. "You must aim to *lie* me into the streets. Well, I ain't even thinking about moving."

"You'll move," Mary said. "You'll be glad to move. And you still won't know nothing 'bout green."

"Then you tell us, Miss Mary," Mrs. Garfield said. "Don't pay Portwood any mind."

Portwood sat down, shaking his head hopelessly. "Now she's bound to lie. Mrs. Garfield, you done *guaranteed* she go' lie. And just look at her," he said, his voice rising indignantly, "sitting there looking like a lady preacher or something!"

"Portwood, I done tole you 'bout your way of talking," Mary began, but suddenly the stern façade of her face collapsed and they were all laughing.

"Hush, y'all," Mary said, her eyes gleaming. "Hush!"

"Don't try to laugh out of it," Portwood said, "I maintain these youngsters nowadays is green. They black and trying to git to heaven in a Cadillac. They think their education proves that we old southern folks is fools who don't know nothing 'bout life or loving or nothing 'bout living in the world. They green, I tell you! How we done come this far and lived this long if we didn't learn nothing 'bout life? Answer me that!"

"Now, Portwood," Mrs. Garfield said gently, "They're not that bad, the world just looks different to their eyes."

"Don't tell me, I see 'em when they get off the trains. Long as I been a Red Cap I've seen thousands of 'em, and dam' nigh everyone of 'em is green. And just cause these here is rooming with you, Moms, don't make 'em no different. Here you done fixed this fine Thanksgiving dinner and they caint hardly finish it for rushing off somewhere. Too green to be polite. Don't even know there ain't no other ole fool woman like you renting rooms in Harlem who'll treat 'em like kinfolks. Don't tell me 'bout . . ."

"Shh," Mrs. Garfield said, as the sound of voices leaving the elevator came to them, "they might be coming back."

They listened. The voices grew gaily up the hall, then blending with a remote peel of chimes, faded beyond a further wall. Mrs. Garfield sighed as they looked at one another guiltily.

"Shucks," Portwood said, "by now they just about beating the door down, trying to get into that dance. Like I was telling y'all . . ."

"Hush, Portwood!" Mary said. "What *green?*" She said singing full-throatedly now, her voice suddenly folk-toned and deep with echoes of sermons and blue trombones, "Lawd *I* was green. That's what I'm trying to tell you. Y'all hear me? *I, Me, Mary Raaaam-bo,* was green."

"You telling me?" Portwood laughed. "Is you telling *me?*" Nevertheless he leaned forward with Mrs. Garfield now, surrendering once more to Mary's once-upon-a-time antiphonal spell, waiting to respond to her stated theme: green.

"Here y'all," she said, beckoning for their glasses with one hand and lifting the decanter with the other. "Git some wine in y'all's stomachs so's it can warm y'alls' old-time blood."

They drank ceremoniously with lowered eyes, waiting for Mary's old contralto to resume its flight, its tragic-comic ascendence.

"Sho, I was green," she continued. "Green as anybody what ever left the farm and come to town. Shucks, here you criticizing those youngsters for rushing to the dance 'cause they hope to win that auto—that ain't nothing, not to what I done. Cause like them chillun and everybody else, I was after money. And I was full grown, too. Times was hard. My husband had done died and I couldn't get nothing but part-time work and didn't nobody have enough to eat. My daughter Lucy and me couldn't even afford a ten cents movies so we could go forget about it. So Lawd, this evening we're sitting in the window watching the doings down in the streets. Y'all know how it gits round here in the summertime, after it has been hot all day and has cooled off a bit: Folks out strolling or hanging on the stoops and hollering out the windows, chillun yelling and ripping and romping and begging for pennies to buy that there shaved ice with the red sirup poured over it. Dogs barking—y'all know how it is round here in the summertime. All that talk and noise and Negroes laughing loud and juke boxes blaring and like-a-that. Well, it's 'bout that time on one of them kinda days, and one of them store-front churches is just beginning to jump. You can hear them clapping their hands and shouting and the tambourines is a-shaking and a-beating, and that ole levee camp trombone they has is going *Wah-wah, Wah-wah, Wah-wah-wah!* Y'all know, just like it really has something to do with the good Lawd's business—when all of a sudden two autos decides to see which is the toughest."

"A wreck?" Portwood said. "What the newspapers call a *collision?*"

"That's it," Mary said, sipping her wine, "one of the biggest smashups you ever seen. Here we is up in the window on the fourth floor and it's happening right down below us. Why, it's like two big bulls has done charged and run head-on. I tell you, Mrs. Garfield, it was something! Here they is," she said, shifting two knives upon the cloth, "one's coming thisa way, and the other's coming thata way, and when they gits right here, WHAM! They done come together and something flies out of there like a cannon ball. Then for a second it gets real quiet. It's like everybody done stopped to take a breath at the same time—all except those clapping hands and tambourines and that ole nasty-mouthed trombone (that fool was sounding like he done took over and started preaching the gospel by now). Then, Lawd," she said, rocking forward for emphasis, "*glass is falling, dust is rising, women* is screaming—Oh, such a commotion. Then all of a sudden all you can hear is Negroes' feet slapping the sidewalks . . ."

"Never mind them feet," Portwood said, "what was it that flew out of there?"

"I'm fixing to tell you now, fool. When the cars come together me and Lucy sees that thing bust outa there like a comet and fly off to one side somewhere. Lucy said, 'Mama, did you see what I seen?' 'Come on, chile,' I says, 'Let's us get ourselfs on down there!' And good people, that's when we started to move! Lawd, we flew down them stairs. I didn't even take time to pull off my apron or my house shoes. Just come a-jumping. Oh, it was a sight, I tell you. Everybody and his brother standing round trying to see if anybody was killed and measuring the skid marks and waiting for the ambulance to come—the man coulda died before that ambulance got there——"

"Well, how about it, Moms, was anybody hurt?"

"Yes, they was, but I ain't your mama, an ole rusty Negro like you! Sho' they was hurt. One man was all cut up and bleeding and the other knocked cold as a big deep freeze. They thought he was dead.

"But me and Lucy don't waste no time with none of that. We gets busy looking for what we seen shoot out of them cars. I whispers, 'Chile, where did it hit?' And she points over near the curb. And sho 'nough, when I starts slow-dragging my leg along the gutter my foot hits against something heavy, and when I hears it clink together my heart almost flies out of my mouth . . ."

"My Lord, Miss Mary! What was it?" Mrs. Garfield said, her eyes intense. "You don't mean to tell me it was——"

Mary gave her a flat look. "I'm goin' to tell you," she said, taking a taste of wine. "I give y'all my word I'm gon' tell you—I calls to Lucy, 'Gal, come over here a minute,' justa looking 'round to see if anybody'd seen me. And she come and I whispers to her, 'Now don't let on we found anything, just get on the other side of me and make like you trying to kick me on the foot. Go on, gal,' I says, 'Don't argue with me—And watch out for my bunion!' And Lawd, she kicks that bag and this time I'm sho, 'cause I hear that sweet metal-like sound. 'What you think it is' I says and she leans close to me, eyes done got round as silver dollars, says, 'Mother' (always called me *mother* steada 'mama,' when she was excited or trying to be proper or something) says, 'Mother, that's money!' 'Shhh, fool,' I tole her, 'you don't have to tell *eve'ybody*.'

" 'But, Mother, what are we going to do?'

" 'Just stand still a secon', I says. 'Just quiet down. Don't move. Take it easy! Make out like you watching what they doing over yonder with those cars. Gimme time to figure this thing out . . .' "

She laughed. "Lawd, I was sweating by the gallon. Here I am standing in the street with my foot on a bag full of somebody's money! I don't know what to do. By now the police is all around us and I don't know when whichever one of them men who was hurt is gonna rise up and start yelling for it. I tell you, I musta lost five pounds in five minutes, trying to figure out the deal."

"Miss Mary, I wish I could have seen you," Mrs. Garfield said.

"Well, I'm glad you didn't; I was having trouble enough. Oh it was agonizing. Everytime somebody walks toward us I almost faint. And Lucy, she's turning this-away and that-away, real fast, like she's trying to invent a new dance. 'Do something, Mother,' she says. 'Please hurry up and do something!' Till finally I caint stand it and just flops down on the curbstone and kicks the bag kinda up under my skirts. Lawd, today!" she sang, then halted to inspect Portwood, who, with his head on his arms, laughed in silent glee. "What's the matter with you, fool?"

"Go on, tell the lie," Portwood said. "Don't mind poor me. You really had larceny in your heart that day."

"Well," Mary grinned, "'bout this time old Miz Brazelton, a meddlesome ole lady who lived across the hall from me, she comes up talking 'bout, 'Why, Miss Mary, don't you know a woman of your standing in the community oughtn't to be sitting on the curb like some ole common nobody?' Like all Mary Rambo's got to do is worry 'bout what somebody might think about her—I looks and I knows the only way to git rid of the fool is to bawl her out. 'Look here, Miz Brazelton,' I says, 'this here's my own ole rusty tub I'm sitting on and long as I can haul it 'round without your help I guess I can put it down wherever I please . . .' "

"You a rough woman, Moms," Portwood said with deep resonance, his face a judicial frown. "Rough!"

"I done tole you 'bout calling me Moms!" Mary warned.

"Just tell the lie," Portwood said. "Then what happen?"

"I know that type," Mrs. Garfield said. "With them you do sometimes have to be radical."

"You know it too?" Mary said. "Radical sho is the word. You shoulda seen her face. I really didn't want to hurt that ole woman's feelings, but right then I had to git shed of the fool.

"Well, she leaves and I'm still sitting there fighting with myself over what I oughta do. Should I report what we'd found, or just take it on upstairs? Not that I meant to be dishonest, you know, but like everybody else in New York if something-for-nothing comes along, I wanted to be the one to git it. Besides, anybody fool enough to have that much money riding around with him in a car *deserves* to lose it."

"He sho dam' do," Portwood said. "He *dam'* sho do!"

"Well, all at once Lucy shakes me and here comes the ambulance, justa screaming.

" 'Mother, we better go,' Lucy says. And me I don't know *what* to do. By now the cops is pushing folks around and I knows soon as they see me they bound to find out what kinda egg this is I'm nesting on. Then all of a sudden it comes over me that I'm still wearing my apron! Lawd, I reaches down and touches that bag and my heart starts to going ninety miles a minute. It feels like a heapa money! And when I touches that thick cloth bag you can hear it clinking together. 'Lucy, chile,' I whispers, 'stand right in front of me while the ole lady rolls this heavy stuff up in her apron . . .' "

"Oh, Miss Mary," Mrs. Garfield said, shaking her head, "You'd given in to the devil."

"I'm in his arms, girl, in his hairy arms! And Lucy in on the deal. She's hurrying me up and I picks up that bag and no sooner'n I do, here comes a cop!"

"Oh my Jesus, Miss Mary!" cried Mrs. Garfield.

"Woman," said Mary, "you don't know; you have no *idea*. He's one of these tough-looking young cops, too. One of them that thinks he has to beat you up just to prove he's in command of things. Here he comes, swinging up to Lucy like a red sledge hammer, telling folks to move along— Ain't seen *me*, cause I'm still sitting down. And when he comes up to Lucy I starts to moaning like I'm sick: 'Please, mister officer,' I says, kinda hiding my face, 'we just fixin' to leave.' Well, suh, his head shoots round Lucy like a turkey gobbler's and he sees me. Says, 'What's the matter, madam, wuz you in this wreck?'—and in a real nice voice too. Then Lucy—Lawd, that Lucy was smart; up to that time I didn't know my chile could lie. But Lucy looks the cop dead in the eye and says, 'Officer, we be going in a minute. My mother here is kinda nauchus from looking at all that blood.' "

"Oh, Miss Mary, she didn't say that!"

"She sho did, and it worked! Why the cop bends down and tries to help me to my feet and I says, 'Thank you, officer, just let me rest here a second and I be all right.' Well, suh, he leaves us and goes on off. But by now I got the bag in my apron and gets up moaning and groaning and starts out across the street, kinda bent over like, you know, with Lucy helping me along. Lawd, that bag feels like a thousand pounds. And everytime I takes a step it gets heavier. And on top of that, looks like we never going to cross the street, cause everybody in the block is stopping us to ask what's wrong: 'You sick Miss Mary?'; 'Lucy, what done happen to your mother?'; 'Do she want a doctor?'; 'Po' thing, she done got herself overexcited'—and all likea that. Shucks! I'm overexcited, all right, tha bag's 'bout to give me a nervous breakdown!

"When we finally make it up to the apartment, I'm so beat that I just flops into a chair and sits there panting. Don't even take the bag outa my apron, and Lucy, she's having a fit. 'Open it up, Mother, let's see what's in it,' she says. But I figures we better wait, cause after all, they might miss the money and come searching for it. You see, after I done worked so hard gitting it up there, I had decided to keep it sho 'nough . . ."

"You had given in to the devil," Mrs. Garfield said.

"Who?" said Mary, reaching for the wine, "I'm way, *way* past the giving-in stage."

"This world is surely a trial," Mrs. Garfield mused. "It truly is."

"And you can say that again," said Mary, "cause it's the agonizing truth."

"What did you do then, Miss Mary?"

"Pass me your glass, Portwood," Mary said, reaching for the decanter.

"Never mind the wine," said Portwood, covering his glass with his hand. "Get back to what *happened!*"

"Well, we goes to the bathroom—wait, don't say it!" she warned, giving Portwood a frown. "We goes to the bathroom and I gits up on a chair and drops that bag dead into the flush box."

"Now Miss Mary, really!"

"Girl, yes! I knowed wouldn't nobody think to look for it up there. It coulda been hid up in heaven somewhere. Sho! I dropped it in there, then I sent Lucy on back downstairs to see if anybody'd missed it. She musta hung 'round there for over an hour. Police and the newspaper people come and made pictures and asked a heapa questions and everything, but nothing 'bout the bag. Even after the wreckers come and dragged that pile of brand new junk away—still nothing 'bout the bag."

"Everything going in y'all's favor," Portwood said.

"Uhhuh, everything going our way."

"Y'all had it made, Moms," Portwood said, "Why you never tole this lie before?"

"The devil is truly powerful," Mrs. Garfield said, "Almost as powerful as the Lord. Even so, it's strange nobody missed *that* much money!"

"Now that's what me and Lucy thought . . ."

Portwood struck the table, "What I want to know is how much money was in the bag?"

"I'm coming to that in a second," Mary said.

"Yeah, but why you taking so long?"

"Who's telling this lie, Portwood, me or you?" said Mary.

"You was 'til you got off the track."

"Don't forget your manners, Portwood," Mrs. Garfield said.

"I'm not, but looks like to me y'all think money ought to be as hard to get in a lie somebody's telling as it is to get carrying folks' bags."

"Or as 'tis to git you to hush your mouth," said Mary. "Anyway, we didn't count it right then. We was scaird. I knowed I was doing wrong, holding on to something wasn't really mine. But that wasn't stopping me."

"Y'all was playing a little finders-keepers," Portwood said, resting back.

"Yeah, and concentrating on the keeping part."

"But why didn't you just *look* at the money, Miss Mary?"

"Cause we mighta been tempted to spend some of it, girl."

"Yeah, and y'all mighta give yourself away," Portwood said.

"Ain't it the truth! And that bag was powerful enough as it was. It was really working on us. Me and Lucy just sitting 'round like two ole hens on a nest, trying to guess how much is in it. Then we tries to figure whether it was dollars or fifty-centies. Finally we decides that it caint be less'n five or ten dollar gold pieces to weigh so much."

"But how on earth could you resist looking at it?" Mrs. Garfield said.

"Scaird, chile; scaird; We was like a couple kids who somebody's done give a present and tole 'em it would disappear if they opened it before Christmas. And know something else, neither one of us ever had to go to the bathroom so much as when us had that bag up there in that flush box. I got to flushing it just to hear it give out that fine clinking sound."

Portwood groaned, "I know you was gon' lie," he said. "I *knowed* it."

"Hush, man, hush!" Mary laughed. "I know our neighbors musta got sick and tired of hearing us flush that thing. But I tell you, everytime I pulled the chain it was like ringing up money in the cash register! I tell you, it was disintegrating! Whew! I'd go in there and stay a while and come out. Next thing I know there'd be Lucy going in. Then we got shamed and started slipping past one another. She'd try to keep hid from me, and me from her. I tell you, that stuff was working on us like a dose of salts! Why, after a few days I got so I couldn't work, just sat 'round thinking 'bout that doggone bag. And naturally, I done most of my thinking up there on the throne."

"Didn't I tell you she was tuning up to lie," Portwood laughed. "If she don't stop I'm dead gon' call the police."

"This here's the agonizing truth I'm telling y'all," said Mary.

"I wouldn't have been able to stand it, Miss Mary. I would have had to get it over with."

"They shoulda been looking for it by now," Portwood said, "all that money."

"That's what us thought," said Mary. "And we got to figuring why they didn't. First we figgers maybe it was because the man who was hurt so bad had died. But then we seen in the papers that he got well . . ."

"Maybe they was gangsters," Portwood said.

"Yeah, we thought of that too; gangsters or bootleggers."

"Yeah, yeah, either one of them coulda been carrying all that money—or gamblers even."

"Sho they could. Me and Lucy figgered that maybe they thought the cops had took the money or that they was trying to find it theyselves on the q.t., y'know."

"Miss Mary, you were either very brave or very reckless."

"Neither one, girl," Mary said, "just broke and hongry. And don't talk about brave, shucks, we was scaird to answer the doorbell at night. Let me tell you, we was doing some tall figuring. Finally I got so I couldn't eat and Lucy couldn't sleep. We was evil as a coupla lady bears at cubbing time."

"You just couldn't stand all that prosperity, huh, Moms?"

"It was a burden, all right. And everytime we pulled the chain it got a few dollars more so."

Mrs. Garfield smiled. "Mr. Garfield often said that the possession of great wealth brought with it the slings and arrows of outrageous responsibility."

"Mrs. Garfield," Mary mused, "you know you had you a right smart man in him? You really did. And looks like when you got stuff saved up like that you got the responsibility of keeping some of it circulating. Even without looking at it we got to figuring how to spend it. Lucy, she wants to go into business. Why she *almost* persuaded me to see about buying a building and opening a restaurant! And as if *that* wasn't enough trouble to git into, she decides she's goin' take the third floor and open her a beauty shop. Oh, we had it all planned!" She shook her head.

"And y'all still ain't looked at it," Portwood said.

"Still ain't seen a thing."

"Dam!"

"You had marvelous self-control," Mrs. Garfield said.

"Yeah, I did," Mary said, "until that day Lucy went to the dentist. Seems I just couldn't hold out no longer. Seems like I got to thinking 'bout that bag and couldn't stop. I looked at the newspaper and all those ads. Reminded me of things I wanted to buy; looked out the window and saw autos; I tried to read the Bible and as luck would have it I opened it to where it says something 'bout 'Store ye up riches in heaven,' or 'Cast your bread upon the waters.' It really had me on a merry-go-round. I just had to take a peep! So I went and pulled down all the shades and started the water running in the tub like I was taking me a bath—turned on every faucet in the house—then I climbed up there with a pair of scissors and reached in and raised that bag up and just looked at it awhile.

"It had done got *cooold!* It come up *cooold,* with the water dripping off it like some old bucket been deep down in a well. Done turned green with canker, y'all!! I just couldn't resist it no longer. I really couldn't, I took them scissors and snipped me a piece outa that bag and took me a good, *looong* look. And let me tell you, dear people, after I looked I was so excited I had to get down from there and put myself to bed. My nerves just couldn't take it . . ."

"It surely must have been an experience, Miss Mary."

"Woman, you don't know. You really don't know. You hear me? *I had to go to bed!"*

"Heck, with that much money you could afford to go to bed," said Portwood.

"Wait, le'me tell you. I'm laying up there moaning and groaning when here come Lucy and she's in one of her talking moods. Soon as I seen her I knowed pretty soon she was going to want to talk 'bout that bag and I truly dreaded telling her that I'd done looked into it without her. I says, 'Baby, I don't feel so good. You talk to me later' . . . But y'all think that stopped her? Shucks, all she does is to go get me a bottle of cold beer she done brought me and start to running her mouth again. And, just like I knowed she was gon' do, she finally got round to talking 'bout that bag. What ought we to buy *first,* she wants to know. Lawd, that pore chile, whenever she got her mind set on a thing! Well suh, I took me a big swoller of beer and just lay there like I was thinking awhile."

"You were really good companions," Mrs. Garfield said. "There is nothing like young people to make life rich and promising. Especially if they're your own children. If only Mr. Garfield and I . . ."

"Mrs. Garfield, let her finish this lie," Portwood said, "*then* we can talk about you and Mr. Garfield."

"Oh, of course," Mrs. Garfield said, "I'm sorry, Miss Mary, you know I didn't really mean to interrupt."

"Pay that pore fool no min'," Mary said. "I wish I had Lucy with me right this minit!"

"Is this lie about money or chillun," Portwood said. "Y'all here'bout to go serious. I want to know what you tole Lucy *then.* What did y'all start out to buy?"

"If you hadn't started monkeying with Mrs. Garfield you'da learned by now," Mary said. "Well, after I lay there and thought awhile I tole her, 'Well, baby, if you want to know the truth 'bout what I think, *I* think we oughta buy us an auto.'

"Well suh, you coulda knocked her over with a feather. 'A car!' she says, 'why Mother, I didn't know you was interested in a car. We don't want to be like these ole ignorant Negroes who buy cars and don't have anything to go with it and no place to keep it,' she says. Says, 'I'm certainly surprised at you, Mother. I never would've dreamed you wanted a *car,* not the very first thing.'

"Oh, she was running off a mile a minute. And looking at me like she done caught me kissing the preacher or the iceman or somebody! 'We want to be practical,' she says, 'We don't want to throw our money away . . .'

"Well, it almost killed me. 'Lucy, honey,' I says, 'that's just what your mama's trying to do, be practical. That's why I say let's git us an auto.'

" 'But, Mama,' she says, 'a car isn't practical at all.'

" 'Oh yes it is,' I says, 'Cause how else is we gon' use two sets of auto chains?'——

"And do y'all know," said Mary, sitting up suddenly and balancing the tips of her fingers on her knees, her face a mask of incredulity, "I had to hop outa bed and catch that chile before she swayed dead away in a faint!"

"Yeah," Portwood laughed, falling back in his chair, "and you better hop up from there and catch me."

Mrs. Garfield's voice rose up girlishly, "Oh Miss Mary," she laughed, "you're just fooling."

Mary's bosom heaved, "I wish I was, girl," she said, "I sho wish I was."

"How 'bout that? Tire chains," Portwood said. "All that larceny for some dam' tire chain!"

"Fool," said Mary, "didn't I tell you you didn't know nothing 'bout green? There *I* was thinking I done found me a bird nest on the ground. C'mon now," she said chuckling at the gullibility of all mankind, "let's us finish the wine."

Portwood winked at Mrs. Garfield. "Hey, Moms, tell us something . . ."

"I ain't go' tell you again that I ain't yo' mama," said Mary.

"I just want you to tell us one last thing . . ."

Mary looked at him warily, "What is it? I got no more time for your foolishness now, I got to git up from here and fix for them chillun."

"Never mind them youngsters," said Portwood, "just tell us if you ever dreamed lucky?"

Mary grinned, "Ain't I just done tole you?" she said. "Sho I did, but I woke up cold in hand. Just the same though," she added thoughtfully, "I still hope them youngsters win that there auto."

"Yes," Mrs. Garfield said, "And wouldn't it be a comfort, Miss Mary? Just to know that they *can* win one, I mean . . . ?"

Mary said that it certainly would be.

1954

"Did You Ever Dream Lucky?" belongs to a tradition of humorous storytelling that is characteristically American. Margaret Atwood, a Canadian, has defined that tradition more clearly than many American humorists could.

"American humor is a different kettle of fish": Margaret Atwood

American humour is a different kettle of fish. Classically, it has been Tall Tale or Wooden Nutmeg humour. The three roles available are the con-man or sharpie, sucker or dupe, and audience, and the idea is for the sharpie to put one over on the dupe, with the audience admiring the con-man's superior cunning and laughing at the dupe's gullibility. In Tall Tale, the audience itself plays dupe until the tallness of the tale is finally revealed. A simple con-man story is Mark Twain's famous Jumping Frog tale; a more complicated rendition is the episode in Owen Wister's *Virginian,* where the cowboy hero wins his duel, not with pistols but by telling an absurd story and sucking the villain into believing it. The "audience" is both the reading audience and an audience of "cultivated" easterners who have gathered to listen. Both audiences are flattered by being able to perceive themselves as more astute than the dupe. Then there's the King and the Duke and their Royal Nonesuch in *Huckleberry Finn,* with the audience in the book playing dupe and the reading audience laughing; and the Connecticut Yankee, putting things over on the "gentlemen" of King Arthur's Court. "Gentlemen" get short shrift in American humour; in fact they are distrusted as generally as they are in the rest of American literature, and are likely to be exposed as fakes, pretenders, snobs or ninnies. Real admiration is reserved for the con-men, who are just as likely to have a "regional" accent and play their tricks on city slickers as they are to be travelling salesmen pulling a fast one on the farmer's daughter (a wonderful variation occurs in Flannery O'Connor's story of the Bible salesman who steals the crippled woman's wooden leg). Faulkner's Compsons are Southern Gentlemen and have a kind of crumbling nobility, but it's the lowbrow Snopeses who make the sharp horse trades and end up with the money.

One of the charms of James Thurber is that he reverses the roles: in "Sitting in the Catbird Seat," the potential dupe turns the tables on the con-lady, and time and again the ineffectual Walter Mittys end up, if not top dog, at least unduped.

In American humour the desired pattern is not one of right, correct, "gentlemanly" behaviour; instead it is a pattern suited to a highly competitive, individualistic society: you have to be smart enough to take care of yourself and not let the other guy outsmart you. Better still, you should have the wit to do it to him.

DORIS LESSING

(b. 1919)

TO ROOM NINETEEN

This is a story, I suppose, about a failure in intelligence: the Rawlings' marriage was grounded in intelligence.

They were older when they married than most of their married friends: in their well-seasoned late twenties. Both had had a number of affairs, sweet rather than bitter; and when they fell in love—for they did fall in love—had known each other for some time. They joked that they had saved each other "for the real thing." That they had waited so long (but not too long) for this real thing was to them a proof of their sensible discrimination. A good many of their friends had married young, and now (they felt) probably regretted lost opportunities; while others, still unmarried, seemed to them arid, self-doubting, and likely to make desperate or romantic marriages.

Not only they, but others, felt they were well-matched: their friends' delight was an additional proof of their happiness. They had played the same roles, male and female, in this group or set, if such a wide, loosely connected, constantly changing constellation of people could be called a set. They had both become, by virtue of their moderation, their humour, and their abstinence from painful experience, people to whom others came for advice. They could be, and were, relied on. It was one of those cases of a man and a woman linking themselves whom no one else had ever thought of linking, probably because of their similarities. But then everyone exclaimed: Of course! How right! How was it we never thought of it before!

And so they married amid general rejoicing, and because of their foresight and their sense for what was probable, nothing was a surprise to them.

Both had well-paid jobs. Matthew was a subeditor on a large London newspaper, and Susan worked in an advertising firm. He was not the stuff of which editors or publicised journalists are made, but he was much more than "a subeditor," being one of the essential background people who in fact steady, inspire and make possible the people in the limelight. He was content with this position. Susan had a talent for commercial drawing. She was humorous about the advertisements she was responsible for, but she did not feel strongly about them one way or the other.

Both, before they married, had had pleasant flats, but they felt it unwise to base a marriage on either flat, because it might seem like a submission of personality on the part of the one whose flat it was not. They moved into a new flat in South Kensington on the clear understanding that when their marriage had settled down (a process they knew would not take long, and was in fact more a humorous concession to popular wisdom than what was due to themselves) they would buy a house and start a family.

And this is what happened. They lived in their charming flat for two years, giving parties and going to them, being a popular young married couple, and then Susan became pregnant, she gave up her job, and they bought a house in Richmond. It was typical of this couple that they had a son first, then a daughter, then twins, son and daughter. Everything right, appropriate, and what everyone would wish for, if they could choose. But people did feel these two had chosen; this balanced and sensible family was no more than what was due to them because of their infallible sense for *choosing* right.

And so they lived with their four children in their gardened house in Richmond and were happy. They had everything they had wanted and had planned for.

And yet . . .

Well, even this was expected, that there must be a certain flatness. . . .

Yes, yes, of course, it was natural they sometimes felt like this. Like what?

Their life seemed to be like a snake biting its tail. Matthew's job for the sake of Susan, children, house, and garden—which caravanserai needed a well-paid job to maintain it. And Susan's practical intelligence for the sake of Matthew, the children, the house and the garden—which unit would have collapsed in a week without her.

But there was no point about which either could say: "For the sake of *this* is all the rest." Children? But children can't be a centre of life and a reason for being. They can be a thousand things that are delightful, interesting, satisfying, but they can't be a wellspring to live from. Or they shouldn't be. Susan and Matthew knew that well enough.

Matthew's job? Ridiculous. It was an interesting job, but scarcely a reason for living. Matthew took pride in doing it well, but he could hardly be expected to be proud of the newspaper; the newspaper he read, *his* newspaper, was not the one he worked for.

Their love for each other? Well, that was nearest it. If this wasn't a centre, what was? Yes, it was around this point, their love, that the whole extraordinary structure revolved. For extraordinary it certainly was. Both Susan and Matthew had moments of thinking so, of looking in secret disbelief at this thing they had created: marriage, four children, big house, garden, charwomen, friends, cars . . . and this *thing*, this entity, all of it had come into existence, been blown into being out of nowhere, because Susan loved Matthew and Matthew loved Susan. Extraordinary. So that was the central point, the wellspring.

And if one felt that it simply was not strong enough, important enough, to support it all, well whose fault was that? Certainly neither Susan's nor Matthew's. It was in the nature of things. And they sensibly blamed neither themselves nor each other.

On the contrary, they used their intelligence to preserve what they had created from a painful and explosive world: they looked around them, and took lessons. All around them, marriages collapsing, or breaking, or rubbing along (even worse, they felt). They must not make the same mistakes, they must not.

They had avoided the pitfall so many of their friends had fallen into —of buying a house in the country *for the sake of the children,* so that the husband became a weekend husband, a weekend father, and the wife always careful not to ask what went on in the town flat which they called (in joke) a bachelor flat. No, Matthew was a full-time husband, a full-time father, and at night, in the big married bed in the big married bedroom (which had an attractive view of the river), they lay beside each other talking and he told her about his day, and what he had done, and whom he had met; and she told him about her day (not as interesting, but that was not her fault), for both knew of the hidden resentments and deprivations of the woman who has lived her own life—and above all, has earned her own living—and is now dependent on a husband for outside interests and money.

Nor did Susan make the mistake of taking a job for the sake of her independence, which she might very well have done, since her old firm, missing her qualities of humour, balance, and sense, invited her often to go back. Children needed their mother to a certain age, that both parents knew and agreed on; and when these four healthy wisely brought up children were of the right age, Susan would work again, because she knew, and so did he, what happened to women of fifty at the height of their energy and ability, with grownup children who no longer needed their full devotion.

So here was this couple, testing their marriage, looking after it, treating it like a small boat full of helpless people in a very stormy sea. Well, of course, so it was. . . . The storms of the world were bad, but not too close—which is not to say they were selfishly felt: Susan and Matthew were both well-informed and responsible people. And the inner storms and quicksands were understood and charted. So everything was all right. Everything was in order. Yes, things were under control.

So what did it matter if they felt dry, flat? People like themselves, fed on a hundred books (psychological, anthropological, sociological), could scarcely be unprepared for the dry, controlled wistfulness which is the distinguishing mark of the intelligent marriage. Two people, endowed with education, with discrimination, with judgement, linked together voluntarily from their will to be happy together and to be of use to others— one sees them everywhere, one knows them, one even is that thing oneself:

sadness because so much is after all so little. These two, unsurprised, turned towards each other with even more courtesy and gentle love: this was life, that two people, no matter how carefully chosen, could not be everything to each other. In fact, even to say so, to think in such a way, was banal; they were ashamed to do it.

It was banal, too, when one night Matthew came home late and confessed he had been to a party, taken a girl home and slept with her. Susan forgave him, of course. Except that forgiveness is hardly the word. Understanding, yes. But if you understand something, you don't forgive it, you are the thing itself: forgiveness is for what you *don't* understand. Nor had he *confessed*—what sort of word is that?

The whole thing was not important. After all, years ago they had joked: Of course I'm not going to be faithful to you, no one can be faithful to one other person for a whole lifetime. (And there was the word "faithful"—stupid, all these words, stupid, belonging to a savage old world.) But the incident left both of them irritable. Strange, but they were both bad-tempered, annoyed. There was something unassimilable about it.

Making love splendidly after he had come home that night, both had felt that the idea that Myra Jenkins, a pretty girl met at a party, could be even relevant was ridiculous. They had loved each other for over a decade, would love each other for years more. Who, then, was Myra Jenkins?

Except, thought Susan, unaccountably bad-tempered, she was (is?) the first. In ten years. So either the ten years' fidelity was not important, or she isn't. (No, no, there is something wrong with this way of thinking, there must be.) But if she isn't important, presumably it wasn't important either when Matthew and I first went to bed with each other that afternoon whose delight even now (like a very long shadow at sundown) lays a long, wandlike finger over us. (Why did I say sundown?) Well, if what we felt that afternoon was not important, nothing is important, because if it hadn't been for what we felt, we wouldn't be Mr. and Mrs. Rawlings with four children, et cetera, et cetera. The whole thing is *absurd*—for him to have come home and told me was absurd. For him not to have told me was absurd. For me to care or, for that matter, not to care, is absurd . . . and who is Myra Jenkins? Why, no one at all.

There was only one thing to do, and of course these sensible people did it; they put the thing behind them, and consciously, knowing what they were doing, moved forward into a different phase of their marriage, giving thanks for past good fortune as they did so.

For it was inevitable that the handsome, blond, attractive, manly man, Matthew Rawlings, should be at times tempted (oh, what a word!) by the attractive girls at parties she could not attend because of the four children; and that sometimes he would succumb (a word even more repulsive, if possible) and that she, a goodlooking woman in the big well-tended garden at Richmond, would sometimes be pierced as by an arrow from the sky with bitterness. Except that bitterness was not in order, it was out of court. Did the casual girls touch the marriage? They did not. Rather it was they who knew defeat because of the handsome Matthew Rawlings' marriage body and soul to Susan Rawlings.

In that case why did Susan feel (though luckily not for longer than a few seconds at a time) as if life had become a desert, and that nothing mattered, and that her children were not her own?

Meanwhile her intelligence continued to assert that all was well. What if her Matthew did have an occasional sweet afternoon, the odd affair? For she knew quite well, except in her moments of aridity, that they were very happy, that the affairs were not important.

Perhaps that was the trouble? It was in the nature of things that the adventures and delights could no longer be hers, because of the four children and the big house that needed so much attention. But perhaps she was secretly wishing, and even knowing that she did, that the wildness and the beauty could be his. But he was married to her. She was married to him. They were married inextricably. And therefore the gods could not strike him with the real magic, not really. Well, was it Susan's fault that after he came home from an adventure he looked harassed rather than fulfilled? (In fact, that was how she knew he had been *unfaithful,* because of his sullen air, and his glances at her, similar to hers at him: What is it that I share with this person that shields all delight from me?) But none of it by anybody's fault. (But what did they feel ought to be somebody's fault?) Nobody's fault, nothing to be at fault, no one to blame, no one to offer or to take it . . . and nothing wrong, either, except that Matthew never was really struck, as he wanted to be, by joy; and that Susan was more and more often threatened by emptiness. (It was usually in the garden that she was invaded by this feeling: she was coming to avoid the garden, unless the children or Matthew were with her.) There was no need to use the dramatic words "unfaithful," "forgive," and the rest: intelligence forbade them. Intelligence barred, too, quarrelling, sulking, anger, silences of withdrawal, accusations and tears. Above all, intelligence forbids tears.

A high price has to be paid for the happy marriage with the four healthy children in the large white gardened house.

And they were paying it, willingly, knowing what they were doing. When they lay side by side or breast to breast in the big civilised bedroom overlooking the wild sullied river, they laughed, often, for no particular reason; but they knew it was really because of these two small people, Susan and Matthew, supporting such an edifice of their intelligent love. The laugh comforted them; it saved them both, though from what, they did not know.

They were now both fortyish. The older children, boy and girl, were ten and eight, at school. The twins, six, were still at home. Susan did not have nurses or girls to help her: childhood is short; and she did not regret the hard work. Often enough she was bored, since small children can be boring; she was often very tired; but she regretted nothing. In another decade, she would turn herself back into being a woman with a life of her own.

Soon the twins would go to school, and they would be away from home from nine until four. These hours, so Susan saw it, would be the preparation for her own slow emancipation away from the role of hub-of-the-family into woman-with-her-own-life. She was already planning for the hours of freedom when all the children would be "off her hands." That was the phrase used by Matthew and by Susan and by their friends, for the moment when the youngest child went off to school. "They'll be off your hands, darling Susan, and you'll have time to yourself." So said Matthew, the intelligent husband, who had often enough commended and consoled Susan, standing by her in spirit during the years when her soul was not her own, as she said, but her children's.

What it amounted to was that Susan saw herself as she had been at twenty-eight, unmarried; and then again somewhere about fifty, blossoming from the root of what she had been twenty years before. As if the essential Susan were in abeyance, as if she were in cold storage. Matthew said something like this to Susan one night: and she agreed that it was true—she did feel something like that. What, then, was this essential Susan? She did not know. Put like that it sounded ridiculous, and she did not really feel it. Anyway, they had a long discussion about the whole thing before going off to sleep in each other's arms.

So the twins went off to their school, two bright affectionate children who had no problems about it, since their older brother and sister had trodden this path so successfully before them. And now Susan was going to be alone in the big house, every day of the school term, except for the daily woman who came in to clean.

It was now, for the first time in this marriage, that something happened which neither of them had foreseen.

This is what happened. She returned, at nine-thirty, from taking the twins to the school by car, looking forward to seven blissful hours of freedom. On the first morning she was simply restless, worrying about the twins "naturally enough" since this was their first day away at school. She was hardly able to contain herself until they came back. Which they did happily, excited by the world of school, looking forward to the next day. And the next day Susan took them, dropped them, came back, and found herself reluctant to enter her big and beautiful home because it was as if something was waiting for her there that she did not wish to confront. Sensibly, however, she parked the car in the garage, entered the house, spoke to Mrs. Parkes, the daily woman, about her duties, and went up to her bedroom. She was possessed by a fever which drove her out again, downstairs, into the kitchen, where Mrs. Parkes was making cake and did not need her, and into the garden. There she sat on a bench and tried to calm herself looking at trees, at a brown glimpse of the river. But she was filled with tension, like a panic: as if an enemy was in the garden with her. She spoke to herself severely, thus: All this is quite natural. First, I spent twelve years of my adult life working, *living my own life*. Then I married, and from the moment I became pregnant for the first time I signed myself over, so to

speak, to other people. To the children. Not for one moment in twelve years have I been alone, had time to myself. So now I have to learn to be myself again. That's all.

And she went indoors to help Mrs. Parkes cook and clean, and found some sewing to do for the children. She kept herself occupied every day. At the end of the first term she understood she felt two contrary emotions. First: secret astonishment and dismay that during those weeks when the house was empty of children she had in fact been more occupied (had been careful to keep herself occupied) than ever she had been when the children were around her needing her continual attention. Second: that now she knew the house would be full of them, and for five weeks, she resented the fact she would never be alone. She was already looking back at those hours of sewing, cooking (but by herself) as at a lost freedom which would not be hers for five long weeks. And the two months of term which would succeed the five weeks stretched alluringly open to her—freedom. But what freedom—when in fact she had been so careful *not* to be free of small duties during the last weeks? She looked at herself, Susan Rawlings, sitting in a big chair by the window in the bedroom, sewing shirts or dresses, which she might just as well have bought. She saw herself making cakes for hours at a time in the big family kitchen: yet usually she bought cakes. What she saw was a woman alone, that was true, but she had not felt alone. For instance, Mrs. Parkes was always somewhere in the house. And she did not like being in the garden at all, because of the closeness there of the enemy —irritation, restlessness, emptiness, whatever it was—which keeping her hands occupied made less dangerous for some reason.

Susan did not tell Matthew of these thoughts. They were not sensible. She did not recognise herself in them. What should she say to her dear friend and husband, Matthew? "When I go into the garden, that is, if the children are not there, I feel as if there is an enemy there waiting to invade me." "What enemy, Susan darling?" "Well I don't know, really. . . ." "Perhaps you should see a doctor?"

No, clearly this conversation should not take place. The holidays began and Susan welcomed them. Four children, lively, energetic, intelligent, demanding: she was never, not for a moment of her day, alone. If she was in a room, they would be in the next room, or waiting for her to do something for them; or it would soon be time for lunch or tea, or to take one of them to the dentist. Something to do: five weeks of it, thank goodness.

On the fourth day of these so welcome holidays, she found she was storming with anger at the twins; two shrinking beautiful children who (and this is what checked her) stood hand in hand looking at her with sheer dismayed disbelief. This was their calm mother, shouting at them. And for what? They had come to her with some game, some bit of nonsense. They looked at each other, moved closer for support, and went off hand in hand, leaving Susan holding on to the windowsill of the livingroom, breathing deep, feeling sick. She went to lie down, telling the older children she had a headache. She heard the boy Harry telling the little ones: "It's all right, Mother's got a headache." She heard that *It's all right* with pain.

That night she said to her husband: "Today I shouted at the twins, quite unfairly." She sounded miserable, and he said gently: "Well, what of it?"

"It's more of an adjustment than I thought, their going to school."

"But Susie, Susie darling. . . ." For she was crouched weeping on the bed. He comforted her: "Susan, what is all this about? You shouted at them? What of it? If you shouted at them fifty times a day it wouldn't be more than the little devils deserve." But she wouldn't laugh. She wept. Soon he comforted her with his body. She became calm. Calm, she wondered what was wrong with her, and why she should mind so much that she might, just once, have behaved unjustly with the children. What did it matter? They had forgotten it all long ago: Mother had a headache and everything was all right.

It was a long time later that Susan understood that that night, when she had wept and Matthew had driven the misery out of her with his big solid body, was the last time, ever in their married life, that they had been— to use their mutual language—with each other. And even that was a lie, because she had not told him of her real fears at all.

The five weeks passed, and Susan was in control of herself, and good and kind, and she looked forward to the holidays with a mixture of fear and longing. She did not know what to expect. She took the twins off to school (the elder children took themselves to school) and she returned to the house determined to face the enemy wherever he was, in the house, or the garden or—where?

She was again restless, she was possessed by restlessness. She cooked and sewed and worked as before, day after day, while Mrs. Parkes remonstrated: "Mrs. Rawlings, what's the need for it? I can do that, it's what you pay me for."

And it was so irrational that she checked herself. She would put the car into the garage, go up to her bedroom, and sit, hands in her lap, forcing herself to be quiet. She listened to Mrs. Parkes moving around the house. She looked out into the garden and saw the branches shake the trees. She sat defeating the enemy, restlessness. Emptiness. She ought to be thinking about her life, about herself. But she did not. Or perhaps she could not. As soon as she forced her mind to think about Susan (for what else did she want to be alone for?), it skipped off to thoughts of butter or school clothes. Or it thought of Mrs. Parkes. She realised that she sat listening for the movements of the cleaning woman, following her every turn, bend, thought. She followed her in her mind from kitchen to bathroom, from table to oven, and it was as if the duster, the cleaning cloth, the saucepan, were in her own hand. She would hear herself saying: No, not like that, don't put that there. . . . Yet she did not give a damn what Mrs. Parkes did, or if she did it at all. Yet she could not prevent herself from being conscious of her, every minute. Yes, this was what was wrong with her: she needed, when she was alone, to be really alone, with no one near. She could not endure the knowledge that in ten minutes or in half an hour Mrs. Parkes would call up the stairs: "Mrs. Rawlings, there's no silver polish. Madam, we're out of flour."

So she left the house and went to sit in the garden where she was screened from the house by trees. She waited for the demon to appear and claim her, but he did not.

She was keeping him off, because she had not, after all, come to an end of arranging herself.

She was planning how to be somewhere where Mrs. Parkes would not come after her with a cup of tea, or a demand to be allowed to telephone (always irritating, since Susan did not care who she telephoned or how often), or just a nice talk about something. Yes, she needed a place, or a state of affairs, where it would not be necessary to keep reminding herself: In ten minutes I must telephone Matthew about . . . and at half past three I must leave early for the children because the car needs cleaning. And at ten o'clock tomorrow I must remember. . . . She was possessed with resentment that the seven hours of freedom in every day (during weekdays in the school term) were not free, that never, not for one second, ever, was she free from the pressure of time, from having to remember this or that. She could never forget herself; never really let herself go into forgetfulness.

Resentment. It was poisoning her. (She looked at this emotion and thought it was absurd. Yet she felt it.) She was a prisoner. (She looked at this thought too, and it was no good telling herself it was a ridiculous one.) She must tell Matthew—but what? She was filled with emotions that were utterly ridiculous, that she despised, yet that nevertheless she was feeling so strongly she could not shake them off.

The school holidays came round, and this time they were for nearly two months, and she behaved with a conscious controlled decency that nearly drove her crazy. She would lock herself in the bathroom, and sit on the edge of the bath, breathing deep, trying to let go into some kind of calm. Or she went up into the spare room, usually empty, where no one would expect her to be. She heard the children calling "Mother, Mother," and kept silent, feeling guilty. Or she went to the very end of the garden, by herself, and looked at the slow-moving brown river; she looked at the river and closed her eyes and breathed slow and deep, taking it into her being, into her veins.

Then she returned to the family, wife and mother, smiling and responsible, feeling as if the pressure of these people—four lively children and her husband—were a painful pressure on the surface of her skin, a hand pressing on her brain. She did not once break down into irritation during these holidays, but it was like living out a prison sentence, and when the children went back to school, she sat on a white stone near the flowing river, and she thought: It is not even a year since the twins went to school, since *they were off my hands* (What on earth did I think I meant when I used that stupid phrase?), and yet I'm a different person. I'm simply not myself. I don't understand it.

Yet she had to understand it. For she knew that this structure—big white house, on which the mortgage still cost four hundred a year, a husband, so good and kind and insightful; four children, all doing so nicely; and the garden where she sat; and Mrs. Parkes, the cleaning woman—all this depended on her, and yet she could not understand why, or even what it was she contributed to it.

She said to Matthew in their bedroom: "I think there must be something wrong with me."

And he said: "Surely not, Susan? You look marvellous—you're as lovely as ever."

She looked at the handsome blond man, with his clear, intelligent, blue-eyed face, and thought: Why is it I can't tell him? Why not? And she said: "I need to be alone more than I am."

At which he swung his slow blue gaze at her, and she saw what she had been dreading: Incredulity. Disbelief. And fear. An incredulous blue stare from a stranger who was her husband, as close to her as her own breath.

He said: "But the children are at school and off your hands."

She said to herself: I've got to force myself to say: Yes, but do you realize that I never feel free? There's never a moment I can say to myself: There's nothing I have to remind myself about, nothing I have to do in half an hour, or an hour, or two hours. . . .

But she said: "I don't feel well."

He said: "Perhaps you need a holiday."

She said, appalled: "But not without you, surely?" For she could not imagine herself going off without him. Yet that was what he meant. Seeing her face, he laughed, and opened his arms, and she went into them, thinking: Yes, yes, but why can't I say it? And what is it I have to say?

She tried to tell him, about never being free. And he listened and said: "But Susan, what sort of freedom can you possibly want—short of being dead! Am I ever free? I go to the office, and I have to be there at ten —all right, half past ten, sometimes. And I have to do this or that, don't I? Then I've got to come home at a certain time—I don't mean it, you know I don't—but if I'm not going to be back home at six I telephone you. When can I ever say to myself: I have nothing to be responsible for in the next six hours?"

Susan, hearing this, was remorseful. Because it was true. The good marriage, the house, the children, depended just as much on his voluntary bondage as it did on hers. But why did he not feel bound? Why didn't he chafe and become restless? No, there was something really wrong with her and this proved it.

And that word "bondage"—why had she used it? She had never felt marriage, or the children, as bondage. Neither had he, or surely they wouldn't be together lying in each other's arms content after twelve years of marriage.

No, her state (whatever it was) was irrelevant, nothing to do with her real good life with her family. She had to accept the fact that, after all, she was an irrational person and to live with it. Some people had to live with crippled arms, or stammers, or being deaf. She would have to live knowing she was subject to a state of mind she could not own.

Nevertheless, as a result of this conversation with her husband, there was a new regime next holidays.

The spare room at the top of the house now had a cardboard sign saying: PRIVATE! DO NOT DISTURB on it. (This sign had been drawn in coloured chalks by the children, after a discussion between the parents in which it was decided this was psychologically the right thing.) The family and Mrs. Parkes knew this was "Mother's Room" and that she was entitled to her privacy. Many serious conversations took place between Matthew and the children about not taking Mother for granted. Susan overheard the first, between father and Harry, the older boy, and was surprised at her irritation over it. Surely she could have a room somewhere in that big house and retire into it without such a fuss being made? Without it being so solemnly discussed? Why couldn't she simply have announced: "I'm going to fit out the little top room for myself, and when I'm in it I'm not to be disturbed for anything short of fire"? Just that, and finished; instead of long earnest discussions. When she heard Harry and Matthew explaining it to the twins with Mrs. Parkes coming in—"Yes, well, a family sometimes gets on top of a woman"—she had to go right away to the bottom of the garden until the devils of exasperation had finished their dance in her blood.

But now there was a room, and she could go there when she liked, she used it seldom: she felt even more caged there than in her bedroom. One day she had gone up there after a lunch for ten children she had cooked and served because Mrs. Parkes was not there, and had sat alone for a while looking into the garden. She saw the children stream out from the kitchen and stand looking up at the window where she sat behind the curtains. They were all—her children and their friends—discussing Mother's Room. A few minutes later, the chase of children in some game came pounding up the stairs, but ended as abruptly as if they had fallen over a ravine, so sudden was the silence. They had remembered she was there, and had gone silent in a great gale of "Hush! Shhhhh! Quiet, you'll disturb her. . . ." And they went tiptoeing downstairs like criminal conspirators. When she came down to make tea for them, they all apologised. The twins put their arms around her, from front and back, making a human cage of loving limbs, and promised it would never occur again. "We forgot, Mummy, we forgot all about it!"

What it amounted to was that Mother's Room, and her need for privacy, had become a valuable lesson in respect for other people's rights. Quite soon Susan was going up to the room only because it was a lesson it was a pity to drop. Then she took sewing up there, and the children and Mrs. Parkes came in and out: it had become another family room.

She sighed, and smiled, and resigned herself—she made jokes at her own expense with Matthew over the room. That is, she did from the self she liked, she respected. But at the same time, something inside her howled with impatience, with rage. . . . And she was frightened. One day she found herself kneeling by her bed and praying: "Dear God, keep it away from me, keep him away from me." She meant the devil, for she now thought of it, not caring if she was irrational, as some sort of demon. She imagined him, or it, as a youngish man, or perhaps a middleaged man pretending to be young. Or a man young-looking from immaturity? At any rate, she saw the young-looking face which, when she drew closer, had dry lines about mouth and eyes. He was thinnish, meagre in build. And he had a reddish complexion, and ginger hair. That was he—a gingery, energetic man, and he wore a reddish hairy jacket, unpleasant to the touch.

Well, one day she saw him. She was standing at the bottom of the garden, watching the river ebb past, when she raised her eyes and saw this person, or being, sitting on the white stone bench. He was looking at her, and grinning. In his hand was a long crooked stick, which he had picked off the ground, or broken off the tree above him. He was absent-mindedly, out of an absent-minded or freakish impulse of spite, using the stick to stir around in the coils of a blindworm or a grass snake (or some kind of snake-like creature: it was whitish and unhealthy to look at, unpleasant). The snake was twisting about, flinging its coils from side to side in a kind of dance of protest against the teasing prodding stick.

Susan looked at him, thinking: Who is the stranger? What is he doing in our garden? Then she recognised the man around whom her terrors had crystallised. As she did so, he vanished. She made herself walk over to the bench. A shadow from a branch lay across thin emerald grass, moving jerkily over its roughness, and she could see why she had taken it for a snake, lashing and twisting. She went back to the house thinking: Right, then, so I've seen him with my own eyes, so I'm not crazy after all—there *is* a danger because I've seen him. He is lurking in the garden and sometimes even in the house, and he wants to *get into me and to take me over.*

She dreamed of having a room or a place, anywhere, where she could go and sit, by herself, no one knowing where she was.

Once, near Victoria, she found herself outside a news agent that had Rooms to Let advertised. She decided to rent a room, telling no one. Sometimes she could take the train into Richmond and sit alone in it for an hour or two. Yet how could she? A room would cost three or four pounds a week, and she earned no money, and how could she explain to Matthew that she needed such a sum? What for? It did not occur to her that she was taking it for granted she wasn't going to tell him about the room.

Well, it was out of the question, having a room; yet she knew she must.

One day, when a school term was well established, and none of the children had measles or other ailments, and everything seemed in order, she did the shopping early, explained to Mrs. Parkes she was meeting an old school friend, took the train to Victoria, searched until she found a small quiet hotel, and asked for a room for the day. They did not let rooms by the day, the manageress said, looking doubtful, since Susan so obviously was not the kind of woman who needed a room for unrespectable reasons. Susan made a long explanation about not being well, being unable to shop without frequent rests for lying down. At last she was allowed to rent the room provided she paid a full night's price for it. She was taken up by the manageress and a maid, both concerned over the state of her health . . . which must be pretty bad if, living at Richmond (she had signed her name and address in the register), she needed a shelter at Victoria.

The room was ordinary and anonymous, and was just what Susan needed. She put a shilling in the gas fire, and sat, eyes shut, in a dingy armchair with her back to a dingy window. She was alone. She was alone. She was alone. She could feel pressures lifting off her. First the sounds of traffic came very loud; then they seemed to vanish; she might even have slept a little. A knock on the door: it was Miss Townsend, the manageress, bringing her a cup of tea with her own hands, so concerned was she over Susan's long silence and possible illness.

Miss Townsend was a lonely woman of fifty, running this hotel with all the rectitude expected of her, and she sensed in Susan the possibility of understanding companionship. She stayed to talk. Susan found herself in the middle of a fantastic story about her illness, which got more and more impossible as she tried to make it tally with the large house at Richmond, well-off husband, and four children. Suppose she said instead: Miss Townsend, I'm here in your hotel because I need to be alone for a few hours, above all *alone and with no one knowing where I am*. She said it mentally, and saw, mentally, the look that would inevitably come on Miss Townsend's elderly maiden's face. "Miss Townsend, my four children and my husband are driving me insane, do you understand that? Yes, I can see from the gleam of hysteria in your eyes that comes from loneliness controlled but only just contained that I've got everything in the world you've ever longed for. Well, Miss Townsend, I don't want any of it. You can have it, Miss Townsend. I wish I was absolutely alone in the world, like you. Miss Townsend, I'm besieged by seven devils, Miss Townsend, Miss Townsend, let me stay here in your hotel where the devils can't get me. . . ." Instead of saying all this, she described her anaemia, agreed to try Miss Townsend's remedy for it, which was raw liver, minced, between whole-meal bread, and said yes, perhaps it would be better if she stayed at home and let a friend do shopping for her. She paid her bill and left the hotel, defeated.

At home Mrs. Parkes said she didn't really like it, no, not really, when Mrs. Rawlings was away from nine in the morning until five. The teacher had telephoned from school to say Joan's teeth were paining her, and she hadn't known what to say; and what was she to make for the children's tea, Mrs. Rawlings hadn't said.

All this was nonsense, of course. Mrs. Parkes's complaint was that Susan had withdrawn herself spiritually, leaving the burden of the big house on her.

Susan looked back at her day of "freedom" which had resulted in her becoming a friend of the lonely Miss Townsend, and in Mrs. Parkes's remonstrances. Yet she remembered the short blissful hour of being alone, really alone. She was determined to arrange her life, no matter what it cost, so that she could have that solitude more often. An absolute solitude, where no one knew her or cared about her.

But how? She thought of saying to her old employer: I want you to back me up in a story with Matthew that I am doing part-time work for you. The truth is that . . . But she would have to tell him a lie too, and which lie? She could not say: I want to sit by myself three or four times a week in a rented room. And besides, he knew Matthew, and she could not really ask him to tell lies on her behalf, apart from being bound to think it meant a lover.

Suppose she really took a part-time job, which she could get through fast and efficiently, leaving time for herself. What job? Addressing envelopes? Canvassing?

And there was Mrs. Parkes, working widow, who knew exactly what she was prepared to give to the house, who knew by instinct when her mistress withdrew in spirit from her responsibilities. Mrs. Parkes was one of the servers of this world, but she needed someone to serve. She had to have Mrs. Rawlings, her madam, at the top of the house or in the garden, so that she could come and get support from her: "Yes, the bread's not what it was when I was a girl. . . . Yes, Harry's got a wonderful appetite, I wonder where he puts it all. . . . Yes, it's lucky the twins are so much of a size, they can wear each other's shoes, that's a saving in these hard times. . . . Yes, the cherry jam from Switzerland is not a patch on the jam from Poland, and three times the price . . ." And so on. That sort of talk Mrs. Parkes must have, every day, or she would leave, not knowing herself why she left.

Susan Rawlings, thinking these thoughts, found that she was prowling through the great thicketed garden like a wild cat: she was walking up the stairs, down the stairs, through the rooms into the garden, along the brown running river, back, up through the house, down again. . . . It was a wonder Mrs. Parkes did not think it strange. But, on the contrary, Mrs. Rawlings could do what she liked, she could stand on her head if she wanted, provided she was *there*. Susan Rawlings prowled and muttered through her house, hating Mrs. Parkes, hating poor Miss Townsend, dreaming of her hour of solitude in the dingy respectability of Miss Townsend's hotel bedroom, and she knew quite well she was mad. Yes, she was mad.

She said to Matthew that she must have a holiday. Matthew agreed with her. This was not as things had been once—how they had talked in each other's arms in the marriage bed. He had, she knew, diagnosed her finally as *unreasonable*. She had become someone outside himself that he had to manage. They were living side by side in this house like two tolerably friendly strangers.

Having told Mrs. Parkes—or rather, asked for her permission— she went off on a walking holiday in Wales. She chose the remotest place she knew of. Every morning the children telephoned her before they went off to school, to encourage and support her, just as they had over Mother's Room. Every evening she telephoned them, spoke to each child in turn, and then to Matthew. Mrs. Parkes, given permission to telephone for instructions or advice, did so every day at lunchtime. When, as happened three times, Mrs. Rawlings was out on the mountainside, Mrs. Parkes asked that she should ring back at such-and-such a time, for she would not be happy in what she was doing without Mrs. Rawlings' blessing.

Susan prowled over wild country with the telephone wire holding her to her duty like a leash. The next time she must telephone, or wait to be telephoned, nailed her to her cross. The mountains themselves seemed trammelled by her unfreedom. Everywhere on the mountains, where she met no one at all, from breakfast time to dusk, excepting sheep, or a shepherd, she came face to face with her own craziness, which might attack her in the broadest valleys, so that they seemed too small, or on a mountain top from which she could see a hundred other mountains and valleys, so that they seemed too low, too small, with the sky pressing down too close. She would stand gazing at a hillside brilliant with ferns and bracken, jewelled with running water, and see nothing but her devil, who lifted inhuman eyes at her from where he leaned negligently on a rock, switching at his ugly yellow boots with a leafy twig.

She returned to her home and family, with the Welsh emptiness at the back of her mind like a promise of freedom.

She told her husband she wanted to have an *au pair* girl.[1]

They were in their bedroom, it was late at night, the children slept. He sat, shirted and slippered, in a chair by the window, looking out. She sat brushing her hair and watching him in the mirror. A time-hallowed scene in the connubial bedroom. He said nothing, while she heard the arguments coming into his mind, only to be rejected because every one was *reasonable*.

"It seems strange to get one now; after all, the children are in school most of the day. Surely the time for you to have help was when you were stuck with them day and night. Why don't you ask Mrs. Parkes to cook for you? She's even offered to—I can understand if you are tired of cooking for six people. But you know that an *au pair* girl means all kinds of problems; it's not like having an ordinary char in during the day. . . ."

Finally he said carefully: "Are you thinking of going back to work?"

---

1. A foreign girl or woman who works for a family in exchange for room and board and the chance to learn the language.

"No," she said, "no, not really." She made herself sound vague, rather stupid. She went on brushing her black hair and peering at herself so as to be oblivious of the short uneasy glances her Matthew kept giving her. "Do you think we can't afford it?" she went on vaguely, not at all the old efficient Susan who knew exactly what they could afford.

"It's not that," he said, looking out of the window at dark trees, so as not to look at her. Meanwhile she examined a round, candid, pleasant face with clear dark brows and clear grey eyes. A sensible face. She brushed thick healthy black hair and thought: Yet that's the reflection of a madwoman. How very strange! Much more to the point if what looked back at me was the gingery green-eyed demon with his dry meagre smile. . . . Why wasn't Matthew agreeing? After all, what else could he do? She was breaking her part of the bargain and there was no way of forcing her to keep it: that her spirit, her soul, should live in this house, so that the people in it could grow like plants in water, and Mrs. Parkes remain content in their service. In return for this, he would be a good loving husband, and responsible towards the children. Well, nothing like this had been true of either of them for a long time. He did his duty, perfunctorily; she did not even pretend to do hers. And he had become like other husbands, with his real life in his work and the people he met there, and very likely a serious affair. All this was her fault.

At last he drew heavy curtains, blotting out the trees, and turned to force her attention: "Susan, are you really sure we need a girl?" But she would not meet his appeal at all. She was running the brush over her hair again and again, lifting fine black clouds in a small hiss of electricity. She was peering in and smiling as if she were amused at the clinging hissing hair that followed the brush.

"Yes, I think it would be a good idea, on the whole," she said, with the cunning of a madwoman evading the real point.

In the mirror she could see her Matthew lying on his back, his hands behind his head, staring upwards, his face sad and hard. She felt her heart (the old heart of Susan Rawlings) soften and call out to him. But she set it to be indifferent.

He said: "Susan, the children?" It was an appeal that *almost* reached her. He opened his arms, lifting them palms up, empty. She had only to run across and fling herself into them, onto his hard, warm chest, and melt into herself, into Susan. But she could not. She would not see his lifted arms. She said vaguely: "Well, surely it'll be even better for them? We'll get a French or a German girl and they'll learn the language."

In the dark she lay beside him, feeling frozen, a stranger. She felt as if Susan had been spirited away. She disliked very much this woman who lay here, cold and indifferent beside a suffering man, but she could not change her.

Next morning she set about getting a girl, and very soon came Sophie Traub from Hamburg, a girl of twenty, laughing, healthy, blue-eyed, intending to learn English. Indeed, she already spoke a good deal. In return for a room—"Mother's Room"—and her food, she undertook to do some light cooking, and to be with the children when Mrs. Rawlings asked. She was an intelligent girl and understood perfectly what was needed. Susan said: "I go off sometimes, for the morning or for the day—well, sometimes the children run home from school, or they ring up, or a teacher rings up. I should be here, really. And there's the daily woman. . . ." And Sophie laughed her deep fruity *Fräulein*'s laugh, showed her fine white teeth and her dimples, and said: "You want some person to play mistress of the house sometimes, not so?"

"Yes, that is just so," said Susan, a bit dry, despite herself, thinking in secret fear how easy it was, how much nearer to the end she was than she thought. Healthy Fräulein Traub's instant understanding of their position proved this to be true.

The *au pair* girl, because of her own commonsense, or (as Susan said to herself, with her new inward shudder) because she had been *chosen* so well by Susan, was a success with everyone, the children liking her, Mrs. Parkes forgetting almost at once that she was German, and Matthew finding her "nice to have around the house." For he was now taking things as they came, from the surface of life, withdrawn both as a husband and a father from the household.

One day Susan saw how Sophie and Mrs. Parkes were talking and laughing in the kitchen, and she announced that she would be away until tea time. She knew exactly where to go and what she must look for. She took the District Line to South Kensington, changed to the Circle, got off at Paddington, and walked around looking at the smaller hotels until she was satisfied with one which had FRED'S HOTEL painted on windowpanes that needed cleaning. The facade was a faded shiny yellow, like unhealthy skin. A door at the end of a passage said she must knock; she did, and Fred appeared. He was not at all attractive, not in any way, being fattish, and run-down, and wearing a tasteless striped suit. He had small sharp eyes in a white creased face, and was quite prepared to let Mrs. Jones (she chose the farcical name deliberately, staring him out) have a room three days a week from ten until six. Provided of course that she paid in advance each time she came? Susan produced fifteen shillings (no price had been set by him) and held it out, still fixing him with a bold unblinking challenge she had not known until then she could use at will. Looking at her still, he took up a ten-shilling note from her palm between thumb and forefinger, fingered it; then shuffled up two half-crowns, held out his own palm with these bits of money displayed thereon, and let his gaze lower broodingly at them. They were standing in the passage, a red-shaded light above, bare boards beneath, and a strong smell of floor polish rising about them. He shot his gaze up at her over the still-extended palm, and smiled as if to say: What do you take me for? "I shan't," said Susan, "be using this room for the purposes of making money." He still waited. She added another five shillings, at which he nodded and said: "You pay, and I ask no questions." "Good," said Susan. He now went past her to the stairs, and there waited a moment:

the light from the street door being in her eyes, she lost sight of him momentarily. Then she saw a sober-suited, white-faced, white-balding little man trotting up the stairs like a waiter, and she went after him. They proceeded in utter silence up the stairs of this house where no questions were asked—Fred's Hotel, which could afford the freedom for its visitors that poor Miss Townsend's hotel could not. The room was hideous. It had a single window, with thin green brocade curtains, a three-quarter bed that had a cheap green satin bedspread on it, a fireplace with a gas fire and a shilling meter by it, a chest of drawers, and a green wicker armchair.

"Thank you," said Susan, knowing that Fred (if this was Fred, and not George, or Herbert or Charlie) was looking at her, not so much with curiosity, an emotion he would not own to, for professional reasons, but with a philosophical sense of what was appropriate. Having taken her money and shown her up and agreed to everything, he was clearly disapproving of her for coming here. She did not belong here at all, so his look said. (But she knew, already, how very much she did belong: the room had been waiting for her to join it.) "Would you have me called at five o'clock, please?" and he nodded and went downstairs.

It was twelve in the morning. She was free. She sat in the armchair, she simply sat, she closed her eyes and sat and let herself be alone. She was alone and no one knew where she was. When a knock came on the door she was annoyed, and prepared to show it: but it was Fred himself; it was five o'clock and he was calling her as ordered. He flicked his sharp little eyes over the room—bed, first. It was undisturbed. She might never have been in the room at all. She thanked him, said she would be returning the day after tomorrow, and left. She was back home in time to cook supper, to put the children to bed, to cook a second supper for her husband and herself later. And to welcome Sophie back from the pictures where she had gone with a friend. All these things she did cheerfully, willingly. But she was thinking all the time of the hotel room; she was longing for it with her whole being.

Three times a week. She arrived promptly at ten, looked Fred in the eyes, gave him twenty shillings, followed him up the stairs, went into the room, and shut the door on him with gentle firmness. For Fred, disapproving of her being here at all, was quite ready to let friendship, or at least acquaintanceship, follow his disapproval, if only she would let him. But he was content to go off on her dismissing nod, with the twenty shillings in his hand.

She sat in the armchair and shut her eyes.

What did she *do* in the room? Why, nothing at all. From the chair, when it had rested her, she went to the window, stretching her arms, smiling, treasuring her anonymity, to look out. She was no longer Susan Rawlings, mother of four, wife of Matthew, employer of Mrs. Parkes and of Sophie Traub, with these and those relations with friends, school-teachers, tradesmen. She no longer was mistress of the big white house and garden, owning clothes suitable for this and that activity or occasion. She was Mrs.

Jones, and she was alone, and she had no past and no future. Here I am, she thought, after all these years of being married and having children and playing those roles of responsibility—and I'm just the same. Yet there have been times I thought that nothing existed of me except the roles that went with being Mrs. Matthew Rawlings. Yes, here I am, and if I never saw any of my family again, here would still be . . . how very strange that is! And she leaned on the sill, and looked into the street, loving the men and women who passed, because she did not know them. She looked at the down-trodden buildings over the street, and at the sky, wet and dingy, or sometimes blue, and she felt she had never seen buildings or sky before. And then she went back to the chair, empty, her mind a blank. Sometimes she talked aloud, saying nothing—an exclamation, meaningless, followed by a comment about the floral pattern on the thin rug, or a stain on the green satin coverlet. For the most part, she wool-gathered—what word is there for it?—brooded, wandered, simply went dark, feeling emptiness run deliciously through her veins like the movement of her blood.

This room had become more her own than the house she lived in. One morning she found Fred taking her a flight higher than usual. She stopped, refusing to go up, and demanded her usual room, Number 19. "Well, you'll have to wait half an hour, then," he said. Willingly she descended to the dark disinfectant-smelling hall, and sat waiting until the two, man and woman, came down the stairs, giving her swift indifferent glances before they hurried out into the street, separating at the door. She went up to the room, *her* room, which they had just vacated. It was no less hers, though the windows were set wide open, and a maid was straightening the bed as she came in.

After these days of solitude, it was both easy to play her part as mother and wife, and difficult—because it was so easy: she felt an imposter. She felt as if her shell moved here, with her family, answering to Mummy, Mother, Susan, Mrs. Rawlings. She was surprised no one saw through her, that she wasn't turned out of doors, as a fake. On the contrary, it seemed the children loved her more; Matthew and she "got on" pleasantly, and Mrs. Parkes was happy in her work under (for the most part, it must be confessed) Sophie Traub. At night she lay beside her husband, and they made love again, apparently just as they used to, when they were really married. But she, Susan, or the being who answered so readily and improbably to the name of Susan, was not there: she was in Fred's Hotel, in Paddington, waiting for the easing hours of solitude to begin.

Soon she made a new arrangement with Fred and with Sophie. It was for five days a week. As for the money, five pounds, she simply asked Matthew for it. She saw that she was not even frightened he might ask what for: he would give it to her, she knew that, and yet it was terrifying it could be so, for this close couple, these partners, had once known the destination of every shilling they must spend. He agreed to give her five pounds a week. She asked for just so much, not a penny more. He sounded indifferent about it. It was as if he were paying her, she thought: *paying her off—*

yes, that was it. Terror came back for a moment when she understood this, but she stilled it: things had gone too far for that. Now, every week, on Sunday nights, he gave her five pounds, turning away from her before their eyes could meet on the transaction. As for Sophie Traub, she was to be somewhere in or near the house until six at night, after which she was free. She was not to cook, or to clean; she was simply to be there. So she gardened or sewed, and asked friends in, being a person who was bound to have a lot of friends. If the children were sick, she nursed them. If teachers telephoned, she answered them sensibly. For the five daytimes in the school week, she was altogether the mistress of the house.

One night in the bedroom, Matthew asked: "Susan, I don't want to interfere—don't think that, please—but are you sure you are well?"

She was brushing her hair at the mirror. She made two more strokes on either side of her head, before she replied: "Yes, dear, I am sure I am well."

He was again lying on his back, his blond head on his hands, his elbows angled up and part-concealing his face. He said: "Then Susan, I have to ask you this question, though you must understand, I'm not putting any sort of pressure on you." (Susan heard the word "pressure" with dismay, because this was inevitable; of course she could not go on like this.) "Are things going to go on like this?"

"Well," she said, going vague and bright and idiotic again, so as to escape: "Well, I don't see why not."

He was jerking his elbows up and down, in annoyance or in pain, and, looking at him, she saw he had got thin, even gaunt; and restless angry movements were not what she remembered of him. He said: "Do you want a divorce, is that it?"

At this, Susan only with the greatest difficulty stopped herself from laughing: she could hear the bright bubbling laughter she *would* have emitted, had she let herself. He could only mean one thing: she had a lover, and that was why she spent her days in London, as lost to him as if she had vanished to another continent.

Then the small panic set in again: she understood that he hoped she did have a lover, he was begging her to say so, because otherwise it would be too terrifying.

She thought this out as she brushed her hair, watching the fine black stuff fly up to make its little clouds of electricity, hiss, hiss, hiss. Behind her head, across the room, was a blue wall. She realised she was absorbed in watching the black hair making shapes against the blue. She should be answering him. "Do *you* want a divorce, Matthew?"

He said: "That surely isn't the point, is it?"

"You brought it up, I didn't," she said, brightly, suppressing meaningless tinkling laughter.

Next day she asked Fred: "Have enquiries been made for me?"

He hesitated, and she said: "I've been coming here a year now. I've made no trouble, and you've been paid every day. I have a right to be told."

"As a matter of fact, Mrs. Jones, a man did come asking."

"A man from a detective agency?"

"Well, he could have been, couldn't he?"

"I was asking you . . . . Well, what did you tell him?"

"I told him a Mrs. Jones came every weekday from ten until five or six and stayed in Number 19 by herself."

"Describing me?"

"Well, Mrs. Jones, I had no alternative. Put yourself in my place."

"By rights I should deduct what that man gave you for the information."

He raised shocked eyes: she was not the sort of person to make jokes like this! Then he chose to laugh: a pinkish wet slit appeared across his white crinkled face; his eyes positively begged her to laugh, otherwise he might lose some money. She remained grave, looking at him.

He stopped laughing and said: "You want to go up now?"—returning to the familiarity, the comradeship, of the country where no questions are asked, on which (and he knew it) she depended completely.

She went up to sit in her wicker chair. But it was not the same. Her husband had searched her out. (The world had searched her out.) The pressures were on her. She was here with his connivance. He might walk in at any moment, here, into Room 19. She imagined the report from the detective agency: "A woman calling herself Mrs. Jones, fitting the description of your wife (et cetera, et cetera, et cetera), stays alone all day in Room No. 19. She insists on this room, waits for it if it is engaged. As far as the proprietor knows, she receives no visitors there, male or female." A report something on these lines Matthew must have received.

Well, of course he was right: things couldn't go on like this. He had put an end to it all simply by sending the detective after her.

She tried to shrink herself back into the shelter of the room, a snail pecked out of its shell and trying to squirm back. But the peace of the room had gone. She was trying consciously to revive it, trying to let go into the dark creative trance (or whatever it was) that she had found there. It was no use, yet she craved for it, she was as ill as a suddenly deprived addict.

Several times she returned to the room, to look for herself there, but instead she found the unnamed spirit of restlessness, a pricking fevered hunger for movement, an irritable self-consciousness that made her brain feel as if it had coloured lights going on and off inside it. Instead of the soft dark that had been the room's air, were now waiting for her demons that made her dash blindly about, muttering words of hate; she was impelling herself from point to point like a moth dashing itself against a windowpane, sliding to the bottom, fluttering off on broken wings, then crashing into the invisible barrier again. And again and again. Soon she was exhausted, and she told Fred that for a while she would not be needing the room, she was going on holiday. Home she went, to the big white house by the river. The middle of a weekday, and she felt guilty at returning to her own home when not expected. She stood unseen, looking in at the kitchen window. Mrs.

Parkes, wearing a discarded floral overall of Susan's, was stooping to slide something into the oven. Sophie, arms folded, was leaning her back against a cupboard and laughing at some joke made by a girl not seen before by Susan—a dark foreign girl, Sophie's visitor. In an armchair Molly, one of the twins, lay curled, sucking her thumb and watching the grownups. She must have some sickness, to be kept from school. The child's listless face, the dark circles under her eyes, hurt Susan: Molly was looking at the three grownups working and talking in exactly the same way Susan looked at the four through the kitchen window: she was remote, shut off from them.

But then, just as Susan imagined herself going in, picking up the little girl, and sitting in an armchair with her, stroking her probably heated forehead, Sophie did just that: she had been standing on one leg, the other knee flexed, its foot set against the wall. Now she let her foot in its ribbon-tied red shoe slide down the wall, stood solid on two feet, clapping her hands before and behind her, and sang a couple of lines in German, so that the child lifted her heavy eyes at her and began to smile. Then she walked, or rather skipped, over to the child, swung her up, and let her fall into her lap at the same moment she sat herself. She said "Hopla! Hopla! Molly . . ." and began stroking the dark untidy young head that Molly laid on her shoulder for comfort.

Well. . . . Susan blinked the tears of farewell out of her eyes, and went quietly up through the house to her bedroom. There she sat looking at the river through the trees. She felt at peace, but in a way that was new to her. She had no desire to move, to talk, to do anything at all. The devils that had haunted the house, the garden, were not there; but she knew it was because her soul was in Room 19 in Fred's Hotel: she was not really here at all. It was a sensation that should have been frightening: to sit at her own bedroom window, listening to Sophie's rich young voice sing Germany nursery songs to her child, listening to Mrs. Parkes clatter and move below, and to know that all this had nothing to do with her: she was already out of it.

Later, she made herself go down and say she was home: it was unfair to be here unannounced. She took lunch with Mrs. Parkes, Sophie, Sophie's Italian friend Maria, and her daughter Molly, and felt like a visitor.

A few days later, at bedtime, Matthew said: "Here's your five pounds," and pushed them over at her. Yet he must have known she had not been leaving the house at all.

She shook her head, gave it back to him, and said, in explanation, not in accusation: "As soon as you knew where I was, there was no point."

He nodded, not looking at her. He was turned away from her: thinking, she knew, how best to handle this wife who terrified him.

He said: "I wasn't trying to . . . It's just that I was worried."

"Yes, I know."

"I must confess that I was beginning to wonder . . ."

"You thought I had a lover?"

"Yes, I am afraid I did."

She knew that he wished she had. She sat wondering how to say:

"For a year now I've been spending all my days in a very sordid hotel room. It's the place where I'm happy. In fact, without it I don't exist." She heard herself saying this, and understood how terrified he was that she might. So instead she said: "Well, perhaps you're not far wrong."

Probably Matthew would think the hotel proprietor lied: he would want to think so.

"Well," he said, and she could hear his voice spring up, so to speak, with relief, "in that case I must confess I've got a bit of an affair on myself."

She said, detached and interested: "Really? Who is she?" and saw Matthew's startled look because of this reaction.

"It's Phil. Phil Hunt."

She had known Phil Hunt well in the old unmarried days. She was thinking: No, she won't do, she's too neurotic and difficult. She's never been happy yet. Sophie's much better. Well, Matthew will see that himself, as sensible as he is.

This line of thought went on in silence, while she said aloud: "It's no point telling you about mine, because you don't know him."

Quick, quick, invent, she thought. Remember how you invented all that nonsense for Miss Townsend.

She began slowly, careful not to contradict herself: "His name is Michael" (*Michael What?*)—"Michael Plant." (What a silly name!) "He's rather like you—in looks, I mean." And indeed, she could imagine herself being touched by no one but Matthew himself. "He's a publisher." (Really? Why?) "He's got a wife already and two children."

She brought out this fantasy, proud of herself.

Matthew said: "Are you two thinking of marrying?"

She said, before she could stop herself: "Good God, *no!*"

She realised, if Matthew wanted to marry Phil Hunt, that this was too emphatic, but apparently it was all right, for his voice sounded relieved as he said: "It is a bit impossible to imagine oneself married to anyone else, isn't it?" With which he pulled her to him, so that her head lay on his shoulder. She turned her face into the dark of his flesh, and listened to the blood pounding through her ears saying: I am alone, I am alone, I am alone.

In the morning Susan lay in bed while he dressed.

He had been thinking things out in the night, because now he said: "Susan, why don't we make a foursome?"

Of course, she said to herself, of course he would be bound to say that. If one is sensible, if one is reasonable, if one never allows oneself a base thought or an envious emotion, naturally one says: Let's make a foursome!

"Why not?" she said.

"We could all meet for lunch. I mean, it's ridiculous, you sneaking off to filthy hotels, and me staying late at the office, and all the lies everyone has to tell."

What on earth did I say his name was?—she panicked, then said: "I think it's a good idea, but Michael is away at the moment. When he comes back, though—and I'm sure you two would like each other."

"He's away, is he? So that's why you've been . . ." Her husband put his hand to the knot of his tie in a gesture of male coquetry she would not before have associated with him; and he bent to kiss her cheek with the expression that goes with the words: Oh you naughty little puss! And she felt its answering look, naughty and coy, come onto her face.

Inside she was dissolving in horror at them both, at how far they had both sunk from honesty of emotion.

So now she was saddled with a lover, and he had a mistress! How ordinary, how reassuring, how jolly! And now they would make a foursome of it, and go about to theatres and restaurants. After all, the Rawlings could well afford that sort of thing, and presumably the publisher Michael Plant could afford to do himself and his mistress quite well. No, there was nothing to stop the four of them developing the most intricate relationship of civilised tolerance, all enveloped in a charming afterglow of autumnal passion. Perhaps they would all go off on holidays together? She had known people who did. Or perhaps Matthew would draw the line there? Why should he, though, if he was capable of talking about "foursomes" at all?

She lay in the empty bedroom, listening to the car drive off with Matthew in it, off to work. Then she heard the children clattering off to school to the accompaniment of Sophie's cheerfully ringing voice. She slid down into the hollow of the bed, for shelter against her own irrelevance. And she stretched out her hand to the hollow where her husband's body had lain, but found no comfort there: he was not her husband. She curled herself up in a small tight ball under the clothes: she could stay here all day, all week, indeed, all her life.

But in a few days she must produce Michael Plant, and—but how? She must presumably find some agreeable man prepared to impersonate a publisher called Michael Plant. And in return for which she would—what? Well, for one thing they would make love. The idea made her want to cry with sheer exhaustion. Oh no, she had finished with all that—the proof of it was that the words "make love," or even imagining it, trying hard to revive no more than the pleasures of sensuality, let alone affection, or love, made her want to run away and hide from the sheer effort of the thing. . . . Good Lord, why make love at all? Why make love with anyone? Or if you are going to make love, what does it matter who with? Why shouldn't she simply walk into the street, pick up a man and have a roaring sexual affair with him? Why not? Or even with Fred? What difference did it make?

But she had let herself in for it—an interminable stretch of time with a lover, called Michael, as part of a gallant civilised foursome. Well, she could not, and she would not.

She got up, dressed, went down to find Mrs. Parkes, and asked her for the loan of a pound, since Matthew, she said, had forgotten to leave her money. She exchanged with Mrs. Parkes variations on the theme that husbands are all the same, they don't think, and without saying a word to Sophie, whose voice could be heard upstairs from the telephone, walked to the underground, travelled to South Kensington, changed to the Inner Circle, got out at Paddington, and walked to Fred's Hotel. There she told Fred that she wasn't going on holiday after all, she needed the room. She would have to wait an hour, Fred said. She went to a busy tearoom-cum-restaurant around the corner, and sat watching the people flow in and out the door that kept swinging open and shut, watched them mingle and merge, and separate, felt her being flow into them, into their movement. When the hour was up, she left a half-crown for her pot of tea, and left the place without looking back at it, just as she had left her house, the big, beautiful white house, without another look, but silently dedicating it to Sophie. She returned to Fred, received the key of Number 19, now free, and ascended the grimy stairs slowly, letting floor after floor fall away below her, keeping her eyes lifted, so that floor after floor descended jerkily to her level of vision, and fell away out of sight.

Number 19 was the same. She saw everything with an acute, narrow, checking glance: the cheap shine of the satin spread, which had been replaced carelessly after the two bodies had finished their convulsions under it; a trace of powder on the glass that topped the chest of drawers; an intense green shade in a fold of the curtain. She stood at the window, looking down, watching people pass and pass and pass until her mind went dark from the constant movement. Then she sat in the wicker chair, letting herself go slack. But she had to be careful, because she did not want, today, to be surprised by Fred's knock at five o'clock.

The demons were not here. They had gone forever, because she was buying her freedom from them. She was slipping already into the dark fructifying dream that seemed to caress her inwardly, like the movement of her blood . . . but she had to think about Matthew first. Should she write a letter for the coroner? But what should she say? She would like to leave him with the look on his face she had seen this morning—banal, admittedly, but at least confidently healthy. Well, that was impossible, one did not look like that with a wife dead from suicide. But how to leave him believing she was dying because of a man—because of the fascinating publisher Michael Plant? Oh, how ridiculous! How absurd! How humiliating! But she decided not to trouble about it, simply not to think about the living. If he wanted to believe she had a lover, he would believe it. And he *did* want to believe it. Even when he had found out that there was no publisher in London called Michael Plant, he would think: Oh poor Susan, she was afraid to give me his real name.

And what did it matter whether he married Phil Hunt or Sophie? Though it ought to be Sophie, who was already the mother of those children . . . and what hypocrisy to sit here worrying about the children, when she was going to leave them because she had not got the energy to stay.

She had about four hours. She spent them delightfully, darkly, sweetly, letting herself slide gently, to the edge of the river. Then, with hardly a break in her consciousness, she got up, pushed the thin rug against the door, made sure the windows were tight shut, put two shillings in the meter, and turned on the gas. For the first time since she had been in the room she lay on the hard bed that smelled stale, that smelled of sweat and sex.

She lay on her back on the green satin cover, but her legs were chilly. She got up, found a blanket folded in the bottom of the chest of drawers, and carefully covered her legs with it. She was quite content lying there, listening to the faint soft hiss of the gas that poured into the room, into her lungs, into her brain, as she drifted off into the dark river.

1963

"To Room Nineteen" will strike some readers as irredeemably gloomy, but other readers find in it some signs of hope. It is worthwhile to reconsider the story in light of Doris Lessing's statement (made in her essay "A Small Personal Voice") that she prefers literature that can "enlarge one's perception of life."

"Literature should be committed": Doris Lessing

If there is one thing which distinguishes our literature, it is a confusion of standards and the uncertainty of values. It would be hard, now, for a writer to use Balzacian phrases like "sublime virtue" or "monster of wickedness" without self-consciousness. Words, it seems, can no longer be used simply and naturally. All the great words like love, hate; life, death; loyalty, treachery; contain their opposite meanings and half a dozen shades of dubious implication. Words have become so inadequate to express the richness of our experience that the simplest sentence overheard on a bus reverberates like words shouted against a cliff. One certainty we all accept is the condition of being uncertain and insecure. It is hard to make moral judgements, to use words like good and bad.

Yet I reread Tolstoy, Stendhal, Balzac, and the rest of the old giants continuously. So do most of the people I know, people who are left and right, committed and uncommitted, religious and unreligious, but who have at least this in common, that they read novels as I think they should be read, for illumination, in order to enlarge one's perception of life.

Why? Because we are in search of certainties? Because we want a return to a comparatively uncomplicated world? Because it gives us a sense of safety to hear Balzac's thundering verdicts of guilt or innocence, and to explore with Dostoevsky, for instance in *Crime and Punishment,* the possibilities of moral anarchy, only to find order restored at the end with the simplest statements of faith in forgiveness, expiation, redemption?

Recently I finished reading an American novel which pleased me; it was witty, intelligent, un-self-pitying, courageous. Yet when I put it down I knew I would not reread it. I asked myself why not, what demand I was making on the author that he did not answer. Why was I left dissatisfied with nearly all the contemporary novels I read? Why, if I were reading for my own needs, rather than for the purposes of informing myself about what was going on, would I begin rereading *War and Peace* or *The Red and the Black?*

Put directly, like this, the answer seemed to me clear. I was not looking for a firm reaffirmation of old ethical values, many of which I don't accept; I was not in search of the pleasures of familiarity. I was looking for the warmth, the compassion, the humanity, the love of people which illuminates the literature of the nineteenth century and which makes all these old novels a statement of faith in man himself.

These are qualities which I believe are lacking from literature now.

This is what I mean when I say that literature should be committed. It is these qualities which I demand, and which I believe spring from being committed; for one cannot be committed without belief.

MAVIS GALLANT

(b. 1922)

THE REMISSION

When it became clear that Alec Webb was far more ill than anyone had cared to tell him, he tore up his English life and came down to die on the Riviera. The time was early in the reign of the new Elizabeth, and people were still doing this—migrating with no other purpose than the hope of a merciful sky. The alternative (Alec said to his only sister) meant queueing for death on the National Health Service, lying on a regulation mattress and rubber sheet, hearing the breath of other men dying.

Alec—as obituaries would have it later—was husband to Barbara, father to Will, Molly, and James. It did not occur to him or to anyone else that the removal from England was an act of unusual force that could rend and lacerate his children's lives as well as his own. The difference was that their lives were barely above ground and not yet in flower.

The five Webbs arrived at a property called Lou Mas in the course of a particularly hot September. Mysterious Lou Mas, until now a name on a deed of sale, materialized as a pink house wedged in the side of a hill between a motor road and the sea. Alec identified its style as Edwardian-Riviera. Barbara supposed he must mean the profusion of balconies and parapets, and the slender pillars in the garden holding up nothing. In the new southern light everything looked to her brilliant and moist, like color straight from a paintbox. One of Alec's first gestures was to raise his arm and shield his eyes against this brightness. The journey had exhausted him, she thought. She had received notice in dreams that their change of climates was irreversible, not just Alec but none of them could go back. She did not tell him so, though in better times it might have interested that part of his mind he kept fallow: being entirely rational, he had a prudent respect for second sight.

The children had never been in a house this size. They chased each other and slid along the floors until Alec asked, politely, if they wouldn't mind playing outside, though one of the reasons he had wanted to come here was to be with them for the time remaining. Dispatched to a flagged patio in front of the house, the children looked down on terraces bearing olive trees, then a railway line, then the sea. Among the trees was a cottage standing empty which Barbara had forbidden them to explore. The children were ten, eleven, and twelve, with the girl in the middle. Since they had no school to attend, and did not know any of the people living around them, and as their mother was too busy to invent something interesting for them to do, they hung over a stone balustrade waving and calling to trains, hoping to see an answering wave and perhaps a decapitation. They had often been warned about foolish passengers and the worst that could happen. Their mother came out and put her arms around Will, the eldest. She kissed the top of his head. "Do look at that sea," she said. "Aren't we lucky?" They looked, but the vast, flat sea was a line any of them could have drawn on a sheet of paper. It was there, but no more than there; trains were better—so was the ruined cottage. Within a week James had cut his hand on glass breaking into it, but by then Barbara had forgotten her injunction.

The sun Alec had wanted turned out to be without compassion, and he spent most of the day indoors, moving from room to room, searching for some gray, dim English cave in which to take cover. Often he sat without reading, doing nothing, in a room whose one window, none too clean, looked straight into the blank hill behind the house. Seepage and a residue of winter rainstorms had traced calm yellowed patterns on its walls. He guessed it had once been assigned to someone's hapless, helpless paid companion, who would have marvelled at the thought of its lending shelter to a dying man. In the late afternoon he would return to his bedroom, where, out on the balcony, an angular roof shadow slowly replaced the sun. Barbara unfolded his deck chair on the still burning tiles. He stretched out, opened a book, found the page he wanted, at once closed his eyes. Barbara knelt in a corner, in a triangle of light. She had taken her clothes off, all but a sunhat; bougainvillea grew so thick no one could see. She said, "Would you like me to read to you?" No; he did everything alone, or nearly. He was—always—bathed, shaved, combed, and dressed. His children would not remember him unkempt or dishevelled, though it might not have mattered to them. He did not smell of sweat or sickness or medicine or fear.

When it began to rain, later in the autumn, the children played indoors. Barbara tried to keep them quiet. There was a French school up in the town, but neither Alec nor Barbara knew much about it; and, besides, there was no use settling them in. He heard the children asking for bicycles so they could ride along the motor road, and he heard Barbara saying no, the road was dangerous. She must have changed her mind, for he next heard them discussing the drawbacks and advantages of French bikes. One of the children—James, it was—asked some question about the cost.

"You're not to mention things like that," said Barbara. "You're not to speak of money."

Alec was leaving no money and three children—four, if you counted his wife. Barbara often said she had no use for money, no head for it. "Thank God I'm Irish," she said. "I haven't got rates of interest on the brain." She read Irishness into her nature as an explanation for it, the way some people attributed their gifts and failings to a sign of the zodiac. Anything natively Irish had dissolved long before, leaving only a family custom of Catholicism and another habit, fervent in Barbara's case, of anticlerical passion. Alec supposed she was getting her own back, for a mysterious reason, on ancestors she would not have recognized in Heaven. Her family, the Laceys, had been in Wales for generations. Her brothers considered themselves Welsh.

It was Barbara's three Welsh brothers who had put up the funds for Lou Mas. Houses like this were to be had nearly for the asking, then. They stood moldering at the unfashionable end of the coast, damaged sometimes by casual shellfire, difficult to heat, costly to renovate. What the brothers had seen as valuable in Lou Mas was not the villa, which they had no use for, but the undeveloped seafront around it, for which each of them had a different plan. The eldest brother was a partner in a firm of civil engineers; another managed a resort hotel and had vague thoughts about building one of his own. The youngest, Mike, who was Barbara's favorite, had converted from the R.A.F. to commercial flying. Like Alec, he had been a prisoner of war. The two men had that, but nothing else, in common. Mike was the best travelled of the three. He could see, in place of the pink house with its thick walls and high ceilings, one of the frail, domino-shaped blocks that were starting to rise around the Mediterranean basin, creating a vise of white plaster at the rim of the sea.

Because of United Kingdom income-tax laws, which made it awkward for the Laceys to have holdings abroad, Alec and Barbara had been registered as owners of Lou Mas, with Desmond, the engineer, given power of attorney. This was a manageable operation because Alec was entirely honorable, while Barbara did not know a legal document from the ace of diamonds. So that when the first scouts came round from the local British colony to find out what the Webbs were like and Barbara told them Lou Mas belonged to her family she was speaking the truth. Her visitors murmured that they had been very fond of the Vaughan-Thorpes and had been sorry to see them go—a reference to the previous owners, whose grandparents had built Lou Mas. Barbara did not suppose this to be a snub: she simply wondered why it was that a war out of which her brothers had emerged so splendidly should have left Alec, his sister, and the unknown Vaughan-Thorpes worse off than before.

The scouts reported that Mr. Webb was an invalid, that the children were not going to school, that Mrs. Webb must at one time have been pretty, and that she seemed to be spending a good deal of money, either her husband's or her own. When no improvements were seen in the house, the grounds, or the cottage, it began to be taken for granted that she had been squandering, on trifles, rather more than she had.

Her visitors were mistaken: Barbara never spent more than she had, but only the total of all she could see. What she saw now was a lump of money like a great block of marble, from which she could chip as much as she liked. It had come by way of Alec's sister. Alec's obstinate refusal to die on National Health had meant that his death had somehow to be paid for. Principle was a fine thing, one of Barbara's brother's remarked, but it came high. Alec's earning days were done for. He had come from a long line of medium-rank civil servants who had never owned anything except the cottages to which they had eventually retired, and which their heirs inevitably sold. Money earned, such as there was, disappeared in the sands of their male progeny's education. Girls were expected to get married. Alec's sister, now forty-four, had not done so, though she was no poorer or plainer than most. "I am better off like this," she had told Alec, perhaps once too often. She was untrained, unready, unfitted for any life save that of a woman civilian's in wartime; peace had no use for her, just as the postwar seemed too fast, too hard, and too crowded to allow for Alec. Her only asset was material: a modest, cautiously invested sum of money settled on her by a godparent, the income from which she tried to add to by sewing. Christening robes had been her special joy, but fewer babies were being baptized with pomp, while nylon was gradually replacing the silks and lawns she worked with such care. Nobody wanted the bother of ironing flounces and tucks in a world without servants.

Barbara called her sister-in-law "the mouse." She had small brown eyes; was vegetarian; prayed every night of her life for Alec and for the parents who had not much loved her. "If they would just listen to me," she was in the habit of saying—about Alec and Barbara, for instance. She never complained about her compressed existence, which seemed to her the only competent one at times; at least it was quiet. When Alec told her that he was about to die, and wanted to emigrate, and had been provided with a house but with nothing to run it on, she immediately offered him half her capital. He accepted in the same flat way he had talked about death—out of his driving need, she supposed, or because he still held the old belief that women never need much. She knew she had made an impulsive gesture, perhaps a disastrous one, but she loved Alec and did not want to add to her own grief. She was assured that anything left at the end would be returned enriched and amplified by some sort of nimble investment, but as Alec and his family intended to live on the capital she did not see how this could be done.

Alec knew that his sister had been sacrificed. It was merely another of the lights going out. Detachment had overtaken him even before the journey south. Mind and body floated on any current that chose to bear them.

For the first time in her life Barbara had enough money, and no one to plague her with useless instructions. While Alec slept, or seemed to, she knelt in the last triangle of sun on the balcony reading the spread-out pages of the *Continental Daily Mail*. It had been one thing to have no head for money when there was none to speak of; the present situation called for percipience and wit. Her reading informed her that dollars were still stronger than pounds. (Pounds were the decaying cottage, dollars the Edwardian house.) Alec's background and training made him find the word "dollars" not overnice, perhaps alarming, but Barbara had no class prejudice to hinder her. She had already bought dollars for pounds, at giddy loss, feeling each time she had put it over on banks and nations, on snobs, on the financial correspondent of the *Mail,* on her own clever brothers. (One of the Webbs' neighbors, a retired Army officer, had confided to Alec that he was expecting the Russians to land in the bay below their villas at any time. He intended to die fighting on his doorstep; however, should anything happen to prevent his doing so, he had kept a clutch of dollars tucked in the pocket of an old dressing gown so that he and his mother could buy their way out.)

In Alec's darkened bedroom she combed her hair with his comb. Even if he survived he would have no foothold on the nineteen-fifties. She, Barbara, had been made for her time. This did not mean she wanted to live without him. Writing to one of her brothers, she advised him to open a hotel down here. Servants were cheap—twenty or thirty cents an hour, depending on whether you worked the official or the free-market rate. In this letter her brother heard Barbara's voice, which had stayed high and breathless though she must have been thirty-four. He wondered if this was the sort of prattle poor dying old Alec had to listen to there in the south.

"South" was to Alec a place of the mind. He had not deserted England, as his sad sister thought, but moved into one of its oldest literary legends, the Mediterranean. His part of this legend was called Rivabella. Actually, "Rivebelle" was written on maps and road signs, for the area belonged to France—at least, for the present. It had been tugged between France and Italy so often that it now had a diverse, undefinable character and seemed to be remote from any central authority unless there were elections or wars. At its heart was a town sprawled on the hill behind Lou Mas and above the motor road. Its inhabitants said "Rivabella"; they spoke, among themselves, a Ligurian dialect with some Spanish and Arabic expressions mixed in, though their children went to school and learned French and that they descended from a race with blue eyes. What had remained constant to Rivabella was its poverty, and the groves of ancient olive trees that only the strictest of laws kept the natives from cutting down, and the look and character of the people. Confined by his illness, Alec would never meet more of these than about a dozen; they bore out the expectation set alight by his reading, seeming to him classless and pagan, poetic and wise, imbued with an instinctive understanding of light, darkness, and immortality. Barbara expected them to be cunning and droll, which they were, and to steal from her, which they did, and to love her, which they seemed to. Only the children were made uneasy by these strange new adults, so squat and ill-favored, so quarrelsome and sly, so destructive of nature and pointlessly cruel to animals. But, then, the children had not read much, were unfamiliar with films, and had no legends to guide them.

Barbara climbed up to the town quite often during the first weeks, looking for a doctor for Alec, for a cook and maid, for someone to give lessons to the children. There was nothing much to see except a Baroque church from which everything removable had long been sold to antiquarians, and a crumbling palace along the very dull main street. In one of the palace rooms she was given leave to examine some patches of peach-colored smudge she was told were early Renaissance frescoes. Some guidebooks referred to these, with the result that a number of the new, hardworking breed of postwar traveller panted up a steep road not open to motor traffic only to find that the palace belonged to a cranky French countess who lived alone with her niece and would not let anyone in. (Barbara, interviewing the niece for the post of governess, had been admitted but was kept standing until the countess left the room.) Behind the palace she discovered a town hall with a post office and a school attached, a charming small hospital —where a doctor was obtained for Alec—and a walled graveyard. Only the graveyard was worth exploring; it contained Victorian English poets who had probably died of tuberculosis in the days when an enervating climate was thought to be good for phthisis, and Russian aristocrats who had owned some of the English houses, and Garibaldian adventurers who, like Alec, had never owned a thing. Most of these graves were overgrown and neglected, with the headstones all to one side, and wild grasses grown taller than roses. The more recent dead seemed to be commemorated by marble plaques on a high concrete wall; these she did not examine. What struck her about this place was its splendid view: she could see Lou Mas, and quite far into Italy, and of course over a vast stretch of the sea. How silly of all those rich foreigners to crowd down by the shore, with the crashing noise of the railway. I would have built up here in a minute, she thought.

Alec's new doctor was young and ugly and bit his nails. He spoke good English, and knew most of the British colony, to whose colds, allergies, and perpetually upset stomachs he ministered. British ailments were nursery ailments; what his patients really wanted was to be tucked up next to a nursery fire and fed warm bread-and-milk. He had taken her to be something like himself—an accomplice. "My husband is anything but childish," she said gently. She hesitated before trotting out her usual Irish claim, for she was not quite certain what he meant.

"Rivabella has only two points of cultural interest," he said. "One is the market on the church square. The other is the patron saint, St. Damian. He appears on the church roof, dressed in armor, holding a flaming sword in the air. He does this when someone in Rivabella seems to be in danger." She saw, in the way he looked at her, that she had begun her journey south a wife and mother whose looks were fading, and arrived at a place where her face seemed exotic. Until now she had thought only that a normal English family had taken the train, and the caricature of one had descended. It amounted to the same thing—the eye of the beholder.

From his balcony Alec saw the hill as a rough triangle, with a few straggling farms beneath the gray and umber town (all he could discern was its color) and the apex of graveyard. This, in its chalky whiteness, looked like an Andalusian or a North African village washed up on the wrong part of the coast. It was alien to the lush English gardens and the foreign villas, which tended to pinks, and beiges, and to a deep shade known as Egyptian red. Within those houses was a way of being he sensed and understood, for it was a smaller, paler version of colonial life, with chattering foreign servants who might have been budgerigars, and hot puddings consumed under brilliant sunlight. Rules of speech and regulations for conduct were probably observed, as in the last days of the dissolving Empire. Barbara had told him of one: it was bad form to say "Rivebelle" for "Rivabella," for it showed one hadn't known about the place in its rich old days, or even that Queen Victoria had mentioned "*pretty* little Rivabella" to the Crown Princess of Prussia in one of her affectionate letters.

"All snobs," said Barbara. "Thank God I'm Irish," though there was something she did in a way mind: saying "Rivebelle" had been one of her first mistakes. Another had been hiring a staff without taking advice. She was also suspected of paying twice the going rate, which was not so much an economic blunder as a social affront. "All snobs" was not much in the way of ammunition, but, then, none of the other villas could claim a cook, a maid, a laundress, a gardener, and a governess marching down from Rivabella, all of them loyal, devoted, cheerful, hardworking, and kind.

She wrote to her pilot brother, the one she loved, telling him how self-reliant people seemed to be here, what pride they took in their jobs, how their philosophy was completely alien to the modern British idea of strife and grab. "I would love it if you would come and stay for a while. We have more rooms than we know what to do with. You and I could talk." But no one came. None of them wanted to have to watch poor old Alec dying.

The children would recall later on that their cook had worn a straw hat in the kitchen, so that steam condensing on the ceiling would not drop on her head, and that she wore the same hat to their father's funeral. Barbara would remind them about the food. She had been barely twenty at the beginning of the war, and there were meals for which she had never stopped feeling hungry. Three times a day, now, she sat down to cream and butter and fresh bread, new-laid eggs, jam you could stand a spoon in: breakfasts out of a storybook from before the war. As she preferred looking at food to eating it, it must have been the *idea* of her table spread that restored richness to her skin, lustre to her hair. She had been all cream and gold, once, but war and marriage and Alec's illness and being hard up and some other indefinable disappointment had skimmed and darkened her. And yet she felt shot through with happiness sometimes, or at least by a piercing clue as to what bliss might be. This sensation, which she might have controlled more easily in another climate, became so natural, so insistent, that she feared sometimes that its source might be religious and that she would need to reject—out of principle—the felicity it promised. But no; she was, luckily, too earthbound for such nonsense. She could experience sudden felicity merely seeing her cook arrive with laden baskets, or the gardener crossing the terrace with a crate of flowering plants. (He would bed these out under the olive trees, where they perished rapidly.) Lou Mas at such times seemed to shrink to a toy house she might lift and carry; she would remember what it had been like when the children were babies still, and hers alone.

Carrying Alec's breakfast tray, she came in wearing the white dressing gown that had been his sister's parting gift to her. Her hair, which she now kept thick and loose, was shades lighter than it had been in England. He seemed barely to see her. But, then, everything dazzled him now. She buttered toast for him, and spread it with jam, saying, "Do try it, darling. You will never taste jam like this again." Of course, it thundered with prophecy. Her vision blurred—not because of tears, for she did not cry easily. It was as if a sheet of pure water had come down with an enormous crashing sound, cutting her off from Alec.

Now that winter was here, he moved with the sun instead of away from it. Shuffling to the balcony, he leaned on her shoulder. She covered him with blanket, gave him a book to read, combed his hair. He had all but stopped speaking, though he made an effort for strangers. She thought, What would it be like to be shot dead? Only the lingering question contained in a nightmare could account for this, but her visionary dreams had left her, probably because Alec's fate, and so to some measure her own, had been decided once and for all. Between house and sea the gardener crouched with a trowel in his hand. His work consisted of bedding-out, and his imagination stopped at salvia: the ground beneath the olive trees was dark red with them. She leaned against the warm parapet and thought of what he might see should he look up—herself, in white, with her hair blazing in the sun. But when he lifted his face it was only to wipe sweat from it with the shirt he had taken off. A dream of loss came back: she had been ordered to find new names for refugee children whose names had been forgotten. In real life, she had wanted her children to be called Giles, Nigel, and Samantha, but Alec had interfered. All three had been conceived on his wartime leaves, before he was taken prisoner. The children had her gray eyes, her skin that freckled, her small bones and delicate features (though Molly showed signs of belonging to a darker, sturdier race), but none of them had her richness, her shine. They seemed to her and perhaps to each other thin and dry, like Alec.

Everything Mademoiselle said was useless or repetitive. She explained, " 'Lou Mas' means 'the farm,' " which the children knew. When they looked out the dining-room window she remarked, "You can see Italy." She came early in order to share their breakfast; the aunt she lived with, the aunt with the frescoes, kept all the food in their palace locked up. "What do you take me for?" she sometimes asked them, tragically, of some small thing, such as their not paying intense attention. She was not teaching them much, only some French, and they were picking this up faster now than she could instruct. Her great-grandfather had been a French volunteer against Garibaldi (an Italian bandit, she explained); her grandfather was founder of a nationalist movement; her father had been murdered on the steps of his house at the end of the war. She was afraid of Freemasons, Socialists, Protestants, and Jews, but not of drowning or falling from a height or being attacked by a mad dog. When she discovered that the children had been christened (Alec having considered baptism a rational start to agnostic life), she undertook their religious education, which was not at all what Barbara was paying for.

After lunch, they went upstairs to visit Alec. He lay on his deck chair, tucked into blankets, as pale as clouds. James suddenly wailed out, believing he was singing, "We'll ring all the bells and kill all the Protestants." Silence, then James said, "Are there any left? Any Protestants?"

"I am left, for one," said his father.

"It's a good thing we came down here, then," said the child calmly. "They couldn't get at you."

Mademoiselle said, looking terrified, "It refers to old events in France."

"It wouldn't have mattered." His belief had gone to earth as soon as he had realized that the men he admired were in doubt. His conversation, like his reading, was increasingly simple. He was reading a book about gardening. He held it close to his face. Daylight tired him; it was like an intruder between memory and the eye. He read, "Nerine. Guernsey Lily. Ord. Amaryllidacae. First introduced, 1680." Introduced into England, that meant. "Oleander, 1596. East Indian Rose Bay, 1770. Tamarind Tree, 1633. Chrysanthemum, 1764." So England had flowered, become bedecked, been bedded-out.

The book had been given him by a neighbor. The Webbs not only had people working for them, and delicious nursery food to eat, and a garden running down to the sea, but distinguished people living on either side —Mr. Edmund Cranefield of Villa Osiris to the right, and Mrs. Massie at Casa Scotia on the left. To reach their houses you had to climb thirty steps to the road then descend more stairs on their land. Mr. Cranefield had a lift, which looked like a large crate stood on its side. Within it was a kitchen chair. He sat on the chair and was borne up to the road on an electric rail. No one had ever seen him doing this. When he went to Morocco during the worst of the winter, he had the lift disconnected and covered with rugs, the pond drained and the fish put in tanks, and his two peacocks, who screamed every dawn as if a fox were at them, boarded for a high fee with a private zoo. Casa Scotia belonged to Mrs. Massie, who was lame, wore a tweed cape, never went out without a hat, walked with a stick, and took a good twenty minutes to climb her steps.

Mr. Cranefield was a novelist, Mrs. Massie the author of a whole shelf of gardening books. Mr. Cranefield never spoke of his novels or offered to lend them; he did not even say what their titles were. "You must tell me every one!" Barbara cried, as if she were about to rush out and return with a wheelbarrow full of books by Mr. Cranefield.

He sat upstairs with Alec, and they talked about different things, quite often about the war. Just as Barbara was beginning to imagine Mr. Cranefield did not like her, he invited her to tea. She brought Molly along for protection, but soon saw he was not drawn to women—at least, not in the way she supposed men to be. She wondered then if she should keep Will and James away from him. He showed Barbara and Molly the loggia where he worked on windless mornings; a strong mistral had once blown one hundred and forty pages across three gardens—some were even found in a hedge at Casa Scotia. On a table were oval picture frames holding the likeness of a fair girl and a fair young man. Looking more closely, Barbara saw they were illustrations cut out of magazines. Mr. Cranefield said, "They are the pair I write about. I keep them there so that I never make a mistake."

"Don't they bore you?" said Barbara.

"Look at all they have given me." But the most dispossessed peasant, the filthiest housemaid, the seediest nail-biting doctor in Rivabella had what he was pointing out—the view, the sea. Of course, a wave of the hand cannot take in everything; he probably had more than this in reserve. He turned to Molly and said kindly, "When you are a little older you can do some typing for me," because it was his experience that girls liked doing that—typing for Mr. Cranefield while waiting for someone to marry. Girls were fond of him: he gave sound advice about love affairs, could read the future in handwriting. Molly knew nothing about him, then, but she would recall later on how Mr. Cranefield, who had invented women deep-sea divers, women test pilots, could not imagine—in his innocence, in his manhood—anything more thrilling to offer a girl when he met one than "You can type."

Barbara broke in, laughing: "She is only eleven."

This was true, but it seemed to Molly a terrible thing to say.

Mrs. Massie was not shy about bringing *her* books around. She gave several to Alec, among them *Flora's Gardening Encyclopaedia*, seventeenth edition, considered her masterpiece. All her books were signed "Flora," though it was not her name. She said about Mr. Cranefield, "Edmund is a great, pampered child. Spoiled by adoring women all his life. Not by me." She sat straight on the straightest chair, her hands clasped on her stick. "I do my own typing. My own gardening, too," though she did say to James and Will, "You can help in the garden for pocket money, if you like."

In the spring, the second Elizabeth was crowned. Barbara ordered a television set from a shop in Nice. It was the first the children had seen. Two men carried it with difficulty down the steps from the road, and soon became tired of lifting it from room to room while Barbara decided where she wanted it. She finally chose a room they kept shut usually; it had a raised platform at one end and until the war had been the site of amateur theatricals. The men set the box down on the stage and began fiddling with antennae and power points, while the children ran about arranging rows of chairs. One of the men said they might not have a perfect view of the Queen the next day, the day of the Coronation, because of Alps standing in the way. The children sat down and stared at the screen. Horizontal lightning streaked across its face. The men described implosion, which had killed any number of persons all over the world. They said that should the socket and plug begin to smoke, Barbara was to make a dash for the meter box and pull out the appropriate fuse.

"The appropriate fuse?" said Barbara. The children minded sometimes about the way she laughed at everything.

When the men had gone, they trooped upstairs to tell Alec about the Alps and implosion. He was resting in preparation for tomorrow's ceremony, which he would attend. It was clear to Molly that her father would not be able to get up and run if there was an accident. Kneeling on the warm tiles (this was in June) she pressed her face to his hand. Presently he slipped the hand away to turn a page. He was reading more of the book Mrs. Massie had pounded out on her 1929 Underwood—four carbons, single-spaced, no corrections, every page typed clean: "Brussels Sprouts—see Brassica." Brassica must be English, Alec thought. That was why he withdrew his hand—to see about Brassica. What use was his hand to Molly or her anxiety to him now? Why hold her? Why draw her into his pale world? She was a difficult, dull, clumsy child, something of a moper when her brothers teased her but sulky and tough when it came to Barbara. He had watched Barbara, goaded by Molly, lose control of herself and slap the girl's face, and he had heard Molly's pitiful credo: "You can't hurt me. My vaccination hurt worse than that." "Hurt more," Alec in silence had amended. "Hurt me *more* than that."

He found Brassica. It was Borecole, Broccoli, Cabbage, Cauliflower. His eyes slid over the rest of what it was until, "Native to Europe—BRITAIN," which Mrs. Massie had typed in capital letters during the war, with a rug around her legs in unheated Casa Scotia, waiting for the Italians or the Germans or the French to take her away to internment in a lorry. He was closer in temper to Mrs. Massie than to anyone else except his sister, though he had given up priorities. His blood was white (that was how he saw it), and his lungs and heart were bleached, too, and starting to disintegrate like snowflakes. He was a pale giant, a drained Gulliver, cast up on the beach, open territory for invaders. (Barbara and Will were sharing a paperback about flying saucers, whose occupants had built Stonehenge.) Alec's intrepid immigrants, his microscopic colonial settlers had taken over. He had been easy to subdue, being courteous by nature, diffident by choice. He had been a civil servant then a soldier; had expected the best, relied on good behavior; had taken to prison camp thin books about Calabria and Greece; had been evasive, secretive, brave, unscrupulous only sometimes— had been English and middle class, in short.

That night Alec had what the doctor called "a crisis" and Alec termed "a bad patch." There was no question of his coming down for Coronation the next day. The children thought of taking the television set up to him, but it was too heavy, and Molly burst into tears thinking of implosion and accidents and Alec trapped. In the end the Queen was crowned in the little theatre, as Barbara had planned, in the presence of Barbara and the children, Mr. Cranefield and Mrs. Massie, the doctor from Rivabella, a neighbor called Major Lamprey and his old mother, Mrs. Massie's housekeeper, Barbara's cook and two of her grandchildren, and Mademoiselle. One after the other these people turned their heads to look at Alec, gasping in the doorway, holding on to the frame. His hair was carefully combed and parted low on one side, like Mr. Cranefield's, and he had dressed completely, though he had a scarf around his neck instead of a tie. He was the last, the very last, of a kind. Not British but English. Not Christian so much as Anglican. Not Anglican but giving the benefit of the doubt. His children would never feel what he had felt, suffer what he had suffered, relinquish what he had done without so that this sacrament could take place. The new Queen's voice flowed easily over the Alps—thin, bored, ironed flat by the weight of what she had to remember—and came as far as Alec, to whom she owed her crown. He did not think that, precisely, but what had pulled him to his feet, made him stand panting for life in the doorway, would not occur to James or Will or Molly—not then, or ever.

He watched the rest of it from a chair. His breathing bothered the others: it made their own seem too quiet. He ought to have died that night. It would have made a reasonable ending. This was not a question of getting rid of Alec (no one wanted that) but of being able to say later, "He got up and dressed to see the Coronation." However, he went on living.

A nurse came every day, the doctor almost as often. He talked quietly to Barbara in the garden. A remission as long as this was unknown to him; it smacked of miracles. When Barbara would not hear of that, he said that Alec was holding on through willpower. But Alec was not holding on. His invaders had pushed him off the beach and into a boat. The stream was white and the shoreline, too. Everything was white, and he moved peacefully. He had glimpses of his destination—a room where the hems of thin curtains swept back and forth on a bare floor. His vision gave him green bronze doors sometimes; he supposed they were part of the same room.

He could see his children, but only barely. He had guessed what the boys might become—one a rebel, one turned inward. The girl was a question mark. She was stoic and sentimental, indifferent sometimes to pleasure and pain. Whatever she was or could be or might be, he had left her behind. The boys placed a row of bricks down the middle of the room they shared. In the large house they fought for space. They were restless and noisy, untutored and bored. "I'll always have a packet of love from my children," Barbara had said to a man once (not Alec).

At the start of their second winter one of the Laceys came down to investigate. This was Ron, the hotelkeeper. He had dark hair and was thin and pale and walked softly. When he understood that what Barbara had written about servants and dollars was true, he asked to see the accounts. There were none. He talked to Barbara without raising his voice; that day she let everyone working for her go with the exception of the cook, whom Ron had said she was to keep because of Alec. He seemed to feel he was in a position of trust, for he ordered her—there was no other word for it—to place the children at once in the Rivabella town school: Lou Mas was costing the Lacey brothers enough in local taxes—they might as well feel they were getting something back. He called his sister "Bab" and Alec "Al." The children's parents suddenly seemed to them strangers.

When Ron left, Barbara marched the children up to Rivabella and made them look at the church. They had seen it, but she made them look again. She held the mistaken belief that religion was taught in French state schools, and she wanted to arm them. The children knew by now that what their mother called "France" was not really France down here but a set of rules, a code for doing things, such as how to recite the multiplication table or label a wine. Instead of the northern saints she remembered, with their sorrowful preaching, there was a southern St. Damian holding up a blazing sword. Any number of persons had seen him; Mademoiselle had, more than once.

"I want you to understand what superstition is," said Barbara, in clear, carrying English. "Superstition is what is wrong with Uncle Ron. He believes what he can't see, and what he sees he can't believe in. Now, imagine intelligent people saying they've seen this—this apparition. This St. George, or whatever." The church had two pink towers, one bearing a cross and the other a weather vane. St. Damian usually hovered between them. "In armor," said Barbara.

To all three children occurred "Why not?" Protect me, prayed the girl. Vanquish, said Will. Lead, ordered the youngest, seeing only himself in command. He looked around the square and said to his mother, "Could we go, soon, please? Because people are looking."

That winter Molly grew breasts; she thought them enormous, though each could have been contained easily in a small teacup. Her brothers teased her. She went about with her arms crossed. She was tall for her age, and up in the town there was always some man staring. Elderly neighbors pressed her close. Major Lamprey, calling on Alec, kissed her on the mouth. He smelled of gin and pipe smoke. She scrubbed her teeth for minutes afterward. When she began to menstruate, Barbara said, "Now, Molly, you are to keep away from men," as if she weren't trying to.

The boys took their bicycles and went anywhere they wanted. In the evening they wheeled round and round the church square. Above them were swallows, on the edge of the square men and boys. Both were starting to speak better French than English, and James spoke dialect better than French. Molly disliked going up to Rivabella, unless she had to. She helped Barbara make the beds and wash the dishes and she did her homework and then very often went over to talk to Mr. Cranefield. She discovered, by chance, that he had another name—E. C. Arden. As E. C. Arden he was the author of a series of thumbed, comfortable novels (it was Mrs. Massie who lent Molly these), one of which, called *Belinda at Sea*, was Molly's favorite book of any kind. It was about a girl who joined the crew of a submarine, disguised as a naval rating, and kept her identity a secret all the way to Hong Kong. In the end, she married the submarine commander, who apparently had loved her all along. Molly read *Belinda at Sea* three or four times without ever mentioning to Mr. Cranefield she knew he was E. C. Arden. She thought it was a matter of deep privacy and that it was up to him to speak of it first. She did, however, ask what he thought of the saint on the church roof, using the name Barbara had, which was St. George.

"What," said Mr. Cranefield. "That Ethiopian?"

The girl looked frightened—not of Ethiopians, certainly, but of confusion as to person, the adult world of muddle. Even Mr. Cranefield was *also* E. C. Arden, creator of Belinda.

Mr. Cranefield explained, kindly, that up at Rivabella they had made a patron saint out of a mixture of St. Damian, who was an intellectual, and St. Michael, who was not, and probably a local pagan deity as well. St. Michael accounted for the sword, the pagan for the fire. Reliable witnesses had seen the result, though none of these witnesses were British. "We aren't awfully good at seeing saints," he said. "Though we do have an eye for ghosts."

Another thing still troubled Molly, but it was not a matter she could mention: she did not know what to do about her bosom—whether to try to hold it up in some way or, on the contrary, bind it flat. She had been granted, by the mistake of a door's swinging wide, an upsetting glimpse of Mrs. Massie changing out of a bathing suit, and she had been worried about the future shape of her own body ever since. She pored over reproductions of statues and paintings in books belonging to Mr. Cranefield. The Eves and Venuses represented were not reassuring—they often seemed to be made of India rubber. There was no one she could ask. Barbara was too dangerous; the mention of a subject such as this always made her go too far and say things Molly found unpleasant.

She did remark to both Mrs. Massie and Mr. Cranefield that she hated the Rivabella school. She said, "I would give anything to be sent home to England, but I can't leave my father."

After a long conversation with Mrs. Massie, Mr. Cranefield agreed to speak to Alec. Interfering with other people was not his way, but Molly struck him as being pathetic. Something told him that Molly was not useful leverage with either parent and so he mentioned Will first: Will would soon be fourteen, too old for the school at Rivabella. Unless the Webb children were enrolled, and quickly, in good French establishments—say, in lycées at Nice—they would become unfit for anything save menial work in a foreign language they could not speak in an educated way. Of course, the ideal solution would be England, if Alec felt he could manage that.

Alec listened, sitting not quite straight in his chair, wearing a dressing gown, his back to a window. He found all light intolerable now. Several times he lifted his hand as if he were trying to see through it. No one knew why Alec made these odd gestures; some people thought he had gone slightly mad because death was too long in coming. He parted his lips and whispered, "French school . . . If you would look after it," and then, "I would be grateful."

Mr. Cranefield dropped his voice too, as if the gray of the room called for hush. He asked if Alec had thought of appointing a guardian for them. The hand Alec seemed to want transparent waved back and forth, stiffly, like a shut ivory fan.

All that Barbara said to Mr. Cranefield was "Good idea," once he had assured her French high schools were not priest-ridden.

"It might have occurred to *her* to have done something about it," said Mrs. Massie, when this was repeated.

"Things do occur to Barbara," said Mr. Cranefield. "But she doesn't herself get the drift of them."

The only disturbing part of the new arrangement was that the children had been assigned to separate establishments, whose schedules did not coincide; this meant they would not necessarily travel in the same bus. Molly had shot up as tall as Will now. Her hair was dark and curled all over her head. Her bones and her hands and feet were going to be larger, stronger, than her mother's and brothers'. She looked, already, considerably older than her age. She was obstinately innocent, turning her face away when Barbara, for her own good, tried to tell her something about men.

Barbara imagined her willful, ignorant daughter being enticed, trapped, molested, impregnated, and disgraced. *And* ending up wondering how it happened, Barbara thought. She saw Molly's seducer, brutish and dull. I'd get him by the throat, she said to herself. She imagined the man's strong neck and her own small hands, her brittle bird-bones. She said, "You are never, ever to speak to a stranger on the bus. You're not to get in a car with a man—not even if you know him."

"I don't know any man with a car."

"You could be waiting for a bus on a dark afternoon," said Barbara. "A car might pull up. Would you like a lift? No, you must answer. No and no and no. It is different for the boys. There are the two of them. They could put up a fight."

"Nobody bothers boys," said Molly.

Barbara drew breath but for once in her life said nothing.

Alec's remission was no longer just miraculous—it had become unreasonable. Barbara's oldest brother hinted that Alec might be better off in England, cared for on National Health: they were paying unholy taxes for just such a privilege. Barbara replied that Alec had no use for England, where the Labour government had sapped everyone's self-reliance. He believed in having exactly the amount of suffering you could pay for, no less and no more. She knew this theory did not hold water, because the Laceys and Alec's own sister had done the paying. It was too late now; they should have thought a bit sooner; and Alec was too ravaged to make a new move.

The car that, inevitably, pulled up to a bus stop in Nice was driven by a Mr. Wilkinson. He had just taken Major Lamprey and the Major's old mother to the airport. He rolled his window down and called to Molly, through pouring rain, "I say, aren't you from Lou Mas?"

If he sounded like a foreigner's Englishman, like a man in a British joke, it was probably because he had said so many British-sounding lines in films set on the Riviera. Eric Wilkinson was the chap with the strong blue eyes and ginger mustache, never younger than thirty-four, never as much as forty, who flashed on for a second, just long enough to show there was an Englishman in the room. He could handle a uniform, a dinner jacket, tails, a monocle, a cigarette holder, a swagger stick, a polo mallet, could open a cigarette case without looking like a gigolo, could say without being an ass about it, "Bless my soul, wasn't that the little Maharani?" or even, "Come along, old boy—fair play with Monica, now!" Foreigners meeting him often said, "That is what the British used to be like, when they were still all right, when the Riviera was still fit to live in." But the British who knew him were apt to glaze over: "You mean Wilkinson?" Mrs. Massie and Mr. Crane-field said, "Well, Wilkinson, what are you up to now?" There was no harm to him: his one-line roles did not support him, but he could do anything, even cook. He used his car as a private taxi, driving people to airports, meeting them when they came off cruise ships. He was not a chauffeur, never said "sir," and at the same time kept a certain distance, was not shy about money changing hands—no fake pride, no petit-bourgeois demand for a slipped envelope. Good-natured. Navy blazer. Summer whites in August. Wore a tie that carried a message. What did it stand for? A third-rate school? A disgraced, disbanded regiment? A club raided by the police? No one knew. Perhaps it was the symbol of something new alto-gether. "Still playing in those films of yours, Wilkinson?" He would flash on and off—British gent at roulette, British Army officer, British diplomat, British political agent, British anything. Spoke his line, fitted his monocle, pressed the catch on his cigarette case. His ease with other people was genuine, his financial predicament unfeigned. He had never been married, and had no children that he knew of.

"By Jove, it's nippy," said Wilkinson, when Molly had settled beside him, her books on her lap.

What made her do this—accept a lift from a murderer of school-girls? First, she had seen him somewhere safe once—at Mr. Cranefield's. Also, she was wet through, and chilled to the heart. Barbara kept refusing or neglecting or forgetting to buy her the things she needed: a lined rain-coat, a jersey the right size. (The boys were wearing hand-me-down clothes from England now, but no one Barbara knew of seemed to have a daugh-ter.) The sleeves of her old jacket were so short that she put her hands in her pockets, so that Mr. Wilkinson would not despise her. He talked to Molly as he did to everyone, as if they were of an age, informing her that Major Lam-prey and his mother were flying to Malta to look at a house. A number of people were getting ready to leave the South of France now; it had become so seedy and expensive, and all the wrong people were starting to move in.

"What kind of wrong people?" She sat tense beside him until he said, "Why, like Eric Wilkinson, I should think," and she laughed when his own laugh said she was meant to. He was nice to her; even later, when she thought she had reason to hate him, she would remember that Wilkinson had been nice. He drove beyond his destination—a block of flats that he waved at in passing and that Molly in a confused way supposed he owned. They stopped in the road behind Lou Mas; she thanked him fervently, and then, struck with something, sat staring at him: "Mr. Wilkinson," she said. "Please—I am not allowed to be in cars with men alone. In case someone happened to see us, would you mind just coming and meeting my mother? Just so she can see who you are?"

"God bless my soul," said Wilkinson, sincerely.

Once, Alec had believed that Barbara was not frightened by any-thing, and that this absence of fear was her principal weakness. It was true that she had begun drifting out of her old life now, as calmly as Alec drifted away from life altogether. Her mock phrase for each additional Lou Mas catastrophe had become "the usual daily developments." The usual devel-opments over seven rainy days had been the departure of the cook, who took with her all she could lay her hands on, and a French social-security fine that had come down hard on the remains of her marble block of money, reducing it to pebbles and dust. She had never filled out employer's forms for the people she had hired, because she had not known she was supposed to and none of them had suggested it; for a number of reasons having to do with government offices and tax files, none of them had wanted even this modest income to be registered anywhere. As it turned out, the gardener had also been receiving unemployment benefits, which, unfairly, had increased the amount of the fine Barbara had to pay. Rivabella turned out to be just as grim and bossy as England—worse, even, for it kept up a cam-ouflage of wine and sunshine and olive trees and of amiable southern idiots who, if sacked, thought nothing of informing on one.

She sat at the dining-room table, wearing around her shoulders a red cardigan Molly had outgrown. On the table were the Sunday papers Alec's sister continued to send faithfully from England, and Alec's lunch tray, exactly as she had taken it up to him except that everything on it was now cold. She glanced up and saw the two of them enter—one stricken and guilty-looking, the other male, confident, smiling. The recognition that leaped between Barbara and Wilkinson was the last thing that Wilkinson in his right mind should have wanted, and absolutely everything Barbara now desired and craved. Neither of them heard Molly saying, "Mummy, this is Mr. Wilkinson. Mr. Wilkinson wants to tell you how he came to drive me home."

It happened at last that Alec had to be taken to the Rivabella hospital, where the local poor went when it was not feasible to let them die at home. Eric Wilkinson, new family friend, drove his car as far as it could go along a winding track, after which they placed Alec on a stretcher; and Wilkinson, Mr. Cranefield, Will, and the doctor carried him the rest of the way. A soft April rain was falling, from which they protected Alec as they could. In the rain the doctor wept unnoticed. The others were silent and absorbed. The hospital stood near the graveyard—shamefully near, Wilkinson finally remarked, to Mr. Cranefield. Will could see the cemetery from his father's new window, though to do so he had to lean out, as he'd imagined passengers doing and having their heads cut off in the train game long ago. A concession was made to Alec's status as owner of a large villa, and he was given a private room. It was not a real sickroom but the place where the staff went to eat and drink when they took time off. They cleared away the plates and empty wine bottles and swept up most of the crumbs and wheeled a bed in.

The building was small for a hospital, large for a house. It had been the winter home of a Moscow family, none of whom had come back after 1917. Alec lay flat and still. Under a drift of soot on the ceiling he could make out a wreath of nasturtiums and a bluebird with a ribbon in its beak.

At the window, Will said to Mr. Cranefield, "We can see Lou Mas from here, and even your peacocks."

Mr. Cranefield fretted, "They shouldn't be in the rain."

Alec's neighbors came to visit. Mrs. Massie, not caring who heard her (one of the children did), said to someone she met on the hospital staircase, "Alec is a gentleman and always will be, but Barbara . . . Barbara." She took a rise of the curved marble stairs at a time. "If the boys were girls they'd be sluts. As it is, they are ruffians. Their old cook saw one of them stoning a cat to death. And now there is Wilkinson. Wilkinson." She moved on alone, repeating his name.

Everyone was saying "Wilkinson" now. Along with "Wilkinson" they said "Barbara." You would think that having been married to one man who was leaving her with nothing, leaving her dependent on family charity, she would have looked around, been more careful, picked a reliable kind of person. "A foreigner, say," said Major Lamprey's mother, who had not cared for Malta. Italians love children, even other people's. She might have chosen—you know—one of the cheerful sort, with a clean shirt and a clean white handkerchief, proprietor of a linen shop. The shop would have kept Barbara out of mischief.

No one could blame Wilkinson, who had his reasons. Also, he had said all those British-sounding lines in films, which in a way made him all right. Barbara had probably said she was Irish once too often. "What can you expect?" said Mrs. Massie. "Think how they were in the war. They keep order when there is someone to bully them. Otherwise . . ." The worst she had to say about Wilkinson was that he was preparing to flash on as the colonel of a regiment in a film about desert warfare; it had been made in the hilly country up behind Monte Carlo.

"Not a grain of sand up there," said Major Lamprey. He said he wondered what foreigners thought they meant by "desert."

"A colonel!" said Mrs. Massie.

"Why not?" said Mr. Cranefield.

"They must think he looks it," said Major Lamprey. "Gets a fiver a day, I'm told, and an extra fiver when he speaks his line. He says, 'Don't underestimate Rommel.' For a fiver I'd say it," though he would rather have died.

The conversation veered to Wilkinson's favor. Wilkinson was merry; told irresistible stories about directors, unmalicious ones about film stars; repeated comic anecdotes concerning underlings who addressed him as "Guv." "I wonder who they can be?" said Mrs. Massie. "It takes a Wilkinson to find them." Mr. Cranefield was more indulgent; he had to be. A sardonic turn of mind would have been resented by E. C. Arden's readers. The blond-headed pair on his desk stood for a world of triumphant love, with which his readers felt easy kinship. The fair couple, though competent in any domain, whether restoring a toppling kingdom or taming a tiger, lived on the same plane as all human creatures except England's enemies. They raised the level of existence—raised it, and flattened it.

Mr. Cranefield—as is often and incorrectly said of children—lived in a world of his own, too, in which he kept everyone's identity clear. He did not confuse St. Damian with an Ethiopian, or Wilkinson with Raffles, or Barbara with a slut. This was partly out of the habit of neatness and partly because he could not make up his mind to live openly in the world he wanted, which was a homosexual one. He said about Wilkinson and Barbara and the blazing scandal at Lou Mas, "I am sure there is no harm in it. Barbara has too much to manage alone, and it is probably better for the children to have a man about the place."

When Wilkinson was not travelling, he stayed at Lou Mas. Until now his base had been a flat he'd shared with a friend who was a lawyer and who was also frequently away. Wilkinson left most of his luggage behind; there was barely enough of his presence to fill a room. For a reason no one understood Barbara had changed everyone's room around: she and Molly slept where Alec had been, the boys moved to Barbara's room, and Wilkinson was given Molly's bed. It seemed a small bed for so tall a man.

Molly had always slept alone, until now. Some nights, when Wilkinson was sleeping in her old room, she would waken just before dawn and find that her mother had disappeared. Her feeling at the sight of the empty bed was one of panic. She would get up, too, and go in to Will and shake him, saying, "She's disappeared."

"No, she hasn't. She's with Wilkinson." Nevertheless, he would rise and stumble, still nearly sleeping, down the passage—Alec's son, descendant of civil servants, off on a mission.

Barbara slept with her back against Wilkinson's chest. Outside, Mr. Cranefield's peacocks greeted first light by screaming murder. Years from now, Will would hear the first stirrings of dawn and dream of assassinations. Wilkinson never moved. Had he shown he was awake, he might have felt obliged to say a suitable one-liner—something like "I say, old chap, you are a bit of a trial, you know."

Will's mother picked up the nightgown and robe that lay white on the floor, pulled them on, flung her warm hair back, tied her sash—all without haste. In the passage, the door shut on the quiet Wilkinson, she said tenderly, "Were you worried?"

"Molly was."

Casual with her sons, she was modest before her daughter. Changing to a clean nightdress, she said, "Turn the other way." Turning, Molly saw her mother, white and gold, in the depths of Alec's mirror. Barbara had her arms raised, revealing the profile of a breast with at its tip the palest wash of rose, paler than the palest pink flower. (Like a Fragonard, Barbara had been told, like a Boucher—not by Alec.) What Molly felt now was immense relief. It was not the fate of every girl to turn into India rubber. But in no other way did she wish to resemble her mother.

Like the residue left by winter rains, awareness of Barbara and Wilkinson seeped through the house. There was a damp chill about it that crept to the bone. One of the children, Will, perceived it as torment. Because of the mother defiled, the source of all such knowledge became polluted, probably forever. The boys withdrew from Barbara, who had let the weather in. James imagined ways of killing Wilkinson, though he drew the line at killing Barbara. He did not want her dead, but different. The mother he wanted did not stand in public squares pointing crazily up to invisible saints, or begin sleeping in one bed and end up in another.

Barbara felt that they were leaving her; she put the blame on Molly, who had the makings of a prude, and who, at worst, might turn out to be something like Alec's sister. Barbara said to Molly, "I had three children before I was twenty-three, and I was alone, and there were all the air-raids. The life I've tried to give you and the boys has been so different, so happy, so free." Molly folded her arms, looked down at her shoes. Her height, her grave expression, her new figure gave her a bogus air of maturity: she was only thirteen, and she felt like a pony flicked by a crop. Barbara tried to draw near: "My closest friend is my own daughter," she wanted to be able to say. "I never do a thing without talking it over with Molly." So she would have said, laughing, her bright head against Molly's darker hair, if only Molly had given half an inch.

"What a cold creature you are," Barbara said, sadly. "You live in an ice palace. There is so little happiness in life unless you let it come near. I always at least had an *idea* about being happy." The girl's face stayed shut and locked. All that could cross it now was disappointment.

One night when Molly woke Will, he said, "I don't care where she is." Molly went back to bed. Fetching Barbara had become a habit. She was better off in her room alone.

When they stopped coming to claim her, Barbara perceived it as mortification. She gave up on Molly, for the moment, and turned to the boys, sat curled on the foot of their bed, sipping wine, telling stories, offering to share her cigarette, though James was still twelve. James said, "He told us it was dangerous to smoke in bed. People have died that way." "He" meant Alec. Was this all James would remember? That he had warned about smoking in bed?

James, who was embarrassed by this attempt of hers at making them equals, thought she had an odd smell, like a cat. To Will, at another kind of remove, she stank of folly. They stared at her, as if measuring everything she still had to mean in their lives. This expression she read as she could. Love for Wilkinson had blotted out the last of her dreams and erased her gift of second sight. She said unhappily to Wilkinson, "My children are prigs. But, then, they are only half mine."

Mademoiselle, whom the children now called by her name—Geneviève—still came to Lou Mas. Nobody paid her, but she corrected the children's French, which no longer needed correcting, and tried to help with their homework, which amounted to interference. They had always in some way spared her; only James, her favorite, sometimes said, "No, I'd rather work alone." She knew now that the Webbs were poor, which increased her affection: their descent to low water equalled her own. Sometimes she brought a packet of biscuits for their tea, which was a dull affair now the cook had gone. They ate the biscuits straight from the paper wrapping: nobody wanted to wash an extra plate. Wilkinson, playing at British something, asked about her aunt. He said "Madame la Comtesse." When he had gone, she cautioned the children not to say that but simply "your aunt." But as Geneviève's aunt did not receive foreigners, save for a few such as Mrs. Massie, they had no reason to ask how she was. When Geneviève realized from something said that Wilkinson more or less lived at Lou Mas, she stopped coming to see them. The Webbs had no further connection with Rivabella then except for their link with the hospital, where Alec still lay quietly, still alive.

Barbara went up every day. She asked the doctor, "Shouldn't he be having blood transfusions—something of that kind?" She had never been in a hospital except to be born and to have her children. She was remembering films she had seen, bottles dripping liquids, needles taped to the crook of an arm, nursing sisters wheeling oxygen tanks down white halls.

The doctor reminded her that this was Rivabella—a small town where half the population lived without employment. He had been so sympathetic at first, so slow to present a bill. She could not understand what had changed him; but she was hopeless at reading faces now. She could scarcely read her children's.

She bent down to Alec, so near that her eyes would have seemed enormous had he been paying attention. She told him the name of the scent she was wearing; it reminded her and perhaps Alec, too, of jasmine. Eric had brought it back from a dinner at Monte Carlo, given to promote this very perfume. He was often invited to these things, where he represented the best sort of Britishness. "Eric is being the greatest help," she said to Alec, who might have been listening. She added, for it had to be said some time, "Eric has very kindly offered to stay at Lou Mas."

Mr. Cranefield and Mrs. Massie continued to plod up the hill, she with increasing difficulty. They brought Alec what they thought he needed. But he had no addictions, no cravings, no use for anything now but his destination. The children were sent up evenings. They never knew what to say or what he could hear. They talked as if they were still eleven or twelve, when Alec had stopped seeing them grow.

To Mr. Cranefield they looked like imitations of English children—loud, humorless, dutiful, clear. "James couldn't come with us tonight," said Molly. "He was quite ill, for some reason. He brought his dinner up." All three spoke the high, thin English of expatriate children who, unknowingly, mimic their mothers. The light bulb hanging crooked left Alec's face in shadow. When the children had kissed Alec and departed, Mr. Cranefield could hear them taking the hospital stairs headlong, at a gallop. The children were young and alive, and Alec was forty-something and nearly always sleeping. Unequal chances, Mr. Cranefield thought. They can't really beat their breasts about it. When Mrs. Massie was present, she never failed to say, "Your father is tired," though nobody knew if Alec was tired or not.

The neighbors pitied the children. Meaning only kindness, Mr. Cranefield reminded Molly that one day she would type, Mrs. Massie said something more about helping in the garden. That was how everyone saw them now—grubbing, digging, lending a hand. They had become Wilkinson's second-hand kin but without his panache, his ease in adversity. They were Alec's offspring: stiff. Humiliated, they overheard and garnered for memory: "We've asked Wilkinson to come over and cook up a curry. He's hours in the kitchen, but I must say it's worth every penny." "We might get Wilkinson to drive us to Rome. He doesn't charge all that much, and he's such good company." Always Wilkinson, never Eric, though that was what

Barbara had called him from their first meeting. To the children he was, and remained, "Mr. Wilkinson," friend of both parents, occasional guest in the house.

The rains of their third southern spring were still driving hard against the villa when Barbara's engineer brother wrote to say they were letting Lou Mas. Everything dripped wet as she stood near a window, with bougainvillea soaked and wild-looking on one side of the pane and steam forming on the other, to read this letter. The new tenants were a family of planters who had been forced to leave Malaya; it had a connection with political events, but Barbara's life was so full now that she never looked at the papers. They would be coming there in June, which gave Barbara plenty of time to find another home. He—her brother—had thought of giving her the Lou Mas cottage, but he wondered if it would suit her, inasmuch as it lacked electric light, running water, an indoor lavatory, most of its windows, and part of its roof. This was not to say it could not be fixed up for the Webbs in the future, when Lou Mas had started paying for itself. Half the rent obtained would be turned over to Barbara. She would have to look hard, he said, before finding brothers who were so considerate of a married sister. She and the children were not likely to suffer from the change, which might even turn out to their moral advantage. Barbara supposed this meant that Desmond—the richest, the best-educated, the most easily flabbergasted of her brothers—was still mulling over the description of Lou Mas Ron must have taken back.

With Wilkinson helping, the Webbs moved to the far side of the hospital, on a north-facing slope, away from the sea. Here the houses were tall and thin with narrow windows, set in gardens of raked gravel. Their neighbors included the mayor, the more prosperous shopkeepers, and the coach of the local football team. Barbara was enchanted to find industrial activity she had not suspected—a thriving ceramics factory that produced figurines of monks whose heads were mustard pots, dogs holding thermometers in their paws, and the patron saint of Rivabella wearing armor of pink, orange, mauve, or white. These were purchased by tourists who had trudged up to the town in the hope of seeing early Renaissance frescoes.

Barbara had never missed a day with Alec, not even the day of the move. She held his limp hand and told him stories. When he was not stunned by drugs, or too far lost in his past, he seemed to be listening. Sometimes he pressed her fingers. He seldom spoke more than a word at a time. Barbara described to him the pleasures of moving, and how pretty the houses were on the north side, with their gardens growing gnomes and shells and tinted bottles. Why make fun of such people, she asked his still face. They probably knew, by instinct, how to get the best out of life. She meant every word, for she was profoundly in love and knew that Wilkinson would never leave her except for a greater claim. She combed Alec's hair and bathed him; Wilkinson came whenever he could to shave Alec and cut his nails and help Barbara change the bedsheets; for it was not the custom of the hospital staff to do any of this.

Sometimes Alec whispered, "Diana," who might have been either his sister or Mrs. Massie. Barbara tried to remember her old prophetic dreams, from that time when, as compensation for absence of passion, she had been granted second sight. In none had she ever seen herself bending over a dying man, listening to him call her by another woman's name.

They lived, now, in four dark rooms stuffed with furniture, some of it useful. Upstairs resided the widow of the founder of the ceramics factory. She had been bought out at a loss at the end of the war, and disapproved of the new line of production, especially the monks. She never interfered, never asked questions—simply came down once a month to collect her rent, which was required in cash. She did tell the children that she had never seen the inside of an English villa, but did not seem to think her exclusion was a slight; she took her bearings from a very small span of the French middle-class compass.

Barbara and Wilkinson made jokes about the French widow-lady, but the children did not. To replace their lopped English roots they had grown the sensitive antennae essential to wanderers. They could have drawn the social staircase of Rivabella on a blackboard, and knew how low a step, now, had been assigned to them. Barbara would not have cared. Wherever she stood now seemed to suit her. On her way home from the hospital she saw two men, foreigners, stop and stare and exchange remarks about her. She could not understand the language they spoke, but she saw they had been struck by her beauty. One of them seemed to be asking the other, "Who can she be?" In their new home she took the only bedroom—an imposing matrimonial chamber. When Wilkinson was in residence he shared it as a matter of course. The boys slept on a pull-out sofa in the dining room, and Molly had a couch in a glassed-in verandah. The verandah contained their landlady's rubber plants, which Molly scrupulously tended. The boys had stopped quarrelling. They would never argue or ever say much to each other again. Alec's children seemed to have been collected under one roof by chance, like strays, or refugees. Their narrow faces, their gray eyes, their thinness and dryness, were similar, but not alike; a stranger would not necessarily have known they were of the same father and mother. The boys still wore second-hand clothes sent from England; this was their only connection with English life.

On market days Molly often saw their old housemaid or the laundress. They asked for news of Alec, which made Molly feel cold and shy. She was dressed very like them now, in a cotton frock and roped-soled shoes from a market stall. "Style is all you need to bring it off," Barbara had assured her, but she had none, at least not that kind. It was Molly who chose what the family would eat, who looked at prices and kept accounts and counted her change. Barbara was entirely busy with Alec at the hospital, and with Wilkinson at home. With love, she had lost her craving for nursery breakfasts. She sat at table smoking, watching Wilkinson telling stories. When Wilkinson was there, he did much of the cooking. Molly was grateful for that.

The new people at Lou Mas had everyone's favor. If there had been times when the neighbors had wondered how Barbara and Alec could possibly have met, the Malayan planter and his jolly wife were an old novel known by heart. They told about jungle terrorists, and what the British ought to be doing, and they described the owner of Lou Mas—a Welshman who was planning to go into politics. Knowing Barbara to be Irish, no one could place the Welshman. The story started up that Barbara's family were bankrupt and had sold Lou Mas to a Welsh war profiteer.

Mrs. Massie presented the new people with *Flora's Gardening Ency-clopaedia.* "It is by way of being a classic," she said. "Seventeen editions. I do all my typing myself."

"Ah, well, poor Barbara," everyone said now. What could you expect? Luckily for her, she had Wilkinson. Wilkinson's star was rising. "Don't underestimate Rommel" had been said to some effect—there was a mention in the *Sunday Telegraph.* "Wilkinson goes everywhere. He's invited to everything at Monte Carlo. He must positively live on lobster salad." "Good for old Wilkinson. Why shouldn't he?" Wilkinson had had a bad war, had been a prisoner somewhere.

Who imagined that story, Mr. Cranefield wondered. Some were mixing up Wilkinson with the dying Alec, others seemed to think Alec was already dead. By August it had become established that Wilkinson had been tortured by the Japanese and had spent the years since trying to leave the memory behind. He never mentioned what he'd been through, which was to his credit. Barbara and three kids must have been the last thing he wanted, but that was how it was with Wilkinson—too kind for his own good, all too ready to lend a hand, to solve a problem. Perhaps, rising, he would pull the Webbs with him. Have you seen that girl hanging about in the market? You can't tell her from the butcher's child.

From Alec's bedside Barbara wrote a long letter to her favorite brother, the pilot, Mike. She told about Alec, "sleeping so peacefully as I write," and described the bunch of daisies Molly had put in a jug on the windowsill, and how well Will had done in his finals ("He will be the family intellectual, a second Alec"), and finally she came round to the matter of Wilkinson: "You probably saw the rave notice in the *Telegraph,* but you had no way of knowing of course it was someone I knew. Well, here is the whole story. Please, Mike, do keep it to yourself for the moment, you know how Ron takes things sometimes." Meeting Eric had confirmed her belief there was something in the universe more reasonable than God—at any rate more logical. Eric had taken a good look at the Lou Mas cottage and thought something might be done with it after all. "You will adore Eric," she promised. "He is marvellous with the children and so kind to Alec," which was true.

"Are you awake, love?" She moistened a piece of cotton with mineral water from a bottle that stood on the floor (Alec had no table) and wet his lips with it, then took his hand, so light it seemed hollow, and held it in her own, telling him quietly about the Lou Mas cottage, where he would occupy a pleasant room overlooking the sea. He flexed his fingers; she bent close: "Yes, dear; what is it, dear?" For the first time since she'd known him he said, "Mother." She waited; but no, that was all. She saw herself on his balcony at Lou Mas in her white dressing gown, her hair in the sun, saw what the gardener would have been struck by if only he had looked up. She said to herself, "I gave Alec three beautiful children. That is what he is thanking me for now."

Her favorite brother had been away from England when her letter came, so that it was late in September when he answered to call her a bitch, a trollop, a crook, and a fool. He was taking up the question of her gigolo boyfriend with the others. They had been supporting Alec's family for three years. If she thought they intended to take on her lover (this written above a word scratched out); and here the letter ended. She went white, as her children did, easily. She said to Wilkinson, "Come and talk in the car, where we can be quiet," for they were seldom alone.

She let him finish reading, then said, in a voice that he had never heard before but that did not seem to surprise him—"I grew up blacking my brothers' boots. Alec was the first man who ever held a door open for me."

He said, "Your brothers all did well," without irony, meaning there was that much to admire.

"Oh," she said, "If you are comparing their chances with Alec's, if that's what you mean—the start Alec had. Well, poor Alec. Yes, a better start. I often thought, Well, there it is with him, that's the very trouble—a start too good."

This exchange, this double row of cards faceup, seemed all they intended to reveal. They instantly sat differently, she straighter, he more relaxed.

Wilkinson said, "Which one of them actually owns Lou Mas?"

"Equal shares, I think. Though Desmond has power of attorney and makes all the decisions. Alec and I *own* Lou Mas, but only legally. They put it in our name because we were emigrating. It made it easier for them, with all the taxes. We had three years, and not a penny in rent."

Wilkinson said, in a kind of anguish, "Oh, God bless my soul."

It was Wilkinson's English lawyer friend in Monte Carlo who drew up the papers with which Alec signed his share of Lou Mas over to Barbara and Alec and Barbara revoked her brother's power of attorney. Alec, his obedient hand around a pen and the hand firmly held in Barbara's, may have known what he was doing but not why. The documents were then put in the lawyer's safe to await Alec's death, which occurred not long after.

The doctor, who had sat all night at the bedside, turning Alec's head so that he would not strangle vomiting (for that was not the way he wished him to die), heard him breathing deeply and ever more deeply and then no longer. Alec's eyes were closed, but the doctor pressed the lids with his fingers. Believing in his own and perhaps Alec's damnation, he stood for a long time at the window while the roof and towers of the church became clear and flushed with rose; then the red rim of the sun emerged, and turned yellow, and it was as good as day.

There was only one nurse in the hospital, and a midwife on another floor. Summoning both, he told them to spread a rubber sheet under Alec, and wash him, and put clean linen on the bed.

At that time, in that part of France, scarcely anyone had a telephone. The doctor walked down the slope on the far side of Rivabella and presented himself unshaven to Barbara in her nightdress to say that Alec was dead. She dressed and came at once; there was no one yet in the streets to see her and to ask who she was. Eric followed, bringing the clothes in which Alec would be buried. All he could recall of his prayers, though he would not have said them around Barbara, were the first words of the Collect: "Almighty God, unto whom all hearts be open, all desires known, and from whom no secrets are hid."

Barbara had a new friend—her French widowed landlady. It was she who arranged to have part of Barbara's wardrobe dyed black within twenty-four hours, who lent her a black hat and gloves and a long crêpe veil. Barbara let the veil down over her face. Her friend, whose veil was tied round her hat and floated behind her, took Barbara by the arm, and they walked to the cemetery and stood side by side. The Webbs' former servants were there, and the doctor, and the local British colony. Some of the British thought the other woman in black must be Barbara's Irish mother: only the Irish poor or the Royal Family ever wore mourning of that kind.

The graveyard was so cramped and small, so crowded with dead from the time of Garibaldi and before, that no one else could be buried. The coffins of the recent dead were stored in cells in a thick concrete wall. The cells were then sealed, and a marble plaque affixed in lieu of a tombstone. Alec had to be lifted to shoulder level, which took the strength of several persons—the doctor, Mr. Cranefield, Barbara's brothers, and Alec's young sons. (Wilkinson would have helped, but he had already wrenched his shoulder quite badly carrying the coffin down the hospital steps.) Molly thrust her way into this crowd of male mourners. She said to her mother, "Not you—you never loved him."

God knows who might have heard that, Barbara thought.

Actually, no one had, except for Mrs. Massie. Believing it to be true, she dismissed it from memory. She was composing her own obituary: "Two generations of gardeners owed their . . ." "Two generations of readers owed their gardens . . ."

"Our Father," Alec's sister said, hoping no one would notice and mistake her for a fraud. Nor did she wish to have a scrap of consideration removed from Barbara, whose hour this was. Her own loss was beyond remedy, and so not worth a mention. There was no service—nothing but whispering and silence. To his sister, it was as if Alec had been left, stranded and alone, in a train stalled between stations. She had not seen him since the day he left England, and had refused to look at him dead. Barbara was aware of Diana, the mouse, praying like a sewing machine somewhere behind her. She clutched the arm of the older widow and thought, I know, I know, but she can get a job, can't she? I was working when I met Alec, wasn't I? But what Diana Webb meant by "work" was the fine stitching her own mother had done to fill time, not for a living. In Diana's hotel room was a box containing the most exquisite and impractical child's bonnet and coat made from some of the white silk Alec had sent her from India, before the war. Perhaps a luxury shop in Monte Carlo or one of Barbara's wealthy neighbors would be interested. Perhaps there was an Anglican clergyman with a prosperous parish. She opened her eyes and saw that absolutely no one in the cemetery looked like Alec—not even his sons.

The two boys seemed strange, even to each other, in their dark, new suits. The word "father" had slipped out of their grasp just now. A marble plaque on which their father's name was misspelled stood propped against the wall. The boys looked at it helplessly.

Is that all? People began wondering. What happens now?

Barbara turned away from the wall and, still holding the arm of her friend, led the mourners out past the gates.

It was I who knew what he wanted, the doctor believed. He had told me long before. Asked me to promise, though I refused. I heard his last words. The doctor kept telling himself this. "I heard his last words"— though Alec had not said anything, had merely breathed, then stopped.

"Her father was a late Victorian poet of some distinction," Mrs. Massie's obituary went on.

Will, who was fifteen, was no longer a child, did not look like Alec, spoke up in that high-pitched English of his: "Death is empty without God." Now where did that come from? Had he heard it? Read it? Was he performing? No one knew. Later, he would swear that at that moment a vocation had come to light, though it must have been born with him—bud within the bud, mind within the mind. I will buy back your death, he would become convinced he had said to Alec. Shall enrich it; shall refuse the southern glare, the southern void. I shall pay for your solitude, your humiliation. Shall demand for myself a stronger life, a firmer death. He thought, later, that he had said all this, but he had said and thought only five words.

As they shuffled out, all made very uncomfortable by Will, Mrs. Massie leaned half on her stick and half on James, observing, "You were such a little boy when I saw you for the first time at Lou Mas." Because his response was silence, she supposed he was waiting to hear more. "You three must stick together now. The Three Musketeers." But they were already apart.

Major Lamprey found himself walking beside the youngest of the Laceys. He told Mike what he told everyone now—why he had not moved to Malta. It was because he did not trust the Maltese. "Not that one can

trust anyone here," he said. "Even the major belongs to an anarchist movement, I've been told. Whatever happens, I intend to die fighting on my own
doorstep."

The party was filing down a steep incline. "You will want to be with
your family," Mrs. Massie said, releasing James and leaning half her weight
on Mr. Cranefield instead. They picked up with no trouble a conversation
dropped the day before. It was about how Mr. Cranefield—rather, his
other self, E. C. Arden—was likely to fare in the second half of the nineteen-fifties: "It is a question of your not being too modern and yet not slipping back," Mrs. Massie said. "I never have to worry. Gardens don't
change."

"I am not worried about new ideas," he said. "Because there are
none. But words, now. 'Permissive.' "

"What's that?"

"It was in the *Observer* last Sunday. I suppose it means something.
Still. One musn't. One can't. There are limits."

Barbara met the mayor coming the other way, too late, carrying a
wreath with a purple ribbon on which was written, in gold, "From the
Municipality—Sincere Respects." Waiting for delivery of the wreath had
made him tardy. "For a man who never went out, Alec made quite an
impression," Mrs. Massie remarked.

"His funeral was an attraction," said Mr. Cranefield.

"Can one call that a funeral?" She was still thinking about her own.

Mike Lacey caught up to his sister. They had once been very close.
As soon as she saw him she stood motionless, bringing the line behind her to
a halt. He said he knew this was not the time or place, but he had to let her
know she was not to worry. She would always have a roof over her head.
They felt responsible for Alec's children. There were vague plans for fixing
up the cottage. They would talk about it later on.

"Ah, Mike," she said. "That is so kind of you." Using both hands
she lifted the veil so that he could see her clear gray eyes.

The procession wound past the hospital and came to the church
square. Mr. Cranefield had arranged a small after-funeral party, as a favor
to Barbara, who had no real home. Some were coming and some were not;
the latter now began to say goodbye. Geneviève, whose face was like a pink
sponge because she had been crying so hard, flung herself at James, who let
her embrace him. Over his governess's dark shoulder he saw the faces of
people who had given him second-hand clothes, thus (he believed) laying
waste to his life. He smashed their faces to particles, left the particles dancing in the air like midges until they dissolved without a sound. Wait, he was
thinking. Wait, wait.

Mr. Cranefield wondered if Molly was going to become her
mother's hostage, her moral bail—if Barbara would hang on to her to show
that Alec's progeny approved of her. He remembered Molly's small, anxious face, and how worried she had been about St. George. "You will grow
up, you know," he said, which was an odd thing to say, since she was quite

tall. They walked down the path Wilkinson had not been able to climb in his car. She stared at him. "I mean, when you grow up you will be free." She shook her head. She knew better than that now, at fourteen: there was no freedom except to cease to love. She would love her brothers when they had stopped thinking much about her: women's fidelity. This would not keep her from fighting them, inch by inch, over money, property, remnants of the past: women's insecurity. She would hound them and pester them about Alec's grave, and Barbara's old age, and where they were all to be buried: women's sense of order. They would by then be another James, an alien Will, a different Molly.

Mr. Cranefield's attention slipped from Molly to Alec to the funeral, to the extinction of one sort of Englishman and the emergence of another. Most people looked on Wilkinson as a prewar survival, what with his I say's and By Jove's, but he was really an English mutation, a new man, wearing the old protective coloring. Alec would have understood his language, probably, but not the person behind it. A landscape containing two male figures came into high relief in Mr. Cranefield's private image of the world, as if he had been lent trick spectacles. He allowed the vision to fade. Better to stick to the blond pair on his desk; so far they had never let him down. I am not impulsive, or arrogant, he explained to himself. No one would believe the truth about Wilkinson even if he were to describe it. I shall not insist, he decided, or try to have the last word. I am not that kind of fool. He breathed slowly, as one does when mortal danger has been averted.

The mourners attending Mr. Cranefield's party reached the motor road and began to straggle across: it was a point of honor for members of the British colony to pay absolutely no attention to cars. The two widows had fallen back, either so that Barbara could make an entrance, or because the older woman believed it would not be dignified for her to exhibit haste. A strong west wind flattened the black dresses against their breasts and lifted their thick veils.

How will he hear me, Molly wondered. You could speak to someone in a normal grave, for earth is porous and seems to be life, of a kind. But how to speak across marble? Even if she were to place her hands flat on the marble slab, it would not absorb a fraction of human warmth. She had to tell him what she had done—how it was she, Molly, who had led the intruder home, let him in, causing Alec, always courteous, to remove himself first to the hospital, then farther on. Disaster, the usual daily development, had to have a beginning. She would go back to the cemetery, alone, and say it, whether or not he could hear. The disaster began with two sentences: "Mummy, this is Mr. Wilkinson. Mr. Wilkinson wants to tell you how he happened to drive me home."

Barbara descended the steps to Mr. Cranefield's arm in arm with her new friend, who was for the first time about to see the inside of an English house. "Look at that," said the older widow. One of the peacocks had taken shelter from the wind in Mr. Cranefield's electric lift. A minute earlier Alec's sister had noticed, too, and had thought something that seemed irrefutable: no power on earth would ever induce her to eat a peacock.

Who is to say I never loved Alec, said Barbara, who loved Wilkinson. He was high-handed, yes, laying down the law as long as he was able, but he was always polite. Of course I loved him. I still do. He will have to be buried properly, where we can plant something—white roses. The mayor told me that every once in a while they turn one of the Russians out, to make room. There must be a waiting list. We could put Alec's name on it. Alec gave me three children. Eric gave me Lou Mas.

Entering Mr. Cranefield's, she removed her dark veil and hat and revealed her lovely head, like the sun rising. Because the wind had started blowing leaves and sand, Mr. Cranefield's party had to be moved indoors from the loggia. This change occasioned some confusion, in which Barbara did not take part; neither did Wilkinson, whose wrenched shoulder was making him feel ill. She noticed her children helping, carrying plates of small sandwiches and silver buckets of ice. She approved of this; they were obviously well brought up. The funeral had left Mr. Cranefield's guests feeling hungry and thirsty and rather lonely, anxious to hold on to a glass and to talk to someone. Presently their voices rose, overlapped, and created something like a thick woven fabric of blurred design, which Alec's sister (who was not used to large social gatherings) likened to a flying carpet. It was now, with Molly covertly watching her, that Barbara began in the most natural way in the world to live happily ever after. There was nothing willful about this: she was simply borne in a single direction, though she did keep seeing for a time her black glove on her widowed friend's black sleeve.

Escorting lame Mrs. Massie to a sofa, Mr. Cranefield said they might as well look on the bright side. (He was still speaking about the second half of the nineteen-fifties.) Wilkinson, sitting down because he felt sick, and thinking the remark was intended for him, assured Mr. Cranefield, truthfully, that he had never looked anywhere else. It then happened that every person in the room, at the same moment, spoke and thought of something other than Alec. This lapse, this inattention, lasting no longer than was needed to say "No, thank you" or "Oh, really?" or "Yes, I see," was enough to create the dark gap marking the end of Alec's span. He ceased to be, and it made absolutely no difference after that whether or not he was forgotten.

1979

We sometimes seem to know the people in a novella like Mavis Gallant's "The Remission" better than we know the people in our own family. In Aspects of the Novel *E. M. Forster explains this strange phenomenon, beginning with a summary of the views of the French literary critic Alain.*

"People in a novel can be understood completely": E. M. Forster

[Alain] asserts that each human being has two sides, appropriate to history and fiction. All that is observable in a man—that is to say his actions and such of his spiritual existence as can be deduced from his actions—falls into the domain of history. But his romanceful or romantic side (sa partie romanesque ou romantique) includes "the pure passions, that is to say the dreams, joys, sorrows and self-communings which politeness or shame prevent him from mentioning"; and to express this side of human nature is one of the chief functions of the novel. "What is fictitious in a novel is not so much the story as the method by which thought develops into action, a method which never occurs in daily life. . . . History, with its emphasis on external causes, is dominated by the notion of fatality, whereas there is no fatality in the novel; there, everything is founded on human nature, and the dominating feeling is of an existence where everything is intentional, even passions and crimes, even misery."

This is perhaps a roundabout way of saying what every British schoolboy knew, that the historian records whereas the novelist must create. Still, it is a profitable roundabout, for it brings out the fundamental difference between people in daily life and people in books. In daily life we never understand each other, neither complete clairvoyance nor complete confessional exists. We know each other approximately, by external signs, and these serve well enough as a basis for society and even for intimacy. But people in a novel can be understood completely by the reader, if the novelist wishes; their inner as well as their outer life can be exposed. And this is why they often seem more definite than characters in history, or even our own friends; we have been told all about them that can be told; even if they are imperfect or unreal they do not contain any secrets, whereas our friends do and must, mutual secrecy being one of the conditions of life upon this globe.

NADINE GORDIMER

(b. 1923)

THE CATCH

His thin strong bony legs passed by at eye level every morning as they lay, stranded on the hard smooth sand. Washed up thankfully out of the swirl and buffet of the city, they were happy to lie there, but because they were accustomed to telling the time by their nerves' response to the different tensions of the city—children crying in flats, lorries going heavily, and bicycles jangling for early morning, skid of tyres, sound of frying, and the human insect noise of thousands talking and walking and eating at midday —the tensionless shore keyed only to the tide gave them a sense of timelessness that, however much they rejoiced mentally, troubled their habit-impressed bodies with a lack of pressure. So the sound of his feet, thudding nearer over the sand, passing their heads with the deep sound of a man breathing in the heat above the rolled-up, faded trousers, passing away up the beach and shrinking into the figure of an Indian fisherman, began to be something to be waited for. His coming and going divided the morning into three; the short early time before he passed, the time when he was actually passing, and the largish chunk of warm midday that followed when he had gone.

After a few days, he began to say good morning, and looking up they found his face, a long head with a shining dark dome surrounded with curly hair given a stronger liveliness by the sharp coarse strokes of grey hairs, the beautiful curved nose handed out so impartially to Indians, dark eyes slightly bloodshot from the sun, a wide muscular mouth smiling on strong uneven teeth that projected slightly like the good useful teeth of an animal. But it was by his legs they would have known him; the dark, dull-skinned feet with the few black hairs on the big toe, the long hard shaft of the shin tightly covered with smooth shining skin, the pull of the tendons at his ankle like the taut ropes that control the sails of a ship.

They idly watched him go, envious of his fisherman's life not because they could ever really have lived it themselves, but because it had about it the frame of their holiday freedom. They looked at him with the curious respect people feel for one who has put a little space between himself and the rest of the world. 'It's a good life,' said the young man, the words not quite hitting the nail of this respect. 'I can just see *you* . . .,' said the girl, smiling. She saw him in his blue creased suit, carrying a bottle of gin wrapped in brown paper, a packet of bananas, and the evening paper.

'He's got a nice open face,' said the young man. 'He wouldn't have a face like that if he worked as a waiter at the hotel.'

But when they spoke to him one morning when he was fishing along the surf for chad right in front of them, they found that he like themselves was only on holiday from a more complicated pattern of life. He worked five or six miles away at the sugar refinery, and this was his annual two weeks. He spent it fishing, he told them, because that was what he liked to do with his Sundays. He grinned his strong smile, lifting his chin out to sea as he swung his spoon glittering into the coming wave. They stood by like children, tugging one another back when he cast his line, closing in to peer with their hands behind their backs when he pulled in the flat silver fish and pushed the heads into the sand. They asked him questions, and he answered with a kind of open pleasure, as if discounting his position as a man of skill, a performer before an audience, out of friendliness. And they questioned animatedly, feeling the knowledge that he too was on holiday was a sudden intimacy between them, like the discovery between strangers that they share a friend. The fact that he was an Indian troubled them hardly at all. They almost forgot he *was* an Indian. And this too, though they did not know it, produced a lightening of the heart, a desire to do conversational frolics with a free tongue the way one stretches and kicks up one's legs in the sun after confinement in a close dark room.

'Why not get the camera?' said the girl, beginning to help with the fish as they were brought in. And the young man went away over the sand and came back adjusting the complications of his gadget with the seriousness of the amateur. He knelt in the wet sand that gave beneath his weight with a wet grinding, trying to catch the moment of skill in the fisherman's face. The girl watched quietly, biting her lip for the still second when the camera blinked. Aware but not in the least self-conscious of the fact that he was the subject, the Indian went on with his fishing, now and then parenthetically smiling his long-toothed smile.

The tendrils of their friendship were drawn in sharply for a moment when, putting his catch into a sack, he inquired naturally, 'Would you like to buy one for lunch, sir?' Down on his haunches with a springy strand of hair blowing back and forth over his ear, he could not know what a swift recoil closed back through the air over his head. He wanted to sell something. Disappointment as much as a satisfied dig in the ribs from opportunist prejudice stiffened them momentarily. Of course, he was not in quite the same position as themselves, after all. They shifted their attitude slightly.

'Well, we live at the hotel, you see,' said the girl.

He tied the mouth of the sack and looked up with a laugh. 'Of course!' he smiled, shaking his head. 'You couldn't cook it.' His lack of embarrassment immediately made things easy.

'Do you ever sell fish to the hotel?' asked the young man. 'We must keep a look out for it.'

'No—no, not really,' said the Indian. 'I don't sell much of my fish —mostly we eat it up there,' he lifted his eyebrows to the hills, brilliant with cane. 'It's only sometimes I sell it.'

The girl felt the dismay of having mistaken a privilege for an imposition. 'Oh well,' she smiled at him charmingly, 'that's a pity. Anyway, I suppose the hotel has to be sure of a regular supply.'

'That's right,' he said. 'I only fish in my spare time.'

He was gone, firmly up the beach, his strong feet making clefts in the sand like the muscular claws of a big strong-legged bird.

'You'll see the pictures in a few days,' shouted the girl. He stopped and turned with a grin. 'That's nothing,' he said. 'Wait till I catch something big. Perhaps soon I'll get something worth taking.'

He was 'their Indian'. When they went home they might remember the holiday by him as you might remember a particular holiday as the one when you used to play with a spaniel on the beach every day. It would be, of course, a nameless spaniel, an ownerless spaniel, an entertaining creature existing nowhere in your life outside that holiday, yet bound with absolute intimacy within that holiday itself. And, as an animal becomes more human every day, so every day the quality of their talk with the Indian had to change; the simple question-and-answer relation that goes with the celluloid pop of a ping-pong ball and does so well for all inferiors, foreigners and children became suddenly a toy (the Indian was grown-up and might smile at it). They did not know his name, and now, although they might have asked the first day and got away with it, it was suddenly impossible, because he didn't ask them theirs. So their you's and he's and I's took on the positiveness of names, and yet seemed to deepen their sense of communication by the fact that they introduced none of the objectivity that names must always bring. He spoke to them quite a lot about Johannesburg, to which he assumed they must belong, as that was his generalization of city life, and he knew, sympathetically, that they were city people. And although they didn't live there, but somewhere near on a smaller pattern, they answered as if they did. They also talked a little of his life; or rather of the processes of the sugar refinery from which his life depended. They found it fascinating.

'If I were working, I'd try and arrange for you to come and see it,' he said, pausing, with his familiar taking his own time, and then looking directly smiling at them, his head tilted a little, the proud, almost rueful way one looks at two attractive children. They responded to his mature pleasure in them with a diffusion of warm youth that exuded from their skin as sweat is released at the touch of fear. 'What a fascinating person he is!' they would say to one another, curious.

But mostly they talked about fishing, the sea, and the particular stretch of coast on which they were living. The Indian knew the sea—at home the couple would have said he 'loved' it—and from the look of it he could say whether the water would be hot or cold, safe or nursing an evil grievance of currents, evenly rolling or sucking at the land in a fierce backwash. He knew, as magically to them as a diviner feeling the pull of water beneath the ground, where the fish would be when the wind blew from the east, when it didn't blow at all, and when clouds covered in from the hills to the horizon. He stood on the slippery rocks with them and saw as they did, a great plain of heaving water, empty and unreadable as infinity; but *he* saw a hard greedy life going on down in there, shining plump bodies gaping swiftly close together through the blind green, tentacles like dark hands feeling over the deep rocks. And he would say, coming past them in his salt-stiff old trousers that seemed to put to shame clothes meekly washed in soap and tap-water, 'Over there at the far rocks this morning.'

They saw him most days; but always only in the morning. By afternoon they had had enough of the beach, and wanted to play golf on the closely green course that mapped inland through the man-high cane as though a barber had run a pair of clippers through a fine head of hair, or to sit reading old hotel magazines on the porch whose windows were so bleared with salt air that looking through them was like seeing with the opaque eyes of an old man. The beach was hot and far away; one day after lunch when a man came up from the sand and said as he passed their chairs, 'There's someone looking for you down there. An Indian's caught a huge salmon and he says you've promised to photograph it for him,'—they sat back and looked at one another with a kind of lazy exasperation. They felt weak and unwilling, defeating interest.

'Go on,' she said. 'You must go.'

'It had to be right after lunch,' he grumbled, smiling.

'Oh go on,' she insisted, head tilted. She herself did not move, but remained sitting back with her chin dropped to her chest, while he fetched the camera and went jogging off down the steep path through the bush. She pictured the salmon. She had never seen a salmon: it would be pink and powerfully agile; how big? She could not imagine.

A child came racing up from the beach, all gasps. 'Your husband says,' saying it word for word, 'he says you must come down right away and you must bring the film with you. It's in the little dressing-table drawer under his handkerchiefs.' She swung out of her chair as if she had been ready to go. The small boy ran before her all the way down to the beach, skidding on the stony path. Her husband was waving incoherently from the sand, urgent and excited as a waving flag. Not understanding, she began to hurry too.

'Like this!' he was shouting. 'Like this! Never seen anything like it! It must weigh eighty pounds—' his hands sized out a great hunk of air.

'But where?' she cried impatiently, not wanting to be told, but to see.

'It's right up the beach. He's gone to fetch it. I'd forgotten the film was finished, so when I got there, it was no use. I had to come back, and he said he'd lug it along here.' Yet he hadn't been able to leave the beach to get the film himself; he wanted to be there to show the fish to anyone who came along; he couldn't have borne to have someone see it without him, who had seen it first.

At last the Indian came round the paw of the bay, a tiny black stick-shape detected moving alive along the beached waterline of black drift-sticks, and as he drew nearer he took on a shape, and then, more distinctly, the shape divided, another shape detached itself from the first, and there he was—a man hurrying heavily with a huge fish slung from his shoulder to his heels. 'O-o-h!' cried the girl, knuckle of her first finger caught between her teeth. The Indian's path wavered, as if he staggered under the weight, and his forearms and hands, gripping the mouth of the fish, were bent stiff as knives against his chest. Long strands of grey curly hair blew over from the back of his head along his bright high forehead, that held the sun in a concentric blur of light on its domed prominence.

'Go and help him,' the girl said to her husband, shaming him. He was standing laughing proudly, like a spectator watching the winner come in at a race. He was startled he hadn't gone himself: 'Shall I?' he said, already going.

They staggered up with the fish between them, panting heavily, and dropped the dead weight of the great creature with a scramble and thud upon the sand. It was as if they had rescued someone from the sea. They stood back that they might feel the relief of their burden, and the land might receive the body. But what a beautiful creature lay there! Through the powdering of sand, mother-of-pearl shone up. A great round glass eye looked out.

'Oh, get the sand off it!' laughed the girl. 'Let's see it properly.'

Exhausted as he was, he belonged to the fish, and so immediately the Indian dragged it by the tail down to the rill of the water's edge, and they cupped water over it with their hands. Water cleared it like a cloth wiping a film from a diamond; out shone the magnificent fish, stiff and handsome in its mail of scales, glittering a thousand opals of colour, set with two brilliant deep eyes all hard clear beauty and not marred by the capability of expression which might have made a reproach of the creature's death; a king from another world, big enough to shoulder a man out of the way; dead, captured, astonishing.

The child came up and put his forefinger on its eye. He wrinkled his nose, smiling and pulling a face, shoulders rising. 'It can't see!' he said joyously. The girl tried it; smooth, firm, resilient eye; like a butterfly wing bright under glass.

They all stood, looking down at the fish, that moved very slightly in the eddy of sand as the thin water spread out softly round its body and then drew gently back. People made for them across the sand. Some came down from the hotel; the piccanin caddies left the golf course. Interest spread like a net, drawing in the few, scattered queer fish of the tiny resort, who avoided one another in a gesture of jealous privacy. They came to stand and stare, prodding a tentative toe at the real fish, scooped out of his sea. The men tried to lift it, making terse suggestions about its weight. A hundred, seventy, sixty-five they said with assurance. Nobody really knew. It was a wonderful fish. The Indian, wishing to take his praise modestly, busied himself with practical details, explaining with serious charm, as if he were quoting a book or someone else's experience, how such a fish was landed, and how rarely it was to be caught on that part of the coast. He kept his face averted, down over the fish, like a man fighting tears before strangers.

'Will it bite? Will it bite?' cried the children, putting their hands inside its rigid white-lipped mouth and shrieking. 'Now that's enough,' said a mother.

'Sometimes there's a lovely stone, here,' the Indian shuffled nearer on his haunches, not touching but indicating with his brown finger a place just above the snout. He twisted his head to the girl. 'If I find it in this one, I'll bring it for you. It makes a lovely ring.' He was smiling to her.

'I want a picture taken with the fish,' she said determinedly, feeling the sun very hot on her head.

Someone had to stand behind her, holding it up. It was exactly as tall as she was; the others pointed with admiration. She smiled prettily, not looking at the fish. Then the important pictures were to be taken: the Indian and his fish.

'Just a minute,' he said, surprisingly, and taking a comb out of his pocket, carefully smoothed back his hair under his guiding hand. He lifted the fish by the gills with a squelch out of the wet sand, and some pictures were taken. 'Like this?' he kept saying anxiously, as he was directed by the young man to stand this way or that.

He stood tense, as if he felt oppressed by the invisible presence of some long-forgotten backdrop and palmstand. 'Smile!' demanded the man and the girl together, anxiously. And the sight of them, so concerned for his picture, released him to smile what was inside him, a strong, wide smile of pure achievement, that gathered up the unequal components of his face —his slim fine nose, his big ugly horse-teeth, his black crinkled-up eyes, and scribbled boldly a brave moment of whole man.

After the pictures had been taken, the peak of interest had been touched; the spectators' attention, quick to rise to a phenomenon, tended to sink back to its level of ordinary, more dependable interests. Wonderment at the fish could not be sustained in its purely specific projection; the remarks became more general and led to hearsay stories of other catches, other unusual experiences. As for the Indian, he had neglected his fish for his audience long enough. No matter how it might differ as an experience, as a fish it did not differ from other fish. He worried about it being in the full hot sun, and dragged it a little deeper into the sea so that the wavelets might flow over it. The mothers began to think that the sun was too hot for their children, and straggled away with them. Others followed, talking about the fish, shading the backs of their necks with their hands. 'Half past two,' said someone. The sea glittered with broken mirrors of hurtful light. 'What do you think you'd get for it?' asked the young man, slowly fitting his camera into its case.

'I'll get about two-pound-ten.' The Indian was standing with his hands on hips, looking down at the fish as if sizing it up.

So he *was* going to sell it! 'As much as that?' said the girl in surprise. With a slow, deliberate movement that showed that the sizing up had been a matter of weight rather than possible ⸱   he tried carrying the fish under his arm. But his whole body ben⸱   o its weight. He let it slither to the sand

'Are you going to try the hotel?' she asked; she expected something from the taste of this fish, a flavour of sentiment.

He smiled, understanding her. 'No,' he said indulgently, 'I might. But I don't think they'd take it. I'll try somewhere else. *They* might want it.' His words took in vaguely the deserted beach, the one or two tiny holiday cottages. 'But where else?' she insisted. It irritated her although she smiled, this habit of other races of slipping out of one's questioning, giving vague but adamant assurances of sureties which were supposed to be hidden but that one knew perfectly well did not exist at all. 'Well, there's the boarding-house at Bailey's River—the lady there knows me. She often likes to take my fish.'

Bailey's River was the next tiny place, about a mile away over the sands. 'Well, I envy them their eating!' said the girl, giving him her praise again. She had taken a few steps back over the sand, ready to go; she held out her hand to draw her husband away. 'When will I see the picture?' the Indian stayed them eagerly. 'Soon, soon, soon!' they laughed. And they left him, kneeling beside his fish and laughing with them.

'I don't know how he's going to manage to carry that great thing all the way to Bailey's,' said the young man. He was steering his wife along with his hand on her little nape. 'It's only a mile!' she said. 'Ye-es! But—?' 'Oh, they're strong. They're used to it,' she said, shaking her feet free of the sand as they reached the path.

When they got back to the hotel, there was a surprise for them. As though the dam of their quiet withdrawal had been fuller than they thought, fuller than they could withstand, they found themselves toppling over into their old stream again, that might run on pointlessly and busy as the brook for ever and ever. Three friends from home up-country were there, come on an unexpected holiday to a farm a mile or two inland. They had come to look them up, as they would no doubt every day of the remainder of the holiday; and there would be tennis, and picnic parties, and evenings when they would laugh on the veranda round a table spiked with bottles and glasses. And so they were swept off from something too quiet and sure to beckon them back, looking behind them for the beckon, but already twitching to the old familiar tune. The visitors were shown the hotel bedroom, and walked down the broken stone steps to the first tee of the little golf course. They were voracious with the need to make use of everything they saw; bouncing on the beds, hanging out of the window, stamping on the tee, and assuring that they'd be there with their clubs in the morning.

After a few rounds of drinks at the close of the afternoon, the young man and his wife suddenly felt certain that they had had a very dead time indeed up till now, and the unquiet gnaw of the need to 'make the best'

—of time, life, holidays, anything—was gleefully hatched to feed on them again. When someone suggested that they all go into Durban for dinner and a cinema, they were excited. 'All in our car!' the girl cried. 'Let's all go together.'

The women had to fly off to the bedroom to prepare themselves to meet the city, and while the men waited for them, talking quieter and closer on the veranda, the sun went down behind the cane, the pale calm sea thinned into the horizon and turned long straight shoals of light foam to glass on the sand, pocked, farther up, by shadow. When they drove off up the dusty road between the trees they were steeped in the first dark. White stones stood out; as they came to the dip in the road where the stream ran beneath, they saw someone sitting on the boulder that marked the place, and as they slowed and bumped through, the figure moved slightly with a start checked before it could arrest their attention. They were talking. 'What was that?' said one of the women, without much interest. 'What?' said the young man, braking in reflex. 'It's just an old Indian with a sack or something,' someone else broke off to say. The wife, in the front seat, turned:

'Les!' she cried. 'It's him, with the fish!'

The husband had pulled up the car, skidded a little sideways on the road, its two shafts of light staring up among the trees. He sat looking at his wife in consternation. 'But I wonder what's the matter?' he said. 'I don't know!' she shrugged, in a rising tone. 'Who is it?' cried someone from the back.

'An Indian fisherman. We've spoken to him on the beach. He caught a huge salmon today.'

'We know him well,' said the husband; and then to her: 'I'd better back and see what's wrong.' She looked down at her handbag. 'It's going to make us awfully late, if you hang about,' she said. 'I won't hang about!' He reversed in a long jerk, annoyed with her or the Indian, he did not know. He got out, banging the door behind him. They all twisted, trying to see through the rear window. A silence had fallen in the car; the woman started to hum a little tune, faded out. The wife said with a clear little laugh: 'Don't think we're crazy. This Indian is really quite a personality. We forgot to tell you about the fish—it happened only just before you came. Everyone was there looking at it—the most colossal thing I've ever seen. And Les took some pictures of him with it; I had one taken too?'

'So why the devil's the silly fool sitting there with the thing?'

She shrugged. 'God knows,' she said, staring at the clock.

The young husband appeared at the window; he leaned conspiratorially into the waiting faces, with an unsure gesture of the hand. 'He's stuck,' he explained with a nervous giggle. 'Can't carry the thing any farther.' A little way behind him the figure of the Indian stood uncertainly, supporting the long dark shape of the fish. 'But why didn't he sell it?' said the wife, exasperated. 'What can *we* do about it?'

'Taking it home as a souvenir, of course,' said a man, pleased with his joke. But the wife was staring, accusing, at the husband. 'Didn't he try to sell it?' He gestured impatiently. 'Of course. But what does it matter? Fact is, he couldn't sell the damn thing, and now he can't carry it home.' 'So what do you want to do about it?' her voice rose indignantly. 'Sit here all night?' 'Shh,' he frowned. He said nothing. The others kept the studiedly considerate silence of strangers pretending not to be present at a family argument. Her husband's silence seemed to be forcing her to speak. 'Where does he live?' she said in resigned exasperation. 'Just off the main road,' said the husband, pat.

She turned with a charmingly exaggerated sense of asking a favour. 'Would you mind awfully if we gave the poor old thing a lift down the road?' 'No. No . . . Good Lord, no,' they said in a rush. 'There'll be no time to have dinner,' someone whispered.

'Come on and get in,' the young man called over his shoulder, but the Indian still hung back, hesistant. '*Not* the fish!' whispered the wife urgently after her husband. 'Put the fish in the boot!'

They heard the wrench of the boot being opened, the thud of the lid coming down again. Then the Indian stood with the young husband at the door of the car. When he saw her, he smiled at her quickly.

'So your big catch is more trouble than it's worth,' she said brightly. The words seemed to fall hard upon him; his shoulders dropped as if he suddenly realized his stiff tiredness; he smiled and shrugged.

'Jump in,' said the husband heartily, opening the door of the driver's seat and getting in himself. The Indian hesitated, his hand on the back door. The three in the back made no move.

'No, there's no room there,' said the girl clearly, splintering the pause. 'Come round the other side and get in the front.' Obediently the fisherman walked through the headlights—a moment of his incisive face against the light—and opened the door at her side.

She shifted up. 'That's right,' she said, as he got in.

His presence in the car was as immediate as if he had been drawn upon the air. The sea-starched folds of his trousers made a slight harsh rubbing noise against the leather of the seat, his damp old tweed jacket smelled of warm wool, showed fuzzy against the edge of light. He breathed deeply and slowly beside her. In her clear voice she continued to talk to him, to ask him about his failure to sell the fish.

'The catch was more trouble than it was worth,' he said once, shaking his head, and she did not know whether he had just happened to say what she herself had said, or whether he was consciously repeating her words to himself.

She felt a stab of cold uncertainty, as if she herself did not know what she had said, did not know what she had meant, or might have meant. Nobody else talked to the Indian. Her husband drove the car. She was furious with them for leaving it all to her: the listening of the back of the car was as rude and blatant as staring.

'What will you do with the salmon now?' she asked brightly, and 'I'll probably give it away to my relations,' he answered obediently.

When they got to a turn-off a short distance along the main road, the Indian lifted his hand and said quickly, 'Here's the place, thank you.' His hand sent a little whiff of fish into the air. The car scudded into the dust at the side of the road, and as it did so, the door swung open and he was out.

He stood there as if his body still held the position he had carefully disciplined himself to in the car, head hunched a bit, hands curled as if he had had a cap he might perhaps have held it before him, pinned there by the blurs of faces looking out at him from the car. He seemed oddly helpless, standing while the young husband opened the boot and heaved the fish out.

'I must thank you very much,' he kept saying seriously. 'I must thank you.'

'That's all right,' the husband smiled, starting the car with a roar. The Indian was saying something else, but the revving of the engine drowned it. The girl smiled down to him through the window, but did not turn her head as they drove off.

'The things we get ourselves into!' she said, spreading her skirt on the seat. She shook her head and laughed a high laugh. 'Shame! The poor thing! What on earth can he do with the great smelly fish now?'

And as if her words had touched some chord of hysteria in them all, they began to laugh, and she laughed with them, laughed till she cried, gasping all the while, 'But what have I said? Why are you laughing at me? What have I said?'

1952

Like Henry James and Doris Lessing, Nadine Gordimer is remarkably successful in developing the inner lives of her characters. The political context in which she creates this development is worth noting: many of her central characters are, like her, middle-class South African whites, confronting or failing to confront the injustices of their society. In an interview with Jannika Hurwitt, she discusses her method of characterization.

"Perhaps I know us too well through myself": Nadine Gordimer

Hurwitt: I noticed that almost all of the white women in your *Selected Stories* are physically and mentally both highly unattractive and middle-class. Does this reflect the way in which you view white colonialists in your country?

Gordimer: I don't make such judgments about people. After all, I'm a white colonial woman myself, of colonial descent. Perhaps I know us too well through myself. But if somebody is partly frivolous or superficial, has moments of cruelty or self-doubt, I don't write them off, because I think that absolutely everybody has what are known as human failings. My black characters are not angels either. All this role-playing that is done in a society like ours—it's done in many societies, but it's more noticeable in ours—sometimes the role is forced upon you. You fall into it. It's a kind of song-and-dance routine, and you find yourself, and my characters find themselves, acting out these preconceived, ready-made roles. But, of course, there are a large number of white women of a certain kind in the kind of society that I come from who . . . well, the best one can say of them is that one can excuse them because of their ignorance of what they have allowed themselves to become. I see the same kind of women here in the U.S. You go into one of the big stores here and you can see these extremely well-dressed, often rather dissatisfied-looking, even sad-looking middle-aged women, rich, sitting trying on a dozen pairs of shoes; and you can see they're sitting there for the morning. And it's a terribly agonizing decision, but maybe the heel should be a little higher or maybe . . . should I get two pairs? And a few blocks away it's appalling to see in what poverty and misery other people are living in this city, New York. Why is it that one doesn't criticize that American woman the same way one does her counterpart in South Africa? For me, the difference is that the rich American represents class difference and injustice, while in South Africa the injustice is based on both class *and* race prejudice.

Hurwitt: Is it intentional that so often the physical details of characters are not brought home strongly in your work? One gets a very strong sense of the mind's workings in major characters, but often a very limited sense of what they actually look like.

Gordimer: I think that physical descriptions of people should be minimal. There are exceptions—take Isaac Bashevis Singer. He very often starts off a story by giving you a full physical description. If you look very closely at the description, of course it's extremely good. He stamps character on a twist of the nose or a tuft of red beard. My own preference is for physical description to come piecemeal at times when it furthers other elements in the text. For instance, you might describe a character's eyes when another character is looking straight into them so it would be natural . . . a feature of that particular moment in the narrative. There might be another scene later, where the character whose eyes you've described is under tension, and is showing it by tapping her foot or picking at a hangnail—so if there was something particular about her hands, that would be the time to talk about them. I'm telling you this as if it were something to be planned. It isn't. It comes at the appropriate moment.

JOSÉ DONOSO

(b. 1924)

PASEO

translated from the Spanish by Lorraine O'Grady Freeman

1

This happened when I was very young, when my father and Aunt Mathilda, his maiden sister, and my uncles Gustav and Armand were still living. Now they are all dead. Or I should say, I prefer to think they are all dead: it is too late now for the questions they did not ask when the moment was right, because events seemed to freeze all of them into silence. Later they were able to construct a wall of forgetfulness or indifference to shut out everything, so that they would not have to harass themselves with impotent conjecture. But then, it may not have been that way at all. My imagination and my memory may be deceiving me. After all, I was only a child then, with whom they did not have to share the anguish of their inquiries, if they made any, nor the result of their discussions.

What was I to think? At times I used to hear them closeted in the library, speaking softly, slowly, as was their custom. But the massive door screened the meaning of their words, permitting me to hear only the grave and measured counterpoint of their voices. What was it they were saying? I used to hope that, inside there, abandoning the coldness which isolated each of them, they were at last speaking of what was truly important. But I had so little faith in this that, while I hung around the walls of the vestibule near the library door, my mind became filled with the certainty that they had chosen to forget, that they were meeting only to discuss, as always, some case in jurisprudence relating to their specialty in maritime law. Now I think that perhaps they were right in wanting to blot out everything. For why should one live with the terror of having to acknowledge that the streets of a city can swallow up a human being, leaving him without life and without death, suspended as it were, in a dimension more dangerous than any dimension with a name?

One day, months after, I came upon my father watching the street from the balcony of the drawing room on the second floor. The sky was close, dense, and the humid air weighed down the large, limp leaves of the ailanthus trees. I drew near my father, eager for an answer that would contain some explanation.

"What are you doing here, Papa?" I murmured.

When he answered, something closed over the despair on his face, like the blow of a shutter closing on a shameful scene.

"Don't you see? I'm smoking . . ." he replied.

And he lit a cigarette.

It wasn't true. I knew why he was peering up and down the street, his eyes darkened, lifting his hand from time to time to stroke his smooth chestnut whiskers: it was in hope of seeing them reappear, returning under the trees of the sidewalk, the white bitch trotting at heel.

Little by little I began to realize that not only my father but all of them, hiding from one another and without confessing even to themselves what they were doing, haunted the windows of the house. If someone happened to look up from the sidewalk he would surely have seen the shadow of one or another of them posted beside a curtain, or faces aged with grief spying out from behind the window panes.

In those days the street was paved with quebracho[1] wood, and under the ailanthus trees a clangorous streetcar used to pass from time to time. The last time I was there neither the wooden pavements nor the streetcars existed any longer. But our house was still standing, narrow and vertical like a little book pressed between the bulky volumes of new buildings, with shops on the ground level and a crude sign advertising knitted undershirts covering the balconies of the second floor.

When we lived there all the houses were tall and slender like our own. The block was always happy with the games of children playing in the patches of sunshine on the sidewalks, and with the gossip of the servant girls on their way back from shopping. But our house was not happy. I say it that way, "it was not happy" instead of "it was sad," because that is exactly what I mean to say. The word "sad" would be wrong because it has too definite a connotation, a weight and a dimension of its own. What took place in our house was exactly the opposite: an absence, a lack, which because it was unacknowledged was irremediable, something that, if it weighed, weighed by not existing.

My mother died when I was only four years old, so the presence of a woman was deemed necessary for my care. As Aunt Mathilda was the only woman in the family and she lived with my uncles Armand and Gustav, the three of them came to live at our house, which was spacious and empty.

Aunt Mathilda discharged her duties towards me with that propriety which was characteristic of everything she did. I did not doubt that she

_____

1. A variety of South American tree with very hard wood.

loved me, but I could never feel it as a palpable experience uniting us. There was something rigid in her affections, as there was in those of the men of the family. With them, love existed confined inside each individual, never breaking its boundaries to express itself and bring them together. For them to show affection was to discharge their duties to each other perfectly, and above all not to inconvenience, never to inconvenience. Perhaps to express love in any other way was unnecessary for them now, since they had so long a history together, had shared so long a past. Perhaps the tenderness they felt in the past had been expressed to the point of satiation and found itself stylized now in the form of certain actions, useful symbols which did not require further elucidation. Respect was the only form of contact left between those four isolated individuals who walked the corridors of the house which, like a book, showed only its narrow spine to the street.

I, naturally, had no history in common with Aunt Mathilda. How could I, if I was no more than a child then who could not understand the gloomy motivations of his elders? I wished that their confined feeling might overflow and express itself in a fit of rage, for example, or with some bit of foolery. But she could not guess this desire of mine because her attention was not focused on me: I was a person peripheral to her life, never central. And I was not central because the entire center of her being was filled up with my father and my uncles. Aunt Mathilda was born the only woman, an ugly woman moreover, in a family of handsome men, and on realizing that for her marriage was unlikely, she dedicated herself to looking out for the comfort of those three men, by keeping house for them, by taking care of their clothes and providing their favorite dishes. She did these things without the least servility, proud of her role because she did not question her brothers' excellence. Furthermore, like all women, she possessed in the highest degree the faith that physical well-being is, if not principal, certainly primary, and that to be neither hungry nor cold nor uncomfortable is the basis for whatever else is good. Not that these defects caused her grief, but rather they made her impatient, and when she saw affliction about her she took immediate steps to remedy what, without doubt, were errors in a world that should be, that had to be, perfect. On another plane, she was intolerant of shirts which were not stupendously well-ironed, of meat that was not of the finest quality, of the humidity that owing to someone's carelessness had crept into the cigar-box.

After dinner, following what must have been an ancient ritual in the family, Aunt Mathilda went upstairs to the bedrooms, and in each of her brothers' rooms she prepared the beds for sleeping, parting the sheets with her bony hands. She spread a shawl at the foot of the bed for that one, who was subject to chills, and placed a feather pillow at the head of this one, for he usually read before going to sleep. Then, leaving the lamps lighted beside those enormous beds, she came downstairs to the billiard room to join the men for coffee and for a few rounds, before, as if bewitched by her, they retired to fill the empty effigies of the pajamas she had arranged so carefully upon the white, half-opened sheets.

But Aunt Mathilda never opened my bed. Each night, when I went up to my room, my heart thumped in the hope of finding my bed opened with the recognizable dexterity of her hands. But I had to adjust myself to the less pure style of the servant girl who was charged with doing it. Aunt Mathilda never granted me that mark of importance because I was not her brother. And not to be "one of my brothers" seemed to her a misfortune of which many people were victims, almost all in fact, including me, who after all was only the son of one of them.

Sometimes Aunt Mathilda asked me to visit her in her room where she sat sewing by the tall window, and she would talk to me. I listened attentively. She spoke to me about her brothers' integrity as lawyers in the intricate field of maritime law, and she extended to me her enthusiasm for their wealth and reputation, which I would carry forward. She described the embargo on a shipment of oranges, told of certain damages caused by miserable tugboats manned by drunkards, of the disastrous effects that arose from the demurrage of a ship sailing under an exotic flag. But when she talked to me of ships her words did not evoke the hoarse sounds of ships' sirens that I heard in the distance on summer nights when, kept awake by the heat, I climbed to the attic, and from an open window watched the far-off floating lights, and those blocks of darkness surrounding the city that lay forever out of reach for me because my life was, and would ever be, ordered perfectly. I realize now that Aunt Mathilda did not hint at this magic because she did not know of it. It had no place in her life, as it had no place in the life of anyone destined to die with dignity in order afterward to be installed in a comfortable heaven, a heaven identical to our house. Mute, I listened to her words, my gaze fastened on the white thread that, as she stretched it against her black blouse, seemed to capture all of the light from the window. I exulted at the world of security that her words projected for me, that magnificent straight road which leads to a death that is not dreaded since it is exactly like this life, without anything fortuitous or unexpected. Because death was not terrible. Death was the final incision, clean and definitive, nothing more. Hell existed, of course, but not for us. It was rather for chastising the other inhabitants of the city and those anonymous seamen who caused the damages that, when the cases were concluded, filled the family coffers.

Aunt Mathilda was so removed from the idea of fear that, since I now know that love and fear go hand in hand, I am tempted to think that in those days she did not love anyone. But I may be mistaken. In her rigid way she may have been attached to her brothers by a kind of love. At night, after supper, they gathered in the billiard room for a few games. I used to go in with them. Standing outside that circle of imprisoned affections, I watched for a sign that would show me the ties between them did exist, and did, in fact, bind. It is strange that my memory does not bring back anything but shades of indeterminate grays in remembering the house, but when I evoke that hour, the strident green of the table, the red and white of the balls and the little cube of blue chalk become inflamed in my memory, illumined by the low lamp whose shade banished everything else into dusk. In one of the family's many rituals, the voice of Aunt Mathilda rescued each of the brothers by turn from the darkness, so that they might make their plays.

"Now, Gustav . . ."

And when he leaned over the green table, cue in hand, Uncle Gustav's face was lit up, brittle as paper, its nobility contradicted by his eyes, which were too small and spaced too close together. Finished playing, he returned to the shadow, where he lit a cigar whose smoke rose lazily until it was dissolved in the gloom of the ceiling. Then his sister said: "All right, Armand . . ."

And the soft, timid face of Uncle Armand, with his large sky-blue eyes concealed by gold-rimmed glasses, bent down underneath the light. His game was generally bad because he was "the baby," as Aunt Mathilda sometimes referred to him. After the comments aroused by his play he took refuge behind his newspaper and Aunt Mathilda said: "Pedro, your turn . . ."

I held my breath when I saw him lean over to play, held it even more tightly when I saw him succumb to his sister's command. I prayed, as he got up, that he would rebel against the order established by his sister's voice. I could not see that this order was in itself a kind of rebellion, constructed by them as a protection against chaos, so that they might not be touched by what can be neither explained nor resolved. My father, then, leaned over the green cloth, his practiced eye gauging the exact distance and positions of the billiards. He made his play, and making it, he exhaled in such a way that his mustache stirred about his half-opened mouth. Then he handed me his cue so I might chalk it with the blue cube. With this minimal role that he assigned to me, he let me touch the circle that united him with the others, without letting me take part in it more than tangentially.

Now it was Aunt Mathilda's turn. She was the best player. When I saw her face, composed as if from the defects of her brothers' faces, coming out of the shadow, I knew that she was going to win. And yet . . . had I not seen her small eyes light up that face so like a brutally clenched fist, when by chance one of them succeeded in beating her? That spark appeared because, although she might have wished it, she would never have permitted herself to let any of them win. That would be to introduce the mysterious element of love into a game that ought not to include it, because affection should remain in its place, without trespassing on the strict reality of a carom shot.

2

I never did like dogs. One may have frightened me when I was very young, I don't know, but they have always displeased me. As there were no dogs at home and I went out very little, few occasions presented themselves to make me uncomfortable. For my aunt and uncles and for my father, dogs, like all the rest of the animal kingdom, did not exist. Cows, of course, supplied the cream for the dessert that was served in a silver dish on Sundays. Then there were the birds that chirped quite agreeably at twilight in the branches of the elm tree, the only inhabitant of the small garden at the rear of the house. But animals for them existed only in the proportion in which they contributed to the pleasure of human beings. Which is to say that dogs, lazy as city dogs are, could not even dent their imagination with a possibility of their existence.

Sometimes, on Sunday, Aunt Mathilda and I used to go to Mass early to take communion. It was rare that I succeeded in concentrating on the sacrament, because the idea that she was watching me without looking generally occupied the first place of my conscious mind. Even when her eyes were directed to the altar, or her head bowed before the Blessed Sacrament, my every movement drew her attention to it. And on leaving the church she told me with sly reproach that it was without doubt a flea trapped in the pews that prevented me from meditating, as she had suggested, that death is the good foreseen end, and from praying that it might not be painful, since that was the purpose of masses, novenas and communions.

This was such a morning. A fine drizzle was threatening to turn into a storm, and the quebracho pavements extended their shiny fans, notched with streetcar rails, from sidewalk to sidewalk. As I was cold and in a hurry to get home I stepped up the pace beside Aunt Mathilda, who was holding her black mushroom of an umbrella above our heads. There were not many people in the street since it was so early. A dark-complexioned gentleman saluted us without lifting his hat, because of the rain. My aunt was in the process of telling me how surprised she was that someone of mixed blood had bowed to her with so little show of attention, when suddenly, near where we were walking, a streetcar applied its brakes with a screech, making her interrupt her monologue. The conductor looked out through his window:

"Stupid dog!" he shouted.

We stopped to watch.

A small white bitch escaped from between the wheels of the streetcar and, limping painfully, with her tail between her legs, took refuge in a doorway as the streetcar moved on again.

"These dogs," protested Aunt Mathilda. "It's beyond me how they are allowed to go around like that."

Continuing on our way, we passed by the bitch huddled in the corner of a doorway. It was small and white, with legs which were too short for its size and an ugly pointed snout that proclaimed an entire genealogy of misalliances: the sum of unevenly matched breeds which for generations had been scouring the city, searching for food in the garbage cans and among the refuse of the port. She was drenched, weak, trembling with cold or fever. When we passed in front of her I noticed that my aunt looked at the bitch, and the bitch's eyes returned her gaze.

We continued on our way home. Several steps further I was on the point of forgetting the dog when my aunt surprised me by abruptly turning around and crying out: "Psst! Go away!"

She had turned in such absolute certainty of finding the bitch following us that I trembled with the mute question which arose from my surprise: How did she know? She couldn't have heard her, since she was following us at an appreciable distance. But she did not doubt it. Perhaps the look that had passed between them of which I saw only the mechanics— the bitch's head raised slightly toward Aunt Mathilda, Aunt Mathilda's slightly inclined toward the bitch—contained some secret commitment? I do not know. In any case, turning to drive away the dog, her peremptory "psst" had the sound of something like a last effort to repel an encroaching destiny. It is possible that I am saying all this in the light of things that happened later, that my imagination is embellishing with significance what was only trivial. However, I can say with certainty that in that moment I felt a strangeness, almost a fear of my aunt's sudden loss of dignity in condescending to turn around and confer rank on a sick and filthy bitch.

We arrived home. We went up the stairs and the bitch stayed down below, looking up at us from the torrential rain that had just been unleashed. We went inside, and the delectable process of breakfast following communion removed the white bitch from my mind. I have never felt our house so protective as that morning, never rejoiced so much in the security derived from those old walls that marked off my world.

In one of my wanderings in and out of the empty sitting rooms, I pulled back the curtain of a window to see if the rain promised to let up. The storm continued. And, sitting at the foot of the stairs still scrutinizing the house, I saw the white bitch. I dropped the curtain so that I might not see her there, soaked through and looking like one spellbound. Then, from the dark outer rim of the room, Aunt Mathilda's low voice surprised me. Bent over to strike a match to the kindling wood already arranged in the fireplace, she asked: "Is it still there?"

"What?"

I knew what.

"The white bitch . . ."

I answered yes, that it was.

3

It must have been the last storm of the winter, because I remember quite clearly that the following days opened up and the nights began to grow warmer.

The white bitch stayed posted on our doorstep scrutinizing our windows. In the mornings, when I left for school, I tried to shoo her away, but barely had I boarded the bus when I would see her reappear around the corner or from behind the mailbox. The servant girls also tried to frighten her away, but their attempts were as fruitless as mine, because the bitch never failed to return.

Once, we were all saying goodnight at the foot of the stairs before going up to bed. Uncle Gustav had just turned off the lights, all except the one on the stairway, so that the large space of the vestibule had become peopled with the shadowy bodies of furniture. Aunt Mathilda, who was entreating Uncle Armand to open the window of his room so a little air could come in, suddenly stopped speaking, leaving her sentence unfinished, and the movements of all of us, who had started to go up, halted.

"What is the matter?" asked Father, stepping down one stair.

"Go on up," murmured Aunt Mathilda, turning around and gazing into the shadow of the vestibule.

But we did not go up.

The silence of the room was filled with the sweet voice of each object: a grain of dirt trickling down between the wallpaper and the wall, the creaking of polished woods, the quivering of some loose crystal. Someone, in addition to ourselves, was where we were. A small white form came out of the darkness near the service door. The bitch crossed the vestibule, limping slowly in the direction of Aunt Mathilda, and without even looking at her, threw herself down at her feet.

It was as though the immobility of the dog enabled us to move again. My father came down two stairs. Uncle Gustav turned on the light. Uncle Armand went upstairs and shut himself in his room.

"What is this?" asked my father.

Aunt Mathilda remained still.

"How could she have come in?" she asked aloud.

Her question seemed to acknowledge the heroism implicit in having either jumped walls in that lamentable condition, or come into the basement through a broken pane of glass, or fooled the servants' vigilance by creeping through a casually opened door.

"Mathilda, call one of the girls to take her away," said my father, and went upstairs followed by Uncle Gustav.

We were left alone looking at the bitch. She called a servant, telling the girl to give her something to eat and the next day to call a veterinarian.

"Is she going to stay in the house?" I asked.

"How can she walk in the street like that?" murmured Aunt Mathilda. "She has to get better so we can throw her out. And she'd better get well soon because I don't want animals in the house."

Then she added: "Go upstairs to bed."

She followed the girl who was carrying the dog out.

I sensed that ancient drive of Aunt Mathilda's to have everything go well about her, that energy and dexterity which made her sovereign of immediate things. Is it possible that she was so secure within her limitations that for the only necessity was to overcome imperfections, errors not of intention or motive, but of condition? If so, the white bitch was going to get well. She would see to it because the animal had entered the radius of her power. The veterinarian would bandage the broken leg under her watchful eye, and protected by rubber gloves and an apron, she herself would take charge of cleaning the bitch's pustules with disinfectant that would make her howl. But Aunt Mathilda would remain deaf to those howls, sure that whatever she was doing was for the best.

And so it was. The bitch stayed in the house. Not that I saw her, but I could feel the presence of any stranger there, even though confined to the lower reaches of the basement. Once or twice I saw Aunt Mathilda with the rubber gloves on her hands, carrying a vial full of red liquid. I found a plate with scraps of food in a passage of the basement where I went to look for the bicycle I had just been given. Weakly, buffered by walls and floors, at times the suspicion of a bark reached my ears.

One afternoon I went down to the kitchen. The bitch came in, painted like a clown with red disinfectant. The servants threw her out without paying her any mind. But I saw that she was not hobbling any longer, that her tail, limp before, was curled up like a feather, leaving her shameless bottom in plain view.

That afternoon I asked Aunt Mathilda: "When are you going to throw her out?"

"Who?" she asked.

She knew perfectly well.

"The white bitch."

"She's not well yet," she replied.

Later I thought of insisting, of telling her that surely there was nothing now to prevent her from climbing the garbage cans in search of food. I didn't do it because I believe it was the same night that Aunt Mathilda, after losing the first round of billiards, decided that she did not feel like playing another. Her brothers went on playing, and she, ensconced in the leather sofa, made a mistake in calling their names. There was a moment of confusion. Then the thread of order was quickly picked up again by the men, who knew how to ignore an accident if it was not favorable to them. But I had already seen.

It was as if Aunt Mathilda were not there at all. She was breathing at my side as she always did. The deep, silencing carpet yielded under her feet as usual and her tranquilly crossed hands weighed on her skirt. How is it possible to feel with the certainty I felt then the absence of a person whose heart is somewhere else? The following nights were equally troubled by the invisible slur of her absence. She seemed to have lost all interest in the game and left off calling her brothers by their names. They appeared not to notice it. But they must have, because their games became shorter and I noticed an infinitesimal increase in the deference with which they treated her.

One night, as we were going out of the dining room, the bitch appeared in the doorway and joined the family group. The men paused before they went into the library so that their sister might lead the way to the billiard room, followed this time by the white bitch. They made no comment, as if they had not seen her, beginning their game as they did every night.

The bitch sat down at Aunt Mathilda's feet. She was very quiet. Her lively eyes examined the room and followed the players' strategies as if all of that amused her greatly. She was fat now and had a shiny coat. Her whole body, from her quivering snout to her tail ready to waggle, was full of an abundant capacity for fun. How long had she stayed in the house? A month? Perhaps more. But in that month Aunt Mathilda had forced her to get well, caring for her not with displays of affection but with those hands of hers which could not refrain from mending what was broken. The leg was well. She had disinfected, fed and bathed her, and now the white bitch was whole.

In one of his plays Uncle Armand let the cube of blue chalk fall to the floor. Immediately, obeying an instinct that seemed to surge up from her picaresque past, the bitch ran toward the chalk and snatched it with her mouth away from Uncle Armand, who had bent over to pick it up. Then followed something surprising: Aunt Mathilda, as if suddenly unwound, burst into a peal of laughter that agitated her whole body. We remained frozen. On hearing her laugh, the bitch dropped the chalk, ran towards her with tail waggling aloft, and jumped up onto her lap. Aunt Mathilda's laugh relented, but Uncle Armand left the room. Uncle Gustav and my father went on with the game: now it was more important than ever not to see, not to see anything at all, not to comment, not to consider oneself alluded to by these events.

I did not find Aunt Mathilda's laugh amusing, because I may have felt the dark thing that had stirred it up. The bitch grew calm sitting on her lap. The cracking noises of the balls when they hit seemed to conduct Aunt Mathilda's hand first from its place on the edge of the sofa, to her skirt, and then to the curved back of the sleeping animal. On seeing that expressionless hand reposing there, I noticed that the tension which had kept my aunt's features clenched before, relented, and that a certain peace was now softening her face. I could not resist. I drew closer to her on the sofa, as if to a newly kindled fire. I hoped that she would reach out to me with a look or include me with a smile. But she did not.

4

When I arrived from school in the afternoon, I used to go directly to the back of the house and, mounting my bicycle, take turn after turn around the narrow garden, circling the pair of cast-iron benches and the elm tree. Behind the wall, the chestnut trees were beginning to display their light spring down, but the seasons did not interest me, for I had too many serious things to think about. And since I knew that no one came down into the garden until the suffocation of midsummer made it imperative, it seemed to be the best place for meditating about what was going on inside the house.

One might have said that nothing was going on. But how could I remain calm in the face of the entwining relationship which had sprung up between my aunt and the white bitch? It was as if Aunt Mathilda, after having resigned herself to an odd life of service and duty, had found at last her equal. And as women-friends do, they carried on a life full of niceties and pleasing refinements. They ate bonbons that came in boxes wrapped frivolously with ribbons. My aunt arranged tangerines, pineapples and grapes in tall crystal bowls, while the bitch watched her as if on the point of criticizing her taste or offering a suggestion.

Often when I passed the door of her room, I heard a peal of laughter like the one which had overturned the order of her former life that night. Or I heard her engage in a dialogue with an interlocutor whose voice I did not hear. It was a new life. The bitch, the guilty one, slept in a hamper near her bed, an elegant, feminine hamper, ridiculous to my way of thinking, and followed her everywhere except into the dining room. Entrance there was forbidden her, but waiting for her friend to come out again, she followed her to the billiard room and sat at her side on the sofa or on her lap, exchanging with her from time to time complicitory glances.

How was it possible? I used to ask myself: why had she waited until now to go beyond herself and establish a dialogue? At times she appeared insecure about the bitch, fearful that, in the same way she had arrived one fine day, she might also go, leaving her with all this new abundance weighing on her hands. Or did she still fear for her health? These ideas, which now seem to clear, floated blurred in my imagination while I listened to the gravel of the path crunching under the wheels of my bicycle. What was not blurred, however, was my vehement desire to become gravely ill, to see if I might also succeed in harvesting some kind of relationship. Because the bitch's illness had been the cause of everything. If it had not been for that, my aunt might have never joined in league with her. But I had a constitution of iron, and furthermore it was clear that Aunt Mathilda's heart did not have room for more than one love at a time.

My father and my uncles did not seem to notice any change. The bitch was very quiet and, abandoning her street ways, seemed to acquire manners more worthy of Aunt Mathilda. But still, she had somehow preserved all the sauciness of a female of the streets. It was clear that the hardships of her life had not been able to cloud either her good humor or her taste for adventure which, I felt, lay dangerously dormant inside her. For the men of the house it proved easier to accept her than to throw her out, since this would have forced them to revise their canons of security.

One night, when the pitcher of lemonade had already made its appearance on the console table of the library, cooling that corner of the shadow, and the windows had been thrown open to the air, my father halted abruptly at the doorway of the billiard room.

"What is that?" he exclaimed, looking at the floor.

José Donoso   *493*

The three men stopped in consternation to look at a small, round pool on the waxed floor.

"Mathilda!" called Uncle Gustav.

She went to look and then reddened with shame. The bitch had taken refuge under the billiard table in the adjoining room. Walking over to the table my father saw her there, and changing direction sharply, he left the room, followed by his brothers.

Aunt Mathilda went upstairs. The bitch followed her. I stayed in the library with a glass of lemonade in my hand, and looked out at the summer sky, listening to some far-off siren from the sea, and to the murmur of the city stretched out under the stars. Soon I heard Aunt Mathilda coming down. She appeared with her hat on and with her keys chinking in her hand.

"Go up and go to bed," she said. "I'm going to take her for a walk on the street so that she can do her business."

Then she added something strange: "It's such a lovely night."

And she went out.

From that night on, instead of going up after dinner to open her brothers' beds, she went to her room, put her hat tightly on her head and came downstairs again, chinking her keys. She went out with the bitch without explaining anything to anyone. And my uncles and my father and I stayed behind in the billiard room, and later we sat on the benches of the garden, with all the murmuring of the elm tree and the clearness of the sky weighing down on us. These nocturnal walks of Aunt Mathilda's were never spoken of by her brothers. They never showed any awareness of the change that had occurred inside our house.

In the beginning Aunt Mathilda was gone at the most for twenty minutes or half an hour, returning to take whatever refreshment there was and to exchange some trivial commentary. Later, her sorties were inexplicably prolonged. We began to realize, or I did at least, that she was no longer a woman taking her dog out for hygienic reasons: outside there, in the streets of the city, something was drawing her. When waiting, my father furtively eyed his pocket watch, and if the delay was very great Uncle Gustav went up to the second floor pretending he had forgotten something there, to spy for her from the balcony. But still they did not speak. Once, when Aunt Mathilda stayed out too long, my father paced back and forth along the path that wound between the hydrangeas. Uncle Gustav threw away a cigar which he could not light to his satisfaction, then another, crushing it with the heel of his shoe. Uncle Armand spilled a cup of coffee. I watched them, hoping that at long last they would explode, that they would finally say something to fill the minutes that were passing by one after another, getting longer and longer and longer without the presence of Aunt Mathilda. It was twelve-thirty when she arrived.

"Why are you all waiting up for me?" she asked, smiling.

She was holding her hat in her hand, and her hair, ordinarily so well-groomed, was mussed. I saw that a streak of mud was soiling her shoes.

"What happened to you?" asked Uncle Armand.

"Nothing," came her reply, and with it she shut off any right of her brothers to meddle in those unknown hours that were now her life. I say they were her life because, during the minutes she stayed with us before going up to her room with the bitch, I perceived an animation in her eyes, an excited restlessness like that in the eyes of the animal: it was as though they had been washed in scenes to which even our imagination lacked access. Those two were accomplices. The night protected them. They belonged to the murmuring sound of the city, to the sirens of the ships which, crossing the dark or illuminated streets, the houses and factories and parks, reached my ears.

Her walks with the bitch continued for some time. Now we said good night immediately after dinner, and each one went up to shut himself in his room, my father, Uncle Gustav, Uncle Armand and I. But no one went to sleep before she came in, late, sometimes terribly late, when the light of dawn was already striking the top of our elm. Only after hearing her close the door of her bedroom did the pacing with which my father measured his room cease, or was the window in one of his brothers' rooms finally closed to exclude that fragment of the night which was no longer dangerous.

Once I heard her come up very late, and as I thought I heard her singing softly, I opened my door and peeked out. When she passed my room, with the white bitch nestled in her arms, her face seemed to me surprisingly young and unblemished, even though it was dirty, and I saw a rip in her skirt. I went to bed terrified, knowing this was the end.

I was not mistaken. Because one night, shortly after, Aunt Mathilda took the dog out for a walk after dinner, and did not return.

We stayed awake all night, each one in his room, and she did not come back. No one said anything the next day. They went—I presume—to their office, and I went to school. She wasn't home when we came back and we sat silently at our meal that night. I wonder if they found out something definite that very first day. But I think not, because we all, without seeming to, haunted the windows of the house, peering into the street.

"Your aunt went on a trip," the cook answered me when I finally dared to ask, if only her.

But I knew it was not true.

Life continued in the house just as if Aunt Mathilda were still living there. It is true that they used to gather in the library for hours and hours, and closeted there they may have planned ways of retrieving her out of that night which had swallowed her. Several times a visitor came who was clearly not of our world, a plainclothesman perhaps, or the head of a stevedore's union come to pick up indemnification for some accident. Sometimes their voices rose a little, sometimes there was a deadened quiet, sometimes their voices became hard, sharp, as they fenced with the voice I did not know. But the library door was too thick, too heavy for me to hear what they were saying.

trans. 1969

José Donoso   495

"Paseo" is a story that invites the reader to find symbolic meanings for certain details. Straining after symbolic reading can often lead the reader astray, however. Flannery O'Connor, whose fiction is comparable to José Donoso's in its use of symbolism, wrote very clearly on the way that symbols accumulate meaning in a story.

"Letting the wooden leg accumulate meaning": Flannery O'Connor

In good fiction, certain of the details will tend to accumulate meaning from the action of the story itself, and when this happens they become symbolic in the way they work. I once wrote a story called "Good Country People," in which a lady Ph.D. has her wooden leg stolen by a Bible salesman whom she has tried to seduce. Now I'll admit that, paraphrased in this way, the situation is simply a low joke. The average reader is pleased to observe anybody's wooden leg being stolen. But without ceasing to appeal to him and without making any statements of high intention, this story does manage to operate at another level of experience, by letting the wooden leg accumulate meaning. Early in the story, we're presented with the fact that the Ph.D. is spiritually as well as physically crippled. She believes in nothing but her own belief in nothing, and we perceive that there is a wooden part of her soul that corresponds to her wooden leg. Now of course this is never stated. The fiction writer states as little as possible. The reader makes this connection from things he is shown. He may not even know that he makes the connection, but the connection is there nevertheless and it has its effect on him. As the story goes on, the wooden leg continues to accumulate meaning. The reader learns how the girl feels about her leg, how her mother feels about it, and how the country woman on the place feels about it; and finally, by the time the Bible salesman comes along, the leg has accumulated so much meaning that it is, as the saying goes, loaded. And when the Bible salesman steals it, the reader realizes that he has taken away part of the girl's personality and has revealed her deeper affliction to her for the first time.

If you want to say that the wooden leg is a symbol, you can say that. But it is a wooden leg first, and as a wooden leg it is absolutely necessary to the story. It has its place on the literal level of the story, but it operates in depth as well as on the surface. It increases the story in every direction, and this is essentially the way a story escapes being short.

FLANNERY O'CONNOR

(1925–1964)

A GOOD MAN IS HARD TO FIND

The grandmother didn't want to go to Florida. She wanted to visit some of her connections in east Tennessee and she was seizing every chance to change Bailey's mind. Bailey was the son she lived with, her only boy. He was sitting on the edge of his chair at the table, bent over the orange sports section of the *Journal*. "Now look here, Bailey," she said, "see here, read this," and she stood with one hand on her thin hip and the other rattling the newspaper at his bald head. "Here this fellow that calls himself The Misfit is aloose from the Federal Pen and headed toward Florida and you read here what it says he did to these people. Just you read it. I wouldn't take my children in any direction with a criminal like that aloose in it. I couldn't answer to my conscience if I did."

Bailey didn't look up from his reading so she wheeled around then and faced the children's mother; a young woman in slacks, whose face was as broad and innocent as a cabbage and was tied around with a green head-kerchief that had two points on the top like rabbit's ears. She was sitting on the sofa, feeding the baby his apricots out of a jar. "The children have been to Florida before," the old lady said. "You all ought to take them somewhere else for a change so they would see different parts of the world and be broad. They never have been to east Tennessee."

The children's mother didn't seem to hear her, but the eight-year-old boy, John Wesley, a stocky child with glasses, said, "If you don't want to go to Florida, why dontcha stay at home?" He and the little girl, June Star, were reading the funny papers on the floor.

"She wouldn't stay at home to be queen for a day," June Star said without raising her yellow head.

"Yes, and what would you do if this fellow, The Misfit, caught you?" the grandmother asked.

"I'd smack his face," John Wesley said.

"She wouldn't stay at home for a million bucks," June Star said. "Afraid she'd miss something. She has to go everywhere we go."

"All right, Miss," the grandmother said. "Just remember that the next time you want me to curl your hair."

June Star said her hair was naturally curly.

The next morning the grandmother was the first one in the car, ready to go. She had her big black valise that looked like the head of a hippopotamus in one corner, and underneath it she was hiding a basket with Pitty Sing, the cat, in it. She didn't intend for the cat to be left alone in the house for three days because he would miss her too much and she was afraid he might brush against one of the gas burners and accidentally asphyxiate himself. Her son, Bailey, didn't like to arrive at a motel with a cat.

She sat in the middle of the back seat with John Wesley and June Star on either side of her. Bailey and the children's mother and the baby sat in the front and they left Atlanta at eight forty-five with the mileage on the car at 55890. The grandmother wrote this down because she thought it would be interesting to say how many miles they had been when they got back. It took them twenty minutes to reach the outskirts of the city.

The old lady settled herself comfortably, removing her white cotton gloves and putting them up with her purse on the shelf in front of the back window. The children's mother still had on slacks and still had her head tied up in a green kerchief, but the grandmother had on a navy blue straw sailor hat with a bunch of white violets on the brim and a navy blue dress with a small white dot in the print. Her collar and cuffs were white organdy trimmed with lace and at her neckline she had pinned a purple spray of cloth violets containing a sachet. In case of an accident, anyone seeing her dead on the highway would know at once that she was a lady.

She said she thought it was going to be a good day for driving, neither too hot nor too cold, and she cautioned Bailey that the speed limit was fifty-five miles an hour and that the patrolmen hid themselves behind billboards and small clumps of trees and sped out after you before you had a chance to slow down. She pointed out interesting details of the scenery: Stone Mountain; the blue granite that in some places came up to both sides of the highway; the brilliant red clay banks slightly streaked with purple; and the various crops that made rows of green lace-work on the ground. The trees were full of silver-white sunlights and the meanest of them sparkled. The children were reading comic magazines and their mother had gone back to sleep.

"Let's go through Georgia fast so we won't have to look at it much," John Wesley said.

"If I were a little boy," said the grandmother, "I wouldn't talk about my native state that way. Tennessee has the mountains and Georgia has the hills."

"Tennessee is just a hillbilly dumping ground," John Wesley said, "and Georgia is a lousy state too."

"You said it," June Star said.

"In my time," said the grandmother, folding her thin veined fingers, "children were more respectful of their native states and their parents and everything else. People did right then. Oh look at the cute little pickaninny!" she said and pointed to a Negro child standing in the door of a shack. "Wouldn't that make a picture, now?" she asked and they all turned and looked at the little Negro out of the back window. He waved.

"He didn't have any britches on," June Star said.

"He probably didn't have any," the grandmother explained. "Little niggers in the country don't have things like we do. If I could paint, I'd paint that picture," she said.

The children exchanged comic books.

The grandmother offered to hold the baby and the children's mother passed him over the front seat to her. She set him on her knee and bounced him and told him about the things they were passing. She rolled her eyes and screwed up her mouth and stuck her leathery thin face into his smooth bland one. Occasionally he gave her a faraway smile. They passed a large cotton field with five or six graves fenced in the middle of it, like a small island. "Look at the graveyard!" the grandmother said, pointing it out. "That was the old family burying ground. That belonged to the plantation."

"Where's the plantation?" John Wesley asked.

"Gone With the Wind," said the grandmother. "Ha. Ha."

When the children finished all the comic books they had brought, they opened the lunch and ate it. The grandmother ate a peanut butter sandwich and an olive and would not let the children throw the box and the paper napkins out the window. When there was nothing else to do they played a game by choosing a cloud and making the other two guess what shape it suggested. John Wesley took one the shape of a cow and June Star guessed a cow and John Wesley said, no, an automobile, and June Star said he didn't play fair, and they began to slap each other over the grandmother.

The grandmother said she would tell them a story if they would keep quiet. When she told a story, she rolled her eyes and waved her head and was very dramatic. She said once when she was a maiden lady she had been courted by a Mr. Edgar Atkins Teagarden from Jasper, Georgia. She said he was a very good-looking man and a gentleman and that he brought her a watermelon every Saturday afternoon with his initials cut in it, E.A.T. Well, one Saturday, she said, Mr. Teagarden brought the watermelon and there was nobody at home and he left it on the front porch and returned in his buggy to Jasper, but she never got the watermelon, she said, because a nigger boy ate it when he saw the initials, E.A.T.! This story tickled John Wesley's funny bone and he giggled and giggled but June Star didn't think it was any good. She said she wouldn't marry a man that just brought her a watermelon on Saturday. The grandmother said she would have done well to marry Mr. Teagarden because he was a gentleman and had bought Coca-Cola stock when it first came out and that he had died only a few years ago, a very wealthy man.

They stopped at The Tower for barbecued sandwiches. The Tower was a part-stucco and part-wood filling station and dance hall set in a clearing outside of Timothy. A fat man named Red Sammy Butts ran it and there were signs stuck here and there on the building and for miles up and down the highway saying, TRY RED SAMMY'S FAMOUS BARBECUE. NONE LIKE FAMOUS RED SAMMY'S! RED SAM! THE FAT BOY WITH THE HAPPY LAUGH. A VETERAN! RED SAMMY'S YOUR MAN!

Red Sammy was lying on the bare ground outside The Tower with his head under a truck while a gray monkey about a foot high, chained to a small chinaberry tree, chattered nearby. The monkey sprang back into the tree and got on the highest limb as soon as he saw the children jump out of the car and run toward him.

Inside, The Tower was a long dark room with a counter at one end and tables at the other and dancing space in the middle. They all sat down at a broad table next to the nickelodeon and Red Sam's wife, a tall burnt-brown woman with hair and eyes lighter than her skin, came and took their order. The children's mother put a dime in the machine and played "The Tennessee Waltz," and the grandmother said that tune always made her want to dance. She asked Bailey if he would like to dance but he only glared at her. He didn't have a naturally sunny disposition like she did and trips made him nervous. The grandmother's brown eyes were very bright. She swayed her head from side to side and pretended she was dancing in her chair. June Star said play something she could tap to so the children's mother put in another dime and played a fast number and June Star stepped out onto the dance floor and did her tap routine.

"Ain't she cute?" Red Sam's wife said, leaning over the counter. "Would you like to come be my little girl?"

"No, I certainly wouldn't," June Star said. "I wouldn't live in a broken-down place like this for a million bucks!" and she ran back to the table.

"Ain't she cute?" the woman repeated, stretching her mouth politely.

"Aren't you ashamed?" hissed the grandmother.

Red Sam came in and told his wife to quit lounging on the counter and hurry up with these people's order. His khaki trousers reached just to his hip bones and his stomach hung over them like a sack of meal swaying under his shirt. He came over and sat down at a table nearby and let out a combination sigh and yodel. "You can't win," he said. "You can't win," and he wiped his sweating red face off with a gray handkerchief. "These days you don't know who to trust," he said. "Ain't that the truth?"

"People are certainly not nice like they used to be," said the grandmother.

"Two fellers come in here last week," Red Sammy said, "driving a Chrysler. It was an old beat-up car but it was a good one and these boys looked all right to me. Said they worked at the mill and you know I let them fellers charge the gas they bought? Now why did I do that?"

"Because you're a good man!" the grandmother said at once.

"Yes'm, I suppose so," Red Sam said as if he were struck with this answer.

His wife brought the orders, carrying the five plates all at once without a tray, two in each hand and one balanced on her arm. "It isn't a soul in this green world of God's that you can trust," she said. "And I don't count nobody out of that, not nobody," she repeated, looking at Red Sammy.

"Did you read about that criminal, The Misfit, that's escaped?" asked the grandmother.

"I wouldn't be a bit surprised if he didn't attack this place right here," said the woman. "If he hears about it being here, I wouldn't be none surprised to see him. If he hears it's two cent in the cash register, I wouldn't be a tall surprised if he. . . ."

"That'll do," Red Sam said. "Go bring these people their Co'-Colas," and the woman went off to get the rest of the order.

"A good man is hard to find," Red Sammy said. "Everything is getting terrible. I remember the day you could go off and leave your screen door unlatched. Not no more."

He and the grandmother discussed better times. The old lady said that in her opinion Europe was entirely to blame for the way things were now. She said the way Europe acted you would think we were made of money and Red Sam said it was no use talking about it, she was exactly right. The children ran outside into the white sunlight and looked at the monkey in the lacy chinaberry tree. He was busy catching fleas on himself and biting each one carefully between his teeth as if it were a delicacy.

They drove off again into the hot afternoon. The grandmother took cat naps and woke up every few minutes with her own snoring. Outside of Toombsboro she woke up and recalled an old plantation that she had visited in this neighborhood once when she was a young lady. She said the house had six white columns across the front and that there was an avenue of oaks leading up to it and two little wooden trellis arbors on either side in front where you sat down with your suitor after a stroll in the garden. She recalled exactly which road to turn off to get to it. She knew that Bailey would not be willing to lose any time looking at an old house, but the more she talked about it, the more she wanted to see it once again and find out if the little twin arbors were still standing. "There was a secret panel in this house," she said craftily, not telling the truth but wishing that she were, "and the story went that all the family silver was hidden in it when Sherman[1] came through but it was never found. . . ."

"Hey!" John Wesley said. "Let's go see it! We'll find it! We'll poke all the wood work and find it! Who lives there? Where do you turn off at? Hey Pop, can't we turn off there?"

"We never have seen a house with a secret panel!" June Star shrieked. "Let's go to the house with the secret panel! Hey, Pop, can't we go see the house with the secret panel!"

"It's not far from here, I know," the grandmother said. "It wouldn't take over twenty minutes."

Bailey was looking straight ahead. His jaw was as rigid as a horseshoe. "No," he said.

The children began to yell and scream that they wanted to see the house with the secret panel. John Wesley kicked the back of the front seat and June Star hung over her mother's shoulder and whined desperately

_____
1. William T. Sherman (1820–1891), American Union General who blazed a trail of destruction through the South during the Civil War.

into her ear that they never had any fun even on their vacation, that they could never do what THEY wanted to do. The baby began to scream and John Wesley kicked the back of the seat so hard that his father could feel the blows in his kidney.

"All right!" he shouted and drew the car to a stop at the side of the road. "Will you all shut up? Will you all shut up for one second? If you don't shut up, we won't go anywhere."

"It would be very educational for them," the grandmother murmured.

"All right," Bailey said, "but get this. This is the only time we're going to stop for anything like this. This is the one and only time."

"The dirt road that you have to turn down is about a mile back," the grandmother directed. "I marked it when we passed."

"A dirt road," Bailey groaned.

After they had turned around and were headed toward the dirt road, the grandmother recalled other points about the house, the beautiful glass over the front doorway and the candle lamp in the hall. John Wesley said that the secret panel was probably in the fireplace.

"You can't go inside this house," Bailey said. "You don't know who lives there."

"While you all talk to the people in front, I'll run around behind and get in a window," John Wesley suggested.

"We'll all stay in the car," his mother said.

They turned onto the dirt road and the car raced roughly along in a swirl of pink dust. The grandmother recalled the times when there were no paved roads and thirty miles was a day's journey. The dirt road was hilly and there were sudden washes in it and sharp curves on dangerous embankments. All at once they would be on a hill, looking down over the blue tops of trees for miles around, then the next minute, they would be in a red depression with the dust-coated trees looking down on them.

"This place had better turn up in a minute," Bailey said, "or I'm going to turn around."

The road looked as if no one had traveled on it in months.

"It's not much farther," the grandmother said and just as she said it, a horrible thought came to her. The thought was so embarrassing that she turned red in the face and her eyes dilated and her feet jumped up, upsetting her valise in the corner. The instant the valise moved, the newspaper top she had over the basket under it rose with a snarl and Pitty Sing, the cat, sprang onto Bailey's shoulder.

The children were thrown to the floor and their mother, clutching the baby, was thrown out the door onto the ground; the old lady was thrown into the front seat. The car turned over once and landed right-side-up in a gulch on the side of the road. Bailey remained in the driver's seat with the cat—gray-striped with a broad white face and an orange nose—clinging to his neck like a caterpillar.

As soon as the children saw they could move their arms and legs, they scrambled out of the car, shouting, "We've had an ACCIDENT!" The grandmother was curled up under the dashboard, hoping she was injured so that Bailey's wrath would not come down on her all at once. The horrible thought she had had before the accident was that the house she had remembered so vividly was not in Georgia but in Tennessee.

Bailey removed the cat from his neck with both hands and flung it out the window against the side of a pine tree. Then he got out of the car and started looking for the children's mother. She was sitting against the side of the red gutted ditch, holding the screaming baby, but she only had a cut down her face and a broken shoulder. "We've had an ACCIDENT!" the children screamed in a frenzy of delight.

"But nobody's killed," June Star said with disappointment as the grandmother limped out of the car, her hat still pinned to her head but the broken front brim standing up at a jaunty angle and the violet spray hanging off the side. They all sat down in the ditch, except the children, to recover from the shock. They were all shaking.

"Maybe a car will come along," said the children's mother hoarsely.

"I believe I have injured an organ," said the grandmother, pressing her side, but no one answered her. Bailey's teeth were clattering. He had on a yellow sport shirt with bright blue parrots designed in it and his face was as yellow as the shirt. The grandmother decided that she would not mention that the house was in Tennessee.

The road was about ten feet above and they could see only the tops of the trees on the other side of it. Behind the ditch they were sitting in there were more woods, tall and dark and deep. In a few minutes they saw a car some distance away on top of a hill, coming slowly as if the occupants were watching them. The grandmother stood up and waved both arms dramatically to attract their attention. The car continued to come on slowly, disappeared around a bend and appeared again, moving even slower, on top of the hill they had gone over. It was a big black battered hearselike automobile. There were three men in it.

It came to a stop just over them and for some minutes, the driver looked down with a steady expressionless gaze to where they were sitting, and didn't speak. Then he turned his head and muttered something to the other two and they got out. One was a fat boy in black trousers and a red sweat shirt with a silver stallion embossed on the front of it. He moved around on the right side of them and stood staring, his mouth partly open in a kind of loose grin. The other had on khaki pants and a blue striped coat and a gray hat pulled down very low, hiding most of his face. He came around slowly on the left side. Neither spoke.

The driver got out of the car and stood by the side of it, looking down at them. He was an older man than the other two. His hair was just beginning to gray and he wore silver-rimmed spectacles that gave him a scholarly look. He had a long creased face and didn't have on any shirt or undershirt. He had on blue jeans that were too tight for him and was holding a black hat and a gun. The two boys also had guns.

"We've had an ACCIDENT!" the children screamed.

The grandmother had the peculiar feeling that the bespectacled man was someone she knew. His face was as familiar to her as if she had known him all her life but she could not recall who he was. He moved away from the car and began to come down the embankment, placing his feet carefully so that he wouldn't slip. He had on tan and white shoes and no socks, and his ankles were red and thin. "Good afternoon," he said. "I see you all had you a little spill."

"We turned over twice!" said the grandmother.

"Oncet," he corrected. "We see it happen. Try their car and see will it run, Hiram," he said quietly to the boy with the gray hat.

"What you got that gun for?" John Wesley asked. "Whatcha gonna do with that gun?"

"Lady," the man said to the children's mother, "would you mind calling them children to sit down by you? Children make me nervous. I want all you all to sit down right together there were you're at."

"What are you telling us what to do for?" June Star asked.

Behind them the line of woods gaped like a dark open mouth. "Come here," said their mother.

"Look here now," Bailey began suddenly, "we're in a predicament! We're in. . . ."

The grandmother shrieked. She scrambled to her feet and stood staring.

"You're The Misfit!" she said. "I recognized you at once!"

"Yes'm," the man said, smiling slightly as if he were pleased in spite of himself to be known, "but it would have been better for all of you, lady, if you hadn't of reckernized me."

Bailey turned his head sharply and said something to his mother that shocked even the children. The old lady began to cry and The Misfit reddened.

"Lady," he said, "don't you get upset. Sometimes a man says things he don't mean. I don't reckon he meant to talk to you thataway."

"You wouldn't shoot a lady, would you?" the grandmother said and removed a clean handkerchief from her cuff and began to slap at her eyes with it.

The Misfit pointed the toe of his shoe into the ground and made a little hole and then covered it up again. "I would hate to have to," he said.

"Listen," the grandmother almost screamed, "I know you're a good man. You don't look a bit like you have common blood. I know you must come from nice people!"

"Yes mam," he said, "finest people in the world." When he smiled he showed a row of strong white teeth. "God never made a finer woman than my mother and my daddy's heart was pure gold," he said. The boy with the red sweat shirt had come around behind them and was standing with his gun at his hip. The Misfit squatted down on the ground. "Watch them children, Bobby Lee," he said. "You know they make me nervous."

He looked at the six of them huddled together in front of him and he seemed to be embarrassed as if he couldn't think of anything to say. "Ain't a cloud in the sky," he remarked, looking up at it. "Don't see no sun but don't see no cloud neither."

"Yes, it's a beautiful day," said the grandmother. "Listen," she said, "you shouldn't call yourself The Misfit because I know you're a good man at heart. I can just look at you and tell."

"Hush!" Bailey yelled. "Hush! Everybody shut up and let me handle this!" He was squatting in the position of a runner about to sprint forward but he didn't move.

"I pre-chate that, lady," The Misfit said and drew a little circle in the ground with the butt of his gun.

"It'll take a half a hour to fix this here car," Hiram called, looking over the raised hood of it.

"Well, first you and Bobby Lee get him and that little boy to step over yonder with you," The Misfit said, pointing to Bailey and John Wesley. "The boys want to ask you something," he said to Bailey. "Would you mind stepping back in them woods there with them?"

"Listen," Bailey began, "we're in a terrible predicament! Nobody realizes what this is," and his voice cracked. His eyes were as blue and intense as the parrots in his shirt and he remained perfectly still.

The grandmother reached up to adjust her hat brim as if she were going to the woods with him but it came off in her hand. She stood staring at it and after a second she let it fall on the ground. Hiram pulled Bailey up by the arm as if he were assisting an old man. John Wesley caught hold of his father's hand and Bobby Lee followed. They went off toward the woods and just as they reached the dark edge, Bailey turned and supporting himself against a gray naked pine trunk, he shouted, "I'll be back in a minute, Mamma, wait on me!"

"Come back this instant!" his mother shrilled but they all disappeared into the woods.

"Bailey Boy!" the grandmother called in a tragic voice but she found she was looking at The Misfit squatting on the ground in front of her. "I just know you're a good man," she said desperately. "You're not a bit common!"

"Nome, I ain't a good man," The Misfit said after a second as if he had considered her statement carefully, "but I ain't the worst in the world neither. My daddy said I was a different breed of dog from my brothers and sisters. 'You know,' Daddy said, 'it's some that can live their whole life out without asking about it and it's others has to know why it is, and this boy is one of the latters. He's going to be into everything!'" He put on his black hat and looked up suddenly and then away deep into the woods as if he were embarrassed again. "I'm sorry, I don't have on a shirt before you ladies," he said, hunching his shoulders slightly. "We buried our clothes that we had on when we escaped and we're just making do until we can get better. We borrowed these from some folks we met," he explained.

"That's perfectly all right," the grandmother said. "Maybe Bailey has an extra shirt in his suitcase."

"I'll look and see terreckly," The Misfit said.

"Where are they taking him?" the children's mother screamed.

"Daddy was a card himself," The Misfit said. "You couldn't put anything over on him. He never got in trouble with the Authorities though. Just had the knack of handling them."

"You could be honest too if you'd only try," said the grandmother. "Think how wonderful it would be to settle down and live a comfortable life and not have to think about somebody chasing you all the time."

The Misfit kept scratching in the ground with the butt of his gun as if he were thinking about it. "Yes'm, somebody is always after you," he murmured.

The grandmother noticed how thin his shoulder blades were just behind his hat because she was standing up looking down on him. "Do you ever pray?" she asked.

He shook his head. All she saw was the black hat wiggle between his shoulder blades. "Nome," he said.

There was a pistol shot from the woods, followed closely by another. Then silence. The old lady's head jerked around. She could hear the wind move through the tree tops like a long satisfied insuck of breath. "Bailey Boy!" she called.

"I was a gospel singer for a while," The Misfit said. "I been most everything. Been in the arm service, both land and sea, at home and abroad, been twict married, been an undertaker, been with the railroads, plowed Mother Earth, been in a tornado, seen a man burnt alive oncet," and he looked up at the children's mother and the little girl who were sitting close together, their faces white and their eyes glassy; "I even seen a woman flogged," he said.

"Pray, pray," the grandmother began, "pray, pray. . . ."

"I never was a bad boy that I remember of," The Misfit said in an almost dreamy voice, "but somewheres along the line I done something wrong and got sent to the penitentiary. I was buried alive," and he looked up and held her attention to him by a steady stare.

"That's when you should have started to pray," she said. "What did you do to get sent to the penitentiary that first time?"

"Turn to the right, it was a wall," The Misfit said, looking up again at the cloudless sky. "Turn to the left, it was a wall. Look up it was a ceiling, look down it was a floor. I forget what I done, lady. I set there and set there, trying to remember what it was I done and I ain't recalled it to this day. Oncet in a while, I would think it was coming to me, but it never come."

"Maybe they put you in by mistake," the old lady said vaguely.

"Nome," he said. "It wasn't no mistake. They had the papers on me."

"You must have stolen something," she said.

The Misfit sneered slightly. "Nobody had nothing I wanted," he said. "It was a head-doctor at the penitentiary said what I had done was kill my daddy but I known that for a lie. My daddy died in nineteen ought nineteen of the epidemic flu and I never had a thing to do with it. He was buried in the Mount Hopewell Baptist churchyard and you can go there and see for yourself."

"If you would pray," the old lady said, "Jesus would help you."

"That's right," The Misfit said.

"Well then, why don't you pray?" she asked trembling with delight suddenly.

"I don't want no hep," he said. "I'm doing all right by myself."

Bobby Lee and Hiram came ambling back from the woods. Bobby Lee was dragging a yellow shirt with bright blue parrots in it.

"Throw me that shirt, Bobby Lee," The Misfit said. The shirt came flying at him and landed on his shoulder and he put it on. The grandmother couldn't name what the shirt reminded her of. "No, lady," The Misfit said while he was buttoning it up, "I found out the crime don't matter. You can do one thing or you can do another, kill a man or take a tire off his car, because sooner or later you're going to forget what it was you done and just be punished for it."

The children's mother had begun to make heaving noises as if she couldn't get her breath. "Lady," he asked, "would you and that little girl like to step off yonder with Bobby Lee and Hiram and join your husband?"

"Yes, thank you," the mother said faintly. Her left arm dangled helplessly and she was holding the baby, who had gone to sleep, in the other. "Hep that lady up, Hiram," The Misfit said as she struggled to climb out of the ditch, "and Bobby Lee, you hold onto that little girl's hand."

"I don't want to hold hands with him," June Star said. "He reminds me of a pig."

The fat boy blushed and laughed and caught her by the arm and pulled her off into the woods after Hiram and her mother.

Alone with The Misfit, the grandmother found that she had lost her voice. There was not a cloud in the sky nor any sun. There was nothing around her but woods. She wanted to tell him that he must pray. She opened and closed her mouth several times before anything came out. Finally she found herself saying, "Jesus. Jesus," meaning, Jesus will help you, but the way she was saying it, it sounded as if she might be cursing.

"Yes'm," The Misfit said as if he agreed. "Jesus thrown everything off balance. It was the same case with Him as with me except He hadn't committed any crime and they could prove I had committed one because they had the papers on me. Of course," he said, "they never shown me my papers. That's why I sign myself now. I said long ago, you get you a signature and sign everything you do and keep a copy of it. Then you'll know what you done and you can hold up the crime to the punishment and see do they match and in the end you'll have something to prove you ain't been treated right. I call myself The Misfit," he said, "because I can't make what all I done wrong fit what all I gone through in punishment."

There was a piercing scream from the woods, followed closely by a pistol report. "Does it seem right to you, lady, that one is punished a heap and another ain't punished at all?"

"Jesus!" the old lady cried. "You've got good blood! I know you wouldn't shoot a lady! I know you come from nice people! Pray! Jesus, you ought not to shoot a lady. I'll give you all the money I've got!"

"Lady," The Misfit said, looking beyond her far into the woods, "there never was a body that give the undertaker a tip."

There were two more pistol reports and the grandmother raised her head like a parched old turkey hen crying for water and called, "Bailey Boy, Bailey Boy!" as if her heart would break.

"Jesus was the only One that ever raised the dead," The Misfit continued, "and He shouldn't have done it. He thrown everything off balance. If He did what He said, then it's nothing for you to do but throw away everything and follow Him, and if He didn't then it's nothing for you to do but enjoy the few minutes you got left the best way you can—by killing somebody or burning down his house or doing some other meanness to him. No pleasure but meanness," he said and his voice had become almost a snarl.

"Maybe He didn't raise the dead," the old lady mumbled, not knowing what she was saying and feeling so dizzy that she sank down in the ditch with her legs twisted under her.

"I wasn't there so I can't say He didn't," The Misfit said. "I wisht I had of been there," he said, hitting the ground with his fist. "It ain't right I wasn't there because if I had of been there I would of known. Listen Lady," he said in a high voice, "if I had of been there I would of known and I wouldn't be like I am now." His voice seemed about to crack and the grandmother's head cleared for an instant. She saw the man's face twisted close to her own as if he were going to cry and she murmured, "Why, you're one of my babies. You're one of my own children!" She reached out and touched him on the shoulder. The Misfit sprang back as if a snake had bitten him and shot her three times through the chest. Then he put his gun down on the ground and took off his glasses and began to clean them.

Hiram and Bobby Lee returned from the woods and stood over the ditch, looking down at the grandmother who half sat and half lay in a puddle of blood with her legs crossed under her like a child's and her face smiling up at the cloudless sky.

Without his glasses, The Misfit's eyes were red-rimmed and pale and defenseless-looking. "Take her off and throw her where you thrown the others," he said, picking up the cat that was rubbing itself against his leg.

"She was a talker, wasn't she?" Bobby Lee said, sliding down the ditch with a yodel.

"She would of been a good woman," The Misfit said, "if it had been somebody there to shoot her every minute of her life."

"Some fun!" Bobby Lee said.

"Shut up, Bobby Lee," The Misfit said. "It's no real pleasure in life."

1955

Flannery O'Connor was sometimes irritated by the interpretations imposed on her stories by teachers and literary critics. In remarks made at Hollins College before a reading of "A Good Man is Hard to Find," she cited a teacher who had told his class that the grandmother in the story is "a witch, even down to the cat." Like this teacher's students, O'Connor rejected such an over-simple view.

"Where the real heart of the story lies": Flannery O'Connor

This same teacher was telling his students that morally the Misfit was several cuts above the Grandmother. He had a really sentimental attachment to the Misfit. But then a prophet gone wrong is almost always more interesting than your grandmother, and you have to let people take their pleasures where they find them.

It is true that the old lady is a hypocritical old soul; her wits are no match for the Misfit's, nor is her capacity for grace equal to his; yet I think the unprejudiced reader will feel that the Grandmother has a special kind of triumph in this story which instinctively we do not allow to someone altogether bad.

I often ask myself what makes a story work, and what makes it hold up as a story, and I have decided that it is probably some action, some gesture of a character that is unlike any other in the story, one which indicates where the real heart of the story lies. This would have to be an action or a gesture which was both totally right and totally unexpected; it would have to be one that was both in character and beyond character; it would have to suggest both the world and eternity. The action or gesture I'm talking about would have to be on the anagogical level, that is, the level which has to do with the Divine life and our participation in it. It would be a gesture that transcended any neat allegory and might have been intended or any pat moral categories a reader could make. It would be a gesture which somehow made contact with mystery.

YUKIO MISHIMA

(1925–1970)

SWADDLING CLOTHES

translated from the Japanese by Ivan Morris

He was always busy, Toshiko's husband. Even tonight he had to dash off to an appointment, leaving her to go home alone by taxi. But what else could a woman expect when she married an actor—an attractive one? No doubt she had been foolish to hope that he would spend the evening with her. And yet he must have known how she dreaded going back to their house, unhomely with its Western-style furniture and with the bloodstains still showing on the floor.

Toshiko had been oversensitive since girlhood: that was her nature. As the result of constant worrying she never put on weight, and now, an adult woman, she looked more like a transparent picture than a creature of flesh and blood. Her delicacy of spirit was evident to her most casual acquaintance.

Earlier that evening, when she had joined her husband at a night club, she had been shocked to find him entertaining friends with an account of 'the incident.' Sitting there in his American-style suit, puffing at a cigarette, he had seemed to her almost a stranger.

'It's a fantastic story,' he was saying, gesturing flamboyantly as if in an attempt to outweigh the attractions of the dance band. 'Here this new nurse for our baby arrives from the employment agency, and the very first thing I notice about her is her stomach. It's enormous—as if she had a pillow stuck under her kimono! No wonder, I thought, for I soon saw that she could eat more than the rest of us put together. She polished off the contents of our rice bin like that. . . .' He snapped his fingers. ' "Gastric dilation"—that's how she explained her girth and her appetite. Well, the day before yesterday we heard groans and moans coming from the nursery. We rushed in and found her squatting on the floor, holding her stomach in her two hands, and moaning like a cow. Next to her our baby lay in his cot, scared out of his wits and crying at the top of his lungs. A pretty scene, I can tell you!'

'So the cat was out of the bag?' suggested one of their friends, a film actor like Toshiko's husband.

'Indeed it was! And it gave me the shock of my life. You see, I'd completely swallowed that story about "gastric dilation." Well, I didn't waste any time. I rescued our good rug from the floor and spread a blanket for her to lie on. The whole time the girl was yelling like a stuck pig. By the time the doctor from the maternity clinic arrived, the baby had already been born. But our sitting room was a pretty shambles!'

'Oh, that I'm sure of!' said another of their friends, and the whole company burst into laughter.

Toshiko was dumbfounded to hear her husband discussing the horrifying happening as though it were no more than an amusing incident which they chanced to have witnessed. She shut her eyes for a moment and all at once she saw the newborn baby lying before her: on the parquet floor the infant lay, and his frail body was wrapped in bloodstained newspapers.

Toshiko was sure that the doctor had done the whole thing out of spite. As if to emphasize his scorn for this mother who had given birth to a bastard under such sordid conditions, he had told his assistant to wrap the baby in some loose newspapers, rather than proper swaddling. This callous treatment of the newborn child had offended Toshiko. Overcoming her disgust at the entire scene, she had fetched a brand-new piece of flannel from her cupboard and, having swaddled the baby in it, had lain him carefully in an armchair.

This all had taken place in the evening after her husband had left the house. Toshiko had told him nothing of it, fearing that he would think her oversoft, oversentimental; yet the scene had engraved itself deeply in her mind. Tonight she sat silently thinking back on it, while the jazz orchestra brayed and her husband chatted cheerfully with his friends. She knew that she would never forget the sight of the baby, wrapped in stained newspapers and lying on the floor—it was a scene fit for a butchershop. Toshiko, whose own life had been spent in solid comfort, poignantly felt the wretchedness of the illegitimate baby.

I am the only person to have witnessed its shame, the thought occurred to her. The mother never saw her child lying there in its newspaper wrappings, and the baby itself of course didn't know. I alone shall have to preserve that terrible scene in my memory. When the baby grows up and wants to find out about his birth, there will be no one to tell him, so long as I preserve silence. How strange that I should have this feeling of guilt! After all, it was I who took him up from the floor, swathed him properly in flannel, and laid him down to sleep in the armchair.

They left the night club and Toshiko stepped into the taxi that her husband had called for her. 'Take this lady to Ushigomé,' he told the driver and shut the door from the outside. Toshiko gazed through the window at her husband's smiling face and noticed his strong, white teeth. Then she leaned back in the seat, oppressed by the knowledge that their life together was in some way too easy, too painless. It would have been difficult for her to put her thoughts into words. Through the rear window of the taxi she took a last look at her husband. He was striding along the street toward his Nash car, and soon the back of his rather garish tweed coat had blended with the figures of the passers-by.

The taxi drove off, passed down a street dotted with bars and then by a theatre, in front of which the throngs of people jostled each other on the pavement. Although the performance had only just ended, the lights had already been turned out and in the half dark outside it was depressingly obvious that the cherry blossoms decorating the front of the theatre were merely scraps of white paper.

Even if that baby should grow up in ignorance of the secret of his birth, he can never become a respectable citizen, reflected Toshiko, pursuing the same train of thoughts. Those soiled newspaper swaddling clothes will be the symbol of his entire life. But why should I keep worrying about him so much? Is it because I feel uneasy about the future of my own child? Say twenty years from now, when our boy will have grown up into a fine, carefully educated young man, one day by a quirk of fate he meets that other boy, who then will also have turned twenty. And say that the other boy, who has been sinned against, savagely stabs him with a knife. . . .

It was a warm, overcast April night, but thoughts of the future made Toshiko feel cold and miserable. She shivered on the back seat of the car.

No, when the time comes I shall take my son's place, she told herself suddenly. Twenty years from now I shall be forty-three. I shall go to that young man and tell him straight out about everything—about his newspaper swaddling clothes, and about how I went and wrapped him in flannel.

The taxi ran along the dark wide road that was bordered by the park and by the Imperial Palace moat. In the distance Toshiko noticed the pinpricks of light which came from the blocks of tall office buildings.

Twenty years from now that wretched child will be in utter misery. He will be living a desolate, hopeless, poverty-stricken existence—a lonely rat. What else could happen to a baby who has had such a birth? He'll be wandering through the streets by himself, cursing his father, loathing his mother.

No doubt Toshiko derived a certain satisfaction from her somber thoughts: she tortured herself with them without cease. The taxi approached Hanzomon and drove past the compound of the British Embassy. At that point the famous rows of cherry trees were spread out before Toshiko in all their purity. On the spur of the moment she decided to go and view the blossoms by herself in the dark night. It was a strange decision for a timid and unadventurous young woman, but then she was in a strange state of mind and she dreaded the return home. That evening all sorts of unsettling fancies had burst open in her mind.

She crossed the wide street—a slim, solitary figure in the darkness. As a rule when she walked in the traffic Toshiko used to cling fearfully to her companion, but tonight she darted alone between the cars and a moment later had reached the long narrow park that borders the Palace moat. Chidorigafuchi, it is called—the Abyss of the Thousand Birds.

Tonight the whole park had become a grove of blossoming cherry trees. Under the calm cloudy sky the blossoms formed a mass of solid whiteness. The paper lanterns that hung from wires between the trees had been put out; in their place electric light bulbs, red, yellow, and green, shone dully beneath the blossoms. It was well past ten o'clock and most of the flower-viewers had gone home. As the occasional passers-by strolled through the park, they would automatically kick aside the empty bottles or crush the waste paper beneath their feet.

Newspapers, thought Toshiko, her mind going back once again to those happenings. Bloodstained newspapers. If a man were ever to hear of that piteous birth and know that it was he who had lain there, it would ruin his entire life. To think that I, a perfect stranger, should from now on have to keep such a secret—the secret of a man's whole existence. . . .

Lost in these thoughts, Toshiko walked on through the park. Most of the people still remaining there were quiet couples; no one paid her any attention. She noticed two people sitting on a stone bench beside the moat, not looking at the blossoms, but gazing silently at the water. Pitch black it was, and swathed in heavy shadows. Beyond the moat the somber forest of the Imperial Palace blocked her view. The trees reached up, to form a solid dark mass against the night sky. Toshiko walked slowly along the path beneath the blossoms hanging heavily overhead.

On a stone bench, slightly apart from the others, she noticed a pale object—not, as she had at first imagined, a pile of cherry blossoms, nor a garment forgotten by one of the visitors to the park. Only when she came closer did she see that it was a human form lying on the bench. Was it, she wondered, one of those miserable drunks often to be seen sleeping in public places? Obviously not, for the body had been systematically covered with newspapers, and it was the whiteness of those papers that had attracted Toshiko's attention. Standing by the bench, she gazed down at the sleeping figure.

It was a man in a brown jersey who lay there, curled up on layers of newspapers, other newspapers covering him. No doubt this had become his normal night residence now that spring had arrived. Toshiko gazed down at the man's dirty, unkempt hair, which in places had become hopelessly matted. As she observed the sleeping figure wrapped in its newspapers, she was inevitably reminded of the baby who had lain on the floor in its wretched swaddling clothes. The shoulder of the man's jersey rose and fell in the darkness in time with his heavy breathing.

It seemed to Toshiko that all her fears and premonitions had suddenly taken concrete form. In the darkness the man's pale forehead stood out, and it was a young forehead, though carved with the wrinkles of long poverty and hardship. His khaki trousers had been slightly pulled up; on his sockless feet he wore a pair of battered gym shoes. She could not see his face and suddenly had an overmastering desire to get one glimpse of it.

She walked to the head of the bench and looked down. The man's head was half buried in his arms, but Toshiko could see that he was surprisingly young. She noticed the thick eyebrows and the fine bridge of his nose. His slightly open mouth was alive with youth.

But Toshiko had approached too close. In the silent night the newspaper bedding rustled, and abruptly the man opened his eyes. Seeing the young woman standing directly beside him, he raised himself with a jerk, and his eyes lit up. A second later a powerful hand reached out and seized Toshiko by her slender wrist.

She did not feel in the least afraid and made no effort to free herself. In a flash the thought had struck her. Ah, so the twenty years have already gone by! The forest of the Imperial Palace was pitch dark and utterly silent.

1966

The clash in "Swaddling Clothes" between Western and Japanese values is a theme reflected in much of Yukio Mishima's fiction; it figured importantly in his life as well. In an interview conducted a few months before his death, Mishima discussed the relation between his Japanese spirit and his Westernized way of life.

"There is no fire in our present society": Yukio Mishima

"If you look at my house, it seems completely Westernized," he said after a pause. "But I am living in a double house. You can see only the visible house. But I also live in an invisible house which you cannot see. Let me give you a simple explanation for the Western civilization you see here.

"Here are two floors of a house. How to get from the first to the second floor is the basic problem. In Western culture, the solution is to make a stairway. Then anyone can climb up from the ground floor.

"The stairway is a method—not technique, not civilization, but method inherited from the ancient Greeks. They adopted this method in building their culture.

"Since the 19th century, the Japanese have learned the Western way of using a stairway. We've imported this stairway, this method, from the West and with the method we immediately imported all the trappings of Western civilization to modernize our country.

"But in our own Oriental way of thinking, there is no stairway at all. We never believed in method. It has been said of Noh acting that its highest discipline is a flower. How can you reach a flower? There is no method. You can only try hard by yourself. Independently. A teacher may suggest something but he cannot help you. So it is with climbing to the second floor. You must try hard to climb by your own enthusiasm and ambition. Maybe you will jump up. Maybe you will climb a pillar. But you must decide yourself and not rely on method . . ."

"Another way of thinking is Indian. The Indian meditates about how to reach the second floor and after a while reaches the conclusion that he already is there. That is an illusion. But the Japanese can actually climb to the second floor. . . . But I would like to ask the Japanese people: "We think we have climbed to the second floor. But can we be sure? Can we really certify that this is the second floor? I believe Europeans can certify their results and say they have reached the second floor because they built the stairway. But if we borrow the stairway, the second floor is not our second floor—at best it is borrowed." . . .

Before the war, he said, writers used to serve up the raw stuff of life to tradition-bound Japanese society. Now, the Japanese people feel liberated and free. They are materialistic and wealthy and want nothing but to enjoy life without limitation. Of course, Mishima added, all this freedom and enjoyment is artificial. This is also true of the writer. He has no raw material to offer because his life, too, is "artificial" canned food.

"So I reached the conclusion that we must search for and find something genuine and pure—something 'raw' not only in our minds but in our history. I want to touch fire, but there is no fire in our present society. Who is the one in Greek myth who took fire from the mountain? Yes, Prometheus. I want to be Prometheus."

JOHN BERGER

(b. 1926)

AN INDEPENDENT WOMAN

Catherine seized each man to embrace him. Her long arms pulled him towards her tall body. First Nicolas her brother, then Jean-François the neighbour. She kissed them on both cheeks, near the mouth. At seventy-four, she was just the eldest of the three.

"It's buried one metre deep," said Catherine, "I can hear Mathieu telling me that. One metre deep."

"Where does it cross the field?" shouted Nicolas.

She shrugged her shoulders. "Fifty years is a long time, but I remember him saying it was one metre deep."

Two months ago, when she was helping her brother bring in his second hay, she had told him that the water to the *bassin*[1] beside her house was

---

1. A container, tub for water or for washing in.

no longer flowing. After that, she had refused to mention the subject again. She was going to be dependent on nobody. Yet now the expression in her eyes was excited as though she had willed the two men to come.

"The spring must be at the top," said Jean-François and he began to climb the field, disappearing into the fog.

"Jean-François," she cried out, "come back before I lose sight of you."

Born into another house Catherine would surely have married, but each year of her life more men had left the valley, and she herself had inherited too little to propose to any of them that they remain.

She seized hold of Jean-François by the arm. "You shouldn't have come to give up a whole day."

"We dig one metre deep, at right angles to the line. Begin at the top and come down to the bottom. That way we're bound to arrive at the pipe."

"And the pipe will lead us to the spring! Jésus, Marie and Joseph! We'll have it by midday."

They began digging. Underneath the snow, the ground was still unfrozen.

When Catherine came from the house, carrying in a canvas bag glasses, a jug of hot wine and some bread and cheese, she heard the men before she could see them. At a distance of twenty metres the white fog merged into the white snow on the ground. Each time Jean-François bent his back to strike the pick into the earth, he grunted. And she heard Nicolas scraping his spade so the earth should not stick to it.

She had worked once as a waitress in a café near the Gare de Lyon in Paris. She and her brother Mathieu, the one who had laid the pipe and the one who was killed by the Germans during the Occupation, were the first members of the family ever to earn wages. And to do this they both went to Paris. He was a porter. She was a waitress. Her lasting impression of the capital was one of money continually changing hands. There, without money, you could literally do nothing. Not even drink water. With money you could do anything. He who could buy courage was brave, even if he was a coward.

The two men had dug the trench exactly one metre deep. From time to time they had measured it. It was straight and impeccably cut and cleaned out. On one side was stacked the turf; on the other, the earth. All the stones lifted out were piled in a heap together.

Nicolas scrambled out of the trench and Jean-François plunged his spade into the loose soil, as if in the hope that it would disappear into the centre of the earth. Living by himself in the corner under the mountain, he had the habit of making violent movements; in his solitude such violence was a kind of company. Catherine poured out the hot wine. The men kept the glasses up to their faces between sips, their noses in the steam which smelt of cloves and cinnamon.

"In God's name it must be here," Nicolas grumbled.

"I tell you if it's not in this field, there's no fire in hell."

During the second half of the day Nicolas continued the long trench already begun. Jean-François dug another higher up. And Catherine started digging a third near the pair of apple trees. When she had cut the turf, she kicked the snow off before lifting the pieces up. She disliked having cold hands or feet. At night she took three hot bricks to bed with her, one for each foot and one for the small of her back. As she swung the pick the breath came out of her with a whistle, quite unlike Jean-François' grunt.

After working in the restaurant by the Gare de Lyon she became a maid in a doctor's house. The doctor worked at the hospital of St Antonine and lived a few streets away in the rue Charles V. Her principal jobs were cleaning grates, washing floors and laundering. The first time she laundered, she had asked the cook where the wood ash was kept. "Wood ash!" repeated the cook, incredulous. "To clean the sheets," explained Catherine. The cook told her to go back to her goat shit. It was the first time Catherine heard the word *peasant* used as an insult.

They dug until the fog absorbed the dusk.

Jean-François looked down at his trench which was now a good fifteen metres long.

"Not quite wide enough for a coffin."

"We are all of us thin," said Catherine.

"Three graves, one for each of us."

"A grave for each of us!" roared Nicolas.

When she returned from Paris, Catherine had found her sister-in-law dying of puerperal fever. During the next fifteen years she brought up her two nieces like daughters.

Jean-François abruptly picked up a stone and threw it up the field into the dark.

Catherine began hustling the two men towards the house. Outside the kitchen door she placed a bowl of heated water for them to wash in. She took hold of Jean-François' wrists and placed his hands in the water. Then she draped a towel round his neck.

The last time the three of them had sat round the table in the kitchen was when she believed she might die. The doctor said it was pleurisy. She refused to go to hospital. If she was going to die, she wanted death to pass by the things she knew. Her two rooms were bare, there was neither armchair nor carpets nor curtains. But there were certain objects which were intimate to her: her yellow coffee-pot, the stove which she kept as shiny as a groomed black horse, her high bed, the picture of the Madonna above it, her work-basket. Death must run the gauntlet of these. Each night she laid out her linen and stockings before climbing into the bed, so that Nicolas should know exactly how to dress her for the coffin.

One night when he came to the house, Nicolas noticed the linen laid out.

"What's that for?"

"To dress me in the morning if I shut my umbrella in the night."
She spoke in a hoarse whisper.

At that moment there was a scuffling noise against the door and a voice had intoned, like a lament:

"Four wild boar! I've seen them with my own eyes, charging down the hill!"

Jean-François had stumbled in, clutching a rifle. Drunk, he came up to the bed.

"Catherine, what will we do without you? They tell me you are very sick."

"Is the gun loaded?" she whispered.

He handed it to her and she took out the cartridges.

When she was working at the doctor's house, she had received the letter from Mathieu saying that his wife was ill and that she must return immediately. By leaving so abruptly she lost two months' wages. She protested to the doctor's wife that nobody could foresee illness. For illness there are hospitals, was the reply. Catherine picked up one of the pokers she had polished every morning. The doctor's wife screamed for help. The cook came running to the rescue. She found the mistress of the house clutching the curtains as if she had been surprised naked. And the mad Savoyard maid was standing with a poker in her hand looking at the fire.

"Tomorrow," Jean-François said, "we'll come and cup you. Eh, Nicolas?"

"I might be better off on the other side," she said.

"Seigneur!" screamed her brother. "Stop talking like that. We're coming tomorrow."

When they came, the two men stuffed the stove with wood. She stripped naked to the waist and sat on a chair. "It's not the first time you've seen a woman," she said to Jean-François.

"What difference does that make?" demanded Nicolas. "We're going to cure you."

On the table was a set of glasses with a candle. Jean-François lit the candle, wiped a glass, tore a shred of newspaper, put it in the candle flame and when it was burning, placed it in the glass. Nicolas pressed the rim of the glass hard against his sister's back. Almost immediately the flame went out. The skin beneath her shoulder-blade was white and soft, not very different from when she was a young woman. Tentatively, Nicolas' large hand abandoned the glass to see whether the vacuum would hold it against the flesh. Glass and flesh stayed firm.

Jean-François prepared the fire in a second glass.

"Put it," he said, "where there's plenty of meat."

"Never on the vertebral column," proclaimed Nicolas.

"I said where there's meat!"

They applied five glasses. Her skin rose up inside them like pies in an oven. She held the table with her arms to steady herself against the hurt.

"I don't want you to hear me cry out."

"I'll sing," offered Nicolas.

He sang:

La vie est une rose
La rose piquera . . .

When it came to removing the glasses, Jean-François did it because Nicolas' nails were too broken. He ran his finger-nail round the rim of the glass, making a tiny trench in the flesh, to let the air in.

"Ah," she sighed, as each glass came off. "Thank you, my friend!" Two days later she was cured.

Now together in the same kitchen the three of them were dispirited by the day's work which had yielded nothing.

"They have a machine," mused Jean-François, "for detecting water underground, like a water diviner's stick, only it's electronic. And it finds where water is to twenty centimetres."

"Where?" asked Catherine, on the edge of her chair.

"It costs seventy thousand francs to hire."

"Merde de merde!" said Catherine.

Next morning the three of them surveyed the three trenches. During the night, as if encouraged by their digging, moles had thrown up their own earthworks over most of the field. This made all the digging look less systematic.

"In this earth," roared Nicolas—and between each phrase he struck with his pick—"in this damned earth of this damned field in this damned fog I have a rendez-vous with the Devil!"

By the afternoon they had still not found any sign of any pipe. Occasionally in the kitchen Catherine heard one of their raised voices. She could not distinguish the words but the tone of the shouting was enough to tell her how discouraged they must be. "If they don't find it today, they won't come back tomorrow."

She put more wood on the stove, took her slippers out of the oven and shut the oven door. "I have wasted two of their days," she muttered. She set about preparing some pastry. When it was rolled out, she made small pastry purses, each large enough to hold a five-franc piece. Into the purses she put purée of apples. She made twenty-five.

She packed the pastries with the coffee-pot, *gnôle* and cups into her canvas bag, and strode across the orchard. Before the men became visible through the fog she stopped and adjusted the scarf tied round her head. She held out the bowl of sugar so that each man could sugar his coffee to his taste. She herself poured the *eau-de-vie* plentifully into their cups. The men held them with both hands and gazed around them into the fog.

"Mathieu!" muttered Nicolas. "Mathieu was cunning. He could have laid this pipe at a depth of eighty centimetres and it would still have been safe from the hardest frost. But no! Not Mathieu. He had to lay it at a metre!"

"The moles have eaten the pipe."

"The pipe has gone to La Roche, I tell you!"

Corner by corner, she unfolded the napkin wrapped round the pastries. Baked a light brown, they steamed in the air. The smell made the two men glance at each other and smile with complicity.

"We used to eat them after midnight mass at Christmas," said Nicolas quietly.

"The blood's coming back," said Jean-François.

Between mouthfuls of coffee, they ate them one by one.

When they were finished, Catherine issued her command: "No more work today."

The two men put on their coats and, by an accord of common tact, nobody mentioned tomorrow.

She woke up when it was still dark. She did not expect the men to return for a third day's work. After she had fed the goats and cleaned the stable, the sky was as blue and large as it only is over the mountains. In the valley, through the transparent early-morning mist were church, dairy, cemetery, two cafés, post office: the village. The worst about real fog is that it hangs square like a curtain. Vertical and horizontal. The best about it lifting is that all the slopes are revealed and everything is precipitous.

She went to fetch her water, downhill, across two fields. She had done this ever since the water had dried up. All her father's life and grandfather's life the sound of water had marked the place below where it was easy to fill buckets.

What she feared was the ice. The ice would soon be back. The pine trees, only one hundred metres higher up towards La Roche, were white with hoar-frost, not a needle, not a spider's web had escaped its white load. She feared that when the slope was frozen with ice, she might slip as she carried the buckets, and break a leg, and lie there all day without being found.

"On the other side I'd have no goats to look after, no potatoes to lift, no chickens to feed. I would have all the time in the world, and I could make all the visits I don't make now. Yet I don't want to die out of the house. I want to see death come past the things I've lived with. Then I can concentrate and not be distracted."

In the clear air which no longer muffled sounds, she heard Jean-François' voice, high up, in the field by the orchard.

"I tell you where it is! Here! Here is where I am betting it is! You'll see. I thought about it in the night. This is where it is. Within half a metre of here!"

Leaving the two buckets, she clambered up, shouting, "I don't believe it!"

They did not begin digging where Jean-François had driven in his spade to mark his bet. They systematically extended the long trench which would eventually come to the point he had indicated.

After two hours, Nicolas said: "The earth has been worked here. Fifty years ago maybe, but the earth has been worked here."

The only sign of his impatience was that he wielded the pick with shorter pauses.

"I told you so!"

He pointed, at the bottom of the trench, to a reddish mark in the earth, the size of a small flower.

"Rust!"

"Rust!"

"Catherine!"

The three of them looked down at the pipe at the bottom of the trench.

"It's in perfect condition."

"It's a well-turned pipe."

Jean-François jumped down and scratched at it with his knife.

"The metal is shiny underneath."

"I knew it when we saw the rust."

"It was there all the time," shouted Nicolas.

"The pipe under the field was there all the time."

"Exactly one metre down. Measure it."

Jean-François measured it.

"Exactly one metre."

"All we do now is to follow it."

"The spring should be here."

They stood looking down at the coarse grass.

"We'd have found it yesterday if we'd gone on," Nicolas shouted. He surveyed everything: the snow peaks, the rock-faces, the white forest, the ledges of land, the valley. "You'd have found it, Catherine, if you'd dug another two metres by the apple trees." He gazed up at the spaceless blue sky. "I'd have found it if I'd dug upwards instead of downwards! And Jean-François found it where he said he would!"

Impatiently Catherine started cutting the turf. The two men ambled away, opened their trousers and pissed.

They unearthed the reservoir after half an hour's further digging.

"It's a huge stone," announced Jean-François, "it must be two metres wide, the lid."

Nicolas peered at the flat stone being uncovered. "Where could he have found a stone like that. From La Roche!"

"We'll need crowbars to prise it off."

"Is it all one stone?"

"He placed it well, he knew how to place it, did Mathieu. I told you he was cunning."

"It's going to weigh a ton!"

"How did he get it here?"

"It's huge."

"As huge as a tomb."

"It's Jésus' tomb!"

"Jésus' tomb," repeated Catherine.

John Berger   521

Jean-François scraped at the stone, his unshaven face almost touching it.

"We've got to roll it away."

Catherine went to fetch what bars she could find in the stable. They forced in two to steady it, and they used one to prise with. The flat stone did not shift. All three strained to use all their weight.

"Jésus' . . . tomb!"

"We're opening it."

"Op—en—ing!"

"Up!"

"Up!"

"What's inside?"

Jean-François peered through the narrow space under the prised-up flat stone.

"Shit!"

"He says Jésus' tomb is full of shit!"

"Fifty years of shit!" said Catherine.

"Slide it now."

"Gently."

"There!"

In the great current of their triple laughter, words they had already used surfaced, turned and eddied, disappeared, reappeared and were carried on, submerged by the laughter.

—Jésus, Marie and Joseph!—

—Mathieu knew what he was doing!—

—It was easy for him.—

—It's big enough to dip a sheep in.—

—The tomb of Jésus, that's what it is.—

They plunged in their arms up to their armpits, to find where the outlet pipe was. Their arms came out black. With a bucket they began emptying out the sediment, until the water no longer overspilled.

"Run to the *bassin,* Catherine, and see if it's coming."

"It's coming," she screamed. "It's coming out brown like coffee."

The sun had set before they stopped dredging.

The men carried the tools to the house. Close against the wall, in the shelter of the eaves, water gushed out of the mouth of the pipe. As it fell, it became tangled and silver.

Inside the kitchen it was warm. Catherine strode around the room, particularly between stove and table, serving.

"Sit down, woman!"

"I never expected you to come today," she said.

"Tonight it's going to freeze."

"The water from the spring will never freeze," she said.

"Today is the last day we could have dug."

"This morning I never said you'd both come."

"Catherine, you have always expected too little," Jean-François announced.

"Listen a moment!" roared Nicolas.

The three of them placed their knives on the table and through the window they listened to the frivolous sound of the running water.

1979

John Berger's fiction and art criticism always register his political and moral commitments. In discussing the paintings of Jean Francois Millet, similar in subject to "An Independent Woman," Berger reveals his view of the way great artists can also be moralists.

"By the power of identification with his subjects": John Berger

Millet was a moralist in the only way that a great artist can be: by the power of his identification with his subjects. He chose to paint peasants because he was one, and because—under a somewhat similar influence to the unpolitical realists today— he instinctively hated the false elegance of the beau monde. His genius was the result of the fact that, choosing to paint physical labour, he had the passionate, highly sensuous and sexual temperament that could lead him to intense physical identification. . . . [A]t the age of thirty-five he gave up painting nudes. . . .

Yet there was no inhibited puritanism behind this decision. Millet objected to Boucher because 'he did not paint nude women, but only little creatures undressed'.

As for the nature of Millet's power of identification, this is clearly revealed in one of his remarks about a drawing by Michelangelo.

> When I saw that drawing of his in which he depicts a man in a
> fainting fit—I felt like the subject of it, as though I were racked
> with pain. I suffered with the body, with the limbs, that I saw
> suffer.

In the same way he strode forward with *The Sower,* felt the weight of the hand on a lap even when it was obscured in shadow (see his etching of a *Mother Feeding her Child*), embraced with the harvesters the trusses of hay, straightened his back with the hoers, clenched his leg to steady the log with the wood-cutters, leant his weight against the tree trunk with the shepherdess, sprawled at midday on the ground with the exhausted.

ALICE ADAMS

(b. 1926)

RETURN TRIPS

Some years ago I spent a hot and mostly miserable summer in an ugly yellow hotel on the steep and thickly wooded, rocky coast of northern Yugoslavia, not far from the island of Rab. I was with a man whom I entirely, wildly loved, and he, Paul, loved me, too, but together we suffered the most excruciating romantic agonies, along with the more ordinary daily discomforts of bad food, an uncomfortable, poorly ventilated room with a hard, unyielding bed, and not enough money to get away. Or enough strength: Paul's health was bad. Morosely we stared out over the lovely clear, cool blue water, from our pine forest, to enticing islands that were purplish-gray in the distance. Or else I swam and Paul looked out after me.

Paul's problem was a congenital heart condition, now correctable by surgery, but not so then; he hurt a lot, and the smallest walks could cause pain. Even love, I came to realize, was for Paul a form of torture, although we kept at it—for him suicidally, I guess—during those endless sultry yellow afternoons, on our awful bed, between our harsh, coarse sheets.

I wanted us to marry. I was very young, and very healthy, and my crazy, unreal idea of marriage seemed to include a sort of transfer of strength. I was not quite so silly as to consciously think that marrying me would "cure" Paul, nor did I imagine a lifelong nurse role for myself. It was, rather, a magic belief that if we did a normal thing, something other people did all the time, like getting married, Paul's heart would become normal, too, like other, ordinary hearts.

Paul believed that he would die young, and, nobly, he felt that our marriage would be unfair to me. He also pointed out that whereas he had enough money from a small inheritance for one person, himself, to live on very sparingly, there was really not enough for two, and I would do well to go back to America and to the years of graduate study to which my professor mother wanted to stake me. At that time, largely because of Paul, who was a poet, I thought of studying literature; instead, after he died I turned to history, contemporary American. By now I have written several books; my particular interest is in the Trotskyite movement: its rich history of lonely, occasionally brilliant, contentious voices, its legacy of schisms—an odd choice, perhaps, but the books have been surprisingly popular. You might say, and I hope Paul would, that I have done very well professionally. In any case you could say that Paul won our argument. That fall I went back to graduate school, at Georgetown, and Paul died young, as he said he would, in a hospital in Trieste.

I have said that Paul loved me, and so he did, intensely—he loved me more, it has come to seem to me, than anyone since, although I have had my share, I guess. But Paul loved me with a meticulous attention that included every aspect. Not only my person: at that time I was just a skinny tall young girl with heavy dark hair that was fated to early gray, as my mother's had been. With an old-fashioned name—Emma. Paul loved my hair and my name and whatever I said to him, any odd old memory, or half-formed ambition; he took all my perceptions seriously. He laughed at all my jokes, although his were much funnier. He was even interested in my dreams, which I would sometimes wake and tell him, that summer, in the breathless pre-dawn cool, in the ugly hotel.

And so it is surprising that there was one particular dream that I did not tell him, especially since this dream was so painful and troubling that I remember it still. Much later I even arranged to reënact the dream, an expurgatory ritual of sorts—but that is to get far ahead of my story.

In the dream, then, that I dreamed as I slept with Paul, all those years ago in Yugoslavia, it was very hot, and I was walking down a long, intensely familiar hill, beside a winding white concrete highway. In the valley below was the rambling white house where (long before Yugoslavia) my parents and I had lived for almost five years, in a small Southern town called Hilton. I did not get as far as the house, in the dream; it was so hot, and I was burdened with the most terrific, heavy pain in my chest, a pain that must have come from Paul's actual pain, as the heat in the dream would have come from the actual heat of that summer.

"Oh, I had such an awful dream!" I cried out to Paul, as I burrowed against his sharp back, his fine damp skin.

"What about?" He kissed my hair.

"Oh, I don't know," I said. "I was in Hilton. You know, just before my parents' divorce. Where I had such a good time and my mother hated everything."

Against my hair he murmured, "Your poor mother."

"Yes, but she brings it on herself. She's so difficult. No wonder my father . . . really. And I don't want to go to graduate school."

And so I did not tell Paul my dream, in which I had painfully walked that downhill mile toward the scene of our family's dissolution, and the heady start of my own adolescence. Instead, in a familiar way, Paul and I argued about my future, and as usual I took a few stray shots at my mother.

And Paul died, and I did after all go to graduate school, and then my mother died—quite young, it now seems to me, and long before our war was in any way resolved.

A very wise woman who is considerably older than I am once told me that in her view relationships with people to whom we have been very close can continue to change even after the deaths of those people, and for me I think this has been quite true, with my mother, and in quite another way with Paul.

I am now going back to a very early time, long before my summer with Paul, in Yugoslavia. Before anyone had died. I am going back to Hilton.

When we arrived in Hilton I was eleven, and both my parents were in their early forties, and almost everything that went so darkly and irretrievably wrong among the three of us was implicit in our ages. Nearly adolescent, I was eager for initiation into romantic, sensual mysteries of which I had dim intimations from books. For my mother, the five years from forty-two or forty-three onward were a desolate march into middle age. My father, about ten months younger than my mother—and looking, always, ten years younger—saw his early forties as prime time; he had never felt better in his life. Like me, he found Hilton both romantic and exciting —he had a marvellous time there, as I did, mostly.

My first overtly sensual experience took place one April night on that very stretch of road, the gravelled walk up above the highway that wound down to our house, that I dreamed of in Yugoslavia. I must have been twelve, and a boy who was "walking me home" reached for and took and held my hand, and I felt an overwhelming hot excitement. Holding hands.

About hands:

These days, like most of my friends, I am involved in a marriage, my second, which seems problematical—even more problematical than most of the marriages I see—but then maybe everyone views his or her marriage in this way. Andreas is Greek, by way of Berkeley, to which his parents immigrated in the thirties and opened a student restaurant, becoming successful enough to send their promising son to college there, and later on to medical school. Andreas and I seem to go from friendliness or even love to rage, with a speed that leaves me dizzy, and scared. However, ambivalent as in many ways I am about Andreas, I do very much like—in fact, I love—his hands. They are just plain male hands, rather square in shape, usually callused and very competent. Warm. A doctor, he specializes in kidneys, unromantically enough, but his hands are more like a workman's, a carpenter's. And sometimes even now an accidental meeting of our hands can recall me to affection; his hands remind me of love.

I liked Paul's hands, too, and I remember them still. They were very smooth, and cool.

Back in Hilton, when I was twelve, my mother violently disapproved of my being out at night with boys. Probably sensing just how exciting I found those April nights that smelled of privet and lilacs, and those lean, tall, sweet-talking Southern boys, she wept and raged, despairing and helpless as she recognized the beginning of my life as a sensual woman, coinciding as it probably did with the end of her own.

My feckless father took my side, of course. "Things are different down here, my dear," he told her. "It's a scientific fact that girls, uh, mature much earlier in the South. And when in Rome, you know. I see no harm in Emma's going to a movie with some nice boy, if she promises to be home at a reasonable hour. Ten-thirty?"

"But Emma isn't Southern. She has got to be home by ten!"

My mother filled me with a searing discomfort, a longing to be away from her. Having no idea how much I pitied her, I believed that I hated her.

My father was not only younger than my mother, he was at least a full inch shorter—a small man, compactly built, and handsome. "Has anyone ever told you that you look like that writer fellow, that Scott Fitzgerald?" asked one of the local Hilton ladies, a small brunette, improbably named Popsie Hooker. "Why no, I don't believe anyone ever has," my father lied; he had been told at least a dozen times of that resemblance. "But of course I'm flattered to be compared to such a famous man. Rather a devil, though, I think I've heard," he said, with a wink at Popsie Hooker.

"Popsie Hooker, how remarkably redundant," hopelessly observed my academic mother, to my bored and restless father. They had chosen Hilton rather desperately, as a probably cheap place to live on my father's dwindling Midwestern inheritance; he was never exactly cut out for work, and after divorcing my mother he resolved his problems, or some of them, in a succession of marriages to very rich women.

Popsie Hooker, who was later to play a curious, strong role in my life, at that time interested me not at all; if I had a view of her, it was closer to my mother's than I would have admitted, and for not dissimilar reasons. She was ludicrous, so small and silly, and just a little cheap, with those girlish clothes, all ribbons and bows, and that tinny little laugh. And that accent: Popsie out-Southerned everyone around.

"It's rather like a speech defect," my mother observed, before she stopped mentioning Popsie altogether.

Aside from her smallness and blue-eyed prettiness, Popsie's local claim to fame was her lively correspondence with "famous people," to whom she wrote what were presumably letters of adulation, the puzzle being that these people so often wrote back to her. Popsie was fond of showing off her collection. She had a charming note from Mr. Fitzgerald, and letters from Eleanor Roosevelt, Norma Shearer, Willa Cather, Clare Boothe Luce. No one, least of all my mother, could understand why such people would write to dopey Popsie, nor could I, until many years later, when she began to write to me.

However, I was too busy at that time to pay much attention to my parents or their friends, their many parties at which everyone drank too much; my own burgeoning new life was much more absorbing.

My walks at night with various boys up and down that stretch of highway sometimes came to include a chaste but passionate kiss; this would take place, if at all, on the small secluded dirt road that led down from the highway to our house.

One winter, our fourth year in Hilton, when I was fifteen, in January we had an exceptionally heavy fall of snow, deep and shadowed in the valley where our house was, ladening boughs of pine and fir and entirely covering the privet and quince and boxwood that edged the highway. For several days most of the highway itself lay under snow. Cars labored up and down the hill, singly, at long intervals, wearing unaccustomed chains.

Those nights of snow were marvellous: so cold, the black sky broken with stars as white as snow. My friends and I went sledding; that winter I was strongly taken with a dark boy who looked rather like Paul, now that I try to see him: a thin, bony face, a certain Paul-like intensity. On a dare we sledded down the highway, so perilously exciting! We lay on the sled, I stretched along his back.

We went hurtling down past the back road to my house, past everything. At last on a level area we stopped; on either side of us fields of white seemed to billow and spread off into the shadows, in the cold. Standing there we kissed—and then we began the long slow ascent of the highway, toward my house. He was pulling the sled, and we stopped several times to kiss, to press our upright bodies warmly together.

As we neared and then reached the back road to my house, we saw a car stopped, its headlights on. Guiltily we dropped hands. Dazzled by the light, only as we were almost upon it could I recognize our family car, the only wood-panelled Chrysler in town. In it was my father, kissing someone; their bodies were blotted into one silhouette.

If he saw and recognized us, there was no sign. He could easily not have seen us, or, knowing my father, who was nothing if not observant, I would guess it's more likely he did see us but pretended to himself that he did not, as he pretended not to see that my mother was miserably unhappy, and that I was growing up given to emotional extremes, and to loneliness.

"Stricken" probably comes closest to how I felt: burning rage, a painful, seething shame—emotions that I took to be hatred. "I hate him" is what I thought. Oblivious of the tall boy at my side, I began to walk as fast as I could, clumping heavily through the snow; at the door of my house I muttered what must have been a puzzlingly abrupt good night. Without kissing.

By the time we left Hilton, the summer that I was sixteen, my parents were entirely fed up with Hilton, and with each other. My father thought he could get a job in the Pentagon, in Washington—he knew someone there; and my mother had decided on New York, on graduate school at Columbia; I would go to Barnard.

I was less upset about my parents' separation than I was about leaving Hilton, which was by now to me a magic, enchanted place. In the spring and summer just preceding our departure there were amazing white bursts of dogwood, incredible wisteria and roses.

I wept for my friends, whom I would always love and miss, I thought.

I hated New York. The city seemed violent and confusing, ugly and dirty, loud. Voices in the streets or on subways and busses grated against my ears; everyone spoke so stridently, so harshly. Until I met Paul I was lonely and miserable, and frightened.

I would not have told him of my unease right away, even though Paul and I began as friends. But he must have sensed some rural longings just beneath my New York veneer. He would have; almost from the start Paul felt whatever I felt—he came to inhabit my skin.

In any case, our friendship and then our love affair had a series of outdoor settings. Paul, melancholy and romantic, and even then not well, especially liked the sea, and he liked to look out to islands—which led us, eventually, to Yugoslavia, our desolate summer there.

Not having had an actual lover before, only boys who kissed me, who did not talk much, I was unprepared for the richness of love with Paul —or, rather, I assumed that that was how love was between true intimates. Paul's sensuality was acutely sensitive, and intense; with him I felt both beautiful and loved—indescribably so. You could say that Paul spoiled me for other men, and in a way that is true—he did. But on the other hand Paul knew that he was dying, gradually, and that knowledge must have made him profligate with love. We talked and talked, we read poetry; Paul read Wallace Stevens and Eliot aloud to me, and his own poems, which I thought remarkable. We made jokes, we laughed, we made love.

Since Hilton was only twelve hours from New York by train, and we both liked travel, and trains, in a way it is odd that Paul and I did not go down to Hilton. I know he would have said yes had I suggested a trip. His curiosity about me was infinite; he would have wanted to see a place that I cared so much about. I suppose we would have stayed at the inn, as I was to do later on, when finally I did go back to Hilton. We could have taken a taxi out to what had been my house.

However, for whatever reasons, Paul and I did not go to Hilton. We went to upstate New York and to Connecticut, and out to Long Island.

And, eventually, to Yugoslavia.

Our unhappiness there in the ugly yellow hotel on the beautiful rockbound coast was due not only to Paul's declining health and my unreal but urgent wish to marry. Other problems lay in the sad old truth, well known to most adults but not at that time to us, that conducting a love affair while living apart is quite unlike taking up residence together, even for a summer. In domestic ways we were both quite impossible then—and of course Paul did not get time to change.

I could not cook, and our arrangement with the hotel included the use of a communal kitchen, an allotted space in the refrigerator and time at the stove; my cooking was supposed to save us money, which my burned disasters failed to do. Neither could I sew or iron. I even somehow failed at washing socks. None of this bothered Paul at all; his expectations of me did not run along such lines, but mine, which must have been plucked from the general culture rather than from my own freethinking mother, were strong, and tormenting.

Paul had terrible troubles with the car, a Peugeot that we had picked up in Paris, on our way, and that had functioned perfectly well all across the Italian Alps, until we got to Trieste, where it began to make inexplicable noises, and sometimes not to start. Paul was utterly incapable of dealing with these *crises;* he would shout and rant, even clutch melodramatically at his thin black hair. I dimly sensed that he was reacting to the car's infirmities instead of to his own, which of course I did not say; but I also felt that men were supposed to deal with cars, an insupportable view, I knew even then, and derived from my father, who possessed remarkable mechanical skills.

We were there in Yugoslavia for almost three months in all, from June to September. It was probably in August, near the end of our stay, that I had my dream of going back to Hilton, and walking down the highway to our house—in the heat, with the pain in my heart that must have been Paul's pain. The dream that I did not tell Paul.

And in the fall I went back to America, to Washington, D.C., to study at Georgetown.

And Paul moved up to Trieste, where shortly after Christmas he went into a hospital and died.

Sheer disbelief was my strongest reaction to the news of Paul's death, which came in the form of a garbled cablegram. I could not believe that such an acute and lively intelligence could simply be snuffed out. In a conventional way I wept and mourned his loss: I played music that he had liked—the Hummel trumpet concerto, of which he was especially fond—and I reread "Sunday Morning" and "Four Quartets." But at the same time I never believed that he was entirely gone (I still do not).

Two years after Paul's death, most unexpectedly my mother died, in a senseless automobile accident; she was driving to see friends in Connecticut and swerved on a wet highway to avoid an oncoming truck. I was more horrified, more devastated, really, than I could have believed possible. I went to an analyst. "I haven't even written her for a month!" I cried out, during one dark fifty-minute hour. "How many letters does it take to keep a mother alive?" was the gentle and at least mildly helpful answer. Still, I wrestled with my guilt and with the sheer irresolution of our connection for many, many years.

In my late twenties I married one of my former professors: Lewis —a large, blond, emphatically healthy, outgoing man, as much unlike Paul as anyone I could have found; this occurred to me at the time as an ironic twist that only Paul himself could have appreciated. We lived in New York, where we both now taught.

To sum up very complicated events in a short and simple way: my work prospered, while my marriage did not—and I present these as simultaneous conditions, not causally linked. A happier first marriage could have made for even better work on my part, I sometimes think.

During those years, I thought of my mother with increasing sympathy. This is another simplification, but that is what it came to. She did her best under very difficult, sometimes painful circumstances is one way of putting it.

And I thought of Paul. It was his good-friend aspect that I most missed, I found, in the loneliness of my marriage. I felt, too, always, the most vast regret for what seemed the waste of a life.

And Hilton was very much in my mind.

Sometimes I tried to imagine what my life would have been like if I had never left: I could have studied at the university there, and married one of those lean and sexy sweet-talking boys. And often that seemed a preferable way to have taken.

I divorced Lewis, and I had various "relationships." I wrote and published articles, several books—and I began getting letters from Popsie Hooker. Long, quite enthralling letters. They were often about her childhood, which had been spent on a farm in Illinois—southern Illinois, to be sure, but, still, I thought how my mother would have laughed to hear that Popsie, the near-professional Southerner, was really from Illinois. Popsie wrote to me often, and I answered, being compulsive in that way, and also because I so much enjoyed hearing from her.

Some of her letters were very funny, as when she wrote about the new "rest home" in Hilton, in which certain former enemies were housed in adjacent rooms: "Mary Lou and Henrietta haven't spoken for years and *years,* and there they are. Going over there to visit is like reading a novel, a real long one," Popsie wrote, and she added, "They couldn't get me into one of those places if they carried me there on a stretcher." I gathered that Popsie was fairly rich; several husbands had come and gone, all leaving her well endowed.

We wrote back and forth, Popsie and I, she writing more often than I did, often telling me how much my letters meant to her. Her letters meant a great deal to me, too. I was especially moved when she talked about the seasons down there in Hilton—the weather and what was in bloom; I could remember all of it, so vividly. And I was grateful that she never mentioned my parents, and her own somewhat ambiguous connection with them.

During some of those years, I began an affair with Andreas, the doctor whom I eventually married: a turbulent, difficult, and sometimes rewarding marriage. Andreas is an exceptionally skilled doctor; he is also arrogant, quick-tempered, and inconsiderate, especially of other people's time—like all doctors, I have sometimes thought.

Our conflicts often have to do with schedules: his conference in Boston versus mine in Chicago; his need for a vacation in February versus mine for time to finish a book, just then. And more ordinary arguments:

my dislike of being kept waiting, his wish that I do more cooking. Some-times even now his hot, heavy body next to mine in bed seems alien, unknown, and I wonder what he is doing there, really. At other times, as I have said, I am deeply stirred by an accidental touching of our hands.

At some of our worst moments I think of leaving Andreas; this would be after an especially ugly quarrel, probably fuelled by too much wine, or simply after several weeks of non-communication.

In one such fantasy I do go back to Hilton, and I take up the rest of my life there as a single woman. I no longer teach, I only do research in the library, which is excellent. And I write more books. I imagine that I see a lot of Popsie Hooker; I might even become the sort of "good daughter" to her that I was so far from being to my own mother. And sometimes in this fantasy I buy the house that we used to live in, the rambling house down the highway, in the valley. I have imagined it as neglected, needing paint, new gutters, perhaps even falling apart, everything around it overgrown and gone to seed.

Last June, when I had agreed to give a series of lectures at George-town, Andreas and I made reservations in a small hotel where we had stayed before, not far from the university. We both like Washington; we looked forward to revisiting favorite galleries and restaurants. It was one of the many times when we needed a vacation together, and so, as I might have known would happen, this became impossible: two sick patients got sicker, and although I argued, citing the brilliance and the exceptional compe-tence of his partners (an argument that did not go over very well), Andreas said no, he had to stay in New York, with the kidneys of Mrs. Howell and old Mr. Rosenthal.

I went to Georgetown and to our hotel alone. I called several times, and Andreas and I "made up" what had been a too familiar argument.

In Georgetown, the second day, as I walked alone past those ele-gantly maintained houses, as I glanced into seductively cloistered, luxur-iantly ferned and flowered gardens, some stray scent of privet or a glimpse of a yellow rosebush in full bloom—something reminded me strongly, com-pellingly of Hilton, and I thought, Well, why not? I could take the train and just stay for a couple of days. That much more time away from Andreas might be to the good, just now. I could stay at the Hilton Inn. I could visit Popsie. I could walk down the highway to our house.

And that is what I did, in more or less that order, except that I saved the visit to Popsie for the last, which turned out to be just as well. But right away I stopped at a travel agency on Wisconsin Avenue, and I bought a ticket to Raleigh, treating myself to a roomette for the five-hour trip; I felt that both ceremony and privacy were required.

I had thought that on the train I would be struck by the deep famil-iarity of the landscape; at last, that particular soil, that special growth. But actually it was novelty that held me to my window: the wide flat brown shining rivers that we crossed, with their tacky little marinas, small boats, small boys on the banks. Flooded swamps, overgrown with kudzu vines and honeysuckle. I had the curious illusion that one sometimes gets on trains, of traversing an exotic, hitherto untravelled land. I felt myself to be an explorer.

That night I had an unmemorable dinner alone at the inn—which, having been redone, was all unfamiliar to me. I went to bed early, slept well.

Sometime in the night, though, I did wake up with the strange and slightly scary thought that in a few years I would be as old as my mother was when she died, and I wondered what, if anything, that fact had to do with my coming back to Hilton, after all these years.

The next morning's early air was light and delicate. Dew still shone on the heavy, dark-green shrubbery around the inn, on silver cobwebs, as I set out for my walk—at last! The sky was soft and pale, an eggshell blue. Walking along the still gravelled sidewalk, beside the tarred road that led from the inn out to the highway, I recognized houses; I knew who used to live in almost all of them, and I said those names to myself as I walked along: Hudson, Phipps, Zimmerman, Rogerson, Pittman. I noticed that the old Pittman place was now a fraternity house, with an added sun porch and bright new paint, bright gold Greek letters over the door. In fact, the look of all those houses was one of improvement, upgrading, with their trim lawns, abundant boxwood, their lavish flower beds.

I reached the highway, still on the gravelled walk, and I began the long descent toward my house. The air was still light, and barely warm, although the day to come would be hot. I thought of my dream in Yugoslavia, of this walk, and I smiled, inexplicably happy at just that moment—with no heat, no pain in my heart.

I recognized more houses, and said more names, and I observed that these houses, too, were in splendid shape, all bright and visibly cared for. There was much more green growth than I remembered, the trees were immense, and I thought, Well, of course; they've had time to grow.

No one seeing me as I walked there could know or guess that that was where I used to live, I thought. They would see—a tall thin woman, graying, in early middle age, in a striped gray cotton skirt, gray shirt. A woman looking intently at everything, and smiling to herself.

And then, there before me was our house. But not our house. It, too, had been repainted—all smartened up with bright white paint and long black louvred shutters, now closed against the coming heat and light. Four recent-model sports cars, all imported, were parked in the driveway, giving the place a recreational, non-familiar air. A group of students, I thought; perhaps some club? The surrounding trees were huge; what had been a small and murmurous pine grove at one side of the house now towered over it, thickly green and rustling slightly in a just-arisen morning breeze. No one came out while I stood there, for not very long, but I was sure that there was not a family inside but some cluster of transients—young people, probably, who liked each other and liked the house, but without any deep or permanent attachment.

I continued on my walk, a circle of black roads on which I was pleased to find that I still knew my way, which led at last back to the highway, and up the hill, to the inn.

I had called Popsie Hooker from Washington, and again from the inn, when I got there. She arose from her nap about four in the afternoon, she said, and if I could come out to her house along about then she would be thrilled, just simply thrilled.

By midafternoon it was too hot for another walk, and so I took a taxi out to Popsie's house, in the direction opposite to mine. I arrived about four-thirty, which I assumed to be along about four in Southernese.

Popsie's house, the fruit of one of her later marriages, was by far the most splendid I had yet seen in town: a Georgian house, of ancient soft red brick smartly trimmed in black, with frequent accents of highly polished brass. Magnificent lawns, magnolias, rhododendrons. By the time I got to the door I half expected to be greeted by an array of uniformed retainers—all black, of course.

But it was Popsie herself who opened the door to me—a Popsie barely recognizable, so shrunken and wizened had she become: a small woman withered down to dwarf size, in a black silk dress with grosgrain at her throat, a cameo brooch. She smelled violently of gardenia perfume and of something else that at first I could not place.

"Emma! Emma!" she breathed up into my face, the old blue eyes filming over, and she caught at both my arms and held them in her weak tight grasp. I recognized the second scent, which was sherry.

"You're *late*," she next accused me. "Here I've been expecting you this whole long after*noon*."

I murmured apologies, and together we proceeded down the hallway and into a small parlor, Popsie still clutching my arm, her small fierce weight almost tugging me over sideways.

We sat down. The surfaces in that room were all so cluttered with silver and ivory pieces, inlay, old glass, that it could have been an antique shop, or the parlor of a medium. I told Popsie how happy I was to be there, how wonderful Hilton looked.

"Well, you know, it's become a very fancy place to live. Very *expensive*. Lots of Yankees retiring down here, and fixing up the old houses."

"Uh, where do the poor people live?"

She laughed, a tiny rasp. "Oh, there you go, talking *liberal*, and you just got here. Well, the poor folks, what's left of them, have moved out to Robertsville."

Robertsville was the adjacent town, once predominantly black, and so I next asked, "What about the Negroes?"

"Well, I guess they've just sort of drifted back into the countryside, where they came from. But did you notice all the fancy new stores on Main Street? All the restaurants, and the *clothes*?"

We talked for a while about the new splendors of Hilton, and the rudeness of the new Yankees, who did not even go to church—as I thought, This could not be the woman who has been writing to me. Although of course she was—the same Popsie, half tipsy in the afternoon; she probably spent her sober mornings writing letters. This woman was more like the Popsie of my early years in Hilton, that silly little person, my mother's natural enemy.

Possibly to recall the Popsie of the wonderful letters, I asked about the local rest home. How were things out there?

"Well, I have to tell you. What gripes me the most about that place is that they don't pay any taxes" was Popsie's quick, unhelpful response. "Tax-*free*, and you would not believe the taxes I have to pay on this old place."

"But this place is so beautiful." I did not add, And you have so much money.

"Well, it is right pretty," she acknowledged, dipping her head. "But why must I go on and on paying for it? It's not fair."

Our small chairs were close together in that crowded, stuffy room, so that when Popsie leaned closer yet to me, her bleary eyes peering up into mine, the sherry fumes that came my way were very strong indeed. And Popsie said, "You know, I've always thought you were so beautiful, even if no one else ever thought you were." She peered again. "Where did you get that beauty, do you think? Your mother never was even one bit pretty."

More stiffly than I had meant to, I spoke the truth. "Actually I look quite a lot like my mother," I told her. And I am not beautiful.

Catching a little of my anger, which probably pleased her, Popsie raised her chin. "Well, one thing certain, you surely don't favor your daddy."

"No, I don't. I don't favor him at all." My father had recently moved to La Jolla, California, with another heiress, this one younger than I am, which would have seemed cruel news to give to Popsie.

After a pause, during which I suppose we both could have been said to be marshalling our forces, Popsie and I continued our conversation, very politely, until I felt that I could decently leave.

I told her how much I liked her letters, and she said how she liked mine, and we both promised to write again, very soon—and I wondered if we would.

On the plane to New York, a smooth, clear, easy flight, I was aware of an unusual sense of well-being, which out of habit I questioned. I noted the sort of satisfaction that I might have been expected to feel on finishing a book, except that at the end of books I usually feel drained, exhausted. But now I simply felt well, at peace, and ready for whatever should come next.

Then Paul returned from nowhere to my mind, more strongly than for some time. In an affectionate way I remembered how impossible he was, in terms of daily life, and how much I had loved him—and how he had loved me.

Actually he and Andreas were even more unlike than he and Lewis were, I next thought, and a little wearily I noted my own tendency to extremes, and contrasts. Andreas likes to fix and mend things, including kidneys, of course. He is good with cars. "I come from strong Greek peasant stock" is a thing that he likes to say, and it is true; clearly he does, with his powerful black hair, his arrogant nose. His good strong heart.

We were planning a trip to Greece the following fall. Andreas had gone back as a boy to visit relatives, and later with both his first and second wives. And he and I had meant to go, and now we would.

We planned to fly to Rome, maybe spend a few days there; we both like Rome. But now another route suggested itself: we could fly to Vienna, where we have never been, and then take the train to Trieste, where we could pick up a car and drive down to Greece by way of Yugoslavia. We would drive past the ferry to the island of Rab, and past the road that led to our yellow hotel. I did not imagine driving down to see it; Andreas would be in a hurry, and my past does not interest him much. He would see no need to stop on such an errand.

Nor do I. And besides, that particular ugly, poorly built structure has probably been torn down. Still, I very much like the idea of just being in its vicinity.

1985

In "Return Trips" the thoughts of the protagonist are revealed to us in extraordinary detail. Not every writer of fiction would approve of this technique. Certainly Guy de Maupassant, one of the earliest and best writers on theories of fiction, cannot conceal his preference for stories constructed on a different principle.

"Conceal psychology instead of flaunting it": de Maupassant

Two of these theories have more particularly been the subject of discussion, and set up in opposition to each other instead of being admitted on an equal footing: that of the purely analytical novel, and that of the objective novel.

The partisans of analysis require the writer to devote himself to indicating the smallest evolutions of a soul, and all the most secret motives of our every action, giving but a quite secondary importance to the act and fact in itself. It is but the goal, a simple milestone, the excuse for the book.

According to them, these works, at once exact and visionary, in which imagination merges into observation, are to be written after the fashion in which a philosopher composes a treatise on psychology, seeking out causes in their remotest origin, telling the why and wherefore of every impulse, and detecting every reaction of the soul's movements under the promptings of interest, passion, or instinct.

The partisans of objectivity—odious world—aiming, on the contrary, at giving us an exact presentment of all that happens in life, carefully avoid all complicated explanations, all disquisitions on motive, and confine themselves to let persons and events pass before our eyes. In their opinion, psychology should be concealed in the book, as it is in reality, under the facts of existence.

The novel as conceived of on these lines gains in interest; there is more movement in the narrative, more color, more of the stir of life.

Hence, instead of giving long explanations of the state of mind of an actor in the tale, the objective writer tries to discover the action or gesture which that state of mind must inevitably lead to in that personage, under certain given circumstances. And he makes him so demean himself from one end of the volume to the other, that all his actions, all his movements shall be the expression of his inmost nature, of all his thoughts, and all his impulses or hesitancies. Thus they conceal psychology instead of flaunting it; they use it as the skeleton of the work, just as the invisible bony framework is the skeleton of the human body. The artist who paints our portrait does not display our bones.

GABRIEL GARCÍA MÁRQUEZ

(b. 1928)

A VERY OLD MAN WITH ENORMOUS WINGS
A TALE FOR CHILDREN

translated from the Spanish by Gregory Rabassa

On the third day of rain they had killed so many crabs inside the house that Pelayo had to cross his drenched courtyard and throw them into the sea, because the newborn child had a temperature all night and they thought it was due to the stench. The world had been sad since Tuesday. Sea and sky were a single ash-gray thing and the sands of the beach, which on March nights glimmered like powdered light, had become a stew of mud and rotten shellfish. The light was so weak at noon that when Pelayo was coming back to the house after throwing away the crabs, it was hard for him to see what it was that was moving and groaning in the rear of the courtyard. He had to go very close to see that it was an old man, a very old man, lying face down in the mud, who, in spite of his tremendous efforts, couldn't get up, impeded by his enormous wings.

Frightened by that nightmare, Pelayo ran to get Elisenda, his wife, who was putting compresses on the sick child, and he took her to the rear of the courtyard. They both looked at the fallen body with mute stupor. He was dressed like a ragpicker. There were only a few faded hairs left on his bald skull and very few teeth in his mouth, and his pitiful condition of a drenched great-grandfather had taken away any sense of grandeur he might have had. His huge buzzard wings, dirty and half-plucked, were forever entangled in the mud. They looked at him so long and so closely that Pelayo and Elisenda very soon overcame their surprise and in the end found him familiar. Then they dared speak to him, and he answered in an incomprehensible dialect with a strong sailor's voice. That was how they skipped over the inconvenience of the wings and quite intelligently concluded that he was a lonely castaway from some foreign ship wrecked by the storm. And yet, they called in a neighbor woman who knew everything about life and death to see him, and all she needed was one look to show them their mistake.

"He's an angel," she told them. "He must have been coming for the child, but the poor fellow is so old that the rain knocked him down."

On the following day everyone knew that a flesh-and-blood angel was held captive in Pelayo's house. Against the judgment of the wise neighbor woman, for whom angels in those times were the fugitive survivors of a celestial conspiracy, they did not have the heart to club him to death. Pelayo watched over him all afternoon from the kitchen, armed with his bailiff's club, and before going to bed he dragged him out of the mud and locked him up with the hens in the wire chicken coop. In the middle of the night, when the rain stopped, Pelayo and Elisenda were still killing crabs. A short time afterward the child woke up without a fever and with a desire to eat. Then they felt magnanimous and decided to put the angel on a raft with fresh water and provisions for three days and leave him to his fate on the high seas. But when they went out into the courtyard with the first light of dawn, they found the whole neighborhood in front of the chicken coop having fun with the angel, without the slightest reverence, tossing him things to eat through the openings in the wire as if he weren't a supernatural creature but a circus animal.

Father Gonzaga arrived before seven o'clock, alarmed at the strange news. By that time onlookers less frivolous than those at dawn had already arrived and they were making all kinds of conjectures concerning the captive's future. The simplest among them thought that he should be named mayor of the world. Others of sterner mind felt that he should be promoted to the rank of five-star general in order to win all wars. Some visionaries hoped that he could be put to stud in order to implant on earth a race of winged wise men who could take charge of the universe. But Father Gonzaga, before becoming a priest, had been a robust woodcutter. Standing by the wire, he reviewed his catechism in an instant and asked them to open the door so that he could take a close look at that pitiful man who looked more like a huge decrepit hen among the fascinated chickens. He was lying in a corner drying his open wings in the sunlight among the fruit peels and breakfast leftovers that the early risers had thrown him. Alien to the impertinences of the world, he only lifted his antiquarian eyes and murmured something in his dialect when Father Gonzaga went into the chicken coop and said good morning to him in Latin. The parish priest had his first suspicion of an imposter when he saw that he did not understand the language of God or know how to greet His ministers. Then he noticed that seen close up he was much too human: he had an unbearable smell of the outdoors, the back side of his wings was strewn with parasites and his main feathers had been mistreated by terrestrial winds, and nothing about him measured up to the proud dignity of angels. Then he came out of the chicken coop and in a brief sermon warned the curious against the risks of being ingenuous. He reminded them that the devil had the bad habit of making use of carnival tricks in order to confuse the unwary. He argued that if wings were not the essential element in determining the difference between a hawk and an airplane, they were even less so in the recognition of angels. Nevertheless, he promised to write a letter to his bishop so that the latter would write to his primate so that the latter would write to the Supreme Pontiff in order to get the final verdict from the highest courts.

His prudence fell on sterile hearts. The news of the captive angel spread with such rapidity that after a few hours the courtyard had the bustle of a marketplace and they had to call in troops with fixed bayonets to disperse the mob that was about to knock the house down. Elisenda, her spine all twisted from sweeping up so much marketplace trash, then got the idea of fencing in the yard and charging five cents admission to see the angel.

The curious came from far away. A traveling carnival arrived with a flying acrobat who buzzed over the crowd several times, but no one paid any attention to him because his wings were not those of an angel but, rather, those of a sidereal bat. The most unfortunate invalids on earth came in search of health: a poor woman who since childhood had been counting her heartbeats and had run out of numbers; a Portuguese man who couldn't sleep because the noise of the stars disturbed him; a sleepwalker who got up at night to undo the things he had done while awake; and many others with less serious ailments. In the midst of that shipwreck disorder that made the earth tremble, Pelayo and Elisenda were happy with fatigue, for in less than a week they had crammed their rooms with money and the line of pilgrims waiting their turn to enter still reached beyond the horizon.

The angel was the only one who took no part in his own act. He spent his time trying to get comfortable in his borrowed nest, befuddled by the hellish heat of the oil lamps and sacramental candles that had been placed along the wire. At first they tried to make him eat some mothballs, which, according to the wisdom of the wise neighbor woman, were the food prescribed for angels. But he turned them down, just as he turned down the papal lunches that the penitents brought him, and they never found out whether it was because he was an angel or because he was an old man that in the end he ate nothing but eggplant mush. His only supernatural virtue seemed to be patience. Especially during the first days, when the hens pecked at him, searching for the stellar parasites that proliferated in his wings, and the cripples pulled out feathers to touch their defective parts with, and even the most merciful threw stones at him, trying to get him to rise so they could see him standing. The only time they succeeded in arousing him was when they burned his side with an iron for branding steers, for he had been motionless for so many hours that they thought he was dead. He awoke with a start, ranting in his hermetic[1] language and with tears in his eyes, and he flapped his wings a couple of times, which brought on a whirlwind of chicken dung and lunar dust and a gale of panic that did not seem to be of this world. Although many thought that his reaction had been one not of rage but of pain, from then on they were careful not to annoy him, because the majority understood that his passivity was not that of a hero taking his ease but that of a cataclysm in repose.

Father Gonzaga held back the crowd's frivolity with formulas of maidservant inspiration while awaiting the arrival of a final judgment on the nature of the captive. But the mail from Rome showed no sense of urgency. They spent their time finding out if the prisoner had a navel, if his dialect had any connection with Aramaic,[2] how many times he could fit on the head of a pin, or whether he wasn't just a Norwegian with wings. Those meager letters might have come and gone until the end of time if a providential event had not put an end to the priest's tribulations.

It so happened that during those days, among so many other carnival attractions, there arrived in town the traveling show of the woman who had been changed into a spider for having disobeyed her parents. The admission to see her was not only less than the admission to see the angel, but people were permitted to ask her all manner of questions about her absurd state and to examine her up and down so that no one would ever doubt the truth of her horror. She was a frightful tarantula the size of a ram and with the head of a sad maiden. What was most heart-rending, however, was not her outlandish shape but the sincere affliction with which she recounted the details of her misfortune. While still practically a child she had sneaked out of her parents' house to go to a dance, and while she was coming back through the woods after having danced all night without permission, a fearful thunderclap rent the sky in two and through the crack came the lightning bolt of brimstone that changed her into a spider. Her only nourishment came from the meatballs that charitable souls chose to toss into her mouth. A spectacle like that, full of so much human truth and with such a fearful lesson, was bound to defeat without even trying that of a

_____
1. Occult, mysterious.
2. An ancient Semitic language dating from the seventh century B.C.

haughty angel who scarcely deigned to look at mortals. Besides, the few miracles attributed to the angel showed a certain mental disorder, like the blind man who didn't recover his sight but grew three new teeth, or the paralytic who didn't get to walk but almost won the lottery, and the leper whose sores sprouted sunflowers. Those consolation miracles, which were more like mocking fun, had already ruined the angel's reputation when the woman who had been changed into a spider finally crushed him completely. That was how Father Gonzaga was cured forever of his insomnia and Pelayo's courtyard went back to being as empty as during the time it had rained for three days and crabs walked through the bedrooms.

The owners of the house had no reason to lament. With the money they saved they built a two-story mansion with balconies and gardens and high netting so that crabs wouldn't get in during the winter, and with iron bars on the windows so that angels wouldn't get in. Pelayo also set up a rabbit warren close to town and gave up his job as bailiff for good, and Elisenda bought some satin pumps with high heels and many dresses of iridescent silk, the kind worn on Sunday by the most desirable women in those times. The chicken coop was the only thing that didn't receive any attention. If they washed it down with creolin and burned tears of myrrh inside it every so often, it was not in homage to the angel but to drive away the dungheap stench that still hung everywhere like a ghost and was turning the new house into an old one. At first, when the child learned to walk, they were careful that he not get too close to the chicken coop. But then they began to lose their fears and got used to the smell, and before the child got his second teeth he'd gone inside the chicken coop to play, where the wires were falling apart. The angel was no less standoffish with him than with other mortals, but he tolerated the most ingenious infamies with the patience of a dog who had no illusions. They both came down with chicken pox at the same time. The doctor who took care of the child couldn't resist the temptation to listen to the angel's heart, and he found so much whistling in the heart and so many sounds in his kidneys that it seemed impossible for him to be alive. What surprised him most, however, was the logic of his wings. They seemed so natural on that completely human organism that he couldn't understand why other men didn't have them too.

When the child began school it had been some time since the sun and rain had caused the collapse of the chicken coop. The angel went dragging himself about here and there like a stray dying man. They would drive him out of the bedroom with a broom and a moment later find him in the kitchen. He seemed to be in so many places at the same time that they grew to think that he'd been duplicated, that he was reproducing himself all through the house, and the exasperated and unhinged Elisenda shouted that it was awful living in that hell full of angels. He could scarcely eat and his antiquarian eyes had also become so foggy that he went about bumping into posts. All he had left were the bare cannulae of his last feathers. Pelayo threw a blanket over him and extended him the charity of letting him sleep in the shed, and only then did they notice that he had a temperature at night, and was delirious with the tongue twisters of an old Norwegian. That was one of the few times they became alarmed, for they thought he was going to die and not even the wise neighbor woman had been able to tell them what to do with dead angels.

And yet he not only survived his worst winter, but seemed improved with the first sunny days. He remained motionless for several days in the farthest corner of the courtyard, where no one would see him, and at the beginning of December some large, stiff feathers began to grow on his wings, the feathers of a scarecrow, which looked more like another misfortune of decrepitude. But he must have known the reason for those changes, for he was quite careful that no one should notice them, that no one should hear the sea chanteys that he sometimes sang under the stars. One morning Elisenda was cutting some bunches of onions for lunch when a wind that seemed to come from the high seas blew into the kitchen. Then she went to the window and caught the angel in his first attempts at flight. They were so clumsy that his fingernails opened a furrow in the vegetable patch and he was on the point of knocking the shed down with the ungainly flapping that slipped on the light and couldn't get a grip on the air. But he did manage to gain altitude. Elisenda let out a sigh of relief, for herself and for him, when she saw him pass over the last houses, holding himself up in some way with the risky flapping of a senile vulture. She kept watching him even when she was through cutting the onions and she kept on watching until it was no longer possible for her to see him, because then he was no longer an annoyance in her life but an imaginary dot on the horizon of the sea.

1955

The term "magical realism" is often associated with Gabriel García Márquez's fiction. His account of the origin of this "journalistic trick" is given in an interview with Peter Stone for Paris Review.

"Four hundred and twenty-five elephants in the sky": Gabriel García Márquez

---

  Interviewer: How would you describe the search for a style that you went through after *Leaf Storm* and before you were able to write *One Hundred Years of Solitude?* . . .

García Márquez: . . . After *The Evil Hour* I did not write anything for five years. I had an idea of what I always wanted to do, but there was something missing and I was not sure what it was until one day I discovered the right tone—the tone that I eventually used in *On Hundred Years of Solitude*. It was based on the way my grandmother used to tell her stories. She told things that sounded supernatural and fantastic, but she told them with complete naturalness. When I finally discovered the tone I had to use, I sat down for eighteen months and worked every day.

Interviewer: How did she express the "fantastic" so naturally?

García Márquez: What was most important was the expression she had on her face. She did not change her expression at all when telling her stories, and everyone was surprised. In previous attempts to write *One Hundred Years of Solitude,* I tried to tell the story without believing in it. I discovered that what I had to do was believe in them myself and write them with the same expression with which my grandmother told them: with a brick face.

Interviewer: There also seems to be a journalistic quality to that technique or tone. You describe seemingly fantastic events in such minute detail that it gives them their own reality. Is this something you have picked up from journalism?

García Márquez: That's a journalistic trick which you can also apply to literature. For example, if you say that there are elephants flying in the sky, people are not going to believe you. But if you say that there are four hundred and twenty-five elephants in the sky, people will probably believe you. *One Hundred Years of Solitude* is full of that sort of thing. That's exactly the technique my grandmother used. I remember particularly the story about the character who is surrounded by yellow butterflies. When I was very small there was an electrician who came to the house. I became very curious because he carried a belt with which he used to suspend himself from the electrical posts. My grandmother used to say that every time this man came around, he would leave the house full of butterflies. But when I was writing this, I discovered that if I didn't say the butterflies were yellow, people would not believe it. When I was writing the episode of Remedios the Beauty going to heaven, it took me a long time to make it credible. One day I went out to the garden and saw a woman who used to come to the house to do the wash and she was putting out the sheets to dry and there was a lot of wind. She was arguing with the wind not to blow the sheets away. I discovered that if I used the sheets for Remedios the Beauty, she would ascend. That's how I did it, to make it credible. The problem for every writer is credibility. Anybody can write anything so long as it's believed.

ALICE MUNRO

(b. 1931)

CIRCLE OF PRAYER

Trudy threw a jug across the room. It didn't reach the opposite wall; it didn't hurt anybody, it didn't even break.

This was the jug without a handle—cement-colored with brown streaks on it, rough as sandpaper to the touch—that Dan made the winter he took pottery classes. He made six little handleless cups to go with it. The jug and the cups were supposed to be for sake, but the local liquor store doesn't carry sake. Once, they brought some home from a trip, but they didn't really like it. So the jug Dan made sits on the highest open shelf in the kitchen, and a few odd items of value are kept in it. Trudy's wedding ring and her engagement ring, the medal Robin won for all-round excellence in Grade 8, a long, two-strand necklace of jet beads that belonged to Dan's mother and was willed to Robin. Trudy won't let her wear it yet.

Trudy came home from work a little after midnight; she entered the house in the dark. Just the little stove light was on—she and Robin always left that on for each other. Trudy didn't need any other light. She climbed up on a chair without even letting go of her bag, got down the jug, and fished around inside it.

It was gone. Of course. She had known it would be gone.

She went through the dark house to Robin's room, still with her bag over her arm, the jug in her hand. She turned on the overhead light. Robin groaned and turned over, pulled the pillow over her head. Shamming.

"Your grandmother's necklace," Trudy said. "Why did you do that? Are you insane?"

Robin shammed a sleepy groan. All the clothes she owned, it seemed, old and new and clean and dirty, were scattered on the floor, on the chair, the desk, the dresser, even on the bed itself. On the wall was a huge poster showing a hippopotamus, with the words underneath "Why Was I Born So Beautiful?" And another poster showing Terry Fox running along a rainy highway, with a whole cavalcade of cars behind him. Dirty glasses, empty yogurt containers, school notes, a Tampax still in its wrapper, the stuffed snake and tiger Robin had had since before she went to school, a collage of pictures of her cat Sausage, who had been run over two years ago. Red and blue ribbons that she had won for jumping, or running, or throwing basketballs.

"You answer me!" said Trudy. "You tell me why you did it!"

She threw the jug. But it was heavier than she'd thought, or else at the very moment of throwing it she lost conviction, because it didn't hit the wall; it fell on the rug beside the dresser and rolled on the floor, undamaged.

You threw a jug at me that time. You could have killed me.
Not at you. I didn't throw it at you.
You could have killed me.

Proof that Robin was shamming: She started up in a fright, but it wasn't the blank fright of somebody who'd been asleep. She looked scared, but underneath that childish, scared look was another look—stubborn, calculating, disdainful.

"It was so beautiful. And it was valuable. It belonged to your grandmother."

"I thought it belonged to me," said Robin.

"That girl wasn't even your friend. Christ, you didn't have a good word to say for her this morning."

"You don't know who is my friend!" Robin's face flushed a bright pink and her eyes filled with tears, but her scornful, stubborn expression didn't change. "I knew her. I talked to her. So get out!"

Trudy works at the Home for Mentally Handicapped Adults. Few people call it that. Older people in town still say "the Misses Weir's house," and a number of others, including Robin—and, presumably, most of those her age—call it the Half-Wit House.

The house has a ramp now for wheelchairs, because some of the mentally handicapped may be physically handicapped as well, and it has a swimming pool in the back yard, which caused a certain amount of discussion when it was installed at taxpayers' expense. Otherwise the house looks pretty much the way it always did—the white wooden walls, the dark-green curlicues on the gables, the steep roof and dark screened side porch, and the deep lawn in front shaded by soft maple trees.

This month, Trudy works the four-to-midnight shift. Yesterday afternoon, she parked her car in front and walked up the drive thinking how nice the house looked, peaceful as in the days of the Misses Weir, who must have served iced tea and read library books, or played croquet, whatever people did then.

Always some piece of news, some wrangle or excitement, once you get inside. The men came to fix the pool but they didn't fix it. They went away again. It isn't fixed yet.

"We don't get no use of it, soon summer be over," Josephine said.

"It's not even the middle of June, you're saying summer'll be over,"

Kelvin said. "You think before you talk. Did you hear about the young girl that was killed out in the country?" he said to Trudy.

Trudy had started to mix two batches of frozen lemonade, one pink and one plain. When he said that, she smashed the spoon down on the frozen chunk so hard that some of the liquid spilled over.

"How, Kelvin?"

She was afraid she would hear that a girl was dragged off a country road, raped in the woods, strangled, beaten, left there. Robin goes running along the country roads in her white shorts and T-shirt, a headband on her flying hair. Robin's hair is golden; her legs and arms are golden. Her cheeks and limbs are downy, not shiny—you wouldn't be surprised to see a cloud of pollen delicately floating and settling behind her when she runs. Cars hoot at her and she isn't bothered. Foul threats are yelled at her, and she yells foul threats back.

"Driving a truck," Kelvin said.

Trudy's heart eased. Robin doesn't know how to drive yet.

"Fourteen years old, she didn't know how to drive," Kelvin said. "She got in the truck, and the first thing you know, she ran it into a tree. Where was her parents? That's what I'd like to know. They weren't watching out for her. She got in the truck when she didn't know how to drive and ran it into a tree. Fourteen. That's too young."

Kelvin goes uptown by himself; he hears all the news. He is fifty-two years old, still slim and boyish-looking, well-shaved, with soft, short, clean dark hair. He goes to the barbershop every day, because he can't quite manage to shave himself. Epilepsy, then surgery, an infected bone-flap, many more operations, a permanent mild difficulty with feet and fingers, a gentle head fog. The fog doesn't obscure facts, just motives. Perhaps he shouldn't be in the Home at all, but where else? Anyway, he likes it. He says he likes it. He tells the others they shouldn't complain; they should be more careful, they should behave themselves. He picks up the soft-drink cans and beer bottles that people have thrown into the front yard —though of course it isn't his job to do that.

When Janet came in just before midnight to relieve Trudy, she had the same story to tell.

"I guess you heard about that fifteen-year-old girl?"

When Janet starts telling you something like this, she always starts off with "I guess you heard." *I guess you heard Wilma and Ted are breaking up,* she says. *I guess you heard Alvin Stead had a heart attack.*

"Kelvin told me," Trudy said. "Only he said she was fourteen."

"Fifteen," Janet said. "She must've been in Robin's class at school. She didn't know how to drive. She didn't even get out of the lane."

"Was she drunk?" said Trudy. Robin won't go near alcohol, or dope, or cigarettes, or even coffee, she's so fanatical about what she puts into her body.

"I don't think so. Stoned, maybe. It was early in the evening. She was home with her sister. Their parents were out. Her sister's boyfriend came over—it was his truck, and he either gave her the keys to the truck or she took them. You hear different versions. You hear that they sent her out for something, they wanted to get rid of her, and you hear she just took the keys and went. Anyway, she ran it right into a tree in the lane."

"Jesus," said Trudy.

"I know. It's so idiotic. It's getting so you hate to think about your kids growing up. Did everybody take their medication okay? What's Kelvin watching?"

Kelvin was still up, sitting in the living room watching TV.

"It's somebody being interviewed. He wrote a book about schizophrenics," Trudy told Janet.

Anything he comes across about mental problems, Kelvin has to watch, or try to read.

"I think it depresses him, the more he watches that kind of thing," Janet said. "Do you know I found out today I have to make five hundred roses out of pink Kleenex for my niece Laurel's wedding? For the car. She said I promised I'd make the roses for the car. Well, I didn't. I don't remember promising a thing. Are you going to come over and help me?"

"Sure," said Trudy.

"I guess the real reason I want him to get off the schizophrenics is I want to watch the old *Dallas,*" said Janet. She and Trudy disagree about this. Trudy can't stand to watch those old reruns of *Dallas,* to see the characters, with their younger, plumper faces, going through tribulations and bound up in romantic complications they and the audience have now forgotten all about. That's what's so hilarious, Janet says; it's so unbelievable it's wonderful. All that happens and they just forget about it and go on. But to Trudy it doesn't seem so unbelievable that the characters would go from one thing to the next thing—forgetful, hopeful, photogenic, forever changing their clothes. That it's not so unbelievable is the thing she really can't stand.

Robin, the next morning, said, "Oh, probably. All those people she hung around with drink. They party all the time. They're self-destructive. It's her own fault. Even if her sister told her to go, she didn't have to go. She didn't have to be so stupid."

"What was her name?" Trudy said.

"Tracy Lee," said Robin with distaste. She stepped on the pedal of the garbage tin, lifted rather than lowered the container of yogurt she had just emptied, and dropped it in. She was wearing bikini underpants and a T-shirt that said "If I Want to Listen to an Asshole, I'll Fart."

"That shirt still bothers me," Trudy said. "Some things are disgusting but funny, and some things are more disgusting than funny."

"What's the problem?" said Robin. "I sleep alone."

Trudy sat outside, in her wrapper, drinking coffee while the day got hot. There is a little brick-paved space by the side door that she and Dan always called the patio. She sat there. This is a solar-heated house, with big panels of glass in the south-sloping roof—the oddest-looking house in town. It's odd inside, too, with the open shelves in the kitchen instead of cupboards, and the living room up some stairs, looking out over the fields at the back. She and Dan, for a joke, gave parts of it the most conventional, suburban-sounding names—the patio, the powder room, the master bedroom. Dan always had to joke about the way he was living. He built the house himself—Trudy did a lot of the painting and staining—and it was a success. Rain didn't leak in around the panels, and part of the house's heat really did come from the sun. Most people who have the ideas, or ideals, that Dan has aren't very practical. They can't fix things or make things; they don't understand wiring or carpentry, or whatever it is they need to understand. Dan is good at everything—at gardening, cutting wood, building a house. He is especially good at repairing motors. He used to travel around getting jobs as an auto mechanic, a small-engines repairman. That's how he ended up here. He came here to visit Marlene, got a job as a mechanic, became a working partner in an auto-repair business, and before he knew it —married to Trudy, not Marlene—he was a small-town businessman, a member of the Kinsmen. All without shaving off his nineteen-sixties beard or trimming his hair any more than he wanted to. The town was too small and Dan was too smart for that to be necessary.

Now Dan lives in a townhouse in Richmond Hill with a girl named Genevieve. She is studying law. She was married when she was very young, and has three little children. Dan met her three years ago when her camper broke down a few miles outside of town. He told Trudy about her that night. The rented camper, the three little children hardly more than babies, the lively little divorced mother with her hair in pigtails. Her bravery, her poverty, her plans to enter law school. If the camper hadn't been easily fixed, he was going to invite her and her children to spend the night. She was on her way to her parents' summer place at Pointe au Baril.

"Then she can't be all that poor," Trudy said.

"You can be poor and have rich parents," Dan said.

"No, you can't."

Last summer, Robin went to Richmond Hill for a month's visit. She came home early. She said it was a madhouse. The oldest child has to go to a special reading clinic, the middle one wets the bed. Genevieve spends all her time in the law library, studying. No wonder. Dan shops for bargains, cooks, looks after the children, grows vegetables, drives a taxi on Saturdays and Sundays. He wants to set up a motorcycle-repair business in the garage, but he can't get a permit; the neighbors are against it.

He told Robin he was happy. Never happier, he said. Robin came home firmly grownup—severe, sarcastic, determined. She had some slight, steady grudge she hadn't had before. Trudy couldn't worm it out of her, couldn't tease it out of her; the time when she could do that was over.

Robin came home at noon and changed her clothes. She put on a light, flowered cotton blouse and ironed a pale-blue cotton skirt. She said that some of the girls from the class might be going around to the funeral home after school.

"I forgot you had that skirt," said Trudy. If she thought that was going to start a conversation, she was mistaken.

The first time Trudy met Dan, she was drunk. She was nineteen years old, tall and skinny (she still is), with a wild head of curly black hair (it is cropped short now and showing the gray as black hair does). She was very tanned, wearing jeans and a tie-dyed T-shirt. No brassière and no need. This was in Muskoka in August, at a hotel bar where they had a band. She was camping with girlfriends. He was there with his fiancée, Marlene. He had taken Marlene home to meet his mother, who lived in Muskoka on an island in an empty hotel. When Trudy was nineteen, he was twenty-eight. She danced around by herself, giddy and drunk, in front of the table where he sat with Marlene, a meek-looking blonde with a big pink shelf of bosom all embroidered in little fake pearls. Trudy just danced in front of him until he got up and joined her. At the end of the dance, he asked her name, and took her back and introduced her to Marlene.

"This is Judy," he said. Trudy collapsed, laughing, into the chair beside Marlene's. Dan took Marlene up to dance. Trudy finished off Marlene's beer and went looking for her friends.

"How do you do?" she said to them. "I'm Judy!"

He caught up with her at the door of the bar. He had ditched Marlene when he saw Trudy leaving. A man who could change course quickly, see the possibilities, flare up with new enthusiasm. He told people later that he was in love with Trudy before he even knew her real name. But he told Trudy that he cried when he and Marlene were parting.

"I have feelings," he said. "I'm not ashamed to show them."

Trudy had no feelings for Marlene at all. Marlene was over thirty —what could she expect? Marlene still lives in town, works at the Hydro office, is not married. When Trudy and Dan were having one of their conversations about Genevieve, Trudy said, "Marlene must be thinking I got what's coming to me."

Dan said he had heard that Marlene had joined the Fellowship of Bible Christians. The women weren't allowed makeup and had to wear a kind of bonnet to church on Sundays.

"She won't be able to have a thought in her head but forgiving," Dan said.

Trudy said, "I bet."

This is what happened at the funeral home, as Trudy got the story from both Kelvin and Janet.

The girls from Tracy Lee's class all showed up together after school. This was during what was called the visitation, when the family waited beside Tracy Lee's open casket to receive friends. Her parents were there, her married brother and his wife, her sister, and even her sister's boyfriend who owned the truck. They stood in a row and people lined up to say a few words to them. A lot of people came. They always do, in a case like this. Tracy Lee's grandmother was at the end of the row in a brocade-covered chair. She wasn't able to stand up for very long.

All the chairs at the funeral home are upholstered in this white-and-gold brocade. The curtains are the same, the wallpaper almost matches. There are little wall-bracket lights behind heavy pink glass. Trudy has been there several times and knows what it's like. But Robin and most of these girls had never been inside the place before. They didn't know what to expect. Some of them began to cry as soon as they got inside the door.

The curtains were closed. Soft music was playing—not exactly church music but it sounded like it. Tracy Lee's coffin was white with gold trim, matching all the brocade and the wallpaper. It had a lining of pleated pink satin. A pink satin pillow. Tracy Lee had not a mark on her face. She was not made up quite as usual, because the undertaker had done it. But she was wearing her favorite earrings, turquoise-colored triangles and yellow crescents, two to each ear. (Some people thought that was in bad taste.) On the part of the coffin that covered her from the waist down, there was a big heart-shaped pillow of pink roses.

The girls lined up to speak to the family. They shook hands, they said sorry-for-your-loss, just the way everybody else did. When they got through that, when all of them had let the grandmother squash their cool hands between her warm, swollen, freckled ones, they lined up again, in a straggling sort of way, and began to go past the coffin. Many were crying now, shivering. What could you expect? Young girls.

But they began to sing as they went past. With difficulty at first, shyly, but with growing confidence in their sad, sweet voices, they sang:

> *"Now, while the blossom still clings to the vine,*
> *I'll taste your strawberries, I'll drink your sweet wine—"*

They had planned the whole thing, of course, beforehand; they had got that song off a record. They believed that it was an old hymn.

So they filed past, singing, looking down at Tracy Lee, and it was noticed that they were dropping things into the coffin. They were slipping the rings off their fingers and the bracelets from their arms, and taking the earrings out of their ears. They were undoing necklaces, and bowing to pull chains and long strands of beads over their heads. Everybody gave something. All this jewellery went flashing and sparkling down on the dead girl, to lie beside her in her coffin. One girl pulled the bright combs out of her hair, let those go.

And nobody made a move to stop it. How could anyone interrupt? It was like a religious ceremony. The girls behaved as if they'd been told what to do, as if this was what was always done on such occasions. They sang, they wept, they dropped their jewellery. The sense of ritual made every one of them graceful.

The family wouldn't stop it. They thought it was beautiful.

"It was like church," Tracy Lee's mother said, and her grandmother said, "All those lovely young girls loved Tracy Lee. If they wanted to give their jewellery to show how they loved her, that's their business. It's not anybody else's business. I thought it was beautiful."

Tracy Lee's sister broke down and cried. It was the first time she had done so.

Dan said, "This is a test of love."

Of Trudy's love, he meant. Trudy started singing, "Please release me, let me go—"

She clapped a hand to her chest, danced in swoops around the room, singing. Dan was near laughing, near crying. He couldn't help it; he came and hugged her and they danced together, staggering. They were fairly drunk. All that June (it was two years ago), they were drinking gin, in between and during their scenes. They were drinking, weeping, arguing, explaining, and Trudy had to keep running to the liquor store. Yet she can't remember ever feeling really drunk or having a hangover. Except that she felt so tired all the time, as if she had logs chained to her ankles.

She kept joking. She called Genevieve "Jenny the Feeb."

"This is just like wanting to give up the business and become a potter," she said. "Maybe you should have done that. I wasn't really against it. You gave up on it. And when you wanted to go to Peru. We could still do that."

"All those things were just straws in the wind," Dan said.

"I should have known when you started watching the Ombudsman on TV," Trudy said. "It was the legal angle, wasn't it? You were never so interested in that kind of thing before."

"This will open life up for you, too," Dan said. "You can be more than just my wife."

"Sure. I think I'll be a brain surgeon."

"You're very smart. You're a wonderful woman. You're brave."

"Sure you're not talking about Jenny the Feeb?"

"No, you. You, Trudy. I still love you. You can't understand that I still love you."

Not for years had he had so much to say about how he loved her. He loved her skinny bones, her curly hair, her roughening skin, her way of coming into a room with a stride that shook the windows, her jokes, her clowning, her tough talk. He loved her mind and her soul. He always would. But the part of his life that had been bound up with hers was over.

"That is just talk. That is talking like an idiot!" Trudy said. "Robin, go back to bed!" For Robin in her skimpy nightgown was standing at the top of the steps.

"I can hear you yelling and screaming," Robin said.

"We weren't yelling and screaming," Trudy said. "We're trying to talk about something private."

"What?"

"I told you, it's something private."

When Robin sulked off to bed, Dan said, "I think we should tell her. It's better for kids to know. Genevieve doesn't have any secrets from her kids. Josie's only five, and she came into the bedroom one afternoon—"

Then Trudy did start yelling and screaming. She clawed through a cushion cover. "You stop telling me about your sweet fucking Genevieve and her sweet fucking bedroom and her asshole kids—you shut up, don't tell me anymore! You're just a big dribbling mouth without any brains. I don't care what you do, just shut up!"

Dan left. He packed a suitcase; he went off to Richmond Hill. He was back in five days. Just outside of town, he had stopped the car to pick Trudy a bouquet of wildflowers. He told her he was back for good, it was over.

"You don't say?" said Trudy.

But she put the flowers in water. Dusty pink milkweed flowers that smelled like face powder, black-eyed Susans, wild sweet peas, and orange lilies that must have got loose from old disappeared gardens.

"So you couldn't stand the pace?" she said.

"I knew you wouldn't fall all over me," Dan said. "You wouldn't be you if you did. And what I came back to is you."

She went to the liquor store, and this time bought champagne. For a month—it was still summer—they were back together being happy. She never really found out what had happened at Genevieve's house. Dan said he'd been having a middle-aged fit, that was all. He'd come to his senses. His life was here, with her and Robin.

"You're talking like a marriage-advice column," Trudy said.

"Okay. Forget the whole thing."

"We better," she said. She could imagine the kids, the confusion, the friends—old boyfriends, maybe—that he hadn't been prepared for. Jokes and opinions that he couldn't understand. That was possible. The music he liked, the way he talked—even his hair and his beard—might be out of style.

They went on family drives, picnics. They lay out in the grass behind the house at night, looking at the stars. The stars were a new interest of Dan's; he got a map. They hugged and kissed each other frequently and tried out some new things—or things they hadn't done for a long time —when they made love.

At this time, the road in front of the house was being paved. They'd built their house on a hillside at the edge of town, past the other houses, but trucks were using this street quite a bit now, avoiding the main streets, so the town was paving it. Trudy got so used to the noise and constant vibration she said she could feel herself jiggling all night, even when everything was quiet. Work started at seven in the morning. They woke up at the bottom of a river of noise. Dan dragged himself out of bed then, losing the hour of sleep that he loved best. There was a smell of diesel fuel in the air.

She woke up one night to find him not in bed. She listened to hear noises in the kitchen or the bathroom, but she couldn't. She got up and walked through the house. There were no lights on. She found him sitting outside, just outside the door, not having a drink or a glass of milk or a coffee, sitting with his back to the street.

Trudy looked out at the torn-up earth and the huge stalled machinery. "Isn't the quiet lovely?" she said.

He didn't say anything.

Oh. Oh.

She realized what she'd been thinking when she found his side of the bed empty and couldn't hear him anywhere in the house. Not that he'd left her, but that he'd done worse. Done away with himself. With all their happiness and hugging and kissing and stars and picnics, she could think that.

"You can't forget her," she said. "You love her."

"I don't know what to do."

She was glad just to hear him speak. She said, "You'll have to go and try again."

"There's no guarantee I can stay," he said. "I can't ask you to stand by."

"No," said Trudy. "If you go, that's it."

"If I go, that's it."

He seemed paralyzed. She felt that he might just sit there, repeating what she said, never be able to move or speak for himself again.

"If you feel like this, that's all there is to it," she said. "You don't have to choose. You're already gone."

That worked. He stood up stiffly, came over, and put his arms around her. He stroked her back.

"Come back to bed," he said. "We can rest for a little while yet."

"No. You've got to be gone when Robin wakes up. If we go back to bed, it'll just start all over again."

She made him a thermos of coffee. He packed the bag he had taken with him before. All Trudy's movements seemed skillful and perfect, as they never were, usually. She felt serene. She felt as if they were an old couple, moving in harmony, in wordless love, past injury, past forgiving. Their goodbye was hardly a ripple. She went outside with him. It was between four-thirty and five o'clock; the sky was beginning to lighten and the birds to wake, everything was drenched in dew. There stood the big harmless machinery, stranded in the ruts of the road.

"Good thing it isn't last night—you couldn't have got out," she said. She meant that the road hadn't been navigable. It was just yesterday that they had graded a narrow track for local traffic.

"Good thing," he said.

Goodbye.

"All I want is to know why you did it. Did you just do it for show? Like your father—for show? It's not the necklace so much. But it was a beautiful thing—I love jet beads. It was the only thing we had of your grandmother's. It was your right, but you have no right to take me by surprise like that. I deserve an explanation. I always loved jet beads. Why?"

"I blame the family," Janet says. "It was up to them to stop it. Some of the stuff was just plastic—those junk earrings and bracelets—but what Robin threw in, that was a crime. And she wasn't the only one. There were birthstone rings and gold chains. Somebody said a diamond cluster ring, but I don't know if I believe that. They said the girl inherited it, like Robin. You didn't ever have it evaluated, did you?"

"I don't know if jet is worth anything," Trudy says.

They are sitting in Janet's front room, making roses out of pink Kleenex.

"It's just stupid," Trudy says.

"Well. There is one thing you could do," says Janet. "I don't hardly know how to mention it."

"What?"

"Pray."

Trudy'd had the feeling, from Janet's tone, that she was going to tell her something serious and unpleasant, something about herself—Trudy—that was affecting her life and that everybody knew except her. Now she wants to laugh, after bracing herself. She doesn't know what to say.

"You don't pray, do you?" Janet says.

"I haven't got anything against it," Trudy says. "I wasn't brought up to be religious."

"It's not strictly speaking religious," Janet says. "I mean, it's not connected with any church. This is just some of us that pray. I can't tell you the names of anybody in it, but most of them you know. It's supposed to be secret. It's called the Circle of Prayer."

"Like at high school," Trudy says. "At high school there were secret societies, and you weren't supposed to tell who was in them. Only I wasn't."

"I was in everything going." Janet sighs. "This is actually more on the serious side. Though some people in it don't take it seriously enough, I don't think. Some people, they'll pray that they'll find a parking spot, or they'll pray they get good weather for their holidays. That isn't what it's for. But that's just individual praying. What the Circle is really about is, you phone up somebody that is in it and tell them what it is you're worried about, or upset about, and ask them to pray for you. And they do. And they phone one other person that's in the Circle, and they phone another and it goes all around, and we pray for one person, all together."

Trudy throws a rose away. "That's botched. Is it all women?"

"There isn't any rule it has to be. But it is, yes. Men would be too embarrassed. I was embarrassed at first. Only the first person you phone knows your name, who it is that's being prayed for, but in a town like this nearly everybody can guess. But if we started gossiping and ratting on each other it wouldn't work, and everybody knows that. So we don't. And it does work."

"Like how?" Trudy says.

"Well, one girl banged up her car. She did eight hundred dollars' damage, and it was kind of a tricky situation, where she wasn't sure her insurance would cover it, and neither was her husband—he was raging mad —but we all prayed, and the insurance came through without a hitch. That's only one example."

"There wouldn't be much point in praying to get the necklace back when it's in the coffin and the funeral's this morning," Trudy says.

"It's not up to you to say that. You don't say what's possible or impossible. You just ask for what you want. Because it says in the Bible, 'Ask and it shall be given.' How can you be helped if you won't ask? You can't, that's for sure. What about when Dan left—what if you'd prayed then? I wasn't in the Circle then, or I would have said something to you. Even if I knew you'd resist it, I would have said something. A lot of people resist. Now, even—it doesn't sound too great with that girl, but how do you know, maybe even now it might work? It might not be too late."

"All right," says Trudy, in a hard, cheerful voice. "All right." She pushes all the floppy flowers off her lap. "I'll just get down on my knees right now and pray that I get Dan back. I'll pray that I get the necklace back and I get Dan back, and why do I have to stop there? I can pray that Tracy Lee never died. I can pray that she comes back to life. Why didn't her mother ever think of that?"

Good news. The swimming pool is fixed. They'll be able to fill it tomorrow. But Kelvin is depressed. Early this afternoon—partly to keep them from bothering the men who were working on the pool—he took Marie and Josephine uptown. He let them get ice-cream cones. He told them to pay attention and eat the ice cream up quickly, because the sun was hot and it would melt. They licked at their cones now and then, as if they had all day. Ice cream was soon dribbling down their chins and down their arms. Kelvin had grabbed a handful of paper napkins, but he couldn't wipe it up fast enough. They were a mess. A spectacle. They didn't care. Kelvin told them they weren't so pretty that they could afford to look like that.

"Some people don't like the look of us anyway," he said. "Some people don't even think we should be allowed uptown. People just get used to seeing us and not staring at us like freaks and you make a mess and spoil it."

They laughed at him. He could have cowed Marie if he had her alone, but not when she was with Josephine. Josephine was one who needed some old-fashioned discipline, in Kelvin's opinion. Kelvin had been in places where people didn't get away with anything like they got away with here. He didn't agree with hitting. He had seen plenty of it done, but he didn't agree with it, even on the hand. But a person like Josephine could be shut up in her room. She could be made to sit in a corner, she could be put on bread and water, and it would do a lot of good. All Marie needed was a talking-to—she had a weak personality. But Josephine was a devil.

"I'll talk to both of them," Trudy says. "I'll tell them to say they're sorry."

"I want for them to *be* sorry," Kelvin says. "I don't care if they say they are. I'm not taking them ever again."

Later, when all the others are in bed, Trudy gets him to sit down to play cards with her on the screened veranda. They play Crazy Eights. Kelvin says that's all he can manage tonight; his head is sore.

Uptown, a man said to him, "Hey, which one of them two is your girlfriend?"

"Stupid," Trudy says. "He was a stupid jerk."

The man talking to the first man said, "Which one you going to marry?"

"They don't know you, Kelvin. They're just stupid."

But they did know him. One was Reg Hooper, one was Bud DeLisle. Bud DeLisle that sold real estate. They knew him. They had talked to him in the barbershop; they called him Kelvin. "Hey, Kelvin, which one you going to marry?"

"Nerds," says Trudy. "That's what Robin would say."

"You think they're your friend, but they're not," says Kelvin. "How many times I see that happen."

Trudy goes to the kitchen to put on coffee. She wants to have fresh coffee to offer Janet when she comes in. She apologized this morning, and Janet said all right, I know you're upset. It really is all right. Sometimes you think they're your friend, and they are.

She looks at all the mugs hanging on their hooks. She and Janet shopped all over to find them. A mug with each one's name. Marie, Josephine, Arthur, Kelvin, Shirley, George, Dorinda. You'd think Dorinda would be the hardest name to find, but actually the hardest was Shirley. Even the people who can't read have learned to recognize their own mugs, by color and pattern.

One day, two new mugs appeared, bought by Kelvin. One said Trudy, the other Janet.

"I'm not going to be too overjoyed seeing my name in that lineup," Janet said. "But I wouldn't hurt his feelings for a million dollars."

For a honeymoon, Dan took Trudy to the island on the lake where his mother's hotel was. The hotel was closed down, but his mother still lived there. Dan's father was dead, and she lived there alone. She took a boat

with an outboard motor across the water to get her groceries. She sometimes made a mistake and called Trudy Marlene.

The hotel wasn't much. It was a white wooden box in a clearing by
the shore. Some little boxes of cabins were stuck behind it. Dan and Trudy
stayed in one of the cabins. Every cabin had a wood stove. Dan built a fire
at night to take off the chill. But the blankets were damp and heavy when he
and Trudy woke up in the morning.

Dan caught fish and cooked them. He and Trudy climbed the big
rock behind the cabins and picked blueberries. He asked her if she knew
how to make a piecrust, and she didn't. So he showed her, rolling out the
dough with a whiskey bottle.

In the morning there was a mist over the lake, just as you see in the
movies or in a painting.

One afternoon, Dan stayed out longer than usual, fishing. Trudy
kept busy for a while in the kitchen, rubbing the dust off things, washing
some jars. It was the oldest, darkest kitchen she had ever seen, with wooden
racks for the dinner plates to dry in. She went outside and climbed the rock
by herself, thinking she would pick some blueberries. But it was already
dark under the trees; the evergreens made it dark, and she didn't like the
idea of wild animals. She sat on the rock looking down on the roof of the
hotel, the old dead leaves and broken shingles. She heard a piano being
played. She scrambled down the rock and followed the music around to the
front of the building. She walked along the front veranda and stopped at
a window, looking into the room that used to be the lounge. The room
with the blackened stone fireplace, the lumpy leather chairs, the horrible
mounted fish.

Dan's mother was there, playing the piano. A tall, straight-backed
old woman, with her gray-black hair twisted into such a tiny knot. She
sat and played the piano, without any lights on, in the half-dark, half-
bare room.

Dan had said that his mother came from a rich family. She had
taken piano lessons, dancing lessons; she had gone around the world when
she was a young girl. There was a picture of her on a camel. But she wasn't
playing a classical piece, the sort of thing you'd expect her to have learned.
She was playing "It's Three O'Clock in the Morning." When she got to the
end, she started in again. Maybe it was a special favorite of hers, something
she had danced to in the old days. Or maybe she wasn't satisfied yet that she
had got it right.

Why does Trudy now remember this moment? She sees her young
self looking in the window at the old woman playing the piano. The dim
room, with its oversize beams and fireplace and the lonely leather chairs.
The clattering, faltering, persistent piano music. Trudy remembers that so
clearly and it seems she stood outside her own body, which ached then from
the punishing pleasures of love. She stood outside her own happiness in a
tide of sadness. And the opposite thing happened the morning Dan left.

Then she stood outside her own unhappiness in a tide of what seemed unreasonably like love. But it was the same thing, really, when you got out-side. What are those times that stand out, clear patches in your life—what do they have to do with it? They aren't exactly promises. Breathing spaces. Is that all?

She goes into the front hall and listens for any noise from upstairs. All quiet there, all medicated.

The phone rings right beside her head.

"Are you still there?" Robin says. "You're not gone?"

"I'm still here."

"Can I run over and ride back with you? I didn't do my run earlier because it was so hot."

You threw the jug. You could have killed me.

Yes.

Kelvin, waiting at the card table, under the light, looks bleached and old. There's a pool of light whitening his brown hair. His face sags, waiting. He looks old, sunk into himself, wrapped in a thick bewilderment, nearly lost to her.

"Kelvin, do you pray?" says Trudy. She didn't know she was going to ask him that. "I mean, it's none of my business. But, like for anything specific?"

He's got an answer for her, which is rather surprising. He pulls his face up, as if he might have felt the tug he needed to bring him to the surface.

"If I was smart enough to know what to pray for," he says, "then I wouldn't have to."

He smiles at her, with some oblique notion of conspiracy, offering his halfway joke. It's not meant as comfort, particularly. Yet it radiates—what he said, the way he said it, just the fact that he's there again, radiates, expands the way some silliness can, when you're very tired. In this way, when she was young, and high, a person or a moment could become a lily floating on the cloudy river water, perfect and familiar.

1986

Alice Munro's stories reflect life in small towns in southwest Ontario, a region that retains something of a frontier flavor and encourages independ- ence. Life there may also make a person feel more isolated and vulnerable

than a more cosmopolitan life would. Margaret Atwood, another Canadian writer, has attempted to define the effects of isolation on Canada's fiction.

"Carving out a place and a way of keeping alive": Margaret Atwood

The central symbol for Canada—and this is based on numerous instances of its occurrence in both English and French Canadian literature—is undoubtedly Survival, *la Survivance*. Like the Frontier and The Island, it is a multi-faceted and adaptable idea. For early explorers and settlers, it meant bare survival in the face of "hostile" elements and/or natives: carving out a place and a way of keeping alive. But the word can also suggest survival of a crisis or disaster, like a hurricane or a wreck, and many Canadian poems have this kind of survival as a theme; what you might call 'grim' survival as opposed to 'bare' survival. For French Canada after the English took over it became cultural survival, hanging on as a people, retaining a religion and a language under an alien government. And in English Canada now while the Americans are taking over it is acquiring a similar meaning. There is another use of the word as well: a survival can be a vestige of a vanished order which has managed to persist after its time is past, like a primitive reptile. This version crops up in Canadian thinking too, usually among those who believe that Canada is obsolete.

But the main idea is the first one: hanging on, staying alive. Canadians are forever taking the national pulse like doctors at a sickbed: the aim is not to see whether the patient will live well but simply whether he will live at all. Our central idea is one which generates, not the excitement and sense of adventure or danger which The Frontier holds out, not the smugness and/or sense of security, of everything in its place, which The Island can offer, but an almost intolerable anxiety. Our stories are likely to be tales not of those who made it but of those who made it back, from the awful experience—the North, the snowstorm, the sinking ship—that killed everyone else. The survivor has no triumph or victory but the fact of his survival; he has little after his ordeal that he did not have before, except gratitude for having escaped with his life.

CHINUA ACHEBE

(b. 1930)

CIVIL PEACE

Jonathan Iwegbu counted himself extra-ordinarily lucky. 'Happy survival!' meant so much more to him than just a current fashion of greeting old friends in the first hazy days of peace. It went deep to his heart. He had come out of the war with five inestimable blessings—his head, his wife Maria's head and the heads of three out of their four children. As a bonus he also had his old bicycle—a miracle too but naturally not to be compared to the safety of five human heads.

The bicycle had a little history of its own. One day at the height of the war it was commandeered 'for urgent military action'. Hard as its loss would have been to him he would still have let it go without a thought had he not had some doubts about the genuineness of the officer. It wasn't his disreputable rags, nor the toes peeping out of one blue and one brown canvas shoe, nor yet the two stars of his rank done obviously in a hurry in biro, that troubled Jonathan; many good and heroic soldiers looked the same or worse. It was rather a certain lack of grip and firmness in his manner. So Jonathan, suspecting he might be amenable to influence, rummaged in his raffia bag and produced the two pounds with which he had been going to buy firewood which his wife, Maria, retailed to camp officials for extra stock-fish and corn meal, and got his bicycle back. That night he buried it in the little clearing in the bush where the dead of the camp, including his own youngest son, were buried. When he dug it up again a year later after the surrender all it needed was a little palm-oil greasing. 'Nothing puzzles God,' he said in wonder.

He put it to immediate use as a taxi and accumulated a small pile of Biafran money ferrying camp officials and their families across the four-mile stretch to the nearest tarred road. His standard charge per trip was six pounds and those who had the money were only glad to be rid of some of it in this way. At the end of a fortnight he had made a small fortune of one hundred and fifteen pounds.

Then he made the journey to Enugu and found another miracle waiting for him. It was unbelievable. He rubbed his eyes and looked again and it was still standing there before him. But, needless to say, even that monumental blessing must be accounted also totally inferior to the five heads in the family. This newest miracle was his little house in Ogui Overside. Indeed nothing puzzles God! Only two houses away a huge concrete edifice some wealthy contractor had put up just before the war was a mountain of rubble. And here was Jonathan's little zinc house of no regrets built with mud blocks quite intact! Of course the doors and windows were missing and five sheets off the roof. But what was that? And anyhow he had returned to Enugu early enough to pick up bits of old zinc and wood and soggy sheets of cardboard lying around the neighbourhood before thousands more came out of their forest holes looking for the same things. He got a destitute carpenter with one old hammer, a blunt plane and a few bent and rusty nails in his tool bag to turn this assortment of wood, paper and metal into door and window shutters for five Nigerian shillings or fifty Biafran pounds. He paid the pounds, and moved in with his overjoyed family carrying five heads on their shoulders.

His children picked mangoes near the military cemetery and sold them to soldiers' wives for a few pennies—real pennies this time—and his wife started making breakfast akara balls for neighbours in a hurry to start life again. With his family earnings he took his bicycle to the villages around and bought fresh palm-wine which he mixed generously in his rooms with the water which had recently started running again in the public tap down the road, and opened up a bar for soldiers and other lucky people with good money.

At first he went daily, then every other day and finally once a week, to the offices of the Coal Corporation where he used to be a miner, to find out what was what. The only thing he did find out in the end was that that little house of his was even a greater blessing than he had thought. Some of his fellow ex-miners who had nowhere to return at the end of the day's waiting just slept outside the doors of the offices and cooked what meal they could scrounge together in Bournvita tins. As the weeks lengthened and still nobody could say what was what Jonathan discontinued his weekly visits altogether and faced his palm-wine bar.

But nothing puzzles God. Came the day of the windfall when after five days of endless scuffles in queues and counterqueues in the sun outside the Treasury he had twenty pounds counted into his palms as ex-gratia award for the rebel money he had turned in. It was like Christmas for him and for many others like him when the payments began. They called it (since few could manage its proper official name) *egg-rasher*.

As soon as the pound notes were placed in his palm Jonathan simply closed it tight over them and buried fist and money inside his trouser pocket. He had to be extra careful because he had seen a man a couple of days earlier collapse into near-madness in an instant before that oceanic crowd because no sooner had he got his twenty pounds than some heartless ruffian picked it off him. Though it was not right that a man in such an extremity of agony should be blamed yet many in the queues that day were able to remark quietly at the victim's carelessness, especially after he pulled out the innards of his pocket and revealed a hole in it big enough to pass a thief's head. But of course he had insisted that the money had been in the other pocket, pulling it out too to show its comparative wholeness. So one had to be careful.

Jonathan soon transferred the money to his left hand and pocket so as to leave his right free for shaking hands should the need arise, though by fixing his gaze at such an elevation as to miss all approaching human faces he made sure that the need did not arise, until he got home.

He was normally a heavy sleeper but that night he heard all the neighbourhood noises die down one after another. Even the night watch-man who knocked the hour on some metal somewhere in the distance had fallen silent after knocking one o'clock. That must have been the last thought in Jonathan's mind before he was finally carried away himself. He couldn't have been gone for long, though, when he was violently awakened again.

'Who is knocking?' whispered his wife lying beside him on the floor.

'I don't know,' he whispered back breathlessly.

The second time the knocking came it was so loud and imperious that the rickety old door could have fallen down.

'Who is knocking?' he asked them, his voice parched and trembling.

'Na tief-man and him people,' came the cool reply. 'Make you hopen de door.' This was followed by the heaviest knocking of all.

Maria was the first to raise the alarm, then he followed and all their children.

'*Police-o! Thieves-o! Neighbours-o! Police-o! We are lost! We are dead! Neighbours, are you asleep? Wake up! Police-o!*'

This went on for a long time and then stopped suddenly. Perhaps they had scared the thief away. There was total silence. But only for a short while.

'You done finish?' asked the voice outside. 'Make we help you small. Oya, everybody!'

'*Police-o! Tief-man-so! Neighbours-o! we done loss-o! Police-o! . . .*'

There were at least five other voices besides the leader's.

Jonathan and his family were now completely paralysed by terror. Maria and the children sobbed inaudibly like lost souls. Jonathan groaned continuously.

The silence that followed the thieves' alarm vibrated horribly. Jon-athan all but begged their leader to speak again and be done with it.

'My frien,' said he at long last, 'we don try our best for call dem but I tink say dem all done sleep-o . . . So wetin we go do now? Sometaim you wan call soja? Or you wan make we call dem for you? Soja better pass police. No be so?'

'Na so!' replied his men. Jonathan thought he heard even more voices now than before and groaned heavily. His legs were sagging under him and his throat felt like sandpaper.

'My frien, why you no de talk again. I de ask you say you wan make we call soja?'

'No'.

'Awrighto. Now make we talk business. We no be bad tief. We no like for make trouble. Trouble done finish. War done finish and all the katakata wey de for inside. No Civil War again. This time na Civil Peace. No be so?'

'Na so!' answered the horrible chorus.

'What do you want from me? I am a poor man. Everything I had went with this war. Why do you come to me? You know people who have money. We . . .'

'Awright! We know say you no get plenty money. But we sef no get even anini. So derefore make you open dis window and give us one hundred pound and we go commot. Orderwise we de come for inside now to show you guitar-boy like dis . . .'

A volley of automatic fire rang through the sky. Maria and the children began to weep aloud again.

'Ah, missisi de cry again. No need for dat. We done talk say we na good tief. We just take our small money and go nwayorly. No molest. Abi we de molest?'

'At all!' sang the chorus.

'My friends,' began Jonathan hoarsely. 'I hear what you say and I thank you. If I had one hundred pounds . . .'

'Lookia my frien, no be play we come play for your house. If we make mistake and step for inside you no go like am-o. So derefore . . .'

'To God who made me; if you come inside and find one hundred pounds, take it and shoot me and shoot my wife and children. I swear to God. The only money I have in this life is this twenty-pounds *egg-rasher* they gave me today . . .'

'Ok. Time de go. Make you open dis window and bring the twenty pound. We go manage am like dat.'

There were now loud murmurs of dissent among the chorus: 'Na lie de man de lie; e get plenty money . . . Make we go inside and search properly well . . . Wetin be twenty pound? . . .'

'Shurrup!' rang the leader's voice like a lone shot in the sky and silenced the murmuring at once. 'Are you dere? Bring the money quick!'

'I am coming,' said Jonathan fumbling in the darkness with the key of the small wooden box he kept by his side on the mat.

At the first sign of light as neighbours and others assembled to commiserate with him he was already strapping his five-gallon demijohn to his bicycle carrier and his wife, sweating in the open fire, was turning over akara balls in a wide clay bowl of boiling oil. In the corner his eldest son was rinsing out dregs of yesterday's palm-wine from old beer bottles.

'I count it as nothing,' he told his sympathizers, his eyes on the rope he was tying. 'What is *egg-rasher*? Did I depend on it last week? Or is it greater than other things that went with the war? I say, let *egg-rasher* perish in the flames! Let it go where everything else has gone. Nothing puzzles God.'

1971

An African writer with international stature like Chinua Achebe's natu-rally assumes the role of educator to Europeans and Americans who, Achebe says, tend to assume that there was no African culture until Europeans brought one. His impatience with this assumption was in his mind when he delivered a lecture at the University of Massachusetts, from which this excerpt is taken.

"Yonkers, New York is full of odd customs and superstitions": Chinua Achebe

It was a fine autumn morning at the beginning of this academic year such as encouraged friendliness to passing strangers. Brisk youngsters were hurry-ing in all directions, many of them obviously freshmen in their first flush of enthusiasm. An older man, going the same way as I, turned and remarked to me how very young they came these days. I agreed. Then he asked me if I was a student too. I said no, I was a teacher. What did I teach? African literature. Now that was funny, he said, because he never had thought of Africa as having that kind of stuff, you know. By this time I was walking much faster. "Oh well," I heard him say finally, behind me, "I guess I have to take your course to find out."

A few weeks later I received two very touching letters from high school children in Yonkers, New York, who—bless their teacher—had just read *Things Fall Apart*. One of them was particularly happy to learn about the customs and superstitions of an African tribe.

I propose to draw from these rather trivial encounters rather heavy conclusions which at first sight might seem somewhat out of proportion to them: But only at first sight.

The young fellow from Yonkers, perhaps partly on account of his age but I believe also for much deeper and more serious reasons, is obviously unaware that the life of his own tribesmen in Yonkers, New York, is full of odd customs and superstitions and, like everybody else in his cul-ture, imagines that he needs a trip to Africa to encounter those things.

The other person being fully my own age could not be excused on the grounds of his years. Ignorance might be a more likely reason; but here again I believe that something more willful than a mere lack of information was at work. For did not that erudite British historian and Regius Professor at Oxford, Hugh Trevor Roper, pronounce a few years ago that African his-tory did not exist?

If there is something in these utterances more than youthful experience, more than a lack of factual knowledge, what is it? Quite simply it is the desire—one might indeed say the need—in Western psychology to set up Africa as a foil to Europe, a place of negations at once remote and vaguely familiar in comparison with which Europe's own state of spiritual grace will be manifest.

ELENA PONIATOWSKA

(b. 1933)

A LITTLE FAIRY TALE

translated from the Spanish by Magda Bogin

From time to time we would hear about the wild boar and I would look down at the forest. We lived up above in a house held back by a retaining wall that kept us from falling down onto the sea of trees, but to me they looked so strong that I was sure they would support us with their branches if the wall ever collapsed. I could see them from my window. They were different at different times of day: at noon so thick that the sun's rays bounced off without penetrating them; a single black, ominous tree at night; and at dawn a pale green lake emerging through the mist. In my head I could hear old Madame Dot saying, "The woods are dark," drawing out the "a" of dark into a long, terrifying tunnel. "The woods are daaaaaaark. Very very daaaaaaark." Sofia, who was always the stronger one, or at any rate less morbidly inclined than I, would say, "Don't listen to her. She's old. She just doesn't want us going down to gather wild strawberries." Sofia had a special predilection for the tiny, aromatic strawberries that grow at the foot of trees. She never waited, but ate them on the spot, so that by the time we got back home our basket would be empty. Even on the way uphill she'd still be saying, "Pass me the basket. I'll carry it," finishing them off by the fistful, leaves and all.

I've always liked to put my hands in cracks and crevices; to dig. I can spend hours standing at the sink pulling garbage from the drain, along with leaves, tangled hair, dirt and hardened soap. The closer I get to unclogging it the more excited I become. As the feeling of satisfaction rises through my body, filling my mouth, I think of our revolutionary generals shouting to their men: "Nail them, lay into them, let them have it, kill the sons of bitches," and I feel I'm doing something useful equal to what they did, although I'm not completely sure that what they did was right. In the forest, while Sofia gathered strawberries, I would stop to stroke the rough bark, to plunge my hands into the damp earth, to cut the stems of mushrooms with their fascinating texture; crack; I'd stroke them with my index finger for a long time, watching their skin stiffen like the leaves of certain plants that tighten and close on themselves. "You and your poisons," Sofia would shout with her mouth full. Sometimes I would find a dark black truffle beneath a bed of musty leaves. "You're going to turn into a mushroom," she'd say. But I didn't move. Bent over the earth, crouched on all fours, looking and sniffing, when I found what I was looking for I'd scratch and scratch with a little stick: crack, crack, crack, pulling out the worms and all the other little forest creatures. I pulled them from their dens so I could see them and feel them walk across my palm, so I could feel their sharp little feet. I didn't want to hurt them. When I was done I closed up the holes, fortified their dwelling places, put them back in their homes. I wanted to see them and feel them but that's all. And when Sofia called, "Come here, there are piles of them here!" I never went, because I couldn't tear myself away from the damp moss, the lichen, but above all the moss that is like the earth's softest hair, its childhood down, a sweet delicate fleece that went back and forth across my face.

When the news broke the whole village was stunned. The boar had gored Berta. They brought her up from the woods thin and transparent after a two-day search. She had been wounded in the stomach and died in their arms on the way uphill. She was wearing a white dress and they had found her basket almost full. *She* didn't eat the berries. The boar had bitten her. Or charged her. Or who knows. The long and short of it is that she had bled to death and neither Sofia nor I was allowed to see her. The peasants made her a stretcher out of branches and covered her with foliage. Her whole face was hidden with green leaves so no one would be left with the image, the expression fear had stamped there. For days no one in the village talked of anything but the wild boar and how on Sunday, a holy day, a posse would go down into the forest to avenge her death. Someone had seen the bloody eyes of the beast glowing through the branches. Berta's father would lead the hunters, not her fiancé who had fled drunk and crazed, arms flailing, to Cahors.

"You're not to go into the woods ever again, is that clear, girls?"

For days I circled Madame Dot's windowless house. I wanted to speak to her. But she never came out. I never saw her open the door, and her broom still stood to one side, leaning, in the same place. The pail filled with cobwebs. The chickens cackled untended, left to fend for themselves. Finally one Thursday—Thursdays are always good days, white and round, days for talking—I saw her stooped back just ahead on the path, her shoulders covered by her black shawl.

"Madame Dot, Madame Dot!"

I walked her to her house and she invited me in. The broom was still leaning against the wall. No one had swept. She knew that I wanted to ask about the woods, which is to say, about the wild boar. She offered me a small low chair and I liked having to crouch down to sit in it the way I do when I'm looking for mushrooms in the earth. Outside a cold wind was blowing. She told me in her cracked voice that the boar's eyes were always red and that his hairs stood on end, almost like a porcupine's. She said he was black and thick and weighed a lot in the dark. "He charges like a huge pig." She pulled her shawl across her chest to protect herself from an imaginary attack. "He has hooves like the devil. Didn't you know that the devil has hooves?"

"What I want to know is why he killed Berta."

"For her flower."

"Her flower? What flower?"

"The black flower that grows between a woman's legs."

She saw the terror on my lips and said gently: "Yes, a tiny black flower. You don't have yours yet."

Madame Dot's old nose lengthened into a hook.

"That's what wild boars hunt. That's what they eat."

"Eat?"

"Yes, they tear it out by the roots, once and for all."

I ran out of there as fast as I could and didn't stop for weeks and weeks until I was twenty-three. The day of my wedding was also my birthday. The guests all remarked on the coincidence and offered double congratulations. "How nice to be getting married on the day you were born." They told me I was being born again to love. People are clever. Besides, it was a Sunday, but I prefer Thursdays. Guests like Sundays. My mother in her ramblings always spoke of the week of four Thursdays, and she made up a secret one just for me, in French: *la semaine des quatre jeudis.*[1] But I live in Mexico and have only been to France two times and the French are very exact about their days; they never lose track. On my wedding day she lifted my organdy veil and whispered in my ear, "Now you'll really have your week of four Thursdays."

I thought the veil was holding me aloft and with a smile I stretched out my arms that were swathed in white. He struck head-on from his powerful tuxedo. I saw him coming straight toward me from the dark, his head lowered. I heard the rumble of his hooves. When he was a few yards away I could see his eyes glowing red beneath his thick black eyebrows. On the broad planes of his thinker's brow I saw the erect hairs. Like a porcupine's. He breathed into my face as his moustached mouth drew close. I who had begun to caress the fascinating texture of mushrooms, to feel their damp beneath my fingertips, fell backwards: crack, crack, crack, and when he put his arms around me I fell down, down onto a steep path that descended to the deepest reaches of the woods. My screams must have pierced the thin walls of the hotel because the next morning an old woman with a hooked nose and a broom came rushing toward me. "You must be the new bride."

And just as speedily she handed me a white cup of herb tea. "Drink this. It will clean out your stomach."

I almost spilled it when he entered haughtily on his gleaming

---

1. A week of four Thursdays.

hooves and in the noon heat of Mérida immediately announced, slamming his fist on the table: "It's better to visit the ruins at dusk when the sun is going down."

Without taking her eyes off me the old lady insisted, "Drink your tea. Can't you see you've spilled your honeymoon?"

Then she brought us the menu. "It's almost dinner time. May I recommend tacos stuffed with black beans, with pheasant, venison or wild boar?"

He ordered tacos with wild boar and ate them lost in concentration. I washed down a bowl of lime soup, cleansing myself with its consoling water. The sky had turned purple from the heat.

"Can I bring you anything else?"

"And this old hag—why's she being so attentive?" he asked, wiping his moustache that was rotting in sauce. I didn't know how to tell him that women like me have always had a fairy godmother.

The same scream was heard again that night, but over the years it grew fainter and less frequent. I gave birth to some little bisons who took their first wobbly steps holding on to my arm. Now that my hair has begun to turn white my only wish is to return to the house in the mountains and go down to the forest with my basket; to walk beneath the arching trees, the thick ferns, to tread the ochres and yellows, choose the path, put my hands into the earth, find the truffle and feel the little creatures who make their home in the dense weeds. But I'm afraid it's only an illusion, a fairy tale that I will have to try again in my next incarnation—because we're all given a second chance, aren't we? It's only fair, after all; you can always start over again, meet up with some other animal, a unicorn for example, or a lion with a flat head like in the tapestries or a swan like Leda's that made love to her by covering her with its wings, or a deer. It doesn't always have to be a wild boar, does it? A fairy tale, yes, because it's late now and I don't have what it takes for all this jousting, and the little dog laughed to see such sport, right? and all I know is that they all lived everly happily after and had many children and rode in a carriage, and all the king's horses and all the king's men, do you want me to tell it all over again?

1986

When a contemporary author like Elena Poniatowska calls one of her stories a fairy tale, she is setting up specific expectations in her reader. She may fulfill these expectations, violate them, or do both at once. A very clear explanation of what the expectations are is found in W. H. Auden's introduction to an edition of the Grimms' fairy tales.

"Projection in symbolic images of the life of the psyche": W. H. Auden

A fairy story, as distinct from a merry tale, or an animal story, is a serious tale with a human hero and a happy ending. The progression of its hero is the reverse of the tragic hero's: at the beginning he is either socially obscure or despised as being stupid or untalented, lacking in the heroic virtues, but at the end, he has surprised everyone by demonstrating his heroism and winning fame, riches, and love. Though ultimately he succeeds, he does not do so without a struggle in which his success is in doubt, for opposed to him are not only natural difficulties like glass mountains, or barriers of flame, but also hostile wicked powers, stepmothers, jealous brothers and witches. In many cases, indeed, he would fail were he not assisted by friendly powers who give him instructions or perform tasks for him which he cannot do himself; that is, in addition to his own powers, he needs luck, but this luck is not fortuitous but dependent upon his character and his actions. The tale ends with the establishment of justice; not only are the good rewarded but also the evil are punished. . . .

In the folk tale, as in the Greek epic and tragedy, situation and character are hardly separable; a man reveals what he is in what he does, or what happens to him is a revelation of what he is. In modern literature, what a man is includes all the possibilities of what he may become, so that what he actually does is never a complete revelation. . . .

Broadly speaking, and in most cases, the fairy tale is a dramatic projection in symbolic images of the life of the psyche, and it can travel from one country to another, one culture to another culture, whenever what it has to say holds good for human nature in both, despite their differences. Insofar as the myth is valid, the events of the story and its basic images will appeal irrespective of the artistic value of their narration; a genuine myth, like the Chaplin clown, can always be recognized by the fact that its appeal cuts across all differences between highbrow and lowbrow tastes. Further, no one conscious analysis can exhaust its meaning.

EDNA O'BRIEN

(b. 1936)

SISTER IMELDA

Sister Imelda did not take classes on her first day back in the convent but we spotted her in the grounds after the evening Rosary. Excitement and curiosity impelled us to follow her and try to see what she looked like, but she thwarted us by walking with head bent and eyelids down. All we could be certain of was that she was tall and limber and that she prayed while she walked. No looking at nature for her, or no curiosity about seventy boarders in gaberdine coats and black shoes and stockings. We might just as well have been crows, so impervious was she to our stares and to abortive attempts at trying to say "Hello, Sister."

We had returned from our long summer holiday and we were all wretched. The convent, with its high stone wall and green iron gates enfolding us again, seemed more of a prison than ever—for after our spell in the outside world we all felt very much older and more sophisticated, and my friend Baba and I were dreaming of our final escape, which would be in a year. And so, on that damp autumn evening when I saw the chrysanthemums and saw the new nun intent on prayer I pitied her and thought how alone she must be, cut off from her friends and conversation, with only God as her intangible spouse.

The next day she came into our classroom to take geometry. Her pale, slightly long face I saw as formidable, but her eyes were different, being blue-black and full of verve. Her lips were very purple, as if she had put puce pencil on them. They were the lips of a woman who might sing in a cabaret, and unconsciously she had formed the habit of turning them inward, as if she, too, was aware of their provocativeness. She had spent the last four years—the same span that Baba and I had spent in the convent— at the university in Dublin, where she studied languages. We couldn't understand how she had resisted the temptations of the hectic world and willingly come back to this. Her spell in the outside world made her different from the other nuns; there was more bounce in her walk, more excitement in the way she tackled teaching, reminding us that it was the most important thing in the world as she uttered the phrase "Praise be the Incarnate World." She began each day's class by reading from Cardinal Newman, who was a favorite of hers. She read how God dwelt in light unapproachable, and how with Him there was neither change nor shadow of alteration. It was amazing how her looks changed. Some days, when her eyes were flashing, she looked almost profane and made me wonder what events inside the precincts of the convent caused her to be suddenly so excited. She might have been a girl going to a dance, except for her habit.

"Hasn't she wonderful eyes," I said to Baba. That particular day they were like blackberries, large and soft and shiny.

"Something wrong in her upstairs department," Baba said, and added that with makeup Imelda would be a cinch.

"Still, she has a vocation!" I said, and even aired the idiotic view that I might have one. At certain moments it did seem enticing to become a nun, to lead a life unspotted by sin, never to have to have babies, and to wear a ring that singled one out as the Bride of Christ. But there was the other side to it, the silence, the gravity of it, having to get up two or three times a night to pray and, above all, never having the opportunity of leaving the confines of the place except for the funeral of one's parents. For us boarders it was torture, but for the nuns it was nothing short of doom. Also, we could complain to each other, and we did, food being the source of the greatest grumbles. Lunch was either bacon and cabbage or a peculiar stringy meat followed by tapioca pudding; tea consisted of bread dolloped with lard and occasionally, as a treat, fairly green rhubarb jam, which did not have enough sugar. Through the long curtainless windows we saw the conifer trees and a sky that was scarcely ever without the promise of rain or a downpour.

She was a right lunatic, then, Baba said, having gone to university for four years and willingly come back to incarceration, to poverty, chastity, and obedience. We concocted scenes of agony in some Dublin hostel, while a boy, or even a young man, stood beneath her bedroom window throwing up chunks of clay or whistles or a supplication. In our version of it he was slightly older than her, and possibly a medical student, since medical students had a knack with women, because of studying diagrams and skeletons. His advances, like those of a sudden storm, would intermittently rise and overwhelm her, and the memory of these sudden flaying advances of his would haunt her until she died, and if ever she contracted fever, these secrets would out. It was also rumored that she possessed a fierce temper and that, while a postulant, she had hit a girl so badly with her leather strap that the girl had to be put to bed because of wounds. Yet another black mark against Sister Imelda was that her brother Ambrose had been sued by a nurse for breach of promise.

That first morning when she came into our classroom and modestly introduced herself, I had no idea how terribly she would infiltrate my life, how in time she would be not just one of those teachers or nuns but rather a special one, almost like a ghost who passed the boundaries of common exchange and who crept inside one, devouring so much of one's thoughts, so much of one's passion, invading the place that was called one's heart. She talked in a low voice, as if she did not want her words to go beyond the bounds of the wall, and constantly she stressed the value of work both to enlarge the mind and to discipline the thought. One of her eyelids was red and swollen, as if she was getting a sty. I reckoned that she overmortified herself by not eating at all. I saw in her some terrible premonition of sacrifice which I would have to emulate. Then, in direct contrast, she absently held the stick of chalk between her first and second fingers, the very same as if it were a cigarette, and Baba whispered to me that she might have been a smoker when in Dublin. Sister Imelda looked down sharply at me and said what was the secret and would I like to share it, since it seemed so comical. I said, "Nothing, Sister, nothing," and her dark eyes exuded such vehemence that I prayed she would never have occasion to punish me.

November came and the tiled walls of the recreation hall oozed moisture and gloom. Most girls had sore throats and were told to suffer this inconvenience to mortify themselves in order to lend a glorious hand in that communion of spirit that linked the living with the dead. It was the month of the Suffering Souls in Purgatory, and as we heard of their twofold agony, the yearning for Christ and the ferocity of the leaping flames that burned and charred their poor limbs, we were asked to make acts of mortification. Some girls gave up jam or sweets and some gave up talking, and so in recreation time they were like dummies making signs with thumb and finger to merely say "How are you?" Baba said that saner people were locked in the lunatic asylum, which was only a mile away. We saw them in the grounds, pacing back and forth, with their mouths agape and dribble coming out of them, like melting icicles. Among our many fears was that one of those lunatics would break out and head straight for the convent and assault some of the girls.

Yet in the thick of all these dreads I found myself becoming dreadfully happy. I had met Sister Imelda outside of class a few times and I felt that there was an attachment between us. Once it was in the grounds, when she did a reckless thing. She broke off a chrysanthemum and offered it to me to smell. It had no smell, or at least only something faint that suggested autumn, and feeling this to be the case herself, she said it was not a gardenia, was it? Another time we met in the chapel porch, and as she drew her shawl more tightly around her body, I felt how human she was, and prey to the cold.

In the classroom things were not so congenial between us. Geometry was my worst subject, indeed, a total mystery to me. She had not taught more than four classes when she realized this and threw a duster at me in a rage. A few girls gasped as she asked me to stand up and make a spectacle of myself. Her face had reddened, and presently she took out her handkerchief and patted the eye which was red and swollen. I not only felt a fool but felt in imminent danger of sneezing as I inhaled the smell of chalk that had fallen onto my gym frock. Suddenly she fled from the room, leaving us ten minutes free until the next class. Some girls said it was a disgrace, said I should write home and say I had been assaulted. Others welcomed the few minutes in which to gabble. All I wanted was to run after her and say that I was sorry to have caused her such distemper, because I knew dimly that it was as much to do with liking as it was with dislike. In me then there came a sort of speechless tenderness for her, and I might have known that I was stirred.

"We could get her defrocked," Baba said, and elbowed me in God's name to sit down.

That evening at Benediction I had the most overwhelming surprise. It was a particularly happy evening, with the choir nuns in full soaring form and the rows of candles like so many little ladders to the golden chalice that glittered all the more because of the beams of fitful flame. I was full of tears when I discovered a new holy picture had been put in my prayer book, and before I dared look on the back to see who had given it to me, I felt and guessed that this was no ordinary picture from an ordinary girl friend, that this was a talisman and a peace offering from Sister Imelda. It was a pale-blue picture, so pale that it was almost gray, like the down of a pigeon, and it showed a mother looking down on the infant child. On the back, in her beautiful ornate handwriting, she had written a verse:

> Trust Him when dark doubts assail thee,
> Trust Him when thy faith is small,
> Trust Him when to simply trust Him
> Seems the hardest thing of all.

This was her atonement. To think that she had located the compartment in the chapel where I kept my prayer book and to think that she had been so naked as to write in it and give me a chance to boast about it and to show it to other girls. When I thanked her next day, she bowed but did not speak. Mostly the nuns were on silence and only permitted to talk during class.

In no time I had received another present, a little miniature prayer book with a leather cover and gold edging. The prayers were in French and the lettering so minute it was as if a tiny insect had fashioned them. Soon I was publicly known as her pet. I opened the doors for her, raised the blackboard two pegs higher (she was taller than other nuns), and handed out the exercise books which she had corrected. Now in the margins of my geometry propositions I would find "Good" or "Excellent," when in the past she used to splash "Disgraceful." Baba said it was foul to be a nun's pet and that any girl who sucked up to a nun could not be trusted.

About a month later Sister Imelda asked me to carry her books up four flights of stairs to the cookery kitchen. She taught cookery to a junior class. As she walked ahead of me, I thought how supple she was and how thoroughbred, and when she paused on the landing to look out through the long curtainless window, I too paused. Down below, two women in suede boots were chatting and smoking as they moved along the street with shopping baskets. Nearby a lay nun was on her knees scrubbing the granite steps, and the cold air was full of the raw smell of Jeyes Fluid.[1] There was a potted plant on the landing, and Sister Imelda put her fingers in the earth

---

1. A commercial cleaning fluid.

and went "Tch tch tch," saying it needed water. I said I would water it later on. I was happy in my prison then, happy to be near her, happy to walk behind her as she twirled her beads and bowed to the servile nun. I no longer cried for my mother, no longer counted the days on a pocket calendar until the Christmas holidays.

"Come back at five," she said as she stood on the threshold of the cookery kitchen door. The girls, all in white overalls, were arranged around the long wooden table waiting for her. It was as if every girl was in love with her. Because, as she entered, their faces broke into smiles, and in different tones of audacity they said her name. She must have liked cookery class, because she beamed and called to someone, anyone, to get up a blazing fire. Then she went across to the cast-iron stove and spat on it to test its temperature. It was hot, because her spit rose up and sizzled.

When I got back later, she was sitting on the edge of the table swaying her legs. There was something reckless about her pose, something defiant. It seemed as if any minute she would take out a cigarette case, snap it open, and then archly offer me one. The wonderful smell of baking made me realize how hungry I was, but far more so, it brought back to me my own home, my mother testing orange cakes with a knitting needle and letting me lick the line of half-baked dough down the length of the needle. I wondered if she had supplanted my mother, and I hoped not, because I had aimed to outstep my original world and take my place in a new and hallowed one.

"I bet you have a sweet tooth," she said, and then she got up, crossed the kitchen, and from under a wonderful shining silver cloche she produced two jam tarts with a crisscross design on them where the pastry was latticed over the dark jam. They were still warm.

"What will I do with them?" I asked.

"Eat them, you goose," she said, and she watched me eat as if she herself derived some peculiar pleasure from it, whereas I was embarrassed about the pastry crumbling and the bits of blackberry jam staining my lips. She was amused. It was one of the most awkward yet thrilling moments I had lived, and inherent in the pleasure was the terrible sense of danger. Had we been caught, she, no doubt, would have had to make massive sacrifice. I looked at her and thought how peerless and how brave, and I wondered if she felt hungry. She had a white overall over her black habit and this made her warmer and freer, and caused me to think of the happiness that would be ours, the laissez-faire[2] if we were away from the convent in an ordinary kitchen doing something easy and customary. But we weren't. It was clear to me then that my version of pleasure was inextricable from pain, that they existed side by side and were interdependent, like the two forces of an electric current.

"Had you a friend when you were in Dublin at university?" I asked daringly.

---

2. Freedom from restriction.

"I shared a desk with a sister from Howth and stayed in the same hostel," she said.

But what about boys? I thought, and what of your life now and do you long to go out into the world? But could not say it.

We knew something about the nuns' routine. It was rumored that they wore itchy wool underwear, ate dry bread for breakfast, rarely had meat, cakes, or dainties, kept certain hours of strict silence with each other, as well as constant vigil on their thoughts; so that if their minds wandered to the subject of food or pleasure, they would quickly revert to thoughts of God and their eternal souls. They slept on hard beds with no sheets and hairy blankets. At four o'clock in the morning while we slept, each nun got out of bed, in her habit—which was also her death habit—and chanting, they all flocked down the wooden stairs like ravens, to fling themselves on the tiled floor of the chapel. Each nun—even the Mother Superior—flung herself in total submission, saying prayers in Latin and offering up the moment to God. Then silently back to their cells for one more hour of rest. It was not difficult to imagine Sister Imelda face downward, arms outstretched, prostrate on the tiled floor. I often heard their chanting when I wakened suddenly from a nightmare, because, although we slept in a different building, both adjoined, and if one wakened one often heard that monotonous Latin chanting, long before the birds began, long before our own bell summoned us to rise at six.

"Do you eat nice food?" I asked.

"Of course," she said, and smiled. She sometimes broke into an eager smile, which she did much to conceal.

"Have you ever thought of what you will be?" she asked.

I shook my head. My design changed from day to day.

She looked at her man's silver pocket watch, closed the damper of the range, and prepared to leave. She checked that all the wall cupboards were locked by running her hand over them.

"Sister," I called, gathering enough courage at last—we must have some secret, something to join us together—"what color hair have you?"

We never saw the nuns' hair, or their eyebrows, or ears, as all that part was covered by a stiff white wimple.

"You shouldn't ask such a thing," she said, getting pink in the face, and then she turned back and whispered, "I'll tell you on your last day here, provided your geometry has improved."

She had scarcely gone when Baba, who had been lurking behind some pillar, stuck her head in the door and said, "Christsake, save me a bit." She finished the second pastry, then went around looking in kitchen drawers. Because of everything being locked, she found only some castor sugar in a china shaker. She ate a little and threw the remainder into the dying fire, so that it flared up for a minute with a yellow spluttering flame. Baba showed her jealousy by putting it around the school that I was in the cookery kitchen every evening, gorging cakes with Sister Imelda and telling tales.

Edna O'Brien   575

I did not speak to Sister Imelda again in private until the evening of our Christmas theatricals. She came to help us put on makeup and get into our stage clothes and fancy headgear. These clothes were kept in a trunk from one year to the next, and though sumptuous and strewn with braiding and gold, they smelled of camphor. Yet as we donned them we felt different, and as we sponged pancake makeup onto our faces, we became saucy and emphasized these new guises by adding dark pencil to the eyes and making the lips bright carmine. There was only one tube of lipstick and each girl clamored for it. The evening's entertainment was to comprise scenes from Shakespeare and laughing sketches. I had been chosen to recite Mark Antony's lament over Caesar's body, and for this I was to wear a purple toga, white knee-length socks, and patent buckle shoes. The shoes were too big and I moved in them as if in clogs. She said to take them off, to go barefoot. I realized that I was getting nervous and that in an effort to memorize my speech, the words were getting all askew and flying about in my head, like the separate pieces of a jigsaw puzzle. She sensed my panic and very slowly put her hand on my face and enjoined me to look at her. I looked into her eyes, which seemed fathomless, and saw that she was willing me to be calm and obliging me to be master of my fears, and I little knew that one day she would have to do the same as regards the swoop of my feelings for her. As we continued to stare I felt myself becoming calm and the words were restored to me in their right and fluent order. The lights were being lowered out in the recreation hall, and we knew now that all the nuns had arrived, had settled themselves down, and were eagerly awaiting this annual hotchpotch of amateur entertainment. There was that fearsome hush as the hall went dark and the few spotlights were turned on. She kissed her crucifix and I realized that she was saying a prayer for me. Then she raised her arm as if depicting the stance of a Greek goddess, walking onto the stage, I was fired by her ardor.

Baba could say that I bawled like a bloody bull, but Sister Imelda, who stood in the wings, said that temporarily she had felt the streets of Rome, had seen the corpse of Caesar, as I delivered those poignant, distempered lines. When I came off stage she put her arms around me and I was encased in a shower of silent kisses. After we had taken down the decorations and put the fancy clothes back in the trunk, I gave her two half-pound boxes of chocolates—bought for me illicitly by one of the day girls—and she gave me a casket made from the insides of match boxes and covered over with gilt paint and gold dust. It was like holding moths and finding their powder adhering to the fingers.

"What will you do on Christmas Day, Sister?" I said.

"I'll pray for you," she said.

It was useless to say, "Will you have turkey?" or "Will you have plum pudding?" or "Will you loll in bed?" because I believed that Christmas Day would be as bleak and deprived as any other day in her life. Yet she was radiant as if such austerity was joyful. Maybe she was basking in some secret realization involving her and me.

On the cold snowy afternoon three weeks later when we returned from our holidays, Sister Imelda came up to the dormitory to welcome me back. All the other girls had gone down to the recreation hall to do barn dances and I could hear someone banging on the piano. I did not want to go down and clump around with sixty other girls, having nothing to look forward to, only tea and the Rosary and early bed. The beds were damp after our stay at home, and when I put my hand between the sheets, it was like feeling dew but did not have the freshness of outdoors. What depressed me further was that I had seen a mouse in one of the cupboards, seen its tail curl with terror as it slipped away into a crevice. If there was one mouse, there were God knows how many, and the cakes we hid in secret would not be safe. I was still unpacking as she came down the narrow passage between the rows of iron beds and I saw in her walk such agitation.

"Tut, tut, tut, you've curled your hair," she said, offended.

Yes, the world outside was somehow declared in this perm, and for a second I remembered the scalding pain as the trickles of ammonia dribbled down my forehead and then the joy as the hairdresser said that she would make me look like Movita, a Mexican star. Now suddenly that world and those aspirations seemed trite and I wanted to take a brush and straighten my hair and revert to the dark gawky somber girl that I had been. I offered her iced queen cakes that my mother had made, but she refused them and said she could only stay a second. She lent me a notebook of hers, which she had had as a pupil, and into which she had copied favorite quotations, some religious, some not. I read at random:

> Twice or thrice had I loved thee,
> Before I knew thy face or name.
> So in a voice, so in a shapeless flame,
> Angels affect us oft . . .

"Are you well?" I asked.

She looked pale. It may have been the day, which was wretched and gray with sleet, or it may have been the white bedspreads, but she appeared to be ailing.

"I missed you," she said.

"Me too," I said.

At home, gorging, eating trifle at all hours, even for breakfast, having little ratafias to dip in cups of tea, fitting on new shoes and silk stockings, I wished that she could be with us, enjoying the fire and the freedom.

"You know it is not proper for us to be so friendly."

"It's not wrong," I said.

I dreaded that she might decide to turn away from me, that she might stamp on our love and might suddenly draw a curtain over it, a black crepe curtain that would denote its death. I dreaded it and knew it was going to happen.

"We must not become attached," she said, and I could not say we already were, no more than I could remind her of the day of the revels and the intimacy between us. Convents were dungeons and no doubt about it.

From then on she treated me as less of a favorite. She said my name sharply in class, and once she said if I must cough, could I wait until class had finished. Baba was delighted, as were the other girls, because they were glad to see me receding in her eyes. Yet I knew that the crispness was part of her love, because no matter how callously she looked at me, she would occasionally soften. Reading her notebook helped me, and I copied out her quotations into my own book, trying as accurately as possible to imitate her handwriting.

But some little time later when she came to supervise our study one evening, I got a smile from her as she sat on the rostrum looking down at us all. I continued to look up at her and by slight frowning indicated that I had a problem with my geometry. She beckoned to me lightly and I went up, bringing my copybook and the pen. Standing close to her, and also because her wimple was crooked, I saw one of her eyebrows for the first time. She saw that I noticed it and said did that satisfy my curiosity. I said not really. She said what else did I want to see, her swan's neck perhaps, and I went scarlet. I was amazed that she would say such a thing in the hearing of other girls, and then she said a worse thing, she said that G. K. Chesterton was very forgetful and had once put on his trousers backward. She expected me to laugh. I was so close to her that a rumble in her stomach seemed to be taking place in my own, and about this she also laughed. It occurred to me for one terrible moment that maybe she had decided to leave the convent, to jump over the wall. Having done the theorem for me, she marked it "100 out of 100" and then asked if I had any other problems. My eyes filled with tears, I wanted her to realize that her recent coolness had wrought havoc with my nerves and my peace of mind.

"What is it?" she said.

I could cry, or I could tremble to try to convey the emotion, but I could not tell her. As if on cue, the Mother Superior came in and saw this glaring intimacy and frowned as she approached the rostrum.

"Would you please go back to your desk," she said, "and in future kindly allow Sister Imelda to get on with her duties."

I tiptoed back and sat with head down, bursting with fear and shame. Then she looked at a tray on which the milk cups were laid, and finding one cup of milk untouched, she asked which girl had not drunk her milk.

"Me, Sister," I said, and I was called up to drink it and stand under the clock as a punishment. The milk was tepid and dusty, and I thought of cows on the fairs days at home and the farmers hitting them as they slid and slithered over the muddy streets.

For weeks I tried to see my nun in private; I even lurked outside doors where I knew she was due, only to be rebuffed again and again. I suspected the Mother Superior had warned her against making a favorite of me. But I still clung to a belief that a bond existed between us and that her coldness and even some glares which I had received were a charade, a mask. I would wonder how she felt alone in bed and what way she slept and if she thought of me, or refusing to think of me, if she dreamed of me as I did of her. She certainly got thinner, because her nun's silver ring slipped easily and sometimes unavoidably off her marriage finger. It occurred to me that she was having a nervous breakdown.

One day in March the sun came out, the radiators were turned off, and, though there was a lashing wind, we were told that officially spring had arrived and that we could play games. We all trooped up to the games field and, to our surprise, saw that Sister Imelda was officiating that day. The daffodils in the field tossed and turned; they were a very bright shocking yellow, but they were not as fetching as the little timid snowdrops that trembled in the wind. We played rounders, and when my turn came to hit the ball with the long wooden pound, I crumbled and missed, fearing that the ball would hit me.

"Champ . . ." said Baba, jeering.

After three such failures Sister Imelda said that if I liked I could sit and watch, and when I was sitting in the greenhouse swallowing my shame, she came in and said that I must not give way to tears, because humiliation was the greatest test of Christ's love, or indeed *any* love.

"When you are a nun you will know that," she said, and instantly I made up my mind that I would be a nun and that though we might never be free to express our feelings, we would be under the same roof, in the same cloister, in mental and spiritual conjunction all our lives.

"Is it very hard at first?" I said.

"It's awful," she said, and she slipped a little medal into my gymfrock pocket. It was warm from being in her pocket, and as I held it, I knew that once again we were near and that in fact we had never severed. Walking down from the playing field to our Sunday lunch of mutton and cabbage, everyone chattered to Sister Imelda. The girls milled around her, linking her, trying to hold her hand, counting the various keys on her bunch of keys, and asking impudent questions.

"Sister, did you ever ride a motorbicycle?"

"Sister, did you ever wear seamless stockings?"

"Sister, who's your favorite film star—male?"

"Sister, what's your favorite food?"

"Sister, if you had a wish, what would it be?"

"Sister, what do you do when you want to scratch your head?"

Yes, she had ridden a motorbicycle, and she had worn silk stockings, but they were seamed. She liked bananas best, and if she had a wish, it would be to go home for a few hours to see her parents and her brother.

That afternoon as we walked through the town, the sight of closed shops with porter barrels outside and mongrel dogs did not dispel my refound ecstasy. The medal was in my pocket, and every other second I would touch it for confirmation. Baba saw a Swiss roll in a confectioner's window laid on a doily and dusted with castor sugar, and it made her cry out with hunger and rail against being in a bloody reformatory, surrounded by drips and mopes. On impulse she took her nail file out of her pocket and dashed across to the window to see if she could cut the glass. The prefect rushed up from the back of the line and asked Baba if she wanted to be locked up.

"I am anyhow," Baba said, and sawed at one of her nails, to maintain her independence and vent her spleen. Baba was the only girl who could stand up to a prefect. When she felt like it, she dropped out of a walk, sat on a stone wall, and waited until we all came back. She said that if there was one thing more boring than studying it was walking. She used to roll down her stockings and examine her calves and say that she could see varicose veins coming from this bloody daily walk. Her legs, like all our legs, were black from the dye of the stockings; we were forbidden to bathe, because baths were immoral. We washed each night in an enamel basin beside our beds. When girls splashed cold water onto their chests, they let out cries, though this was forbidden.

After the walk we wrote home. We were allowed to write home once a week; our letters were always censored. I told my mother that I had made up my mind to be a nun, and asked if she could send me bananas when a batch arrived at our local grocery shop. That evening, perhaps as I wrote to my mother on the ruled white paper, a telegram arrived which said that Sister Imelda's brother had been killed in a van while on his way home from a hurling match. The Mother Superior announced it, and asked us to pray for his soul and write letters of sympathy to Sister Imelda's parents. We all wrote identical letters, because in our first year at school we had been given specimen letters for various occasions, and we all referred back to our specimen letter of sympathy.

Next day the town hire-car drove up to the convent, and Sister Imelda, accompanied by another nun, went home for the funeral. She looked as white as a sheet, with eyes swollen, and she wore a heavy knitted shawl over her shoulders. Although she came back that night (I stayed awake to hear the car), we did not see her for a whole week, except to catch a glimpse of her back, in the chapel. When she resumed class, she was peaky and distant, making no reference at all to her recent tragedy.

The day the bananas came I waited outside the door and gave her a bunch wrapped in tissue paper. Some were still a little green, and she said that Mother Superior would put them in the glasshouse to ripen. I felt that Sister Imelda would never taste them; they would be kept for a visiting priest or bishop.

"Oh, Sister, I'm sorry about your brother," I said in a burst.

"It will come to us all, sooner or later," Sister Imelda said dolefully.

I dared to touch her wrist to communicate my sadness. She went quickly, probably for fear of breaking down. At times she grew irritable and had a boil on her cheek. She missed some classes and was replaced in the cookery kitchen by a younger nun. She asked me to pray for her brother's soul and to avoid seeing her alone. Each time as she came down a corridor toward me, I was obliged to turn the other way. Now Baba or some other girl moved the blackboard two pegs higher and spread her shawl, when wet, over the radiator to dry.

I got flu and was put to bed. Sickness took the same bleak course, a cup of hot senna delivered in person by the head nun, who stood there while I drank it, tea at lunchtime with thin slices of brown bread (because it was just after the war, food was still rationed, so the butter was mixed with lard and had white streaks running through it and a faintly rancid smell), hours of just lying there surveying the empty dormitory, the empty iron beds with white counterpanes on each one, and metal crucifixes laid on each white, frilled pillow slip. I knew that she would miss me and hoped that Baba would tell her where I was. I counted the number of tiles from the ceiling to the head of my bed, thought of my mother at home on the farm mixing hen food, thought of my father, losing his temper perhaps and stamping on the kitchen floor with nailed boots, and I recalled the money owing for my school fees and hoped that Sister Imelda would never get to hear of it. During the Christmas holiday I had seen a bill sent by the head nun to my father which said, "Please remit this week without fail." I hated being in bed causing extra trouble and therefore reminding the head nun of the unpaid liability. We had no clock in the dormitory, so there was no way of guessing the time, but the hours dragged.

Marigold, one of the maids, came to take off the counterpanes at five and brought with her two gifts from Sister Imelda—an orange and a pencil sharpener. I kept the orange peel in my hand, smelling it, and planning how I would thank her. Thinking of her I fell into a feverish sleep and was wakened when the girls came to bed at ten and switched on the various ceiling lights.

At Easter Sister Imelda warned me not to give her chocolates, so I got her a flashlamp instead and spare batteries. Pleased with such a useful gift (perhaps she read her letters in bed), she put her arms around me and allowed one cheek to adhere but not to make the sound of a kiss. It made up for the seven weeks of withdrawal, and as I drove down the convent drive with Baba, she waved to me, as she had promised, from the window of her cell.

In the last term at school, studying was intensive because of the examinations which loomed at the end of June. Like all the other nuns, Sister Imelda thought only of these examinations. She crammed us with knowledge, lost her temper every other day, and gritted her teeth whenever the blackboard was too greasy to take the imprint of the chalk. If ever I met her in the corridor, she asked if I knew such and such a thing, and coming down from Sunday games, she went over various questions with us. The fateful examination day arrived and we sat at single desks supervised by some strange woman from Dublin. Opening a locked trunk, she took out the pink examination papers and distributed them around. Geometry was on the fourth day. When we came out from it, Sister Imelda was in the hall with all the answers, so that we could compare our answers with hers. Then she called me aside and we went up toward the cookery kitchen and sat on the stairs while she went over the paper with me, question for question. I knew that I had three right and two wrong, but did not tell her so.

"It is black," she said then, rather suddenly. I thought she meant the dark light where we were sitting.

"It's cool, though," I said.

Summer had come: our white skins baked under the heavy uniform, and dark violet pansies bloomed in the convent grounds. She looked well again, and her pale skin was once more unblemished.

"My hair," she whispered, "is black." And she told me how she had spent her last night before entering the convent. She had gone cycling with a boy and ridden for miles, and they'd lost their way up a mountain, and she became afraid she would be so late home that she would sleep it out the next morning. It was understood between us that I was going to enter the convent in September and that I could have a last fling, too.

Two days later we prepared to go home. There were farewells and outlandish promises, and autograph books signed, and girls trudging up the recreation hall, their cases bursting open with clothes and books. Baba scattered biscuit crumbs in the dormitory for the mice and stuffed all her prayer books under a mattress. Her father promised to collect us at four. I had arranged with Sister Imelda secretly that I would meet her in one of the summerhouses around the walks, where we would spend our last half hour together. I expected that she would tell me something of what my life as a postulant would be like. But Baba's father came an hour early. He had something urgent to do later and came at three instead. All I could do was ask Marigold to take a note to Sister Imelda.

> *Remembrance is all I ask,*
> *But if remembrance should prove a task,*
> *Forget me.*

I hated Baba, hated her busy father, hated the thought of my mother standing in the doorway in her good dress, welcoming me home at last. I would have become a nun that minute if I could.

I wrote to my nun that night and again the next day and then every week for a month. Her letters were censored, so I tried to convey my feelings indirectly. In one of her letters to me (they were allowed one letter a month) she said that she looked forward to seeing me in September. But by September Baba and I had left for the university in Dublin. I stopped writing to Sister Imelda then, reluctant to tell her that I no longer wished to be a nun.

In Dublin we enrolled at the college where she had surpassed herself. I saw her maiden name on a list, for having graduated with special honors, and for days was again sad and remorseful. I rushed out and bought batteries for the flashlamp I'd given her, and posted them without any note enclosed. No mention of my missing vocation, no mention of why I had stopped writing.

One Sunday about two years later, Baba and I were going out to Howth on a bus. Baba had met some businessmen who played golf there and she had done a lot of scheming to get us invited out. The bus was packed, mostly mothers with babies and children on their way to Dollymount Strand. We drove along the coast road and saw the sea, bright green and glinting in the sun, and because of the way the water was carved up into millions of little wavelets, its surface seemed like an endless heap of dark-green broken bottles. Near the shore the sand looked warm and was biscuit-colored. We never swam or sunbathed, we never did anything that was good for us. Life was geared to work and to meeting men, and yet one knew that mating could only lead to one's being a mother and hawking obstreperous children out to the seaside on Sunday. "They know not what they do" could surely be said of us.

We were very made up; even the conductor seemed to disapprove and snapped at having to give change of ten shillings. For no reason at all I thought of our makeup rituals before the school play and how innocent it was in comparison, because now our skins were smothered beneath layers of it and we never took it off at night. Thinking of the convent, I suddenly thought of Sister Imelda, and then, as if prey to a dream, I heard the rustle of serge, smelled the Jeyes Fluid and the boiled cabbage, and saw her pale shocked face in the months after her brother died. Then I looked around and saw her in earnest, and at first thought I was imagining things. But no, she had got on accompanied by another nun and they were settling themselves in the back seat nearest the door. She looked older, but she had the same aloof quality and the same eyes, and my heart began to race with a mixture of excitement and dread. At first it raced with a prodigal strength, and then it began to falter and I thought it was going to give out. My fear of her and my love came back in one fell realization. I would have gone through the window except that it was not wide enough. The thing was how to escape her. Baba gurgled with delight, stood up, and in the most flagrant way looked around to make sure that it was Imelda. She recognized the other nun as one with the nickname of Johnny who taught piano lessons. Baba's first thought was revenge, as she enumerated the punishments they had meted out to us and said how nice it would be to go back and shock them and say, "Mud in your eye, Sisters," or "Get lost," or something worse. Baba could not understand why I was quaking, no more than she could understand why I began to wipe off the lipstick. Above all, I knew that I could not confront them.

"You're going to have to," Baba said.

"I can't," I said.

It was not just my attire; it was the fact of my never having written and of my broken promise. Baba kept looking back and said they weren't saying a word and that children were gawking at them. It wasn't often that nuns traveled in buses, and we speculated as to where they might be going.

"They might be off to meet two fellows," Baba said, and visualized them in the golf club getting blotto and hoisting up their skirts. For me it was no laughing matter. She came up with a strategy: it was that as we approached our stop and the bus was still moving, I was to jump up and go down the aisle and pass them without even looking. She said most likely they would not notice us, as their eyes were lowered and they seemed to be praying.

"I can't run down the bus," I said. There was a matter of shaking limbs and already a terrible vertigo.

"You're going to," Baba said, and though insisting that I couldn't, I had already begun to rehearse an apology. While doing this, I kept blessing myself over and over again, and Baba kept reminding me that there was only one more stop before ours. When the dreadful moment came, I jumped up and put on my face what can only be called an apology of a smile. I followed Baba to the rear of the bus. But already they had gone. I saw the back of their two sable, identical figures with their veils being blown wildly about in the wind. They looked so cold and lost as they hurried along the pavement and I wanted to run after them. In some way I felt worse than if I had con-fronted them. I cannot be certain what I would have said. I knew that there is something sad and faintly distasteful about love's ending, particularly love that has never been fully realized. I might have hinted at that, but I doubt it. In our deepest moments we say the most inadequate things.

1982

Edna O'Brien's stories involve what some readers might dismiss as a very ordinary range of emotions and characters. Ordinary emotions intelligently observed and felt with unusual sensitivity are, in fact, the great strength of O'Brien's fiction. In the following excerpt from an interview with Joseph McCulloch, O'Brien discusses the way that observation and affection can lead to "an extraordinary kind of glory."

"Making it fit for all gracious impressions": Edna O'Brien

I think fear is probably man's greatest handicap. We all have fear: fear of each other, fear of ourselves, fear of failure, fear of living, and of course, the middle-of-the-night fear, which is the fear of dying. I think that fear is a dreadful drawback because it stops us living in the moment. I would like to be robbed of some of my fears. Some of them were founded very much in childhood, on the fear of God and definitely the fear of hell. But along with that, we have a fear I think that we could easily live without and that is the fear of each other. I suppose it comes about because we don't really *meet* each other. One bit of us meets the other bit of the other person, but somehow we find it difficult to be our real selves with other people, and therefore we are, if not *false*, we are diminished and often artificial. And I think fear, like envy, or indeed any other vice, is an extremely contagious thing, and that we owe it to each other to say, 'Yes, you are afraid. Be less afraid!' A lot of it, I imagine, springs from childhood—perhaps parents nowadays are more understanding—but a lot of children are told not to do this or that, not to displease, not to spill, not to fall, and when you have that drummed into you day after day, you become a little fearful and hesitant. And certainly Irish Catholicism is very much founded on the stone of fear and of punishment. I don't know enough about English upbringing or religion; it seems to be a lot more reasonable.

Fear in another form can make one more sensitive. I remember once finding a wonderful quotation: 'Fear intenerates the heart, making it fit for all gracious impressions'; I looked up 'intenerates', which seemed to me a great word, and it said, 'to soften or make tender'. So that every handicap perhaps has something of value in it. I would hate to find that people were fear-*less* because it might mean they were closed. . . .

I vacillate between states of certain love towards people, and paranoia. The times in my life when I have really been with another human being—a man or a woman or a child—and I have really looked at their faces and their necks and their eyelids and their whole being and what their faces say, apart from what their lips are saying, and have observed myself observing that state—I have, at those odd and very, very rare moments, felt that it is really possible to be very near another person. And there is then an extraordinary—it is very subtle—but an extraordinary kind of glory.

GAIL GODWIN

(b. 1937)

DREAM CHILDREN

The worst thing. Such a terrible thing to happen to a young woman. It's a wonder she didn't go mad.

As she went about her errands, a cheerful, neat young woman, a wife, wearing pants with permanent creases and safari jackets and high-necked sweaters that folded chastely just below the line of the small gold hoops she wore in her ears, she imagined people saying this, or thinking it to themselves. But nobody knew. Nobody knew anything, other than that she and her husband had moved here a year ago, as so many couples were moving farther away from the city, the husband commuting, or staying in town during the week—as hers did. There was nobody here, in this quaint, unspoiled village, nestled in the foothills of the mountains, who could have looked at her and guessed that anything out of the ordinary, predictable, auspicious spectrum of things that happen to bright, attractive young women had happened to her. She always returned her books to the local library on time; she bought liquor at the local liquor store only on Friday, before she went to meet her husband's bus from the city. He was something in television, a producer? So many ambitious young couples moving to this Dutch farming village, found in 1690, to restore ruined fieldstone houses and plant herb gardens and keep their own horses and discover the relief of finding oneself insignificant in Nature for the first time!

A terrible thing. So freakish. If you read it in a story or saw it on TV, you'd say no, this sort of thing could never happen in an American hospital.

DePuy, who owned the old Patroon farm adjacent to her land, frequently glimpsed her racing her horse in the early morning, when the mists still lay on the fields, sometimes just before the sun came up and there was a frost on everything. "One woodchuck hole and she and that stallion will both have to be put out of their misery," he told his wife. "She's too reckless. I'll bet you her old man doesn't know she goes streaking to hell across the fields like that." Mrs. DePuy nodded, silent, and went about her business. She, too, watched that other woman ride, a woman not much younger than herself, but with an aura of romance—of tragedy, perhaps. The way she looked: like those heroines in English novels who ride off their bad tempers and unrequited love affairs, clenching their thighs against the flanks of spirited horses with murderous red eyes. Mrs. DePuy, who had ridden since the age of three, recognized something beyond recklessness in that elegant young woman, in her crisp checked shirts and her dove-gray jodhpurs. *She has nothing to fear anymore,* thought the farmer's wife, with sure feminine instinct; she both envied and pitied her. "What she needs is children," remarked DePuy.

"A Dry Sack, a Remy Martin, and . . . let's see, a half-gallon of the Chablis, and I think I'd better take a Scotch . . . and the Mouton-Cadet . . . and maybe a dry vermouth." Mrs. Frye, another farmer's wife, who runs the liquor store, asks if her husband is bringing company for the weekend. "He sure is; we couldn't drink all that by ourselves," and the young woman laughs, her lovely teeth exposed, her small gold earrings quivering in the light. "You know, I saw his name—on the television the other night," says Mrs. Frye. "It was at the beginning of that new comedy show, the one with the woman who used to be on another show with her husband and little girl, only they divorced, you know the one?" "Of course I do. It's one of my husband's shows. I'll tell him you watched it." Mrs. Frye puts the bottles in an empty box, carefully inserting wedges of cardboard between them.

Through the window of her store she sees her customer's pert bottle-green car, some sort of little foreign car with the engine running, filled with groceries and weekend parcels, and that big silver-blue dog sitting up in the front seat just like a human being. "I think that kind of thing is so sad," says Mrs. Frye; "families breaking up, poor little children having to divide their loyalties." "I couldn't agree more," replies the young woman, nodding gravely. Such a personable, polite girl! "Are you sure you can carry that, dear? I can get Earl from the back. . . ." But the girl has it hoisted on her shoulder in a flash, is airily maneuvering between unopened cartons stacked in the aisle, in her pretty boots. Her perfume lingers in Mrs. Frye's store for a half-hour after she has driven away.

After dinner, her husband and his friends drank brandy. She lay in front of the fire, stroking the dog, and listening to Victoria Darrow, the news commentator, in person. A few minutes ago, they had all watched Victoria on TV. "That's right; thirty-nine!" Victoria now whispered to her. "What? That's kind of you. I'm photogenic, thank God, or I'd have been put out to pasture long before. . . . I look five, maybe seven years younger on the screen . . . but the point I'm getting at is, I went to this doctor and he said, 'If you want to do this thing, you'd better go home today and get started.' He told me—did you know this? Did you know that a woman is born with all the eggs she'll ever have, and when she gets to my age, the ones that are left have been rattling around so long they're a little shopworn; then every time you fly you get an extra dose of radioactivity, so those poor eggs. He told me when a woman over forty comes into his office pregnant, his heart sinks; that's why he quit practicing obstetrics, he said; he could still remember the screams of a woman whose baby he delivered . . . she was having natural childbirth and she kept saying, 'Why won't you let me see it, I insist on seeing it,' and so he had to, and he says he can still hear her screaming."

"Oh, what was—what was wrong with it?"

But she never got the answer. Her husband, white around the lips, was standing over Victoria ominously, offering the Remy Martin bottle. "Vicky, let me pour you some more," he said. And to his wife, "I think Blue Boy needs to go out."

"Yes, yes, of course. Please excuse me, Victoria. I'll just be . . ."

Her husband followed her to the kitchen, his hand on the back of her neck. "Are you okay? That stupid yammering bitch. She and her twenty-six-year-old lover! I wish I'd never brought them, but she's been hinting around the studio for weeks."

"But I like them, I like having them. I'm fine. Please go back. I'll take the dog out and come back. Please . . ."

"All right. If you're sure you're okay." He backed away, hands dangling at his sides. A handsome man, wearing a pink shirt with Guatemalan embroidery. Thick black hair and a face rather boyish, but cunning. Last weekend she had sat beside him, alone in this house, just the two of them, and watched him on television: a documentary, in several parts, in which TV "examines itself." There was his double, sitting in an armchair in his executive office, coolly replying to the questions of Victoria Darrow. *"Do you personally watch all the programs you produce, Mr. McNair?"* She watched the man on the screen, how he moved his lips when he spoke, but kept the rest of his face, his body perfectly still. Funny, she had never noticed this before. He managed to say that he did and did not watch all the programs he produced.

Now, in the kitchen, she looked at him backing away, a little like a renegade in one of his own shows—a desperate man, perhaps, who had just killed somebody and is backing away, hands dangling loosely at his sides, Mr. McNair, her husband. That man on the screen. Once a lover above her in bed. That friend who held her hand in the hospital. One hand in hers, the other holding the stopwatch. For a brief instant, all the images coalesce and she feels something again. But once outside, under the galaxies of autumn-sharp stars, the intelligent dog at her heels like some smart gray ghost, she is glad to be free of all that. She walks quickly over the damp grass to the barn, to look in on her horse. She understands something: her husband, Victoria Darrow lead double lives that seem perfectly normal to them. But if she told her husband that she, too, is in two lives, he would become alarmed; he would sell this house and make her move back to the city where he could keep an eye on her welfare.

She is discovering people like herself, down through the centuries, all over the world. She scours books with titles like *The Timeless Moment, The Sleeping Prophet, Between Two Worlds, Silent Union: A Record of Unwilled Communication*; collecting evidence, weaving a sort of underworld net of colleagues around her.

A rainy fall day. Too wet to ride. The silver dog asleep beside her in her special alcove, a padded window seat filled with pillows and books. She is looking down on the fields of dried lithrium, and the fir trees beyond, and the mountains gauzy with fog and rain, thinking, in a kind of terror and ecstasy, about all these connections. A book lies face down on her lap. She has just read the following:

> Theodore Dreiser and his friend John Cowper Powys had been dining at Dreiser's place on West Fifty Seventh Street. As Powys made ready to leave and catch his train to the little town up the Hudson, where he was then living, he told Dreiser, "I'll appear before you here, later in the evening."
>
> Dreiser laughed. "Are you going to turn yourself into a ghost, or have you a spare key?" he asked. Powys said he would return "in some form," he didn't know exactly what kind.
>
> After his friend left, Dreiser sat up and read for two hours. Then he looked up and saw Powys standing in the doorway to the living

room. It was Powys' features, his tall stature, even the loose tweed garments which he wore. Dreiser rose at once and strode toward the figure, saying, "Well, John, you kept your word. Come on in and tell me how you did it." But the figure vanished when Dreiser came within three feet of it.

Dreiser then went to the telephone and called Powys' house in the country. Powys answered. Dreiser told him what had happened and Powys said, "I told you I'd be there and you oughtn't to be surprised." But he refused to discuss how he had done it, if, indeed, he knew how.

"But don't you get frightened, up here all by yourself, alone with all these creaky sounds?" asked Victoria, the next morning.

"No, I guess I'm used to them," she replied, breaking eggs into a bowl. "I know what each one means. The wood expanding and contracting . . . the wind getting caught between the shutter and the latch . . . Sometimes small animals get lost in the stone walls and scratch around till they find their way out . . . or die."

"Ugh. But don't you imagine things? I would, in a house like this. How old? That's almost three hundred years of lived lives, people suffering and shouting and making love and giving birth, under this roof. . . . You'd think there'd be a few ghosts around."

"I don't know," said her hostess blandly. "I haven't heard any. But of course, I have Blue Boy, so I don't get scared." She whisked the eggs, unable to face Victoria. She and her husband had lain awake last night, embarrassed at the sounds coming from the next room. No ghostly moans, those. "Why can't that bitch control herself, or at least lower her voice," he said angrily. He stroked his wife's arm, both of them pretending not to remember. She had bled for an entire year afterward, until the doctor said they would have to remove everything. "I'm empty," she had said when her husband had tried again, after she was healed. "I'm sorry, I just don't feel anything." Now they lay tenderly together on these weekends, like childhood friends, like effigies on a lovers' tomb, their mutual sorrow like a sword between them. She assumed he had another life, or lives, in town. As she had here. Nobody is just one person, she had learned.

"I'm sure I would imagine things," said Victoria. "I would see things and hear things inside my head much worse than an ordinary murderer or rapist."

The wind caught in the shutter latch . . . a small animal dislodging pieces of fieldstone in its terror, sending them tumbling down the inner walls, from attic to cellar . . . a sound like a child rattling a jar full of marbles, or small stones . . .

"I have so little imagination," she said humbly, warming the butter in the omelet pan. She could feel Victoria Darrow's professional curiosity waning from her dull country life, focusing elsewhere.

Cunning!

As a child of nine, she had gone through a phase of walking in her sleep. One summer night, they found her bed empty, and after an hour's hysterical search they had found her in her nightgown, curled up on the flagstones beside the fishpond. She woke, baffled, in her father's tense clutch, the stars all over the sky, her mother repeating over and over again to the night at large, "Oh, my God, she could have drowned!" They took her to a child psychiatrist, a pretty Austrian woman who spoke to her with the same vocabulary she used on grownups, putting the child instantly at ease. "It is not at all uncommon what you did. I have known so many children who take little night journeys from their beds, and then they awaken and don't know what all the fuss is about! Usually these journeys are quite harmless, because children are surrounded by a magical reality that keeps them safe. Yes, the race of children possesses magically sagacious powers! But the grownups, they tend to forget how it once was for them. They worry, they are afraid of so many things. You do not want your mother and father, who love you so anxiously, to live in fear of you going to live with the fishes." She had giggled at the thought. The woman's steady gray-green eyes were trained on her carefully, suspending her in a kind of bubble. Then she had rejoined her parents, a dutiful "child" again, holding a hand up to each of them. The night journeys had stopped.

A thunderstorm one night last spring. Blue Boy whining in his insulated house below the garage. She had lain there, strangely elated by the nearness of the thunderclaps that tore at the sky, followed by instantaneous flashes of jagged light. Wondering shouldn't she go down and let the dog in; he hated storms. Then dozing off again . . .

She woke. The storm had stopped. The dark air was quiet. Something had changed, some small thing—what? She had to think hard before she found it: the hall light, which she kept burning during the week-nights when she was there alone, had gone out. She reached over and switched the button on her bedside lamp. Nothing. A tree must have fallen and hit a wire, causing the power to go off. This often happened here. No problem. The dog had stopped crying. She felt herself sinking into a delicious, deep reverie, the kind that sometimes came just before morning, as if her being broke slowly into tiny pieces and spread itself over the world. It was a feeling she had not known until she had lived by herself in this house: this weightless though conscious state in which she lay, as if in a warm bath, and yet was able to send her thoughts anywhere, as if her mind contained the entire world.

And as she floated in this silent world, transparent and buoyed upon the dream layers of the mind, she heard a small rattling sound, like pebbles being shaken in a jar. The sound came distinctly from the guest room, a room so chosen by her husband and herself because it was the farthest room from their bedroom on this floor. It lay above what had been the old side of the house, built seventy-five years before the new side, which was completed in 1753. There was a bed in it, and a chair, and some plants in the window. Sometimes on weekends when she could not sleep, she went and read there, or meditated, to keep from waking her husband. It was the room where Victoria Darrow and her young lover would not sleep the following fall, because she would say quietly to her husband, "No . . . not that room. I—I've made up the bed in the other room." "What?" he would want to know. "The one next to ours? Right under our noses?"

She did not lie long listening to this sound before she understood it was one she had never heard in the house before. It had a peculiar regularity to its rhythm; there was nothing accidental about it, nothing influenced by the wind, or the nerves of some lost animal. *K-chunk, k-chunk, k-chunk,* it went. At intervals of exactly a half-minute apart. She still remembered how to time such things, such intervals. She was as good as any stopwatch when it came to timing certain intervals.

K-chunk, k-chunk, k-chunk. That determined regularity. Something willed, something poignantly repeated, as though the repetition was a means of consoling someone in the dark. Her skin began to prickle. Often, lying in such states of weightless reverie, she had practiced the trick of sending herself abroad, into rooms of the house, out into the night to check on Blue Boy, over to the barn to look in on her horse, who slept standing up. Once she had heard a rather frightening noise, as if someone in the basement had turned on a faucet, and so she forced herself to "go down," floating down two sets of stairs into the darkness, only to discover what she had known all the time: the hookup system between the hot-water tank and the pump, which sounded like someone turning on the water.

Now she went through the palpable, prickly darkness, without lights, down the chilly hall in her sleeveless gown, into the guest room. Although there was no light, not even a moon shining through the window, she could make out the shape of the bed and then the chair, the spider plants on the window, and a small dark shape in one corner, on the floor, which she and her husband had painted a light yellow.

K-chunk, k-chunk, k-chunk. The shape moved with the noise.

Now she knew what they meant, that "someone's hair stood on end." It was true. As she forced herself across the borders of a place she had never been, she felt, distinctly, every single hair on her head raise itself a millimeter or so from her scalp.

She knelt down and discovered him. He was kneeling, a little cold and scared, shaking a small jar filled with some kind of pebbles. (She later found out, in a subsequent visit, that they were small colored shells, of a triangular shape, called coquinas: she found them in a picture in a child's nature book at the library.) He was wearing pajamas a little too big for him, obviously hand-me-downs, and he was exactly two years older than the only time she had ever held him in her arms.

The two of them knelt in the corner of the room, taking each other in. His large eyes were the same as before: dark and unblinking. He held the small jar close to him, watching her. He was not afraid, but she knew better than to move too close.

She knelt, the tears streaming down her cheeks, but she made no sound, her eyes fastened on that small form. And then the hall light came on silently, as well as the lamp beside her bed, and with wet cheeks and pounding heart she could not be sure whether or not she had actually been out of the room.

But what did it matter, on the level where they had met? He traveled so much farther than she to reach that room. ("*Yes, the race of children possesses magically sagacious powers!*")

She and her husband sat together on the flowered chintz sofa, watching the last ofthe series in which TV purportedly examined itself. She said, "Did you ever think that the whole thing is really a miracle? I mean, here we sit, eighty miles away from your studios, and we turn on a little machine and there is Victoria, speaking to us as clearly as she did last weekend when she was in this very room. Why, it's magic, it's time travel and space travel right in front of our eyes, but because it's been discovered,' because the world understands that it's only little dots that transmit Victoria electrically to us, it's *all right*. We can bear it. Don't you sometimes wonder about all the miracles that haven't been officially approved yet? I mean, who knows, maybe in a hundred years everybody will take it for granted that they can send an image of themselves around in space by some perfectly natural means available to us now. I mean, when you think about it, what *is* space? What *is* time? Where do the so-called boundaries of each of us begin and end? Can anyone explain it?"

He was drinking Scotch and thinking how they had decided not to renew Victoria Darrow's contract. Somewhere on the edges of his mind hovered an anxious, growing certainty about his wife. At the local grocery store this morning, when he went to pick up a carton of milk and the paper, he had stopped to chat with DePuy. "I don't mean to interfere, but she doesn't know those fields," said the farmer. "Last year we had to shoot a mare, stumbled into one of those holes. . . . It's madness, the way she rides."

And look at her now, her face so pale and shining, speaking of miracles and space travel, almost on the verge of tears. . . .

And last night, his first night up from the city, he had wandered through the house, trying to drink himself into this slower weekend pace, and he had come across a pile of her books, stacked in the alcove where, it was obvious, she lay for hours, escaping into science fiction, and the occult.

Now his own face appeared on the screen. "I want to be fair," he was telling Victoria Darrow. "I want to be objective. . . . Violence has always been part of the human makeup. I don't like it anymore than you do, but there it is. I think it's more a question of whether we want to face things as they are or escape into fantasies of how we would like them to be."

Beside him, his wife uttered a sudden bell-like laugh.

("*. . . It's madness, the way she rides.*")

He did want to be fair, objective. She had told him again and again that she liked her life here. And he—well, he had to admit he liked his own present setup.

"I am a pragmatist," he was telling Virginia Darrow on the screen. He decided to speak to his wife about her riding and leave her alone about the books. She had the right to some escape, if anyone did. But the titles: *Marvelous Manifestations, The Mind Travellers, A Doctor Looks at Spiritualism, The Other Side . . .* Something revolted in him, he couldn't help it; he felt an actual physical revulsion at this kind of thinking. Still it was better than some other escapes. His friend Barnett, the actor, who said at night he went from room to room, after his wife was asleep, collecting empty glasses. ("Once I found one by the Water Pik, a second on the ledge beside the tub, a third on the back of the john, and a fourth on the floor beside the john. . . .")

He looked sideways at his wife, who was absorbed, it seemed, in watching him on the screen. Her face was tense, alert, animated. She did not look mad. She wore slim gray pants and a loose-knit pullover made of some silvery material, like a knight's chain mail. The lines of her profile were clear and silvery themselves, somehow sexless and pure, like a child's profile. He no longer felt lust when he looked at her, only a sad determination to protect her. He had a mistress in town, whom he loved, but he had explained, right from the beginning, that he considered himself married for the rest of his life. He told this woman the whole story. "And I am implicated in it. I could never leave her." An intelligent, sensitive woman, she had actually wept and said, "Of course not."

He always wore the same pajamas, a shade too big, but always clean. Obviously washed again and again in a machine that went through its cycles frequently. She imagined his "other mother," a harassed woman with several children, short on money, on time, on dreams—all the things she herself had too much of. The family lived, she believed, somewhere in Florida, probably on the west coast. She had worked that out from the little coquina shells: their bright colors, even in moonlight shining through a small window with spider plants in it. His face and arms had been sun-tanned early in the spring and late into the autumn. They never spoke or touched. She was not sure how much of this he understood. She tried and failed to remember where she herself had gone, in those little night journeys to the fishpond. Perhaps he never remembered afterward, when he woke up, clutching his jar, in a roomful of brothers and sisters. Or with a worried mother or father come to collect him, asleep by the sea. Once she had a very clear dream of the whole family, living in a trailer, with palm trees. But that was a dream; she recognized its difference in quality from those truly magic times when, through his own childish powers, he somehow found a will strong enough, or innocent enough, to project himself upon her still-floating consciousness, as clearly and as believably as her own husband's image on the screen.

There had been six of those times in six months. She dared to look forward to more. So unafraid he was. The last time was the day after Victoria Darrow and her young lover and her own good husband had returned to the city. She had gone farther with the child than ever before. On a starry-clear, cold September Monday, she had coaxed him down the stairs and out of the house with her. He held to the banisters, a child unused to stairs, and yet she knew there was no danger; he floated in his own dream with her. She took him to see Blue Boy. Who disappointed her by whining and backing away in fear. And then to the barn to see the horse. Who perked up his ears and looked interested. There was no touching, of course, no touching or speaking. Later she wondered if horses, then, were more magical than dogs. If dogs were more "realistic." She was glad the family was poor, the mother harassed. They could not afford any expensive child psychiatrist who would hypnotize him out of his night journeys.

He loved her. She knew that. Even if he never remembered her in his other life.

"At last I was beginning to understand what Teilhard de Chardin meant when he said that man's true home is the mind. I understood that when the mystics tell us that the mind is a place, they *don't mean it as a metaphor.* I found these new powers developed with practice. I had to detach myself from my ordinary physical personality. The intelligent part of me had to remain wide awake, and move down into this world of thoughts, dreams and memories. After several such journeyings I understood something else: dream and reality aren't competitors, but reciprocal sources of consciousness." This she read in a "respectable book," by a "respectable man," a scientist, alive and living in England, only a few years older than herself. She looked down at the dog, sleeping on the rug. His lean silvery body actually ran as he slept! Suddenly his muzzle lifted, the savage teeth snapped. Where was he "really" now? Did the dream rabbit in his jaws know it was a dream? There was much to think about, between her trips to the nursery.

Would the boy grow, would she see his body slowly emerging from its child's shape, the arms and legs lengthening, the face thinning out into a man's—like a certain advertisement for bread she had seen on TV where a child grows up, in less than a half-minute of sponsor time, right before the viewer's eyes. Would he grow into a man, grow a beard . . . outgrow the nursery region of his mind where they had been able to meet?

And yet, some daylight part of his mind must have retained an image of her from that single daylight time they had looked into each other's eyes.

The worst thing, such an awful thing to happen to a young woman . . . She was having this natural childbirth, you see, her husband in the delivery room with her, and the pains were coming a half-minute apart, and the doctor had just said, "This is going to be a breeze, Mrs. McNair," and they never knew exactly what went wrong, but all of a sudden the pains stopped and they had to go in after the baby without even time to give her a saddle block or any sort of anesthetic. . . . They must have practically had to tear it out of her . . . the husband fainted. The baby was born dead, and they gave her a heavy sedative to put her out all night.

When she woke the next morning, before she had time to remember what had happened, a nurse suddenly entered the room and laid a baby in her arms. "Here's your little boy," she said cheerfully, and the woman thought, with a profound, religious relief, *So that other nightmare was a dream,* and she had the child at her breast feeding him before the nurse realized her mistake and rushed back into the room, but they had to knock the poor woman out with more sedatives before she would let the child go. She was screaming and so was the little baby and they clung to each other till she passed out.

They would have let the nurse go, only it wasn't entirely her fault. The hospital was having a strike at the time; some of the nurses were outside picketing and this nurse had been working straight through for forty-eight hours, and when she was questioned afterward she said she had just mixed up the rooms, and yet, she said, when she had seen the woman and the baby clinging to each other like that, she had undergone a sort of revelation in her almost hallucinatory exhaustion: the nurse said she saw that all children and mothers were interchangeable, that nobody could own anybody or anything, anymore than you could own an idea that happened to be passing through the air and caught on your mind, or anymore than you owned the rosebush that grew in your back yard. There were only mothers and children, she realized; though, afterward, the realization faded.

It was the kind of freakish thing that happens once in a million times, and it's a wonder the poor woman kept her sanity.

In the intervals, longer than those measured by any stopwatch, she waited for him. In what the world accepted as "time," she shopped for groceries, for clothes; she read; she waved from her bottle-green car to Mrs. Frye, trimming the hedge in front of the liquor store, to Mrs. DePuy, hanging out her children's pajamas in the back yard of the old Patroon farm. She rode her horse through the fields of the waning season, letting him have his head; she rode like the wind, a happy, happy woman. She rode faster than fear because she was a woman in a dream, a woman anxiously awaiting her child's sleep. The stallion's hoofs pounded the earth. Oiling his tractor, DePuy resented the foolish woman and almost wished for a woodchuck hole to break that arrogant ride. Wished deep in a violent level of himself he never knew he had. For he was a kind, distracted father and husband, a practical, hard-working man who would never descend deeply into himself. Her body, skimming through time, felt weightless to the horse.

Was she a woman riding a horse and dreaming she was a mother who anxiously awaited her child's sleep; or was she a mother dreaming of herself as a free spirit who could ride her horse like the wind because she had nothing to fear?

I am a happy woman, that's all I know. Who can explain such things?

Gail Godwin's mother, a divorcee, supported her family partly by writing fiction for women's magazines. The formula for such fiction, as Godwin points out, is quite restrictive, and the desire to avoid it became one of Godwin's motives as a writer.

"Stories they still feel obliged to suppress": Gail Godwin

GIRL MEETS MAN. MUTUAL ATTRACTION. THINGS DEVELOP. A PROBLEM ARISES. CONFLICT AND DOUBT. RESOLUTION OF CONFLICT. FINAL EMBRACE. The formula was unvarying. All the stories that bought my clothes, my storybook dolls, my subscriptions to children's magazines, were contained by, were imprisoned in that plot. Did my young divorced mother, while typing in that sun-filled breakfast nook, ever have moments of bitter irony when she was tempted to rip out the "happily ever after" lie she was perpetrating, and roll a fresh sheet into the carriage and tell her own story? It would have been much more interesting. But who would have bought it? Not *Love Short Stories,* nor any of the other pulps—nor any of the "slicks" for women, either. When you write for the market, you lock yourself willingly into the prison of your times: a lesson I learned early. Now I sit in my dentist's office and leaf through women's magazines whose fictional terrains support, quite matter-of-factly, divorced mothers, unmarried mothers, even well-to-do suburban wives who may or may not "keep" that unplanned-for last child. And I think of the writers of these stories, safely within the ideologies of their *zeitgeist,* and I wonder what parts of their own stories they still feel obliged to suppress, what dark blossomings of their imaginations still lie outside the realm of the current "market"? Yes, even in these "liberated" times.

It is this realm that I fight; it is the dark blossomings, the suppressed (or veiled) truths that I court. Not always successfully. Like my mother, I, too, am the child of my times.

JOYCE CAROL OATES

(b. 1938)

WHERE ARE YOU GOING,
WHERE HAVE YOU BEEN?

To Bob Dylan

Her name was Connie. She was fifteen and she had a quick nervous giggling habit of craning her neck to glance into mirrors or checking other people's faces to make sure her own was all right. Her mother, who noticed everything and knew everything and who hadn't much reason any longer to look at her own face, always scolded Connie about it. "Stop gawking at yourself, who are you? You think you're so pretty?" she would say. Connie would raise her eyebrows at these familiar complaints and look right through her mother, into a shadowy vision of herself as she was right at that moment: she knew she was pretty and that was everything. Her mother had been pretty once too, if you could believe those old snapshots in the album, but now her looks were gone and that was why she was always after Connie.

"Why don't you keep your room clean like your sister? How've you got your hair fixed—what the hell stinks? Hair spray? You don't see your sister using that junk."

Her sister June was twenty-four and still lived at home. She was a secretary in the high school Connie attended, and if that wasn't bad enough —with her in the same building—she was so plain and chunky and steady that Connie had to hear her praised all the time by her mother and her mother's sisters. June did this, June did that, she saved money and helped clean the house and cooked and Connie couldn't do a thing, her mind was all filled with trashy daydreams. Their father was away at work most of the time and when he came home he wanted supper and he read the newspaper at supper and after supper he went to bed. He didn't bother talking much to them, but around his bent head Connie's mother kept picking at her until Connie wished her mother were dead and she herself were dead and it were all over. "She makes me want to throw up sometimes," she complained to her friends. She had a high, breathless, amused voice which made everything she said sound a little forced, whether it was sincere or not.

There was one good thing: June went places with girlfriends of hers, girls who were just as plain and steady as she, and so when Connie wanted to do that her mother had no objections. The father of Connie's best girlfriend drove the girls the three miles to town and left them off at a shopping plaza, so that they could walk through the stores or go to a movie, and when he came to pick them up again at eleven he never bothered to ask what they had done.

They must have been familiar sights, walking around that shopping plaza in their shorts and flat ballerina slippers that always scuffed the side-walk, with charm bracelets jingling on their thin wrists; they would lean together to whisper and laugh secretly if someone passed by who amused or interested them. Connie had long dark blond hair that drew anyone's eye to it, and she wore part of it pulled up on her head and puffed out and the rest of it she let fall down her back. She wore a pullover jersey blouse that looked one way when she was at home and another way when she was away from home. Everything about her had two sides to it, one for home and one for anywhere that was not home: her walk that could be childlike and bob-bing, or languid enough to make anyone think she was hearing music in her head, her mouth which was pale and smirking most of the time, but bright and pink on these evenings out, her laugh which was cynical and drawling at home—"Ha, ha, very funny"—but high-pitched and nervous anywhere else, like the jingling of the charms on her bracelet.

Sometimes they did go shopping or to a movie, but sometimes they went across the highway, ducking fast across the busy road, to a drive-in res-taurant where older kids hung out. The restaurant was shaped like a big bottle, though squatter than a real bottle, and on its cap was a revolving fig-ure of a grinning boy who held a hamburger aloft. One night in midsum-mer they ran across, breathless with daring, and right away someone leaned out a car window and invited them over, but it was just a boy from high school they didn't like. It made them feel good to be able to ignore him. They went up through the maze of parked and cruising cars to the bright-lit, fly-infested restaurant, their faces pleased and expectant as if they were entering a sacred building that loomed out of the night to give them what haven and what blessing they yearned for. They sat at the counter and crossed their legs at the ankles, their thin shoulders rigid with excitement, and listened to the music that made everything so good: the music was always in the background like music at a church service, it was something to depend upon.

A boy named Eddie came in to talk with them. He sat backward on his stool, turning himself jerkily around in semicircles and then stopping and turning again, and after a while he asked Connie if she would like some-thing to eat. She said she did and so she tapped her friend's arm on her way out—her friend pulled her face up into a brave droll look—and Connie said she would meet her at eleven, across the way. "I just hate to leave her like that," Connie said earnestly, but the boy said that she wouldn't be alone for long. So they went out to his car and on the way Connie couldn't help but let her eyes wander over the windshields and faces all around her, her face gleaming with a joy that had nothing to do with Eddie or even this place; it might have been the music. She drew her shoulders up and sucked in her breath with the pure pleasure of being alive, and just at that moment she happened to glance at a face just a few feet from hers. It was a boy with shaggy black hair, in a convertible jalopy painted gold. He stared at her and then his lips widened into a grin. Connie slit her eyes at him and turned away, but she couldn't help glancing back and there he was still watching her. He wagged a finger and laughed and said, "Gonna get you, baby," and Connie turned away again without Eddie noticing anything.

She spent three hours with him, at the restaurant where they ate hamburgers and drank Cokes in wax cups that were always sweating, and then down an alley a mile or so away, and when he left her off at five to eleven only the movie house was still open at the plaza. Her girlfriend was there, talking with a boy. When Connie came up the two girls smiled at each other and Connie said, "How was the movie?" and the girl said, "*You* should know." They rode off with the girl's father, sleepy and pleased, and Connie couldn't help but look at the darkened shopping plaza with its big empty parking lot and its signs that were faded and ghostly now, and over at the drive-in restaurant where cars were still circling tirelessly. She couldn't hear the music at this distance.

Next morning June asked her how the movie was and Connie said, "So-so."

She and that girl and occasionally another girl went out several times a week that way, and the rest of the time Connie spent around the house—it was summer vacation—getting in her mother's way and thinking, dreaming, about the boys she met. But all the boys fell back and dissolved into a single face that was not even a face, but an idea, a feeling, mixed up with the urgent insistent pounding of the music and the humid night air of July. Connie's mother kept dragging her back to the daylight by finding things for her to do or saying, suddenly, "What's this about the Pettinger girl?"

And Connie would say nervously, "Oh, her. That dope." She always drew thick clear lines between herself and such girls, and her mother was simple and kindly enough to believe her. Her mother was so simple, Connie thought, that it was maybe cruel to fool her so much. Her mother went scuffling around the house in old bedroom slippers and complained over the telephone to one sister about the other, then the other called up and the two of them complained about the third one. If June's name was mentioned her mother's tone was approving, and if Connie's name was mentioned it was disapproving. This did not really mean she disliked Connie and actually Connie thought that her mother preferred her to June because she was prettier, but the two of them kept up a pretense of exasperation, a sense that they were tugging and struggling over something of little value to either of them. Sometimes, over coffee, they were almost friends, but something would come up—some vexation that was like a fly buzzing suddenly around their heads—and their faces went hard with contempt.

One Sunday Connie got up at eleven—none of them bothered with church—and washed her hair so that it could dry all day long, in the sun. Her parents and sisters were going to a barbecue at an aunt's house and Connie said no, she wasn't interested, rolling her eyes to let her mother know just what she thought of it. "Stay home alone then," her mother said sharply. Connie sat out back in a lawn chair and watched them drive away, her father quiet and bald, hunched around so that he could back the car out, her mother with a look that was still angry and not at all softened through the windshield, and in the back seat poor old June all dressed up as if she didn't know what a barbecue was, with all the running yelling kids and the flies. Connie sat with her eyes closed in the sun, dreaming and dazed with the warmth about her as if this were a kind of love, the caresses of love, and her mind slipped over onto thoughts of the boy she had been with the night before and how nice he had been, how sweet it always was, not the way someone like June would suppose but sweet, gentle, the way it was in movies and promised in songs; and when she opened her eyes she hardly knew where she was, the back yard ran off into weeds and a fence line of trees and behind it the sky was perfectly blue and still. The asbestos "ranch house" that was now three years old startled her—it looked small. She shook her head as if to get awake.

It was too hot. She went inside the house and turned on the radio to drown out the quiet. She sat on the edge of her bed, barefoot, and listened for an hour and a half to a program called XYZ Sunday Jamboree, record after record of hard, fast, shrieking songs she sang along with, interspersed by exclamations from "Bobby King": "An' look here you girls at Napoleon's—Son and Charley want you to pay real close attention to this song coming up!"

And Connie paid close attention herself, bathed in a glow of slow-pulsed joy that seemed to rise mysteriously out of the music itself and lay languidly about the airless little room, breathed in and breathed out with each gentle rise and fall of her chest.

After a while she heard a car coming up the drive. She sat up at once, startled, because it couldn't be her father so soon. The gravel kept crunching all the way in from the road—the driveway was long—and Connie ran to the window. It was a car she didn't know. It was an open jalopy, painted a bright gold that caught the sunlight opaquely. Her heart began to pound and her fingers snatched at her hair, checking it, and she whispered "Christ, Christ," wondering how bad she looked. The car came to a stop at the side door and the horn sounded four short taps as if this were a signal Connie knew.

She went into the kitchen and approached the door slowly, then hung out the screen door, her bare toes curling down off the step. There were two boys in the car and now she recognized the driver: he had shaggy, shabby black hair that looked crazy as a wig and he was grinning at her.

"I ain't late, am I?" he said.

"Who the hell do you think you are?" Connie said.

"Toldja I'd be out, didn't I?"

"I don't even know who you are."

She spoke sullenly, careful to show no interest or pleasure, and he spoke in a fast bright monotone. Connie looked past him to the other boy, taking her time. He had fair brown hair, with a lock that fell onto his forehead. His sideburns gave him a fierce, embarrassed look, but so far he hadn't even bothered to glance at her. Both boys wore sunglasses. The driver's glasses were metallic and mirrored everything in miniature.

"You wanta come for a ride?" he said.

Connie smirked and let her hair fall loose over one shoulder.

"Don'tcha like my car? New paint job," he said. "Hey."

"What?"

"You're cute."

She pretended to fidget, chasing flies away from the door.

"Don'tcha believe me, or what?" he said.

"Look, I don't even know who you are," Connie said in disgust.

"Hey, Ellie's got a radio, see. Mine's broke down." He lifted his friend's arm and showed her the little transistor the boy was holding, and now Connie began to hear the music. It was the same program that was playing inside the house.

"Bobby King?" she said.

"I listen to him all the time. I think he's great."

"He's kind of great," Connie said reluctantly.

"Listen, that guy's *great*. He knows where the action is."

Connie blushed a little, because the glasses made it impossible for her to see just what this boy was looking at. She couldn't decide if she liked him or if he was just a jerk, and so she dawdled in the doorway and wouldn't come down or go back inside. She said, "What's all that stuff painted on your car?"

"Can'tcha read it?" He opened the door very carefully, as if he was afraid it might fall off. He slid out just as carefully, planting his feet firmly on the ground, the tiny metallic world in his glasses slowing down like gelatine hardening and in the midst of it Connie's bright green blouse. "This here is my name, to begin with," he said. ARNOLD FRIEND was written in tarlike black letters on the side, with a drawing of a round grinning face that reminded Connie of a pumpkin, except it wore sunglasses. "I wanta introduce myself, I'm Arnold Friend and that's my real name and I'm gonna be your friend, honey, and inside the car's Ellie Oscar, he's kinda shy." Ellie brought his transistor radio up to his shoulder and balanced it there. "Now these numbers are a secret code, honey," Arnold Friend explained. He read off the numbers 33, 19, 17 and raised his eyebrows at her to see what she thought of that, but she didn't think much of it. The left rear fender had been smashed and around it was written, on the gleaming gold background: DONE BY CRAZY WOMAN DRIVER. Connie had to laugh at that. Arnold Friend was pleased at her laughter and looked up at her. "Around the other side's a lot more—you wanta come and see them?"

"No."

"Why not?"

"Why should I?"

"Don'tcha wanta see what's on the car? Don'tcha wanta go for a ride?"

"I don't know."

"Why not?"

"I got things to do."

"Like what?"

"Things."

He laughed as if she had said something funny. He slapped his thighs. He was standing in a strange way, leaning back against the car as if he were balancing himself. He wasn't tall, only an inch or so taller than she would be if she came down to him. Connie liked the way he was dressed, which was the way all of them dressed: tight faded jeans stuffed into black, scuffed boots, a belt that pulled his waist in and showed how lean he was, and a white pullover shirt that was a little soiled and showed the hard small muscles of his arms and shoulders. He looked as if he probably did hard work, lifting and carrying things. Even his neck looked muscular. And his face was a familiar face, somehow: the jaw and chin and cheeks slightly darkened, because he hadn't shaved for a day or two, and the nose long and hawklike, sniffing as if she were a treat he was going to gobble up and it was all a joke.

"Connie, you ain't telling the truth. This is your day set aside for a ride with me and you know it," he said, still laughing. The way he straightened and recovered from his fit of laughing showed that it had been all fake.

"How do you know what my name is?" she said suspiciously.

"It's Connie."

"Maybe and maybe not."

"I know my Connie," he said, wagging his finger. Now she remembered him even better, back at the restaurant, and her cheeks warmed at the thought of how she sucked in her breath just at the moment she passed him —how she must have looked at him. And he had remembered her. "Ellie and I come out here especially for you," he said. "Ellie can sit in back. How about it?"

"Where?"

"Where what?"

"Where're we going?"

He looked at her. He took off the sunglasses and she saw how pale the skin around his eyes was, like holes that were not in shadow but instead in light. His eyes were like chips of broken glass that catch the light in an amiable way. He smiled. It was as if the idea of going for a ride somewhere, to some place, was a new idea to him.

"Just for a ride, Connie sweetheart."

"I never said my name was Connie," she said.

"But I know what it is. I know your name and all about you, lots of things," Arnold Friend said. He had not moved yet but stood still leaning back against the side of his jalopy. "I took a special interest in you, such a pretty girl, and found out all about you like I know your parents and sister are gone somewheres and I know where and how long they're going to be gone, and I know who you were with last night, and your best girlfriend's name is Betty. Right?"

He spoke in a simple lilting voice, exactly as if he were reciting the words to a song. His smile assured her that everything was fine. In the car Ellie turned up the volume on his radio and did not bother to look around at them.

"Ellie can sit in the back seat," Arnold Friend said. He indicated his friend with a casual jerk of his chin, as if Ellie did not count and she should not bother with him.

"How'd you find out all that stuff?" Connie said.

"Listen: Betty Schultz and Tony Fitch and Jimmy Pettinger and Nancy Pettinger," he said, in a chant. "Raymond Stanley and Bob Hutter—"

"Do you know all those kids?"

"I know everybody."

"Look, you're kidding. You're not from around here."

"Sure."

"But—how come we never saw you before?"

"Sure you saw me before," he said. He looked down at his boots, as if he were a little offended. "You just don't remember."

"I guess I'd remember you," Connie said.

"Yeah?" He looked up at this, beaming. He was pleased. He began to mark time with the music from Ellie's radio, tapping his fists lightly together. Connie looked away from his smile to the car, which was painted so bright it almost hurt her eyes to look at it. She looked at that name. ARNOLD FRIEND. And up at the front fender was an expression that was familiar—MAN THE FLYING SAUCERS. It was an expression kids had used the year before, but didn't use this year. She looked at it for a while as if the words meant something to her that she did not yet know.

"What're you thinking about? Huh?" Arnold Friend demanded. "Not worried about your hair blowing around in the car, are you?"

"No."

"Think I maybe can't drive good?"

"How do I know?"

"You're a hard girl to handle. How come?" he said. "Don't you know I'm your friend? Didn't you see me put my sign in the air when you walked by?"

"What sign?"

"My sign." And he drew an X in the air, leaning out toward her. They were maybe ten feet apart. After his hand fell back to his side the X was still in the air, almost visible. Connie let the screen door close and stood perfectly still inside it, listening to the music from her radio and the boy's blend together. She stared at Arnold Friend. He stood there so stiffly relaxed, pretending to be relaxed, with one hand idly on the door handle as if he were keeping himself up that way and had no intention of ever moving again. She recognized most things about him, the tight jeans that showed his thighs and buttocks and the greasy leather boots and the tight shirt, and even that slippery friendly smile of his, that sleepy dreamy smile that all the boys used to get across ideas they didn't want to put into words. She recognized all this and also the singsong way he talked, slightly mocking, kidding, but serious and a little melancholy, and she recognized the way he tapped one fist against the other in homage of the perpetual music behind him. But all these things did not come together.

She said suddenly, "Hey, how old are you?"

His smile faded. She could see then that he wasn't a kid, he was much older—thirty, maybe more. At this knowledge her heart began to pound faster.

"That's a crazy thing to ask. Can'tcha see I'm your own age?"

"Like hell you are."

"Or maybe a coupla years older, I'm eighteen."

"Eighteen?" she said doubtfully.

He grinned to reassure her and lines appeared at the corners of his mouth. His teeth were big and white. He grinned so broadly his eyes became slits and she saw how thick the lashes were, thick and black as if painted with a black tarlike material. Then he seemed to become embarrassed, abruptly, and looked over his shoulder at Ellie. "*Him,* he's crazy," he said. "Ain't he a riot, he's a nut, a real character." Ellie was still listening to the music. His sunglasses told nothing about what he was thinking. He wore a bright orange shirt unbuttoned halfway to show his chest, which was a pale, bluish chest and not muscular like Arnold Friend's. His shirt collar was turned up all around and the very tips of the collar pointed out past his chin as if they were protecting him. He was pressing the transistor radio up against his ear and sat there in a kind of daze, right in the sun.

"He's kinda strange," Connie said.

"Hey, she says you're kinda strange! Kinda strange!" Arnold Friend cried. He pounded on the car to get Ellie's attention. Ellie turned for the first time and Connie saw with shock that he wasn't a kid either—he had a fair, hairless face, cheeks reddened slightly as if the veins grew too close to the surface of his skin, the face of a forty-year-old baby. Connie felt a wave of dizziness rise in her at this sight and she stared at him as if waiting for something to change the shock of the moment, make it all right again. Ellie's lips kept shaping words, mumbling along with the words blasting in his ear.

"Maybe you two better go away," Connie said faintly.

"What? How come?" Arnold Friend cried. "We come out here to take you for a ride. It's Sunday." He had the voice of the man on the radio now. It was the same voice, Connie thought. "Don'tcha know it's Sunday all day and honey, no matter who you were with last night today you're with Arnold Friend and don't you forget it!—Maybe you better step out here," he said, and this last was in a different voice. It was a little flatter, as if the heat was finally getting to him.

"No. I got things to do."

"Hey."

"You two better leave."

"We ain't leaving until you come with us."

"Like hell I am—"

"Connie, don't fool around with me. I mean, I mean, don't fool *around*," he said, shaking his head. He laughed incredulously. He placed his sunglasses on top of his head, carefully, as if he were indeed wearing a wig, and brought the stems down behind his ears. Connie stared at him, another wave of dizziness and fear rising in her so that for a moment he wasn't even in focus but was just a blur, standing there against his gold car, and she had the idea that he had driven up the driveway all right but had come from nowhere before that and belonged nowhere and that everything about him and even about the music that was so familiar to her was only half real.

"If my father comes and sees you—"

"He ain't coming. He's at a barbecue."

"How do you know that?"

"Aunt Tillie's. Right now they're—uh—they're drinking. Sitting around," he said vaguely, squinting as if he were staring all the way to town and over to Aunt Tillie's back yard. Then the vision seemed to get clear and he nodded energetically. "Yeah. Sitting around. There's your sister in a blue dress, huh? And high heels, the poor sad bitch—nothing like you, sweetheart! And your mother's helping some fat woman with the corn, they're cleaning the corn—husking the corn—"

"What fat woman?" Connie cried.

"How do I know what fat woman, I don't know every goddam fat woman in the world!" Arnold laughed.

"Oh, that's Mrs. Hornby . . . Who invited her?" Connie said. She felt a little light-headed. Her breath was coming quickly.

"She's too fat. I don't like them fat. I like them the way you are, honey," he said, smiling sleepily at her. They stared at each other for a while, through the screen door. He said softly, "Now what you're going to do is this: you're going to come out that door. You're going to sit up front with me and Ellie's going to sit in the back, the hell with Ellie, right? This isn't Ellie's date. You're my date. I'm your lover, honey."

"What? You're crazy—"

"Yes, I'm your lover. You don't know what that is, but you will," he said. "I know that too. I know all about you. But look: it's real nice and you couldn't ask for nobody better than me, or more polite. I always keep my word. I'll tell you how it is, I'm always nice at first, the first time. I'll hold you so tight you won't think you have to try to get away or pretend anything because you'll know you can't. And I'll come inside you where it's all secret and you'll give in to me and you'll love me—"

"Shut up! You're crazy!" Connie said. She backed away from the door. She put her hands against her ears as if she'd heard something terrible, something not meant for her. "People don't talk like that, you're crazy," she muttered. Her heart was almost too big now for her chest and its pumping made sweat break out all over her. She looked out to see Arnold Friend pause and then take a step toward the porch lurching. He almost fell. But, like a clever drunken man, he managed to catch his balance. He wobbled in his high boots and grabbed hold of one of the porch posts.

"Honey?" he said. "You still listening?"

"Get the hell out of here!"

"Be nice, honey. Listen."

"I'm going to call the police—"

He wobbled again and out of the side of his mouth came a fast spat curse, an aside not meant for her to hear. But even this "Christ!" sounded forced. Then he began to smile again. She watched this smile come, awkward as if he were smiling from inside a mask. His whole face was a mask, she thought wildly, tanned down onto his throat but then running out as if he had plastered makeup on his face but had forgotten about his throat.

"Honey—? Listen, here's how it is. I always tell the truth and I promise you this: I ain't coming in that house after you."

"You better not! I'm going to call the police if you—if you don't—"

"Honey," he said, talking right through her voice, "honey, I'm not coming in there but you are coming out here. You know why?"

She was panting. The kitchen looked like a place she had never seen before, some room she had run inside but which wasn't good enough, wasn't going to help her. The kitchen window had never had a curtain, after three years, and there were dishes in the sink for her to do—probably —and if you ran your hand across the table you'd probably feel something sticky there.

"You listening, honey? Hey?"

"—going to call the police—"

"Soon as you touch the phone I don't need to keep my promise and can come inside. You won't want that."

She rushed forward and tried to lock the door. Her fingers were shaking. "But why lock it," Arnold Friend said gently, talking right into her face. "It's just a screen door. It's just nothing." One of his boots was at a strange angle, as if his foot wasn't in it. It pointed out to the left, bent at the ankle. "I mean, anybody can break through a screen door and glass and wood and iron or anything else if he needs to, anybody at all and specially Arnold Friend. If the place got lit up with a fire honey you'd come runnin' out into my arms, right into my arms an' safe at home—like you knew I was your lover and'd stopped fooling around. I don't mind a nice shy girl but I don't like no fooling around." Part of those words were spoken with a slight rhythmic lilt, and Connie somehow recognized them—the echo of a song from last year, about a girl rushing into her boyfriend's arms and coming home again—

Connie stood barefoot on the linoleum floor, staring at him. "What do you want?" she whispered.

"I want you," he said.

"What?"

"Seen you that night and thought, that's the one, yes sir. I never needed to look any more."

"But my father's coming back. He's coming to get me. I had to wash my hair first—" She spoke in a dry, rapid voice, hardly raising it for him to hear.

"No, your Daddy is not coming and yes, you had to wash your hair and you washed it for me. It's nice and shining and all for me, I thank you, sweetheart," he said, with a mock bow, but again he almost lost his balance. He had to bend and adjust his boots. Evidently his feet did not go all the way down; the boots must have been stuffed with something so that he would seem taller. Connie stared out at him and behind him Ellie in the car, who seemed to be looking off toward Connie's right into nothing. This Ellie said, pulling the words out of the air one after another as if he were just discovering them, "You want me to pull out the phone?"

"Shut your mouth and keep it shut," Arnold Friend said, his face red from bending over or maybe from embarrassment because Connie had seen his boots. "This ain't none of your business."

"What—what are you doing? What do you want?" Connie said. "If I call the police they'll get you, they'll arrest you—"

"Promise was not to come in unless you touch that phone, and I'll keep that promise," he said. He resumed his erect position and tried to force his shoulders back. He sounded like a hero in a movie, declaring something important. He spoke too loudly and it was as if he were speaking to someone behind Connie. "I ain't made plans for coming in that house where I don't belong but just for you to come out to me, the way you should. Don't you know who I am?"

"You're crazy," she whispered. She backed away from the door but did not want to go into another part of the house, as if this would give him permission to come through the door. "What do you . . . You're crazy, you . . ."

"Huh? What're you saying, honey?"

Her eyes darted everywhere in the kitchen. She could not remember what it was, this room.

"This is how it is, honey; you come out and we'll drive away, have a nice ride. But if you don't come out we're gonna wait till your people come home and then they're all going to get it."

"You want that telephone pulled out?" Ellie said. He held the radio away from his ear and grimaced, as if without the radio the air was too much for him.

"I toldja shut up, Ellie," Arnold Friend said, "you're deaf, get a hearing aid, right? Fix yourself up. This little girl's no trouble and's gonna be nice to me, so Ellie keep to yourself, this ain't your date—right? Don't

hem in on me. Don't hog. Don't crush. Don't bird dog. Don't trail me,"
he said in a rapid meaningless voice, as if he were running through all the
expressions he'd learned but was no longer sure which one of them was in
style, then rushing on to new ones, making them up with his eyes closed,
"Don't crawl under my fence, don't squeeze in my chipmunk hole, don't
sniff my glue, suck my popsicle, keep your own greasy fingers on yourself!"
He shaded his eyes and peered in at Connie, who was backed against the
kitchen table. "Don't mind him honey he's just a creep. He's a dope.
Right? I'm the boy for you and like I said you come out here nice like a lady
and give me your hand, and nobody else gets hurt, I mean, your nice old
bald-headed daddy and your mummy and your sister in her high heels.
Because listen: why bring them in this?"

"Leave me alone," Connie whispered.

"Hey, you know that old woman down the road, the one with the
chickens and stuff—you know her?"

"She's dead!"

"Dead? What? You know her?" Arnold Friend said.

"She's dead—"

"Don't you like her?"

"She dead—she's—she isn't there any more—"

"But don't you like her, I mean, you got something against her?
Some grudge or something?" Then his voice dipped as if he were conscious
of a rudeness. He touched the sunglasses perched on top of his head as if to
make sure they were still there. "Now you be a good girl."

"What are you going to do?"

"Just two things, or maybe three," Arnold Friend said. "But I
promise it won't last long and you'll like me the way you get to like people
you're close to. You will. It's all over for you here, so come on out. You
don't want your people in any trouble, do you?"

She turned and bumped against a chair or something, hurting her
leg, but she ran into the back room and picked up the telephone. Something roared in her ear, a tiny roaring, and she was so sick with fear that she
could do nothing but listen to it—the telephone was clammy and very heavy
and her fingers groped down to the dial but were too weak to touch it. She
began to scream into the phone, into the roaring. She cried out, she cried
for her mother, she felt her breath start jerking back and forth in her lungs
as if it were something Arnold Friend were stabbing her with again and
again with no tenderness. A noisy sorrowful wailing rose all about her and
she was locked inside it the way she was locked inside this house.

After a while she could hear again. She was sitting on the floor with
her wet back against the wall.

Arnold Friend was saying from the door, "That's a good girl. Put
the phone back."

She kicked the phone away from her.

"No, honey. Pick it up. Put it back right."

She picked it up and put it back. The dial tone stopped.

"That's a good girl. Now you come outside."

She was hollow with what had been fear, but what was now just an emptiness. All that screaming had blasted it out of her. She sat, one leg cramped under her, and deep inside her brain was something like a pinpoint of light that kept going and would not let her relax. She thought, I'm not going to see my mother again. She thought, I'm not going to sleep in my bed again. Her bright green blouse was all wet.

Arnold Friend said, in a gentle-loud voice that was like a stage voice. "The place where you came from ain't there any more, and where you had in mind to go is canceled out. This place you are now—inside your daddy's house—is nothing but a cardboard box I can knock down any time. You know that and always did know it. You hear me?"

She thought, I have got to think. I have to know what to do.

"We'll go out to a nice field, out in the country here where it smells so nice and it's sunny," Arnold Friend said. "I'll have my arms tight around you so you won't need to try to get away and I'll show you what love is like, what it does. The hell with this house! It looks solid all right," he said. He ran a fingernail down the screen and the noise did not make Connie shiver, as it would have the day before. "Now put your hand on your heart, honey. Feel that? That feels solid too, but we know better, be nice to me, be sweet like you can because what else is there for a girl like you but to be sweet and pretty and give in?—and get away before her people come back?"

She felt her pounding heart. Her hand seemed to enclose it. She thought for the first time in her life that it was nothing that was hers, that belonged to her, but just a pounding, living thing inside this body that wasn't really hers either.

"You don't want them to get hurt," Arnold Friend went on. "Now get up, honey. Get up all by yourself."

She stood.

"Now turn this way. That's right. Come over here to me—Ellie, put that away, didn't I tell you? You dope. You miserable creepy dope," Arnold Friend said. His words were not angry but only part of an incantation. The incantation was kindly. "Now come out through the kitchen to me honey, and let's see a smile, try it, you're a brave sweet little girl and now they're eating corn and hot dogs cooked to bursting over an outdoor fire, and they don't know one thing about you and never did and honey you're better than them because not a one of them would have done this for you."

Connie felt the linoleum under her feet; it was cool. She brushed her hair back out of her eyes. Arnold Friend let go of the post tentatively and opened his arms for her, his elbows pointing in toward each other and his wrists limp, to show that this was an embarrassed embrace and a little mocking, he didn't want to make her self-conscious.

She put out her hand against the screen. She watched herself push the door slowly open as if she were safe back somewhere in the other doorway, watching this body and this head of long hair moving out into the sunlight where Arnold Friend waited.

"My sweet little blue-eyed girl," he said, in a half-sung sigh that had nothing to do with her brown eyes but was taken up just the same by the vast sunlit reaches of the land behind him and on all sides of him, so much land that Connie had never seen before and did not recognize except to know that she was going to it.

1970

When she discusses her intentions as a writer, Joyce Carol Oates shows us that she is equally anxious to avoid simple spontaneity (the unreflective reporting of emotions and events) and strict rationality (the production of stories that are embodied ideas). A story like "Where Are You Going, Where Have You Been?" may exemplify her notion that a story, like a dream, can be suspended somewhere between logic and effusion.

"The short story is a dream verbalized": Joyce Carol Oates

In our time, in the Seventies, we are chided for being too intellectual, too clinical, if we do not surrender to the tyranny of the Present. Our art, if it is careful, if it makes a rational and even calculated point, is considered a betrayal of the spontaneous joy of life—living—which is always non-rational or anti-rational, as if only the more primitive levels of our brains are truly human. All this is a mistake. More than that, it is a waste: it is a waste that intelligent people should earnestly deny their intelligence, extolling the impulsive and the sensuous and the "original." In making a blunt distinction between a life of action and a life of reflection, Sartre is insisting that the materials of life cannot become translated immediately into the materials of art; the two belong to entirely different dimensions.

Any remarks about the short story made by a writer of short stories are bound to be autobiographical, if they are at all honest. For me the short story is an absolutely undecipherable fact. Years ago I believed that art was rational, at bottom, that it could be seen to "make sense," that it had a definite relationship with philosophical inquiry, though its aim was not necessarily to resolve philosophical doubt. Now I am not so sure: certain short stories, certain works of fiction, are obviously more rational than others, more reducible to an essence. But others are mysterious and fluid and unpossessible, like certain people. The short story is a dream verbalized, arranged in space and presented to the world, imagined as a sympathetic audience (and not, as the world really is, a busy and indifferent crowd): the dream is said to be some kind of manifestation of desire, so the short story must also represent a desire, perhaps only partly expressed, but the most interesting thing about it is its mystery.

TONI CADE BAMBARA

(b. 1939)

THE LESSON

Back in the days when everyone was old and stupid or young and foolish and me and Sugar were the only ones just right, this lady moved on our block with nappy hair and proper speech and no makeup. And quite naturally we laughed at her, laughed the way we did at the junk man who went about his business like he was some big-time president and his sorry-ass horse his secretary. And we kinda hated her too, hated the way we did the winos who cluttered up our parks and pissed on our handball walls and stank up our hallways and stairs so you couldn't halfway play hide-and-seek without a goddamn gas mask. Miss Moore was her name. The only woman on the block with no first name. And she was black as hell, cept for her feet, which were fish-white and spooky. And she was always planning these boring-ass things for us to do, us being my cousin, mostly, who lived on the block cause we all moved North the same time and to the same apartment then spread out gradual to breathe. And our parents would yank our heads into some kinda shape and crisp up our clothes so we'd be presentable for travel with Miss Moore, who always looked like she was going to church, though she never did. Which is just one of the things the grownups talked about when they talked behind her back like a dog. But when she came calling with some sachet she'd sewed up or some gingerbread she'd made or some book, why then they'd all be too embarrassed to turn her down and we'd get handed over all spruced up. She'd been to college and said it was only right that she should take responsibility for the young ones' education, and she not even related by marriage or blood. So they'd go for it. Specially Aunt Gretchen. She was the main gofer in the family. You got some ole dumb shit foolishness you want somebody to go for, you send for Aunt Gretchen. She been screwed into the go-along for so long, it's a blood-deep natural thing with her. Which is how she got saddled with me and Sugar and Junior in the first place while our mothers were in a la-de-da apartment up the block having a good ole time.

So this one day Miss Moore rounds us all up at the mailbox and it's puredee hot and she's knockin herself out about arithmetic. And school suppose to let up in summer I heard, but she don't never let up. And the starch in my pinafore scratching the shit outta me and I'm really hating this nappy-head bitch and her goddamn college degree. I'd much rather go to the pool or to the show where it's cool. So me and Sugar leaning on the mailbox being surly, which is a Miss Moore word. And Flyboy checking out what everybody brought for lunch. And Fat Butt already wasting his pea-nut-butter-and-jelly sandwich like the pig he is. And Junebug punchin on Q.T.'s arm for potato chips. And Rosie Giraffe shifting from one hip to the other waiting for somebody to step on her foot or ask her if she from Georgia so she can kick ass, preferably Mercedes'. And Miss Moore asking us do we know what money is, like we a bunch of retards. I mean real money, she say, like it's only poker chips or monopoly papers we lay on the grocer. So right away I'm tired of this and say so. And would much rather snatch Sugar and go to the Sunset and terrorize the West Indian kids and take their hair ribbons and their money too. And Miss Moore files that remark away for next week's lesson on brotherhood, I can tell. And finally I say we oughta get to the subway cause it's cooler and besides we might meet some cute boys. Sugar done swiped her mama's lipstick, so we ready.

So we heading down the street and she's boring us silly about what things cost and what our parents make and how much goes for rent and how money ain't divided up right in this country. And then she gets to the part about we all poor and live in the slums, which I don't feature. And I'm ready to speak on that, but she steps out in the street and hails two cabs just like that. Then she hustles half the crew in with her and hands me a five-dollar bill and tells me to calculate 10 percent tip for the driver. And we're off. Me and Sugar and Junebug and Flyboy hangin out the window and hollering to everybody, putting lipstick on each other cause Flyboy a faggot anyway, and making farts with our sweaty armpits. But I'm mostly trying to figure how to spend this money. But they all fascinated with the meter ticking and Junebug starts laying bets as to how much it'll read when Flyboy can't hold his breath no more. Then Sugar lays bets as to how much it'll be when we get there. So I'm stuck. Don't nobody want to go for my plan, which is to jump out at the next light and run off to the first bar-b-que we can find. Then the driver tells us to get the hell out cause we there already. And the meter reads eighty-five cents. And I'm stalling to figure out the tip and Sugar say give him a dime. And I decide he don't need it bad as I do, so later for him. But then he tries to take off with Junebug foot still in the door so we talk about his mama something ferocious. Then we check out that we on Fifth Avenue and everybody dressed up in stockings. One lady in a fur coat, hot as it is. White folks crazy.

"This is the place," Miss Moore say, presenting it to us in the voice she uses at the museum. "Let's look in the windows before we go in."

"Can we steal?" Sugar asks very serious like she's getting the ground rules squared away before she plays. "I beg your pardon," say Miss Moore, and we fall out. So she leads us around the windows of the toy store and me and Sugar screamin, "This is mine, that's mine, I gotta have that, that was made for me, I was born for that," till Big Butt drowns us out.

"Hey, I'm goin to buy that there."

"That there? You don't even know what it is, stupid."

"I do so," he say punchin on Rosie Giraffe. "It's a microscope."

"Whatcha gonna do with a microscope, fool?"

"Look at things."

"Like what, Ronald?" ask Miss Moore. And Big Butt ain't got the first notion. So here go Miss Moore gabbing about the thousands of bacteria in a drop of water and the somethinorother in a speck of blood and the million and one living things in the air around us is invisible to the naked eye. And what she say that for? Junebug go to town on that "naked" and we rolling. Then Miss Moore ask what it cost. So we all jam into the window smudgin it up and the price tag say $300. So then she ask how long'd take for Big Butt and Junebug to save up their allowances. "Too long," I say. "Yeh," adds Sugar, "outgrown it by that time." And Miss Moore say no, you never outgrow learning instruments. "Why, even medical students and interns and," blah, blah, blah. And we ready to choke Big Butt for bringing it up in the first damn place.

"This here costs four hundred eighty dollars," say Rosie Giraffe. So we pile up all over her to see what she pointin out. My eyes tell me it's a chunk of glass cracked with something heavy, and different-color inks dripped into the splits, then the whole thing put into a oven or something. But for $480 it don't make sense.

"That's a paperweight made of semi-precious stones fused together under tremendous pressure," she explains slowly, with her hands doing the mining and all the factory work.

"So what's a paperweight?" asks Rosie Giraffe.

"To weigh paper with, dumbbell," say Flyboy, the wise man from the East.

"Not exactly," say Miss Moore, which is what she say when you warm or way off too. "It's to weigh paper down so it won't scatter and make your desk untidy." So right away me and Sugar curtsy to each other and then to Mercedes who is more the tidy type.

"We don't keep paper on top of the desk in my class," say Junebug, figuring Miss Moore crazy or lyin one.

"At home, then," she say. "Don't you have a calendar and a pencil case and a blotter and a letter-opener on your desk at home where you do your homework?" And she know damn well what our homes look like cause she nosys around in them every chance she gets.

"I don't even have a desk," say Junebug. "Do we?"

"No. And I don't get no homework neither," says Big Butt.

"And I don't even have a home," say Flyboy like he do at school to keep the white folks off his back and sorry for him. Send this poor kid to camp posters, is his specialty.

"I do," says Mercedes. "I have a box of stationery on my desk and a picture of my cat. My godmother bought the stationery and the desk. There's a big rose on each sheet and the envelopes smell like roses."

"Who wants to know about your smelly-ass stationery," say Rosie Giraffe fore I can get my two cents in.

"It's important to have a work area all your own so that . . ."

Toni Cade Bambara   613

"Will you look at this sailboat, please," say Flyboy, cuttin her off and pointin to the thing like it was his. So once again we tumble all over each other to gaze at this magnificent thing in the toy store which is just big enough to maybe sail two kittens across the pond if you strap them to the posts tight. We all start reciting the price tag like we in assembly. "Hand-crafted sailboat of fiberglass at one thousand one hundred ninety-five dollars."

"Unbelievable," I hear myself say and am really stunned. I read it again for myself just in case the group recitation put me in a trance. Same thing. For some reason this pisses me off. We look at Miss Moore and she lookin at us, waiting for I dunno what.

"Who'd pay all that when you can buy a sailboat set for a quarter at Pop's, a tube of glue for a dime, and a ball of string for eight cents? It must have a motor and a whole lot else besides," I say. "My sailboat cost me about fifty cents."

"But will it take water?" say Mercedes with her smart ass.

"Took mine to Alley Pond Park once," say Flyboy. "String broke. Lost it. Pity."

"Sailed mine in Central Park and it keeled over and sank. Had to ask my father for another dollar."

"And you got the strap," laugh Big Butt. "The jerk didn't even have a string on it. My old man wailed on his behind."

Little Q.T. was staring hard at the sailboat and you could see he wanted it bad. But he too little and somebody'd just take it from him. So what the hell. "This boat for kids, Miss Moore?"

"Parents silly to buy something like that just to get all broke up," say Rosie Giraffe.

"That much money it should last forever," I figure.

"My father'd buy it for me if I wanted it."

"Your father, my ass," say Rosie Giraffe getting a chance to finally push Mercedes.

"Must be rich people shop here," say Q.T.

"You are a very bright boy," say Flyboy. "What was your first clue?" And he rap him on the head with the back of his knuckles, since Q.T. the only one he could get away with. Though Q.T. liable to come up behind you years later and get his licks in when you half expect it.

"What I want to know is," I says to Miss Moore though I never talk to her, I wouldn't give the bitch that satisfaction, "is how much a real boat costs? I figure a thousand'd get you a yacht any day."

"Why don't you check that out," she says, "and report back to the group?" Which really pains my ass. If you gonna mess up a perfectly good swim day least you could do is have some answers. "Let's go in," she say like she got something up her sleeve. Only she don't lead the way. So me and Sugar turn the corner to where the entrance is, but when we get there I kinda hang back. Not that I'm scared, what's there to be afraid of, just a toy store. But I feel funny, shame. But what I got to be shamed about? Got as much right to go in as anybody. But somehow I can't seem to get hold of the door, so I step away from Sugar to lead. But she hangs back too. And I look at her and she looks at me and this is ridiculous. I mean, damn, I have never ever been shy about doing nothing or going nowhere. But then Mercedes steps up and then Rosie Giraffe and Big Butt crowd in behind and shove, and next thing we all stuffed into the doorway with only Mercedes squeezing past us, smoothing out her jumper and walking right down the aisle. Then the rest of us tumble in like a glued-together jigsaw done all wrong. And people lookin at us. And it's like the time me and Sugar crashed into the Catholic church on a dare. But once we got in there and everything so hushed and holy and the candles and the bowin and the handkerchiefs on all the drooping heads, I just couldn't go through with the plan. Which was for me to run up to the altar and do a tap dance while Sugar played the nose flute and messed around in the holy water. And Sugar kept givin me the elbow. Then later teased me so bad I tied her up in the shower and turned it on and locked her in. And she'd be there till this day if Aunt Gretchen hadn't finally figured I was lyin about the boarder takin a shower.

Same thing in the store. We all walkin on tiptoe and hardly touchin the games and puzzles and things. And I watched Miss Moore who is steady watchin us like she waitin for a sign. Like Mama Drewery watches the sky and sniffs the air and takes note of just how much slant is in the bird formation. Then me and Sugar bump smack into each other, so busy gazing at the toys, 'specially the sailboat. But we don't laugh and go into out fat-lady bump-stomach routine. We just stare at that price tag. Then Sugar run a finger over the whole boat. And I'm jealous and want to hit her. Maybe not her, but I sure want to punch somebody in the mouth.

"Watcha bring us here for, Miss Moore?"

"You sound angry, Sylvia. Are you mad about something?" Givin me one of them grins like she tellin a grown-up joke that never turns out to be funny. And she's lookin very closely at me like maybe she plannin to do my portrait from memory. I'm mad, but I won't give her that satisfaction. So I slouch around the store bein very bored and say, "Let's go."

Me and Sugar at the back of the train watchin the tracks whizzin by large then small then gettin gobbled up in the dark. I'm thinkin about this tricky toy I saw in the store. A clown that somersaults on a bar then does chin-ups just cause you yank lightly at his leg. Cost $35. I could see me askin my mother for a $35 birthday clown. "You wanna who that costs what?" she'd say, cocking her head to the side to get a better view of the hole in my head. Thirty-five dollars could buy new bunk beds for Junior and Gretchen's boy. Thirty-five dollars and the whole household could go visit Granddaddy Nelson in the country. Thirty-five dollars would pay for the rent and the piano bill too. Who are these people that spend that much for performing clowns and $1000 for toy sailboats? What kinda work they do and how they live and how come we ain't in on it? Where we are is who we are, Miss Moore always pointin out. But it don't necessarily have to be that way, she always adds then waits for somebody to say that poor people have to wake up and demand their share of the pie and don't none of us know what kind of pie she talking about in the first damn place. But she ain't so smart cause I still got her four dollars from the taxi and she sure ain't gettin it. Messin up my day with this shit. Sugar nudges me in my pocket and winks.

Miss Moore lines us up in front of the mailbox where we started from, seem like years ago, and I got a headache for thinkin so hard. And we lean all over each other so we can hold up under the draggy ass lecture she always finishes us off with at the end before we thank her for borin us to tears. But she just looks at us like she readin tea leaves. Finally she say, "Well, what did you think of F.A.O. Schwarz?"

Rosie Giraffe mumbles, "White folks crazy."

"I'd like to go there again when I get my birthday money," says Mercedes, and we shove her out the pack so she has to lean on the mailbox by herself.

"I'd like a shower. Tiring day," say Flyboy.

Then Sugar surprises me by sayin, "You know, Miss Moore, I don't think all of us here put together eat in a year what that sailboat costs." And Miss Moore lights up like somebody goosed her. "And?" she say, urging Sugar on. Only I'm standin on her foot so she don't continue.

"Imagine for a minute what kind of society it is in which some people can spend on a toy what it would cost to feed a family of six or seven. What do you think?"

"I think," say Sugar pushing me off her feet like she never done before, cause I whip her ass in a minute, "that this is not much of a democracy if you ask me. Equal chance to pursue happiness means an equal crack at the dough, don't it?" Miss Moore is besides herself and I am disgusted with Sugar's treachery. So I stand on her foot one more time to see if she'll shove me. She shuts up, and Miss Moore looks at me, sorrowfully I'm thinkin. And somethin weird is goin on, I can feel it in my chest.

"Anybody else learn anything today?" lookin dead at me. I walk away and Sugar has to run to catch up and don't even seem to notice when I shrug her arm off my shoulder.

"Well, we got four dollars anyway," she says.

"Uh hunh."

"We could go to Hascombs and get half a chocolate layer and then go to the Sunset and still have plenty money for potato chips and ice cream sodas."

"Uh hunh."

"Race you to Hascombs," she say.

We start down the block and she gets ahead which is O.K. by me cause I'm going to the West End and then over to the Drive to think this day through. She can run if she want to and even run faster. But ain't nobody gonna beat me at nuthin.

1972

616   Short Fiction

Some of Toni Cade Bambara's subjects, in the hands of another writer, could develop into political invective. The poverty of the children in "The Lesson" is, after all, serious business. Bambara's own explanation of why she avoids turning a story into a merely political statement gives us some insight into her goals as a writer.

"I can't get happy writing ugly weird": Toni Cade Bambara

The greatest challenge in writing, then, in the earlier stages was to strike a balance between candor, honesty, integrity, and truth—terms that are fairly synonymous for crossword puzzlers and thesaurus ramblers but hard to equate as living actions. Speaking one's mind, after all, does not necessarily mean one is in touch with the truth or even with the facts. Being honest and frank in terms of my own where—where I'm at a given point in my political/spiritual/etc. development—is not necessarily in my/our interest to utter, not necessarily in the interest of health, wholesomeness. Certain kinds of poisons, for example—rage, bitterness, revenge—don't need to be in the atmosphere, not to mention in my mouth. I don't, for example, hack up racists and stuff them in metaphorical boxes. I do not wish to lend them energy, for one thing. Though certainly there are "heavies" that people my stories. But I don't, for example, conjure up characters for the express purpose of despising them, of breaking their humps in public. I used to be astounded at Henry James et al., so nice nasty about it too, soooo refined. Gothic is of no interest to me. I try not to lend energy to building grotesqueries, depicting morbid relationships, dramatizing perversity. Folks come up to me 'lowing as how since I am a writer I would certainly want to hear blah, blah, blah, blah. They dump shit all over me, tell me about every ugly overheard and lived-through nightmare imaginable. They've got the wrong writer. The kid can't use it. I straightaway refer them to the neighborhood healer, certain that anyone so intoxicated would surely welcome a cleansing. But they persist—"Hey, this is for real, square business. The truth." I don't doubt that the horror tales are factual. I don't even doubt that ugly is a truth for somebody . . . somehow. But I'm not convinced that ugly is *the* truth that can save us, redeem us. The old folks teach that. Be triflin' and ugly and they say, "Deep down, gal, you know that ain't right," appealing to a truth about our deep-down nature. Good enough for me. Besides, I can't get happy writing ugly weird. If I'm not laughing while I work, I conclude that I am not communicating nourishment, since laughter is the most sure-fire healant I know. I don't know all my readers, but I know well for whom I write. And I want for them no less than I want for myself—wholesomeness.

MARGARET ATWOOD

(b. 1939)

RAPE FANTASIES

The way they're going on about it in the magazines you'd think it was just invented, and not only that but it's something terrific, like a vaccine for cancer. They put it in capital letters on the front cover, and inside they have these questionnaires like the ones they used to have about whether you were a good enough wife or an endomorph or an ectomorph, remember that? with the scoring upside down on page 73, and then these numbered do-it-yourself dealies, you know? RAPE, TEN THINGS TO DO ABOUT IT, like it was ten new hairdos or something. I mean, what's so new about it?

So at work they all have to talk about it because no matter what magazine you open, there it is, staring you right between the eyes, and they're beginning to have it on the television, too. Personally I'd prefer a June Allyson movie anytime but they don't make them anymore and they don't even have them that much on the Late Show. For instance, day before yesterday, that would be Wednesday, thank god it's Friday as they say, we were sitting around in the women's lunch room—the *lunch* room, I mean you'd think you could get some peace and quiet in there—and Chrissy closes up the magazine she's been reading and says, "How about it, girls, do you have rape fantasies?"

The four of us were having our game of bridge the way we always do, and I had a bare twelve points counting the singleton with not that much of a bid in anything. So I said one club, hoping Sondra would remember about the one club convention, because the time before when I used that she thought I really meant clubs and she bid us up to three, and all I had was four little ones with nothing higher than a six, and we went down two and on top of that we were vulnerable. She is not the world's best bridge player. I mean, neither am I but there's a limit.

Darlene passed but the damage was done, Sondra's head went round like it was on ball bearings and she said, "*What* fantasies?"

"Rape fantasies," Chrissy said. She's a receptionist and she looks like one; she's pretty but cool as a cucumber, like she's been painted all over with nail polish, if you know what I mean. Varnished. "It says here all women have rape fantasies."

"For Chrissake, I'm eating an egg sandwich," I said, "and I bid one club and Darlene passed."

"You mean, like some guy jumping you in an alley or something," Sondra said. She was eating her lunch, we all eat our lunches during the game, and she bit into a piece of that celery she always brings and started to chew away on it with this thoughtful expression in her eyes and I knew we might as well pack it in as far as the game was concerned.

"Yeah, sort of like that," Chrissy said. She was blushing a little, you could see it even under her makeup.

"I don't think you should go out alone at night," Darlene said, "you put yourself in a position," and I may have been mistaken but she was looking at me. She's the oldest, she's forty-one though you wouldn't know it and neither does she, but I looked it up in the employees' file. I like to guess a person's age and then look it up to see if I'm right. I let myself have an extra pack of cigarettes if I am, though I'm trying to cut down. I figure it's harmless as long as you don't tell. I mean, not everyone has access to that file, it's more or less confidential. But it's all right if I tell you, I don't expect you'll ever meet her, though you never know, it's a small world. Anyway.

"For *heaven's* sake, it's only *Toronto,*" Greta said. She worked in Detroit for three years and she never lets you forget it, it's like she thinks she's a war hero or something, we should all admire her just for the fact that she's still walking this earth, though she was really living in Windsor the whole time, she just worked in Detroit. Which for me doesn't really count. It's where you sleep, right?

"Well, do you?" Chrissy said. She was obviously trying to tell us about hers but she wasn't about to go first, she's cautious, that one.

"I certainly don't," Darlene said, and she wrinkled up her nose, like this, and I had to laugh. "I think it's disgusting." She's divorced, I read that in the file too, she never talks about it. It must've been years ago anyway. She got up and went over to the coffee machine and turned her back on us as though she wasn't going to have anything more to do with it.

"Well," Greta said. I could see it was going to be between her and Chrissy. They're both blondes, I don't mean that in a bitchy way but they do try to outdress each other. Greta would like to get out of Filing, she'd like to be a receptionist too so she could meet more people. You don't meet much of anyone in Filing except other people in Filing. Me, I don't mind it so much, I have outside interests.

"Well," Greta said, "I sometimes think about, you know my apartment? It's got this little balcony, I like to sit out there in the summer and I have a few plants out there. I never bother that much about locking the door to the balcony, it's one of those sliding glass ones, I'm on the eighteenth floor for heaven's sake, I've got a good view of the lake and the CN Tower and all. But I'm sitting around one night in my housecoat, watching TV with my shoes off, you know how you do, and I see this guy's feet, coming down past the window, and the next thing you know he's standing on the balcony, he's let himself down by a rope with a hook on the end of it from the floor above, that's the nineteenth, and before I can even get up off the chesterfield he's inside the apartment. He's all dressed in black with black gloves on"—I knew right away what show she got the black gloves off because I saw the same one—"and then he, well, you know."

"You know what?" Chrissy said, but Greta said, "And afterwards he tells me that he goes all over the outside of the apartment building like that, from one floor to another, with his rope and his hook . . . and then he goes out to the balcony and tosses his rope, and he climbs up it and disappears."

"Just like Tarzan," I said, but nobody laughed.

"Is that all?" Chrissy said. "Don't you ever think about, well, I think about being in the bathtub, with no clothes on . . ."

"So who takes a bath in their clothes?" I said, you have to admit it's stupid when you come to think of it, but she just went on, ". . . with lots of bubbles, what I use is Vitabath, it's more expensive but it's so relaxing, and my hair pinned up, and the door opens and this fellow's standing there . . ."

"How'd he get in?" Greta said.

"Oh, I don't know, through a window or something. Well, I can't very well get out of the bathtub, the bathroom's too small and besides he's blocking the doorway, so I just lie there, and he starts to very slowly take his own clothes off, and then he gets into the bathtub with me."

"Don't you scream or anything?" said Darlene. She'd come back with her cup of coffee, she was getting really interested. "I'd scream like bloody murder."

"Who'd hear me?" Chrissy said. "Besides, all the articles say it's better not to resist, that way you don't get hurt."

"Anyway you might get bubbles up your nose," I said, "from the deep breathing," and I swear all four of them looked at me like I was in bad taste, like I'd insulted the Virgin Mary or something. I mean, I don't see what's wrong with a little joke now and then. Life's too short, right?

"Listen," I said, "those aren't *rape* fantasies. I mean, you aren't getting *raped*, it's just some guy you haven't met formally who happens to be more attractive than Derek Cummins"—he's the Assistant Manager, he wears elevator shoes or at any rate they have these thick soles and he has this funny way of talking, we call him Derek Duck—"and you have a good time. Rape is when they've got a knife or something and you don't want to."

"So what about you, Estelle," Chrissy said, she was miffed because I laughed at her fantasy, she thought I was putting her down. Sondra was miffed too, by this time she'd finished her celery and she wanted to tell about hers, but she hadn't got in fast enough.

"All right, let me tell you one," I said. "I'm walking down this dark street at night and this fellow comes up and grabs my arm. Now it so happens that I have a plastic lemon in my purse, you know how it always says you should carry a plastic lemon in your purse? I don't really do it, I tried it once but the darn thing leaked all over my checkbook, but in this fantasy I have one, and I say to him, 'You're intending to rape me, right?' and he nods, so I open my purse to get the plastic lemon, and I can't find it! My purse is full of all this junk, Kleenex and cigarettes and my change purse and my lipstick and my driver's license, you know the kind of stuff; so I ask him to hold out his hands, like this, and I pile all this junk into them and down at the bottom there's the plastic lemon, and I can't get the top off. So

I hand it to him and he's very obliging, he twists the top off and hands it back to me, and I squirt him in the eye."

I hope you don't think that's too vicious. Come to think of it, it is a bit mean, especially when he was so polite and all.

"*That's* your rape fantasy?" Chrissy says. "I don't believe it."

"She's a card," Darlene says, she and I are the ones that've been here the longest and she never will forget the time I got drunk at the office party and insisted I was going to dance under the table instead of on top of it, I did a sort of Cossack number but then I hit my head on the bottom of the table—actually it was a desk—when I went to get up, and I knocked myself out cold. She's decided that's the mark of an original mind and she tells everyone new about it and I'm not sure that's fair. Though I did do it.

"I'm being totally honest," I say. I always am and they know it. There's no point in being anything else, is the way I look at it, and sooner or later the truth will come out so you might as well not waste the time, right? "You should hear the one about the Easy-Off Oven Cleaner."

But that was the end of the lunch hour, with one bridge game shot to hell, and the next day we spent most of the time arguing over whether to start a new game or play out the hands we had left over from the day before, so Sondra never did get a chance to tell about her rape fantasy.

It started me thinking though, about my own rape fantasies. Maybe I'm abnormal or something, I mean I have fantasies about handsome strangers coming in through the window too, like Mr. Clean, I wish one would, please god somebody without flat feet and big sweat marks on his shirt, and over five feet five, believe me being tall is a handicap though it's getting better, tall guys are starting to like someone whose nose reaches higher than their belly button. But if you're being totally honest you can't count those as rape fantasies. In a real rape fantasy, what you should feel is this anxiety, like when you think about your apartment building catching on fire and whether you should use the elevator or the stairs or maybe just stick your head under a wet towel, and you try to remember everything you've read about what to do but you can't decide.

For instance, I'm walking along this dark street at night and this short, ugly fellow comes up and grabs my arm, and not only is he ugly, you know, with a sort of puffy nothing face, like those fellows you have to talk to in the bank when your account's overdrawn—of course I don't mean they're all like that—but he's absolutely covered in pimples. So he gets me pinned against the wall, he's short but he's heavy, and he starts to undo himself and the zipper gets stuck. I mean, one of the most significant moments in a girl's life, it's almost like getting married or having a baby or something, and he sticks the zipper.

So I say, kind of disgusted, "Oh for Chrissake," and he starts to cry. He tells me he's never been able to get anything right in his entire life, and this is the last straw, he's going to go jump off a bridge.

"Look," I say, I feel so sorry for him, in my rape fantasies I always end up feeling sorry for the guy, I mean there has to be something *wrong* with them, if it was Clint Eastwood it'd be different but worse luck it never is. I was the kind of little girl who buried dead robins, know what I mean? It used to drive my mother nuts, she didn't like me touching them, because of the germs I guess. So I say, "Listen, I know how you feel. You really should do something about those pimples, if you got rid of them you'd be quite good looking, honest; then you wouldn't have to go around doing stuff like this. I had them myself once," I say, to comfort him, but in fact I did, and it ends up I give him the name of my old dermatologist, the one I had in high school, that was back in Leamington, except I used to go to St. Catharines for the dermatologist. I'm telling you, I was really lonely when I first came here; I thought it was going to be such a big adventure and all, but it's a lot harder to meet people in a city. But I guess it's different for a guy.

Or I'm lying in bed with this terrible cold, my face is all swollen up, my eyes are red and my nose is dripping like a leaky tap, and this fellow comes in through the window and *he* has a terrible cold too, it's a new kind of flu that's been going around. So he says, "I'b goig do rabe you"—I hope you don't mind me holding my nose like this but that's the way I imagine it —and he lets out this terrific sneeze, which slows him down a bit, also I'm no object of beauty myself, you'd have to be some kind of pervert to want to rape someone with a cold like mine, it'd be like raping a bottle of LePages mucilage the way my nose is running. He's looking wildly around the room, and I realize it's because he doesn't have a piece of Kleenex! "Id's ride here," I say, and I pass him the Kleenex, god knows why he even bothered to get out of bed, you'd think if you were going to go around climbing in windows you'd wait till you were healthier, right? I mean, that takes a certain amount of energy. So I ask him why doesn't he let me fix him a Neo-Citran and scotch, that's what I always take, you still have the cold but you don't feel it, so I do and we end up watching the Late Show together. I mean, they aren't all sex maniacs, the rest of the time they must lead a normal life. I figure they enjoy watching the Late Show just like anybody else.

I do have a scarier one though . . . where the fellow says he's hearing angel voices that're telling him he's got to kill me, you know, you read about things like that all the time in the papers. In this one I'm not in the apartment where I live now, I'm back in my mother's house in Leamington and the fellow's been hiding in the cellar, he grabs my arm when I go downstairs to get a jar of jam and he's got hold of the axe too, out of the garage, that one is really scary. I mean, what do you say to a nut like that?

So I start to shake but after a minute I get control of myself and I say, is he sure the angel voices have got the right person, because I hear the same angel voices and they've been telling me for some time that I'm going to give birth to the reincarnation of St. Anne who in turn has the Virgin Mary and right after that comes Jesus Christ and the end of the world, and he wouldn't want to interfere with that, would he? So he gets confused and listens some more, and then he asks for a sign and I show him my vaccination mark, you can see it's sort of an odd-shaped one, it got infected because I scratched the top off, and that does it, he apologizes and climbs out the coal chute again, which is how he got in in the first place, and I say to myself there's some advantage in having been brought up a Catholic even though I haven't been to church since they changed the service into English, it just isn't the same, you might as well be a Protestant. I must write to Mother and tell her to nail up that coal chute, it always has bothered me. Funny, I couldn't tell you at all what this man looks like but I know exactly what kind of shoes he's wearing, because that's the last I see of him, his shoes going up the coal chute, and they're the old-fashioned kind that lace up the ankles, even though he's a young fellow. That's strange, isn't it?

Let me tell you though I really sweat until I see him safely out of there and I go upstairs right away and make myself a cup of tea. I don't think about that one much. My mother always said you shouldn't dwell on unpleasant things and I generally agree with that, I mean, dwelling on them doesn't make them go away. Though not dwelling on them doesn't make them go away either, when you come to think of it.

Sometimes I have these short ones where the fellow grabs my arm but I'm really a Kung-Fu expert, can you believe it, in real life I'm sure it would just be a conk on the head and that's that, like getting your tonsils out, you'd wake up and it would be all over except for the sore places, and you'd be lucky if your neck wasn't broken or something, I could never even hit the volleyball in gym and a volleyball is fairly large, you know?—and I just go *zap* with my fingers into his eyes and that's it, he falls over, or I flip him against a wall or something. But I could never really stick my fingers in anyone's eyes, could you? It would feel like hot jello and I don't even like cold jello, just thinking about it gives me the creeps. I feel a bit guilty about that one, I mean how would you like walking around knowing someone's been blinded for life because of you?

But maybe it's different for a guy.

The most touching one I have is when the fellow grabs my arm and I say, sad and kind of dignified, "You'd be raping a corpse." That pulls him up short and I explain that I've just found out I have leukemia and the doctors have only given me a few months to live. That's why I'm out pacing the streets alone at night, I need to think, you know, come to terms with myself. I don't really have leukemia but in the fantasy I do, I guess I chose that particular disease because a girl in my grade four class died of it, the whole class sent her flowers when she was in the hospital. I didn't understand then that she was going to die and I wanted to have leukemia too so I could get flowers. Kids are funny, aren't they? Well, it turns out that he has leukemia himself, and *he* only has a few months to live, that's why he's going around raping people, he's very bitter because he's so young and his life is being taken from him before he's really lived it. So we walk along gently under the street lights, it's spring and sort of misty, and we end up going for coffee, we're happy we've found the only other person in the world who can understand what we're going through, it's almost like fate, and after a while we just sort of look at each other and our hands touch, and he comes back with me and moves into my apartment and we spend our last months together before we die, we just sort of don't wake up in the morning, though I've never decided which one of us gets to die first. If it's him I have to go on and fantasize about the funeral, if it's me I don't have to worry about that, so it just about depends on how tired I am at the time. You may not believe this but sometimes I even start crying. I cry at the ends of movies, even the ones that aren't all that sad, so I guess it's the same thing. My mother's like that too.

The funny thing about these fantasies is that the man is always someone I don't know, and the statistics in the magazines, well, most of them anyway, they say it's often someone you do know, at least a little bit, like your boss or something—I mean, it wouldn't be *my* boss, he's over sixty and I'm sure he couldn't rape his way out of a paper bag, poor old thing, but it might be someone like Derek Duck, in his elevator shoes, perish the thought—or someone you just met, who invites you up for a drink, it's getting so you can hardly be sociable anymore, and how are you supposed to meet people if you can't trust them even that basic amount? You can't spend your whole life in the Filing Department or cooped up in your own apartment with all the doors and windows locked and the shades down. I'm not what you would call a drinker but I like to go out now and then for a drink or two in a nice place, even if I am by myself, I'm with Women's Lib on that even though I can't agree with a lot of other things they say. Like here for instance, the waiters all know me and if anyone, you know, bothers me. . . . I don't know why I'm telling you all this, except I think it helps you get to know a person, especially at first, hearing some of the things they think about. At work they call me the office worry wart, but it isn't so much like worrying, it's more like figuring out what you should do in an emergency, like I said before.

Anyway, another thing about it is that there's a lot of conversation, in fact I spend most of my time, in the fantasy that is, wondering what I'm going to say and what he's going to say, I think it would be better if you could get a conversation going. Like, how could a fellow do that to a person he's just had a long conversation with, once you let them know you're human, you have a life too, I don't see how they could go ahead with it, right? I mean, I know it happens but I just don't understand it, that's the part I really don't understand.

1977

Margaret Atwood likes to call herself a storyteller rather than a writer of fiction. Her reason is that she sees a clear connection between her writing and the oral storytelling she grew up with.

"All literature, like music, is oral by nature":
Margaret Atwood

Think of a simple joke; now think of the same joke told, first well and then badly. It's the timing, isn't it? And the gestures, the embellishments, the tangents, the occasion, the expression on the face of the teller, and whether you like him or not. Literary critics talking about fiction may call these things style, voice and narrative technique and so forth, but you can trace them all back to that moment when the tribe or the family is sitting around the fire or the dinner table and the story-teller decides to add something, leave something out or vary the order of telling in order to make the story a little better. Writing on the page is after all just a notation, and all literature, like all music, is oral by nature.

Neither of my parents are writers, but both of them are very good story-tellers; and since they're both from Nova Scotia, I'd like to illustrate one kind of story. . . .

I used to hear around the dinner table when I was growing up. Anyone from rural Nova Scotia is well-steeped in what we now call the oral tradition but which they didn't call anything of the sort. Sometimes they called these stories "yarns"; sometimes they didn't call them anything. They were just things that had once happened.

For instance, there was the ingenious man who lived down around the South Shore and built a circular barn for his cows. The cows spent the night facing outwards, with their rear ends all facing inwards towards the centre of the circle, which made mucking out the barn more efficient. Each cow had its own door, and the doors, equidistant around the perimeter of the circle, were worked by a central pulley. Every morning people would gather from miles around to watch the cows being let out of the barn. At the sound of a horn, the doors would all fly upwards at once, and the cows, urged on by little boys with switches, would squirt out of the barn like drops from a lemon. Or so my father said.

GARRISON KEILLOR

(b. 1942)

THE TIP-TOP CLUB

The idea of pouring warm soapy water into overshoes and wearing them around the house to give yourself a relaxing footbath while you work is one that all fans of WLT's "The Tip-Top Club" seem to have remembered over the years, along with the idea that if you're depressed you should sit down and write a letter to yourself praising all of your good qualities, and the idea of puffing cigarette smoke at violets to prevent aphids.

Every evening, Sunday through Thursday, at 10:00 P.M. ("and now . . . direct from the Tip-Top studio in downtown Minneapolis . . ."), WLT played the Tip-Top theme song—

> Whenever you feel blue, think of something nice to do;
> That's the motto of the Tip-Top crew.
> Don't let it get you down, wear a smile and not a frown,
> And you'll be feeling tip-top too.

—and Bud Swenson came on the air with his friendly greeting: "Good evening, Tip-Toppers, and welcome to *your* show. This is your faithful recording secretary, chief cook and bottle-washer, Bud Swenson, calling the Club to order and waiting to hear from you." And of the hundreds of calls that came in on the Tip-Top line (847-8677, or T-I-P-T-O-P-S), and of the fifty or sixty that actually got on the air, many were from listeners who simply wanted Bud to know they were doing fine, feeling good, and enjoying the show. "And—oh, yes," they might add, "we got our boots on," referring to overshoes.

Every night, Bud got at least one request for a copy of the poem a woman had written about writing a letter to yourself. It was called "Dear Me," it was a hundred and eight lines long, WLT mailed out 18,000 copies of it in the six months after it was written (May 18, 1956), and it began:

> When I look around these days
> And hear blame instead of praise
> (For to bless is so much harder than to damn),
> It makes me feel much better
> To write myself a letter
> And tell myself how good I really am.
>
> Dear Me, Sorry it's been
> So long since I took pen
> In hand and scribbled off a word or two.
> I'm busy with my work and such,
> But I need to keep in touch
> Cause the very closest friend I have is you.
>
> Through times of strife and toil,
> You've always remained loyal
> And stuck with me when other friends were far,
> And because we are so close,
> I think of you the most
> And of just how near and dear to me you are.

As for puffing smoke at violets, it touched off a debate that lasted for years. For months after it was suggested by an elderly woman, Bud got call after call from listeners who said that smoke-puffing would *not* discourage aphids; that even if it would, there are *better* ways to discourage aphids; and, worse, that it might encourage young people to take up smoking.

The pro-puffers replied hotly that: (1) you don't have to *inhale* in order to *puff* on a plant; (2) the treatment should be given only once a week or so; and (3) anyone who wants to smoke probably will go ahead and do it *anyway,* violets or *no* violets.

As time passed, the issue became confused in the minds of some Tip-Toppers, who came to think that Bud himself was a smoker (he was not). To the very end (November 26, 1969), he got calls from listeners wanting to know if he didn't agree with them that smoking is a filthy habit. (He did.)

At Bud's retirement party, Roy Elmore, Jr., president of WLT, presented him with twenty-five potted violet plants, one for each year of service.

Controversy was the very thing that distinguished "The Tip-Top Club." It had none. Edgar Elmore, the founder of WLT, abhorred controversy, and the terms of his will bound his heir, Roy Jr., to abhor it also. Though Edgar never heard Bud's show, having died in 1940, eleven years before the Club was formed, he certainly would have enjoyed it very much, as Roy Jr. told Bud frequently. No conversation about religion or politics was permitted, nor were callers allowed to be pessimistic or moody on the air. If a person started in to be moody, he or she was told firmly and politely to hang up and *listen* to the show and it would cheer him or her up. Few had to be told.

Vacations and pets were favorite Tip-Top topics, along with household hints, children, gardening, memories of long ago, favorite foods, great persons, good health and how to keep it, and of course the weather. Even when the weather was bad, even in times of national crisis, the Tip-Toppers always came up with cheerful things to talk about.

One reason for the show's cheery quality and the almost complete absence of crank calls was Bud's phone policy. After the first year he never divulged the Tip-Top phone number over the air (nor, for that matter, over the phone). In fact, it was an unlisted number, and one could obtain it only from another Tip-Topper. This tended to limit participation to those who understood the rules and accepted them.

The main reason for the show's cheery quality was Bud himself and his radio personality. His voice wasn't deep but his style of speaking was warm and reassuring, and he always tried to look on the bright side, even as host of "The Ten o'Clock News" (starting July 1, 1944). On the newscast, Bud played up features and human-interest stories and he skimmed over what he called "the grim stuff." He might devote fifteen seconds to a major earthquake and three minutes to a story about a chimpanzee whose finger paintings had been exhibited at a New York gallery and fooled all the critics. His approach offended a few listeners ("the *New York Times* crowd," he called them), but most people liked it. Bud pulled in fifty or sixty fan letters a week, more than all other WLT newscasters combined.

Garrison Keillor   627

After reading a few headlines, he'd say, "Oh, here's something you might be interested in," and he'd tell about a dog that had actually learned to sing and sing on key, or read a story about the world's largest known tomato, or about a three-year-old kid who was a whiz at chess; and then he'd talk about a dog that *he* knew, or a kid *he* knew, or a tomato *he* had seen, and then he'd say, "Well, I don't know. Let me know what *you* think."

At first, some letters said, "What happened to the news?" but they quickly dwindled. ("Anger doesn't last," Roy Jr. said. "Only love is lasting. Angry people spout off once and then get over it. The people who love you are loyal to the end.") Most of the letters were about a story Bud had read: the letter writer described a similar experience that *he* had had, or quoted a poem or a saying that the story had reminded *her* of—and Bud made sure to read every one of those letters on the air. One day in the winter of 1950, Roy Jr. said, "It's time to close down the News. You need a new shingle."

According to Bud, the Tip-Top Club was the idea of a woman in St. Paul. "We love your show," she wrote in January 1951, "and feel that truly it is our show too. When I listen, as I do every night, I feel as if I am among friends and we are all members of a club that gathers around our radios. We share ideas and experiences, we inspire each other with beautiful thoughts, and I only wish I could meet personally every one of the wonderful people who also write to you, for when they write to you, they are truly writing to me also."

Bud read her letter on the air, and listeners responded favorably to the idea of a club. (Since he had often referred to his stories as "News-Toppers," Bud suggested the name Tip-Top Club and it stuck.)

Nobody at WLT quite remembers who came up with the phone idea. WLT had been doing remote broadcasts over telephone lines for years, starting with the "WLT Barn Dance and Bean Feed" in 1938; all that needed to be done to put a telephone signal on the air was wrap the bare end of one wire around the bare end of another. One night, Bud's engineer, Harlan, did just that, and a woman's voice came on describing dark thunderstorm clouds moving east toward Minneapolis.

"Is it raining there yet?" asked Bud.

"No," she said, "but it will be, any minute now. But I've got my boots on!"

Roy Jr. was leery of the phone idea from the start. "Every foul-mouth in town will be slobbering into his telephone for the chance to get on the air," he told Bud. "Every creep who writes on toilet walls, every dummy, every drunken son-of-a-bitch from hell to breakfast. We'll be running a nuthouse. We'll lose our license in a week."

Then Harlan came forward with his tape loop. Harlan was one who seldom cracked a smile, but when WLT bought its first tape recorders, two big Ampexes, in 1949, he was like a boy with a new toy. He recorded everything on tape, and he played around with it, and his favorite game was to play around with Bud's voice. At first, he got a kick out of playing Bud's voice at a faster speed so he sounded like a hysterical woman; then backward, which sounded like Russian; then slower, so Bud sounded drunk; and then Harlan became fascinated with editing Bud. With a razor blade in hand, Harlan went through thousands of feet of Bud tape, finding a word here and a word there, and a vowel sound here and a consonant there, making new words, and snipping and splicing hundreds of little bits of tape to form a few sentences spoken in Bud's own voice, in which Bud spoke, in his own warm and reassuring tones, about having carnal relations with dogs, cats, tomatoes, small boys, chimpanzees, overshoes, fruit jars, lawn mowers. It was disgusting, and also an amazing feat of patience. In two years, Harlan assembled just three minutes of Bud.

Harlan solved the problem of loonies by the simple trick of threading a continuous loop of tape through two machines sitting side by side. Bud and his telephone caller could be recorded on the first machine, which fed the tape to the second machine, which played it back on the air three seconds later. If the caller said something not befitting the show, Harlan, listening to the first machine, would have three seconds in which to turn off the second. "Can't beat it," said Harlan. "I hit the button and they die like rats."

Nevertheless, Roy Jr. was on hand for the first taped show and supervised the Stop button personally. "I trust you," he told Harlan, "but the way you talk, you might not notice profanity until it is too late." Bud explained the tape loop on the air and invited calls as Roy Jr. hunched over the machine, his finger in position, like a ship's gunner waiting for incoming aircraft. The first caller was a man who wanted to know more about the loop and if it might have useful applications in the home. He got flustered in mid-call and stopped. On his radio at home, he heard his own voice, delayed by tape, saying what he had said three seconds before. "Please turn your radio down," Bud said. It was a line that he was to repeat thousands of times in the next eighteen years.

"This has been an historic event," Roy Jr. said proudly when the show was over. He had cut off just two calls, the first one after the words "What in hell—" and the second at the mention of the Pope ("Probably nothing, but I wasn't about to take chances," he explained to Harlan).

Most of the calls were about the tape loop, with all callers favoring its use, howbeit with some trepidation that a mechanical failure or employee carelessness might lead to tragedy. Several were worried that certain persons might try to fool Bud, opening their calls with a few innocuous remarks and then slipping in a fast one. ("Thanks for the tip," said Bud. "I'm confident we can handle them.")

Communists, people agreed, might be particularly adept at subverting the tape loop. Communists, one man reported, learned these techniques at special schools, including how to insinuate their beliefs into a conversation without anyone being the wiser. ("Appreciate your concern, sir, and, believe me, we'll be on guard.")

It was three weeks before Roy Jr. turned over the guard duty to Harlan and Alice the switchboard girl. Alice was to screen all callers: no kids, no foreign accents, and nobody who seemed unusually intense or determined to get on the air. Harlan was the second line of defense. Roy Jr. instructed him to listen carefully to each call and try to anticipate what the caller was driving at; and if the conversation should drift toward deep waters—hit the button. No politics. No religion except for general belief in the Almighty, thankfulness for His gifts, wonder at His creation, etc. No criticism of others, not even the caller's kith and kin. Roy Jr. didn't want them to get dragged into family squabbles and maybe have to give equal time to a miffed husband or mother-in-law giving *their* side of it. No promotion of products, services, clubs, fund drives, or events.

"What's left to talk about?" Harlan wondered. "Not a goddamn helluva lot."

And, at first, the Tip-Toppers seemed unsure of what to talk about too. "Just thought I'd call and say hi," one would say. "Great. What are you doing tonight?" Bud would ask. "Oh, not much," the caller would reply. "Just sitting here listening to the show."

Gradually, though, they loosened up, and when Bud said to a caller, "Tell me about yourself," the caller generally did. Most Tip-Toppers seemed to be older persons leading quiet lives and keeping busy with hobbies and children and grandchildren, and, judging from the interest in household hints, their homes were neat as a pin and in good repair. They were unfailingly courteous ("The distinguished gentleman who spoke earlier on cats was very well-informed on most points, but I feel he may have overlooked the fact that cats will not shed if brushed regularly"), and soon Harlan was taking his finger off the button and relaxing in the control room and even leaving for a smoke now and then. The few nuts who called in Alice soon recognized by voice—she enjoyed talking with them, and after a few conversations they always asked for her and not for Bud. They sent her gifts, usually pamphlets or books but occasionally a box of cookies or a cake, which, on Harlan's advice, she did not eat. Three months went by, and not a single nut got past the loop; Roy Jr. raised Bud's salary and even gave him a contract—six months with an option of renewing for three more.

"It is so pleasant in this day and age when we are subjected to so much dissension and mud-slinging to take a rest and listen to a show that follows the old adage 'If you can't say something nice, don't say anything at all,'" a woman wrote to Bud. "I am a faithful listener-in and now have a telephone in my bedroom so that I can participate after turning in. I go to sleep listening to the show, and I believe I sleep better knowing it is there."

Sleep was a major item on the Tip-Top agenda: how much is needed? how to get it? what position is best? Many scorned the eight-hour quota as wasteful and self-indulgent and said four or five is enough for any adult. "The secret of longevity is to stay out of bed," said one oldster.

Most members disagreed; they felt they needed more sleep, and one call asking for a cure for insomnia would set off an avalanche of sleep tips—warm milk, a hot bath, a brisk walk, a brief prayer, a mild barbiturate —each of which had gotten the caller through some difficult nights. A doctor (he called in often, usually to settle somebody's hash on the value of vitamins, chiropractic medicine, and vegetarian diets) offered the opinion that worry causes 95 percent of all sleeplessness. He suggested that Tip-Toppers who go to bed with restless thoughts should fill their minds instead with pleasant memories and plans for vacations.

As for vacations, there were strong voices in the Club who argued that a Minnesotan's vacation money should be kept at home, not spent abroad. The rest of the world, it was said, could be seen perfectly well in the pages of the *National Geographic*. There was general agreement, however, that the purpose of a vacation is to rest and enjoy yourself and not necessarily to visit family members or to catch up on work around the house.

Housework was important, though, a sure antidote for grief and worry and feeling sorry for yourself. To scrub a floor or paint a wall or make a pie was better than going to a psychiatrist. At the same time, there was no use taking more time than necessary to get the job done, and every job had its shortcuts. "What's a quick way to get bubble gum out of hair?" a woman would ask, and minutes later, a legion of women who had faced that very problem would rally to her side. Give the Club a problem, and in short order the Club solved it, whether it be a wobbly table, a grape-juice stain, or a treacherous stair tread, and then it suggested two or three things you could do in the time you had saved, such as making lovely and useful gifts from egg cartons, Popsicle sticks, and bottle caps.

And then there were hobbies. Bud often asked callers, particularly the shyer ones, to talk about their hobbies. He *never* asked about their occupations, not after the first few times: the answers were always apologetic-sounding—"Oh, I'm just a truck driver," or "Oh, I just work for the Post Office." But ask someone what he did in his spare time and the answer might be good for five or ten minutes.

Club members tended to be collectors. It seemed as if every object of which there was more than one sort, type, shape, brand, color, or configuration was the object of some collector's affection. "I have matchbook covers from more than thirty-five countries." "Some of my fruit jars have been appraised at ten dollars and more." "I hope someday to open a license-plate museum." "I plan to donate my nails to the historical society."

Bird-watching, a sort of collecting, was also popular, and Bud had to put a damper on the bird people, they were so fanatical. One might call in and say, "I wonder if anyone out there can help me identify a bird I heard this morning. Its call sounded something like this—" and then whistle, "*twee-twee, twee-twee,*" and suddenly Alice was swamped with calls, some identifying the bird, some saying they had heard it too and didn't know what it was either, and others wondering if the bird's call perhaps wasn't more of a "*twee-it, twee-it.*"

Five nights a week, from 10:00 P.M. to sign-off, Bud sat in Studio B behind a table, the earphones clamped on, and scribbled notes on a pad as one Tip-Topper after another poured it out. After the first few months of the tape loop, he quit reading news stories, and after the Club had hit full stride, telephonically speaking, he himself said very little, aside from an occasional question. He became a listener. For eighteen years, from 1951 to 1969, he sat in the same chair, in the same position (slightly hunched, head down and supported with one hand, the other hand writing, feet on the floor), and heard the same stuff, until he seemed to lose whatever personality he had in the beginning. He became neutral. "A goddamn ghost," Harlan said. "When he comes in, I don't even see him anymore. He don't really exist, except on the air."

At the age of sixty-five, he quietly retired. He didn't mention his retirement on "The Tip-Top Club." Tip-Toppers didn't know he was gone until they tuned in one night and heard Wayne Bargy. Wayne was the only WLT announcer willing to take the show. Others had subbed for Bud before when he took vacations and they noted a certain snideness, a meanness, among the Tip-Toppers, who implied in their conversations that the new man, while adequate, was certainly no Bud. "Bud would *know* that," a caller might say. "Bud wouldn't have said that." "Maybe I'll talk to Bud about it. When is Bud coming back?"

So one night out of the clear blue it was "The Tip-Top Club with Wayne Bargy," and one can only imagine the shock that Bud's fans felt to hear a new theme song (Simon and Garfunkel's "Sounds of Silence") instead of the old Tip-Top song, and then Wayne Bargy delivering a tribute to Bud as if Bud were dead. He called him "an innovator" and "a genius" and "a man who was totally concerned about others." "I loved him," said Wayne. "He was a totally understanding, giving type of man. He was someone I could always talk to about my problems.

"Friends, I know you're as disappointed as I am that Bud won't be here with us anymore, and let me tell you, I'd give anything if he were, and I want to be honest with you and admit that I've never done this type of show before and I don't know how good I am at talking with people, and maybe some of you will even wonder what I'm doing in the radio business and I have to admit that you may have a point there, but I would rather be honest about this than sit here and pretend that I'm somebody that I'm not, because I think that honesty has a place in radio, I don't think a radio personality has to be some sort of star or an idol or anything, I think he can be a real person, and even if I should fail and would quit this show tomorrow, I'd still be satisfied knowing I had done it my way and not tried to be like somebody else."

The Tip-Toppers heard him out; there was a minute or so of lull at the switchboard (perhaps they were too dazed to dial, or else they were composing carefully what they would say); and then the first wave struck. Even Harlan was surprised by the abuse Wayne got.

First call: "Why wait until tomorrow? Why not quit tonight?" (Wayne: "Thanks for calling.") A man said, "Oh, don't worry that we'll consider you a star, Wayne. Don't worry about that for one minute!" (Wayne: "Okay, I won't.") A woman said it was the worst night of her life. (Wayne:

"It's hard for all of us.") "You make me absolutely sick. You're the biggest mistake they've made down there!" ("I appreciate your honesty, sir. I don't necessarily agree with that statement, but I think it's important that you feel you can be honest with me.")

By midnight, Wayne had logged almost a hundred calls, most of them quite brief and most cut off by Harlan. The longest exchange was with a woman who wanted to know where Bud was. Wayne said that Bud had retired.

> SHE: Then I'd like his number.
> HE: I'm sorry?
> SHE: I want Bud's phone number.
> HE: I—ma'am, I wish I could give you that but I can't, it's against company policy. We don't give out announcers' home numbers to the general public.
> SHE: Well, *I'm* not the general public. I'm Grace Ritter and he knows me even if you don't.
> HE: I'm sorry, but—
> SHE: And this is his show, and I think he has a right to know what you're doing to it! (CLICK)

During the midnight newscast, Roy Jr. called and told Wayne he was doing great. "I knew it'd be tough sledding the first night," he said, "but you stick in there. They're sore about Bud, but in three weeks they'll get tired and give up and all you'll get is flowers."

It didn't work that way. For one thing, Wayne had little interest in the old Tip-Top topics. He was divorced and lived in an efficiency apartment (no lawn to keep up, no maintenance responsibilities) and had no pets or children. His major interest was psychology. "People fascinate me," he said. ("You don't fascinate *me*," someone said.) He read psychology books and talked about them on the air. He said that he was undergoing therapy, and it had helped him to understand himself better. ("What's to understand?")

His other interests were eating out in foreign restaurants, attending films, and planning a trip to the Far East. ("How about leaving tomorrow?") Occasionally, he got a friendly caller who also liked Szechuan cuisine or Carl Rogers or Woody Allen movies, and he reached out and hung onto that call for dear life. Those calls would last for fifteen, twenty minutes, as if the caller were an old college chum he hadn't heard from in ages, but when he hung up, the Tip-Toppers were waiting, more determined than ever.

> THEM: This show is so boring. You talk about stuff that nobody but you is interested in.
> HIM: I really think you're mistaken about that, at least I hope you are, but more importantly, I think that I would have no business

being here if I *didn't* talk about things that interest me, because, when all is said and done, I do have to be myself.

THEM: That's the problem, Wayne. Yourself. You're dull.

HIM: Well, I grant you I'm not slick or polished, and I'm not a comedian, but that's not my job. Basically, I'm a communicator, and whatever my faults or failures in relating to people, I do try to be positive.

THEM: You're positively boring.

HIM: Well, let's talk about that. Define your terms. What do you mean by "boring"?

What they meant was Wayne Bargy. For all he said about keeping an open mind ("You got a hole in your head, Wayne!") and not condemning others but trying to understand people who may be different from ourselves ("You're different from everybody, Wayne! You're a different species!"), the Club kept a united front against him.

One night, Wayne casually mentioned that it was his first anniversary hosting the show. The switchboard sizzled. One man said it was time for Club members to take action, and before Harlan could cut him off he announced a time and a place for the meeting.

Word came back that the Tip-Toppers had elected officers and were putting together a mailing list for a monthly newsletter. It was said the Club was assigning members to "listening squads" with each squad assigned two hours of "Wayne duty" a week. The squad members were responsible for listening to the show and calling in frequently. The newsletter printed a list of things to say.

It was harder on Harlan than on Wayne. Harlan had started to assemble a special Wayne Bargy tape, but he had no time to work on it. What with Wayne giving out the phone number every fifteen minutes, the show was attracting oddballs, in addition to the legions of Tip-Toppers, and Harlan was cutting calls off the air by the dozens. One night, after Wayne had talked about his divorce (he said that he and his wife didn't "relate to each other sexually"), there passed a long half hour during which no call was fit to broadcast. "I was slapping them down like barnyard flies. We were up to our ears in crazies," said Harlan. "Finally, my fingers got sore, and Alice pulled the plug on the switchboard and her and me sat down and had a cup of coffee and left that poor dumb SOB sit and die by himself."

Wayne talked a long time that night. He said he'd had a typical middle-class upbringing until he went to college, which opened his mind up to new possibilities. He said he had gone into radio because it had tremendous possibilities for creative communication. This show was a tremendous opportunity to get people to open up their minds. He viewed himself as an educator of sorts.

"I'll be honest," he said. "The past year has been rough. There's a lot of anger and violence out there—and I don't say people shouldn't feel that way, but I do feel people should be willing to change. Life is change.

We all change. I've changed. Frankly, when I started doing this show, I didn't come off very well. I didn't communicate well. I had a hard time relating to working-class people. I think I've improved. I'm learning. I've put my feelings on the line, and I've benefited from it. I'm going to keep on trying."

He did keep on trying, and the Tip-Toppers kept calling—"We won't go away, Wayne!" they said, and he said, "I don't want you to go away. I want you to stay and let's get to know each other." That summer WLT did a survey that showed that most of the Tip-Top Club audience was over forty (72 percent), the least desirable age group to advertisers, and in July the station switched the Tip-Top slot to what it called "a modified middle-of-the-road pop-rock format" with a disc jockey who never talked except to give time, temperature, and commercials. His name was Michael Keske, but he never said it on the air.

1983

In the preface to Happy To Be Here, *the collection of stories from which "The Tip-Top Club" is taken, Garrison Keillor tells the story of his attempts to write a long, serious novel in which the characters seemed "vaguely ill and unhappy." The novel was never finished, but the stories embody much of what Keillor learned from his "heroes."*

"Three pages sharp and funny about the lives of geese": Garrison Keillor

Meanwhile, I wrote these stories.

I've been reluctant to collect them in a book because they were written in revolt against a book and out of admiration for a magazine, *The New Yorker,* which I first saw in 1956 in the Anoka Public Library. Our family subscribed to *Reader's Digest, Popular Mechanics, National Geographic, Boys' Life,* and *American Home.* My people weren't much for literature, and they were dead set against conspicuous wealth, so a magazine in which classy paragraphs marched down the aisle between columns of diamond necklaces and French cognacs was not a magazine they welcomed into their home. I was more easily dazzled than they and to me *The New Yorker* was a fabulous sight, an immense glittering ocean liner off the coast of Minnesota, and I loved to read it. I bought copies and smuggled them home, though with a clear conscience, for what I most admired was not the decor or the tone of the thing but rather the work of some writers, particularly *The New Yorker*'s great infield of Thurber, Liebling, Perelman, and White.

They were my heroes: four older gentlemen, one blind, one fat, one delicate, and one a chicken rancher, and in my mind they took the field against the big mazumbos of American Literature, and I cheered for them. I cheer for them now, all dead except Mr. White, and still think (as I thought then) that it is more worthy in the eyes of God and better for us as a people if a writer make three pages sharp and funny about the lives of geese than to make three hundred flat and flabby about God or the American people.

ALICE WALKER

(b. 1944)

EVERYDAY USE

---

for your grandmamma

I will wait for her in the yard that Maggie and I made so clean and wavy yesterday afternoon. A yard like this is more comfortable than most people know. It is not just a yard. It is like an extended living room. When the hard clay is swept clean as a floor and the fine sand around the edges lined with tiny, irregular grooves, anyone can come and sit and look up into the elm tree and wait for the breezes that never come inside the house.

Maggie will be nervous until after her sister goes: she will stand hopelessly in corners, homely and ashamed of the burn scars down her arms and legs, eying her sister with a mixture of envy and awe. She thinks her sister has held life always in the palm of one hand, that "no" is a word the world never learned to say to her.

You've no doubt seen those TV shows where the child who has "made it" is confronted, as a surprise, by her own mother and father, tottering in weakly from backstage. (A pleasant surprise, of course: What would they do if parent and child came on the show only to curse out and insult each other?) On TV mother and child embrace and smile into each other's faces. Sometimes the mother and father weep, the child wraps them in her arms and leans across the table to tell how she would not have made it without their help. I have seen these programs.

Sometimes I dream a dream in which Dee and I are suddenly brought together on a TV program of this sort. Out of a dark and soft-seated limousine I am ushered into a bright room filled with many people. There I meet a smiling, gray, sporty man like Johnny Carson who shakes my hand and tells me what a fine girl I have. Then we are on the stage and Dee is embracing me with tears in her eyes. She pins on my dress a large orchid, even though she has told me once that she thinks orchids are tacky flowers.

In real life I am a large, big-boned woman with rough, man-working hands. In the winter I wear flannel nightgowns to bed and overalls during the day. I can kill and clean a hog as mercilessly as a man. My fat keeps me hot in zero weather. I can work outside all day, breaking ice to get water for washing; I can eat pork liver cooked over the open fire minutes after it comes steaming from the hog. One winter I knocked a bull calf straight in the brain between the eyes with a sledge hammer and had the meat hung up to chill before nightfall. But of course all this does not show on television. I am the way my daughter would want me to be: a hundred pounds lighter, my skin like an uncooked barley pancake. My hair glistens in the hot bright lights. Johnny Carson has much to do to keep up with my quick and witty tongue.

But that is a mistake. I know even before I wake up. Who ever knew a Johnson with a quick tongue? Who can even imagine me looking a strange white man in the eye? It seems to me I have talked to them always with one foot raised in flight, with my head turned in whichever way is farthest from them. Dee, though. She would always look anyone in the eye. Hesitation was no part of her nature.

"How do I look, Mama?" Maggie says, showing just enough of her thin body enveloped in pink skirt and red blouse for me to know she's there, almost hidden by the door.

"Come out into the yard," I say.

Have you ever seen a lame animal, perhaps a dog run over by some careless person rich enough to own a car, sidle up to someone who is ignorant enough to be kind to him? That is the way my Maggie walks. She has been like this, chin on chest, eyes on ground, feet in shuffle, ever since the fire that burned the other house to the ground.

Dee is lighter than Maggie, with nicer hair and a fuller figure. She's a woman now, though sometimes I forget. How long ago was it that the other house burned? Ten, twelve years? Sometimes I can still hear the flames and feel Maggie's arms sticking to me, her hair smoking and her dress falling off her in little black papery flakes. Her eyes seemed stretched open, blazed open by the flames reflected in them. And Dee. I see her standing off under the sweet gum tree she used to dig gum out of; a look of concentration on her face as she watched the last dingy gray board of the house fall in toward the red-hot brick chimney. Why don't you do a dance around the ashes? I'd wanted to ask her. She had hated the house that much.

I used to think she hated Maggie, too. But that was before we raised the money, the church and me, to send her to Augusta to school. She used to read to us without pity; forcing words, lies, other folks' habits, whole lives upon us two, sitting trapped and ignorant underneath her voice. She washed us in a river of make-believe, burned us with a lot of knowledge we didn't necessarily need to know. Pressed us to her with the serious way she read, to shove us away at just the moment, like dimwits, we seemed about to understand.

Dee wanted nice things. A yellow organdy dress to wear to her graduation from high school; black pumps to match a green suit she'd made from an old suit somebody gave me. She was determined to stare down any disaster in her efforts. Her eyelids would not flicker for minutes at a time. Often I fought off the temptation to shake her. At sixteen she had a style of her own: and knew what style was.

I never had an education myself. After second grade the school was closed down. Don't ask me why: in 1927 colored asked fewer questions than they do now. Sometimes Maggie reads to me. She stumbles along good-naturedly but can't see well. She knows she is not bright. Like good looks and money, quickness passed her by. She will marry John Thomas (who has mossy teeth in an earnest face) and then I'll be free to sit here and I guess just sing church songs to myself. Although I never was a good singer. Never could carry a tune. I was always better at a man's job. I used to love to milk till I was hooked in the side in '49. Cows are soothing and slow and don't bother you, unless you try to milk them the wrong way.

I have deliberately turned my back on the house. It is three rooms, just like the one that burned, except the roof is tin; they don't make shingle roofs any more. There are no real windows, just some holes cut in the sides, like the portholes in a ship, but not round and not square, with rawhide holding the shutters up on the outside. This house is in a pasture, too, like the other one. No doubt when Dee sees it she will want to tear it down. She wrote me once that no matter where we "choose" to live, she will manage to come see us. But she will never bring her friends. Maggie and I thought about this and Maggie asked me, "Mama, when did Dee ever *have* any friends?"

She had a few. Furtive boys in pink shirts hanging about on wash-day after school. Nervous girls who never laughed. Impressed with her they worshiped the well-turned phrase, the cute shape, the scalding humor that erupted like bubbles in lye. She read to them.

When she was courting Jimmy T she didn't have much time to pay to us, but turned all her faultfinding power on him. He *flew* to marry a cheap city girl from a family of ignorant flashy people. She hardly had time to recompose herself.

When she comes I will meet—but there they are!

Maggie attempts to make a dash for the house, in her shuffling way, but I stay her with my hand. "Come back here," I say. And she stops and tries to dig a well in the sand with her toe.

It is hard to see them clearly through the strong sun. But even the first glimpse of leg out of the car tells me it is Dee. Her feet were always neat-looking, as if God himself had shaped them with a certain style. From the other side of the car comes a short, stocky man. Hair is all over his head a foot long and hanging from his chin like a kinky mule tail. I hear Maggie suck in her breath. "Uhnnnh," is what it sounds like. Like when you see the wriggling end of a snake just in front of your foot on the road. "Uhnnnh."

Dee next. A dress down to the ground, in this hot weather. A dress so loud it hurts my eyes. There are yellows and oranges enough to throw back the light of the sun. I feel my whole face warming from the heat waves it throws out. Earrings gold, too, and hanging down to her shoulders. Bracelets dangling and making noises when she moves her arm up to shake the folds of the dress out of her armpits. The dress is loose and flows, and as she walks closer, I like it. I hear Maggie go "Uhnnnh" again. It is her sister's hair. It stands straight up like the wool on a sheep. It is black as night and around the edges are two long pigtails that rope about like small lizards disappearing behind her ears.

"Wa-su-zo-Tean-o!" she says, coming on in that gliding way the dress makes her move. The short stocky fellow with the hair to his navel is all grinning and he follows up with "Asalamalakim,[1] my mother and sister!" He moves to hug Maggie but she falls back, right up against the back of my chair. I feel her trembling there and when I look up I see the perspiration falling off her chin.

"Don't get up," says Dee. Since I am stout it takes something of a push. You can see me trying to move a second or two before I make it. She turns, showing white heels through her sandals, and goes back to the car. Out she peeks next with a Polaroid. She stoops down quickly and lines up picture after picture of me sitting there in front of the house with Maggie cowering behind me. She never takes a shot without making sure the house is included. When a cow comes nibbling around the edge of the yard she snaps it and me and Maggie *and* the house. Then she puts the Polaroid in the back seat of the car, and comes up and kisses me on the forehead.

Meanwhile Asalamalakim is going through motions with Maggie's hand. Maggie's hand is as limp as a fish, and probably as cold, despite the sweat, and she keeps trying to pull it back. It looks like Asalamalakim wants to shake hands but wants to do it fancy. Or maybe he don't know how people shake hands. Anyhow, he soon gives up on Maggie.

"Well," I say. "Dee."

"No, Mama," she says. "Not 'Dee,' Wangero Leewanika Kemanjo!"

"What happened to 'Dee'?" I wanted to know.

"She's dead," Wangero said. "I couldn't bear it any longer, being named after the people who oppress me."

"You know as well as me you was named after your aunt Dicie," I said. Dicie is my sister. She named Dee. We called her "Big Dee" after Dee was born.

"But who was *she* named after?" asked Wangero.

"I guess after Grandma Dee," I said.

"And who was she named after?" asked Wangero.

---

1. A Muslim greeting sounded phonetically. Likewise, Wa-su-zo-Tean-o is an African greeting.

"Her mother," I said, and saw Wangero was getting tired. "That's about as far back as I can trace it," I said. Though, in fact, I probably could have carried it back beyond the Civil War through the branches.

"Well," said Asalamalakim, "there you are."

"Uhnnnh," I heard Maggie say.

"There I was not," I said, "before 'Dicie' cropped up in our family, so why should I try to trace it that far back?"

He just stood there grinning, looking down on me like somebody inspecting a Model A car. Every once in a while he and Wangero sent eye signals over my head.

"How do you pronounce this name?" I asked.

"You don't have to call me by it if you don't want to," said Wangero.

"Why shouldn't I?" I asked. "If that's what you want us to call you, we'll call you."

"I know it might sound awkward at first," said Wangero.

"I'll get used to it," I said. "Ream it out again."

Well, soon we got the name out of the way. Asalamalakim had a name twice as long and three times as hard. After I tripped over it two or three times he told me to just call him Hakim-a-barber. I wanted to ask him was he a barber, but I didn't really think he was, so I didn't ask.

"You must belong to those beef-cattle peoples down the road," I said. They said "Asalamalakim" when they met you, too, but they didn't shake hands. Always too busy: feeding the cattle, fixing the fences, putting up salt-lick shelters, throwing down hay. When the white folks poisoned some of the herd the men stayed up all night with rifles in their hands. I walked a mile and a half just to see the sight.

Hakim-a-barber said, "I accept some of their doctrines, but farming and raising cattle is not my style." (They didn't tell me, and I didn't ask, whether Wangero (Dee) had really gone and married him.)

We sat down to eat and right away he said he didn't eat collards and pork was unclean. Wangero, though, went on through the chitlins and corn bread, the greens and everything else. She talked a blue streak over the sweet potatoes. Everything delighted her. Even the fact that we still used the benches her daddy made for the table when we couldn't afford to buy chairs.

"Oh, Mama!" she cried. Then turned to Hakim-a-barber. "I never knew how lovely these benches are. You can feel the rump prints," she said, running her hands underneath her and along the bench. Then she gave a sigh and her hand closed over Grandma Dee's butter dish. "That's it!" she said. "I knew there was something I wanted to ask you if I could have." She jumped up from the table and went over in the corner where the churn stood, the milk in it clabber by now. She looked at the churn and looked at it.

"This churn top is what I need," she said. "Didn't Uncle Buddy whittle it out of a tree you all used to have?"

"Yes," I said.

"Uh huh," she said happily. "And I want the dasher, too."

"Uncle Buddy whittle that, too?" asked the barber.

Dee (Wangero) looked up at me.

"Aunt Dee's first husband whittled the dash," said Maggie so low you almost couldn't hear her. "His name was Henry, but they called him Stash."

"Maggie's brain is like an elephant's," Wangero said, laughing. "I can use the churn top as a centerpiece for the alcove table," she said, sliding a plate over the churn, "and I'll think of something artistic to do with the dasher."

When she finished wrapping the dasher the handle stuck out. I took it for a moment in my hands. You didn't even have to look close to see where hands pushing the dasher up and down to make butter had left a kind of sink in the wood. In fact, there were a lot of small sinks; you could see where thumbs and fingers had sunk into the wood. It was beautiful light yellow wood, from a tree that grew in the yard where Big Dee and Stash had lived.

After dinner Dee (Wangero) went to the trunk at the foot of my bed and started rifling through it. Maggie hung back in the kitchen over the dishpan. Out came Wangero with two quilts. They had been pieced by Grandma Dee and then Big Dee and me had hung them on the quilt frames on the front porch and quilted them. One was in the Lone Star pattern. The other was Walk Around the Mountain. In both of them were scraps of dresses Grandma Dee had worn fifty and more years ago. Bits and pieces of Grandpa Jarrell's Paisley shirts. And one teeny faded blue piece, about the size of a penny matchbox, that was from Great Grandpa Ezra's uniform that he wore in the Civil War.

"Mama," Wangero said sweet as a bird. "Can I have these old quilts?"

I heard something fall in the kitchen, and a minute later the kitchen door slammed.

"Why don't you take one or two of the others?" I asked. "These old things was just done by me and Big Dee from some tops your grandma pieced before she died."

"No," said Wangero. "I don't want those. They are stitched around the borders by machine."

"That'll make them last better," I said.

"That's not the point," said Wangero. "These are all pieces of dresses Grandma used to wear. She did all this stitching by hand. Imagine!" She held the quilts securely in her arms, stroking them.

"Some of the pieces, like those lavender ones, come from old clothes her mother handed down to her," I said, moving up to touch the quilts. Dee (Wangero) moved back just enough so that I couldn't reach the quilts. They already belonged to her.

"Imagine!" she breathed again, clutching them closely to her bosom.

"The truth is," I said, "I promised to give them quilts to Maggie, for when she marries John Thomas."

She gasped like a bee had stung her.

"Maggie can't appreciate these quilts!" she said. "She'd probably be backward enough to put them to everyday use."

"I reckon she would," I said. "God knows I been saving 'em for long enough with nobody using 'em. I hope she will!" I didn't want to bring up how I had offered Dee (Wangero) a quilt when she went away to college. Then she had told me they old-fashioned, out of style.

"But they're *priceless*!" she was saying now, furiously; for she has a temper. "Maggie would put them on the bed and in five years they'd be in rags. Less than that!" "She can always make some more," I said. "Maggie knows how to quilt."

Dee (Wangero) looked at me with hatred. "You just will not understand. The point is these quilts, *these* quilts!"

"Well," I said, stumped. "What would you do with them?"

"Hang them," she said. As if that was the only thing you *could* do with quilts.

Maggie by now was standing in the door. I could almost hear the sound her feet made as they scraped over each other.

"She can have them, Mama," she said, like somebody used to never winning anything, or having anything reserved for her. "I can 'member Grandma Dee without the quilts."

I looked at her hard. She had filled her bottom lip with checkerberry snuff and it gave her face a kind of dopey, hangdog look. It was Grandma Dee and Big Dee who taught her how to quilt herself. She stood there with her scarred hands hidden in the folds of her skirt. She looked at her sister with something like fear but she wasn't mad at her. This was Maggie's portion. This was the way she knew God to work.

When I looked at her like that something hit me in the top of my head and ran down to the soles of my feet. Just like when I'm in church and the spirit of God touches me and I get happy and shout. I did something I never had done before: hugged Maggie to me, then dragged her on into the room, snatched the quilts out of Miss Wangero's hands and dumped them into Maggie's lap. Maggie just sat there on my bed with her mouth open.

"Take one or two of the others," I said to Dee.

But she turned without a word and went out to Hakim-a-barber.

"You just don't understand," she said, as Maggie and I came out to the car.

"What don't I understand?" I wanted to know.

"Your heritage," she said. And then she turned to Maggie, kissed her, and said, "You ought to try to make something of yourself, too, Maggie. It's really a new day for us. But from the way you and Mama still live you'd never know it."

She put on some sunglasses that hid everything above the tip of her nose and her chin.

Maggie smiled; maybe at the sunglasses. But a real smile, not scared. After we watched the car dust settle I asked Maggie to bring me a dip of snuff. And then the two of us sat there just enjoying, until it was time to go in the house and go to bed.

1973

The contrast between the way that Dee and her mother view the world in "Everyday Life" comes largely from the differences between them in age, experience, and hardship. In a 1981 interview with Kay Bonetti, Walker discussed a somewhat comparable contrast of age and experience between two reknowned singers.

. . . But Bessie did have it harder, and did have it longer: Alice Walker

I was reading another book yesterday by Ellen Willis, who writes the rock column in *The New Yorker,* and for the *Voice*—the *Village Voice.* Here's a woman who has spent her whole life listening to rock and roll, and loves it, and knows every record ever cut, and so forth. And yet she talks about how it took her years and years and years and years to understand—because she played a Bessie Smith record over and over, and she played one of Bessie's songs called, I think, "Electric Chair Blues"—that Bessie was able to put more energy and more integrity and more substance in one line of that song than Janis Joplin was able to put in all the songs that she sang, and many of them of course were Bessie's songs.

Now why is that?

It certainly can't be said that Janis did not have energy, in her own struggle, you know. But Bessie did have it harder, and did have it longer, and had to really surmount, in her life, the things that really Janis succumbed to. I regret very much that Janis Joplin didn't live to be an old woman. Think of what she would have been able to sing, if she had been an old woman, singing.

LESLIE MARMON SILKO

(b. 1948)

LULLABY

The sun had gone down but the snow in the wind gave off its own light. It came in thick tufts like new wool—washed before the weaver spins it. Ayah reached out for it like her own babies had, and she smiled when she remembered how she had laughed at them. She was an old woman now, and her life had become memories. She sat down with her back against the wide cottonwood tree, feeling the rough bark on her back bones; she faced east and listened to the wind and snow sing a high-pitched Yeibechei song. Out of the wind she felt warmer, and she could watch the wide fluffy snow fill in her tracks, steadily, until the direction she had come from was gone. By the light of the snow she could see the dark outline of the big arroyo a few feet away. She was sitting on the edge of Cebolleta Creek, where in the springtime the thin cows would graze on grass already chewed flat to the ground. In the wide deep creek bed where only a trickle of water flowed in the summer, the skinny cows would wander, looking for new grass along winding paths splashed with manure.

Ayah pulled the old Army blanket over her head like a shawl. Jimmie's blanket—the one he had sent to her. That was a long time ago and the green wool was faded, and it was unraveling on the edges. She did not want to think about Jimmie. So she thought about the weaving and the way her mother had done it. On the tall wooden loom set into the sand under a tamarack tree for shade. She could see it clearly. She had been only a little girl when her grandma gave her the wooden combs to pull the twigs and burrs from the raw, freshly washed wool. And while she combed the wool, her grandma sat beside her, spinning a silvery strand of yarn around the smooth cedar spindle. Her mother worked at the loom with yarns dyed bright yellow and red and gold. She watched them dye the yarn in boiling black pots full of beeweed petals, juniper berries, and sage. The blankets her mother made were soft and woven so tight that rain rolled off them like birds' feathers. Ayah remembered sleeping warm on cold windy nights, wrapped in her mother's blankets on the hogan's sandy floor.

The snow drifted now, with the northwest wind hurling it in gusts. It drifted up around her black overshoes—old ones with little metal buckles. She smiled at the snow which was trying to cover her little by little. She could remember when they had no black rubber overshoes; only the high buckskin leggings that they wrapped over their elkhide moccasins. If the snow was dry or frozen, a person could walk all day and not get wet; and in the evenings the beams of the ceiling would hang with lengths of pale buckskin leggings, drying out slowly.

She felt peaceful remembering. She didn't feel cold any more.

Jimmie's blanket seemed warmer than it had ever been. And she could remember the morning he was born. She could remember whispering to her mother, who was sleeping on the other side of the hogan, to tell her it was time now. She did not want to wake the others. The second time she called to her, her mother stood up and pulled on her shoes; she knew. They walked to the old stone hogan together, Ayah walking a step behind her mother. She waited alone, learning the rhythms of the pains while her mother went to call the old woman to help them. The morning was already warm even before dawn and Ayah smelled the bee flowers blooming and the young willow growing at the springs. She could remember that so clearly, but his birth merged into the births of the other children and to her it became all the same birth. They named him for the summer morning and in English they called him Jimmie.

It wasn't like Jimmie died. He just never came back, and one day a dark blue sedan with white writing on its doors pulled up in front of the boxcar shack where the rancher let the Indians live. A man in a khaki uniform trimmed in gold gave them a yellow piece of paper and told them that Jimmie was dead. He said the Army would try to get the body back and then it would be shipped to them; but it wasn't likely because the helicopter had burned after it crashed. All of this was told to Chato because he could understand English. She stood inside the doorway holding the baby while Chato listened. Chato spoke English like a white man and he spoke Spanish too. He was taller than the white man and he stood straighter too. Chato didn't explain why; he just told the military man they could keep the body if they found it. The white man looked bewildered; he nodded his head and he left. Then Chato looked at her and shook his head, and then he told her, "Jimmie isn't coming home anymore," and when he spoke, he used the words to speak of the dead. She didn't cry then, but she hurt inside with anger. And she mourned him as the years passed, when a horse fell with Chato and broke his leg, and the white rancher told them he wouldn't pay Chato until he could work again. She mourned Jimmie because he would have worked for his father then; he would have saddled the big bag horse and ridden the fence lines each day, with wire cutters and heavy gloves, fixing the breaks in the barbed wire and putting the stray cattle back inside again.

She mourned him after the white doctors came to take Danny and Ella away. She was at the shack alone that day they came. It was back in the days before they hired Navajo women to go with them as interpreters. She recognized one of the doctors. She had seen him at the children's clinic at Cañoncito about a month ago. They were wearing khaki uniforms and they waved papers at her and a black ball-point pen, trying to make her understand their English words. She was frightened by the way they looked at the children, like the lizard watches the fly. Danny was swinging on the tire swing on the elm tree behind the rancher's house, and Ella was toddling around the front door, dragging the broomstick horse Chato made for her. Ayah could see they wanted her to sign the papers, and Chato had taught her to sign her name. It was something she was proud of. She only wanted them to go, and to take their eyes away from her children.

She took the pen from the man without looking at his face and she signed the papers in three different places he pointed to. She stared at the ground by their feet and waited for them to leave. But they stood there and began to point and gesture at the children. Danny stopped swinging. Ayah could see his fear. She moved suddenly and grabbed Ella into her arms; the child squirmed, trying to get back to her toys. Ayah ran with the baby toward Danny; she screamed for him to run and then she grabbed him around his chest and carried him too. She ran south into the foothills of juniper trees and black lava rock. Behind her she heard the doctors running, but they had been taken by surprise, and as the hills became steeper and the cholla cactus were thicker, they stopped. When she reached the top of the hill, she stopped to listen in case they were circling around her. But in a few minutes she heard a car engine start and they drove away. The children had been too surprised to cry while she ran with them. Danny was shaking and Ella's little fingers were gripping Ayah's blouse.

She stayed up in the hills for the rest of the day, sitting on a black lava boulder in the sunshine where she could see for miles all around her. The sky was light blue and cloudless, and it was warm for late April. The sun warmth relaxed her and took the fear and anger away. She lay back on the rock and watched the sky. It seemed to her that she could walk into the sky, stepping through clouds endlessly. Danny played with little pebbles and stones, pretending they were birds eggs and then little rabbits. Ella sat at her feet and dropped fistfuls of dirt into the breeze, watching the dust and particles of sand intently. Ayah watched a hawk soar high above them, dark wings gliding; hunting or only watching, she did not know. The hawk was patient and he circled all afternoon before he disappeared around the high volcanic peak the Mexicans called Guadalupe.

Late in the afternoon, Ayah looked down at the gray boxcar shack with the paint all peeled from the wood; the stove pipe on the roof was rusted and crooked. The fire she had built that morning in the oil drum stove had burned out. Ella was asleep in her lap now and Danny sat close to her, complaining that he was hungry; he asked when they would go to the house. "We will stay up here until your father comes," she told him, "because those white men were chasing us." The boy remembered then and he nodded at her silently.

If Jimmie had been there he could have read those papers and explained to her what they said. Ayah would have known then, never to sign them. The doctors came back the next day and they brought a BIA[1] policeman with them. They told Chato they had her signature and that was all they needed. Except for the kids. She listened to Chato sullenly; she hated him when he told her it was the old woman who died in the winter, spitting blood; it was her old grandma who had given the children this disease.

---

1. Bureau of Indian Affairs.

"They don't spit blood," she said coldly. "The whites lie." She held Ella and Danny close to her, ready to run to the hills again. "I want a medicine man first," she said to Chato, not looking at him. He shook his head. "It's too late now. The policeman is with them. You signed the paper." His voice was gentle.

It was worse than if they had died: to lose the children and to know that somewhere, in a place called Colorado, in a place full of sick and dying strangers, her children were without her. There had been babies that died soon after they were born, and one that died before he could walk. She had carried them herself, up to the boulders and great pieces of the cliff that long ago crashed down from Long Mesa; she laid them in the crevices of sandstone and buried them in fine brown sand with round quartz pebbles that washed down the hills in the rain. She had endured it because they had been with her. But she could not bear this pain. She did not sleep for a long time after they took her children. She stayed on the hill where they had fled the first time, and she slept rolled up in the blanket Jimmie had sent her. She carried the pain in her belly and it was fed by everything she saw: the blue sky of their last day together and the dust and pebbles they played with; the swing in the elm tree and broomstick horse choked life from her. The pain filled her stomach and there was no room for food or for her lungs to fill with air. The air and the food would have been theirs.

She hated Chato, not because he let the policeman and doctors put the screaming children in the government car, but because he had taught her to sign her name. Because it was like the old ones always told her about learning their language or any of their ways: it endangered you. She slept alone on the hill until the middle of November when the first snows came. Then she made a bed for herself where the children had slept. She did not lie down beside Chato again until many years later, when he was sick and shivering and only her body could keep him warm. The illness came after the white rancher told Chato he was too old to work for him anymore, and Chato and his old woman should be out of the shack by the next afternoon because the rancher had hired new people to work there. That had satisfied her. To see how the white man repaid Chato's years of loyalty and work. All of Chato's fine-sounding English talk didn't change things.

It snowed steadily and the luminous light from the snow gradually diminished into the darkness. Somewhere in Cebolleta a dog barked and other village dogs joined with it. Ayah looked in the direction she had come, from the bar where Chato was buying the wine. Sometimes he told her to go on ahead and wait; and then he never came. And when she finally went back looking for him, she would find him passed out at the bottom of the wooden steps to Azzie's Bar. All the wine would be gone and most of the money too, from the pale blue check that came to them once a month in a government envelope. It was then that she would look at his face and his hands, scarred by ropes and the barbed wire of all those years, and she would think, this man is a stranger; for forty years she had smiled at him and cooked his food, but he remained a stranger. She stood up again, with the snow almost to her knees, and she walked back to find Chato.

Leslie Marmon Silko   647

It was hard to walk in the deep snow and she felt the air burn in her lungs. She stopped a short distance from the bar to rest and readjust the blanket. But this time he wasn't waiting for her on the bottom step with his old Stetson hat pulled down and his shoulders hunched up in his long wool overcoat.

She was careful not to slip on the wooden steps. When she pushed the door open, warm air and cigarette smoke hit her face. She looked around slowly and deliberately, in every corner, in every dark place that the old man might find to sleep. The bar owner didn't like Indians in there, especially Navajos, but he let Chato come in because he could talk Spanish like he was one of them. The men at the bar stared at her, and the bartender saw that she left the door open wide. Snowflakes were flying inside like moths and melting into a puddle on the oiled wood floor. He motioned to her to close the door, but she did not see him. She held herself straight and walked across the room slowly, searching the room with every step. The snow in her hair melted and she could feel it on her forehead. At the far corner of the room, she saw red flames at the mica window of the old stove door; she looked behind the stove just to make sure. The bar got quiet except for the Spanish polka music playing on the jukebox. She stood by the stove and shook the snow from her blanket and held it near the stove to dry. The wet wool smell reminded her of new-born goats in early March, brought inside to warm near the fire. She felt calm.

In past years they would have told her to get out. But her hair was white now and her face was wrinkled. They looked at her like she was a spider crawling slowly across the room. They were afraid; she could feel the fear. She looked at their faces steadily. They reminded her of the first time the white people brought her children back to her that winter. Danny had been shy and hid behind the thin white woman who brought them. And the baby had not known her until Ayah took her into her arms, and then Ella had nuzzled close to her as she had when she was nursing. The blonde woman was nervous and kept looking at a dainty gold watch on her wrist. She sat on the bench near the small window and watched the dark snow clouds gather around the mountains; she was worrying about the unpaved road. She was frightened by what she saw inside too: the strips of venison drying on a rope across the ceiling and the children jabbering excitedly in a language she did not know. So they stayed for only a few hours. Ayah watched the government car disappear down the road and she knew they were already being weaned from these lava hills and from this sky. The last time they came was in early June, and Ella stared at her the way the men in the bar were now staring. Ayah did not try to pick her up; she smiled at her instead and spoke cheerfully to Danny. When he tried to answer her, he could not seem to remember and he spoke English words with the Navajo. But he gave her a scrap of paper that he had found somewhere and carried in his pocket; it was folded in half, and he shyly looked up at her and said it was a bird. She asked Chato if they were home for good this time. He spoke to the white woman and she shook her head. "How much longer?" he asked, and she said she didn't know; but Chato saw how she stared at the boxcar shack. Ayah turned away then. She did not say good-bye.

She felt satisfied that the men in the bar feared her. Maybe it was her face and the way she held her mouth with teeth clenched tight, like there was nothing anyone could do to her now. She walked north down the road, searching for the old man. She did this because she had the blanket, and there would be no place for him except with her and the blanket in the old adobe barn near the arroyo. They always slept there when they came to Cebolleta. If the money and the wine were gone, she would be relieved because then they could go home again; back to the old hogan with a dirt roof and rock walls where she herself had been born. And the next day the old man could go back to the few sheep they still had, to follow along behind them, guiding them, into dry sandy arroyos where sparse grass grew. She knew he did not like walking behind old ewes when for so many years he rode big quarter horses and worked with cattle. But she wasn't sorry for him; he should have known all along what would happen.

There had not been enough rain for their garden in five years; and that was when Chato finally hitched a ride into the town and brought back brown boxes of rice and sugar and big tin cans of welfare peaches. After that, at the first of the month they went to Cebolleta to ask the postmaster for the check; and then Chato would go to the bar and cash it. They did this as they planted the garden every May, not because anything would survive the summer dust, but because it was time to do this. The journey passed the days that smelled silent and dry like the caves above the canyon with yellow painted buffaloes on their walls.

He was walking along the pavement when she found him. He did not stop or turn around when he heard her behind him. She walked beside him and she noticed how slowly he moved now. He smelled strong of woodsmoke and urine. Lately he had been forgetting. Sometimes he called her by his sister's name and she had been gone for a long time. Once she had found him wandering on the road to the white man's ranch, and she asked him why he was going that way; he laughed at her and said, "You know they can't run that ranch without me," and he walked on determined, limping on the leg that had been crushed many years before. Now he looked at her curiously, as if for the first time, but he kept shuffling along, moving slowly along the side of the highway. His gray hair had grown long and spread out on the shoulders of the long overcoat. He wore the old felt hat pulled down over his ears. His boots were worn out at the toes and he had stuffed pieces of an old red shirt in the holes. The rags made his feet look like little animals up to their ears in snow. She laughed at his feet; the snow muffled the sound of her laugh. He stopped and looked at her again. The wind had quit blowing and the snow was falling straight down; the southeast sky was beginning to clear and Ayah could see a star.

Leslie Marmon Silko   *649*

"Let's rest awhile," she said to him. They walked away from the road and up the slope to the giant boulders that had tumbled down from the red sandrock mesa throughout the centuries of rainstorms and earth tremors. In a place where the boulders shut out the wind, they sat down with their backs against the rock. She offered half of the blanket to him and they sat wrapped together.

The storm passed swiftly. The clouds moved east. They were massive and full, crowding together across the sky. She watched them with the feeling of horses—steely blue-gray horses startled across the sky. The powerful haunches pushed into the distances and the tail hairs streamed white mist behind them. The sky cleared. Ayah saw that there was nothing between her and the stars. The light was crystalline. There was no shimmer, no distortion through earth haze. She breathed the clarity of the night sky; she smelled the purity of the half moon and the stars. He was lying on his side with his knees pulled up near his belly for warmth. His eyes were closed now, and in the light from the stars and the moon, he looked young again.

She could see it descend out of the night sky: an icy stillness from the edge of the thin moon. She recognized the freezing. It came gradually, sinking snowflake by snowflake until the crust was heavy and deep. It had the strength of the stars in Orion, and its journey was endless. Ayah knew that with the wine he would sleep. He would not feel it. She tucked the blanket around him, remembering how it was when Ella had been with her; and she felt the rush so big inside her heart for the babies. And she sang the only song she knew to sing for babies. She could not remember if she had ever sung it to her children, but she knew that her grandmother had sung it and her mother had sung it:

> The earth is your mother,
>   she holds you.
> The sky is your father,
>   he protects you.
> Sleep,
> sleep.
> Rainbow is your sister,
>   she loves you.
> The winds are your brothers,
>   they sing to you.
> Sleep,
> sleep.
> We are together always
> We are together always
> There never was a time
> when this
> was not so.

1981

The sense of place is very important in Leslie Marmon Silko's fiction. In an interview with Dexter Fisher, conducted on the Laguna Indian reservation where she grew up, Silko described her feeling that our ordinary way of thinking about geography fails to show the relation between the people and their landscape.

"A little bit better understanding of place": Leslie Marmon Silko

Fisher: What do you like to read?

Silko: Everything! I love Milton and Shakespeare, especially the tragedies. I don't have much patience with a lot of contemporary literature, because there's a lot of crap going around.

Fisher: Has there been any one major influence on your writing?

Silko: The major influence has been growing up around here and listening to people and to the way the stories just keep coming.

Fisher: Let's go back for a minute to the notion of context. It is obvious from your short stories that environment, particularly the landscape here at Laguna, is important. What do you think people should know about context before they read your stories?

Silko: Well, nothing really. I don't know. Maybe if there are words like *arroyo* that aren't clear, those could be explained. That's irritating. I used to get irritated with T. S. Eliot and all his Greek. I would wish that people would have a little bit better understanding of place, that in geography classes they would teach how people live in Bethel, Alaska, and Laguna, New Mexico, or Iowa City, etc. It's as if what you see on television takes the place of a geography class. Instead, in Bethel, people live without indoor plumbing, and there's one truck that comes around to deliver water and another one to pick up the waste products. What I would ideally wish for is that people had just a general familiarity, a sense of the history, when the Spaniards came in, just American history, for Christ's sake, but they don't. It can be turned around on us; for example, I don't think people here know much about New York subways. I think what's horrifying is that we're made to believe that the television lifestyle and geography are one, and we're really so diverse.

It's sad. Anyway, that's all my stories really need. Included in geography should be the way people live, some of their attitudes, their point of view, so if you have even just a smattering of Pueblo point of view, that helps. It's not much.

LEIGH ALLISON WILSON

(b. 1957)

THE RAISING

1

Of the eight matrons perched like pigeons around two identical card tables, Mrs. Bertram Eastman was the lone childless woman. Her husband, in whom—she was sure—the fault lay, only confounded this burden she'd borne for thirty years, fixing a funny look on his face every time the subject came up and saying, in a voice soft as solemnity itself, "Spare the child and spare the rod, Mrs. Eastman." But he was like that, a nitwit, and half the time she never knew what he was talking about. Still, being a woman of industry, Mrs. Eastman took up the slack of impotence by becoming an expert on children and motherhood. She was renowned in the gin rummy set, in the Daughters of the Confederacy set, and perhaps in the whole area of East Tennessee, renowned and widely quoted for her running commentary on child-rearing.

"A child is like a new boot," she'd say and pause with the dramatic flair of a born talker. "You take that boot and wear it and at first it blisters your foot, pains you all over, but the time comes it fits like a glove and you got a dutiful child on your hands." What she had missed in experience, Mrs. Eastman overcame with pithy insight; what she lacked as human collateral in a world of procreation, Mrs. Eastman guaranteed with sheer volume. She was a specialist in armchair mothering.

A steady hum of a general nature had settled over the women playing at both tables, punctuated by an occasional snap of a card, but like a foghorn in the midst of a desert the voice of Mrs. Eastman rose and fell in every ear. She was explaining, for the third time since seven o'clock, the circumstances that led to Little Darryl, the Melungeon orphan boy, who would come to live at her house the very next morning. A child! In her own home! She couldn't get over it. Her brain worked at the idea with a violence akin to despair turning upside-down and her hair, from some internal cue, dropped onto her forehead a large, stiff curl that flopped from side to side as if to let off steam. Mrs. Eastman, although not fat, was a formidable personage, stout and big-boned and not unlike the bouncer in a hard-bitten country bar. Mr. Eastman was the tiniest man in Hawklen County. Just yesterday he had come home and told her, out of the blue, that he was bringing Little Darryl out from Eastern State and into their home—one two three and like a bolt of electricity she was a mother. She couldn't get over it.

Little Darryl was thirteen years old and of "origin unknown," a poor abandoned charity case dumped from orphanage to orphanage since the day his faceless mother—unfit and unwed, Mrs. Eastman knew for a certainty—dropped him off in the middle of the canned-goods section of the Surgoinsville A&P. He was discovered beside the creamed corn, eating an unhealthy peanut butter and jelly sandwich. The "origin unknown" part delighted Mrs. Eastman: Little Darryl would be *her* child, sprung as mysteriously and as certainly into her care as a baby of her own making. O, she would make a lawyer out of him, distill the taint of his blood like meltwater. She would recreate the boy in her own image and watch him tower among men in her old age.

"Smart as a *whip*, the social worker told Mr. Eastman," Mrs. Eastman said in a loud, confidential voice. At her table were old Mrs. Cowan, the Methodist preacher's wife; Mrs. Jenkins, the wife of the Jenkins Hardware Jenkinses; and Mrs. Talley, wife of Hubert Talley, the local butcher. Mrs. Eastman had given each one advice, off and on, for thirty years, from Mrs. Talley's redheaded boy who was thirty years old and no good, right down to Mrs. Jenkins's six-year-old who still sucked her thumb and was a "mistake."

"You said that ten minutes ago, Eloise," Mrs. Jenkins told Mrs. Eastman, "and you said he was a genius before that." Mrs. Jenkins was playing North to Mrs. Eastman's South. "You said he was a genius that wasn't understood and you ain't even met him yet."

"Made him a lawyer already, too," said Mrs. Talley, looking calmly over Mrs. Jenkins's shoulder, her lips screwed up in concentration.

"Ida Mae Talley!" cried Mrs. Jenkins. "Put you in the East and straightway you cheat left and right."

"For your general information," Mrs. Eastman said and tossed her curl, like a hook, back up into her beehive hairdo, "for your edification, Little Darryl scored in the 'excessively bright' range on three different tests."

"I am most certainly not cheating," said Mrs. Talley. "I seen those kings three minutes ago."

"God loves all the little children, smart and stupid, black and white," old Mrs. Cowan said with a smile so bright that her lips appeared to retreat back into her gums. She was the simple-minded member of the women's club although, somehow, her children had grown up to be wildly successful bankers and businessmen in the county, as if to intimate that children, even life, were too muddled a factor to control entirely. For this reason old Mrs. Cowan said nothing that was really heard, did nothing that was really seen, and existed in the main as a hand in gin rummy, or as a how-de-do on the Methodist Church steps every Sunday morning. She was incapable of taking sound advice, given in good faith, by even the best of friends. Deep in her bowels Mrs. Eastman believed her to be the most wicked woman of her acquaintance, the most deceitful as well as the most dangerous, and to hold, somewhere behind her idiocy, a hidden ace in the hole.

"God may be well and good on Sundays," Mrs. Eastman said, leveling her eyes like shotgun bores toward old Mrs. Cowan's western position. "But God Hisself don't have to raise no boy geniuses at a moment's notice. Pass me one of those green mints, Vivian." She stretched her free hand toward Mrs. Jenkins. "The white ones give me the morning sickness."

"They come in the same box, Eloise. Green and white. In the same damn box." Mrs. Jenkins, whose mints and home provided this evening's entertainment for the club, shut her cards with a click, laid them carefully facedown on the table, then folded her arms like hemp cord and stared at Mrs. Eastman. She looked ready to pounce in panther fashion across the table, to defend her territory with a beast's wit. Mrs. Eastman had on her patient expression, the one she recommended for children with colic.

"I only meant to point out that I *read* somewheres that they put more dye in the white mints than they do in the green, that's all. They start out gray and add twice't the dye to turn them white. Scientific fact. Twenty schoolchildren alone have died in Detroit, Michigan, from a pound of white mints. Now think about *that*."

"All I know," said Mrs. Jenkins, rising clumsily from her chair, "is we've had these same mints for fifteen years and I never heard a word till now. I'm going to put whip cream on my Jell-O if you'll excuse me."

"I didn't read it till last week," Mrs. Eastman called over her shoulder, then she lowered her voice until only the whole room could hear: "Don't either of you tell a dead man, but she's on par*tic*ular edge tonight strictly because her boy was found pig drunk, with a hair ribbon in his mouth, underneath the II-E overpass. No clothes on him anywhere."

"O," said old Mrs. Cowan. "He was the finest acolyte our church ever had."

"No more he ain't," Mrs. Eastman said happily. "Comes of no discipline."

"Now, now," Mrs. Talley said, watching herself thumb through Mrs. Jenkins's cards. "You ain't exactly the one, Eloise"—here she paused to exchange one of her cards with one in the other pile—"you ain't exactly the one to pass judgment on a drunk, now are you?"

"Well, Mrs. Ida *Mae* Talley." Mrs. Eastman sneered on the "Mae." "Are you sinuating that my husband is a drunk?"

"That's for you to know, Eloise," she said, "and me to hear over coffee."

The truth of the matter was that, although Mr. Eastman sat in his law office with the door shut to clients and associates alike and drank corn whiskey from a Dixie cup, reading obscure poetry and even more obscure philosophy from dusty, dead-looking bindings, he was not a drunk. He was merely partial to alcohol, had told Mrs. Eastman more than once that he and whiskey were blood-related, on better terms with one another than anyone living or dead he'd ever known. Mrs. Eastman believed him through a rare faculty of reflexive apathy, a sixth sense she applied to all situations beyond her ken and control. Once, when Mr. Eastman brought home a litter of eight mongrel dogs, payment for services rendered from one of his poverty clients (who were the only ones he seemed to have, crowded into his office anteroom with chickens and moonshine and quart jars full of pennies clutched under their arms, the room always a three-ring circus to the point that each newly hired legal secretary had but to walk in the door before she quit and walked back out), Mrs. Eastman, in a reflex as immediate as a sneeze, stepped on the dogs' tails, ate the dogs' fur in her potatoes and greens, got nipped on the calves in the middle of dogfights, and she never knew the difference. The dogs existed only as the vaguest of doubts in her mind, much as the person and behavior of Mr. Eastman, and eventually, one by one, the dogs skulked emphatically from the premises and trotted off westward, as if in search of something that either would caress them passionately or kick them viciously. Leave bad enough alone, Mrs. Eastman always said, as well as, Never look a gifted horse in the mouth.

"Leave bad enough alone *I* always say," Mrs. Eastman told Mrs. Talley. "If I had a boy thirty year old and still at home, I wouldn't make no sinuations on nobody else."

"The best, O! O!" said old Mrs. Cowan, almost luringly. "The best acolyte we ever had."

Both women stared at her.

"Attention ladies!" Mrs. Jenkins called from the kitchen door. She held a tray of eight green Jell-O molds, each topped with pear-shaped smidgens of whipped cream. "Laura June here wants to say goodnight," she said. "Say goodnight, Laura June." Laura June, who was under the tray in her mother's hands, just stood and looked stupidly at the seven crooked smiles fastened maternally on the faces of the women's club. Under her arm showed the hind legs and tail of a tabby cat, and she wore a pink nightgown, hiked up at the waist from the furious squirms of the cat. Because her thumb was plunged up to the knuckle into her mouth, Laura June had difficulty saying goodnight, so she just stood and stared, stupidly, at all the smiles.

"That there is what I call a real teddy bear," Mrs. Talley said sweetly. "What's that there teddy bear's name, honey?"

Laura June turned her head in the direction of Mrs. Talley, squinting her eyes, and the cat, as though synchronized puppetlike to her movements, turned its head around and squinted at the women with two uneven green eyes that matched the color of the Jell-O. One of its eyes had an ugly yellow pustule on the rim, making the whole eye look like an open wound in the act of rankling. Laura June unplugged her mouth long enough to say "Name's Darryl Lee Roy," then she quickly plugged the thumb back, as if any second something more important might fall out into the open.

"Why isn't that just the cutest thing!" Mrs. Eastman cried and clapped her hands in the air over the card table. "Come over here, honey, Mama Eastman has a secret for you." Laura June stayed put; the cat blinked its eyes and only one of them opened again. It appeared to be winking suggestively at Mrs. Eastman. "I have a little boy coming to my house that has the very same name," she said. "Little Darryl."

"Time for Laura June to go to bed," said Mrs. Jenkins. "Go to bed, Laura June." Laura June turned obediently toward a door across the room and stalked stiff-legged across the wooden slats with the cat's head bouncing behind her like a gibbous growth. At the door she stopped, facing the room, and caught Mrs. Eastman's eye. There was an expression of malignancy on her face. She dropped the thumb and the hand wandered with a will of its own to the side of her face where it started to scratch a cheek. It might have been a large, pink spider dropped incredibly there to spin a cobweb.

"It's a lie!" she shouted abruptly and the cat meowed and then both were gone into the dark recesses of the house.

2

The mountains spliced at the southernmost tip of the city limits, then diverged northward to form the east and west boundaries of Hawklenville where Mr. Bertram Eastman lived. An ambitious person could climb to the top of that southern splice—named Devil's Nose by the first Methodist settlers—could sit on one of the numerous granite slabs found there, and he would notice that the town appears to be a discolored blemish in the middle of a dark green arrowhead. If that person were ambitious indeed, he would climb a tree and see the land beyond the mountains, land welling out for miles, green with tobacco, brown with freshly tilled soil, and still farther, the cusp of something huge and dusky-blue. But he would see no people. Though these mountains were the town's sole measure of eminent height, a stranger well-versed in the world would point out that they were only foothills, mere knurls in the great body of the Appalachians. Still, from their summits, one could see no people. They are *that* high, Mr. Eastman often said, but quietly and mostly to himself, they are high enough.

From his small back porch, or from what might have been a porch had he chosen to call it one, preferring the word *veranda* because it "sounded like a sigh," Mr. Eastman was watching the last tendrils of light skid away over the top of the mountains. Mr. Eastman, a man not balding but bald, sat in a plastic lawn chair and sipped corn whiskey from a Dixie cup. His shoulders cocked slightly forward and his head tilted slightly backward, giving him the appearance (as the more flexible gossips of the town were quick to mimic) of neither coming nor going. At the moment, though, he was poised over a precipice, at the edge of something, and somehow the boy, Little Darryl, was the nub to which his mind clung. Tomorrow he would come and tomorrow something—he didn't know what—something would happen, for tomorrow Little Darryl would come.

Beads of sweat, tiny as dewdrops, eased from the crown of his head and slid unhindered down the back of his neck. So quickly did they fall, and so brazenly, they could have been the tears of a brokenhearted old woman too tired for pretense. Night had fallen and the mountains crouched against the sky, darker even than the night.

Experience had taught Mr. Eastman that the mountains themselves were deceptive, mute purveyors of nothing but bulk. To the tourist, as he had been when he first brought his wife to the town, they were beautiful, rumpled across the horizon like an immense and living snake. He recalled an incident from those earlier days. They had been walking down Main Street, he and his newly-wed wife, he arm in arm with a woman who was so striking and so lovely, all the more so because of her height and his lack of it, that he thought he might be crushed under the weight of his own pride. They had walked in silence for many minutes, nodding sociably at the passerby, when he noticed the mountains around them, as though for the first time.

"They are like a great undulating serpent, Eloise," he told her, and he was trying to profess his love for her and for their new home. Her eyes almost the color of ripe raspberries, she looked first at the mountains, then down at him, and she stared into his face with an expression that may have been utter tenderness. At last she fluttered her eyelashes and, looking vaguely toward the mountains, said: "Do tell." The mountains were no longer beautiful to Mr. Eastman, hadn't been perhaps from the incident on: and neither was his wife. No longer did he see the mountains surge upward as living things, no longer was the town, nor the county of Hawklen, a place where north and south and west and east converged into only one thing: the place to be. He had been deceived.

This boy, this Little Darryl, would be his salvation.

"Yoo-hoo!" came his wife's voice through the entranceway, through the hallway, through the kitchen and onto the back veranda where he started, like a frightened sparrow, in the lawn chair. "I'm home!"

Mr. Eastman bent down and set his Dixie cup on the floor, then he placed his hands, one grottoed in the bowl of the other, into his lap. Patiently, keenly, like a man for whom time was as yet unborn, he waited to be found out by his wife. An excess of amplified noise, her greeting was meant for the house and not for him, but in a short time she would work her way through every room until she found him out. She was tenacious in that way, could find anything lost, stolen, or converted, except the truth. She had a gift of activity at its most inessential whereabouts, a kind of feverish sprinting in place that left her wrung-out and triumphant and as blind as a newt. Mr. Eastman believed he was safe from her, his wife of thirty years, because, when you got right down to it, she didn't know shit from apple butter; and without distinctions the rage to live was merely a delirious murmur. Despite the sounds of a bull ox, Mrs. Eastman, he felt, was a murmurer.

"*There* you are," Mrs. Eastman said and poked her head between the screen door and the door frame. It hung there in space like a giant full moon whose face had a coarse, sketchy expression. The least cloud would obscure any resemblance to humanity it may have had. Or so it seemed to Mr. Eastman who sat quietly with his hands in his lap.

"Here I am," Mr. Eastman said.

Here and there across the backyard a group of crickets screeched to one another in duets, in off-beat duets, in those insistent and eerie cries of utterly invisible creatures involved in communication. *Cheezit!* they said. *Cheezit!*

"Listen to those bugs," Mrs. Eastman said and stepped onto the veranda. She let the screen door slam shut behind her, its springs squealing, and the crickets paused for a measure, then started back up again. With her hands fastened securely onto her hips, elbows akimbo, she peered out into the backyard in order to pin down the source of the sound coming from everywhere and nowhere. "I declare they sound like they're in painful love. Bugs do fall in love and set up house together just like anybody. It's nature is what it is." Mr. Eastman said nothing and sat tight, as if he were just hanging in a closet without any insides; he wanted to pat his wife kindly on the cheek or else smack her very hard in the middle of her face. But he did nothing at all, could have been dead except for the heart pounding madly between the places he breathed.

"Buddy Ruth Quarles run off this morning with that retarded taxicab driver. Took almost everything they owned. In case you're interested." She slapped and killed a periwinkle green insect, then continued on in a cheerful tone. A dollop of hair ticked coquettishly onto her forehead. "Took the TV, took the radio, took the silverware. Took the sofa and the phonograph. Took ever light bulb in the house. Didn't take that half-grown boy of hers. Last anybody saw of Mr. Quarles, he took off down II-E with a butcher knife, wearing a pair of socks and green pants. He had to borrow the butcher knife. Mr. Eastman, are you listening to me?"

"No, Mrs. Eastman," he said. "I am not."

"Ida Mae said she hadn't known the taxicab driver but three weeks, and him so simple to begin with. They did it with a U-Haul hitched to the taxicab."

"Mrs. Eastman," said Mr. Eastman.

"Can't figure out, though, what she *sees* in him. He had that wart in the corner of his eye. Puckered and bobbed ever time he opened his mouth. I can't figure it. And him so simple too."

Mr. Eastman reached for his Dixie cup, squinting out into the night settled over his yard. It appeared to him to be the inside of a huge windowless box set on its side out in the middle of nowhere. The stars, pricking out relentlessly, didn't fit into his picture.

"I foretold it long ago. Time and again I said, If he don't kill her first, he won't never know where she'll be or what she's doing there. I foretold it twice in the past two years. If she's not six feet under, I said, no telling where she is. There you have it."

"Perhaps she's happy, Mrs. Eastman."

"Well *I like that!*" Mrs. Eastman cried and stomped three paces to the edge of the veranda, then stomped the three paces back. She was furious, looking at him as she might at some bear who still hibernated in the chafe of summer, and her hair bristled like burs along the top of her head. "Happy, Mr. Eastman, is what those bugs have. Any *nor*mal human being might know that already. Any *nor*mal human being might know that happy is a word the government made up. What will our son think? I'll tell you what he'll think, he'll think his daddy's shoes are too little to grow into, that's what. You'll be a stigmatism to him all the days of his life!"

Again, Mr. Eastman sat tight. Thought and action in his wife, usually by tongue but sometimes otherwise, were almost simultaneous in her, rather like thunder and lightning, and Mr. Eastman was forever surprised by the coincidence. For him there was by necessity a gap between the two, first deep thought and much later decisive action. And it was true: it had taken him thirty years to secure a son.

"Do you hear me, Bertram Eastman?" she asked. Stomping up and back, her hair at loose ends, her shadow stomping crabbed and backward behind her through the light from the house, she made Mr. Eastman want to shout; want to scream out madly; made him want to take the box of his backyard and the night and his wife and fling the whole of them over that impenetrable black scar of the mountains. Instead he said absolutely nothing and, too, the silence within him grew absolute.

"Do you *hear* me?"

"I hear you very well, Mrs. Eastman."

"Our son is a responsibility. He's a responsibility for bad and for worse, for sickness and disease, forever and forever, till the dead do us part. He's responsibility is what this boy's made of."

"I know what little boys are made of," he said, raising himself to leave. So soaked with sweat was the back of his collar that it crept toward his collarbone and felt like a cold hand at his throat. Out in the yard the crickets seemed to have gone mad in the interim of their conversation. *Cheezit! cheezit! cheezit!* they sang. Chee-*zit!* If his wife said anything, he couldn't hear her for the crickets.

3

Little Darryl's people, the Melungeons, came from Goins Hollow, a cul-de-sac at the base of Devil's Nose from whence there was only one exit: a deep green bottleneck steeped in poison ivy and ridden with underbrush and so utterly hidden that the inhabitants themselves were known to leave and never return, set suddenly adrift in the outside world. Brown-eyed and maize-colored, they wedlocked themselves, cheated on themselves, coalesced with abandon, and produced either geniuses or idiots. They had no in-betweens. They loved each other or they killed each other, and still they endured in Goins Hollow; their endurance preceded the first Methodist settlers by many hand-counted years. On a vivid autumn day the smoke of their fires, beckoning upward like unformed fingers, was clearly visible from the town of Hawklenville, but not one soul in Hawklenville ever looked at it.

The Melungeon blood, although not their experience, was fecund as a loam in the body of Little Darryl, the orphan, and by the age of five he knew the appetites of a very old man. He knew when to lie outright and when to tell a lie honestly, when to cheat and when to win fairly. He knew when to be given and when to steal someone blind. He even knew when to attack a problem face-forward, and when to beat a noble retreat into the next county. He was thirteen years old, of a conspicuous unknown origin, and he had lived in nine separate orphanages, one of which burned down mysteriously.

"They got the papers that's stuck to me," Little Darryl told the orphan boys who sat roosting on the next cot, "and there ain't nothing but for me to go with them. They got the papers."

"You could burn them papers," suggested the littlest boy, writhing himself in embarrassment so that the row of boys tilted sideways like a wave washing through. Each little boy had a scar of some kind on some part of his body, and each boy loved Little Darryl with a passion that drew blood. He had seen to that.

"You would, would you," said Little Darryl and leaned over and flipped the littlest boy's nose until he bellowed out. "They got the machines that can resurrect a million a me. You burn one paper and they make ten more. You burn ten papers and they fill a library with them. You burn down a library and they fill the whole shittin' world with paper. They got you up one side and down the other."

"You could run away from here," a boy with a cauliflower ear said, "could run to Kingdom Come from here."

The littlest boy sniffed and said: "That's what I meant back then."

"I already done that once't," Little Darryl said. "They come at me with three cop cars and six guns. They had the papers that's stuck to me. The highest mountain and the lowest hole, they got you if they got them papers that they think is you."

"*I* don't have no papers on *me*," said the boy with a cauliflower ear. He let out a yell and thumped his chest to prove himself. All the little boys fell to scuffling, then they cheered and the cot skittered a few inches along the floor.

"It's because you ain't never done nothing worth the proving of it," Little Darryl said and smacked the boy on his cauliflower ear. They all settled down after that.

"These here people I ain't never seen nor seen their house might think they know what my paper says, but they don't know me. I reckon I got the upper hand under them, I reckon I know who I am." Little Darryl puffed himself up with air, standing slack-kneed on the bed with his shoes on. "I seen worse predicaments." The little boys stared up at him with the expressions of crows strung on a telephone wire. They flapped their arms and stared. "I seen the worser and the worst and they's nothing I seen that could make me forget myself in it. Pain's nothing to the forgetting yourself from it. I know who I am."

"Darryl!" cried the social worker. "Get your shoes off that bed and on the floor." She had on a pink polyester pantsuit that clung to her legs and gave the appearance of a second skin shedding off from the waist down.

"Boooo," said all the little boys, punching each other.

"It's my bed," Little Darryl said. "I'll stand on my own bed with anything on."

"You go home today and you know it. Effective at seven o'clock A.M. it wasn't your bed any more."

"I'll stand on anybody's bed with anything on."

"Let's go," the social worker said grimly. With her free arm cocked in a triangle just above her waist, she held open the door and looked as if the least movement would make her pants disappear. The little boys waited expectantly, booing softly.

"I seen worse than you look on Monday morning," said Little Darryl and got down off the bed. The little boys cheered, scuffled, grew into a wad of arms and legs on top of the cot. At the door Little Darryl looked back into the dormitory room, then he spat viciously on the floor.

"I seen even worser," he said, but the little boys, scuffling, didn't look up again.

4

"Excessively bright! Excessively bright!" Mrs. Eastman sang aloud, scattering motes of dust helter-skelter with her mud-colored featherduster. The dust settled down again just inches ahead of Mrs. Eastman's movement across the table. "O my boy, O yes *my* boy, O he is ex—*press*—ive—ly—bright!"

Up at cock's crow that morning (the cock one of Mr. Eastman's poverty payments), Mrs. Eastman rampaged through the dawn inside her house with a vengeance and a joy. She had attacked her floors and her ceilings, her walls, her knickknacks. She'd made, then unmade, then made again her beds. She did the same with Little Darryl. First he was a lawyer, then he was a president, then he was a brain surgeon. Nothing suited. She couldn't get over it, she was electrified. And when the doorbell rang she thought she'd liked to have had a heart murmur. With the hand that held the duster pressed against her chest, she prayed to God and sneezed violently. Dust floated everywhere like tiny messengers. A feeling came to her, at the base of her spine, and it said, Practice makes perfect! Pretty is as pretty does! These were the exact sentiments she had expressed, intuitively, to the women's club off and on for thirty years: real mothering would be her forte. She sneezed once more and felt powerful.

By the second ring from the doorbell Mrs. Eastman was prepared, so much so that when she opened the door she had on her wisdom expression, the one she recommended for children with homesickness. On her porch stood a pair of pink polyester pants and Little Darryl, who wore an oversized Prince Albert coat, collar turned up, and a brown fedora hat, brim turned down. His eyes peeped out from under his hat as though from inside a tank turret. Mrs. Eastman said the first thing to come to her mind.

"I didn't know he was such a colored child," she said and smiled maternally. The eyes inside the hat seemed to look through Mrs. Eastman and onto the entranceway carpet. "I could've mistook you for a pickaninny, little boy," she said sweetly.

"They's two people said that to me before and lived," said Little Darryl.

"I'll be running right along," the social worker told Mrs. Eastman, "if you'll just sign these documents. I already stopped by your husband's office."

"The outside of it looked more like one of them goddamn saloons to me," Little Darryl snarled, spitting through his teeth at a fly on the porch. "Smell't of it, too."

"We don't curse in this home, Darryl. We are gentlemen and ladies in this home. Gentlemen and ladies don't curse or spit."

He looked at her, his eyes slightly askew.

"Sign here," said the social worker, and Mrs. Eastman did.

"You might think that's me right there," Little Darryl said through his teeth. Mrs. Eastman could have sworn it came from the paper itself. "But I know where I stand."

"Why of course you do!" Mrs. Eastman cried. "You're on the doorstep of your very own home!" She gave Little Darryl a hug, agitated by the goodness welling inside her like a carbonation, and he stood stiffly as a hanged man.

"From now on you touch me by permission," he said out of a corner of his mouth.

When they looked up the social worker was long gone.

"Food," said Mrs. Eastman. "You must be hungry, little boys are always hungry. They are hungry until they reach the age of twenty and then they are modern afterward."

"I've eat but I could do it again if it was a roast beef with string beans."

Without another word Mrs. Eastman clucked and herded Little Darryl into the kitchen of her house. On his way he picked up two china cats, pilfering them into the pocket of his Prince Albert. A look of sublime pleasure, which Mrs. Eastman mistook for good adjustment, showed above the coat collar. He sidled up to a kitchen window, gazed sullenly onto the backyard with a hooded pucker around his eyes.

"Gentlemen don't wear hats on in their homes," said Mrs. Eastman. Her hands gripped and sliced on the roast as if performing an emergency operation on a still-live body.

"Lady," said Little Darryl, his eyes directed toward the backyard.

"I don't like you. I don't like your house, I don't like your husband. The onliest thing to keep me from the murder of you is if'n you pretend you don't see hear smell feel nor taste me. Do you understand me in that head a hair?"

"But I'm your mother." Mrs. Eastman paused, an expression of some awful recognition shrouding her nose and eyes and mouth. "Pretty is as pretty does," she said.

"You're nuts," he said, "and my mother was a thought my daddy thought for about three seconds. Serve me that roast beef with ketchup on it." He sat down at the table, pulling out a jackknife; the silver spoon and knife already on a place mat, he put in his pocket. He left the fork where it was.

"God loves all the little children," Mrs. Eastman said and her voice sounded very far away. "Black and white, smart and stupid."

"Serve it with ketchup and some mayo on the side, lady." In a rapid, choppy movement Little Darryl flipped open the jackknife and let the blade hang, for an instant, in the air like an unkept promise. "That God of yourn loves because they got the papers on Him a million years ago. You don't a bit more know who He is than you think you know who I am. I know worser."

"You!" screeched Mrs. Eastman. "You're a mistake!" Her hair and nerves were all unstrung. "I'm not your mother, you won't be a lawyer, you won't be." She couldn't think, and immediately, in a reflexive action, she shifted gears into the vaguest of doubts. Outside the rooster crooned an offbeat love song. "I'm going to call my husband," said Mrs. Eastman, dispassionately.

"Serve me the roast beef first," Little Darryl said, and Mrs. Eastman did, filling a plate with greasy slices that hunkered on top of each other in an orgy of flesh. "I ain't afraid of nobody that'd marry you."

While Mrs. Eastman was gone Little Darryl ate the roast beef and when he finished he roamed around, pocketing certain valuables. Inside the refrigerator he found a hamhock. He put it inside the coat, down near the waistline. Inside a drawer he found the silverware, and he put it all, including a soup ladle, into the front left pocket of the Prince Albert. It bulged outward like a cancerous tumor. He put the remains of the roast beef and a bottle of ketchup into the front right pocket. By the time Mrs. Eastman got back, there was very little left in her kitchen.

"He's on his way home," Mrs Eastman told him, as if the matter were settled at last.

"Whoopee," said Little Darryl. He clinked when he spoke. "You're going to have to go upstairs." Briefly, but certainly, he flashed the jackknife in front of Mrs. Eastman. It caused her to remember a story she'd heard quite a time ago. "You're going to have to show me where your jewry is up there. I'll take my chances with them papers this time."

"You're just a little boy," Mrs. Eastman said. "Just a little children."

"They's bigger than me that's less. Upstairs, lady."

Mrs. Eastman breathed heavily up the stairs, and she felt her heart make little leaps, as though it might creep onto her tongue and expose something. Each crack in the wood of the floor struck her as the place to be, each piece of dust looked like the safest of sizes, and she studied them with the vigilance of a scientist. In the bedroom she had a horrible thought.

"You wouldn't hurt a lady would you?" she asked, but Little Darryl was already rooting through her dressing table. "You wouldn't hurt a lady *would you?*" she asked, a little louder. She got up on her bed and held tightly as a tick to the wood of the headboard. "*Would you?*"

Little Darryl turned around, his hands full of rings and bracelets and necklaces that dangled like liquids through his fingers. Along the lines of his face there slithered a configuration of sheer hatred.

"Lady," he said, almost tenderly, "I wouldn't touch a hair a your head for anything anywhere," and then he disappeared out of the bedroom.

"Rape!" Mrs. Eastman cried, but her heart wasn't in it.

When Mr. Eastman came home all he could hear were his wife's screams, and all he could see was a brown figure in the distance, the plumes of a rooster sticking out like an exhaust under its arms, and all he could think would be forever silent.

1983

The characters in Leigh Allison Wilson's story are developed largely through what Flannery O'Connor calls their "manners—good and bad" and especially their speech. O'Connor's description of the uses and abuses of Southern speech and demeanor provide a useful perspective for discussing "The Raising."

"There is a whole book in that one sentence": Flannery O'Connor

There are two qualities that make fiction. One is the sense of mystery and the other is the sense of manners. You get the manners from the texture of existence that surrounds you. The great advantage of being a Southern writer is that we don't have to go anywhere to look for manners; bad or good, we've got them in abundance. We in the South live in a society that is rich in contradiction, rich in irony, rich in contrast, and particularly rich in its speech. . . .

There is nothing worse than the writer who doesn't *use* the gifts of the region, but wallows in them. Everything becomes so Southern that it's sickening, so local that it is unintelligible, so literally reproduced that it conveys nothing. The general gets lost in the particular instead of being shown through it.

However, when the life that actually surrounds us is totally ignored, when our patterns of speech are absolutely overlooked, then something is out of kilter. The writer should then ask himself if he is not reaching out for a kind of life that is artificial to him.

An idiom characterizes a society, and when you ignore the idiom, you are very likely ignoring the whole social fabric that could make a meaningful character. You can't cut characters off from their society and say much about them as individuals. You can't say anything meaningful about the mystery of a personality unless you put that personality in a believable and significant social context. And the best way to do this is through the character's own language. When the old lady in one of Andrew Lytle's stories says contemptuously that she has a mule that is older than Birmingham, we get in that one sentence a sense of a society and its history. A great deal of the Southern writer's work is done for him before he begins, because our history lives in our talk. In one of Eudora Welty's stories a character says, "Where I come from, we use fox for yard dogs and owls for chickens, but we sing true." Now there is a whole book in that one sentence; and when the people of your section can talk like that, and you ignore it, you're just not taking advantage of what's yours.

POETRY

ANTH

To Shape Our Perception of the World:
The Art of Poetry

Poetry, like all art, has three lives. The first begins and ends in the process of composition, during which the poem seems not so much *made* as *discovered*. Randall Jarrell, discussing the composition of "The Woman at the Washington Zoo," talks about things that "came into" the poem, as if of their own free will, and began to arrange themselves in patterns plain "even to the writer." Maxine Kumin, too, talks as though a poem were alive and formidable: ". . . I sit back like the old hunter, waiting for the bear to pass this way." For some poets only this first life of the poem is truly interesting; they do not reread their old poems.

The second life of a poem comes when a reader or listener experiences through the poem a discovery comparable to the poet's. Jarrell's poem is told from the perspective of a government office worker in a navy-blue dress, a dull dress acceptable to the "Deputy Chief Assistant." At the Washington zoo she sees Indian women in brilliant saris watching a brilliantly spotted leopard, and she connects the bright colors in a phrase: "They look back at the leopard like the leopard." Jarrell's poem allows us to see in that moment what the woman sees, to discover an image that links humans and animals and reminds us of the joy of color and movement, sometimes lost in over-civilized life. Much of the pleasure of a poem comes from its ability to provide us

with these discoveries. As the critic and scientist Jacob
Bronowski points out, the same sort of pleasure can
come to us when we look at a painting or read about a
scientific theory:

> The poem or the discovery exists in two
> moments of vision: the moment of appreciation
> as much as that of creation; for the appreciator
> must see the movement, wake to the echo
> which is started in the creation of the work. In
> the moment of appreciation we live again the
> moment when the creator saw and held the
> hidden likeness. When a simile takes us aback
> and persuades us together, when we find a
> juxtaposition in a picture both odd and
> intriguing, when a theory is at once fresh and
> convincing, we do not merely nod over some-
> one else's work. We re-enact the creative act,
> and we ourselves make the discovery again.

The second life of the poem, then, comes when the
reader becomes a partner of the poet, a co-creator.

The third life is probably the most important.
It is the poem's life after we make our first discovery of
it, after we cease to "study" it or consciously to appreciate it. The music that moves us most stays with us when
it is not being played, and poetry that counts for most is

that which comes back to us unbidden, months after we see the printed page. In this third life the poem may accumulate unexpected meanings and may be fragmented and distorted by a faulty memory, but it is *alive*. It becomes part of the internal monologue that plays constantly through our heads, shaping our perception of the world, of language, of other poems.

The first life of poetry does not depend on our active participation, but the second and third lives obviously do. How can we become partners with the poet, discovering in the poem something akin to what he or she discovered? How can we savor and articulate the discovery? There are certainly no pat answers to these questions: every reader must eventually find his or her own way. There are, however, at least five approaches that have frequently helped readers discover what they might otherwise have missed.

- Read the poem in light of related poems.
- Read the poem in light of poems not obviously related.
- Read the poem in light of other poems by the same author.
- Read the poem in light of its internal contrasts.
- Live with the poem.

READ THE POEM IN LIGHT OF RELATED POEMS

Sometimes poems come into focus best when we see them in the context of other poems. Take, for example, this short one by Gary Snyder, published under the title "Hitch Haiku":

> After weeks of watching the roof leak
>   I fixed it tonight
>   by moving a single board.

In itself, the poem looks like a moderately interesting sentence, arranged into lines for no particular reason. There is more to it than this, as anyone willing to read other haiku will quickly learn.

In Japan, haiku have a strong second and third life. The Japanese sometimes play a parlor game in which fragments of several haiku are written on slips of paper and put into a box. A player draws a slip of paper, reads out the fragment, and attempts to reconstruct the entire poem from memory. Successful players can do so because the haiku is a living and popular art form. Educated people, rather than buying mass-produced greeting cards, frequently compose haiku to send to friends. They model the haiku, loosely or closely, seriously or humorously, on the great haiku of the past.

Non-Japanese readers rarely achieve the depth of understanding that Japanese readers have. But we quickly learn that many haiku deal with a sudden insight and that many are concerned with the relation between nature and human beings. A fairly easy haiku to translate and understand was written by Chiyo (1703–1775):

> Morning glories
>   have captured the well bucket;
>   I go to a neighbor for water.

Chiyo approaches her well and discovers that she cannot get a drink without tearing morning glory vines off the bucket. She does not have to tell us that the vines are in glorious full bloom; if they were not, there would be no conflict. She does not need to tell us that it is summer and that she is thirsty; the morning glory blooms in summer and she is approaching the well. The poem hesitates for a moment between the second and third line: is Chiyo's choice between destroying the morning glory and going thirsty? No, there is another course: "go to a neighbor for water." No one who has watched a contemporary suburb eat its way into woodland can fail to see the larger implications of the morning glory and the bucket. What we might particularly note in relation to Snyder's haiku, however, is that the poem presents the poet as a person suddenly in a quandary and just as suddenly out of it.

Those who know a great deal about haiku find Chiyo's work beautiful but say that it lacks the overtones, the suggestions of large meaning, that we find in a poem like this one by Kohyo (dates uncertain):

> The stick that strikes at it:
>   Onto the tip settles
>   the dragonfly.

Anyone who has spent a summer afternoon trying to dislodge a dragonfly from the tip of a fishing rod will recognize the situation here. But what are we to make of it? If we look at the situation from the point of view of the person who must be swinging the stick, this appears to be a poem about a futile effort. The stick is too slow, too clumsy to have a chance of actually striking the almost bodiless dragonfly. Here is a quandary which, unlike Chiyo's, has no solution. It suggests a whole class of efforts certain to fail: to try with gritted teeth to find happiness, to try to capture the natural world without destroying it, to resist the advance of age, to try to force the conscious mind to deal with things only the unconscious mind can reach. We certainly cannot say that Kohyo had any of these problems in his mind when he composed the poem, but they are the sort of problems often touched on in haiku (and in Zen Buddhism, to which haiku is allied). The touch is often very light, as in this poem by Issa (1762–1826):

> A butterfly, a child:
>   When she crawls, it flies, and when
>   she crawls, it flies . . .

Now we are ready to return to Gary Snyder's poem. Like Chiyo and Kohyo, Snyder presents himself as a person with a problem. It is a rainy season (". . . weeks of watching the roof leak"), and he would like to have a snug roof overhead. Snyder might wish that he could take the attitude that Matsuo Basho (1644–94) did:

> Not even a hat on—
>   will I get soaked by the cold rain?
>   No matter.

Snyder is, however, a twentieth-century American. The roof leaks; this *does* matter. It needs to be fixed, but roof problems are notoriously tricky. Perhaps if he starts on this one, he will waste time and effort and make the situation worse. At any rate, he lets the problem get under his skin (*weeks* of watching the roof leak). Then one night he goes up on the roof and fixes it, "by moving a *single* board"! It was that simple all along, even simpler than Chiyo's quandary with the morning glory; the problem had more to do with his lack of faith than with his roof. We are inclined to read the poem this way because the reading is consistent with what we have seen in other haiku by Japanese poets. In them, the poet figures humbly, humorously: a woman defeated by a morning glory vine, a man outflanked by a dragonfly, a man who forgets his hat. All things considered, Snyder's poem reads better if we assume that he is laughing at himself (he did use the title "Hitch Haiku," after all), presenting himself as a man who frets needlessly until he sees how simple things can be.

English poetry in some eras has operated in forms nearly as tightly knit as the Japanese haiku tradition. From Geoffrey Chaucer's time to William Wordsworth's, a poet could write a complaint or an aubade, for instance, and assume that his readers or listeners would recognize it for what it was and appreciate its relationship, serious or comic, to other poems in the same tradition. Since Wordsworth's time, poets have tended to avoid such narrowly defined forms or types, but most begin their careers imitating poets they particularly admire, and their early enthusiasms affect their later work. If it is hard to talk about the relation of a modern poem to its genre, it is often easier to talk about it in relation to a loose tradition of poetic apprenticeship and admiration. The contemporary poet Frank O'Hara, for instance, is very explicit in naming his poetic forebears: "after all, only Whitman and Crane and Williams, of the American poets, are better than the movies." Louise Bogan prefers the French symbolists (including Charles Baudelaire), the English metaphysicals (including John Donne), Emily Dickinson, and William Butler Yeats. Just as we read Gary Snyder's poem better when we looked at it in the light of poems by Basho, Kohyo, and Chiyo, we can often read an O'Hara poem better in light of Whitman, Crane, and Williams; a Bogan poem in light of Dickinson, Yeats, and other members of the poetic family she adopted.

READ THE POEM IN LIGHT OF OTHER POEMS NOT OBVIOUSLY RELATED

Sometimes we may feel uncomfortable about comparing two poems because we are not sure that they belong together. The best assumption is that, ultimately, all poems belong together. As Robert Frost says,

> A poem is best read in the light of all other poems ever written. We read A the better to read B (we have to start somewhere; we may get very little out of A). We read B the better to read C, C the better to read D, D the better to go back and get something more out of A. Progress is not the aim, but circulation. The thing is to get among the poems where they hold each other apart in their places as the stars do.

An apparently outlandish comparison sometimes helps us see both of the compared poems more clearly. Take, for example, "The Moment," a fairly recent poem by Patricia Hampl:

> Standing by the parking-ramp elevator
> a week ago, sunk, stupid with sadness.
> Black slush puddled on the cement floor,
> the place painted a killer-pastel
> as in an asylum.
> A number 1, big as a person,
> was stencilled on the cinder block:
> Remember your level.
> The toneless bell sounded.
> Doors opened, nobody inside.
> Then, who knows why, a rod of light
> at the base of my skull flashed
> to every outpost of my far-flung body—
> *I've got my life back.*
> It was nothing, just the present moment
> occurring for the first time in months.
> My head translated light,
> my eyes spiked with tears.
> The awful green walls, I could have stroked them.
> The dirt, the moving cube I stepped into—
> it was all beautiful,
> everything that took me up.

Here is a poem that we might like immediately but feel uneasy about because it seems (by the standards we have learned in school) to be too explicit, too detailed, too "up front." The critic Helen Vendler once observed that contemporary American poetry is often *very* spontaneous. There is "a kind of trancelike looseness of construction, as though the poet had taped his own telephone conversation." This looseness may attract us to a poem or put us off it.

As I thought about Hampl's poem, another poem kept tugging at my memory and finally got my attention: Shakespeare's Sonnet 29.

> When, in disgrace with fortune and men's eyes,
> I all alone beweep my outcast state,
> And trouble deaf heaven with my bootless cries,
> And look upon myself, and curse my fate,
> Wishing myself like to one more rich in hope,
> Featured like him, like him with friends possessed,
> Desiring this man's art and that man's scope,
> With what I most enjoy contented least;
> Yet in these thoughts myself almost despising,
> Haply I think on thee—and then my state,
> Like to the lark at break of day arising
> From sullen earth, sings hymns at heaven's gate;
> From thy sweet love remembered such wealth brings
> That then I scorn to change my state with kings.

It is very unlikely that Hampl wrote her poem with Shakespeare's consciously in mind, but in some ways the poems are remarkably similar. The most striking thing is the physical movement of the lark in Shakespeare and the elevator in Hampl, both symbolizing an emotional lift. From "sunk, stupid with sadness" or "in disgrace with fortune and men's eyes," the poet's spirit rises. "My head translated light, /my eyes spiked with tears," says Hampl; "my state . . . sings hymns at heaven's gate," says Shakespeare. The similarity is striking enough to make us notice another similarity: the manifest emotion of the poems. Many poets approach emotion very indirectly. With them, it is a principle of taste not to wear one's heart on one's sleeve. Neither Shakespeare's sonnet nor Hampl's poem leaves any doubt about its underlying emotions.

By now we have seen enough similarity to turn to the obvious difference: Shakespeare's poem is more formal in its pattern and more artificial in its diction. Laced into the sonnet form and purified of language or imagery outside the traditional range of "poetry," Shakespeare's poem handles the emotion with what Adrienne Rich calls the "asbestos gloves" of formalism. For some readers, this formality is a fatal flaw: the Victorian essayist William Hazlitt, for instance, said that "if Shakespeare had written nothing but his sonnets . . . he would . . . have been assigned to the class of cold, artificial writers, who had no genuine sense of nature or passion." On the other hand, readers like W. H. Auden feel that

> . . . those sonnets which express passionate emotions, whether of adoration or anger or grief or disgust, owe a very great deal of their effect precisely to Shakespeare's artifice, for without the restraint and distancing which the rhetorical devices provide, the intensity and immediacy of the emotion might have produced, not a poem, but an embarrassing "human document."

Shall we ask poetry *include* or to *purify?* Do we want it to be as faithful to the world ("nature and passion") as possible? Or do we want poetry to have the balance, restraint, unity, and sense of tradition we associate with works of art? We *want* both, of course, and perhaps all poets strive to give both simultaneously.

They have to start somewhere. They can start with the established order of art and reach out to include the raw material of life, or they can start with the raw material and try to find a new order in it. Either method involves great risks. Hampl chooses the risks of inclusiveness, and her poem's strengths are just the things that make it potentially "embarrassing."

In Shakespeare's poem, the poet is lifted from his gloom by love of another human being: a familiar human experience, but also a poetic convention. In Hampl's poem, she is totally alone and happens out of gloom for reasons that are never explained: a situation that might be at least as common (particularly in twentieth-century America), but one not often associated with poetry. Similarly, Hampl's poem includes imagery is that neither dreamy nor pastoral. When Shakespeare's sonnet turns to joy, we have the sudden appearance of "the lark at break of day arising/ From sullen earth." But joy comes to Patricia Hampl amid images realistic enough to embarrass some poetic sensibilities: a parking ramp, black slush, cement floor, green walls, stencilled signs, a toneless bell. In this unpoetic setting, Hampl does not *talk* like a poet—not, that is, like the stereotyped poet with a plume in one hand and a rose in the other. Most of the language is flat ("Doors opened, nobody inside") or loose and prosy ("a killer-pastel," "who knows why").

All this gives the poem the feeling of an unblinkingly honest personal report, but does not (by my standards) reduce it to the sort of "human document" Auden wants to avoid. Sometimes the imagery—visual, tactile, auditory—makes the underground parking garage seem as complete a hell as the rock-bound, many-leveled one the poet Dante described five centuries ago.

> A number 1, big as a person,
> was stencilled on the cinder block:
> Remember your level.
> The toneless bell sounded.
> Doors opened, nobody inside.

And so the poet's movement out of that very real and very contemporary setting seems an echo of the ascents from hell that have always fascinated poets:

> The awful green walls, I could have stroked them.
> The dirt, the moving cube I stepped into—
> it was all beautiful,
> everything that took me up.

Randall Jarrell says that the challenge of poetry is to say something that is simultaneously very old (since the truths that count are unchanging) and very new (since we can only see those truths by the light of our own day). A comparison of a modern poem like Patricia Hampl's with an older poem like Shakespeare's sometimes helps us to see the interaction of old and new.

READ THE POEM IN THE LIGHT OF OTHER POEMS BY THE SAME AUTHOR

Among the first Louise Glück poems I read seriously was "Still Life":

> Father has his arm around Tereze.
> She squints. My thumb
> is in my mouth: my fifth autumn.
> Near the copper beech
> the spaniel dozes in shadows.
> Not one of us does not avert his eyes.
>
> Across the lawn, in full sun, my mother
> stands behind her camera.

I immediately liked something about the poem: like Glück, I was a child in the heyday of the unsophisticated box camera. I remember these ritual occasions, posing in full sun in stiff poses suitable for family albums. Now I, too, look at the results with nostalgia. That was all I saw in the poem until one afternoon a friend and I read through several of Glück's poems together.

A half-dozen of the poems we read are collected on pages 1200–1205, where you can read them for yourself. I think you will find, as we did, that simple nostalgia is not at all characteristic of Glück's poetry. In poems like "For My Mother," "The Apple Tree," and "Metamorphosis," we get a view of the difficulties, pains, and separations of family life:

> In the dark room your son sleeps.
> The walls are green, the walls

are spruce and silence.
I wait to see how he will leave me.

This is not the view of the happy, inseparable family that the photo album is supposed to present, and when we think again about "Still Life" we realize what a disturbing poem it is.

Through the first six lines the picture seems a standard one: young family squinting into the sun, with dog and beech tree. Then, significantly set off by the blank line, a reminder of who is *not* in the picture: the mother, from whose perspective, we suddenly realize, we have been viewing the entire scene. This is the family as the mother sees it, as she tries to preserve it, on film at least, for reasons no one else seems quite to understand. "Not one of us does not avert his eyes" now seems a more sinister line; the mother gazes intently through the viewfinder at a family that does not look back at her.

When I realized this much, I saw a dimension of the poem that had entirely escaped me on first reading. When she looks at the photograph, Glück (now a grown woman, now—in fact—a mother) is seeing the family as her mother had seen it thirty years before. She is seeing *herself*, even, through her mother's eyes, as a thumb-sucking five-year-old who will inevitably grow up, move away, call less frequently, become a stranger, become a mother herself of a daughter who will grow up to repeat the cycle. The sad look into the past and future is captured in the moment of looking at the photograph. Until we read the poem in light of other Glück poems, however, much of it escapes us.

READ THE POEM IN LIGHT OF ITS INTERNAL CONTRASTS

As we see very clearly in "Still Life," "The Moment," and Sonnet 29, poems often articulate a tension: the family versus the mother, the public world versus the private relationship, the gritty surroundings versus the internal joy. Sometimes the best way into a poem is to begin by identifying a key tension. Here, for example, is a poem by Emily Dickinson in which the tension is expressed clearly in rhythm and rhyme:

A Bird came down the Walk—
He did not know I saw—
He bit an Angleworm in halves
And ate the fellow, raw,

And then he drank a Dew
From a convenient Grass—
And then hopped sidewise to the Wall
To let a Beetle pass—

He glanced with rapid eyes
That hurried all around—
They looked like frighted Beads, I thought—
He stirred his Velvet Head

Like one in danger, Cautious,
I offered him a Crumb
And he unrolled his feathers
And rowed him softer home—

Than Oars divide the Ocean,
Too silver for a seam—
Or Butterflies, off Banks of Noon
Leap, plashless as they swim.

The contrast between the nursery-rhyme quality of first half of the poem and the more complex second half strikes us immediately . The first two stanzas are built on the same pattern: lines in iambic meter (ta-TUM, ta-Tum, ta-Tum—mechanically—with an extra foot in the third line of the stanza). The obvious full rhymes would delight a five-year-old: *saw/raw* and *grass/pass* remind me of Mother Goose's *dock/clock* and *muffet/tuffet*. The little anthropomorphized bird, too, is straight from the nursery: reminiscent of Peter Rabbit on and off his best behavior. Even those of us whose experience with poetry is very limited know exactly where we stand through the second stanza.

Then we discover that we are not standing where the poem is. The third stanza misses the expected rhyme almost entirely (is *around/head* a rhyme at all?) and the poem staggers into the fourth stanza with what textbooks call an enjambment:

They looked like frighted Beads, I thought—
He stirred his Velvet Head

Like one in danger, Cautious,
I offered him a Crumb

Even the syntax has become unclear. Who is cautious, the bird or the poet, or both? The poem seems to be reeling as if it had been boxed on the ears. The mechanical iambic meter is blurred by an occasional extra syllable at the end ("Like one in danger, Cautious"), and when the rhymes return, they are unpredictable slant rhymes (*crumb/home, seam/swim*). The form that had been so confident and comfortable has shifted, and the effect is somewhat eerie—like the effect of music shifting to a minor key.

The difference in form between the first and second half of the poem corresponds to a difference in the way the bird is viewed. At first it is a comical mechanical thing, as birds tend to be on the ground, or as we tend to see them. But when the bird flies it becomes something else again, and we begin to see the mystery of it.

Contrasts within the poem need not involve meter or rhyme, of course. William Stafford's "Traveling Through the Dark" is written in a free verse virtually indistinguishable from the prose, so it does not provide an opportunity for such a dramatic change in form:

> Traveling through the dark I found a deer
> dead on the edge of the Wilson River road.
> It is usually best to roll them into the canyon:
> that road is narrow; to swerve might make more dead.
>
> By glow of the tail-light I stumbled back of the car
> and stood by the heap, a doe, a recent killing;
> she had stiffened already, almost cold.
> I dragged her off; she was large in the belly.
>
> My fingers touching her side brought me the reason—
> her side was warm; her fawn lay there waiting,
> alive, still, never to be born.
> Beside that mountain road I hesitated.
>
> The car aimed ahead its lowered parking lights;
> under the hood purred the steady engine.
> I stood in the glare of the warm exhaust turning red;
> around our group I could hear the wilderness listen.
>
> I thought hard for all of us—my only swerving—,
> then pushed her over the edge into the river.

The great tension is between two realities, two systems of life. On one hand are efficiency and responsibility, unglamorous virtues that we learn to admire when we face danger or loss. The protagonist's statement that "to swerve might make more dead" could be the motto of the dedicated soldier, reformer, or surgeon, all of whom occasionally need to view life with utter detachment in order to serve their cause. On the other hand, there are emotions warmer than efficiency and deeper than good judgment. Where on the scale of rational decision making is the protagonist to weight what he feels when he touches the doe's side: ". . . her fawn lay there waiting,/alive, still, never to be born"? Stafford's poem is strong because he does full justice to both sides of the conflict.

Another tension is at work in the style of the poem. Stafford has a large theme here, one that could fly off into sentimentality in one direction ("What a torment life is for us sensitive souls who are alert to brutality!") or into philosophical cliches in another (ditto). To avoid these failings, he stays very close to literal reality. The incident takes place on the Wilson River road, which runs from Portland to Tillamook and which the state calls Highway 6. Many of the Oregonians who drive it would say, in precisely the same words, that they had to "swerve" to avoid a "heap" in the road, or that "it is usually best to roll them into the canyon." The flat accuracy of Stafford's language and setting provide a background against which a few passages assume a particularly sharp profile. Take, for example, these lines from the fourth quatrain:

> The car aimed ahead its lowered parking lights;
> under the hood purred the steady engine.
> I stood in the glare of the warm exhaust turning red . . .

Immediately after the description of the dead doe, warmed from the inside by a living fawn, we get this description of a truly dead object, an automobile, the embodiment of efficiency. But so restrained has Stafford's language been to this point that little touches—"aimed," "purred the steady engine," "the warm exhaust turning red"—make the automobile seem like a living thing, slightly demonic. The effect is not flashy: the car never stops being a car, but the poems steps up its emotional intensity. Now we are ready to see the larger emotions and thoughts that the restrained language of this poem opens out on. Now we will read Stafford's "I thought hard for all of us—my only swerving" with a sense that "all of us" reaches beyond one man, one doe, one car and whatever passengers may be in it, and that "swerving" has acquired new meaning. We may go back to the title of the poem and realize that Stafford's plain title "Traveling Through the Dark" symbolizes the terrifying freedom of a life in which we have to make moral choices by the faint light of our human judgement.

LIVE WITH THE POEM

The faint light of judgement leaves some poems unilluminated, and we should leave this introduction with a reminder that poems often affect us for reasons we will never understand. Full appreciation of poetry has to go beyond fully conscious appreciation, and many poems need to be lived with over a period of weeks or months while they do their work unanalyzed. Here I can only give an example from my own experience. Six months ago I discovered the following poem:

The Castle of my Heart

Cleanse and refresh the castle of my heart
Where I have lived for long with little joy.
For Falsest Danger, with its counterpart
Sorrow, has made this siege its long employ.

Now lift the siege, for in your bravest part
Full power exists, most eager for employ;
Cleanse and refresh the castle of my heart
Where I have lived for long with little joy.

Do not let Peril play its lordly part;
Show up the bad game's bait, and its employ.

Nor, for a moment, strut as future's toy.
Advance, and guard your honor and my art.

Cleanse and refresh the castle of my heart.

There is little to say about the poem. It is in the form of a rondel, an elaborate French invention in which both lines and rhymes rearrange themselves from stanza to stanza like keys juggled on a key ring. It was composed by Charles D'Orleans, probably after his release in 1440 from twenty-five years of captivity as an English prisoner of war. Louise Bogan translated it from the French in 1966, when she was sixty-eight years old and nearing the end of a life remarkable for its devotion to art, its fierce independence, and its frequent solitude. She never published the translation.

There are things about the poem I do not understand. It seems to be a prayer, but how odd it is to say that "full power" exists in God's "bravest part" (as if there were a cowardly part) or that He "strut[s] as future's toy." When I try to reason about the poem, I cannot tell if it is addressed to God or to some part of the poet's soul or to another person, a lover, real or imagined. Perhaps it is all three simultaneously. Finally this difficulty makes no difference, since the poem works on me without my having to understand it completely. What makes a difference is that almost every day the poem comes back to me in fragments. Sometimes when I recite the lines I think of the literal castles, smelly and unromantic, where Charles D'Orleans "lived for long with little joy." Sometimes I think of Louise Bogan's poetry, austere and beautiful and undervalued ("Advance, and guard your honor and my art"). Generally, however, I let the music of the poem do its work without interference. "Cleanse and refresh the castle of my heart": it is a craftsman's line, but it is also something more. It is a prayer that seems to rise spontaneously from a part of us that analysis cannot reach.

WILLIAM SHAKESPEARE

(1564–1616)

[NOT MARBLE, NOR THE GILDED MONUMENTS]

Not marble, nor the gilded monuments
Of princes shall outlive this pow'rful rhyme,
But you shall shine more bright in these conténts
Than unswept stone, besmear'd with sluttish time.
When wasteful war shall statues overturn,   5
And broils root out the work of masonry,
Nor Mars his sword nor war's quick fire shall burn
The living record of your memory.
'Gainst death and all-oblivious enmity
Shall you pace forth; your praise shall still find room   10
Even in the eyes of all posterity
That wear this world out to the ending doom.
   So, till the judgment that yourself arise,
    You live in this, and dwell in lovers' eyes.

(Sonnet 55) 1609

[SINCE BRASS, NOR STONE, NOR EARTH, NOR BOUNDLESS SEA]

Since brass, nor stone, nor earth, nor boundless sea
But sad mortality o'er-sways their power,
How with this rage shall beauty hold a plea,
Whose action is no stronger than a flower?
O how shall summer's honey breath hold out   5
Against the wreckful siege of batt'ring days,
When rocks impregnable are not so stout,
Nor gates of steel so strong, but Time decays?
O fearful meditation! where, alack,
Shall Time's best jewel from Time's chest lie hid?   10
Or what strong hand can hold his swift foot back?
Or who his spoil of beauty can forbid?

Sonnet 55: 4 *sluttish:* dirty and slovenly;   6 *broils:* quarrels, battles;   7 *Nor . . . nor:* neither
. . . nor;   *Mars his:* Mars';   9 *all-oblivious:* all-obliterating   Sonnet 65: 10 *chest:* treasure
chest

O, none, unless this miracle have might,
That in black ink my love may still shine bright.

(Sonnet 65) 1609

[THAT TIME OF YEAR THOU MAYST IN ME BEHOLD]

That time of year thou mayst in me behold
When yellow leaves, or none, or few, do hang
Upon those boughs which shake against the cold,
Bare ruin'd choirs, where late the sweet birds sang.
In me thou seest the twilight of such day   5
As after sunset fadeth in the west,
Which by and by black night doth take away,
Death's second self, that seals up all in rest.
In me thou seest the glowing of such fire,
That on the ashes of his youth doth lie,   10
As the deathbed whereon it must expire,
Consum'd with that which it was nourish'd by.
   This thou perceiv'st, which makes thy love more
   strong,
   To love that well which thou must leave ere long.

(Sonnet 73) 1609

[O, NEVER SAY THAT I WAS FALSE OF HEART]

O, never say that I was false of heart,
Though absence seem'd my flame to qualify;
As easy might I from myself depart
As from my soul, which in thy breast doth lie:
That is my home of love; if I have ranged   5
Like him that travels I return again,
Just to the time, not with the time exchang'd,
So that myself bring water for my stain.
Never believe, though in my nature reign'd
All frailties that besiege all kinds of blood,   10
That it could so preposterously be stain'd,
To leave for nothing all thy sum of good;

Sonnet 109: 2 *qualify:* to diminish or make less complete; 7 *just . . . time:* faithful to the appointed time; *altered:* changed; 10 *blood:* temperament; 12 *for:* in exchange for

For nothing this wide universe I call,
Save thou, my rose; in it thou art my all.

(Sonnet 109) 1609

[WHEN MY LOVE SWEARS THAT SHE IS MADE OF TRUTH]

When my love swears that she is made of truth,
I do believe her, though I know she lies,
That she might think me some untutor'd youth,
Unlearnéd in the world's false subtleties.
Thus vainly thinking that she thinks me young,   5
Although she knows my days are past the best,
Simply I credit her false-speaking tongue:
On both sides thus is simple truth suppress'd.
But wherefore says she not she is unjust?
And wherefore say not I that I am old?   10
Oh, love's best habit is in seeming trust,
And age in love loves not t' have years told.
    Therefore I lie with her and she with me,
    And in our faults by lies we flattered be.

(Sonnet 138) 1609

O MISTRESS MINE, WHERE ARE YOU ROAMING?

O mistress mine, where are you roaming?
Oh, stay and hear! your true Love's coming,
    That can sing both high and low:
Trip no further, pretty sweeting;
Journeys end in lovers' meeting,   5
    Every wise man's son doth know.

What is love? 'tis not hereafter;
Present mirth hath present laughter;
    What's to come is still unsure:
In delay there lies no plenty: 10
Then come kiss me, sweet-and-twenty,
    Youth's a stuff will not endure.

1599

Sonnet 138: 1 *truth:* faithfulness;   7 *simply:* naively;   9 *unjust:* unfaithful

COME AWAY, COME AWAY, DEATH

Come away, come away, death,
   And in sad cypress let me be laid.
Fly away, fly away, breath;
   I am slain by a fair cruel maid.
My shroud of white, stuck all with yew,   5
      O, prepare it!
My part of death, no one so true
      Did share it.

Not a flower, not a flower sweet,
   On my black coffin let there be strown.   10
Not a friend, not a friend greet
   My poor corpse, where my bones shall be thrown.
A thousand thousand sighs to save,
      Lay me, O, where
Sad true lover never find my grave,   15
      To weep there!

1602

FEAR NO MORE THE HEAT O' THE SUN

Fear no more the heat o' the sun,
   Nor the furious winter's rages;
Thou thy worldly task hast done,
   Home art gone, and ta'en thy wages:
Golden lads and girls all must,   5
As chimney-sweepers, come to dust.

Fear no more the frown o' the great;
   Thou art past the tyrant's stroke;
Care no more to clothe and eat;
   To thee the reed is as the oak: 10
The scepter, learning, physic, must
All follow this, and come to dust.

Fear no more the lightning flash,
   Nor the all-dreaded thunder stone;
Fear not slander, censure rash;   15
   Thou hast finished joy and moan:
All lovers young, all lovers must
Consign to thee, and come to dust.

No exorciser harm thee!
Nor no witchcraft charm thee!   20
Ghost unlaid forbear thee!

Nothing ill come near thee!
Quiet consummation have;
And renownéd be thy grave!

1611

Shakespeare's lyrics do what they do so well that they periodically become a reference point in debates about what poetry ought to be doing. In the 1930s such influential poets as T. S. Eliot and Ezra Pound were writing poems more intellectual, ironic, and "objective" than the lyrics Shakespeare had written so well. A. E. Housman delivered his address on "The Name and Nature of Poetry" partly in answer to such poets. A dismayed proponent of the new poetry reported that he would have to work fifteen years to undo the damage Housman had done in one hour.

"That is nonsense, but it is ravishing poetry": A. E. Housman

Poetry is not the thing said but a way of saying it. Can it then be isolated and studied by itself? For the combination of language with its intellectual content, its meaning, is as close a union as can well be imagined. Is there such a thing as pure unmingled poetry, poetry independent of meaning?

. . . Even Shakespeare, who had so much to say, would sometimes pour out his loveliest poetry in saying nothing.

> Take O take those lips away
>   That so sweetly were forsworn,
> And those eyes, the break of day,
>   Lights that do misled the morn;
> But my kisses bring again,
>   bring again,
> Seals of love, but seal'd in vain,
>   seal'd in vain.

That is nonsense, but it is ravishing poetry. When Shakespeare fills such poetry with thought, and thought which is worthy of it, as in 'Fear no more the heat o' the sun' or 'O mistress mine, where are you roaming?' those songs, the very summits of lyrical achievement, are indeed greater and more moving poems, but I hardly know how to call them more poetical.

. . . Poetry indeed seems to me more physical than intellectual. A year or two ago, in common with others, I received from America a request that I would define poetry. I replied that I could no more define poetry than a terrier can define a rat, but that I thought we both recognised the object by the symptoms which it provokes in us. One of these symptoms was described in connexion with another object by Elipaz the Temanite: 'A spirit passed before my face: the hair of my flesh stood up.' Experience has taught me, when I am shaving in the morning, to keep watch over my thoughts, because, if a line of poetry strays into my memory, my skin bristles so that the razor ceases to act. This particular symptom is accompanied by a shiver down the spine; there is another which consists in a constriction of the throat and a precipitation of water to the eyes; and there is a third which I can only describe by borrowing a phrase from one of Keats's last letters, where he says, speaking of Fanny Brawne, 'everything that reminds me of her goes through me like a spear'. The seat of this sensation is the pit of the stomach.

Of course, Shakespeare is not the only poet cited in discussions of the pure lyric. It might be useful to compare his poems to other lyrics that have from time to time been praised for their purity.

Francesco Petrarch

(1304–1374)

THE SOOTE SEASON, THAT BUD AND BLOME FURTH BRINGES

translated from the Italian by Henry Howard, Earl of Surrey

The soote season, that bud and blome furth bringes,
With grene hath clad the hill and eke the vale;
The nightingale with fethers new she singes;
The turtle to her make hath tolde her tale.
Somer is come, for every spray nowe springes;   5
The hart hath hong his olde hed on the pale;
The buck in brake his winter cote he flings;
The fishes flote with newe repaired scale;
The adder all her sloughe awaye she slinges;
The swift swalow pursueth the flyes smale;   10
The busy bee her honye now she minges.
Winter is worne, that was the flowers bale.

The Soote Season: 2 *eke:* also; 4 *turtle:* turtledove; 11 *minges:* discharges.

And thus I see among these pleasant thinges
Eche care decayes, and yet my sorrow springes.

1557

François Villon

(1431–1463)

A BALLADE OF DEAD LADIES

translated from the French by Dante Gabriel Rossetti

Tell me now in what hidden way is
   Lady Flora the lovely Roman?
Where's Hipparchia, and where is Thais,
   Neither of them the fairer woman?
   Where is Echo, beheld of no man,   5
Only heard on river and mere,
   She whose beauty was more than human? . . .
But where are the snows of yester-year?

Where's Heloise, the learned nun,
   For whose sake, Abeillard, I ween,   10
Lost manhood and put priesthood on?
   (From Love he won such dule and teen!)
   And where, I pray you, is the Queen
Who willed that Buridan should steer
   Sewed in a sack's mouth down the Seine? . . .   15
But where are the snows of yester-year?

White Queen Blanche, like a queen of lilies,
   With a voice like any mermaiden,

Ballade of Dead Ladies: 2 *Lady Flora:* a famous Roman courtesan;   3 *Hipparchia:* possibly the pupil of the Greek philosopher Crates who left her wealthy family to live with him;   *Thais:* an Athenian courtesan and mistress of Alexander the Great;   5 *Echo:* a nymph of immortal beauty, whose unrequited love for Narcissus caused her to pine away until only her voice remained.   9 *Heloise:* pupil of Abeillard, the twelfth century philosopher. When Abeillard became her lover and secret husband, Heloise's uncle had him castrated.   13 *Queen . . . Buridan:* Jeanne of Navarre, who seduced Parisian students and then cast them into the river. Buridan, a philosopher and professor at the University, supposedly won her favor and then arranged for a barge of hay to rescue him from the Seine. Buridan's involvement is purely legendry, however, as he was only five years old at the time of the Queen's death.   17 *Queen Blanche:* possible Blanche of Castille, mother of Saint Louis, or Blanche of Burgundy, wife of Charles IV and condemned for adultry.

Bertha Broadfoot, Beatrice, Alice,
    And Ermengarde the lady of Maine,   20
    And that good Joan whom Englishmen
At Rouen doomed and burned her there,
    Mother of God, where are they then? . . .
But where are the snows of yester-year?

Nay, never ask this week, fair lord,   25
    Where they are gone, nor yet this year,
Except with this for an overword,
    But where are the snows of yester-year?

ca. 1461

Anonymous

WESTERN WIND

Western wind, when will thou blow,
    The small rain down can rain?
Christ, if my love were in my arms
    And I in my bed again!

ca. 1500

Thomas Wyatt

(1503–1542)

THEY FLEE FROM ME

They flee from me, that sometime did me seek,
With naked foot stalking in my chamber.
I have seen them, gentle, tame, and meek,
That now are wild, and do not remember
That sometime they put themselves in danger   5
To take bread at my hand; and now they range,
Busily seeking with a continual change.

---

19 *Bertha Broadfoot, Beatrice, Alice:* heroines of the medieval *Chanson de Geste;* Bertha was also the mother of Charlemagne.   20 *Ermengarde:* the heiress of Maine who was forced to marry Folque of Anjou, who later murdered her.   21 *Joan:* Joan of Arc, the fifteenth century French national heroine.

Thanked be Fortune it hath been otherwise,
Twenty times better; but once in special,
In thin array, after a pleasant guise,   10
When her loose gown from her shoulders did fall,
And she me caught in her arms long and small,
And therewith all sweetly did me kiss
And softly said, "Dear heart, how like you this?"

It was no dream, I lay broad waking.   15
But all is turned, thorough my gentleness,
Into a strange fashion of forsaking;
And I have leave to go, of her goodness,
And she also to use newfangleness.
But since that I so kindely am served,   20
I fain would know what she hath deserved.

                                                    1557

George Gordon, Lord Byron

(1788–1824)

WHEN WE TWO PARTED

When we two parted
In silence and tears,
Half broken-hearted,
To sever for years,
Pale grew thy cheek and cold,   5
Colder thy kiss;
Truly that hour foretold
Sorrow to this!

The dew of the morning
Sunk chill on my brow;   10
It felt like the warning
Of what I feel now.
Thy vows are all broken,
And light is thy fame:
I hear thy name spoken   15
And share in its shame.

They name thee before me,
A knell to mine ear;
A shudder comes o'er me—
Why wert thou so dear?   20

They know not I knew thee
Who knew thee too well:
Long, long shall I rue thee
Too deeply to tell.

In secret we met: 25
In silence I grieve
That thy heart could forget,
Thy spirit deceive.
If I should meet thee
After long years,   30
How should I greet thee?—
With silence and tears.

1808

Gustavo Adolfo Bécquer

(1836–1870)

WILL NOT COME BACK *(Volverán[1])*

adapted and translated from the Spanish by Robert Lowell

Dark swallows will doubtless come back killing
the injudicious nightflies with a clack of the beak;
but these that stopped full flight to see your beauty
and my good fortune . . . as if they knew our names —
they'll not come back. The thick lemony honeysuckle,   5
climbing from the earthroot to your window,
will open more beautiful blossoms to the evening;
but these . . . like dewdrops, trembling, shining, falling,
the tears of day—they'll not come back. . . .
Some other love will sound his fireword for you   10
and wake your heart, perhaps, from its cool sleep;
but silent, absorbed, and on his knees,
as men adore God at the altar, as I love you —
don't blind yourself, you'll not be loved like that.

1871, trans. 1961

_____

1. The title is Lowell's. Bécquer's poem is untitled in Spanish, although from its first
line—"Volverán las oscuras golondrinas"—it has come to be known as "Volverán." In
this free translation (which he called an "imitation") Lowell has also altered the stanzaic
form of the poem.

Gustavo Adolfo Bécquer   **691**

Thomas Hardy

(1840–1928)

WEATHERS

1

This is the weather the cuckoo likes,
   And so do I;
When showers betumble the chestnut spikes,
   And nestlings fly:
And the little brown nightingale bills his best,   5
And they sit outside at 'The Travellers' Rest,'
And maids come forth sprig-muslin drest,
And citizens dream of the south and west,
   And so do I.

2

This is the weather the shepherd shuns,   10
   And so do I;
When beeches drip in browns and duns,
   And thresh, and ply;
And hill-hid tides throb, throe on throe,
And meadow rivulets overflow,   15
And drops on gate-bars hang in a row,
And rooks in families homeward go,
   And so do I.

1922

JOHN DONNE

(1572–1631)

THE RELIC

When my grave is broke up again
Some second guest to entertain
(For graves have learned that woman-head,
To be to more than one a bed)
   And he that digs it spies   5

A bracelet of bright hair about the bone,
    Will he not let us alone,
And think that there a loving couple lies,
Who thought that this device might be some way
To make their souls, at the last busy day,   10
Meet at this grave, and make a little stay?

    If this fall in a time, or land,
    Where mis-devotion doth command,
    Then he that digs us up will bring
    Us to the Bishop and the King   15
        To make us relics; then
Thou shalt be a Mary Magdalen, and I
        A something else thereby;
All women shall adore us, and some men;
And, since at such time miracles are sought,   20
I would have that age by this paper taught
What miracles we harmless lovers wrought.
    First, we loved well and faithfully,
    Yet knew not what we loved, nor why;
    Difference of sex no more we knew,   25
    Than our guardian angels do;
        Coming and going, we
Perchance might kiss, but not between those meals;
        Our hands ne'er touched the seals
Which nature, injured by late law, sets free.   30
These miracles we did; but now, alas,
All measure, and all language, I should pass,
Should I tell what a miracle she was.

                                        1633

THE CANONIZATION

For God's sake, hold your tongue, and let me love,
    Or chide my palsy, or my gout,
My five gray hairs, or ruined fortune flout,
    With wealth your state, your mind with arts improve,
        Take you a course, get you a place,   5
        Observe his honor, or his grace,
Or the King's real, or his stamped face
    Contemplate; what you will, approve,
    So you will let me love.

The Relic: 13 *mis-devotion:* idolatry;   *Canonization:* 7 *stamped face:* the likeness on a coin;
8 *approve:* try out

John Donne   *693*

Alas, alas, who's injured by my love?   10
    What merchant's ships have my sighs drowned?
Who says my tears have overflowed his ground?
      When did my colds a forward spring remove?
        When did the heats which my veins fill
        Add one more to the plaguy bill?   15
Soldiers find wars, and lawyers find out still
    Litigious men, which quarrels move,
    Though she and I do love.

Call us what you will, we are made such by love;
    Call her one, me another fly,   20
We're tapers too, and at our own cost die,
      And we in us find the eagle and the dove.
        The phoenix riddle hath more wit
        By us; we two being one, are it.
So, to one neutral thing both sexes fit.   25
    We die and rise the same, and prove
    Mysterious by this love.

We can die by it, if not live by love,
    And if unfit for tombs and hearse
Our legend be, it will be fit for verse;   30
      And if no piece of chronicle we prove,
        We'll build in sonnets pretty rooms;
        As well a well-wrought urn becomes
The greatest ashes, as half-acre tombs,
      And by these hymns, all shall approve   35
    Us *canonized* for Love.

And thus invoke us: "You, whom reverend love
    Made one another's hermitage;
You, to whom love was peace, that now is rage;
      Who did the whole world's soul extract, and drove   40
        Into the glass of your eyes
        (So made such mirrors, and such spies,
That they did all to you epitomize)
    Countries, towns, courts: beg from above
    A pattern of your love!"   45

1633

---

15 *plaguy bill:* the list of those dead from the plague; Donne is possibly referring to the plague of 1592 which struck London while he was living there;   22 *eagle . . . dove:* the powerful and the meek; the two also represent righteousness and mercy which, in medieval literature, produced peace;   23 *phoenix:* a mythical bird which was both male and female, and which self-procreated by burning in fire and then rising again from the ashes

A VALEDICTION: FORBIDDING MOURNING

As virtuous men pass mildly away,
   And whisper to their souls to go,
Whilst some of their sad friends do say,
   "The breath goes now," and some say, "No,"

So let us melt, and make no noise,   5
   No tear-floods, nor sigh-tempests move;
'Twere profanation of our joys
   To tell the laity our love.

Moving of the earth brings harms and fears,
   Men reckon what it did and meant;   10
But trepidation of the spheres,
   Though greater far, is innocent.

Dull sublunary lovers' love
   (Whose soul is sense) cannot admit
Absence, because it doth remove   15
   Those things which elemented it.

But we, by a love so much refined
   That our selves know not what it is,
Inter-assured of the mind,
   Care less, eyes, lips, and hands to miss.   20

Our two souls therefore, which are one,
   Though I must go, endure not yet
A breach, but an expansion,
   Like gold to airy thinness beat.

If they be two, they are two so   25
   As stiff twin compasses are two:
Thy soul, the fixed foot, makes no show
   To move, but doth, if the other do;

And though it in the center sit,
   Yet when the other far doth roam,   30
It leans, and hearkens after it,
   And grows erect, as that comes home.

Such wilt thou be to me, who must,
   Like the other foot, obliquely run;
Thy firmness makes my circle just,   35
   And makes me end where I begun.

1633

Valediction: 12 *innocent:* innocuous

THE GOOD-MORROW

I wonder, by my troth, what thou and I
Did, till we loved? were we not weaned till then?
But sucked on country pleasures, childishly?
Or snorted we in the Seven Sleepers' den?
'Twas so; but this, all pleasures fancies be.   5
If ever any beauty I did see,
Which I desired, and got, 'twas but a dream of thee.

And now good-morrow to our waking souls,
Which watch not one another out of fear;
For love, all love of other sights controls,   10
And makes one little room an everywhere.
Let sea-discoverers to new worlds have gone,
Let maps to others, worlds on worlds have shown,
Let us possess one world, each hath one, and is one.

My face in thine eye, thine in mine appears,   15
And true plain hearts do in the faces rest;
Where can we find two better hemispheres,
Without sharp north, without declining west?
Whatever dies was not mixed equally;
If our two loves be one, or, thou and I   20
Love so alike that none do slacken, none can die.

1633

THE SUN RISING

Busy old fool, unruly sun,
    Why dost thou thus,
Through windows, and through curtains, call on us?
Must to thy motions lovers' seasons run?
    Saucy pedantic wretch, go chide   5
    Late schoolboys, and sour prentices,
  Go tell court-huntsmen that the King will ride,
  Call country ants to harvest offices;
Love, all alike, no season knows, nor clime,
Nor hours, days, months, which are the rags of time.   10

    Thy beams, so reverend and strong
    Why shouldst thou think?

Good-morrow: 4 *Seven Sleepers:* according to legend, seven Christian youths who took refuge in
a cave to escape persecution during the rule of Decius; they awakened two centuries later.
Sun Rising: 6 *prentices:* apprentices;

I could eclipse and cloud them with a wink,
But that I would not lose her sight so long:
    If her eyes have not blinded thine,   15
    Look, and tomorrow late, tell me
  Whether both the Indias of spice and mine
  Be where thou leftst them, or lie here with me.
Ask for those kings whom thou saw'st yesterday,
And thou shalt hear, All here in one bed lay.   20

    She's all states, and all princes I,
    Nothing else is.
Princes do but play us; compared to this,
All honor's mimic, all wealth alchemy.
    Thou, sun, art half as happy as we,   25
    In that the world's contracted thus;
  Thine age asks ease, and since thy duties be
  To warm the world, that's done in warming us.
Shine here to us, and thou art everywhere;
This bed thy center is, these walls thy sphere.   30

                                        1633

THE FLEA

Mark but this flea, and mark in this
How little that which thou deny'st me is;
It sucked me first, and now sucks thee,
And in this flea our two bloods mingled be;
Thou know'st that this cannot be said   5
A sin, nor shame, nor loss of maidenhead,
    Yet this enjoys before it woo,
    And pampered swells with one blood made of two,
    And this, alas, is more than we would do.

Oh stay, three lives in one flea spare,   10
Where we almost, yea more than married are.
This flea is you and I, and this
Our marriage bed, and marriage temple is;
Though parents grudge, and you, we're met
And cloistered in these living walls of jet.   15
    Though use make you apt to kill me,
    Let not to that, self-murder added be,
    And sacrilege, three sins in killing three.

Cruel and sudden, hast thou since
Purpled thy nail in blood of innocence?   20

---

17 *Indias:* the East Indies, known for its spices, and the West Indies, known for its gold mines.

Wherein could this flea guilty be,
Except in that drop which it sucked from thee?
Yet thou triumph'st, and say'st that thou
Find'st not thyself, nor me, the weaker now;
  'Tis true; then learn how false, fears be;   25
   Just so much honor, when thou yield'st to me,
   Will waste, as this flea's death took life from thee.

1633

[DEATH BE NOT PROUD, THOUGH SOME HAVE CALLED THEE]

Death be not proud, though some have called thee
Mighty and dreadful, for thou art not so;
For those whom thou think'st thou dost overthrow
Die not, poor death, nor yet canst thou kill me.
From rest and sleep, which but thy pictures be,   5
Much pleasure; then from thee much more must flow,
And soonest our best men with thee do go,
Rest of their bones, and soul's delivery.
Thou art slave to fate, chance, kings, and desperate
   men,
And dost with poison, war, and sickness dwell;   10
And poppy or charms can make us sleep as well,
And better than thy stroke; why swell'st thou then?
One short sleep past, we wake eternally,
And death shall be no more; death, thou shalt die.

(Holy Sonnet 10) 1633

[BATTER MY HEART, THREE-PERSONED GOD; FOR YOU]

Batter my heart, three-personed God; for You
As yet but knock, breathe, shine, and seek to mend;
That I may rise and stand, o'erthrow me, and bend
Your force, to break, blow, burn, and make me new.
I, like an usurped town, to another due,   5
Labor to admit You, but Oh, to no end!
Reason, Your viceroy in me, me should defend,
But is captived, and proves weak or untrue.
Yet dearly I love You, and would be loved fain,
But am betrothed unto Your enemy: 10
Divorce me, untie or break that knot again,
Take me to You, imprison me, for I,

Except You enthrall me, never shall be free,
Nor ever chaste, except You ravish me.

(Holy Sonnet 14) 1633

A HYMN TO GOD THE FATHER

Wilt Thou forgive that sin where I begun,
   Which is my sin, though it were done before?
Wilt Thou forgive that sin through which I run,
   And do run still, though still I do deplore?
     When Thou hast done, Thou hast not done,   5
       For I have more.

Wilt Thou forgive that sin by which I have won
   Others to sin? and made my sin their door?
Wilt Thou forgive that sin which I did shun
   A year or two, but wallowed in a score?   10
     When Thou hast done, Thou hast not done,
       For I have more.

I have a sin of fear, that when I have spun
   My last thread, I shall perish on the shore;
Swear by Thy self, that at my death Thy Son   15
   Shall shine as he shines now and heretofore;
     And, having done that, Thou hast done,
       I fear no more.

1633

HYMN TO GOD MY GOD,
IN MY SICKNESS

Since I am coming to that holy room
   Where, with Thy choir of saints for evermore,
I shall be made Thy music; as I come
   I tune the instrument here at the door,
   And what I must do then, think here before.   5

Whilst my physicians by their love are grown
   Cosmographers, and I their map, who lie
Flat on this bed, that by them may be shown
   That this is my southwest discovery
   Per fretum febris, by these straits to die,   10

Hymn: 9 *southwest discovery:* the Straits of Magellan;   10 *Per fretum febris:* through the raging,
or strait, of fever.

I joy, that in these straits, I see my West;
    For, though their currents yield return to none,
What shall my West hurt me? As West and East
    In all flat maps (and I am one) are one,
    So death doth touch the resurrection.   15

Is the Pacific Sea my home? Or are
    The Eastern riches? Is Jerusalem?
Anyan, and Magellan, and Gibraltar,
    All straits, and none but straits, are ways to them,
    Whether where Japhet dwelt, or Cham, or Shem.   20

We think that Paradise and Calvary,
    Christ's cross, and Adam's tree, stood in one place;
Look, Lord, and find both Adams met in me;
    As the first Adam's sweat surrounds my face,
    May the last Adam's blood my soul embrace.   25

So, in his purple wrapped, receive me, Lord;
    By these his thorns give me his other crown;
And, as to others' souls I preached Thy word,
    Be this my text, my sermon to mine own;
    Therefore that he may raise the Lord throws down.   30

1635

Shakespeare's songs and sonnets approach pure lyricism, but the "metaphysical" poems of some of his contemporaries and immediate successors (including John Donne and George Herbert) replace direct, simple themes with subjects and ideas far more subtle and emotionally complex. A poet like A. E. Housman is naturally unsympathetic to this sort of poetry; a poet like T. S. Eliot admires it.

"Such discoveries are no more poetical than anagrams": A. E. Housman

There was a whole age of English in which the place of poetry was usurped by something very different which possessed the proper and specific name

---

18 *Anyan:* the Bering Strait;   20 *Japhet, Cham, Shem:* the sons of Noah who populated Europe, Africa, and Asia respectively

of wit: wit not in its modern sense, but as defined by Johnson, 'a combination of dissimilar images, or discovery of occult resemblances in things apparently unlike'. Such discoveries are no more poetical than anagrams; such pleasure as they give is purely intellectual and is intellectually frivolous; but this was the pleasure principally sought and found in poems by the intelligentsia of fifty years and more of the seventeenth century. Some of the writers who purveyed it to their contemporaries were, by accident, considerable poets; and though their verse was generally inharmonious, and apparently cut into lengths and tied into faggots by deaf mathematicians, some little of their poetry was beautiful and even superb. But it was not by this that they captivated and sought to captivate. Simile and metaphor, things inessential to poetry, were their great engrossing preoccupation, and were prized the more in proportion as they were further fetched. They did not mean these accessories to be helpful, to make their sense clearer or their conceptions more vivid; they hardly even meant them for ornament, or cared whether an image had any independent power to please: their object was to startle by novelty and amuse by ingenuity a public whose one wish was to be so startled and amused. The pleasure, however luxurious, of hearing St Mary Magdalene's eyes described as

> Two walking baths, two weeping motions,
> Portable and compendious oceans,

was not a poetic pleasure; and poetry, as a label for this particular commodity, is not appropriate.

"Feel their thought as immediately as the odour of a rose": T. S. Eliot

The difference [between a passage by Herbert and one by Tennyson] is not a simple difference of degree between poets. It is something which had happened to the mind of England between the time of Donne or Lord Herbert of Cherbury and the time of Tennyson and Browning; it is the difference between the intellectual poet and the reflective poet. Tennyson and Browning are poets, and they think; but they do not feel their thought as immediately as the odour of a rose. A thought to Donne was an experience; it modified his sensibility. When a poet's mind is perfectly equipped for its work, it is constantly amalgamating disparate experience; the ordinary man's experience is chaotic, irregular, fragmentary. The latter falls in love, or reads Spinoza, and these two experiences have nothing to do with each other, or with the noise of the typewriter or the smell of cooking; in the mind of the poet these experiences are always forming new wholes.

*The sort of wit that blends emotion and thought and brings together unex-
pected images is certainly alive in contemporary poetry, as we see in the following poems by Alan Dugan, Adrienne Rich, and Sandra McPherson.*

Alan Dugan

(b. 1923)

LOVE SONG: I AND THOU

Nothing is plumb, level, or square:
   the studs are bowed, the joists
are shaky by nature, no piece fits
   any other piece without a gap
or pinch, and bent nails   5
   dance all over the surfacing
like maggots. By Christ
   I am no carpenter. I built
the roof for myself, the walls
   for myself, the floors   10
for myself, and got
   hung up in it myself. I
danced with a purple thumb
   at this house-warming, drunk
with my prime whiskey: rage.   15
   Oh I spat rage's nails
into the frame-up of my work:
   it held. It settled plumb,
level, solid, square and true
   for that great moment. Then   20
it screamed and went on through,
   skewing as wrong the other way.
God damned it. This is hell,
   but I planned it, I sawed it,
I nailed it, and I   25
   will live in it until it kills me.
I can nail my left palm
   to the left-hand crosspiece but
I can't do everything myself.
   I need a hand to nail the right,   30
a help, a love, a you, a wife.

1961

Adrienne Rich

(b. 1929)

TWO SONGS

1

Sex, as they harshly call it,
I fell into this morning
at ten o'clock, a drizzling hour
of traffic and wet newspapers.
I thought of him who yesterday   5
clearly didn't
turn me to a hot field
ready for plowing,
and longing for that young man
piercéd me to the roots   10
bathing every vein, etc.
All day he appears to me
touchingly desirable,
a prize one could wreck one's peace for.
I'd call it love if love   15
didn't take so many years
but lust too is a jewel
a sweet flower and what
pure happiness to know
all our high-toned questions   20
breed in a lively animal.

2

That "old last act"!
And yet sometimes
all seems post coitum triste
and I a mere bystander.   25
Somebody else is going off,
getting shot to the moon.
Or, a moon-race!
Split seconds after
my opposite number lands   30
I make it—
we lie fainting together
at a crater-edge
heavy as mercury in our moonsuits

till he speaks—   35
in a different language
yet one I've picked up
through cultural exchanges . . .
we murmur the first moonwords:
Spasibo. Thanks. O.K.   40

1964

Sandra McPherson

(b. 1943)

7,22,66

Which doesn't belong in this group of three?—
Soap, Bible, stationery.
Two deal with creation;
So obviously the soap

Doesn't blend—   5
It can't wash away the fate
Of three of us trying to belong
To one another.

But on our honeymoon, from the key's first turn,
I thought the misfit was the Bible.   10
I was already with child
Beside the Gideon cover with its torch.

Fresh out of the shower, you judged each queen
For softness; I packed the stationery.
Even while we lay still,   15
Fog closed the window.

From the Port Townsend double on heavy pilings,
Tides growing barnacles and starfish
Under the bed, we did not take God's Word
For a souvenir.   20

Rustling an atlas, catching the morning ferry,
You went on with me, into a life that had stolen you,
Asking that night for a decent room for two,
And puzzling out the number on its key.

1983

JOHN MILTON

(1608–1674)

[WHEN I CONSIDER HOW MY LIGHT IS SPENT]

When I consider how my light is spent
  Ere half my days, in this dark world and wide,
  And that one talent which is death to hide
  Lodged with me useless, though my soul more bent
To serve therewith my Maker, and present   5
  My true account, lest he returning chide;
  "Doth God exact day-labor, light denied?"
  I fondly ask; but Patience to prevent
That murmur, soon replies, "God doth not need
  Either man's work or his own gifts; who best   10
  Bear his mild yoke, they serve him best. His state
Is kingly. Thousands at his bidding speed
  And post o'er land and ocean without rest:
  They also serve who only stand and wait."

1652

ON THE LATE MASSACRE IN PIEDMONT

Avenge, O Lord, thy slaughtered saints, whose bones
  Lie scattered on the Alpine mountains cold,
  Even them who kept thy truth so pure of old
  When all our fathers worshiped stocks and stones,
Forget not: in thy book record their groans   5
  Who were thy sheep and in their ancient fold
  Slain by the bloody Piedmontese that rolled
  Mother with infant down the rocks. Their moans
The vales redoubled to the hills, and they

Massacre: The massacre of the Vaudois, a protestant sect founded by Peter Valdres in the twelfth century, resulted from a dispute over land rights involving villages bordering France and Italy. In 1655 the Duke of Savoy sent the Marquis of Pianezza to expel the Vaudois, and when the villagers fled, Pianezza pursued and massacred nearly 2,000 of them. Cromwell took up the Vaudois cause and had Milton write letters of protest to several European countries. Meanwhile, the Vaudois regained strength and won several battles against the Piedmontese troops. A treaty which restored the ancient rights of the Vaudois was signed within months of the massacre. 8 *Mother with infant:* an account of the massacre by one of Cromwell's agents records three separate incidents in which a woman and her child were hurled down the rocks to their deaths.

To Heaven. Their martyred blood and ashes sow   10
   O'er all th' Italian fields where still doth sway
The triple tyrant: that from these may grow
   A hundredfold, who having learnt thy way
   Early may fly the Babylonian woe.

1655

[METHOUGHT I SAW]

Methought I saw my late espoused saint
   Brought to me like Alcestis from the grave,
   Whom Jove's great son to her glad husband gave,
   Rescued from Death by force, though pale and faint.
Mine, as whom washed from spot of child-bed taint   5
   Purification in the Old Law did save,
   And such, as yet once more I trust to have
   Full sight of her in heaven without restraint,
Came vested all in white, pure as her mind.
   Her face was veiled; yet to my fancied sight   10
   Love, sweetness, goodness, in her person shined
So clear as in no face with more delight.
   But O, as to embrace me she inclined,
   I waked, she fled, and day brought back my night.

ca. 1658

from PARADISE LOST, Book IX

Satan, having compassed the earth, with meditated guile returns as a mist by night into Paradise, enters into the serpent sleeping. Adam and Eve in the morning go forth to their labours, which Eve proposes to divide in several places, each labouring apart: Adam consents not, alleging the dangers lest that enemy, of whom they were forewarned, should attempt her found alone. Eve loth to be thought not circumspect or firm enough, urges her going apart, the rather desirous to make trial of her strength; Adam at last yields. [Milton's summary]

Oft he to her his charge of quick return
Repeated; she to him as oft engaged   400

---

12 *tyrant:* the Pope with his three-tiered crown;   14 *Babylonian:* Puritans often identified Roman Catholicism with the Babylon of *Revelation. Methought:* 2 *Alcestis:* in Euripides' *Alcestis,* she gives her life for her husband; Hercules ("Jove's great son") brings her back to life by wrestling with death.   6 *purification:* Old Testament purification of a woman after childbirth

To be returned by noon amid the bower,
And all things in best order to invite
Noontide repast, or afternoon's repose.
O much deceived, much failing, hapless Eve,
Of thy presumed return! Event perverse!   405
Thou never from that hour in Paradise
Found'st either sweet repast, or sound repose;
Such ambush hid among sweet flowers and shades
Waited with hellish rancor imminent
To intercept thy way, or send thee back   410
Despoiled of innocence, of faith, of bliss.
For now, and since first break of dawn, the fiend,
Mere serpent in appearance, forth was come,
And on his quest, where likeliest he might find
The only two of mankind, but in them   415
The whole included race, his purposed prey.
In bower and field he sought, where any tuft
Of grove or garden-plot more pleasant lay,
Their tendance or plantation for delight;
By fountain or by shady rivulet   420
He sought them both, but wished his hap might find
Eve separate; he wished, but not with hope
Of what so seldom chanced; when to his wish,
Beyond his hope, Eve separate he spies,
Veiled in a cloud of fragrance, where she stood,   425
Half spied, so thick the roses bushing round
About her glowed, oft stooping to support
Each flower of slender stalk, whose head though gay
Carnation, purple, azure, or specked with gold,
Hung drooping unsustained, them she upstays   430
Gently with myrtle band, mindless the while
Herself, though fairest unsupported flower,
From her best prop so far, and storm so nigh.
Nearer he drew, and many a walk traversed
Of stateliest covert, cedar, pine, or palm;   435
Then voluble and bold, now hid, now seen
Among thick-woven arborets and flowers
Embordered on each bank, the hand of Eve:
Spot more delicious than those gardens feigned
Or of revived Adonis, or renowned   440
Alcinous, host of old Laertes' son,

Paradise Lost: 419 *tendance:* object of care;   436 *voluble:* gliding easily; rolling;   438 *hand:*
handiwork;   440 *Adonis:* a youth loved by Venus and killed by a boar; his death and revival are
celebrated in seasonal rites.   441 *Alcinous:* king of Phaeacia who entertained Odysseus;
Odysseus was "stopped still" by the beauty of his garden. *Laertes' son:* Odysseus; Laertes gave
up kingship to take up gardening.

Or that, not mystic, where the sapient king
Held dalliance with his fair Egyptian spouse.
Much he the place admired, the person more.
As one who long in populous city pent, 445
Where houses thick and sewers annoy the air,
Forth issuing on a summer's morn to breathe
Among the pleasant villages and farms
Adjoined, from each thing met conceives delight,
The smell of grain, or tedded grass, or kine, 450
Or dairy, each rural sight, each rural sound:
If chance with nymphlike step fair virgin pass,
What pleasing seemed, for her now pleases more,
She most, and in her look sums all delight.
Such pleasure took the serpent to behold 455
This flowery plat, the sweet recess of Eve
Thus early, thus alone; her heavenly form
Angelic, but more soft, and feminine,
Her graceful innocence, her every air
Of gesture or least action overawed 460
His malice, and with rapine sweet bereaved
His fierceness of the fierce intent it brought:
That space the evil one abstracted stood
From his own evil, and for the time remained
Stupidly good, of enmity disarmed, 465
Of guile, of hate, of envy, of revenge.
But the hot Hell that always in him burns,
Though in mid Heaven, soon ended his delight,
And tortures him now more, the more he sees
Of pleasure not for him ordained: then soon 470
Fierce hate he recollects, and all his thoughts
Of mischief, gratulating, thus excites:
    "Thoughts, whither have ye led me? with what sweet
Compulsion thus transported to forget
What hither brought us? hate, not love, nor hope 475
Of Paradise for Hell, hope here to taste
Of pleasure, but all pleasure to destroy,
Save what is in destroying; other joy
To me is lost. Then let me not let pass
Occasion which now smiles; behold alone 480
The woman, opportune to all attempts,
Her husband, for I view far round, not nigh,
Whose higher intellectual more I shun,
And strength, of courage haughty, and of limb

---

442 *sapient king:* Solomon, another Old Testament figure led to sin by love of his wife.
456 *plat:* patch of ground;   472 *gratulating:* expressing joy;

Poetry

Heroic built, though of terrestrial mold; 485
Foe not informidable, exempt from wound,
I not; so much hath Hell debased, and pain
Enfeebled me, to what I was in Heaven.
She fair, divinely fair, fit love for gods,
Not terrible, though terror be in love 490
And beauty, not approached by stronger hate,
Hate stronger, under show of love well feigned,
The way which to her ruin now I tend."
    So spake the enemy of mankind, enclosed
In serpent, inmate bad, and toward Eve 495
Addressed his way, not with indented wave,
Prone on the ground, as since, but on his rear,
Circular base of rising folds, that towered
Fold above fold a surging maze; his head
Crested aloft, and carbuncle his eyes; 500
With burnished neck of verdant gold, erect
Amidst his circling spires, that on the grass
Floated redundant. Pleasing was his shape,
And lovely; never since of serpent kind
Lovelier, not those that in Illyria changed 505
Hermione and Cadmus, or the god
In Epidaurus; nor to which transformed
Ammonian Jove, or Capitoline was seen,
He with Olympias, this with her who bore
Scipio, the height of Rome. With tract oblique 510
At first, as one who sought access, but feared
To interrupt, sidelong he works his way.
As when a ship by skillful steersman wrought
Nigh river's mouth or foreland, where the wind
Veers oft, as oft so steers, and shifts her sail: 515
So varied he, and of his tortuous train
Curled many a wanton wreath in sight of Eve,
To lure her eye: she busied heard the sound
Of rustling leaves, but minded not, as used
To such disport before her through the field, 520
From every beast, more duteous at her call,
Than at Circean call the herd disguised.
He bolder now, uncalled before her stood:

---

500 *carbuncle:* red garnet, a mineral associated with the underworld;   505: *Illyria:* the
Adriatic region;   506 *Hermione* . . . Cadmus: both were metamorphosed into serpents;
507 *Epidaurus:* a god of medicine who, in serpent form, went to Rome to stop the plague;
508 *Ammonian Jove:* while in serpent form, fathered Alexander the Great *Capitoline:* Jupiter
Capitolinus, who took a serpent form to father Scipio, the greatest general of the Roman
Republic;   509 *Olympias:* mother of Alexander the Great;   522 *Circean:* allegorically, any
form of excess which reduces men to beasts.

But as in gaze admiring; oft he bowed
His turret crest, and sleek enameled neck,   525
Fawning, and licked the ground whereon she trod.
His gentle dumb expression turned at length
The eye of Eve to mark his play: he, glad
Of her attention gained, with serpent tongue
Organic, or impulse of vocal air,   530
His fraudulent temptation thus began.
    "Wonder not, sovereign mistress, if perhaps
Thou canst, who art sole wonder; much less arm
Thy looks, the heaven of mildness, with disdain,
Displeased that I approach thee thus, and gaze   535
Insatiate, I thus single, nor have feared
Thy awful brow, more awful thus retired.
Fairest resemblance of thy Maker fair,
Thee all things living gaze on, all things thine
By gift, and thy celestial beauty adore   540
With ravishment beheld, there best beheld
Where universally admired: but here
In this enclosure wild, these beasts among,
Beholders rude, and shallow to discern
Half what in thee is fair, one man except,   545
Who sees thee? (and what is one?) who shouldst be
   seen
A goddess among gods, adored and served
By angels numberless, thy daily train."

*Eve, wondering to hear the Serpent speak, asks how he attained to human
speech and such understanding, not till now; the Serpent answers that by
tasting of a certain tree in the garden he attained both to speech and reason,
till then void of both. Eve requires him to bring her to that tree, and finds it
to be the tree of knowledge forbidden. The Serpent now grown bolder, with
many wiles and arguments induces her at length to eat; she, pleased with the
taste, deliberates a while whether to impart thereof to Adam or not, at last
brings him of the fruit; relates what persuaded her to eat thereof. Adam at
first amazed, but perceiving her lost, resolves through vehemence of love to
perish with her and, extenuating the trespass, eats also of the fruit. [Milton's summary]*

In recompense (for such compliance bad
Such recompense best merits), from the bough   995
She gave him of that fair enticing fruit
With liberal hand; he scrupled not to eat,
Against his better knowledge, not deceived,
But fondly overcome with female charm.

Earth trembled from her entrails, as again   1000
In pangs, and Nature gave a second groan,
Sky lowered, and muttering thunder, some sad drops
Wept at completing of the mortal sin
Original; while Adam took no thought,
Eating his fill, nor Eve to iterate   1005
Her former trespass feared, the more to soothe
Him with her loved society; that now
As with new wine intoxicated both,
They swim in mirth, and fancy that they feel
Divinity within them breeding wings   1010
Wherewith to scorn the Earth. But that false fruit
Far other operation first displayed,
Carnal desire inflaming; he on Eve
Began to cast lacivous eyes, she him
As wantonly repaid; in lust they burn,   1015
Till Adam thus 'gan Eve to dalliance move:
    "Eve, now I see thou art exact of taste,
And elegant, of sapience no small part,
Since to each meaning savor we apply,
And palate call judicious. I the praise   1020
Yield thee, so well this day thou hast purveyed.
Much pleasure we have lost, while we abstained
From this delightful fruit, nor known till now
True relish, tasting; if such pleasure be
In things to us forbidden, it might be wished,   1025
For this one tree had been forbidden ten.
But come; so well refreshed, now let us play,
As meet is, after such delicious fare;
For never did thy beauty, since the day
I saw thee first and wedded thee, adorned   1030
With all perfections, so enflame my sense
With ardor to enjoy thee, fairer now
Than ever, bounty of this virtuous tree."
    So said he, and forbore not glance or toy
Of amorous intent, well understood   1035
Of Eve, whose eye darted contagious fire.
Her hand he seized, and to a shady bank,
Thick overhead with verdant roof embowered
He led her, nothing loath; flowers were the couch,
Pansies, and violets, and asphodel,   1040
And hyacinth—Earth's freshest, softest lap.

————

1018 *sapience:* the Latin word *sapere* means both "to taste" and "to be wise";   1036 *Of:* by

John Milton   711

There they their fill of love and love's disport
Took largely, of their mutual guilt the seal,
The solace of their sin, till dewy sleep
Oppressed them, wearied with their amorous play.   1045
    Soon as the force of that fallacious fruit,
That with exhilarating vapor bland
About their spirits had played, and inmost powers
Made err, was now exhaled, and grosser sleep
Bred of unkindly fumes, with conscious dreams   1050
Encumbered, now had left them, up they rose
As from unrest, and each the other viewing,
Soon found their eyes how opened, and their minds
How darkened. Innocence, that as a veil
Had shadowed them from knowing ill, was gone;   1055
Just confidence, and native righteousness,
And honor from about them, naked left
To guilty Shame; he covered, but his robe
Uncovered more. So rose the Danite strong,
Herculean Samson, from the harlot-lap   1060
Of Philstean Dalilah, and waked
Shorn of his strength; they destitute and bare
Of all their virtue. Silent, and in face
Confounded, long they sat, as strucken mute;
Till Adam, though not less than Eve abashed,   1065
At length gave utterance to these words constrained:
    "O Eve, in evil hour thou didst give ear
To that false worm, of whomsoever taught
To counterfeit man's voice, true in our fall,
False in our promised rising; since our eyes   1070
Opened we find indeed, and find we know
Both good and evil, good lost, and evil got:
Bad fruit of knowledge, if this be to know,
Which leaves us naked thus, of honor void,
Of innocence, of faith, of purity,   1075
Our wonted ornaments now soiled and stained,
And in our faces evident the signs
Of foul concupiscence; whence evil store,
Even shame, the last of evils; of the first
Be sure then. How shall I behold the face   1080
Henceforth of God or angel, erst with joy
And rapture so oft beheld? Those heavenly shapes
Will dazzle now this earthly with their blaze
Insufferably bright. O might I here

1050 *unkindly:* unnatural

In solitude live savage, in some glade   1085
Obscured, where highest woods, impenetrable
To star or sunlight, spread their umbrage broad,
And brown as evening! Cover me, ye pines,
Ye cedars, with innumerable boughs
Hide me, where I may never see them more!   1090
But let us now, as in bad plight, devise
What best may for the present serve to hide
The parts of each from other, that seem most
To shame obnoxious, and unseemliest seen;
Some tree whose broad smooth leaves together sewed,   1095
And girded on our loins, may cover round
Those middle parts, that this newcomer, Shame,
There sit not, and reproach us as unclean."
    So counseled he, and both together went
Into the thickest wood; there soon they chose   1100
The figtree, not that kind for fruit renowned,
But such as at this day, to Indians known,
In Malabar or Deccan spreads her arms
Branching so broad and long, that in the ground
The bended twigs take root, and daughters grow   1105
About the mother tree, a pillared shade
High overarched, and echoing walks between;
There oft the Indian herdsman, shunning heat,
Shelters in cool, and tends his pasturing herds
At loopholes cut through thickest shade. Those leaves 1110
They gathered, broad as Amazonian targe,
And with what skill they had, together sewed,
To gird their waist; vain covering, if to hide
Their guilt and dreaded shame! O how unlike
To that first naked glory! Such of late   1115
Columbus found th' American, so girt
With feathered cincture, naked else and wild
Among the trees on isles and woody shores.
Thus fenced, and, as they thought, their shame in part
Covered, but not at rest or ease of mind,   1120
They sat them down to weep; nor only tears
Rained at their eyes, but high winds worse within
Began to rise, high passions, anger, hate,
Mistrust, suspicion, discord, and shook sore
Their inward state of mind, calm region once   1125
And full of peace, now tossed and turbulent:
For Understanding ruled not, and the Will

1094 *obnoxious:* exposed

Heard not her lore, both in subjection now
To sensual Appetite, who, from beneath
Usurping over sovereign Reason, claimed   1130
Superior sway. From thus distempered breast,
Adam, estranged in look and altered style,
Speech intermitted thus to Eve renewed:
     "Would thou hadst hearkened to my words, and
          stayed
With me, as I besought thee, when that strange   1135
Desire of wandering, this unhappy morn,
I know not whence possessed thee! we had then
Remained still happy, not as now, despoiled
Of all our good, shamed, naked, miserable.
Let none henceforth seek needless cause to approve   1140
The faith they owe; when earnestly they seek
Such proof, conclude, they then begin to fail."
     To whom, soon moved with touch of blame, thus
          Eve:
"What words have passed thy lips, Adam severe?
Imput'st thou that to my default, or will   1145
Of wandering, as thou call'st it, which who knows
But might as ill have happened, thou being by,
Or to thyself perhaps? Hadst thou been there,
Or here th' attempt, thou couldst not have discerned
Fraud in the serpent, speaking as he spake;   1150
No ground of enmity between us known,
Why he should mean me ill, or seek to harm?
Was I to have never parted from thy side?
As good have grown there still a lifeless rib.
Being as I am, why didst not thou, the head,   1155
Command me absolutely not to go,
Going into such danger, as thou saidst?
Too facile then, thou didst not much gainsay,
Nay, didst permit, approve, and fair dismiss.
Hadst thou been firm and fixed in thy dissent,   1160
Neither had I transgressed, nor thou with me."
     To whom, then first incensed, Adam replied:
"Is this the love, is this the recompense
Of mine to thee, ingrateful Eve, expressed
Immutable when thou were lost, not I,   1165
Who might have lived and joyed immortal bliss,
Yet willingly chose rather death with thee?
And am I now upbraided as the cause

––––––––––

1140 *approve:* prove;   1141 *owe:* own

Of thy transgressing? not enough severe,
It seems, in thy restraint! What could I more?   1170
I warned thee, I admonished thee, foretold
The danger, and the lurking enemy
That lay in wait: beyond this had been force,
And force upon free will hath here no place.
But confidence then bore thee on, secure   1175
Either to meet no danger, or to find
Matter of glorious trial; and perhaps
I also erred in overmuch admiring
What seemed in thee so perfect, that I thought
No evil durst attempt thee! but I rue   1180
That error now, which is become my crime,
And thou th' accuser. Thus it shall befall
Him who, to worth in women overtrusting,
Lets her will rule; restraint she will not brook,
And, left to herself, if evil thence ensue,   1185
She first his weak indulgence will accuse."
   Thus they in mutual accusation spent
The fruitless hours, but neither self-condemning;
And of their vain contést, appeared no end.

1667

*John Milton's great stature among English poets has not kept readers from
finding fault with some aspects of his poetry. Some readers, like T. S. Eliot,
have objected that Milton's language and imagery are vague. Others like
Samuel Taylor Coleridge have found in the supposed vagueness some unexpected virtues.*

"The most important fact about Milton . . . is his blindness": T. S. Eliot

The most important fact about Milton, for my purpose, is his blindness. I
do not mean that to go blind in middle life is itself enough to determine the
whole nature of a man's poetry. Blindness must be considered in conjunction with Milton's personality and character, and the peculiar education
which he received. It must also be considered in connection with his devotion to, and expertness in, the art of music. Had Milton been a man of very
keen senses—I mean of *all* the five senses—his blindness would not have

mattered so much. But for a man whose sensuousness, such as it was, had been withered early by book-learning, and whose gifts were naturally aural; it mattered a great deal. It would seem, indeed, to have helped him to concentrate on what he could do best.

At no period is the visual imagination conspicuous in Milton's poetry. . . . Milton's images do not give a sense of particularity, nor are the separate words developed in significance. His language is, if one may use the term without disparagement, *artificial* and *conventional*.

> *O'er the smooth enamel'd green . . .*

> *. . . paths of this drear wood*
> *The nodding horror of whose shady brows*
> *Threats the forlorn and wandering passenger.*

('Shady brow' here is a diminution of the value of the two words from their use in the line from *Dr. Faustus*

> *Shadowing more beauty in their airy brows.*)

The imagery in *L'Allegro* and *Il Penseroso* is all general:

> *While the ploughman near at hand,*
> *Whistles o'er the furrowed land,*
> *And the milkmaid singeth blithe,*
> *And the mower whets his scythe,*
> *And every shepherd tells his tale,*
> *Under the hawthorn in the dale.*

It is not a particular ploughman, milkmaid, and shepherd that Milton sees (as Wordsworth might see them); the sensuous effect of these verses is entirely on the ear, and is joined to the concepts of ploughman, milkmaid, and shepherd.

"This is *creation* rather then *painting*": Samuel Taylor Coleridge

The poet should paint to the imagination, not to the fancy; and I know no happier case to exemplify the distinction between these two faculties. Masterpieces of the former mode of poetic painting abound in the writings of Milton, ex. gr.

> "The fig-tree; not that kind for fruit renown'd,
> But such as at this day, to Indians known,
> In Malabar or Decan spreads her arms

Branching so broad and long, that in the ground
The bended twigs take root, *and daughters grow*
About the mother tree, a pillar'd shade
High over-arch'd, and ECHOING WALKS BETWEEN:
There oft the Indian Herdsman, shunning heat,
Shelters in cool, and tends his pasturing herds
At loop holes cut through thickest shade.''

Paradise Lost, ix, 1100

This is *creation* rather than *painting*, or if painting, yet such, and with such co-presence of the whole picture flash'd at once upon the eye, as the sun paints in a camera obscura. But the poet must likewise understand and command what Bacon calls the *vestigia communia* of the senses, the latency of all in each, and more especially as by a magical *penna duplex,* the excitement of vision by sound and the exponents of sound. Thus "THE ECHOING WALKS BETWEEN," may be almost said to reverse the fable in tradition of the head of Memnon, in the Egyptian statue. Such may be deservedly entitled the *creative words* in the world of imagination.

ANDREW MARVELL

(1621–1678)

EYES AND TEARS

1

How wisely nature did decree,
With the same eyes to weep and see!
That, having viewed the object vain,
They might be ready to complain.

2

And, since the self-deluding sight,   5
In a false angle takes each height;
These tears which better measure all,
Like wat'ry lines and plummets fall.

3

Two tears, which sorrow long did weigh
Within the scales of either eye,   10

Eyes and Tears: 8 *plummet:* a plumb, a weight suspended to establish a vertical line

Andrew Marvell **717**

And then paid out in equal poise,
Are the true price of all my joys.

4

What in the world most fair appears,
Yea even laughter, turns to tears:
And all the jewels which we prize,   15
Melt in these pendants of the eyes.

5

I have through every garden been,
Amongst the red, the white, the green;
And yet, from all the flow'rs I saw,
No honey, but these tears could draw.   20

6

So the all-seeing sun each day
Distils the world with chemic ray;
But finds the essence only showers,
Which straight in pity back he pours.

7

Yet happy they whom grief doth bless,   25
That weep the more, and see the less:
And, to preserve their sight more true,
Bathe still their eyes in their own dew.

8

So Magdalen, in tears more wise
Dissolved those captivating eyes,   30
Whose liquid chains could flowing meet
To fetter her Redeemer's feet.

9

Not full sails hasting loaden home,
Nor the chaste lady's pregnant womb,
Nor Cynthia teeming shows so fair,   35
As two eyes swoll'n with weeping are.

10

The sparkling glance that shoots desire,
Drenched in these waves, does lose its fire.
Yea oft the Thund'rer pity takes
And here the hissing lightning slakes.   40

---

11 *poise:* equal weight;   22 *chemic:* chemical or alchemic

11

The incense was to heaven dear,
Not as a perfume, but a tear.
And stars show lovely in the night,
But as they seem the tears of light.

12

Ope then mine eyes your double sluice,   45
And practise so your noblest use.
For others too can see, or sleep;
But only human eyes can weep.

13

Now like two clouds dissolving, drop,
And at each tear in distance stop: 50
Now like two fountains trickle down;
Now like two floods o'erturn and drown.

14

Thus let your streams o'erflow your springs,
Till eyes and tears be the same things:
And each the other's difference bears;   55
These weeping eyes, those seeing tears.

1681

THE DEFINITION OF LOVE

1

My Love is of a birth as rare
   As 'tis, for object, strange and high;
It was begotten by Despair,
   Upon Impossibility.

2

Magnanimous Despair alone   5
   Could show me so divine a thing,
Where feeble Hope could ne'er have flown,
   But vainly flapped its tinsel wing.

3

And yet I quickly might arrive
   Where my extended soul is fixed;   10
But Fate does iron wedges drive,
   And always crowds itself betwixt.

For Fate with jealous eye does see
   Two perfect loves, nor lets them close;
Their union would her ruin be,   15
   And her tyrannic pow'r depose.

5

And therefore her decrees of steel
   Us as the distant poles have placed,
(Though Love's whole world on us doth
      wheel),
   Not by themselves to be embraced,   20

6

Unless the giddy heaven fall,
   And earth some new convulsion tear,
And, us to join, the world should all
   Be cramped into a planisphere.

7

As lines, so loves oblique, may well   25
   Themselves in every angle greet:
But ours, so truly parallel,
   Though infinite, can never meet.

8

Therefore the love which us doth bind,
   But Fate so enviously debars,   30
Is the conjunction of the mind,
   And opposition of the stars.

1681

A DIALOGUE BETWEEN
THE SOUL AND BODY

Soul. O, who shall from this dungeon raise
     A soul enslaved so many ways?
     With bolts of bones, that fettered stands
     In feet, and manacled in hands;
     Here blinded with an eye, and there   5
     Deaf with the drumming of an ear;
     A soul hung up, as 'twere, in chains

Definition of Love: 25 *planisphere:* a flat representation of a sphere with the poles united;

Of nerves, and arteries, and veins;
Tortured, besides each other part,
In a vain head, and double heart?   10

Body. O, who shall me deliver whole
From bonds of this tyrannic soul?
Which, stretched upright, impales me so
That mine own precipice I go;
And warms and moves his needless
      frame,   15
(A fever could but do the same,)
And, wanting where its spite to try,
Has made me live to let me die
A body that could never rest
Since this ill spirit it possessed.   20

Soul. What magic could me thus confine
Within another's grief to pine?
Where, whatsoever it complain,
I feel, that cannot feel, the pain;
And all my care itself employs,   25
That to preserve which me destroys;
Constrained not only to endure
Diseases, but, what's worse, the cure;
And, ready oft the port to gain,
Am shipwrecked into health again.   30

Body. But Physic yet could never reach
The maladies thou me dost teach;
Whom first the cramp of hope does tear,
And then the palsy shakes of fear;
The pestilence of love does heat,   35
Or hatred's hidden ulcer eat;
Joy's cheerful madness does perplex,
Or sorrow's other madness vex;
Which knowledge forces me to know,
And memory will not forego;   40
What but a soul could have the wit
To build me up for sin so fit?
So architects do square and hew
Green trees that in the forest grew.

1681

TO HIS COY MISTRESS

Had we but world enough, and time,
This coyness, lady, were no crime.

We would sit down, and think which way
To walk, and pass our long love's day.
Thou by the Indian Ganges' side   5
Shouldst rubies find: I by the tide
Of Humber would complain. I would
Love you ten years before the flood,
And you should, if you please, refuse
Till the conversion of the Jews;   10
My vegetable love should grow
Vaster than empires and more slow;
An hundred years should go to praise
Thine eyes, and on thy forehead gaze;
Two hundred to adore each breast,   15
But thirty thousand to the rest;
An age at least to every part,
And the last age should show your heart.
For, lady, you deserve this state,
Nor would I love at lower rate.   20
    But at my back I always hear
Time's winged chariot hurrying near,
And yonder all before us lie
Deserts of vast eternity.
Thy beauty shall no more be found,   25
Nor, in thy marble vault, shall sound
My echoing song; then worms shall try
That long-preserved virginity,
And your quaint honour turn to dust,
And into ashes all my lust: 30
The grave's a fine and private place,
But none, I think, do there embrace.
    Now therefore, while the youthful hue
Sits on thy skin like morning dew,
And while thy willing soul transpires   35
At every pore with instant fires,
Now let us sport us while we may,
And now, like am'rous birds of prey,
Rather at once our time devour,
Than languish in his slow-chapped power.   40
Let us roll all our strength and all
Our sweetness up into one ball,
And tear our pleasures with rough strife,
Through the iron gates of life;

Mistress: 4 *Humber:* a small river which runs through Marvell's hometown of Hull;   29 *quaint:*
fastidious

Thus, though we cannot make our sun   45
Stand still, yet we will make him run.

BERMUDAS

Where the remote Bermudas ride,
In the ocean's bosom unespied,
From a small boat, that rowed along,
The listening winds received this song:

   "What should we do but sing His praise,   5
That led us through the wat'ry maze,
Unto an isle so long unknown,
And yet far kinder than our own?

Where He the huge sea-monsters wracks,
That lift the deep upon their backs;   10
He lands us on a grassy stage,
Safe from the storms, and prelate's rage.
He gave us this eternal spring,
Which here enamels every thing,
And sends the fowls to us in care,   15
On daily visits through the air;
He hangs in shades the orange bright,
Like golden lamps in a green night,
And does in the pom'granates close
Jewels more rich than Ormus shows;   20
He makes the figs our mouths to meet,
And throws the melons at our feet;
But apples plants of such a price.
No tree could ever bear them twice;
With cedars chosen by His hand,   25
From Lebanon, He stores the land,
And makes the hollow seas, that roar,
Proclaim the ambergris on shore;
He cast (of which we rather boast)
The Gospel's pearl upon our coast,   30
And in these rocks for us did frame
A temple where to sound His name.
Oh! let our voice His praise exalt,

Bermudas: Inspired by the Puritan zeal and cheerfulness of his friends, the Oxenbridges,
Marvell wrote "Bermudas" while he was a guest in their house. The Oxenbridges returned to
England in 1641 after two extended stays in the islands.   20 *Ormus:* a trading center for
pearls and jewels in the Persian gulf;   23 *apples:* pineapples

Andrew Marvell   723

Till it arrive at Heaven's vault,
Which, thence (perhaps) rebounding, may   35
Echo beyond the Mexique Bay."

    Thus sung they, in the English boat,
An holy and a cheerful note;
And all the way, to guide their chime,
With falling oars they kept the time.   40

1681

Andrew Marvell's poetic reputation was not great at the time of his death (it was overshadowed by his political reputation). In the eighteenth and nineteenth centuries, he was thought of as a distinctly minor poet. Three hundred years after his birth, however, his reputation rose because the rising generation of poets (and especially T. S. Eliot) found in his work qualities they wished to emulate in their own.

"Tough reasonableness beneath a slight lyric grace": T. S. Eliot

The wit of the Caroline poets . . . is more than a technical accomplishment, or the vocabulary and syntax of an epoch; it is, what we have designated tentatively as wit, a tough reasonableness beneath a slight lyric grace . . . . There is here an equipoise, a balance and proportion of tones, which, while it cannot raise Marvell to the level of Dryden or Milton, extorts an approval which these poets do not receive from us, and bestows a pleasure at least different in kind than what they can often give. It is what makes Marvell a classic; or a classic at least in a sense in which Gray and Collins are not; for the latter, with all their accredited purity, are comparatively poor in shades of feeling to contrast and unite.

    . . . With our eye still on Marvell, we can say that wit is not erudition; it is sometimes stifled by erudition, as in much of Milton. It is not cynicism, though it has a kind of toughness which may be confused with cynicism by the tender-minded. It is confused with erudition because it belongs to an educated mind, rich in generations of experience. It involves, probably, a recognition, implicit in the expression of every experience, of the other kinds of experience which are possible, which we find as clearly in

---

36 *Mexique Bay:* Gulf of Mexico

the greatest as in poets like Marvell. . . . [T]hat precise taste of Marvell's . . . finds for him the proper degree of seriousness for every subject which he treats . . . . But later poets, who would have been the better for Marvell's quality, were without it; even Browning seems oddly immature, in some way, beside Marvell. And nowadays we find occasionally good irony, or satire, which lacks wit's internal equilibrium, because their voices are essential protests against some outside sentimentality or stupidity; or we find serious poets who seem afraid of acquiring wit, lest they lose intensity. The quality which Marvell had, this modest and certainly impersonal virtue—whether we call it wit or reason, or even urbanity— . . . . is something precious and needed and apparently extinct; it is what should preserve the reputation of Marvell.

The "tough reasonableness" that Eliot admires in Marvell involves a sensibility opposed to the "pure unmingled poetry" that A. E. Housman admires in Shakespeare. The following group of poems, some closely related to Marvell's theme in "To His Coy Mistress," range nearly from one end of the Housman/Eliot spectrum to the other.

Robert Herrick

(1591–1674)

TO THE VIRGINS,
TO MAKE MUCH OF TIME

Gather ye rosebuds while ye may,
   Old time is still a-flying;
And this same flower that smiles today
   Tomorrow will be dying.

The glorious lamp of heaven, the sun,   5
   The higher he's a-getting,
The sooner will his race be run,
   And nearer he's to setting.

That age is best which is the first,
   When youth and blood are warmer;   10
But being spent, the worse, and worst
   Times still succeed the former.

Then be not coy, but use your time.
   And, while ye may, go marry;

For, having lost but once your prime,   15
    You may forever tarry.

                                        1648

Archibald MacLeish

(1892–1982)

YOU, ANDREW MARVELL

And here face down, beneath the sun
And here upon earth's noonward height
To feel the always coming on
The always rising of the night

To feel creep up the curving east   5
The earthy chill of dusk and slow
Upon those under lands the vast
And ever climbing shadow grow

And strange at Ecbatan the trees
Take leaf by leaf the evening strange   10
The flooding dark about their knees
The mountains over Persia change

And now at Kermanshah the gate
Dark empty and the withered grass
And through the twilight now the late   15
Few travelers in the westward pass

And Baghdad darken and the bridge
Across the silent river gone
And through Arabia the edge
Of evening widen and steal on   20

And deepen on Palmyra's street
The wheel rut in the ruined stone
And Lebanon fade out and Crete
High through the clouds and overblown

And over Sicily the air   25
Still flashing with the landward gulls
And loom and slowly disappear
The sails above the shadowy hulls

And Spain go under and the shore
Of Africa the gilded sand   30

And evening vanish and no more
The low pale light across that land

Nor now the long light on the sea

And here face downward in the sun
To feel how swift how secretly   35
The shadow of the night comes on. . .

1930

Dorothy Parker
(1893–1967)

THE FLAW IN PAGANISM

Drink and dance and laugh and lie,
   Love, the reeling midnight through.
For tomorrow we shall die!
   (But, alas, we never do.)

1931

May Swenson
(b. 1919)

Body my house
my horse my hound
what will I do
when you are fallen

Where will I sleep   5
How will I ride
What will I hunt

Where can I go
without my mount
all eager and quick   10
How will I know
in thicket ahead

is danger or treasure
when Body my good
bright dog is dead   15

How will it be
to lie in the sky
without roof or door
and wind for an eye

With cloud for shift   20
how will I hide?

1966

Richard Wilbur

(b. 1921)

A LATE AUBADE

You could be sitting now in a carrel
Turning some liver-spotted page,
Or rising in an elevator-cage
Toward Ladies' Apparel.

You could be planting a raucous bed   5
Of salvia, in rubber gloves,
Or lunching through a screed of someone's loves
With pitying head,

Or making some unhappy setter
Heel, or listening to a bleak   10
Lecture on Schoenberg's serial technique.
Isn't this better?

Think of all the time you are not
Wasting, and would not care to waste,
Such things, thank God, not being to your taste.   15
Think what a lot

Of time, by woman's reckoning,
You've saved, and so may spend on this,
You who had rather lie in bed and kiss
Than anything.   20

It's almost noon, you say? If so,
Times flies, and I need not rehearse

The rosebuds-theme of centuries of verse.
If you *must* go,

Wait for a while, then slip downstairs   25
And bring us up some chilled white wine,
And some blue cheese, and crackers, and some fine
Ruddy-skinned pears.

1969

ALEXANDER POPE

(1688–1744)

SOUND AND SENSE

But most by Numbers judge a Poet's song,
And smooth or rough, with them, is right or wrong;
In the bright Muse tho' thousand charms conspire,
Her Voice is all these tuneful fools admire;
Who haunt *Parnassus* but to please their ear,   5
Not mend their minds; as some to Church repair,
Not for the doctrine, but the music there.
These equal syllables alone require,
Tho' oft' the ear the open vowels tire;
While expletives their feeble aid do join;   10
And ten low words oft' creep in one dull line;
While they ring round the same unvary'd chimes,
With sure returns of still-expected rhymes.
Where-e'er you find *the cooling western breeze*,
In the next line, it *whispers thro' the trees;*   15
If crystal streams *with pleasing murmurs creep,*
The reader's threaten'd (not in vain) with *sleep.*
Then, at the last, and only couplet fraught
With some unmeaning thing they call a Thought,
A needless *Alexandrine* ends the song,   20
That like a wounded snake, drags its slow length along.
Leave such to tune their own dull rhimes, and know
What's roundly smooth, or languishingly slow;
And praise the easy vigor of a line,

Criticism: 1 *Numbers:* versification;   5 *Parnassus:* a mountain in Greece sacred to the Muses

Where *Denham's* strength, and *Waller's* sweetness join.　25
True ease in writing comes from art, not chance,
As those move easiest who have learn'd to dance.
'Tis not enough no harshness gives offence,
The sound must seem an echo to the sense.
Soft is the strain when *Zephyr* gently blows,　30
And the smooth stream in smoother numbers flows;
But when loud surges lash the sounding shore,
The hoarse, rough verse should like the torrent roar.
When *Ajax* strives, some rock's vast weight to throw,
The line too labours, and the words move slow;　35
Not so, when swift *Camilla* scours the plain,
Flies o'er th' unbending corn, and skims along the
　　main.
Hear how *Timotheus'* various lays surprize,
And bid alternate passions fall and rise!

(Essay on Criticism, part 2, ll. 337–374)　*1711*

THE GAME OF OMBRE

Close by those meads, for ever crown'd with flow'rs,
Where *Thames* with pride surveys his rising tow'rs,
There stands a structure of majestic frame,
Which from the neighb'ring *Hampton* takes its name.
Here *Britain's* statesman oft' the fall foredoom　5
Of foreign tyrants, and of nymphs at home;
Here thou, great *Anna!* whom three realms obey,
Dost sometimes counsel take—and sometimes Tea.
　Hither the heroes and the nymphs resort,
To taste a while the pleasures of a Court;　10
In various talk th' instructive hours they past,
Who gave the ball, or paid the visit last:
One speaks the glory of the *British* Queen,

---

25 *Denham and Waller:* seventeenth century poets; Pope claimed that the Elizabethans could produce "nothing so even, sweet, and flowing, as Mr. Waller; nothing so majestic, so correct, as Sir John Denham."　30 *Zephyr:* the west wind;　34 *Ajax:* hero in Virgil's *Aeneid* known for his roughness and strength;　36 *Camilla:* female warrior in Virgil's *Aeneid* whose life was saved when her father attached her to a javelin and hurled her across a river;　38 *Timotheus:* a bard known for his music which was so passionate it could drive one to rage or tranquility *Ombre:* Ombre is a three-handed card game in which the player naming trumps tries to take more tricks than the other two players combined. When spades are trumps, the three highest ranked cards (the Matadores) are the ace of spades (Spadille), the deuce of spades (Manille), and the ace of clubs (Basto). Thereafter, the cards rank as in bridge, except that in non-trump suits, aces are low.　2 *Thames:* a river in Southern England which runs through London. 4 *Hampton:* a section of London surrounding Hampton Court, the largest of royal palaces. 7 *Anna:* Queen Anne, ruler of Great Britain and Ireland.

And one describes a charming *Indian* screen;
A third interprets motions, looks, and eyes;   15
At ev'ry word a reputation dies.
Snuff, or the fan, supply each pause of chat,
With singing, laughing, ogling, and all that.
    Mean while declining from the noon of day,
The sun obliquely shoots his burning ray;   20
The hungry Judges soon the sentence sign,
And wretches hang that Jury-men may dine;
The merchant from th' *Exchange* returns in peace,
And the long labours of the Toilet cease.—
Belinda now, whom thirst of fame invites,   25
Burns to encounter two adventrous Knights,
At *Ombre* singly to decide their doom;
And swells her breast with conquests yet to come.
Strait the three bands prepare in arms to join,
Each band the number of the sacred nine.   30
Soon as she spreads her hand, th' aerial guard
Descend, and sit on each important card:
First *Ariel* perch'd upon a Matadore,
Then each, according to the rank they bore;
For *Sylphs,* yet mindful of their ancient race,   35
Are, as when women, wondrous fond of place.
    Behold, four Kings in majesty rever'd,
With hoary whiskers and a forky beard:
And four fair Queens whose hands sustain a flow'r,
Th' expressive emblem of their softer pow'r;   40
Four Knaves in garbs succinct, a trusty band,
Caps on their heads, and halberds in their hand
And particolour'd troops, a shining train,
Draw forth to combat on the velvet plain.
    The skilful nymph reviews her force with care;   45
Let Spades be trumps, she said, and trumps they were.
    Now move to war her sable Matadores,
In show like leaders of the swarthy Moors.
Spadillio first, unconquerable Lord!
Led off two captive trumps, and swept the board.   50
As many more *Manillio* forc'd to yield,
And march'd a victor from the verdant field.
Him *Basto* follow'd, but his fate more hard
Gain'd but one trump and one *Plebeian* card.
With his broad sabre next, a chief in years,   55
The hoary Majesty of Spades appears;
Puts forth one manly leg, to sight reveal'd;
The rest, his many-colour'd robe conceal'd.
The rebel-Knave, who dares his prince engage,

Proves the just victim of his royal rage.   60
Ev'n mighty *Pam* that Kings and Queens o'erthrew,
And mow'd down armies in the fights of *Lu,*
Sad chance of war! now, destitute of aid,
Falls undistinguish'd by the victor Spade!
    Thus far both armies to *Belinda* yield;   65
Now to the Baron fate inclines the field.
His warlike *Amazon* her host invades,
Th' imperial consort of the crown of Spades.
The Club's black Tyrant first her victim dy'd,
Spite of his haughty mien, and barb'rous pride: 70
What boots the regal circle on his head,
His giant limbs, in state unwieldy spread;
That long behind he trails his pompous robe,
And, of all monarchs, only grasps the globe?
    The Baron now his Diamonds pours apace;   75
Th' embroider'd King who shows but half his face,
And his refulgent Queen, with pow'rs combin'd,
Of broken troops an easy conquest find.
Clubs, Diamonds, Hearts, in wild disorder seen,
With throngs promiscuous strow the level green.   80
Thus when dispers'd a routed army runs,
Of *Asia*'s troops, and *Africa*'s sable sons,
With like confusion different nations fly,
In various habits, and of various dye,
The pierc'd battalions dis-united fall,   85
In heaps on heaps; one fate o'erwhelms them all.
    The Knave of Diamonds tries his wily arts,
And wins (oh shameful chance) the Queen of Hearts.
At this, the blood the virgin's cheek forsook,
A livid paleness spreads o'er all her look;   90
She sees, and trembles at th' approaching ill,
Just in the jaws of ruin, and *Codille.*
And now, (as oft' in some distemper'd state)
On one nice Trick depends the gen'ral fate.
An Ace of Hearts steps forth: The King unseen   95
Lurk'd in her hand, and mourn'd his captive Queen:
He springs to vengeance with an eager pace,
And falls like thunder on the prostrate Ace.
The nymph exulting fills with shouts the sky,
The walls, the woods, and long canals reply.   100
    Oh thoughtless mortals! ever blind to fate,
Too soon dejected, and too soon elate!

---

61 *Pam:* Knave of Clubs; strongest card in the card game Loo (Lu).   67 *Amazon:* Queen of Spades;   92 *Codille:* defeat, failure to take five tricks of nine.

Sudden, these honours shall be snatch'd away,
And curs'd for ever this victorious day.

(The Rape of the Lock, canto 3, ll. 1–104) 1714

TO A YOUNG LADY

On her leaving the Town after the Coronation

As some fond virgin, whom her mother's care
Drags from the town to wholsom country air,
Just when she learns to roll a melting eye,
And hear a spark, yet think no danger nigh;
From the dear man unwilling she must sever,   5
Yet takes one kiss before she parts for ever.
Thus from the world fair *Zephalinda* flew,
Saw others happy, and with sighs withdrew;
Not that their pleasures caus'd her discontent,
She sigh'd not that They stay'd, but that She went.   10
    She went, to plain-work and to purling brooks,
Old-fashion'd halls, dull aunts, and croaking rooks,
She went from Op'ra, park, assembly, play,
To morning walks, and pray'rs three hours a day:
To part her time 'twixt reading and Bohea,   15
To muse, and spill her solitary Tea,
Or o'er cold coffee trifle with the spoon,
Count the slow clock, and dine exact at noon;
Divert her eyes with pictures in the fire,
Hum half a tune, tell stories to the squire;   20
Up to her godly garret after sev'n,
These starve and pray, for that's the way to heav'n.
    Some Squire, perhaps, you take delight to rack;
Whose game is Whisk, whose treat a toast in sack,
Who visits with a gun, presents you birds,   25
Then gives a smacking buss, and cries—No words!
Or with his hound comes hollowing from the stable,
Makes love with nods, and knees beneath a table;
Whose laughs are hearty, tho' his jests are coarse,
And loves you best of all things—but his horse.   30
    In some fair evening, on your elbow laid,
You dream of triumphs in the rural shade;

To a Young Lady: This poem was written for Teresa Blout, the sister of Pope's close friend, Martha Blout. The coronation suggested was that of George I in 1714. 4 *spark:* a fop or beau; 7 *Zephalinda:* a fanciful name adopted by Teresa Blout. 15 *Bohea:* an expensive tea; 26 *buss:* kiss;

In pensive thought recall the fancy'd scene,
See Coronations rise on ev'ry green,
Before you pass th' imaginary sights   35
Of Lords, and Earls, and Dukes, and garter'd Knights;
While the spread Fan o'ershades your closing eyes;
Then give one flirt, and all the vision flies.
Thus vanish sceptres, coronets, and balls,
And leave you in lone woods, or empty walls.   40
    So when your slave, at some dear, idle time,
(Not plagu'd with headachs, or the want of rhime)
Stands in the streets, abstracted from the crew,
And while he seems to study, thinks of you:
Just when his fancy points your sprightly eyes,   45
Or sees the blush of *Parthenissa* rise,
Gay pats my shoulder, and you vanish quite;
Streets, chairs, and coxcombs, rush upon my sight;
Vext to be still in town, I knit my brow,
Look sow'r, and hum a song—as you may now.   50

                                    1717

TIMON'S VILLA

At *Timon*'s Villa let us pass a day,
Where all cry out, 'What sums are thrown away!'
So proud, so grand; of that stupendous air,
Soft and *Agreeable* come never there.
Greatness, with *Timon*, dwells in such a draught   5
As brings all *Brobdignag* before your thought.
To compass this, his building is a Town,
His pond an Ocean, his parterre a Down:
Who but must laugh, the Master when he sees,
A puny insect, shiv'ring at a breeze!   10
Lo! what huge heaps of littleness around!
The whole, a labour'd quarry above ground.
Two *Cupids* squirt before: a Lake behind
Improves the keenness of the Northern wind.
His Gardens next your admiration call,   15
On ev'ry side you look, behold the Wall!
No pleasing Intricacies intervene,
No artful wildness to perplex the scene;
Grove nods at grove, each Alley has a brother,

---

46 *Parthenissa:* Martha Blout;   47 *Gay:* the poet, John Gay *Timon's Villa:* Pope presents in
the person of Timon a synthesis of several wealthy men whose estates grossly insulted good
taste.   6 *Brobdignag:* the land of giants in Swift's *Gulliver's Travels* (1726);

And half the platform just reflects the other.   20
The suff'ring eye inverted Nature sees,
Trees cut to Statues, Statues thick as trees,
With here a Fountain, never to be play'd,
And there a Summer-house, that knows no shade.
Here *Amphitrite* sails thro' myrtle bow'rs;   25
There *Gladiators* fight, or die in flow'rs;
Un-water'd see the drooping sea-horse mourn,
And swallows roost in *Nilus'* dusty Urn.
    My Lord advances with majestic mien,
Smit with the mighty pleasure, to be seen: 30
But soft—by regular approach—not yet—
First thro' the length of yon hot Terrace sweat;
And when up ten steep slopes you've dragg'd your
    thighs,
Just at his Study-door he'll bless your eyes.
    His *Study*? with what Authors is it stor'd?   35
In Books, not Authors, curious is my Lord;
To all their *dated Backs* he turns you round:
These *Aldus* printed, those *Da Suëil* has bound.
Lo some are *Vellom,* and the rest as good
For all his Lordship knows, but they are Wood.   40
For *Locke* or *Milton* 'tis in vain to look,
These shelves admit not any modern book.
    And now the Chappel's silver bell you hear,
That summons you to all the pride of Pray'r:
Light quirks of Musick, broken and uneven,   45
Make the soul dance upon a Jig to Heav'n.
On painted Ceilings you devoutly stare,
Where sprawl the Saints of *Verrio,* or *Laguerre,*
On gilded clouds in fair expansion lie,
And bring all Paradise before your eye.   50
To rest, the Cushion and soft Dean invite,
Who never mentions Hell to ears polite.
    But hark! the chiming Clocks to dinner call;
A hundred footsteps scrape the marble Hall:
The rich Buffet well-colour'd *Serpents* grace,   55
And gaping *Tritons* spew to wash your face.
Is this a dinner? this a Genial room?
No, 'tis a Temple, and a Hecatomb;

---

25 *Amphitrite:* Greek goddess of the sea, Poseiden's wife;   28 *Nilus' . . . urn:* the urn from
which the river god Nile should pour water;   38 *Aldus, Da Sueil, Vellum:* European men
prominent in the book-making business;   48 *Verrio, Laguerre:* fashionable court artists;
56 *Tritons:* like mermaids, half human and half fish; water was ejected from their open
mouths into a fountain;

A solemn Sacrifice, perform'd in state,
You drink by measure, and to minutes eat.   60
So quick retires each flying course, you'd swear
Sancho's dread Doctor and his Wand were there.
Between each Act the trembling salvers ring,
From soup to sweetwine, and *God bless the King.*
In plenty starving, tantaliz'd in state,   65
And complaisantly help'd to all I hate,
Treated, caress'd, and tir'd, I take my leave,
Sick of his civil Pride from Morn to Eve;
I curse such lavish cost, and little skill,
And swear no Day was ever past so ill.   70
 Yet hence the *Poor* are cloath'd, the *Hungry* fed;
Health to himself, and to his Infants bread
The Lab'rer bears: What his hard Heart denies,
His charitable Vanity supplies.

(*Epistle to Richard Boyle, Earl of Burlington, ll. 1–73*) *1731*

*The "tough reasonableness" of Andrew Marvell's poetry became, in the dec-
ades that followed, something almost exactly opposed to the metaphysical wit
of Donne and Herbert. By the time of Alexander Pope, reasonableness had
become devotion to Reason, and wit had come to mean taste and judgment:*

> *Some to conceit alone their taste confine,*
> *And glittering thoughts struck out at every line;*
> *Pleased with a work where nothing's just or fit;*
> *One glaring chaos and wild heap of wit.*
> *Poets, like painters, thus, unskilled to trace*
> *The naked Nature and the living grace,*
> *With gold and jewels cover every part,*
> *And hide with ornaments their want of art.*
> *True wit is nature to advantage dress'd:*
> *What oft was thought, but ne'er so well express'd.*
>
> *Essay on Criticism, ll. 289–298*

*As the century wore on and the first stirring of the Romantic revolution began, some
people began to question whether Pope, for all his brilliance, was a poet at all. The
reputation of the neoclassical poets sank in the nineteenth and the early twentieth*

---

62 *Sancho's . . . wand:* In Cervantes' *Don Quixote,* the doctor steals away the food Sancho
longs for

centuries, for reasons well stated by A. E. Housman in "The Name and Nature of Poetry" (1933).

"Man had ceased to live from the depths of his nature": A. E. Housman

The literature of the eighteenth century in England is an admirable and most enjoyable thing. It has a greater solidity of excellence than any before or after; and although the special task and characteristic achievement of the age was the invention and establishment of a healthy, workmanlike, athletic prose, to supersede the cumbrous and decorated and self-admiring prose of a Milton or a Jeremy Taylor, and to become a trustworthy implement for accurate thinking and the serious pursuit of truth, yet in verse also it created masterpieces, and perhaps no English poem of greater than lyric length, not even 'The Nonne's Priest's Tale' or 'The Ancient Mariner', is quite so perfect as 'The Rape of the Lock'. But the human faculty which dominated the eighteenth century and informed its literature was the intelligence, and that involved, as Arnold says, 'some repressing and silencing of poetry', 'some touch of frost to the imaginative life of the soul'. Man had ceased to live from the depths of his nature; he occupied himself for choice with thoughts which do not range beyond the sphere of the understanding; he lighted the candles and drew down the blind to shut out that patroness of poets, the moon. The writing of poetry proceeded, and much of the poetry written was excellent literature; but excellent literature which is also poetry is not therefore excellent poetry, and the poetry of the eighteenth century was most satisfactory when it did not try to be poetical. . . .

To poets of the eighteenth century high and impassioned poetry did not come spontaneously, because the feelings which foster its birth were not then abundant and urgent in the inner man; but they girt up their loins and essayed a lofty strain at the bidding of ambition. The way to write real poetry, they thought, must be to write something as little like prose as possible; they devised for the purpose what was called a 'correct and splendid diction', which consisted in always using the wrong word instead of the right, and plastered it as ornament, with no thought of propriety, on whatever they desired to dignify. It commanded notice and was not easy to mistake; so the public mind soon connected it with the notion of poetry and came in course of time to regard it as alone poetical.

WILLIAM BLAKE

(1757–1827)

THE LAMB

    Little Lamb, who made thee?
    Dost thou know who made thee?
Gave thee life & bid thee feed,
By the stream & o'er the mead;
Gave thee clothing of delight,   5
Softest clothing wooly bright;
Gave thee such a tender voice,
Making all the vales rejoice!
    Little Lamb who made thee?
    Dost thou know who made thee?   10

    Little Lamb I'll tell thee,
    Little Lamb I'll tell thee!
He is called by thy name,
For he calls himself a Lamb:
He is meek & he is mild,   15
He became a little child:
I a child & thou a lamb,
We are calléd by his name.
    Little Lamb God bless thee.
    Little Lamb God bless thee.   20

(Songs of Innocence) *1789*

THE CHIMNEY SWEEPER

When my mother died I was very young,
And my father sold me while yet my tongue
Could scarcely cry " 'weep! 'weep! 'weep! 'weep!"
So your chimneys I sweep & in soot I sleep.

There's little Tom Dacre, who cried when his head   5
That curl'd like a lambs back, was shav'd, so I said,
"Hush, Tom! never mind it, for when your head's bare,
You know that the soot cannot spoil your white hair."

And so he was quiet, & that very night,
As Tom was a-sleeping he had such a sight!   10
That thousands of sweepers, Dick, Joe, Ned, & Jack,
Were all of them lock'd up in coffins of black;

And by came an Angel who had a bright key,
And he open'd the coffins & set them all free;
Then down a green plain, leaping, laughing they run,   15
And wash in a river and shine in the Sun;

Then naked & white, all their bags left behind,
They rise upon clouds, and sport in the wind.
And the Angel told Tom, if he'd be a good boy,
He'd have God for his father & never want joy.   20

And so Tom awoke; and we rose in the dark
And got with our bags & our brushes to work.
Tho' the morning was cold, Tom was happy & warm;
So if all do their duty, they need not fear harm.

(Songs of Innocence)   1789

THE LITTLE BLACK BOY

My mother bore me in the southern wild,
And I am black, but O! my soul is white;
White as an angel is the English child:
But I am black as if bereav'd of light.

My mother taught me underneath a tree,   5
And sitting down before the heat of day,
She took me on her lap and kissèd me,
And pointing to the east, began to say:

"Look on the rising sun: there God does live,
And gives his light, and gives his heat away;   10
And flowers and trees and beasts and men receive
Comfort in morning, joy in the noon day.

"And we are put on earth a little space,
That we may learn to bear the beams of love,
And these black bodies and this sun-burnt face   15
Is but a cloud, and like a shady grove.

"For when our souls have learn'd the heat to bear,
The cloud will vanish; we shall hear his voice,
Saying: 'Come out from the grove, my love & care,
And round my golden tent like lambs rejoice.' "   20

Thus did my mother say, and kissèd me;
And thus I say to little English boy:
When I from black and he from white cloud free,
And round the tent of God like lambs we joy,

I'll shade him from the heat till he can bear   25
To lean in joy upon our father's knee;
And then I'll stand and stroke his silver hair,
And be like him, and he will then love me.

(Songs of Innocence) 1789

THE TYGER

Tyger! Tyger! burning bright
In the forests of the night,
What immortal hand or eye
Could frame thy fearful symmetry?

In what distant deeps or skies   5
Burnt the fire of thine eyes?
On what wings dare he aspire?
What the hand, dare seize the fire?

And what shoulder, & what art,
Could twist the sinews of thy heart?   10
And when thy heart began to beat,
What dread hand? & what dread feet?

What the hammer? what the chain?
In what furnace was thy brain?
What the anvil? what dread grasp   15
Dare its deadly terrors clasp?

When the stars threw down their spears,
And water'd heaven with their tears,
Did he smile his work to see?
Did he who made the Lamb make thee?   20

Tyger! Tyger! burning bright
In the forests of the night,
What immortal hand or eye
Dare frame thy fearful symmetry?

(Songs of Experience) 1794

THE SICK ROSE

O Rose, thou art sick.
The invisible worm
That flies in the night
In the howling storm

Has found out thy bed
Of crimson joy,   5
And his dark secret love
Does thy life destroy.

(Songs of Experience) 1794

A POISON TREE

I was angry with my friend:
I told my wrath, my wrath did end.
I was angry with my foe:
I told it not, my wrath did grow.

And I waterd it in fears,   5
Night & morning with my tears;
And I sunnéd it with smiles,
And with soft deceitful wiles.

And it grew both day and night,
Till it bore an apple bright.   10
And my foe beheld it shine,
And he knew that it was mine,

And into my garden stole,
When the night had veild the pole;
In the morning glad I see   15
My foe outstretchd beneath the tree.

(Songs of Experience) 1794

LONDON

I wander thro' each charter'd street,
Near where the charter'd Thames does flow,
And mark in every face I meet
Marks of weakness, marks of woe.

In every cry of every man,   5
In every Infant's cry of fear,
In every voice, in every ban,
The mind-forg'd manacles I hear.

How the Chimney-sweeper's cry
Every blackning Church appalls;   10

"London": 1 *charter'd:* legally authorized, or hired out

And the hapless Soldier's sigh
Runs in blood down Palace walls.

But most thro' midnight streets I hear
How the youthful Harlot's curse
Blasts the new-born Infant's tear,   15
And blights with plagues the Marriage hearse.

                        (Songs of Experience) 1794

AUGURIES OF INNOCENCE

To see a World in a Grain of Sand
And a Heaven in a Wild Flower
Hold Infinity in the palm of your hand
And Eternity in an hour
A Robin Red breast in a Cage   5
Puts all Heaven in a Rage
A dove house filld with doves & Pigeons
Shudders Hell thro all its regions
A dog starvd at his Masters Gate
Predicts the ruin of the State   10
A Horse misusd upon the Road
Calls to Heaven for Human blood
Each outcry of the hunted Hare
A fibre from the Brain does tear
A Skylark wounded in the wing   15
A Cherubim does cease to sing
The Game Cock clipd & armd for fight
Does the Rising Sun affright
Every Wolfs & Lions howl
Raises from Hell a Human Soul   20
The wild deer wandring here & there
Keeps the Human Soul from Care
The Lamb misusd breeds Public strife
And yet forgives the Butchers Knife
    The Bat that flits at close of Eve   25
Has left the Brain that wont Believe
The Owl that calls upon the Night
Speaks the Unbelievers fright
He who shall hurt the little Wren
Shall never be belovd by Men   30
He who the Ox to wrath has movd
Shall never be by Woman lovd

———

16 *plagues:* evils of prostitution

The wanton Boy that kills the Fly
Shall feel the Spiders enmity
He who torments the Chafers sprite   35
Weaves a Bower in endless Night
The Catterpiller on the Leaf
Repeats to thee thy Mothers grief
Kill not the Moth nor Butterfly
For the Last Judgment draweth nigh   40
He who shall train the Horse to War
Shall never pass the Polar Bar
The Beggers Dog & Widows Cat
Feed them & thou wilt grow fat
The Gnat that sings his Summers song   45
Poison gets from Slanders tongue
The poison of the Snake & Newt
Is the sweat of Envys Foot
The Poison of the Honey Bee
Is the Artists Jealousy   50
The Princes Robes & Beggars Rags
Are Toadstools on the Misers Bags
A truth thats told with bad intent
Beats all the Lies you can invent
It is right it should be so   55
Man was made for Joy & Woe
And when this we rightly know
Thro the World we safely go
Joy & Woe are woven fine
A Clothing for the Soul divine   60
Under every grief & pine
Runs a joy with silken twine
The Babe is more than swadling Bands
Throughout all these Human Lands
Tools were made & Born were hands   65
Every Farmer Understands
Every Tear from Every Eye
Becomes a Babe in Eternity
This is caught by Females bright
And returned to its own delight   70
The Bleat the Bark Bellow & Roar
Are Waves that Beat on Heavens Shore
The Babe that weeps the Rod beneath
Writes Revenge in realms of death
The Beggars Rags fluttering in Air   75

————————
"Auguries of Innocence":35 *Chafers:* beetles

Does to Rags the Heavens tear
The Soldier armd with Sword & Gun
Palsied strikes the Summers Sun
The poor Mans Farthing is worth more
Than all the Gold on Africs Shore   80
One Mite wrung from the Labrers hands
Shall buy & sell the Misers Lands
Or if protected from on high
Does that whole Nation sell & buy
He who mocks the Infants Faith   85
Shall be mock'd in Age & Death
He who shall teach the Child to Doubt
The rotting Grave shall neer get out
He who respects the Infants faith
Triumphs over Hell & Death   90
The Childs Toys & the Old Mans Reasons
Are the Fruits of the Two seasons
The Questioner who sits so sly
Shall never know how to Reply
He who replies to words of Doubt   95
Doth put the Light of Knowledge out
The Strongest Poison ever known
Came from Caesars Laurel Crown
Nought can deform the Human Race
Like to the Armours iron brace   100
When Gold & Gems adorn the Plow
To peaceful Arts shall Envy Bow
A Riddle or the Crickets Cry
Is to Doubt a fit Reply
The Emmets Inch & Eagles Mile   105
Make Lame Philosophy to smile
He who Doubts from what he sees
Will neer Believe do what you Please
If the Sun & Moon should doubt
Theyd immediately Go out   110
To be in a Passion you Good many do
But no Good if a Passion is in you
The Whore & Gambler by the State
Licencd build that Nations Fate
The Harlots cry from Street to Street   115
Shall weave Old Englands winding Sheet
The Winners Shout the Losers Curse
Dance before dead Englands Hearse

---

105 *Emmets:* ants

Every Night & every Morn
Some to Misery are Born   120
Every Morn & every Night
Some are Born to sweet delight
Some are Born to sweet delight
Some are Born to Endless Night
We are led to Believe a Lie   125
When we see not Thro the Eye
Which was Born in a Night to perish in a Night
When the Soul Slept in Beams of Light
God Appears & God is Light
To those poor Souls who dwell in Night   130
But does a Human Form Display
To those Who Dwell in Realms of day

1800–1808

AND DID THOSE FEET

And did those feet in ancient time
Walk upon England's mountains green?
And was the holy Lamb of God
On England's pleasant pastures seen?

And did the Countenance Divine   5
Shine forth upon our clouded hills?
And was Jerusalem builded here,
Among these dark Satanic Mills?

Bring me my Bow of burning gold:
Bring me my Arrows of desire: 10
Bring me my Spear: O clouds unfold!
Bring me my Chariot of fire!

I will not cease from Mental Fight,
Nor shall my Sword sleep in my hand,
Till we have built Jerusalem   15
In England's green & pleasant Land.

1804

When William Blake was writing his Songs of Innocence *and* Songs of
Experience, *most other poets were still writing verse in the style of Alexander Pope. Eighteenth-century critics were inclined to talk about poetry as*

William Blake   **745**

a sort of dignified clothing for the poet's thoughts, which were what really mattered. Blake and a few of his contemporaries wrote poetry on entirely different principles, ones that appeal more strongly to readers like A. E. Housman.

"Insurgent against the centralised tyranny of the intellect": A. E. Housman

---

Meaning is of the intellect, poetry is not. If it were, the eighteenth century would have been able to write it better. As matters actually stand, who are the English poets of that age in whom pre-eminently one can hear and recognise the true poetic accent emerging clearly from the contemporary dialect? These four: Collins, Christopher Smart, Cowper, and Blake. And what other characteristic had these four in common? They were mad. Remember Plato: 'He who without the Muses' madness in his soul comes knocking at the door of poesy and thinks that art will make him anything fit to be called a poet, finds that the poetry which he indites in his sober senses is beaten hollow by the poetry of madmen.'. . .

Collins and Cowper, though they saw the inside of madhouses, are not supposed to have written any of their poetry there; and Blake was never mad enough to be locked up. But elements of their nature were more or less insurgent against the centralised tyranny of the intellect, and their brains were not thrones on which the great usurper could sit secure. And so it strangely came to pass that in the eighteenth century, the age of prose and of unsound or unsatisfying poetry, there sprang up one well of the purest inspiration. For me the most poetical of all poets is Blake. I find his lyrical note as beautiful as Shakespeare's and more beautiful than anyone else's; and I call him more poetical than Shakespeare, even though Shakespeare has so much more poetry, because poetry in him preponderates more than in Shakespeare over everything else, and instead of being confounded in a great river can be drunk pure from a slender channel of its own. Shakespeare is rich in thought, and his meaning has power of itself to move us, even if the poetry were not there: Blake's meaning is often unimportant or virtually non-existent, so that we can listen with all our hearing to his celestial tune.

Housman's view of Blake does him justice as a poet, but it makes him seem a sort of idiot savant, unaware of what he was doing and not likely to affect the thought of any of his readers. It is worthwhile, therefore, to compare Blake not only with the poems of the "mad poets" of the eighteenth century but also with the hymns he consciously imitated (or parodied) and with the poems of a modern American admirer, Richard Eberhart.

Isaac Watts

(1674–1748)

A CRADLE HYMN

Hush, my dear, lie still and slumber;
Holy angels guard thy bed!
Heavenly blessings without number
Gently falling on thy head.

Sleep, my babe; thy food and raiment,   5
House and home thy friends provide;
All without thy care or payment,
All thy wants are well supplied.

How much better thou'rt attended
Than the Son of God could be,   10
When from Heaven he descended,
And became a child like thee!

Soft and easy is thy cradle;
Coarse and hard thy Saviour lay,
When his birth-place was a stable,   15
And his softest bed was hay.

Blessed Babe! what glorious features,
Spotless fair, divinely bright!
Must he dwell with brutal creatures?
How could angels bear the sight?   20

Was there nothing but a manger
Curséd sinners could afford,
To receive the heavenly Stranger?
Did they thus affront their Lord?

Soft, my child; I did not chide thee,   25
Though my song might sound too hard;
'Tis thy { Nurse that Mother } sits beside thee
And her arm shall be thy guard.

Yet to read the shameful story,
How the Jews abused their King,   30
How they served the Lord of Glory,
Makes me angry while I sing.

See the kinder shepherds round him,
Telling wonders from the sky;

There they sought him, there they found him,   35
With his Virgin-Mother by.

See the lovely Babe a-dressing;
Lovely Infant, how he smiled!
When he wept, the Mother's blessing
Soothed and hushed the holy Child.   40

Lo, he slumbers in his manger,
Where the hornéd oxen fed;
Peace, my darling, here's no danger,
Here's no ox anear thy bed.

'Twas to save thee, child, from dying,   45
Save my dear from burning flame,
Bitter groans, and endless crying,
That my blest Redeemer came.

Mayst thou live to know and fear him,
Trust and love him all thy days!   50
Then go dwell forever near him,
See his face, and sing his praise!

I could give thee thousand kisses,
Hoping what I most desire;
Not a mother's fondest wishes   55
Can to greater joys aspire.

1720

Charles Wesley

(1707–1788)

GENTLE JESUS

Gentle Jesus, meek and mild,
Look upon a little child;
Pity my simplicity,
Suffer me to come to Thee.

Lamb of God, O look to Thee;   5
Thou shalt my example be:
Thou art gentle, meek and mild;
Thou wast once a little child.

Fain I would be as Thou art;
Give me Thine obedient heart: 10

Thou art pitiful and kind;
Let me have Thy loving mind.

Loving Jesus, gentle Lamb,
In Thy gracious hands I am;
Make me, Saviour, what Thou art,   15
Live Thyself within my heart.

                    Amen.

                    1742

Christopher Smart

(1722–1771)

[FOR I WILL CONSIDER MY CAT JEOFFRY]

For I will consider my Cat Jeoffry.
For he is the servant of the Living God, duly and daily
    serving him.
For at the first glance of the glory of God in the East he
    worships in his way.
For is this done by wreathing his body seven times
    round with elegant quickness.
For then he leaps up to catch the musk, which is the
    blessing of God upon his prayer.   5
For he rolls upon prank to work it in.
For having done duty and received blessing he begins
    to consider himself.
For this he performs in ten degrees.
For first he looks upon his forepaws to see if they are
    clean.
For secondly he kicks up behind to clear away there.   10
For thirdly he works it upon stretch with the forepaws
    extended.
For fourthly he sharpens his paws by wood.
For fifthly he washes himself.
For sixthly he rolls upon wash.
For seventhly he fleas himself, that he may not be
    interrupted upon the beat.   15
For eighthly he rubs himself against a post.
For ninthly he looks up for his instructions.
For tenthly he goes in quest of food.

For having considered God and himself he will consider
   his neighbor.
For if he meets another cat he will kiss her in kindness.   20
For when he takes his prey he plays with it to give it a
   chance.
For one mouse in seven escapes by his dallying.
For when his day's work is done his business more
   properly begins.
For he keeps the Lord's watch in the night against the
   adversary.
For he counteracts the powers of darkness by his
   electrical skin and glaring eyes.   25
For he counteracts the Devil, who is death, by brisking
   about the life.
For in his morning orisons he loves the sun and the sun
   loves him.
For he is of the tribe of Tiger.
For the Cherub Cat is a term of the Angel Tiger.
For he has the subtlety and hissing of a serpent, which
   in goodness he suppresses.   30
For he will not do destruction if he is well-fed, neither
   will he spit without provocation.
For he purrs in thankfulness when God tells him he's a
   good Cat.
For he is an instrument for the children to learn
   benevolence upon.
For every house is incomplete without him, and a
   blessing is lacking in the spirit.
For the Lord commanded Moses concerning the cats at
   the departure of the Children of Israel from Egypt.   35
For every family had one cat at least in the bag.
For the English Cats are the best in Europe.
For he is the cleanest in the use of his forepaws of any
   quadruped.
For the dexterity of his defense is an instance of the
   love of God to him exceedingly.
For he is the quickest to his mark of any creature.   40
For he is tenacious of his point.
For he is a mixture of gravity and waggery.
For he knows that God is his Saviour.
For there is nothing sweeter than his peace when at
   rest.
For there is nothing brisker than his life when in
   motion.   45
For he is of the Lord's poor, and so indeed is he called

by benevolence perpetually—Poor Jeoffry! poor
Jeoffry! the rat has bit thy throat.
For I bless the name of the Lord Jesus that Jeoffry is
better.
For the divine spirit comes about his body to sustain it
in complete cat.
For his tongue is exceeding pure so that it has in purity
what it wants in music.
For he is docile and can learn certain things.   50
For he can sit up with gravity, which is patience upon
approbation.
For he can fetch and carry, which is patience in
employment.
For he can jump over a stick, which is patience upon
proof positive.
For he can spraggle upon waggle at the word of
command.
For he can jump from an eminence into his master's
bosom.   55
For he can catch the cork and toss it again.
For he is hated by the hypocrite and miser.
For the former is afraid of detection.
For the latter refuses the charge.
For he camels his back to bear the first notion of
business.   60
For he is good to think on, if a man would express
himself neatly.
For he made a great figure in Egypt for his signal
services.
For he killed the Icneumon rat, very pernicious by
land.
For his ears are so acute that they sting again.
For from this proceeds the passing quickness of his
attention.   65
For by stroking of him I have found out electricity.
For I perceived God's light about him both wax and
fire.
For the electrical fire is the spiritual substance which
God sends from heaven to sustain the bodies both of
man and beast.
For God has blessed him in the variety of his
movements.

"*Jubilate Agno*": 73 *Icneumon rat:* A mongoose-like rodent, which preys upon small mammals

For, though he cannot fly, he is an excellent clamberer.   70
For his motions upon the face of the earth are more
   than any other quadruped.
For he can tread to all the measures upon the music.
For he can swim for life.
For he can creep.

(from Jubilate Agno)   ca. 1760

William Cowper

(1731–1800)

LINES WRITTEN DURING A PERIOD OF INSANITY

Hatred and vengeance, my eternal portion,
Scarce can endure delay of execution,
Wait, with impatient readiness, to seize my
              Soul in a moment.

Damned below Judas: more abhorred than he was,   5
Who for a few pence sold his holy Master.
Twice-betrayed Jesus me, the last delinquent,
              Deems the profanest.

Man disavows, and Deity disowns me:
Hell might afford my miseries a shelter;   10
Therefore hell keeps her ever-hungry mouths all
              Bolted against me.

Hard lot! encompassed with a thousand dangers;
Weary, faint, trembling with a thousand terrors;
I'm called, if vanquished, to receive a sentence   15
              Worse than Abiram's.

Him the vindictive rod of angry justice
Sent quick and howling to the center headlong;
I, fed with judgment, in a fleshly tomb, am
              Buried above ground.   20

1774

"*Lines*": 16 *Abriam:* Abiram is swallowed by the arth in Numbers 16:33

Richard Eberhart

(b. 1904)

FOR A LAMB

I saw on the slant hill a putrid lamb,
Propped with daisies. The sleep looked deep,
The face nudged in the green pillow
But the guts were out for crows to eat.

Where's the lamb? whose tender plaint   5
Said all for the mute breezes.
Say he's in the wind somewhere,
Say, there's a lamb in the daisies.

1937

IN A HARD INTELLECTUAL LIGHT

In a hard intellectual light
I will kill all delight,
And I will build a citadel
Too beautiful to tell

O too austere to tell   5
And far too beautiful to see,
Whose evident distance
I will call the best of me.

And this light of intellect
Will shine on all my desires,   10
It will my flesh protect
And flare my bold constant fires,

For the hard intellectual light
Will lay the flesh with nails.
And it will keep the world bright   15
And close the body's soft jails.

And from this fair edifice
I shall see, as my eyes blaze,
The moral grandeur of man
Animating all his days.   20

And peace will marry purpose,
And purity married to grace

Will make the human absolute
As sweet as the human face.

Until my hard vision blears,   25
And Poverty and Death return
In organ music like the years,
Making the spirit leap, and burn

For the hard intellectual light
That kills all delight   30
And brings the solemn, inward pain
Of truth into the heart again.

1937

WILLIAM WORDSWORTH

(1770–1850)

LINES

*Composed a Few Miles Above Tintern Abbey on Revisiting
the Banks of the Wye During a Tour. July 13, 1798*

Five years have passed; five summers, with the length
Of five long winters! and again I hear
These waters, rolling from their mountain-springs
With a soft inland murmur. Once again
Do I behold these steep and lofty cliffs,   5
That on a wild secluded scene impress
Thoughts of more deep seclusion; and connect
The landscape with the quiet of the sky.
The day is come when I again repose
Here, under this dark sycamore, and view   10
These plots of cottage ground, these orchard tufts,
Which at this season, with their unripe fruits,
Are clad in one green hue, and lose themselves
'Mid groves and copses. Once again I see
These hedgerows, hardly hedgerows, little lines   15
Of sportive wood run wild; these pastoral farms,
Green to the very door; and wreaths of smoke
Sent up, in silence, from among the trees!
With some uncertain notice, as might seem
Of vagrant dwellers in the houseless woods,   20

Or of some Hermit's cave where by his fire
The Hermit sits alone.

                These beauteous forms,
Through a long absence, have not been to me
As is a landscape to a blind man's eye;   25
But oft, in lonely rooms, and 'mid the din
Of towns and cities, I have owed to them,
In hours of weariness, sensations sweet,
Felt in the blood, and felt along the heart;
And passing even into my purer mind,   30
With tranquil restoration—feelings too
Of unremembered pleasure; such, perhaps,
As have no slight or trivial influence
On that best portion of a good man's life,
His little, nameless, unremembered, acts   35
Of kindness and of love. Nor less, I trust,
To them I may have owed another gift,
Of aspect more sublime; that blessed mood,
In which the burthen of the mystery,
In which the heavy and the weary weight   40
Of all this unintelligible world,
Is lightened—that serene and blessed mood,
In which the affections gently lead us on—
Until, the breath of this corporeal frame
And even the motion of our human blood   45
Almost suspended, we are laid asleep
In body, and become a living soul;
While with an eye made quiet by the power
Of harmony, and the deep power of joy,
We see into the life of things.   50

                If this
Be but a vain belief, yet, oh! how oft—
In darkness and amid the many shapes
Of joyless daylight; when the fretful stir
Unprofitable, and the fever of the world,   55
Have hung upon the beatings of my heart—
How oft, in spirit, have I turned to thee,
O sylvan Wye! thou wanderer through the woods,
How often has my spirit turned to thee!

  And now, with gleams of half-extinguished thought,   60
With many recognitions dim and faint,
And somewhat of a sad perplexity,
The picture of the mind revives again;
While here I stand, not only with the sense

Of present pleasure, but with pleasing thoughts   65
That in this moment there is life and food
For future years. And so I dare to hope,
Though changed, no doubt, from what I was when first
I came among these hills; when like a roe
I bounded o'er the mountains, by the sides   70
Of the deep rivers, and the lonely streams,
Wherever nature led—more like a man
Flying from something that he dreads than one
Who sought the thing he loved. For nature then
(The coarser pleasures of my boyish days,   75
And their glad animal movements all gone by)
To me was all in all.—I cannot paint
What then I was. The sounding cataract
Haunted me like a passion; the tall rock,
The mountain, and the deep and gloomy wood,   80
Their colors and their forms, were then to me
An appetite; a feeling and a love,
That had no need of a remoter charm,
By thought supplied, nor any interest
Unborrowed from the eye.—That time is past,   85
And all its aching joys are now no more,
And all its dizzy raptures. Not for this
Faint I, nor mourn nor murmur; other gifts
Have followed; for such loss, I would believe,
Abundant recompense. For I have learned   90
To look on nature, not as in the hour
Of thoughtless youth; but hearing oftentimes
The still, sad music of humanity,
Nor harsh nor grating, though of ample power
To chasten and subdue. And I have felt   95
A presence that disturbs me with the joy
Of elevated thoughts; a sense sublime
Of something far more deeply interfused,
Whose dwelling is the light of setting suns,
And the round ocean and the living air,   100
And the blue sky, and in the mind of man:
A motion and a spirit, that impels
All thinking things, all objects of all thought,
And rolls through all things. Therefore am I still
A lover of the meadows and the woods,   105
And mountains; and of all that we behold
From this green earth; of all the mighty world
Of eye, and ear—both what they half create,
And what perceive; well pleased to recognize
In nature and the language of the sense   110

The anchor of my purest thoughts, the nurse,
The guide, the guardian of my heart, and soul
Of all my moral being.

                   Nor perchance,
If I were not thus taught, should I the more   115
Suffer my genial spirits to decay:
For thou art with me here upon the banks
Of this fair river; thou my dearest Friend,
My dear, dear Friend; and in thy voice I catch
The language of my former heart, and read   120
My former pleasures in the shooting lights
Of thy wild eyes. Oh! yet a little while
May I behold in thee what I was once,
My dear, dear Sister! and his prayer I make,
Knowing that Nature never did betray   125
The heart that loved her; 'tis her privilege,
Through all the years of this our life, to lead
From joy to joy: for she can so inform
The mind that is within us, so impress
With quietness and beauty, and so feed   130
With lofty thoughts, that neither evil tongues,
Rash judgments, nor the sneers of selfish men,
Nor greetings where no kindness is, nor all
The dreary intercourse of daily life,
Shall e'er prevail against us, or disturb   135
Our cheerful faith, that all which we behold
Is full of blessings. Therefore let the moon
Shine on thee in thy solitary walk;
And let the misty mountain winds be free
To blow against thee: and, in after years,   140
When these wild ecstasies shall be matured
Into a sober pleasure; when thy mind
Shall be a mansion for all lovely forms,
Thy memory be as a dwelling place
For all sweet sounds and harmonies; oh! then,   145
If solitude, or fear, or pain, or grief
Should be thy portion, with what healing thoughts
Of tender joy wilt thou remember me,
And these my exhortations! Nor, perchance—
If I should be where I no more can hear   150
Thy voice, nor catch from thy wild eyes these gleams
Of past existence—wilt thou then forget
That on the banks of this delightful stream

"*Lines*": 119 *Friend:* his sister Dorothy

William Wordsworth   **757**

We stood together; and that I, so long
A worshiper of Nature, hither came   155
Unwearied in that service; rather say
With warmer love—oh! with far deeper zeal
Of holier love. Nor wilt thou then forget,
That after many wanderings, many years
Of absence, these steep woods and lofty cliffs,   160
And this green pastoral landscape, were to me
More dear, both for themselves and for thy sake!

1798

SHE DWELT AMONG THE UNTRODDEN WAYS

She dwelt among the untrodden ways
   Beside the springs of Dove,
A maid whom there were none to praise
   And very few to love:

A violet by a mossy stone   5
   Half hidden from the eye!
—Fair as a star, when only one
   Is shining in the sky.

She lived unknown, and few could know
   When Lucy ceased to be;   10
But she is in her grave, and, oh,
   The difference to me!

1800

STRANGE FITS OF PASSION HAVE I KNOWN

Strange fits of passion have I known:
And I will dare to tell,
But in the Lover's ear alone,
What once to me befell.

When she I loved looked every day   5
Fresh as a rose in June,
I to her cottage bent my way,
Beneath an evening-moon.

Upon the moon I fixed my eye,
All over the wide lea;   10

With quickening pace my horse drew nigh
Those paths so dear to me.

And now we reached the orchard-plot;
And, as we climbed the hill,
The sinking moon to Lucy's cot   15
Came near, and nearer still.

In one of those sweet dreams I slept,
Kind Nature's gentlest boon!
And all the while my eyes I kept
On the descending moon.   20

My horse moved on; hoof after hoof
He raised, and never stopped:
When down behind the cottage roof,
At once, the bright moon dropped.

What fond and wayward thoughts will slide   25
Into a Lover's head!
"O mercy!" to myself I cried,
"If Lucy should be dead!"

1800

THERE WAS A BOY

   There was a Boy: ye knew him well, ye cliffs
And islands of Winander!—many a time
At evening, when the earliest stars began
To move along the edges of the hills,
Rising or setting, would he stand alone   5
Beneath the trees or by the glimmering lake,
And there, with fingers interwoven, both hands
Pressed closely palm to palm, and to his mouth
Uplifted, he, as through an instrument,
Blew mimic hootings to the silent owls,   10
That they might answer him; and they would shout
Across the watery vale, and shout again,
Responsive to his call, with quivering peals,
And long halloos and screams, and echoes loud,
Redoubled and redoubled, concourse wild   15
Of jocund din; and, when a lengthened pause
Of silence came and baffled his best skill,
Then sometimes, in that silence while he hung
Listening, a gentle shock of mild surprise
Has carried far into his heart the voice   20
Of mountain torrents; or the visible scene

Would enter unawares into his mind,
With all its solemn imagery, its rocks,
Its woods, and that uncertain heaven, received
Into the bosom of the steady lake.   25

   This Boy was taken from his mates, and died
In childhood, ere he was full twelve years old.
Fair is the spot, most beautiful the vale
Where he was born; the grassy churchyard hangs
Upon a slope above the village school,   30
And through that churchyard when my way has led
On summer evenings, I believe that there
A long half hour together I have stood
Mute, looking at the grave in which he lies!

1800

THE WORLD IS TOO MUCH WITH US

The world is too much with us; late and soon,
Getting and spending, we lay waste our powers;
Little we see in Nature that is ours;
We have given our hearts away, a sordid boon!
This Sea that bares her bosom to the moon,   5
The winds that will be howling at all hours,
And are up-gathered now like sleeping flowers,
For this, for everything, we are out of tune;
It moves us not.—Great God! I'd rather be
A Pagan suckled in a creed outworn;   10
So might I, standing on this pleasant lea,
Have glimpses that would make me less forlorn;
Have sight of Proteus rising from the sea;
Or hear old Triton blow his wreathéd horn.

1807

COMPOSED UPON WESTMINSTER
BRIDGE, SEPTEMBER 3, 1802

Earth has not anything to show more fair:
Dull would he be of soul who could pass by
A sight so touching in its majesty;

"*The World is Too Much With Us*": 13 *Proteus:* a sea god in Greek mythology   14 *Triton:* a
gigantic god in Greek mythology; he dwelt on the ocean floor and blew a shell trumpet to
raise or quiet storms.

This City now doth, like a garment, wear
The beauty of the morning; silent, bare,   5
Ships, towers, domes, theaters, and temples lie
Open unto the fields, and to the sky;
All bright and glittering in the smokeless air.
Never did sun more beautifully steep
In his first splendor, valley, rock, or hill;   10
Ne'er saw I, never felt, a calm so deep!
The river glideth at his own sweet will:
Dear God! the very houses seem asleep;
And all that mighty heart is lying still!

1807

RESOLUTION AND INDEPENDENCE

1

There was a roaring in the wind all night;
The rain came heavily and fell in floods;
But now the sun is rising calm and bright;
The birds are singing in the distant woods;
Over his own sweet voice the Stock-dove broods;   5
The Jay makes answer as the Magpie chatters;
And all the air is filled with pleasant noise of waters.

2

All things that love the sun are out of doors;
The sky rejoices in the morning's birth;
The grass is bright with rain-drops;—on the moors   10
The hare is running races in her mirth;
And with her feet she from the plashy earth
Raises a mist; that, glittering in the sun,
Runs with her all the way, wherever she doth run.

3

I was a Traveller then upon the moor;   15
I saw the hare that raced about with joy;
I heard the woods and distant waters roar;
Or heard them not, as happy as a boy:
The pleasant season did my heart employ:
My old remembrances went from me wholly;   20
And all the ways of men, so vain and melancholy.

4

But, as it sometimes chanceth, from the might
Of joy in minds that can no further go,

William Wordsworth   **761**

As high as we have mounted in delight
In our dejection do we sink as low;   25
To me that morning did it happen so;
And fears and fancies thick upon me came;
Dim sadness—and blind thoughts, I knew not, nor
    could name.

                            5

I heard the sky-lark warbling in the sky;
And I bethought me of the playful hare: 30
Even such a happy Child of earth am I;
Even as these blissful creatures do I fare;
Far from the world I walk, and from all care;
But there may come another day to me—
Solitude, pain of heart, distress, and poverty.   35

                            6

My whole life I have lived in pleasant thought,
As if life's business were a summer mood;
As if all needful things would come unsought
To genial faith, still rich in genial good;
But how can He expect that others should   40
Build for him, sow for him, and at his call
Love him, who for himself will take no heed at all?

                            7

I thought of Chatterton, the marvellous Boy,
The sleepless Soul that perished in his pride;
Of Him who walked in glory and in joy   45
Following his plough, along the mountain-side:
By our own spirits are we deified:
We Poets in our youth begin in gladness;
But thereof come in the end despondency and
    madness.

                            8

Now, whether it were by peculiar grace,   50
A leading from above, a something given,
Yet it befell that, in this lonely place,
When I with these untoward thoughts had striven,

"*Resolution and Independence*": 44 *Chatterton:* Thomas Chatterton (1752–1770); after a brief
period of literary success, he declined into poverty and committed suicide at age 17.
45 *Him:* Robert Burns (1759–1796), the great Scottish lyric poet who grew up doing heavy
farm labor and died at the height of his career.

Beside a pool bare to the eye of heaven
I saw a Man before me unawares: 55
The oldest man he seemed that ever wore grey hairs.

9

As a huge stone is sometimes seen to lie
Couched on the bald top of an eminence;
Wonder to all who do the same espy,
By what means it could thither come, and whence;   60
So that it seems a thing endued with sense:
Like a sea-beast crawled forth, that on a shelf
Of rock or sand reposeth, there to sun itself;

10

Such seemed this Man, not all alive nor dead,
Nor all asleep—in his extreme old age: 65
His body was bent double, feet and head
Coming together in life's pilgrimage;
As if some dire constraint of pain, or rage
Of sickness felt by him in times long past,
A more than human weight upon his frame had cast.   70

11

Himself he propped, limbs, body, and pale face,
Upon a long grey staff of shaven wood:
And, still as I drew near with gentle pace,
Upon the margin of that moorish flood
Motionless as a cloud the old Man stood,   75
That heareth not the loud winds when they call;
And moveth all together, if it move at all.

12

At length, himself unsettling, he the pond
Stirred with his staff, and fixedly did look
Upon the muddy water, which he conned,   80
As if he had been reading in a book:
And now a stranger's privilege I took;
And, drawing to his side, to him did say,
"This morning gives us promise of a glorious day."

13

A gentle answer did the old Man make,   85
In courteous speech which forth he slowly drew:
And him with further words I thus bespake,
"What occupation do you there pursue?
This is a lonesome place for one like you."

Ere he replied, a flash of mild surprise   90
Broke from the sable orbs of his yet-vivid eyes.

14

His words came feebly, from a feeble chest,
But each in solemn order followed each,
With something of a lofty utterance drest—
Choice word and measured phrase, above the reach   95
Of ordinary men; a stately speech;
Such as grave Livers do in Scotland use,
Religious men, who give to God and man their dues.

15

He told, that to these waters he had come
To gather leeches, being old and poor: 100
Employment hazardous and wearisome!
And he had many hardships to endure:
From pond to pond he roamed, from moor to moor;
Housing, with God's good help, by choice or chance;
And in this way he gained an honest maintenance.   105

16

The old Man still stood talking by my side;
But now his voice to me was like a stream
Scarce heard; nor word from word could I divide;
And the whole body of the Man did seem
Like one whom I had met with in a dream;   110
Or like a man from some far region sent,
To give me human strength, by apt admonishment.

17

My former thoughts returned: the fear that kills;
And hope that is unwilling to be fed;
Cold, pain, and labor, and all fleshly ills;   115
And mighty Poets in their misery dead.
—Perplexed, and longing to be comforted,
My question eagerly did I renew,
"How is it that you live, and what is it you do?"

18

He with a smile did then his words repeat;   120
And said that, gathering leeches, far and wide
He travelled; stirring thus about his feet
The waters of the pools where they abide.

---

98 *grave Livers:* those who live serious lives

"Once I could meet with them on every side;
But they have dwindled long by slow decay;   125
Yet still I persevere, and find them where I may."

                        19

While he was talking thus, the lonely place,
The old Man's shape, and speech—all troubled me:
In my mind's eye I seemed to see him pace
About the weary moors continually,   130
Wandering about alone and silently.
While I these thoughts within myself pursued,
He, having made a pause, the same discourse renewed.

                        20

And soon with this he other matter blended,
Cheerfully uttered, with demeanor kind,   135
But stately in the main; and, when he ended,
I could have laughed myself to scorn to find
In that decrepit Man so firm a mind.
"God," said I, "be my help and stay secure;
I'll think of the Leech-gatherer on the lonely moor!"   140

                                    1807

ODE: INTIMATIONS OF IMMORTALITY
FROM RECOLLECTIONS
OF EARLY CHILDHOOD

The child is father of the man;
And I could wish my days to be
Bound each to each by natural piety.

                        1

There was a time when meadow, grove, and stream,
The earth, and every common sight,
     To me did seem
   Apparelled in celestial light,
The glory and the freshness of a dream.   5
It is not now as it hath been of yore;—
     Turn whereso'er I may,
       By night or day,
The things which I have seen I now can see no more.

                        2

     The rainbow comes and goes,   10
     And lovely is the rose;

The moon doth with delight
  Look round her when the heavens are bare;
    Waters on a starry night
    Are beautiful and fair;   15
  The sunshine is a glorious birth;
  But yet I know, where'er I go,
That there hath passed away a glory from the earth.

3

Now, while the birds thus sing a joyous song,
  And while the young lambs bound   20
    As to the tabor's sound,
To me alone there came a thought of grief:
A timely utterance gave that thought relief,
    And I again am strong:
The cataracts blow their trumpets from the steep;   25
No more shall grief of mine the season wrong;
I hear the echoes through the mountains throng,
The winds come to me from the fields of sleep,
    And all the earth is gay;
      Land and sea   30
  Give themselves up to jollity,
    And with the heart of May
Doth every beast keep holiday;—
    Thou child of joy,
Shout round me, let me hear thy shouts, thou happy
  shepherd-boy!   35

4

Ye blessed creatures, I have heard the call
  Ye to each other make; I see
The heavens laugh with you in your jubilee;
  My heart is at your festival,
    My head hath its coronal,   40
The fullness of your bliss, I feel—I feel it all.
    O evil day! if I were sullen
    While earth herself is adorning,
      This sweet May-morning,
    And the children are culling   45
      On every side,
  In a thousand valleys far and wide,
    Fresh flowers; while the sun shines warm,
And the babe leaps up on his mother's arm:—
    I hear, I hear, with joy I hear!   50
    —But there's a tree, of many, one,
A single field which I have looked upon,

Both of them speak of something that is gone:
> The pansy at my feet
> Doth the same tale repeat: 55
Whither is fled the visionary gleam?
Where is it now, the glory and the dream?

5

Our birth is but a sleep and a forgetting:
The soul that rises with us, our life's star,
> Hath had elsewhere its setting, 60
> And cometh from afar:
> Not in entire forgetfulness,
> And not in utter nakedness,
But trailing clouds of glory do we come
> From God, who is our home: 65
Heaven lies about us in our infancy!
Shades of the prison-house begin to close
> Upon the growing boy,
> But he
Beholds the light, and whence it flows, 70
> He sees it in his joy;
The youth, who daily farther from the east
> Must travel, still is Nature's priest,
> And by the vision splendid
> Is on his way attended; 75
At length the man perceives it die away,
And fade into the light of common day.

6

Earth fills her lap with pleasures of her own;
> Yearnings she hath in her own natural kind;
And, even with something of a mother's mind,
> And no unworthy aim, 80
> The homely nurse doth all she can
To make her foster-child, her inmate man,
> Forget the glories he hath known,
And that imperial palace whence he came. 85

7

Behold the child among his new-born blisses,
A six years' darling of a pigmy size!
See, where 'mid work of his own hand he lies,
Fretted by sallies of his mother's kisses,
With light upon him from his father's eyes! 90
See, at his feet, some little plan or chart,
Some fragment from his dream of human life,

Shaped by himself with newly-learnèd art;
    A wedding or a festival,
    A mourning or a funeral;   95
      And this hath now his heart,
      And unto this he frames his song:
      Then will he fit his tongue
To dialogues of business, love, or strife;
      But it will not be long   100
      Ere this be thrown aside,
      And with new joy and pride
The little actor cons another part;
Filling from time to time his "humorous stage"
With all the persons, down to palsied age,   105
That life brings with her in her equipage;
      As if his whole vocation
      Were endless imitation.

8

Thou, whose exterior semblance doth belie
      Thy soul's immensity;   110
Thou best philosopher, who yet dost keep
Thy heritage, thou eye among the blind,
That, deaf and silent, read'st the eternal deep,
Haunted for ever by the eternal mind,—
      Mighty prophet! Seer blest!   115
      On whom those truths do rest,
Which we are toiling all our lives to find,
In darkness lost, the darkness of the grave;
Thou, over whom thy immortality
Broods like the day, a master o'er a slave,   120
A presence which is not to be put by;
Thou little child, yet glorious in the might
Of heaven-born freedom on thy being's height,
Why with such earnest pains dost thou provoke
The years to bring the inevitable yoke,   125
Thus blindly with thy blessedness at strife?
Full soon thy soul shall have her earthly freight,
And custom lie upon thee with a weight,
Heavy as frost, and deep almost as life!

9

    O joy! that in our embers   130
    Is something that doth live,
    That nature yet remembers
    What was so fugitive!

The thought of our past years in me doth breed
Perpetual benediction: not indeed   135
For that which is most worthy to be blest—
Delight and liberty, the simple creed
Of childhood, whether busy or at rest,
With new-fledged hope still fluttering in his breast:—
    Not for these I raise   140
      The song of thanks and praise;
   But for those obstinate questionings
   Of sense and outward things,
   Fallings from us, vanishings;
   Blank misgivings of a creature   145
Moving about in worlds not realized,
High instincts before which our mortal Nature
Did tremble like a guilty thing surprised:
   But for those first affections,
    Those shadowy recollections,   150
  Which, be they what they may,
Are yet the fountain-light of all our day,
Are yet a master-light of all our seeing;
  Uphold us, cherish, and have power to make
Our noisy years seem moments in the being   155
Of the eternal silence: truths that wake,
    To perish never:
Which neither listlessness, nor mad endeavour,
    Nor man nor boy,
Nor all that is at enmity with joy,   160
Can utterly abolish or destroy!
  Hence in a season of calm weather
    Though inland far we be,
Our souls have sight of that immortal sea
    Which brought us hither,   165
  Can in a moment travel thither,
And see the children sport upon the shore,
And hear the mighty waters rolling evermore.

10

Then sing, ye birds, sing, sing a joyous song!
    And let the young lambs bound   170
    As to the tabor's sound!
We in thought will join your throng,
  Ye that pipe and ye that play,
  Ye that through your hearts today
  Feel the gladness of the May!   175
What though the radiance which was once so bright

Be now for ever taken from my sight,
   Though nothing can bring back the hour
Of splendour in the grass, of glory in the flower;
      We will grieve not, rather find   180
      Strength in what remains behind;
      In the primal sympathy
      Which having been must ever be;
      In the soothing thoughts that spring
      Out of human suffering;   185
      In the faith that looks through death,
In years that bring the philosophic mind.

11

And O ye fountains, meadows, hills, and groves,
Forbode not any severing of our loves!
Yet in my heart of hearts I feel your might;   190
I only have relinquished one delight
To live beneath your more habitual sway.
I love the brooks which down their channels fret,
Even more than when I tripped lightly as they;
The innocent brightness of a new-born day   195
      Is lovely yet;
The clouds that gather round the setting sun
Do take a sober colouring from an eye
That hath kept watch o'er man's mortality;
Another race hath been, and other palms are won.   200
Thanks to the human heart by which we live,
Thanks to its tenderness, its joys, and fears,
To me the meanest flower that blows can give
Thoughts that do often lie too deep for tears.

1807

MY HEART LEAPS UP

My heart leaps up when I behold
   A rainbow in the sky:
So was it when my life began;
So is it now I am a man;
So be it when I shall grow old,   5
   Or let me die!
The Child is father of the Man;
And I could wish my days to be
Bound each to each by natural piety.

1807

William Wordsworth was among the most revolutionary figures in the history of English poetry. Pope and the other major writers of the Age of Reason had built a citadel of literary taste based on what we would now call sophistication: their poems were typically formal, emotionally cool, and skeptical about human nature—distinctly the products of the city and the university. Wordsworth introduced (or reintroduced) England to poetry that rejected sophistication, looked to nature for inspiration, and attempted a more direct expression of basic human emotions. The impetus for this Romantic revolution was political and psychological as well as artistic, as we can see in the following excerpts from a letter to John Wilson and from the preface to Lyrical Ballads.

"I answer, from within; by stripping our own hearts naked": William Wordsworth

You begin what you say . . . with this observation, that nothing is a fit subject for poetry which does not please. But here follows a question. Does not please whom? Some have little knowledge of natural imagery of any kind, and, of course, little relish for it; some are disgusted with the very mention of the words "pastoral poetry," "sheep," or "shepherds"; some cannot tolerate a poem with a ghost or any supernatural agency in it; others would shrink from an animated description of the pleasures of love, as from a thing carnal and libidinous; some cannot bear to see delicate and refined feelings ascribed to men in low conditions of society, because their vanity and self-love tell them that these belong only to themselves and men like themselves in dress, station, and way of life; others are disgusted with the naked language of some of the most interesting passions of men, because either it is indelicate, or gross, or vulgar. . . . I return then to the question, please whom? or what? I answer, human nature, as it has been and ever will be. But where are we to find the best measure of this? I answer, from within; by stripping our own hearts naked, and by looking out of ourselves towards men who lead the simplest lives, and those most according to nature; men who have never known false refinements, wayward and artificial desires, false criticisms, effeminate habits of thinking and feeling, or who, having known these things, have outgrown them. This latter class is the most to be depended upon, but it is very small in number. . . . You have given me praise for having reflected faithfully in my Poems the feelings of human nature. I would fain hope that I have done so. But a great Poet ought to do more than this: he ought, to a certain degree, to rectify men's feelings, to give them new compositions of feeling, to render their feelings more sane, pure, and permanent, in short, more consonant to nature, that is, to eternal nature, and the great moving spirit of things. He ought to travel before men occasionally as well as at their sides.

"Poetry is the spontaneous overflow of powerful feelings": William Wordsworth

I have said that Poetry is the spontaneous overflow of powerful feelings: it takes its origin from emotion recollected in tranquillity: the emotion is contemplated till by a species of reaction the tranquillity gradually disappears, and an emotion, kindred to that which was before the subject of contemplation, is gradually produced, and does itself actually exist in the mind. In this mood successful composition generally begins, and in a mood similar to this it is carried on; but the emotion, of whatever kind and in whatever degree, from various causes is qualified by various pleasures, so that in describing any passions whatsoever, which are voluntarily described, the mind will upon the whole be in a state of enjoyment. Now, if Nature be thus cautious in preserving in a state of enjoyment a being thus employed, the Poet ought to profit by the lesson thus held forth to him, and ought especially to take care, that whatever passions he communicates to his Reader, those passions, if his Reader's mind be sound and vigorous, should always be accompanied with an overbalance of pleasure. Now the music of harmonious metrical language, the sense of difficulty overcome, and the blind association of pleasure which has been previously received from works of rhyme or metre of the same or similar construction, an indistinct perception perpetually renewed of language closely resembling that of real life, and yet, in the circumstance of metre, differing from it so widely, all these imperceptibly make up a complex feeling of delight, which is of the most important use in tempering the painful feeling which will always be found intermingled with powerful descriptions of the deeper passions.

SAMUEL TAYLOR COLERIDGE

(1772–1834)

THE AEOLIAN HARP

Composed at Clevedon, Somersetshire

My pensive Sara! thy soft cheek reclined
Thus on mine arm, most soothing sweet it is
To sit beside our Cot, our Cot o'ergrown
With white-flowered Jasmin, and the broad-leaved
   Myrtle,
(Meet emblems they of Innocence and Love!)   5
And watch the clouds, that late were rich with light,
Slow saddening round, and mark the star of eve
Serenely brilliant (such should Wisdom be)
Shine opposite! How exquisite the scents
Snatched from yon bean-field! and the world *so*
   hushed!   10
The stilly murmur of the distant Sea
Tells us of silence.

           And that simplest Lute,
Placed length-ways in the clasping casement, hark!
How by the desultory breeze caressed,   15
Like some coy maid half yielding to her lover,
It pours such sweet upbraiding, as must needs

Tempt to repeat the wrong! And now, its strings
Boldlier swept, the long sequacious notes
Over delicious surges sink and rise,   20
Such a soft floating witchery of sound
As twilight Elfins make, when they at eve
Voyage on gentle gales from Fairy-Land,
Where Melodies round honey-dropping flowers,
Footless and wild, like birds of Paradise,   25
Nor pause, nor perch, hovering on untamed wing!
O! the one Life within us and abroad,
Which meets all motion and becomes its soul,
A light in sound, a sound-like power in light,
Rhythm in all thought, and joyance everywhere—   30
Methinks, it should have been impossible
Not to love all things in a world so filled;
Where the breeze warbles, and the mute still air
Is Music slumbering on her instrument.

And thus, my Love! as on the midway slope   35
Of yonder hill I stretch my limbs at noon,
Whilst through my half-closed eyelids I behold
The sunbeams dance, like diamonds, on the main,
And tranquil muse upon tranquility:
Full many a thought uncalled and undetained,   40
And many idle flitting phantasies,
Traverse my indolent and passive brain,
As wild and various as the random gales
That swell and flutter on this subject Lute!

    And what if all of animated nature   45
Be but organic Harps diversely framed,
That tremble into thought, as o'er them sweeps
Plastic and vast, one intellectual breeze,
At once the Soul of each, and God of all?
    But thy more serious eye a mild reproof   50
Darts, O belovéd Woman! nor such thoughts
Dim and unhallowed dost thou not reject,
And biddest me walk humbly with my God.
Meek Daughter in the family of Christ!
Well hast thou said and holily dispraised   55
These shapings of the unregenerate mind;
Bubbles that glitter as they rise and break
On vain Philosophy's aye-babbling spring.
For never guiltless may I speak of him,
The Incomprehensible! save when with awe   60
I praise him, and with Faith that inly *feels;*
Who with his saving mercies healéd me,
A sinful and most miserable man,
Wildered and dark, and gave me to possess
Peace, and this Cot, and thee, heart-honored Maid!   65

1796

KUBLA KHAN

Or a vision in a dream. A Fragment

In Xanadu did Kubla Khan
A stately pleasure dome decree:
Where Alph, the sacred river, ran

"*Kubla Han*": 1 *Xamdu:* Xanadu, where Kublai Khan had his summer capital. *Kubla Khan:* Kublai Khan, the first Mongol Emperor of China, visited and served by Marco Polo during the thirteenth century.

Through caverns measureless to man
   Down to a sunless sea.   5
So twice five miles of fertile ground
With walls and towers were girdled round:
And there were gardens bright with sinuous rills,
Where blossomed many an incense-bearing tree;
And here were forests ancient as the hills,   10
Enfolding sunny spots of greenery.

But oh! that deep romantic chasm which slanted
Down the green hill athwart a cedarn cover!
A savage place! as holy and enchanted
As e'er beneath a waning moon was haunted   15
By woman wailing for her demon lover!
And from this chasm, with ceaseless turmoil seething,
As if this earth in fast thick pants were breathing,
A mighty fountain momently was forced:
Amid whose swift half-intermitted burst   20
Huge fragments vaulted like rebounding hail,
Or chaffy grain beneath the thresher's flail:
And 'mid these dancing rocks at once and ever
It flung up momently the sacred river.
Five miles meandering with a mazy motion   25
Through wood and dale the sacred river ran,
Then reached the caverns measureless to man,
And sank in tumult to a lifeless ocean:
And 'mid this tumult Kubla heard from far
Ancestral voices prophesying war!   30

   The shadow of the dome of pleasure
   Floated midway on the waves;
   Where was heard the mingled measure
   From the fountain and the caves.
It was a miracle of rare device,   35
A sunny pleasure dome with caves of ice!

   A damsel with a dulcimer
   In a vision once I saw:
   It was an Abyssinian maid,
   And on her dulcimer she played,   40
   Singing of Mount Abora.
   Could I revive within me
   Her symphony and song,
   To such a deep delight 'twould win me,

---

39 *Abyssinian:* Ethiopian   41 *Mount Abora:* Mount Amara in Abyssinia, referred to by Milton
in *Paradise Lost* 4: 281.

That with music loud and long,   45
I would build that dome in air,
That sunny dome! those caves of ice!
And all who heard should see them there,
And all should cry, Beware! Beware!
His flashing eyes, his floating hair!   50
Weave a circle round him thrice,
And close your eyes with holy dread,
For he on honey-dew hath fed,
And drunk the milk of Paradise.

1797

THE RIME OF THE ANCIENT MARINER

Part 1

*An ancient Mariner
meeteth three Gallants
bidden to a wedding-feast,
and detaineth one.*

It is an ancient Mariner
And he stoppeth one of three.
—"By thy long gray beard and glittering eye
Now wherefore stopp'st thou me?

The Bridegroom's doors are opened wide,   5
And I am next of kin;
The guests are met, the feast is set:
May'st hear the merry din."

He holds him with his skinny hand,
"There was a ship," quoth he.   10
"Hold off! unhand me, graybeard loon!"
Eftsoons his hand dropped he.

*The Wedding-Guest is
spellbound by the eye of the
old seafaring man, and
constrained to hear his
tale.*

He holds him with his glittering eye—
The Wedding Guest stood still,
And listens like a three years' child: 15
The Mariner hath his will.

The Wedding Guest sat on a stone:
He cannot choose but hear;
And thus spake on that ancient man,
The bright-eyed Mariner.   20

"The ship was cheered, the harbor cleared,
Merrily did we drop

"*Rime of the Ancient Mariner*": 13 *Eftsoons:* at once

Below the kirk, below the hill,
Below the lighthouse top.

The Sun came up upon the left,   25
Out of the sea came he!
And he shone bright, and on the right
Went down into the sea.

Higher and higher every day,
Till over the mast at noon—"   30
The Wedding Guest here beat his breast,
For he heard the loud bassoon.

The bride hath paced into the hall,
Red as a rose is she;
Nodding their heads before her goes   35
The merry minstrelsy.

The Wedding Guest he beat his breast,
Yet he cannot choose but hear;
And thus spake on that ancient man,
The bright-eyed Mariner.   40

"And now the STORM-BLAST came, and he
Was tyrannous and strong;
He struck with his o'ertaking wings,
And chased us south along.

With sloping masts and dipping prow,   45
As who pursued with yell and blow
Still treads the shadow of his foe,
And forward bends his head,
The ship drove fast, loud roared the blast,
And southward aye we fled.   50

And now there came both mist and snow,
And it grew wondrous cold:
And ice, mast-high, came floating by,
As green as emerald.

And through the drifts the snowy clifts   55
Did send a dismal sheen:
Nor shapes of men nor beasts we ken—
The ice was all between.

The ice was here, the ice was there,
The ice was all around: 60

---

23 *kirk:* church   55 *clifts:* fissures

It cracked and growled, and roared and howled,
Like noises in a swound!

At length did cross an Albatross,
Through the fog it came;
As if it had been a Christian soul,   65
We hailed it in God's name.

It ate the food it ne'er had eat,
And round and round it flew.
The ice did split with a thunder-fit;
The helmsman steered us through!   70

And a good south wind sprung up behind;
The Albatross did follow,
And every day, for food or play,
Came to the mariners' hollo!

In mist or cloud, on mast or shroud,   75
It perched for vespers nine;
Whiles all the night, through fog-smoke white,
Glimmered the white Moon-shine."

"God save thee, ancient Mariner!
From the fiends, that plague thee thus!—   80
Why look'st thou so?"—With my crossbow
I shot the ALBATROSS.

Part 2

The Sun now rose upon the right:
Out of the sea came he,
Still hid in mist, and on the left   85
Went down into the sea.

And the good south wind still blew behind,
But no sweet bird did follow,
Nor any day for food or play
Came to the mariners' hollo!   90

And I had done a hellish thing,
And it would work 'em woe:
For all averred, I had killed the bird
That made the breeze to blow.
Ah wretch! said they, the bird to slay,   95
That made the breeze to blow!

---

62 *swound:* swoon

But when the fog cleared
off, they justify the same,
and thus make themselves
accomplices in the crime.

Nor dim nor red, like God's own head,
The glorious Sun uprist:
Then all averred, I had killed the bird
That brought the fog and mist.   100
'Twas right, said they, such birds to slay,
That bring the fog and mist.

The fair breeze continues;
the ship enters the Pacific
Ocean, and sails
northward, even till it
reaches the Line. The ship
hath been suddenly
becalmed.

The fair breeze blew, the white foam flew,
The furrow followed free;
We were the first that ever burst   105
Into that silent sea.

Down dropped the breeze, the sails dropped down,
'Twas sad as sad could be;
And we did speak only to break
The silence of the sea!   110

All in a hot and copper sky,
The bloody Sun, at noon,
Right up above the mast did stand,
No bigger than the Moon.

Day after day, day after day,   115
We stuck, nor breath nor motion;
As idle as a painted ship
Upon a painted ocean.

And the Albatross begins
to be avenged.

Water, water, everywhere,
And all the boards did shrink;   120
Water, water, everywhere,
Nor any drop to drink.

The very deep did rot: O Christ!
That ever this should be!
Yea, slimy things did crawl with legs   125
Upon the slimy sea.

A Spirit had followed
them; one of the invisible
inhabitants of this planet,
neither departed souls nor
angels; concerning whom
the learned Jew, Josephus,
and the Platonic
Constantinopolitan,
Michael Psellus, may be
consulted. They are very
numerous, and there is no
climate or element without
one or more.

About, about, in reel and rout
The death-fires danced at night;
The water, like a witch's oils,
Burnt green, and blue and white.   130

And some in dreams assuréd were
Of the Spirit that plagued us so;
Nine fathom deep he had followed us
From the land of mist and snow.

And every tongue, through utter drought,   135
Was withered at the root;

We could not speak, no more than if
We had been choked with soot.

*The ship-mates, in their
sore distress, would fain
throw the whole guilt on
the ancient Mariner: in
sign whereof they hang the
dead sea-bird round his
neck.*

Ah! well-a-day! what evil looks
Had I from old and young!   140
Instead of the cross, the Albatross
About my neck was hung.

*The ancient Mariner
beholdeth a sign in the element afar off.*

Part 3

There passed a weary time. Each throat
Was parched, and glazed each eye.
A weary time! a weary time!   145
How glazed each weary eye,
When looking westward, I beheld
A something in the sky.

At first it seemed a little speck,
And then it seemed a mist;   150
It moved and moved, and took at last
A certain shape, I wist.

A speck, a mist, a shape, I wist!
And still it neared and neared:
As if it dodged a water sprite,   155
It plunged and tacked and veered.

*At its nearer approach, it
seemeth him to be a ship;
and at a dear ransom he
freeth his speech from the
bonds of thirst.*

With throats unslaked, with black lips bake
We could nor laugh nor wail;
Through utter drought all dumb we stood!
I bit my arm, I sucked the blood,   160
And cried, A sail! a sail!

With throats unslaked, with black lips bake
Agape they heard me call:
A flash of joy;
Gramercy! they for joy did grin,
And all at once their breath drew in,   165
As they were drinking all.

*And horror follows. For
can it be a ship that comes
onward without wind or
tide?*

See! see! (I cried) she tacks no more!
Hither to work us weal;
Without a breeze, without a tide,
She steadies with upright keel!   170

The western wave was all aflame.
The day was well nigh done!
Almost upon the western wave

---

155 *sprite:* a spirit which haunted the water   157 *unslaked:* parched   164 *Gramercy:*
exclamation of surprise and thanks   168 *weal:* good

Rested the broad bright Sun;
When that strange shape drove suddenly   175
Betwixt us and the Sun.

*It seemeth him but the
skeleton of a ship:*

And straight the Sun was flecked with bars,
(Heaven's Mother send us grace!)
As if through a dungeon grate he peered
With broad and burning face.   180

Alas! (though I, and my heart beat loud)
How fast she nears and nears!
Are those *her* sails that glance in the Sun,
Like restless gossameres?

*And its ribs are seen as
bars on the face of the
setting Sun. The
Spectre-Woman and her
Death-mate, and no other
on board the skeleton-ship.
Like vessel, like crew.*

Are those *her* ribs through which the Sun   185
Did peer, as through a grate?
And is that Woman all her crew?
Is that a DEATH? and are there two?
Is DEATH that woman's mate?

Her lips were red, *her* looks were free,   190
Her locks were yellow as gold:
Her skin was as white as leprosy,
The Nightmare LIFE-IN-DEATH was she,
Who thicks man's blood with cold.

*Death and Life-in-Death
have diced for the ship's
crew, and she (the latter)
winneth the ancient
Mariner.*

The naked hulk alongside came,   195
And the twain were casting dice;
"The game is done! I've won! I've won!"
Quoth she, and whistles thrice.

*No twilight within the
courts of the Sun.*

The Sun's rim dips; the stars rush out:
At one stride comes the dark;   200
With far-heard whisper, o'er the sea,
Off shot the specter-bark.

At the rising of the Moon,

We listened and looked sideways up!
Fear at my heart, as at a cup,
My lifeblood seemed to sip!   205
The stars were dim, and thick the night,
The steersman's face by his lamp gleamed white;
From the sails the dew did drip—
Till clomb above the eastern bar
The hornéd Moon, with one bright star   210
Within the nether tip.

One after another,

One after one, by the star-dogged Moon,
Too quick for groan or sigh,
Each turned his face with ghastly pang,
And cursed me with his eye.   215

Samuel Taylor Coleridge   **781**

Four times fifty living men,
(And I heard nor sigh nor groan)
With heavy thump, a lifeless lump,
They dropped down one by one.

*But Life-in-Death begins
her work on the ancient
Mariner.*

The souls did from their bodies fly—   220
They fled to bliss or woe!
And every soul, it passed me by,
Like the whizz of my cross-bow!

Part 4

*The Wedding-Guest
feareth that a Spirit is
talking to him;*

"I fear thee, ancient Mariner!
I fear thy skinny hand!   225
And thou art long, and lank, and brown,
As is the ribbed sea-sand.

*But the ancient Mariner
assureth him of his bodily
life, and proceedeth to
relate his horrible
penance.*

I fear thee and thy glittering eye,
And thy skinny hand, so brown."—
Fear not, fear not, thou Wedding Guest!   230
This body dropped not down.

Alone, alone, all, all alone,
Alone on a wide wide sea!
And never a saint took pity on
My soul in agony.   235

*He despiseth the creatures
of the calm.*

The many men, so beautiful!
And they all dead did lie:
And a thousand thousand slimy things
Lived on; and so did I.

*And envieth that they
should live, and so many
lie dead.*

I looked upon the rotting sea,   240
And drew my eyes away;
I looked upon the rotting deck,
And there the dead men lay.

I looked to heaven, and tried to pray;
But or ever a prayer had gushed,   245
A wicked whisper came, and made
My heart as dry as dust.

I closed my lids, and kept them close,
And the balls like pulses beat,
For the sky and the sea, and the sea and the sky   250
Lay like a load on my weary eye,
And the dead were at my feet.

*But the curse liveth for
him in the eye of the dead
men.*

The cold sweat melted from their limbs,
Nor rot nor reek did they:

The look with which they looked on me   255
Had never passed away.

An orphan's curse would drag to hell
A spirit from on high;
But oh! more horrible than that
Is the curse in a dead man's eye!   260
Seven days, seven nights, I saw that curse,
And yet I could not die.

The moving Moon went up the sky,
And nowhere did abide:
Softly she was going up,   265
And a star or two beside—

Her beams bemocked the sultry main,
Like April hoar-frost spread;
But where the ship's huge shadow lay,
The charmèd water burnt alway   270
A still and awful red.

Beyond the shadow of the ship,
I watched the water snakes:
They moved in tracks of shining white,
And when they reared, the elfish light   275
Fell off in hoary flakes.

Within the shadow of the ship
I watched their rich attire:
Blue, glossy green, and velvet black,
They coiled and swam; and every track   280
Was a flash of golden fire.

O happy living things! no tongue
Their beauty might declare:
A spring of love gushed from my heart,

And I blessed them unaware: 285
Sure my kind saint took pity on me,
And I blessed them unaware.

The self-same moment I could pray;
And from my neck so free
The Albatross fell off, and sank   290
Like lead into the sea.

Part 5

Oh sleep! it is a gentle thing,
Beloved from pole to pole!

To Mary Queen the praise be given!
She sent the gentle sleep from Heaven,   295
That slid into my soul.

*By grace of the holy
Mother, the ancient Mari-
ner is refreshed with rain.*

The silly buckets on the deck,
That had so long remained,
I dreamt that they were filled with dew;
And when I awoke, it rained.   300

My lips were wet, my throat was cold,
My garments all were dank;
Sure I had drunken in my dreams,
And still my body drank.

I moved, and could not feel my limbs: 305
I was so light—almost
I thought that I had died in sleep,
And was a blessèd ghost.

*He heareth sounds and
seeth strange sights and
commotions in the sky and
the element.*

And soon I heard a roaring wind:
It did not come anear;   310
But with its sound it shook the sails,
That were so thin and sere.

The upper air burst into life!
And a hundred fire-flags sheen,
To and fro they were hurried about!   315
And to and fro, and in and out,
The wan stars danced between.

And the coming wind did roar more loud,
And the sails did sigh like sedge;
And the rain poured down from one black cloud;   320
The Moon was at its edge.

The thick black cloud was cleft, and still
The Moon was at its side:
Like waters shot from some high crag,
The lightning fell with never a jag,   325
A river steep and wide.

The loud wind never reached the ship,
Yet now the ship moved on!
Beneath the lightning and the Moon
The dead men gave a groan.   330

*The bodies of the ship's
crew are inspired and the
ship moves on;*

They groaned, they stirred, they all uprose,
Nor spake, nor moved their eyes;

---

298 *silly:* simple; here useless   314 *sheen:* shone

It had been strange, even in a dream,
To have seen those dead men rise.

The helmsman steered, the ship moved on;   335
Yet never a breeze up-blew;
The mariners all 'gan work the ropes,
Where they were wont to do;
They raised their limbs like lifeless tools—
We were a ghastly crew.   340

The body of my brother's son
Stood by me, knee to knee:
The body and I pulled at one rope,
But he said nought to me.

But not by the souls of the men, nor by daemons of earth or middle air, but by a blessed troop of angelic spirits, sent down by the invocation of the guardian saint.

"I fear thee, ancient Mariner!"   345
Be calm, thou Wedding Guest!
'Twas not those souls that fled in pain,
Which to their corses came again,
But a troop of spirits blest:

For when it dawned—they dropped their arms,   350
And clustered round the mast;
Sweet sounds rose slowly through their mouths,
And from their bodies passed.

Around, around, flew each sweet sound,
Then darted to the Sun;   355
Slowly the sounds came back again,
Now mixed, now one by one.

Sometimes a-dropping from the sky
I heard the sky-lark sing;
Sometimes all little birds that are,   360
How they seemed to fill the sea and air
With their sweet jargoning!

And now 'twas like all instruments,
Now like a lonely flute;
And now it is an angel's song,   365
That makes the heavens be mute.

It ceased; yet still the sails made on
A pleasant noise till noon,
A noise like of a hidden brook
In the leafy month of June,   370
That to the sleeping woods all night
Singeth a quiet tune.

---

348 *corses:* corpses

Till noon we quietly sailed on,
Yet never a breeze did breathe:
Slowly and smoothly went the ship,   375
Moved onward from beneath.

Under the keel nine fathom deep,
From the land of mist and snow,
The spirit slid: and it was he
That made the ship to go.   380
The sails at noon left off their tune,
And the ship stood still also.

The Sun, right up above the mast,
Had fixed her to the ocean:
But in a minute she 'gan stir,   385
With a short uneasy motion—
Backwards and forwards half her length
With a short uneasy motion.

Then like a pawing horse let go,
She made a sudden bound: 390
It flung the blood into my head,
And I fell down in a swound.

How long in that same fit I lay,
I have not to declare;
But ere my living life returned,   395
I heard and in my soul discerned
Two voices in the air.

"Is it he?" quoth one, "Is this the man?
By him who died on cross,
With his cruel bow he laid full low   400
The harmless Albatross.

The spirit who bideth by himself
In the land of mist and snow,
He loved the bird that loved the man
Who shot him with his bow."   405

The other was a softer voice,
As soft as honey-dew:
Quoth he, "The man hath penance done,
And penance more will do."

Part 6

FIRST VOICE
"But tell me, tell me! speak again,   410
Thy soft response renewing—

What makes that ship drive on so fast?
What is the ocean doing?"

SECOND VOICE

"Still as a slave before his lord,
The ocean hath no blast;   415
His great bright eye most silently
Up to the Moon is cast—

If he may know which way to go;
For she guides him smooth or grim.
See, brother, see! how graciously   420
She looketh down on him."

FIRST VOICE

The Mariner hath been
cast into a trance; for the
angelic power causeth the
vessel to drive northward
faster than human life
could endure.

"But why drives on that ship so fast,
Without or wave or wind?"

SECOND VOICE

"The air is cut away before,
And closes from behind.   425

Fly, brother, fly! more high, more high!
Or we shall be belated:
For slow and slow that ship will go,
When the Mariner's trance is abated."

The supernatural motion
is retarded; the Mariner
awakes, and his penance
begins anew.

I woke, and we were sailing on   430
As in a gentle weather:
'Twas night, calm night, the moon was high;
The dead men stood together.

All stood together on the deck,
For a charnel-dungeon fitter: 435
All fixed on me their stony eyes,
That in the Moon did glitter.

The pang, the curse, with which they died,
Had never passed away:
I could not draw my eyes from theirs,   440
Nor turn them up to pray.

The curse is finally
expiated.

And now this spell was snapped: once more
I viewed the ocean green,
And looked far forth, yet little saw
Of what had else been seen—   445

Like one, that on a lonesome road
Doth walk in fear and dread,
And having once turned round walks on,
And turns no more his head;

Because he knows, a frightful fiend   450
Doth close behind him tread.

But soon there breathed a wind on me,
Nor sound nor motion made:
Its path was not upon the sea,
In ripple or in shade.   455

It raised my hair, it fanned my cheek
Like a meadow-gale of spring—
It mingled strangely with my fears,
Yet it felt like a welcoming.

Swiftly, swiftly flew the ship,   460
Yet she sailed softly too:
Sweetly, sweetly blew the breeze—
On me alone it blew.

And the ancient Mariner beholdeth his native country.

Oh! dream of joy! is this indeed
The lighthouse top I see?   465
Is this the hill? is this the kirk?
Is this mine own countree?

We drifted o'er the harbor-bar,
And I with sobs did pray—
O let me be awake, my God!   470
Or let me sleep alway.

The harbor-bay was clear as glass,
So smoothly it was strewn!
And on the bay the moonlight lay,
And the shadow of the Moon.   475

The rock shone bright, the kirk no less,
That stands above the rock:
The moonlight steeped in silentness
The steady weathercock.

And the bay was white with silent light,   480
Till rising from the same,
Full many shapes, that shadows were,
In crimson colors came.

The angelic spirits leave the dead bodies,

A little distance from the prow
Those crimson shadows were: 485
I turned my eyes upon the deck—
Oh, Christ! what saw I there!

And appear in their own forms of light.

Each corse lay flat, lifeless and flat,
And, by the holy rood!

A man all light, a seraph-man,   490
On every corse there stood.

This seraph-band, each waved his hand;
It was a heavenly sight!
They stood as signals to the land,
Each one a lovely light;   495

This seraph-band, each waved his hand,
No voice did they impart—
No voice; but oh! the silence sank
Like music on my heart.

But soon I heard the dash of oars,   500
I heard the Pilot's cheer;
My head was turned perforce away
And I saw a boat appear.

The Pilot and the Pilot's boy,
I heard them coming fast: 505
Dear Lord in Heaven! it was a joy
The dead men could not blast.

I saw a third—I heard his voice:
It is the Hermit good!
He singeth loud his godly hymns   510
That he makes in the wood.
He'll shrieve my soul, he'll wash away
The Albatross's blood.

Part 7

The Hermit of the Wood,   This Hermit good lives in that wood
Which slopes down to the sea.   515
How loudly his sweet voice he rears!
He loves to talk with marineres
That come from a far countree.

He kneels at morn, and noon, and eve—
He hath a cushion plump: 520
It is the moss that wholly hides
The rotted old oak stump.

The skiff-boat neared: I heard them talk,
"Why, this is strange, I trow!
Where are those lights so many and fair,   525
That signal made but now?"

Approacheth the ship with   "Strange, by my faith!" the Hermit said—
wonder.   "And they answered not our cheer!

The planks looked warped! and see those sails,
How thin they are and sere!   530
I never saw aught like to them,
Unless perchance it were

Brown skeletons of leaves that lag
My forest-brook along;
When the ivy tod is heavy with snow,   535
And the owlet whoops to the wolf below,
That eats the she-wolf's young."

"Dear Lord! it hath a fiendish look,"
The Pilot made reply,
"I am a-feared"—"Push on, push on!"   540
Said the Hermit cheerily.

The boat came closer to the ship,
But I nor spake nor stirred;
The boat came close beneath the ship,
And straight a sound was heard.   545

The ship suddenly sinketh. Under the water it rumbled on,
Still louder and more dread:
It reached the ship, it split the bay;
The ship went down like lead.

The ancient Mariner is   Stunned by that loud and dreadful sound,   550
saved in the Pilot's boat. Which sky and ocean smote,
Like one that hath been seven days drowned
My body lay afloat;
But swift as dreams, myself I found
Within the Pilot's boat.   555

Upon the whirl, where sank the ship,
The boat spun round and round;
And all was still, save that the hill
Was telling of the sound.

I moved my lips—the Pilot shrieked   560
And fell down in a fit;
The holy Hermit raised his eyes,
And prayed where he did sit.

I took the oars: the Pilot's boy,
Who now doth crazy go,   565
Laughed loud and long, and all the while

---

535 *tod:* bushy clump

His eyes went to and fro.
"Ha! ha!" quoth he, "full plain I see,
The Devil knows how to row."

And now, all in my own countree,   570
I stood on the firm land!
The Hermit stepped forth from the boat,
And scarcely he could stand.

"O shrieve me, shrieve me, holy man!"
The Hermit crossed his brow.   575
"Say quick," quoth he, "I bid thee say—
What manner of man art thou?"

Forthwith this frame of mine was wrenched
With a woeful agony,
Which forced me to begin my tale;   580
And then it left me free.

Since then, at an uncertain hour,
That agony returns:
And till my ghastly tale is told,
This heart within me burns.   585

I pass, like night, from land to land;
I have strange power of speech;
That moment that his face I see,
I know the man that must hear me:
To him my tale I teach.   590

What loud uproar bursts from that door!
The wedding guests are there:
But in the garden-bower the bride
And bridemaids singing are:
And hark the little vesper bell,   595
Which biddeth me to prayer!

O Wedding Guest! this soul hath been
Alone on a wide wide sea:
So lonely 'twas, that God himself
Scarce seeméd there to be.   600

O sweeter than the marriage feast,
'Tis sweeter far to me,
To walk together to the kirk
With a goodly company!

To walk together to the kirk,   605
And all together pray,
While each to his great Father bends,

Samuel Taylor Coleridge   **791**

Old men, and babes, and loving friends
And youths and maidens gay!

Farewell, farewell! but this I tell   610
To thee, thou Wedding Guest!
He prayeth well, who loveth well
Both man and bird and beast.

He prayeth best, who loveth best
All things both great and small;   615
For the dear God who loveth us,
He made and loveth all.

The Mariner, whose eye is bright,
Whose beard with age is hoar,
Is gone: and now the Wedding Guest   620
Turned from the bridegroom's door.

He went like one that hath been stunned,
And is of sense forlorn:
A sadder and a wiser man,
He rose the morrow morn.   625

1797–1798

FROST AT MIDNIGHT

   The Frost performs its secret ministry,
Unhelped by any wind. The owlet's cry
Came loud—and hark, again! loud as before
The inmates of my cottage, all at rest,
Have left me to that solitude, which suits   5
Abstruser musings: save that at my side
My cradled infant slumbers peacefully.
'Tis calm indeed! so calm, that it disturbs
And vexes meditation with its strange
And extreme silentness. Sea, hill, and wood,   10
This populous village! Sea, and hill, and wood,
With all the numberless goings-on of life,
Inaudible as dreams! the thin blue flame
Lies on my low-burnt fire, and quivers not;
Only that film, which fluttered on the grate,   15
Still flutters there, the sole unquiet thing.
Methinks its motion in this hush of nature

---

624 *forlorn:* deprived, denied *"Frost at Midnight":* 7 *infant:* Coleridge's son Hartley
15 *film:* an ember or ash lingering on the grate; according to folklore, it foretell the arrival of
an unexpected guest, a stranger

Gives it dim sympathies with me who live,
Making it a companionable form,
Whose puny flaps and freaks the idling Spirit   20
By its own mood interprets, everywhere
Echo or mirror seeking of itself,
And makes a toy of Thought.

                              But O! how oft,
How oft, at school, with most believing mind,   25
Presageful, have I gazed upon the bars,
To watch that fluttering *stranger!* and as oft
With unclosed lids, already had I dreamt
Of my sweet birthplace, and the old church tower,
Whose bells, the poor man's only music, rang   30
From morn to evening, all the hot Fair-day,
So sweetly, that they stirred and haunted me
With a wild pleasure, falling on mine ear
Most like articulate sounds of things to come!
So gazed I, till the soothing things, I dreamt,   35
Lulled me to sleep, and sleep prolonged my dreams!
And so I brooded all the following morn,
Awed by the stern preceptor's face, mine eye
Fixed with mock study on my swimming book:
Save if the door half opened, and I snatched   40
A hasty glance, and still my heart leaped up,
For still I hoped to see the *stranger's* face,
Townsman, or aunt, or sister more beloved,
My playmate when we both were clothed alike!

   Dear Babe, that sleepest cradled by my side,   45
Whose gentle breathings, heard in this deep calm,
Fill up the interspersèd vacancies
And momentary pauses of the thought!
My babe so beautiful! it thrills my heart
With tender gladness, thus to look at thee,   50
And think that thou shalt learn far other lore,
And in far other scenes! For I was reared
In the great city, pent 'mid cloisters dim,
And saw nought lovely but the sky and stars.
But *thou*, my babe! shalt wander like a breeze   55
By lakes and sandy shores, beneath the crags
Of ancient mountain, and beneath the clouds,
Which image in their bulk both lakes and shores
And mountain crags: so shalt thou see and hear

---

26 *presageful:* foretelling   38 *preceptor's:* schoolmaster's

The lovely shapes and sounds intelligible   60
Of that eternal language, which thy God
Utters, who from eternity doth teach
Himself in all, and all things in himself.
Great universal Teacher! he shall mold
Thy spirit, and by giving make it ask.   65

   Therefore all seasons shall be sweet to thee,
Whether the summer clothe the general earth
With greenness, or the redbreast sit and sing
Betwixt the tufts of snow on the bare branch
Of mossy apple tree, while the nigh thatch   70
Smokes in the sun-thaw; whether the eave-drops fall
Heard only in the trances of the blast,
Or if the secret ministry of frost
Shall hang them up in silent icicles,
Quietly shining to the quiet Moon.   75

1798

Samuel Taylor Coleridge was in some ways a more radical rebel against eighteenth-century taste than Wordsworth himself. While Wordsworth kept returning to nature and strong emotion as the source of poetry, Coleridge looked primarily to a poetic unity above the tangle of the natural world, created by the imagination. Coleridge's theories eventually became more intricate than his poems, but we can see their kernel in his comment on the origins of Lyrical Ballads.

"To Procure for These Shadows of Imagination That Willing Suspension of Disbelief": Samuel Taylor Coleridge

During the first year that Mr. Wordsworth and I were neighbours, our conversations turned frequently on the two cardinal points of poetry, the power of exciting the sympathy of the reader by a faithful adherence to the truth of nature, and the power of giving the interest of novelty by the modifying colors of imagination. The sudden charm, which accidents of light and shade, which moon-light or sun-set diffused over a known and familiar

---

67 *general:* generative

landscape, appeared to represent the practicability of combining both. These are the poetry of nature. The thought suggested itself (to which of us I do not recollect) that a series of poems might be composed of two sorts. In the one, the incidents and agents were to be, in part at least, supernatural; and the excellence aimed at was to consist in the interesting of the affections by the dramatic truth of such emotions, as would naturally accompany such situations, supposing them real. And real in *this* sense they have been to every human being who, from whatever source of delusion, has at any time believed himself under supernatural agency. For the second class, subjects were to be chosen from ordinary life; the characters and incidents were to be such, as will be found in every village and its vicinity, where there is a meditative and feeling mind to seek after them, or to notice them, when they present themselves.

In this idea originated the plan of the "Lyrical Ballads"; in which it was agreed, that my endeavours should be directed to persons and characters supernatural, or at least romantic; yet so as to transfer from our inward nature a human interest and a semblance of truth sufficient to procure for these shadows of imagination that willing suspension of disbelief for the moment, which constitutes poetic faith. With this view I wrote "The Ancient Mariner," and was preparing among other poems, "The Dark Ladie," and the "Christabel," in which I should have more nearly realized my ideal, than I had done in my first attempt.

JOHN KEATS

(1795–1821)

WHEN I HAVE FEARS THAT I MAY CEASE TO BE

When I have fears that I may cease to be
   Before my pen has gleaned my teeming brain,
Before high-pilèd books, in charactery,
   Hold like rich garners the full ripened grain;
When I behold, upon the night's starred face;   5
   Huge cloudy symbols of a high romance,
And think that I may never live to trace
   Their shadows, with the magic hand of chance;
And when I feel, fair creature of an hour,
   That I shall never look upon thee more,   10
Never have relish in the faery power
   Of unreflecting love;—then on the shore

Of the wide world I stand alone, and think
Till Love and Fame to nothingness do sink.

1818

ODE ON MELANCHOLY

1

No, no, go not to Lethe, neither twist
   Wolf's-bane, tight-rooted, for its poisonous wine;
Nor suffer thy pale forehead to be kissed
   By nightshade, ruby grape of Proserpine;
Make not your rosary of yew-berries,   5
   Nor let the beetle, nor the death-moth be
      Your mournful Psyche, nor the downy owl
A partner in your sorrow's mysteries;
   For shade to shade will come too drowsily,
      And drown the wakeful anguish of the soul.   10

2

But when the melancholy fit shall fall
   Sudden from heaven like a weeping cloud,
That fosters the droop-headed flowers all,
   And hides the green hill in an April shroud;
Then glut thy sorrow on a morning rose,   15
   Or on the rainbow of the salt sand-wave,
      Or on the wealth of globèd peonies;
Or if thy mistress some rich anger shows,
   Emprison her soft hand, and let her rave,
      And feed deep, deep upon her peerless eyes.   20

3

She dwells with Beauty—Beauty that must die;
   And Joy, whose hand is ever at his lips
Bidding adieu; and aching Pleasure nigh,
   Turning to poison while the bee-mouth sips:
Ay, in the very temple of Delight   25
   Veiled Melancholy has her sovran shrine,
      Though seen of none save him whose strenuous
tongue
   Can burst Joy's grape against his palate fine:

"Ode on Melancholy": 1 *Lethe:* in Greek mythology, one of the rivers of Hades. Those who drank from it forgot their former lives. 4 *Proserpine:* queen of Hades 7 *Psyche:* personification of the soul in Greek mythology, often symbolized by a butterfly

His soul shall taste the sadness of her might,
  And be among her cloudy trophies hung.   30

                                    1819

LA BELLE DAME SANS MERCI

Ah, what can ail thee, wretched wight,
  Alone and palely loitering;
The sedge is withered from the lake,
  And no birds sing.

Ah, what can ail thee, wretched wight,   5
  So haggard and so woe-begone?
The squirrel's granary is full,
  And the harvest's done.

I see a lily on thy brow
  With anguish moist and fever dew,   10
And on thy cheek a fading rose
  Fast withereth too.

I met a lady in the meads,
  Full beautiful, a faery's child:
Her hair was long, her foot was light,   15
  And her eyes were wild.

I set her on my pacing steed,
  And nothing else saw all day long;
For sideways would she lean, and sing
  A faery's song.   20

I made a garland for her head,
  And bracelets too, and fragrant zone;
She looked at me as she did love,
  And made sweet moan.

She found me roots of relish sweet,   25
  And honey wild, and manna dew,
And sure in language strange she said,
  I love thee true.

She took me to her elfin grot,
  And there she gazed and sighèd deep,   30
And there I shut her wild sad eyes—
  So kissed to sleep.

And there we slumbered on the moss,
  And there I dreamed, ah woe betide

The latest dream I ever dreamed   35
    On the cold hill side.

I saw pale kings, and princes too,
    Pale warriors, death-pale were they all;
Who cried—"La belle Dame sans merci
    Hath thee in thrall!"   40

I saw their starved lips in the gloom,
    With horrid warning gapèd wide,
And I awoke, and found me here
    On the cold hill side.

And this is why I sojourn here,   45
    Alone and palely loitering,
Though the sedge is withered from the lake,
    And no birds sing.

                                                                    1819

ODE TO A NIGHTINGALE

1

My heart aches, and a drowsy numbness pains
    My sense, as though of hemlock I had drunk,
Or emptied some dull opiate to the drains
    One minute past, and Lethe-wards had sunk:
'Tis not through envy of thy happy lot,   5
    But being too happy in thine happiness,—
        That thou, light-wingèd Dryad of the trees,
            In some melodious plot
    Of beechen green, and shadows numberless,
        Singest of summer in full-throated ease.   10

2

O, for a draught of vintage! that hath been
    Cool'd a long age in the deep-delvèd earth,
Tasting of Flora and the country green,
    Dance, and Provençal song, and sunburnt mirth!
O for a breaker full of the warm South,   15
    Full of the true, the blushful Hippocrene,
        With beaded bubbles winking at the brim,
            And purple-stainèd mouth;

"*Ode to a Nightingale*": 4 *Lethe-wards:* toward the river in Hades whose water brings forgetfulness   13 *Flora:* Roman goddess of flowers   16 *Hippocrene:* in Greek mythology, a fountain
sacred to the Muses and the source of poetic inspiration

That I might drink, and leave the world unseen,
   And with thee fade away into the forest dim: 20

3

Fade far away, dissolve, and quite forget
  What thou among the leaves hast never known,
The weariness, the fever, and the fret
  Here, where men sit and hear each other groan;
Where palsy shakes a few, sad, last gray hairs,   25
   Where youth grows pale, and spectre-thin, and dies;
    Where but to think is to be full of sorrow
      And leaden-eyed despairs,
    Where Beauty cannot keep her lustrous eyes,
      Or new Love pine at them beyond tomorrow.   30

4

Away! away! for I will fly to thee,
  Not charioted by Bacchus and his pards,
But on the viewless wings of Poesy,
  Though the dull brain perplexes and retards:
Already with thee! tender is the night,   35
  And haply the Queen-Moon is on her throne,
    Clustered around by all her starry fays;
      But here there is no light,
  Save what from heaven is with the breezes blown
    Through verdurous glooms and winding mossy
ways.   40

5

I cannot see what flowers are at my feet,
  Nor what soft incense hangs upon the boughs,
But, in embalmèd darkness, guess each sweet
  Wherewith the seasonable month endows
The grass, the thicket, and the fruit-tree wild;   45
  White hawthorn, and the pastoral eglantine;
    Fast fading violets covered up in leaves;
      And mid-May's eldest child,
The coming musk-rose, full of dewy wine,
    The murmurous haunt of flies on summer eves.   50

6

Darkling I listen; and for many a time
  I have been half in love with easeful Death,

---

32 *Bacchus:* Greek god of wine   *pards:* leopards

Called him soft names in many a musèd rhyme,
    To take into the air my quiet breath;
Now more than ever seems it rich to die,   55
    To cease upon the midnight with no pain,
    While thou art pouring forth thy soul abroad
        In such an ecstasy!
Still wouldst thou sing, and I have ears in vain—
    To thy high requiem become a sod.   60

7

Thou wast not born for death, immortal Bird!
    No hungry generations tread thee down;
The voice I hear this passing night was heard
    In ancient days by emperor and clown:
Perhaps the self-same song that found a path   65
    Through the sad heart of Ruth, when, sick for home,
        She stood in tears amid the alien corn;
            The same that oft-times hath
Charmed magic easements, opening on the foam
    Of perilous seas, in faery lands forlorn.   70

8

Forlorn! the very word is like a bell
    To toll me back from thee to my sole self!
Adieu! the fancy cannot cheat so well
    As she is famed to do, deceiving elf.
Adieu! adieu! thy plaintive anthem fades   75
    Past the near meadows, over the still stream,
        Up the hill-side; and now 'tis buried deep
            In the next valley-glades:
    Was it a vision, or a waking dream?
        Fled is that music:—Do I wake or sleep?   80

1820

ODE ON A GRECIAN URN

1

Thou still unravished bride of quietness,
    Thou foster-child of silence and slow time,
Sylvan historian, who canst thus express
    A flowery tale more sweetly than our rhyme:

------

66 *Ruth:* the Old Testament account can be found in Ruth 2:1-7

What leaf-fringèd legend haunts about thy shape   5
    Of deities or mortals, or of both.
        In Tempe or the dales of Arcady?
    What men or gods are these? what maidens loth?
What mad pursuit? What struggle to escape?
        What pipes and timbrels? What wild ecstasy?   10

2

Heard melodies are sweet, but those unheard
    Are sweeter; therefore, ye soft pipes, play on;
Not to the sensual ear, but, more endeared,
    Pipe to the spirit ditties of no tone:
Fair youth, beneath the trees, thou canst not leave   15
    Thy song, nor ever can those trees be bare;
        Bold Lover, never, never canst thou kiss,
Though winning near the goal—yet, do not grieve;
    She cannot fade, though thou hast not thy bliss,
        For ever wilt thou love, and she be fair!   20

3

Ah, happy, happy boughs! that cannot shed
    Your leaves, nor ever bid the Spring adieu;
And, happy melodist, unwearièd,
    For ever piping songs for ever new;
More happy love! more happy, happy love!   25
    For ever warm and still to be enjoyed,
        For ever panting, and for ever young;
All breathing human passion far above,
    That leaves a heart high-sorrowful and cloyed,
        A burning forehead, and a parching tongue.   30

4

Who are these coming to the sacrifice?
    To what green altar, O mysterious priest,
Lead'st thou that heifer lowing at the skies,
    And all her silken flanks with garlands drest?
What little town by river or sea shore,   35
    Or mountain-built with peaceful citadel,
        Is emptied of this folk, this pious morn?
And, little town, thy streets for evermore
    Will silent be; and not a soul to tell
        Why thou art desolate, can e'er return.   40

"Ode on a Grecian Urn": 7 *Tempe:* a beautiful and sublime valley in eastern Greece   *Arcady:*
Arcadia, an isolated region in Greece known for its rustic simplicity

O Attic shape! Fair attitude! with brede
  Of marble men and maidens overwrought,
With forest branches and the trodden weed;
  Thou, silent form, dost tease us out of thought
As doth eternity: Cold Pastoral!   45
  When old age shall this generation waste,
    Thou shalt remain, in midst of other woe
Than ours, a friend to man, to whom thou say'st,
  "Beauty is truth, truth beauty—that is all
    Ye know on earth, and all ye need to know."   50

                                        1820

TO AUTUMN

1

Season of mists and mellow fruitfulness,
  Close bosom-friend of the maturing sun:
Conspiring with him how to load and bless
  With fruit the vines that round the thatch-eves run;
To bend with apples the mossed cottage-trees,   5
  And fill all fruit with ripeness to the core;
    To swell the gourd, and plump the hazel shells
With a sweet kernel; to set budding more,
  And still more, later flowers for the bees,
  Until they think warm days will never cease,   10
    For Summer has o'er-brimmed their clammy cells.

2

Who hath not seen thee oft amid thy store?
  Sometimes whoever seeks abroad may find
Thee sitting careless on a granary floor,
  Thy hair soft-lifted by the winnowing wind;   15
Or on a half-reaped furrow sound asleep,
  Drowsed with the fume of poppies, while thy hook
    Spares the next swath and all its twinèd flowers:
And sometimes like a gleaner thou dost keep
  Steady thy laden head across a brook;   20
  Or by a cider-press, with patient look,
    Thou watchest the last oozings hours by hours.

3

Where are the songs of Spring? Ay, where are they?
  Think not of them, thou hast thy music too,—

While barrèd clouds bloom the soft-dying day,   25
And touch the stubble-plains with rosy hue;
Then in a wailful choir the small gnats mourn
    Among the river sallows, borne aloft
        Or sinking as the light wind lives or dies;
And full-grown lambs loud bleat from hilly bourn;   30
    Hedge-crickets sing; and now with trebel soft
    The red-breast whistles from a garden-croft;
    And gathering swallows twitter in the skies.

1820

Born a generation after Wordsworth and Coleridge, John Keats responded strongly to their emphasis on the sensuous dimension of poetry. So strong, in fact, was this response that some readers have doubted that there was anything beneath the beautifully wrought surface. William Butler Yeats, for instance, gives us this picture of Keats:

> I see a schoolboy, when I think of him,
> With face and nose pressed to a sweetshop window,
> For certainly he sank into his grave,
> His senses and his heart unsatisfied;
> And made—being poor, ailing and ignorant,
> Shut out from all the luxury of the world,
> The coarse-bred son of a livery stable keeper—
> Luxuriant song.
>
> *Ego Dominus Tuus*

Keats's letters, including the following one to John Taylor, show the deeper thought other readers find at work in the poems.

"This Chamber of Maiden Thought becomes gradually darken'd": John Keats

. . . axioms in philosophy are not axioms until they are proved upon our pulses. We read fine things but never feel them to the full until we have gone the same steps as the Author. . . .

"To Autumn": 28 *sallows:* low-growing willows   30 *bourn:* realm or domain

I compare human life to a large Mansion of Many Apartments, two of which I can only describe, the doors of the rest being as yet shut upon me. The first we step into we call the infant or thoughtless Chamber, in which we remain as long as we do not think—We remain there a long while, and notwithstanding the doors of the second Chamber remain wide open, showing a bright appearance, we care not to hasten to it; but are at length imperceptibly impelled by the awakening of this thinking principle within us—we no sooner get into the second Chamber, which I call the Chamber of Maiden-Thought, than we become intoxicated with the light and atmosphere, we see nothing but pleasant wonders, and think of delaying there for ever in delight: However among the effects this breathing is father of is that tremendous one of sharpening one's vision into the heart and nature of Man —of convincing one's nerves that the world is full of Misery and Heartbreak, Pain, Sickness and oppression—whereby this Chamber of Maiden Thought becomes gradually darken'd and at the same time on all sides of it many *doors* are set open—but all dark—all leading to dark passages—We see not the balance of good and evil. We are in a Mist. *We* are now in that state—We feel the 'burden of the Mystery'. To this Point was Wordsworth come, as far as I can conceive when he wrote *Tintern Abbey* and it seems to me that his genius is explorative of those dark Passages. Now if we live, and go on thinking, we too shall explore them—he is a Genius and superior to us, in so far as he can, more than we, make discoveries, and shed a light in them—Here I must think Wordsworth is deeper than Milton— though I think it has depended more upon the general and gregarious advance of intellect, than individual greatness of Mind.

ALFRED, LORD TENNYSON

(1809–1892)

MARIANA

'Mariana in the moated grange.'
        MEASURE FOR MEASURE

With blackest moss the flower-plots
    Were thickly crusted, one and all:
The rusted nails fell from the knots
    That held the pear to the gable-wall.
The broken sheds look'd sad and strange: 5
    Unlifted was the clinking latch;
    Weeded and worn the ancient thatch
Upon the lonely moated grange.

She only said, 'My life is dreary,
    He cometh not,' she said;
She said, 'I am aweary, aweary,
    I would that I were dead!'   10

Her tears fell with the dews at even;
    Her tears fell ere the dews were dried;
She could not look on the sweet heaven,   15
    Either at morn or eventide.
After the flitting of the bats,
    When thickest dark did trance the sky,
    She drew her casement-curtain by,
And glanced athwart the glooming flats.   20
        She only said, 'The night is dreary,
            He cometh not,' she said;
        She said, 'I am aweary, aweary,
            I would that I were dead!'

Upon the middle of the night,   25
    Waking she heard the night-fowl crow:
The cock sung out an hour ere light:
    From the dark fen the oxen's low
Came to her: without hope of change,
    In sleep she seem'd to walk forlorn,   30
    Till cold winds woke the gray-eyed morn
About the lonely moated grange.
        She only said, 'The day is dreary,
            He cometh not,' she said;
        She said, 'I am aweary, aweary,   35
            I would that I were dead!'

About a stone-cast from the wall
    A sluice with blacken'd waters slept,
And o'er it many, round and small,
    The cluster'd marish-mosses crept.   40
Hard by a poplar shook alway,
    All silver-green with gnarled bark:
    For leagues no other tree did mark
The level waste, the rounding gray.
        She only said, 'My life is dreary,   45
            He cometh not,' she said;
        She said, 'I am aweary, aweary,
            I would that I were dead!'

And ever when the moon was low,
    And the shrill winds were up and away,   50
In the white curtain, to and fro,
    She saw the gusty shadow sway.

But when the moon was very low,
    And wild winds bound within their cell,
    The shadow of the poplar fell   55
Upon her bed, across her brow.
        She only said, 'The night is dreary,
            He cometh not,' she said;
        She said, 'I am aweary, aweary,
            I would that I were dead!'   60

All day within the dreamy house,
    The doors upon their hinges creak'd;
The blue fly sung in the pane, the mouse
Behind the mouldering wainscot shriek'd,
Or from the crevice peer'd about.   65
    Old faces glimmer'd thro' the doors,
    Old footsteps trod the upper floors,
Old voices called her from without.
        She only said, 'My life is dreary,
            He cometh not,' she said;   70
        She said, 'I am aweary, aweary,
            I would that I were dead!'

The sparrow's chirrup on the roof,
    The slow clock ticking, and the sound
Which to the wooing wind aloof   75
    The poplar made, did all confound
Her sense; but most she loathed the hour
    When the thick-moted sunbeam lay
    Athwart the chambers, and the day
Was sloping toward his western bower.   80
        Then, said she, 'I am very dreary,
            He will not come,' she said;
        She wept, 'I am aweary, aweary,
            Oh God, that I were dead!'

1830

THE KRAKEN

Below the thunders of the upper deep;
Far, far beneath in the abysmal sea,
His ancient, dreamless, uninvaded sleep
The Kraken sleepeth: faintest sunlights flee
About his shadowy sides: above him swell   5

"*The Kraken*": *Kraken:* a mythical Norwegian sea-beast; see also Revelation 13:1

Huge sponges of millennial growth and height;
And far away into the sickly light,
From many a wondrous grot and secret cell
Unnumber'd and enormous polypi
Winnow with giant arms the slumbering green.   10
There hath he lain for ages and will lie
Battening upon huge seaworms in his sleep,
Until the latter fire shall heat the deep;
Then once by man and angels to be seen,
In roaring he shall rise and on the surface die.   15

1830

THE LOTOS-EATERS

"Courage!" he said, and pointed toward the land,
"This mounting wave will roll us shoreward soon."
In the afternoon they came unto a land
In which it seeméd always afternoon.
All round the coast the languid air did swoon,   5
Breathing like one that hath a weary dream.
Full-faced above the valley stood the moon;
And, like a downward smoke, the slender stream
Along the cliff to fall and pause the fall did seem.

A land of streams! some, like a downward smoke,   10
Slow-dropping veils of thinnest lawn, did go;
And some through wavering lights and shadows broke,
Rolling a slumbrous sheet of foam below.
They saw the gleaming river seaward flow
From the inner land; far off, three mountain-tops,   15
Three silent pinnacles of aged snow,
Stood sunset-flushed; and, dewed with showery drops,
Up-clomb the shadowy pine above the woven copse.

The charméd sunset lingered low adown
In the red West; through mountain clefts the dale   20
Was seen far inland, and the yellow down
Bordered with palm, and many a winding vale
And meadow, set with slender galingale;
A land where all things always seemed the same!
And round about the keel with faces pale,   25

9 *polypi:* sea animals such as the octopus or hydra   13 *fire:* that which destroys the earth; see
Revelation 16:8–9   *"The Lotos-Eaters":* Lotos-Eaters: based on Homer's *Odyssey* Book
9: 82–104   1 *he:* Odysseus   23 *galingale:* a reed with rough-edged leaves

Dark faces pale against that rosy flame,
The mild-eyed melancholy Lotos-eaters came.

Branches they bore of that enchanted stem,
Laden with flower and fruit, whereof they gave
To each, but whoso did receive of them   30
And taste, to him the gushing of the wave
Far far away did seem to mourn and rave
On alien shores; and if his fellow spake,
His voice was thin, as voices from the grave;
And deep-asleep he seemed, yet all awake,   35
And music in his ears his beating heart did make.

They sat them down upon the yellow sand,
Between the sun and moon upon the shore;
And sweet it was to dream of fatherland,
Of child, and wife, and slave; but evermore   40
Most weary seemed the sea, weary the oar,
Weary the wandering fields of barren foam.
Then someone said, "We will return no more;"
And all at once they sang, "Our island home
Is far beyond the wave; we will no longer roam."   45

Choric Song

1

There is sweet music here that softer falls
Than petals from blown roses on the grass,
Or night-dews on still waters between walls
Of shadowy granite, in a gleaming pass;
Music that gentlier on the spirit lies,   50
Than tired eyelids upon tired eyes;
Music that brings sweet sleep down from the blissful
    skies.
Here are cool mosses deep,
And through the moss the ivies creep,
And in the stream the long-leaved flowers weep,   55
And from the craggy ledge the poppy hangs in sleep.

2

Why are we weighed upon with heaviness,
And utterly consumed with sharp distress
While all things else have rest from weariness?
All things have rest: why should we toil alone,   60
We only toil, who are the first of things,
And make perpetual moan,
Still from one sorrow to another thrown;

Nor ever fold our wings,
And cease from wanderings,   65
Nor steep our brows in slumber's holy balm;
Nor harken what the inner spirit sings,
"There is no joy but calm!"—
Why should we only toil, the roof and crown of things?

3

Lo! in the middle of the wood,   70
The folded leaf is wooed from out the bud
With winds upon the branch, and there
Grows green and broad, and takes no care,
Sun-steeped at noon, and in the moon
Nightly dew-fed; and turning yellow   75
Falls, and floats adown the air.
Lo! sweetened with the summer light,
The full-juiced apple, waxing over-mellow,
Drops in a silent autumn night.
All its allotted length of days   80
The flower ripens in its place,
Ripens and fades, and falls, and hath no toil,
Fast-rooted in the fruitful soil.

4

Hateful is the dark-blue sky,
Vaulted o'er the dark-blue sea.   85
Death is the end of life; ah, why
Should life all labor be?
Let us alone. Time driveth onward fast
And in a little while our lips are dumb.
Let us alone. What is it that will last?   90
All things are taken from us, and become
Portions and parcels of the dreadful past.
Let us alone. What pleasure can we have
To war with evil? Is there any peace
In ever climbing up the climbing wave?   95
All things have rest, and ripen toward the grave
In silence—ripen, fall, and cease:
Give us long rest or death, dark death, or dreamful
    ease.

5

How sweet it were, hearing the downward stream,
With half-shut eyes ever to seem   100
Falling asleep in a half-dream!
To dream and dream, like yonder amber light,

Which will not leave the myrrh-bush on the height;
To hear each other's whispered speech;
Eating the Lotos day by day   105
To watch the crisping ripples on the beach,
And tender curving lines of creamy spray;
To lend our hearts and spirits wholly
To the influence of mild-minded melancholy;
To muse and brood and live again in memory,   110
With those old faces of our infancy
Heaped over with a mound of grass,
Two handfuls of white dust, shut in an urn of brass!

6

Dear is the memory of our wedded lives,
And dear the last embraces of our wives   115
And their warm tears; but all hath suffered change;
For surely now our household hearths are cold,
Our sons inherit us, our looks are strange,
And we should come like ghosts to trouble joy.
Or else the island princes over-bold   120
Have eat our substance, and the minstrel sings
Before them of the ten years' war in Troy,
And our great deeds, as half-forgotten things.
Is there confusion in the little isle?
Let what is broken so remain.   125
The Gods are hard to reconcile;
'Tis hard to settle order once again.
There *is* confusion worse than death,
Trouble on trouble, pain on pain,
Long labor unto aged breath,   130
Sore tasks to hearts worn out by many wars
And eyes grown dim with gazing on the pilot-stars.

7

But, propt on beds of amaranth and moly,
How sweet—while warm airs lull us, blowing lowly—
With half-dropt eyelid still,   135
Beneath a heaven dark and holy,
To watch the long bright river drawing slowly
His waters from the purple hill—
To hear the dewy echoes calling
From cave to cave through the thick-twined vine—   140
To watch the emerald-colored water falling

---

133 *amaranth:* an imaginary flower that never fades   *moly:* a magical herb given to Odysseus
by Hermes to protect him from Circe, the witch

Through many a woven acanthus-wreath divine!
Only to hear and see the far-off sparkling brine,
Only to hear were sweet, stretched out beneath the
    pine.

8

The Lotos blooms below the barren peak,   145
The Lotos blows by every winding creek;
All day the wind breathes low with mellower tone;
Through every hollow cave and alley lone
Round and round the spicy downs the yellow Lotos-
    dust is blown.
We have had enough of action, and of motion we,   150
Rolled to starboard, rolled to larboard, when the surge
    was seething free,
Where the wallowing monster spouted his foam-foun-
    tains in the sea.
Let us swear an oath, and keep it with an equal mind,
In the hollow Lotos-land to live and lie reclined
On the hills like Gods together, careless of mankind.   155
For they lie beside their nectar, and the bolts are
    hurled
Far below them in the valleys, and the clouds are lightly
    curled
Round their golden houses, girdled with the gleaming
    world;
Where they smile in secret, looking over wasted lands,
Blight and famine, plague and earthquake, roaring
    deeps and fiery sands,   160
Clanging fights, and flaming towns, and sinking ships,
    and praying hands.
But they smile, they find a music centered in a doleful
    song
Steaming up, a lamentation and an ancient tale of
    wrong,
Like a tale of little meaning though the words are
    strong;
Chanted from an ill-used race of men that cleave the
    soil,   165
Sow the seed, and reap the harvest with enduring toil,
Storing yearly little dues of wheat, and wine and oil;
Till they perish and they suffer—some, 'tis whispered
    —down in hell
Suffer endless anguish, others in Elysian valleys dwell,

---

169 *Elysian valleys:* the abode of the blessed after death

Resting weary limbs at last on beds of asphodel.   170
Surely, surely, slumber is more sweet than toil, the
    shore
Than labor in the deep mid-ocean, wind and wave and
    oar;
O, rest ye, brother mariners, we will not wander more.

1842

ULYSSES

It little profits that an idle king,
By this still hearth, among these barren crags,
Matched with an aged wife, I mete and dole
Unequal laws unto a savage race,
That hoard, and sleep, and feed, and know not me.   5
I cannot rest from travel; I will drink
Life to the lees. All times I have enjoyed
Greatly, have suffered greatly, both with those
That loved me, and alone; on shore, and when
Through scudding drifts the rainy Hyades   10
Vext the dim sea. I am become a name;
For always roaming with a hungry heart
Much have I seen and known—cities of men
And manners, climates, councils, governments,
Myself not least, but honored of them all,—   15
And drunk delight of battle with my peers,
Far on the ringing plains of windy Troy.
I am a part of all that I have met;
Yet all experience is an arch wherethrough
Gleams that untraveled world whose margin fades   20
For ever and for ever when I move.
How dull it is to pause, to make an end,
To rust unburnished, not to shine in use!
As though to breathe were life! Life piled on life
Were all too little, and of one to me   25
Little remains; but every hour is saved
From that eternal silence, something more,
A bringer of new things; and vile it were
For some three suns to store and hoard myself,
And this gray spirit yearning in desire   30

"Ulysses": Ulysses: also known as Odysseus. Tennyson wrote this poem just after the death of
his close friend, Arthur Hallam. It is based on Homer's *Odyssey* Book 11: 100–137, and on
Dante's *Inferno* Canto 26   10 *Hyades*: a group of stars; their rising with the sun was associated
with the beginning of the rainy season

To follow knowledge like a sinking star,
Beyond the utmost bound of human thought.
    This is my son, mine own Telemachus,
To whom I leave the scepter and the isle,
Well-loved of me, discerning to fulfill   35
This labor, by slow prudence to make mild
A rugged people, and through soft degrees
Subdue them to the useful and the good.
Most blameless is he, centered in the sphere
Of common duties, decent not to fail   40
In offices of tenderness, and pay
Meet adoration to my household gods,
When I am gone. He works his work, I mine.
    There lies the port; the vessel puffs her sail;
There gloom the dark, broad seas. My mariners,   45
Souls that have toiled, and wrought, and thought with
    me,
That ever with a frolic welcome took
The thunder and the sunshine, and opposed
Free hearts, free foreheads—you and I are old;
Old age hath yet his honor and his toil.   50
Death closes all; but something ere the end,
Some work of noble note, may yet be done,
Not unbecoming men that strove with gods.
The lights begin to twinkle from the rocks;
The long day wanes; the slow moon climbs; the deep   55
Moans round with many voices. Come, my friends,
'Tis not too late to seek a newer world.
Push off, and sitting well in order smite
The sounding furrows; for my purpose holds
To sail beyond the sunset, and the baths   60
Of all the western stars, until I die.
It may be that the gulfs will wash us down;
I may be we shall touch the Happy Isles,
And see the great Achilles, whom we knew.
Though much is taken, much abides; and though   65
We are not now that strength which in old days
Moved earth and heaven, that which we are, we are,
One equal temper of heroic hearts,
Made weak by time and fate, but strong in will
To strive, to seek, to find, and not to yield.

1842

---

63 *Happy Isles:* islands supposedly west of the known world where the souls of the virtuous
meet after death   64 *Achilles:* in Greek mythology, one of the chief heroes of the
Trojan War

'BREAK, BREAK, BREAK . . .'

Break, break, break,
    On thy cold gray stones, O Sea!
And I would that my tongue could utter
    The thoughts that arise in me.

O well for the fisherman's boy,   5
    That he shouts with his sister at play!
O well for the sailor lad,
    That he sings in his boat on the bay!

And the stately ships go on
    To their haven under the hill;   10
But O for the touch of a vanish'd hand,
    And the sound of a voice that is still!

Break, break, break,
    At the foot of thy crags, O Sea!
But the tender grace of a day that is dead   15
    Will never come back to me.

1842

TEARS, IDLE TEARS

    Tears, idle tears, I know not what they mean,
Tears from the depth of some divine despair
Rise in the heart, and gather to the eyes,
In looking on the happy autumn-fields,
And thinking of the days that are no more.   5

    Fresh as the first beam glittering on a sail,
That brings our friends up from the underworld,
Sad as the last which reddens over one
That sinks with all we love below the verge;
So sad, so fresh, the days that are no more.   10

Ah, sad and strange as in dark summer dawns
The earliest pipe of half-awakened birds
To dying ears, when unto dying eyes
The casement slowly grows a glimmering square;
So sad, so strange, the days that are no more.   15

    Dear as remembered kisses after death,
And sweet as those by hopeless fancy feigned
On lips that are for others; deep as love,
Deep as first love, and wild with all regret;
O Death in Life, the days that are no more!   20

1847

814   *Poetry*

NOW SLEEPS THE CRIMSON PETAL

Now sleeps the crimson petal, now the white;
Nor waves the cypress in the palace walk;

Nor winks the gold fin in the porphyry font.
The firefly wakens; waken thou with me.

Now droops the milk-white peacock like a ghost,   5
And like a ghost she glimmers on to me.

Now lies the Earth all Danaë to the stars,
And all thy heart lies open unto me.

Now slides the silent meteor on, and leaves
A shining furrow, as thy thoughts in me.   10

Now folds the lily all her sweetness up,
And slips into the bosom of the lake.
So fold thyself, my dearest, thou, and slip
Into my bosom and be lost in me.

1847

'COME DOWN, O MAID . . .'

'Come down, O maid, from yonder mountain height:
What pleasure lives in height (the shepherd sang)
In height and cold, the splendour of the hills?
But cease to move so near the Heavens, and cease
To glide a sunbeam by the blasted Pine,   5
To sit a star upon the sparkling spire;
And come, for Love is of the valley, come,
For Love is of the valley, come thou down
And find him; by the happy threshold, he,
Or hand in hand with Plenty in the maize,   10
Or red with spirted purple of the vats,
Or foxlike in the vine; nor cares to walk
With Death and Morning on the silver horns,
Nor wilt thou snare him in the white ravine,
Nor find him dropt upon the firths of ice,   15
That huddling slant in furrow-cloven falls
To roll the torrent out of dusky doors:
But follow; let the torrent dance thee down
To find him in the valley; let the wild
Lean-headed Eagles yelp alone, and leave   20

"Now Sleeps the Crimson Petal": 7 *Danaë*: in Greek mythology, while Danae was imprisoned in a tower, she was visited by Zeus in the form of a shower of gold

Alfred, Lord Tennyson   **815**

The monstrous ledges there to slope, and spill
Their thousand wreaths of dangling water-smoke,
That like a broken purpose waste in air:
So waste not thou; but come; for all the vales
Await thee; azure pillars of the hearth   25
Arise to thee; the children call, and I
Thy shepherd pipe, and sweet is every sound,
Sweeter thy voice, but every sound is sweet;
Myriads of rivulets hurrying thro' the lawn,
The moan of doves in immemorial elms,   30
And murmuring of innumerable bees.'

                                              1847

from IN MEMORIAM

2

Old Yew, which graspest at the stones
     That name the under-lying dead,
     Thy fibres net the dreamless head,
Thy roots are wrapt about the bones.

The seasons bring the flower again.   5
     And bring the firstling to the flock;
     And in the dusk of thee, the clock
Beats out the little lives of men.

O not for thee the glow, the bloom,
     Who changest not in any gale,   10
     Nor branding summer suns avail
To touch thy thousand years of gloom:

And gazing on thee, sullen tree,
     Sick for thy stubborn hardihood,
     I seem to fail from out my blood   15
And grow incorporate into thee.

7

Dark house, by which once more I stand
     Here in the long unlovely street,
     Doors, where my heart was used to beat
So quickly, waiting for a hand.

A hand that can be clasp'd no more—   5
     Behold me, for I cannot sleep,
     And like a guilty thing I creep
At earliest morning to the door.

He is not here; but far away
  The noise of life begins again,
  And ghastly thro' the drizzling rain
On the bald street breaks the blank day.   10

11

Calm is the morn with a sound,
  Calm as to suit a calmer grief,
  And only thro' the faded leaf
The chestnut pattering to the ground:

Calm and deep peace on this high wold,   5
  And on these dews that drench the furze,
  And all the silvery gossamers
That twinkle into green and gold:

Calm and still light on yon great plain
  That sweeps with all its autumn bowers,   10
  And crowded farms and lessening towers,
To mingle with the bounding main:

Calm and deep peace in this wide air,
  These leaves that redden to the fall;
  And in my heart, if calm at all,   15
If any calm, a calm despair:

Calm on the seas, and silver sleep,
  And waves that sway themselves in rest,
  And dead calm in that noble breast
Which heaves but with the heaving deep.   20

20

The lesser griefs that may be said,
  That breathe a thousand tender vows,
  Are but as servants in a house
Where lies the master newly dead;

Who speak their feeling as it is,   5
  And weep the fulness from the mind:
  'It will be hard,' they say, 'to find
Another service such as this.'

My lighter moods are like to these,
  That out of words a comfort win;   10
  But there are other griefs within,
And tears that at their fountain freeze;

For by the hearth the children sit
  Cold in that atmosphere of Death,

Alfred, Lord Tennyson   **817**

And scarce endure to draw the breath,   15
Or like to noiseless phantoms flit:

But open converse is there none,
   So much the vital spirits sink
   To see the vacant chair, and think,
'How good! how kind! and he is gone.'   20

39

Old warder of these buried bones,
   And answering now my random stroke
   With fruitful cloud and living smoke,
Dark yew, that graspest at the stones

And dippest toward the dreamless head,   5
   To thee too comes the golden hour
   When flower is feeling after flower;
But Sorrow—fixt upon the dead,

And darkening the dark graves of men,—
   What whisper'd from her lying lips?   10
   Thy gloom is kindled at the tips,
And passes into gloom again.

1850

After he became Poet Laureate in 1850, Lord Tennyson became increasingly identified with the "authorized" view of Victorian life. Many of his later poems were patriotic, optimistic, and very popular; few of these are now read. His twentieth-century readers, led by such influential poets as T. S. Eliot, have found the other side of Tennyson far more interesting.

"The saddest of all English poets . . . the most instinctive rebel": T. S. Eliot

---

In ending we must go back to the beginning and remember that *In Memoriam* would not be a great poem, or Tennyson a great poet, without the technical accomplishment. Tennyson is the great master of metric as well as of melancholia; I do not think any poet in English has ever had a finer ear for vowel sound, as well as a subtler feeling for some moods of anguish:

Dear as remember'd kisses after death,
And sweet as those by hopeless fancy feign'd
On lips that are for others; deep as love,
Deep as first love, and wild with all regret.

And this technical gift of Tennyson's is no slight thing. Tennyson lived in a time which was already acutely time-conscious: a great many things seemed to be happening, railways were being built, discoveries were being made, the face of the world was changing. That was a time busy in keeping up to date. It had, for the most part, no hold on permanent things, on permanent truths about man and God and life and death. The surface of Tennyson stirred about with his time; and he had nothing to which to hold fast except his unique and unerring feeling for the sounds of words. But in this he had something that no one else had. Tennyson's surface, his technical accomplishment, is intimate with his depths: what we most quickly see about Tennyson is that which moves between the surface and the depths, that which is of slight importance. By looking innocently at the surface we are most likely to come to the depths, to the abyss of sorrow. Tennyson is not only a minor Virgil, he is also with Virgil as Dante saw him, a Virgil among the Shades, the saddest of all English poets, among the Great in Limbo, the most instinctive rebel against the society in which he was the most perfect conformist.

ROBERT BROWNING

(1812–1889)

MY LAST DUCHESS

Ferrara

That's my last duchess painted on the wall,
Looking as if she were alive. I call
That piece a wonder, now: Frà Pandolf's hands
Worked busily a day, and there she stands.
Will't please you sit and look at her? I said   5
"Frà Pandolf" by design, for never read
Strangers like you that pictured countenance,

"My Last Duchess": Ferrara: a center of culture during the early Italian Renaissance   3 *Frà Pandolf:* an imaginary artist, intended to represent a number of early Renaissance painters; "Frà" (brother) was the title given to monks and friars

The depth and passion of its earnest glance,
But to myself they turned (since none puts by
The curtain I have drawn for you, but I)   10
And seemed as they would ask me, if they durst,
How such a glance came there; so, not the first
Are you to turn and ask thus. Sir, 'twas not
Her husband's presence only, called that spot
Of joy into the Duchess' cheek: perhaps   15
Frà Pandolf chanced to say "Her mantle laps
"Over my lady's wrist too much," or "Paint
"Must never hope to reproduce the faint
"Half-flush that dies along her throat": such stuff
Was courtesy, she thought, and cause enough   20
For calling up that spot of joy. She had
A heart—how shall I say?— too soon made glad,
Too easily impressed; she like whate'er
She looked on, and her looks went everywhere.
Sir, 'twas all one! My favor at her breast,   25
The dropping of the daylight in the West,
The bough of cherries some officious fool
Broke in the orchard for her, the white mule
She rode with round the terrace—all and each
Would draw from her alike the approving speech,   30
Or blush, at least. She thanked men—good! but
     thanked
Somehow—I know not how—as if she ranked
My gift of a nine-hundred-years-old name
With anybody's gift. Who'd stoop to blame
This sort of trifling? Even had you skill   35
In speech—which I have not—to make your will
Quite clear to such an one, and say, "Just this
"Or that in you disgusts me; here you miss,
"Or there exceed the mark"—and if she let
Herself be lessoned so, nor plainly set   40
Her wits to yours, forsooth, and made excuse,
—E'en then would be some stooping; and I choose
Never to stoop. Oh sir, she smiled, no doubt,
Whene'er I passed her; but who passed without
Much the same smile? This grew; I gave commands;   45
Then all smiles stopped together. There she stands
As if alive. Will 't please you rise? We'll meet
The company below, then. I repeat,
The Count your master's known munificence
Is ample warrant that no just pretense   50
Of mine for dowry will be disallowed;
Though his fair daughter's self, as I avowed

At starting, is my object. Nay, we'll go
Together down, sir. Notice Neptune, though,
Taming a sea-horse, thought a rarity,   55
Which Claus of Innsbruck cast in bronze for me!

1842

MEETING AT NIGHT

1

THE grey sea and the long black land;
And the yellow half-moon large and low;
And the startled little waves that leap
In fiery ringlets from their sleep,
As I gain the cove with pushing prow,   5
And quench its speed i' the slushy sand.

2

Then a mile of warm sea-scented beach;
Three fields to cross till a farm appears;
A tap at the pane, the quick sharp scratch
And blue spurt of a lighted match,   10
And a voice less loud, thro' its joys and fears,
Than the two hearts beating each to each!

1845

FRA LIPPO LIPPI

I am poor brother Lippo, by your leave!
You need not clap your torches to my face.
Zooks, what's to blame? you think you see a monk!
What, 'tis past midnight, and you go the rounds,
And here you catch me at an alley's end   5
Where sportive ladies leave their doors ajar?
The Carmine's my cloister: hunt it up,
Do—harry out, if you must show your zeal,
Whatever rat, there, haps on his wrong hole,
And nip each softling of a wee white mouse,   10
Weke, weke, that's crept to keep him company!

---

54 *Neptune:* in Roman mythology, the god of the sea   56 *Claus of Innsbruck:* another
imaginary artist   *"Fra Lippo Lippi"*: *Fra Lippo Lippi:* (1406–1469); a Florentine artist and
Carmelite monk. Browning obtained most of his information from Giorgio Vasari's gossipy
Lives of the Painters.   3 *Zooks:* an exclamation of vexation or surprise

Aha, you know your betters! Then, you'll take
Your hand away that's fiddling on my throat,
And please to know me likewise. Who am I?
Why, one, sir, who is lodging with a friend   15
Three streets off—he's a certain . . . how d'ye call?
Master—a . . . Cosimo of the Medici,
I' the house that caps the corner. Boh! you were best!
Remember and tell me, the day you're hanged,
How you affected such a gullet's gripe!   20
But you, sir, it concerns you that your knaves
Pick up a manner nor descredit you:
Zooks, are we pilchards, that they sweep the streets
And count fair prize what comes into their net?
He's Judas to a tittle, that man is!   25
Just such a face! Why, sir, you make amends.
Lord, I'm not angry! Bid your hangdogs go
Drink out this quarter-florin to the health
Of the munificent House that harbors me
(And many more beside, lads! more beside!)   30
And all's come square again. I'd like his face—
His, elbowing on his comrade in the door
With the pike and lantern—for the slave that holds
John Baptist's head a-dangle by the hair
With one hand ("Look you, now," as who should say) 35
And his weapon in the other, yet unwiped!
It's not your chance to have a bit of chalk,
A wood-coal or the like? or you should see!
Yes, I'm the painter, since you style me so.
What, brother Lippo's doings, up and down,   40
You know them and they take you? like enough!
I saw the proper twinkle in your eye—
'Tell you, I liked your looks at very first.
Let's sit and set things straight now, hip to haunch.
Here's spring come, and the nights one makes up
     bands   45
To roam the town and sing out carnival,
And I've been three weeks shut within my mew,
A-painting for the great man, saints and saints
And saints again. I could not paint all night—
Ouf! I leaned out of window for fresh air.   50
There came a hurry of feet and little feet,
A sweep of lute-strings, laughs, and whifts of song—

---

17 *Cosimo of the Medici:* a Florentine banker who practically ruled Florence by his wealth, also
a patron of the arts   23 *pilchards:* common Mediterranean fish

Flower o' the broom,
Take away love, and our earth is a tomb!
Flower o' the quince,   55
I let Lisa go, and what good in life since?
Flower o' the thyme—and so on. Round they went.
Scarce had they turned the corner when a titter
Like the skipping of rabbits by moonlight—
    three slim shapes,
And a face that looked up . . . zooks, sir, flesh and
    blood,   60
That's all I'm made of! Into shreds it went,
Curtain and counterpane and coverlet,
All the bed-furniture—a dozen knots,
There was a ladder! Down I let myself,
Hands and feet, scrambling somehow, and so dropped,   65
And after them. I came up with the fun
Hard by Saint Laurence, hail fellow, well met—
Flower o' the rose,
If I've been merry, what matter who knows?
And so as I was stealing back again   70
To get to bed and have a bit of sleep
Ere I rise up to-morrow and go work
On Jerome knocking at his poor old breast
With his great round stone to subdue the flesh,
You snap me of the sudden. Ah, I see!   75
Though your eye twinkles still, you shake your head—
Mine's shaved—a monk, you say—the sting's in that!
If Master Cosimo announced himself,
Mum's the word naturally; but a monk!
Come, what am I a beast for? tell us, now!   80
I was a baby when my mother died
And father died and left me in the street.
I starved there, God knows how, a year or two
On fig-skins, melon-parings, rinds and shucks,
Refuse and rubbish. One fine frosty day,   85
My stomach being empty as your hat,
The wind doubled me up and down I went.
Old Aunt Lapaccia trussed me with one hand,
(Its fellow was a stinger as I knew)
And so along the wall, over the bridge,   90
By the straight cut to the convent. Six words there,
While I stood munching my first bread that month:

---

67 *Saint Laurence:* San Lorenzo, a church in Florence   73 *Jerome:* Saint Jerome (340–420)
whom Lippi painted for Cosimo   88 *Aunt Lapaccia:* Lippi's aunt who placed him in the
Carmelite monastery after he was orphaned

"So, boy, you're minded," quoth the good fat father
Wiping his own mouth, 't was refection-time—
"To quit this very miserable world?   95
"Will you renounce" . . . "the mouthful of bread?"
   thought I;
By no means! Brief, they made a monk of me;
I did renounce the world, its pride and greed,
Palace, farm, villa, shop and banking-house,
Trash, such as these poor devils of Medici   100
Have given their hearts to—all at eight years old.
Well, sir, I found in time, you may be sure,
'T was not for nothing—the good bellyful,
The warm serge and the rope that goes all round,
And day-long blessed idleness beside!   105
"Let's see what the urchin's fit for"—that came next.
Not overmuch their way, I must confess.
Such a to-do! They tried me with their books:
Lord, they'd have taught me Latin in pure waste!
Flower o' the clove,   110
All the Latin I construe is, "amo" I love!
But, mind you, when a boy starves in the streets
Eight years together, as my fortune was,
Watching folk's faces to know who will fling
The bit of half-stripped grape-bunch he desires,   115
And who will curse or kick him for his pains—
Which gentleman processional and fine,
Holding a candle to the Sacrament,
Will wink and let him lift a plate and catch
The droppings of the wax to sell again,   120
Or holla for the Eight and have him whipped—
How say I? nay, which dog bites, which lets drop
His bone from the heap of offal in the street—
Why, soul and sense of him grow sharp alike,
He learns the look of things, and none the less   125
For admonition from the hunger-pinch.
I had a store of such remarks, be sure,
Which, after I found leisure, turned to use.
I drew men's faces on my copy-books,
Scrawled them within the antiphonary's marge,   130
Joined legs and arms to the long music-notes,
Found eyes and nose and chin for A's and B's,
And made a string of pictures of the world
Betwixt the ins and outs of verb and noun,
On the wall, the bench, the door. The monks looked
   black.   135
"Nay," quoth the Prior, "turn him out, d'ye say?

"In no wise. Lose a crow and catch a lark.
"What if at last we get our man of parts,
"We Carmelites, like those Camaldolese
"And Preaching Friars, to do our church up fine   140
"And put the front on it that ought to be!"
And hereupon he bade me daub away.
Thank you! my head being crammed, the walls a blank,
Never was such prompt disemburdening.
First, every sort of monk, the black and white,   145
I drew them, fat and lean: then, folk at church,
From good old gossips waiting to confess
Their cribs of barrel-droppings, candle-ends—
To the breathless fellow at the altar-foot,
Fresh from his murder, safe and sitting there   150
With the little children round him in a row
Of admiration, half for his beard and half
For that white anger of his victim's son
Shaking a fist at him with one fierce arm,
Signing himself with the other because of Christ   155
(Whose sad face on the cross sees only this
After the passion of a thousand years)
Till some poor girl, her apron o'er her head,
(Which the intense eyes looked through) came at eve
On tiptoe, said a word, dropped in a loaf,   160
Her pair of earrings and a bunch of flowers
(The brute took growling), prayed, and so was gone.
I painted all, then cried " 'Tis ask and have;
"Choose, for more's ready!"—laid the ladder flat,
And showed my covered bit of cloister-wall.   165
The monks closed in a circle and praised loud
Till checked, taught what to see and not to see,
Being simple bodies—"That's the very man!
"Look at the boy who stoops to pat the dog!
"That woman's like the Prior's niece who comes   170
"To care about his asthma: it's the life!"
But there my triumph's straw-fire flared and funked;
Their betters took their turn to see and say:
The Prior and the learned pulled a face
And stopped all that in no time. "How? what's here?   175
"Quite from the mark of painting, bless us all!
"Faces, arms, legs and bodies like the true
"As much as pea and pea! it's devil's-game!

---

139 *Camaldolese:* Benedictine religious order   140 *Preaching Friars:* Dominican religious
order

"Your business is not to catch men with show,
"With homage to the perishable clay,   180
"But lift them over it, ignore it all,
"Make them forget there's such a thing as flesh.
"Your business is to paint the souls of men—
"Man's soul, and it's a fire, smoke . . . no, it's not
"It's vapor done up like a new-born babe—   185
"(In that shape when you die it leaves your mouth)
"It's . . . well, what matters talking, it's the soul!
"Give us no more of body than shows soul!
"Here's Giotto, with his Saint a-praising God,
"That sets us praising—why not stop with him?   190
"Why put all thoughts of praise out of our head
"With wonder at lines, colors, and what not?
"Paint the soul, never mind the legs and arms!
"Rub all out, try at it a second time.
"Oh, that white smallish female with the breasts,   195
"She's just my niece . . . Herodias, I would say—
"Who went and danced and got men's heads cut off!
"Have it all out!" Now, is this sense, I ask?
A fine way to paint soul, by painting body
So ill, the eye can't stop there, must go further   200
And can't fare worse! Thus, yellow does for white
When what you put for yellow's simply black,
And any sort of meaning looks intense
When all beside itself means and looks nought.
Why can't a painter lift each foot in turn,   205
Left foot and right foot, go a double step,
Make his flesh liker and his soul more like,
Both in their order? Take the prettiest face,
The Prior's niece . . . patron-saint—is it so pretty
You can't discover if it means hope, fear,   210
Sorrow or joy? won't beauty go with these?
Suppose I've made her eyes all right and blue,
Can't I take breath and try to add life's flash,
And then add soul and heighten them threefold?
Or say there's beauty with no soul at all—   215
(I never saw it—put the case the same—)
If you get simple beauty and nought else,
You get about the best thing God invents:
That's somewhat: and you'll find the soul you have
    missed,

---

189 *Giotto:* (1276–1337); an early medieval Italian painter, sculptor, and architect who became one of the leaders of the Italian Renaissance   196 *Herodias:* see Matthew 14:1–12

Within yourself, when you return him thanks.
"Rub all out!" Well, well, there's my life, in short,
And so the thing has gone on ever since.
I'm grown a man no doubt, I've broken bounds:
You should not take a fellow eight years old
And make him swear to never kiss the girls.   225
I'm my own master, paint now as I please—
Having a friend, you see, in the Corner-house!
Lord, it's fast holding by the rings in front—
Those great rings serve more purposes than just
To plant a flag in, or tie up a horse!   230
And yet the old schooling sticks, the old grave eyes
Are peeping o'er my shoulder as I work,
The heads shake still—"It's art's decline, my son!
"You're not of the true painters, great and old;
"Brother Angelico's the man, you'll find;   235
"Brother Lorenzo stands his single peer:
"Fag on at flesh, you'll never make the third!"
Flower o' the pine,
You keep your mistr . . . manners, and I'll stick to mine!
I'm not the third, then: bless us, they must know!   240
Don't you think they're the likeliest to know,
They with their Latin? So, I swallow my rage,
Clench my teeth, suck my lips in tight, and paint
To please them—sometimes do and sometimes don't;
For, doing most, there's pretty sure to come   245
A turn, some warm eve finds me at my saints—
A laugh, a cry, the business of the world—
(Flower o' the peach,
Death for us all, and his own life for each!)
And my whole soul revolves, the cup runs over,   250
The world and life's too big to pass for a dream,
And I do these wild things in sheer despite,
And play the fooleries you catch me at,
In pure rage! The old mill-horse, out at grass
After hard years, throws up his stiff heels so,   255
Although the miller does not preach to him
The only good of grass is to make chaff.
What would men have? Do they like grass or no—
May they or mayn't they? all I want's the thing
Settled for ever one way. As it is,   260
You tell too many lies and hurt yourself:

---

235 *Angelico . . . Lorenzo:* Fra Angelico (1387–1455) and Lorenzo Monaco (1370–1425);
both painters of the traditional, acceptable medieval style

You don't like what you only like too much,
You do like what, if given you at your word,
You find abundantly detestable.
For me, I think I speak as I was taught;   265
I always see the garden and God there
A-making man's wife: and, my lesson learned,
The value and significance of flesh,
I can't unlearn ten minutes afterwards.

       You understand me: I'm a beast, I know.   270
But see, now—why, I see as certainly
As that the morning-star's about to shine,
What will hap some day. We've a youngster here
Comes to our convent, studies what do,
Slouches and stares and lets no atom drop: 275
His name is Guidi—he'll not mind the monks—
They call him Hulking Tom, he lets them talk—
He picks my practice up—he'll paint apace,
I hope so—though I never live so long,
I know what's sure to follow. You be judge!   280
You speak no Latin more than I, belike;
However, you're my man, you've seen the world
—The beauty and the wonder and the power,
The shapes of things, their colors, lights and shades,
Changes, surprises—and God made it all!   285
—For what? Do you feel thankful, ay or no,
For this fair town's face, yonder river's line,
The mountain round it and the sky above,
Much more the figures of man, woman, child,
These are the frame to? What's it all about?   290
To be passed over, despised? or dwelt upon,
Wondered at? oh, this last of course!—you say.
But why not do as well as say, paint these
Just as they are, careless what comes of it?
God's works—paint anyone, and count it crime   295
To let a truth slip. Don't object, "His works
"Are here already; nature is complete:
"Suppose you reproduce her (which you can't)
"There's no advantage! you must beat her, then."
For, don't you mark? we're made so that we love   300
First when we see them painted, things we have passed
Perhaps a hundred times nor cared to see;

---

276 *Guidi:* Tommaso Guidi or Masaccio (1401–1429) was probably a teacher, rather than
pupil of Lippi; he revolted against the medieval theory of art and was called the father of
modern painting.

And so they are better, painted—better to us,
Which is the same thing. Art was given for that;   305
God uses us to help each other so,
Lending our minds out. Have you noticed, now,
Your cullion's hanging face? A bit of chalk,
And trust me but you should, though! How much
      more,
If I drew higher things with the same truth!

1855

ANDREA DEL SARTO

Called "The Faultless Painter"

But do not let us quarrel any more,
No, my Lucrezia; bear with me for once:
Sit down and all shall happen as you wish.
You turn your face, but does it bring your heart?
I'll work then for your friend's friend, never fear,   5
Treat his own subject after his own way,
Fix his own time, accept too his own price,

And shut the money into this small hand
When next it takes mine. Will it? tenderly?
Oh, I'll content him—but tomorrow, Love!   10
I often am much wearier than you think,
This evening more than usual, and it seems
As if—forgive now—should you let me sit
Here by the window with your hand in mine
And look a half-hour forth on Fiesole,   15
Both of one mind, as married people use,
Quietly, quietly the evening through
I might get up tomorrow to my work
Cheerful and fresh as ever. Let us try.
Tomorrow, how you shall be glad for this!   20
Your soft hand is a woman of itself,
And mine the man's bared breast she curls inside.
Don't count the time lost, neither; you must serve
For each of the five pictures we require:

"Andrea del Sarto": Andrea del Sarto: (1486–1531); a Florentine painter famous for his
religious frescoes. In 1517 he married Lucrezia de Fede and then spent one year painting for
the French King Francis at Fontainebleau. Lucrezia supposedly persuaded Andrea to leave
the king without finishing the work he was paid to do. Browning obtained most of his
information from Vasari's *Lives of the Painters.* 15 *Fiesole:* a small town on a hill above
Florence

It saves a model. So! keep looking so—
My serpenting beauty, rounds on rounds!   25
—How could you ever prick those perfect ears,
Even to put the pearl there! oh, so sweet—
My face, my moon, my everybody's moon,
Which everybody looks on and calls his,   30
And, I suppose, is looked on by in turn,
While she looks no one's: very dear, no less.
You smile? why, there's my picture ready made,
There's what we painters call our harmony!
A common grayness silvers everything,   35
All in a twilight, you and I alike
—You, at the point of your first pride in me
(That's gone you know)—but I, at every point;
My youth, my hope, my art, being all toned down
To yonder sober pleasant Fiesole.   40
There's the bell clinking from the chapel-top;
That length of convent-wall across the way
Holds the trees safer, huddled more inside;
The last monk leaves the garden, days decrease,
And autumn grows, autumn in everything   45
Eh? the whole seems to fall into a shape
As if I saw alike my work and self
And all that I was born to be and do,
A twilight-piece. Love, we are in God's hand.
How strange now, looks the life he makes us lead;   50
So free we seem, so fettered fast we are!
I feel he laid the fetter: let it lie!
This chamber for example turn your head—
All that's behind us! You don't understand
Nor care to understand about my art,   55
But you can hear at least when people speak:
And that cartoon, the second from the door
—It is the thing, Love! so such things should be—
Behold Madonna! I am bold to say.
I can do with my pencil what I know,   60
What I see, what at bottom of my heart
I wish for, if I ever wish so deep—
Do easily, too when I say, perfectly,
I do not boast, perhaps: yourself are judge,
Who listened to the Legate's talk last week,   65
And just as much they used to say in France.
At any rate 'tis easy, all of it!

————

65 *Legate:* the Pope's representative or deputy

No sketches first, no studies, that's long past:
I do what many dream of, all their lives,
—Dream? strive to do, and agonize to do,   70
And fail in doing. I could count twenty such
On twice your fingers, and not leave this town,
Who strive—you don't know how the others strive
To paint a little thing like that you smeared
Carelessly passing with your robes afloat—   75
Yet do much less, so much less, Someone says,
(I know his name, no matter)—so much less!
Well, less is more, Lucrezia: I am judged.
There burns a truer light of God in them,
In their vexed beating stuffed and stopped-up brain,   80
Heart, or whate'er else, than goes on to prompt
This low-pulsed forthright craftsman's hand of mine.
Their works drop groundward, but themselves, I know,
Reach many a time a heaven that's shut to me,
Enter and take their place there sure enough,   85
Though they come back and cannot tell the world.
My works are nearer heaven, but I sit here.
The sudden blood of these men! at a word—
Praise them, it boils, or blame them, it boils too.
I, painting from myself and to myself,   90
Know what I do, am unmoved by men's blame
Or their praise either. Somebody remarks
Morello's outline there is wrongly traced,
His hue mistaken; what of that? or else,
Rightly traced and well ordered; what of that?   95
Speak as they please, what does the mountain care?
Ah, but a man's reach should exceed his grasp,
Or what's a heaven for? All is silver-gray
Placid and perfect with my art: the worse!
I know both what I want and what might gain,   100
And yet how profitless to know, to sigh
"Had I been two, another and myself,
Our head would have o'erlooked the world!"
   No doubt.
Yonder's a work now, of that famous youth   105
The Urbinate who died five years ago.
('Tis copied, George Vasari sent it me.)
Well, I can fancy how he did it all,
Pouring his soul, with kings and popes to see,

---

93 *Morello:* a peak of the Apennine Mountains near Florence   106 *Urbinate:* Raphael Sanzio
(1483–1520), originally from Urbino

Reading, that heaven might so replenish him,   110
Above and through his art—for it gives way;
That arm is wrongly put—and there again—
A fault to pardon in the drawing's lines,
Its body, so to speak: its soul is right,
He means right—that, a child may understand.   115
Still, what an arm! and I could alter it:
But all the play, the insight and the stretch—
Out of me, out of me! And wherefore out?
Had you enjoined them on me, given me soul,
We might have risen to Rafael, I and you!   120
Nay, Love, you did give all I asked, I think—
More than I merit, yes, by many times.
But had you—oh, with the same perfect brow,
And perfect eyes, and more than perfect mouth,
And the low voice my soul hears, as a bird   125
The fowler's pipe, and follows to the snare—
Had you, with these the same, but brought a mind!
Some women do so. Had the mouth there urged
"God and the glory! never care for gain.
The present by the future, what is that?   130
Live for fame, side by side with Agnolo!
"Rafael is waiting: up to God, all three!"
I might have done it for you. So it seems:
Perhaps not. All is as God over-rules.
Beside, incentives come from the soul's self;   135
The rest avail not. Why do I need you?
What wife had Rafael, or has Agnolo?
In this world, who can do a thing, will not;
And who would do it, cannot, I perceive:
Yet the will's somewhat—somewhat, too, the power—   140
And thus we half-men struggle. At the end,
God, I conclude, compensates, punishes.
'Tis safer for me, if the award be strict,
That I am something underrated here,
Poor this long while, despised, to speak the truth.   145
I dared not, do you know, leave home all day,
For fear of chancing on the Paris lords.
The best is when they pass and look aside;
But they speak sometimes; I must bear it all.
Well may they speak! That Francis, that first time,   150
And that long festal year at Fontainebleau!
I surely then could sometimes leave the ground,
Put on the glory, Rafael's daily wear,

————

131 *Agnolo:* Michelangelo (1475–1564), the great Florentine painter and sculptor

In that humane great monarch's golden look—
One finger in his beard or twisted curl   155
Over his mouth's good mark that made the smile,
One arm about my shoulder, round my neck,
The jingle of his gold chain in my ear,
I painting proudly with his breath on me,
All his court round him, seeing with his eyes,   160
Such frank French eyes, and such a fire of souls
Profuse, my hand kept plying by those hearts—
And, best of all, this, this, this face beyond,
This in the background, waiting on my work,
To crown the issue with a last reward!   165
A good time, was it not, my kingly days?
And had you not grown restless . . . but I know—
'Tis done and past; 'twas right, my instinct said;
Too live the life grew, golden and not gray,
And I'm the weak-eyed bat no sun should tempt   170
Out of the grange whose four walls make his world
How could it end in any other way?
You called me, and I came home to your heart.
The triumph was—to reach and stay there; since
I reached it ere the triumph, what is lost?   175
Let my hands frame your face in your hair's gold,
You beautiful Lucrezia that are mine!
"Rafael did this, Andrea painted that;
"The Roman's is the better when you pray,
"But still the other's Virgin was his wife—"   180
Men will excuse me. I am glad to judge
Both pictures in your presence; clearer grows
My better fortune, I resolve to think.
For, do you now, Lucrezia, as God lives,
Said one day Agnolo, his very self,   185
To Rafael . . . I have known it all these years . . .
(When the young man was flaming out his thoughts
Upon a palace-wall for Rome to see,
Too lifted up in heart because of it)
"Friend, there's a certain sorry little scrub   190
Goes up and down our Florence, none cares how,
Who, were he set to plan and execute
As you are, pricked on by your popes and kings,
Would bring the sweat into that brow of yours!"
To Rafael's! And indeed the arm is wrong.   195
I hardly dare . . . yet, only you to see,
Give the chalk here—quick, thus the line should go!

---

179 *Roman:* the Pope, for whom Raphael spent his last years painting

Ay, but the soul! he's Rafael! rub it out!
Still, all I care for, if he spoke the truth,
(What he? why, who but Michel Agnolo?   200
Do you forget already words like those?)
If really there was such a chance, so lost,
Is, whether you're—not grateful—but more pleased.
Well, let me think so. And you smile indeed!
This hour has been an hour! Another smile?   205
If you would sit thus by me every night
I should work better, do you comprehend?
I mean that I should earn more, give you more,
See, it is settled dusk now; there's a star;
Morello's gone, the watch-lights show the wall,   210
The cue-owls speak the name we call them by.
Come from the window, love—come in, at last,
Inside the melancholy little house
We built to be so gay with. God is just.
King Francis may forgive me: oft at nights   215
When I look up from painting, eyes tired out,
The walls become illumined, brick from brick
Distinct, instead of mortar, fierce bright gold,
That gold of his I did cement them with!
Let us but love each other. Must you go?   220
That Cousin here again? he waits outside?
Must see you—you, and not with me? Those loans?
More gaming debts to pay? you smiled for that?
Well, let smiles buy me! have you more to spend?
While hand and eye and something of a heart   225
Are left me, work's my ware, and what's it worth?
I'll pay my fancy. Only let me sit
The gray remainder of the evening out,
Idle, you call it, and muse perfectly
How I could paint, were I but back in France,   230
One picture, just one more—the Virgin's face,
Not yours this time! I want you at my side
To hear them—that is, Michel Agnolo—
Judge all I do and tell you of its worth.
Will you? Tomorrow, satisfy your friend.   235
I take the subjects for his corridor,
Finish the portrait out of hand—there, there,
And throw him in another thing or two
If he demurs; the whole should prove enough
To pay for this same Cousin's freak. Beside,   240
What's better and what's all I care about,
Get you the thirteen scudi for the ruff!
Love, does that please you? Ah, but what does he,

The Cousin! what does he to please you more?
   I am grown peaceful as old age tonight.   245
I regret little, I would change still less.
Since there my past life lies, why alter it?
The very wrong to Francis! it is true
I took his coin, was tempted and complied,
And built this house and sinned, and all is said.   250
My father and my mother died of want.
Well, had I riches of my own? you see
How one gets rich! Let each one bear his lot.
They were born poor, lived poor, and poor they died:
And I have labored somewhat in my time   255
And not been paid profusely. Some good son
Paint my two hundred pictures—let him try!
No doubt, there's something strikes a balance. Yes,
You loved me quite enough, it seems tonight.
This must suffice me here. What would one have?   260
In heaven, perhaps, new chances, one more chance—
Four great walls in the New Jerusalem,
Meted on each side by the angel's reed,
For Leonard, Rafael, Agnolo and me
To cover—the three first without a wife,   265
While I have mine! So—still they overcome
Because there's still Lucrezia—as I choose.

Again the Cousin's whistle! Go, my Love.

1855

TWO IN THE CAMPAGNA

1

I wonder do you feel today
   As I have felt since, hand in hand,
We sat down on the grass, to stray
   In spirit better through the land,
This morn of Rome and May?   5

2

For me, I touched a thought, I know,
   Has tantalized me many times,
(Like turns of thread the spiders throw
   Mocking across our path) for rhymes
To catch and let go.   10

———

262 *New Jerusalem:* see Revelation 21:10–21

3

Help me to hold it! First it left
    The yellowing fennel, run to seed
There, branching from the brickwork's cleft,
    Some old tomb's ruin: yonder weed
Took up the floating weft,   15

4

Where one small orange cup amassed
    Five beetles—blind and green they grope
Among the honey-meal: and last,
    Everywhere on the grassy slope
I traced it. Hold it fast!   20

5

The champaign with its endless fleece
    Of feathery grasses everywhere!
Silence and passion, joy and peace,
    An everlasting wash of air—
Rome's ghost since her decease.   25

6

Such life here, through such lengths of hours,
    Such miracles performed in play,
Such primal naked forms of flowers,
    Such letting nature have her way
While heaven looks from its towers!   30

7

How say you? Let us, O my dove,
    Let us be unashamed of soul,
As earth lies bare to heaven above!
    How is it under our control
To love or not to love?   35

8

I would that you were all to me,
    You that are just so much, no more.
Nor yours nor mine, nor slave nor free!
    Where does the fault lie? What the core
O' the wound, since wound must be?   40

9

I would I could adopt your will,
    See with your eyes, and set my heart
Beating by yours, and drink my fill

At your soul's springs—your part my part
In life, for good and ill.   45

10

No. I yearn upward, touch you close,
   Then stand away. I kiss your cheek,
Catch your soul's warmth—I pluck the rose
   And love it more than tongue can speak—
Then the good minute goes.   50

11

Already how am I so far
   Out of that minute? Must I go
Still like the thistle-ball, no bar,
   Onward, whenever light winds blow,
Fixed by no friendly star?   55

12

Just when I seemed about to learn!
   Where is the thread now? Off again!
That old trick! Only I discern—
   Infinite passion, and the pain
Of finite hearts that yearn.   60

1855

While Tennyson was in some ways devoting his energy to being as English as possible, his contemporary Robert Browning was being resolutely foreign. Many of his poems are set in Italy, and few satisfied the widespread English taste for simple, musical lyrics. Nonetheless, his reputation grew greater as the nineteenth century progressed, and his influence on twentieth-century poetry—English and European—has been much greater than Tennyson's.

"At once lyric and epic, chronicle and romance, elegy and hymn": Eugenio Montale

translated from the Italian by Jonathan Galassi

It would be ridiculous to claim that Browning deserves vindication, since his reputation—entrusted in his own country to clubs of extremely intransigent faithful—has never languished. But Browning's reputation certainly has two aspects, and in Italy, even an ugly aspect. Translated (in his best work) many years ago, illustrated with flowery lithography, he was the preferred poet of inconsolable widows and girls with broken hearts; he was the poet who is bound in Florentine leather and put next to the *Vita Nuova* in the bookcase, over which of course hangs a three-color print representing Dante's encounter with Beatrice. He was, or he soon became, an Art Nouveau-style archaelogical-sentimental poet, the poet of the English who live in Florence, dine in the *buche,* and are happy if they can rent an apartment two doors down from "Casa Guidi Windows." The true Browning is very different; he is the beloved poet of the exiles and imagists of thirty years ago, those who at the same time reevaluated Byron's *Don Juan,* those in short—Pound & Co.—who did not accept the limits of the lyric genre in writing their own lyrics, but who dreamed of a poetry that was at once lyric and epic, chronicle and romance, elegy and hymn, satire and invective. I know this is a polemical interpretation; one can't make Browning into a simple precursor of Pound's *Cantos* and Joyce's interior monologue. It is possible that prosperity will choose those poems of his which conform most closely to the requirements of the lyric genre—the purest ones, in short— and will reject the integralist requirements of our contemporaries. It is possible, even probable, that the vast poetic *reportage* attempted by the new English lyric poets, from Auden on, will prove to be vitiated at the base and that the lyric will once again come to be considered what it is, a contemplative genre par excellence which is always tending toward a limit of purity. But Browning will survive even in pieces. Is it possible to say this of others today?

One thing that has attracted readers to Browning is his use of the dramatic monologue, a form that frees the poet from the convention of speaking in his own voice. The attraction of this form to twentieth-century poets (see, for example, "The Love Song of J. Alfred Prufrock") is that it allows them to be simultaneously objective and subjective, to assume the personality of the narrator without having to claim that the personality is (entirely) their own. We can get a sense of how this arrangement affects the poem by comparing Browning's work to two other poems on a Browningesque theme: one subjective, one objective.

Walter James Turner

(1889–1946)

HYMN TO HER UNKNOWN

In despair at not being able to rival the creations of
  God
I thought on her

Whom I saw on the twenty-fourth of August nineteen
    thirty-four
Having tea on the fifth story of Swan and Edgar's
In Piccadilly Circus.   5

She sat facing me with an older woman and a younger
And a little boy aged about five;
I could see that she was his mother,
Also she wore a wedding-ring and one set with
    diamonds.

She was about twenty-five years old,   10
Slim, graceful, disciplined;
She had none of the mannerisms of the suburbs,
No affectations, a low clear speech, good manners,
Hair thick and undyed.

She knew that she was beautiful and exceedingly
    attractive,   15
Every line of her dress showed it;
She was cool and determined and laughed heartily,
A wide mouth with magnificent teeth.

And having said this I come to the beginning of my
    despair,
Despair that I in no way can describe her   20
Or bring before the eyes of the present or the future
This image that I saw.

Hundreds and hundreds of women do I see
But rarely a woman on whom my eyes linger
As the eyes of Venus lingered on Adonis.   25

What is the use of being a poet?
Is it not a farce to call an artist a creator,
Who can create nothing, not even re-present what his
    eyes have seen?

She never showed a sign that she saw me
But I knew and she knew that I knew—   30
Our eyes fleeting past, never meeting directly
Like that vernal twinkling of butterflies
To which Coleridge compared Shakespeare's *Venus and
    Adonis.*

And, like Venus, I lavished my love upon her.
I dallied with her hair, her delicate skin and smooth
    limbs,   35

"*Hymn to Her Unknown*": 5 *Piccadilly Circus:* an intersection on Piccadilly, a great thorough-fare in London   25 *Venus . . . Adonis:* in Greek mythology, Venus, the goddess of love and beauty, was struck by Cupid's arrow and suddenly fell in love with the young mortal Adonis.

On her arms were heavy thick bangles
Like the ropes of my heart's blood.

Could I express the ecstasy of my adoration?
Mating with her were itself a separation!
Only our bodies fusing in a flame of crystal   40
Burning in an infinite empyrean
Until all the blue of the limitless heaven were drunken
In one globe of united perfection
Like a bubble that is all the oceans of the world
    ascending
To the fire that is the fire of fires, transcending   45
The love of God, the love of God, the love of God—
Ah! my pitiful efforts now ending
I remember a bough of coral
Flower of the transparent sea

Delicate pink as though a ray of the sun descending   50
Pathless into the ocean
Printed the foot of Venus
Where bloomed this asphodel.

                                        1936

Bertolt Brecht

(1898–1956)

A FILM OF THE COMEDIAN CHAPLIN

translated from the German by Michael Hamburger

Into a bistro on the Boulevard St. Michel
One rainy autumn day a young painter came
Drank four or five of those green spirits and bored
The billiard players with the story of a stirring reunion
With a former mistress, a delicate creature   5
Now the wife of a wealthy butcher.
"Quick, gentlemen," he urged, "please hand me the
    chalk you're using
For your cues!" and kneeling on the floor

"*A Film of the Comedian Chaplin*": 1 *Boulevard St. Michel:* the Latin Quarter in Paris, inhabited
by university students and known for its bohemian lifestyle, street sellers, book shops, and
jazz music

With a tremulous hand he tried to draw her picture
Hers, the beloved of another time, despairingly   10
Rubbing out what he had drawn, beginning again,
Stopping once more, combining
Other features and mumbling: "Only yesterday I knew
    them."
Cursing clients tripped over him, the angry landlord
Took hold of him by the collar and threw him out, but   15
Tireless on the pavement, shaking his head, with the
    chalk he
Hunted those fading features.

trans. 1971

WALT WHITMAN

(1819–1892)

from SONG OF MYSELF

5

I believe in you my soul, the other I am must not abase
    itself to you,
And you must not be abased to the other.

Loafe with me on the grass, loose the stop from your
    throat,
Not words, not music or rhyme I want, not custom or
    lecture, not even the best,
Only the lull I like, the hum of your valvèd voice.   5

I mind how once we lay such a transparent summer
    morning,
How you settled your head athwart my hips and gently
    turn'd over upon me,
And parted the shirt from my bosom-bone, and
    plunged your tongue to my bare-stript heart,
And reach'd till you felt my beard, and reach'd till you
    held my feet.   10

Swiftly arose and spread around me the peace and
    knowledge that pass all the argument of the earth,
And I know that the hand of God is the promise of my
    own,
And I know that the spirit of God is the brother of my
    own,

And that all the men ever born are also my brothers,
    and the women my sisters and lovers,
And that a kelson of the creation is love,
And limitless are leaves stiff or drooping in the fields,
And brown ants in the little wells beneath them,
And mossy scabs of the worm fence, heap'd stones,
    elder, mullein and poke-weed.   20

1855

from LEAVES OF GRASS

11

Twenty-eight young men bathe by the shore,
Twenty-eight young men, and all so friendly,
Twenty-eight years of womanly life, and all so
    lonesome.

She owns the fine house by the rise of the bank,
She hides handsome and richly drest aft the blinds of
    the window.   5

Which of the young men does she like the best?
Ah the homeliest of them is beautiful to her.

Where are you off to, lady? for I see you,
You splash in the water there, yet stay stock still in your
    room.

Dancing and laughing along the beach came the
    twenty-ninth bather,   10
The rest did not see her, but she saw them and loved
    them.

The beards of the young men glistened with wet, it ran
    from their long hair,
Little streams passed all over their bodies.

An unseen hand also passed over their bodies,
It descended tremblingly from their temples and ribs.   15

The young men float on their backs, their white bellies
    swell to the sun. . . . they do not ask who seizes
    fast to them,
They do not know who puffs and declines with pendant
    and bending arch,
They do not think whom they souse with spray.

1855

"*Song of Myself*": 16 *kelson:* a line of timber which holds the floorboards to the keel, the
principal structure of a ship which runs through its center

I think I could turn and live awhile with the animals. . . .
   they are so placid and self-contained,
I stand and look at them sometimes half the day long.

They do not sweat and whine about their condition,
They do not lie awake in the dark and weep for their
   sins,   5
They do not make me sick discussing their duty to God,
Not one is dissatisfied. . . . not one is demented with
   the mania of owning things,
Not one kneels to another nor to his kind that lived
   thousands of years ago,   10
Not one is respectable or industrious over the whole
   earth.
So they show their relations to me and I accept them;
They bring me tokens of myself. . . . they evince them
   plainly in their possession.

I do not know where they got those tokens,   15
I must have passed that way untold times ago and
   negligently dropt them,
Myself moving forward then and now and forever,
Gathering and showing more always and with velocity,
Infinite and omnigenous and the like of these among
   them;   20
Not too exclusive toward the reaches of my
   remembrancers,
Picking out here one that shall be my amie,
Choosing to go with him on brotherly terms.

A gigantic beauty of a stallion, fresh and responsive to
   my caresses,
Head high in the forehead and wide between the ears,   25
Limbs glossy and supple, tail dusting the ground,
Eyes well apart and full of sparkling wicked-
   ness: . . . ears finely cut and flexibly moving.

His nostrils dilate. . . . my heels embrace him. . . . his
   well built limbs tremble with pleasure. . . . we speed
   around and return.   30

I but use you a moment and then I resign you stallion. . . . and do not need your paces, and outgallop
   them,
And myself as I stand or sit pass faster than you.

1855

Walt Whitman   *843*

THE WOUND-DRESSER

1

An old man bending I come among new faces,
Years looking backward resuming in answer to
    children,
Come tell us old man, as from young men and maidens
    that love me,
(Arous'd and angry, I'd thought to beat the alarum,
    and urge relentless war,
But soon my fingers fail'd me, my face droop'd and I
    resign'd myself,   5
To sit by the wounded and soothe them, or silently
    watch the dead;)
Years hence of these scenes, of these furious passions,
    these chances,
Of unsurpass'd heroes, (was one side so brave? the
    other was equally brave;)
Now be witness again, paint the mightiest armies of
    earth,
Of those armies so rapid so wondrous what saw you to
    tell us?   10
What stays with you latest and deepest? of curious
    panics,
Of hard-fought engagements or sieges tremendous
    what deepest remains?

2

O maidens and young men I love and that love me,
What you ask of my days those the strangest and
    sudden your talking recalls,
Soldier alert I arrive after a long march cover'd with
    sweat and dust,   15
In the nick of time I come, plunge in the fight, loudly
    shout in the rush of successful charge,
Enter the captur'd works—yet lo, like a swift-running
    river they fade,
Pass and are gone they fade—I dwell not on soldiers'
    perils or soldiers' joys,
(Both I remember well—many the hardships, few the
    joys, yet I was content.)
But in silence, in dreams' projections,   20
While the world of gain and appearance and mirth goes
    on,
So soon what is over forgotten, and waves wash the
    imprints off the sand,

With hinged knees returning I enter the doors, (while
    for you up there,
Whoever you are, follow without noise and be of strong
    heart.)

Bearing the bandages, water and sponge,   25
Straight and swift to my wounded I go,
Where they lie on the ground after the battle brought
    in,
Where their priceless blood reddens the grass the
    ground,
Or to the rows of the hospital tent, or under the roof'd
    hospital,
To the long rows of cots up and down each side I
    return,   30
To each and all one after another I draw near, not one
    do I miss,
An attendant follows holding a tray, he carries a refuse
    pail,
Soon to be fill'd with clotted rags and blood, emptied,
    and fill'd again.

I onward go, I stop,
With hinged knees and steady hand to dress wounds,   35
I am firm with each, the pangs are sharp yet
    unavoidable,
One turns to me his appealing eyes—poor boy! I never
    knew you,
Yet I think I could not refuse this moment to die for
    you, if that would save you.

3

On, on I go, (open doors of time! open hospital doors!)
The crush'd head I dress, (poor crazed hand tear not
    the bandage away,)   40
The neck of the cavalry-man with the bullet through
    and through I examine,
Hard the breathing rattles, quite glazed already the
    eye, yet life struggles hard,
(Come sweet death! be persuaded O beautiful death!
In mercy come quickly.)

From the stump of the arm, the amputated hand,
I undo the clotted lint, remove the slough, wash off the
    matter and blood,   45
Back on his pillow the soldier bends with curv'd neck
    and side-falling head,

His eyes are closed, his face is pale, he dares not look
  on the bloody stump,
And has not yet look'd on it.

I dress a wound in the side, deep, deep,
But a day or two more, for see the frame all wasted and
  sinking,   50
And the yellow-blue countenance see.

I dress the perforated shoulder, the foot with the
  bullet-wound,
Cleanse the one with a gnawing and putrid gangrene,
  so sickening, so offensive,
While the attendant stands behind aside me holding
  the tray and pail.

I am faithful, I do not give out,   55
The fractur'd thigh, the knee, the wound in the
  abdomen,
These and more I dress with impassive hand, (yet deep
  in my breast a fire, a burning flame.)

                    4

Thus in silence in dreams' projections,
Returning, resuming, I thread my way through the
  hospitals,
The hurt and wounded I pacify with soothing hand,   60
I sit by the restless all the dark night, some are so
  young,
Some suffer so much, I recall the experience sweet and
  sad,
(Many a soldier's loving arms about this neck have
  cross'd and rested,
Many a soldier's kiss dwells on these bearded lips.)

                                        1865

WHEN I HEARD THE LEARN'D ASTRONOMER

When I heard the learn'd astronomer,
When the proofs, the figures, were ranged in columms
  before me,
When I was shown the charts and diagrams, to add,
  divide, and measure them,
When I sitting heard the astronomer where he lectured
  with much applause in the lecture-room,
How soon unaccountable I became tired and sick,   5

Till rising and gliding out I wander'd off by myself,
In the mystical moist night-air, and from time to time,
Look'd up in perfect silence at the stars.

1865

A NOISELESS PATIENT SPIDER

A noiseless patient spider,
I mark'd where on a little promontory it stood is
   isolated,
Mark'd how to explore the vacant vast surrounding,
It launch'd forth filament, filament, filament, out of
   itself,
Ever unreeling them, ever tirelessly speeding them.   5

And you O my soul where you stand,
Surrounded, detached, in measureless oceans of space,
Ceaselessly musing, venturing, throwing, seeking the
   spheres to connect them,
Till the bridge you will need be form'd, till the ductile
   anchor hold,
Till the gossamer thread you fling catch somewhere, O
   my soul.   10

1868

*The impact of Walt Whitman's poetry has inspired a wide range of imitators
and admirers. In the 1880s, William Butler Yeats was proving himself a
poetic rebel by walking around Dublin with a copy of* Leaves *of* Grass *in
his pocket. Later Pablo Neruda of Chile and Federico García Lorca of
Spain were profoundly affected by their encounters with Whitman's work.
More recently John Berryman, Allen Ginsberg, and Frank O'Hara have
acknowledged his influence. Besides poems by Berryman, Ginsberg, and
O'Hara, we include below critical estimates of Whitman's work by two poets
who are not themselves Whitman followers.*

"Walt Whitman: He had his nerve:" Randall Jarrell

Whitman is more coordinate and parallel than anybody, is *the* poet of parallel present participles, of twenty verbs joined by a single subject: all this

helps to give his work its feeling of raw hypnotic reality, of being that world which also streams over us joined only by *ands,* until we supply the subordinating conjunctions; and since as children we see the *ands* and not the *becauses,* this method helps to give Whitman some of the freshness of childhood. How inexhaustibly interesting the world is in Whitman! Arnold all his life kept wishing that he could see the world "with a plainness as near, as flashing" as that with which Moses and Rebekah and the Argonauts saw it. He asked with elegiac nostalgia, "Who can see the green earth any more / As she was by the sources of Time?"—and all the time there was somebody alive who saw it so, as plain and near and flashing, and with a kind of calm, pastoral, Biblical dignity and elegance as well, sometimes. The *thereness* and *suchness* of the world are incarnate in Whitman as they are in few other writers.

They might have put on his tombstone WALT WHITMAN: HE HAD HIS NERVE. He is the rashest, the most inexplicable and unlikely—the most impossible, one wants to say—of poets. He somehow *is* in a class by himself, so that one compares him with other poets about as readily as one compares *Alice* with other books. (Even his free verse has a completely different effect from anybody else's.) Who would think of comparing him with Tennyson or Browning or Arnold or Baudelaire?—it is Homer, or the sagas, or something far away and long ago, that comes to one's mind only to be dismissed; for sometimes Whitman *is* epic, just as *Moby Dick* is, and it surprises us to be able to use truthfully this word that we have misused so many times.

"Most of the time he's making a speech": W. S. Merwin

ED FOLSOM: . . . I'm wondering if some of that positivism in Whitman is that he refused ever to set his past aside and begin again?

WSM: . . . Both Whitman's strength and his weakness is that he is basically a rhetorical poet. And he's rhetorical not only in the obvious sense that all poetry is rhetorical, but in the sense of rhetoric as public speech: you decide on a stance and then you bring in material to flesh out that stance, to give details to your position. This is one of the things that makes me uneasy about Whitman. The stance is basically *there;* and much of the poetry simply adds detail to it. So many of the moments in Whitman that I really love are exceptions to this. Yet to my mind, these exceptions occur far too infrequently. Most of the time he's making a speech. The whole *Leaves of Grass* in a sense is a speech. It's a piece of emotional propaganda about an emotional approach to a historical moment. It's almost set up in a way which makes it impossible for it to develop, to deepen, or to reflect on itself and come out with sudden new perspectives.

Certainly that urge to write propaganda is one I not only understand but sympathize with. But I think it's an urge that doesn't often make poetry. Of course poetry should never be completely devoid of the desire to make something happen—it would only be decoration then—and that desire to make something happen is the part of you that is writing propaganda: so it's always there. After all, there is a kind of desperate hope built into poetry now; one really wants, hopelessly, to save the world and one tries to say everything that can be said for the things that one loves, while there's still time. But I don't think it can be messianic, you know; poets can't go out and preach on the street corners to save the world.

EF: What about some of the poems of the "Drum Taps" period like the "Wound Dresser"?

WSM: They're some of my favorite passages, because his theory won't support him there. He's simply paying attention to what he sees in front of him. I find those poems both sharper and more moving than many other things in Whitman.

John Berryman

(1914–1972)

from THE DREAM SONGS

4

Filling her compact & delicious body
with chicken paprika, she glanced at me
twice.
Fainting with interest, I hungered back
and only the fact of her husband & four other people   5
kept me from springing on her

or falling at her little feet and crying
'You are the hottest one for years of night
Henry's dazed eyes
have enjoyed, Brilliance. I advanced upon   10
(despairing) my spumoni.—Sir Bones: is stuffed,
de world, wif feeding girls.

—Black hair, complexion Latin, jewelled eyes
downcast . . . The slob beside her   feasts . . . What
    wonders is she sitting on, over there?   15
The restaurant buzzes. She might as well be on Mars.
Where did it all go wrong? There ought to be a law
    against Henry.
—Mr. Bones: there is.

Life, friends, is boring. We must not say so.
After all, the sky flashes, the great sea yearns,
we ourselves flash and yearn,
and moreover my mother told me as a boy
(repeatedly) 'Ever to confess you're bored   5
means you have no

Inner Resources.' I conclude now I have no
inner resources, because I am heavy bored.
Peoples bore me,
literature bores me, especially great literature,   10
Henry bores me, with his plights & gripes
as bad as achilles,

who loves people and valiant art, which bores me.
And the tranquil hills, & gin, look like a drag
and somehow a dog   15
has taken itself & its tail considerably away
into mountains or sea or sky, leaving
behind: me, wag.

1964

Allen Ginsberg

(b. 1926)

A SUPERMARKET IN CALIFORNIA

What thoughts I have of you tonight, Walt
Whitman, for I walked down the sidestreets under the
trees with a headache self-conscious looking at the full
moon.
In my hungry fatigue, and shopping for
images, I went into the neon fruit supermarket, dreaming of your enumerations!   5
What peaches and what penumbras! Whole
families shopping at night! Aisles full of husbands!
Wives in the avocados, babies in the tomatoes!—and
you, Garcia Lorca, what were you doing down by the
watermelons?

I saw you, Walt Whitman, childless, lonely old
grubber, poking among the meats in the refrigerator
and eyeing the grocery boys.   10

I heard you asking questions of each: Who
killed the pork chops?
What price bananas? Are you my Angel?
      I wandered in and out of the brilliant stacks of
cans following you, and followed in my imagination by
the store detective. 15
      We strode down the open corridors together in
our solitary fancy tasting artichokes, possessing every
frozen delicacy, and never passing the cashier.

      Where are we going, Walt Whitman? The
doors close in an hour.
Which way does your beard point tonight? 20
      (I touch your book and dream of our odyssey
in the supermarket and feel absurd.)
      Will we walk all night through solitary streets?
The trees add shade to shade, lights out in the houses,
we'll both be lonely.
      Will we stroll dreaming of the lost America of
love past blue automobiles in driveways, home to our
silent cottage? 25
      Ah, dear father, graybeard, lonely old courage-
teacher, what America did you have when Charon quit
poling his ferry and you got out on a smoking bank and
stood watching the boat disappear on the black waters
of Lethe?

1956

Frank O'Hara

(1926–1966)

STEPS

How funny you are today New York
like Ginger Rogers in *Swingtime*
and St. Bridget's steeple leaning a little to the left

"*A Supermarket in California*": 27 *Charon:* in classical mythology, the ferryman who carried
the dead to Hades across the river Styx   29 *Lethe:* an underworld river which causes those
who drink from it to forget their former lives
"*Steps*": 2 *Ginger Rogers:* (1911–   ); an actress known best for dancing with Fred Astaire.
Swing Time was produced in 1936

here I have just jumped out of a bed full of V-days
(I got tired of D-days) and blue you there still   5
accepts me foolish and free
all I want is a room up there
and you in it

and even the traffic halt so thick is a way
for people to rub up against each other   10
and when their surgical appliances lock
they stay together
for the rest of the day (what a day)
I go by to check a slide and I say
that painting's not so blue   15

where's Lana Turner
she's out eating
and Garbo's backstage at the Met
everyone's taking their coat off
so they can show a rib-cage to the rib-watchers   20
and the park's full of dancers with their tights and
    shoes
in little bags
who are often mistaken for worker-outers at the West
    Side Y
why not
the Pittsburgh Pirates shout because they won   25
and in a sense we're all winning
we're alive

the apartment was vacated by a gay couple
who moved to the country for fun
they moved a day too soon   30
even the stabbings are helping the population
    explosion
though in the wrong country
and all those liars have left the U N
the Seagram Building's no longer rivalled in interest
not that we need liquor (we just like it)   35

and the little box is out on the sidewalk
next to the delicatessen
so the old man can sit on it and drink beer

---

16 *Lana Turner:* (1920–   ); an American actress and sex symbol, known as "The Sweater
Girl"   18 *Garbo:* Greta Garbo (1905–   ), a Swedish actress, came to America in 1925; she
won an Academy Award in 1954   *Met:* Metropolitan Opera   34 *Seagram Building:* an
architectural masterpiece of Philip Johnson and Ludwig Mies van der Rohe; it is the
headquarters of Seagram's distilling company.

and get knocked off it by his wife later in the day
while the sun is still shining   40

oh god it's wonderful
to get out of bed
and drink too much coffee
and smoke too many cigarettes
and love you so much   45

1964

WHY I AM NOT A PAINTER

I am not a painter, I am a poet.
Why? I think I would rather be
a painter, but I am not. Well,
for instance, Mike Goldberg
is starting a painting. I drop in.   5
"Sit down and have a drink" he
says. I drink; we drink. I look
up. "You have SARDINES in it."
"Yes, it needed something there."
"Oh." I go and the days go by   10
and I drop in again. The painting
is going on, and I go, and the days
go by. I drop in. The painting is
finished. "Where's SARDINES?"   15
All that's left is just
letters, "It was too much," Mike says.
But me? One day I am thinking of
a color: orange. I write a line
about orange. Pretty soon it is a   20
whole page of words, not lines.
Then another page. There should be
so much more, not of orange, of
words, of how terrible orange is
and life. Days go by. It is even in   25
prose, I am a real poet. My poem
is finished and I haven't mentioned
orange yet. It's twelve poems, I call
it ORANGES. And one day in a gallery
I see Mike's painting, called SARDINES.   30

1971

CHARLES BAUDELAIRE

(1821–1867)

TO THE READER

translated from the French by Robert Lowell

Infatuation, sadism, lust, avarice
possess our souls and drain the body's force;
we spoonfeed our adorable remorse,
like whores or beggars nourishing their lice.

Our sins are mulish, our confessions lies;   5
we play to the grandstand with our promises,
we pray for tears to wash our filthiness,
importantly pissing hogwash through our styes.

The devil, watching by our sickbeds, hissed
old smut and folk-songs to our soul, until   10
the soft and precious metal of our will
boiled off in vapor for this scientist.

Each day his flattery makes us eat a toad,
and each step forward is a step to hell,
unmoved, though previous corpses and their smell   15
asphyxiate our progress on this road.

Like the poor lush who cannot satisfy,
we try to force our sex with counterfeits,
die drooling on the deliquescent tits,
mouthing the rotten orange we suck dry.   20

Gangs of demons are boozing in our brain—
ranked, swarming, like a million warrior-ants,
they drown and choke the cistern of our wants;
each time we breathe, we tear our lungs with pain.

If poison, arson, sex, narcotics, knives   25
have not yet ruined us and stitched their quick,
loud patterns on the canvas of our lives,
it is because our souls are still too sick.

Among the vermin, jackals, panthers, lice,
gorillas and tarantulas that suck   30
and snatch and scratch and defecate and fuck
in the disorderly circus of our vice,

there's one more ugly and abortive birth.
It makes no gestures, never beats its breast,

yet it would murder for a moment's rest,   35
and willingly annihilate the earth.

It's BOREDOM. Tears have glued its eyes together.
You know it well, my Reader. This obscene
beast chain-smokes yawning for the guillotine—
you—hypocrite Reader—my double—my brother!   40

1857, trans. 1961

CORRESPONDENCES

translated from the French by Richard Howard

The pillars of Nature's temple are alive
and sometimes yield perplexing messages;
forests of symbols between us and the shrine
remark our passage with accustomed eyes.

Like long-held echoes, blending somewere else   5
into one deep and shadowy unison
as limitless as darkness and as day,
the sounds, the scents, the colors correspond.

There are odors succulent as young flesh,
sweet as flutes, and green as any grass,   10
while others—rich, corrupt and masterful—

possess the power of such infinite things
as incense, amber, benjamin and musk,
to praise the senses' raptures and the mind's.

1857, trans. 1982

BY ASSOCIATION

translated from the French by Richard Howard

These warm fall nights I breathe, eyes closed, the scent
of your welcoming breasts, and thereupon appears
the coast of maybe Malabar—some paradise
besotted by the sun's monotonous fire;

an idle isle where Nature grants to men   5
with bodies slim and strong, to women who
meet your eye with amazing willingness,
the rarest trees, the ripest fruit; and then,

guided by your fragrance to enchanted ground,
I glimpse a harbor filled with masts and sails   10
still troubled by the slow-receding tide,

Charles Baudelaire   **855**

while the aroma of green tamarinds
dilates my nostrils as it drifts to sea
and mingles in my soul with the sailors' song.

                                        1857, trans. 1982

A PHANTOM

translated from the French by Richard Howard

1 The Shadows

Dejection has its catacombs
to which Fate has abandoned me;
no light comes, and I am left
with Night, a sullen cell-mate—

as if a scoffing God had forced   5
my hand to fresco . . . silhouettes!
Here with grisly appetite
I grill and devour my heart,

but then a shape looms, shining,
and as it moves it modifies: 10
a lovely . . . something—is there not

all the East in its easy way?
I know my visitor! *She* comes,
black—yet how that blackness glows!

2 The Perfume

Reader, you know how a church can reek   15
from one grain of incense you inhale
with careful greed—remember the smell?
Or the stubborn musk of an old sachet?

The spell is cast, the magic works,
and the present is the past—restored!   20
So a lover from beloved flesh
plucks subtle flowers of memory . . .

In bed her heavy resilient hair
—a living censer, like a sachet—
released its animal perfume,   25

and from discarded underclothes
still fervent with her sacred body's
form, there rose a scent of fur.

3 The Frame

As the fine frame completes a canvas
(even one from a master's hand),   30
adding an indefinable magic
by dividing art from mere nature,

so jewels, mirrors, metals, gold
invariably suited her loveliness—
none violated the lustre she had,   35
and each thing seemed to set her off.

You might have said, sometimes, she thought
objects longed to make love to her,
so greedily she slaked her nakedness

on the kisses of linen sheets and silk,
revealing with each movement all   40
the unstudied grace of a marmoset.

4 The Portrait

Look what Death and Disease have made
of our old flame: a heap of ashes.
My god, how horrible! What's left
of eyes so soft yet so intense,   45

of kisses stronger than any drug,
of a mouth that used to drown my heart,
of all our glowing exaltation?
Precious little—barely a sketch

fading in a solitude like mine,   50
erased a little more each day
by disrespectful Time that wipes
out Life and Art; yet even Time
cannot force me to forget Her
who was my glory and my Joy!   55

1857, trans. 1982

THE KING OF THE RAINY COUNTRY

translated from the French by Edna St. Vincent Millay

A rainy country this, that I am monarch of,—
A rich but powerless king, worn-out while yet a boy;
For whom in vain the falcon falls upon the dove;

Not even his starving people's groans can give him joy;
Scorning his tutors, loathing his spaniels, finding stale 5
His favourite jester's quips, yawning at the droll tale.
His bed, for all its *fleurs de lis,* looks like a tomb;
The ladies of the court, attending him, to whom
He, being a prince, is handsome, see him lying there
Cold as a corpse, and lift their shoulders in despair: 10
No garment they take off, no garter they leave on
Excites the gloomy eye of this young skeleton.
The royal alchemist, who makes him gold from lead,
The baser element from out the royal head
Cannot extract; nor can those Roman baths of blood, 15
For some so efficacious, cure the hebetude
Of him, along whose veins, where flows no blood at all,
For ever the slow waters of green Lethe crawl.

1857, trans. 1932

THE LITTLE OLD WOMEN

to Victor Hugo

translated from the French by Richard Howard

1

In murky corners of old cities where
everything—horror too—is magical,
I study, servile to my moods, the odd
and charming refuse of humanity.

These travesties were women once—Laïs 5
or Eponine! Love them, pathetic freaks,
hunchbacked and crippled—for they still have souls!
In ragged skirts and threadbare finery

they creep, tormented by the wicked gusts,
cowering each time an omnibus 10
thunders past, and clutching a reticule
as if it were a relic sewn with spells.

Whether they mince like marionettes or drag
themselves along like wounded animals,
they dance—against their will, the creatures dance— 15
sad bells on which a merciless Devil tugs.

"*The King of the Rainy Country*": 7 *fleurs de lis:* lilies   16 *hebetude:* lethargy or dullness of the mind   18 *Lethe:* the mythic, underworld river of forgetfulness
"*The Little Old Women*": 5 *Laïs . . . Eponine:* Greek courtesans known for their beauty

They waver, but their eyes are gimlet-sharp
and gleam like holes where water sleeps at night—
the eyes of a child, a little girl who laughs
in sacred wonder at whatever shines!   20

—The coffins of old women are often the size
of a child's, have you ever noticed? Erudite
Death, by making the caskets match, suggests
a tidy symbol, if in dubious taste,

and when I glimpse one of these feeble ghosts   25
at grips with Paris and its murderous swarm,
it always seems to me the poor old thing
is slowly crawling toward a second crib;

or else those ill-assorted limbs propose
a problem in geometry: to fit   30
so many crooked corpses, how many times
must the workman alter a coffin's shape?

Those eyes are cisterns fed by a million tears,
or crucibles cracked by an ore that has gone cold:
irresistible their sovereignty   35
to one who suckled at disaster's dugs!

                                    2

A Vestal at defunct *Frascati*'s shrine;
a priestess of Thalia whose memory survives
only in one long-dead prompter's mind;
the profligate of *Tivoli* in her prime;   40

this one a martyr to her fatherland,
that one her husband's victim, and one more
doomed by her son to a Madonna's grief—
all could make a river of their tears.

And all beguile me, but especially   45
those who, honeying their pain, implore
Addiction that had once lent them its wings:
'Mighty Hippogriff, let me fly again!'

                                    3

Little old women! I remember one
I had trailed for hours, until the sky   50
went scarlet as a wound, and she sat down
lost in thought on a public-garden bench,

---

37 *Frascati:* a central Italian town known for its palaces of the Roman aristocracy   38 *Thalia:*
in Greek mythology, the Muse of comedy and idyllic poetry   40 *Tivoli:* a central Italian town
known for its temples and famous villas

Charles Baudelaire   859

listening to the tunes our soldiers play—
brazen music for daylight's waning gold
(and yet such martial measures stir the soul, 55
granting a kind of glory to the crowd) . . .

Upright and proud she sat, and greedily
drank in the military airs, her eyes
like some old eagle's brightening beneath
the absent laurel on her marble brow! 60

4

And so you wander, stoic and inured
to all the uproar of the heedless town:
broken-hearted mothers, trollops, saints,
whose names were once the order of the day,

embodiments of glory and of grace! 65
Who knows you now? From doorways, derelicts
murmur obscene endearments as you pass,
and mocking children caper at your heels . . .

Poor wizened spooks, ashamed to be alive,
you hug the walls, sickly and timorous, 70
and no one greets you, no one says goodbye
to rubbish ready for eternity!

But I who at a distance follow you
and anxiously attend your failing steps
as if I had become your father—mine 75
are secret pleasures you cannot suspect!

I see first love in bloom upon your flesh,
dark or luminous I see your vanished days—
my teeming heart exults in all your sins
and all your virtues magnify my soul! 80

Flotsam, my family—ruins, my race!
Each night I offer you a last farewell!
Where will you be tomorrow, ancient Eves
under God's undeviating paw?

1861, trans. 1982

THE ALBATROSS

translated from the French by Richard Wilbur

Often, for pastime, mariners will ensnare
The albatross, that vast sea-bird who sweeps

On high companionable pinion where
Their vessel glides upon the bitter deeps.

Torn from his native space, this captive king   5
Flounders upon the deck in stricken pride,
And pitiably lets his great white wing
Drag like a heavy paddle at his side.

This rider of winds, how awkward he is, and weak!
How droll he seems, who was all grace of late!   10
A sailor pokes a pipestem into his beak;
Another, hobbling, mocks his trammeled gait.

The Poet is like this monarch of the clouds,
Familiar of storms, of stars, and of all high things;
Exiled on earth amidst its hooting crowds,
He cannot walk, borne down by his giant wings.   15

1861, trans. 1955

*About the time that Whitman in America was expressing an all-embracing
exuberance, the Frenchman Charles Baudelaire was expressing a darker
view of life. The common view of the poet as a "bohemian" outsider stems
partly from the "dandyism" Baudelaire expresses in the following passage
from his journal, an attitude adopted by the later French symbolists Arthur
Rimbaud, Paul Verlaine, and Stéphane Mallarmé.*

"I will never have the charity of a physician": Charles Baudelaire

translated from the French by David Paul

. . . universal ruin, or universal progress—I don't care which you call it—
will manifest itself not so much in political institutions, as in the debasement
of the human heart. Need I say that what is left of political systems will
struggle feebly in the clutches of universal animality, and that governments,
in order to hold on to their power, will be forced to resort to means that
would make our humanity today, hardened as it is, shudder with horror?
Then the son will run away from his family not at eighteen, but at twelve
years of age, emancipated by his gluttonous precocity; he will run away, not
in search of heroic adventures, not to deliver some captive maiden from a
prison tower, nor to immortalize some garret with the sublimity of his
thought, but in order to found his own business, get rich, and set up in com-

petition with his infamous papa. Then, anything resembling virtue, anything at all indeed which is not a rage for money, will be deemed contemptible, ridiculous. Your spouse, your chaste better half, oh Bourgeois, she who provides the legitimate poetry of your life, will introduce an irreproachable infamy into her legality, become the loving and vigilant guardian of your strong-boxes, and be none other than the perfect ideal of the kept woman. Your daughter, prematurely nubile, will dream in her cradle of selling herself for a million. And you yourself, Bourgeois—even less of a poet than you are today—you will find no cause for reproach in that. For there are things in man which prosper and strengthen in proportion as other qualities shrink and grow enfeebled; and thanks to the progress of these times, there will be nothing left of your compassion but your bowels! These times are perhaps quite near; who knows if they are not already come, and the coarsening of our natures is the only obstacle that prevents us from truly appreciating the atmosphere we are now breathing!

For my part, though I feel a ridiculous touch of the prophet in me sometimes, I know I will never have the charity of a physician. Astray in this foul world, shoved by the crowd, I feel like one prematurely worn out, who sees, in the depths of time behind him only bitterness and disappointment, ahead only a tumult with nothing new in it, whether of enlightenment or suffering. In the evening, when such a man has snatched from fate a few pleasant hours, and lulled by the digestive process, forgetting the past—as far as he can—content with the moment and resigned to the future, exhilarated by his own nonchalance and dandyism, proud to be not quite as base as those who pass by, he can say, as he gazes at the smoke of his cigar: How should I care what become of these conscious entities?

EMILY DICKINSON

(1830–1886)

[I LIKE A LOOK OF AGONY]

I like a look of Agony,
Because I know it's true—
Men do not sham Convulsion,
Nor simulate, a Throe—

The Eyes glaze once—and that is Death—   5
Impossible to feign
The Beads upon the Forehead
By homely Anguish strung.

1861

[WILD NIGHTS—WILD NIGHTS!]

Wild Nights—Wild Nights!
Were I with thee
Wild Nights should be
Our luxury!

Futile—the Winds—   5
To a Heart in port—
Done with the Compass—
Done with the Chart!

Rowing in Eden—
Ah, the Sea!   10
Might I but moor—Tonight—
In Thee!

1861

[OF BRONZE—AND BLAZE—]

Of Bronze—and Blaze—
The North—Tonight—
So adequate—it forms—
So preconcerted with itself
So distant—to alarms—   5
An Unconcern so sovreign
To Universe, or me—
Infects my simple spirit
With Taints of Majesty—
Till I take vaster attitudes—   10
And strut upon my stem—
Disdaining Men, and Oxygen,
For Arrogance of them—

My Splendors, are Managerie—
But their Competeless Show   15
Will entertain the Centuries
When I, am long ago,
An Island in dishonored Grass—
Whom none but Daisies, know.

1861

[THE SOUL SELECTS HER OWN
SOCIETY—]

The Soul selects her own Society—
Then—shuts the Door—

To her divine Majority—
Present no more—

Unmoved—she notes the Chariots—pausing—   5
At her low Gate—
Unmoved—an Emperor be kneeling
Upon her Mat—

I've known her—from an ample nation—
Choose One—   10
Then—close the Valves of her attention—
Like Stone—

                                        1862

[WHAT SOFT—CHERUBIC CREATURES—]

What Soft—Cherubic Creatures—
These Gentlewomen are—

One would as soon assault a Plush—
Or violate a Star—

Such Dimity Convictions—   5
A Horror so refined
Of freckled Human Nature—
Of Deity—ashamed—

It's such a common—Glory—
A Fisherman's—Degree—   10
Redemption—Brittle Lady—
Be so—ashamed of Thee—

                                        1862

[I DIED FOR BEAUTY—BUT WAS SCARCE]

I died for Beauty—but was scarce
Adjusted in the Tomb
When One who died for Truth, was lain
In an adjoining Room—

He questioned softly "Why I failed"?   5
"For Beauty", I replied—
"And I—for Truth—Themself are One—
We Brethren, are", He said—

And so, as Kinsmen, met a Night—
We talked between the Rooms—
Until the Moss had reached our lips—
And covered up—our names—

                                        1862

[IT WAS NOT DEATH, FOR I STOOD UP]

It was not Death, for I stood up,
And all the Dead, lie down—
It was not Night, for all the Bells
Put out their Tongues, for Noon.

It was not Frost, for on my Flesh   5
I felt Siroccos—crawl—
Nor Fire—for just my Marble feet
Could keep a Chancel, cool—

And yet, it tasted, like them all,
The Figures I have seen   10
Set orderly, for Burial,
Reminded me, of mine—

As if my life were shaven,
And fitted to a frame,
And could not breathe without a key,   15
And 'twas like Midnight, some—

When everything that ticked—has stopped—
And Space stares all around—
Or Grisly frosts—first Autumn morns,
Repeat the Beating Ground—   20

But, most, like Chaos—Stopless—cool—
Without a Chance, or Spar—
Or even a Report of Land—
To justify Despair.

                                        1862

[THE HEART ASKS
PLEASURE—FIRST—]

The Heart asks Pleasure—first—
And then—Excuse from Pain—
And then—those little Anodynes
That deaden suffering—

                                        Emily Dickinson   865

And then—to go to sleep—   5
And then—if it should be
The will of its Inquisitor
The privilege to die—

                                                            1862

[BECAUSE I COULD NOT STOP FOR DEATH—]

Because I could not stop for Death—
He kindly stopped for me—
The Carriage held but just Ourselves—
And Immortality.

We slowly drove—He knew no haste   5
And I had put away
My labor and my leisure too,
For His Civility—

We passed the School, where Children strove
As Recess—in the Ring—   10
We passed the Fields of Gazing Grain—
We passed the Setting Sun—

Or rather—He passed Us—
The Dews drew quivering and chill—
For only Gossamer, my Gown—   15
My Tippet—only Tulle—

We paused before a House that seemed
A Swelling of the Ground—
The Roof was scarcely visible—
The Cornice—in the Ground—   20

Since then—'tis Centuries—and yet
Feels shorter than the Day
I first surmised the Horses' Heads
Were toward Eternity—

                                                            1863

[MY LIFE HAD STOOD—A LOADED GUN—]

My Life had stood—a Loaded Gun—
In Corners—till a Day
The Owner passed—identified—
And carried Me away—

And now We roam in Sovereign Woods—   5
And now We hunt the Doe—
And every time I speak for Him—
The Mountains straight reply—

And do I smile, such cordial light
Upon the Valley glow—   10
It is as a Vesuvian face
Had let its pleasure through—

And when at Night—Our good Day done—
I guard My Master's Head—
'Tis better than the Eider-Duck's   15
Deep Pillow—to have shared—

To foe of His—I'm deadly foe—
None stir the second time—
On whom I lay a Yellow Eye—
Or an emphatic Thumb—   20

Though I than He—may longer live
He longer must—than I—
For I have but the power to kill,
Without—the power to die—

                                        1863

[A NARROW FELLOW IN THE GRASS]

A narrow Fellow in the Grass
Occasionally rides—
You may have met Him—did you not
His notice sudden is—

The Grass divides as with a Comb—   5
A spotted shaft is seen—
And then it closes at your feet
And opens further on—

He likes a Boggy Acre
A Floor too cool for Corn—   10
Yet when a Boy, and Barefoot—
I more than once at Noon
Have passed, I thought, a Whip lash
Unbraiding in the Sun
When stooping to secure it   15
It wrinkled, and was gone—

Several of Nature's People
I know, and they know me—

I feel for them a transport
Of cordiality—

But never met this Fellow
Attended, or alone
Without a tighter breathing
And Zero at the Bone—

20

1865

[MY LIFE CLOSED TWICE BEFORE ITS CLOSE—]

My life closed twice before its close—
It yet remains to see
If Immortality unveil
A third event to me

So huge, so hopeless to conceive   5
As these that twice befell.
Parting is all we know of heaven,
And all we need of hell.

1865

Though Emily Dickinson is sometimes seen as an American Romantic poet, she can hardly be considered a disciple of Wordworth or Keats. If we had to name the poet whose work shaped hers most strongly, it would probably be the hymnist Isaac Watts, whose quatrain of four iambic feet gives the basic rhythm to most of her poems. A simple hymnist, however, she was not, and readers soon find that the apparently simple form undergoes a metamorphosis to reflect strong tensions: religious feelings versus skepticism, Romantic optimism versus disillusioned wit, strong emotions versus formal restraint. Most of her work was unpublished in her lifetime, known only to a small circle of correspondents; but when Amherst, Massachusetts, celebrated its bicentenary, it became clear that Dickinson had become the town's most famous citizen. Louis Bogan and Richard Wilbur were among those paying tribute to her.

"Now and again they bring eternity into focus": Louise Bogan

Poets down the centuries, visited by that power which the ancients call *the Muse,* have described their experience in much the same way as the mystic describes his ecstatic union with Divine Truth. This experience has been rendered at length, and dramatically, by Dante, as well as by St. John of the Cross; and certain poems in the literature of every language attest to moments when, for the poet, "the deep and primal life which he shares with all creation has been roused from its sleep." And both poets and mystics have described with great poignance that sense of deprivation and that shutting away from grace which follows the loss of the vision (or of the inspiring breath), which is called, in the language of mysticism, "the dark night of the soul."

Certainly one of the triumphs brought about by the emergence of the Romantic spirit, in English poetry, at the end of the eighteenth century, was a freeing and an enlargement of poetic vision, and in the nineteenth century we come upon a multiplication of poets whose spiritual perceptions were acute. . . . By examining the work of these poets—to whom the imagination, the creative spirit of man, was of utmost importance—we find that the progress of the mystic toward illumination, and of the poet toward the full depth and richness of his insight, is much alike. Both work from the world of reality, toward the realm of Essence; from the microcosm to the macrocosm. Both have an intense and accurate sense of their surroundings; there is nothing vague or floating in their perception of reality; it is indeed as though they saw "through, not with, the eye." And they are filled with love for the beauty they perceive in the world of time—"this remarkable world" as Emily Dickinson called it; and concerning death they are neither fearful nor morbid—how could they be, since they feel immortality behind it? They document life's fearful limitations from which they suffer, but they do not mix self-pity with the account of their suffering (which they describe, like their joy, in close detail). They see the world in a grain of sand and Heaven in a wild flower; and now and again they bring eternity into focus, as it were, in a phrase of the utmost clarity. In the work of Emily Dickinson such moments of still and halted perception are many. The slant of light on a winter day, the still brilliance of a summer noon, the sound of the wind before the rain—she speaks of these, and we share the shock of insight, the slight dislocation of serial events, the sudden shift from the Manifold into the One.

"She became an unsteady congregation of one": Richard Wilbur

At some point Emily Dickinson sent her whole Calvinist vocabulary into exile, telling it not to come back until it would subserve her own sense of things.

Of course, that is not a true story, but it is a way of saying what I find most remarkable in Emily Dickinson. She inherited a great and overbearing vocabulary, which, had she used it submissively, would have forced her to express an established theology and psychology. But she would not let that vocabulary write her poems for her. There lies the real difference between a poet like Emily Dickinson and a fine versifier like Isaac Watts. To be sure, Emily Dickinson also wrote in the meters of hymnody, and paraphrased the Bible, and made her poems turn on great words like Immortality and Salvation and Election. But in her poems those great words are not merely being themselves; they have been adopted, for expressive purposes; they have been taken personally, and therefore redefined. . . .

At the age of seventeen, after a series of revival meetings at Mount Holyoke Seminary, Emily Dickinson found that she must refuse to become a professing Christian. To some modern minds this may seem to have been a sensible and necessary step; and surely it was a step toward becoming such a poet as she became. But for her, no pleasure in her own integrity could then eradicate the feeling that she had betrayed a deficiency, a want of grace. In her letters to Abiah Root she tells of the enhancing effect of conversion on her fellow-students, and says of herself in a famous passage:

> I am one of the lingering bad ones, and so do I slink away, and pause and ponder, and ponder and pause, and do work without knowing why, not surely for this brief world, and more sure it is not for heaven, and I ask what this message *means* that they ask for so very eagerly: *you* know of this depth and fulness, will you try to tell me about it?

There is humor in that, and stubbornness, and a bit of characteristic lurking pride: but there is also an anguished sense of having separated herself, through some dry incapacity, from spiritual community, from purpose, and from magnitude of life. As a child of evangelical Amherst, she inevitably thought of purposive, heroic life as requiring a vigorous faith. Out of such a thought she later wrote:

> The abdication of Belief
> Makes the Behavior small—
> Better an ignis fatuus
> Than no illume at all—

That hers *was* a species of religious personality goes without saying; but by her refusal of such ideas as original sin, redemption, hell, and election, she made it impossible for herself—as Whicher observed—"to share the religious life of her generation." She became an unsteady congregation of one.

CHRISTINA ROSSETTI

(1830–1894)

IN AN ARTIST'S STUDIO

One face looks out from all his canvases,
    One selfsame figure sits or walks or leans:
    We found her hidden just behind those screens,
That mirror gave back all her loveliness.
A queen in opal or in ruby dress,   5
    A nameless girl in freshest summer-greens,
    A saint, an angel—every canvas means
The same one meaning, neither more nor less.
He feeds upon her face by day and night,
    And she with true kind eyes looks back on him,   10
Fair as the moon and joyful as the light:
    Not wan with waiting, not with sorrow dim;
Not as she is, but was when hope shone bright;
    Not as she is, but as she fills his dream.

1861

SONG

When I am dead, my dearest,
    Sing no sad songs for me;
Plant thou no roses at my head,
    Nor shady cypress tree:
Be the green grass above me   5
    With showers and dewdrops wet;
And if thou wilt, remember,
    And if thou wilt, forget.

I shall not see the shadows,
    I shall not feel the rain;   10
I shall not hear the nightingale
    Sing on, as if in pain:
And dreaming through the twilight
    That doth not rise nor set,
Haply I may remember,   15
    And haply may forget.

1862

L.E.L.

"Whose heart was breaking for a little love."

Downstairs I laugh, I sport and jest with all:
    But in my solitary room above
I turn my face in silence to the wall;
    My heart is breaking for a little love.
        Tho' winter frosts are done,   5
        And birds pair every one,
And leaves peep out, for springtide is begun.

I feel no spring, while spring is wellnigh blown,
    I find no nest, while nests are in the grove:
Woe's me for mine own heart that dwells alone,   10
    My heart that breaketh for a little love.
        While golden in the sun
        Rivulets rise and run,
While lilies bud, for springtide is begun.

All love, are loved, save only I; their hearts   15
    Beat warm with love and joy, beat full thereof:
They cannot guess, who play the pleasant parts,
    My heart is breaking for a little love.
        While beehives wake and whirr,
        And rabbit thins his fur,   20
In living spring that sets the world astir.

I deck myself with silks and jewelry,
    I plume myself like any mated dove:
They praise my rustling show, and never see
    My heart is breaking for a little love.   25
        While sprouts green lavender
        With rosemary and myrrh,
For in quick spring the sap is all astir.

Perhaps some saints in glory guess the truth,
    Perhaps some angels read it as they move,   30
And cry one to another full of ruth,
    "Her heart is breaking for a little love."
        Tho' other things have birth,
        And leap and sing for mirth,
When springtime wakes and clothes and feeds the
    earth.   35

"L.E.L.": L.E.L. Letitia Elizabeth Landon (1802–38), a popular poet

Yet saith a saint: "Take patience for thy scathe;"
  Yet saith an angel: "Wait, for thou shalt prove
True best is last, true life is born of death,
  O thou, heart-broken for a little love.
  Then love shall fill thy girth,   40
  And love make fat thy dearth,
When new spring builds new heaven and clean new
  earth."

1863

GOOD FRIDAY

Am I a stone and not a sheep
  That I can stand, O Christ, beneath Thy Cross,
  To number drop by drop Thy Blood's slow loss,
And yet not weep?

Not so those women loved   5
  Who with exceeding grief lamented Thee;
  Not so fallen Peter weeping bitterly;
Not so the thief was moved;

Not so the Sun and Moon
  Which hid their faces in a starless sky,   10
A horror of great darkness at broad noon—
  I, only I.

Yet give not o'er,
  But seek Thy sheep, true Shepherd of the flock;
Greater than Moses, turn and look once more   15
  And smite a rock.

1864

LIFE AND DEATH

Life is not sweet. One day it will be sweet
  To shut our eyes and die:
Nor feel the wild flowers blow, nor birds dart by
  With flitting butterfly,
Nor grass grow long above our heads and feet,   5
Nor hear the happy lark that soars sky high,
Nor sigh that spring is fleet and summer fleet,
  Nor mark the waxing wheat,
Nor know who sits in our accustomed seat.

Life is not good. One day it will be good   10
    To die, then live again;
To sleep meanwhile: so not to feel the wane
Of shrunk leaves dropping in the wood,
Nor hear the foamy lashing of the main,
Nor mark the blackened bean-fields, nor where stood   15
    Rich ranks of golden grain
Only dead refuse stubble clothe the plain:
Asleep from risk, asleep from pain.

1866

BY THE SEA

Why does the sea moan evermore?
    Shut out from heaven it makes its moan,
It frets against the boundary shore;
    All earth's full rivers cannot fill
    The sea, that drinking thirsteth still.   5

Sheer miracles of loveliness
    Lie hid in its unlooked-on bed:
Anemones, salt, passionless,
    Blow flower-like; just enough alive
    To blow and multiply and thrive.   10

Shells quaint with curve, or spot, or spike,
    Encrusted live things argus-eyed,
All fair alike, yet all unlike,
    Are born without a pang, and die
    Without a pang, and so pass by.   15

1866

. . . THEY DESIRE A BETTER COUNTRY . . .

1

I would not if I could undo my past,
    Tho' for its sake my future is a blank;
    My past for which I have myself to thank,
For all its faults and follies first and last.
I would not cast anew the lot once cast,   5
    Or launch a second ship for one that sank,
    Or drug with sweets the bitterness I drank,
Or break by feasting my perpetual fast.
I would not if I could: for much more dear

Is one remembrance than a hundred joys,   10
More than a thousand hopes in jubilee;

2

What seekest thou, far in the unknown land?
   In hope I follow joy gone on before;
   In hope and fear persistent more and more,
As the dry desert lengthens out its sand.   15
Whilst day and night I carry in my hand
   The golden key to ope the golden door
   Of golden home; yet mine eye weepeth sore,
For long the journey is that makes no stand.
And who is this that veiled doth walk with thee?   20
   Lo, this is Love that walketh at my right;
      One exile holds us both, and we are bound
   To selfsame home-joys in the land of light.
Weeping thou walkest with him; weepeth he?—
      Some sobbing weep, some weep and make no
      sound.   25

3

A dimness of a glory glimmers here
   Thro' veils and distance from the space remote,
   A faintest far vibration of a note
Reaches to us and seems to bring us near;
Causing our face to glow with braver cheer,   30
   Making the serried mist to stand afloat,
   Subduing languor with an antidote,
And strengthening love almost to cast out fear:
Till for one moment golden city walls
   Rise looming on us, golden walls of home,   35
Light of our eyes until the darkness falls;
   Then thro' the outer darkness burdensome
I hear again the tender voice that calls,
   "Follow me hither, follow, rise, and come."

1869

PASSING AND GLASSING

   All things that pass
   Are woman's looking-glass;
They show her how her bloom must fade,
And she herself be laid
With withered roses in the shade;   5
   With withered roses and the fallen peach,

Unlovely, out of reach
    Of summer joy that was.

    All things that pass
    Are woman's tiring-glass;   10
The faded lavender is sweet,
Sweet the dead violet
Culled and laid by and cared for yet;
The dried-up violets and dried lavender
Still sweet, may comfort her,   15
    Nor need she cry Alas!

    All things that pass
    Are wisdom's looking-glass;
Being full of hope and fear, and still
Brimful of good or ill,   20
According to our work and will;
    For there is nothing new beneath the sun;
    Our doings have been done,
        And that which shall be was.

                                        1881

*Christina Rossetti's poems reveal a tension between the sensuous appeal
notable among the pre-Raphaelites (including her brother Dante Gabriel
Rossetti and Algernon Charles Swinburne) and a deep religious commitment. Virginia Woolf's well-known tribute to Rossetti's work shows a clear
insight into this conflict.*

"When you struck your harp many strings sounded together": Virginia Woolf

O Christina Rossetti, I have humbly to confess that though I know many of
your poems by heart, I have not read your works from cover to cover. I
have not followed your course and traced your development. I doubt
indeed that you developed very much. You were an instinctive poet. You
saw the world from the same angle always. Years and the traffic of the mind
with men and books did not affect you in the least. You carefully ignored
any book that could shake your faith or any human being who could trouble
your instincts. You were wise perhaps. Your instinct was so sure, so direct,
so intense that it produced poems that sing like music in one's ears—like a
melody by Mozart or an air by Gluck. Yet for all its symmetry, yours was a

complex song. When you struck your harp many strings sounded together. Like all instinctives you had a keen sense of the visual beauty of the world. Your poems are full of gold dust and "sweet geraniums' varied brightness"; your eye noted incessantly how rushes are "velvet-headed", and lizards have a "strange metallic mail"—your eye, indeed, observed with a sensual pre-Raphaelite intensity that must have surprised Christina the Anglo-Catholic. But to her you owed perhaps the fixity and sadness of your muse. The pressure of a tremendous faith circles and clamps together these little songs. Perhaps they owe to it their solidity. Certainly they owe to it their sadness—your God was a harsh God, your heavenly crown was set with thorns. No sooner have you feasted on beauty with your eyes than your mind tells you that beauty is vain and beauty passes. Death, oblivion, and rest lap round your songs with their dark wave. And then, incongruously, a sound of scurrying and laughter is heard. There is the patter of animals' feet and the odd guttural notes of rooks and the snufflings of obtuse furry animals grunting and nosing. For you were not a pure saint by any means. You pulled legs; you tweaked noses. You were at war with all humbug and pretence. Modest as you were, still you were drastic, sure of your gift, convinced of your vision. A firm hand pruned your lines; a sharp ear tested their music. Nothing soft, otiose, irrelevant cumbered your pages. In a word, you were an artist.

GERARD MANLEY HOPKINS

(1844–1889)

THE WINDHOVER

To Christ Our Lord

I caught this morning morning's minion, king-
    dom of daylight's dauphin, dapple-dawn-drawn
        Falcon, in his riding
    Of the rolling level underneath him steady air, and
        striding
High there, how he rung upon the rein of a wimpling
        wing
In his ecstasy! then off, off forth on swing,   5
    As a skate's heel sweeps smooth on a bow-bend: the
        hurl and gliding
    Rebuffed the big wind. My heart in hiding

"The Windhover": Windhover: a kestrel or small hawk

Stirred for a bird,—the achieve of, the mastery of the
    thing!

Brute beauty and valour and act, oh, air, pride, plume,
        here
    Buckle! AND the fire that breaks from thee then, a
        billion   10
Times told lovelier, more dangerous, O my chevalier!

    No wonder of it: sheer plod makes plough down
        sillion
Shine, and blue-bleak embers, ah my dear,
    Fall, gall themselves, and gash gold-vermilion.

                                        1877

PIED BEAUTY

Glory be to God for dappled things—
    For skies of couple-colour as a brinded cow;
        For rose-moles all in stipple upon trout that swim;
Fresh-firecoal chestnut-falls; finches' wings;
    Landscape plotted and pieced—fold, fallow, and
        plough,   5
        And all trades, their gear and tackle and trim.
All things counter, original, spare, strange;
    Whatever is fickle, freckled (who knows how?)
        With swift, slow; sweet, sour; adazzle, dim;
He fathers-forth whose beauty is past change: 10
                    Praise him.

                                        1877

GOD'S GRANDEUR

The world is charged with the grandeur of God.
    It will flame out, like shining from shook foil;
    It gathers to a greatness, like the ooze of oil
Crushed. Why do men then now not reck his rod?
Generations have trod, have trod, have trod;   5
    And all is seared with trade; bleared, smeared with
        toil;

---

12 *sillion:* the ridge between furrows of a plowed field   *"Pied Beauty"*: 2 *brinded:* streaked
"God's Grandeur": 2 *shook foil:* Hopkins explained that he meant gold leaf and compared it to
lightning   4 *reck his rod:* pay attention to the commands of God

And wears man's smudge and shares man's smell: the
   soil
Is bare now, nor can foot feel, being shod.

And for all this, nature is never spent;
   There lives the dearest freshness deep down things;   10
And though the last lights off the black West went
   Oh, morning, at the brown brink eastward,
      springs—
Because the Holy Ghost over the bent
   World broods with warm breast and with ah! bright
      wings.

1877

THE SEA AND THE SKYLARK

On ear and ear two noises too old to end
   Trench—right, the tide that ramps against the shore;
   With a flood or a fall, low lull-off or all roar,
Frequenting there while moon shall wear and wend.

Left hand, off land, I hear the lark ascend,   5
   His rash-fresh re-winded new-skeinèd score
   In crisps of curl off wild winch whirl, and pour
And pelt music, till none's to spill nor spend.

How these two shame this shallow and frail town!
   How ring right out our sordid turbid time,   10
Being pure! We, life's pride and cared-for crown,

   Have lost that cheer and charm of earth's past prime:
Our make and making break, are breaking, down
   To man's last dust, drain fast towards man's first
      slime.

1877

THOU ART INDEED JUST, LORD

Justus quidem tu es, Domine, si disputem tecum:
verum justa loquar ad te: Quare
via impiorum prosperatur?

Thou art indeed just, Lord, if I contend
With thee; but, sir, so what I plead is just.

"*Thou Art Indeed Just, Lord*": *Justus quidem . . . prosperatur:* "Righteous art thou, O Lord, when
I plead with thee: yet let me talk with thee of thy judgments: Wherefore doth the way of the
wicked prosper?" Jeremiah 12:1

Why do sinners' ways prosper? and why must
Disappointment all I endeavour end?
    Wert thou my enemy, O thou my friend,   5
How wouldst thou worse, I wonder, than thou dost
Defeat, thwart me? Oh, the sots and thralls of lust
Do in spare hours more thrive than I that spend,
Sir, life upon thy cause. See, banks and brakes
Now, leavèd how thick! lacèd they are again   10
With fretty chervil, look, and fresh wind shakes
Them; birds build—but not I build; no, but strain,
Time's eunuch, and not breed one work that wakes.
Mine, O thou lord of life, send my roots rain.

1889

*The poetry of Gerard Manley Hopkins is hymnlike in more ways than one.
It is full of the bright side of a deep religious faith and is written (as Hopkins said in a letter to his brother) to be "performed" aloud. Hopkins
believed that his much-discussed "sprung rhythm" was part of a long tradition of oral poetry, a tradition that includes both nursery rhymes and the Old
English "The Seafarer."*

"We feel the poem opening out": Richard Wilbur

That is what the cataloguing impulse almost always expresses—a longing to
possess the whole world, and to praise it, or at least to feel it. We see this
most plainly and perfectly in the Latin canticle *Benedicite, omnia opera
domini*. The first verses of that familiar canticle are:

> O all ye Works of the Lord, bless ye the Lord: praise him,
>   and magnify him for ever.
> O ye Angels of the Lord, bless ye the Lord: praise him,
>   and magnify him for ever.
> O ye Heavens, bless ye the Lord: praise him and magnify
>   him for ever.
> O ye Waters that be above the firmament, bless ye the Lord:
>   praise him and magnify him forever.

---

9 *brakes:* an area overgrown with brushwood 11 *fretty chervil:* cow-parsley, which has
ornamental, lacy leaves 13 *eunuch:* see Matthew 19:12

I need not go on to the close, because I am sure that you all know the logic of what follows. All the works of the Lord are called upon in turn—the sun, moon, and stars, the winds and several weathers of the sky, the creatures of earth and sea, and lastly mankind. There is nothing left out. The canticle may not speak of crushed laurel leaves and sycamores, but it does say more comprehensively, "O all ye Green Things upon the Earth, bless ye the Lord"; it may not speak of foxes and of young cows in a mountain stream, but it does say, "O all ye Beasts and Cattle, bless ye the Lord.". . .

It is interesting to compare the strategy of the *Benedicite* to that of another and more personal poem of catalogue and praise, Gerard Manley Hopkins's "curtal sonnet" "Pied Beauty.". . . As in the old canticle, God is praised first and last; but what lies between is very different. Hopkins does not give us an inventory of the creation; rather, he sets out to celebrate one kind of beauty—pied beauty, the beauty of things that are patchy, partico-lored, variegated. And in his tally of variegated things there is no hierarchy or other logic: his mind jumps, seemingly at random, from sky to trout to chestnuts to finches, and finally, by way of landscape, to the gear and tackle of the various trades. The poem *sets out*, then, to give scattered examples of a single class of things; and yet in its final effect this is a poem of universal praise. Why does it work out that way?

It works that way, for one thing, because of the randomness which I have just pointed out; when a catalogue has a random air, when it seems to have been assembled by chance, it implies a vast reservoir of other things that might just as well have been mentioned. In the second place, Hopkins's poem may begin with dappled things, but when we come to "gear and tackle and trim," the idea of variegation is far less clear, and seems to be yielding to that of *character*. When, in the next line, Hopkins thanks God for "All things counter, original, spare, strange," we feel the poem opening out toward the celebration of the rich and quirky particularity of all things whatever.

"The darling child of speech, of lips and spoken utterance": Gerard Manley Hopkins

Every art then and every work of art has its own play or performance. The play or performance of a stageplay is the playing it on the boards, the stage: reading it, much more writing it, is not its performance. The performance of a symphony is not the scoring it however elaborately; it is in the concert room, by the orchestra, and then and there only. A picture is performed, or performs, when anyone looks at it in the proper and intended light. A house performs when it is now built and lived in. To come nearer: books play, perform, or are played and performed when they are read; and ordi-narily by one reader, alone, to himself, with the eyes only. Now we are getting to it, George. Poetry was originally meant for either singing or reciting; a record was kept of it; the record could be, was, read, and that in time by one reader, alone, to himself, with the eyes only. This reacted on the art: what was to be performed under these conditions, for these conditions ought to be and was composed and calculated. Sound-effects were intended, wonderful combinations even; but they bear the marks of having been meant for the whispered, not even whispered, merely mental perform-ance of the closet, the study, and so on. You follow, Edward Joseph? You do: then we are there. This is not the true nature of poetry, the darling child of speech, of lips and spoken utterance: it must be spoken; *till it is spo-ken it is not performed*, it does not perform, it is not itself.

ANONYMOUS

THE SEAFARER

translated from the Anglo-Saxon by Ezra Pound

May I, for my own self, song's truth reckon,
Journey's jargon, how I in harsh days
Hardship endured oft.
Bitter breast-cares have I abided,
Known on my keel many a care's hold,   5
And dire sea-surge, and there I oft spent
Narrow nightwatch nigh the ship's head
While she tossed close to cliffs. Coldly afflicted.
My feet were by frost benumbed.
Chill its chains are; chafing sighs   10
Hew my heart round and hunger begot
Mere-weary mood. Lest man know not
That he on dry land loveliest liveth,
List how I, care-wretched, on ice-cold sea,
Weathered the winter, wretched outcast   15
Deprived of my kinsmen;
Hung with hard ice-flakes, where hail-scur flew,
There I heard naught save the harsh sea
And ice-cold wave, at whiles the swan cries,
Did for my games the gannet's clamour,   20
Sea-fowls' loudness was for me laughter,
The mews' singing all my mead-drink.
Storms, on the stone-cliffs beaten, fell on the stern
In icy feathers; full oft the eagle screamed
With spray on his pinion.   25

Not any protector

May make merry man faring needy.
This he little believes, who aye in winsome life
Abides 'mid burghers some heavy business,
Wealthy and wine-flushed, how I weary oft   30
Must bide above brine.
Neareth nightshade, snoweth from north,
Frost froze the land, hail fell on earth then,
Corn of the coldest. Nathless there knocketh now
The heart's thought that I on high streams   35
The salt-wavy tumult traverse alone.
Moaneth alway my mind's lust
That I fare forth, that I afar hence
Seek out a foreign fastness.
For this there's no mood-lofty man over earth's midst,   40
Not though he be given his good, but will have in his
     youth greed;
Nor his deed to the daring, nor his king to the faithful
But shall have his sorrow for sea-fare
Whatever his lord will.
He hath not heart for harping, nor in ring-having   45
Nor winsomeness to wife, nor world's delight
Nor any whit else save the wave's slash,
Yet longing comes upon him to fare forth on the water.
Bosque taketh blossom, cometh beauty of berries,
Fields to fairness, land fares brisker,   50
All this admonisheth man eager of mood,
The heart turns to travel so that he then thinks
On flood-ways to be far departing.
Cuckoo calleth with gloomy crying,
He singeth summerward, bodeth sorrow,   55
The bitter heart's blood. Burgher knows not—
He the prosperous man—what some perform
Where wandering them widest draweth.
So that but now my heart burst from my breastlock,
My mood 'mid the mere-flood,   60
Over the whale's acre, would wander wide.
On earth's shelter cometh oft to me,
Eager and ready, the crying lone-flyer,
Whets for the whale-path the heart irresistibly,
O'er tracks of ocean; seeing that anyhow   65
My lord deems to me this dead life
On loan and on land, I believe not
That any earth-weal eternal standeth
Save there be somewhat calamitous
That, ere a man's tide go, turn it to twain.   70

Gerard Manley Hopkins   **883**

Disease or oldness or sword-hate
Beats out the breath from doom-gripped body.
And for this, every earl whatever, for those speaking
    after—
Laud of the living, boasteth some last word,
That he will work ere he pass onward,   75
Frame on the fair earth 'gainst foes his malice,
Daring ado, . . .
So that all men shall honour him after
And his laud beyond them remain 'mid the English,
Aye, for ever, a lasting life's-blast,   80
Delight 'mid the doughty.
                        Days little durable,
And all arrogance of earthen riches,
There come now no kings nor Cæsars
Nor gold-giving lords like those gone.   85
Howe'er in mirth most magnified,
Whoe'er lived in life most lordliest,
Drear all this excellence, delights undurable!
Waneth the watch, but the world holdeth.
Tomb hideth trouble. The blade is layed low.   90
Earthly glory ageth and seareth.
No man at all going the earth's gait,
But age fares against him, his face paleth,
Grey-haired he groaneth, knows gone companions,
Lordly men, are to earth o'ergiven,   95
Nor may he then the flesh-cover, whose life ceaseth,
Nor eat the sweet nor feel the sorry,
Nor stir hand nor think in mid heart,
And though he strew the grave with gold,
His born brothers, their buried bodies   100
Be an unlikely treasure hoard.

                        c. 600, trans. 1912

A. E. HOUSMAN

(1859–1936)

LOVELIEST OF TREES, THE CHERRY NOW

Loveliest of trees, the cherry now
Is hung with bloom along the bough,

And stands about the woodland ride
Wearing white for Eastertide.

Now, of my threescore years and ten,   5
Twenty will not come again,
And take from seventy springs a score,
It only leaves me fifty more.

And since to look at things in bloom
Fifty springs are little room,   10
About the woodlands I will go
To see the cherry hung with snow.

1896

TO AN ATHLETE DYING YOUNG

The time you won your town the race
We chaired you through the market-place;
Man and boy stood cheering by,
And home we brought you shoulder-high.

To-day, the road all runners come,   5
Shoulder-high we bring you home,
And set you at your threshold down,
Townsman of a stiller town.

Smart lad, to slip betimes away
From fields where glory does not stay   10
And early though the laurel grows
It withers quicker than the rose.

Eyes the shady night has shut
Cannot see the record cut,
And silence sounds no worse than cheers   15
After earth has stopped the ears:

Now you will not swell the rout
Of lads that wore their honours out,
Runners whom renown outran
And the name died before the man.   20

So set, before its echoes fade,
The fleet foot on the sill of shade,
And hold to the low lintel up
The still-defended challenge-cup.

And round that early-laurelled head   25
Will flock to gaze the strengthless dead,

A. E. Housman   **885**

And find unwithered on its curls
The garland briefer than a girl's.

1896

TERENCE, THIS IS STUPID STUFF

'Terence, this is stupid stuff:
You eat your victuals fast enough;
There can't be much amiss, 'tis clear,
To see the rate you drink your beer.
But oh, good Lord, the verse you make,   5
It gives a chap the belly-ache.
The cow, the old cow, she is dead;
It sleeps well, the horned head:
We poor lads, 'tis our turn now
To hear such tunes as killed the cow.   10
Pretty friendship 'tis to rhyme
Your friends to death before their time
Moping melancholy mad:
Come, pipe a tune to dance to, lad.'

Why, if 'tis dancing you would be,   15
There's brisker pipes than poetry.
Say, for what were hop-yards meant,
Or why was Burton built on Trent?
Oh many a peer of England brews
Livelier liquor than the Muse,   20
And malt does more than Milton can
To justify God's ways to man.
Ale, man, ale's the stuff to drink
For fellows whom it hurts to think:
Look into the pewter pot   25
To see the world as the world's not.
And faith, 'tis pleasant till 'tis past:
The mischief is that 'twill not last.
Oh I have been to Ludlow fair
And left my necktie God knows where,   30
And carried half-way home, or near,
Pints and quarts of Ludlow beer:
Then the world seemed none so bad,
And I myself a sterling lad;
And down in lovely muck I've lain,   35
Happy till I woke again.
Then I saw the morning sky:
Heigho, the tale was all a lie;
The world, it was the old world yet,

I was I, my things were wet,   40
And nothing now remained to do
But begin the game anew.

    Therefore, since the world has still
Much good, but much less good than ill,
And while the sun and moon endure   45
Luck's a chance, but trouble's sure,
I'd face it as a wise man would,
And train for ill and not for good.
'Tis true, the stuff I bring for sale
Is not so brisk a brew as ale: 50
Out of a stem that scored the hand
I wrung it in a weary land.
But take it: if the smack is sour,
The better for the embittered hour;
It should do good to heart and head   55
When your soul is in my soul's stead;
And I will friend you, if I may,
In the dark and cloudy day.

    There was a king reigned in the East:
There, when kings will sit to feast,   60
They get their fill before they think
With poisoned meat and poisoned drink.
He gathered all that springs to birth
From the many-venomed earth;
First a little, thence to more   65
He sampled all her killing store;
And easy, smiling, seasoned sound,
Sate the king when healths went round.
They put arsenic in his meat
And stared aghast to watch him eat;   70
They poured strychnine in his cup
And shook to see him drink it up:
They shook, they stared as white's their shirt:
Them it was their poison hurt.
—I tell the tale that I heard told.   75
Mithridates, he died old.

                                             1896

IS MY TEAM PLOUGHING

'Is my team ploughing,
   That I was used to drive
And hear the harness jingle
   When I was man alive?'

Ay, the horses trample,
    The harness jingles now; 5
No change though you lie under
    The land you used to plough.

'Is football playing
    Along the river shore, 10
With lads to chase the leather,
    Now I stand up no more?'

Ay, the ball is flying,
    The lads play heart and soul;
The goal stands up, the keeper 15
    Stands up to keep the goal.

'Is my girl happy,
    That I thought hard to leave,
And has she tired of weeping
    As she lies down at eve?' 20

Ay, she lies down lightly,
    She lies not down to weep:
Your girl is well contented.
    Be still, my lad, and sleep.

'Is my friend hearty, 25
    Now I am thin and pine,
And has he found to sleep in
    A better bed than mine?'

Yes, lad, I lie easy,
    I lie as lads would choose; 30
I cheer a dead man's sweetheart,
    Never ask me whose.

1896

ON MOONLIT HEATH

On moonlit heath and lonesome bank
    The sheep beside me graze;
And yon the gallows used to clank
    Fast by the four cross ways.

A careless shepherd once would keep 5
    The flocks by moonlight there,

And high amongst the glimmering sheep
    The dead man stood on air.

They hang us now in Shrewsbury jail:
    The whistles blow forlorn,   10
And trains all night groan on the rail
    To men that die at morn.

There sleeps in Shrewsbury jail to-night,
    Or wakes, as may betide,
A better lad, if things went right,   15
    Than most that sleep outside.

And naked to the hangman's noose
    The morning clocks will ring
A neck God made for other use
    Than strangling in a string.   20

And sharp the link of life will snap,
    And dead on air will stand
Heels that held up as straight a chap
    As treads upon the land.

So here I'll watch the night and wait   25
    To see the morning shine,
When he will hear the stroke of eight
    And not the stroke of nine;

And wish my friend as sound a sleep
    As lads I did not know,   30
That shepherded the moonlit sheep
    A hundred years ago.

1896

COULD MAN BE DRUNK FOR EVER

Could man be drunk for ever
    With liquor, love, or fights,
Lief should I rouse at morning
    And lief lie down of nights.

But men at whiles are sober   5
    And think by fits and starts,
And if they think, they fasten
    Their hands upon their hearts.

1922

A. E. Housman   **889**

WHEN FIRST MY WAY

When first my way to fair I took
   Few pence in purse had I,
And long I used to stand and look
   At things I could not buy.

Now times are altered: if I care   5
   To buy a thing, I can;
The pence are here and here's the fair,
   But where's the lost young man?

—To think that two and two are four
   And neither five nor three   10
The heart of man has long been sore
   And long 'tis like to be.

1922

STARS, I HAVE SEEN THEM FALL

Stars, I have seen them fall,
   But when they drop and die
No star is lost at all
   From all the star-sown sky.
The toil of all that be   5
   Helps not the primal fault;
It rains into the sea,
   And still the sea is salt.

1936

A. E. Housman's anti-intellectual attitude toward poetry (see p. 686) made him cut a peculiar figure in the literary world. Professionally, he was a Latin professor who entered into hair-splitting scholarly disputes with great gusto. As a poet, on the other hand, he seemed distrustful of intellectualization, or uninterested in it. These peculiar attitudes and a very distinctive style made him a subject of controversy and sometimes parody, as the following poems show. The Dorothy Parker poem may not deliberately echo Housman, but it has in extreme form Housman's blend of humor and dourness.

Ezra Pound

(1885–1972)

MR. HOUSMAN'S MESSAGE

O woe, woe,
People are born and die,
We also shall be dead pretty soon
Therefore let us act as if we were
                  dead already.   5

The bird sits on the hawthorn tree
But he dies also, presently.
Some lads get hung, and some get shot.
Woeful is this human lot.
             Woe! woe, etcetera. . . .   10

London is a woeful place,
Shropshire is much pleasanter.
Then let us smile a little space
Upon fond nature's morbid grace.
         Oh, Woe, woe, woe, etcetera. . . .   15

1911

Hugh Kingsmill

(1889–1949)

WHAT, STILL ALIVE

What, still alive at twenty-two,
A clean upstanding chap like you?
Sure, if your throat 'tis hard to slit,
Slit your girl's, and swing for it.

Like enough, you won't be glad,   5
When they come to hang you, lad:
But bacon's not the only thing
That's cured by hanging from a string.

So, when the spilt ink of the night
Spreads o'er the blotting pad of light,   10

Lads whose job is still to do
Shall whet their knives, and think of you.

ca. 1927

Dorothy Parker

(1893–1967)

THOUGHT FOR A SUNSHINY MORNING

It costs me never a stab nor squirm
To tread by chance upon a worm.
"Aha, my little dear," I say,
"Your clan will pay me back one day."

1928

W. H. Auden

(1907–1973)

A. E. HOUSMAN

No one, not even Cambridge, was to blame
(Blame if you like the human situation):
Heart-injured in North London, he became
The Latin Scholar of his generation.

Deliberately he chose the dry-as-dust.   5
Kept tears like dirty postcards in a drawer;
Food was his public love, his private lust
Something to do with violence and the poor.

In savage foot-notes on unjust editions
He timidly attacked the life he led,   10
And put the money of his feelings on

The uncritical relations of the dead,
Where only geographical divisions
Parted the coarse hanged soldier from the don.

1939

WILLIAM BUTLER YEATS

(1865–1939)

THE LAKE ISLE OF INNISFREE

I will arise and go now, and go to Innisfree,
And a small cabin build there, of clay and wattles made:
Nine bean-rows will I have there, a hive for the
    honey-bee,
And live alone in the bee-loud glade.

And I shall have some peace there, for peace comes
    dropping slow,   5
Dropping from the veils of the morning to where the
    cricket sings;
There midnight's all a glimmer, and noon a purple
    glow,
And evening full of the linnet's wings.

I will arise and go now, for always night and day
I hear lake water lapping with low sounds by the shore;   10
While I stand on the roadway, or on the pavements
    gray,
I hear it in the deep heart's core.

1892

THE FOLLY OF BEING COMFORTED

One that is ever kind said yesterday:
'Your well-beloved's hair has threads of grey,
And little shadows come about her eyes;
Time can but make it easier to be wise
Though now it seems impossible, and so   5
All that you need is patience.'
                       Heart cries, 'No,
I have not a crumb of comfort, not a grain.
Time can but make her beauty over again:
Because of that great nobleness of hers   10
The fire that stirs about her, when she stirs,
Burns but more clearly. O she had not these ways
When all the wild summer was in her gaze.'

O heart! O heart! if she'd but turn her head,
You'd know the folly of being comforted.

1903

THE WILD SWANS AT COOLE

The trees are in their autumn beauty,
The woodland paths are dry,
Under the October twilight the water
Mirrors a still sky;
Upon the brimming water among the stones   5
Are nine-and-fifty swans.

The nineteenth autumn has come upon me
Since I first made my count;
I saw, before I had well finished,
All suddenly mount   10
And scatter wheeling in great broken rings
Upon their clamorous wings.

I have looked upon those brilliant creatures,
And now my heart is sore.
All's changed since I, hearing at twilight,   15
The first time on this shore,
The bell-beat of their wings above my head,
Trod with a lighter tread.

Unwearied still, lover by lover,
They paddle in the cold   20
Companionable streams or climb the air;
Their hearts have not grown old;
Passion or conquest, wander where they will,
Attend upon them still.

But now they drift on the still water,   25
Mysterious, beautiful;
Among what rushes will they build,
By what lake's edge or pool
Delight men's eyes when I awake some day
To find they have flown away?   30

1917

THE SCHOLARS

Bald heads forgetful of their sins,
Old, learned, respectable bald heads
Edit and annotate the lines
That young men, tossing on their beds,
Rhymed out in love's despair   5
To flatter beauty's ignorant ear.

All shuffle there; all cough in ink;
All wear the carpet with their shoes;
All think what other people think;
All know the man their neighbor knows.   10
Lord, what would they say
Did their Catullus walk that way?

1917

THE CAT AND THE MOON

The cat went here and there
And the moon spun round like a top,
And the nearest kin of the moon,
The creeping cat, looked up.
Black Minnaloushe stared at the moon,   5
For, wander and wail as he would,
The pure cold light in the sky
Troubled his animal blood.
Minnaloushe runs in the grass
Lifting his delicate feet.   10
Do you dance, Minnaloushe, do you dance?
When two close kindred meet,
What better than call a dance?
Maybe the moon may learn,
Tired of that courtly fashion,   15
A new dance turn.
Minnaloushe creeps through the grass
From moonlit place to place,
The sacred moon overhead
Has taken a new phase.   20
Does Minnaloushe know that his pupils
Will pass from change to change,
And that from round to crescent,
From crescent to round they range?
Minnaloushe creeps through the grass   25
Alone, important and wise,
And lifts to the changing moon
His changing eyes.

1918

"*The Cat and the Moon*": *The Cat and the Moon:* appears in Yeats's play by the same name
5 *Minnaloushe:* a black Persian cat belonging to a friend of Yeats

THE SECOND COMING

Turning and turning in the widening gyre
The falcon cannot hear the falconer;
Things fall apart; the centre cannot hold;
Mere anarchy is loosed upon the world,
The blood-dimmed tide is loosed, and everywhere   5
The ceremony of innocence is drowned;
The best lack all conviction, while the worst
Are full of passionate intensity.

Surely some revelation is at hand;
Surely the Second Coming is at hand.   10
The Second Coming! Hardly are those words out
When a vast image out of *Spiritus Mundi*
Troubles my sight: somewhere in sands of the desert
A shape with lion body and the head of a man,
A gaze blank and pitiless as the sun,   15
Is moving its slow thighs, while all about it

Reel shadows of the indignant desert birds.
The darkness drops again; but now I know
That twenty centuries of stony sleep
Were vexed to nightmare by a rocking cradle,   20
And what rough beast, its hour come round at last,
Slouches towards Bethlehem to be born?

1921

LEDA AND THE SWAN

A sudden blow: the great wings beating still
Above the staggering girl, her thighs caressed
By the dark webs, her nape caught in his bill,
He holds her helpless breast upon his breast.

How can those terrified vague fingers push   5
The feathered glory from her loosening thighs?
And how can body, laid in that white rush,
But feel the strange heart beating where it lies?

A shudder in the loins engenders there
The broken wall, the burning roof and tower   10
And Agamemnon dead.

"*The Second Coming*": 12 *Spiritus Mundi:* "The Spirit of the World"; the psychic pool of
images which all human minds share and draw from   "*Leda and the Swan*": *Leda:* impregnated
by Zeus in the form of a swan, became the mother of Helen of Troy

                    Being so caught up,
So mastered by the brute blood of the air,
Did she put on his knowledge with his power
Before the indifferent beak could let her drop?   15

                                        1924

SAILING TO BYZANTIUM

1

That is no country for old men. The young
In one another's arms, birds in the trees,
—Those dying generations—at their song,
The salmon-falls, the mackerel-crowded seas,
Fish, flesh, or fowl, commend all summer long   5
Whatever is begotten, born, and dies.
Caught in that sensual music all neglect
Monuments of unageing intellect.

2

An aged man is but a paltry thing,
A tattered coat upon a stick, unless   10
Soul clap its hands and sing, and louder sing
For every tatter in its mortal dress,
Nor is there singing school but studying
Monuments of its own magnificence;
And therefore I have sailed the seas and come   15
To the holy city of Byzantium.

3

O sages standing in God's holy fire
As in the gold mosaic of a wall,
Come from the holy fire, perne in a gyre,
And be the singing-masters of my soul.   20
Consume my heart away; sick with desire
And fastened to a dying animal
It knows not what it is; and gather me
Into the artifice of eternity.

4

Once out of nature I shall never take   25
My bodily form from any natural thing,

"Sailing to Byzantium": Byzantium: for a BBC broadcast in 1931, Yeats wrote: "Byzantium was
the center of European civilization and the source of its spiritual philosophy, so I symbolize
the search for spiritual life by a journey to that city."

But such a form as Grecian goldsmiths make
Of hammered gold and gold enamelling
To keep a drowsy Emperor awake;
Or set upon a golden bough to sing   30
To lords and ladies of Byzantium
Of what is past, or passing, or to come.

1928

AMONG SCHOOL CHILDREN

1

I walk through the long schoolroom questioning;
A kind old nun in a white hood replies;
The children learn to cipher and to sing,
To study reading-books and histories,
To cut and sew, be neat in everything   5
In the best modern way—the children's eyes
In momentary wonder stare upon
A sixty-year-old smiling public man.

2

I dream of a Ledaean body, bent
Above a sinking fire, a tale that she   10
Told of a harsh reproof, or trivial event
That changed some childish day to tragedy—
Told, and it seemed that our two natures blent
Into a sphere from youthful sympathy,
Or else, to alter Plato's parable,   15
Into the yolk and white of the one shell.

3

And thinking of that fit of grief or rage
I look upon one child or t'other there
And wonder if she stood so at that age—
For even daughters of the swan can share   20
Something of every paddler's heritage—
And had that color upon cheek or hair,

"*Among School Children*": 9 *Ledaean*: "like Helen of Troy," Leda's daughter   15 *Plato's parable*: in his *Symposium*, Plato explains the origin of love between men and women: once the two sexes were united in one body, with four arms and legs, which moved by rolling; it was so big and powerful that the gods decided each one had to be divided "as you might divide an egg with a hair." Each half was unhappy and longed for the other, however, and this longing is love.

And thereupon my heart is driven wild:
She stands before me as a living child.

4

Her present image floats into the mind—   25
Did Quattrocento finger fashion it
Hollow of cheek as though it drank the wind
And took a mess of shadows for its meat?
And I though never of Ledaean kind
Had pretty plumage once—enough of that,   30
Better to smile on all that smile, and show
There is a comfortable kind of old scarecrow.

5

What youthful mother, a shape upon her lap
Honey of generation had betrayed,
And that must sleep, shriek, struggle to escape   35
As recollection or the drug decide,
Would think her son, did she but see that shape
With sixty or more winters on its head,
A compensation for the pang of his birth,
Or the uncertainty of his setting forth?   40

6

Plato thought nature but a spume that plays
Upon a ghostly paradigm of things;
Solider Aristotle played the taws
Upon the bottom of a king of kings;
World-famous golden-thighed Pythagoras   45
Fingered upon a fiddle-stick or strings
What a star sang and careless Muses heard:
Old clothes upon old sticks to scare a bird.

7

Both nuns and mothers worship images,
But those the candles light are not as those   50
That animate a mother's reveries,
But keep a marble or a bronze repose.
And yet they too break hearts—O Presences
That passion, piety or affection knows,

---

26 *Quattrocento:* the 1400's in Italy, which was one of the greatest times of artistic creation
41 *Aristotle:* in contrast to Plato, who located reality in Ideal forms, Aristotle believed reality
was found in the natural world.   43 *Pythagoras:* a sixth century philosopher and mathematician who believed that the underlying truth of things was numerical; his mathematical theory
of music led to the legend that he possessed a golden bone which allowed him to hear the
music of the spheres.

And that all heavenly glory symbolize—   55
O self-born mockers of man's enterprise;

8

Labor is blossoming or dancing where
The body is not bruised to pleasure soul,
Nor beauty born out of its own despair,
Nor blear-eyed wisdom out of midnight oil.   60
O chestnut-tree, great-rooted blossomer,
Are you the leaf, the blossom or the bole?
O body swayed to music, O brightening glance,
How can we know the dancer from the dance?

1928

CRAZY JANE TALKS WITH THE BISHOP

I met the Bishop on the road
And much said he and I.
'Those breasts are flat and fallen now,
Those veins must soon be dry;
Live in a heavenly mansion,   5
Not in some foul sty.'

'Fair and foul are near of kin,
And fair needs foul,' I cried.
'My friends are gone, but that's a truth
Nor grave nor bed denied,   10
Learned in bodily lowliness
And in the heart's pride.

'A women can be proud and stiff
When on love intent;
But Love has pitched his mansion in   15
The place of excrement;
For nothing can be sole or whole
That has not been rent.'

1933

Certainly one of the key figures in defining the character of poetry in the first half of the twentieth century, William Butler Yeats edited The Oxford Book of Modern Verse *in 1936. In the introduction, he explained the new generation's movement away from the influence of such nineteenth-century figures as Gerard Manley Hopkins and Thomas Hardy.*

"The new generation was in revolt": William Butler Yeats

All these writers were, in the eye of the new generation, in so far as they were known, Victorian, and the new generation was in revolt. But one writer, almost unknown to the general public—I remember somebody saying at his death 'no newspaper has given him an obituary notice'—had its entire uncritical admiration, Walter Pater. That is why I begin this book with the famous passage from his essay on Leonardo da Vinci. Only by printing it in *vers libre* can one show its revolutionary importance. Pater was accustomed to give each sentence a separate page of manuscript, isolating and analysing its rhythm; Henley wrote certain 'hospital poems,' not included in this book, in *vers libre,* but did not permit a poem to arise out of its own rhythm as do Turner and Pound at their best and as, I contend, Pater did. [T]his passage . . . dominated a generation, a domination so great that all over Europe from that day to this men shrink from Leonardo's masterpiece as from an over-flattered woman. . . .

The revolt against Victorianism meant to the young poet a revolt against irrelevant descriptions of nature, the scientific and moral discursiveness of *In Memoriam*—'When he should have been broken-hearted', said Verlaine, 'he had many reminiscences'—the political eloquence of Swinburne, the psychological curiosity of Browning, and the poetical diction of everybody. Poets said to one another over their black coffee—a recently imported fashion—'We must purify poetry of all that is not poetry', and by poetry they meant poetry as it had been written by Catullus, a great name at that time, by the Jacobean writers, by Verlaine, by Baudelaire. Poetry was a tradition like religion and liable to corruption, and it seemed that they could best restore it by writing lyrics technically perfect, their emotion pitched high, and as Pater offered instead of moral earnestness life lived as 'a pure gem-like flame' all accepted him for master.

Yeats's arrangement into lines of the above-mentioned Walter Pater sentence was printed as the first "poem" in The Oxford Book of Modern Verse.

Walter Pater

(1839–1894)

MONA LISA

She is older than the rocks among which she sits;
Like the Vampire,

She has been dead many times,
And learned the secrets of the grave;
And has been a diver in deep seas,   5
And keeps their fallen day about her;
And trafficked for strange webs with Eastern
    merchants;
And, as Leda,
Was the mother of Helen of Troy,
And, as St. Anne,   10
Was the mother of Mary;
And all this has been to her but as the sound of lyres
    and flutes,
And lives
Only in the delicacy
With which it has moulded the changing lineaments,   15
And tinged the eyelids and the hands.

                                          1939

If Yeats was in some ways a typical "modern" poet, he was also very different from his contemporaries, in ways touched on in this passage from his autobiography.

"An infallible church of poetic tradition": William Butler Yeats

I was unlike others of my generation in one thing only. I am very religious, and deprived by Huxley and Tyndall, whom I detested, of the simple-minded religion of my childhood, I had made a new religion, almost an infallible church of poetic tradition, of a fardel of stories, and of personages, and of emotions, inseparable from their first expression, passed on from generation to generation by poets and painters with some help from philosophers and theologians. I wished for a world, where I could discover this tradition perpetually, and not in pictures and in poems only, but in tiles round the chimney-piece and in the hangings that kept out the draft. I had even created a dogma: "Because those imaginary people are created out of the deepest instinct of man, to be his measure and his norm, whatever I can imagine those mouths speaking may be the nearest I can go to truth." When I listened they seemed always to speak of one thing only: they, their loves, every incident of their lives, were steeped in the supernatural. Could even Titian's "Ariosto" that I loved beyond other portraits have its grave look, as if waiting for some perfect final event, if the painters before Titian had not learned portraiture, while painting into the corner of compositions full of saints and Madonnas, their kneeling patrons? At seventeen years old I was already an old-fashioned brass cannon full of shot, and nothing had kept me from going off but a doubt as to my capacity to shoot straight.

EDWIN ARLINGTON ROBINSON

(1869–1935)

RICHARD CORY

Whenever Richard Cory went down town,
  We people on the pavement looked at him:
He was a gentleman from sole to crown,
  Clean favored, and imperially slim.

And he was always quietly arrayed,   5
  And he was always human when he talked;
But still he fluttered pulses when he said,
  "Good-morning," and he glittered when he walked.

And he was rich—yes, richer than a king,
  And admirably schooled in every grace: 10
In fine, we thought that he was everything
  To make us wish that we were in his place.

So on we worked, and waited for the light,
  And went without the meat, and cursed the bread;
And Richard Cory, one calm summer night,   15
  Went home and put a bullet through his head.

1897

MINIVER CHEEVY

Miniver Cheevy, child of scorn,
  Grew lean while he assailed the seasons;
He wept that he was ever born,
  And he had reasons.

Miniver loved the days of old   5
  When swords were bright and steeds were prancing;

The vision of a warrior bold
   Would set him dancing.

Miniver sighed for what was not,
   And dreamed, and rested from his labors;   10
He dreamed of Thebes and Camelot,
   And Priam's neighbors.

Miniver mourned the ripe renown
   That made so many a name so fragrant;
He mourned Romance, now on the town,   15
   And Art, a vagrant.

Miniver loved the Medici,
   Albeit he had never seen one;
He would have sinned incessantly
   Could he have been one.   20

Miniver cursed the commonplace
   And eyed a khaki suit with loathing;
He missed the medieval grace
   Of iron clothing.

Miniver scorned the gold he sought,   25
   But sore annoyed was he without it;
Miniver thought, and thought, and thought,
   And thought about it.

Miniver Cheevy, born too late,
   Scratched his head and kept on thinking;   30
Miniver coughed, and called it fate,
   And kept on drinking.

                                        1910

EROS TURANNOS

She fears him, and will always ask
   What fated her to choose him;
She meets in his engaging mask
   All reasons to refuse him;
But what she meets and what she fears   5
Are less than are the downward years,

"*Miniver Cheevy*": 11 *Thebes:* a Greek city and the site of many mythical events, including the
stories of Oedipus, Antigone, and the Sphinx   *Camelot:* The legendary location of King
Arthur's court   12 *Priam:* King of Troy during the Trojan War   17 *Medici:* merchant princes
of the Italian Renaissance who by their wealth ruled Florence for nearly 200 years. They are
known for their cruelty and as patrons of the arts.   "*Eros Turannos*": *Eros Turannos:* "love the
tyrant"

Drawn slowly to the foamless weirs
   Of age, were she to lose him.

Between a blurred sagacity
   That once had power to sound him,   10
And Love, that will not let him be
   The Judas that she found him,
Her pride assuages her almost,
As if it were alone the cost.—
He sees that he will not be lost,   15
   And waits and looks around him.

A sense of ocean and old trees
   Envelops and allures him;
Tradition, touching all he sees,
   Beguiles and reassures him;   20
And all her doubts of what he says
Are dimmed with what she knows of days—
Till even prejudice delays
   And fades, and she secures him

The falling leaf inaugurates   25
   The reign of her confusion:
The pounding wave reverberates
   The dirge of her illusion;
And home, where passion lived and died,
Becomes a place where she can hide,   30
While all the town and harbor side
   Vibrate with her seclusion.

We tell you, tapping on our brows,
   The story as it should be,—
As if the story of a house   35
   Were told, or ever could be;
We'll have no kindly veil between
Her visions and those we have seen,—
As if we guessed what hers have been,
   Or what they are or would be.   40

Meanwhile we do no harm; for they
   That with a god have striven,
Not hearing much of what we say,
   Take what the god has given;
Though like waves breaking it may be   45
Or like a changed familiar tree,
Or like a stairway to the sea
   Where down the blind are driven.

1916

THE MILL

The miller's wife had waited long,
    The tea was cold, the fire was dead;
And there might yet be nothing wrong
    In how he went and what he said:
"There are no millers any more,"   5
    Was all that she had heard him say;
And he had lingered at the door
    So long that it seemed yesterday.

Sick with a fear that had no form
    She knew that she was there at last;   10
And in the mill there was a warm
    And mealy fragrance of the past.
What else there was would only seem
    To say again what he had meant;
And what was hanging from a beam   15
    Would not have heeded where she went.

And if she thought it followed her,
    She may have reasoned in the dark
That one way of the few there were
    Would hide her and would leave no mark: 20
Black water, smooth above the weir
    Like starry velvet in the night,
Though ruffled once, would soon appear
    The same as ever to the sight.

1920

MR. FLOOD'S PARTY

Old Eben Flood, climbing alone one night
Over the hill between the town below
And the forsaken upland hermitage
That held as much as he should ever know
On earth again of home, paused warily.   5
The road was his with not a native near;
And Eben, having leisure, said aloud,
For no man else in Tilbury Town to hear:

'Well, Mr. Flood, we have the harvest moon
Again, and we may not have many more;   10
The bird is on the wing, the poet says,
And you and I have said it here before.

Drink to the bird.' He raised up to the light
The jug that he had gone so far to fill,
And answered huskily: 'Well, Mr. Flood,   15
Since you propose it, I believe I will.'

Alone, as if enduring to the end
A valiant armor of scarred hopes outworn,
He stood there in the middle of the road
Like Roland's ghost winding a silent horn.   20
Below him, in the town among the trees,
Where friends of other days had honored him,
A phantom salutation of the dead
Rang thinly till old Eben's eyes were dim.

Then, as a mother lays her sleeping child   25
Down tenderly, fearing it may awake,
He set the jug down slowly at his feet
With trembling care, knowing that most things break;
And only when assured that on firm earth
It stood, as the uncertain lives of men   30
Assuredly did not, he paced away,
And with his hand extended paused again:

'Well, Mr. Flood, we have not met like this
In a long time; and many a change has come
To both of us, I fear, since last it was   35
We had a drop together. Welcome home!'
Convivially returning with himself,
Again he raised the jug up to the light;
And with an acquiescent quaver said:
'Well, Mr. Flood, if you insist, I might.   40

'Only a very little, Mr. Flood—
For auld lang syne. No more, sir; that will do.'
So, for the time, apparently it did,
And Eben evidently thought so too;
For soon amid the silver loneliness   45
Of night he lifted up his voice and sang,
Secure, with only two moons listening,
Until the whole harmonious landscape rang—

'For auld lang syne.' The weary throat gave out,
The last word wavered, and the song was done.   50

"*Mr. Flood's Party*": 20 *Roland:* from the medieval *Song of Roland;* Roland was a commander
in Charlemagne's army, defeated because he was too proud to sound his horn for help
42 *auld lang syne:* "old long since"; the good old days

He raised again the jug regretfully
And shook his head, and was again alone.
There was not much that was ahead of him,
And there was nothing in the town below—
Where strangers would have shut the many doors   55
That many friends had opened long ago.

1921

THE SHEAVES

Where long the shadows of the wind had rolled,
Green wheat was yielding to the change assigned;
And as by some vast magic undivined
The world was turning slowly into gold.
Like nothing that was ever bought or sold   5
It waited there, the body and the mind;
And with a mighty meaning of a kind
That tells the more the more it is not told.

So in a land where all days are not fair,
Fair days went on till on another day   10
A thousand golden sheaves were lying there,
Shining and still, but not for long to stay—
As if a thousand girls with golden hair
Might rise from where they slept and go away.

1925

Edwin Arlington Robinson was master of a tone related to A. E. Housman's in some ways, but distinctly his own. No one has identified this tone more accurately than Robert Frost.

"Never having let grief go further than it could in play": Robert Frost

---

The first poet I ever sat down with to talk about poetry was Ezra Pound. It was in London in 1913. The first poet we talked about, to the best of my recollection, was Edwin Arlington Robinson. I was fresh from America and from having read *The Town Down the River*. Beginning at that book, I have slowly spread my reading of Robinson twenty years backward and forward, about equally in both directions.

I remember the pleasure with which Pound and I laughed over the fourth "thought" in

> Miniver thought, and thought, and thought,
> And thought about it.

Three "thoughts" would have been "adequate" as the critical praise-word then was. There would have been nothing to complain of, if it had been left at three. The fourth made the intolerable touch of poetry. With the fourth, the fun began. . . .

There is more to it than the number of "thoughts." There is the way the last one turns up by surprise round the corner, the way the shape of the stanza is played with, the easy way the obstacle of verse is turned to advantage. The mischief is in it.

> One pauses half afraid—
> To say for certain that he played

a man as sorrowful as Robinson. His death was sad to those who knew him, but nowhere near as sad as the lifetime of poetry to which he attuned our ears. Nevertheless, I say his much-admired restraint lies wholly in his never having let grief go further than it could in play. So far shall grief go, so far shall philosophy go, so far shall confidences go, and no further. Taste may set the limit. Humor is a surer dependence.

ROBERT FROST

(1874–1963)

HOME BURIAL

He saw her from the bottom of the stairs
Before she saw him. She was starting down,
Looking back over her shoulder at some fear.
She took a doubtful step and then undid it
To raise herself and look again. He spoke   5
Advancing toward her: "What is it you see
From up there always?—for I want to know."
She turned and sank upon her skirts at that,
And her face changed from terrified to dull.

He said to gain time: "What is it you see?" 10
Mounting until she cowered under him.
"I will find out now—you must tell me, dear."
She, in her place, refused him any help,
With the least stiffening of her neck and silence.
She let him look, sure that he wouldn't see, 15
Blind creature; and awhile he didn't see.
But at last he murmured, "Oh," and again, "Oh."

"What is it—what?" she said.

            "Just that I see."

"You don't," she challenged. "Tell me what it is." 20

"The wonder is I didn't see at once.
I never noticed it from here before.
I must be wonted to it—that's the reason.
The little graveyard where my people are!
So small the window frames the whole of it. 25
Not so much larger than a bedroom, is it?
There are three stones of slate and one of marble,
Broad shouldered little slabs there in the sunlight
On the sidehill. We haven't to mind *those*.
But I understand: it is not the stones, 30
But the child's mound———"

           "Don't, don't, don't,
  don't," she cried.

She withdrew, shrinking from beneath his arm
That rested on the banister, and slid downstairs; 35
And turned on him with such a daunting look,
He said twice over before he knew himself:
"Can't a man speak of his own child he's lost?"

"Not you!—Oh, where's my hat? Oh, I don't need it!
I must get out of here. I must get air.— 40
I don't know rightly whether any man can."

"Amy! Don't go to someone else this time.
Listen to me. I won't come down the stairs."
He sat and fixed his chin between his fists.
"There's something I should like to ask you, dear." 45

"You don't know how to ask it."

            "Help me, then."

Her fingers moved the latch for all reply.

"My words are nearly always an offense.
I don't know how to speak of anything   50
So as to please you. But I might be taught,
I should suppose. I can't say I see how.
A man must partly give up being a man
With womenfolk. We could have some arrangement
By which I'd bind myself to keep hands off   55
Anything special you're a-mind to name.
Though I don't like such things 'twixt those that love.
Two that don't love can't live together without them.
But two that do can't live together with them."
She moved the latch a little. "Don't—don't go.   60
Don't carry it to someone else this time.
Tell me about it if it's something human.
Let me into your grief. I'm not so much
Unlike other folks as your standing there
Apart would make me out. Give me my chance.   65
I do think, though, you overdo it a little.
What was it brought you up to think it the thing
To take your mother-loss of a first child
So inconsolably—in the face of love.
You'd think his memory might be satisfied——"   70

"There you go sneering now!"

                        "I'm not, I'm not!
You make me angry. I'll come down to you.
God, what a woman! And it's come to this,
A man can't speak of his own child that's dead."   75

"You can't because you don't know how to speak.
If you had any feelings, you that dug
With your own hand—how could you?—his little
   grave;
I saw you from that very window there,
Making the gravel leap and leap in air,   80
Leap up, like that, like that, and land so lightly
And roll back down the mound beside the hole.
I thought, Who is that man? I didn't know you.
And I crept down the stairs and up the stairs
To look again, and still your spade kept lifting.   85
Then you came in. I heard your rumbling voice
Out in the kitchen, and I don't know why,
But I went near to see with my own eyes.
You could sit there with the stains on your shoes
Of the fresh earth from your own baby's grave   90

And talk about your everyday concerns.
You had stood the spade up against the wall
Outside there in the entry, for I saw it."

"I shall laugh the worst laugh I ever laughed.
I'm cursed. God, if I don't believe I'm cursed."   95

"I can repeat the very words you were saying:
'Three foggy mornings and one rainy day
Will rot the best birch fence a man can build.'
Think of it, talk like that at such a time!
What had how long it takes a birch to rot   100
To do with what was in the darkened parlor?
You *couldn't* care! The nearest friends can go
With anyone to death, comes so far short
They might as well not try to go at all.
No, from the time when one is sick to death,   105
One is alone, and he dies more alone.
Friends make pretense of following to the grave,
But before one is in it, their minds are turned
And making the best of their way back to life
And living people, and things they understand.   110
But the world's evil. I won't have grief so
If I can change it. Oh, I won't, I won't!"

"There, you have said it all and you feel better.
You won't go now. You're crying. Close the door.
The heart's gone out of it: why keep it up?   115
Amy! There's someone coming down the road!"

"*You*—oh, you think the talk is all. I must go—
Somewhere out of this house. How can I make you—"

"If—you—do!" She was opening the door wider.
"Where do you mean to go? First tell me that.   120
I'll follow and bring you back by force. I *will*!—"

1914

THE WOOD-PILE

Out walking in the frozen swamp one gray day,
I paused and said, "I will turn back from here.
No, I will go on farther—and we shall see."
The hard snow held me, save where now and then
One foot went through. The view was all in lines   5
Straight up and down of tall slim trees

Too much alike to mark or name a place by
So as to say for certain I was here
Or somewhere else: I was just far from home.
A small bird flew before me. He was careful   10
To put a tree between us when he lighted,
And say no word to tell me who he was
Who was so foolish as to think what *he* thought.
He thought that I was after him for a feather—
The white one in his tail; like one who takes   15
Everything said as personal to himself.
One flight out sideways would have undeceived him.
And then there was a pile of wood for which
I forgot him and let his little fear
Carry him off the way I might have gone,   20
Without so much as wishing him good-night.
He went behind it to make his last stand.
It was a cord of maple, cut and split
And piled—and measured, four by four by eight.
And not another like it could I see.   25
No runner tracks in this year's snow looped near it.
And it was older sure than this year's cutting,
Or even last year's or the year's before.
The wood was gray and the bark warping off it
And the pile somewhat sunken. Clematis   30
Had wound strings round and round it like a bundle.
What held it, though, on one side was a tree
Still growing, and on one a stake and prop,
These latter about to fall. I thought that only
Someone who lived in turning to fresh tasks   35
Could so forget his handiwork on which
He spent himself, the labor of his ax,
And leave it there far from a useful fireplace
To warm the frozen swamp as best it could
With the slow smokeless burning of decay.   40

1914

NOTHING GOLD CAN STAY

Nature's first green is gold,
Her hardest hue to hold.
Her early leaf's a flower;
But only so an hour.
Then leaf subsides to leaf.   5
So Eden sank to grief,

So dawn goes down to day.
Nothing gold can stay.

1916

STOPPING BY WOODS ON A SNOWY EVENING

Whose woods these are I think I know.
His house is in the village though;
He will not see me stopping here
To watch his woods fill up with snow.

My little horse must think it queer   5
To stop without a farmhouse near
Between the woods and frozen lake
The darkest evening of the year.

He gives his harness bells a shake
To ask if there is some mistake.   10
The only other sound's the sweep
Of easy wind and downy flake.

The woods are lovely, dark and deep.
But I have promises to keep,
And miles to go before I sleep,   15
And miles to go before I sleep.

1923

ACQUAINTED WITH THE NIGHT

I have been one acquainted with the night.
I have walked out in rain—and back in rain.
I have outwalked the furthest city light.

I have looked down the saddest city lane.
I have passed by the watchman on his beat   5
And dropped my eyes, unwilling to explain.

I have stood still and stopped the sound of feet
When far away an interrupted cry
Came over houses from another street,

But not to call me back or say good-bye;   10
And further still at an unearthly height,
One luminary clock against the sky

Proclaimed the time was neither wrong nor right.
I have been one acquainted with the night.

1928

NEITHER OUT FAR NOR IN DEEP

The people along the sand
All turn and look one way.
They turn their back on the land.
They look at the sea all day.

As long as it takes to pass   5
A ship keeps raising its hull;
The wetter ground like glass
Reflects a standing gull.

The land may vary more;
But wherever the truth may be—   10
The water comes ashore,
And the people look at the sea.

They cannot look out far.
They cannot look in deep.
But when was that ever a bar   15
To any watch they keep?

1932

PROVIDE, PROVIDE

The witch that came (the withered hag)
To wash the steps with pail and rag,
Was once the beauty Abishag,

The picture pride of Hollywood.
Too many fall from great and good   5
For you to doubt the likelihood.

Die early and avoid the fate.
Or if predestined to die late,
Make up your mind to die in state.

Make the whole stock exchange your own!   10
If need be occupy a throne,
Where nobody can call *you* crone.

"*Provide, Provide*": 3 Abishag: A woman who comforted King David in his old age; see 1 Kings
1:1–4

Robert Frost   *915*

Some have relied on what they knew;
Others on being simply true.
What worked for them might work for you.   15

No memory of having starred
Atones for later disregard,
Or keeps the end from being hard.

Better to go down dignified
With boughten friendship at your side   20
Than none at all. Provide, provide!

1936

DEPARTMENTAL

An ant on the tablecloth
Ran into a dormant moth
Of many times his size.
He showed not the least surprise.
His business wasn't with such.   5
He gave it scarcely a touch,
And was off on his duty run.
Yet if he encountered one
Of the hive's enquiry squad
Whose work is to find out God   10
And the nature of time and space,
He would put him onto the case.
Ants are a curious race;
One crossing with hurried tread
The body of one of their dead   15
Isn't given a moment's arrest—
Seems not even impressed.
But he no doubt reports to any
With whom he crosses antennae,
And they no doubt report   20
To the higher-up at court.
Then word goes forth in Formic:
"Death's come to Jerry McCormic,
Our selfless forager Jerry.
Will the special Janizary   25
Whose office it is to bury
The dead of the commissary
Go bring him home to his people.

_____

"Departmental": 25 *Janizary*: a janissary, a soldier in an elite guard of Turkish troops

Lay him in state on a sepal.
Wrap him for shroud in a petal.   30
Embalm him with ichor of nettle.
This the word of your Queen."
And presently on the scene
Appears a solemn mortician;
And taking formal position,   35
With feelers calmly atwiddle,
Seizes the dead by the middle,
And heaving him high in air,
Carries him out of there.
No one stands round to stare.   40
It is nobody else's affair.

It couldn't be called ungentle.
But how thoroughly departmental.

1936

THE GIFT OUTRIGHT

The land was ours before we were the land's.
She was our land more than a hundred years
Before we were her people. She was ours
In Massachusetts, in Virginia,
But we were England's, still colonials,   5
Possessing what we still were unpossessed by,
Possessed by what we now no more possessed.
Something we were withholding made us weak
Until we found it was ourselves
We were withholding from our land of living,   10
And forthwith found salvation in surrender.
Such as we were we gave ourselves outright
(The deed of gift was many deeds of war)
To the land vaguely realizing westward,
But still unstoried, artless, unenhanced,   15
Such as she was, such as she would become.

1942

Robert Frost, born in a generation full of poetic experimenters, clung to tra-
ditional meter and poetic form and wrote many poems about the rural land-
scape, the most traditional of subjects. Frost had his reasons for doing so,

and articulated them often and well, as in the excerpt below from "The Constant Symbol." Some of Frost's readers, however, would agree with Galway Kinnell that beneath the technical accomplishment and commitment to form there was something deeper and darker in Frost that accounts for the power of his best poetry.

"An epitome of the great predicament": Robert Frost

There are many other things I have found myself saying about poetry, but the chiefest of these is that it is metaphor, saying one thing and meaning another, saying one thing in terms of another, the pleasure of ulteriority. Poetry is simply made of metaphor. So also is philosophy—and science, too, for that matter, if it will take the soft impeachment from a friend. Every poem is a new metaphor inside or it is nothing. And there is a sense in which all poems are the same old metaphor always.

Every single poem written regular is a symbol small or great of the way the will has to pitch into commitments deeper and deeper to a rounded conclusion and then be judged for whether any original intention it had has been strongly spent or weakly lost; be it in art, politics, school, church, business, love, or marriage—in a piece of work or in a career. Strongly spent is synonymous with kept. . . .

The bard has said in effect, Unto these forms did I commend the spirit. It may take him a year after the act to confess he only betrayed the spirit with a rhymster's cleverness and to forgive his enemies the critics for not having listened to his oaths and protestations to the contrary. Had he anything to be true to? Was he true to it? Did he use good words? You couldn't tell unless you made out what idea they were supposed to be good for. Every poem is an epitome of the great predicament; a figure of the will braving alien entanglements.

Take the President in the White House. A study of the success of his intention might have to go clear back to when as a young politician, youthfully step-careless, he made the choice between the two parties of our system. He may have stood for a moment wishing he knew of a third party nearer the ideal; but only for a moment, since he was practical. And in fact he may have been so little impressed with the importance of his choice that he left his first commitment to be made for him by his friends and relatives. It was only a small commitment anyway, like a kiss. He can scarcely remember how much credit he deserved personally for the decision it took. Calculation is usually no part in the first step in any walk. And behold him now a statesman so multifariously closed in on with obligations and answerabilities that sometimes he loses his august temper. He might as well have got himself into a sestina royal. . . .

There's an indulgent smile I get for the recklessness of the unnecessary commitment I made when I came to the first line in the second stanza of a poem in this book called "Stopping by Woods on a Snowy Evening." I was riding too high to care what trouble I incurred. And it was all right so long as I didn't suffer deflection.

Galway Kinnell

(b. 1927)

FOR ROBERT FROST

1

Why do you talk so much
Robert Frost? One day
I drove up to Ripton to ask,

I stayed the whole day
And never got the chance   5
To put the question.

I drove off at dusk
Worn out and aching
In both ears. Robert Frost,

Were you shy as a boy?   10
Do you go on making up
For some long stint of solitude?

Is it simply that talk
Doesn't have to be metered and rhymed?
Or is gab distracting from something worse?   15

2

I saw you once on the TV,
Unsteady at the lectern,
The flimsy white leaf
Of hair standing straight up
In the wind, among top hats,   20
Old farmer and son
Of worse winters than this,
Stopped in the first dazzle

"*For Robert Frost*": 3 *Ripton:* a town in Vermont where Frost lived   16 *TV:* Frost appeared on the televised inauguration of John F. Kennedy, January 20, 1961, for which he recited his "The Gift Outright."

Of the District of Columbia,
Suddenly having to pay   25
For the cheap onionskin,
The worn-out ribbon, the eyes
Wrecked from writing poems
For us—stopped,
Lonely before millions,   30
The paper jumping in your grip,
And as the Presidents
Also on the platform
Began flashing nervously
Their Presidential smiles   35
For the harmless old guy,
And poets watching on the TV
Started thinking, Well that's
The end of *that* tradition,

And the managers of the event   40
Said, Boys this is it,
The sonofabitch poet
Is gonna croak,
Putting the paper aside
You drew forth   45
From your great faithful heart
The poem.

3

Once, walking in winter in Vermont,
In the snow, I followed a set of footprints
That aimed for the woods. At the verge   50
I could make out, "far in the pillared dark,"
An old creature in a huge, clumsy overcoat,
Lifting his great boots through the drifts,
Going as if to die among "those dark trees"
Of his own country. I watched him go,   55

Past a house, quiet, warm and light,
A farm, a countryside, a woodpile in its slow
Smokeless burning, alder swamps ghastly white,
Tumultuous snows, blanker whitenesses,
Into the pathless woods, one eye weeping,   60
The dark trees, for which no saying is dark enough,
Which mask the gloom and lead on into it,
The bare, the withered, the deserted.

There were no more cottages.
Soft bombs of dust falling from the boughs,   65

The sun shining no warmer than the moon,
He had outwalked the farthest city light,
And there, clinging to the perfect trees,
A last leaf. What was it?
What was that whiteness?—white, uncertain—   70
The night too dark to know.

4

He turned. *Love,*
Love of things, duty, he said.
And made his way back to the shelter
No longer sheltering him, the house   75
Where everything real was turning to words,

Where he would think on the white wave,
Folded back, that rides in place on the obscure
Pouring of this life to the sea—
And invent on the broken lips of darkness   80
The seal of form and the *mot juste*.

5

Poet of the country of white houses,
Of clearings going out to the dark wall of woods
Frayed along the skyline, you who nearly foreknew
The next lines of poems you suddenly dropped,   85
Who dwelt in access to that which other men
Have burnt all their lives to get near, who heard
The high wind, in gusts, seething
From far off, headed through the trees exactly
To this place where it must happen, who spent   90
Your life on the point of giving away your heart
To the dark trees, the dissolving woods,
Into which you go at last, heart in hand, deep in:
When we think of a man who was cursed
Neither with the mystical all-lovingness of Walt
     Whitman   95
Nor with Melville's anguish to know and to suffer,
And yet cursed . . . a man, what shall I say,
Vain, not fully convinced he was dying, whose calling
Was to set up in the wilderness of his country,
At whatever cost, a man, who would be his own man,   100
We think of you. And from the same doorway
At which you lived, between the house and the woods,

---

81 *mot juste:* right, exact word (French)

We see your old footprints going away across
The great Republic, Frost, up memorized slopes,
Down hills floating by heart on the bulldozed land.   105

1964

RAINER MARIA RILKE

(1875–1926)

ARIEL

(After reading Shakespeare's Tempest*)*

translated from the German by Stephen Mitchell

Once, somewhere, somehow, you had set him free
with that sharp jolt which as a young man tore you
out of your life and vaulted you to greatness.
Then he grew willing; and, since then, he serves,
after each task impatient for his freedom.   5
And half imperious, half almost ashamed,
you make excuses, say that you still need him
for this and that, and, ah, you must describe
how you helped him. Yet you feel, yourself,
that everything held back by his detention   10
is missing from the air. How sweet, how tempting:
to let him go—to give up all your magic,
submit yourself to destiny like the others,
and know that his light friendship, without strain now,
with no more obligations, anywhere,   15
an intensifying of this space you breathe,
is working in the element, thoughtlessly.
Henceforth dependent, never again empowered
to shape the torpid mouth into that call
at which he dived. Defenseless, aging, poor,   20
and yet still breathing *him* in, like a fragrance
spread endlessly, which makes the invisible
complete for the first time. Smiling that you ever
could summon him and feel so much at home
in that vast intimacy. Weeping too, perhaps,   25
when you remember how he loved and yet
wished to leave you: always both, at once.

(Have I let go already? I look on,
terrified by this man who has become
a duke again. How easily he draws   30
the wire through his head and hangs himself
up with the other puppets; then steps forward
to ask the audience for their applause
and their indulgence. . . . What consummate power:
to lay aside, to stand there nakedly   35
with no strength but one's own, "which is most faint.")

1913, trans. 1982

EXPOSED ON THE CLIFFS OF
THE HEART

translated from the German by Stephen Mitchell

Exposed on the cliffs of the heart. Look, how tiny
   down there,
look: the last village of words and, higher,
(but how tiny) still one last
farmhouse of feeling. Can you see it?
Exposed on the cliffs of the heart. Stoneground   5
under your hands. Even here, though,
something can bloom; on a silent cliff-edge
an unknowing plant blooms, singing, into the air.
But the one who knows? Ah, he began to know
and is quiet now, exposed on the cliffs of the heart.   10
While, with their full awareness,
many sure-footed mountain animals pass
or linger. And the great sheltered bird flies, slowly
circling, around the peak's pure denial.—But
without a shelter, here on the cliffs of the heart. . . .   15

1914, trans. 1982

DUINO ELEGIES: IX

translated from the German by Stephen Mitchell

Why, if this interval of being can be spent serenely
in the form of a laurel, slightly darker than all
other green, with tiny waves on the edges
of every leaf (like the smile of a breeze)—: why then
have to be human—and, escaping from fate,   5
keep longing for fate? . . .

Oh *not* because happiness

exists,
that too-hasty profit snatched from approaching loss.
Not out of curiosity, not as practice for the heart, which
would exist in the laurel too.   10

But because *truly* being here is so much; because
    everything here
apparently needs us, this fleeting world, which in some
    strange way
keeps calling to us. Us, the most fleeting of all.
Once for each thing. Just once; no more. And we too,
just once. And never again. But to have been   15
this once, completely, even if only once:
to have been at one with the earth, seems beyond
    undoing.

And so we keep pressing on, trying to achieve it,
trying to hold it firmly in our simple hands,
in our overcrowded gaze, in our speechless heart.   20
Trying to become it.—Whom can we give it to? We
    would
hold on to it all, forever . . . Ah, but what can we take
    along
into that other realm? Not the art of looking,
which is learned so slowly, and nothing that happened
    here. Nothing.
The sufferings, then. And, above all, the heaviness,   25
and the long experience of love,—just what is wholly
unsayable. But later, among the stars,
what good is it—*they* are *better* as they are: unsayable.
For when the traveler returns from the mountain-slopes
    into the valley,
he brings, not a handful of earth, unsayable to others,
    but instead   30
some word he has gained, some pure word, the yellow
    and blue
gentian. Perhaps we are *here* in order to say: house,
bridge, fountain, gate, pitcher, fruit-tree, window—
at most: column, tower. . . . But to *say* them, you must
    understand,
oh to say them *more* intensely than the Things
    themselves   35
ever dreamed of existing. Isn't the secret intent
of this taciturn earth, when it forces lovers together,
that inside their boundless emotion all things may
    shudder with joy?

Threshold: what it means for two lovers
to be wearing down, imperceptibly, the ancient
    threshold of their door—   40
they too, after the many who came before them
and before those to come. . . . , lightly.

Here is the time for the *sayable, here* is its homeland.
Speak and bear witness. More than ever
the Things that we might experience are vanishing, for   45
what crowds them out and replaces them is an imageless
    act.
An act under a shell, which easily cracks open as soon
    as
the business inside outgrows it and seeks new limits.
Between the hammers our heart
endures, just as the tongue does   50
between the teeth and, despite that,
still is able to praise.

Praise this world to the angel, not the unsayable one,
you can't impress *him* with glorious emotion; in the
    universe
where he feels more powerfully, you are a novice. So
    show him   55
something simple which, formed over generations,
lives as our own, near our hand and within our gaze.
Tell him of Things. He will stand astonished; as *you*
    stood
by the rope-maker in Rome or the potter along the
    Nile.
Show him how happy a Thing can be, how innocent
    and ours,   60
how even lamenting grief purely decides to take form,
serves as a Thing, or dies into a Thing—, and blissfully
escapes far beyond the violin.—And these Things,
which live by perishing, know you are praising them;
    transient,
they look to us for deliverance: us, the most transient
    of all.   65
They want us to change them, utterly, in our invisible
    heart,
within—oh endlessly—within us! Whoever we may be
    at last.

Earth, isn't this what you want: to arise within us,
invisible? Isn't it your dream
to be wholly invisible someday?—O Earth: invisible!   70
What, if not transformation, is your urgent command?

Earth, my dearest, I will. Oh believe me, you no longer
need your springtimes to win me over—one of them,
ah, even one, is already too much for my blood.
Unspeakably I have belonged to you, from the first.   75
You were always right, and your holiest inspiration
is our intimate companion, Death.

Look, I am living. On what? Neither childhood nor
      future
grows any smaller . . . . . Superabundant being
wells up in my heart.   80

                                        1922, trans. 1982

ARCHAIC TORSO OF APOLLO

translated from the German by Stephen Mitchell

We cannot know his legendary head
with eyes like ripening fruit. And yet his torso
is still suffused with brilliance from inside,
like a lamp, in which his gaze, now turned to low,

gleams in all its power. Otherwise   5
the curved breast could not dazzle you so, nor could
a smile run through the placid hips and thighs
to that dark center where procreation flared.

Otherwise the stone would seem defaced
beneath the translucent cascade of the shoulders   10
and would not glisten like a wild beast's fur:

would not, from all the borders of itself,
burst like a star; for here there is no place
that does not see you. You must change your life.

                                        1927, trans. 1982

EVENING

translated from the German by Stephen Mitchell

The sky puts on the darkening blue coat
held for it by a row of ancient trees;

"Archaic Torso of Apollo": Apollo: one of the greatest classical gods; he was identified with the
sun, but was also the god of healing, music, and poetry, and the leader of the Muses

you watch: and the lands grow distant in your sight,
one journeying to heaven, one that falls;

and leave you, not at home in either one,   5
not quite so still and dark as the darkened houses,
not calling to eternity with the passion
of what becomes a star each night, and rises;

and leave you (inexpressibly to unravel)
your life, with its immensity and fear,   10
so that, now bounded, now immeasurable,
it is alternately stone in you and star.

1927, trans. 1982

THE PANTHER

In the Jardin des Plantes, Paris

translated from the German by Stephen Mitchell

His vision, from the constantly passing bars,
has grown so weary that it cannot hold
anything else. It seems to him there are
a thousand bars; and behind the bars, no world.

As he paces in cramped circles, over and over,   5
the movement of his powerful soft strides
is like a ritual dance around a center
in which a mighty will stands paralyzed.

Only at times, the curtain of the pupils
lifts, quietly—. An image enters in,   10
rushes down through the tensed, arrested muscles,
plunges into the heart and is gone.

1927, trans. 1982

In Rainer Maria Rilke, as in Emily Dickinson and William Butler Yeats, there is a strain of mysticism. The poet is so strongly attuned to the inner life that he seems almost to experience the world with another set of senses, or to see in his experience messages that would elude anyone else. Rilke's "Letters to a Young Poet" show that this extraordinary sensibility can isolate the poet both from his fellow humans and from nature. The appended poems by Kathleen Raine and Gloria Fuertes reflect sensibilities similar to Rilke's.

"The senses with which we could have grasped them are atrophied": Rainer Maria Rilke

And to speak of solitude again, it becomes always clearer that this is at bottom not something that one can take or leave. We *are* solitary. We may delude ourselves and act as though this were not so. That is all. But how much better it is to realize that we are so, yes, even to begin by assuming it. We shall indeed turn dizzy then; for all points upon which our eye has been accustomed to rest are taken from us, there is nothing near any more and everything far is infinitely far. A person removed from his own room, almost without preparation and transition, and set upon the height of a great mountain range, would feel something of the sort: an unparalleled insecurity, an abandonment to something inexpressible would almost annihilate him. He would think himself falling or hurled out into space, or exploded into a thousand pieces: what a monstrous lie his brain would have to invent to catch up with and explain the state of his senses! So for him who becomes solitary all distances, all measures change; of these changes many take place suddenly, and then, as with the man on the mountaintop, extraordinary imaginings and singular sensations arise that seem to grow out beyond all bearing. But it is necessary for us to experience *that* too. We must assume our existence as *broadly* as we in any way can; everything, even the unheard-of, must be possible in it. That is at bottom the only courage that is demanded of us: to have courage for the most strange, the most singular and the most inexplicable that we may encounter. That mankind has in this sense been cowardly has done life endless harm; the experiences that are called "visions," the whole so-called "spirit-world," death, all those things that are so closely akin to us, have by daily parrying been so crowded out of life that the senses with which we could have grasped them are atrophied. To say nothing of God.

Kathleen Raine

(b. 1908)

STATUES

They more than we are what we are:
Serenity and joy
We lost or never found,
The forms of heart's desire,
We gave them what we could not keep;   5
We made them what we cannot be.

Their kingdom is our dream, but who can say
If they or we
Are dream or dreamer, signet or clay?
If the most perfect be most true,   10
These faces pure, these bodies poised in thought
Are substance of our form
And we the confused shadows cast.

Growing toward their prime they take our years away,
And from our deaths they rise   15
Immortal in the life we lose.
The gods consume us, but restore
More than we were:
We love, that they may be,
They are, that we may know.   20

1965

Gloria Fuertes

(b. 1918)

PAINTED WINDOWS

translated from the Spanish by Philip Levine

I lived in a house
with two real windows and the other two painted on.
Those painted windows caused my first sorrow.
I'd touch the sides of the hall
trying to reach the windows from inside.   5
I spent my whole childhood wanting
to lean out and see what could be seen
from the windows that weren't there.

trans. 1984

WALLACE STEVENS

(1879–1955)

SUNDAY MORNING

1

Complacencies of the peignoir, and late
Coffee and oranges in a sunny chair,
And the green freedom of a cockatoo
Upon a rug mingle to dissipate
The holy hush of ancient sacrifice.   5
She dreams a little, and she feels the dark
Encroachment of that old catastrophe,
As a calm darkens among water-lights.
The pungent oranges and bright, green wings
Seem things in some procession of the dead   10
Winding across wide water, without sound.
The day is like wide water, without sound,
Stilled for the passing of her dreaming feet
Over the seas, to silent Palestine,
Dominion of the blood and sepulchre.   15

2

Why should she give her bounty to the dead?
What is divinity if it can come
Only in silent shadows and in dreams?
Shall she not find in comforts of the sun,
In pungent fruit and bright, green wings, or else   20
In any balm or beauty of the earth,
Things to be cherished like the thought of heaven?
Divinity must live within herself:
Passions of rain, or moods in falling snow;
Grievings in loneliness, or unsubdued   25
Elations when the forest blooms; gusty
Emotions on wet roads on autumn nights;
All pleasures and all pains, remembering
The bough of summer and the winter branch.
These are the measures destined for her soul.   30

3

Jove in the clouds had his inhuman birth.
No mother suckled him, no sweet land gave
Large-mannered motions to his mythy mind

He moved among us, as a muttering king,
Magnificent, would move among his hinds,   35
Until our blood, commingling, virginal,
With heaven, brought such requital to desire
The very hinds discerned it, in a star.
Shall our blood fail? Or shall it come to be
The blood of paradise? And shall the earth   40
Seem all of paradise that we shall know?
The sky will be much friendlier then than now,
A part of labor and a part of pain,
And next in glory to enduring love,
Not this dividing and indifferent blue.   45

4

She says, "I am content when wakened birds,
Before they fly, test the reality
Of misty fields, by their sweet questionings;
But when the birds are gone, and their warm fields
Return no more, where, then, is paradise?"   50
There is not any haunt of prophecy,
Nor any old chimera of the grave,
Neither the golden underground, nor isle
Melodious, where spirits gat them home,
Nor visionary south, nor cloudy palm   55
Remote on heaven's hill, that has endured
As April's green endures; or will endure
Like her remembrance of awakened birds,
Or her desire for June and evening, tipped
By the consummation of the swallow's wings.   60

5

She says, "But in contentment I still feel
The need of some imperishable bliss."
Death is the mother of beauty; hence from her,
Alone, shall come fulfilment to our dreams
And our desires. Although she strews the leaves   65
Of sure obliteration on our paths,
The path sick sorrow took, the many paths
Where triumph rang its brassy phrase, or love
Whispered a little out of tenderness,
She makes the willow shiver in the sun   70
For maidens who were wont to sit and gaze
Upon the grass, relinquished to their feet.
She causes boys to pile new plums and pears
On disregarded plate. The maidens taste
And stray impassioned in the littering leaves.   75

Is there no change of death in paradise?
Does ripe fruit never fall? Or do the boughs
Hang always heavy in that perfect sky,
Unchanging, yet so like our perishing earth,
With rivers like our own that seek for seas   80
They never find, the same receding shores
That never touch with inarticulate pang?
Why set the pear upon those river-banks
Or spice the shores with odors of the plum?
Alas, that they should wear our colors there,   85
The silken weavings of our afternoons,
And pick the strings of our insipid lutes!
Death is the mother of beauty, mystical,
Within whose burning bosom we devise
Our earthy mothers waiting, sleeplessly.   90

7

Supple and turbulent, a ring of men
Shall chant in orgy on a summer morn
Their boisterous devotion to the sun,
Not as a god, but as a god might be,
Naked among them, like a savage source.   95
Their chant shall be a chant of paradise,
Out of their blood, returning to the sky;
And in their chant shall enter, voice by voice,
The windy lake wherein their lord delights,
The trees, like serafin, and echoing hills,   100
That choir among themselves long afterward.
They shall know well the heavenly fellowship
Of men that perish and of summer morn.
And whence they came and whither they shall go
The dew upon their feet shall manifest.   105

8

She hears, upon that water without sound,
A voice that cries, "The tomb in Palestine
Is not the porch of spirits lingering.
It is the grave of Jesus, where he lay."
We live in an old chaos of the sun,   110
Or old dependency of day and night,
Or island solitude, unsponsored, free,
Of that wide water, inescapable.
Deer walk upon our mountains, and the quail
Whistle about us their spontaneous cries;   115

Sweet berries ripen in the wilderness;
And, in the isolation of the sky,
At evening, casual flocks of pigeons make
Ambiguous undulations as they sink,
Downward to darkness, on extended wings.   120

1923

THE EMPEROR OF ICE-CREAM

Call the roller of big cigars,
The muscular one, and bid him whip
In kitchen cups concupiscent curds.
Let the wenches dawdle in such dress
As they are used to wear, and let the boys   5
Bring flowers in last month's newspapers.
Let be be finale of seem.
The only emperor is the emperor of ice-cream.

Take from the dresser of deal,
Lacking the three glass knobs, that sheet   10
On which she embroidered fantails once
And spread it so as to cover her face.
If her horny feet protrude, they come
To show how cold she is, and dumb.
Let the lamp affix its beam.   15
The only emperor is the emperor of ice-cream.

1923

ANECDOTE OF THE JAR

I placed a jar in Tennessee,
And round it was, upon a hill.
It made the slovenly wilderness
Surround that hill.

The wilderness rose up to it,   5
And sprawled around, no longer wild.
The jar was round upon the ground
And tall and of a port in air.

It took dominion everywhere.
The jar was gray and bare.   10
It did not give of bird or bush,
Like nothing else in Tennessee.

1923

DISILLUSIONMENT OF TEN O'CLOCK

The houses are haunted
By white night-gowns
None are green,
Or purple with green rings,
Or green with yellow rings,   5
Or yellow with blue rings.
None of them are strange,
With socks of lace
And beaded ceintures.
People are not going   10
To dream of baboons and periwinkles.
Only, here and there, an old sailor,
Drunk and asleep in his boots,
Catches tigers
In red weather.   15

1923

STUDY OF TWO PEARS

1

Opusculum paedagogum
The pears are not viols,
Nudes or bottles.
They resemble nothing else.

2

They are yellow forms   5
Composed of curves
Bulging toward the base.
They are touched red.

3

They are not flat surfaces
Having curved outlines.   10
They are round
Tapering toward the top.

4

In the way they are modelled
There are bits of blue.

"*Study of Two Pears*": 1 *Opusculum paedagogum:* a little study, a practice piece

A hard dry leaf hangs   15
From the stem.

                 5

The yellow glistens.
It glistens with various yellows,
Citrons, oranges and greens
Flowering over the skin.   20

                 6

The shadows of the pears
Are blobs on the green cloth.
The pears are not seen
As the observer wills.

                                              1942

PAGE FROM A TALE

In the hard brightness of that winter day
The sea was frozen solid and Hans heard,
By his drift-fire, on the shore, the difference
Between loud water and loud wind, between that
Which has no accurate syllables and that   5
Which cries *so blau* and cries again *so lind*
Und so lau, between sound without meaning and
    speech,
Of clay and wattles made as it ascends
And *hear it* as it falls *in the deep heart's core*
A steamer lay near him, foundered in the ice.   10
So blau, so blau . . . Hans listened by the fire.
New stars that were a foot across came out
And shone. *And a small cabin build there.*
So lind. The wind blazed as they sang. *So lau.*
The great ship, Balayne, lay frozen in the sea.   15
The one-foot stars were couriers of its death
To the wild limits of its habitation.
These were not tepid stars of torpid places
But bravest at midnight and in lonely spaces,
They looked back at Hans' look with savage faces.   20
The wet weed sputtered, the fire died down, the cold
Was like a sleep. The sea was a sea he dreamed.

"Page from a Tale": 6 *so blau:* so blue (German)   *so lind:* so gentle (German)   7 *Und so lau:* and so lukewarm (German)   8 *Of clay and wattles made:* See W. B. Yeats's "The Lake Isle of Innisfree"

Yet Hans lay wide awake. *And live alone*
In the bee-loud glade. Lights on the steamer moved.
Men would be starting at dawn to walk ashore.   25
They would be afraid of the sun: what it might be,
Afraid of the country angels of those skies,
The finned flutterings and gaspings of the ice,
As if whatever in water strove to speak
Broke dialect in a break of memory.   30

The sun might rise and it might not and if
It rose, ashen and red and yellow, each
Opaque, in orange circlet, nearer than it
Had ever been before, no longer known,
No more that which most of all brings back the known,   35
But that which destroys it completely by this light
For that, or a motion not in the astronomies,
Beyond the habit of sense, anarchic shape
Afire—it might and it might not in that
Gothic blue, speed home its portents to their ends.   40

It might become a wheel spoked red and white
In alternate stripes converging at a point
Of flame on the line, with a second wheel below,
Just rising, accompanying, arranged to cross,
Through weltering illuminations, humps   45
Of billows, downward, toward the drift-fire shore.
It might come bearing, out of chaos, kin
Smeared, smoked, and drunken of thin potencies,
Lashing at images in the atmosphere,
Ringed round and barred, with eyes held in their
    hands,   50
And capable of incapably evil thought:
Slight gestures that could rend the palpable ice,
Or melt Arcturus to ingots dropping drops,
Or spill night out in brilliant vanishings,
Whirlpools of darkness in whirlwinds of light . . .   55
The miff-maff-muff of water, the vocables
Of the wind, the glassily-sparkling particles
Of the mind—They would soon climb down the side of
    the ship.
They would march single file, with electric lamps, alert
For a tidal undulation underneath.   60

                                        1950

———

53   *Arcturus:* an orange star, sixth brightest in the sky, situated between the thighs of Boötes

Wallace Stevens was widely admired by his fellow poets, but their admiration was in some ways very hard to articulate. Part of this difficulty stems from the restraint and subtlety of Stevens's work. Horace Gregory, reviewing Harmonium, *once said that "the expression of the face is indicated in the lifting of an eyebrow." Among the clearest expressions of where this subtlety leaves us are Marianne Moore's and Randall Jarrell's.*

"The difference between the grand and the grandiose": Marianne Moore

The poet commits himself to that one integrity: antipathy to falsity. But "the imagination always makes use of the familiar," Mr. Stevens says, "to produce the unfamiliar," and "a deliberately commonplace costume" clothes themes far from commonplace, as we see in this metaphor of the shawl ("Final Soliloquy of the Interior Paramour"):

> Light the first light of evening, as in a room
> In which we rest and, for small reason, think
> The world imagined is the ultimate good.
>
> . . . .
>
> Within a single thing, a single shawl
> Wrapped tightly round us, since we are poor, a warmth,
> A light, a power, the miraculous influence.

A single shawl—Imagination's—is wrapped tightly round us since we are poor. Wallace Stevens embeds his secrets, inventing disguises which assure him freedom to speak out; and poverty is one of his favorites. In "Page from a Tale" (*The Auroras of Autumn*), Hans is poor and chilly—Hans "by his drift-fire" near "a steamer . . . foundered in the ice," warmed by fires of his imagining, "a beggar in a bad time" "opening the door of his mind" to the aurora borealis, "to flames." . . .

For poverty, poetry substitutes a spiritual happiness in which the intangible is more real than the visible and earth is innocent, "not a guilty dream" but a "holiness, in which we are awake as peacefully as if we lay asleep." One sees "new stars . . . a foot across" come out; . . .

Amid grandeurs of this sort, surrounded by the imagination's "mercies," one knows the difference between the grand and the grandiose. With a metaphysician, an ogre, a grammarian, a nomad, an eel, as disguise for intensity, one is safe from "harangue," "ado," and the ambitious page.

"He is the poet of well-being": Randall Jarrell

At the bottom of Stevens's poetry there is wonder and delight, the child's or animal's or savage's—man's—joy in his own existence, and thankfulness for it. He is the poet of well-being: "One might have thought of sight, but who could think/Of what it sees, for all the ill it sees?" This sigh of awe, of wondering pleasure, is underneath all these poems that show us the "celestial possible," everything that has not yet been transformed into the infernal impossibilities of our everyday earth. Stevens is full of the natural or Aristotelian virtues; he is, in the terms of Hopkins's poem, all windhover and no Jesuit. There is about him, under the translucent glazes, a Dutch solidity and weight; he sits surrounded by all the good things of this earth, with rosy cheeks and fresh clear blue eyes, eyes not going out to you but shining in their place, like fixed stars—or else he moves off, like the bishop in his poem, "globed in today and tomorrow." If he were an animal he would be, without a doubt, that rational, magnanimous, voluminous animal, the elephant.

WILLIAM CARLOS WILLIAMS
(1883–1963)

THE RED WHEELBARROW

so much depends
upon

a red wheel
barrow

glazed with rain   5
water

beside the white
chickens.

1923

QUEEN-ANN'S-LACE

Her body is not so white as
anemone petals nor so smooth—nor

so remote a thing. It is a field
of the wild carrot taking
the field by force; the grass   5
does not raise above it.
Here is no question of whiteness,
white as can be, with a purple mole
at the center of each flower.
Each flower is a hand's span   10
of her whiteness. Wherever
his hand has lain there is
a tiny purple blemish. Each part
is a blossom under his touch
to which the fibers of her being   15
stem one by one, each to its end,
until the whole field is a
white desire, empty, a single stem,
a cluster, flower by flower,
a pious wish to whiteness gone over—   20
or nothing.

1925

THE BOTTICELLIAN TREES

The alphabet of
the trees

is fading in the
song of the leaves

the crossing   5
bars of the thin

letters that spelled
winter

and the cold
have been illumined   10

with
pointed green

by the rain and sun—
The strict simple

principles of   15
straight branches

are being modified
by pinched-out

ifs of color, devout
conditions

the smiles of love—
. . . . . .

until the stript
sentences

move as a woman's
limbs under cloth   25

and praise from secrecy
quick with desire

love's ascendancy
in summer—   30

In summer the song
sings itself

above the muffled words—

1931

THIS IS JUST TO SAY

I have eaten
the plums
that were in
the icebox

and which   5
you were probably
saving
for breakfast

Forgive me
they were delicious   10
so sweet
and so cold

1934

TO A POOR OLD WOMAN

munching a plum on
the street a paper bag
of them in her hand

They taste good to her
They taste good   5

to her. They taste
good to her

You can see it by
the way she gives herself
to the one half   10
sucked out in her hand

Comforted
a solace of ripe plums
seeming to fill the air
They taste good to her   15

1938

YOUNG WOMAN AT A WINDOW

She sits with
tears on

her cheek
her cheek on

her hand   5
the child

in her lap
his nose

pressed
to the glass   10

1951

THE YELLOW FLOWER

What shall I say, because talk I must?
        That I have found a cure
            for the sick?

I have found no cure
        for the sick   5
                but this crooked flower
which only to look upon
        all men
                are cured. This
is that flower   10
        for which all men
                sing secretly their hymns
of praise. This

is that sacred
       flower!   15

Can this be so?
     A flower so crooked
         and obscure? It is
a mustard flower,
     and not a mustard flower,   20
         a single spray
topping the deformed stem
     of fleshy leaves
         in this freezing weather
under glass.   25

An ungainly flower and
     an unnatural one,
         in this climate; what
can be the reason
     that it has picked me out   30
         to hold me, openmouthed,
rooted before this window
     in the cold,
         my will
drained from me   35
     so that I have only eyes
         for these yellow,
twisted petals   .   ?

That the sight,
     though strange to me,   40
         must be a common one,
is clear: there are such flowers
     with such leaves
         native to some climate
which they can call   45
     their own.

But why the torture
     and the escape through
         the flower? It is
as if Michelangelo   50
     had conceived the subject
         of his *Slaves* from this
—or might have done so.
     And did he not make
         the marble bloom? I   55
am sad
     as he was sad
         in his heroic mood.

But also
    I have eyes   60
        that are made to see and if
they see ruin for myself
    and all that I hold
        dear, they see
also   65
    through the eyes
        and through the lips
and tongue the power
    to free myself
        and speak of it, as   70
Michelangelo through his hands
    had the same, if greater,
        power.

Which leaves, to account for,
    the tortured bodies   75
        of
the slaves themselves
    and
        the tortured body of my flower
which is not a mustard flower at all   80
    but some unrecognized
        and unearthly flower
for me to naturalize
    and acclimate
        and choose it for my own.   85

1954

William Carlos Williams's influence on contemporary American poetry has been enormous, not only because his poems were so widely admired but because his attitude toward poetry drew to him followers tired of poetry in the European tradition. This attitude shows in the following quotations drawn from various interviews.

"Speaking straight ahead about what concerned us": William Carlos Williams

"Forcing twentieth-century America into a sonnet—gosh, how I hate sonnets—is like putting a crab into a square box. You've got to cut his legs off to make him fit. When you get through, you don't have a crab any more."

William Carlos Williams   **943**

* * * *

We were speaking straight ahead about what concerned us, and if I could have overheard what I was saying then, that would have given me a hint of how to phrase myself, to say what I had to say. Not after the establishment, but speaking straight ahead. I would gladly have traded what I have tried to say, for what came off my tongue, naturally. . . . I couldn't speak like the academy. It had to be modified by the conversation about me. As Marianne Moore used to say, a language dogs and cats could understand. So I think she agrees with me fundamentally. Not the speech of English country people, which would have something artificial about it; not that, but language modified by *our* environment; the American environment.

* * * *

The commonest situations in the world have the very essence of poetry if looked at correctly. If I take a dirty old woman in the street, it is not necessary to put her in the situation of a princess. All poets have a tendency to dress up an ordinary person, as Yeats does. It has to be a special treatment to be poetic, and I don't acknowledge this at all. I'd rather look at an old woman paring her nails as the essence of the "anti-poetic."

* * * *

I had a violent feeling that Eliot had betrayed what I believed in. He was looking backward; I was looking forward. He was a conformist, with wit, learning which I did not possess. He knew French, Latin, Arabic, God knows what. I was interested in that. But I felt he had rejected America and I refused to be rejected and so my reaction was violent. I realized the responsibility I must accept. I knew he would influence all subsequent American poets and take them out of my sphere. I had envisaged a new form of poetic composition, a form for the future. It was a shock to me that he was so tremendously successful; my contemporaries flocked to him— away from what I wanted. It forced me to be successful.

Not every poet is convinced, however, that Williams's influence has been benign. Robert Bly speaks for several others when he questions some of Williams's assumptions about what poetry should do.

"General remarks mixed with bits of glass and paper bags": Robert Bly

William Carlos Williams's work shows a similar attachment to objects. "No ideas but in things!" he said. His poems show great emotional life mingled with the drive of the intelligence to deal with outward things—but no inward life, if by inward life we mean an interest in spiritual development. Williams was a noble man, of all the poets in his generation the warmest and most human. Still, his ideas contained something destructive: there is in them a drive toward the extinction of personality. Williams's "No ideas but

944   *Poetry*

in things!" is a crippling program. Besides the ideas in things there are ideas in images and in feelings. True, bits of broken glass are preferable for poetry to fuzzy generalities such as virtue or patriotism. But images like Lorca's "black horses and dark people are riding over the deep roads of the guitar" also contain ideas and give birth to ideas. Williams asked poetry to confine itself to wheelbarrows, bottlecaps, weeds—with the artist "limited to the range of his contact with the objective world." Keeping close to the surface becomes an obsession. The effect of Williams's thought, therefore, was to narrow the language of poetry—to narrow it to general remarks mixed with bits of glass and paper bags, with what Pound called "natural objects." Williams says, "The good poetry is where the vividness comes up true like in prose but better. That's poetry."

> *BETWEEN WALLS*
> The back wings
> of the
>
> hospital where
> nothing
>
> will grow lie
> cinders
>
> in which shine
> the broken
>
> pieces of a green
> bottle

In that Williams poem the personality and the imagination are merely two among many guests. The imagination has to exist as best it can in a poem crowded with objects. In the bare poems of some of Williams's followers the personality of the poet is diffused among lampposts and matchfolders, and vanishes. The poet appears in the poem only as a disembodied anger or an immovable eye.

MARIANNE MOORE

(1887–1972)

POETRY

I, too, dislike it: there are things that are important
      beyond all this fiddle.
  Reading it, however, with a perfect contempt for it,
      one discovers in

it after all, a place for the genuine.   5
    Hands that can grasp, eyes
    that can dilate, hair that can rise
        if it must, these things are important not
            because a

high-sounding interpretation can be put upon them
            but because they are   10
useful. When they become so derivative as to
            become unintelligible,
    the same thing may be said for all of us, that we
        do not admire what
        we cannot understand: the bat   15
            holding on upside down or in quest of something
                to

eat, elephants pushing, a wild horse taking a roll, a
        tireless wolf under a tree, the immovable critic
        twitching his skin like a horse that feels a flea,
        the base-
ball fan, the statistician—   20
    nor is it valid
        to discriminate against 'business documents and

school-books'; all these phenomena are important.
        One must make a distinction
    however: when dragged into prominence by half
            poets, the result is not poetry,   25
    nor till the poets among us can be
        'literalists of
        the imagination'—above
            insolence and triviality and can present   30

for inspection, imaginary gardens with real toads in
            them, shall we have
    it. In the meantime, if you demand on the one hand,
    the raw material of poetry in
        all its rawness and   35
        that which is on the other hand
            genuine, then you are interested in poetry.

                                        1921

SILENCE

My father used to say,
"Superior people never make long visits,
have to be shown Longfellow's grave
or the glass flowers at Harvard.

Self-reliant like the cat—   5
that takes its prey to privacy,
the mouse's limp tail hanging like a shoelace from its
    mouth—
they sometimes enjoy solitude,
and can be robbed of speech
by speech which has delighted them.   10
The deepest feeling always shows itself in silence;
not in silence, but restraint."
Nor was he insincere in saying, "Make my house your
    inn."
Inns are not residences.

                                                    1921

THE FISH

wade
through black jade.
    Of the crow-blue mussel shells, one keeps
    adjusting the ash heaps;
        opening and shutting itself like   5

an
injured fan.
    The barnacles which encrust the side
    of the wave, cannot hide
        there for the submerged shafts of the   10

sun,
split like spun
    glass, move themselves with spotlight swiftness
into the crevices—
    in and out, illuminating   15

the
turquoise sea
    of bodies. The water drives a wedge
    of iron through the iron edge
        of the cliff; whereupon the stars,   20

pink
rice-grains, ink-
    bespattered jellyfish, crabs like green
    lilies, and submarine
        toadstools, slide each on the other.   25

All
external
    marks of abuse are present on this

                                        Marianne Moore   947

      defiant edifice—
         all the physical features of   30

ac-
cident—lack
   of cornice, dynamite grooves, burns, and
      hatchet strokes, these things stand
         out on it; the chasm side is   35

dead.
Repeated
   evidence has proved that it can live
   on what can not revive
      its youth. The sea grows old in it.   40

                                                    1921

PETER

   Strong and slippery,
built for the midnight grass-party
confronted by four cats, he sleeps his time away—
the detached first claw on the foreleg corresponding
to the thumb, retracted to its tip; the small tuft of
      fronds   5
or katydid-legs above each eye numbering all units
in each group; the shadbones regularly set about the
      mouth
to droop or rise in unison like porcupine-quills.
He lets himself be flattened out by gravity,
as seaweed is tamed and weakened by the sun,   10
compelled when extended, to lie stationary.
Sleep is the result of his delusion that one must
do as well as one can for oneself,
sleep—epitome of what is to him the end of life.
Demonstrate on him how the lady placed a forked stick   15
on the innocuous neck-sides of the dangerous southern
      snake.
One need not try to stir him up; his prune-shaped head
and alligator-eyes are not party to the joke.
Lifted and handled, he may be dangled like an eel
or set up on the forearm like a mouse;   20
his eyes bisected by pupils of a pin's width,
are flickeringly exhibited, then covered up.
May be? I should have said might have been;
when he has been got the better of in a dream—
as in a fight with nature or with cats, we all know it.   25
Profound sleep is not with him a fixed illusion.

Springing about with froglike accuracy, with jerky cries
when taken in hand, he is himself again;
to sit caged by the rungs of a domestic chair
would be unprofitable—human. What is the good of
    hypocrisy?   30
it is permissible to choose one's employment,
to abandon the nail, or roly-poly,
when it shows signs of being no longer a pleasure,
to score the nearby magazine with a double line of
    strokes.
He can talk but insolently says nothing. What of it?   35
 When one is frank, one's very presence is a
    compliment.
It is clear that he can see the virtue of naturalness,
that he does not regard the published fact as a
    surrender.
As for the disposition invariably to affront,
an animal with claws should have an opportunity to use
    them.   40
The eel-like extension of trunk into tail is not an
    accident.
To leap, to lengthen out, divide the air, to purloin, to
    pursue.
To tell the hen: fly over the fence, go in the wrong way
in your perturbation—this is life;
to do less would be nothing but dishonesty.   45

                                                    1935

FOUR QUARTZ CRYSTAL CLOCKS

There are four vibrators, the world's exactest clocks;
    and these quartz timepieces that tell
time intervals to other clocks,
    these worksless clocks work well;
independently the same, kept in   5
    the 41 Bell
        Laboratory time

vault. Checked by a comparator with Arlington,
    they punctualize the "radio,
cinéma," and "presse"—a group the   10
    Giraudoux truth-bureau

"*Four Quartz Crystal Clocks*": 11 *Jean Giraudoux* (1882–1944); a French novelist and
dramatist

of hoped-for accuracy has termed
    "instruments of truth." We know—
        as Jean Giraudoux says

certain Arabs have not heard—that Napoleon   15
    is dead; that a quartz prism when
the temperature changes, feels
    the change and that the then
electrified alternate edges
        oppositely charged, threaten   20
            careful timing; so that

this water-clear crystal as the Greeks used to say,
    this "clear ice" must be kept at the
same coolness. Repetition, with
    the scientist, should be   25
synonymous with accuracy.
    The lemur-student can see
        that an aye-aye is not

an angwan-tibo, potto, or loris. The sea-
    side burden should not embarrass   30
the bell-boy with the buoy-ball
    endeavoring to pass
hotel patronesses; nor could a
    practiced ear confuse the glass
        eyes for taxidermists   35

with eyeglasses from the optometrist. And as
    MEridian-seven one-two
one-two gives, each fifteenth second
    in the same voice, the new
data—"The time will be" so and so   40
    you realize that "when you
        hear the signal," you'll be

hearing Jupiter or jour pater, the day god—
    the salvaged son of Father Time—
telling the cannibal Chronos   45
    (eater of his proxime
newborn progeny) that punctuality
    is not a crime.

1941

---

28 *aye-aye:* a lemur   29 *angwan-tibo:* a small African primate   *potto:* a small African
primate   *loris:* a small Asian primate   43 *jour pater:* "day father"; Jupiter is the god of day
and son of Time   45 *Chronos:* devoured all his children except Jupiter (air), Neptune (water),
and Pluto (the grave), which Time cannot consume

ELEPHANTS

Uplifted and waved till immobilized
wistaria-like, the opposing opposed
mouse-gray twined proboscises' trunk formed by two
trunks, fights itself to a spiraled inter-nosed

deadlock of dyke-enforced massiveness. It's a   5
knock-down drag-out fight that asks no quarter? Just
a pastime, as when the trunk rains on itself
the pool siphoned up; or when—since each must

provide his forty-pound bough dinner—he broke
the leafy branches. These templars of the Tooth,   10
these matched intensities, take master care of
master tools. One, sleeping with the calm of youth,

at full length in the half-dry sun-flecked stream-bed,
rests his hunting-horn-curled trunk on shallowed
    stone.
The sloping hollow of the sleeper's body   15
cradles the gently breathing eminence's prone

mahout, asleep like a lifeless six-foot
frog, so feather light the elephant's stiff
ear's unconscious of the crossed feet's weight. And the
defenseless human thing sleeps as sound as if   20

incised with hard wrinkles, embossed with wide ears,
invincibly tusked, made safe by magic hairs!
As if, as if, it is all ifs; we are at
much unease. But magic's masterpiece is theirs—

Houdini's serenity quelling his fears.   25
Elephant-ear-witnesses-to-be of hymns
and glorias, these ministrants all gray or
gray with white on legs or trunk, are a pilgrims'

pattern of revery not reverence—a
religious procession without any priests,   30
the centuries-old carefullest unrehearsed
play. Blessed by Buddha's Tooth, the obedient beasts

themselves as toothed temples blessing the street, see
the white elephant carry the cushion that

"Elephants": 17 *mahout:* the elephant keeper and driver   27 *glorias:* hymns of praise
32 *Buddha's Tooth:* Ceylonese elephants guard the tooth-relic of the Buddha, "the Enlightened
one," in Kandy, a mountain city

carries the casket that carries the Tooth.   35
Amenable to what, matched with him, are gnat

trustees, he does not step on them as the white-
canopied blue-cushioned Tooth is augustly
and slowly returned to the shrine. Though white is
the color of worship and of mourning, he   40

is not here to worship and he is too wise
to mourn—a life prisoner but reconciled.
With trunk tucked up compactly—the elephant's
sign of defeat—he resisted, but is the child

of reason now. His straight trunk seems to say: when   45
what we hoped for came to nothing, we revived.
As loss could not ever alter Socrates'
tranquillity, equanimity's contrived

by the elephant. With the Socrates of
animals as with Sophocles the Bee, on whose   50
tombstone a hive was incised, sweetness tinctures
his gravity. His held-up foreleg for use

as a stair, to be climbed or descended with
the aid of his ear, expounds the brotherhood
of creatures to man the encroacher, by the   55
small word with the dot, meaning know—the verb bŭd.

These knowers "arouse the feeling that they are
allied to man" and can change roles with their trustees.
Hardship makes the soldier; then teachableness
makes him the philosopher—as Socrates,   60

prudently testing the suspicious thing, knew
the wisest is he who's not sure that he knows.
Who rides on a tiger can never dismount;
asleep on an elephant, that is repose.

                                                    1944

*In Marianne Moore's poems, animals and things are viewed with a clarity
that some readers have found too precise, too cold, too clinical. Robert Bly,
for instance, has complained that the animals in Moore's poems are always*

---

47 *Socrates:* (470–399 B.C.); one of the earliest and greatest of Greek philosophers, known as
a seeker of virtue and tranquillity   56 *bŭd:* the Sanskrit verb for "knowing"

really trophies of animals, suitable for display in a living room. The most enthusiastic readers of Marianne Moore's poetry, however, respond to the concentration and affection she lavishes on the things of the world.

"Nothing loses its identity because of the composition": William Carlos Williams

There are two elements essential to Miss Moore's scheme of composition, the hard and unaffected concept of the apple itself as an idea, then its edge-to-edge contact with the things which surround it—the coil of a snake, leaves at various depths, or as it may be; and without connectives unless it be poetry, the inevitable connective, if you will. . . .
. . .

There must be edges. This casts some light I think on the simplicity of design in much of Miss Moore's work. There must be recognizable edges against the ground which cannot, as she might desire it, be left entirely white. Prose would be all black, a complete black painted or etched over, but solid.

There is almost no overlaying at all. The effect is of every object sufficiently uncovered to be easily recognizable. This simplicity, with the light coming through from between the perfectly plain masses, is however extremely bewildering to one who has been accustomed to look upon the usual "poem," the commonplace opaque board covered with vain curlicues. They forget, those who would read Miss Moore aright, that white circular discs grouped closely edge to edge upon a dark table make black six-pointed stars.

The "useful result" is an accuracy to which this simplicity of design greatly adds. The effect is for the effect to remain "true"; nothing loses its identity because of the composition, but the parts in their assembly remain quite as "natural" as before they were gathered. There is no "sentiment"; the softening effect of word upon word is nil; everything is in the style. To make this ten times evident is Miss Moore's constant care. There seems to be almost too great a wish to be transparent and it is here if anywhere that Miss Moore's later work will show a change, I think.

"Four coarse, grayish hairs in a piece of Kleenex": Elizabeth Bishop

I got to Madison Square Garden very early—we had settled on the hour because we wanted to see the animals before the show began—but Marianne was there ahead of me. She was loaded down: two blue cloth bags, one on each arm, and two huge brown paper bags, full of something. I was given one of these. They contained, she told me, stale brown bread for the elephants, because stale brown bread was one of the things they liked best to eat. (I later suspected that they might like stale white bread just as much but that Marianne had been thinking of their health.) As we went in and down to the lower level, where we could hear (and smell) the animals, she told me her preliminary plan for the circus. Her brother, Warner, had given her an elephant-hair bracelet, of which she was very fond, two or three strands of black hairs held together with gold clasps. One of the elephant hairs had fallen out and been lost. As I probably knew, elephant hairs grow only on the tops of the heads of very young elephants. In her bag, Marianne had a pair of strong nail scissors. I was to divert the adult elephants with the bread, and, if we were lucky, the guards wouldn't observe her at the end of the line where the babies were, and she could take out her scissors and snip a few hairs from a baby's head, to repair her bracelet.

She was quite right; the elephants adored stale brown bread and started trumpeting and pushing up against each other to get it. I stayed at one end of the line, putting slices of bread into the trunks of the older elephants, and Miss Moore went rapidly down to the other end, where the babies were. The large elephants were making such a to-do that a keeper did come up my way, and out of the corner of my eye I saw Miss Moore leaning forward over the rope on tiptoe, scissors in hand. Elephant hairs are tough; I thought she would never finish her hair-cutting. But she did, and triumphantly we handed out the rest of the bread and set off to see the other animals. She opened her bag and showed me three or four coarse, grayish hairs in a piece of Kleenex.

T. S. ELIOT

(1888–1965)

THE LOVE SONG OF J. ALFRED PRUFROCK

S'io credesse che mia risposta fosse
A persona che mai tornasse al mondo,
Questa fiamma staria senza piu scosse.
Ma perciocche giammai di questo fondo

"The Love Song of J. Alfred Prufrock": *S'io credesse . . . rispondo:* from Dante's *Inferno,* Canto 27: 61–66; Guido de Montefeltro, enclosed in a flame, tells Dante of the shame of his evil life: "If I thought that my reply would be to one who would ever return to the world [and tell others], this flame would move no more [with his speech]; but since no one has ever returned alive from such depth, if what I hear is true, I will answer without fear of being further disgraced."

Non torno vivo alcun, s'i'odo il vero,
Senza tema d'infamia ti rispondo.

Let us go then, you and I,
When the evening is spread out against the sky
Like a patient etherized upon a table;
Let us go, through certain half-deserted streets,
The muttering retreats   5
Of restless nights in one-night cheap hotels
And sawdust restaurants with oyster-shells:
Streets that follow like a tedious argument
Of insidious intent
To lead you to an overwhelming question . . .   10
Oh, do not ask, "What is it?"
Let us go and make our visit.

In the room the women come and go
Talking of Michelangelo.

The yellow fog that rubs its back upon the
     window-panes   15
The yellow smoke that rubs its muzzle on the
     window-panes
Licked its tongue into the corners of the evening,
Lingered upon the pools that stand in drains,
Let fall upon its back the soot that falls from chimneys,
Slipped by the terrace, made a sudden leap,   20
And seeing that it was a soft October night,
Curled once about the house, and fell asleep.

And indeed there will be time
For the yellow smoke that slides along the street,
Rubbing its back upon the window-panes;   25
There will be time, there will be time
To prepare a face to meet the faces that you meet;
There will be time to murder and create,
And time for all the works and days of hands
That lift and drop a question on your plate;   30
Time for you and time for me,
And time yet for a hundred indecisions,
And for a hundred visions and revisions,
Before the taking of a toast and tea.

In the room the women come and go   35
Talking of Michelangelo.

_____

14 *Michelangelo:* the great sixteenth century painter and sculptor

T. S. Eliot   *955*

And indeed there will be time
To wonder, "Do I dare?" and, "Do I dare?"
Time to turn back and descend the stair,
With a bald spot in the middle of my hair—   40
[They will say: "How his hair is growing thin!"]
My morning coat, my collar mounting firmly to the
    chin,
My necktie rich and modest, but asserted by a simple
    pin—
[They will say: "But how his arms and legs are thin!"]
Do I dare   45
Disturb the universe?
In a minute there is time
For decisions and revisions which a minute will reverse.

For I have known them all already, known them all:
Have known the evenings, mornings, afternoons,   50
I have measured out my life with coffee spoons;
I know the voices dying with a dying fall
Beneath the music from a farther room.
    So how should I presume?

And I have known the eyes already, known them all—   55
The eyes that fix you in a formulated phrase,
And when I am formulated, sprawling on a pin,
When I am pinned and wriggling on the wall,
Then how should I begin
To spit out all the butt-ends of my days and ways?   60
    And how should I presume?

And I have known the arms already, known them all—
Arms that are braceleted and white and bare

[But in the lamplight, downed with light brown hair!]
Is it perfume from a dress   65
That makes me so digress?
Arms that lie along a table, or wrap about a shawl.
    And should I then presume?
    And how should I begin?

                .   .   .   .   .

Shall I say, I have gone at dusk through narrow streets   70
And watched the smoke that rises from the pipes
Of lonely men in shirt-sleeves, leaning out of windows?

    .   .   .

I should have been a pair of ragged claws
Scuttling across the floors of silent seas.

                .   .   .   .   .

And the afternoon, the evening, sleeps so peacefully!   75
Smoothed by long fingers,
Asleep . . . tired . . . or it malingers,
Stretched on the floor, here beside you and me.
Should I, after tea and cakes and ices,
Have the strength to force the moment to its crisis?   80
But though I have wept and fasted, wept and prayed,
Though I have seen my head [grown slightly bald]
   brought in upon a platter,
I am no prophet—and here's no great matter;
I have seen the moment of my greatness flicker,   85
And I have seen the eternal Footman hold my coat, and
   snicker,
And in short, I was afraid.

And would it have been worth it, after all,
After the cups, the marmalade, the tea,
Among the porcelain, among some talk of you and me,   90
Would it have been worth while,
To have bitten off the matter with a smile,
To have squeezed the universe into a ball
To roll it toward some overwhelming question,
To say: "I am Lazarus, come from the dead,   95
Come back to tell you all, I shall tell you all"—
If one, settling a pillow by her head,
   Should say· "That is not what I meant at all.
   That is not it, at all."

And would it have been worth it, after all,   100
Would it have been worth while,
After the sunsets and the dooryards and the sprinkled
   streets,
After the novels, after the teacups, after the skirts that
   trail along the floor—
And this, and so much more?—
It is impossible to say just what I mean!   105
But as if a magic lantern threw the nerves in patterns
   on a screen:
Would it have been worth while
If one, settling a pillow or throwing off a shawl,
And turning toward the window, should say:
   "That is not it at all,   110
   That is not what I meant, at all."

          ·   ·   ·   ·   ·

No! I am not Prince Hamlet, nor was meant to be;
Am an attendant lord, one that will do
To swell a progress, start a scene or two,

Advise the prince; no doubt, an easy tool,   115
Deferential, glad to be of use,
Politic, cautious, and meticulous;
Full of high sentence, but a bit obtuse;
At times, indeed, almost ridiculous—
Almost, at times, the Fool.   120

I grow old . . . I grow old . . .
I shall wear the bottoms of my trousers rolled.

Shall I part my hair behind? Do I dare to eat a peach?
I shall wear white flannel trousers, and walk upon the
    beach.
I have heard the mermaids singing, each to each.   125

I do not think that they will sing to me.

I have seen them riding seaward on the waves
Combing the white hair of the waves blown back
When the wind blows the water white and black.

We have lingered in the chambers of the sea   130
By sea-girls wreathed with seaweed red and brown
Till human voices wake us, and we drown.

                                    1915

LA FIGLIA CHE PIANGE

O quam te memorem virgo . . .

   Stand on the highest pavement of the stair—
Lean on a garden urn—
Weave, weave the sunlight in your hair—
Clasp your flowers to you with a pained surprise—
Fling them to the ground and turn   5
With a fugitive resentment in your eyes:
But weave, weave the sunlight in your hair.

   So I would have had him leave,
So I would have had her stand and grieve,
So he would have left   10
As the soul leaves the body torn and bruised,
As the mind deserts the body it has used.
I should find

"*La Figlia Che Piange*": *La Figlia Che Piange:* "the young girl weeping" (Italian)   *O quam . . .
virgo:* "Maiden, how shall I name thee?"; spoken by Aeneas when he encountered his mother,
Venus, in Virgil's *Aeneid* 1:327.

Some way incomparably light and deft,
Some way we both should understand,   15
Simple and faithless as a smile and shake of the hand.

    She turned away, but with the autumn weather
Compelled my imagination many days,
Many days and many hours:
Her hair over her arms and her arms full of flowers.   20
And I wonder how they should have been together!
I should have lost a gesture and a pose.
Sometimes these cogitations still amaze
The troubled midnight and the noon's repose.

1917

JOURNEY OF THE MAGI

'A cold coming we had of it,
Just the worst time of the year
For a journey, and such a long journey:
The ways deep and the weather sharp,
The very dead of winter.'   5
And the camels galled, sore-footed, refractory,
Lying down in the melting snow.
There were times we regretted
The summer palaces on slopes, the terraces,
And the silken girls bringing sherbet.   10
Then the camel men cursing and grumbling
And running away, and wanting their liquor and
    women,
And the night-fires going out, and the lack of shelters,
And the cities hostile and the towns unfriendly
And the villages dirty and charging high prices: 15
A hard time we had of it.
At the end we preferred to travel all night,
Sleeping in snatches,
With the voices singing in our ears, saying
That this was all folly.   20

Then at dawn we came down to a temperate valley,
Wet, below the snow line, smelling of vegetation;
With a running stream and a water-mill beating the
    darkness,

"Journey of the Magi": *Magi*: the Wise Men who visited Christ in Chapter 2 of Matthew   *[First 5 lines]* Eliot is quoting from Bishop Lancelot Andrewe's Christmas sermon of 1622.

And three trees on the low sky,
And an old white horse galloped away in the meadow.   25
Then we came to a tavern with vine-leaves over the
    lintel,
Six hands at an open door dicing for pieces of silver,
And feet kicking the empty wine-skins.
But there was no information, and so we continued
And arrived at evening, not a moment too soon   30
Finding the place; it was (you may say) satisfactory.

All this was a long time ago, I remember,
And I would do it again, but set down
This set down
This: were we led all that way for   35
Birth or Death? There was a Birth, certainly,
We had evidence and no doubt. I had seen birth and
    death,
But had thought they were different; this Birth was
Hard and bitter agony for us, like Death, our death.
We returned to our places, these Kingdoms,   40
But no longer at ease here, in the old dispensation,
With an alien people clutching their gods.
I should be glad of another death.

                                                    1927

ANIMULA

'Issues from the hand of God, the simple soul'
To a flat world of changing lights and noise,
To light, dark, dry or damp, chilly or warm;
Moving between the legs of tables and of chairs,
Rising or falling, grasping at kisses and toys,   5
Advancing boldly, sudden to take alarm,
Retreating to the corner of arm and knee,
Eager to be reassured, taking pleasure
In the fragrant brilliance of the Christmas tree,
Pleasure in the wind, the sunlight and the sea;   10
Studies the sunlit pattern on the floor
And running stags around a silver tray;
Confounds the actual and the fanciful,
Content with playing-cards and kings and queens,

"Animula": Animula: "a little soul" (Latin)   1 *Issues . . . soul:* taken from Dante's *Purgatorio*,
Canto 16: 85–93; in response to Dante's question about the origin of evil, Marco Lombardo
locates it in man, particularly in evil leaders

What the fairies do and what the servants say.   15
The heavy burden of the growing soul
Perplexes and offends more, day by day;
Week by week, offends and perplexes more
With the imperatives of 'is and seems'
And may and may not, desire and control.   20
The pain of living and the drug of dreams
Curl up the small soul in the window seat
Behind the *Encyclopedia Britannica.*
Issues from the hand of time the simple soul
Irresolute and selfish, misshapen, lame,   25
Unable to fare forward or retreat,
Fearing the warm reality, the offered good,
Denying the importunity of the blood,
Shadow of its own shadows, spectre in its own gloom,
Leaving disordered papers in a dusty room;   30
Living first in the silence after the viaticum.

    Pray for Guiterriez, avid of speed and power,
For Boudin, blown to pieces,
For this one who made a great fortune,
And that one who went in his own way.   35
Pray for Floret, by the boarhound slain between the
    yew trees,
Pray for us now and at the hour of our birth.

1929

THE HOLLOW MEN

Mistah Kurtz—he dead.

A penny for the Old Guy

1

We are the hollow men
We are the stuffed men
Leaning together
Headpiece filled with straw. Alas!
Our dried voices, when   5

---

32 *Guiterriez . . . Boudin . . . Floret:* Eliot claims all are "entirely imaginary"   *"The Hollow Men": Mistah Kurtz—he dead:* from Joseph Conrad's *The Heart of Darkness;* Kurtz is a "lost violent soul"   *A penny . . . Guy:* In the annual celebration of Guy Fawkes Day, children beg money for fireworks to set off in honor of the defeat of Fawkes's "gunpowder plot" against King James I

We whisper together
Are quiet and meaningless
As wind in dry grass
Or rats' feet over broken glass
In our dry cellar   10

    Shape without form, shade without color,
Paralysed force, gesture without motion;

    Those who have crossed
With direct eyes, to death's other Kingdom
Remember us—if at all—not as lost   15
Violent souls, but only
As the hollow men
The stuffed men.

2

Eyes I dare not meet in dreams
In death's dream kingdom   20
These do not appear:
There, the eyes are
Sunlight on a broken column
There, is a tree swinging
And voices are   25
In the wind's singing
More distant and more solemn
Than a fading star.

    Let me be no nearer
In death's dream kingdom   30
Let me also wear
Such deliberate disguises
Rat's coat, crowskin, crossed staves
In a field
Behaving as the wind behaves   35
No nearer—

    Not that final meeting
In the twilight kingdom

3

This is the dead land
This is cactus land   40
Here the stone images
Are raised, here they receive
The supplication of a dead man's hand
Under the twinkle of a fading star.

            Is it like this   45
In death's other kingdom
Waking alone
At the hour when we are
Trembling with tenderness
Lips that would kiss   50
Form prayers to broken stone.

                              4

The eyes are not here
There are no eyes here
In this valley of dying stars
In this hollow valley   55
This broken jaw of our lost kingdoms

      In this last of meeting places
We grope together
And avoid speech
Gathered on this beach of the tumid river   60

      Sightless, unless
The eyes reappear
As the perpetual star
Multifoliate rose
Of death's twilight kingdom   65
The hope only
Of empty men.

                              5

Here we go round the prickly pear
Prickly pear, prickly pear
Here we go round the prickly pear   70
At five o'clock in the morning.

      Between the idea
And the reality
Between the motion
And the act   75
Falls the shadow
      For Thine is the Kingdom.

      Between the conception
And the creation
Between the emotion   80
And the response
Falls the Shadow
      Life is very long.

Between the desire
And the spasm   85
Between the potency
And the existence
Between the essence
And the descent
Falls the Shadow.   90
        For Thine is the Kingdom.

    For Thine is
Life is
For Thine is the

    This is the way the world ends   95
This is the way the world ends
This is the way the world ends
Not with a bang but a whimper.

                                        1936

T. S. Eliot's emphasis on the separation of the poet's personality from the poem itself has caused considerable controversy. Some poets agree that their job is not to describe an emotion, but to create an "objective correlative" of the emotion. Poet and reader, experiencing the correlative, will have the emotion rise from it. Other poets find Eliot's methods too cold, too distanced.

"I could not endure the grey middle-tint": William Butler Yeats

---

Eliot has produced his great effect upon his generation because he has described men and women that get out of bed or into it from mere habit; in describing this life that has lost heart his own art seems grey, cold, dry. He is an Alexander Pope, working without apparent imagination, producing his effects by a rejection of all rhythms and metaphors used by the more popular romantics rather than by the discovery of his own, this rejection giving his work an unexaggerated plainness that has the effect of novelty. He has the rhythmical flatness of the *Essay on Man*—despite Miss Sitwell's advocacy I see Pope as Blake and Keats saw him—later, in *The Waste Land*, amid much that is moving in symbol and imagery there is much monotony of accent:

When lovely woman stoops to folly and
Paces about her room again, alone,
She smooths her hair with automatic hand,
And puts a record on the gramophone.

I was affected, as I am by these lines, when I saw for the first time a painting by Manet. I longed for the vivid colour and light of Rousseau and Courbet, I could not endure the grey middle-tint—and even to-day Manet gives me an incomplete pleasure; he had left the procession. Nor can I put the Eliot of these poems among those that descend from Shakespeare and the translators of the Bible. I think of him as satirist rather than poet. Once only does that early work speak in the great manner:

The host with someone indistinct
Converses at the door apart,
The nightingales are singing near
The Convent of the Sacred Heart,

And sang within the bloody wood
When Agamemnon cried aloud,
And let their liquid siftings fall
To stain the stiff dishonoured shroud.

Not until *The Hollow Men* and *Ash-Wednesday,* where he is helped by the short lines, and in the dramatic poems where his remarkable sense of actor, chanter, scene, sweeps him away, is there rhythmical animation.

"A continual self-sacrifice, a continual extinction of personality": T. S. Eliot

The progress of an artist is a continual self-sacrifice, a continual extinction of personality.

There remains to define this process of depersonalization and its relation to the sense of tradition. It is in this depersonalization that art may be said to approach the condition of science. I shall, therefore, invite you to consider, as a suggestive analogy, the action which takes place when a bit of finely filiated platinum is introduced into a chamber containing oxygen and sulphur dioxide. . . .

When the two gases . . . are mixed in the presence of a filament of platinum, they form sulphurous acid. This combination takes place only if the platinum is present; nevertheless the newly formed acid contains no trace of platinum, and the platinum itself is apparently unaffected; has remained inert, neutral, and unchanged. The mind of the poet is the shred of platinum. It may partly or exclusively operate upon the experience of the man himself; but, the more perfect the artist, the more completely separate in him will be the man who suffers and the mind which creates; the more perfectly will the mind digest and transmute the passions which are its material.

The experience, you will notice, the elements which enter the presence of the transforming catalyst, are of two kinds: emotions and feelings. The effect of a work of art upon the person who enjoys it is an experience different in kind from any experience not of art. It may be formed out of one emotion, or may be a combination of several; and various feelings, inhering for the writer in particular words or phrases or images, may be added to compose the final result. Or great poetry may be made without the direct use of any emotion whatever: composed out of feelings solely. . . .

The poet's mind is in fact a receptacle for seizing and storing up numberless feelings, phrases, images, which remain there until all the particles which can unite to form a new compound are present together.

If you compare several representative passages of the greatest poetry you see how great is the variety of types of combination, and also how completely any semi-ethical criterion of 'sublimity' misses the mark. For it is not the 'greatness', the intensity, of the emotions, the components, but the intensity of the artistic process, the pressure, so to speak, under which the fusion takes place, that counts.

EDNA ST. VINCENT MILLAY

(1892–1950)

RECUERDO

We were very tired, we were very merry—
We had gone back and forth all night on the ferry.
It was bare and bright, and smelled like a stable—
But we looked into a fire, we leaned across a table,
We lay on a hill-top underneath the moon;   5
And the whistles kept blowing, and the dawn came
    soon.

We were very tired, we were very merry—
We had gone back and forth all night on the ferry;
And you ate an apple, and I ate a pear,

———
"Recuerdo": Recuerdo: "reminiscence" (Spanish)

From a dozen of each we had bought somewhere;　　10
And the sky went wan, and the wind came cold,
And the sun rose dripping, a bucketful of gold.

We were very tired, we were very merry,
We had gone back and forth all night on the ferry.
We hailed, "Good morrow, mother!" to a shawl-
　　covered head,　　　　　　　　　　　　　15
And bought a morning paper, which neither of us read;
And she wept, "God bless you!" for the apples and
　　pears,
And we gave her all our money but our subway fares.

1920

SPRING

To what purpose, April, do you return again?
Beauty is not enough.
You can no longer quiet me with the redness
Of little leaves opening stickily.
I know what I know.　　　　　　　　　　　　5
The sun is hot on my neck as I observe
The spikes of the crocus.
The smell of the earth is good.
It is apparent that there is no death.
But what does that signify?　　　　　　　　　10
Not only under ground are the brains of men
Eaten by maggots.
Life in itself
Is nothing,
An empty cup, a flight of uncarpeted stairs.　　15
It is not enough that yearly, down this hill,
April
Comes like an idiot, babbling and strewing flowers.

1921

LOVE IS NOT ALL: IT IS NOT MEAT
NOR DRINK

Love is not all: it is not meat nor drink
Nor slumber nor a roof against the rain;
Nor yet a floating spar to men that sink
And rise and sink and rise and sink again;
Love can not fill the thickened lung with breath,　　5

Nor clean the blood, nor set the fractured bone;
Yet many a man is making friends with death
Even as I speak, for lack of love alone.
It well may be that in a difficult hour,
Pinned down by pain and moaning for release,   10
Or nagged by want past resolution's power,
I might be driven to sell your love for peace,
Or trade the memory of this night for food.
It well may be. I do not think I would.

1931

FROM A TRAIN WINDOW

Precious in the light of the early sun the Housatonic
Between its not unscalable mountains flows.
Precious in the January morning the shabby fur of the
    cat-tails by the stream.
The farmer driving his horse to the feed-store for a
    sack of cracked corn
Is not in haste; there is no whip in the socket.   5

Pleasant enough, gay even, by no means sad
Is the rickety graveyard on the hill. Those are not
    cypress trees
Perpendicular among the lurching slabs, but cedars
    from the neighbourhood,
Native to this rocky land, self-sown. Precious
In the early light, reassuring   10
Is the grave-scarred hillside.
As if after all, the earth might know what it is about.

1934

THE OAK-LEAVES

Yet in the end, defeated too, worn out and ready to fall,
Hangs from the drowsy tree with cramped and desper-
    ate stem above the ditch the last leaf of all.

There is something to be learned, I guess, from looking
    at the dead leaves under the living tree;
Something to be set to a lusty tune and learned and
    sung, it well might be;
Something to be learned—though I was ever a ten-
    o'clock scholar at this school—   5
Even perhaps by me.

But my heart goes out to the oak-leaves that are the last
    to sigh
"Enough," and loose their hold;
They have boasted to the nudging frost and to the
    two-and-thirty winds that they would never die,
Never even grow old.   10
(These are those russet leaves that cling
All winter, even into the spring,
To the dormant bough, in the wood knee-deep in snow
    the only coloured thing.)

1934

CHILDHOOD IS THE KINGDOM WHERE NOBODY DIES

Childhood is not from birth to a certain age and at a
    certain age
The child is grown, and puts away childish things.
Childhood is the kingdom where nobody dies.

Nobody that matters, that is. Distant relatives of
    course
Die, whom one never has seen or has seen for an hour,   5
And they gave one candy in a pink-and-green striped
    bag, or a jack-knife,
And went away, and cannot really be said to have lived
    at all.

And cats die. They lie on the floor and lash their tails,
And their reticent fur is suddenly all in motion
With fleas that one never knew were there,   10
Polished and brown, knowing all there is to know,
Trekking off into the living world.
You fetch a shoe-box, but it's much too small, because
    she won't curl up now:
So you find a bigger box, and bury her in the yard, and
    weep.   15

But you do not wake up a month from then, two
    months,
A year from then, two years, in the middle of the night
And weep, with your knuckles in your mouth, and say
    Oh, God! Oh, God!
Childhood is the kingdom where nobody dies that
    matters,—mothers and fathers don't die.

And if you have said, "For heaven's sake, must you
    always be kissing a person?"   20
Or, "I do wish to gracious you'd stop tapping on the
    window with your thimble!"
Tomorrow, or even the day after tomorrow if you're
    busy having fun,
Is plenty of time to say, "I'm sorry, mother."

To be grown up is to sit at the table with people who
    have died, who neither listen nor speak;
Who do not drink their tea, though they always said   25
Tea was such a comfort.

Run down into the cellar and bring up the last jar of
    raspberries; they are not tempted.
Flatter them, ask them what was it they said exactly
That time, to the bishop, or to the overseer, or to Mrs.
    Mason;   30
They are not taken in.
Shout at them, get red in the face, rise,
Drag them up out of their chairs by their stiff shoulders
    and shake them and yell at them;
They are not startled, they are not even embarrassed;
    they slide back into their chairs.

Your tea is cold now.   35
You drink it standing up,
And leave the house.

1934

MODERN DECLARATION

I, having loved ever since I was a child a few things,
    never having wavered
In these affections; never through shyness in the
    houses of the rich or in the presence of clergymen
    having denied these loves;   5
Never when worked upon by cynics like chiropractors
    having grunted or clicked a vertebra to the discredit
    of these loves;
Never when anxious to land a job having diminished
    them by a conniving smile; or when befuddled by
    drink
Jeered at them through heartache or lazily fondled the   10
 fingers of their alert enemies; declare

That I shall love you always.
No matter what party is in power;
No matter what temporarily expedient combination of
    allied interests wins the war;   15
Shall love you always.

1939

AN ANCIENT GESTURE

I thought, as I wiped my eyes on the corner of my
    apron:
Penelope did this too.
And more than once: you can't keep weaving all day
And undoing it all through the night;
Your arms get tired, and the back of your neck gets
    tight;   5
And along towards morning, when you think it will
    never be light,
And your husband has been gone, and you don't know
    where, for years,
Suddenly you burst into tears;
There is simply nothing else to do.   10

And I thought, as I wiped my eyes on the corner of my
    apron:
This is an ancient gesture, authentic, antique,
In the very best tradition, classic, Greek;
Ulysses did this too.
But only as a gesture,—a gesture which implied   15
To the assembled throng that he was much too moved
    to speak.
He learned it from Penelope . . .
Penelope, who really cried.

1954

Edna St. Vincent Millay's early poetry appealed to a wide audience in the
1920s, when women were emerging from traditional roles and asserting a
new independence of thought and action. Serious readers of her later poetry
seldom doubted her talent, but some wondered whether her themes matured
as she grew older. Louise Bogan, her contemporary, reviewed the poems in
Wine from These Grapes *(1934) with great enthusiasm, feeling that*

Millay had made "a successful passage from the emotions and point of view of a rebellious girl to that of a maturely contemplative woman." Reviewing Huntsman, What Quarry? *(1939), she was somewhat disappointed.*

"Is it not possible for a woman to come to terms with herself?": Louise Bogan

It is difficult to say what a woman poet should concern herself with as she grows older, because woman poets who have produced an impressively bulky body of work are few. But is there any reason to believe that a woman's spiritual fibre is less sturdy than a man's? Is it not possible for a woman to come to terms with herself, if not with the world; to withdraw more and more, as time goes on, her own personality from her productions; to stop childish fears of death and eschew charming rebellions against facts? Certainly some fragments of Sappho are more "mature" than others. And Christina Rossetti, who lived an anonymous life and somewhat resembled, according to the cruel wit of Max Beerbohm, "a pew-opener," explored regions which Miss Millay has not yet entered. And there is the case of Emily Dickinson.

Miss Millay has always fought, and is still fighting, injustice. She is still subject to moods of self-disgust as well as to moods of mutiny against mankind's infringements on its own human decency. Once or twice she contemplates a truce which "slackens the mind's allegiance to despair." And twice—in the poem just quoted and in the recessively titled "The Princess Recalls Her One Adventure"—she writes as beautiful lyrics as she has ever written. But what has happened to the kind of development announced in *Wine from These Grapes*, the most kindly disposed reader cannot say. If Miss Millay should give up for good the idea that "wisdom" and "peace" are stuffy concepts, perhaps that development might be renewed.

WILFRED OWEN

(1893–1918)

ANTHEM FOR DOOMED YOUTH

What passing-bells for these who die as cattle?
   Only the monstrous anger of the guns.
   Only the stuttering rifles' rapid rattle
Can patter out their hasty orisons.

No mockeries now for them; no prayers nor bells,   5
   Nor any voice of mourning save the choirs—
The shrill, demented choirs of wailing shells;
   And bugles calling for them from sad shires.

What candles may be held to speed them all?
   Not in the hands of boys, but in their eyes   10
Shall shine the holy glimmers of good-byes.
   The pallor of girls' brows shall be their pall;
Their flowers the tenderness of patient minds,
And each slow dusk a drawing-down of blinds.

1920

ARMS AND THE BOY

Let the boy try along this bayonet-blade
How cold steel is, and keen with hunger of blood;
Blue with all malice, like a madman's flash;
And thinly drawn with famishing for flesh.

Lend him to stroke these blind, blunt bullet-heads   5
Which long to nuzzle in the hearts of lads,
Or give him cartridges of fine zinc teeth,
Sharp with the sharpness of grief and death.

For his teeth seem for laughing round an apple
There lurk no claws behind his fingers supple;   10
And God will grow no talons at his heels,
Nor antlers through the thickness of his curls.

1920

DULCE ET DECORUM EST

Bent double, like old beggars under sacks,
Knock-kneed, coughing like hags, we crushed through
   sludge,
Till on the haunting flares we turned our backs
And towards our distant rest began to trudge.
Men marched asleep. Many had lost their boots   5
But limped on, blood-shod. All went lame; all blind;
Drunk with fatigue; deaf even to the hoots
Of tired, outstripped Five-Nines that dropped behind.

"Dulce et Decorum Est": 8 *Five-Nines:* 5.9 caliber shells

Gas! Gas! Quick, boys!—An ecstasy of fumbling,
Fitting the clumsy helmets just in time;   10
But someone still was yelling out and stumbling
And flound'ring like a man in fire or lime . . .
Dim, through the misty panes and thick green light,
As under a green sea, I saw him drowning.

In all my dreams, before my helpless sight,   15
He plunges at me, guttering, choking, drowning.

If in some smothering dreams you too could pace
Behind the wagon that we flung him in,
And watch the white eyes writhing in his face,
His hanging face, like a devil's sick of sin;   20
If you could hear, at every jolt, the blood
Come gargling from the froth-corrupted lungs,
Obscene as cancer, bitter as the cud
Of vile, incurable sores on innocent tongues,—
My friend, you would not tell with such high zest   25
To children ardent for some desperate glory,
The old Lie: Dulce et decorum est
Pro patria mori.

                                                    1920

DISABLED

He sat in a wheeled chair, waiting for dark,
And shivered in his ghastly suit of grey,
Legless, sewn short at elbow. Through the park
Voices of boys rang saddening like a hymn,
Voices of play and pleasure after day,   5
Till gathering sleep had mothered them from him.

About this time Town used to swing so gay
When glow-lamps budded in the light blue trees,
And girls glanced lovelier as the air grew dim,—
In the old times, before he threw away his knees.   10
Now he will never feel again how slim
Girls' waists are, or how warm their subtle hands;
All of them touch him like some queer disease.

There was an artist silly for his face,
For it was younger than his youth, last year.   15
Now, he is old; his back will never brace;
He's lost his color very far from here,

———————
27–28 *Dulce . . . mori:* "It is sweet and honorable to die for one's country" – Horace

Poured it down shell-holes till the veins ran dry,
And half his lifetime lapsed in the hot race,
And leap of purple spurted from his thigh.   20

One time he liked a blood-smear down his leg,
After the matches, carried shoulder-high
It was after football, when he'd drunk a peg.
He thought he'd better join.—He wonders why.
Someone had said he'd look a god in kilts,   25
That's why; and may be, too, to please his Meg;
Aye, that was it, to please the giddy jilts
He asked to join. He didn't have to beg;
Smiling they wrote his lie; aged nineteen years.
Germans he scarcely thought of; all their guilt,   30
And Austria's, did not move him. And no fears
Of Fear came yet. He thought of jeweled hilts
For daggers in plaid socks; of smart salutes;
And care of arms; and leave; and pay arrears;
Esprit de corps; and hints for young recruits.   35
And soon, he was drafted out with drums and cheers.

Some cheered him home, but not as crowds cheer
     Goal.
Only a solemn man who brought him fruits
Thanked him; and then inquired about his soul.
Now, he will spend a few sick years in Institutes,   40
And do what things the rules consider wise,
And take whatever pity they may dole.
Tonight he noticed how the women's eyes
Passed from him to the strong men that were whole.
How cold and late it is! Why don't they come   45
And put him into bed? Why don't they come?

1920

*The poet who writes about war has two great obstacles to overcome. First, a
subject so public may not produce poems that either writer or reader can feel
as personal statements. Second, the poet's theme is predictable: rarely (in
this century at least) will we find poems in praise of war, and it is difficult to
write a fresh poem deploring what has so often been deplored before. If we*

"*Disabled*": 23 *peg:* a shot of liquor   27 *jilts:* women who discard their lovers   37 *cheer
Goal:* that is, cheer for a goal in a soccer match

look at several war poems together, we get a sense of the different ways poets have overcome these obstacles.

Niccolò Degli Albizzi

(13th century)

PROLONGED SONNET
WHEN THE TROOPS
WERE RETURNING FROM MILAN

translated from the Italian by Dante Gabriel Rossetti

If you could see, fair brother, how dead beat
   The fellows look who come through Rome to-day,—
   Black-yellow smoke-dried visages,—you'd say
   They thought their haste at going all too fleet.
Their empty victual-wagons up the street   5
   Over the bridge dreadfully sound and sway;
   Their eyes, as hanged men's, turning the wrong way;
   And nothing on their backs, or heads, or feet.
One sees the ribs and all the skeletons
   Of their gaunt horses; and a sorry sight   10
   Are the torn saddles, crammed with straw and
      stones.
They are ashamed, and march throughout the night,
   Stumbling, for hunger, on their marrowbones;
   Like barrels rolling, jolting, in this plight.
   Their arms all gone, not even their swords are saved;   15
   And each as silent as a man being shaved.

ca. 1300

Walt Whitman

(1819–1892)

I SAW THE VISION OF ARMIES

I saw the vision of armies;
And I saw, as in noiseless dreams, hundreds of
   battle-flags;

Borne through the smoke of the battles, and pierc'd
   with missiles, I saw them,
And carried hither and yon through the smoke, and
   torn and bloody;

And at last but a few shreds of the flags left on the
   staffs, (and all in silence,)   5
And the staffs all splinter'd and broken.

I saw battle-corpses, myriads of them,
And the white skeletons of young men—I saw them;
I saw the debris and debris of all dead soldiers;
But I saw they were not as was thought;   10
They themselves were fully at rest—they suffer'd not;
The living remain'd and suffer'd—the mother suffer'd,
And the wife and the child, and the musing comrade
   suffer'd,
And the armies that remained suffer'd.

1865

Thomas Hardy

(1840–1928)

CHANNEL FIRING

That night your great guns, unawares,
Shook all our coffins as we lay,
And broke the chancel window-squares,
We thought it was the Judgment-day

And sat upright. While drearisome   5
Arose the howl of wakened hounds:
The mouse let fall the altar-crumb,
The worms drew back into the mounds,

The glebe cow drooled. Till God called, "No;
It's gunnery practice out at sea   10
Just as before you went below;
The world is as it used to be:

"All nations striving strong to make
Red war yet redder. Mad as hatters

"*Channel Firing*": 9 *glebe:* a small plot of land granted to a clergyman

They do no more for Christés sake   15
Than you who are helpless in such matters.

"That this is not the judgment-hour
For some of them's a blessed thing,
For if it were they'd have to scour
Hell's floor for so much threatening. . . .   20

"Ha, ha. It will be warmer when
I blow the trumpet (if indeed
I ever do; for you are men,
And rest eternal sorely need)."

So down we lay again. "I wonder,   25
Will the world ever saner be,"
Said one, "than when He sent us under
In our indifferent century!"

And many a skeleton shook his head.—
"Instead of preaching forty year,"   30
My neighbour Parson Thirdly said,
"I wish I had stuck to pipes and beer."

Again the guns disturbed the hour,
Roaring their readiness to avenge,
As far inland as Stourton Tower,   35
And Camelot, and starlit Stonehenge.

1914

Arthur Rimbaud

(1854–1891)

THE SLEEPER OF THE VALLEY

translated from the French by Robert Lowell

The swollen river sang through the green hole,
and madly hooked white tatters on the grass.

---

35 *Stourton Tower:* in the ninth century, King Alfred's Tower   36 *Camelot:* the legendary site of King Arthur's court   *Stonehenge:* Hardy associated this prehistoric circle of stones with legendary prophets and sorcerors, the Druids

Light escaladed the hot hills. The whole
valley bubbled with sunbeams like a beer-glass.

The conscript was open-mouthed; his bare head   5
and neck swam in the bluish water cress.
He slept. The mid-day soothed his heaviness,
sunlight was raining into his green bed,

and baked the bruises from his body, rolled
as a sick child might hug itself asleep . . .   10
Oh Nature, rock him warmly, he is cold.

The flowers no longer make his hot eyes weep.
The river sucks his hair. His blue eye rolls.
He sleeps. In his right side are two red holes.

1870, trans. 1961

Joy Davidman

(1915–1960)

SNOW IN MADRID

Softly, so casual,
Lovely, so light, so light,
The cruel sky lets fall
Something one does not fight.

How tenderly to crown   5
The brutal year
The clouds send something down
That one need not fear.

Men before perishing
See with unwounded eye   10
For once a gentle thing
Fall from the sky.

1938

"*Snow in Madrid*": *Madrid:* the Nationalist forces in the Spanish Civil War bombed Madrid in
1937.

Anthony Hecht

(b. 1923)

"MORE LIGHT! MORE LIGHT!"

for Heinrich Blücher and Hannah Arendt

Composed in the Tower before his execution
These moving verses, and being brought at that time
Painfully to the stake, submitted, declaring thus:
"I implore my God to witness that I have made no
  crime."

Nor was he forsaken of courage, but the death was
  horrible,   5
The sack of gunpowder failing to ignite.
His legs were blistered sticks on which the black sap
Bubbled and burst as he howled for the Kindly Light.

And that was but one, and by no means one of the
  worst;
Permitted at least his pitiful dignity;   10
And such as were by, made prayers in the name of
  Christ,
That shall judge all men, for his soul's tranquillity.

We move now to outside a German wood.
Three men are there commanded to dig a hole
In which the two Jews are ordered to lie down   15
And be buried alive by the third, who is a Pole.

Not light from the shrine at Weimar beyond the hill
Nor light from heaven appeared. But he did refuse.
A Luger settled back deeply in its glove.
He was ordered to change places with the Jews.   20

Much casual death had drained away their souls.
The thick dirt mounted toward the quivering chin.

"More Light! More Light!": *More light:* The last words spoken by the German poet Goethe
before he died   *Heinrich Blucher and Hannah Arendt:* German husband and wife who
emigrated to the United States in 1941; she is known as the author of several books on
totalitarianism.   1 *Tower:* Tower of London   8 *Kindly Light:* "Lead, Kindly Light" is a hymn
written by John Henry Newman in 1833.   17 *Weimar:* the setting of the poem is Buchen-
wald, a Nazi concentration camp north of Weimar; Goethe spent most of his life in Weimar,
which is now the site of the Goethe National Museum.   19 *Luger:* a German automatic pistol

When only the head was exposed the order came
To dig him out again and to get back in.

No light, no light in the blue Polish eye.   25
When he finished a riding boot packed down the earth.
The Luger hovered lightly in its glove.
He was shot in the belly and in three hours bled to
   death.

1961

Denise Levertov

(b. 1923)

LIFE AT WAR

The disasters numb within us
caught in the chest, rolling
in the brain like pebbles. The feeling
resembles lumps of raw dough

weighing down a child's stomach on baking day.   5
Or Rilke said it, 'My heart . . .
Could I say of it, it overflows
with bitterness . . . but no, as though

its contents were simply balled into
formless lumps, thus   10
do I carry it about.'
The same war

continues.
We have breathed the grits of it in, all our lives,
our lungs are pocked with it,   15
the mucous membrane of our dreams
coated with it, the imagination
filmed over with the gray filth of it:

the knowledge that humankind,

delicate Man, whose flesh   20
responds to a caress, whose eyes
are flowers that perceive the stars,

whose music excels the music of birds,
whose laughter matches the laughter of dogs,
whose understanding manifests designs   25
fairer than the spider's most intricate web,

still turns without surprise, with mere regret
to the scheduled breaking open of breasts whose milk
runs out over the entrails of still-alive babies,
transformation of witnessing eyes to pulp-fragments,   30
implosion of skinned penises into carcass-gulleys.

We are the humans, men who can make;
whose language imagines *mercy,*
lovingkindness; we have believed one another
mirrored forms of a God we felt as good—   35

who do these acts, who convince ourselves
it is necessary; these acts are done
to our own flesh; burned human flesh
is smelling in Viet Nam as I write.

Yes, this is the knowledge that jostles for space   40
in our bodies along with all we
go on knowing of joy, of love;

our nerve filaments twitch with its presence
day and night,
nothing we say has not the husky phlegm of it in the
    saying,   45
nothing we do has the quickness, the sureness,
the deep intelligence living at peace would have.

                                        1965

E. E. CUMMINGS

(1894–1962)

All in green went my love riding

All in green went my love riding
on a great horse of gold
into the silver dawn.

four lean hounds crouched low and smiling
the merry deer ran before.   5

Fleeter be they than dappled dreams
the swift sweet deer
the red rare deer.

Four red roebuck at a white water
the cruel bugle sang before.   10

Horn at hip went my love riding
riding the echo down
into the silver dawn.

four lean hounds crouched low and smiling
the level meadows ran before.   15

Softer be they than slippered sleep
the lean lithe deer
the fleet flown deer.

Four fleet does at a gold valley
the famished arrow sang before.   20

Bow at belt went my love riding
riding the mountain down
into the silver dawn.

four lean hounds crouched low and smiling
the sheer peaks ran before.   25

Paler be they than daunting death
the sleek slim deer
the tall tense deer.

Four tall stags at a green mountain
the lucky hunter sang before.   30

All in green went my love riding
on a great horse of gold
into the silver dawn.

four lean hounds crouched low and smiling
my heart fell dead before.   35

1923

the cambridge ladies who live in furnished souls

the Cambridge ladies who live in furnished souls
are unbeautiful and have comfortable minds
(also, with the church's protestant blessings
daughters, unscented shapeless spirited)

they believe in Christ and Longfellow, both dead,   5
are invariably interested in so many things—
at the present writing one still finds
delighted fingers knitting for the is it Poles?
perhaps. While permanent faces coyly bandy
scandal of Mrs. N and Professor D   10
. . . . the Cambridge ladies do not care, above
Cambridge if sometimes in its box of
sky lavender and cornerless, the
moon rattles like a fragment of angry candy

                                            1923

In Just-

in Just-
spring   when the world is mud-
luscious the little
lame balloonman

whistles   far   and wee   5

and eddieandbill come
running from marbles and
piracies and it's
spring

when the world is puddle-wonderful   10

the queer
old balloonman whistles
far   and   wee
and bettyandisbel come dancing

from hop-scotch and jump-rope and   15

it's
spring
and
    the

            goat-footed   20
balloonMan   whistles

"the cambridge ladies": 5 *Longfellow:* Henry Wadsworth Longfellow (1807–1882), the first
American poet of international reputation. He was known for his moralistic and romantic
narrative poetry.

far
and
wee

1923

Buffalo Bill's

Buffalo Bill's
defunct
       who used to
       ride a watersmooth-silver
                     stallion   5
and break onetwothreefourfive pigeonsjustlikethat
                              Jesus

he was a handsome man
              and what i want to know is
how do you like your blueeyed boy   10
Mister Death

1923

Somewhere i have never travelled, gladly beyond

somewhere i have never travelled,gladly beyond
any experience,your eyes have their silence:
in your most frail gesture are things which enclose me,
or which i cannot touch because they are too near

your slightest look easily will unclose me   5
though i have closed myself as fingers,
you open always petal by petal myself as Spring opens
(touching skilfully,mysteriously) her first rose

or if your wish be to close me,i and
my life will shut very beautifully,suddenly,   10
as when the heart of this flower imagines
the snow carefully everywhere descending;

nothing which we are to perceive in this world equals
the power of your intense fragility:whose texture
compels me with the colour of its countries,   15
rendering death and forever with each breathing

(i do not know what it is about you that closes
and opens;only something in me understands

the voice of your eyes is deeper than all roses)
nobody,not even the rain,has such small hands   20

                                        1931

i sing of Olaf glad and big

i sing of Olaf glad and big
whose warmest heart recoiled at war:
a conscientious object-or

his wellbelovéd colonel (trig
westpointer most succinctly bred)   5
took erring Olaf soon in hand;
but—though an host of overjoyed
noncoms (first knocking on the head
him) do through icy waters roll
that helplessness which others stroke   10
with brushes recently employed
anent this muddy toiletbowl,
while kindred intellects evoke
allegiance per blunt instruments—
Olaf (being to all intents   15
a corpse and wanting any rag
upon what God unto him gave)
responds, without getting annoyed
"I will not kiss your f.ing flag"

straightway the silver bird looked grave   20
(departing hurriedly to shave)

but—though all kinds of officers
(a yearning nation's blueeyed pride)
their passive prey did kick and curse
until for wear their clarion   25
voices and boots were much the worse,
and egged the firstclassprivates on
his rectum wickedly to tease

by means of skilfully applied
bayonets roasted hot with heat—   30
Olaf (upon what were once knees)
does almost ceaselessly repeat
"there is some s. I will not eat"

our president,being of which
assertions duly notified   35
threw the yellowsonofabitch
into a dungeon,where he died

Christ (of His mercy infinite)
i pray to see; and Olaf,too

preponderatingly because   40
unless statistics lie he was
more brave than me:more blond than you.

1931

r-p-o-p-h-e-s-s-a-g-r

         r-p-o-p-h-e-s-s-a-g-r
     who
a)s w(e loo)k
upnowgath
       PPEGORHRASS   5
              eringint(o-
aThe):l
    eA
      !p:
S   a   10
        (r
rIvInG   .gRrEaPsPhOs)
                 to
rea(be)rran(com)gi(e)ngly
,grasshopper;   15

1935

*A poet as innovative as E. E. Cummings was naturally watched with inter-
est by fellow poets. Among the more thoughtful comments on his work are
those by Louise Bogan and Randall Jarrell.*

"Vital material that Victorian taste had outlawed": Louise Bogan

---

Cummings, whose relation to the 1914–1918 war was close and cruel,
brought into American postwar poetry a bittersweet mixture of satire and
sentiment. His typographical experiments, which gave him an early notoriety, today seem less important than his persistent attempts to break taboos

—to bring back into formal verse vital material that Victorian taste had outlawed. Today, as we read Cummings's lyric output from beginning to end, we are struck by the directness with which he has presented himself— his adolescent daydreams as well as his more mature desires; his small jealousies and prejudices, along with his big hatreds; his negative malice and his fears, beside his positive hopes. His awareness of tradition, too, comes out plainly; he has reworked traditional forms as often as he has invented new ones, turning not only the sonnet to his own purposes but also the ballad, the nursery rhyme, the epigrammatic quatrain, and the incantatory rune. His habit of projecting a continuing present, avoiding any expression of remorse or regret, gave a glitter to his middle period; nothing in it casts a shadow. The pathos of his later elegies is all the more remarkable because no one could foresee its occurrence. But it is his satire that remains focal and sharp as his main contribution to the reinvigoration of modern verse. His targets have been, for the most part, well chosen, and he has made his stand clear—for the rights and value of the individual as opposed to the demands of the crowd and the standards of the machine. He scornfully stuck to his guns in times of crisis, when many of his contemporaries were deserting theirs. It is this underlying passion for simple justice that has given Cummings the power to uncover, point to, and stigmatize those dead areas of custom as only a satirist can effectively do it.

"He sits at the Muse's door making mobiles": Randall Jarrell

So many critics have been more than just to Cummings's virtues—who could overlook so much life, individuality, charm, freshness, ingenuity?— that I should like to be unjust about his faults. Some of his sentimentality, his easy lyric sweetness I enjoy in the way one enjoys a rather commonplace composer's half-sweet, half-cloying melodies, but much of it is straight ham, straight corn. All too often Cummings splits man into a delicate unique Ariel, drifting through dew like moonlight, and into a Brooklyn Caliban who says, to prostitutes, dese, dem and dose. Some of all that Sex is there to shock, but more of it is there for its own sweet sake. And there is so much love—love infinite and eternal; love in the movie moonlight, after the prop champagne—that one values all the more the real love affair in Cummings's play *Him.*

To Cummings words are things, exciting things excitingly manipulable: he sits at the Muse's door making mobiles. He is a magical but shallow rhetorician who specializes in turning inside out, fooling around with the rhetoric of popular songs, advertisements, bad romantic poetry. He invents a master stroke, figures out the formula for it, and repeats it fifty times. The best rhetoric is less interested in itself, more interested in what it describes, than Cummings's.

Some of Cummings's humor is genuinely funny, some is crude and expected. He is, alas! a monotonous poet. Everything a poem does is, to old readers, expected. "Type Four," they murmur. "Well done!" Then they yawn. "Change in all things is sweet," said Aristotle; "They must often change who would be constant in happiness or wisdom," said Confucius; "Change the name of Arkansas? Never!" said Senator James Kimbrough Jones. Would that Cummings had listened to Aristotle and Confucius.

What I like least about Cummings's poems is their pride in Cummings and their contempt for most other people; the difference between the *I* and *you* of the poems, and other people, is the poems' favorite subject. All his work thanks God that he is not as other men are; none of it says, "Lord, be merciful to me, a sinner."

Although Louise Bogan may be right about the relative unimportance of Cummings's typographical experiments, they have attracted a great deal of attention. It might be useful to examine them in the light of other "concrete" poems written before and after Cummings's own.

George Herbert

(1593–1633)

EASTER-WINGS

Lord, who createdst man in wealth and store,
  Though foolishly he lost the same,
    Decaying more and more
      Till he became
        Most poor: 5

        With thee
      Oh let me rise
    As larks, harmoniously,
  And sing this day thy victories:
Then shall the fall further the flight in me.   10

My tender age in sorrow did begin:
  And still with sicknesses and shame
    Thou didst so punish sin,
      That I became
        Most thin.   15

With thee
Let me combine.
And feel thy victory:
For, if I imp my wing on thine,
Affliction shall advance the flight in me.   20

1633

May Swenson

(b. 1919)

HOW EVERYTHING HAPPENS (Based on a Study of the Wave)

                                             happen.
                                          to
                                       up
                                 stacking
                             is   5
                    something
When nothing is happening

When it happens
                 something
                          pulls   10
                             back
                               not
                                 to
                                   happen.
When   has happened.   15
      pulling back   stacking up
            happens

        has happened   stacks up.
When it   something   nothing
                        pulls back while   20

Then nothing is happening.

                             happens.
                          and
                     forward
                 pushes   25
              up

<pre>
                    stacks
        something
Then
</pre>

EUGENIO MONTALE

(1896–1981)

THE WALL

translated from the Italian by Maurice English

To lie in shadow on the lawn
By a crumbling wall, pale and withdrawn,
And spy in the weeds the gliding snake
And hear the rustle blackbirds make—

To watch in the cracked earth and the grass   5
Battalions of red ants at drill,
That break and form ranks, pass and repass
In busy marches on some tiny hill—

To catch, each time the leaves blow free,
The faint and pulsing motion of the sea,   10
While ceaseless, tremulous and shrill,
The cicadas chatter on the bald hill—

Rising, to wander in bewilderment
With the sun's dazzle, and the sorry thought
How all our life, and all its labors spent,   15
Are like a man upon a journey sent
Along a wall that's sheer and steep and endless, dressed
With bits of broken bottles on its crest.

1956, trans. 1961

from THE MOTETS

translated from the Italian by Dana Gioia

1

You know this: I must lose you again and cannot.
Every action, every cry strikes me
like a well-aimed shot, even the salt spray

Eugenio Montale   **991**

that spills over the harbor walls
and makes spring   5
dark against the gates of Genoa.

Country of ironwork and ship masts
like a forest in the dust of evening.
A long drone comes from the open spaces
scraping like a nail on a windowpane. I look   10
for the sign I have lost, the only pledge
I had from you.
              Now hell is certain.

10

Why are you waiting? The squirrel in the pine tree
beats its torch-like tail on the bark.   15
Half of the moon is sinking with one horn
touching the sun and fading. The day is finished.

The lazy smoke is startled by a breeze
but gathers itself to cover you.
Nothing will end, or everything, if you,   20
the flash of lightning, leave the cloud.

12

I run my hand across your forehead
to wipe away the ice
that formed there as you crossed
the highest clouds. Your wings   25
have been torn by cyclones.
You wake in sudden starts.

Noon: and the black shadows of the medlars
stretch themselves across the square,
a cold sun   30
persists in heaven, and the other
shadows turning in the alley
don't know that you are here.

13

The gondola that glides
forward in the dark   35
splendor of its polished
tar and poppies, the insinuating
song that rises from beyond
the heaps of rigging, the tall
doors that close behind you,   40
and the smiles of the masqueraders
who run away in packs—

only one evening out of many,
but my night goes deeper still.
Down there a pale mass   45
writhing in the water startles
me awake and makes me
like the self-absorbed old man
fishing for eels on the bank.

14

The reed that sheds its   50
soft, red crescent
in the spring; the gravel path
above the gulley where dragonflies
are hovering on the slow
dark current; the dog,   55
breathless, coming home
with a bundle in its mouth.

Today there is nothing here
which I can recognize:
only there   60
where the reflection burns
more fiercely, and the clouds
are sinking, there beyond the eyes
which are so far away
by now, only these   65
two beams of light
that cross.

And time passes.

1939, trans. 1985

THE EEL

translated from the Italian by Robert Lowell

The eel, the North Sea siren,
who leaves dead-pan Icelandic gods
and the Baltic for our Mediterranean,
our estuaries, our rivers
who lances through their profound places,   5
and flinty portages, from branch to branch,
twig to twig, thinning down now,
ever snaking inward, worming
for the granite's heartland, threading
delicate capillaries of slime—   10

Eugenio Montale   **993**

and in the Romagna one morning
the blaze of the chestnut blossoms
ignites its smudge in the dead water
pooled from chiselings
of the Apennines. . .   15
the eel, a whipstock, a Roman candle,
love's arrow on earth, which only
reaches the paradise of fecundity
through our gullies and fiery, charred streams;
a green spirit, potent only   20
where desolation and arson burn;
a spark that says everything
begins where everything is clinker;
this buried rainbow, this iris, twin sister
of the one you set in your eye's target center   25
to shine on the sons of men,
on us, up to our gills in your life-giving mud—
can you call her *Sister?*

1956, trans. 1961

LITTLE TESTAMENT

translated from the Italian by Robert Lowell

This thing the night flashes
like marshlight through the skull of my mind,
this pearl necklace snail's trail,
this ground glass, diamond-dust sparkle—
it is not the lamp in any church or office,   5
tended by some adolescent altar boy,
Communist or papist,
in black or red.
I have only this rainbow
to leave you, this testimonial   10
of a faith, often invaded,
of a hope that burned more slowly
than a green log on the fire.
Keep its spectrum in your pocket-mirror,
when every lamp goes out,   15
when hell's orchestra trembles,
and the torch-bearing Lucifer
lands on some bowsprit
in the Thames, Hudson or Seine—
rotating his hard coal wings,   20
half lopped by fatigue, to tell you, "Now."

It's hardly an heirloom or charm
that can tranquillize monsoons
with the transparent spider web of contemplation—
but an autobiography can only survive in ashes,   25
persistence is extinction.
It is certainly a sign: whoever has seen it,
will always return to you.
Each knows his own: his pride
was not an escape, his humility   30
was not a meanness, his obscure
earth-bound flash
was not the fizzle of a wet match.

1956, trans. 1961

THE SUNFLOWER

translated from the Italian by Maurice English

Bring me the sunflower to plant in my garden here
Where the salt of the flung spray has parched a space,
And all day long to the blue and mirroring air
Let it turn the ardor of its yellow face.

These dark things to the source of brightness turn,   5
In a flow of colors into music flowing, spend
Themselves forever. Thus to burn
Is consummation, of all ends the end.

Bring me within your hands that flower which yearns
Up to the ultimate transparent white   10
Where all of life into its essence burns:
Bring me that flower impassioned of the light.

1965, trans. 1985

LA BELLE DAME SANS MERCI

translated from the Italian by G. Singh

To be sure the cantonal seagulls
waited in vain for the crumbs
I used to throw on your balcony,
that you might hear their cries even when asleep.

Today neither of us turns up for the appointment,   5
our breakfast grows cold among piles
of my useless books and your various relics:
calendars, jewel cases, medicine
bottles and creams.

Your astounding face lingers still,   10
carved against the morning's chalky
background; but a life without wings
can't reach it and its suffocated fire
is no more than the flash of a lighter.

1970, trans. 1985

from XENIA II

translated from the Italian by G. Singh

5

With my arm in yours I have descended at least a
    million stairs,
and now that you aren't here, a void opens at each step.
Even so our long journey has been brief.
Mine continues still, though I've no more use
for connections, bookings, traps,   5
and the disenchantment of him who believes
that the real is what one sees.

I have descended millions of stairs with my arm in
    yours,
not, of course, that with four eyes one might see better.
I descended them because I knew   10
that even though so bedimmed
yours were the only true eyes.

1971, trans. 1976

Like Baudelaire (see page 861), but for very different reasons, Eugenio Montale saw himself at cross-purposes with the spirit of his time. He spoke sometimes with great bitterness about a society that seemed to be running away from its past and encouraging its members to forget their own histories.

"Man is the product of industry and industry is the product of man": Eugenio Montale

translated from the Italian by Jonathan Galassi

It is useless, then, to haunt the archives, libraries, or museums; if we keep in mind that a new humanism has been discovered, in which man is the product of industry and industry is the product of man (and so the circle is closed), what real interest can the humanism of times less advanced than our own hold for us?

We should add that while it is silly and dangerous to detest the present the past can be detested with impunity: it doesn't react or take revenge, it doesn't compromise anyone. We can expect dirty tricks from the future: we need to keep all the windows open so it won't surprise us. It is with good reason, then, that we speak of "open-ended" works of art, as men's minds are already open and no longer blocked or closed by the rubble of the past. A closed work is a piece of the past which claims to go back in time, an operation destined to fail because time is irreversible. The work of man, and not only the work of art, must be so open that it dies at the very instant of its creation. Practically speaking, the instant will not be a literal flash of lightning, it may last a bit longer; but it is clear that if we produced objects that insisted on a long life they would be harmful to the economy (and to morale).

Contemporary man is like a sailor who must continually throw into the sea a ballast which has become dangerous: a ballast not only of things but of memories and regrets. An insignificant object can become a concentration of the past for us and thus assume a totemic function. For many years I carried with me a rusty metal shoehorn I was so ashamed of that when I stayed in a hotel I'd hide it so the maid wouldn't see it. It was the only thing that had been with me since childhood. One day in Venice I forgot where I had hidden it, or rather forgot the shoehorn itself, and I never had the courage to inquire about it. In all probability it is sleeping today at the bottom of the lagoon. Still, I feel remorse, and when they tell me that a cosmonaut has circled the globe six, ten, or sixty times, I think the greatest discovery would be the one that would bring me back my old rusty shoehorn. I know perfectly well that if the shoehorn were to reappear on my table I would feel more terror than joy. Consciously or not, I rid myself of it. I must therefore accept the assistance of chance and continue to live without that magic, silent, rusty Oliphant, as I must confess that I have dared to replace it with a red plastic model which I now set out in plain view and could lose without regret.

LOUISE BOGAN

(1897–1970)

MEDUSA

I had come to the house, in a cave of trees,
Facing a sheer sky.
Everything moved,—a bell hung ready to strike,
Sun and reflection wheeled by.

When the bare eyes were before me   5
And the hissing hair,
Held up at a window, seen through a door.
The stiff bald eyes, the serpents on the forehead
Formed in the air.

This is a dead scene forever now.   10
Nothing will ever stir.
The end will never brighten it more than this,
Nor the rain blur.

The water will always fall, and will not fall,
And the tipped bell make no sound.   15
The grass will always be growing for hay
Deep on the ground.

And I shall stand here like a shadow
Under the great balanced day,
My eyes on the yellow dust, that was lifting in the wind,   20
And does not drift away.

                                        1923

THE ENGINE

The secure pulses of the heart
Drive and rock in dark precision,
Though life brings fever to the mouth
And the eyes vision.

Whatever joy the body takes,   5
Whatever sound the voice makes purer,

"Medusa": *Medusa:* In Greek mythology whoever looked upon the face of this serpent-haired
sorceress was turned to stone.

Will never cause their beat to faint
Or become surer.

These perfect chambers, and their springs,
So fitly sealed against remorse   10
That keep the lifting shaft of breath
To its cool course,

Cannot delay, and cannot dance—
Until, wrung out to the last drop,
The brain, knowing time and love, must die,   15
And they must stop.

1931

TO MY BROTHER

Killed: Chaumont Wood, October 1918

O you so long dead,
You masked and obscure,
I can tell you, all things endure:
The wine and the bread;

The marble quarried for the arch;   5
The iron become steel;
The spoke broken from the wheel;
The sweat of the long march;

The haystacks cut through like loaves,
And the hundred flowers from the seed.   10

All things indeed,
Though struck by the hooves

Of disaster, of time due,
Of fell loss and gain,
All things remain,   15
I can tell you, this is true,

Though burned down to stone,
Though lost from the eye,
I can tell you, and not lie—
Save of peace alone.   20

1935

COME, BREAK WITH TIME

Come, break with time,
You who were lorded

By a clock's chime
So ill afforded.
If time is allayed   5
Be not afraid.

I shall break, if I will.
Break, since you must.
Time has its fill,
Sated with dust.   10
Long the clock's hand
Burned like a brand.

Take the rocks' speed
And earth's heavy measure.
Let buried seed   15
Drain out time's pleasure,
Take time's decrees.
Come, cruel ease.

1941

THE DREAM

O God, in the dream the terrible horse began
To paw at the air, and make for me with his blows.
Fear kept for thirty-five years poured through his
   mane,
And retribution equally old, or nearly, breathed
   through his nose.

Coward complete, I lay and wept on the ground   5
When some strong creature appeared, and leapt for
   the rein.
Another woman, as I lay half in a swound,
Leapt in the air, and clutched at the leather and chain.

Give him, she said, something of yours as a charm.
Throw him, she said, some poor thing you alone claim.   10
No, no, I cried, he hates me; he's out for harm,
And whether I yield or not, it is all the same.

But, like a lion in a legend, when I flung the glove
Pulled from my sweating, my cold right hand,
The terrible beast, that no one may understand,   15
Came to my side, and put down his head in love.

1941

EVENING IN THE SANITARIUM

The free evening fades, outside the windows fastened
    with decorative iron grilles.
The lamps are lighted; the shades drawn; the nurses are
    watching a little.
It is the hour of the complicated knitting on the safe
    bone needles; of the games of anagrams and bridge;
The deadly game of chess; the book held up like a mask.

The period of the wildest weeping, the fiercest delu-
    sion, is over.   5
The women rest their tired half-healed hearts; they are
    almost well.
Some of them will stay almost well always: the blunt-
    faced woman whose thinking dissolved
Under academic discipline; the manic-depressive girl
Now leveling off; one paranoiac afflicted with jealousy.
Another with persecution. Some alleviation has been
    possible.   10

O fortunate bride, who never again will become elated
    after childbirth!
O lucky older wife, who has been cured of feeling
    unwanted!
To the suburban railway station you will return, return,
To meet forever Jim home on the 5:35.
You will be again as normal and selfish and heartless as
    anybody else.   15

There is life left: the piano says it with its octave smile.
The soft carpets pad the thump and splinter of the
    suicide to be.
Everything will be splendid: the grandmother will not
    drink habitually.
The fruit salad will bloom on the plate like a bouquet
And the garden produce the blue-ribbon aquilegia.   20
The cats will be glad; the fathers feel justified; the
    mothers relieved.

The sons and husbands will no longer need to pay the
    bills.
Childhoods will be put away, the obscene nightmare
    abated.

At the ends of the corridors the baths are running.
Mrs. C. again feels the shadow of the obsessive idea.   25

Miss R. looks at the mantel-piece, which must mean
   something.

1941

ZONE

We have struck the regions wherein we are keel or reef
The wind breaks over us,
And against high sharp angles almost splits into words
And these are of fear or grief.

Like a ship, we have struck expected latitudes   5
Of the universe, in March.
Through one short segment's arch
Of the zodiac's round
We pass,
Thinking: Now we hear   10
What we heard last year,
And bear the wind's rude touch
And its ugly sound
Equally with so much
We have learned how to bear.   15

1941

THE DRAGONFLY

You are made of almost nothing
But of enough
To be great eyes
And diaphanous double vans;
To be ceaseless movement,   5
Unending hunger
Grappling love.

Link between water and air,
Earth repels you.
Light touches you only to shift into iridescence   10
Upon your body and wings.
Twice-born, predator,
You split into the heat.
Swift beyond calculation or capture
You dart into the shadow   15
Which consumes you.

You rocket into the day.
But at last, when the wind flattens the grasses,
For you, the design and purpose stop.

And you fall
With the other husks of summer.

1961

Louise Bogan once said of lyric poetry, "The chances of getting away with pure fakery within it are very small. One cannot fib—it shows. One cannot manipulate—it spoils." Her most enthusiastic readers respond strongly to the intellectual and emotional honesty of her work.

"Intense, proud, strong willed, never hysterical or silly": Theodore Roethke

Two of the charges most frequently levelled against poetry by women are lack of range—in subject matter, in emotional tone—and lack of a sense of humor. And one could, in individual instances among writers of real talent, add other aesthetic and moral shortcomings: the spinning-out; the embroidering of trivial themes; a concern with the mere surfaces of life—that special province of the feminine talent in prose—hiding from the real agonies of the spirit; refusing to face up to what existence is; lyric or religious posturing; running between the boudoir and the altar, stamping a tiny foot against God; or lapsing into a sententiousness that implies the author has re-invented integrity; carrying on excessively about Fate, about time; lamenting the lot of the woman; caterwauling; writing the same poem about fifty times, and so on.

But Louise Bogan is something else. True, a very few of her earliest poems bear the mark of fashion, but for the most part she writes out of the severest lyrical tradition in English. Her real spiritual ancestors are Campion, Jonson, the anonymous Elizabethan song writers. The word order is usually direct, the plunge straight into the subject, the music rich and subtle (she has one of the best ears of our time), and the subject invariably given its due and no more. As a result, her poems, even the less consequential, have a finality, a comprehensiveness, the sense of being all of a piece, that we demand from the short poem at its best. . . .

One definition of a serious lyric—it may come from Stanley Kunitz —would call it a revelation of a tragic personality. Behind the Bogan poems is a woman intense, proud, strong-willed, never hysterical or silly; who scorns the open unabashed caterwaul so usual with the love poet, male or female; who never writes a serious poem until there is a genuine "upwelling" from the unconscious; who shapes emotion into an inevitable-seeming, an endurable, form.

For love, passion, its complexities, its tensions, its betrayals, is one of Louise Bogan's chief themes. And this love, along with marriage itself, is a virtual battle-ground. But the enemy is respected, the other is there, given his due; the experience, whatever its difficulties, shared.

FEDERICO GARCÍA LORCA

(1899–1936)

FAREWELL

translated from the Spanish by W. S. Merwin

If I die,
leave the balcony open.

The little boy is eating oranges.
(From my balcony I can see him.)

The reaper is harvesting the wheat.   5
(From my balcony I can hear him.)

If I die,
leave the balcony open!

1921–24, trans. 1955

SONG OF THE BARREN ORANGE TREE

translated from the Spanish by W. S. Merwin

Woodcutter.
Cut my shadow from me.
Free me from the torment
of seeing myself without fruit.

Why was I born among mirrors?   5
The day walks in circles around me,
and the night copies me
in all its stars.

I want to live without seeing myself.
And I will dream that ants   10

and thistleburrs are my
leaves and my birds.

Woodcutter.
Cut my shadow from me.
Free me from the torment   15
of seeing myself without fruit.

1921–24, trans. 1955

THE FAITHLESS WIFE

*translated from the Spanish by Stephen Spender and J. L.
Gili*

So I took her to the river
believing she was a maiden,
but she already had a husband.
It was on Saint James's night
and almost as if I was obliged to.   5
The lanterns went out
and the crickets lighted up.
In the farthest street corners
I touched her sleeping breasts,
and they opened to me suddenly   10
like spikes of hyacinth.
The starch of her petticoat
sounded in my ears
like a piece of silk
rent by ten knives.   15
Without silver light on their foliage
the trees had grown larger
and a horizon of dogs
barked very far from the river.

Past the blackberries,   20
the reeds and the hawthorn,
underneath her cluster of hair
I made a hollow in the earth.
I took off my tie.
She took off her dress.   25
I my belt with the revolver.
She her four bodices.

"The Faithless Wife": 4 *Saint James's night:* The feast of the patron saint of Spain is celebrated
on November 27

Nor nard nor mother-o'-pearl
have skin so fine,
nor does glass with silver   30
shine with such brilliance.
Her thighs slipped away from me
like startled fish,
half full of fire,
half full of cold.   35
That night I ran
on the best of roads
mounted on a nacre mare
without bridle or stirrups.
As a man, I won't repeat   40
the things she said to me.
The light of understanding
has made me most discreet.
Smeared with sand and kisses
I took her away from the river.   45
The swords of the lilies
battled with the air.

I behaved like what I am.
Like a proper gypsy.
I gave her a large sewing basket,   50
of straw-coloured satin,
and I did not fall in love
for although she had a husband
she told me she was a maiden
when I took her to the river.   55

1924–27, trans. 1955

BALLAD OF THE SPANISH CIVIL GUARD

translated from the Spanish by A. L. Lloyd

Black are the horses.
The horseshoes are black.
On the dark capes glisten
stains of ink and of wax.
Their skulls are leaden,   5
which is why they don't weep.
With their patent-leather souls

"*Ballad of the Spanish Civil Guard*": *Spanish Civil Guard:* founded to maintain order in remote areas, became in the 1920s and 1930s an instrument of political repression

they come down the street.
Hunchbacked and nocturnal,
where they go, they command   10
silences of dark rubber
and fears like fine sand.
They pass where they want,
and they hide in their skulls
a vague astronomy   15
of shapeless pistols.
Oh, city of gypsies!
Your corners hung with banners.
The moon and the pumpkin
with mazard berries preserved.   20
Oh, city of gypsies!
Who could see you and forget?
City of musk and sorrow,
with your cinnamon towers.

And at the fall of night,   25
the night benighted by nightfall,
the gypsies within their smithies
were forging suns and arrows.
A badly wounded stallion
was knocking at all the doors.   30
Near Jerez de la Frontera,
loud crowded the cocks of crystal!
Naked, the wind turns
the corner of the surprise
in the silver-dark night   35
the night benighted by nightfall.

The Virgin and St. Joseph
have lost their castanets,
and they search for the gypsies
to see if they have found them.   40
The Virgin comes dressed
in the robe of a Mayoress
made of chocolate paper
with an almond necklace.
St. Joseph moves his arms   45
under a silken cloak.

And, with three sultans of Persia,
behind marches Pedro Domecq.

_____

31 *Jerez de la Frontera:* a city in Andalusia (SW Spain) notable for the production of sherry
48 *Pedro Domecq:* creator of a sherry made at Jerez de la Frontera

Federico García Lorca   **1007**

The half-moon was dreaming
the ecstasy of a crane.   50
Standards and street-lamps
invade the flat roofs.
Dancers without hips
are sobbing in the mirrors.
Water and shadow, shadow and water   55
by Jerez de la Frontera.

Oh, city of gypsies!
Your corners decked with banners.
Put out your green lights,
the Civil Guard is coming!   60
O, city of gypsies!
Who could see you and forget?
(Leave her far from the sea
with no combs for her hairdress.)

They ride in double file   65
towards the festive streets,
the rustle of everlastings
invades their cartridge belts.
They ride in ranks of two,
a double nocturne in serge.   70
The sky, so they fancy,
is a show-case of spurs.

The city, free from fear,
multiplied its doors.
Forty Civil Guards   75
took them by storm.
The clocks ceased to strike
and the bottles of brandy,
to arouse no suspicion,
wore the mask of November.   80
Among the weathervanes
rose a flight of long screams.
The sabres cut the breeze
that the hooves trampled on.
Along the streets of shadow   85
old gypsy women run
with their somnolent horses
and their jars full of coins.
And up the steep streets
the sinister capes fleer,   90
leaving behind them swift
whirlwinds of shears.

The gypsies are all gathered
by the Bethlehem gate.
St. Joseph, full of wounds,   95
enshrouds a young maid.
Stubborn and sharp, the guns
clatter the whole night through,
while the Virgin is healing children
with drops of star spume.   100
But the Guardia Civil
comes scattering fires
by which, young and naked,
the imagination is seared.
Rosa of the Camborios   105
sits moaning by her door.
Her two breasts, cut off,
are lying on a tray.
And other girls flee,
pursued by their braids,   110
through the air in which roses
of black powder are bursting.
When all the tile roofs
were but furrows in the soil,
the dawn shrugged her shoulders   115
in a long stony profile.

Oh, city of gypsies!
The Civil Guard rides away
through a tunnel of silence,
while around you are flames.   120

Oh, city of gypsies!
Who could see you and forget?
Let them seek you on my brow.
The play of moon and sand.

1924–27, trans. 1955

NEW YORK: OFFICE AND
DENUNCIATION

translated from the Spanish by Betty Jean Craige

 Beneath the multiplications
there is a drop of duck's blood;
beneath the divisions
there is a drop of sailor's blood;
beneath the sums, a river of young blood;   5

Federico García Lorca **1009**

A river that comes singing
through the bedrooms of the suburbs,
and it is silver, cement, or breeze
in the false dawn of New York.
Mountains exist. I know.   10
And glasses for higher learning.
I know. But I have not come to see the sky.
I have come to see the turbid blood.
The blood that carries the machines to the waterfalls
and the spirit to the snake's tongue.   15
Everyday there are killed in New York
four million ducks,
five million pigs,
two thousand pigeons for the pleasure of the dying,
one million cows,   20
one million lambs
and two million roosters,
that leave the sky in smithereens.
It is better to sob sharpening the knife
or murder the dogs   25
in the fascinating hunts,
than to endure in the early morning
the interminable milk trains,
the interminable trains of blood
and the trains of handcuffed roses   30
for the merchants of perfume.
The ducks and the pigeons,
and the pigs and the lambs
leave their drops of blood
beneath the multiplications,   35
and the terrible bawling of the jammed-together cows
fills the valley with pain
where the Hudson gets drunk on oil.
I denounce all the people
who are ignorant of the other half,   40
I denounce the irredeemable half
that raises its mountains of cement
where beat the hearts
of animals now forgotten
and where we all shall fall   45
in the last feast of the blasting drills,
I spit in your face.
The other half listens to me
devouring, urinating, flying in their purity,
like the children of the doorways   50
who carry old sticks

to the holes where are rusting
the antennae of insects.
It is not hell, it is the street.
It is not death, it is the fruit store.   55
There is a world of broken rivers
and unreachable distances
in the paw of that cat
broken by the automobile,
and I hear the song of the earthworm   60
in the hearts of many little girls.
Rust, rot, shuddering earth.
Earth, yourself, who swim
through the numbers of the office.
What shall I do? Set the landscape in order?   65
Set in order the loves that will later be photographs,
that will later be pieces of wood
and mouthfuls of blood?
St. Ignatius of Loyola
murdered a small rabbit   70
and still his lips grieve
in the towers of the churches.
No, no, no, no; I denounce.
I denounce the conspiracy
of these deserted offices   75
that do not radiate agony,
that erase the programs of the jungle,
and I offer up myself to be eaten
by the jammed-together cows
when their bawling fills the valley   80
where the Hudson gets drunk on oil.

1929–30, trans. 1966

LAMENT FOR IGNACIO SÁNCHEZ MEJÍAS

translated from the Spanish by Stephen Spender and J. L. Gili

1. *Cogida and Death*

At five in the afternoon.
It was exactly five in the afternoon.
A boy brought the white sheet

"*Lament for Ignacio Sánchez Mejías*": *Ignacio Sánchez Mejías:* a famous bullfighter and a friend of Garcia Lorca's, killed in the ring in September 1934

at five in the afternoon.
A frail of lime ready prepared   5
at five in the afternoon.
The rest was death, and death alone
at five in the afternoon.

The wind carried away the cottonwool
at five in the afternoon.   10
And the oxide scattered crystal and nickel
at five in the afternoon.
Now the dove and the leopard wrestle
at five in the afternoon.
And a thigh with a desolate horn   15
at five in the afternoon.
The bass-string struck up
at five in the afternoon.
Arsenic bells and smoke
at five in the afternoon.   20
Groups of silence in the corners
at five in the afternoon.
And the bull alone with a high heart!
at five in the afternoon.
When the sweat of snow was coming   25
at five in the afternoon.
when the bull ring was covered in iodine
at five in the afternoon.
death laid eggs in the wound
at five in the afternoon.   30
At five in the afternoon.
Exactly at five o'clock in the afternoon.

A coffin on wheels is his bed
at five in the afternoon.
Bones and flutes resound in his ears   35
at five in the afternoon.
Now the bull was bellowing through his forehead
at five in the afternoon.
The room was iridescent with agony
at five in the afternoon.   40
In the distance the gangrene now comes
at five in the afternoon.
Horn of the lily through green groins
at five in the afternoon.
The wounds were burning like suns   45
at five in the afternoon.
and the crowd was breaking the windows
at five in the afternoon.

At five in the afternoon.
Ah, that fatal five in the afternoon!   50
It was five by all the clocks!
It was five in the shade of the afternoon!

2. *The Spilled Blood*

I will not see it!

Tell the moon to come
for I do not want to see the blood   55
of Ignacio on the sand.

I will not see it!

The moon wide open.
Horse of still clouds,
and the grey bull ring of dreams   60
with willows in the barreras.

I will not see it!

Let my memory kindle!
Warn the jasmines
of such minute whiteness!   65

I will not see it!

The cow of the ancient world
passed her sad tongue
over a snout of blood
spilled on the sand,   70
and the bulls of Guisando,
partly dead and partly stone,
bellowed like two centuries
sated with treading the earth.
No.   75
I do not want to see it!
I will not see it!

Ignacio goes up the tiers
with all his death on his shoulders.
He sought for the dawn   80
but the dawn was no more.
He seeks for his confident profile
and the dream bewilders him.
He sought for his beautiful body
and encountered his opened blood.   85
I will not see it!
I do not want to hear it spurt
each time with less strength:

that spurt that illuminates
the tiers of seats, and spills   90
over the corduroy and the leather
of a thirsty multitude.
Who shouts that I should come near!
Do not ask me to see it!

His eyes did not close   95
when he saw the horns near,
but the terrible mothers
lifted their heads.
And across the ranches,
an air of secret voices rose,   100
shouting to celestial bulls,
herdsmen of pale mist.
There was no prince in Seville
who could compare with him,
nor sword like his sword   105
nor heart so true.
Like a river of lions
was his marvellous strength,
and like a marble torso
his firm drawn moderation.   110
The air of Andalusian Rome
gilded his head
where his smile was a spikenard
of wit and intelligence.
What a great torero in the ring!   115
What a good peasant in the sierra!
How gentle with the sheaves!
How hard with the spurs!
How tender with the dew!
How dazzling in the fiesta!   120
How tremendous with the final
banderillas of darkness!

But now he sleeps without end.
Now the moss and the grass
open with sure fingers   125
the flower of his skull.
And now his blood comes out singing;
singing along marshes and meadows,
sliding on frozen horns,
faltering soulless in the mist,   130
stumbling over a thousand hoofs

---

112 *Andalusian Rome:* the Spanish province of Andalusia was part of the Roman Empire

like a long, dark, sad tongue,
to form a pool of agony
close to the starry Guadalquivir.
Oh, white wall of Spain!   135
Oh, black bull of sorrow!
Oh, hard blood of Ignacio!
Oh, nightingale of his veins!
No.
I will not see it!   140
No chalice can contain it,
no swallows can drink it,
no frost of light can cool it,
nor song nor deluge of white lilies,
no glass can cover it with silver.   145
No.
I will not see it!

3. *The Laid Out Body*

Stone is a forehead where dreams grieve
without curving waters and frozen cypresses.
Stone is a shoulder on which to bear Time   150
with trees formed of tears and ribbons and planets.

I have seen grey showers move towards the waves
raising their tender riddled arms,
to avoid being caught by the lying stone
which loosens their limbs without soaking the blood.   155

For stone gathers seed and clouds,
skeleton larks and wolves of penumbra:
but yields not sounds nor crystals nor fire,
only bull rings and bull rings and more bull rings
    without walls.

Now, Ignacio the well born lies on the stone.   160
All is finished. What is happening? Contemplate his
    face:
death has covered him with pale sulphur
and has placed on him the head of a dark minotaur.

All is finished. The rain penetrates his mouth.
The air, as if mad, leaves his sunken chest,   165
and Love, soaked through with tears of snow,
warms itself on the peak of the herd.

What are they saying? A stenching silence settles down.
We are here with a body laid out which fades away,

---

135 *Guadalquivir:* river that enters the Atlantic near Cadiz

with a pure shape which had nightingales 170
and we see it being filled with depthless holes.

Who creases the shroud? What he says is not true!
Nobody sings here, nobody weeps in the corner,
nobody pricks the spurs, nor terrifies the serpent.
Here I want nothing else but the round eyes 175
to see this body without a chance of rest.

Here I want to see those men of hard voice.
Those that break horses and dominate rivers;
those men of sonorous skeleton who sing
with a mouth full of sun and flint. 180

Here I want to see them. Before the stone.
Before this body with broken reins.
I want to know from them the way out
for this captain strapped down by death.

I want them to show me a lament like a river 185
which will have sweet mists and deep shores,
to take the body of Ignacio where it loses itself
without hearing the double panting of the bulls.

Loses itself in the round bull ring of the moon
which feigns in its youth a sad quiet bull: 190
loses itself in the night without song of fishes
and in the white thicket of frozen smoke.

I don't want them to cover his face with handkerchiefs
that he may get used to the death he carries.
Go, Ignacio; feel not the hot bellowing. 195
Sleep, fly, rest: even the sea dies!

4. *Absent Soul*

The bull does not know you, nor the fig tree,
nor the horses, nor the ants in your own house.
The child and the afternoon do not know you
because you have died for ever. 200

The back of the stone does not know you,
nor the black satin in which you crumble.
Your silent memory does not know you
because you have died for ever.

The autumn will come with small white snails, 205
misty grapes and with clustered hills,
but no one will look into your eyes
because you have died for ever.

Because you have died for ever,
like all the dead of the Earth,   210
like all the dead who are forgotten
in a heap of lifeless dogs.

Nobody knows you. No. But I sing of you.
For posterity I sing of your profile and grace.
Of the signal maturity of your understanding.   215
Of your appetite for death and the taste of its mouth.
Of the sadness of your once valiant gaiety.

It will be a long time, if ever, before there is born
an Andalusian so true, so rich in adventure.
I sing of his elegance with words that groan,   220
and I remember a sad breeze through the olive trees.

1935, trans. 1955

GACELA OF UNFORESEEN LOVE

translated from the Spanish by W. S. Merwin

No one understood the perfume
of the dark magnolia of your womb.
No one knew that you tormented
a hummingbird of love between your teeth.

A thousand Persian ponies fell asleep   5
in the moonlit plaza of your forehead,
while through four nights I embraced
your waist, enemy of the snow.

Between plaster and jasmines, your glance
was a pale branch of seeds.   10
I sought in my heart to give you
the ivory letters that say *always,*

always, always: garden of my agony,
your body elusive always,
the blood of your veins in my mouth,   15
your mouth already lightless for my death.

1936, trans. 1955

"Gacela of Unforeseen Love": Gacela: a short, rhymed, fixed verse form used in Arabic poetry

Federico García Lorca   **1017**

The tone of Federico García Lorca's poetry is different from that of a restrained poet like Edwin Arlington Robinson. It is the style of the **duende,** *which we might translate as "spirit" or "spell" or "ghost" or "soul." No translation can do the term as much justice as García Lorca's own description of it.*

"A ten-fingered hand around the nailed but stormy feet of a Christ": Federico García Lorca

translated from the Spanish by Christopher Maurer

The Andalusian singer Pastora Pavón, "La Niña de los Peines," dark Hispanic genius whose powers of fantasy are equal to those of Goya or Rafael el Gallo, was once singing in a little tavern in Cádiz. For a while she played with her voice of shadow, of beaten tin, her moss-covered voice, braiding it into her hair or soaking it in wine or letting it wander away to the farthest, darkest bramble patches. No use. Nothing. The audience remained silent.

In the same room was Ignacio Espeleta, handsome as a Roman tortoise, who had once been asked, "How come you don't work?" and had answered, with a smile worthy of Argantonius, "Work? I'm from Cádiz!" And there was Hot Elvira, aristocrat, Sevillian whore, direct descendant of Soledad Vargas, who in 1930 refused to marry a Rothschild because he was not of equal blood. And the Floridas, whom the people take to be butchers but who are really millennial priests who still sacrifice bulls to Geryon. And in one corner sat the formidable bull rancher Don Pablo Murube, with the air of a Cretan mask. When Pastora Pavón finished singing there was total silence, until a tiny man, one of those dancing manikins that rise suddenly out of brandy bottles, sarcastically murmured "¡Viva Paris!" as if to say: "Here we care nothing about ability, technique, skill. Here we are after something else."

As though crazy, torn like a medieval weeper, La Niña de los Peines got to her feet, tossed off a big glass of firewater and began to sing with a scorched throat, without voice, without breath or color, but with duende. She was able to kill all the scaffolding of the song and leave way for a furious, enslaving duende, friend of sand winds, who made the listeners rip their clothes with the same rhythm as do the blacks of the Antilles when, in the "lucumí" rite, they huddle in heaps before the statue of Santa Bárbara.

La Niña de los Peines had to tear her voice because she knew she had an exquisite audience, one which demanded not forms but the marrow of forms, pure music with a body so lean it could stay in the air. She had to rob herself of skill and security, send away her muse and become helpless, that her duende might come and deign to fight her hand to hand. And how she sang! Her voice was no longer playing, it was a jet of blood worthy of her pain and her sincerity, and it opened like a ten-fingered hand around the nailed but stormy feet of a Christ by Juan de Juni.

The duende's arrival always means a radical change in forms. It brings to old planes unknown feelings of freshness, with the quality of something newly created, like a miracle, and it produces an almost religious enthusiasm.

In all Arabic music, whether dance, song, or elegy, the duende's arrival is greeted with energetic cries of Allah! Allah!, which is so close to the Olé of the bullfight that who knows if it is not the same thing? And in all the songs of the south of Spain the duende is greeted with sincere cries of ¡Viva Dios!—deep and tender human cry of communication with God through the five senses, thanks to the duende, who shakes the body and voice of the dancer. It is a real and poetic evasion of this world, as pure as that of the strange seventeenth-century poet Pedro Soto de Rojas with his seven gardens, or that of John Climacus with his tremulous ladder of lamentation.

LANGSTON HUGHES

(1902–1967)

THE NEGRO SPEAKS OF RIVERS

I've known rivers:
I've known rivers ancient as the world and older than
   the flow of human blood in human veins.

My soul has grown deep like the rivers.

I bathed in the Euphrates when dawns were young.   5
I built my hut near the Congo and it lulled me to sleep.
I look upon the Nile and raised the pyramids above it.
I heard the singing of the Mississippi when Abe Lincoln
   went down to New Orleans, and I've seen its muddy
   bosom turn all golden in the sunset.   10

I've known rivers:
Ancient, dusky rivers.

My soul has grown deep like the rivers.

1921

EPILOGUE

I, too, sing America.

I am the darker brother.
They send me to eat in the kitchen
When company comes,
But I laugh,   5
And eat well,
And grow strong.

Tomorrow,
I'll sit at the table
When company comes.   10
Nobody'll dare
Say to me,
"Eat in the kitchen,"
Then.

Besides,   15
They'll see how beautiful I am
And be ashamed,—

I, too, am America.

1926

AFRO-AMERICAN FRAGMENT

So long,
So far away
Is Africa,
Not even memories alive
Save those that history books create,   5
Save those that songs
Beat back into the blood—
Beat out of blood with words sad-sung
In strange un-Negro tongue—
So long,   10
So far away
Is Africa.

Subdued and time-lost
Are the drums—and yet
Through some vast mist of race   15
There comes this song
I do not understand,
This song of atavistic land,

Of bitter yearnings lost
Without a place—   20
So long,
So far away
Is Africa's
Dark face.

1930

HARLEM SWEETIES

Have you dug the spill
Of Sugar Hill?
Cast your gims
On this sepia thrill:
Brown sugar lassie,   5
Caramel treat,
Honey-gold baby
Sweet enough to eat.
Peach-skinned girlie,
Coffee and cream,   10
Chocolate darling
Out of a dream.
Walnut tinted
Or cocoa brown,
Pomegranate-lipped   15
Pride of the town.
Rich cream-colored
To plum-tinted black,
Feminine sweetness
In Harlem's no lack.   20
Glow of the quince
To blush of the rose.
Persimmon bronze
To cinnamon toes.
Blackberry cordial,   25
Virginia Dare wine—
All those sweet colors
Flavor Harlem of mine!
Walnut or cocoa,
Let me repeat: 30
Caramel, brown sugar,
A chocolate treat.

———————

"*Harlem Sweeties*": 2 *Sugar Hill:* in Hughes's time, a wealthy section of Harlem   3 *gims:* eyes,
possibly a variant of the slang word "glims"

Molasses taffy,
Coffee and cream,
Licorice, clove, cinnamon   35
To a honey-brown dream.
Ginger, wine-gold,
Persimmon, blackberry,
All through the spectrum
Harlem girls vary—   40
So if you want to know beauty's
Rainbow-sweet thrill,
Stroll down luscious,
Delicious, *fine* Sugar Hill.

1942

THEME FOR ENGLISH B

The instructor said,

> *Go home and write*
> *a page tonight.*
> *And let that page come out of you—*
> *Then, it will be true.*   5

I wonder if it's that simple?
I am twenty-two, colored, born in Winston-Salem.
I went to school there, then Durham, then here
to this college on the hill above Harlem.
I am the only colored student in my class.   10
The steps from the hill lead down into Harlem,
through a park, then I cross St. Nicholas,
Eighth Avenue, Seventh, and I come to the Y,
the Harlem Branch Y, where I take the elevator
up to my room, sit down, and write this page: 15

It's not easy to know what is true for you or me
at twenty-two, my age. But I guess I'm what
I feel and see and hear, Harlem, I hear you:
hear you, hear me—we two—you, me, talk on this
    page.
(I hear New York, too.) Me—who?   20
Well, I like to eat, sleep, drink, and be in love.
I like to work, read, learn, and understand life.
I like a pipe for a Christmas present,

"*Theme for English B*": 9 *college:* Columbia University

or records—Bessie, bop, or Bach.
I guess being colored doesn't make me *not* like   25
the same things other folks like who are other races.
So will my page be colored that I write?
Being me, it will not be white.
But it will be
a part of you, instructor.   30
You are white—
yet a part of me, as I am a part of you.
That's American.
Sometimes perhaps you don't want to be a part of me.
Nor do I often want to be a part of you.   35
But we are, that's true!
As I learn from you,
I guess you learn from me—
although you're older—and white—
and somewhat more free.   40

This is my page for English B.

1950

HARLEM

What happens to a dream deferred?

  Does it dry up
  like a raisin in the sun?
  Or fester like a sore—
  And then run?   5
  Does it stink like rotten meat?
  Or crust and sugar over—
  like a syrupy sweet?

  Maybe it just sags
  like a heavy load.   10

  Or does it explode?

1951

SAME IN BLUES

I said to my baby,
Baby, take it slow.
I can't, she said, I can't!
I got to go!

---

24 *Bessie:* Bessie Smith (1894–1937), the great blues singer

> *There's a certain*
> *amount of traveling*
> *in a dream deferred.*   5

Lulu said to Leonard,
I want a diamond ring.
Leonard said to Lulu,   10
You won't get a goddamn thing!

> *A certain*
> *amount of nothing*
> *in a dream deferred.*

Daddy, daddy, daddy,   15
All I want is you.
You can have me, baby—
but my lovin' days is through.

> *A certain*
> *amount of impotence*   20
> *in a dream deferred.*

Three parties
On my party line—
But that third party,
Lord, ain't mine!   25

> *There's liable*
> *to be confusion*
> *in a dream deferred.*

From river to river,
Uptown and down,   30
There's liable to be confusion
when a dream gets kicked around.

1951

While E. E. Cummings was breaking away from the traditions of English verse by taking up forbidden subject matter and developing novel treatments, Langston Hughes was breaking from tradition by making poetry based on the life, language, and culture of Harlem. Among the readers who

had a mixed response to Hughes's experiments was Countee Cullen, another great figure of the Harlem Renaissance.

"I regard these jazz poems as interlopers": Countee Cullen

If I have the least powers of prediction, the first section of this book, *The Weary Blues,* will be most admired, even if less from intrinsic poetical worth than because of its dissociation from the traditionally poetic. Never having been one to think all subjects and forms proper for poetic consideration, I regard these jazz poems as interlopers in the company of the truly beautiful poems in other sections of the book. They move along with the frenzy and electric heat of a Methodist or Baptist revival meeting, and affect me in much the same manner. The revival meeting excites me, cooling and flushing me with alternate chills and fevers of emotion; so do these poems. But when the storm is over, I wonder if the quiet way of communing is not more spiritual for the God-seeking heart; and in the light of reflection I wonder if jazz poems really belong to that dignified company, that select and austere circle of high literary expression which we call poetry. Surely, when in *Negro Dancers* Mr. Hughes says

> Me an' ma baby's
> Got two mo' ways,
> Two mo' ways to do de buck!

he voices, in lyrical, thumb-at-nose fashion the happy careless attitude, akin to poetry, that is found in certain types. And certainly he achieves one of his loveliest lyrics in *Young Singer.* Thus I find myself straddling a fence. It needs only *The Cat and The Saxaphone,* however, to knock me over completely on the side of bewilderment, and incredulity. This creation is a *tour de force* of its kind, but is it a poem:

> EVERYBODY
>
> Half-pint,—
> Gin?
> No, make it
>
> LOVES MY BABY
>
> corn. You like
> don't you, honey?
> BUT MY BABY. . . . .

In the face of accomplished fact, I cannot say *This will never do,* but I feel that it ought never to have been done.

Taken as a group the selections in this book seem one-sided to me. They tend to hurl this poet into the gaping pit that lies before all Negro writers, in the confines of which they become racial artists instead of artists pure and simple. There is too much emphasis here on strictly Negro themes; and this is probably an added reason for my coldness toward the jazz poems—they seem to set a too definite limit upon an already limited field.

Dull books cause no schisms, raise no dissensions, create no parties. Much will be said of *The Weary Blues* because it is a definite achievement, and because Mr. Hughes, in his own way, with a first book that cannot be dismissed as merely *promising*, has arrived.

"To express our individual dark-skinned selves without fear or shame": Langston Hughes

---

One of the most promising of the young Negro poets said to me once, "I want to be a poet—not a Negro poet," meaning, I believe, "I want to write like a white poet"; meaning subconsciously, "I would like to be a white poet"; meaning behind that, "I would like to be white." And I was sorry the young man said that, for no great poet has ever been afraid of being himself. And I doubted then that, with his desire to run away spiritually from his race, this boy would ever be a great poet. But this is the mountain standing in the way of any true Negro art in America—this urge within the race toward whiteness, the desire to pour racial individuality into the mold of American standardization, and to be as little Negro and as much American as possible. . . .

Let the blare of Negro jazz bands and the bellowing voice of Bessie Smith singing Blues penetrate the closed ears of the colored near-intellectuals until they listen and perhaps understand. Let Paul Robeson singing Water Boy, and Rudolph Fisher writing about the streets of Harlem, and Jean Toomer holding the heart of Georgia in his hands, and Aaron Douglas drawing strange black fantasies cause the smug Negro middle class to turn from their white, respectable, ordinary books and papers to catch a glimmer of their own beauty. We younger Negro artists who create now intend to express our individual dark-skinned selves without fear or shame. If white people are pleased we are glad. If they are not, it doesn't matter. We know we are beautiful. And ugly too. The tom-tom cries and the tom-tom laughs. If colored people are pleased we are glad. If they are not, their displeasure doesn't matter either. We build our temples for tomorrow, strong as we know how, and we stand on top of the mountain, free within ourselves.

COUNTEE CULLEN

(1903–1946)

INCIDENT

Once riding in old Baltimore,
   Heart-filled, head-filled with glee,
I saw a Baltimorean
Keep looking straight at me.

Now I was eight and very small,   5
   And he was no whit bigger,
And so I smiled, but he poked out
   His tongue and called me, "Nigger."

I saw the whole of Baltimore
   From May until December: 10
Of all the things that happened there
   That's all that I remember.

1925

YET DO I MARVEL

I doubt not God is good, well-meaning, kind,
And did He stoop to quibble could tell why
The little buried mole continues blind,
Why flesh that mirrors Him must some day die,
Make plain the reason tortured Tantalus   5
Is baited by the fickle fruit, declare
If merely brute caprice dooms Sisyphus
To struggle up a never-ending stair.
Inscrutable His ways are, and immune
To catechism by a mind too strewn   10
With petty cares to slightly understand
What awful brain compels His awful hand.
Yet do I marvel at this curious thing:
To make a poet black, and bid him sing!

1925

"*Yet Do I Marvel*": 5 *Tantalus:* a mythical king punished by having to stand up to his chin in water under a loaded fruit tree; both fruit and water retreated whenever he reached to satisfy his hunger or thirst   7 *Sisyphus:* a mythical king condemned in Hades to roll a huge stone up a hill perpetually; whenever he reached the top of the hill, the stone rolled back down

TO JOHN KEATS, POET, AT SPRINGTIME

I cannot hold my peace, John Keats;
There never was a spring like this;
It is an echo, that repeats
My last year's song and next year's bliss.
I know, in spite of all men say   5
Of Beauty, you have felt her most.
Yea, even in your grave her way
Is laid. Poor, troubled, lyric ghost,
Spring never was so fair and dear
As Beauty makes her seem this year.   10

I cannot hold my peace, John Keats;
I am as helpless in the toil
Of Spring as any lamb that bleats
To feel the solid earth recoil
Beneath his puny legs. Spring beats   15
Her tocsin call to those who love her,
And lo! the dogwood petals cover
Her breast with drifts of snow, and sleek
White gulls fly screaming to her, and hover
About her shoulders, and kiss her cheek,   20
While white and purple lilacs muster
A strength that bears them to a cluster
Of color and odor; for her sake
All things that slept are now awake.

And you and I, shall we lie still,   25
John Keats, while Beauty summons us?
Somehow I feel your sensitive will
Is pulsing up some tremulous
Sap road of a maple tree, whose leaves
Grow music as they grow, since your   30
Wild voice is in them, a harp that grieves
For life that opens death's dark door.
Though dust, your fingers still can push
The Vision Splendid to a birth,
Though now they work as grass in the hush   35
Of the night on the broad sweet page of the earth.

"John Keats is dead," they say, but I
Who hear your full insistent cry
In bud and blossom, leaf and tree,
Know John Keats still writes poetry.   40
And while my head is earthward bowed

To read new life sprung from your shroud,
Folks seeing me must think it strange
That merely spring should so derange
My mind. They do not know that you,   45
John Keats, keep revel with me, too.

1925

FOR A POET

I have wrapped my dreams in a silken cloth,
And laid them away in a box of gold;
Where long will cling the lips of the moth,
I have wrapped my dreams in a silken cloth;
I hide no hate; I am not even wroth   5
Who found earth's breath so keen and cold;
I have wrapped my dreams in a silken cloth,
And laid them away in a box of gold.

1925

FROM THE DARK TOWER

To Charles S. Johnson

We shall not always plant while others reap
The golden increment of bursting fruit,
Not always countenance, abject and mute,
That lesser men should hold their brothers cheap;
Not everlastingly while others sleep   5
Shall we beguile their limbs with mellow flute,
Not always bend to some more subtle brute;
We were not made eternally to weep.

The night whose sable breast relieves the stark,
White stars is no less lovely being dark,   10
And there are buds that cannot bloom at all
In light, but crumple, piteous, and fall;
So in the dark we hide the heart that bleeds,
And wait, and tend our agonizing seeds.

1927

BLACK MAJESTY

These men were kings, albeit they were black,
Christophe and Dessalines and L'Ouverture;
Their majesty has made me turn my back
Upon a plaint I once shaped to endure.
These men were black, I say, but they were crowned   5
And purple-clad, however brief their time.
Stifle your agony; let grief be drowned;
We know joy had a day once and a clime.

Dark gutter-snipe, black sprawler-in-the-mud,
A thing men did a man may do again.   10
What answer filters through your sluggish blood
To these dark ghosts who knew so bright a reign?
"Lo, I am dark, but comely," Sheba sings.
"And we were black," three shades reply, "but kings."

1929

ONLY THE POLISHED SKELETON

The heart has need of some deceit
    To make its pistons rise and fall;
For less than this it would not beat,
    Nor flush the sluggish vein at all.

With subterfuge and fraud the mind   5
    Must fend and parry thrust for thrust,
With logic brutal and unkind
    Beat off the onslaughts of the dust.

Only the polished skeleton,
    Of flesh relieved and pauperized,   10
Can rest at ease and think upon
    The worth of all it so despised.

1935

*Although Countee Cullen rejected the idea that black poets should limit
themselves to poems about race, many of his most familiar poems protest the
treatment and status of American blacks in the 1920s and 30s. Poetry about*

"*Black Majesty*": 2 *Christophe:* Henri Christophe (1767–1820), king of Haiti (1811–1820), was
the most trusted general of L'Ouverture   *Dessalines:* Jean Dessalines (1758–1806), emperor
of Haiti (1805–06), was second in command under L'Ouverture and known for his cruelty
L'Ouverture: Dominique Toussaint L'Ouverture (1743–1803), president of Haiti (1801–02),
stripped the French commissioners of their power and temporarily revolutionized the social
conditions for the black Haitians

injustice, like war poetry (see pages 971–982), always runs the danger of becoming too cliché-riddled and predictable to be effective. The collection of poems below shows a range of approaches to keeping the poetry fresh.

Percy Bysshe Shelley

(1792–1822)

OZYMANDIAS

I met a traveler from an antique land
Who said: Two vast and trunkless legs of stone
Stand in the desert. . . . Near them, on the sand,
Half sunk, a shattered visage lies, whose frown,
And wrinkled lip, and sneer of cold command,   5
Tell that its sculptor well those passions read
Which yet survive, stamped on these lifeless things,
The hand that mocked them, and the heart that fed:
And on the pedestal these words appear:
"My name is Ozymandias, King of Kings: 10
Look on my works, ye Mighty, and despair!"
Nothing beside remains. Round the decay
Of that colossal wreck, boundless and bare
The lone and level sands stretch far away.

1817

Dennis Brutus

(b. 1924)

NIGHTSONG: CITY

Sleep well, my love, sleep well:
the harbour lights glaze over restless docks.
police cars cockroach through the tunnel streets

from the shanties creaking iron-sheets
violence like a bug-infested rag is tossed   5
and fear is immanent as sound in the wind-swung bell;

the long day's anger pants from sand and rocks;
but for this breathing night at least,
my land, my love, sleep well.

1963

Carter Revard

(b. 1931)

DISCOVERY OF THE NEW WORLD

The creatures that we met this morning
marveled at our green skins
and scarlet eyes.
They lack antennae
and can't be made to grasp   5
your proclamation that they are
our lawful food and prey and slaves,
nor can they seem to learn
their body-space is needed to materialize
our oxygen-absorbers—   10
which they conceive are breathing
and thinking creatures whom they implore
at first as angels, then as devils,
when they are being snuffed out
by an absorber swelling   15
into their space.
Their history bled from one this morning,
while we were tasting his brain,
in holographic rainbows,
which we assembled into quite an interesting   20
set of legends—
that's all it came to, though
the colors were quite lovely before we
poured them into our time;
the blue shift bleached away   25
meaningless circumstances, and they would not fit
any of our truth-matrices—
there was, however,
a curious visual echo in their history
of our own coming to their earth;   30
a certain General Sherman said
about one group of them precisely what
we have been telling you about these creatures:
it is our destiny to asterize this planet,
and they WILL not be asterized,   35
so they must be wiped out.
WE NEED their space and nitrogen
which they do not know how to *use*,
nor will they breathe ammonia, as we do;

yet they will not give up their "air" unforced,   40
so it is clear,
    whatever our "agreements" made this
                 morning,
we'll have to kill them all:
    the more we cook this orbit,
the fewer next time round.   45
We've finished lazing all their crops and stores,
we've killed their meat-slaves, now
    they'll have to come into our pens
and we can use them for our final studies
    of how our heart attacks and cancers spread
              among them,   50
    since they seem not immune to these.
—If we didn't have this mission it might be sad
    to see such helpless creatures die
chanting their sacred psalms and bills of rights; but
           never fear
    the riches of this globe are ours   55
and worth whatever pains others may have to
           feel.
    We'll soon have it cleared
completely, as it now is, at the poles, and then
    we will be safe, and rich, and happy here, forever.

1975

Wole Soyinka

(b. 1934)

TELEPHONE CONVERSATION

The price seemed reasonable, location
Indifferent. The landlady swore she lived
Off premises. Nothing remained
But self-confession. 'Madam,' I warned,
'I hate a wasted journey—I am African.'   5
Silence. Silenced transmission of
Pressurized good-breeding. Voice, when it came,
Lipstick coated, long gold-rolled
Cigarette-holder pipped. Caught I was, foully.
'HOW DARK?'. . . I had not misheard. . . .'ARE YOU
    LIGHT   10

OR VERY DARK?' Button B. Button A. Stench
Of rancid breath of public hide-and-speak.
Red booth. Red pillar-box. Red double-tiered
Omnibus squelching tar. It *was* real! Shamed
By ill-mannered silence, surrender   15
Pushed dumbfoundment to beg simplification.
Considerate she was, varying the emphasis—
'ARE YOU DARK? OR VERY LIGHT?' Revelation came.
'You mean—like plain or milk chocolate?'
Her assent was clinical, crushing in its light   20
Impersonality. Rapidly, wave-length adjusted.
I chose. 'West African sepia'—and as afterthought,
'Down in my passport.' Silence for spectroscopic
Flight of fancy, till truthfulness clanged her accent
Hard on the mouthpiece. 'WHAT'S THAT?' conceding   25
'DON'T KNOW WHAT THAT IS.' 'Like brunette.'
'THAT'S DARK, ISN'T IT?' 'Not altogether.
Facially, I am brunette, but madam, you should see
The rest of me. Palm of my hand, soles of my feet
Are a peroxide blonde. Friction, caused—   30
Foolishly madam—by sitting down, has turned
My bottom raven black—One moment
    madam!'—sensing
Her receiver rearing on the thunderclap
About my ears—'Madam,' I pleaded, 'wouldn't you
    rather
See for yourself?'   35

1960

Olga Broumas

(b. 1949)

CINDERELLA

. . . the joy that isn't shared
I heard, dies young.
    Anne Sexton, 1928–1974

"*Telephone Conversation*": 13–14 *Red . . . Omnibus:* phone booths, post office "pillars" and buses in London are painted red in London

Apart from my sisters, estranged
from my mother, I am a woman alone
in a house of men
who secretly
call themselves princes, alone   5
with me usually, under cover of dark. I am the one
    allowed in

to the royal chambers, whose small foot conveniently
fills the slipper of glass. The woman writer, the lady
umpire, the madam chairman, anyone's wife.
I know what I know.   10
And I once was glad

of the chance to use it, even alone
in a strange castle, doing overtime on my own, cracking
the royal code. The princes spoke
in their fathers' language, were eager to praise me   15
my nimble tongue. I am a woman in a state of siege,
    alone

as one piece of laundry, strung on a windy clothesline a
mile long. A woman co-opted by promises: the lure
of a job, the ruse of a choice, a woman forced
to bear witness, falsely   20
against my kind, as each
other sister was judged inadequate, bitchy,
    incompetent,
jealous, too thin, too fat. I know what I know.
What sweet bread I make

for myself in this prosperous house   25
is dirty, what good soup I boil turns
in my mouth to mud. Give
me my ashes. A cold stove, a cinder-block pillow, wet
canvas shoes in my sisters', my sisters' hut. Or I swear

I'll die young   30
like those favored before me, hand-picked each one
for her joyful heart.

1977

PABLO NERUDA

(1904–1973)

HERE I LOVE YOU

translated from the Spanish by W. S. Merwin

Here I love you.
In the dark pines the wind disentangles itself.
The moon glows like phosphorous on the vagrant waters.
Days, all one kind, go chasing each other.

The snow unfurls in dancing figures.   5
A silver gull slips down from the west.
Sometimes a sail. High, high stars.

Oh the black cross of a ship.
Alone.
Sometimes I get up early and even my soul is wet.   10
Far away the sea sounds and resounds.
This is a port.
Here I love you.

Here I love you and the horizon hides you in vain.
I love you still among these cold things.   15
Sometimes my kisses go on those heavy vessels
that cross the sea towards no arrival.
I see myself forgotten like those old anchors.
The piers sadden when the afternoon moors there.
My life grows tired, hungry to no purpose.   20
I love what I do not have. You are so far.
My loathing wrestles with the slow twilights.
But night comes and starts to sing to me.

The moon turns its clockwork dream.
The biggest stars look at me with your eyes.   25
And as I love you, the pines in the wind
want to sing your name with their leaves of wire.

1924, trans. 1969

RITUAL OF MY LEGS

translated from the Spanish by Donald Walsh

For a long time I have stayed looking at my long legs,
with infinite and curious tenderness, with my accus-
    tomed passion,

1036   Poetry

as if they had been the legs of a divine woman,
deeply sunk in the abyss of my thorax:
and, to tell the truth, when time, when time passes   5
over the earth, over the roof, over my impure head,
and it passes, time passes, and in my bed I do not feel at
   night
that a woman is breathing sleeping naked and at my
   side,
then strange, dark things take the place of the absent
   one,
vicious, melancholy thoughts   10
sow heavy possibilities in my bedroom,
and thus, then, I look at my legs as if they belonged to
   another body
and were stuck strongly and gently to my insides.

Like stems or feminine adorable things,
from the knees they rise, cylindrical and thick,   15
with a disturbed and compact material of existence
like brutal, thick goddess arms,
like trees monstrously dressed as human beings,
like fatal, immense lips thirsty and tranquil,
they are, there, the best part of my body: 20
the entirely substantial part, without complicated
   content
of senses or tracheas or intestines or ganglia
nothing but the pure, the sweet, and the thick part of
   my own life
nothing but form and volume existing,
guarding life, nevertheless, in a complete way.   25

People cross through the world nowadays
scarcely remembering that they possess a body and life
   within it,
and there is fear, in the world there is fear of the words
   that designate the body,
and one talks favorably of clothes,
it is possible to speak of trousers, of suits,   30
and of women's underwear (of "ladies'" stockings and
   garters)
as if the articles and the suits went completely empty
   through the streets
and a dark and obscene clothes closet occupied the
   world.

Suits have existence, color, form, design,
and a profound place in our myths, too much of a
   place,   35

there is too much furniture and there are too many
    rooms in the world
and my body lives downcast among and beneath so
    many things,
with an obsession of slavery and chains.

Well, my knees, like knots,
private, functional, evident,   40
separate neatly the halves of my legs:
and really two different worlds, two different sexes
are not so different as the two halves of my legs.

From the knee to the foot a hard form,
mineral, coldly useful, appears,   45
a creature of bone and persistence,
and the ankles are now nothing but the naked purpose,
exactitude and necessity definitively disposed.

Without sensuality, short and hard, and masculine,
my legs exist, there, and endowed   50
with muscular groups like complementary animals,
and there too a life, a solid, subtle, sharp life
endures without trembling, waiting and performing.

At my feet ticklish
and hard like the sun, and open like flowers,   55
and perpetual, magnificent soldiers
in the gray war of space,
everything ends, life definitively ends at my feet,
what is foreign and hostile begins there:
the names of the world, the frontier and the remote,   60
the substantive and the adjectival too great for my heart
originate there with dense and cold constancy.

Always,
manufactured products, stockings, shoes,
or simply infinite air.   65
There will be between my feet and the earth
stressing the isolated and solitary part of my being,
something tenaciously involved between my life and the
    earth,
something openly unconquerable and unfriendly.

1933, trans. 1973

HORSES

translated from the Spanish by Alastair Reid

From the window I saw the horses.

I was in Berlin, in winter. The light
was without light, the sky skyless.

The air white like a moistened loaf.

From my window, I could see a deserted arena,   5
a circle bitten out by the teeth of winter.

All at once, led out by a single man,
ten horses were stepping, stepping into the snow.

Scarcely had they rippled into existence
like flame, than they filled the whole world of my eyes,   10
empty till now. Faultless, flaming,
they stepped like ten gods on broad, clean hoofs,
their manes recalling a dream of salt spray.

Their rumps were globes, were oranges.

Their colour was amber and honey, was on fire.   15

Their necks were towers
carved from the stone of pride,
and in their furious eyes, sheer energy
showed itself, a prisoner inside them.

And there, in the silence, at the mid-   20
point of the day, in a dirty, disgruntled winter,
the horses' intense presence was blood,
was rhythm, was the beckoning light of all being.

I saw, I saw, and seeing, I came to life.
There was the unwitting fountain, the dance of gold,
    the sky,   25
the fire that sprang to life in beautiful things.

I have obliterated that gloomy Berlin winter.

I shall not forget the light from these horses.

1958, trans. 1972

LOVE

translated from the Spanish by Alastair Reid

So many days, oh so many days
seeing you so tangible and so close,
how do I pay, with what do I pay?

The bloodthirsty spring
has awakened in the woods.   5
The foxes start from their earths,

Pablo Neruda   **1039**

the serpents drink the dew,
and I go with you in the leaves
between the pines and the silence,
asking myself how and when   10
I will have to pay for my luck.

Of everything I have seen,
it's you I want to go on seeing;
of everything I've touched,
it's your flesh I want to go on touching.   15
I love your orange laughter.
I am moved by the sight of you sleeping.

What am I to do, love, loved one?
I don't know how others love
or how people loved in the past.   20
I live, watching you, loving you.
Being in love is my nature.

You please me more each afternoon.

Where is she? I keep on asking
if your eyes disappear.   25
How long she's taking! I think, and I'm hurt.
I feel poor, foolish and sad,
and you arrive and you are lightning
glancing off the peach trees.

That's why I love you and yet not why.   30
There are so many reasons, and yet so few,
for love has to be so,
involving and general,
particular and terrifying,
honoured and yet in mourning,   35
flowering like the stars,
and measureless as a kiss.

1958, trans. 1972

SWEETNESS, ALWAYS

translated from the Spanish by Alastair Reid

Why such harsh machinery?
Why, to write down the stuff
and people of every day,
must poems be dressed up in gold,
in old and fearful stone?   5

I want verses of felt or feather
which scarcely weigh, mild verses
with the intimacy of beds
where people have loved and dreamed.
I want poems stained   10
by hands and everydayness.

Verses of pastry which melt
into milk and sugar in the mouth,
air and water to drink,
the bites and kisses of love.   15
I long for eatable sonnets,
poems of honey and flour.

Vanity keeps prodding us
to lift ourselves skyward
or to make deep and useless   20
tunnels underground.
So we forget the joyous
love-needs of our bodies.
We forget about pastries.
We are not feeding the world.   25

In Madras a long time since,
I saw a sugary pyramid,
a tower of confectionery—
one level after another,
and in the construction, rubies,   30
and other blushing delights,
medieval and yellow.

Someone dirtied his hands
to cook up so much sweetness.

Brother poets from here   35
and there, from earth and sky,
from Medellín, from Veracruz,
Abyssinia, Antofagasta,
do you know the recipe for honeycombs?

Let's forget about all that stone.   40

Let your poetry fill up
the equinoctial pastry shop
our mouths long to devour—
all the children's mouths
and the poor adults' also.   45
Don't go on without seeing,
relishing, understanding
all these hearts of sugar.

Don't be afraid of sweetness.

With us or without us,   50
sweetness will go on living
and is infinitely alive,
forever being revived,
for it's in a man's mouth,
whether he's eating or singing,   55
that sweetness has its place.

1958, trans. 1972

LOVE SONNET VI

translated from the Spanish by Stephen Tapscott

Lost in the forest, I broke off a dark twig
and lifted its whisper to my thirsty lips:
maybe it was the voice of the rain crying,
a cracked bell, or a torn heart.

Something from far off: it seemed   5
deep and secret to me, hidden by the earth,
a shout muffled by huge autumns,
by the moist half-open darkness of the leaves.

And there, awaking from the dreaming forest, the
    hazel-sprig
sang under my tongue, its drifting fragrance   10
climbed up through my conscious mind

as if suddenly the roots I had left behind
cried out to me, the land I had lost with my
    childhood—
and I stopped, wounded by the wandering scent.

1960, trans. 1985

THE DANGER

translated from the Spanish by Ben Belitt

Careful, they said: don't slip
on the wax of the ballroom:

"*Sweetness, Always*": 26 *Madras:* an industrial city in India   37 *Medellín:* a city in Columbia
notable for its coffee industry   37 *Veracruz:* one of Mexico's chief seaports   38 *Abyssinia:*
Ethiopia   38 *Antofagasta:* industrial city on Chile's Pacific coast

look out for the ice and the rain and the mud.
Right, we all answered: this winter
we'll live without slippage!   5
And what happened? Under our feet
we felt something give way
and there we were, flat on our fannies:

in the blood of a century.

It seeped under the typist-stenographers,   10
the sweep of the snowdrifts,
staircases of marble;
it crossed meadows and cities,
editor's desks and theaters,
warehouses of ashes,   15
the colonel's grilled windows—
blood flowed in the ditches,
spurted from one war to another,
millions of corpses whose eyes
saw nothing but blood.   20

All this happened just as I tell it.

Maybe others will live out their lives with
no more than an occasional spill on the ice.

I live with this horror; when I tumble,
I go down into blood.   25

1969, trans. 1974

The poet Howard Moss once said in irritation that everyone being published in America in the 1970s was trying to sound like a translation of Pablo Neruda. Both Robert Bly's prose comment from an introduction to Neruda's poems and his elegy touch on the qualities that have made Neruda so appealing as a model.

"His imagination sees the hidden connections between conscious and unconscious": Robert Bly

We tend to associate the modern imagination with the jerky imagination, which starts forward, stops, turns around, switches from subject to subject. In Neruda's poems, the imagination drives forward, joining the entire poem in a rising flow of imaginative energy. In the underworld of the consciousness, in the thickets where Freud, standing a short distance off, pointed out incest bushes, murder trees, half-buried primitive altars, and unburied bodies, Neruda's imagination moves with utter assurance, sweeping from one spot to another almost magically. The starved emotional lives of notary publics he links to the whiteness of flour, sexual desire to the shape of shoes, death to the barking sound where there is no dog. His imagination sees the hidden connections between conscious and unconscious substances with such assurance that he hardly bothers with metaphors—he links them by tying their hidden tails. He is a new kind of creature moving about under the surface of everything. Moving under the earth, he knows everything from the bottom up (which is the right way to learn the nature of a thing) and therefore is never at a loss for its name. Compared to him, most American poets resemble blind men moving gingerly along the ground from tree to tree, from house to house, feeling each thing for a long time, and then calling out "House!" when we already know it is a house.

Neruda has confidence in what is hidden. The Establishment respects only what the light has fallen on, but Neruda likes the unlit just as well. He writes of small typists without scorn, and of the souls of huge, sleeping snakes.

He violates the rules for behavior set up by the wise. The conventionally wise assure us that to a surrealist the outer world has no reality—only his inner flow of images is real. Neruda's work demolishes this banality. Neruda's poetry is deeply surrealist, and yet entities of the outer world like the United Fruit Company have greater force in his poems than in those of any strictly "outward" poet alive. Once a poet takes a political stand, the wise assure us that he will cease writing good poetry. Neruda became a Communist in the middle of his life and has remained one: at least half of his greatest work, one must admit, was written after that time. He has written great poetry at all times of his life.

Finally, many critics in the United States insist the poem must be hard-bitten, impersonal, and rational, lest it lack sophistication. Neruda is wildly romantic, and more sophisticated than Hulme or Pound could dream of being. He has few literary theories. Like Vallejo, Neruda wishes to help humanity, and tells the truth for that reason.

Robert Bly

(b. 1926)

MOURNING PABLO NERUDA

Water is practical,
especially

in August.
Faucet water
falls   5
into the buckets
I carry
to the young
willow trees
whose leaves   10
have been eaten
off
by grasshoppers.
Or this jar of water
that lies   15
next to me
on the car seat
as I drive
to my shack.
When I look down,   20
the seat all
around the jar
is dark,
for water doesn't intend
to give, it gives   25
anyway
and the jar of water
lies
there quivering
as I drive   30
through a countryside
of granite quarries,
stones
soon to be shaped
into blocks for the dead,   35
the only
thing they have
left that is theirs.

For the dead remain inside
us, as water   40
remains inside granite—
hardly at all—
for their job is to
go
away,   45
and not come back,
even when we ask them,

but water
comes to us—
it doesn't care   50
about us; it goes
around us, on the way
to the Minnesota River,
to the Mississippi River,
to the Gulf,   55
always closer
to where
it has to be.

No one lays flowers
on the grave   60
of water,
for it is not
here,
it is
gone.   65

1981

W. H. AUDEN

(1907–1973)

MUSÉE DES BEAUX ARTS

About suffering they were never wrong,
The Old Masters: how well they understood
Its human position; how it takes place
While someone else is eating or opening a window or
    just walking dully along;
How, when the aged are reverently, passionately
    waiting   5
For the miraculous birth, there always must be
Children who did not specially want it to happen,
    skating
On a pond at the edge of the wood:
They never forgot
That even the dreadful martyrdom must run its course   10
Anyhow in a corner, some untidy spot

Where the dogs go on with their doggy life and the
  torturer's horse
Scratches its innocent behind on a tree.

In Breughel's *Icarus,* for instance: how everything turns
  away
Quite leisurely from the disaster; the ploughman may   15
Have heard the splash, the forsaken cry,
But for him it was not an important failure; the sun
  shone
As it had to on the white legs disappearing into the
  green
Water; and the expensive delicate ship that must have
  seen
Something amazing, a boy falling out of the sky,   20
Had somewhere to get to and sailed calmly on.

                              1938

THE SPHINX

Did it once issue from the carver's hand
Healthy? Even the earliest conqueror saw
The face of a sick ape, a bandaged paw,
An ailing lion crouched on dirty sand.

We gape, then go uneasily away: 5
It does not like the young nor love nor learning.
Time hurt it like a person: it lies turning
A vast behind on shrill America,

And witnesses. The huge hurt face accuses
And pardons nothing, least of all success: 10
What counsel it might offer it refuses
To those who face akimbo its distress.

'Do people like me?' *No.* The slave amuses
The lion. 'Am I to suffer always?' *Yes.*

                              1940

"Musée des Beaux Arts": 14 *Icarus:* This painting (c. 1558) depicts a scene from Greek
mythology. The craftsman Daedalus made wax wings on which both he and his son Icarus
were to escape imprisonment. Ignoring his father's warnings Icarus flew too near the sun and
his wings melted, so that he fell to death in the sea. In the painting Icarus is a tiny figure in
the background, only his legs visible above the surface of a bay busy with ships and boats. In
the foreground a ploughman and shepherd are at work

THE UNKNOWN CITIZEN

(To JS/07/M/378 This Marble Monument Is Erected by the State)

He was found by the Bureau of Statistics to be
One against whom there was no official complaint,
And all the reports on his conduct agree
That, in the modern sense of an old-fashioned word, he
    was a saint,
For in everything he did he served the Greater
    Community.   5
Except for the War till the day he retired
He worked in a factory and never got fired,
But satisfied his employers, Fudge Motors Inc.
Yet he wasn't a scab or odd in his views,
For his Union reports that he paid his dues,   10
(Our report on his Union shows it was sound)
And our Social Psychology workers found
That he was popular with his mates and liked a drink.
The Press are convinced that he bought a paper every
    day
And that his reactions to advertisements were normal
    in every way.   15
Policies taken out in his name prove that he was fully
    insured.
And his Health-card shows he was once in hospital but
    left it cured.
Both Producers Research and High-Grade Living
    declare
He was fully sensible to the advantages of the Install-
    ment Plan
And had everything necessary to the Modern Man,   20
A phonograph, a radio, a car and a frigidaire.
Our researchers into Public Opinion are content
That he held the proper opinions for the time of year;
When there was peace, he was for peace; when there
    was war, he went.
He was married and added five children to the
    population,   25
Which our Eugenist says was the right number for a
    parent of his generation,
And our teachers report that he never interfered with
    their education.
Was he free? Was he happy? The question is absurd:
Had anything been wrong, we should certainly have
    heard.

1940

IN MEMORY OF W. B. YEATS

1

He disappeared in the dead of winter:
The brooks were frozen, the airports almost deserted,
The snow disfigured the public statues;
The mercury sank in the mouth of the dying day.
O all the instruments agree   5
The day of his death was a dark cold day.

Far from his illness
The wolves ran on through the evergreen forests,
The peasant river was untempted by the fashionable
    quays;
By mourning tongues   10
The death of the poet was kept from his poems.

But for him it was his last afternoon as himself,
An afternoon of nurses and rumours;
The provinces of his body revolted,
The squares of his mind were empty,   15
Silence invaded the suburbs,
The current of his feeling failed: he became his
    admirers.

Now he is scattered among a hundred cities
And wholly given over to unfamiliar affections;
To find his happiness in another kind of wood   20
And be punished under a foreign code of conscience.
The words of a dead man
Are modified in the guts of the living.

But in the importance and noise of tomorrow
When the brokers are roaring like beasts on the floor
    of the Bourse,   25
And the pour have the sufferings to which they are
    fairly accustomed,
And each in the cell of himself is almost convinced of
    his freedom;
A few thousand will think of this day
As one thinks of a day when one did something slightly
    unusual.
O all the instruments agree   30
The day of his death was a dark cold day.

2

You were silly like us: your gift survived it all;
The parish of rich women, physical decay,
Yourself; mad Ireland hurt you into poetry.

W. H. Auden   **1049**

Now Ireland has her madness and her weather still,   35
For poetry makes nothing happen: it survives
In the valley of its saying where executives
Would never want to tamper; it flows south
From ranches of isolation and the busy griefs,
Raw towns that we believe and die in; it survives,   40
A way of happening, a mouth.

3

Earth, receive an honoured guest;
William Yeats is laid to rest:
Let the Irish vessel lie
Emptied of its poetry.   45

Time that is intolerant
Of the brave and innocent,
And indifferent in a week
To a beautiful physique,

Worships language and forgives   50
Everyone by whom it lives;
Pardons cowardice, conceit,
Lays its honours at their feet.

Time that with this strange excuse
Pardoned Kipling and his views,   55
And will pardon Paul Claudel,
Pardons him for writing well.

In the nightmare of the dark
All the gods of Europe bark,
And the living nations wait,   60
Each sequestered in its hate;

Intellectual disgrace
Stares from every human face,
And the seas of pity lie
Locked and frozen in each eye.   65

Follow, poet, follow right
To the bottom of the night,
With your unconstraining voice
Still persuade us to rejoice;

With the farming of a verse   70
Make a vineyard of the curse,
Sing of human unsuccess
In a rapture of distress;

In the deserts of the heart
Let the healing fountain start,   75

In the prison of his days
Teach the free man how to praise.

1940

SPAIN, 1937

Yesterday all the past. The language of size
Spreading to China along the trade-routes; the
    diffusion
        Of the counting-frame and the cromlech;
Yesterday the shadow-reckoning in the sunny climates.

Yesterday the assessment of insurance by cards,   5
The divination of water; yesterday the invention
        Of cart-wheels and clocks, the taming of
Horses; yesterday the bustling world of navigators.

Yesterday the abolition of fairies and giants;
The fortress like a motionless eagle eyeing the valley,   10
        The chapel built in the forest;
Yesterday the carving of angels and of frightening
    gargoyles.

The trial of heretics among the columns of stone;
Yesterday the theological feuds in the taverns
        And the miraculous cure at the fountain;   15
Yesterday the Sabbath of Witches. But to-day the
    struggle.

Yesterday the installation of dynamos and turbines;
The construction of railways in the colonial desert;
        Yesterday the classic lecture
On the origin of Mankind. But to-day the struggle.   20
Yesterday the belief in the absolute value of Greek;
The fall of the curtain upon the death of a hero;
        Yesterday the prayer to the sunset,
And the adoration of madmen. But to-day the
    struggle.

As the poet whispers, startled among the pines   25
Or, where the loose waterfall sings, compact, or upright
        On the crag by the leaning tower:
'O my vision. O send me the luck of the sailor.'

"*Spain, 1937*": *1937:* the Spanish Civil War, precursor to World War II in its brutal conflict
between fascism and communism, was at its height in 1937   16 *Sabbath of Witches:* a painting
by the Spanish painter Francisco José de Goya Lucientes (1746–1828).

And the investigator peers through his instruments
At the inhuman provinces, the virile bacillus   30
        Or enormous Jupiter finished:
'But the lives of my friends. I inquire, I inquire.'

And the poor in their fireless lodgings dropping the sheets
Of the evening paper: 'Our day is our loss. O show us
        History the operator, the   35
Organizer, Time the refreshing river.'

And the nations combine each cry, invoking the life
That shapes the individual belly and orders
        The private nocturnal terror:
'Did you not found once the city state of the sponge,   40

'Raise the vast military empires of the shark
And the tiger, establish the robin's plucky canton?
        Intervene, O descend as a dove or
A furious papa or a mild engineer: but descend.'

And the life, if it answers at all, replies from the heart   45
And the eyes and the lungs, from the shops and squares of
        the city:
        'O no, I am not the Mover,
Not to-day, not to you. To you I'm the
Yes-man, the bar-companion, the easily-duped: 50
I am whatever you do; I am your vow to be
        Good, your humorous story;
I am your business voice; I am your marriage.

'What's your proposal? To build the Just City? I will.
I agree. Or is it the suicide pact, the romantic   55
        Death? Very well, I accept, for
I am your choice, your decision: yes, I am Spain.'

Many have heard it on remote peninsulas,
On sleepy plains, in the aberrant fishermen's islands,
        In the corrupt heart of the city;   60
Have heard and migrated like gulls or the seeds of a
        flower.

They clung like burrs to the long expresses that lurch
Through the unjust lands, through the night, through the
        alpine tunnel;
        They floated over the oceans;   65
They walked the passes: they came to present their lives.

On that arid square, that fragment nipped off from hot
Africa, soldered so crudely to inventive Europe,
        On that tableland scored by rivers,
Our fever's menacing shapes are precise and alive.   70

To-morrow, perhaps, the future: the research on
    fatigue
And the movements of packers; the gradual exploring
      of all the
        Octaves of radiation;
To-morrow the enlarging of consciousness by diet and
      breathing.   75

To-morrow the rediscovery of romantic love;
The photographing of ravens; all the fun under
        Liberty's masterful shadow;
To-morrow the hour of the pageant-master and the
    musician.
To-morrow, for the young, the poets exploding like bombs, 80
The walks by the lake, the winter of perfect communion;
        To-morrow the bicycle races
Through the suburbs on summer evenings: but to-day
    the struggle.

To-day the inevitable increase in the chances of death;
The conscious acceptance of guilt in the fact of murder; 85
        To-day the expending of powers
On the flat ephemeral pamphlet and the boring meeting.

To-day the makeshift consolations; the shared cigarette;
The cards in the candle-lit barn and the scraping concert,
        The masculine jokes; to-day the   90
 Fumbled and unsatisfactory embrace before hurting.

The stars are dead; the animals will not look:
We are left alone with our day, and the time is short and
        History to the defeated
May say Alas but cannot help or pardon.   95

                                        1940

LUTHER

With conscience cocked to listen for the thunder,
He saw the Devil busy in the wind,
Over the chiming steeples and then under
The doors of nuns and doctors who had sinned.

What apparatus could stave off disaster   5
Or cut the brambles of man's error down?
Flesh was a silent dog that bites its master,
World a still pond in which its children drown.

The fuse of Judgement spluttered in his head:
'Lord, smoke these honeyed insects from their hives.   10

All works, Great Men, Societies are bad.
The Just shall live by Faith . . .' he cried in dread.

And men and women of the world were glad,
Who'd never cared or trembled in their lives.

1945

VOLTAIRE AT FERNEY

Perfectly happy now, he looked at his estate.
An exile making watches glanced up as he passed
And went on working; where a hospital was rising fast,
A joiner touched his cap; an agent came to tell
Some of the trees he'd planted were progressing well.   5
The white alps glittered. It was summer. He was very
   great.

Far off in Paris where his enemies
Whispered that he was wicked, in an upright chair
A blind old woman longed for death and letters. He
   would write,
"Nothing is better than life." But was it? Yes, the fight   10
Against the false and the unfair
Was always worth it. So was gardening. Civilize.

Cajoling, scolding, scheming, cleverest of them all,
He'd had the other children in a holy war
Against the infamous grown-ups; and, like a child, been
   sly   15
And humble, when there was occasion for
The two-faced answer or the plain protective lie,
But, patient like a peasant, waited for their fall.

And never doubted, like D'Alembert, he would win:
Only Pascal was a great enemy, the rest
Were rats already poisoned; there was much, though,
   to be done,   20
And only himself to count upon.
Dear Diderot was dull but did his best;
Rousseau, he'd always known, would blubber and give
   in.

"*Voltaire at Ferney*": *Voltaire:* the great French philosopher (1694–1778) whose rationalism led him to attack bigotry, cruelty, tyranny, and the church. Among his allies were the encyclopedists Diderot and D'Alembert. Jean-Jacques Rousseau (1712–1778), once an ally to the encyclopedists, turned against them partly because he was influenced by the writings of Blaise Pascal (1623–1662), the great mathematician and advocate of religious faith

Night fell and made him think of women: Lust
Was one of the great teachers; Pascal was a fool.   25
How Emilie had loved astronomy and bed;
Pimpette had loved him too, like scandal; he was glad.
He'd done his share of weeping for Jerusalem: As a
    rule,
It was the pleasure-haters who became unjust.

Yet, like a sentinel, he could not sleep. The night was
    full of wrong,   30
Earthquakes and executions: Soon he would be dead,
And still all over Europe stood the horrible nurses
Itching to boil their children. Only his verses
Perhaps could stop them: He must go on working:
    Overhead,
The uncomplaining stars composed their lucid song.   35

1948

THE SHIELD OF ACHILLES

    She looked over his shoulder
        For vines and olive trees,
    Marble well-governed cities
        And ships upon untamed seas,
    But there on the shining metal   5
        his hands had put instead
    An artificial wilderness
        And a sky like lead.

A plain without a feature, bare and brown,
    No blade of grass, no sign of neighborhood,   10
Nothing to eat and nowhere to sit down,
    Yet, congregated on its blankness, stood
    An unintelligible multitude,
A million eyes, a million boots in line,
Without expression, waiting for a sign.   15

Out of the air a voice without a face
    Proved by statistics that some cause was just
In tones as dry and level as the place:
    No one was cheered and nothing was discussed;
    Column by column in a cloud of dust   20

"The Shield of Achilles": Shield of Achilles: In Homer's *Iliad,* after Patroclus is killed wearing his
friend Achilles' armor, Hephaestos, the blacksmith of the gods, makes him new armor,
including a beautiful shield on which are portrayed the earth, sea, and heavens

They marched away enduring a belief
Whose logic brought them, somewhere else, to grief.

      She looked over his shoulder
         For ritual pieties,
      White flower-garlanded heifers,   25
         Libation and sacrifice,
      But there on the shining metal
         Where the altar should have been,
      She saw by his flickering forge-light
         Quite another scene.   30

Barbed wire enclosed an arbitrary spot
   Where bored officials lounged (one cracked a joke)
And sentries sweated for the day was hot:
   A crowd of ordinary decent folk
   Watched from without and neither moved nor spoke   35
As three pale figures were led forth and bound
To three posts driven upright in the ground.

The mass and majesty of this world, all
   That carries weight and always weighs the same
Lay in the hands of others; they were small   40
   And could not hope for help and no help came:
   What their foes liked to do was done, their shame
Was all the worst could wish; they lost their pride
And died as men before their bodies died.

      She looked over his shoulder   45
         For athletes at their games,
      Men and women in a dance
         Moving their sweet limbs
      Quick, quick, to music,
         But there on the shining shield   50
      His hands had set no dancing-floor
         But a weed-choked field.

A ragged urchin, aimless and alone,
   Loitered about that vacancy, a bird
Flew up to safety from his well-aimed stone: 55
   That girls are raped, that two boys knife a third,
   Were axioms to him, who'd never heard
Of any world where promises were kept,
Or one could weep because another wept.

      The thin-lipped armorer,   60
         Hephaestos hobbled away,
      Thetis of the shining breasts
         Cried out in dismay

At what the god had wrought
   To please her son, the strong   65
   Iron-hearted man-slaying Achilles
   Who would not live long.

1952

The range of W. H. Auden's poetic subjects, styles, and tones is so wide that some readers have found it disturbing. Some have been particularly distressed by the contrast between the poet committed to social justice and the poet of light verse and poetic gamesmanship. When Auden edited The Oxford Book of Light Verse, *he wrote in the introduction a statement that can help us reconcile these two Audens.*

"Poetry which is at the same time light and adult": W. H. Auden

Wordsworth's case is paralleled by the history of most of the Romantic poets, both of his day and of the century following. Isolated in an amorphous society with no real communal ties, bewildered by its complexity, horrified by its ugliness and power, and uncertain of an audience, they turned away from the life of their time to the contemplation of their own emotions and the creation of imaginary worlds, Wordsworth to Nature, Keats and Mallarmé to a world of pure poetry, Shelley to a future Golden Age, Baudelaire and Hölderlin to a past,

> . . . ces époques nues
> Dont Phoebus se plaisait à dorer les statues.

Instead of the poet regarding himself as an entertainer, he becomes the prophet, 'the unacknowledged legislator of the world', or the Dandy who sits in the café, 'proud that he is less base than the passers-by, saying to himself as he contemplates the smoke of his cigar: "What does it matter to me what becomes of my perceptions?"'

   This is not, of course, to condemn the Romantic poets, but to

---

"Poetry . . . light and adult": ces époques . . . statues: ". . . those naked ages/When Phoebus loved to gild statues." The quotation is from Baudelaire's *Flowers of Evil* and is part of a poem contrasting the ancient world's pleasure in healthy, naked young bodies with modern prudery and degeneracy."   *"What does . . . perceptions":* the quotation is from Baudelaire's *Intimate Journals.*

explain why they wrote the kind of poetry they did, why their best work is personal, intense, often difficult, and generally rather gloomy.

The release from social pressure was, at first, extremely stimulating. The private world was a relatively unexplored field, and the technical discoveries made were as great as those being made in industry. But the feeling of excitement was followed by a feeling of loss. For if it is true that the closer bound the artist is to his community the harder it is for him to see with a detached vision, it is also true that when he is too isolated, though he may see clearly enough what he does see, that dwindles in quantity and importance. He 'knows more and more about less and less'. It is significant that so many of these poets either died young like Keats, or went mad like Hölderlin, or ceased producing good work like Wordsworth, or gave up writing altogether like Rimbaud—'I must ask forgiveness for having fed myself on lies, and let us go. . . . One must be absolutely modern.' For the private world is fascinating, but it is exhaustible. Without a secure place in society, without an intimate relation between himself and his audience, without, in fact, those conditions which make for Light Verse, the poet finds it difficult to grow beyond a certain point. . . .

The problem for the modern poet, as for every one else to-day, is how to find or form a genuine community, in which each has his valued place and can feel at home. The old pre-industrial community and culture are gone and cannot be brought back. Nor is it desirable that they should be. They were too unjust, too squalid, and too custom-bound. Virtues which were once nursed unconsciously by the forces of nature must now be recovered and fostered by a deliberate effort of the will and the intelligence. In the future, societies will not grow of themselves. They will either be made consciously or decay. A democracy in which each citizen is as fully conscious and capable of making a rational choice, as in the past has been possible only for the wealthier few, is the only kind of society which in the future is likely to survive for long.

In such a society, and in such alone, will it be possible for the poet, without sacrificing any of his subtleties of sensibility or his integrity, to write poetry which is simple, clear, and gay.

For poetry which is at the same time light and adult can only be written in a society which is both integrated and free.

THEODORE ROETHKE

(1908–1963)

MY PAPA'S WALTZ

The whiskey on your breath
Could make a small boy dizzy;
But I hung on like death:
Such waltzing was not easy.

We romped until the pans   5
Slid from the kitchen shelf;
My mother's countenance
Could not unfrown itself.

The hand that held my wrist
Was battered on one knuckle;   10
At every step you missed
My right ear scraped a buckle.

You beat time on my head
With a palm caked hard by dirt,
Then waltzed me off to bed   15
Still clinging to your shirt.

1942

BIG WIND

Where were the greenhouses going,
Lunging into the lashing
Wind driving water
So far down the river
All the faucets stopped?   5
So we drained the manure-machine
For the steam plant,
Pumping the stale mixture
Into the rusty boilers,
Watching the pressure gauge   10
Waver over to red,
As the seams hissed
And the live steam
Drove to the far
End of the rose-house,   15
Where the worst wind was,

Creaking the cypress window-frames,
Cracking so much thin glass
We stayed all night,
Stuffing the holes with burlap;   20
But she rode it out,
That old rose-house,
She hove into the teeth of it,
The core and pith of that ugly storm,
Ploughing with her stiff prow,   25
Bucking into the wind-waves
That broke over the whole of her,
Flailing her sides with spray,
Flinging long strings of wet across the roof-top,
Finally veering, wearing themselves out, merely   30
Whistling thinly under the wind-vents;
She sailed until the calm morning,
Carrying her full cargo of roses.

                                                    1948

ROOT CELLAR

Nothing would sleep in that cellar, dank as a ditch,
Bulbs broke out of boxes hunting for chinks in the
   dark,
Shoots dangled and drooped,
Lolling obscenely from mildewed crates,
Hung down long yellow evil necks, like tropical snakes.   5
And what a congress of stinks!
Roots ripe as old bait,
Pulpy stems, rank, silo-rich,
Leaf-mold, manure, lime, piled against slippery planks
Nothing would give up life: 10
Even the dirt kept breathing a small breath.

                                                    1948

CHILD ON TOP OF A GREENHOUSE

The wind billowing out the seat of my britches,
My feet crackling splinters of glass and dried putty,
The half-grown chrysanthemums staring up like accusers,
Up through the streaked glass, flashing with sunlight,
A few white clouds all rushing eastward,   5
A line of elms plunging and tossing like horses,
And everyone, everyone pointing up and shouting!

                                                    1948

FRAU BAUMAN, FRAU SCHMIDT, AND FRAU SCHWARTZE

Gone the three ancient ladies
Who creaked on the greenhouse ladders,
Reaching up white strings
To wind, to wind
The sweet-pea tendrils, the smilax,   5
Nasturtiums, the climbing
Roses, to straighten
Carnations, red
Chrysanthemums; the stiff
Stems, jointed like corn,   10
They tied and tucked,—
These nurses of nobody else.
Quicker than birds, they dipped
Up and sifted the dirt;
They sprinkled and shook;   15
They stood astride pipes,
Their skirts billowing out wide into tents,
Their hands twinkling with wet;
Like witches they flew along rows
Keeping creation at ease;   20
With a tendril for needle
They sewed up the air with a stem;
They teased out the seed that the cold kept asleep,—
All the coils, loops, and whorls.
They trellised the sun; they plotted for more than
      themselves   25

I remember how they picked me up, a spindly kid,
Pinching and poking my thin ribs
Till I lay in their laps, laughing,
Weak as a whiffet;
Now, when I'm alone and cold in my bed,   30
They still hover over me,
These ancient leathery crones,
With their bandannas stiffened with sweat,
And their thorn-bitten wrists,
And their snuff-laden breath blowing lightly over me in
      my first sleep.   35

                                    1953

I KNEW A WOMAN

I knew a woman, lovely in her bones,
When small birds sighed, she would sigh back at them;

Ah, when she moved, she moved more ways than one:
The shapes a bright container can contain!
Of her choice virtues only gods should speak,   5
Or English poets who grew up on Greek
(I'd have them sing in chorus, cheek to cheek).

How well her wishes went! She stroked my chin,
She taught me Turn, and Counter-turn, and Stand;
She taught me Touch, that undulant white skin;   10
I nibbled meekly from her proffered hand;
She was the sickle; I, poor I, the rake,
Coming behind her for her pretty sake
(But what prodigious mowing we did make).

Love likes a gander, and adores a goose: 15
Her full lips pursed, the errant note to seize;
She played it quick, she played it light and loose,
My eyes, they dazzled at her flowing knees;
Her several parts could keep a pure repose,
Or one hip quiver with a mobile nose   20
(She moved in circles, and those circles moved).

Let seed be grass, and grass turn into hay:
I'm martyr to a motion not my own;
What's freedom for? To know eternity.
I swear she cast a shadow white as stone.   25
But who would count eternity in days?
These old bones live to learn her wanton ways:
(I measure time by how a body sways).

1954

Louise Bogan once remarked that Theodore Roethke and Robert Lowell are alike in their fascination with memories that stretch back to childhood, but unalike in their methods. Roethke, she said, combines "a close recording of the actual with a kind of lyrical incantation" absent from Lowell. Roethke himself has discussed this "lyrical incantation" in "Some Remarks on Rhythm."

"I Knew a Woman": 9 *Turn . . . Stand:* in classical Greek drama, divisions of a Pindaric ode, corresponding to the movement of the chorus as it chanted the lines

"Mother Goose, or the traditional kind of thing, is almost infallible": Theodore Roethke

What do *I* like? Listen:

> Hinx, minx, the old witch winks!
> The fat begins to fry!
> There's nobody home but Jumping Joan,
> And father, and mother, and I.

Now what makes that "catchy," to use Mr. Frost's word? For one thing: the rhythm. Five stresses out of a possible six in the first line, though maybe "old" doesn't take quite as strong a stress as the others. And three—keep noticing that magic number—internal rhymes, *hinx, minx, winks*. And notice too the apparent mysteriousness of the action: something happens right away—the old witch winks and she sets events into motion. The fat begins to fry, literally and symbolically. She commands—no old fool witch this one. Notice that the second line, "The fat begins to fry," is absolutely regular metrically. It's all iambs, a thing that often occurs when previous lines are sprung or heavily counterpointed. The author doesn't want to get too far from his base, from his ground beat. The third line varies again with an anapaest and variations in the "o" and "u" sounds. "There's nobody home but Jumping Joan." Then the last line—anapaest lengthening the line out to satisfy the ear, "And father, and mother, and I." Sometimes we are inclined to feel that Mother Goose, or the traditional kind of thing, is almost infallible as memorable speech—the phrase is Auden's. . . .

It's nonsense, of course, to think that memorableness in poetry comes solely from rhetorical devices, or the following of certain sound patterns, or contrapuntal rhythmical effects. We all know that poetry is shot through with appeals to the unconsciousness, to the fears and desires that go far back into our childhood, into the imagination of the race. And we know that some words, like *hill, plow, mother, window, bird, fish*, are so drenched with human association, they sometimes can make even bad poems evocative.

ELIZABETH BISHOP

(1911-1979)

THE PRODIGAL

The brown enormous odor he lived by
was too close, with its breathing and thick hair,
for him to judge. The floor was rotten; the sty
was plastered halfway up with glass-smooth dung.
Light-lashed, self-righteous, above moving snouts,   5
the pigs' eyes followed him, a cheerful stare—
even to the sow that always ate her young—
till, sickening, he leaned to scratch her head.
But sometimes mornings after drinking bouts
(he hid the pints behind a two-by-four),   10
the sunrise glazed the barnyard mud with red;
the burning puddles seemed to reassure.
And then he thought he almost might endure
his exile yet another year or more.

But evenings the first star came to warn.   15
The farmer whom he worked for came at dark
to shut the cows and horses in the barn
beneath their overhanging clouds of hay,
with pitchforks, faint forked lightnings, catching light,
safe and companionable as in the Ark.   20
The pigs stuck out their little feet and snored.
The lantern—like the sun, going away—
laid on the mud a pacing aureole.

Carrying a bucket along a slimy board,
he felt the bats' uncertain staggering flight,   25
his shuddering insights, beyond his control,
touching him. But it took him a long time
finally to make his mind up to go home.

1951

"The Prodigal": Prodigal: See Luke 15:11–32.

FILLING STATION

Oh, but it is dirty!
—this little filling station,
oil-soaked, oil-permeated
to a disturbing, over-all
black translucency.   5
Be careful with that match!

Father wears a dirty,
oil-soaked monkey suit
that cuts him under the arms,
and several quick and saucy   10
and greasy sons assist him
(it's a family filling station),
all quite thoroughly dirty.

Do they live in the station?
It has a cement porch   15
behind the pumps, and on it
a set of crushed and grease-
impregnated wickerwork;
on the wicker sofa
a dirty dog, quite comfy.   20

Some comic books provide
the only note of color—
of certain color. They lie
upon a big dim doily
draping a taboret   25
(part of the set), beside
a big hirsute begonia.

Why the extraneous plant?
Why the taboret?
Why, oh why, the doily?   30
(Embroidered in daisy stitch
with marguerites, I think,
and heavy with gray crochet.)

Somebody embroidered the doily.
Somebody waters the plant,   35
or oils it, maybe. Somebody
arranges the rows of cans
so that they softly say:
ESSO—SO—SO—SO
to high-strung automobiles.   40
Somebody loves us all.

1955

Elizabeth Bishop   1065

THE ARMADILLO

(For Robert Lowell)

This is the time of year
when almost every night
the frail, illegal fire balloons appear.
Climbing the mountain height,

rising toward a saint   5
still honored in these parts,
the paper chambers flush and fill with light
that comes and goes, like hearts.

Once up against the sky it's hard
to tell them from the stars—   10
planets, that is—the tinted ones:
Venus going down, or Mars,

or the pale green one. With a wind,
they flare and falter, wobble and toss;
but if it's still they steer between   15
the kite sticks of the Southern Cross,

receding, dwindling, solemnly
and steadily forsaking us,
or, in the downdraft from a peak,
suddenly turning dangerous.   20

Last night another big one fell.
It splattered like an egg of fire
against the cliff behind the house.
The flame ran down. We saw the pair

of owls who nest there flying up   25
and up, their whirling black-and-white
strained bright pink underneath, until
they shrieked up out of sight.

The ancient owls' nest must have burned.
Hastily, all alone,   30
a glistening armadillo left the scene,
rose-flecked, head down, tail down,

and then a baby rabbit jumped out,
short-eared, to our surprise.
So soft!—a handful of intangible ash   35
with fixed, ignited eyes.

Too pretty, dreamlike mimicry!
O falling fire and piercing cry

and panic, and a weak mailed fist
clenched ignorant against the sky!   40

1965

QUESTIONS OF TRAVEL

There are too many waterfalls here; the crowded
   streams
hurry too rapidly down to the sea,
and the pressure of so many clouds on the
   mountaintops
makes them spill over the sides in soft slow-motion,
turning to waterfalls under our very eyes.   5
—For if those streaks, those mile-long, shiny,
   tearstains,
aren't waterfalls yet,
in a quick age or so, as ages go here,
they probably will be.
But if the streams and clouds keep travelling, travelling,
   travelling,   10
the mountains look like the hulls of capsized ships,
slime-hung and barnacled.

Think of the long trip home.
Should we have stayed at home and thought of here?
Where should we be today?   15
Is it right to be watching strangers in a play
in this strangest of theatres?
What childishness is it that while there's a breath of life
in our bodies, we are determined to rush
to see the sun the other way around?   20
The tiniest green hummingbird in the world?
To stare at some inexplicable old stonework,
inexplicable and impenetrable,
at any view,
instantly seen and always, always delightful?   25
Oh, must we dream our dreams
and have them, too?
And have we room
for one more folded sunset, still quite warm?

But surely it would have been a pity   30
not to have seen the trees along this road,
really exaggerated in their beauty,
not to have seen them gesturing
like noble pantomimists, robed in pink.

—Not to have had to stop for gas and heard   35
the sad, two-noted, wooden tune
of disparate wooden clogs
carelessly clacking over
a grease-stained filling-station floor.
(In another country the clogs would all be tested.   40
Each pair there would have identical pitch.)
—A pity not to have heard
the other, less primitive music of the fat brown bird
who sings above the broken gasoline pump
in a bamboo church of Jesuit baroque: 45
three towers, five silver crosses.
—Yes, a pity not to have pondered,
blurr'dly and inconclusively,
on what connection can exist for centuries
between the crudest wooden footwear   50
and, careful and finicky,
the whittled fantasies of wooden cages.
—Never to have studied history in
the weak calligraphy of songbirds' cages.
—And never to have had to listen to rain   55
so much like politicians' speeches:
two hours of unrelenting oratory
and then a sudden golden silence
in which the traveller takes a notebook, writes:

"Is it lack of imagination that makes us come   60
to imagined places, not just stay at home?
Or could Pascal have been not entirely right
about just sitting quietly in one's room?

Continent, city, country, society:
the choice is never wide and never free.   65
And here, or there . . . No. Should we have stayed at home,
wherever that may be?"

1965

IN THE WAITING ROOM

In Worcester, Massachusetts,
I went with Aunt Consuelo
to keep her dentist's appointment

———
"*Questions of Travel*": 62 *Pascal:* The French geometrician and philosopher (1623–1662)
secluded himself in the Jansenist monastery of Port Royal after 1654.

and sat and waited for her
in the dentist's waiting room.   5
It was winter. It got dark
early. The waiting room
was full of grown-up people,
arctics and overcoats,
lamps and magazines.   10
My aunt was inside
what seemed like a long time
and while I waited I read
the *National Geographic*
(I could read) and carefully   15
studied the photographs:
the inside of a volcano,
black, and full of ashes;
then it was spilling over
in rivulets of fire.   20
Osa and Martin Johnson
dressed in riding breeches,
laced boots, and pith helmets.
A dead man slung on a pole
—"Long Pig," the caption said.   25
Babies with pointed heads
wound round and round with string;
black, naked women with necks
wound round and round with wire
like the necks of light bulbs.   30
Their breasts were horrifying.
I read it right straight through.
I was too shy to stop.
And then I looked at the cover:
the yellow margins, the date.   35

Suddenly, from inside,
came an *oh!* of pain
—Aunt Consuelo's voice—
not very loud or long.
I wasn't at all surprised;   40
even then I knew she was
a foolish, timid woman.
I might have been embarrassed,
but wasn't. What took me
completely by surprise   45
was that it was *me:*
my voice, in my mouth.
Without thinking at all

I was my foolish aunt,
I—we—were falling, falling,   50
our eyes glued to the cover
of the *National Geographic,*
February, 1918.

I said to myself: three days
and you'll be seven years old.   55
I was saying it to stop
the sensation of falling off
the round, turning world
into cold, blue-black space.
But I felt: you are an *I,*   60
you are an *Elizabeth,*
you are one of *them.*
Why should you be one, too?
I scarcely dared to look
to see what it was I was.   65
I gave a sidelong glance
—I couldn't look any higher—
at shadowy gray knees,
trousers and skirts and boots
and different pairs of hands   70
lying under the lamps.
I knew that nothing stranger
had ever happened, that nothing
stranger could ever happen.
Why should I be my aunt,   75
or me, or anyone?
What similarities—
boots, hands, the family voice
I felt in my throat, or even
the *National Geographic*   80
and those awful hanging breasts–
held us all together
or made us all just one?
How—I didn't know any
word for it—how "unlikely". . .   85
How had I come to be here,
like them, and overhear
a cry of pain that could have
got loud and worse but hadn't?

The waiting room was bright   90
and too hot. It was sliding
beneath a big black wave,
another, and another.

Then I was back in it.
The War was on. Outside,   95
in Worcester, Massachusetts,
were night and slush and cold,
and it was still the fifth
of February, 1918.

1976

CRUSOE IN ENGLAND

A new volcano has erupted,
the papers say, and last week I was reading
where some ship saw an island being born:

at first a breath of steam, ten miles away;
and then a black fleck—basalt, probably—   5
rose in the mate's binoculars
and caught on the horizon like a fly.
They named it. But my poor old island's still
un-rediscovered, un-renamable.
None of the books has ever got it right.   10

Well, I had fifty-two
miserable, small volcanoes I could climb
with a few slithery strides—
volcanoes dead as ash heaps.
I used to sit on the edge of the highest one   15
and count the others standing up,
naked and leaden, with their heads blown off.
I'd think that if they were the size
I thought volcanoes should be, then I had
become a giant;   20
and if I had become a giant,
I couldn't bear to think what size
the goats and turtles were,
or the gulls, or the over-lapping rollers
—a glittering hexagon of rollers   25
closing and closing in, but never quite,
glittering and glittering, though the sky
was mostly overcast.

My island seemed to be
a sort of cloud-dump. All the hemisphere's   30
left-over clouds arrived and hung

"*Crusoe in England*": Crusoe: shipwrecked hero of Daniel Defoe's *Robinson Crusoe* (1719)

above the craters—their parched throats
were hot to touch.
Was that why it rained so much?
And why sometimes the whole place hissed?   35
The turtles lumbered by, high-domed,
hissing like teakettles.
(And I'd have given years, or taken a few,
for any sort of kettle, of course.)
The folds of lava, running out to sea,   40
would hiss. I'd turn. And then they'd prove
to be more turtles.

The beaches were all lava, variegated,
black, red, and white, and gray;
the marbled colors made a fine display.   45
And I had waterspouts. Oh,
half a dozen at a time, far out,
they'd come and go, advancing and retreating,
their heads in cloud, their feet in moving patches
of scuffed-up white.   50
Glass chimneys, flexible, attenuated,
sacerdotal beings of glass . . . I watched
the water spiral up in them like smoke.
Beautiful, yes, but not much company.

I often gave way to self-pity.   55
"Do I deserve this? I suppose I must.
I wouldn't be here otherwise. Was there
a moment when I actually chose this?
I don't remember, but there could have been."
What's wrong about self-pity, anyway?   60
With my legs dangling down familiarly
over a crater's edge, I told myself
"Pity should begin at home." So the more
pity I felt, the more I felt at home.

The sun set in the sea; the same odd sun   65
rose from the sea,
and there was one of it and one of me.
The island had one kind of everything:
one tree snail, a bright violet-blue
with a thin shell, crept over everything,   70
over the one variety of tree,
a sooty, scrub affair.
Snail shells lay under these in drifts
and, at a distance,
you'd swear that they were beds of irises.   75

There was one kind of berry, a dark red.
I tried it, one by one, and hours apart.
Sub-acid, and not bad, no ill effects;
and so I made home-brew. I'd drink
the awful, fizzy, stinging stuff   80
that went straight to my head
and play my home-made flute
(I think it had the weirdest scale on earth)
and, dizzy, whoop and dance among the goats.
Home-made, home-made! But aren't we all?   85
I felt a deep affection for
the smallest of my island industries.
No, not exactly, since the smallest was
a miserable philosophy.

Because I didn't know enough.   90
Why didn't I know enough of something?
Greek drama or astronomy? The books
I'd read were full of blanks;
the poems—well, I tried
reciting to my iris-beds,   95
"They flash upon that inward eye,
which is the bliss . . ." The bliss of what?
One of the first things that I did
when I got back was look it up.

The island smelled of goat and guano.   100
The goats were white, so were the gulls,
and both too tame, or else they thought
I was a goat, too, or a gull.
Baa, baa, baa and *shriek, shriek, shriek,*
baa . . . shriek . . . baa . . . I still can't shake   105
them from my ears; they're hurting now.
The questioning shrieks, the equivocal replies
over a ground of hissing rain
and hissing, ambulating turtles
got on my nerves.   110

When all the gulls flew up at once, they sounded
like a big tree in a strong wind, its leaves.
I'd shut my eyes and think about a tree,
an oak, say, with real shade, somewhere.
I'd heard of cattle getting island-sick.   115
I thought the goats were.
One billy-goat would stand on the volcano
I'd christened *Mont d'Espoir* or *Mount Despair*
(I'd time enough to play with names),

and bleat and bleat, and sniff the air.   120
I'd grab his beard and look at him.
His pupils, horizontal, narrowed up
and expressed nothing, or a little malice.
I got so tired of the very colors!
One day I dyed a baby goat bright red   125
with my red berries, just to see
something a little different.
And then his mother wouldn't recognize him.

Dreams were the worst. Of course I dreamed of food
and love, but they were pleasant rather   130
than otherwise. But then I'd dream of things
like slitting a baby's throat, mistaking it
for a baby goat. I'd have
nightmares of other islands
stretching away from mine, infinities   135
of islands, islands spawning islands,
like frogs' eggs turning into polliwogs
of islands, knowing that I had to live
on each and every one, eventually,
for ages, registering their flora,   140
their fauna, their geography.

Just when I thought I couldn't stand it
another minute longer, Friday came.
(Accounts of that have everything all wrong.)
Friday was nice.   145
Friday was nice, and we were friends.
If only he had been a woman!
I wanted to propagate my kind,
and so did he, I think, poor boy.
He'd pet the baby goats sometimes,   150
and race with them, or carry one around.
—Pretty to watch; he had a pretty body.
And then one day they came and took us off.

Now I live here, another island,
that doesn't seem like one, but who decides?   155
My blood was full of them; my brain
bred islands. But that archipelago
has petered out. I'm old.
I'm bored, too, drinking my real tea,
surrounded by uninteresting lumber.   160
The knife there on the shelf—
it reeked of meaning, like a crucifix.
It lived. How many years did I
beg it, implore it, not to break?

I knew each nick and scratch by heart,   165
the bluish blade, the broken tip,
the lines of wood-grain on the handle . . .
Now it won't look at me at all.
The living soul has dribbled away.
My eyes rest on it and pass on.   170

The local museum's asked me to
leave everything to them:
the flute, the knife, the shrivelled shoes,
my shedding goatskin trousers
(moths have got in the fur),   175
the parasol that took me such a time
remembering the way the ribs should go.
It still will work but, folded up,
looks like a plucked and skinny fowl.
How can anyone want such things?   180
—And Friday, my dear Friday, died of measles
seventeen years ago come March.

                                    1976

ONE ART

The art of losing isn't hard to master;
so many things seem filled with the intent
to be lost that their loss is no disaster.

Lose something every day. Accept the fluster
of lost door keys, the hour badly spent.   5
The art of losing isn't hard to master.

Then practice losing farther, losing faster:
places, and names, and where it was you meant
to travel. None of these will bring disaster.

I lost my mother's watch. And look! my last, or   10
next-to-last, of three loved houses went.
The art of losing isn't hard to master.

I lost two cities, lovely ones. And, vaster,
some realms I owned, two rivers, a continent.
I miss them, but it wasn't a disaster.   15

—Even losing you (the joking voice, a gesture
I love) I shan't have lied. It's evident
the art of losing's not too hard to master
though it may look like (*Write* it!) like disaster.

                                    1976

The attentive observation that makes Elizabeth Bishop's poems so unusual also shows in her reading of other poets. Poet and translator Dana Gioia, who took Bishop's class in modern poetry at Harvard in 1975, gives us an account of Bishop's attitude toward William Carlos Williams's work in particular and poetry in general.

"She wanted us to see poems, not ideas": Dana Gioia

We began with poems from "Spring and All," by William Carlos Williams. We worked through each poem as slowly as if it had been written in a foreign language, and Miss Bishop provided a detailed commentary: biographical information, publication dates, geographical facts, and personal anecdotes about her meetings with the poet. She particularly admired the passage with which Williams opened the title poem of "Spring and All":

> By the road to the contagious hospital
> under the surge of the blue
> mottled clouds driven from the
> northeast—a cold wind. Beyond, the
> waste of broad, muddy fields
> brown with dried weeds, standing
>   and fallen
>
> patches of standing water
> the scattering of tall trees
>
> All along the road the reddish
> purplish, forked, upstanding, twiggy
> stuff of bushes and small trees
> with dead, brown leaves under them
> leafless vines

It took us about an hour to work through this straightforward passage, not because Miss Bishop had any thesis to prove but because it reminded her of so many things—wildflowers, New Jersey, the medical profession, modern painting. Her remarks often went beyond the point at hand, but frequently she made some phrase or passage we might have overlooked in the poem come alive through a brilliant, unexpected observation. . . .

The poem of Williams' that she enjoyed talking about most was "The Sea-Elephant," which begins:

Trundled from
the strangeness of the sea—
a kind of
heaven—

Ladies and Gentlemen!
the greatest
sea-monster ever exhibited
alive

the gigantic
sea-elephant! O wallow
of flesh where
are

there fish enough for
that
appetite stupidity
cannot lessen?

One thing she found particularly fascinating about the poem was the way Williams made transitions. The poem moves quickly from one voice to the next, from one mood to another. It switches effortlessly from wonder to pathos, then to burlesque, and then back to wonder. I think this was the side of Williams' work closest to Bishop's own poetry. She, too, was a master of swift, unexpected transitions, and her poems move as surprisingly from amusement to wonder, from quiet pathos to joy. But with "The Sea-Elephant" the subject alone was enough to light up her interest. She loved talking about exotic animals or flowers, and, not surprisingly, she proved formidably well informed about sea elephants. And she admitted that for her the high point of the poem was the word that Williams invented to imitate the sea elephant's roar: "Blouaugh." It was music to her ears. . . . She never articulated her philosophy in class, but she practiced it so consistently that it is easy—especially now, a decade later—to see what she was doing. She wanted us to see poems, not ideas. Poetry was the particular way the world could be talked about only in verse, and here, as one of her fellow-Canadians once said, the medium was the message. One did not interpret poetry; one experienced it. Showing us how to experience it clearly, intensely, and, above all, directly was the substance of her teaching. One did not need a sophisticated theory. One needed only intelligence, intuition, and a good dictionary. There was no subtext, only the text. A painter among Platonists, she preferred observation to analysis, and poems to poetry.

RANDALL JARRELL

(1914–1965)

THE DEATH OF THE BALL TURRET GUNNER

From my mother's sleep I fell into the State,
And I hunched in its belly till my wet fur froze.
Six miles from earth, loosed from its dream of life,
I woke to black flak and the nightmare fighters.
When I died they washed me out of the turret with a
    hose.   5

1944

THE SNOW-LEOPARD

His pads furring the scarp's rime,
Weightless in greys and ecru, gliding
Invisibly, incuriously
As the crystals of the cirri wandering
A mile below his absent eyes,   5
The leopard gazes at the caravan.

The yaks groaning with tea, the burlaps
Lapping and lapping each stunned universe
That gasps like a kettle for its thinning life
Are pools in the interminable abyss   10
That ranges up through ice, through air, to night.
Raiders of the unminding element,
The last cold capillaries of their kind,
They move so slowly they are motionless
To any eye less stubborn than a man's. . . .   15
From the implacable jumble of the blocks
The grains dance icily, a scouring plume,
Into the breath, sustaining, unsustainable,
They trade to that last stillness for their death.
They sense with misunderstanding horror, with desire,   20
Behind the world their blood sets up in mist
The brute and geometrical necessity:
The leopard waving with a grating purr
His six-foot tail; the leopard, who looks sleepily—

Cold, fugitive, secure—at all that he knows,   25
At all that he is: the heart of heartlessness.

                                        1945

NESTUS GURLEY

Sometimes waking, sometimes sleeping,
Late in the afternoon, or early
In the morning, I hear on the lawn,
On the walk, on the lawn, the soft quick step.
The sound half song, half breath: a note or two   5
That with a note or two would be a tune.
It is Nestus Gurley.

It is an old
Catch or snatch or tune
In the Dorian mode: the mode of the horses   10
That stand all night in the fields asleep
Or awake, the mode of the cold
Hunter, Orion, wheeling upside-down,
All space and stars, in cater-cornered Heaven.
When, somewhere under the east,   15
The great march begins, with birds and silence;
When, in the day's first triumph, dawn
Rides over the houses, Nestus Gurley
Delivers to me my lot.

As the sun sets, I hear my daughter say: 20
"He has four routes and makes a hundred dollars."
Sometimes he comes with dogs, sometimes with
     children,
Sometimes with dogs and children.
He collects, today.
I hear my daughter say: 25
"Today Nestus has got on his derby."
And he says, after a little: "It's two-eighty."
"How could it be two-eighty?"
"Because this month there're five Sundays: it's
     two-eighty."

He collects, delivers. Before the first, least star   30
Is lost in the paling east; at evening
While the soft, side-lit, gold-leafed day
Lingers to see the stars, the boy Nestus
Delivers to me the Morning Star, the Evening Star
—Ah no, only the Morning *News,* the Evening *Record*   35

Of what I have done and what I have not done
Set down and held against me in the Book
Of Death, on paper yellowing
Already, with one morning's sun, one evening's sun.

Sometimes I only dream him. He brings then   40
News of a different morning, a judgment not of men.
The bombers have turned back over the Pole,
Having met a star. . . . I look at that new year
And, waking, think of our Moravian Star
Not lit yet, and the pure beeswax candle   45
With its red flame-proofed paper pompom
Not lit yet, and the sweetened
Bun we brought home from the love-feast, still not
     eaten,
And the song the children sang: *O Morning Star*—

And at this hour, to the dew-hushed drums   50
Of the morning, Nestus Gurley
Marches to me over the lawn; and the cat Elfie,
Furred like a musk-ox, coon-tailed, gold-leaf-eyed,
Looks at the paper boy without alarm
But yawns, and stretches, and walks placidly   55
Across the lawn to his ladder, climbs it, and begins to
     purr.

I let him in,
Go out and pick up from the grass the paper hat
Nestus has folded: this tricorne fit for a Napoleon
Of our days and institutions, weaving   60
Baskets, being bathed, receiving
Electric shocks, Ranwolfia. . . . I put it on
—Ah no, only unfold it.
There is dawn inside; and I say to no one
About—   65
            it is a note or two
That with a note or two would—
                                    say to no one
About nothing: "He delivers dawn."

When I lie coldly   70
—Lie, that is, neither with coldness nor with warmth—
In the darkness that is not lit by anything,
In the grave that is not lit by anything
Except our hope: the hope
That is not proofed against anything, but pure   75
And shining as the first, least star
That is lost in the east on the morning of Judgment—

May I say, recognizing the step
Or tune or breath. . . .
                        recognizing the breath,   80
May I say, "It is Nestus Gurley."

                                        1960

FIELD AND FOREST

When you look down from the airplane you see lines,
Roads, ruts, braided into a net or web—
Where people go, what people do: the ways of life.

Heaven says to the farmer: 'What's your field?'
And he answers: 'Farming,' with a field,   5
Or: 'Dairy-farming,' with a herd of cows.
They seem a boys' toy cows, seen from this high.

Seen from this high,
The fields have a terrible monotony.

But between the lighter patches there are dark ones.   10
A farmer is separated from a farmer
By what farmers have in common: forests,
Those dark things—what the fields were to begin with.
At night a fox comes out of the forest, eats his
     chickens.
At night the deer come out of the forest, eat his crops. 15

If he could he'd make farm out of all the forest,
But it isn't worth it: some of it's marsh, some rocks,
There are things there you couldn't get rid of
With a bulldozer, even—not with dynamite.
Besides, he likes it. He had a cave there, as a boy;   20
He hunts there now. It's a waste of land,
But it would be a waste of time, a waste of money,
To make it into anything but what it is.

At night, from the airplane, all you see is lights,
A few lights, the lights of houses, headlights,   25
And darkness. Somewhere below, beside a light,
The farmer, naked, takes out his false teeth:
He doesn't eat now. Takes off his spectacles:
He doesn't see now. Shuts his eyes:
If he were able to he'd shut his ears,   30
And as it is, he doesn't hear with them.
Plainly, he's taken out his tongue: he doesn't talk.
His arms and legs: at least, he doesn't move them.

They are knotted together, curled up, like a child's.
And after he has taken off the thoughts   35
It has taken him his life to learn,
He takes off, last of all, the world.

When you take off everything what's left? A wish,
A blind wish; and yet the wish isn't blind,
What the wish wants to see, it sees.   40

There in the middle of the forest is the cave
And there, curled up inside it, is the fox.
He stands looking at it.
Around him the fields are sleeping: the fields dream.
At night there are no more farmers, no more farms.   45
At night the fields dream, the fields *are* the forest.
The boy stands looking at the fox
As if, if he looked long enough—
                                    he looks at it.
Or is it the fox that's looking at the boy?   50
The trees can't tell the two of them apart.

                                    1966

IN MONTECITO

In a fashionable suburb of Santa Barbara,
Montecito, there visited me one night at midnight
A scream with breasts. As it hung there in the sweet air
That was always the right temperature, the contractors
Who had undertaken to dismantle it, stripped off   5
The lips, let the air out of the breasts.
                                    People disappear
Even in Montecito. Greenie Taliaferro,
In her white maillot, her good figure almost firm,
Her old pepper-and-salt hair stripped by the
     hairdresser   10
To nothing and dyed platinum—Greenie has left her
     Bentley.
They have thrown away her electric toothbrush,
     someone else slips
The key into the lock of her safety-deposit box
At the Crocker-Anglo Bank, her seat at the cricket
     matches
Is warmed by buttocks less delectable than hers.   15
Greenie's girdle is empty.
                         A scream hangs there in the night:
They strip off the lips, let the air out of the breasts,

And Greenie has gone into the Greater Montecito
That surrounds Montecito like the echo of a scream.   20

1966

Randall Jarrell's description of the writing of "The Woman at the Washington Zoo" is one of the most thorough and lucid accounts ever written of the way that poets work. It also gives us insight into themes important to all of Jarrell's poetry and criticism.

"I wrote, as they say in suits, 'acting as next friend' ": Randall Jarrell

Late in the summer of 1956 my wife and I moved to Washington. We lived with two daughters, a cat, and a dog, in Chevy Chase; every day I would drive to work through Rock Creek Park, past the zoo. I worked across the street from the Capitol, at the Library of Congress. I knew Washington fairly well, but had never lived there; I had been in the army, but except for that had never worked for the government.

Some of the new and some of the old things there—I was often reminded of the army—had a good deal of effect on me: after a few weeks I began to write a poem. I have most of what I wrote, though the first page is gone; the earliest lines are:

> any color
> My print, that has clung to its old colors
> Through many washings; this dull null
> Navy I wear to work, and wear from work, and so
> ~~And so to bed~~   To bed
> With no complaint, no comment—neither from my chief,
> nor
> The Deputy Chief Assistant, ~~from~~ his chief,
> Nor   nor
> ~~From~~ Congressmen, ~~from~~ their constituents—
> thin
> Only I complain; this ~~poor~~ worn serviceable . . .

The woman talking is a near relation of women I was seeing there in Washington—some at close range, at the Library—and a distant relation of women I had written about before, in "The End of the Rainbow" and "Cinderella" and "Seele im Raum." She is a kind of aging machine part. I wrote, as they say in suits, "acting as next friend"; I had for her the sympathy of an aging machine part. (If I was also something else, that was just personal; and she also was something else.) I felt that one of these hundreds of thousands of government clerks might feel all her dresses one dress, a faded navy-blue print, and that dress her body. This work or life uniform of hers excites neither complaint, nor comment, nor the mechanically protective *No comment* of the civil servant; excites them neither from her "chief," the Deputy Chief Assistant, nor from his, nor from any being on any level of that many-leveled machine: all the system is silent, except for her own cry, which goes unnoticed just as she herself goes unnoticed. (I had met a Deputy Chief Assistant, who saw nothing remarkable in the title.) The woman's days seem to her the going-up-to-work and coming-down-from-work of a worker; each ends in *And so to bed*, the diarist's conclusive unvarying entry in the daybook of his life.

These abruptly opening lines are full of duplications and echoes, like what they describe. And they are wrong in the way in which beginnings are wrong: either there is too much of something or it is not yet there. The lines break off with *this worn serviceable*—the words can apply either to her dress or to her body, but anything so obviously suitable to the dress must be intended for the body. *Body that no sunlight dyes, no hand suffuses,* the page written the next day goes on; then after a space there is *Dome-shadowed, withering among columns, / Wavy upon the pools of fountains, small beside statues* . . . No sun colors, no hand suffuses with its touch, this used, still-useful body. It is subdued to the element it works in: is shadowed by the domes, grows old and small and dry among the columns, of the buildings of the capital; becomes a reflection, its material identity lost, upon the pools of the fountains of the capital; is dwarfed beside the statues of the capital—as year by year it passes among the public places of this city of space and trees and light, city sinking beneath the weight of its marble, city of graded voteless workers.

The word *small*, as it joins the reflections in the pools, the trips to the public places, brings the poem to its real place and subject—to its title, even: next there is *small and shining*, then (with the star beside it that means *use, don't lose*) *small, far-off, shining in the eyes of animals;* the woman ends at the zoo, looking so intently into its cages that she sees her own reflection in *the eyes of animals, these wild ones trapped / As I am trapped but not, themselves, the trap* . . . The lines have written above them *The Woman at the Washington Zoo*.

The next page has the title and twelve lines:

This print, that has kept the memory of color
Alive through many cleanings; this dull null
Navy I wear to work, and wear from work, and so
To bed (with no complaints, no comment: neither from my chief,

The Deputy Chief Assistant, nor her chief,
Nor his, nor Congressmen, nor their constituents
~~wan~~
—Only I complain); this ~~plain~~, worn, serviceable
        sunlight
Body that no ~~sunset~~ dyes, no hand suffuses
But, dome-shadowed, withering among columns,
Wavy beneath fountains—small, far-off, shining
~~wild~~
In the eyes of animals, these beings trapped
As I am trapped but not, themselves, the trap . . .

Written underneath this, in the rapid, ugly, disorganized handwriting of most of the pages, is *bars of my body burst blood breath breathing—lives aging but without knowledge of age / Waiting in their safe prisons for death, knowing not of death;* immediately this is changed into two lines, *Aging, but without knowledge of their age, / Kept safe here, knowing not of death, for death*—and out at the side, scrawled heavily, is: *O bars of my own body, open, open!* She recognizes herself in the animals—and recognizes herself, also, in the cages.

Written across the top of this page is *2nd and 3rd alphabets.* Streets in Washington run through a one-syllable, a two-syllable, and a three-syllable (Albermarle, Brandywine, Chesapeake . . .) alphabet, so that people say about an address: "Let's see, that's in the second alphabet, isn't it?" It made me think of Kronecker's "God made the integers, all else is the work of man"; but it seemed right for Washington to have alphabets of its own—I made up the title of a detective story, *Murder in the Second Alphabet.* The alphabets were a piece of Washington that should have fitted into the poem, but didn't; but the zoo was a whole group of pieces, a little Washington, into which the poem itself fitted.

Rock Creek Park, with its miles of heavily wooded hills and valleys, its rocky stream, is like some National Forest dropped into Washington by mistake. Many of the animals of the zoo are in unroofed cages back in its ravines. My wife and I had often visited the zoo, and now that we were living in Washington we went to it a great deal. We had made friends with a lynx that was very like our cat that had died the spring before, at the age of sixteen. We would feed the lynx pieces of liver or scraps of chicken and turkey; we fed liver, sometimes, to two enormous white timber wolves that lived at the end of one ravine. Eager for the meat, they would stand up against the bars on their hind legs, taller than a man, and stare into our eyes; they reminded me of Akela, white with age, in *The Jungle Books,* and of the wolves who fawn at the man Mowgli's brown feet in "In the Rukh." In one of the buildings of the zoo there was a lioness with two big cubs; when the keeper came she would come over, purring her bass purr, to rub her head against the bars almost as our lynx would rub his head against the turkey skin, in rapture, before he finally gulped it down. In the lions' building there were two black leopards; when you got close to them you saw they had not lost the spots of the ordinary leopards—were the ordinary leopards, but spotted black on black, dingy somehow.

On the way to the wolves one went by a big unroofed cage of foxes curled up asleep; on the concrete floor of the enclosure there would be scattered two or three white rats—stiff, quite untouched—that the foxes had left. (The wolves left their meat, too—big slabs of horse meat, glazing, covered with flies.) Twice when I came to the foxes' cage there was a turkey buzzard that had come down for the rats; startled at me, he flapped up heavily, with a rat dangling underneath. (There are usually vultures circling over the zoo; nearby, at the tennis courts of the Sheraton-Park, I used to see vultures perched on the tower of WTTG, above the court on which Defense Secretary McElroy was playing doubles—so that I would say to myself, like Peer Gynt: "Nature is witty.") As a child, coming around the bend of a country road, I had often seen a turkey buzzard, with its black wings and naked red head, flap heavily up from the mashed body of a skunk or possum or rabbit.

A good deal of this writes itself on the next page, almost too rapidly for line endings or punctuation: *to be and never know I am   when the vulture buzzard comes for the white rat that the foxes left   May he take off his black wings, the red flesh of his head, and step to me as man—a man at whose brown feet the white wolves fawn—to whose hand of power / The lioness stalks, leaving her cubs playing / and rubs her head along the bars as he strokes it.* Along the side of the page, between these lines, two or three words to a line, is written *the animals who are trapped but are not themselves the trap   black leopards   spots, light and darkened, hidden except to the close eyes of love, in their life-long darkness, so I in decent black, navy blue.*

As soon as the zoo came into the poem, everything else settled into it and was at home there; on this page it is plain even to the writer that all the things in the poem come out of, and are divided between, color and color-lessness. Colored women and colored animals and colored cloth—all that the woman sees as her own opposite—come into the poem to begin it. Beside the typed lines are many hurried phrases, most of them crossed out: *red and yellow as October maples   rosy, blood seen through flesh in summer colors wild and easy natural   leaf-yellow cloud-rose leopard-yellow, cloth from another planet   the leopards look back at their wearers, hue for hue   the women look back at the leopard.* And on the back of the vulture's page there is a flight of ideas, almost a daydream, coming out of these last phrases: *we have never mistaken you for the others   among the legations one of a different architecture women, saris of a different color   envoy   impassive clear bulletproof glass lips, through the clear glass of a rose sedan color of blood   you too are represented on this earth . . .*

One often sees on the streets of Washington—fairly often sees at the zoo—what seem beings of a different species: women from the embassies of India and Pakistan, their sallow skin and black hair leopard-like, their yellow or rose or green saris exactly as one imagines the robes of Greek statues before the statues had lost their colors. It was easy for me to see the saris as cloth from another planet or satellite; I have written about a sick child who wants "a ship from some near star / To land in the yard and beings to come out / And think to me: 'So this is where you are!' " and about an old man who says that it is his ambition to be the pet of visitors from another planet; as an old reader of science fiction, I am used to looking at the sun red over the hills, the moon white over the ocean, and saying to my wife in a sober voice: "It's like another planet." After I had worked a little longer, the poem began as it begins now:

> The saris go by me from the embassies.
>
> Cloth from the moon. Cloth from another planet.
> They look back at the leopard like the leopard.
>
> And I . . . This print of mine, that has kept its color
> Alive through so many cleanings; this dull null
> Navy I wear to work, and wear from work, and so
> To my bed, so to my grave, with no
> Complaints, no comment: neither from my chief,
> The Deputy Chief Assistant, nor his chief—
> Only I complain; this serviceable
> Body that no sunlight dyes, no hand suffuses
> But, dome-shadowed, withering among columns,
> Wavy beneath fountains—small, far-off, shining
> In the eyes of animals, these beings trapped
> As I am trapped but not, themselves, the trap,
> Aging, but without knowledge of their age,
> Kept safe here, knowing not of death, for death
> —Oh, bars of my own body, open, open!

It is almost as if, once all the materials of the poem were there, the middle and end of the poem made themselves, as the beginning seemed to make itself. After the imperative *open, open!* there is a space, and the middle of the poem begins evenly—since her despair is beyond expression—in a statement of accomplished fact: *The world goes by my cage and never sees me.* Inside the mechanical official cage of her life, her body, she lives invisibly; no one feeds this animal, reads out its name, pokes a stick through the bars at it—the cage is empty. She feels that she is even worse off than the other animals of the zoo: they are still wild animals—since they do not know how to change into domesticated animals, beings that are their own cages—and they are surrounded by a world that does not know how to surrender them, still thinks them part of itself. This natural world comes through or over the bars of the cages, on its continual visits to those within: to those who are not machine parts, convicts behind the bars of their penitentiary, but wild animals—the free beasts come to their imprisoned brothers and never know that they are not also free. Written on the back of one page, crossed out, is *Come still, you free;* on the next page this becomes:

> The world goes by my cage and never sees me.
> And there come not to me, as come to these,
> The wild ~~ones~~ beasts, sparrows pecking the llamas' grain,
> Pigeons ~~fluttering to~~ settling on the bears' bread,
>   turkey-buzzards
> ~~Coming with grace first, then with horror Vulture seizing~~
>   Tearing the meat the flies have clouded . . .

In saying mournfully that the wild animals do not come to her as they come to the animals of the zoo, she is wishing for their human equivalent to come to her. But she is right in believing that she has become her own cage—she has changed so much, in her manless, childless, fleshless existence, that her longing wish has inside it an increasing repugnance and horror: the innocent sparrows *pecking* the llamas' grain become larger in the pigeons *settling on* (not *fluttering to*) the bears' bread; and these grow larger and larger, come (with grace first, far off in the sky, but at last with horror) as turkey buzzards seizing, no, *tearing* the meat the flies have clouded. She herself is that stale leftover flesh, nauseating just as what comes to it is horrible and nauseating. The series *pecking, settling on,* and *tearing* has inside it a sexual metaphor: the stale flesh that no one would have is taken at last by the turkey buzzard with his naked red neck and head.

Her own life is so terrible to her that, to change, she is willing to accept even this, changing it as best she can. She says: *Vulture* [it is a euphemism that gives him distance and solemnity], *when you come for the white rat that the foxes left* [to her the rat is so plainly herself that she does not need to say so; the small, white, untouched thing is more accurately what she is than was the clouded meat—but, also, it is euphemistic, more nearly bearable], *take off the red helmet of your head* [the bestiality, the obscene sexuality of the flesh-eating death-bird is really—she hopes or pretends or desperately is sure—merely external, *clothes,* an intentionally frightening war garment like a Greek or Roman helmet], *the black wings that have shadowed me* [she feels that their inhuman colorless darkness has always, like the domes of the inhuman city, shadowed her; the wings are like a black parody of the wings the Swan Brothers wear in the fairy tale, just as the whole costume is like that of the Frog Prince or the other beast-princes of the stories] *and step* [as a human being, not fly as an animal] *to me as* [what you really are under the disguising clothing of red flesh and black feathers] *man*—not the machine part, the domesticated animal that is its own cage, but man as he was first, still must be, is: the animals' natural lord,

> The wild brother at whose feet the white wolves fawn,
> To whose hand of power the great lioness
> Stalks, purring . . .

And she ends the poem when she says to him:

> You know what I was,
> You see what I am: change me, change me!

Here is the whole poem:

THE WOMAN AT THE WASHINGTON ZOO

The saris go by me from the embassies.

Cloth from the moon. Cloth from another planet.
They look back at the leopard like the leopard.

And I . . .
                        This print of mine, that has kept its color
Alive through so many cleanings; this dull null
Navy I wear to work, and wear from work, and so
To my bed, so to my grave, with no
Complaints, no comment: neither from my chief,
The Deputy Chief Assistant, nor his chief—
Only I complain; this serviceable
Body that no sunlight dyes, no hand suffuses
But, dome-shadowed, withering among columns,
Wavy beneath fountains—small, far-off, shining
In the eyes of animals, these beings trapped
As I am trapped but not, themselves, the trap,
Aging, but without knowledge of their age,
Kept safe here, knowing not of death, for death
—Oh, bars of my own body, open, open!

The world goes by my cage and never sees me.
And there come not to me, as come to these,
The wild beasts, sparrows pecking the llamas' grain,
Pigeons settling on the bears' bread, buzzards
Tearing the meat the flies have clouded . . .
                                    Vulture,
When you come for the white rat that the foxes left,
Take off the red helmet of your head, the black
Wings that have shadowed me, and step to me as man,
The wild brother at whose feet the white wolves fawn,
To whose hand of power the great lioness
Stalks, purring . . .
                        You know what I was,
You see what I am: change me, change me!

Randall Jarrell   **1089**

DYLAN THOMAS

(1914–1953)

THE FORCE THAT THROUGH THE GREEN FUSE DRIVES THE FLOWER

The force that through the green fuse drives the flower
Drives my green age; that blasts the roots of trees
Is my destroyer.
And I am dumb to tell the crooked rose
My youth is bent by the same wintry fever.   5

The force that drives the water through the rocks
Drives my red blood; that dries the mouthing streams
Turns mine to wax.
And I am dumb to mouth unto my veins
How at the mountain spring the same mouth sucks.   10

The hand that whirls the water in the pool
Stirs the quicksand; that ropes the blowing wind
Hauls my shroud sail.
And I am dumb to tell the hanging man
How of my clay is made the hangman's lime.   15

The lips of time leech to the fountain head;
Love drips and gathers, but the fallen blood
Shall calm her sores.
And I am dumb to tell a weather's wind
How time has ticked a heaven round the stars.   20

And I am dumb to tell the lover's tomb
How at my sheet goes the same crooked worm.

1934

THE HUNCHBACK IN THE PARK

The hunchback in the park
A solitary mister
Propped between trees and water
From the opening of the garden lock
That lets the trees and water enter   5
Until the Sunday somber bell at dark

Eating bread from a newspaper
Drinking water from the chained cup

That the children filled with gravel
In the fountain basin where I sailed my ship   10
Slept at night in a dog kennel
But nobody chained him up.

Like the park birds he came early
Like the water he sat down
And Mister they called Hey mister   15
The truant boys from the town
Running when he had heard them clearly
On out of sound

Past lake and rockery
Laughing when he shook his paper   20
Hunchbacked in mockery
Through the loud zoo of the willow groves
Dodging the park keeper
With his stick that picked up leaves.

And the old dog sleeper   25
Alone between nurses and swans
While the boys among willows
Made the tigers jump out of their eyes
To roar on the rockery stones
And the groves were blue with sailors   30

Made all day until bell time
A woman figure without fault
Straight as a young elm
Straight and tall from his crooked bones
That she might stand in the night   35
After the locks and chains

All night in the unmade park
After the railings and shrubberies
The birds the grass the trees the lake
And the wild boys innocent as strawberries   40
Had followed the hunchback
To his kennel in the dark.

                                             1942

POEM IN OCTOBER

It was my thirtieth year to heaven
Woke to my hearing from harbor and neighbor wood
    And the mussel pooled and the heron
            Priested shore

        The morning beckon   5
With water praying and call of seagull and rook
And the knock of sailing boats on the net webbed wall
        Myself to set foot
             That second
In the still sleeping town and set forth.   10

        My birthday began with the water-
Birds and the birds of the winged trees flying my name
        Above the farms and the white horses
             And I rose
        In rainy autumn   15
And walked abroad in a shower of all my days.
High tide and the heron dived when I took the road
        Over the border
             And the gates
of the town closed as the town awoke.   20

        A springful of larks in a rolling
Cloud and the roadside bushes brimming with whistling
        Blackbirds and the sun of October
             Summery
        On the hill's shoulder,   25
Here were fond climates and sweet singers suddenly
Come in the morning where I wandered and listened
        To the rain wringing
             Wind blow cold
In the wood faraway under me.   30

        Pale rain over the dwindling harbor
And over the sea wet church the size of a snail
        With its horns through mist and the castle
             Brown as owls
        But all the gardens   35
Of spring and summer were blooming in the tall tales
Beyond the border and under the lark full cloud.
        There could I marvel
             My birthday
Away but the weather turned around.   40

        It turned away from the blithe country
And down the other air and the blue altered sky
        Streamed again a wonder of summer
             With apples
        Pears and red currants   45
And I saw in the turning so clearly a child's
Forgotten mornings when he walked with his mother
        Through the parables

Of sun light
And the legends of the green chapels   50

And the twice told fields of infancy
That his tears burned my cheeks and his heart moved in
mine.
These were the woods the river and sea
Where a boy
In the listening   55
Summertime of the dead whispered the truth of his joy
To the trees and the stones and the fish in the tide.
And the mystery
Sang alive
Still in the water and singingbirds.   60

And there could I marvel my birthday
Away but the weather turned around. And the true
Joy of the long dead child sang burning
In the sun.
It was my thirtieth   65
Year to heaven stood there then in the summer noon
Though the town below lay leaved with October blood.
O may my heart's truth
Still be sung
On this high hill in a year's turning.   70

1946

OVER SIR JOHN'S HILL

Over Sir John's hill,
The hawk on fire hangs still;
In a hoisted cloud, at drop of dusk, he pulls to his claws
And gallows, up the rays of his eyes the small birds of
    the bay
And the shrill child's play   5
Wars
Of the sparrows and such who swansing, dusk, in
    wrangling hedges.
And blithely they squawk
To fiery tyburn over the wrestle of elms until
The flashed the noosed hawk   10
Crashes, and slowly the fishing holy stalking heron
In the river Towy below bows his tilted headstone.

Flash, and the plumes crack,
And a black cap of jack-

Daws Sir John's just hill dons, and again the gulled
    birds hare   15
To the hawk on fire, the halter height, over Towy's fins,
In a whack of wind.
There
Where the elegiac fisherbird stabs and paddles
In the pebbly dab-filled   20
Shallow and sedge, and 'dilly dilly,' calls the loft hawk,
'Come and be killed,'
I open the leaves of the water at a passage
Of psalms and shadows among the pincered sandcrabs
    prancing

And read, in a shell,   25
Death clear as a buoy's bell:
All praise of the hawk on fire in hawk-eyed dusk be
    sung,
When his viperish fuse hangs looped with flames under
    the brand
Wing, and blest shall
Young   30
Green chickens of the bay and bushes cluck, 'dilly dilly,
Come let us die.'
We grieve as the blithe birds, never again, leave shingle
    and elm,
The heron and I,
I young Aesop fabling to the near night by the dingle   35
Of eels, saint heron hymning in the shell-hung distant

Crystal harbour vale
Where the sea cobbles sail,
And wharves of water where the walls dance and the
    white cranes stilt.
It is the heron and I, under judging Sir John's elmed   40
Hill, tell-tale the knelled
Guilt
Of the led-astray birds whom God, for their breast of
    whistles,
Have mercy on,
God in his whirlwind silence save, who marks the
    sparrows hail,   45
For their souls' song.
Now the heron grieves in the weeded verge. Through
    windows
Of dusk and water I see the tilting whispering

Heron, mirrored, go,
As the snapt feathers snow,   50

Fishing in the tear of the Towy. Only a hoot owl
Hollows, a grassblade blown in cupped hands, in the
    looted elms
And no green cocks or hens
Shout
Now on Sir John's hill. The heron, ankling the scaly   55
Lowlands of the waves
Makes all the music; and I who hear the tune of the
    slow,
Wear-willow river, grave,
Before the lunge of the night, the notes on this
    time-shaken
Stone for the sake of the souls of the slain birds sailing.   60

1950

POEM ON HIS BIRTHDAY

   In the mustardseed sun,
By full tilt river and switchback sea
   Where the cormorants scud,
In his house on stilts high among beaks
   And palavers of birds   5
This sandgrain day in the bent bay's grave
   He celebrates and spurns
His driftwood thirty-fifth wind turned age;
   Herons spire and spear.

   Under and round him go   10
Flounders, gulls, on their cold, dying trails,
   Doing what they are told,
Curlews aloud in the congered waves
   Work at their ways to death,
And the rhymer in the long tongued room,   15
   Who tolls his birthday bell,
Toils towards the ambush of his wounds;
   Herons, steeple stemmed, bless.

   In the thistledown fall,
He sings towards anguish; finches fly   20
   In the claw tracks of hawks
On a seizing sky; small fishes glide
   Through wynds and shells of drowned
Ship towns to pastures of otters. He
   In his slant, racking house   25
And the hewn coils of his trade perceives
   Herons walk in their shroud,

The livelong river's robe
Of minnows wreathing around their prayer;
   And far at sea he knows,   30
Who slaves to his crouched, eternal end
   Under a serpent cloud,
Dolphins dive in their turnturtle dust,
   The rippled seals streak down
To kill and their own tide daubing blood   35
   Slides good in the sleek mouth.

   In a cavernous, swung
Wave's silence, wept white angelus knells.
   Thirty-five bells sing struck
On skull and scar where his loves lie wrecked,   40
   Steered by the falling stars.
And to-morrow weeps in a blind cage
   Terror will rage apart
Before chains break to a hammer flame
   And love unbolts the dark   45

   And freely he goes lost
In the unknown, famous light of great
   And fabulous, dear God.
Dark is a way and light is a place,
   Heaven that never was   50
Nor will be ever is always true,
   And, in that brambled void,
Plenty as blackberries in the woods
   The dead grow for His joy.

There he might wander bare   55
With the spirits of the horseshoe bay
   Or the stars' seashore dead,
Marrow of eagles, the roots of whales
   And wishbones of wild geese,
With blessed, unborn God and His Ghost,   60
   And every soul His priest,
Gulled and chanter in young Heaven's fold
   Be at cloud quaking peace,

   But dark is a long way.
He, on the earth of the night, alone   65
   With all the living, prays,
Who knows the rocketing wind will blow
   The bones out of the hills,
And the scythed boulders bleed, and the last
   Rage shattered waters kick   70
Masts and fishes to the still quick stars,
   Faithlessly unto Him

Who is the light of old
And air shaped Heaven where souls grow wild
　　As horses in the foam:　　　　　　　　　　　　75
Oh, let me midlife mourn by the shrined
　　And druid herons' vows
The voyage to ruin I must run
　　Dawn ships clouted aground,
Yet, though I cry with tumbledown tongue,　　　　80
　　Count my blessings aloud:

Four elements and five
Senses, and man a spirit in love
　　Tangling through this spun slime
To his nimbus bell cool kingdom come　　　　　　85
　　And the lost, moonshine domes,
And the sea that hides his secret selves
　　Deep in its black, base bones,
Lulling of spheres in the seashell flesh,
　　And this last blessing most,　　　　　　　　90

That the closer I move
To death, one man through his sundered hulks,
　　The louder the sun blooms
And the tusked, ramshackling sea exults;
　　And every wave of the way　　　　　　　　95
And gale I tackle, the whole world then,
　　With more triumphant faith
That ever was since the world was said,
　　Spins its morning of praise,

　I hear the bouncing hills　　　　　　　　　100
Grow larked and greener at berry brown
　　Fall and the dew larks sing
Taller this thunderclap spring, and how
　　More spanned with angels ride
The mansouled fiery islands! Oh,　　　　　　105
　　Holier then their eyes,
And my shining men no more alone
　　As I sail out to die.

1951

DO NOT GO GENTLE INTO THAT GOOD NIGHT

Do not go gentle into that good night,
Old age should burn and rave at close of day;
Rage, rage against the dying of the light.

Though wise men at their end know dark is right,
Because their words had forked no lightning they   5
Do not go gentle into that good night.

Good men, the last wave by, crying how bright
Their frail deeds might have danced in a green bay,
Rage, rage against the dying of the light.

Wild men who caught and sang the sun in flight,   10
And learn, too late, they grieved it on its way,
Do not go gentle into that good night.

Grave men, near death, who see with blinding sight
Blind eyes could blaze like meteors and be gay,
Rage, rage against the dying of the light.   15

And you, my father, there on the sad height,
Curse, bless, me now with your fierce tears, I pray.
Do not go gentle into that good night.
Rage, rage against the dying of the light.

1952

Dylan Thomas's poetry, sometimes surrealist, sometimes traditional, often exuberant, is so different from the sort of poetry William Carlos Williams advocated and wrote that Williams's appreciation of it has special meaning.

"You might call it drunken poetry, it smacks of the divine": William Carlos Williams

Politer verse, more in the english style, appears to have been impossible for Thomas, it's a constitutional matter, in which a man has no choice. At least I don't think it was a choice that was open to him. Thomas was a lyric poet and, I think, a great one. Such memorable poems as "Over Sir John's Hill" and, even more to be emphasized, "On His Birthday," are far and away beyond the reach of any contemporary english or american poet. Not only in the contrapuntal metaphors which he uses, the fuguelike overlay of his language does he excel but he is outstanding in the way he packs the thought in among the words. For it is not all sound and image, but the ability to think is there also with a flaming conviction that clinches each point as the images mount. The clarity of his thought is not obscured by his images but rather emphasized.

The wind does "whack" as the hawk which is "on fire" hangs still in the sky. This devotional poem which in its packed metaphors shows a man happy in his fate though soon to die shows Dylan Thomas in a triumphant mood, exultant. What else can a man say or be? He carries the image through to a definite conclusion and as a lyric poet at his best does show the sparks of light which convinces us that he means what he says. He includes the whole world in his benisons.

The second poem, "Poem on His Birthday," is demonic, you have to chortle with glee at some of the figures. But it is the way the metaphors are identified with the meaning to emphasize it and to universalize and dignify it that is the proof of the poet's ability. You may not like such poems but prefer a more reasoned mode but this is impassioned poetry, you might call it drunken poetry, it smacks of the divine—as Dylan Thomas does also.

The analytic spirit that might have made him backtrack and reconsider, building a rational system of thought and technique, was not his. He had passion and a heart which carried him where he wanted to go but it cannot be said that he did not choose what he wanted.

GWENDOLYN BROOKS

(b. 1917)

A STREET IN BRONZEVILLE:
SOUTHEAST CORNER

The School of Beauty's a tavern now.
The Madam is underground.
Out at Lincoln, among the graves
Her own is early found.
Where the thickest, tallest monument   5
Cuts grandly into the air
The Madam lies, contentedly.
Her fortune, too, lies there,
Converted into cool hard steel
And right red velvet lining;   10
While over her tan impassivity
Shot silk is shining.

1945

WE REAL COOL

The Pool Players.
Seven at the Golden Shovel.

We real cool. We
Left school. We

Lurk late. We
Strike straight. We

Sing sin. We   5
Thin gin. We

Jazz June. We
Die soon.

1957–1958

THE CHICAGO DEFENDER SENDS A
MAN TO LITTLE ROCK

Fall, 1957

In Little Rock the people bear
Babes, and comb and part their hair
And watch the want ads, put repair
To roof and latch. While wheat toast burns
A woman waters multiferns.   5

Time upholds or overturns
The many, tight, and small concerns.

In Little Rock the people sing
Sunday hymns like anything,
Through Sunday pomp and polishing.   10

And after testament and tunes,
Some soften Sunday afternoons
With lemon tea and Lorna Doones.

I forecast
And I believe   15

"*The Chicago Defender Sends a Man to Little Rock*": *Little Rock:* The desegregation of Central
High in Little Rock, Arkansas, in 1957 was resisted by both the local population and state
authorities. President Eisenhower eventually had to send in federal troops to maintain order.

Come Christmas Little Rock will cleave
To Christmas tree and trifle, weave,
From laugh and tinsel, texture fast.

In Little Rock is baseball; Barcarolle.
That hotness in July . . . the uniformed figures raw and
   implacable   20
And not intellectual,
Batting the hotness or clawing the suffering dust.
The Open Air Concert, on the special twilight
   green. . . .
When Beethoven is brutal or whispers to lady-like air.
Blanket-sitters are solemn, as Johann troubles to lean   25
To tell them what to mean. . . .

There is love, too, in Little Rock. Soft women softly
Opening themselves in kindness,
Or, pitying one's blindness,
Awaiting one's pleasure   30
In azure
Glory with anguished rose at the root. . . .
To wash away old semi-discomfitures.
They re-teach purple and unsullen blue.
The wispy soils go. And uncertain   35
Half-havings have they clarified to sures.

In Little Rock they know
Not answering the telephone is a way of rejecting life,
That it is our business to be bothered, is our business
To cherish bores or boredom, be polite   40
To lies and love and many-faceted fuzziness.

I scratch my head, massage the hate-I-had.
I blink across my prim and pencilled pad.
The saga I was sent for is not down.
Because there is a puzzle in this town.   45
The biggest News I do not dare
Telegraph to the Editor's chair:
"They are like people everywhere."

The angry Editor would reply
In hundred harryings of Why.   50

And true, they are hurling spittle, rock,
Garbage and fruit in Little Rock.
And I saw coiling storm a-writhe
On bright madonnas. And a scythe
Of men harassing brownish girls.   55

(The bows and barrettes in the curls
And braids declined away from joy.)

I saw a bleeding brownish boy. . . .

The lariat lynch-wish I deplored.

The loveliest lynchee was our Lord.   60

1960

THE BLACKSTONE RANGERS

1

AS SEEN BY DISCIPLINES

There they are.
Thirty at the corner.
Black, raw, ready.
Sores in the city
that do not want to heal.   5

2

THE LEADERS

Jeff. Gene. Geronimo. And Bop.
They cancel, cure and curry.
Hardly the dupes of the downtown thing
the cold bonbon,
the rhinestone thing. And hardly   10
in a hurry.
Hardly Belafonte, King,
Black Jesus, Stokely, Malcolm X or Rap.
Bungled trophies.
Their country is a Nation on no map.   15

Jeff, Gene, Geronimo and Bop
in the passionate noon,
in bewitching night
are the detailed men, the copious men.

"*The Blackstone Rangers*": *Blackstone Rangers:* a Chicago street gang

They curry, cure,   20
they cancel, cancelled images whose Concerts
are not divine, vivacious; the different tins
are intense last entries; pagan argument;
translations of the night.

The Blackstone bitter bureaus   25
(bureaucracy is footloose) edit, fuse
unfashionable damnations and descent;
and exulting, monstrous hand on monstrous hand,
construct, strangely, a monstrous pearl or grace.

3

GANG GIRLS

A Rangerette

Gang Girls are sweet exotics.   30
Mary Ann
uses the nutrients of her orient,
but sometimes sighs for Cities of blue and jewel
beyond her Ranger rim of Cottage Grove.
(Bowery Boys, Disciples, Whip-Birds will   35
dissolve no margins, stop no savory sanctities.)

Mary is
a rose in a whiskey glass.

Mary's
Februaries shudder and are gone. Aprils   40
fret frankly, lilac hurries on.
Summer is a hard irregular ridge.
October looks away.
And that's the Year!
                Save for her bugle-love.   45
Save for the bleat of not-obese devotion.
Save for Somebody Terribly Dying, under
the philanthropy of robins. Save for her Ranger
bringing
an amount of rainbow in a string-drawn bag.   50
"Where did you get the diamond?" Do not ask:
but swallow, straight, the spirals of his flask
and assist him at your zipper; pet his lips
and help him clutch you.

Love's another departure.   55
Will there be any arrivals, confirmations?
Will there be gleaning?

Mary, the Shakedancer's child
from the rooming-flat, pants carefully, peers at
her laboring lover. . . .   60
            Mary! Mary Ann!
Settle for sandwiches! settle for stocking caps!
for sudden blood, aborted carnival,
the props and niceties of non-loneliness—
the rhymes of Leaning.   65

                                                      1968

RIOT

A riot is the language of the unheard.
            —Martin Luther King

John Cabot, out of Wilma, once a Wycliffe,
all whitebluerose below his golden hair,
wrapped richly in right linen and right wool,
almost forgot his Jaguar and Lake Bluff;
almost forgot Grandtully (which is The   5
Best Thing That Ever Happened To Scotch); almost
forgot the sculpture at the Richard Gray
and Distelheim; the kidney pie at Maxim's,
the Grenadine de Boeuf at Maison Henri.

Because the Negroes were coming down the street.   10

Because the Poor were sweaty and unpretty
(not like Two Dainty Negroes in Winnetka)

and they were coming toward him in rough ranks.
In seas. In windsweep. They were black and loud.
And not detainable. And not discreet.   15

Gross. Gross. *"Que tu es grossier!"* John Cabot
itched instantly beneath the nourished white
that told his story of glory to the World.
"Don't let It touch me! the blackness! Lord!" he
      whispered
to any handy angel in the sky.   20

But, in a thrilling announcement, on It drove
and breathed on him: and touched him. In that breath

_____

"*Riot*": 4 *Lake Bluff:* township in Chicago   7–8 *Richard Gray . . . Distelheim:* art galleries
8–9 *Maxim's . . . Maison Henri:* restaurants   12 *Winnetka:* township in Chicago   16 *Que tue
es grossier!:* You (singular) are gross! (French)

the fume of pig foot, chitterling and cheap chili,
malign, mocked John. And, in terrific touch, old
averted doubt jerked forward decently,   25
cried "Cabot! John! You are a desperate man,
and the desperate die expensively today."

John Cabot went down in the smoke and fire
and broken glass and blood, and he cried "Lord!
Forgive these nigguhs that know not what they do."   30

1969

THE CHICAGO PICASSO

August 15, 1967
"Mayor Daley tugged a white ribbon, loosing the blue percale wrap. A hearty cheer
went up as the covering slipped off the big steel sculpture that looks at once like a
bird and a woman."

—Chicago *Sun-Times*

(Seiji Ozawa leads the Symphony.
The Mayor smiles.
And 50,000 See.)

Does man love Art? Man visits Art, but squirms.
Art hurts. Art urges voyages—   5
and it is easier to stay at home,
the nice beer ready.
    In commonrooms
we belch, or sniff, or scratch.
Are raw.   10

But we must cook ourselves and style ourselves for Art,
    who
is a requiring courtesan.
We squirm.
We do not hug the Mona Lisa.
We   15
may touch or tolerate
an astounding fountain, or a horse-and-rider.
At most, another Lion.

Observe the tall cold of a Flower
which is as innocent and as guilty,   20
as meaningful and as meaningless as any
other flower in the western field.

1973

In midcareer, Gwendolyn Brooks's work underwent a change. Her first fame had been established on the basis of A Street in Bronzeville *(1945) and the Pulitzer Prize-winning* Annie Allen *(1949). In these early collections, racial and social themes are usually one face of lyrics multifaceted as cut glass. The later poems deal more directly with race. In her autobiography,* Report from Part One, *Brooks gives an account of a critical moment in the change.*

"A surprised queenhood in the new black sun": Gwendolyn Brooks

Until 1967 my own blackness did not confront me with a shrill spelling of itself. I knew that I was what most people were calling "a Negro;" I called myself that, although always the word fell awkwardly on a poet's ear; I had never liked the sound of it (Caucasian has an ugly sound, too, while the name Indian is beautiful to look at and to hear.) *And* I knew that people of my coloration and distinctive history had been bolted to trees and sliced or burned or shredded; knocked to the back of the line; provided with separate toilets, schools, neighborhoods; denied, when possible, voting rights; hounded, hooted at, or shunned, or patronizingly patted. . . . Yet, although almost secretly, I had always felt that to be black was good. Sometimes, there would be an approximate whisper around me: *others* felt, it seemed, that to be black was good. The translation would have been something like "Hey—being black is *fun.*" Or something like "Hey—our folks have got stuff to be proud of!" Or something like "Hey—since we are so good why aren't we treated like the other 'Americans?' "

Suddenly there was New Black to meet. In the spring of 1967 I met some of it at the Fisk University Writers' Conference in Nashville. Coming from white white white South Dakota State College I arrived in Nashville, Tennessee, to give one more "reading." But blood-boiling surprise was in store for me. First, I was aware of a general energy, an electricity, in look, walk, speech, *gesture* of the young blackness I saw all about me. I had been "loved" at South Dakota State College. Here, I was coldly Respected. . . . I didn't know what to make of what surrounded me, of what with hot sureness began almost immediately to invade me. *I* had never been, before, in the general presence of such insouciance, such live firmness, such confident vigor, such determination to mold or carve something DEFINITE.

Up against the wall, white man! was the substance of the Baraka shout, at the evening reading he shared with fierce Ron Milner among intoxicating drum-beats, heady incense and organic underhumming. Up against the wall! And a pensive (until that moment) white man of thirty or thirty three abruptly shot himself into the heavy air, screaming "Yeah! *Yeah!* Up against the wall, Brother! KILL 'EM ALL! KILL 'EM *ALL!*"

I thought that was interesting. . . .

I—who have "gone the gamut" from an almost angry rejection of my dark skin by some of my brainwashed brothers and sisters to a surprised queenhood in the new black sun—am qualified to enter at least the kindergarten of new consciousness now. New consciousness and trudge-toward-progress.

I have hopes for myself.

ROBERT LOWELL

(1917–1977)

THE DRUNKEN FISHERMAN

Wallowing in this bloody sty,
I cast for fish that pleased my eye
(Truly Jehovah's bow suspends
No pots of gold to weight its ends);
Only the blood-mouthed rainbow trout   5
Rose to my bait. They flopped about
My canvas creel until the moth
Corrupted its unstable cloth.

A calendar to tell the day;
A handkerchief to wave away   10
The gnats; a couch unstuffed with storm
Pouching a bottle in one arm;
A whiskey bottle full of worms;
And bedroom slacks: are these fit terms
To mete the worm whose molten rage   15
Boils in the belly of old age?

Once fishing was a rabbit's foot—
O wind blow cold, O wind blow hot,
Let suns stay in or suns step out:
Life danced a jig on the sperm-whale's spout—   20
The fisher's fluent and obscene
Catches kept his conscience clean.

Children, the raging memory drools
Over the glory of past pools.

1944

WAKING IN THE BLUE

The night attendant, a B. U. sophomore,
rouses from the mare's-nest of his drowsy head
propped on *The Meaning of Meaning*.
He catwalks down our corridor.
Azure day   5
makes my agonized blue window bleaker.
Crows maunder on the petrified fairway.
Absence! My heart grows tense
as though a harpoon were sparring for the kill.
(This is the house for the "mentally ill.")   10

What use is my sense of humor?
I grin at Stanley, now sunk in his sixties,
once a Harvard all-American fullback,
(if such were possible!)
still hoarding the build of a boy in his twenties,   15
as he soaks, a ramrod
with the muscle of a seal
in his long tub,
vaguely urinous from the Victorian plumbing.
A kingly granite profile in a crimson golf-cap,   20
worn all day, all night,
he thinks only of his figure,
of slimming on sherbet and ginger ale—
more cut off from words than a seal.

This is the way day breaks in Bowditch Hall at
    McLean's;   25
the hooded night lights bring out "Bobbie,"
Porcellian '29,
a replica of Louis XVI
without the wig—
redolent and roly-poly as a sperm whale,   30
as he swashbuckles about in his birthday suit
and horses at chairs.

"*Waking in the Blue*": 1 *B.U.:* Boston University   25 *McLean's:* a private mental hospital in
Belmont, Massachusetts   27 *Porcellian:* an exclusive club at Harvard

These victorious figures of bravado ossified young.

In between the limits of day,
hours and hours go by under the crew haircuts   35
and slightly too little nonsensical bachelor twinkle
of the Roman Catholic attendants.
(There are no Mayflower
screwballs in the Catholic Church.)

After a hearty New England breakfast,   40
I weigh two hundred pounds
this morning. Cock of the walk,
I strut in my turtle-necked French sailor's jersey
before the metal shaving mirrors,

and see the shaky future grow familiar   45
in the pinched, indigenous faces
of these thoroughbred mental cases,
twice my age and half my weight.
We are all old-timers,
each of us holds a locked razor.   50

1959

FOR THE UNION DEAD

"Relinquunt omnia
servare rem publicam."

The old South Boston Aquarium stands
in a Sahara of snow now. Its broken windows are
     boarded.
The bronze weathervane cod has lost half its scales.
The airy tanks are dry.

Once my nose crawled like a snail on the glass;   5
my hand tingled
to burst the bubbles
drifting from the noses of the cowed, compliant fish.

My hand draws back, I often sigh still
for the dark downward and vegetating kingdom   10

"For the Union Dead": Reliquunt . . . publicam: "They gave up everything to preserve the
Republic." A slightly different form of this quotation appears on the monument on Boston
Common dedicated to Colonel Robert Gould Shaw (1837–1863) and the Negro troops he led
in an assault on Fort Wagner, South Carolina, on July 18, 1863.

of the fish and reptile. One morning last March,
I pressed against the new barbed and galvanized

fence on the Boston Common. Behind their cage,
yellow dinosaur steamshovels were grunting
as they cropped up tons of mush and grass   15
to gouge their underworld garage.

Parking spaces luxuriate like civic
sandpiles in the heart of Boston.
A girdle of orange, Puritan-pumpkin colored girders
braces the tingling Statehouse,   20

shaking over the excavations, as it faces Colonel Shaw
and his bell-cheeked Negro infantry
on St. Gaudens' shaking Civil War relief,
propped by a plank splint against the garage's
    earthquake.

Two months after marching through Boston,   25
half the regiment was dead;
at the dedication,
William James could almost hear the bronze Negroes
    breathe.

Their monument sticks like a fishbone
in the city's throat.   30
Its Colonel is as lean
as a compass-needle.

He has an angry wrenlike vigilance,
a greyhound's gentle tautness;
he seems to wince at pleasure,   35
and suffocate for privacy.

He is out of bounds now. He rejoices in man's lovely,
peculiar power to choose life and death—
when he leads his black soldiers to death,
he cannot bend his back.   40

On a thousand small town New England greens,
the old white churches hold their air
of sparse, sincere rebellion; frayed flags
quilt the graveyards of the Grand Army of the
    Republic.

The stone statues of the abstract Union Soldier   45
grow slimmer and younger each year—
wasp-wasted, they doze over muskets
and muse through their sideburns . . .

Shaw's father wanted no monument
except the ditch,   50
where his son's body was thrown
and lost with his "niggers."

The ditch is nearer.
There are no statues for the last war here;
on Boylston Street, a commercial photograph   55
shows Hiroshima boiling

over a Mosler Safe, the "Rock of Ages"
that survived the blast. Space is nearer.
When I crouch to my television set,
the drained faces of Negro school-children rise like
    balloons.   60

Colonel Shaw
is riding on his bubble,
he waits
for the blessed break.

The Aquarium is gone. Everywhere,   65
giant finned cars nose forward like fish;
a savage servility
slides by on grease.

                                                            1959

NIGHT SWEAT

Work-table, litter, books and standing lamp,
plain things, my stalled equipment, the old broom—
but I am living in a tidied room,
for ten nights now I've felt the creeping damp
float over my pajamas' wilted white . . .   5
Sweet salt embalms me and my head is wet,
everything streams and tells me this is right;
my life's fever is soaking in night sweat—
one life, one writing! But the downward glide
and bias of existing wrings us dry—   10
always inside me is the child who died,
always inside me is his will to die—
one universe, one body . . . in this urn
the animal night sweats of the spirit burn.
Behind me! You! Again I feel the light   15
lighten my leaded eyelids, while the gray
skulled horses whinny for the soot of night.

I dabble in the dapple of the day,
a heap of wet clothes, seamy, shivering,
I see my flesh and bedding washed with light,   20
my child exploding into dynamite,
my wife . . . your lightness alters everything,
and tears the black web from the spider's sack,
as your heart hops and flutters like a hare.
Poor turtle, tortoise, if I cannot clear   25
the surface of these troubled waters here,
absolve me, help me, Dear Heart, as you bear
this world's dead weight and cycle on your back.

                                        1964

THE NEO-CLASSICAL URN

I rub my head and find a turtle shell
stuck on a pole,
each hair electrical
with charges, and the juice alive
with ferment. Bubbles drive   5
the motor, always purposeful . . .
Poor head!
How its skinny shell once hummed,
as I sprinted down the colonnade
of bleaching pines, cylindrical   10
clipped trunks without a twig between them. Rest!
I could not rest. At full run on the curve,
I left the caste stone statue of a nymph,
her soaring armpits and her one bare breast,
gray from the rain and graying in the shade,   15
as on, on, in sun, the pathway now a dyke,
I swerved between two water bogs,
two seines of moss, and stooped to snatch
the painted turtles on dead logs.

In that season of joy;   20
my turtle catch
was thirty-three,
dropped splashing in our garden urn,
like money in the bank,
the plop and splash   25
of turtle on turtle,
fed raw gobs of hash . . .

Oh neo-classical white urn, Oh nymph,
Oh lute! The boy was pitiless who strummed

their elegy,   30
for as the month wore on,
the turtles rose,
and popped up dead on the stale scummed
surface—limp wrinkled heads and legs withdrawn
in pain. What pain? A turtle's nothing. No   35
grace, no cerebration, less free will
than the mosquito I must kill—
nothings! Turtles! I rub my skull,
that turtle shell,
and breathe their dying smell,   40
still watch their crippled last survivors pass,
and hobble humpbacked through the grizzled grass.

                                        1964

EPILOGUE

Those blessed structures, plot and rhyme—
why are they no help to me now
I want to make
something imagined, not recalled?
I hear the noise of my own voice: 5
The painter's vision is not a lens,
it trembles to caress the light.
But sometimes everything I write
with the threadbare art of my eye
seems a snapshot,   10
lurid, rapid, garish, grouped,
heightened from life,
yet paralyzed by fact.
All's misalliance.
Yet why not say what happened?   15
Pray for the grace of accuracy
Vermeer gave to the sun's illumination
stealing like the tide across a map
to his girl solid with yearning.
We are poor passing facts,   20
warned by that to give
each figure in the photograph
his living name.

                                        1975

_____

"*Epilogue*": 17 *Vermeer:* Jan Vermeer (1632–1675), the Dutch painter; the reference is
probably to his painting "The Letter"

Robert Lowell, like William Butler Yeats, was never completely satisfied with his poetry and searched restlessly for an appropriate style. Early in his career he became a master of highly formal verse. In Life Studies *(1959) he broke with formalism and treated autobiographical subjects in a free verse that approached prose. Later, he returned to a somewhat more reserved and formal style. In an interview with Fredrick Seidel, Lowell discussed the relationship between the formality of verse and the informality of prose.*

"Prose is in many ways better off than poetry": Robert Lowell

But there's another point about this mysterious business of prose and poetry, form and content, and the reason for breaking forms. I don't think there's any very satisfactory answer. I seesaw back and forth between something highly metrical and something free; there isn't any one way to write. But it seems to me we've gotten into a sort of Alexandrian age. Poets of my generation and particularly younger ones have gotten terribly proficient at these forms. They write a very musical, difficult poem with tremendous skill, perhaps there's never been such skill. Yet the writing seems divorced from the culture. It's become too much something specialized that can't handle much experience. It's become a craft, purely a craft, and there must be some breakthrough back into life. Prose is in many ways better off than poetry. It's quite hard to think of a young poet who has the vitality, say, of Salinger or Saul Bellow. Yet prose tends to be very diffuse. The novel is really a much more difficult form than it seems; few people have the wind to write anything that long. Even a short story demands almost poetic perfection. Yet, on the whole, prose is less cut off from life than poetry is. Now, some of this Alexandrian poetry is very brilliant, you would not have it changed at all. But I thought it was getting increasingly stifling. I couldn't get my experience into tight metrical forms.

RICHARD WILBUR

(b. 1921)

PRAISE IN SUMMER

Obscurely yet most surely called to praise,
As sometimes summer calls us all, I said
The hills are heavens full of branching ways
Where star-nosed moles fly overhead the dead;
I said the trees are mines in air, I said   5
See how the sparrow burrows in the sky!
And then I wondered why this mad *instead*
Perverts our praise to uncreation, why
Such savor's in this wrenching things awry.
Does sense so stale that it must needs derange   10
The world to know it? To a praiseful eye
Should it not be enough of fresh and strange
That trees grow green, and moles can course in clay,
And sparrows sweep the ceiling of our day?

1947

THE DEATH OF A TOAD

A toad the power mower caught,
Chewed and clipped off a leg, with a hobbling hop has got
To the garden verge, and sanctuaried him
Under the cineraria leaves, in the shade
Of the ashen heartshaped leaves, in a dim,   5
Low, and a final glade.

The rare original heartsblood goes,
Spends on the earthen hide, in the folds and wizening, flows
In the gutters of the banked and staring eyes. He lies
As still as if he would return to stone,   10
And soundlessly attending, dies
Toward some deep monotone,

Toward misted and ebullient seas
And cooling shores, toward lost Amphibia's emperies.
Day dwindles, drowning, and at length is gone   15
In the wide and antique eyes, which still appear
To watch, across the castrate lawn,
The haggard daylight steer.

1950

Richard Wilbur   **1115**

STILL, CITIZEN SPARROW

Still, citizen sparrow, this vulture which you call
Unnatural, let him but lumber again to air
Over the rotten office, let him bear
The carrion ballast up, and at the tall

Tip of the sky lie cruising. Then you'll see   5
That no more beautiful bird is in heaven's height,
No wider more placid wings, no watchfuller flight
He shoulders nature there, the frightfully free,

The naked-headed one. Pardon him, you
Who dart in the orchard aisles, for it is he   10
Devours death, mocks mutability,
Has heart to make an end, keeps nature new.

Thinking of Noah, childheart, try to forget
How for so many bedlam hours his saw
Soured the song of birds with its wheezy gnaw,   15
And the slam of his hammer all the day beset

The people's ears. Forget that he could bear
To see the towns like coral under the keel,
And the fields so dismal deep. Try rather to feel
How high and weary it was, on the waters where   20

He rocked his only world, and everyone's.
Forgive the hero, you who would have died
Gladly with all you knew; he rode that tide
To Ararat; all men are Noah's sons.

1950

AFTER THE LAST BULLETINS

After the last bulletins the windows darken
And the whole city founders readily and deep,
Sliding on all its pillows
To the thronged Atlantis of personal sleep,

And the wind rises. The wind rises and bowls   5
The day's litter of news in the alleys. Trash
Tears itself on the railings,
Soars and falls with a soft crash,

"*After the Last Bulletins*": 4 *Atlantis:* a legendary island located northwest of Africa in the
Atlantic Ocean that supposedly sank into the sea after its people became corrupt and greedy.
The island is often portrayed in literature as a utopian world

Tumbles and soars again. Unruly flights
Scamper the park, and taking a statue for dead   10
Strike at the positive eyes,
Batter and flap the stolid head

And scratch the noble name. In empty lots
Our journals spiral in a fierce noyade
Of all we thought to think,   15
Or caught in corners cramp and wad

And twist our words. And some from gutters flail
Their tatters at the tired patrolman's feet,
Like all that fisted snow
That cried beside his long retreat   20

Damn you! damn you! to the emperor's horse's heels.
Oh none too soon through the air white and dry
Will the clear announcer's voice
Beat like a dove, and you and I

From the heart's anarch and responsible town   25
Return by subway-mouth to life again,
Bearing the morning papers,
And cross the park where saintlike men

White and absorbed with stick and bag remove
The litter of the night, and footsteps rouse   30
with confident morning sound
The songbirds in the public boughs.

1953

THE UNDEAD

 Even as children they were late sleepers,
Preferring their dreams, even when quick with monsters,
  To the world with all its breakable toys,
   Its compacts with the dying;

  From the stretched arms of withered trees   5
They turned, fearing contagion of the mortal,
  And even under the plums of summer
   Drifted like winter moons.

 Secret, unfriendly, pale, possessed
Of the one wish, the thirst for mere survival,   10
  They came, as all extremists do
   In time, to a sort of grandeur:

Richard Wilbur **1117**

Now, to their Balkan battlements
Above the vulgar town of their first lives,
    They rise at the moon's rising. Strange   15
        That their utter self-concern

    Should, in the end, have left them selfless:
Mirrors fail to perceive them as they float
    Through the great hall and up the staircase;
        Nor are the cobwebs broken.   20

    Into the pallid night emerging,
Wrapped in their flapping capes, routinely maddened
    By a wolf's cry, they stand for a moment
        Stoking the mind's eye

    With lewd thoughts of the pressed flowers   25
And bric-a-brac of rooms with something to lose,—
    Of love-dismembered dolls, and children
        Buried in quilted sleep.

    Then they are off in a negative frenzy,
Their black shapes cropped into sudden bats   30
    That swarm, burst, and are gone. Thinking
        Of a thrush cold in the leaves

    Who has sung his few summers truly,
Or an old scholar resting his eyes at last,
    We cannot be much impressed with vampires,   35
        Colorful though they are;

    Nevertheless their pain is real,
And requires our pity. Think how sad it must be
    To thirst always for a scorned elixir,
        The salt quotidian blood   40

    Which, if mistrusted, has no savor;
To prey on life forever and not possess it,
    As rock-hollows, tide after tide,
        Glassily strand the sea.

1961

ALL THAT IS

Twilight approaches, with its last brief spot-lit
Galaxies of midges, its first star,
And having put in doubt its bats or swallows,
Enters the eastern suburbs. There the hedged
Air darkens like a fast-reducing broth,   5

Simmering the shapes of things. And counter to
Those topiary whims, those *carceri*,
That cypress dye which taints the arbor vitae,
Bright squares flash on in staggered patterns, block
By block, some few blacked out by lowered shades.   10
Meanwhile, through evening traffic and beneath
Checkered façades, a many-lighted bus,
Pausing or turning at the intersections,
Goes intricately home. One passenger
Already folds his paper to the left-   15
Hand lower corner of the puzzles page,
As elsewhere other hands are doing, whether
At kitchen tables under frazzled light,
In plumped-up sickbed, or the easy chair
Near which a facetted decanter glows.   20
Above this séance, in the common dark
Between the street lamps and the jotted sky,
What now takes shape? It is a ghostly grille
Through which, as often, we begin to see
The confluence of the Oka and the Aare.   25

Is it a vision? Does the eye make out
A flight of ernes, rising from aits or aeries,
Whose shadows track across a harsh terrain
Of esker and arête? At waterside,
Does the shocked eeler lay his lampreys by,   30
Sighting a Reo driven by an edile?
And does the edile, from his running board,
Step down to meet a ranee? Does she end
By reading to him from the works of Elia?
No, there are no such chance encounters here   35
As you imagined once, O Lautréamont,
No all-reflecting prism-grain of sand
Nor eyeful such as Markandeya got
When, stumbled into vacancy, he saw
A lambent god reposing on the sea,   40
Full of the knitted light of all that is.
It is a puzzle which, as puzzles do,
Dreams that there is no puzzle. It is a rite
Of finitude, a picture in whose frame

"*All That Is*": 25 *Oka:* River in central European USSR   *Aare:* River in central and northern
Switzerland, flowing to the Rhine   31 *edile: aedile:* an official of ancient Rome   34 *Elia:*
pseudonym used by Charles Lamb (1775–1834), the English essayist, critic, and humorist
36 *Lautréamont:* (1846–1870); French poet who became a model for the Surrealists
38 *Markandeya:* (1924–   ); Anglo-Indian novelist

Roc, oast, and Inca decompose at once   45
Into the ABCs of every day.
A door is rattled shut, a deadbolt thrown.
Under some clipped euonymus, a mushroom,
Bred of an old and deep mycelium
As hidden as the webwork of the world,   50
Strews on the shifty night-wind, rising now,
A cast of spores as many as the stars.

1985

Like Amy Clampitt, Richard Wilbur writes poetry different in tone and per-
spective than many poets of his generation. Louise Bogan says that he is
apparently free by temperament "from the persistent presence of anguish
and anxiety" characteristic of so many of the poets who came onto the scene
after World War II and thus able to indulge in poetry that is bright and
clear even when it approaches mysteries. Randall Jarrell, however, finds
the poetry too indulgent, too light.

"Mr. Wilbur almost always settles for six or eight yards": Randall Jarrell

When you read "The Death of a Toad," a poem that begins *A toad the power*
mower caught,/ Chewed and clipped off a leg, with a hobbling hop has got/ To the
garden verge, you stop to shudder at the raw being of the world, at all that *a*
hobbling hop has brought to life—*that* toad is real, all right. But when you
read on, when Mr. Wilbur says that the toad *dies/Toward some deep mono-*
tone,/ Toward misted and ebullient seas/ And cooling shores, toward lost Amphi-
bia's emperies, you think with a surge of irritation and dismay, "So it was all
only an excuse for some Poetry.". . . .

　　　　Most of his poetry consents too easily to its own unnecessary limitations. An unusually reflective half-back told me that as a run develops there
is sometimes a moment when you can "settle for six or eight yards, or else
take a chance and get stopped cold or, if you're lucky, go the whole way."
Mr. Wilbur almost always settles for six or eight yards; and so many
reviewers have praised him for this that in his second book he takes fewer
risks than in his first. (He is like one of those Southern girls to whom every-

---

45 *Roc:* a legendary bird of prey of enormous size and strength   *oast:* a kiln for drying hops,
malt, or tobacco

body north of Baltimore has said, "Whatever you do, *don't* lose that lovely Southern accent of yours"; after a few years they sound like Amos and Andy.) If I were those reviewers I would quote to Mr. Wilbur something queer and true that Blake said on the same subject: "You never know what is enough unless you know what is more than enough." Mr. Wilbur never goes too far, but he never goes far enough. In the most serious sense of the word he is not a very satisfactory poet. And yet he seems the best of the quite young poets writing in this country. . . .

AMY CLAMPITT

(b. 1923)

THE BURNING CHILD

After a few hours' sleep, the father had a dream that his child was standing beside his bed, caught him by the arm and whispered reproachfully: "Father, don't you see I'm burning?"

—Freud, *The Interpretation of Dreams*

Dreamwork, the mnemonic flicker
of the wave of lost particulars—
whose dream, whose child, where, when, all lost
except the singed reprieve, its fossil ardor
burnished to a paradigm of grief,   5
half a century before the cattle cars,
the shunted parceling—*links, rechts*—
in a blaspheming parody of judgment
by the Lord of burning: the bush, the lava flow,
the chariot, the pillar. What is, even so,   10
whatever breathes but a reprieve, a risk,
a catwalk stroll between the tinder
and the nurture whose embrace is drowning?

The dream redacted cannot sleep; it whimpers
so relentlessly of lost particulars, I can't   15
help thinking of the dreamer as your father,
sent for by the doctors the night he said the *Sh'ma*

_____

"*The Burning Child*": 7 *links, rechts:* left, right (German)   17 *Sh'ma:* Shema Yihsrael, "Hear, O Israel"

over the dim phoenix-nest of scars
you were, survivor
pulled from behind a blazing gas tank   20
that summer on the Cape, those many years
before we two, by a shuttlecock-and-battle-
dore, a dreamworklike accretion of nitwit
trouvées, were cozened into finding how
minute particulars might build themselves   25
into a house that almost looks substantial:
just as I think of how, years earlier,
the waves at Surfside on Nantucket, curveting
like herded colts, subsiding, turned
against my staggering thighs, a manacle   30
of iron cold I had to be pulled out of. Drowning,
since, has seemed a native region's ocean,
that anxiety whose further shores are lurid
with recurrences of burning.

The people herded from the cattle cars   35
first into barracks, then to killing chambers,
stripped of clothes, of names, of chattels—all those
of whom there would remain so few particulars:
I think of them, I think of how your mother's
people made the journey, and of how   40
                              unlike
    my own forebears who made the journey,
    when the rush was on, aboard a crowded
    train from Iowa to California, where,
    hedged by the Pacific's lunging barricades,   45
    they brought into the world the infant
    who would one day be my father, and
    (or the entire astonishment, for me, of
    having lived until this moment would
    have drowned unborn, unburied without   50
    ever having heard of Surfside) chose
    to return, were free to stay or go
    back home, go anywhere at all—
                              not one
outlived the trip whose terminus was burning.   55

The catwalk shadows of the cave, the whimper
of the burning child, the trapped
reprieve of nightmare between the
tinder and the nurture whose
embrace is drowning.   60

                                        1979

BEACH GLASS

While you walk the water's edge,
turning over concepts
I can't envision, the honking buoy
serves notice that at any time
the wind may change,   5
the reef-bell clatters
its treble monotone, deaf as Cassandra
to any note but warning. The ocean,
cumbered by no business more urgent
than keeping open old accounts   10
that never balanced,
goes on shuffling its millenniums
of quartz, granite, and basalt.
                        It behaves
toward the permutations of novelty—   15
driftwood and shipwreck, last night's
beer cans, spilt oil, the coughed-up
residue of plastic—with random
impartiality, playing catch or tag
or touch-last like a terrier,   20
turning the same thing over and over,
over and over. For the ocean, nothing
is beneath consideration.
                        The houses
of so many mussels and periwinkles   25
have been abandoned here, it's hopeless
to know which to salvage. Instead
I keep a lookout for beach glass—
amber of Budweiser, chrysoprase
of Almadén and Gallo, lapis   30
by way of (no getting around it,
I'm afraid) Phillips'
Milk of Magnesia, with now and then a rare
translucent turquoise or blurred amethyst
of no known origin.   35
                        The process
goes on forever: they came from sand,
they go back to gravel,
along with the treasuries

"*Beach Glass*": 7 *Cassandra:* in Greek mythology, the Trojan princess and prophetess who
warned Troy of the wooden horse of the Greeks   29 *chrysoprase:* brilliant to light green

of Murano, the buttressed   40
astonishments of Chartres,
which even now are readying
for being turned over and over as gravely
and gradually as an intellect
engaged in the hazardous   45
redefinition of structures
no one has yet looked at.

                                                1980

LINDENBLOOM

Before midsummer density
opaques with shade the checker-
tables underneath, in daylight
unleafing lindens burn
green-gold a day or two,   5
no more, with intimations
of an essence I saw once,
in what had been the pleasure-
garden of the popes
at Avignon, dishevel   10

into half (or possibly three-
quarters of) a million
hanging, intricately
tactile, blond bell-pulls
of bloom, the in-mid-air   15
resort of honeybees'
hirsute cotillion
teasing by the milligram
out of those necklaced
nectaries, aromas   20
so intensely subtle,
strollers passing under
looked up confused,
as though they'd just
heard voices, or   25
inhaled the ghost
of derelict splendor

---

40 *Murano:* island and town northeast of Venice, famous for its glass manufacturing and
cathedrals   41 *Chartres:* a city in northern France famous for its cathedral
"Lindenbloom": 10 *Avignon:* a city in southeast France. During the thirteenth and fourteenth
centuries, Roman popes, facing instability in the Vatican, fled to Avignon and made it a papal
territory

and/or of seraphs shaken
into pollen dust
no transubstantiating   30
pope or antipope could sift
or quite precisely ponder.

1981

THE WOODLOT

Clumped murmuring above a sump of loam—
grass-rich, wood-poor—that first the plow,
then the inventor (his name plowed under
somewhere in the Patent Office) of barbed wire,
taught, if not fine manners, how at least to follow   5
the surveyor's rule, the woodlot nodes of willow,
evergreen or silver maple gave the prairie grid
what little personality it had.
                           Who could
have learned fine manners where the air,   10
that rude nomad, still domineered,
without a shape it chose to keep,
oblivious of section lines, in winter
whisking its wolfish spittle to a froth
that turned whole townships into   15
one white wallow? Barbed wire
kept in the cattle but would not abrade
the hide or draw the blood
of gales hurled gnashing like seawater over fences'
laddered apertures, rigging the landscape   20
with the perspective of a shipwreck. Land-chained,
the blizzard paused to caterwaul
at every windbreak, a rage the worse
because it was in no way personal.
                        Against   25
the involuted tantrums of spring and summer—
sackfuls of ire, the frightful udder
of the dropped mammocumulus
become all mouth, a lamprey
swigging up whole farmsteads, suction   30
dislodging treetrunks like a rotten tooth—
luck and a cellarhole were all
a prairie dweller had to count on.

"The Woodlot": 28 *mammocumulus:* mammatocumulus, a cumulus storm cloud with breast-shaped protuberances below

Whether

the inventor of barbed wire was lucky   35
finally in what he found himself
remembering, who knows? Did he
ever, even once, envision
the spread of what he'd done
across a continent: whale-song's   40
taut dulcimer still thrumming as it strung together
orchard, barnyard, bullpen, feedlot,
windbreak: wire to be clambered over,
crawled through or slid under, shepherded—
the heifers staring—to an enclosure   45
whose ceiling's silver-maple tops
stir overhead, uneasy, in the interminably
murmuring air? Deep in it,under
appletrees like figures in a ritual, violets
are thick, a blue cellarhole   50
of pure astonishment.
It is
the earliest memory. Before it,
I/you, whatever that conundrum may yet
prove to be, amounts to nothing.   55

1981

DANCERS EXERCISING

Frame within frame, the evolving conversation
is dancelike, as though two could play
at improvising snowflakes'
six-feather-vaned evanescence,
no two ever alike. All process   5
and no arrival: the happier we are,
the less there is for memory to take hold of,
or—memory being so largely a predilection
for the exceptional—come to a halt
in front of. But finding, one evening   10
on a street not quite familiar,
inside a gated
November-sodden garden, a building
of uncertain provenance,
peering into whose vestibule we were   15
arrested—a frame within a frame,
a lozenge of impeccable clarity—
by the reflection, no, not
of our two selves, but of

dancers exercising in a mirror,   20
at the center
of that clarity, what we saw
was not stillness
but movement: the perfection
of memory consisting, it would seem,   25
in the never-to-be completed.
We saw them mirroring themselves,
never guessing the vestibule
that defined them, frame within frame,
contained two other mirrors.   30

1981

ANO PRINIOS

Transport was what we'd come in search of.
A hill village where no bus goes—
we caught a lift there in a pickup truck,
hopped down onto cobblestones. Dank plane trees,
root, branch and foliage, engulfed the square.   5
The mountain slope behind spoke, murmurous,
in tongues of torrents. In what was actually
someone's living room, a small bar at the back,
two men sat by the window, drinking coffee.
We asked for ouzo. Olives on a bed of herbs   10
came with it, and feta, freshly made.
What next? Conversation halted, stumbling,
drew repeated blanks. The woman of the house
sat half-retired, hands busy, needle-glint
releasing a slow rill of thread lace.   15
What it was for—a tablecloth, a baby's
christening robe perhaps—I tried to ask,
she tried to tell me, but the filament fell short.
The plane trees dripped. The old man,
the proprietor, moved in and out. A course   20
we hadn't asked for—two fishes, mountain trout
they must have been, served on a single plate—
was set between us: seasoned with leeks,
I could not guess what else, the ridged
flesh firm and delicate.   25
Later, as I came from the latrine,
the old man, intercepting, showed me

"Ano Prinios": A small Greek village

the rooms we might have slept in—hangings
vivid over whitewash, the blankets rough.
A disappointed avarice—how could we, savoring   30
a poverty rarer than any opulence, begin
to grasp how dear our fickle custom was?—
gloomed, hurtful as a bruise, on
our departure: the rooted and the footloose
each looking past the other, for something missed.   35
A scruple over how to deal with matters so
fundamental, and so unhandsome, restrained me,
for two years and more, from writing
of what happened in between: how happiness
asperged, redeemed, made the occasion   40
briefly articulate. One of the coffee-drinkers,
having vanished, came back in. He brought,
dripping as from a fountain, a branch just severed
from some fruit tree, loaded with drupes
that were, though still green, delectable.   45
Turning to the woman, I asked what
they were called in Greek. She answered,
"Damaskēno." Damson, damask, damascene:
the word hung, still hangs there,
glistening among its cognates.   50

                                        1987

MAN FEEDING PIGEONS

It was the form of the thing, the unmanaged
symmetry of it, of whatever it was
he convoked as he knelt on the sidewalk
and laid out from his unfastened briefcase
a benefaction of breadcrumbs—this band   5

arriving of the unhoused and opportune
we have always with us, composing
as they fed, heads together, wing tip
and tail edge serrated like chicory
(that heavenly weed, that cerulean   10

commoner of waste places) but with a
glimmer in it, as though the winged
beings of all the mosaics of Ravenna
had gotten the message somehow and come
flying in to rejoin the living: plump-   15

contoured as the pomegranates and pears
in a Della Robbia holiday wreath that had

put on the bloom, once again, of the soon
to perish, to begin to decay, to reënter
that dance of freewheeling dervishes,   20

the breakdown of order: it was the form
of the thing, if a thing is what it was,
and not the merest wisp of a part of
a process—this unravelling inkling
of the envisioned, of states of being   25

past alteration, of all that we've
never quite imagined except by way of
the body: the winged proclamations,
the wheelings, the stairways, the
vast, concentric, paradisal rose.   30

1987

*Amy Clampitt's career has been complicated by her absolute independence
from the poetic fashions. Some of the great poets of her generation created
an audience with a taste for poetry that was confessional and hard-edged.
Her own interest was in poetry richer in sound, less openly confessional, and
more openly tied to the literature and culture of the past. So unfashionable
were these standards that when Clampitt began to write seriously, she had no
anticipation of the popularity she has enjoyed in recent years. Echos of this
unusual poetic career appear in a 1986 interview with Laura Fairchild.*

"I still heard them and I could not shut them out": Amy Clampitt

Fairchild: Your work seems to have a special emphasis on sound. Are you
           particularly interested in the aural tradition of verse?

Clampitt: Aural tradition—I'm not sure that I would say that. Certainly
           the sound is what I start out with. I write for the ear. I don't
           really know what I've got until I've read it aloud to someone. I
           can't read things aloud to myself. . . .

                As I was growing up the poetry that appealed to me was
           certainly aural. For a while I had a crush on Swinburne. I got
           over it. I decided there was a little bit too much mellifluousness
           there. It goes so smoothly that you hardly notice that he's say-
           ing anything, and he is saying something. I never wanted to

sound so pretty that no one would think that there was any meaning to it. Just lately I've been attacked very harshly by a reviewer who said, "All her prosodies tend toward cacophony." (*Laughing*) . . . I guess I know what she means. I don't try to be pretty all the time. I kind of like all of these mouth-filling, bumpy sounds. English is full of them.

Fairchild: What about all this use of allusion? Do you feel that poetry should help to preserve literary and cultural history?

Clampitt: I was writing for quite a while without any sense that I would ever be published at all, out of what I heard in my head. I can't exactly say what I was doing. But certainly all of those voices out of the past were there. I still heard them and I could not shut them out. I'm feeling now somewhat chastened by a couple of reviews objecting to so many literary allusions. The truth is I am not an academic; I am not a scholar at all. I just get excited about books. But it may be that the best poetry does come out of direct experience. That I am drawn by subjects that go back into previous literature may be a sign of something reprehensible, I don't know.

I'm fascinated by Greek literature. And although I'm not good at it at all, I've studied classical Greek. I decided it was worth doing, to take an intensive course; we go through Attic grammar in one semester. I liked Homer. There is something about the worn-smooth sense you get line by line, although the sound of Greek is rather harsh. It has a lot of diphthongs, it has a lot of consonants, and so they kind of jamb against each other. I'm drawn by that kind of harsh sound. It's harsh and at the same time tempered in some kind of way that no other literature I know has. It's just wonderful to be reading and to feel that you are going back through time to the sources of things.

Travelling in Greece was more exciting to me than anything. There is so much to be found in Homer that no one has yet surpassed, the sad knowledge of what human beings are really like, told in this very straightforward and unpretentious way—grown men acting like children. They still do.

MAXINE KUMIN

(b. 1925)

MORNING SWIM

Into my empty head there come
a cotton beach, a dock wherefrom

I set out, oily and nude
through mist, in chilly solitude

There was no line, no roof or floor   5
to tell the water from the air.

Night fog thick as terry cloth
closed me in its fuzzy growth.

I hung my bathrobe on two pegs.
I took the lake between my legs.   10

Invaded and invader, I
went overhand on that flat sky.

Fish twitched beneath me, quick and tame.
In their green zone they sang my name

and in the rhythm of the swim   15
I hummed a two-four-time show hymn.

I hummed *Abide with Me.* The beat
rose in the fine thrash of my feet,

rose in the bubbles I put out
slantwise, trailing through my mouth.   20

My bones drank water; water fell
through all my doors. I was the well

that fed the lake that met my sea
in which I sang *Abide with Me.*

1965

MAKING THE JAM WITHOUT YOU

For Judy

Old daughter, small traveler
asleep in a German featherbed

under the eaves in a postcard town
of turrets and towers,
I am putting a dream in your head.   5

Listen! Here it is afternoon.
The rain comes down like bullets.
I stand in the kitchen,
that harem of good smells
where we have bumped hips and   10
cracked the cupboards with our talk
while the stove top danced with pots
and it was not clear who did
the mothering. Now I am
crushing blackberries   15
to make the annual jam
in a white cocoon of steam.

Take it, my sleeper. Redo it
in any of your three
languages and nineteen years.   20
Change the geography.
Let there be a mountain,
the fat cows on it belled
like a cathedral. Let
there be someone beside you   25
as you come upon the ruins
of a schloss, all overgrown
with a glorious thicket,
its brambles soft as wool.
Let him bring the buckets   30
crooked on his angel arms
and may the berries, vaster
than any forage in
the mild hills of New Hampshire,
drop in your pail, plum size,   35
heavy as the eyes
of an honest dog
and may you bear them
home together to a square
white unreconstructed kitchen   40
not unlike this one.

Now may your two heads
touch over the kettle,
over the blood of the berries
that drink up sugar and sun,   45
over that tar-thick boil

love cannot stir down.
More plainly than
the bric-a-brac of shelves
filling with jelly glasses,   50
more surely than
the light driving through them
trite as rubies, I see him
as pale as paraffin beside you.
I see you cutting   55
fresh baked bread to spread it
with the bright royal fur.

At this time
I lift the flap of your dream
and slip out thinner than a sliver   60
as your two mouths open
for the sweet stain of purple.

1970

THE LONGING TO BE SAVED

When the barn catches fire
I am wearing the wrong negligee.
It hangs on me like a gunny sack.
I get the horses out, but they
wrench free, wheel, dash back   5
and three or four trips are required.
Much whinnying and rearing as well.
This happens whenever I travel.

At the next stopover, the children take off
their doctor and lawyer disguises   10
and turn back into little lambs.
They cower at windows from which flames
shoot like the tattered red cloth
of dimestore devil suits. They refuse
to jump into my waiting arms, although   15
I drilled them in this technique, years ago.

Finally they come to their senses and leap
but each time, the hoop holds my mother.
Her skin is as dry and papery
as a late onion. I take her   20
into my bed, an enormous baby
I do not especially want to keep.

Three nights of such disquiet
in and out of dreams as thin as acetate

until, last of all, it's you   25
trapped in the blazing fortress.
I hold the rope as you slide from danger.
It's tricky in high winds and drifting snow.
Your body swaying in space
grows heavier, older, stranger   30

and me in the same gunny sack
and the slamming sounds as the gutted building burns.
Now the family's out, there's no holding back.
I go in to get my turn.

                                        1978

THE ENVELOPE

It is true, Martin Heidegger, as you have written,
I *fear to cease,* even knowing that at the hour
of my death my daughters will absorb me, even
knowing they will carry me about forever
inside them, an arrested fetus, even as I carry   5
the ghost of my mother under my navel, a nervy
little androgynous person, a miracle
folded in lotus position.

Like those old pear-shaped Russian dolls that open
at the middle to reveal another and another, down   10
to the pea-sized, irreducible minim,
may we carry our mothers forth in our bellies.
May we, borne onward by our daughters, ride
in the Envelope of Almost-Infinity,
that chain letter good for the next twenty-five   15
thousand days of their lives.

                                        1978

IN APRIL, IN PRINCETON

They are moving the trees in Princeton.
Full-grown and burlapped, aboard two-ton

"*The Envelope*": 1 *Martin Heidegger:* (1889–1976); German philosopher and proponent of
existentialism

trucks, great larches go up the main artery
—once the retreat route of Washington's army—
to holes in the ground I know nothing of.   5
They are moving the trees for money and love.

They are changing the grass in Princeton
as well. They are bringing it in from sod farms
rolled tight as a church-wedding carpet, unrolled
on the lawn's raw skin in place of the old   10
onion grass, acid moss, dandelions.
The eye rests, approving. Order obtains.

There is no cure for beauty so replete
it hurts in Princeton. In April, here's such light
and such benevolence that winter   15
is overlooked, like bad table manners.
Peach, pear, and cherry bloom. The mockingbirds
seize the day, a bunch of happy drunkards

and mindful it will pass, I hurry each noon
to yoga in the Hillel Reading Room   20
where Yahweh and Krishna intersect in Princeton;
where, under my navel in lotus position
by sending fresh *prana* to the center
albeit lunchless, the soul may enter.

Here, let me not forget Antonin Artaud   25
who feared to squat, lest his immortal soul
fly out of his anus and disappear
from the madhouse in thin air.
Let me remember how I read those words
in my square white office, its windows barred   30

by sunlight through dust motes, my own asylum
for thoughts unsorted as to phylum.
Cerulean-blue rug softening the floor,
desk, chair, books, nothing more
except for souls aloft—Artaud's, perhaps,   35
and mine—drifting like the waxy cups

of white magnolias that drop their porcelain
but do not shatter, in April, in Princeton.

1982

_____

"*In April, In Princeton*": 23 *prana*: Pranavayu, the wind of life (Hindu)   25 *Antonin Artaud*:
(1896–1948); French director and playwright who founded the "theater of cruelty"

AT A PRIVATE SHOWING IN 1982

For Gillian Anderson

This loving attention to the details:
faces by Bosch and Bruegel,
the mélange of torture tools,
the carpentry of the stake,
the Catherine wheel,   5
the bars, spires, gibbets, pikes—
I confess my heart sank
when they brought out the second reel . . .

Anorectic Jeanne d'Arc,
how long it takes her   10
to burn to death in this picture!
When monks fast, it is called ascetic.
The film beamed on the dining-room wall
of an old brownstone
undergoing gentrification on Capitol Hall,   15
glass shards and daffodils
on alternate lawns,
harpsichord, bare board table,
cheese, nuts, jug wine,

and striding across the screen,   20
hauntingly young, unbowed,
not yet absurd, not yet insane,
Antonin Artaud in a bit part:
the "good" priest,
the one who declaims   25
"You are persecuting a saint!"
but does not offer
to die beside her.

And how is any of this
different today,   30
except now in color, and talky—
this prurient close
examination of pain,
fanaticism, terror?

"At a Private Showing": 2 *Bosch:* Hieronymous Bosch (1450–1515), a Dutch painter whose
works, such as *The Garden of Earthly Delights,* include graphic representations of the torments
of hell   *Bruegel:* Pieter Brueghel (1525–1569), a painter from the Netherlands whose
engravings are adaptations of Bosch's works   5 *Catherine wheel:* an instrument of torture on
which the victim was bound and broken   9 *Jeanne d'Arc:* Joan of Arc (1412–1431), the
French nationalistic heroine   22 *Antonin Artaud:* (1896–1948); French director and
playwright who founded the "theater of cruelty"

Though the judges dress   35
like World War I British
soldiers in tin helmets
and Sam Browne belts,
though the music exactly
matches the mouthed words,   40
though Jeanne's
enormous wounded-doe's eyes
roll up or shut down
in hope, in anguish,
though Renée Falconetti,   45
who plays this part, was merely
a comic-stage actress
and never shows up on celluloid again,

though Artaud
tonsured for the set   50
walks the streets of Paris
in costume in 1928
and is mocked by urchins
and is peppered with catcalls,
what does it profit us?   55

Artaud will die in the madhouse
in terror for his immortal soul,
Falconetti will drop out of sight,
an émigrée in the Argentine,
we few will finish the wine   60
and skulk out on this spring night
together, unsafe on Capitol Hill.

1985

An unfriendly critic once remarked that Maxine Kumin's poetry comes from "a special world, unmistakably upper middle-class, comfortable, urbane, safe in its place at the center of things." Certainly the experiences she writes about are often those open to a relatively small group, but it is dangerous to dismiss them too lightly. "At a Private Showing in 1982," for instance, grew out of a private screening of "Jeanne D'Arc," a 1928 silent film by Carl Dreyer. All this seems comfortable enough. The film, however, is influenced by Antonin Artaud's idea of a "theater of cruelty" that will bring humans face-to-face with their brutal nature. Kumin's comments on the poem help us see how she tries to span the gap between her comfortable life and the sometimes uncomfortable world.

"To act *as if* bearing witness matters": Maxine Kumin

Increasingly, the poems that we write are poems about the death of society, the collapse of the planet, the end of everything human we have been taught to believe in, to build from, to aspire toward. I use the plural pronoun because I think my moral dilemma as a poet is rapidly becoming every artist's dilemma. Thanks to modern technology, we can watch the world's local wars on television. We can see the torture and the killings in color, even as they happen. Salvador is an example, but it is only one of many mind-numbing grisly situations around the world. What use do we make of this pounding on the doors of our perception, this battering of rationality? Why do we persist with our poems of anger and lament, even as we know that poetry "makes nothing happen"?

I write these poems because I have to. I wrestle with my own notions of human depravity in this, and in other poems, not because I think the poem can change our foreign policy, soften the heart of the military-industrial complex that feeds on first-strike potential propaganda, or arouse the citizenry to acts of civil disobedience for peace, but because, for my own sanity (and yours, and yours), I must live the dream out to the end. It is important to act *as if* bearing witness matters. To write about the monstrous sense of alienation the poet feels in this culture of polarized hatreds is a way of staying sane. With the poem, I reach out to an audience equally at odds with official policy, and I celebrate our mutual humanness in an inhuman world.

In the poem under discussion, raw feeling was not enough. Had it not been for the presence of Artaud in the film, I wonder if I would have been able to complete the poem. He was the catalyst in an earlier poem of mine, called "In April, in Princeton," a very formal set piece written in matching stanzas of three couplets apiece on which I had imposed the added constraint of finding a way to insert the words "in Princeton" in each stanza. It had begun as a kind of ornament, an act of fealty for the semester I had spent so happily in that luscious, wealthy community. But Artaud, whose work I had been reading in my big, bare office, invaded and saved the poem. To encounter him young, strong, and sane in this old film was a tender reexperiencing of the bond I had felt some years earlier when I read the sad drama of his death in the madhouse.

ROBERT BLY

(b. 1926)

MY FATHER'S WEDDING 1924

Today, lonely for my father, I saw
a log, or branch,
long, bent, ragged, bark gone.
I felt lonely for my father when I saw it.
It was the log   5
that lay near my uncle's old milk wagon.

Some men live with an invisible limp,
stagger, or drag
a leg. Their sons are often angry.
Only recently I thought: 10
Doing what you want . . .
Is that like limping? Tracks of it show in sand.

Have you seen those giant bird-
men of Bhutan?
Men in bird masks, with pig noses, dancing,   15
teeth like a dog's, sometimes
dancing on one bad leg!
They do what they want, the dog's teeth say that!

But I grew up without dogs' teeth,
showed a whole body,   20
left only clear tracks in sand.
I learned to walk swiftly, easily,
no trace of a limp.
I even leaped a little. Guess where my defect is!

Then what? If a man, cautious   25
hides his limp,
Somebody has to limp it! Things
do it; the surroundings limp.
House walls get scars,
the car breaks down; matter, in drudgery, takes it up.   30

On my father's wedding day,
no one was there
to hold him. Noble loneliness
held him. Since he never asked for pity
his friends thought he   35
was whole. Walking alone, he could carry it.

He came in limping. It was a simple
wedding, three
or four people. The man in black,
lifting the book, called for order.   40
And the invisible bride
stepped forward, before his own bride.

He married the invisible bride, not his own.
In her left
breast she carried the three drops   45
that wound and kill. He already had
his barklike skin then,
made rough especially to repel the sympathy

he longed for, didn't need, and wouldn't accept.
They stopped. So   50
the words are read. The man in black
speaks the sentence. When the service
is over, I hold him
in my arms for the first time and the last.

After that he was alone   55
and I was alone.
No friends came; he invited none.
His two-story house he turned
into a forest,
where both he and I are the hunters.   60

1981

FOR MY SON NOAH, TEN YEARS OLD

Night and day arrive, and day after day goes by,
and what is old remains old, and what is young remains
    young, and grows old.
The lumber pile does not grow younger, nor the
    two-by-fours lose their darkness,
but the old tree goes on, the barn stands without help
    so many years;
The advocate of darkness and night is not lost.   5

The horse steps up, swings on one leg, turns its body,
the chicken flapping claws onto the roost, its wings
    whelping and walloping,
but what is primitive is not to be shot out into the night
    and the dark.
And slowly the kind man comes closer, loses his rage,
    sits down at table.

So I am proud only of those days that pass in undivided
    tenderness,   10
when you sit drawing, or making books, stapled, with
    messages to the world,
or coloring a man with fire coming out of his hair.
Or we sit at a table, with small tea carefully poured.
So we pass our time together, calm and delighted.

1981

WORDS RISING

I open my journal, write a few
sounds with green ink, and suddenly
fierceness enters me, stars
begin to revolve, and pick up
alligator dust from under the ocean.   5
The music comes, I feel the bushy
tail of the Great Bear
reach down and brush the seafloor.

All those lives we lived in the sunlit
shelves of the Dordogne, the thousand   10
tunes we sang to the skeletons
of Papua, the many times
we died—wounded—under the cloak
of an animal's sniffing, all of these
return, and the grassy nights   15
we ran for hours in the moonlight.

Watery syllables come welling up.
Anger that barked and howled in the cave,
the luminous head of barley
the priest holds up, growls   20
from under fur, none of that is lost.
The old earth fragrance remains
in the word "and." We experience
"the" in its lonely suffering.

We are bees then; our honey is language.   25
Now the honey lies stored in caves

"*Words Rising*": 10 *Dordogne:* region of central France containing significant remains of
Stone Age man, including the cave paintings at Lascaux   12 *Papua:* formerly the name for
British New Guinea; now the entire country is named Papua New Guinea

beneath us, and the sound of words
carries what we do not.
When a man or woman feeds a few words
with private grief, the shames we knew   30
before we could invent the wheel,
then words grow. We slip out

into farmyards, where rabbits lie
stretched out on the ground for buyers.
Wicker baskets and hanged men   35
come to us as stanzas and vowels.
We see a crowd with dusty
palms turned up inside each
verb. There are eternal vows
held inside the word "Jericho."   40

Blessings then on the man who labors
in his tiny room, writing stanzas on the lamb;
blessings on the woman who picks the brown
seeds of solitude in afternoon light
out of the black seeds of loneliness.   45
And blessings on the dictionary maker, huddled among
his bearded words, and on the setter of songs
who sleeps at night inside his violin case.

1981

IN RAINY SEPTEMBER

In rainy September, when leaves grow down to the dark,
I put my forehead down to the damp, seaweed-smelling sand.
The time has come. I have put off choosing for years,
perhaps whole lives. The fern has no choice but to live;
for this crime it receives earth, water, and night.   5

We close the door. "I have no claim on you."
Dusk comes. "The love I have had with you is enough."
We know we could live apart from one another.
The sheldrake floats apart from the flock.
The oaktree puts out leaves alone on the lonely hillside. 10

Men and women before us have accomplished this.
I would see you, and you me, once a year.
We would be two kernels, and not be planted.

---

40 *Jericho:* God promised the city of Jericho to Joshua; see Joshua 6:2

We stay in the room, door closed, lights out.
I weep with you without shame and without honor.   15

1984

THE INDIGO BUNTING

I go to the door often.
Night and summer. Crickets
lift their cries.
I know you are out.
You are driving   5
late through the summer night.

I do not know what will happen.
I have no claim on you.
I am one star
you have as guide; others   10
love you, the night
so dark over the Azores.

You have been working outdoors,
gone all week. I feel you
in this lamp lit   15
so late. As I reach for it
I feel myself
driving through the night.

I love a firmness in you
that disdains the trivial   20
and regains the difficult.
You become part then
of the firmness of night,
the granite holding up walls.

There were women in Egypt who   25
supported with their firmness the stars
as they revolved,
hardly aware
of the passage from night
to day and back to night.   30

I love you where you go
through the night, not swerving,
clear as the indigo
bunting in her flight,

passing over two
thousand miles of ocean.

35

1985

Robert Bly came to poetic maturity in an era when poets like T. S. Eliot, William Carlos Williams, and Marianne Moore were predominant. He, however, did not adopt their "objectivist" views of poetry. Instead, he looked for inspiration to non-English-speaking poets, notably Federico García Lorca, Rainer Maria Rilke, and Pablo Neruda. Following their example, he sought to produce poetry that would "transfer an intuition from poet to reader" rather than direct the reader's attention to objects which would carry the emotions "in dehydrated form."

"Remembering forgotten relations is then one of the great joys": Robert Bly

The image belongs with the simile, the metaphor, and the analogy as an aspect of metaphorical language. Shelley said: "Metaphorical language marks the before unapprehended relations of things." Owen Barfield remarks in his marvelous book called *Poetic Diction* (which is about many other things as well) that he would like to alter only one detail in Shelley's sentence. He would change "before unapprehended relations" to "forgotten relations." Ancient man stood in the center of a wheel of relations coming to the human being from objects. The Middle Ages were aware of a relationship between a woman's body and a tree, and Jung reproduces in one of his books an old plate showing a woman taking a baby from a tree trunk. That would be an example of a forgotten relationship recently retrieved; and Greek myths, when studied, turn up others. Many relationships then have been forgotten—by us. They can be recovered. "For though they were never yet apprehended they were at one time seen," Barfield says. "And imagination can see them again." Whenever a poet through imagination discovers a true analogy, he or she is bringing up into consciousness a relationship that has been forgotten for centuries; the object is then not only more seen, but the poet receives a permanent addition to his knowledge.

   The power of the image is the power of seeing resemblances, a discipline important to the growth of intelligence, and essential to a poet's intelligence. Emerson said of true analogies:

It is easily seen that there is nothing lucky or capricious in these analogies, but that they are constant, and pervade nature. These are not the dreams of a few poets, here and there, but man is an analogist, and studies relations in all objects. He is placed in the center of beings, and a ray of relation passes from every other being to him.

Remembering forgotten relationships is then one of the great joys that comes from making up poetry. Of course not every image the mind makes up is a true one, and we have the right to ask of every image in a poem: Does this image help us to remember a forgotten relationship, or is it merely a silly juxtaposition, which is amusing and no more?

W. S. MERWIN

(b. 1927)

GRANDMOTHER WATCHING AT HER WINDOW

There was always the river or the train
Right past the door, and someone might be gone
Come morning. When I was a child I mind
Being held up at a gate to wave
Good-bye, good-bye to I didn't know who,   5
Gone to the War, and how I cried after.
When I married I did what was right
But I knew even that first night
That he would go. And so shut my soul tight
Behind my mouth, so he could not steal it   10
When he went. I brought the children up clean
With my needle, taught them that stealing
Is the worst sin; knew if I loved them
They would be taken away, and did my best
But must have loved them anyway   15
For they slipped through my fingers like stitches.
Because God loves us always, whatever
We do. You can sit all your life in churches
And teach your hands to clutch when you pray
And never weaken, but God loves you so dearly   20
Just as you are, that nothing you are can stay,
But all the time you keep going away, away.

1960

NOAH'S RAVEN

Why should I have returned?
My knowledge would not fit into theirs.
I found untouched the desert of the unknown,
Big enough for my feet. It is my home.
It is always beyond them. The future   5
Splits the present with the echo of my voice.
Hoarse with fulfilment, I never made promises.

1963

FOR THE ANNIVERSARY OF MY DEATH

Every year without knowing it I have passed the day
When the last fires will wave to me
And the silence will set out
Tireless traveller
Like the beam of a lightless star   5
Then I will no longer
Find myself in life as in a strange garment
Surprised at the earth
And the love of one woman
And then shamelessness of men   10
As today writing after three days of rain
Hearing the wren sing and the falling cease
And bowing not knowing to what

1967

THE LAST ONE

Well they'd made up their minds to be everywhere
      because why not.
Everywhere was theirs because they thought so.
They with two leaves they whom the birds despise.
In the middle of stones they made up their minds.
They started to cut.   5

Well they cut everything because why not.
Everything was theirs because they thought so.
It fell into its shadows and they took both away.
Some to have some for burning.

"Noah's Raven": See Genesis 8:7–9; God sent out a raven before the dove

Well cutting everything they came to the water.   10
They came to the end of the day there was one left
    standing.
They would cut it tomorrow they went away.
The night gathered in the last branches.
The shadow of the night gathered in the shadow on the
    water.
The night and the shadow put on the same head.   15
And it said Now.

Well in the morning they cut the last one.
Like the others the last one fell into its shadow.
It fell into its shadow on the water.
They took it away its shadow stayed on the water.   20

Well they shrugged they started trying to get the
    shadow away.
They cut right to the ground the shadow stayed whole.
They laid boards on it the shadow came out on top.
They shone lights on it the shadow got blacker and
    clearer.
They exploded the water the shadow rocked.   25
They built a huge fire on the roots.
They sent up black smoke between the shadow and the
    sun.
The new shadow flowed without changing the old one.
They shrugged they went away to get stones.

They came back the shadow was growing.   30
They started setting up stones it was growing.
They looked the other way it went on growing.
They decided they would make a stone out of it.
They took stones to the water they poured them into
    the shadow.
They poured them in they poured them in the stones
    vanished.   35
The shadow was not filled it went on growing.
That was one day.

The next day was just the same it went on growing.
They did all the same things it was just the same.
They decided to take its water from under it.   40
They took away water they took it away the water went
    down.
The shadow stayed where it was before.
It went on growing it grew onto the land.
They started to scrape the shadow with machines.
When it touched the machines it stayed on them.   45

They started to beat the shadow with sticks.
Where it touched the sticks it stayed on them.
They started to beat the shadow with hands.
Where it touched the hands it stayed on them.
That was another day.   50

Well the next day started about the same it went on
     growing.
They pushed lights into the shadow.
Where the shadow got onto them they went out.
They began to stomp on the edge it got their feet.
And when it got their feet they fell down.   55
It got into eyes the eyes went blind.

The ones that fell down it grew over and they vanished.
The ones that went blind and walked into it vanished.
The ones that could see and stood still
It swallowed their shadows.   60
Then it swallowed them too and they vanished.
Well the others ran.

The ones that were left went away to live if it would let
     them.
They went as far as they could.
The lucky ones with their shadows.   65

1968

THE DIFFERENT STARS

I could never have come to the present without you
remember that
from whatever stage we may again
watch it appear

with its lines clear   5
pain
having gone from there

so that we may well wonder
looking back on us here what tormented us
what great difficulty invisible   10
in a time that by then looks simple
and is irrevocable

pain having come from there
my love
I tend to think of division as the only evil   15
when perhaps it is merely my own

that unties
one day the veins one the arteries
that prizes less
as it receives than as it loses   20
that breaks the compasses
cannot be led or followed
cannot choose what to carry
into grief
even   25
unbinds will unbind
unbinds our hands
pages of the same story
what is it
they say can turn even this into wisdom   30
and what is wisdom if it is not
now
in the loss that has not left this place

oh if we knew
if we knew what we needed if we even knew   35
the stars would look to us to guide them

                                                   1970

THE JUDGMENT OF PARIS

For Anthony Hecht

Long afterwards
the intelligent could deduce what had been offered
and not recognized
and they suggest that bitterness should be confined
to the fact that the gods chose for their arbiter   5
a mind and character so ordinary
albeit a prince

and brought up as a shepherd
a calling he must have liked
for he had returned to it   10

when they stood before him
the three

"The Judgment of Paris": In Greek mythology, Paris was the son of Priam, King of Troy. Asked
to decide who was the fairest among Athena, Juno, and Aphrodite, Paris chose Aphrodite,
who promised him the fairest woman for his wife. By abducting Helen of Troy, whom
Aphrodite had destined for him, Paris caused the Trojan War.

naked feminine deathless
and he realized that he was clothed
in nothing but mortality   15
the strap of his quiver of arrows crossing
between his nipples
making it seem stranger

and he knew he must choose
and on that day   20

the one with the gray eyes spoke first
and whatever she said he kept
thinking he remembered
but remembered it woven with confusion and fear
the two faces that he called father   25
the first sight of the palace
where the brothers were strangers

and the dogs watched him and refused to know him
she made everything clear she was dazzling she
offered it to him   30
to have for his own but what he saw
was the scorn above her eyes
and her words of which he understood few
all said to him *Take wisdom*
take power   35
you will forget anyway

the one with the dark eyes spoke
and everything she said
he imagined he had once wished for
but in confusion and cowardice   40
the crown
of his father the crowns the crowns bowing to him
his name everywhere like grass
only he and the sea
triumphant   45
she made everything sound possible she was
dazzling she offered it to him
to hold high but what he saw
was the cruelty around her mouth
and her words of which he understood more   50
all said to him *Take pride*
take glory
you will suffer anyway

the third one the color of whose eyes
later he could not remember   55

spoke last and slowly and
of desire and it was his
though up until then he had been
happy with his river nymph
here was his mind   60
filled utterly with one girl gathering
yellow flowers
and no one like her
the words
made everything seem present   65
almost present
present
they said to him *Take*
her
you will lose her anyway   70

it was only when he reached out to the voice
as though he could take the speaker
herself
that his hand filled with
something to give   75
but to give to only one of the three
an apple as it is told
discord itself in a single fruit its skin
already carved
To the fairest   80

then a mason working above the gates of Troy
in the sunlight thought he felt the stone
shiver

in the quiver on Paris's back the head
of the arrow for Achilles' heel   85
smiled in its sleep

and Helen stepped from the palace to gather
as she would do every day in that season
from the grove the yellow ray flowers tall
as herself   90

Whose roots are said to dispel pain

1970

EMIGRÉ

You will find it is
much as you imagined

in some respects
which no one can predict
you will be homesick   5
at times for something you can describe
and at times without being able to say
what you miss
just as you used to feel when you were at home

some will complain from the start   10
that you club together
with your own kind
but only those who have
done what you have done
conceived of it longed for it   15
lain awake waiting for it
and have come out with
no money no papers nothing
at your age
know what you have done   20
what you are talking about
and will find you a roof and employers

others will say from the start
that you avoid
those of your country   25
for a while
as your country becomes
a category in the new place
and nobody remembers the same things
in the same way   30
and you come to the problem
of what to remember after all
and of what is your real
language
where does it come from what does it   35
sound like
who speaks it

if you cling to the old usage
do you not cut yourself off
from the new speech   40
but if you rush to the new lips
do you not fade like a sound cut off
do you not dry up like a puddle
is the new tongue to be trusted

what of the relics of your childhood   45
should you bear in mind pieces

of dyed cotton and gnawed wood
lint of voices untranslatable stories
summer sunlight on dried paint
whose color continues to fade in the   50
growing brightness of the white afternoon
ferns on the shore of the transparent lake
or should you forget them
as you float between ageless languages
and call from one to the other who you are   55

1986

HISTORY

Only I never came back

the gates stand open
where I left the barnyard in the evening
as the owl was bringing the mouse home
in the gold sky   5
at the milking hour
and I turned to the amber hill and followed
along the gray fallen wall
by the small mossed oaks and the bushes of rusting
arches bearing the ripe   10
blackberries into the long shadow
and climbed the ancient road
through the last songs of the blackbirds

passing the last live farms
their stones running with dark liquid   15
and the ruined farms their windows without frames
facing away
looking out across the pastures of dead shepherds
whom nobody ever knew
grown high with the dry flowers of a late summer   20
their empty doorways gazing
toward the arms of the last oaks
and at night their broken chimneys watching
the cold of the meteors
the beams had fallen together   25
to rest in brown herds around the fireplaces
and in the shade of black trees the houses were full
of their own fragrance at last
mushrooms and owls
and the song of the cicadas   30

there was a note on a page
made at the time
and the book was closed
and taken on a journey
into a country where no one   35
knew the language
no one could read
even the address
inside the cover
and there the book was   40
of course lost

it was a book full of words to remember
this is how we manage without them
this is how they manage
without us   45

I was not going to be long

1986

W. S. Merwin, like Robert Bly, has been profoundly affected by poetry that comes from outside the Anglo-American tradition. We see in the excerpt below (from a conversation with Ed Folsom and Cary Nelson) that many of his poems are nonetheless attempts to find the layers that underlie a life lived on the apparently stable surface of twentieth-century America.

"Our lives are maimed and truncated accordingly": W. S. Merwin

I don't think it's possible for me to see or to approach that subject—it never has been—without . . . this feeling of inhabiting a palimpsest. However long the culture may have left, we are not just sitting here on a Sunday afternoon. Insofar as there is any historical or temporal continuity at all, that continuity involves these many layers, many of them invisible, and they are not different at all from the repressed, pressed, and forgotten layers of our own experience. And if we really are so dishonest and so mutilated that we can't make any sense of the world, or come to any terms with them, then our lives are maimed and truncated accordingly—our imaginative lives and probably our physical lives too. You know I've felt various things about that over the years and very often the rage that you, Ed, said that your father felt

when he saw what was happening to the soil of this country—I can imagine
feeling it about the soil, too. For a while I used to think of it in terms of two
myths, two Western myths, one of them the myth of Orpheus obviously—
the important thing there is that Orpheus is singing with the animals all
around him listening—and one can take that as a myth of arrogation or as a
myth of harmony. It's both, you know, it is homocentric but it's also inclu-
sive, and everything is there in the act of singing. And the other is the myth
of Phaeton, who says "Daddy, I want to drive those horses," and ends up
with a holocaust . . . and the beginning of racism. It's probably not as simple as that, but at one point I kept seeing it in terms of those two myths—
harmonious interaction with the living world, or envy and exploitation of
it. . . .

       You know, one can begin to see differently the great phony myth of
the "winning of the West"—it was the *destruction* of the West. It *was* heroic,
but it was heroic in an incredibly cramped and vicious way. People did suffer and were magnificent, but they were also broken and cruel, and in the
long run incredibly destructive, irreversibly destructive. What we've done
to this continent is something *unbelievable*—to think that one species could
have done this in a hundred years. Right where we're sitting. And this is
our lives. This is not something to have an opinion about, this is what we
live with, this is our bodies and our minds, this is what our words come out
of, and we should know.

ADRIENNE RICH

(b. 1929)

AUNT JENNIFER'S TIGERS

Aunt Jennifer's tigers prance across a screen,
Bright topaz denizens of a world of green.
They do not fear the men beneath the tree;
They pace in sleek chivalric certainty.

Aunt Jennifer's fingers fluttering through her wool   5
Find even the ivory needle hard to pull.
The massive weight of Uncle's wedding band
Sits heavily upon Aunt Jennifer's hand.

When Aunt is dead, her terrified hands will lie
Still ringed with ordeals she was mastered by.   10
The tigers in the panel that she made
Will go on prancing, proud and unafraid.

1951

LOVE IN THE MUSEUM

Now will you stand for me, in this cool light,
Infanta reared in ancient etiquette,
A point-lace queen of manners—at your feet,
The doll-like royal dog demurely set
Upon a chequered floor of black and white.   5

Or be a Louis' mistress, by Boucher,
Lounging on cushions, silken feet asprawl
Upon a couch where casual cupids play,
While on your arms and shoulders seems to fall
The tired extravagance of a sunset day.   10

Or let me think I pause beside a door
And see you in a bodice by Vermeer,
Where light falls quartered on the polished floor
And rims the line of water tilting clear
Out of an earthen pitcher as you pour.   15

But art requires a distance; let me be
Always the connoisseur of your perfection.
Stay where the spaces of the gallery
Flow calm between your pose and my inspection,
Lest one imperfect gesture make demands   20
As troubling as the touch of human hands.

1954

ORION

Far back when I went zig-zagging
through tamarack pastures
you were my genius, you
my cast-iron Viking, my helmed
lion-heart king in prison.   5
Years later now you're young

my fierce half-brother, staring
down from that simplified west
your breast open, your belt dragged down
by an oldfashioned thing, a sword   10

"*Love in the Museum*": 2 *Infanta:* probably refers to "The Maids of Honor," a painting by
Diego Rodriquez Velázquez (1599–1660), the Spanish painter   6 *Boucher:* François Boucher
(1703–1770), the French painter; the painting is probably his "Young Girl Resting"
12 *Vermeer:* Jan Vermeer (1632–1675), the Dutch painter; the painting is probably his "Girl
Pouring Milk"   "*Orion*": *Orion:* a giant and hunter favored by the goddess Diana, who placed
him among the stars where he appears with his dog Sirius

the last bravado you won't give over
though it weighs you down as you stride

and the stars in it are dim
and maybe have stopped burning.
But you burn, and I know it;   15
as I throw back my head to take you in
an old transfusion happens again:
divine astronomy is nothing to it.

Indoors I bruise and blunder,
break faith, leave ill enough   20
alone, a dead child born in the dark.
Night cracks up over the chimney,
pieces of time, frozen geodes
come showering down in the grate.

A man reaches behind my eyes   25
and finds them empty
a woman's head turns away
from my head in the mirror
children are dying my death
and eating crumbs of my life.   30

Pity is not your forte.
Calmly you ache up there
pinned aloft in your crow's nest,
my speechless pirate!
You take it all for granted   35
and when I look you back

it's with a starlike eye
shooting its cold and egotistical spear
where it can do least damage.
Breathe deep! No hurt, no pardon   40
out here in the cold with you
you with your back to the wall.

                                                    1965

GABRIEL

There are no angels   yet
here comes an angel   one

"*Gabriel*": *Gabriel:* the angel who announced the birth of John the Baptist to Zachary (Luke
1:11–20) and the birth and life of Christ to Mary (Luke 1:26–38)

with a man's face   young
shut-off   the dark
side of the moon   turning to me   5
and saying: I am the plumed
                serpent   the beast
                with fangs of fire   and a gentle
                heart

But he doesn't say that   His message   10
drenches his body
he'd want to kill me
for using words to name him

I sit in the bare apartment
reading   15
words stream past me   poetry
twentieth-century rivers
disturbed surfaces   reflecting clouds
reflecting wrinkled neon
but clogged   and mostly   20
nothing alive left
in their depths

The angel is barely
speaking   to me
Once in a horn of light   25
he stood   or someone like him
salutations in gold-leaf
ribboning from his lips
Today again   the hair streams
to his shoulders   30
the eyes reflect something
like a lost country   or so I think
but the ribbon has reeled itself
up
    he isn't giving   35
or taking any shit
We glance miserably
across the room   at each other

It's true   there are moments
closer and closer together   40
when words stick   in my throat
                        'the art of love'
                        'the art of words'
I get your message Gabriel
just   will you stay looking   45

straight at me
awhile longer

1969

PLANETARIUM

Thinking of Caroline Herschel (1750–1848)
astronomer, sister of William; and others.

A woman in the shape of a monster
a monster in the shape of a woman
the skies are full of them

a woman   'in the snow
among the Clocks and instruments   5
or measuring the ground with poles'

in her 98 years to discover
8 comets

she whom the moon ruled
like us   10
levitating into the night sky
riding the polished lenses

Galaxies of women, there
doing penance for impetuousness
ribs chilled   15
in those spaces   of the mind

An eye,

    'virile, precise and absolutely certain'
    from the mad webs of Uranusborg
                              encountering the NOVA   20
every impulse of light exploding
from the core
as life flies out of us

    Tycho whispering at last   25
    'Let me not seem to have lived in vain'

What we see, we see
and seeing is changing

the light that shrivels a mountain
and leaves a man alive   30

Heartbeat of the pulsar
Heart sweating through my body

The radio impulse
pouring in from Taurus

    I am bombarded yet   I stand   35

I have been standing all my life in the
direct path of a battery of signals
the most accurately transmitted most
untranslatable language in the universe
I am a galactic cloud so deep   so invo-   40
luted that a light wave could take 15
years to travel through me   And has
taken   I am an instrument in the shape
of a woman trying to translate pulsations
into images   for the relief of the body   45
and the reconstruction of the mind.

                                                    1971

DIVING INTO THE WRECK

First having read the book of myths,
and loaded the camera,
and checked the edge of the knife-blade,
I put on
the body-armor of black rubber   5
the absurd flippers
the grave and awkward mask.
I am having to do this
not like Cousteau with his
assiduous team   10
aboard the sun-flooded schooner
but here alone.

There is a ladder.
The ladder is always there
hanging innocently   15
close to the side of the schooner.
We know what it is for,
we who have used it.
Otherwise
it's a piece of maritime floss   20
some sundry equipment.

"Diving into the Wreck": 9 *Cousteau:* Jacques Yves Cousteau (1906–   ), the French
underwater explorer, film producer, and author

I go down.
Rung after rung and still
the oxygen immerses me
the blue light   25
the clear atoms
of our human air.
I go down.
My flippers cripple me,
I crawl like an insect down the ladder   30
and there is no one
to tell me when the ocean
will begin.

First the air is blue and then
it is bluer and then green and then   35
black I am blacking out and yet
my mask is powerful
it pumps my blood with power
the sea is another story
the sea is not a question of power   40
I have to learn alone
to turn my body without force
in the deep element.

And now: it is easy to forget
what I came for   45
among so many who have always
lived here
swaying their crenellated fans
between the reefs
and besides   50
you breathe differently down here.

I came to explore the wreck.
The words are purposes.
The words are maps.
I came to see the damage that was done   55
and the treasures that prevail.
I stroke the beam of my lamp
slowly along the flank
of something more permanent
than fish or weed   60

the thing I came for:
the wreck and not the story of the wreck
the thing itself and not the myth
the drowned face always staring
toward the sun   65

the evidence of damage
worn by salt and sway into this threadbare beauty
the ribs of the disaster
curving their assertion
among the tentative haunters.   70

This is the place.
And I am here, the mermaid whose dark hair
streams black, the merman in his armored body
We circle silently
about the wreck   75
we dive into the hold.
I am she: I am he

whose drowned face sleeps with open eyes
whose breasts still bear the stress
whose silver, copper, vermeil cargo lies   80
obscurely inside barrels
half-wedged and left to rot
we are the half-destroyed instruments
that once held to a course
the water-eaten log   85
the fouled compass

We are, I am, you are
by cowardice or courage
the one who find our way
back to this scene   90
carrying a knife, a camera
a book of myths
in which
our names do not appear.

1973

FRAME

Winter twilight. She comes out of the laboratory, last class of the day
a pile of notebooks slung in her knapsack, coat
zipped high against the already swirling
evening sleet. The wind is wicked and the   5
busses slower than usual. On her mind
is organic chemistry and the issue
of next month's rent and will it be possible to
bypass the professor with the coldest eyes
to get a reference for graduate school,   10
and whether any of them, even those who smile

can see, looking at her, a biochemist
or a marine biologist, which of the faces
can she trust to see her at all, either today
or in any future. The busses are worm-slow in the   15
quickly gathering dark. *I don't know her. I am*
standing though somewhere just outside the frame
of all this, trying to see. At her back
the newly finished building suddenly looks
like shelter, it has glass doors, lighted halls   20
presumably heat. The wind is wicked. She throws a
glance down the street, sees no bus coming and runs
up the newly constructed steps into the newly
constructed hallway. *I am standing all this time*
just beyond the frame, trying to see. She runs   25
her hand through the crystals of sleet about to melt
on her hair. She shifts the weight of the books
on her back. It isn't warm here exactly but it's
out of that wind. Through the glass
door panels she can watch for the bus through the
   thickening   30
weather. Watching so, she is not
watching for the white man who watches the building
who has been watching her. This is Boston 1979.
I am standing somewhere at the edge of the frame
watching the man, we are both white, who watches the
   building   35
telling her to move on, get out of the hallway.
I can hear nothing because I am not supposed to be present
   but I can see her gesturing
out toward the street at the wind-raked curb
I see her drawing her small body up   40
against the implied charges. The man
goes away. Her body is different now.
It is holding together with more than a hint of fury
and more than a hint of fear. She is smaller, thinner
more fragile-looking than I am. *But I am not supposed*
   to be   45
there. I am just outside the frame
of this action when the anonymous white man
returns with a white police officer. Then she starts
to leave into the windraked night but already
the policeman is going to work, the handcuffs are
   on her   50
wrists he is throwing her down his knee has gone into
her breast he is dragging her down the stairs *I am*
   unable

to hear a sound of all this all that I know is what
I can see from this position there is no soundtrack
to go with this and I understand at once   55
it is meant to be in silence that this happens
in silence that he pushes her into the car
banging her head in silence that she cries out
in silence that she tries to explain she was only
waiting for a bus   60
in silence that he twists the flesh of her thigh
with his nails in silence that her tears begin to flow
that she pleads with the other policeman as if
he could be trusted to see her at all
in silence that in the precinct she refuses to give her
    name   65
in silence that they throw her into the cell
in silence that she stares him
straight in the face in silence that he sprays her
in her eyes with Mace in silence that she sinks her teeth
into his hand in silence that she is charged   70
with trespass assault and battery in
silence that at the sleet-swept corner her bus
passes without stopping and goes on
in silence. What I am telling you
is told by a white woman who they will say   75
was never there. I say I am there.

                                                 1980

*Adrienne Rich's essay "When We Dead Awaken" describes a change in her
attitude toward being a female poet comparable in many ways to Gwendolyn
Brooks's changed attitude toward being a black poet (see page 1106). It
also shows the relationship between this change and the style of the poems in
various stages of Rich's career.*

"I had been taught that poetry should be "universal" . . . non-female": Adrienne Rich

I know that my style was formed first by male poets: by the men I was reading as an undergraduate—Frost, Dylan Thomas, Donne, Auden, MacNeice,

Stevens, Yeats. What I chiefly learned from them was craft.* But poems are like dreams: in them you put what you don't know you know. Looking back at poems I wrote before I was twenty-one, I'm startled because beneath the conscious craft are glimpses of the split I even then experienced between the girl who wrote poems, who defined herself in writing poems, and the girl who was to define herself by her relationships with men. "Aunt Jennifer's Tigers" (1951), written while I was a student, looks with deliberate detachment at this split. . . . In writing this poem, composed and apparently cool as it is, I thought I was creating a portrait of an imaginary woman. But this woman suffers from the opposition of her imagination, worked out in tapestry, and her life-style, "ringed with ordeals she was mastered by." It was important to me that Aunt Jennifer was a person as distinct from myself as possible—distanced by the formalism of the poem, by its objective, observant tone—even by putting the woman in a different generation.

In those years formalism was part of the strategy—like asbestos gloves, it allowed me to handle materials I couldn't pick up bare-handed.

In the late fifties I was able to write, for the first time, directly about experiencing myself as a woman. The poem was jotted in fragments during children's naps, brief hours in a library, or at 3:00 A.M. after rising with a wakeful child. I despaired of doing any continuous work at this time. Yet I began to feel that my fragments and scraps had a common consciousness and a common theme, one which I would have been very unwilling to put on paper at an earlier time because I had been taught that poetry should be "universal," which meant, of course, nonfemale. Until then I had tried very much *not* to identify myself as a female poet. Over two years I wrote a ten-part poem called "Snapshots of a Daughter-in-Law" (1958–60), in a longer looser mode than I'd ever trusted myself with before. It was an extraordinary relief to write that poem. It strikes me now as too literary, too dependent on allusion; I hadn't found the courage yet to do without authorities, or even to use the pronoun "I"—the woman in the poem is always "she." One section of it, No. 2, concerns a woman who thinks she is going mad; she is haunted by voices telling her to resist and rebel, voices which she can hear but not obey.

2

Banging the coffee-pot into the sink
she hears the angels chiding, and looks out
past the raked gardens to the sloppy sky.
Only a week since They said: *Have no patience.*

————
*A.R., 1978: Yet I spent months, at sixteen, memorizing and writing imitations of Millay's sonnets: and in notebooks of that period I find what are obviously attempts to imitate Dickinson's metrics and verbal compression. I knew H.D. only through anthologized lyrics; her epic poetry was not then available to me.

The next time it was: *Be insatiable.*
Then: *Save yourself; others you cannot save.*
Sometimes she's let the tapstream scald her arm,
a match burn to her thumbnail,

or held her hand above the kettle's snout
right in the woolly steam. They are probably angels,
since nothing hurts her anymore, except
each morning's grit blowing into her eyes.

SYLVIA PLATH

(1932–1963)

BLACK ROOK IN RAINY WEATHER

On the stiff twig up there
Hunches a wet black rook
Arranging and rearranging its feathers in the rain.
I do not expect miracle
Or an accident   5

To set the sight on fire
In my eye, nor seek
Any more in the desultory weather some design,
But let spotted leaves fall as they fall,
Without ceremony, or portent   10

Although, I admit, I desire,
Occasionally, some backtalk
From the mute sky, I can't honestly complain:
A certain minor light may still
Leap incandescent   15

Out of kitchen table or chair
As if a celestial burning took
Possession of the most obtuse objects now and then—
Thus hallowing an interval
Otherwise inconsequent   20

By bestowing largesse, honor,
One might say love. At any rate, I now walk
Wary (for it could happen
Even in this dull, ruinous landscape); skeptical,
Yet politic; ignorant   25

Of whatever angel may choose to flare
Suddenly at my elbow. I only know that a rook
Ordering its black features can so shine
As to seize my senses, haul
My eyelids up, and grant   30

A brief respite from fear
Of total neutrality. With luck,
Trekking stubborn through this season
Of fatigue, I shall
Patch together a content   35

Of sorts. Miracles occur,
If you care to call those spasmodic
Tricks of radiance miracles. The wait's begun again,
The long wait for the angel,
For that rare, random descent.   40

1960

MEDALLION

By the gate with star and moon
Worked into the peeled orange wood
The bronze snake lay in the sun

Inert as a shoelace; dead
But pliable still, his jaw   5
Unhinged and his grin crooked,

Tongue a rose-colored arrow.
Over my hand I hung him.
His little vermilion eye

Ignited with a glassed flame   10
As I turned him in the light;
When I split a rock one time

The garnet bits burned like that.
Dust dulled his back to ochre
The way sun ruins a trout.   15

Yet his belly kept its fire
Going under the chainmail,
The old jewels smoldering there

In each opaque belly-scale:
Sunset looked at through milk glass.   20
And I saw white maggots coil

Thin as pins in the dark bruise
Where his innards bulged as if
He were digesting a mouse.

Knifelike, he was chaste enough,   25
Pure death's-metal. The yardman's
Flung brick perfected his laugh.

1960

TULIPS

The tulips are too excitable; it is winter here.
Look how white everything is, how quiet, how
    snowed-in!
I am learning peacefulness, lying by myself quietly
As the light lies on these white walls, this bed, these
    hands.
I am nobody; I have nothing to do with explosions.   5
I have given my name and my day-clothes up to the
    nurses
And my history to the anesthetist and my body to
    surgeons.

They have propped my head between the pillow and
    the sheet-cuff
Like an eye between two white lids that will not shut.
Stupid pupil, it has to take everything in.   10
The nurses pass and pass; they are no trouble;
They pass the way gulls pass inland in their white caps,
Doing things with their hands, one just the same as
    another,
So it is impossible to tell how many there are.

My body is a pebble to them; they tend it as water   15
Tends to the pebbles it must run over, smoothing them
    gently.
They bring me numbness in their bright needles, they
    bring me sleep.
Now I have lost myself, I am sick of baggage—
My patent-leather overnight case like a black pillbox,
My husband and child smiling out of the family photo.   20
Their smiles catch onto my skin, little smiling hooks.

I have let things slip, a thirty-year-old cargo boat
Stubbornly hanging onto my name and address.
They have swabbed me clear of my loving associations,

Scared and bare on the green plastic-pillowed trolley,   25
I watched my tea set, my bureaus of linen, my books
Sink out of sight, and the water went over my head.
I am a nun now; I have never been so pure.

I didn't want any flowers, I only wanted
To lie with my hands turned up and be utterly empty.   30
How free it is, you have no idea how free!
The peacefulness is so big it dazes you,
And it asks nothing—a name tag, a few trinkets.
It is what the dead close on, finally; I imagine them
Shutting their mouths on it, like a Communion tablet.   35

The tulips are too red in the first place; they hurt me.
Even through the gift paper I could hear them breathe
Lightly, through their white swaddlings, like an awful
    baby.
Their redness talks to my wound, it corresponds.
They are subtle: they seem to float, though they weigh
    me down,   40
Upsetting me with their sudden tongues and their
    color,
A dozen red lead sinkers round my neck.

Nobody watched me before; now I am watched.
The tulips turn to me and the window behind me,
Where, once a day, the light slowly widens and slowly
    thins,   45
And I see myself, flat, ridiculous, a cut-paper shadow
Between the eye of the sun and the eyes of the tulips,
And I have no face. I have wanted to efface myself.
The vivid tulips eat my oxygen.

Before they came, the air was calm enough,   50
Coming and going, breath by breath, without any fuss.
Then the tulips filled it up like a loud noise.
Now the air snags and eddies round them the way a
    river
Snags and eddies round a sunken rust-red engine.
They concentrate my attention that was happy   55
Playing and resting without committing itself.

The walls, also, seem to be warming themselves.
The tulips should be behind bars, like dangerous
    animals;
They are opening like the mouth of some great African
    cat,
And I am aware of my heart: it opens and closes   60

Its bowl of red blooms out of sheer love of me.
The water I taste is warm and salt, like the sea,
And comes from a country far away as health.

1961

THE ARRIVAL OF THE BEE BOX

I ordered this, this clean wood box
Square as a chair and almost too heavy to lift.
I would say it was the coffin of a midget
Or a square baby
Were there not such a din in it.   5

The box is locked, it is dangerous.
I have to live with it overnight
And I can't keep away from it.
There are no windows, so I can't see what is in there.
There is only a little grid, no exit.   10

I put my eye to the grid.
It is dark, dark,
With the swarmy feeling of African hands
Minute and shrunk for export,
Black on black, angrily clambering.   15

How can I let them out?
It is the noise that appalls me most of all,
The unintelligible syllables.
It is like a Roman mob,
Small, taken one by one, but my god, together!   20

I lay my ear to furious Latin.
I am not a Caesar.
I have simply ordered a box of maniacs.
They can be sent back.
They can die, I need feed them nothing, I am the
    owner.   25

I wonder how hungry they are.
I wonder if they would forget me
If I just undid the locks and stood back and turned into
    a tree.
There is the laburnum, its blond colonnades,
And the petticoats of the cherry.   30

They might ignore me immediately
In my moon suit and funeral veil.
I am no source of honey

So why should they turn on me?
Tomorrow I will be sweet God, I will set them free.   35

The box is only temporary.

1962

CUT

for Susan O'Neill Roe

What a thrill——
My thumb instead of an onion.
The top quite gone
Except for a sort of a hinge

Of skin,   5
A flap like a hat,
Dead white.
Then that red plush.

Little pilgrim,
The Indian's axed your scalp.   10
Your turkey wattle
Carpet rolls

Straight from the heart.
I step on it,
Clutching my bottle   15
Of pink fizz.

A celebration, this is.
Out of a gap
A million soldiers run,
Redcoats, every one.   20

Whose side are they on?
O my
Homunculus, I am ill.
I have taken a pill to kill

The thin   25
Papery feeling.
Saboteur,
Kamikaze man——

The stain on your
Gauze Ku Klux Klan   30
Babushka
Darkens and tarnishes and when

The balled
Pulp of your heart
Confronts its small   35
Mill of silence

How you jump——
Trepanned veteran,
Dirty girl,
Thumb stump.   40

1965

DADDY

You do not do, you do not do
Any more, black shoe
In which I have lived like a foot
For thirty years, poor and white,
Barely daring to breathe or Achoo.   5

Daddy, I have had to kill you.
You died before I had time——
Marble-heavy, a bag full of God,
Ghastly statue with one grey toe
Big as a Frisco seal   10

And a head in the freakish Atlantic
Where it pours bean green over blue
In the waters off beautiful Nauset.
I used to pray to recover you.
Ach, du.   15

In the German tongue, in the Polish town
Scraped flat by the roller
Of wars, wars, wars.
But the name of the town is common.
My Polack friend   20

Says there are a dozen or two.
So I never could tell where you
Put your foot, your root,
I never could talk to you.
The tongue stuck in my jaw.   25

It stuck in a barb wire snare.
Ich, ich, ich, ich,

———————

"*Daddy*": 15 *ach, du:* ah, you (German)   27 *Ich, ich, ich, ich:* I, I, I, I (German)

I could hardly speak.
I thought every German was you.
And the language obscene   30

An engine, an engine
Chuffing me off like a Jew.
A Jew to Dachau, Auschwitz, Belsen.
I began to talk like a Jew.
I think I may well be a Jew.   35

The snows of the Tyrol, the clear beer of Vienna
Are not very pure or true.
With my gypsy ancestress and my weird luck
And my Taroc pack and my Taroc pack
I may be a bit of a Jew.   40

I have always been scared of *you*,
With your Luftwaffe, your gobbledygoo.
And your neat moustache
And your Aryan eye, bright blue.
Panzer-man, panzer-man, O You——   45

Not God but a swastika
So black no sky could squeak through.
Every woman adores a Fascist,
The boot in the face, the brute
Brute heart of a brute like you.   50

You stand at the blackboard, daddy,
In the picture I have of you,
A cleft in your chin instead of your foot
But no less a devil for that, no not
Any less the black man who   55

Bit my pretty red heart in two.
I was ten when they buried you.
At twenty I tried to die
And get back, back, back to you.
I thought even the bones would do.   60

But they pulled me out of the sack,
And they stuck me together with glue.
And then I knew what to do.
I made a model of you,
A man in black with a Meinkampf look   65

_____

33 *Dachau, Auschwitz, Belsen:* German concentration camps   36 *Tyrol:* Tirol, a west Austrian
alpine province   65 *Meinkampf:* Mein Kampf (My Battle), Hitler's political autobiography

And a love of the rack and the screw.
And I said I do, I do.
So daddy, I'm finally through.
The black telephone's off at the root,
The voices just can't worm through.   70

If I've killed one man, I've killed two——
The vampire who said he was you
And drank my blood for a year,
Seven years, if you want to know.
Daddy, you can lie back now.   75

There's a stake in your fat black heart
And the villagers never liked you.
They are dancing and stamping on you.
They always *knew* it was you.
Daddy, daddy, you bastard, I'm through.   80

1965

LADY LAZARUS

I have done it again.
One year in every ten
I manage it——

A sort of walking miracle, my skin
Bright as a Nazi lampshade,   5
My right foot

A paperweight
My face a featureless, fine
Jew linen.

Peel off the napkin   10
O my enemy.
Do I terrify?——

The nose, the eye pits, the full set of teeth?
The sour breath
Will vanish in a day.   15

Soon, soon the flesh
The grave cave ate will be
At home on me

"*Lady Lazarus*": *Lazarus:* Jesus raised Lazarus from the dead; see John 11:44

And I a smiling woman.
I am only thirty.
And like the cat I have nine times to die.

20

This is Number Three.
What a trash
To annihilate each decade.

What a million filaments.
The peanut-crunching crowd
Shoves in to see

25

Them unwrap me hand and foot——
The big strip tease.
Gentleman, ladies,

30

These are my hands,
My knees.
I may be skin and bone,

Nevertheless, I am the same, identical woman.
The first time it happened I was ten.
It was an accident.

35

The second time I meant
To last it out and not come back at all.
I rocked shut

As a seashell.
They had to call and call
And pick the worms off me like sticky pearls.

40

Dying
Is an art, like everything else.
I do it exceptionally well.

45

I do it so it feels like hell.
I do it so it feels real.
I guess you could say I've a call.

It's easy enough to do it in a cell.
It's easy enough to do it and stay put.
It's the theatrical

50

Comeback in broad day
To the same place, the same face, the same brute
Amused shout:

"A miracle!"
That knocks me out.
There is a charge

55

For the eyeing of my scars, there is a charge
For the hearing of my heart——
It really goes. 60

And there is a charge, a very large charge,
For a word or a touch
Or a bit of blood

Or a piece of my hair or my clothes.
So, so, Herr Doktor. 65
So, Herr Enemy.

I am your opus,
I am your valuable,
The pure gold baby

That melts to a shriek. 70
I turn and burn.
Do not think I underestimate your great concern.

Ash, ash—
You poke and stir.
Flesh, bone, there is nothing there—— 75

A cake of soap,
A wedding ring,
A gold filling.

Herr God, Herr Lucifer,
Beware 80
Beware.

Out of the ash
I rise with my red hair
And I eat men like air.

1965

Though Sylvia Plath was one of the most skillful nature poets of the twen-
tieth century, her reputation has been largely shaped by her anguished con-
fessional poetry. Even poets whose own work is very different in approach
from Plath's have admired this poetry. "Some of it," Amy Clampitt says,
"is so beautiful that I'm drawn to it in spite of the confessional tone." Rich-
ard Wilbur's description of a meeting with Plath tells us a great deal about
both poets.

Richard Wilbur

(b. 1921)

COTTAGE STREET, 1953

Framed in her phoenix fire-screen, Edna Ward
Bends to the tray of Canton, pouring tea
For frightened Mrs. Plath; then, turning toward
The pale, slumped daughter, and my wife, and me,

Asks if we would prefer it weak or strong.   5
Will we have milk or lemon, she enquires?
The visit seems already strained and long.
Each in his turn, we tell her our desires.

It is my office to exemplify
The published poet in his happiness,   10
Thus cheering Sylvia, who has wished to die;
But half-ashamed, and impotent to bless,

I am a stupid life-guard who has found,
Swept to his shallows by the tide, a girl
Who, far from shore, has been immensely drowned,   15
And stares through water now with eyes of pearl.

How large is her refusal; and how slight
The genteel chat whereby we recommend
Life, of a summer afternoon, despite
The brewing dusk which hints that it may end.   20

And Edna Ward shall die in fifteen years,
After her eight-and-eighty summers of
Such grace and courage as permit no tears,
The thin hand reaching out, the last word *love*,

Outliving Sylvia who, condemned to live,   25
Shall study for a decade, as she must,
To state at last her brilliant negative
In poems free and helpless and unjust.

1976

LUCILLE CLIFTON

(b. 1936)

THE LOST BABY POEM

the time i dropped your almost body down
down to meet the waters under the city
and run one with the sewage to the sea
what did i know about waters rushing back
what did i know about drowning   5
or being drowned

you would have been born into winter
in the year of the disconnected gas
and no car   we would have made the thin
walk over Genesee hill into the Canada wind   10
to watch you slip like ice into strangers' hands
you would have fallen naked as snow into winter
if you were here i could tell you these
and some other things

if i am ever less than a mountain   15
for your definite brothers and sisters
let the rivers pour over my head
let the sea take me for a spiller
of seas   let black men call me stranger
always   for your never named sake   20

1972

GOD'S MOOD

these daughters are bone,
they break.
He wanted stone girls
and boys with branches for arms
that He could lift His life with   5
and be lifted by.
these sons are bone.

He is tired of years that keep turning into age
and flesh that keeps widening.
He is tired of waiting for His teeth to   10
bite Him and walk away.

He is tired of bone,
it breaks.
He is tired of eve's fancy and
adam's whining ways.   15

                                                         1974

SHE UNDERSTANDS ME

it is all blood and breaking,
blood and breaking. the thing
drops out of its box squalling
into the light. they are both squalling,
animal and cage. her bars lie wet, open   5
and empty and she has made herself again
out of flesh out of dictionaries,
she is always emptying and it is all
the same wound the same blood the same breaking.

                                                         1974

[THERE IS A GIRL INSIDE]

there is a girl inside.
she is randy as a wolf.
she will not walk away
and leave these bones
to an old woman.   5

she is a green tree
in a forest of kindling.
she is a green girl
in a used poet.

she has waited   10
patient as a nun
for the second coming,
when she can break through gray hairs
into blossom

and her lovers will harvest   15
honey and thyme
and the woods will be wild
with the damn wonder of it.

                                                         1977

FOR THE MUTE

they will blow from your mouth one morning
like from a shook bottle
and you will try to keep them for
tomorrow's conversation but
your patience will be broken when the   5
bottle bursts
and you will spill all of your
extraordinary hearings for there are
too many languages for
one mortal tongue.   10

1978

FOR THE LAME

happen you will rise,
lift from grounded in a spin
and begin to forget the geography
of fixed things.
happen you will walk past   5
where you meant to stay,
happen you will wonder at the way
it seemed so marvelous to move.

1980

TO JOAN

joan
did you never hear
in the soft rushes of france
merely the whisper of french grass
rubbing against leathern   5
sounding now like a windsong
now like a man?
did you never wonder
oh fantastical joan,
did you never cry in the sun's face   10
unreal unreal? did you never run

"To Joan": Joan: Joan of Arc (1412–1431), who said that she was being instructed directly by "voices" from heaven, including the archangel Michael, successfully led French forces to battle against the English in the siege of Orleans

villageward
hands pushed out toward your apron?
and just as you knew that your mystery
was broken for all time   15
did they not fall then
soft as always
into your ear
calling themselves Michael
among beloved others?   20
and you
sister   sister
did you not then sigh
my voices   my voices   of course?

1980

PERHAPS

i am going blind.
my eyes exploding,
seeing more than is there
until they burst into nothing

or going deaf, these sounds   5
the feathered hum of silence

or going away from my self, the cool
fingers of lace on my skin
the fingers of madness

or perhaps   10
in the palace of time
our lives are a circular stair
and i am turning

1980

There is an absolute confidence and independence about the voice that we hear in Lucille Clifton's poetry. It seems not to depend on the voice of any particular literary predecessor (though she does acknowledge the importance of Walt Whitman). Instead it seems to come directly from a life lived among people who talk well and frankly and deeply.

"Also the inward feeling and meaning of things": Lucille Clifton

When I was 5 years old I forgot my piece. It was the annual Christmas program of Macedonia Baptist Church—a splendid affair—and all of the young Sunday school members had been given poems and recitations to memorize. I forgot mine. I remember standing there on stage in my new Christmas dress, trying not to cry as the church mothers smiled, nodded and murmured encouragement from the front row.

"Go 'head, baby."

"Say it now, Luc."

"Come on now, baby."

But I couldn't remember, and to hide my deep humiliation, my embarrassment, I became sullen, angry.

"I don' wanna."

And I stood there with my mouth poked out.

It was a scandal! This fresh young nobody baby standing in front of the Lord in His own house talking about what she don't want! I could feel the disapproval pouring over my new dress. Then, like a great tidal wave from the ocean of God, my sanctified mother poured down the Baptist aisle, huge as love, her hand outstretched toward mine.

"Come on, baby," she smiled, then turned to address the church: "She don't have to do nothing she don't want to do."

And I was at the same time empowered and made free. . . .

In November of 1984 my beloved husband of almost 30 years died. I am making it because of my daughters, my sons, my woman friends. When I retreat into my room to just sit and stare or cry I can hear my mama speak through my four daughters. "She don't have to act strong if she don't want to." And they still love me.

We talk a lot, these four women and I, but then we always did. They grew up hearing stories I heard from mama and aunts and the old mothers of the church. It was, it is, the way we have continued in this country, passing on our own and the wider history and culture of America. Not just of Black America, of all of it, so that we know what life was like among Black people as well as white ones during slavery time because we heard and overheard the tales of Ole Miz and what happened when. It has been, it is, our strength, this talking and listening, because we have traditionally shared not only the outward cold and definite facts, but also the inward feeling and meaning of things.

ROBERT HASS

(b. 1941)

PALO ALTO: THE MARSHES

For Mariana Richardson (1830–1891)

1

She dreamed along the beaches of this coast.
Here where the tide rides in to desolate
the sluggish margins of the bay,
sea grass sheens copper into distances.
Walking, I recite the hard   5
explosive names of birds:
egret, killdeer, bittern, tern.
Dull in the wind and early morning light,
the striped shadows of the cattails
twitch like nerves.   10

2

Mud, roots, old cartridges, and blood.
High overhead, the long silence of the geese.

3

"We take no prisoners," John Fremont said
and took California for President Polk.
That was the Bear Flag War.   15
She watched it from the Mission San Rafael,
named for the archangel (the terrible one)
who gently laid a fish across the eyes
of saintly, miserable Tobias
that he might see.   20
The eyes of fish. The land
shimmers fearfully.
No archangels here, no ghosts,
and terns rise like seafoam
from the breaking surf.   25

4

Kit Carson's antique .45, blue,
new as grease. The roar
flings up echoes,
row on row of shrieking avocets.

The blood of Francisco de Haro,   30
Ramon de Haro, José de los Reyes Berryessa
runs darkly to the old ooze.

                         5

The star thistles: erect, surprised,

                         6

and blooming
violet caterpillar hairs. One   35
of the de Haros was her lover,
the books don't say which.
They were twins.

                         7

In California in the early spring
there are pale yellow mornings
when the mist burns slowly into day.   40
The air stings
like autumn, clarifies
like pain.

                         8

Well I have dreamed this coast myself.   45
Dreamed Mariana, since here father owned the land
where I grew up. I saw her picture once:
a wraith encased in a high-necked black silk
dress so taut about the bones there were hardly ripples
for the light to play in. I knew her eyes   50
had watched the hills seep blue with lupine after rain,
seen the young peppers, heavy and intent,
first rosy drupes and then the acrid fruit,
the ache of spring. Black as her hair
the unreflecting venom of those eyes   55
is an aftermath I know, like these brackish,
russet pools a strange life feeds in
or the old fury of land grants, maps,
and deeds of trust. A furious dun-
colored mallard knows my kind   60
and skims across the edges of the marsh
where the dead bass surface
and their flaccid bellies bob.

                         9

A chill tightens the skin
around my bones. The other California   65

and its bitter absent ghosts
dance to a stillness in the air:
the Klamath tribe was routed and they disappeared.
Even the dust seemed stunned,
tools on the ground, fishnets.   70
Fires crackled, smouldering.
No movement but the slow turning
of the smoke, no sound but jays
shrill in the distance and flying further off.
The flicker of lizards, dragonflies.   75
And beyond the dry flag-woven lodges
a faint persistent slapping.
Carson found ten wagonloads
of fresh-caught salmon, silver
in the sun. The flat eyes stared.   80
Gills sucked the thin annulling air.
They flopped and shivered,
ten wagonloads. Kit Carson
burned the village to the ground.
They rode some twenty miles that day   85
and still they saw the black smoke
smear the sky above the pines.

10

Here everything seems clear,
firmly etched against the pale
smoky sky: sedge, flag, owl's clover,   90
rotting wharves. A tanker lugs silver
bomb-shaped napalm tins toward
port at Redwood City. Again,
my eye performs
the lobotomy of description.   95
Again, almost with yearning,
I see the malice of her ancient eyes.
The mud flats hiss as the tide turns.
They say she died in Redwood City,
cursing "the goddamned Anglo-Yankee yoke."   100

11

The otters are gone from the bay
and I have seen five horses
easy in the grassy marsh
beside three snowy egrets.

Bird cries and the unembittered sun,   105
wings and the white bodies of the birds,

it is morning. Citizens are rising
to murder in their moral dreams.

1973

HEROIC SIMILE

When the swordsman fell in Kurosawa's *Seven Samurai*
in the gray rain,
in Cinemascope and the Tokugawa dynasty,
he fell straight as a pine, he fell
as Ajax fell in Homer   5
in chanted dactyls and the tree was so huge
the woodsman returned for two days
to that lucky place before he was done with the sawing
and on the third day he brought his uncle.

They stacked logs in the resinous air,   10
hacking the small limbs off,
tying those bundles separately.
The slabs near the root
were quartered and still they were awkwardly large;
the logs from midtree they halved: 15
ten bundles and four great piles of fragrant wood,
moons and quarter moons and half moons
ridged by the saw's tooth.

The woodsman and the old man his uncle
are standing in midforest   20
on a floor of pine silt and spring mud.
They have stopped working
because they are tired and because
I have imagined no pack animal
or primitive wagon. They are too canny   25
to call in neighbors and come home
with a few logs after three days' work.
They are waiting for me to do something
or for the overseer of the Great Lord
to come and arrest them.   30

How patient they are!
The old man smokes a pipe and spits.
The young man is thinking he would be rich
if he were already rich and had a mule.
Ten days of hauling   35
and on the seventh day they'll probably
be caught, go home empty-handed

or worse. I don't know
whether they're Japanese or Mycenaean
and there's nothing I can do.   40
The path from here to that village
is not translated. A hero, dying,
gives off stillness to the air.
A man and a woman walk from the movies
to the house in the silence of separate fidelities.   45
There are limits to imagination.

1978

MEDITATION AT LAGUNITAS

All the new thinking is about loss.
In this it resembles all the old thinking.
The idea, for example, that each particular erases
the luminous clarity of a general idea. That the clown-
faced woodpecker probing the dead sculpted trunk   5
of that black birch is, by his presence,
some tragic falling off from a first world
of undivided light. Or the other notion that,
because there is in this world no one thing
to which the bramble of *blackberry* corresponds,   10
a word is elegy to what it signifies.
We talked about it late last night and in the voice
of my friend, there was a thin wire of grief, a tone
almost querulous. After a while I understood that,
talking this way, everything dissolves: *justice,*   15
pine, hair, woman, you and *I.* There was a woman
I made love to and I remembered how, holding
her small shoulders in my hands sometimes,
I felt a violent wonder at her presence
like a thirst for salt, for my childhood river   20
with its island willows, silly music from the pleasure
    boat,
muddy places where we caught the little orange-silver
    fish
called *pumpkinseed.* It hardly had to do with her.
Longing, we say, because desire is full
of endless distances. I must have been the same to her.   25
But I remember so much, the way her hands dismantled
    bread,
the thing her father said that hurt her, what
she dreamed. There are moments when the body is as
    numinous

as words, days that are the good flesh continuing.
Such tenderness, those afternoons and evenings,   30
saying *blackberry, blackberry, blackberry.*

1978

SANTA LUCIA

1

Art & love: he camps outside my door,
innocent, carnivorous. As if desire
were actually a flute, as if the little song
transcend, transcend could get you anywhere.
He brings me wine; he believes in the arts   5
and uses them for beauty. He brings me
vinegar in small earthen pots, postcards
of the hillsides by Cézanne desire has left
alone, empty farms in August and the vague
tall chestnut trees at Jas de Bouffan, fetal   10
sandstone rifted with mica from the beach.
He brings his body, wolfish, frail,
all brown for summer like croissant crusts
at La Seine in the Marina, the bellies
of pelicans I watched among white dunes   15
under Pico Blanco on the Big Sur coast.
It sickens me, this glut & desperation.

2

Walking the Five Springs trail, I tried to think.
Dead-nettle, thimbleberry. The fog heaved in
between the pines, violet sparrows made curves   20
like bodies in the ruined air. *All women
are masochists.* I was so young, believing
every word they said. *Dürer is second-rate.*
Dürer's Eve feeds her apple to the snake;
snaky tresses, cat at her feet, at Adam's foot   25
a mouse. Male fear, male eyes and art. The art
of love, the eyes I use to see myself

"*Santa Lucia*": *Santa Lucia:* or Saint Lucy (c. 283–303), patroness of those suffering from
distemper of the eyes. When a nobleman wished to marry her because of her beautiful eyes,
she tore them out and gave them to him so that she might remain a virgin. She died by the
sword when she refused to marry a pagan suitor and was denounced as a Christian
8 *Cézanne:* Paul Cézanne, French painter (1839–1906) whose works include "Chestnut Trees
at Jas de Bouffan" (c. 1885).   23 *Dürer:* Albrecht Dürer, German painter and engraver
(1471–1528). His panels of *Adam* and *Eve* were painted in 1507.

in love. Ingres, pillows. I think the erotic
is not sexual, only when you're lucky.
That's where the path forks. It's not the riddle   30
of desire that interests me; it is the riddle
of good hands, chervil in a windowbox,
the white pages of a book, someone says
I'm tired, someone turning on the light.

3

Streaked in the window, the city wavers   35
but the sky is empty, clean. Emptiness
is strict; that pleases me. I do cry out.
Like everyone else, I thrash, am splayed.
Oh, oh, oh, oh. Eyes full of wonder.
Guernica. Ulysses on the beach. I see   40
my body is his prayer. I see my body.
Walking in the galleries at the Louvre,
I was, each moment, naked & possessed.
Tourists gorged on goosenecked Florentine girls
by Pollaiuolo. He sees me like a painter.   45
I hear his words for me: white, gold.
I'd rather walk the city in the rain.
Dog shit, traffic accidents. Whatever god
there is dismembered in his Chevy.
A different order of religious awe: 50
agony & meat, everything plain afterwards.

4

Santa Lucia: eyes jellied on a plate.
The thrust of serpentine was almost green
all through the mountains where the rock cropped out.
I liked sundowns, dusks smelling of madrone,   55
the wildflowers, which were not beautiful,
fierce little wills rooting in the yellow
grass year after year, thirst in the roots,

---

28 *Ingres:* Jean Auguste Dominique Ingres, French painter (1780–1867) notable for his
voluptuous portraits of reclining women   40 *Guernica:* Name of a 1937 painting by Pablo
Picasso depicting the horrors of the bombing of the peaceful market town of Guernica by
Spanish Nationalist and Germans during the Spanish Civil War   40 *Ulysses on the beach:* In
Homer's *Odyssey,* Odysseus is washed up naked on the beach at Phaecia, where he sees the
beautiful princess Nausicaa and begs her assistance. Haas may be alluding to a painting
entitled *Ulysse et Nausicaa* by J. A. Benouville.   45 *Polliauolo:* The Florentine Pollaiuolo
brothers, Antonio (c. 1432–1478) and Piero (c. 1443–1496), often collaborated on paintings.
This reference is probably to the long-necked woman in their *Portrait of a Lady.*   52 *eyes . . .
plate:* Santa Lucia is often portrayed with a sword at her throat and her extracted eyes on a
tray.

mineral. They have intelligence
of hunger. Poppies lean to the morning sun,   60
lupine grows thick in the rockface, self-heal
at creekside. He wants to fuck. Sweet word.
All suction. I want less. Not that I fear
the huge dark of sex, the sharp sweet light,
light if it were water raveling, rancor,   65
tenderness like rain. What I want happens
not when the deer freezes in the shade
and looks at you and you hold very still
and meet her gaze but in the moment after
when she flicks her ears & starts to feed again.   70

1978

OLD DOMINION

The shadows of late afternoon and the odors
of honeysuckle are a congruent sadness.
Everything is easy but wrong. I am walking
across thick lawns under maples in borrowed tennis
    whites.
It is like the photographs of Randall Jarrell   5
I stared at on the backs of books in college.
He looked so sad and relaxed in the pictures.
He was translating Chekhov and wore tennis whites.
It puzzled me that in his art, like Chekhov's,
everyone was lost, that the main chance was never
    seized   10
because it is only there as a thing to be dreamed of
or because someone somewhere had set the old words
to the old tune: we live by habit and it doesn't hurt.
Now the *thwack . . . thwack* of tennis balls being hit
reaches me and it is the first sound of an ax   15
in the cherry orchard or the sound of machine guns
where the young terrorists are exploding
among poor people on the streets of Los Angeles.
I begin making resolutions: to take risks, not to stay
in the south, to somehow do honor to Randall Jarrell,   20
never to kill myself. Through the oaks I see the courts,
the nets, the painted boundaries, and the people in
    tennis
whites who look so graceful from this distance.

1978

WEED

Horse is Lorca's word, fierce as wind,
or melancholy, gorgeous, Andalusian:
   white horse grazing near the river dust;
and parsnip is hopeless,
   second cousin to the rhubarb   5
which is already second cousin
   to an apple pie. Marrying the words
to the coarse white umbels sprouting
   on the first of May is history
but conveys nothing; it is not the veined   10
   body of Queen Anne's lace
I found, bored, in a spring classroom
   from which I walked hands tingling
for the breasts that are meadows in New Jersey
   in 1933; it is thick, shaggier, and the name   15
is absurd. It speaks of durable
   unimaginative pleasures: reading Balzac,
fixing the window sash, rising
   to a clean kitchen, the fact
that the car starts & driving to work   20
   through hills where the roadside thickens
with the green ungainly stalks,
   the bracts and bright white flowerets
      of horse-parsnips.

1978

Robert Hass brings together threads that connect several contemporary poets. Like Amy Clampitt and Maxine Kumin, he reminds us of the historical underlayers of the present moment. Like Robert Bly and W. S. Merwin, he is an enthusiastic reader of poets from other cultures. He also writes lucid prose about the values that connect him with poets of all periods.

"We are clued to the hope of a shapeliness in things": Robert Hass

---

I've been trying to think about form in poetry and my mind keeps returning to a time in the country in New York when I was puzzled that my son Leif was getting up a little earlier every morning. I had to get up with him, so it exasperated me. I wondered about it until I slept in his bed one night. His window faced east. At six-thirty I woke to brilliant sunlight. The sun had risen. . . .

The first fact of the world is that it repeats itself. I had been taught to believe that the freshness of children lay in their capacity for wonder at the vividness and strangeness of the particular, but what is fresh in them is that they still experience the power of repetition, from which our first sense of the power of mastery comes. Though *predictable* is an ugly little word in daily life, in our first experience of it we are clued to the hope of a shapeliness in things. To see that power working on adults, you have to catch them out: the look of foolish happiness on the faces of people who have just sat down to dinner is their knowledge that dinner will be served.

Probably, that is the psychological basis for the power and the necessity of artistic form. I think of our children when they first came home from the hospital, wide, staring eyes, wet mouths, fat, uncontrollable tongues. I thought they responded when I bent over their cribs because they were beginning to recognize me. Now I think it was because they were coming to recognize themselves. They were experiencing in the fluidity of things a certain orderliness: footsteps, a face, the smell of hair and tobacco, cooing syllables. One would gradually have the sense that looking-out-of-the-eyes was a point around which phenomena organized themselves; thinking *this is going to happen* and having it happen might be, then, the authentic source of the experience of being, of identity, that word which implies that a lot of different things are the same thing.

"A long slow hurtle through the forms of things": Robert Hass

Images haunt. There is a whole mythology built on this fact: Cézanne painting till his eyes bled, Wordsworth wandering the Lake Country hills in an impassioned daze. Blake describes it very well, and so did the colleague of Tu Fu who said to him, "It is like being alive twice." Images are not quite ideas, they are stiller than that, with less implication outside themselves. And they are not myth, they do not have that explanatory power; they are nearer to pure story. Nor are they always metaphors; they do not say this is that, they say this is. In the nineteenth century one would have said that what compelled us about them was a sense of the eternal. And it is something like that, some feeling in the arrest of the image that what perishes and what lasts forever have been brought into conjunction, and accompanying that sensation is a feeling of release from the self. Antonio Machado wrote, *"Hoy es siempre todavía."* Yet today is always. And Czeslaw Miłosz, *"Tylko trwa wieczna chwila."* Only the moment is eternal.

For me, at least, there is a delicate balance in this matter. Walking through the rooms of my house on a moonlit August night, with a sharp sense of my children each at a particular moment in their lives and changing, with three or four shed, curled leaves from a Benjamin fig on the floor of the dining room and a spider, in that moonlight, already set to work in one of them, and the dark outline of an old Monterey pine against the sky outside the window, the one thing about the house that seems not to have changed in the years of my living in it, it is possible to feel my life, in a quiet ecstatic helplessness, as a long slow hurtle through the forms of things. I think I resist that sensation because there is a kind of passivity in it; I suppose that I fear it would make me careless of those things that need concentration to attend to.

SHARON OLDS

(b. 1942)

THE ELDER SISTER

When I look at my elder sister now
I think how she had to go first, down through the
birth canal, to force her way
head-first through the tiny channel,
the pressure of Mother's muscles on her brain,   5
the tight walls scraping her skin.
Her face is still narrow from it, the long
hollow cheeks of a Crusader on a tomb,
and her inky eyes have the look of someone who has
been in prison a long time and   10
knows they can send her back. I look at her
body and think how her breasts were the first to
    rise, slowly, like swans on a pond.
By the time mine came along, they were just
two more birds in the flock, and when the hair   15
rose on the white mound of her flesh, like
threads of water out of the ground, it was the
first time, but when mine came
they knew about it. I used to think
only in terms of her harshness, sitting and   20
pissing on me in bed, but now I
see I had her before me always
like a shield. I look at her wrinkles, her clenched

jaws, her frown-lines—I see they are
the dents on my shield, the blows that did not reach
   me.   25
She protected me, not as a mother
protects a child, with love, but as a
hostage protects the one who makes her
escape as I made my escape, with my sister's
body held in front of me.   30

1984

THE VICTIMS

When Mother divorced you, we were glad. She took it and
took it, in silence, all those years and then
kicked you out, suddenly, and her
kids loved it. Then you were fired, and we
grinned inside, the way people grinned when   5
Nixon's helicopter lifted off the South
Lawn for the last time. We were tickled
to think of your office taken away,
your secretaries taken away,
your lunches with three double bourbons,   10
your pencils, your reams of paper. Would they take your
suits back, too, those dark
carcasses hung in your closet, and the black
noses of your shoes with their large pores?
She had taught us to take it, to hate you and take it   15
until we pricked with her for your
annihilation, Father. Now I
pass the bums in doorways, the white
slugs of their bodies gleaming through slits in their
suits of compressed silt, the stained   20
flippers of their hands, the underwater
fire of their eyes, ships gone down with the
lanterns lit, and I wonder who took it and
took it from them in silence until they had
given it all away and had nothing   25
left but this.

1984

BATHING THE NEW BORN

I love with a fearful love to remember the
first baths I gave this boy—

my second child, so my hands knew what to do,
I laid the tiny torso along my
left forearm, nape of the noodle   5
neck in the crook of my elbow, hips
tiny as a bird's hips against my wrist, and the
thigh the thickness of a thick pencil held
loosely in the loop of my thumb and forefinger, the
sign that means perfect. I'd soap him slowly, the   10
long thin cold feet, the
scrotum tight and wrinkled as a rosy
shell so new it was flexible yet, the
miniature underweight athlete's chest, the
gummy furze of the scalp. If I got him too   15
soapy he'd get so slippery he'd
slide in my grip like an armful of white
buttered noodles, but I'd hold him not too tight,
I knew I was so good for him, and I'd
talk to him the whole time, I'd   20
tell him about his wonderful body
and the wonderful soap, the whole world made of love,
and he'd look up at me, one week old,
his eyes still wide and apprehensive of his
new life. I love that time   25
when you croon and croon to them, you can see the
calm slowly entering them, you can
feel it in your anchoring hand, the
small necklace of the spine against the
muscle of your forearm, you feel the fear   30
leaving their bodies, he lay in the blue
oval plastic baby tub and
looked at me in wonder and began to
move his silky limbs at will in the water.

                                        1984

SEX WITHOUT LOVE

How do they do it, the ones who make love
without love? Beautiful as dancers,
gliding over each other like ice-skaters
over the ice, fingers hooked
inside each other's bodies, faces   5
red as steak, wine, wet as the
children at birth whose mothers are going to
give them away. How do they come to the
come to the   come to the   God   come to the

still waters, and not love
the one who came there with them, light
rising slowly as steam off their joined
skin? These are the true religious,
the purists, the pros, the ones who will not
accept a false Messiah, love the   15
priest instead of the God. They do not
mistake the lover for their own pleasure,
they are like great runners: they know they are alone
with the road surface, the cold, the wind,
the fit of their shoes, their over-all cardio-   20
vascular health—just factors, like the partner
in the bed, and not the truth, which is the
single body alone in the universe
against its own best time.

1985

THE RACE

When I got to the airport I rushed up to the desk
and they told me the flight was cancelled. The doctors had
said my father would not live through the night
and the flight was cancelled. A young man with a
dark blond moustache told me   5
another airline had a non-stop
leaving in seven minutes—see that
elevator over there well go
down to the first floor, make a right you'll
see a yellow bus, get off at the   10
second Pan Am terminal—I
ran, I who have no sense of direction
raced exactly where he'd told me, like a fish
slipping upstream deftly against the
flow of the river. I jumped off that bus with my   15
heavy bags and ran, the bags
wagged me from side to side as if to
prove I was under the claims of the material, I
ran up to a man with a white flower on his breast,
I who always go to the end of the line, I said   20
Help me. He looked at my ticket, he said make a
left and then a right go up the moving stairs and then
run. I raced up the moving stairs
two at a time, at the top I saw the
long hollow corridor and   25
then I took a deep breath, I said

goodbye to my body, goodbye to comfort, I
used my legs and heart as if I would
gladly use them up for this, to
touch him again in this life. I ran and the   30
big heavy dark bags
banged me, wheeled and swam around me like
planets in wild orbits—I have seen
pictures of women running down roads with their
belongings tied in black scarves   35
grasped in their fists, running under serious
gray historical skies—I blessed my
long legs he gave me, my strong
heart I abandoned to its own purpose, I
ran to Gate 17 and they were   40
just lifting the thick white
lozenge of the door to fit it into the
socket of the plane. Like the man who is not
too rich, I turned to the side and
slipped through the needle's eye, and then I   45
walked down the aisle toward my father. The jet was
full and people's hair was shining, they were
smiling, the interior of the plane was filled with a
mist of gold endorphin light,
I wept as people weep when they enter heaven,   50
in massive relief. We lifted up
gently from one tip of the continent and
did not stop until we set down lightly on the
other edge, I walked into his room and
watched his chest rise slowly and   55
sink again, all night
I watched him breathe.

1985

SUMMER SOLSTICE, NEW YORK CITY

By the end of the longest day of the year he could not
    stand it,
he went up the iron stairs through the roof of the
    building
and over the soft, tarry surface
to the edge, put one leg over the complex green tin
    cornice
and said if they came a step closer that was it.   5
Then the huge machinery of the earth began to work
    for his life,

the cops came in their suits blue-gray as the sky on a
   cloudy evening,
and one put on a bulletproof vest, a
black shell around his own life,
life of his children's father, in case   10
the man was armed, and one, slung with a
rope like the sign of his bounden duty,
came up out of a hole in the top of the neighboring
   building,
like the gold hole they say is in the top of the head,
and began to lurk toward the man who wanted to die.   15
The tallest cop approached him directly,
softly, slowly, talking to him, talking, talking,
while the man's leg hung over the lip of the next world,
and the crowd gathered in the street, silent, and the
dark hairy net with its implacable grid was   20
unfolded near the curb and spread out and
stretched as the sheet is prepared to receive at a birth.
Then they all came a little closer
where he squatted next to his death, his shirt
glowing its milky glow like something   25
growing in a dish at night in the dark in a lab, and then
everything stopped
as his body jerked and he
stepped down from the parapet and went toward them
and they closed on him, I thought they were going to   30
beat him up, as a mother whose child has been
lost will scream at the child when it's found, they
took him by the arms and held him up and
leaned him against the wall of the chimney and the
tall cop lit a cigarette   35
in his own mouth, and gave it to him, and
then they all lit cigarettes, and the
red glowing ends burned like the
tiny campfires we lit at night
back at the beginning of the world.   40

1986

Perhaps because the nineteenth century produced so much sentimental poetry
about romantic love and family relationships, twentieth-century poets have
approached these subjects very carefully, often very obliquely. In 1947

Tess Gallagher

(b. 1943)

EACH BIRD WALKING

Not while, but long after he had told me,
I thought of him, washing his mother, his
bending over the bed and taking back
the covers. There was a basin of water
and he dipped a washrag in and   5
out of the basin, the rag
dripping a little onto the sheet as he
turned from the bedside to the nightstand
and back, there being no place

on her body he shouldn't touch because   10
he had to and she helped him, moving
the little she could, lifting so he could
wipe under her arms, a dipping motion
in the hollow. Then working up from
the feet, around the ankles, over the   15
knees. And this last, opening
her thighs and running the rag firmly
and with the cleaning thought
up through her crotch, between the lips,
over the V of thin hairs—   20

as though he were a mother
who had the excuse of cleaning to touch
with love and indifference,
the secret parts of her child, to graze
the sleepy sexlessness in its waiting   25
to find out what to do for the sake
of the body, for the sake of what only
the body can do for itself.

So his hand, softly at the place
of his birth-light. And she, eyes deepened   30
and closed in the dim room.
And because he told me her death was
important to his being with her,
I could love him another way. Not
of the body alone, or of its making,   35
but carried in the white spires of trembling
until what spirit, what breath we were
was shaken from us. Small then,
the word *holy*.

He turned her on her stomach   40
and washed the blades of her shoulders, the
small of the back. "That's good," she said,
"that's enough."
On our lips that morning, the tart juice
of the mothers, so strong in remembrance, no   45
asking, no giving, and what you said, this
being the end of our loving, so as not to hurt
the closer one to you, made me look
to see what was left of us
with our sex taken away. "Tell me," I said,   50
"something I can't forget." Then the story of
your mother, and when you finished
I said, "That's good, that's enough."

1984

LOUISE GLÜCK

(b. 1943)

FOR MY MOTHER

It was better when we were
together in one body.
Thirty years. Screened
through the green glass
of your eye, moonlight   5
filtered into my bones
as we lay
in the big bed, in the dark,
waiting for my father.

Thirty years. He closed   10
your eyelids with
two kisses. And then spring
came and withdrew from me
the absolute
knowledge of the unborn,   15
leaving the brick stoop
where you stand, shading
your eyes, but it is
night, the moon
is stationed in the beech tree,   20
round and white among
the small tin markers of the stars:
Thirty years. A marsh
grows up around the house.
Schools of spores circulate   25
behind the shades, drift through
gauze flutterings of vegetation.

                                                            1975

THE APPLE TREES

Your son presses against me
his small intelligent body.

I stand beside his crib
as in another dream
you stood among trees hung   5
with bitten apples
holding out your arms.
I did not move
but saw the air dividing
into panes of color—at the very last   10
I raised him to the window saying
See what you have made
and counted out the whittled ribs,
the heart on its blue stalk
as from among the trees   15
the darkness issued:

In the dark room your son sleeps.
The walls are green, the walls
are spruce and silence.
I wait to see how he will leave me.   20
Already on his hand the map appears

as though you carved it there,
the dead fields, women rooted to the river.

                                                    1975

METAMORPHOSIS

1. Night

The angel of death flies
low over my father's bed.
Only my mother sees. She and my father
are alone in the room.

She bends over him to touch   5
his hand, his forehead. She is
so used to mothering
that now she strokes his body
as she would the other children's,
first gently, then   10
inured to suffering.

Nothing is any different.
Even the spot on the lung
was always there.

2. Metamorphosis

My father has forgotten me   15
in the excitement of dying.
Like a child who will not eat,
he takes no notice of anything.

I sit at the edge of his bed
while the living circle us   20
like so many tree stumps.

Once, for the smallest
fraction of an instant, I thought
he was alive in the present again;
then he looked at me   25
as a blind man stares
straight into the sun, since
whatever it could do to him
is done already.

Then his flushed face   30
turned away from the contract.

3. For My Father

I'm going to live without you
as I learned once
to live without my mother.
You think I don't remember that?   35
I've spent my whole life trying to remember.

Now, after so much solitude,
death doesn't frighten me,
not yours, not mine either.
And those words, *the last time,*   40
have no power over me. I know
intense love always leads to mourning.

For once, your body doesn't frighten me.
From time to time, I run my hand over your face
lightly, like a dustcloth.   45
What can shock me now? I feel
no coldness that can't be explained.
Against your cheek, my hand is warm
and full of tenderness.

1985

THE TRIUMPH OF ACHILLES

In the story of Patroclus
no one survives, not even Achilles
who was nearly a god.
Patroclus resembled him; they wore
the same armor.   5

Always in these friendships
one serves the other, one is less than the other:
the hierachy
is always apparent, though the legends
cannot be trusted—   10
their source is the survivor,
the one who has been abandoned.

What were the Greek ships on fire
compared to this loss?

In his tent, Achilles   15
grieved with his whole being
and the gods saw

he was a man already dead, a victim
of the part that loved,
the part that was mortal.   20

1985

HORSE

What does the horse give you
that I cannot give you?

I watch you when you are alone,
when you ride into the field behind the dairy,
your hands buried in the mare's   5
dark mane.

Then I know what lies behind your silence:
scorn, hatred of me, of marriage. Still,
you want me to touch you; you cry out
as brides cry, but when I look at you I see   10
there are no children in your body.
Then what is there?

Nothing, I think. Only haste
to die before I die.

In a dream, I watched you ride the horse   15
over the dry fields and then
dismount: you two walked together;
in the dark, you had no shadows.
But I felt them coming toward me
since at night they go anywhere,   20
they are their own masters.

Look at me. You think I don't understand?
What is the animal
if not passage out of this life?

1985

NIGHT SONG

Look up into the light of the lantern.
Don't you see? The calm of darkness
is the horror of heaven.

We've been apart too long, too painfully separated.
How can you bear to dream,   5
to give up watching? I think you must be dreaming,
your face is full of mild expectancy.

I need to wake you, to remind you that there isn't a
    future.
That's why we're free. And now some weakness in me
has been cured forever, so I'm not compelled   10
to close my eyes, to go back, to rectify—

The beach is still; the sea, cleansed of its superfluous
    life,
opaque, rocklike. In mounds, in vegetal clusters,
seabirds sleep on the jetty. Terns, assassins—

You're tired; I can see that.   15
We're both tired, we have acted a great drama.
Even our hands are cold, that were like kindling.
Our clothes are scattered on the sand; strangely
    enough,
they never turned to ashes.

I have to tell you what I've learned, that I know now   20
what happens to the dreamers.
They don't feel it when they change. One day
they wake, they dress, they are old.

Tonight I'm not afraid
to feel the revolutions. How can you want sleep   25
when passion gives you that peace?
You're like me tonight, one of the lucky ones.
You'll get what you want. You'll get your oblivion.

1985

*The critic Helen Vendler points out that Louise Glück's poems are often
"cryptic narratives," pared to the bare minimum so that the reader must
construct plot, character, theme, and action. Glück's own account of the
writing of "Night Song" shows the same sort of cryptic quality from the
poet's perspective: the suprisingly indirect relation between the external
events that stimulate a poem and the "messages" the poet is "equipped to
receive."*

"These are, in the deepest sense, ordinary experiences": Louise Glück

In April of 1980, my house was destroyed by fire. . . . Gradually, certain benefits became apparent. I felt grateful; the vivid sense of escape conferred on daily life an aura of blessedness. I felt lucky to wake up, lucky to make the beds, lucky to grind the coffee. There was also, after a period of devastating grief, a strange exhilaration. Having nothing, I was no longer hostage to possessions. . . .

That first summer after the fire was a period of rare happiness. I mean, by that word, not ecstasy but another state, one more balanced, serene, attentive. . . .

It was clear to me long ago that any hope I had of writing real poetry depended on my living through common experiences. The privileged, the too-protected, the mandarin in my nature would have to be checked. At the same time, I was wary of drama, of disaster too deliberately courted: I have always been too at ease with extremes. What had to be cultivated, beyond a necessary neutrality, was the willingness to be identified with others. . . .

Major experiences vary in form—what reader and writer learn to do is recognize analogies. I watched my house burn—in the category of major losses, this made only the most modest start. Nor was it unexpected: I had spent twenty years waiting to undergo the losses I knew to be inevitable. I was obsessed with loss; not surprisingly, I was also acquisitive, possessive. The two tendencies fed each other; every impulse to extend my holdings increased the fundamental anxiety. Actual loss, loss of mere property, was a release, an abrupt transition from anticipation to expertise. In passing, I learned something about fire, about its appetite. I watched the destruction of all that had been, all that would not be again, and all that remained took on a radiance.

These are, in the deepest sense, ordinary experiences. On the subject of change, of loss, we all attain to authority. In my case, the timing was efficient. I was in my late thirties; perhaps I'd learned all I could about preparation, about gathering. The next lesson is abandon, letting go.

Perhaps, too, in all this there were other messages to be heard. And perhaps "Night Song" sounds much more of a piece with my other work than this suggests. It wouldn't surprise me. It seems these are the messages I'm equipped to receive.

DRAMA

DRAMA

ANTH

"To Hold the Mirror Up to Nature": The Art of Drama

An attractive hypothesis about the relation of drama to fiction is that a play is a short story told by acting it out. If we put the hypothesis to the test, however, we are forced to discard or change it. We might try, for example, to "dramatize" a passage that comes about five hundred words into Anton Chekhov's story "The Lady with the Pet Dog." We have learned that the principal character, Dmitry Dmitrich Gurov, is a married man under forty, "bored and ill at ease" in the presence of men, who has been repeatedly unfaithful to his wife and who regards women as "the inferior race."

> One evening while he was dining in the public garden the lady in the beret walked up without haste to take the next table. Her expression, her gait, her dress, and the way she did her hair told him that she belonged to the upper class, that she was married, that she was in Yalta for the first time and alone, and that she was bored there. The stories told of the immorality in Yalta are to a great extent untrue; he despised them, and knew that such stories were made up for the most part by persons who would have been glad to sin themselves if they had had the chance; but when the lady sat down at the next table three paces from him, he recalled these stories of easy con-

quests, of trips to the mountains, and the
tempting thought of a swift, fleeting liaison, a
romance with an unknown woman of whose
very name he was ignorant suddenly took hold
of him.

He beckoned invitingly to the Pomeranian, and when the dog approached him,
shook his finger at it. The Pomeranian
growled; Gurov threatened it again.

The lady glanced at them and at once
dropped her eyes.

"He doesn't bite," she said and
blushed.

"May I give him a bone?" he asked;
and when she nodded he inquired affably,
"Have you been in Yalta long?"

"About five days."

"And I am dragging out the second
week here."

There was a short silence.

"Time passes quickly, and yet it is so
dull here!" she said, not looking at him.

A great dramatist as well as a great fiction writer, Chekhov has given us promising material here: external
action that need only be converted into stage directions,

some practical hints for costuming and set. Here is the
scene as we might work it up in an adaptation for the stage.

> *[A public garden, with tables, about half of them occupied, at which*
> *people sit eating. Gurov occupies a table alone. Anna, a fair-haired*
> *young lady of medium height, fashionably dressed, enters with a Pomer-*
> *anian on a leash. She sits at the table next to Gurov, about fifteen feet*
> *away. Gurov drops his hand to his side and wiggles his fingers to attract*
> *the dog's attention. When the dog approaches, he shakes his finger at it.*
> *The dog growls and Gurov shakes his finger again. Anna glances at*
> *Gurov and drops her eyes.]*

Anna: (*blushing*). He doesn't bite.

Gurov: May I give him a bone? (*Anna nods.*) (*affably*) Have you been in
          Yalta long?

Anna: About five days.

Gurov: I am dragging out the second week here.

Anna   (*after a short pause, not looking at him*). Time passes quickly and yet it
          is so dull here.

In some ways this is not a bad bit of scriptwriting: the presence of
the dog not only creates an interesting bit of stage business but leads naturally to dialogue that reveals something about the characters of Gurov and
Anna. The problem, however, is that the Gurov our viewers will see on
stage is not the same one that we read about in the story. They can see by
the way that he entices the dog and then shakes his finger at it that Gurov is
trying to find a way to draw the lady into conversation. But they may—if
they have watched enough romantic movies, they probably will—assume
that Gurov is a bachelor who has seen an unmarried woman. Even if we
show him to be married (perhaps we could bring on a waiter at the beginning of the scene to deliver a letter from his wife?), there will be nothing to
show his contempt for women or his habit of using them to fill up the emptiness of his life.

How can we show Gurov's inner life to the audience? Three tactics
come to mind. We could supply Gurov with a confidant to whom he could
talk about his feelings, but this method can work only if the character has a
confiding nature, which Gurov does not. He confides in neither men nor
women: his isolation is essential to his character. We could have him
address an occasional aside directly to the audience. After Anna says,
"Time passes quickly, and yet it is so dull here," for instance, he might say,
"And so it is as I thought: here is a woman ripe for a fleeting affair." But a
character who confides in the audience hardly seems isolated, and asides
like these would make the play seem like a comedy or even a farce rather
than the serious story Chekhov has provided us. We might write another

scene in which Gurov, alone on the stage, reveals his thoughts in a soliloquy. But soliloquies require characters (like Hamlet) who are inclined to search their souls: Gurov's soul-searching will come later in the story, when he discovers that he has one to search.

A good playwright could find a way around some of these difficulties of presenting a character's psychological state in dramatic form[1] but some of them are inherent in the form of drama. A play depends upon external actions and on words spoken while standing in a particular place: it is a physical art form. This physical form imposes some limitations on drama, but it also opens up possibilities, for action, spoken words, and a sense of place are powerful tools.

THE SOCIAL NATURE OF DRAMA: GREEK DRAMA

Toward the end of "The Lady with the Pet Dog," Chekhov says this: "The personal life of every individual is based on secrecy, and perhaps it is partly for that reason that civilized man is so nervously anxious that personal privacy should be respected." This statement is profoundly true, but it does not exhaust the truth. Humans are public creatures as well as private ones, and "the personal life of every individual" comes largely from a relation to the society in which he or she lives. Private musing, joys, and heartaches have tremendous weight; so too do external actions and words spoken aloud to the community.

The ancient Greeks very strongly felt the importance of this public side of human nature, nowhere more clearly expressed than in Aristotle's statement that "Man is a political animal." Translation here obscures Aristotle's meaning slightly. It might be better to say that a human is a creature of the *polis,* the community: from it the individual derives the values and understanding that allow a fully human life; to it the individual is ultimately answerable. Aristotle admits that the individual may sometimes be separated from the *polis* by accident, but insists that "the person who by nature, not accident, does not belong to the polis is either a wild animal or a god."

Implied in this emphasis on "political" life is the Greek love of talk, gesture, games, debate, public worship, song, dance: all the things that bind people together in ways that have nothing to do with privacy. The Greek view did not assume that life's true center was in private relations that were separated by a wide moat from an alien public life. The Greek public life penetrated what we would view as private sanctuaries. This penetration is crucial to Greek drama, as we can see in a play like Sophocles' *Antigone,* where the grief of a sister for the death of her brother raises an enormous public issue: duty to the *polis* versus duty to the gods.

---

1. See, for example, Samuel Beckett's play *Krapp's Last Tape.*

Euripides' *Medea*, too, treats in a surprisingly "political" way a subject most of us would see as extremely personal. Medea, discovering that her husband is abandoning her to form a more convenient marriage to the daughter of the king of Corinth, is enraged by the betrayal. The play's opening exposition, delivered by the nurse to Medea's children, reminds the audience of these facts. Then the audience hears Medea crying out ("Ah, wretch! Ah, lost in my sufferings,/I wish, I wish I might die.") from her house. A chorus of Corinthian women enters to console Medea, but also—very much in the Greek fashion—to investigate the situation and discuss it. While they are talking with the nurse, they hear Medea's loud complaints and comment on them.

> *Chorus:* O God and Earth and Heaven!
> Did you hear what a cry was that
> Which the sad wife sings?
> Poor foolish one, why should you long
> For that appalling rest?
> The final end of death comes fast.
> No need to pray for that.
> Suppose your man gives honour
> To another woman's bed.
> It often happens. Don't be hurt.
> God will be your friend in this.
> You must not waste away
> Grieving too much for him who shared your bed.

When this play was originally performed the chorus would have entered the orchestra (the circle at the base of the amphitheater) by the same aisles the Athenian audience had used to get to their seats. Coming literally from the people, the chorus naturally represents the reactions of the *polis*. Characters often try to win the approval from the chorus, just as in Athenian trials, accused and accuser would argue for the approval of a large citizen-jury.

In ancient performances, the chorus sometimes spoke as a single character (perhaps through the chorus leader), but more often it sang and danced its lines to the accompaniment of a flute. We should try to imagine the chorus's speech of consolation as a song matched with a slow, sweeping dance across the orchestra. At the same time, we should remember that the song announces a judgment: Medea should curb her passion and remember that others have felt a similar affliction.

Meanwhile Medea, about whom this judgment has been made, has still not appeared. She speaks again from the skene, the low building behind the orchestra, recalling what she has done to deserve the loyalty of her husband, Jason: she has betrayed her country and killed her own brother to help Jason win fame and fortune. The nurse calls on the gods to remember the oaths Jason is breaking by betraying Medea. Then the chorus speaks again.

Chorus: . . . But go inside and bring her
    Out of the house to us,
    And speak kindly to her: hurry,
    Before she wrongs her own.
    This passion of hers moves to something great.

The nurse goes somewhat reluctantly to get her mistress, pausing on the way to wish that poets could write songs to put an end to "grief,/Bitter grief, from which death and disaster/Cheat the hopes of a house." The chorus, alone on stage, sings and dances a somber reminder of Medea's troubles and then the protagonist herself enters:

Medea: Women of Corinth, I have come outside to you
    Lest you should be indignant with me; for I know
    That many people are overproud, . . .
    But on me this thing has fallen so unexpectedly,
    It has broken my heart. I am finished. I let go
    All my life's joy. . . .
    Of all things which are living and can form a judgment
    We women are the most unfortunate creatures.
    Firstly, with an excess of wealth it is required
    For us to buy a husband and take for our bodies
    A master; for not to take one is even worse. . . .
    And if we work out all this well and carefully,
    And the husband lives with us and lightly bears his yoke,
    Then life is enviable. If not, I'd rather die.
    A man, when he's tired of the company in his home,
    Goes out of the house and puts an end to his boredom
    And turns to a friend or companion of his own age.
    But we are forced to keep our eyes on one alone.
    What they say of us is that we have a peaceful time
    Living at home, while they do the fighting in war.
    How wrong they are! I would very much rather stand
    Three times in the front of battle than bear one child.
    Yet what applies to me does not apply to you.
    You have a country. Your family home is here.
    You enjoy life and the company of your friends.
    But I am deserted, a refugee, thought nothing of
    By my husband,—something he won in a foreign land.
    I have no mother or brother, nor any relation
    With whom I can take refuge in this sea of woe.
    This much then is the service I would beg from you:
    If I can find the means or devise any scheme
    To pay my husband back for what he has done to me,—
    Him and his father-in-law and the girl who married him,—
    Just to keep silent. For in other ways a woman

Is full of fear, defenseless, dreads the sight of cold
Steel; but, when once she is wronged in the matter of love,
No other soul can hold so many thoughts of blood.

Chorus: This I will promise. You are in the right, Medea
In paying your husband back. I am not surprised at you
For being sad.

Medea has given a stirring speech, and one full of passion, but not in Chekhov's sense a *personal* speech. Always her emphasis is on the central questions of the *polis:* justice, equity, propriety, participation in (or exclusion from) the life of the community. Her complaint is not in a sense peculiar to herself: she talks about "we women" or "a woman," as if what she feels might be felt (sometimes must be felt) by all the women in the chorus or by any stranger in the polis. And the chorus is temporarily won over.

Consider for a moment the circumstances in which this scene was originally enacted. The amphitheater in Athens held an audience of almost 14,000 and of course was in the open air. The average theatergoer was two hundred feet from the actors. So far away were the actors that they wore oversized masks with exaggerated facial expressions, stood in elevator shoes about six inches high, and dressed in bold stylized costumes (Medea's would have declared her at great distance to be a regal woman from the East). Built into the masks of the actors was a sort of megaphone that allowed their voices to carry to the back rows—provided, of course, that they spoke very loudly. None of this can have encouraged an easy identification with Medea as an individual human. But shoulder to shoulder with the average spectator and quite visible to him in the broad daylight were the members of his community, listening intently to Medea's speech, weighing its justice, considering the treatment of women and strangers in the *polis,* watching as the play unfolds the horrifying effects of pride and unchecked passion. In this context a Greek tragedy gathers a force that a short story, read silently by a single reader, can never have. Works like *Medea* and *Antigone* are "social documents," as Arthur Miller says, "not just piddling private conversations."

Adding to this force of public performance was the atmosphere of the spring festival of Dionysius, during which the drama was performed. Religious in origin, the festival had become in the days of Sophocles and Euripides a celebration of the glory of the Athenian *polis,* a very civic event. All citizens attended the plays: those who could not afford the price of admission were admitted at the expense of the city. The cost of the production was borne as a civic duty and honor by a rich man the *polis* elected. The city was small enough that the theatergoer would have known the producer, the playwright, the actors, and the members of the chorus. The audience must have felt on the day of a performance that "we" were coming together to enjoy, consider, and argue about a thing "we" all valued and were building together: a shared understanding of life.

TRANSPARENT DECEPTION: ELIZABETHAN DRAMA

The whole of the Globe, Shakespeare's theater in London, could have fit in the orchestra of the theater in Athens. The change in scale signals a change in all aspects of drama. English public theaters in the time of Elizabeth I (1558–1603) and James I (1603–25) were not places where the whole society gathered for a religious and civic celebration. They were places where a fraction of the city's population paid for entertainment, just as they paid for it at the Bear Garden, which stood so close to the Globe that the roar of the bears sometimes competed with the voices of the actors. An Elizabethan tragedian did not have the Athenian's advantages in achieving high seriousness and civic involvement.

On the other hand, whether writing tragedy or comedy, the Elizabethan playwright reaped advantages from the smaller theater. A full house at the Globe might have consisted of about two thousand people, some six hundred "groundlings" standing in the "yard" that surrounded the stage on three sides, more wealthy patrons seated in the galleries built one above the other a bit further back, a few seated on the stage itself. Those seated on the stage could see the wrinkles around an actor's eyes. Even those seated in the back of the third gallery would only be about sixty feet away: close enough to see ordinary gestures—shrugging the shoulders, clenching the fists, running fingers nervously through the hair. Under these circumstances plays could assume a sort of realism they had never had in the ancient world. A man[2] standing on platform shoes, wearing a carved mask, and chanting in a voice that could be heard a hundred yards away might *represent* Medea to an Athenian audience willing to use its imagination. But a man dressed in fairly ordinary costume, his features mobile and expressive and his voice varying naturally in volume and inflection might *impersonate* Prince Hamlet so well that the audience would for a moment see life itself on the stage. In *Hamlet*, in fact, the Prince tells a group of actors that the purpose of drama is "to hold, as 't were, the mirror up to nature." The older style of acting, he says, is quite out of fashion:

> O! there be players, that I have seen play,—and heard others
> praise, and that highly,—not to speak it profanely, that, neither
> having the accent of Christians, not the gait of Christian, pagan,
> nor man, have so strutted, and bellowed, that I have thought some
> of nature's journeymen had made men, and not made them well,
> they imitated humanity so abominably.

Holding the mirror up to nature was not, however, the whole mission of Elizabethan theater, and one of the pleasures of the period's drama

---

2. Men and boys played women's roles in both Greek and Elizabethan theater.

is the dazzling counterpoint between the imitated reality on stage and the actual reality of a London afternoon in a bustling theater. Like the Athenian amphitheater, Elizabethan public theaters were open to the sky, and the spectators could see each other quite as well as they could see the players. In fact, the audience was part of the attraction. One observer reported that "in the playhouses at London, it is the fashion of youths to go first into the yard, and there to carry their eye through every gallery" in search of beautiful women. When they find them "thither they fly, and press as near to the fairest as they can" where "they dally with their garments to pass the time." The awareness of other spectators was so strong that playwrights occasionally incorporated references to the audience in their plays. In his speech to the players, Hamlet says, "O! it offends me to the soul to hear a robustious periwig-pated fellow tear a passion to tatters, to very rags, to split the ears of the groundlings; who, for the most part, are capable of nothing but inexplicable dumb shows, and noise. . . ." The groundlings, standing within a few yards of the player delivering these lines, *must* have reacted, visibly if not audibly, and the people in the galleries must have watched for the groundlings' reactions as if they were part of the play. At the beginning of *The Careless Shepherd,* a play produced in a theater much like the Globe, two supposed spectators rise up from their seats at the edge of the stage and talk about moving into the gallery. A third "spectator" gets up and follows them, commenting that he knew that they would have preferred to sit on stage "To show their cloak and Sute," and that they were undoubtedly moving into the gallery only because they feared they might have creditors in the audience.

In reading some passages of Shakespearean drama, we can sense the pleasure playwright, players, and audience felt when they could do acrobatics on the tightwire stretched between the Elizabethan fascination with realism and Elizabethan frankness about the play as an entirely fictional entertainment. In *Twelfth Night,* for example, Viola disguises herself as a boy and becomes a page to Orsino, Duke of Illyria. The audience, knowing that all women on the Elizabethan stage were played by boys, has an interesting idea to play with: the boy had been dressed as a woman to play Viola, now Viola decides to dress as a eunuch named Cesario. Very well. Dressed as Cesario, she becomes a page to Orsino, with whom she secretly falls in love. Orsino, not knowing these things, makes Cesario/Viola a messenger to speak words of love to Olivia. Now the audience is quite aware that two boy actors are about to play a love scene in which one is pretending to be a woman and the other is pretending to be a woman pretending to be a boy. Viola/Cesario arrives at Olivia's house where Olivia, her face covered, is standing with her maid, Maria:

Viola: The honorable lady of the house, which is she?

Olivia: Speak to me, I shall answer for her. Your will?

Viola: Most radiant, exquisite, and unmatchable beauty—I pray you tell me if this be the lady of the house, for I never saw her. I would be loath to cast away my speech; for, besides that it is excellently well penn'd, I have taken great pains to con it. Good beauties, let me sustain no scorn; I am very comptible, even to the least sinister usage.

Olivia: Whence came you, sir?

Viola: I can say little more than I have studied, and that question's out of my part. Good gentle one, give me modest assurance if you be the lady of the house, that I may proceed in my speech.

Olivia: Are you a comedian?

Viola: No, my profound heart; and yet (by the very fangs of malice I swear) I am not that I play. Are you the lady of the house?

Olivia: If I do not usurp myself, I am.

When the boy playing Viola says that she/he has taken "great pains to con" an "excellently well penned" speech, the audience can step into the illusion of the play and hear Viola talking about her relation to her writer/master Orsino, but can also step outside the illusion to hear the boy actor talking about his relation to the playwright. When she/he swears that she is "not that I play," the levels of revealed make-believe are deliciously complicated:

- Cesario must pretend to be Olivia's lover, though he is not.
- Viola must pretend to be Cesario, though she is not.
- Viola must act as though she does not love Orsino, though she does.
- The boy actor must pretend to be Viola, though he is not.

All these levels of illusion are plain to the audience and are part of the comedy. And yet for all the humor that comes from admitting that the play is a performance, the characters eventually develop such definite personalities that the audience comes to believe in them.

Viola: Most certain, if you are she, you do usurp yourself; for what is yours to bestow is not yours to reserve. But this is from my commission; I will on with my speech in your praise, and then show you the heart of my message.

Olivia: Come to what is important in 't: I forgive you the praise.

Viola: Alas, I took great pains to study it, and 'tis poetical.

Olivia: It is the more like to be feign'd, I pray you keep it in. I heard you were saucy at my gates, and allow'd your approach, rather to wonder at you than to hear you. If you be not mad, be gone. If you have reason, be brief. 'Tis not that time of moon with me to make one in so skipping a dialogue.

Maria:	Will you hoist sail, sir? Here lies your way.
Viola:	No, good swabber, I am to hull here a little longer. Some mollification of your giant, sweet lady. Tell me your mind—I am a messenger.
Olivia:	Sure you have some hideous matter to deliver, when the courtesy of it is so fearful. Speak your office.
Viola:	It alone concerns your ear. I bring no overture of war, no taxation of homage. I hold the olive in my hand; my words are as full of peace as matter.
Olivia:	Yet you began rudely. What are you? What would you?
Viola:	The rudeness that hath appear'd in me have I learn'd from my entertainment. What I am, and what I would, are as secret as maidenhead: to your ears, divinity; to any other's, profanation.
Olivia:	Give us the place alone. We will hear this divinity. [*Exeunt* Maria and Attendants.] Now, sir, what is your text?
Viola:	Most sweet lady—
Olivia:	A comfortable doctrine, and much may be said of it. Where lies your text?
Viola:	In Orsino's bosom.
Olivia:	In his bosom? In what chapter of his bosom?
Viola:	To answer by the method, in the first of his heart.
Olivia:	O, I have read it; it is heresy. Have you no more to say?
Viola:	Good madam, let me see your face.
Olivia:	Have you any commission from your lord to negotiate with my face? You are now out of your test; but we will draw the curtain, and show you the picture. Look you, sir, such a one I was this present. [*Unveiling*] Is't not well done?
Viola:	Excellently done, if God did all.
Olivia:	'Tis in grain, sir, 'twill endure wind and weather.

The wit of this dialogue absorbs the audience's attention, and two extraordinarily interesting characters begin to emerge—intelligent, sharp-tongued, resourceful, hard-shelled, and (as we later learn) tender-hearted women. The boys stand in women's costumes in broad daylight on the bare stage, with no curtain to hide their exits and entrances, no scenery in the background, and very few stage props. But they "imitate humanity" so convincingly that the audience can sometimes forget the stage and the spectators. The playwright reminds us that they are only actors, and yet slowly they seem to assume a reality more intense than that of the groundlings or the spectators on stools at the edge of the stage. This sort of magic is characteristic of Shakespearean drama and distinguishes it both from the ritual drama of Athens and the realistic drama of the nineteenth and twentieth centuries.

TOTAL ILLUSION: REALISTIC DRAMA IN THIS CENTURY

Realism in drama is difficult to define and depends partly on a system of contrasts. In the context of Greek drama, with its larger-than-human scale, its dance and song, and its masked actors, Medea may have seemed a surprisingly realistic character because her emotions seem to imitate those of actual humans. But if the same actor represented Medea by the same methods at the Globe theater, where gestures and speech were more natural and the range of emotions wider and more fluid, Medea would be less convincing than the bombastic players Prince Hamlet criticizes. On a typical twentieth-century stage, however, an actor playing Viola or Hamlet in the Elizabethan fashion would not strike us as remarkably realistic.[3] We would probably find that he or she delivered the lines with too much attention to their poetry and too little attention to motivation, and we would be distracted by the soliloquies, asides, and gestures addressed frankly to the audience. The way that Elizabethan actors hovered between artifice and reality is consistent with the way their parts are written. These characters speak far more cleverly than anyone we have met, and their lives, filled with unlikely events, are lived at an emotional pitch no one ever sustains for long. They are created for a theater where the literal reproduction of reality was neither possible nor desirable.

After the seventeenth century, theater became increasingly an indoor business, and an indoor theater gave directors an opportunity to control the audience's perceptions more completely than before. The standard theater acquired a proscenium, the arch at the stage front through which the audience looks, a curtain to cover the proscenium between acts, and footlights that made the actors highly visible while leaving the audience in the dark. With the addition of carefully contrived scenery, it became possible to reproduce the visible world on stage, sometimes with breathtaking accuracy. When in 1898 the curtain went up on the Moscow Art Theatre's production of Anton Chekhov's *The Seagull*, the audience saw a convincing outdoor scene: a dark summer evening, the distant sounds of a drunkard singing and a dog howling, the croaking of frogs, the crake of a marsh bird,

---

3. I am not saying that the plays do not work on the modern stage, of course: they are still among the most popular plays ever written. The point is that one rarely leaves a contemporary Shakespearean performance thinking how much Hamlet and Ophelia resemble the couple next door, or how we meet Violas every day.

the tolling of a distant church bell, flashes of lightning, faint thunder in the distance. By the light of a lantern on top of a lamppost, the audience could see trees and bushes surrounding a clearing in which a workman was humming a tune as he hammered a nail into a crude stage for an amateur play. A white sheet was draped across the front of the stage the workman is building. A man smoking a cigarette and a woman cracking nuts strolled in from the right and began a conversation, sometimes facing directly away from the audience as they talked. The illusion was so nearly perfect that the auditorium in which the spectators sat now seemed to look into a real world, extending indefinitely into space. Midway through the first act, the white sheet came down and the audience saw a lake gleaming in the moonlit distance.

In a sense, this production of *The Seagull* was the logical culmination of three centuries of movement toward realistic theater. In another sense, it was an absolute revolution, one we associate with the writer Chekhov and the actor/directors Constantine Stanislavsky and Vladimir Nemirovich-Danchenko. These three men, objecting to the artificial conventions of the nineteenth-century Russian theater,[4] began to build a drama on new principles. Ultimately, the aim of the spectacularly realistic setting of plays like *The Seagull* was to make possible a new sort of drama, one where actors seemed to stand in the real world and act like real people. In the old drama actors addressed their lines to the audience and used conventional gestures and intonations to convey their emotions; when they were not talking they simply waited for their next line to come up. In the new drama the actors addressed their comments to each other, listened to the responses, and adopted whatever gestures, accents, and intonations seemed realistic for a person of the character's region, education, and disposition. In the old drama, there were recognizable stars in the play, stars who would bow to the audience and receive an ovation the minute they came onstage. In the new drama, the actor was completely subordinated to the character, and the star of one play might have the smallest part in another. In the old theater, the script presented characters who were in many ways larger than life, involved in extraordinarily dramatic situations, and expressing extraordinarily strong and unmixed emotions. In the new drama, the scale had shrunk to truly human proportions. The characters were people as ordinary as ourselves.

A Moscow Art Theatre production of a Chekhov play was so bold a departure into realism that it put everyone's nerves on edge. Was there an audience for drama about genuinely ordinary people? *The Seagull* opened with a cast so edgy that the actors took tranquilizers and made signs of the cross before they made their entrances. Stanislavsky managed to sit through the performance, but his legs twitched so violently that he had to hold them with both hands. Nemirovich-Danchenko stood out in the foyer

---

4. Russian theater had lagged behind, for instance, the Norwegian theater of Ibsen.

for the whole first act, dreading a bad reaction. Chekhov was in Yalta, very ill with tuberculosis, and his sister had warned the company that a failure of the play might be his deathblow. Stanislavsky's description of the company's mood at the end of the last act deserves quotation:

> There was a gravelike silence. Knipper fainted on stage. All of us could hardly keep our feet. In the throes of despair we began moving to our dressing rooms. Suddenly there was a roar in the auditorium, and a shriek of joy or fright on the stage. The curtain was lifted, fell, was lifted again, showing the whole auditorium our amazed and astounded immovability. It fell again, it rose; it fell, it rose, and we could not even gather enough sense to bow.

At the end of the performance Nemirovich-Danchenko suggested to the audience that Chekhov be sent a congratulatory telegram. The ovation was enormous and prolonged.

This success made it possible for Chekhov to write still more realistic drama of the sort we find in *The Three Sisters*, where the dialogue is lifelike to the point of imitating the pointlessness of everyday conversation.

Fedotik: I will now show you a new kind of solitaire. . . .

[He lays out the cards.
They *bring in the samovar;* Anfisa *stands by it; a little later* Natasha *comes in and begins to straighten things on the table;* Solyony *enters, is greeted, and sits down at the table.*]

Vershinin: What a wind!

Masha: Yes. I'm bored with winter. I've forgotten what summer's like.

Irina: I'm going to go out, I can see it. We're going to get to Moscow!

Fedotik: No it's not—see, that eight's on the deuce of spades. (*He laughs*) So, you're not going to get to Moscow.

Chebutykin: (*Reading the newspaper*) Tsitsikar. Smallpox is raging here.

Anfisa: (*Going up to* Masha): Masha, have some tea, darling. (*To* Vershinin) Please, your honor. . . . Excuse me, sir, I've forgotten your name. . . .

Masha: Bring it over here, nurse. I'm not going there.

Irina: Nurse!

Anfisa: Coming-g!

Natasha: (*To* Solyony): Babies, little babies still at the breast—they understand perfectly. "Good morning, Bobik!" I say. "Good morning, sweetheart!" Then he looks up at me in a very special way. You think I'm just saying that because I'm a mother, but that isn't so, no indeed it isn't so! He really is the most amazing child.

Solyony: If that child were mine I'd fry him in frying pan and then eat him.

[He picks up his glass goes into the living room, and sits down in a corner.]

Natasha: *(Covering her face with her hands):* Rude, common man!

Masha: If you're happy you don't notice whether it's summer or winter. It seems to me that if I were in Moscow I wouldn't care what the weather was like.

Despite the success of *The Seagull*, the script of *The Three Sisters* once again challenged the nerves of the Moscow Art Theatre. Some of the dismayed actors and actresses complained that it was not a play, that it could not be acted. It seemed to be an uncomposed photograph of life rather than an orderly imitation of it. Eventually, actors and audiences discovered in Chekhov's dialogue a "music of life"[5] that reveals individual characters and also portrays the connections and disconnections of the small society on stage. Chekhov's music, so different from the literal music of Greek or Elizabethan drama, gave order to the realistic action of the play.

    A word of warning about realism is in order at this point. The historical accident that gave us Greek drama before Elizabethan, and Elizabethan drama before Chekovian realism, might deceive us into thinking that the theater has progressed toward a goal. Progress is hardly the issue. Some of today's playwrights have more in common with Euripides than with Chekhov. Some very deliberately turn their back on the capacity of twentieth-century stagecraft (or cinematography) to produce a fictional world as detailed as the everyday world. Even Chekhov complained that technical realism could interfere with drama: when characters are too busy slapping mosquitoes to establish the reality of an outdoor setting, the heart of the play can be overlooked. Although complete illusions of reality are easier to create now than they were at the turn of the century, many playwrights have stepped back from extreme realism in setting or performance and preferred the more symbolic patterns we associate with Greek drama or the half-illusion we associate with Elizabethan drama.

---

5. The phrase is Nemirovich-Danchenko's. He is referring particularly to the way that Chekhov writes dialogue full of pauses "in which were expressed unspoken feelings, insinuations as to character, the semitones. The atmosphere gradually deepened, gathered itself into one harmonious whole, became, as it were, the music of life."

READING THE PLAY SILENTLY

Obviously, a play we read silently cannot have exactly the same impact on the reader that a performed play does. As silent readers we gain because we can approach the text at our own pace, rereading passages that are difficult or interesting and carefully comparing one scene to another. We lose because we cannot get a complete sense of the action onstage, the sound of the performance, or the interaction between audience and players. The loss, however, need not be complete. We may not be able, like Stanislavsky, to write out a mise en scène as long as the script itself, but we can take some useful steps.

First, we can pay attention to the setting and to the degree of detailed realism the author seems to expect in the set. In Greek or Shakespearean drama, where scenery and stage properties were severely limited, much of the setting was conveyed in the language of the play. Thus, at the beginning of *Hamlet,* two sentries help create a setting by their words:

Bernardo: 'Tis now struck twelve: get thee to bed, Francisco.

Francisco: For this relief much thanks: 'tis bitter cold,
And I am sick at heart.

We get the time, temperature, and general mood conveyed in dialogue. Chekhov and Stanislavsky would probably have done the same work visually, but the Shakespearean stage could not be darkened or converted visually to the gloomy walls of Elsinore castle.

In a play where setting is written into dialogue, we are not likely to overlook it, but many novice readers fail to read the description most modern playwrights insert before the action begins. At the beginning of *Death of a Salesman,* for instance, Arthur Miller spends over six hundred words describing the set in a way that also defines the play's relation to reality. The kitchen of Willy Loman's house should seem "actual enough," with a kitchen table, three chairs, and a refrigerator, but "no other fixtures are seen." In the other rooms of the house are a few pieces of actual furniture. But most of the walls are missing, so that actors can occasionally walk right through them when the action is not in the present time. Around the house are "towering, angular shapes" that as the lights come up are revealed as "a solid vault of apartment building around the small, fragile-seeming home." This both is and is not the real world. Miller says that the set should have "the air of a dream rising out of reality." He is preparing the audience for a type of drama intermediate between Chekhov's realism and the Greek theater of ideas and symbolic actions. Spectators can take all this in subconsciously, but as readers we need to give it conscious thought.

Second, we can notice the skill the playwright uses in marshaling the resources and circumventing the limitations of dramatic form. In the first hundred lines of *Twelfth Night* Shakespeare manages to give the audience music, poetic language, the background information on two story lines, a bit of imaginary geography, and the description of a shipwreck: all through the mouths of characters who have motives to say what they say. Twice in *The Three Sisters* Chekhov manages to solve the technical problem mentioned at the beginning of this chapter, that of getting an essentially uncommunicative character into a situation where he will reveal his innermost thoughts. Andrei talks freely to Ferapont in Act 2 because Ferapont is too hard of hearing to understand him, and Chebutykin gets so drunk in Act 2 that he begins to talk to himself in what he thinks is an empty room. This sort of virtuosity deserves to be consciously savored.

Third, we can take time early to get the firmest possible grip on the identity of the characters: to know their ages, relations to each other, and general dispositions well enough that a statement by one of them would seem different to us if it were put in the mouth of another character. Modern playwrights often help us by a thumbnail description in the list of characters that precedes the text of the play. In *Crimes of the Heart* Beth Henley gives brief physical descriptions when the character enters, and also makes the initial words and actions typical. Chick Boyle, for instance, opens the play shouting:

Chick's Voice: Lenny! Oh, Lenny. Lenny *quickly blows out the candle and stuffs the cookie and candle into her dress pocket.* Chick, *twenty-nine, enters from the back door. She is a brightly dressed matron with yellow hair and shiny red lips.*

Lenny: Hi! I saw your car pull up.

Chick: Well, did you see today's paper?

> Lenny *nods.*

Chick: It's just too awful? It's just way too awful! How I'm gonna continue holding my head up high in this community, I do not know. Did you remember those pantyhose for me?

Lenny: They're in the sack.

Chick: Well, thank goodness, at least I'm not gonna have to go into town wearing holes in my stockings. *She gets the package, tears it open, and proceeds to take off one pair of stockings and put on another throughout the following scene. There should be something lightly grotesque about this woman changing her stockings in the kitchen.*

We should pause a moment to fix our image of Chick: a twenty-nine-year-old woman, brightly dressed, with red lipstick, struggling into pantyhose and talking about holding her head up in this community. The essential Chick is all there, and every subsequent speech she makes is more interesting if we can keep the image clearly in mind.

The image is crucial to drama. Medea with the bloody corpses of her children escaping in a chariot drawn by dragons, the pompous Malvolio appearing onstage with his trousers rolled up to reveal yellow stockings and crossed garters, Chekhov's three sisters embracing in the garden of the home they must soon leave: these images move us whether we see them on a literal stage or only on the stage of our imagination. As a boy, the eighteenth-century writer Samuel Johnson sat in the basement kitchen of his house, reading plays by firelight. When he read the opening scenes of *Hamlet,* the ghost scenes worked so vividly on his imagination that he ran up the stairs onto the street so "that he might have people about him." If we could all read with this sort of intensity, we would not need textbooks or classrooms to learn what drama is about.

SOPHOCLES

(496–406 B.C.)

ANTIGONE

translated from the Greek by Elizabeth Wyckoff

CHARACTERS

Antigone
Ismene
Chorus of Theban Elders
Creon
A Guard
Haemon
Teiresias
A Messenger
Eurydice

Scene: Thebes, before the royal palace.

(Antigone and Ismene emerge from its great central door.)

Antigone: My sister, my Ismene, do you know
    of any suffering from our father sprung
    that Zeus does not achieve for us survivors?
    There's nothing grievous, nothing free from doom,
    not shameful, not dishonored, I've not seen.   5
    Your sufferings and mine.
    And now, what of this edict which they say
    the commander has proclaimed to the whole people?
    Have you heard anything? Or don't you know
    that the foes' trouble comes upon our friends?   10
  Ismene: I've heard no word, Antigone, of our friends.
    Not sweet nor bitter, since that single moment
    when we two lost two brothers
    who died on one day by a double blow.
    And since the Argive army[1] went away   15
    this very night, I have no further news
    of fortune or disaster for myself.

---

1. The army from Argos had been led against Thebes by Antigone's brother Polyneices. Her other brother, Eteocles, had helped lead the defense.

Antigone: I knew it well, and brought you from the house
    for just this reason, that you alone may hear.
    Ismene: What is it? Clearly some news has clouded you.   20
Antigone: It has indeed. Creon will give the one
    of our two brothers honor in the tomb;
    the other none.
    Eteocles, with just entreatment treated,
    as law provides he has hidden under earth   25
    to have full honor with the dead below.
    But Polyneices' corpse who died in pain,
    they say he has proclaimed to the whole town
    that none may bury him and none bewail,
    but leave him unwept, untombed, a rich sweet sight   30
    for the hungry birds' beholding.
    Such orders they say the worthy Creon gives
    to you and me—yes, yes, I say to *me*—
    and that he's coming to proclaim it clear
    to those who know it not.   35
    Further: he has the matter so at heart
    that anyone who dares attempt the act
    will die by public stoning in the town.
    So there you have it and you soon will show
    if you are noble, or fallen from your descent.   40
    Ismene: If things have reached this stage, what can I do,
    poor sister, that will help to make or mend?
Antigone: Think will you share my labor and my act.
    Ismene: What will you risk? And where is your intent?
Antigone: Will you take up that corpse along with me?   45
    Ismene: To bury him you mean, when it's forbidden?
Antigone: My brother, and yours, though you may wish he were not.
    I never shall be found to be his traitor.
    Ismene: O hard of mind! When Creon spoke against it!
Antigone: It's not for him to keep me from my own.   50
    Ismene: Alas. Remember, sister, how our father
    perished abhorred, ill-famed.
    Himself with his own hand, through his own curse
    destroyed both eyes.
    Remember next his mother and his wife   55
    finishing life in the shame of the twisted strings.[2]
    And third two brothers on a single day,
    poor creatures, murdering, a common doom
    each with his arm accomplished on the other.

---

2. Oedipus blinded himself when he learned that he had unknowingly killed his father, Laius, and married his mother, Jocasta. Jocasta hanged herself.

And now look at the two of us alone.   60
We'll perish terribly if we force law
and try to cross the royal vote and power.
We must remember that we two are women
so not to fight with men.
And that since we are subject to strong power   65
we must hear these orders, or any that may be worse.
So I shall ask of them beneath the earth
forgiveness, for in these things I am forced,
and shall obey the men in power. I know
that wild and futile action makes no sense.   70

Antigone: I wouldn't urge it. And if now you wished
to act, you wouldn't please me as a partner.
Be what you want to; but that man shall I
bury. For me, the doer, death is best.
Friend shall I lie with him, yes friend with friend,   75
when I have dared the crime of piety.
Longer the time in which to please the dead
than that for those up here.
There shall I lie forever. You may see fit
to keep from honor what the gods have honored.   80

  Ismene: I shall do no dishonor. But to act
against the citizens. I cannot.

Antigone: That's your protection. Now I go, to pile
the burial-mound for him, my dearest brother.

  Ismene: Oh my poor sister. How I fear for you!   85

Antigone: For me, don't borrow trouble. Clear your fate.

  Ismene: At least give no one warning of this act;
you keep it hidden, and I'll do the same.

Antigone: Dear God! Denounce me. I shall hate you more
if silent, not proclaiming this to all.   90

  Ismene: You have a hot mind over chilly things.

Antigone: I know I please those whom I most should please.

  Ismene: If but you can. You crave what can't be done.

Antigone: And so, when strength runs out, I shall give over.

  Ismene: Wrong from the start, to chase what cannot be.   95

Antigone: If that's your saying, I shall hate you first,
and next the dead will hate you in all justice.
But let me and my own ill-counselling
suffer this terror. I shall suffer nothing
as great as dying with a lack of grace.   100

  Ismene: Go, since you want to. But know this: you go
senseless indeed, but loved by those who love you.

*(Ismene returns to the palace; Antigone leaves by one of the side entrances. The
Chorus now enters from the other side.)*

Chorus: Sun's own radiance, fairest light ever shone on the gates of
Thebes,
then did you shine, O golden day's
eye, coming over Dirce's stream,   105
on the Man who had come from Argos with all his armor
running now in headlong fear as you shook his bridle free.

   He was stirred by the dubious quarrel of Polyneices.
   So, screaming shrill,
   like an eagle over the land he flew,   110
   covered with white-snow wing,
   with many weapons,
   with horse-hair crested helms.

He who had stood above our halls, gaping about our seven gates,
with that circle of thirsting spears.   115
Gone, without our blood in his jaws,
before the torch took hold on our tower-crown.
Rattle of war at his back; hard the fight for the dragon's foe.

   The boasts of a proud tongue are for Zeus to hate.
   So seeing them streaming on   120
   in insolent clangor of gold,
   he struck with hurling fire him who rushed
   for the high wall's top,
   to cry conquest abroad.

Swinging, striking the earth he fell   125
fire in hand, who in mad attack,
had raged against us with blasts of hate.
He failed. He failed of his aim.
For the rest great Ares[3] dealt his blows about,
first in the war-team.   130

   The captains stationed at seven gates
   fought with seven and left behind
   their brazen arms as an offering
   to Zeus who is turner of battle.
   All but those wretches, sons of one man,   135
   one mother's sons, who sent their spears
   each against each and found the share
   of a common death together.

Great-named Victory comes to us
answering Thebes' warrior-joy.   140
Let us forget the wars just done

_____

3. God of war

and visit the shrines of the gods.
All, with night-long dance which Bacchus[4] will lead,
who shakes Thebes' acres.

(Creon enters from the palace.)

Now here he comes, the king of the land,   145
Creon, Menoeceus' son,
newly named by the gods' new fate.
What plan that beats about his mind
has made him call this council-session,
sending his summons to all?   150

Creon: My friends, the very gods who shook the state
with mighty surge have set it straight again.
So now I sent for you, chosen from all,
first that I knew you constant in respect
to Laius' royal power; and again   155
when Oedipus had set the state to rights,
and when he perished, you were faithful still
in mind to the descendants of the dead.
When they two perished by a double fate,
on one day struck and striking and defiled   160
each by his own hand, now it comes that I
hold all the power and the royal throne
through close connection with the perished men.
You cannot learn of any man the soul,
the mind, and the intent until he shows   165
his practise of the government and law.
For I believe that who controls the state
and does not hold to the best plans of all,
but locks his tongue up through some kind of fear,
that he is worst of all who are or were.   170
And he who counts another greater friend
than his own fatherland, I put him nowhere.
So I—may Zeus all-seeing always know it—
could not keep silent as disaster crept
upon the town, destroying hope of safety.   175
Nor could I count the enemy of the land
friend to myself, not I who know so well
that she it is who saves us, sailing straight,
and only so can we have friends at all.
With such good rules shall I enlarge our state.   180
And now I have proclaimed their brother-edict.
In the matter of the sons of Oedipus,

---

4. God of wine; the great Greek tragedies were performed at festivals dedicated to him.

citizens, know: Eteocles who died,
defending this our town with champion spear,
is to be covered in the grave and granted   185
all holy rites we give the noble dead.
But his brother Polyneices whom I name
the exile who came back and sought to burn
his fatherland, the gods who were his kin,
who tried to gorge on blood he shared, and lead   190
the rest of us as slaves—
it is announced that no one in this town
may give him burial or mourn for him.
Leave him unburied, leave his corpse disgraced,
a dinner for the birds and for the dogs.   195
Such is my mind. Never shall I, myself,
honor the wicked and reject the just.
The man who is well-minded to the state
from me in death and life shall have his honor.

Chorus: This resolution, Creon, is your own,   200
in the matter of the traitor and the true.
For you can make such rulings as you will
about the living and about the dead.

Creon: Now you be sentinels of the decree.

Chorus: Order some younger man to take this on.   205

Creon: Already there are watchers of the corpse.

Chorus: What other order would you give us, then?

Creon: Not to take sides with any who disobey.

Chorus: No fool is fool as far as loving death.

Creon: Death is the price. But often we have known   210
men to be ruined by the hope of profit.

(Enter, from the side, a guard.)

Guard: Lord, I can't claim that I am out of breath
from rushing here with light and hasty step,
for I had many haltings in my thought
making me double back upon my road.   215
My mind kept saying many things to me:
"Why go where you will surely pay the price?"
"Fool, are you halting? And if Creon learns
from someone else, how shall you not be hurt?"
Turning this over, on I dilly-dallied.   220
And so a short trip turns itself to long.
Finally, though, my coming here won out.
If what I say is nothing, still I'll say it.
For I come clutching to one single hope
that I can't suffer what is not my fate.   225

Creon: What is it that brings on this gloom of yours?

Guard: I want to tell you first about myself.
    I didn't do it, didn't see who did it.
    It isn't right for me to get in trouble.
Creon: Your aim is good. You fence the fact around.   230
    It's clear you have some shocking news to tell.
Guard: Terrible tidings make for long delays.
Creon: Speak out the story, and then get away.
Guard: I'll tell you. Someone left the corpse just now,
    burial all accomplished, thirsty dust   235
    strewn on the flesh, the ritual complete.
Creon: What are you saying? What man has dared to do it?
Guard: I wouldn't know. There were no marks of picks,
    no grubbed-out earth. The ground was dry and hard,
    no trace of wheels. The doer left no sign.   240
    When the first fellow on the day-shift showed us,
    we all were sick with wonder.
    For he was hidden, not inside a tomb,
    light dust upon him, enough to turn the curse,
    no wild beast's track, nor track of any hound   245
    having been near, nor was the body torn.
    We roared bad words about, guard against guard,
    and came to blows. No one was there to stop us.
    Each man had done it, nobody had done it
    so as to prove it on him—we couldn't tell.   250
    We were prepared to hold to red-hot iron,
    to walk through fire, to swear before the gods
    we hadn't done it, hadn't shared the plan,
    when it was plotted or when it was done.
    And last, when all our sleuthing came out nowhere,   255
    one fellow spoke, who made our heads to droop
    low toward the ground. We couldn't disagree.
    We couldn't see a chance of getting off.
    He said we had to tell you all about it.
    We couldn't hide the fact.   260
    So he won out. The lot chose poor old me
    to win the prize. So here I am unwilling,
    quite sure you people hardly want to see me.
    Nobody likes the bringer of bad news.
Chorus: Lord, while he spoke, my mind kept on debating.   265
    Isn't this action possibly a god's?
Creon: Stop now, before you fill me up with rage,
    or you'll prove yourself insane as well as old.
    Unbearable, your saying that the gods
    take any kindly forethought for this corpse.   270
    Would it be they had hidden him away,

honoring his good service, his who came
to burn their pillared temples and their wealth,
even their land, and break apart their laws?
Or have you seen them honor wicked men?   275
It isn't so.
No, from the first there were some men in town
who took the edict hard, and growled against me,
who hid the fact that they were rearing back,
not rightly in the yoke, no way my friends.   280
These are the people—oh it's clear to me—
who have bribed these men and brought about the deed.
No current custom among men as bad
as silver currency. This destroys the state;
this drives men from their homes; this wicked teacher   285
drives solid citizens to acts of shame.
It shows men how to practise infamy
and know the deeds of all unholiness.
Every least hireling who helped in this
brought about then the sentence he shall have.   290
But further, as I still revere great Zeus,
understand this, I tell you under oath,
if you don't find the very man whose hands
buried the corpse, bring him for me to see,
not death alone shall be enough for you   295
till living, hanging, you make clear the crime.
For any future grabbings you'll have learned
where to get pay, and that it doesn't pay
to squeeze a profit out of every source.
For you'll have felt that more men come to doom   300
through dirty profits than are kept by them.
Guard: May I say something? Or just turn and go?
Creon: Aren't you aware your speech is most unwelcome?
Guard: Does it annoy your hearing or your mind?
Creon: Why are you out to allocate my pain?   305
Guard: The doer hurts your mind. I hurt your ears.
Creon: You are a quibbling rascal through and through.
Guard: But anyhow I never did the deed.
Creon: And you the man who sold your mind for money!
Guard: Oh!   310
How terrible to guess, and guess at lies!
Creon: Go pretty up your guesswork. If you don't
show me the doers you will have to say
that wicked payments work their own revenge.
Guard: Indeed, I pray he's found, but yes or no,   315
taken or not as luck may settle it,

you won't see me returning to this place.
Saved when I neither hoped nor thought to be,
I owe the gods a mighty debt of thanks.

(Creon enters the palace. The Guard leaves by the way he came.)

Chorus: Many the wonders but nothing walks stranger than man.   320
           This thing crosses the sea in the winter's storm,
           making his path through the roaring waves.
           And she, the greatest of gods, the earth—
           ageless she is, and unwearied—he wears her away
           as the ploughs go up and down from year to year   325
           and his mules turn up the soil.

           Gay nations of birds he snares and leads,
           wild beast tribes and the salty brood of the sea,
           with the twisted mesh of his nets, this clever man.
           He controls with craft the beasts of the open air,   330
           walkers on hills. The horse with his shaggy mane
           he holds and harnesses, yoked about the neck,
           and the strong bull of the mountain.

           Language, and thought like the wind
           and the feelings that make the town,   335
           he has taught himself, and shelter against the cold,
           refuge from rain. He can always help himself.
           He faces no future helpless. There's only death
           that he cannot find an escape from. He has contrived
           refuge from illnesses once beyond all cure.   340

           Clever beyond all dreams
           the inventive craft that he has
           which may drive him one time or another to well or ill.
           When he honors the laws of the land and the gods' sworn right
           high indeed is his city; but stateless the man   345
           who dares to dwells with dishonor. Not by my fire,
           never to share my thoughts, who does these things.

(The Guard enters with Antigone.)

           My mind is split at this awful sight.
           I know her. I cannot deny
           Antigone is here.   350
           Alas, the unhappy girl,
           her unhappy father's child.
           Oh what is the meaning of this?
           It cannot be you that they bring
           for breaking the royal law,   355
           caught in open shame.

Guard: This is the woman who has done the deed.
　　　We caught her at the burying. Where's the king?

(Creon enters.)

　Chorus: Back from the house again just when he's needed.
　Creon: What must I measure up to? What has happened?　　　　360
　Guard: Lord, one should never swear off anything.
　　　Afterthought makes the first resolve a liar.
　　　I could have vowed I wouldn't come back here
　　　after your threats, after the storm I faced.
　　　But joy that comes beyond the wildest hope　　　　365
　　　is bigger than all other pleasure known.
　　　I'm here, though I swore not to be, and bring
　　　this girl. We caught her burying the dead.
　　　This time we didn't need to shake the lots;
　　　mine was the luck, all mine.　　　　370
　　　So now, lord, take her, you, and question her
　　　and prove her as you will. But I am free.
　　　And I deserve full clearance on this charge.
　Creon: Explain the circumstance of the arrest.
　Guard: She was burying the man. You have it all.　　　　375
　Creon: Is this the truth? And do you grasp its meaning?
　Guard: I saw her burying the very corpse you had forbidden. Is this
　　　adequate?
　Creon: How was she caught and taken in the act?
　Guard: It was like this: when we got back again　　　　380
　　　struck with those dreadful threatenings of yours,
　　　we swept away the dust that hid the corpse.
　　　We stripped it back to slimy nakedness.
　　　And then we sat to windward on the hill
　　　so as to dodge the smell.　　　　385
　　　We poked each other up with growling threats
　　　if anyone was careless of his work.
　　　For some time this went on, till it was noon.
　　　The sun was high and hot. Then from the earth
　　　up rose a dusty whirlwind to the sky,　　　　390
　　　filling the plain, smearing the forest-leaves,
　　　clogging the upper air. We shut our eyes,
　　　sat and endured the plague the gods had sent.
　　　So the storm left us after a long time.
　　　We saw the girl. She cried the sharp and shrill　　　　395
　　　cry of a bitter bird which sees the nest
　　　bare where the young birds lay.
　　　So this same girl, seeing the body stripped,
　　　cried with great groanings, cried a dreadful curse
　　　upon the people who had done the deed.　　　　400

Soon in her hands she brought the thirsty dust,
and holding high a pitcher of wrought bronze
she poured the three libations for the dead.
We saw this and surged down. We trapped her fast;
and she was calm. We taxed her with the deeds   405
both past and present. Nothing was denied.
And I was glad, and yet I took it hard.
One's own escape from trouble makes one glad;
but bringing friends to trouble is hard grief.
Still, I care less for all these second thoughts   410
than for the fact that I myself am safe.
   Creon: You there, whose head is drooping to the ground,
    do you admit this, or deny you did it?
Antigone: I say I did it and I don't deny it.
   Creon *(to the Guard):* Take yourself off wherever you wish to go   415
    free of a heavy charge.
   Creon *(to Antigone):* You—tell me not at length but in a word.
    You knew the order not to do this thing?
Antigone: I knew, of course I knew. The word was plain.
   Creon: And still you dared to overstep these laws?   420
Antigone: For me it was not Zeus who made that order.
    Nor did that Justice who lives with the gods below
    mark out such laws to hold among mankind.
    Nor did I think your orders were so strong
    that you, a mortal man, could over-run   425
    the gods' unwritten and unfailing laws.
    Not now, nor yesterday's, they always live,
    and no one knows their origin in time.
    So not through fear of any man's proud spirit
    would I be likely to neglect these laws,   430
    draw on myself the gods' sure punishment.
    I knew that I must die; how could I not?
    even without your warning. If I die
    before my time, I say it is a gain.
    Who lives in sorrows many as are mine   435
    how shall he not be glad to gain his death?
    And so, for me to meet this fate, no grief.
    But if I left that corpse, my mother's son,
    dead and unburied I'd have cause to grieve
    as now I grieve not.   440
    And if you think my acts are foolishness
    the foolishness may be in a fool's eye.
   Chorus: The girl is bitter. She's her father's child.
    She cannot yield to trouble; nor could he.
   Creon: These rigid spirits are the first to fall.   445
    The strongest iron, hardened in the fire,

most often ends in scraps and shatterings.
Small curbs bring raging horses back to terms.
Slave to his neighbor, who can think of pride?
This girl was expert in her insolence   450
when she broke bounds beyond established law.
Once she had done it, insolence the second,
to boast her doing, and to laugh in it.
I am no man and she the man instead
if she can have this conquest without pain.   455
She is my sister's child, but were she child
of closer kin than any at my hearth,
she and her sister should not so escape
their death and doom. I charge Ismene too.
She shared the planning of this burial.   460
Call her outside. I saw her in the house,
maddened, no longer mistress of herself.
The sly intent betrays itself sometimes
before the secret plotters work their wrong.
I hate it too when someone caught in crime   465
then wants to make it seem a lovely thing.

Antigone: Do you want more than my arrest and death?

Creon: No more than that. For that is all I need.

Antigone: Why are you waiting? Nothing that you say
fits with my thought. I pray it never will.   470
Nor will you ever like to hear my words.
And yet what greater glory could I find
than giving my own brother funeral?
All these would say that they approved my act
did fear not mute them.   475
(A king is fortunate in many ways,
and most, that he can act and speak at will.)

Creon: None of these others see the case this way.

Antigone: They see, and do not say. You have them cowed.

Creon: And you are not ashamed to think alone?   480

Antigone: No, I am not ashamed. When was it shame
to serve the children of my mother's womb?

Creon: It was not your brother who died against him, then?

Antigone: Full brother, on both sides, my parents' child.

Creon: Your act of grace, in his regard, is crime.   485

Antigone: The corpse below would never say it was.

Creon: When you honor him and the criminal just alike?

Antigone: It was a brother, not a slave, who died.

Creon: Died to destroy this land the other guarded.

Antigone: Death yearns for equal law for all the dead.   490

Creon: Not that the good and bad draw equal shares.

Antigone: Who knows that this is holiness below?

Sophocles   **1239**

Creon: Never the enemy, even in death, a friend.
Antigone: I cannot share in hatred, but in love.
   Creon: Then go down there, if you must love, and love   495
     the dead. No woman rules me while I live.

(Ismene is brought from the palace under guard.)

 Chorus: Look there! Ismene is coming out.
     She loves her sister and mourns,
     with clouded brow and bloodied cheeks,
     tears on her lovely face.   500
   Creon: You, lurking like a viper in the house,
     who sucked me dry. I looked the other way
     while twin destruction planned against the throne.
     Now tell me, do you say you shared this deed?
     Or will you swear you didn't even know?   505
 Ismene: I did the deed, if she agrees I did.
     I am accessory and share the blame.
Antigone: Justice will not allow this. You did not
     wish for a part, nor did I give you one.
 Ismene: You are in trouble, and I'm not ashamed   510
     to sail beside you into suffering.
Antigone: Death and the dead, they know whose act it was.
     I cannot love a friend whose love is words.
 Ismene: Sister, I pray, don't fence me out from honor,
     from death with you, and honor done the dead.   515
Antigone: Don't die along with me, nor make your own
     that which you did not do. My death's enough.
 Ismene: When you are gone what life can be my friend?
Antigone: Love Creon. He's your kinsman and your care.
 Ismene: Why hurt me, when it does yourself no good?   520
Antigone: I also suffer, when I laugh at you.
 Ismene: What further service can I do you now?
Antigone: To save yourself. I shall not envy you.
 Ismene: Alas for me. Am I outside your fate?
Antigone: Yes. For you chose to live when I chose death.   525
 Ismene: At least I was not silent. You were warned.
Antigone: Some will have thought you wiser. Some will not.
 Ismene: And yet the blame is equal for us both.
Antigone: Take heart. You live. My life died long ago.
     And that has made me fit to help the dead.   530
   Creon: One of these girls has shown her lack of sense
     just now. The other had it from her birth.
 Ismene: Yes, lord. When people fall in deep distress
     their native sense departs, and will not stay.
   Creon: You chose your mind's distraction when you chose   535
     to work out wickedness with this wicked girl.

Ismene: What life is there for me to live without her?
  Creon: Don't speak of her. For she is here no more.
Ismene: But will you kill your own son's promised bride?
  Creon: Oh, there are other furrows for his plough.   540
Ismene: But where the closeness that has bound these two?
  Creon: Not for my sons will I choose wicked wives.
Ismene: Dear Haemon, your father robs you of your rights.
  Creon: You and your marriage trouble me too much.
Ismene: You will take away his bride from your own son?   545
  Creon: Yes. Death will help me break this marriage off.
Chorus: It seems determined that the girl must die.
  Creon: You helped determine it. Now, no delay!
          Slaves, take them in. They must be women now.
          No more free running.   550
          Even the bold will fly when they see Death
          drawing in close enough to end their life.

(Antigone and Ismene are taken inside.)

Chorus: Fortunate they whose lives have no taste of pain.
          For those whose house is shaken by the gods
          escape no kind of doom. It extends to all the kin   555
          like the wave that comes when the winds of Thrace
          run over the dark of the sea.
          The black sand of the bottom is brought from the depth;
          the beaten capes sound back with a hollow cry.

          Ancient the sorrow of Labdacus'[5] house, I know.   560
          Dead men's grief comes back, and falls on grief.
          No generation can free the next.
          One of the gods will strike. There is no escape.
          So now the light goes out
          for the house of Oedipus, while the bloody knife   565
          cuts the remaining root. Folly and Fury have done this.

          What madness of man, O Zeus, can bind your power?
          Not sleep can destroy it who ages all,
          nor the weariless months the gods have set. Unaged in time
          monarch you rule of Olympus' gleaming light.   570
          Near time, far future, and the past,
          one law controls them all:
          any greatness in human life brings doom.

          Wandering hope brings help to many men.
          But others she tricks from their giddy loves,   575

———
5. Father of Laius, thus grandfather of Oedipus.

and her quarry knows nothing until he has walked into flame.
Word of wisdom it was when someone said,
"The bad becomes the good
to him a god would doom."
Only briefly is that one from under doom.   580

(Haemon enters from the side.)

    Here is your one surviving son.
    Does he come in grief at the fate of his bride,
    in pain that he's tricked of his wedding?
Creon: Soon we shall know more than a seer could tell us.
    Son, have you heard the vote condemned your bride?   585
    And are you here, maddened against your father,
    or are we friends, whatever I may do?
Haemon: My father, I am yours. You keep me straight
    with your good judgment, which I shall ever follow.
    Nor shall a marriage count for more with me   590
    than your kind leading.
Creon: There's my good boy. So should you hold at heart
    and stand behind your father all the way.
    It is for this men pray they may beget
    households of dutiful obedient sons,   595
    who share alike in punishing enemies,
    and give due honor to their father's friends.
    Whoever breeds a child that will not help
    what has he sown but trouble for himself,
    and for his enemies laughter full and free?   600
    Son, do not let your lust mislead your mind,
    all for a woman's sake, for well you know
    how cold the thing he takes into his arms
    who has a wicked woman for his wife.
    What deeper wounding than a friend no friend?   605
    Oh spit her forth forever, as your foe.
    Let the girl marry somebody in Hades.
    Since I have caught her in the open act,
    the only one in town who disobeyed,
    I shall not now proclaim myself a liar,   610
    but kill her. Let her sing her song of Zeus
    who guards the kindred.
    If I allow disorder in my house
    I'd surely have to licence it abroad.
    A man who deals in fairness with his own,   615
    he can make manifest justice in the state.
    But he who crosses law, or forces it,
    or hopes to bring the rulers under him,
    shall never have a word of praise from me.

The man the state has put in place must have   620
obedient hearing to his least command
when it is right, and even when it's not.
He who accepts this teaching I can trust,
ruler, or ruled, to function in his place,
to stand his ground even in the storm of spears,   625
a mate to trust in battle at one's side.
There is no greater wrong than disobedience.
This ruins cities, this tears down our homes,
this breaks the battle-front in panic-rout.
If men live decently it is because   630
discipline saves their very lives for them.
So I must guard the men who yield to order,
not let myself be beaten by a woman.
Better, if it must happen, that a man
should overset me.   635
I won't be called weaker than womankind.
Chorus: We think—unless our age is cheating us—
that what you say is sensible and right.
Haemon: Father, the gods have given men good sense,
the only sure possession that we have.   640
I couldn't find the words in which to claim
that there was error in your late remarks.
Yet someone else might bring some further light.
Because I am your son I must keep watch
on all men's doing where it touches you,   645
their speech, and most of all, their discontents.
Your presence frightens any common man
from saying things you would not care to hear.
But in dark corners I have heard them say
how the whole town is grieving for this girl,   650
unjustly doomed, if ever woman was,
to die in shame for glorious action done.
She would not leave her fallen, slaughtered brother
there, as he lay, unburied, for the birds
and hungry dogs to make an end of him.   655
Isn't her real desert a golden prize?
This is the undercover speech in town.
Father, your welfare is my greatest good.
What loveliness in life for any child
outweighs a father's fortune and good fame?   660
And so a father feels his children's faring.
Then, do not have one mind, and one alone
that only your opinion can be right.
Whoever thinks that he alone is wise,
his eloquence, his mind, above the rest,   665

come the unfolding, shows his emptiness.
A man, though wise, should never be ashamed
of learning more, and must unbend his mind.
Have you not seen the trees beside the torrent,
the ones that bend them saving every leaf,   670
while the resistant perish root and branch?
And so the ship that will not slacken sail,
the sheet drawn tight, unyielding, overturns.
She ends the voyage with her keel on top.
No, yield your wrath, allow a change of stand.   675
Young as I am, if I may give advice,
I'd say it would be best if men were born
perfect in wisdom, but that failing this
(which often fails) it can be no dishonor
to learn from others when they speak good sense.   680

Chorus: Lord, if your son has spoken to the point
you should take his lesson. He should do the same.
Both sides have spoken well.

Creon: At my age I'm to school my mind by his?
This boy instructor is my master, then?   685

Haemon: I urge no wrong. I'm young, but you should watch
my actions, not my years, to judge of me.

Creon: A loyal action, to respect disorder?

Haemon: I wouldn't urge respect for wickedness.

Creon: You don't think she is sick with that disease?   690

Haemon: Your fellow-citizens maintain she's not.

Creon: Is the town to tell me how I ought to rule?

Haemon: Now there you speak just like a boy yourself.

Creon: Am I to rule by other mind than mine?

Haemon: No city is property of a single man.   695

Creon: But custom gives possession to the ruler.

Haemon: You'd rule a desert beautifully alone.

Creon (to the Chorus): It seems he's firmly on the woman's side.

Haemon: If you're a woman. It is you I care for.

Creon: Wicked, to try conclusions with your father.   700

Haemon: When you conclude unjustly, so I must.

Creon: Am I unjust, when I respect my office?

Haemon: You tread down the gods' due. Respect is gone.

Creon: Your mind is poisoned. Weaker than a woman!

Haemon: At least you'll never see me yield to shame.   705

Creon: Your whole long argument is but for her.

Haemon: And you, and me, and for the gods below.

Creon: You shall not marry her while she's alive.

Haemon: Then she shall die. Her death will bring another.

Creon: Your boldness has made progress. Threats, indeed!   710

Haemon: No threat, to speak against your empty plan.

Creon: Past due, sharp lessons for your empty brain.
Haemon: If you weren't father, I should call you mad.
Creon: Don't flatter me with "father," you woman's slave.
Haemon: You wish to speak but never wish to hear.   715
Creon: You think so? By Olympus, you shall not
    revile me with these tauntings and go free.
    Bring out the hateful creature; she shall die
    full in his sight, close at her bridegroom's side.
Haemon: Not at my side her death, and you will not   720
    ever lay eyes upon my face again.
    Find other friends to rave with after this.

(Haemon leaves, by one of the side entrances.)

Chorus: Lord, he has gone with all the speed of rage.
    When such a man is grieved his mind is hard.
Creon: Oh, let him go, plan superhuman action.   725
    In any case the girls shall not escape.
Chorus: You plan for both the punishment of death?
Creon: Not her who did not do it. You are right.
Chorus: And what death have you chosen for the other?
Creon: To take her where the foot of man comes not.   730
    There shall I hide her in a hollowed cave
    living, and leave her just so much to eat
    as clears the city from the guilt of death.
    There, if she prays to Death, the only god
    of her respect, she may manage not to die.   735
    Or she may learn at last and even then
    how much too much her labor for the dead.

(Creon returns to the palace.)

Chorus: Love unconquered in fight, love who falls on our havings.
    You rest in the bloom of a girl's unwithered face.
    You cross the sea, you are known in the wildest lairs.   740
    Not the immortal gods can fly,
    nor men of a day. Who has you within him is mad.

    You twist the minds of the just. Wrong they pursue and are
      ruined.
    You made this quarrel of kindred before us now.
    Desire looks clear from the eyes of a lovely bride: 745
    power as strong as the founded world.
    For there is the goddess at play with whom no man can fight.

(Antigone is brought from the palace under guard.)

    Now I am carried beyond all bounds.
    My tears will not be checked.

I see Antigone depart   750
    to the chamber where all men sleep.
Antigone: Men of my fathers' land, you see me go
    my last journey. My last sight of the sun,
    then never again. Death who brings all to sleep
    takes me alive to the shore   755
    of the river underground.
    Not for me was the marriage-hymn nor will anyone start the song
    at a wedding of mine. Acheron[6] is my mate.
  Chorus: With praise as your portion you go
    in fame to the vault of the dead.   760
    Untouched by wasting disease,
    not paying the price of the sword,
    of your own motion you go.
    Alone among mortals will you descend
    in life to the house of Death.   765
Antigone: Pitiful was the death that stranger died,
    our queen once, Tantalus'[7] daughter. The rock
    it covered her over, like stubborn ivy it grew.
    Still, as she wastes, the rain
    and snow companion her.   770
    Pouring down from her mourning eyes comes the water that
    soaks the stone.
    My own putting to sleep a god has planned like hers.
  Chorus: God's child and god she was.
    We are born to death.   775
    Yet even in death you will have your fame,
    to have gone like a god to your fate,
    in living and dying alike.
Antigone: Laughter against me now. In the name of our fathers' gods,
    could you not wait till I went? Must affront be thrown in my face? 780
    O city of wealthy men.
    I call upon Dirce's[8] spring,
    I call upon Thebes' grove in the armored plain,
    to be my witnesses, how with no friend's mourning,
    by what decree I go to the fresh-made prison-tomb.   785
    Alive to the place of corpses, an alien still,
    never at home with the living nor with the dead.
  Chorus: You went to the furthest verge
    of daring, but there you found

---

6. Underworld River of Sorrow
7. Niobe, whose boasting drove Apollo and Artemis to kill her 14 children; Niobe was
   transformed into a stone from which a stream of water flowed.
8. For her cruelty to Antiope, a princess of Thebes, Dirce was brutally killed and her body
   thrown into a spring.

the high foundation of justice, and fell. 790
Perhaps you are paying your father's pain.
Antigone: You speak of my darkest thought, my pitiful father's fame,
spread through all the world, and the doom that haunts our
house,
the royal house of Thebes.
My mother's marriage-bed. 795
Destruction where she lay with her husband-son,
my father. These are my parents and I their child.
I go to stay with them. My curse is to die unwed.
My brother, you found your fate when you found your bride,
found it for me as well. Dead, you destroy my life. 800
Chorus: You showed respect for the dead.
So we for you: but power
is not to be thwarted so.
Your self-sufficiency has brought you down.
Antigone: Unwept, no wedding-song, unfriended, now I go 805
the road laid down for me.
No longer shall I see this holy light of the sun.
No friend to bewail my fate.

(Creon enters from the palace.)

Creon: When people sing the dirge for their own deaths
ahead of time, nothing will break them off 810
if they can hope that this will buy delay.
Take her away at once, and open up
the tomb I spoke of. Leave her there alone.
There let her choose: death, or a buried life.
No stain of guilt upon us in this case, 815
but she is exiled from our life on earth.
Antigone: O tomb, O marriage-chamber, hollowed out
house that will watch forever, where I go.
To my own people, who are mostly there;
Persephone has taken them to her. 820
Last of them all, ill-fated past the rest,
shall I descend, before my course is run.
Still when I get there I may hope to find
I come as a dear friend to my dear father,
to you, my mother, and my brother too. 825
All three of you have known my hand in death.
I washed your bodies, dressed them for the grave,
poured out the last libation at the tomb.
Last, Polyneices knows the price I pay
for doing final service to his corpse. 830
And yet the wise will know my choice was right.
Had I had children or their father dead,

I'd let them moulder. I should not have chosen
in such a case to cross the state's decree.
What is the law that lies behind these words?   835
One husband gone, I might have found another,
or a child from a new man in first child's place,
but with my parents hid away in death,
no brother, ever, could spring up for me.
Such was the law by which I honored you.   840
But Creon thought the doing was a crime,
a dreadful daring, brother of my heart.
So now he takes and leads me out by force.
No marriage-bed, no marriage-song for me,
and since no wedding, so no child to rear.   845
I go, without a friend, struck down by fate,
live to the hollow chambers of the dead.
What divine justice have I disobeyed?
Why, in my misery, look to the gods for help?
Can I call any of them my ally?   850
I stand convicted of impiety,
the evidence my pious duty done.
Should the gods think that this is righteousness,
in suffering I'll see my error clear.
But if it is the others who are wrong   855
I wish them no greater punishment than mine.

Chorus: The same tempest of mind
      as ever, controls the girl.
  Creon: Therefore her guards shall regret
      the slowness with which they move.   860
Antigone: That word comes close to death.
  Creon: You are perfectly right in that.
Antigone: O town of my fathers in Thebes' land,
      O gods of our house.
      I am led away at last.   865
      Look, leaders of Thebes,
      I am last of your royal line,
      Look what I suffer, at whose command,
      because I respected the right.

(Antigone is led away. The slow procession should begin during the preceding
passage.)

Chorus: Danaë[9] suffered too.   870
      She went from the light to the brass-built room,

---

9. Danaë was locked in a room by her father so that she could not conceive the son destined
   to kill him. Zeus took the form of a shower to impregnate her.

chamber and tomb together. Like you, poor child,
she was of great descent, and more, she held and kept
the seed of the golden rain which was Zeus.
Fate has terrible power.   875
You cannot escape it by wealth or war.
No fort will keep it out, no ships outrun it.

Remember the angry king,
son of Dryas,[10] who raged at the god and paid,
pent in a rock-walled prison. His bursting wrath   880
slowly went down. As the terror of madness went,
he learned of his frenzied attack on the god.
Fool, he had tried to stop
the dancing women possessed of god,
the fire of Dionysus, the songs and flutes.   885

Where the dark rocks divide
sea from sea in Thrace
is Salmydessus whose savage god
beheld the terrible blinding wounds
dealt to Phineus'[11] sons by their father's wife.   890
Dark the eyes that looked to avenge their mother.
Sharp with her shuttle she struck, and blooded her hands.

Wasting they wept their fate,
settled when they were born
to Cleopatra, unhappy queen.   895
She was a princess too, of an ancient house,
reared in the cave of the wild north wind, her father.
Half a goddess but, child, she suffered like you.

(Enter, from the side, Teiresias, the blind prophet, led by a boy attendant.)

Teiresias: Elders of Thebes, we two have come one road,
two of us looking through one pair of eyes.   900
This is the way of walking for the blind.
 Creon: Teiresias, what news has brought you here?
Teiresias: I'll tell you. You in turn must trust the prophet.
 Creon: I've always been attentive to your counsel.
Teiresias: And therefore you have steered this city straight.   905
 Creon: So I can say how helpful you have been.
Teiresias: But now you are balanced on a razor's edge.
 Creon: What is it? How I shudder at your words!

———

10. Lycurgus; for insulting Bacchus and opposing worship of him, Lycurgus was driven mad
and killed his own son. He was eventually torn to pieces by wild horses.
11. King Phineus divorced and imprisoned his first wife, Cleopatra, in order to marry Idaea.
Idaea then persuaded Phineus that his sons by Cleopatra had violated her, and put their eyes
out.

Teiresias: You'll know, when you hear the signs that I have marked
    I sat where every bird of heaven comes 910
    in my old place of augury, and heard
    bird-cries I'd never known. They screeched about
    goaded by madness, inarticulate.
    I marked that they were tearing one another
    with claws of murder. I could hear the wing-beats. 915
    I was afraid, so straight away I tried
    burnt sacrifice upon the flaming altar.
    No fire caught my offerings. Slimy ooze
    dripped on the ashes, smoked and sputtered there.
    Gall burst its bladder, vanished into vapor; 920
    the fat dripped from the bones and would not burn.
    These are the omens of the rites that failed,
    as my boy here has told me. He's my guide
    as I am guide to others.
    Why has this sickness struck against the state? 925
    Through your decision.
    All of the altars of the town are choked
    with leavings of the dogs and birds; their feast
    was on that fated, fallen Polyneices.
    So the gods will have no offering from us, 930
    not prayer, nor flame of sacrifice. The birds
    will not cry out a sound I can distinguish,
    gorged with the greasy blood of that dead man.
    Think of these things, my son. All men may err
    but error once committed, he's no fool 935
    nor yet unfortunate, who gives up his stiffness
    and cures the trouble he has fallen in.
    Stubbornness and stupidity are twins.
    Yield to the dead. Why goad him where he lies?
    What use to kill the dead a second time? 940
    I speak for your own good. And I am right.
    Learning from a wise counsellor is not pain
    if what he speaks are profitable words.
Creon: Old man, you all, like bowmen at a mark,
    have bent your bows at me. I've had my share 945
    of seers. I've been an item in your accounts.
    Make profit, trade in Lydian silver-gold,
    pure gold of India; that's your chief desire.
    But you will never cover up that corpse.
    Not if the very eagles tear their food 950
    from him, and leave it at the throne of Zeus.
    I wouldn't give him up for burial
    in fear of that pollution. For I know
    no mortal being can pollute the gods.

O old Teiresias, human beings fall;   955
    the clever ones the furthest, when they plead
    a shameful case so well in hope of profit.
Teiresias: Alas!
    What man can tell me, has he thought at all . . .
  Creon: What hackneyed saw is coming from your lips?   960
Teiresias: How better than all wealth is sound good counsel.
  Creon: And so is folly worse than anything.
Teiresias: And you're infected with that same disease.
  Creon: I'm reluctant to be uncivil to a seer . . .
Teiresias: You're that already. You have said I lie.   965
  Creon: Well, the whole crew of seers are money-mad.
Teiresias: And the whole tribe of tyrants grab at gain.
  Creon: Do you realize you are talking to a king?
Teiresias: I know. Who helped you save this town you hold?
  Creon: You're a wise seer, but you love wickedness.   970
Teiresias: You'll bring me to speak the unspeakable, very soon.
  Creon: Well, speak it out. But do not speak for profit.
Teiresias: No, there's no profit in my words for you.
  Creon: You'd better realise that you can't deliver
    my mind, if you should sell it, to the buyer.   975
Teiresias: Know well, the sun will not have rolled its course
    many more days, before you come to give
    corpse for these corpses, child of your own loins.
    For you've confused the upper and lower worlds.
    You sent a life to settle in a tomb;   980
    you keep up here that which belongs below
    the corpse unburied, robbed of its release.
    Not you, nor any god that rules on high
    can claim him now.
    You rob the nether gods of what is theirs.   985
    So the pursuing horrors lie in wait
    to track you down. The Furies sent by Hades[12]
    and by all gods will even you with your victims.
    Now say that I am bribed! At no far time
    shall men and women wail within your house.   990
    And all the cities that you fought in war
    whose sons had burial from wild beasts, or dogs,
    or birds that brought the stench of your great wrong
    back to each hearth, they move against you now.
    A bowman, as you said, I send my shafts,   995
    now you have moved me, straight. You'll feel the wound.

---

12. *Furies:* avenging spirits who punished crimes beyond the reach of human justice; *Hades:*
god of the underworld.

Boy, take me home now. Let him spend his rage
on younger men, and learn to calm his tongue,
and keep a better mind than now he does.

(Exit.)

Chorus: Lord, he has gone. Terrible prophecies!   1000
And since the time when I first grew grey hair
his sayings to the city have been true.
 Creon: I also know this. And my mind is torn.
To yield is dreadful. But to stand against him.
Dreadful to strike my spirit to destruction.   1005
Chorus: Now you must come to counsel, and take advice.
 Creon: What must I do? Speak, and I shall obey.
Chorus: Go free the maiden from that rocky house.
Bury the dead who lies in readiness.
 Creon: This is your counsel? You would have me yield?   1010
Chorus: Quick as you can. The gods move very fast
when they bring ruin on misguided men.
 Creon: How hard, abandonment of my desire.
But I can fight necessity no more.
Chorus: Do it yourself. Leave it to no one else.   1015
 Creon: I'll go at once. Come, followers, to your work.
You that are here round up the other fellows.
Take axes with you, hurry to that place
that overlooks us.
Now my decision has been overturned   1020
shall I, who bound her, set her free myself.
I've come to fear it's best to hold the laws
of old tradition to the end of life.

(Exit.)

Chorus: God of the many names, Semele's golden child,
Child of Olympian thunder, Italy's lord.   1025
Lord of Eleusis, where all men come
to mother Demeter's plain.
Bacchus, who dwell in Thebes,
by Ismenus' running water,
where wild Bacchic women[13] are at home,   1030
on the soil of the dragon seed.

Seen in the glaring flame, high on the double mount,
with the nymphs of Parnassus at play on the hill,
seen by Kastalia's flowing stream.
You come from the ivied heights,   1035

---

13. The Maenads, frenzied devotees of Bacchus.

from green Euboea's shore.
In immortal words we cry
your name, lord, who watch the ways,
the many ways of Thebes.

This is your city, honored beyond the rest,   1040
the town of your mother's miracle-death.
Now, as we wrestle our grim disease,
come with healing step from Parnassus' slope
or over the moaning sea.

Leader in dance of the fire-pulsing stars,   1045
overseer of the voices of night,
child of Zeus, be manifest,
with due companionship of Maenad maids
whose cry is but your name.

(Enter one of those who left with Creon, as messenger.)

Messenger: Neighbors of Cadmus, and Amphion's[14] house,   1050
there is no kind of state in human life
which I now dare to envy or to blame.
Luck sets it straight, and luck she overturns
the happy or unhappy day by day.
No prophecy can deal with men's affairs.   1055
Creon was envied once, as I believe,
for having saved this city from its foes
and having got full power in this land.
He steered it well. And he had noble sons.
Now everything is gone.   1060
Yes, when a man has lost all happiness,
he's not alive. Call him a breathing corpse.
Be very rich at home. Live as a king.
But once your joy has gone, though these are left
they are smoke's shadow to lost happiness.   1065
Chorus: What is the grief of princes that you bring?
Messenger: They're dead. The living are responsible.
Chorus: Who died? Who did the murder? Tell us now.
Messenger: Haemon is gone. One of his kin drew blood.
Chorus: But whose arm struck? His father's or his own?   1070
Messenger: He killed himself. His blood is on his father.
Chorus: Seer, all too true the prophecy you told!
Messenger: This is the state of things. Now make your plans.

---

14. *Cadmus:* founder of Thebes; *Amphion:* son of Antiope who killed Dirce to avenge his
mother. As King of Thebes, Amphion played such beautiful music that he moved stones to
build a wall around the city. Married to Niobe, he took his own life when their children were
killed.

(Enter, from the palace, Eurydice.)

   Chorus: Eurydice is with us now, I see.
         Creon's poor wife. She may have come by chance.   1075
         She may have heard something about her son.
  Eurydice: I heard your talk as I was coming out
         to greet the goddess Pallas with my prayer.
         And as I moved the bolts that held the door
         I heard of my own sorrow.   1080
         I fell back fainting in my women's arms.
         But say again just what the news you bring.
         I, whom you speak to, have known grief before.
Messenger: Dear lady, I was there, and I shall tell,
         leaving out nothing of the true account.   1085
         Why should I make it soft for you with tales
         to prove myself a liar? Truth is right.
         I followed your husband to the plain's far edge,
         where Polyneices' corpse was lying still
         unpitied. The dogs had torn him all apart.   1090
         We prayed the goddess of all journeyings,
         and Pluto, that they turn their wrath to kindness,
         we gave the final purifying bath,
         then burned the poor remains on new-cut boughs,
         and heaped a high mound of his native earth.   1095
         Then turned we to the maiden's rocky bed,
         death's hollow marriage-chamber.
         But, still far off, one of us heard a voice
         in keen lament by that unblest abode.
         He ran and told the master. As Creon came   1100
         he heard confusion crying. He groaned and spoke:
         "Am I a prophet now, and do I tread
         the saddest of all roads I ever trod?
         My son's voice crying! Servants, run up close,
         stand by the tomb and look, push through the crevice   1105
         where we built the pile of rock, right to the entry.
         Find out if that is Haemon's voice I hear
         or if the gods are tricking me indeed."
         We obeyed the order of our mournful master
         In the far corner of the tomb we saw   1110
         her, hanging by the neck, caught in a noose
         of her own linen veiling.
         Haemon embraced her as she hung, and mourned
         his bride's destruction, dead and gone below,
         his father's actions, the unfated marriage.   1115
         When Creon saw him, he groaned terribly,
         and went toward him, and called him with lament:

"What have you done, what plan have you caught up,
what sort of suffering is killing you?
Come out, my child, I do beseech you, come!"   1120
The boy looked at him with his angry eyes,
spat in his face and spoke no further word.
He drew his sword, but as his father ran,
he missed his aim. Then the unhappy boy,
in anger at himself, leant on the blade.   1125
It entered, half its length, into his side.
While he was conscious he embraced the maiden,
holding her gently. Last, he gasped out blood,
red blood on her white cheek.
Corpse on a corpse he lies. He found his marriage.   1130
Its celebration in the halls of Hades.
So he has made it very clear to men
that to reject good counsel is a crime.

(Eurydice returns to the house.)

    Chorus: What do you make of this? The queen has gone
        in silence. We know nothing of her mind.   1135
Messenger: I wonder at her, too. But we can hope
        that she has gone to mourn her son within
        with her own women, not before the town.
        She knows discretion. She will do no wrong.
    Chorus: I am not sure. This muteness may portend   1140
        as great disaster as a loud lament.
Messenger: I will go in and see if some deep plan
        hides in her heart's wild pain. You may be right.
        There can be heavy danger in mute grief.

*(The messenger goes into the house. Creon enters with his followers. They are
carrying Haemon's body on a bier.)*

    Chorus: But look, the king draws near.   1145
        His own hand brings
        the witness of his crime,
        the doom he brought on himself.
    Creon: O crimes of my wicked heart,
        harshness bringing death.   1150
    You see the killer, you see the kin he killed.
    My planning was all unblest.
    Son, you have died too soon.
    Oh, you have gone away
    through my fault, not your own.   1155
    Chorus: You have learned justice, though it comes too late.
    Creon: Yes, I have learned in sorrow. It was a god who struck,

who has weighted my head with disaster; he drove me to wild
    strange ways,
his heavy heel on my joy.
Oh sorrows, sorrows of men.   1160

(Re-enter the messenger, from a side door of the palace.)

Messenger: Master, you hold one sorrow in your hands
    but you have more, stored up inside the house.
   Creon: What further suffering can come on me?
Messenger: Your wife has died. The dead man's mother in deed,
    poor soul, her wounds are fresh.   1165
   Creon: Hades, harbor of all,
    you have destroyed me now.
    Terrible news to hear, horror the tale you tell.
    I was dead, and you kill me again.
    Boy, did I hear you right?   1170
    Did you say the queen was dead,
    slaughter on slaughter heaped?

(The central doors of the palace begin to open.)

   Chorus: Now you can see. Concealment is all over.

(The doors are open, and the corpse of Eurydice is revealed.)

   Creon: My second sorrow is here. Surely no fate remains
    which can strike me again. Just now, I held my son in my arms. 1175
    And now I see her dead.
    Woe for the mother and son.
Messenger: There, by the altar, dying on the sword,
    her eyes fell shut. She wept her older son
    who died before, and this one. Last of all   1180
    she cursed you as the killer of her children.
   Creon: I am mad with fear. Will no one strike
    and kill me with cutting sword?
    Sorrowful, soaked in sorrow to the bone!
Messenger: Yes, for she held you guilty in the death   1185
    of him before you, and the elder dead.
   Creon: How did she die?
Messenger: Struck home at her own heart
    when she had heard of Haemon's suffering.
   Creon: This is my guilt, all mine. I killed you, I say it clear. 1190
    Servants, take me away, out of the sight of men.
    I who am nothing more than nothing now.
   Chorus: Your plan is good—if any good is left.
    Best to cut short our sorrow.
   Creon: Let me go, let me go. May death come quick,   1195
    bringing my final day.
    O let me never see tomorrow's dawn.

Chorus: That is the future's. We must look to now.
    What will be is in other hands than ours.
 Creon: All my desire was in that prayer of mine. 1200
Chorus: Pray not again. No mortal can escape
    the doom prepared for him.
 Creon: Take me away at once, the frantic man who killed
    my son, against my meaning. I cannot rest.
    My life is warped past cure. My fate has struck me down. 1205

(Creon and his attendants enter the house.)

Chorus: Our happiness depends
    on wisdom all the way.
    The gods must have their due.
    Great words by men of pride
    bring greater blows upon them. 1210
    So wisdom comes to the old.

In 1944 the French playwright Jean Anouilh rewrote Sophocles's Antigone. *His version was not a simple translation or adaptation, but a rein-
terpretation of Antigone's story. The passage below is part of a long speech
Creon makes to Antigone soon after she is captured. It gives a sufficient
glimpse of Anouilh's Creon to allow us to see how the character differs from
and conforms to Sophocles's Creon.*

"I stand here with both feet firm on the ground": Jean Anouilh

You come of people for whom the human vestment is a kind of straitjacket:
it cracks at the seams. You spend your lives wriggling to get out of it. Nothing less than a cosy tea party with death and destiny will quench your thirst.
The happiest hour of your father's life came when he listened greedily to
the story of how, unknown to himself, he had killed his own father and
dishonored the bed of his own mother. Drop by drop, word by word, he
drank in the dark story that the gods had destined him first to live and then
to hear. How avidly men and women drink the brew of such a tale when
their names are Oedipus—and Antigone! And it is so simple, afterwards, to
do what your father did, to put out one's eyes and take one's daughter begging on the highways.
    Let me tell you, Antigone: those days are over for Thebes. Thebes
has a right to a king without a past. My name, thank God, is only Creon. I
stand here with both feet firm on the ground; with both hands in my

pockets; and I have decided that so long as I am king—being less ambitious than your father was—I shall merely devote myself to introducing a little order into this absurd kingdom; if that is possible.

Don't think that being a king seems to me romantic. It is my trade; a trade a man has to work at every day; and like every other trade, it isn't all beer and skittles. But since it is my trade, I take it seriously. And if, tomorrow, some wild and bearded messenger walks in from some wild and distant valley—which is what happened to your dad—and tells me that he's not quite sure who my parents were, but thinks that my wife Eurydice is actually my mother, I shall ask him to do me the kindness to go back where he came from; and I shan't let a little matter like that persuade me to order my wife to take a blood test and the police to let me know whether or not my birth certificate was forged. Kings, my girl, have other things to do than to surrender themselves to their private feelings. *[He looks at her and smiles.]* Hand *you* over to be killed! *[He rises, moves to end of table and sits on the top of table.]* I have other plans for you. You're going to marry Haemon; and I want you to fatten up a bit so that you can give him a sturdy boy. Let me assure you that Thebes needs that boy a good deal more than it needs your death. You will go to your room, now, and do as you have been told; and you won't say a word about this to anybody. Don't fret about the guards: I'll see that their mouths are shut. And don't annihilate me with those eyes. I know that you think I am a brute, and I'm sure you must consider me very prosaic. But the fact is, I have always been fond of you, stubborn though you always were. Don't forget that the first doll you ever had came from me.

EURIPIDES

(480–406 B.C.)

MEDEA

translated from the Greek by Rex Warner

CHARACTERS

*Medea, princess of Colchis and wife of
Jason, son of Aeson, king of Iolcus
Two children of Medea and Jason
Creon, king of Corinth
Aegeus, king of Athens
Nurse to Medea
Tutor to Medea's children
Messenger
Chorus of Corinthian Women*

Scene: *In front of Medea's house in Corinth. Enter from the house
Medea's nurse.*

Nurse: How I wish the Argo never had reached the land
      Of Colchis,[1] skimming through the blue Symplegades,
      Nor ever had fallen in the glades of Pelion
      The smitten fir-tree to furnish oars for the hands
      Of heroes who in Pelias' name attempted   5
      The Golden Fleece! For then my mistress Medea
      Would not have sailed for the towers of the land of Iolcus,
      Her heart on fire with passionate love for Jason;
      Nor would she have persuaded the daughters of Pelias
      To kill their father, and now be living here   10
      In Corinth with her husband and children. She gave
      Pleasure to the people of her land of exile,
      And she herself helped Jason in every way.
      This is indeed the greatest salvation of all—
      For the wife not to stand apart from the husband.   15
      But now there's hatred everywhere, Love is diseased.

---

1. In order to obtain his rightful crown from his uncle Pelias, Jason had to sail to Colchis and
   return with the Golden Fleece. With his band of followers, Jason launched from the city of
   Iolcus in his ship, the *Argo.* Arriving at Colchis, Jason persuaded Medea, the king's daughter
   and a sorceress, to help him secure the Fleece. He then married her and the two fled to
   Corinth.

For, deserting his own children and my mistress,
Jason has taken a royal wife to his bed,
The daughter of the ruler of this land, Creon.
And poor Medea is slighted, and cries aloud on the   20
Vows they made to each other, the right hands clasped
In eternal promise. She calls upon the gods to witness
What sort of return Jason has made to her love.
She lies without food and gives herself up to suffering,
Wasting away every moment of the day in tears.   25
So it has gone since she knew herself slighted by him.
Not stirring an eye, not moving her face from the ground,
No more than either a rock or surging sea water
She listens when she is given friendly advice.
Except that sometimes she twists back her white neck and   30
Moans to herself, calling out on her father's name,
And her land, and her home betrayed when she came away with
A man who now is determined to dishonor her.
Poor creature, she has discovered by her sufferings
What it means to one not to have lost one's country.   35
She has turned from the children and does not like to see them.
I am afraid she may think of some dreadful thing,
For her heart is violent. She will never put up with
The treatment she is getting. I know and fear her
Lest she may sharpen a sword and thrust to the heart,   40
Stealing into the palace where the bed is made,
Or even kill the king and the new-wedded groom,
And thus bring a greater misfortune on herself.
She's a strange woman. I know it won't be easy
To make an enemy of her and come off best.   45
But here the children come. They have finished playing.
They have no thought at all of their mother's trouble.
Indeed it is not usual for the young to grieve.

*Enter from the right the slave who is the tutor to Medea's two small children. The
children follow him.*

    Tutor: You old retainer of my mistress' household,
        Why are you standing here all alone in front of the   50
        Gates and moaning to yourself over your misfortune?
        Medea could not wish you to leave her alone.
    Nurse: Old man, and guardian of the children of Jason,
        If one is a good servant, it's a terrible thing
        When one's master's luck is out; it goes to one's heart. 55
        So I myself have got into such a state of grief
        That a longing stole over me to come outside here
        And tell the earth and air of my mistress' sorrows.
    Tutor: Has the poor lady not given up her crying?

Nurse: Given up? She's at the start, not halfway through her tears. 60
Tutor: Poor fool—if I may call my mistress such a name—
How ignorant she is of troble more to come.
Nurse: What do you mean, old man? You needn't fear to speak.
Tutor: Nothing. I take back the words which I used just now.
Nurse: Don't, by your beard, hide this from me, your
fellow-servant. 65
If need be, I'll keep quiet about what you tell me.
Tutor: I heard a person saying, while I myself seemed
Not to be paying attention, when I was at the place
Where the old draught-players sit, by the holy fountain,
That Creon, ruler of the land, intends to drive 70
These children and their mother in exile from Corinth.
But whether what he said is really true or not
I do not know. I pray that it may not be true.
Nurse: And will Jason put up with it that his children
Should suffer so, though he's no friend to their mother? 75
Tutor: Old ties give place to new ones. As for Jason, he
No longer has a feeling for this house of ours.
Nurse: It's black indeed for us, when we add new to old
Sorrows before even the present sky has cleared.
Tutor: But you be silent, and keep all this to yourself. 80
It is not the right time to tell our mistress of it.
Nurse: Do you hear, children, what a father he is to you?
I wish he were dead—but no, he is still my master.
Yet certainly he has proved unkind to his dear ones.
Tutor: What's strange in that? Have you only just discovered 85
That everyone loves himself more than his neighbor?
Some have good reason, others get something out of it.
So Jason neglects his children for the new bride.
Nurse: Go indoors, children. That will be the best thing.
And you, keep them to themselves as much as possible. 90
Don't bring them near their mother in her angry mood
For I've seen her already blazing her eyes at them
As though she meant some mischief and I am sure that
She'll not stop raging until she has struck at someone.
May it be an enemy and not a friend she hurts! 95

Medea is heard inside the house.

Medea: Ah, wretch! Ah, lost in my sufferings,
I wish, I wish I might die.
Nurse: What did I say, dear children? Your mother
Frets her heart and frets it to anger.
Run away quickly into the house, 100
And keep well out of her sight.
Don't go anywhere near, but be careful

Of the wildness and bitter nature
Of that proud mind.
Go now! Run quickly indoors.   105
It is clear that she soon will put lightning
In that cloud of her cries that is rising
With a passion increasing. O, what will she do,
Proud-hearted and not to be checked on her course,
A soul bitten into with wrong?   110

The Tutor takes the children into the house.

  Medea: Ah, I have suffered
What should be wept for bitterly. I hate you,
Children of a hateful mother. I curse you
And your father. Let the whole house crash.
  Nurse: Ah, I pity you, you poor creature.   115
How can your children share in their father's
Wickedness? Why do you hate them? Oh children,
How much I fear that something may happen!
Great people's tempers are terrible, always
Having their own way, seldom checked,   120
Dangerous they shift from mood to mood.
How much better to have been accustomed
To live on equal terms with one's neighbors.
I would like to be safe and grow old in a
Humble way. What is moderate sounds best,   125
Also in practice *is* best for everyone.
Greatness brings no profit to people.
God indeed, when in anger, brings
Greater ruin to great men's houses.

*Enter, on the right, a Chorus of Corinthian women. They have come to inquire
about Medea and to attempt to console her.*

  Chorus: I heard the voice, I heard the cry   131→130
Of Colchis' wretched daughter.
Tell me, mother, is she not yet
At rest? Within the double gates
Of the court I heard her cry. I am sorry
For the sorrow of this home. O, say, what has happened?   135
  Nurse: There is no home. It's over and done with.
Her husband holds fast to his royal wedding,
While she, my mistress, cries out her eyes
There in her room, and takes no warmth from
Any word of any friend.   140
  Medea: O, I wish
That lightning from heaven would split my head open.
Oh, what use have I now for life?

I would find my release in death
And leave hateful existence behind me.   145
Chorus: O God and Earth and Heaven!
Did you hear what a cry was that
Which the sad wife sings?
Poor foolish one, why should you long
For that appalling rest?   150
The final end of death comes fast.
No need to pray for that.
Suppose your man gives honor
To another woman's bed.
It often happens. Don't be hurt.   155
God will be your friend in this.
You must not waste away
Grieving too much for him who shared your bed.
Medea: Great Themis, lady Artemis,[2] behold
The things I suffer, though I made him promise,   160
My hateful husband. I pray that I may see him,
Him and his bride and all their palace shattered
For the wrong they dare to do me without cause.
Oh, my father! Oh, my country! In what dishonor
I left you, killing my own brother for it.   165
Nurse: Do you hear what she says, and how she cries
Oh Themis, the goddess of Promises, and on Zeus,
Whom we believe to be the Keeper of Oaths?
Of this I am sure, that no small thing
Will appease my mistress' anger.   170
Chorus: Will she come into our presence?
Will she listen when we are speaking
To the words we say?
I wish she might relax her rage
And temper of her heart.   175
My willingness to help will never
Be wanting to my friends.
But go inside and bring her
Out of the house to us,
And speak kindly to her: hurry,   180
Before she wrongs her own.
This passion of hers moves to something great.
Nurse: I will, but I doubt if I'll manage
To win my mistress over.
But still I'll attempt it to please you.   185
Such a look she will flash on her servants

---

2. *Themis:* goddess of justice; *Artemis:* goddess of the moon and protector of women

If any comes near with a message,
Like a lioness guarding her cubs.
It is right, I think, to consider
Both stupid and lacking in foresight   190
Those poets of old who wrote songs
For revels and dinners and banquets,
Pleasant sounds for men living at ease;
But none of them all has discovered
How to put to an end with their singing   195
Or musical instruments grief,
Bitter grief, from which death and disaster
Cheat the hopes of a house. Yet how good
If music could cure men of this! But why raise
To no purpose the voice at a banquet? For *there* is   200
Already abundance of pleasure for men
With a joy of its own.

The Nurse goes into the house.

   Chorus: I heard a shriek that is laden with sorrow.
      Shrilling out her hard grief she cries out
      Upon him who betrayed both her bed and her marriage.   205
      Wronged, she calls on the gods,
      On the justice of Zeus, the oath sworn,
      Which brought her away
      To the opposite shore of the Greeks
      Through the gloomy salt straits to the gateway   210
      Of the salty unlimited sea.

Medea, attended by servants, comes out of the house.

   Medea: Women of Corinth, I have come outside to you
      Lest you should be indignant with me; for I know
      That many people are overproud, some when alone,
      And others when in company. And those who live   215
      Quietly, as I do, get a bad reputation.
      For a just judgment is not evident in the eyes
      When a man at first sight hates another, before
      Learning his character, being in no way injured;
      And a foreigner especially must adapt himself.   220
      I'd not approve of even a fellow-countryman
      Who by pride and want of manners offends his neighbors.
      But on me this thing has fallen so unexpectedly,
      It has broken my heart. I am finished. I let go
      All my life's joy. My friends, I only want to die.   225
      It was everything to me to think well of one man,
      And he, my own husband, has turned out wholly vile.
      Of all things which are living and can form a judgment

We women are the most unfortunate creatures.
Firstly, with an excess of wealth it is required   230
For us to buy a husband and take for our bodies
A master; for not to take one is even worse.
And now the question is serious whether we take
A good or bad one; for there is no easy escape
For a woman, nor can she say no to her marriage.   235
She arrives among new modes of behavior and manners,
And needs prophetic power, unless she has learned at home,
How best to manage him who shares the bed with her.
And if we work out all this well and carefully,
And the husband lives with us and lightly bears his yoke,   240
Then life is enviable. If not, I'd rather die.
A man, when he's tired of the company in his home,
Goes out of the house and puts an end to his boredom
And turns to a friend or companion of his own age.
But we are forced to keep our eyes on one alone.   245
What they say of us is that we have a peaceful time
Living at home, while they do the fighting in war.
How wrong they are! I would very much rather stand
Three times in the front of battle than bear one child.
Yet what applies to me does not apply to you.   250
You have a country. Your family home is here.
You enjoy life and the company of your friends.
But I am deserted, a refugee, thought nothing of
By my husband—something he won in a foreign land.
I have no mother or brother, nor any relation   255
With whom I can take refuge in this sea of woe.
This much then is the service I would beg from you:
If I can find the means or devise any scheme
To pay my husband back for what he has done to me—
Him and his father-in-law and the girl who married him—   260
Just to keep silent. For in other ways a woman
Is full of fear, defenseless, dreads the sight of cold
Steel; but, when once she is wronged in the matter of love,
No other soul can hold so many thoughts of blood.
Chorus: This I will promise. You are in the right, Medea,   265
In paying your husband back. I am not surprised at you
For being sad.
But look! I see our King Creon[3]
Approaching. He will tell us of some new plan.

Enter, from the right, Creon, with attendants.

————

3. In ancient Greece, "Creon" was synonymous with "king"; there, the king of Thebes.

Creon: You, with that angry look, so set against your husband,   270
    Medea, I order you to leave my territories
    An exile, and take along with you your two children,
    And not to waste time doing it. It is my decree,
    And I will see it done. I will not return home
    Until you are cast from the boundaries of my land.   275
Medea: Oh, this is the end for me. I am utterly lost.
    Now I am in the full force of the storm of hate
    And have no harbor from ruin to reach easily.
    Yet still, in spite of it all, I'll ask the question:
    What is your reason, Creon, for banishing me?   280
Creon: I am afraid of you—why should I dissemble it?—
    Afraid that you may injure my daughter mortally.
    Many things accumulate to support my feeling.
    You are a clever woman, versed in evil arts,
    And are angry at having lost your husband's love.   285
    I hear that you are threatening, so they tell me,
    To do something against my daughter and Jason
    And me, too. I shall take my precautions first.
    I tell you, I prefer to earn your hatred now
    Than to be soft-hearted and afterward regret it.   290
Medea: This is not the first time, Creon. Often previously
    Through being considered clever I have suffered much.
    A person of sense ought never to have his children
    Brought up to be more clever than the average.
    For, apart from cleverness bringing them no profit,   295
    It will make them objects of envy and ill-will.
    If you put new ideas before the eyes of fools
    They'll think you foolish and worthless into the bargain;
    And if you are thought superior to those who have
    Some reputation for learning, you will become hated.   300
    I have some knowledge myself of how this happens;
    For being clever, I find that some will envy me,
    Others object to me. Yet all my cleverness
    Is not so much.
              Well, then, are you frightened, Creon,   305
    That I should harm you? There is no need. It is not
    My way to transgress the authority of a king.
    How have you injured me? You gave your daughter away
    To the man you wanted. Oh, certainly I hate
    My husband, but you, I think, have acted wisely;   310
    Nor do I grudge it you that your affairs go well.
    May the marriage be a lucky one! Only let me
    Live in this land. For even though I have been wronged,
    I will not raise my voice, but submit to my betters.
Creon: What you say sounds gentle enough. Still in my heart   315

I greatly dread that you are plotting some evil,
And therefore I trust you even less than before.
A sharp-tempered woman, or, for that matter, a man,
Is easier to deal with than the clever type
Who holds her tongue. No. You must go. No need for more   320
Speeches. The thing is fixed. By no manner of means
Shall you, an enemy of mine, stay in my country.

Medea: I beg you. By your knees, by your new-wedded girl.

Creon: Your words are wasted. You will never persuade me.

Medea: Will you drive me out, and give no heed to my prayers?   325

Creon: I will, for I love my family more than you.

Medea: O my country! How bitterly now I remember you!

Creon: I love my country too—next after my children.

Medea: Oh what an evil to men is passionate love!

Creon: That would depend on the luck that goes along with it.   330

Medea: O God, do not forget who is the cause of this!

Creon: Go. It is no use. Spare me the pain of forcing you.

Medea: I'm spared no pain. I lack no pain to be spared me.

Creon: Then you'll be removed by force by one of my men.

Medea: No, Creon, not that! But do listen, I beg you.   335

Creon: Woman, you seem to want to create a disturbance.

Medea: I *will* go into exile. *This* is not what I beg for.

Creon: Why then this violence and clinging to my hand?

Medea: Allow me to remain here just for this one day,
So I may consider where to live in my exile,   340
And look for support for my children, since their father
Chooses to make no kind of provision for them.
Have pity on them! You have children of your own.
It is natural for you to look kindly on them.
For myself I do not mind if I go into exile.   345
It is the children being in trouble that I mind.

Creon: There is nothing tyrannical about my nature,
And by showing mercy I have often been the loser.
Even now I know that I am making a mistake.
All the same you shall have your will. But this I tell you,   350
That if the light of heaven tomorrow shall see you,
You and your children in the confines of my land,
You die. This word I have spoken is firmly fixed.
But now, if you must stay, stay for this day alone.
For in it you can do none of the things I fear.   355

Exit Creon with his attendants.

Chorus: Oh, unfortunate one! Oh, cruel!
Where will you turn? Who will help you?
What house or what land to preserve you
From ill can you find?

Medea, a god has thrown suffering   360
        Upon you in waves of despair.
    Medea: Things have gone badly every way. No doubt of that
        But not these things this far, and don't imagine so.
        There are still trials to come for the new-wedded pair,
        And for their relations pain that will mean something.   365
        Do you think that I would ever have fawned on that man
        Unless I had some end to gain or profit in it?
        I would not even have spoken or touched him with my hands.
        But he has got to such a pitch of foolishness
        That, though he could have made nothing of all my plans   370
        By exiling me, he has given me this one day
        To stay here, and in this I will make dead bodies
        Of three of my enemies—father, the girl, and my husband.
        I have many ways of death which I might suit to them,
        And do not know, friends, which one to take in hand;   375
        Whether to set fire underneath their bridal mansion,
        Or sharpen a sword and thrust it to the heart,
        Stealing into the palace where the bed is made.
        There is just one obstacle to this. If I am caught
        Breaking into the house and scheming against it,   380
        I shall die, and give my enemies cause for laughter.
        It is best to go by the straight road, the one in which
        I am most skilled, and make away with them by poison.
        So be it then.
        And now suppose them dead. What town will receive me?   385
        What friend will offer me a refuge in his land,
        Or the guaranty of his house and save my own life?
        There is none. So I must wait a little time yet,
        And if some sure defense should then appear for me,
        In craft and silence I will set about this murder.   390
        But if my fate should drive me on without help,
        Even though death is certain, I will take the sword
        Myself and kill, and steadfastly advance to crime.
        It shall not be—I swear it by her, my mistress,
        Whom most I honor and have chosen as partner,   395
        Hecate,[4] who dwells in the recesses of my hearth—
        That any man shall be glad to have injured me.
        Bitter I will make their marriage for them and mournful,
        Bitter the alliance and the driving me out of the land.
        Ah, come, Medea, in your plotting and scheming   400
        Leave nothing untried of all those things which you know.
        Go forward to the dreadful act. The test has come

———————

4. Goddess of sorcery and witchcraft.

For resolution. You see how you are treated. Never
Shall you be mocked by Jason's Corinthian wedding,
Whose father was noble, whose grandfather Helius.[5]   405
You have the skill. What is more, you were born a woman,
And women, though most helpless in doing good deeds,
Are of every evil the cleverest of contrivers.
Chorus: Flow backward to your sources, sacred rivers,
And let the world's great order be reversed.   410
It is the thoughts of *men* that are deceitful,
Their pledges that are loose.

Story shall now turn my condition to a fair one,
Women are paid their due.
No more shall evil-sounding fame be theirs.   415

Cease now, you muses of the ancient singers,
To tell the tale of my unfaithfulness;
For not on us did Phoebus,[6] lord of music,
Bestow the lyre's divine
Power, for otherwise I should have sung an answer   420
To the other sex. Long time
Has much to tell of us, and much of them.

You sailed away from your father's home,
With a heart on fire you passed
The double rocks of the sea.   425
And now in a foreign country
You have lost your rest in a widowed bed,
And are driven forth, a refugee
In dishonor from the land.

Good faith has gone, and no more remains   430
In great Greece a sense of shame.
It has flown away to the sky.
No father's house for a haven
Is at hand for you now, and another queen
Of your bed has dispossessed you and   435
Is mistress of your home.

Enter Jason, with attendants.

Jason: This is not the first occasion that I have noticed
How hopeless it is to deal with a stubborn temper.
For, with reasonable submission to our ruler's will,
You might have lived in this land and kept your home.   440
As it is you are going to be exiled for your loose speaking.

———————

5. God of the sun.
6. Phoebus means "bright," the sun personified as well as the epithet of Apollo, the sun god.

Not that I mind myself. You are free to continue
Telling everyone that Jason is a worthless man.
But as to your talk about the king, consider
Yourself most lucky that exile is your punishment.   445
I, for my part, have always tried to calm down
The anger of the king, and wished you to remain.
But you will not give up your folly, continually
Speaking ill of him, and so you are going to be banished.
All the same, and in spite of your conduct, I'll not desert   450
My friends, but have come to make some provision for you,
So that you and the children may not be penniless
Or in need of anything in exile. Certainly
Exile brings many troubles with it. And even
If you hate me, I cannot think badly of you.   455
Medea: O coward in every way—that is what I call you,
With bitterest reproach for your lack of manliness,
You have come, you, my worst enemy, have come to me!
It is not an example of overconfidence
Or of boldness thus to look your friends in the face,   460
Friends you have injured—no, it is the worst of all
Human diseases, shamelessness. But you did well
To come, for I can speak ill of you and lighten
My heart, and you will suffer while you are listening.
And first I will begin from what happened first.   465
I saved your life, and every Greek knows I saved it,
Who was a shipmate of yours aboard the Argo,
When you were sent to control the bulls that breathed fire
And yoke them, and when you would sow that deadly field.
Also that snake, who encircled with his many folds   470
The Golden Fleece and guarded it and never slept,
I killed, and so gave you the safety of the light.
And I myself betrayed my father and my home,
And came with you to Pelias' land of Iolcus.
And then, showing more willingness to help than wisdom,   475
I killed him, Pelias, with a most dreadful death
At his own daughters' hands, and took away your fear.
This is how I behaved to you, you wretched man,
And you forsook me, took another bride to bed,
Though you had children; for, if that had not been,   480
You would have had an excuse for another wedding.
Faith in your word has gone. Indeed, I cannot tell
Whether you think the gods whose names you swore by then
Have ceased to rule and that new standards are set up,
Since you must know you have broken your word to me.   485
O my right hand, and the knees which you often clasped
In supplication, how senselessly I am treated

By this bad man, and how my hopes have missed their mark!
Come, I will share my thoughts as though you were a friend—
You! Can I think that you would ever treat me well?   490
But I will do it, and these questions will make you
Appear the baser. Where am I to go? To my father's?
Him I betrayed and his land when I came with you.
To Pelias' wretched daughters? What a fine welcome
They would prepare for me who murdered their father!   495
For this is my position—hated by my friends
At home, I have, in kindness to you, made enemies
Of others whom there was no need to have injured.
And how happy among Greek women you have made me
On your side for all this! A distinguished husband   500
I have—for breaking promises. When in misery
I am cast out of the land and go into exile,
Quite without friends and all alone with my children,
That will be a fine shame for the new-wedded groom,
For his children to wander as beggars and she who saved him.   505
O God, you have given to mortals a sure method
Of telling the gold that is pure from the counterfeit;
Why is there no mark engraved upon men's bodies,
By which we could know the true ones from the false ones?
Chorus: It is a strange form of anger, difficult to cure,   510
    When two friends turn upon each other in hatred.
  Jason: As for me, it seems I must be no bad speaker.
    But, like a man who has a good grip of the tiller,
    Reef up his sail, and so run away from under
    This mouthing tempest, women, of your bitter tongue.   515
    Since you insist on building up your kindness to me,
    My view is that Cypris[7] was alone responsible
    Of men and gods for the preserving of my life.
    You are clever enough—but really I need not enter
    Into the story of how it was love's inescapable   520
    Power that compelled you to keep my person safe.
    On this I will not go into too much detail.
    In so far as you helped me, you did well enough.
    But on this question of saving me, I can prove
    You have certainly got from me more than you gave.   525
    Firstly, instead of living among barbarians,
    You inhabit a Greek land and understand our ways,
    How to live by law instead of the sweet will of force.
    And all the Greeks considered you a clever woman.
    You were honored for it; while, if you were living at   530

---

7. Aphrodite, goddess of love and beauty.

The ends of the earth, nobody would have heard of you.
For my part, rather than stores of gold in my house
Or power to sing even sweeter songs than Orpheus,[8]
I'd choose the fate that made me a distinguished man.
There is my reply to your story of my labors.   535
Remember it was you who started the argument.
Next for your attack on my wedding with the princess:
Here I will prove that, first, it was a clever move,
Secondly, a wise one, and, finally, that I made it
In your best interests and the children's. Please keep calm.   540
When I arrived here from the land of Iolcus,
Involved, as I was, in every kind of difficulty,
What luckier chance could I have come across than this,
An exile to marry the daughter of the king?
It was not—the point that seems to upset you—that I   545
Grew tired of your bed and felt the need of a new bride;
Nor with any wish to outdo your number of children.
We have enough already. I am quite content.
But—this was the main reason—that we might live well,
And not be short of anything. I know that all   550
A man's friends leave him stone-cold if he becomes poor.
Also that I might bring my children up worthily
Of my position, and, by producing more of them
To be brothers of yours, we would draw the families
Together and all be happy. You need no children.   555
And it pays me to do good to those I have now
By having others. Do you think this a bad plan?
You wouldn't if the love question hadn't upset you.
But you women have got into such a state of mind
That, if your life at night is good, you think you have   560
Everything; but, if in that quarter things go wrong,
You will consider your best and truest interests
Most hateful. It would have been better far for men
To have got their children in some other way, and women
Not to have existed. Then life would have been good.   565
Chorus: Jason, though you have made this speech of yours look well,
        Still I think, even though others do not agree,
        You have betrayed your wife and are acting badly.
Medea: Surely in many ways I hold different views
        From others, for I think that the plausible speaker   570
        Who is a villain deserves the greatest punishment.
        Confident in his tongue's power to adorn evil,
        He stops at nothing. Yet he is not really wise.
        As in your case. There is no need to put on the airs

---

8. Poet and musician whose music moved even inanimate objects.

Of a clever speaker, for one word will lay you flat.   575
  If you were not a coward, you would not have married
  Behind my back, but discussed it with me first.
Jason: And you, no doubt, would have furthered the proposal.
  If I had told you of it, you who even now
  Are incapable of controlling your bitter temper.   580
Medea: It was not that. No, you thought it was not respectable
  As you got on in years to have a foreign wife.
Jason: Make sure of this: it was not because of a woman
  I made the royal alliance in which I now live,
  But, as I said before, I wished to preserve you   585
  And breed a royal progeny to be brothers
  To the children I have now, a sure defense to us.
Medea: Let me have no happy future that brings pain with it,
  Or prosperity which is upsetting to the mind!
Jason: Change your ideas of what you want, and show more sense. 590
  Do not consider painful what is good for you,
  Nor, when you are lucky, think yourself unfortunate.
Medea: You can insult me. You have somewhere to turn to.
  But I shall go from this land into exile, friendless.
Jason: It was what you chose yourself. Don't blame others for it.   595
Medea: And how did I choose it? Did I betray my husband?
Jason: You called down wicked curses on the king's family.
Medea: A curse, that is what I am become to your house too.
Jason: I do not propose to go into all the rest of it;
  But, if you wish for the children or for yourself   600
  In exile to have some of my money to help you,
  Say so, for I am prepared to give with open hand,
  Or to provide you with introductions to my friends
  Who will treat you well. You are a fool if you do not
  Accept this. Cease your anger and you will profit.   605
Medea: I shall never accept the favors of friends of yours,
  Nor take a thing from you, so you need not offer it.
  There is no benefit in the gifts of a bad man.
Jason: Then, in any case, I call the gods to witness that
  I wish to help you and the children in every way,   610
  But you refuse what is good for you. Obstinately
  You push away your friends. You are sure to suffer for it.
Medea: Go! No doubt you hanker for your virginal bride,
  And are guilty of lingering too long out of her house.
  Enjoy your wedding. But perhaps—with the help of God—   615
  You will make the kind of marriage that you will regret.

Jason goes out with his attendants.

Chorus: When love is in excess
  It brings a man no honor
  Nor any worthiness.

But if in moderation Cypris comes,   620
There is no other power at all so gracious.
O goddess, never on me let loose the unerring
Shaft of your bow in the poison of desire.

Let my heart be wise.
It is the gods' best gift.   625
On me let mighty Cypris
Inflict no wordy wars or restless anger
To urge my passion to a different love.
But with discernment may she guide women's weddings,
Honoring most what is peaceful in the bed.   630

O country and home,
Never, never may I be without you,
Living the hopeless life,
Hard to pass through and painful,
Most pitiable of all.   635
Let death first lay me low and death
Free me from this daylight.
There is no sorrow above
The loss of a native land.

I have seen it myself,   640
Do not tell of a secondhand story.
Neither city nor friend
Pitied you when you suffered
The worst of sufferings.
O let him die ungraced whose heart   645
Will not reward his friends,
Who cannot open an honest mind
No friend will he be of mine.

Enter Aegeus, king of Athens, an old friend of Medea.

Aegeus: Medea, greeting! This is the best introduction
       Of which men know for conversation between friends.   650
Medea: Greeting to you too, Aegeus, son of King Pandion.[9]
       Where have you come from to visit this country's soil?
Aegeus: I have just left the ancient oracle of Phoebus.
Medea: And why did you go to earth's prophetic center?
Aegeus: I went to inquire how children might be born to me.   655
Medea: Is it so? Your life still up to this point is childless?
       Yes. By the fate of some power we have no children.
Medea: Have you a wife, or is there none to share your bed?
Aegeus: There is. Yes, I am joined to my wife in marriage.

---

9. King of Athens.

Medea: And what did Phoebus say to you about children?   660
Aegeus: Words too wise for a mere man to guess their meaning.
Medea: It is proper for me to be told the god's reply?
Aegeus: It is. For sure what is needed is cleverness.
Medea: Then what was his message? Tell me, if I may hear.
Aegeus: I am not to loosen the hanging foot of the wine-skin . . .   665
Medea: Until you have done something, or reached some country?
Aegeus: Until I return again to my hearth and house.
Medea: And for what purpose have you journeyed to this land?
Aegeus: There is a man called Pittheus, king of Troezen.
Medea: A son of Pelops,[10] they say, a most righteous man.   670
Aegeus: With him I wish to discuss the reply of the god.
Medea: Yes. He is wise and experienced in such matters.
Aegeus: And to me also the dearest of all my spear-friends.
Medea: Well, I hope you have good luck, and achieve your will.
Aegeus: But why this downcast eye of yours, and this pale cheek?   675
Medea: O Aegeus, my husband has been the worst of all to me.
Aegeus: What do you mean? Say clearly what has caused this grief.
Medea: Jason wrongs me, though I have never injured him.
Aegeus: What has he done? Tell me about it in clearer words.
Medea: He has taken a wife to his house, supplanting me.   680
Aegeus: Surely he would not dare to do a thing like that.
Medea: Be sure he has. Once dear, I now am slighted by him.
Aegeus: Did he fall in love? Or is he tired of your love?
Medea: He was greatly in love, this traitor to his friends.
Aegeus: Then let him go, if, as you say, he is so bad.   685
Medea: A passionate love—for an alliance with the king.
Aegeus: And who gave him his wife? Tell me the rest of it.
Medea: It was Creon, he who rules this land of Corinth.
Aegeus: Indeed, Medea, your grief was understandable.
Medea: I am ruined. And there is more to come: I am banished.   690
Aegeus: Banished? By whom? Here you tell me of a new wrong.
Medea: Creon drives me an exile from the land of Corinth.
Aegeus: Does Jason consent? I cannot approve of this.
Medea: He pretends not to, but he will put up with it.
    Ah, Aegeus, I beg and beseech you, by your beard   695
    And by your knees I am making myself your suppliant,
    Have pity on me, have pity on your poor friend,
    And do not let me go into exile desolate,
    But receive me in your land and at your very hearth.
    So may your love, with God's help, lead to the bearing   700
    Of children, and so may you yourself die happy.

---

10. *Pittheus:* grandfather of Theseus, founder of Athens; *Pelops:* son of Tantalus who killed, boiled, and served his son to the gods at the banquet. Pelops was later restored to life.

You do not know what a chance you have come on here.
I will end your childlessness, and I will make you able
To beget children. The drugs I know can do this.

Aegeus: For many reasons, woman, I am anxious to do   705
This favor for you. First, for the sake of the gods,
And then for the birth of children which you promise,
For in that respect I am entirely at my wits' end.
But this is my position: if you reach my land,
I, being in my rights, will try to befriend you.   710
But this much I must warn you of beforehand:
I shall not agree to take you out of this country;
But if you by yourself can reach my house, then you
Shall stay there safely. To none will I give you up
But from this land you must make your escape yourself,   715
For I do not wish to incur blame from my friends.

Medea: It shall be so. But, if I might have a pledge from you
For this, then I would have from you all I desire.

Aegeus: Do you not trust me? What is it rankles with you?

Medea: I trust you, yes. But the house of Pelias hates me,   720
And so does Creon. If you are bound by this oath,
When they try to drag me from your land, you will not
Abandon me; but if our pact is only words,
With no oath to the gods, you will be lightly armed,
Unable to resist their summons. I am weak,   725
While they have wealth to help them and a royal house.

Aegeus: You show much foresight for such negotiations.
Well, if you will have it so, I will not refuse.
For, both on my side this will be the safest way
To have some excuse to put forward to your enemies,   730
And for you it is more certain. You may name the gods.

Medea: Swear by the plain of Earth, and Helius, father
Of my father, and name together all the gods. . .

Aegeus: That I will act or not act in what way? Speak.

Medea: That you yourself will never cast me from your land,   735
Nor, if any of my enemies should demand me,
Will you, in your life, willingly hand me over.

Aegeus: I swear by the Earth, by the holy light of Helius,
By all the gods, I will abide by this you say.

Medea: Enough. And, if you fail, what shall happen to you?   740

Aegeus: What comes to those who have no regard for heaven.

Medea: Go on your way. Farewell. For I am satisfied.
And I will reach your city as soon as I can,
Having done the deed I have to do and gained my end.

Aegeus goes out.

Chorus: May Hermes, god of travelers,   745
Escort you, Aegeus, to your home!

And may you have the things you wish
So eagerly; for you
Appear to me to be a generous man.

Medea: God, and God's daughter, justice, and light of Helius!   750
Now, friends, has come the time of my triumph over
My enemies, and now my foot is on the road.
Now I am confident they will pay the penalty.
For this man, Aegeus, has been like a harbor to me
In all my plans just where I was most distressed.   755
To him I can fasten the cable of my safety
When I have reached the town and fortress of Pallas.[11]
And now I shall tell to you the whole of my plan.
Listen to these words that are not spoken idly.
I shall send one of my servants to find Jason   760
And request him to come once more into my sight.
And when he comes, the words I'll say will be soft ones.
I'll say that I agree with him, that I approve
The royal wedding he has made, betraying me.
I'll say it was profitable, an excellent idea.   765
But I shall beg that my children may remain here:
Not that I would leave in a country that hates me
Children of mine to feel their enemies' insults,
But that by a trick I may kill the king's daughter.
For I will send the children with gifts in their hands   770
To carry to the bride, so as not to be banished—
A finely woven dress and a golden diadem.
And if she takes them and wears them upon her skin
She and all who touch the girl will die in agony;
Such poison will I lay upon the gifts I send.   775
But there, however, I must leave that account paid.
I weep to think of what a deed I have to do
Next after that; for I shall kill my own children.
My children, there is none who can give them safety.
And when I have ruined the whole of Jason's house,   780
I shall leave the land and flee from the murder of my
Dear children, and I shall have done a dreadful deed.
For it is not bearable to be mocked by enemies.
So it must happen. What profit have I in life?
I have no land, no home, no refuge from my pain.   785
My mistake was made the time I left behind me
My father's house, and trusted the words of a Greek,
Who, with heaven's help, will pay me the price for that.
For those children he had from me he will never
See alive again, nor will he on his new bride   790

_____

11. A shrine in Athens.

Beget another child, for she is to be forced
To die a most terrible death by these my poisons.
Let no one think me a weak one, feeble-spirited,
A stay-at-home, but rather just the opposite,
One who can hurt my enemies and help my friends;   795
For the lives of such persons are most remembered.
Chorus: Since you have shared the knowledge of your plan with us,
I both wish to help you and support the normal
Ways of mankind, and tell you not to do this thing.
Medea: I can do no other thing. It is understandable   800
For you to speak thus. You have not suffered as I have.
Chorus: But can you have the heart to kill your flesh and blood?
Medea: Yes, for this is the best way to wound my husband.
Chorus: And you, too. Of women you will be most unhappy.
Medea: So it must be. No compromise is possible.   805

She turns to the Nurse.

    Go, you, at once, and tell Jason to come to me.
You I employ on all affairs of greatest trust.
Say nothing of these decisions which I have made,
If you love your mistress, if you were born a woman.
Chorus: From of old the children of Erechtheus[12] are   810
Splendid, the sons of blessed gods. They dwell
In Athens' holy and unconquered land,
Where famous Wisdom feeds them and they pass gaily
Always through that most brilliant air where once, they say,
That golden Harmony gave birth to the nine   815
Pure Muses of Pieria.

And beside the sweet flow of Cephisus' stream,
Where Cypris sailed, they say, to draw the water,
And mild soft breezes breathed along her path,
And on her hair were flung the sweet-smelling garlands   820
Of flowers of roses by the Lovers, the companions
Of Wisdom, her escort, the helpers of men
In every kind of excellence.

How then can these holy rivers
Or this holy land love you,   825
Or the city find you a home,
You, who will kill your children,
You, not pure with the rest?
O think of the blow at your children
And think of the blood that you shed.   830
O, over and over I beg you,

---

12. Mythical king of Athens who killed some of his own children to save the city.

By your knees I beg you do not
Be the murderess of your babes!

O where will you find the courage
Or the skill of hand and heart,   835
When you set yourself to attempt
A deed so dreadful to do?
How, when you look upon them,
Can you tearlessly hold the decision
For murder? You will not be able,   840
When your children fall down and implore you,
You will not be able to dip
Steadfast your hand in their blood.

Enter Jason with attendants.

  Jason: I have come at your request. Indeed, although you are
Bitter against me, this you shall have: I will listen   845
To what new thing you want, woman, to get from me.
  Medea: Jason, I beg you to be forgiving toward me
For what I said. It is natural for you to bear with
My temper, since we have had much love together.
I have talked with myself about this and I have   850
Reproached myself. "Fool," I said, "why am I so mad?
Why am I set against those who have planned wisely?
Why make myself an enemy of the authorities
And of my husband, who does the best thing for me
By marrying royalty and having children who   855
Will be as brothers to my own? What is wrong with me?
Let me give up anger, for the gods are kind to me.
Have I not children, and do I not know that we
In exile from our country must be short of friends?"
When I considered this I saw that I had shown   860
Great lack of sense, and that my anger was foolish.
Now I agree with you. I think that you are wise
In having this other wife as well as me, and I
Was mad. I should have helped you in these plans of yours,
Have joined in the wedding, stood by the marriage bed,   865
Have taken pleasure in attendance on your bride.
But we women are what we are—perhaps a little
Worthless; and you men must not be like us in this,
Nor be foolish in return when we are foolish.
Now, I give in, and admit that then I was wrong.   870
I have come to a better understanding now.

She turns toward the house.

Children, come here, my children, come outdoors to us!
Welcome your father with me, and say goodbye to him,

And with your mother, who just now was his enemy,
Join again in making friends with him who loves us.   875

Enter the children, attended by the Tutor.

We have made peace, and all our anger is over.
Take hold of his right hand—O God, I am thinking
Of something which may happen in the secret future.
O children, will you just so, after a long life,
Hold out your loving arms at the grave? O children,   880
How ready to cry I am, how full of foreboding!
I am ending at last this quarrel with your father,
And, look my soft eyes have suddenly filled with tears.

Chorus: And the pale tears have started also in my eyes.
O may the trouble not grow worse than now it is!   885

Jason: I approve of what you say. And I cannot blame you
Even for what you said before. It is natural
For a woman to be wild with her husband when he
Goes in for secret love. But now your mind has turned
To better reasoning. In the end you have come to   890
The right decision, like the clever woman you are.
And of you, children, your father is taking care.
He has made, with God's help, ample provision for you.
For I think that a time will come when you will be
The leading people in Corinth with your brothers.   895
You must grow up. As to the future, your father
And those of the gods who love him will deal with that.
I want to see you, when you have become young men,
Healthy and strong, better men than my enemies.
Medea, why are your eyes all wet with pale tears?   900
Why is your cheek so white and turned away from me?
Are not these words of mine pleasing for you to hear?

Medea: It is nothing. I was thinking about these children.

Jason: You must be cheerful. I shall look after them well.

Medea: I will be. It is not that I distrust your words,   905
But a woman is a frail thing, prone to crying.

Jason: But why then should you grieve so much for these children?

Medea: I am their mother. When you prayed that they might live
I felt unhappy to think that these things will be.
But come, I have said something of the things I meant   910
To say to you, and now I will tell you the rest.
Since it is the king's will to banish me from here—
And for me, too, I know that this is the best thing,
Not to be in your way by living here or in
The king's way, since they think me ill-disposed to them—   915
I then am going into exile from this land;
But do you, so that you may have the care of them,
Beg Creon that the children may not be banished.

Jason: I doubt if I'll succeed, but still I'll attempt it.

Medea: Then you must tell your wife to beg from her father 920
  That the children may be reprieved from banishment.

Jason: I will, and with her I shall certainly succeed.

Medea: If she is like the rest of us women, you will.
  And I, too, will take a hand with you in this business,
  For I will send her some gifts which are far fairer, 925
  I am sure of it, than those which now are in fashion,
  A finely woven dress and a golden diadem,
  And the children shall present them. Quick, let one of you
  Servants bring here to me that beautiful dress.

One of her attendants goes into the house.

  She will be happy not in one way, but in a hundred, 930
  Having so fine a man as you to share her bed,
  And with this beautiful dress which Helius of old,
  My father's father, bestowed on his descendants.

Enter attendant carrying the poisoned dress and diadem.

  There, children, take these wedding presents in your hands.
  Take them to the royal princess, the happy bride, 935
  And give them to her. She will not think little of them.

Jason: No, don't be foolish, and empty your hands of these.
  Do you think the palace is short of dresses to wear?
  Do you think there is no gold there? Keep them, don't give them
  Away. If my wife considers me of any value, 940
  She will think more of me than money, I am sure of it.

Medea: No, let me have my way. They say the gods themselves
  Are moved by gifts, and gold does more with men than words.
  Hers is the luck, her fortune that which god blesses;
  She is young and a princess; but for my children's reprieve 945
  I would give my very life, and not gold only.
  Go children, go together to that rich palace,
  Be suppliants to the new wife of your father,
  My lady, beg her not to let you be banished.
  And give her the dress—for this is of great importance, 950
  That she should take the gift into her hand from yours.
  Go, quick as you can. And bring your mother good news
  By your success of those things which she longs to gain.

Jason goes out with his attendants, followed by the Tutor and the children carrying the poisoned gifts.

Chorus: Now there is no hope left for the children's lives.
  Now there is none. They are walking already to murder. 955
  The bride, poor bride, will accept the curse of the gold,
  Will accept the bright diadem.

Around her yellow hair she will set that dress
Of death with her own hands.

The grace and the perfume and glow of the golden robe   960
Will charm her to put them upon her and wear the wreath,
And now her wedding will be with the dead below,
Into such a trap she will fall,
Poor thing, into such a fate of death and never
Escape from under that curse.   965

You, too, O wretched bridegroom, making your match with
       kings,
You do not see that you bring
Destruction on your children and on her,
Your wife, a fearful death.
Poor soul, what a fall is yours!   970
In your grief, too, I weep, mother of little children,
You who will murder your own,
In vengeance for the loss of married love
Which Jason has betrayed
As he lives with another wife.   975

Enter the Tutor with the children.

   Tutor: Mistress, I tell you that these children are reprieved,
        And the royal bride has been pleased to take in her hands
        Your gifts. In that quarter the children are secure.
        But come,
        Why do you stand confused when you are fortunate?   980
        Why have you turned round with your cheek away from me?
        Are not these words of mine pleasing for you to hear?
Medea: Oh! I am lost!
 Tutor: That word is not in harmony with my tidings.
Medea: I am lost, I am lost!   985
 Tutor: Am I in ignorance telling you
     Of some disaster, and not the good news I thought?
Medea: You have told what you have told. I do not blame you.
 Tutor: Why then this downcast eye, and this weeping of tears?
Medea: Oh, I am forced to weep, old man. The gods and I,   990
     I in a kind of madness, have contrived all this.
 Tutor: Courage! You, too, will be brought home by your children.
Medea: Ah, before that happens I shall bring others home.
 Tutor: Others before you have been parted from their children.
     Mortals must bear in resignation their ill luck.   995
Medea: That is what I shall do. But go inside the house,
     And do for the children your usual daily work.

The Tutor goes into the house. Medea turns to her children.

O children, O my children, you have a city,
You have a home, and you can leave me behind you,
And without your mother you may live there forever. 1000
But I am going into exile to another land
Before I have seen you happy and taken pleasure in you,
Before I have dressed your brides and made your marriage beds
And held up the torch at the ceremony of wedding.
Oh, what a wretch I am in this my self-willed thought! 1005
What was the purpose, children, for which I reared you?
For all my travail and wearing myself away?
They were sterile, those pains I had in the bearing of you.
Oh surely once the hopes in you I had, poor me,
Were high ones: you would look after me in old age, 1010
And when I died would deck me well with your own hands;
A thing which all would have done. Oh but now it is gone,
That lovely thought. For, once I am left without you,
Sad will be the life I'll lead and sorrowful for me.
And you will never see your mother again with 1015
Your dear eyes, gone to another mode of living.
Why, children, do you look upon me with your eyes?
Why do you smile so sweetly that last smile of all?
Oh, Oh, what can I do? My spirit has gone from me,
Friends, when I saw that bright look in the children's eyes. 1020
I cannot bear to do it. I renounce my plans.
I had before. I'll take my children away from
This land. Why should I hurt their father with the pain
They feel, and suffer twice as much of pain myself?
No, no, I will not do it. I renounce my plans. 1025
Ah, what is wrong with me? Do I want to let go
My enemies unhurt and be laughed at for it?
I must face this thing. Oh, but what a weak woman
Even to admit to my mind these soft arguments.
Children, go into the house. And he whom laws forbids 1030
To stand in attendance at my sacrifices,
Let him see to it. I shall not mar my handiwork.
Oh! Oh!
Do not, O my heart, you must not do these things!
Poor heart, let them go, have pity upon the children. 1035
If they live with you in Athens they will cheer you.
No! By Hell's avenging furies it shall not be—
This shall never be, that I should suffer my children
To be the prey of my enemies' insolence.
Every way is it fixed. The bride will not escape. 1040
No, the diadem is now upon her head; and she,
The royal princess, is dying in the dress, I know it.
But—for it is the most dreadful of roads for me

To tread, and them I shall send on a more dreadful still—
I wish to speak to the children.   1045

She calls the children to her.

                                    Come, children, give
Me your hands, give your mother your hands to kiss them.
Oh the dear hands, and O how dear are these lips to me,
And the generous eyes and the bearing of my children!
I wish you happiness, but not here in this world.   1050
What is here your father took. Oh how good to hold you!
How delicate the skin, how sweet the breath of children!
Go, go! I am no longer able, no longer
To look upon you. I am overcome by sorrow.

The children go into the house.

I know indeed what evil I intend to do,   1055
But stronger than all my afterthoughts is my fury,
Fury that brings upon mortals the greatest evils.

She goes out to the right, toward the royal palace.

Chorus: Often before
I have gone through more subtle reasons,
And have come upon questionings greater   1060
Than a woman should strive to search out.
But we too have a goddess to help us
And accompany us into wisdom.
Not all of us. Still you will find
Among many women a few,   1065
And our sex is not without learning.
This I say, that those who have never
Had children, who know nothing of it,
In happiness have the advantage
Over those who are parents.   1070
The childless, who never discover
Whether children turn out as a good thing
Or as something to cause pain, are spared
Many troubles in lacking this knowledge.
And those who have in their homes   1075
The sweet presence of children, I see that their lives
Are all wasted away by their worries.
First they must think how to bring them up well and
How to leave them something to live on.
And then after this whether all their toil   1080
Is for those who will turn out good or bad,
Is still an unanswered question.
And of one more trouble, the last of all,

That is common to mortals I tell.
For suppose you have found them enough for their living,   1085
Suppose that the children have grown into youth
And have turned out good, still, if God so wills it,
Death will away with your children's bodies,
And carry them off into Hades.
What is our profit, then, that for the sake of   1090
Children the gods should pile upon mortals
After all else
This most terrible grief of all?

Enter Medea, from the spectators' right.

  Medea: Friends, I can tell you that for long I have waited
For the event. I stare toward the place from where   1095
The news will come. And now, see one of Jason's servants
Is on his way here, and that labored breath of his
Shows he has tidings for us, and evil tidings.

Enter, also from the right, the Messenger.

Messenger: Medea, you have done such a dreadful thing,
So outrageous, run for your life, take what you can,   1100
A ship to bear you hence or chariot on land.
  Medea: And what is the reason deserves such flight as this?
Messenger: She is dead, only just now, the royal princess,
And Creon dead, too, her father, by your poisons.
  Medea: The finest words you have spoken. Now and hereafter   1105
I shall count you among my benefactors and friends.
Messenger: What! Are you right in the mind? Are you not mad,
Woman? The house of the king is outraged by you.
Do you enjoy it? Not afraid of such doings?
  Medea: To what you say I on my side have something too   1110
To say in answer. Do not be in a hurry, friend,
But speak. How did they die? You will delight me twice
As much again if you say they died in agony.
Messenger: When those two children, born of you, had entered in,
Their father with them, and passed into the bride's house,   1115
We were pleased, we slaves who were distressed by your wrongs.
All through the house we were talking of but one thing,
How you and your husband had made up your quarrel.
Some kissed the children's hands and some their yellow hair,
And I myself was so full of my joy that I   1120
Followed the children into the women's quarters.
Our mistress, whom we honor now instead of you,
Before she noticed that your two children were there,
Was keeping her eye fixed eagerly on Jason.
Afterwards, however, she covered up her eyes,   1125

Her cheek paled, and she turned herself away from him,
So disgusted was she at the children's coming there.
But your husband tried to end the girl's bad temper,
And said "You must not look unkindly on your friends.
Cease to be angry. Turn your head to me again.   1130
Have as your friends the same ones as your husband has.
And take these gifts, and beg your father to reprieve
These children from their exile. Do it for my sake."
She, when she saw the dress, could not restrain herself.
She agreed with all her husband said, and before   1135
He and the children had gone far from the palace,
She took the gorgeous robe and dressed herself in it,
And put the golden crown around her curly locks,
And arranged the set of the hair in a shining mirror,
And smiled at the lifeless image of herself in it.   1140
Then she rose from her chair and walked about the room,
With her gleaming feet stepping most soft and delicate,
All overjoyed with the present. Often and often
She would stretch her foot out straight and look along it.
But after it was a fearful thing to see.   1145
The color of her face changed, and she staggered back,
She ran, and her legs trembled, and she only just
Managed to reach a chair without falling flat down.
An aged woman servant who, I take it, thought
This was some seizure of Pan[13] or another god,   1150
Cried out "God bless us," but that was before she saw
The white foam breaking through her lips and her rolling
The pupils of her eyes and her face all bloodless.
Then she raised a different cry from that "God bless us,"
A huge shriek, and the women ran, one to the king,   1155
One to the newly wedded husband to tell him
What had happened to his bride; and with frequent sound
The whole of the palace rang as they were running.
One walking quickly round the course of a race-track
Would now have turned the bend and be close to the goal,   1160
When she, poor girl, opened her shut and speechless eye,
And with a terrible groan she came to herself.
For a twofold pain was moving up against her.
The wreath of gold that was resting around her head
Let forth a fearful stream of all-devouring fire,   1165
And the finely woven dress your children gave to her,
Was fastening on the unhappy girl's fine flesh.
She leapt up from the chair, and all on fire she ran,

---

13. God of nature known to incite fear among mortals.

Shaking her hair now this way and now that, trying
To hurl the diadem away; but fixedly   1170
The gold preserved its grip, and, when she shook her hair,
Then more and twice as fiercely the fire blazed out.
Till, beaten by her fate, she fell down to the ground,
Hard to be recognized except by a parent.
Neither the setting of her eyes was plain to see,   1175
Nor the shapeliness of her face. From the top of
Her head there oozed out blood and fire mixed together.
Like the drops on pine-bark, so the flesh from her bones
Dropped away, torn by the hidden fang of the poison.
It was a fearful sight; and terror held us all   1180
From touching the corpse. We had learned from what had
    happened.
But her wretched father, knowing nothing of the event,
Came suddenly to the house, and fell upon the corpse,
And at once cried out and folded his arms about her,
And kissed her and spoke to her, saying, "O my poor child,   1185
What heavenly power has so shamefully destroyed you?
And who has set me here like an ancient sepulcher,
Deprived of you? O let me die with you, my child!"
And when he had made an end of his wailing and crying,
Then the old man wished to raise himself to his feet;   1190
But, as the ivy clings to the twigs of the laurel,
So he stuck to the fine dress, and he struggled fearfully.
For he was trying to lift himself to his knee,
And she was pulling him down, and when he tugged hard
He would be ripping his aged flesh from his bones.   1195
At last his life was quenched, and the unhappy man
Gave up the ghost, no longer could hold up his head.
There they lie close, the daughter and the old father,
Dead bodies, an event he prayed for in his tears.
As for your interests, I will say nothing of them,   1200
For you will find your own escape from punishment.
Our human life I think and have thought a shadow,
And I do not fear to say that those who are held
Wise among men and who search the reasons of things
Are those who bring the most sorrow on themselves.   1205
For of mortals there is no one who is happy.
If wealth flows in upon one, one may be perhaps
Luckier than one's neighbor, but still not happy.

exit

    Chorus: Heaven, it seems, on this day has fastened many
            Evils on Jason, and Jason has deserved them.   1210
            Poor girl, the daughter of Creon, how I pity you

And your misfortunes, you who have gone quite away
    To the house of Hades because of marrying Jason.
Medea: Women, my task is fixed: as quickly as I may
    To kill my children, and start away from this land,   1215
    And not, by wasting time, to suffer my children
    To be slain by another hand less kindly to them.
    Force every way will have it they must die, and since
    This must be so, then I, their mother, shall kill them.
    Oh, arm yourself in steel, my heart! Do not hang back   1220
    From doing this fearful and necessary wrong.
    Oh, come, my hand, poor wretched hand, and take the sword,
    Take it, step forward to this bitter starting point,
    And do not be a coward, do not think of them,
    How sweet they are, and how you are their mother. Just for   1225
    This one short day be forgetful of your children,
    Afterward weep; for even though you will kill them,
    They were very dear—Oh, I am an unhappy woman!

With a cry she rushes into the house.

Chorus: O Earth, and the far shining
    Ray of the Sun, look down, look down upon   1230
    This poor lost woman, look, before she raises
    The hand of murder against her flesh and blood.
    Yours was the golden birth from which
    She sprang, and now I fear divine
    Blood may be shed by men.   1235
    O heavenly light, hold back her hand,
    Check her, and drive from out the house
    The bloody Fury raised by fiends of Hell.
    Vain waste, your care of children;
    Was it in vain you bore the babes you loved,   1240
    After you passed the inhospitable strait
    Between the dark blue rocks, Symplegades?
    O wretched one, how has it come,
    This heavy anger on your heart,
    This cruel bloody mind?   1245
    For God from mortals asks a stern
    Price for the stain of kindred blood
    In like disaster falling on their homes.

A cry from one of the children is heard.

Chorus: Do you hear the cry, do you hear the children's cry?
    O you hard heart, O woman fated for evil!   1250
One of the Children (from within):
    What can I do and how escape my mother's hands?

Another child (from within):
> O my dear brother, I cannot tell. We are lost.

Chorus: Shall I enter the house? Oh, surely I should
> Defend the children from murder.

A Child (from within):
> O help us, in God's name, for now we need your help.   1255
> Now, now we are close to it. We are trapped by the sword.

Chorus: O your heart must have been made of rock or steel,
> You who can kill
> With your own hand the fruit of your own womb.
> Of one alone I have heard, one woman alone   1260
> Of those of old who laid her hands on her children,
> Ino, sent mad by heaven when the wife of Zeus
> Drove her out from her home and made her wander;
> And because of the wicked shedding of blood
> Of her own children she threw   1265
> Herself, poor wretch, into the sea and stepped away
> Over the sea-cliff to die with her two children.
> What horror more can be? O women's love,
> So full of trouble,
> How many evils have you caused already!   1270

Enter Jason, with attendants.

Jason: You women, standing close in front of this dwelling,
> Is she, Medea, she who did this dreadful deed,
> Still in the house, or has she run away in flight?
> For she will have to hide herself beneath the earth,
> Or raise herself on wings into the height of air,   1275
> If she wishes to escape the royal vengeance.
> Does she imagine that, having killed our rulers,
> She will herself escape uninjured from this house?
> But I am thinking not so much of her as for
> The children—her the king's friends will make to suffer   1280
> For what she did. So I have come to save the lives
> Of my boys, in case the royal house should harm them
> While taking vengeance for their mother's wicked deed.

Chorus: O Jason, if you but knew how deeply you are
> Involved in sorrow, you would not have spoken so.   1285

Jason: What is it? That she is planning to kill me also?

Chorus: Your children are dead, and by their own mother's hand.

Jason: What! That is it? O woman, you have destroyed me!

Chorus: You must make up your mind your children are no more.

Jason: Where did she kill them? Was it here or in the house?   1290

Chorus: Open the gates and there you will see them murdered.

Jason: Quick as you can unlock the doors, men, and undo

The fastenings and let me see this double evil,
My children dead and her—Oh her I will repay.

*His attendants rush to the door. Medea appears above the house in a chariot drawn
by dragons. She has the dead bodies of her children with her.*

   Medea: Why do you batter these gates and try to unbar them,   1295
          Seeking the corpses and for me who did the deed?
          You may cease your trouble, and, if you have need of me,
          Speak, if you wish. You will never touch me with your hand,
          Such a chariot has Helius, my father's father,
          Given me to defend me from my enemies.   1300
   Jason: You hateful thing, you woman most utterly loathed
          By the gods and me and by all the race of mankind,
          You who have had the heart to raise a sword against
          Your children, you, their mother, and left me childless—
          You have done this, and do you still look at the sun   1305
          And at the earth, after these most fearful doings?
          I wish you dead. Now I see it plain, though at that time
          I did not, when I took you from your foreign home
          And brought you to a Greek house, you, an evil thing,
          A traitress to your father and your native land.   1310
          The gods hurled the avenging curse of yours on me.
          For your own brother you slew at your own hearthside,
          And then came aboard that beautiful ship, the Argo.
          And that was your beginning. When you were married
          To me, your husband, and had borne children to me,   1315
          For the sake of pleasure in the bed you killed them.
          There is no Greek woman who would have dared such deeds,
          Out of all those whom I passed over and chose you
          To marry instead, a bitter destructive match,
          A monster, not a woman, having a nature   1320
          Wilder than that of Scylla[14] in the Tuscan sea.
          Ah! no, not if I had ten thousand words of shame
          Could I sting you. You are naturally so brazen.
          Go, worker in evil, stained with your children's blood.
          For me remains to cry aloud upon my fate,   1325
          Who will get no pleasure from my newly wedded love,
          And the boys whom I begot and brought up, never
          Shall I speak to them alive. Oh, my life is over!
   Medea: Long would be the answer which I might have made to
          These words of yours, if Zeus the father did not know   1330
          How I have treated you and what you did to me.
          No, it was not to be that you should scorn my love,

_____

14. A sea nymph changed into a dangerous rock, facing the whirlpool Charybdis.

And pleasantly live your life through, laughing at me;
Nor would the princess, nor he who offered the match,
Creon, drive me away without paying for it.   1335
So now you may call me a monster, if you wish,
A Scylla housed in the caves of the Tuscan sea.
I too, as I had to, have taken hold of your heart.

Jason: You feel the pain yourself. You share in my sorrow.
Medea: Yes, and my grief is gain when you cannot mock it.   1340
Jason: O children, what a wicked mother she was to you!
Medea: They died from a disease they caught from their father.
Jason: I tell you it was not my hand that destroyed them.
Medea: But it was your insolence, and your virgin wedding.
Jason: And just for the sake of that you chose to kill them.   1345
Medea: Is love so small a pain, do you think, for a woman?
Jason: For a wise one, certainly. But you are wholly evil.
Medea: The children are dead. I say this to make you suffer.
Jason: The children, I think, will bring down curses on you.
Medea: The gods know who was the author of this sorrow.
Jason: Yes, the gods know indeed, they know your loathsome   1350
heart.
Medea: Hate me. But I tire of your barking bitterness.
Jason: And I of yours. It is easier to leave you.
Medea: How then? What shall I do? I long to leave you too.
Jason: Give me the bodies to bury and to mourn them.   1355
Medea: No, that I will not. I will bury them myself,
Bearing them to Hera's[15] temple on the promontory;
So that no enemy may evilly treat them
By tearing up their grave. In this land of Corinth
I shall establish a holy feast and sacrifice   1360
Each year for ever to atone for the blood guilt.
And I myself go to the land of Erechtheus
To dwell in Aegeus' house, the son of Pandion.
While you, as is right, will die without distinction,
Struck on the head by a piece of the Argo's timber,   1365
And you will have seen the bitter end of my love.

Jason: May a Fury for the children's sake destroy you,
And justice, Requitor of blood.
Medea: What heavenly power lends an ear
To a breaker of oaths, a deceiver?   1370
Jason: Oh, I hate you, murderess of children.
Medea: Go to your palace. Bury your bride.
Jason: I go, with two children to mourn for.
Medea: Not yet do you feel it. Wait for the future.

---

15. Wife and sister of Zeus, king of gods.

<pre>
 Jason: Oh, children I loved!   1375
Medea: I loved them, you did not.
 Jason: You loved them, and killed them.
Medea: To make you feel pain.
 Jason: Oh, wretch that I am, how I long
        To kiss the dear lips of my children!   1380
Medea: Now you would speak to them, now you would kiss them.
        Then you rejected them.
 Jason: Let me, I beg you,
        Touch my boys' delicate flesh.
Medea: I will not. Your words are all wasted.   1385
 Jason: O God, do you hear it, this persecution,
        These my sufferings from this hateful
        Woman, this monster, murderess of children?
        Still what I can do that I will do:
        I will lament and cry upon heaven,   1390
        Calling the gods to bear me witness
        How you have killed my boys and prevent me from
        Touching their bodies or giving them burial.
        I wish I had never begot them to see them
        Afterward slaughtered by you.   1395
Chorus: Zeus in Olympus is the overseer
        Of many doings. Many things the gods
        Achieve beyond our judgment. What we thought
        Is not confirmed and what we thought not god
        Contrives. And so it happens in this story.
</pre>

Curtain

*The introduction of the major characters is crucial in establishing the tone
and theme of a play. We can get a clear sense of the effect created by Euripides' introduction of Medea by comparing it to the following fragments of
the opening scenes of Seneca's* Medea *(circa 50 A.D.) and Jean Anouilh's*
Medea *(1946).*

"Ye crime-avenging furies, come": Seneca

Scene:—Before the house of *Jason* in Corinth. The palace of
Creon is near.

ACT ONE

Scene I

(Enter Medea.*)*

> *Medea:* Ye gods of wedlock, thou the nuptial couch's guard,
>   Lucina, thou from whom that tamer of the deep,
>   The Argo's pilot, learned to guide his pristine bark,
>   And Neptune, thou stern ruler of the ocean's depths,
>   And Titan, by whose rays the shining day is born,
>   Thou triformed maiden Hecate, whose conscious beams
>   With splendour shine upon the mystic worshippers—
>   Upon ye all I call, the powers of heaven, the gods
>   By whose divinity false Jason swore; and ye
>   Whose aid Medea may more boldly claim, thou world
>   Of endless night, th' antipodes of heavenly realms,
>   Ye damnéd ghosts, thou lord of hades' dark domain,
>   Whose mistress was with trustier pledge won to thy side—
>   Before ye all this baleful prayer I bring: Be near!
>   Be near! Ye crime-avenging furies, come and loose
>   Your horrid locks with serpent coils entwined, and grasp
>   With bloody hands the smoking torch; be near as once
>   Ye stood in dread array beside my wedding couch.
>   Upon this new-made bride destruction send, and death
>   Upon the king and all the royal line! But he,
>   My husband, may he live to meet some heavier doom;
>   This curse I imprecate upon his head; may he,
>   Through distant lands, in want, in exile wander, scorned
>   And houseless.

"I hate their feast days. I hate their joy": Jean Anouilh

When the curtain rises, Medea *and the* Nurse *are seen squatting on the ground before a wagon. Vague music and singing are heard in the distance. They listen.*

> *Medea:* Do you hear it?
> *Nurse:* What?
> *Medea:* Happiness. Prowling around.
> *Nurse:* They are singing in the village. Today may be a feast day for them.
> *Medea:* I hate their feast days. I hate their joy.
> *Nurse:* It does not concern us. [*A silence.*] At home our feast days came earlier. In June. The girls put flowers in their hair and the boys paint their faces red with their blood, and then in the

small hours of the morning, after the first sacrifices, they begin
to fight. How handsome our Colchis boys look when they fight!

Medea: Be still.

Nurse: Afterward they spend all day taming wild animals. And in
the evening they set large fires before your father's palace—
large yellow bonfires made with herbs that smelled so strongly.
Have you forgotten the fragrance of our native plants, child?

Medea: Be still. Not another word, good woman.

Nurse: Ah, I am old now and the way is so long. . . . Why, why did
we leave, Medea?

Medea [shouts]: We left because I loved Jason, because I stole from
my father for him, because I killed my brother for him! Be still,
good woman. Be still. Do you think it is wise to repeat these
things over and over again?

Nurse: You had a palace with walls of gold and now we squat here
like two beggars before a fire which always dies out.

Medea: Go and fetch some wood.

The Nurse *gets up moaning and walks away.*

WILLIAM SHAKESPEARE

(1564–1616)

TWELFTH NIGHT, or WHAT YOU WILL

edited by G. Blakemore Evans

CHARACTERS

Orsino, Duke of Illyria
Sebastian, brother to Viola
Antonio, a sea captain, friend to Sebastian
Sea Captain, friend to Viola
Valentine ⎫
Curio ⎬ *gentlemen attending on the Duke*
Sir Toby Belch, uncle to Olivia
Sir Andrew Aguecheek
Malvolio, steward to Olivia
Fabian ⎫
Feste, a clown ⎬ *servants to Olivia*

Olivia, a rich countess
Viola, sister to Sebastian
Maria, Olivia's gentlewoman

Lords, Priests, Sailors, Officers, Musicians, Gentlewoman,
    Servant, and other Attendants

Scene: A city in Illyria, and the sea-coast near it.

ACT I

Scene I

Enter Orsino, *Duke of Illyria,* Curio, *and other* Lords: [Musicians *attending*].

    Duke: If music be the food of love, play on,
        Give me excess of it; that surfeiting,

Words and passages enclosed in square brackets in the text above are either emendations of the copy-text or additions to it. The Textual Notes immediately following the play cite the earliest authority for every such change or insertion and supply the reading of the copy-text wherever it is emended in this edition.

I.i. Location: The Duke's palace.   o.s.d. *Illyria:* a country extending along the east coast of the Adriatic, in large part approximating modern Jugoslavia.   1. *music . . . love:* Cf. *Antony and Cleopatra,* II.v. 1–2, "music, moody food / Of us that trade in love." The whole speech is concerned, using a figure of nausea (surfeiting), with the insatiable, but paradoxically quickly sated, quality of love as Orsino here sees it—a kind of glutton that devours dainties only to vomit them up. In a real sense, the play is about a rectification of this view of love.

The appetite may sicken, and so die.
That strain again, it had a dying fall;
O, it came o'er my ear like the sweet sound   5
That breathes upon a bank of violets,
Stealing and giving odor. Enough, no more,
'Tis not so sweet now as it was before.
O spirit of love, how quick and fresh art thou,
That notwithstanding thy capacity   10
Receiveth as the sea, nought enters there,
Of what validity and pitch soe'er,
But falls into abatement and low price
Even in a minute. So full of shapes is fancy
That it alone is high fantastical.   15

Curio: Will you go hunt, my lord?
Duke: What, Curio?
Curio: The hart.
Duke: Why, so I do, the noblest that I have.
O, when mine eyes did see Olivia first,
Methought she purg'd the air of pestilence!
That instant was I turn'd into a hart,   20
And my desires, like fell and cruel hounds,
E'er since pursue me.

Enter Valentine.

                    How now, what news from her?
Valentine: So please my lord, I might not be admitted,
But from her handmaid do return this answer:
The element itself, till seven years' heat,   25
Shall not behold her face at ample view;
But like a cloistress she will veiled walk,
And water once a day her chamber round
With eye-offending brine; all this to season
A brother's dead love, which she would keep fresh   30
And lasting in her sad remembrance.
Duke: O, she that hath a heart of that fine frame

---

3. *appetite:* i.e. love's appetite for music.   4. *fall:* cadence.   9. *quick:* lively, vigorous. *fresh:*
keen.   10. *capacity:* power to take in.   12. *validity:* value. *pitch:* high worth (a term from
falconry, designating the highest point of a hawk's flight; or perhaps *validity and pitch* is better
taken as a hendiadys, meaning "high valuation."   13. *abatement:* depreciation. *price:*
esteem.   14. *shapes:* fanciful forms. *fancy:* love.   15. *it . . . fantastical:* it carries imagination
to unique heights.   16. *hart:* Orsino plays on *heart.*   20–22. *turn'd . . . me:* Alluding to the
story of Actaeon who, having seen Diana naked, was turned into a stag, whereupon his own
hounds hunted him down and killed him.   21. *fell:* fierce.   25. *element:* sky. *heat:* course (?)
or progress of the sun through the zodiac (?).   26. *ample:* unrestricted.   27. *cloistress:*
cloistered nun.   29. *season:* preserve (with play on preserving food in brine).   30. *A brother's*
dead love: a dead brother's love (referring both to her love for him and the memory of his for
her).   32. *frame:* framing, construction.

To pay this debt of love but to a brother,
How will she love when the rich golden shaft
Hath kill'd the flock of all affections else   35
That live in her; when liver, brain, and heart,
These sovereign thrones, are all supplied and fill'd
Her sweet perfections with one self king!
Away before me to sweet beds of flow'rs,
Love-thoughts lie rich when canopied with bow'rs.   *Exeunt.* 40

Scene II

Enter Viola, *a* Captain, *and* Sailors.

   Viola: What country, friends, is this?
Captain: This is Illyria, lady.
   Viola: And what should I do in Illyria?
     My brother he is in Elysium.
     Perchance he is not drown'd—what think you, sailors?   5
Captain: It is perchance that you yourself were saved.
   Viola: O my poor brother! and so perchance may he be.
Captain: True, madam, and to comfort you with chance,
     Assure yourself, after our ship did split,
     When you, and those poor number saved with you,   10
     Hung on our driving boat, I saw your brother,
     Most provident in peril, bind himself
     (Courage and hope both teaching him the practice)
     To a strong mast that liv'd upon the sea;
     Where like [Arion] on the dolphin's back,   15
     I saw him hold acquaintance with the waves
     So long as I could see.
   Viola: For saying so, there's gold.
     Mine own escape unfoldeth to my hope,
     Whereto thy speech serves for authority,   20
     The like of him. Know'st thou this country?

---

34. *golden shaft:* Cupid's gold-tipped arrow, which caused love. He had also a lead-tipped
arrow, which produced loathing.   35. *affections else:* other emotions (than love) (?) or other
loves (?).   36. *liver . . . heart:* The supposed seats of the passions (and especially love),
thought or judgment, and the feelings or sentiments respectively.   37. *supplied:* Synonymous
with *fill'd.*   37–38. *and . . . perfections:* and her sweet perfections filled.   38. *one self king:*
one and the same lord, the person whom she loves wholly.

I.ii. Location: The sea-coast.   4. *Elysium:* i.e. heaven. The classical name is used to play on
Illyria.   5–6. *Perchance . . .perchance:* perhaps . . . by mere chance.   8. *chance:* i.e. a
favorable possibility.   11. *driving:* drifting.   12. *Most provident:* showing great foresight.
14. *liv'd:* i.e. remained afloat.   15. *Arion . . . back:* Arion, a Greek poet and musician, on a
voyage from Sicily to Greece charmed dolphins with his singing and playing on the lyre. When
he leaped overboard to escape murder by the sailors, he was saved by a dolphin on whose
back he rode to shore.   19. *unfoldeth:* discloses.   21. *like of him:* i.e. chance that he escaped
likewise.

Captain: Ay, madam, well, for I was bred and born
          Not three hours' travel from this very place.
    Viola: Who governs here?
Captain: A noble duke, in nature as in name.   25
    Viola: What is his name?
Captain: Orsino.
    Viola: Orsino! I have heard my father name him.
          He was a bachelor then.
Captain: And so is now, or was so very late;   30
          For but a month ago I went from hence,
          And then 'twas fresh in murmur (as you know
          What great ones do, the less will prattle of)
          That he did seek the love of fair Olivia.
    Viola: What's she?   35
Captain: A virtuous maid, the daughter of a count
          That died some twelvemonth since, then leaving her
          In the protection of his son, her brother,
          Who shortly also died; for whose dear love,
          They say, she hath abjur'd the [company]   40
          And [sight] of men.
    Viola: O that I serv'd that lady,
          And might not be delivered to the world
          Till I had made mine own occasion mellow
          What my estate is!
Captain: That were hard to compass,
          Because she will admit no kind of suit,   45
          No, not the Duke's.
    Viola: There is a fair behavior in thee, captain,
          And though that nature with a beauteous wall
          Doth oft close in pollution, yet of thee
          I will believe thou hast a mind that suits   50
          With this thy fair and outward character.
          I prithee (and I'll pay thee bounteously)
          Conceal me what I am, and be my aid
          For such disguise as haply shall become
          The form of my intent. I'll serve this duke;   55
          Thou shalt present me as an eunuch to him,
          It may be worth thy pains; for I can sing
          And speak to him in many sorts of music

---

32. _murmur:_ rumor. 42–44. _might . . . is:_ that my position in life _(estate)_ might not be
revealed to the world until the moment is ripe for me. 44. _compass:_ achieve. 46. _not:_ not
even. 47. _behavior:_ appearance and conduct, the "outward character" of line 51.
54. _become:_ be suitable to. 55. _form . . . intent:_ nature of my purpose (with _form_ in the sense
of "shape" looking back to _disguise,_ line 54). 56. _as an eunuch:_ i.e. as a _castrato_ or male
soprano singer; thus her high voice will not be incongruous with her male disguise. Actually,
Viola becomes his page.

That will allow me very worth his service.
What else may hap, to time I will commit,   60
Only shape thou thy silence to my wit.
Captain: Be you his eunuch, and your mute I'll be;
When my tongue blabs, then let mine eyes not see.
Viola: I thank thee. Lead me on.   *Exeunt.*

Scene III

Enter Sir Toby [Belch] *and* Maria.

Sir Toby: What a plague means my niece to take the death of her
brother thus? I am sure care's an enemy to life.

Maria: By my troth, Sir Toby, you must come in earlier a' nights.
Your cousin, my lady, takes great exceptions to your ill hours.

Sir Toby: Why, let her except before excepted.   5

Maria: Ay, but you must confine yourself within the modest limits
of order.

Sir Toby: Confine? I'll confine myself no finer than I am. These
clothes are good enough to drink in, and so be these boots too;
and they be not, let them hang themselves in their own straps.   10

Maria: That quaffing and drinking will undo you. I heard my lady
talk of it yesterday; and of a foolish knight that you brought in
one night here to be her wooer.

Sir Toby: Who, Sir Andrew Aguecheek?

Maria: Ay, he.   15

Sir Toby: He's as tall a man as any's in Illyria.

Maria: What's that to th' purpose?

Sir Toby: Why, he has three thousand ducats a year.

Maria: Ay, but he'll have but a year in all these ducats. He's a very
fool and a prodigal.   20

Sir Toby: Fie, that you'll say so! He plays o' th' viol-de-gamboys, and
speaks three or four languages word for word without book,
and hath all the good gifts of nature.

Maria: He hath indeed, almost natural; for besides that he's a
fool, he's a great quarreller; and but that he hath the gift of a   25

---

59. *allow . . . service:* cause me to be acknowledged as worthy to serve him.   61. *shape:*
fashion. *wit:* plan, device.   62. *mute:* i.e. silent servant (suggested by *eunuch*, both being
servants in the Turkish court).

I.iii. Location: Olivia's house.   3. *a':* of.   4. *cousin:* kinswoman.   5. *except before excepted:* A
quibble on the legal phrase *exceptis excipiendis* = with the exceptions aforesaid. Sir Toby
apparently means that Olivia's objections are an old story and that she is welcome to go on
making them.   6. *modest:* moderate.   7. *order:* orderly conduct.   8. *confine:* Quibbling on
the sense "dress."   10. *and:* if.   11. *undo you:* be the ruin of you.   14. *Aguecheek:*
Suggestive of a thin, pale face, like that of a man with ague.   16. *tall:* valiant, stalwart.
19. *he'll . . . ducats:* i.e. he'll run through his estate in a year (at the rate he's going). *very:* true,
utter.   21. *viol-de-gamboys: viola da gamba* ("leg-viol"), the bass of the viol family.   22. *without book:* by memory.   24. *almost natural:* almost like a "natural" or halfwit.

coward to allay the gust he hath in quarrelling, 'tis thought
among the prudent he would quickly have the gift of a grave.

Sir Toby: By this hand, they are scoundrels and substractors that say
so of him. Who are they?

Maria: They that add moreov'r, he's drunk nightly in your 30
company.

Sir Toby: With drinking healths to my niece. I'll drink to her as long
as there is a passage in my throat, and drink in Illyria. He's a
coward and a coystrill that will not drink to my niece till his
brains turn o' th' toe like a parish-top. What, wench! *Castiliano* 35
vulgo! for here comes Sir Andrew Agueface.

Enter Sir Andrew [Aguecheek].

Sir Andrew: Sir Toby Belch! How now, Sir Toby Belch?

Sir Toby: Sweet Sir Andrew!

Sir Andrew: Bless you, fair shrew.

Maria: And you too, sir.   40

Sir Toby: Accost, Sir Andrew, accost.

Sir Andrew: What's that?

Sir Toby: My niece's chambermaid.

[Sir Andrew:] Good Mistress Accost, I desire better acquaintance.

Maria: My name is Mary, sir.   45

Sir Andrew: Good Mistress Mary Accost—

Sir Toby: You mistake, knight. "Accost is front her, board her, woo
her, assail her.

Sir Andrew: By my troth, I would not undertake her in this company.
Is that the meaning of "accost"?   50

Maria: Fare you well, gentlemen.

Sir Toby: And thou let part so, Sir Andrew, would thou mightst
never draw sword again.

Sir Andrew: And you part so, mistress, I would I might never draw
sword again. Fair lady, do you think you have fools in hand?   55

Maria: Sir, I have not you by th' hand.

---

26. *gust:* relish, gusto.   28. *substractors:* i.e. detractors.   34. *coystrill:* knave.   35. *parish-top:*
Parishes kept large tops for the amusement and exercise of their people in winter; they were
made to spin by means of whips.   35–36. *Castiliano vulgo:* Meaning uncertain; perhaps
Maria is urged to act with the proverbial gravity and decorum of the Castilians to impress Sir
Andrew.   36. *Agueface:* Perhaps a slip on Shakespeare's part which was later received into
the text as an intentional jest.   41. *Accost:* address (her). Sir Toby's gloss (lines 47–48)
includes the several suggestive connotations of the word.   43. *chambermaid:* lady in waiting.
In a household like Olivia's such a term does not imply low social position. Maria is clearly a
gentle woman.   47. *board:* approach closely (as in boarding a ship in naval warfare.
48. *assail:* i.e. attack with offers of love. Both *board* and *assail* illustrate the common practice
of applying the language of war to amorous activity.   49. *undertake:* have to do (a word
frequently used in a bawdy sense).   52. *And . . . so:* i.e. if you let her go thus.   55. *have . . .
hand:* are dealing with fools.

Sir Andrew: Marry, but you shall have—and here's my hand.

   Maria: Now, sir, thought is free. I pray you bring your hand to th' butt'ry-bar, and let it drink.

Sir Andrew: Wherefore, sweetheart? What's your metaphor?   60

   Maria: It's dry, sir.

Sir Andrew: Why, I think so. I am not such an ass but I can keep my hand dry. But what's your jest?

   Maria: A dry jest, sir.

Sir Andrew: Are you full of them?   65

   Maria: Ay, sir, I have them at my fingers' ends. Marry, now I let go your hand, I am barren.   *Exit Maria.*

   Sir Toby: O knight, thou lack'st a cup of canary. When did I see thee so put down?

Sir Andrew: Never in your life I think, unless you see canary put me   70 down. Methinks sometimes I have no more wit than a Christian or an ordinary man has; but I am a great eater of beef, and I believe that does harm to my wit.

   Sir Toby: No question.

Sir Andrew: And I thought that, I'd forswear it. I'll ride home to- 75 morrow, Sir Toby.

   Sir Toby: *Pourquoi,* my dear knight?

Sir Andrew: What is *"pourquoi"*? Do, or not do? I would I had bestow'd that time in the tongues that I have in fencing, dancing, and bear-baiting. O had I but follow'd the arts!   80

   Sir Toby: Then hadst thou had an excellent head of hair.

Sir Andrew: Why, would that have mended my hair?

   Sir Toby: Past question, for thou seest it will not [curl by] nature.

Sir Andrew: But it becomes [me] well enough, does't not?

   Sir Toby: Excellent, it hangs like flax on a distaff; and I hope to see a 85 huswife take thee between her legs, and spin it off.

Sir Andrew: Faith, I'll home to-morrow, Sir Toby. Your niece will not

---

57. *Marry:* indeed (a weakened oath, "by the Virgin Mary"). *you shall have:* An unfortunate choice of words.   58. *thought is free:* i.e. I may think what I like (proverbial); an unreassuring answer to his question in line 55.   59. *butt'ry-bar:* entrance to the buttery, the room where butts of air and wine were stored and from which drinks were dispensed.   61. *dry:* (1) thirsty; (2) lacking in moisture (a dry hand was associated with age and impotence).   62–63. *I . . . dry:* Alluding to a proverb to the effect that even a fool knows enough to come in out of the rain.   64. *dry jest:* (1) ironic joke; (2) barren old laughingstock.   66. *at . . . ends:* (1) in readiness; (2) held by my hand.   67. *barren:* i.e. destitute of dry jests.   68. *canary:* a sweet wine from the Canary Islands.   69. *put down:* confounded, overcome.   70–71. *put me down:* make me drunk.   73. *I . . . wit:* This reflects a current belief.   75. *forswear:* swear off. 77. *Pourquoi:* why.   79. *bestow'd:* employed. *tongues:* languages.   80. *follow'd the arts:* applied myself to learning.   82. *mended:* improved.   83. *it . . . nature:* Sir Toby's jest takes advantage of the phonetic similarity of *tongues* and *tongs* (= curling-tongs) and of a second meaning of *arts,* "artificial methods."   85. *distaff:* three-foot cleft staff used in spinning wool or flax.   86. *huswife . . . off:* With second meaning involving *huswife* (housewife) in the sense "hussy, whore" and a reference to loss of hair from venereal disease.

be seen, or if she be, it's four to one she'll none of me. The
Count himself here hard by woos her.

Sir Toby: She'll none o' th' Count. She'll not match above her 90
degree, neither in estate, years, nor wit; I have heard her
swear't. Tut, there's life in't, man.

Sir Andrew: I'll stay a month longer. I am a fellow o' th' strangest mind
i' th' world; I delight in masques and revels sometimes
altogether. 95

Sir Toby: Art thou good at these kickshawses, knight?

Sir Andrew: As any man in Illyria, whatsoever he be, under the degree
of my betters, and yet I will not compare with an old man.

Sir Toby: What is thy excellence in a galliard, knight?

Sir Andrew: Faith, I can cut a caper. 100

Sir Toby: And I can cut the mutton to't.

Sir Andrew: And I think I have the back-trick simply as strong as any
man in Illyria.

Sir Toby: Wherefore are these things hid? Wherefore have these
gifts a curtain before 'em? Are they like to take dust, like Mis- 105
tress Mall's picture? Why dost thou not go to church in a galliard, and come home in a coranto? My very walk should be a
jig. I would not so much as make water but in a sink-a-pace.
What dost thou mean? Is it a world to hide virtues in? I did
think by the excellent constitution of thy leg, it was form'd 110
under the star of a galliard.

Sir Andrew: Ay, 'tis strong; and it does indifferent well in a [dun-]-
color'd stock. Shall we [set] about some revels?

Sir Toby: What shall we do else? were we not born under Taurus?

Sir Andrew: Taurus? That['s] sides and heart. 115

Sir Toby: No, sir, it is legs and thighs. Let me see thee caper. Ha,
higher! Ha, ha, excellent! *Exeunt.*

---

89. *hard by:* near by. 90–91. *above her degree:* with her superior. 91. *estate:* social
position. 96. *kickshawses:* elegant trifles (the singular *kickshaws* is an anglicization of French
quelque chose). 97–98. *under . . . betters:* except for those that excel me. 98. *old man:*
experienced man, expert (?). 99. *galliard:* a lively dance in triple time. 100. *cut a caper:*
execute a leap. Sir Toby's reply quibbles on *caper* as a condiment often served with mutton.
102. *back-trick:* steps taken backwards in the galliard. 105. *like:* likely. *take:* gather.
105–106. *Mistress Mall's picture:* A topical allusion has been suspected, but the reference is
probably general (*Mall* = Moll). Pictures were often protected from fading by curtains; see
I.v.198. 107. *coranto:* a quick running dance. *should:* would. 108. *sink-a-pace:* cinquepace
(French *cinque-pas*), a dance resembling the galliard. 109. *virtues:* talents, accomplishments.
There is probably an allusion here to Jesus' parable of the talents (Matthew 25:14-30).
111. *star . . . galliard:* i.e. star favorable to dancing. Cf. Beatrice's "There was a star danc'd,
and under that was I born" (*Much Ado*, II.i.335) 112. *indifferent:* moderately. 113. *stock:*
stocking. 114. *Taurus:* the zodiacal sign that according to a few authorities controls "legs
and thighs" (line 116), but neck and throat according to the majority. 115. *sides and heart:*
Sir Andrew errs as usual; the sign for this region is Leo.

Scene IV

Enter Valentine, *and* Viola *in man's attire.*

Valentine: If the Duke continue these favors towards you, Cesario,
you are like to be much advanc'd; he hath known you but three
days, and already you are no stranger.

Viola: You either fear his humor or my negligence, that you call in
question the continuance of his love. Is he inconstant, sir, in   5
his favors?

Valentine: No, believe me.

Enter Duke, Curio, *and* Attendants.

Viola: I thank you. Here comes the Count.

Duke: Who saw Cesario, ho?

Viola: On your attendance, my lord, here.   10

Duke: Stand you awhile aloof. Cesario,
Thou know'st no less but all. I have unclasp'd
To thee the book even of my secret soul.
Therefore, good youth, address thy gait unto her,
Be not denied access, stand at her doors,   15
And tell them, there thy fixed foot shall grow
Till thou have audience.

Viola: Sure, my noble lord,
If she be so abandon'd to her sorrow
As it is spoke, she never will admit me.

Duke: Be clamorous, and leap all civil bounds,   20
Rather than make unprofited return.

Viola: Say I do speak with her, my lord, what then?

Duke: O then, unfold the passion of my love,
Surprise her with discourse of my dear faith;
It shall become thee well to act my woes: 25
She will attend it better in thy youth
Than in a nuntio's of more grave aspect.

Viola: I think not so, my lord.

Duke: Dear lad, believe it;
For they shall yet belie thy happy years,
That say thou art a man. Diana's lip   30
Is not more smooth and rubious; thy small pipe

I.iv. Location: The Duke's palace.   4. *his humor . . . negligence:* change of mood on his part
or neglect of duty on mine.   10. *On your attendance:* waiting to attend upon you.   11. *you:*
Addressed to all except Viola-Cesario.   14. *address thy gait:* go.   17. *audience:* a hearing (of
the Duke's love-suit).   20. *civil bounds:* i.e. bounds of good manners.   21. *unprofited:*
profitless.   24. *Surprise:* overpower. *dear:* loving, heartfelt.   26. *attend:* heed, give ear to.
27. *nuntio's:* messenger's.   29. *yet:* as yet.   31. *rubious:* ruby-red. *pipe:* throat.

Is as the maiden's organ, shrill and sound,
And all is semblative a woman's part.
I know thy constellation is right apt
For this affair. Some four or five attend him—   35
All, if you will; for I myself am best
When least in company. Prosper well in this,
And thou shalt live as freely as thy lord,
To call his fortunes thine
Viola: I'll do my best
To woo your lady. [*Aside.*] Yet a barful strife!   40
Whoe'er I woo, myself would be his wife.   *Exeunt.*

Scene V

Enter Maria *and* Clown [Feste].

Maria: Nay, either tell me where thou hast been, or I will not open
my lips so wide as a bristle may enter, in way of thy excuse. My
lady will hang thee for thy absence.

Clown: Let her hang me! He that is well hang'd in this world needs
to fear no colors.   5

Maria: Make that good.

Clown: He shall see none to fear.

Maria: A good lenten answer. I can tell thee where that saying
was born, of "I fear no colors."

Clown: Where, good Mistress Mary?   10

Maria: In the wars, and that may you be bold to say in your
foolery.

Clown: Well, God give them wisdom that have it; and those that are
fools, let them use their talents.

Maria: Yet you will be hang'd for being so long absent, or to be   15
turn'd away—is not that as good as a hanging to you?

Clown: Many a good hanging prevents a bad marriage; and for
turning away, let summer bear it out.

Maria: You are resolute then?

Clown: Not so, neither, but I am resolv'd on two points—   20

------

32. *shrill and sound:* high and clear (uncracked).   33. *semblative:* resembling. *part:* role (cf.
act, line 25).   34. *constellation:* i.e. nature (as determined by position of the stars at one's
birth).   38. *freely:* generously.   40. *barful strife:* i.e. an endeavor to which there is (for me) a
serious impediment.

I.v. Location: Olivia's house.   o.s.d. *Feste:* This name is known only from II.iv.11.   5. *fear no
colors:* Proverbial for "fear nothing" (*colors* = worldy deceptions). Feste puns on *collars* =
hangman's nooses.   8. *lenten:* meagre (in wit).   11. *In the wars:* Maria quibbles on *colors* in
the sense "military standards."   14. *talents:* (1) natural abilities; (2) talons (with a pun on *fools /
fowls*).   16. *turn'd away:* With a play on *turned off* = hanged.   17. *for:* as for.   18. *let . . . out:*
let the fact that summer is coming make it endurable.   20. *points:* Maria's rejoinder quibbles
on the sense "laces support the breeches or hose."

Maria: That if one break, the other will hold; or if both break, your gaskins fall.

Clown: Apt, in good faith, very apt. Well, go thy way, if Sir Toby would leave drinking, thou wert as witty a piece of Eve's flesh as any in Illyria. 25

Maria: Peace, you rogue, no more o' that. Here comes my lady. Make your excuse wisely, you were best. *[Exit.]*

Enter Lady Olivia *with* Malvolio *[and* Attendants].

Clown: Wit, and't be thy will, put me into good fooling! Those wits that think they have thee do very oft prove fools; and I that am sure I lack thee, may pass for a wise man. For what says Quina- 30 palus? "Better a witty fool than a foolish wit."—God bless thee, lady!

Olivia: Take the fool away.

Clown: Do you not hear, fellows? Take away the lady.

Olivia: Go to, y' are a dry fool; I'll no more of you. Besides, you 35 grow dishonest.

Clown: Two faults, madonna, that drink and good counsel will amend; for give the dry fool drink, then is the fool not dry; bid the dishonest man mend himself: if he mend, he is no longer dishonest; if he cannot, let the botcher mend him. Any thing 40 that's mended is but patch'd; virtue that transgresses is but patch'd with sin, and sin that amends is but patch'd with vir- tue. If that this simple syllogism will serve, so; if it will not, what remedy? As there is no true cuckold but calamity, so beauty's a flower. The lady bade take away the fool, therefore 45 I say again, take her away.

Olivia: Sir, I bade them take away you.

Clown: Misprision in the highest degree! Lady, "*Cucullus non facit monachum*": that's as much to say as I wear not motley in my brain. Good madonna, give me leave to prove you a fool. 50

Olivia: Can you do it?

---

22. *gaskins:* breeches. 23. *go thy way:* run along. 24–25. *thou . . . Illyria:* i.e. you'd make him a good match. 28. *and't:* if it. *good fooling:* good form for jesting. 29. *thee:* i.e. wit. 30–31. *Quinapalus:* Feste's invention. 35. *Go to:* a conventional phrase of reproof. *dry:* dull, stale. 36. *dishonest:* wanton, wicked. 37. *madonna:* my lady (Italian *mia donna*). 39. *mend:* reform. 40. *let . . . him:* let him be mended by someone who can do the job (*botcher* = one who mends shoes or clothes, a cobbler or a tailor). 41–43. *virtue . . . virtue:* Feste warns that he, like all men, will be imperfect after he reforms, as he was before. *Patch'd* plays on Feste's motley, the conventional parti-colored dress for jesters. 43. *so:* well and good. 44. *what remedy:* i.e. there's nothing more I can say or do. 44–45. *As . . . flower:* A difficult passage. Dover Wilson explains: "Olivia has wedded calamity by taking her vow, and has proved herself a fool, since women are proverbially unfaithful to their weeds and beauty fades like the flower." 48. *Misprision:* mistaking one thing for another. 48–49. *Cucullus . . . monachum:* the cowl does not make the monk.

Clown: Dexteriously, good madonna.

Olivia: Make your proof.

Clown: I must catechize you for it, madonna. Good my mouse of
virtue, answer me.   55

Olivia: Well, sir, for want of other idleness, I'll bide your proof.

Clown: Good madonna, why mourn'st thou?

Olivia: Good fool, for my brother's death.

Clown: I think his soul is in hell, madonna.

Olivia: I know his soul is in heaven, fool.   60

Clown: The more fool, madonna, to mourn for your brother's
soul, being in heaven. Take away the fool, gentlemen.

Olivia: What think you of this fool, Malvolio? doth he not mend?

Malvolio: Yes, and shall do till the pangs of death shake him. Infirmity, that decays the wise, doth ever make the better fool.   65

Clown: God send you, sir, a speedy infirmity, for the better
increasing your folly! Sir Toby will be sworn that I am no fox,
but he will not pass his word for twopence that you are no fool.

Olivia: How say you to that, Malvolio?

Malvolio: I marvel your ladyship takes delight in such a barren ras- 70
cal. I saw him put down the other day with an ordinary fool
that has no more brain than a stone. Look you now, he's out of
his guard already. Unless you laugh and minister occasion to
him, he is gagg'd. I protest I take these wise men that crow so
at these set kind of fools no better than the fools' zanies.   75

Olivia: O, you are sick of self-love, Malvolio, and taste with a distemper'd appetite. To be generous, guiltless, and of free disposition, is to take those things for bird-bolts that you deem
cannon-bullets. There is no slander in an allow'd fool, though
he do nothing but rail; nor no railing in a known discreet man,   80
though he do nothing but reprove.

Clown: Now Mercury indue thee with leasing, for thou speak'st
well of fools!

Enter Maria.

---

52. *Dexteriously:* dexterously (a true variant, not Feste's coinage). 54–55. *Good . . . virtue:*
my good virtuous mouse. The transpositions in *Good my* is common in forms of address (e.g.
good my lord). 56. *other idleness:* any other way of wasting time. 62. *being:* when it is.
63. *mend:* equivalent to "become a better fool"; Olivia uses it in the sense "become a more
amusing fool," Malvolio in the sense "become more and more foolish." 67. *fox:* crafty
fellow. 68. *pass:* pledge. 71. *with:* by. 72–73. *out . . . guard:* without a witty riposte (a
figure from fencing). 73. *minister occasion:* give opportunity, provide openings. 74. *protest:*
declare, avow. 75. *set kind:* artificial sort. *fools' zanies:* fools' fools. A zany (a character in the
commedia dell'arte) was a clown's attendant who aped his master on stage. 76. *of:* with. *self-
love:* The key to Malvolio's character. 76–77. *distemper'd:* unhealthy. 77. *free:* open.
78. *bird-bolts:* blunt-headed arrows for shooting birds. The passage has reference to the
proverb "A fool's bolt is soon shot." 79. *allow'd:* given license to speak his mind.
80. *known discreet:* of recognized judgment. 82. *Mercury:* god of guile and trickery. *leasing:*
lying.

Maria: Madam, there is at the gate a young gentleman much
  desires to speak with you.   85
Olivia: From the Count Orsino, is it?
Maria: I know not, madam. 'Tis a fair young man, and well
  attended.
Olivia: Who of my people hold him in delay?
Maria: Sir Toby, madam, your kinsman.   90
Olivia: Fetch him off, I pray you, he speaks nothing but madman;
  fie on him! [*Exit Maria.*] Go you, Malvolio; if it be a suit from
  the Count, I am sick, or not at home—what you will, to dismiss
  it. (*Exit Malvolio.*) Now you see, sir, how your fooling grows
  old, and people dislike it.   95
Clown: Thou hast spoke for us, madonna, as if thy eldest son
  should be a fool; whose skull Jove cram with brains! for—here
  he comes—one of thy kin has a most weak *pia mater.*

Enter Sir Toby.

Olivia: By mine honor, half drunk. What is he at the gate, cousin?
Sir Toby: A gentleman.   100
Olivia: A gentleman? What gentleman?
Sir Toby: 'Tis a gentleman here—a plague o' these pickle-herring!
  How now, sot?
Clown: Good Sir Toby!
Olivia: Cousin, cousin, how have you come so early by this   105
  lethargy?
Sir Toby: Lechery! I defy lechery. There's one at the gate.
Olivia: Ay, marry, what is he?
Sir Toby: Let him be the devil and he will, I care not; give me faith
  say I. Well, it's all one.   *Exit.* 110
Olivia: What's a drunken man like, fool?
Clown: Like a drown'd man, a fool, and a madman. One draught
  above heat makes him a fool, the second mads him, and a third
  drowns him.
Olivia: Go thou and seek the crowner, and let him sit o' my coz;   115
  for he's in the third degree of drink, he's drown'd. Go look
  after him.
Clown: He is but mad yet, madonna, and the fool shall look to the
  madman.   [*Exit.*]

Enter Malvolio.

---

91. *madman:* i.e. mad talk.   95. *old:* i.e. stale (cf. line 35).   98. *pia mater:* brain (properly,
the membrane enveloping the brain).   99. *What:* what sort of man.   102. *a plague . . .
pickle-herring:* Sir Toby thus excuses a belch.   103. *sot:* fool.   106. *lethargy:* stupor.
109. *give me faith:* As protection in confrontation with the devil.   110. *it's all one:* no matter.   113. *above heat:* i.e. above the point of feeling a pleasant warmth.   115. *crowner:*
coroner. *sit . . . coz:* i.e. hold an inquest on my kinsman.

Malvolio: Madam, yond young fellow swears he will speak with you.   120
I told him you were sick; he takes on him to understand so
much, and therefore comes to speak with you.   I told him you
were asleep; he seems to have a foreknowledge of that too, and
therefore comes to speak with you.   What is to be said to him,
lady? he's fortified against any denial.   125

Olivia: Tell him he shall not speak with me.

Malvolio: H'as been told so; and he says he'll stand at your door like a
sheriff's post, and be the supporter to a bench, but he'll speak
with you.

Olivia: What kind o' man is he?   130

Malvolio: Why, of mankind.

Olivia: What manner of man?

Malvolio: Of very ill manner: he'll speak with you, will you or no.

Olivia: Of what personage and years is he?

Malvolio: Not yet old enough for a man, nor young enough for a boy;   135
as a squash is before 'tis a peascod, or a codling when 'tis
almost an apple.   'Tis with him in standing water, between boy
and man.   He is very well-favor'd, and he speaks very shrewishly.   One would think his mother's milk were scarce out of him.

Olivia: Let him approach.   Call in my gentlewoman.   140

Malvolio: Gentlewoman, my lady calls.   *Exit.*

Enter Maria.

Olivia: Give me my veil; come throw it o'er my face.
We'll once more hear Orsino's embassy.

Enter [Viola].

Viola: The honorable lady of the house, which is she?

Olivia: Speak to me, I shall answer for her.   Your will?   145

Viola: Most radiant, exquisite, and unmatchable beauty—I pray
you tell me if this be the lady of the house, for I never saw her.
I would be loath to cast away my speech; for besides that it is
excellently well penn'd, I have taken great pains to con it.
Good beauties, let me sustain no scorn; I am very comptible,   150
even to the least sinister usage.

Olivia: Whence came you, sir?

Viola: I can say little more than I have studied, and that ques-

---

122. *therefore:* for that very reason.   127. *H'as:* he has.   128. *sheriff's post:* a decorative post
set up outside the sheriff's office.   131. *of mankind:* of the human race, i.e. just an ordinary
man.   134. *personage:* physical appearance.   136. *squash:* unripe pea pod.   *peascod:* pea
pod.   *codling:* unripe apple.   137. *in standing water:* i.e. at the turn of the tide.   138. *well-
favor'd:* handsome.   138–39. *shrewishly:* ill-temperedly, sharply.   148. *cast away:* waste (by
delivering it to the wrong person).   149. *con:* memorize.   150. *comptible:* sensitive,
susceptible.   151. *least sinister usage:* slightest uncivil treatment.

tion's out of my part. Good gentle one, give me modest assurance if you be the lady of the house, that I may proceed in my 155
speech.

Olivia: Are you a comedian?

Viola: No, my profound heart; and yet (by the very fangs of malice I swear) I am not that I play. Are you the lady of the house?

Olivia: If I do not usurp myself, I am. 160

Viola: Most certain, if you are she, you do usurp yourself; for
what is yours to bestow is not yours to reserve. But this is from
my commission; I will on with my speech in your praise, and
then show you the heart of my message.

Olivia: Come to what is important in't. I forgive you the praise. 165

Viola: Alas, I took great pains to study it, and 'tis poetical.

Olivia: It is the more like to be feign'd, I pray you keep it in. I
heard you were saucy at my gates, and allow'd your approach
rather to wonder at you than to hear you. If you be not mad,
be gone. If you have reason, be brief. 'Tis not that time of 170
moon with me to make one in so skipping a dialogue.

Maria: Will you hoist sail, sir? Here lies your way.

Viola: No, good swabber, I am to hull here a little longer. Some
mollification for your giant, sweet lady. Tell me your mind—I
am a messenger. 175

Olivia: Sure you have some hideous matter to deliver, when the
courtesy of it is so fearful. Speak your office.

Viola: It alone concerns your ear. I bring no overture of war, no
taxation of homage; I hold the olive in my hand; my words are
as full of peace as matter. 180

Olivia: Yet you began rudely. What are you? What would you?

Viola: The rudeness that hath appear'd in me have I learn'd from
my entertainment. What I am, and what I would, are as secret
as maidenhead: to your ears, divinity; to any other's,
profanation. 185

---

154. *out . . . part:* not in my lines. *modest:* befitting. 157. *comedian:* actor (continuing the
theatrical metaphor of line 154). 158. *my profound heart:* my very wise lady (?). 160. *do . . .
myself:* am not an impostor. 161. *usurp yourself:* possess yourself wrongfully (by refusing to
give yourself to a husband). 162–63. *from my commission:* i.e. beyond my instructions.
165. *forgive you:* excuse you from. 167. *keep it in:* do not utter it. 169. *not mad:* i.e. not
utterly mad (?). Some editors emend to *but mad* (Staunton conjecture). 170. *reason:* your
wits. 170–71. *time of moon:* Certain phases of the moon were supposed to have a bad
influence, particularly on lunacy. 171. *make one:* take part. *skipping:* flighty. 173. *swabber:*
Continuing Maria's nautical metaphor. A swabber was a petty officer charged with keeping
the decks clean. *hull:* drift with sails furled. 174. *mollification:* appeasement. *your giant:*
Referring ironically to Maria, who is apparently diminutive (see II.v.11, III.ii.56), and
alluding to giants as guardians of ladies in romantic tales. *Tell . . . mind:* Assigned by many
editors (following Warburton) to Olivia. 176–77. *when . . . fearful:* i.e. when what should be
the courteous manner of its introduction is so threatening (?). 177. *office:* business.
179. *taxation of homage:* demand for tribute. 180. *matter:* significant meaning. 183. *entertainment:* manner of reception. 184. *maidenhead:* virginity.

Olivia: Give us the place alone, we will hear this divinity. [*Exeunt
    Maria and Attendants.*] Now, sir, what is your text?
  Viola: Most sweet lady—
Olivia: A comfortable doctrine, and much may be said of it.
    Where lies your text?   190
  Viola: In Orsino's bosom.
Olivia: In his bosom? In what chapter of his bosom?
  Viola: To answer by the method, in the first of his heart.
Olivia: O, I have read it; it is heresy. Have you no more to say?
  Viola: Good madam, let me see your face.   195
Olivia: Have you any commission from your lord to negotiate with
    my face? You are now out of your text; but we will draw the
    curtain, and show you the picture. Look you, sir, such a one I
    was this present. [*Unveiling.*] Is't not well done?
  Viola: Excellently done, if God did all.   200
Olivia: 'Tis in grain, sir, 'twill endure wind and weather.
  Viola: 'Tis beauty truly blent, whose red and white Nature's own
    sweet and cunning hand laid on.
      Lady, you are the cruell'st she alive
      If you will lead these graces to the grave,   205
      And leave the world no copy.
Olivia: O, sir, I will not be so hard-hearted. I will give out divers
    schedules of my beauty. It shall be inventoried, and every par-
    ticle and utensil labell'd to my will: as *item,* two lips, indifferent
    red; *item,* two grey eyes, with lids to them; *item,* one neck, one 210
    chin, and so forth. Were you sent hither to praise me?
  Viola: I see you what you are, you are too proud;
      But if you were the devil, you are fair.
      My lord and master loves you. O, such love
      Could be but recompens'd, though you were crown'd   215
      The nonpareil of beauty.
Olivia: How does he love me?

---

187. *what . . . text:* Picking up *divinity* (line 184), Olivia suggests that Viola-Cesario is going to
proceed like a preacher in setting forth the text of a sermon. She continues this figure, with
Viola's coorporation, through line 194.   189. *comfortable:* full of comfort.   193. *by the
method:* according to the accepted form in beginning a sermon.   197. *out of:* wandering
from.   198–99. *such . . . present:* Olivia begins as if displaying a portrait of herself painted at
an earlier time, then ends with "at the present time" *(this present).*   200. *if . . . all:* if it is all
natural (unaided by cosmetics).   201. *'Tis in grain:* it is fast-dyed, i.e. it won't wash off.
202. *blent:* blended.   203. *cunning:* skilled.   204–206. *Lady . . . copy:* Reminiscent of the
argument in Shakespeare's first seventeen sonnets.   204. *she:* woman.   206. *copy:* i.e. a
child inheriting your beauty. Olivia plays on the sense "transcript, record."   208. *schedules:*
itemized lists, inventories.   208–209. *particle and utensil:* particular and item.   209. *labell'd:*
attached. *item:* a term (= also) usually preceding each item after the first (signalled by
imprimis = in the first place) in a list, but sometimes, as here, preceding the first as well. *indifferent:* moderately.   211. *praise:* With a quibble on "appraise."   213. *if:* even if. *the devil:*
The supreme example of pride.   215. *Could . . . though:* could be no more than evenly repaid
even though.   216. *nonpareil:* one that has no equal.

Viola: With adorations, fertile tears,
　　With groans that thunder love, with sighs of fire.
Olivia: Your lord does know my mind, I cannot love him,
　　Yet I suppose him virtuous, know him noble,　　　　　　　　　220
　　Of great estate, of fresh and stainless youth;
　　In voices well divulg'd, free, learn'd, and valiant,
　　And in dimension, and the shape of nature,
　　A gracious person. But yet I cannot love him.
　　He might have took his answer long ago.　　　　　　　　　　　225
Viola: If I did love you in my master's flame,
　　With such a suff'ring, such a deadly life,
　　In your denial I would find no sense,
　　I would not understand it.
Olivia:　　　　　　　　　　　　　　Why, what would you?
Viola: Make me a willow cabin at your gate,　　　　　　　　　230
　　And call upon my soul within the house;
　　Write loyal cantons of contemned love,
　　And sing them loud even in the dead of night;
　　Hallow your name to the reverberate hills,
　　And make the babbling gossip of the air　　　　　　　　　　235
　　Cry out "Olivia!" O, you should not rest
　　Between the elements of air and earth
　　But you should pity me!
Olivia:　　　　　　　　　　　　You might do much.
　　What is your parentage?
Viola: Above my fortunes, yet my state is well:　　　　　　　240
　　I am a gentleman.
Olivia:　　　　　　　　　　　Get you to your lord.
　　I cannot love him; let him send no more—
　　Unless (perchance) you come to me again
　　To tell me how he takes it. Fare you well.
　　I thank you for your pains. Spend this for me.　　　　　　　245
Viola: I am no fee'd post, lady; keep your purse;
　　My master, not myself, lacks recompense.
　　Love make his heart of flint that you shall love,
　　And let your fervor like my master's be
　　Plac'd in contempt! Farewell, fair cruelty.　　　　　*Exit.*　250

---

217. *fertile:* abundant, ever-flowing.　221. *stainless:* unstained.　222. *In . . . divulg'd:* well
reputed by general opinion (*voices*).　223. *dimension . . . nature:* form and physique.
224. *gracious person:* pleasing figure of a man.　226. *flame:* passion.　227. *deadly:* death-
like.　230. *willow cabin:* hut of willow boughs. Willow was the symbol of unrequited love.
231. *my soul:* i.e. Olivia.　232. *cantons:* cantos, songs. *contemned:* despised, scornfully
rejected.　234. *Hallow:* halloo, shout. *reverberate:* resounding.　235. *babbling . . . air:* echo.
237. *Between . . . earth:* i.e. anywhere on the face of the earth.　238. *But:* but that.
240. *state:* condition.　246. *fee'd post:* messenger who should be tipped.　248. *Love . . . love:*
may love give a heart of flint to the man you fall in love with.　250. *cruelty:* cruel person.

Olivia: "What is your parentage?"
    "Above my fortunes, yet my state is well:
    I am a gentleman." I'll be sworn thou art;
    Thy tongue, thy face, thy limbs, actions, and spirit
    Do give thee fivefold blazon. Not too fast! soft, soft!   255
    Unless the master were the man. How now?
    Even so quickly may one catch the plague?
    Methinks I feel this youth's perfections
    With an invisible and subtle stealth
    To creep in at mine eyes. Well, let it be.   260
    What ho, Malvolio!

Enter Malvolio.

Malvolio: Here, madam, at your service.
  Olivia: Run after that same peevish messenger,
    The [County's] man. He left this ring behind him,
    Would I or not. Tell him I'll none of it.
    Desire him not to flatter with his lord,   265
    Nor hold him up with hopes: I am not for him.
    If that the youth will come this way to-morrow,
    I'll give him reasons for't. Hie thee, Malvolio.
Malvolio: Madam, I will.   *Exit.*
  Olivia: I do I know not what, and fear to find   270
    Mine eye too great a flatterer for my mind.
    Fate, show thy force: ourselves we do not owe;
    What is decreed must be; and be this so.   *[Exit.]*

ACT II

Scene I

Enter Antonio *and* Sebastian.

  Antonio: Will you stay no longer? nor will you not that I go with you?
  Sebastian: By your patience, no. My stars shine darkly over me. The
    malignancy of my fate might perhaps distemper yours; there-
    fore I shall crave of you your leave, that I may bear my evils

---

255. *give . . . blazon:* i.e. proclaim you a gentleman five times over as surely as if they were coats of arms. A blazon is a heraldic description of armorial bearings. *soft:* stay.
260. *creep . . .eyes:* It was a conventional idea that love entered through the eyes.   262. *peevish:* pettish, childish.   263. *County's:* Count's, i.e. Duke's.   265. *flatter with:* encourage. 268. Hie: hasten.   270–71. *fear . . .mind:* am afraid I shall find that my eyes (i.e. senses) have seduced my mind.   272. *owe:* own, control.
II.i. Location: The sea-coast.   2. *patience:* sufferance.   3. *malignancy:* virulent condition, (1) in its medical sense = deadly contagion, (2) in its astrological sense = evil stellar influence. *distemper:* infect.

alone. It were a bad recompense for your love, to lay any of 5
them on you.

Antonio: Let me yet know of you whither you are bound.

Sebastian: No, sooth, sir; my determinate voyage is mere extravagancy. But I perceive in you so excellent a touch of modesty,
that you will not extort from me what I am willing to keep in; 10
therefore it charges me in manners the rather to express
myself. You must know of me then, Antonio, my name is Sebastian, which I call'd Rodorigo; my father was that Sebastian of
Messaline, whom I know you have heard of. He left behind him
myself and a sister, both born in an hour. If the heavens had 15
been pleas'd, would we had so ended! But you, sir, alter'd that,
for some hour before you took me from the breach of the sea
was my sister drown'd.

Antonio: Alas the day!

Sebastian: A lady, sir, though it was said she much resembled me, was 20
yet of many accounted beautiful; but though I could not with
such estimable wonder overfar believe that, yet thus far I will
boldly publish her: she bore a mind that envy could not but call
fair. She is drown'd already, sir, with salt water, though I seem
to drown her remembrance again with more. 25

Antonio: Pardon me, sir, your bad entertainment.

Sebastian: O good Antonio, forgive me your trouble.

Antonio: If you will not murther me for my love, let me be your
servant.

Sebastian: If you will not undo what you have done, that is, kill him 30
whom you have recover'd, desire it not. Fare ye well at once;
my bosom is full of kindness, and I am yet so near the manners
of my mother, that upon the least occasion more mine eyes will
tell tales of me. I am bound to the Count Orsino's court.
Farewell. *Exit.* 35

Antonio: The gentleness of all the gods go with thee!
I have many enemies in Orsino's court,
Else would I very shortly see thee there.
But come what may, I do adore thee so
That danger shall seem sport, and I will go. *Exit.* 40

---

8. *sooth:* truly (shortened form of *in sooth*). *determinate:* intended. 8–9. *mere extravagancy:*
utter vagabondage. 9. *touch:* feeling. 10. *willing . . . in:* desirous of keeping secret.
11. *it charges me:* it is incumbent on me. *in manners:* by the requirements of good manners, in
courtesy. 14. *Messaline:* Not identified. 15. *in an hour:* within the same hour.
17. *breach . . . sea:* breaking waves, surf. 22. *such estimable wonder:* estimation reflecting so
much admiration. 23. *publish:* proclaim. *envy:* i.e. even malice. 26. *your bad entertainment:*
the humble hospitality I have offered you. 28. *murther me:* i.e. be the cause of my death.
31. *recover'd:* rescued. 32. *kindness:* natural feeling, i.e. a brother's grief. 32–33. *yet . . .
mother:* i.e. still so newly a man. Such apologies by men for womanish tears are numerous in
Shakespeare.

Scene II

Enter Viola *and* Malvolio *at several doors.*

Malvolio: Were you not ev'n now with the Countess Olivia?

Viola: Even now, sir; on a moderate pace I have since arriv'd but
  hither.

Malvolio: She returns this ring to you, sir. You might have sav'd me
  my pains, to have taken it away yourself. She adds moreover, 5
  that you should put your lord into a desperate assurance she
  will none of him. And one thing more, that you be never so
  hardy to come again in his affairs, unless it be to report your
  lord's taking of this. Receive it so.

Viola: She took the ring of me, I'll none of it. 10

Malvolio: Come, sir, you peevishly threw it to her, and her will is, it
  should be so return'd. If it be worth stooping for, there it lies,
  in your eye; if not, be it his that finds it. *Exit.*

Viola: I left no ring with her. What means this lady?
  Fortune forbid my outside have not charm'd her! 15
  She made good view of me; indeed so much
  That methought her eyes had lost her tongue,
  For she did speak in starts distractedly.
  She loves me sure, the cunning of her passion
  Invites me in this churlish messenger. 20
  None of my lord's ring? Why, he sent her none.
  I am the man! If it be so, as 'tis,
  Poor lady, she were better love a dream.
  Disguise, I see thou art a wickedness
  Wherein the pregnant enemy does much. 25
  How easy is it for the proper-false
  In women's waxen hearts to set their forms!
  Alas, [our] frailty is the cause, not we,
  For such as we are made [of,] such we be.
  How will this fadge? My master loves her dearly, 30
  And I (poor monster) fond as much on him;
  And she (mistaken) seems to dote on me.
  What will become of this? As I am man,

II.ii. Location: A street. o.s.d. *several:* separate. 2. *on:* at. 5. *to have taken:* by taking.
6. *desperate assurance:* certainty without hope of change. 8. *hardy:* bold. 9. *taking of this:* i.e.
reception of Olivia's message of rejection. 12. *so return'd:* i.e. thrown back at you. 13. *in
your eye:* in plain view. 15. *forbid . . . not:* Modern idiom would omit *not*. 16. *made . . . me:*
examined me closely. 17. *lost:* i.e. made her lose. 18. *in starts:* by fits and starts. *distractedly:* disjointedly. 20. *in:* by means of, through. 25. *the pregnant enemy:* the devil, always
ready (to take advantage of our evil for his own evil ends). 26. *proper-false:* i.e. men who are
handsome but false. 27. *waxen:* i.e. impressionable. The image is from sealing. *set their
forms:* stamp their images. 28. *frailty:* human weakness. 29. *such . . . of:* i.e. frail flesh.
30. *fadge:* work out, come off. 31. *monster:* i.e. being both a man and woman. *fond:* dote.

My state is desperate for my master's love;
As I am woman (now alas the day!),   35
What thriftless sighs shall poor Olivia breathe!
O time, thou must untangle this, not I,
It is too hard a knot for me t' untie.   *[Exit.]*

Scene III

Enter Sir Toby *and* Sir Andrew.

> *Sir Toby:* Approach, Sir Andrew. Not to be a-bed after midnight is
> to be up betimes, and *"deliculo surgere,"* thou know'st—
>
> *Sir Andrew:* Nay, by my troth, I know not; but I know, to be up late is to
> be up late.
>
> *Sir Toby:* A false conclusion. I hate it as an unfill'd can. To be up 5
> after midnight and to go to bed then, is early; so that to go to
> bed after midnight is to go to bed betimes. Does not our lives
> consist of the four elements?
>
> *Sir Andrew:* Faith, so they say, but I think it rather consists of eating
> and drinking.   10
>
> *Sir Toby:* Th' art a scholar; let us therefore eat and drink. Marian, I
> say, a stoup of wine!

Enter Clown.

> *Sir Andrew:* Here comes the fool, i' faith.
>
> *Clown:* How now, my hearts? Did you never see the picture of "we
> three"?   15
>
> *Sir Toby:* Welcome, ass. Now let's have a catch.
>
> *Sir Andrew:* By my troth, the fool has an excellent breast. I had rather
> than forty shillings I had such a leg, and so sweet a breath to
> sing, as the fool has. In sooth, thou wast in very gracious fool-
> ing last night, when thou spok'st of Pigrogromitus, of the 20
> Vapians passing the equinoctial of Queubus. 'Twas very good,
> i' faith. I sent thee sixpence for thy leman; hadst it?
>
> *Clown:* I did impeticos thy gratillity; for Malvolio's nose is no

---

36. *thriftless:* unprofitable.

II.iii. Location: Olivia's house.   2. *betimes:* in good season. *deliculo surgere:* From a well-
known Latin maxim, *Diluculo surgere saluberrimum est,* "to get up at dawn is very healthful."
3. *by my troth:* on my word.   5. *can:* tankard.   8. *four elements:* earth, water, air, and fire,
supposed the constitnents of all created things.   11. *Th' art a scholar:* i.e. I'll accept your
authority on that point.   12. *stoup:* large drinking-cup.   14–15. *picture of "we three":* i.e. a
picture of two fools or ass-heads inscribed "we three," the viewer being the third.   16. *catch:*
round.   17. *breast:* i.e. breath, voice.   18. *leg:* graceful bow or obeisance (?) or fine leg for
dancing (?). Relevance uncertain.   19. *gracious:* delightful.   20–21. *Pigrogromitus . . .
Queubus:* Feste's mock scholarship.   21. *equinoctial:* equator.   22. *leman:* sweetheart.
23. *impeticos:* impetticoat, i.e. pocket (?) or, possibly, spend on a woman (?). *gratillity:* little tip
(invented diminutive of *gratuity*).

whipstock. My lady has a white hand, and the Mermidons are
no bottle-ale houses.   25
Sir Andrew: Excellent! Why, this is the best fooling, when all is done.
Now a song.
Sir Toby: Come on, there is sixpence for you. Let's have a song.
Sir Andrew: There's a testril of me too. If one knight give a—
Clown: Would you have a love-song, or a song of good life?   30
Sir Toby: A love-song, a love-song.
Sir Andrew: Ay, ay. I care not for good life.

Clown sings.

    O mistress mine, where are you roaming?
    O, stay and hear, your true-love's coming,
       That can sing both high and low.   35
    Trip no further, pretty sweeting;
    Journeys end in lovers meeting,
       Every wise man's son doth know.

Sir Andrew: Excellent good, i' faith.
Sir Toby: Good, good.   40

Clown [sings].

    What is love? 'Tis not hereafter;
    Present mirth hath present laughter;
       What's to come is still unsure.
    In delay there lies no plenty,
    Then come kiss me sweet and twenty;   45
       Youth's a stuff will not endure.

Sir Andrew: A mellifluous voice, as I am true knight.
Sir Toby: A contagious breath.
Sir Andrew: Very sweet and contagious, i' faith.
Sir Toby: To hear by the nose, it is dulcet in contagion. But shall we   50
make the welkin dance indeed? Shall we rouse the night-owl in
a catch that will draw three souls out of one weaver? Shall we
do that?

---

24. *whipstock:* whip handle, i.e. whip. The apparent meaning is that Malvolio's nose is stuck
into everything but is no real deterrent. *has . . . hand:* is gently bred (?) or has ladylike tastes
(?). *Mermidons:* Presumably a tavern, with a sign displaying Myrmidons (Achilles' troop).
25. *bottle-ale houses:* i.e. low-class taverns.   29. *testril:* sixpence (invented diminutive of *tester;*
Sir Andrew seems to be aping Feste, with absurd effect).   30. *of good life:* conducive to virtue,
edifying. 36. *sweeting:* sweet one.   37. *in lovers meeting:* when lovers meet.   43. *still:* ever,
always.   46. *sweet and twenty:* sweet and twenty more times sweet. *Twenty* is used as an
intensive.   48. *contagious breath:* (1) catchy song; (2) bad breath.   50. *To . . . contagion:* if we
could both hear and smell with our noses, we could call it sweetly stinking.   51. *welkin:*
heavens, i.e. heavenly bodies.   52. *draw three souls:* It was a conventional notion that music
could draw the soul from the body. These three singers will have three times that
effect. *weaver:* Weavers were supposedly given to singing psalms.

Sir Andrew: And you love me, let's do't. I am dog at a catch.

    Clown: By'r lady, sir, and some dogs will catch well.   55

Sir Andrew: Most certain. Let our catch be "Thou knave."

    Clown: "Hold thy peace, thou knave," knight? I shall be constrain'd in't to call thee knave, knight.

Sir Andrew: 'Tis not the first time I have constrain'd one to call me knave. Begin, fool. It begins, "Hold thy peace."   60

    Clown: I shall never begin if I hold my peace.

Sir Andrew: Good, i' faith. Come, begin.   *Catch sung.*

Enter Maria.

    Maria: What a caterwauling do you keep here! If my lady have not called up her steward Malvolio and bid him turn you out of doors, never trust me.   65

  Sir Toby: My lady's a Cataian, we are politicians, Malvolio's a Peg-a-Ramsey, and [*sings*] "Three merry men be we." Am I not consanguineous? Am I not of her blood? Tilly-vally! Lady! [*Sings.*] "There dwelt a man in Babylon, lady, lady."

    Clown: Beshrew me, the knight's in admirable fooling.   70

Sir Andrew: Ay, he does well enough if he be dispos'd, and so do I too. He does it with a better grace, but I do it more natural.

  Sir Toby: [*Sings.*] "O' the twelf day of December"—

    Maria: For the love o' God, peace!

Enter Malvolio.

  Malvolio: My masters, are you mad? Or what are you? Have you no 75 wit, manners, nor honesty, but to gabble like tinkers at this time of night? Do ye make an alehouse of my lady's house, that ye squeak out your coziers' catches without any mitigation or remorse of voice? Is there no respect of place, persons, nor time in you?   80

  Sir Toby: We did keep time, in our catches. Sneck up!

  Malvolio: Sir Toby, I must be round with you. My lady bade me tell

---

54. *dog:* i.e. very good, expert.   55. *By'r lady:* by Our Lady.   56. *"Thou knave.":* The words of the catch are: "Hold thy peace, thou knave; and I prithee hold thy peace." Each singer in turn thus calls another a knave.   59–60. *constrain'd . . . knave:* compelled someone to challenge me to a duel (but as usual Sir Andrew's form of words is unfortunate).   63. *keep:* keep up.   66. *Cataian:* Cathayan (i.e., Chinese); slang for one whose word cannot be trusted (?). *politicians:* schemers, intriguers.   66–67. *Peg-a-Ramsey:* A term of contempt, alluding to a character in a coarse ballad.   67. *"Three . . . we.":* A fragment of an old song. 68. *Tilly-vally! Lady!:* fiddle-faddle, lady indeed! Perhaps Sir Toby is annoyed by Maria's "my lady" instead of "your cousin" as elsewhere.   69. *There . . . lady:* The first line of the *Ballad of Constant Susanna,* with the song's "burden" (*lady, lady*) added.   70. *Beshrew me:* a mild oath (originally = curse me).   71. *dispos'd:* inclined to mirth.   72. *natural:* (1) naturally; (2) like a fool.   73. *"O' . . . December":* The opening line of another ballad (*twelf* = twelfth). 76. *honesty:* decorum, decency.   78. *coziers':* cobblers'.   78–79. *mitigation or remorse:* i.e. softening.   79 *respect:* regard.   81. *Sneck up:* go hang.   82. *round:* plain-spoken.

you, that though she harbors you as her kinsman, she's nothing
allied to your disorders. If you can separate yourself and your
misdemeanors, you are welcome to the house; if not, and it   85
would please you to take leave of her, she is very willing to bid
you farewell.

Sir Toby: [*Sings.*] "Farewell, dear heart, since I must needs be
    gone."

Maria: Nay, good Sir Toby.   90

Clown: [*Sings.*] "His eyes do show his days are almost done."

Malvolio: Is't even so?

Sir Toby: [*Sings.*] "But I will never die."

Clown: Sir Toby, there you lie.

Malvolio: This is much credit to you.   95

Sir Toby: [*Sings.*] "Shall I bid him go?"

Clown: [*Sings.*] "What and if you do?"

Sir Toby: [*Sings.*] "Shall I bid him go, and spare not?"

Clown: [*Sings.*] "O no, no, no, no, you dare not."

Sir Toby: [*To Clown.*] Out o' tune, sir! ye lie. *[To Malvolio.]* Art any   100
    more than a steward? Dost thou think because thou art virtu-
    ous there shall be no more cakes and ale?

Clown: Yes, by Saint Anne, and ginger shall be hot i' th' mouth too.

Sir Toby: Th' art i' th' right. Go, sir, rub your chain with crumbs. A
    stope of wine, Maria!   105

Malvolio: Mistress Mary, if you priz'd my lady's favor at any thing
    more than contempt, you would not give means for this uncivil
    rule. She shall know of it, by this hand.   *Exit.*

Maria: Go shake your ears.

Sir Andrew: 'Twere as good a deed as to drink when a man's a-hungry,   110
    to challenge him the field, and then to break promise with him,
    and make a fool of him.

Sir Toby: Do't, knight. I'll write thee a challenge, or I'll deliver thy
    indignation to him by word of mouth.

Maria: Sweet Sir Toby, be patient for to-night. Since the youth of   115
    the Count's was to-day with my lady, she is much out of quiet.
    For Monsieur Malvolio, let me alone with him. If I do not gull

---

83. *harbors you:* allows you residence.   83–84. *nothing allied:* no kin at all.   88–89. *Farewell
. . . gone:* From the ballad *Corydon's Farewell to Phillis.* The subsequent lines sung by Sir Toby
and Feste are slightly adapted to the occasion.   94. *Sir . . . Lie:* It seems likely that Feste sings
this line too.   97. *and if:* if.   100. *Out o' tune:* i.e. false (quibbling on *false* as in "a false
note," but with intended meaning "lying"); like the following *ye lie,* a reference to Feste's
"you dare not [bid him go]."   102. *cakes and ale:* Proverbial for revelry.   103. *ginger:* A
common addition to ale.   104. *rub . . . crumbs:* i.e. polish your steward's chain (a reminder of
his position as a servant).   105. *stope:* stoup.   107. *give means:* i.e. provide drinks.
108. *rule:* course of conduct.   109. *Go . . . ears:* Implying that Malvolio is an ass.
111. *field:* i.e. duelling-ground.   117. *let . . . him:* leave him to me. *gull:* befool.

him into an ayword, and make him a common recreation, do
not think I have wit enough to lie straight in my bed. I know I
can do it.   120

Sir Toby: Possess us, possess us, tell us something of him.

Maria: Marry, sir, sometimes he is a kind of puritan.

Sir Andrew: O, if I thought that, I'd beat him like a dog!

Sir Toby: What, for being a puritan? Thy exquisite reason, dear
knight?   125

Sir Andrew: I have no exquisite reason for't, but I have reason good
enough.

Maria: The dev'l a puritan that he is, or any thing constantly but a
time-pleaser, an affection'd ass, that cons state without book,
and utters it by great swarths; the best persuaded of himself, so 130
cramm'd (as he thinks) with excellencies, that it is his grounds
of faith that all that look on him love him; and on that vice in
him will my revenge find notable cause to work.

Sir Toby: What wilt thou do?

Maria: I will drop in his way some obscure epistles of love, where- 135
in by the color of his beard, the shape of his leg, the manner of
his gait, the expressure of his eye, forehead, and complexion,
he shall find himself most feelingly personated. I can write very
like my lady your niece; on a forgotten matter we can hardly
make distinction of our hands.   140

Sir Toby: Excellent, I smell a device.

Sir Andrew: I have't in my nose too.

Sir Toby: He shall think by the letters that thou wilt drop that they
come from my niece, and that she's in love with him.

Maria: My purpose is indeed a horse of that color.   145

Sir Andrew: And your horse now would make him an ass.

Maria: Ass, I doubt not.

Sir Andrew: O, 'twill be admirable!

Maria: Sport royal, I warrant you. I know my physic will work

---

118. *an ayword:* a byword or proverb (*ay* = ever). The F1 form is here retained, since
Shakespeare seems to have been the first to use the phrase and its etymology is doubtful.
Editors (following Rowe) usually read *a nayword,* a form that occurs twice in *The Merry Wives
of Windsor,* where, however, the sense required seems to be "password." *common recreation:*
general laughingstock.   121. *Possess:* tell, inform.   122. *puritan:* i.e. one who professes to be
extremely precise in morals; frequently (as Malvolio has just shown himself to be), one who is
complacent about his own moral superiority and highly censorious of the lapses or fancied
lapses of others. Apparently Sir Andrew in line 124 takes Maria to be charging him with
being a member of the Puritan party in the Anglican Church, and Maria in line 128 rejects
the idea.   124. *exquisite:* ingenious.   128. *constantly:* consistently, steadily.   129. *time-
pleaser:* self-seeking flatterer. *affection'd:* full of affectation. *cons . . . book:* commits to memory
the speech and behavior of the great.   130. *utters:* (1) repeats; (2) discharges. *swarths:*
swaths, i.e. masses. *the best . . . himself:* having the highest opinion of himself.
131–32. *grounds of faith:* firm belief.   137. *expressure:* expressive quality.   138. *feelingly
personated:* exactly represented.   140. *hands:* handwriting.   146. *Ass:* A quibble on *as / ass* (
= Sir Andrew).   149. *physic:* medicine.

with him. I will plant you two, and let the fool make a third,   150
where he shall find the letter; observe his construction of it.
For this night, to bed, and dream on the event. *Farewell. Exit.*

Sir Toby: Good night, Penthesilea.

Sir Andrew: Before me, she's a good wench.

Sir Toby: She's a beagle true-bred, and one that adores me. What o'   155
that?

Sir Andrew: I was ador'd once too.

Sir Toby: Let's to bed, knight. Thou hadst need send for more
money.

Sir Andrew: If I cannot recover your niece, I am a foul way out.   160

Sir Toby: Send for money, knight; if thou hast her not i' th' end, call
me cut.

Sir Andrew: If I do not, never trust me, take it how you will.

Sir Toby: Come, come, I'll go burn some sack, 'tis too late to go to
bed now. Come, knight, come, knight.   *Exeunt.*   165

Scene IV

Enter Duke, Viola, Curio, *and others.*

Duke: Give me some music. Now good morrow, friends.
Now, good Cesario, but that piece of song,
That old and antique song we heard last night;
Methought it did relieve my passion much,
More than light airs and recollected terms   5
Of these most brisk and giddy-paced times.
Come, but one verse.

Curio: He is not here, so please your lordship, that should sing it.

Duke: Who was it?

Curio: Feste the jester, my lord, a fool that the Lady Olivia's   10
father took much delight in. He is about the house.

Duke: Seek him out, and play the tune the while.
                                    [Exit Curio.] Music plays.
Come hither, boy. If ever thou shalt love,
In the sweet pangs of it remember me;

----

150. *fool . . . third:* Actually it is not Feste but Fabian who makes the third (see II.v). Maria's words imply that Feste is no longer present. He last speaks at line 103; perhaps Malvolio waves him out as he leaves at line 108.   151. *construction:* interpretation.   152. *event:* outcome.   153. *Penthesilea:* queen of the Amazons (an ironical allusion to Maria's size). 154. *Before me:* i.e. on my soul (formed on the pattern of such oaths as *before God* and *before heaven*).   155. *beagle:* small hunting-dog.   157. *I . . . too:* A line that suddenly, as elsewhere in Shakespeare, reveals the human being in a hitherto ridiculous figure of fun.   160. *recover:* win (with a suggestion of making good on his expenditure, as in *recover a debt*). *foul way out:* wretchedly out of pocket.   162. *cut:* a horse with a docked tail.   164. *burn some sack:* prepare some warm sack (Spanish wine) and sugar.

II.iv. Location: The Duke's palace.   2. *but:* just (let us have).   3. *antique:* quaint.   5. *light:* trivial (?) or quick in tempo (?). *recollected:* Meaning uncertain; variously explained as "refined," "studied," "farfetched," and so on.

For such as I am, all true lovers are, 15
Unstaid and skittish in all motions else,
Save in the constant image of the creature
That is belov'd. How dost thou like this tune?

Viola: It gives a very echo to the seat
Where Love is thron'd.

Duke: Thou dost speak masterly. 20
My life upon't, young though thou art, thine eye
Hath stay'd upon some favor that it loves.
Hath it not, boy?

Viola: A little, by your favor.

Duke: What kind of woman is't?

Viola: Of your complexion.

Duke: She is not worth thee then. What years, i' faith? 25

Viola: About your years, my lord.

Duke: Too old, by heaven. Let still the woman take
An elder than herself, so wears she to him;
So sways she level in her husband's heart.
For, boy, however we do praise ourselves, 30
Our fancies are more giddy and unfirm,
More longing, wavering, sooner lost and worn,
Than women's are.

Viola: I think it well, my lord.

Duke: Then let thy love be younger than thyself,
Or thy affection cannot hold the bent; 35
For women are as roses, whose fair flow'r
Being once display'd, doth fall that very hour.

Viola: And so they are; alas, that they are so!
To die, even when they to perfection grow!

Enter Curio *and* Clown.

Duke: O fellow, come, the song we had last night. 40
Mark it, Cesario, it is old and plain.
The spinsters and the knitters in the sun,
And the free maids that weave their thread with bones,

---

16. *Unstaid and skittish:* giddy and fickle. *motions else:* other thoughts and feelings.
18–19. *gives . . . thron'd:* i.e. it expresses what the heart feels.   20. *masterly:* like one who has had experience (of love).   22. *stay'd upon:* attended (?) or lingered upon (?). *favor:* face.
23. *by your favor:* if you please (a polite phrase), but with obvious quibbles on "near your face" and "thanks to you."   24. *complexion:* appearance, good looks.   27. *still:* ever, always.   28. *wears:* adapts herself (like a garment adjusting itself to the wearer).   29. *sways:* (1) holds sway; (2) swings. *level:* in perfect balance.   31. *fancies:* loves. *unfirm:* fickle.
32. *worn:* spent.   33. *think it well:* think so too.   35. *hold the bent:* maintain its fullness and intensity (as a bow is kept bent to its full extent under high tension).   37. *display'd:* fully opened.   39. *even when:* just when.   40. *fellow:* here, a familiar term of address to one of lower station (without derogatory implication).   42. *spinsters:* spinning-women.   43. *free:* carefree. *weave . . . bones:* make bone or thread lace with bone bobbins.

Do use to chant it. It is silly sooth,
And dallies with the innocence of love,   45
Like the old age.
    Clown: Are you ready, sir?
    Duke: Ay, prithee sing.   *Music.*

    THE SONG

[Clown]: Come away, come away, death,
    And in sad cypress let me be laid.   50
  [Fly] away, [fly] away, breath,
    I am slain by a fair cruel maid.
  My shroud of white, stuck all with yew,
       O, prepare it!
  My part of death, no one so true   55
       Did share it.

  Not a flower, not a flower sweet
    On my black coffin let there be strown.
  Not a friend, not a friend greet
    My poor corpse, where my bones shall be thrown.   60
  A thousand thousand sighs to save,
       Lay me, O, where
  Sad true lover never find my grave,
       To weep there.

    Duke: There's for thy pains.   65
  Clown: No pains, sir, I take pleasure in singing, sir.
    Duke: I'll pay thy pleasure then.
  Clown: Truly, sir, and pleasure will be paid, one time or another.
    Duke: Give me now leave to leave thee.
  Clown: Now the melancholy god protect thee, and the tailor make 70
thy doublet of changeable taffeta, for thy mind is a very
opal. I would have men of such constancy put to sea, that
their business might be every thing and their intent every
where, for that's it that always makes a good voyage of nothing.
Farewell.   *Exit.* 75

---

44. *Do use:* are accustomed. *silly sooth:* simple truth. 45. *dallies:* plays lovingly. 46. *Like
. . . age:* as in the good old days. 49. *Come away:* come hither. 50. *cypress:* i.e. a coffin of
cypress wood, or a bier covered with cypress boughs. Cypress trees, like yews (line 53), were
often planted in graveyards and were emblematic of death. 55–56. *My . . . it:* i.e. I had to
enact alone my role of dying, unsupported by one of equal constancy. 68. *pleasure . . .
another:* i.e. indulgence exacts payment sooner or later. 69. *leave to leave:* permission to take
leave of. 70. *the melancholy god:* i.e. the god to whom you pay your devotion. Feste clearly
implies that Orsino's melancholy is a self-indulgence. 71. *doublet:* close-fitting
jacket. *changeable taffata:* taffeta (thin silk) woven of threads of different colors, so that its
color shifts with movement. 72–75. *I . . . nothing:* Intended ironically; men of such
changeable mind arrive at no destination and bring nothing home.

Duke: Let all the rest give place.

[*Curio and Attendants retire.*]

Once more, Cesario,

Get thee to yond same sovereign cruelty.

Tell her, my love, more noble than the world,

Prizes not quantity of dirty lands;

The parts that fortune hath bestow'd upon her,   80

Tell her, I hold as giddily as fortune;

But 'tis that miracle and queen of gems

That nature pranks her in attracts my soul.

Viola: But if she cannot love you, sir?

Duke: [I] cannot be so answer'd.

Viola: Sooth, but you must.   85

Say that some lady, as perhaps there is,

Hath for your love as great a pang of heart

As you have for Olivia. You cannot love her;

You tell her so. Must she not then be answer'd?

Duke: There is no woman's sides   90

Can bide the beating of so strong a passion

As love doth give my heart; no woman's heart

So big, to hold so much; they lack retention.

Alas, their love may be call'd appetite,

No motion of the liver, but the palate,   95

That suffer surfeit, cloyment, and revolt,

But mine is all as hungry as the sea,

And can digest as much. Make no compare

Between that love a woman can bear me

And that I owe Olivia.

Viola: Ay, but I know—   100

Duke: What dost thou know?

Viola: Too well what love women to men may owe:

In faith, they are as true of heart as we.

My father had a daughter lov'd a man

As it might be perhaps, were I a woman,   105

I should your lordship.

Duke: And what's her history?

---

76. *give place:* withdraw.   77. *sovereign cruelty:* supremely cruel person, "cruell'st she alive" (I.v.204).   80. *parts:* worldly goods.   81. *hold . . . fortune:* esteem as lightly as fortune does (which could sweep them away in a moment).   82. *miracle . . . gems:* i.e. her beauty. 83. *nature:* As contrasted with fortune. *pranks:* adorns.   87. *for your love:* for love of you. 89. *be answer'd:* accept your answer.   90–91. *There . . . Olivia:* True to his changeable nature, the Duke now contradicts the opinion he voiced in lines 30–31.   91. *bide:* endure. 93. *retention:* power of retaining.   95. *No . . . liver:* no impulse of the liver, i.e. not the passion of true love. *the palate:* i.e. a motion of the palate, a sensual appetite.   96. *suffer:* experience. *cloyment:* satiety. *revolt:* revulsion of appetite. Cf. lines 94–98 with Orsino's opening speech in I.i; there is considerable irony in what he here attributes to women's love and what to his own.   99. *owe:* bear.

Viola: A blank, my lord; she never told her love,
　　　　But let concealment like a worm i' th' bud
　　　　Feed on her damask cheek; she pin'd in thought,
　　　　And with a green and yellow melancholy   110
　　　　She sate like Patience on a monument,
　　　　Smiling at grief. Was not this love indeed?
　　　　We men may say more, swear more, but indeed
　　　　Our shows are more than will; for still we prove
　　　　Much in our vows, but little in our love.   115
Duke: But died thy sister of her love, my boy?
Viola: I am all the daughters of my father's house.
　　　　And all the brothers too—and yet I know not.
　　　　Sir, shall I to this lady?
Duke:　　　　　　　　　Ay, that's the theme,
　　　　To her in haste; give her this jewel; say   120
　　　　My love can give no place, bide no denay.   *Exeunt.*

Scene V

Enter Sir Toby, Sir Andrew, *and* Fabian.

　Sir Toby: Come thy ways, Signior Fabian.
　　Fabian: Nay, I'll come. If I lose a scruple of this sport, let me be
　　　　boil'd to death with melancholy.
　Sir Toby: Wouldst thou not be glad to have the niggardly rascally
　　　　sheep-biter come by some notable shame?   5
　　Fabian: I would exult, man. You know he brought me out o' favor
　　　　with my lady about a bear-baiting here.
　Sir Toby: To anger him we'll have the bear again, and we will fool
　　　　him black and blue, shall we not, Sir Andrew?
Sir Andrew: And we do not, it is pity of our lives.   10

Enter Maria.

　Sir Toby: Here comes the little villain. How now, my metal of India?
　　Maria: Get ye all three into the box-tree; Malvolio's coming down
　　　　this walk. He has been yonder i' the sun practicing behavior to

---

109. *damask:* pink and white, like a damask rose.   110. *green and yellow:* pale and sallow.
111. *sate:* sat. *like . . . monument:* like a sculptured figure of Patience on a tomb.   114. *more than will:* greater than our desire. *still:* ever, always.   121. *give . . . denay:* yield no ground and endure no denial.

II.v. Location: Olivia's garden.   1. *Come they ways:* come along.   2. *Nay:* Implying that Sir Toby need not urge. *scruple:* tiniest bit.   3. *boil'd . . . melancholy:* With a pun on *boil/bile* (pronounced alike). Black bile was the cause of melancholy.   5. *sheep-biter:* i.e. malicious sneak.   7. *bear-baiting:* A type of entertainment that Malvolio would naturally disapprove of (with some reason).   8. *fool:* mock.   9. *black and blue:* i.e. thoroughly (used figuratively with *fool* instead of the usual *beat*).   10. *it . . . lives:* "life won't be worth living" (Kittredge).
11. *metal of India:* i.e. gold; here = girl worth her weight in gold.   13. *behavior:* courtly manners.

his own shadow this half hour. Observe him, for the love of mockery; for I know this letter will make a contemplative idiot 15 of him. Close, in the name of jesting! [*The men hide themselves.*] Lie thou there [*throws down a letter*]; for here comes the trout that must be caught with tickling.   *Exit.*

Enter Malvolio.

   Malvolio: 'Tis but fortune, all is fortune. Maria once told me she did affect me, and I have heard herself come thus near, that should 20 she fancy, it should be one of my complexion. Besides, she uses me with a more exalted respect than any one else that follows her. What should I think on't?

    Sir Toby: Here's an overweening rogue!

    Fabian: O, peace! Contemplation makes a rare turkey-cock of 25 him. How he jets under his advanc'd plumes!

Sir Andrew: 'Slight, I could so beat the rogue!

    Sir Toby: Peace, I say!

   Malvolio: To be Count Malvolio!

    Sir Toby: Ah, rogue!   30

Sir Andrew: Pistol him, pistol him!

    Sir Toby: Peace, peace!

   Malvolio: There is example for't: The lady of the Strachy married the yeoman of the wardrobe.

Sir Andrew: Fie on him, Jezebel!   35

    Fabian: O, peace! now he's deeply in. Look how imagination blows him.

   Malvolio: Having been three months married to her, sitting in my state—

    Sir Toby: O, for a stone-bow, to hit him in the eye!   40

   Malvolio: Calling my officers about me, in my branch'd velvet gown; having come from a day-bed, where I have left Olivia sleeping—

    Sir Toby: Fire and brimstone!

    Fabian: O, peace, peace!   45

15–16. *make . . . him:* make him sit and daydream like an idiot staring into space.   16. *Close:* keep hidden.   18. *tickling:* (1) stroking under the gills (trout were actually taken by this means); (2) flattery.   19. *she:* i.e. Olivia.   19–20. *did affect:* was fond of.   21. *fancy:* fall in love.   22–23. *follows her:* is in her service.   24. *overweening:* arrogant, presumptuous. 25. *Contemplation:* Looking back to lines 15–16.   26. *jets:* struts. *advanc'd:* raised. 27. *'Slight:* by God's light.   33. *example:* precedent. *Lady . . . Strachy:* Not certainly identified.   34. *yeoman . . . wardrobe:* servant in charge of clothing and linen in a nobleman's household.   35. *Jezebel:* the cruel and arrogant wife of Ahab, king of Israel (the application of the word to Malvolio is typical of Sir Andrew).   36–37. *blows him:* puffs him up. 39. *state:* chair of state (as Count).   40. *stone-bow:* crossbow that shot stones instead of arrows.   41. *officers:* household staff. *branch'd:* figured with a pattern of leaves or flowers. 42. *day-bed:* couch.

Malvolio: And then to have the humor of state; and after a demure travel of regard—telling them I know my place as I would they should do theirs—to ask for my kinsman Toby—

Sir Toby: Bolts and shackles!

Fabian: O, peace, peace, peace! Now, now.   50

Malvolio: Seven of my people, with an obedient start, make out for him. I frown the while, and perchance wind up my watch, or play with my—some rich jewel. Toby approaches; curtsies there to me—

Sir Toby: Shall this fellow live?   55

Fabian: Though our silence be drawn from us with cars, yet peace.

Malvolio: I extend my hand to him thus, quenching my familiar smile with an austere regard of control—

Sir Toby: And does not Toby take you a blow o' the lips then?

Malvolio: Saying, "Cousin Toby, my fortunes, having cast me on your   60 niece, give me this prerogative of speech"—

Sir Toby: What, what?

Malvolio: "You must amend your drunkenness."

Sir Toby: Out, scab!

Fabian: Nay, patience, or we break the sinews of our plot!   65

Malvolio: "Besides, you waste the treasure of your time with a foolish knight"—

Sir Andrew: That's me, I warrant you.

Malvolio: "One Sir Andrew"—

Sir Andrew: I knew 'twas I, for many do call me fool.   70

Malvolio: What employment have we here?   *[Taking up the letter.]*

Fabian: Now is the woodcock near the gin.

Sir Toby: O, peace, and the spirit of humors intimate reading aloud to him!

Malvolio: By my life, this is my lady's hand. These be her very c's, her   75 u's, and her t's, and thus makes she her great P's. It is, in contempt of question, her hand.

---

46. *have . . . state:* i.e. adopt the manner of the great.   46–47. *after . . . regard:* having gravely allowed my eyes to travel from one to another.   47. *telling:* indicating to.   51. *with . . . start:* in obedient haste. *make out:* sally forth.   53. *my— . . . jewel:* Malvolio is on the verge of saying "my chain" (his insignia of office as steward) but catches himself in time.   56. *with cars.* The general meaning is clearly "by main force." *Cars* is sometimes explained as meaning "carts" (with citation of III.ii.50, "oxen and wain-ropes cannot hale them together"), but Shakespeare elsewhere uses *car* only in the sense *chariot,* usually with reference to the sun-god's chariot; Johnson therefore proposed emending to *carts.* Possibly a reference to some form of torture is intended; the line would then mean "it is torture to remain silent" and would present a witty reversal of the usual purpose of torture, which is to draw speech from the silent. The emendation most often adopted, however, is Hanmer's *by th' ears,* which implies reluctance or resistance on the part of what is drawn.   57. *familiar:* friendly. 58. *austere . . . control:* look of stern authority.   59. *take:* give.   64. *scab:* scurvy fellow. *employment:* business.   72. *woodcock:* A proverbially stupid bird, easily caught. *gin:* trap, snare (short form of *engine* = contrivance).   73. *humors:* caprice.   75–76. *c's . . . t's:* Malvolio has unwittingly spelled out *cut,* slang for the female pudenda. The "joke" is compounded by *great P's,* line 76.   76. *great:* capital.   76–77. *in . . . question:* beyond dispute.

Sir Andrew: Her c's, her u's, and her t's: why that?

Malvolio: [*Reads.*] "To the unknown belov'd, this, and my good
wishes":—her very phrases! By your leave, wax. Soft! And the   80
impressure her Lucrece, with which she uses to seal. 'Tis my
lady. To whom should this be?

Fabian: This wins him, liver and all.

Malvolio: [*Reads.*]

"Jove knows I love.
    But who?   85
Lips, do not move;
    No man must know."

"No man must know." What follows? The numbers alter'd!
"No man must know." If this should be thee, Malvolio?

Sir Toby: Marry, hand thee, brock!   90

Malvolio: [*Reads.*]

"I may command where I adore,
    But silence, like a Lucrece knife,
With bloodless stroke my heart doth gore;
    M. O. A. I. doth sway my life."

Fabian: A fustian riddle!   95

Sir Toby: Excellent wench, say I.

Malvolio: "M. O. A. I. doth sway my life." Nay, but first let me see,
let me see, let me see.

Fabian: What dish a' poison has she dress'd him!

Sir Toby: And with what wing the [staniel] checks at it!   100

Malvolio: "I may command where I adore." Why, she may command me: I serve her, she is my lady. Why, this is evident to any
formal capacity, there is no obstruction in this. And the end—
what should that alphabetical position portend? If I could
make that resemble something in me! Softly! M. O. A. I.—   105

Sir Toby: O ay, make up that. He is now at a cold scent.

Fabian: Sowter will cry upon't for all this, though it be as rank as a
fox.

Malvolio: M—Malvolio; M—why, that begins my name.

---

80. *By your leave:* with your permission (addressed to the seal as he breaks it). *Soft:* not so fast,
wait a moment.   81. *impressure:* device impressed on the wax. *Lucrece:* i.e. a figure of the
virtuous Roman matron Lucretia, who stabbed herself after her rape by Tarquin—an emblem
of chastity. *uses:* is accustomed.   83. *wins:* conquers. *liver:* i.e. his love.   88. *The numbers
alter'd:* the metre changed.   90. *brock:* badger, i.e. stinker.   95. *fustian:* worthless, nonsensical.   99. *What:* what a. *dress'd:* prepared.   100. *wing:* flight, i.e. speed. *staniel:* inferior
hawk. *checks:* is diverted from its proper quarry by an inferior prey, i.e. is led astray.
103. *formal capacity:* normal understanding. *Obstruction:* obstacle, difficulty.   104. *alphabetical position:* arrangement of letters.   106. *O, ay:* Sir Toby seems to echo two of the letters that
Malvolio has just read (*ay* is spelled *I*, as usual in F1). *make up that:* piece that together, work
that out. *cold scent:* faint, hence difficult, trail.   107. *Sowter:* a hound's name; literally,
cobbler, i.e. bungler. *cry upon't:* give tongue as if he had found the scent.
107–08. *though . . . fox:* though the deception is as easy to smell out as a stinking *(rank)* fox.

Fabian: Did not I say he would work it out? The cur is excellent at 110
   faults.
Malvolio: M—but then there is no consonancy in the sequel that suf-
   fers under probation: A should follow, but O does.
Fabian: And O shall end, I hope.
Sir Toby: Ay, or I'll cudgel him, and make him cry O! 115
Malvolio: And then I comes behind.
Fabian: Ay, and you had any eye behind you, you might see more
   detraction at your heels than fortunes before you.
Malvolio: M. O. A. I. This simulation is not as the former; and yet, to
   crush this a little, it would bow to me, for every one of these let- 120
   ters are in my name. Soft, here follows prose.

   [*Reads.*] "If this fall into thy hand, revolve. In my stars I am
   above thee, but be not afraid of greatness. Some are [born]
   great, some [achieve] greatness, and some have greatness
   thrust upon 'em. Thy Fates open their hands, let thy blood and 125
   spirit embrace them, and to inure thyself to what thou art like
   to be, cast thy humble slough and appear fresh. Be opposite
   with a kinsman, surly with servants; let thy tongue tang arguments of state; put thyself into the trick of singularity. She thus
   advises thee that sighs for thee. Remember who commended 130
   thy yellow stockings, and wish'd to see thee ever cross-garter'd:
   I say, remember. Go to, thou art made if thou desir'st to be so;
   if not, let me see thee a steward still, the fellow of servants, and
   not worthy to touch Fortune's fingers. Farewell. She that
   would alter services with thee, 135
              The Fortunate-Unhappy."

   Daylight and champian discovers not more. This is open. I will
   be proud, I will read politic authors, I will baffle Sir Toby, I will
   wash off gross acquaintance, I will be point-devise the very

---

110–11. *excellent at faults:* not put off the trail by breaks in the scent (with ironic implication
that he is very likely to pick up a false scent).   112. *consonancy:* agreement,
correspondence. *sequel:* i.e. following letter(s).   112–13. *suffers:* endures, stands up. *probation:* testing, examination.   113. *O:* i.e. a hangman's noose.   118. *detraction:* defamation.
119. *simulation:* representation, disguised meaning.   120. *crush:* force. *bow to:* (1) yield its
meaning to; (2) point to, indicate.   122. *revolve:* consider. *stars:* fortunates, i.e. rank and
wealth.   125. *open their hands:* i.e. are ready to give.   125–26. *let . . . them:* i.e. welcome their
gifts with the whole force of your being. *Blood and spirit* = either "body and soul" or "passion
and mettle."   126. *inure:* accustom.   127. *cast . . . slough:* cast off your lowly demeanor.
The figure is of a snake sloughing off its old skin. *opposite:* quarrelsome.   128. *tang:* sound
loud with.   128–29. *arguments of state:* political topics, matters of statecraft. *trick:* custom,
habit.   129. *put . . . singularity:* cultivate individuality, adopt eccentric habits.   131. *cross-
garter'd:* wearing the garters crossed at the back so that in front they pass both above and
below the knee.   133. *still:* always (so also in line 151).   135. *alter services:* exchange duties,
i.e. make you master and myself your servant.   137. *champian:* champaign, open
country. *discovers:* reveals. *open:* evident, obvious.   138. *proud:* lofty. *politic authors:* writers
on political science. *baffle:* treat with disdain.   139. *wash off:* rid myself of. *gross:* low. *point-
devise:* correctly in every detail, precisely.

man. I do not now fool myself, to let imagination jade me; for 140
every reason excites to this, that my lady loves me. She did
commend my yellow stockings of late, she did praise my leg
being cross-garter'd, and in this she manifests herself to my
love, and with a kind of injunction drives me to these habits of
her liking. I thank my stars, I am happy. I will be strange, 145
stout, in yellow stockings, and cross-garter'd, even with the
swiftness of putting on. Jove and my stars be prais'd! Here is
yet a postscript.

[*Reads.*] "Thou canst not choose but know who I am. If thou
entertain'st my love, let it appear in thy smiling; thy smiles 150
become thee well. Therefore in my presence still smile, dear
my sweet, I prithee."

Jove, I thank thee. I will smile, I will do every thing that thou
wilt have me.   *Exit.*

 Fabian: I will not give my part of this sport for a pension of thou- 155
  sands to be paid from the Sophy.
 Sir Toby: I could marry this wench for this device—
Sir Andrew: So could I too.
 Sir Toby: And ask no other dowry with her but such another jest.

Enter Maria.

Sir Andrew: Nor I neither.   160
 Fabian: Here comes my noble gull-catcher.
 Sir Toby: Wilt thou set thy foot o' my neck?
Sir Andrew: Or o' mine either?
 Sir Toby: Shall I play me freedom at tray-trip, and become thy
  bond-slave?   165
Sir Andrew: I' faith, or I either?
 Sir Toby: Why, thou hast put him in such a dream, that when the
  image of it leaves him he must run mad.
 Maria: Nay, but say true, does it work upon him?
 Sir Toby: Like aqua-vitae with a midwife.   170
 Maria: If you will then see the fruits of the sport, mark his first
  approach before my lady. He will come to her in yellow stockings, and 'tis a color she abhors, and cross-garter'd, a fashion
  she detests; and he will smile upon her, which will now be so

---

140. *I . . . me:* I am not foolishly allowing imagination to trick me.   141. *every . . . this:* every
piece of evidence urges this conclusion.   145. *happy:* blessed by fortune. *strange:* distant,
reserved.   146. *stout:* haughty.   147, 153. *Jove.* Here and elsewhere (III.iv.67, 73, and
particularly IV. ii.10), possibly a replacement for an original *God,* to comply with the
anti-profanity statute of 1606.   150. *entertain'st:* acceptest.   156. *Sophy:* the Shah of
Persia.   161. *gull-catcher:* tricker of credulous fools.   162. *set . . . neck:* i.e. as a symbol of
conquest.   164. *play:* gamble. *tray-trip:* a game of dice in which the best throw was three (*tray*
= *trey*).   170. *aqua-vitae:* brandy or other spirits.

unsuitable to her disposition, being addicted to a melancholy as   175
she is, that it cannot but turn him into a notable contempt. If
you will see it, follow me.

    Sir Toby: To the gates of Tartar, thou most excellent devil of wit!

Sir Andrew: I'll make one too.   *Exeunt.*

ACT III

Scene I

Enter Viola, *and* Clown [*with a tabor*].

    Viola: 'Save thee, friend, and thy music! Dost thou live by thy
tabor?

    Clown: No, sir, I live by the church.

    Viola: Art thou a churchman?

    Clown: No such matter, sir. I do live by the church; for I do live at   5
my house, and my house doth stand by the church.

    Viola: So thou mayst say the [king] lies by a beggar, if a beggar
dwells near him; or the church stands by thy tabor, if thy tabor
stand by the church.

    Clown: You have said, sir. To see this age! A sentence is but a   10
chev'ril glove to a good wit. How quickly the wrong side may be
turn'd outward!

    Viola: Nay, that's certain. They that dally nicely with words may
quickly make them wanton.

    Clown: I would therefore my sister had had no name, sir.   15

    Viola: Why, man?

    Clown: Why, sir, her name's a word, and to dally with that word
might make my sister wanton. But indeed, words are very rascals since bonds disgrac'd them.

    Viola: Thy reason, man?   20

    Clown: Troth, sir, I can yield you none without words, and words
are grown so false, I am loath to prove reason with them.

    Viola: I warrant thou art a merry fellow, and car'st for nothing.

---

178. *Tartar:* Tartarus, hell.   179. *make one:* go along.

III.i. Location: Olivia's garden.   o.s.d. *tabor:* small drum.   1. *'Save:* God save.   *music:* Feste
probably has also a pipe (played with the help of one hand while the tabor was beaten with the
other).   3. *live by:* earn a living by. Feste quibbles on "dwell near."   4. *churchman:* man in
holy orders.   7. *So . . . beggar:* in the same fashion you could say what would be taken to
mean "the king lies with a beggar." (Similarly, *stands by,* line 8, could be taken to mean "is supported by.")   10. *A sentence:* any utterance.   11. *chev'ril:* kidskin (soft and pliable).
13. *dally nicely:* play sophistically.   13–14. *make them wanton:* allow them to get out of hand.
17. *dally:* toy amorously.   18. *wanton:* unchaste. Dover Wilson suggests a pun on *want one,*
i.e. lack a (good) name.   19. *bonds disgrac'd them:* Quibbling on *bonds* as (1) sworn statements
(in place of a man's plain word or promise); (2) fetters (betokening criminality).   22. *reason:*
"the reasonableness of any proposition" (Kittredge).   23. *car'st for nothing:* dost not worry
about anything. Feste then proceeds to play on other meanings of *care.*

Clown: Not so, sir, I do care for something; but in my conscience, sir, I do not care for you. If that be to care for nothing, sir, I would it would make you invisible.   25

Viola: Art not thou the Lady Olivia's fool?

Clown: No, indeed, sir, the Lady Olivia has no folly. She will keep no fool, sir, till she be married, and fools are as like husbands as pilchers are to herrings, the husband's the bigger. I am indeed   30 not her fool, but her corrupter of words.

Viola: I saw thee late at the Count Orsino's.

Clown: Foolery, sir, does walk about the orb like the sun, it shines every where. I would be sorry, sir, but the fool should be as oft with your master as with my mistress. I think I saw your wisdom   35 there.

Viola: Nay, and thou pass upon me, I'll no more with thee. Hold, there's expenses for thee.

Clown: Now Jove, in his next commodity of hair, send thee a beard!   40

Viola: By my troth, I'll tell thee, I am almost sick for one—[*aside*] though I would not have it grow on my chin. Is thy lady within?

Clown: Would not a pair of these have bred, sir?

Viola: Yes, being kept together, and put to use.

Clown: I would play Lord Pandarus of Phrygia, sir, to bring a   45 Cressida to this Troilus.

Viola: I understand you, sir. 'Tis well begg'd.

Clown: The matter, I hope, is not great, sir—begging but a beggar: Cressida was a beggar. My lady is within, sir. I will conster to them whence you come; who you are, and what you would,   50 are out of my welkin—I might say "element," but the word is overworn.   *Exit.*

Viola: This fellow is wise enough to play the fool,

---

24. *in my conscience:* to let you into a secret.   25–26. *I . . . invisible.* Viola ought to be invisible, by Feste's process of thought, since if he cares for something and does not care for Viola, then Viola is nothing.   30. *pilchers:* pilchards, small fish resembling herring. 32. *late:* recently.   33. *orb:* earth, as the centre about which the sun courses *(walks)* in the Ptolemaic system.   34. *but:* unless.   35. *your wisdom:* An ironic form of address on the model of *your honor* or *your worship.*   37. *pass upon me:* fence with me (using sharp words as your weapon). *Hold:* take this.   38. *expenses:* something for you to spend.   39–40. *Jove . . . beard.* Feste follows the usual practice of one who received alms by invoking God's blessing on the giver.   39. *commodity:* consignment, lot.   41. *one:* a beard, i.e. a man (Orsino).   42. *my chin:* The stress belongs on *my.*   43. *pair of these:* i.e. two coins. *bred:* multiplied.   44. *put to use:* loaned at interest.   45. *Pandarus:* Cressida' suncle, and the go-between in her love affair with Troilus.   48. *The matter:* i.e. the amount begged.   49. *Cressida . . . beggar.* Alluding to the tradition stemming from Henryson's *Testament of Cresseid* that Cressida became a leper and a beggar. *conster:* construe, explain.   51. *welkin, element. Element* in the sense "sky" is synonymous with *welkin*, but it can have other senses as well, as of course it has in the phrase *out of my element* (= here "outside the range of my information"). Feste gives a final example of how words can be made "wanton."   53. *play the fool.* Feste, like Touchstone in *As You Like It,* is a shrewd, sharp person who makes his living by playing the fool; he is not, like the Fool in *King Lear*, a "natural" or halfwit.

And to do that well craves a kind of wit.
He must observe their mood on whom he jests,   55
The quality of persons, and the time;
And like the haggard, check at every feather
That comes before his eye. This is a practice
As full of labor as a wise man's art;
For folly that he wisely shows is fit,   60
But wise [men], folly-fall'n, quite taint their wit.

Enter Sir Toby *and* Sir Andrew.

    Sir Toby: 'Save you, gentleman.
      Viola: And you, sir.
Sir Andrew: *Dieu vous garde, monsieur.*
      Viola: *Et vous aussi; votre serviteur.*   65
Sir Andrew: I hope, sir, you are, and I am yours.
    Sir Toby: Will you encounter the house? My niece is desirous you
      should enter, if you trade be to her.
      Viola: I am bound to your niece, sir; I mean she is the list of my
      voyage.   70
    Sir Toby: Taste your legs, sir, put them to motion.
      Viola: My legs do better understand me, sir, than I understand
      what you mean by bidding me taste my legs.
    Sir Toby: I mean, to go, sir, to enter.
      Viola: I will answer you with gait and entrance—but we are   75
      prevented.

Enter Olivia *and* Gentlewoman.

      Most excellent accomplish'd lady, the heavens rain odors on
      you!
Sir Andrew: That youth's a rare courtier—"rain odors," well.
      Viola: My matter hath no voice, lady, but to your own most preg-   80
      nant and vouchsafed ear.
Sir Andrew: "Odors," "pregnant," and "vouchsafed"; I'll get 'em all
      three all ready.

---

54. *wit:* intelligence.   55. *their mood:* the mood of those.   56. *quality:* character.
57. *haggard:* a hawk taken in maturity and hence difficult to train. check. See the note on
II.v.100.   58. *practice:* exercise of skill.   59. *art:* skill.   60. *wisely shows:* assumes judiciously. *fit:* proper.   61. *folly-fall'n:* lapsed into folly. *taint:* discredit.   64. *Dieu . . .
monsieur:* God keep you, sir.   65. *Et . . . serviteur:* And you too; your servant.   67. *encounter:*
Pedantry for "enter."   68. *trade:* business. The word suggests to Viola a trading voyage.
69. *I . . . to:* i.e. my destination is. *list:* limit, utmost point.   71. *Taste:* i.e. make trial of,
test.   73. *understand me:* stand under me, hold me up.   75. *gait and entrance:* going and
entering (answering to go and enter in line 74); with a play on "gate and entrance."
76. *prevented:* anticipated.   80. *hath no voice:* cannot be spoken.   82. *pregnant and vouchsafed:* receptive and graciously bestowed.   83. *all ready:* i.e. all ready for use in future
conversation.

Olivia: Let the garden door be shut, and leave me to my hearing.
  [*Exeunt all but Olivia and Viola.*] Give me your hand, sir.   85
  Viola: My duty, madam, and most humble service.
Olivia: What is your name?
  Viola: Cesario is your servant's name, fair princess.
Olivia: My servant, sir. 'Twas never merry world
  Since lowly feigning was call'd compliment.   90
  Y' are servant to the Count Orsino, youth.
  Viola: And he is yours, and his must needs be yours:
  Your servant's servant is your servant, madam.
Olivia: For him, I think not on him. For his thoughts,
  Would they were blanks, rather than fill'd with me.   95
  Viola: Madam, I come to whet your gentle thoughts
  On his behalf.
Olivia: O, by your leave, I pray you:
  I bade you never speak again of him;
  But would you undertake another suit,
  I had rather hear you to solicit that   100
  Than music from the spheres.
  Viola: Dear lady—
Olivia: Give me leave, beseech you. I did send,
  After the last enchantment you did here,
  A ring in chase of you; so did I abuse
  Myself, my servant, and I fear me you.   105
  Under your hard construction must I sit,
  To force that on you in a shameful cunning
  Which you knew none of yours. What might you think?
  Have you not set mine honor at the stake,
  And baited it with all th' unmuzzled thoughts   110
  That tyrannous heart can think? To one of your receiving
  Enough is shown; a cypress, not a bosom,
  Hides my heart. So let me hear you speak.
  Viola: I pity you.
Olivia: That's a degree to love.

---

84. *hearing:* audience, interview.   89. *'Twas . . . world:* life has never been as pleasant (proverbial).   90. *lowly feigning:* pretending humility, i.e. calling oneself "your servant." *was call'd:* was first called, began to be called.   94. *For: as for.*   98. *by your leave:* a polite phrase of interruption: "please say no more" (so also *Give me leave,* line 103).   101. *music . . . spheres:* A reference to the notion that the revolution of the spheres in which the heavenly bodies were fixed produced ravishing music, inaudible to human ears.   103. *enchantment you did:* charm you worked, spell you cast.   104. *abuse:* dishonor.   106. *construction:* interpretation.   107. *To force:* for forcing.   109. *at the stake.* The figure in 109–10 is from bear-baiting; Olivia's honor is set upon by Cesario's thoughts as the bear is set upon by dogs to tear and worry it.   111. *tyrannous:* cruel. *receiving:* power to apprehend.   112. *cypress:* a nearly transparent black fabric.   114. *degree:* step; *grize* in line 115 is a synonym.

Viola: No, not a grize; for 'tis a vulgar proof   115
        That very oft we pity enemies.
Olivia: Why then methinks 'tis time to smile again.
        O world, how apt the poor are to be proud!
        If one should be a prey, how much the better
        To fall before the lion than the wolf!   *Clock strikes.*   120
        The clock upbraids me with the waste of time.
        Be not afraid, good youth, I will not have you,
        And yet when wit and youth is come to harvest,
        Your wife is like to reap a proper man.
        There lies your way, due west.
Viola: Then westward-ho!   125
        Grace and good disposition attend your ladyship!
        You'll nothing, madam, to my lord by me?
Olivia: Stay!
        I prithee tell me what thou think'st of me.
Viola: That you do think you are not what you are.   130
Olivia: If I think so, I think the same of you.
Viola: Then think you right: I am not what I am.
Olivia: I would you were as I would have you be.
Viola: Would it be better, madam, than I am?
        I wish it might, for now I am your fool.   135
Olivia: [*Aside.*] O, what a deal of scorn looks beautiful
        In the contempt and anger of his lip!
        A murd'rous guilt shows not itself more soon
        Than love that would seem hid: love's night is noon.—
        Cesario, by the roses of the spring,   140
        By maidhood, honor, truth, and every thing,
        I love thee so, that maugre all thy pride,
        Nor wit nor reason can my passion hide.
        Do not extort thy reasons from this clause,
        For that I woo, thou therefore hast no cause;   145

---

115. *'tis . . . proof:* i.e. everybody knows from experience.   117. *then:* i.e. if you are my
enemy. *smile:* i.e. abandon love and its pangs.   118. *apt: ready.*   *119. should be:* were to be.
120. *lion . . . wolf:* i.e. Orsino . . . Cesario.   122. *have you:* have you for a husband.
123. *proper:* worthy.   124. *due west:* i.e. where the sun disappears from sight; a clear dismissal.   125. *westward-ho:* the cry of watermen on the Thames when they were about to put
off westward.   126. *good disposition:* a tranquil mind.   130. *That . . . what you are:* i.e. that
you are mistaken in supposing you are in love with a man, not a woman.   131. *If . . . you:*
Presumably she interprets his remark as meaning that she is mad but doesn't know it.
135. *now . . . fool:* i.e. you have put me into a foolish position (in a sense that she cannot
guess).   136. *deal:* large amount.   139. *love's . . . noon:* love's attempted secrecy is like broad
daylight to everybody else.   142. *maugre:* in spite of.   143. *Nor:* neither.   144–45. *Do . . .
cause:* do not wrest reasons for not loving me from this proposition that because I woo, you
have no cause to accept my love.

But rather reason thus with reason fetter:
Love sought is good, but given unsought is better.
  Viola: By innocence I swear, and by my youth,
    I have one heart, one bosom, and one truth,
    And that no woman has, nor never none   150
    Shall mistress be of it, save I alone.
    And so adieu, good madam, never more
    Will I my master's tears to you deplore.
  Olivia: Yet come again; for thou perhaps mayst move
    That heart which now abhors, to like his love.   *Exeunt.* 155

Scene II

Enter Sir Toby, Sir Andrew, *and* Fabian.

Sir Andrew: No, faith, I'll not stay a jot longer.
  Sir Toby: Thy reason, dear venom, give thy reason.
    Fabian: You must needs yield your reason, Sir Andrew.
Sir Andrew: Marry, I saw your niece do more favors to the Count's ser-
    vingman than ever she bestow'd upon me. I saw't i' th' 5
    orchard.
  Sir Toby: Did she see [thee] the while, old boy? tell me that.
Sir Andrew: As plain as I see you now.
    Fabian: This was a great argument of love in her toward you.
Sir Andrew: 'Slight! will you make an ass o' me?   10
    Fabian: I will prove it legitimate, sir, upon the oaths of judgment
    and reason.
  Sir Toby: And they have been grand-jurymen since before Noah was
    a sailor.
    Fabian: She did show favor to the youth in your sight only to exas- 15
    perate you, to awake your dormouse valor, to put fire in your
    heart, and brimstone in your liver. You should then have
    accosted her, and with some excellent jests, fire-new from the
    mint, you should have bang'd the youth into dumbness. This
    was look'd for at your hand, and this was balk'd. The double 20
    gilt of this opportunity you let time wash off, and you are now
    sail'd into the north of my lady's opinion, where you will hang

---

146. *rather . . . fetter:* instead bind together these two reasons (to accept my love).
147. *Love . . . better:* Olivia will receive a love that she sued for, which is good; Cesario will
receive a love for which he did not have to sue, which is better.   153. *deplore:* lament,
describe.

III.ii. Location: Olivia's house.   2. *venom:* venomous one.   6. *orchard:* garden.   9. *argument:* evidence.   11. *oaths:* i.e. sworn testimony.   13. *grand-jurymen:* i.e. experts in
evaluating evidence.   16. *dormouse:* i.e. sleepy.   18. *fire-new:* brand-new.   20. *balk'd:*
neglected, let slip.   20–21. *double gilt:* double plating with gold; perhaps referring to Sir
Andrew's double opportunity to prove his love and valor.   22. *north:* i.e. cold regions (of dis-
favor).

like an icicle on a Dutchman's beard, unless you do redeem it by
some laudable attempt either of valor or policy.

Sir Andrew: And't be any way, it must be with valor, for policy I hate. I 25
had as lief be a Brownist as a politician.

Sir Toby: Why then build me thy fortunes upon the basis of valor.
Challenge me the Count's youth to fight with him, hurt him in
eleven places—my niece shall take note of it, and assure thyself,
there is no love-broker in the world can more prevail in man's 30
commendation with woman than report of valor.

Fabian: There is no way but this, Sir Andrew.

Sir Andrew: Will either of you bear me a challenge to him?

Sir Toby: Go, write it in a martial hand, be curst and brief. It is no
matter how witty, so it be eloquent and full of invention. Taunt 35
him with the license of ink. If thou thou'st him some thrice, it
shall not be amiss; and as many lies as will lie in thy sheet of
paper, although the sheet were big enough for the bed of Ware
in England, set 'em down. Go about it. Let there be gall
enough in thy ink, though thou write with a goose-pen, no mat- 40
ter. About it.

Sir Andrew: Where shall I find you?

Sir Toby: We'll call thee at the cubiculo. Go.   *Exit Sir Andrew.*

Fabian: This is a dear manikin to you, Sir Toby.

Sir Toby: I have been dear to him, lad, some two thousand strong, or 45
so.

Fabian: We shall have a rare letter from him; but you'll not
deliver't?

Sir Toby: Never trust me then; and by all means stir on the youth to
an answer. I think oxen and wain-ropes cannot hale them 50
together. For Andrew, if he were open'd and you find so much
blood in his liver as will clog the foot of a flea, I'll eat the rest of
th' anatomy.

---

23. *icicle . . . beard:* Perhapes an allusion to William Barentz, a Dutchman who travelled to the
Arctic in 1596–97 and wrote an account of his experiences which was entered in the
Stationers' Register in June 1598 (earliest extant edition, 1609).   25. *policy:* cunning,
strategy.   26. *Brownist:* a follower of Robert Browne, founder of the Congregationalist
sect. *politician:* contriver, schemer.   27. *build me:* build (a colloquialism); cf. *Challenge me,*
line 28.   30. *love-broker:* go-between in love matters.   31. *report:* reputation.   34. *curst:*
bad-tempered, insulting.   35. *so:* provided that, so long as. *invention:* imagination. (Sir Toby
is being intentionally contradictory in lines 34–35.   36. *with . . . ink:* i.e. with the freedom
that writing affords (arising in this case from its comparative safety). *If . . . him:* Thou instead
of *you* was the form of address used to friends and to social inferiors, hence an insult to a
comparative stranger.   38. *bed of Ware:* This bed (which may be seen in the Victoria and
Albert Museum, London) is eleven feet square.   39. *gall:* (1) an ingredient of ink; (2)
acrimony.   40. *goose-pen:* quill pen made from a goose feather (with an implication that the
letter will be couched in foolish terms).   43. *call thee:* call for you. *cubiculo:* little chamber.
44. *dear . . . you:* puppet dear to you (referring to Sir Toby's manipulation of him).   45. *dear:*
expensive.   49. *then:* i.e. if I don't.   50. *wain-ropes:* wagon ropes. *hale:* drag.   52. *blood . . .
liver:* Cowards were thought to have white (bloodless) livers.   53. *anatomy:* a medical term
meaning either "body" or "skeleton." In view of Sir Andrew's thinness, Sir Toby may intend
the latter.

Fabian: And his opposite, the youth, bears in his visage no great
  presage of cruelty.   55

Enter Maria.

   Sir Toby: Look where the youngest wren of [nine] comes.
   Maria: If you desire the spleen, and will laugh yourselves into
     stitches, follow me. Yond gull Malvolio is turn'd heathen, a
     very renegado; for there is no Christian that means to be sav'd
     by believing rightly can ever believe such impossible passages of 60
     grossness. He's in yellow stockings.
   Sir Toby: And cross-garter'd?
   Maria: Most villainously; like a pedant that keeps a school i' th'
     church. I have dogg'd him like his murtherer. He does obey
     every point of the letter that I dropp'd to betray him. He does   65
     smile his face into more lines than is in the new map, with the
     augmentation of the Indies; you have not seen such a thing as
     'tis. I can hardly forbear hurling things at him. I know my lady
     will strike him. If she do, he'll smile, and take't for a great
     favor.   70
   Sir Toby: Come bring us, bring us where he is.   *Exeunt omnes.*

Scene III

Enter Sebastian *and* Antonio.

   Sebastian: I would not by my will have troubled you,
     But since you make your pleasure of your pains,
     I will no further chide you.
   Antonio: I could not stay behind you. My desire
     (More sharp than filed steel) did spur me forth,   5
     And not all love to see you (though so much
     As might have drawn one to a longer voyage)
     But jealousy what might befall your travel,
     Being skilless in these parts; which to a stranger,
     Unguided and unfriended, often prove   10
     Rough and unhospitable. My willing love,

---

54. *opposite:* adversary. 56. *youngest . . . nine:* i.e. the very smallest of wrens. 57. *the spleen:*
extreme mirth. The spleen was regarded as the source of immoderate or uncontrollable
laughter. 58. *gull:* dupe. 59. *renegado:* regegade, i.e. renouncer of his religion.
60–61. *such . . . grossness:* such obviously impossible expressions (as the letter contains).
63. *pedant:* schoolmaster (the point of the reference to his holding a school in the church is
unexplained). 65. *betray:* expose, ensnare. 66–67. *lines . . . Indies.* Probably referring to a
map prepared by Edward Wright, Richard Hakluyt, and John Davis, and printed in 1600. It
was the first English map based on Mercator's projection, and therefore showed North
America *(the Indies)* as proportionately larger than in earlier maps. It is crisscrossed by numerous rhumb lines.

III.iii. Location: A street. 6. *all:* entirely, only. 8. *jealousy:* suspicion, anxiety. 9. *skilless
in:* unfamiliar with.

The rather by these arguments of fear,
Set forth in your pursuit.
Sebastian: My kind Antonio,
I can no other answer make but thanks,
And thanks; and ever oft good turns   15
Are shuffled off with such uncurrent pay;
But were my worth as is my conscience firm,
You should find better dealing. What's to do?
Shall we go see the reliques of this town?
  Antonio: To-morrow, sir; best first go see your lodging.   20
Sebastian: I am not weary, and 'tis long to night;
I pray you let us satisfy our eyes
With the memorials and the things of fame
That do renown this city.
  Antonio: Would you'ld pardon me.
I do not without danger walk these streets.   25
Once in a sea-fight 'gainst the Count his galleys
I did some service, of such note indeed,
That were I ta'en here, it would scarce be answer'd.
Sebastian: Belike you slew great number of his people?
  Antonio: Th' offense is not of such a bloody nature,   30
Albeit the quality of the time and quarrel
Might well have given us bloody argument.
It might have since been answer'd in repaying
What we took from them, which for traffic's sake
Most of our city did. Only myself stood out,   35
For which if I be lapsed in this place
I shall pay dear.
Sebastian: Do not then walk too open.
  Antonio: It doth not fit me. Hold, sir, here's my purse.
In the south suburbs at the Elephant
Is best to lodge. I will bespeak our diet,   40
Whiles you beguile the time, and feed your knowledge
With viewing of the town. There shall you have me.

---

15. *And . . . turns:* A much-emended line. Sense can be made of it by taking *ever oft* as "it has always been true that frequently," but the awkwardness of this and the metrical deficiency of the line strongly suggest corruption. Most editors adopt Theobald's *And thanks, and ever thanks: and oft good turns.* 16. *shuffled off:* shrugged off. *uncurrent pay:* payment in worthless money, i.e. mere thanks. An uncurrent coin is one not accepted as legal tender. 17. *worth:* wealth. *conscience:* awareness (of my indebtedness). 19. *reliques:* relics of the past, ancient monuments (see line 23). 24. *renown:* make famous. 26. *Count his:* Count's. 28. *it . . . answer'd:* it would be difficult for me to make a defense. 29. *Belike:* probably. 31. *quality:* i.e. circumstances. 32. *bloody argument:* occasion for bloodshed. 34. *for traffic's sake:* in order to resume trading. 36. *lapsed:* caught napping, taken by surprise (literally, slipped). 38. *fit:* behoove. 39. *Elephant:* the name of an inn. 40. *bespeak our diet:* order our food. 42. *have me:* know where to find me.

Sebastian: Why I your purse?

  Antonio: Haply your eye shall light upon some toy
      You have desire to purchase; and your store   45
      I think is not for idle markets, sir.

Sebastian: I'll be your purse-bearer, and leave you
      For an hour.

  Antonio: To th' Elephant.

Sebastian: I do remember.   *Exeunt.*

Scene IV

Enter Olivia *and* Maria.

    Olivia: [*Aside.*] I have sent after him; he says he'll come.
        How shall I feast him? What bestow of him?
        For youth is bought more oft than begg'd or borrow'd.
        I speak too loud.—
        Where's Malvolio? He is sad and civil,   5
        And suits well for a servant with my fortunes.
        Where is Malvolio?

  Maria: He's coming, madam, but in very strange manner. He is
      sure possess'd, madam.

    Olivia: Why, what's the matter? does he rave?   10

  Maria: No, madam, he does nothing but smile. Your ladyship
      were best to have some guard about you, if he come, for sure
      the man is tainted in 's wits.

    Olivia: Go call him hither.

Enter Malvolio.

                    I am as mad as he,
        If sad and merry madness equal be.   15
        How now, Malvolio?

  Malvolio: Sweet lady, ho, ho.

    Olivia: Smil'st thou? I sent for thee upon a sad occasion.

  Malvolio: Sad, lady? I could be sad. This does make some obstruc-
      tion in the blood, this cross-gartering, but what of that? If it 20
      please the eye of one, it is with me as the very true sonnet is,
      "Please one, and please all."

    Olivia: Why, how dost thou, man? What is the matter with thee?

---

44. *Haply:* perchance. *toy:* trifle.   45. *store:* supply of money.   46. *idle markets:* luxuries.

III.iv. Location: Olivia's garden.   1. *he . . . come:* In view of lines 52–53, this apparently means 'if he says he'll come."   5. *sad:* sober, serious (so also in line 18). *civil:* seemly, decorous.   6. *suits:* accords.   9. *possess'd:* i.e. possessed of an evil spirit.   10. *rave:* talk incoherently.   13. *tainted:* infected, disordered.   21. *sonnet:* poem.   22. *Please . . .all:* i.e. if I please you, I please everyone I care to please (the first line and refrain of a popular ballad published in 1592).

Malvolio: Not black in my mind, though yellow in my legs. It did
come to his hands, and commands shall be executed. I think we 25
do know the sweet Roman hand.

   Olivia: Wilt thou go to bed, Malvolio?

Malvolio: To bed? Ay, sweet heart, and I'll come to thee.

   Olivia: God comfort thee! Why dost thou smile so, and kiss thy
hand so oft? 30

   Maria: How do you, Malvolio?

Malvolio: At your request! Yes, nightingales answer daws.

   Maria: Why appear you with this ridiculous boldness before my
lady?

Malvolio: "Be not afraid of greatness": 'twas well writ. 35

   Olivia: What mean'st thou by that, Malvolio?

Malvolio: "Some are born great"—

   Olivia: Ha?

Malvolio: "Some achieve greatness"—

   Olivia: What say'st thou? 40

Malvolio: "And some have greatness thrust upon them."

   Olivia: Heaven restore thee!

Malvolio: "Remember who commended thy yellow stockings"—

   Olivia: Thy yellow stockings?

Malvolio: "And wish'd to see thee cross-garter'd." 45

   Olivia: Cross-garter'd?

Malvolio: "Go to, thou art made, if thou desir'st to be so"—

   Olivia: Am I made?

Malvolio: "If not, let me see thee a servant still."

   Olivia: Why, this is very midsummer madness. 50

Enter Servant.

   Servant: Madam, the young gentleman of the Count Orsino's is
return'd. I could hardly entreat him back. He attends your
ladyship's pleasure.

   Olivia: I'll come to him. [*Exit Servant.*] Good Maria, let this fellow be look'd to. Where's my cousin Toby? Let some of my 55
people have a special care of him. I would not have him miscarry for the half of my dowry.   *Exit* [*with Maria*].

---

24. *Not . . . legs:* Meaning not entirely clear. *To wear yellow hose* meant "to be jealous," and
Malvolio may mean "Though I wear yellow on my legs, my thoughts are not black, i.e. I don't
wear yellow because I am jealous." His main intent, of course, is to call attention to the
stockings. 26. *Roman hand:* The Italian script, resembling our own, which was beginning to
replace the English or secretary hand. 32. *At . . . daws:* i.e. am I to notice a question from
you? O, certainly, a nightingale should answer a crow. (Malvolio is being "surly with servants,"
as instructed.) 50. *midsummer madness:* Proverbial; the midsummer moon was traditionally
associated with insanity. 52. *attends:* awaits. 54–55. *fellow:* man (used of a servant or social
inferior, without contemptuous sense). 56–57. *miscarry:* come to harm.

Malvolio: O ho, do you come near me now? No worse man than Sir
Toby to look to me! This concurs directly with the letter: she
sends him on purpose, that I may appear stubborn to him; for 60
she incites me to that in the letter. "Cast thy humble slough,"
says she; "be opposite with a kinsman, surly with servants; let
thy tongue [tang] with arguments of state; put thyself into the
trick of singularity"; and consequently sets down the manner
how: as a sad face, a reverend carriage, a slow tongue, in the 65
habit of some sir of note, and so forth. I have lim'd her, but it is
Jove's doing, and Jove make me thankful! And when she went
away now, "Let this fellow be look'd to"; "fellow"! not "Malvolio," nor after my degree, but "fellow." Why, every thing
adheres together, that no dram of a scruple, no scruple of a 70
scruple, no obstacle, no incredulous or unsafe circumstance—
What can be said? Nothing that can be can come between me
and the full prospect of my hopes. Well, Jove, not I, is the doer
of this, and he is to be thank'd.

Enter Sir Toby, Fabian, *and* Maria.

Sir Toby: Which way is he, in the name of sanctity? If all the devils of 75
hell be drawn in little, and Legion himself possess'd him, yet I'll
speak to him.
Fabian: Here he is, here he is. How is't with you, sir?
[Sir Toby:] How is't with you, man?
Malvolio: Go off, I discard you. Let me enjoy my private. Go off. 80
Maria: Lo, how hollow the fiend speaks within him! Did not I tell
you? Sir Toby, my lady prays you to have a care of him.
Malvolio: Ah ha, does she so?
Sir Toby: Go to, go to; peace, peace, we must deal gently with him.
Let me alone. How do you, Malvolio? How is't with you? 85
What, man, defy the devil! Consider, he's an enemy to
mankind.
Malvolio: Do you know what you say?

---

58. *come near:* begin to understand. 60. *stubborn:* rude, harsh. 61. *incites:* encourages.
64. *consequently:* thereafter. 65. *reverend:* dignified. *slow tongue:* deliberate manner of
speaking. 66. *habit . . . note:* attire of a kind suitable for a distinguished gentleman. *lim'd:*
caught as with birdlime (a sticky substance spread on bushes to ensnare small birds).
68. *fellow:* Malvolio takes the word to mean "companion." 69. *after my degree:* according to
my place, i.e. "steward." 70. *adheres together:* hangs together. *dram:* small quantity
(one-eighth of a fluid ounce). *scruple:* (1) doubt; (2) smallest quantity, (one-third of a dram).
71. *incredulous:* incredible. *unsafe:* uncertain. 73. *prospect:* range, scope. 75. *in . . .
sanctity:* in the name of all that is holy. 76. *drawn in little:* contracted into small compass (so
that they could all find room in Malvolio's bosom). *Legion:* Alluding to Mark 5:8–9: "For he
[Jesus] said unto him, Come out of the man, thou unclean spirit. And he asked him, What is
thy name? And he answered, saying, My name is Legion: for we are many" (Geneva).
80. *discard:* cast off, want nothing to do with. *private:* privacy. 81. *hollow:* deep, resounding
(adverbial). 82. *have . . . of:* be attentive to, take care of. 85. *Let me alone:* leave him to
me. 86. *defy:* renounce.

William Shakespeare   1341

Maria: La you, and you speak ill of the devil, how he takes it at
heart! Pray God he be not bewitch'd!   90
Fabian: Carry his water to th' wise woman.
Maria: Marry, and it shall be done to-morrow morning if I live.
My lady would not lose him for more than I'll say.
Malvolio: How now, mistress?
Maria: O Lord!   95
Sir Toby: Prithee hold thy peace, this is not the way. Do you not see
you move him? Let me alone with him.
Fabian: No way but gentleness, gently, gently. The fiend is rough,
and will not be roughly us'd.
Sir Toby: Why, how now, my bawcock? How dost thou, chuck?   100
Malvolio: Sir!
Sir Toby: Ay, biddy, come with me. What, man, 'tis not for gravity to
play at cherry-pit with Sathan. Hang him, foul collier!
Maria: Get him to say his prayers, good Sir Toby, get him to pray.
Malvolio: My prayers, minx!   105
Maria: No, I warrant you, he will not hear of godliness.
Malvolio: Go hang yourselves all! You are idle shallow things, I am
not of your element. You shall know more hereafter.   *Exit.*
Sir Toby: Is't possible?
Fabian: If this were play'd upon a stage now, I could condemn it as   110
an improbable fiction.
Sir Toby: His very genius hath taken the infection of the device,
man.
Maria: Nay, pursue him now, lest the device take air, and taint.
Fabian: Why, we shall make him mad indeed.   115
Maria: The house will be the quieter.
Sir Toby: Come, we'll have him in a dark room and bound. My niece
is already in the belief that he's mad. We may carry it thus, for
our pleasure and his penance, till our very pastime, tir'd out of
breath, prompt us to have mercy on him; at which time we will 120
bring the device to the bar and crown thee for a finder of madmen. But see, but see.

---

89. *La you:* an exclamation. *and:* if, when.   90. *bewitch'd:* Demoniac possession was
sometimes attributed to witchcraft.   91. *water:* urine (for analysis).   97. *move him:* make him
angry.   98. *rough:* violent.   99. *us'd:* treated.   100. *bawcock:* fine fellow (from French *beau
coq*). *chuck:* chick (a term of endearment).   102. *biddy:* child's name for a chicken. *gravity:* a
grave man.   103. *cherry-pit:* a child's game in which cherry stones are thrown into a hole. Sir
Toby provokingly talks to Malvolio as if he were a child and at the same time warns him that
his soul is in danger. *foul collier:* filthy coal-miner. Devils were always represented as
coal-black, and they worked in hell-pit.   105. *minx:* impudent woman.   107. *idle:* foolish.
I . . . element: i.e. I do not belong to your earthy level. *know more:* hear about this.
112. *genius:* governing principle of his being (literally, attendant spirit).   114. *take . . . taint:*
(1) be exposed to (noxious) air and corrupt; (2) become known and be spoiled.
117. *dark . . . bound.* A common treatment at this time for the insane.   118. *carry it:* keep it
going.   121. *bar:* i.e. bar of judgment.

Enter Sir Andrew.

    Fabian: More matter for a May morning.

Sir Andrew: Here's the challenge, read it. I warrant there's vinegar
    and pepper in't.   125

    Fabian: Is't so saucy?

Sir Andrew: Ay, is't! I warrant him. Do but read.

    Sir Toby: Give me. [*Reads.*] "Youth, whatsoever thou art, thou art
        but a scurvy fellow."

    Fabian: Good, and valiant.   130

    Sir Toby: [*Reads.*] "Wonder not, nor admire not in thy mind, why I
        do call thee so, for I will show thee no reason for't."

    Fabian: A good note, that keeps you from the blow of the law.

    Sir Toby: [*Reads.*] "Thou com'st to the Lady Olivia, and in my sight
        she uses thee kindly. But thou liest in thy throat, that is not the 135
        matter I challenge thee for."

    Fabian: Very brief, and to exceeding good sense—less.

    Sir Toby: [*Reads.*] "I will waylay thee going home, where if it be thy
        chance to kill me"—

    Fabian: Good.   140

    Sir Toby: [*Reads.*] "Thou kill'st me like a rouge and a villain."

    Fabian: Still you keep o' th' windy side of the law; good.

    Sir Toby: [*Reads.*] "Fare thee well, and God have mercy upon one of
        our souls! He may have mercy upon mine, but my hope is bet-
        ter, and so look to thyself. Thy friend as thou usest him, and 145
        thy sworn enemy, Andrew Aguecheek." If this letter move him
        not, his legs cannot. I'll give't him.

    Maria: You may have very fit occasion for't; he is now in some
        commerce with my lady, and will by and by depart.

    Sir Toby: Go, Sir Andrew, scout me for him at the corner of the 150
        orchard like a bum-baily. So soon as ever thou seest him, draw,
        and as thou draw'st, swear horrible; for it comes to pass oft that
        a terrible oath, with a swaggering accent sharply twang'd off,
        gives manhood more approbation than ever proof itself would
        have earn'd him. Away!   155

---

123. *matter . . . morning:* material for a May-day comedy.   126. *saucy:* (1) highly spiced; (2)
insolent.   127. *I warrant him:* I guarantee he (Cesario) will be taken care of.   131. *admire:*
marvel.   133. *A . . . law:* i.e. a carefully worded challenge, that safeguards you from a charge
of slander.   135. *in thy throat:* in the most heinous degree.   142. *windy side:* windward, i.e.
safe (because, as before, the abuse is too feeble to be defamatory, but perhaps also because
like a rogue and a villain can be taken to modify *me*, not *thou*).   145. *Thy . . . him:* your friend
insofar as you behave in a friendly fashion toward him.   146. *move him:* stir him up (with
following quibble).   148. *fit:* convenient.   149. *commerce:* dealing, business. *will . . . depart:*
is on the verge of departing.   150. *scout me:* keep watch.   151. *bum-baily:* petty sheriff's
officer who arrested for debt.   154. *gives . . .approbation:* gives valor a higher reputation. i.e.
gives a man a higher reputation for valor. *proof:* actual trial, performance.

Sir Andrew Nay, let me alone for swearing.   *Exit.*

Sir Toby: Now will not I deliver his letter; for the behavior of the
young gentleman gives him out to be of good capacity and
breeding; his employment between his lord and my niece confirms no less. Therefore this letter, being so excellently igno-   160
rant, will breed no terror in the youth; he will find it comes
from a clodpole. But, sir, I will deliver his challenge by word of
mouth, set upon Aguecheek a notable report of valor, and
drive the gentleman (as I know his youth will aptly receive it)
into a most hideous opinion of his rage, skill, fury, and impe-   165
tuosity. This will so fright them both that they will kill one
another by the look, like cockatrices.

Enter Olivia *and* Viola.

Fabian: Here he comes with your niece. Give them way till he take
leave, and presently after him.
Sir Toby: I will meditate the while upon some horrid message for a   170
challenge.   *[Exeunt Sir Toby, Fabian, and Maria.]*
Olivia: I have said too much unto a heart of stone,
And laid mine honor too unchary on't.
There's something in me that reproves my fault;
But such a headstrong potent fault it is   175
That it but mocks reproof.
Viola: With the same havior that your passion bears
Goes on my master's griefs.
Olivia: Here, wear this jewel for me, 'tis my picture.
Refuse it not, it hath no tongue to vex you;   180
And I beseech you come again to-morrow.
What shall you ask of me that I'll deny,
That honor, sav'd, may upon asking give?
Viola: Nothing but this—your true love for my master.
Olivia: How with mine honor may I give him that   185
Which I have given to you?
Viola: I will acquit you.
Olivia: Well, come again to-morrow. Fare thee well.
A fiend like thee might bear my soul to hell.   *[Exit.]*

Enter Sir Toby *and* Fabian.

---

156. *let . . . swearing:* have no fears about my ability to swear.   158. *gives him out:* declares
him. *capacity:* ability.   161. *find:* detect, see.   162. *clodpole:* knucklehead (variant form of
clodpoll).   164. *youth:* i.e. inexperience. *aptly receive it:* readily credit the report.   166. *cockatrices:* basilisks, fabulous serpents that were supposedly able to kill by their glance alone.
168. *Give them way:* stay out of their way.   169. *presently:* immediately.   173. *laid:*
hazarded. *unchary:* carelessly.   175. *potent:* powerful.   177. *havior:* behavior.   179. *jewel:*
Used of any product of the jeweller's art; here a brooch or locket with Olivia's picture set in
it.   183. *sav'd:* i.e. without injury to itself, safely.   187. *acquit:* waive all claim to.   189. *like
thee:* in your likeness. *might:* i.e. could without resistance from me.

Sir Toby: Gentleman, God save thee!

    Viola: And you, sir. 190

Sir Toby: That defense thou hast, betake thee to't. Of what nature the wrongs are thou hast done him, I know not; but thy intercepter, full of despite, bloody as the hunter, attends thee at the orchard-end. Dismount thy tuck, be yare in thy preparation, for thy assailant is quick, skillful, and deadly. 195

    Viola: You mistake, sir, I am sure; no man hath any quarrel to me. My remembrance is very free and clear from any image of offense done to any man.

Sir Toby: You'll find it otherwise, I assure you; therefore, if you hold your life at any price, betake you to your guard; for your oppo- 200 site hath in him what youth, strength, skill, and wrath can furnish man withal.

    Viola: I pray you, sir, what is he?

Sir Toby: He is knight, dubb'd with unhatch'd rapier, and on carpet consideration, but he is a devil in private brawl. Souls and 205 bodies hath he divorc'd three, and his incensement at this moment is so implacable, that satisfaction can be none but by pangs of death and sepulchre. Hob, nob, is his word; give't or take't.

    Viola: I will return again into the house, and desire some conduct 210 of the lady. I am no fighter. I have heard of some kind of men that put quarrels purposely on others, to taste their valor. Belike this is a man of that quirk.

Sir Toby: Sir, no; his indignation derives itself out of a very [competent] injury; therefore get you on, and give him his desire. Back 215 you shall not to the house, unless you undertake that with me which with as much safety you might answer him; therefore on, or strip your sword stark naked; for meddle you must, that's certain, or forswear to wear iron about you.

    Viola: This is as uncivil as strange. I beseech you do me this cour- 220 teous office, as to know of the knight what my offense to him is. It is something of my negligence, nothing of my purpose.

---

191. *That defense:* whatever skill in fencing.   193. *intercepter:* ambusher. *despite:* contempt and hatred.   193. *bloody . . . hunter:* i.e. as intent on bloodshed as the hunting dog tracking down its prey.   194. *Dismount thy tuck:* draw your rapier. *yare:* ready, brisk.   196. *quarrel to:* reason to quarrel with.   197. *remembrance:* memory.   200. *price:* value.   200–01. *opposite:* adversary.   202. *withal:* with.   204. *unhatch'd:* unhacked, undented (i.e. never used in battle).   204–05. *on carpet consideration:* A carpet knighthood was one not given on the battlefield for services performed there, hence often one given for political reasons; *consideration* suggests a bought knighthood.   208. *Hob, nob:* have it, have it not; i.e. "give't or take't." *word:* motto.   210. *conduct:* protective escort.   212. *taste:* make trial of. 214–15. *competent:* sufficient.   216. *that:* i.e. a duel.   218. *strip . . . naked:* draw your sword now (and fight with me). *meddle:* have to do, be involved. Cf. line 240, where *not meddle with* = have nothing to do with.   219. *forswear . . . you:* renounce your right to wear a sword. 221. *know of:* ascertain from.   222. *of:* arising from. *purpose:* intention.

Sir Toby: I will do so. Signior Fabian, stay you by this gentleman till
my return. *Exit Sir Toby.*
Viola: Pray you, sir, do you know of this matter? 225
Fabian: I know the knight is incens'd against you, even to a mortal
arbitrement, but nothing of the circumstance more.
Viola: I beseech you, what manner of man is he?
Fabian: Nothing of that wonderful promise, to read him by his
form, as you are like to find him in the proof of his valor. He is 230
indeed, sir, the most skillful, bloody, and fatal opposite that you
could possibly have found in any part of Illyria. Will you walk
towards him? I will make your peace with him if I can.
Viola: I shall be much bound to you for't. I am one that had
rather go with sir priest than sir knight. I care not who knows 235
so much of my mettle. *Exeunt.*

Enter Sir Toby *and* Sir Andrew.

Sir Toby: Why, man, he's a very devil, I have not seen such a firago.
I had a pass with him, rapier, scabbard, and all; and he gives me
the stuck in with such a mortal motion that it is inevitable; and
on the answer, he pays you as surely as your feet hit the ground 240
they step on. They say he has been fencer to the Sophy.
Sir Andrew: Pox on't, I'll not meddle with him.
Sir Toby: Ay, but he will not now be pacified. Fabian can scarce hold
him yonder.
Sir Andrew: Plague on't, and I thought he had been valiant, and so 245
cunning in fence, I'd have seen him damn'd ere I'd have chal-
leng'd him. Let him let the matter slip, and I'll give him my
horse, grey Capilet.
Sir Toby: I'll make the motion. Stand here, make a good show on't;
this shall end without the perdition of souls. [*Aside.*] Marry, 250
I'll ride your horse as well as I ride you.

Enter Fabian *and* Viola.

[*To Fabian:*] I have his horse to take up the quarrel. I have persuaded
him the youth's a devil.

226–27. *to . . . arbitrement:* to a point requiring settlement by a duel to the death.   229–
30. *read . . . form:* judge him by his appearance.   235. *sir priest.* Priests were often adressed
by the courtesy title *sir.*   236. *mettle:* temperament.   237. *firago:* virago. Schmidt suggests
that Sir Toby uses this word, applicable only to a woman (its original meaning is "acting like a
man"), as a linguistic joke on Sir Andrew, who has not studied languages (I.iii.92–93); if so,
there is a joke on Sir Toby also.   238. *pass:* bout. *gives me:* gives.   239. *stuck in:* stoccado (or
stoccato), thrust.   240. *answer:* return hit. *pays:* repays.   245. *and . . . been:* if I had
supposed he was.   248. *Capilet:* a name meaning, "little horse." It is typical of Sir Andrew's
imagination that he should name a little horse "little horse."   249. *motion:* offer.
make . . .show: put a good face.   250. *perdition of souls:* loss of lives.   252. *take up:* settle.

Fabian: He is as horribly conceited of him; and pants and looks
　　pale, as if a bear were at his heels.　　　　　　　　　　　　255
Sir Toby: [*To Viola.*] There's no remedy, sir, he will fight with you for
　　's oath sake.　Marry, he hath better bethought him of his quar-
　　rel, and he finds that now scarce to be worth talking of; there-
　　fore draw, for the supportance of his vow.　He protests he will
　　not hurt you.　　　　　　　　　　　　　　　　　　　　　260
Viola: [*Aside.*] Pray God defend me!　A little thing would make
　　me tell them how much I lack of a man.
Fabian: Give ground if you see him furious.
Sir Toby: Come, Sir Andrew, there's no remedy, the gentleman will
　　for his honor's sake have one bout with you.　He cannot by the　265
　　duello avoid it; but he has promis'd me, as he is a gentleman
　　and a soldier, he will not hurt you.　Come on, to't.
Sir Andrew: Pray God he keep his oath!

Enter Antonio.

Viola: I do assure you, 'tis against my will.　　　　*[They draw.]*
Antonio: Put up your sword.　If this young gentleman　　　270
　　Have done offense, I take the fault on me;
　　If you offend him, I for him defy you.
Sir Toby: You, sir?　Why, what are you?
Antonio: One, sir, that for his love dares yet do more
　　Than you have heard him brag to you he will.　　　　275
Sir Toby: Nay, if you be an undertaker, I am for you.—　*[They draw.]*

Enter Officers.

Fabian: O good Sir Toby, hold! here come the officers.
Sir Toby: [*To Antonio.*] I'll be with you anon.
　　　　　　　　　　[Steps aside to avoid the Officers.]
Viola: Pray, sir, put your sword up, if you please.
Sir Andrew: Marry, will I, sir; and for that I promis'd you, I'll be as　280
　　good as my word.　He will bear you easily, and reins well.
1. Officer: This is the man, do thy office.
2. Officer: Antonio, I arrest thee at the suit of Count Orsino.
Antonio: You do mistake me, sir.
1. Officer: No, sir, no jot.　I know your favor well,　　　285
　　Though now you have no sea-cap on your head.
　　Take him away, he knows I know him well.

---

254. *He . . . him:* i.e. the youth has as dreadful a conception of Sir Andrew.　256–57. *for's:*
for his.　257–58. *bethought . . . quarrel:* considered the grounds for his challenge.
259. *supportance:* upholding. *protests:* solemnly promises.　266. *duello:* the code of duelling.
276. *undertaker:* i.e. one who takes up a challenge for another.　278. *be . . . anon:* be back
right away.　280. *that . . . you:* i.e. the horse Capilet (about which of course Viola knows
nothing).　281. *easily:* smoothly.　282. *office:* duty, function.　285. *favor:* face.

Antonio: I must obey. *[To Viola.]* This comes with seeking you;
　　　But there's no remedy, I shall answer it.
　　　What will you do, now my necessity　　　　　　　　　　　290
　　　Makes me to ask you for my purse? It grieves me
　　　Much more for what I cannot do for you
　　　Than what befalls myself. You stand amaz'd,
　　　But be of comfort.
2. Officer: Come, sir, away.　　　　　　　　　　　　　　　　295
　Antonio: I must entreat of you some of that money.
　　Viola: What money, sir?
　　　For the fair kindness you have show'd me here,
　　　And part being prompted by your present trouble,
　　　Out of my lean and low ability　　　　　　　　　　　　300
　　　I'll lend you something. My having is not much;
　　　I'll make division of my present with you.
　　　Hold, there's half my coffer.
　Antonio:　　　　　　　　　　Will you deny me now?
　　　Is't possible that my deserts to you
　　　Can lack persuasion? Do not tempt my misery,　　　　305
　　　Lest that it make me so unsound a man
　　　As to upbraid you with those kindnesses
　　　That I have done for you.
　　Viola:　　　　　　　　　I know of none,
　　　Nor know I you by voice or any feature.
　　　I hate ingratitude more in a man　　　　　　　　　　　310
　　　Than lying, vainness, babbling, drunkenness,
　　　Or any taint of vice whose strong corruption
　　　Inhabits our frail blood.
　Antonio:　　　　　　　　　O heavens themselves!
　2. Officer: Come, sir, I pray you go.
　Antonio: Let me speak a little. This youth that you see here　　315
　　　I snatch'd one half out of the jaws of death,
　　　Reliev'd him with such sanctity of love,
　　　And to his image, which methought did promise
　　　Most venerable worth, did I devotion.
　1. Officer: What's that to us? The time goes by; away!　　　320
　Antonio: But O, how vild an idol proves this god!
　　　Thou hast, Sebastian, done good feature shame.

---

289. *answer it:* i.e. make what defence I can. 293. *amaz'd:* bewildered. 299. *part:* in part. 300. *ability:* means. 301. *My having:* what I possess. 302. *present:* ready money. 303. *coffer:* store of wealth (literally, strong-box). 305. *lack persuasion:* fail to persuade you. *tempt:* try too far. 306. *unsound:* unhealthy (used figuratively). 311. *vainness:* vanity. *babbling:* foolish, loose talk. 312. *any . . . vice:* the taint of any fault. 316. *one . . . death:* out of the jaws of death which had half-swallowed him. 317. *such:* Used here with intensive force. 318. *his image:* what he appeared to be (with play on *image* in the sense "religious statue"). 319. *venerable worth:* worthiness of veneration. 321. *vild:* vile. 322. *Thou . . . shame:* Alluding to the belief that physical beauty is a reflection of spiritual beauty. *feature:* physical form.

In nature there's no blemish but the mind;
None can be call'd deform'd but the unkind.
Virtue is beauty, but the beauteous evil   325
Are empty trunks o'erflourish'd by the devil.
1. Officer: The man grows mad, away with him! Come, come, sir.
Antonio: Lead me on.   *Exit [with Officers].*
Viola: Methinks his words do from such passion fly
That he believes himself; so do not I.   330
Prove true, imagination, O, prove true,
That I, dear brother, be now ta'en for you!
Sir Toby: Come hither, knight; come hither, Fabian; we'll whisper
o'er a couplet or two of most sage saws.
Viola: He nam'd Sebastian. I my brother know   335
Yet living in my glass; even such and so
In favor was my brother, and he went
Still in this fashion, color, ornament,
For him I imitate. O, if it prove,
Tempests are kind and salt waves fresh in love.   340
                                                         [Exit.]

Sir Toby: A very dishonest paltry boy, and more a coward than a
  hare. His dishonesty appears in leaving his friend here in
  necessity, and denying him; and for his cowardship, ask Fabian.
Fabian: A coward, a most devout coward, religious in it.
Sir Andrew: 'Slid, I'll after him again, and beat him.   345
Sir Toby: Do, cuff him soundly, but never draw thy sword.
Sir Andrew: And I do not—   *[Exit.]*
Fabian: Come, let's see the event.
Sir Toby: I dare lay any money 'twill be nothing yet.   *Exeunt.*

ACT IV

Scene I

Enter Sebastian *and* Clown.

Clown: Will you make me believe that I am not sent for you?
Sebastian: Go to, go to, thou art a foolish fellow,
Let me be clear of thee.
Clown: Well held out, i' faith! No, I do not know you, nor I am not

---

324. *unkind:* unnatural. The unnatural quality with which he is charging the supposed
Sebastian is of course ingratitude.   326. *trunks o'erflourish'd:* (1) chests covered over with
elaborate carvings; (2) bodies made externally beautiful.   330. *so . . . I:* [I do not believe
myself, i.e. I don't quite dare to believe what all this suggests to me (that my brother is alive).
334. *saws:* sayings, maxims.   335–36. *I . . . glass:* I know that the appearance of my brother
is still alive every time I look in a mirror (i.e. I am the living image of my brother).   337–
38. *went Still in:* always wore.   339. *prove:* prove true.   341. *dishonest:* dishonorable. *more a
coward:* more cowardly.   345. *'Slid:* by God's eyelid.   347. *And:* if.   348. *event:* outcome.
349. *yet:* now as before(?) or nevertheless (?) or after all (?).

IV.i. Location: Before Olivia's house.   3. *clear:* rid.   4. *held out:* persisted in.

sent to you by my lady, to bid you come speak with her, nor your 5
name is not Master Cesario, nor this is not my nose neither:
nothing that is so is so.

Sebastian: I prithee vent thy folly somewhere else,
Thou know'st not me.

Clown: Vent my folly! He has heard that word of some great man, 10
and now applies it to a fool. Vent my folly! I am afraid this
great lubber the world will prove a cockney. I prithee now
ungird thy strangeness, and tell me what I shall vent to my lady.
Shall I vent to her that thou art coming?

Sebastian: I prithee, foolish Greek, depart from me. 15
There's money for thee. If you tarry longer,
I shall give worse payment.

Clown: By my troth, thou hast an open hand. These wise men that
give fools money get themselves a good report—after fourteen
years' purchase. 20

Enter Sir Andrew, Sir Toby *and* Fabian.

Sir Andrew: Now, sir, have I met you again? There's for you.
[Strikes Sebastian.]

Sebastian: Why, there's for thee, and there, and there. *[Strikes Sir
Andrew.]* Are all the people mad?
[Draws his dagger.]

Sir Toby: Hold, sir, or I'll throw your dagger o'er the house.
[Seizes Sebastian's arm.]

Clown: This will I tell my lady straight; I would not be in some of 25
your coats for twopence. *[Exit.]*

Sir Toby: Come on, sir, hold!

Sir Andrew: Nay, let him alone. I'll go another way to work with him;
I'll have an action of battery against him, if there be any law in
Illyria. Though I strook him first, yet it's no matter for that. 30

Sebastian: Let go thy hand.

Sir Toby: Come, sir, I will not let you go. Come, my young soldier,
put up your iron; you are well flesh'd. Come on.

Sebastian: I will be free from thee. *[Breaks away and draws his sword.]*
What wouldst thou now? If thou dar'st tempt me further, draw 35
thy sword.

Sir Toby: What, what? Nay then I must have an ounce or two of this
malapert blood from you. *[Draws.]*

Enter Olivia.

---

11. *vent thy folly:* utter your foolish talk. *Vent* was in common use, and it is hard to understand
why Feste chooses to think it affected. 12. *lubber:* clumsy stupid fellow, lout. *cockney:*
overnice, effeminate fellow. 13. *ungird thy strangeness:* put off your pretense of being a
stranger. 15. *Greek:* i.e. jester.

Olivia: Hold, Toby, on thy life I charge thee hold!
Sir Toby: Madam—   40
    Olivia: Will it be ever thus? Ungracious wretch,
    Fit for the mountains and the barbarous caves,
    Where manners ne'er were preach'd! Out of my sight!
    Be not offended, dear Cesario.
    Rudesby, be gone!   *[Exeunt Sir Toby, Sir Andrew, and Fabian.]*
                 I prithee, gentle friend,   45
    Let thy fair wisdom, not thy passion, sway
    In this uncivil and unjust extent
    Against thy peace. Go with me to my house,
    And hear thou there how many fruitless pranks
    This ruffian hath botch'd up, that thou thereby   50
    Mayst smile at this. Thou shalt not choose but go,
    Do not deny. Beshrew his soul for me,
    He started one poor heart of mine, in thee.
Sebastian: What relish is in this? How runs the stream?
    Or I am mad, or else this is a dream.   55
    Let fancy still my sense in Lethe steep;
    If it be thus to dream, still let me sleep!
    Olivia: Nay, come, I prithee. Would thou'dst be rul'd by me!
    Sebastian: Madam, I will.
    Olivia: O, say so, and so be!   *Exeunt.*

Scene II

Enter Maria *and* Clown.

    Maria: Nay, I prithee put on this gown and this beard, make him
        believe thou art Sir Topas the curate, do it quickly. I'll call Sir
        Toby the whilst.   *[Exit.]*
    Clown: Well, I'll put it on, and I will dissemble myself in't, and I
        would I were the first that ever dissembled in such a gown. I am 5
        not tall enough to become the function well, nor lean enough
        to be thought a good student; but to be said an honest man and

---

52. *Beshrew:* Here much closer to its original sense "curse" than in II.iii.70. 53. *He . . . thee:*
"He that offends thee, attacks one of my hearts, or as the ancients expressed it, half my heart"
(Johnson). There may also be a glancing play on *hart,* suggested by *started.* 54. *relish:* taste,
i.e. quality, nature. 55. *Or:* either. 56. *fancy:* imagination. *Lethe:* the river of forgetfulness
in the underworld.

IV.ii. Location: Olivia's house. 2. *Sir Topas:* Shakespeare may have borrowed the name
from Chaucer's "Rime of Sir Thopas" in *The Canterbury Tales.* On *Sir* see the note to
III.iv.235. 3. *the whilst:* in the meantime. 4. *dissemble:* disguise. 5. *dissembled:* created a
false impression, concealed his true nature. 6. *tall:* The sense here is probably "large,
well-fleshed," in contrast to *lean,* line 7. Feste seems to be glancing jestingly at two traditional
notions, that clerics are given to the pleasures of the table and that scholars lead ascetic
lives. *become . . . well:* grace the priestly office. 7. *studient:* scholar (a variant form of *student,*
not Feste's inverent. Most scholars were churchmen. *said:* known as.

a good house-keeper goes as fairly as to say a careful man and a
great scholar. The competitors enter.

Enter Sir Toby [*and* Maria].

Sir Toby: Jove bless thee, Master Parson.   10
    Clown: *Bonos dies,* Sir Toby: for as the old hermit of Prague, that
        never saw pen and ink, very wittily said to a niece of King Gor-
        boduc, "That that is is"; so I, being Master Parson, am Master
        Parson; for what is "that" but "that," and "is" but "is"?
Sir Toby: To him, Sir Topas.   15
    Clown: What ho, I say! Peace in this prison!
Sir Toby: The knave counterfeits well; a good knave.
Malvolio: (*Within.*) Who calls there?
    Clown: Sir Topas the curate, who comes to visit Malvolio the
        lunatic.   20
Malvolio: Sir Topas, Sir Topas, good Sir Topas, go to my lady.
    Clown: Out, hyperbolical fiend! how vexest thou this man! Talkest
        thou nothing but of ladies?
Sir Toby: Well said, Master Parson.
Malvolio: Sir Topas, never was man thus wrong'd. Good Sir Topas, 25
        do not think I am mad; they have laid me here in hideous
        darkness.
    Clown: Fie, thou dishonest Sathan! I call thee by the most modest
        terms, for I am one of those gentle ones that will use the devil
        himself with courtesy. Say'st thou that house is dark?   30
Malvolio: As hell, Sir Topas.
    Clown: Why, it hath bay windows transparent as barricadoes, and
        the [clerestories] toward the south north art as lustrous as
        ebony; and yet complainest thou of obstruction?
Malvolio: I am not mad, Sir Topas, I say to you this house is dark.   35
    Clown: Madman, thou errest. I say there is not darkness but igno-
        rance, in which thou art more puzzled than the Egyptians in
        their fog.
Malvolio: I say this house is as dark as ignorance, though ignorance
        were as dark as hell; and I say there was never man thus abus'd. 40
        I am no more mad than you are; make the trial of it in any con-
        stant question.

---

8. *good house-keeper:* good manager of his household. *goes as fairly:* sounds as well. *careful:*
highly respected duties.   9. *competitors:* partners, confederates.   11. *Bonos dies:* for *bonus
dies,* good day. *hermit of Prague:* Now that Feste is a priest invents is a man of religion.
12. *wittily:* cleverly.   12–13. *Gorboduc:* a legendary king of England.   22. *hyperbolical:* vehement (a rhetorical term, meaning "exaggerated in style"). *fiend:* i.e. the devil by whom
Malvolio is possessed.   28. *modest:* moderate.   30. *house:* i.e. room.   32. *barricadoes:* barri-
cades.   33. *clerestories:* windows in the upper wall.   34. *obstruction:* shutting out of light.
37. *puzzled:* greatly perplexed.   37–38. *Egyptians . . . fog:* An allusion to Exodus 10:22,
"And Moses stretched forth his hand toward heaven; and there was a black darkness in all the
land of Egypt three days" (Geneva).   41–42. *constant question:* topic for rational discourse.

Clown: What is the opinion of Pythagoras concerning wild-fowl?

Malvolio: That the soul of our grandam might happily inhabit a bird.

Clown: What think'st thou of his opinion?   45

Malvolio: I think nobly of the soul, and no way approve his opinion.

Clown: Fare thee well. Remain thou still in darkness. Thou shalt
hold th' opinion of Pythagoras ere I will allow of thy wits, and
fear to kill a woodcock lest thou dispossess the soul of thy grandam. Fare thee well.   50

Malvolio: Sir Topas, Sir Topas!

Sir Toby: My most exquisite Sir Topas!

Clown: Nay, I am for all waters.

Maria: Thou mightst have done this without thy beard and gown,
he sees thee not.   55

Sir Toby: To him in thine own voice, and bring me word now thou
find'st him. I would we were well rid of this knavery. If he may
be conveniently deliver'd, I would he were, for I am now so far
in offense with my niece that I cannot pursue with any safety
this sport [t'] the upshot. Come by and by to my chamber.   60

Exit [with Maria].

Clown: *[Sings.]*

"Hey , Robin, jolly Robin,
Tell me how thy lady does."

Malvolio: Fool!   65

Clown: "My lady is unkind, perdie."

Malvolio: Fool!

Clown: "Alas, why is she so?"

Malvolio: Fool, I say!

Clown: "She loves another"—Who calls, ha?

Malvolio: Good fool, as ever thou wilt deserve well at my hand, help
me to a candle, and pen, ink, and paper. As I am a gentleman, I 70
will live to be thankful to thee for't.

Clown: Master Malvolio?

Malvolio: Ay, good fool.

Clown: Alas, sir, how fell you besides your five wits?

Malvolio: Fool, there was never man so notoriously abus'd; I am as 75
well in my wits, fool, as thou art.

---

43. *Pythagoras . . . wild-fowl:* Referring to the Pythagorean doctrine of transmigration of
souls.   44. *happily:* haply, perchance.   48. *allow . . . wits:* grant that you are sane.
49. *woodcock:* Proverbial for its stupidity.   52. *exquisite:* consummately accomplished.
53. *for all waters:* i.e. ready for anything (a phrase of unknown origin).   58. *deliver'd:* set
free.   58–59. *far in offense:* deeply in disgrace.   60. *upshot:* conclusion (the decisive shot in
an archery contest).   61–62. *Hey . . . does:* These lines, with 66, 68, 70, are from an old song,
a version of which is attributed to Sir Thomas Wyatt.   66. *perdie:* indeed (a weakened oath,
like French *pardieu,* literally "by God").   74. *besides:* out of. *five wits:* Usually listed as
common wit (common sense), fantasy, memory, judgment, and imagination.   75. *notoriously
abus'd:* egregiously misused.

Clown: But as well! Then you are mad indeed, if you be no better
   in your wits than a fool.

Malvolio: They have here propertied me, keep me in darkness, send
   ministers to me, asses, and do all they can to face me out of my   80
   wits.

Clown: Advise you what you say; the minister is here.—Malvolio,
   Malvolio, thy wits the heavens restore! Endeavor thyself to
   sleep, and leave thy vain bibble babble.

Malvolio: Sir Topas!   85

Clown: Maintain no words within, good fellow.—Who, I, sir? Not
   I, sir. God buy you, good Sir Topas.—Marry, amen.—I will,
   sir, I will.

Malvolio: Fool, fool, fool, I say!

Clown: Alas, sir, be patient. What say you, sir? I am shent for   90
   speaking to you.

Malvolio: Good fool, help me to some light and some paper. I tell
   thee I am as well in my wits as any man in Illyria.

Clown: Well-a-day that you were, sir!

Malvolio: By this hand, I am. Good fool, some ink, paper, and light;   95
   and convey what I will set down to my lady. It shall advantage
   thee more than ever the bearing of letter did.

Clown: I will help you to't. But tell me true, are you not mad
   indeed, or do you but counterfeit?

Malvolio: Believe me I am not, I tell thee true.   100

Clown: Nay, I'll ne'er believe a madman till I see his brains. I will
   fetch you light and paper and ink.

Malvolio: Fool, I'll require it in the highest degree. I prithee be
   gone.

Clown: *[Sings.]*

   I am gone,sir,   105
   And anon, sir,
      I'll be with you again;
   In a trice,
   Like to the old Vice,
      Your need to sustain;   110

---

79. *propertied me:* i.e. stowed me away like a piece of furniture (perhaps with play on stage
properties).   80–81. *face . . . wits:* brazenly deny that I am sane.   82. *Advise you:* consider
well.   83–84. *Malvolio . . . babble:* Feste here impersonates Sir Topas again, and in his next
speech takes both parts in a dialogue between Sir Topas and himself.   83. *Endeavor thyself:*
strive.   87. *God buy you:* God be with you, goodby.   90. *shent:* rebuked.   94. *Well-a-day:*
alas.   96. *advantage:* benefit.   108. *trice:* moment.   109. *Vice:* the comic character in the
morality plays and interludes in which he often beat the Devil with his "dagger of lath" and
threatened to trim his long nails with it. Feste here compares himself to the Vice (whose role
was an ancestor of the Clown's role), and his impudent remarks to the devil by whom Malvolio
is supposedly possessed are by implication addressed to Malvolio himself.

Who with dagger of lath,
In his rage and his wrath,
   Cries, ah, ha! to the devil;
Like a mad lad,
Pare thy nails, dad. 115
   Adieu, goodman devil. *Exit.*

Scene III

Enter Sebastian.

Sebastian: This is the air, that is the glorious sun,
   This pearl she gave me, I do feel't and see't,
   And though 'tis wonder that enwraps me thus,
   Yet 'tis not madness. Where's Antonio then?
   I could not find him at the Elephant, 5
   Yet there he was, and there I found this credit,
   That he did range the town to seek me out.
   His counsel now might do me golden service,
   For though my soul disputes well with my sense,
   That this may be some error, but no madness, 10
   Yet doth this accident and flood of fortune
   So far exceed all instance, all discourse,
   That I am ready to distrust mine eyes,
   And wrangle with my reason that persuades me
   To any other trust but that I am mad, 15
   Or else the lady's mad; yet if 'twere so,
   She could not sway her house, command her followers.
   Take and give back affairs, and their dispatch,
   With such a smooth, discreet, and stable bearing
   As I perceive she does. There's something in't 20
   That is deceivable. But here the lady comes.

Enter Olivia *and* Priest.

Olivia: Blame not this haste of mine. If you mean well,
   Now go with me, and with this holy man,
   Into the chantry by; there, before him,

---

116. *goodman devil:* A final insult to Malvolio, who is addressed by the title proper for those below the rank of gentleman.

IV.iii. Location: Olivia's garden. 6. *was:* had been. *found this credit:* learned that they believed as follows. 7. *range:* go about. 9. *my soul . . . sense:* i.e. my reason and my senses both maintain (*disputes with* = "argues together with"). 11. *accident . . . fortune:* chance occurrence and (i.e. which is a brimming over of good fortune. 12. *instance:* example, precedent. *discourse:* reasoning, logic. 15. *trust:* belief, conviction. 17. *sway:* rule, manage. *followers:* servants. 18. *Take . . . dispatch:* i.e. take business in hand and give instructions for its prompt execution. *Take* governs *affairs; give back* governs *dispatch.* 19. *discreet:* judicious. 21. *deceivable:* deceptive. 24. *chantry:* a small private chapel where mass was sung daily for the souls of the dead. *by:* near by.

And underneath that consecrated roof,   25
Plight me the full assurance of your faith,
That my most jealous and too doubtful soul
May live at peace. He shall conceal it
Whiles you are willing it shall come to note,
What time we will our celebration keep   30
According to my birth. What do you say?
Sebastian: I'll follow this good man, and go with you,
And having sworn truth, ever will be true.
Olivia: Then lead the way, good father, and heavens so shine
That they may fairly note this act of mine!   *Exeunt.* 35

ACT V

Scene I

Enter Clown *and* Fabian.

Fabian: Now as thou lov'st me, let me see his letter.
Clown: Good Master Fabian, grant me another request.
Fabian: Any thing.
Clown: Do not desire to see this letter.
Fabian: This is to give a dog and in recompense desire my dog 5
   again.

Enter Duke, Viola, Curio, *and* Lords.

Duke: Belong you to the Lady Olivia, friends?
Clown: Ay, sir, we are some of her trappings.
Duke: I know thee well; how dost thou, my good fellow?
Clown: Truly, sir, the better for my foes and the worse for my 10
   friends.
Duke: Just the contrary: the better for thy friends.
Clown: No, sir, the worse.
Duke: How can that be?
Clown: Marry, sir, they praise me, and make an ass of me. Now my 15
   foes tell me plainly I am an ass; so that by my foes, sir, I profit in

---

26. *Plight:* pledge. The ceremony in question here is the betrothal, regarded as a binding contract; the marriage will be solemnized later (lines 30–31).   27. *jealous:* mistrustful (variant form of *jealous*). *doubtful:* apprehensive.   29. *Whiles:* until. *come to note:* become publicly known.   30. *What:* at which.   31. *birth:* rank, social position.

V.i. Location: Before Olivia's house.   5–6. *This . . . again:* Manningham in his *Diary* (in which the Middle Temple performance of *Twelfth Night* is recorded; see the introduction) relates a similar incident involving Queen Elizabeth and a Dr. Bullein, her kinsman, the owner of the dog. But whether Shakespeare knew of the incident is uncertain.

the knowledge of myself, and by my friends I am abus'd; so that, conclusions to be as kisses, if your four negatives make your two affirmatives, why then the worse for my friends and the better for my foes.   20

Duke: Why, this is excellent.

Clown: By my troth, sir, no; though it please you to be one of my friends.

Duke: Thou shalt not be the worse for me, there's gold.

Clown: But that it would be double-dealing, sir, I would you could · 25 make it another.

Duke: O, you give me ill counsel.

Clown: Put your grace in your pocket, sir, for this once, and let your flesh and blood obey it.

Duke: Well, I will be so much a sinner to be a double-dealer. 30 There's another.

Clown: *Primo, secundo, tertio,* is a good play, and the old saying is, the third pays for all. The triplex, sir, is a good tripping measure, or the bells of Saint Bennet, sir, may put you in mind— one, two, three.   35

Duke: You can fool no more money out of me at this throw. If you will let your lady know I am here to speak with her, and bring her along with you, it may awake my bounty further.

Clown: Marry, sir, lullaby to your bounty till I come again. I go, sir, but I would not have you to think that my desire of having is 40 the sin of covetousness; but as you say, sir, let your bounty take a nap, I will awake it anon.   *Exit.*

Enter Antonio *and* Officers.

Viola: Here comes the man, sir, that did rescue me.

Duke: That face of his I do remember well, Yet when I saw it last, it was besmear'd   45 As black as Vulcan in the smoke of war.

---

17. *abus'd:* deceived.   17–20. *so . . .foes:* This jest has never been satisfactorily paraphrased. Dover Wilson's explication may be given as one of many: "a kiss is made by four lips (contraries or negatives) brought together by two ardent mouths (affirmatives); if conclusions are like this, says Feste, then the conclusion that I am not an ass is only half the value of the conclusion that I am one."   25. *But:* except for the fact. *double-dealing:* (1) duplicity; (2) giving two coins.   28. *Put . . . pocket:* (1) pocket up (set aside) your virtue; (2) let your Grace dip into your purse (with further sense in *grace* of "favor" or "generosity").   29. *flesh and blood:* frail human nature. *it:* i.e. the "ill counsel."   32. *Primo, secundo, tertio:* Perhaps with reference to a game of dice, perhaps to a child's game.   33. *the third . . . all:* Proverbial; cf. "The third time's the charm." *triplex:* triple time in music.   34. *Saint Bennet:* Saint Benedict; possibly alluding to the London parish church of St. Bennet Hithe on Paul's Wharf, just across the Thames from the Globe.   36. *fool:* (1) befool, cheat; (2) obtain by your jester's wit. *throw:* (1) time; (2) throw of the dice.   46. *Vulcan:* the smith of the gods, blackened by the smoky fire in his smithy.

A baubling vessel was he captain of,
For shallow draught and bulk unprizable,
With which such scathful grapple did he make
With the most noble bottom of our fleet,   50
That very envy, and the tongue of loss,
Cried fame and honor on him. What's the matter?
1. Officer: Orsino, this is that Antonio
That took the *Phoenix* and her fraught from Candy,
And this is he that did the *Tiger* board,   55
When your young nephew Titus lost his leg.
Here in the streets, desperate of shame and state,
In private brabble did we apprehend him.
Viola: He did me kindness, sir, drew on my side,
But in conclusion put strange speech upon me.   60
I know not what 'twas but distraction.
Duke: Notable pirate, thou salt-water thief!
What foolish boldness brought thee to their mercies
Whom thou in terms so bloody and so dear
Hast made thine enemies?
Antonio: Orsino, noble sir,   65
Be pleas'd that I shake off these names you give me.
Antonio never yet was thief or pirate,
Though I confess, on base and ground enough,
Orsino's enemy. A witchcraft drew me hither:
That most ingrateful boy there by your side   70
From the rude sea's enrag'd and foamy mouth
Did I redeem; a wrack past hope he was.
His life I gave him, and did thereto add
My love, without retention or restraint,
All his in dedication. For his sake   75
Did I expose myself (pure for his love)
Into the danger of this adverse town,
Drew to defend him when he was beset;
Where being apprehended, his false cunning
(Not meaning to partake with me in danger)   80

---

47. *baubling:* trifling, toylike.   48. *For . . . unprizable:* valueless because of its shallow
draught and small size. For another *bauble / shallow / bulk* cluster see *Troilus and Cressida,* I.
iii.34–37.   49. *scathful:* damaging.   50. *bottom:* ship.   51. *envy:* enmity, i.e. (we) his
enemies. *loss:* i.e. the losers.   54. *fraught:* freight, cargo   *from Candy:* returning from Candia
(Crete).   57. *desperate . . . state:* i.e. with reckless disregard of disgrace and danger. *Shame*
refers perhaps to his involvement in a street brawl, *state* to his dangerous position as a public
enemy.   58. *brabble:* brawl.   59. *drew . . . side:* drew his sword in my defense.   60. *put . . .
me:* spoke very strangely to me.   61. *but distraction:* unless it was insanity.   62. *Notable:*
notorious.   64. *in terms:* in a manner. *dear:* grievous.   66. *Be pleas'd:* permit.   68. *base and
ground:* The nouns are synonyms.   72. *wrack:* wreck.   74. *retention:* reservation.   76. *pure:*
solely.   77. *Into:* to. *adverse:* hostile.   80. *Not . . . partake:* having no intention of sharing.

Taught him to face me out of his acquaintance,
And grew a twenty years removed thing
While one would wink; denied me mine own purse,
Which I had recommended to his use
Not half an hour before.
Viola: How can this be?   85
Duke: When came he to this town?
Antonio: To-day, my lord; and for three months before,
No int'rim, not a minute's vacancy,
Both day and night did we keep company.

Enter Olivia *and* Attendants.

Duke: Here comes the Countess, now heaven walks on earth.   90
But for thee, fellow—fellow, thy words are madness.
Three months this youth hath tended upon me,
But more of that anon. Take him aside.
Olivia: What would my lord, but that he may not have,
Wherein Olivia may seem serviceable?   95
Cesario, you do not keep promise with me.
Viola: Madam—
Duke: Gracious Olivia—
Olivia: What do you say, Cesario? Good my lord—
Viola: My lord would speak, my duty hushes me.   100
Olivia: If it be aught to the old tune, my lord,
It is as fat and fulsome to mine ear
As howling after music.
Duke: Still so cruel?
Olivia: Still so constant, lord.
Duke: What, to perverseness? You uncivil lady.   105
To whose ingrate and unauspicious altars
My soul the faithfull'st off'rings have breath'd out
That e'er devotion tender'd! What shall I do?
Olivia: Even what it please my lord, that shall become him.
Duke: Why should I not (had I the heart to do it),   110
Like to th' Egyptian thief at point of death,
Kill what I love? (a savage jealousy

---

81. *face . . . acquaintance:* deny brazenly that he knew me.   82–83. *grew . . . wink:* in the twinkling of an eye became as distant as if we had not seen each other for twenty years. 84. *recommended:* commended, committed.   88. *vacancy:* gap, interval.   94. *but . . . have:* i.e. except what I cannot give him (i.e. her love).   95. *seem serviceable:* show her duty. 102. *fat and fulsome:* gross and distasteful.   105. *uncivil:* inhumane.   106. *ingrate:* ungrateful. *unauspicious:* unpropitious.   108. *tender'd:* offered.   111. *Egyptian thief:* Referring to an episode in Heliodorus' *Ethiopica* in which Thyamis, an Egyptian robber captain who has taken Chariclea captive and fallen in love with her, finds himself in danger of death at his enemies' hands and attempts to kill Chariclea first.

That sometime savors nobly), but hear me this:
Since you to non-regardance cast my faith,
And that I partly know the instrument   115
That screws me from my true place in your favor,
Live you the marble-breasted tyrant still.
But this your minion, whom I know you love,
And whom, by heaven I swear, I tender dearly,
Him will I tear out of that cruel eye,   120
Where he sits crowned in his master's spite.
Come, boy, with me, my thoughts are ripe in mischief.
I'll sacrifice the lamb that I do love,
To spite a raven's heart within a dove.
Viola: And I most jocund, apt, and willingly,   125
To do you rest, a thousand deaths would die.
Olivia: Where goes Cesario?
Viola: After him I love
More than I love these eyes, more than my life,
More by all mores than e'er I shall love wife.
If I do feign, you witnesses above   130
Punish my life for tainting of my love!
Olivia: Ay me, detested! how am I beguil'd!
Viola: Who does beguile you? who does do you wrong?
Olivia: Hast thou forgot thyself? Is it so long? Call forth the holy
father.
Duke: Come, away!   135
Olivia: Whither, my lord? Cesario, husband, stay.
Duke: Husband?
Olivia: Ay, husband. Can he that deny?
Duke: Her husband, sirrah?
Viola: No, my lord, not I.
Olivia: Alas, it is the baseness of thy fear
That makes thee strangle thy propriety.   140
Fear not, Cesario, take thy fortunes up,
Be that thou know'st thou art, and then thou art
As great as that thou fear'st.

Enter Priest.

                    O, welcome, father!

---

113. *savors nobly:* has a noble quality about it.   114. *non-regardance:* disregard, neglect. *faith:* constancy.   115. *that:* Repeating the sense of *Since*, line 114.   116. *screws:* forces.
117. *marble-breasted:* stony-hearted.   118. *minion:* darling.   119. *tender:* regard.
121. *in . . . spite:* in defiance of his master.   125. *apt:* ready.   126. *do you rest:* give you peace.   129. *mores:* (such) comparisons.   131. *tainting . . . love:* bringing my love into discredit.   132. *detested:* renounced, rejected.   138. *sirrah:* form of address to an inferior.
140. *strangle thy propriety:* i.e. disown your identity as my husband.   141. *take . . . up:* receive your fortune.   143. *that thou fear'st:* i.e. Orsino.

Father, I charge thee by thy reverence
Here to unfold, though lately we intended 145
To keep in darkness what occasion now
Reveals before 'tis ripe, what thou dost know
Hath newly pass'd between this youth and me.
Priest: A contract of eternal bond of love,
Confirm'd by mutual joinder of your hands, 150
Attested by the holy close of lips,
Strength'ned by interchangement of your rings,
And all the ceremony of this compact
Seal'd in my function, by my testimony;
Since when, my watch hath told me, toward my grave 155
I have travell'd but two hours.
Duke: O thou dissembling cub! what wilt thou be
When time hath sow'd a grizzle on thy case?
Or will not else thy craft so quickly grow,
That thine own trip shall be thine overthrow? 160
Farewell, and take her, but direct thy feet
Where thou and I (henceforth) may never meet.
Viola: My lord, I do protest—
Olivia: O, do not swear!
Hold little faith, though thou hast too much fear.

Enter Sir Andrew.

Sir Andrew: For the love of God, a surgeon! Send one presently to Sir 165
Toby.
Olivia: What's the matter?
Sir Andrew: H'as broke my head across, and has given Sir Toby a
bloody coxcomb too. For the love of God, your help! I had
rather than forty pound I were at home. 170
Olivia: Who has done this, Sir Andrew?
Sir Andrew: The Count's gentleman, one Cesario. We took him for a
coward, but he's the very devil incardinate.
Duke: My gentleman, Cesario?
Sir Andrew: 'Od's lifelings, here he is! You broke my head for nothing, 175
and that that I did, I was set on to do't by Sir Toby.
Viola: Why do you speak to me? I never hurt you.

---

147. *occasion:* necessity. 148. *newly:* recently. 150. *joinder:* joining. 151. *close:* union.
154. *Seal'd:* ratified, attested. *in my function:* i.e. by my authority as priest. 158. *a grizzle:*
grey hair. *case:* skin (of a fox); Orsino is thus calling Viola-Cesario a fox-cub. 160. *trip:*
attempt to trip up (or trap) another. 163. *protest:* avow, swear. 164. *Hold little:* keep a little. 165. *presently:* immediately. 168. *H'as . . . across:* he has given me a cut on the head.
169. *coxcomb:* head (with a suggestion of the cap traditionally worn by the professional fool in
its applicability to Sir Toby and Sir Andrew). 173. *incardinate:* Apparently Sir Andrew's slip
for *incarnate.* 175. *'Od's lifelings:* by God's little lives.

You drew your sword upon me without cause,
But I bespake you fair, and hurt you not.

Enter Sir Toby *and* Clown.

Sir Andrew: If a bloody coxcomb be a hurt, you have hurt me. I think   180
you set nothing by a bloody coxcomb. Here comes Sir Toby
halting—you shall hear more. But if he had not been in drink,
he would have tickled you othergates than he did.
      Duke: How now, gentleman? how is't with you?
   Sir Toby: That's all one. H'as hurt me, and there's th' end on't. Sot,   185
didst see Dick surgeon, sot?
     Clown: O, he's drunk, Sir Toby, an hour agone; his eyes were set at
eight i' th' morning.
   Sir Toby: Then he's a rogue, and a passy-measures [pavin]. I hate a
drunken rogue.   190
     Olivia: Away with him! Who hath made this havoc with them?
Sir Andrew: I'll help you, Sir Toby, because we'll be dress'd together.
   Sir Toby: Will you help?—an ass-head and a coxcomb and a knave, a
thin-fac'd knave, a gull!
     Olivia: Get him to bed, and let his hurt be look'd to.   195

[Exeunt Clown, Fabian, Sir Toby, and Sir Andrew.]

Enter Sebastian.

Sebastian: I am sorry, madam, I have hurt your kinsman,
But had it been the brother of my blood,
I must have done no less with wit and safety.
You throw a strange regard upon me, and by that
I do perceive it hath offended you.   200
Pardon me, sweet one, even for the vows
We made each other but so late ago.
      Duke: One face, one voice, one habit, and two persons,
A natural perspective, that is and is not!
Sebastian: Antonio, O my dear Antonio!   205
How have the hours rack'd and tortur'd me,

179. *bespake you fair:* spoke courteously to you.   181. *set nothing by:* regard as nothing.
182. *halting:* limping. *But if:* if only. *in drink:* drunk.   183. *tickled:* chastised. *othergates:*
otherwise.   185. *That's all one:* no matter. *there's . . . on't:* that's that. *Sot:* fool.   187. *set:*
extinguished (as in *the sun sets*), i.e. closed.   189. *passy-measures pavin:* Naylor explains
passy-measures (from Italian *passamezzo*) as a dance tune with "strains" consisting of eight bars
each (hence suggested to Sir Toby by Feste's "set at eight"). The pavin or pavan(e) was a slow
and stately dance. Sir Toby obviously expects no speedy aid from Dick surgeon.   192. *be
dress'd:* have our wounds cared for.   193. *coxcomb:* fool.   194. *gull:* dupe.   198. *with . . .
safety:* i.e. with due regard for my own safety.   199. *throw . . . me:* look at me as if I were a
stranger.   203. *habit:* dress.   204. *natural perspective:* i.e. an optical illusion produced by
nature, not by a perspective glass (an optical device that makes the viewer see an object
differently). *that . . . not:* i.e. that must be an illusion and yet is not.

Since I have lost thee!
Antonio: Sebastian are you?
Sebastian: Fear'st thou that, Antonio?
  Antonio: How have you made division of yourself?
        An apple, cleft in two, is not more twin   210
        Than these two creatures. Which is Sebastian?
    Olivia: Most wonderful!
Sebastian: Do I stand there? I never had a brother;
        Nor can there be that deity in my nature
        Of here and every where. I had a sister,   215
        Whom the blind waves and surges have devour'd.
        Of charity, what kin are you to me?
        What countryman? What name? What parentage?
      Viola: Of Messaline; Sebastian was my father,
        Such a Sebastian was my brother too;   220
        So went he suited to his watery tomb.
        If spirits can assume both form and suit,
        You come to fright us.
Sebastian: A spirit I am indeed,
        But am in that dimension grossly clad
        Which from the womb I did participate.   225
        Were you a woman, as the rest goes even,
        I should my tears let fall upon your cheek,
        And say, "Thrice welcome, drowned Viola!"
      Viola: My father had a mole upon his brow.
Sebastian: And so had mine.   230
      Viola: And died that day when Viola from her birth
        Had numb'red thirteen years.
Sebastian: O, that record is lively in my soul!
        He finished indeed his mortal act
        That day that made my sister thirteen years.   235
      Viola: If nothing lets to make us happy both
        But this my masculine usurp'd attire,
        Do not embrace me till each circumstance
        Of place, time, fortune, do cohere and jump
        That I am Viola—which to confirm,   240
        I'll bring you to a captain in this town,
        Where lie my maiden weeds; by whose gentle help
        I was preserv'd to serve this noble count.

---

214. *deity:* divine attribute.   215. *here . . . where:* omnipresence.   216. *blind:* ruthless.
217. *Of charity:* (tell me) out of kindness.   221. *suited:* dressed.   224. *in . . . clad:* clothed in
that corporeal frame.   225. *participate:* share existence with.   226. *as . . . even:* i.e. as (is
likely since) all the rest accords. A common type of ellipsis; for another example see line
252.   233. *lively:* vivid.   236. *lets:* hinders.   239. *cohere:* agree. *jump:* coincide, agree.
242. *Where:* at whose house. *weeds:* clothes.

All the occurrence of my fortune since
Hath been between this lady and this lord.   245
Sebastian: [To Olivia.] So comes it, lady, you have been mistook;
But Nature to her bias drew in that.
You would have been contracted to a maid,
Nor are you therein, by my life, deceiv'd,
You are betroth'd both to a maid and man.   250
Duke: Be not amaz'd, right noble is his blood.
If this be so, as yet the glass seems true,
I shall have share in this most happy wrack.
[To Viola.] Boy, thou hast said to me a thousand times
Thou never shouldst love woman like to me.   255
Viola: And all those sayings will I over swear,
And all those swearings keep as true in soul
As doth that orbed continent the fire
That severs day from night.
Duke: Give me thy hand,
And let me see thee in thy woman's weeds.   260
Viola: The captain that did bring me first on shore
Hath my maid's garments. He upon some action
Is now in durance, at Malvolio's suit,
A gentleman, and follower of my lady's.
Olivia: He shall enlarge him; fetch Malvolio hither.   265
And yet, alas, now I remember me,
They say, poor gentleman, he's much distract.

Enter Clown *with a letter, and* Fabian.

A most extracting frenzy of mine own
From my remembrance clearly banish'd his.
How does he, sirrah?   270
Clown: Truly, madam, he holds Belzebub at the stave's end as well
as a man in his case may do. H'as here writ a letter to you; I
should have given't you to-day morning. But as a madman's
epistles are no gospels, so it skills not much when they are
deliver'd.   275

---

247. *Nature . . . that:* i.e. your nature was true to its own bent when you fell in love with one
who is the perfect likeness of me.   248. *contracted:* betrothed.   250. *maid:* virgin (here
applied to a man).   251. *amaz'd:* astounded, dazed (a much stronger word than in modern
usage).   252. *glass:* i.e. the "natural perspective" of line 204.   256. *over:* again.
258. *As . . . fire:* i.e. as the sun's sphere keeps the fire. *Continent* = container.   262. *action:*
legal charge.   263. *durance:* prison.   265. *enlarge:* release.   266. *remember me:* recall.
267. *distract:* distracted, out of his wits.   268. *extracting frenzy:* i.e. madness that took other
things out of my mind.   269. *his:* i.e. remembrance of his frenzy.   271. *holds . . . end:* keeps
the devil (who possesses him) at a distance. "To hold the devil at stave's end" was proverbial.
273–74. *a madman's . . . gospels:* i.e. a madman's letters are not to be taken as gospel truth
(with play on the reading of appointed passages from the epistles and the gospels in a church
service).   274. *it . . . much:* doesn't matter much.

Olivia: Open't and read it.

Clown: Look then to be well edified when the fool delivers the madman. *[Reads madly.]* "By the Lord, madam,"—

Olivia: How now, art thou mad?

Clown: No, madam, I do but read madness. And your ladyship   280
will have it as it ought to be, you must allow *vox.*

Olivia: Prithee read i' thy right wits.

Clown: So I do, madonna; but to read his right wits is to read thus;
therefore perpend, my princess, and give ear.

Olivia: [To Fabian.] Read it you, sirrah.   285

Fabian: (Reads.) "By the Lord, madam, you wrong me, and the
world shall know it. Though you have put me into darkness,
and given your drunken cousin rule over me, yet have I the
benefit of my senses as well as your ladyship. I have your own
letter that induc'd me to the semblance I put on; with the which   290
I doubt not but to do myself much right, or you much shame.
Think of me as you please. I leave my duty a little unthought of,
and speak out of my injury.
The madly-us'd Malvolio."

Olivia: Did he write this?   295

Clown: Ay, madam.

Duke: This savors not much of distraction.

Olivia: See him deliver'd, Fabian, bring him hither. *[Exit Fabian.]*
My lord, so please you, these things further thought on,
To think me as well a sister as a wife,   300
One day shall crown th' alliance on't, so please you,
Here at my house and at my proper cost.

Duke: Madam, I am most apt t' embrace your offer.
[To Viola.] Your master quits you; and for your service done
him,   305
So much against the mettle of your sex,
So far beneath your soft and tender breeding,
And since you call'd me master for so long,
Here is my hand—you shall from this time be
Your master's mistress.

Olivia: A sister! you are she.

Enter [Fabian *with*] Malvolio.

Duke: Is this the madman?

---

277. *delivers:* presents, speaks the words of.   280. *And:* if.   281. *vox:* voice, i.e. dramatic
reading.   284. *perpend:* consider.   290. *the which:* i.e. the letter (as proof).   292. *my duty:*
the duty I owe you as your servant.   298. *deliver'd:* released.   300. *think . . . wife:* regard me
as favorably as a sister-in-law as you would have as a wife.   301. *crown . . . on't:* i.e. see the
performance of the two weddings that will create that relationship.   302. *proper cost:* own
expense.   303. *apt:* ready.   304. *quits:* frees, withdraws all claim to.   306. *mettle:*
disposition.

Olivia: Ay, my lord, this same.
      How now, Malvolio?
Malvolio: Madam, you have done me wrong,
      Notorious wrong.
    Olivia: Have I, Malvolio? No.
Malvolio: Lady, you have. Pray you peruse that letter.
      You must not now deny it is your hand;   315
      Write from it if you can, in hand or phrase,
      Or say 'tis not your seal, not your invention.
      You can say none of this. Well, grant it then,
      And tell me, in the modesty of honor,
      Why you have given me such clear lights of favor,   320
      Bade me come smiling and cross-garter'd to you,
      To put on yellow stockings, and to frown
      Upon Sir Toby and the lighter people;
      And acting this in an obedient hope,
      Why have you suffer'd me to be imprison'd,   325
      Kept in a dark house, visited by the priest,
      And made the most notorious geck and gull
      That e'er invention play'd on? Tell me why!
    Olivia: Alas, Malvolio, this is not my writing,
      Though I confess much like the character;   330
      But out of question 'tis Maria's hand.
      And now I do bethink me, it was she
      First told me thou wast mad. Then cam'st in smiling,
      And in such forms which here were presuppos'd
      Upon thee in the letter. Prithee be content.   335
      This practice hath most shrewdly pass'd upon thee;
      But when we know the grounds and authors of it,
      Thou shalt be both the plaintiff and the judge
      Of thine own cause.
    Fabian: Good madam, here me speak,
      And let no quarrel nor no brawl to come   340
      Taint the condition of this present hour,
      Which I have wond'red at. In hope it shall not,
      Most freely I confess, myself and Toby
      Set this device against Malvolio here,
      Upon some stubborn and uncourteous parts   345
      We had conveiv'd against him. Maria writ

---

316. *from it:* differently. *hand or phrase:* handwriting or phraseology.   317. *invention:*
composition.   319. *in . . . honor:* with the sense of propriety of an honorable person.
320. *clear lights:* i.e. sure signs.   323. *lighter:* lesser.   327. *geck:* fool.   328. *invention:*
devising.   331. *out of:* beyond.   333. *cam'st:* cam'st thou.   334. *which:* as. *presuppos'd:* suggested beforehand.   336. *shrewdly:* grievously. *pass'd upon:* imposed upon.   342. *wond'red:*
marvelled.   345. *Upon:* (which) in consequence of. *stubborn:* rude, haughty. *parts:* acts.
346. *conceiv'd:* devised.

The letter at Sir Toby's great importance,
In recompense whereof he hath married her.
How with a sportful malice it was follow'd
May rather pluck on laughter than revenge,   350
If that the injuries be justly weigh'd
That have on both sides pass'd.
   Olivia: Alas, poor fool, how have they baffled thee!
   Clown: Why, "some are born great, some achieve greatness, and
some have greatness thrown upon them." I was one, sir, in this 355
enterlude—one Sir Topas, sir, but that's all one. "By the Lord,
fool, I am not mad." But do you remember? "Madam, why
laugh you at such a barren rascal? And you smile not, he's
gagg'd." And thus the whirligig of time brings in his revenges.
   Malvolio: I'll be reveng'd on the whole pack of you.   *[Exit.]* 360
   Olivia: He hath been most notoriously abus'd.
   Duke: Pursue him, and entreat him to a peace;
He hath not told us of the captain yet.
When that is known, and golden time convents,
A solemn combination shall be made   365
Of our dear souls. Mean time, sweet sister,
We will not part from hence. Cesario, come—
For so you shall be while you are a man;
But when in other habits you are seen,
Orsino's mistress, and his fancy's queen. *Exeunt [all but Clown].* 370

Clown sings.

When that I was and a little tine boy,
   With hey ho, the wind and the rain,
A foolish thing was but a toy,
   For the rain it raineth every day.

But when I came to man's estate,   375
   With hey ho, etc.
'Gainst knaves and thieves men shut their gate,
   For the rain, etc.

But when I came, alas, to wive,
   With hey ho, etc.   380

---

347. *importance:* importunity.   349. *sportful:* jesting. *follow'd:* carried through.   350. *pluck on:* draw on, induce.   353. *baffled thee:* put you down.   356. *enterlude:* interlude, i.e. comedy.   359. *whirligig of time:* time's circling course. A whirligig is a spinning top or toy. 361. *He . . . abus'd:* Olivia thus repeats Malvolio's own judgment at IV.ii.75.   363. *captain:* See lines 240–43, 261–64.   364. *convents:* suits.   365. *combination:* marriage.   371. *tine:* tiny. Cf. with lines 389 ff. the song in *King Lear,* III.ii.74–77, in which the variant spelling *tine* again appears.   373. *A . . . toy:* i.e. my mischief was not taken seriously.   377. *'Gainst . . . gate:* i.e. my mischief caused men to shut their doors against me as a knave and a thief.

By swaggering could I never thrive,
    For the rain, etc.

But when I came unto my beds,
    With hey ho, etc.

With toss-pots still had drunken heads,   385
    For the rain, etc.

A great while ago the world begun,
    [With] hey ho, etc.

But that's all one, our play is done,
    And we'll strive to please you every day.   *[Exit.]* 390

That drama is meant to be acted by players on a stage—that it is written to be brought literally to life before an audience—is easy enough to forget when we sit solitary, silent, reading the printed page. The "sport and play" of words, especially the words of Shakespeare, can overtake us, and we can feel that the play's essence is imprinted on our consciousness. But many nuances, intonations, and downright interpretations can only be conveyed by voice and gesture, thus the reader's understanding is often different from that of the viewer. As Virginia Woolf reminds us in a review of a performance of Twelfth Night, *to see the play enacted is to be made "to pause and think about it," to recognize that playwrights write "for the body and the mind simultaneously."*

"The word is given a body as well as a soul": Virginia Woolf

Certainly there is a good deal to be said for reading *Twelfth Night* in the book if the book can be read in a garden, with no sound but the thud of an apple falling to the earth, or of the wind ruffling the branches of the trees. For one thing there is time—time not only to hear "the sweet sound that breathes upon a bank of violets" but to unfold the implications of that very subtle speech as the Duke winds into the nature of love. There is time, too, to make a note in the margin; time to wonder at queer jingles like "that live in her; when liver, brain, and heart" . . . "and of a foolish knight that you brought in one night" and to ask oneself whether it was from them that was born the lovely, "And what should I do in Illyria? My brother he is in Elysium." For Shakespeare is writing, it seems, not with the whole of his mind

---

381. *swaggering:* bullying, blustering.   383. *unto my beds:* to old age (?)   385. *toss-pots:* drunkards.

mobilized and under control but with feelers left flying that sport and play with words so that the trail of a chance word is caught and followed recklessly. From the echo of one word is born another word, for which reason, perhaps, the play seems as we read it to tremble perpetually on the brink of music. They are always calling for songs in *Twelfth Night,* "O fellow come, the song we had last night." Yet Shakespeare was not so deeply in love with words but that he could turn and laugh at them. "They that do dally with words do quickly make them wanton." There is a roar of laughter and out burst Sir Toby, Sir Andrew, Maria. Words on their lips are things that have meaning; that rush and leap out with a whole character packed in a little phrase. When Sir Andrew says "I was adored once," we feel that we hold him in the hollow of our hands; a novelist would have taken three volumes to bring us to that pitch of intimacy. And Viola, Malvolio, Olivia, the Duke —the mind so brims and spills over with all that we know and guess about them as they move in and out among the lights and shadows of the mind's stage that we ask why should we imprison them within the bodies of real men and women? Why exchange this garden for the theatre? The answer is that Shakespeare wrote for the stage and presumably with reason. . . .

The play gains immensely in robustness, in solidity. The printed word is changed out of all recognition when it is heard by other people. We watch it strike upon this man or woman; we see them laugh or shrug their shoulders, or turn aside to hide their faces. The word is given a body as well as a soul. Then again as the actors pause, or topple over a barrel, or stretch their hands out, the flatness of the print is broken up as by crevasses or precipices; all the proportions are changed. Perhaps the most impressive effect in the play is achieved by the long pause which Sebastian and Viola make as they stand looking at each other in a silent ecstasy of recognition. The reader's eye may have slipped over that moment entirely. Here we are made to pause and think about it; and are reminded that Shakespeare wrote for the body and for the mind simultaneously.

But now that the actors have done their proper work of solidifying and intensifying our impressions, we begin to criticize them more minutely and to compare their version with our own. We make Mr. Quartermaine's Malvolio stand beside our Malvolio. And to tell the truth, wherever the fault may lie, they have very little in common. Mr. Quartermaine's Malvolio is a splendid gentleman, courteous, considerate, well bred; a man of parts and humour who has no quarrel with the world. He has never felt a twinge of vanity or a moment's envy in his life. If Sir Toby and Maria fool him he sees through it, we may be sure, and only suffers it as a fine gentleman puts up with the games of foolish children. Our Malvolio, on the other hand, was a fantastic complex creature, twitching with vanity, tortured by ambition. There was cruelty in his teasing, and a hint of tragedy in his defeat; his final threat had a momentary terror in it. But when Mr. Quartermaine says "I'll be revenged on the whole pack of you," we feel merely that the powers of the law will be soon and effectively invoked. What, then, becomes of Olivia's "He hath been most notoriously abused"? Then there is Olivia.

Madame Lopokova has by nature that rare quality which is neither to be had for the asking nor to be subdued by the will—the genius of personality. She has only to float on to the stage and everything round her suffers, not a sea change, but a change into light, into gaiety; the birds sing, the sheep are garlanded, the air rings with melody and human beings dance towards each other on the tips of their toes possessed of an exquisite friendliness, sympathy and delight. But our Olivia was a stately lady; of sombre complexion, slow moving, and of few sympathies. She could not love the Duke nor change her feeling. Madame Lopokova loves everybody. She is always changing. Her hands, her face, her feet, the whole of her body, are always quivering in sympathy with the moment. She could make the moment, as she proved when she walked down the stairs with Sebastian, one of intense and moving beauty; but she was not our Olivia. . . .

Nevertheless, the play has served its purpose. It has made us compare our Malvolio with Mr. Quartermaine's; our Olivia with Madame Lopokova's; our reading of the whole play with Mr. Guthrie's; and since they all differ, back we must go to Shakespeare. We must read *Twelfth Night* again.

WILLIAM SHAKESPEARE

(1564–1616)

THE TRAGEDY OF HAMLET, PRINCE OF DENMARK

edited by G. Blakemore Evans

CHARACTERS

Claudius, King of Denmark
Hamlet, son to the late King Hamlet, and nephew to the
    present King
Polonius, Lord Chamberlain
Horatio, friend to Hamlet
Laertes, son to Polonius
Voltemand ⎤
Cornelius ⎥
Rosencrantz ⎥
Guildenstern ⎬ courtiers
Osric ⎥
Gentleman ⎦
Marcellus ⎤ officers
Barnardo ⎦
Francisco, a soldier
Reynaldo, servant to Polonius
Fortinbras, Prince of Norway
Norwegian Captain
Doctor of Divinity
Players
Two Clowns, gravediggers
English Ambassadors
Gertrude, Queen of Denmark, and mother to Hamlet
Ophelia, daughter ot Polonius
Ghost of Hamlet's Father
Lords, Ladies, Officers, Soldiers, Sailors, Messengers, and
    Attendants

Scene: Denmark

Words and passages enclosed in square brackets in the text above are either emendations of the copy-text or additions to it. The Textual Notes immediately following the play cite the earliest authority for every such change or insertion and supply the reading of the copy-text wherever it is emended in this edition.

ACT I

Scene I

Enter Barnardo *and* Francisco, *two sentinels, [meeting].*

Barnardo: Who's there?

Francisco: Nay, answer me. Stand and unfold yourself.

Barnardo: Long live the King!

Francisco: Barnardo.

Barnardo: He.   5

Francisco: You come most carefully upon your hour.

Barnardo: 'Tis now strook twelf. Get thee to bed, Francisco.

Francisco: For this relief much thanks. 'Tis bitter cold,
       And I am sick at heart.

Barnardo: Have you had quiet guard?

Francisco: Not a mouse stirring.   10

Barnardo: Well, good night.
       If you do meet Horatio and Marcellus,
       The rivals of my watch, bid them make haste.

Enter Horatio *and* Marcellus.

Francisco: I think I hear them. Stand ho! Who is there?

   Horatio: Friends to this ground.

Marcellus: And liegemen to the Dane.   15

Francisco: Give you good night.

Marcellus: O, farewell, honest [soldier].
       Who hath reliev'd you?

Francisco: Barnardo hath my place.
       Give you good night.   *Exit* Francisco.

Marcellus: Holla, Barnardo!

Barnardo: Say—
       What, is Horatio there?

   Horatio: A piece of him.

Barnardo: Welcome, Horatio, welcome, good Marcellus.   20

   Horatio: What, has this thing appear'd again to-night?

Barnardo: I have seen nothing.

Marcellus: Horatio says 'tis but our fantasy,
       And will not let belief take hold of him
       Touching this dreaded sight twice seen of us;   25
       Therefore I have entreated him along,

I.i. Location: Elsinore. A guard-platform of the castle.   2. *answer me:* i.e. *you* answer *me.*
Francisco is on watch; Barnardo has come to relieve him.   *unfold yourself:* make known who
you are.   3. *Long . . . King:* Perhaps a password, perhaps simply an utterance to allow the
voice to be recognized.   7. *strook twelf:* struck twelve.   9. *sick at heart:* in low spirits.
13. *rivals:* partners.   15. *liegemen . . . Dane:* loyal subjects to the King of Denmark.
16. *Give:* God give.   23. *fantasy:* imagination.

With us to watch the minutes of this night,
That if again this apparition come,
He may approve our eyes and speak to it.
Horatio: Tush, tush, 'twill not appear.
Barnardo: Sit down a while,   30
          And let us once again assail your ears,
          That are so fortified against our story,
          What we have two nights seen.
Horatio: Well, sit we down,
          And let us hear Barnardo speak of this.
Barnardo: Last night of all,   35
          When yond same star that's westward from the pole
          Had made his course t' illume that part of heaven
          Where now it burns, Marcellus and myself,
          The bell then beating one—

Enter Ghost.

   Marcellus: Peace, break thee off! Look where it comes again!   40
   Barnardo: In the same figure like the King that's dead.
   Marcellus: Thou art a scholar, speak to it, Horatio.
   Barnardo: Looks 'a not like the King? Mark it, Horatio.
     Horatio: Most like; it [harrows] me with fear and wonder.
   Barnardo: It would be spoke to.
   Marcellus: Speak to it, Horatio.   45
     Horatio: What art thou that usurp'st this time of night,
          Together with that fair and warlike form
          In which the majesty of buried Denmark
          Did sometimes march? By heaven I charge thee speak!
   Marcellus: It is offended.
   Barnardo: See, it stalks away!   50
     Horatio: Stay! Speak, speak, I charge thee speak!   *Exit* Ghost.
   Marcellus: 'Tis gone, and will not answer.
   Barnardo: How now, Horatio? you tremble and look pale.
          Is not this something more than fantasy?
          What think you on't?   55
     Horatio: Before my God, I might not this believe
          Without the sensible and true avouch
          Of mine own eyes.
   Marcellus: Is it not like the King?
     Horatio: As thou art to thyself.

---

29. *approve:* corroborate.   36. *pole:* pole star.   37. *his:* its (the commonest form of the
neuter possessive singular in Shakespeare's day).   41. *like:* in the likeness of.   42. *a scholar:*
i.e. one who knows how best to address it.   43. *'a:* he.   45. *It . . . to:* A ghost had to be
spoken to before it could speak.   46. *usurp'st:* The ghost, a supernatural being, has invaded
the realm of nature.   48. *majesty . . . Denmark:* late King of Denmark.   49. *sometimes:*
formerly.   57. *sensible:* relating to the senses.   *avouch:* guarantee.

Such was the very armor he had on   60
When he the ambitious Norway combated.
So frown'd he once when in an angry parle
He smote the sledded [Polacks] on the ice.
'Tis strange.
Marcellus: Thus twice before, and jump at this dead hour,   65
With martial stalk hath he gone by our watch.
Horatio: In what particular thought to work I know not,
But in the gross and scope of mine opinion,
This bodes some strange eruption to our state.
Marcellus: Good now, sit down, and tell me, he that knows,   70
Why this same strict and most observant watch
So nightly toils the subject of the land,
And [why] such daily [cast] of brazen cannon,
And foreign mart for implements of war,
Why such impress of shipwrights, whose sore task   75
Does not divide the Sunday from the week,
What might be toward, that this sweaty haste
Doth make the night joint-laborer with the day:
Who is't that can inform me?
Horatio: That can I,
At least the whisper goes so: our last king,   80
Whose image even but now appear'd to us,
Was, as you know, by Fortinbras of Norway,
Thereto prick'd on by a most emulate pride,
Dar'd to the combat; in which our valiant Hamlet
(For so this side of our known world esteem'd him)   85
    Did slay this Fortinbras, who, by a seal'd compact
Well ratified by law and heraldry,
Did forfeit (with his life) all [those] his lands
Which he stood seiz'd of, to the conqueror;
Against the which a moi'ty competent   90
Was gaged by our king, which had [return'd]
To the inheritance of Fortinbras,
Had he been vanquisher; as by the same comart
And carriage of the article [design'd],
His fell to Hamlet. Now, sir, young Fortinbras,   95

---

61. *Norway:* King of Norway.   62. *parle:* parley.   63. *sledded:* using sleds or sledges.
Polacks: Poles.   65. *jump:* precisely.   67-68. *In . . . opinion:* while I have no precise theory
about it, my general feeling is that. *Gross* = wholeness, totality; *scope* = range.   69. *eruption:*
upheaval.   72. *toils:* causes to work. *subject:* subjects.   74. *foreign mart:* dealing with foreign
markets.   75. *impress:* forced service.   77. *toward:* in preparation.   83. *emulate:* emulous,
proceeding from rivalry.   87. *law and heraldry:* heraldic law (governing combat). *Heraldy* is a
variant of *heraldry.*   89. *seiz'd of:* possessed of.   90. *moi'ty:* portion. *competent:* adequate, i.e.
equivalent.   91. *gaged:* pledged. *had:* would have.   92. *inheritance:* possession.   93. *comart:*
bargain.   94. *carriage:* tenor. *design'd:* drawn up.

Of unimproved mettle hot and full,
Hath in the skirts of Norway here and there
Shark'd up a list of lawless resolutes
For food and diet to some enterprise
That hath a stomach in't, which is no other,   100
As it doth well appear unto our state,
But to recover of us, by strong hand
And terms compulsatory, those foresaid lands
So by his father lost; and this, I take it,
Is the main motive of our preparations,   105
The source of this our watch, and the chief head
Of this post-haste and romage in the land.
Barnardo: I think it be no other but e'en so.
Well may it sort that this portentous figure
Comes armed through our watch so like the King   110
That was and is the question of these wars.
Horatio: A mote it is to trouble the mind's eye.
In the most high and palmy state of Rome,
A little ere the mightiest Julius fell,
The graves stood [tenantless] and the sheeted dead   115
Did squeak and gibber in the Roman streets.
As stars with trains of fire, and dews of blood,
Disasters in the sun; and the moist star
Upon whose influence Neptune's empire stands
Was sick almost to doomsday with eclipse.   120
And even the like precurse of [fear'd] events,
As harbingers preceding still the fates
And prologue to the omen coming on,
Have heaven and earth together demonstrated
Unto our climatures and countrymen.   125

Enter Ghost.

But soft, behold! lo where it comes again!

                                            It spreads his arms.
I'll cross it though it blast me. Stay, illusion!

---

96. *unimproved:* untried (?) or not directed to any useful end (?).   97. *skirts:* outlying
territories.   98. *Shark'd up:* gathered up hastily and indiscriminately.   100. *stomach:* relish
of danger (?) or demand for courage (?).   106. *head:* source.   107. *romage:* rummage,
bustling activity.   109. *sort:* fit. *portentous:* ominous.   116. One or more lines may have been
lost between this line and the next.   118. *Disasters:* ominous signs. *moist star:* moon.
119. *Neptune's empire stands:* the seas are dependent.   120. *sick . . . doomsday:* i.e. almost
totally darkened. When the Day of Judgment is imminent, says Matthew 24:29, "the moon
shall not give her light." *eclipse:* There were a solar and two total lunar eclipses visible in
England in 1598; they caused gloomy speculation.   121. *precurse:* foreshadowing.
122. *harbingers:* advance messengers. *still:* always.   123. *omen:* i.e. the events portended.
125. *climatures:* regions.   126 s.d. *his:* its.   127. *cross it:* cross its path, confront it directly.
blast: wither (by supernatural means).

If thou hast any sound or use of voice,
Speak to me.
If there be any good thing to be done   130
That may to thee do ease, and grace to me,
Speak to me.
If thou art privy to thy country's fate,
Which happily foreknowing may avoid,
O speak!   135
Or if thou hast uphoarded in thy life
Extorted treasure in the womb of earth,
For which, they say, your spirits oft walk in death,
Speak of it, stay and speak! *(The cock crows.)* Stop it,
Marcellus.   140
Marcellus: Shall I strike it with my partisan?
 Horatio: Do, if it will not stand.
Barnardo: 'Tis here!
 Horatio: 'Tis here!
Marcellus: 'Tis gone!   [*Exit* Ghost.]
We do it wrong, being so majestical,
To offer it the show of violence,
For it is as the air, invulnerable,   145
And our vain blows malicious mockery.
Barnardo: It was about to speak when the cock crew.
 Horatio: And then it started like a guilty thing
Upon a fearful summons. I have heard
The cock, that is the trumpet to the morn,   150
Doth with his lofty and shrill-sounding throat
Awake the god of day, and at his warning,
Whether in sea or fire, in earth or air,
Th' extravagant and erring spirit hies
To his confine, and of the truth herein   155
This present object made probation.
Marcellus: It faded on the crowing of the cock.
Some say that ever 'gainst that season comes
Wherein our Saviour's birth is celebrated,
This bird of dawning singeth all night long,   160
And then they say no spirit dare stir abroad,
The nights are wholesome, then no planets strike,
No fairy takes, nor witch hath power to charm,
So hallowed, and so gracious, is that time.

---

134. *happily:* haply, perhaps.   138. *your:* Colloquial and impersonal; cf. I.v.167, IV.iii.20,
22. Most editors adopt *you* from F1.   141. *partisan:* long-handled spear.   146. *malicious
mockery:* mockery of malice, i.e. empty pretenses of harming it.   150. *trumpet:* trumpeter.
154. *extravagant:* wandering outside its proper bounds. *erring:* wandering abroad. *hies:*
hastens.   156. *object:* sight. *probation:* proof.   158. *'gainst:* just before.   162. *strike:* exert
malevolent influence.   163. *takes:* bewitches, charms.   164. *gracious:* blessed.

Horatio: So have I heard and do in part believe it.   165
            But look, the morn in russet mantle clad
            Walks o'er the dew of yon high eastward hill.
            Break we our watch up, and by my advice
            Let us impart what we have seen to-night
            Unto young Hamlet, for, upon my life,   170
            This spirit, dumb to us, will speak to him.
            Do you consent we shall acquaint him with it,
            As needful in our loves, fitting our duty?
Marcellus: Let's do't, I pray, and I this morning know
            Where we shall find him most convenient.   *Exeunt.* 175

Scene II

Flourish.   Enter Claudius, King of Denmark, Gertrude the Queen; Council:
as Polonius; *and his son* Laertes, Hamlet, *cum aliis [including* Voltemand *and*
Cornelius].

King: Though yet of Hamlet our dear brother's death
            The memory be green, and that it us befitted
            To bear our hearts in grief, and our whole kingdom
            To be contracted in one brow of woe,
            Yet so far hath discretion fought with nature   5
            That we with wisest sorrow think on him
            Together with remembrance of ourselves.
            Therefore our sometime sister, now our queen,
            Th' imperial jointress to this warlike state,
            Have we, as 'twere with a defeated joy,   10
            With an auspicious, and a dropping eye,
            With mirth in funeral, and with dirge in marriage,
            In equal scale weighing delight and dole,
            Taken to wife; nor have we herein barr'd
            Your better wisdoms, which have freely gone   15
            With this affair along. For all, our thanks.
            Now follows that you know young Fortinbras,
            Holding a weak supposal of our worth,
            Or thinking by our late dear brother's death
            Our state to be disjoint and out of frame,   20
            Co-leagued with this dream of his advantage,
            He hath not fail'd to pester us with message

---

166. *russet:* coarse greyish-brown cloth.
I.ii. Location: The castle.   o.s.d. *Flourish:* trumpet fanfare. *cum aliis:* with others.
2. *befitted:* would befit.   4. *contracted in:* (1) reduced to; (2) knit or wrinkled in. *brow of woe:*
mournful brow.   9. *jointress:* joint holder.   10. *defeated:* impaired.   11. *auspicious . . .*
dropping: cheerful . . . weeping.   15. *freely:* fully, without reservation.   17. *know:* be
informed, learn.   18. *supposal:* conjecture, estimate.   21. *Co-leagued:* joined.   22. *pester*
. . . message: trouble me with persistent messages (the original sense of *pester* is "overcrowd").

Importing the surrender of those lands
Lost by his father, with all bands of law,
To our most valiant brother. So much for him.   25
Now for ourself, and for this time of meeting,
Thus much the business is: we have here writ
To Norway, uncle of young Fortinbras—
Who, impotent and bedred, scarcely hears
Of this his nephew's purpose—to suppress   30
His further gait herein, in that the levies,
The lists, and full proportions are all made
Out of his subject; and we here dispatch
You, good Cornelius, and you, Voltemand,
For bearers of this greeting to old Norway,   35
Giving to you no further personal power
To business with the King, more than the scope
Of these delated articles allow.   *[Giving a paper.]*
Farewell, and let your haste commend your duty.
Cornelius, Voltemand: In that, and all things, will we show our duty.   40
    King: We doubt it nothing; heartily farewell.
                                    [Exeunt Voltemand and Cornelius.]
And now, Laertes, what's the news with you?
You told us of some suit, what is't, Laertes?
You cannot speak of reason to the Dane
And lose your voice. What wouldst thou beg, Laertes,   45
    That shall not be my offer, not thy asking?
The head is not more native to the heart,
The hand more instrumental to the mouth,
Than is the throne of Denmark to thy father.
What wouldst thou have, Laertes?
    Laertes: My dread lord,   50
Your leave and favor to return to France,
From whence though willingly I came to Denmark
To show my duty in your coronation,
Yet now I must confess, that duty done,
My thoughts and wishes bend again toward France,   55
And bow them to your gracious leave and pardon.
    King: Have you your father's leave? What says Polonius?
Polonius: H'ath, my lord, wrung from me my slow leave
    By laborsome petition, and at last
    Upon his will I seal'd my hard consent.   60

---

23. *Importing:* having as import.   24. *bands:* bonds, binding terms.   29. *impotent and bedred:*
feeble and bedridden.   31. *gait:* proceeding.   31-33. *in . . . subject:* since the troops are all
drawn from his subjects.   38. *delated:* extended, detailed (a variant of *dilated*).   41. *nothing:*
not at all.   45. *lose:* waste.   47. *native:* closely related.   48. *instrumental:* serviceable.
51. *leave and favor:* gracious permission.   56. *pardon:* permission to depart.   58. *H'ath:* he
hath.   60. *hard:* reluctant.

I do beseech you give him leave to go.
   King: Take thy fair hour, Laertes, time be thine,
      And thy best graces spend it at thy will!
      But now, my cousin Hamlet, and my son—
Hamlet: *[Aside.]* A little more than kin, and less than kind.   65
   King: How is it that the clouds still hang on you?
Hamlet: Not so, my lord, I am too much in the sun.
  Queen: Good Hamlet, cast thy nighted color off,
      And let thine eye look like a friend on Denmark.
      Do not for ever with thy vailed lids   70
      Seek for thy noble father in the dust.
      Thou know'st 'tis common, all that lives must die,
      Passing through nature to eternity.
Hamlet: Ay, madam, it is common.
  Queen: If it be,
      Why seems it so particular with thee?   75
Hamlet: Seems, madam? nay, it is, I know not "seems."
      'Tis not alone my inky cloak, [good] mother,
      Nor customary suits of solemn black,
      Nor windy suspiration of forc'd breath,
      No, nor the fruitful river in the eye,   80
      Nor the dejected havior of the visage,
      Together with all forms, moods, [shapes] of grief,
      That can [denote] me truly. These indeed seem,
      For they are actions that a man might play,
      But I have that within which passes show,   85
      These but the trappings and the suits of woe.
   King: 'Tis sweet and commendable in your nature, Hamlet,
      To give these mourning duties to your father.
      But you must know your father lost a father,
      That father lost, lost his, and the survivor bound   90
      In filial obligation for some term
      To do obsequious sorrow. But to persever
      In obstinate condolement is a course
      Of impious stubbornness, 'tis unmanly grief,
      It shows a will most incorrect to heaven,   95
      A heart unfortified, or mind impatient,
      An understanding simple and unschool'd:
      For what we know must be, and is as common

---

64. *cousin:* kinsman (used in familiar address to any collateral relative more distant than a brother or sister; here to a nephew).   65. *A little . . . kind:* closer than a nephew, since you are my mother's husband; yet more distant than a son, too (and not well disposed to you). 67. *sun:* With obvious quibble on *son.*   70. *vailed:* downcast.   72. *common:* general, universal.   75. *particular:* individual, personal.   80. *fruitful:* copious.   92. *obsequious:* proper to obsequies.   93. *condolement:* grief.   95. *incorrect:* unsubmissive.

As any the most vulgar thing to sense,
Why should we in our peevish opposition   100
Take it to heart? Fie, 'tis a fault to heaven,
A fault against the dead, a fault to nature,
To reason most absurd, whose common theme
Is death of fathers, and who still hath cried,
From the first corse till he that died to-day,   105
"This must be so." We pray you throw to earth
This unprevailing woe, and think of us
As of a father, for let the world take note
You are the most immediate to our throne,
And with no less nobility of love   110
Than that which dearest father bears his son
Do I impart toward you. For your intent
In going back to school in Wittenberg,
It is most retrograde to our desire,
And we beseech you bend you to remain   115
Here in the cheer and comfort of our eye,
Our chiefest courtier, cousin, and our son.
Queen: Let not thy mother lose her prayers, Hamlet,
I pray thee stay with us, go not to Wittenberg.
Hamlet: I shall in all my best obey you, madam.   120
King: Why, 'tis a loving and a fair reply.
Be as ourself in Denmark. Madam, come.
This gentle and unforc'd accord of Hamlet
Sits smiling to my heart, in grace whereof,
No jocund health that Denmark drinks to-day,   125
But the great cannon to the clouds shall tell,
And the King's rouse the heaven shall bruit again,
Respeaking earthly thunder. Come away.
                          Flourish.   Exeunt all but Hamlet.
Hamlet: O that this too too sallied flesh would melt,
Thaw, and resolve itself into a dew!   130
Or that the Everlasting had not fix'd
His canon 'gainst [self-]slaughter! O God, God,
How [weary], stale, flat, and unprofitable
Seem to me all the uses of this world!
Fie on't, ah fie! 'tis an unweeded garden   135
That grows to seed, things rank and gross in nature
Possess it merely. That it should come [to this]!

---

99. *any . . . sense:* what is perceived to be commonest.   101. *to:* against.   103. *absurd:*
contrary.   107. *unprevailing:* unavailing.   111. *dearest:* most loving.   112. *impart:* i.e.
impart love.   127. *rouse:* bumper, drink. *bruit:* loudly declare.   129. *sallied:* sullied. See the
Textual Notes. Many editors prefer the F1 reading, *solid.*   132. *canon:* law.   134. *uses:*
customs.   137. *merely:* utterly.

But two months dead, nay, not so much, not two.
So excellent a king, that was to this
Hyperion to a satyr, so loving to my mother   140
That he might not beteem the winds of heaven
Visit her face too roughly. Heaven and earth,
Must I remember? Why, she should hang on him
As if increase of appetite had grown
By what it fed on, and yet, within a month—   145
Let me not think on't! Frailty, thy name is woman!—
A little month, or ere those shoes were old
With which she followed my poor father's body,
Like Niobe, all tears—why, she, [even she]—
O God, a beast that wants discourse of reason   150
Would have mourn'd longer—married with my uncle,
My father's brother, but no more like my father
Than I to Hercules. Within a month,
Ere yet the salt of most unrighteous tears
Had left the flushing in her galled eyes,   155
She married—O most wicked speed: to post
With such dexterity to incestious sheets,
It is not, nor it cannot come to good,
But break my heart, for I must hold my tongue.

Enter Horatio, Marcellus, *and* Barnardo.

   Horatio: Hail to your lordship!
   Hamlet: I am glad to see you well.   160
      Horatio—or I do forget myself.
   Horatio: The same, my lord, and your poor servant ever.
   Hamlet: Sir, my good friend—I'll change that name with you.
      And what make you from Wittenberg, Horatio? Marcellus.
  Marcellus: My good lord.   165
   Hamlet: I am very glad to see you. *[To Barnardo.]* Good even,
      sir.—
      But what, in faith, make you from Wittenberg?
   Horatio: A truant disposition, good my lord.
   Hamlet: I would not hear your enemy say so,   170
      Nor shall you do my ear that violence
      To make it truster of your own report
      Against yourself. I know you are no truant.

---

139. *to:* in comparison with.   140. *Hyperion:* the sun-god.   141. *beteem:* allow.   147. *or ere:*
before.   149. *Niobe:* She wept endlessly for her children, whom Apollo and Artemis had
killed.   150. *wants . . . reason:* lacks the power of reason (which distinguishes men from
beasts).   154. *unrighteous:* i.e. hypocritical.   155. *flushing:* redness. *galled:* inflamed.
157. *incestious:* incestuous. The marriage of a man to his brother's widow was so regarded
until long after Shakespeare's day.   163. *change:* exchange.   164. *what . . . from:* what are
you doing away from.   169. *truant disposition:* inclination to play truant.

But what is your affair in Elsinore?
We'll teach you to drink [deep] ere you depart.   175
Horatio: My lord, I came to see your father's funeral.
Hamlet: I prithee do not mock me, fellow student,
  I think it was to [see] my mother's wedding.
Horatio: Indeed, my lord, it followed hard upon.
Hamlet: Thrift, thrift, Horatio, the funeral bak'd meats   180
  Did coldly furnish forth the marriage tables.
  Would I had met my dearest foe in heaven
  Or ever I had seen that day, Horatio!
  My father—methinks I see my father.
Horatio: Where, my lord?   185
Hamlet: In my mind's eye, Horatio.
Horatio: I saw him once, 'a was a goodly king.
Hamlet: 'A was a man, take him for all in all,
  I shall not look upon his like again.
Horatio: My lord, I think I saw him yesternight.
Hamlet: Saw, who?   190
Horatio: My lord, the King your father.
Hamlet: The King my father?
Horatio: Season your admiration for a while
  With an attent ear, till I may deliver,
  Upon the witness of these gentlemen,   195

  This marvel to you.
Hamlet: For God's love let me hear!
Horatio: Two nights together had these gentlemen,
  Marcellus and Barnardo, on their watch,
  In the dead waste and middle of the night,
  Been thus encount'red: a figure like your father,   200
  Armed at point exactly, cap-a-pe,
  Appears before them, and with solemn march
  Goes slow and stately by them; thrice he walk'd
  By their oppress'd and fear-surprised eyes
  Within his truncheon's length, whilst they, distill'd   205
  Almost to jelly with the act of fear,
  Stand dumb and speak not to him. This to me
  In dreadful secrecy impart they did,
  And I with them the third night kept the watch,

---

177. *studient:* student.   181. *coldly:* when cold.   182. *dearest:* most intensely hated.
183. *Or:* ere, before.   193. *Season:* temper. *admiration:* wonder.   194. *deliver:* report.
199. *waste:* empty expanse.   201. *at point exactly:* in every particular. *cap-a-pe:* from head to
foot.   204. *fear-surprised:* overwhelmed by fear.   205. *truncheon:* short staff carried as a
symbol of military command.   206. *act:* action, operation.   208. *dreadful:* held in awe, i.e.
solemnly sworn.

Where, as they had delivered, both in time, 210
Form of the thing, each word made true and good,
The apparition comes. I knew your father,
These hands are not more like.

Hamlet: But where was this?

Marcellus: My lord, upon the platform where we watch.

Hamlet: Did you not speak to it?

Horatio: My lord, I did, 215
But answer made it none. Yet once methought
It lifted up it head and did address
Itself to motion like as it would speak;
But even then the morning cock crew loud,
And at the sound it shrunk in haste away 220
And vanish'd from our sight.

Hamlet: 'Tis very strange.

Horatio: As I do live, my honor'd lord, 'tis true,
And we did think it writ down in our duty
To let you know of it.

Hamlet: Indeed, [indeed,] sirs. But this troubles me. 225
Hold you the watch to-night?

Marcellus, Barnardo: We do, my lord.

Hamlet: Arm'd, say you?

Marcellus, Barnardo: Arm'd, my lord.

Hamlet: From top to toe?

Marcellus, Barnardo: My lord, from head to foot.

Hamlet: Then saw you not his face. 230

Horatio: O yes, my lord, he wore his beaver up.

Hamlet: What, look'd he frowningly?

Horatio: A countenance more
In sorrow than in anger.

Hamlet: Pale, or red?

Horatio: Nay, very pale.

Hamlet: And fix'd his eyes upon you?

Horatio: Most constantly.

Hamlet: I would I had been there. 235

Horatio: It would have much amaz'd you.

Hamlet: Very like, [very like]. Stay'd it long?

Horatio: While one with moderate haste might tell a hundreth.

Both [Marcellus, Barnardo]: Longer, longer.

Horatio: Not when I saw't.

Hamlet: His beard was grisl'd, no? 240

---

213. *are . . . like:* i.e. do not resemble each other more closely than the apparition resembled him. 217. *it:* its. 217-18. *address . . . motion:* begin to make a gesture. 231. *beaver:* visor. 238. *tell a hundreth:* count a hundred. 240. *grisl'd:* grizzled, mixed with grey.

Horatio: It was, as I have seen it in his life,
    A sable silver'd.
Hamlet: I will watch to-night,
    Perchance 'twill walk again.
Horatio: I warr'nt it will.
Hamlet: If it assume my noble father's person,
    I'll speak to it though hell itself should gape   245
    And bid me hold my peace. I pray you all,
    If you have hitherto conceal'd this sight,
    Let it be tenable in your silence still,
    And whatsomever else shall hap tonight,
    Give it an understanding but no tongue.   250
    I will requite your loves. So fare you well.
    Upon the platform 'twixt aleven and twelf
    I'll visit you.
All: Our duty to your honor.
Hamlet: Your loves, as mine to you; farewell.

                         Exeunt [all but Hamlet].

    My father's spirit—in arms! All is not well,   255
    I doubt some foul play. Would the night were come!
    Till then sit still, my soul. [Foul] deeds will rise,
    Though all the earth o'erwhelm them, to men's eyes.   *Exit.*

Scene III

Enter Laertes *and* Ophelia, *his sister.*

Laertes: My necessaries are inbark'd. Farewell.
    And, sister, as the winds give benefit
    And convey [is] assistant, do not sleep,
    But let me hear from you.
Ophelia: Do you doubt that?
Laertes: For Hamlet, and the trifling of his favor,   5
    Hold it a fashion and a toy in blood,
    A violet in the youth of primy nature,
    Forward, not permanent, sweet, not lasting,
    The perfume and suppliance of a minute—
    No more.
Ophelia: No more but so?
Laertes: Think it no more: 10
    For nature crescent does not grow alone

---

248. *tenable:* held close.　252. *aleven:* eleven.　256. *doubt:* suspect.

I.iii. Location: Polonius' quarters in the castle.　1. *inbark'd:* embarked, abroad.　3. *convey is assistant:* means of transport is available.　6. *a fashion:* i.e. standard behavior for a young man. *toy in blood:* idle fancy of youthful passion.　7. *primy:* springlike.　8. *Forward:* early of growth.　9. *suppliance:* pastime.　11. *crescent:* growing, increasing.

In thews and [bulk], but as this temple waxes,
The inward service of the mind and soul
Grows wide withal. Perhaps he loves you now,
And now no soil nor cautel doth besmirch   15
The virtue of his will, but you must fear,
His greatness weigh'd, his will is not his own,
[For he himself is subject to his birth:]
He may not, as unvalued persons do,
Carve for himself, for on his choice depends   20
The safety and health of this whole state,
And therefore must his choice be circumscrib'd
Unto the voice and yielding of that body
Whereof he is the head. Then if he says he loves you,
It fits your wisdom so far to believe it   25
As he in his particular act and place
May give his saying deed, which is no further
Than the main voice of Denmark goes withal.
Then weigh what loss your honor may sustain
If with too credent ear you list his songs,   30
Or lose your heart, or your chaste treasure open
                           To his unmast'red importunity.
Fear it, Ophelia, fear it, my dear sister,
And keep you in the rear of your affection,
Out of the shot and danger of desire.   35
The chariest maid is prodigal enough
If she unmask her beauty to the moon.
Virtue itself scapes not calumnious strokes.
The canker galls the infants of the spring
Too oft before their buttons be disclos'd,   40
And in the morn and liquid dew of youth
Contagious blastments are most imminent.
Be wary then, best safety lies in fear:
Youth to itself rebels, though none else near.
Ophelia: I shall the effect of this good lesson keep   45
As watchman to my heart. But, good my brother,
Do not, as some ungracious pastors do,
Show me the steep and thorny way to heaven,
Whiles, [like] a puff'd and reckless libertine,

---

12. *thews:* muscles, sinews.   12–14. *as . . . withal:* as the body develops, the powers of mind
and spirit grow along with it.   15. *soil:* stain. *cautel:* deceit.   16. *will:* desire.   17. *His
greatness weigh'd:* considering his princely status.   19. *unvalued:* of low rank.   20. *Carve for
himself:* indulge his own wishes.   23. *voice:* vote, approval. *yielding:* consent. *that body:* i.e. the
state.   26. *in . . . place:* i.e. acting as he must act in the position he occupies.   28. *main:*
general. *goes withal:* accord with.   30. *credent:* credulous.   35. *shot:* range.   39. *canker:*
canker-worm.   40. *buttons:* buds. *disclos'd:* opened.   42. *blastments:* withering blights.
44. *to:* of.   47. *ungracious:* graceless.   49. *puff'd:* bloated.

Himself the primrose path of dalliance treads,   50
And reaks not his own rede.
Laertes: O, fear me not.

Enter Polonius.

I stay too long—but here my father comes.
A double blessing is a double grace,
Occasion smiles upon a second leave.
Polonius: Yet here, Laertes? Aboard, aboard, for shame!   55
The wind sits in the shoulder of your sail,
And you are stay'd for. There—*[laying his hand on* Laertes'
head] my blessing with thee!
And these few precepts in thy memory
Look thou character. Give thy thoughts no tongue,   60
Nor any unproportion'd thought his act.
Be thou familiar, but by no means vulgar:
Those friends thou hast, and their adoption tried,
Grapple them unto thy soul with hoops of steel,
But do not dull thy palm with entertainment   65
Of each new-hatch'd, unfledg'd courage. Beware
Of entrance to a quarrel, but being in,
Bear't that th' opposed may beware of thee.
Give every man thy ear, but few thy voice,
Take each man's censure, but reserve thy judgment.   70
Costly thy habit as thy purse can buy,
But not express'd in fancy, rich, not gaudy,
For the apparel oft proclaims the man,
And they in France of the best rank and station
[Are] of a most select and generous chief in that.   75
Neither a borrower nor a lender [be],
For [loan] oft loses both itself and friend,
And borrowing dulleth [th'] edge of husbandry.
This above all: to thine own self be true,
And it must follow, as the night the day,   80
Thou canst not then be false to any man.
Farewell, my blessing season this in thee!
Laertes: Most humbly do I take my leave, my lord.
Polonius: The time invests you, go, your servants tend.

---

51. *reaks:* recks, heeds. *rede:* advice. *fear me not:* don't worry about me. 54. *Occasion:* opportunity (here personified, as often). *smiles upon:* i.e. graciously bestows. 60. *character:* inscribe. 61. *unproportion'd:* unfitting. 62. *familiar:* affable, sociable. *vulgar:* friendly with everybody. 63. *their adoption tried:* their association with you tested and proved. 66. *courage:* spirited, young blood. 68. *Bear't that:* manage it in such a way that. 70. *Take:* listen to. *censure:* opinion. 75. *generous:* noble. *chief:* eminence (?). But the line is probably corrupt. Perhaps *of* a is intrusive, in which case *chief* = chiefly. 78. *husbandry:* thrift. 82. *season:* preserve (?) or ripen, make fruitful (?). 84. *invests:* besieges. *tend:* wait.

Laertes: Farewell, Ophelia, and remember well   85
    What I have said to you.
Ophelia: 'Tis in my memory lock'd,
    And you yourself shall keep the key of it.
Laertes: Farewell.   *Exit* Laertes.
Polonius: What is't, Ophelia, he hath said to you?
Ophelia: So please you, something touching the Lord Hamlet.
Polonius: Marry, well bethought.   90
    'Tis told me, he hath very oft of late
    Given private time to you, and you yourself
    Have of your audience been most free and bounteous.
    If it be so—as so 'tis put on me,
    And that in way of caution—I must tell you,   95
    You do not understand yourself so clearly
    As it behooves my daughter and your honor.
    What is between you? Give me up the truth.
Ophelia: He hath, my lord, of late made many tenders
    Of his affection to me.   100
Polonius: Affection, puh! You speak like a green girl,
    Unsifted in such perilous circumstance.
    Do you believe his tenders, as you call them?
Ophelia: I do not know, my lord, what I should think.
Polonius: Marry, I will teach you: think yourself a baby   105
    That you have ta'en these tenders for true pay,
    Which are not sterling. Tender yourself more dearly,
    Or (not to crack the wind of the poor phrase,
    [Wringing] it thus) you'll tender me a fool.
Ophelia: My lord, he hath importun'd me with love   110
    In honorable fashion.
Polonius: Ay, fashion you may call it. Go to, go to.
Ophelia: And hath given countenance to his speech, my lord,
    With almost all the holy vows of heaven.
Polonius: Ay, springes to catch woodcocks. I do know,   115
    When the blood burns, how prodigal the soul
    Lends the tongue vows. These blazes, daughter,
    Giving more light than heat, extinct in both
    Even in their promise, as it is a-making,
    You must not take for fire. From this time   120
    Be something scanter of your maiden presence,

---

90. *Marry:* indeed (originally the name of the Virgin Mary used as an oath).   94. *put on:* told
to.   99. *tenders:* offers.   102. *Unsifted:* untried.   106. *tenders:* With play on the sense
"money offered in payment" (as in *legal tender*).   107. *Tender:* hold, value.   109. *Wringing:*
straining, forcing to the limit. *tender . . . fool:* (1) show me that you are a fool; (2) make me look
like a fool; (3) present me with a (bastard) grandchild.   112. *fashion:* See note on line 6.
113. *countenance:* authority.   115. *springes:* snares. *woodcocks:* Proverbially gullible birds.

Set your entreatments at a higher rate
Than a command to parle. For Lord Hamlet,
Believe so much in him, that he is young,
And with a larger teder may he walk   125
Than may be given you. In few, Ophelia,
Do not believe his vows, for they are brokers,
Not of that dye which their investments show,
But mere [implorators] of unholy suits,
Breathing like sanctified and pious bonds,   130
The better to [beguile]. This is for all:
I would not, in plain terms, from this time forth
Have you so slander any moment leisure
As to give words or talk with the Lord Hamlet.
Look to't, I charge you. Come your ways.   135
    Ophelia: I shall obey, my lord.   *Exeunt.*

[Scene IV]

Enter Hamlet, Horatio, *and* Marcellus.

    Hamlet: The air bites shrowdly, it is very cold.
    Horatio: It is [a] nipping and an eager air.
    Hamlet: What hour now?
    Horatio: I think it lacks of twelf.
  Marcellus: No, it is strook.
    Horatio: Indeed? I heard it not. It then draws near the season   5
    Wherein the spirit held his wont to walk.

A flourish of trumpets, and two pieces goes off [within].

    What does this mean, my lord?
    Hamlet: The King doth wake to-night and takes his rouse,
    Keeps wassail, and the swagg'ring up-spring reels;
    And as he drains his draughts of Rhenish down,   10
    The kettle-drum and trumpet thus bray out
    The triumph of his pledge.

122-23. *Set . . . parle:* place a higher value on your favors; do not grant interviews simply because he asks for them. Polonius uses a military figure: *entreatments* = negotiations for surrender; *parle* = parley, discuss terms.   124. *so . . . him:* no more than this with respect to him.   125. *larger teder:* longer tether.   127. *brokers:* procurers.   128. *Not . . . show:* not of the color that their garments (*investments*) exhibit, i.e. not what they seem.   129. *mere:* out-and-out.   130. *bonds:* (lover's) vows or assurances. Many editors follow Theobald in reading *bawds.*   133. *slander:* disgrace. *moment:* momentary.   135. *Come your ways:* come along.

I.iv. Location: The guard-platform of the castle.   1. *shrowdly:* shrewdly, wickedly.   2. *eager:* sharp.   6. s.d. *pieces:* cannon.   8. *doth . . . rouse:* i.e. holds revels far into the night.
9. *wassail:* carousal. *up-spring:* wild dance.   10. *Rhenish:* Rhine wine.   12. *triumph . . . pledge:* accomplishment of his toast (by draining his cup at a single draught).

Horatio: Is it a custom?
  Hamlet: Ay, marry is't,
            But to my mind, though I am native here
            And to the manner born, it is a custom   15
            More honor'd in the breach than the observance.
            This heavy-headed revel east and west
            Makes us traduc'd and tax'd of other nations.
            They clip us drunkards, and with swinish phrase
            Soil our addition, and indeed it takes   20
            From our achievements, though perform'd at height,
            The pith and marrow of our attribute.
            So, oft it chances in particular men,
            That for some vicious mole of nature in them,
            As in their birth, wherein they are not guilty   25
            (Since nature cannot choose his origin),
            By their o'ergrowth of some complexion
            Oft breaking down the pales and forts of reason,
            Or by some habit, that too much o'er-leavens
            The form of plausive manners—that these men,   30
            Carrying, I say, the stamp of one defect,
            Being nature's livery, or fortune's star,
            His virtues else, be they as pure as grace,
            As infinite as man may undergo,
            Shall in the general censure take corruption   35
            From that particular fault: the dram of [ev'l]
            Doth all the noble substance of a doubt
            To his own scandal.

Enter Ghost.

  Horatio: Look, my lord, it comes!
  Hamlet: Angels and ministers of grace defend us!
            Be thou a spirit of health, or goblin damn'd,   40
            Bring with thee airs from heaven, or blasts from hell,
            Be thy intents wicked, or charitable,

---

15. *manner:* custom (of carousing).   16. *More . . . observance:* which it is more honorable to
break than to observe.   18. *tax'd of:* censured by.   19. *clip:* clepe, call.   20. *addition:* titles
of honor.   21. *at height:* most excellently.   22. *attribute:* reputation.   23. *particular:*
individual.   24. *vicious . . . nature:* small natural blemish.   26. *his:* its.   27. *By . . .*
complexion: by the excess of some one of the humors (which were thought to govern the
disposition).   28. *pales:* fences.   29. *o'er-leavens:* makes itself felt throughout (as leaven
works in the whole mass of dough).   30. *plausive:* pleasing.   32. *Being . . . star:* i.e. whether
they were born with it, or got it by misfortune. *Star* means "blemish."   34. *undergo:* carry the
weight of, sustain.   35. *general censure:* popular opinion.   36. *dram:* minute amount. *ev'l:*
evil, with a pun on *eale,* "yeast" (cf. *o'er-leavens* in line 29).   37. *of a doubt:* A famous crux, for
which many emendations have been suggested, the most widely accepted being Steevens' *often*
dout (i.e. extinguish).   38. *To . . . scandal:* i.e. so that it all shares in the disgrace.   40. *of*
health: wholesome, good.

Thou com'st in such a questionable shape
That I will speak to thee. I'll call thee Hamlet,
King, father, royal Dane. O, answer me!   45
Let me not burst in ignorance, but tell
Why thy canoniz'd bones, hearsed in death,
Have burst their cerements; why the sepulchre,
Wherein we saw thee quietly [inurn'd,]
Hath op'd his ponderous and marble jaws   50
To cast thee up again. What may this mean,
That thou, dead corse, again in complete steel
Revisits thus the glimpses of the moon,
Making night hideous, and we fools of nature
So horridly to shake our disposition   55
With thoughts beyond the reaches of our souls?
Say why is this? wherefore? what should we do?

           [Ghost] *beckons* [Hamlet].

Horatio: It beckons you to go away with it,
  As if it some impartment did desire
  To you alone.
Marcellus: Look with what courteous action   60
  It waves you to a more removed ground,
  But do not go with it.
Horatio: No, by no means.
Hamlet: It will not speak, then I will follow it.
Horatio: Do not, my lord.
Hamlet: Why, what should be the fear?
  I do not set my life at a pin's fee,   65
  And for my soul, what can it do to that,
  Being a thing immortal as itself?
  It waves me forth again, I'll follow it.
Horatio: What if it tempt you toward the flood, my lord,
  Or to the dreadful summit of the cliff   70
  That beetles o'er his base into the sea,
  And there assume some other horrible form
  Which might deprive your sovereignty of reason,
  And draw you into madness? Think of it.
  The very place puts toys of desperation,   75
  Without more motive, into every brain
  That looks so many fadoms to the sea
  And hears it roar beneath.

---

43. *questionable:* inviting talk. 47. *canoniz'd:* buried with the prescribed rites. 48. *cerements:* grave-clothes. 52. *complete steel:* full armor. 53. *Revisits:* The -*s* ending in the second person singular is common. 54. *fools of nature:* the children (or the dupes) of a purely natural order, baffled by the supernatural. 55. *disposition:* nature. 59. *impartment:* communication. 65. *fee:* worth. 73. *deprive . . . reason:* unseat reason from the rule of your mind. 75. *toys of desperation:* fancies of desperate action, i.e. inclinations to jump off. 77. *fadoms:* fathoms.

Hamlet:	It waves me still.—	
	Go on, I'll follow thee.	
Marcellus:	You shall not go, my lord.	
Hamlet:	Hold off your hands.	80
Horatio:	Be rul'd, you shall not go.	
Hamlet:	My fate cries out,	

And makes each petty artere in this body
As hardy as the Nemean lion's nerve.
Still am I call'd. Unhand me, gentlemen.   85
By heaven, I'll make a ghost of him that lets me!
I say away!—Go on, I'll follow thee.

Exeunt Ghost *and* Hamlet.

Horatio:	He waxes desperate with [imagination].	
Marcellus:	Let's follow. 'Tis not fit thus to obey him.	
Horatio:	Have after. To what issue will this come?	90
Marcellus:	Something is rotten in the state of Denmark.	
Horatio:	Heaven will direct it.	
Marcellus:	Nay, let's follow him. *Exeunt.*	

[Scene V]

Enter Ghost *and* Hamlet.

Hamlet:	Whither wilt thou lead me? Speak, I'll go no further.	
Ghost:	Mark me.	
Hamlet:	I will.	
Ghost:	My hour is almost come	

When I to sulph'rous and tormenting flames
Must render up myself.

Hamlet:	Alas, poor ghost!	
Ghost:	Pity me not, but lend thy serious hearing	5

To what I shall unfold.

Hamlet:	Speak, I am bound to hear.	
Ghost:	So art thou to revenge, when thou shalt hear.	
Hamlet:	What?	
Ghost:	I am thy father's spirit,	

Doom'd for a certain term to walk the night,   10
And for the day confin'd to fast in fires,
Till the foul crimes done in my days of nature
Are burnt and purg'd away. But that I am forbid
To tell the secrets of my prison-house,
I could a tale unfold whose lightest word   15
Would harrow up thy soul, freeze thy young blood,

---

83. *artere:* variant spelling of *artery;* here, ligament, sinew.   84. *Nemean lion:* Slain by
Hercules as one of his twelve labors. *nerve:* sinew.   86. *lets:* hinders.   92. *it:* i.e. the issue.
I.v. Location: On the battlements of the castle.   11. *fast:* do penance.   12. *crimes:* sins.

Make thy two eyes like stars start from their spheres,
Thy knotted and combined locks to part,
And each particular hair to stand an end,
Like quills upon the fearful porpentine. 20
But this eternal blazon must not be
To ears of flesh and blood. List, list, O, list!
If thou didst ever thy dear father love—

Hamlet: O God!

  Ghost: Revenge his foul and most unnatural murther. 25

Hamlet: Murther!

  Ghost: Murther most foul, as in the best it is,
But this most foul, strange, and unnatural.

Hamlet: Haste me to know't, that I with wings as swift
As meditation, or the thoughts of love, 30
May sweep to my revenge.

  Ghost: I find thee apt,
And duller shouldst thou be than the fat weed
That roots itself in ease on Lethe wharf,
Wouldst thou not stir in this. Now, Hamlet, hear:
'Tis given out that, sleeping in my orchard, 35
A serpent stung me, so the whole ear of Denmark
Is by a forged process of my death
Rankly abus'd; but know, thou noble youth,
The serpent that did sting thy father's life
Now wears his crown.

Hamlet: O my prophetic soul! 40
My uncle?

  Ghost: Ay, that incestuous, that adulterate beast,
With witchcraft of his wits, with traitorous gifts—
O wicked wit and gifts that have the power
So to seduce!—won to his shameful lust 45
The will of my most seeming virtuous queen.
O Hamlet, what [a] falling-off was there
From me, whose love was of that dignity
That it went hand in hand even with the vow
I made to her in marriage, and to decline 50
Upon a wretch whose natural gifts were poor
To those of mine!
But virtue, as it never will be moved,

---

17. *spheres:* eye-sockets; with allusion to the revolving spheres in which, according to the
Ptolemaic astronomy, the stars were fixed. 19. *an end:* on end. 20. *fearful porpentine:*
frightened porcupine. 21. *eternal blazon:* revelation of eternal things. 30. *meditation:*
thought. 33. *Lethe:* river of Hades, the water of which made the drinker forget the past.
wharf: bank. 35. *orchard:* garden. 37. *forged process:* false account. 38. *abus'd:* deceived.
42. *adulterate:* adulterous.

Though lewdness court it in a shape of heaven,
So [lust], though to a radiant angel link'd,   55
Will [sate] itself in a celestial bed
And prey on garbage.
But soft, methinks I scent the morning air,
Brief let me be. Sleeping within my orchard,
My custom always of the afternoon,   60
Upon my secure hour thy uncle stole,
With juice of cursed hebona in a vial,
And in the porches of my ears did pour
The leprous distillment, whose effect
Holds such an enmity with blood of man   65
That swift as quicksilver it courses through
The natural gates and alleys of the body,
And with a sudden vigor it doth [posset]
And curd, like eager droppings into milk,
The thin and wholesome blood. So did it mine,   70
And a most instant tetter bark'd about,
Most lazar-like, with vile and loathsome crust
All my smooth body.
Thus was I, sleeping, by a brother's hand
Of life, of crown, of queen, at once dispatch'd,   75
Cut off even in the blossoms of my sin,
Unhous'led, disappointed, unanel'd,
No reck'ning made, but sent to my account
With all my imperfections on my head.
O, horrible, O, horrible, most horrible!   80
If thou hast nature in thee, bear it not,
Let not the royal bed of Denmark be
A couch for luxury and damned incest.
But howsomever thou pursues this act,
Taint not thy mind, nor let thy soul contrive   85
Against thy mother aught. Leave her to heaven,
And to those thorns that in her bosom lodge
To prick and sting her. Fare thee well at once!
The glow-worm shows the matin to be near,
And gins to pale his uneffectual fire.   90
Adieu, adieu, adieu! remember me.   *[Exit.]*
    Hamlet: O all you host of heaven! O earth! What else?

---

54. *shape of heaven:* angelic form.   61. *secure:* carefree.   62. *hebona:* ebony (which Shakespeare, following a literary tradition, and perhaps also associating the word with *henbane,* thought the name of a poison).   68. *posset:* curdle.   69. *eager:* sour.   71. *tetter:* scabby eruption. *bark'd:* formed a hard covering, like bark on a tree.   72. *lazar-like:* leper-like.   75. *at once:* all at the same time. *dispatch'd:* deprived.   77. *Unhous'led:* without the Eucharist. *disappointed:* without (spiritual) preparation. *unanel'd:* unanointed, without extreme unction.   81. *nature:* natural feeling.   83. *luxury:* lust.   89. *matin:* morning.   90. *gins:* begins.

And shall I couple hell? O fie, hold, hold, my heart,
And you, my sinows, grow not instant old,
But bear me [stiffly] up. Remember thee!   95
Ay, thou poor ghost, whiles memory holds a seat
In this distracted globe. Remember thee!
Yea, from the table of my memory
I'll wipe away all trivial fond records,
All saws of books, all forms, all pressures past   100
That youth and observation copied there,
And thy commandement all alone shall live
Within the book and volume of my brain,
Unmix'd with baser matter. Yes, by heaven!
O most pernicious woman!   105
O villain, villain, smiling, damned villain!
My tables—meet it is I set it down
That one may smile, and smile, and be a villain!
At least I am sure it may be so in Denmark.   *[He writes.]*
So, uncle, there you are. Now to my word.   110
It is "Adieu, adieu! remember me."
I have sworn't.
 Horatio: *[Within.]* My lord, my lord!
 Marcellus: *[Within.]*   Lord Hamlet!

Enter Horatio *and* Marcellus.

 Horatio: Heavens secure him!
 Hamlet: So be it!
Marcellus: Illo, ho, ho, my lord!   115
 Hamlet: Hillo, ho, ho, boy! Come, [bird,] come.
Marcellus: How is't, my noble lord?
 Horatio: What news, my lord?
 Hamlet: O, wonderful!
 Horatio: Good my lord, tell it.
 Hamlet: No, you will reveal it.
 Horatio: Not I, my lord, by heaven.
Marcellus: Nor I, my lord.   120
 Hamlet: How say you then, would heart of man once think it?—
  But you'll be secret?
      Both [Horatio, Marcellus]:
    Ay, by heaven, [my lord].
 Hamlet: There's never a villain dwelling in all Denmark
  But he's an arrant knave.

---

94. *sinows:* sinews.   97. *globe:* head.   98. *table:* writing tablet.   99. *fond:* foolish.
100. *saws:* wise sayings. *forms:* shapes, images. *pressures:* impressions.   110. *word:* i.e. word of
command from the Ghost.   116. *Hillo . . . come:* Hamlet answers Marcellus' halloo with a
falconer's cry.

Horatio: There needs no ghost, my lord, come from the grave   125
    To tell us this.
Hamlet: Why, right, you are in the right,
    And so, without more circumstance at all,
    I hold it fit that we shake hands and part,
    You, as your business and desire shall point you,
    For every man hath business and desire,   130
    Such as it is, and for my own poor part,
    I will go pray.
Horatio: These are but wild and whirling words, my lord.
Hamlet: I am sorry they offend you, heartily,
    Yes, faith, heartily.
Horatio: There's no offense, my lord.   135
Hamlet: Yes, by Saint Patrick, but there is, Horatio,
    And much offense too. Touching this vision here,
    It is an honest ghost, that let me tell you.
    For your desire to know what is between us,
    O'ermaster't as you may. And now, good friends,   140
    As you are friends, scholars, and soldiers,
    Give me one poor request.
Horatio: What is't, my lord, we will.
Hamlet: Never make known what you have seen to-night.
                              Both [Horatio, Marcellus]:
    My lord, we will not.
Hamlet: Nay, but swear't.
Horatio: In faith,   145
    My lord, not I.
Marcellus: Nor I, my lord, in faith.
Hamlet: Upon my sword.
Marcellus: We have sworn, my lord, already.
Hamlet: Indeed, upon my sword, indeed.
                              Ghost cries under the stage.
Ghost: Swear.
Hamlet: Ha, ha, boy, say'st thou so? Art thou there, truepenny?   150
    Come on, you hear this fellow in the cellarage,
    Consent to swear.
Horatio: Propose the oath, my lord.
Hamlet: Never to speak of this that you have seen,
    Swear by my sword.
Ghost: *[Beneath.]* Swear.   155
Hamlet: *Hic et ubique?* Then we'll shift our ground.
    Come hither, gentlemen,

---

127. *circumstance:* ceremony.   138. *honest:* true, genuine.   143. *What is't:* whatever it is.
147. *Upon my sword:* i.e. on the cross formed by the hilt.   150. *truepenny:* trusty fellow.
156. *Hic et ubique:* here and everywhere.

And lay your hands again upon my sword.
Swear by my sword
Never to speak of this that you have heard.   160
    Ghost: [Beneath.]   Swear by his sword.
  Hamlet: Well said, old mole, canst work i' th' earth so fast?
A worthy pioner! Once more remove, good friends.
  Horatio: O day and night, but this is wondrous strange!
  Hamlet: And therefore as a stranger give it welcome.   165
There are more things in heaven and earth, Horatio,
Than are dreamt of in your philosophy.
But come—
Here, as before, never, so help you mercy,
How strange or odd some'er I bear myself—   170
As I perchance hereafter shall think meet
To put an antic disposition on—
That you, at such times seeing me, never shall,
With arms encumb'red thus, or this headshake,
Or by pronouncing of some doubtful phrase,   175
As "Well, well, we know," or "We could, and if we would,"
Or "If we list to speak," or "There be, and if they might,"
Or such ambiguous giving out, to note
That you know aught of me—this do swear,
So grace and mercy at your most need help you.   180
    Ghost: [Beneath.]   Swear.   *[They swear.]*
  Hamlet: Rest, rest, perturbed spirit! So, gentlemen,
With all my love I do commend me to you,
And what so poor a man as Hamlet is
May do t' express his love and friending to you,   185
God willing, shall not lack. Let us go in together,
And still your fingers on your lips, I pray.
The time is out of joint—O cursed spite,
That ever I was born to set it right!
Nay, come, let's go together.   *Exeunt.* 190

ACT II

Scene I

Enter old Polonius *with his man* [Reynaldo].

  Polonius: Give him this money and these notes, Reynaldo.
  Reynaldo: I will, my lord.

---

163. *pioner:* digger, miner (variant of *pioneer*).   165. *as . . . welcome:* give it the welcome due
in courtesy to strangers.   167. *your:* See note on I.i.138. *philosophy:* i.e. natural philosophy,
science.   172. *put . . . on:* behave in some fantastic manner, act like a madman.
174. *encumb'red:* folded.   176. *and if:* if.   177. *list:* cared, had a mind.   178. *note:*
indicate.   187. *still:* always.   190. *Nay . . . together:* They are holding back to let him go first.

II.i. Location: Polonius' quarters in the castle.

Polonius: You shall do marvell's wisely, good Reynaldo,
         Before you visit him, to make inquire
         Of his behavior.
Reynaldo: My lord, I did intend it.   5
Polonius: Marry, well said, very well said. Look you, sir,
         Inquire me first what Danskers are in Paris,
         And how, and who, what means, and where they keep,
         What company, at what expense; and finding
         By this encompassment and drift of question   10
         That they do know my son, come you more nearer
         Than your particular demands will touch it.
         Take you as 'twere some distant knowledge of him,
         As thus, "I know his father and his friends,
         And in part him." Do you mark this, Reynaldo?   15
Reynaldo: Ay, very well, my lord.
Polonius: "And in part him—but," you may say, "not well.
         But if't be he I mean, he's very wild,
         Addicted so and so," and there put on him
         What forgeries you please: marry, none so rank   20
         As may dishonor him, take heed of that,
         But, sir, such wanton, wild, and usual slips
         As are companions noted and most known
         To youth and liberty.
Reynaldo: As gaming, my lord.
Polonius: Ay, or drinking, fencing, swearing, quarreling,   25
         Drabbing—you may go so far.
Reynaldo: My lord, that would dishonor him.
Polonius: Faith, as you may season it in the charge:
         You must not put another scandal on him,
         That he is open to incontinency—   30
         That's not my meaning. But breathe his faults so quaintly
         That they may seem the taints of liberty,
         The flash and outbreak of a fiery mind,
         A savageness in unreclaimed blood,
         Of general assault.
Reynaldo: But, my good lord—   35
Polonius: Wherefore should you do this?
Reynaldo: Ay, my lord,
         I would know that.
Polonius: Marry, sir, here's my drift,

----

3. *marvell's:* marvellous(ly).   7. *Danskers:* Danes.   8. *keep:* lodge.   10. *encompassment:*
circuitousness. *drift of question:* directing of the conversation.   12. *particular demands:* direct
questions.   20. *forgeries:* invented charges.   22. *wanton:* sportive.   26. *Drabbing:* whoring.
28. *Faith:* Most editors read *Faith, no,* following F1; this makes easier sense. *season:* qualify,
temper.   30. *open to incontinency:* habitually profligate.   31. *quaintly:* artfully.   33. *unre-
claimed:* untamed.   34. *Of general assault:* i.e. to which young men are generally subject.

And I believe it is a fetch of wit:
You laying these slight sallies on my son,
As 'twere a thing a little soil'd [wi' th'] working,   40
Mark you,
Your party in converse, him you would sound,
Having ever seen in the prenominate crimes
The youth you breathe of guilty, be assur'd
He closes with you in this consequence: 45
"Good sir," or so, or "friend," or "gentleman,"
According to the phrase or the addition
Of man and country.
Reynaldo: Very good, my lord.
Polonius: And then, sir, does 'a this—'a does—what was I about
to say?   50
By the mass, I was about to say something.
Where did I leave?
Reynaldo: At "closes in the consequence."
Polonius: At "closes in the consequence," ay, marry.
He closes thus: "I know the gentleman.
I saw him yesterday, or th' other day,   55
Or then, or then, with such or such, and as you say,
There was 'a gaming, there o'ertook in 's rouse,
There falling out at tennis"; or, perchance,
"I saw him enter such a house of sale,"
Videlicet, a brothel, or so forth. See you now,   60
Your bait of falsehood take this carp of truth,
And thus do we of wisdom and of reach,
With windlasses and with assays of bias,
By indirections find directions out;
So by my former lecture and advice   65
Shall you my son. You have me, have you not?
Reynaldo: My lord, I have.
Polonius: God buy ye, fare ye well.
Reynaldo: Good my lord.
Polonius: Observe his inclination in yourself.
Reynaldo: I shall, my lord.   70
Polonius: And let him ply his music.

---

38. *fetch of wit:* ingenious device.   39. *sallies:* sullies, blemishes.   40. *soil'd . . . working:* i.e.
shopworn.   43. *Having:* if he has. *prenominate crimes:* aforementioned faults.   45. *closes:*
falls in. *in this consequence:* as follows.   47. *addition:* style of address.   57. *o'ertook in 's rouse:*
overcome by drink.   62. *reach:* capacity, understanding.   63. *windlasses:* roundabout
methods. *assays of bias:* indirect attempts (a figure from the game of bowls, in which the player
must make allowance for the curving course his bowl will take toward its mark).   64. *directions:* the way things are going.   66. *have me:* understand me.   67. *God buy ye:* good-bye (a
contraction of *God be with you*).   69. *in:* by. Polonius asks him to observe Laertes directly, as
well as making inquiries.   71. *let him ply:* see that he goes on with.

Reynaldo: Well, my lord.
Polonius: Farewell.   *Exit Reynaldo.*

Enter Ophelia.

                          How now, Ophelia, what's the matter?
    Ophelia: O my lord, my lord, I have been so affrighted!
    Polonius: With what, i' th' name of God?
    Ophelia: My lord, as I was sewing in my closet,   75
        Lord Hamlet, with his doublet all unbrac'd,
        No hat upon his head, his stockins fouled,
        Ungart'red, and down-gyved to his ankle,
        Pale as his shirt, his knees knocking each other,
        And with a look so piteous in purport   80
        As if he had been loosed out of hell
        To speak of horrors—he comes before me.
    Polonius: Mad for thy love?
    Ophelia: My lord, I do not know,
        But truly I do fear it.
    Polonius: What said he?
    Ophelia: He took me by the wrist, and held me hard,   85
        Then goes he to the length of all his arm,
        And with his other hand thus o'er his brow,
        He falls to such perusal of my face
        As 'a would draw it. Long stay'd he so.
        At last, a little shaking of mine arm,   90
        And thrice his head thus waving up and down,
        He rais'd a sigh so piteous and profound
        As it did seem to shatter all his bulk
        And end his being. That done, he lets me go,
        And with his head over his shoulder turn'd,   95
        He seem'd to find his way without his eyes,
        For out a' doors he went without their helps,
        And to the last bended their light on me.
    Polonius: Come, go with me. I will go seek the King.
        This is the very ecstasy of love,   100
        Whose violent property fordoes itself,
        And leads the will to desperate undertakings
        As oft as any passions under heaven
        That does afflict our natures. I am sorry—
        What, have you given him any hard words of late?   105
    Ophelia: No, my good lord, but as you did command

---

75. *closet:* private room.   76. *unbrac'd:* unlaced.   77. *stockins fouled:* stockings dirty.
78. *down-gyved:* hanging down like fetters on a prisoner's legs.   93. *bulk:* body.   100. *ecstasy:* madness.   101. *property:* quality. *fordoes:* destroys.

I did repel his letters, and denied
His access to me.

Polonius: That hath made him mad.
I am sorry that with better heed and judgment
I had not coted him. I fear'd he did but trifle   110
And meant to wrack thee, but beshrew my jealousy!
By heaven, it is as proper to our age
To cast beyond ourselves in our opinions,
As it is common for the younger sort
To lack discretion. Come, go we to the King.   115
This must be known, which, being kept close, might move
More grief to hide, than hate to utter love.
Come.   *Exeunt.*

Scene II

Flourish.   Enter King *and* Queen, Rosencrantz *and* Guildenstern *[cum aliis].*

King: Welcome, dear Rosencrantz and Guildenstern!
Moreover that we much did long to see you,
The need we have to use you did provoke
Our hasty sending. Something have you heard
Of Hamlet's transformation; so call it,   5
Sith nor th' exterior nor the inward man
Resembles that it was. What it should be,
More than his father's death, that thus hath put him
So much from th' understanding of himself,
I cannot dream of. I entreat you both   10
That, being of so young days brought up with him,
And sith so neighbored to his youth and havior,
That you voutsafe your rest here in our court
Some little time, so by your companies
To draw him on to pleasures, and to gather   15
So much as from occasion you may glean,
Whether aught to us unknown afflicts him thus,
That, open'd, lies within our remedy.
Queen: Good gentlemen, he hath much talk'd of you,
And sure I am two men there is not living   20
To whom he more adheres. If it will please you

---

110. *coted:* observed.   111. *beshrow:* beshrew, plague take. *jealousy:* suspicious mind.
112. *proper . . . age:* characteristic of men of my age.   113. *cast beyond ourselves:* overshoot,
go too far (by way of caution).   116. *close:* secret.   116-17. *move . . . love:* cause more
grievous consequences by its concealment than we shall incur displeasure by making it known.

II.ii. Location: The castle.   2. *Moreover . . . you:* besides the fact that we wanted to see you
for your own sakes.   6. *Sith:* since.   11. *of:* from.   13. *voutsafe your rest:* vouchsafe to
remain.   21. *more adheres:* is more attached.

To show us so much gentry and good will
As to expend your time with us a while
For the supply and profit of our hope,
Your visitation shall receive such thanks   25
As fits a king's remembrance.
Rosencrantz: Both your Majesties
Might, by the sovereign power you have of us,
Put your dread pleasures more into command
Than to entreaty.
Guildenstern: But we both obey,
And here give up ourselves, in the full bent,   30
To lay our service freely at your feet,
To be commanded.
   King: Thanks, Rosencrantz and gentle Guildenstern.
   Queen: Thanks, Guildenstern and gentle Rosencrantz.
And I beseech you instantly to visit   35
My too much changed son. Go some of you
And bring these gentlemen where Hamlet is.
Guildenstern: Heavens make our presence and our practices
Pleasant and helpful to him!
   Queen: Ay, amen!

Exeunt Rosencrantz *and* Guildenstern *[with some Attendants].*
Enter Polonius.

Polonius: Th' embassadors from Norway, my good lord,   40
Are joyfully return'd.
   King: Thou still hast been the father of good news.
Polonius: Have I, my lord? I assure my good liege
I hold my duty as I hold my soul,
Both to my God and to my gracious king;   45
And I do think, or else this brain of mine
Hunts not the trail of policy so sure
As it hath us'd to do, that I have found
The very cause of Hamlet's lunacy.
   King: O, speak of that, that do I long to hear.   50
Polonius: Give first admittance to th' embassadors;
My news shall be the fruit to that great feast.
   King: Thyself do grace to them, and bring them in.
                                        [*Exit* Polonius.]
He tells me, my dear Gertrude, he hath found
The head and source of all your son's distemper.   55

---

22. *gentry:* courtesy.   24. *supply and profit:* support and advancement.   30. *in . . . bent:* to
our utmost.   40. *embassadors:* ambassadors.   42. *still:* always.   43. *liege:* sovereign.
47. *policy:* statecraft.   52. *fruit:* dessert.   55. *head:* Synonymous with *source. distemper:*
(mental) illness.

Queen: I doubt it is no other but the main,
His father's death and our [o'erhasty] marriage.

Enter [Polonius *with* Voltemand *and* Cornelius, *the*] *Embassadors.*

King: Well, we shall sift him.—Welcome, my good friends!
Say, Voltemand, what from our brother Norway?
Voltemand: Most fair return of greetings and desires.   60
Upon our first, he sent out to suppress
His nephew's levies, which to him appear'd
To be a preparation 'gainst the Polack;
But better look'd into, he truly found
It was against your Highness. Whereat griev'd,   65
That so his sickness, age, and impotence
Was falsely borne in hand, sends out arrests
On Fortinbras, which he, in brief, obeys,
Receives rebuke from Norway, and in fine,
Makes vow before his uncle never more   70
To give th' assay of arms against your Majesty.
Whereon old Norway, overcome with joy,
Gives him threescore thousand crowns in annual fee,
And his commission to employ those soldiers,
So levied, as before, against the Polack,   75
With an entreaty, herein further shown,   *[Giving a paper.]*
That it might please you to give quiet pass
Through your dominions for this enterprise,
On such regards of safety and allowance
As therein are set down.
King: It likes us well,   80
And at our more considered time we'll read,
Answer, and think upon this business.
Mean time, we thank you for your well-took labor.
Go to your rest, at night we'll feast together.
Most welcome home!   *Exeunt Embassadors [and Attendants].*
Polonius: This business is well ended.   85
My liege, and madam, to expostulate
What majesty should be, what duty is,
Why day is day, night night, and time is time,
Were nothing but to waste night, day, and time;
Therefore, [since] brevity is the soul of wit,   90
And tediousness the limbs and outward flourishes,
I will be brief. Your noble son is mad:

---

56. *doubt:* suspect. *main:* main cause.   61. *Upon our first:* at our first representation.
65. *griev'd:* aggrieved, offended.   67. *borne in hand:* taken advantage of.   69. *in fine:* in the
end.   71. *assay:* trial.   79. *On . . . allowance:* with such safeguards and provisos.   80. *likes:*
pleases.   81. *consider'd:* suitable for consideration.   86. *expostulate:* expound.   90. *wit:*
understanding, wisdom.

Mad call I it, for to define true madness,
What is't but to be nothing else but mad?
But let that go.
Queen: More matter with less art.   95
Polonius: Madam, I swear I use no art at all.
That he's mad, 'tis true, 'tis true 'tis pity,
And pity 'tis 'tis true—a foolish figure,
But farewell it, for I will use no art.
Mad let us grant him then, and now remains   100
That we find out the cause of this effect,
Or rather say, the cause of this defect,
For this effect defective comes by cause:
Thus it remains, and the remainder thus.
Perpend.   105
I have a daughter—have while she is mine—
Who in her duty and obedience, mark,
Hath given me this. Now gather, and surmise.

[Reads the salutation of the letter.]
"To the celestial and my soul's idol, the most beautified
Ophelia"—   110
That's an ill phrase, a vile phrase, "beautified" is a vile
phrase. But you shall hear. Thus:
"In her excellent white bosom, these, etc."
Queen: Came this from Hamlet to her?
Polonius: Good madam, stay awhile. I will be faithful.   115

[Reads the] letter.
"Doubt thou the stars are fire,
Doubt that the sun doth move,
Doubt truth to be a liar,
But never doubt I love.
O dear Ophelia, I am ill at these numbers. I have not art to 120
reckon my groans, but that I love thee best, O most best,
believe it. Adieu.
Thine evermore, most dear lady,
whilst this machine is to him, Hamlet."
This in obedience hath my daughter shown me,   125
And more [above], hath his solicitings,
As they fell out by time, by means, and place,
All given to mine ear.
King: But how hath she
Receiv'd his love?

---

95. *art:* i.e. rhetorical art.   98. *figure:* figure of speech.   103. *For . . . cause:* for this effect
(which shows as a defect in Hamlet's reason) is not merely accidental, and has a cause we may
trace.   105. *Perpend:* consider.   109. *beautified:* beautiful (not an uncommon usage).
118. *Doubt:* suspect.   120. *ill . . . numbers:* bad at versifying.   121. *reckon:* count (with a
quibble on *numbers*).   124. *machine:* body.   126. *more above:* furthermore.

Polonius: What do you think of me?

   King: As of a man faithful and honorable.   130

Polonius: I would fain prove so. But what might you think,

     When I had seen this hot love on the wing—

     As I perceiv'd it (I must tell you that)

     Before my daughter told me—what might you,

     Or my dear Majesty your queen here, think,   135

     If I had play'd the desk or table-book,

     Or given my heart a [winking,] mute and dumb,

     Or look'd upon this love with idle sight,

     What might you think? No, I went round to work,

     And my young mistress thus I did bespeak: 140

     "Lord Hamlet is a prince out of thy star;

     This must not be"; and then I prescripts gave her,

     That she should lock herself from [his] resort,

     Admit no messengers, receive no tokens.

     Which done, she took the fruits of my advice;   145

     And he repell'd, a short tale to make,

     Fell into a sadness, then into a fast,

     Thence to a watch, thence into a weakness,

     Thence to [a] lightness, and by this declension,

     Into the madness wherein now he raves,   150

     And all we mourn for.

   King: Do you think ['tis] this?

  Queen: It may be, very like.

Polonius: Hath there been such a time—I would fain know that—

     That I have positively said, "'Tis so,"

     When it prov'd otherwise?

   King: Not that I know.   155

Polonius: *[Points to his head and shoulder.]* Take this from this, if

     this be otherwise.

     If circumstances lead me, I will find

     Where truth is hid, though it were hid indeed

     Within the centre.

   King: How may we try it further?   160

Polonius: You know sometimes he walks four hours together

     Here in the lobby.

  Queen: So he does indeed.

Polonius: At such a time I'll loose my daughter to him.

     Be you and I behind an arras then,

---

131. *fain:* willingly, gladly.   136. *play'd . . . table-book:* i.e. noted the matter secretly.
137. *winking:* closing of the eyes.   138. *idle sight:* noncomprehending eyes.   139. *round:*
straightforwardly.   140. *bespeak:* address.   141. *star:* i.e. sphere, lot in life.   145. *took . . . of:*
profited by, i.e. carried out.   146. *repell'd:* repulsed.   148. *watch:* sleeplessness.
149. *lightness:* lightheadedness.   159. *centre:* i.e. of the earth (which in the Ptolemaic system
is also the centre of the universe).   163. *arras:* hanging tapestry.

Mark the encounter: if he love her not,   165
And be not from his reason fall'n thereon,
Let me be no assistant for a state,
But keep a farm and carters.
    King: We will try it.

Enter Hamlet *[reading on a book.]*

  Queen: But look where sadly the poor wretch comes reading.
Polonius: Away, I do beseech you, both away.   170
    I'll board him presently.   *Exeunt* King *and* Queen.
                        O, give me leave,
    How does my good Lord Hamlet?
  Hamlet: Well, God-a-mercy.
Polonius: Do you know me, my lord?
  Hamlet: Excellent well, you are a fishmonger.   175
Polonius: Not I, my lord.
  Hamlet: Then I would you were so honest a man.
Polonius: Honest, my lord?
  Hamlet: Ay, sir, to be honest, as this world goes, is to be one man
    pick'd out of ten thousand.   180
Polonius: That's very true, my lord.
  Hamlet: For if the sun breed maggots in a dead dog, being a good
    kissing carrion—Have you a daughter?
Polonius: I have, my lord.
  Hamlet: Let her not walk i' th' sun. Conception is a blessing, but   185
    as your daughter may conceive, friend, look to't.
Polonius: *[Aside.]* How say you by that? still harping on my daugh-
    ter. Yet he knew me not at first, 'a said I was a fishmonger. 'A
    is far gone. And truly in my youth I suff'red much extremity
    for love—very near this. I'll speak to him again.—What do   190
    you read, my lord?
  Hamlet: Words, words, words.
Polonius: What is the matter, my lord?
  Hamlet: Between who?
Polonius: I mean, the matter that you read, my lord.   195
  Hamlet: Slanders, sir; for the satirical rogue says here that old
    men have grey beards, that their faces are wrinkled, their eyes
    purging thick amber and plumtree gum, and that they have a
    plentiful lack of wit, together with most weak hams; all which,
    sir, though I most powerfully and potently believe, yet I hold   200

---

166. *thereon:* because of that.   171. *board:* accost. *presently:* at once.   173. *God-a-mercy:*
thank you.   175. *fishmonger:* Usually explained as slang for "bawd," but no evidence has been
produced for such a usage in Shakespeare's day.   182–83. *good kissing carrion:* flesh good
enough for the sun to kiss.   185. *Conception:* understanding (with following play on the sense
"conceiving a child").   193. *matter:* subject; but Hamlet replies as if he had understood
Polonius to mean "cause for a quarrel."

it not honesty to have it thus set down, for yourself, sir, shall grow old as I am, if like a crab you could go backward.

Polonius: [Aside.] Though this be madness, yet there is method in't.—Will you walk out of the air, my lord?

Hamlet: Into my grave.   205

Polonius: Indeed that's out of the air. [Aside.] How pregnant sometimes his replies are! a happiness that often madness hits on, which reason and [sanity] could not so prosperously be deliver'd of. I will leave him, [and suddenly contrive the means of meeting between him] and my daughter.—My lord,   210 I will take my leave of you.

Hamlet: You cannot take from me any thing that I will not more willingly part withal—except my life, except my life, except my life.

Polonius: Fare you well, my lord.   215

Hamlet: These tedious old fools!

Enter Guildenstern *and* Rosencrantz.

Polonius: You go to seek the Lord Hamlet, there he is.

Rosencrantz: [To Polonius.] God save you, sir!   [Exit Polonius.]

Guildenstern: My honor'd lord!

Rosencrantz: My most dear lord!   220

Hamlet: My [excellent] good friends! How dost thou, Guilden-stern? Ah, Rosencrantz! Good lads, how do you both?

Rosencrantz: As the indifferent children of the earth.

Guildenstern: Happy, in that we are not [over-]happy, on Fortune's [cap] we are not the very button.   225

Hamlet: Nor the soles of her shoe?

Rosencrantz: Neither, my lord.

Hamlet: Then you live about her waist, or in the middle of her favors?

Guildenstern: Faith, her privates we.   230

Hamlet: In the secret parts of Fortune? O, most true, she is a strumpet. What news?

Rosencrantz: None, my lord, but the world's grown honest.

Hamlet: Then is doomsday near. But your news is not true. [Let me question more in particular. What have you, my good   235 friends, deserv'd at the hands of Fortune, that she sends you to prison hither?

Guildenstern: Prison, my lord?

Hamlet: Denmark's a prison.

---

201. *honesty:* a fitting thing.   203. *method:* orderly arrangement, sequence of ideas. *out . . . air:* Outdoor air was thought to be bad for invalids.   206. *pregnant:* apt.   209. *suddenly:* at once.   223. *indifferent:* average.   230. *privates:* (1) intimate friends; (2) genitalia. 232. *strumpet:* A common epithet for Fortune, because she grants favors to all men.

Rosencrantz: Then is the world one. 240

Hamlet: A goodly one, in which there are many confines, wards, and dungeons, Denmark being one o' th' worst.

Rosencrantz: We think not so, my lord.

Hamlet: Why then 'tis none to you; for there is nothing either good or bad, but thinking makes it so. To me it is a prison. 245

Rosencrantz: Why then your ambition makes it one. 'Tis too narrow for your mind.

Hamlet: O God, I could be bounded in a nutshell, and count myself a king of infinite space—were it not that I have bad dreams. 250

Guildenstern: Which dreams indeed are ambition, for the very substance of the ambitious is merely the shadow of a dream.

Hamlet: A dream itself is but a shadow.

Rosencrantz: Truly, and I hold ambition of so airy and light a quality that it is but a shadow's shadow. 255

Hamlet: Then are our beggars bodies, and our monarchs and outstretch'd heroes the beggars' shadows. Shall we to th' court? for, by my fay, I cannot reason.

Both [Rosencrantz, Guildenstern]:
We'll wait upon you.

Hamlet: No such matter. I will not sort you with the rest of my 260 servants; for to speak to you like an honest man, I am most dreadfully attended.] But in the beaten way of friendship, what make you at Elsinore?

Rosencrantz: To visit you, my lord, no other occasion.

Hamlet: Beggar that I am, I am [even] poor in thanks—but I 265 thank you, and sure, dear friends, my thanks are too dear a halfpenny. Were you not sent for? is it your own inclining? is it a free visitation? Come, come, deal justly with me. Come, come—nay, speak.

Guildenstern: What should we say, my lord? 270

Hamlet: Any thing but to th' purpose. You were sent for, and there is a kind of confession in your looks, which your modesties have not craft enough to color. I know the good King and Queen have sent for you.

Rosencrantz: To what end, my lord? 275

Hamlet: That you must teach me. But let me conjure you, by the

---

241. *wards:* cells.   256. *bodies:* i.e. not shadows (since they lack ambition).   256–57. *outstretch'd:* i.e. with their ambition extended to the utmost (and hence producing stretched-out or elongated shadows).   258. *fay:* faith.   259. *wait upon you:* attend you thither.   260. *sort:* associate.   262. *dreadfully:* execrably.   266–67. *too . . . halfpenny:* too expensive priced at a halfpenny, i.e. not worth much.   268. *justly:* honestly.   271. *but:* Ordinarily punctuated with a comma preceding, to give the sense "provided that it is"; but Q2 has no comma, and Hamlet may intend, or include, the sense "except."   272–73. *modesties:* sense of shame.

rights of our fellowship, by the consonancy of our youth, by
the obligation of our ever-preserv'd love, and by what more
dear a better proposer can charge you withal, be even and
direct with me, whether you were sent for or no!   280

Rosencrantz: [*Aside to Guildenstern.*] What say you?

Hamlet: [*Aside.*] Nay then I have an eye of you!—If you love me,
hold not off.

Guildenstern: My lord, we were sent for.

Hamlet: I will tell you why, so shall my anticipation prevent your   285
discovery, and your secrecy to the King and Queen moult no
feather. I have of late—but wherefore I know not—lost all
my mirth, forgone all custom of exercises; and indeed it goes
so heavily with my disposition, that this goodly frame, the
earth, seems to me a sterile promontory; this most excellent   290
canopy, the air, look you, this brave o'erhanging firmament,
this majestical roof fretted with golden fire, why, it appeareth
nothing to me but a foul and pestilent congregation of
vapors. What [a] piece of work is a man, how noble in reason,
how infinite in faculties, in form and moving, how express   295
and admirable in action, how like an angel in apprehension,
how like a god! the beauty of the world; the paragon of animals; and yet to me what is this quintessence of dust? Man
delights not me—nor women neither, though by your smiling
you seem to say so.   300

Rosencrantz: My lord, there was no such stuff in my thoughts.

Hamlet: Why did ye laugh then, when I said, "Man delights not
me"?

Rosencrantz: To think, my lord, if you delight not in man, what lenten
entertainment the players shall receive from you. We coted   305
them on the way, and hither are they coming to offer you
service.

Hamlet: He that plays the king shall be welcome—his Majesty
shall have tribute on me, the adventerous knight shall use his
foil and target, the lover shall not sigh gratis, the humorous   310
man shall end his part in peace, [the clown shall make those

---

277. *consonancy . . . youth:* similarity of our ages.   279. *charge:* urge, adjure. *even:* frank,
honest (cf. modern "level with me").   282. *of:* on.   285–86. *prevent your discovery:* forestall
your disclosure (of what the King and Queen have said to you in confidence).   286–87. *moult
no feather:* not be impaired in the least.   288. *custom of exercises:* my usual athletic activities.
291. *brave:* splendid.   292. *fretted:* ornamented as with fretwork.   294. *piece of work:*
masterpiece.   295. *how infinite . . . god:* See the Textual Notes for the different punctuation
in F1.   295. *express:* exact.   298. *quintessence:* finest and purest extract.   304–05. *lenten
entertainment:* meagre reception.   305. *coted:* outstripped.   309. *on:* of, from. *adventerous:*
adventurous, i.e. wandering in search of adventure.   310. *foil and target:* light fencing sword
and small shield. *gratis:* without reward. *humorous:* dominated by some eccentric trait (like the
melancholy Jaques in *As You Like It*).

laugh whose lungs are [tickle] a' th' sere,] and the lady shall
say her mind freely, or the [blank] verse shall halt for't. What
players are they?

Rosencrantz: Even those you were wont to take such delight in, the tra-   315
gedians of the city.

Hamlet: How chances it they travel? Their residence, both in reputation and profit, was better both ways.

Rosencrantz: I think their inhibition comes by the means of the late
innovation.   320

Hamlet: Do they hold the same estimation they did when I was in
the city? Are they so follow'd?

Rosencrantz: No indeed are they not.

[Hamlet: How comes it? do they grow rusty?

Rosencrantz: Nay, their endeavor keeps in the wonted pace; but there   325
is, sir, an aery of children, little eyases, that cry out on the top
of question, and are most tyrannically clapp'd for't. These
are now the fashion, and so [berattle] the common stages—
so they call them—that many wearing rapiers are afraid of
goose-quills and dare scarce come thither.   330

Hamlet: What, are they children? Who maintains 'em? How are
they escoted? Will they pursue the quality no longer than
they can sing? Will they not say afterwards, if they should
grow themselves to common players (as it is [most like], if
their means are [no] better), their writers do them wrong, to   335
make them exclaim against their own succession?

Rosencrantz: Faith, there has been much to do on both sides, and the
nation holds it no sin to tarre them to controversy. There was

---

312. *tickle . . . sere:* i.e. easily made to laugh (literally, describing a gun that goes off easily; *sere* = a catch in the gunlock; *tickle* = easily affected, highly sensitive to stimulus).   313. *halt:* limp, come off lamely (the verse will not scan if she omits indecent words).   319. *inhibition:* hindrance (to playing in the city). The word could be used of an official prohibition. See next note.   320. *innovation:* Shakespeare elsewhere uses this word of a political uprising or revolt, and lines 319-20 are often explained as meaning that the company had been forbidden to play in the city as the result of some disturbance. It is commonly conjectured that the allusion is to the Essex rebellion of 1601, but it is known that Shakespeare's company, though to some extent involved on account of the special performance of *Richard II* they were commissioned to give on the eve of the rising, were not in fact punished by inhibition. A second interpretation explains *innovation* as referring to the new theatrical vogue described in lines 326 ff., and conjectures that *inhibition* may allude to a Privy Council order of 1600 restricting the number of London playhouses to two and the number of performances to two a week.   324-44. *How . . . too:* This passage refers topically to the "War of the Theatres" between the child actors and their poet Jonson on the one side, and on the other the adults, with Dekker, Marston, and possibly Shakespeare as spokesmen, in 1600-1601.   326. *aery:* nest. *eyases:* unfledged hawks.   326-27. *cry . . . question:* cry shrilly above others in controversy.   327. *tyranically:* outrageously.   328. *berattle:* cry down, satirize. *common stages:* public theatres (the children played at the Blackfriars, a private theatre).   330. *goose-quills:* pens (of satirical playwrights).   332. *escoted:* supported. *quality:* profession (of acting).   332-33. *no . . . sing:* i.e. only until their voices change.   336. *succession:* future.   337. *to do:* ado.   338. *tarre:* incite.

for a while no money bid for argument, unless the poet and
the player went to cuffs in the question.   340

Hamlet: Is't possible?

Guildenstern: O, there has been much throwing about of brains.

Hamlet: Do the boys carry it away?

Rosencrantz: Ay, that they do, my lord—Hercules and his load too.]

Hamlet: It is not very strange, for my uncle is King of Denmark,   345
and those that would make mouths at him while my father
liv'd, give twenty, forty, fifty, a hundred ducats a-piece for his
picture in little. 'Sblood, there is something in this more than
natural, if philosophy could find it out.

A flourish [for the Players].

Guildenstern: There are the players.   350

Hamlet: Gentlemen, you are welcome to Elsinore. Your hands,
come then: th' appurtenance of welcome is fashion and ceremony. Let me comply with you in this garb, [lest my] extent
to the players, which, I tell you, must show fairly outwards,
should more appear like entertainment than yours. You are   355
welcome; but my uncle-father and aunt-mother are deceiv'd.

Guildenstern: In what, my dear lord?

Hamlet: I am but mad north-north-west. When the wind is south-
erly I know a hawk from a hand-saw.

Enter Polonius.

Polonius: Well be with you, gentlemen!   360

Hamlet: *[Aside to them.]* Hark you, Guildenstern, and you too—at
each ear a hearer—that great baby you see there is not yet
out of his swaddling-clouts.

Rosencrantz: Happily he is the second time come to them, for they say
an old man is twice a child.   365

Hamlet: I will prophesy, he comes to tell me of the players, mark
it. *[Aloud.]* You say right, sir, a' Monday morning, 'twas then
indeed.

Polonius: My lord, I have news to tell you.

Hamlet: My lord, I have news to tell you. When Roscius was an   370
actor in Rome—

---

339. *argument:* plot of a play.   340. *in the question:* i.e. as part of the script.   343. *carry it
away:* win.   344. *Hercules . . . too:* Hercules in the course of one of his twelve labors
supported the world for Atlas; the children do better, for they carry away the world and
Hercules as well. There is an allusion to the Globe playhouse, which reportedly had for its
sign the figure of Hercules upholding the world.   346. *mouths:* derisive faces.   348. *'Sblood:*
by God's (Christ's) blood.   353. *comply:* observe the formalities. *garb:* fashion, manner. *my
extent:* i.e. the degree of courtesy I show.   354-55. *more . . . yours:* seem to be a warmer
reception than I have given you.   359. *hawk, hand-saw:* Both cutting-tools; but also both
birds, if *hand-saw* quibbles on *henshaw,* "heron," a bird preyed upon by the hawk.
363. *swaddling-clouts:* swaddling clothes.   364. *Happily:* haply, perhaps.   365. *twice:* i.e. for
the second time.   370. *Roscius:* the most famous of Roman actors (died 62 B.C.). News about
him would be stale news indeed.

Polonius: The actors are come hither, my lord.

Hamlet: Buzz, buzz!

Polonius: Upon my honor—

Hamlet: "Then came each actor on his ass"— 375

Polonius: The best actors in the world, either for tragedy, comedy, history, pastoral, pastoral-comical, historical-pastoral, [tragical-historical, tragical-comical-historical-pastoral,] scene individable, or poem unlimited; Seneca cannot be too heavy, nor Plautus too light, for the law of writ and the liberty: these 380 are the only men.

Hamlet: O Jephthah, judge of Israel, what a treasure hadst thou!

Polonius: What a treasure had he, my lord?

Hamlet: Why—

"One fair daughter, and no more, 385
    The which he loved passing well."

Polonius: [*Aside.*] Still on my daughter.

Hamlet: Am I not i' th' right, old Jephthah?

Polonius: If you call me Jephthah, my lord, I have a daughter that I love passing well. 390

Hamlet: Nay, that follows not.

Polonius: What follows then, my lord?

Hamlet: Why—

"As by lot, God wot,"
and then, you know, 395
"It came to pass, as most like it was"—
the first row of the pious chanson will show you more, for look where my abridgment comes.

Enter the Players, *[four or five].*

You are welcome, masters, welcome all. I am glad to see thee well. Welcome, good friends. O, old friend! why, thy face is 400 valanc'd since I saw thee last; com'st thou to beard me in Denmark? What, my young lady and mistress! by' lady, your ladyship is nearer to heaven than when I saw you last, by the altitude of a chopine. Pray God your voice, like a piece of

---

373. *Buzz:* exclamation of impatience at someone who tells news already known.   378–79. *scene individable:* play observing the unity of place.   379. *poem unlimited:* play ignoring rules such as the three unities.   *Seneca:* Roman writer of tragedies.   380. *Plautus:* Roman writer of comedies.   *for . . . liberty:* for strict observance of the rules, or for freedom from them (with possible allusion to the location of playhouses, which were not built in properties under city jurisdiction, but in the "liberties"—land once monastic and now outside the jurisdiction of the city authorities).   381. *only:* very best (a frequent use).   382. *Jephthah . . . Israel:* title of a ballad, from which Hamlet goes on to quote. For the story of Jephthah and his daughter, see Judges 11.   397. *row:* stanza. *chanson:* song, ballad.   398. *abridgment:* (1) interruption; (2) pastime.   401. *valanc'd:* fringed, i.e. bearded. *beard:* confront boldly (with obvious pun).   402. *by' lady:* by Our Lady.   404. *chopine:* thick-soled shoe.

uncurrent gold, be not crack'd within the ring. Masters, you 405
are all welcome. We'll e'en to't like [French] falc'ners—fly at
any thing we see; we'll have a speech straight. Come give us a
taste of your quality, come, a passionate speech.

[1.] Player: What speech, my good lord?

Hamlet: I heard thee speak me a speech once, but it was never 410
acted, or if it was, not above once; for the play, I remember,
pleas'd not the million, 'twas caviary to the general, but it was
—as I receiv'd it, and others, whose judgments in such
matters cried in the top of mine—an excellent play, well
digested in the scenes, set down with as much modesty as 415
cunning. I remember one said there were no sallets in the
lines to make the matter savory, nor no matter in the phrase
that might indict the author of affection, but call'd it an
honest method, as wholesome as sweet, and by very much
more handsome than fine. One speech in't I chiefly lov'd, 420
'twas Aeneas' [tale] to Dido, and thereabout of it especially
when he speaks of Priam's slaughter. If it live in your
memory, begin at this line—let me see, let me see:
"The rugged Pyrrhus, like th' Hyrcanian beast—"
'Tis not so, it begins with Pyrrhus: 425
"The rugged Pyrrhus, he whose sable arms,
Black as his purpose, did the night resemble
When he lay couched in th' ominous horse,
Hath now this dread and black complexion smear'd
With heraldy more dismal: head to foot 430
Now is he total gules, horridly trick'd
With blood of fathers, mothers, daughters, sons,
Bak'd and impasted with the parching streets,
That lend a tyrannous and a damned light
To their lord's murther. Roasted in wrath and fire, 435
And thus o'er-sized with coagulate gore,
With eyes like carbuncles, the hellish Pyrrhus

---

405. *crack'd . . . ring:* i.e. broken to the point where you can no longer play female roles. A
coin with a crack extending far enough in from the edge to cross the circle surrounding the
stamp of the sovereign's head was unacceptable in exchange (*uncurrent*).   407. *straight:*
straightway.   408. *quality:* professional skill.   412. *caviary . . . general:* caviare to the
common people, i.e. too choice for the multitude.   414. *cried . . . of:* were louder than, i.e.
carried more authority than.   416. *sallets:* salads, i.e. spicy jokes.   417. *savory:* zesty.
418. *affection:* affectation.   420. *fine:* showily dressed (in language).   422. *Priam's
slaughter:* the slaying of Priam (at the fall of Troy).   424. *Pyrrhus:* another name for Neopto-
lemus, Achilles' son. *Hyrcanian beast:* Hyrcania in the Caucasus was notorious for its tigers.
426. *sable arms:* The Greeks within the Trojan horse had blackened their skin so as to be
inconspicuous when they emerged at night.   430. *heraldy:* heraldry. *dismal:* ill-boding.
431. *gules:* red (heraldic term). *trick'd:* adorned.   433. *Bak'd:* caked. *impasted:* crusted. *with
. . . streets:* i.e. by the heat from the burning streets.   436. *o'er-sized:* covered over as with a
coat of sizing.   437. *carbuncles:* jewels believed to shine in the dark.

Old grandsire Priam seeks."
So proceed you.

Polonius: 'Fore God, my lord, well spoken, with good accent and   440
good discretion.

[1.] Player: "Anon he finds him
Striking too short at Greeks. His antique sword,
Rebellious to his arm, lies where it falls,
Repugnant to command. Unequal match'd,   445
Pyrrhus at Priam drives, in rage strikes wide,
But with the whiff and wind of his fell sword
Th' unnerved father falls. [Then senseless Ilium,]
Seeming to feel this blow, with flaming top
Stoops to his base, and with a hideous crash   450
Takes prisoner Pyrrhus' ear; for lo his sword,
Which was declining on the milky head
Of reverent Priam, seem'd i' th' air to stick.
So as a painted tyrant Pyrrhus stood
[And,] like a neutral to his will and matter,   455
Did nothing.
But as we often see, against some storm,
A silence in the heavens, the rack stand still,
The bold winds speechless, and the orb below
As hush as death, anon the dreadful thunder   460
Doth rend the region; so after Pyrrhus' pause,
A roused vengeance sets him new a-work,
And never did the Cyclops' hammers fall
On Mars's armor forg'd for proof eterne
With less remorse than Pyrrhus' bleeding sword   465
Now falls on Priam.
Out, out, thou strumpet Fortune! All you gods,
In general synod take away her power!
Break all the spokes and [fellies] from her wheel,
And bowl the round nave down the hill of heaven   470
As low as to the fiends!"

Polonius: This is too long.

Hamlet: It shall to the barber's with your beard. Prithee say on,
he's for a jig or a tale of bawdry, or he sleeps. Say on, come to
Hecuba.   475

---

445. *Repugnant:* resistant, hostile.   447. *fell:* cruel.   448. *unnerved:* drained of strength.
senseless: insensible. *Ilium:* the citadel of Troy.   453. *reverent:* reverend, aged.   455. *like* . . .
matter: i.e. poised midway between intention and performance.   457. *against:* just before.
458. *rack:* cloud-mass.   461. *region:* i.e. air.   463. *Cyclops:* giants who worked in Vulcan's
smithy, where armor was made for the gods.   464. *proof eterne:* eternal endurance.
465. *remorse:* pity.   469. *fellies:* rims.   470. *nave:* hub.   474. *jig:* song-and-dance entertainment performed after the main play.

[1.] Player: "But who, ah woe, had seen the mobled queen"—
    Hamlet: "The mobled queen"?
    Polonius: That's good, ["[mobled] queen" is good].
[1.] Player: "Run barefoot up and down, threat'ning the flames
            With bisson rheum, a clout upon that head   480
            Where late the diadem stood, and for a robe,
            About her lank and all o'er-teemed loins,
            A blanket, in the alarm of fear caught up—
            Who this had seen, with tongue in venom steep'd,
            'Gainst Fortune's state would treason have pronounc'd.   485
            But if the gods themselves did see her then,
            When she saw Pyrrhus make malicious sport
            In mincing with his sword her [husband's] limbs,
            The instant burst of clamor that she made,
            Unless things mortal move them not at all,   490
            Would have made milch the burning eyes of heaven,
            And passion in the gods."
    Polonius: Look whe'er he has not turn'd his color and has tears in 's
            eyes. Prithee no more.
    Hamlet: 'Tis well, I'll have thee speak out the rest of this soon. 495
            Good my lord, will you see the players well bestow'd? Do you
            hear, let them be well us'd, for they are the abstract and brief
            chronicles of the time. After your death you were better have
            a bad epitaph than their ill report while you live.
    Polonius: My lord, I will use them according to their desert.   500
    Hamlet: God's bodkin, man, much better: use every man after his
            desert, and who shall scape whipping? Use them after your
            own honor and dignity—the less they deserve, the more
            merit is in your bounty. Take them in.
    Polonius: Come, sirs.   *[Exit.]* 505
    Hamlet: Follow him, friends, we'll hear a play to-morrow. *[Exeunt*
            all the Players but the First.] Dost thou hear me, old friend?
            Can you play "The Murther of Gonzago"?
[1.] Player: Ay, my lord.
    Hamlet: We'll ha't to-morrow night. You could for need study a 510
            speech of some dozen lines, or sixteen lines, which I would
            set down and insert in't, could you not?
[1.] Player: Ay, my lord.
    Hamlet: Very well. Follow that lord, and look you mock him not.
            [Exit First Player.] My good friends, I'll leave you [till] night. 515
            You are welcome to Elsinore.

---

476. *mobled:* muffled. 480. *bisson rheum:* blinding tears. *clout:* cloth. 482. *o'er-teemed:*
worn out by childbearing. 485. *state:* rule, government. 491. *milch:* moist (literally,
milky). 492. *passion:* grief. 493. *Look . . . not:* i.e. note how he has. 496. *bestow'd:* lodged.
us'd: treated. 501. *God's bodkin:* by God's (Christ's) little body. 510. *for need:* if necessary.

Rosencrantz: Good my lord!
    Hamlet: Ay so, God buy to you. it]
                     Exeunt [Rosencrantz and Guildenstern].

Now I am alone.
O, what a rogue and peasant slave am I!   520
Is it not monstrous that this player here,
But in a fiction, in a dream of passion,
Could force his soul so to his own conceit
That from her working all the visage wann'd,
Tears in his eyes, distraction in his aspect,   525
A broken voice, an' his whole function suiting
With forms to his conceit? And all for nothing,
For Hecuba!
What's Hecuba to him, or he to [Hecuba],
That he should weep for her? What would he do   530
    Had he the motive and [the cue] for passion
That I have? He would drown the stage with tears,
And cleave the general ear with horrid speech,
Make mad the guilty, and appall the free,
Confound the ignorant, and amaze indeed   535
The very faculties of eyes and ears. Yet I,
A dull and muddy-mettled rascal, peak
Like John-a-dreams, unpregnant of my cause,
And can say nothing; no, not for a king,
Upon whose property and most dear life   540
A damn'd defeat was made. Am I a coward?
Who calls me villain, breaks my pate across,
Plucks off my beard and blows it in my face,
Tweaks me by the nose, gives me the lie i' th' throat
As deep as to the lungs? Who does me this?   545
Hah, 'swounds, I should take it; for it cannot be
But I am pigeon-liver'd, and lack gall
To make oppression bitter, or ere this
I should 'a' fatted all the region kites
With this slave's offal. Bloody, bawdy villain!   550
Remorseless, treacherous, lecherous, kindless villain!
Why, what an ass am I! This is most brave,
That I, the son of a dear [father] murthered,

---

523. *conceit:* imaginative conception.   526. *his whole function:* the operation of his whole
body.   527. *forms:* actions, expressions.   534. *free:* innocent.   535. *amaze:* confound.
537. *muddy-mettled:* dull-spirited. *peak:* mope.   538. *John-a-dreams:* a sleepy fellow. *unpreg-*
nant of: unquickened by.   541. *defeat:* destruction.   544-45. *gives . . . lungs:* calls me a liar in
the extremest degree.   546. *'swounds:* by God's (Christ's) wounds. *should:* would certainly.
547. *am . . . gall:* i.e. am constitutionally incapable of resentment. That doves were mild
because they had no gall was a popular belief.   549. *region kites:* kites of the air.   550. *offal:*
entrails.   551. *kindless:* unnatural.

Prompted to my revenge by heaven and hell,
Must like a whore unpack my heart with words,   555
And fall a-cursing like a very drab,
A stallion. Fie upon't, foh!
About, my brains! Hum—I have heard
That guilty creatures sitting at a play
Have by the very cunning of the scene   560
Been strook so to the soul, that presently
They have proclaim'd their malefactions:
For murther, though it have no tongue, will speak
With most miraculous organ. I'll have these players
Play something like the murther of my father   565
Before mine uncle. I'll observe his looks,
I'll tent him to the quick. If 'a do blench,
I know my course. The spirit that I have seen
May be a [dev'l], and the [dev'l] hath power
T' assume a pleasing shape, yea, and perhaps,   570
Out of my weakness and my melancholy,
As he is very potent with such spirits,
Abuses me to damn me. I'll have grounds
More relative than this—the play's the thing
Wherein I'll catch the conscience of the King.   *Exit.* 575

ACT III

Scene I

Enter King, Queen, Polonius, Ophelia, Rosencrantz, Guildenstern, Lords.

    King: An' can you by no drift of conference
      Get from him why he puts on this confusion,
      Grating so harshly all his days of quiet
      With turbulent and dangerous lunacy?
 Rosencrantz: He does confess he feels himself distracted,   5
      But from what cause 'a will by no means speak.
Guildenstern: Nor do we find him forward to be sounded,
      But with a crafty madness keeps aloof
      When we would bring him on to some confession
      Of his true state.
    Queen: Did he receive you well?   10

---

557. *stallion:* male whore. Most editors adopt the F1 reading *scullion,* "kitchen menial."
558. *About:* to work.   561. *presently:* at once, then and there.   567. *tent:* probe. *blench:*
flinch.   572. *spirits:* states of temperament.   573. *Abuses:* deludes.   574. *relative:* closely
related (to fact), i.e. conclusive.

III.i. Location: The castle. See the Textual Notes for the Q1 version of parts of this scene.
1. *An':* and. *drift of conference:* leading on of conversation.   7. *forward:* readily willing.
sounded: plumbed, probed.   8. *crafty madness:* i.e. mad craftiness, the shrewdness that mad
people sometimes exhibit.

Rosencrantz: Most like a gentleman.
Guildenstern: But with much forcing of his disposition.
Rosencrantz: Niggard of question, but of our demands
　　　　　Most free in his reply.
　　Queen:　　　　　　　　Did you assay him
　　　　　To any pastime?　　　　　　　　　　　　　　　　15
Rosencrantz: Madam, it so fell out that certain players
　　　　　We o'erraught on the way; of these we told him,
　　　　　And there did seem in him a kind of joy
　　　　　To hear of it. They are here about the court,
　　　　　And as I think, they have already order　　　　　20
　　　　　This night to play before him.
　　Polonius:　　　　　　　　　　　'Tis most true,
　　　　　And he beseech'd me to entreat your Majesties
　　　　　To hear and see the matter.
　　King: With all my heart, and it doth much content me
　　　　　To hear him so inclin'd.　　　　　　　　　　　25
　　　　　Good gentlemen, give him a further edge,
　　　　　And drive his purpose into these delights.
Rosencrantz: We shall, my lord.　　*Exeunt Rosencrantz and Guildenstern.*
　　King:　　　　　　　　　Sweet Gertrude, leave us two,
　　　　　For we have closely sent for Hamlet hither,
　　　　　That he, as 'twere by accident, may here　　　　30
　　　　　Affront Ophelia. Her father and myself,
　　　　　We'll so bestow ourselves that, seeing unseen,
　　　　　We may of their encounter frankly judge,
　　　　　And gather by him, as he is behav'd,
　　　　　If't be th' affliction of his love or no　　　　　35
　　　　　That thus he suffers for.
　　Queen:　　　　　　　　I shall obey you.
　　　　　And for your part, Ophelia, I do wish
　　　　　That your good beauties be the happy cause
　　　　　Of Hamlet's wildness. So shall I hope your virtues
　　　　　Will bring him to his wonted way again,　　　　40
　　　　　To both your honors.
Ophelia:　　　　　　　　Madam, I wish it may.　　*[Exit Queen.]*
Polonius: Ophelia, walk you here.—Gracious, so please you,
　　　　　We will bestow ourselves. *[To Ophelia.]* Read on this book,
　　　　　That show of such an exercise may color
　　　　　Your [loneliness]. We are oft to blame in this—　　45
　　　　　'Tis too much prov'd—that with devotion's visage

---

12. *disposition:* inclination.　13. *question:* conversation. *demands:* questions.　14. *assay:*
attempt to win.　17. *o'erraught:* passed (literally, overreached).　26. *edge:* stimulus.
27. *into:* on to.　29. *closely:* privately.　31. *Affront:* meet.　33. *frankly:* freely.　44. *exercise:*
i.e. religious exercise (as the next sentence makes clear).　44-45. *color Your loneliness:* make
your solitude seem natural.　46. *too much prov'd:* too often proved true.

And pious action we do sugar o'er
The devil himself.
King: [Aside.] O, 'tis too true!
                How smart a lash that speech doth give my conscience!
                The harlot's cheek, beautied with plast'ring art,   50
                Is not more ugly to the thing that helps it
                Than is my deed to my most painted word.
                O heavy burthen!
Polonius: I hear him coming. Withdraw, my lord.
                                                    [Exeunt King and Polonius.]

Enter Hamlet.

Hamlet: To be, or not to be, that is the question: 55
                Whether 'tis nobler in the mind to suffer
                The slings and arrows of outrageous fortune,
                Or to take arms against a sea of troubles,
                And by opposing, end them. To die, to sleep—
                No more, and by a sleep to say we end   60
                The heart-ache and the thousand natural shocks
                That flesh is heir to; 'tis a consummation
                Devoutly to be wish'd. To die, to sleep—
                To sleep, perchance to dream—ay, there's the rub,
                For in that sleep of death what dreams may come,   65
                When we have shuffled off this mortal coil,
                Must give us pause; there's the respect
                That makes calamity of so long life:
                For who would bear the whips and scorns of time,
                Th' oppressor's wrong, the proud man's contumely,   70
                The pangs of despis'd love, the law's delay,
                The insolence of office, and the spurns
                That patient merit of th' unworthy takes,
                When he himself might his quietus make
                With a bare bodkin; who would fardels bear,   75
                To grunt and sweat under a weary life,
                But that the dread of something after death,
                The undiscover'd country, from whose bourn
                No traveller returns, puzzles the will,
                And makes us rather bear those ills we have,   80

---

47. *action:* demeanor.   51. *to . . . it:* in comparison with the paint that makes it look
beautiful.   55-89. See the Textual Notes for the version of this soliloquy in Q1.   56. *suffer:*
submit to, endure patiently.   62. *consummation:* completion, end.   64. *rub:* obstacle (a term
from the game of bowls).   66. *shuffled off:* freed ourselves from. *this mortal coil:* the turmoil
of this mortal life.   67. *respect:* consideration.   68. *of . . . life:* so long-lived.   69. *time:* the
world.   74. *his quietus make:* write paid to his account.   75. *bare bodkin:* mere dagger. *fardels:*
burdens.   78. *undiscover'd:* not disclosed to knowledge; about which men have no information. *bourn:* boundary, i.e. region.   79. *puzzles:* paralyzes.

Than fly to others that we know not of?
Thus conscience does make cowards [of us all],
And thus the native hue of resolution
Is sicklied o'er with the pale cast of thought,
And enterprises of great pitch and moment   85
With this regard their currents turn awry,
And lose the name of action.—Soft you now,
The fair Ophelia. Nymph, in thy orisons
Be all my sins rememb'red.

Ophelia: Good my lord,
How does your honor for this many a day?   90

Hamlet: I humbly thank you, well, [well, well].

Ophelia: My lord, I have remembrances of yours
That I have longed long to redeliver.
I pray you now receive them.

Hamlet: No, not I,
I never gave you aught.   95

Ophelia: My honor'd lord, you know right well you did,
And with them words of so sweet breath compos'd
As made these things more rich. Their perfume lost,
Take these again, for to the noble mind
Rich gifts wax poor when givers prove unkind.   100
There, my lord.

Hamlet: Ha, ha! are you honest?

Ophelia: My lord?

Hamlet: Are you fair?

Ophelia: What means your lordship?   105

Hamlet: That if you be honest and fair, [your honesty] should
admit no discourse to your beauty.

Ophelia: Could beauty, my lord, have better commerce than with
honesty?

Hamlet: Ay, truly, for the power of beauty will sooner transform 110
honesty from what it is to a bawd than the force of honesty
can translate beauty into his likeness. This was sometime a
paradox, but now the time gives it proof. I did love you once.

Ophelia: Indeed, my lord, you made me believe so.

Hamlet: You should not have believ'd me, for virtue cannot so   115
[inoculate] our old stock but we shall relish of it. I lov'd you
not.

---

82. *conscience:* reflection (but with some of the modern sense, too).   83. *native hue:* natural
(ruddy) complexion.   84. *pale cast:* pallor. *thought:* i.e. melancholy thought, brooding.
85. *pitch:* loftiness (a term from falconry, signifying the highest point of a hawk's flight).
88. *orisons:* prayers.   102. *honest:* chaste.   112. *sometime:* formerly.   113. *paradox:* tenet
contrary to accepted belief.   115-16. *virtue . . . it:* virtue, engrafted on our old stock (of
viciousness), cannot so change the nature of the plant that no trace of the original will remain.

Ophelia: I was the more deceiv'd.

Hamlet: Get thee [to] a nunn'ry, why wouldst thou be a breeder of sinners? I am myself indifferent honest, but yet I could 120 accuse me of such things that it were better my mother had not borne me: I am very proud, revengeful, ambitious, with more offenses at my beck than I have thoughts to put them in, imagination to give them shape, or time to act them in. 125 What should such fellows as I do crawling between earth and heaven? We are arrant knaves, believe none of us. Go thy ways to a nunn'ry. Where's your father?

Ophelia: At home, my lord.

Hamlet: Let the doors be shut upon him, that he may play the fool 130 no where but in 's own house. Farewell.

Ophelia: O, help him, you sweet heavens!

Hamlet: If thou dost marry, I'll give thee this plague for thy dowry: be thou as chaste as ice, as pure as snow, thou shalt not escape calumny. Get thee to a nunn'ry, farewell. Or if thou wilt needs marry, marry a fool, for wise men know well 135 enough what monsters you make of them. To a nunn'ry, go, and quickly too. Farewell.

Ophelia: Heavenly powers, restore him!

Hamlet: I have heard of your paintings, well enough. God hath given you one face, and you make yourselves another. You jig 140 and amble, and you [lisp,] you nickname God's creatures and make your wantonness [your] ignorance. Go to, I'll no more on't, it hath made me mad. I say we will have no moe marriage. Those that are married already (all but one) shall live, the rest shall keep as they are. To a nunn'ry, go.   *Exit.* 145

Ophelia: O, what a noble mind is here o'erthrown!
The courtier's, soldier's, scholar's, eye, tongue, sword,
Th' expectation and rose of the fair state,
The glass of fashion and the mould of form,
Th' observ'd of all observers, quite, quite down!   150
And I, of ladies most deject and wretched,
That suck'd the honey of his [music] vows,
Now see [that] noble and most sovereign reason
Like sweet bells jangled out of time, and harsh;
That unmatch'd form and stature of blown youth   155

---

120. *indifferent honest:* tolerably virtuous.   136. *monsters:* Alluding to the notion that the husbands of unfaithful wives grew horns. *you:* you women.   141. *You . . . creatures:* i.e. you walk and talk affectedly.   142. *make . . . ignorance:* excuse your affectation as ignorance. 143. *moe:* more.   148. *expectation:* hope. *rose:* ornament. *fair:* Probably proleptic: "(the kingdom) made fair by his presence."   149. *glass:* mirror. *mould of form:* pattern of (courtly) behavior.   150. *observ'd . . . observers:* Shakespeare uses *observe* to mean not only "behold, mark attentively" but also "pay honor to."   155. *blown:* in full bloom.

Blasted with ecstasy. O, woe is me
T' have seen what I have seen, see what I see!

[Ophelia withdraws.]

Enter King *and* Polonius.

> *King:* Love? his affections do not that way tend,
> Nor what he spake, though it lack'd form a little,
> Was not like madness. There's something in his soul   160
> O'er which his melancholy sits on brood,
> And I do doubt the hatch and the disclose
> Will be some danger; which for to prevent,
> I have in quick determination
> Thus set it down: he shall with speed to England   165
> For the demand of our neglected tribute.
> Haply the seas, and countries different,
> With variable objects, shall expel
> This something-settled matter in his heart,
> Whereon his brains still beating puts him thus   170
> From fashion of himself. What think you on't?
> *Polonius:* It shall do well; but yet do I believe
> The origin and commencement of his grief
> Sprung from neglected love. *[Ophelia comes forward.]* How
> now, Ophelia?   175
> You need not tell us what Lord Hamlet said,
> We heard it all. My lord, do as you please,
> But if you hold it fit, after the play
> Let his queen-mother all alone entreat him
> To show his grief. Let her be round with him,   180
> And I'll be plac'd (so please you) in the ear
> Of all their conference. If she find him not,
> To England send him, or confine him where
> Your wisdom best shall think.
> *King:*   It shall be so.
> Madness in great ones must not [unwatch'd] go.   *Exeunt.* 185

Scene II

Enter Hamlet *and three of the* Players.

> *Hamlet:* Speak the speech, I pray you, as I pronounc'd it to you,
> trippingly on the tongue, but if you mouth it, as many of our

---

156. *Blasted:* withered. *ecstasy:* madness.   158. *affections:* inclinations, feelings.   162. *doubt:*
fear. *disclose:* Synonymous with *hatch;* see also V.i.263.   166. *neglected:* unrequited.
173. *his grief:* what is troubling him. *round:* blunt, outspoken.   182. *find him:* learn the truth
about him.

III.ii. Location: The castle.   2. *mouth:* pronounce with exaggerated distinctness or declama-
tory effect.

players do, I had as live the town-crier spoke my lines. Nor do
not saw the air too much with your hand, thus, but use all
gently, for in the very torrent, tempest, and, as I may say, 5
whirlwind of your passion, you must acquire and beget a temperance that may give it smoothness. O, it offends me to the
soul to hear a robustious periwig-pated fellow tear a passion
to totters, to very rags, to spleet the ears of the groundlings,
who for the most part are capable of nothing but inexplicable 10
dumb shows and noise. I would have such a fellow whipt for
o'erdoing Termagant, it out-Herods Herod, pray you avoid
it.
  [1.] *Player:* I warrant your honor.
    Hamlet: Be not too tame neither, but let your own discretion be 15
your tutor. Suit the action to the word, the word to the
action, with this special observance, that you o'erstep not the
modesty of nature: for any thing so o'erdone is from the purpose of playing, whose end, both at the first and now, was and
is, to hold as 'twere the mirror up to nature: to show virtue 20
her feature, scorn her own image, and the very age and body
of the time his form and pressure. Now this overdone, or
come tardy off, though it makes the unskillful laugh, cannot
but make the judicious grieve; the censure of which one must
in your allowance o'erweigh a whole theatre of others. O, 25
there be players that I have seen play—and heard others
[praise], and that highly—not to speak it profanely, that, neither having th' accent of Christians nor the gait of Christian,
pagan, nor man, have so strutted and bellow'd that I have
thought some of Nature's journeymen had made men, and 30
not made them well, they imitated humanity so abominably.
  [1.] *Player:* I hope we have reform'd that indifferently with us, [sir].
    Hamlet: O, reform it altogether. And let those that play your
clowns speak no more than is set down for them, for there be
of them that will themselves laugh to set on some quantity of 35
barren spectators to laugh too, though in the mean time
some necessary question of the play be then to be consider'd.
That's villainous, and shows a most pitiful ambition in the
fool that uses it. Go make you ready.   *[Exeunt Players.]*

---

3. *live:* lief, willingly.   9. *totters:* tatters. *spleet:* split.   *groundlings:* those who paid the lowest
admission price and stood on the ground in the "yard" or pit of the theatre.   10. *capable of:*
able to take in.   12. *Termagant:* a supposed god of the Saracens, whose role in medieval
drama, like that of Herod (line 12), was noisy and violent.   18. *modesty:* moderation. *from:*
contrary to.   21. *scorn:* i.e. that which is worthy of scorn.   22. *pressure:* impression (as of a
seal), exact image.   23. *tardy:* inadequately.   24. *censure:* judgment. *which one:* (even) one of
whom.   26. *allowance:* estimation.   27. *profanely:* irreverently.   30-31. *some . . . abominably:*
i.e. they were so unlike men that it seemed Nature had not made them herself, but had
delegated the task to mediocre assistants.   32. *indifferently:* pretty well.   35. *of them:* some
of them.   39. *fool:* (1) stupid person; (2) actor playing a fool's role. *uses it:* See the Textual
Notes for an interesting passage following these words in Q1.

Enter Polonius, Guildenstern, *and* Rosencrantz.

     How now, my lord? Will the King hear this piece of work?   40
  Polonius: And the Queen too, and that presently.
    Hamlet: Bid the players make haste.   *[Exit Polonius.]*
     Will you two help to hasten them?
 Rosencrantz: Ay, my lord.   *Exeunt they two.*
    Hamlet: What ho, Horatio!   45

Enter Horatio.

    Horatio: Here, sweet lord, at your service.
    Hamlet: Horatio, thou art e'en as just a man
     As e'er my conversation cop'd withal.
    Horatio: O my dear lord—
    Hamlet: Nay, do not think I flatter,
     For what advancement may I hope from thee   50
     That no revenue hast but thy good spirits
     To feed and clothe thee? Why should the poor be flatter'd?
     No, let the candied tongue lick absurd pomp,
     And crook the pregnant hinges of the knee
     Where thrift may follow fawning. Dost thou hear?   55
     Since my dear soul was mistress of her choice
     And could of men distinguish her election,
     Sh' hath seal'd thee for herself, for thou hast been
     As one in suff'ring all that suffers nothing,
     A man that Fortune's buffets and rewards   60
     Hast ta'en with equal thanks; and blest are those
     Whose blood and judgment are so well co-meddled,
     That they are not a pipe for Fortune's finger
     To sound what stop she please. Give me that man
     That is not passion's slave, and I will wear him   65
     In my heart's core, ay, in my heart of heart,
     As I do thee. Something too much of this.
     There is a play to-night before the King,
     One scene of it comes near the circumstance
     Which I have told thee of my father's death.   70
     I prithee, when thou seest that act afoot,
     Even with the very comment of thy soul
     Observe my uncle. If his occulted guilt
     Do not itself unkennel in one speech,
     It is a damned ghost that we have seen,   75

---

40. *piece of work:* masterpiece (said jocularly).   41. *presently:* at once.   47. *thou . . . man:* i.e. you come as close to being what a man should be (*just* = exact, precise).   48. *my . . . withal:* my association with people has brought me into contact with.   53. *candied:* sugared, i.e. flattering. *absurd:* tasteless (Latin sense).   54. *pregnant:* moving readily.   55. *thrift:* thriving, profit.   62. *blood:* passions. *co-meddled:* mixed, blended.   66. *my heart of heart:* the heart of my heart.   72. *very . . . soul:* your most intense critical observation.   73. *occulted:* hidden.   74. *unkennel:* bring into the open.   75. *damned ghost:* evil spirit, devil.

And my imaginations are as foul
As Vulcan's stithy. Give him heedful note,
For I mine eyes will rivet to his face,
And after we will both our judgments join
In censure of his seeming.

Horatio: Well, my lord.   80
If 'a steal aught the whilst this play is playing,
And scape [detecting], I will pay the theft.

[Sound a flourish. Danish march.] Enter Trumpets and Kettle-drums, King,
Queen, Polonius, Ophelia, *[Rosencrantz, Guildenstern, and other* Lords
attendant, with his Guard *carrying torches].*

Hamlet: They are coming to the play. I must be idle;
    Get you a place.
    King: How fares our cousin Hamlet?   85
Hamlet: Excellent, i' faith, of the chameleon's dish: I eat the air,
    promise-cramm'd—you cannot feed capons so.
    King: I have nothing with this answer, Hamlet, these words are
    not mine.
Hamlet: No, nor mine now. *[To Polonius.]* My lord, you play'd 90
    once i' th' university, you say?
Polonius: That did I, my lord, and was accounted a good actor.
Hamlet: What did you enact?
Polonius: I did enact Julius Caesar. I was kill'd i' th' Capitol;
    Brutus kill'd me.   95
    Hamlet: It was a brute part of him to kill so capital a calf there. Be
    the players ready?
Rosencrantz: Ay, my lord, they stay upon your patience.
    Queen: Come hither, my dear Hamlet, sit by me.
Hamlet: No, good mother, here's metal more attractive.   100
                                        [Lying down at Ophelia's *feet.]*
Polonius: *[To the King.]* O ho, do you mark that?
    Hamlet: Lady, shall I lie in your lap?
Ophelia: No, my lord.
[Hamlet: I mean, my head upon your lap?
Ophelia: Ay, my lord.]   105
    Hamlet: Do you think I meant country matters?
Ophelia: I think nothing, my lord.
    Hamlet: That's a fair thought to lie between maids' legs.

---

77. *stithy:* forge.   79. *censure . . . seeming:* reaching a verdict on his behavior.   83. *be idle:*
act foolish, pretend to be crazy.   85. *fares:* Hamlet takes up this word in another sense.
86. *chameleon's dish:* Chameleons were thought to feed on air. Hamlet says that he subsists on
an equally nourishing diet, the promise of succession. There is probably a pun on *air/heir.*
88. *have nothing with:* do not understand.   89. *mine:* i.e. an answer to my question.
96. *part:* action.   106. *country matters:* indecency.

Ophelia: What is, my lord?

Hamlet: Nothing. 110

Ophelia: You are merry, my lord.

Hamlet: Who, I?

Ophelia: Ay, my lord.

Hamlet: O God, your only jig-maker. What should a man do but
be merry, for look you how cheerfully my mother looks, and 115
my father died within 's two hours.

Ophelia: Nay, 'tis twice two months, my lord.

Hamlet: So long? Nay then let the dev'l wear black, for I'll have a
suit of sables. O heavens, die two months ago, and not forgotten yet? Then there's hope a great man's memory may 120
outlive his life half a year, but, by'r lady, 'a must build
churches then, or else shall 'a suffer not thinking on, with the
hobby-horse, whose epitaph is, "For O, for O, the hobby-
horse is forgot."

The trumpets sounds. Dumb show follows.
Enter a King and a Queen [very lovingly], the Queen embracing him and he her.
[She kneels and makes show of protestation unto him.] He takes her up and declines
his head upon her neck. He lies him down upon a bank of flowers. She, seeing him
asleep, leaves him. Anon comes in another man, takes off his crown, kisses it, pours
poison in the sleeper's ears, and leaves him. The Queen returns, finds the King
dead, makes passionate action. The pois'ner with some three or four [mutes] come
in again, seem to condole with her. The dead body is carried away. The pois'ner
woos the Queen with gifts; she seems harsh [and unwilling] awhile, but in the end
accepts love. *[Exeunt.]*

Ophelia: What means this, my lord? 125

Hamlet: Marry, this' [miching] mallecho, it means mischief.

Ophelia: Belike this show imports the argument of the play.

Enter Prologue.

Hamlet: We shall know by this fellow. The players cannot keep
[counsel], they'll tell all.

Ophelia: Will 'a tell us what this show meant? 130

Hamlet: Ay, or any show that you will show him. Be not you
asham'd to show, he'll not shame to tell you what it means.

Ophelia: You are naught, you are naught. I'll mark the play.

---

114. *only:* very best. *jig-maker:* one who composed or played in the farcical song-and-dance
entertainments that followed plays. 116. *'s:* this. 118-19. *let . . . sables:* i.e. to the devil
with my garments; after so long a time I am ready for the old man's garb of sables (fine fur).
122. *not thinking on:* not being thought of, i.e. being forgotten. 123-24. *For . . . forgot:* line
from a popular ballad lamenting puritanical suppression of such country sports as the
May-games, in which the hobby-horse, a character costumed to resemble a horse, traditionally
appeared. 126. *this' miching mallecho:* this is sneaking mischief. 127. *argument:* subject,
plot. 129. *counsel:* secrets. 131. *Be not you:* if you are not. 133. *naught:* wicked.

Prologue: For us, and for our tragedy,
　　　　Here stooping to your clemency, 135
　　　　We beg your hearing patiently.　　　　　　　*[Exit.]*
　　Hamlet: Is this a prologue, or the posy of a ring?
　　Ophelia: 'Tis brief, my lord.
　　Hamlet: As woman's love.

Enter [two Players,] King and Queen.

[Player] King: Full thirty times hath Phoebus' cart gone round 140
　　　　Neptune's salt wash and Tellus' orbed ground,
　　　　And thirty dozen moons with borrowed sheen
　　　　About the world have times twelve thirties been,
　　　　Since love our hearts and Hymen did our hands
　　　　Unite comutual in most sacred bands. 145
[Player] Queen: So many journeys may the sun and moon
　　　　Make us again count o'er ere love be done!
　　　　But woe is me, you are so sick of late,
　　　　So far from cheer and from [your] former state,
　　　　That I distrust you. Yet though I distrust, 150
　　　　Discomfort you, my lord, it nothing must,
　　　　[For] women's fear and love hold quantity,
　　　　In neither aught, or in extremity.
　　　　Now what my [love] is, proof hath made you know,
　　　　And as my love is siz'd, my fear is so. 155
　　　　Where love is great, the littlest doubts are fear;
　　　　Where little fears grow great, great love grows there.
[Player] King: Faith, I must leave thee, love, and shortly too;
　　　　My operant powers their functions leave to do,
　　　　And thou shalt live in this fair world behind, 160
　　　　Honor'd, belov'd, and haply one as kind
　　　　For husband shalt thou—
[Player] Queen: 　　　　　　　　O, confound the rest!
　　　　Such love must needs be treason in my breast.
　　　　In second husband let me be accurs'd!
　　　　None wed the second but who kill'd the first. 165
　　Hamlet: *[Aside.]* That's wormwood!
[Player Queen:] The instances that second marriage move
　　　　Are base respects of thrift, but none of love.

---

137. *posy . . . ring:* verse motto inscribed in a ring (necessarily short). 140-58. See the Textual Notes for the corresponding lines in Q1. 140. *Phoebus' cart:* the sun-god's chariot. 141. *Tellus:* goddess of the earth. 144. *Hymen:* god of marriage. 145. *bands:* bonds. 150. *distrust:* fear for. 152. *hold quantity:* are related in direct proportion. 154. *proof:* experience. 159. *operant:* active, vital. *leave to do:* cease to perform. 163. *confound the rest:* may destruction befall what you are about to speak of—a second marriage on my part. 167. *instances:* motives. *move:* give rise to. 168. *respects of thrift:* considerations of advantage.

A second time I kill my husband dead,
When second husband kisses me in bed. 170

[Player] King: I do believe you think what now you speak,
But what we do determine, oft we break.
Purpose is but the slave to memory,
Of violent birth, but poor validity,
Which now, the fruit unripe, sticks on the tree, 175
But fall unshaken when they mellow be.
Most necessary 'tis that we forget
To pay ourselves what to ourselves is debt.
What to ourselves in passion we propose,
The passion ending, doth the purpose lose. 180
The violence of either grief or joy
Their own enactures with themselves destroy.
Where joy most revels, grief doth most lament;
Grief [joys], joy grieves, on slender accident.
This world is not for aye, nor 'tis not strange 185
That even our loves should with our fortunes change:
For 'tis a question left us yet to prove,
Whether love lead fortune, or else fortune love.
The great man down, you mark his favorite flies,
The poor advanc'd makes friends of enemies. 190
And hitherto doth love on fortune tend,
For who not needs shall never lack a friend,
And who in want a hollow friend doth try,
Directly seasons him his enemy.
But orderly to end where I begun, 195
Our wills and fates do so contrary run
That our devices still are overthrown,
Our thoughts are ours, their ends none of our own:
So think thou wilt no second husband wed,
But die thy thoughts when thy first lord is dead. 200

[Player] Queen: Nor earth to me give food, nor heaven light,
Sport and repose lock from me day and night,
To desperation turn my trust and hope,
[An] anchor's cheer in prison be my scope!
Each opposite that blanks the face of joy 205
Meet what I would have well and it destroy!

---

174. *validity:* strength, power to last. 177-78. *Most . . . debt:* i.e. such resolutions are debts
we owe to ourselves, and it would be foolish to pay such debts. 179. *passion:* violent
emotion. 181-82. *The violence . . . destroy:* i.e. both violent grief and violent joy fail of their
intended acts because they destroy themselves by their very violence. 184. *slender accident:*
slight occasion. 194. *seasons:* ripens, converts into. 197. *devices:* devisings, intentions. *still:*
always. 204. *anchor's cheer:* hermit's fare. *my scope:* the extent of my comforts. 205. *blanks:*
blanches, makes pale (a symptom of grief).

Both here and hence pursue me lasting strife,
If once I be a widow, ever I be a wife!

Hamlet: If she should break it now!

[Player] King: 'Tis deeply sworn. Sweet, leave me here a while,   210
My spirits grow dull, and fain I would beguile
The tedious day with sleep.   *[Sleeps.]*

[Player] Queen: Sleep rock thy brain,
and never come mischance between us twain!   *Exit.*

Hamlet: Madam, how like you this play?

Queen: The lady doth protest too much, methinks.   215

Hamlet: O but she'll keep her word.

King: Have you heard the argument? is there no offense in't?

Hamlet: No, no, they do but jest, poison in jest—no offense i' th'
world.

King: What do you call the play?   220

Hamlet: "The Mouse-trap." Marry, how? tropically: this play is
the image of a murther done in Vienna; Gonzago is the
duke's name, his wife, Baptista. You shall see anon. 'Tis a
knavish piece of work, but what of that? Your Majesty, and
we that have free souls, it touches us not. Let the gall'd jade 225
winch, our withers are unwrung.

Enter Lucianus.

This is one Lucianus, nephew to the king.

Ophelia: You are as good as a chorus, my lord.

Hamlet: I could interpret between you and your love, if I could
see the puppets dallying.   230

Ophelia: You are keen, my lord, you are keen.

Hamlet: It would cost you a groaning to take off mine edge.

Ophelia: Still better, and worse.

Hamlet: So you mistake your husbands. Begin, murtherer, leave
thy damnable faces and begin. Come, the croaking raven 235
doth bellow for revenge.

Lucianus: Thoughts black, hands apt, drugs fit, and time agreeing,
[Confederate] season, else no creature seeing,

---

217. *offense:* offensive matter (but Hamlet quibbles on the sense "crime"). 218. *jest:* i.e.
pretend. 221. *tropically:* figuratively (with play on *trapically*—which is the reading of
Q1—and probably with allusion to the children's saying *marry trap,* meaning "now you're
caught"). 222. *image:* representation. 225. *free souls:* clear consciences. 225. *gall'd jade:*
chafed horse. 226. *winch:* wince. *withers:* ridge between a horse's shoulders. *unwrung:* not
rubbed sore. 228. *chorus:* i.e. one who explains the forthcoming action. 229–30. *I . . .
dallying:* I could speak the dialogue between you and your lover like a puppet-master (with an
indecent jest). 231. *keen:* bitter, sharp. 233. *better, and worse:* i.e. more pointed and less
decent. 234. *So:* i.e. "for better, for worse," in the words of the marriage service. *mistake:* i.e.
mis-take, take wrongfully. Their vows, Hamlet suggests, prove false. 235. *faces:* facial
expressions 235-36. *the croaking . . . revenge:* Misquoted from an old play, *The True Tragedy
of Richard III.* 238. *Confederate season:* the time being my ally.

Thou mixture rank, of midnight weeds collected,
With Hecat's ban thrice blasted, thrice [infected],   240
Thy natural magic and dire property
On wholesome life usurps immediately.

[Pours the poison in his ears.]

Hamlet: 'A poisons him i' th' garden for his estate. His name's
    Gonzago, the story is extant, and written in very choice Ital-
    ian. You shall see anon how the murtherer gets the love of 245
    Gonzago's wife.

Ophelia: The King rises.

[Hamlet: What, frighted with false fire?]

Queen: How fares my lord?

Polonius: Give o'er the play.   250

King: Give me some light. Away!

Polonius: Lights, lights, lights!

Exeunt all but Hamlet *and* Horatio.

Hamlet: "Why, let the strooken deer go weep,
      The hart ungalled play,
    For some must watch while some must sleep,   255
      Thus runs the world away."
    Would not this, sir, and a forest of feathers—if the rest of my
    fortunes turn Turk with me—with [two] Provincial roses on
    my raz'd shoes, get me a fellowship in a cry of players?

Horatio: Half a share.   260

Hamlet: A whole one, I.
    "For thou dost know, O Damon dear,
      This realm dismantled was
    Of Jove himself, and now reigns here
      A very, very"—pajock.   265

Horatio: You might have rhym'd.

Hamlet: O good Horatio, I'll take the ghost's word for a thousand
    pound. Didst perceive?

Horatio: Very well, my lord.

Hamlet: Upon the talk of the pois'ning?   270

Horatio: I did very well note him.

Hamlet: Ah, ha! Come, some music! Come, the recorders!

---

240. *Hecat's ban:* the curse of Hecate, goddess of witchcraft.   248. *false fire:* i.e. a blank
cartridge.   253. *strooken:* struck, i.e. wounded.   254. *ungalled:* unwounded.   255. *watch:*
stay awake.   257. *feathers:* the plumes worn by tragic actors.   258. *turn Turk:* i.e. go to the
bad.   *Provincial roses:* rosettes designed to look like a variety of French rose.   259. *raz'd:*
with decorating slashing. *fellowship:* partnership.   *cry:* company.   263. *dismantled:* divested,
deprived.   265. *pajock:* peacock (substituting for the rhyme-word *ass*). The natural history of
the time attributed many vicious qualities to the peacock.

> For if the King like not the comedy,
> Why then belike he likes it not, perdy.
> Come, some music! 275

Enter Rosencrantz *and* Guildenstern.

Guildenstern: Good my lord, voutsafe me a word with you.
Hamlet: Sir, a whole history.
Guildenstern: The King, sir—
Hamlet: Ay, sir, what of him? 280
Guildenstern: Is in his retirement marvellous distemp'red.
Hamlet: With drink, sir?
Guildenstern: No, my lord, with choler.
Hamlet: Your wisdom should show itself more richer to signify this to the doctor, for for me to put him to his purgation 285 would perhaps plunge him into more choler.
Guildenstern: Good my lord, put your discourse into some frame, and [start] not so wildly from my affair.
Hamlet: I am tame, sir. Pronounce.
Guildenstern: The Queen, your mother, in most great affliction of 290 spirit, hath sent me to you.
Hamlet: You are welcome.
Guildenstern: Nay, good my lord, this courtesy is not of the right breed. If it shall please you to make me a wholesome answer, I will do your mother's commandement; if not, your pardon 295 and my return shall be the end of [my] business.
Hamlet: Sir, I cannot.
Rosencrantz: What, my lord?
Hamlet: Make you a wholesome answer—my wit's diseas'd. But, sir, such answer as I can make, you shall command, or rather, 300 as you say, my mother. Therefore no more, but to the matter: my mother, you say—
Rosencrantz: Then thus she says: your behavior hath strook her into amazement and admiration.
Hamlet: O wonderful son, that can so stonish a mother! But is 305 there no sequel at the heels of this mother's admiration? Impart.
Rosencrantz: She desires to speak with you in her closet ere you go to bed.
Hamlet: We shall obey, were she ten times our mother. Have you 310 any further trade with us?

---

274. *perdy:* assuredly (French *pardieu,* "by God"). 283. *choler:* anger (but Hamlet willfully takes up the word in the sense "biliousness"). 285. *put . . . purgation:* i.e. prescribe for what's wrong with him. 287. *frame:* logical structure. 294. *wholesome:* sensible, rational. 295. *pardon:* permission for departure. 304. *amazement and admiration:* bewilderment and wonder. 305. *stonish:* astound. 308. *closet:* private room.

Rosencrantz: My lord, you once did love me.

    Hamlet: And do still, by these pickers and stealers.

Rosencrantz: Good my lord, what is your cause of distemper? You do surely bar the door upon your own liberty if you deny your 315 griefs to your friend.

    Hamlet: Sir, I lack advancement.

Rosencrantz: How can that be, when you have the voice of the King himself for your succession in Denmark?

    Hamlet: Ay, sir, but "While the grass grows"—the proverb is 320 something musty.

Enter the Players *with recorders.*

O, the recorders! Let me see one.—To withdraw with you— why do you go about to recover the wind of me, as if you would drive me into a toil?

Guildenstern: O my lord, if my duty be too bold, my love is too 325 unmannerly.

    Hamlet: I do not well understand that. Will you play upon this pipe?

Guildenstern: My lord, I cannot.

    Hamlet: I pray you. 330

Guildenstern: Believe me, I cannot.

    Hamlet: I do beseech you.

Guildenstern: I know no touch of it, my lord.

    Hamlet: It is as easy as lying. Govern these ventages with your fingers and [thumbs], give it breath with your mouth, and it 335 will discourse most eloquent music. Look you, these are the stops.

Guildenstern: But these cannot I command to any utt'rance of harmony. I have not the skill.

    Hamlet: Why, look you now, how unworthy a thing you make of 340 me! You would play upon me, you would seem to know my stops, you would pluck out the heart of my mystery, you would sound me from my lowest note to [the top of] my compass; and there is much music, excellent voice, in this little organ, yet cannot you make it speak. 'Sblood, do you think I 345 am easier to be play'd on than a pipe? Call me what instrument you will, though you fret me, [yet] you cannot play upon me.

---

313. *pickers and stealers:* hands; which, as the Catechism says, we must keep "from picking and stealing."   320. *proverb:* i.e. "While the grass grows, the steed starves."   321. *something musty:* somewhat stale.   323. *recover the wind:* get to windward.   324. *toil:* snare.   334. *ventages:* stops.   345. *organ:* instrument.   347. *fret:* (1) finger (an instrument); (2) vex.

Enter Polonius.

        God bless you, sir.

Polonius: My lord, the Queen would speak with you, and presently.   350

Hamlet: Do you see yonder cloud that's almost in shape of a
    camel?

Polonius: By th' mass and 'tis, like a camel indeed.

Hamlet: Methinks it is like a weasel.

Polonius: It is back'd like a weasel.   355

Hamlet: Or like a whale.

Polonius: Very like a whale.

Hamlet: Then I will come to my mother by and by. *[Aside.]* They
    fool me to the top of my bent.—I will come by and by.

[Polonius]: I will say so.   *[Exit.]* 360

Hamlet: "By and by" is easily said. Leave me, friends.

                                [Exeunt all but Hamlet.*]*

'Tis now the very witching time of night,
When churchyards yawn and hell itself [breathes] out
Contagion to this world. Now could I drink hot blood,
And do such [bitter business as the] day   365
Would quake to look on. Soft, now to my mother.
O heart, lose not thy nature! let not ever
The soul of Nero enter this firm bosom,
Let me be cruel, not unnatural;
I will speak [daggers] to her, but use none.   370
My tongue and soul in this be hypocrites—
How in my words somever she be shent,
To give them seals never my soul consent!   *Exit.*

Scene III

Enter King, Rosencrantz, *and* Guildenstern.

King: I like him not, nor stands it safe with us
    To let his madness range. Therefore prepare you.
    I your commission will forthwith dispatch,
    And he to England shall along with you.
    The terms of our estate may not endure   5
    Hazard so near 's as doth hourly grow
    Out of his brows.

Guildenstern: We will ourselves provide.

---

350. *presently:* at once.   358-59. *They . . . bent:* they make me play the fool to the limit of my
ability.   *by and by:* at once.   362. *witching:* i.e. when the powers of evil are at large.
367. *nature:* natural affection, filial feeling.   368. *Nero:* Murderer of his mother.
372. *shent:* rebuked.   373. *give them seals:* confirm them by deeds.

III.iii. Location: The castle.   1. *him:* i.e. his state of mind, his behavior.   3. *dispatch:* have
drawn up.   5. *terms:* conditions, nature. *our estate:* my position (as king).   7. *his brows:* the
madness visible in his face (?)

Most holy and religious fear it is
To keep those many many bodies safe
That live and feed upon your Majesty.   10
Rosencrantz: The single and peculiar life is bound
With all the strength and armor of the mind
To keep itself from noyance, but much more
That spirit upon whose weal depends and rests
The lives of many. The cess of majesty   15
Dies not alone, but like a gulf doth draw
What's near it with it. Or it is a massy wheel
Fix'd on the summit of the highest mount,
To whose [huge] spokes ten thousand lesser things
Are mortis'd and adjoin'd, which when it falls,   20
Each small annexment, petty consequence,
Attends the boist'rous [ruin]. Never alone
Did the King sigh, but [with] a general groan.
King: Arm you, I pray you, to this speedy viage,
For we will fetters put about this fear,   25
Which now goes too free-footed.
Rosencrantz: We will haste us.

Exeunt Gentlemen [Rosencrantz *and* Guildenstern].

Enter Polonius.

Polonius: My lord, he's going to his mother's closet.
Behind the arras I'll convey myself
To hear the process. I'll warrant she'll tax him home,
And as you said, and wisely was it said,   30
'Tis meet that some more audience than a mother,
Since nature makes them partial, should o'erhear
The speech, of vantage. Fare you well, my liege,
I'll call upon you ere you go to bed,
And tell you what I know.
King: Thanks, dear my lord.   35

Exit [Polonius].

O, my offense is rank, it smells to heaven,
It hath the primal eldest curse upon't,
A brother's murther. Pray can I not,
Though inclination be as sharp as will.

---

8. *fear:* concern.   11. *single and peculiar:* individual and private.   13. *noyance:* injury.
15. *cess:* cessation, death.   16. *gulf:* whirlpool.   20. *mortis'd:* fixed.   22. *Attends:* accompanies. *ruin:* fall.   24. *Arm:* prepare. *viage:* voyage.   25. *fear:* object of fear.   29. *process:*
course of the talk. *tax him home:* take him severely to task.   33. *of vantage:* from an advantageous position (?) or in addition (?).   36-72. See the Textual Notes for the corresponding
lines in Q1.   37. *primal eldest curse:* i.e. God's curse on Cain, who also slew his brother.
39. *Though . . . will:* though my desire is as strong as my resolve to do so.

My stronger guilt defeats my strong intent,   40
And, like a man to double business bound,
I stand in pause where I shall first begin,
And both neglect. What if this cursed hand
Were thicker than itself with brother's blood,
Is there not rain enough in the sweet heavens   45
To wash it white as snow? Whereto serves mercy
But to confront the visage of offense?
And what's in prayer but this twofold force,
To be forestalled ere we come to fall,
Or [pardon'd] being down? then I'll look up.   50
My fault is past, but, O, what form of prayer
Can serve my turn? "Forgive me my foul murther"?
That cannot be, since I am still possess'd
Of those effects for which I did the murther:
My crown, mine own ambition, and my queen.   55
May one be pardon'd and retain th' offense?
In the corrupted currents of this world
Offense's gilded hand may [shove] by justice,
And oft 'tis seen the wicked prize itself
Buys out the law, but 'tis not so above: 60
There is no shuffling, there the action lies
In his true nature, and we ourselves compell'd,
Even to the teeth and forehead of our faults,
To give in evidence. What then? What rests?
Try what repentance can. What can it not?   65
Yet what can it, when one can not repent?
O wretched state! O bosom black as death!
O limed soul, that struggling to be free
Art more engag'd! Help, angels! Make assay,
Bow, stubborn knees, and heart, with strings of steel,   70
Be soft as sinews of the new-born babe!
All may be well.   *[He kneels.]*

Enter Hamlet.

Hamlet: Now might I do it [pat], now 'a is a-praying;
     And now I'll do't—and so 'a goes to heaven,
     And so am I [reveng'd]. That would be scann'd: 75

---

41. *bound:* committed.   43. *neglect:* omit.   46-47. *Whereto . . . offense:* i.e. what function has
mercy except when there has been sin.   56. *th' offense:* i.e. the "effects" or fruits of the
offense.   57. *currents:* courses.   58. *gilded:* i.e. bribing.   59. *wicked prize:* rewards of vice.
61. *shuffling:* evasion. *the action lies:* the charge comes for legal consideration.   63. *Even . . .
forehead:* i.e. fully recognizing their features, extenuating nothing.   64. *rests:* remains.
68. *limed:* caught (as in birdlime, a sticky substance used for catching birds).   69. *engag'd:*
entangled.   75. *would be scann'd:* must be carefully considered.

A villain kills my father, and for that
I, his sole son, do this same villain send
To heaven.
Why, this is [hire and salary], not revenge.
'A took my father grossly, full of bread,   80
With all his crimes broad blown, as flush as May,
And how his audit stands who knows save heaven?
But in our circumstance and course of thought
'Tis heavy with him. And am I then revenged,
To take him in the purging of his soul,   85
When he is fit and season'd for his passage?
No!
Up, sword, and know thou a more horrid hent:
When he is drunk asleep, or in his rage,
Or in th' incestious pleasure of his bed,   90
At game a-swearing, or about some act
That has no relish of salvation in't—
Then trip him, that his heels may kick at heaven,
And that his soul may be as damn'd and black
As hell, whereto it goes. My mother stays,   95
This physic but prolongs thy sickly days.   *Exit.*
King: *[Rising.]* My words fly up, my thoughts remain below:
Words without thoughts never to heaven go.   *Exit.*

Scene IV

Enter [Queen] Gertrude *and* Polonius.

Polonius: 'A will come straight. Look you, lay home to him.
Tell him his pranks have been too broad to bear with,
And that your Grace hath screen'd and stood between
Much heat and him. I'll silence me even here;
Pray you be round [with him].   5
Queen: I'll [warr'nt] you, fear me not. Withdraw,
I hear him coming.   [Polonius *hides behind the arras.*]

Enter Hamlet.

Hamlet: Now, mother, what's the matter?
Queen: Hamlet, thou hast thy father much offended.
Hamlet: Mother, you have my father much offended.   10

---

80. *grossly:* in a gross state; not spiritually prepared.   81. *crimes:* sins. *broad blown:* in full
bloom. *flush:* lusty, vigorous.   82. *audit:* account.   83. *in . . . thought:* i.e. to the best of our
knowledge and belief.   88. *Up:* into the sheath. *know . . . hent:* be grasped at a more dreadful
time.   92. *relish:* trace.   96. *physic:* (attempted) remedy, i.e. prayer.

III.iv. Location: The Queen's closet in the castle.   1. *lay . . . him:* reprove him severely.
2. *broad:* unrestrained.   5. *round:* plain-spoken.   6. *fear me not:* have no fears about my handling of the situation.

Queen: Come, come, you answer with an idle tongue.

Hamlet: Go, go, you question with a wicked tongue.

Queen: Why, how now, Hamlet?

Hamlet: What's the matter now?

Queen: Have you forgot me?

Hamlet: No, by the rood, not so:

You are the Queen, your husband's brother's wife,   15

And would it were not so, you are my mother.

Queen: Nay, then I'll set those to you that can speak.

Hamlet: Come, come, and sit you down, you shall not boudge;

You go not till I set you up a glass

Where you may see the [inmost] part of you.   20

Queen: What wilt thou do? Thou wilt not murther me?

Help ho!

Polonius: *[Behind.]* What ho, help!

Hamlet: *[Drawing.]* How now? A rat? Dead, for a ducat, dead!

                              [Kills Polonius *through the arras.]*

Polonius: *[Behind.]* O, I am slain.

Queen: O me, what hast thou done?   25

Hamlet: Nay, I know not, is it the King?

Queen: O, what a rash and bloody deed is this!

Hamlet: A bloody deed! almost as bad, good mother,

As kill a king, and marry with his brother.

Queen: As kill a king!

Hamlet: Ay, lady, it was my word.   30

                         [Parts the arras and discovers Polonius.]

Thou wretched, rash, intruding fool, farewell!

I took thee for thy better. Take thy fortune;

Thou find'st to be too busy is some danger.—

Leave wringing of your hands. Peace, sit you down,

And let me wring your heart, for so I shall   35

If it be made of penetrable stuff,

If damned custom have not brass'd it so

That it be proof and bulwark against sense.

Queen: What have I done, that thou dar'st wag thy tongue

In noise so rude against me?

Hamlet: Such an act   40

That blurs the grace and blush of modesty,

Calls virtue hypocrite, takes off the rose

From the fair forehead of an innocent love

And sets a blister there, makes marriage vows

---

11. *idle:* foolish.   14. *rood:* cross.   18. *boudge:* budge.   24. *for a ducat:* I'll wager a ducat. 33. *busy:* officious, meddlesome.   37. *damned custom:* i.e. the habit of ill-doing. *brass'd:* hardened, literally, plated with brass.   38. *proof:* armor. *sense:* feeling.   44. *blister:* brand of shame.

As false as dicers' oaths, O, such a deed   45
As from the body of contraction plucks
The very soul, and sweet religion makes
A rhapsody of words. Heaven's face does glow
O'er this solidity and compound mass
With heated visage, as against the doom;   50
Is thought-sick at the act.
Queen: Ay me, what act,
    That roars so loud and thunders in the index?
Hamlet: Look here upon this picture, and on this,
    The counterfeit presentment of two brothers.
    See what a grace was seated on this brow: 55
    Hyperion's curls, the front of Jove himself,
    An eye like Mars, to threaten and command,
    A station like the herald Mercury
    New lighted on a [heaven-]kissing hill,
    A combination and a form indeed,   60
    Where every god did seem to set his seal
    To give the world assurance of a man.
    This was your husband. Look you now what follows:
    Here is your husband, like a mildewed ear,
    Blasting his wholesome brother. Have you eyes?   65
    Could you on this fair mountain leave to feed,
    And batten on this moor? ha, have you eyes?
    You cannot call it love, for at your age
    The heyday in the blood is tame, it's humble,
    And waits upon the judgment, and what judgment   70
    Would step from this to this? Sense sure you have,
    Else could you not have motion, but sure that sense
    Is apoplex'd, for madness would not err,
    Nor sense to ecstasy was ne'er so thrall'd
    But it reserv'd some quantity of choice   75
    To serve in such a difference. What devil was't
    That thus hath cozen'd you at hoodman-blind?
    Eyes without feeling, feeling without sight,
    Ears without hands or eyes, smelling sans all,

---

46. *contraction:* the making of contracts, i.e. the assuming of solemn obligation.   47. *religion:*
i.e. sacred vows.   48. *rhapsody:* miscellaneous collection, jumble. *glow:* i.e. with anger.
49. *this . . . mass:* i.e. the earth. *Compound* = compounded of the four elements.   50. *as . . .
doom:* as if for Judgment Day.   52. *index:* i.e. table of contents. The index was formerly
placed at the beginning of a book.   54. *counterfeit presentment:* painted likenesses.
56. *Hyperion's:* the sun-god's. *front:* forehead.   58. *station:* bearing.   64. *ear:* i.e. of grain.
67. *batten:* gorge.   69. *heyday:* excitement.   71. *Sense:* sense perception, the five senses.
73. *apoplex'd:* paralyzed.   73-76. *madness . . . difference:* i.e. madness itself could not go so far
astray, nor were the senses ever so enslaved by lunacy that they did not retain the power to
make so obvious a distinction.   77. *cozen'd:* cheated. *hoodman-blind:* blindman's bluff.
79. *sans:* without.

Or but a sickly part of one true sense   80
Could not so mope. O shame, where is thy blush?
Rebellious hell,
If thou canst mutine in a matron's bones,
To flaming youth let virtue be as wax
And melt in her own fire. Proclaim no shame   85
When the compulsive ardure gives the charge,
Since frost itself as actively doth burn,
And reason [panders] will.
        Queen: O Hamlet, speak no more!
Thou turn'st my [eyes into my very] soul,
And there I see such black and [grained] spots   90
As will [not] leave their tinct.
        Hamlet: Nay, but to live
In the rank sweat of an enseamed bed,
Stew'd in corruption, honeying and making love
Over the nasty sty!
        Queen: O, speak to me no more!
These words like daggers enter in my ears.   95
No more, sweet Hamlet!
        Hamlet: A murtherer and a villain!
A slave that is not twentith part the [tithe]
Of your precedent lord, a Vice of kings,
A cutpurse of the empire and the rule,
That from a shelf the precious diadem stole,   100
And put it in his pocket—
        Queen: No more!

Enter Ghost [*in his night-gown*].

        Hamlet: A king of shreds and patches—
Save me, and hover o'er me with your wings,
You heavenly guards! What would your gracious figure?
        Queen: Alas, he's mad!   105
        Hamlet: Do you not come your tardy son to chide,
That, laps'd in time and passion, lets go by
Th' important acting of your dread command?
O, say!

---

81. *mope:* be dazed.   83. *mutine:* rebel.   85-88. *Proclaim . . . will:* do not call it sin when the
hot blood of youth is responsible for lechery, since here we see people of calmer age on fire
for it; and reason acts as procurer for desire, instead of restraining it. *Ardure* = ardor.
90. *grained:* fast-dyed, indelible.   91. *leave their tinct:* lose their color.   92. *enseamed:*
greasy.   97. *twentith:* twentieth.   98. *precedent:* former. *Vice:* buffoon (like the Vice of the
morality plays).   101s.d. *night-gown:* dressing gown.   102. *of . . . patches:* clownish (alluding
to the motley worn by jesters) (?) or patched-up, beggarly (?).   107. *laps'd . . . passion:*
"having suffered time to slip and passion to cool" (Johnson).   108. *important:* urgent.

Ghost: Do not forget! This visitation   110
   Is but to whet thy almost blunted purpose.
   But look, amazement on thy mother sits,
   O, step between her and her fighting soul.
   Conceit in weakest bodies strongest works,
   Speak to her, Hamlet.
Hamlet: How is it with you, lady?   115
Queen: Alas, how is't with you,
   That you do bend your eye on vacancy,
   And with th' incorporal air do hold discourse?
   Forth at your eyes your spirits wildly peep,
   And as the sleeping soldiers in th' alarm,   120
   Your bedded hair, like life in excrements,
   Start up and stand an end. O gentle son,
   Upon the heat and flame of thy distemper
   Sprinkle cool patience. Whereon do you look?
Hamlet: On him, on him! look you how pale he glares!   125
   His form and cause conjoin'd, preaching to stones,
   Would make them capable.—Do not look upon me,
   Lest with this piteous action you convert
   My stern effects, then what I have to do
   Will want true color—tears perchance for blood.   130
Queen: To whom do you speak this?
Hamlet: Do you see nothing there?
Queen: Nothing at all, yet all that is I see.
Hamlet: Nor did you nothing hear?
Queen: No, nothing but ourselves.
Hamlet: Why, look you there, look how it steals away!
   My father, in his habit as he lived!   135
   Look where he goes, even now, out at the portal! *Exit* Ghost.
Queen: This is the very coinage of your brain,
   This bodiless creation ecstasy
   Is very cunning in.
Hamlet: [Ecstasy?]
   My pulse as yours doth temperately keep time,   140
   And makes as healthful music. It is not madness
   That I have utt'red. Bring me to the test,
   And [I] the matter will reword, which madness
   Would gambol from. Mother, for love of grace,

---

112. *amazement:* utter bewilderment.   114. *Conceit:* imagination.   120. *in th' alarm:* when
the call to arms is sounded.   121. *excrements:* outgrowths; here, hair (also used of nails).
122. *an end:* on end.   124. *patience:* self-control.   126. *His . . . cause:* his appearance and
what he has to say.   127. *capable:* sensitive, receptive.   128. *convert:* alter.   129. *effects:*
(purposed) actions.   130. *want true color:* lack its proper appearance.   135. *habit:* dress.
137-216. See the Textual Notes for the conclusion of the scene in Q1.   138. *ecstasy:*
madness.   144. *gambol:* start, jerk away.

Lay not that flattering unction to your soul,   145
That not your trespass but my madness speaks;
It will but skin and film the ulcerous place,
Whiles rank corruption, mining all within,
Infects unseen. Confess yourself to heaven,
Repent what's past, avoid what is to come,   150
And do not spread the compost on the weeds
To make them ranker. Forgive me this my virtue,
For in the fatness of these pursy times
Virtue itself of vice must pardon beg,
Yea, curb and woo for leave to do him good.   155
Queen: O Hamlet, thou hast cleft my heart in twain.
Hamlet: O, throw away the worser part of it,
And [live] the purer with the other half.
Good night, but go not to my uncle's bed—
Assume a virtue, if you have it not.   160
That monster custom, who all sense doth eat,
Of habits devil, is angel yet in this,
That to the use of actions fair and good
He likewise gives a frock or livery
That aptly is put on. Refrain [to-]night,   165
And that shall lend a kind of easiness
To the next abstinence, the next more easy;
For use almost can change the stamp of nature,
And either [....] the devil or throw him out
With wondrous potency. Once more good night,   170
And when you are desirous to be blest,
I'll blessing beg of you. For this same lord,
                                            [*Pointing to* Polonius.]
I do repent; but heaven hath pleas'd it so
To punish me with this, and this with me,
That I must be their scourge and minister.   175
I will bestow him, and will answer well
The death I gave him. So again good night.
I must be cruel only to be kind.
This bad begins and worse remains behind.
One word more, good lady.

---

145. *flattering unction:* soothing ointment.   151. *compost:* manure.   153. *pursy:* puffy, out of condition.   155. *curb and woo:* bow and entreat.   161. *all . . . eat:* wears away all natural feeling.   162. *Of habits devil:* i.e. though it acts like a devil in establishing bad habits. Most editors read (in lines 161-62) *eat / Of habits evil,* following Theobald.   164-165. *frock . . . on:* i.e. a "habit" or customary garment, readily put on without need of any decision.   168. *use:* habit.   169. A word seems to be wanting after *either;* for conjectures see the Textual Notes. 171. *desirous . . . blest:* i.e. repentant.   175. *scourge and minister:* the agent of heavenly justice against human crime. *Scourge* suggests a permissive cruelty (Tamburlaine was the "scourge of God"), but "woe to him by whom the offense cometh"; the scourge must suffer for the evil it performs.   176. *bestow:* dispose of. *answer:* answer for.   179. *behind:* to come.

Queen: What shall I do?   180
Hamlet: Not this, by no means, that I bid you do:
      Let the bloat king tempt you again to bed,
      Pinch wanton on your cheek, call you his mouse,
      And let him, for a pair of reechy kisses,
      Or paddling in your neck with his damn'd fingers,   185
      Make you to ravel all this matter out,
      That I essentially am not in madness,
      But mad in craft. 'Twere good you let him know,
      For who that's but a queen, fair, sober, wise,
      Would from a paddock, from a bat, a gib,   190
      Such dear concernings hide? Who would do so?
      No, in despite of sense and secrecy,
      Unpeg the basket on the house's top,
      Let the birds fly, and like the famous ape,
      To try conclusions in the basket creep,   195
      And break your own neck down.
Queen: Be thou assur'd, if words be made of breath,
      And breath of life, I have no life to breathe
      What thou hast said to me.
Hamlet: I must to England, you know that?
Queen: Alack,   200
      I had forgot. 'Tis so concluded on.
Hamlet: There's letters seal'd, and my two schoolfellows,
      Whom I will trust as I will adders fang'd,
      They bear the mandate, they must sweep my way
      And marshal me to knavery. Let it work,   205
      For 'tis the sport to have the enginer
      Hoist with his own petar, an't shall go hard
      But I will delve one yard below their mines,
      And blow them at the moon. O, 'tis most sweet
      When in one line two crafts directly meet.   210
      This man shall set me packing;
      I'll lug the guts into the neighbor room.
      Mother, good night indeed. This counsellor
      Is now most still, most secret, and most grave,
      Who was in life a foolish prating knave.   215
      Come, sir, to draw toward an end with you.
      Good night, mother.
                  Exeunt [*severally*, Hamlet *tugging in* Polonius].

---

184. *reechy:* filthy.   190. *paddock:* toad. *gib:* tom-cat.   191. *dear concernings:* matters of intense concern.   193. *Unpeg the basket:* open the door of the cage.   194. *famous ape:* The actual story has been lost.   195. *conclusions:* experiments (to see whether he too can fly if he enters the cage and then leaps out).   196. *down:* by the fall.   205. *knavery:* some knavish scheme against me.   206. *enginer:* deviser of military "engines" or contrivances.   207. *Hoist with:* blown up by. *petar:* petard, bomb.   210. *crafts:* plots.   211. *packing:* (1) taking on a load; (2) leaving in a hurry.   216. *draw . . . end:* finish my conversation.

ACT IV

Scene I

Enter King *and* Queen *with* Rosencrantz *and* Guildenstern.

    King: There's matter in these sighs, these profound heaves—
        You must translate, 'tis fit we understand them.
        Where is your son?
    Queen: Bestow this place on us a little while.
                 [*Exeunt* Rosencrantz *and* Guildenstern.]
        Ah, mine own lord, what have I seen to-night!   5
    King: What, Gertrude? How does Hamlet?
    Queen: Mad as the sea and wind when both contend
        Which is the mightier. In his lawless fit,
        Behind the arras hearing something stir,
        Whips out his rapier, cries, "A rat, a rat!"   10
        And in this brainish apprehension kills
        The unseen good old man.
    King: O heavy deed!
        It had been so with us had we been there.
        His liberty is full of threats to all,
        To you yourself, to us, to every one.   15
        Alas, how shall this bloody deed be answer'd?
        It will be laid to us, whose providence
        Should have kept short, restrain'd, and out of haunt
        This mad young man; but so much was our love,
        We would not understand what was most fit,   20
        But like the owner of a foul disease,
        To keep it from divulging, let it feed
        Even on the pith of life. Where is he gone?
    Queen: To draw apart the body he hath kill'd,
        O'er whom his very madness, like some ore   25
        Among a mineral of metals base,
        Shows itself pure: 'a weeps for what is done.
    King: O Gertrude, come away!
        The sun no sooner shall the mountains touch,
        But we will ship him hence, and this vile deed   30
        We must with all our majesty and skill
        Both countenance and excuse. Ho, Guildenstern!

Enter Rosencrantz *and* Guildenstern.

IV.i. Location: The castle.   11. *brainish apprehension:* crazy notion.   16. *answer'd:* i.e.
satisfactorily accounted for to the public.   17. *providence:* foresight.   18. *short:* on a short
leash. *out of haunt:* away from other people.   22. *divulging:* being revealed.   25. *ore:* vein of
gold.   26. *mineral:* mine.

Friends both, go join you with some further aid:
Hamlet in madness hath Polonius slain,
And from his mother's closet hath he dragg'd him,   35
Go seek him out, speak fair, and bring the body
Into the chapel. I pray you haste in this.
                    [*Exeunt* Rosencrantz *and* Guildenstern.]
Come, Gertrude, we'll call up our wisest friends
And let them know both what we mean to do
And what's untimely done, [....]   40
Whose whisper o'er the world's diameter,
As level as the cannon to his blank,
Transports his pois'ned shot, may miss our name,
And hit the woundless air. O, come away!
My soul is full of discord and dismay.   *Exeunt.* 45

Scene II

Enter Hamlet.

   Hamlet: Safely stow'd.
[Gentlemen: (Within.) Hamlet! Lord Hamlet!]
  [Hamlet:] But soft, what noise? Who calls on Hamlet? O, here they
     come.

Enter Rosencrantz *and* [Guildenstern].

Rosencrantz: What have you done, my lord, with the dead body?   5
   Hamlet: [Compounded] it with dust, whereto 'tis kin.
Rosencrantz: Tell us where 'tis, that we may take it thence,
    And bear it to the chapel.
   Hamlet: Do not believe it.
Rosencrantz: Believe what?   10
   Hamlet: That I can keep your counsel and not mine own. Besides,
    to be demanded of a spunge, what replication should be
    made by the son of a king?
Rosencrantz: Take you me for a spunge, my lord?
   Hamlet: Ay, sir, that soaks up the King's countenance, his   15
    rewards, his authorities. But such officers do the King best
    service in the end: he keeps them, like [an ape] an apple, in
    the corner of his jaw, first mouth'd, to be last swallow'd.
    When he needs what you have glean'd, it is but squeezing
    you, and, spunge, you shall be dry again.   20

----

40. Some words are wanting at the end of the line. Capell's conjecture, *so, haply, slander,*
probably indicates the intended sense of the passage.   42. *As level:* with aim as good. *blank:*
target.   44. *woundless:* incapable of being hurt.

IV.ii. Location: The castle.   12. *demanded of:* questioned by. *spunge:* sponge.   *replication:*
reply.   15. *countenance:* favor.

Rosencrantz: I understand you not, my lord.

Hamlet: I am glad of it, a knavish speech sleeps in a foolish ear.

Rosencrantz: My lord, you must tell us where the body is, and go with
us to the King.

Hamlet: The body is with the King, but the King is not with the 25
body. The King is a thing—

Guildenstern: A thing, my lord?

Hamlet: Of nothing, bring me to him. [Hide fox, and all after.]

Exeunt.

Scene III

Enter King *and two or three.*

King: I have sent to seek him, and to find the body.
How dangerous is it that this man goes loose!
Yet must not we put the strong law on him.
He's lov'd of the distracted multitude,
Who like not in their judgment, but their eyes, 5
And where 'tis so, th' offender's scourge is weigh'd,
But never the offense. To bear all smooth and even,
This sudden sending him away must seem
Deliberate pause. Diseases desperate grown
By desperate appliance are reliev'd, 10
Or not at all.

Enter Rosencrantz.

How now, what hath befall'n?

Rosencrantz: Where the dead body is bestow'd, my lord,
We cannot get from him.

King: But where is he?

Rosencrantz: Without, my lord, guarded, to know your pleasure.

King: Bring him before us.

Rosencrantz: Ho, bring in the lord. 15

They [Hamlet *and* Guildenstern] *enter.*

King: Now, Hamlet, where's Polonius?

Hamlet: At supper.

---

22. *sleeps:* is meaningless.   25-26. *The body . . . the body:* Possibly alluding to the legal fiction
that the king's dignity is separate from his mortal body.   28. *Of nothing:* of no account. Cf.
"Man is like a thing of nought, his time passeth away like a shadow" (Psalm 144:4 in the
Prayer Book version). "Hamlet at once insults the King and hints that his days are numbered"
(Dover Wilson).   *Hide . . . after:* Probably a cry in some game resembling hide-and-seek.

IV.iii. Location: The castle.   4. *distracted:* unstable.   6. *scourge:* i.e. punishment.   7. *bear:*
manage.   8-9. *must . . . pause:* i.e. must be represented as a maturely considered decision.

King: At supper? where?

Hamlet: Not where he eats, but where 'a is eaten; a certain convo- 20
cation of politic worms are e'en at him. Your worm is your
only emperor for diet: we fat all creatures else to fat us, and
we fat ourselves for maggots; your fat king and your lean beggar is but variable service, two dishes, but to one table—
that's the end.

King: Alas, alas!   25

Hamlet: A man may fish with the worm that hath eat of a king, and
eat of the fish that hath fed of that worm.

King: What dost thou mean by this?

Hamlet: Nothing but to show you how a king may go a progress
through the guts of a beggar.   30

King: Where is Polonius?

Hamlet: In heaven, send thither to see; if your messenger find him
not there, seek him i' th' other place yourself. But if indeed
you find him not within this month, you shall nose him as you
go up the stairs into the lobby.   35

King: [To Attendants.] Go seek him there.

Hamlet: 'A will stay till you come.   *[Exeunt Attendants.]*

King: Hamlet, this deed, for thine especial safety—
Which we do tender, as we dearly grieve
For that which thou hast done—must send thee hence   40
[With fiery quickness]; therefore prepare thyself,
The bark is ready, and the wind at help,
Th' associates tend, and every thing is bent
For England.

Hamlet: For England.

King: Ay, Hamlet.

Hamlet: Good.

King: So is it, if thou knew'st our purposes.   45

Hamlet: I see a cherub that sees them. But come, for England!
Farewell, dear mother.

King: Thy loving father, Hamlet.

Hamlet: My mother: father and mother is man and wife, man and
wife is one flesh—so, my mother. Come, for England! *Exit.* 50

King: Follow him at foot, tempt him with speed aboard.
Delay it not, I'll have him hence to-night.
Away, for every thing is seal'd and done
That else leans on th' affair. Pray you make haste.

---

20. *politic:* crafty, prying; "such worms as might breed in a politician's corpse" (Dowden).
e'en: even now. 21. *for diet:* with respect to what it eats. 23. *variable service:* different
courses of a meal. 29. *progress:* royal journey of state. 39. *tender:* regard with tenderness,
hold dear. *dearly:* with intense feeling. 42. *at help:* favorable. 43. *Th':* thy. *tend:* await. *bent:*
made ready. 46. *I . . . them:* i.e. heaven sees them. 51. *at foot:* at his heels, close behind.
54. *leans on:* relates to.

And, England, if my love thou hold'st at aught—   55
As my great power thereof may give thee sense,
Since yet thy cicatrice looks raw and red
After the Danish sword, and thy free awe
Pays homage to us—thou mayst not coldly set
Our sovereign process, which imports at full,   60
By letters congruing to that effect,
The present death of Hamlet. Do it, England,
For like the hectic in my blood he rages,
And thou must cure me. Till I know 'tis done,
How e'er my haps, my joys [were] ne'er [begun].   *Exit.* 65

Scene IV

Enter Fortinbras *with his army over the stage.*

Fortinbras: Go, captain, from me greet the Danish king.
Tell him that by his license Fortinbras
Craves the conveyance of a promis'd march
Over his kingdom. You know the rendezvous.
If that his Majesty would aught with us,   5
We shall express our duty in his eye,
And let him know so.
       Captain: I will do't, my lord.
       Fortinbras: Go softly on.   [*Exeunt all but the* Captain.]

Enter Hamlet, Rosencrantz, [Guildenstern,] *etc.*

       Hamlet: Good sir, whose powers are these?
       Captain: They are of Norway, sir.   10
       Hamlet: How purpos'd, sir, I pray you?
       Captain: Against some part of Poland.
       Hamlet: Who commands them, sir?
       Captain: The nephew to old Norway, Fortinbras.
       Hamlet: Goes it against the main of Poland, sir,   15
Or for some frontier?
       Captain: Truly to speak, and with no addition,
We go to gain a little patch of ground
That hath in it no profit but the name.
To pay five ducats, five, I would not farm it;   20

---

55. *England:* King of England.   57. *cicatrice:* scar.   58-59. *thy . . . Pays:* your fear makes you pay voluntarily.   59. *coldly set:* undervalue, disregard.   60. *process:* command.   61. *congruing to:* in accord with.   62. *present:* immediate.   63. *hectic:* continuous fever.   65. *haps:* fortunes.

IV.iv. Location: The Danish coast, near the castle.   3. *conveyance of:* escort for.   6. *eye:* presence.   8. *softly:* slowly.   9. *powers:* forces.   15. *main:* main territory.   20. *To pay:* i.e. for an annual rent of. *farm:* lease.

Nor will it yield to Norway or the Pole
A ranker rate, should it be sold in fee.
Hamlet: Why then the Polack never will defend it.
Captain: Yes, it is already garrison'd.
Hamlet: Two thousand souls and twenty thousand ducats   25
Will not debate the question of this straw.
This is th' imposthume of much wealth and peace,
That inward breaks, and shows no cause without
Why the man dies. I humbly thank you, sir.
Captain: God buy you, sir.   *[Exit.]*
Rosencrantz: Will't please you go, my lord?   30
Hamlet: I'll be with you straight—go a little before.
                              [Exeunt all but Hamlet.*]*
How all occasions do inform against me,
And spur my dull revenge! What is a man,
If his chief good and market of his time
Be but to sleep and feed? a beast, no more.   35
Sure He that made us with such large discourse,
Looking before and after, gave us not
That capability and godlike reason
To fust in us unus'd. Now whether it be
Bestial oblivion, or some craven scruple   40
Of thinking too precisely on th' event—
A thought which quarter'd hath but one part wisdom
And ever three parts coward—I do not know
Why yet I live to say, "This thing's to do,"
Sith I have cause, and will, and strength, and means   45
To do't. Examples gross as earth exhort me:
Witness this army of such mass and charge,
Led by a delicate and tender prince,
Whose spirit with divine ambition puff'd
Makes mouths at the invisible event,   50
Exposing what is mortal and unsure
To all that fortune, death, and danger dare,
Even for an egg-shell. Rightly to be great
Is not to stir without great argument,
But greatly to find quarrel in a straw   55
When honor's at the stake. How stand I then,
That have a father kill'd, a mother stain'd,

---

22. *ranker:* higher. *in fee:* outright.   26. *Will not debate:* i.e. will scarcely be enough to fight
out.   27. *imposthume:* abscess.   32. *inform against:* denounce, accuse.   34. *market:*
purchase, profit.   36. *discourse:* reasoning power.   39. *fust:* grow mouldy.   40. *oblivion:*
forgetfulness.   41. *event:* outcome.   46. *gross:* large, obvious.   47. *mass and charge:* size and
expense.   50. *Makes mouths at:* treats scornfully. *invisible:* i.e. unforeseeable.   54. *Is not to:*
i.e. is *not* not to. *argument:* cause.   55. *greatly:* nobly.

Excitements of my reason and my blood,
And let all sleep, while to my shame I see
The imminent death of twenty thousand men,   60
That for a fantasy and trick of fame
Go to their graves like beds, fight for a plot
Whereon the numbers cannot try the cause,
Which is not tomb enough and continent
To hide the slain? O, from this time forth,   65
My thoughts be bloody, or be nothing worth!   *Exit.*

Scene V

Enter Horatio, [Queen] Gertrude, *and a* Gentleman.

    Queen: I will not speak with her.
  Gentleman: She is importunate, indeed distract.
      Her mood will needs be pitied.
    Queen: What would she have?
  Gentleman: She speaks much of her father, says she hears
      There's tricks i' th' world, and hems, and beats her heart,   5
      Spurns enviously at straws, speaks things in doubt
      That carry but half sense. Her speech is nothing,
      Yet the unshaped use of it doth move
      The hearers to collection; they yawn at it,
      And botch the words up fit to their own thoughts,   10
      Which as her winks and nods and gestures yield them,
      Indeed would make one think there might be thought,
      Though nothing sure, yet much unhappily.
    Horatio: 'Twere good she were spoken with, for she may strew
      Dangerous conjectures in ill-breeding minds.   15
  [Queen:] Let her come in.   *[Exit* Gentleman.]
      [Aside.] To my sick soul, as sin's true nature is,
      Each toy seems prologue to some great amiss,
      So full of artless jealousy is guilt,
      It spills itself in fearing to be spilt.   20

Enter Ophelia [*distracted, with her hair down, playing on a lute*].

    Ophelia: Where is the beauteous majesty of Denmark?

---

58. *Excitements of:* urgings by.   61. *fantasy:* caprice. *trick:* trifle.   63. *Whereon . . . cause:*
which isn't large enough to let the opposing armies engage upon it.   64. *continent:* container.

IV.v. Location: The castle.   1–20. See the Textual Notes for the lines that replace these in
Q1.   6. *Spurns . . . straws:* spitefully takes offense at trifles. *in doubt:* obscurely.   7. *Her
speech:* what she says.   8. *unshaped use:* distracted manner.   9. *collection:* attempts to gather
the meaning. *yawn at:* gape eagerly (as if to swallow). Most editors adopt the F1 reading *aim
at.*   10. *botch:* patch.   11. *Which:* i.e. the words.   12. *thought:* inferred, conjectured.
15. *ill-breeding:* conceiving ill thoughts, prone to think the worst.   18. *toy:* trifle. *amiss:*
calamity.   19. *artless jealousy:* uncontrolled suspicion.   20. *spills:* destroys.

Queen: How now, Ophelia?

Ophelia: "How should I your true-love know   *She sings.*
    From another one?
By his cockle hat and staff,   25
    And his sandal shoon."

Queen: Alas, sweet lady, what imports this song?

Ophelia: Say you? Nay, pray you mark.
"He is dead and gone, lady,   *Song.*
    He is dead and gone,   30
At his head a grass-green turf,
    At his heels a stone."
  O ho!

Queen: Nay, but, Ophelia—

Ophelia: Pray you mark.   35
  [Sings.] "White his shroud as the mountain snow"—

Enter King.

Queen: Alas, look here, my lord.

Ophelia: "Larded all with sweet flowers,   *Song.*
Which bewept to the ground did not go
    With true-love showers."   40

King: How do you, pretty lady?

Ophelia: Well, God dild you! They say the owl was a baker's
    daughter. Lord, we know what we are, but know not what
    we may be. God be at your table!

King: Conceit upon her father.   45

Ophelia: Pray let's have no words of this, but when they ask you
    what it means, say you this:
"To-morrow is Saint Valentine's day,   *Song.*
    All in the morning betime,
And I a maid at your window,   50
    To be your Valentine.

"Then up he rose and donn'd his clo'es,
    And dupp'd the chamber-door,
Let in the maid, that out a maid
    Never departed more."   55

23-24. These lines resemble a passage in an earlier ballad beginning "As you came from the holy land / Of Walsingham." Probably all the song fragments sung by Ophelia were familiar to the Globe audience, but only one other line (185) is from a ballad still extant.   25. *cockle hat:* hat bearing a cockle shell, the badge of a pilgrim to the shrine of St. James of Compostela in Spain. *staff:* Another mark of a pilgrim.   26. *shoon:* shoes (already an archaic form in Shakespeare's day).   38. *Larded:* adorned.   39. *not:* Contrary to the expected sense, and unmetrical; explained as Ophelia's alteration of the line to accord with the facts of Polonius' burial (see line 83).   42. *dild:* yield, reward. *owl:* Alluding to the legend of a baker's daughter whom Jesus turned into an owl because she did not respond generously to his request for bread.   45. *Conceit:* fanciful brooding.   53. *dupp'd:* opened.

King: Pretty Ophelia!

Ophelia: Indeed without an oath I'll make an end on't.

        [*Sings.*]   "By Gis, and by Saint Charity,
                    Alack, and fie for shame!
             Young men will do't if they come to't,   60
                    By Cock, they are to blame.

             "Quoth she, 'Before you tumbled me,
                    You promis'd me to wed.'"

    (He answers.)

             "'So would I 'a' done, by yonder sun,   65
                    And thou hadst not come to my bed.'"

King: How long hath she been thus?

Ophelia: I hope all will be well. We must be patient, but I cannot
choose but weep to think they would lay him i' th' cold
ground. My brother shall know of it, and so I thank you for   70
your good counsel. Come, my coach! Good night, ladies,
good night. Sweet ladies, good night, good night.   *[Exit.]*

King: Follow her close, give her good watch, pray you.

                            [*Exit* Horatio.]

    O, this is the poison of deep grief, it springs
    All from her father's death—and now behold!   75
    O Gertrude, Gertrude,
    When sorrows come, they come not single spies,
    But in battalions: first, her father slain;
    Next, your son gone, and he most violent author
    Of his own just remove; the people muddied,   80
    Thick and unwholesome in [their] thoughts and whispers
    For good Polonius' death; and we have done but greenly
    In hugger-mugger to inter him; poor Ophelia
    Divided from herself and her fair judgment,
    Without the which we are pictures, or mere beasts;   85
    Last, and as much containing as all these,
    Her brother is in secret come from France,
    Feeds on this wonder, keeps himself in clouds,
    And wants not buzzers to infect his ear
    With pestilent speeches of his father's death,   90
    Wherein necessity, of matter beggar'd,
    Will nothing stick our person to arraign
    In ear and ear. O my dear Gertrude, this,

---

58. *Gis:* contraction of *Jesus.* 61. *Cock:* corruption of *God.* 66. *And:* if. 77. *spies:* i.e.
soldiers sent ahead of the main force to reconnoiter, scouts. 80. *muddied:* confused.
82. *greenly:* unwisely. 83. *In hugger-mugger:* secretly and hastily. 88. *in clouds:* i.e. in
cloudy surmise and suspicion (rather than the light of fact). 89. *wants:* lacks. *buzzers:*
whispering informers. 92. *of matter beggar'd:* destitute of facts. 92–93. *nothing . . . arraign:*
scruple not at all to charge me with the crime.

Like to a murd'ring-piece, in many places
Gives me superfluous death.   *A noise within.*
[*Queen:*   Alack, what noise is this?]   95
  King: Attend!
Where is my Swissers? Let them guard the door.

Enter a Messenger.

    What is the matter?
  Messenger: Save yourself, my lord!
The ocean, overpeering of his list,
Eats not the flats with more impiteous haste   100
Than young Laertes, in a riotous head,
O'erbears your officers. The rabble call him lord,
And as the world were now but to begin,
Antiquity forgot, custom not known,
The ratifiers and props of every word,   105
[They] cry, "Choose we, Laertes shall be king!"
Caps, hands, and tongues applaud it to the clouds,
"Laertes shall be king, Laertes king!"   *A noise within.*
  Queen: How cheerfully on the false trail they cry!
O, this is counter, you false Danish dogs!   110

Enter Laertes *with others.*

    King: The doors are broke.
  Laertes: Where is this king? Sirs, stand you all without.
    All: No, let 's come in.
  Laertes: I pray you give me leave.
    All: We will, we will.
  Laertes: I thank you, keep the door. [*Exeunt* Laertes' *followers.*]   115
      O thou vile king,
      Give me my father!
    Queen: Calmly, good Laertes.
  Laertes: That drop of blood that's calm proclaims me bastard,
Cries cuckold to my father, brands the harlot
Even here between the chaste unsmirched brow   120
Of my true mother.
    King: What is the cause, Laertes,
That thy rebellion looks so giant-like?
Let him go, Gertrude, do not fear our person:
There's such divinity doth hedge a king
That treason can but peep to what it would,   125

---

94. *murd'ring-piece:* cannon firing a scattering charge.   98. *Swissers:* Swiss guards.
99. *overpeering . . . list:* rising higher than its shores.   101. *in . . . head:* with a rebellious
force.   103. *as:* as if.   105. *word:* pledge, promise.   110. *counter:* on the wrong scent (literally, following the scent backward).   123. *fear:* fear for.   125. *would:* i.e. would like to do.

Acts little of his will. Tell me, Laertes,
Why thou art thus incens'd. Let him go, Gertrude.
Speak, man.

Laertes: Where is my father?

  King: Dead.

  Queen: But not by him.

  King: Let him demand his fill.   130

Laertes: How came he dead? I'll not be juggled with.
    To hell, allegiance! vows, to the blackest devil!
    Conscience and grace, to the profoundest pit!
    I dare damnation. To this point I stand,
    That both the worlds I give to negligence,   135
    Let come what comes, only I'll be reveng'd
    Most throughly for my father.

  King: Who shall stay you?

Laertes: My will, not all the world's:
    And for my means, I'll husband them so well,
    They shall go far with little.

  King: Good Laertes,   140
    If you desire to know the certainty
    Of your dear father, is't writ in your revenge
    That, swoopstake, you will draw both friend and foe,
    Winner and loser?

Laertes: None but his enemies.

  King: Will you know them then?   145

Laertes: To his good friends thus wide I'll ope my arms,
    And like the kind life-rend'ring pelican,
    Repast them with my blood.

  King: Why, now you speak
    Like a good child and a true gentleman.
    That I am guiltless of your father's death,   150
    And am most sensibly in grief for it,
    It shall as level to your judgment 'pear
    As day does to your eye.

                                   A noise within: "Let her come in!"

Laertes: How now, what noise is that?

Enter Ophelia.

    O heat, dry up my brains! tears seven times salt   155
    Burn out the sense and virtue of mine eye!

---

135. *both . . . negligence:* i.e. I don't care what the consequences are in this world or in the
next.   137. *throughly:* thoroughly.   138. *world's:* i.e. world's will.   143. *swoopstake:*
sweeping up everything without discrimination (modern *sweepstake*).   147. *pelican:* The
female pelican was believed to draw blood from her own breast to nourish her young.
149. *good child:* faithful son.   151. *sensibly:* feelingly.   152. *level:* plain.   156. *virtue:*
faculty.

By heaven, thy madness shall be paid with weight
[Till] our scale turn the beam. O rose of May!
Dear maid, kind sister, sweet Ophelia!
O heavens, is't possible a young maid's wits   160
Should be as mortal as [an old] man's life?
[Nature is fine in love, and where 'tis fine,
It sends some precious instance of itself
After the thing it loves.]

Ophelia: "They bore him barefac'd on the bier,   *Song.* 165
   [Hey non nonny, nonny, hey nonny,]
  And in his grave rain'd many a tear"—
Fare you well, my dove!

Laertes: Hadst thou thy wits and didst persuade revenge,
It could not move thus.   170

Ophelia: You must sing, "A-down, a-down," and you call him a-
down-a. O how the wheel becomes it! It is the false steward,
that stole his master's daughter.

Laertes: This nothing's more than matter.

Ophelia: There's rosemary, that's for remembrance; pray you,   175
love, remember. And there is pansies, that's for thoughts.

Laertes: A document in madness, thoughts and remembrance
fitted.

Ophelia: [*To* Claudius.] There's fennel for you, and columbines.
[*To* Gertrude.] There's rue for you, and here's some for me;   180
we may call it herb of grace a' Sundays. You may wear your
rue with a difference. There's a daisy. I would give you some
violets, but they wither'd all when my father died. They say 'a
made a good end—
[*Sings.*] "For bonny sweet Robin is all my joy."   185

Laertes: Thought and afflictions, passion, hell itself,
She turns to favor and to prettiness.

Ophelia: "And will 'a not come again?   *Song.*
  And will 'a not come again?
   No, no, he is dead,   190
   Go to thy death-bed,
  He never will come again.

---

162. *fine in:* refined or spiritualized by.   163. *instance:* proof, token. So delicate is Ophelia's
love for her father that her sanity has pursued him into the grave.   169. *persuade:* argue
logically for.   171-72. *and . . . a-down-a:* "if he indeed agrees that Polonius is 'a-down,' i.e.
fallen low" (Dover Wilson).   172. *wheel:* refrain (?) or spinning-wheel, at which women sang
ballads (?).   174. *matter:* lucid speech.   177. *A document in madness:* a lesson contained in
mad talk.   179. *fennel, columbines:* Symbols respectively of flattery and ingratitude.
180. *rue:* Symbolic of sorrow and repentance.   182. *with a difference:* i.e. to represent a
different cause of sorrow. *Difference* is a term from heraldry, meaning a variation in a coat of
arms made to distinguish different members of a family.   182-83. *daisy, violets:* Symbolic
respectively of dissembling and faithfulness. It is not clear who are the recipients of these.
186. *Thought:* melancholy.   187. *favor:* grace, charm.

"His beard was as white as snow,
[All] flaxen was his pole,
 He is gone, he is gone,   195
 And we cast away moan,
God 'a' mercy on his soul!"

And of all Christians' souls, [I pray God]. God buy you.

                    [Exit.]

Laertes: Do you [see] this, O God?
  King: Laertes, I must commune with your grief,   200
   Or you deny me right. Go but apart,
   Make choice of whom your wisest friends you will,
   And they shall hear and judge 'twixt you and me.
   If by direct or by collateral hand
   They find us touch'd, we will our kingdom give,   205
   Our crown, our life, and all that we call ours,
   To you in satisfaction; but if not,
   Be you content to lend your patience to us,
   And we shall jointly labor with your soul
   To give it due content.
Laertes: Let this be so.   210
   His means of death, his obscure funeral—
   No trophy, sword, nor hatchment o'er his bones,
   No noble rite nor formal ostentation—
   Cry to be heard, as 'twere from heaven to earth,
   That I must call't in question.
  King: So you shall,   215
   And where th' offense is, let the great axe fall.
   I pray you go with me.   *Exeunt.*

Scene VI

Enter Horatio *and others.*

  Horatio: What are they that would speak with me?
Gentleman: Sea-faring men, sir. They say they have letters for you.
  Horatio: Let them come in.   *[Exit* Gentleman.*]*
   I do not know from what part of the world
   I should be greeted, if not from Lord Hamlet.   5

Enter Sailors.

 [1.] Sailor: God bless you, sir.

---

194. *flaxen:* white. *pole:* poll, head. 204. *collateral:* i.e. indirect. 205. *touch'd:* guilty.
212. *trophy:* memorial. *hatchment:* heraldic memorial tablet. 213. *formal ostentation:* fitting
and customary ceremony. 214. *That:* so that.

IV.vi. Location: The castle. See the Textual Notes for a scene unique to Q1.

Horatio: Let him bless thee too.

[1.] Sailor: 'A shall, sir, and['t] please him. There's a letter for you, sir—it came from th' embassador that was bound for England—if your name be Horatio, as I am let to know it is. 10

Horatio: [*Reads.*] "Horatio, when thou shalt have overlook'd this, give these fellows some means to the King, they have letters for him. Ere we were two days old at sea, a pirate of very warlike appointment gave us chase. Finding ourselves too slow of sail, we put on a compell'd valor, and in the grapple I 15 boarded them. On the instant they got clear of our ship, so I alone became their prisoner. They have dealt with me like thieves of mercy, but they knew what they did: I am to do a [good] turn for them. Let the King have the letters I have sent, and repair thou to me with as much speed as thou woul- 20 dest fly death. I have words to speak in thine ear will make thee dumb, yet are they much too light for the [bore] of the matter. These good fellows will bring thee where I am. Rosencrantz and Guildenstern hold their course for England, of them I have much to tell thee. Farewell. 25

> [He] that thou knowest thine,
>> Hamlet."

Come, I will [give] you way for these your letters,
And do't the speedier that you may direct me
To him from whom you brought them.   *Exeunt.*

Scene VII

Enter King *and* Laertes.

King: Now must your conscience my acquittance seal,
    And you must put me in your heart for friend,
    Sith you have heard, and with a knowing ear,
    That he which hath your noble father slain
    Pursued my life.

Laertes: It well appears. But tell me 5
    Why you [proceeded] not against these feats
    So criminal and so capital in nature,
    As by your safety, greatness, wisdom, all things else
    You mainly were stirr'd up.

King: O, for two special reasons,
    Which may to you perhaps seem much unsinow'd, 10

---

18. *thieves of mercy:* merciful thieves.   22. *bore:* calibre, size (gunnery term).

IV.vii. Location: The castle.   1. *my acquittance seal:* ratify my acquittal, i.e. acknowledge my innocence in Polonius' death.   6. *feats:* acts.   8. *safety:* i.e. regard for your own safety.
9. *mainly:* powerfully.   10. *unsinow'd:* unsinewed, i.e. weak.

But yet to me th' are strong. The Queen his mother
Lives almost by his looks, and for myself—
My virtue or my plague, be it either which—
She is so [conjunctive] to my life and soul,
That, as the star moves not but in his sphere,   15
I could not but by her. The other motive,
Why to a public count I might not go,
Is the great love the general gender bear him,
Who, dipping all his faults in their affection,
Work like the spring that turneth wood to stone,   20
Convert his gyves to graces, so that my arrows,
Too slightly timber'd for so [loud a wind],
Would have reverted to my bow again,
But not where I have aim'd them.
Laertes: And so have I a noble father lost,   25
A sister driven into desp'rate terms,
Whose worth, if praises may go back again,
Stood challenger on mount of all the age
For her perfections—but my revenge will come.
King: Break not your sleeps for that. You must not think   30
That we are made of stuff so flat and dull
That we can let our beard be shook with danger
And think it pastime. You shortly shall hear more.
I lov'd your father, and we love ourself,
And that, I hope, will teach you to imagine—   35

Enter a Messenger *with letters.*

[How now? What news?
Messenger: Letters, my lord, from Hamlet:]
These to your Majesty, this to the Queen.
King: From Hamlet? Who brought them?
Messenger: Sailors, my lord, they say, I saw them not.
They were given me by Claudio. He receiv'd them   40
Of him that brought them.
King: Laertes, you shall hear them.
—Leave us.   [*Exit* Messenger.]
[*Reads.*] "High and mighty, You shall know I am set naked on
your kingdom. To-morrow shall I beg leave to see your kingly

---

13. *either which:* one or the other.   14. *conjunctive:* closely joined.   15. *in his sphere:* by the
movement of the sphere in which it is fixed (as the Ptolemaic astronomy taught).   17. *count:*
reckoning.   18. *the general gender:* everybody.   21. *gyves:* fetters.   26. *terms:* condition.
27. *go back again:* i.e. refer to what she was before she went mad.   28. *on mount:* pre-eminent.   30. *for that:* i.e. for fear of losing your revenge.   31. *flat:* spiritless.   32. *let . . .
shook:* To ruffle or tweak a man's beard was an act of insolent defiance that he could not disregard without loss of honor. Cf. II.ii.543. *with:* by.   43. *naked:* destitute.

eyes, when I shall, first asking you pardon thereunto, recount   45
the occasion of my sudden [and more strange] return.
                              [Hamlet.]"
What should this mean? Are all the rest come back?
Or is it some abuse, and no such thing?

Laertes: Know you the hand?

   King: 'Tis Hamlet's character. "Naked"!   50
And in a postscript here he says "alone."
Can you devise me?

Laertes: I am lost in it, my lord. But let him come,
It warms the very sickness in my heart
That I [shall] live and tell him to his teeth,   55
"Thus didst thou."

   King: If it be so, Laertes—
As how should it be so? how otherwise?—
Will you be rul'd by me?

Laertes: Ay, my lord,
So you will not o'errule me to a peace.

   King: To thine own peace. If he be now returned   60
As [checking] at his voyage, and that he means
No more to undertake it, I will work him
To an exploit, now ripe in my device,
Under the which he shall not choose but fall;
And for his death no wind of blame shall breathe,   65
But even his mother shall uncharge the practice,
And call it accident.

Laertes: My lord, I will be rul'd,
The rather if you could devise it so
That I might be the organ.

   King: It falls right.
You have been talk'd of since your travel much,   70
And that in Hamlet's hearing, for a quality
Wherein they say you shine. Your sum of parts
Did not together pluck such envy from him
As did that one, and that, in my regard,
Of the unworthiest siege.

Laertes: What part is that, my lord?   75

   King: A very riband in the cap of youth,
Yet needful too, for youth no less becomes

---

45. *pardon thereunto:* permission to do so.   48. *abuse:* deceit.   50. *character:* handwriting.
52. *devise me:* explain it to me.   57. *As . . . otherwise:* How can he have come back? Yet he
obviously has.   59. *So:* provided that.   61. *checking at:* turning from (like a falcon diverted
from its quarry by other prey).   66. *uncharge the practice:* adjudge the plot no plot, i.e. fail to
see the plot.   67. *organ:* instrument, agent.   71. *quality:* skill.   72. *Your . . . parts:* all your
(other) accomplishments put together.   74. *unworthiest:* i.e. least important (with no
implication of unsuitableness). *siege:* status, position.

The light and careless livery that it wears
Than settled age his sables and his weeds,
Importing health and graveness. Two months since   80
Here was a gentleman of Normandy:
I have seen myself, and serv'd against, the French,
And they can well on horseback, but this gallant
Had witchcraft in't, he grew unto his seat,
And to such wondrous doing brought his horse,   85
As had he been incorps'd and demi-natur'd
With the brave beast. So far he topp'd [my] thought,
That I in forgery of shapes and tricks
Come short of what he did.
Laertes: A Norman was't?
  King: A Norman.   90
Laertes: Upon my life, Lamord.
  King: The very same.
Laertes: I know him well. He is the brooch indeed
          And gem of all the nation.
    King: He made confession of you,
          And gave you such a masterly report   95
          For art and exercise in your defense,
          And for your rapier most especial,
          That he cried out 'twould be a sight indeed
          If one could match you. The scrimers of their nation
          He swore had neither motion, guard, nor eye,   100
          If you oppos'd them. Sir, this report of his
          Did Hamlet so envenom with his envy
          That he could nothing do but wish and beg
          Your sudden coming o'er to play with you.
          Now, out of this—
Laertes: What out of this, my lord?   105
    King: Laertes, was your father dear to you?
          Or are you like the painting of a sorrow,
          A face without a heart?
Laertes: Why ask you this?
    King: Not that I think you did not love your father,
          But that I know love is begun by time,   110
          And that I see, in passages of proof,
          Time qualifies the spark and fire of it.

---

79. *weeds:* (characteristic) garb.   80. *Importing . . . graveness:* signifying prosperity and
dignity.   83. *can . . . horseback:* are excellent riders.   86. *incorps'd:* made one body.
demi-natur'd: i.e. become half of a composite animal.   88. *forgery:* mere imagining.
93. *brooch:* ornament (worn in the hat).   94. *made . . . you:* acknowledged your excellence.
99. *scrimers:* fencers.   104. *sudden:* speedy.   110. *time:* i.e. a particular set of circumstances.   111. *in . . . proof:* i.e. by the test of experience, by actual examples.   112. *qualifies:*
moderates.

There lives within the very flame of love
A kind of week or snuff that will abate it,
And nothing is at a like goodness still,   115
For goodness, growing to a plurisy,
Dies in his own too much. That we would do,
We should do when we would; for this "would" changes,
And hath abatements and delays as many
As there are tongues, are hands, are accidents,   120
And then this "should" is like a spendthrift's sigh,
That hurts by easing. But to the quick of th' ulcer:
Hamlet comes back. What would you undertake
To show yourself indeed your father's son
More than in words?
Laertes: To cut his throat i' th' church.   125
   King: No place indeed should murther sanctuarize,
      Revenge should have no bounds. But, good Laertes,
      Will you do this, keep close within your chamber.
      Hamlet return'd shall know you are come home.
      We'll put on those shall praise your excellence,   130
      And set a double varnish on the fame
      The Frenchman gave you, bring you in fine together,
      And wager o'er your heads. He, being remiss,
      Most generous, and free from all contriving,
      Will not peruse the foils, so that with ease,   135
      Or with a little shuffling, you may choose
      A sword unbated, and in a [pass] of practice
      Requite him for your father.
Laertes: I will do't,
      And for [that] purpose I'll anoint my sword.
      I bought an unction of a mountebank,   140
      So mortal that, but dip a knife in it,
      Where it draws blood, no cataplasm so rare,
      Collected from all simples that have virtue
      Under the moon, can save the thing from death
      That is but scratch'd withal. I'll touch my point   145

---

114. *week:* wick.   115. *nothing . . . still:* nothing remains forever at the same pitch of
perfection.   116. *plurisy:* plethora (a variant spelling of *pleurisy,* which was erroneously
related to *plus,* stem *plur-,* "more, overmuch."   117. *too much:* excess.   121. *spendthrift's
sigh:* A sigh was supposed to draw blood from the heart.   122. *hurts by easing:* injures us at the
same time that it gives us relief.   126. *sanctuarize:* offer asylum to.   128. *Will . . . this:* if you
want to undertake this.   130. *put on those:* incite those who.   131. *double varnish:* second
coat of varnish.   132. *in fine:* finally.   133. *remiss:* careless, overtrustful.   134. *generous:*
noble-minded. *free . . . contriving:* innocent of sharp practices.   135. *peruse:* examine.
136. *shuffling:* cunning exchange.   137. *unbated:* not blunted. *pass of practice:* tricky thrust.
140. *unction:* ointment. *mountebank:* travelling quack-doctor.   141. *mortal:* deadly.
142. *cataplasm:* poultice.   143. *simples:* medicinal herbs. *virtue:* curative power.

With this contagion, that if I gall him slightly,
It may be death.
King: Let's further think of this,
Weigh what convenience both of time and means
May fit us to our shape. If this should fail,
And that our drift look through our bad performance,   150
'Twere better not assay'd; therefore this project
Should have a back or second, that might hold
If this did blast in proof. Soft, let me see.
We'll make a solemn wager on your cunnings—
I ha't!   155
When in your motion you are hot and dry—
As make your bouts more violent to that end—
And that he calls for drink, I'll have preferr'd him
A chalice for the nonce, whereon but sipping,
If he by chance escape your venom'd stuck,   160
Our purpose may hold there. But stay, what noise?

Enter Queen.

Queen: One woe doth tread upon another's heel,
So fast they follow. Your sister's drown'd, Laertes.
Laertes: Drown'd! O, where?
Queen: There is a willow grows askaunt the brook,   165
That shows his hoary leaves in the glassy stream,
Therewith fantastic garlands did she make
Of crow-flowers, nettles, daisies, and long purples
That liberal shepherds give a grosser name,
But our cull-cold maids do dead men's fingers call them. 170
There on the pendant boughs her crownet weeds
Clamb'ring to hang, an envious sliver broke,
When down her weedy trophies and herself
Fell in the weeping brook. Her clothes spread wide,
And mermaid-like awhile they bore her up,   175
Which time she chaunted snatches of old lauds,
As one incapable of her own distress,
Or like a creature native and indued
Unto that element. But long it could not be

---

146. *gall:* graze. 149. *fit . . . shape:* i.e. suit our purposes best. 150. *drift:* purpose. *look through:* become visible, be detected. 152. *back or second:* i.e. a second plot in reserve for emergency. 153. *blast in proof:* blow up while being tried (an image from gunnery). 157. *As:* i.e. and you should. 158. *preferr'd:* offered to. Most editors adopt the F1 reading *prepar'd.* 159. *nonce:* occasion. 160. *stuck:* thrust (from *stoccado,* a fencing term). 165. *askaunt:* sideways over. 166. *hoary:* grey-white. 167. *Therewith:* i.e. with willow branches. 168. *long purples:* wild orchids. 169. *liberal:* free-spoken. 170. *cull-cold:* chaste. 171. *crownet:* made into coronets. 172. *envious sliver:* malicious branch. 176. *lauds:* hymns. 177. *incapable:* insensible. 178. *indued:* habituated.

Till that her garments, heavy with their drink,   180
　　　Pull'd the poor wretch from her melodious lay
　　　To muddy death.
Laertes:　　　　　　　　Alas, then she is drown'd?
　Queen:　Drown'd, drown'd.
Laertes:　Too much of water hast thou, poor Ophelia,
　　　And therefore I forbid my tears; but yet   185
　　　It is our trick, Nature her custom holds,
　　　Let shame say what it will; when these are gone,
　　　The woman will be out. Adieu, my lord,
　　　I have a speech a' fire that fain would blaze,
　　　But that this folly drowns it.   *Exit.*
　King:　　　　　　　　Let's follow, Gertrude.   190
　　　How much I had to do to calm his rage!
　　　Now fear I this will give it start again,
　　　Therefore let's follow.   *Exeunt.*

ACT V

Scene I

Enter two Clowns [*with spades and mattocks*].

1. Clown: Is she to be buried in Christian burial when she willfully
　　　seeks her own salvation?
2. Clown: I tell thee she is, therefore make her grave straight. The
　　　crowner hath sate on her, and finds it Christian burial.
1. Clown: How can that be, unless she drown'd herself in her own   5
　　　defense?
2. Clown: Why, 'tis found so.
1. Clown: It must be [*se offendendo*], it cannot be else. For here lies
　　　the point: if I drown myself wittingly, it argues an act, and an
　　　act hath three branches—it is to act, to do, to perform;   10
　　　[argal], she drown'd herself wittingly.
2. Clown: Nay, but hear you, goodman delver—
1. Clown: Give me leave. Here lies the water; good. Here stands
　　　the man; good. If the man go to this water and drown him-
　　　self, it is, will he, nill he, he goes, mark you that. But if the   15
　　　water come to him and drown him, he drowns not himself;

---

186. *It:* i.e. weeping. *trick:* natural way.   187. *these:* these tears.   188. *The woman . . . out:*
my womanish traits will be gone for good.

V.i. Location: A churchyard.   o.s.d. *Clowns:* rustics.   3. *straight:* immediately. *crowner:*
coroner.   8. *se offendendo:* blunder for *se defendendo,* "in self-defense."   11. *argal:* blunder
for *ergo,* "therefore."   13-18. *Here . . . life:* Alluding to a very famous suicide case, that of Sir
James Hales, a judge who drowned himself in 1554; it was long cited in the courts. The clown
gives a garbled account of the defense summing-up and the verdict.   15. *nill he:* will he not.

argal, he that is not guilty of his own death shortens not his
own life.

2. Clown: But is this law?

1. Clown: Ay, marry, is't—crowner's quest law.   20

2. Clown: Will you ha' the truth an't? If this had not been a gentlewoman, she should have been buried out a' Christian burial.

1. Clown: Why, there thou say'st, and the more pity that great folk
should have count'nance in this world to drown or hang
themselves, more than their even-Christen. Come, my   25
spade. There is no ancient gentlemen but gard'ners,
ditchers, and grave-makers; they hold up Adam's profession.

2. Clown: Was he a gentleman?

1. Clown: 'A was the first that ever bore arms.

[*2. Clown:* Why, he had none.   30

1. Clown: What, art a heathen? How dost thou understand the
Scripture? The Scripture says Adam digg'd; could he dig
without arms?] I'll put another question to thee. If thou
answerest me not to the purpose, confess thyself—

2. Clown: Go to.   35

1. Clown: What is he that builds stronger than either the mason, the
shipwright, or the carpenter?

2. Clown: The gallows-maker, for that outlives a thousand tenants.

1. Clown: I like thy wit well, in good faith. The gallows does well;
but how does it well? It does well to those that do ill. Now   40
thou dost ill to say the gallows is built stronger than the
church; argal, the gallows may do well to thee. To't again,
come.

2. Clown: Who builds stronger than a mason, a shipwright, or a
carpenter?   45

1. Clown: Ay, tell me that, and unyoke.

2. Clown: Marry, now I can tell.

1. Clown: To't.

2. Clown: Mass, I cannot tell.

Enter Hamlet *and* Horatio [*afar off*].

1. Clown: Cudgel thy brains no more about it, for your dull ass will   50
not mend his pace with beating, and when you are ask'd this
question next, say "a grave-maker": the houses he makes lasts
till doomsday. Go get thee in, and fetch me a sup of liquor.

[*Exit Second* Clown. *First* Clown *digs.*]

"In youth when I did love, did love,   *Song.*

Methought it was very sweet,   55

---

20. *quest:* inquest.   25. *even-Christen:* fellow-Christians.   30. *none:* i.e. no coat of arms.
46. *unyoke:* i.e. cease to labor, call it a day.   49. *Mass:* by the mass.

> To contract—O—the time for—a—my behove,
>   O, methought there—a—was nothing—a—meet."

Hamlet: Has this fellow no feeling of his business? 'a sings in
grave-making.

Horatio: Custom hath made it in him a property of easiness.   60

Hamlet: 'Tis e'en so, the hand of little employment hath the
daintier sense.

1. Clown: "But age with his stealing steps   *Song.*
        Hath clawed me in his clutch,
    And hath shipped me into the land,   65
        As if I had never been such."

[Throws up a shovelful of earth with a skull in it.]

Hamlet: That skull had a tongue in it, and could sing once. How
the knave jowls it to the ground, as if 'twere Cain's jaw-bone,
that did the first murder! This might be the pate of a politician, which this ass now o'erreaches, one that would circum-   70
vent God, might it not?

Horatio: It might, my lord.

Hamlet: Or of a courtier, which could say, "Good morrow, sweet
lord! How dost thou, sweet lord?" This might be my Lord
Such-a-one, that prais'd my Lord Such-a-one's horse when 'a   75
[meant] to beg it, might it not?

Horatio: Ay, my lord.

Hamlet: Why, e'en so, and now my Lady Worm's, chopless, and
knock'd about the [mazzard] with a sexton's spade. Here's
fine revolution, and we had the trick to see't. Did these   80
bones cost no more the breeding, but to play at loggats with
them? Mine ache to think on't.

1. Clown: "A pickaxe and a spade, a spade,   *Song.*
        For and a shrouding sheet:
    O, a pit of clay for to be made   85
        For such a guest is meet."   *[Throws up another skull.]*

Hamlet: There's another. Why may not that be the skull of a lawyer? Where be his quiddities now, his quillities, his cases, his
tenures, and his tricks? Why does he suffer this mad knave

---

56. *contract . . . behove:* shorten, i.e. spend agreeably . . . advantage. The song, punctuated by
the grunts of the clown as he digs, is a garbled version of a poem by Thomas Lord Vaux,
entitled "The Aged Lover Renounceth Love." 60. *Custom:* habit. *a property of easiness:* i.e.
a thing he can do with complete ease of mind. 62. *daintier sense:* more delicate sensitivity.
68. *jowls:* dashes. 69-70. *politician:* schemer, intriguer. 70. *o'erreaches:* gets the better of
(with play on the literal sense). 70-71. *circumvent God:* bypass God's law. 78. *chopless:* lacking
the lower jaw. 79. *mazzard:* head. 80. *revolution:* change. *and:* if. *trick:* knack, ability.
80-81. *Did . . . cost:* were . . . worth. 81. *loggats:* a game in which blocks of wood were
thrown at a stake. 88. *quiddities:* subtleties, quibbles. *quillities:* fine distinctions.
89. *tenures:* titles to real estate.

now to knock him about the sconce with a dirty shovel, and 90
will not tell him of his action of battery? Hum! This fellow
might be in 's time a great buyer of land, with his statutes, his
recognizances, his fines, his double vouchers, his recoveries.
[Is this the fine of his fines, and the recovery of his recoveries,] to have his fine pate full of fine dirt? Will [his] vouchers 95
vouch him no more of his purchases, and [double ones too],
than the length and breadth of a pair of indentures? The very
conveyances of his lands will scarcely lie in this box, and must
th' inheritor himself have no more, ha?

Horatio: Not a jot more, my lord. 100

Hamlet: Is not parchment made of sheep-skins?

Horatio: Ay, my lord, and of calves'-skins too.

Hamlet: They are sheep and calves which seek out assurance in
that. I will speak to this fellow. Whose grave's this, sirrah?

1. Clown: Mine, sir. 105

[*Sings.*] "[O], a pit of clay for to be made
[For such a guest is meet]."

Hamlet: I think it be thine indeed, for thou liest in't.

1. Clown: You lie out on't, sir, and therefore 'tis not yours; for my
part, I do not lie in't, yet it is mine. 110

Hamlet: Thou dost lie in't, to be in't and say it is thine. 'Tis for the
dead, not for the quick; therefore thou liest.

1. Clown: 'Tis a quick lie, sir, 'twill away again from me to you.

Hamlet: What man dost thou dig it for?

1. Clown: For no man, sir. 115

Hamlet: What woman then?

1. Clown: For none neither.

Hamlet: Who is to be buried in't?

1. Clown: One that was a woman, sir, but, rest her soul, she's dead.

Hamlet: How absolute the knave is! we must speak by the card, or 120
equivocation will undo us. By the Lord, Horatio, this three
years I have took note of it: the age is grown so pick'd that the
toe of the peasant comes so near the heel of the courtier, he
galls his kibe. How long hast thou been grave-maker?

1. Clown: Of [all] the days i' th' year, I came to't that day that our 125
last king Hamlet overcame Fortinbras.

---

90. *sconce:* head. 92–93. *statutes, recognizances:* bonds securing debts by attaching land and
property. 93. *fines . . . recoveries:* procedures for converting an entailed estate to freehold.
93. *double vouchers:* documents guaranteeing title to real estate, signed by two persons.
94. *fine:* end. 97. *pair of indentures:* legal document cut into two parts which fitted together
on a serrated edge. Perhaps Hamlet thus refers to the two rows of teeth in the skull, or to the
bone sutures. 98. *conveyances:* documents relating to transfer of property. *this box:* i.e. the
skull itself. 99. *inheritor:* owner. 104. *sirrah:* term of address to inferiors. 120. *absolute:*
positive. *by the card:* by the compass, i.e. punctiliously. 121. *equivocation:* ambiguity.
122. *pick'd:* refined. 124. *galls his kibe:* rubs the courtier's chilblain.

Hamlet: How long is that since?

1. Clown: Cannot you tell that? Every fool can tell that. It was that
very day that young Hamlet was born—he that is mad, and
sent into England. 130

Hamlet: Ay, marry, why was he sent into England?

1. Clown: Why, because 'a was mad. 'A shall recover his wits there,
or if 'a do not, 'tis no great matter there.

Hamlet: Why?

1. Clown: 'Twill not be seen in him there, there the men are as mad 135
as he.

Hamlet: How came he mad?

1. Clown: Very strangely, they say.

Hamlet: How strangely?

1. Clown: Faith, e'en with losing his wits. 140

Hamlet: Upon what ground?

1. Clown: Why, here in Denmark. I have been sexton here, man
and boy, thirty years.

Hamlet: How long will a man lie i' th' earth ere he rot?

1. Clown: Faith, if 'a be not rotten before 'a die—as we have many 145
pocky corses, that will scarce hold the laying in—'a will last
you some eight year or nine year. A tanner will last you nine
year.

Hamlet: Why he more than another?

1. Clown: Why, sir, his hide is so tann'd with his trade that 'a will 150
keep out water a great while, and your water is a sore decayer
of your whoreson dead body. Here's a skull now hath lien
you i' th' earth three and twenty years.

Hamlet: Whose was it?

1. Clown: A whoreson mad fellow's it was. Whose do you think it 155
was?

Hamlet: Nay, I know not.

1. Clown: A pestilence on him for a mad rogue! 'a pour'd a flagon
of Rhenish on my head once. This same skull, sir, was, sir,
Yorick's skull, the King's jester. 160

Hamlet: This? *[Takes the skull.]*

1. Clown: E'en that.

Hamlet: Alas, poor Yorick! I knew him, Horatio, a fellow of infinite jest, of most excellent fancy. He hath bore me on his
back a thousand times, and now how abhorr'd in my imagina- 165
tion it is! my gorge rises at it. Here hung those lips that I
have kiss'd I know not how oft. Where be your gibes now,
your gambols, your songs, your flashes of merriment, that
were wont to set the table on a roar? Not one now to mock

---

146. *pocky:* rotten with venereal disease. *hold . . . in:* last out the burial.

your own grinning—quite chop-fall'n. Now get you to my 170
lady's [chamber], and tell her, let her paint an inch thick, to
this favor she must come; make her laugh at that. Prithee,
Horatio, tell me one thing.

Horatio: What's that, my lord?

Hamlet: Dost thou think Alexander look'd a' this fashion i' th' 175
earth?

Horatio: E'en so.

Hamlet: And smelt so? pah!   *[Puts down the skull.]*

Horatio: E'en so, my lord.

Hamlet: To what base uses we may return, Horatio! Why may not 180
imagination trace the noble dust of Alexander, till 'a find it
stopping a bunghole?

Horatio: 'Twere to consider too curiously, to consider so.

Hamlet: No, faith, not a jot, but to follow him thither with mod-
esty enough and likelihood to lead it: Alexander died, Alex- 185
ander was buried, Alexander returneth to dust, the dust is
earth, of earth we make loam, and why of that loam whereto
he was converted might they not stop a beer-barrel?
Imperious Caesar, dead and turn'd to clay,
Might stop a hole to keep the wind away.   190
O that that earth which kept the world in awe
Should patch a wall t' expel the [winter's] flaw!
But soft, but soft awhile, here comes the King,

Enter King, Queen, Laertes, *and [a* Doctor of Divinity, *following] the corse,
[with* Lords *attendant].*

The Queen, the courtiers. Who is this they follow?
And with such maimed rites? This doth betoken   195
The corse they follow did with desp'rate hand
Foredo it own life. 'Twas of some estate.
Couch we a while and mark.   *[Retiring with* Horatio.*]*

Laertes: What ceremony else?

Hamlet: That is Laertes, a very noble youth. Mark.   200

Laertes: What ceremony else?

Doctor: Her obsequies have been as far enlarg'd
As we have warranty. Her death was doubtful,
And but that great command o'ersways the order,
She should in ground unsanctified been lodg'd   205

---

170. *chop-fall'n:* (1) lacking the lower jaw; (2) downcast.   172. *favor:* appearance.
183. *curiously:* closely, minutely.   184–185. *modesty:* moderation.   187. *loam:* a mixture of
moistened clay with sand, straw, etc.   189. *Imperious:* imperial.   192. *flaw:* gust.
195. *maimed rites:* lack of customary ceremony.   197. *Foredo:* fordo, destroy. *it:* its. *estate:*
rank.   198. *Couch we:* let us conceal ourselves.   203. *doubtful:* i.e. the subject of an "open
verdict."   204. *order:* customary procedure.   205. *should:* would certainly.

Till the last trumpet; for charitable prayers,
[Shards,] flints, and pebbles should be thrown on her.
Yet here she is allow'd her virgin crants,
Her maiden strewments, and the bringing home
Of bell and burial.   210

Laertes: Must there no more be done?

Doctor: No more be done:
We should profane the service of the dead
To sing a requiem and such rest to her
As to peace-parted souls.

Laertes: Lay her i' th' earth,
And from her fair and unpolluted flesh   215
May violets spring! I tell thee, churlish priest,
A minist'ring angel shall my sister be
When thou liest howling.

Hamlet: What, the fair Ophelia!

Queen: *[Scattering flowers.]*   Sweets to the sweet, farewell!
I hop'd thou shouldst have been my Hamlet's wife.   220
I thought thy bride-bed to have deck'd, sweet maid,
And not have strew'd thy grave.

Laertes: O, treble woe
Fall ten times [treble] on that cursed head
Whose wicked deed thy most ingenious sense
Depriv'd thee of! Hold off the earth a while,   225
Till I have caught her once more in mine arms.

                                    [Leaps in the grave.]
Now pile your dust upon the quick and dead,
Till of this flat a mountain you have made
T' o'ertop old Pelion, or the skyish head
Of blue Olympus.   230

Hamlet: [Coming forward.]   What is he whose grief
Bears such an emphasis, whose phrase of sorrow
Conjures the wand'ring stars and makes them stand
Like wonder-wounded hearers? This is I,
Hamlet the Dane!   *[Hamlet leaps in after Laertes.]* 235

Laertes: The devil take thy soul!   *[Grappling with him.]*

Hamlet: Thou pray'st not well.
I prithee take thy fingers from my throat.
For though I am not splenitive [and] rash,

---

206. *for:* instead of.   208. *crants:* garland.   209. *maiden strewments:* flowers scattered on the grave of an unmarried girl.   209–10. *bringing . . . burial:* i.e. burial in consecrated ground, with the bell tolling.   213. *requiem:* dirge.   219. *Sweets:* flowers.   224. *ingenious:* intelligent.   229–230. *Pelion, Olympus:* mountains in northeastern Greece.   232. *emphasis, phrase:* Rhetorical terms, here used in disparaging reference to Laertes' inflated language.   233. *Conjures:* puts a spell upon. *wand'ring stars:* planets.   235. *the Dane:* This title normally signifies the King.   238. *splenitive:* impetuous.

Yet have I in me something dangerous,
Which let thy wisdom fear. Hold off thy hand!   240
King: Pluck them asunder.
Queen: Hamlet, Hamlet!
All: Gentlemen!
Horatio: Good my lord, be quiet.

[*The Attendants part them, and they come out of the grave.*]

Hamlet: Why, I will fight with him upon this theme
Until my eyelids will no longer wag.
Queen: O my son, what theme?   245
Hamlet: I lov'd Ophelia. Forty thousand brothers
Could not with all their quantity of love
Make up my sum. What wilt thou do for her?
King: O, he is mad, Laertes.
Queen: For love of God, forbear him.   250
Hamlet: 'Swounds, show me what thou't do.
Woo't weep, woo't fight, woo't fast, woo't tear thyself?
Woo't drink up eisel, eat a crocadile?
I'll do't. Dost [thou] come here to whine?
To outface me with leaping in her grave?   255
Be buried quick with her, and so will I.
And if thou prate of mountains, let them throw
Millions of acres on us, till our ground,
Singeing his pate against the burning zone,
Make Ossa like a wart! Nay, and thou'lt mouth,   260
I'll rant as well as thou.
Queen: This is mere madness,
And [thus] a while the fit will work on him;
Anon, as patient as the female dove,
When that her golden couplets are disclosed,
His silence will sit drooping.
Hamlet: Hear you, sir,   265
What is the reason that you use me thus?
I lov'd you ever. But it is no matter.
Let Hercules himself do what he may,
The cat will mew, and dog will have his day.   *Exit* Hamlet.
King: I pray thee, good Horatio, wait upon him.   270
                                        [*Exit*] Horatio.

---

251. *thou't:* thou wilt.   252. *Woo't:* wilt thou.   253. *eisel:* vinegar. *crocadile:* crocodile.
257. *if . . . mountains:* Referring to lines 227–30.   259. *burning zone:* sphere of the sun.
260. *Ossa:* another mountain in Greece, near Pelion and Olympus. *mouth:* talk bombast
(synonymous with *rant* in the next line).   262. *mere:* utter.   263. *patient:* calm.   264. *golden
couplets:* pair of baby birds, covered with yellow down. *disclosed:* hatched.   268–69. *Let . . .
day:* i.e. nobody can prevent another from making the scenes he feels he has a right to.

[*To* Laertes.]   Strengthen your patience in our last night's
    speech,
We'll put the matter to the present push.—
Good Gertrude, set some watch over your son.
This grave shall have a living monument.   275
An hour of quiet [shortly] shall we see,
Till then in patience our proceeding be.   *Exeunt.*

Scene II

Enter Hamlet *and* Horatio.

    Hamlet: So much for this, sir, now shall you see the other—
            You do remember all the circumstance?
    Horatio: Remember it, my lord!
    Hamlet: Sir, in my heart there was a kind of fighting
            That would not let me sleep. [Methought] I lay   5
            Worse than the mutines in the [bilboes]. Rashly—
            And prais'd be rashness for it—let us know
            Our indiscretion sometime serves us well
            When our deep plots do pall, and that should learn us
            There's a divinity that shapes our ends,   10
            Rough-hew them how we will—
    Horatio: That is most certain.
    Hamlet: Up from my cabin,
            My sea-gown scarf'd about me, in the dark
            Grop'd I to find out them, had my desire,
            Finger'd their packet, and in fine withdrew   15
            To mine own room again, making so bold,
            My fears forgetting manners, to [unseal]
            Their grand commission; where I found, Horatio—
            Ah, royal knavery!—an exact command,
            Larded with many several sorts of reasons,   20
            Importing Denmark's health and England's too,
            With, ho, such bugs and goblins in my life,

271–76. See the Textual Notes for the lines that replace these in Q1.   271. *in:* i.e. by
recalling.   272. *present push:* immediate test.   275. *living:* enduring (?) or in the form of a
lifelike effigy (?).

V.ii. Location: The castle.   1. *see the other:* i.e. hear the other news I have to tell you (hinted at
in the letter to Horatio, IV.vi.24-25).   6. *mutines:* mutineers (but the term *mutiny* was in
Shakespeare's day used of almost any act of rebellion against authority). *bilboes:* fetters
attached to a heavy iron bar. *Rashly:* on impulse.   7. *know:* recognize, acknowledge.   9. *pall:*
lose force, come to nothing. *learn:* teach.   10. *shapes our ends:* gives final shape to our
designs.   11. *Rough-hew them:* block them out in initial form.   15. *Finger'd:* filched,
"pinched."   20. *Larded:* garnished.   21. *Importing:* relating to.   22. *bugs . . . life:* terrifying
things in prospect if I were permitted to remain alive. *Bugs* = bugaboos.

That, on the supervise, no leisure bated,
No, not to stay the grinding of the axe,
My head should be strook off.
Horatio: Is't possible?   25
Hamlet: Here's the commission, read it at more leisure.
But wilt thou hear now how I did proceed?
Horatio: I beseech you.
Hamlet: Being thus benetted round with [villainies],
Or I could make a prologue to my brains,   30
They had begun the play. I sat me down,
Devis'd a new commission, wrote it fair.
I once did hold it, as our statists do,
A baseness to write fair, and labor'd much
How to forget that learning, but, sir, now   35
It did me yeman's service. Wilt thou know
Th' effect of what I wrote?
Horatio: Ay, good my lord.
Hamlet: An earnest conjuration from the King,
As England was his faithful tributary,
As love between them like the palm might flourish,   40
As peace should still her wheaten garland wear
And stand a comma 'tween their amities,
And many such-like [as's] of great charge,
That on the view and knowing of these contents,
Without debatement further, more or less,   45
He should those bearers put to sudden death,
Not shriving time allow'd.
Horatio: How was this seal'd?
Hamlet: Why, even in that was heaven ordinant.
I had my father's signet in my purse,
Which was the model of that Danish seal;   50
Folded the writ up in the form of th' other,
[Subscrib'd] it, gave't th' impression, plac'd it safely,
The changeling never known. Now the next day
Was our sea-fight, and what to this was sequent
Thou knowest already.   55

---

23. *supervise:* perusal. *bated:* deducted (from the stipulated speediness).   24. *stay:* wait for.
30. *Or:* before.   32. *fair:* i.e. in a beautiful hand (such as a professional scribe would use).
33. *statists:* statesmen, public officials.   34. *A baseness:* i.e. a skill befitting men of low rank.
36. *yeman's:* yeoman's, i.e. solid, substantial.   37. *effect:* purport, gist.   42. *comma:*
connective, link.   43. *as's . . . charge:* (1) weighty clauses beginning with *as;* (2) asses with
heavy loads.   47. *shriving time:* time for confession and absolution.   48. *ordinant:* in charge,
guiding.   50. *model:* small copy.   52. *Subscrib'd:* signed.   53. *changeling:* i.e. Hamlet's
letter, substituted secretly for the genuine letter, as fairies substituted their children for
human children. *never known:* never recognized as a substitution (unlike the fairies'
changelings).

Horatio: So Guildenstern and Rosencrantz go to't.
Hamlet: [Why, man, they did make love to this employment,]
    They are not near my conscience. Their defeat
    Does by their own insinuation grow.
    'Tis dangerous when the baser nature comes   60
    Between the pass and fell incensed points
    Of mighty opposites.
Horatio: Why, what a king is this!
Hamlet: Does it not, think thee, stand me now upon—
    He that hath kill'd my king and whor'd my mother,
    Popp'd in between th' election and my hopes,   65
    Thrown out his angle for my proper life,
    And with such coz'nage—is't not perfect conscience
    [To quit him with this arm? And is't not to be damn'd,
    To let this canker of our nature come
    In further evil?   70
Horatio: It must be shortly known to him from England
    What is the issue of the business there.
Hamlet: It will be short; the interim's mine,
    And a man's life's no more than to say "one."
    But I am very sorry, good Horatio,   75
    That to Laertes I forgot myself,
    For by the image of my cause I see
    The portraiture of his. I'll [court] his favors.
    But sure the bravery of his grief did put me
    Into a tow'ring passion.
Horatio: [Peace, who comes here?]   80

Enter [young Osric,] *a courtier.*

    Osric: Your lordship is right welcome back to Denmark.
    Hamlet: I [humbly] thank you, sir.—Dost know this water-fly?
    Horatio: No, my good lord.
    Hamlet: Thy state is the more gracious, for 'tis a vice to know him.
    He hath much land, and fertile; let a beast be lord of beasts, 85
    and his crib shall stand at the King's mess. 'Tis a chough, but,
    as I say, spacious in the possession of dirt.

---

56. *go to't:* i.e. are going to their death. 58. *defeat:* ruin, overthrow. 59. *insinuation:*
winding their way into the affair. 60. *baser:* inferior. 61. *pass:* thrust. *fell:* fierce.
62. *stand . . . upon:* i.e. rest upon me as a duty. 65. *election:* i.e. as King of Denmark.
66. *angle:* hook and line. *proper:* very. 67. *coz'nage:* trickery. 68. *quit him:* pay him back.
69. *canker:* cancerous sore. 69-70. *come In:* grow into. 74. *a man's . . . more:* i.e. to kill a
man takes no more time. *say "one":* Perhaps this is equivalent to "deliver one sword thrust";
see line 257 below, where Hamlet says "One" as he makes the first hit. 77. *image:* likeness.
79. *bravery:* ostentatious expression. 82. *water-fly:* i.e. tiny, vainly agitated creature.
84. *gracious:* virtuous. 85-86. *let . . . mess:* i.e. if a beast owned as many cattle as Osric, he
could feast with the King. 86. *chough:* jackdaw, a bird that could be taught to speak.

Osric: Sweet lord, if your lordship were at leisure, I should impart a thing to you from his Majesty.

Hamlet: I will receive it, sir, with all diligence of spirit. [Put] your 90
bonnet to his right use, 'tis for the head.

Osric: I thank your lordship, it is very hot.

Hamlet: No, believe me, 'tis very cold, the wind is northerly.

Osric: It is indifferent cold, my lord, indeed.

Hamlet: But yet methinks it is very [sultry] and hot [for] my 95
complexion.

Osric: Exceedingly, my lord, it is very sultry—as 'twere—I cannot tell how. My lord, his Majesty bade me signify to you that
'a has laid a great wager on your head. Sir, this is the
matter— 100

Hamlet: I beseech you remember.

[Hamlet *moves him to put on his hat.*]

Osric: Nay, good my lord, for my ease, in good faith. Sir, here is
newly come to court Laertes, believe me, an absolute [gentleman], full of most excellent differences, of very soft society,
and great showing; indeed, to speak sellingly of him, he is the 105
card or calendar of gentry; for you shall find in him the continent of what part a gentleman would see.

Hamlet: Sir, his definement suffers no perdition in you, though I
know to divide him inventorially would dozy th' arithmetic of
memory, and yet but yaw neither in respect of his quick sail; 110
but in the verity of extolment, I take him to be a soul of great
article, and his infusion of such dearth and rareness as, to
make true diction of him, his semblable is his mirror, and who
else would trace him, his umbrage, nothing more.

Osric: Your lordship speaks most infallibly of him. 115

Hamlet: The concernancy, sir? Why do we wrap the gentleman in
our more rawer breath?

Osric: Sir?

---

91. *bonnet:* hat. 94. *indifferent:* somewhat. 95. *complexion:* temperament. 102. *for my ease:* i.e. I am really more comfortable with my hat off (a polite insistence on maintaining ceremony). 103. *absolute:* complete, possessing every quality a gentleman should have. 104. *differences:* distinguishing characteristics, personal qualities. *soft:* agreeable. 105. *great showing:* splendid appearance. *sellingly:* i.e. like a seller to a prospective buyer; in a fashion to do full justice. Most editors follow Q3 in reading *feelingly* = with exactitude, as he deserves. 106. *card or calendar:* chart or register, i.e. compendious guide. *gentry:* gentlemanly behavior. 106–07. *the continent . . . part:* one who contains every quality. 108. *perdition:* loss. 109. *dozy:* make dizzy. 110. *yaw:* keep deviating erratically from its course (said of a ship). *neither:* for all that. *in respect of:* compared with. 111. *in . . . extolment:* to praise him truly. 112. *article:* scope (?) or importance (?). *infusion:* essence, quality. *dearth:* scarceness. 113. *make true diction:* speak truly. *his semblable:* his only likeness or equal. 113–14. *who . . . him:* anyone else who tries to follow him. 114. *umbrage:* shadow. 116. *concernancy:* relevance. 117. *more rawer breath:* i.e. words too crude to describe him properly.

Horatio: Is't not possible to understand in another tongue? You will to't, sir, really.   120

Hamlet: What imports the nomination of this gentleman?

Osric: Of Laertes?

Horatio: His purse is empty already: all 's golden words are spent.

Hamlet: Of him, sir.

Osric: I know you are not ignorant—   125

Hamlet: I would you did, sir, yet, in faith, if you did, it would not much approve me. Well, sir?

Osric: You are not ignorant of what excellence Laertes is—

Hamlet: I dare not confess that, lest I should compare with him in excellence, but to know a man well were to know himself.   130

Osric: I mean, sir, for [his] weapon, but in the imputation laid on him by them, in his meed he's unfellow'd.

Hamlet: What's his weapon?

Osric: Rapier and dagger.

Hamlet: That's two of his weapons—but well.   135

Osric: The King, sir, hath wager'd with him six Barbary horses, against the which he has impawn'd, as I take it, six French rapiers and poniards, with their assigns, as girdle, [hangers], and so. Three of the carriages, in faith, are very dear to fancy, very responsive to the hilts, most delicate carriages,   140 and of very liberal conceit.

Hamlet: What call you the carriages?

Horatio: I knew you must be edified by the margent ere you had done.

Osric: The [carriages], sir, are the hangers.   145

Hamlet: The phrase would be more germane to the matter if we could carry a cannon by our sides; I would it [might be] hangers till then. But on: six Barb'ry horses against six French swords, their assigns, and three liberal-conceited carriages; that's the French bet against the Danish. Why is this   150 all [impawn'd, as] you call it?

Osric: The King, sir, hath laid, sir, that in a dozen passes between yourself and him, he shall not exceed you three hits;

---

119. *in another tongue:* i.e. when someone else is the speaker.   119–20. *You . . . really:* i.e. you can do it if you try.   121. *nomination:* naming, mention.   127. *approve:* commend. 129–30. *compare . . . excellence:* i.e. seem to claim the same degree of excellence for myself. 130. *but:* The sense seems to require *for. himself:* i.e. oneself.   131–32. *in . . . them:* i.e. in popular estimation.   132. *meed:* merit.   137. *impawn'd:* staked.   138. *assigns:* appurtenances. *hangers:* straps on which the swords hang from the girdle.   139. *carriages:* properly, gun-carriages; here used affectedly in place of *hangers.*   140. *fancy:* taste. *very responsive to:* matching well.   141. *liberal conceit:* elegant design.   143. *must . . . margent:* would require enlightenment from a marginal note.   152. *laid:* wagered.   153. *he . . . hits:* Laertes must win by at least eight to four (if none of the "passes" or bouts are draws), since at seven to five he would be only two up.

he hath laid on twelve for nine; and it would come to immediate trial, if your lordship would vouchsafe the answer.   155

Hamlet: How if I answer no?

   Osric: I mean, my lord, the opposition of your person in trial.

Hamlet: Sir, I will walk here in the hall. If it please his Majesty, it
is the breathing time of day with me. Let the foils be brought,
the gentleman willing, and the King hold his purpose, I will 160
win for him and I can; if not, I will gain nothing but my shame
and the odd hits.

   Osric: Shall I deliver you so?

Hamlet: To this effect, sir—after what flourish your nature will.

   Osric: I commend my duty to your lordship.   165

Hamlet: Yours. *[Exit* Osric.*]* ['A] does well to commend it himself,
there are no tongues else for 's turn.

Horatio: This lapwing runs away with the shell on his head.

Hamlet: 'A did [comply], sir, with his dug before 'a suck'd it. Thus
has he, and many more of the same breed that I know the 170
drossy age dotes on, only got the tune of the time, and out of
an habit of encounter, a kind of [yesty] collection, which carries them through and through the most [profound] and
[winnow'd] opinions, and do but blow them to their trial, the
bubbles are out.   175

Enter a Lord.

   Lord: My lord, his Majesty commended him to you by young
Osric, who brings back to him that you attend him in the hall.
He sends to know if your pleasure hold to play with Laertes,
or that you will take longer time.

Hamlet: I am constant to my purposes, they follow the King's 180
pleasure. If his fitness speaks, mine is ready; now or whensoever, provided I be so able as now.

   Lord: The King and Queen and all are coming down.

Hamlet: In happy time.

---

154. *he . . . nine:* Not satisfactorily explained despite much discussion. One suggestion is that
Laertes has raised the odds against himself by wagering that out of twelve bouts he will win
nine.   155. *answer:* encounter (as Hamlet's following quibble forces Osric to explain in his
next speech).   159. *breathing . . . me:* my usual hour for exercise.   164. *after what flourish:*
with whatever embellishment of language.   165. *commend my duty:* offer my dutiful respects
(but Hamlet picks up the phrase in the sense "praise my manner of bowing").   168. *lapwing:*
a foolish bird which upon hatching was supposed to run with part of the eggshell still over its
head. (Osric has put his hat on at last.)   169. *comply . . . dug:* bow politely to his mother's
nipple.   171. *drossy:* i.e. worthless. *tune . . . time:* i.e. fashionable ways of talk. *habit of
encounter:* mode of social intercourse.   172. *yesty:* yeasty, frothy. *collection:* i.e. anthology of
fine phrases.   174. *winnow'd:* sifted, choice. *opinions:* judgments. *blow . . . trial:* test them by
blowing on them, i.e. make even the least demanding trial of them.   175. *out:* blown away (?)
or at an end, done for (?).   181. *If . . . ready:* i.e. if this is a good moment for him, it is for me
also.

Lord: The Queen desires you to use some gentle entertainment 185
    to Laertes before you fall to play.

Hamlet: She well instructs me.   [*Exit* Lord.]

Horatio: You will lose, my lord.

Hamlet: I do not think so; since he went into France I have been in
    continual practice. I shall win at the odds. Thou wouldst not 190
    think how ill all's here about my heart—but it is no matter.

Horatio: Nay, good my lord—

Hamlet: It is but foolery, but it is such a kind of [gain-]giving, as
    would perhaps trouble a woman.

Horatio: If your mind dislike any thing, obey it. I will forestall 195
    their repair hither, and say you are not fit.

Hamlet: Not a whit, we defy augury. There is special providence
    in the fall of a sparrow. If it be [now], 'tis not to come; if it be
    not to come, it will be now; if it be not now, yet it [will] come
    —the readiness is all. Since no man, of aught he leaves, 200
    knows what is't to leave betimes, let be.

*A table prepar'd, [and flagons of wine on it. Enter] Trumpets, Drums, and Officers
with cushions, foils, daggers; King, Queen, Laertes, [Osric,] and all the State.*

King: Come, Hamlet, come, and take this hand from me.
                   [*The* King *puts* Laertes' *hand into* Hamlet's.]

Hamlet: Give me your pardon, sir. I have done you wrong,
    But pardon't as you are a gentleman.
    This presence knows, 205
    And you must needs have heard, how I am punish'd
    With a sore distraction. What I have done
    That might your nature, honor, and exception
    Roughly awake, I here proclaim was madness.
    Was't Hamlet wrong'd Laertes? Never Hamlet! 210
    If Hamlet from himself be ta'en away,
    And when he's not himself does wrong Laertes,
    Then Hamlet does it not, Hamlet denies it.
    Who does it then? His madness. If't be so,
    Hamlet is of the faction that is wronged, 215
    His madness is poor Hamlet's enemy.
    [Sir, in this audience,]
    Let my disclaiming from a purpos'd evil
    Free me so far in your most generous thoughts,

---

185. *gentle entertainment:* courteous greeting.   193. *gain-giving:* misgiving.   197–98. *special
. . . sparrow:* See Matthew 10:29.   200. *of aught:* i.e. whatever.   201. *knows . . . betimes:*
knows what is the best time to leave.   202 s.d. *State:* nobles.   205. *presence:* assembled
court.   206. *punish'd:* afflicted.   208. *exception:* objection.   218. *my . . . evil:* my declaration that I intended no harm.   219. *Free:* absolve.

That I have shot my arrow o'er the house   220
    And hurt my brother.
Laertes: I am satisfied in nature,
    Whose motive in this case should stir me most
    To my revenge, but in my terms of honor
    I stand aloof, and will no reconcilement
    Till by some elder masters of known honor   225
    I have a voice and president of peace
    To [keep] my name ungor'd. But [till] that time
    I do receive your offer'd love like love,
    And will not wrong it.
Hamlet: I embrace it freely,
    And will this brothers' wager frankly play.   230
    Give us the foils. [Come on.]
Laertes: Come, one for me.
Hamlet: I'll be your foil, Laertes; in mine ignorance
    Your skill shall like a star i' th' darkest night
    Stick fiery off indeed.
Laertes: You mock me, sir.
Hamlet: No, by this hand.   235
  King: Give them the foils, young Osric. Cousin Hamlet,
    You know the wager?
Hamlet: Very well, my lord.
    Your Grace has laid the odds a' th' weaker side.
  King: I do not fear it, I have seen you both;
    But since he is [better'd], we have therefore odds.   240
Laertes: This is too heavy; let me see another.
Hamlet: This likes me well. These foils have all a length?
                                   [Prepare to play.]
  Osric: Ay, my good lord.
  King: Set me the stoups of wine upon that table.
    If Hamlet give the first or second hit,   245
    Or quit in answer of the third exchange,
    Let all the battlements their ord'nance fire.
    The King shall drink to Hamlet's better breath,
    And in the cup an [union] shall he throw,

---

222. *in nature:* so far as my personal feelings are concerned.   223. *in . . . honor:* i.e. as a man
governed by an established code of honor.   226–27. *have . . . ungor'd:* can secure an opinion
backed by precedent that I can make peace with you without injury to my reputation.
230. *brothers':* i.e. amicable, as if between brothers. *frankly:* freely, without constraint.
232. *foil:* thin sheet of metal placed behind a jewel to set it off.   233. *Stick . . . off:* blaze out
in contrast.   238. *laid the odds:* i.e. wagered a higher stake (horses to rapiers).   240. *is*
better'd: has perfected his skill. *odds:* i.e. the arrangement that Laertes must take more bouts
than Hamlet to win.   242. *likes:* pleases. *a length:* the same length.   244. *stoups:* tankards.
246. *quit . . . exchange:* pays back wins by Laertes in the first and second bouts by taking the
third.   249. *union:* an especially fine pearl.

Richer than that which four successive kings   250
In Denmark's crown have worn. Give me the cups,
And let the kettle to the trumpet speak,
The trumpet to the cannoneer without,
The cannons to the heavens, the heaven to earth,
"Now the King drinks to Hamlet." Come begin;   255
                                          Trumpets the while.
And you, the judges, bear a wary eye.
Hamlet: Come on, sir.
Laertes: Come, my lord.

                              [*They play and* Hamlet *scores a hit.*]

Hamlet: One.
Laertes: No.
Hamlet: Judgment.
  Osric: A hit, a very palpable hit.
Laertes: Well, again.
   King: Stay, give me drink. Hamlet, this pearl is thine,
         Here's to thy health! Give him the cup.   260
Drum, trumpets [sound] flourish. A piece goes off [within].
Hamlet: I'll play this bout first, set it by a while.
         Come. [*They play again.*] Another hit; what say you?
Laertes: [A touch, a touch,] I do confess't.
   King: Our son shall win.
  Queen: He's fat, and scant of breath.
         Here, Hamlet, take my napkin, rub thy brows.   265
         The Queen carouses to thy fortune, Hamlet.
Hamlet: Good madam!
   King: Gertrude, do not drink.
  Queen: I will, my lord, I pray you pardon me.
   King: [*Aside.*] It is the pois'ned cup, it is too late.
Hamlet: I dare not drink yet, madam; by and by.   270
  Queen: Come, let me wipe thy face.
Laertes: My lord, I'll hit him now.
   King: I do not think't.
Laertes: [*Aside.*] And yet it is almost against my conscience.
Hamlet: Come, for the third, Laertes, you do but dally.
         I pray you pass with your best violence;   275
         I am sure you make a wanton of me.
Laertes: Say you so? Come on.   [*They play.*]
  Osric: Nothing, neither way.
Laertes: Have at you now!
         [Laertes *wounds* Hamlet; *then, in scuffling, they change rapiers.*]

---

252. *kettle:* kettle-drum. 264. *fat:* sweaty. 266. *carouses:* drinks a toast. 276. *make . . .*
me: i.e. are holding back in order to let me win, as one does with a spoiled child (*wanton*).

King:	Part them, they are incens'd.
Hamlet:	Nay, come again.

[Hamlet *wounds* Laertes. *The* Queen *falls.*]

Osric: Look to the Queen there ho!   280

Horatio: They bleed on both sides. How is it, my lord?

Osric: How is't, Laertes?

Laertes: Why, as a woodcock to mine own springe, Osric:
    I am justly kill'd with mine own treachery.

Hamlet: How does the Queen?

King: She sounds to see them bleed.   285

Queen: No, no, the drink, the drink—O my dear Hamlet—
    The drink, the drink! I am pois'ned.   *[Dies.]*

Hamlet: O villainy! Ho, let the door be lock'd!
    Treachery! Seek it out.

Laertes: It is here, Hamlet. [Hamlet,] thou art slain.   290
    No med'cine in the world can do thee good;
    In thee there is not half an hour's life.
    The treacherous instrument is in [thy] hand,
    Unbated and envenom'd. The foul practice
    Hath turn'd itself on me. Lo here I lie,   295
    Never to rise again. Thy mother's pois'ned.
    I can no more—the King, the King's to blame.

Hamlet: The point envenom'd too!
    Then, venom, to thy work.   [*Hurts the* King.]

All: Treason! treason!   300

King: O, yet defend me, friends, I am but hurt.

Hamlet: Here, thou incestious, [murd'rous], damned Dane,
    Drink [off] this potion! Is [thy union] here?
    Follow my mother!   [King *dies.*]

Laertes: He is justly served,
    It is a poison temper'd by himself.   305
    Exchange forgiveness with me, noble Hamlet.
    Mine and my father's death come not upon thee,
    Nor thine on me!   *[Dies.]*

Hamlet: Heaven make thee free of it! I follow thee.
    I am dead, Horatio. Wretched queen, adieu!   310
    You that look pale, and tremble at this chance,
    That are but mutes or audience to this act,
    Had I but time—as this fell sergeant, Death,
    Is strict in his arrest—O, I could tell you—
    But let it be. Horatio, I am dead,   315

---

283. *springe:* snare. 285. *sounds:* swoons. 294. *Unbated:* not blunted. *foul practice:* vile plot. 299. s.d. *Hurts:* wounds. 305. *temper'd:* mixed. 309. *make thee free:* absolve you. 312. *mutes or audience:* silent spectators. 313. *fell:* cruel. *sergeant:* sheriff's officer.

Thou livest. Report me and my cause aright
To the unsatisfied.
Horatio: Never believe it;
I am more an antique Roman than a Dane.
Here's yet some liquor left.
Hamlet: As th' art a man,
Give me the cup. Let go! By heaven, I'll ha't!   320
O God, Horatio, what a wounded name,
Things standing thus unknown, shall I leave behind me!
If thou didst ever hold me in thy heart,
Absent thee from felicity a while,
And in this harsh world draw thy breath in pain   325
To tell my story.   *A march afar off [and a shot within]*
What warlike noise is this?
[Osric *goes to the door and returns.*]
Osric: Young Fortinbras, with conquest come from Poland,
To th' embassadors of England gives
This warlike volley.
Hamlet: O, I die, Horatio,
The potent poison quite o'er-crows my spirit.   330
I cannot live to hear the news from England,
But I do prophesy th' election lights
On Fortinbras, he has my dying voice.
So tell him, with th' occurrents more and less
Which have solicited—the rest is silence.   *[Dies.]* 335
Horatio: Now cracks a noble heart. Good night, sweet prince,
And flights of angels sing thee to thy rest!   *[March within.]*
Why does the drum come hither?

Enter Fortinbras *with the* [English] *Embassadors,* [*with Drum, Colors, and Attendants*].

Fortinbras: Where is this sight?
Horatio: What is it you would see?
If aught of woe or wonder, cease your search.   340
Fortinbras: This quarry cries on havoc. O proud death,
What feast is toward in thine eternal cell,
That thou so many princes at a shot
So bloodily hast strook?
[1.] Embassador: The sight is dismal,
And our affairs from England come too late.   345
The ears are senseless that should give us hearing,

---

317. *antique Roman:* i.e. one who will commit suicide on such an occasion.   330. *o'ercrows:*
triumphs over (a term derived from cockfighting). *spirit:* vital energy.   333. *voice:* vote.
334. *occurrents:* occurrences.   335. *solicited:* instigated.   341. *This . . . havoc:* this heap of
corpses proclaims a massacre.   342. *toward:* in preparation.

To tell him his commandment is fulfill'd,
That Rosencrantz and Guildenstern are dead.
Where should we have our thanks?
Horatio: Not from his mouth,
Had it th' ability of life to thank you.   350
He never gave commandement for their death.
But since so jump upon this bloody question,
You from the Polack wars, and you from England,
Are here arrived, give order that these bodies
High on a stage be placed to the view,   355
And let me speak to [th'] yet unknowing world
How these things came about. So shall you hear
Of carnal, bloody, and unnatural acts,
Of accidental judgments, casual slaughters,
Of deaths put on by cunning and [forc'd] cause,   360
And in this upshot, purposes mistook
Fall'n on th' inventors' heads: all this can I
Truly deliver.
Fortinbras: Let us haste to hear it,
And call the noblest to the audience.
For me, with sorrow I embrace my fortune.   365
I have some rights, of memory in this kingdom,
Which now to claim my vantage doth invite me.
Horatio: Of that I shall have also cause to speak,
And from his mouth whose voice will draw [on] more.
But let this same be presently perform'd   370
Even while men's minds are wild, lest more mischance
On plots and errors happen.
Fortinbras: Let four captains
Bear Hamlet like a soldier to the stage,
For he was likely, had he been put on,
To have prov'd most royal; and for his passage,   375
The soldiers' music and the rite of war
Speak loudly for him.
Take up the bodies. Such a sight as this
Becomes the field, but here shows much amiss.
Go bid the soldiers shoot.   380

Exeunt [marching; after the which a peal of ordinance are shot off].

-----

349. *his:* i.e. the King's.   352. *jump:* precisely, pat. *question:* matter.   355. *stage:* platform.
359. *judgments:* retributions. *casual:* happening by chance.   360. *put on:* instigated.   366. *of
memory:* unforgotten.   367. *my vantage:* i.e. my opportune presence at a moment when the
throne is empty.   369. *his . . . more:* the mouth of one (Hamlet) whose vote will induce others
to support your claim.   370. *presently:* at once.   371. *wild:* distraught.   374. *put on:* put to
the test (by becoming king).   375. *passage:* death.   379. *Becomes . . . amiss:* befits the
battlefield, but appears very much out of place here.

Shakespearean tragedy differs so greatly from Greek tragedy and from modern tragedy that it is hard to find a single adequate definition of the genre. Most of us, if forced to attempt a definition, would be tempted to say that a tragedy is a sad play, one that ends in disaster. But as Arthur Miller points out, sadness (pathos) is not quite the issue. His much more penetrating definition of tragedy provides a particularly useful way to think about Hamlet.

"The knowledge that man . . . is capable of flowering on this earth": Arthur Miller

It is my view—or my prejudice—that when a man is seen whole and round and so characterized, when he is allowed his life on the stage over and beyond the mould and purpose of the story, hope will show its face in his, just as it does, even so dimly, in life. As the old saying has it, there is some good in the worst of us. I think that the tragedian, supposedly the saddest of citizens, can never forget this fact, and must strive always to posit a world in which that good might have been allowed to express itself instead of succumbing to the evil. I began by saying that tragedy would probably never be wholly defined. I end by offering you a definition. It is not final for me, but at least it has the virtue of keeping mere pathos out.

You are witnessing a tragedy when the characters before you are wholly and intensely realized, to the degree that your belief in their reality is all but complete. The story in which they are involved is such as to force their complete personalities to be brought to bear upon the problem, to the degree that you are able to understand not only why they are ending in sadness, but how they might have avoided their end. The demeanor, so to speak, of the story is most serious—so serious that you have been brought to the state of outright fear for the people involved, as though for yourself.

And all this, not merely so that your senses shall have been stretched and your glands stimulated, but that you may come away with the knowledge that man, by reason of his intense effort and desire, which you have just seen demonstrated, is capable of flowering on this earth.

Tragedy arises when we are in the presence of a man who has missed accomplishing his joy. But the joy must be there, the promise of the right way of life must be there. Otherwise pathos reigns, and an endless, meaningless, and essentially untrue picture of man is created—man helpless under the falling piano, man wholly lost in a universe which by its very nature is too hostile to be mastered.

WILLIAM SHAKESPEARE

(1564–1616)

MEASURE FOR MEASURE

edited by G. Blakemore Evans

CHARACTERS

Vincentio, the Duke
Angelo, the Deputy
Escalus, an ancient lord
Claudio, a young gentleman
Lucio, a fantastic
Two other like Gentlemen
Provost
Thomas ⎫
Peter ⎭ *two friars*
[Justice]
[Varrius]
Elbow, a simple constable
Froth, a foolish gentleman
[Pompey,] clown, [servant to Mistress Overdone]
Abhorson, an executioner
Barnardine, a dissolute prisoner
[Servant]
Isabella, sister to Claudio
Mariana, betrothed to Angelo
Juliet, beloved of Claudio
Francisca, a nun
Mistress Overdone, a bawd
[Lords, Officers, Citizens, Boy, and Attendants]

The Scene: *Vienna* [and its environs]

ACT I

Scene I

Enter Duke, Escalus, Lords, [*and* Attendants].

Words and passages enclosed in square brackets in the text above are either emendations of the copy-text or additions to it. The Textual Notes immediately following the play cite the earliest authority for every such change or insertion and supply the reading of the copy-text wherever it is emended in this edition.

I.i. Location: Vienna. The Duke's palace.

Duke: Escalus.

Escalus: My lord.

Duke: Of government the properties to unfold
Would seem in me t' affect speech and discourse,
Since I am put to know that your own science   5
Exceeds, in that, the lists of all advice
My strength can give you. Then no more remains
But that, to your sufficiency, as your worth is able,
And let them work. The nature of our people,
Our city's institutions, and the terms   10
For common justice, y' are as pregnant in
As art and practice hath enriched any
That we remember. There is our commission,
From which we would not have you warp. Call hither,
I say, bid come before us Angelo.   *[Exit an Attendant.]* 15
What figure of us think you he will bear?
For you must know, we have with special soul
Elected him our absence to supply,
Lent him our terror, dress'd him with our love,
And given his deputation all the organs   20
Of our own pow'r. What think you of it?

Escalus: If any in Vienna be of worth
To undergo such ample grace and honor,
It is Lord Angelo.

Enter Angelo.

Duke: Look where he comes.

Angelo: Always obedient to your Grace's will,   25
I come to know your pleasure.

Duke: Angelo:
There is a kind of character in thy life,

---

3. *Of . . . unfold:* to expound the qualities required for governing well.   4. *seem . . . discourse:* i.e. make me appear to be fond of talking for its own sake.   5. *put to know:* forced to recognize. *science:* expert knowledge.   6. *lists:* boundaries.   7. *strength:* capability. 8–9. *But . . . work:* A crux that has inspired many emendations, none satisfactory. To provide a referent for *them,* commentators have explained *sufficiency . . . worth* as "authority . . . qualifications" (or "qualifications . . . authority"), but in fact both words probably mean "qualifications." There is now wide agreement that a lacuna exists after *sufficiency,* or, less probably, after *able.*   9–11. *The nature . . . justice:* i.e. our social, political, and judicial usages. *Terms* probably means "modes of procedure." The Duke shifts in this sentence to the "royal" plural.   11. *pregnant:* ready, i.e. well versed.   12. *art:* study, theory.   14. *warp:* deviate.   16. *What . . . bear:* i.e. how do you think he will represent me as my deputy. The figure is of the royal likeness stamped on wax or metal to validate a seal or a coin.   17. *soul:* conviction (that the choice is right) (?).   18. *Elected . . . supply:* chosen him to fill my place in my absence.   19. *Lent . . . love:* i.e. bestowed on him the royal attributes that inspire terror and those that inspire love. Cf. the list of the "servants" of kings in *Henry VIII,* V.v. 48: "peace, plenty, love, truth, terror."   20. *his deputation:* to him as my deputy. *organs:* instruments.   23. *undergo:* sustain, bear up.   27. *character:* writing, i.e. clear indication

That to th' observer doth thy history
Fully unfold. Thyself and thy belongings
Are not thine own so proper as to waste   30
Thyself upon thy virtues, they on thee.
Heaven doth with us as we with torches do,
Not light them for themselves; for if our virtues
Did not go forth of us, 'twere all alike
As if we had them not. Spirits are not finely touch'd   35
But to fine issues; nor Nature never lends
The smallest scruple of her excellence,
But like a thrifty goddess, she determines
Herself the glory of a creditor,
Both thanks and use. But I do bend my speech   40
To one that can my art in him advertise.
Hold therefore, Angelo:
In our remove be thou at full ourself.
Mortality and mercy in Vienna
Live in thy tongue and heart. Old Escalus,   45
Though first in question, is thy secondary.
Take thy commission.
 Angelo: Now, good my lord,
Let there be some more test made of my mettle
Before so noble and so great a figure
Be stamp'd upon it.
 Duke: No more evasion.   50
We have with a leaven'd and prepared choice
Proceeded to you; therefore take your honors.
Our haste from hence is of so quick condition
That it prefers itself, and leaves unquestion'd
Matters of needful value. We shall write to you,   55
As time and our concernings shall importune,

28–29. *to . . . unfold:* i.e. enables an observer to predict what your future behavior will be.
This is Johnson's explanation, strongly supported by *2 Henry IV*, III.i.80–85.   29. *belongings:*
qualities, attributes (the *virtues* of line 31).   30. *proper:* exclusively.   *waste:* expend.   34. *all
alike:* precisely the same.   35. *finely touch'd:* excellently endowed (with play on testing gold
for fineness by means of a touchstone).   36. *issues:* purposes, ends.   37. *scruple:* a very small
unit of weight.   38. *determines:* allots (to).   39. *glory:* proud due.   40. *use:* interest.
41. *can . . . advertise:* can instruct that part of me now vested in him, i.e. knows more about
how to govern than I can tell him (cf. lines 5–7). *Advertise* is accented on the second syllable.
42. *Hold:* i.e. maintain your worthiness (?) or take this (the document, as in lines 13, 47) (?).
43. *remove:* absence.   *at full:* Perhaps with play on *part* in line 41.   44. *Mortality and mercy:*
i.e. authority to pronounce sentence of death and freedom to temper justice with mercy. Cf.
terror . . . love in line 19.   45. *tongue and heart:* With reference to *Mortality* and *mercy*
respectively.   46. *first in question:* i.e. first appointed.   48. *mettle:* In Elizabethan English
mettle and *metal* were variants of the same word, with primary meaning "substance." Here the
sense now spelled *metal* carries on the coining imagery of lines 16, 35–36.   51. *leaven'd:* i.e.
pervaded by the gradual working of judgment (like the action of yeast in dough).   53. *so
quick condition:* so urgent a nature.   54. *prefers:* advances, gives priority to.   *unquestion'd:*
undiscussed, uninvestigated.   56. *our concernings:* matters of concern to us.   *importune:* urge,
require.

How it goes with us, and do look to know
What doth befall you here. So fare you well.
To th' hopeful execution do I leave you
Of your commissions.

Angelo: Yet give leave, my lord,   60
That we may bring you something on the way.

Duke: My haste may not admit it,
Nor need you (on mine honor) have to do
With any scruple. Your scope is as mine own,
So to enforce or qualify the laws   65
As to your soul seems good. Give me your hand,
I'll privily away. I love the people,
But do not like to stage me to their eyes;
Though it do well, I do not relish well
Their loud applause and aves vehement;   70
Nor do I think the man of safe discretion
That does affect it. Once more fare you well.

Angelo: The heavens give safety to your purposes!

Escalus: Lead forth and bring you back in happiness!

Duke: I thank you. Fare you well.   *Exit.*   75

Escalus: I shall desire you, sir, to give me leave
To have free speech with you; and it concerns me
To look into the bottom of my place.
A pow'r I have, but of what strength and nature
I am not yet instructed.   80

Angelo: 'Tis so with me. Let us withdraw together,
And we may soon our satisfaction have
Touching that point.

Escalus: I'll wait upon your honor.   *Exeunt.*

Scene II

Enter Lucio *and two other* Gentlemen.

Lucio: If the Duke with the other dukes come not to composition with the King of Hungary, why then all the
dukes fall upon the King.

---

57. *look to know:* expect to be informed of.   59. *hopeful:* A transferred modifier, rightly
describing the Duke's expectations.   61. *bring . . . way:* escort you some distance on your
way.   64. *scruple:* misgiving.   *scope:* freedom to act; here, breadth of authority (a word that
occurs five times in this play).   65. *enforce or qualify:* i.e. apply with greater or lesser
severity.   67–72. *I . . . it:* Usually taken to allude to King James's dislike of effusive English
crowds. See II.iv.24–30.   68. *stage me:* make public show of myself.   69. *do well:* i.e. show
their good will.   70. *aves:* acclamations (Latin *ave,* "hail," connected with acclaim of
Caesar).   71. *safe discretion:* sound judgment.   72. *does affect:* is fond of.   73. *give safety to:*
protect, safeguard.   77. *free:* frank.   78. *look . . . place:* determine how far my duties and
authority extend.   82. *satisfaction:* dispelling of uncertainty.   83. *wait upon:* attend,
accompany.

I.ii. Location: A street.   1–2. *composition:* agreement, treaty.

1. Gentleman: Heaven grant us its peace, but not the King of
Hungary's!   5
2. Gentleman: Amen.
Lucio: Though conclud'st like the sanctimonious pirate,
that went to sea with the Ten Commandements, but
scrap'd one out of the table.
2. Gentleman: "Thou shalt not steal"?   10
Lucio: Ay, that he raz'd.
1. Gentleman: Why, 'twas a commandement to command the captain and all the rest from their functions; they put forth
to steal. There's not a soldier of us all, that in the
thanksgiving before meat, do relish the petition well   15
that prays for peace.
2. Gentleman: I never heard any soldier dislike it.
Lucio: I believe thee; for I think thou never wast where
grace was said.
2. Gentleman: No? a dozen times at least.   20
1. Gentleman: What? in metre?
Lucio: In any proportion, or in any language.
1 Gentleman: I think, or in any religion.
Lucio: Ay, why not? Grace is grace, despite of all controversy; as for example, thou thyself art a wicked villain, 25
despite of all grace.
1. Gentleman: Well; there went but a pair of shears between us.
Lucio: I grant; as there may between the lists and the velvet. Thou art the list.
1. Gentleman: And thou the velvet—thou art good velvet; thou'rt a 30
three-pil'd piece, I warrant thee. I had as lief be a list of
an English kersey as be pil'd, as thou art pil'd, for a
French velvet. Do I speak feelingly now?

---

4. *its:* With the exception of one occurrence in *2 Henry VI* (III.ii.393), this is Shakespeare's
earliest recorded use of *its*, in a total of eleven. Elsewhere, save for an occasional appearance
of *it* (as in *King Lear*, I.iv.216), he uses *his* as the possessive form of *it*.   7. *sanctimonious:* The
earliest example of the modern ironic sense listed in *O.E.D.*: the word's only other occurrence
in Shakespeare—*sanctimonious ceremonies* in *The Tempest*, IV.i.16—shows the original
straightforward meaning "marked by sanctity."   8. *Commandements:* A variant spelling,
perhaps here (as often in verse) quadrisyllabic.   9. *table:* tablet (referring to the tablets of
stone on which the Ten Commandments were traditionally represented).   11. *raz'd:* erased,
"scrap'd out."   13. *functions:* professional duties. Leisi sees an extended wordplay on *steal*
stale (= urinate), *functions*, and *put forth*.   17. *dislike:* express dislike of.   22. *proportion:*
form.   24–26. *Grace . . . grace.* Lucio shifts the sense of *grace* to "God's grace": grace
remains grace despite all the debates about its nature—just as, to cite a parallel, in you villainy
remains villainy despite the availability of grace.   27. *Well:* Often used to show that note has
been taken of an insult; cf. line 55.   *there . . . us:* we are cut from the same cloth (proverbial).   28. *lists:* selvages, plain strips along the edge (from the basic sense "boundaries" seen
in I.i.6).   31. *three-pil'd:* having a pile or nap of triple thickness.   *lief:* willingly.   32. *kersey:*
plain woollen fabric (named for Kersey in Suffolk, where it was first made).   *pil'd:* Lucio
plays on *piled*, "napped," and *pilled*, "bald." Loss of hair was an effect of the treatment for
syphilis, which was called the "French disease"—hence *French velvet* in line 33.   33. *speak*
feelingly: speak to the purpose, i.e. touch the quick; but Lucio quibbles on "speak painfully"
(i.e. because his mouth is affected by the lesions of venereal disease).

Lucio: I think thou dost; and indeed with most painful feel-
　　　　　　ing of thy speech. I will, out of thine own confession, 35
　　　　　　learn to begin thy health; but, whilst I live, forget to
　　　　　　drink after thee.
1. Gentleman: I think I have done myself wrong, have I not?
2. Gentleman: Yes, that thou hast; whether thou art tainted or free.

Enter Bawd [Mistress Overdone].

Lucio: Behold, behold, where Madam Mitigation comes! 40
[1. Gentleman:] I have purchas'd many diseases under her roof as
　　　　　　come to—
2. Gentleman: To what, I pray?
Lucio: Judge.
2. Gentleman: To three thousand dolors a year. 45
1. Gentleman: Ay, and more.
Lucio: A French crown more.
1. Gentleman: Thou art always figuring diseases in me; but thou art
　　　　　　full of error, I am sound.
Lucio: Nay, not (as one would say) healthy; but so sound as 50
　　　　　　things that are hollow. Thy bones are hollow; impiety
　　　　　　has made a feast of thee.
1. Gentleman: How now, which of your hips has the most profound
　　　　　　sciatica?
Mistress Overdone: Well, well; there's one yonder arrested and carried 55
　　　　　　to prison was worth five thousand of you all.
2. Gentleman: Who's that, I pray thee?
Mistress Overdone: Marry, sir, that's Claudio, Signior Claudio.
1. Gentleman: Claudio to prison? 'tis not so.
Mistress Overdone: Nay, but I know 'tis so. I saw him arrested; saw him 60
　　　　　　carried away; and which is more, within these three days
　　　　　　his head to be chopp'd off.
Lucio: But after all this fooling, I would not have it so. Art
　　　　　　thou sure of this?
Mistress Overdone: I am too sure of it; and it is for getting Madam 65
　　　　　　Julietta with child.
Lucio: Believe me, this may be. He promis'd to meet me

---

36. *begin thy health:* begin drinking to your health.   36–37. *forget . . . thee:* remember not to
drink out of your glass.   38. *done myself wrong:* i.e. laid myself open to that.   39. *tainted:*
infected (in which case he has "done himself wrong" in a different sense).   44. *Mitigation:* So
called because she allays sexual desire.   45. *dolors:* (1) pains; (2) dollars (continental coins).
47. *French crown:* (1) French gold coin; (2) bald head (in consequence of the "French
disease").   48. *figuring:* (1) reckoning (with reference to the preceding lines); (2) imagining.
50. *sound:* resounding.   51. *Thy . . . hollow:* Another effect of syphilis.   53. *How now:*
Probably addressed to Mrs. Overdone; "How now" is a casual greeting, and sciatica (another
supposed effect of venereal disease) is elsewhere associated with bawds.   55. *one yonder:* a
man back there (not limited to what is in view).   *carried:* conducted.   58. *Marry:* indeed
(originally the name of the Virgin Mary used as an oath).   *after . . . fooling:* to return to
seriousness.

two hours since, and he was ever precise in
promise-keeping.
2. *Gentleman:* Beside, you know, it draws something near to the 70
speech we had to such a purpose.
1. *Gentleman:* But most of all agreeing with the proclamation.
Lucio: Away! let's go learn the truth of it.

Exit [with Gentlemen].

Mistress Overdone: Thus, what with the war, what with the sweat, what
with the gallows, and what with poverty, I am 75
custom-shrunk.

Enter Clown [Pompey].

How now? what's the news with you?
Pompey: Yonder man is carried to prison.
Mistress Overdone: Well; what has he done?
Pompey: A woman. 80
Mistress Overdone: But what's his offense?
Pompey: Groping for trouts in a peculiar river.
Mistress Overdone: What? is there a maid with child by him?
Pompey: No; but there's a woman with maid by him.
You have not heard of the proclamation, have you? 85
Mistress Overdone: What proclamation, man?
Pompey: All houses in the suburbs of Vienna must be
pluck'd down.
Mistress Overdone: And what shall become of those in the city?
Pompey: They shall stand for seed. They had gone down too, 90
but that a wise burgher put in for them.
Mistress Overdone: But shall all our houses of resort in the suburbs be
pull'd down?
Pompey: To the ground, mistress.

70–71. *draws . . . purpose:* fits fairly closely with the conversation we had about that situation
(i.e. the relation between Claudio and Juliet? or the increasing rigor of law enforcement?).
72. *proclamation:* Apparently the public announcement of the revived penalty for fornication.   74. *sweat:* sweating sickness, a form of the plague (which had been rampant in 1603
and until the middle of 1604).   76. *custom-shrunk:* short on customers.   78. *Yonder man:* This
cannot be anyone but Claudio, since later we hear repeatedly that he is the first and still the
only victim of the new dispensation. Mrs. Overdone's ignorance of his arrest (an event which
she herself has announced shortly before), together with other obvious discrepancies, has
been made the basis of various theories of revision.   79. *done:* Pompey quibbles on the slang
sense "copulated" (a sense to which Mrs. Overdone's name is related).   82. *peculiar:* private
(i.e. where fishing is against the law).   84. *with maid:* Playing on *maid* = young fish (suggested
by the trouts of line 82).   87. *houses:* i.e. houses of prostitution.   *suburbs:* The site of the
London brothels (which were thus beyond the reach of city regulations).   88. *pluck'd:*
pulled.   90. *stand for seed:* remain standing to assure the continuance of prostitution (like
grain left uncut to provide seed for another season), with a bawdy equivoque.   91. *put . . .
them:* intervened in their behalf (?) or made an offer for their purchase (?).

Mistress Overdone: Why, here's a change indeed in the commonwealth! 95
What shall become of me?

Pompey: Come; fear not you; good counsellors lack no
clients. Though you change your place, you need not
change your trade; I'll be your tapster still. Courage!
there will be pity taken on you. You that have worn your 100
eyes almost out in the service, you will be consider'd.

Mistress Overdone: What's to do here, Thomas tapster? Let's withdraw.

Pompey: Here comes Signior Claudio, led by the Provost to
prison; and there's Madam Juliet.   *Exeunt.*

Enter Provost, Claudio, Juliet, Officers.

Claudio: Fellow, why dost thou show me thus to th' world? 105
Bear me to prison, where I am committed.

Provost: I do it not in evil disposition,
But from Lord Angelo by special charge.

Claudio: Thus can the demigod, Authority,
Make us pay down for our offense by weight   110
The words of heaven: on whom it will, it will;
On whom it will not, so; yet still 'tis just.

[Enter] Lucio *and two* Gentlemen.

Lucio: Why, how now, Claudio? whence comes this
restraint?

Claudio: From too much liberty, my Lucio, liberty: 115
As surfeit is the father of much fast,
So every scope by the immoderate use
Turns to restraint. Our natures do pursue,
Like rats that ravin down their proper bane,
A thirsty evil, and when we drink we die.   120

Lucio: If I could speak so wisely under an arrest, I would
send for certain of my creditors; and yet, to say the
truth, I had as lief have the foppery of freedom as the

---

102. *What's to do here:* what to-do is this.   *Thomas tapster:* A stock name for a tapster; but
Shakespeare may have changed his mind about Pompey's name.   109. *the demigod, Authority:*
Reflecting the Elizabethan view of earthly rulers and magistrates as God's viceregents.
110–11. *pay . . . heaven:* The oddness of *pay down . . . the words of heaven* has provoked various
emendations. Johnson conjectured a lacuna between the two lines. If a period is placed after
weight, lines 109–10. make a complete sentence; *pay down by weight* = pay the precise amount
due.   111. *words of heaven:* Explained as a reference to Romans 9:15: "I will have mercy on
him to whom I will show mercy" (Geneva).   112. *so:* similarly, i.e. it will not.   *still:* always, in
every case.   113–15. *whence . . . restraint:* This is inconsistent with lines 55 ff., where Lucio
learns of Claudio's arrest and its cause.   117. *scope:* freedom (see note on I.i.64).   119. *ravin
down:* devour greedily.   *proper bane:* particular poison.   120. *A thirsty . . die:* Rat poison
does not kill directly; it makes the rat thirsty, and taking water is fatal. So too much liberty
stimulates lust, and the satisfying of lust incurs death.   122. *send . . . creditors:* i.e. take steps
to bring about my own arrest.   123. *foppery:* folly.

                    mortality of imprisonment.   What's thy offense,
                    Claudio?   125
    Claudio: What but to speak of would offend again.
      Lucio: What, is't murder?
    Claudio: No.
      Lucio: Lechery?
    Claudio: Call it so.   130
     Provost: Away, sir, you must go.
    Claudio: One word, good friend. Lucio, a word with you.
      Lucio: A hundred! if they'll do you any good.
                    Is lechery so look'd after?
    Claudio: Thus stands it with me: upon a true contract.   135
                    I got possession of Julietta's bed.
                    You know the lady; she is fast my wife,
                    Save that we do the denunciation lack
                    Of outward order. This we came not to,
                    Only for propagation of a dow'r   140
                    Remaining in the coffer of her friends,
                    From whom we thought it meet to hide our love
                    Till time had made them for us. But it chances
                    The stealth of our most mutual entertainment
                    With character too gross is writ on Juliet.   145
      Lucio: With child, perhaps?
    Claudio: Unhappily, even so.
                    And the new deputy now for the Duke—
                    Whether it be the fault and glimpse of newness,
                    Or whether that the body public be
                    A horse whereon the governor doth ride,   150
                    Who, newly in the seat, that it may know
                    He can command, lets it straight feel the spur;
                    Whether the tyranny be in his place,
                    Or in his eminence that fills it up,

---

124. *mortality:* being subject to death (?) or deadliness (?). Most editors from Rowe onward emend to *morality,* "moralizing talk," which provides an apt antithesis to *foppery* in the sense "idle talk." Shakespeare never uses the word *morality* elsewhere, but he does not use *mortality* in the precise sense required here either.   134. *look'd after:* kept watch upon.   135. *a true contract:* Claudio and Juliet have declared themselves husband and wife in the presence of witnesses. Under the common law such a declaration created a valid marriage *(sponsalia per verba de praesenti),* but the church required a religious ceremony before such a marriage could be consummated without incurring a penalty.   137. *fast:* firmly bound (perhaps with reference to making a contract of marriage by handfasting or joining hands).   138. *denunciation:* public announcement.   140. *propagation:* breeding, bringing to birth. Many editors adopt Malone's conjecture *prorogation,* i.e. delay; but figures of breeding and pregnancy are frequent in the play.   141. *friends:* relatives.   143. *made . . . us:* won them to our side.
145. *character:* writing, letters.   *gross:* large, obvious.   148. *Whether . . . newness:* i.e. whether it is the sudden brilliance *(glimpse)* of his new honor that is to blame.   152. *straight:* straightway.   153. *in his place:* inherent in his office.   154. *eminence:* distinction, superiority.

I stagger in—but this new governor   155
Awakes me all the enrolled penalties
Which have, like unscour'd armor, hung by th' wall
So long that nineteen zodiacs have gone round
And none of them been worn; and for a name
Now puts the drowsy and neglected act   160
Freshly on me—'tis surely for a name.
   Lucio: I warrant it is; and thy head stands so tickle on thy
      shoulders that the milkmaid, if she be in love, may sigh it
      off. Send after the Duke, and appeal to him.
   Claudio: I have done so, but he's not to be found.
I prithee, Lucio, do me this kind service: 165
This day my sister should the cloister enter,
And there receive her approbation.
Acquaint her with the danger of my state;
Implore her, in my voice, that she make friends   170
To the strict deputy; bid herself assay him.
I have great hope in that; for in her youth
There is a prone and speechless dialect,
Such as move men; beside, she hath prosperous art
When she will play with reason and discourse,   175
And well she can persuade.
   Lucio: I pray she may; as well for the encouragement of the
      like, which else would stand under grievous imposition,
      as for the enjoying of thy life, who I would be sorry
      should be thus foolishly lost at a game of tick-tack. I'll to 180
      her.
   Claudio: I thank you, good friend Lucio.
   Lucio: Within two hours.
   Claudio: Come, officer, away!   *Exeunt.*

---

155. *stagger in:* am at a loss to decide.   156. *Awakes me:* awakes (a colloquialism). The
figure is continued in *drowsy,* line 160.   157. *unscour'd:* unpolished, i.e. rusty.   158. *zodiacs
. . . round:* i.e. years have passed.   159. *worn:* i.e. used (continuing the parallel between
penalties and armor; cf. *puts . . . on,* lines 160–61).   *for a name:* for the sake of his reputation.   162. *tickle:* unstable, precariously attached.   163–64. *a milkmaid . . . off:* i.e. the merest breath of wind (a lovesick milkmaid's sigh) will blow it off (?). But the combination of
milkmaid and *head* suggests a common play on *head* = maidenhead (as in IV.ii.4), and the passage may be an elliptical way of saying "a milkmaid, if her virginity were as unstable as your
head, would lose it with her first sigh of love."   167. *approbation:* probation, novice's
status.   170. *in my voice:* i.e. as persuasively as I would.   181. *assay him:* make trial of him (?)
or assail him with words (?). Probably both senses are present: try how he will respond to your
urging.   173. *prone:* eager, ready (?) or apt, expressive (?). Some commentators take the
word to suggest the prostrate or bowed posture of supplication, but Shakespeare never uses
prone in the sense of "recumbent."   174. *move:* Plural after a singular noun modified by two
adjectives; for another example see III.i.128–29.   177–78. *encouragement . . . like:* giving
comfort to offenders like yourself.   178. *which:* who (as often).   *stand . . . imposition:* be subject to very serious accusation.   180. *tick-tack:* a game resembling backgammon, scored by
means of pegs set into holes; here, sexual intercourse.

Scene [III]

Enter Duke *and* Friar Thomas.

> *Duke:* No; holy father, throw away that thought;
> Believe not that the dribbling dart of love
> Can pierce a complete bosom. Why I desire thee
> To give me secret harbor, hath a purpose
> More grave and wrinkled than the aims and ends   5
> Of burning youth.
>
> *Friar Thomas:*   May your Grace speak of it?
> *Duke:* My holy sir, none better knows than you
> How I have ever lov'd the life removed,
> And held in idle price to haunt assemblies
> Where youth, and cost, witless bravery keeps.   10
> I have deliver'd to Lord Angelo
> (A man of stricture and firm abstinence)
> My absolute power and place here in Vienna,
> And he supposes me travell'd to Poland
> (For so I have strew'd it in the common ear,   15
> And so it is receiv'd). Now, pious sir,
> You will demand of me why I do this.
>
> *Friar Thomas:* Gladly, my lord.
> *Duke:* We have strict statutes and most biting laws
> (The needful bits and curbs to headstrong weeds),   20
> Which for this fourteen years we have let slip,
> Even like an o'ergrown lion in a cave,
> That goes not to prey. Now, as fond fathers,
> Having bound up the threat'ning twigs of birch,
> Only to stick it in their children's sight   25
> For terror, not to use, in time the rod

I.iii. Location: A friary.
2. *dribbling:* falling too feebly to pierce its mark.   3. *complete:* fully defended (as if in complete armor, hence invulnerable).   5. *wrinkled:* i.e. befitting one of mature years.
8. *removed:* secluded, private.   9. *in idle price:* as of trifling value.   10. *cost:* lavish expenditure.   *bravery:* display. Many editors improve the metre by inserting *a* before *witless bravery.* *keeps:* maintains. The verb in *-s* with a plural subject is common in Shakespeare.   12. *stricture:* strictness, keeping a tight rein (on oneself).   15. *strew'd:* scattered (an image from sowing seed).   *common:* general.   16. *receiv'd:* accepted, believed.   17. *demand:* ask (without the modern note of peremptoriness).   20. *weeds.* A type of lawlessness, because of their rank growth and resistance to control. Almost all editors, however, find the metaphor too mixed even for Shakespeare, and emend—most often to *steeds* (Theobald), which fits well with *bits and curbs,* but is unlikely to have been mistaken for *weeds* by a compositor. More attractive is *wills* (S. Walker), which with *curb* produces a figure found elsewhere in Shakespeare, e.g. in *The Merchant of Venice,* IV.i.215–17, where *law, curb* (verb), and *will* are found in conjunction.
21. *fourteen:* Cf. *nineteen zodiacs* in I.ii.158. The discrepancy could have arisen from a confusion of *xiv* and *xix* in the manuscript.   *let slip:* allowed to go lax, i.e. left unapplied.
22. *o'ergrown:* grown too fat, hence inactive.   23. *fond:* foolish, doting.   25. it: i.e. the switch made up of the twigs.

[Becomes] more mock'd than fear'd; so our decrees,
Dead to infliction, to themselves are dead,
And liberty plucks justice by the nose;
The baby beats the nurse, and quite athwart   30
Goes all decorum.

Friar Thomas: It rested in your Grace
To unloose this tied-up justice when you pleas'd:
And it in you more dreadful would have seem'd
Than in Lord Angelo.

Duke: I do fear—too dreadful;
Sith 'twas my fault to give the people scope,   35
'Twould be my tyranny to strike and gall them
For what I bid them do; for we bid this be done,
When evil deeds have their permissive pass,
And not the punishment. Therefore indeed, my father,
I have on Angelo impos'd the office,   40
Who may, in th' ambush of my name, strike home,
And yet my nature never in the fight
To do in slander. And to behold his sway,
I will, as 'twere a brother of your order,
Visit both prince and people; therefore I prithee   45
Supply me with the habit, and instruct me
How I may formally in person bear
Like a true friar. Moe reasons for this action
At our more leisure shall I render you;
Only, this one: Lord Angelo is precise;   50
Stands at a guard with envy; scarce confesses
That his blood flows; or that his appetite
Is more to bread than stone: hence shall we see
If power change purpose: what our seemers be. *Exeunt.*

---

28. *Dead . . . dead:* since they are not enforced, are as if non-existent.   29. *liberty:* license.
plucks . . . nose: An action indicating the highest degree of contempt and defiance.
30. *athwart:* contrary, topsyturvey.   31. *decorum:* appropriateness of behavior.   32. *tied-up:*
leashed (but also recalling the bound-up birch twigs).   33. *dreadful:* inspiring a proper terror
of punishment (cf. *terror* in line 26 and, as a royal attribute, in I.i.19).   35. *Sith:* since.
36. *strike and gall:* Recalling respectively "twigs of birch" and "bits and curbs" (*gall* = chafe,
cause physical irritation).   37. *we . . . done:* i.e. it is tantamount to ordering that a thing be
done.   41. *in th' ambush:* under cover.   *home:* to the target.   42. *nature:* i.e. person
(contrasted with *name*).   43. *do in slander:* put in disrepute.   45. *prince:* the one who has
sovereign power, i.e. Angelo.   47. *formally:* in external appearance and demeanor.   *bear:*
comport (myself).   48–49. *Moe . . . more:* more in number . . . greater in amount.
50. *precise:* punctiliously correct in manners and morals; in Shakespeare's day, often applied
to Puritans.   51. *Stands . . with:* maintains a wary defense against (a fencing term).   *envy:*
malice.   52–53. *that . . . stone:* i.e. that he has any sensual desires.   54. *If . . . be:* i.e. whether
possession of power will alter intention, and whether certain persons are what they seem to
be.

Scene [IV]

Enter Isabella *and* Francisca, *a nun.*

> *Isabella:* And have you nuns no farther privileges?
> *Francisca:* Are not these large enough?
> *Isabella:* Yes, truly; I speak not as desiring more,
>   But rather wishing a more strict restraint
>   Upon the sisterhood, the votarists of Saint Clare.   5
> *Lucio:* (*Within.*) Ho! Peace be in this place!
> *Isabella:* Who's that which calls?
> *Francisca:* It is a man's voice. Gentle Isabella,
>   Turn you the key, and know his business of him;
>   You may, I may not; you are yet unsworn.
>   When you have vow'd, you must not speak with men   10
>   But in the presence of the prioress;
>   Then if you speak, you must not show your face,
>   Or if you show your face, you must not speak.
>   He calls again; I pray you answer him.   *[Exit]* 15
> *Isabella:* Peace and prosperity! Who is't that calls?

[*Enter* Lucio.]

> *Lucio:* Hail, virgin, if you be, as those cheek-roses
>   Proclaim you are no less! Can you so stead me
>   As bring me to the sight of Isabella,
>   A novice of this place, and the fair sister   20
>   To her unhappy brother Claudio?
> *Isabella:* Why "her unhappy brother"? let me ask,
>   The rather for I now must make you know
>   I am that Isabella, and his sister.
> *Lucio:* Gentle and fair, your brother kindly greets you.   25
>   Not to be weary with you, he's in prison.
> *Isabella:* Woe me! for what?
> *Lucio:* For that which, if myself might be his judge,
>   He should receive his punishment in thanks:
>   He hath got his friend with child.   30
> *Isabella:* Sir, make me not your story.
> *Lucio:*   'Tis true.
>   I would not—though 'tis my familiar sin

I.iv. Location: A nunnery. *o.s.d. Isabel:* Although commentators on the play always refer to its heroine as Isabella, that form of her name appears only five times in the dialogue (three times in this scene). *Isabel* five times as often though only twice in the stage directions. There is a similar variation of *Juliet / Julietta.*   2. *large:* liberal.   5. *Saint Clare:* thirteenth-century foundress of an order of nuns (the Franciscan "poor Clares") having a rule of extreme austerity.   18. *stead:* help.   26. *weary:* wearisome.   30. *friend:* sweetheart.   31. *story:* i.e. theme for jesting or deception.

With maids to seem the lapwing, and to jest,
Tongue far from heart—play with all virgins so.
I hold you as a thing enskied, and sainted,   35
By your renouncement an immortal spirit,
And to be talk'd with in sincerity,
As with a saint.
Isabella: You do blaspheme the good in mocking me.
  Lucio: Do not believe it. Fewness and truth, 'tis thus: 40
Your brother and his lover have embrac'd.
As those that feed grow full, as blossoming time
That from the seedness the bare fallow brings
To teeming foison, even so her plenteous womb
Expresseth his full tilth and husbandry.   45
Isabella: Some one with child by him? My cousin Juliet?
  Lucio: Is she your cousin?
Isabella: Adoptedly, as school-maids change their names
By vain though apt affection.
  Lucio: She it is.
Isabella: O, let him marry her.
  Lucio: This is the point.   50
The Duke is very strangely gone from hence;
Bore many gentlemen (myself being one)
In hand, and hope of action; but we do learn
By those that know the very nerves of state,
His [givings]-out were of an infinite distance   55
From his true-meant design. Upon his place,
And with full line of his authority,
Governs Lord Angelo, a man whose blood
Is very snow-broth; one who never feels
The wanton stings and motions of the sense;
But doth rebate and blunt his natural edge   60
With profits of the mind: study and fast.
He (to give fear to use and liberty,
Which have for long run by the hideous law,

---

33. *lapwing:* This bird misled predators about the whereabouts of its young by fluttering
about at some distance from the nest.   35. *enskied:* dwelling in heaven.   39. *You . . . me:* in
mockingly calling me a saint you blaspheme against the true saints.   40. *Fewness and truth:* to
speak briefly and truthfully.   43. *seedness:* state or time of being sown.   44. *foison:*
abundance, i.e. harvest.   *plenteous:* fruitful.   45. *tilth:* tillage.   *husbandry:* (1) tillage: (2)
husband's duties. Cf. Sonnet 3.5–6.   48. *change:* exchange.   49. *vain:* idle, i.e. producing
no change in their relationship.   *apt:* i.e. natural to their age.   52–53. *Bore . . . action:* i.e.
mislead them about his intentions so that they kept expecting to see military action; a
telescoping of *bore in hand* (= deluded) and *bore in hope* (= maintained in expectation).
54. *nerves:* sinews, i.e. inner workings.   *state:* policy.   57. *full line:* free range (as of a tether
so long that it imposes no restraint).   58. *snow-broth:* melted snow.   59. *motions:* urgings.
60. *rebate.* Synonymous with *blunt.*   *edge:* keenness of desire.   62. *use and liberty:* license that
has become customary.

As mice by lions) hath pick'd out an act,   65
Under whose heavy sense your brother's life
Falls into forfeit; he arrests him on it,
And follows close the rigor of the statute,
To make him an example. All hope is gone,
Unless you have the grace by your fair prayer   70
To soften Angelo. And that's my pith
Of business 'twixt you and your poor brother.

Isabella: Doth he so seek his life?

  Lucio: H'as censur'd him
Already, and as I hear, the Provost hath
A warrant for's execution.   75

Isabella: Alas, what poor ability's in me
To do him good!

  Lucio: Assay the pow'r you have.

Isabella: My power? Alas, I doubt—

  Lucio: Our doubts are traitors,
And makes us lose the good we oft might win,
By fearing to attempt. Go to Lord Angelo,   80
And let him learn to know, when maidens sue,
Men give like gods; but when they weep and kneel,
All their petitions are as freely theirs
As they themselves would owe them.

Isabella: I'll see what I can do.

  Lucio: But speedily.   85

Isabella: I will about it straight:
No longer staying but to give the Mother
Notice of my affair. I humbly thank you.
Commend me to my brother. Soon at night
I'll send him certain word of my success.   90

  Lucio: I take my leave of you.

Isabella: Good sir, adieu.

                       Exeunt [severally].

ACT II

Scene I

Enter Angelo, Escalus, *and* Servants, Justice.

  Angelo: We must not make a scarecrow of the law,
Setting it up to fear the birds of prey,

---

65. *act:* law.   66. *heavy sense:* severe tenor.   71–72. *my . . . business:* the heart of my errand.   73. *H'as censur'd:* he has passed judgment.   83. *their petitions:* the things they sue for.   84. *owe:* own.   89. *Commend me:* give my loving greetings. *Soon at night:* early this evening.   90. *certain . . . success:* definite word of the outcome.

II.i. Location: A court of justice.   2. *fear:* frighten.

And let it keep one shape, till custom make it
Their perch and not their terror.

Escalus: Ay, but yet
Let us be keen, and rather cut a little,   5
Than fall, and bruise to death. Alas, this gentleman,
Whom I would save, had a most noble father!
Let but your honor know
(Whom I believe to be most strait in virtue)
That in the working of your own affections,   10
Had time coher'd with place, or place with wishing,
Or that the resolute acting of [your] blood
Could have attain'd th' effect of your own purpose,
Whether you had not sometime in your life
Err'd in this point which now you censure him,   15
And pull'd the law upon you.

Angelo: 'Tis one thing to be tempted, Escalus,
Another thing to fall. I not deny
The jury, passing on the prisoner's life,
May in the sworn twelve have a thief or two   20
Guiltier than him they try. What's open made to justice,
That justice seizes. What knows the laws
That thieves do pass on thieves? 'Tis very pregnant,
The jewel that we find, we stoop and take't,
Because we see it; but what we do not see   25
We tread upon, and never think of it.
You may not so extenuate his offense
For I have had such faults; but rather tell me,
When I, that censure him, do so offend,
Let mine own judgment pattern out my death,   30
And nothing come in partial. Sir, he must die.

Enter Provost.

Escalus: Be it as your wisdom will.
Angelo: Where is the Provost?
Provost: Here, if it like your honor.
Angelo: See that Claudio
Be executed by nine to-morrow morning.

---

5. *keen:* sharp.   6. *fall:* Like bludgeons or heavy weights.   *bruise:* i.e. crush.   8. *know:*
consider and decide.   10. *affections:* desires.   12. *that:* i.e. if (repeating the conditional sense
of *Had time,* line 11).   *blood:* passions.   13. *effect:* effectuation, fulfillment.   14. *had not:*
would not have.   15. *which:* for which.   *censure:* condemn.   20. *thief:* Often used in the
more general sense "criminal."   21. *open:* manifest.   22. *What . . . laws:* how can the laws
take cognizance.   23. *pregnant:* readily perceived, obvious.   28. *For:* because.   30. *judgment:* sentence (decreed for Claudio).   *pattern out:* be the precedent for.   31. *come in partial:*
be admitted in my favor.   33. *like:* please.

Bring him his confessor, let him be prepar'd,   35
For that's the utmost of his pilgrimage.   *[Exit Provost.]*
Escalus: Well; heaven forgive him! and forgive us all!
Some rise by sin, and some by virtue fall;
Some run from brakes of ice and answer none,
And some condemned for a fault alone.   40

Enter Elbow, Froth, *Clown* [Pompey], Officers.

Elbow: Come, bring them away. If these be good people in
a commonweal that do nothing but use their abuses in
common houses, I know no law. Bring them away.
Angelo: How now, sir, what's your name? and what's the
matter?   45
Elbow: If it please your honor, I am the poor Duke's
constable, and my name is Elbow. I do lean upon
justice, sir, and do bring in here before your good
honor two notorious benefactors.
Angelo: Benefactors? Well; what benefactors are they? Are   50
they not malefactors?
Elbow: If it please your honor, I know not well what they
are; but precise villains they are, that I am sure of, and
void of all profanation in the world that good Christians
ought to have.   55
Escalus: This comes off well. Here's a wise officer.
Angelo: Go to; what quality are they of? Elbow is your
name? *[A pause.]* Why dost thou not speak, Elbow?
Pompey: He cannot, sir, he's out at elbow.
Angelo: What are you, sir?   60

---

35. *prepar'd:* given spiritual preparation.   36. *utmost . . . pilgrimage:* limit of his life's
journey.   39. *brakes of ice:* A famous crux. Attempts to relate the phrase to punishment in
hell (cf. III.i.123–24), taking *brakes* as "cages" or "means of confinement," are unpersuasive,
since it is clearly the inequalities of temporal justice that Escalus is talking about. Many
editors adopt Rowe's *brakes of vice,* meaning "thickets (i.e. a multiplicity) of crimes," which
provides the expected contrast with a *fault alone,* "a single fault." Others follow Collier in
reading "breaks of ice." In its literal sense this image lacks the element of moral responsibility
that the context requires; but ice is symbolic of virginity (cf. *the very ice of chastity* in *As You Like
It,* III.iv.18; *as chaste as ice* in *Hamlet,* III.i.140), and the reference may be to breaches of
virginity, with *fault* in line 40 meaning "a mere crack," i.e. a slighter sexual offense. *answer
none:* i.e. are not called to account.   41. *away:* along, this way.   42–43. *use . . . houses:*
practice their improprieties in brothels.   45. *matter:* i.e. complaints.   46–47. *poor Duke's
constable:* Elbow intends to depreciate himself, not the Duke.   47. *lean upon.* Probably a
blunder for *uphold* or some such word that means the opposite of what he says; cf. *benefactors*
for *malefactors* in line 50.   53. *precise:* This word has been used of Angelo in I.iii.50. It is not
clear whether Elbow is blundering ("morally strict villain") or not ("neither more nor less
than a villain"); certainly *profanation* is his blunder; but the whole sentence ironically recalls
the Duke's comment on Angelo's icy, almost inhuman virtue.   56. *comes off well:* is well
said.   57. *Go to:* a conventional phrase of rebuke, equivalent to "come, come" (spoken, of
course, to Elbow). *quality:* occupation or station.   59. *out at elbow:* (1) impoverished (in his
wits?); (2) rendered speechless (*out*) at the sound of his name.   60. *What:* of what quality (as in
line 57).

Elbow: He, sir! A tapster, sir; parcel-bawd; one that serves
a bad woman; whose house, sir, was (as they say)
pluck'd down in the suburbs; and now she professes a
hot-house; which, I think, is a very ill house too.

Escalus: How know you that?   65

Elbow: My wife, sir, whom I detest before heaven and your
honor—

Escalus: How? thy wife?

Elbow: Ay, sir; whom I thank heaven is an honest woman.

Escalus: Dost thou detest her therefore?   70

Elbow: I say, sir, I will detest myself also, as well as she, that
this house, if it be not a bawd's house, it is pity of her
life, for it is a naughty house.

Escalus: How dost thou know that, constable?

Elbow: Marry, sir, by my wife, who, if she had been a woman   75
cardinally given, might have been accus'd in fornication,
adultery, and all uncleanliness there.

Escalus: By the woman's means?

Elbow: Ay, sir, by Mistress Overdone's means; but as she
spit in his face, so she defied him.   80

Pompey: Sir, if it please your honor, this is not so.

Elbow: Prove it before these varlets here, thou honorable
man, prove it.

Escalus: Do you hear how he misplaces?

Pompey: Sir, she came in great with child; and longing (saving   85
your honors' reverence) for stew'd pruins. Sir, we had
but two in the house, which at that very distant time
stood, as it were, in a fruit-dish, a dish of some threepence—your honors have seen such dishes; they are not
china dishes, but very good dishes.   90

Escalus: Go to, go to; no matter for the dish, sir.

Pompey: No indeed sir, not of a pin; you are therein in the
right. But to the point. As I say, this Mistress Elbow,
being (as I say) with child, and being great-bellied, and
longing (as I said) for pruins; and having but two in the   95

61. *parcel-bawd:* a part-time bawd. The word *bawd* was used of men as well as women.
63–64. *she . . . hot-house:* i.e. her profession is the operation of a bath-house (but *professes*
already had the meaning "falsely professes," and many brothels masqueraded as bath-
houses). 66. *detest:* blunder for *attest* or *protest,* "avow." 72–73. *pity . . . life:* a very sad
thing for her. Again Elbow says something other than what he intends. 73. *naughty:*
wicked. 76. *cardinally:* blunder for *carnally.* 78. *means:* Elbow takes this to mean
"instrument, agent," i.e. the procurer Pompey. 84. *misplaces:* i.e. transposes *varlets* (=
rascals) and *honorable men.* 85–86. *saving . . . reverence:* conventional phrase of apology preceding an expression that may give offense. 86. *stew'd pruins:* Stewed prunes were a favorite
dish in brothels; hence the term became a slang designation for prostitutes. 87. *distant:*
blunder for *instant (instant time* = precise moment). 92. *pin:* Proverbial for worthlessness,
but here with an equivoque, like *point* in the next line. Pompey's speeches are full of such
ribaldry.

dish (as I said), Master Froth here, this very man, having eaten the rest (as I said) and (as I say) paying for them very honestly; for, as you know, Master Froth, I could not give you threepence again.

Froth: No indeed. 100

Pompey: Very well; you being then (if you be rememb'red) cracking the stones of the foresaid pruins—

Froth: Ay, so I did indeed.

Pompey: Why, very well; I telling you then (if you be rememb'red) that such a one and such a one were past 105 cure of the thing you wot of, unless they kept very good diet, as I told you—

Froth: All this is true.

Pompey: Why, very well then—

Escalus: Come; you are a tedious fool. To the purpose: what 110 was done to Elbow's wife, that he hath cause to complain of? Come me to what was done to her.

Pompey: Sir, your honor cannot come to that yet.

Escalus: No, sir, nor I mean it not.

Pompey: Sir, but you shall come to it, by your honor's leave. 115 And I beseech you, look into Master Froth here, sir; a man of fourscore pound a year; whose father died at Hallowmas. Was't not at Hallowmas, Master Froth?

Froth: All-hallond eve.

Pompey: Why, very well; I hope here be truths. He sir, sitting 120 (as I say) in a lower chair, sir—'twas in the Bunch of Grapes, where indeed you have a delight to sit, have you not?

Froth: I have so, because it is an open room and good for winter. 125

Pompey: Why, very well then; I hope here be truths.

Angelo: This will last out a night in Russia
When nights are longest there. I'll take my leave,
And leave you to the hearing of the cause,
Hoping you'll find good cause to whip them all. 130

Escalus: I think no less. Good morrow to your lordship.

Exit [Angelo].

---

106. *the thing . . . of:* you-know-what; here, venereal disease. 107. *good diet:* strict regimen. 112. *Come me:* come (a colloquialism); but Pompey replies to the sense "let me come," with a bawdy quibble on *come.* 118. *Hallowmas:* All Saints' Day, November 1. 119. *All-hallond eve:* the day before Hallowmas. 121. *lower chair:* Not satisfactorily explained. 121–22. *Bunch of Grapes:* Rooms in taverns were often given names. 124. *open:* public (where a fire would be kept burning in winter). 130. *whip them all:* i.e. find them all guilty. Whipping was a common penalty for bawds and prostitutes. 131. *think no less:* expect that will be the outcome.

Now, sir, come on. What was done to Elbow's wife, once more?

Pompey: Once, sir? There was nothing done to her once.

Elbow: I beseech you, sir, ask him what this man did to my wife. 135

Pompey: I beseech your honor, ask me.

Escalus: Well, sir, what did this gentleman to her?

Pompey: I beseech you, sir, look in this gentleman's face. Good Master Froth, look upon his honor; 'tis for a 140 good purpose. Doth your honor mark his face?

Escalus: Ay, sir, very well.

Pompey: Nay, I beseech you mark it well.

Escalus: Well, I do so.

Pompey: Doth your honor see any harm in his face? 145

Escalus: Why, no.

Pompey: I'll be suppos'd upon a book, his face is the worst thing about him. Good then; if his face be the worst thing about him, how could Master Froth do the constable's wife any harm? I would know that of your honor. 150

Escalus: He's in the right, constable. What say you to it?

Elbow: First, and it like you, the house is a respected house; next, this is a respected fellow; and his mistress is a respected woman. 155

Pompey: By this hand, sir, his wife is a more respected person than any of us all.

Elbow: Varlet, thou liest! thou liest, wicked varlet! The time is yet to come that she was ever respected with man, woman, or child. 160

Pompey: Sir, she was respected with him before he married with her.

Escalus: Which is the wiser here: Justice or Iniquity? Is this true?

Elbow: O thou caitiff! O thou varlet! O thou wicked Han- 165 nibal! I respected with her before I was married to her? If ever I was respected with her, or she with me, let not your worship think me the poor Duke's officer. Prove this, thou wicked Hannibal, or I'll have mine action of batt'ry on thee. 170

147. *suppos'd:* blunder for *depos'd,* i.e. sworn. *book:* Bible. 152. *and it like:* if it please. *respected:* blunder for *suspected* (and so several times in lines 154–66). 157. *By this hand:* A common oath. 162. *Justice or Iniquity:* Elbow and Pompey are referred to in terms of stock characters in the morality plays. 165. *caitiff:* wretch. 169. *Hannibal:* blunder for *cannibal,* i.e. savage; but the pairing of the names of the celebrated generals Pompey and Hannibal would not go unnoted. 170. *batt'ry:* blunder for *slander,* as Escalus points out obliquely.

Escalus: If he took you a box o' th' ear, you might have your
action of slander too.

Elbow: Marry, I thank your good worship for it. What is't
your worship's pleasure I shall do with this wicked
caitiff? 175

Escalus: Truly, officer, because he hath some offenses in
him that thou wouldst discover if thou couldst, let him
continue in his courses till thou know'st what they are.

Elbow: Marry, I thank your worship for it. Thou seest,
thou wicked varlet, now, what's come upon thee. Thou 180
art to continue now, thou varlet, thou art to continue.

Escalus: Where were you born, friend?

Froth: Here in Vienna, sir.

Escalus: Are you of fourscore pounds a year?

Froth: Yes, and't please you, sir. 185

Escalus: So. *[To Pompey.]* What trade are you of, sir?

Pompey: A tapster, a poor widow's tapster.

Escalus: Your mistress' name?

Pompey: Mistress Overdone.

Escalus: Hath she had any more than one husband? 190

Pompey: Nine, sir; Overdone by the last.

Escalus: Nine? Come hither to me, Master Froth. Master
Froth, I would not have you acquainted with tapsters;
they will draw you, Master Froth, and you will hang
them. Get you gone, and let me hear no more of you. 195

Froth: I thank your worship. For mine own part, I never
come into any room in a tap-house, but I am drawn in.

Escalus: Well; no more of it, Master Froth. Farewell. *[Exit
Froth.]* Come you hither to me, Master Tapster.
What's your name, Master Tapster? 200

Pompey: Pompey.

Escalus: What else?

Pompey: Bum, sir.

Escalus: Troth, and your bum is the greatest thing about
you, so that in the beastliest sense you are Pompey the 205
Great. Pompey, you are partly a bawd, Pompey, how-
soever you color it in being a tapster, are you not?

---

171. *took:* struck.   177. *discover:* expose.   181. *continue:* Dover Wilson suggests that Elbow
confuses this with *contain*, i.e. be sexually continent. But perhaps he simply confuses the word
with its opposite, as elsewhere.   191. *Overdone . . . last.* With a bawdy quibble deriving from
do = copulate.   194. *draw:* deplete, drain dry; with a play on Froth's name and the drawing of
liquor, and a second quibble (signalled by *hang* in line 194) on "disembowel" or, alternatively,
"drag to execution" (*draw* was used in both senses in judicial sentences).   *will hang them:* will
be the cause of their being hanged (?) or will have no recourse but to say "Hang them!" (?).
197. *drawn in:* (1) attracted to enter; (2) cheated.   204–05. *your . . . about you:* Probably with
a reference to the fashion of wearing thickly padded trunk-hose.   207. *color:* try to put a
better appearance on.

Come, tell me true, it shall be the better for you.

Pompey: Truly, sir, I am a poor fellow that would live.

Escalus: How would you live, Pompey? by being a bawd? 210
What do you think of the trade, Pompey? Is it a lawful
trade?

Pompey: If the law would allow it, sir.

Escalus: But the law will not allow it, Pompey; nor it shall
not be allow'd in Vienna. 215

Pompey: Does your worship mean to geld and splay all the
youth of the city?

Escalus: No, Pompey.

Pompey: Truly, sir, in my poor opinion, they will to't then.
If your worship will take order for the drabs and the 220
knaves, you need not to fear the bawds.

Escalus: There is pretty orders beginning, I can tell you: it is
but heading and hanging.

Pompey: If you head and hand all that offend that way but
for ten year together, you'll be glad to give out a commission for more heads. If this law hold in Vienna 225
ten year, I'll rent the fairest house in it after threepence
a bay. If you live to see this come to pass, say Pompey
told you so.

Escalus: Thank you, good Pompey; and in requital of your 230
prophecy, hark you: I advise you let me not find you
before me again upon any complaint whatsoever; no,
not for dwelling where you do. If I do, Pompey, I shall
beat you to your tent, and prove a shrewd Caesar to
you; in plain-dealing, Pompey, I shall have you whipt. 235
So for this time, Pompey, fare you well.

Pompey: I thank your worship for your good counsel; [*aside*]
but I shall follow it as the flesh and fortune shall better
determine.
Whip me? No, no, let carman whip his jade, 240
The valiant heart's not whipt out of his trade.   *Exit.*

Escalus: Come hither to me, Master Elbow; come hither,
Master Constable. How long have you been in this
place of constable?

Elbow: Seven year and a half, sir. 245

Escalus: I thought, by the readiness in the office, you had
continu'd in it some time. You say seven years
together?

---

209. *would live:* want to earn a living.   216. *splay:* spay.   220. *take order for:* see to.
222. *heading:* beheading.   224–25. *commission:* mandate.   226. *after:* at the rate of.
227. *bay:* portion of a house lying under one gable or between two party walls.   234. *beat . . .*
Caesar: Alluding to Pompey's defeat by Caesar at Pharsalus in 48 B.C. *Shrewd* = harsh.
240. *carman:* carter.   *jade:* worthless horse.   246. *readiness:* proficiency.

Elbow: And a half, sir.

Escalus: Alas, it hath been great pains to you. They do you 250
    wrong to put you so oft upon't. Are there not men in
    your ward sufficient to serve it?

Elbow: Faith, sir, few of any wit in such matters. As they
    are chosen, they are glad to choose me for them. I do it
    for some piece of money, and go through with all. 255

Escalus: Look you bring me in the names of some six or
    seven, the most sufficient of your parish.

Elbow: To your worship's house, sir?

Escalus: To my house. Fare you well. *[Exit Elbow.]* What's a'
    clock, think you? 260

Justice: Eleven, sir.

Escalus: I pray you home to dinner with me.

Justice: I humbly thank you.

Escalus: It grieve me for the death of Claudio,
    But there's no remedy. 265

Justice: Lord Angelo is severe.

Escalus: It is but needful.
    Mercy is not itself, that oft looks so;
    Pardon is still the nurse of second woe.
    But yet, poor Claudio; there is no remedy.
    Come, sir.   *Exeunt.* 270

Scene II

Enter Provost, Servant.

Servant: He's hearing of a cause; he will come straight.
    I'll tell him of you.

Provost: Pray you do. *[Exit Servant.]* I'll know
    His pleasure, may be he will relent. Alas,
    He hath but as offended in a dream!
    All sects, all ages smack of this vice, and he 5
    To die for't!

Enter Angelo.

Angelo: Now, what's the matter, Provost?

---

251. *put . . . upon't:* make you serve so many times. The constable was elected annually.
252. *sufficient:* suitably qualified.   254. *choose . . . them:* i.e. engage me as their deputy (an
ironic reminder of the Duke's deputizing of Angelo).   255. *piece:* coin.   261. *Eleven, sir:* The
Justice's brief entry into the dialogue after nearly 300 lines of silence has been variously
explained as an afterthought (see the rather awkward attachment of his name to the opening
stage direction) and as evidence of revision.   262. *dinner:* The Elizabethan dinner was at
midday.   267. *Mercy . . . so:* i.e. to extend mercy too often is to prove unmerciful in the long
run (since it encourages wrongdoers).

II.ii. Location: Angelo's house. 4. *He:* i.e. Claudio.   *in a dream:* i.e. without conscious
intent.   5. *sects:* classes.   *vice:* sin.

Provost: Is it your will Claudio shall die to-morrow?

Angelo: Did not I tell thee yea? Hadst thou not order?
   Why dost thou ask again?

Provost: Lest I might be too rash.
   Under your good correction, I have seen   10
   When, after execution, judgment hath
   Repented o'er his doom.

Angelo: Go to; let that be mine.
   Do you your office, or give up your place,
   And you shall well be spar'd.

Provost: I crave your honor's pardon.
   What shall be done, sir, with the groaning Juliet?   15
   She's very near her hour.

Angelo: Dispose of her
   To some more fitter place; and that with speed.

[*Enter* Servant.]

Servant: Here is the sister of the man condemn'd
   Desires access to you.

Angelo: Hath he a sister?

Provost: Ay, my good lord, a very virtuous maid,   20
   And to be shortly of a sisterhood,
   If not already.

Angelo: Well; let her be admitted.   *[Exit Servant.]*
   See you the fornicatress be remov'd.
   Let her have needful but not lavish means;
   There shall be order for't.

Enter Lucio *and* Isabella.

Provost: 'Save your honor!   25

Angelo: Stay a little while. *[To Isabella.]* Y' are welcome;
   what's your will?

Isabella: I am a woeful suitor to your honor,
   Please but your honor hear me.

Angelo: Well; what's your suit?

Isabella: There is a vice that most I do abhor,   30
   And most desire should meet the blow of justice;
   For which I would not plead, but that I must;
   For which I must not plead, but that I am
   At war 'twixt will and will not.

Angelo: Well; the matter?

Isabella: I have a brother is condemn'd to die;   35

---

10. *Under:* subject to.   *seen:* known cases.   12. *doom:* sentence.   *mine:* my responsibility.
16. *Dispose of her:* arrange for her to go.   25. *'Save:* God save.

I do beseech you let it be his fault,
And not my brother.

Provost: *[Aside.]* Heaven give thee moving
graces!

Angelo: Condemn the fault and not the actor of it?
Why, every fault's condemn'd ere it be done.   40
Mine were the very cipher of a function,
To fine the faults whose fine stands in record,
And let go by the actor.

Isabella: O just but severe law!
I had a brother then. Heaven keep your honor!

Lucio: *[Aside to Isabella.]* Give't not o'er so. To him again, 45
entreat him,
Kneel down before him, hang upon his gown;
You are too cold. If you should need a pin,
You could not with more tame a tongue desire it;
To him, I say!   50

Isabella: Must he needs die?

Angelo: Maiden, no remedy.

Isabella: Yes; I do think that you might pardon him,
And neither heaven nor man grieve at the mercy.

Angelo: I will not do't.

Isabella: But can you if you would?

Angelo: Look what I will not, that I cannot do.   55

Isabella: But might you do't, and do the world no wrong,
If so your heart were touch'd with that remorse
As mine is to him?

Angelo: He's sentenc'd; 'tis too late.

Lucio: *[Aside to Isabella.]* You are too cold.

Isabella: Too late? Why, no; I that do speak a word   60
May call it again. Well, believe this,
No ceremony that to great ones 'longs,
Not the king's crown, nor the deputed sword,
The marshal's truncheon, nor the judge's robe,
Become them with one half so good a grace   65
As mercy does.
If he had been as you, and you as he,
You would have slipp'd like him, but he, like you,
Would not have been so stern.

Angelo: Pray you be gone.

---

36. *let . . . fault:* let his fault be condemned.   42. *fine . . . fine:* impose a penalty upon . . .
penalty.   48. *a pin:* i.e. the merest trifle.   53. *might:* could.   55. *Look what:* whatsoever.
57. *remorse:* pity.   62. *ceremony:* symbolic appurtenance.   *'longs:* belongs.   63. *deputed
sword:* i.e. sword of justice, symbolizing an authority deputed by God.   64. *marshal's
truncheon:* military commander's staff of office.   65. *grace:* appropriateness.   67–68. *he . . .
not:* he would not, like you.

Isabella: I would to heaven I had your potency,   70
        And you were Isabel! Should it then be thus?
        No; I would tell what 'twere to be a judge,
        And what a prisoner.
    Lucio: *[Aside to Isabella.]* Ay, touch him;
        there's the vein.
Angelo: Your brother is a forfeit of the law,   75
        And you but waste your words.
Isabella: Alas, alas!
        Why, all the souls that were were forfeit once,
        And He that might the vantage best have took
        Found out the remedy. How would you be
        If He, which is the top of judgment, should   80
        But judge you as you are? O, think on that,
        And mercy then will breathe within your lips,
        Like man new made.
    Angelo: Be you content, fair maid,
        It is the law, not I, condemn your brother.
        Were he my kinsman, brother, or my son,   85
        It should be thus with him: he must die to-morrow.
Isabella: To-morrow? O, that's sudden! Spare him, spare
        him!
        He's not prepar'd for death. Even for our kitchens
        We kill the fowl of season. Shall we serve heaven   90
        With less respect than we do minister
        To our gross selves? Good, good my lord, bethink you:
        Who is it that hath died for this offense?
        There's many have committed it.
    Lucio: *[Aside to Isabella.]* Ay,
        well said.   95
Angelo: The law hath not been dead, though it hath slept.
        Those many had not dar'd to do that evil
        If the first that did th' edict infringe
        Had answer'd for his deed. Now 'tis awake,
        Takes note of what is done, and like a prophet   100

---

70. *potency:* power, authority to act.   72. *tell:* i.e. let people see.   74. *there's the vein:* that's the right style; but also with reference to finding a vein in bloodletting, as *touch* suggests (cf. *As You Like It*, II.vii.94, "you touch'd my vein at first").   78. *vantage:* advantage.   80. *top of judgment:* supreme judge.   82. *breathe within:* (1) come to life within; (2) breathe forth from within.   83. *Like . . . made.* Explained by Malone as referring to man newly created, but by most commentators as referring to man made new by God's redeeming mercy; suggesting also the transformation of Angelo into a different man.   84. *Be you content:* i.e. be satisfied that further objection is vain.   85. *kinsman:* Often used of a relative more remote than a brother or sister, who in turn was more remote than a parent or a child. The nouns in this line are thus in ascending order.   86. *sudden:* (too) soon.   90. *of season:* i.e. of the proper degree of maturity.   *serve:* With a quibble on serving food.   91. *respect:* thoughtful care.   92. *gross:* corporal.   *bethink you:* consider.   99. *answer'd:* paid.   100. *prophet:* fortune-teller.

Looks in a glass that shows what future evils,
Either now, or by remissness new conceiv'd,
And so in progress to be hatch'd and born,
Are now to have no successive degrees,
But here they live, to end.

Isabella: Yet show some pity.   105

Angelo: I show it most of all when I show justice;
For then I pity those I do not know,
Which a dismiss'd offense would after gall,
And do him right that, answering one foul wrong,
Lives not to act another. Be satisfied;   110
Your brother dies to-morrow; be content.

Isabella: So you must be the first that gives this sentence.
And he, that suffers. O, it is excellent
To have a giant's strength; but it is tyrannous
To use it like a giant.

Lucio: *[Aside to Isabella.]* That's well said.   115

Isabella: Could great men thunder
As Jove himself does, Jove would never be quiet,
For every pelting, petty officer
Would use his heaven for thunder,
Nothing but thunder! Merciful heaven,   120
Thou rather with thy sharp and sulphurous bolt
Splits the unwedgeable and gnarled oak
Than the soft myrtle; but man, proud man,
Dress'd in a little brief authority,
Most ignorant of what he's most assur'd   125
(His glassy essence), like an angry ape
Plays such fantastic tricks before high heaven
As makes the angels weep; who, with our spleens,
Would all themselves laugh mortal.

---

101. glass: prospective glass or magic crystal.   102. *Either . . . conceiv'd:* i.e. both those that
are already conceived and those that will be conceived if lax enforcement of law *(remissness)*
continues.   103. *have . . . degrees:* propagate themselves no further.   104. *here:* i.e. in the
potential offenders. Many editors emended to *ere* (following Hanmer) or *where* (Malone).
108. *dismiss'd:* forgiven.   *gall:* injure.   109. *right:* justice.   113. *that suffers:* (the first) that
undergoes the penalty.   114. *like a giant:* i.e. without restraint. If (as Isabella's next speech
suggests) there is an allusion here to the giants who warred against the gods, the phrase would
mean "without the divine attribute of mercy."   116. *great men:* men in high place.   117. *be
quiet:* have any quiet.   118. *pelting:* paltry.   *officer:* official.   121. *bolt:* The damage done by
lightning was formerly attributed to thunderbolts.   122. *Splits:* for *splitst.* A frequent type
of simplification for euphony; cf. *exists*, III.i.20.   124. *brief:* short-lived.   125. *assur'd:*
assured of.   126. *glassy essence:* i.e. man's essential being or rational soul, which, mirror-like
(glassy), will show the man who contemplates it what he is. *Glassy* has probably the additional
sense of "fragile, highly susceptible of damage."   *like . . . ape.* The point is that men who
undertake to act like gods make as ludicrous (or as sad) a spectacle as apes imitating what they
have seen men do.   128. *with our spleens:* if they had spleens like us. The spleen was
regarded as the seat of laughter as well as of irascibility.   129. *themselves laugh mortal:* laugh
themselves into a resemblance of mortals, i.e. laugh as much at men as men laugh at apes (?).

Lucio: *[Aside to Isabella.]* O, to him, to him, wench! he will 130
relent.
He's coming; I perceive't.
Provost: *[Aside.]* Pray heaven she win
him!
Isabella: We cannot weigh our brother with ourself.
Great men may jest with saints; 'tis wit in them,   135
But in the less foul profanation.
Lucio: *[Aside to Isabella.]* Thou'rt i' th' right, girl, more o'
that.
Isabella: That in the captain's but a choleric word,
Which in the soldier is flat blasphemy.   140
Lucio: *[Aside to Isabella.]* Art avis'd o' that? more on't.
Angelo: Why do you put these sayings upon me?
Isabella: Because authority, though it err like others,
Hath yet a kind of medicine in itself.
That skins the vice o' th' top. Go to your bosom,   145
Knock there, and ask your heart what it doth know
That's like my brother's fault. If it confess
A natural guiltiness such as is his,
Let it not sound a thought upon your tongue
Against my brother's life.
Angelo: *[Aside.]* She speaks, and 'tis 150
Such sense that my sense breeds with it.—Fare you well.
Isabella: Gentle my lord, turn back.
Angelo: I will bethink me. Come again to-morrow.
Isabella: Hark how I'll bribe you. Good my lord, turn back.
Angelo: How? bribe me?   155
Isabella: Ay, with such gifts that heaven shall share with you.
Lucio: *[Aside to Isabella.]* You had marr'd all else.
Isabella: Not with fond sicles of the tested gold,
Or stones, whose rate are either rich or poor
As fancy values them; but with true prayers,   160
That shall be up at heaven, and enter there
Ere sun-rise, prayers from preserved souls,

---

132. *coming:* coming round, beginning to yield.   134. *cannot . . . ourself:* refuse to judge
ourselves and other men by the same standard.   135. *may:* can with impunity.   *jest with:* treat
with levity.   139. *captain:* general.   *choleric:* angry.   140. *blasphemy:* defamation.   141. *Art
avis'd o':* are you informed of, have you discovered.   142. *put . . . upon:* apply . . . to.
145. *skins . . . top:* causes a new skin to grow over the sore.   145–49. *Go . . . life.* The same
argument for mercy that Escalus put forward in II.i.8–16.   150–51. *'tis Such sense:* its import
is such.   151. *my sense breeds:* my sensual desire multiplies.   152. *Gentle my lord:* my noble
lord.   156. *that:* as.   157. *had . . . else:* would have spoiled everything otherwise (i.e. if you
had used *bribe* in the normal sense).   158. *fond:* foolish, i.e. foolishly valued.   *sicles:* shekels,
i.e. coins.   *tested:* i.e. purest (as confirmed by the touchstone).   159. *rate are.* The context
establishes a collective sense for *rate;* hence the plural verb.   162. *preserved:* kept safe from
the world.

From fasting maids, whose minds are dedicate
To nothing temporal.

Angelo: Well; come to me to-morrow.

Lucio: [*Aside to Isabella.*] Go to; 'tis well. Away!   165

Isabella: Heaven keep your honor safe!

Angelo: [*Aside.*] Amen!
For I am that way going to temptation,
Where prayers cross.

Isabella: At what hour to-morrow
Shall I attend your lordship?

Angelo: At any time 'fore noon.

Isabella: 'Save your honor!

                    [*Exeunt Isabella, Lucio, and Provost.*]

Angelo: From thee: even from thy virtue.   170
What's this? what's this? Is this her fault, or mine?
The tempter, or the tempted, who sins most, ha?
Not she; nor doth she tempt; but it is I
That, lying by the violet in the sun,
Do as the carrion does, not as the flow'r,   175

Corrupt with virtuous season. Can it be
That modesty may more betray our sense
Than woman's lightness? Having waste ground enough,
Shall we desire to raze the sanctuary
And pitch our evils there? O fie, fie, fie!   180
What dost thou? or what art thou, Angelo?
Dost thou desire her foully for those things
That make her good? O, let her brother live!
Thieves for their robbery have authority
When judges steal themselves. What, do I love her,   185
That I desire to hear her speak again?
And feast upon her eyes? What is't I dream on?
O cunning enemy, that to catch a saint,
With saints dost bait thy hook! Most dangerous
Is that temptation that doth goad us on   190
To sin in loving virtue. Never could the strumpet,
With all her double vigor, art and nature,

---

167. *cross:* thwart, i.e. impede.   169. *'fore noon:* note that this implies a change in the hour of Claudio's execution (see II.i.33–34), but the Provost is given no change of instruction.
176. *Corrupt:* putrefy.   *virtuous season:* season or weather that has power (*virtue*) to make things grow (perhaps with play on *season* = preservative).   177. *sense:* sensual nature.
178. *lightness:* wantonness.   180. *pitch our evils:* Variously explained as "cast our offensive waste matter" or "erect our privies." Those who prefer the second explanation cite *Henry VIII,* II.i.67, "Nor build our evils on the graves of great men," but no certain evidence for *evils* = privies has been found.   184–85. *Thieves . . . themselves:* Cf. II.i.18–23.   192. *art and nature:* i.e. her artifice as a prostitute added to her sexual appeal as a woman.

Once stir my temper; but this virtuous maid
Subdues me quite. Ever till now,
When men were fond, I smil'd and wond'red how. *Exit.* 195

Scene III

Enter Duke *[disguised as a friar] and* Provost, *[meeting].*

 Duke: Hail to you, Provost! so I think you are.
 Provost: I am the Provost. What's your will, good friar?
 Duke: Bound by my charity and my blest order,
  I come to visit the afflicted spirits
  Here in the prison. Do me the common right   5
  To let me see them, and to make me know
  The nature of their crimes, that I may minister
  To them accordingly.
 Provost: I would do more than that, if more were needful.

Enter Juliet.

  Look, here comes one; a gentlewoman of mine, 10
  Who, falling in the flaws of her own youth,
  Hath blister'd her report. She is with child,
  And he that got it, sentenc'd; a young man
  More fit to do another such offense
  Than die for this.   15
 Duke: When must he die?
 Provost: As I do think, to-morrow.
  [To Juliet.] I have provided for you. Stay a while,
  And you shall be conducted.
 Duke: Repent you, fair one, of the sin you carry?
 Juliet: I do; and bear the shame most patiently. 20
 Duke: I'll teach you how you shall arraign your conscience,
  And try your penitence, if it be sound,
  Or hollowly put on.
 Juliet: I'll gladly learn.
 Duke: Love you the man that wrong'd you?
 Juliet: Yes, as I love the woman that wrong'd him. 25
 Duke: So then it seems your most offenseful act
  Was mutually committed?
 Juliet: Mutually.

---

193. *stir my temper:* disturb my mental composure. 194. *Subdues:* overcomes. 195. *fond:* infatuated.

II.iii. Location: A prison. 3. *charity:* obligation to perform works of Christian charity.
5. *the common right:* i.e. the right of all persons in holy orders. 6. *make me know:* inform me.
11. *flaws:* sudden gusts (of passion). 12. *blister'd her report:* blighted her reputation.
13. *got:* begot. 21. *arraign:* accuse, bring to trial. 23. *hollowly:* not sincerely.

Duke: Then was your sin of heavier kind than his.

Juliet: I do confess it, and repent it, father.

Duke: 'Tis meet so, daughter, but lest you do repent   30
    As that the sin hath brought you to this shame,
    Which sorrow is always toward ourselves, not heaven,
    Showing we would not spare heaven as we love it,
    But as we stand in fear—

Juliet: I do repent me as it is an evil,   35
    And take the shame with joy.

Duke: There rest.
    Your partner, as I hear, must die to-morrow,
    And I am going with instruction to him.
    Grace go with you, *Benedicite!*   *Exit.*

Juliet: Must die to-morrow? O injurious love,   40
    That respites me a life whose very comfort
    Is still a dying horror!

Provost: 'Tis pity of him.   *Exeunt.*

Scene IV

Enter Angelo.

Angelo: When I would pray and think, I think and pray
    To several subjects. Heaven hath my empty words,
    Whilst my invention, hearing not my tongue,
    Anchors on Isabel; heaven in my mouth,
    As if I did but only chew his name,   5
    And in my heart the strong and swelling evil
    Of my conception. The state, whereon I studied,
    Is like a good thing, being often read,
    Grown [sere] and tedious; yea, my gravity,
    Wherein (let no man hear me) I take pride,   10
    Could I, with boot, change for an idle plume,
    Which the air beats for vain. O place, O form,
    How often dost thou with thy case, thy habit,

---

28. *heavier:* graver.   31. *As that:* because (so also *as* in lines 33–35).   33. *spare heaven:* i.e. relieve by your repentance the sorrow felt in heaven for sin.   36. *There rest:* continue in that frame of mind.   40. *love:* The result of love, her pregnancy, is presumably what saves her from execution. Many editors adopt Hanmer's emendation *law.*   42. *still:* ever.

II.iv. Location: Angelo's house.   2. *several:* separate.   3. *invention:* imagination.   4–5. *heaven . . . his name. His name* could of course mean "its name" (see the note in I.ii.4), but it seems more likely that *heaven* has here displaced an earlier *God,* in accordance with the statute of 1606 prohibiting the use of God's name in stage performances; so also in line 45, and perhaps elsewhere in the play where the context affords no clue.   6, 7. *swelling . . . conception.* Another pregnancy figure.   7. *The state:* statecraft, politics.   9. *sere:* arid. *gravity:* dignified demeanor.   11. *boot:* advantage.   12. *for vain:* for vanity (with pun on *for vane*). *place . . . form:* rank . . . dignity.

Wrench awe from fools, and tie the wiser souls
To thy false seeming! Blood, thou art blood. 15
Let's write "good angel" on the devil's horn,
'Tis not the devil's crest.

Enter Servant.

                                        How now? who's there?
Servant: One Isabel, a sister, desires access to you.
Angelo: Teach her the way. *[Exit Servant.]* O heavens!
Why does my blood thus muster to my heart, 20
Making both it unable for itself,
And dispossessing all my other parts
Of necessary fitness?
So play the foolish throngs with one that swounds,
Come all to help him, and so stop the air 25
By which he should revive; and even so
The general subject to a well-wish'd king
Quit their own part, and in obsequious fondness
Crowd to his presence, where their untaught love
Must needs appear offense.

Enter Isabella.

                                        How now, fair maid? 30
Isabella: I am come to know your pleasure.
Angelo: That you might know it, would much better please me
Then to demand what 'tis. Your brother cannot live.
Isabella: Even so. Heaven keep your honor!
Angelo: Yet may he live a while; and it may be 35
As long as you or I. Yet he must die.
Isabella: Under your sentence?
Angelo: Yea.
Isabella: When, I beseech you? that in his reprieve,
Longer or shorter, he may be so fitted 40
That his soul sicken not.
Angelo: Ha? fie, these filthy vices! It were as good
To pardon him that hath from nature stol'n
A man already made, as to remit

---

15. *Blood . . . blood:* i.e. under the external trappings lie the basic passions common to all
men. 16. *Let's write:* i.e. say that we write. *good angel.* With a play on Angelo's name.
17. *'Tis . . . crest:* it is no true mark of his identity (as a heraldic crest is), i.e. it doesn't make an
angel of him. 20. *muster to:* assemble in. 21. *it:* i.e. the heart. 24. *swounds:* faints.
26–30. *and . . . offense.* Apparently an allusion to a visit made by James I in March 1604 to
the Royal Exchange in London, where a tremendous throng got out of control and nearly
overwhelmed him. 27. *subject:* body of subjects. 28. *Quit . . . part:* leave their proper
functions. *obsequious fondness:* foolish eagerness to pay homage. 29. *untaught:* ignorant.
40. *fitted:* equipped, prepared. 43–44. *him . . . made:* i.e. a murderer. 44. *remit:* pardon.

Their saucy sweetness that do coin heaven's image   45
In stamps that are forbid. 'Tis all as easy
Falsely to take away a life true made
As to put metal in restrained means
To make a false one.

Isabella: 'Tis set down so in heaven, but not in earth.   50

Angelo: Say you so? Than I shall pose you quickly.
Which had you rather, that the most just law
Now took your brother's life [or,] to redeem him,
Give up your body to such sweet uncleanness
As she that he hath stain'd?

Isabella: Sir, believe this,   55
I had rather give my body than my soul.

Angelo: I talk not of your soul; our compell'd sins
Stand more for number than for accompt.

Isabella: How say you?

Angelo: Nay, I'll not warrant that; for I can speak
Against the thing I say. Answer to this: 60
I (now the voice of the recorded law)
Pronounce a sentence on your brother's life;
Might there not be a charity in sin
To save this brother's life?

Isabella: Please you to do't,
I'll take it as a peril to my soul,   65
It is no sin at all, but charity.

Angelo: Pleas'd you to do't at peril of your soul,
Were equal poise of sin and charity.

Isabella: That I do beg his life, if it be sin,
Heaven let me bear it! You granting of my suit,   70
If that be sin, I'll make it my morn-prayer
To have it added to the faults of mine,
And nothing of your answer.

Angelo: Nay, but hear me,
Your sense pursues not mine. Either you are ignorant,
Or seem so [craftily]; and that's not good.   75

---

45. *saucy sweetness:* lascivious pleasure.   45–46. *coin . . . forbid:* i.e. beget children unlawfully. The image is of counterfeiting coins (*stamps*).   46. *all as:* just as.   48. *metal:* With the same double sense of *metal / mettle* as at I.i.48.   *restrained:* forbidden.   50. *'Tis . . . earth:* i.e. divine law forbids them equally, but in earthly law murder is more heinous.   51. *pose:* put a question to (shortened form of *appose*).   58. *Stand . . . accompt:* are recorded but are not charged against our account.   59–60. *I'll . . . say:* i.e. I don't necessarily subscribe to that view; I can assert any position in order to test you.   64. *Please you:* if you are willing. Isabella thinks he is talking about the possible guilt involved in pardoning Claudio.   68. *Were:* there would be.   *poise:* weight.   73. *nothing:* Perhaps adverbial, "in no way."   *your answer:* what you are answerable for.   74. *Your . . . mine:* i.e. you don't follow my meaning.

Isabella: Let [me] be ignorant, and in nothing good,
          But graciously to know I am no better.
Angelo: Thus wisdom wishes to appear most bright
          When it doth tax itself; as these black masks
          Proclaim an enshield beauty ten times louder   80
          Than beauty could, displayed. But mark me:
          To be received plain, I'll speak more gross:
          Your brother is to die.
Isabella: So.
Angelo: And his offense is so, as it appears,   85
          Accountant to the law upon that pain.
Isabella: True.
Angelo: Admit no other way to save his life
          (As I subscribe not that, nor any other,
          But in the loss of question), that you, his sister,   90
          Finding yourself desir'd of such a person,
          Whose credit with the judge, or own great place,
          Could fetch your brother from the manacles
          Of the all-[binding] law; and that there were
          No earthly mean to save him, but that either   95
          You must lay down the treasures of your body
          To this supposed, or else to let him suffer—
          What would you do?
Isabella: As much for my poor brother as myself:
          That is, were I under the terms of death,   100
          Th' impression of keen whips I'ld wear as rubies,
          And strip myself to death, as to a bed
          That longing have been sick for, ere I'ld yield
          My body up to shame.
Angelo: Then must your brother die.
Isabella: And 'twere the cheaper way: 105
          Better it were a brother died at once,
          Than that a sister, by redeeming him,
          Should die for ever
Angelo: Were not you then as cruel as the sentence
          That you have slander'd so?   110

---

77. *graciously:* by God's grace.   79. *tax itself:* charge itself (with ignorance).   *these black masks.*   The generic use: "the black masks that women wear."   80. *enshield:* enshielded, shielded from view.   82. *received:* understood.   *gross:* obviously, plainly.   86. *Accountant:* accountable.   *pain:* penalty.   90. *in . . . question:* to avoid lack of matter for argument, i.e. for the sake of discussion (?). Singer's proposed change of *loss* to *loose* (= freedom) is tempting. 97. *him:* i.e. Claudio.   100. *the terms:* sentence.   103. *longing have:* If the text is correct, *have* = I have. Of the various emendations proposed, Sisson's *long I have* is perhaps the best.   105. *the cheaper way:* a better bargain.   106. *at once:* once (and then proceeded to eternal life).   108. *die for ever:* incur damnation.   110. *slander'd so:* i.e. accused of the same thing (cruelty).

Isabella: Ignomy in ranson and free pardon
       Are of two houses: lawful mercy
       Is nothing kin to foul redemption.
   Angelo: You seem'd of late to make the law a tyrant,
       And rather prov'd the sliding of your brother   115
       A merriment than a vice.
Isabella: O, pardon me, my lord, it oft falls out,
       To have what we would have, we speak not what we mean.
       I something do excuse the thing I hate,
       For his advantage that I dearly love.   120
   Angelo: We are all frail.
Isabella: Else let my brother die,
       If not a fedary, but only he,
       Owe and succeed thy weakness.
   Angelo: Nay, women are frail too.
Isabella: Ay, as the glasses where they view themselves,   125
       Which are as easy broke as they make forms.
       Women? Help heaven! men their creation mar
       In profiting by them. Nay, call us ten times frail,
       For we are soft as our complexions are,
       And credulous to false prints.
   Angelo: I think it well;   130
       And from this testimony of your own sex
       (Since I suppose we are made to be no stronger
       Than faults may shake our frames), let me be bold.
       I do arrest your words. Be that you are,
       That is a woman; if you be more, you're none;   135
       If you be one (as you are well express'd
       By all external warrants), show it now,
       By putting on the destin'd livery.
Isabella: I have no tongue but one; gentle my lord,
       Let me entreat you speak the former language.   140
   Angelo: Plainly conceive, I love you.

---

111. *Ignomy:* ignominy (a frequent variant). 112. *two houses:* different families. 113. *nothing:* in no way. Cf. *something* (= somewhat) in line 119. 114. *of late:* not long ago.
115. *prov'd:* argued. 116. *A merriment:* something to be taken lightly. 121. *frail:* morally weak, unable to resist temptation. 122. *fedary:* confederate, i.e. one guilty of the same offense. 123. *Owe and succeed:* possess and hold by succession. *thy weakness:* this frailty you speak of (but with an unintended second meaning). 126. *make forms:* (1) reflect images (as referring to mirrors); (2) produce children (as referring to women). The comparison of virginity to glass is a commonplace. 127. *men . . . mar:* Since it is women who create them. 128. *complexions:* constitutions, physical and mental. 129. *credulous:* readily receptive. *false prints:* A recurrence of the figure of lines 45–49. 130. *think it well:* hold the same opinion. 133. *Than:* than that. 134. *arrest your words:* hold you to what you have said. *that:* what. 135. *be more:* i.e. insist on keeping your chastity. *none:* no women (in terms of what you have just said of them). 136. *express'd:* shown to be. 137. *warrants:* assurances. 138. *putting . . . livery:* i.e. accepting the role that women are born to. 139. *tongue:* language.

Isabella: My brother did love Juliet,
And you tell me that he shall die for't.
Angelo: He shall not, Isabel, if you give me love.
Isabella: I know your virtue hath a license in't,   145
Which seems a little fouler than it is,
To pluck on others.
Angelo: Believe me, on mine honor,
My words express my purpose.
Isabella: Ha? little honor to be much believ'd,
And most pernicious purpose! Seeming, seeming!   150
I will proclaim thee, Angelo, look for't!
Sign me a present pardon for my brother,
Or with an outstretch'd throat I'll tell the world aloud
What man thou art.
Angelo: Who will believe thee, Isabel?
My unsoil'd name, th' austereness of my life,   155
My vouch against you, and my place i' th' state,
Will so your accusation overweigh,
That you shall stifle in your own report,
And smell of calumny. I have begun,
And now I give my sensual race the rein.   160
Fit thy consent to my sharp appetite,
Lay by all nicety and prolixious blushes
That banish what they sue for. Redeem thy brother
By yielding up thy body to my will,
Or else he must not only die the death,   165
But thy unkindness shall his death draw out
To ling'ring sufferance. Answer me to-morrow,
Or by the affection that now guides me most,
I'll prove a tyrant to him. As for you,
Say what you can: my false o'erweighs your true.   170

                                                                    Exit.

Isabella: To whom should I complain? Did I tell this,
Who would believe me? O perilous mouths,

---

145. *license:* allowed freedom.   146. *seems . . . fouler:* looks . . . uglier.   147. *pluck on:* draw
on, tempt.   148. *purpose:* true intent.   151. *proclaim thee:* denounce you publicly.
152. *present:* immediate.   153. *with . . . aloud:* This faintly ludicrous image of a cock crowing
loudly shows the pitch of Isabella's excited indignation. The rhetorical fitness of the
hexameter line has been pointed out.   154. *What:* what manner of.   156. *vouch:* sworn
statement.   157. *overweigh:* outweigh.   158. *in . . . report:* in your own story (implying that it
has polluted or poisoned the air) (?) or, with respect to your own reputation (?).   160. *race:*
strain.   *the rein:* free rein.   162. *nicety:* fastidious reserve. prolixious: prolix, i.e. excessive,
tiresome. This word (ordinarily applied to language), taken with the next line, ironically
recalls Claudio's hope that Isabella will succeed by virtue of her youth's "prone and speechless
dialect / Such as move men" (I.ii.173–74).   166. *unkindness:* unnaturalness (as a woman and
as a sister).   167. *sufferance:* suffering (by torture).   168. *affection:* passion.   171. *Did I:* if I
were to.

That bear in them one and the self-same tongue,
Either of condemnation or approof,
Bidding the law make curtsy to their will,   175
Hooking both right and wrong to th' appetite,
To follow as it draws! I'll to my brother.
Though he hath fall'n by prompture of the blood,
Yet hath he in him such a mind of honor
That had he twenty heads to tender down   180
On twenty bloody blocks, he'ld yield them up,
Before his sister should her body stoop
To such abhorr'd pollution.
Then, Isabel, live chaste, and, brother, die;
More than our brother is our chastity.   185
I'll tell him yet of Angelo's request,
And fit his mind to death, for his soul's rest.   *Exit.*

ACT III

Scene I

Enter Duke *[disguised as a friar],* Claudio, *and* Provost.

> *Duke:* So then you hope of pardon from Lord Angelo?
> *Claudio:* The miserable have no other medicine
> But only hope:
> I have hope to live, and am prepar'd to die.
> *Duke:* Be absolute for death: either death or life   5
> Shall thereby be the sweeter. Reason thus with life:
> If I do lose thee, I do lose a thing
> That none but fools would keep. A breath thou art,
> Servile to all the skyey influences,
> That dost this habitation where thou keep'st   10
> Hourly afflict. Merely, thou art death's fool,
> For him thou labor'st by thy flight to shun,
> And yet run'st toward him still. Thou art not noble,
> For all th' accommodations that thou bear'st

---

174. *Either . . . approof:* i.e. now condemning, now sanctioning.   175. *make curtsy:* bow, make
obeisance.   176. *Hooking:* Cf. *Anchor* in line 4.   177. *draws:* drags.   178. *prompture:*
urging.   179. *mind of honor:* honorable mind.

III.i. Location: The prison.

5. *absolute for death:* certain that you must die.   9. *Servile to:* the slave of.   *skyey influences:*
influence of the stars (supposedly a physical emanation or flow, hence the name).

10. *dost.* The subject is *influences.* A singular verb with such a subject is common enough;
here it has been attracted into the second person by the surrounding matter.   *habitation:* (1)
the earth; (2) the body.   *keep'st:* dwellest.   11. *Merely:* utterly.   *fool:* plaything.   13. *still:*
continually.   14. *accommodations:* comforts, sophistications of civilized life. Cf. *King Lear,*
III.iv.106–8, "unaccommodated man is no more but . . . a poor, bare, fork'd animal. . . ."
bear'st: The meaning may be "possessest" or, more narrowly, "wearest," which would make
clothing the dominant idea in *accommodations* (as in the *Lear* passage); but *bear'st* also suggests
bearing a child (in two senses) and leads to the next image.

Are nurs'd by baseness. Thou'rt by no means valiant,   15
For thou dost fear the soft and tender fork
Of a poor worm. Thy best of rest is sleep,
And that thou oft provok'st, yet grossly fear'st
Thy death, which is no more. Thou art not thyself,
For thou exists on many a thousand grains   20
That issue out of dust. Happy thou art not,
For what thou hast not, still thou striv'st to get,
And what thou hast, forget'st. Thou art not certain,
For thy complexion shifts to strange effects,
After the moon. If thou art rich, thou'rt poor,   25
For like an ass, whose back with ingots bows,
Thou bear'st thy heavy riches but a journey,
And death unloads thee. Friend hast thou none,
For thine own bowels, which do call thee [sire],
The mere effusion of thy proper loins,   30
Do curse the gout, sapego, and the rheum
For ending thee no sooner. Thou hast nor youth nor age,
But as it were an after-dinner's sleep,
Dreaming on both, for all thy blessed youth
Becomes as aged, and doth beg the alms   35
Of palsied eld; and when thou art old and rich,
Thou hast neither heat, affection, limb, nor beauty,
To make thy riches pleasant. What's yet in this
That bears the name of life? Yet in this life
Lie hid moe thousand deaths; yet death we fear   40
That makes these odds all even.
    Claudio: I humbly thank you.
To sue to live, I find I seek to die,
And seeking death, find life. Let it come on.
    Isabella: *[Within.]* What ho! Peace here; grace and good
company!   45

---

15. *nurs'd by baseness:* fed by lowly means. Cf. *Antony and Cleopatra*, V.ii.7–8, "which sleeps, and never palates more the dung, / The beggar's nurse and Caesar's." 17. *worm:* snake. 18. *grossly:* stupidly. 19. *not thyself:* not your own, not self-contained and independent. 20. *exists:* See the note on II.ii.122. *grains:* seeds. 23. *certain:* stable, of fixed character. 24. *complexion:* physical and mental constitution. *effects:* manifestations. 25. *After the moon:* (1) influenced by the moon; (2) resembling the moon, constantly changing. 26. *ingots:* bars of precious metal. 29. *bowels:* i.e. offspring. 30. *mere:* very. *proper:* own. 31. *sapego:* serpigo, a disfiguring skin disease. *rheum:* catarrh, running eyes, and other disorders associated with excess bodily fluid. 32. *nor youth:* neither youth. 33–34. *an after-dinner's . . . both.* "Our life . . . resembles our dreams after dinner [i.e. the noonday meal], when the events of the morning are mingled with the designs of the evening" (Johnson). 35. *as aged:* as if aged, i.e. no different from age (since young men must beg for money from their elders, just as feeble old men must look to younger men for physical assistance) (?). The passage may be corrupt and has been variously emended. 36. *eld:* old age. 37. *heat:* vigor, vitality. It was thought that in old age the blood became cold and thick. *affection:* passion. *limb:* i.e. proper use of any bodily member. 41. *makes . . . even:* i.e. removes all these ills. 42. *To sue:* suing.

Provost: Who's there? Come in, the wish deserves a
         welcome.
Duke: Dear sir, ere long I'll visit you again.
Claudio: Most holy sir, I thank you.

Enter Isabella.

Isabella: My business is a word or two with Claudio.   50
Provost: And very welcome. Look, signior, here's your sister.
Duke: Provost, a word with you.
Provost: As many as you please.
Duke: Bring [me] to hear [them] speak, where I may be
         conceal'd.   *[Exeunt Duke and Provost.]* 55
Claudio: Now, sister, what's the comfort?
Isabella: Why,
         As all comforts are: most good, most good indeed.
         Lord Angelo, having affairs to heaven,
         Intends you for his swift ambassador,
         Where you shall be an everlasting leiger;   60
         Therefore your best appointment make with speed,
         To-morrow you set on.
Claudio: Is there no remedy?
Isabella: None, but such remedy as, to save a head,
         To cleave a heart in twain.
Claudio: But is there any?
Isabella: Yes, brother, you may live;   65
         There is a devilish mercy in the judge,
         If you'll implore it, that will free your life,
         But fetter you till death.
Claudio: Perpetual durance?
Isabella: Ay, just, perpetual durance, a restraint,
         [Though] all the world's vastidity you had,   70
         To a determin'd scope.
Claudio: But in what nature?
Isabella: In such a one as, you consenting to't,
         Would bark your honor from that trunk you bear,
         And leave you naked.
Claudio: Let me know the point.
Isabella: O, I do fear thee, Claudio, and I quake,   75
         Lest thou a feverous life shouldst entertain,

---

58. *affairs to:* business with.   60. *leiger:* resident ambassador.   61. *appointment:* preparation.   62. *set on:* set forth.   69. *durance:* confinement.   *just:* exactly.   70. *vastidity:*
vastness (apparently Shakespeare's coinage).   71. *a determin'd scope:* fixed limits, i.e. the
ever-present consciousness of the means by which he had gained his life.   73. *bark:* strip off
(as bark from a tree).   *trunk:* body (with play on "tree trunk").   75. *fear:* fear for.
76. *feverous life.* Cf. "life's fitful fever," *Macbeth,* III.ii.23.   *entertain:* cherish, cling to.

And six or seven winters more respect
Than a perpetual honor. Dar'st thou die?
The sense of death is most in apprehension,
And the poor beetle that we tread upon   80
In corporal sufferance finds a pang as great
As when a giant dies.

Claudio: Why give you me this shame?
Think you I can a resolution fetch
From flow'ry tenderness? If I must die,
I will encounter darkness as a bride,   85
And hug it in mine arms.

Isabella: There spake my brother; there my father's grave
Did utter forth a voice. Yes, thou must die:
Thou art too noble to conserve a life
In base appliances. This outward-sainted deputy,   90
Whose settled visage and deliberate word
Nips youth i' th' head, and follies doth [enew]
As falcon doth the fowl, is yet a devil;
His filth within being cast, he would appear
A pond as deep as hell.

Claudio: The prenzie Angelo?   95

Isabella: O, 'tis the cunning livery of hell,
The damned'st body to invest and cover
In prenzie guards! Dost thou think, Claudio,
If I would yield him my virginity,
Thou mightst be freed!

Claudio: O heavens, it cannot be.   100

Isabella: Yes, he would give't thee, from this rank offense,
So to offend him still. This night's the time

---

77. *respect:* regard, value.   79. *apprehension:* i.e. the idea of it (literally, "taking hold").   80–
82. *the poor . . . dies:* i.e. as for the physical pain of death, a giant feels proportionately no
greater pain than a beetle feels.   83. *a resolution fetch:* achieve resoluteness of mind.
84. *flow'ry tenderness:* soothing flowers of rhetoric.   90. *In base appliances:* by applying ignoble
remedies.   *outward-sainted:* outwardly saintly.   91. *settled visage:* composed and unaltering
expression.   92–93. *Nips . . . head.* The image is of a falcon striking its prey; it continues in
enew = drive prey into the water *(in-eau)* or covert.   94. *cast.* Variously explained as
"vomited," "calculated" (as in *casting accounts),* "examined for diagnosis" (as in *casting urine),*
etc. But in view of *pond* in line 94, the likeliest meaning is "cleared out," as mud and refuse is
cleared out of a ditch or pond and cast up on the bank *(O.E.D., v.,* 28, 29).   *pond.* The linking
of a dirty pond and a hypocritical "settled visage" (line 99) occurs again in *The Merchant of
Venice,* I.i.88–89, where men desirous of a reputation for "wisdom, gravity, profound
conceit" are said to assume "visages" that "cream and mantle like a standing [stagnant]
pool."   95, 98. *prenzie.* A word found nowhere else, and not satisfactorily explained. Among
the many emendations, the two most favored by editors have been *princely* (F2) and *precise*
(Tieck conjecture in Cambridge). Some proposed readings, e.g. *proxy* (Bulloch conjecture in
Cambridge), fit one line but not the other, and some editors adopt different readings in the
two lines.   96. *livery:* distribution of clothing to retainers.   97. *invest:* clothe.   98. *guards:*
trimmings, external trappings.   *Dost thou think:* i.e. can you believe.   101–02. *give't . . . still:*
grant you freedom, in return for my foul offense, to go on offending in the same fashion.

William Shakespeare   1521

That I should do what I abhor to name,
Or else thou diest to-morrow.

Claudio: Thou shalt not do't.

Isabella: O, were it but my life,   105
I'd throw it down for your deliverance
As frankly as a pin.

Claudio: Thanks, dear Isabel.

Isabella: Be ready, Claudio, for your death to-morrow.

Claudio: Yes. Has he affection in him,
That thus can make him bite the law by th' nose,   110
When he would force it? Sure it is no sin,
Or of the deadly seven it is the least.

Isabella: Which is the least?

Claudio: If it were damnable, he being so wise,
Why would he for the momentary trick   115
Be perdurably fin'd? O Isabel!

Isabella: What says my brother?

Claudio: Death is a fearful thing.

Isabella: And shamed life a hateful.

Claudio: Ay, but to die, and go we know not where;
To lie in cold obstruction, and to rot;   120
This sensible warm motion to become
A kneaded clod; and the delighted spirit
To bathe in fiery floods, or to reside
In thrilling region of thick-ribbed ice;
To be imprison'd in the viewless winds   125
And blown with restless violence round about
The pendant world; or to be worse than worst
Of those that lawless and incertain thought
Imagine howling—'tis too horrible!
The weariest and most loathed worldly life   130
That age, ache, [penury], and imprisonment
Can lay on nature is a paradise
To what we fear of death.

Isabella: Alas, alas!

Claudio: Sweet sister, let me live.

---

106. *deliverance:* liberation from prison.   107. *As . . . pin:* as freely as I would throw away a pin.   110. *bite . . . nose:* flout the law. An ironic reversal of the "biting laws" of I.iii.19; cf. also I.iii.29.   111. *force:* enforce.   115. *trick:* trifle.   116. *perdurably fin'd:* punished eternally.   120. *obstruction:* darkness (as in *Twelfth Night*, IV.iii.39) (?). More often explained as stoppage of blood, i.e. cessation of all vital activity.   121. *sensible warm motion:* i.e. body endowed with feeling and heat and movement.   122. *kneaded:* reduced to a common mass (*O.E.D.*).   *delighted:* having (capacity for) delight (?) or now experiencing delight (?).
124. *thrilling:* piercingly cold.   125. *viewless:* invisible.   126–27. *blown . . . world:* Cf. the punishment of sexual offenders in Dante's *Inferno.* Canto V.   126. *restless:* never-resting.
127. *pendant:* hanging in space.   128. *lawless . . . thought:* unrestrained and dubious conjecture.

What sin you do to save a brother's life,   135
Nature dispenses with the deed so far,
That it becomes a virtue.

Isabella: O you beast!
O faithless coward! O dishonest wretch!
Wilt thou be made a man out of my vice?
Is't not a kind of incest, to take life   140
From thine own sister's shame? What should I think?
Heaven shield my mother play'd my father fair!
For such a warped slip of wilderness
Ne'er issu'd from his blood. Take my defiance!
Die, perish! Might but my bending down   145
Reprieve thee from thy fate, it should proceed.
I'll pray a thousand prayers for thy death,
No word to save thee.

Claudio: Nay, hear me, Isabel.

Isabella: O fie, fie, fie!
Thy sin's not accidental, but a trade.   150
Mercy to thee would prove itself a bawd,
'Tis best that thou diest quickly.

Claudio: O, hear me, Isabella!

[Enter Duke disguised as a friar.]

Duke: Vouchsafe a word, young sister, but one word.

Isabella: What is your will?

Duke: Might you dispense with your leisure, I would by and   155
by have some speech with you. The satisfaction I would
require is likewise your own benefit.

Isabella: I have no superfluous leisure; my stay must be stolen
out of other affairs; but I will attend you a while.

[Walks apart.]

Duke: Son, I have overheard what hath pass'd between you   160
and your sister. Angelo had never the purpose to corrupt her; only he hath made an assay of her virtue to
practice his judgment with the disposition of natures.
She (having the truth of honor in her) hath made him
that gracious denial which he is most glad to receive. I   165
am confessor to Angelo, and I know this to be true;

---

136. *dispenses with:* excuses.   139. *made a man:* i.e. given life (with a play on "conceived" or
"born").   142. *shield:* defend.   143. *warped:* deviating from what is natural, deformed,
perverted.   *slip of wilderness:* shoot of a wild stock.   144. *defiance:* rejection, declaration of
enmity.   145. *Might . . . down:* even if a mere bow from me could.   150. *accidental:* a chance
happening.   *trade:* established practice.   151. *prove . . . bawd:* procure further sexual
indulgence for you.   155. *dispense with:* forgo.   159. *attend:* await.   162. *only he hath:* he
has only.   *assay:* test.   163. *disposition:* manner of thought and behavior.   164. *truth:*
integrity.   165. *gracious:* virtuous.

therefore prepare yourself to death. Do not satisfy your
resolution with hopes that are fallible, to-morrow you
must die; go to your knees, and make ready.

Claudio: Let me ask my sister pardon. I am so out of love 170
with life that I will sue to be rid of it.

Duke: Hold you there! Farewell. *[Exit Claudio.]* Provost,
a word with you.

[*Enter* Provost.]

Provost: What's your will, father?

Duke: That now you are come, you will be gone. Leave me 175
a while with the maid. My mind promises with my habit,
no loss shall touch her by my company.

Provost: In good time.   *Exit.*

Duke: *[Turning to Isabella.]* The hand that hath made you
fair hath made you good; the goodness that is cheap in 180
beauty makes beauty brief in goodness; but grace, being
the soul of your complexion, shall keep the body of it
ever fair. The assault that Angelo hath made to you,
fortune hath convey'd to my understanding; and but
that frailty hath examples for his falling, I should 185
wonder at Angelo. How will you do to content this substitute, and to save your brother?

Isabella: I am now going to resolve him. I had rather my
brother die by the law than my son should be unlawfully
born. But O, how much is the good Duke deceiv'd in 190
Angelo! If ever he return, and I can speak to him, I will
open my lips in vain, or discover his government.

Duke: That shall not be much amiss; yet, as the matter now
stands, he will avoid your accusation: he made trial of
you only. Therefore fasten your ear on my advisings: to 195
the love I have in doing good a remedy presents itself. I
do make myself believe that you may most uprighteously
do a poor wrong'd lady a merited benefit; redeem your
brother from the angry law; do no stain to your own gracious person; and much please the absent Duke, if 200
peradventure he shall ever return to have hearing of this
business.

---

167. *to death:* for death.   172. *Hold you there:* continue in that resolution.   176. *habit:* friar's
gown.   178. *In good time.* A phrase of acquiescence, "very well."   180–81. *the goodness . . .
in beauty:* the kindness that beauty is free with (?).   181. *makes . . . goodness:* makes virtue
short-loved in beauty.   182. *complexion:* makeup, nature.   184–85. *but that:* except for the
fact that.   185. *hath examples:* furnishes precedents.   *falling:* This word, taken with Angelo's
name, has prompted the suggestion that an allusion to the fallen angels is intended.
186–87. *substitute:* deputy.   188. *resolve him:* give him a definite answer.   192. *discover:*
expose.   *government:* conduct.   194–95. *avoid . . . only:* i.e. get round your accusation by
saying that he was merely testing you.

Isabella: Let me hear you speak farther. I have spirit to do any thing that appears not foul in the truth of my spirit.

Duke: Virtue is bold, and goodness never fearful. Have 205 you not heard speak of Mariana, the sister of Frederick, the great soldier who miscarried at sea?

Isabella: I have heard of the lady, and good words went with her name.

Duke: She should this Angelo have married; was affianc'd 210 to her [by] oath, and the nuptial appointed; between which time of the contract and limit of the solemnity, her brother Frederick was wrack'd at sea, having in that perish'd vessel the dowry of his sister. But mark how heavily this befell to the poor gentlewoman: there she 215 lost a noble and renown'd brother, in his love toward her ever most kind and natural; with him, the portion and sinew of her fortune, her marriage-dowry; with both, her combinate-husband, this well-seeming Angelo. 220

Isabella: Can this be so? Did Angelo so leave her?

Duke: Left her in her tears, and dried not one of them with his comfort; swallow'd his vows whole, pretending in her discoveries of dishonor; in few, bestow'd her on her own lamentation, which she yet wears for his sake; and he, a 225 marble to her tears, is wash'd with them, but relents not.

Isabella: What a merit were in death to take this poor maid from the world! What corruption in this life, that it will let this man live! But how out of this can she avail?

Duke: It is a rupture that you may easily heal; and the cure 230 of it not only saves your brother, but keeps you from dishonor in doing it.

Isabella: Show me how, good father.

Duke: This forenam'd maid hath yet in her the continu-

---

204. *foul:* ugly.   205. *fearful:* timid.   207. *miscarried:* was lost.   210. *She . . . married.* The closest modern rendering would be "Her was this Angelo to have married." Nominative for accusative in emphatic initial position is not unusual.   210–11. *affianc'd . . . oath.* The contract between Angelo and Mariana, unlike that between Claudio and Juliet, appears to have been *sponsalia per verba de futuro,* a betrothal which could be cancelled by mutual consent or broken for cause by either party at any time before the marriage was solemnized. Mariana's alleged unchastity (line 224) would have been adequate cause if the allegation had been true. Sexual intercourse between a betrothed pair created a valid marriage at common law.   211. *the nuptial appointed:* the wedding day set.   212. *limit . . . solemnity:* day set for solemnizing the marriage.   217. *natural:* i.e. brotherly.   218. *sinew:* i.e. strength, mainstay.   219. *her combinate-husband:* the man bound by oath to be her husband.   223. *swallow'd:* retracted (cf. *eat one's words*).   223–24. *pretending . . . dishonor:* alleging she had been discovered to be unchaste.   224. *in few:* in short.   *bestow'd her on:* gave her over to (with ironic play on "gave her in marriage to").   225. *wears:* makes her habit.   225–26. *a marble:* i.e. impervious.   229. *avail:* benefit.   230. *rupture:* breach (with play on the medical sense, as indicated by *heal* and *cure*).

ance of her first affection; his unjust unkindness 235
(that in all reason should have quench'd her love) hath
(like an impediment in the current) made it more violent
and unruly. Go you to Angelo, answer his requiring
with a plausible obedience, agree with his demands to
the point; only refer yourself to this advantage; first, 240
that your stay with him may not be long; that the time
may have all shadow and silence in it; and the place
answer to convenience. This being granted in course—
and now follows all—we shall advise this wrong'd maid
to stead up your appointment, go in your place. If the 245
encounter acknowledge itself hereafter, it may compel
him to her recompense; and here, by this is your brother
sav'd, your honor untainted, the poor Mariana advan-
tag'd, and the corrupt deputy scal'd. The maid
will I frame, and make fit for his attempt. If you think 250
well to carry this as you may, the doubleness of the benefit defends the deceit from reproof. What think you of
it?

Isabella: The image of it gives me content already, and I trust
it will grow to a most prosperous perfection. 255

Duke: It lies much in your holding up. Haste you speedily
to Angelo; if for this night he entreat you to his bed, give
him promise of satisfaction. I will presently to Saint
Luke's; there, at the moated grange, resides this
dejected Mariana. At that place call upon me, and dis- 260
patch with Angelo, that it may be quickly.

Isabella: I thank you for this comfort. Fare you well, good
father. *Exit. [Manet Duke.]*

[Scene II]

Enter Elbow, *Clown* [Pompey], Officers.

Elbow: Nay, if there be no remedy for it but that you will
needs buy and sell men and women like beasts, we shall
have all the world drink brown and white bastard.

---

235. *unjust unkindness:* unnatural degree of faithlessness.   239. *plausible obedience:*
convincing pretense of obedience.   239–40. *to the point:* in every detail.   240. *refer yourself
to:* commit yourself to, i.e. impose (?) or rely on (?).   *advantage:* favorable condition.   241,
242. *time, place.* It has been suggested that these words are transposed.   242. *shadow:*
darkness.   244. *all:* i.e. the heart of the matter.   245. *stead up:* fulfill in your stead.
246. *encounter:* sexual encounter (as often; cf. line 85).   *acknowledge itself:* make itself known
(by Mariana's pregnancy).   249. *scal'd:* weighed (and found wanting).   250. *frame:* shape,
prepare.   254. *image:* i.e. mental image, idea.   256. *holding up:* sustaining, ability to carry it
through.   259. *moated:* surrounded by a ditch (not necessarily filled with water).   *grange:*
country house.   260. *dejected:* (1) low-spirited; (2) humbled.   260–61. *dispatch:* settle
affairs.   262. s.d. *Manet:* remains.

III.ii. Location: Scene continues.
3. *bastard:* sweet Spanish wine (with obvious pun).

Duke: O heavens, what stuff is here?

Pompey: 'Twas never merry world since of two usuries the 5
      merriest was put down, and the worser allow'd by order
      of law; a furr'd gown to keep him warm; and furr'd with
      fox and lambskins too, to signify that craft, being richer
      than innocency, stands for the facing.

Elbow: Come you way, sir. Bless you, good father friar. 10

Duke: And you, good brother father. What offense hath
      this man made you, sir?

Elbow: Marry, sir, he hath offended the law; and sir, we take
      him to be a thief too, sir, for we have found upon him,
      sir, a strange picklock, which we have sent to the deputy. 15

Duke: Fie, sirrah, a bawd, a wicked bawd!
      The evil that thou causest to be done,
      That is thy means to live. Do thou but think
      What 'tis to cram a maw or clothe a back
      From such a filthy vice; say to thyself, 20
      From their abominable and beastly touches
      I drink, I eat, [array] myself, and live.
      Canst thou believe thy living is a life,
      So stinkingly depending? Go mend, go mend.

Pompey: Indeed, it does sink in some sort, sir; but yet, sir, I 25
      would prove—

Duke: Nay, if the devil have given thee proofs for sin,
      Thou wilt prove his. Take him to prison, officer.
      Correction and instruction must both work
      Ere this rude beast will profit. 30

Elbow: He must before the deputy, sir, he has given him
      warning. The deputy cannot abide a whoremaster. If
      he be a whoremonger, and comes before him, he were
      as good go a mile on his errand.

Duke: That we were all, as some would seem to be, 35
      From our faults, as faults from seeming, free!

---

5. *'Twas . . . world:* things have never gone well (proverbial). *two usuries:* i.e. lending money at interest and fornication, both of which produce increase. 7. *furr'd gown:* Associated with usurers. 8. *fox and lambskins:* Most editors read *on* for *and,* for closer agreement with *facing* (line 9). 9. *stands . . . facing:* sanctions the trimming (with a bawdy equivoque). 10. *father friar:* Friar = brother. The Duke answers Elbow's blunder in kind. 13. *the law:* i.e. not me but the law (a literal-minded reply). *take:* With a quibble on "arrest." A precise equivalent would be *apprehend.* 15. *picklock:* skeleton key. 19. *maw:* stomach. 21. *abominable:* Supposedly derived from *ab homine,* "alien to man, inhuman," a sense here reinforced by *beastly.* 26. *prove:* i.e. try to prove, argue. 27. *proofs for:* arguments in support of. 28. *prove:* turn out to be. 29. *Correction:* punishment. *both work:* operate together, make their joint effect felt. Probably *work* in I.i.9 has the same meaning. 33–34. *he . . . errand:* i.e. things will go hard with him. 35–36. *That . . . free:* would that we were all free of faults, as some make themselves appear, and that faults were free of dissembling. Many editors adopt the F2 reading *Free from* in place of *From* (line 36); this improves the metre but does not alter the sense.

Enter Lucio.

    Elbow: His neck will come to your waist—a cord, sir.

    Pompey: I spy comfort, I cry bail. Here's a gentleman, and a
        friend of mine.

    Lucio: How now, noble Pompey? What, at the wheels of 40
        Caesar? Art thou led in triumph? What, is there none
        of Pygmalion's images newly made woman to be had
        now, for putting the hand in the pocket and extracting
        [it]clutch'd? What reply? Ha? What say'st thou to this
        tune, matter, and method? Is't not drown'd i' th' last 45
        rain? Ha? What say'st thou, Trot? Is the world as it
        was, man? Which is the way? Is it sad, and few words?
        or how? The trick of it?

    Duke: Still thus, and thus; still worse!

    Lucio: How doth my dear morsel, thy mistress? Procures 50
        she still? Ha?

    Pompey: Troth, sir, she hath eaten up all her beef, and she is
        herself in the tub.

    Lucio: Why, 'tis good; it is the right of it; it must be so. Ever
        your fresh whore and your powder'd bawd, an 55
        unshunn'd consequence; it must be so. Art going to
        prison, Pompey?

    Pompey: Yes, faith, sir.

    Lucio: Why, 'tis not amiss, Pompey. Farewell. Go say I
        sent thee thither. For debt, Pompey? or how? 60

    Elbow: For being a bawd, for being a bawd.

    Lucio: Well, then imprison him. If imprisonment be the
        due of a bawd, why, 'tis his right. Bawd is he doubtless,
        and of antiquity too; bawd-born. Farewell, good Pom-
        pey. Commend me to the prison, Pompey. You will 65
        turn good husband now, Pompey, you will keep the
        house.

    Pompey: I hope, sir, your good worship will be my bail.

---

37. *come . . . waist:* come to the condition of your waist, i.e. be encircled by a cord.
40–41. *at . . . triumph.* Cf. II.i. 234–35. The historical Pompey was never led in triumph by
Caesar, though his sons were.   42: *Pygmalion's . . . woman:* Alluding to the legend of the
sculptor Pygmalion's female statue that came to life; with a play on *become a woman* in the sense
"lose one's virginity."   44. *clutch'd:* i.e. grasping a coin.   45–46. *drown'd . . . rain:* i.e. out of
fashion (?).   46. *Trot:* old bawd (ordinarily applied to a woman).   47. *Which . . . way:* how
does the world go. *The trick of it* (line 48) is another way of saying the same thing.   *sad:*
melancholy.   52. *eaten . . . beef:* worn out all her prostitutes.   53. *tub:* (1) pickling-tub (for
beef); (2) sweating-tub (for treating venereal disease).   55. *fresh . . . powder'd:* (1) young; (2)
not preserved . . . (1) made-up; (2) pickled, corned.   56. *unshunn'd:* unshunnable (i.e. the
young whore inevitably turns into the old bawd).   64. *antiquity:* long standing.   65. *Commend.* Playing on the senses "give my regards to" and "commit."   66. *husband:* master of a
household.   66–67. *keep the house:* (1) manage the household; (2) stay indoors.

Lucio: No indeed will I not, Pompey, it is not the wear. I will pray, Pompey, to increase your bondage. If you 70 take it not patiently, why, your mettle is the more. Adieu, trusty Pompey. Bless you, friar.

Duke: And you.

Lucio: Does Bridget paint still, Pompey? Ha?

Elbow: Come your ways, sir, come. 75

Pompey: You will not bail me then, sir?

Lucio: Then, Pompey, nor now. What news abroad, friar? what news?

Elbow: Come you ways, sir, come.

Lucio: Go to kennel, Pompey, go. *[Exeunt Elbow, Pompey,* 80 *and Officers.]* What news, friar, of the Duke?

Duke: I know none. Can you tell me of any?

Lucio: Some say he is with the Emperor of Russia; other some, he is in Rome; but where is he, think you?

Duke: I know not where; but wheresoever, I wish him well. 85

Lucio: It was a mad fantastical trick of him to steal from the state, and usurp the beggary he was never born to. Lord Angelo dukes it well in his absence; he puts transgression to't.

Duke: He does well in't. 90

Lucio: A little more lenity to lechery would do no harm in him. Something too crabbed that way, friar.

Duke: It is too general a vice, and severity must cure it.

Lucio: Yes, in good sooth, the vice is of a great kindred; it is well allied; but it is impossible to extirp it quite, friar, till 95 eating and drinking be put down. They say this Angelo was not made by man and woman after this downright way of creation. Is it true, think you?

Duke: How should he be made then?

Lucio: Some report a sea-maid spawn'd him; some, that he 100 was begot between two stock-fishes. But it is certain that when he makes water his urine is congeal'd ice, that I know to be true; and he is a motion generative, that's infallible.

---

69. *wear:* fashion. 71. *mettle:* (1) spirit; (2) metal, i.e. shackles. 72. *trusty:* faithful. 75. *Come your ways:* come along. 77. *Then:* i.e. neither then. 87. *usurp the beggary:* It is not clear why Lucio should say this. 88–89. *puts transgression to't:* applies extreme measures to lawbreaking. 92. *crabbed:* harsh. 93. *general:* common. 94. *sooth:* truth. *great kindred:* (1) large family; (2) good family (*well allied,* line 95, has the same meanings). 95. *extirp:* extirpate. 97. *downright:* plain, ordinary (with a play on "horizontal"). 99. *should he be:* is he said to have been. 100. *sea-maid:* mermaid. 101. *stock-fishes:* dried cod. 103. *motion:* puppet. *generative:* male (?). Many editors adopt Theobald's *ungenerative* (= sexless); cf. *ungenitur'd* in lines 160–61. 104. *infallible:* certain.

Duke: You are pleasant, sir, and speak apace. 105

Lucio: Why, what a ruthless thing is this in him, for the rebellion of a codpiece to take away the life of a man! Would the Duke that is absent have done this? Ere he would have hang'd a man for the getting a hundred bastards, he would have paid for the nursing a thousand. 110 He had some feeling of the sport; he knew the service, and that instructed him to mercy.

Duke: I never heard the absent Duke much detected for women, he was not inclin'd that way.

Lucio: O, sir, you are deceiv'd. 115

Duke: 'Tis not possible.

Lucio: Who? not the Duke? Yes, your beggar of fifty; and his use was to put a ducat in her clack-dish. The Duke had crotchets in him. He would be drunk too, that let me inform you. 120

Duke: You do him wrong, surely.

Lucio: Sir, I was an inward of his. A shy fellow was the Duke, and I believe I know the cause of his withdrawing.

Duke: What, I prithee, might be the cause?

Lucio: No, pardon; 'tis a secret must be lock'd within the 125 teeth and the lips. But this I can let you understand, the greater file of the subject held the Duke to be wise.

Duke: Wise? Why, no question but he was.

Lucio: A very superficial, ignorant, unweighing fellow.

Duke: Either this is envy in you, folly, or mistaking. The 130 very stream of his life, and the business he hath helm'd, must, upon a warranted need, give him a better proclamation. Let him be but testimonied in his own bringings-forth, and he shall appear to the envious a scholar, a statesman, and a soldier. Therefore you speak unskill- 135 fully; or, if your knowledge be more, it is much dark'ned in your malice.

Lucio: Sir, I know him, and I love him.

---

105. *pleasant:* jocose. *apace:* rapidly, i.e. heedlessly.   107. *codpiece:* baggy appendage at the front of breeches; hence slang for "penis."   110. *nursing:* rearing.   113. *detected for:* accused of.   117. *your:* The indefinite use (but comically applicable, if Lucio but knew it, to the person he is addressing).   118. *use:* custom.   *clack-dish:* beggar's bowl with a wooden cover that could be "clacked" to attract the attention of passers-by.   119. *crotchets:* whims, odd notions.   121. *wrong:* injustice.   122. *inward:* intimate.   *shy:* warily reserved (*O.E.D.*). Used by Shakespeare only here and at V.i.56, where the context helps to define its sense. 123. *withdrawing:* departure, i.e. absence.   127. *greater . . . subject:* majority of his subjects. 129. *unweighing:* injudicious.   130. *envy:* malice.   131. *stream:* course.   *helm'd:* steered, directed.   132. *upon . . . need:* if a warrant were needed.   132–33. *give . . . proclamation:* proclaim him a better man (than you allow).   133–34. *bringings-forth:* achievements. 134. *to the envious:* even to the malicious.   135–36. *unskillfully:* in ignorance.

Duke: Love talks with better knowledge, and knowledge
with [dearer] love.   140

Lucio: Come, sir, I know what I know.

Duke: I can hardly believe that, since you know not what
you speak. But if ever the Duke return (as our prayers
are he may), let me desire you to make your answer
before him. If it be honest you have spoke, you have 145
courage to maintain it. I am bound to call upon you,
and I pray you your name?

Lucio: Sir, my name is Lucio, well known to the Duke.

Duke: He shall know you better, sir, if I may live to report
you.   150

Lucio: I fear you not.

Duke: O, you hope the Duke will return no more; or you
imagine me too unhurtful an opposite. But indeed I can
do you little harm; you'll forswear this again.

Lucio: I'll be hang'd first; thou art deceiv'd in me, friar. 155
But no more of this. Canst thou tell if Claudio die tomorrow, or no?

Duke: Why should he die, sir?

Lucio: Why? For filling a bottle with a tun-dish. I would
the Duke we talk of were return'd again. This ungeni- 160
tur'd agent will unpeople the province with continency.
Sparrows must not build in his house-eaves, because
they are lecherous. The Duke yet would have dark
deeds darkly answer'd, he would never bring them to
light. Would he were return'd! Marry, this Claudio is 165
condemn'd for untrussing. Farewell, good friar, I
prithee pray for me. The Duke (I say to thee again)
would eat mutton on Fridays. He's now past it, yet (and
I say to thee) he would mouth with a beggar, though she
smelt brown bread and garlic. Say that I said so. 170
Farewell.   *Exit.*

Duke: No might nor greatness in mortality
Can censure scape; back-wounding calumny
The whitest virtue strikes. What kind so strong

---

145. *If . . . spoke:* if what you have said is true.   146. *I am bound:* it is my duty.   153. *opposite:*
opponent.   154. *forswear:* deny on oath.   159. *tun-dish:* funnel.   160–61. *ungenitur'd:*
incapable of sex (see the note on line 111).   *agent:* deputy.   162. *Sparrows:* Proverbially
lecherous.   164. *darkly:* secretly.   166. *untrussing:* untying the laces that fastened hose to
doublet, i.e. undressing.   167. *I . . . again:* Here and in lines 168–69 *(and . . . thee)* and 170
(Say . . . so) Lucio brashly underlines his slanders to show his lack of concern about having
them reported to the Duke.   168. *eat . . . Fridays:* eat forbidden meat, i.e. have recourse to
prostitutes. *Mutton* is slang for "whore"; cf. *beef* in line 52.   170. *smelt:* smelt of. *brown bread:*
bread made of flour with most of the bran left in it, hence soon musty.   172. *mortality:*
humankind.   173. *back-wounding:* backbiting.   174. *whitest:* purest.

Can tie the gall up in the slanderous tongue?   175
But who comes here?

Enter Escalus, Provost, *and* [Officers *with*] Bawd [Mistress Overdone].

Escalus: Go, away with her to prison.

Mistress Overdone: Good my lord, be good to me, your honor is accounted a merciful man. Good my lord.

Escalus: Double and treble admonition, and still forfeit in   180
the same kind! This would make mercy swear and play the tyrant.

Provost: A bawd of eleven years' continuance, may it please your honor.

Mistress Overdone: My lord, this is one Lucio's information against me.   185
Mistress Kate Keepdown was with child by him in the Duke's time; he promis'd her marriage. His child is a year and a quarter old come Philip and Jacob. I have kept it myself; and see how he goes about to abuse me!

Escalus: That fellow is a fellow of much license; let him be   190
call'd before us. Away with her to prison! Go to, no more words. *[Exeunt Officers and Mistress Overdone.]*
Provost, my brother Angelo will not be alter'd, Claudio must die to-morrow. Let him be furnish'd with divines, and have all charitable preparation. If my brother   195
wrought by my pity, it should not be so with him.

Provost: So please you, this friar hath been with him, and advis'd him for th' entertainment of death.

Escalus: Good even, good father.

Duke: Bliss and goodness on you!   200

Escalus: Of whence are you?

Duke: Not of this country, though my chance is now
To use it for my time. I am a brother
Of gracious order, late come from the [See],
In special business from his Holiness.   205

Escalus: What news abroad i' th' world?

Duke: None, but that there is so great a fever on goodness,
that the dissolution of it must cure it. Novelty is only in

---

175. *tie . . . up:* restrain the bitterness (or venom).   180–81. *forfeit . . . kind:* found guilty of the same offense.   181–82. *make . . . tyrant:* turn mercy itself to cruelty (with allusion to the raging and ranting of conventional tyrants, notably Herod, in early drama).   188. *Philip and Jacob:* the Feast of St. Philip and St. James, May 1. This was also May-day, celebrated with traditional festivities that were the occasion of much sexual license.   190. *license:* licentiousness.   193. *brother:* i.e. colleague in office, cf. *brother-justice,* line 234.   195. *charitable:* required by Christian charity.   196. *wrought . . . pity:* exercised his function as compassionately as I.   198. *entertainment:* acceptance.   203. *for my time:* to serve my particular occasion.   204. *late:* recently. *the See:* the Holy See, Rome.   208. *the dissolution . . . cure it:* i.e goodness can get rid of the disease only by dying.   208–09. *Novelty . . . request:* newfangledness alone is in demand.

request, and, as it is, as dangerous to be ag'd in any kind
of course, as it is virtuous to be constant in any under-   210
taking. There is scarce truth enough alive to make societies secure, but security enough to make fellowships
accurs'd. Much upon this riddle runs the wisdom of the
world. This news is old enough, yet it is every day's
news. I pray you, sir, of what disposition was the Duke?   215
Escalus: One that, above all other strifes, contended especially to know himself.
   Duke: What pleasure was he given to?
Escalus: Rather rejoicing to see another merry, than merry
at any thing which profess'd to make him rejoice; a gen-   220
tleman of all temperance. But leave we him to his
events, with a prayer they may prove prosperous, and let
me desire to know how you find Claudio prepar'd. I am
made to understand that you have lent him visitation.
   Duke: He professes to have receiv'd no sinister measure   225
from his judge, but most willingly humbles himself to
the determination of justice; yet had he fram'd to himself (by the instruction of his frailty) many deceiving
promises of life, which I (by my good leisure) have dis-
credited to him, and now is he resolv'd to die.   230
Escalus: You have paid the heavens your function, and the
prisoner the very debt of your calling. I have labor'd for
the poor gentleman to the extremest shore of my modesty, but my brother-justice have I found so severe, that
he hath forc'd me to tell him he is indeed Justice.   235
   Duke: If his own life answer the straitness of his proceeding, it shall become him well; wherein if he chance to
fail, he hath sentenc'd himself.
Escalus: I am going to visit the prisoner. Fare you well.

209–10. *as . . . as:* as things stand, (it is) as.   209. *ag'd:* settled, constant.   210. *constant:*
Many editors, following Staunton, emend to *inconstant,* so that *virtuous* (line 210) means
"deemed virtuous by the new scale of values." But the F1 reading makes excellent sense:
"constancy is now as dangerous as it is in actuality virtuous."   *truth:* Perhaps meaning here
"keeping one's plain word," in contrast to the following *security,* "giving security to bind an
obligation." The sentence could then mean "There is hardly enough integrity left alive to
make friendships possible, but enough security demanded to make commercial partnerships
burdensome."   213. *upon this riddle:* after this paradoxical fashion.   215. *disposition:*
inclination, temperament.   216. *strifes:* strivings, endeavors.   220. *which profess'd:* whose
declared purpose was.   221. *temperance:* moderation.   221–22. *his events:* the outcome of his
affairs.   224. *lent him visitation:* bestowed a visit upon him.   225. *sinister measure:* unjust
treatment.   227. *determination:* decision.   227–28. *fram'd to himself:* formed in his mind.
228. *instruction . . . frailty:* prompting of natural human weakness.   229. *by . . . leisure:* as
time gave me opportunity.   230. *resolv'd to die:* resolute for death.   231. *You . . . function:*
Recalling the Duke's remarks in I.i.29 ff.   232. *the very . . . calling:* what you are obligated as
a friar to give him.   233. *shore:* limit.   *modesty:* propriety.   236–37. *answer . . . proceeding:*
matches the strictness of his official acts (cf. line 242).

Duke: Peace be with you!   *[Exeunt Escalus and Provost.]* 240
            He who the sword of heaven will bear
            Should be as holy as severe;
            Pattern in himself to know,
            Grace to stand, and virtue go;
            More nor less to others paying   245
            Than by self-offenses weighing.
            Shame to him whose cruel striking
            Kills for faults of his own liking!
            Twice treble shame on Angelo,
            To weed my vice, and let his grow!   250
            O, what may man within him hide,
            Though angel on the outward side!
            How may likeness made in crimes,
            Making practice on the times,
            To draw with idle spiders' strings   255
            Most ponderous and substantial things!
            Craft against vice I must apply.
            With Angelo to-night shall lie
            His old betrothed (but despised);
            So disguise shall by th' disguised   260
            Pay with falsehood false exacting,
            And perform an old contracting.   *Exit.*

ACT IV

Scene I

Enter Mariana, *and* Boy *singing.*

            SONG

            Take, O, take those lips away,
                That so sweetly were forsworn,
            And those eyes, the break of day,
                Lights that do mislead the morn;
            But my kisses bring again, bring again,   5
            Seals of love, but seal'd in vain, seal'd in vain.

---

241. *sword of heaven:* i.e. authority to execute justice (the "deputed sword" of II.ii.63).
243. *Pattern . . . know:* to find a precedent (for his judgment of others) in his judgment of his own behavior (?).   244. *Grace . . . go:* (to find in himself) grace to stand firm and virtue to go forward (?) or grace to stand firm if virtue fail (in others) (?).   245–46. *More . . . weighing:* allotting neither more nor less to others than is determined by weighing his own offenses. Cf. II.ii.134.   250. *my vice:* i.e. another's sin.   252. *angel.* Another play on Angelo's name. 253–56. *How . . . things.* Not satisfactorily explained. A major obstacle is the meaning of *likeness made in crimes.* Line 254 means "practicing deception on the world." The language of lines 255–56 is clear in itself, but not its grammatical or logical relation to what precedes. Lever's theory that two lines are missing after line 254 may well be correct.   261. *falsehood:* deception, illusion.

IV.i. Location: The moated grange at St. Luke's. 2. *were forsworn:* swore falsely (to be true).
4. *mislead the morn:* i.e. make morning think that the sun has risen.

Enter Duke *[disguised as a friar].*

  Mariana: Break off thy song, and haste thee quick away.
     Here comes a man of comfort, whose advice
     Hath often still'd my brawling discontent. *[Exit Boy.]*
     I cry you mercy, sir, and well could wish   10
     You had not found me here so musical.
     Let me excuse me, and believe me so,
     My mirth it much displeas'd, but pleas'd my woe.
  Duke: 'Tis good; though music oft hath such a charm
     To make bad good, and good provoke to harm.   15
     I pray you tell me, hath any body inquir'd for me here
     to-day? Much upon this time have I promis'd here to
     meet.
  Mariana: You have not been inquir'd after. I have sat here all
     day.   20

Enter Isabel.

  Duke: I do constantly believe you. The time is come even
     now. I shall crave your forbearance a little. May be I
     will call upon you anon for some advantage to yourself.
  Mariana: I am always bound to you.   *Exit.*
  Duke: Very well met, and well come.   25
     What is the news from this good deputy?
  Isabella: He hath a garden circummur'd with brick,
     Whose western side is with a vineyard back'd;
     And to that vineyard is a planched gate,
     That makes his opening with this bigger key.   30
     This other doth command a little door,
     Which from the vineyard to the garden leads;
     There have I made my promise upon the heavy
     Middle of the night to call upon him.
  Duke: But shall you on your knowledge find this way? 35
  Isabella: I have ta'en a due and wary note upon't.
     With whispering and most guilty diligence,
     In action all of precept, he did show me
     The way twice o'er.
  Duke: Are there no other tokens
     Between you 'greed concerning her observance?   40

---

9. *brawling:* clamorous. 10. *cry you mercy:* beg your pardon. 12. *excuse me:* excuse myself
(by saying). 13. *My . . . woe:* i.e. it was a song to ease my grief, not to make me merry.
14. *charm:* magic spell. 15. *make bad good:* make evil attractive. 17. *upon:* about.
21. *constantly:* assuredly. 22. *crave . . . little:* ask you to withdraw for a short time.
24. *bound to you:* in your debt. 25. *well come:* a common variant of *welcome,* and here paral-
leling *well met.* 27. *circummur'd:* walled about. 29. *planched:* made of planks. 36. *wary:*
careful, attentive. 38. *In . . . precept:* i.e. with explanatory gestures. 40. *her observance:* the
conditions she is to observe.

Isabella: No; none but only a repair i' th' dark,
And that I have posses'd him my most stay
Can be but brief; for I have made him know
I have a servant comes with me along,
That stays upon me, whose persuasion is   45
I come about my brother.
Duke: 'Tis well borne up.
I have not yet made known to Mariana
A word of this. What ho, within! come forth!

Enter Mariana.

I pray you be acquainted with this maid,
She comes to do you good.
Isabella: I do desire the like.   50
Duke: Do you persuade yourself that I respect you?
Mariana: Good friar, I know you do, and have found it.
Duke: Take then this your companion by the hand,
Who hath a story ready for your ear.
I shall attend your leisure, but make haste,   55
The vaporous night approaches.
Mariana: Will't please you walk aside?   *Exit [with Isabella].*
Duke: O place and greatness! millions of false eyes
Are stuck upon thee. Volumes of report
Run with these false, and most contrarious quest   60
Upon thy doings; thousand escapes of wit
Make thee the father of their idle dream,
And rack thee in their fancies.

Enter Mariana *and* Isabella.

Welcome, how agreed?
Isabella: She'll take the enterprise upon her, father,
If you advise it.
Duke: It is not my consent,   65
But my entreaty too.

---

41. *repair:* coming.   42. *possess'd:* informed.   *most:* longest possible.   45. *stays upon:* waits
for.   *persuasion:* belief. Cf. *persuade yourself,* line 51.   47. *borne up:* sustained, carried on. Cf.
holding up, III.i.256.   51. *respect you:* have concern for your welfare.   52. *found it:* had
proof of it. Editors have repaired the metrical deficiency of this line by inserting a word (*oft,*
so or *I*) before *have.*   56. *vaporous:* Night mists were considered noxious.   58–63. *O . . .*
fancies: Most commentators agree that these lines, not appropriate to the context, were
originally part of the Duke's soliloquy at III.i.185–188, perhaps preceding line 185.
59. *stuck:* fixed, fastened.   *Volumes:* quantities.   *report:* rumor.   60. *these false:* i.e. these
false (= distorting) eyes.   *contrarious:* A word (probably adverbial here) of many shades of
meaning; the sense here may be that the rumormongers are hostile or perverse, that the
rumors are false or inconsistent with one another or adverse, or all of these.   *quest:* give
tongue (like hunting dogs when they sight their quarry).   61. *escapes:* scapes, transgressions.
62. *idle dream:* foolish fantasy.   63. *rack:* stretch on the rack, i.e. distort, tear apart.
65. *not:* not only.

<pre>
Isabella: Little have you to say
             When you depart from him, but soft and low,
             "Remember now my brother."
Mariana: Fear me not.
   Duke: Nor, gentle daughter, fear you not at all.
             He is your husband on a pre-contract: 70
             To bring you thus together 'tis no sin,
             Sith that the justice of your title to him
             Doth flourish the deceit. Come, let us go,
             Our corn's to reap, for yet our tithe's to show.   *Exeunt.*
</pre>

Scene II

Enter Provost *and Clown* [Pompey].

> *Provost:* Come hither, sirrah; can you cut off a man's head?
>
> *Pompey:* If the man be a bachelor, sir, I can; but if he be a
> married man, he's his wive's head, and I can never cut
> off a woman's head.
>
> *Provost:* Come, sir, leave me your snatches, and yield me a 5
> direct answer. To-morrow morning are to die Claudio
> and Barnardine. Here is in our prison a common exe-
> cutioner, who in his office lacks a helper. If you will take
> it on you to assist him, it shall redeem you from your
> gyves; if not, you shall have your full time of imprison- 10
> ment, and your deliverance with an unpitied whipping,
> for you have been a notorious bawd.
>
> *Pompey:* Sir, I have been an unlawful bawd time out of mind,
> but yet I will be content to be a lawful hangman. I
> would be glad to receive some instruction from my fel- 15
> low partner.
>
> *Provost:* What ho, Abhorson! Where's Abhorson there?

Enter Abhorson.

> *Abhorson:* Do you call, sir?
>
> *Provost:* Sirrah, here's a fellow will help you to-morrow in
> your execution. If you think it meet, compound with 20

---

67. *Little . . . say:* say little (*have you* is imperative).   69. *Fear me not:* i.e. have no fears about
my management of it.   70. *husband . . . pre-contract:* i.e. affianced husband. Cf. Claudio's
"true contract" (I.ii.135), which made him Juliet's actual husband.   72. *title to him:* right to
possess him.   73. *flourish:* make fair, justify.   74. *Our . . . sow:* our grain is still to be reaped,
for the seed that will produce our tithe dues isn't even sown yet, i.e. we have work to do
before we can enjoy the fruits of our endeavor.

IV.ii. Location: The prison. 3. *wive's:* wife's. Cf. Ephesians 5:23: "For the husband is the
wive's head" (Geneva).   4. *head:* i.e. maidenhead.   5. *leave me:* leave, cease (a colloquialism).   *snatches:* quibbles.   7. *common:* public.   8. *office:* duties.   10. *gyves:* shackles; here
(apparently), imprisonment.   11. *deliverance:* release.   *unpitied:* pitiless, severe.   17. *Abhorson.* A telescoping of *abhor* and *whoreson.*   20. *execution.* In view of the context the sense may
be "execution of official duties" rather than "judicial killing," but for an executioner the
distinction is academic.   *compound:* come to an agreement.

him by the year, and let him abide here with you; if not, use him for the present and dismiss him. He cannot plead his estimation with you; he hath been a bawd.

Abhorson: A bawd, sir? fie upon him, he will discredit our mystery. 25

Provost: Go to, sir, you weigh equally; a feather will turn the scale. *Exit.*

Pompey: Pray, sir, by your good favor—for surely, sir, a good favor you have, but that you have a hanging look—do you call, sir, your occupation a mystery? 30

Abhorson: Ay, sir, a mystery.

Pompey: Painting, sir, I have heard say, is a mystery; and your whores, sir, being members of my occupation, using painting, do prove my occupation a mystery; but what mystery there should be in hanging, if I should be 35 hang'd, I cannot imagine.

Abhorson: Sir, it is a mystery.

Pompey: Proof.

Abhorson: Every true man's apparel fits your thief. If it be too little for your thief, your true man thinks it big enough; 40 if it be too big for your thief, your thief thinks it little enough; so every true man's apparel fits your thief.

Enter Provost.

Provost: Are you agreed?

Pompey: Sir, I will serve him; for I do find your hangman is a more penitent trade than your bawd: he doth oft'ner ask 45 forgiveness.

Provost: You, sirrah, provide your block and your axe tomorrow, four a' clock.

Abhorson: Come on, bawd, I will instruct thee in my trade; follow. 50

Pompey: I do desire to learn, sir; and I hope, if you have occa-

---

1. *abide:* lodge.   22. *present:* immediate occasion.   23. *estimation:* worthiness, claim to consideration.   25. *mystery:* skilled craft.   28–29. *favor . . . favor:* leave . . . face.   29. *a hanging look:* (1) a melancholy expression; (2) the look of a hangman.   32. *your:* The indefinite use (as also in lines 39 ff.).   39–42. *Every . . . thief:* Abhorson begins his proof by showing that a thief is a "fitter" of clothes, hence a tailor, hence a member of a mystery. Presumably he would continue by arguing that thieves are "members of [his] occupation" (picking up Pompey's argument in line 33), and that his occupation is therefore a mystery. The argument from clothes is doubtless related to the fact that the clothes of an executed man were the due of the executioner.   39. *true man:* honest man (regularly used in antithesis to *thief*).   40. *big enough:* i.e. a big enough loss.   41–42. *thinks . . . enough:* i.e. doesn't think much of it.   45–46. *ask forgiveness:* The executioner always asked forgiveness of the condemned man.

sion to use me for your own turn, you shall find me yare;
for truly, sir, for your kindness, I owe you a good turn.
Provost: Call hither Barnardine and Claudio.

Exeunt [Abhorson and Pompey].

Th' one has my pity; not a jot the other,   55
Being a murtherer, though he were my brother.

Enter Claudio.

Look, here's the warrant, Claudio, for thy death.
'Tis now dead midnight, and by eight to-morrow
Thou must be made immortal. Where's Barnardine?
Claudio: As fast lock'd up in sleep as guiltless labor   60
When it lies starkly in the traveller's bones.
He will not wake.
Provost: Who can do good on him?
Well, go, prepare yourself. *[Knocking within.]* But hark,
what noise?
Heaven give your spirits comfort! *[Exit Claudio.]* By   65
and by.—
I hope it is some pardon or reprieve
For the most gentle Claudio.

Enter Duke *[disguised as a friar].*

Welcome, father.
Duke: The best and wholesom'st spirits of the night
Envelop you, good Provost! Who call'd here of late?   70
Provost: None since the curfew rung.
Duke: Not Isabel?
Provost: No.
Duke: They will then ere't be long.
Provost: What comfort is for Claudio?
Duke: There's some in hope.
Provost: It is a bitter deputy.

---

52. *use . . . turn:* (1) make use of my professional expertise to serve your own purpose; (2)
employ me for your own hanging (commonly called "turning off"). *yare:* nimble, adroit.
53. *a good turn.* Referring to the proverbial "one good turn deserves another," but with play
on *turn* in its senses of "sexual satisfaction" and "hanging" (as in line 52). 58. *eight:* Cf. *four*
in line 48. The discrepancy has been taken to indicate careless revision, but possibly it is for
Barnardine, who is also to die in the morning (line 7), that the block and axe are to be ready at
four. 61. *starkly:* stiffly. A transferred modifier, rightly describing the "traveller."
traveller's: laborer's (*travel* and *travail* were still variant spellings of a single word). Cf. Eccle-
siastes 5:12, "The sleep of him that travaileth is sweet" (Geneva; "a laboring man" in King
James). 63. *do good on:* bestow a benefit on, aid. 65–66. *By and by:* coming; just a minute
(called out to the one who knocks). 69. *best . . . spirits:* Contrasted with the harmful vapors
alluded to in IV.i.56. 75–76. *is . . . with:* runs precisely parallel with.

Duke: Not so, not so; his life is parallel'd   75
    Even with the stroke and line of his great justice.
    He doth with holy abstinence subdue
    That in himself which he spurs on his pow'r
    To qualify in others. Were he meal'd with that
    Which he corrects, then were he tyrannous,   80
    But this being so, he's just. *[Knocking within.]* Now are
    they come.   *[Exit Provost.]*
    This is a gentle Provost: seldom when
    The steeled jailer is the friend of men.*[Knocking within.]*
    How now? what noise? The spirit's possess'd with haste   85
    That wounds th' unsisting postern with these strokes.

[Enter Provost.*]*

    Provost: There he must stay until the officer
      Arise to let him in; he is call'd up.
    Duke: Have you no countermand for Claudio yet,
      But he must die to-morrow?
    Provost: None, sir, none.   90
    Duke: As near the dawning, Provost, as it is,
      You shall hear more ere morning.
    Provost: Happily
    You something know, yet I believe there comes
    No countermand; no such example have we.
    Besides, upon the very siege of justice   95
    Lord Angelo hath to the public ear
    Profess'd the contrary.

Enter a Messenger.

                   This is his [Lordship's] man.
    [Duke.] And here comes Claudio's pardon.
  Messenger: My lord hath sent you this note, and by me this fur-
    ther charge: that you swerve not from the smallest arti-   100
    cle of it, neither in time, matter, or other circumstance.
    Good morrow; for as I take it, it is almost day.
    Provost: I shall obey him.   *[Exit Messenger.]*
    Duke: *[Aside.]* This is his pardon, purchas'd by such sin
      For which the pardoner himself is in.   105

---

76. *stroke:* Synonymous with *line* in the image evoked by *parallel'd.* But *stroke* also recalls the *cruel striking* of Angelo's justice as it has been described in III.ii.247, and perhaps *stroke and line* has the second meaning "headsman's stroke and hangman's rope."   79. *qualify:* abate. *meal'd:* stained.   83. *gentle:* kindly.   *seldom when:* it rarely happens that.   84. *steeled:* hardened.   86. *unsisting:* shortened form of *unassisting* (?). Of several proposed emendations the best are *unshifting* (Capell) and *resisting* (Collier).   *postern:* small door.   93. *Happily:* haply, perhaps.   94. *example:* precedent.   95. *siege:* seat.

Hence hath offense his quick celerity,
When it is borne in high authority.
When vice makes mercy, mercy's so extended,
That for the fault's love is th' offender friended.
Now, sir, what news?   110

Provost: I told you: Lord Angelo (belike) thinking me remiss
in mine office, awakens me with this unwonted putting-
on, methinks strangely, for he hath not us'd it before.

Duke: Pray you let's hear.

[Prov. Reads] the letter.

"Whatsoever you may hear to the contrary, let Claudio   115
be executed by four of the clock, and in the afternoon
Barnardine. For my better satisfaction, let me have
Claudio's head sent me by five. Let this be duly perform'd, with a thought that more depends on it than we
must yet deliver. Thus fail not to do your office, as you   120
will answer it at your peril."
What say you to this, sir?

Duke: What is that Barnardine who is to be executed in th'
afternoon?

Provost: A Bohemian born; but here nurs'd up and bred, one   125
that is a prisoner nine years old.

Duke: How came it that the absent Duke had not either
deliver'd him to his liberty or executed him? I have
heard it was ever his manner to do so.

Provost: His friends still wrought reprieves for him; and   130
indeed his fact, till now in the government of Lord
Angelo, came not to an undoubtful proof.

Duke: It is now apparent?

Provost: Most manifest, and not denied by himself.

Duke: Hath he borne himself penitently in prison?   135
How seems he to be touch'd?

Provost: A man that apprehends death no more dreadfully
but as a drunken sleep, careless, reakless, and fearless of
what's past, present, or to come; insensible of mortality,
and desperately mortal.   140

Duke: He wants advice.

---

106. *his quick celerity:* Explained as "its lively speed" in order to clear the phrase of the charge
of tautology, but cf. *swift celerity* in V.i.393.   111. *belike:* I suppose.   112–13. *putting-on:*
pressure.   117. *satisfaction:* assurance.   120. *deliver:* declare, make known.   125. *here:* i.e.
in Vienna.   126. *is . . . old:* has been a prisoner for nine years.   130. *wrought:* managed to
obtain.   131. *fact:* deed, i.e. crime.   136. *touch'd:* affected.   137–38. *apprehends . . . as:*
conceives of death as no more dreadful than.   138. *careless:* without anxiety.   *reakless:*
reckless, unconcerned.   139. *insensible of mortality:* with no feeling about what death means
(?).   *desperately mortal:* without hope of escaping execution (?) or in a desperate state of
mortal sin (?).   141. *wants advice:* lacks (spiritual) counsel.

Provost: He will hear none. He hath evermore had the liberty of the prison; give him leave to escape hence, he would not. Drunk many times a day, if not many days entirely drunk. We have very oft awak'd him, as if to 145 carry him to execution, and show'd him a seeming warrant for it; it hath not mov'd him at all.

Duke: More of him anon. There is written in your brow, Provost, honesty and constancy; if I read it not truly, my ancient skill beguiles me; but in the boldness of my cun- 150 ning, I will lay myself in hazard. Claudio, whom here you have warrant to execute, is no greater forfeit to the law than Angelo who hath sentenc'd him. To make you understand this in a manifested effect, I crave but four day's respite; for the which you are to do me both a 155 present and a dangerous courtesy.

Provost: Pray, sir, in what?

Duke: In the delaying death.

Provost: Alack, how may I do it, having the hour limited, and an express command, under penalty, to deliver his head 160 in the view of Angelo? I may make my case as Claudio's, to cross this in the smallest.

Duke: By the vow of mine order I warrant you, if my instructions may be your guide. Let this Barnardine be this morning executed, and his head borne to Angelo. 165

Provost: Angelo hath seen them both, and will discover the favor.

Duke: O, death's a great disguiser, and you may add to it. Shave the head, and tie the beard, and say it was the desire of the penitent to be so bar'd before his death. 170 You know the course is common. If any thing fall to you upon this, more than thanks and good fortune, by the saint whom I profess, I will plead against it with my life.

Provost: Pardon me, good father, it is against my oath.

Duke: Were you sworn to the Duke, or to the deputy? 175

Provost: To him, and to his substitutes.

Duke: You will think you have made no offense, if the Duke avouch the justice of your dealing?

Provost: But what likelihood is in that?

Duke: Not a resemblance, but a certainty; yet since I see 180

---

151. *lay . . . hazard:* risk my all.   154. *in . . . effect:* through concrete evidence, by a clear demonstration.   154–55. *four days' respite.* Cf. *two days* in line 189. It is difficult to account for *four.*   156. *present:* immediate.   159. *limited:* fixed.   161. *cross:* go contrary to. 163. *warrant you:* guarantee you against harm.   166–67. *discover the favor:* recognize the face.   168. *tie.* Not satisfactorily explained. Many editors emended to *trim* or *dye.*   171. *fall to:* befall.   172. *upon:* in consequence of.   178. *avouch:* confirm, uphold.   *justice:* justness.   180. *resemblance:* probability (?).

you fearful, that neither my coat, integrity, nor persuasion can with ease attempt you, I will go further than I meant, to pluck all fears out of you. Look you, sir, here is the hand and seal of the Duke; you know the character, I doubt not, and the signet is not strange to you. 185

Provost: I know them both.

Duke: The contents of this is the return of the Duke. You shall anon over-read it at your pleasure; where you shall find, within these two days he will be here. This is a thing that Angelo knows not, for he this very day 190 receives letters of strange tenor, perchance of the Duke's death, perchance entering into some monastery, but by chance nothing of what is writ. Look, th' unfolding star calls up the shepherd. Put not yourself into amazement how these things should be; all difficulties 195 are but easy when they are known. Call your executioner, and off with Barnardine's head. I will give him a present shrift, and advise him for a better place. Yet you are amaz'd, but this shall absolutely resolve you. Come away, it is almost clear dawn. *Exeunt.* 200

Scene III

Enter Clown [Pompey].

Pompey: I am as well acquainted here as I was in our house of profession. One would think it were Mistress Overdone's own house, for here be many of her old customers. First, here's young Master Rash, he's in for a commodity of brown paper and old ginger, ninescore 5 and seventeen pounds, of which he made five marks ready money. Marry, then ginger was not much in request, for the old women were all dead. Then is there here one Master Caper, at the suit of Master Three-pile the mercer, for some four suits of peach-color'd satin, 10

---

182. *attempt:* tempt.   184–85. *character:* handwriting.   193. *writ:* i.e. written here (?).
193–94. *unfolding star:* morning star, whose appearance tells the shepherd that it is time to release his sheep from the fold.   195. *amazement:* perplexity.   199. *absolutely resolve you:* dispel your doubts completely.

IV.iii. Location: Scene continues. 1. *am . . . acquainted:* have as wide an acquaintance.
4–5. *a commodity . . . ginger:* A moneylender could circumvent the statute limiting interest on loans to ten percent by forcing a borrower to take a substantial part of the loan in some "commodity" at a valuation determined by the lender. Rash has had to agree to a valuation of 197 pounds on merchandise which on resale has brought little more than three pounds (a mark was two-thirds of a pound). 8. *old women.* Traditionally fond of ginger. The sentence has been taken as a reference to the heavy plague mortality in 1603.. 9. *Caper:* i.e. frolic. The names of the prisoners are more or less suggestive of their particular bents. *Three-pile:* See the note on I.ii.31.

which now peaches him a beggar. Then have we here
young Dizzy, and young Master Deep-vow, and Master
Copper-spur, and Master Starve-lackey the rapier and
dagger man, and young Drop-heir that kill'd lusty Pudding, and Master Forthlight the tilter, and brave Master   15
Shoe-tie the great traveller, and wild Half-can that
stabb'd Pots, and I think forty more, all great doers in
our trade, and are now "for the Lord's sake."

Enter Abhorson.

> *Abhorson:* Sirrah, bring Barnardine hither.
> *Pompey:* Master Barnardine! You must rise and be hang'd,   20
> Master Barnardine!
> *Abhorson:* What ho, Barnardine!
> *Barnardine:* (Within.) A pox o' your throats! Who makes that
> noise there? What are you?
> *Pompey:* Your friends, sir, the hangman. You must be so   25
> good, sir, to rise, and be put to death.
> *Barnardine:* [Within.] Away, you rogue, away! I am sleepy.
> *Abhorson:* Tell him he must awake, and that quickly too.
> *Pompey:* Pray, Master Barnardine, awake till you are exe-
> cuted, and sleep afterwards.   30
> *Abhorson:* Go in to him, and fetch him out.
> *Pompey:* He is coming, sir, he is coming. I hear his straw
> rustle.

Enter Barnardine.

> *Abhorson:* Is the axe upon the block, sirrah?
> *Pompey:* Very ready, sir.   35
> *Barnardine:* How now, Abhorson? What's the news with you?
> *Abhorson:* Truly, sir, I would desire you to clap into your
> prayers; for look you, the warrant's come.
> *Barnardine:* You rogue, I have been drinking all night, I am not
> fitted for't.   40
> *Pompey:* O, the better, sir; for he that drinks all night, and is
> hang'd betimes in the morning, may sleep the sounder
> all the next day.

---

11. *peaches him:* accuses him (of being).   15. *Forthlight:* Perhaps an error for *Forthright*, i.e.
straight ahead (as a tilter, or jouster, might ride).   *brave:* showily dressed.   16. *Shoe-tie . . .
traveller:* Gaudy decorations on shoes were a foreign importation.   18. *"for . . . sake":* the cry
with which prisoners, who had to supply their own food and other necessities, besought the
charity of those who passed by their barred windows.   26. *to:* as to.   37. *clap into:* speedily
begin.   42. *betimes:* early.

Enter Duke *[disguised as a friar.]*

Abhorson: Look you, sir, here comes your ghostly father. Do
 we jest now, think you?   45
    Duke: Sir, induc'd by my charity, and hearing how hastily
 you are to depart, I am come to advise you, comfort you,
 and pray with you.
Barnardine: Friar, not I; I have been drinking hard all night, and
 I will have more time to prepare me, or they shall beat   50
 out my brains with billets. I will not consent to die this
 day, that's certain.
    Duke: O sir, you must; and therefore I beseech you
 Look forward on the journey you shall go.
Barnardine: I swear I will not die to-day for any man's   55
 persuasion.
    Duke: But hear you—
Barnardine: Not a word. If you have any thing to say to me, come
 to my ward; for thence will not I to-day.   *Exit.*

Enter Provost.

    Duke: Unfit to live, or die; O gravel heart!   60
 After him, fellows, bring him to the block.
                          [Exeunt Abhorson and Pompey.]
Provost: Now, sir, how do you find the prisoner?
    Duke: A creature unprepar'd, unmeet for death;
 And to transport him in the mind he is
 Were damnable.
Provost: Here in the prison, father,   65
 There died this morning of a cruel fever
 One Ragozine, a most notorious pirate,
 A man of Claudio's years; his beard and head
 Just of his color. What if we do omit
 This reprobate till he were well inclin'd,   70
 And satisfy the deputy with the visage
 of Ragozine, more like to Claudio?
    Duke: O, 'tis an accident that heaven provides!
 Dispatch it presently, the hour draws on
 Prefix'ed by Angelo. See this be done,   75
 And sent according to command, whiles I
 Persuade this rude wretch willingly to die.

---

44. *ghostly:* spiritual.   51. *billets:* blocks of wood, clubs.   59. *ward:* cell.   60. *gravel:*
stony.   64. *transport him:* send him to the next world.   69. *omit:* pass over.   70. *well inclin'd:*
in a proper state of mind.   73. *accident:* event.   74. *Dispatch it presently:* put it into execution
at once.   75. *Prefix'd:* set in advance.

Provost: This shall be done, good father, presently.
But Barnardine must die this afternoon;
And how shall we continue Claudio,   80
To save me from the danger that might come
If he were known alive?
    Duke: Let this be done:
Put them in secret holds, both Barnardine and Claudio.
Ere twice the sun hath made his journal greeting
To yond generation, you shall find   85
Your safety manifested.
    Provost: I am your free dependant.
    Duke: Quick, dispatch, and send the head to Angelo.

                                  Exit [Provost].

Now will I write letters to Angelo
(The Provost, he shall bear them), whose contents   90
Shall witness to him I am near at home;
And that by great injunctions I am bound
To enter publicly. Him I'll desire
To meet me at the consecrated fount,
A league below the city; and from thence,   95
By cold gradation and weal-balanc'd form,
We shall proceed with Angelo.

Enter Provost *[with Ragozine's head].*

    Provost: Here is the head, I'll carry it myself.
    Duke: Convenient is it. Make a swift return,
For I would commune with you of such things   100
That want no ear but yours.
    Provost: I'll make all speed.   *Exit.*
    Isabella: (*Within.*) Peace, ho, be here!
    Duke: The tongue of Isabel. She's come to know
If yet her brother's pardon be come hither.
But I will keep her ignorant of her good,   105
To make her heavenly comforts of despair,
When it is least expected.

---

80. *continue:* keep.   83. *holds:* cells.   84. *journal:* daily.   85. *yond generation:* i.e. men
outside the prison, on whom the sunlight falls (?). Some editors adopt Rowe's *yonder
generation* (to mend the metre); others follow Hanmer in reading *th' under generation,* meaning
either "people under the sun" or "people in the Antipodes" (so that line 84 would mean
either "before two days are past" or "before two nights are past").   87. *free dependant:*
willing follower.   89. *Angelo.* Since in V.i the Duke enters the city with Varrius, it is
conjectured that *Angelo* is an error for *Varrius,* picked up inadvertently from the end of line
88.   92. *by great injunctions:* for compelling reasons (?).   94. *fount:* spring.   96. *cold
gradation:* coolly reasoned steps (?).   *weal-balanc'd form:* formalities required by considerations
of state (?). Most editors follow Rowe in reading *well-balanced form,* "all due formalities."
97. *with:* in the affair of, against.   99. *Convenient:* fitting.   101. *want:* require.   106. *of:* out
of.   107. *it:* i.e comfort.

Isabella:	Ho, by your leave!

Duke: Good morning to you, fair and gracious daughter.

Isabella: The better, given me by so holy a man.

Hath yet the deputy sent my brother's pardon? 110

Duke: He hath releas'd him, Isabel, from the world,

His head is off, and sent to Angelo.

Isabella: Nay, but it is not so.

Duke: It is no other.

Show your wisdom, daughter, in your close patience.

Isabella: O, I will to him, and pluck out his eyes! 115

Duke: You shall not be admitted to his sight.

Isabella: Unhappy Claudio! Wretched Isabel!

Injurious world! Most damned Angelo!

Duke: This nor hurts him, nor profits you a jot.

Forbear it therefore, give your cause to heaven. 120

Mark what I say, which you shall find

By every syllable a faithful verity.

The Duke comes home to-morrow—nay, dry your

eyes—

One of our covent, and his confessor, 125

Gives me this instance: already he hath carried

Notice to Escalus and Angelo,

Who do prepare to meet him at the gates,

There to give up their pow'r. If you can pace your

wisdom 130

In that good path that I would wish it go,

And you shall have your bosom on this wretch,

Grace of the Duke, revenges to your heart,

And general honor.

Isabella: I am directed by you.

Duke: This letter then to Friar Peter give; 135

'Tis that he sent me of the Duke's return.

Say, by this token, I desire his company

At Mariana's house to-night. Her cause and yours

I'll perfect him withal, and he shall bring you

Before the Duke; and to the head of Angelo 140

Accuse him home and home. For my poor self,

---

114. *close patience:* silent fortitude.   117. *Unhappy:* unfortunate.   120. *give:* commit, entrust.   125. *convent:* convent, religious house.   *and:* i.e. who is   126. *instance:* evidence. 129–30. *pace your wisdom:* teach your wisdom to go (a figure from riding).   131. *go.* Some such expression as *do so* must be understood after this word—a not uncommon type of ellipsis.   132. *have your bosom:* have your desire fulfilled.   135. *Peter.* Probably Shakespeare had in mind the friar of I.iii but had forgotten that he is there named Thomas.   139. *perfect him withal:* fully acquaint him with.   140. *head:* i.e. face.   141. *home and home:* to the utmost.

I am combined by a sacred vow,
And shall be absent. Wend you with this letter.
Command these fretting waters from your eyes
With a light heart; trust not my holy order   145
If I pervert your course. Who's here?

Enter Lucio.

Lucio: Good even. Friar, where's the Provost?
Duke: Not within, sir.
Lucio: O pretty Isabella, I am pale at mine heart to see
thine eyes so red; thou must be patient. I am fain to   150
dine and sup with water and bran; I dare not for my
head fill my belly; one fruitful meal would set me to't.
But they say the Duke will be here to-morrow. By my
troth, Isabel, I lov'd thy brother. If the old fantastical
Duke of dark corners had been at home, he had liv'd.   155

[Exit Isabella.]

Duke: Sir, the Duke is marvellous little beholding to your
reports, but the best is, he lives not in them.
Lucio: Friar, thou knowest not the Duke so well as I do; he's
a better woodman than thou tak'st him for.
Duke: Well; you'll answer this one day. Fare ye well.   160
Lucio: Nay, tarry, I'll go along with thee. I can tell thee
pretty tales of the Duke.
Duke: You have told me too many of him already, sir, if
they be true; if not true, none were enough.
Lucio: I was once before him for getting a wench with   165
child.
Duke: Did you such a thing?
Lucio: Yes, marry, did I; but I was fain to forswear it. They
would else have married me to the rotten medlar.
Duke: Sir, your company is fairer than honest. Rest you   170
well.
Lucio: By my troth, I'll go with thee to the lane's end. If
bawdy talk offend you, we'll have very little of it. Nay,
friar, I am a kind of bur, I shall stick.   *Exeunt.*

---

142. *combined:* bound (cf. *combinate-husband,* III.i.219).   144. *fretting:* corrosive.   146. *per-vert:* direct wrongly.   147. *Good even.* A striking discrepancy.   149. *pale . . . heart.* Grief was thought to draw blood from the heart.   150. *fain:* obliged.   151. *bran:* coarse brown bread.   151–52. *for my head:* i.e. for fear of being beheaded.   155. *of dark corners:* Cf. Lucio's earlier allegations of the Duke's secret lechery.   156. *beholding:* beholden, indebted.   157. *he . . . them:* i.e. they do not describe him.   159. *woodman:* forester, i.e. hunter (of women).   160. *answer:* be held answerable.   169. *medlar:* an apple-like fruit that was not edible until it had begun to rot.   170. *fairer:* more amusing.

Scene IV

Enter Angelo *and* Escalus.

Escalus: Every letter he hath writ hath disvouch'd other.

Angelo: In most uneven and distracted manner. His actions
show much like to madness, pray heaven his wisdom be
not tainted! And why meet him at the gates, and [rede-
liver] our authorities there?   5

Escalus: I guess not.

Angelo: And why should we proclaim it in an hour before his
ent'ring, that if any crave redress of injustice, they
should exhibit their petitions in the street?

Escalus: He shows his reason for that: to have a dispatch of   10
complaints, and to deliver us from devices hereafter,
which shall then have no power to stand against us.

Angelo: Well; I beseech you let it be proclaim'd betimes i' th'
morn. I'll call you at your house. Give notice to such
men of sort and suit as are to meet him.   15

Escalus: I shall, sir. Fare you well.

Angelo: Good night.   *Exit [Escalus].*
This deed unshapes me quite, makes me unpregnant
And dull to all proceedings. A deflow'red maid!
And by an eminent body that enforc'd   20
The law against it! But that her tender shame
Will not proclaim against her maiden loss,
How might she tongue me! Yet reason dares her no,
For my authority bears of a credent bulk,
That no particular scandal once can touch   25
But it confounds the breather. He should have liv'd,
Save that his riotous youth with dangerous sense
Might in the times to come have ta'en revenge,
By so receiving a dishonor'd life
With ransom of such shame. Would yet he had liv'd!   30
Alack, when once our grace we have forgot,
Nothing goes right—we would, and we would not. *Exit.*

IV.iv. Location: Angelo's house. 1. *disvouch'd:* disavowed.   2. *uneven:* irregular.   3. *wisdom
. . . tainted:* reason . . . impaired.   6. *guess not:* cannot guess.   7. *in an hour:* "leaving a clear
hour" (Lever).   10. *dispatch:* speedy settlement.   11. *devices:* contrived charges.   15. *sort:*
rank.   *suit:* following (?) or service at court (?).   18. *unpregnant:* unready, unapt.   20. *body:*
person.   *enforc'd:* executed rigorously.   21. *But that:* were it not that.   22. *her maiden loss:*
the loss of her virginity.   23. *tongue:* i.e. denounce.   *dares her no.* Not satisfactorily
explained, but the sense is clear: reason forbids it.   24. *bears of a:* bears a (cf. *allows of, accept
of,* etc.). Some editors read *bears a* for metrical reasons.   *credent bulk:* massive credibility,
great power to win belief.   25. *no particular scandal:* no scandal whatever (*particular* = single,
as in V.i.245).   26. *But . . . breather:* without destroying the one who uttered it.   *Should:*
would.   27. *sense:* passion (?) or perceptiveness (?).   29. *By:* at, for.

Scene V

Enter Duke *[in his own habit] and* Friar Peter.

> *Duke:* These letters at fit time deliver me. *[Giving letters.]*
> The Provost knows our purpose and our plot.
> The matter being afoot, keep your instruction,
> And hold you ever to our special drift,
> Though sometimes you do blench from this to that, 5
> As cause doth minister. Go call at Flavio's house,
> And tell him where I stay. Give the like notice
> To Valentius, Rowland, and to Crassus,
> And bid them bring the trumpets to the gate.
> But send me Flavius first.
>
> *Friar Peter:* It shall be speeded well.*[Exit.]* 10

Enter Varrius.

> *Duke:* I thank thee, Varrius, thou hast made good haste.
> Come, we will walk. There's other of our friends
> Will greet us here anon. My gentle Varrius! *Exeunt.*

Scene VI

Enter Isabella *and* Mariana.

> *Isabella:* To speak so indirectly I am loath.
> I would say the truth, but to accuse him so,
> That is your part. Yet I am advis'd to do it,
> He says, to veil full purpose.
>
> *Mariana:* Be rul'd by him.
> *Isabella:* Besides, he tells me that if peradventure 5
> He speak against me on the adverse side,
> I should not think it strange, for 'tis a physic
> That's bitter to sweet end.

Enter [Friar] Peter.

> *Mariana:* I would Friar Peter—
> *Isabella:* O, peace, the friar is come.
> *Friar Peter:* Come, I have found you out a stand most fit, 10
> Where you may have such vantage on the Duke,
> He shall not pass you. Twice have the trumpets
> sounded;

IV.v. Location: Fields outside the town. 1. *deliver me:* deliver for me. 3. *keep:* keep to, follow. 4. *drift:* course, intention. 5. *blench:* turn aside. 6. *minister:* give occasion. 9. *trumpets:* trumpeters.

IV.vi. Location: A street near the city gate. 3. *advis'd:* well-advised. 10. *stand:* place to stand. 11. *have . . . on:* be in so favorable a position for accosting.

The generous and gravest citizens
Have hent the gates, and very near upon   15
The Duke is ent'ring; therefore hence away!   *Exeunt.*

ACT V

Scene I

[Flourish.] Enter Duke, Varrius, Lords, Angelo, Escalus, Lucio, [Provost,
Officers,] Citizens *at several doors.*

Duke: My very worthy cousin, fairly met!
   Our old and faithful friend, we are glad to see you.
Angelo, Escalus: Happy return be to your royal Grace!
Duke: Many and hearty thankings to you both.
   We have made inquiry of you, and we hear   5
   Such goodness of your justice, that our soul
   Cannot but yield you forth to public thanks,
   Forerunning more requital.
Angelo: You make my bonds still
   greater.
Duke: O, your desert speaks loud, and I should wrong it   10
   To lock it in the wards of covert bosom,
   When it deserves with characters of brass
   A forted residence 'gainst the tooth of time
   And razure of oblivion. Give [me] your hand,
   And let the subject see, to make them know   15
   That outward courtesies would fain proclaim
   Favors that keep within. Come, Escalus,
   You must walk by us on our other hand;
   And good supporters are you.

Enter [Friar] Peter *and* Isabella.

Friar Peter: Now is your time: speak loud, and kneel before him. 20
Isabella: Justice, O royal Duke! Vail your regard
   Upon a wrong'd—I would fain have said a maid!
   O worthy Prince, dishonor not your eye
   By throwing it on any other object,
   Till you have heard me in my true complaint,   25

---

14. *generous and gravest:* noblest and worthiest (the superlative ending of *gravest* governs both
adjectives).   15. *hent:* taken places at.   *very near upon:* at just about this time.
V.i. Location: The city gate. 1. *cousin.* Form of address by a sovereign to one of his lords.
6. *goodness:* good reports.   7. *yield . . . thanks:* i.e. offer you public thanks.   8. *more requital:*
greater reward.   *bonds:* obligations.   11. *wards:* cells.   *covert bosom:* private thoughts and
feelings.   12. *characters:* letters, inscription.   13. *forted:* fortified.   *tooth of time:* Time
devours all things.   14. *razure:* obliteration.   16. *fain:* gladly.   17. *keep:* dwell.   19. *supporters:* A heraldic term, designating the figures at either side of the shield.   21. *Vail your
regard:* bend your look.

And given me justice, justice, justice, justice!
Duke: Relate your wrongs. In what? By whom? Be brief.
Here is Lord Angelo shall give you justice;
Reveal yourself to him.
Isabella: O worthy Duke,
You bid me seek redemption of the devil.   30
Hear me yourself; for that which I must speak
Must either punish me, not being believ'd,
Or wring redress from you. Hear me, O hear me, here.
Angelo: My lord, her wits, I fear me, are not firm.
She hath been a suitor to me for her brother,   35
Cut off by course of justice—
Isabella: By course of justice!
Angelo: And she will speak most bitterly and strange.
Isabella: Most strange! but yet most truly will I speak:
That Angelo's forsworn, is it not strange?
That Angelo's a murtherer, is't not strange?   40
That Angelo is an adulterous thief,
An hypocrite, a virgin-violator,
Is it not strange? and strange?
Duke: Nay, it is ten times
strange.
Isabella: It is not truer he is Angelo   45
Than this is all as true as it is strange;
Nay, it is ten times true, for truth is truth
To th' end of reck'ning.
Duke: Away with her! Poor soul,
She speaks this in th' infirmity of sense.
Isabella: O Prince, I conjure thee, as thou believ'st   50
There is another comfort than this world,
That thou neglect me not, with that opinion
That I am touch'd with madness. Make not impossible
That which but seems unlike; 'tis not impossible
But one the wicked'st caitiff on the ground,   55
May seem as shy, as grave, as just, as absolute
As Angelo. Even so may Angelo,
In all his dressings, caracts, titles, forms,
Be an arch-villain. Believe it, royal Prince,
If he be less, he's nothing, but he's more,   60
Had I more name for badness.
Duke: By mine honesty,

---

29. *Reveal yourself:* i.e. disclose your suit.   46. *all as:* just as.   49. *sense:* intellect, reason.
50. *conjure:* adjure.   53. *Make:* deem.   54. *unlike:* unlikely.   55. *one the wicked'st:* the most
wicked (an old idiom).   *caitiff:* wretch.   56. *shy.* See the note on III.ii.122.   *absolute:*
without defect.   58. *dressings . . . forms:* robes of office, insignia, titles, ceremonies.   60. *If
. . . nothing:* i.e. he could be less a villain than he is, yet wicked.   61. *more:* i.e. worse (than
arch-villain).

If she be mad, as I believe no other,
Her madness hath the oddest frame of sense,
Such a dependancy of thing on thing,
As e'er I heard in madness.

Isabella: O gracious Duke, 65
Harp not on that; nor do not banish reason
For inequality, but let your reason serve
To make the truth appear, where it seems hid,
And hide the false seems true.

Duke: Many that are not mad
Have sure more lack of reason. What would you say? 70

Isabella: I am the sister of one Claudio,
Condemn'd upon the act of fornication
To lose his head, condemn'd by Angelo.
I (in probation of a sisterhood)
Was sent to by my brother; one Lucio 75
As then the messenger—

Lucio: That's I, and't like your Grace.
I came to her from Claudio, and desir'd her
To try her gracious fortune with Lord Angelo,
For her poor brother's pardon.

Isabella: That's he indeed. 80

Duke: [To Lucio.] You were not bid to speak.

Lucio: No, my good lord,
Nor wish'd to hold my peace.

Duke: I wish you now then.
Pray you take note of it; and when you have
A business for yourself, pray heaven you then
Be perfect.

Lucio: I warrant your honor. 85

Duke: The warrant's for yourself; take heed to't.

Isabella: This gentleman told somewhat of my tale—

Lucio: Right.

Duke: It may be right, but you are i' the wrong
To speak before your time. Proceed.

---

63. *frame of sense:* rational form.   64. *dependancy . . . thing:* logical order.   66. *that:* i.e.
madness.   66–67. *do . . . inequality:* i.e. do not declare my reason gone because of discrepancy
(between her report of Angelo and the general report) (?). This interpretation seems
preferable to those that take *reason* as referring to the Duke's reason and *inequality* as "injustice" or "partiality" or "disparity" (between Isabella's status and Angelo's); it permits Isabella
a more respectful address to her sovereign and furnishes an effective contrast rather than
mere repetition in *reason / your reason:* "Do not adjudge me lacking in reason, but rather
employ your own reason to find out the truth."   69. *hide:* remove from sight.   *seems:* that
seems.   72. *upon:* in consequence of.   74. *probation:* novitiate.   81. *wish'd:* asked, bidden
(cf. *desir'd* in line 77).   *wish you now:* bid you now to do so.   84. *A business for yourself:* a
matter in which you are involved.   *perfect:* fully prepared.   85. *warrant:* assure. The Duke
quibbles on the sense "warrant for arrest."

Isabella: I went   90
To this pernicious caitiff deputy—
Duke: That's somewhat madly spoken.
Isabella: Pardon it,
The phrase is to the matter.
Duke: Mended again. The matter; proceed.
Isabella: In brief, to set the needless process by—   95
How I persuaded, how I pray'd, and kneel'd,
How he refell'd me, and how I replied
(For this was of much length)—the vild conclusion
I now begin with grief and shame to utter.
He would not, but by gift of my chaste body   100
To his concupiscible intemperate lust,
Release my brother; and after much debatement,
My sisterly remorse confutes mine honor,
And I did yield to him; but the next morn betimes,
His purpose surfeiting, he sends a warrant   105
For my poor brother's head.
Duke: This is most likely!
Isabella: O that it were as like as it is true!
Duke: By heaven, fond wretch, thou know'st not what
thou speak'st,
Or else thou art suborn'd against his honor   110
In hateful practice. First, his integrity
Stands without blemish; next, it imports no reason
That with such vehemency he should pursue
Faults proper to himself. If he had so offended,
He would have weigh'd thy brother by himself,   115
And not have cut him off. Some one hath set you on;
Confess the truth, and say by whose advice
Thou cam'st here to complain.
Isabella: And is this all?
Then, O you blessed ministers above,
Keep me in patience, and with ripened time   120
Unfold the evil which is here wrapp'd up
In countenance! Heaven shield your Grace from woe,
As I, thus wrong'd, hence unbelieved go!
Duke: I know you'ld fain be gone. An officer!

---

93. *to the matter:* to the point, germane.   94. *Mended:* i.e. speaking sanely.   *The matter:* get to
the point (since you say it is to the point).   95. *set . . . by:* omit unnecessary details of the
story.   96. *persuaded:* pleaded.   97. *refell'd:* refuted.   98. *vild:* vile (a variant form).
103. *remorse:* pity.   109. *fond:* foolish.   111. *practice:* conspiracy.   112. *it . . . reason:* it is
irrational.   113. *pursue:* persecute.   114. *proper to himself:* that he himself possessed.
115. *weigh'd . . . himself.* Cf.II.ii.134, III.ii.246.   119. *ministers:* angels.   121. *Unfold:*
unwrap, disclose.   122. *In countenance:* in the Duke's authority (?) or by the Duke's allowance
(?).

To prison with her! Shall we thus permit   125
A blasting and a scandalous breath to fall
On him so near us? This needs must be a practice.
Who knew of your intent and coming hither?

Isabella: One that I would were here, Friar Lodowick.

Duke: A ghostly father, belike. Who knows that Lodowick?   130

Lucio: My lord, I know him, 'tis a meddling friar.
I do not like the man; had he been lay, my lord,
For certain words he spake against your Grace
In your retirement, I had swing'd him soundly.

Duke: Words against me? This' a good friar, belike!   135
And to set on this wretched woman here
Against our substitute! Let this friar be found.

Lucio: But yesternight, my lord, she and that friar,
I saw them at the prison. A saucy friar,
A very scurvy fellow.   140

Friar Peter: Blessed be your royal Grace!
I have stood by, my lord, and I have heard
Your royal ear abus'd. First, hath this woman
Most wrongfully accus'd your substitute,
Who is as free from touch or soil with her   145
As she from one ungot.

Duke: We did believe no less.
Know you that Friar Lodowick that she speaks of?

Friar Peter: I know him for a man divine and holy,
Not scurvy, nor a temporary meddler,
As he's reported by this gentleman;   150
And on my trust, a man that never yet
Did (as he vouches) misreport your Grace.

Lucio: My lord, most villainously, believe it.

Friar Peter: Well; he in time may come to clear himself;
But at this instant he is sick, my lord,   155
Of a strange fever. Upon his mere request,
Being come to knowledge that there was complaint
Intended 'gainst Lord Angelo, came I hither,
To speak as from his mouth, what he with his oath
And all probation will make up full clear,   160
Whensoever he's convented. First, for this woman,

---

126. *blasting:* blighting (like a destructive wind). 131. *meddling:* Perhaps (as often) with an implication of sexual impropriety; cf. *saucy* (line 139), which can mean both "impudent" and "lecherous." 134. *swing'd:* beaten (from *swinge*). 135. *This':* this is. 143. *abus'd:* deceived. 145. *touch or soil:* impure contact. 146. *ungot:* unbegotten. 149. *temporary meddler:* meddler in temporal affairs. 152. *as he vouches:* i.e. as Lucio affirms. 156. *Upon . . . request:* solely at his request. 157. *Being . . . knowledge:* since he had learned. 160. *probation:* proof. 161. *convented:* summoned.

To justify this worthy nobleman,
So vulgarly and personally accus'd,
Her shall you hear disproved to her eyes,
Till she herself confess it.

Duke: Good friar, let's hear it.   165

[Isabella is carried off guarded.]

Do you not smile at this, Lord Angelo?
O heaven, the vanity of wretched fools!
Give us some seats. Come, cousin Angelo,
In this I'll be impartial. Be you judge
Of your own cause.

Enter Mariana *[veiled].*

                                Is this the witness, friar?   170
First, let her show [her] face, and after speak.

Mariana: Pardon, my lord, I will not show my face
Until my husband bid me.

Duke: What, are you married?

Mariana: No, my lord.   175

Duke: Are you a maid?

Mariana: No, my lord.

Duke: A widow then?

Mariana: Neither, my lord.

Duke: Why, you are nothing then: neither maid, widow,   180
nor wife?

Lucio: My lord, she may be a punk; for many of them are
neither maid, widow, nor wife.

Duke: Silence that fellow. I would he had some cause
To prattle for himself.   185

Lucio: Well, my lord.

Mariana: My lord, I do confess I ne'er was married,
And I confess besides I am no maid.
I have known my husband, yet my husband
Knows not that ever he knew me.   190

Lucio: He was drunk then, my lord, it can be no better.

Duke: For the benefit of silence, would thou wert so too!

Lucio: Well, my lord.

Duke: This is not witness for Lord Angelo.

Mariana: Now I come to't, my lord.   195
She that accuses him of fornication,
In self-same manner doth accuse my husband,
And charges him, my lord, with such a time

---

163. *vulgarly:* publicly.   167. *vanity:* folly.   168. *be impartial:* not take part.   179. *Neither:*
nor that either.   182. *punk:* prostitute.   184–85. *some . . . himself:* some necessity to speak
in his own defense.   189. *known:* known carnally.   198. *with . . . time:* with committing the
offense at the very time.

1556   **Drama**

When I'll depose I had him in mine arms
With all th' effect of love.   200
    Angelo: Charges she moe than me?
    Mariana: Not that I know.
    Duke: No? You say your husband.
    Mariana: Why, just, my lord, and that is Angelo,
Who thinks he knows that he ne'er knew my body,
But knows he thinks that he knows Isabel's.   205
    Angelo: This is a strange abuse. Let's see thy face.
    Mariana: My husband bids me, now I will unmask.

                                   [Unveiling.]

That is that face, thou cruel Angelo,
Which once thou swor'st was worth the looking on;
This is the hand which, with a vow'd contract,   210
Was fast belock'd in thine; this is the body
That took away the match from Isabel,
And did supply thee at thy garden-house
In her imagin'd person.
    Duke: Know you this woman?
    Lucio: Carnally, she says.
    Duke: Sirrah, no more!   215
    Lucio: Enough, my lord.
    Angelo: My lord, I must confess I know this woman,
And five years since there was some speech of marriage
Betwixt myself and her; which was broke off,
Partly for that her promised proportions   220
Came short of composition, but in chief
For that her reputation was disvalued
In levity. Since which time of five years
I never spake with her, saw her, nor heard from her,
Upon my faith and honor.
    Mariana: Noble Prince,   225
As there comes light from heaven, and words from
breath,
As there is sense in truth, and truth in virtue,
I am affianc'd this man's wife as strongly
As words could make up vows; and, my good lord,   230
But Tuesday night last gone, in 's garden-house,
He knew me as a wife. As this is true,

---

199. *depose:* testify on oath.   200. *effect:* manifestations.   201. *moe:* more (persons).
203. *just:* just so, exactly.   211. *fast belock'd:* See note on I.ii.137.   212. *match:* appointed
meeting (but also with reference to the marriage thus consummated).   213. *supply thee:* (1) fill
her place with you; (2) satisfy your wants.   222. *for that:* because.   *proportions:* portion,
dowry.   *composition:* the agreed amount.   223. *disvalued:* debased.   224. *levity:* lightness,
wantonness.

Let me in safety raise me from my knees,
Or else for ever be confixed here,
A marble monument!

Angelo: I did not smile till now.   235
Now, good my lord, give me the scope of justice,
My patience here is touch'd. I do perceive
These poor informal women are no more
But instruments of some more mightier member
That sets them on. Let me have way, my lord,   240
To find this practice out.

Duke: Ay, with my heart,
And punish them to your height of pleasure.
Thou foolish friar, and thou pernicious woman,
Compact with her that's gone, think'st thou thy oaths,
Though they would swear down each particular saint,   245
Were testimonies against his worth and credit
That's seal'd in approbation? You, Lord Escalus,
Sit with my cousin; lend him your kind pains
To find out this abuse, whence 'tis deriv'd.
There is another friar that set them on,   250
Let him be sent for.

Friar Peter: Would he were here, my lord, for he indeed
Hath set the women on to this complaint.
Your Provost knows the place where he abides,
And he may fetch him.

Duke: Go, do it instantly. *[Exit Provost.]* 255
And you, my noble and well-warranted cousin,
Whom it concerns to hear this matter forth,
Do with your injuries as seems you best,
In any chastisement. I for a while will leave you;
But stir not you till you have well determin'd   260
Upon these slanderers.

Escalus: My lord, we'll do it throughly.
                                                    Exit [Duke].

Signior Lucio, did not you say you knew that Friar
Lodowick to be a dishonest person?

Lucio. *Cucullus non facit monachum:* honest in nothing but

---

233. *confixed:* firmly fixed.   234. *marble:* immovable.   236. *scope:* full authority.
237. *touch'd:* wounded, i.e. tried beyond its limit.   238. *informal:* distracted.   244. *Compact:*
leagued.   245. *each particular:* every single.   247. *seal'd in approbation.* "Angelo's faith has
been tried, approved, and sealed in testimony of that approbation, and . . . is no more to be
called in question" (Johnson).   257. *forth:* to the end, thoroughly.   258. *with your injuries:*
with respect to the wrongs done you.   260. *determin'd:* reached a judgment.   262. *throughly:*
thoroughly.   264. *Cucullus . . . monachum:* the hood does not make the monk (proverbial).
Lucio does not know how truly he speaks.

in his clothes, and one that hath spoke most villainous 265
speeches of the Duke.

Escalus: We shall entreat you to abide here till he come, and
enforce them against him. We shall find this friar a
notable fellow.

Lucio: As any in Vienna, on my word. 270

Escalus: Call that same Isabel here once again, I would speak
with her. *[Exit an Attendant.]* Pray you, my lord, give me
leave to question, you shall see how I'll handle her.

Lucio: Not better than he, by her own report.

Escalus: Say you? 275

Lucio: Marry, sir, I think if you handled her privately she
would sooner confess; perchance publicly she'll be
asham'd.

Enter Duke *[in his friar's habit],* Provost, [Officers *with*] Isabella.

Escalus: I will go darkly to work with her.

Lucio: That's the way; for women are light at midnight. 280

Escalus: Come on, mistress. Here's a gentlewoman denies all
that you have said.

Lucio: My lord, here comes the rascal I spoke of, here with
the Provost.

Escalus: In very good time. Speak not you to him till we call 285
upon you.

Lucio: Mum.

Escalus: Come, sir, did you set these women on to slander
Lord Angelo? They have confess'd you did.

Duke: 'Tis false. 290

Escalus: How! know you where you are?

Duke: Respect to your great place! and let the devil
Be sometime honor'd for his burning throne!
Where is the Duke? 'tis he should hear me speak.

Escalus: The Duke's in us; and we will hear you speak: 295
Look you speak justly.

Duke: Boldly, at least. But O, poor souls,
Come you to seek the lamb here of the fox,
Good night to your redress! Is the Duke gone?
Then is your cause gone too. The Duke's unjust 300
Thus to retort your manifest appeal,

---

267. *enforce them:* put them strongly.   268. *notable:* notorious.   272. *give.* Probably with
conditional sense: "if you will give."   279. *darkly:* secretly, cunningly.   280. *light at
midnight:* i.e. wanton in the dark.   290. *'Tis false:* Equivocal: apparently a denial that he set
the women on, but actually a denial that Angelo has been slandered, i.e. charged falsely.
292–93. *let . . . throne.* The Duke ironically extends the principle to its logical conclusion.
296. *justly:* truthfully.   298. *Come you:* if you come.   301. *retort:* throw back, refuse to
accept.   *manifest:* obviously just.

And put your trial in the villain's mouth
Which here you come to accuse.

Lucio: This is the rascal; this is he I spoke of.

Escalus: Why, thou unreverend and unhallowed friar,   305
Is't not enough thou hast suborn'd these women
To accuse this worthy man, but in foul mouth,
And in the witness of his proper ear,
To call him villain, and then to glance from him
To th' Duke himself, to tax him with injustice?   310
Take him hence; to th' rack with him! We'll touze you
Joint by joint, but we will know his purpose.
What? "unjust"?

Duke: Be not so hot. The Duke
Dare no more stretch this finger of mine than he
Dare rack his own. His subject am I not,   315
Nor here provincial. My business in this state
Made me a looker-on here in Vienna,
Where I have seen corruption boil and bubble,
Till it o'errun the stew; laws for all faults,
But faults so countenanc'd, that the strong statutes   320
Stand like the forfeits in a barber's shop,
As much in mock as mark.

Escalus: Slander to th' state!
Away with him to prison.

Angelo: What can you vouch
Against him, Signior Lucio? Is this the man
That you did tell us of?

Lucio: 'Tis he, my lord.   325
Come hither, goodman bald-pate, do you know me?

Duke: I remember you, sir, by the sound of your voice; I
met you at the prison, in the absence of the Duke.

Lucio: O, did you so? And do you remember what you said
of the Duke?   330

Duke: Most notedly, sir.

302–3. *the villain's mouth Which:* the mouth of the villain whom.   308. *in . . . ear:* in his own
hearing.   309. *glance:* ricochet.   311. *touze:* tear, jerk.   313. *hot:* hasty.   316. *provincial:*
subject to local religious authority.   319. *stew:* (1) pot; (2) brothel.   320. *countenanc'd:*
tolerated.   321. *forfeits . . . shop:* Usually explained as extracted teeth (barber-surgeons also
pulled teeth), which like disused laws have lost their power to bite. But the comparison is
forced and gives a weak sense for line 322. More likely is the earlier explanation that barbers
hung up in their shops, which were often thronged, a list of penalties for various kinds of
misbehavior. Hart (*Notes and Queries,* July 1908, p. 64) cites from *Plain Percival:* "Speake a
blooddy word in a Barbers shop, you make a forfet" (quoted by Lever).   322. *As . . . mark:* i.e.
as often broken as observed.   326. *goodman:* term of address, here ironic, to one below the
rank of a gentleman.   *bald-pate:* Lucio supposes that there is a tonsure under the Duke's
hood.

Lucio: Do you so, sir? And was the Duke a fleshmonger, a
fool, and a coward, as you then reported him to be?

Duke: You must, sir, change persons with me, ere you make
that my report. You indeed spoke so of him, and much   335
more, much worse.

Lucio: O thou damnable fellow! Did not I pluck thee by the
nose for thy speeches?

Duke: I protest I love the Duke as I love myself.

Angelo: Hark how the villain would close now, after his trea-   340
sonable abuses!

Escalus: Such a fellow is not to be talk'd withal.
  Away with him to prison! Where is the Provost?
  Away with him to prison! Lay bolts enough upon him.
  Let him speak no more. Away with those giglets too,   345
  and with the other confederate companion!
                          [The Provost lays hands on the Duke.]

Duke: Stay, sir, stay a while.

Angelo: What, resists he? Help him, Lucio.

Lucio: Come, sir, come, sir, come, sir; foh, sir, why, you
  bald-pated, lying rascal, you must be hooded, must   350
  you? Show your knave's visage, with a pox to you! Show
  your sheep-biting face, and be hang'd an hour! Will't
  not off? *[Pulls off the friar's hood.]*

Duke: Thou art the first knave that e'er mad'st a duke.
  First, Provost, let me bail these gentle three.   355
  [To Lucio.] Sneak not away, sir, for the friar and you
  Must have a word anon.—Lay hold on him.

Lucio: This may prove worse than hanging.

Duke: *[To Escalus.]* What you have spoke I pardon. Sit
  you down,   360
  We'll borrow place of him.—Sir, by your leave.
                          [Takes Angelo's seat.]
  Hast thou or word, or wit, or impudence,
  That yet can do thee office? If thou hast,
  Rely upon it till my tale be heard,
  And hold no longer out.

Angelo: O my dread lord,   365
  I should be guiltier than my guiltiness,
  To think I can be undiscernible,

---

339. *protest:* affirm.   340. *close:* come to terms.   345. *giglets:* wantons.   346. *confederate
companion:* i.e. Friar Peter.   351–52. *Show . . . face.* Probably alluding to the fable of the wolf
in sheep's clothing.   352. *hang'd an hour:* Presumably a jocular version of "hanged";
examples of "hanged awhile" have been cited. For another reference to the hanging of an
animal, see *The Merchant of Venice,* IV.i.133–35, "Thy currish spirit / Govern'd a wolf, who
hang'd for human slaughter, / Even from the gallows did his fell soul fleet. . . ."   355. *gentle
three:* i.e. Isabella, Mariana, and Friar Peter.   361. *We'll:* The royal plural.

When I perceive your Grace, like pow'r divine,
Hath look'd upon my passes. Then, good Prince,
No longer session hold upon my shame,   370
But let my trial be mine own confession.
Immediate sentence then, and sequent death,
Is all the grace I beg.
    Duke: Come hither, Mariana.
Say: wast thou e'er contracted to this woman?
Angelo: I was, my lord.   375
    Duke: Go take her hence, and marry her instantly.
Do you the office, friar, which consummate,
Return him here again. Go with him, Provost.
            Exeunt [Angelo, Mariana, Friar Peter, Provost].
Escalus: My lord, I am more amaz'd at his dishonor
Than at the strangeness of it.
    Duke: Come hither, Isabel,   380
Your friar is now your prince. As I was then
Advertising and holy to your business,
Not changing heart with habit, I am still
Attorneyed at your service.
    Isabella: O, give me pardon,
That I, your vassal, have employ'd and pain'd   385
Your unknown sovereignty!
    Duke: You are pardon'd, Isabel;
And now, dear maid, be you as free to us.
Your brother's death I know sits at your heart;
And you may marvel why I obscur'd myself,
Laboring to save his life, and would not rather   390
Make rash remonstrance of my hidden pow'r
Than let him so be lost. O most kind maid,
It was the swift celerity of his death,
Which I did think with slower foot came on,
That brain'd my purpose. But peace be with him!   395
That life is better life, past fearing death,
Than that which lives to fear. Make it your comfort,
So happy is your brother.

Enter Angelo, Mariana, [Friar] Peter, Provost.

    Isabella: I do, my lord.
    Duke: For this new-married man approaching here,
Whose salt imagination yet hath wrong'd   400

---

369. *passes:* transgressions.   382. *Advertising:* attentive.   *holy:* devoted.   383. *habit:*
attire.   384. *Attorneyed at:* acting as agent in.   385. *pain'd:* given trouble to.   387. *free to:*
i.e. quick to pardon.   391. *rash remonstrance:* quick manifestation.   393. *swift celerity.* See the
note on IV.ii.106.   395. *brain'd:* dashed out the brains of, brought to a shattering end.
398. *So:* thus, in this way.   400. *salt:* lecherous.

Your well-defended honor, you must pardon
For Mariana's sake; but as he adjudg'd your brother—
Being criminal, in double violation
Of sacred chastity and of promise-breach,
Thereon dependant, for your brother's life—   405
The very mercy of the law cries out
Most audible, even from his proper tongue,
"An Angelo for Claudio, death for death!"
Haste still pays haste, and leisure answers leisure;
Like doth quit like, and *Measure* still *for Measure*.   410
Then, Angelo, thy fault's thus manifested;
Which though thou wouldst deny, denies thee vantage.
We do condemn thee to the very block
Where Claudio stoop'd to death, and with like haste.
Away with him!

Mariana: O my most gracious lord,   415
I hope you will not mock me with a husband!

Duke: It is your husband mock'd you with a husband.
Consenting to the safeguard of your honor,
I thought your marriage fit; else imputation,
For that he knew you, might reproach your life,   420
And choke your good to come. For his possessions,
Although by [confiscation] they are ours,
We do enstate and widow you with all,
To buy you a better husband.

Mariana: O my dear lord,
I crave no other, nor no better man.   425

Duke: Never crave him, we are definitive.

Mariana: *[Kneeling.]* Gently my liege—

Duke: You do but lose your labor.
Away with him to death! *[To Lucio.]* Now, sir, to you.

Mariana: O my good lord! Sweet Isabel, take my part!
Lend me your knees, and all my life to come   430
I'll lend you all my life to do you service.

Duke: Against all sense you do importune her.

---

402. *adjudg'd:* condemned.   404. *promise-breach . . . for:* breaking his promise, conditional
on the former action, to save. Strict syntax would require *promise* in place of *promise-breach.*
406. *very mercy.* Angelo's crime is such that not only justice but mercy itself demands his
death.   407. *proper:* own.   409. *Haste . . . haste:* haste is always repaid with haste.
410. *quit:* requite, retaliate with.   *Measure . . . Measure:* Cf. Matthew 7:2: "with what judgment ye judge, ye shall be judged, and with what measure ye mete, it shall be measured unto
you again" (Geneva).   412. *though . . . deny:* even if you wished to deny it (which Angelo does
not wish to do).   *vantage:* i.e. a lesser penalty than was imposed on Claudio.   416. *mock . . .
husband:* i.e. tantalize me by offering and then immediately withdrawing, the gift of a
husband.   419. *imputation:* imputation of sin.   423. *enstate . . . you:* i.e. endow you by virtue
of a widow's rights.   426. *we are definitive:* my decision is final.   427. *liege:* sovereign.
431–32. *all sense:* rationality and natural feeling.

Should she kneel down in mercy of this fact,
Her brother's ghost his paved bed would break,
And take her hence in horror.

Mariana: Isabel!   435
Sweet Isabel, do yet but kneel by me.
Hold up your hands, say nothing; I'll speak all.
They say best men are moulded out of faults,
And for the most, become much more the better
For being a little bad; so may my husband.   440
O Isabel! will you not lend a knee?

Duke: He dies for Claudio's death.

Isabella: [Kneeling.]   Most bounteous sir:
Look, if it please you, on this man condemn'd
As if my brother liv'd. I partly think
A due sincerity governed his deeds,   445
Till he did look on me. Since it is so,
Let him not die. My brother had but justice,
In that he did the thing for which he died;
For Angelo,
His act did not o'ertake his bad intent,   450
And must be buried but as an intent
That perish'd by the way. Thoughts are no subjects,
Intents but merely thoughts.

Mariana: Merely, my lord.

Duke: Your suit's unprofitable; stand up, I say.
I have bethought me of another fault.   455
Provost, how came it Claudio was beheaded
At an unusual hour?

Provost: It was commanded so.

Duke: Had you a special warrant for the deed?

Provost: No, my good lord; it was by private message.

Duke: For which I do discharge you of your office;   460
Give up your keys.

Provost: Pardon me, noble lord,
I thought it was a fault, but knew it not,
Yet did repent me, after more advice,
For testimony whereof, one in the prison,
That should by private order else have died,   465
I have reserv'd alive.

Duke: What's he?

Provost: His name is
Barnardine.

---

433. *in . . . fact:* to beg mercy for this crime.   434. *his paved bed:* the stone paving above his grave.   452. *no subjects:* i.e. not answerable to authority.   462. *knew it not:* was not certain of it.   463. *more advice:* further consideration.

Duke: I would thou hadst done so by Claudio.
Go fetch him hither, let me look upon him.

[Exit Provost.]

Escalus: I am sorry, one so learned and so wise   470
As you, Lord Angelo, have still appear'd,
Should slip so grossly, both in the heat of blood
And lack of temper'd judgment afterward.
Angelo: I am sorry that such sorrow I procure,
And so deep sticks it in my penitent heart   475
That I crave death more willingly than mercy:
'Tis my deserving, and I do entreat it.

Enter Barnardine *and* Provost, Claudio *[muffled]*, Julietta.

Duke: Which is that Barnardine?
Provost: This, my lord.
Duke: There was a friar told me of this man.
Sirrah, thou art said to have a stubborn soul   480
That apprehends no further than this world,
And squar'st thy life according. Thou'rt condemn'd,
But for those earthly faults, I quit them all,
And pray thee take this mercy to provide
For better times to come. Friar, advise him,   485
I leave him to your hand. What muffled fellow's that?
Provost: This is another prisoner that I sav'd,
Who should have died when Claudio lost his head,
As like almost to Claudio as himself.

[Unmuffles Claudio.]

Duke: *[To Isabella.]* If he be like your brother, for his sake   490
Is he pardon'd, and for your lovely sake,
Give me your hand, and say you will be mine,
He is my brother too. But fitter time for that.
By this Lord Angelo perceives he's safe;
Methinks I see a quick'ning in his eye.   495
Well, Angelo, your evil quits you well.
Look that you love your wife; her worth worth yours.
I find an apt remission in myself;
And yet here's one in place I cannot pardon.
[To Lucio.] You, sirrah, that knew me for a fool, a   500
coward,
One all of luxury, an ass, a madman,

---

471. *still:* always (heretofore).   473. *temper'd:* balanced.   481. *apprehends:* understands.
482. *squar'st:* shapest.   483. *quit:* remit.   492. *Give:* if you will give.   495. *quick'ning:*
renewal of life.   496. *quits you well:* (1) is well rewarded; (2) is requited with good (in contrast
to "measure for measure").   497. *her . . . yours:* making your worth equal to hers (?).
498. *apt remission:* readiness to pardon.   499. *in place:* at hand, before me.   501. *luxury:*
lechery.

Wherein have I so deserv'd you,
That you extol me thus?

Lucio: Faith, my lord, I spoke it but according to the trick.   505
 If you will hang me for it, you may; but I had rather it
 would please you I might be whipt.

Duke: Whipt first, sir, and hang'd after.
 Proclaim it, Provost, round about the city,
 If any woman wrong'd by this lewd fellow   510
 (As I have heard him swear himself there's one
 Whom he begot with child), let her appear,
 And he shall marry her. The nuptial finish'd,
 Let him be whipt and hang'd.

Lucio: I beseech your Highness do not marry me to a   515
 whore. Your Highness said even now I made you a
 duke; good my lord, do not recompense me in making
 me a cuckold.

Duke: Upon mine honor, thou shalt marry her.
 Thy slanders I forgive, and therewithal   520
 Remit thy other forfeits. Take him to prison,
 And see our pleasure herein executed.

Lucio: Marrying a punk, my lord, is pressing to death,
 whipping, and hanging.

Duke: Slandering a prince deserves it.   525

                    [Exeunt Officers with Lucio.]

 She, Claudio, that you wrong'd, look you restore.
 Joy to you, Mariana! Love her, Angelo!
 I have confess'd her, and I know her virture.
 Thanks, good friend Escalus, for thy much goodness,
 There's more behind that is more gratulate.   530
 Thanks, Provost, for thy care and secrecy,
 We shall employ thee in a worthier place.
 Forgive him, Angelo, that brought you home
 The head of Ragozine for Claudio's,
 Th' offense pardons itself. Dear Isabel,   535
 I have a motion much imports your good,
 Whereto if you'll a willing ear incline,
 What's mine is yours, and what is yours is mine.
 So bring us to our palace, where we'll show
 What's yet behind, that['s] meet you all should know.   540

                                            [Exeunt.]

---

505. *trick:* fashion.   520. *therewithal:* in addition.   523. *pressing to death.* One accused of
felony who refused to plead guilty or not guilty was secured on his back and weights were
piled on him in increasing number until he pleaded or died.   528. *confess'd her:* been her
confessor.   530. *behind:* beyond, i.e. to come (so also in line 540).   533–35. *Forgive . . . itself:*
This distinction between the offender and the offense recalls II.ii.35–43.   536. *a motion:*
something to propose.   539. *bring:* accompany.   *show:* make known.

Shakespeare's Measure for Measure *is based on* Promos and Cassandra *by George Whetstone. Some of Shakespeare's scenes are so close to Whetstone's that we can look at them side-by-side and evaluate the touches that make Shakespeare's play the more interesting of the two. Whetstone's Act 3, Scene 4, is the basis for Shakespeare's Act 3, Scene 1. In Shakespeare's version Andrugio becomes Claudio, and Cassandra becomes Isabella.*

"Sister, that wise men love we often see": George Whetstone

Scena IV: Andrugio *out of prison,* Cassandra *on the stage.*

Andrugio: My Cassandra, what news? Good sister, show!
Cassandra: All things conclude thy death, Andrugio.
    Prepare thyself. To hope, it were in vain.
Andrugio: My death, alas! What raised this new disdain?
Cassandra: Not justice' zeal in wicked Promos, sure.
Andrugio: Sweet, show the cause I must this doom endure.
Cassandra: If thou dost live, I must my honor lose.
    Thy ransom is to Promos' fleshly will
    That I do yield; than which I rather choose
    With torments sharp myself he first should kill.
    Thus am I bent. Thou seest thy death at hand.
    O would my life would satisfy his ire;
    Cassandra then would cancel soon thy bond.
Andrugio: And may it be a judge of his account
    Can spot his mind with lawless love or lust?
    But more, may he doom any fault with death
    When in such fault he finds himself injust?
    Sister, that wise men love we often see,
    And where love rules, 'gainst thorns doth reason spurn.
    But whoso loves, if he rejected be,
    His passing love to peevish hate will turn.
    Dear sister, then note how my fortune stands:
    That Promos love, the like is oft in use;
    And sith he crave this kindness of your hands,
    Think this; if you his pleasure do refuse,
    I in his rage, poor wretch, shall sing *peccavi*
    Here are two evils; the best, hard to digest;
    But where as things are driven unto necessity,
    There are we bid of both evils choose the least.
Cassandra: And of these evils the least I hold is death,

To shun whose darts, we can no mean devise;
Yet honor lives when death has done his worst.
Thus fame than life is far more emprise.

Andrugio: Nay, Cassandra, if thou thyself submit,
To save my life, to Promos' fleshly will,
Justice will say thou dost no crime commit;
For in forced faults is no intent of ill.

Cassandra: How so th' intent is construed in offence,
The proverb says, that ten good turns lie dead,
And one ill deed, ten times beyond pretense,
By envious tongues report abroad doth spread.
Andrugio, so my fame shall valued be.
Despite will blaze my crime, but not the cause.
And thus, although I fain would set thee free,
Poor wench, I fear the gripe of slander's paws.

Andrugio: Nay, Sweet sister, more slander would infame
Your spotless life, to reave your brother's breath,
When you have power for to enlarge the same,
Once in your hands doth lie my life and death.
Way that I am, the selfsame flesh you are.
Think, I once gone, our house will go to wrack.
Know forced faults for slander need not care.
Look you for blame if I quail through your lack.
Consider well my great extremity.
If otherwise this doom I could revoke,
I would not spare, for any jeopardy,
To free thee, wench, from this same heavy yoke.
But, ah, I see else no way saves my life.
And yet his hope may further thy consent.
He said he may percase make thee his wife,
And 'tis likely he cannot be content
With one night's joy; if love he after seeks,
And I discharged, if thou aloof then be,
Before he lose thyself, that so he leeks
No doubt but he to marriage will agree.

Cassandra: And shall I stick to stoop to Promos' will,
Since my brother enjoyeth life thereby?
No, although it doth my credit kill,
Ere that he should, myself would choose to die.
My Andrugio, take comfort in distress,
Cassandra is won thy ransom great to pay;
Such care she hath thy thralldom to release
As she consents her honor for to slay.
Farewell, I must my virgin's weeds forsake
And like a page to Promos lewd repair.

Andrugio: My good sister, to God I thee betake,
To whom I pray that comfort change thy care.

HENRIK IBSEN

(1828–1906)

HEDDA GABLER

translated from the Norwegian by Jens Arup

CHARACTERS

*Jörgen Tesman, the holder to a University Fellowship in
  cultural history*
Mrs. Hedda Tesman, his wife
Miss Juliane Tesman, his aunt
Mrs. Elvsted
Mr. Brack, a judge
Ejlert Lövborg
Berte, the Tesmans' maid

The action takes place in Tesman's villa on the west side of the
town.

ACT ONE

*A spacious, handsome, and tastefully appointed reception room, decorated in dark
colours. In the back wall there is a wide doorway with the hangings pulled back.
This opening leads to a smaller room in the same style as the reception room. In the
wall to the right of the outer room is a folding door leading to the hall. In the opposite wall, to the left, is a glass door, also with the curtains drawn aside. Through
the windows we see part of a covered verandah outside, and trees in autumn colours. In the foreground stands an oval table, covered with a heavy cloth, and with
chairs around it. Downstage by the right wall are a large, dark, porcelain stove, a
high-backed armchair, an upholstered footrest, and two stools. Up in the right-
hand corner, a corner sofa and a small round table. Downstage on the left, a little
away from the wall, a sofa. Above the glass door, a piano. On either side of the
doorway at the back is a whatnot with objects in terra-cotta and majolica.—By the
back wall of the inner room are a sofa, a table, and a couple of chairs. Over this sofa
hangs the portrait of a handsome, elderly man in the uniform of a general. Over the
table, a hanging lamp with a matte, milky-white glass shade.—All around the
reception room there are numerous bunches of flowers arranged in vases and
glasses. More lie on the tables. The floors of both rooms are covered with thick carpets.—Morning light. The sun is shining in at the glass door.*

Miss Juliane Tesman, *with hat and parasol, comes in from the hall, followed by*
Berte, *who carries a bunch of flowers wrapped in paper.* Miss Tesman *is a good-*

looking lady of benevolent aspect, some 65 years old, neatly but simply dressed in a grey costume: Berte *is a serving-maid getting on in years, with a plain and somewhat countrified exterior.*

Miss Tesman: *[stops just inside the room, listens and speaks softly]* Well, I declare! I don't believe they are up yet!

Berte: *[similarly sudbued]* Why, that's what I said, Miss. So late the steamer was last night. And then afterwards! Gracious . . . all the things the young mistress wanted unpacked before she could get off to bed.

Miss Tesman: Well, well . . . let them have a good rest and welcome. But we'll give them a breath of the fresh morning air when they do come down.

[She crosses to the glass door and throws it wide open.]

Berte: *[by the table, not knowing what to do with the flowers in her hand]* I'm sure there isn't a decent place left for them. Maybe I'd better put them here, Miss.

[She places the flowers on the front of the piano.]

Miss Tesman: And so now you've got yourself a new mistress, Berte my dear. The Lord knows, I found it more than hard to let you go.

Berte: *[Close to tears]* And what about me then, Miss? What am I to say! For so many years now I've been with you and Miss Rina.

Miss Tesman: We must make the best of it, Berte. There's really no other way. Jörgen must have you in the house with him, you see. He simply must. You've always looked after him, ever since he was a little boy.

Berte: Yes but, Miss, I get so worried about her, too, lying at home. The poor dear, she's quite helpless. And then with that new girl, now! She'll never learn to make things right for the poor lady, she won't.

Miss Tesman: Oh, I'll soon get her into the way of it. And I'll see to most things myself, you may be sure. You needn't be so anxious for my poor sister's sake, my dear Berte.

Berte: Yes, but then there's another thing too, Miss. I'm really so scared I'll never give satisfaction to the young mistress.

Miss Tesman: Oh, Heavens . . . just to begin with of course there might be this and that. . . .

Berte: Because she's ever so particular.

Miss Tesman: Why, of course she is. General Gabler's daughter. The way she was used to having things in the General's time. Do you remember her riding along the road with her father? In that long black habit? And with a feather in her hat?

Berte: I should think I would remember! . . . But I declare, I never once dreamed they'd make a match of it, her and Mr. Jörgen, not in those days I didn't.

Miss Tesman: Nor I. . . . But now here's a point, Berte, while I remember it: you mustn't say mister about Jörgen from now on. He's a doctor.

Berte: Yes, the lady did say about that too . . . last night . . . soon as they came in at the door. Is it really true then, Miss?

Miss Tesman: Why certainly it's true. Just fancy, Berte . . . they made him a doctor abroad. Now, on the journey, you know. And I never knew the first thing about it . . . till he told me down there on the quay.

Berte: Well, I should think he could get to be anything at all, he could. He's that clever. But I'd never have thought he'd have taken to doctoring people, too.

Miss Tesman: Oh no, he's not that sort of doctor. . . . *[She nods significantly.]* And by the way, you'll probably have to call him something even finer pretty soon.

Berte: Well I never! What sort of thing, Miss?

Miss Tesman: *[smiles]* Hm . . . wouldn't you like to know! . . . *[Emotionally.]* Ah, dear God . . . if my sainted brother could look up from the grave and see what's become of his little boy! *[She looks around.]* But what's this, Berte . . . why on earth have you done that? Taken all the loose covers off?

Berte: The lady told me to do it. She doesn't like loose covers on the chairs, she said.

Miss Tesman: But will they be coming in here . . . I mean for every day?

Berte: That's what it sounded like. The lady, that is. As for himself . . . the doctor . . . he didn't say anything.

[Jörgen Tesman *enters from the right of the inner room, humming a tune and carrying an open, empty suitcase. He is a man of 33, of middle height and youthful appearance; slightly plump, his face round, open, and cheerful. Fair hair and beard. He wears glasses, and is dressed in comfortable, slightly slovenly, indoor clothes.*]

Miss Tesman: Good morning, good morning, Jörgen!

Tesman: *[in the doorway]* Aunt Julle! Dear Aunt Julle! *[Goes over and pumps her hand.]* Come all this way . . . so early in the morning! Eh?

Miss Tesman: Well, of course I had to come and see how you've all settled in.

Tesman: And you never even had a proper night's rest!

Miss Tesman: Oh, that won't do me any harm.

Tesman: Well, well, and you managed all right getting home from the quay, I hope? Eh?

Miss Tesman: Oh yes, I did very well . . . thank Heavens. Mr. Brack was so very kind as to take me right to the door.

Tesman: We were so dreadfully sorry we couldn't take you in the cab. But you could see for yourself. . . . Hedda had so many cases that had to come.

Miss Tesman: Yes, she really did have a great many cases.

Berte: [*to* Tesman]: Should I maybe go in and ask the mistress whether she wants me for anything?

Tesman: No thank you, Berte . . . I don't think you'd better. If there is anything she'll ring, she said.

Berte: [*crossing to the right*] All right, then. I'll put it up in the loft.

Tesman: Hey, wait a moment . . . take this along, will you.

Berte: [*taking the suitcase*]

[*She goes out at the hall door.*]

Tesman: Just think, Auntie . . . the whole of that case was crammed full of nothing but notes. It's quite incredible, really, all the things I managed to dig up round about in those old archives. Fantastic old things that no one knew anything about. . . .

Miss Tesman: Well to be sure, I don't expect you wasted your time on your honeymoon, did you, Jörgen?

Tesman: I can assure you I didn't. But do take your hat off, Auntie. There now! Let me undo that ribbon. Eh?

Miss Tesman: [*as he does so*] Oh, my dear . . . it's just as though you were home with us still.

Tesman: [*turning the hat around in his hand*] My, my . . . that's a fine and fancy hat you've given yourself!

Miss Tesman: I bought it because of Hedda.

Tesman: Because of Hedda? Eh?

Miss Tesman: Yes, so Hedda won't be ashamed of me, if we should happen to walk together in the street.

Tesman: [*patting her cheek*] You always think of everything, don't you, Auntie Julle. [*He puts the hat on a chair by the table.*] And now . . . there we are . . . now we'll sit down on the sofa here. And we'll have a little chat until Hedda turns up.

[*They sit down. She puts her parasol in the corner by the sofa.*]

Miss Tesman: [*takes both his hands and looks at him*] How wonderfully good it is to see you here again, as well as ever, and full of life, Jörgen! Ah . . . sainted Joachim's little boy!

Tesman: For me too! To be with you again, Auntie Julle! You've always been both father and mother to me.

Miss Tesman: Yes, I know you'll always have a soft spot in your heart for your old aunts.

Tesman: But there's absolutely no improvement in Auntie Rina. Eh?

Miss Tesman: Oh no, dear . . . we don't expect any, poor thing. She just lies there as she has done all these years. But God grant that I may keep her a little while yet! I don't know what I'd do without her, Jörgen. Especially now, you know, when I haven't got you to cope with any more.

Tesman: [patting her back] There now, Auntie . . . !

Miss Tesman: [suddenly switching to another tone] Well just think of it, so now you're a married man, Jörgen! . . . And to think that you'd be the one to walk off with Hedda Gabler! The lovely Hedda Gabler. Imagine it! So many admirers she always had around her!

Tesman: [hums a bit and smirks] Yes, I dare say there are one or two of my good friends who wouldn't mind being in my shoes. Eh?

Miss Tesman: And then that you were able to take such a honeymoon, too! Five months . . . almost six. . . .

Tesman: Oh well . . . for me it was a sort of academic trip too, you know. I had to look through all those old records. And the books I had to plough through!

Miss Tesman: Yes, I suppose you did. [Lowers her voice confidentially.] But tell me, now, Jörgen . . . isn't there anything . . . any other news you can tell me?

Tesman: From the trip, you mean?

Miss Tesman: Yes.

Tesman: Well, I don't think there's much I didn't get into my letters. I was given a doctorate . . . but I told you about that last night.

Miss Tesman: Oh, all those things, yes. But I mean to say . . . haven't you any . . . as it were . . . any prospects of . . . ?

Tesman: Prospects?

Miss Tesman: Oh, good Heavens, Jörgen . . . after all I am your old aunt!

Tesman: Why certainly I can talk of prospects.

Miss Tesman: Oh!

Tesman: I have the best prospect in the world of becoming professor, one of these days.

Miss Tesman: Oh yes, professor. . . .

Tesman: Or . . . I may as well say I'm certain to get it. But dear Auntie Julle . . . you know all this yourself!

Miss Tesman: [suppressing a smile] Why, to be sure I do. You're quite right. [Changing the subject.] . . . But you were telling me about the journey. . . . It must have cost a pretty penny, Jörgen?

Tesman: Oh well, the cost . . . that big fellowship helped quite a bit, you know.

Miss Tesman: But I just can't imagine how you could make it do for both of you.

Tesman: No, I suppose that would need a bit of imagination. Eh?

Miss Tesman: And then when you're travelling with a lady. That makes everything so very much more expensive, I'm told.

Tesman: Oh of course . . . it's bound to make a bit of difference. But Hedda had to have that trip, Aunt! She really had to. I couldn't do less.

Miss Tesman: No, I suppose not. A honeymoon trip, that seems to be part of the trimmings, these days. . . . But tell me now . . . have you had a good look round the house?

Tesman: Indeed I have. I've been up and about since dawn.

Miss Tesman: Well, and how do you like it all?

Tesman: Very much! Oh, very much indeed! There's just one thing, I don't quite know what we're going to do about those two empty rooms, you know, between the back room there and Hedda's bedroom.

Miss Tesman: [with a smile] Ah, my dear Jörgen, you might find a use for them . . . when the time comes.

Tesman: Why yes, Auntie Julle, you've got something there! As I gradually add to my collection of books, then. . . . Eh?

Miss Tesman: Precisely, my dear boy. I was thinking of your books.

Tesman: Most of all I'm pleased for Hedda, though. Before we got engaged she always said that old Lady Falk's villa was the only house she'd really like to live in.

Miss Tesman: Yes, think of it . . . and then just after you'd gone away it came up for sale.

Tesman: Yes, Aunt Julle, we really were lucky. Eh?

Miss Tesman: But expensive, my dear Jörgen! It'll be a terrible expense for you . . . all this.

Tesman: [looks at her rather crestfallen] Why yes, I suppose it will, Auntie?

Miss Tesman: Oh my dear!

Tesman: How much, do you think? Approximately? Eh?

Miss Tesman: I simply can't tell you, before all the bills have come in.

Tesman: Oh well, luckily Brack was able to get very favourable terms for me. He said as much when he wrote to Hedda.

Miss Tesman: Yes, don't you worry about that, my boy. . . . Anyway, I've given security for the furniture and all the carpets.

Tesman: Security? You have? But Auntie Julle . . . what sort of security could you offer?

Miss Tesman: I made out a mortgage on the annuity.

   Tesman: *[leaps up].* What! On your . . . and Aunt Rina's annuity!

Miss Tesman: Well, there didn't seem to be any other way of doing it, you know.

   Tesman: *[places himself in front of her]* But have you gone out of your mind, Auntie! That annuity . . . you and Aunt Rina, it's the only thing you've got to live on.

Miss Tesman: There now . . . don't get so excited about it. It's just a formality, you know. Mr. Brack said so too, and he's a judge. He was the one who helped me to arrange the whole thing. Just a formality, he said.

   Tesman: Yes, that's all very well. But all the same . . .

Miss Tesman: And now you're getting your own salary to draw on. And good gracious, if we did have to spend a little . . . ? A helping hand, just to begin with . . . ? Why, we'd be only too happy.

   Tesman: Oh, Auntie . . . you'll never stop sacrificing yourself for me!

Miss Tesman: *[rises and puts her hands on his shoulders]* Isn't it the only joy I have in this world, to help you along your road, my darling boy? You, who have neither father nor mother to look to? And now we're very nearly there, my boy! There were some black days among the rest. But, thanks be to God, you've made good, Jörgen!

   Tesman: Yes, it's queer, really, the way it all turned out.

Miss Tesman: Yes . . . and the people who stood in your way . . . and wanted to keep you back . . . you outran them all. They've fallen by the wayside, Jörgen! And your most dangerous adversary, he fell lower than any of them, he did. . . . And now he must lie on the bed he's made for himself . . . the poor depraved creature.

   Tesman: Have you heard anything of Ejlert? Since I went off, I mean.

Miss Tesman: Only that he's supposed to have published a new book.

   Tesman: What's that! Ejlert Lövborg? Just recently, you mean? Eh?

Miss Tesman: Yes, so they say. Do you think it's likely to amount to anything much? Now when your new book arrives . . . that'll be another matter, Jörgen! What's it going to be about?

   Tesman: It will be an account of the domestic crafts of mediaeval Brabant.

Miss Tesman: Just think . . . and you can write about things like that!

   Tesman: Incidentally, it may be quite a while before I get it finished. There are all these extensive collections of material, you know, they all have to be sorted out first.

Miss Tesman: Yes, collecting things and sorting them out . . . you've always been good at that. You're not Joachim's son for nothing!

Tesman: I'm ever so keen to get going on it. Especially now, with my own comfortable and charming house to sit and work in.

Miss Tesman: Ah, and most of all, now that you've won the wife of your heart, dear Jörgen.

Tesman: [embracing her] Oh yes, Auntie Julle! Hedda . . . that's the most wonderful thing of all! *[Looks towards the doorway.]* But here she is, isn't she? Eh?

[Hedda *comes in from the left of the back room. She is a lady of 29. Her face and her figure are aristocratic and elegant in their proportions. Her complexion is of an even pallor. Her eyes are steel grey, and cold, clear, and dispassionate. Her hair is an attractive medium brown in colour, but not particularly ample. She is dressed in a tasteful, somewhat loose-fitting morning gown.*]

Miss Tesman: [goes to meet her] Good morning, dear Hedda! A very good morning to you!

Hedda: [offers her hand] Good morning, dear Miss Tesman! Such an early visit. So very kind.

Miss Tesman: [appearing somewhat put out] Well, and did the young mistress sleep well in her new home?

Hedda: Thank you, I slept tolerably well.

Tesman: [laughs] Tolerably! That's a good one, Hedda! You were sleeping like a log, you were, when I got up.

Hedda: How fortunate. But then, Miss Tesman, one always has to get used to new things. Bit by bit. *[Looks towards the windows.]* Ugh . . . the maid's been and opened the verandah door. The place is flooded with sunlight.

Miss Tesman: [moving towards the door] Well, let's shut it.

Hedda: Oh no, don't do that! Dear Tesman, go and draw the curtains. That gives a softer light.

Tesman: [at the door] So be it . . . so be it. . . . There you are, Hedda . . . now you've got both shade and fresh air.

Hedda: Yes, we can do with a bit of fresh air. All these blessed flowers. . . . But dear Miss Tesman . . . won't you take a seat?

Miss Tesman: No, thank you very much. Now I know everything's all right . . . thanks be to God! And I'd better be thinking of getting home again. To her, lying and waiting so patiently, poor dear.

Tesman: You'll give her my love, won't you. And say I'll pop in to see her later in the day.

Miss Tesman: Yes, yes, I'll tell her. Oh, here's another thing, Jörgen . . . *[She feels in her skirt pocket.]* I almost went and forgot it. I've got a little something for you.

Tesman: What can it be, Aunt? Eh?

Miss Tesman: [*extracts a flat object wrapped in newspaper and hands it to him*] There you are, my boy.

Tesman: [*opens it*] Oh my goodness! . . . So you kept them for me, Auntie Julle! Hedda! Now isn't that nice of her, Hedda! Eh?

Hedda: [*by the right-hand whatnot*] Of course, dear. What is it?

Tesman: My old house shoes! My slippers, Hedda!

Hedda: Ah yes. You mentioned them quite frequently on the trip, I remember.

Tesman: Yes, I did miss them so. [*He goes to her.*] Here, just take a look at them, Hedda!

Hedda: [*crossing to the stove*] Thank you, they wouldn't appeal to me.

Tesman: [*following her*] Think of it . . . Aunt Rina lay there and embroidered them for me. Weak as she was. Oh, you can't imagine how many memories they have for me.

Hedda: [*by the table*] But not for me, particularly.

Miss Tesman: Why, Hedda's quite right about that, Jörgen.

Tesman: Yes, but I do think, now that she's one of the family . . .

Hedda: [*interrupts*] We'll never be able to manage with that maid, Tesman.

Miss Tesman: Not manage with Berte?

Tesman: My dear . . . why on earth should you say that? Eh?

Hedda: [*points*] Look at that! She's left her old hat lying on the chair there.

Tesman: [*appalled, drops the slippers on the floor*] But . . . but Hedda . . . !

Hedda: Just think . . . somebody might come in and see it.

Tesman: No but Hedda . . . that . . . that's Auntie Julle's hat!

Hedda: Is it?

Miss Tesman: [*takes the hat*] Yes indeed it's mine. And as it happens it isn't so very old either, my dear young lady.

Hedda: I really didn't look at it so very closely, Miss Tesman.

Miss Tesman: [*ties on the hat*] As a matter of fact I'm wearing it for the very first time. And that's God's truth.

Tesman: And an awfully fine hat it is too. Really smart!

Miss Tesman: Oh, that's as it may be, my dear Jörgen. [*Looks around.*] And my parasol . . . ? Here it is. [*She takes it.*] Because that happens to be mine too. [*Under her breath.*] Not Berte's.

Tesman: A new hat and a new parasol! Think of that, Hedda!

Hedda: Yes, really charming.

Tesman: Yes, aren't they just? Eh? But Aunt, take a good look at Hedda before you go! Charming's the word for her, eh?

Miss Tesman: Oh my dear, that's nothing new. Hedda's been lovely all her life.

[She nods and starts across to the right.]

    Tesman: [following her] Yes, but have you noticed how well and bonny she looks? I declare she's filled out beautifully on the trip.

    Hedda: [moves irritably] Oh, do you have to . . . !

    Miss Tesman: [has stopped and turned] Filled out?

    Tesman: Yes, Aunte Julle, you don't notice it so much when she's wearing that dress. But I . . . well, I have occasion to. . . .

    Hedda: [at the verandah door, impatiently] Oh, you don't have occasion for anything!

    Tesman: It must be the mountain air in the Tyrol. . . .

    Hedda: [curtly interrupting] I'm exactly the same as I was when we left.

    Tesman: Yes, that's what you say. But you aren't, you know. Can't you see it too, Auntie?

    Miss Tesman: [she has folded her hands and gazes at Hedda] Lovely . . . lovely . . . lovely Hedda. [She goes to Hedda, *takes her head and inclines it towards her with both hands, and kisses her hair.*] God bless you and keep you, Hedda Tesman. For Jörgen's sake.

    Hedda: [frees herself] Oh . . . ! Leave me be!

    Miss Tesman: [in quiet rapture] Every single day I'll come and visit you both.

    Tesman: Yes, Auntie, that'll be wonderful! Eh?

    Miss Tesman: Goodbye . . . goodbye!

[She goes out at the hall door. Tesman *follows her out. The door stays half open, and we hear* Tesman *repeating his message of love to Aunt Rina, and thanking again for the slippers.]*

While this is going on Hedda *walks about the room, raises her arms and clenches her fists as though in a frenzy. Then she draws the curtains back from the verandah door, stands there and looks out.*

[After a while Tesman *comes back and shuts the door behind him.]*

    Tesman: [picking up the slippers from the floor] What are you looking at, Hedda?

    Hedda: [calm and collected once more] I'm just looking at the leaves on the trees. They're so yellow. And so withered.

    Tesman: [rewraps the slippers and lays them on the table] Yes, well, it's September now, you know.

    Hedda: [ill at ease again] Why yes . . . already it's . . . it's September.

    Tesman: Don't you think Aunt Julle was odd, dear? Almost affected? What can have got into her, do you think? Eh?

    Hedda: Well, I hardly know her. Isn't she usually like that?

    Tesman: Why, no, not like she was just now.

Hedda: [*leaving the window*] Do you think she was very put out about that hat business?

Tesman: Oh, not so particularly. Perhaps a little just for a moment. . . .

Hedda: Well, what manner of behaviour is that, anyway, flinging her hat just anywhere in the drawing-room! It's not done.

Tesman: Well, you may be quite sure that Aunt Julle won't do it again.

Hedda: Oh, never mind. I'll propitiate her.

Tesman: Oh my dear, sweet Hedda, if only you would!

Hedda: When you go down there later you can invite her over for this evening.

Tesman: Yes, certainly I will. And there's another thing, Hedda, that would make her so very happy.

Hedda: Well?

Tesman: Couldn't you bring yourself to give her a kiss when you meet? For my sake, Hedda? Eh?

Hedda: Oh, don't ask me, Tesman, for God's sake. I've told you before, I just couldn't. I'll try to call her Aunt. And she'll have to be content with that.

Tesman: Oh well . . . I just thought, now that you belong to the family, you . . .

Hedda: Hm . . . I'm not at all sure . . .

[*She goes upstage towards the doorway.*]

Tesman: [*after a pause*] Is there anything the matter with you, Hedda? Eh?

Hedda: I was just looking at my old piano. It doesn't go with the rest of the things.

Tesman: As soon as I get my first cheque, we'll see about getting it changed.

Hedda: Oh no . . . not changed. I don't want to part with it. We'd better put it in the back room, there. And then we can get another one for this room. At a suitable moment, I mean.

Tesman: [*rather put out*] Yes . . . I suppose that would be an alternative.

Hedda: [*takes the bunch of flowers from the piano*] These flowers weren't here last night when we arrived.

Tesman: Aunt Julle probably brought them.

Hedda: [*looks into the bouquet*] A card. [*Takes it out and reads.*] 'Will come again later today.' Can you guess who it's from?

Tesman: No. Who is it from? Eh?

Hedda: It says 'Mrs. Carl Elvsted'.

Tesman: Really! Mrs. Elvsted! Miss Rysing, as she used to be.

Hedda: Exactly. That woman with the provoking hair that everyone made such a fuss of. An old flame of yours, too, I'm
told.

Tesman: *[laughs]* Oh, it didn't last long. And besides, that was
before I met you, Hedda. But just think . . . that she should
be back in town.

Hedda: It's odd that she should come here. I hardly know her,
apart from school.

Tesman: No, and I haven't seen her for . . . oh good Lord, it must
be years. I don't know how she can bear to be stuck right up
there, so many miles away. Eh?

Hedda: *[thinks a moment, then suddenly speaks]* I say, Tesman . . .
wasn't it up there somewhere that he went . . . that . . . Ejlert
Lövborg?

Tesman: Yes, it must be just about there.

*[Berte *appears at the hall door.]*

Berte: She's here again, ma'am, the lady who looked in with the
flowers earlier on. *[She points.]* The ones you're holding,
ma'am.

Hedda: She is, is she. Well, be so good as to let her in.

*[Berte *opens the door to* Mrs. Elvsted *and goes out herself.—*Mrs. Elvsted *is a
slight woman with soft, attractive features. Her eyes are light blue, large, round,
and somewhat protruding, with a scared, questioning expression. Her hair is strikingly fair, almost whitish-yellow, and unusually rich and wavy. She is a couple of
years younger than* Hedda. *She wears a dark going-out dress, tastefully styled but
not quite in the latest fashion.]*

Hedda: *[goes to meet her in a friendly manner.]* Good morning, my
dear Mrs. Elvsted. How nice to see you once again.

Mrs. Elvsted: *[nervous, trying to control herself]* Yes, it's a long time now
since we met.

Tesman: *[offering his hand]* And since we met, too. Eh?

Hedda: Thank you for your lovely flowers. . . .

Mrs. Elvsted: Oh, thank you. . . . I would have come here at once, yesterday afternoon. But then I heard you were abroad. . . .

Tesman: You've just arrived in town? Eh?

Mrs. Elvsted: Yes. I got in about lunch time yesterday. Oh, I was quite
in despair when I heard you were away.

Hedda: In despair! Buy why?

Tesman: But my dear Mrs. Rysing—Mrs. Elvsted I mean to say . . .

Hedda: I hope there isn't anything wrong?

Mrs. Elvsted: Yes, there is. And I don't know another soul here, not
anyone I could turn to, apart from you.

Hedda: *[puts the flowers on the table]* Come . . . we'll sit down here
on the sofa. . . .

Mrs. Elvsted: Oh, I can hardly keep still, let alone sit down!
Hedda: Of course you can. Come along.

[She persuades Mrs. Elvsted *on to the sofa, and sits beside her.]*

Tesman: Well? What is it then . . . ?
Hedda: It is something that's happened up at your place?
Mrs. Elvsted: Well . . . it both is and yet isn't. Oh, I do so hope you won't misunderstand me.
Hedda: Well, in that case you'd better tell us all about it, from the beginning, Mrs. Elvsted.
Tesman: After all, that's the reason why you came. Eh?
Mrs. Elvsted: Yes . . . yes of course it is. And so I'd better tell you . . . if you don't already know it . . . that Ejlert Lövborg is also in town.
Hedda: Lövorg is . . . !
Tesman: What, Ejlert Lövborg back again! Think of that, Hedda!
Hedda: Yes, yes, I heard!
Mrs. Elvsted: He's been here now for about a week. Think of it . . . a whole week! In this dangerous place. Alone! And all the bad influences there are here.
Hedda: But . . . excuse me, Mrs. Elvsted, but how can this possibly concern you?
Mrs. Elvsted: *[gives her a scared look, then speaks quickly]* He used to come and teach the children.
Hedda: Your children?
Mrs. Elvsted: My husband's. I haven't got any.
Hedda: Stepchildren, then.
Mrs. Elvsted: Yes.
Tesman: *[slightly incoherent]* But was he sufficiently . . . I don't quite know how to put it . . . sort of . . . well, regular in his life and habits, so that he could be trusted with . . . ? Eh?
Mrs. Elvsted: For the last two years, there's been nothing that anyone could hold against him.
Tesman: Hasn't there really? Think of that, Hedda!
Hedda: Yes, I'm listening.
Mrs. Elvsted: Nothing at all, I assure you. Not in any way. But all the same. . . . Now that I know he's down here . . . in the big city. . . . And with so much money in his pocket. I'm so dreadfully worried about him.
Tesman: Well, why didn't he stay where he was, then? With you and your husband? Eh?
Mrs. Elvsted: When the book came out, you see, he just couldn't contain himself any more, up there.
Tesman: Why yes of course . . . Aunt Julle said he'd published a new book.
Mrs. Elvsted: Yes, a big new book, dealing with cultural development

. . . sort of altogether. It's a fortnight ago, now. And then when it sold so many copies . . . and caused such an enormous stir . . .

Tesman: Did it? Did it indeed? I suppose it was something he had tucked away from his good period, then.

Mrs. Elvsted: From before, you mean?

Tesman: Yes.

Mrs. Elvsted: No, he wrote the whole thing while he was with us. Just now . . . during the last year.

Tesman: Well, that really is good news, Hedda! Think of that!

Mrs. Elvsted: Oh yes, if only everything's all right!

Hedda: Have you seen him here in town?

Mrs. Elvsted: No, not yet. It was so difficult, trying to discover his address. But this morning I got it at last.

Hedda: [*gives her a searching glance*] You know, it seems a little odd that your husband . . . hm . . .

Mrs. Elvsted: [*with a nervous start*] That my husband? What?

Hedda: That he should send you down to town on this errand. That he didn't come in himself to look after his friend.

Mrs. Elvsted: Oh no, no . . . my husband doesn't have the time. And then there was . . . some shopping I had to do.

Hedda: [*with a little smile*] Oh, well, that's different, then.

Mrs. Elvsted: [*gets up quickly, ill at ease*] And now I beg of you, Mr. Tesman, please . . . receive Ejlert Lövborg well, if he comes here! And he's sure to. I know . . . you were such good friends before. And then you're both interested in the same subject. The same field of studies . . . so far as I understand it.

Tesman: Well, it used to be before, anyway.

Mrs. Elvsted: Yes, and that's why I ask you so particularly, . . . please do . . . please would you keep an eye on him as well. You will, won't you Mr. Tesman . . . you promise you will.

Tesman: Yes of course, I'll be only too happy, Mrs. Rysing . . .

Hedda: Elvsted.

Tesman: I'll certainly do absolutely everything I can for Ejlert. You may be sure of that.

Mrs. Elvsted: Oh, how very kind you are! [*She presses his hands.*] Thank you, Mr. Tesman, thank you! [*Alarmed.*] Yes, because my husband is so particularly fond of him!

Hedda: [*rising*] You ought to write to him, Tesman. Perhaps he won't come on his own initiative.

Tesman: Yes, wouldn't that be the best idea, Hedda? Eh?

Hedda: And the sooner the better. You'd better do it now, at once.

Mrs. Elvsted: [*beseechingly*] Yes, if only you would!

Tesman: I'll do it right away. Do you have his address, Mrs. . . . Mrs. Elvsted?

Mrs. Elvsted: Yes. *[She takes a piece of paper from her pocket and hands it to him.]* I wrote it there.

Tesman: Good, good. I'll go in, then . . . *[He looks around].* Oh yes, what happened to . . . ? Oh, there they are.

[He picks up the packet with the slippers and is about to go.]

  Hedda: Now be sure to write something really warm and friendly. A good long letter.

Tesman: Yes, I'll do that.

Mrs. Elvsted: But for goodness' sake don't say that I asked you to invite him!

  Tesman: No, of course not . . . that goes without saying. Eh?

[He goes out to the right through the back room.]

  Hedda: *[goes over to* Mrs. Elvsted, *smiles, and speaks in a low voice]* There! Two birds with one stone.

Mrs. Elvsted: What do you mean by that?

  Hedda: Couldn't you see that I wanted him to leave us?

Mrs. Elvsted: Yes, to write the letter . . .

  Hedda: And so that I could speak to you alone.

Mrs. Elvsted: *[flustered]* What, about all this?

  Hedda: Exactly.

Mrs. Elvsted: *[scared]* But there isn't anything else, Mrs. Tesman! Really, nothing more to say!

  Hedda: Oh there is indeed. There's a great deal more. That's perfectly obvious. Come here . . . we'll sit down and have a nice talk about it.

[She forces Mrs. Elvsted *into the armchair by the stove, and sits down herself on one of the stools.]*

Mrs. Elvsted: *[anxious, looking at her watch]* But Mrs. Tesman, please . . . I should have left long ago.

  Hedda: Oh, you can't be in such an enormous hurry. . . . Well, then. Now you tell me a bit about your life at home.

Mrs. Elvsted: Oh, that's just the one thing I really didn't want to talk about.

  Hedda: But you can tell me, my dear . . . ? After all, we were at school together.

Mrs. Elvsted: Yes, but you were in the class above me. Oh, I was dreadfully frightened of you in those days!

  Hedda: Frightened? Of me?

Mrs. Elvsted: Oh, dreadfully frightened. When we met on the steps you always used to pull my hair.

  Hedda: No, did I really?

Mrs. Elvsted: Yes, and you once said you were going to burn it off.

  Hedda: Oh, that was just something I said, you know.

Mrs. Elvsted: Yes, but I was such a fool in those days. . . . And anyway, since then . . . we've grown such miles apart. We don't meet the same sort of people at all.

Hedda: Well, we must try to bridge the gap again. We spoke freely to each other at school, at least, and we always called each other by our Christian names. . . .

Mrs. Elvsted: Oh, I'm sure you're wrong about that.

Hedda: Oh no I'm not! I remember it perfectly. And so we'll be good friends again, like we were in the old days. *[She moves her chair closer.]* There! *[She kisses her cheek.]* From now on you're to call me Hedda.

Mrs. Elvsted: *[presses and pats her hand]* Oh, you're so kind and good to me! I'm just not used to such kind treatment.

Hedda: There, now! And I'm going to call you my darling Thora.

Mrs. Elvsted: I'm called Thea.

Hedda: Quite right. Of course. Thea, I meant. *[Looks at her sympathetically.]* And so you're not accustomed to kind treatment, my poor Thea? Not even in your own home?

Mrs. Elvsted: Oh, if only I had a home! But I haven't got one. Never had one.

Hedda: *[looks at her a little]* I rather thought it must be something like that.

Mrs. Elvsted: *[stares helplessly in front of her]* Yes . . . yes . . . yes.

Hedda: I don't quite remember how it was, now. But didn't you go up there in the first place as Mr. Elvsted's housekeeper?

Mrs. Elvsted: Oh, actually I was meant to be a governess. But his wife . . . in those days . . . she was an invalid . . . and usually stayed in bed. So I had to look after the house as well.

Hedda: But then . . . after that . . . you became the mistress of the house.

Mrs. Elvsted: *[heavily]* Yes, I became his wife.

Hedda: Let me see. . . . About how long ago would that be, now?

Mrs. Elvsted: That I got married?

Hedda: Yes.

Mrs. Elvsted: That was five years ago.

Hedda: That's right, five years it must be.

Mrs. Elvsted: Oh, those five years . . . ! Well, the last two or three at least. Oh, if only you knew, Mrs. Tesman . . .

Hedda: *[hits her lightly on the hand]* Mrs. Tesman? Now that's naughty, Thea.

Mrs. Elvsted: Oh no, I'm sorry . . . Hedda. I'll try. But if only you could imagine what it was like. . . .

Hedda: *[casually]* Ejlert Lövborg's been up there about three years, hasn't he?

Mrs. Elvsted: *[looks at her uncertainly]* Ejlert Lövborg? Yes . . . so he has.

Hedda: Did you know him before that? From town?

Mrs. Elvsted: Hardly at all. Well, that is . . . I'd heard of him, of course.

Hedda: But then up there . . . he used to come to your house quite often?

Mrs. Elvsted: Yes, he came over every day. He had to come and read with the children. Because in the long run I couldn't manage it all by myself.

Hedda: No indeed, I can imagine. . . . And your husband . . . ? I suppose he travels quite a bit in his position?

Mrs. Elvsted: Well, of course . . . he's in charge of the whole administration of the district, so he has to keep an eye on things.

Hedda: [leaning against the arm of the chair] Thea . . . poor, sweet Thea . . . now you must tell me all about it . . . as it really is.

Mrs. Elvsted: Well, what do you want to know?

Hedda: Tell me, what's your husband really like, Thea? I mean, well . . . to be with? Does he treat you well?

Mrs. Elvsted: [evasively] He thinks he does everything for the best.

Hedda: It just seems to me that he must be a little old for you. Over twenty years older, isn't he?

Mrs. Elvsted: [roused] Oh, that as well. Just everything about him! There's simply nothing . . . we just haven't a thought in common. We don't share a thing, he and I.

Hedda: But isn't he fond of you all the same? In his own way?

Mrs. Elvsted: Oh, I don't know what he is. I think he just finds me useful. And then it doesn't cost much to keep me. I'm cheap.

Hedda: That's foolish of you.

Mrs. Elvsted: [shakes her head] Can't be anything else. Not with him. I don't believe he thinks of anyone except himself. And then perhaps a bit the children.

Hedda: And then he's fond of Ejlert Lövborg, Thea.

Mrs. Elvsted: [looks at her] Of Ejlert Lövborg! What gives you that idea?

Hedda: But my dear . . . it seems to me that when he sends you all this way to town to look for him . . . *[Smiles almost imperceptibly.]* And besides, you told Tesman so yourself.

Mrs. Elvsted: [with a nervous laugh] Did I? Well, I suppose I did. *[A subdued outburst.]* No . . . I may as well make a clean breast of it at once! It's bound to come out anyway, in the end.

Hedda: But Thea, my dear . . . ?

Mrs. Elvsted: Brief and to the point, then! I never told my husband I was leaving.

Hedda: What are you saying! Didn't he know you were leaving!

Mrs. Elvsted: Of course not. Anyway he wasn't at home. He'd gone on a tour of inspection. Oh, I just couldn't bear it any longer, Hedda! Not another minute! So terribly alone I'd have been, up there, from now on.

Hedda: Well? And then?

Mrs. Elvsted: I just packed up a few of my belongings. The essentials. Without letting anyone see. And then I left.

Hedda: Just like that?

Mrs. Elvsted: Yes. And took the train to town.

Hedda: But my dear, sweet Thea . . . I don't know how you dared!

Mrs. Elvsted: [gets up from the chair and walks across the floor] Well what on earth else would you have me do?

Hedda: But what do you think your husband will say when you go back?

Mrs. Elvsted: Back up there?

Hedda: Yes, yes.

Mrs. Elvsted: I'll never go back up there.

Hedda: [gets up, and goes closer to her] Then you've really . . . in all seriousness . . . run away from it all?

Mrs. Elvsted: Yes. I didn't think there was anything else I could do.

Hedda: And then . . . that you left so openly.

Mrs. Elvsted: Oh, there's no hiding that sort of thing, anyway.

Hedda: But what do you think people will say about you, Thea?

Mrs. Elvsted: Oh, they'll just have to say what they please. [She sits depressed and exhausted on the sofa.] I simply had to do what I did.

Hedda: [after a short pause] And what's going to happen to you now? What are you going to do with yourself?

Mrs. Elvsted: I don't know yet. I just know that I must live here, where Ejlert Lövborg's living. . . . If I have to live at all.

Hedda: [moves a chair across from the table, sits by her and strokes her hands] Tell me, Thea . . . how did it come about, this . . . this familiarity between you and Ejlert Lövborg?

Mrs. Elvsted: Oh, it just happened, bit by bit. I got a sort of control over him.

Hedda: Really?

Mrs. Elvsted: He left off his old ways. Not because I asked him to. I never dared to do that. But he knew all right that I didn't like that sort of thing. And then he gave it up.

Hedda: [concealing an involuntary sneer] And so you've reclaimed the prodigal . . . as they say . . . little Thea.

Mrs. Elvsted: Well, that's what he says, anyway. And he . . . for his part . . . he's made me into a sort of real person. Taught me to think . . . and to understand quite a lot of things.

Hedda: Did he give you lessons too, then?

Mrs. Elvsted: No, not lessons, like that. But he talked to me. Talked of so fantastically many things. And then came that beautiful, happy time, when I shared his work! Was allowed to help him!

Hedda: He let you help him?

Mrs. Elvsted: Yes! When he wrote anything, we always had to do it together.

Hedda: Like two good companions, then.

Mrs. Elvsted: [animated] Companions! Yes, imagine, Hedda . . . that's what he used to say! . . . Oh, I ought to be so wonderfully happy. But I can't be, quite. For I can't be sure that it will really last.

Hedda: Are you still so uncertain of him, then?

Mrs. Elvsted: [heavily] There's the shadow of a woman who stands between us.

Hedda: [looks at her with keen interest] Who might that be?

Mrs. Elvsted: Don't know. Someone or other from . . . from his past. Someone he can't really forget.

Hedda: What has he told you . . . about this?

Mrs. Elvsted: He's only ever once . . . sort of indirectly . . . touched on it.

Hedda: Well! And what did he say?

Mrs. Elvsted: He said that when they parted, she threatened to shoot him with a pistol.

Hedda: [cold and collected] Oh rubbish! People don't have such things here.

Mrs. Elvsted: No. And that's why I think it must be that red-haired singer, whom he once . . .

Hedda: Yes, I suppose that's possible.

Mrs. Elvsted: Because I can remember someone telling me that she carried a loaded pistol.

Hedda: Oh well . . . then it must be her, then.

Mrs. Elvsted: [wrings her hands] Yes but just think, Hedda . . . now I hear that that woman . . . she's in town again! Oh . . . I'm quite distracted. . . .

Hedda: [glancing towards the back room] Sh! Here's Tesman coming. *[Gets up, and whispers.]* Thea . . . all this must be just between you and me.

Mrs. Elvsted: [jumping up] Oh yes . . . yes! For God's sake . . . !

[Jörgen Tesman, with a letter in his hand, comes from the right of the inner room.]

Tesman: There now . . . the epistle is signed and sealed.

Hedda: That's splendid. But I think Mrs. Elvsted wants to go now. I won't be a moment. I'm just going as far as the garden gate.

Tesman: Oh Hedda . . . do you think Berte could see to this?

Hedda: [takes the letter] I'll tell her.

[Berte comes in from the hall.]

Berte: Mr. Brack is here and says please may he come in.

Hedda: Yes, ask Mr. Brack to step inside. And then . . . I say, . . .
then put this letter in the post box.

Berte: [takes the letter] Yes, ma'am.

[She opens the door for Mr. Brack, and goes out herself. Brack is a gentleman of
45. Stocky, but well-built and elastic in his movements. His face roundish, with a
good profile. Hair short, still almost black, and carefully dressed. Eyes lively and
playful. Thick eyebrows, thick moustaches cut short at the ends. He is dressed in a
stylish walking suit, perhaps a little too youthful in cut for a man of his age. He
uses an eyeglass, which he now and again allows to fall.]

Brack: [bowing, his hat in his hand] Is it permissible to call so early
in the day?

Hedda: Of course it is.

Tesman: [takes his hand] We're always glad to see you. [He introduces.] Mr. Brack . . . Miss Rysing. . . .

Hedda: Oh . . . !

Brack: [bows] Ah . . . delighted to make your acquaintance. . . .

Hedda: [looks at him and laughs] How charming to view you by
daylight, Mr. Brack!

Brack: You find me . . . perhaps a little changed?

Hedda: Yes, you look rather younger, I think.

Brack: Accept my humble gratitude.

Tesman: But what do you say to Hedda, then! Eh? Isn't she blossoming? She's positively . . .

Hedda: Oh, pray leave me out of this. You'd do better to thank
Mr. Brack for all the trouble he's taken . . .

Brack: Oh, not at all . . . I do assure you it was a pleasure. . . .

Hedda: Yes, you're a loyal soul. But my friend's standing here
and trying to get away. Au revoir, Mr. Brack. I'll be back in a
moment.

[Mutual leave-taking. Mrs. Elvsted and Hedda leave by the hall door.]

Brack: Well, now . . . and does everything come up to the lady's
expectations?

Tesman: Oh yes, and we can't thank you enough. That is . . . a little shifting back and forth may be necessary, I gather. And
there are one or two things missing. We'll doubtless have to
acquire a few trifles yet.

Brack: Oh, will you? Really?

Tesman: But we won't be putting you to any further trouble.
Hedda said she'd take care of the necessary purchases herself. . . . But I say, shan't we sit down? Eh?

Brack: Thank you, just for a moment. [Sits by the table.] There's a
little matter I'd like to talk to you about, my dear Tesman.

Tesman: Oh? Ah, I'm with you! [He sits down.] The entertainment
has its serious side, no doubt. Eh?

Brack: Oh, as yet there's no tearing hurry about the financial side. Though incidentally, I should be happier if we'd arranged things a little more modestly.

Tesman: But that would have been quite out of the question! Think of Hedda, man! You, who know her so well. . . . I couldn't possibly have expected her to put up with a genteel suburb!

Brack: Ah, no . . . there's the rub.

Tesman: And then . . . fortunately . . . it can't be long before I get that appointment.

Brack: Well, you know . . . these things have a habit of taking their time.

Tesman: Perhaps you've heard some more about it? Eh?

Brack: Nothing in any way definite, but . . . *[He breaks off.]* Oh, by the way, I do have one piece of news for you.

Tesman: Oh?

Brack: Your old friend Ejlert Lövborg is back in town.

Tesman: I know that already.

Brack: Oh? How did you come to know it?

Tesman: She told us, the lady who just went out with Hedda.

Brack: She did. What was her name again? I didn't quite catch . . .

Tesman: Mrs. Elvsted.

Brack: Aha . . . so that's who it was, then. Yes . . . I believe he stayed with them up there.

Tesman: And just think . . . I was so delighted to hear that he's become quite a sober citizen again!

Brack: Yes, that's what they say.

Tesman: And he's supposed to have published a new book. Eh?

Brack: Yes, by God he has!

Tesman: And what's more, it's been very well received!

Brack: It's been quite exceptionally well received.

Tesman: Just think . . . isn't that wonderfully good news? That fellow, with all his extraordinary talents. . . . I was terribly convinced that he'd gone to the dogs for good.

Brack: Yes, pretty nearly everyone thought the same.

Tesman: But I just can't imagine what he's going to do with himself now! What on earth can he possibly find to live on? Eh?

[During the last speech, Hedda *has come in from the hall.]*

Hedda: [to Brack, *laughing a little scornfully]* Tesman's for ever worrying about what people are going to find to live on.

Tesman: Oh Heavens . . . we're sitting here talking about poor Ejlert Lövborg, my dear.

Hedda: [looks at him quickly] Oh yes? [Sits down in the armchair by the stove and asks indifferently.] What's the matter with him?

Tesman: Well . . . he must have spent all the money he inherited ages ago. And I don't suppose he can write a new book every year. Eh? Well, then . . . I really can't for the life of me see how he's going to exist at all.

Brack: Perhaps I could tell you a little about that.

Tesman: Oh?

Brack: You must remember that he's got relations with quite a lot of influence.

Tesman: Oh well, his relations . . . I'm afraid they've disowned him entirely.

Brack: They used to regard him as the white hope of the family.

Tesman: Yes, they used to, yes! But he's been and dished all that himself.

Hedda: Who knows? *[She smiles faintly.]* Up at the Elvsteds' they've been busy reclaiming him. . . .

Brack: And then there's this new book he's written. . . .

Tesman: Oh well, I hope to goodness they will help him to get something. I've just written to him. Oh, Hedda, I asked him to come round this evening.

Brack: But my dear Tesman, you're coming to my bachelor party this evening. You promised last night on the quay.

Hedda: Had you forgotten, Tesman?

Tesman: Yes, by all that's holy.

Brack: In any case, I think you may rely on him to find an excuse.

Tesman: Why should you think that? Eh?

Brack: *[a little hesitantly, rising and leaning his hands on the back of the chair]* My dear Tesman. . . . And you too, madam. . . . I can no longer allow you to remain in ignorance of something that . . . that . . .

Tesman: Something to do with Ejlert . . . ?

Brack: Both him and yourself.

Tesman: But come on then, Mr. Brack!

Brack: You ought to prepare yourself for the discovery that your appointment may not come quite as soon as you hope and expect.

Tesman: *[jumps up in alarm]* Has something happened to delay it? Eh?

Brack: The appointment to the professorship might conceivably be contested by another candidate. . . .

Tesman: Another candidate! Think of that, Hedda!

Hedda: *[leans further back in her chair]* Ah, yes . . . yes!

Tesman: But who on earth! Surely not . . . ?

Brack: Quite correct. Ejlert Lövborg.

Tesman: *[clasps his hands together]* No, no . . . this is quite unthinkable! Quite impossible! Eh?

Brack: Hm . . . we may very well find it happening, all the same.

Tesman: Oh but my dear sir . . . but that would be quite incredibly inconsiderate of him! *[He flings his arms about.]* Yes, because . . . just think . . . I'm a married man! We got married on our expectations, Hedda and I. Been and borrowed vast sums. We're in debt to Auntie Julle, too! Because, good God . . . the post was as good as promised to me. Eh?

Brack: Come, come, come . . . you'll most probably get it, too. But only after a bit of competition.

Hedda: *[immobile in her chair]* Just think, Tesman . . . it'll be quite a sporting event.

Tesman: But my dearest Hedda, how can you take it all so calmly!

Hedda: *[as before]* Oh, I don't at all. I await the result with breathless expectation.

Brack: Well, anyway, Mrs. Tesman, it's as well that you should know how matters stand. I mean . . . before you embark on those little purchases you apparently threaten to make.

Hedda: This can't change anything so far as that's concerned.

Brack: No? Well, that's all right, then. I'll say goodbye! *[To Tesman.]* When I take my constitutional this afternoon I'll step in and fetch you, shall I?

Tesman: Oh yes, yes . . . I hardly know where I am.

Hedda: *[reclining, stretching out her hand]* Goodbye, Mr. Brack! We look forward to your return.

Brack: Many thanks. Goodbye, goodbye.

Tesman: *[escorting him to the door]* Goodbye, my dear Mr. Brack! You really must excuse all this. . . .

[Brack goes out at the hall door.]

Tesman: *[trails across the floor]* Ah, Hedda . . . one should never go building castles in the air. Eh?

Hedda: *[looks at him and smiles]* And do you?

Tesman: Yes . . . it can't be denied . . . it was idiotically romantic to go and get married, and buy a house, just on expectations alone.

Hedda: You may be right about that.

Tesman: Well . . . at least we have got our lovely house, Hedda! Just think . . . the house we'd both set our hearts on. Our dream house, I might almost call it. Eh?

Hedda: *[rises slowly and tiredly]* The agreement was that we were to live a social life. Entertain.

Tesman: Yes, oh Heavens . . . I was so looking forward to it! Just think, to see you as the hostess . . . presiding over a select group of friends! Eh? . . . Well, well, well . . . for the time being we'll just have to be the two of us, Hedda. Just see Aunt Julle once in a while. . . . Oh, for you everything should have been so very . . . very different . . . !

Hedda: And I suppose I won't get my footman just yet awhile.

Tesman: Oh no . . . a manservant, you must see that that's quite out of the question.

Hedda: And the saddle-horse I was to have had . . .

Tesman: [appalled] The saddle-horse!

Hedda: . . . I suppose I daren't even think of that, now.

Tesman: No, God preserve us . . . that goes without saying!

Hedda: [moving across] Oh, well . . . I've got one thing at least that I can pass the time with.

Tesman: [ecstatic] Oh, thank the good Lord for that! And what might that be, Hedda? Eh?

Hedda: [at the centre doorway, looking at him with concealed contempt] My pistols . . . Jörgen.

Tesman: [alarmed] Pistols!

Hedda: [with cold eyes] General Gabler's pistols.

[She goes out to the left through the back room.]

Tesman: [runs to the doorway and shouts after her] No, for the love of God, my darling Hedda . . . don't touch those dangerous contraptions! For my sake, Hedda! Eh?

ACT TWO

The room at the Tesmans' as in the first Act, except that the piano has been removed and an elegant little writing-desk with a book-shelf put in its place. A small table has been placed by the sofa on the left. Most of the flowers have been removed. Mrs. Elvsted's bunch of flowers stands on the large table in the foreground. . . . It is afternoon.

Hedda, *now dressed to receive visitors, is alone in the room. She is standing by the open glass door, loading a revolver-type pistol. Its companion lies in an open case on the writing-desk.*

Hedda: [looks down into the garden and shouts] Hullo again, Mr. Brack!

Brack: [down in the garden some distance away] Good afternoon to you, Mrs. Tesman!

Hedda: [raises the pistol and takes aim] I'm going to shoot you, sir!

Brack: [shouting down below] No-no-no! Don't stand there aiming right at me!

Hedda: That's what comes of sneaking round the back!

[She fires.]

Brack: [closer] Are you quite mad . . . !

Hedda: Oh good Lord . . . did I hit you perhaps?

Brack: [still outside] Stop fooling about, I tell you!

Hedda: Come inside then, Mr. Brack.

[Mr. Brack, *already dressed for the evening's occasion, comes in through the glass door. He carries a light overcoat on his arm.*]

Brack: What the devil . . . do you still play at that game? What are you shooting at?

Hedda: Oh, I just stand here and shoot into the blue.

Brack: [eases the pistol out of her hand] By your leave, my lady. *[Looks at it.]* Ah yes . . . I seem to recognize this fellow. *[Looks around.]* Now then, where's the case? Ah, here. *[He replaces the pistol and shuts the case.]* And now we won't play with those toys any more today.

Hedda: Well, what in God's name do you want me to do with myself?

Brack: Haven't you had any visitors?

Hedda: [shuts the verandah door] Not a soul. I suppose the crowd are all in the country still.

Brack: And Tesman's not in either, perhaps?

Hedda: [at the writing-desk, puts the pistol case in the drawer] No. As soon as he'd eaten he ran off to the aunts. He didn't expect you so soon.

Brack: Hm . . . and I didn't think of that. Stupid of me.

Hedda: [turns her head and looks at him] Why stupid?

Brack: Because then I could have come out here . . . even a little earlier.

Hedda: [crosses the floor] And then you'd have found no one at all. I've been in my room, changing after lunch.

Brack: And isn't there the minutest chink in the door that would have permitted communication?

Hedda: Why, you forgot to arrange one of those.

Brack: That was also stupid of me.

Hedda: Well, we'd better sit down here then. And wait. Because Tesman won't be home in a hurry.

Brack: Well, well, good Heavens, I shall be patient.

[Hedda *sits in the corner of the sofa.* Brack *lays his coat over the nearest chair and seats himself, but keeps his hat in his hand. A short pause. They look at one another.*]

Hedda: Well?

Brack: [in the same tone] Well?

Hedda: I asked first.

Brack: [leans forward slightly] Well, my lady, what do you say to a comfortable little gossip.

Hedda: [leans further back in the sofa] Doesn't it seem to you that it's an eternity since we talked together? Oh . . . I don't count those few words last night and this morning.

Brack: But . . . between ourselves? Just the two of us, you mean?

Hedda: Well, yes. More or less.

Brack: I've gone around here day after day longing for you to come back again.

Hedda: And for the matter of that, I've been longing for the same thing.

Brack: You have? Really, my lady? And I was convinced you were having a wonderful time on the trip!

Hedda: Oh, magnificent!

Brack: But Tesman was always saying so in his letters.

Hedda: Yes, he was! He's absolutely in his element if he's given leave to grub around in libraries. And sit copying out ancient parchments . . . or whatever they are.

Brack: [a little maliciously] After all, that is his particular *raison d'être*. Part of it, anyway.

Hedda: Yes, that's it. So it was all very fine for him. . . . But for me! Oh no, my dear Brack . . . for me it was horribly tedious!

Brack: [sympathizing] Was it really as bad as all that?

Hedda: Oh yes, use your imagination . . . ! For six months on end, never meeting anyone who knew anybody in our circle. Who could talk about our own affairs.

Brack: Well, no . . . I'd have felt the want of that myself.

Hedda: And then the most unbearable thing of all . . .

Brack: Well?

Hedda: . . . everlastingly having to be together with . . . with the self-same person. . . .

Brack: [nods assentingly] Day in and day out . . . yes. Think of it . . . at all possible times of the . . .

Hedda: I said everlastingly.

Brack: So be it. But I should have thought that in the case of our estimable Tesman, it would have been possible to . . .

Hedda: Tesman is . . . an academic, my dear sir.

Brack: Undeniably.

Hedda: And academics aren't a bit amusing as travelling-companions. Not in the long run, anyway.

Brack: Not even . . . the academic with whom one happens to be . . . in love?

Hedda: Ugh . . . don't use that glutinous word!

Brack: [pulled up] What's this, my lady!

Hedda: [half laughingly, half bitterly] Well, you ought to have a try at it! Hearing about the history of civilization day in and day out. . . .

Brack: Everlastingly.

Hedda: Yes-yes-yes! and then this stuff about mediaeval domestic crafts . . . ! That's the most sickening of the lot!

Brack: [looks at her inquiringly] But, tell me . . . how am I then to account for the fact that . . . ? Hm. . . .

Hedda: That Jörgen Tesman and I made a match of it, you mean?

Brack: Well, let's put it that way.

Hedda: Oh, Heavens, does it seem to you so strange, then?

Brack: Both yes and no . . . my lady.

Hedda: I'd really danced myself tired, my dear sir. I had had my day . . . *[She gives a little shudder.]* Oh, no . . . I'm not going to say that. Nor think it, either.

Brack: With respect, madam, you've no reason to.

Hedda: Oh . . . reason. . . . *[She sums him up with her look.]* And Jörgen Tesman . . . you must allow that he's a most worthy person in every way.

Brack: Oh, solid worth. Heaven preserve us.

Hedda: And I can't see that there's anything specifically ridiculous about him. . . . Or what do you say?

Brack: Ridiculous? No-o . . . I wouldn't say that exactly. . . .

Hedda: Well. But then he's a most diligent research worker, at any rate! . . . And after all, he might get somewhere with it in time, in spite of everything.

Brack: *[looks at her a little uncertainly]* But I thought you believed, like everybody else, that he'd make a really outstanding man.

Hedda: *[with a tired expression]* Yes, so I did. . . . And then when he came along and was so pathetically eager to be allowed to support me. . . . I don't really see why I shouldn't let him?

Brack: Well of course, if you put it like that. . . .

Hedda: It was more than any of my other gallant friends were prepared to do, dear Mr. Brack.

Brack: *[laughs]* Ah, I regret I can't answer for all the others. But as for myself, as you know I've always observed a . . . a certain respect for the bonds of holy matrimony. In a general sort of way, my lady.

Hedda: *[banteringly]* Well no, I never really had any very high hopes of you.

Brack: I demand no more than a nice intimate circle of acquaintances, where I can rally round with advice and assistance, and where I'm allowed to come and go as . . . as a trusted friend. . . .

Hedda: Of the master of the house, you mean?

Brack: *[inclines his head]* Candidly . . . of the lady, for choice. But naturally of the man as well. D'you know . . . this sort of . . . let me put it, this sort of triangular relationship . . . it's really highly convenient for all concerned.

Hedda: Yes, I'd have been glad of a third on the trip, often enough. Ugh . . . sitting there, just two people alone in the compartment . . . !

Brack: Fortunately, the nuptial journey is at an end. . . .

Hedda: *[shakes her head]* The journey'll be a long one . . . a long one yet. I've just come to a stopping-place on the line.

Brack: Well, then you jump out. And move around a little, my
    lady.

Hedda: I'll never jump out.

Brack: Are you quite sure?

Hedda: Yes. Because there's always someone there who'll . . .

Brack: *[laughing].* . . . who'll look at your legs, you mean?

Hedda: Exactly.

Brack: Oh well, good Lord. . . .

Hedda: *[with a gesture of dismissal]* Don't like it. . . . Then I'd
    sooner stay where I am . . . in the compartment. Two people
    alone together.

Brack: Well then, if somebody else climbs into the compartment.

Hedda: Ah yes . . . that's quite another thing!

Brack: A trusted and sympathetic friend . . .

Hedda: . . . who can converse on all manner of lively topics . . .

Brack: . . . and who's not in the least academic!

Hedda: *[with an audible sigh]* Yes, that really is a relief.

Brack: *[hears the front door opening and listens]* The triangle is
    completed.

Hedda: *[half aloud]* And the train drives on.

*[Jörgen Tesman, in a grey walking suit and with a soft hat, comes in from the
hall. He has quite a number of unbound books under his arm and in his pockets.]*

Tesman: *[goes up to the table by the corner sofa]* Poof . . . hot work
    dragging all these around. *[He puts down the books.]* To put it
    elegantly, I'm sweating, Hedda. Why, what's this . . . you're
    here already, Mr. Brack? Eh? Berte didn't tell me anything
    about that.

Brack: *[gets up]* I came up through the garden.

Hedda: What are those books you've got there?

Tesman: *[turns a few pages]* Oh, new academic publications that I
    simply had to have.

Hedda: Academic publications?

Brack: Aha, they're academic publications, Mrs. Tesman.

[Brack and Hedda exchange a knowing smile.]

Hedda: Do you need still more academic publications?

Tesman: Oh yes, my dear Hedda . . . can't get too many of those.
    One must keep up with everything that's written.

Hedda: Yes, I suppose one must.

Tesman: *[searching among the books]* And look here . . . here we are,
    I've got hold of Ejlert Lövborg's new book, too. *[He holds it
    out.]* Perhaps you'd like to have a look at it, Hedda? Eh?

Hedda: No thank you. Or . . . yes, perhaps I will, later on.

Tesman: I glanced at a few pages on my way up.

Brack: Well, and what did you think of it, then? . . . From the academic point of view?

Tesman: I think it's remarkable how soberly he's argued it. He never used to write like this before. *[Gathers up the books.]* But now I'm going to go in with all this. It'll be a joy to cut the pages . . . ! And then I'll have to get into some other clothes. *[To* Brack.*]* I take it we don't have to leave straight away, do we? Eh?

Brack: No indeed . . . there's no hurry for a long while yet.

Tesman: Ah well, I'll take my time then. *[Goes with the books, but stops in the doorway and turns.]* Oh, while I think of it, Hedda . . . Aunt Julle won't be able to come this evening.

Hedda: Won't she? Is it because of that affair with the hat, perhaps?

Tesman: Oh, good gracious! How can you think that of Auntie Julle? Just think . . . ! But the thing is Aunt Rina's so very ill, you see.

Hedda: She always is.

Tesman: Yes, but today she was quite exceptionally bad, poor thing.

Hedda: Well, then it's only reasonable that the other one should stay with her. I'll have to make the best of it.

Tesman: And you can't imagine, Hedda, how overjoyed Aunt Julle was in spite of everything . . . because you looked so well from the trip!

Hedda: *[half under her breath, getting up]* Oh, these everlasting aunts!

Tesman: Eh?

Hedda: *[crossing to the glass door]* Nothing.

Tesman: Oh, all right then.

[He goes out through the back room to the right.]

Brack: What was that about a hat?

Hedda: Oh, it was to do with Miss Tesman this morning. She'd put her hat down there on the chair. *[Looks at him and smiles.]* And I pretended I thought it was the maid's.

Brack: *[shakes his head]* But my dearest lady, how could you do such a thing! To that harmless old soul!

Hedda: *[nervously, walking across]* Oh, you know how it is . . . these things just suddenly come over me. And then I can't resist them. *[Flings herself down in the armchair by the stove.]* Oh, I don't know myself how to explain it.

Brack: *[behind the armchair]* You're not really happy . . . that's probably what it is.

Hedda: [*looking straight ahead*] And I don't really know why I should be . . . happy. Or perhaps you might be able to tell me?

Brack: Yes . . . among other things, because you've got just the home you wanted.

Hedda: [*looks up at him and laughs*] Do you also believe that fairy story?

Brack: Why, isn't there anything in it?

Hedda: Oh yes . . . there's something in it.

Brack: Well?

Hedda: There's this much in it, that I used Tesman as an escort to take me home from evening parties last summer. . . .

Brack: Ah, regrettably . . . I had to go quite a different way.

Hedda: True enough, you were going a rather different way, last summer.

Brack: [*laughs*] Touché, my lady! Well . . . but you and Tesman, then . . . ?

Hedda: Yes, well then we came past this house one evening. And Tesman, poor fellow, was floundering and dithering. Because he couldn't think of anything to talk about. So I felt sorry for the poor erudite man. . . .

Brack: [*smiles sceptically*] Did you? Hm. . . .

Hedda: Yes, by your leave, sir, I did. And then . . . to help him along a bit . . . I happened to say, just on the impulse, that I'd like to live here in this villa.

Brack: No more than that?

Hedda: Not that particular evening.

Brack: But afterwards, then?

Hedda: Ah yes. My impulsiveness had its consequences, my dear Mr. Brack.

Brack: Unfortunately . . . impulsiveness does that only too frequently, my lady.

Hedda: Thank you! But in this ardour for Lady Falk's villa Jörgen Tesman and I met in mutual understanding, you see! It brought on engagement and marriage and honeymoon and the whole lot. Ah well, Mr. Brack . . . as one makes one's bed one must lie on it . . . I almost said.

Brack: But this is delicious! And perhaps you didn't really care about the place at all?

Hedda: No, God knows I did not.

Brack: Well, but now, then? Now that we've arranged everything a bit comfortably for you!

Hedda: Ugh . . . I think it smells of lavender and pot-pourri in all the rooms. . . . But perhaps Auntie Julle brought that smell in with her.

Brack: [laughs] No, I think it's more probably a relic of the late lamented Lady Falk.

Hedda: Yes, it has a sort of odour of death. Like a bouquet the day after a ball. *[Clasps her hands at the back of her neck, leans back in the chair and looks at him.]* Ah, dear Mr. Brack . . . you just can't imagine how excruciatingly bored I'll be, out here.

Brack: Don't you think that for you too, my lady, life might have something or other up its sleeve?

Hedda: Anything . . . in any way inviting?

Brack: Well of course that would be best.

Hedda: Lord knows what sort of thing that would be. I often wonder whether . . . *[She breaks off.]* But that wouldn't be any good either.

Brack: Who knows? Let me hear about it.

Hedda: Whether I could get Tesman to go in for politics, I mean.

Brack: [laughs] Tesman! Oh now seriously . . . anything like politics, he wouldn't be any . . . manner of use at that.

Hedda: No, I don't suppose he would. . . . But don't you think I might get him to do it, all the same?

Brack: Well . . . what possible satisfaction could that give you? When he's no good? Why should you want him to?

Hedda: Because I'm bored, d'you hear! *[After a pause.]* So you think it would be quite out of the question for Tesman to end up as Prime Minister?

Brack: Hm . . . you know, my lady . . . to do that he'd have to be quite a rich man, for a start.

Hedda: [rises impatiently] Yes, there we have it! It's these paltry circumstances I've landed up in . . . ! *[She moves across.]* That's what makes life so pitiful! So positively ludicrous! . . . Because that's what it is.

Brack: I think it's something else that's the trouble.

Hedda: What, then?

Brack: You've never had to go through any really stirring experience.

Hedda: Anything serious, you mean?

Brack: Yes, I suppose one could put it that way too. But now . . . it might come.

Hedda: [tosses her head] Oh, you're thinking of all the commotion about this wretched professorship! But that'll be Tesman's own affair. I'm not going to give it a thought.

Brack: No-no, well we won't talk about that. But then when you're faced with . . . what I may . . . perhaps a little pompously . . . refer to as a sacred and . . . and exacting responsibility? *[Smiles.]* A new responsibility, my little lady.

Hedda: [angry] Be quiet! You'll never see anything of the sort!

Brack: [carefully] We'll talk about it in a year's time . . . at the very latest.

Hedda: [shortly] I've no aptitude for any such thing, Mr. Brack. No responsibilities for me, thank you!

Brack: Why shouldn't you, like most other women, have a natural aptitude for a vocation that . . . ?

Hedda: [at the glass door] Oh, be quiet, I say! . . . I've often thought there's only one thing in the world I'm any good at.

Brack: [moves closer] And what might that be, may I venture to ask?

Hedda: [standing and looking out] Boring myself to death. So now you know. [Turns, looks towards the inner room, and laughs.] Ah yes, right enough! Here comes the professor.

Brack: [cautioning her in a low voice] Now, now, now, my lady!

[Jörgen Tesman, *dressed for the party, holding his gloves and his hat, comes in from the right of the back room.*]

Tesman: Hedda . . . did Ejlert Lövborg send to say he wasn't coming? Eh?

Hedda: No.

Tesman: Well then, you'll see, he'll be here in a moment.

Brack: Do you really think he'll come?

Tesman: Yes, I'm almost sure of it. Because I don't think you can have been right about what you said this morning.

Brack: Oh?

Tesman: Well at any rate Auntie Julle said she couldn't see how he could possibly think of putting himself up against me, as things are. Think of that!

Brack: Well, then everything's perfectly all right.

Tesman: [puts his hat, with the gloves inside, on a chair to the right] Yes, but you won't mind if we give him as long as possible.

Brack: Oh, we've got any amount of time. Nobody'll be coming to my place until seven or half past.

Tesman: Well, we can keep Hedda company until then. And see what happens. Eh?

Hedda: [carrying Brack's overcoat and hat over to the corner sofa] And if the worst comes to the worst Mr. Lövborg can always stay here with me.

Brack: [wants to carry his things himself] Allow me, Mrs. Tesman! . . . What do you mean by the worst?

Hedda: If he won't go with you and Tesman.

Tesman: [looks at her uncertainly] But, dearest Hedda . . . do you think it would be quite the thing for him to stay with you? Eh? Remember Aunt Julle can't come.

Hedda: No, but Mrs. Elvsted's coming. And we'll all three have a nice cup of tea together.

Tesman: Oh well, then, that's quite all right!

Brack: [*smiles*] And perhaps that arrangement would be the most wholesome thing for him.

Hedda: How so?

Brack: Oh, come, Mrs. Tesman, you've twitted me often enough about my little bachelor parties. Only to be recommended, wasn't it, to men of the most steadfast principles?

Hedda: But surely Mr. Lövborg is steadfast enough now. A prodigal reformed. . . .

[Berte *appears at the hall door.*]

Berte: Ma'am, there's a gentleman who wants to come in. . . .

Hedda: Let him come.

Tesman: [*quietly*] I'm sure it's him! Think of it!

[Ejlert Lövborg *comes in from the hall. He is slim and lean; the same age as Tesman, but looks older and a little haggard. Hair and beard dark brown, face longish and pale, patches of colour on either cheekbone. He is dressed in an elegant, black, and quite new suit. Dark gloves and a top hat in his hands. He remains standing close to the door and bows hurriedly. He seems a little embarrassed.*]

Tesman: [*goes to him and pumps his hand*] My dear Ejlert . . . so we meet again in spite of everything!

Lövborg: [*speaks in a low voice*] Thanks for the letter, Tesman. [*Approaches* Hedda.] May I take your hand as well, Mrs. Tesman?

Hedda: [*taking the hand he offers*] So pleased you came, Mr. Lövborg. [*With a gesture.*] I wonder if you two gentlemen . . . ?

Lövborg: [*with a slight inclination*] Mr. Brack, I believe.

Brack: [*following suit*] How do you do. Some years ago now. . . .

Tesman: [*to* Lövborg, *his hands on* Lövborg's *shoulders*] And now you must behave just as if you were at home, Ejlert! Isn't that right, Hedda? . . . And I hear you're going to settle here in town again? Eh?

Lövborg: That is so.

Tesman: Well, and why not indeed? Hey listen . . . I've got hold of your new book. But I just haven't had a moment to read it yet.

Lövborg: You might as well save yourself the bother.

Tesman: Why do you say that?

Lövborg: Because there's nothing much to it.

Tesman: Oh but . . . what a thing for you to say!

Brack: But it's been enormously praised, they tell me.

Lövborg: That was just what I wanted. So I wrote a book that nobody could disagree with.

Brack: Very sensible.

Tesman: Yes but, my dear Ejlert . . . !

Lövborg: Because I'm trying now to build up a position for myself. Starting over again.

Tesman: [a bit embarrassed] Why yes, I suppose you are? Eh?

Lövborg: [smiles, puts down his hat and pulls a packet wrapped in paper from his coat pocket] But when this one comes out . . . Jörgen Tesman . . . then you're to read it. Because this is the real thing. I put some of myself into this one.

Tesman: Really? And what's that about?

Lövborg: It's the continuation.

Tesman: The continuation? Of what?

Lövborg: Of the book.

Tesman: The new one?

Lövborg: Of course.

Tesman: Yes but, my dear Ejlert . . . it carries on right to the present day!

Lövborg: That is so. And this one deals with the future.

Tesman: With the future! But ye gods, we don't know anything about that!

Lövborg: No. But there are one or two things to be said about it, all the same. [Opens the packet.] Here, look at this. . . .

Tesman: But that isn't your writing.

Lövborg: I dictated it. [Turns the leaves.] It's in two sections. The first is about the social forces involved, and this other bit . . . [He ruffles the pages further on.] . . . that's about the future course of civilization.

Tesman: Amazing! It just wouldn't enter my head to write about anything like that.

Hedda: [at the glass door, drumming her fingers on the pane] Hm. . . . No-no.

Lövborg: [wraps up the papers again, and puts the packet on the table] I brought it along so that I could read you a bit this evening.

Tesman: Well yes, that was frightfully decent of you, old man. But this evening . . . ? [Looks at Brack.] I don't really know if we can manage it. . . .

Lövborg: Well, some other time then. There's no hurry.

Brack: I ought to tell you, Mr. Lövborg . . . there's going to be a little entertainment at my place this evening. More or less in honour of Tesman, you understand. . . .

Lövborg: [looks for his hat] Ah . . . in that case I won't . . .

Brack: No, just a moment. Wouldn't you do me the very great honour of joining us?

Lövborg: [shortly and firmly] No, I'm afraid I can't. Thank you very much indeed.

Brack: Oh, come along! Do be persuaded. We'll be quite a small and select gathering. And I guarantee that it'll be 'lively', as my la— . . . as Mrs. Tesman expresses it.

Lövborg: I don't doubt it. But all the same . . .

Brack: Then you could bring along your manuscript and read to Tesman over at my place. There are plenty of rooms.

Tesman: Yes, just think, Ejlert . . . what about that! Eh?

Hedda: [intervenes] But my dear, when Mr. Lövborg doesn't want to! I'm sure that Mr. Lövborg would far sooner stay where he is and take a bit of supper with me.

Lövborg: [looks at her] With you, Mrs. Tesman?

Hedda: And then with Mrs. Elvsted.

Lövborg: Oh. . . . *[Casually.]* I met her for a moment this afternoon.

Hedda: Did you? Well, she's coming out here. And so you'll almost have to stay, Mr. Lövborg. Because otherwise there'll be no one to see her home.

Lövborg: That's true. Well, thank you very much, Mrs. Tesman . . . I'll stay here then.

Hedda: Then I'll just have a word with the maid. . . .

[She goes to the hall door and rings. Berte *comes in.* Hedda *speaks to her quietly and points towards the inner room.* Berte *nods and goes out again.]*

Tesman: [while this is going on, to Lövborg*]* Tell me, Ejlert . . . is it this new subject . . . this business about the future . . . that you'll be lecturing about?

Lövborg: Yes.

Tesman: Because I heard at the bookseller's that you're giving a series of lectures here this autumn.

Lövborg: I am. You mustn't hold it against me, Tesman.

Tesman: No, no, of course I wouldn't dream of it. But . . . ?

Lövborg: I can see that for you this must be rather an embarrassment.

Tesman: [dejected] Oh well, I can't possibly expect you to . . .

Lövborg: But I shall wait till you've received your appointment.

Tesman: You'll wait till . . . ! Yes but . . . yes but . . . aren't you going to compete for it? Eh?

Lövborg: No. I only intend to outshine you. In reputation.

Tesman: But, good Heavens . . . so Auntie Julle was right after all! There . . . I said she would be! Hedda! Just think, Hedda . . . Ejlert Lövborg isn't going to stand in our way at all!

Hedda: [shortly] Our way? Leave me out of it.

[She goes upstage towards the back room, where Berte *is placing a tray with decanters and glasses on the table.* Hedda *nods her approval and comes forward again.* Berte *goes out.]*

Tesman: [while this is going on] Well, Mr. Brack, what about that! . . . What do you say? Eh?

Brack: Well, I say that honour and reputation . . . hm . . . these
   things certainly have their appeal. . . .

Tesman: Yes of course they do. But all the same . . .

Hedda: *[looks at* Tesman *with a cold smile]* You stand there looking
   as if you'd been struck by lightning.

Brack: And it was quite a thunderstorm that passed over us, Mrs.
   Tesman.

Hedda: *[points to the back room]* Now, would all you gentlemen like
   to go inside and take a glass of cold punch?

Brack: *[looks at his watch]* By way of an hors d'oeuvre? That
   wouldn't be a bad idea.

Tesman: Excellent, Hedda! Just what we need! I really feel in the
   mood for something now.

Hedda: You'll have some too, Mr. Lövborg.

Lövborg: *[dismissing the subject]* No thank you. Not for me.

Brack: But good Lord . . . there's nothing lethal about cold
   punch, let me tell you.

Lövborg: Not perhaps for everyone.

Hedda: Well then, I'll entertain Mr. Lövborg in the meanwhile.

Tesman: All right, dear Hedda, you do that.

*[*Tesman *and* Brack *go into the inner room, sit down, drink punch, smoke cigarettes, and carry on an animated conversation during the following scene.* Ejlert
Lövborg *remains standing by the stove.* Hedda *goes to the desk.]*

Hedda: *[in a slightly loud voice]* And now if you like I'll show you
   some photographs. We took an excursion through the Tyrol
   . . . Tesman and I . . . on our way home.

*[She produces an album, and, laying it on the small table, sits down at the upper
end of the sofa.* Ejlert Lövborg *comes closer, stops, and looks at her. Then he takes
a chair and sits on her left, with his back to the inner room.]*

Hedda: *[opens the album]* Do you see this range of mountains, Mr.
   Lövborg? That is the Ortler Group. Tesman wrote it under-
   neath the picture. There you are: The Ortler Group at
   Meran.

Lövborg: *[who has not once taken his eyes off her, says softly and slowly].*
   Hedda . . . Gabler!

Hedda: *[with a quick sidelong glance at him]* Now! Sh!

Lövborg: *[softly repeats]* Hedda Gabler!

Hedda: *[looks in the album]* That was once my name. When . . .
   when we two used to know each other.

Lövborg: And from now on . . . and for the rest of my life . . . I must
   stop saying Hedda Gabler.

Hedda: *[still turning the pages]* Yes, you must. And I think you'd
   better start practising at once. The sooner the better, I
   should say.

Lövborg: [*with bitterness in his voice*] Hedda Gabler married. And married to . . . Jörgen Tesman!

Hedda: Yes . . . that's the way of it.

Lövborg: Oh Hedda . . . darling Hedda, how could you throw yourself away like that?

Hedda: [*with a sharp look*] Now. None of that!

Lövborg: None of what?

[Tesman *comes in and goes towards the sofa.*]

Hedda: [*hears him coming and says indifferently*] And this, Mr. Lövborg, was taken in the Ampezzo Valley. Just look at those rock formations. [*Looks amiably up at* Tesman.] What were those peculiar mountains called, dear?

Tesman: Let me look. Ah, those are the Dolomites.

Hedda: That's right! . . . those are the Dolomites, Mr. Lövborg.

Tesman: Oh, Hedda . . . I just wanted to ask if you wouldn't like a little punch in here all the same? For yourself at least. Eh?

Hedda: Yes, thank you very much. And maybe a few cakes.

Tesman: No cigarettes?

Hedda: No.

Tesman: Very good.

[He goes into the back room and away to the right. Brack *sits within, occasionally keeping an eye on* Hedda *and* Lövborg.]

Lövborg: [*quietly, as before*] Answer me then, dearest Hedda, how could you go and do such a thing?

Hedda: [*apparently immersed in the album*] If you continue to address me like that I shan't speak to you at all.

Lövborg: Even when we're alone, won't you let me?

Hedda: I can't dictate your thoughts, Mr. Lövborg. But you will speak to me with respect.

Lövborg: Ah, I see. Because of your love . . . for Jörgen Tesman.

Hedda: [*glances sideways at him and smiles*] Love? That's good!

Lövborg: Not love, then!

Hedda: But no kind of unfaithfulness! I'll have none of that.

Lövborg: Hedda . . . answer one single question. . . .

Hedda: Sh!

[Tesman, *with a tray, comes in from the back room.*]

Tesman: Here we are! This is what you've been waiting for!

[He puts the tray on the table.]

Hedda: Why don't you leave that to the maid?

Tesman: [*fills the glasses*] Because I think it's such fun to wait on you, Hedda.

Hedda: But now you've filled them both. And Mr. Lövborg doesn't want . . .

Tesman: No, but Mrs. Elvsted must be here soon.

Hedda: Oh yes, that's true . . . Mrs. Elvsted. . . .

Tesman: Had you forgotten her? Eh?

Hedda: We're so taken up with this. *[Shows him a picture.]* Do you remember that little village?

Tesman: Ah, that's the one below the Brenner Pass! That was where we stayed the night . . .

Hedda: . . . and met all those lively summer visitors.

Tesman: Yes, that's the place. Just think . . . if only you could have been with us, Ejlert! Well then!

[He goes in again and sits down by Brack.*]*

Lövborg: Answer me just this one question, Hedda . . .

Hedda: Well?

Lövborg: Was there no love in your relationship to me either? Not a trace . . . not a suspicion of love in that either?

Hedda: Can there have been, I wonder? My memory is that we were two good companions. Really sincere friends. *[Smiles.]* You were especially candid.

Lövborg: You were the one who wanted it like that.

Hedda: When I think back to that time, wasn't there something beautiful, something attractive . . . something courageous too, it seems to me . . . about this . . . this secret intimacy, this companionship that no one even dreamed of.

Lövborg: There was, Hedda, wasn't there! . . . When I came up to your father's in the afternoons. . . And the General used to sit by the window, reading the papers . . . his back towards us . . .

Hedda: And we sat in the corner sofa . . .

Lövborg: Always with the same magazine in front of us . . .

Hedda: Yes . . . for want of an album.

Lövborg: Yes, Hedda . . . and then when I used to confess to you . . . ! Told you things about myself that none of the others knew at that time. Sat there and admitted that I'd been out on the razzle for whole days and nights. For days on end. Oh, Hedda . . . what power was it in you that forced me to reveal all those things?

Hedda: Do you think it was a power in me?

Lövborg: Well, how else can I explain it? And all those . . . those roundabout questions you used to put to me . . .

Hedda: And which you were so quick to understand. . . .

Lövborg: That you could sit and ask like that! Quite confidently!

Hedda: Roundabout questions, if you please.

Lövborg: Yes, but confidently all the same. Cross-examine me about . . . about all those things!

Hedda: And that you could answer, Mr. Lövborg.

Lövborg: Yes, that's just what I find so incredible . . . now afterwards. But tell me then, Hedda . . . wasn't it love at the back of it all? Wasn't it on your part a desire to absolve me . . . when I came to you and confessed? Wasn't that a part of it?

Hedda: No, not exactly.

Lövborg: Why did you do it, then?

Hedda: Do you find it so hard to understand that a young girl . . . when it can happen like that . . . in secret . . .

Lövborg: Well?

Hedda: That she should want to find out about a world that . . .

Lövborg: That . . . ?

Hedda: . . . that she isn't supposed to know anything about?

Lövborg: So that was it!

Hedda: That as well . . . I rather think it was that as well.

Lövborg: Our common lust for life. But then why couldn't that at least have gone on?

Hedda: That was your own fault.

Lövborg: It was you who broke it off.

Hedda: Yes, because there was an imminent danger that the game would become a reality. Shame on you, Ejlert Lövborg, how could you offer such violence to . . . to your confidential companion!

Lövborg: *[presses his fists together]* Oh, why didn't you play it out! Why didn't you shoot me down, as you threatened!

Hedda: I'm too much afraid of a scandal.

Lövborg: Yes, Hedda, at bottom you're a coward.

Hedda: An awful coward. *[In a different tone.]* Which was lucky for you. And now you've consoled yourself so beautifully up at the Elvsteds'.

Lövborg: I know what Thea's told you.

Hedda: And perhaps you told her something about us?

Lövborg: Not a word. She's too stupid to understand anything like that.

Hedda: Stupid?

Lövborg: She's stupid about things like that.

Hedda: And I'm a coward. *[Leans a little closer to him, and without meeting his eyes says softly.]* But now I'm going to confess something to you.

Lövborg: *[in suspense]* What?

Hedda: That I didn't dare to shoot you . . .

Lövborg: Yes!

Hedda: . . . that wasn't my worst cowardice . . . that evening. . . .

Lövborg: [*looks at her for a moment, takes her meaning, and whispers passionately*] Oh Hedda! Hedda Gabler! Now I think I see what it was that lay behind our companionship! You and I . . . ! So it was your lust for life . . .

Hedda: [*quietly, with a sharp glance at him*] Have a care! Don't assume any such thing!

[*It has started to get dark. The hall door is opened by* Berte.]

Hedda: [*claps the album shut and cries out with a smile*] At last! Thea, my dear . . . come in then!

[*Mrs. Elvsted comes in from the hall. She is dressed for a social occasion. The door shuts behind her.*]

Hedda: [*on the sofa, stretching out her arms towards* Mrs. Elvsted] Dearest Thea . . . you can't imagine how I've been longing for you to come!

[*Mrs. Elvsted, in passing, exchanges a greeting with the gentlemen in the inner room; then crosses to the table and gives* Hedda *her hand. Ejlert Lövborg has stood up. He and* Mrs. Elvsted *exchange a nod of greeting without speaking.*]

Mrs. Elvsted: Shouldn't I go in and have a word with your husband?

Hedda: Oh, don't worry. Let them stay where they are. They'll be gone soon.

Mrs. Elvsted: Are they going?

Hedda: Yes, they're going out on the spree.

Mrs. Elvsted: [*quickly, to* Lövborg] But not you?

Lövborg: No.

Hedda: Mr. Lövborg . . . he'll stay here with us.

Mrs. Elvsted: [*takes a chair and makes to sit down beside* Lövborg] Oh, it's good to be here!

Hedda: No you don't, Thea my pet! Not there! You come over here like a good girl. I want to be in the middle.

Mrs. Elvsted: All right, just as you please.

[*She goes round the table and sits on the sofa on* Hedda's *right.* Lövborg *resumes his chair.*]

Lövborg: [*after a little pause, to* Hedda] Isn't she lovely to sit and look at?

Hedda: [*passes a hand lightly over* Mrs. Elvsted's *hair*] Just to look at?

Lövborg: Yes. Because we two . . . she and I . . . we're really good companions. We trust each other completely. And so we can sit and talk together in full confidence.

Hedda: Nothing roundabout, Mr. Lövborg?

Lövborg: Oh, well . . .

Mrs. Elvsted: [*quietly, clinging to* Hedda] Oh, how happy I am, Hedda!

Because, do you know what he also says . . . he says I've inspired him, too.

Hedda: [*looking at her with a smile*] Does he really say that, Thea?

Lövborg: And then she has the courage to act, Mrs. Tesman!

Mrs. Elvsted: Oh Heavens . . . me, courage!

Lövborg: Infinite courage . . . for her companion.

Hedda: Oh courage . . . oh yes! If only one had that.

Lövborg: What, then, do you mean?

Hedda: Then life might be liveable, in spite of everything. [*Switches to another tone.*] But now, Thea my dear . . . now you must let me give you a glass of cold punch.

Mrs. Elvsted: No thank you . . . I never drink anything like that.

Hedda: Well, then you must, Mr. Lövborg.

Lövborg: Thank you, not for me either.

Mrs. Elvsted: No, he doesn't either!

Hedda: [*looks at him steadily*] But when I want you to?

Lövborg: Makes no difference.

Hedda: [*laughs*] And so I've got no power over you at all? Is that it?

Lövborg: Not where that's concerned.

Hedda: But quite seriously, I do think you should have some all the same. For your own sake.

Mrs. Elvsted: Oh, but Hedda . . . !

Lövborg: How do you mean?

Hedda: Or rather, because of other people.

Lövborg: Oh?

Hedda: Otherwise people might so easily get the idea that you're not . . . really confident, really sure of yourself.

Mrs. Elvsted: [*quietly*] Oh, no Hedda, no . . . !

Lövborg: People can think whatever they like . . . for the time being.

Mrs. Elvsted: [*happy*] Yes, that's right!

Hedda: It was so obvious with Mr. Brack just now.

Lövborg: What do you mean?

Hedda: He smiled so contemptuously when you didn't dare to join them in there at the table.

Lövborg: Didn't I dare! I quite naturally preferred to stay here and talk to you.

Mrs. Elvsted: Of course he did, Hedda!

Hedda: Well, Mr. Brack wasn't to know that. And I also saw the way he smiled and glanced at Tesman when you didn't dare to go along to this wretched little party, either.

Lövborg: Dare! Do you say I didn't dare?

Hedda: I don't. But that's the way Mr. Brack understood it.

Lövborg: Let him.

Hedda: So you're not going?

Lövborg: I'll stay with you and Thea.

Mrs. Elvsted: Yes, Hedda . . . of course he's going to stay!

Hedda: [nods and smiles approvingly at Lövborg] Firm as a rock, then. A man who is steadfast in his principles. Well, that's how a man should be! [Turns to Mrs. Elvsted and pats her.] There, wasn't that what I said this morning when you came in here in such a state of desperation. . . .

Lövborg: [pulled up] Desperation?

Mrs. Elvsted: [in a panic] Hedda . . . oh but Hedda . . . !

Hedda: Just look at him! There isn't the slightest need for you to go about in mortal terror . . . [She breaks off.] There! Now we can all be lively!

Lövborg: [shocked] But . . . what is all this, Mrs. Tesman?

Mrs. Elvsted: Oh God, oh God, Hedda! What are you saying? What are you trying to do?

Hedda: Hush, now! That odious Mr. Brack has got his eye on you.

Lövborg: So you were in mortal terror. On my account.

Mrs. Elvsted: [quietly wailing] Oh, Hedda . . . now you've really made me unhappy!

Lövborg: [looks at her steadily for a moment. His face is tense] So that was my companion's confident belief in me.

Mrs. Elvsted: [piteously] Oh, my dear, you must let me explain . . . !

Lövborg: [takes one of the full punch glasses, raises it, and says quietly, in a hoarse voice] Your health, Thea!

[He empties the glass, puts it down, and picks up the other.]

Mrs. Elvsted: [quietly] Oh Hedda, Hedda . . . how could you have wanted this to happen?

Hedda: I wanted it? Don't be absurd!

Lövborg: And yours too, Mrs. Tesman! Thanks for the truth. Here's to it!

[He drinks and makes to refill the glass.]

Hedda: [putting her hand on his arm] Now, now . . . no more for the moment. Remember you're going to a party.

Mrs. Elvsted: No, no, no!

Hedda: Quiet! They're sitting there looking at you.

Lövborg: [puts down the glass] Thea . . . be honest with me. . . .

Mrs. Elvsted: Yes!

Lövborg: Did your husband know you were coming down to look for me?

Mrs. Elvsted: [wrings her hands] Oh Hedda . . . did you hear what he asked me?

Lövborg: Did you arrange it between you that you should come to town to keep an eye on me? Or maybe it was the old man

himself who suggested it? Aha, now I've got it . . . he wanted
me back in the office again! Or was he short of a fourth at
cards?

Mrs. Elvsted: [quietly, painfully] Oh Lövborg, Lövborg . . . !

Lövborg: [grabs a glass and starts to fill it] And here's one to old
Elvsted, too!

Hedda: [firmly] No more now. Remember you're going out to
read to Tesman.

Lövborg: [quietly, putting down the glass] I'm sorry, Thea. I've made
a fool of myself. Taking it like that, I mean. Don't be angry
with me, my dear . . . dear companion. I'll show you . . . both
you and the others . . . that however worthless I may have
been in the past, I . . . I've found my feet again! With your
help, Thea.

Mrs. Elvsted: [ecstatically happy again] Oh, thank God . . . !

[In the meanwhile Brack has been looking at his watch. He and Tesman get up
and come into the drawing-room.]

Brack: [taking his hat and coat] Well, Mrs. Tesman, our time is up.

Hedda: I suppose it is.

Lövborg: [getting up] Mine too, Mr. Brack.

Mrs. Elvsted: [quietly and imploringly] Oh Lövborg . . . don't do it!

Hedda: [pinches her arm] They can hear you!

Mrs. Elvsted: [crying out faintly] Ow!

Lövborg: [to Brack]. You were so kind as to invite me.

Brack: Oh, so you've changed your mind?

Lövborg: Yes, if I may.

Brack: A very great pleasure. . . .

Lövborg: [pockets his manuscript and addresses Tesman] Because there
are one or two things I'd like to show you before I hand it in.

Tesman: Just think . . . that'll be wonderful! . . . But I say, Hedda,
how will you get Mrs. Elvsted home then? Eh?

Hedda: Oh, we'll manage somehow.

Lövborg: [looking at the ladies]. Mrs. Elvsted? Why, naturally I'll
come back and fetch her. [Goes closer.] Somewhere about ten
o'clock, Mrs. Tesman. Will that suit you?

Hedda: Yes, that'll be splendid.

Tesman: Oh well, then everything's in order. But you mustn't
expect me so early, Hedda.

Hedda: Oh that's all right. Just you stay as long as . . . ever you
like.

Mrs. Elvsted: [with suppressed anxiety]. Mr. Lövborg . . . I'll stay here
then, till you come.

Lövborg: [his hat in his hand]. Why of course.

Brack: And now, gentlemen, let the revels commence! I trust it
will be lively, as a certain lovely lady has it.

Hedda: Ah, if only that lovely lady could come along as an invisible onlooker . . . !

Brack: Why invisible?

Hedda: So as to hear a little of your liveliness . . . unexpurgated, Mr. Brack.

Brack: [laughs]. Ah, now that's something I wouldn't recommend to the lovely lady!

Tesman: [also laughing]. That's a good one, Hedda! Think of that!

Brack: Well, goodbye, goodbye, ladies!

Lövborg: [bowing in departure]. About ten, then.

[Brack, Lövborg, *and* Tesman *go out at the hall door. Simultaneously* Berte *comes in from the back room with a lighted lamp, which she places on the large table, and goes out the way she came.]*

Mrs. Elvsted: [has got up, and wanders uneasily about the room]. Hedda . . . Hedda . . . how is all this going to end!

Hedda: Ten o'clock . . . and back he'll come. I can just seen him. With vine leaves in his hair. Flushed and confident. . . .

Mrs. Elvsted: Yes, oh I do so hope it's like that.

Hedda: And then, my dear . . . then he'll be master of himself again. He'll be a free man for the rest of his life.

Mrs. Elvsted: Oh yes, oh God . . . if only he would come back, just as you see him.

Hedda: He'll come . . . just exactly like that! *[She gets up and goes closer to her.]* You may doubt him as much as you please. I believe in him. And then we'll be able to see . . .

Mrs. Elvsted: You've got some reason for all this, Hedda!

Hedda: Yes, I have. For once in my life I want to feel that I control a human destiny.

Mrs. Elvsted: But surely you do already?

Hedda: I don't, and I never have done.

Mrs. Elvsted: But what about your husband?

Hedda: Yes, that would really be something, wouldn't it. Oh, if only you knew how destitute I am. And you're allowed to be so rich! *[She passionately grips* Mrs. Elvsted *in her arms.]* I think I'll burn your hair off after all.

Mrs. Elvsted: Let me go! Let me go! I'm frightened of you, Hedda!

Berte: [in the doorway]. Everything's ready, ma'am, in the dining-room.

Hedda: Good. We're coming.

Mrs. Elvsted: No, no, no! I'd sooner go home alone! Now, at once!

Hedda: Nonsense! First you're going to have some tea, you little goose. And then . . . at ten o'clock . . . then Ejlert Lövborg will come . . . with vine leaves in his hair.

[She pulls Mrs. Elvsted *towards the doorway almost by main force.]*

ACT THREE

The room at the Tesmans'. The curtains are drawn across the centre doorway, and also at the glass door. The lamp, with a shade, and half turned down, is alight on the table. The door of the stove stands open; the fire within has almost burnt itself out.

Mrs. Elvsted, wrapped in a large shawl and with her feet on a footstool, is reclining in the armchair close to the stove. Hedda, still fully dressed, is lying asleep on the sofa with a rug over her.

Mrs. Elvsted: *[after a pause, starts up in the chair and listens anxiously. Then she sinks back wearily and wails quietly]* Still not back! Oh God . . . oh God . . . still not back!

[Berte comes tiptoeing carefully in at the hall door. She carries a letter in her hand.]

Mrs. Elvsted: *[turns and whispers urgently]* Well . . . has anybody come?
    Berte: *[quietly]* Yes, a young woman just came with this letter.
Mrs. Elvsted: *[quickly, stretching out her hand]* A letter! Give it to me!
    Berte: No, ma'am, it's for Dr. Tesman.
Mrs. Elvsted: Oh. . . .
    Berte: It was Miss Tesman's maid who brought it. I'll put it on the table here.
Mrs. Elvsted: Yes, do that.
    Berte: *[puts down the letter]* Perhaps I'd best put out the lamp. It's smoking a bit.
Mrs. Elvsted: Yes, put it out. It'll soon be light now.
    Berte: *[dousing the lamp]* It's broad daylight.
Mrs. Elvsted: Yes, daylight! And still not back . . . !
    Berte: Oh, bless you, ma'am . . . I knew this would happen.
Mrs. Elvsted: You knew it?
    Berte: Yes, when I saw that a certain person was back in town. . . . And then when he went off with them. We know what to expect of that gentleman.
Mrs. Elvsted: Not so loud. You'll wake Mrs. Tesman.
    Berte: *[looks at the sofa and sighs]* Oh the poor dear . . . let her have her sleep. . . . Shan't I put a bit more on the fire?
Mrs. Elvsted: Thank you, not on my account.
    Berte: All right, then.

[She goes out quietly at the hall door.]

    Hedda: *[is woken by the closing of the door and looks up]* What's that . . . !
Mrs. Elvsted: It was just the maid. . . .
    Hedda: *[looks around]* Here . . . ! Oh yes, I remember . . . *[Sits up on the sofa, stretches and rubs her eyes.]* What's the time, Thea?

Mrs. Elvsted: *[looks at her watch]* It's gone seven.

Hedda: When did Tesman come in?

Mrs. Elvsted: He isn't back yet.

Hedda: Not back yet?

Mrs. Elvsted: *[getting up]* No one came at all.

Hedda: And we sat there watching and waiting till four in the morning. . . .

Mrs. Elvsted: *[wringing her hands]* Oh, and how I did wait for him!

Hedda: *[yawns, and speaks with her hand over her mouth]* Ah well . . . we could have saved ourselves the trouble.

Mrs. Elvsted: Did you sleep at all?

Hedda: Oh yes . . . I think I slept quite well. Didn't you?

Mrs. Elvsted: Not a wink. I just couldn't, Hedda! It was quite impossible.

Hedda: *[gets up and goes towards her]* Now, now, now! There's nothing to worry about. It's quite obvious what's happened.

Mrs. Elvsted: Well, what has happened, then? Just tell me that!

Hedda: Well, naturally, they must have carried on till all hours at Mr. Brack's . . .

Mrs. Elvsted: Yes, Oh God . . . I suppose they did. But all the same . . .

Hedda: And then of course Tesman didn't want to come home and make a din and ring the bell in the middle of the night. *[Laughs.]* Perhaps he didn't want to show himself either . . . right on top of a night like that.

Mrs. Elvsted: But for goodness' sake . . . where else could he have gone?

Hedda: He obviously went along up to the aunts to sleep it off there. They still have his old room.

Mrs. Elvsted: No, there at least he can't be. Because just now a letter came for him from Miss Tesman. It's lying there.

Hedda: Oh? *[Looks at the writing on the envelope.]* Yes, it's from Auntie Julle all right, in her own fair hand. Well, he must have stopped over at Mr. Brack's, then. And Ejlert Lövborg, he's sitting there reading aloud . . . with vine leaves in his hair.

Mrs. Elvsted: Oh, Hedda, you're just saying all this, you don't really believe it yourself.

Hedda: You really are a little ninny, Thea.

Mrs. Elvsted: Yes, I suppose I am, really.

Hedda: And you look tired to death.

Mrs. Elvsted: Yes, I am tired to death.

Hedda: And so you're to do as I tell you. You're to go into my room and lie down on the bed for a little while.

Mrs. Elvsted: Oh no, no . . . anyway I wouldn't sleep.

Hedda: Of course you would.

Mrs. Elvsted: Yes, but your husband must be back soon. And then I must hear at once . . .

Hedda: I'll let you know when he comes.

Mrs. Elvsted: Do you promise me, Hedda?

Hedda: Yes, yes, that's all right. Just you go in and sleep till then.

Mrs. Elvsted: Thank you. Well, I'll try, then.

[She goes out through the inner room.]

[Hedda goes over to the glass door and draws the curtains aside. Full daylight streams into the room. She then takes a small looking-glass from the desk, inspects herself and arranges her hair. Then she crosses to the hall door and presses the bell.]

[After a short while Berte *comes to the door.]*

Berte: Did you ring, ma'am?

Hedda: Yes, be so good as to put some more on the stove. I'm cold.

Berte: Gracious . . . straight away, ma'am . . . I'll have it hot in a moment.

[She rakes the embers together and puts in a piece of wood.]

Berte: *[stops and listens]* That was the front door, ma'am.

Hedda: Then go and attend to it. I'll look after the fire myself.

Berte: It'll soon burn up.

[She goes out at the hall door.]

[Hedda kneels on the footstool and puts more wood into the stove.]

[After a little while Jörgen Tesman *comes in from the hall. He looks tired and rather serious. Creeps on tiptoe towards the doorway, and is about to slip in through the curtains.]*

Hedda: *[at the stove, without looking up]* Good morning.

Tesman: *[turning]* Hedda! *[Comes closer.]* But what on earth . . . are you up already! Eh?

Hedda: Yes, I was up very early this morning.

Tesman: And I was so sure you'd be sound asleep still! Think of that, Hedda!

Hedda: Don't talk so loudly. Mrs. Elvsted is lying down in my room.

Tesman: Did Mrs. Elvsted stay the night!

Hedda: Well, nobody came to fetch her.

Tesman: No, I suppose not.

Hedda: *[shuts the stove door and gets up]* Well, and did you have a good time at Mr. Brack's?

Tesman: Were you worried about me? Eh?

Hedda: Good gracious no . . . I wouldn't dream of it. But I asked if you'd had a good time.

Tesman: Yes, I suppose. For once in a way. . . . But most to begin with, I thought. Then Ejlert read to me. We got there an hour too soon . . . think of that! And Brack had to arrange things. But then Ejlert read to me.

Hedda: [sits to the right of the table] Well? Tell me about it. . . .

Tesman: [sits on a stool by the stove] Oh Hedda, you've no idea, it's going to be ever so good! One of the most remarkable books ever written, I'd almost say. Think of that!

Hedda: Yes, yes, I don't care so much about that . . .

Tesman: There's something I'm bound to confess, Hedda. When he'd finished reading . . . something ugly came over me.

Hedda: Something ugly?

Tesman: I sat and envied Ejlert that he'd been able to write such a thing. Think of that, Hedda!

Hedda: Yes, yes, I'm thinking.

Tesman: And then to know that . . . with all his talents . . . unfortunately he's quite beyond hope of reform, all the same.

Hedda: I suppose you mean he's got more courage than the rest?

Tesman: No, good Lord . . . he just can't keep himself under control at all, you know.

Hedda: Well, and what happened then . . . in the end?

Tesman: Yes, well, I'd almost have described it as an orgy, Hedda.

Hedda: Did he have vine leaves in his hair?

Tesman: Vine leaves? No, I didn't see anything like that. But he made a long and incoherent speech about the woman who had inspired him in his work. Yes, that's how he expressed it.

Hedda: Did he say who that was?

Tesman: No, he didn't. But I can only imagine that it must have been Mrs. Elvsted. You mark my words!

Hedda: Well . . . and where did you part company with him?

Tesman: On the way back to town. We broke up . . . the last of us . . . all together. And Brack came along too to get some fresh air. And then, you see, we agreed that we'd better see Ejlert home. Well, you know, he had quite a few drinks inside him!

Hedda: I suppose he had.

Tesman: But now comes the most remarkable thing, Hedda! Or the saddest, I suppose I should say. Oh . . . I'm almost ashamed . . . on Ejlert's behalf . . . to tell you about it. . . .

Hedda: Well, then . . . ?

Tesman: Yes, well as we were going along, you see, I happened to fall back a bit behind the others. Just for a minute or two . . . think of it!

Hedda: Yes, yes, good Lord, but . . . ?

Tesman: And then as I was hurrying along to catch up . . . well, do you know what I found in the gutter? Eh?

Hedda: How on earth should I know?

Tesman: Don't tell anyone, will you, Hedda. Do you hear? Promise me that, for Ejlert's sake! *[He pulls a packet wrapped in paper out of his coat pocket.]* Just think . . . I found this.

Hedda: Isn't that the packet he had with him here yesterday?

Tesman: That's it, it's his precious, irreplaceable manuscript! And he's just gone along and dropped it . . . without noticing. Just think of it, Hedda! It's quite pathetic. . . .

Hedda: But why didn't you give the packet back to him at once?

Tesman: No, I didn't dare to do that . . . when he was in that condition . . .

Hedda: Didn't you tell any of the others that you'd found it either?

Tesman: Oh no, no. You must see I couldn't have done that, for Ejlert's sake.

Hedda: So nobody knows at all that you've got Ejlert Lövborg's papers?

Tesman: No. And no one must get to know it.

Hedda: What did you talk to him about, afterwards?

Tesman: I didn't get to talk to him at all. Because as we got into the town we quite lost him . . . him and two or three others. Think of that!

Hedda: Oh? I suppose they saw him home, then.

Tesman: Yes, so it seemed. And Brack went off, too.

Hedda: And what did you get up to then . . . afterwards?

Tesman: Oh, I went with some of the others, and one of the fellows took us up to his place and gave us morning coffee. Or night coffee, I suppose I should say. Eh? But now as soon as I've rested a bit . . . and when poor old Ejlert has had a chance to sleep it off . . . I must go in and give him this.

Hedda: [stretches out her hand for the packet] No . . . don't give it back! Not straight away, I mean. Let me read it first.

Tesman: No, my dear, sweet Hedda, I swear I just daren't do that.

Hedda: You daren't?

Tesman: No . . . because you can just imagine, he'll be quite desperate when he wakes up and finds he's lost his manuscript. Because this is the only copy he's got, you know! He told me so himself.

Hedda: [looks at him keenly] But can't a thing like that be rewritten? Over again, I mean?

Tesman: No, I don't think that would do at all. Because the inspiration . . . you see . . .

Hedda: Yes, yes . . . that's it, I suppose . . . *[Casually.]* Oh, by the way . . . there's a letter for you.

Tesman: A letter? Just think . . . !

Hedda: [passes it to him]. It came early this morning.

Tesman: From Auntie Julle! What can it be? *[He puts the manu-*

script down on the other stool, opens the letter, glances through it, and jumps up.] Oh, Hedda . . . she writes that poor Auntie Rina is at the point of death!

Hedda: Well, it was to be expected.

Tesman: And if I want to see her again, I must hurry. I'll rush over at once.

Hedda: [suppressing a smile]. You'll rush, will you?

Tesman: Oh Hedda, my dearest . . . if only I could persuade you to come too! Just think!

Hedda: [gets up and answers tiredly but firmly]. No, no, don't ask me. I don't want to look at sickness and death. I must be free of everything that's ugly.

Tesman: Oh well, for God's sake then . . . ! *[Rushes about.]* My hat . . . ! My coat . . . ? Oh, in the hall. . . . Oh, I do so hope I'm not going to be too late, Hedda? Eh?

Hedda: You'd better rush, then. . . .

[Berte appears at the hall door.]

Berte: Mr. Brack is outside and asks if he can come in.

Tesman: Now! No, I can't possibly see him now.

Hedda: But I can. *[To Berte.]* Ask Mr. Brack to come inside.

[Berte goes.]

Hedda: [quickly, whispering] The papers, Tesman!

[She whips the packet off the stool.]

Tesman: Yes, give them to me!

Hedda: No, no, I'll look after them till you come back.

[She goes to the desk and puts the packet in the bookshelf. Tesman stands there in a flap, unable to get his gloves on.]

[Mr. Brack comes in from the hall.]

Hedda: [nods to him] Well, you are an early bird.

Brack: Yes, am I not? *[To Tesman.]* Are you going out again?

Tesman: Yes, I have to go to the aunts. Just think . . . the one who's ill, she's dying, poor thing.

Brack: Good Lord, is she really? But then you musn't stand here talking to me. At such a serious moment. . . .

Tesman: Yes, I really must rush. . . . Goodbye! Goodbye!

[He hurries out at the hall door.]

Hedda: [comes closer] It seems it was decidedly lively at your place last night, Mr. Brack.

Brack: I haven't even had time to change my clothes, my lady.

Hedda: You haven't either?

Brack: As you see. But what has Tesman told you of the events of the night?

Hedda: Oh, nothing much. That he went somewhere and drank coffee.

Brack: Yes, I know about that coffee party. Ejlert Lövborg wasn't there though, I believe?

Hedda: No, they'd seen him home first.

Brack: Tesman too?

Hedda: No, but a few of the others, he said.

Brack: [smiles]. Jörgen Tesman really is a credulous soul, my lady.

Hedda: Yes, God knows he is. But is there something behind all this?

Brack: Yes, you might say there is.

Hedda: Well! Let's sit down, dear Mr. Brack. Then you'll tell it better.

[She sits to the left of the table. Brack sits down at the table close to her.]

Hedda: Well, then?

Brack: There were particular reasons why I wanted to keep track of my guests . . . or rather, of certain of my guests last night.

Hedda: And perhaps Ejlert Lövborg was among them?

Brack: I have to confess . . . he was.

Hedda: Now you really begin to intrigue me. . . .

Brack: Do you know where he and a few of the others spent what was left of the night, my lady?

Hedda: Tell me . . . if it bears telling.

Brack: Oh yes, it may be told. Well, they adorned a particularly animated soirée.

Hedda: One of the lively kind?

Brack: One of the very liveliest.

Hedda: A bit more about about this, Mr. Brack . . .

Brack: Lövborg had also been invited earlier. I happened to know about it. But at that time he declined the invitation. Because now he's put on a new man, as you know.

Hedda: Up at the Elvsteds', yes. But he went all the same?

Brack: Well you see, my lady . . . most unfortunately the inspiration took him up at my place last night. . . .

Hedda: Yes, the spirit did move him, so I'm told.

Brack: Moved him somewhat vehemently. And, well . . . then he had second thoughts about it, I assume. Because we men, you know, we're not always so firm in our principles as we ought to be.

Hedda: Oh, I don't doubt that you provide an exception, Mr. Brack. But Lövborg . . . ?

Brack: Well, to cut a long story short . . . he finally adjourned to Mademoiselle Diana's salon.

Hedda: Mademoiselle Diana's?

Brack: Mademoiselle Diana was giving the aforesaid soirée. For a select circle of friends and admirers.

Hedda: Is that a red-haired woman?

Brack: Most decidedly.

Hedda: A sort of a . . . singer?

Brack: Oh yes . . . among other things. And moreover a mighty huntress . . . of men . . . my lady. You must have heard of her. Ejlert Lövborg was one of her most ardent champions . . . in the days of his glory.

Hedda: And how did it all end, then?

Brack: Not altogether amicably, it appears. Mademoiselle Diana, I understand, passed from the tenderest possible welcome to actual violence.

Hedda: Against Lövborg?

Brack: Yes. He maintained that she, or one of the members of her entourage, had robbed him. He said that he'd lost a pocket-book. And other things as well. In short, he appears to have kicked up the devil of a row.

Hedda: And what happened then?

Brack: What happened then was a general mêlée, involving both ladies and gentlemen. Fortunately the police arrived at last.

Hedda: The police came, too?

Brack: Yes. But I fear this will have been a costly interlude for that imbecile Lövborg.

Hedda: Oh!

Brack: Apparently he put up a spirited resistance. Struck an officer of the law over the head, and tore his tunic. So he had to go along to the police station too.

Hedda: How do you know all this?

Brack: The police told me themselves.

Hedda: *[looking away]* So that was how it was. He didn't have vine leaves in his hair.

Brack: Vine leaves, my lady?

Hedda: *[in a different voice]* But tell me now, Mr. Brack . . . why should you show such an elaborate interest in Ejlert Lövborg?

Brack: In the first place, I can't be altogether indifferent if it comes out, when the case is heard, that he came straight from my place.

Hedda: There'll be a court case, then?

Brack: Naturally. but it isn't really that so much. No, the fact is I felt it my duty, as a friend of the house, to give you and your husband a full account of his nocturnal escapades.

Hedda: And why should you feel that, Mr. Brack?

Brack: Well, I have a pretty shrewd suspicion that he intends to use you as a sort of screen.

Hedda: Why, what gives you that idea?

Brack: Oh good Heavens . . . we're not blind, my lady. Use your eyes! This Mrs. Elvsted person, she won't be leaving town in such a hurry.

Hedda: Well, and if there is anything between those two, I suppose there are plenty of other places where they can meet.

Brack: No private household. From now on every decent home will be closed to Ejlert Lövborg once again.

Hedda: And mine ought to be too, you mean?

Brack: Yes. I must admit I'd find it extremely awkward if this fellow were to become a constant visitor here. If this superfluous and . . . and unsuitable individual were to insinuate himself into . . .

Hedda: Into the triangle?

Brack: Just so. For me it would be like becoming homeless.

Hedda: [looks at him with a smile] So . . . you want to be the only cock in the yard, is that it?

Brack: [nods slowly and lowers his voice] Yes, that's what I want. And I'll fight for that end . . . with every means at my disposal.

Hedda: [her smile fading] You're quite a formidable person . . . when it comes to the point.

Brack: You think so?

Hedda: Yes, I'm beginning to think so, now. And I'm content . . . so long as you don't have any sort of hold over me.

Brack: [laughs equivocally] Ah yes, my lady . . . you may be right about that. Who knows, in such a case I might be capable of . . . one thing and another.

Hedda: Really, Mr. Brack! You sound almost as though you mean to threaten me.

Brack: [rising] Oh, far from it! This triangle . . . well, you know, it's best when it's fortified and defended by mutual consent.

Hedda: I agree with you.

Brack: Well, now I've said what I wanted to say. And I'd better see about getting back home. Goodbye, my lady!

[He moves towards the glass door.]

Hedda: [getting up] Are you going through the garden?

Brack: Yes, it's a bit nearer for me.

Hedda: Yes, and then it's round the back way.

Brack: Very true. I've no objection to going round the back way. At times it can be quite stimulating.

Hedda: When there's target practice going on, you mean?

Brack: [at the door, laughing] Oh, nobody shoots their tame farmyard cocks!

Hedda: [also laughing] Ah no, when they've only got one of them. . . .

[Laughing, they nod their farewells. He leaves. She shuts the door behind him.]

[Hedda stands for a moment with a serious expression, looking out. Then she crosses to the centre doorway and looks in through the curtains. Then moves to the desk, takes Lövborg's packet out of the bookcase, and is about to look at the papers. Berte's voice, raised in altercation, is heard from the hall. Hedda turns and listens. Then she quickly locks the manuscript away in a drawer and puts the key on the writing-pad.]

[Ejlert Lövborg, wearing his overcoat and holding his hat, flings open the hall door. He looks somewhat confused and excited.]

Lövborg: [turned towards the hall] And I tell you that I must go in! And that's that!

[He shuts the door, turns, and sees Hedda. He controls himself at once, and bows.]

Hedda: [at the desk] Well, Mr. Lövborg, you're a little late in calling for Thea.

Lövborg: Or a little early in calling on you. I apologize.

Hedda: How do you know she's still here?

Lövborg: They told me at her lodgings that she'd been out all night.

Hedda: [crosses to the table] Did you notice anything in particular when they told you that?

Lövborg: [looks at her questioningly] Notice anything?

Hedda: I mean, did they seem to be drawing any inferences at all?

Lövborg: [suddenly understands] Oh yes, of course, you're right! I'm dragging her down with me! But as it happens I didn't notice anything. . . . I suppose Tesman isn't up yet?

Hedda: No . . . I don't think . . .

Lövborg: When did he come in?

Hedda: Very late.

Lövborg: Did he tell you anything?

Hedda: Yes, he said it was a very gay party at Mr. Brack's.

Lövborg: Nothing else?

Hedda: No, I don't think so. But I was frightfully sleepy. . . .

[Mrs. Elvsted comes in through the curtains at the back.]

Mrs. Elvsted: [comes towards him] Oh, Lövborg! At last . . . !

Lövborg: Yes, at last. And too late.

Mrs. Elvsted: [looks at him anxiously] What's too late?

Lövborg: Everything's too late now. I'm finished.

Mrs. Elvsted: Oh, no, no . . . don't say that!

Lövborg: You'll say the same yourself when you hear. . . .

Mrs. Elvsted: I don't want to hear anything!

Hedda: Perhaps you'd prefer to speak to her alone? Because if so I'll go.

Lövborg: No, stay . . . I beg you to stay.

Mrs. Elvsted: But I don't want to hear about it, I tell you!

Lövborg: I'm not going to talk about what happened last night.

Mrs. Elvsted: What is it then . . . ?

Lövborg: It's just this, that it's all over between us now.

Mrs. Elvsted: All over!

Hedda: [involuntarily] I knew it!

Lövborg: Because I have no use for you any more, Thea.

Mrs. Elvsted: And you can stand there and say that! No use for me any more! Can't I help you now as I did before? Aren't we going to go on working together?

Lövborg: I don't intend to do any more work.

Mrs. Elvsted: [yielding to despair] What am I to do with my life, then?

Lövborg: You must try to live your life as though you had never known me.

Mrs. Elvsted: Oh, but I can't!

Lövborg: See if you can, Thea. You must go back home. . . .

Mrs. Elvsted: [in rebellion] That I'll never do! Wherever you are, that's where I want to be! I won't be packed off like this! I want to be right here! To be together with you when the book comes out.

Hedda: [half aloud, tensely] Ah yes . . . the book!

Lövborg: [looks at her] My book and Thea's. Because that's what it is.

Mrs. Elvsted: Yes, that's what I feel that it is. And therefore I have a right to be together with you when it comes! I want to see you praised and honoured again. And the joy . . . I want to share the joy of it with you.

Lövborg: Thea . . . our book will never be published.

Hedda: Ah!

Mrs. Elvsted: Not published!

Lövborg: It's impossible now.

Mrs. Elvsted: [in dreadful foreboding] Lövborg . . . what have you done to the manuscript!

Hedda: [looks at him in suspense] Yes, the manuscript . . . ?

Mrs. Elvsted: Where is it!

Lövborg: Oh Thea. . . . Don't ask me to tell you that.

Mrs. Elvsted: Yes, yes, I want to know. I've got the right to know. At once.

Lövborg: The manuscript. . . . Well, then . . . I've torn the manuscript into a thousand pieces.

Mrs. Elvsted: [shrieks] Oh no, no . . . !

Hedda: [involuntarily] But that's not . . . !

Lövborg: *[looks at her]* Not true, you think?

   Hedda: *[collects herself]* Oh well . . . of course. If you say so your-self. But it sounded so fantastic. . . .

Lövborg: True all the same.

Mrs. Elvsted: *[wrings her hands]* Oh God . . . oh God, Hedda . . . torn his own work to pieces!

Lövborg: I've torn my own life to pieces. So I might as well tear up my life's work as well.

Mrs. Elvsted: And you did that last night!

Lövborg: Yes, I tell you. Into a thousand pieces. And scattered them out in the fjord. A long way out. At least the water's clean and salt out there. They'll drift with the current and the wind. And after a while they'll sink. Deeper and deeper. Like I will, Thea.

Mrs. Elvsted: I want you to know, Lövborg, what you've done to the book. . . . For the rest of my life it'll be for me as though you'd killed a little child.

Lövborg: You're right. It was like killing a child.

Mrs. Elvsted: But how could you then . . . ! The child was mine, it was also mine.

   Hedda: *[almost inaudibly]* The child . . .

Mrs. Elvsted: *[sighs deeply]* So there's an end of it. Well, I'm leaving now, Hedda.

   Hedda: But you're not going back . . . ?

Mrs. Elvsted: Oh, I don't know myself what I'll do. There's nothing but darkness ahead of me.

[She goes out at the hall door.]

   Hedda: *[stands for a while and waits]* So you're not going to take her home, Mr. Lövborg?

Lövborg: I? Through the streets? And let everybody see her walk-ing with me?

   Hedda: Well, I don't know what else happened last night. But was it so utterly irrevocable?

Lövborg: It won't stop at last night. I know that well enough. But then there's another thing, I just can't be bothered with that kind of a life either. Not now again. She's broken my cour-age, and my defiance.

   Hedda: *[looking straight ahead]* So that silly little fool has had her fingers in a man's destiny. *[Looks at him.]* But how could you treat her so callously, all the same?

Lövborg: Oh, don't say I was callous!

   Hedda: To destroy everything that's filled her mind and her heart for all this long time! Don't you call that callous?

Lövborg: I can tell you the truth, Hedda.

Hedda: The truth?

Lövborg: Promise me first . . . give me your word that Thea will never know what I'm going to tell you now.

Hedda: I give you my word.

Lövborg: Well. Then I'll tell you that what I was saying just now wasn't the truth.

Hedda: About the manuscript?

Lövborg: Yes. I didn't tear it up. And I didn't throw it in the fjord, either.

Hedda: No. . . . But . . . where is it then?

Lövborg: I've destroyed it all the same. Destroyed it utterly, Hedda!

Hedda: I don't understand this.

Lövborg: Thea said that for her it was as though I had killed a child.

Hedda: Yes . . . so she did.

Lövborg: But to kill his child . . . that's not the worst thing a father can do.

Hedda: Not the worst?

Lövborg: No. I wanted to spare Thea the worst.

Hedda: And what is this worst thing, then?

Lövborg: Look, Hedda, suppose a man . . . in the early hours of the morning . . . came home to his child's mother after a wild and senseless debauch and said: now listen . . . I've been here and I've been there. To all sorts of places. And I had our child along with me. All over the place. And I've lost him. Just like that. Christ alone knows where he's got to, or who's got hold of him.

Hedda: Oh but . . . when all's said and done . . . this was only a book. . . .

Lövborg: Thea's soul was in that book.

Hedda: Yes, I can understand that.

Lövborg: And so you must understand also that Thea and I . . . that there isn't any future for us any more.

Hedda: And what are you going to do, then?

Lövborg: Nothing. Just put an end to it all. The sooner the better.

Hedda: [takes a step towards him] Ejlert Lövborg . . . listen to me. . . . Couldn't you let it happen . . . beautifully?

Lövborg: Beautifully? [Smiles.] Crowned with vine leaves, as you used to imagine?

Hedda: Oh no. I don't believe in those vine leaves any more. But beautifully all the same! Just for this once! . . . Goodbye. You must go now. And never come here again.

Lövborg: Goodbye, Mrs. Tesman. And remember me to your husband.

[He is about to leave.]

Hedda: No, wait! I want to give you something to remember me by.

[She goes to the desk and opens the drawer, and takes out the pistol case. Then she comes back to Lövborg *with one of the pistols.]*

    Lövborg: *[looks at her]* That! Is that what you want me to have?
    Hedda: *[nods slowly]* Do you recognize it? It was aimed at you, once.
    Lövborg: You should have used it then.
    Hedda: Well . . . ! You use it now.
    Lövborg: *[sticking the pistol in his breast pocket]* Thank you.
    Hedda: And beautifully, Ejlert Lövborg. Promise me that!
    Lövborg: Goodbye, Hedda Gabler.

[He goes out at the hall door.]

*[*Hedda *listens at the door for a moment. Then she goes to the desk and takes out the packet with the manuscript, peeps inside the wrappers for a moment, takes some of the leaves half way out and looks at them. Then she takes it all over to the armchair by the stove and sits down. After a while she opens the stove door, and unwraps the packet.]*

    Hedda: *[throws one of the folded sheets into the fire and whispers to herself]* Now I'm burning your child, Thea! With your curly hair! *[Throws a few more sheets into the stove.]* Your child and Ejlert Lövborg's. *[Throws in the rest.]* I'm burning . . . burning your child.

ACT FOUR

The same room at the Tesmans'. It is evening. The outer room is in darkness. The lamp over the table in the inner room is alight. The curtains at the glass door are drawn.

Hedda, *dressed in black, is walking aimlessly about the darkened room. Then she goes into the inner room and is lost to view to the left of the doorway. A few chords from the piano are heard. Then she emerges again and goes back into the reception room.*

Berte *comes in from the right of the inner room, carrying a lighted lamp, which she places on the table by the corner sofa in the reception room. Her eyes show signs of weeping, and she has black bands in her cap. Goes out quietly and carefully to the right.* Hedda *crosses to the glass door, draws the curtains aside a little, and looks out into the darkness.*

After a little while Miss Tesman *comes in from the hall, dressed in mourning and wearing a hat and veil.* Hedda *goes to meet her and gives her her hand.*

Miss Tesman: Yes, Hedda, I come dressed in the colour of mourning.
    For now my poor sister has passed away at last.

Hedda: I am already aware of it, as you see. Tesman sent me a note.

Miss Tesman: Yes, he promised he would. But I felt all the same that here to Hedda . . . in this house of life . . . I must bring the tidings of death myself.

Hedda: That was extremely kind of you.

Miss Tesman: Oh, but Rina shouldn't have been taken just now. This is no time for mourning, not in Hedda's house.

Hedda: [avoiding the subject] She died quite peacefully, Miss Tesman?

Miss Tesman: Oh, she passed over so quietly . . . and so gently. And it was such a blessed joy to her that she could see Jörgen once again. And could say goodbye to him properly. He isn't home yet?

Hedda: No. He wrote that I wasn't to expect him straight away. But do sit down.

Miss Tesman: No, thank you, my dear . . . dear Hedda. I should have liked to. But I have so little time. Now I have to attend to her and prepare her as well as I may. She shall go to her grave looking her best.

Hedda: Is there nothing I can do?

Miss Tesman: Oh, you mustn't think of it! No, that's not fit work for Hedda Tesman's hands. Nor a fit subject for her thoughts, either. Not at this time.

Hedda: Oh thoughts . . . they can't be curbed so easily. . . .

Miss Tesman: [continuing] Ah yes, dear God, that's how it goes. We'll be sewing linen for poor Rina; and soon there'll be sewing to be done here too, I fancy. But that'll be of a different kind . . . thanks be to God.

[Jörgen Tesman *comes in at the hall door.*]

Hedda: Well, so you're here at last.

Tesman: You here, Auntie Julle? With Hedda? Think of that!

Miss Tesman: I was just going away again, my dear boy. Well, and did you manage to see to it all?

Tesman: Oh, I'm awfully afraid I'll have forgotten the half of it. I'll have to dash over and see you again tomorrow. I'm all at sixes and sevens today. I just can't think straight.

Miss Tesman: But Jörgen, my own boy, you mustn't take it like that.

Tesman: I mustn't? Well, how else, then?

Miss Tesman: You must be glad, even in your grief. Glad of what has come to pass. As I am.

Tesman: Oh yes, yes. You're thinking of Auntie Rina.

Hedda: It will be a little lonely for you now, Miss Tesman.

Miss Tesman: Why yes, just to begin with. But not for so very long, I sincerely hope. Poor Rina's little room won't be left empty, you may be sure of that!

Tesman: Oh? Who are you thinking of putting in there, then? Eh?

Miss Tesman: Oh, there's always some poor invalid or other who needs a bit of care and attention, unfortunately.

Hedda: Would you really take on another burden of that kind?

Miss Tesman: Burden! Oh, God forgive you, child . . . this hasn't been a burden to me.

Hedda: But in the case of a total stranger . . .

Miss Tesman: Oh, you soon get friendly with people when they're sick. And besides, I also do need to have someone to live for. Ah well, God is good . . . and I fancy there'll soon be a few things for an old aunt to do here in this house, too.

Hedda: Oh, don't think about us.

Tesman: Yes, just think how fine it would be if we all three. . . . Yes . . . if only . . .

Hedda: If only . . . ?

Tesman: [ill at ease] Oh, never mind. It'll all turn out all right, I expect. Let's hope so. Eh?

Miss Tesman: Well, well. I expect you young people have lots of things you want to talk about. [Smiles.] And perhaps Hedda has something to tell you, too, Jörgen. Goodbye, my dears! I must get back home to Rina. [She turns at the door.] Yes, dear God, how strange to think! Now Rina's both here with me, and also with sainted Joachim.

Tesman: Yes, just think of that, Auntie Julle! Eh?

[Miss Tesman *goes out at the hall door.*]

Hedda: [coldly appraising Tesman] I almost think you're more upset about this death than she is.

Tesman: Oh, it's not just Aunt Rina. I'm so frightfully worried about Ejlert.

Hedda: [quickly] Have you heard anything about him?

Tesman: I was going to run over to see him this afternoon, to tell him that the manuscript's in good hands.

Hedda: Well? Didn't you catch him?

Tesman: No. He wasn't at home. But afterwards I met Mrs. Elvsted, and she said he'd been here early this morning.

Hedda: Yes, just after you left.

Tesman: And that he said that he'd torn up the manuscript. Eh?

Hedda: Yes, that's what he said.

Tesman: But, good Heavens above, the man must have been raving! And then you didn't dare to let him have it back, I suppose, Hedda?

Hedda: No, he didn't get it.

Tesman: But you did tell him we'd got it?

Hedda: No. *[Quickly.]* Did you tell Mrs. Elvsted?

Tesman: No. I didn't like to. But you ought to have said it to him. Just think, he might go and do something desperate! Give me the manuscript, Hedda! I'll rush over with it at once. Where have you got it?

Hedda: [cold and immobile, supporting herself on the armchair] I haven't got it any more.

Tesman: You haven't got it! But for God's sake . . . what do you mean?

Hedda: I've burnt it up . . . all of it.

Tesman: [jumps up in alarm] Burnt . . . you've burnt it! Burnt Ejlert Lövborg's manuscript!

Hedda: Don't shout like that. The maid might hear you.

Tesman: Burnt! But good God! . . . No, no, no . . . this is quite impossible!

Hedda: Well, it's true, for all that.

Tesman: Yes, but . . . do you know what it is that you've done, Hedda? It's a felony . . . it's misappropriation of lost property! Think of that! Yes, you just go and ask Mr. Brack, he'll tell you.

Hedda: I think you'd be well advised not to talk about it . . . either to Mr. Brack or anyone else.

Tesman: But how could you go and do anything so utterly fantastic! How on earth did you come to do such a thing? What got into you? Answer me, Hedda! Eh?

Hedda: [suppressing an almost imperceptible smile] I did it for your sake, Jörgen.

Tesman: For my sake!

Hedda: When you came home this morning and told me how he'd read to you . . .

Tesman: Yes, yes, what about it?

Hedda: You admitted that you envied him for it.

Tesman: Oh Heavens above, I didn't mean it so literally.

Hedda: All the same. I couldn't bear the thought that someone else should put you in the shade.

Tesman: [exclaiming, torn between doubt and happiness] Hedda . . . oh gracious . . . is this really true! . . . Yes, but . . . yes, but . . . I never knew you loved me like that, Hedda, not in that way. Think of that!

Hedda: Well, then I suppose I'd better tell you that . . . that just at this time . . . *[Breaks off passionately.]* Oh no, no . . . you can go and ask your Auntie Julle. She'll tell you all about it.

Tesman: Oh, I almost think I know what it is, Hedda! *[Claps his hands together.]* Oh good Heavens . . . is it really possible! Eh!

Hedda: Don't shout like that. The maid can hear you.

Tesman: [laughing in the excess of his joy] The maid! Oh, Hedda,

you really are priceless! The maid . . . why that's Berte! I'll go
out and tell Berte myself!

Hedda: [clenches her hands as though in desperation] Oh, it'll kill me
. . . it'll kill me, all this!

Tesman: All what, Hedda? Eh?

Hedda: [coldly, in control again] All this . . . farce . . . Jörgen.

Tesman: Farce? But it's just that I'm so happy. But, perhaps. . . .
Well, perhaps I'd better not tell Berte, then.

Hedda: Oh yes . . . why not do the thing properly.

Tesman: No, no, not just yet. But at least I'll have to tell Aunt
Julle. And that you've started to call me Jörgen, too! Think
of it. Oh, Auntie Julle really will be pleased!

Hedda: When she hears that I've burnt Ejlert Lövborg's papers
. . . for your sake?

Tesman: Oh, good Lord yes . . . the papers! No, of course, nobody
must get to know about that. But your burning zeal on my
behalf, Hedda . . . Auntie Julle really must hear about that! I
say though, I wonder, is that sort of thing usual with young
wives, d'you think? Eh?

Hedda: I think it would be a good idea if you asked Auntie Julle
about that, too.

Tesman: Yes, yes, I'll do that some time. [Looks uneasy and thoughtful again.] No, but this business with the manuscript! Good
Lord, it's . . . it's quite awful, really, to think of poor Ejlert.

[Mrs. Elvsted, *dressed as for her first visit, with hat and coat, comes in at the hall
door.*]

Mrs. Elvsted: [greets them hurriedly and speaks in agitation] Oh my dear
Hedda, do excuse me for coming back again.

Hedda: What's happened to you, Thea?

Tesman: Is it something to do with Ejlert Lövborg again? Eh?

Mrs. Elvsted: Oh yes . . . I'm so dreadfully afraid that he may have met
with an accident.

Hedda: [grips Mrs. Elvsted's *arm*] Oh . . . do you think so!

Tesman: Oh, but good Heavens . . . why should you think that,
Mrs. Elvsted?

Mrs. Elvsted: Oh, yes, I heard them talking about him at the lodging
house . . . just as I came in. There are the most incredible
rumours about him going around today.

Tesman: Yes, just think, I heard something too! And yet I can testify that he went straight off home to bed. Think of that!

Hedda: Well . . . what were they saying then, at the boarding
house?

Mrs. Elvsted: Oh, I didn't really discover anything at all. Either
because they didn't really know the particulars or else. . . .

They all stopped talking when they saw me. And I didn't dare to ask.

Tesman: [*anxiously pacing around*] We can only hope . . . we can only hope you were mistaken, Mrs. Elvsted!

Mrs. Elvsted: No, no I'm sure it was him they were talking about. And then I heard one of them say something that sounded like hospital or . . .

Tesman: Hospital!

Hedda: Oh no . . . that can't be possible!

Mrs. Elvsted: Oh, I was so horribly frightened for him. And then I went up to his lodgings and asked after him there.

Hedda: You could bring yourself to do that, Thea!

Mrs. Elvsted: Well, and what else was I to do? Because it seemed to me I just couldn't go on, not knowing.

Tesman: But I suppose you didn't find him there, either? Eh?

Mrs. Elvsted: No. And the people knew nothing whatever about him. He hadn't been home since yesterday afternoon, they said.

Tesman: Yesterday! Fancy their saying that!

Mrs. Elvsted: Oh God, I'm so sure that something must have happened to him!

Tesman: I say, Hedda . . . what if I go into town, and make a few inquiries round about . . . ?

Hedda: No, no . . . you'd better not get mixed up in this.

[*Mr. Brack, carrying his hat in his hand, comes in at the hall door, which Berte opens and closes again behind him. He looks serious and bows without speaking.*]

Tesman: Oh, Mr. Brack, you're here are you? Eh?

Brack: Yes, I had to come up and see you again this evening.

Tesman: I can see that you've heard from Aunt Julle.

Brack: Yes, I also received her message.

Tesman: Isn't it terribly sad? Eh?

Brack: Oh, my dear Tesman, that's as you choose to take it.

Tesman: [*looks at him uneasily*] Is there something else, perhaps?

Brack: Yes, there is.

Hedda: [*in suspense*] Bad news, Mr. Brack?

Brack: Also as you choose to take it, Mrs. Tesman.

Mrs. Elvsted: [*in a spontaneous outburst*] Oh, it's to do with Ejlert Lövborg!

Brack: [*looks at her*] Why should you think that, madam? Perhaps you know something already . . . ?

Mrs. Elvsted: [*confused*] No, no, I know absolutely nothing; but . . .

Tesman: Well, good gracious man, let's have it then!

Brack: [*shrugs his shoulders*] Well then . . . I regret to say . . . Ejlert Lövborg has been taken to the hospital. He is not expected to live.

Mrs. Elvsted: *[crying out]* Oh my God, my God . . . !

Tesman: To the hospital! And not expected . . . !

Hedda: *[involuntarily]* So soon . . . !

Mrs. Elvsted: *[wailing]* And we . . . we weren't even reconciled when we parted, Hedda!

Hedda: *[whispers]* Now Thea . . . Thea!

Mrs. Elvsted: *[taking no notice of her]* I must go to him! I must see him alive!

Brack: It's no use, madam. No one is allowed to see him.

Mrs. Elvsted: Oh, but at least tell me what's happened to him! What's the matter with him?

Tesman: Surely he can't have . . . himself . . . ! Eh?

Hedda: Yes, I'm certain he did.

Mrs. Elvsted: Oh Hedda . . . how can you . . . !

Brack: *[who is watching her all the time]* Regrettably your guess is correct, Mrs. Tesman.

Mrs. Elvsted: Oh, but how dreadful!

Tesman: Did it himself! Think of that!

Hedda: Shot himself!

Brack: Correctly guessed again, Mrs. Tesman.

Mrs. Elvsted: *[trying to pull herself together]* When did this happen, Mr. Brack?

Brack: This afternoon. Between three and four.

Tesman: Yes, but, good Lord . . . where did he do it, then? Eh?

Brack: *[a little uncertainly]* Where? Well, I . . . suppose it was at his lodgings.

Mrs. Elvsted: No, that can't be right. I was there myself at about half past six.

Brack: Well, somewhere else then. I don't exactly know about that. I just know that he was found. . . . He had shot himself . . . in the breast.

Mrs. Elvsted: Oh, but how dreadful! That he should end like that!

Hedda: *[to Brack]* He was shot in the breast?

Brack: Yes . . . as I said.

Hedda: Not in the temple?

Brack: In the breast, Mrs. Tesman.

Hedda: Well . . . the breast is good, too.

Brack: I beg your pardon, Mrs. Tesman?

Hedda: *[evasively]* Oh no . . . nothing.

Tesman: And the wound may be fatal, you say? Eh?

Brack: The wound will undoubtedly be fatal. Most probably it's all over already.

Mrs. Elvsted: Yes, yes, I feel that it is! It's all over! All over! Oh, Hedda . . . !

Tesman: Yes but tell me then . . . how did you come to hear of all this?

Brack: *[briefly]* Through the police, a . . . man there I had to see.

Hedda: *[triumphantly]* At last . . . a really courageous act!

Tesman: *[alarmed]* But good Lord . . . what are you saying, Hedda?

Hedda: I say that there is beauty in this deed.

Brack: Hm, Mrs. Tesman . . .

Tesman: Beauty! Think of that!

Mrs. Elvsted: Oh, Hedda, how can you call a thing like that beautiful?

Hedda: Ejlert Lövborg has settled accounts with himself. He had the courage to do . . . what had to be done.

Mrs. Elvsted: Oh no, it couldn't possibly have been like that! He must have done what he did in a fit of madness.

Tesman: In desperation, it must have been!

Hedda: It wasn't like that. I am quite certain of it.

Mrs. Elvsted: Yes, it was! A fit of madness! Like when he tore our book to pieces!

Brack: *[pulled up]* The book? The manuscript, you mean? Did he tear it to pieces?

Mrs. Elvsted: Yes, he did that last night.

Tesman: *[whispering softly]* Oh Hedda, we'll never get clear of this.

Brack: Hm, how very extraordinary.

Tesman: *[drifting about the stage]* Think of it! That Ejlert should end his life like that! And not even to leave behind him the work that would have made his name immortal. . . .

Mrs. Elvsted: Oh, if only it could be put together again!

Tesman: Yes, if only it could! I'd give anything on earth . . .

Mrs. Elvsted: Perhaps it can, Mr. Tesman.

Tesman: What do you mean?

Mrs. Elvsted: *[searching in her skirt pocket]* Look here. I kept the notes, all the notes he used when he dictated.

Hedda: *[a step closer]* Ah . . . !

Tesman: You kept them, Mrs. Elvsted! Eh?

Mrs. Elvsted: Yes, they're all here. I took them with me when I left. And they've just stayed in my pocket. . . .

Tesman: Oh, let me see them!

Mrs. Elvsted: *[gives him a handful of small papers]* But they're in such a muddle. All just anyhow.

Tesman: Just think, if we could manage it all the same! Perhaps if we two were to have a go at it between us . . .

Mrs. Elvsted: Oh, yes, let's try at least . . .

Tesman: It must be done! It shall be done! I'll devote my life to this work!

Hedda: You, Jörgen? Your life?

Tesman: Yes, or at any rate the time I have at my disposal. My own material will just have to wait. Hedda . . . you understand me? Eh? I owe this to Ejlert's memory.

Hedda: Perhaps you do.

Tesman: And now, my dear Mrs. Elvsted, we must pull ourselves together. God knows, there's no point in crying over spilt milk. Eh? We must try to contemplate the matter calmly. . . .

Mrs. Elvsted: Yes, Mr. Tesman, I'll do my best.

Tesman: Well, come along then. We must look at these jottings at once. Now, where shall we sit? Here? No, there, in the back room. You'll excuse us, Mr. Brack! You come along with me, Mrs. Elvsted.

Mrs. Elvsted: Oh God . . . if only it could be done!

*[*Tesman *and* Mrs. Elvsted *go into the inner room. She removes her hat and coat. They both sit at the table under the hanging lamp, and immerse themselves in an eager examination of the papers.* Hedda *goes across to the stove and sits in the armchair. After a while* Mr. Brack *joins her.]*

Hedda: *[softly]* Ah, Mr. Brack . . . what a sense of release it gives, this affair of Ejlert Lövborg.

Brack: Release, my lady? Well, of course, for him it's a release. . . .

Hedda: I mean, for me. It's a liberation to know that an act of spontaneous courage is yet possible in this world. An act that has something of unconditional beauty.

Brack: *[smiles]* Hm . . . my very dear lady . . .

Hedda: Oh, I know what you're going to say. Because you're something of an academic too, in your own line, like . . . well!

Brack: *[looks at her steadily]* Ejlert Lövborg was more to you perhaps than you are willing to admit, even to yourself. Or am I mistaken?

Hedda: I don't answer that kind of question. I just know that Ejlert Lövborg had the courage to live his life in his own fashion. And then now . . . this! This beautiful act. That he had the courage to take his leave of life . . . so early.

Brack: It pains me, my lady . . . but I am compelled to disabuse you of a beautiful illusion.

Hedda: Illusion?

Brack: Which you would in any case have been deprived of fairly soon.

Hedda: And what might that be?

Brack: He didn't shoot himself . . . intentionally.

Hedda: Not intentionally!

Brack: No. This business with Ejlert Lövborg didn't happen quite as I described it.

Hedda: *[in suspense]* Did you keep something back? What is it?

Brack: For the sake of that poor Mrs. Elvsted I made use of a few circumlocutions.

Hedda: What, then?

Brack: In the first place, he is already dead.

Hedda: At the hospital?

Brack: Yes. Without recovering consciousness.

Hedda: And what else?

Brack: That the affair did not take place at his lodgings.

Hedda: Well, that doesn't really make any difference.

Brack: Does it not? Because as it happens . . . Ejlert Lövborg was found shot in . . . in Mademoiselle Diana's boudoir.

Hedda: [is about to jump up, but sinks back again] No, that's impossible, Mr. Brack! He can't have gone there again today!

Brack: He went there this afternoon. He wanted to recover something that he said they'd taken. He was talking wildly about a child that had been lost. . . .

Hedda: Oh . . . so that was why . . .

Brack: I imagined that he might have been referring to his manuscript. But that he apparently destroyed himself. So it must have been his pocket-book, then.

Hedda: I suppose so. . . . And so . . . he was found there.

Brack: Yes, there. With a discharged pistol in his breast pocket. The bullet had wounded him fatally.

Hedda: In the breast.

Brack: No . . . he was shot in the abdomen.

Hedda: [looks up with an expression of revulsion] That as well! Oh. . . . Everything I touch seems destined to turn into something mean and farcical.

Brack: There is a further detail, my lady. Another circumstance that might be classified as somewhat distasteful.

Hedda: And what's that?

Brack: The pistol that was found on his body . . .

Hedda: [holding her breath] Well! What about it!

Brack: It must have been stolen.

Hedda: [jumps up] Stolen! No! That isn't true!

Brack: There is no possible alternative. He must have stolen it. . . . Sh!

[Tesman *and* Mrs. Elvsted *have got up from the table in the inner room and come out to the reception room.*]

Tesman: [with papers in both hands] Oh, Hedda . . . it's almost impossible for me to see in there under the lamp. Think of that!

Hedda: Yes, I'm thinking.

Tesman: Do you think we might be allowed to sit at your desk for a bit? Eh?

Hedda: Yes, of course you can. [Quickly] No, wait a moment! Let me clear away some of these things first.

Tesman: Oh, don't worry about that, Hedda. There's plenty of room.

Henrik Ibsen 1635

Hedda: No, no, let me take all these away. I'll put them on the piano. There you are!

[She has pulled an object, covered with sheets of music, out of the bookcase; she adds a few more sheets and carries the whole pile off to the left of the inner room. Tesman puts the papers on the desk, and brings over the lamp from the corner table. He and Mrs. Elvsted sit down and proceed with their work. Hedda returns.]

Hedda: [behind Mrs. Elvsted's chair, lightly caressing her hair] Well, Thea, my sweet . . . and how is the Ejlert Lövborg memorial getting on?

Mrs. Elvsted: [looks up at her, discouraged] Oh goodness . . . it's going to be dreadfully difficult to sort it out.

Tesman: It must be possible. It simply has to be. And this . . . putting other people's papers in order . . . that's just the sort of thing I'm good at.

[Hedda goes across to the stove and sits on one of the stools. Brack stands over her, leaning against the armchair.]

Hedda: [whispers] What were you saying about the pistol?

Brack: [quietly] That it must have been stolen.

Hedda: And why must it have been?

Brack: Because any other explanation ought to be impossible, my lady.

Hedda: Indeed.

Brack: [looks at her] Ejlert Lövborg was evidently here this morning. Isn't that so?

Hedda: Yes.

Brack: Were you alone with him?

Hedda: Yes, for a while.

Brack: And did you not leave the room while he was here?

Hedda: No.

Brack: Think carefully. Were you not out of the room even for a moment?

Hedda: Yes, perhaps just for a moment . . . out in the hall.

Brack: And where was the case with your pistols during this time?

Hedda: It was locked in . . .

Brack: Well, my lady?

Hedda: The case was standing over there on the writing table.

Brack: Have you looked at it since then to see whether both pistols are still in place?

Hedda: No.

Brack: You don't need to look. I saw the pistol that was found on Lövborg. And I recognized it immediately, from yesterday. And from before that, too.

Hedda: Have you got the pistol?

Brack: No, it is in the hands of the police.

Hedda: And what will the police do with it?

Brack: Try to discover who owns it.

Hedda: And do you think they will be successful?

Brack: [bends over her and whispers] No, Hedda Gabler . . . not if I hold my tongue.

Hedda: [looks at him apprehensively] And if you don't . . . what then?

Brack: [shrugs his shoulders] There is always the possibility that the pistol was stolen.

Hedda: [with determination] I'd sooner die!

Brack: [smiles] People say such things. But they don't do them.

Hedda: [without answering] And so . . . as the pistol was not stolen. And when the owner is discovered. What happens then?

Brack: There will be an unpleasant scandal . . . Hedda.

Hedda: A scandal!

Brack: Yes, a scandal . . . the one thing you are afraid of. You will of course be required to go into the witness box. Both you and Mademoiselle Diana. She will have to explain how the event took place. Whether the wound was inflicted accidentally or deliberately. Was he about to pull the pistol out of his pocket in order to threaten her? And did it then go off? Or did she seize the pistol out of his hand, shoot him down, and then stick the weapon back in his pocket? I wouldn't put it past her. She's a spirited wench, is this Mademoiselle Diana.

Hedda: But all this revolting business has nothing to do with me.

Brack: No. But you will be obliged to tell the court why you gave Ejlert Lövborg the pistol. And what inference will be drawn from the fact that you did give it to him?

Hedda: [lowers her head] That's true. I didn't think of that.

Brack: Well, fortunately there is nothing to fear so long as I keep silence.

Hedda: [looks up at him] And so I am in your power, Mr. Brack. From now on I am at your mercy.

Brack: [whispers more softly] Dearest Hedda . . . believe me . . . I shall not abuse the position.

Hedda: In your power, all the same. Subject to your will and your demands. No longer free! *[She gets up violently.]* No! That's a thought that I'll never endure! Never.

Brack: [looks at her half tauntingly] One generally acquiesces in what is inevitable.

Hedda: [returns the look] Perhaps you're right.

[She crosses to the writing desk.]

Hedda: [suppresses an involuntary smile, and imitates Tesman's *intonation]* Well? Is it going to work out, Jörgen? Eh?

Tesman: Heaven knows, my love. At any rate it's going to take us months.

Hedda: [as before] Well, think of that! *[She passes her fingers lightly through* Mrs. Elvsted's *hair.]* Isn't this strange for you, Thea? Now you're sitting here together with Tesman . . . as you used to sit with Ejlert Lövborg.

Mrs. Elvsted: Oh yes, oh God . . . if only I could inspire your husband in the same way.

Hedda: Oh, I expect it will come . . . in time.

Tesman: Yes, d'you know what, Hedda . . . it really does seem to me that I'm beginning to feel something of the sort. But you go and sit down again, now, with Mr. Brack.

Hedda: And is there nothing I can do to help you two?

Tesman: No, nothing at all. *[Turns his head.]* We'll just have to rely on you, dear Mr. Brack, to keep Hedda company!

Brack: *[with a look to* Hedda*]* It will be a pleasure indeed.

Hedda: Thank you. But tonight I'm tired. I'm going to go in and lie down a bit on the sofa.

Tesman: Yes, you do that my dear. Eh?

*[*Hedda *goes into the inner room and pulls the curtains together behind her. A short pause. Suddenly she is heard to play a wild dance tune on the piano.]*

Mrs. Elvsted: *[starts up from her chair]* Oh . . . what's that!

Tesman: *[runs to the doorway]* But Hedda, my dear . . . don't play dance music, not tonight! Do think of Aunt Rina! And of Ejlert, too!

Hedda: *[puts her head out between the curtains]* And of Aunt Julle. And of all the rest of them. . . . I shall be silent in future.

[She draws the curtains together again.]

Tesman: *[at the desk]* I don't think it's good for her to see us at this melancholy task. I'll tell you what, Mrs. Elvsted . . . you'll have to move in to Aunt Julle's. Then I'll come up in the evenings. And then we can sit and work there. Eh?

Mrs. Elvsted: Yes, perhaps that would be the best. . . .

Hedda: *[from the inner room]* I can hear what you're saying, Tesman. And how am I supposed to survive the evenings out here?

Tesman: *[leafing through the papers]* Oh, I expect Mr. Brack will be kind enough to look in now and again.

Brack: *[in the armchair, shouts cheerfully]* I'll gladly come every single evening, Mrs. Tesman! Don't you worry, we'll have a fine time out here together!

Hedda: *[clearly and distinctly]* Yes, you're looking forward to that, aren't you, Mr. Brack? Yourself as the only cock in the yard. . . .

[A shot is heard within. Tesman, Mrs. Elvsted, *and* Brack *all start to their feet.]*

Tesman: Oh, now she's playing about with those pistols again.

[He pulls the curtains aside and runs in. Mrs. Elvsted *follows.* Hedda *lies stretched out dead on the sofa. Confusion and shouting.* Berte, *in alarm, comes in from the right.]*

> Tesman: *[yelling at* Brack*]* Shot herself! Shot herself in the temple! Think of that!
> Brack: *[half prostrate in the armchair]* But, good God Almighty . . . people don't do such things!

Though Henrik Ibsen is generally thought of as a master of the "well-formed play," some readers have thought that Hedda Gabler *is imperfectly plotted. W. H. Auden, for instance, says that the play "fails because nothing important has been damaged. Lövborg's book . . . will be duly pieced together by Tesman and Mrs. Elvsted, so it doesn't matter the author and the original M.S. being destroyed, and Hedda's suicide is a positive convenience. If the notes couldn't be deciphered* or *were represented as mediocre we should be nearer to tragedy." If there is an answer to Auden's criticism, it may lie in Ibsen's own explanation of how he focuses his attention.*

"I must penetrate into the last wrinkle of his soul": Henrik Ibsen

Before I write down one word, I have to have the character in mind through and through. I must penetrate into the last wrinkle of his soul. I always proceed from the individual; the stage setting, the dramatic ensemble, all of that comes naturally and does not cause me any worry, as soon as I am certain of the individual in every aspect of his humanity. But I have to have his exterior in mind also, down to the last button, how he stands and walks, how he conducts himself, what his voice sounds like. Then I do not let him go until his fate is fulfilled.

As a rule, I make three drafts of my dramas which differ very much from each other in characterization, not in action. When I proceed to the first sketch of the material I feel as though I had the degree of acquaintance with my characters that one acquires on a railway journey; one has met and chatted about this or that. With the next draft I see everything more clearly, I know characters just about as one would know them after a few weeks' stay in a spa; I have learned the fundamental traits in their characters as well their little peculiarities; yet it is not impossible that I might make an error in some essential matter. In the last draft, finally, I stand at the limit of knowledge; I know my people from close and long association— they are my intimate friends, who will not disappoint me in any way; in the manner in which I see them now, I shall always see them.

ANTON CHEKHOV

(1860–1904)

THE THREE SISTERS

Translated from the Russian by Randall Jarrell

CHARACTERS

Prozorov, Andrei Sergeevich
Natalya [Natasha] Ivanovna, his fiancée, then his wife
Olga ⎫
Masha ⎬ his sisters
Irina ⎭
Kulygin, Fyodor Ilich, a high school teacher, husband of
  Masha
Vershinin, Alexander Ignatyevich, Lieutenant Colonel,
  Battery Commander
Tuzenbach, Nikolai Lvovich, Baron, Lieutenant
Solyony, Vasili Vasilevich, Staff Captain
Chebutykin, Ivan Romanovich, Military Doctor
Fedotik, Alexei Petrovich, Second Lieutenant
Rode, Vladimir Karlovich, Second Lieutenant
Ferapont, janitor from the county board, an old man
Anfisa, nurse, an old woman of eighty

The action takes place in a provincial city.

ACT 1

The living room in the house of the Prozorovs—*a row of columns separates it from a large dining room at the back. Midday; outside it is sunny and bright. In the dining room the table is being set for lunch.* Olga, *in the dark blue uniform of a teacher in a girls' high school, is correcting papers, standing or walking to and fro.* Masha, *in a black dress, her hat on her knees, is sitting reading a book.* Irina, *in a white dress, stands lost in thought.*

> *Olga:* Just a year ago, a year ago on this very day, Father died— on your birthday, Irina, on the fifth of May. It was very cold, the snow was falling. I thought I'd never live through it; you had fainted, and lay there as if you were dead. But now a year's gone by and we can remember it calmly; you're already wearing white, your face is radiant. . . .

[The clock strikes twelve]

And the clock struck just the same way then. *(A pause)* I remember that as they took Father there the band was playing, they fired a volley over his grave. He was a general, he was in command of a whole brigade, and yet there weren't many people. Of course, it was raining. Raining hard—rain and snow.

Irina: Why think about it?

[Behind the columns, in the dining room, Baron Tuzenbach, Chebutykin, and Solyony appear]

Olga: It's warm today, we can have the windows wide open—and yet there still aren't any leaves on the birches. They gave Father his brigade, we left Moscow with him, eleven years ago, and I remember distinctly that in Moscow at this time, at the start of May, everything is already in bloom; it's warm, everything is bathed in sunshine. That was eleven years ago, and yet I remember it all as if we'd left it yesterday. Oh, God! When I woke up this morning I saw that everything was light, that it was spring, and I thought my heart would burst with joy. I longed so passionately to go home.

Chebutykin: The devil it is!

Tuzenbach: Of course, it's all nonsense. *(Masha, brooding over her book, softly whistles a tune)*

Olga: Don't *whistle*, Masha! How can you? *(A pause)* Being at school every day and then giving lessons all afternoon—it makes my head ache all the time, the thoughts I have are an old woman's thoughts already. Really and truly, these four years I've been at the high school I've felt the strength and the youth being squeezed out of me day by day, drop by drop. And just one dream grows stronger and stronger.

Irina: To go back to Moscow! To sell the house, finish up everything here, and—off to Moscow!

Olga: Yes! As soon as we possibly can, to Moscow! *(Chebutykin and Tuzenbach laugh)*

Irina: Brother will probably be a professor, he won't be living here anyway. The only thing wrong is poor Masha.

Olga: Masha's going to come and spend the whole summer in Moscow every summer. *(Masha softly begins to whistle a tune)*

Irina: Please God, it will all come out right! *(She looks out of the window)* It's such a beautiful day, I don't know why I feel so happy. This morning I remembered it's my birthday, and all at once I felt joyful and remembered my childhood, when Mother was still alive. And what marvelous thrilling thoughts I had—what thoughts!

Olga: You're radiant today—I've never seen you lovelier. And Masha looks lovely, too. And Andrei would be good-looking, only he's got so fat; it isn't a bit becoming. And I've got older and so much thinner—I suppose it's because I get so cross at the girls at school. Today now, I'm free, I'm at home, my head doesn't ache, I feel so much younger to myself than I did yesterday. I'm only twenty-eight. . . . It's all good, it's all as God means it to be, but it seems to me that if I were married and stayed home all day it would be better. *(A pause)* I'd love my husband.

Tuzenbach: You talk such nonsense I'm sick of listening to you. *(Coming into the living room)* I forgot to tell you. Today you are to be visited by our new battery commander. His name's Vershinin.

Olga: Really? I'm delighted.

Irina: Is he old?

Tuzenbach: No, not very. Forty or so—forty-five at the most. He seems quite nice—and he's certainly no fool. Only he talks a lot.

Irina: Is he interesting?

Tuzenbach: Yes, interesting enough—only there's a wife, a mother-in-law, and two little girls. What's more, she's his second wife. He goes around calling on people and telling them he has a wife and two little girls. He'll tell you that. His wife isn't exactly all there: she has long braids like a girl's, talks only of lofty things, philosophizes, and regularly tries to commit suicide—to annoy her husband, evidently. If I were Vershinin I'd have left such a woman long ago, but he puts up with it and just complains.

Solyony: *(Entering the living room with* Chebutykin) With one hand I can only lift sixty pounds, but with two hands I can lift a hundred and eighty-two—two hundred, even. From that I deduce that two men aren't twice as strong, they're three times as strong as one man . . . or even stronger. . . .

Chebutykin: *(Reading a newspaper as he comes in)* For falling hair: Two ounces of naphtha in half a pint of alcohol . . . dissolve and apply daily. *(He writes it down in his notebook)* Let's make a note of it! *(To* Solyony) So remember what I told you, you want to cork the bottle tight and push a glass tube down through the cork. Then you take a pinch of alum, plain ordinary alum—

Irina: Ivan Romanich, dear Ivan Romanich!

Chebutykin: What is it, my child, my treasure?

Irina: Tell me, why is it I'm so happy today? As if I were sailing along with the wide blue sky over me and great white birds floating across it. Why is that? Why?

Chebutykin: *(Kissing both her hands tenderly)* My white bird . . .

Irina: When I woke up this morning and got up and bathed, all at once I felt as if everything in the world were clear to me, and I understood the way one ought to live. Dear Ivan Romanich, I understand everything. A man must work, must make his

bread by the sweat of his brow, it doesn't matter who he is—
and it is in this alone that he can find the purpose and meaning
of his life, his happiness, his ecstasies. Oh, how good it is to be
a workman who gets up at dawn and breaks stones in the street,
or a shepherd, or a schoolteacher who teaches children, or a
locomotive engineer! My God, it's better to be an ox, it's better to be a plain horse, and *work,* than to be a girl who wakes up
at twelve o'clock, has coffee in bed, and then takes two hours to
get dressed. . . . Oh, how awful that is! Sometimes I—I *thirst*
for work the way on a hot day you thirst for water. And if I
don't get up early and work, give me up forever, Ivan
Romanich!

Chebutykin: *(Tenderly)* I will, I will.

    Olga: Father trained us to get up at seven. Now Irina wakes up at
seven and lies there till nine at least, and thinks about something. And she does look so serious! *(Laughing)*

    Irina: You're so used to considering me a child that you're sur-
prised I should ever be serious. I am twenty!

Tuzenbach: That thirst for work—good God, how well I understand it!
I've never worked a day in my life. I was born in Petersburg,
cold, lazy Petersburg—born into a family that never knew what
work or worry meant. I remember that when I'd get home
from cadet school a footman would pull my boots off for me,
and I'd do something idiotic and my mother would look at me
in awe, and then be surprised when everybody else didn't. I've
been sheltered from work. But they've hardly succeeded in
sheltering me forever—hardly! The time has come: a thunder-
cloud is hanging over us all, a great healthy storm is gathering;
it's coming, it's already almost upon us, and is going to sweep
out of our society the laziness, the indifference, the contempt
for work, the rotten boredom. I'll work—and in another
twenty-five or thirty years everybody will work. Everybody!

Chebutykin: *I'm* not going to work.

Tuzenbach: You don't count.

    Solyony: In another twenty-five years, thank God, you won't be here
on this earth. In two or three years either you'll get apoplexy
or I'll lose control of myself and put a bullet through your
head, my angel. *(He takes a little bottle of perfume from his pocket
and sprinkles it over his chest and hands)*

Chebutykin: I really never have done a thing. Since I left the university
I haven't lifted a finger, I haven't opened a book—I just read
the newspapers. *(He takes another newspaper out of his pocket)*
Here we are. I know from the papers that there was, say, some-
body named Dobrolyubov, but what he wrote I don't know.
God only knows. *(A knock is heard from the floor below)* Listen.
They want me downstairs, somebody's come to see me. . . .

I'm coming right away. Wait a minute. . . . *(He goes out hurriedly, combing his beard)*

Irina: He's up to something.

Tuzenbach: Yes. He went out looking solemn—plainly, he's about to bring you a present.

Irina: What a nuisance!

Olga: Yes, it's awful. He's always doing something silly.

Masha: By the curved seastrand a green oak stands, / A chain of gold upon it . . . *(She gets up and hums softly)*

Olga: You're not very cheerful today, Masha. (Masha, *humming, puts on her hat)* Where are you going?

Masha: Home.

Irina: That's strange.

Tuzenbach: To walk out on a birthday party!

Masha: What's the difference? I'll be back this evening. Good-bye, my darling. . . . *(She kisses* Irina*)* I'll wish all over again: may you always be well and happy! In the old days, when Father was alive, there'd always be thirty or forty officers here on our birthdays, there was lots of noise, and today there's a man and a half and it's as silent as the tomb. . . . I'm going. I'm depressed today, I feel miserable—don't you listen to me. *(She smiles through her tears)* We'll talk afterwards—good-bye till then, dearest, I'm going.

Irina: *(Discontentedly)* Oh, how can you be so . . .

Olga: *(In tears)* I understand you, Masha.

Solyony: If a man philosophizes, you get philosophy or, anyway, something that looks like philosophy; but if a woman philosophizes, or two do, you might just as well suck your thumb.

Masha: And what is that supposed to mean, you terribly dreadful man?

Solyony: Nothing. Before he'd time to get his breath / The bear was hugging him to death. *(A pause)*

Masha: *(To* Olga, *angrily)* Don't sit there sniveling!

[Enter Anfisa *and* Ferapont *with a cake]*

Anfisa: In here, uncle. Come on in, your feet are clean. *(To* Irina*)* From the county board, from Mikhail Ivanich Protopopov—a cake.

Irina: Thank you. And thank him for me, please.

Ferapont: How's that?

Irina: *(Louder)* Thank him!

Anfisa: Come on, Ferapont Spiridonich. Come on. . . .

[She goes out with Ferapont*]*

Masha: I don't like that Protopopov, that Mikhail Potapich or Ivanich or whatever it is. He ought not to be invited.

Irina: I didn't invite him.

Masha: That's fine!

[Chebutykin *enters, behind him an orderly with a silver samovar; there is a hum of amazement and displeasure*]

Olga: [*Covering her face with her hands*] A samovar! This is awful!

[*She goes to the table in the dining room*]

Irina: Darling Ivan Romanich, what can have possessed you?

Tuzenbach: (*Laughing*) I told you so.

Masha: Ivan Romanich, you're simply shameless.

Chebutykin: My darlings, my blessed girls, you are all that I have left, to me you are the most precious treasures that there are upon this earth. Soon I'll be sixty years old: I'm an old man, a lonely worthless old man. The only good that there is in me is my love for you—if it weren't for you I should have left this world long ago. (*To* Irina) My darling, my own little girl, I've known you since the day you were born. . . . I carried you in these arms. . . . I loved your sainted mother. . . .

Irina: But why such expensive presents?

Chebutykin: (*Through his tears, angrily*) Expensive presents! Oh, get out! (*To the* Orderly) Carry the samovar over there. (*Mimicking*) Expensive presents!

[*The* Orderly *carries the samovar into the dining room*]

Anfisa: [*Walking through the living room*] My dears, there's a strange colonel. He's already taken off his overcoat, children, he's coming in here. Irina darling, now you be a nice polite little girl. (*As she goes out*) And it was time for lunch hours ago. . . . The Lord have mercy!

Tuzenbach: It must be Vershinin.

[Vershinin *enters*]

Tuzenbach: Lieutenant Colonel Vershinin!

Vershinin: I have the honor of introducing myself: Vershinin. I'm so glad, so very glad to be here in your house at last. But how you've grown! My, my!

Irina: Do sit down. We're delighted.

Vershinin: How glad I am! How glad I am! But surely there are three of you sisters. I remember—three little girls. I can't remember your faces any longer, but your father, Colonel Prozorov, had three little girls—that I remember distinctly; I saw them with my own eyes. How time does fly! My, my, how time does fly!

Tuzenbach: Alexander Ignatyevich is from Moscow.

Irina: From Moscow? You're from Moscow?

Vershinin: Yes, from Moscow. Your father, God bless him, was a battery commander there, and I was an officer in the same brigade. *(To* Masha*)* Now that I—it seems to me I do remember your face a little.

Masha: Yours—I—no!

Irina: Olga! Olga! *(She calls into the dining room)* Olga! Come here!

[Olga *comes in from the dining room]*

Irina: It seems Colonel Vershinin's from Moscow.

Vershinin: You must be Olga Sergeevna, the eldest. . . . And you're Marya. . . . And you're Irina, the youngest.

Olga: You're from Moscow?

Vershinin: Yes, I went to school in Moscow and went into the service in Moscow, I was stationed there for many years, and finally they gave me a battery here and I've moved here, as you see. I don't exactly remember you, I just remember that there were you three sisters. But I remember your father so well: if I shut my eyes I can see him standing there as plain as life. I used to come to see you in Moscow. . . .

Olga: It seemed to me I remembered everybody, and now all at once. . . .

Vershinin: My name is Alexander Ignatyevich.

Irina: Alexander Ignatyevich, so you're from Moscow! What a surprise!

Olga: We're about to move there, you know.

Irina: We'll be there by this fall, we expect. It's our home town, we were born there. . . . On Old Basmanny Street. *(They both laugh with delight)*

Masha: We've met someone from home—and so unexpectedly! *(Animatedly)* Now I remember! Remember, Olga, they used to talk to us about "the love-sick major." You were a lieutenant then, and in love with somebody, and for some reason they'd all call you major to tease you.

Vershinin: (Laughing) That's it! That's it! The love-sick major. That was it!

Masha: You just had a moustache then. But how old you've got! *(Tearfully)* How old you've got!

Vershinin: Yes, when they used to call me the love-sick major I was young, I was in love. It's different now.

Olga: But you still haven't a single gray hair. You've got older, but you're still not old.

Vershinin: Just the same, I'm forty-two. Has it been long since you left Moscow?

Irina: Eleven years. Oh, Masha, what are you crying for, you crazy thing? *(Through her tears)* You've made me cry, too.

Masha: I'm all right. What street did you live on?

Vershinin: On Old Basmanny.

Olga: We did, too.

Vershinin: For a while I lived on Nyemetski Street. From there I used to go back and forth to the Red Barracks. On the way there's a gloomy-looking bridge, you can hear the water under it. A lonely man gets melancholy there. *(A pause)* But here you've such a broad, such a splendid river! A wonderful river!

Olga: Yes . . . only it's so cold. It's so cold here, and there're mosquitoes.

Vershinin: How can you say that? You have such a splendid, healthy, Russian climate here. The forest, the river . . . and there're birches here, too. Dear, modest birches—of all the trees I love birches best. It's good to live here. The only queer thing, the railroad station is ten miles away. . . . And nobody knows why.

Solyony: I know why. *(Everyone looks at him)* Because if the station were here it wouldn't be way off there; and if it's way off there, then of course it can't be here. *(An awkward silence)*

Tuzenbach: He's a joker, Vasili Vasilich.

Olga: Now I've remembered you. I remember.

Vershinin: I knew your mother.

Chebutykin: She was a lovely woman, bless her soul.

Irina: Mother is buried in Moscow.

Olga: In the Novo Devichy. . . .

Masha: Imagine, I'm already beginning to forget her face. And the same way, they won't remember us. They'll forget us.

Vershinin: Yes. They'll forget us. That is our fate, there is nothing we can do about it. Everything that seems to us serious, significant, profoundly important—the time will come when it will be forgotten or will seem unimportant. . . . *(A pause)* And what's so interesting is that there's no way for us to know what it is that's going to seem great and important, and what it is that's going to seem pitiful and ridiculous. Take Copernicus or Columbus, for instance—didn't their discoveries seem useless or ridiculous at first, and some fool's empty nonsense seem the truth? And it may be that the life we lead now, the life we reconcile ourselves to so easily, will seem strange some day, uncomfortable, unintelligent, not clean enough—perhaps, even, wrong.

Tuzenbach: Who knows? Or perhaps our life will be called great and be remembered with respect. We don't torture people any more, we've no more executions and invasions—but just the same, how much suffering there is still!

Solyony: (In a high-pitched voice) He-ere, chicky, chicky, chicky!
Don't feed the baron chicken feed, just let him philosophize.

Tuzenbach: Vasili Vasilich, leave me alone, please. *(He sits down in another place)* After all, this sort of thing gets to be boring.

Solyony: (In a high-pitched voice) He-ere, chicky, chicky, chicky!

Tuzenbach: The suffering we see now—there's still so much of it—itself is a sign that our society has reached a certain level of moral development. . . .

Vershinin: Yes, yes, of course.

Chebutykin: You said just now, Baron, that they'll call our life great: just the same, people are very small. *(He stands up)* Look how small I am. If anybody were to say that my life is something great, something that makes sense, he'd just be saying it to make me feel good.

[Behind the scene someone is playing the violin]

Masha: That's Andrei playing, our brother.

Irina: He's the scholar of the family. We expect he'll be a professor someday. Father was a military man, but his son has chosen an academic career.

Masha: Father wanted him to.

Olga: We've been teasing him all morning. It looks as if he's a little bit in love.

Irina: With one of the local girls. She'll probably be here before long.

Masha: The way she does dress! It's not that her clothes are ugly or old-fashioned, somehow they're just pathetic. Some sort of queer gaudy yellowish skirt with a cheap fringe on it—and a red blouse. And her cheeks scrubbed till they shine! Andrei isn't in love with her—I refuse to admit it, he does have some taste—he's just making fun of us, playing some sort of joke on us. I heard yesterday that she's going to marry Protopopov, the chairman of the county board. That would be perfect. *(Through the side door)* Andrei, come in here! Just for a minute, darling!

[Andrei enters]

Olga: This is my brother, Andrei Sergeevich.

Vershinin: Vershinin.

Andrei: Prozorov. *(He wipes the sweat off his face)* You're our new battery commander?

Olga: Just imagine, Alexander Ignatyevich is from Moscow.

Andrei: You are? Well then, I congratulate you—my sisters won't give you a moment's peace.

Vershinin: I've already succeeded in boring your sisters.

Irina: Look at the frame Andrei gave me today! *(Showing the frame)* He made it himself.

Vershinin: (Looking at the frame and not knowing what to say) Yes. It's . . . it's a thing . . .

[Andrei *waves his hand in disgust and walks away*]

Olga: He's our scholar, and he plays the violin, and he can make *anything* with his fretsaw. In fact, he's a kind of universal expert. Don't go away, Andrei! That's the way he is, always going off by himself. Come back here!

[Masha *and* Irina *take him by the arms and, laughing, lead him back*]

Masha: Come along! Come along!

Andrei: Please let me alone.

Masha: Isn't he absurd! They used to call Alexander Ignatyevich the love-sick major, and he never got angry, not even once.

Vershinin: Not even once!

Masha: I think we ought to call you the love-sick violinist!

Irina: Or the love-sick professor!

Olga: He's in love! Our little Andrei's in love!

Irina: (Applauding) Bravo! Bravo! Encore! Our little Andrei's in love!

Chebutykin: (Coming up behind Andrei *and putting both hands around his waist)* Male and female created He them! *(He laughs. He still has the newspaper.)*

Andrei: Well, that's enough, that's enough. . . . *(He wipes his face)* I couldn't sleep all night and this morning I'm not quite myself, as the phrase goes. I read till four o'clock and then went to bed, but it wasn't any use. I'd think of something, and then think of something else—and it gets light so early here: the sunlight simply pours into my bedroom. This summer while I'm here there's this English book I want to translate . . .

Vershinin: You read English?

Andrei: Yes. Father, God bless him, absolutely loaded us down with education. It's absurd, it's idiotic, but just the same I've got to admit that after his death I began to gain weight—in a year I've got fat like this, just as if my body had taken the chance to break loose from him. Thanks to Father my sisters and I know French, German, and English, and Irina even knows Italian. But what's the use of that?

Masha: In this town knowing three languages is a useless luxury. Not even a luxury but a sort of useless appendage, like a sixth finger. We know a lot that isn't any use.

Vershinin: Really now! *(He laughs)* You know a lot that isn't any use! I don't think that there is a town, that there can be a town, so boring and so dismal that it doesn't need intelligent, cultivated people. Suppose that among the hundred thousand inhabitants of this town—this obviously crude, obviously backward place—suppose that there're only three people like you. It's plain that you won't be able to get the better of the darkness and ignorance around you; as you go on living, little by little you'll have to give up, you'll be lost in this crowd of a hundred thousand human beings, their life will choke you out. But you'll have been here, you'll not disappear without a trace: later on others like you will come, perhaps only six at first, then twenty, and so on, until at last people like you will be in the majority. In two or three hundred years life on earth will be unimaginably wonderful. Mankind needs such a life—and if it isn't here yet then we must look forward to it, wait, dream of it, prepare for it; and to do that we must see and know more than our fathers and grandfathers saw and knew. *(He laughs)* And you say you know a lot that isn't any use!

Masha: *(Taking off her hat)* I'm staying to lunch.

Irina: *(Sighing)* Really, all that ought to be written down.

[Andrei *is not there; he has gone out unnoticed*]

Tuzenbach: After many years, you say, life on earth will be beautiful, wonderful. That is true. But to have a share in it now, even from a distance, we must get ready for it, we must work.

Vershinin: Yes. *(He gets up)* But what a lot of flowers you have! *(He looks around)* And this beautiful house. I envy you! My whole life has been spent in little apartments with two chairs, a sofa, and a stove that keeps smoking all the time. It's just such flowers as these that have been missing in my life. *(He rubs his hands together)* Well, there's nothing to be done about it now. . . .

Tuzenbach: Yes, we must work. Probably you're thinking: the German is getting sentimental. But I give you my word of honor, I'm Russian, I can't even speak German. My father's Orthodox. . . . *(A pause)*

Vershinin: I often think, suppose it were possible for us to begin life over again—and consciously, this time. If only the first life, the one we've lived through already, were a rough draft, so to speak, and the other the final copy! I believe that each of us would try above all not to repeat himself—or at least would create a different set of circumstances for his life, would manage to live in a house like this, with flowers, with plenty of light. . . . I have a wife and two little girls, and not only that, my wife's an invalid, and so forth and so on—well, if I were to begin life over again, I'd never get married. . . . Never, never!

[Kulygin *enters, in a schoolteacher's uniform*]

    Kulygin: (*Going up to* Irina) Dear sister, allow me to congratulate you on the day of your birth—and to wish for you, sincerely and from the bottom of my heart, health and everything else that's appropriate for a girl of your age. And to offer you as a gift this little book. (*He hands her a book*) An insignificant little book, written only because I had nothing else to do, but just the same, read it. Good morning, gentlemen! (*To* Vershinin) Kulygin, teacher in the local high school, court councillor. (*To* Irina) In this book you will find a list of everyone who has graduated from our high school in the last fifty years. *Feci, quod potui, faciant meliora potentes.*[1] (*He kisses* Masha)

    Irina: But you gave me one Easter!

    Kulygin: (*He laughs*) Impossible! Well, in that case give it back—or better still, give it to the colonel. Take it, Colonel. Some day when you're bored, read it.

    Vershinin: Thank you. (*He is about to leave*) I'm extremely glad to have made your acquaintance—

    Olga: You're leaving? No, no!

    Irina: Surely you'll stay and have lunch with us. Please.

    Olga: I beg you.

    Vershinin: I can see I've happened in on a party for your birthday. Forgive me, I didn't know—I haven't congratulated you.

[*He goes into the dining room with* Olga]

    Kulygin: Today, gentlemen, is a Sunday, a day of rest, so let us rest, let us rejoice, each in accordance with his age and position. The rugs must be taken up for the summer and put away till winter . . . with moth balls or naphthalene. . . . The Romans were healthy because they knew both how to work and how to rest, they had *mens sana in corpore sano.*[2] Their lives were organized into a definite routine. Our principal is fond of saying that the most important thing in any life is its routine. . . . That which loses its routine loses its very existence—and it is exactly the same in our everyday life. (*He takes* Masha *by the waist, laughing*) Masha loves me. My wife loves me. And the curtains too, along with the carpets. I am gay today, in the very best of spirits. Masha, at four o'clock today we are due at the principal's. An outing has been arranged for the teachers and their families.

    Masha: I'm not going.

---

1. "Do what you can, let those who are able do better." (Latin)
2. "A sound mind in a sound body." (Latin)

Kulygin: *(Aggrieved)* But dear Masha, why?

Masha: We'll talk about it later. . . . *(Angrily)* Oh, all right, I'll go, only please leave me alone. . . .

[She walks away]

Kulygin: And afterwards we're to spend the evening at the principal's. In spite of the precarious condition of his health, that man tries above all else to be sociable. A stimulating, an outstanding personality! Yesterday after the faculty meeting he said to me, "I am tired, Fyodor Ilich! I am tired!" *(He looks at the clock on the wall, then at his watch)* Your clock is seven minutes fast. "Yes," he said, "I am tired!"

[Behind the scene a violin is playing]

Olga: Ladies and gentlemen, please come to lunch. There's a meat pie.

Kulygin: Ah, Olga, my dear Olga! Yesterday I worked from early morning till eleven o'clock at night, and I was tired, literally exhausted—and today I am happy. *(He goes into the dining room by the table)* Ah, my dear . . .

Chebutykin: *(Putting the newspaper into his pocket and combing his beard)* A meat pie? Splendid!

Masha: *(To* Chebutykin, *sternly)* Only—listen to me!—nothing to drink today. Do you hear? It's bad for you.

Chebutykin: Oh, come on, that's ancient history. I haven't been drunk for two years. *(Impatiently)* And, my dear girl, what's the difference anyway?

Masha: Difference or no difference, don't you dare drink! Don't you dare! *(Angrily, but so that her husband doesn't hear)* Oh, damnation, damnation! for another whole evening to sit and be bored to death at that principal's!

Tuzenbach: If I were you I just wouldn't go. It's perfectly simple.

Chebutykin: Don't you go, my darling!

Masha: Yes, don't you go! . . . A damnable life! an insufferable life!

[She goes into the dining room]

Chebutykin: *(Going after her)* Now, now!

Solyony: *(Going into the dining room)* He-ere, chicky, chicky, chicky!

Tuzenbach: That's enough, Vasili Vasilich. Stop it!

Solyony: He-ere, chicky, chicky, chicky!

Kulygin: *(Cheerfully)* Your health, Colonel! I am a pedagogue, you know, and here in this house I'm one of the family, Masha's husband. . . . She is kind—so kind. . . .

Vershinin: I'll have some of this dark vodka here. *(Drinking)* Your health! *(To* Olga) I feel so good here at your house! . . .

[Only Irina *and* Tuzenbach *are left in the living room]*

Irina: Masha's not in a very good humor today. She was married
when she was eighteen, and he seemed to her the most intelligent of men. It's different now. He's the kindest of men, but
not the most intelligent.

Olga: *(Impatiently)* Andrei, *please* come on. After all! . . .

Andrei: *(Offstage)* This minute.

[He comes in and goes over to the table]

Tuzenbach: What are you thinking about?

Irina: This: I don't like that Solyony of yours, I'm afraid of him.
Everything he says is so stupid. . . .

Tuzenbach: He's a strange man. I'm sorry for him and irritated at him
too, but mostly I'm sorry for him. It seems to me he's shy. . . .
When he's alone with you he's quite intelligent and pleasant,
but when there're other people around he's rude, a sort of
bully. Don't go, let's let them sit down without us. Let me be
near you a little. What are you thinking about? *(A pause)*
You're twenty, I'm not thirty yet. How many years we still have
left—so many days, row on row of them, all full of my love for
you. . . .

Irina: Nikolai Lvovich, don't talk to me about love.

Tuzenbach: *(Not listening)* I long so passionately to live, to struggle, to
work—and because I love you, Irina, the longing's stronger
than ever: it's as if you were meant to be so beautiful, and life
seems to me just as beautiful. What are you thinking about?

Irina: You say life is beautiful. Yes, but suppose it only seems that
way! For us three sisters life hasn't been beautiful, it's—it's
choked us out, the way weeds choke out grass. I'm crying. . . .
(She quickly wipes her eyes and smiles) I mustn't cry. We must
work, work. We're so unhappy, we take such a gloomy view of
life, because we don't work. We come from people who
despised work.

*[Natalya (Natasha) Ivanovna enters; she has on a pink dress and a bright green
belt]*

Natasha: They've already sat down to the table. . . . I'm late. . . . *(As
she goes by it she looks into the mirror and tidies herself)* My hair
seems to be all right. . . . *(Seeing* Irina) Many happy returns of
the day, dear Irina Sergeevna! *(She gives her a vigorous and prolonged kiss)* You've got such a lot of visitors, I really do feel
embarrassed. . . . How do you do, Baron!

Olga: *(Entering the living room)* Why, here's Natalya Ivanovna!
How are you, dear?

[They kiss]

Natasha: Many happy returns! You've got so much company I really
do feel terribly embarrassed.

Olga: You mustn't, it's only the family. *(In an undertone, alarmed)*
You have on a green belt! Dear, that's too bad—

Natasha: What's wrong, is it bad luck?

Olga: No, it's just that it doesn't go with . . . somehow it looks a
little strange.

Natasha: (In a tearful voice) It—it does? But it isn't really green, it's
more a sort of a neutral shade.

[She follows Olga *into the dining room. In the dining room they sit down to lunch;
there is no one left in the living room.]*

Kulygin: I wish you, Irina, a good fiancé! It's time you were getting
married.

Chebutykin: Natalya Ivanovna, I wish you a fiancé too.

Kulygin: Natalya Ivanovna already has a fiancé.

Masha: I'll have a little drink! What the—life's a bed of roses!
Come on, take a chance!

Kulygin: For that you get a C-minus in deportment.

Vershinin: This liqueur's good—what's it made of?

Solyony: Cockroaches.

Irina: Ugh! How disgusting!

Olga: For dinner we're having roast turkey and apple pie. Thank
the Lord, I'll be home all day today and home all evening. Everybody must come this evening.

Vershinin: Let me come this evening, too.

Olga: Please do.

Natasha: They certainly don't wait to be asked twice around here.

Chebutykin: Male and female created He them! *(He laughs)*

Andrei: (Angrily) Oh, stop it, everybody! Don't you ever get tired
of it?

[Fedotik and Rode *enter with a big basket of flowers]*

Fedotik: Look, they're already having lunch. . . .

Rode: (Loudly and affectedly) Already having lunch? That's right,
they're already having lunch.

Fedotik: Hold still a minute! *(He takes a photograph)* One! Wait, just
one more! *(He takes another photograph)* Two! Now it's all right.

*[They pick up the basket and go on into the dining room, where they are greeted
noisily]*

Rode: (Loudly) Many happy returns! I wish you everything, everything! It's wonderful out today, absolutely magnificent. I've
been out all morning with the high school boys, on a hike. I
teach the gym class at the high school, you know.

Fedotik: You can move, Irina Sergeevna, you can move now. *(He takes a photograph)* You look simply beautiful today. *(He takes a top out of his pocket)* By the way, here's a little top. . . . It makes the most wonderful sound. . . .

Irina: How *nice!*

Masha: By the curved seastrand a green oak stands,
A chain of gold upon it . . .
A chain of gold upon it . . . *(Tearfully)* What am I saying that for? It's been going through my head all day. . . .

Kulygin: Thirteen at table!

Rode: *(Loudly)* But surely, ladies and gentlemen, you do not actually take such superstitions as these seriously? *(Laughter)*

Kulygin: If there're thirteen at table it means that one of them's in love. It's not you by any chance, Ivan Romanovich? *(Laughter)*

Chebutykin: I'm an old reprobate, but why Natalya Ivanovna is so embarrassed I simply can't imagine.

[Loud laughter. Natalya *runs out of the dining room into the living room;* Andrei *follows her.]*

Andrei: Please don't pay any attention to them! Wait. . . . Don't go, please don't. . . .

Natasha: I'm ashamed. . . . I don't know what's the matter with me, and they're all making fun of me. I know it's bad manners for me to leave the table like this, but I just can't help it. . . . I just can't. . . .

[She covers her face with her hands]

Andrei: Dear, I beg you, I implore you, don't let them upset you. Honestly, they're only joking, they mean well. They have such kind hearts—my darling, my dearest, they're all such good, kindhearted people, they love both of us. Come over here by the window, they can't see us here. . . . *(He looks around)*

Natasha: I'm just not used to being in society!

Andrei: Ah, youth, marvelous, beautiful youth! My darling, my dearest, please don't be upset! Believe me, believe me. . . . I'm so happy, so in love—I'm so blissfully happy. . . . Oh, they can't see us! They can't see us at all! Why I first fell in love with you, when I first fell in love with you—I don't know . . . My dearest, my darling, my innocent one, be my wife! I love you, love you as nobody ever—

[They kiss.

Two Officers *come in and seeing the two kissing, stop in amazement.]*

CURTAIN

ACT 2

The scene is that of the first act. It is eight o'clock at night. The faint sound of an accordion comes up from the street. The room is dark. Natalya Ivanovna *enters in a dressing gown, with a candle; she walks over and stops at the door of* Andrei's *room.*

Natasha: Andrei . . . dear, what are you doing? Reading? Nothing, I just . . . *(She goes to another door, opens it, looks inside, and then shuts it)* No, there isn't one. . . .

Andrei: *(Entering with a book in his hand)* What, Natasha?

Natasha: I was looking to see whether there's a light. . . . Now it's carnival week the servants are simply impossible, you have to be on the lookout every minute to make sure nothing goes wrong. Last night at midnight I went through the dining room, and there on the table was a lighted candle! Now, who lit it? I still haven't been able to get a straight answer. *(She puts down her candle)* What time is it?

Andrei: *(Looking at his watch)* Quarter after eight.

Natasha: And Olga and Irina not in yet. They aren't in yet. Still hard at work, poor things! Olga at the teachers' council and Irina at the telegraph office. . . . *(She sighs)* I was saying to your sister just this morning, "Irina darling," I said, "you simply must take better care of yourself." But she just won't listen. . . . Quarter after eight, you said? I'm worried, I'm afraid our Bobik just isn't well. Why is he so cold? Yesterday he had a temperature and today he's cold all over. . . . I am so worried!

Andrei: It's all right, Natasha. The boy's all right.

Natasha: Just the same, I think we'd better put him on a diet. I *am* worried. And tonight at almost ten o'clock those carnival people are going to be here, they said—it would be better if they didn't come, Andrei dear.

Andrei: I don't know. They *have* been asked, you know.

Natasha: This morning the little thing woke up and looked at me, and all of a sudden he gave a big smile: he knew me! "Good morning, Bobik!" I said. "Good morning, sweetheart!" And he laughed. . . . Babies understand, they understand perfectly. So Andrei dear, I'm going to tell them they mustn't let those carnival people in.

Andrei: *(Indecisively)* But that's up to my sisters, you know. This is their house.

Natasha: Yes, theirs too. I'll speak to them. They're so kind. . . . *(She starts to leave)* I've ordered cottage cheese for your supper. The doctor says you mustn't eat anything but cottage cheese or you won't ever get any thinner. *(She stops)* Bobik is *cold.* I'm afraid he must be cold in that room of his. At least till it's warm weather, we ought to put him in a different room.

For instance, Irina's room is a perfect room for a child, it's dry and the sun simply pours in all day long. I must speak to her about it. She could stay in Olga's room with her, for the time being. . . . It won't make any difference to her, she's never at home in the daytime anyway, she only spends the night there. . . . *(A pause)* Andrei-Wandrei, why don't you say something?

Andrei: I was just thinking. . . . Anyway, there isn't anything to say. . . .

Natasha: Uh-huh. . . . There was something I meant to tell you about. . . . Now I remember: Ferapont's here from the county board, he wants to see you.

Andrei: *(Yawning)* Send him on in.

[Natasha *goes out.* Andrei, *stooping over the candle she has left, reads his book.* Ferapont *comes in; he is in a worn-out old overcoat, the collar turned up, a scarf over his ears.*]

Andrei: How are you, Ferapont, old man? What have you got to tell me?

Ferapont: The chairman's sent you a little book and some kind of paper. Here . . . *(He gives a book and an envelope to* Andrei*)*

Andrei: Thanks. That's fine. But what did you come so late for? It's already past eight, you know.

Ferapont: How's that?

Andrei: *(Louder)* I said you're late, it's past eight.

Ferapont: That's right. I got here when it was still light but they wouldn't let me in. The master's busy, they said. Well, if you're busy you're busy, I'm not in any hurry. *(Thinking that* Andrei *has said something)* How's that?

Andrei: Nothing. *(He examines the book)* Tomorrow's Friday, we don't have any meeting, but I'll come anyway. . . . I'll do something. It's boring at home. *(A pause)* Ferapont, old man, it's funny how life changes, how it fools you. Today out of pure boredom, just because I hadn't anything else to do, I picked up this book here, some old university lectures, and I couldn't help laughing. . . . Good God! I'm the secretary of the county board, the board Protopopov's the head of; I'm the secretary, and the very most I can ever hope for is—to be a member of the board! I a member of a county board—I who dream every night that I'm a professor at the University of Moscow, a famous scholar of whom all Russia is proud!

Ferapont: I couldn't rightly say . . . I'm a little hard of hearing. . . .

Andrei: If you could hear as you ought I might not be talking to you like this. I've got to talk to somebody and my wife doesn't understand me, I'm afraid of my sisters, somehow—I'm afraid they'll make fun of me, make me feel ashamed. . . . You know,

I don't drink, I don't like cafés, but . . . good old Ferapont, what I'd give to be sitting in Moscow right now, at Testov's or the Great Muscovite!

Ferapont: In Moscow, there was a contractor at the board the other day that said so, there were some merchants eating pancakes, and it seems as how one of them ate forty pancakes and he died. It was either forty or fifty. I don't remember.

Andrei: In Moscow you sit in the main room at a restaurant, you don't know anybody and nobody knows you, but just the same you don't feel like a stranger. And here you know everybody and everybody knows you, and you're a stranger, a stranger . . . a stranger and lonely.

Ferapont: How's that? *(A pause)* And the contractor said—maybe he was lying, though—that there's a rope stretched all the way across Moscow.

Andrei: What for?

Ferapont: I couldn't rightly say. The contractor said so.

Andrei: That's nonsense. *(He reads)* Have you ever been to Moscow?

Ferapont: *(After a pause)* I never have. It wasn't God's will I should. *(A pause)* Shall I go now?

Andrei: You can go. Good-bye. (Ferapont *goes out*) Good-bye. *(Reading)* In the morning come back and get these papers. . . . You can go. . . . *(A pause)* He's gone. *(The bell rings)* Yes, it's a nuisance. . . .

[He stretches and walks slowly into his room. Behind the scene the Nurse *is singing, rocking the baby.* Masha *and* Vershinin *enter. While they talk, a* Maid *is lighting the lamp and candles.]*

Masha: I don't know. *(A pause)* I don't know. Of course, a lot of it is just habit. For instance, after Father's death it took us a long time to get used to not having orderlies in the house. But even if you disregard habit, it's only fair to say that—maybe it's not so in other places—that in our town the nicest people, the decentest people, the best-mannered people, really are the ones in the army.

Vershinin: I'm thirsty. I'd certainly like some tea.

Masha: It'll be here before long. They married me when I was eighteen, and I was afraid of my husband because he was a teacher and I was barely out of school. He seemed terribly learned to me then, intelligent, and important. It's different now, unfortunately.

Vershinin: I see . . . yes.

Masha: I'm not talking about my husband, I'm used to him, but among civilians in general there're so many coarse, unpleasant, ill-bred people. Coarseness upsets me—insults me; when I see that a man isn't polite enough, isn't refined or delicate enough, I suffer. When I'm with the teachers, my husband's colleagues, I'm simply miserable.

Vershinin: Yes. . . . But it seems to me it doesn't make any difference —whether they're army men or civilians, they're equally uninteresting . . . in this town, at any rate. It makes no difference! If you listen to one of the local intellectuals, civilian or military, all you ever hear is that he's sick and tired of his wife, sick and tired of his house, sick and tired of his estate, sick and tired of his horses. . . . When it comes to lofty ideas, thinking on an exalted plane, a Russian is extraordinary, but will you tell me why it is he aims so low in life? Why?

Masha: Why?

Vershinin: Why is a Russian always sick and tired of his children, sick and tired of his wife? And why are his wife and children always sick and tired of him?

Masha: You're a little depressed today.

Vershinin: Perhaps. I didn't have any dinner—I've had nothing to eat since breakfast. One of my daughters isn't exactly well, and when my little girls are ill I get anxious about them, my conscience torments me for having given them such a mother. If you could have seen her today! What a miserable creature! We began quarreling at seven in the morning, and at nine I slammed the door and walked away. . . . *(A pause)* I never mention it to anybody—it's strange, it's only to you that I complain. *(He kisses her hand)* Don't be angry with me. If it weren't for you I'd have no one—no one. *(A pause)*

Masha: Listen to the chimney! Just before Father died there was a howling in the chimney—there, just like that!

Vershinin: You're superstitious?

Masha: Yes.

Vershinin: That's strange. *(He kisses her hand)* You're a splendid woman, a wonderful woman. Splendid, wonderful! It's dark in here, but I can see how your eyes sparkle.

Masha: *(Moving to another chair)* The light's better over here.

Vershinin: I love, love, love . . . love your eyes, the way you move, I see them in my dreams. . . . Splendid, wonderful woman!

Masha: *(Laughing softly)* When you talk to me like that, somehow, I don't know why, I laugh, even when it frightens me. But don't do it again, please don't. . . . *(In a low voice)* No, you can, though—it doesn't make any difference to me. . . . *(She covers her face with her hands)* It doesn't make any difference to me. Someone's coming. Talk about something else.

[Irina and Tuzenbach come in through the dining room]

Tuzenbach: I've got three last names, my name is Baron Tuzenbach-

Krone-Altschauer, and yet I'm Russian and Orthodox, just like you. There's hardly anything German left in me—nothing, maybe, except the patience and obstinacy with which I keep boring you. Every single night I see you home.

Irina: I'm so tired!

Tuzenbach: And every single day for ten years, for twenty years, I'll come to the telegraph office and see you home, as long as you don't drive me away. . . . *(Seeing* Masha *and* Vershinin, *delightedly)* Oh, it's you! How are you!

Irina: Here I am, home at last! *(To* Masha*)* Just before I left a lady came in—she was wiring her brother in Saratov that her son had died today, and she couldn't manage to remember the address. So she sent it without any address, just to Saratov. She was crying. And for no reason whatsoever, I was rude to her. I said, "I simply haven't the time." It was so stupid! Are the carnival people coming tonight?

Masha: Yes.

Irina: *(Sitting down in an armchair)* I'll rest. I'm so tired.

Tuzenbach: *(Smiling)* When you come home from work you seem so young and so unhappy. . . . *(A pause)*

Irina: I'm tired. No, I don't like working there, I don't like it.

Masha: You've got thinner . . . *(She begins to whistle)* And younger, and your face looks like a little boy's.

Tuzenbach: That's the way she does her hair.

Irina: I must try to find some other job, this one's not right for me. What I longed for so, what I dreamed about, is exactly what's missing. It's work without poetry, without sense, even . . . *(A knock on the floor)* The Doctor's knocking. . . . *(To* Tuzenbach*)* You knock, dear. . . . I can't . . . I'm so tired. *(Tuzenbach knocks on the floor)* He'll be right up. Some way or other we've got to do something about it. Yesterday he and Andrei were at the club, and they lost again. They say Andrei lost two hundred rubles.

Masha: *(Indifferently)* Well, there's nothing we can do about it now.

Irina: Two weeks ago he lost, in December he lost. If only he'd hurry up and lose everything, maybe then we'd get out of this town. My God, every night I dream of Moscow, it's as if I were possessed. *(She laughs)* We're moving there in June, from now to June leaves—February, March, April, May . . . almost half a year!

Masha: The only thing is, Natasha mustn't hear anything about what he's lost.

Irina: I don't think it makes any difference to her.

[Chebutykin, *just out of bed—He has taken a nap after dinner—enters the dining room combing his beard, then sits down at the table and takes a newspaper from his pocket]*

Masha: So, he arrives. . . . Has he paid anything on his apartment?

Irina: (Laughing) No. For eight months, not a kopeck. Evidently he's forgotten.

Masha: (Laughing) How grandly he sits there! *(Everybody laughs. A pause.)*

Irina: Why are you so silent, Alexander Ignatich?

Vershinin: I don't know. I'd like some tea. I'd sell my soul for a glass of tea! I've had nothing to eat since breakfast. . . .

Chebutykin: Irina Sergeevna!

Irina: What is it?

Chebutykin: Please come here. *Venez ici!* (Irina *goes and sits down at the table*) I simply cannot do without you.

Vershinin: Well, if they won't give us any tea, at least let's philosophize.

Tuzenbach: Yes, let's. What about?

Vershinin: What about? Let's dream . . . for instance, about the life that will come after us, in two or three hundred years.

Tuzenbach: Well, after us they'll fly in balloons, their clothes will be different, they'll discover a sixth sense, maybe, and then develop it; but life will stay the same, a difficult life, full of mysteries, and happy. And in a thousand years people will be sighing, the same as now: "Ah, life is hard!"—and along with that, exactly the same as now, they'll be frightened of death and not want to die.

Vershinin: (After a moment's thought) How shall I put it? It seems to me that everything on earth must change, little by little, and that it is already changing before our eyes. In two or three hundred, in a thousand years—the length of time doesn't matter—a new and happy life will come. We can have no share in it, of course, but we are living for it, working for it, yes, suffering for it: we are creating it—and in that and in that alone is the aim of our existence and, if you wish, our happiness. (Masha *laughs softly*)

Tuzenbach: What's the matter with you?

Masha: I don't know. All day today, ever since morning, I've been laughing.

Vershinin: I finished school there where you did, I didn't go on to the Academy; I read a lot, but I don't know how to choose the books, and what I read, maybe, isn't exactly what I need to read. But the longer I live the more I want to know. My hair's getting gray, I'm an old man, almost, and yet I know so little, oh, so little! Still, though, it seems to me that what matters most, what's absolutely essential—that I do know, and know very well. If only I could make you see that there *is* no happiness, that there should not be, and that there will not be, for us. . . . We must only work and work, and happiness—that is the lot of our remote descendants. *(A pause)* Not mine but, at least, that of the descendants of my descendants.

[Fedotik and Rode appear in the dining room; they sit down and softly begin to sing, one of them playing on the guitar.]

Tuzenbach: According to you, we ought not even to dream of happiness! But suppose I *am* happy?

Vershinin: No.

Tuzenbach: *(Throwing up his hands and laughing)* Obviously we don't understand each other. Well, how am I going to convince you? *(Masha laughs softly)*

Tuzenbach: *(Showing her his finger)* Laugh! *(To Vershinin)* Not just in two or three hundred but in a million years, even, life will be the same: it doesn't change, it goes on the same as ever, obeying laws of its own—laws that are none of our business or, anyhow, that we'll never be able to discover. Migratory birds, cranes for instance, fly and fly, and no matter what thoughts, great or small, wander into their heads, they'll still keep on flying, they don't know where, they don't know why. They fly and will fly, no matter what philosophers appear among them; and they can philosophize as much as they please, just so long as they still fly.

Masha: But still, it means something?

Tuzenbach: Means something. . . . Look, it's snowing. What does that mean? *(A pause)*

Masha: It seems to me a man must believe or search for some belief, or else his life is empty, empty. . . . To live and not know why the cranes fly, why children are born, why there are stars in the sky. . . . Either you know what you're living for or else it's all nonsense, hocus-pocus.

Vershinin: Still, it's a pity one's youth is over.

Masha: Gogol says: Life on this earth is a dull proposition, gentlemen! I give up.

Chebutykin: *(Reading a newspaper)* Balzac was married in Berdichev. *(Irina softly begins to sing)* I really ought to write that down in my book. *(He writes it down)* Balzac was married in *Berdichev.* *(He reads his newspaper)*

Irina: *(Pensively, as she lays out the cards for solitaire)* Balzac was married in Berdichev.

Tuzenbach: The die is cast. You know, I've handed in my resignation, Marya Sergeevna.

Masha: So I hear. But I don't see anything good about that. I don't like civilians.

Tuzenbach: What's the difference? *(He gets up)* I'm not handsome, what sort of soldier am I? Well, anyway, what's the difference?. . . I'm going to work. If only for one day in my life, work so that I come home at night, fall in bed exhausted, and go right to sleep. *(He goes into the dining room)* Surely workmen must sleep soundly!

Fedotik: I got these crayons for you—on Moscow Street, at Pyzi-
kov's. . . . And this little penknife. . . .

Irina: You keep on treating me as if I were a little girl, but I'm
grown up now, you know. . . . *(Taking the crayons and the knife,
joyfully)* How lovely!

Fedotik: And I bought myself a knife. . . . Look. . . . One blade,
two, three, this is to clean your ears with, a pair of scissors, this
is to clean your nails with. . . .

Rode: *(Loudly)* Doctor, how old are you?

Chebutykin: I? Thirty-two. *(Laughter)*

Fedotik: I will now show you a new kind of solitaire. . . .

[He lays out the cards.

They bring in the samovar; Anfisa *stands by it; a little later* Natasha *comes in and
begins to straighten things on the table;* Solyony *enters, is greeted, and sits down at
the table.]*

Vershinin: What a wind!

Masha: Yes. I'm bored with winter. I've forgotten what summer's
like.

Irina: I'm going to go out, I can see it. We're going to get to
Moscow!

Fedotik: No it's not—see, that eight's on the deuce of spades. *(He
laughs)* So you're not going to get to Moscow.

Chebutykin: *(Reading the newspaper)* Tsitsikar. Smallpox is raging here.

Anfisa: *(Going up to* Masha*)* Masha, have some tea, darling. *(To*
Vershinin*)* Please, your honor. . . . Excuse me, sir, I've forgotten your name. . . .

Masha: Bring it over here, nurse. I'm not going there.

Irina: Nurse!

Anfisa: Coming-g!

Natasha: *(To* Solyony*)* Babies, little babies still at the breast—they
understand perfectly. "Good morning, Bobik!" I say. "Good
morning, sweetheart!" Then he looks up at me in a very special
way. You think I'm just saying that because I'm a mother, but
that isn't so, no indeed it isn't so! He really is the most amazing
child.

Solyony: If that child were mine I'd fry him in a frying pan and then
eat him.

[He picks up his glass, goes into the living room, and sits down in a corner]

Natasha: *(Covering her face with her hands)* Rude, common man!

Masha: If you're happy you don't notice whether it's summer or
winter. It seems to me that if I were in Moscow I wouldn't care
what the weather was like.

Vershinin: The other day I was reading the diary of some French cabinet minister—he's been sent to prison because of that Panama

affair. With what rapture, with what delight he describes the birds he sees from the window of his cell . . . birds he'd never noticed in the days when he was a minister. Now that they've let him out again, of course, it's the same as it used to be: he doesn't notice the birds. Just as when you live in Moscow again, you won't notice it. We aren't happy, we never will be, we only long to be.

Tuzenbach: *(Picking up a box from the table)* What's become of the candy?

Irina: Solyony ate it.

Tuzenbach: All of it?

Anfisa: *(Serving tea)* A letter for you, sir.

Vershinin: For me? *(He takes the letter)* From my daughter. *(He reads)* Yes, of course. . . . Forgive me, Marya Sergeevna, I'll slip out quietly. No tea for me. *(He gets up, disturbed)* The same old story. . . .

Masha: What is it? It's not a secret?

Vershinin: *(In a low voice)* My wife's poisoned herself again. I must go. I'll slip out so no one will notice. All this is horribly unpleasant. *(He kisses* Masha's *hand)* My good, darling, wonderful woman. . . . I'll just slip out quietly. . . .

Anfisa: Where on earth's he going now? After I've poured out his tea. . . . If he isn't a . . .

Masha: *(Losing her temper)* Stop it! Bothering everybody to death, you never give us a moment's peace. . . . *(She goes over to the table with her cup)* I'm bored with you, old woman!

Anfisa: What are you so mad about? Darling girl!

Andrei's Voice: *(Offstage)* Anfisa!

Anfisa: *(Mimicking him)* Anfisa! There he sits . . .

[She goes out]

Masha: *(By the table in the dining room, angrily)* Let me sit down! *(She mixes up the cards on the table)* Sprawling all over the place with your cards. Drink your tea!

Irina: Masha, you're just mean.

Masha: Well if I'm mean don't talk to me. Don't bother me!

Chebutykin: *(Laughing)* Don't bother her, don't bother her. . . .

Masha: You're sixty years old and yet you behave like a spoiled child, always jabbering the devil knows what. . . .

Natasha: *(She sighs)* Dear Masha, why *must* you use such expressions in conversation? With your looks you'd be simply fascinating in society if only it weren't for these—I'm going to be frank with you—for these expressions of yours. Excuse me for mentioning it, Masha, but your manners *are* a little coarse.

Tuzenbach: (*Trying to keep from laughing*) Give me . . . Give me . . . It seems to me there's some cognac somewhere. . . .

Natasha: It looks like my little Bobik isn't asleep any more, he's waked up. He isn't well today. I must go to him, excuse me. . . .

[She goes out]

Irina: And where's Alexander Ignatich gone?

Masha: Home. Something about his wife again—something odd.

Tuzenbach: (*Going over to* Solyony *with a decanter of cognac*) You always sit by yourself thinking about something, and there's no telling what it is. Come on, let's make peace. Let's have some cognac. (*They drink*) I'll have to play the piano all night tonight, I expect—all sorts of trash. . . . Well, come what may!

Solyony: Why make peace? I'm not mad at you.

Tuzenbach: You always give me the feeling that something's gone wrong between us. You're a strange character, you've got to admit it.

Solyony: (*Declaiming*) I am strange, and yet, who is not strange? Ah, be not wroth, Aleko!

Tuzenbach: You see! How'd that Aleko get in? (*A pause*)

Solyony: When I'm alone with anybody I'm all right, I'm just like everybody else, but when there are people around I get depressed and shy and . . . just talk nonsense. But just the same, I'm more honest and sincere than lots of people—lots and lots of people. And I can prove it.

Tuzenbach: I'm always getting angry at you, you keep bothering me so when there're other people around, but I like you just the same . . . why I don't know. . . . Come what may, I'm going to get drunk tonight. Let's have another!

Solyony: Yes, let's! (*He drinks*) I never have had anything against you, Baron. But I have a disposition like Lermontov's. . . . (*In a low voice*) I even look a little like Lermontov . . . so I'm told. . . . (*He takes a bottle of perfume from his pocket and sprinkles some over his hands*)

Tuzenbach: I've sent in my resignation. Finished! For five years I've been thinking about it and at last I've made up my mind. I'm going to work.

Solyony: (*Declaiming*) Ah, be not wroth, Aleko. . . . Forget, forget thy dreams. . . .

[While they are talking Andrei *comes in quietly, a book in his hand, and sits down by a candle]*

Tuzenbach: I'm going to work.

Chebutykin: (*Coming into the living room with* Irina) And besides that, they had real Caucasian food for me—onion soup, and for the meat course *chekhartma.*

Solyony: *Cheremsha* isn't meat at all, it's a vegetable like an onion.

Chebutykin: No indeed, my angel. . . . *Chekhartma* isn't onion, it's roast lamb.

Solyony: And I tell you, *cheremsha*'s onion.

Chebutykin: And I tell you, *chekhartma*'s lamb.

Solyony: And I tell you, *cheremsha*'s onion.

Chebutykin: What's the use of arguing with you! You never were in the Caucasus, you never ate any *chekhartma.*

Solyony: I never ate it because I hate it. *Cheremsha* smells—it smells like garlic.

Andrei: *(Imploringly)* That's enough, gentlemen! I beg you.

Tuzenbach: When are the carnival people coming?

Irina: They promised about nine—and that means any minute.

Tuzenbach: *(Embracing* Andrei *and singing)* "O my porch, O my porch, O my new porch . . ."[3]

Andrei: *(Dancing and singing)* "My new porch, my maple porch . . ."

Chebutykin: *(Dancing)* "Porch with my new trellis!" *(Laughter)*

Tuzenbach: *(Embracing* Andrei*)* Ah, the devil take it, let's have a drink! Old Andrei, let's drink to our eternal friendship! And Andrei, I'm going right along to Moscow with you, to the University.

Solyony: To which university? There's two universities in Moscow.

Andrei: There's one university in Moscow.

Solyony: And I tell you, there're two.

Andrei: There can be three for all I care. The more the better.

Solyony: There's two universities in Moscow! *(Murmurs of protest; people say, "Sh!")* There're two universities in Moscow, the old one and the new one. And if you don't want to listen to me, if my words annoy you, then I don't have to talk. I can even go in the other room. . . .

[He goes out through one of the doors]

Tuzenbach: Bravo, bravo! *(He laughs)* Get ready, ladies and gentlemen, I'm about to sit down at the piano! That Solyony, he's a funny one!

[He sits down at the piano and plays a waltz]

Masha: *(Waltzing by herself)* The Ba-ron's drunk, the Ba-ron's drunk, the Ba-a-ron is dru-unk! *(Natasha comes in)*

Natasha: *(To* Chebutykin*)* Ivan Romanich!

---

3. See Randall Jarrell's comment, p. 1697.

[*She speaks about something with* Chebutykin, *then quietly goes out.* Chebutykin *touches* Tuzenbach *on the shoulder and whispers to him.*]

Irina: What's the matter?

Chebutykin: It's time we were going. Good-bye.

Tuzenbach: Good night. Time we were going.

Irina: But—but what do you mean? What about the carnival people?

Andrei: (*Embarrassed*) There aren't going to be any carnival people. You see, my dear, Natasha says that Bobik doesn't feel very good, and so . . . To tell the truth, I don't know anything about it, it doesn't make any difference to me.

Irina: (*Shrugging her shoulders*) Bobik doesn't feel good!

Masha: Oh, what's the difference! If they run us out, then we've got to go. (*To* Irina) There's nothing wrong with Bobik, there's something wrong with her. . . . Here! (*She taps her forehead*) Common little creature!

[Andrei *goes into his room;* Chebutykin *follows him; in the dining room they are saying good-bye*]

Fedotik: What a shame! I was counting on spending the evening, but if the little baby's sick then of course . . . Tomorrow I'll bring him a little toy. . . .

Rode: (*Loudly*) I took a long nap this afternoon on purpose, just because I thought I was going to get to dance all night. Why, it's only nine o'clock!

Masha: Let's go on out and talk things over there. We'll decide about everything.

[*Sounds of "Good night!" "Good-bye!"* Tuzenbach *is heard laughing gaily. Everyone goes out.* Anfisa *and a* Maid *clear the table and put out the lights. The* Nurse *is heard singing.* Andrei, *in a hat and overcoat, and* Chebutykin *come in.*]

Chebutykin: I never did manage to get married, because life's gone by me like lightning, and because I was crazy about your mother and she was married. . . .

Andrei: People shouldn't get married. They shouldn't because it's boring.

Chebutykin: Maybe so, maybe so, but the loneliness! You can philosophize as much as you please, but loneliness is a terrible thing, Andrei boy. . . . Though on the other hand, really . . . of course, it doesn't make any difference one way or the other!

Andrei: Let's hurry.

Chebutykin: What's the hurry? We'll make it.

Andrei: I'm afraid my wife might stop me.

Chebutykin: Oh!

    Andrei: Tonight I won't play any myself, I'll just sit and watch. I
        don't feel very good. . . . Sometimes I feel as if I had asthma—
        what should I do for it, Ivan Romanich?

Chebutykin: Why ask me? *I* don't remember, Andrei boy. I don't
        know. . . .

    Andrei: Let's go out through the kitchen.

[They go out. A ring, then another ring; voices and laughter. Irina *enters.]*

    Irina: What's that?

    Anfisa: (Whispering) The carnival people! *(Another ring)*

    Irina: Nurse dear, tell them there isn't anyone at home. They'll
        have to excuse us.

*[*Anfisa *goes out.* Irina *walks back and forth, lost in thought; she seems disturbed.*
Solyony *comes in.]*

    Solyony: (Perplexed) Nobody here. . . . Where is everybody?

    Irina: Gone home.

    Solyony: That's funny. You're alone here?

    Irina: Alone. *(A pause)* Good-bye.

    Solyony: A little while ago I lost control of myself, I wasn't tactful.
        But you are different from the rest of them, you are exalted,
        pure, you see the truth. . . . You are the only one there is that
        can understand me. I love you so, I'll love you to the end of—

    Irina: Good-bye. Go away.

    Solyony: I can't live without you. *(Following her)* Oh, my ideal!
        (Through his tears) Oh, bliss! Those marvelous, glorious,
        incredible eyes—eyes like no other woman's I've ever seen. . . .

    Irina: (Coldly) Stop it, Vasili Vasilich!

    Solyony: For the first time I'm speaking to you of love, and it's as if I
        were no longer on this earth, but on another planet. *(He runs
        his hand across his forehead)* Well, it doesn't make any differ-
        ence. I can't make you love me, of course. . . . But rivals,
        happy rivals—I can't stand those . . . can't stand them. I swear
        to you by all that is holy, I shall kill any rival. . . . Oh, wonder-
        ful one!

*[*Natasha *comes in, a candle in her hand. She looks into one room, then into
another, but walks by her husband's door without stopping.]*

    Natasha: There Andrei is. Let him read! Excuse me, Vasili Vasilich,
        I hadn't any idea you were in here. I'm not dressed.

    Solyony: It doesn't make any difference to me. Good-bye!

[He goes out]

Natasha: And you're tired, dear—my poor little girl! *(She kisses* Irina*)* If only you would go to bed a little earlier!
   Irina: Is Bobik asleep?
Natasha: Asleep. But not sound asleep. By the way, dear, I keep meaning to speak to you about it, but either you're not home or else I haven't the time. . . . It seems to me that it's so cold and damp for Bobik in the nursery he has now. And your room is simply ideal for a child. My darling, my precious, do move in with Olga for a while!
   Irina: (Not understanding) Where?

[A troika with bells is heard driving up to the house]

Natasha: You and Olga will be in one room, for the time being, and your room will be for Bobik. He's such a little dear, this morning I said to him, "Bobik, you're mine! Mine!" And he looked up at me with those darling little eyes of his. *(A ring)* That must be Olga. How late she is!

[A Maid *comes in and whispers in* Natasha*'s ear]*

Natasha: Protopopov! What a funny man! Protopopov's here and wants me to go for a ride in his troika with him. *(She laughs)* Men are so funny! *(A ring)* Someone else's come. I suppose I might go, just for a few minutes. *(To the* Maid*)* Tell him just a minute. . . . *(A ring)* There's that doorbell again, it must be Olga.

[She goes out]

[The Maid *runs out;* Irina *sits thinking;* Kulygin *and* Olga *enter,* Vershinin *just behind]*

   Kulygin: Well, this is a fine state of affairs! And they said they were going to have a party!
Vershinin: Strange. I left a little while ago, a half hour ago, and they were expecting the carnival people.
   Irina: They've all gone.
   Kulygin: And Masha's gone too? Where's she gone? And why's Protopopov waiting down there in his troika? Who's he waiting for?
   Irina: Don't ask questions. . . . I'm tired.
   Kulygin: Little crosspatch!
   Olga: The meeting lasted till just this minute. I'm exhausted. Our headmistress is ill and I've had to take her place. My head, how my head aches, my head . . . *(She sits down)* Andrei lost two hundred rubles yesterday, playing cards. Everybody in town is talking about it. . . .

Kulygin: Yes, and I got tired at the meeting, too.

Vershinin: My wife decided to give me a scare just now, she almost poisoned herself. Everything's turned out all right, and I certainly am glad—I can relax now. . . . Then of course, we ought to leave? Well then, let me wish you good-bye. Fyodor Ilich, come somewhere with me! I can't go home tonight, I absolutely can't. . . . Come on!

Kulygin: I am tired. I'm not going. *(He gets up)* I am tired. Has my wife gone home?

Irina: I suppose so.

Kulygin: (Kissing Irina's *hand)* Good-bye. Tomorrow and the day after tomorrow I'm going to rest all day long. Good-bye! *(He goes)* I surely would like some tea. I'd been counting on spending the evening in congenial company and—*O, fallacem hominum spem!* Accusative of exclamation. . . .

Vershinin: It means I go by myself.

[He goes out with Kulygin, *whistling]*

Olga: My head aches, my head . . . Andrei's lost—everybody in town's talking about it. . . . I'll go lie down. *(She starts to go)* Tomorrow I'm free. . . . O my God, what a relief that is! Tomorrow I'm free, the day after tomorrow I'm free. . . . My head aches, my head . . .

[She goes out]

Irina: (Alone) They've all gone. There's no one left.

[An accordion is heard in the street, the Nurse *is singing in the next room]*

Natasha: (Crossing the dining room in a fur coat and cap, followed by a Maid*)* I'll be back in half an hour. I'll only go for a short drive.

[She goes out]

Irina: (Alone, yearningly) To Moscow! To Moscow! To Moscow!

CURTAIN

ACT 3

Olga's *and* Irina's *room. To the left and right are beds, with screens around them. It is past two o'clock in the morning. Offstage a fire bell is being rung, for a fire that began a long time ago. No one in the house has gone to bed yet.* Masha *is lying on the sofa, dressed as usual in a black dress.* Olga *and* Anfisa *come in.*

Anfisa: They're down there now, just sitting by the stairs. I said, "Come upstairs. Please," I said, "you can't just sit here like this!"—they were crying. "Papa," they said, "we don't know where he is—" they said, "Maybe he's burned to death." What a thing to think of! And there're some people in the yard—they're not dressed either. . . .

Olga: (*Taking dresses from a wardrobe*) Here, this gray one, take it . . . and this one here . . . the blouse, too. . . . And this skirt—take it, nurse dear. . . . My God, what a thing to happen—all Kirsanov Street's burned down, evidently. . . . Take this. . . . Take this. . . . (*She piles the clothes in* Anfisa's *arms*) The Vershinins, poor things, certainly did get a fright. . . . Their house nearly burned down. They must spend the night here with us. . . . We can't send them home. . . . Poor Fedotik's had everything he owns burnt, there isn't a thing left. . . .

Anfisa: You'll have to call Ferapont, Olga darling, or else I can't carry it. . . .

Olga: (*Ringing*) Nobody answers. (*She calls through the door*) Come here, whoever's down there. (*A window, red with the glow of the fire, can be seen through the open door; the fire department is heard going past the house*) How terrible it all is! And how sick of it I am!

[Ferapont *comes in*]

Olga: Here, take these downstairs. . . . The Kelotilin girls are down there by the staircase—give them to them. Give them this, too. . . .

Ferapont: Yes'm. In the year '12 Moscow burned too.[4] Good God Almighty! The Frenchmen were flabbergasted.

Olga: Go on, get along. . . .

Ferapont: Yes'm.

[*He goes out*]

Olga: Nurse darling, give it all away. We don't need anything, give it all away, nurse. . . . I'm so tired I can hardly stand on my feet. . . . We *can't* allow the Vershinins to go home. The little girls can sleep in the living room, and put Alexander Ignatich downstairs at the Baron's . . . Fedotik at the Baron's, too, or else in our dining room. . . . The Doctor's drunk, terribly drunk, just as if he'd done it on purpose—we can't put anyone in with him. And put Vershinin's wife in the living room too.

Anfisa: (*Wearily*) Olga darling, don't drive me away! Don't drive me away!

———

4. In 1812, when the French invaded Russia, the Moscovites burned down their own city.

Olga: You're talking nonsense, nurse. Nobody's driving you away.

Anfisa: (Laying her head on Olga's breast) My own, treasure, I do the best I can, I do work. . . . I'm getting weak, they'll all say, "Get out!" And where is there for me to go? Where? Eighty years old . . . my eighty-second year. . . .

Olga: You sit down, nurse darling. . . . You're tired, poor thing. . . . *(She gets her to sit down)* Rest, my darling. How pale you look!

[Natasha *enters*]

Natasha: They're saying we ought to organize a committee right away to aid the victims of the fire. Well, why not? It's a fine idea. After all, we ought to help the poor, that's the duty of the rich. Bobik and Baby Sophie are both sound asleep—sleeping as if nothing had happened! . . . There're people here everywhere, wherever you go the house is full of them. And there's all this flu in town now, I'm so afraid the children may catch it.

Olga: (Not listening to her) From this room you can't see the fire, it's peaceful here. . . .

Natasha: Uh-huh. . . . I must be a sight. *(In front of the mirror)* They keep saying I've gained. . . . And it's not so! It's not a bit so! And Masha's fast asleep—dead tired, poor thing. . . . *(To* Anfisa, *coldly)* Don't you dare sit down in my presence! Get up! Get out of here! (Anfisa *goes out. A pause)* What you keep that old woman for I simply do not understand!

Olga: (Taken aback) I beg your pardon, I don't understand either. . . .

Natasha: She's around here for no reason whatsoever. She's a peasant, she ought to be in the country where she belongs. . . . It's simply spoiling them! I like for everything in the house to have its proper place! There ought not to be these useless people cluttering up the house. *(She strokes* Olga's *cheek)* Poor girl, you're tired. Our headmistress is tired. When my little Sophie gets to be a big girl and goes to the high school, I'm going to be so afraid of you.

Olga: I'm not going to be headmistress.

Natasha: You're sure to be, Olga. It's already settled.

Olga: I won't accept. I can't . . . I'm not strong enough. . . . *(She drinks some water)* You were so rude to nurse just now. Forgive me, I just haven't the strength to bear it. . . . It's getting all black before my eyes. . . .

Natasha: (Agitated) Forgive me, Olga, forgive me. . . . I didn't mean to upset you.

[Masha *gets up, takes her pillow, and goes out angrily*]

Olga: Try to understand, dear . . . perhaps we've been brought up in an unusual way, but I can't bear this. This sort of thing depresses me so, I get sick. . . . I just despair!

Natasha: Forgive me, forgive me. *(She kisses her)*

Olga: The least rudeness, even, an impolite word—it upsets me. . . .

Natasha: Sometimes I do say more than I should, that's so, but you must admit, my dear, she *could* live in the country.

Olga: She's been with us thirty years already.

Natasha: But now she just can't do anything, you know that! Either I don't understand you or you don't want to understand me. She's not fit for any work, she just sleeps or sits.

Olga: Well, let her sit.

Natasha: *(Surprised)* What do you mean, let her sit? Why, she's a servant. *(Tearfully)* I simply cannot understand you, Olga. I've got a nurse, a wet nurse, we've got a maid, we've got a cook. . . . What do we have to have that old woman for too? What *for?*

[Behind the scene a fire alarm rings]

Olga: Tonight I have aged ten years.

Natasha: We've got to settle things, Olga. You're at the high school, I'm at home; you have the teaching, and I have the housekeeping. And if I say something about the servants, I know what I'm talking about: *I—know—what—I'm—talking—about* . . . and tomorrow morning that old thief, that old wretch *(She stamps her foot)*, that witch is going to be out of this house! Don't you dare irritate me! Don't you dare! *(Collecting herself)* Honestly, if you don't move downstairs we'll be quarreling like this for the rest of our lives. This is awful!

[Kulygin comes in]

Kulygin: Where's Masha? It's time to go home. They say the fire's dying down. *(He stretches)* In spite of all the wind, only one block's burned—at first it looked as if the whole town would burn. *(He sits down)* I am exhausted, Olga my dear. . . . I often think if it hadn't been Masha I'd have married you, Olga dear. You have such a generous nature. . . . I am exhausted. *(He listens for something)*

Olga: What is it?

Kulygin: As if he'd done it on purpose, the Doctor's got drunk, he's terribly drunk. As if he'd done it on purpose! *(He gets up)* I do believe he's coming up here. . . . Hear him? Yes, up here. . . . *(He laughs)* If he isn't the . . . I'll hide. *(He goes to the wardrobe and stands between it and the wall)* What a rascal!

Olga: For two years he doesn't drink, and now all of a sudden he goes and gets drunk. . . .

[She follows Natasha *to the back of the room.*

Chebutykin *enters; without staggering, like a sober person, he crosses the room, stops, looks around, then goes to the washbasin and begins to wash his hands]*

Chebutykin: (*Gloomily*) The devil take every one of them . . . every one of them. . . . They think I'm a doctor, know how to treat anything there is, and I don't know a thing, I've forgotten everything I ever did know, I remember nothing, absolutely nothing.

*[*Olga *and* Natasha *leave the room without his noticing]*

Chebutykin: The devil take them. Last Wednesday I treated a woman at Zasyp—dead, and it's my fault she's dead. Yes. . . . Twenty-five years ago I used to know a little something, but now I don't remember a thing. One single thing. Maybe I'm not a man at all, but just look like one—maybe it just looks like I've got arms and legs and a head. Maybe I don't even exist, and it only looks like I walk and eat and sleep. (*He cries*) Oh, if only I didn't exist! (*He stops crying; gloomily*) The devil only knows. . . . Day before yesterday they were talking at the club; they talked about Shakespeare, Voltaire. . . . I haven't read them, I never have read them at all, but I looked like I'd read them. And the others did too, the same as me. So cheap! So low! And that woman I killed Wednesday—she came back to me, and it all came back to me, and everything inside me felt all twisted, all vile, all nauseating. . . . I went and got drunk. . . .

*[*Irina, Vershinin, *and* Tuzenbach *come in;* Tuzenbach *is wearing new and stylish civilian clothes]*

Irina: Let's sit in here. Nobody will be coming in here.
Vershinin: If it hadn't been for the soldiers the whole town would have burnt up. Brave men, those! (*He rubs his hands with pleasure*) The salt of the earth! Ah, those are first-rate men!
Kulygin: (*Going up to them*) What's the time, gentlemen?
Tuzenbach: Going on four. It's getting light.
Irina: They're all sitting there in the dining room, nobody thinks of leaving, and that Solyony of yours sits there. . . . (*To* Chebutykin) Oughtn't you to go to bed, Doctor?
Chebutykin: Doesn't matter. . . . Thank you. . . . (*He combs his beard*)
Kulygin: (*Laughing*) You're tight, Ivan Romanich! (*He slaps him on the back*) Bravo! *In vino veritas,*[5] as the ancients used to say.

---

5. "In wine there is truth." (Latin)

Tuzenbach: Everybody keeps asking me to get up a concert to help the people whose houses burned.

Irina: Yes, but who's there to . . . ?

Tuzenbach: We could arrange one if we wanted to. Marya Sergeevna, in my opinion, is a wonderful pianist.

Kulygin: Yes indeed, wonderful.

Irina: She's forgotten how, by now. She hasn't played for three years—four.

Tuzenbach: Here in this town there is not a soul who understands music, not a single soul; but I, I do understand it, and I give you my word of honor that Marya Sergeevna plays magnificently, almost with genius.

Kulygin: You're right, Baron. I love her very much, Masha. She's wonderful.

Tuzenbach: To be able to play so beautifully and all the time to know that no one, no one, understands you!

Kulygin: (*Sighing*) Yes. . . . But would it be proper for her to appear in a public concert? (*A pause*) Really, gentlemen, I know nothing about it. Perhaps it would be quite all right. You have to admit that our principal is a fine man, in fact a very fine man, very intelligent, too; but his views *are* a little . . . Of course, it isn't any of his affair, but just the same, if you think I ought to, I'll speak to him about it.

[Chebutykin *picks up a porcelain clock and examines it*]

Vershinin: I got all covered with dirt at the fire—I look pretty disreputable. (*A pause*) Yesterday just by accident I heard someone say that they may be sending our brigade a long way off—some of them said to Poland, some of them said to Siberia, to Chita.

Tuzenbach: I heard that too. Well, what is there you can do? The town will be completely empty.

Irina: And we'll leave too!

Chebutykin: (*Drops the clock, smashing it*) To smithereens!

[*A pause; everyone looks embarrassed and upset*]

Kulygin: (*Picking up the pieces*) To break such an expensive thing—oh, Ivan Romanich, Ivan Romanich! You get a zero-minus in deportment!

Irina: That's Mother's clock.

Chebutykin: Maybe. . . . If it's Mother's, then it's Mother's. Maybe I didn't break it but it only looks like I broke it. Maybe it only looks like we exist, and really we don't. I don't know anything, nobody knows anything. (*At the door*) What are you staring at? Natasha's having an affair with Protopopov, and you don't see that. You sit there and see nothing, and Natasha's having an affair with Protopopov. . . . *(Singing)* "Tell me how you like this little present!"

[*He goes out*]

Vershinin: Yes. . . . *(He laughs)* How strange all this is, in reality! When the fire started I rushed home; I got there, looked around . . . the house was safe and sound, not in any danger at all, but there my two little girls were, standing in the doorway in just their underwear, their mother gone, people rushing around, horses running by, dogs, and my little girls' faces were so anxious and terrified and beseeching and—I don't know what; it wrung my heart to look at those faces. My God, I thought, what these girls still have to go through in the rest of their lives, in all the years to come! I picked them up and ran, and I kept thinking one thing: what they still have to live through in this world! *(Fire alarm; a pause)* I got here and here was their mother—she was shouting, she got angry.

[Masha *comes in with the pillow and sits down on the sofa*]

Vershinin: And while my little girls were standing in the doorway in just their underwear, and the street was red with the fire, the noise was terrible, I started thinking that it's almost what happened long ago, when the enemy attacked unexpectedly, looting and burning. . . . And yet, in reality, what a difference there is between what things are now and what they were then! And when a little more time has passed, two or three hundred years, people will look in horror and mockery at this life we live now, and everything we do now will seem to them clumsy, and difficult, and terribly uncomfortable and strange. Oh, what life will be like then! What life will be like then! *(He laughs)* Sorry, I've started philosophizing again. But do let me go on, ladies and gentlemen. I feel terribly like philosophizing, I'm in just the right frame of mind. *(A pause)* Looks like they're all asleep. So I say: What life will be like then! Can you imagine! Here in this town there are only three of your kind now, but in the generations to come there will be more and more and more; the time will come when everything will get to be the way you want it to be, everybody will live like you, and then after a while you yourselves will be out-of-date, there'll be people born who'll be better than you. . . . *(He laughs)* I'm in a most peculiar frame of mind tonight. I want like the devil to live. *(He sings)* "Unto love all ages bow, its pangs are blest . . ."

Masha: Da-da-dum . . .

Vershinin: Da-dum . . .

Masha: Da-da-da?

Vershinin: Da-da-da! *(He laughs)*

[Fedotik comes in]

> Fedotik: *(Dancing)* Burnt to ashes! Burnt to ashes! Everything I had in this world! *(Laughter)*
>
> Irina: What kind of joke is that? Is it really all burnt?
>
> Fedotik: *(Laughing)* Every single last thing! There's not one thing left! The guitar's burnt, and the camera burnt, and all my letters are burnt. . . . And I meant to give you a little notebook, and it's burnt too. . . .

[Solyony enters]

> Irina: No, please go away, Vasili Vasilich. You can't come in here.
>
> Solyony: But why is it the Baron can and I can't?
>
> Vershinin: We ought to be going, really. How's the fire?
>
> Solyony: They say it's dying down. No, it's a very strange thing to me, why is it the Baron can and I can't? *(He takes out a bottle of perfume and sprinkles it on himself)*
>
> Vershinin: Da-da-dum?
>
> Masha: Da-dum!
>
> Vershinin: *(Laughing, to Solyony)* Let's go on in the dining room.
>
> Solyony: All right, but there'll be a note made of this. "This moral could be made more clear. But 'twould annoy the geese, I fear."[6] *(He looks at Tuzenbach)* He-ere, chicky, chicky, chicky!

[He goes out with Vershinin and Fedotik]

> Irina: That Solyony! There's smoke all over everything. . . . *(In surprise)* The Baron's asleep! Baron! Baron!
>
> Tuzenbach: *(Waking up)* I'm tired, only I . . . the brickyard . . . I'm not delirious, I really am going to start work there soon. . . . I've already talked it over with them. *(To Irina, tenderly)* You're so pale and beautiful and enchanting. . . . It seems to me your paleness brightens the dark air like light . . . You're sad, you're dissatisfied with life. . . . Oh, come away with me, let's go and work together!
>
> Masha: Nikolai Lvovich, go away from here!
>
> Tuzenbach: *(Laughing)* You're here? I didn't see you. *(He kisses Irina's hand)* Good-bye, I'm going. I look at you now, and it reminds me of how long ago on your birthday you were so happy and cheerful, and talked about the joy of work. . . . And what a happy life I saw before me then! Where is it? *(He kisses her hand)* You have tears in your eyes. Go to bed, it's already getting light. . . . It's beginning to be morning. . . . If only I might give my life for you!

---

6. The concluding lines of "The Geese," by Ivan Andreyevich Krylov (1768–1844).

Masha: Nikolai Lvovich, go away! Why, really, what . . .

Tuzenbach: I'm going.

[He goes out]

Masha: *(Lying down)* Are you asleep, Fyodor?

Kulygin: What?

Masha: You should go home.

Kulygin: My darling Masha, my precious Masha . . .

Irina: She's worn out. . . . Let her rest, Fyodor dear.

Kulygin: I'll go in just a minute. My good, wonderful wife . . . I love you, my only one. . . .

Masha: *(Angrily)* Amo, amas, amat, amamus, amatis, amant.[7]

Kulygin: *(Laughing)* No, really, she's amazing. I've been married to you for seven years, and it seems as if we were married only yesterday. Word of honor! No, really, you're an amazing woman. I am satisfied, I am satisfied, I am satisfied!

Masha: Bored, bored, bored! . . . *(She sits up)* I can't get it out of my head. It's simply revolting. It sticks in my head like a nail, I can't keep quiet about it any longer. I mean about Andrei . . . he's mortgaged this house at the bank and his wife's got hold of all the money. But the house doesn't belong just to him, it belongs to the four of us! He ought to know that if he's a decent man.

Kulygin: Must you, Masha? What's it to you? Poor Andrei's in debt to everybody—well, God help him!

Masha: Just the same, it's revolting. *(She lies down)*

Kulygin: You and I aren't poor. I work, I go to the high school, I give lessons afterwards. . . . I'm an honest man . . . a simple man. . . . *Omnia mea mecum porto,*[8] as the saying goes.

Masha: I don't need anything, but the injustice of it nauseates me. *(A pause)* Go on, Fyodor.

Kulygin: *(Kissing her)* You're tired, rest for half an hour, and I'll sit there and wait. . . . Sleep. . . . *(He starts to leave)* I am satisfied, I am satisfied, I am satisfied.

[He goes out]

Irina: No, really, how petty our Andrei's become, how lifeless and old he's got, at the side of that woman! Once he was preparing to be a professor, a scholar, and yesterday he was boasting that he's finally managed to get made a member of the county board. He a member, Protopopov chairman. . . . Everybody in town is talking about it, laughing at it, and he's the

---

7. "I love, you love," etc. (Latin)
8. "All that is mine I carry with me." (Latin)

only one that knows nothing, that sees nothing. . . . And now everybody's run off to the fire, and he sits there in his room and doesn't pay any attention to anything, he just plays the violin. *(Nervously)* Oh, it's awful, awful, awful! *(She cries)* I can't stand any more, I can't stand it! . . . I can't, I can't. . . .

[Olga *comes in and begins to straighten her dressing table*]

Irina: *(Sobbing loudly)* Throw me out, throw me out, I can't stand any more!

Olga: *(Alarmed)* What is it, what is it? Darling!

Irina: *(Sobbing)* Where? Where's it all gone? Where is it? Oh, my God, my God! I've forgotten everything, forgotten . . . it's all mixed up in my head, I don't remember what *window* is in Italian, or—or *ceiling*. . . . I'm forgetting everything, every day I forget, and life goes by and won't ever come back, won't ever, we'll never go to Moscow, we won't ever . . . now I see that we won't ever . . .

Olga: Darling, darling . . .

Irina: *(Trying to control herself)* Oh, I'm miserable . . . I can't work, I'm not ever going to work. That's enough, that's enough! First I worked at the telegraph office, now I work at the county board, and I hate and despise every last thing they have me do. . . . I'm already almost twenty-four, I've been working for years and years already, my brain is drying up, I'm getting thin, getting ugly, getting old, and there's nothing, nothing—there isn't the least satisfaction of any kind—and the years are going by, and every day, over and over, everything's getting farther away from any real life, beautiful life, everything's going farther and farther into some abyss. . . . I am in despair, I can't understand how I'm alive, how I haven't killed myself long ago. . . .

Olga: Don't cry, my own little girl, don't cry. . . . I suffer, too.

Irina: I'm not crying, I'm not crying. . . . That's enough. . . . See, now I'm not crying any more. . . . That's enough, that's enough!

Olga: Darling, I tell you as your sister, as your friend: If you want my advice, marry the Baron!

[Irina *weeps silently*]

Olga: You know you respect him, you think so much of him. . . . He's ugly, it's true, but he's such an honest man, such a good man. . . . You know, people don't marry for love, but for duty. At least, I think so, and I would marry without being in love. If someone proposed to me, no matter who it was, I'd marry him, as long as he was a decent man. I'd marry an old man, even. . . .

Irina: I was always waiting till we moved to Moscow, I'd meet the real one there—I used to dream about him, love him. . . . But it's all turned out nonsense, all nonsense!

Olga: (Embracing her sister) My dear, beautiful sister, I understand it all: When Baron Nikolai Lvovich left the army and came to see us in his civilian clothes, he looked so homely to me I absolutely started to cry. . . . He said, "Why are you crying?" How could I tell him! But if it were God's will he should marry you, I'd be happy. That would be different, you know, completely different.

[Natasha, with a candle, comes out of the door on the right, crosses the stage, and goes out through the door on the left, without speaking]

Masha: (Sitting up) She walks like the one that started the fire.

Olga: Masha, you're silly. The silliest one in the whole family—that's you. Please forgive me. *(A pause)*

Masha: I want to confess, dear sisters. Inside I—I can't keep on this way any longer. I'll confess to you and then never again to anybody, never again. . . . In a minute I'll say it. *(In a low voice)* It's my secret, but you ought to know it. . . . I can't keep quiet any longer. . . . *(A pause)* I love, love . . . I love that man. . . . The one you just saw. . . . Oh, why not say it? In one word, I love Vershinin.

Olga: (Going behind her screen) Stop it. Anyway, I don't hear you.

Masha: What is there I can do? *(She holds her head in her hands)* At first he seemed strange to me, then I felt sorry for him . . . then I fell in love with him, fell in love with his voice, his words, his misfortunes, his two little girls. . . .

Olga: (Behind the screen) Anyway, I don't hear you. Whatever silly things you're saying, anyway, I don't hear you.

Masha: Oh, you're so silly, Olga. I love him—it means, it's my fate. It means, it's my lot. . . . And he loves me. . . . It's all so strange. Yes? It isn't good? *(She takes* Irina *by the hand and draws her close to her)* Oh my darling, how are we going to live our lives, what is going to become of us? When you read some novel then it all seems so old and so easy to understand, but when you're in love yourself you see that no one knows anything, and everyone has to decide for himself. . . . My darlings, my sisters, I've confessed to you, now I'll be silent. . . . From now on I'll be like Gogol's madman . . . silence . . . silence . . .

[Andrei comes in, followed by Ferapont]

Andrei: (Angrily) What is it you want? I don't understand.

Ferapont: (Standing in the doorway, impatiently) Andrei Sergeevich, I've told you ten times already.

Andrei: In the first place, to you I am not Andrei Sergeevich, but
   your honor!
Ferapont: The firemen, your honor, want to know if you'll please let
   them go to the river through your garden. Because the way it
   is they have to go around and around, they're getting all worn
   out.
Andrei: All right. Tell them all right.

[Ferapont leaves]

Andrei: What a bore! . . . Where's Olga? *(Olga comes out from
   behind the screen)* I've come to get the key to the cupboard from
   you, I've lost mine. You've got one of those little keys. . . .
   *(Olga hands him the key, without speaking. Irina goes behind her
   screen. A pause)* What a tremendous fire! It's started to die
   down now. . . . The devil, that Ferapont made me lose my
   temper—that was stupid to say that. . . . Your honor. . . . *(A
   pause)* Why don't you say something, Olga? *(A pause)* It's
   about time you stopped this silliness . . . pouting like this without rhyme or reason. . . . Masha, you're here, Irina's here,
   well, that's just fine—let's get things settled once and for all.
   What is it you've got against me? What is it?
Olga: Let it go now, Andrei dear. We'll straighten things out
   tomorrow. *(In an agitated voice)* What a dreadful night!
Andrei: *(In great confusion and embarrassment)* Don't get all upset.
   I'm asking you perfectly calmly: What is it you've got against
   me? Come right out with it.

Vershinin's Voice: *(Offstage)* Da-da-dum!

Masha: *(In a loud voice, getting up)* Da-da-dah! *(To Olga)* Good-
   bye, Olga, God bless you! *(She goes behind the screen and kisses
   Irina)* Have a good sleep. . . . Good-bye, Andrei. Leave them
   alone now, they're worn out. . . . Tomorrow we can straighten
   things out.

[She goes out]

Olga: That's right, Andrei dear, let's put it off until tomorrow. . . . *(She goes behind the screen on her side of the room)* It's
   time to go to sleep.
Andrei: I'll only say this much and go. Right away. . . . In the first
   place, you've got something against Natasha, my wife, and I've
   seen that from the very first day we were married. Natasha is a
   splendid, honest person, straightforward and sincere—that is
   my opinion. I love and respect my wife—respect her, you
   understand, and I demand that others respect her too. I
   repeat, she's an honest, sincere person, and anything you've

got against her, if I may say so, is just your imagination. . . . *(A pause)* In the second place, you seem to be angry with me because I'm not a professor, don't in some way advance knowledge. But I am in the service of the government, I am a member of the county board, and this service of mine is to me just as sacred and lofty as the service of knowledge. I am a member of the county board and I am proud of it, if you want to know. . . . *(A pause)* In the third place. . . . I have something else to say. . . . I've mortgaged the house without your permission. . . . For that I am to blame, I admit it, and I beg you to forgive me. My debts forced me to. . . . Thirty-five thousand. . . . I no longer play cards, gave them up long ago, but the main thing I can say to justify myself is this, that you—that you're girls, you get a pension, I, though, didn't get . . . earnings, so to speak. . . . *(A pause)*

Kulygin: *(At the door)* Isn't Masha here? *(Anxiously)* But where is she? This is strange. . . .

[He goes out]

Andrei: They won't listen. Natasha's a splendid, honest person. *(He walks up and down silently, then stops)* When I got married I thought we'd be happy . . . all of us happy . . . but my God! . . . *(He cries)* My dearest sisters, darling sisters, don't believe me, don't believe . . .

[He goes out]

Kulygin: *(at the door anxiously)* Where's Masha? Isn't Masha here? What an extraordinary thing!

[He goes out]

[Fire alarm; the stage is empty]

Irina: *(Behind the screen)* Olga! Who's that knocking on the floor?

Olga: It's the Doctor, it's Ivan Romanich. He's drunk.

Irina: What a miserable night! *(A pause)* Olga! *(She looks out from behind the screen)* Did you hear? They're taking the brigade away from us, sending it way off somewhere.

Olga: It's only a rumor.

Irina: Then we'll be left all alone. . . . Olga!

Olga: Well?

Irina: Dearest sister, darling sister, I respect the Baron, I admire the Baron, he's a marvelous person, I'll marry him, I agree, only let's go to Moscow! Let's go, oh please let's go! There's nothing in this world better than Moscow! Let's go, Olga! Let's go!

CURTAIN

ACT 4

The old garden of the Prozorovs' *house. At the end of a long avenue of fir trees there is the river. On the other bank of the river is a forest. To the right of the house there is a terrace. Here on a table there are bottles and glasses; it is evident that they have just been drinking champagne. Occasionally people from the street cut through the garden to get to the river; five or six soldiers go through, walking fast.* Chebutykin, *in a genial mood which does not leave him during the act, is sitting in an easy chair in the garden; he wears his uniform cap and is holding a walking stick.* Irina, Kulygin *with a decoration around his neck and with no moustache, and* Tuzenbach *are standing on the terrace saying good-bye to* Fedotik *and* Rode, *who are coming down the steps; both officers are in parade uniform.*

Tuzenbach: *(Embracing* Fedotik*)* You're a fine man, we got along so well together. *(He embraces* Rode*)* One more time. . . . Good-bye, old man. . . .

Irina: *Au revoir!*

Fedotik: It isn't *au revoir,* it's good-bye; we'll never see each other again!

Kulygin: Who knows? *(He wipes his eyes and smiles)* Here I've started crying.

Irina: Some day or other we'll meet again.

Fedotik: In ten years—fifteen? By then we'll hardly recognize each other, we'll say "How do you do" coldly. . . . *(He takes a photograph)* Stand still. . . . One more time, it's the last time.

Rode: *(Embracing* Tuzenbach*)* We'll never see each other again. . . . *(He kisses* Irina's *hand)* Thank you for everything, for everything!

Fedotik: *(Annoyed)* Oh, stand still!

Tuzenbach: Please God, we'll see each other again. Write us now. Be sure to write us.

Rode: *(Looking around the garden)* Good-bye, trees! *(He shouts)* Yoo-hoo! *(A pause)* Good-bye, echo!

Kulygin: With any luck you'll get married there in Poland. . . . Your Polish wife will hug you and call you *kochany!*[9] *(He laughs)*

Fedotik: *(Looking at his watch)* We've less than an hour left. Solyony's the only one from our battery that's going on the barge, the rest of us are going with the enlisted men. Three batteries are leaving today, three more tomorrow—and then peace and quiet will descend on the town.

Tuzenbach: And awful boredom.

Rode: But where's Marya Sergeevna?

Kulygin: Masha's in the garden.

Fedotik: We must say good-bye to her.

---

9. Beloved. (Polish)

Rode: Good-bye. We must go, otherwise I'll start crying. *(He hurriedly embraces* Tuzenbach *and* Kulygin, *and kisses* Irina's *hand)* It was so nice living here.

Fedotik: *(To* Kulygin*)* This is for you to remember us by . . . a note-book with a pencil. . . . We'll go on down to the river this way. . . .

[They go off, both looking back]

Rode: *(Shouting)* Yoo-hoo!

Fedotik: *(Shouting)* Good-bye!

[At the back of the stage Fedotik *and* Rode *meet* Masha *and say good-bye to her; she goes off with them]*

Irina: They're gone. . . .

[She sits down on the bottom step of the terrace]

Chebutykin: And forgot to say good-bye to me.

Irina: And what about you?

Chebutykin: Well, I forgot, somehow. Anyway, I'll be seeing them again soon, I'm leaving tomorrow. Yes. . . . Only one more day. In a year more they'll retire me, I'll come back again and live out the rest of my days near you. . . . Only one more year and I get my pension. . . . *(He puts a newspaper in his pocket, takes a news-paper out of his pocket)* I'll come back here to you and lead a completely new life. I'll get to be such a sober, Gu-Gu-God-fearing, respectable man.

Irina: Yes, you really ought to, my dove. Somehow or other you ought.

Chebutykin: Yes. I feel so. *(He begins to sing softly)* Ta-ra-ra-boom-de-aye . . . / Sit on a log I may . . .

Kulygin: You're incorrigible, Ivan Romanich! You're incorrigible!

Chebutykin: Yes, if only I had *you* for a teacher! Then I'd reform.

Irina: Fyodor's shaved off his moustache. I can't bear to look at him.

Kulygin: And what of it?

Chebutykin: I could say what that face of yours looks like now—but I don't dare.

Kulygin: Well, what of it? It's the accepted thing, it's the *modus vivendi*. . . . Our principal's shaved off his moustache, so when they made me the assistant principal I shaved mine off too. Nobody likes it, but it doesn't make any difference to me. I am satisfied. With a moustache or without a moustache, I am satisfied. . . .

[He sits down.

Andrei *walks across the back of the stage, wheeling a baby carriage with the baby asleep in it.]*

    Irina: Ivan Romanich, my dove, my darling, I'm terribly worried. You were on the boulevard yesterday, tell me, what happened there?

Chebutykin: What happened? Nothing. Piffle! *(He reads the newspaper)* What's the difference!

    Kulygin: What they say is that Solyony and the Baron met each other yesterday on the boulevard, up by the theater—

Tuzenbach: Stop it! Why, really, what . . .

[He waves his hand and goes into the house]

    Kulygin: Up by the theater . . . Solyony started bothering the Baron, and the Baron wouldn't stand for it, he said something insulting . . .

Chebutykin: I don't know. It's all nonsense.

    Kulygin: There was a teacher in some seminary that wrote *Nonsense!* on a theme, and the pupil thought it was *Nonesuch!*—thought it was Latin. *(He laughs)* Amazingly funny! They say it looks like Solyony's in love with Irina, and he hates the Baron. . . . That's understandable. Irina is a very nice girl. She's quite like Masha, even—always thinking about something. Only you have a milder disposition, Irina. Though as a matter of fact Masha has a fine disposition too. I love her, Masha.

[At the rear of the garden, behind the stage, someone shouts: "Yoo-hoo!"]

    Irina: *(Shivering)* Somehow everything frightens me today. *(A pause)* I've got everything packed already, I'm sending my things off right after dinner. The Baron and I are getting married tomorrow, tomorrow we leave for the brickyard, and day after tomorrow I'll already be at school, the new life will have begun. Somehow God will help me! When I passed my teacher's examination I wept for joy . . . so grateful . . . *(A pause)* In a little while the horse and the cart will be here for my things. . . .

    Kulygin: That's all right, only somehow it isn't serious. It's all just ideas, and hardly anything really serious. Still, though, I wish you luck from the bottom of my heart.

Chebutykin: *(With emotion)* My dearest, my treasure. . . . My wonderful girl. . . . You have gone on far ahead, I'll never catch up with you. I'm left behind like a bird that's grown old, too old to fly. Fly on, my dears, fly on and God be with you! *(A pause)* It's a shame you shaved off your moustache, Fyodor Ilich.

    Kulygin: That's enough from you! *(He sighs)* Well, the soldiers leave today, and then everything will be the way it used to be. No matter what they say, Masha is a good, honest woman, I love her very much, and I'm thankful for my fate. . . . People have such different fates. . . . There's a man named Kozyrev that works in the tax department here. He went to school with me, but they expelled him from high school because he just couldn't manage to understand *ut consecutivum*.[10] Now he's terribly poor, sick, and when we meet each other I say to him, "Hello, *ut consecutivum!*" Yes, he says, that's it, *consecutivum*, and he coughs. . . . And I've been lucky all my life, I've even got the Order of Stanislav Second Class, I myself am teaching others, now, that *ut consecutivum*. Of course, I'm an intelligent man, more intelligent than lots of people, but happiness doesn't consist in that. . . .

[Inside the house someone plays "The Maiden's Prayer" on the piano]

    Irina: Tomorrow evening I won't be hearing that "Maiden's Prayer" any more, I won't be meeting that Protopopov. . . . *(A pause)* And Protopopov's sitting there in the living room—he's come today too. . . .

  Kulygin: The headmistress still hasn't arrived?

    Irina: No. They've sent for her. If only you knew how hard it is for me to live here alone, without Olga. . . . She lives at the high school; she's the headmistress, all day she's busy with her job, and I'm alone, I'm bored, there's nothing to do, I hate the very room I live in. . . . So I just made up my mind: If it's fated for me not to live in Moscow, then that's that. It means, it's fate. There's nothing to be done about it. . . . It's all in God's hands, that's the truth. Nikolai Lvovich proposed to me. . . . Well? I thought it over and made up my mind. He's a good man, it really is extraordinary how good . . . and all at once it was as if my soul had wings, I was happy, I felt all relieved, I wanted to work all over again, to work! . . . Only something happened yesterday, there's something mysterious hanging over me. . . .

Chebutykin: Nonesuch. Nonsense.

  Natasha: *(At the window)* The headmistress!

  Kulygin: The headmistress has arrived. Let's go on in.

[He and Irina *go into the house]*

Chebutykin: *(Reading the newspaper and singing softly to himself)* Ta-ra-ra-boom-de-aye . . . / Sit on a log I may . . .

[Masha comes up; Andrei *passes across the back of the stage wheeling the baby carriage]*

---

10. A grammatical construction in Latin

Masha: He sits there. There he sits.

Chebutykin: So what?

Masha: (Sitting down) Nothing. . . . *(A pause)* Did you love my mother?

Chebutykin: Very much.

Masha: And she loved you?

Chebutykin: (After a pause) I don't remember any more.

Masha: Is my man here? That's the way our cook Marfa used to talk about her policeman—my man. Is my man here?

Chebutykin: Not yet.

Masha: When you get happiness in snatches, in shreds, and then lose it the way I'm losing it, little by little you get coarse, you get furious. *(She points to her breast)* In here I'm boiling. . . . *(She looks at* Andrei, *who again crosses the stage with the baby carriage)* There's that little brother of ours, our Andrei. . . . All our hopes vanished. Once upon a time there was a great bell, thousands of people were raising it, ever so much work and money had gone into it, and all of a sudden it fell and broke. All of a sudden, for no reason at all. And that's Andrei.

Andrei: Aren't they ever going to quiet down in the house? What a hubbub!

Chebutykin: In a little. *(He looks at his watch)* I've got an old-fashioned watch, it strikes. . . . *(He winds the watch, it strikes)* The first and the second and the fifth batteries leave at one o'clock sharp. *(A pause)* And I leave tomorrow.

Masha: For good?

Chebutykin: I don't know. Maybe I'll be back in a year. Except . . . the devil knows. . . . What's the difference! . . .

[Somewhere in the distance a harp and violin are playing]

Andrei: The town will be deserted. It will be as if they'd put all the lights out. *(A pause)* Something happened yesterday up by the theater—everybody's talking about it, but I haven't any idea.

Chebutykin: Nothing. Just nonsense. Solyony started bothering the Baron, and he got mad and insulted him, and finally Solyony had to challenge him to a duel. *(He looks at his watch)* It's already about time. . . . At half past twelve, in the state forest over there, the one you can see across the river. . . . Piff-Paff! *(He laughs)* Solyony's got the idea he's Lermontov, and even writes little poems. A joke is a joke, but this is his third duel already.

Masha: Whose?

Chebutykin: Solyony's.

Masha: And the Baron?

Chebutykin: What about the Baron? *(A pause)*

Masha: It's all mixed up in my head. . . . Just the same, I say it isn't right to allow them to. He might wound the Baron or even kill him.

Chebutykin: The Baron's a good man, but one baron more, one baron less—what's the difference?

[Someone shouts from beyond the garden: "Yoo-hoo!"]

You wait. That's Skvortsov shouting, one of the seconds. He's in the boat. *(A pause)*

Andrei: In my opinion, to take part in a duel, to be present at one even in the capacity of a doctor, is simply immoral.

Chebutykin: It only looks that way. . . . We're not here, there's nothing in this world, we don't exist, it looks like we exist. . . . And what's the difference anyway!

Masha: That's how it is—the whole day long they talk, talk. . . . *(She walks away)* To live in a climate where you have to expect it to snow every minute—and then on top of it, that's the way they talk. *(She stops)* I won't go into that house, I can't bear it. . . . Tell me when Vershinin comes. . . . *(She goes off along the avenue of trees)* And the birds are flying south already. . . . Swans or geese. . . . *(She looks up)* My beautiful ones, my happy ones. . . .

[She goes out]

Andrei: Our house will be deserted. The officers are leaving, you're leaving, my sister's getting married, and I'll be the only one left.

Chebutykin: And your wife?

[Ferapont comes in with some papers]

Andrei: A wife's a wife. She's honest, sincere—well, kind, but at the same time there's something in her that makes her a kind of blind, petty, hairy animal. In any case, she's not a human being. I'm saying this to you as my friend, the only one I can really talk to. I love Natasha, that's so, but sometimes she seems to me astonishingly vulgar, and then I just despair, I can't understand why I love her as much as I do—or anyway, did. . . .

Chebutykin: *(Getting up)* Brother, I'm going away tomorrow, we may never see each other again, so here's my advice to you. Put on your hat, take your walking stick in your hand, and get out . . . get out, keep going, don't ever look back. And the farther you go the better.

[Solyony walks across the back of the stage, along with two Officers; seeing Chebutykin, he turns toward him—the other Officers walk on]

Solyony: Doctor, it's time! It's already half past twelve. *(He shakes hands with* Andrei)

Chebutykin: In a minute. I'm sick of all of you. *(To* Andrei) If anybody wants me, Andrei boy, tell them I'll be back in a minute. . . . *(He sighs)* Oh—oh—oh!

Solyony: Before he'd time to get his breath /
The bear was hugging him to death. *(He goes with him)* What are you groaning about, old man?

Chebutykin: Well . . .

Solyony: How're you feeling?

Chebutykin: *(Angrily)* As snug as a bug in a rug!

Solyony: The old man's unduly excited. I'm only going to indulge myself a little, I'll just shoot him like a snipe. *(He takes out a bottle of perfume and sprinkles it on his hands)* I've used up the whole bottle today, and they still smell. They smell like a corpse. *(A pause)* So. . . . Remember the poem? "But he, the rebel, seeks the storm /
As if in tempests there were peace . . ."[11]

Chebutykin: Uh-huh. "Before he'd time to get his breath
The bear was hugging him to death."

[He and Solyony *go out.*

People shout, "Yoo-hoo! Yoo-hoo!" Andrei *and* Ferapont *come in.]*

Ferapont: Papers to sign. . . .

Andrei: *(Nervously)* Leave me alone! Leave me alone! *I beg you!*

[He goes off with the carriage]

Ferapont: But that's what papers are for, you know, to sign.

[He goes to the back of the stage.

Irina *and* Tuzenbach *come in; he is wearing a straw hat.* Kulygin *crosses the stage, calling: "Yoo-hoo, Masha! Yoo-hoo!"]*

Tuzenbach: I believe he's the only person in town that's glad the soldiers are leaving.

Irina: That's understandable. *(A pause)* The town's getting all empty.

Tuzenbach: *(After looking at his watch)* Dear, I'll be back in a minute.

Irina: Where are you going?

Tuzenbach: I have to go in to town, to—to say good-bye to my friends.

Irina: That's not so. . . . Nikolai, why are you so upset today? *(A pause)* What happened yesterday, by the theater?

---

11. Concluding lines of "The Sail" by Mikhail Yuryevich Lermontov (1814–1841).

Tuzenbach: (*With a movement of impatience*) In an hour I'll come back and be with you again. (*He kisses her hands*) My beloved . . . (*He looks into her face*) For five years now I've been in love with you, and still I can't get used to it, and you seem more beautiful to me all the time. What marvelous, wonderful hair! What eyes! Tomorrow I'll take you away, we'll work, we'll be rich, my dreams will come true. You'll be happy. Only there's one thing wrong, just one thing wrong: you don't love me!

Irina: It isn't in my power! I'll be your wife, I'll be faithful and obedient, but it's not love, oh, what is there I can do? (*She cries*) I never have been in love in my life, not even once. Oh, I've dreamed so about love, dreamed about love so long now, day and night, but my soul is like some expensive piano that's locked and the key lost. (*A pause*) You look so worried.

Tuzenbach: I didn't sleep all night. There isn't anything in my life terrible enough to frighten me, only that lost key tortures me, it won't let me sleep. Say something to me. (*A pause*) Say something to me. . . .

Irina: What? What is there to say? What?

Tuzenbach: Something.

Irina: That's enough, that's enough! . . . (*A pause*)

Tuzenbach: What senseless things, what idiotic little things suddenly, for no reason, start to matter in your life! You laugh at them the way you did before, you know they're senseless, and yet you go on and on and haven't the strength to stop. Oh, let's not talk about it! I'm happy. It's as if I were seeing for the first time in my life these firs and maples and birches, and they are all looking at me curiously and waiting. What beautiful trees, and how beautiful life ought to be under them! (*A shout: "Yoohoo!"*) I must go, it's already time. . . . See that tree, it's dried up, but the wind moves it with the others just the same. So it seems to me that if I die, still, some way or other I'll have a share in life. Good-bye, my darling. . . . (*He kisses her hands*) The papers you gave me are on my table under the calendar.

Irina: I'm going with you.

Tuzenbach: (*Uneasily*) No, no! (*He goes away quickly, then stops by the avenue of trees*) Irina!

Irina: What?

Tuzenbach: (*Not knowing what to say*) I didn't have any coffee this morning. Tell them to make me some. . . .

[*He goes out quickly.*

Irina *stands lost in thought, then goes to the back of the stage and sits down in the swing.*

Andrei *comes in with the baby carriage;* Ferapont *appears.*]

Ferapont: Andrei Sergeevich, they're not my papers, you know, they're the government's. I didn't think them up.

Andrei: Oh, where's it gone, what's become of it—my past, when I was young and gay and clever, when I had such beautiful dreams, such beautiful thoughts, when my present and future were bright with hope? Why is it that, almost before we've begun to live, we get boring, drab, uninteresting, lazy, indifferent, useless, unhappy? . . . Our town's been in existence for two hundred years, there's a hundred thousand people living in it, and there's not one of them that's not exactly the same as the others; there never has been in it, either in the past or in the present, a single saint, a single scholar, a single artist, a single person famous enough for anybody to envy him or try to be like him. . . . They just eat, drink, sleep, and then die. . . . And some more are born and they too eat, drink, sleep, and so as not to die of boredom they fill their lives with nasty gossip, vodka, cards, affairs, and the wives deceive their husbands and the husbands lie and pretend they don't see anything, and a kind of inexorable vulgarity oppresses the children, and the divine spark within them dies, and they become the same pitiful, absolutely identical corpses that their mothers and fathers were before them. . . . *(To* Ferapont, *angrily)* What do you want?

Ferapont: What? Papers to sign.

Andrei: I'm sick of you.

Ferapont: A while ago the doorman at the courthouse was saying—in Petersburg last winter, he says, it seems as how it was two hundred degrees below zero.

Andrei: The present's disgusting, but on the other hand, when I think of the future—oh, then it's so good! I feel so light, so free: Off there in the distance the light dawns, I see freedom, I see my children and myself freed from laziness, from vodka, from goose with cabbage, from naps after dinner, from all this laziness and cowardice. . . .

Ferapont: It seems as how two thousand people were frozen to death. He says people were terrified. Either it was Petersburg or Moscow, I don't remember.

Andrei: *(Suddenly overcome with tenderness)* My own darling sisters, my wonderful sisters . . . *(Tearfully)* Masha, my own sister . . .

Natasha: Who's that making all that noise out there? Is that you, Andrei? You'll wake Baby Sophie! You know you ought not to make any noise, Sophie's asleep. You're as clumsy as a bear. If you want to talk, then give the baby carriage and the baby to someone else! Ferapont, take the baby carriage from your master.

Ferapont: Yes'm.

Andrei: (Embarrassed) I was speaking in a low voice.

Natasha: (Behind the window, petting Bobik) Bobik! Naughty Bobik! Bad Bobik!

Andrei: (Glancing through the papers) All right, I'll look them over and sign the ones that have to be signed, and you can take them back to the board. . . .

[He goes into the house, reading the papers.

Ferapont pushes the baby carriage toward the back of the garden.]

Natasha: Bobik, tell Mother what's her name! You darling, you darling! And who's that over there? That's Aunt Olga. Say to your Aunt Olga: "How do you do, Olga!"

[Two street Musicians, *a* Man *and a* Girl, *come in and begin to play on a violin and harp;* Vershinin, Olga, *and* Anfisa *come out of the house and listen silently for a moment;* Irina *comes up]*

Olga: Our garden's like a vacant lot, they walk right through it. Nurse dear, give the musicians something.

Anfisa: (Giving something to the Musicians) Good-bye and God bless you! *(The* Musicians *bow and go out)* Poor things! If you've enough to eat you don't go around playing. *(To* Irina) Good morning, little Irina! *(She kisses her)* M-m-m-m, child, the life I lead! the life I lead! At the high school in a lovely government apartment, there with little Olga—that's what the Lord has vouchsafed me in my old age! Sinner that I am, never in my whole life have I lived the way I live now! . . . A big apartment, a government one, and I've a little room all to myself, a little bed—all government property! I go to sleep at night and—O Lord! Mother of God, there's nobody in the whole world happier than I am!

Vershinin: We're leaving right away, Olga Sergeevna. It's time I was going. *(A pause)* I wish you everything, everything. . . . Where is Marya Sergeevna?

Irina: She's somewhere in the garden. I'll go look for her.

Vershinin: Please do. I haven't much time.

Anfisa: I'll go look too. *(She calls)* Little Masha, yoo-hoo! *(She goes with* Irina *toward the back of the garden)* Yoo-hoo! Yoo-hoo!

Vershinin: Everything comes to an end. And so we too must part. *(He looks at his watch)* The town gave us a sort of lunch, we drank champagne, the mayor made a speech, I ate and listened, but my soul was here with you. . . . *(He looks around the garden)* I'll miss you.

Olga: Shall we see each other again, someday?

Vershinin: Most likely not. *(A pause)* My wife and my two little girls will be staying for two months more; please, if anything should happen, if they should need anything . . .

Olga: Yes, yes, of course. Don't even think about it. *(A pause)* By tomorrow there won't be a single soldier left in town, it will all be only a memory—and of course a new life will begin for us. . . . *(A pause)* Nothing turns out the way we want it to. I didn't want to be a headmistress, and just the same I've become one. It means we won't live in Moscow. . . .

Vershinin: Well. . . . Thank you for everything. Forgive me if anything wasn't what it should have been. . . . I've talked a lot, such a lot—and forgive me for that, don't hold it against me. . . .

Olga: *(Wiping her eyes)* Why doesn't Masha come on . . .

Vershinin: What is there left for me to say to you, in farewell? What's left to philosophize about? . . . *(He laughs)* Life is hard. It seems to many of us lonely and hopeless—but just the same you've got to admit it's gradually getting clearer and lighter, and plainly the time isn't too far away when it will be entirely bright. *(He looks at his watch)* It's time for me to leave, it's time! In the old days mankind was busy with wars, its whole existence was filled with campaigns, invasions, conquests, but nowadays we've outlived all that. It's left behind an enormous vacuum which, so far, there is nothing to fill; mankind is passionately searching for it and of course will find it. Ah, if only it would come more quickly! *(A pause)* You know, if only industry could be added to education, and education to industry . . . *(He looks at his watch)* But it's time I was going. . . .

Olga: Here she comes.

Vershinin: I came to say good-bye. . . .

[Olga *goes off a little to the side, in order to let them say good-bye*]

Masha: *(Looking into his face)* Good-bye. . . . *(A long kiss)*

Olga: There, there . . . (Masha *is sobbing violently*)

Vershinin: Write me. . . . Don't forget me! Let me go . . . it's time. . . . Olga Sergeevna, take her, I'm already . . . it's time . . . I'm late . . .

[Moved, *he kisses* Olga's *hands, then once again embraces* Masha *and quickly goes out*]

Olga: There, Masha, there. . . . Stop, darling. . . .

[Kulygin *enters*]

Kulygin: *(Embarrassed)* It's all right, let her cry, let her. . . . My good Masha, my sweet Masha. . . . You're my wife, and I'm happy, no matter what happens. . . . I don't complain, I don't reproach you for a single thing. There's Olga, she'll be our witness. . . . Let's start over and live the way we used to, and I won't by so much as a single word, by the least hint . . .

Masha: *(Stifling her sobs)* By the curved seastrand a green oak stands, /
A chain of gold upon it . . . a chain of gold upon it . . . I'm going out of my mind. . . . By the curved seastrand . . . a green oak . . .

Olga: Hush, Masha. . . . Hush. . . . Give her some water.

Masha: I'm not crying any more. . . .

Kulygin: She's not crying any more. . . . She's a good girl. . . .

[A muffled, far-off shot is heard]

Masha: By the curved seastrand a green oak stands, /
A chain of gold upon it . . . a green cat . . . a green oak . . . I'm all mixed up. . . . *(She takes a drink of water)* My life's all wrong. I don't want anything any more. . . . I'll be all right in a minute. . . . What difference is anything anyway? . . . What does it mean, *by the curved seastrand*? Why do I keep saying that? My thoughts are all mixed up.

[Irina *enters*]

Olga: Hush, Masha. Now you're being a sensible girl. . . . Let's go on in. . . .

Masha: *(Angrily)* I won't go in there. *(She sobs, but immediately stops herself)* I don't go in that house any more, and I won't now. . . .

Irina: Let's just sit together for a while and not say anything. . . . Tomorrow I'm going, you know. . . .

Kulygin: Yesterday I took this moustache and beard away from one of the boys in my class. . . . *(He puts on the moustache and beard)* I look just like the German teacher. . . . *(He laughs)* Don't I? They're funny, those boys. . . .

Masha: You really do look just like that German of yours.

Olga: *(Laughing)* You do. (Masha *cries*)

Irina: There, Masha, there!

Kulygin: Just like . . .

[Natasha *comes in*]

Natasha: *(To the maid)* What? Protopopov's going to sit with Baby Sophie, and Andrei Sergeevich can take Bobik for a ride. Children are so much trouble. . . . *(To Irina)* Irina, you're leaving tomorrow—such a pity! Do stay at least one week more! *(She catches sight of Kulygin and shrieks; he laughs and takes off his moustache and beard)* What on earth—get out, how you did scare me! *(To Irina)* I'll miss you—do you think having you leave is going to be easy for me? I've told them to put Andrei and his violin in your room—let him saw away in there!—and we're going to put Baby Sophie in his room. That wonderful, marvelous child! What a girl! Today she looked up at me with the most extraordinary expression in her eyes and—"Mama!"

Kulygin: A beautiful child, that's so.

Natasha: So tomorrow I'll be all alone here. *(She sighs)* First of all I'm going to have them chop down all those fir trees along the walk, and then that maple. . . . In the evening it's so ugly. . . . *(To* Irina*)* Dear, that belt isn't a bit becoming to you. . . . It's in bad taste—you need something a little brighter. . . . And I'm having them plant darling little flowers everywhere—how they will smell! *(Sternly)* What's this fork doing lying around on this bench? *(She goes into the house; to the* Maid*)* Will you tell me what this fork is doing lying around on this bench? *(She shouts)* Don't you dare talk back to me!

Kulygin: There she goes again!

[*Behind the scene a band is playing a march; everybody listens*]

    Olga: They are leaving.

[*She goes away.*

Chebutykin *comes in.*]

    Masha: Our friends are leaving. Well, let's wish them a happy journey! *(To her husband)* We must go home. Where are my hat and cape?

    Kulygin: I took them indoors. . . . I'll get them right away.

[*He goes into the house*]

    Olga: Yes, now we can all go home. It's time.

Chebutykin: Olga Sergeevna!

    Olga: What is it? *(A pause)* What is it?

Chebutykin: Nothing. . . . I don't know how to tell you. . . . *(He whispers in her ear)*

    Olga: *(Alarmed)* It's not possible!

Chebutykin: Yes. . . . What a mess! . . . I'm worn out, I'm sick and tired of it. I don't want to say another word. . . . *(Irritably)* Anyway, what's the difference!

    Masha: What's happened?

    Olga: *(Putting her arms around* Irina*)* This is a terrible day. I don't know how to tell you, my darling. . . .

    Irina: What? Tell me right away, what? For God's sake! *(She cries)*

Chebutykin: A little while ago the Baron was killed in a duel.

    Irina: *(Crying softly)* I knew, I knew. . . .

Chebutykin: (Sitting down on a bench at the back of the stage) I'm worn out. . . . *(He takes a newspaper out of his pocket)* Let 'em cry. . . . *(He sings softly)* Ta-ra-ra-boom-de-aye . . . / Sit on a log I may . . . What's the difference anyway? *(The* Three Sisters *stand nestled against one another)*

Masha: Oh, how the music is playing! They are leaving us, one is really gone, really, gone forever and ever; we'll stay here alone, to begin our life over again. We must live . . . we must live . . .

Irina: (Putting her head on Olga's *breast)* The time will come when everyone will know why all this is, what these sufferings are for, there will be no more secrets—but in the meantime we must live . . . must work, only work! Tomorrow I'll go away alone, I'll teach in the school and give my life to those who'll need it, perhaps. It's fall now, soon the winter will come and cover everything with snow, and I will work, I will work . . .

Olga: (Putting her arms around both her sisters) The music is playing so gaily, so eagerly, and one wants so to live! Oh, my God! Time will pass, and we shall be gone forever, they will forget us —they'll forget our faces, our voices, and how many of us there were, but our sufferings will change into joy for those who will live after us, happiness and peace will come on earth, and they'll be reminded and speak tenderly of those who are living now, they will bless them. Oh, dear sisters, our life isn't over yet. We shall live! The music is playing so gaily, so joyfully, and it seems as though a little more and we shall know why we live, why we suffer. . . . If only we knew, if only we knew!

[The music grows fainter and fainter; Kulygin, *smiling happily, brings the hat and cape;* Andrei *pushes* Bobik *across the stage in the baby carriage]*

Chebutykin: (Singing softly) Ta-ra-ra-boom-de-aye. Sit on a log I may . . . *(He reads the newspaper)* What's the difference anyway! What's the difference!

Olga: If only we knew, if only we knew!

CURTAIN

The realism of Anton Chekhov's plays, their mixture of themes and moods, makes them sometimes almost as hard to interpret as life itself. When The Three Sisters *was first read by the actors of the Moscow Arts Theater, for example, they felt primarily its note of melancholy and took it for a tragedy. Chekhov, who was present at the reading, was embarrassed and troubled*

because he saw the play as a comedy. Randall Jarrell, who translated the play in 1964, saw it neither as a tragedy nor a comedy but emphasized its blend of loneliness and music.

"To the lonely man the world is a desert": Randall Jarrell

Loneliness (hardly a value or a philosophy) becomes a sort of ghost that haunts Andrei all the time, Irina until she gets older, and Solyony under cover of his Lermontov personality. Loneliness pervaded Chekhov's own life in similar ways. He wrote someone, "I positively cannot live without guests. When I am alone, for some reason I become terrified, just as though I were in a frail little boat on a great ocean." . . .

For years he wore a seal ring with these words: "To the lonely man the world is a desert." He keeps us conscious of the loneliness underneath the general animation. At the birthday party in Act I, there is Vershinin's line about the gloomy-looking bridge in Moscow where the water under it could be heard: "It makes a lonely man feel sad." Later on we hear again when Chebutykin tells Andrei about being unmarried, even if marriage is boring: "But the loneliness! You can philosophize as much as you please, but loneliness is a terrible thing, Andrei. . . ." With the "good-bye trees" and "good-bye echo" and the embraces, tears, *au revoir*'s and farewells, loneliness has built up like entropy as the good social group—that partly kept people from being lonely—has been broken into by the inferior outside world. The organized enclave of Act I, after being invaded by the relatively unorganized environment, loses its own organization like a physical system and runs down to almost nothing . . . Andrei.

The musical side of Russian life, and Chekhov, comes into the play in every act: Masha whistles, the carnival people play offstage, Chebutykin sings nervously after the duel. Specifically, Act I opens with Olga remembering the band's funeral march after the father's death and Act IV ends with the band playing a march as the brigade leaves and Olga has her last, summarizing speech. The "yoo-hoos" beforehand have imparted a faintly musical nostalgia to the scene, too. In Acts I and II there are guitar and piano and singing. "My New Porch" is a song everyone knows like "Old MacDonald Had a Farm," so that when Tuzenbach starts it off, even lonely Andrei and old Chebutykin can carry it along. Masha and Vershinin's duet becomes a witty—but entirely different—parallel of this formula. The camaraderie at the bottom of the first is countered with the romantic insinuation of the second. "Unto love all ages bow, its pangs are blest . . ." leaves nothing in doubt, and when Masha sings a refrain of this and Vershinin adds another, they make a musical declaration of love. This is an excellent preparation for Act III when, after Masha's love confession, it would have been awkward for Vershinin and her to appear together on stage. Their intimacy is even strengthened, in our minds, by his off-stage song to Masha which she hears, comprehends, and answers in song before leaving the stage to join him.

There was always a piano in Chekhov's house, and having someone play helped him to write when he got stuck. Rhythms came naturally to him, and just as he has varied them in the lines of *The Three Sisters*—from the shortest (sounds, single words) to the arias and big set speeches—similarly there is a rhythmic pattern like that on a railway platform where all the people know each other and little groups leave, say good-bye, meet.

SAMUEL BECKETT

(b. 1906)

KRAPP'S LAST TAPE

A late evening in the future.

Krapp's den.

Front centre a small table, the two drawers of which open towards audience.

Sitting at the table, facing front, i.e. across from the drawers, a bearish old man: Krapp.

Rusty black narrow trousers too short for him. Rusty black sleeveless waistcoat, four capacious pockets. Heavy silver watch and chain. Grimy white shirt open at neck, no collar. Surprising pair of dirty white boots, size ten at least, very narrow and pointed.

White face. Purple nose. Disordered grey hair. Unshaven.

Very near-sighted (but unspectacled). Hard of hearing.

Cracked voice. Distinctive intonation.

Laborious walk.

On the table a tape-recorder with microphone and a number of cardboard boxes containing reels of recorded tapes.

Table and immediately adjacent area in strong white light. Rest of stage in darkness.

Krapp remains a moment motionless, heaves a great sigh, looks at his watch, fumbles in his pockets, takes out an envelope, puts it back, fumbles, takes out a small bunch of keys, raises it to his eyes, chooses a key, gets up and moves to front of table. He stoops, unlocks first drawer, peers into it, feels about inside it, takes out a reel of tape, peers at it, puts it back, locks drawer, unlocks second drawer, peers into it, feels about inside it, takes out a large banana, peers at it, locks drawer, puts keys back in his pocket. He turns, advances to edge of stage, halts, strokes banana, peels it, drops skin at his feet, puts end of banana in his mouth and remains motionless, staring vacuously before him. Finally he bites off the end, turns aside and begins pacing to and fro at edge of stage, in the light, i.e. not more than four or five paces either way, meditatively eating banana. He treads on skin, slips, nearly falls, recovers himself, stoops and peers at skin and finally pushes it, still stooping, with his foot over the edge of stage into pit. He resumes his pacing, finishes banana, returns to table, sits down, remains a moment motionless, heaves a great sigh, takes keys from his pockets, raises them to his eyes, chooses key, gets up and moves to front of table, unlocks second drawer, takes out a second large banana, peers at it, locks drawer, puts back keys in his pocket, turns, advances to edge of stage, halts, strokes banana, peels it, tosses skin into pit, puts end of banana in his mouth and remains motion-less, staring vacuously before him. Finally he has an idea, puts banana in his waistcoat pocket, the end emerging, and goes with all the speed he can muster back-stage into darkness. Ten seconds. Loud pop of cork. Fifteen seconds. He comes back into light carrying an old ledger and sits down at table. He lays ledger on table, wipes his mouth, wipes his hands on the front of his waistcoat, brings them smartly together and rubs them.

Krapp: *(briskly.)* Ah! *(He bends over ledger, turns the pages, finds the entry he wants, reads.)* Box . . . thrree . . . spool . . . five. *(He raises his head and stares front. With relish.)* Spool! *(Pause.)* Spooool! *(Happy smile. Pause. He bends over table, starts peering and poking at the boxes.)* Box . . . thrree . . . thrree . . . four . . . two . . . *(with surprise)* nine! good God! . . . seven . . . ah! the little rascal! *(He takes up box, peers at it.)* Box thrree. *(He lays it on table, opens it and peers at spools inside.)* Spool . . . *(he peers at ledger)* . . . five . . . *(he peers at spools)* . . . five . . . five . . . ah! the little scoundrel! *(He takes out a spool, peers at it.)* Spool five. *(He lays it on table, closes box three, puts it back with the others, takes up the spool.)* Box thrree, spool five. *(He bends over the machine, looks up. With relish.)* Spooool! *(Happy smile. He bends, loads spool on machine, rubs his hands.)* Ah! *(He peers at ledger, reads entry at foot of page.)* Mother at rest at last . . . Hm . . . The black ball . . . *(He raises his head, stares blankly front. Puzzled.)* Black ball? . . . *(He peers again at ledger, reads.)* The dark nurse . . . *(He raises his head, broods, peers again at ledger, reads.)* Slight improvement in bowel condition . . . Hm . . . Memorable . . . what? *(He peers closer.)* Equinox, memorable equinox. *(He raises his head, stares blankly front. Puzzled.)* Memorable equinox? . . . *(Pause. He shrugs his shoulders, peers again at ledger, reads.)* Farewell to—*(he turns the page)*—love.

He raises his head, broods, bends over machine, switches on and assumes listening posture, i.e. leaning forward, elbows on table, hand cupping ear towards machine, face front.

Tape: *(strong voice, rather pompous, clearly Krapp's at a much earlier time.)* Thirty-nine today, sound as a—*(Settling himself more comfort-ably he knocks one of the boxes off the table, curses, switches off, sweeps boxes and ledger violently to the ground, winds tape back to beginning, switches on, resumes posture.)* Thirty-nine today, sound as a bell, apart from my old weakness, and intellectually I have now every reason to suspect at the . . . *(hesitates)* . . . crest of the wave—or thereabouts. Celebrated the awful occasion, as in recent years, quietly at the Winehouse. Not a soul. Sat before the fire with closed eyes, separating the grain from the husks. Jotted down a few notes, on the back of an envelope. Good to be back in my den, in my old rags. Have just eaten I regret to say three bananas and only with difficulty refrained from a fourth. Fatal things for a man with my condition. *(Vehemently.)* Cut 'em out! *(Pause.)* The new light above my table is a great improvement. With all this darkness round me I feel less alone. *(Pause.)* In a way. *(Pause.)* I love to get up and move about in it, then back here to . . . *(hesitates)* . . . me. *(Pause.)* Krapp.

Pause.

The grain, now what I wonder do I mean by that, I mean . . . *(hesitates)* . . . I suppose I mean those things worth having when all the dust has—when all *my* dust has settled. I close my eyes and try and imagine them.

Pause.

Krapp closes his eyes briefly.

Extraordinary silence this evening, I strain my ears and do not hear a sound. Old Miss McGlome always sings at this hour. But not tonight. Songs of her girlhood, she says. Hard to think of her as a girl. Wonderful woman though. Connaught, I fancy. *(Pause.)* Shall I sing when I am her age, if I ever am? No. *(Pause.)* Did I sing as a boy? No. *(Pause.)* Did I ever sing? No.

Pause.

Just been listening to an old year, passages at random. I did not check in the book, but it must be at least ten or twelve years ago. At that time I think I was still living on and off with Bianca in Kedar Street. Well out of that, Jesus yes! Hopeless business. *(Pause.)* Not much about her, apart from a tribute to her eyes. Very warm. I suddenly saw them again. *(Pause.)* Incomparable! *(Pause.)* Ah well . . . *(Pause.)* These old P.M.s are gruesome, but I often find them—*(Krapp switches off, broods, switches on)*—a help before embarking on a new . . . *(hesitates)* . . . retrospect. Hard to believe I was ever that young whelp. The voice! Jesus! And the aspirations! *(Brief laugh in which Krapp joins.)* And the resolutions! *(Brief laugh in which Krapp joins.)* To drink less, in particular. *(Brief laugh of Krapp alone.)* Statistics. Seventeen hundred hours, out of the preceding eight thousand odd, consumed on licensed premises alone. More than 20%, say 40% of his waking life. *(Pause.)* Plans for a less . . . *(hesitates)* . . . engrossing sexual life. Last illness of his father. Flagging pursuit of happiness. Unattainable laxation. Sneers at what he calls his youth and thanks to God that it's over. *(Pause.)* False ring there. *(Pause.)* Shadows of the opus . . . magnum. Closing with a—*(brief laugh)*—yelp to Providence. *(Prolonged laugh in which Krapp joins.)* What remains of all that misery? A girl in a shabby green coat, on a railway-station platform? No?

Pause.

When I look—

Krapp switches off, broods, looks at his watch, gets up, goes backstage into darkness. Ten seconds. Pop of cork. Ten seconds. Second cork. Ten seconds. Third cork. Ten seconds. Brief burst of quavering song.

Krapp: *(sings).*   Now the day is over,
                      Night is drawing nigh-igh,
                      Shadows—

Fit of coughing. He comes back into light, sits down, wipes his mouth, switches on, resumes his listening posture.

Tape: —back on the year that is gone, with what I hope is perhaps a glint of the old eye to come, there is of course the house on the canal where mother lay a-dying, in the late autumn, after her long viduity *(Krapp gives a start)*, and the—*(Krapp switches off, winds back tape a little, bends his ear closer to machine, switches on)*—a-dying, after her long viduity, and the—

Krapp switches off, raises his head, stares blankly before him. His lips move in the syllables of "viduity." No sound. He gets up, goes backstage into darkness, comes back with an enormous dictionary, lays it on table, sits down and looks up the word.

Krapp: *(reading from dictionary.)* State—or condition of being—or remaining—a widow—or widower. *(Looks up. Puzzled.)* Being— or remaining? . . . *(Pause. He peers again at dictionary. Reading.)* "Deep weeds of viduity" . . . Also of an animal, especially a bird . . . the vidua or weaver-bird . . . Black plumage of male . . . *(He looks up. With relish.)* The vidua-bird!

Pause. He closes dictionary, switches on, resumes listening posture.

Tape: —bench by the weir from where I could see her window. There I sat, in the biting wind, wishing she were gone. *(Pause.)* Hardly a soul, just a few regulars, nursemaids, infants, old men, dogs. I got to know them quite well—oh by appearance of course I mean! One dark young beauty I recollect particularly, all white and starch, incomparable bosom, with a big black hooded perambulator, most funereal thing. Whenever I looked in her direction she had her eyes on me. And yet when I was bold enough to speak to her—not having been introduced—she threatened to call a policeman. As if I had designs on her virtue! *(Laugh. Pause.)* The face she had! The eyes! Like . . . *(hesitates)* . . . chrysolite! *(Pause.)* Ah well . . . *(Pause.)* I was there when—*(Krapp switches off, broods, switches on again)*—the blind went down, one of those dirty brown roller affairs, throwing a ball for a little white dog, as chance would have it. I happened to look up and there it was. All over and done with, at last. I sat on for a few moments with the ball in my hand and the dog yelping and pawing at me. *(Pause.)* Moments. Her moments, my moments. *(Pause.)* The dog's moments. *(Pause.)* In the end I held it out to him and he took it in his mouth, gently, gently. A small, old, black, hard, solid rubber ball. *(Pause.)* I might have kept it. *(Pause.)* But I gave it to the dog.

Pause.

Ah well . . .

Pause.

Spiritually a year of profound gloom and indigence until that memorable night in March, at the end of the jetty, in the howling wind, never to be forgotten, when suddenly I saw the whole thing. The vision, at last. This I fancy is what I have chiefly to record this evening, against the day when my work will be done and perhaps no place left in my memory, warm or cold, for the miracle that . . . *(hesitates)* . . . for the fire that set it alight. What I suddenly saw then was this, that the belief I had been going on all my life, namely— *(Krapp switches off impatiently, winds tape forward, switches on again)* —great granite rocks the foam flying up in the light of the lighthouse and the wind-gauge spinning like a propellor, clear to me at last that the dark I have always struggled to keep under is in reality my most—*(Krapp curses, switches off, winds tape forward, switches on again)*—unshatterable association until my dissolution of storm and night with the light of the understanding and the fire —*(Krapp curses louder, switches off, winds tape forward, switches on again)*—my face in her breasts and my hand on her. We lay there without moving. But under us all moved, and moved us, gently, up and down, and from side to side.

Pause.

Past midnight. Never knew such silence. The earth might be uninhabited.

Pause.

Here I end—

Krapp switches off, winds tape back, switches on again.

—upper lake, with the punt, bathed off the bank, then pushed out into the stream and drifted. She lay stretched out on the floorboards with her hands under her head and her eyes closed. Sun blazing down, bit of a breeze, water nice and lively. I noticed a scratch on her thigh and asked her how she came by it. Picking gooseberries, she said. I said again I thought it was hopeless and no good going on, and she agreed, without opening her eyes. *(Pause.)* I asked her to look at me and after a few moments—*(pause)*—after a few moments she did, but the eyes just slits, because of the glare. I bent over her to get them in the shadow and they opened. *(Pause. Low.)* Let me in. *(Pause.)* We drifted in among the flags and stuck. The way they went down, sighing, before the stem! *(Pause.)* I lay down across her with my face in her breasts and my hand on her. We lay there without moving. But under us all moved, and moved us, gently, up and down, and from side to side.

Pause.

Past midnight. Never knew—

Krapp switches off, broods. Finally he fumbles in his pockets, encounters the banana, takes it out, peers at it, puts it back, fumbles, brings out the envelope, fumbles, puts back envelope, looks at his watch, gets up and goes backstage into darkness. Ten seconds. Sound of bottle against glass, then brief siphon. Ten seconds. Bottle against glass alone. Ten seconds. He comes back a little unsteadily into light, goes to front of table, takes out keys, raises them to his eyes, chooses key, unlocks first drawer, peers into it, feels about inside, takes out reel, peers at it, locks drawer, puts keys back in his pocket, goes and sits down, takes reel off machine, lays it on dictionary, loads virgin reel on machine, takes envelope from his pocket, consults back of it, lays it on table, switches on, clears his throat and begins to record.

Krapp: Just been listening to that stupid bastard I took myself for thirty years ago, hard to believe I was ever as bad as that. Thank God that's all done with anyway. *(Pause.)* The eyes she had! *(Broods, realizes he is recording silence, switches off, broods. Finally.)* Everything there, everything, all the—*(Realizes this is not being recorded, switches on.)* Everything there, everything on this old muckball, all the light and dark and famine and feasting of . . . *(hesitates)* . . . the ages! *(In a shout.)* Yes! *(Pause.)* Let that go! Jesus! Take his mind off his homework! Jesus! *(Pause. Weary.)* Ah well, maybe he was right. *(Pause.)* Maybe he was right. *(Broods. Realizes. Switches off. Consults envelope.)* Pah! *(Crumples it and throws it away. Broods. Switches on.)* Nothing to say, not a squeak. What's a year now? The sour cud and the iron stool. *(Pause.)* Revelled in the word spool. *(With relish.)* Spooool! Happiest moment of the past half million. *(Pause.)* Seventeen copies sold, of which eleven at trade price to free circulating libraries beyond the seas. Getting known. *(Pause.)* One pound six and something, eight I have little doubt. *(Pause.)* Crawled out once or twice, before the summer was cold. Sat shivering in the park, drowned in dreams and burning to be gone. Not a soul. *(Pause.)* Last fancies. *(Vehemently.)* Keep 'em under! *(Pause.)* Scalded the eyes out of me reading *Effie* again, a page a day, with tears again. Effie . . . (Pause.) Could have been happy with her, up there on the Baltic, and the pines, and the dunes. (Pause.) Could I? (Pause.) And she? (Pause.) Pah! (Pause.) Fanny came in a couple of times. Bony old ghost of a whore. Couldn't do much, but I suppose better than a kick in the crutch. The last time wasn't so bad. How do you manage it, she said, at your age? I told her I'd been saving up for her all my life. (Pause.) Went to Vespers once, like when I was in short trousers. (Pause. Sings.)

> Now the day is over,
> Night is drawing nigh-igh,
> Shadows—(coughing, then almost inaudible)—of the evening
> Steal across the sky.

(Gasping.) Went to sleep and fell off the pew. (Pause.) Sometimes wondered in the night if a last effort mightn't—(Pause.) Ah finish your booze now and get to your bed. Go on with this drivel in the morning. Or leave it at that. (Pause.) Leave it at that. (Pause.) Lie propped up in the dark—and wander. Be again in the dingle on a Christmas Eve, gathering holly, the red-berried. (Pause.) Be again on Croghan on a Sunday morning, in the haze, with the bitch, stop and listen to the bells. (Pause.) And so on. (Pause.) Be again, be again. (Pause.) All that old misery. (Pause.) Once wasn't enough for you. (Pause.) Lie down across her.

Long pause. He suddenly bends over machine, switches off, wrenches off tape, throws it away, puts on the other, winds it forward to the passage he wants, switches on, listens staring front.

Tape: —gooseberries, she said. I said again I thought it was hopeless and no good going on, and she agreed, without opening her eyes. (Pause.) I asked her to look at me and after a few moments— (pause)—after a few moments she did, but the eyes just slits, because of the glare. I bent over her to get them in the shadow and they opened. (Pause. Low.) Let me in. (Pause.) I lay down across her with my face in her breasts and my hand on her. We lay there without moving. But under us all moved, and moved us, gently, up and down, and from side to side.

Pause.

Krapp's lips move. No sound.

Past midnight. Never knew such silence. The earth might be uninhabited.

Pause.

Here I end this reel. Box—(pause)—three, spool—(pause)—five. (Pause.) Perhaps my best years are gone. When there was a chance of happiness. But I wouldn't want them back. Not with the fire in me now. No, I wouldn't want them back.

Krapp motionless staring before him. The tape runs on in silence.
CURTAIN

The "absurdist" plays of Samuel Beckett show characters whose lives seem to be reduced to a least common denominator rather than enlarged to the dimensions we associate with tragedy. The result according to some critics is a fine mixture of tragic and comic elements; other critics find Beckett's view of life too bleak to rise above mere pathos. Arthur Miller's distinction between the tragic and the pathetic can help us clarify the issue, regardless of which side we finally take.

"We forsake literature when we are content to chronicle disaster": Arthur Miller

Let me put it this way. When Mr. B., while walking down the street, is struck on the head by a falling piano, the newspapers call this a tragedy. In fact, of course, this is only the pathetic end of Mr. B. Not only because of the accidental nature of his death; that is elementary. It is pathetic because it merely arouses our feelings of sympathy, sadness, and possibly of identification. What the death of Mr. B. does not arouse is the tragic feeling.

To my mind the essential difference, and the precise difference, between tragedy and pathos is that tragedy brings us not only sadness, sympathy, identification and even fear; it also, unlike pathos, brings us knowledge or enlightenment.

But what sort of knowledge? In the largest sense, it is knowledge pertaining to the right way of living in the world. The manner of Mr. B.'s death was not such as to illustrate any principle of living. In short, there was no illumination of the ethical in it. And to put it all in the same breath, the reason we confuse the tragic with the pathetic, as well as why we create so few tragedies, is twofold: in the first place many of our writers have given up trying to search out the right way of living, and secondly, there is not among us any commonly accepted faith in a way of life that will give us not only material gain but satisfaction.

Our modern literature has filled itself with an attitude which implies that despite suffering, nothing important can really be learned by man that might raise him to a happier condition. The probing of the soul has taken the path of behaviorism. By this method it is sufficient for an artist simply to spell out the anatomy of disaster. Man is regarded as essentially a dumb animal moving through a preconstructed maze toward his inevitable sleep.

Such a concept of man can never reach beyond pathos, for enlightenment is impossible within it, life being regarded as an immutably disastrous fact. Tragedy, called a more exalted kind of consciousness, is so called because it makes us aware of what the character might have been. But to say or strongly imply what a man might have been requires of the author a soundly based, completely believed vision of man's great possibilities. As Aristotle said, the poet is greater than the historian because he presents not only things as they were, but foreshadows what they might have been. We forsake literature when we are content to chronicle disaster.

ARTHUR MILLER

(b. 1915)

DEATH OF A SALESMAN

CHARACTERS

Willy Loman
Linda
Biff
Happy
Bernard
The Woman
Charley
Uncle Ben
Howard Wagner
Jenny
Stanley
Miss Forsythe
Letta

The action takes place in Willy Loman's house and yard and in various places he visits in the New York and Boston of today.

Throughout the play, in the stage directions, left and right mean stage left and stage right.

ACT ONE

A melody is heard, played upon a flute. It is small and fine, telling of grass and trees and the horizon. The curtain rises.

Before us is the Salesman's house. We are aware of towering, angular shapes behind it, surrounding it on all sides. Only the blue light of the sky falls upon the house and forestage; the surrounding area shows an angry glow of orange. As more light appears, we see a solid vault of apartment houses around the small, fragile-seeming home. An air of the dream clings to the place, a dream rising out of reality. The kitchen at center seems actual enough, for there is a kitchen table with three chairs, and a refrigerator. But no other fixtures are seen. At the back of the kitchen there is a draped entrance, which leads to the living-room. To the right of the kitchen, on a level raised two feet, is a bedroom furnished only with a brass bedstead and a straight chair. On a shelf over the bed a silver athletic trophy stands. A window opens onto the apartment house at the side.

Behind the kitchen, on a level raised six and a half feet, is the boys' bedroom, at present barely visible. Two beds are dimly seen, and at the back of the room a dormer window. (This bedroom is above the unseen living-room.) At the left a stairway curves up to it from the kitchen.

The entire setting is wholly or, in some places, partially transparent. The roof-line of the house is one-dimensional; under and over it we see the apartment buildings. Before the house lies an apron, curving beyond the forestage into the orchestra. This forward area serves as the back yard as well as the locale of all Willy's imaginings and of his city scenes. Whenever the action is in the present the actors observe the imaginary wall-lines, entering the house only through its door at the left. But in the scenes of the past these boundaries are broken, and characters enter or leave a room by stepping "through" a wall onto the forestage.

From the right, Willy Loman, the Salesman, enters, carrying two large sample cases. The flute plays on. He hears but is not aware of it. He is past sixty years of age, dressed quietly. Even as he crosses the stage to the doorway of the house, his exhaustion is apparent. He unlocks the door, comes into the kitchen, and thankfully lets his burden down, feeling the soreness of his palms. A word-sigh escapes his lips—it might be "Oh, boy, oh, boy." He closes the door, then carries his cases out into the living-room, through the draped kitchen doorway.

Linda, his wife, has stirred in her bed at the right. She gets out and puts on a robe, listening. Most often jovial, she has developed an iron repression of her exceptions to Willy's behavior—she more than loves him, she admires him, as though his mercurial nature, his temper, his massive dreams and little cruelties, served her only as sharp reminders of the turbulent longings within him, longings which she shares but lacks the temperament to utter and follow to their end.

    Linda, (hearing Willy outside the bedroom, calls with some trepidation): Willy!

    Willy: It's all right. I came back.

    Linda: Why? What happened? (Slight pause.) Did something happen, Willy?

    Willy: No, nothing happened.

    Linda: You didn't smash the car, did you?

    Willy, (with casual irritation): I said nothing happened. Didn't you hear me?

    Linda: Don't you feel well?

    Willy: I'm tired to the death. (The flute has faded away. He sits on the bed beside her, a little numb.) I couldn't make it. I just couldn't make it, Linda.

    Linda, (very carefully, delicately): Where were you all day? You look terrible.

    Willy: I got as far as a little above Yonkers. I stopped for a cup of coffee. Maybe it was the coffee.

Linda: What?

Willy, (after a pause): I suddenly couldn't drive any more. The car kept going off onto the shoulder, y'know?

Linda, (helpfully): Oh. Maybe it was the steering again. I don't think Angelo knows the Studebaker.

Willy: No, it's me, it's me. Suddenly I realize I'm goin' sixty miles an hour and I don't remember the last five minutes. I'm—I can't seem to—keep my mind to it.

Linda: Maybe it's your glasses. You never went for your new glasses.

Willy: No, I see everything. I came back ten miles an hour. It took me nearly four hours from Yonkers.

Linda, (resigned): Well, you'll just have to take a rest, Willy, you can't continue this way.

Willy: I just got back from Florida.

Linda: But you didn't rest your mind. Your mind is overactive, and the mind is what counts, dear.

Willy: I'll start out in the morning. Maybe I'll feel better in the morning. *(She is taking off his shoes.)* These goddam arch supports are killing me.

Linda: Take an aspirin. Should I get you an aspirin? It'll soothe you.

Willy, (with wonder): I was driving along, you understand? And I was fine. I was even observing the scenery. You can imagine, me looking at scenery, on the road every week of my life. But it's so beautiful up there, Linda, the trees are so thick, and the sun is warm. I opened the windshield and just let the warm air bathe over me. And then all of a sudden I'm goin' off the road! I'm tellin' ya, I absolutely forgot I was driving. If I'd've gone the other way over the white line I might've killed somebody. So I went on again—and five minutes later I'm dreamin' again, and I nearly— *(He presses two fingers against his eyes.)* I have such thoughts, I have such strange thoughts.

Linda: Willy, dear. Talk to them again. There's no reason why you can't work in New York.

Willy: They don't need me in New York. I'm the New England man. I'm vital in New England.

Linda: But you're sixty years old. They can't expect you to keep traveling every week.

Willy: I'll have to send a wire to Portland. I'm supposed to see Brown and Morrison tomorrow morning at ten o'clock to show the line. Goddammit, I could sell them! *(He starts putting on his jacket.)*

Linda, (taking the jacket from him): Why don't you go down to the place tomorrow and tell Howard you've simply got to work in New York? You're too accommodating, dear.

Willy: If old man Wagner was alive I'd a been in charge of New York now! That man was a prince, he was a masterful man. But that boy of his, that Howard, he don't appreciate. When I went north the first time, the Wagner Company didn't know where New England was!

Linda: Why don't you tell those things to Howard, dear?

Willy, (encouraged): I will, I definitely will. Is there any cheese?

Linda: I'll make you a sandwich.

Willy: No, go to sleep. I'll take some milk. I'll be up right away. The boys in?

Linda: They're sleeping. Happy took Biff on a date tonight.

Willy, (interested): That so?

Linda: It was so nice to see them shaving together, one behind the other, in the bathroom. And going out together. You notice? The whole house smells of shaving lotion.

Willy: Figure it out. Work a lifetime to pay off a house. You finally own it, and there's nobody to live in it.

Linda: Well, dear, life is a casting off. It's always that way.

Willy: No, no, some people—some people accomplish something. Did Biff say anything after I went this morning?

Linda: You shouldn't have criticized him, Willy, especially after he just got off the train. You mustn't lose your temper with him.

Willy: When the hell did I lose my temper? I simply asked him if he was making any money. Is that a criticism?

Linda: But, dear, how could he make any money?

Willy, (worried and angered): There's such an undercurrent in him. He became a moody man. Did he apologize when I left this morning?

Linda: He was crestfallen, Willy. You know how he admires you. I think if he finds himself, then you'll both be happier and not fight any more.

Willy: How can he find himself on a farm? Is that a life? A farmhand? In the beginning, when he was young, I thought, well, a young man, it's good for him to tramp around, take a lot of different jobs. But it's more than ten years now and he has yet to make thirty-five dollars a week!

Linda: He's finding himself, Willy.

Willy: Not finding yourself at the age of thirty-four is a disgrace!

Linda: Shh!

Willy: The trouble is he's lazy, goddammit!

Linda: Willy, please!

Willy: Biff is a lazy bum!

Linda: They're sleeping. Get something to eat. Go on down.

Willy: Why did he come home? I would like to know what brought him home.

Linda: I don't know. I think he's still lost, Willy. I think he's very lost.

Willy: Biff Loman is lost. In the greatest country in the world a young man with such—personal attractiveness, gets lost. And such a hard worker. There's one thing about Biff—he's not lazy.

Linda: Never.

Willy, (with pity and resolve): I'll see him in the morning; I'll have a nice talk with him. I'll get him a job selling. He could be big in no time. My God! Remember how they used to follow him around in high school? When he smiled at one of them their faces lit up. When he walked down the street . . . *(He loses himself in reminiscences.)*

Linda, (trying to bring him out of it): Willy, dear, I got a new kind of American-type cheese today. It's whipped.

Willy: Why do you get American when I like Swiss?

Linda: I just thought you'd like a change—

Willy: I don't want a change! I want Swiss cheese. Why am I always being contradicted?

Linda, (with a covering laugh): I thought it would be a surprise.

Willy: Why don't you open a window in here, for God's sake?

Linda, (with infinite patience): They're all open, dear.

Willy: The way they boxed us in here. Bricks and windows, windows and bricks.

Linda: We should've bought the land next door.

Willy: The street is lined with cars. There's not a breath of fresh air in the neighborhood. The grass don't grow any more, you can't raise a carrot in the back yard. They should've had a law against apartment houses. Remember those two beautiful elm trees out there? When I and Biff hung the swing between them?

Linda: Yeah, like being a million miles from the city.

Willy: They should've arrested the builder for cutting those down. They massacred the neighborhood. *(Lost):* More and more I think of those days, Linda. This time of year it was lilac and wisteria. And then the peonies would come out, and the daffodils. What fragrance in this room!

Linda: Well, after all, people had to move somewhere.

Willy: No, there's more people now.

Linda: I don't think there's more people. I think—

Willy: There's more people! That's what's ruining this country! Population is getting out of control. The competition is maddening! Smell the stink from that apartment house! And another one on the other side . . . How can they whip cheese?

On Willy's *last line,* Biff *and* Happy *raise themselves up in their beds, listening.*

Linda: Go down, try it. And be quiet.

Willy, (turning to Linda, *guiltily):* You're not worried about me, are you, sweetheart?

Biff: What's the matter?

Happy: Listen!

Linda: You've got too much on the ball to worry about.

Willy: You're my foundation and my support, Linda.

Linda: Just try to relax, dear. You make mountains out of molehills.

Willy: I won't fight with him any more. If he wants to go back to Texas, let him go.

Linda: He'll find his way.

Willy: Sure. Certain men just don't get started till later in life. Like Thomas Edison, I think. Or B. F. Goodrich. One of them was deaf. *(He starts for the bedroom doorway.)* I'll put my money on Biff.

Linda: And Willy—if it's warm Sunday we'll drive in the country. And we'll open the windshield, and take lunch.

Willy: No, the windshields don't open on the new cars.

Linda: But you opened it today.

Willy: Me? I didn't. *(He stops.)* Now isn't that peculiar! Isn't that a remarkable— *(He breaks off in amazement and fright as the flute is heard distantly.)*

Linda: What, darling?

Willy: That is the most remarkable thing.

Linda: What, dear?

Willy: I was thinking of the Chevvy. *(Slight pause.)* Nineteen twenty-eight . . . when I had that red Chevvy— *(Breaks off.)* That funny? I coulda sworn I was driving that Chevvy today.

Linda: Well, that's nothing. Something must've reminded you.

Willy: Remarkable. Ts. Remember those days? The way Biff used to simonize that car? The dealer refused to believe there was eighty thousand miles on it. *(He shakes his head.)* Heh! *(To* Linda*):* Close your eyes, I'll be right up. *(He walks out of the bedroom.)*

Happy, (to Biff*):* Jesus, maybe he smashed up the car again!

Linda, (calling after Willy*):* Be careful on the stairs, dear! The cheese is on the middle shelf! *(She turns, goes over to the bed, takes his jacket, and goes out of the bedroom.)*

Arthur Miller   1713

Light has risen on the boys' room. Unseen, Willy *is heard talking to himself,* "*Eighty thousand miles," and a little laugh.* Biff *gets out of bed, comes downstage a bit, and stands attentively.* Biff *is two years older than his brother* Happy, *well built, but in these days bears a worn air and seems less self-assured. He has suc- ceeded less, and his dreams are stronger and less acceptable than* Happy's. *Happy is tall, powerfully made. Sexuality is like a visible color on him, or a scent that many women have discovered. He, like his brother, is lost, but in a different way, for he has never allowed himself to turn his face toward defeat and is thus more con- fused and hard-skinned, although seemingly more content.*

> *Happy, (getting out of bed):* He's going to get his license taken away if he keeps that up. I'm getting nervous about him, y'know, Biff?
>
> *Biff:* His eyes are going.
>
> *Happy:* No, I've driven with him. He sees all right. He just doesn't keep his mind on it. I drove into the city with him last week. He stops at a green light and then it turns red and he goes. *(He laughs.)*
>
> *Biff:* Maybe he's color-blind.
>
> *Happy:* Pop? Why he's got the finest eye for color in the busi- ness. You know that.
>
> *Biff, (sitting down on his bed):* I'm going to sleep.
>
> *Happy:* You're not still sour on Dad, are you, Biff?
>
> *Biff:* He's all right, I guess.
>
> *Willy, (underneath them, in the living-room):* Yes, sir, eighty thou- sand miles—eighty-two thousand!
>
> *Biff:* You smoking?
>
> *Happy, (holding out a pack of cigarettes):* Want one?
>
> *Biff, (taking a cigarette):* I can never sleep when I smell it.
>
> *Willy:* What a simonizing job, heh!
>
> *Happy, (with deep sentiment):* Funny, Biff, y'know? Us sleeping in here again? The old beds. *(He pats his bed affectionately.)* All the talk that went across those two beds, huh? Our whole lives.
>
> *Biff:* Yeah. Lotta dreams and plans.
>
> *Happy, (with a deep and masculine laugh):* About five hundred women would like to know what was said in this room.

They share a soft laugh.

> *Biff:* Remember that big Betsy something—what the hell was her name—over on Bushwick Avenue?
>
> *Happy, (combing his hair):* With the collie dog!
>
> *Biff:* That's the one. I got you in there, remember?
>
> *Happy:* Yeah, that was my first time—I think. Boy, there was a pig! *(They laugh, almost crudely.)* You taught me everything I know about women. Don't forget that.

Biff: I bet you forgot how bashful you used to be. Especially with girls.

Happy: Oh, I still am, Biff.

Biff: Oh, go on.

Happy: I just control it, that's all. I think I got less bashful and you got more so. What happened, Biff? Where's the old humor, the old confidence? *(He shakes* Biff's *knee. Biff gets up and moves restlessly about the room.)* What's the matter?

Biff: Why does Dad mock me all the time?

Happy: He's not mocking you, he—

Biff: Everything I say there's a twist of mockery on his face. I can't get near him.

Happy: He just wants you to make good, that's all. I wanted to talk to you about Dad for a long time, Biff. Something's— happening to him. He—talks to himself.

Biff: I noticed that this morning. But he always mumbled.

Happy: But not so noticeable. It got so embarrassing I sent him to Florida. And you know something? Most of the time he's talking to you.

Biff: What's he say about me?

Happy: I can't make it out.

Biff: What's he say about me?

Happy: I think the fact that you're not settled, that you're still kind of up in the air . . .

Biff: There's one or two other things depressing him, Happy.

Happy: What do you mean?

Biff: Never mind. Just don't lay it all to me.

Happy: But I think if you just got started—I mean—is there any future for you out there?

Biff: I tell ya, Hap, I don't know what the future is. I don't know—what I'm supposed to want.

Happy: What do you mean?

Biff: Well, I spent six or seven years after high school trying to work myself up. Shipping clerk, salesman, business of one kind or another. And it's a measly manner of existence. To get on that subway on the hot mornings in summer. To devote your whole life to keeping stock, or making phone calls, or selling or buying. To suffer fifty weeks of the year for the sake of a two-week vacation, when all you really desire is to be outdoors, with your shirt off. And always to have to get ahead of the next fella. And still—that's how you build a future.

Happy: Well, you really enjoy it on a farm? Are you content out there?

Biff, (with rising agitation): Hap, I've had twenty or thirty different kinds of jobs since I left home before the war, and it always turns out the same. I just realized it lately. In Nebraska when I herded cattle, and the Dakotas, and Arizona, and now in Texas. It's why I came home now, I guess, because I realized it. This farm I work on, it's spring there now, see? And they've got about fifteen new colts. There's nothing more inspiring or—beautiful than the sight of a mare and a new colt. And it's cool there now, see? Texas is cool now, and it's spring. And whenever spring comes to where I am, I suddenly get the feeling, my God, I'm not gettin' anywhere! What the hell am I doing, playing around with horses, twenty-eight dollars a week! I'm thirty-four years old, I oughta be makin' my future. That's when I come running home. And now, I get here, and I don't know what to do with myself. *(After a pause)*: I've always made a point of not wasting my life, and everytime I come back here I know that all I've done is to waste my life.

Happy: You're a poet, you know that, Biff? You're a—you're an idealist!

Biff: No, I'm mixed up very bad. Maybe I oughta get married. Maybe I oughta get stuck into something. Maybe that's my trouble. I'm like a boy. I'm not married, I'm not in business, I just—I'm like a boy. Are you content, Hap? You're a success, aren't you? Are you content?

Happy: Hell, no!

Biff: Why? You're making money, aren't you?

Happy, (moving about with energy, expressiveness): All I can do now is wait for the merchandise manager to die. And suppose I get to be merchandise manager? He's a good friend of mine, and he just built a terrific estate on Long Island. And he lived there about two months and sold it, and now he's building another one. He can't enjoy it once it's finished. And I know that's just what I would do. I don't know what the hell I'm workin' for. Sometimes I sit in my apartment —all alone. And I think of the rent I'm paying. And it's crazy. But then, it's what I always wanted. My own apartment, a car, and plenty of women. And still, goddammit, I'm lonely.

Biff, (with enthusiasm): Listen, why don't you come out West with me?

Happy: You and I, heh?

Biff: Sure, maybe we could buy a ranch. Raise cattle, use our muscles. Men built like we are should be working out in the open.

Happy, (avidly): The Loman Brothers, heh?

Biff, (with vast affection): Sure, we'd be known all over the counties!

Happy, (enthralled): That's what I dream about, Biff. Sometimes I want to just rip my clothes off in the middle of the store and outbox that goddam merchandise manager. I mean I can outbox, outrun, and outlift anybody in that store, and I have to take orders from those common, petty sons-of-bitches till I can't stand it any more.

Biff: I'm tellin' you, kid, if you were with me I'd be happy out there.

Happy, (enthused): See, Biff, everybody around me is so false that I'm constantly lowering my ideals . . .

Biff: Baby, together we'd stand up for one another, we'd have someone to trust.

Happy: If I were around you—

Biff: Hap, the trouble is we weren't brought up to grub for money. I don't know how to do it.

Happy: Neither can I!

Biff: Then let's go!

Happy: The only thing is—what can you make out there?

Biff: But look at your friend. Builds an estate and then hasn't the peace of mind to live in it.

Happy: Yeah, but when he walks into the store the waves part in front of him. That's fifty-two thousand dollars a year coming through the revolving door, and I got more in my pinky finger than he's got in his head.

Biff: Yeah, but you just said—

Happy: I gotta show some of those pompous, self-important executives over there that Hap Loman can make the grade. I want to walk into the store the way he walks in. Then I'll go with you, Biff. We'll be together yet, I swear. But take those two we had tonight. Now weren't they gorgeous creatures?

Biff: Yeah, yeah, most gorgeous I've had in years.

Happy: I get that any time I want, Biff. Whenever I feel disgusted. The only trouble is, it gets like bowling or something. I just keep knockin' them over and it doesn't mean anything. You still run around a lot?

Biff: Naa. I'd like to find a girl—steady, somebody with substance.

Happy: That's what I long for.

Biff: Go on! You'd never come home.

Happy: I would! Somebody with character, with resistance! Like Mom, y'know? You're gonna call me a bastard when I tell you this. That girl Charlotte I was with tonight is engaged to be married in five weeks. *(He tries on his new hat.)*

Biff: No kiddin'!

Happy: Sure, the guy's in line for the vice-presidency of the store. I don't know what gets into me, maybe I just have an overdeveloped sense of competition or something, but I went and ruined her, and furthermore I can't get rid of her. And he's the third executive I've done that to. Isn't that a crummy characteristic? And to top it all, I go to their weddings! *(Indignantly, but laughing)*: Like I'm not supposed to take bribes. Manufacturers offer me a hundred-dollar bill now and then to throw an order their way. You know how honest I am, but it's like this girl, see. I hate myself for it. Because I don't want the girl, and, still I take it and—I love it!

    Biff: Let's go to sleep.

Happy: I guess we didn't settle anything, heh?

    Biff: I just got one idea that I think I'm going to try.

Happy: What's that?

    Biff: Remember Bill Oliver?

Happy: Sure, Oliver is very big now. You want to work for him again?

    Biff: No, but when I quit he said something to me. He put his arm on my shoulder, and he said, "Biff, if you ever need anything, come to me."

Happy: I remember that. That sounds good.

    Biff: I think I'll go to see him. If I could get ten thousand or even seven or eight thousand dollars I could buy a beautiful ranch.

Happy: I bet he'd back you. 'Cause he thought highly of you, Biff. I mean, they all do. You're well liked, Biff. That's why I say to come back here, and we both have the apartment. And I'm tellin' you, Biff, any babe you want . . .

    Biff: No, with a ranch I could do the work I like and still be something. I just wonder though. I wonder if Oliver still thinks I stole that carton of basketballs.

Happy: Oh, he probably forgot that long ago. It's almost ten years. You'e too sensitive. Anyway, he didn't really fire you.

    Biff: Well, I think he was going to. I think that's why I quit. I was never sure whether he knew or not. I know he thought the world of me, though. I was the only one he'd let lock up the place.

  Willy, (below): You gonna wash the engine, Biff?

Happy: Shh!

Biff *looks at* Happy, *who is gazing down, listening.* Willy *is mumbling in the parlor.*

    Happy: You hear that?

They listen. Willy *laughs warmly.*

> Biff, *(growing angry):* Doesn't he know Mom can hear that?
> Willy: Don't get your sweater dirty, Biff!

A look of pain crosses Biff's *face.*

> Happy: Isn't that terrible? Don't leave again, will you? You'll
> find a job here. You gotta stick around. I don't know what
> to do about him, it's getting embarrassing.
> Willy: What a simonizing job!
> Biff: Mom's hearing that!
> Willy: No kiddin', Biff, you got a date? Wonderful!
> Happy: Go on to sleep. But talk to him in the morning, will you?
> Biff, *(reluctantly getting into bed):* With her in the house.
> Brother!
> Happy, *(getting into bed):* I wish you'd have a good talk with him.

The light on their room begins to fade.

> Biff, *(to himself in bed):* That selfish, stupid . . .
> Happy: Sh . . . Sleep, Biff.

Their light is out. Well before they have finished speaking, Willy's *form is dimly
seen below in the darkened kitchen. He opens the refrigerator, searches in there,
and takes out a bottle of milk. The apartment houses are fading out, and the entire
house and surroundings become covered with leaves. Music insinuates itself as the
leaves appear.*

> Willy: Just wanna be careful with those girls, Biff, that's all.
> Don't make any promises. No promises of any kind.
> Because a girl, y'know, they always believe what you tell 'em,
> and you're very young, Biff, you're too young to be talking
> seriously to girls.

Light rises on the kitchen. Willy, *talking, shuts the refrigerator door and comes
downstage to the kitchen table. He pours milk into a glass. He is totally immersed
in himself, smiling faintly.*

> Willy: Too young entirely, Biff. You want to watch your school-
> ing first. Then when you're all set, there'll be plenty of girls
> for a boy like you. *(He smiles broadly at a kitchen chair.)* That
> so? The girls pay for you? *(He laughs.)* Boy, you must really
> be makin' a hit.

Willy *is gradually addressing—physically—a point offstage, speaking through
the wall of the kitchen, and his voice has been rising in volume to that of a normal
conversation.*

> Willy: I been wondering why you polish the car so careful. Ha!
> Don't leave the hubcaps, boys. Get the chamois to the hub-

caps. Happy, use newspaper on the windows, it's the easiest thing. Show him how to do it, Biff! You see, Happy? Pad it up, use it like a pad. That's it, that's it, good work. You're doin' all right, Hap. *(He pauses, then nods in approbation for a few seconds, then looks upward.)* Biff, first thing we gotta do when we get time is clip that big branch over the house. Afraid it's gonna fall in a storm and hit the roof. Tell you what. We get a rope and sling her around, and then we climb up there with a couple of saws and take her down. Soon as you finish the car, boys, I wanna see ya. I got a surprise for you, boys.

    Biff, (offstage): Whatta ya got, Dad?

Willy: No, you finish first. Never leave a job till you're finished —remember that. *(Looking toward the "big trees"):* Biff, up in Albany I saw a beautiful hammock. I think I'll buy it next trip, and we'll hang it right between those two elms. Wouldn't that be something? Just swingin' there under those branches. Boy, that would be . . .

Young Biff *and* Young Happy *appear from the direction* Willy *was addressing.* Happy *carries rags and a pail of water.* Biff, *wearing a sweater with a block "S,"* carries a football.

    Biff, (pointing in the direction of the car offstage): How's that, Pop, professional?

Willy: Terrific. Terrific job, boys. Good work, Biff.

Happy: Where's the surprise, Pop?

Willy: In the back seat of the car.

Happy: Boy! *(He runs off.)*

    Biff: What is it, Dad? Tell me, what'd you buy?

Willy, (laughing, cuffs him): Never mind, something I want you to have.

    Biff, (turns and starts off): What is it, Hap?

Happy, (offstage): It's a punching bag!

    Biff: Oh, Pop!

Willy: It's got Gene Tunney's signature on it!

Happy *runs onstage with a punching bag.*

    Biff: Gee, how'd you know we wanted a punching bag?

Willy: Well, it's the finest thing for the timing.

Happy, (lies down on his back and pedals with his feet): I'm losing weight, you notice, Pop?

Willy, (to Happy*):* Jumping rope is good too.

    Biff: Did you see the new football I got?

Willy, (examining the ball): Where'd you get a new ball?

    Biff: The coach told me to practice my passing.

Willy: That so? And he gave you the ball, heh?

Biff: Well, I borrowed it from the locker room. *(He laughs confidentially.)*

Willy, (laughing with him at the theft): I want you to return that.

Happy: I told you he wouldn't like it!

Biff, (angrily): Well, I'm bringing it back!

Willy, (stopping the incipient argument, to Happy*):* Sure, he's gotta practice with a regulation ball, doesn't he? *(To* Biff*):* Coach'll probably congratulate you on your initiative!

Biff: Oh, he keeps congratulating my initiative all the time, Pop.

Willy: That's because he likes you. If somebody else took that ball there'd be an uproar. So what's the report, boys, what's the report?

Biff: Where'd you go this time, Dad? Gee we were lonesome for you.

Willy, (pleased, puts an arm around each boy and they come down to the apron): Lonesome, heh?

Biff: Missed you every minute.

Willy: Don't say? Tell you a secret, boys. Don't breathe it to a soul. Someday I'll have my own business, and I'll never have to leave home any more.

Happy: Like Uncle Charley, heh?

Willy: Bigger than Uncle Charley! Because Charley is not— liked. He's liked, but he's not—well liked.

Biff: Where'd you go this time, Dad?

Willy: Well, I got on the road, and I went north to Providence. Met the Mayor.

Biff: The Mayor of Providence!

Willy: He was sitting in the hotel lobby.

Biff: What'd he say?

Willy: He said, "Morning!" And I said, "You got a fine city here, Mayor." And then he had coffee with me. And then I went to Waterbury. Waterbury is a fine city. Big clock city, the famous Waterbury clock. Sold a nice bill there. And then Boston—Boston is the cradle of the Revolution. A fine city. And a couple of other towns in Mass., and on to Portland and Bangor and straight home!

Biff: Gee, I'd love to go with you sometime, Dad.

Willy: Soon as summer comes.

Happy: Promise?

Willy: You and Hap and I, and I'll show you all the towns. America is full of beautiful towns and fine, upstanding people. And they know me, boys, they know me up and down New England. The finest people. And when I bring you fellas up, there'll be open sesame for all of us, 'cause one thing, boys: I have friends. I can park my car in any street in

New England, and the cops protect it like their own. This summer, heh?

Biff and Happy, (together): Yeah! You bet!

Willy: We'll take our bathing suits.

Happy: We'll carry your bags, Pop!

Willy: Oh, won't that be something! Me comin' into the Boston stores with you boys carryin' my bags. What a sensation!

Biff *is prancing around, practicing passing the ball.*

Willy: You nervous, Biff, about the game?

Biff: Not if you're gonna be there.

Willy: What do they say about you in school, now that they made you captain?

Happy: There's a crowd of girls behind him every time the classes change.

Biff, (taking Willy's *hand):* This Saturday, Pop, this Saturday —just for you, I'm going to break through for a touchdown.

Happy: You're supposed to pass.

Biff: I'm takin' one play for Pop. You watch me, Pop, and when I take off my helmet, that means I'm breakin' out. Then you watch me crash through that line!

Willy, (kisses Biff*):* Oh, wait'll I tell this in Boston!

Bernard *enters in knickers. He is younger than* Biff, *earnest and loyal, a worried boy.*

Bernard: Biff, where are you? You're supposed to study with me today.

Willy: Hey, looka Bernard. What're you lookin' so anemic about, Bernard?

Bernard: He's gotta study, Uncle Willy. He's got Regents next week.

Happy, (tauntingly, spinning Bernard *around):* Let's box, Bernard!

Bernard: Biff! *(He gets away from* Happy.*)* Listen, Biff, I heard Mr. Birnbaum say that if you don't start studyin' math he's gonna flunk you, and you won't graduate. I heard him!

Willy: You better study with him, Biff. Go ahead now.

Bernard: I heard him!

Biff: Oh, Pop, you didn't see my sneakers! *(He holds up a foot for* Willy *to look at.)*

Willy: Hey, that's a beautiful job of printing!

Bernard, (wiping his glasses): Just because he printed University of Virginia on his sneakers doesn't mean they've got to graduate him, Uncle Willy!

Willy, (angrily): What're you talking about? With scholarships to three universities they're gonna flunk him?

Bernard: But I heard Mr. Birnbaum say—

Willy: Don't be a pest, Bernard! *(To his boys):* What an anemic!

Bernard: Okay, I'm waiting for you in my house, Biff.

Bernard *goes off.* The Lomans *laugh.*

Willy: Bernard is not well liked, is he?

Biff: He's liked, but he's not well liked.

Happy: That's right, Pop.

Willy: That's just what I mean. Bernard can get the best marks in school, y'understand, but when he gets out in the business world, y'understand, you are going to be five times ahead of him. That's why I thank Almighty God you're both built like Adonises. Because the man who makes an appearance in the business world, the man who creates personal interest, is the man who gets ahead. Be liked and you will never want. You take me, for instance. I never have to wait in line to see a buyer. "Willy Loman is here!" That's all they have to know, and I go right through.

Biff: Did you knock them dead, Pop?

Willy: Knocked 'em cold in Providence, slaughtered 'em in Boston.

Happy, (on his back, pedaling again): I'm losing weight, you notice, Pop?

Linda *enters, as of old, a ribbon in her hair, carrying a basket of washing.*

Linda, (with youthful energy): Hello, dear!

Willy: Sweetheart!

Linda: How'd the Chevvy run?

Willy: Chevrolet, Linda, is the greatest car ever built. *(To the boys):* Since when do you let your mother carry wash up the stairs?

Biff: Grab hold there, boy!

Happy: Where to, Mom?

Linda: Hang them up on the line. And you better go down to your friends, Biff. The cellar is full of boys. They don't know what to do with themselves.

Biff: Ah, when Pop comes home they can wait!

Willy, (laughs appreciatively): You better go down and tell them what to do, Biff.

Biff: I think I'll have them sweep out the furnace room.

Willy: Good work, Biff.

Biff, (goes through wall-line of kitchen to doorway at back and calls down): Fellas! Everybody sweep out the furnace room! I'll be right down!

Arthur Miller   1723

Voices: All right! Okay, Biff.

    Biff: George and Sam and Frank, come out back! We're hangin' up the wash! Come on, Hap, on the double! *(He and Happy carry out the basket.)*

Linda: The way they obey him!

Willy: Well, that's training, the training. I'm tellin' you, I was sellin' thousands and thousands, but I had to come home.

Linda: Oh, the whole block'll be at that game. Did you sell anything?

Willy: I did five hundred gross in Providence and seven hundred gross in Boston.

Linda: No! Wait a minute, I've got a pencil. *(She pulls pencil and paper out of her apron pocket.)* That makes your commission . . . Two hundred—my God! Two hundred and twelve dollars!

Willy: Well, I didn't figure it yet, but . . .

Linda: How much did you do?

Willy: Well, I—I did—about a hundred and eighty gross in Providence. Well, no—it came to—roughly two hundred gross on the whole trip.

Linda, (without hesitation): Two hundred gross. That's . . . *(She figures.)*

Willy: The trouble was that three of the stores were half closed for inventory in Boston. Otherwise I woulda broke records.

Linda: Well, it makes seventy dollars and some pennies. That's very good.

Willy: What do we owe?

Linda: Well, on the first there's sixteen dollars on the refrigerator—

Willy: Why sixteen?

Linda: Well, the fan belt broke, so it was a dollar eighty.

Willy: But it's brand new.

Linda: Well, the man said that's the way it is. Till they work themselves in, y'know.

They move through the wall-line into the kitchen.

    Willy: I hope we didn't get stuck on that machine.

    Linda: They got the biggest ads of any of them!

    Willy: I know, it's a fine machine. What else?

    Linda: Well, there's nine-sixty for the washing machine. And for the vacuum cleaner there's three and a half due on the fifteenth. Then the roof, you got twenty-one dollars remaining.

    Willy: It don't leak, does it?

Linda: No, they did a wonderful job. Then you owe Frank for the carburetor.

Willy: I'm not going to pay that man! That goddam Chevrolet, they ought to prohibit the manufacture of that car!

Linda: Well, you owe him three and a half. And odds and ends, comes to around a hundred and twenty dollars by the fifteenth.

Willy: A hundred and twenty dollars! My God, if business don't pick up I don't know what I'm gonna do!

Linda: Well, next week you'll do better.

Willy: Oh, I'll knock 'em dead next week. I'll go to Hartford. I'm very well liked in Hartford. You know, the trouble is, Linda, people don't seem to take to me.

They move onto the forestage.

Linda: Oh, don't be foolish.

Willy: I know it when I walk in. They seem to laugh at me.

Linda: Why? Why would they laugh at you? Don't talk that way, Willy.

Willy moves to the edge of the stage. Linda *goes into the kitchen and starts to darn stockings.*

Willy: I don't know the reason for it, but they just pass me by. I'm not noticed.

Linda: But you're doing wonderful, dear. You're making seventy to a hundred dollars a week.

Willy: But I gotta be at it ten, twelve hours a day. Other men— I don't know—they do it easier. I don't know why—I can't stop myself—I talk too much. A man oughta come in with a few words. One thing about Charley. He's a man of few words, and they respect him.

Linda: You don't talk too much, you're just lively.

Willy, (smiling): Well, I figure, what the hell, life is short, a couple of jokes. *(To himself):* I joke too much! *(The smile goes.)*

Linda: Why? You're—

Willy: I'm fat. I'm very—foolish to look at, Linda. I didn't tell you, but Christmas time I happened to be calling on F.H. Stewarts, and a salesman I know, as I was going in to see the buyer I heard him say something about—walrus. And I—I cracked him right across the face. I won't take that. I simply will not take that. But they do laugh at me. I know that.

Linda: Darling . . .

Willy: I gotta overcome it. I know I gotta overcome it. I'm not dressing to advantage, maybe.

Linda: Willy, darling, you're the handsomest man in the
world—

Willy: Oh, no, Linda.

Linda: To me you are. *(Slight pause.)* The handsomest.

From the darkness is heard the laughter of a woman. Willy *doesn't turn to it, but it continues through* Linda's *lines.*

Linda: And the boys, Willy. Few men are idolized by their children the way you are.

Music is heard as behind a scrim, to the left of the house, The Woman, *dimly seen, is dressing.*

Willy, (with great feeling): You're the best there is, Linda, you're
a pal, you know that? On the road—on the road I want to
grab you sometimes and just kiss the life outa you.

The laughter is loud now, and he moves into a brightening area at the left, where The Woman *has come from behind the scrim and is standing, putting on her hat, looking into a "mirror" and laughing.*

Willy: 'Cause I get so lonely—especially when business is bad
and there's nobody to talk to. I get the feeling that I'll
never sell anything again, that I won't make a living for you,
or a business, a business for the boys. *(He talks through* The
Woman's *subsiding laughter;* The Woman *primps at the "mirror.")* There's so much I want to make for—

The Woman: Me? You didn't make me, Willy. I picked you.

Willy, (pleased): You picked me?

The Woman, (who is quite proper-looking, Willy's *age):* I did. I've been
sitting at that desk watching all the salesmen go by, day in,
day out. But you've got such a sense of humor, and we do
have such a good time together, don't we?

Willy: Sure, sure. *(He takes her in his arms.)* Why do you have to
go now?

The Woman: It's two o'clock . . .

Willy: No, come on in! *(He pulls her.)*

The Woman: . . . my sisters'll be scandalized. When'll you be back?

Willy: Oh, two weeks about. Will you come up again?

The Woman: Sure thing. You do make me laugh. It's good for me.
(She squeezes his arm, kisses him.) And I think you're a wonderful man.

Willy: You picked me, heh?

The Woman: Sure. Because you're so sweet. And such a kidder.

Willy: Well, I'll see you next time I'm in Boston.

The Woman: I'll put you right through to the buyers.

Willy, (slapping her bottom): Right. Well, bottoms up!

The Woman, (slaps him gently and laughs): You just kill me, Willy. *(He suddenly grabs her and kisses her roughly.)* You kill me. And thanks for the stockings. I love a lot of stockings. Well, good night.

> Willy: Good night. And keep your pores open!
> The Woman: Oh, Willy!

The Woman *bursts out laughing, and* Linda's *laughter blends in.* The Woman *disappears into the dark. Now the area at the kitchen table brightens.* Linda *is sitting where she was at the kitchen table, but now is mending a pair of her silk stockings.*

> Linda: You are, Willy. The handsomest man. You've got no reason to feel that—
> Willy, *(coming out of* The Woman's *dimming area and going over to* Linda*)*: I'll make it all up to you, Linda, I'll—
> Linda: There's nothing to make up, dear. You're doing fine, better than—
> Willy, *(noticing her mending)*: What's that?
> Linda: Just mending my stockings. They're so expensive—
> Willy, *(angrily, taking them from her)*: I won't have you mending stockings in this house! Now throw them out!

Linda *puts the stockings in her pocket.*

> Bernard, *(entering on the run)*: Where is he? If he doesn't study!
> Willy, *(moving to the forestage, with great agitation)*: You'll give him the answers!
> Bernard: I do, but I can't on a Regents! That's a state exam! They're liable to arrest me!
> Willy: Where is he? I'll whip him, I'll whip him!
> Linda: And he'd better give back that football, Willy, it's not nice.
> Willy: Biff! Where is he? Why is he taking everything?
> Linda: He's too rough with the girls, Willy. All the mothers are afraid of him!
> Willy: I'll whip him!
> Bernard: He's driving the car without a license!

The Woman's *laugh is heard.*

> Willy: Shut up!
> Linda: All the mothers—
> Willy: Shut up!
> Bernard, *(backing quietly away and out)*: Mr. Birnbaum says he's stuck up.
> Willy: Get outa here!
> Bernard: If he doesn't buckle down he'll flunk math! *(He goes off.)*
> Linda: He's right, Willy, you've gotta—
> Willy, *(exploding at her)*: There's nothing the matter with him!

You want him to be a worm like Bernard? He's got spirit, personality . . .

As he speaks, Linda, *almost in tears, exits into the living-room.* Willy *is alone in the kitchen, wilting and staring. The leaves are gone. It is night again, and the apartment houses look down from behind.*

Willy: Loaded with it. Loaded! What is he stealing? He's giving it back, isn't he? Why is he stealing? What did I tell him? I never in my life told him anything but decent things.

Happy *in pajamas has come down the stairs;* Willy *suddenly becomes aware of* Happy's *presence.*

Happy: Let's go now, come on.
Willy, *(sitting down at the kitchen table):* Huh! Why did she have to wax the floors herself? Everytime she waxes the floors she keels over. She knows that!
Happy: Shh! Take it easy. What brought you back tonight?
Willy: I got an awful scare. Nearly hit a kid in Yonkers. God! Why didn't I go to Alaska with my brother Ben that time! Ben! That man was a genius, that man was success incarnate! What a mistake! He begged me to go.
Happy: Well, there's no use in—
Willy: You guys! There was a man started with the clothes on his back and ended up with diamond mines!
Happy: Boy, someday I'd like to know how he did it.
Willy: What's the mystery? The man knew what he wanted and went out and got it! Walked into a jungle, and comes out, the age of twenty-one, and he's rich! The world is an oyster, but you don't crack it open on a mattress!
Happy: Pop, I told you I'm gonna retire you for life.
Willy: You'll retire me for life on seventy goddam dollars a week? And your women and your car and your apartment, and you'll retire me for life! Christ's sake, I couldn't get past Yonkers today! Where are you guys, where are you? The woods are burning! I can't drive a car!

Charley *has appeared in the doorway. He is a large man, slow of speech, laconic, immovable. In all he says, despite what he says, there is pity, and, now, trepidation. He has a robe over pajamas, slippers on his feet. He enters the kitchen.*

Charley: Everything all right?
Happy: Yeah, Charley, everything's . . .
Willy: What's the matter?
Charley: I heard some noise. I thought something happened. Can't we do something about the walls? You sneeze in here, and in my house hats blow off.
Happy: Let's go to bed, Dad. Come on.

Charley *signals to* Happy *to go.*

   Willy: You go ahead, I'm not tired at the moment.

  Happy, *(to* Willy)*:* Take it easy, huh? *(He exits.)*

   Willy: What're you doin' up?

Charley, *(sitting down at the kitchen table opposite* Willy)*:* Couldn't sleep good. I had a heartburn.

   Willy: Well, you don't know how to eat.

Charley: I eat with my mouth.

   Willy: No, you're ignorant. You gotta know about vitamins and things like that.

Charley: Come on, let's shoot. Tire you out a little.

   Willy, *(hesitantly)*: All right. You got cards?

Charley, *(taking a deck from his pocket)*: Yeah, I got them. Some-place. What is it with those vitamins?

   Willy, *(dealing)*: They build up your bones. Chemistry.

Charley: Yeah, but there's no bones in a heartburn.

   Willy: What are you talkin' about? Do you know the first thing about it?

Charley: Don't get insulted.

   Willy: Don't talk about something you don't know anything about.

They are playing. Pause.

Charley: What're you doin' home?

   Willy: A little trouble with the car.

Charley: Oh. *(Pause.)* I'd like to take a trip to California.

   Willy: Don't say.

Charley: You want a job?

   Willy: I got a job, I told you that. *(After a slight pause)*: What the hell are you offering me a job for?

Charley: Don't get insulted.

   Willy: Don't insult me.

Charley: I don't see no sense in it. You don't have to go on this way.

   Willy: I got a good job. *(Slight pause.)* What do you keep comin' in here for?

Charley: You want me to go?

   Willy, *(after a pause, withering)*: I can't understand it. He's going back to Texas again. What the hell is that?

Charley: Let him go.

   Willy: I got nothin' to give him, Charley, I'm clean, I'm clean.

Charley: He won't starve. None a them starve. Forget about him.

   Willy: Then what have I got to remember?

Charley: You take it too hard. To hell with it. When a deposit bottle is broken you don't get your nickel back.

Willy: That's easy enough for you to say.

Charley: That ain't easy for me to say.

Willy: Did you see the ceiling I put up in the living-room?

Charley: Yeah, that's a piece of work. To put up a ceiling is a mystery to me. How do you do it?

Willy: What's the difference?

Charley: Well, talk about it.

Willy: You gonna put up a ceiling?

Charley: How could I put up a ceiling?

Willy: Then what the hell are you bothering me for?

Charley: You're insulted again.

Willy: A man who can't handle tools is not a man. You're disgusting.

Charley: Don't call me disgusting, Willy.

Uncle Ben, *carrying a valise and an umbrella, enters the forestage from around the right corner of the house. He is a stolid man, in his sixties, with a mustache and an authoritative air. He is utterly certain of his destiny, and there is an aura of far places about him. He enters exactly as* Willy *speaks.*

Willy: I'm getting awfully tired, Ben.

Ben's *music is heard.* Ben *looks around at everything.*

Charley: Good, keep playing; you'll sleep better. Did you call me Ben?

Ben *looks at his watch.*

Willy: That's funny. For a second there you reminded me of my brother Ben.

Ben: I only have a few minutes. *(He strolls, inspecting the place.* Willy *and* Charley *continue playing.)*

Charley: You never heard from him again, heh? Since that time?

Willy: Didn't Linda tell you? Couple of weeks ago we got a letter from his wife in Africa. He died.

Charley: That so.

Ben, (chuckling): So this is Brooklyn, eh?

Charley: Maybe you're in for some of his money.

Willy: Naa, he had seven sons. There's just one opportunity I had with that man . . .

Ben: I must make a train, William. There are several properties I'm looking at in Alaska.

Willy: Sure, sure! If I'd gone with him to Alaska that time, everything would've been totally different.

Charley: Go on, you'd froze to death up there.

Willy: What're you talking about?

Ben: Opportunity is tremendous in Alaska, William. Surprised you're not up there.

Willy: Sure, tremendous.

Charley: Heh?

Willy: There was the only man I ever met who knew the answers.

Charley: Who?

Ben: How are you all?

Willy, (taking a pot, smiling): Fine, fine.

Charley: Pretty sharp tonight.

Ben: Is Mother living with you?

Willy: No, she died a long time ago.

Charley: Who?

Ben: That's too bad. Fine specimen of a lady, Mother.

Willy, (to Charley*):* Heh?

Ben: I'd hoped to see the old girl.

Charley: Who died?

Ben: Heard anything from Father, have you?

Willy, (unnerved): What do you mean, who died?

Charley, (taking a pot): What're you talkin' about?

Ben, (looking at his watch): William, it's half-past eight!

Willy, (as though to dispel his confusion he angrily stops Charley's *hand):* That's my build!

Charley: I put the ace—

Willy: If you don't know how to play the game I'm not gonna throw my money away on you!

Charley, (rising): It was my ace, for God's sake!

Willy: I'm through, I'm through!

Ben: When did Mother die?

Willy: Long ago. Since the beginning you never knew how to play cards.

Charley, (picks up the cards and goes to the door): All right! Next time I'll bring a deck with five aces.

Willy: I don't play that kind of game!

Charley, (turning to him): You ought to be ashamed of yourself!

Willy: Yeah?

Charley: Yeah! *(He goes out.)*

Willy, (slamming the door after him): Ignoramus!

Ben, (as Willy *comes toward him through the wall-line of the kitchen):* So you're William.

Willy, (shaking Ben's *hand):* Ben! I've been waiting for you so long! What's the answer? How did you do it?

Ben: Oh, there's a story in that.

Linda *enters the forestage, as of old, carrying the wash basket.*

Linda: Is this Ben?

Ben, (gallantly): How do you do, my dear.

Linda: Where've you been all these years? Willy's always wondered why you—

Willy, (pulling Ben *away from her impatiently):* Where is Dad? Didn't you follow him? How did you get started?

Ben: Well, I don't know how much you remember.

Willy: Well, I was just a baby, of course, only three or four years old—

Ben: Three years and eleven months.

Willy: What a memory, Ben!

Ben: I have many enterprises, William, and I have never kept books.

Willy: I remember I was sitting under the wagon in—was it Nebraska?

Ben: It was South Dakota, and I gave you a bunch of wild flowers.

Willy: I remember you walking away down some open road.

Ben, (laughing): I was going to find Father in Alaska.

Willy: Where is he?

Ben: At that age I had a very faulty view of geography, William. I discovered after a few days that I was heading due south, so instead of Alaska, I ended up in Africa.

Linda: Africa!

Willy: The Gold Coast!

Ben: Principally diamond mines.

Linda: Diamond mines!

Ben: Yes, my dear. But I've only a few minutes—

Willy: No! Boys! Boys! *(Young* Biff *and* Happy *appear.)* Listen to this. This is your Uncle Ben, a great man! Tell my boys, Ben!

Ben: Why, boys, when I was seventeen I walked into the jungle, and when I was twenty-one I walked out. *(He laughs.)* And by God I was rich.

Willy, (to the boys): You see what I been talking about? The greatest things can happen!

Ben, (glancing at his watch): I have an appointment in Ketchikan Tuesday week.

Willy: No, Ben! Please tell about Dad. I want my boys to hear. I want them to know the kind of stock they spring from. All I remember is a man with a big beard, and I was in Mamma's lap, sitting around a fire, and some kind of high music.

Ben: His flute. He played the flute.

Willy: Sure, the flute, that's right!

New music is heard, a high, rollicking tune.

Ben: Father was a very great and a very wild-hearted man. We would start in Boston, and he'd toss the whole family into the wagon, and then he'd drive the team right across the country; through Ohio, and Indiana, Michigan, Illinois, and all the Western states. And we'd stop in the towns and sell the flutes that he'd made on the way. Great inventor, Father. With one gadget he made more in a week than a man like you could make in a lifetime.

Willy: That's just the way I'm bringing them up, Ben—rugged, well liked, all-around.

Ben: Yeah? *(To* Biff*):* Hit that, boy—hard as you can. *(He pounds his stomach.)*

Biff: Oh, no, sir!

Ben, (taking boxing stance): Come on, get to me! *(He laughs.)*

Willy: Go to it, Biff! Go ahead, show him!

Biff: Okay! *(He cocks his fists and starts in.)*

Linda, (to Willy*):* Why must he fight, dear?

Ben, (sparring with Biff*):* Good boy! Good boy!

Willy: How's that, Ben, heh?

Happy: Give him the left, Biff!

Linda: Why are you fighting?

Ben: Good boy! *(Suddenly comes in, trips* Biff, *and stands over him, the point of his umbrella poised over* Biff's *eye.)*

Linda: Look out, Biff!

Biff: Gee!

Ben, (patting Biff's *knee):* Never fight fair with a stranger, boy. You'll never get out of the jungle that way. *(Taking* Linda's *hand and bowing):* It was an honor and a pleasure to meet you, Linda.

Linda, (withdrawing her hand coldly, frightened): Have a nice—trip.

Ben, (to Willy*):* And good luck with your—what do you do?

Willy: Selling.

Ben: Yes. Well . . . *(He raises his hand in farewell to all.)*

Willy: No, Ben, I don't want you to think . . . *(He takes* Ben's *arm to show him.)* It's Brooklyn, I know, but we hunt too.

Ben: Really, now.

Willy: Oh, sure, there's snakes and rabbits and—that's why I moved out here. Why, Biff can fell any one of these trees in no time! Boys! Go right over to where they're building the apartment house and get some sand. We're gonna rebuild the entire front stoop right now! Watch this, Ben!

Happy, (as he and Biff *run off):* I lost weight, Pop, you notice?

Charley *enters in knickers, even before the boys are gone.*

Charley: Listen, if they steal any more from that building the watchman'll put the cops on them!

Linda, (to Willy*):* Don't let Biff . . .

Ben *laughs lustily.*

> *Willy:* You shoulda seen the lumber they brought home last week. At least a dozen six-by-tens worth all kinds a money.
>
> *Charley:* Listen, if that watchman—
>
> *Willy:* I gave them hell, understand. But I got a couple of fearless characters there.
>
> *Charley:* Willy, the jails are full of fearless characters.
>
> > *Ben,* (clapping Willy *on the back, with a laugh at* Charley)*:* And the stock exchange, friend!
> >
> > *Willy,* (joining in Ben's *laughter)*: Where are the rest of your pants?
>
> *Charley:* My wife bought them.
>
> *Willy:* Now all you need is a golf club and you can go upstairs and go to sleep. *(To* Ben)*:* Great athlete! Between him and his son Bernard they can't hammer a nail!
>
> *Bernard,* (rushing in)*:* The watchman's chasing Biff!
>
> *Willy,* (angrily)*:* Shut up! He's not stealing anything!
>
> *Linda,* (alarmed, hurrying off left)*:* Where is he? Biff, dear! *(She exits.)*
>
> *Willy,* (moving toward the left, away from Ben)*:* There's nothing wrong. What's the matter with you?
>
> > *Ben:* Nervy boy. Good!
>
> *Willy,* (laughing)*:* Oh, nerves of iron, that Biff!
>
> *Charley:* Don't know what it is. My New England man comes back and he's bleedin', they murdered him up there.
>
> *Willy:* It's contacts, Charley, I got important contacts!
>
> *Charley,* (sarcastically)*:* Glad to hear it, Willy. Come in later, we'll shoot a little casino. I'll take some of your Portland money. *(He laughs at* Willy *and exits.)*
>
> *Willy* (turning to Ben)*:* Business is bad, it's murderous. But not for me, of course.
>
> > *Ben:* I'll stop by on my way back to Africa.
>
> *Willy,* (longingly)*:* Can't you stay a few days? You're just what I need, Ben, because I—I have a fine position here, but I—well, Dad left when I was such a baby and I never had a chance to talk to him and I still feel—kind of temporary about myself.
>
> > *Ben:* I'll be late for my train.

They are at opposite ends of the stage.

> *Willy:* Ben, my boys—can't we talk? They'd go into the jaws of hell for me, see, but I—
>
> > *Ben:* William, you're being first-rate with your boys. Outstanding, manly chaps!
>
> *Willy,* (hanging on to his words)*:* Oh, Ben, that's good to hear!

Because sometimes I'm afraid that I'm not teaching them the right kind of— Ben, how should I teach them?

Ben, (giving great weight to each word, and with a certain vicious audacity): William, when I walked into the jungle, I was seventeen. When I walked out I was twenty-one. And, by God, I was rich! *(He goes off into darkness around the right corner of the house.)*

Willy: . . . was rich! That's just the spirit I want to imbue them with! To walk into a jungle! I was right! I was right! I was right!

Ben *is gone, but* Willy *is still speaking to him as* Linda, *in nightgown and robe, enters the kitchen, glances around for* Willy, *then goes to the door of the house, looks out and sees him. Comes down to his left. He looks at her.*

Linda: Willy, dear? Willy?

Willy: I was right!

Linda: Did you have some cheese? *(He can't answer.)* It's very late, darling. Come to bed, heh?

Willy, (looking straight up): Gotta break your neck to see a star in this yard.

Linda: You coming in?

Willy: Whatever happened to that diamond watch fob? Remember? When Ben came from Africa that time? Didn't he give me a watch fob with a diamond in it?

Linda: You pawned it, dear. Twelve, thirteen years ago. For Biff's radio correspondence course.

Willy: Gee, that was a beautiful thing. I'll take a walk.

Linda: But you're in your slippers.

Willy, (starting to go around the house at the left): I was right! I was! *(Half to* Linda, *as he goes, shaking his head):* What a man! There was a man worth talking to. I was right!

Linda, (calling after Willy): But in your slippers, Willy!

Willy *is almost gone when* Biff, *in his pajamas, comes down the stairs and enters the kitchen.*

Biff: What is he doing out there?

Linda: Sh!

Biff: God Almighty, Mom, how long has he been doing this?

Linda: Don't, he'll hear you.

Biff: What the hell is the matter with him?

Linda: It'll pass by morning.

Biff: Shouldn't we do anything?

Linda: Oh, my dear, you should do a lot of things, but there's nothing to do, so go to sleep.

Happy *comes down the stair and sits on the steps.*

Happy: I never heard him so loud, Mom.

Linda: Well, come around more often; you'll hear him. *(She sits down at the table and mends the lining of* Willy's *jacket.)*

Biff: Why didn't you ever write me about this, Mom?

Linda: How would I write to you? For over three months you had no address.

Biff: I was on the move. But you know I thought of you all the time. You know that, don't you, pal?

Linda: I know, dear, I know. But he likes to have a letter. Just to know that there's still a possibility for better things.

Biff: He's not like this all the time, is he?

Linda: It's when you come home he's always the worst.

Biff: When I come home?

Linda: When you write you're coming, he's all smiles, and talks about the future, and—he's just wonderful. And then the closer you seem to come, the more shaky he gets, and then, by the time you get here, he's arguing, and he seems angry at you. I think it's just that maybe he can't bring himself to —to open up to you. Why are you so hateful to each other? Why is that?

Biff, (evasively): I'm not hateful, Mom.

Linda: But you no sooner come in the door than you're fighting!

Biff: I don't know why. I mean to change. I'm tryin', Mom, you understand?

Linda: Are you home to stay now?

Biff: I don't know. I want to look around, see what's doin'.

Linda: Biff, you can't look around all your life, can you?

Biff: I just can't take hold, Mom. I can't take hold of some kind of a life.

Linda: Biff, a man is not a bird, to come and go with the springtime.

Biff: Your hair . . . *(He touches her hair.)* Your hair got so gray.

Linda: Oh, it's been gray since you were in high school. I just stopped dyeing it, that's all.

Biff: Dye it again, will ya? I don't want my pal looking old. *(He smiles.)*

Linda: You're such a boy! You think you can go away for a year and . . . You've got to get it into your head now that one day you'll knock on this door and there'll be strange people here—

Biff: What are you talking about? You're not even sixty, Mom.

Linda: But what about your father?

Biff, (lamely): Well, I meant him too.

Happy: He admires Pop.

Linda: Biff, dear, if you don't have any feeling for him, then you can't have any feeling for me.

Biff: Sure I can, Mom.

Linda: No. You can't just come to see me, because I love him. *(With a threat, but only a threat, of tears):* He's the dearest man in the world to me, and I won't have anyone making him feel unwanted and low and blue. You've got to make up your mind now, darling, there's no leeway any more. Either he's your father and you pay him that respect, or else you're not to come here. I know he's not easy to get along with—nobody knows that better than me—but . . .

Willy, (from the left, with a laugh): Hey, hey, Biffo!

Biff, (starting to go out after Willy*):* What the hell is the matter with him? *(*Happy *stops him.)*

Linda: Don't—don't go near him!

Biff: Stop making excuses for him! He always, always wiped the floor with you. Never had an ounce of respect for you.

Happy: He's always had respect for—

Biff: What the hell do you know about it?

Happy, (surlily): Just don't call him crazy!

Biff: He's got no character— Charley wouldn't do this. Not in his own house—spewing out that vomit from his mind.

Happy: Charley never had to cope with what he's got to.

Biff: People are worse off than Willy Loman. Believe me, I've seen them!

Linda: Then make Charley your father, Biff. You can't do that, can you? I don't say he's a great man. Willy Loman never made a lot of money. His name was never in the paper. He's not the finest character that ever lived. But he's a human being, and a terrible thing is happening to him. So attention must be paid. He's not to be allowed to fall into his grave like an old dog. Attention, attention must be finally paid to such a person. You called him crazy—

Biff: I didn't mean—

Linda: No, a lot of people think he's lost his—balance. But you don't have to be very smart to know what his trouble is. The man is exhausted.

Happy: Sure!

Linda: A small man can be just as exhausted as a great man. He works for a company thirty-six years this March, opens up unheard-of territories to their trademark, and now in his old age they take his salary away.

Happy, (indignantly): I didn't know that, Mom.

Linda: You never asked, my dear! Now that you get your spending money someplace else you don't trouble your mind with him.

Happy: But I gave you money last—

Linda: Christmas time, fifty dollars! To fix the hot water it cost ninety-seven fifty! For five weeks he's been on straight commission, like a beginner, an unknown!

Biff: Those ungrateful bastards!

Linda: Are they any worse than his sons? When he brought them business, when he was young, they were glad to see him. But now his old friends, the old buyers that loved him so and always found some order to hand him in a pinch— they're all dead, retired. He used to be able to make six, seven calls a day in Boston. Now he takes his valises out of the car and puts them back and takes them out again and he's exhausted. Instead of walking he talks now. He drives seven hundred miles, and when he gets there no one knows him any more, no one welcomes him. And what goes through a man's mind, driving seven hundred miles home without having earned a cent? Why shouldn't he talk to himself? Why? When he has to go to Charley and borrow fifty dollars a week and pretend to me that it's his pay? How long can that go on? How long? You see what I'm sitting here and waiting for? And you tell me he has no character? The man who never worked a day but for your benefit? When does he get the medal for that? Is this his reward—to turn around at the age of sixty-three and find his sons, who he loved better than his life, one a philandering bum—

Happy: Mom!

Linda: That's all you are, my baby! *(To* Biff*):* And you! What happened to the love you had for him? You were such pals! How you used to talk to him on the phone every night! How lonely he was till he could come home to you!

Biff: All right, Mom. I'll live here in my room, and I'll get a job. I'll keep away from him, that's all.

Linda: No, Biff. You can't stay here and fight all the time.

Biff: He threw me out of this house, remember that.

Linda: Why did he do that? I never knew why.

Biff: Because I know he's a fake and he doesn't like anybody around who knows!

Linda: Why a fake? In what way? What do you mean?

Biff: Just don't lay it all at my feet. It's between me and him —that's all I have to say. I'll chip in from now on. He'll settle for half my pay check. He'll be all right. I'm going to bed. *(He starts for the stairs.)*

Linda: He won't be all right.

Biff, (turning on the stairs, furiously): I hate this city and I'll stay here. Now what do you want?

Linda: He's dying. Biff.

Happy *turns quickly to her, shocked.*

Biff, *(after a pause):* Why is he dying?

Linda: He's been trying to kill himself.

Biff, *(with great horror):* How?

Linda: I live from day to day.

Biff: What're you talking about?

Linda: Remember I wrote you that he smashed up the car again? In February?

Biff: Well?

Linda: The insurance inspector came. He said that they have evidence. That all these accidents in the last year —weren't—weren't—accidents.

Happy: How can they tell that? That's a lie.

Linda: It seems there's a woman . . . *(She takes a breath as)*

{ *Biff,* *(sharply but contained):* What woman?
{ *Linda,* *(simultaneously):* . . . and this woman . . .

Linda: What?

Biff: Nothing. Go ahead.

Linda: What did you say?

Biff: Nothing. I just said what woman?

Happy: What about her?

Linda: Well, it seems she was walking down the road and saw his car. She says that he wasn't driving fast at all, and that he didn't skid. She says he came to that little bridge, and then deliberately smashed into the railing, and it was only the shallowness of the water that saved him.

Biff: Oh, no, he probably just fell asleep again.

Linda: I don't think he fell asleep.

Biff: Why not?

Linda: Last month . . . *(With great difficulty):* Oh, boys, it's so hard to say a thing like this! He's just a big stupid man to you, but I tell you there's more good in him than in many other people. *(She chokes, wipes her eyes.)* I was looking for a fuse. The lights blew out, and I went down the cellar. And behind the fuse box—it happened to fall out—was a length of rubber pipe—just short.

Happy: No kidding?

Linda: There's a little attachment on the end of it. I knew right away. And sure enough, on the bottom of the water heater there's a new little nipple on the gas pipe.

Happy, *(angrily):* That—jerk.

Biff: Did you have it taken off?

Linda: I'm—I'm ashamed to. How can I mention it to him? Every day I go down and take away that little rubber pipe. But, when he comes home, I put it back where it was. How can I insult him that way? I don't know what to do. I live from day to day, boys. I tell you, I know every thought in his mind. It sounds so old-fashioned and silly, but I tell you he put his whole life into you and you've turned your backs on him. *(She is bent over in the chair, weeping, her face in her hands.)* Biff, I swear to God! Biff, his life is in your hands!

Happy, (to Biff): How do you like that damned fool!

Biff, (kissing her): All right, pal, all right. It's all settled now. I've been remiss. I know that, Mom. But now I'll stay, and I swear to you, I'll apply myself. *(Kneeling in front of her, in a fever of self-reproach):* It's just—you see, Mom, I don't fit in business. Not that I won't try. I'll try, and I'll make good.

Happy: Sure you will. The trouble with you in business was you never tried to please people.

Biff: I know, I—

Happy: Like when you worked for Harrison's. Bob Harrison said you were tops, and then you go and do some damn fool thing like whistling whole songs in the elevator like a comedian.

Biff, (against Happy*):* So what? I like to whistle sometimes.

Happy: You don't raise a guy to a responsible job who whistles in the elevator!

Linda: Well, don't argue about it now.

Happy: Like when you'd go off and swim in the middle of the day instead of taking the line around.

Biff, (his resentment rising): Well, don't you run off? You take off sometimes, don't you? On a nice summer day?

Happy: Yeah, but I cover myself!

Linda: Boys!

Happy: If I'm going to take a fade the boss can call any number where I'm supposed to be and they'll swear to him that I just left. I'll tell you something that I hate to say, Biff, but in the business world some of them think you're crazy.

Biff, (angered): Screw the business world!

Happy: All right, screw it! Great, but cover yourself!

Linda: Hap, Hap!

Biff: I don't care what they think! They've laughed at Dad for years, and you know why? Because we don't belong in this nuthouse of a city! We should be mixing cement on some open plain, or—or carpenters. A carpenter is allowed to whistle!

Willy *walks in from the entrance of the house, at left.*

Willy: Even your grandfather was better than a carpenter. *(Pause. They watch him.)* You never grew up. Bernard does not whistle in the elevator, I assure you.

Biff, (as though to laugh Willy *out of it):* Yeah, but you do, Pop.

Willy: I never in my life whistled in an elevator! And who in the business world thanks I'm crazy?

Biff: I didn't mean it like that, Pop. Now don't make a whole thing out of it, will ya?

Willy: Go back to the West! Be a carpenter, a cowboy, enjoy yourself!

Linda: Willy, he was just saying—

Willy: I heard what he said!

Happy, (trying to quiet Willy*):* Hey, Pop, come on now . . .

Willy, (continuing over Happy's *line):* They laugh at me, heh? Go to Filene's, go to the Hub, go to Slattery's, Boston. Call out the name Willy Loman and see what happens! Big shot!

Biff: All right, Pop.

Willy: Big!

Biff: All right!

Willy: Why do you always insult me?

Biff: I didn't say a word. *(To* Linda*):* Did I say a word?

Linda: He didn't say anything, Willy.

Willy, (going to the doorway of the living-room): All right, good night, good night.

Linda: Willy, dear, he just decided . . .

Willy, (to Biff*):* If you get tired hanging around tomorrow, paint the ceiling I put up in the living-room.

Biff: I'm leaving early tomorrow.

Happy: He's going to see Bill Oliver, Pop.

Willy, (interestedly): Oliver? For what?

Biff, (with reserve, but trying, trying): He always said he'd stake me. I'd like to go into business, so maybe I can take him up on it.

Linda: Isn't that wonderful?

Willy: Don't interrupt. What's wonderful about it? There's fifty men in the City of New York who'd stake him. *(To* Biff*):* Sporting goods?

Biff: I guess so. I know something about it and—

Willy: He knows something about it! You know sporting goods better than Spalding, for God's sake! How much is he giving you?

Biff: I don't know, I didn't even see him yet, but—

Willy: Then what're you talkin' about?

Biff, (getting angry): Well, all I said was I'm gonna see him, that's all!

Willy, (turning away): Ah, you're counting your chickens again.

Biff, (starting left for the stairs): Oh, Jesus, I'm going to sleep!

Willy, (calling after him): Don't curse in this house!

Biff, (turning): Since when did you get so clean?

Happy, (trying to stop them): Wait a . . .

Willy: Don't use that language to me! I won't have it!

Happy, (grabbing Biff, *shouts):* Wait a minute! I got an idea. I got a feasible idea. Come here, Biff, let's talk this over now, let's talk some sense here. When I was down in Florida last time, I thought of a great idea to sell sporting goods. It just came back to me. You and I, Biff—we have a line, the Loman Line. We train a couple of weeks, and put on a couple of exhibitions, see?

Willy: That's an idea!

Happy: Wait! We form two basketball teams, see? Two water-polo teams. We play each other. It's a million dollars' worth of publicity. Two brothers, see? The Loman Brothers. Displays in the Royal Palms—all the hotels. And banners over the ring and the basketball court: "Loman Brothers." Baby, we could sell sporting goods!

Willy: That is a one-million-dollar idea!

Linda: Marvelous!

Biff: I'm in great shape as far as that's concerned.

Happy: And the beauty of it is, Biff, it wouldn't be like a business. We'd be out playin' ball again . . .

Biff, (enthused): Yeah, that's . . .

Willy: Million-dollar . . .

Happy: And you wouldn't get fed up with it, Biff. It'd be the family again. There'd be the old honor, and comradeship, and if you wanted to go off for a swim or somethin'—well, you'd do it! Without some smart cooky gettin' up ahead of you!

Willy: Lick the world! You guys together could absolutely lick the civilized world.

Biff: I'll see Oliver tomorrow. Hap, if we could work that out . . .

Linda: Maybe things are beginning to—

Willy, (wildly enthused, to Linda*):* Stop interrupting! *(To* Biff*):* But don't wear sport jacket and slacks when you see Oliver.

Biff: No, I'll—

Willy: A business suit, and talk as little as possible, and don't crack any jokes.

Biff: He did like me. Always liked me.

Linda: He loved you!

Willy, (to Linda*):* Will you stop! *(To* Biff*):* Walk in very serious. You are not applying for a boy's job. Money is to pass. Be quiet, fine, and serious. Everybody likes a kidder, but nobody lends him money.

Happy: I'll try to get some myself, Biff. I'm sure I can.

Willy: I see great things for you kids, I think your troubles are over. But remember, start big and you'll end big. Ask for fifteen. How much you gonna ask for?

Biff: Gee, I don't know—

Willy: And don't say "Gee." "Gee" is a boy's word. A man walking in for fifteen thousand dollars does not say "Gee!"

Biff: Ten, I think, would be top though.

Willy: Don't be so modest. You always started too low. Walk in with a big laugh. Don't look worried. Start off with a couple of your good stories to lighten things up. It's not what you say, it's how you say it—because personality always wins the day.

Linda: Oliver always thought the highest of him—

Willy: Will you let me talk?

Biff: Don't yell at her, Pop, will ya?

Willy, (angrily): I was talking, wasn't I?

Biff: I don't like you yelling at her all the time, and I'm tellin' you, that's all.

Willy: What're you, takin' over this house?

Linda: Willy—

Willy, (turning on her): Don't take his side all the time, goddammit!

Biff, (furiously): Stop yelling at her!

Willy, (suddenly pulling on his cheek, beaten down, guilt ridden): Give my best to Bill Oliver—he may remember me. *(He exits through the living-room doorway.)*

Linda, (her voice subdued): What'd you have to start that for? *(Biff turns away.)* You see how sweet he was as soon as you talked hopefully? *(She goes over to Biff.)* Come up and say good night to him. Don't let him go to bed that way.

Happy: Come on, Biff, let's buck him up.

Linda: Please, dear. Just say good night. It takes so little to make him happy. Come. *(She goes through the living-room doorway, calling upstairs from within the living-room):* Your pajamas are hanging in the bathroom, Willy!

Happy, (looking toward where Linda *went out):* What a woman! They broke the mold when they made her. You know that, Biff?

Biff: He's off salary. My God, working on commission!

Happy: Well, let's face it: he's no hot-shot selling man. Except that sometimes, you have to admit, he's a sweet personality.

Biff, (deciding): Lend me ten bucks, will ya? I want to buy some new ties.

Happy: I'll take you to a place I know. Beautiful stuff. Wear one of my striped shirts tomorrow.

Biff: She got gray. Mom got awful old. Gee, I'm gonna go in to Oliver tomorrow and knock him for a—

Happy: Come on up. Tell that to Dad. Let's give him a whirl. Come on.

Biff, (steamed up): You know, with ten thousand bucks, boy!

Happy, (as they go into the living-room): That's the talk, Biff, that's the first time I've heard the old confidence out of you! *(From within the living-room, fading off):* You're gonna live with me, kid, and any babe you want just say the word . . . *(The last lines are hardly heard. They are mounting the stairs to their parents' bedroom.)*

Linda, (entering her bedroom and addressing Willy, *who is in the bathroom. She is straightening the bed for him):* Can you do anything about the shower? It drips.

Willy, (from the bathroom): All of a sudden everything falls to pieces! Goddam plumbing, oughta be sued, those people. I hardly finished putting it in and the thing . . . *(His words rumble off.)*

Linda: I'm just wondering if Oliver will remember him. You think he might?

Willy, (coming out of the bathroom in his pajamas): Remember him? What's the matter with you, you crazy? If he'd've stayed with Oliver he'd be on top by now! Wait'll Oliver gets a look at him. You don't know the average caliber any more. The average young man today—*(he is getting into bed)* —is got a caliber of zero. Greatest thing in the world for him was to bum around.

Biff *and* Happy *enter the bedroom. Slight pause.*

Willy, (stops short, looking at Biff*):* Glad to hear it, boy.

Happy: He wanted to say good night to you, sport.

Willy, (to Biff*):* Yeah. Knock him dead, boy. What'd you want to tell me?

Biff: Just take it easy, Pop. Good night. *(He turns to go.)*

Willy, (unable to resist): And if anything falls off the desk while you're talking to him—like a package or something—don't you pick it up. They have office boys for that.

Linda: I'll make a big breakfast—

Willy: Will you let me finish? *(To* Biff*):* Tell him you were in the business in the West. Not farm work.

Biff: All right, Dad.

Linda: I think everything—

Willy, (going right through her speech): And don't undersell yourself. No less than fifteen thousand dollars.

Biff, (unable to bear him): Okay. Good night, Mom. *(He starts moving.)*

Willy: Because you got a greatness in you, Biff, remember that. You got all kinds a greatness . . . *(He lies back, exhausted.* Biff *walks out.)*

Linda, *(calling after* Biff*)*: Sleep well, darling!

Happy: I'm gonna get married, Mom. I wanted to tell you.

Linda: Go to sleep, dear.

Happy, *(going)*: I just wanted to tell you.

Willy: Keep up the good work. *(Happy exits.)* God . . . remember that Ebbets Field game? The championship of the city?

Linda: Just rest. Should I sing to you?

Willy: Yeah. Sing to me. *Linda hums a soft lullaby.* When that team came out—he was the tallest, remember?

Linda: Oh, yes. And in gold.

Biff *enters the darkened kitchen, takes a cigarette, and leaves the house. He comes downstage into a golden pool of light. He smokes, staring at the night.*

Willy: Like a young god. Hercules—something like that. And the sun, the sun all around him. Remember how he waved to me? Right up from the field, with the representatives of three colleges standing by? And the buyers I brought, and the cheers when he came out—Loman, Loman, Loman! God Almighty, he'll be great yet. A star like that, magnificent, can never really fade away!

The light on Willy *is fading. The gas heater begins to glow through the kitchen wall, near the stairs, a blue flame beneath red coils.*

Linda, *(timidly)*: Willy dear, what has he got against you?

Willy: I'm so tired. Don't talk any more.

Biff *slowly returns to the kitchen. He stops, stares toward the heater.*

Linda: Will you ask Howard to let you work in New York?

Willy: First thing in the morning. Everything'll be all right.

Biff *reaches behind the heater and draws out a length of rubber tubing. He is horrified and turns his head toward* Willy's *room, still dimly lit, from which the strains of* Linda's *desperate but monotonous humming rise.*

Willy, *(staring through the window into the moonlight)*: Gee, look at the moon moving between the buildings!

Biff *wraps the tubing around his hand and quickly goes up the stairs.*

CURTAIN

ACT TWO

Music is heard, gay and bright. The curtain rises as the music fades away. Willy, *in shirt sleeves, is sitting at the kitchen table, sipping coffee, his hat in his lap.* Linda *is filling his cup when she can.*

Willy: Wonderful coffee. Meal in itself.

Linda: Can I make you some eggs?

Willy: No. Take a breath.

Linda: You look so rested, dear.

Willy: I slept like a dead one. First time in months. Imagine, sleeping till ten on a Tuesday morning. Boys left nice and early, heh?

Linda: They were out of here by eight o'clock.

Willy: Good work!

Linda: It was so thrilling to see them leaving together. I can't get over the shaving lotion in this house!

Willy, (smiling): Mmm—

Linda: Biff was very changed this morning. His whole attitude seemed to be hopeful. He couldn't wait to get downtown to see Oliver.

Willy: He's heading for a change. There's no question, there simply are certain men that take longer to get—solidified. How did he dress?

Linda: His blue suit. He's so handsome in that suit. He could be a—anything in that suit!

Willy *gets up from the table.* Linda *holds his jacket for him.*

Willy: There's no question, no question at all. Gee, on the way home tonight I'd like to buy some seeds.

Linda, (laughing): That'd be wonderful. But not enough sun gets back there. Nothing'll grow any more.

Willy: You wait, kid, before it's all over we're gonna get a little place out in the country, and I'll raise some vegetables, a couple of chickens . . .

Linda: You'll do it yet, dear.

Willy *walks out of his jacket.* Linda *follows him.*

Willy: And they'll get married, and come for a weekend. I'd build a little guest house. 'Cause I got so many fine tools. All I'd need would be a little lumber and some peace of mind.

Linda: (joyfully) I sewed the lining . . .

Willy: I could build two guest houses, so they'd both come. Did he decide how much he's going to ask Oliver for?

Linda, (getting him into the jacket): He didn't mention it, but I imagine ten or fifteen thousand. You going to talk to Howard today?

Willy: Yeah. I'll put it to him straight and simple. He'll just have to take me off the road.

Linda: And Willy, don't forget to ask for a little advance, because we've got the insurance premium. It's the grace period now.

Willy: That's a hundred . . . ?

Linda: A hundred and eight, sixty-eight. Because we're a little
   short again.
Willy: Why are we short?
Linda: Well, you had the motor job on the car . . .
Willy: That goddam Studebaker!
Linda: And you got one more payment on the refrigerator . . .
Willy: But it just broke again!
Linda: Well, it's old, dear.
Willy: I told you we should've bought a well-advertised
   machine. Charley bought a General Electric and it's twenty
   years old and it's still good, that son-of-a-bitch.
Linda: But, Willy—
Willy: Whoever heard of a Hastings refrigerator? Once in my
   life I would like to own something outright before it's broken! I'm always in a race with the junkyard! I just finished
   paying for the car and it's on its last legs. The refrigerator
   consumes belts like a goddam maniac. They time those
   things. They time them so when you finally paid for them,
   they're used up.
Linda, (buttoning up his jacket as he unbuttons it): All told, about
   two hundred dollars would carry us, dear. But that includes
   the last payment on the mortgage. After this payment,
   Willy, the house belongs to us.
Willy: It's twenty-five years!
Linda: Biff was nine years old when we bought it.
Willy: Well, that's a great thing. To weather a twenty-five year
   mortgage is—
Linda: It's an accomplishment.
Willy: All the cement, the lumber, the reconstruction I put in
   this house! There ain't a crack to be found in it any more.
Linda: Well, it served its purpose.
Willy: What purpose? Some stranger'll come along, move in,
   and that's that. If only Biff would take this house, and raise
   a family . . . *(He starts to go.)* Good-by, I'm late.
Linda, (suddenly remembering): Oh, I forgot! You're supposed
   to meet them for dinner.
Willy: Me?
Linda: At Frank's Chop House on Forty-eighth near Sixth
   Avenue.
Willy: Is that so! How about you?
Linda: No, just the three of you. They're gonna blow you to a
   big meal!
Willy: Don't say! Who thought of that?
Linda: Biff came to me this morning, Willy, and he said, "Tell
   Dad, we want to blow him to a big meal." Be there six
   o'clock. You and your two boys are going to have dinner.

Willy: Gee whiz! That's really somethin'. I'm gonna knock Howard for a loop, kid. I'll get an advance, and I'll come home with a New York job. Goddammit, now I'm gonna do it!

Linda: Oh, that's the spirit, Willy!

Willy: I will never get behind a wheel the rest of my life!

Linda: It's changing, Willy, I can feel it changing!

Willy: Beyond a question. G'by, I'm late. *(He starts to go again.)*

Linda, (calling after him as she runs to the kitchen table for a handkerchief): You got your glasses?

Willy, (feels for them, then comes back in): Yeah, yeah, got my glasses.

Linda, (giving him the handkerchief): And a handkerchief.

Willy: Yeah, handkerchief.

Linda: And your saccharine?

Willy: Yeah, my saccharine.

Linda: Be careful on the subway stairs.

She kisses him, and a silk stocking is seen hanging from her hand. Willy *notices it.*

Willy: Will you stop mending stockings? At least while I'm in the house. It gets me nervous. I can't tell you. Please.

Linda *hides the stocking in her hand as she follows* Willy *across the forestage in front of the house.*

Linda: Remember, Frank's Chop House.

Willy, (passing the apron): Maybe beets would grow out there.

Linda, (laughing): But you tried so many times.

Willy: Yeah. Well, don't work hard today. *(He disappears around the right corner of the house.)*

Linda: Be careful!

As Willy *vanishes,* Linda *waves to him. Suddenly the phone rings. She runs across the stage and into the kitchen and lifts it.*

Linda: Hello? Oh, Biff! I'm so glad you called, I just . . . Yes, sure, I just told him. Yes, he'll be there for dinner at six o'clock, I didn't forget. Listen, I was just dying to tell you. You know that little rubber pipe I told you about? That he connected to the gas heater? I finally decided to go down the cellar this morning and take it away and destroy it. But it's gone! Imagine? He took it away himself, it isn't there! *(She listens.)* When? Oh, then you took it. Oh—nothing, it's just that I'd hoped he'd taken it away himself. Oh, I'm not worried, darling, because this morning he left in such high spirits, it was like the old days! I'm not afraid any more. Did Mr. Oliver see you? . . . Well, you wait there then. And make a nice impression on him, darling. Just don't perspire too much before you see him. And have a nice time with Dad. He may have big news too! . . . That's right, a New York job. And be sweet to him tonight, dear. Be loving to him. Because he's only a little boat looking for a harbor. *(She is trembling with sorrow and joy.)* Oh, that's wonderful, Biff, you'll save his life. Thanks, darling. Just put your arm around him when he comes into the restaurant. Give him a smile. That's the boy . . . Good-by, dear. . . . You got your comb? . . . That's fine. Good-by, Biff dear.

In the middle of her speech, Howard Wagner, *thirty-six, wheels on a small type-writer table on which is a wire-recording machine and proceeds to plug it in. This is on the left forestage. Light slowly fades on* Linda *as it rises on* Howard. *How-ard is intent on threading the machine and only glances over his shoulder as* Willy *appears.*

Willy: Pst! Pst!
Howard: Hello, Willy, come in.
Willy: Like to have a little talk with you, Howard.
Howard: Sorry to keep you waiting. I'll be with you in a minute.
Willy: What's that, Howard?
Howard: Didn't you ever see one of these? Wire recorder.
Willy: Oh. Can we talk a minute?
Howard: Records things. Just got delivery yesterday. Been driving me crazy, the most terrific machine I ever saw in my life. I was up all night with it.
Willy: What do you do with it?
Howard: I bought it for dictation, but you can do anything with it. Listen to this. I had it home last night. Listen to what I picked up. The first one is my daughter. Get this. *(He flicks the switch and "Roll out the Barrel" is heard being whistled.)* Listen to that kid whistle.
Willy: That is lifelike, isn't it?
Howard: Seven years old. Get that tone.
Willy: Ts, ts. Like to ask a little favor if you . . .

The whistling breaks off, and the voice of Howard's *daughter is heard.*

His Daughter: "Now you, Daddy."
Howard: She's crazy for me! *(Again the same song is whistled.)* That's me! Ha! *(He winks.)*
Willy: You're very good!

The whistling breaks off again. The machine runs silent for a moment.

Howard: Sh! Get this now, this is my son.
His Son: "The capital of Alabama is Montgomery; the capital of

Arizona is Phoenix; the capital of Arkansas is Little Rock; the capital of California is Sacramento . . ." *(and on, and on.)*

Howard, (holding up five fingers): Five years old, Willy!

Willy: He'll make an announcer some day!

His Son, (continuing): "The capital . . ."

Howard: Get that—alphabetical order! *(The machine breaks off suddenly.)* Wait a minute. The maid kicked the plug out.

Willy: It certainly is a—

Howard: Sh, for God's sake!

His Son: "It's nine o'clock, Bulova watch time. So I have to go to sleep."

Willy: That really is—

Howard: Wait a minute! The next is my wife.

They wait.

Howard's Voice: "Go on, say something." *(Pause.)* "Well, you gonna talk?"

His Wife: "I can't think of anything."

Howard's Voice: "Well, talk—it's turning."

His Wife, (shyly, beaten): "Hello." *(Silence.)* "Oh, Howard, I can't talk into this . . ."

Howard, (snapping the machine off): That was my wife.

Willy: That is a wonderful machine. Can we—

Howard: I tell you, Willy, I'm gonna take my camera, and my bandsaw, and all my hobbies, and out they go. This is the most fascinating relaxation I ever found.

Willy: I think I'll get one myself.

Howard: Sure, they're only a hundred and a half. You can't do without it. Supposing you wanna hear Jack Benny, see? But you can't be at home at that hour. So you tell the maid to turn the radio on when Jack Benny comes on, and this automatically goes on with the radio . . .

Willy: And when you come home you . . .

Howard: You can come home twelve o'clock, one o'clock, any time you like, and you get yourself a Coke and sit yourself down, throw the switch, and there's Jack Benny's program in the middle of the night!

Willy: I'm definitely going to get one. Because lots of times I'm on the road, and I think to myself, what I must be missing on the radio!

Howard: Don't you have a radio in the car?

Willy: Well, yeah, but who ever thinks of turning it on?

Howard: Say, aren't you supposed to be in Boston?

Willy: That's what I want to talk to you about, Howard. You got a minute? *(He draws a chair in from the wing.)*

Howard: What happened? What're you doing here?

Willy: Well . . .

Howard: You didn't crack up again, did you?

Willy: Oh, no. No . . .

Howard: Geez, you had me worried there for a minute. What's the trouble?

Willy: Well, tell you the truth, Howard. I've come to the decision that I'd rather not travel any more.

Howard: Not travel! Well, what'll you do?

Willy: Remember, Christmas time, when you had the party here? You said you'd try to think of some spot for me here in town.

Howard: With us?

Willy: Well, sure.

Howard: Oh, yeah, yeah. I remember. Well, I couldn't think of anything for you, Willy.

Willy: I tell ya, Howard. The kids are all grown up, y'know. I don't need much any more. If I could take home—well, sixty-five dollars a week, I could swing it.

Howard: Yeah, but Willy, see I—

Willy: I tell ya why, Howard. Speaking frankly and between the two of us, y'know—I'm just a little tired.

Howard: Oh, I could understand that, Willy. But you're a road man, Willy, and we do a road business. We've only got a half-dozen salesmen on the floor here.

Willy: God knows, Howard, I never asked a favor of any man. But I was with the firm when your father used to carry you in here in his arms.

Howard: I know that, Willy, but—

Willy: Your father came to me the day you were born and asked me what I thought of the name of Howard, may he rest in peace.

Howard: I appreciate that, Willy, but there just is no spot here for you. If I had a spot I'd slam you right in, but I just don't have a single solitary spot.

He looks for his lighter. Willy *has picked it up and gives it to him. Pause.*

Willy, (with increasing anger): Howard, all I need to set my table is fifty dollars a week.

Howard: But where am I going to put you, kid?

Willy: Look, it isn't a question of whether I can sell merchandise, is it?

Howard: No, but it's a business, kid, and everybody's gotta pull his own weight.

Willy, (desperately): Just let me tell you a story, Howard—

Howard: 'Cause you gotta admit, business is business.

Willy, (angrily): Business is definitely business, but just listen for a minute. You don't understand this. When I was a boy —eighteen, nineteen—I was already on the road. And there was a question in my mind as to whether selling had a future for me. Because in those days I had a yearning to go to Alaska. See, there were three gold strikes in one month in Alaska, and I felt like going out. Just for the ride, you might say.

Howard, (barely interested): Don't say.

Willy: Oh, yeah, my father lived many years in Alaska. He was an adventurous man. We've got quite a little streak of self-reliance in our family. I thought I'd go out with my older brother and try to locate him, and maybe settle in the North with the old man. And I was almost decided to go, when I met a salesman in the Parker House. His name was Dave Singleman. And he was eighty-four years old, and he'd drummed merchandise in thirty-one states. And old Dave, he'd go up to his room, y'understand, put on his green velvet slippers—I'll never forget—and pick up his phone and call the buyers, and without ever leaving his room, at the age of eighty-four, he made his living. And when I saw that, I realized that selling was the greatest career a man could want. 'Cause what could be more satisfying than to be able to go, at the age of eighty-four, into twenty or thirty different cities, and pick up a phone, and be remembered and loved and helped by so many different people? Do you know? when he died—and by the way he died the death of a salesman, in his green velvet slippers in the smoker of the New York, New Haven and Hartford, going into Boston— when he died, hundreds of salesmen and buyers were at his funeral. Things were sad on a lotta trains for months after that. *(He stands up.* Howard *has not looked at him.)* In those days there was personality in it, Howard. There was respect, and comradeship, and gratitude in it. Today, it's all cut and dried, and there's no chance for bringing friendship to bear—or personality. You see what I mean? They don't know me any more.

Howard, (moving away, to the right): That's just the thing, Willy.

Willy: If I had forty dollars a week—that's all I'd need. Forty dollars, Howard.

Howard: Kid, I can't take blood from a stone, I—

Willy, (desperation is on him now): Howard, the year Al Smith was nominated, your father came to me and—

Howard, (starting to go off): I've got to see some people, kid.

Willy, (stopping him): I'm talking about your father! There were promises made across this desk! You mustn't tell me you've got people to see—I put thirty-four years into this firm, Howard, and now I can't pay my insurance! You can't eat the orange and throw the peel away—a man is not a piece of fruit! *(After a pause):* Now pay attention. Your father—in 1928 I had a big year. I averaged a hundred and seventy dollars a week in commissions.

Howard, *(impatiently):* Now, Willy, you never averaged—

Willy, *(banging his hand on the desk):* I averaged a hundred and seventy dollars a week in the year of 1928! And your father came to me—or rather, I was in the office here—it was right over this desk—and he put his hand on my shoulder—

Howard, *(getting up):* You'll have to excuse me, Willy, I gotta see some people. Pull yourself together. *(Going out):* I'll be back in a little while.

On Howard's *exit, the light on his chair grows very bright and strange.*

Willy: Pull myself together! What the hell did I say to him? My God, I was yelling at him! How could I! *(Willy breaks off, staring at the light, which occupies the chair, animating it. He approaches this chair, standing across the desk from it.)* Frank, Frank, don't you remember what you told me that time? How you put your hand on my shoulder, and Frank . . . *(He leans on the desk and as he speaks the dead man's name he accidentally switches on the recorder, and instantly)*

Howard's Son: ". . . of New York is Albany. The capital of Ohio is Cincinnati, the capital of Rhode Island is . . ." *(The recitation continues.)*

Willy, *(leaping away with fright, shouting):* Ha! Howard! Howard! Howard!

Howard, *(rushing in):* What happened?

Willy, *(pointing at the machine, which continues nasally, childishly, with the capital cities):* Shut it off! Shut it off!

Howard, *(pulling the plug out):* Look, Willy . . .

Willy, *(pressing his hands to his eyes):* I gotta get myself some coffee. I'll get some coffee . . .

Willy *starts to walk out.* Howard *stops him.*

Howard, *(rolling up the cord):* Willy, look . . .

Willy: I'll go to Boston.

Howard: Willy, you can't go to Boston for us.

Willy: Why can't I go?

Howard: I don't want you to represent us. I've been meaning to tell you for a long time now.

Willy: Howard, are you firing me?

Howard: I think you need a good long rest, Willy.

Willy: Howard—

Howard: And when you feel better, come back, and we'll see if we can work something out.

Willy: But I gotta earn money, Howard. I'm in no position to—

Howard: Where are your sons? Why don't your sons give you a hand?

Willy: They're working on a very big deal.

Howard: This is no time for false pride, Willy. You go to your sons and you tell them that you're tired. You've got two great boys, haven't you?

Willy: Oh, no question, no question, but in the meantime . . .

Howard: Then that's that, heh?

Willy: All right, I'll go to Boston tomorrow.

Howard: No, no.

Willy: I can't throw myself on my sons. I'm not a cripple!

Howard: Look, kid, I'm busy this morning.

Willy, (grasping Howard's *arm):* Howard, you've got to let me go to Boston!

Howard, (hard, keeping himself under control): I've got a line of people to see this morning. Sit down, take five minutes, and pull yourself together, and then go home, will ya? I need the office, Willy. *(He starts to go, turns, remembering the recorder, starts to push off the table holding the recorder.)* Oh, yeah. Whenever you can this week, stop by and drop off the samples. You'll feel better, Willy, and then come back and we'll talk. Pull yourself together, kid, there's people outside.

Howard *exits, pushing the table off left.* Willy *stares into space, exhausted. Now the music is heard—*Ben's *music—first distantly, then closer, closer. As* Willy *speaks,* Ben *enters from the right. He carries valise and umbrella.*

Willy: Oh, Ben, how did you do it? What is the answer? Did you wind up the Alaska deal already?

Ben: Doesn't take much time if you know what you're doing. Just a short business trip. Boarding ship in an hour. Wanted to say good-by.

Willy: Ben, I've got to talk to you.

Ben, (glancing at his watch): Haven't the time, William.

Willy, (crossing the apron to Ben*):* Ben, nothing's working out. I don't know what to do.

Ben: Now, look here, William. I've bought timberland in Alaska and I need a man to look after things for me.

Willy: God, timberland! Me and my boys in those grand outdoors!

Ben: You've a new continent at your doorstep, William. Get out of these cities, they're full of talk and time payments and courts of law. Screw on your fists and you can fight for a fortune up there.

Willy: Yes, yes! Linda, Linda!

Linda *enters as of old, with the wash.*

Linda: Oh, you're back?

Ben: I haven't much time.

Willy: No, wait! Linda, he's got a proposition for me in Alaska.

Linda: But he's got— *(To Ben):* He's got a beautiful job here.

Willy: But in Alaska, kid, I could—

Linda: You're doing well enough, Willy!

Ben, (to Linda): Enough for what, my dear?

Linda, (frightened of Ben *and angry at him):* Don't say those things to him! Enough to be happy right here, right now. *(To* Willy, *while* Ben *laughs):* Why must everybody conquer the world? You're well liked, and the boys love you, and someday—*(to* Ben)—why, old man Wagner told him just the other day that if he keeps it up he'll be a member of the firm, didn't he, Willy?

Willy: Sure, sure. I am building something with this firm, Ben, and if a man is building something he must be on the right track, mustn't he?

Ben: What are you building? Lay your hand on it. Where is it?

Willy, (hesitantly): That's true, Linda, there's nothing.

Linda: Why? *(To* Ben): There's a man eighty-four years old—

Willy: That's right, Ben, that's right. When I look at that man I say, what is there to worry about?

Ben: Bah!

Willy: It's true, Ben. All he has to do is go into any city, pick up the phone, and he's making his living and you know why?

Ben, (picking up his valise): I've got to go.

Willy, (holding Ben *back):* Look at this boy!

Biff, *in his high school sweater, enters carrying suitcase.* Happy *carries* Biff's *shoulder guards, gold helmet, and football pants.*

Willy: Without a penny to his name, three great universities are begging for him, and from there the sky's the limit, because it's not what you do, Ben. It's who you know and the smile on your face! It's contacts, Ben, contacts! The whole wealth of Alaska passes over the lunch table at the Commodore Hotel, and that's the wonder, the wonder of this country, that a man can end with diamonds here on the basis of being liked! *(He turns to Biff.)* And that's why when you get out on that field today it's important. Because thousands of people will be rooting for you and loving you. *(To Ben, who has again begun to leave):* And Ben! when he walks into a business office his name will sound out like a bell and all the doors will open to him! I've seen it, Ben, I've seen it a thousand times! You can't feel it with your hand like timber, but it's there!

Ben: Good-by, William.

Willy: Ben, am I right? Don't you think I'm right? I value your advice.

Ben: There's a new continent at your doorstep, William. You could walk out rich. Rich! *(He is gone.)*

Willy: We'll do it here, Ben! You hear me? We're gonna do it here!

Young Bernard *rushes in. The gay music of the Boys is heard.*

Bernard: Oh, gee, I was afraid you left already!

Willy: Why? What time is it?

Bernard: It's half-past one!

Willy: Well, come on, everybody! Ebbets Field next stop! Where's the pennants? *(He rushes through the wall-line of the kitchen and out into the living-room.)*

Linda, (to Biff): Did you pack fresh underwear?

Biff, (who has been limbering up): I want to go!

Bernard: Biff, I'm carrying your helmet, ain't I?

Happy: No, I'm carrying the helmet.

Bernard: Oh, Biff, you promised me.

Happy: I'm carrying the helmet.

Bernard: How am I going to get in the locker room?

Linda: Let him carry the shoulder guards. *(She puts her coat and hat on in the kitchen.)*

Bernard: Can I, Biff? 'Cause I told everybody I'm going to be in the locker room.

Happy: In Ebbets Field it's the clubhouse.

Bernard: I meant the clubhouse. Biff!

Happy: Biff!

Biff, (grandly, after a slight pause): Let him carry the shoulder guards.

Happy, (as he gives Bernard the shoulder guards): Stay close to us now.

Willy *rushes in with the pennants.*

Willy, (handing them out): Everybody wave when Biff comes out on the field. *(Happy and Bernard run off.)* You set now, boy?

The music has died away.

> *Biff:* Ready to go, Pop. Every muscle is ready.
>
> *Willy, (at the edge of the apron):* You realize what this means?
>
> *Biff:* That's right, Pop.
>
> *Willy, (feeling Biff's muscles):* You're comin' home this after-noon captain of the All-Scholastic Championship Team of the City of New York.
>
> *Biff:* I got it, Pop. And remember, pal, when I take off my helmet, that touchdown is for you.
>
> *Willy:* Let's go! *(He is starting out, with his arm around Biff, when Charley enters, as of old, in knickers.)* I got no room for you, Charley.
>
> *Charley:* Room? For what?
>
> *Willy:* In the car.
>
> *Charley:* You goin' for a ride? I wanted to shoot some casino.
>
> *Willy, (furiously):* Casino? *(Incredulously):* Don't you realize what today is?
>
> *Linda:* Oh, he knows, Willy. He's just kidding you.
>
> *Willy:* That's nothing to kid about!
>
> *Charley:* No, Linda, what's goin' on?
>
> *Linda:* He's playing in Ebbets Field.
>
> *Charley:* Baseball in this weather?
>
> *Willy:* Don't talk to him. Come on, come on! *(He is pushing them out.)*
>
> *Charley:* Wait a minute, didn't you hear the news?
>
> *Willy:* What?
>
> *Charley:* Don't you listen to the radio? Ebbets Field just blew up.
>
> *Willy:* You go to hell! *(Charley laughs. Pushing them out):* Come on, come on! We're late.
>
> *Charley, (as they go):* Knock a homer, Biff, knock a homer!
>
> *Willy, (the last to leave, turning to Charley):* I don't think that was funny, Charley. This is the greatest day of his life.
>
> *Charley:* Willy, when are you going to grow up?
>
> *Willy:* Yeah, heh? When this game is over, Charley, you'll be laughing out of the other side of your face. They'll be call-ing him another Red Grange. Twenty-five thousand a year.
>
> *Charley, (kidding):* Is that so?
>
> *Willy:* Yeah, that's so.
>
> *Charley:* Well, then, I'm sorry, Willy. But tell me something.
>
> *Willy:* What?
>
> *Charley:* Who is Red Grange?
>
> *Willy:* Put up your hands. Goddam you, put up your hands!

Charley, *chuckling, shakes his head and walks away, around the left corner of the stage.* Willy *follows him. The music rises to a mocking frenzy.*

> Willy: Who the hell do you think you are, better than everybody else? You don't know everything, you big, ignorant, stupid . . . Put up your hands!

Light rises, on the right side of the forestage, on a small table in the reception room of Charley's *office. Traffic sounds are heard.* Bernard, *now mature, sits whistling to himself. A pair of tennis rackets and an overnight bag are on the floor beside him.*

> Willy, *(offstage):* What are you walking away for? Don't walk away! If you're going to say something say it to my face! I know you laugh at me behind my back. You'll laugh out of the other side of your goddam face after this game. Touchdown! Touchdown! Eighty thousand people! Touchdown! Right between the goal posts.

Bernard *is a quiet, earnest, but self-assured young man.* Willy's *voice is coming from right upstage now.* Bernard *lowers his feet off the table and listens.* Jenny, *his father's secretary, enters.*

> Jenny, *(distressed):* Say, Bernard, will you go out in the hall?
> Bernard: What is that noise? Who is it?
> Jenny: Mr. Loman. He just got off the elevator.
> Bernard, *(getting up):* Who's he arguing with?
> Jenny: Nobody. There's nobody with him. I can't deal with him any more, and your father gets all upset everytime he comes. I've got a lot of typing to do, and your father's waiting to sign it. Will you see him?
> Willy, *(entering):* Touchdown! Touch— *(He sees* Jenny.) Jenny, Jenny, good to see you. How're ya? Workin'? Or still honest?
> Jenny: Fine. How've you been feeling?
> Willy: Not much any more, Jenny. Ha, ha! *(He is surprised to see the rackets.)*
> Bernard: Hello, Uncle Willy.
> Willy, *(almost shocked):* Bernard! Well, look who's here! *(He comes quickly, guiltily, to* Bernard *and warmly shakes his hand.)*
> Bernard: How are you? Good to see you.
> Willy: What are you doing here?
> Bernard: Oh, just stopped by to see Pop. Get off my feet till my train leaves. I'm going to Washington in a few minutes.
> Willy: Is he in?
> Bernard: Yes, he's in his office with the accountant. Sit down.
> Willy, *(sitting down):* What're you going to do in Washington?
> Bernard: Oh, just a case I've got there, Willy.

Willy: That so? *(Indicating the rackets):* You going to play tennis there?

Bernard: I'm staying with a friend who's got a court.

Willy: Don't say. His own tennis court. Must be fine people, I bet.

Bernard: They are, very nice. Dad tells me Biff's in town.

Willy, (with a big smile): Yeah, Biff's in. Working on a very big deal, Bernard.

Bernard: What's Biff doing?

Willy: Well, he's been doing very big things in the West. But he decided to establish himself here. Very big. We're having dinner. Did I hear your wife had a boy?

Bernard: That's right. Our second.

Willy: Two boys! What do you know!

Bernard: What kind of a deal has Biff got?

Willy: Well, Bill Oliver—very big sporting-goods man—he wants Biff very badly. Called him in from the West. Long distance, carte blanche, special deliveries. Your friends have their own private tennis court?

Bernard: You still with the old firm, Willy?

Willy, (after a pause): I'm—I'm overjoyed to see how you made the grade, Bernard, overjoyed. It's an encouraging thing to see a young man really—really— Looks very good for Biff —very— *(He breaks off, then):* Bernard— *(He is so full of emotion, he breaks off again.)*

Bernard: What is it, Willy?

Willy, (small and alone): What—what's the secret?

Bernard: What secret?

Willy: How—how did you? Why didn't he ever catch on?

Bernard: I wouldn't know that, Willy.

Willy, (confidentially, desperately): You were his friend, his boyhood friend. There's something I don't understand about it. His life ended after that Ebbets Field game. From the age of seventeen nothing good ever happened to him.

Bernard: He never trained himself for anything.

Willy: But he did, he did. After high school he took so many correspondence courses. Radio mechanics; television; God knows what, and never made the slightest mark.

Bernard, (taking off his glasses): Willy, do you want to talk candidly?

Willy, (rising, faces Bernard): I regard you as a very brilliant man, Bernard. I value your advice.

Bernard: Oh, the hell with the advice, Willy. I couldn't advise you. There's just one thing I've always wanted to ask you. When he was supposed to graduate, and the math teacher flunked him—

Willy: Oh, that son-of-a-bitch ruined his life.

Arthur Miller   **1759**

Bernard: Yeah, but, Willy, all he had to do was go to summer school and make up that subject.

Willy: That's right, that's right.

Bernard: Did you tell him not to go to summer school?

Willy: Me? I begged him to go. I ordered him to go!

Bernard: Then why wouldn't he go?

Willy: Why? Why! Bernard, that question has been trailing me like a ghost for the last fifteen years. He flunked the subject, and laid down and died like a hammer hit him!

Bernard: Take it easy, kid.

Willy: Let me talk to you—I got nobody to talk to. Bernard, Bernard, was it my fault? Y'see? It keeps going around in my mind, maybe I did something to him. I got nothing to give him.

Bernard: Don't take it so hard.

Willy: Why did he lay down? What is the story there? You were his friend!

Bernard: Willy, I remember, it was June, and our grades came out. And he'd flunked math.

Willy: That son-of-a-bitch!

Bernard: No, it wasn't right then. Biff just got very angry, I remember, and he was ready to enroll in summer school.

Willy, (surprised): He was?

Bernard: He wasn't beaten by it at all. But then, Willy, he disappeared from the block for almost a month. And I got the idea that he'd gone up to New England to see you. Did he have a talk with you then?

Willy *stares in silence.*

Bernard: Willy?

Willy, (with a strong edge of resentment in his voice): Yeah, he came to Boston. What about it?

Bernard: Well, just that when he came back—I'll never forget this, it always mystifies me. Because I'd thought so well of Biff, even though he'd always taken advantage of me. I loved him, Willy, y'know? And he came back after that month and took his sneakers—remember those sneakers with "University of Virginia" printed on them? He was so proud of those, wore them every day. And he took them down in the cellar, and burned them up in the furnace. We had a fist fight. It lasted at least half an hour. Just the two of us, punching each other down in the cellar, and crying right through it. I've often thought of how strange it was that I knew he'd given up his life. What happened in Boston, Willy?

Willy *looks at him as at an intruder.*

>   *Bernard:* I just bring it up because you asked me.
>   *Willy, (angrily):* Nothing. What do you mean, "What hap-
>   pened?" What's that got to do with anything?
>   *Bernard:* Well, don't get sore.
>   *Willy:* What are you trying to do, blame it on me? If a boy lays
>   down is that my fault?
>   *Bernard:* Now, Willy, don't get—
>   *Willy:* Well, don't—don't talk to me that way! What does that
>   mean, "What happened?"

Charley *enters. He is in his vest, and he carries a bottle of bourbon.*

>   *Charley:* Hey, you're going to miss that train. *(He waves the bottle.)*
>   *Bernard:* Yeah, I'm going. *(He takes the bottle.)* Thanks, Pop. *(He
>   picks up his rackets and bag.)* Good-by, Willy, and don't worry
>   about it. You know, "If at first you don't succeed . . ."
>   *Willy:* Yes, I believe in that.
>   *Bernard:* But sometimes, Willy, it's better for a man just to walk
>   away.
>   *Willy:* Walk away?
>   *Bernard:* That's right.
>   *Willy:* But if you can't walk away?
>   *Bernard, (after a slight pause):* I guess that's when it's tough.
>   *(Extending his hand):* Good-by, Willy.
>   *Willy, (shaking* Bernard's *hand):* Good-by, boy.
>   *Charley, (an arm on* Bernard's *shoulder):* How do you like this kid?
>   Gonna argue a case in front of the Supreme Court.
>   *Bernard, (protesting):* Pop!
>   *Willy, (genuinely shocked, pained, and happy):* No! The Supreme
>   Court!
>   *Bernard:* I gotta run. 'By, Dad!
>   *Charley:* Knock 'em dead, Bernard!

Bernard *goes off.*

>   *Willy, (as* Charley *takes out his wallet):* The Supreme Court!
>   And he didn't even mention it!
>   *Charley, (counting out money on the desk):* He don't have to—he's
>   gonna do it.
>   *Willy:* And you never told him what to do, did you? You never
>   took any interest in him.
>   *Charley:* My salvation is that I never took any interest in anything.
>   There's some money—fifty dollars. I got an accountant
>   inside.
>   *Willy:* Charley, look . . . *(With difficulty):* I got my insurance to

pay. If you can manage it—I need a hundred and ten dollars.

Charley *doesn't reply for a moment; merely stops moving.*

>   *Willy:* I'd draw it from my bank but Linda would know, and I . . .
>   *Charley:* Sit down, Willy.
>   *Willy, (moving toward the chair):* I'm keeping an account of everything, remember. I'll pay every penny back. *(He sits.)*
>   *Charley:* Now listen to me, Willy.
>   *Willy:* I want you to know I appreciate . . .
>   *Charley, (sitting down on the table):* Willy, what're you doin'? What the hell is goin' on in your head?
>   *Willy:* Why? I'm simply . . .
>   *Charley:* I offered you a job. You can make fifty dollars a week. And I won't send you on the road.
>   *Willy:* I've got a job.
>   *Charley:* Without pay? What kind of a job is a job without pay? *(He rises.)* Now, look, kid, enough is enough. I'm no genius but I know when I'm being insulted.
>   *Willy:* Insulted!
>   *Charley:* Why don't you want to work for me?
>   *Willy:* What's the matter with you? I've got a job.
>   *Charley:* Then what're you walkin' in here every week for?
>   *Willy, (getting up):* Well, if you don't want me to walk in here—
>   *Charley:* I am offering you a job.
>   *Willy:* I don't want your goddam job!
>   *Charley:* When the hell are you going to grow up?
>   *Willy, (furiously):* You big ignoramus, if you say that to me again I'll rap you one! I don't care how big you are! *(He's ready to fight.)*

Pause.

>   *Charley, (kindly, going to him):* How much do you need, Willy?
>   *Willy:* Charley, I'm strapped. I'm strapped. I don't know what to do. I was just fired.
>   *Charley:* Howard fired you?
>   *Willy:* That snotnose. Imagine that? I named him. I named him Howard.
>   *Charley:* Willy, when're you gonna realize that them things don't mean anything? You named him Howard, but you can't sell that. The only thing you got in this world is what you can sell. And the funny thing is that you're a salesman, and you don't know that.
>   *Willy:* I've always tried to think otherwise, I guess. I always felt that if a man was impressive, and well liked, that nothing—

Charley: Why must everybody like you? Who liked J. P. Morgan? Was he impressive? In a Turkish bath he'd look like a butcher. But with his pockets on he was very well liked. Now listen, Willy, I know you don't like me, and nobody can say I'm in love with you, but I'll give you a job because—just for the hell of it, put it that way. Now what do you say?

Willy: I—I just can't work for you, Charley.

Charley: What're you, jealous of me?

Willy: I can't work for you, that's all, don't ask me why.

Charley, (angered, takes out more bills): You been jealous of me all your life, you damned fool! Here, pay your insurance. *(He puts the money in* Willy's *hand.)*

Willy: I'm keeping strict accounts.

Charley: I've got some work to do. Take care of yourself. And pay your insurance.

Willy, (moving to the right): Funny, y'know? After all the highways, and the trains, and the appointments, and the years, you end up worth more dead than alive.

Charley: Willy, nobody's worth nothin' dead. *(After a slight pause):* Did you hear what I said?

Willy *stands still, dreaming.*

Charley: Willy!

Willy: Apologize to Bernard for me when you see him. I didn't mean to argue with him. He's a fine boy. They're all fine boys, and they'll end up big—all of them. Someday they'll all play tennis together. Wish me luck, Charley. He saw Bill Oliver today.

Charley: Good luck.

Willy, (on the verge of tears): Charley, you're the only friend I got. Isn't that a remarkable thing? *(He goes out.)*

Charley: Jesus!

Charley *stares after him a moment and follows. All light blacks out. Suddenly raucous music is heard, and a red glow rises behind the screen at right.* Stanley, *a young waiter, appears, carrying a table, followed by* Happy, *who is carrying two chairs.*

Stanley, (putting the table down): That's all right, Mr. Loman, I can handle it myself. *(He turns and takes the chairs from* Happy *and places them at the table.)*

Happy, (glancing around): Oh, this is better.

Stanley: Sure, in the front there you're in the middle of all kinds a noise. Whenever you got a party, Mr. Loman, you just tell me and I'll put you back here. Y'know, there's a lotta people they don't like it private, because when they go out they like to see a lotta action around them because they're sick and tired to stay in the house by theirself. But I know you, you ain't from Hackensack. You know what I mean?

Happy, (sitting down): So how's it coming, Stanley?

Stanley: Ah, it's a dog's life. I only wish during the war they'd a took me in the Army. I coulda been dead by now.

Happy: My brother's back, Stanley.

Stanley: Oh, he come back, heh? From the Far West.

Happy: Yeah, big cattle man, my brother, so treat him right. And my father's coming too.

Stanley: Oh, your father too!

Happy: You got a couple of nice lobsters?

Stanley: Hundred per cent, big.

Happy: I want them with the claws.

Stanley: Don't worry, I don't give you no mice. *(Happy laughs.)* How about some wine? It'll put a head on the meal.

Happy: No. You remember, Stanley, that recipe I brought you from overseas? With the champagne in it?

Stanley: Oh, yeah, sure. I still got it tacked up yet in the kitchen. But that'll have to cost a buck apiece anyways.

Happy: That's all right.

Stanley: What'd you, hit a number or somethin'?

Happy: No, it's a little celebration. My brother is—I think he pulled off a big deal today. I think we're going into business together.

Stanley: Great! That's the best for you. Because a family business, you know what I mean?—that's the best.

Happy: That's what I think.

Stanley: 'Cause what's the difference? Somebody steals? It's in the family. Know what I mean? *(Sotto voce):* Like this bartender here. The boss is goin' crazy what kinda leak he's got in the cash register. You put it in but it don't come out.

Happy, (raising his head): Sh!

Stanley: What?

Happy: You notice I wasn't lookin' right or left, was I?

Stanley: No.

Happy: And my eyes are closed.

Stanley: So what's the—?

Happy: Strudel's comin'.

Stanley, (catching on, looks around): Ah, no, there's no—

He breaks off as a furred, lavishly dressed girl enters and sits at the next table. Both follow her with their eyes.

Stanley: Geez, how'd ya know?

Happy: I got radar or something. *(Staring directly at her profile):* Oooooooo . . . Stanley.

Stanley: I think that's for you, Mr. Loman.

Happy: Look at that mouth. Oh, God. And the binoculars.

Stanley: Geez, you got a life, Mr. Loman.

Happy: Wait on her.

Stanley, (going to the girl's table): Would you like a menu, ma'am?

Girl: I'm expecting someone, but I'd like a—

Happy: Why don't you bring her—excuse me, miss, do you mind? I sell champagne, and I'd like you to try my brand. Bring her a champagne, Stanley.

Girl: That's awfully nice of you.

Happy: Don't mention it. It's all company money. *(He laughs.)*

Girl: That's a charming product to be selling, isn't it?

Happy: Oh, gets to be like everything else. Selling is selling, y'know.

Girl: I suppose.

Happy: You don't happen to sell, do you?

Girl: No, I don't sell.

Happy: Would you object to a compliment from a stranger? You ought to be on a magazine cover.

Girl, (looking at him a little archly): I have been.

Stanley *comes in with a glass of champagne.*

Happy: What'd I say before, Stanley? You see? She's a cover girl.

Stanley: Oh, I could see, I could see.

Happy, (to the Girl*):* What magazine?

Girl: Oh, a lot of them. *(She takes the drink.)* Thank you.

Happy: You know what they say in France, don't you? "Champagne is the drink of the complexion"—Hya, Biff!

Biff *has entered and sits with* Happy.

Biff: Hello, kid. Sorry I'm late.

Happy: I just got here. Uh, Miss—?

Girl: Forsythe.

Happy: Miss Forsythe, this is my brother.

Biff: Is Dad here?

Happy: His name is Biff. You might've heard of him. Great football player.

Girl: Really? What team?

Happy: Are you familiar with football?

Girl: No, I'm afraid I'm not.

Happy: Biff is quarterback with the New York Giants.

Girl: Well, that is nice, isn't it? *(She drinks.)*

Happy: Good health.

Girl: I'm happy to meet you.

Happy: That's my name. Hap. It's really Harold, but at West Point they called me Happy.

Girl, (now really impressed): Oh, I see. How do you do? *(She turns her profile.)*

   Biff: Isn't Dad coming?

Happy: You want her?

   Biff: Oh, I could never make that.

Happy: I remember the time that idea would never come into your head. Where's the old confidence, Biff?

   Biff: I just saw Oliver—

Happy: Wait a minute. I've got to see that old confidence again. Do you want her? She's on call.

   Biff: Oh, no. *(He turns to look at the* Girl.*)*

Happy: I'm telling you. Watch this. *(Turning to the* Girl*):* Honey? *(She turns to him.)* Are you busy?

   Girl: Well, I am . . . but I could make a phone call.

Happy: Do that, will you, honey? And see if you can get a friend. We'll be here for a while. Biff is one of the greatest football players in the country.

   Girl, (standing up): Well, I'm certainly happy to meet you.

Happy: Come back soon.

   Girl: I'll try.

Happy: Don't try, honey, try hard.

The Girl *exits.* Stanley *follows, shaking his head in bewildered admiration.*

Happy: Isn't that a shame now? A beautiful girl like that? That's why I can't get married. There's not a good woman in a thousand. New York is loaded with them, kid!

   Biff: Hap, look—

Happy: I told you she was on call!

   Biff, (strangely unnerved): Cut it out, will ya? I want to say something to you.

Happy: Did you see Oliver?

   Biff: I saw him all right. Now look, I want to tell Dad a couple of things and I want you to help me.

Happy: What? Is he going to back you?

   Biff: Are you crazy? You're out of your goddam head, you know that?

Happy: Why? What happened?

   Biff, (breathlessly): I did a terrible thing today, Hap. It's been the strangest day I ever went through. I'm all numb, I swear.

Happy: You mean he wouldn't see you?

   Biff: Well, I waited six hours for him, see? All day. Kept sending my name in. Even tried to date his secretary so she'd get me to him, but no soap.

Happy: Because you're not showin' the old confidence, Biff. He remembered you, didn't he?

Biff, (stopping Happy *with a gesture):* Finally, about five o'clock, he comes out. Didn't remember who I was or anything. I felt like such an idiot, Hap.

Happy: Did you tell him my Florida idea?

Biff: He walked away. I saw him for one minute. I got so mad I could've torn the walls down! How the hell did I ever get the idea I was a salesman there? I even believed myself that I'd been a salesman for him! And then he gave me one look and—I realized what a ridiculous lie my whole life has been! We've been talking in a dream for fifteen years. I was a shipping clerk.

Happy: What'd you do?

Biff, (with great tension and wonder): Well, he left, see. And the secretary went out. I was all alone in the waiting-room. I don't know what came over me, Hap. The next thing I know I'm in his office—paneled walls, everything. I can't explain it. I—Hap, I took his fountain pen.

Happy: Geez, did he catch you?

Biff: I ran out. I ran down all eleven flights. I ran and ran and ran.

Happy: That was an awful dumb—what'd you do that for?

Biff, (agonized): I don't know, I just—wanted to take something, I don't know. You gotta help me, Hap, I'm gonna tell Pop.

Happy: You crazy? What for?

Biff: Hap, he's got to understand that I'm not the man somebody lends that kind of money to. He thinks I've been spiting him all these years and it's eating him up.

Happy: That's just it. You tell him something nice.

Biff: I can't.

Happy: Say you got a lunch date with Oliver tomorrow.

Biff: So what do I do tomorrow?

Happy: You leave the house tomorrow and come back at night and say Oliver is thinking it over. And he thinks it over for a couple of weeks, and gradually it fades away and nobody's the worse.

Biff: But it'll go on forever!

Happy: Dad is never so happy as when he's looking forward to something!

Willy *enters.*

Happy: Hello, scout!

Willy: Gee, I haven't been here in years!

Stanley *has followed* Willy *in and sets a chair for him.* Stanley *starts off but* Happy *stops him.*

Happy: Stanley!

Stanley *stands by, waiting for an order.*

Biff, *(going to* Willy *with guilt, as to an invalid):* Sit down, Pop. You want a drink?

Willy: Sure, I don't mind.

Biff: Let's get a load on.

Willy: You look worried.

Biff: N-no. *(To* Stanley*):* Scotch all around. Make it doubles.

Stanley: Doubles, right. *(He goes.)*

Willy: You had a couple already, didn't you?

Biff: Just a couple, yeah.

Willy: Well, what happened, boy? *(Nodding affirmatively, with a smile):* Everything go all right?

Biff, *(takes a breath, then reaches out and grasps* Willy's *hand):* Pal . . . *(He is smiling bravely, and* Willy *is smiling too.)* I had an experience today.

Happy: Terrific, Pop.

Willy: That so? What happened?

Biff, *(high, slightly alcoholic, above the earth):* I'm going to tell you everything from first to last. It's been a strange day. *(Silence. He looks around, composes himself as best he can, but his breath keeps breaking the rhythm of his voice.)* I had to wait quite a while for him, and—

Willy: Oliver?

Biff: Yeah, Oliver. All day, as a matter of cold fact. And a lot of—instances—facts, Pop, facts about my life came back to me. Who was it, Pop? Who ever said I was a salesman with Oliver?

Willy: Well, you were.

Biff: No, Dad, I was a shipping clerk.

Willy: But you were practically—

Biff, *(with determination):* Dad, I don't know who said it first, but I was never a salesman for Bill Oliver.

Willy: What're you talking about?

Biff: Let's hold on to the facts tonight, Pop. We're not going to get anywhere bullin' around. I was a shipping clerk.

Willy, *(angrily):* All right, now listen to me—

Biff: Why don't you let me finish?

Willy: I'm not interested in stories about the past or any crap of that kind because the woods are burning, boys, you understand? There's a big blaze going on all around. I was fired today.

Biff, *(shocked):* How could you be?

Willy: I was fired, and I'm looking for a little good news to tell your mother, because the woman has waited and the woman has suffered. The gist of it is that I haven't got a story left in my head, Biff. So don't give me a lecture about facts and aspects. I am not interested. Now what've you got to say to me?

Stanley *enters with three drinks. They wait until he leaves.*

Willy: Did you see Oliver?

   Biff: Jesus, Dad!

Willy: You mean you didn't go up there?

Happy: Sure he went up there.

   Biff: I did. I—saw him. How could they fire you?

Willy, (on the edge of his chair): What kind of a welcome did he give you?

   Biff: He won't even let you work on commission?

Willy: I'm out! *(Driving):* So tell me, he gave you a warm welcome?

Happy: Sure, Pop, sure!

   Biff, (driven): Well, it was kind of—

Willy: I was wondering if he'd remember you. *(To* Happy*):* Imagine, man doesn't see him for ten, twelve years and gives him that kind of a welcome!

Happy: Damn right!

   Biff, (trying to return to the offensive): Pop, look—

Willy: You know why he remembered you, don't you? Because you impressed him in those days.

   Biff: Let's talk quietly and get this down to the facts, huh?

Willy, (as though Biff *had been interrupting):* Well, what happened? It's great news, Biff. Did he take you into his office or'd you talk in the waiting-room?

   Biff: Well, he came in, see, and—

Willy, (with a big smile): What'd he say? Betcha he threw his arm around you.

   Biff: Well, he kinda—

Willy: He's a fine man. *(To* Happy*):* Very hard man to see, y'know.

Happy, (agreeing): Oh, I know.

Willy, (to Biff*):* Is that where you had the drinks?

   Biff: Yeah, he gave me a couple of—no, no!

Happy, (cutting in): He told him my Florida idea.

Willy: Don't interrupt. *(To* Biff*):* How'd he react to the Florida idea?

   Biff: Dad, will you give me a minute to explain?

Willy: I've been waiting for you to explain since I sat down here! What happened? He took you into his office and what?

   Biff: Well—I talked. And—and he listened, see.

Willy: Famous for the way he listens, y'know. What was his answer?

  Biff: His answer was— *(He breaks off, suddenly angry.)* Dad, you're not letting me tell you what I want to tell you!

Willy, *(accusing, angered):* You didn't see him, did you?

  Biff: I did see him!

Willy: What'd you insult him or something? You insulted him, didn't you?

  Biff: Listen, will you let me out of it, will you just let me out of it!

Happy: What the hell!

Willy: Tell me what happened!

  Biff, *(to* Happy*):* I can't talk to him!

A single trumpet note jars the ear. The light of green leaves stains the house, which holds the air of night and a dream. Young Bernard *enters and knocks on the door of the house.*

Young Bernard: Operator's Voice:

Young Bernard, (frantically): Mrs. Loman, Mrs. Loman!

  Happy: Tell him what happened!

  Biff, *(to* Happy*):* Shut up and leave me alone!

Willy: No, no! You had to go and flunk math!

  Biff: What math? What're you talking about?

Young Bernard: Mrs. Loman, Mrs. Loman!

Linda *appears in the house, as of old.*

  Willy, *(wildly):* Math, math, math!

  Biff: Take it easy, Pop!

Young Bernard: Mrs. Loman!

  Willy, *(furiously):* If you hadn't flunked you'd've been set by now!

  Biff: Now, look, I'm gonna tell you what happened, and you're going to listen to me.

Young Bernard: Mrs. Loman!

  Biff: I waited six hours—

Happy: What the hell are you saying?

  Biff: I kept sending in my name but he wouldn't see me. So finally he . . . *(He continues unheard as light fades low on the restaurant.)*

Young Bernard: Biff flunked math!

  Linda: No!

Young Bernard: Birnbaum flunked him! They won't graduate him!

  Linda: But they have to. He's gotta go to the university. Where is he? Biff! Biff!

Young Bernard: No, he left. He went to Grand Central.

Linda: Grand— You mean he went to Boston!

Young Bernard: Is Uncle Willy in Boston?

Linda: Oh, maybe Willy can talk to the teacher. Oh, the poor, poor boy!

Light on house area snaps out.

Biff, (*at the table, now audible, holding up a gold fountain pen*): . . . so I'm washed up with Oliver, you understand? Are you listening to me?

Willy, (*at a loss*): Yeah, sure. If you hadn't flunked—

Biff: Flunked what? What're you talking about?

Willy: Don't blame everything on me! I didn't flunk math— you did! What pen?

Happy: That was awful dumb, Biff, a pen like that is worth—

Willy, (*seeing the pen for the first time*): You took Oliver's pen?

Biff, (*weakening*): Dad, I just explained it to you.

Willy: You stole Bill Oliver's fountain pen!

Biff: I didn't exactly steal it! That's just what I've been explaining to you!

Happy: He had it in his hand and just then Oliver walked in, so he got nervous and stuck it in his pocket!

Willy: My God, Biff!

Biff: I never intended to do it, Dad!

Operator's Voice: Standish Arms, good evening!

Willy, (*shouting*): I'm not in my room!

Biff, (*frightened*): Dad, what's the matter? (*He and* Happy *stand up.*)

Operator: Ringing Mr. Loman for you!

Willy: I'm not there, stop it!

Biff, (*horrified, gets down on one knee before* Willy): Dad, I'll make good, I'll make good. (Willy *tries to get to his feet.* Biff *holds him down.*) Sit down now.

Willy: No, you're no good, you're no good for anything.

Biff: I am, Dad, I'll find something else, you understand? Now don't worry about anything. (*He holds up* Willy's *face*): Talk to me, dad.

Operator: Mr. Loman does not answer. Shall I page him?

Willy, (*attempting to stand, as though to rush and silence the* Operator): No, no, no!

Happy: He'll strike something, Pop.

Willy: No, no . . .

Biff, (*desperately, standing over* Willy): Pop, listen! Listen to me! I'm telling you something good. Oliver talked to his partner about the Florida idea. You listening? He—he talked to his partner, and he came to me . . . I'm going to be all right, you hear? Dad, listen to me, he said it was just a question of the amount!

Willy: Then you . . . got it?

Happy: He's gonna be terrific, Pop!

Willy, (trying to stand): Then you got it, haven't you? You got it! You got it!

Biff, (agonized, holds Willy down): No, no. Look, Pop. I'm supposed to have lunch with them tomorrow. I'm just telling you this so you'll know that I can still make an impression, Pop. And I'll make good somewhere, but I can't go tomorrow, see?

Willy: Why not? You simply—

Biff: But the pen, Pop!

Willy: You give it to him and tell him it was an oversight!

Happy: Sure, have lunch tomorrow!

Biff: I can't say that—

Willy: You were doing a crossword puzzle and accidentally used his pen!

Biff: Listen, kid, I took those balls years ago, now I walk in with his fountain pen? That clinches it, don't you see? I can't face him like that! I'll try elsewhere.

Page's Voice: Paging Mr. Loman!

Willy: Don't you want to be anything?

Biff: Pop, how can I go back?

Willy: You don't want to be anything, is that what's behind it?

Biff, (now angry at Willy for not crediting his sympathy): Don't take it that way! You think it was easy walking into that office after what I'd done to him? A team of horses couldn't have dragged me back to Bill Oliver!

Willy: Then why'd you go?

Biff: Why did I go? Why did I go! Look at you! Look at what's become of you!

Off left, The Woman *laughs.*

Willy: Biff, you're going to go to that lunch tomorrow, or—

Biff: I can't go. I've got no appointment!

Happy: Biff, for . . . !

Willy: Are you spiting me?

Biff: Don't take it that way! Goddammit!

Willy, (strikes Biff and falters away from the table): You rotten little louse! Are you spiting me?

The Woman: Someone's at the door, Willy!

Biff: I'm no good, can't you see what I am?

Happy, (separating them): Hey, you're in a restaurant! Now cut it out, both of you! (The girls enter.) Hello, girls, sit down.

The Woman *laughs, off left.*

Miss Forsythe: I guess we might as well. This is Letta.
  The Woman: Willy, are you going to wake up?
       Biff, (ignoring Willy): How're ya, miss, sit down. What do you
         drink?
Miss Forsythe: Letta might not be able to stay long.
     Letta: I gotta get up very early tomorrow. I got jury duty. I'm
        so excited! Were you fellows ever on a jury?
      Biff: No, but I been in front of them! *(The girls laugh.)* This is
        my father.
     Letta: Isn't he cute? Sit down with us, Pop.
   Happy: Sit him down, Biff!
      Biff, (going to him): Come on, slugger, drink us under the
        table. To hell with it! Come on, sit down, pal.

On Biff's *last insistence,* Willy *is about to sit.*

 The Woman, (now urgently): Willy, are you going to answer the door!

The Woman's *call pulls* Willy *back. He starts right, befuddled.*

      Biff: Hey, where are you going?
    Willy: Open the door.
      Biff: The door?
    Willy: The washroom . . . the door . . . where's the door?
      Biff, (leading Willy *to the left):* Just go straight down.

Willy *moves left.*

 The Woman: Willy, Willy, are you going to get up, get up, get up, get
      up?

Willy *exits left.*

     Letta: I think it's sweet you bring your daddy along.
Miss Forsythe: Oh, he isn't really your father!
      Biff, (at left, turning to her resentfully): Miss Forsythe, you've
        just seen a prince walk by. A fine, troubled prince. A hard-
        working, unappreciated prince. A pal, you understand? A
        good companion. Always for his boys.
     Letta: That's so sweet.
   Happy: Well, girls, what's the program? We're wasting time.
      Come on, Biff. Gather round. Where would you like to go?
      Biff: Why don't you do something for him?
   Happy: Me!
      Biff: Don't you give a damn for him, Hap?
   Happy: What're you talking about? I'm the one who—
      Biff: I sense it, you don't give a good goddam about him. *(He*

takes the rolled-up hose from his pocket and puts it on the table in front of Happy.) Look what I found in the cellar, for Christ's sake. How can you bear to let it go on?

Happy: Me? Who goes away? Who runs off and—

Biff: Yeah, but he doesn't mean anything to you. You could help him—I can't! Don't you understand what I'm talking about? He's going to kill himself, don't you know that?

Happy: Don't I know it! Me!

Biff: Hap, help him! Jesus . . . help him . . . Help me, help me, I can't bear to look at his face! (*Ready to weep, he hurries out, up right.*)

Happy, (*starting after him*): Where are you going?

Miss Forsythe: What's he so mad about?

Happy: Come on, girls, we'll catch up with him.

Miss Forsythe, (as Happy *pushes her out*): Say, I don't like that temper of his!

Happy: He's just a little overstrung, he'll be all right!

Willy, (*off left, as* The Woman *laughs*): Don't answer! Don't answer!

Letta: Don't you want to tell your father—

Happy: No, that's not my father. He's just a guy. Come on, we'll catch Biff, and, honey, we're going to paint this town! Stanley, where's the check! Hey, Stanley!

They exit. Stanley *looks toward left.*

Stanley, (*calling to* Happy *indignantly*): Mr. Loman! Mr. Loman!

Stanley *picks up a chair and follows them off. Knocking is heard off left.* The Woman *enters, laughing.* Willy *follows her. She is in a black slip; he is buttoning his shirt. Raw, sensuous music accompanies their speech.*

Willy: Will you stop laughing? Will you stop?

The Woman: Aren't you going to answer the door? He'll wake the whole hotel.

Willy: I'm not expecting anybody.

The Woman: Whyn't you have another drink, honey, and stop being so damn self-centered?

Willy: I'm so lonely.

The Woman: You know you ruined me, Willy? From now on, whenever you come to the office, I'll see that you go right through to the buyers. No waiting at my desk any more, Willy. You ruined me.

Willy: That's nice of you to say that.

The Woman: Gee, you are self-centered! Why so sad? You are the saddest, self-centeredest soul I ever did see-saw. (*She laughs. He kisses her.*) Come on inside, drummer boy. It's silly to be dressing in the middle of the night. *(As knocking is heard):* Aren't you going to answer the door?

Willy: They're knocking on the wrong door.

The Woman: But I felt the knocking. And he heard us talking in here. Maybe the hotel's on fire!

Willy, (his terror rising): It's a mistake.

The Woman: Then tell him to go away!

Willy: There's nobody there.

The Woman: It's getting on my nerves, Willy. There's somebody standing out there and it's getting on my nerves!

Willy, (pushing her away from him): All right, stay in the bathroom here, and don't come out. I think there's a law in Massachusetts about it, so don't come out. It may be that new room clerk. He looked very mean. So don't come out. It's a mistake, there's no fire.

The knocking is heard again. He takes a few steps away from her, and she vanishes into the wing. The light follows him, and now he is facing Young Biff, *who carries a suitcase.* Biff *steps toward him. The music is gone.*

Biff: Why didn't you answer?

Willy: Biff! What are you doing in Boston?

Biff: Why didn't you answer? I've been knocking for five minutes, I called you on the phone—

Willy: I just heard you. I was in the bathroom and had the door shut. Did anything happen home?

Biff: Dad—I let you down.

Willy: What do you mean?

Biff: Dad . . .

Willy: Biffo, what's this about? *(Putting his arm around Biff):* Come on, let's go downstairs and get you a malted.

Biff: Dad, I flunked math.

Willy: Not for the term?

Biff: The term. I haven't got enough credits to graduate.

Willy: You mean to say Bernard wouldn't give you the answers?

Biff: He did, he tried, but I only got a sixty-one.

Willy: And they wouldn't give you four points?

Biff: Birnbaum refused absolutely. I begged him, Pop, but he won't give me those points. You gotta talk to him before they close the school. Because if he saw the kind of man you are, and you just talked to him in your way, I'm sure he'd come through for me. The class came right before practice, see, and I didn't go enough. Would you talk to him? He'd like you, Pop. You know the way you could talk.

Willy: You're on. We'll drive right back.

Biff: Oh, Dad, good work! I'm sure he'll change it for you!

Willy: Go downstairs and tell the clerk I'm checkin' out. Go right down.

Biff: Yes, sir! See, the reason he hates me, Pop—one day he was late for class so I got up at the blackboard and imitated him. I crossed my eyes and talked with a lithp.

Willy, (laughing): You did? The kids like it?

Biff: They nearly died laughing!

Willy: Yeah? What'd you do?

Biff: The thquare root of thixthy twee is . . . *(Willy bursts out laughing;* Biff *joins him.)* And in the middle of it he walked in!

Willy *laughs and* The Woman *joins in offstage.*

Willy, (without hesitation): Hurry downstairs and—

Biff: Somebody in there?

Willy: No, that was next door.

The Woman *laughs offstage.*

Biff: Somebody got in your bathroom!

Willy: No, it's the next room, there's a party—

The Woman, (enters, laughing. She lisps this): Can I come in? There's something in the bathtub, Willy, and it's moving!

Willy *looks at* Biff, *who is staring open-mouthed and horrified at* The Woman.

Willy: Ah—you better go back to your room. They must be finished painting by now. They're painting her room so I let her take a shower here. Go back, go back . . . *(He pushes her.)*

The Woman, (resisting): But I've got to get dressed, Willy, I can't—

Willy: Get out of here! Go back, go back . . . *(Suddenly striving for the ordinary):* This is Miss Francis, Biff, she's a buyer. They're painting her room. Go back, Miss Francis, go back . . .

The Woman: But my clothes, I can't go out naked in the hall!

Willy, (pushing her offstage): Get outa here! Go back, go back!

Biff *slowly sits down on his suitcase as the argument continues offstage.*

The Woman: Where's my stockings? You promised me stockings, Willy!

Willy: I have no stockings here!

The Woman: You had two boxes of size nine sheers for me, and I want them!

Willy: Here, for God's sake, will you get outa here!

The Woman, (enters holding a box of stockings): I just hope there's nobody in the hall. That's all I hope. *(To Biff):* Are you football or baseball?

Biff: Football.

The Woman, (angry, humiliated): That's me too. G'night. *(She snatches her clothes from* Willy, *and walks out.)*

Willy, (after a pause): Well, better get going. I want to get to the school first thing in the morning. Get my suits out of the closet. I'll get my valise. (Biff *doesn't move.)* What's the matter? (Biff *remains motionless, tears falling.)* She's a buyer. Buys for J. H. Simmons. She lives down the hall— they're painting. You don't imagine— *(He breaks off. After a pause):* Now listen, pal, she's just a buyer. She sees merchandise in her room and they have to keep it looking just so . . . *(Pause. Assuming command):* All right, get my suits. (Biff *doesn't move.)* Now stop crying and do as I say. I gave you an order. Biff, I gave you an order! Is that what you do when I give you an order? How dare you cry! *(Putting his arm around* Biff): Now look, Biff, when you grow up you'll understand about these things. You mustn't—you mustn't overemphasize a thing like this. I'll see Birnbaum first thing in the morning.

Biff: Never mind.

Willy, (getting down beside Biff): Never mind! He's going to give you those points. I'll see to it.

Biff: He wouldn't listen to you.

Willy: He certainly will listen to me. You need those points for the U. of Virginia.

Biff: I'm not going there.

Willy: Heh? If I can't get him to change that mark you'll make it up in summer school. You've got all summer to—

Biff, (his weeping breaking from him): Dad . . .

Willy, (infected by it): Oh, my boy . . .

Biff: Dad . . .

Willy: She's nothing to me, Biff. I was lonely, I was terribly lonely.

Biff: You—you gave her Mama's stockings! *(His tears break through and he rises to go.)*

Willy, (grabbing for Biff): I gave you an order!

Biff: Don't touch me, you—liar!

Willy: Apologize for that!

Biff: You fake! You phony little fake! You fake! *(Overcome, he turns quickly and weeping fully goes out with his suitcase.)* Willy *is left on the floor on his knees.)*

Willy: I gave you an order! Biff, come back here or I'll beat you! Come back here! I'll whip you!

Stanley *comes quickly in from the right and stands in front of* Willy.

Willy, (shouts at Stanley): I gave you an order . . .

Stanley: Hey, let's pick it up, pick it up, Mr. Loman. *(He helps* Willy *to his feet.)* Your boys left with the chippies. They said they'll see you home.

A second waiter watches some distance away.

Willy: But we were supposed to have dinner together.

Music is heard, Willy's *theme.*

Stanley: Can you make it?

Willy: I'll—sure, I can make it. *(Suddenly concerned about his clothes):* Do I—I look all right?

Stanley: Sure, you look all right. *(He flicks a speck off* Willy's *lapel.)*

Willy: Here—here's a dollar.

Stanley: Oh, your son paid me. It's all right.

Willy, (putting it in Stanley's *hand):* No, take it. You're a good boy.

Stanley: Oh, no, you don't have to . . .

Willy: Here—here's some more, I don't need it any more. *(After a slight pause):* Tell me—is there a seed store in the neighborhood?

Stanley: Seeds? You mean like to plant?

As Willy *turns,* Stanley *slips the money back into his jacket pocket.*

Willy: Yes. Carrots, peas . . .

Stanley: Well, there's hardware stores on Sixth Avenue, but it may be too late now.

Willy, (anxiously): Oh, I'd better hurry. I've got to get some seeds. *(He starts off to the right.)* I've got to get some seeds, right away. Nothing's planted. I don't have a thing in the ground.

Willy *hurries out as the light goes down.* Stanley *moves over to the right after him, watches him off. The other waiter has been staring at* Willy.

Stanley, (to the waiter): Well, whatta you looking at?

The waiter picks up the chairs and moves off right. Stanley *takes the table and follows him. The light fades on this area. There is a long pause, the sound of the flute coming over. The light gradually rises on the kitchen, which is empty.* Happy *appears at the door of the house, followed by* Biff. Happy *is carrying a large bunch of long-stemmed roses. He enters the kitchen, looks around for* Linda. *Not seeing her, he turns to* Biff, *who is just outside the house door, and makes a gesture with his hands, indicating "Not here, I guess." He looks into the living-room and freezes. Inside,* Linda, *unseen, is seated,* Willy's *coat on her lap. She rises ominously and quietly and moves toward* Happy, *who backs up into the kitchen, afraid.*

Happy: Hey, what're you doing up? *(*Linda *says nothing but moves* *toward him implacably.)* Where's Pop? *(He keeps backing to the right, and now* Linda *is in full view in the doorway to the living-room.)* Is he sleeping?

  Linda: Where were you?

  Happy, *(trying to laugh it off):* We met two girls, Mom, very fine types. Here, we brought you some flowers. *(Offering them to her):* Put them in your room, Ma.

She knocks them to the floor at Biff's *feet. He has now come inside and closed the door behind him. She stares at* Biff, *silent.*

  Happy: Now what'd you do that for? Mom, I want you to have some flowers—

  Linda, *(cutting* Happy *off, violently to* Biff): Don't you care whether he lives or dies?

  Happy, *(going to the stairs):* Come upstairs, Biff.

    Biff, *(with a flare of disgust, to* Happy): Go away from me! *(To* Linda): What do you mean, lives or dies? Nobody's dying around here, pal.

  Linda: Get out of my sight! Get out of here!

    Biff: I wanna see the boss.

  Linda: You're not going near him!

    Biff: Where is he? *(He moves into the living-room and* Linda *follows.)*

  Linda, *(shouting after* Biff): You invite him for dinner. He looks forward to it all day—(Biff *appears in his parents' bedroom, looks around, and exits)*—and then you desert him there. There's no stranger you'd do that to!

  Happy: Why? He had a swell time with us. Listen, when I— (Linda *comes back into the kitchen)*—desert him I hope I don't outlive the day!

  Linda: Get out of here!

  Happy: Now look, Mom . . .

  Linda: Did you have to go to women tonight? You and your lousy rotten whores!

Biff *re-enters the kitchen.*

  Happy: Mom, all we did was follow Biff around trying to cheer him up! *(To* Biff): Boy, what a night you gave me!

  Linda: Get out of here, both of you, and don't come back! I don't want you tormenting him any more. Go on now, get your things together! *(To* Biff): You can sleep in his apartment. *(She starts to pick up the flowers and stops herself.)* Pick up this stuff, I'm not your maid any more. Pick it up, you bum, you!

Happy *turns his back to her in refusal.* Biff *slowly moves over and gets down on his knees, picking up the flowers.*

Linda: You're a pair of animals! Not one, not another living soul would have had the cruelty to walk out on that man in a restaurant!

Biff, (not looking at her): Is that what he said?

Linda: He didn't have to say anything. He was so humiliated he nearly limped when he came in.

Happy: But, Mom, he had a great time with us—

Biff, (cutting him off violently): Shut up!

Without another word, Happy *goes upstairs.*

Linda: You! You didn't even go in to see if he was all right!

Biff, (still on the floor in front of Linda, *the flowers in his hand; with self-loathing):* No. Didn't. Didn't do a damned thing. How do you like that, heh? Left him babbling in a toilet.

Linda: You louse. You . . .

Biff: Now you hit it on the nose! *(He gets up, throws the flowers in the wastebasket.)* The scum of the earth, and you're looking at him!

Linda: Get out of here!

Biff: I gotta talk to the boss, Mom. Where is he?

Linda: You're not going near him. Get out of this house!

Biff, (with absolute assurance, determination): No. We're gonna have an abrupt conversation, him and me.

Linda: You're not talking to him!

Hammering is heard from outside the house, off right. Biff *turns toward the noise.*

Linda, (suddenly pleading): Will you please leave him alone?

Biff: What's he doing out there?

Linda: He's planting the garden!

Biff, (quietly): Now? Oh, my God!

Biff *moves outside,* Linda *following. The light dies down on them and comes up on the center of the apron as* Willy *walks into it. He is carrying a flashlight, a hoe, and a handful of seed packets. He raps the top of the hoe sharply to fix it firmly, and then moves to the left, measuring off the distance with his foot. He holds the flashlight to look at the seed packets, reading off the instructions. He is in the blue of night.*

Willy: Carrots . . . quarter-inch apart. Rows . . . one-foot rows. *(He measures it off.)* One foot. *(He puts down a package and measures off.)* Beets. *(He puts down another package and measures again.)* Lettuce. *(He reads the package, puts it down.)* One foot—*(He breaks off as* Ben *appears at the right and moves slowly down to him.)* What a proposition, ts, ts. Terrific, terrific. 'Cause she's suffered, Ben, the woman has suffered. You understand me? A man can't go out the way he came in, Ben, a man has to to add up to something. You can't, you can't—(Ben *moves toward him as though to inter-rupt.*) You gotta consider, now. Don't answer so quick. Remember, it's a guaranteed twenty-thousand-dollar proposition. Now look, Ben, I want you to go through the ins and outs of this thing with me. I've got nobody to talk to, Ben, and the woman has suffered, you hear me?

Ben, *(standing still, considering):* What's the proposition?

Willy: It's twenty thousand dollars on the barrelhead. Guaranteed, gilt-edged, you understand?

Ben: You don't want to make a fool of yourself. They might not honor the policy.

Willy: How can they dare refuse? Didn't I work like a coolie to meet every premium on the nose? And now they don't pay off? Impossible!

Ben: It's called a cowardly thing, William.

Willy: Why? Does it take more guts to stand here the rest of my life ringing up a zero?

Ben, *(yielding):* That's a point, William. *(He moves, thinking, turns.)* And twenty thousand—that *is* something one can feel with the hand, it is there.

Willy, *(now assured, with rising power):* Oh, Ben, that's the whole beauty of it! I see it like a diamond, shining in the dark, hard and rough, that I can pick up and touch in my hand. Not like—like an appointment! This would not be another damned-fool appointment, Ben, and it changes all the aspects. Because he thinks I'm nothing, see, and so he spites me. But the funeral— *(Straightening up):* Ben, that funeral will be massive! They'll come from Maine, Massachusetts, Vermont, New Hampshire! All the old-timers with the strange license plates—that boy will be thunder-struck, Ben, because he never realized—I am known! Rhode Island, New York, New Jersey—I am known, Ben, and he'll see it with his eyes once and for all. He'll see what I am, Ben! He's in for a shock, that boy!

Ben, *(coming down to the edge of the garden):* He'll call you a coward.

Willy, *(suddenly fearful):* No, that would be terrible.

Ben: Yes. And a damned fool.

Willy: No, no, he mustn't, I won't have that! *(He is broken and desperate.)*

Ben: He'll hate you, William.

The gay music of the Boys is heard.

Willy: Oh, Ben, how do we get back to all the great times? Used to be so full of light, and comradeship, the sleigh-riding in winter, and the ruddiness on his cheeks. And always some kind of good news coming up, always something nice coming up ahead. And never even let me carry the valises in the house, and simonizing, simonizing that little red car! Why, why can't I give him something and not have him hate me?

Ben: Let me think about it. *(He glances at his watch.)* I still have a little time. Remarkable proposition, but you've got to be sure you're not making a fool of yourself.

Ben *drifts off upstage and goes out of sight.* Biff *comes down from the left.*

Willy, *(suddenly conscious of* Biff, *turns and looks up at him, then begins picking up the packages of seeds in confusion):* Where the hell is that seed? *(Indignantly):* You can't see nothing out here! They boxed in the whole goddam neighborhood!

Biff: There are people all around here. Don't you realize that?

Willy: I'm busy. Don't bother me.

Biff, *(taking the hoe from* Willy): I'm saying good-by to you, Pop. *(Willy looks at him, silent, unable to move.)* I'm not coming back any more.

Willy: You're not going to see Oliver tomorrow?

Biff: I've got no appointment, Dad.

Willy: He put his arm around you, and you've got no appointment?

Biff: Pop, get this now, will you? Everytime I've left it's been a fight that sent me out of here. Today I realized something about myself and I tried to explain it to you and I—I think I'm just not smart enough to make any sense out of it for you. To hell with whose fault it is or anything like that. *(He takes* Willy's *arm.)* Let's just wrap it up, heh? Come on in, we'll tell Mom. *(He gently tries to pull* Willy *to left.)*

Willy, *(frozen, immobile, with guilt in his voice):* No, I don't want to see her.

Biff: Come on! *(He pulls again, and* Willy *tries to pull away.)*

Willy, *(highly nervous):* No, no, I don't want to see her.

Biff, *(tries to look into* Willy's *face, as if to find the answer there):* Why don't you want to see her?

Willy, *(more harshly now):* Don't bother me, will you?

Biff: What do you mean, you don't want to see her? You don't want them calling you yellow, do you? This isn't your fault; it's me, I'm a bum. Now come inside! *(Willy strains to get away.)* Did you hear what I said to you?

Willy *pulls away and quickly goes by himself into the house.* Biff *follows.*

Linda, *(to* Willy): Did you plant, dear?

Biff, *(at the door, to* Linda): All right, we had it out. I'm going and I'm not writing any more.

Linda, *(going to* Willy *in the kitchen):* I think that's the best way, dear. 'Cause there's no use drawing it out, you'll just never get along.

Willy *doesn't respond.*

Biff: People ask where I am and what I'm doing, you don't know, and you don't care. That way it'll be off your mind and you can start brightening up again. All right? That clears it, doesn't it? (Willy *is silent, and* Biff *goes to him.)* You gonna wish me luck, scout? *(He extends his hand.)* What do you say?

Linda: Shake his hand, Willy.

Willy, *(turning to her, seething with hurt):* There's no necessity to mention the pen at all, y'know.

Biff, *(gently):* I've got no appointment, Dad.

Willy, *(erupting fiercely):* He put his arm around . . . ?

Biff: Dad, you're never going to see what I am, so what's the use of arguing? If I strike oil I'll send you a check. Meantime forget I'm alive.

Willy, *(to* Linda): Spite, see?

Biff: Shake hands, Dad.

Willy: Not my hand.

Biff: I was hoping not to go this way.

Willy: Well, this is the way you're going. Good-by.

Biff *looks at him a moment, then turns sharply and goes to the stairs.*

Willy, *(stops him with):* May you rot in hell if you leave this house!

Biff, *(turning):* Exactly what is it that you want from me?

Willy: I want you to know, on the train, in the mountains, in the valleys, wherever you go, that you cut down your life for spite!

Biff: No, no.

Willy: Spite, spite, is the word for your undoing! And when you're down and out, remember what did it. When you're rotting somewhere beside the railroad tracks, remember, and don't you dare blame it on me!

Biff: I'm not blaming it on you!

Willy: I won't take the rap for this, you hear?

Happy *comes down the stairs and stands on the bottom step, watching.*

Biff: That's just what I'm telling you!

Willy, *(sinking into a chair at the table, with full accusation):* You're trying to put a knife in me—don't think I don't know what you're doing!

Biff: All right, phony! Then let's lay it on the line. *(He whips the rubber tube out of his pocket and puts it on the table.)*

Happy: You crazy—

Linda: Biff! *(She moves to grab the hose, but* Biff *holds it down with his hand.)*

Biff: Leave it there! Don't move it!

Willy, (not looking at it): What is that?

Biff: You know goddam well what that is.

Willy, (caged, wanting to escape): I never saw that.

Biff: You saw it. The mice didn't bring it into the cellar! What is this supposed to do, make a hero out of you? This supposed to make me sorry for you?

Willy: Never heard of it.

Biff: There'll be no pity for you, you hear it? No pity!

Willy, (to Linda): You hear the spite!

Biff: No, you're going to hear the truth—what you are and what I am!

Linda: Stop it!

Willy: Spite!

Happy, (coming down toward Biff): You cut it now!

Biff, (to Happy): The man don't know who we are! The man is gonna know! *(To* Willy): We never told the truth for ten minutes in this house!

Happy: We always told the truth!

Biff, (turning on him): You big blow, are you the assistant buyer? You're one of the two assistants to the assistant, aren't you?

Happy: Well, I'm practically—

Biff: You're practically full of it! We all are! And I'm through with it. *(To* Willy): Now hear this, Willy, this is me.

Willy: I know you!

Biff: You know why I had no address for three months? I stole a suit in Kansas City and I was in jail. *(To* Linda, *who is sobbing):* Stop crying. I'm through with it.

Linda *turns away from them, her hands covering her face.*

Willy: I suppose that's my fault!

Biff: I stole myself out of every good job since high school!

Willy: And whose fault is that?

Biff: And I never got anywhere because you blew me so full of hot air I could never stand taking orders from anybody! That's whose fault it is!

Willy: I hear that!

Linda: Don't, Biff!

Biff: It's goddam time you heard that! I had to be boss big shot in two weeks, and I'm through with it!

Willy: Then hang yourself! For spite, hang yourself!

   Biff: No! Nobody's hanging himself, Willy! I ran down eleven flights with a pen in my hand today. And suddenly I stopped, you hear me? And in the middle of that office building, do you hear this? I stopped in the middle of that building and I saw—the sky. I saw the things that I love in this world. The work and the food and time to sit and smoke. And I looked at the pen and said to myself, what the hell am I grabbing this for? Why am I trying to become what I don't want to be? What am I doing in an office, making a contemptuous, begging fool of myself, when all I want is out there, waiting for me the minute I say I know who I am! Why can't I say that, Willy? *(He tries to make* Willy *face him, but* Willy *pulls away and moves to the left.)*

Willy, *(with hatred, threateningly):* The door of your life is wide open!

   Biff: Pop! I'm a dime a dozen, and so are you!

Willy, *(turning on him now in an uncontrolled outburst):* I am not a dime a dozen! I am Willy Loman, and you are Biff Loman!

Biff *starts for* Willy, *but is blocked by* Happy. *In his fury,* Biff *seems on the verge of attacking his father.*

   Biff: I am not a leader of men, Willy, and neither are you. You were never anything but a hard-working drummer who landed in the ash can like all the rest of them! I'm one dollar an hour, Willy! I tried seven states and couldn't raise it. A buck an hour! Do you gather my meaning? I'm not bringing home any prizes any more, and you're going to stop waiting for me to bring them home!

Willy, *(directly to* Biff*):* You vengeful, spiteful mut!

Biff *breaks from* Happy. Willy, *in fright, starts up the stairs.* Biff *grabs him.*

   Biff, *(at the peak of his fury):* Pop, I'm nothing! I'm nothing, Pop. Can't you understand that? There's no spite in it any more. I'm just what I am, that's all.

Biff's *fury has spent itself, and he breaks down, sobbing, holding on to* Willy, *who dumbly fumbles for* Biff's *face.*

   Willy, *(astonished):* What're you doing? What're you doing? *(To* Linda*):* Why is he crying?

   Biff, *(crying, broken):* Will you let me go, for Christ's sake? Will you take that phony dream and burn it before something happens? *(Struggling to contain himself, he pulls away and moves to the stairs.)* I'll go in the morning. Put him—put him to bed. *(Exhausted,* Biff *moves up the stairs to his room.)*

Arthur Miller 1785

Willy, *(after a long pause, astonished, elevated):* Isn't that—isn't that remarkable? Biff—he likes me!

Linda: He loves you, Willy!

Happy, *(deeply moved):* Always did, Pop.

Willy: Oh, Biff! *(Staring wildly):* He cried! Cried to me. *(He is choking with his love, and now cries out his promise):* That boy —that boy is going to be magnificent!

Ben *appears in the light just outside the kitchen.*

Ben: Yes, outstanding, with twenty thousand behind him.

Linda, *(sensing the racing of his mind, fearfully, carefully):* Now come to bed, Willy. It's all settled now.

Willy, *(finding it difficult not to rush out of the house):* Yes, we'll sleep. Come on. Go to sleep, Hap.

Ben: And it does take a great kind of a man to crack the jungle.

In accents of dread, Ben's *idyllic music starts up.*

Happy, *(his arm around* Linda*):* I'm getting married, Pop, don't forget it. I'm changing everything. I'm gonna run that department before the year is up. You'll see, Mom. *(He kisses her.)*

Ben: The jungle is dark but full of diamonds, Willy.

Willy *turns, moves, listening to* Ben.

Linda: Be good. You're both good boys, just act that way, that's all.

Happy: 'Night, Pop. *(He goes upstairs.)*

Linda, *(to* Willy*):* Come, dear.

Ben, *(with greater force):* One must go in to fetch a diamond out.

Willy, *(to* Linda, *as he moves slowly along the edge of the kitchen, toward the door):* I just want to get settled down, Linda. Let me sit alone for a little.

Linda, *(almost uttering her fear):* I want you upstairs.

Willy, *(taking her in his arms):* In a few minutes, Linda. I couldn't sleep right now. Go on, you look awful tired. *(He kisses her.)*

Ben: Not like an appointment at all. A diamond is rough and hard to the touch.

Willy: Go on now. I'll be right up.

Linda: I think this is the only way, Willy.

Willy: Sure, it's the best thing.

Ben: Best thing!

Willy: The only way. Everything is gonna be—go on, kid, get to bed. You look so tired.

Linda: Come right up.

Willy: Two minutes.

Linda *goes into the living-room, then reappears in her bedroom.* Willy *moves just outside the kitchen door.*

Willy: Loves me. *(Wonderingly):* Always loved me. Isn't that a remarkable thing? Ben, he'll worship me for it!

Ben, (with promise): It's dark there, but full of diamonds.

Willy: Can you imagine that magnificence with twenty thousand dollars in his pocket?

Linda, (calling from her room): Willy! Come up!

Willy, (calling into the kitchen): Yes! Yes. Coming! It's very smart, you realize that, don't you, sweetheart! Even Ben sees it. I gotta go, baby. 'By! 'By! *(Going over to Ben, almost dancing):* Imagine? When the mail comes he'll be ahead of Bernard again!

Ben: A perfect proposition all around.

Willy: Did you see how he cried to me? Oh, if I could kiss him, Ben!

Ben: Time, William, time!

Willy: Oh, Ben, I always knew one way or another we were gonna make it, Biff and I!

Ben, (looking at his watch): The boat. We'll be late. *(He moves slowly off into the darkness.)*

Willy, (elegiacally, turning to the house): Now when you kick off, boy, I want a seventy-yard boot, and get right down the field under the ball, and when you hit, hit low and hit hard, because it's important, boy. *(He swings around and faces the audience.)* There's all kinds of important people in the stands, and the first thing you know . . . *(Suddenly realizing he is alone):* Ben! Ben, where do I . . . ? *(He makes a sudden movement of search.)* Ben, how do I . . . ?

Linda, (calling): Willy, you coming up?

Willy, (uttering a gasp of fear, whirling about as if to quiet her): Sh! *(He turns around as if to find his way; sounds, faces, voices, seem to be swarming in upon him and he flicks at them, crying),* Sh! Sh! *(Suddenly music, faint and high, stops him. It rises in intensity, almost to an unbearable scream. He goes up and down on his toes, and rushes off around the house.)* Shhh!

Linda: Willy?

There is no answer. Linda *waits.* Biff *gets up off his bed. He is still in his clothes.* Happy *sits up.* Biff *stands listening.*

Linda, (with real fear): Willy, answer me! Willy!

There is the sound of a car starting and moving away at full speed.

> *Linda:* No!
> *Biff,* (*rushing down the stairs*): Pop!

As the car speeds off, the music crashes down in a frenzy of sound, which becomes the soft pulsation of a single cello string. Biff *slowly returns to his bedroom. He and* Happy *gravely don their jackets.* Linda *slowly walks out of her room. The music has developed into a dead march. The leaves of day are appearing over everything.* Charley *and* Bernard, *somberly dressed, appear and knock on the kitchen door.* Biff *and* Happy *slowly descend the stairs to the kitchen as* Charley *and* Bernard *enter. All stop a moment when* Linda, *in clothes of mourning, bearing a little bunch of roses, comes through the draped doorway into the kitchen. She goes to* Charley *and takes his arm. Now all move toward the audience, through the wall-line of the kitchen. At the limit of the apron,* Linda *lays down the flowers, kneels, and sits back on her heels. All stare down at the grave.*

REQUIEM

> *Charley:* It's getting dark, Linda.

Linda *doesn't react. She stares at the grave.*

> *Biff:* How about it, Mom? Better get some rest, heh? They'll be closing the gate soon.

Linda *makes no move. Pause.*

> *Happy,* (*deeply angered*): He had no right to do that. There was no necessity for it. We would've helped him.
> *Charley,* (*grunting*): Hmmm.
> *Biff:* Come along, Mom.
> *Linda:* Why didn't anybody come?
> *Charley:* It was a very nice funeral.
> *Linda:* But where are all the people he knew? Maybe they blame him.
> *Charley:* Naa. It's a rough world, Linda. They wouldn't blame him.
> *Linda:* I can't understand it. At this time especially. First time in thirty-five years we were just about free and clear. He only needed a little salary. He was even finished with the dentist.
> *Charley:* No man only needs a little salary.
> *Linda:* I can't understand it.
> *Biff:* There were a lot of nice days. When he'd come home from a trip; or on Sundays, making the stoop; finishing the cellar; putting on the new porch; when he built the extra bathroom; and put up the garage. You know something, Charley, there's more of him in that front stoop than in all the sales he ever made.

Charley: Yeah. He was a happy man with a batch of cement.

Linda: He was so wonderful with his hands.

Biff: He had the wrong dreams. All, all wrong.

Happy, (almost ready to fight Biff): Don't say that!

Biff: He never knew who he was.

Charley, (stopping Happy's *movement and reply.* To Biff): Nobody dast blame this man. You don't understand: Willy was a salesman. And for a salesman, there is no rock bottom to the life. He don't put a bolt to a nut, he don't tell you the law or give you medicine. He's a man way out there in the blue, riding on a smile and a shoeshine. And when they start not smiling back—that's an earthquake. And then you get yourself a couple of spots on your hat, and you're finished. Nobody dast blame this man. A salesman is got to dream, boy. It comes with the territory.

Biff: Charley, the man didn't know who he was.

Happy, (infuriated): Don't say that!

Biff: Why don't you come with me, Happy?

Happy: I'm not licked that easily. I'm staying right in this city, and I'm gonna beat this racket! (He looks at Biff, *his chin set.*) The Loman Brothers!

Biff: I know who I am, kid.

Happy: All right, boy. I'm gonna show you and everybody else that Willy Loman did not die in vain. He had a good dream. It's the only dream you can have—to come out number-one man. He fought it out here, and this is where I'm gonna win it for him.

Biff, (with a hopeless glance at Happy, *bends toward his mother*): Let's go, Mom.

Linda: I'll be with you in a minute. Go on, Charley. (He hesitates.) I want to, just for a minute. I never had a chance to say good-by.

Charley *moves away, followed by* Happy. Biff *remains a slight distance up and left of* Linda. *She sits there, summoning herself. The flute begins, not far away, playing behind her speech.*

Linda: Forgive me, dear. I can't cry. I don't know what it is, but I can't cry. I don't understand it. Why did you ever do that? Help me, Willy, I can't cry. It seems to me that you're just on another trip. I keep expecting you. Willy, dear, I can't cry. Why did you do it? I search and search and I search, and I can't undrstand it, Willy. I made the last payment on the house today. Today, dear. And there'll be nobody home. (A sob rises in her throat.) We're free and clear. (Sobbing more fully, released): We're free. (Biff comes slowly toward her.) We're free . . . We're free . . .

Biff *lifts her to her feet and moves out up right with her in his arms.* Linda *sobs quietly.* Bernard *and* Charley *come together and follow them, followed by* Happy. *Only the music of the flute is left on the darkening stage as over the house the hard towers of the apartment buildings rise into sharp focus, and*

THE CURTAIN FALLS

Arthur Miller's drama seems to bring two planes of experience together. On one hand, he is committed to a realistic and often unflattering portrayal of society, and his plays often show his impatience with the less humane aspects of American capitalism. On the other hand, he shares a vision of life that links him with the Greek tragedians, whose characters were certainly not the sort of "common men" who inhabit the social world Miller sets out to explore. In "Tragedy and the Common Man," Miller discusses the elements of tragedy that link a character like Willy Loman to a character like Antigone.

"A man's total compulsion to evaluate himself justly": Arthur Miller

As a general rule, to which there may be exceptions unknown to me, I think the tragic feeling is evoked in us when we are in the presence of a character who is ready to lay down his life, if need be, to secure one thing—his sense of personal dignity. From Orestes to Hamlet, Medea to Macbeth, the underlying struggle is that of the individual attempting to gain his "rightful" position in his society.

Sometimes he is one who has been displaced from it, sometimes one who seeks to attain it for the first time, but the fateful wound from which the inevitable events spiral is the wound of indignity, and its dominant force is indignation. Tragedy, then, is the consequence of a man's total compulsion to evaluate himself justly.

In the sense of having been initiated by the hero himself, the tale always reveals what has been called his "tragic flaw," a failing that is not peculiar to grand or elevated characters. Nor is it necessarily a weakness. The flaw, or crack in the character, is really nothing—and need be nothing —but his inherent unwillingness to remain passive in the face of what he conceives to be a challenge to his dignity, his image of his rightful status. Only the passive, only those who accept their lot without active retaliation, are "flawless." Most of us are in that category.

But there are among us today, as there always have been, those who act against the scheme of things that degrades them, and in the process of action everything we have accepted out of fear or insensitivity or ignorance is shaken before us and examined, and from this total onslaught by an individual against the seemingly stable cosmos surrounding us—from this total examination of the "unchangeable" environment—comes the terror and the fear that is classically associated with tragedy.

HAROLD PINTER

(b. 1930)

THE DUMB WAITER

Scene: A basement room. Two beds, flat against the back wall. A serving hatch, closed, between the beds. A door to the kitchen and lavatory, left. A door to a passage, right.

Ben *is lying on a bed, left, reading a paper.* Gus *is sitting on a bed, right, tying his shoelaces, with difficulty. Both are dressed in shirts, trousers and braces.*

Silence.

Gus *ties his laces, rises, yawns and begins to walk slowly to the door, left. He stops, looks down, and shakes his foot.*

Ben *lowers his paper and watches him.* Gus *kneels and unties his shoelace and slowly takes off the shoe. He looks inside it and brings out a flattened matchbox. He shakes it and examines it. Their eyes meet.* Ben *rattles his paper and reads.* Gus *puts the matchbox in his pocket and bends down to put on his shoe. He ties his lace, with difficulty.* Ben *lowers his paper and watches him.* Gus *walks to the door, left, stops, and shakes the other foot. He kneels, unties his shoelace, and slowly takes off the shoe. He looks inside it and brings out a flattened cigarette packet. He shakes it and examines it. Their eyes meet.* Ben *rattles his paper and reads.* Gus *puts the packet in his pocket, bends down, puts on his shoe and ties the lace.*

He wanders off, left.

Ben *slams the paper down on the bed and glares after him. He picks up the paper and lies on his back, reading.*

Silence.

A lavatory chain is pulled twice off, left, but the lavatory does not flush.

Silence.

Gus *re-enters, left, and halts at the door, scratching his head.* Ben *slams down the paper.*
Ben: Kaw!

He picks up the paper.

What about this? Listen to this!

He refers to the paper.

A man of eighty-seven wanted to cross the road. But there was a lot of traffic, see? He couldn't see how he was going to squeeze through. So he crawled under a lorry.

Gus: He what?

Ben: He crawled under a lorry. A stationary lorry.

Gus: No?

Ben: The lorry started and ran over him.

Gus: Go on!

Ben: That's what it says here.

Gus: Get away.

Ben: It's enough to make you want to puke, isn't it?

Gus: Who advised him to do a thing like that?

Ben: A man of eighty-seven crawling under a lorry!

Gus: It's unbelievable.

Ben: It's down here in black and white.

Gus: Incredible.

Silence.

Gus *shakes his head and exits.* Ben *lies back and reads. The lavatory chain is pulled once off left, but the lavatory does not flush.*

Ben *whistles at an item in the paper.*

Gus *re-enters.*

I want to ask you something.

Ben: What are you doing out there?

Gus: Well, I was just—

Ben: What about the tea?

Gus: I'm just going to make it.

Ben: Well, go on, make it.

Gus: Yes, I will. *(He sits in a chair. Ruminatively.)* He's laid on some very nice crockery this time, I'll say that. It's sort of striped. There's a white stripe.

Ben *reads.*

It's very nice. I'll say that.

Ben *turns the page.*

You know, sort of round the cup. Round the rim. All the rest of it's black, you see. Then the saucer's black, except for right in the middle, where the cup goes, where it's white.

Ben *reads.*

Then the plates are the same, you see. Only they've got a black stripe—the plates—right across the middle. Yes, I'm quite taken with the crockery.

Ben: (still reading). What do you want plates for? You're not going to eat.

Gus: I've brought a few biscuits.

Ben: Well, you'd better eat them quick.

Gus: I always bring a few biscuits. Or a pie. You know I can't drink tea without anything to eat.

Ben: Well, make the tea then, will you? Time's getting on.

Gus *brings out the flattened cigarette packet and examines it.*

Gus: You got any cigarettes? I think I've run out.

He throws the packet high up and leans forward to catch it.

I hope it won't be a long job, this one.

Aiming carefully, he flips the packet under his bed.

Oh, I wanted to ask you something.

Ben: (slamming his paper down). Kaw!

Gus: What's that?

Ben: A child of eight killed a cat!

Gus: Get away.

Ben: It's a fact. What about that, eh? A child of eight killing a cat!

Gus: How did he do it?

Ben: It was a girl.

Gus: How did she do it?

Ben: She—

He picks up the paper and studies it.

It doesn't say.

Gus: Why not?

Ben: Wait a minute. It just says—Her brother, aged eleven, viewed the incident from the toolshed.

Gus: Go on!

Ben: That's bloody ridiculous.

Pause.

Gus: I bet he did it.

Ben: Who?

Gus: The brother.

Ben: I think you're right.

Pause.

(Slamming down the paper.) What about that, eh? A kid of eleven killing a cat and blaming it on his little sister of eight! It's enough to—

He breaks off in disgust and seizes the paper. Gus *rises.*

Gus: What time is he getting in touch?

Ben *reads.*

What time is he getting in touch?

Ben: What's the matter with you? It could be any time. Any time.
Gus: *(moves to the foot of* Ben's *bed).* Well, I was going to ask you
    something.
Ben: What?
Gus: Have you noticed the time that tank takes to fill?
Ben: What tank?
Gus: In the lavatory.
Ben: No. Does it?
Gus: Terrible.
Ben: Well, what about it?
Gus: What do you think's the matter with it?
Ben: Nothing.
Gus: Nothing?
Ben: It's got a deficient ballcock, that's all.
Gus: A deficient what?
Ben: Ballcock.
Gus: No? Really?
Ben: That's what I should say.
Gus: Go on! That didn't occur to me.

Gus *wanders to his bed and presses the mattress.*

    I didn't have a very restful sleep today, did you? It's not much of a
    bed. I could have done with another blanket too. *(He catches sight of
    a picture on the wall.)* Hello, what's this? *(Peering at it.)* "The First
    Eleven." Cricketers. You seen this, Ben?
Ben: *(reading).* What?
Gus: The first eleven.
Ben: What?
Gus: There's a photo here of the first eleven.
Ben: What first eleven?
Gus: *(studying the photo).* It doesn't say.
Ben: What about that tea?
Gus: They all look a bit old to me.

Gus *wanders downstage, looks out front, then all about the room.*

    I wouldn't like to live in this dump. I wouldn't mind if you had a
    window, you could see what it looked like outside.
Ben: What do you want a window for?
Gus: Well, I like to have a bit of a view, Ben. It whiles away the time.

He walks about the room.

    I mean, you come into a place when it's still dark, you come into a
    room you've never seen before, you sleep all day, you do your job,
    and then you go away in the night again.

Pause.

I like to get a look at the scenery. You never get the chance in this job.

Ben: You get your holidays, don't you?

Gus: Only a fortnight.

Ben: (lowering the paper). You kill me. Anyone would think you're working every day. How often do we do a job? Once a week? What are you complaining about?

Gus: Yes, but we've got to be on tap though, haven't we? You can't move out of the house in case a call comes.

Ben: You know what your trouble is?

Gus: What?

Ben: You haven't got any interests.

Gus: I've got interests.

Ben: What? Tell me one of your interests.

Pause.

Gus: I've got interests.

Ben: Look at me. What have I got?

Gus: I don't know. What?

Ben: I've got my woodwork. I've got my model boats. Have you ever seen me idle? I'm never idle. I know how to occupy my time, to its best advantage. Then when a call comes, I'm ready.

Gus: Don't you ever get a bit fed up?

Ben: Fed up? What with?

Silence.

Ben *reads.* Gus *feels in the pocket of his jacket, which hangs on the bed.*

Gus: You got any cigarettes? I've run out.

The lavatory flushes off left.

There she goes.

Gus *sits on his bed.*

No, I mean, I say the crockery's good. It is. It's very nice. But that's about all I can say for this place. It's worse than the last one. Remember that last place we were in? Last time, where was it? At least there was a wireless there. No, honest. He doesn't seem to bother much about our comfort these days.

Ben: When are you going to stop jabbering?

Gus: You'd get rheumatism in a place like this, if you stay long.

Ben: We're not staying long. Make the tea, will you? We'll be on the job in a minute.

Gus *picks up a small bag by his bed and brings out a packet of tea. He examines it and looks up.*

Gus: Eh, I've been meaning to ask you.

Ben: What the hell is it now?

Gus: Why did you stop the car this morning, in the middle of that road?

Ben: (lowering the paper). I thought you were asleep.

Gus: I was, but I woke up when you stopped. You did stop, didn't you?

Pause.

> In the middle of that road. It was still dark, don't you remember? I looked out. It was all misty. I thought perhaps you wanted to kip, but you were sitting up dead straight, like you were waiting for something.

Ben: I wasn't waiting for anything.

Gus: I must have fallen asleep again. What was all that about then? Why did you stop?

Ben: (picking up the paper). We were too early.

Gus: Early? *(He rises.)* What do you mean? We got the call, didn't we, saying we were to start right away. We did. We shoved out on the dot. So how could we be too early?

Ben: (quietly). Who took the call, me or you?

Gus: You.

Ben: We were too early.

Gus: Too early for what?

Pause.

> You mean someone had to get out before we got in?

He examines the bedclothes.

> I thought these sheets didn't look too bright. I thought they ponged a bit. I was too tired to notice when I got in this morning. Eh, that's taking a bit of a liberty, isn't it? I don't want to share my bed-sheets. I told you things were going down the drain. I mean, we've always had clean sheets laid on up till now. I've noticed it.

Ben: How do you know those sheets weren't clean?

Gus: What do you mean?

Ben: How do you know they weren't clean? You've spent the whole day in them, haven't you?

Gus: What, you mean it might be my pong? *(He sniffs sheets.)* Yes. *(He sits slowly on bed.)* It could be my pong, I suppose. It's difficult to tell. I don't really know what I pong like, that's the trouble.

Ben: (referring to the paper). Kaw!

Gus: Eh, Ben.

Ben: Kaw!

Gus: Ben.

Ben: What?

Gus: What town are we in? I've forgotten.

Ben: I've told you. Birmingham.

Gus: Go on!

He looks with interest about the room.

> That's in the Midlands. The second biggest city in Great Britain. I'd never have guessed.

He snaps his fingers.

> Eh, it's Friday today, isn't it? It'll be Saturday tomorrow.

Ben: What about it?

Gus: *(excited).* We could go and watch the Villa.

Ben: They're playing away.

Gus: No, are they? Caarr! What a pity.

Ben: Anyway, there's no time. We've got to get straight back.

Gus: Well, we have done in the past, haven't we? Stayed over and watched a game, haven't we? For a bit of relaxation.

Ben: Things have tightened up, mate. They've tightened up.

Gus *chuckles to himself.*

Gus: I saw the Villa get beat in a cup tie once. Who was it against now? White shirts. It was one-all at half-time. I'll never forget it. Their opponents won by a penalty. Talk about drama. Yes, it was a disputed penalty. Disputed. They got beat two-one, anyway, because of it. You were there yourself.

Ben: Not me.

Gus: Yes, you were there. Don't you remember that disputed penalty?

Ben: No.

Gus: He went down just inside the area. Then they said he was just acting. I didn't think the other bloke touched him myself. But the referee had the ball on the spot.

Ben: Didn't touch him! What are you talking about? He laid him out flat!

Gus: Not the Villa. The Villa don't play that sort of game.

Ben: Get out of it.

Pause.

Gus: Eh, that must have been here, in Birmingham.

Ben: What must?

Gus: The Villa. That must have been here.

Ben: They were playing away.

Gus: Because you know who the other team was? It was the Spurs. It was Tottenham Hotspur.

Ben: Well, what about it?

Gus: We've never done a job in Tottenham.

Ben: How do you know?

Gus: I'd remember Tottenham.

Ben *turns on his bed to look at him.*

Ben: Don't make me laugh, will you?

Ben *turns back and reads.* Gus *yawns and speaks through his yawn.*

Gus: When's he going to get in touch?

Pause.

> Yes, I'd like to see another football match. I've always been an
> ardent football fan. Here, what about coming to see the Spurs
> tomorrow?

Ben: *(tonelessly).* They're playing away.
Gus: Who are?
Ben: The Spurs.
Gus: Then they might be playing here.
Ben: Don't be silly.
Gus: If they're playing away they might be playing here. They might be
playing the Villa.
Ben: *(tonelessly).* But the Villa are playing away.

Pause. An envelope slides under the door, right. Gus *sees it. He stands, looking
at it.*

Gus: Ben.
Ben: Away. They're all playing away.
Gus: Ben, look here.
Ben: What?
Gus: Look.

Ben *turns his head and sees the envelope. He stands.*

Ben: What's that?
Gus: I don't know.
Ben: Where did it come from?
Gus: Under the door.
Ben: Well, what is it?
Gus: I don't know.

They stare at it.

Ben: Pick it up.
Gus: What do you mean?
Ben: Pick it up!

Gus *slowly moves towards it, bends and picks it up.*

> What is it?
Gus: An envelope.
Ben: Is there anything on it?
Gus: No.

Ben: Is it sealed?
Gus: Yes.
Ben: Open it.
Gus: What?
Ben: Open it!

Gus opens it and looks inside.

What's in it?

Gus empties twelve matches into his hand.

Gus: Matches.
Ben: Matches?
Gus: Yes.
Ben: Show it to me.

Gus passes the envelope. Ben *examines it.*

Nothing on it. Not a word.
Gus: That's funny, isn't it?
Ben: It came under the door?
Gus: Must have done.
Ben: Well, go on.
Gus: Go on where?
Ben: Open the door and see if you can catch anyone outside.
Gus: Who, me?
Ben: Go on!

Gus stares at him, puts the matches in his pocket, goes to his bed and brings a revolver from under the pillow. He goes to the door, opens it, looks out and shuts it.

Gus: No one.

He replaces the revolver.

Ben: What did you see?
Gus: Nothing.
Ben: They must have been pretty quick.

Gus takes the matches from pocket and looks at them.

Gus: Well, they'll come in handy.
Ben: Yes.
Gus: Won't they?
Ben: Yes, you're always running out, aren't you?
Gus: All the time.
Ben: Well, they'll come in handy then.
Gus: Yes.
Ben: Won't they?
Gus: Yes, I could do with them. I could do with them too.
Ben: You could, eh?

Gus: Yes.

Ben: Why?

Gus: We haven't got any.

Ben: Well, you've got some now, haven't you?

Gus: I can light the kettle now.

Ben: Yes, you're always cadging matches. How many have you got there?

Gus: About a dozen.

Ben: Well, don't lose them. Red too. You don't even need a box.

Gus *probes his ear with a match.*

    (Slapping his hand). Don't waste them! Go on, go and light it.

Gus: Eh?

Ben: Go and light it.

Gus: Light what?

Ben: The kettle.

Gus: You mean the gas.

Ben: Who does?

Gus: You do.

Ben: *(his eyes narrowing).* What do you mean, I mean the gas?

Gus: Well, that's what you mean, don't you? The gas.

Ben: *(powerfully).* If I say go and light the kettle I mean go and light the kettle.

Gus: How can you light a kettle?

Ben: It's a figure of speech! Light the kettle. It's a figure of speech!

Gus: I've never heard it.

Ben: Light the kettle! It's common usage!

Gus: I think you've got it wrong.

Ben: *(menacing).* What do you mean?

Gus: They say put on the kettle.

Ben: *(taut).* Who says?

They stare at each other, breathing hard.

    (Deliberately.) I have never in all my life heard anyone say put on the kettle.

Gus: I bet my mother used to say it.

Ben: Your mother? When did you last see your mother?

Gus: I don't know, about—

Ben: Well, what are you talking about your mother for?

They stare.

    Gus, I'm not trying to be unreasonable. I'm just trying to point out something to you.

Gus: Yes, but—

Ben: Who's the senior partner here, me or you?

Gus: You.

Ben: I'm only looking after your interests, Gus. You've got to learn, mate.

Gus: Yes, but I've never heard—

Ben: (*vehemently*). Nobody says light the gas! What does the gas light?

Gus: What does the gas—?

Ben: (*grabbing him with two hands by the throat, at arm's length*). THE KET-TLE, YOU FOOL!

Gus *takes the hands from his throat.*

Gus: All right, all right.

Pause.

Ben: Well, what are you waiting for?

Gus: I want to see if they light.

Ben: What?

Gus: The matches.

He takes out the flattened box and tries to strike.

No.

He throws the box under the bed.

Ben *stares at him.*

Gus *raises his foot.*

Shall I try it on here?

Ben *stares.* Gus *strikes a match on his shoe. It lights.*

Here we are.

Ben: (*wearily*). Put on the bloody kettle, for Christ's sake.

Ben *goes to his bed, but, realising what he has said, stops and half turns. They look at each other.* Gus *slowly exits, left.* Ben *slams his paper down on the bed and sits on it, head in hands.*

Gus: (*entering*). It's going.

Ben: What?

Gus: The stove.

Gus *goes to his bed and sits.*

I wonder who it'll be tonight.

Silence.

Eh, I've been wanting to ask you something.

Ben: (*putting his legs on the bed*). Oh, for Christ's sake.

Gus: No. I was going to ask you something.

He rises and sits on Ben's *bed.*

Ben: What are you sitting on my bed for?

Gus sits.

What's the matter with you? You're always asking me questions. What's the matter with you?

Gus: Nothing.

Ben: You never used to ask me so many damn questions. What's come over you?

Gus: No, I was just wondering.

Ben: Stop wondering. You've got a job to do. Why don't you just do it and shut up?

Gus: That's what I was wondering about.

Ben: What?

Gus: The job.

Ben: What job?

Gus: (*tentatively*). I thought perhaps you might know something.

Ben looks at him.

I thought perhaps you—I mean—have you got any idea—who it's going to be tonight?

Ben: Who what's going to be?

They look at each other.

Gus: (*at length*). Who it's going to be.

Silence.

Ben: Are you feeling all right?

Gus: Sure.

Ben: Go and make the tea.

Gus: Yes, sure.

Gus exits, left, Ben looks after him. He then takes his revolver from under the pillow and checks it for ammunition. Gus re-enters.

The gas has gone out.

Ben: Well, what about it?

Gus: There's a meter.

Ben: I haven't got any money.

Gus: Nor have I.

Ben: You'll have to wait.

Gus: What for?

Ben: For Wilson.

Gus: He might not come. He might just send a message. He doesn't always come.

Ben: Well, you'll have to do without it, won't you?

Gus: Blimey.

Ben: You'll have a cup of tea afterwards. What's the matter with you?
Gus: I like to have one before.

Ben *holds the revolver up to the light and polishes it.*

Ben: You'd better get ready anyway.
Gus: Well, I don't know, that's a bit much, you know, for my money.

He picks up a packet of tea from the bed and throws it into the bag.

I hope he's got a shilling, anyway, if he comes. He's entitled to have. After all, it's his place, he could have seen there was enough gas for a cup of tea.
Ben: What do you mean, it's his place?
Gus: Well, isn't it?
Ben: He's probably only rented it. It doesn't have to be his place.
Gus: I know it's his place. I bet the whole house is. He's not even laying on any gas now either.

Gus *sits on his bed.*

It's his place all right. Look at all the other places. You go to this address, there's a key there, there's a teapot, there's never a soul in sight—*(He pauses.)* Eh, nobody ever hears a thing, have you ever thought of that? We never get any complaints, do we, too much noise or anything like that? You never see a soul, do you?—except the bloke who comes. You ever noticed that? I wonder if the walls are sound-proof. *(He touches the wall above his bed.)* Can't tell. All you do is wait, eh? Half the time he doesn't even bother to put in an appearance, Wilson.
Ben: Why should he? He's a busy man.
Gus: *(thoughtfully).* I find him hard to talk to, Wilson. Do you know that, Ben?
Ben: Scrub round it, will you?

Pause.

Gus: There are a number of things I want to ask him. But I can never get round to it, when I see him.

Pause.

I've been thinking about the last one.
Ben: What last one?
Gus: That girl.

Ben *grabs the paper, which he reads.*

(Rising, looking down at Ben*).* How many times have you read that paper?

Ben *slams the paper down and rises.*

Ben: (angrily). What do you mean?

Gus: I was just wondering how many times you'd—

Ben: What are you doing, criticising me?

Gus: No, I was just—

Ben: You'll get a swipe round your earhole if you don't watch your step.

Gus: Now look here, Ben—

Ben: I'm not looking anywhere! *(He addresses the room.)* How many times have I—! A bloody liberty!

Gus: I didn't mean that.

Ben: You just get on with it, mate. Get on with it, that's all.

Ben *gets back on the bed.*

Gus: I was just thinking about that girl, that's all.

Gus *sits on his bed.*

> She wasn't much to look at, I know, but still. It was a mess though, wasn't it? What a mess. Honest, I can't remember a mess like that one. They don't seem to hold together like men, women. A looser texture, like. Didn't she spread, eh? She didn't half spread. Kaw! But I've been meaning to ask you.

Ben *sits up and clenches his eyes.*

> Who clears up after we've gone? I'm curious about that. Maybe they just leave them there, eh? What do you think? How many jobs have we done? Blimey, I can't count them. What if they never clear anything up after we've gone.

Ben: (pityingly). You mutt. Do you think we're the only branch of this organisation? Have a bit of common. They got departments for everything.

Gus: What cleaners and all?

Ben: You birk!

Gus: No, it was that girl made me start to think—

There is a loud clatter and racket in the bulge of wall between the beds, of something descending. They grab their revolvers, jump up and face the wall. The noise comes to a stop. Silence. They look at each other. Ben gestures sharply towards the wall. Gus approaches the wall slowly. He bangs it with his revolver. It is hollow. Ben moves to the head of his bed, his revolver cocked. Gus puts his revolver on his bed and pats along the bottom of the centre panel. He finds a rim. He lifts the panel. Disclosed is a serving-hatch, a "dumb waiter." A wide box is held by pulleys. Gus peers into the box. He brings out a piece of paper.

Ben: What is it?

Gus: You have a look at it.

Ben: Read it.

Gus: (reading). Two braised steak and chips. Two sago puddings. Two teas without sugar.
Ben: Let me see that. (He takes the paper.)
Gus: (to himself). Two teas without sugar.
Ben: Mmnn.
Gus: What do you think of that?
Ben: Well—

The box goes up. Ben levels his revolver.

Gus: Give us a chance! They're in a hurry, aren't they?

Ben re-reads the note. Gus looks over his shoulder.

That's a bit—that's a bit funny, isn't it?
Ben: (quickly). No. It's not funny. It probably used to be a café here, that's all. Upstairs. These places change hands very quickly.
Gus: A café?
Ben: Yes.
Gus: What, you mean this was the kitchen, down here?
Ben: Yes, they change hands overnight, these places. Go into liquidation. The people who run it, you know, they don't find it a going concern, they move out.
Gus: You mean the people who ran this place didn't find it a going concern and moved out?
Ben: Sure.
Gus: WELL, WHO'S GOT IT NOW?

Silence.

Ben: What do you mean, who's got it now?
Gus: Who's got it now? If they moved out, who moved in?
Ben: Well, that all depends—

The box descends with a clatter and bang. Ben levels his revolver. Gus goes to the box and brings out a piece of paper.

Gus: (reading). Soup of the day. Liver and onions. Jam tart.

A pause. Gus looks at Ben. Ben takes the note and reads it. He walks slowly to the hatch. Gus follows. Ben looks into the hatch but not up it. Gus puts his hand on Ben's shoulder. Ben throws it off. Gus puts his finger to his mouth. He leans on the hatch and swiftly looks up it. Ben flings him away in alarm. Ben looks at the note. He throws his revolver on the bed and speaks with decision.

Ben: We'd better send something up.
Gus: Eh?
Ben: We'd better send something up.
Gus: Oh! Yes. Yes. Maybe you're right.

They are both relieved at the decision.

Ben: (*purposefully*). Quick! What have you got in that bag?
Gus: Not much.

Gus goes to the hatch and shouts up it.

   Wait a minute!
Ben: Don't do that!

Gus examines the contents of the bag and brings them out, one by one.

Gus: Biscuits. A bar of chocolate. Half a pint of milk.
Ben: That all?
Gus: Packet of tea.
Ben: Good.
Gus: We can't send the tea. That's all the tea we've got.
Ben: Well, there's no gas. You can't do anything with it, can you?
Gus: Maybe they can send us down a bob.
Ben: What else is there?
Gus: (*reaching into bag*). One Eccles cake.
Ben: One Eccles cake?
Gus: Yes.
Ben: You never told me you had an Eccles cake.
Gus: Didn't I?
Ben: Why only one? Didn't you bring one for me?
Gus: I didn't think you'd be keen.
Ben: Well, you can't send up one Eccles cake, anyway.
Gus: Why not?
Ben: Fetch one of those plates.
Gus: All right.

Gus goes towards the door, left, and stops.

   Do you mean I can keep the Eccles cake then?
Ben: Keep it?
Gus: Well, they don't know we've got it, do they?
Ben: That's not the point.
Gus: Can't I keep it?
Ben: No, you can't. Get the plate.

Gus exits, left. Ben *looks in the bag. He brings out a packet of crisps. Enter* Gus *with a plate.*

   (*Accusingly, holding up the crisps*). Where did these come from?
Gus: What?
Ben: Where did these crisps come from?
Gus: Where did you find them?
Ben: (*hitting him on the shoulder*). You're playing a dirty game, my lad!
Gus: I only eat those with beer!
Ben: Well, where were you going to get the beer?

Gus: I was saving them till I did.
Ben: I'll remember this. Put everything on the plate.

They pile everything on to the plate. The box goes up without the plate.

Wait a minute!

They stand.

Gus: It's gone up.
Ben: It's all your stupid fault, playing about!
Gus: What do we do now?
Ben: We'll have to wait till it comes down.

Ben *puts the plate on the bed, puts on his shoulder holster, and starts to put on his tie.*

You'd better get ready.

Gus *goes to his bed, puts on his tie, and starts to fix his holster.*

Gus: Hey, Ben.
Ben: What?
Gus: What's going on here?

Pause.

Ben: What do you mean?
Gus: How can this be a café?
Ben: It used to be a café.
Gus: Have you seen the gas stove?
Ben: What about it?
Gus: It's only got three rings.
Ben: So what?
Gus: Well, you couldn't cook much on three rings, not for a busy place like this.
Ben: (*irritably*). That's why the service is slow!

Ben *puts on his waistcoat.*

Gus: Yes, but what happens when we're not here? What do they do then? All these menus coming down and nothing going up. It might have been going on like this for years.

Ben *brushes his jacket.*

What happens when we go?

Ben *puts on his jacket.*

They can't do much business.

The box descends. They turn about. Gus goes to the hatch and brings out a note.

Gus: (*reading*). Macaroni Pastitsio. Ormitha Macarounada.

Ben: What was that?
Gus: Macaroni Pastitsio. Ormitha Macarounada.
Ben: Greek dishes.
Gus: No.
Ben: That's right.
Gus: That's pretty high class.
Ben: Quick before it goes up.

Gus *puts the plate in the box.*

Gus: *(calling up the hatch).* Three McVitie and Price! One Lyons Red
    Label! One Smith's Crisps! One Eccles cake! One Fruit and Nut!
Ben: Cadbury's.
Gus: *(up the hatch).* Cadbury's!
Ben: *(handing the milk).* One bottle of milk.
Gus: *(up the hatch).* One bottle of milk! Half a pint! *(He looks at the
    label.)* Express Dairy! *(He puts the bottle in the box.)*

The box goes up.

    Just did it.
Ben: You shouldn't shout like that.
Gus: Why not?
Ben: It isn't done.

Ben *goes to his bed.*

    Well, that should be all right, anyway, for the time being.
Gus: You think so, eh?
Ben: Get dressed, will you? It'll be any minute now.

Gus *puts on his waistcoat.* Ben *lies down and looks up at the ceiling.*

Gus: This is some place. No tea and no biscuits.
Ben: Eating makes you lazy, mate. You're getting lazy, you know that?
    You don't want to get slack on your job.
Gus: Who me?
Ben: Slack, mate, slack.
Gus: Who me? Slack?
Ben: Have you checked your gun? You haven't even checked your
    gun. It looks disgraceful, anyway. Why don't you ever polish it?

Gus *rubs his revolver on the sheet.* Ben *takes out a pocket mirror and straightens
his tie.*

Gus: I wonder where the cook is. They must have had a few, to cope
    with that. Maybe they had a few more gas stoves. Eh! Maybe there's
    another kitchen along the passage.
Ben: Of course there is! Do you know what it takes to make an
    Ormitha Macarounada?
Gus: No, what?

Ben: An Ormitha—! Buck your ideas up, will you?
Gus: Takes a few cooks, eh?

Gus *puts his revolver in its holster.*

The sooner we're out of this place the better.

He puts on his jacket.

Why doesn't he get in touch? I feel like I've been here years. *(He takes his revolver out of its holster to check the ammunition.)* We've never let him down though, have we? We've never let him down. I was thinking only the other day, Ben. We're reliable, aren't we?

He puts his revolver back in its holster.

Still, I'll be glad when it's over tonight.

He brushes his jacket.

I hope the bloke's not going to get excited tonight, or anything. I'm feeling a bit off. I've got a splitting headache.

Silence.

The box descends. Ben *jumps up.*

Gus *collects the note.*

(Reading.) One Bamboo Shoots, Water Chestnuts and Chicken. One Char Siu and Beansprouts.
Ben: Beansprouts?
Gus: Yes.
Ben: Blimey.
Gus: I wouldn't know where to begin.

He looks back at the box. The packet of tea is inside it. He picks it up.

They've sent back the tea.
Ben: (anxious). What'd they do that for?
Gus: Maybe it isn't tea-time.

The box goes up. Silence.

Ben: (throwing the tea on the bed, and speaking urgently). Look here.
We'd better tell them.
Gus: Tell them what?
Ben: That we can't do it, we haven't got it.
Gus: All right then.
Ben: Lend us your pencil. We'll write a note.

Gus, *turning for a pencil, suddenly discovers the speaking-tube, which hangs on the right wall of the hatch facing his bed.*

Gus: What's this?

Ben: What?

Gus: This.

Ben: *(examining it).* This? It's a speaking-tube.

Gus: How long has that been there?

Ben: Just the job. We should have used it before, instead of shouting up there.

Gus: Funny I never noticed it before.

Ben: Well, come on.

Gus: What do you do?

Ben: See that? That's a whistle.

Gus: What, this?

Ben: Yes, take it out. Pull it out.

Gus *does so.*

That's it.

Gus: What do we do now?

Ben: Blow into it.

Gus: Blow?

Ben: It whistles up there if you blow. Then they know you want to speak. Blow.

Gus *blows. Silence.*

Gus: *(tube at mouth).* I can't hear a thing.

Ben: Now you speak! Speak into it!

Gus *looks at* Ben, *then speaks into the tube.*

Gus: The larder's bare!

Ben: Give me that!

He grabs the tube and puts it to his mouth.

(Speaking with great deference.) Good evening. I'm sorry to—bother you, but we just thought we'd better let you know that we haven't got anything left. We sent up all we had. There's no more food down here.

He brings the tube slowly to his ear.

What?

To mouth.

What?

To ear. He listens. To mouth.

No, all we had we sent up.

To ear. He listens. To mouth.

Oh, I'm very sorry to hear that.

To ear. He listens. To Gus.

The Eccles cake was stale.

He listens. To Gus.

The chocolate was melted.

He listens. To Gus.

The milk was sour.

Gus: What about the crisps?

Ben: *(listening)*. The biscuits were mouldy.

He glares at Gus. Tube to mouth.

Well, we're very sorry about that.

Tube to ear.

What?

To mouth.

What?

To ear.

Yes. Yes.

To mouth.

Yes certainly. Certainly. Right away.

To ear. The voice has ceased. He hangs up the tube.

(Excitedly). Did you hear that?

Gus: What?

Ben: You know what he said? Light the kettle! Not put on the kettle! Not light the gas! But light the kettle!

Gus: How can we light the kettle?

Ben: What do you mean?

Gus: There's no gas.

Ben: *(clapping hand to head)*. Now what do we do?

Gus: What did he want us to light the kettle for?

Ben: For tea. He wanted a cup of tea.

Gus: *He* wanted a cup of tea! What about me? I've been wanting a cup of tea all night!

Ben: *(despairingly)*. What do we do now?

Gus: What are we supposed to drink?

Ben *sits on his bed, staring.*

What about us?

Ben *sits.*

I'm thirsty too. I'm starving. And he wants a cup of tea. That beats the band, that does.

Ben *lets his head sink on to his chest.*

I could do with a bit of sustenance myself. What about you? You look as if you could do with something too.

Gus *sits on his bed.*

We send him up all we've got and he's not satisfied. No, honest, it's enough to make the cat laugh. Why did you send him up all that stuff? *(Thoughtfully.)* Why did I send it up?

Pause.

Who knows what he's got upstairs? He's probably got a salad bowl. They must have something up there. They won't get much from down here. You notice they didn't ask for any salads? They've probably got a salad bowl up there. Cold meat, radishes, cucumbers. Watercress. Roll mops.

Pause.

Hardboiled eggs.

Pause.

The lot. They've probably got a crate of beer too. Probably eating my crisps with a pint of beer now. Didn't have anything to say about those crisps, did he? They do all right, don't worry about that. You don't think they're just going to sit there and wait for stuff to come up from down here, do you? That'll get them nowhere.

Pause.

They do all right.

Pause.

And he wants a cup of tea.

Pause.

That's past a joke, in my opinion.

He looks over at Ben, *rises, and goes to him.*

What's the matter with you? You don't look too bright. I feel like an Alka-Seltzer myself.

Ben *sits up.*

Ben: *(in a low voice).* Time's getting on.
Gus: I know. I don't like doing a job on an empty stomach.
Ben: *(wearily).* Be quiet a minute. Let me give you your instructions.

Gus: What for? We always do it the same way, don't we?
Ben: Let me give you your instructions.

Gus *sighs and sits next to* Ben *on the bed. The instructions are stated and repeated automatically.*

When we get the call, you go over and stand behind the door.
Gus: Stand behind the door.
Ben: If there's a knock on the door you don't answer it.
Gus: If there's a knock on the door I don't answer it.
Ben: But there won't be a knock on the door.
Gus: So I won't answer it.
Ben: When the bloke comes in—
Gus: When the bloke comes in—
Ben: Shut the door behind him.
Gus: Shut the door behind him.
Ben: Without divulging your presence.
Gus: Without divulging my presence.
Ben: He'll see me and come towards me.
Gus: He'll see you and come towards you.
Ben: He won't see you.
Gus: (absently). Eh?
Ben: He won't see you.
Gus: He won't see me.
Ben: But he'll see me.
Gus: He'll see you.
Ben: He won't know you're there.
Gus: He won't know you're there.
Ben: He won't know *you're* there.
Gus: He won't know I'm there.
Ben: I take out my gun.
Gus: You take out your gun.
Ben: He stops in his tracks.
Gus: He stops in his tracks.
Ben: If he turns round—
Gus: If he turns round—
Ben: You're there.
Gus: I'm here.

Ben *frowns and presses his forehead.*

You've missed something out.
Ben: I know. What?
Gus: I haven't taken my gun out, according to you.
Ben: You take your gun out—
Gus: After I've closed the door.
Ben: After you've closed the door.
Gus: You've never missed that out before, you know that?

Ben: When he sees you behind him—
Gus: Me behind him—
Ben: And me in front of him—
Gus: And you in front of him—
Ben: He'll feel uncertain—
Gus: Uneasy.
Ben: He won't know what to do.
Gus: So what will he do?
Ben: He'll look at me and he'll look at you.
Gus: We won't say a word.
Ben: We'll look at him.
Gus: He won't say a word.
Ben: He'll look at us.
Gus: And we'll look at him.
Ben: Nobody says a word.

Pause.

Gus: What do we do if it's a girl?
Ben: We do the same.
Gus: Exactly the same?
Ben: Exactly.

Pause.

Gus: We don't do anything different?
Ben: We do exactly the same.
Gus: Oh.

Gus *rises, and shivers.*

   Excuse me.

He exits through the door on the left. Ben *remains sitting on the bed, still.*
The lavatory chain is pulled once off left, but the lavatory does not flush.
Silence.
Gus *re-enters and stops inside the door, deep in thought. He looks at* Ben, *then walks slowly across to his own bed. He is troubled. He stands, thinking. He turns and looks at* Ben. *He moves a few paces towards him.*

   (Slowly in a low, tense voice.) Why did he send us matches if he knew there was no gas?

Silence.

Ben *stares in front of him.* Gus *crosses to the left side of* Ben, *to the foot of his bed, to get to his other ear.*

   Ben. Why did he send us matches if he knew there was no gas?

Ben *looks up.*

Why did he do that?

Ben: Who?

Gus: Who sent us those matches?

Ben: What are you talking about?

Gus *stares down at him.*

Gus: (thickly). Who is it upstairs?

Ben: (nervously). What's one thing to do with another?

Gus: Who is it, though?

Ben: What's one thing to do with another?

Ben *fumbles for his paper on the bed.*

Gus: I asked you a question.

Ben: Enough!

Gus: (with growing agitation). I asked you before. Who moved in? I
    asked you. You said the people who had it before moved out. Well,
    who moved in?

Ben: (hunched). Shut up.

Gus: I told you, didn't I?

Ben: (standing). Shut up!

Gus: (feverishly). I told you before who owned this place, didn't I? I
    told you.

Ben *hits him viciously on the shoulder.*

    I told you who ran this place, didn't I?

Ben *hits him viciously on the shoulder.*

    (Violently.) Well, what's he playing all these games for? That's what I
    want to know. What's he doing it for?

Ben: What games?

Gus: (passionately, advancing). What's he doing it for? We've been
    through our tests, haven't we? We got right through our tests, years
    ago, didn't we? We took them together, don't you remember, didn't
    we? We've proved ourselves before now, haven't we? We've always
    done our job. What's he doing all this for? What's the idea? What's
    he playing these games for?

The box in the shaft comes down behind them. The noise is this time accompanied by
a shrill whistle, as it falls. Gus rushes to the hatch and seizes the note.

    (Reading.) Scampi!

He crumples the note, picks up the tube, takes out the whistle, blows and speaks.

    WE'VE GOT NOTHING LEFT! NOTHING! DO YOU UNDERSTAND?

Ben *seizes the tube and flings* Gus *away. He follows* Gus *and slaps him hard,
back-handed, across the chest.*

Ben: Stop it! You maniac!
Gus: But you heard!
Ben: *(savagely).* That's enough! I'm warning you!

Silence.

Ben *hangs the tube. He goes to his bed and lies down. He picks up his paper and* *reads.*

Silence.

The box goes up.

They turn quickly, their eyes meet. Ben *turns to his paper.*

Slowly Gus *goes back to his bed, and sits.*

Silence.

The hatch falls back into place.

They turn quickly, their eyes meet. Ben *turns back to his paper.*

Silence.

Ben *throws his paper down.*

Ben: Kaw!

He picks up the paper and looks at it.

   Listen to this!

Pause.

   What about that, eh?

Pause.

   Kaw!

Pause.

   Have you ever heard such a thing?
Gus: *(dully).* Go on!
Ben: It's true.
Gus: Get away.
Ben: It's down here in black and white.
Gus: *(very low).* Is that a fact?
Ben: Can you imagine it.
Gus: It's unbelievable.
Ben: It's enough to make you want to puke, isn't it?
Gus: *(almost inaudible).* Incredible.

Ben *shakes his head. He puts the paper down and rises. He fixes the revolver in* *his holster.*

Gus *stands up. He goes towards the door on the left.*

Ben: Where are you going?

Gus: I'm going to have a glass of water.

He exits. Ben *brushes dust off his clothes and shoes. The whistle in the speaking-tube blows. He goes to it, takes the whistle out and puts the tube to his ear. He listens. He puts it to his mouth.*

Ben: Yes.

To ear. He listens. To mouth.

   Straight away. Right.

To ear. He listens. To mouth.

   Sure we're ready.

To ear. He listens. To mouth.

   Understood. Repeat. He has arrived and will be coming in straight away. The normal method to be employed. Understood.

To ear. He listens. To mouth.

   Sure we're ready.

To ear. He listens. To mouth.

   Right.

He hangs the tube up.

   Gus!

He takes out a comb and combs his hair, adjusts his jacket to diminish the bulge of the revolver. The lavatory flushes off left. Ben *goes quickly to the door, left.*

   Gus!

The door right opens sharply. Ben *turns, his revolver levelled at the door.*
Gus *stumbles in.*
He is stripped of his jacket, waistcoat, tie, holster and revolver.
He stops, body stooping, his arms at his sides.
He raises his head and looks at Ben.
A long silence.
They stare at each other.

CURTAIN

Harold Pinter is often seen as one of the leaders of the "theater of the absurd," which breaks with conventional realism of presentation and shows characters overwhelmed by the meaninglessness of life. Comments made in

an interview with Lawrence Bensky show, however, that beneath Pinter's absurdism are two clear organizing principles: an interest in working out a story within the limits of stage production and a recurring theme of "dominance and subservience."

"There are your characters stuck on the stage": Harold Pinter

Interviewer: Do you get impatient with the limitations of writing for the theater?

Pinter: No. It's quite different; the theater's much the most difficult kind of writing for me, the most naked kind, you're so entirely restricted. I've done some film work, but for some reason or other I haven't found it very easy to satisfy myself on an original idea for a film. *Tea Party,* which I did for television, is actually a film, cinematic, I wrote it like that. Television and films are simpler than the theater—if you get tired of a scene you just drop it and go on to another one. (I'm exaggerating, of course.) What *is* so different about the stage is that you're just *there,* stuck—there are your characters stuck on the stage, you've got to live with them and deal with them. I'm not a very inventive writer in the sense of using the technical devices other playwrights do—look at Brecht! I can't use the stage the way he does, I just haven't got that kind of imagination, so I find myself stuck with these characters who are either sitting or standing, and they've either got to walk out of a door, or come in through a door, and that's about all they can do.

Interviewer: And talk.

Pinter: Or keep silent.

*

Interviewer: Why do you think the conversations in your plays are so effective?

Pinter: I don't know. I think possibly it's because people fall back on anything they can lay their hands on verbally to keep away from the danger of knowing and of being known.

*

Interviewer: There's a sense of terror and a threat of violence in most of your plays. Do you see the world as an essentially violent place?

Pinter: The world *is* a pretty violent place, it's as simple as that, so any violence in the plays comes out quite naturally. It seems to me an essential and inevitable factor.

Harold Pinter   1819

I think what you're talking about began in *The Dumb Waiter,* which from my point of view is a relatively simple piece of work. The violence is really only an expression of the question of dominance and subservience, which is possibly a repeated theme in my plays. I wrote a short story a long time ago called "The Examination," and my ideas of violence carried on from there. That short story dealt very explicitly with two people in one room having a battle of an unspecified nature, in which the question was one of who was dominant at what point and how they were going to be dominant and what tools they would use to achieve dominance and how they would try to undermine the other person's dominance. A threat is constantly there: it's got to do with this question of being in the uppermost position, or attempting to be. That's something of what attracted me to do the screenplay of *The Servant,* which was someone else's story, you know. I wouldn't call this violence so much as a battle for positions, it's a very common, everyday thing.

ATHOL FUGARD

(b. 1932)

"MASTER HAROLD"
. . . AND THE BOYS

CHARACTERS

Hally
Sam
Willie

The St. George's Park Tea Room on a wet and windy Port Elizabeth afternoon.

Tables and chairs have been cleared and are stacked on one side except for one which stands apart with a single chair. On this table a knife, fork, spoon and side plate in anticipation of a simple meal, together with a pile of comic books.

Other elements: a serving counter with a few stale cakes under glass and a not very impressive display of sweets, cigarettes and cool drinks, etc.; a few cardboard advertising handouts—Cadbury's Chocolate, Coca-Cola—and a blackboard on which an untrained hand has chalked up the prices of Tea, Coffee, Scones, Milkshakes—all flavors—and Cool Drinks; a few sad ferns in pots; a telephone; an old-style jukebox.

There is an entrance on one side and an exit into a kitchen on the other.

Leaning on the solitary table, his head cupped in one hand as he pages through one of the comic books, is Sam. *A black man in his mid-forties. He wears the white coat of a waiter. Behind him on his knees, mopping down the floor with a bucket of water and a rag, is* Willie. *Also black and about the same age as* Sam. *He has his sleeves and trousers rolled up.*

The year: 1950

Willie: *(Singing as he works)*
    "She was scandalizin' my name,
    She took my money
    She called me honey
    But she was scandalizin' my name.
    Called it love but was playin' a game . . ."

(He gets up and moves the bucket. Stands thinking for a moment, then, raising his arms to hold an imaginary partner, he launches into an intricate ballroom dance step. Although a mildly comic figure, he reveals a reasonable degree of accomplishment)

Hey, Sam.

(Sam, absorbed in the comic book, does not respond)

Hey, Boet Sam!

(Sam looks up)

I'm getting it. The quickstep. Look now and tell me. *(He repeats the step)* Well?

Sam: *(Encouragingly)* Show me again.

Willie: Okay, count for me.

Sam: Ready?

Willie: Ready.

Sam: Five, six, seven, eight . . . (Willie *starts to dance*) A-n-d one two three four . . . and one two three four. . . . *(Ad libbing as* Willie *dances)* Your shoulders, Willie . . . your shoulders! Don't look down! Look happy, Willie! Relax, Willie!

Willie: *(Desperate but still dancing)* I am relax.

Sam: No, you're not.

Willie: *(He falters)* Ag no man, Sam! Mustn't talk. You make me make mistakes.

Sam: But you're too stiff.

Willie: Yesterday I'm not straight . . . today I'm too stiff!

Sam: Well, you are. You asked me and I'm telling you.

Willie: Where?

Sam: Everywhere. Try to glide through it.

Willie: Glide?

Sam: Ja, make it smooth. And give it more style. It must look like you're enjoying yourself.

Willie: *(Emphatically)* I wasn't.

Sam: Exactly.

Willie: How can I enjoy myself? No straight, too stiff and now it's also glide, give it more style, make it smooth. . . . Haai! Is hard to remember all those things, Boet Sam.

Sam: That's your trouble. You're trying too hard.

Willie: I try hard because it *is* hard.

Sam: But don't let me see it. The secret is to make it look easy. Ballroom must look happy, Willie, not like hard work. It must . . . Ja! . . . it must look like romance.

Willie: Now another one! What's romance?

Sam: Love story with happy ending. A handsome man in tails, and in his arms, smiling at him, a beautiful lady in evening dress!

Willie: Fred Astaire, Ginger Rogers.

  Sam: You got it. Tapdance or ballroom, it's the same. Romance. In two weeks' time when the judges look at you and Hilda, they must see a man and a woman who are dancing their way to a happy ending. What I saw was you holding her like you were frightened she was going to run away.

Willie: Ja! Because that is what she wants to do! I got no romance left for Hilda anymore, Boet Sam.

  Sam: Then pretend. When you put your arms around Hilda, imagine she is Ginger Rogers.

Willie: With no teeth? You try.

  Sam: Well, just remember, there's only two weeks left.

Willie: I know, I know! *(To the jukebox)* I do it better with music. You got sixpence for Sarah Vaughan?

  Sam: That's a slow foxtrot. You're practicing the quickstep.

Willie: I'll practice slow foxtrot.

  Sam: *(Shaking his head)* It's your turn to put money in the jukebox.

Willie: I only got bus fare to go home. *(He returns disconsolately to his work)* Love story and happy ending! She's doing it all right, Boet Sam, but is not me she's giving happy endings. Fuckin' whore! Three nights now she doesn't come practice. I wind up gramophone, I get record ready and I sit and wait. What happens? Nothing. Ten o'clock I start dancing with my pillow. You try and practice romance by yourself, Boet Sam. Struesgod, she doesn't come tonight I take back my dress and ballroom shoes and I find me new partner. Size twenty-six. Shoes size seven. And now she's also making trouble for me with the baby again. Reports me to Child Wellfed, that I'm not giving her money. She lies! Every week I am giving her money for milk. And how do I know is my baby? Only his hair looks like me. She's fucking around all the time I turn my back. Hilda Samuels is a bitch! *(Pause)* Hey, Sam!

  Sam: Ja.

Willie: You listening?

  Sam: Ja.

Willie: So what you say?

  Sam: About Hilda?

Willie: Ja.

  Sam: When did you last give her a hiding?

Willie: *(Reluctantly)* Sunday night.

  Sam: And today is Thursday.

Willie: *(He knows what's coming)* Okay.

  Sam: Hiding on Sunday night, then Monday, Tuesday and Wednesday she doesn't come to practice . . . and you are asking me why?

Willie: I said okay, Boet Sam!

  Sam: You hit her too much. One day she's going to leave you for good.

Willie: So? She makes me the hell-in too much.

   Sam: *(Emphasizing his point)* *Too* much and *too* hard. You had the same trouble with Eunice.

Willie: Because she also make the hell-in, Boet Sam. She never got the steps right. Even the waltz.

   Sam: Beating her up every time she makes a mistake in the waltz? *(Shaking his head)* No, Willie! That takes the pleasure out of ballroom dancing.

Willie: Hilda is not too bad with the waltz, Boet Sam. Is the quickstep where the trouble starts.

   Sam: *(Teasing him gently)* How's your pillow with the quickstep?

Willie: *(Ignoring the tease)* Good! And why? Because it got no legs. That's her trouble. She can't move them quick enough, Boet Sam. I start the record and before halfway Count Basie is already winning. Only time we catch up with him is when gramophone runs down.

(Sam laughs)

     Haaikona, Boet Sam, is not funny.

   Sam: *(Snapping his fingers)* I got it! Give her a handicap.

Willie: What's that?

   Sam: Give her a ten-second start and then let Count Basie go. Then I put my money on her. Hot favorite in the Ballroom Stakes: Hilda Samuels ridden by Willie Malopo.

Willie: *(Turning away)* I'm not talking to you no more.

   Sam: *(Relenting)* Sorry, Willie . . .

Willie: It's finish between us.

   Sam: Okay, okay . . . I'll stop.

Willie: You can also fuck off.

   Sam: Willie, listen! I want to help you!

Willie: No more jokes?

   Sam: I promise.

Willie: Okay. Help me.

   Sam: *(His turn to hold an imaginary partner)* Look and learn. Feet together. Back straight. Body relaxed. Right hand placed gently in the small of her back and wait for the music. Don't start worrying about making mistakes or the judges or the other competitors. It's just you, Hilda and the music, and you're going to have a good time. What Count Basie do you play?

Willie: "You the cream in my coffee, you the salt in my stew."

   Sam: Right. Give it to me in strict tempo.

Willie: Ready?

   Sam: Ready.

Willie: A-n-d . . . *(Singing)*

     "You the cream in my coffee.

You the salt in my stew.
You will always be my necessity.
I'd be lost without you. . . ." *(etc.)*

(Sam *launches into the quickstep. He is obviously a much more accomplished dancer than* Willie. Hally *enters. A seventeen-year-old white boy. Wet raincoat and school case. He stops and watches* Sam. *The demonstration comes to an end with a flourish. Applause from* Hally *and* Willie)

Hally: Bravo! No question about it. First place goes to Mr. Sam Semela.

Willie: *(In total agreement)* You was gliding with style, Boet Sam.

Hally: *(Cheerfully)* How's it, chaps?

Sam: Okay, Hally.

Willie: *(Springing to attention like a soldier and saluting)* At your service, Master Harold!

Hally: Not long to the big event, hey!

Sam: Two weeks.

Hally: You nervous?

Sam: No.

Hally: Think you stand a chance?

Sam: Let's just say I'm ready to go out there and dance.

Hally: It looked like it. What about you, Willie?

(Willie *groans*)

What's the matter?

Sam: He's got leg trouble.

Hally: *(Innocently)* Oh, sorry to hear that, Willie.

Willie: Boet Sam! You promised. (Willie *returns to his work*)

(Hally *deposits his school case and takes off his raincoat. His clothes are a little neglected and untidy: black blazer with school badge, gray flannel trousers in need of an ironing, khaki shirt and tie, black shoes.* Sam *has fetched a towel for* Hally *to dry his hair*)

Hally: God, what a lousy bloody day. It's coming down cats and dogs out there. Bad for business, chaps . . . *(Conspiratorial whisper)* . . . but it also means we're in for a nice quiet afternoon.

Sam: You can speak loud. Your Mom's not here.

Hally: Out shopping?

Sam: No. The hospital.

Hally: But it's Thursday. There's no visiting on Thursday afternoons. Is my Dad okay?

Sam: Sounds like it. In fact, I think he's going home.

Hally: *(Stopped short by* Sam's *remark)* What do you mean?

Sam: The hospital phoned.

Hally: To say what?

Sam: I don't know. I just heard your Mom talking.

Hally: So what makes you say he's going home?

Sam: It sounded as if they were telling her to come and fetch him.

(Hally *thinks about what* Sam *has said for a few seconds*)

Hally: When did she leave?

Sam: About an hour ago. She said she would phone you. Want to eat?

(Hally *doesn't respond*)

Hally, want your lunch?

Hally: I suppose so. (*His mood has changed*) What's on the menu? . . . as if I don't know.

Sam: Soup, followed by meat pie and gravy.

Hally: Today's?

Sam: No.

Hally: And the soup?

Sam: Nourishing pea soup.

Hally: Just the soup. (*The pile of comic books on the table*) And these?

Sam: For your Dad. Mr. Kempston brought them.

Hally: You haven't been reading them, have you?

Sam: Just looking.

Hally: (*Examining the comics*) Jungle Jim . . . Batman and Robin . . . Tarzan . . . God, what rubbish! Mental pollution. Take them away.

(Sam *exits waltzing into the kitchen.* Hally *turns to* Willie)

Hally: Did you hear my Mom talking on the telephone, Willie?

Willie: No, Master Hally. I was at the back.

Hally: And she didn't say anything to you before she left?

Willie: She said I must clean the floors.

Hally: I mean about my Dad.

Willie: She didn't say nothing to me about him, Master Hally.

Hally: (*With conviction*) No! It can't be. They said he needed at least another three weeks of treatment. Sam's definitely made a mistake. (*Rummages through his school case, finds a book and settles down at the table to read*) So, Willie!

Willie: Yes, Master Hally! Schooling okay today?

Hally: Yes, okay. . . . (*He thinks about it*) . . . No, not really. Ag, what's the difference? I don't care. And Sam says you've got problems.

Willie: Big problems.

Hally: Which leg is sore?

(Willie *groans*)

Both legs.

Willie: There is nothing wrong with my legs. Sam is just making jokes.

Hally: So then you *will* be in the competition.

Willie: Only if I can find me a partner.

Hally: But what about Hilda?

  Sam: *(Returning with a bowl of soup)* She's the one who's got trouble with her legs.

Hally: What sort of trouble, Willie?

  Sam: From the way he describes it, I think the lady has gone a bit lame.

Hally: Good God! Have you taken her to see a doctor?

  Sam: I think a vet would be better.

Hally: What do you mean?

  Sam: What do you call it again when a racehorse goes very fast?

Hally: Gallop?

  Sam: That's it!

Willie: Boet Sam!

Hally: "A gallop down the homestretch to the winning post." But what's that got to do with Hilda?

  Sam: Count Basie always gets there first.

(Willie *lets fly with his slop rag. It misses* Sam *and hits* Hally)

Hally: *(Furious)* For Christ's sake, Willie! What the hell do you think you're doing!

Willie: Sorry, Master Hally, but it's him. . . .

Hally: Act your bloody age! *(Hurls the rag back at* Willie) Cut out the nonsense now and get on with your work. And you too, Sam. Stop fooling around.

(Sam *moves away*)

    No. Hang on. I haven't finished! Tell me exactly what my Mom said.

  Sam: I have. "When Hally comes, tell him I've gone to the hospital and I'll phone him."

Hally: She didn't say anything about taking my Dad home?

  Sam: No. It's just that when she was talking on the phone . . .

Hally: *(Interrupting him)* No, Sam. They can't be discharging him. She would have said so if they were. In any case, we saw him last night and he wasn't in good shape at all. Staff nurse even said there was talk about taking more X-rays. And now suddenly today he's better? If anything, it sounds more like a bad turn to me . . . which I sincerely hope it isn't. Hang on . . . how long ago did you say she left?

  Sam: Just before two . . . *(His wrist watch)* . . . hour and a half.

Hally: I know how to settle it. *(Behind the counter to the telephone. Talking as he dials)* Let's give her ten minutes to get to the hospital, ten minutes to load him up, another ten, at the most, to get home and another ten to get him inside. Forty minutes. They should have been home for at least half an hour already. *(Pause—he waits with the receiver to his ear)* No reply, chaps. And you know why? Because she's at his bedside in hospital helping him pull through a bad turn. You definitely heard wrong.

  Sam: Okay.

(As far as Hally *is concerned, the matter is settled. He returns to his table, sits down and divides his attention between the book and his soup.* Sam *is at his school case and picks up a textbook)*

  Modern Graded Mathematics for Standards Nine and Ten. *(Opens it at random and laughs at something he sees)* Who is this supposed to be?

Hally: Old fart-face Prentice.

  Sam: Teacher?

Hally: Thinks he is. And believe me, that is not a bad likeness.

  Sam: Has he seen it?

Hally: Yes.

  Sam: What did he say?

Hally: Tried to be clever, as usual. Said I was no Leonardo da Vinci and that bad art had to be punished. So, six of the best, and his are bloody good.

  Sam: On your bum?

Hally: Where else? The days when I got them on my hands are gone forever, Sam.

  Sam: With your trousers down!

Hally: No. He's not quite that barbaric.

  Sam: That's the way they do it in jail.

Hally: *(Flicker of morbid interest)* Really?

  Sam: Ja. When the magistrate sentences you to "strokes with a light cane."

Hally: Go on.

  Sam: They make you lie down on a bench. One policeman pulls down your trousers and holds your ankles, another one pulls your shirt over your head and holds your arms . . .

Hally: Thank you! That's enough.

  Sam: . . . and the one that gives you the strokes talks to you gently and for a long time between each one. *(He laughs)*

Hally: I've heard enough, Sam! Jesus! It's a bloody awful world when you come to think of it. People can be real bastards.

  Sam: That's the way it is, Hally.

Hally: It doesn't *have* to be that way. There is something called progress, you know. We don't exactly burn people at the stake anymore.

  Sam: Like Joan of Arc.

Hally: Correct. If she was captured today, she'd be given a fair trial.

  Sam: And then the death sentence.

Hally: *(A world-weary sigh)* I know, I know! I oscillate between hope and despair for this world as well, Sam. But things will change, you wait and see. One day somebody is going to get up and give history a kick up the backside and get it going again.

Sam: Like who?

Hally: (*After thought*) They're called social reformers. Every age, Sam, has got its social reformer. My history book is full of them.

Sam: So where's ours?

Hally: Good question. And I hate to say it, but the answer is: I don't know. Maybe he hasn't even been born yet. Or is still only a babe in arms at his mother's breast. God, what a thought.

Sam: So we just go on waiting.

Hally: Ja, looks like it. (*Back to his soup and the book*)

Sam: (*Reading from the textbook*) "Introduction: In some mathematical problems only the magnitude . . ." (*He mispronounces the word "magnitude"*)

Hally: (*Correcting him without looking up*) Magnitude.

Sam: What's it mean?

Hally: How big it is. The size of the thing.

Sam: (*Reading*) ". . . magnitude of the quantities is of importance. In other problems we need to know whether these quantities are negative or positive. For example, whether there is a debit or credit bank balance . . ."

Hally: Whether you're broke or not.

Sam: ". . . whether the temperature is above or below Zero . . ."

Hally: Naught degrees. Cheerful state of affairs! No cash and you're freezing to death. Mathematics won't get you out of that one.

Sam: "All these quantities are called . . ." (*Spelling the word*) . . . s-c-a-l . . .

Hally: Scalars.

Sam: Scalars! (*Shaking his head with a laugh*) You understand all that?

Hally: (*Turning a page*) No. And I don't intend to try.

Sam: So what happens when the exams come?

Hally: Failing a maths exam isn't the end of the world, Sam. How many times have I told you that examination results don't measure intelligence?

Sam: I would say about as many times as you've failed one of them.

Hally: (*Mirthlessly*) Ha, ha, ha.

Sam: (*Simultaneously*) Ha, ha, ha.

Hally: Just remember Winston Churchill didn't do particularly well at school.

Sam: You've also told me that one many times.

Hally: Well, it just so happens to be the truth.

Sam: (*Enjoying the word*) Magnitude! Magnitude! Show me how to use it.

Hally: (*After thought*) An intrepid social reformer will not be daunted by the magnitude of the task he has undertaken.

Sam: (Impressed) Couple of jaw-breakers in there!

Hally: I gave you three for the price of one. Intrepid, daunted and magnitude. I did that once in an exam. Put five of the words I had to explain in one sentence. It was half a page long.

Sam: Well, I'll put my money on you in the English exam.

Hally: Piece of cake. Eighty percent without even trying.

Sam: (Another textbook from Hally's *case)* And history?

Hally: So-so. I'll scrape through. In the fifties if I'm lucky.

Sam: You didn't do too badly last year.

Hally: Because we had World War One. That at least had some action. You try to find that in the South African Parliamentary system.

Sam: (Reading from the history textbook) "Napoleon and the principle of equality." Hey! This sounds interesting. "After concluding peace with Britain in 1802, Napoleon used a brief period of calm to in-sti-tute . . ."

Hally: Introduce.

Sam: ". . . many reforms. Napoleon regarded all people as equal before the law and wanted them to have equal opportunities for advancement. All ves-ti-ges of the feu-dal system with its oppression of the poor were abolished." Vestiges, feudal system and abolished. I'm all right on oppression.

Hally: I'm thinking. He swept away . . . abolished . . . the last remains . . . vestiges . . . of the bad old days . . . feudal system.

Sam: Ha! There's the social reformer we're waiting for. He sounds like a man of some magnitude.

Hally: I'm not so sure about that. It's a damn good title for a book, though. A man of magnitude!

Sam: He sounds pretty big to me, Hally.

Hally: Don't confuse historical significance with greatness. But maybe I'm being a bit prejudiced. Have a look in there and you'll see he's two chapters long. And hell! . . . has he only got dates, Sam, all of which you've got to remember! This campaign and that campaign, and then, because of all the fighting, the next thing is we get Peace Treaties all over the place. And what's the end of the story? Battle of Waterloo, which he loses. Wasn't worth it. No, I don't know about him as a man of magnitude.

Sam: Then who would you say was?

Hally: To answer that, we need a definition of greatness, and I suppose that would be somebody who . . . somebody who benefited all mankind.

Sam: Right. But like who?

Hally: (He speaks with total conviction) Charles Darwin. Remember him? That big book from the library. *The Origin of the Species.*

Sam: Him?

Hally: Yes. For his Theory of Evolution.

  Sam: You didn't finish it.

Hally: I ran out of time. I didn't finish it because my two weeks was up. But I'm going to take it out again after I've digested what I read. It's safe. I've hidden it away in the Theology section. Nobody ever goes in there. And anyway who are you to talk? You hardly even looked at it.

  Sam: I tried. I looked at the chapters in the beginning and I saw one called "The Struggle for an Existence." Ah ha, I thought. At last! But what did I get? Something called the mistiltoe which needs the apple tree and there's too many seeds and all are going to die except one . . . ! No, Hally.

Hally: *(Intellectually outraged)* What do you mean, No! The poor man had to start somewhere. For God's sake, Sam, he revolutionized science. Now we know.

  Sam: What?

Hally: Where we come from and what it all means.

  Sam: And that's a benefit to mankind? Anyway, I still don't believe it.

Hally: God, you're impossible. I showed it to you in black and white.

  Sam: Doesn't mean I got to believe it.

Hally: It's the likes of you that kept the Inquisition in business. It's called bigotry. Anyway, that's my man of magnitude. Charles Darwin! Who's yours?

  Sam: *(Without hesitation)* Abraham Lincoln.

Hally: I might have guessed as much. Don't get sentimental, Sam. You've never been a slave, you know. And anyway we freed your ancestors here in South Africa long before the Americans. But if you want to thank somebody on their behalf, do it to Mr. William Wilberforce. Come on. Try again. I want a real genius.

(Now enjoying himself, and so is Sam. Hally *goes behind the counter and helps himself to a chocolate)*

  Sam: William Shakespeare.

Hally: *(No enthusiasm)* Oh. So you're also one of them, are you? You're basing that opinion on only one play, you know. You've only read my *Julius Caesar* and even I don't understand half of what they're talking about. They should do what they did with the old Bible: bring the language up to date.

  Sam: That's all you've got. It's also the only one *you've* read.

Hally: I know. I admit it. That's why I suggest we reserve our judgment until we've checked up on a few others. I've got a feeling, though, that by the end of this year one is going to be enough for me, and I can give you the names of twenty-nine other chaps in the Standard Nine class of the Port Elizabeth Technical College who feel the same. But if you want him, you can have him. My turn now. *(Pacing)* This is a damned good exercise, you know! It started off looking like a simple question and here it's got us really probing into the intellectual heritage of our civilization.

Sam: So who is it going to be?

Hally: My next man . . . and he gets the title on two scores: social reform and literary genius . . . is Leo Nikolaevich Tolstoy.

Sam: That Russian.

Hally: Correct. Remember the picture of him I showed you?

Sam: With the long beard.

Hally: *(Trying to look like Tolstoy)* And those burning, visionary eyes. My God, the face of a social prophet if ever I saw one! And remember my words when I showed it to you? Here's a *man,* Sam!

Sam: Those were words, Hally.

Hally: Not many intellectuals are prepared to shovel manure with the peasants and then go home and write a "little book" called *War and Peace.* Incidentally, Sam, he was somebody else who, to quote, ". . . did not distinguish himself scholastically."

Sam: Meaning?

Hally: He was also no good at school.

Sam: Like you and Winston Churchill.

Hally: *(Mirthlessly)* Ha, ha, ha.

Sam: *(Simultaneously)* Ha, ha, ha.

Hally: Don't get clever, Sam. That man freed his serfs of his own free will.

Sam: No argument. He was a somebody, all right. I accept him.

Hally: I'm sure Count Tolstoy will be very pleased to hear that. Your turn. Shoot. *(Another chocolate from behind the counter)* I'm waiting, Sam.

Sam: I've got him.

Hally: Good. Submit your candidate for examination.

Sam: Jesus.

Hally: *(Stopped him dead in his tracks)* Who?

Sam: Jesus Christ.

Hally: Oh, come on, Sam!

Sam: The Messiah.

Hally: Ja, but still . . . No, Sam. Don't let's get started on religion. We'll just spend the whole afternoon arguing again. Suppose I turn around and say Mohammed?

Sam: All right.

Hally: You can't have them both on the same list!

Sam: Why not? You like Mohammed, I like Jesus.

Hally: I *don't* like Mohammed. I never have. I was merely being hypothetical. As far as I'm concerned, the Koran is as bad as the Bible. No. Religion is out! I'm not going to waste my time again arguing with you about the existence of God. You know perfectly well I'm an atheist . . . and I've got homework to do.

Sam: Okay, I take him back.

Hally: You've got time for one more name.

Sam: *(After thought)* I've got one I know we'll agree on. A simple straightforward great Man of Magnitude . . . and no arguments. And *he* really *did* benefit all mankind.

Hally: I wonder. After your last contribution I'm beginning to doubt whether anything in the way of an intellectual agreement is possible between the two of us. Who is he?

Sam: Guess.

Hally: Socrates? Alexandre Dumas? Karl Marx? Dostoevsky? Nietzsche?

(Sam *shakes his head after each name)*

Give me a clue.

Sam: The letter P is important . . .

Hally: Plato!

Sam: . . . and his name begins with an F.

Hally: I've got it. Freud and Psychology.

Sam: No. I didn't understand him.

Hally: That makes two of us.

Sam: Think of mouldy apricot jam.

Hally: *(After a delighted laugh)* Penicillin and Sir Alexander Fleming! And the title of the book: *The Microbe Hunters. (Delighted)* Splendid, Sam! Splendid. For once we are in total agreement. The major breakthrough in medical science in the Twentieth Century. If it wasn't for him, we might have lost the Second World War. It's deeply gratifying, Sam, to know that I haven't been wasting my time in talking to you. *(Strutting around proudly)* Tolstoy may have educated his peasants, but I've educated you.

Sam: Standard Four to Standard Nine.

Hally: Have we been at it as long as that?

Sam: Yep. And my first lesson was geography.

Hally: *(Intrigued)* Really? I don't remember.

Sam: My room there at the back of the old Jubilee Boarding House. I had just started working for your Mom. Little boy in short trousers walks in one afternoon and asks me seriously: "Sam, do you want to see South Africa?" Hey man! Sure I wanted to see South Africa!

Hally: Was that me?

Sam: . . . So the next thing I'm looking at a map you had just done for homework. It was your first one and you were very proud of yourself.

Hally: Go on.

Sam: Then came my first lesson. "Repeat after me, Sam: Gold in the Transvaal, mealies in the Free State, sugar in Natal and grapes in the Cape." I still know it!

Hally: Well, I'll be buggered. So that's how it all started.

Sam: And your next map was one with all the rivers and the mountains they came from. The Orange, the Vaal, the Limpopo, the Zambezi . . .

Hally: You've got a phenomenal memory!

Sam: You should be grateful. That is why you started passing your exams. You tried to be better than me.

(They laugh together. Willie *is attracted by the laughter and joins them)*

Hally: The old Jubilee Boarding House. Sixteen rooms with board and lodging, rent in advance and one week's notice. I haven't thought about it for donkey's years . . . and I don't think that's an accident. God, was I glad when we sold it and moved out. Those years are not remembered as the happiest ones of an unhappy childhood.

Willie: (Knocking on the table and trying to imitate a woman's voice) "Hally, are you there?"

Hally: Who's that supposed to be?

Willie: "What you doing in there, Hally? Come out at once!"

Hally: (To Sam) What's he talking about?

Sam: Don't you remember?

Willie: "Sam, Willie . . . is he in there with you boys?"

Sam: Hiding away in our room when your mother was looking for you.

Hally: (Another good laugh) Of course! I used to crawl and hide under your bed! But finish the story, Willie. Then what used to happen? You chaps would give the game away by telling her I was in there with you. So much for friendship.

Sam: We couldn't lie to her. She knew.

Hally: Which meant I got another rowing for hanging around the "servants' quarters." I think I spent more time in there with you chaps than anywhere else in that dump. And do you blame me? Nothing but bloody misery wherever you went. Somebody was always complaining about the food, or my mother was having a fight with Micky Nash because she'd caught her with a petty officer in her room. Maud Meiring was another one. Remember those two? They were prostitutes, you know. Soldiers and sailors from the troopships. Bottom fell out of the business when the war ended. God, the flotsam and jetsam that life washed up on our shores! No joking, if it wasn't for your room, I would have been the first certified ten-year-old in medical history. Ja, the memories are coming back now. Walking home from school and thinking: "What can I do this afternoon?" Try out a few ideas, but sooner or later I'd end up in there with you fellows. I bet you I could still find my way to your room with my eyes closed. *(He does exactly that)* Down the corridor . . . telephone on the right, which my Mom

keeps locked because somebody is using it on the sly and not paying . . . past the kitchen and unappetizing cooking smells . . .
around the corner into the backyard, hold my breath again
because there are more smells coming when I pass your lavatory,
then into that little passageway, first door on the right and into
your room. How's that?

Sam: Good. But, as usual, you forgot to knock.

Hally: Like that time I barged in and caught you and Cynthia . . . at it.
Remember? God, was I embarrassed! I didn't know what was
going on at first.

Sam: Ja, that taught you a lesson.

Hally: And about a lot more than knocking on doors, I'll have you
know, and I don't mean geography either. Hell, Sam, couldn't you
have waited until it was dark?

Sam: No.

Hally: Was it that urgent?

Sam: Yes, and if you don't believe me, wait until your time comes.

Hally: No, thank you. I am not interested in girls. *(Back to his memories
. . . Using a few chairs he recreates the room as he lists the items)* A gray
little wall . . . and I now know why the mattress sags so much! . . .
Willie's bed . . . it's propped up on bricks because one leg is broken
. . . that wobbly little table with the washbasin and jug of water . . .
Yes! . . . stuck to the wall above it are some pin-up pictures from
magazines. Joe Louis . . .

Willie: Brown Bomber. World Title. *(Boxing pose)* Three rounds and
knockout.

Hally: Against who?

Sam: Max Schmeling.

Hally: Correct. I can also remember Fred Astaire and Ginger Rogers,
and Rita Hayworth in a bathing costume which always made me
hot and bothered when I looked at it. Under Willie's bed is an old
suitcase with all his clothes in a mess, which is why I never hide
there. Your things are neat and tidy in a trunk next to your bed,
and on it there is a picture of you and Cynthia in your ballroom
clothes, your first silver cup for third place in a competition and an
old radio which doesn't work anymore. Have I left out anything?

Sam: No.

Hally: Right, so much for the stage directions. Now the characters.
(Sam and Willie move to their appropriate positions in the bedroom)
Willie is in bed, under his blankets with his clothes on, complaining
non-stop about something, but we can't make out a word of what
he's saying because he's got his head under the blankets as well.
You're on your bed trimming your toenails with a knife—not a very
edifying sight—and as for me . . . What am I doing?

Sam: You're sitting on the floor giving Willie a lecture about being a
good loser while you get the checker board and pieces ready for a

game. Then you go to Willie's bed, pull off the blankets and make him play with you first because you know you're going to win, and that gives you the second game with me.

Hally: And you certainly were a bad loser, Willie!

Willie: Haai!

Hally: Wasn't he, Sam? And so slow! A game with you almost took the whole afternoon. Thank God I gave up trying to teach you how to play chess.

Willie: You and Sam cheated.

Hally: I never saw Sam cheat, and mine were mostly the mistakes of youth.

Willie: Then how is it you two was always winning?

Hally: Have you ever considered the possibility, Willie, that it was because we were better than you?

Willie: Every time better?

Hally: Not every time. There were occasions when we deliberately let you win a game so that you would stop sulking and go on playing with us. Sam used to wink at me when you weren't looking to show me it was time to let you win.

Willie: So then you two didn't play fair.

Hally: It was for your benefit, Mr. Malopo, which is more than being fair. It was an act of self-sacrifice. *(To* Sam) But you know what my best memory is, don't you?

Sam: No.

Hally: Come on, guess. If your memory is so good, you must remember it as well.

Sam: We got up to a lot of tricks in there, Hally.

Hally: This one was special, Sam.

Sam: I'm listening.

Hally: It started off looking like another of those useless nothing-to-do afternoons. I'd already been down to Main Street looking for adventure, but nothing had happened. I didn't feel like climbing trees in the Donkin Park or pretending I was a private eye and following a stranger . . . so as usual: See what's cooking in Sam's room. This time it was you on the floor. You had two thin pieces of wood and you were smoothing them down with a knife. It didn't look particularly interesting, but when I asked you what you were doing, you just said, "Wait and see, Hally. Wait . . . and see" . . . in that secret sort of way of yours, so I knew there was a surprise coming. You teased me, you bugger, by being deliberately slow and not answering my questions!

(Sam *laughs*)

And whistling while you worked away! God, it was infuriating! I could have brained you! It was only when you tied them together in a cross and put that down on the brown paper that I realized what you were doing. "Sam is making a kite?" And when I asked you and you said "Yes" . . . ! *(Shaking his head with disbelief)* The sheer audacity of it took my breath away. I mean, seriously, what the hell does a black man know about flying a kite? I'll be honest with you, Sam, I had no hopes for it. If you think I was excited and happy, you got another guess coming. In fact, I was shit-scared that we were going to make fools of ourselves. When we left the boarding house to go up onto the hill, I was praying quietly that there wouldn't be any other kids around to laugh at us.

Sam: *(Enjoying the memory as much as* Hally*)* Ja, I could see that.

Hally: I made it obvious, did I?

Sam: Ja. You refused to carry it.

Hally: Do you blame me? Can you remember what the poor thing looked like? Tomato-box wood and brown paper! Flour and water for glue! Two of my mother's old stockings for a tail, and then all those bits and pieces of string you made me tie together so that we could fly it! Hell, no, that was now only asking for a miracle to happen.

Sam: Then the big argument when I told you to hold the string and run with it when I let go.

Hally: I was prepared to run, all right, but straight back to the boarding house.

Sam: *(Knowing what's coming)* So what happened?

Hally: Come on, Sam, you remember as well as I do.

Sam: I want to hear it from you.

(Hally *pauses. He wants to be as accurate as possible*)

Hally: You went a little distance from me down the hill, you held it up ready to let it go. . . . "This is it," I thought. "Like everything else in my life, here comes another fiasco." Then you shouted, "Go, Hally!" and I started to run. *(Another pause)* I don't know how to describe it, Sam. Ja! The miracle happened! I was running, waiting for it to crash to the ground, but instead suddenly there was something alive behind me at the end of the string, tugging at it as if it wanted to be free. I looked back . . . *(Shakes his head)* . . . I still can't believe my eyes. It was flying! Looping around and trying to climb even higher into the sky. You shouted to me to let it have more string. I did, until there was none left and I was just holding that piece of wood we had tied it to. You came up and joined me. You were laughing.

Sam: So were you. And shouting, "It works, Sam! We've done it!"

Hally: And we had! I was so proud of us! It was the most splendid thing I had ever seen. I wished there were hundreds of kids around to watch us. The part that scared me, though, was when you showed me how to make it dive down to the ground and then just when it was on the point of crashing, swoop up again!

Athol Fugard 1837

Sam: You didn't want to try yourself.

Hally: Of course not! I would have been suicidal if anything had happened to it. Watching you do it made me nervous enough. I was quite happy just to see it up there with its tail fluttering behind it. You left me after that, didn't you? You explained how to get it down, we tied it to the bench so that I could sit and watch it, and you went away. I wanted you to stay, you know. I was a little scared of having to look after it by myself.

Sam: *(Quietly)* I had work to do, Hally.

Hally: It was sort of sad bringing it down, Sam. And it looked sad again when it was lying there on the ground. Like something that had lost its soul. Just tomato-box wood, brown paper and two of my mother's old stockings! But, hell, I'll never forget that first moment when I saw it up there. I had a stiff neck the next day from looking up so much.

(Sam *laughs.* Hally *turns to him with a question he never thought of asking before)*

Why did you make that kite, Sam?

Sam: *(Evenly)* I can't remember.

Hally: Truly?

Sam: Too long ago, Hally.

Hally: Ja, I suppose it was. It's time for another one, you know.

Sam: Why do you say that?

Hally: Because it feels like that. Wouldn't be a good day to fly it, though.

Sam: No. You can't fly kites on rainy days.

Hally: *(He studies* Sam. *Their memories have made him conscious of the man's presence in his life)* How old are you, Sam?

Sam: Two score and five.

Hally: Strange, isn't it?

Sam: What?

Hally: Me and you.

Sam: What's strange about it?

Hally: Little white boy in short trousers and a black man old enough to be his father flying a kite. It's not every day you see that.

Sam: But why strange? Because the one is white and the other black?

Hally: I don't know. Would have been just as strange, I suppose, if it had been me and my Dad . . . cripple man and a little boy! Nope! There's no chance of me flying a kite without it being strange. *(Simple statement of fact—no self-pity)* There's a nice little short story there. "The Kite-Flyers." But we'd have to find a twist in the ending.

Sam: Twist?

Hally: Yes. Something unexpected. The way it ended with us was too straightforward . . . me on the bench and you going back to work. There's no drama in that.

Willie: And me?

Hally: You?

Willie: Yes me.

Hally: You want to get into the story as well, do you? I got it! Change the title: "Afternoons in Sam's Room" . . . expand it and tell all the stories. It's on its way to being a novel. Our days in the old Jubilee. Sad in a way that they're over. I almost wish we were still in that little room.

Sam: We're still together.

Hally: That's true. It's just that life felt the right size in there . . . not too big and not too small. Wasn't so hard to work up a bit of courage. It's got so bloody complicated since then.

(The telephone rings. Sam *answers it)*

Sam: St. George's Park Tea Room . . . Hello, Madam . . . Yes, Madam, he's here. . . . Hally, it's your mother.

Hally: Where is she phoning from?

Sam: Sounds like the hospital. It's a public telephone.

Hally: (Relieved) You see! I told you. *(The telephone)* Hello, Mom . . . Yes . . . Yes no fine. Everything's under control here. How's things with poor old Dad? . . . Has he had a bad turn? . . . What? . . . Oh, God! . . . Yes, Sam told me, but I was sure he'd made a mistake. But what's this all about, Mom? He didn't look at all good last night. How can he get better so quickly? . . . Then very obviously you must say no. Be firm with him. You're the boss. . . . You know what it's going to be like if he comes home. . . . Well then, don't blame me when I fail my exams at the end of the year. . . . Yes! How am I expected to be fresh for school when I spend half the night massaging his gammy leg? . . . So am I! . . . So tell him a white lie. Say Dr. Colley wants more X-rays of his stump. Or bribe him. We'll sneak in double tots of brandy in future. . . . What? . . . Order him to get back into bed at once! If he's going to behave like a child, treat him like one. . . . All right, Mom! I was just trying to . . . I'm sorry. . . . I said I'm sorry. . . . Quick, give me your number. I'll phone you back. *(He hangs up and waits a few seconds)* Here we go again! *(He dials)* I'm sorry, Mom. . . . Okay . . . But now listen to me carefully. All it needs is for you to put your foot down. Don't take no for an answer. . . . Did you hear me? And whatever you do, don't discuss it with him. . . . Because I'm frightened you'll give in to him. . . . Yes, Sam gave me lunch. . . . I ate all of it! . . . No, Mom, not a soul. It's still raining here. . . . Right, I'll tell them. I'll just do some homework and then lock up. . . . But remember now, Mom. Don't listen to anything he says. And phone me back and let me know what happens. . . . Okay. Bye, Mom. *(He hangs up. The men are staring at him)* My Mom says that when you're finished with the floors you must do the windows. *(Pause)* Don't misunderstand me, chaps. All I want is for him to get better. And if he was, I'd be the first person to say: "Bring him home." But he's not, and we can't give him the medical care and attention he needs at home. That's what hospitals are there for. *(Brusquely)* So don't just stand there! Get on with it!

(Sam clears Hally's table)

You heard right. My Dad wants to go home.

Sam: Is he better?

Hally: (Sharply) No! How the hell can he be better when last night he was groaning with pain? This is not an age of miracles!

Sam: Then he should stay in hospital.

Hally: (Seething with irritation and frustration) Tell me something I don't know, Sam. What the hell do you think I was saying to my Mom? All I can say is fuck-it-all.

Sam: I'm sure he'll listen to your Mom.

Hally: You don't know what she's up against. He's already packed his shaving kit and pajamas and is sitting on his bed with his crutches, dressed and ready to go. I know him when he gets in that mood. If she tries to reason with him, we've had it. She's no match for him when it comes to a battle of words. He'll tie her up in knots. *(Trying to hide his true feelings)*

Sam: I suppose it gets lonely for him in there.

Hally: With all the patients and nurses around? Regular visits from the Salvation Army? Balls! It's ten times worse for him at home. I'm at school and my mother is here in the business all day.

Sam: He's at least got you at night.

Hally: (Before he can stop himself) And we've got him! Please! I don't want to talk about it anymore. *(Unpacks his school case, slamming down books on the table)* Life is just a plain bloody mess, that's all. And people are fools.

Sam: Come on, Hally.

Hally: Yes, they are! They bloody well deserve what they get.

Sam: Then don't complain.

Hally: Don't try to be clever, Sam. It doesn't suit you. Anybody who thinks there's nothing wrong with this world needs to have his head examined. Just when things are going along all right, without fail someone or something will come along and spoil everything. Somebody should write that down as a fundamental law of the Universe. The principle of perpetual disappointment. If there is a God who created this world, he should scrap it and try again.

Sam: All right, Hally, all right. What you got for homework?

Hally: Bullshit, as usual. *(Opens an exercise book and reads)* "Write five hundred words describing an annual event of cultural or historical significance."

Sam: That should be easy enough for you.

Hally: And also plain bloody boring. You know what he wants, don't you? One of their useless old ceremonies. The commemoration of the 1820 Settlers, or if it's going to be culture, Carols by Candlelight every Christmas.

Sam: It's an impressive sight. Make a good description, Hally. All those candles glowing in the dark and the people singing hymns.

Hally: And it's called religious hysteria. *(Intense irritation)* Please, Sam! Just leave me alone and let me get on with it. I'm not in the mood for games this afternoon. And remember my Mom's orders . . . you're to help Willie with the windows. Come on now, I don't want any more nonsense in here.

Sam: Okay, Hally, okay.

(Hally *settles down to his homework; determined preparations . . . pen, ruler, exercise book, dictionary, another cake . . . all of which will lead to nothing*)

(Sam *waltzes over to* Willie *and starts to replace tables and chairs. He practices a ballroom step while doing so.* Willie *watches. When* Sam *is finished,* Willie *tries*) Good! But just a little bit quicker on the turn and only move in to her after she's crossed over. What about this one?

(*Another step. When* Sam *is finished,* Willie *again has a go*)

Much better. See what happens when you just relax and enjoy yourself? Remember that in two weeks' time and you'll be all right.

Willie: But I haven't got partner, Boet Sam.

Sam: Maybe Hilda will turn up tonight.

Willie: No, Boet Sam. *(Reluctantly)* I gave her a good hiding.

Sam: You mean a bad one.

Willie: Good bad one.

Sam: Then you mustn't complain either. Now you pay the price for losing your temper.

Willie: I also pay two pounds ten shilling entrance fee.

Sam: They'll refund you if you withdraw now.

Willie: *(Appalled)* You mean, don't dance?

Sam: Yes.

Willie: No! I wait too long and I practice too hard. If I find me new partner, you think I can be ready in two weeks? I ask Madam for my leave now and we practice every day.

Sam: Quickstep non-stop for two weeks. World record, Willie, but you'll be mad at the end.

Willie: No jokes, Boet Sam.

Sam: I'm not joking.

Willie: So then what?

Sam: Find Hilda. Say you're sorry and promise you won't beat her again.

Willie: No.

  Sam: Then withdraw. Try again next year.

Willie: No.

  Sam: Then I give up.

Willie: Haaikona, Boet Sam, you can't.

  Sam: What do you mean, I can't? I'm telling you: I give up.

Willie: *(Adamant)* No! *(Accusingly)* It was you who start me ballroom
   dancing.

  Sam: So?

Willie: Before that I use to be happy. And is you and Miriam who
   bring me to Hilda and say here's partner for you.

  Sam: What are you saying, Willie?

Willie: You!

  Sam: But me what? To blame?

Willie: Yes.

  Sam: Willie . . . ? *(Bursts into laughter)*

Willie: And now all you do is make jokes at me. You wait. When Miriam leaves you is my turn to laugh. Ha! Ha! Ha!

  Sam: *(He can't take* Willie *seriously any longer)* She can leave me
   tonight! I know what to do. *(Bowing before an imaginary partner)*
   May I have the pleasure? *(He dances and sings)*
   "Just a fellow with his pillow . . .
   Dancin' like a willow . . .
   In an autumn breeze . . ."

Willie: There you go again!

(Sam goes on dancing and singing)

   Boet Sam!

  Sam: There's the answer to your problem! Judges' announcement in
   two weeks' time: "Ladies and gentlemen, the winner in the open
   section . . . Mr. Willie Malopo and his pillow!"

(This is too much for a now really angry Willie. *He goes for* Sam, *but the latter is
too quick for him and puts* Hally's *table between the two of them)*

 Hally: *(Exploding)* For Christ's sake, you two!

Willie: *(Still trying to get at* Sam*)* I donner you, Sam! Struesgod!

  Sam: *(Still laughing)* Sorry, Willie . . . Sorry . . .

 Hally: Sam! Willie! *(Grabs his ruler and gives* Willie *a vicious whack on
   the bum)* How the hell am I supposed to concentrate with the two
   of you behaving like bloody children!

Willie: Hit him too!

 Hally: Shut up, Willie.

Willie: He started jokes again.

 Hally: Get back to your work. You too, Sam. *(His ruler)* Do you want
   another one, Willie?

(Sam and Willie *return to their work. Hally uses the opportunity to escape from his unsuccessful attempt at homework. He struts around like a little despot, ruler in hand, giving vent to his anger and frustration)*

Suppose a customer had walked in then? Or the Park Superintendent. And seen the two of you behaving like a pair of hooligans. That would have been the end of my mother's license, you know. And your jobs! Well, this is the end of it. From now on there will be no more of your ballroom nonsense in here. This is a business establishment, not a bloody New Brighton dancing school. I've been far too lenient with the two of you. *(Behind the counter for a green cool drink and a dollop of ice cream. He keeps up his tirade as he prepares it)* But what really makes me bitter is that I allow you chaps a little freedom in here when business is bad and what do you do with it? The foxtrot! Specially you, Sam. There's more to life than trotting around a dance floor and I thought at least you knew it.

Sam: It's a harmless pleasure, Hally. It doesn't hurt anybody.

Hally: It's also a rather simple one, you know.

Sam: You reckon so? Have you ever tried?

Hally: Of course not.

Sam: Why don't you? Now.

Hally: What do you mean? Me dance?

Sam: Yes. I'll show you a simple step—the waltz—then you try it.

Hally: What will that prove?

Sam: That it might not be as easy as you think.

Hally: I didn't say it was easy. I said it was simple—like in simple-minded, meaning mentally retarded. You can't exactly say it challenges the intellect.

Sam: It does other things.

Hally: Such as?

Sam: Make people happy.

Hally: *(The glass in his hand)* So do American cream sodas with ice cream. For God's sake, Sam, you're not asking me to take ballroom dancing serious, are you?

Sam: Yes.

Hally: *(Sigh of defeat)* Oh, well, so much for trying to give you a decent education. I've obviously achieved nothing.

Sam: You still haven't told me what's wrong with admiring something that's beautiful and then trying to do it yourself.

Hally: Nothing. But we happen to be talking about a foxtrot, not a thing of beauty.

Sam: But that is just what I'm saying. If you were to see two champions doing, two masters of the art . . . !

Hally: Oh, God, I give up. So now it's also art!

Sam: Ja.

Hally: There's a limit, Sam. Don't confuse art and entertainment.

Sam: So then what is art?

Hally: You want a definition?

Sam: Ja.

Hally: *(He realizes he has got to be careful. He gives the matter a lot of thought before answering)* Philosophers have been trying to do that for centuries. What is Art? What is Life? But basically I suppose it's . . . the giving of meaning to matter.

Sam: Nothing to do with beautiful?

Hally: It goes beyond that. It's the giving of form to the formless.

Sam: Ja, well, maybe it's not art, then. But I still say it's beautiful.

Hally: I'm sure the word you mean to use is entertaining.

Sam: *(Adamant)* No. Beautiful. And if you want proof, come along to the Centenary Hall in New Brighton in two weeks' time.

(The mention of the Centenary Hall draws Willie *over to them)*

Hally: What for? I've seen the two of you prancing around in here often enough.

Sam: *(He laughs)* This isn't the real thing, Hally. We're just playing around in here.

Hally: So? I can use my imagination.

Sam: And what do you get?

Hally: A lot of people dancing around and having a so-called good time.

Sam: That all?

Hally: Well, basically it is that, surely.

Sam: No, it isn't. Your imagination hasn't helped you at all. There's a lot more to it than that. We're getting ready for the championships, Hally, not just another dance. There's going to be a lot of people, all right, and they're going to have a good time, but they'll only be spectators, sitting around and watching. It's just the competitors out there on the dance floor. Party decorations and fancy lights all around the walls! The ladies in beautiful evening dresses!

Hally: My mother's got one of those, Sam, and quite frankly, it's an embarrassment every time she wears it.

Sam: *(Undeterred)* Your imagination left out the excitement.

(Hally *scoffs)*

Oh, yes. The finalists are not going to be out there just to have a good time. One of those couples will be the 1950 Eastern Province Champions. And your imagination left out the music.

Willie: Mr. Elijah Gladman Guzana and his Orchestral Jazzonions.

Sam: The sound of the big band, Hally. Trombone, trumpet, tenor and alto sax. And then, finally, your imagination also left out the climax of the evening when the dancing is finished, the judges have stopped whispering among themselves and the Master of Ceremonies collects their scorecards and goes up onto the stage to announce the winners.

Hally: All right. So you make it sound like a bit of a do. It's an occasion. Satisfied?

Sam: (Victory) So you admit that!

Hally: Emotionally yes, intellectually no.

Sam: Well, I don't know what you mean by that, all I'm telling you is that it is going to be *the* event of the year in New Brighton. It's been sold out for two weeks already. There's only standing room left. We've got competitors coming from Kingwilliamstown, East London, Port Alfred.

(Hally *starts pacing thoughtfully*)

Hally: Tell me a bit more.

Sam: I thought you weren't interested . . . intellectually.

Hally: (Mysteriously) I've got my reasons.

Sam: What do you want to know?

Hally: It takes place every year?

Sam: Yes. But only every third year in New Brighton. It's East London's turn to have the championships next year.

Hally: Which, I suppose, makes it an even more significant event.

Sam: Ah ha! We're getting somewhere. Our "occasion" is now a "significant event."

Hally: I wonder.

Sam: What?

Hally: I wonder if I would get away with it.

Sam: But what?

Hally: (To the table and his exercise book) "Write five hundred words describing an annual event of cultural or historical significance." Would I be stretching poetic license a little too far if I called your ballroom championships a cultural event?

Sam: You mean . . . ?

Hally: You think we could get five hundred words out of it, Sam?

Sam: Victor Sylvester has written a whole book on ballroom dancing.

Willie: You going to write about it, Master Hally?

Hally: Yes, gentlemen, that is precisely what I am considering doing. Old Doc Bromely—he's my English teacher—is going to argue with me, of course. He doesn't like natives. But I'll point out to him that in strict anthropological terms the culture of a primitive black society includes its dancing and singing. To put my thesis in a nutshell: The war-dance has been replaced by the waltz. But it still amounts to the same thing: the release of primitive emotions through movement. Shall we give it a go?

Sam: I'm ready.

Willie: Me also.

Hally: Ha! This will teach the old bugger a lesson. *(Decision taken)* Right. Let's get ourselves organized. *(This means another cake on the table. He sits)* I think you've given me enough general atmosphere, Sam, but to build the tension and suspense I need facts. *(Pencil poised)*

Willie: Give him facts, Boet Sam.

Hally: What you called the climax . . . how many finalists?

  Sam: Six couples.

Hally: *(Making notes)* Go on. Give me the picture.

  Sam: Spectators seated right around the hall. *(Willie becomes a spectator)*

Hally: . . . and it's a full house.

  Sam: At one end, on the stage, Gladman and his Orchestral Jazzonions. At the other end is a long table with the three judges. The six finalists go onto the dance floor and take up their positions. When they are ready and the spectators have settled down, the Master of Ceremonies goes to the microphone. To start with, he makes some jokes to get the people laughing . . .

Hally: Good touch! *(As he writes)* ". . . creating a relaxed atmosphere which will change to one of tension and drama as the climax is approached."

  Sam: *(Onto a chair to act out the M.C.)* "Ladies and gentlemen, we come now to the great moment you have all been waiting for this evening. . . . The finals of the 1950 Eastern Province Open Ballroom Dancing Championships. But first let me introduce the finalists! Mr. and Mrs. Welcome Tchabalala from Kingwilliamstown . . ."

Willie: *(He applauds after every name)* Is when the people clap their hands and whistle and make a lot of noise, Master Hally.

  Sam: "Mr. Mulligan Njikelane and Miss Nomhle Nkonyeni of Grahamstown; Mr. and Mrs. Norman Nchinga from Port Alfred; Mr. Fats Bokolane and Miss Dina Plaatjies from East London; Mr. Sipho Dugu and Mrs. Mable Magada from Peddie; and from New Brighton our very own Mr. Willie Malopo and Miss Hilda Samuels."

(Willie can't believe his ears. He abandons his role as spectator and scrambles into position as a finalist)

Willie: Relaxed and ready to romance!

  Sam: The applause dies down. When everybody is silent, Gladman lifts up his sax, nods at the Orchestral Jazzonions . . .

Willie: Play the jukebox please, Boet Sam!

  Sam: I also only got bus fare, Willie.

Hally: Hold it, everybody. *(Heads for the cash register behind the counter)* How much is in the till, Sam?

  Sam: Three shillings. Hally . . . your Mom counted it before she left.

(Hally hesitates)

Hally: Sorry, Willie. You know how she carried on the last time I did it. We'll just have to pool our combined imaginations and hope for the best. *(Returns to the table)* Back to work. How are the points scored, Sam?

Sam: Maximum of ten points each for individual style, deportment, rhythm and general appearance.

Willie: Must I start?

Hally: Hold it for a second, Willie. And penalties?

Sam: For what?

Hally: For doing something wrong. Say you stumble or bump into somebody . . . do they take off any points?

Sam: *(Aghast)* Hally . . . !

Hally: When you're dancing. If you and your partner collide into another couple.

(Hally can get no further. Sam has collapsed with laughter. He explains to Willie)

Sam: If me and Miriam bump into you and Hilda . . .

(Willie joins him in another good laugh)

Hally, Hally . . . !

Hally: *(Perplexed)* Why? What did I say?

Sam: There's no collisions out there, Hally. Nobody trips or stumbles or bumps into anybody else. That's what that moment is all about. To be one of those finalists on that dance floor is like . . . like being in a dream about a world in which accidents don't happen.

Hally: *(Genuinely moved by Sam's image)* Jesus, Sam! That's beautiful!

Willie: *(Can endure waiting no longer)* I'm starting! *(Willie dances while Sam talks)*

Sam: Of course it is. That's what I've been trying to say to you all afternoon. And it's beautiful because that is what we want life to be like. But instead, like you said, Hally, we're bumping into each other all the time. Look at the three of us this afternoon: I've bumped into Willie, the two of us have bumped into you, you've bumped into your mother, she bumping into your Dad. . . . None of us knows the steps and there's no music playing. And it doesn't stop with us. The whole world is doing it all the time. Open a newspaper and what do you read? America has bumped into Russia, England is bumping into India, rich man bumps into poor man. Those are big collisions, Hally. They make for a lot of bruises. People get hurt in all that bumping, and we're sick and tired of it now. It's been going on for too long. Are we never going to get it right? . . . Learn to dance life like champions instead of always being just a bunch of beginners at it?

Hally: (*Deep and sincere admiration of the man*) You've got a vision, Sam!

Sam: Not just me. What I'm saying to you is that everybody's got it. That's why there's only standing room left for the Centenary Hall in two weeks' time. For as long as the music lasts, we are going to see six couples get it right, the way we want life to be.

Hally: But is that the best we can do, Sam . . . watch six finalists dreaming about the way it should be?

Sam: I don't know. But it starts with that. Without the dream we won't know what we're going for. And anyway I reckon there are a few people who have got past just dreaming about it and are trying for something real. Remember that thing we read once in the paper about the Mahatma Gandhi? Going without food to stop those riots in India?

Hally: You're right. He certainly was trying to teach people to get the steps right.

Sam: And the Pope.

Hally: Yes, he's another one. Our old General Smuts as well, you know. He's also out there dancing. You know, Sam, when you come to think of it, that's what the United Nations boils down to . . . a dancing school for politicians!

Sam: And let's hope they learn.

Hally: (*A little surge of hope*) You're right. We mustn't despair. Maybe there's some hope for mankind after all. Keep it up, Willie. (*Back to his table with determination*) This is a lot bigger than I thought. So what have we got? Yes, our title: "A World Without Collisions."

Sam: That sounds good! "A World Without Collisions."

Hally: Subtitle: "Global Politics on the Dance Floor." No. A bit too heavy, hey? What about "Ballroom Dancing as a Political Vision"?

(*The telephone rings. Sam answers it*)

Sam: St. George's Park Tea Room. . . . Yes, Madam . . . Hally, it's your Mom.

Hally: (*Back to reality*) Oh, God, yes! I'd forgotten all about that. Shit! Remember my words, Sam? Just when you're enjoying yourself, someone or something will come along and wreck everything.

Sam: You haven't heard what she's got to say yet.

Hally: Public telephone?

Sam: No.

Hally: Does she sound happy or unhappy?

Sam: I couldn't tell. (*Pause*) She's waiting, Hally.

Hally: (*To the telephone*) Hello, Mom . . . No, everything is okay here. Just doing my homework. . . . What's your news? . . . You've what? . . . (*Pause. He takes the receiver away from his ear for a few seconds. In the course of* Hally's *telephone conversation,* Sam *and* Willie *discretely position the stacked tables and chairs.* Hally *places the receiver back to his ear*) Yes, I'm still here. Oh, well, I give up now. Why did you do it, Mom? . . . Well, I just hope you know what you've let us in for. . . . *(Loudly)* I said I hope you know what you've let us in for! It's the end of the peace and quiet we've been having. *(Softly)* Where is he? *(Normal voice)* He can't hear us from in there. But for God's sake, Mom, what happened? I told you to be firm with him. . . . Then you and the nurses should have held him down, taken his crutches away. . . . I know only too well he's my father! . . . I'm not being disrespectful, but I'm sick and tired of emptying stinking chamberpots full of phlegm and piss. . . . Yes, I do! When you're not there, he asks *me* to do it. . . . If you really want to know the truth, that's why I've got no appetite for my food. . . . Yes! There's a lot of things you don't know about. For your information, I still haven't got that science textbook I need. And you know why? He borrowed the money you gave me for it. . . . Because I didn't want to start another fight between you two. . . . He says that every time. . . . All right, Mom! *(Viciously)* Then just remember to start hiding your bag away again, because he'll be at your purse before long for money for booze. And when he's well enough to come down here, you better keep an eye on the till as well, because that is also going to develop a leak. . . . Then don't complain to me when he starts his old tricks. . . . Yes, you do. I get it from you on one side and from him on the other, and it makes life hell for me. I'm not going to be the peacemaker any-more. I'm warning you now: when the two of you start fighting again, I'm leaving home. . . . Mom, if you start crying, I'm going to put down the receiver. . . . Okay . . . *(Lowering his voice to a vicious whisper)* Okay, Mom. I heard you. *(Desperate)* No. . . . Because I don't want to. I'll see him when I get home! Mom! . . . *(Pause. When he speaks again, his tone changes completely. It is not simply pre-tense. We sense a genuine emotional conflict)* Welcome home, chum! . . . What's that? . . . Don't be silly, Dad. You being home is just about the best news in the world. . . . I bet you are. Bloody depressing there with everybody going on about their ailments, hey! . . . How you feeling? . . . Good . . . Here as well, pal. Com-ing down cats and dogs. . . . That's right. Just the day for a kip and a toss in your old Uncle Ned. . . . Everything's just hunky-dory on my side, Dad. . . . Well, to start with, there's a nice pile of comics for you on the counter. . . . Yes, old Kemple brought them in. *Batman and Robin, Submariner* . . . just your cup of tea . . . I will. . . . Yes, we'll spin a few yarns tonight. . . . Okay, chum, see you in a little while. . . . No, I promise. I'll come straight home. . . . *(Pause—his mother comes back on the phone)* Mom? Okay. I'll lock up now. . . . What? . . . Oh, the brandy . . . Yes, I'll remember! . . . I'll put it in my suitcase now, for God's sake. I know well enough what will happen if he doesn't get it. . . . *(Places a bottle of brandy on the counter)* I *was* kind to him, Mom. I didn't say anything nasty! . . . All right. Bye. *(End of telephone conversation. A desolate* Hally *doesn't move. A strained silence)*

Sam: *(Quietly)* That sounded like a bad bump, Hally.

Hally: *(Having a hard time controlling his emotions. He speaks carefully)* Mind your own business, Sam.

Sam: Sorry. I wasn't trying to interfere. Shall we carry on? Hally? *(He indicates the exercise book. No response from* Hally)

Willie: *(Also trying)* Tell him about when they give out the cups, Boet Sam.

Sam: Ja! That's another big moment. The presentation of the cups after the winners have been announced. You've got to put that in.

(Still no response from Hally)

Willie: A big silver one, Master Hally, called floating trophy for the champions.

Sam: We always invite some big-shot personality to hand them over. Guest of honor this year is going to be His Holiness Bishop Jabulani of the All African Free Zionist Church.

(Hally gets up abruptly, goes to his table and tears up the page he was writing on)

Hally: So much for a bloody world without collisions.

Sam: Too bad. It was on its way to being a good composition.

Hally: Let's stop bullshitting ourselves, Sam.

Sam: Have we been doing that?

Hally: Yes! That's what all our talk about a decent world has been . . . just so much bullshit.

Sam: We did say it was still only a dream.

Hally: And a bloody useless one at that. Life's a fuck-up and it's never going to change.

Sam: Ja, maybe that's true.

Hally: There's no maybe about it. It's a blunt and brutal fact. All we've done this afternoon is waste our time.

Sam: Not if we'd got your homework done.

Hally: I don't give a shit about my homework, so, for Christ's sake, just shut up about it. *(Slamming books viciously into his school case)* Hurry up now and finish your work. I want to lock up and get out of here. *(Pause)* And then go where? Home-sweet-fucking-home. Jesus, I hate that word.

(Hally goes to the counter to put the brandy bottle and comics in his school case. After a moment's hesitation, he smashes the bottle of brandy. He abandons all further attempts to hide his feelings. Sam *and* Willie *work away as unobtrusively as possible)*

Do you want to know what is really wrong with your lovely little dream, Sam? It's not just that we are all bad dancers. That does happen to be perfectly true, but there's more to it than just that. You left out the cripples.

Sam: Hally!

Hally: (*Now totally reckless*) Ja! Can't leave them out, Sam. That's why we always end up on our backsides on the dance floor. They're also out there dancing . . . like a bunch of broken spiders trying to do the quickstep! (*An ugly attempt at laughter*) When you come to think of it, it's a bloody comical sight. I mean, it's bad enough on two legs . . . but one and a pair of crutches! Hell, no, Sam. That's guaranteed to turn that dance floor into a shambles. Why you shaking your head? Picture it, man. For once this afternoon let's use our imaginations sensibly.

Sam: Be careful, Hally.

Hally: Of what? The truth? I seem to be the only one around here who is prepared to face it. We've had the pretty dream, it's time now to wake up and have a good long look at the way things really are. Nobody knows the steps, there's no music, the cripples are also out there tripping up everybody and trying to get into the act, and it's all called the All-Comers-How-to-Make-a-Fuckup-of-Life Championships. (*Another ugly laugh*) Hang on, Sam! The best bit is still coming. Do you know what the winner's trophy is? A beautiful big chamber-pot with roses on the side, and it's full to the brim with piss. And guess who I think is going to be this year's winner.

Sam: (*Almost shouting*) Stop now!

Hally: (*Suddenly appalled by how far he has gone*) Why?

Sam: Hally? It's your father you're talking about.

Hally: So?

Sam: Do you know what you've been saying?

(Hally *can't answer. He is rigid with shame.* Sam *speaks to him sternly*)

No, Hally, you mustn't do it. Take back those words and ask for forgiveness! It's a terrible sin for a son to mock his father with jokes like that. You'll be punished if you carry on. Your father is your father, even if he is a . . . cripple man.

Willie: Yes, Master Hally. Is true what Sam say.

Sam: I understand how you are feeling, Hally, but even so . . .

Hally: No, you don't!

Sam: I think I do.

Hally: And I'm telling you you don't. Nobody does. (*Speaking carefully as his shame turns to rage at* Sam) It's your turn to be careful, Sam. Very careful! You're treading on dangerous ground. Leave me and my father alone.

Sam: I'm not the one who's been saying things about him.

Hally: What goes on between me and my Dad is none of your business!

Sam: Then don't tell me about it. If that's all you've got to say about him, I don't want to hear.

(For a moment Hally *is at loss for a response)*

Hally: Just get on with your bloody work and shut up.
  Sam: Swearing at me won't help you.
Hally: Yes, it does! Mind your own fucking business and shut up!
  Sam: Okay. If that's the way you want it, I'll stop trying.

(He turns away. This infuriates Hally *even more)*

Hally: Good. Because what you've been trying to do is meddle in something you know nothing about. All that concerns you in here, Sam, is to try and do what you get paid for—keep the place clean and serve the customers. In plain words, just get on with your job. My mother is right. She's always warning me about allowing you to get too familiar. Well, this time you've gone too far. It's going to stop right now.

(No response from Sam*)*

You're only a servant in here, and don't forget it.

(Still no response. Hally *is trying hard to get one)*

And as far as my father is concerned, all you need to remember is that he is your boss.
  Sam: (Needled at last) No, he isn't. I get paid by your mother.
Hally: Don't argue with me, Sam!
  Sam: Then don't say he's my boss.
Hally: He's a white man and that's good enough for you.
  Sam: I'll try to forget you said that.
Hally: Don't! Because you won't be doing me a favor if you do. I'm telling you to remember it.

(A pause. Sam *pulls himself together and makes one last effort)*

  Sam: Hally, Hally . . . ! Come on now. Let's stop before it's too late. You're right. We *are* on dangerous ground. If we're not careful, somebody is going to get hurt.
Hally: It won't be me.
  Sam: Don't be so sure.
Hally: I don't know what you're talking about, Sam.
  Sam: Yes, you do.
Hally: (Furious) Jesus, I wish you would stop trying to tell me what I do and what I don't know.

(Sam gives up. He turns to *Willie)*

  Sam: Let's finish up.
Hally: Don't turn your back on me! I haven't finished talking.

(He grabs Sam *by the arm and tries to make him turn around.* Sam *reacts with a flash of anger)*

Sam: Don't do that, Hally! *(Facing the boy)* All right, I'm listening. Well? What do you want to say to me?

Hally: *(Pause as* Hally *looks for something to say)* To begin with, why don't you also start calling me Master Harold, like Willie.

Sam: Do you mean that?

Hally: Why the hell do you think I said it?

Sam: And if I don't?

Hally: You might just lose your job.

Sam: *(Quietly and very carefully)* If you make me say it once, I'll never call you anything else again.

Hally: So? *(The boy confronts the man)* Is that meant to be a threat?

Sam: Just telling you what will happen if you make me do that. You must decide what it means to you.

Hally: Well, I have. It's good news. Because that is exactly what Master Harold wants from now on. Think of it as a little lesson in respect, Sam, that's long overdue, and I hope you remember it as well as you do your geography. I can tell you now that somebody who will be glad to hear I've finally given it to you will be my Dad. Yes! He agrees with my Mom. He's always going on about it as well. "You must teach the boys to show you more respect, my son."

Sam: So now you can stop complaining about going home. Everybody is going to be happy tonight.

Hally: That's perfectly correct. You see, you mustn't get the wrong idea about me and my Dad, Sam. We also have our good times together. Some bloody good laughs. He's got a marvelous sense of humor. Want to know what our favorite joke is? He gives out a big groan, you see, and says: "It's not fair, is it, Hally?" Then I have to ask: "What, chum?" And then he says: "A nigger's arse" . . . and we both have a good laugh.

(The men stare at him with disbelief)

What's the matter, Willie? Don't you catch the joke? You always were a bit slow on the uptake. It's what is called a pun. You see, fair means both light in color and to be just and decent. *(He turns to* Sam*)* I thought *you* would catch it, Sam.

Sam: Oh ja, I catch it all right.

Hally: But it doesn't appeal to your sense of humor.

Sam: Do you really laugh?

Hally: Of course.

Sam: To please him? Make him feel good?

Hally: No, for heaven's sake! I laugh because I think it's a bloody good joke.

Sam: You're really trying hard to be ugly, aren't you? And why drag poor old Willie into it? He's done nothing to you except show you the respect you want so badly. That's also not being fair, you know . . . and *I* mean just or decent.

Willie: It's all right, Sam. Leave it now.

Sam: It's me you're after. You should just have said "Sam's arse" . . . because that's the one you're trying to kick. Anyway, how do you know it's not fair? You've never seen it. Do you want to? *(He drops his trousers and underpants and presents his backside for* Hally's *inspection)* Have a good look. A real Basuto arse . . . which is about as nigger as they can come. Satisfied? *(Trousers up)* Now you can make your Dad even happier when you go home tonight. Tell him I showed you my arse and he is quite right. It's not fair. And if it will give him an even better laugh next time, I'll also let *him* have a look. Come, Willie, let's finish up and go.

(Sam and Willie *start to tidy up the tea room.* Hally *doesn't move. He waits for a moment when* Sam *passes him)*

Hally: (Quietly) Sam . . .

(Sam stops and looks expectantly at the boy. Hally *spits in his face. A long and heartfelt groan from* Willie. *For a few seconds* Sam *doesn't move)*

Sam: (Taking out a handkerchief and wiping his face) It's all right, Willie.

(To Hally)

Ja, well, you've done it . . . Master Harold. Yes, I'll start calling you that from now on. It won't be difficult anymore. You've hurt yourself, Master Harold. I saw it coming. I warned you, but you wouldn't listen. You've just hurt yourself *bad.* And you're a coward, Master Harold. The face you should be spitting in is your father's . . . but you used mine, because you think you're safe inside your fair skin . . . and this time I don't mean just or decent. *(Pause, then moving violently towards* Hally) Should I hit him, Willie?

Willie: (Stopping Sam) No, Boet Sam.

Sam: (Violently) Why not?

Willie: It won't help, Boet Sam.

Sam: I don't want to help! I want to hurt him.

Willie: You also hurt yourself.

Sam: And if he had done it to you, Willie?

Willie: Me? Spit at me like I was a dog? *(A thought that had not occurred to him before. He looks at* Hally) Ja. Then I want to hit him. I want to hit him hard!

(A dangerous few seconds as the men stand staring at the boy. Willie *turns away, shaking his head)*

But maybe all I do is go cry at the back. He's little boy, Boet Sam. Little *white* boy. Long trousers now, but he's still little boy.

Sam: *(His violence ebbing away into defeat as quickly as it flooded)* You're right. So go on, then: groan again, Willie. You do it better than me. *(To* Hally*)* You don't know all of what you've just done . . . Master Harold. It's not just that you've made me feel dirtier than I've ever been in my life . . . I mean, how do I wash off yours and your father's filth? . . . I've also failed. A long time ago I promised myself I was going to try and do something, but you've just shown me . . . Master Harold . . . that I've failed. *(Pause)* I've also got a memory of a little white boy when he was still wearing short trousers and a black man, but they're not flying a kite. It was the old Jubilee days, after dinner one night. I was in my room. You came in and just stood against the wall, looking down at the ground, and only after I'd asked you what you wanted, what was wrong, I don't know how many times, did you speak and even then so softly I almost didn't hear you. "Sam, please help me to go and fetch my Dad." Remember? He was dead drunk on the floor of the Central Hotel Bar. They'd phoned for your Mom, but you were the only one at home. And do you remember how we did it? You went in first by yourself to ask permission for me to go into the bar. Then I loaded him onto my back like a baby and carried him back to the boarding house with you following behind carrying his crutches. *(Shaking his head as he remembers)* A crowded Main Street with all the people watching a little white boy following his drunk father on a nigger's back! I felt for that little boy . . . Master Harold. I felt for him. After that we still had to clean him up, remember? He'd messed in his trousers, so we had to clean him up and get him into bed.

Hally: *(Great pain)* I love him, Sam.

Sam: I know you do. That's why I tried to stop you from saying these things about him. It would have been so simple if you could have just despised him for being a weak man. But he's your father. You love him and you're ashamed of him. You're ashamed of so much! . . . And now that's going to include yourself. That was the promise I made to myself: to try and stop that happening. *(Pause)* After we got him to bed you came back with me to my room and sat in a corner and carried on just looking down at the ground. And for days after that! You hadn't done anything wrong, but you went around as if you owed the world an apology for being alive. I didn't like seeing that! That's not the way a boy grows up to be a man! . . . But the one person who should have been teaching you what that means was the cause of your shame. If you really want to know, that's why I made you that kite. I wanted you to look up, be proud of something, of yourself . . . *(Bitter smile at the memory)* . . .

and you certainly were that when I left you with it up there on the hill. Oh, ja . . . something else! . . . If you ever do write it as a short story, there *was* a twist in our ending. I couldn't sit down there and stay with you. It was a "Whites Only" bench. You were too young, too excited to notice then. But not anymore. If you're not careful . . . Master Harold . . . you're going to be sitting up there by yourself for a long time to come, and there won't be a kite in the sky. (Sam *has got nothing more to say. He exits into the kitchen, taking off his waiter's jacket*)

Willie: Is bad. Is all all bad in here now.

Hally: (*Books into his school case, raincoat on*) Willie . . . (*It is difficult to speak*) Will you lock up for me and look after the keys?

Willie: Okay.

(Sam *returns.* Hally *goes behind the counter and collects the few coins in the cash register. As he starts to leave . . .*)

   Sam: Don't forget the comic books.

(Hally *returns to the counter and puts them in his case. He starts to leave again*)

   Sam: (*To the retreating back of the boy*) Stop . . . Hally . . .

(Hally *stops, but doesn't turn to face him*)

   Hally . . . I've got no right to tell you what being a man means if I don't behave like one myself, and I'm not doing so well at that this afternoon. Should we try again, Hally?

Hally: Try what?

   Sam: Fly another kite, I suppose. It worked once, and this time I need it as much as you do.

Hally: It's still raining, Sam. You can't fly kites on rainy days, remember.

   Sam: So what do we do? Hope for better weather tomorrow?

Hally: (*Helpless gesture*) I don't know. I don't know anything anymore.

   Sam: You sure of that, Hally? Because it would be pretty hopeless if that was true. It would mean nothing has been learnt in here this afternoon, and there was a hell of a lot of teaching going . . . one way or the other. But anyway, I don't believe you. I reckon there's one thing you know. You don't *have* to sit up there by yourself. You know what that bench means now, and you can leave it any time you choose. All you've got to do is stand up and walk away from it.

(Hally *leaves.* Willie *goes up quietly to* Sam)

Willie: Is okay, Boet Sam. You see. Is . . . (*He can't find any better words*) . . . is going to be okay tomorrow. (*Changing his tone*) Hey, Boet Sam! (*He is trying hard*) You right. I think about it and you

right. Tonight I find Hilda and say sorry. And make promise I
won't beat her no more. You hear me, Boet Sam?

Sam: I hear you, Willie.

Willie: And when we practice I relax and romance with her from
beginning to end. Non-stop! You watch! Two weeks' time: "First
prize for promising newcomers: Mr. Willie Malopo and Miss Hilda
Samuels." *(Sudden impulse)* To hell with it! I walk home. *(He goes
to the jukebox, puts in a coin and selects a record. The machine comes to
life in the gray twilight, blushing its way through a spectrum of soft,
romantic colors)* How did you say it, Boet Sam? Let's dream. *(Willie sways with the music and gestures for Sam to dance)*

(Sarah Vaughan sings)

> "Little man you're crying,
> I know why you're blue,
> Someone took your kiddy car away;
> Better go to sleep now,
> Little man you've had a busy day." *(etc. etc.)*

You lead. I follow.

(The men dance together)

> "Johnny won your marbles,
> Tell you what we'll do;
> Dad will get you new ones right away;
> Better go to sleep now,
> Little man you've had a busy day."

Lawrence Christon, sitting in the audience when Master Harold . . . and
the Boys *opened in Los Angeles, reported that "the audience made a sound
as though it had been punched in the gut" when Hally spit in Sam's face.
This action, so powerful on stage, is imported directly from a moment in
Athol Fugard's own life, recorded in one of his notebooks.*

"Shame . . . overwhelmed me the second after I had done that": Athol Fugard

Sam Semela—Basuto—with the family fifteen years. Meeting him again
when he visited Mom set off string of memories.

The kite which he produced for me one day during those early years when Mom ran the Jubilee Hotel and he was a waiter there. He had made it himself: brown paper, its ribs fashioned from thin strips of tomato-box plank which he had smoothed down, a paste of flour and water for glue. I was surprised and bewildered that he had made it for me.

I vaguely recall shyly 'haunting' the servants' quarters in the well of the hotel—cold, cement-grey world—the pungent mystery of the dark little rooms—a world I didn't understand. Frightened to enter any of the rooms. Sam, broad-faced, broader based—he smelled of woodsmoke. The 'kaffir smell' of South Africa is the smell of poverty—woodsmoke and sweat.

Later, when he worked for her at the Park café, Mom gave him the sack: '. . . he became careless. He came late for work. His work went to hell. He didn't seem to care no more.' I was about thirteen and served behind the counter while he waited on table.

Realise now he was the most significant—the only—friend of my boyhood years. On terrible windy days when no-one came to swim or walk in the park, we would sit together and talk. Or I was reading—Introductions to Eastern Philosophy or Plato and Socrates—and when I had finished he would take the book back to New Brighton.

Can't remember now what precipitated it, but one day there was a rare quarrel between Sam and myself. In a truculent silence we closed the café, Sam set off home to New Brighton on foot and I followed a few minutes later on my bike. I saw him walking ahead of me and, coming out of a spasm of acute loneliness, as I rode up behind him I called his name, he turned in mid-stride to look back and, as I cycled past, I spat in his face. Don't suppose I will ever deal with the shame that overwhelmed me the second after I had done that.

WOLE SOYINKA

(b. 1934)

THE SWAMP DWELLERS

CHARACTERS

> Alu, an old woman
> Makuri, her husband
> A Beggar
> Kadiye, priest
> Igwezu, son to Alu
> A Drummer
> Attendants to Kadiye

A village in the swamps.

Frogs, rain and other swamp noises.

The scene is a hut on stilts, built on one of the scattered semi-firm islands in the swamps. Two doors on the left lead into other rooms, and the one on the right leads outside. The walls are marsh stakes plaited with hemp ropes.

The room is fairly large, and is used both as the family workshop and as the 'parlour' for guests. About the middle of the right half of the stage is a barber's swivel chair, a very ancient one. On a small table against the right wall is a meagre row of hairdressing equipment—a pair of clippers, scissors, local combs, lather basin and brush, razor—not much else. A dirty white voluminous agbada serves for the usual customer's sheet.

Makuri, an old man of about sixty, stands by the window, looking out. Near the left down-stage are the baskets he makes from the rushes which are strewn in front of him. Up-stage left, his equally aged wife, Alu, sits on a mat, busy at her work, unravelling the patterns in dyed 'adire' cloths. Alu appears to suffer more than the normal viciousness of the swamp flies. She has a flick by her side which she uses frequently, yelling whenever a bite has caught her unawares.

It is near dusk, and there is a gentle wash of rain outside.

    Alu: Can you see him?
Makuri: See who?
    Alu: My son Igwezu. Who else?
Makuri: I did not come to look for him. Came only to see if the rain
      looks like stopping.
    Alu: Well, does it?
Makuri: *[grunts.]*

Alu: [*goes back to her work. Then—*] It is time he was back. He went hours and hours ago.

Makuri: He knows the way. He's a grown-up man, with a wife.

Alu: [*flaring up with aged lack of heat.*] If you had any good at all in you, you'd go and look for him.

Makuri: And catch my death of cramp? Not likely . . . And anyway, [*getting warmer*] what's preventing you from going?

Alu: I want to be here when he gives me the news. I don't want to fall down dead out in the open.

Makuri: The older you get, the more of a fraud you become. Every day for the past ten years, you've done nothing but swear that your son was dead in the marshes. And now you sit there like a crow and tell me that you're waiting for news about him.

Alu: [*stubbornly.*] I know he's dead.

Makuri: Then what do you want Igwezu to tell you?

Alu: I only want to know if . . . I only want to ask him . . . I . . . I . . . He shouldn't have rushed off like that . . . dashing off like a mad-man before anyone could ask him a thing.

Makuri: [*insistently.*] Before anyone could ask him WHAT?

Alu: [*flares up again.*] You're always trying to make me a liar.

Makuri: I don't have to make you one.

Alu: Bah! Frog-face! [*Resumes her work.*] . . . Dropped his bundle and rushed off before I could ask him a thing . . . And to think he could have found him after all. To think he could have found him in the city . . .

Makuri: Dead men don't go to the city. They go to hell.

Alu: I know one dead man who is sitting right here instead of going quietly to hell.

Makuri: Now see who is calling who . . .

Alu: You're so useless now that it takes you nearly a whole week to make one basket . . . and to think you don't even cut your own rushes!

Makuri: If you had to get up so often to shave the heads of the whole village . . . and most of them crusted with kraw-kraw so that a man has to scrape and scrape until . . .

Alu: [*yells suddenly and slaps herself on the arm.*]

Makuri: [*looks at her for a moment.*] Ha! Don't tell me now that a fly has been trying to suck blood from your dried-up veins.

Alu: If you had enough blood to hold you up, you'd prove it by going to look for your own son, and bring him home to supper.

Makuri: He'll come home when he's hungry.

Alu: Suppose he's lost his way? Suppose he went walking in the swamps and couldn't find his way back?

Makuri: [*in bewilderment.*] Him? Get lost? Woman, isn't it your son we're speaking of? The one who was born here, and has lived here all his life?

Alu: But he has been away now for some time. You cannot expect him to find his way about so quickly.

Makuri: No, no. Of course not. The poor child has been away for eight . . . whole . . . months . . . ! Tch, tch. You'd drive a man to drown himself in the swamps—just to get away from your fussing.

Alu: [puts aside her work and rises.] I'm going after him. I don't want to lose him too. I don't want him missing his foothold and vanishing without a cry, without a chance for anyone to save him.

Makuri: Stay where you are.

[Alu *crosses to doorpost and looks out.]*

Alu: I'm going out to shout his name until he hears me. I had another son before the mire drew him into the depths. I don't want Igwezu going the same way.

Makuri: [follows her.] You haven't lost a son yet in the slough, but you will soon if you don't stop calling down calamities on their heads.

Alu: It's not what I say. The worst has happened already. Awuchike was drowned.

Makuri: You're a blood-thirsty woman. Awuchike got sick of this place and went into the city. That's where you'll find him, fadding it out with the gentlemen. But you'll be satisfied with nothing less than a festering corpse beneath the mire . . .

Alu: It's the truth.

Makuri: It's a lie. All the young men go into the big town to try their hand at making money . . . only some of them remember their folk and send word once in a while.

Alu: You'll see. When Igwezu returns, you'll find that he never saw a trace of him.

Makuri: And if he didn't? The city is a large place. You could live there all your life and never meet half the people in it.

Alu: They are twins. Their close birth would have drawn them together even if they were living at the opposite ends of the town.

Makuri: Bah!

Alu: Bah to yourself. Nobody has ever seen him. Nobody has ever heard of him, and yet you say to me . . .

Makuri: Nobody? Did you say nobody?

Alu: No one that really knew him. No one that could swear it was he.

Makuri: [despairingly.] No one. No one that could swear . . . Ah, what a woman you are for deceiving yourself.

Alu: No one knows. Only the Serpent can tell. Only the Serpent of the swamps, the Snake that lurks beneath the slough.

Makuri: The serpent be . . . ! Bah! You'll make me voice a sacrilege before I can stop my tongue. The traders came. They came one year, and they came the next. They looked at Igwezu and asked, Has he a twin? Has he a twin brother who lives in the town?

Alu: There are many people who look alike.

Makuri: [*sits down and takes up his work.*] Well, I'll not perform the death rites for a son I know to be living.

Alu: If you felt for him like a true father, you'd know he was dead. But you haven't any feelings at all. Anyone would think they weren't your own flesh and blood.

Makuri: Well, I have only your own word for that.

Alu: Ugh! You always did have a dirty tongue.

Makuri: [*slyly.*] The land is big and wide, Alu, and you were often out by yourself, digging for crabs. And there were all those shifty-eyed traders who came to hunt for crocodile skins . . . Are you sure they didn't take your own skin with them . . . you old crocodile!

Alu: And if they did?

Makuri: Poor luck to them. They couldn't have minded much which crocodile they took.

Alu: You're asking . . . Ayi! [*Slaps off a fly and continues more furiously.*] You're asking to have your head split and the wind let out.

Makuri: And to think . . .

Alu: [*makes a move to rise.*] And I'll do it for you if you carry on the same . . .

Makuri: Now, now, Alu. You know I didn't mean a word of that.

[Alu *tightens her lips and resumes her work.*]

[*In a hurriedly placating tone.*] There wasn't a woman anywhere more faithful than you, Alu; I never had a moment of worry in the whole of my life . . . [*His tone grows more sincere.*] Not every man can look his wife in the face and make that boast, Alu. Not every man can do it.

[Alu *remains inflexible.*]

And the chances you could have taken. Those traders—everyone of them wanted you to go back with him; promised he'd make you live like a lady, clothe you in silks and have servants to wait on your smallest wants . . . You don't belong here, they used to tell you. Come back with us to the city where men know the value of women . . . No, there was no doubt about it. You could have had your choice of them. You turned their heads like a pot of cane brew.

[Alu *begins to smile in spite of herself.*]

Makuri: And the way I would go walking with you, and I could hear their heads turning round, and one tongue hanging out and say-

ing to the other, Now I wonder what she sees in him . . . Poor
fools . . . if only they knew. If only they could see me take you out
into the mangrove, and I so strong that I could make you gripe
and sweat and sink your teeth into my cheeks.

Alu: You were always one for boasting.

Makuri: And you with your eyes shut so tight that I thought the skin
would tear itself. Your eyes always shut, so that up till this day,
you cannot tell what I looked like when the spirit took me, and I
waxed as hot as the devil himself.

Alu: Be quiet.

Makuri: You never feared the swamp then. You could walk across it
day and night and go to sleep in the middle of it . . . Alu, do you
remember our wedding night?

Alu: *[pleased just the same.]* We're past that kind of talk now. Have
you no shame?

Makuri: Come on, my own Alu. Tell old Makuri what you did on the
night of our wedding.

Alu: No.

Makuri: You're a stubborn old hen . . . Won't you even tell how you
dragged me from the house and we went across the swamps,
though it was so dark that I could not see the whites of your eyes?

Alu: *[stubbornly.]* I do not remember.

Makuri: And you took me to the point where the streams meet, and
there you said . . . *[Pauses.]*

Alu: *[shyly.]* Well, it was my mother who used to say it.

Makuri: Tell me just the same . . . just as you said it that night when I
thought they were your own words.

Alu: My memory is not so good . . . but . . .

Makuri: It will come. Think slowly.

Alu: *[with a shy smile.]* She said I had to say it on my bridal bed.

Makuri: Just where we stood. Go on, say it again.

Alu: 'Where the rivers meet, there the marriage must begin. And
the river bed itself is the perfect bridal bed.'

Makuri: *[thoughtfully.]* Ay-ii . . . The bed of the river itself . . . the bed
of the river . . . *[Bursts suddenly into what appears to be illogical
laughter.]*

Alu: Eh? Why? What are you laughing at now?

Makuri: *[futile effort to control himself.]* Ay—ya-ya! The river bed . . .
[Bursts out laughing again.]

Alu: Are you well, Makuri?

Makuri: Ay—ii! You must be really old, Alu. If you don't remember
this, you're too old to lie on another river-bed.

Alu: I don't . . . What are you . . . ?

Makuri: Think hard, woman. Do you not remember? We did not
know that the swamp came up as far as that part of the stream
. . . The ground . . . gave . . . way beneath us!

Alu: *[beginning to laugh.]* It is all beginning to come back . . . yes, yes, so it did. So it did!

Makuri: And can you remember that you were left kicking in the mire . . . ha ha!

Alu: *[no longer amused.]* I was? I suppose you never even got your fingers muddy?

Makuri: Well, I jumped up in time, didn't I? But you went down just as you were, flat on your back. And there I stood looking at you . . .

Alu: Ay. Gawking and yelling your head off with laughter. I can remember now.

Makuri: You'd have laughed too if you had stood where I did and seen what could be seen of you.

Alu: Call yourself a man? And all my ribs bruised because you stood on me trying to get me out.

Makuri: If you hadn't been thrashing about so much, I'd have got you out much quicker . . .

[Alu has tightened her lips again. Bends rigidly over her work. Pause.]

Makuri: The whole village said that the twins were the very colour of the swamp . . . eh . . . Alu?

[Alu remains deaf to him.]

Makuri: Ah well . . . Those were the days . . . those days were really good. Even when times were harsh and the swamp overran the land, we were able to laugh with the Serpent . . . *[Continues to work.]* . . . but these young people . . . They are no sooner born than they want to get out of the village as if it carried a plague . . . *[Looks up suddenly.]* I bet none of them has ever taken his woman into the swamps.

Alu: They have more sense than that. *[She says this with an effort and immediately resumes her frigidity.]*

Makuri: It is not sense they have . . . not sense at all. Igwezu was hardly joined to his wife before he took her off into the city. What would a girl like Desala do in a place like that, I ask you. What would she find to do in the city?

Alu: *[primly.]* If you'd kept your eyes about you, you would have known that she made him promise to take her there before she would wed him.

Makuri: It ruins them. The city ruins them. What do they seek there except money? They talk to the traders, and then they cannot sit still . . . There was Gonushi's son for one . . . left his wife and children . . . not a word to anyone.

Alu: *[almost between her teeth.]* It was the swamp . . . He went the same way as my son . . .

Makuri: *[throwing down his basket.]* Woman . . . !

[He is interrupted by the sound of footsteps on the planks outside.]

Makuri: That must be Igwezu now.

    Alu: Thank heavens. It will soon be dark.

Makuri: You'd better make the most of him. He might be going back tomorrow.

    Alu: Why should he?

Makuri: He came for his crops. Now that he knows they've been ruined by the floods, he'll be running back to the city.

    Alu: He will stay a few days at least.

Makuri: *[licking his lips.]* With a full-bosomed woman like Desala waiting for him in the city . . . ? You must be getting old.

    Alu: It's a let-down for him—coming all the way back and finding no harvest.

Makuri: Now don't you start. We've had worse years before this.

    Alu: *[flaring.]* But you haven't journeyed three days only to be cheated of your crops . . .

[The footsteps are right at the door. There is a knock on the wall.]

    Alu: That's a queer mood he's in. Why is he knocking?

Makuri: It's not Igwezu . . . I didn't think they were his footsteps. *[Goes towards the door and pulls aside the door matting.]* A good evening to you, stranger.

Voice Off-Stage: Allah protect you.

Makuri: Were you sent to me? Come in. Come into the house.

[The caller enters, feeling his way with a staff.]

Makuri: *[picks up the bundle from the floor.]* Alu, take this bundle out of here . . . And bring some light. It is too dark in here.

Beggar: No, no. Not on my account. It makes no difference whatever to me.

Makuri: *[in a bewildered manner.]* Oh . . . oh . . . I understand. *[Takes hold of the other end of the staff and leads him to the swivel chair.]* Sit here . . . Ah. *[Touches the stranger's forehead, and then his, saying devoutly—]* Blessed be the afflicted of the gods.

Beggar: Allah grant everlasting peace to this house.

[The blind man is tall and straight. It is obvious from his dress that he is a stranger to these parts. He wears a long, tubular gown, white, which comes below his calf, and a little skull cap. Down one ear hangs a fairly large ear-ring, and he wears a thick ring on one of his fingers. He has a small beard, which, with the skull cap, accentuates the length of his face and emphasizes its ebony-carving nature.

His feet are muddy above the ankles. The rest of him is lightly wet. His bearing is of quiet dignity.]

Makuri: You have journeyed far?

Beggar: Very far. I came all the way down the river.

Makuri: Walking?

Beggar: Most of the way. Wherever it was possible, I walked. But sometimes, I was forced to accept a lift from the ferries.

Makuri: [*looks rapidly down his legs.*] Alu! Some water for the man to wash his feet.

Alu: [*coming in with the taper.*] Give me time. I can't do everything at once, can I? [*Lights the oil lamps which are hanging from the rafters. Goes back again.*]

Makuri: Have you met anyone in the village? Were you directed here?

Beggar: No. This happened to be the first house on my way . . . Are you the head of this house?

Makuri: Y-yes, yes I am.

Beggar: Then it is with you I must speak.

Makuri: We haven't much, but you can have shelter for the night, and food for . . .

Beggar: I have not come to beg for alms.

Makuri: Oh? Do you know anyone here?

Beggar: No. I come from far away in the North. Have you ever heard of Bukanji?

Makuri: Bukanji? Bukan . . . ? Ah, is that not the village of beggars?

Beggar: So it is known by the rest of the world . . . the village of beggars . . . but I have not come to beg.

Makuri: Bukanji! That is a march of several weeks!

Beggar: I have been journeying for longer than that. I resolved to follow the river as far as it went, and never turn back. If I leave here, it will be to continue in the same direction.

Makuri: But this is the end—this is where the river ends!

Beggar: No, friend. There are many more miles left of this river.

Makuri: Yes, yes . . . But the rest is all swamp. Between here and the sea, you'll not find a human soul.

Beggar: I must stay here or walk on. I have sworn to tread only where the soil is moist.

Makuri: You'll not get far in that direction. This is the end. This is as far as human beings can go, even those who have the use of their sight.

Beggar: Then I must stay here.

Makuri: What do you want?

Beggar: Work.

Makuri: Work?

Beggar: Yes, work. I wish to work on the soil. I wish to knead it between my fingers.

Makuri: But you're blind. Why don't you beg like others? There is no true worshipper who would deny you his charity.

Beggar: I want a home, and I wish to work with my hands.

Makuri: [*in utter bewilderment.*] You . . . the afflicted of the gods! Do you really desire to work, when even the least devout lives under the strict injunction of hospitality towards you?

Beggar: [*getting up.*] No more, no more. All the way down the river the natives read me the code of the afflicted, according to their various faiths. Some fed and clothed me. Others put money in my hands, food and drink in my bag. With some, it was the children and their stones, and sometimes the dogs followed me and whetted their teeth on my ankles . . . Good-bye. I shall follow the river to the end.

Makuri: Wait. You are very hasty. Did you never learn that the blind man does not hurry for fear he out-walks his guide? Sit down again . . . Alu! Alu! When is that supper coming?

Alu: [*from inside.*] What supper? The last time it was water for washing his feet.

Makuri: Well, hurry . . . [*Helps the blind man back into the chair.*] There . . . Now tell me all about your journey . . . Did you come through any of the big cities?

Beggar: One or two, but I did not stop there. I walked right through them without a halt.

Makuri: And you have been on the road for . . . how long did you say?

Beggar: I have lost all count of time. To me, one day is just like another . . . ever since my sight became useless.

Makuri: It must be strange . . . living in perpetual dark.

Beggar: I did not have many years to enjoy the benefit of the eyes. Four or five years at the most, and then . . . You have heard of the fly sickness?

Makuri: [*shaking his head.*] Who hasn't? Who hasn't?

Beggar: It is fatal to cattle. The human beings fall ill and suffer agonies. When the sickness is over, the darkness begins . . . At first, it is mystifying and then . . . [*smiles.*] When it happened to me, I thought I was dead and that I had gone to a paradise where my earthly eyes were unsufficing.

Makuri: You did? If it had been Old Makuri, he would have thought that he was in the darkest corner of hell.

Beggar: [*smiling still.*] But I was only a child, and I knew that I had committed no sins. Moreover, my faith promises paradise for all true believers—paradise in the company of Muhammad and all the prophets . . . [*Becoming serious.*] Those few moments were the happiest in my life. Any moment, I thought, and my eyes would be opened to the wonders around me. I heard familiar voices, and I rejoiced, because I thought that they were dead also, and were in paradise with me . . . And then slowly, the truth came to me, and I knew that I was living—but blind.

Makuri: The gods be merciful.

Beggar: Even before anyone told me, I knew exactly what I had to do to live. A staff, a bowl, and I was out on the roads begging for alms from travellers, singing my prayers, pouring out blessings upon them which were not mine to give . . .

Makuri: No, my friend. The blessings were yours. My faith teaches me that every god shakes a beggar by the hand, and his gifts are passed into his heart so that every man he blesses . . .

Beggar: Ah, but did I bless them from the heart? Were they not so many that I blessed without thought, and took from whatever hand was willing, however vile it was? Did I know if the alms came from a pure heart or from a robber and taker of lives, from the devout, or the profane . . . ? I thanked and blessed them equally, even before I had the time to discover the size of their bounty . . . *[Begins to nod his head in time to his chanting.]*

[His chanting is tonal. No clear words.

Faint drumming can now be heard off-stage. The Beggar *hears it and stops abruptly, listening hard for the sound.]*

Beggar: Have you a festivity in the village tonight?

Makuri: No. Why?

Beggar: I can hear drumming.

Makuri: *[after listening for a moment.]* It must be the frogs. There is a whole city of them in the marshes.

Beggar: No, this is drumming. And it is coming this way . . . yes, it is drawing nearer.

Makuri: Y—yes . . . I think I can hear it now . . . Alu!

Alu: *[from inside]* What now?

Makuri: Can you hear the drumming?

Alu: What drumming?

Makuri: That means you can't. *[Confidentially.]* She was deaf the day she was born. *[Goes to the door and looks out.]* They are not within sight yet, whoever it is . . . Ah, I know who it must be . . . My son.

Beggar: You have a son?

Makuri: Yes. He only came back today. He has been in the city making money.

Beggar: So he is wealthy?

Makuri: We don't know yet. He hardly said a word to anyone before he rushed off again to see what the floods had done to his farm . . . The man is a fool. I told him there wasn't a thing to see except the swamp water, but he rushed out like a madman, dropping his bundle on the floor. He said he had to see for himself before he would believe it.

Beggar: Was there much damage to the farm?

Makuri: Much damage? Not a grain was saved, not one tuber in the soil . . . And what the flood left behind was poisoned by the oil in the swamp water. *[Shakes his head.]* . . . It is hard for him, coming back for a harvest that isn't there.

Beggar: But it is possible then. It is possible to plant on this land in spite of the swamp?

Makuri: [straining his eyes into the dark outside.] Oh yes. There are little bits of land here and there where a man can sow enough to keep his family, and even take to the market . . . Not much, but . . . I can't see them . . . But I'm sure it is he. He must have run into one of the drummers and been merry-making all afternoon. You can trust Luyaka to drum him back to his own house in welcome.

Beggar: Is there land here which a man can till? Is there any land to spare for a man who is willing to give his soul to the soil?

Makuri: [shakes his head.] No, friend. All the land that can take the weight of a hoe is owned by someone in the village. Even the few sheep and goats haven't any land on which to graze. They have to be fed on cassava and other roots.

Beggar: But if a man is willing to take a piece of the ground and redeem it from the swamp—will they let him? If a man is willing to drain the filth away and make the land yield coco-yams and lettuce—will they let him?

Makuri: [stares wildly.] Mind what you are saying, son. Mind what profanities you utter in this house.

Beggar: [surprised.] I merely ask to be given a little of what land is useless to the people.

Makuri: You wish to rob the Serpent of the Swamps? You wish to take the food out of his mouth?

Beggar: The Serpent? The Serpent of the Swamps?

Makuri: The land that we till and live on has been ours from the beginning of time. The bounds are marked by ageless iroko trees that have lived since the birth of the Serpent, since the birth of the world, since the start of time itself. What is ours is ours. But what belongs to the Serpent may never be taken away from him.

Beggar: I beg your forgiveness. *[Rises.]* I have not come to question your faith. Allah reward you for your hospitality . . . I must continue my journey . . .

Makuri: Wait. *[He listens for a moment to the drumming which is now nearly just outside the door.]* That is the drummer of the priest . . . *[Enter* Alu *running.]* Alu, is that not the priest's salutations coming from the drums?

Alu: Yes. It must be the Kadiye.

Makuri: It is. It is . . . Well, don't stand there. Get the place fit to receive him . . . Clear away all the litter . . .

[Alu begins to tidy the room hastily. She takes away Makuri's *baskets and rushes, returns to fetch her own things and takes them out of the room. She trims the lamp wicks and takes away any oddments lying around.]*

Makuri: And see if there is any brew in the attic. The Kadiye might like some.

Alu: [grumbling.] Take this away . . . Prepare supper . . . See if
    there is any brew in the . . . Why don't you try and do something
    to help . . . !

Makuri: Do you want me to be so ill-mannered as to leave my guest by
    himself? . . . *[Takes the blind man by the arm and leads him towards
    his stool.]* . . . You mustn't pay any attention to that ill-tempered
    hen . . . She always gets in a flutter when the Kadiye honours our
    house. *[Picks up his stool and moves off towards* Alu's *corner.]* . . .
    He's probably come to offer prayers of thanks for the safe return
    of our son . . . He's our holy man, the Servant and Priest of the
    Serpent of the Swamp . . . *[Puts down the stool.]* Here. Sit down
    here. We must continue our talk when he is gone.

[The drummer is now at the door, and footsteps come up the gangway.]

The drummer is the first to enter. He bows in backwards, drumming praises of the
Kadiye. *Next comes the Kadiye himself, a big, voluminous creature of about fifty,
smooth-faced except for little tufts of beard around his chin. His head is shaved
clean. He wears a kind of loin-cloth, white, which comes down to below his knees
and a flap of which hangs over his left arm. He is bare above the waist. At least
half of the* Kadiye's *fingers are ringed. He is followed by a servant, who brushes
the flies off him with a horse-tail flick.]*

Makuri: [places his arm across his chest and bows.] My house is open to
    you, Kadiye. You are very welcome.

[The Kadiye *places a hand on his head.]*
[Alu hurries into the room and kneels. The Kadiye *blesses her also.]*

Kadiye: [looks at the Beggar *who remains sitting. Signs to the drummer to
    stop.]* Did Igwezu bring a friend with him?

Makuri: No, Kadiye. This is a stranger who called at my house for
    charity. He is blind.

Kadiye: The gods protect you, friend.

Beggar: Allah shield you from all evil.

Kadiye: [startled.] Allah? is he from the North?

Makuri: He is. He journeyed all the way from Bukanji.

Kadiye: Ah, from Bukanji *[To the servant.]* Kundigu, give the man
    something.

[The servant brings out a purse and approaches the Beggar. *When he is about a
foot away, the* Beggar, *without a change of expression turns his bowl upside down.
The servant stands puzzled and looks to his master for further instructions.* Kadiye
*looks quickly away, and the servant tries to turn the bowl inside up. But the Beg-
gar keeps it firmly downwards. The servant looks backwards at the* Kadiye—*who
by now has hemmed and begun to talk to* Makuri—*slips the money into his own
pocket, pulls the strings shut and returns to his place.]*

Kadiye: Ahem . . . Where is your son? I hear he has returned.

Makuri: Yes he has. He went out in the afternoon to see his . . . He must have been detained by old friends and their sympathizing.

Kadiye: Yes, it is a pity. But then, he is not the only one. Others lost even more than he did . . . And anyway, he has probably made himself a fortune in the city . . . Hasn't he?

Makuri: I don't know. He hasn't told us . . . Won't you sit here . . . ?

Kadiye: [*sits on the swivel chair.*] They all do. They all make money.

Makuri: Well, I only hope he has. He'll need something on which he can fall back.

Kadiye: [*patting the arm of the chair.*] Didn't he send you this chair within a few weeks of his arriving in the city?

Makuri: Yes, he did. He's a man for keeping his word. Before he left, he said to me, With the first money I make, I am going to buy you one of those chairs which spin like a top. And you can put your customers in it and spin them until they are giddy.

Kadiye: [*pushing his toes into the ground to turn the chair.*] Ay—It is comfortable.

Makuri: It is. When I have no customers, I sit in it myself. It is much better than a rocking chair . . . Alu!

Alu: Coming.

Makuri: When are we having something to drink? Are you going to keep us waiting all night . . . ? [*Back to the* Kadiye—*]* And when they were bringing it over the water, it knocked a hole in the bottom of the canoe and nearly sank it . . . But that wasn't all. The carrier got stuck in the swamps and they had to dig him out . . . Alu!

Alu: [*comes out with a gourd and a number of calabash-cups.*] Here it is . . . There is no need to split your guts with shouting.

Makuri: [*takes the gourd from her and serves the drinks.* Alu *takes it round. She curtseys to the* Kadiye *when she hands him his cup.* Makuri *takes a smell at the liquor before he begins to pour it out.*] A-a-ah! You'll find this good, Kadiye . . .

Kadiye: Has it been long fermenting?

Makuri: Months and months. I pulped the canes nearly . . .

Alu: You did?

Makuri: If you'd only give me a chance, woman! . . . I was going to say that my son pulped the canes before he left for the city.

Alu: [*looking out of the door in between serving the drinks.*] I wish he'd come. I wish he'd hurry up and come home. It is so dark and the swamps are . . .

Makuri: [*impatiently.*] Here, here, take this to the drummer and stop your cackling. It will be his own fault if he doesn't come and we finish the lot. Pah! He's probably used to drinking bottled beer by now, instead of thriving on good wholesome cane brew, fermented in the froth of the swamp itself.

[Everyone now has a drink, except the Beggar, *who, in spite of a dumb persuasive attempt by* Alu, *refuses a cup. The* Kadiye *waits for* Makuri *to come and taste his drink.]*

Makuri: *[taking the cup from the* Kadiye.*]* If my face belies my thoughts, may the venom grip at once. *[Drinks a mouthful and hands it back.]*

Kadiye: The protection of the heavens be on us all. *[Drinks and smacks his lips. Then he looks round the room and announces gravely—]* The rains have stopped.

Makuri: *[shakes his head in distrust.]* They have stopped too often Kadiye. It is only a lull.

Kadiye: No. They have stopped finally. My soothsayers have confirmed it. The skies are beginning to open: what few clouds there are, are being blown along the river.

Makuri: *[shrugs, without much enthusiasm.]* The gods be praised.

Kadiye: The floods are over . . . The river will recede and we can plant again . . . I am now released of my vow.

Makuri: Your vow, Kadiye?

Kadiye: Yes. When the floods began and the swamps overran the land, I vowed to the Serpent that I would neither shave nor wash until the rains ceased altogether . . .

Makuri: *[drops his cup.]* I had no idea . . . is that the reason for your visit?

Kadiye: Yes, of course. Did you not guess?

Makuri: *[getting out the lather.]* I will only be a moment . . .

Kadiye: No, old man, I shall wait for your son.

Makuri: For Igwezu? . . . As you please, Kadiye . . . I hope he still remembers his trade. It must be a long time since he last wielded a razor.

Kadiye: Be it as it may, his hand is steadier than yours.

Makuri: *[replacing the lather.]* True. True . . . We must all get old some time.

Kadiye: Has he been out long?

Makuri: All day . . . But he should be back any moment now. He must be drinking with his friends . . . they haven't seen him for a whole season, and they won't let him go in a hurry . . .

Alu: He ought to be back by now. Who of his friends could have kept him so long?

Kadiye: Did he bring his wife?

Alu: No. He wouldn't want to expose her to the flooded roads and other discomforts of the journey.

Makuri: *[disgustedly.]* Ah! They're soft. This younger generation is as soft as . . .

Alu: Aw, shut up in a while. Igwezu himself was lucky to get here at all. He would have had to turn back at the river if it wasn't for old Wazuri who is still ferrying travellers across the swollen stream. All the other fishermen have hung up their boats with their nets. *[Goes into the house.]*

Makuri: And isn't that what I am telling you? As soon as the floods came, the younger men ran home to their wives. But not Wazuri! He's as old as the tortoise himself, but he keeps the paddle in his hand.

[The servant comes up and whispers in Kadiye's *ear.]*

Kadiye: Ah yes ... I nearly forgot. *[Drains his cup and gives it to Makuri.]* I must go first to Daruga. His son is going to be circumcised tonight and he wants me to say the usual prayers ... I'll call again on my way back. *[Rises, the servant helping him.]*

Makuri: Just as you please, Kadiye. And if Igwezu returns I shall tell him to prepare for you.

Kadiye: I shall send a man to find him out ... *[Rubs his chin.]* This nest is beginning to attract the swamp flies. I must get it off tonight.

[Goes out, preceded by his drummer who drums him out as before, bowing backwards.]

Makuri: *[who has held the matting aside for them. Looks after them as the drumming dies away. Sighs.]* What a day! What a day! The whole world seems to have picked the same day to drop into my house ... *[Stops suddenly as he is smitten by a recollection ...]* The pot-bellied pig! So I am too old to shave him now, am I? Too old! Why he's nearly as old as the Serpent himself ... Bah! I hope Igwezu has been celebrating with his friends and comes home drunk. He-he! We'll see who has the steady hand then. We'll see who goes from here with his chin all slashed and bleeding ... He-he ... *[Stops again, thinking hard ...]* Now where was I before ... ? Alu!

Alu: *[enters simultaneously with a bowl of warm water.]* If you want to bellow, go out into the swamp and talk to the frogs.

Makuri: Aha, is that the water? No, no, bring it over here ... Come on, my friend ... come over here. It will be easier to wash your feet sitting in this chair ... *[Leads him to the swivel chair ...]* Do you realize it? You've brought good luck with you.

Beggar: Have I?

Makuri: Well, didn't you hear what the Kadiye said? The rains have stopped ... the floods are over. You must carry luck with your staff.

Beggar: Yes, I could feel the air growing lighter, and the clouds clearing over my head. I think the worst of your season is over.

Makuri: I hope so. Only once or twice in my whole lifetime have we had it so bad.

Beggar: How thankful we would have been for the excess that you had
here. If we had had the hundredth part of the fall you had, I
would not be sitting under your roof this moment.
Makuri: Is it really dry up country?
Beggar: *[Smiles indulgently.]* A little worse than that.
Makuri: Drought? Did you have a drought?

[While the Beggar *is speaking,* Alu *squats down and washes his feet. When this is
finished, she wipes them dry, takes a small jar from one of the shelves, and rubs his
feet with some form of ointment.]*

Beggar: We are used to droughts. Our season is one long continuous
drought . . . But we were used to it. Even when it rained, the soil
lets the water run through it and join some stream in the womb of
the earth. All that we knew, and were content to live on alms . . .
Until one day, about a year or more ago . . .

[There is only the gentle lapping of the water in the bowl. Makuri *has brought his
stool and is sitting on the left side of the chair, looking up at the* Beggar.]*

. . . then we had more rain than I had ever known in my life. And
the soil not only held the water, but it began to show off a leaf
here and there . . . even on kola trees which had been stunted
from birth. Wild millet pushed its way through the soil, and little
tufts of elephant grass appeared from seeds which had lain forgotten season upon season . . . Best of all, hope began to spring
in the heart of everyone . . . It was true that the land had lain
barren for generations, that the fields had yielded no grain for
the lifetime of the eldest in the village. We had known nothing
but the dryness of the earth. Dry soil. Dry crumbs of
dust. Clouds of dust even when there was no wind, but only a vulture flying low and flapping its wings over the earth . . . But now
. . . we could smell the sweetness of lemon leaves, and the feel of
the fronds of desert palm was a happiness which we had never
known . . . The thought was no sooner born than we set to work
before the soil changed its mind and released its moisture. We
deserted the highways and marched on this land, hoes and mattocks in hand—and how few of these there were! The village had
been long unused to farming, and there was no more than a
handful of hoes. But we took our staffs and drove them into the
earth. We sharpened stakes and pricked the sand and the pebble
until they bled . . . And it seemed as if the heavens rejoiced in
our labour, for their blessings were liberal, and their goodwill on
our side. The rains came when we wanted. And the sun shone
and the seeds began to ripen.

*[*Igwezu *enters quietly, and remains by the door, unobserved.]*

Nothing could keep us from the farms from the moment that the shoots came through the surface, and all through the months of waiting. We went round the plantains and rubbed our skins against them, lightly, so that the tenderest bud could not be hurt. This was the closest that we had ever felt to one another. This was the moment that the village became a clan, and the clan a household, and even that was taken by Allah in one of his large hands and kneaded together with the clay of the earth. We loved the sound of a man's passing footsteps as if the rustle of his breath it was that gave life to the sprouting wonder around us. We even forgot to beg, and lived on the marvel of this new birth of the land, and the rich smell of its goodness . . . But it turned out to have been an act of spite. The feast was not meant for us, —but for the locusts.

Makuri: [involuntarily.] Locusts!

Beggar: They came in hordes, and squatted on the land. It only took an hour or two, and the village returned to normal.

Alu: [moaning.] Ay-ii, Ay-ii . . .

[Makuri *buries his head in his hands.*]

Beggar: I headed away from my home, and set my face towards the river. When I said to the passing stranger, Friend, set my face towards the river, he replied, which river? But I only said to him, Towards any river, towards any stream; set my face towards the sea itself. But let there be water, because I am sick of the dryness.

Makuri: Ay-ii, the hands of the gods are unequal. Their gifts become the burden of . . .

[Alu, *who has now finished her task, takes the bowl and rises. She is startled by suddenly seeing* Igwezu, *and she drops the bowl in her fright.*]

Alu: My son!

Makuri: Hm? Oh, he's back at last . . . [*Wakes suddenly to the dropped bowl, shouts—*] But was that a reason for you to be drowning the whole house? Now go and wipe it up instead of gawking at the man . . . Come on here, Igwezu. Come and sit down.

Beggar: [rising.] Your son? Is that the son you spoke of?

Makuri: Yes . . . Now hurry up. Hurry up and dry the place.

[The Beggar *feels for his staff and moves out of the chair.* Igwezu *sits down. He appears indifferent to his surroundings.*]

Makuri: What held you? Have you been carousing?

Igwezu: No. I went for a walk by myself.

Makuri: All afternoon?

[Igwezu *nods.*]

Do you mean to tell me . . . ? *[anxiously.]* Son, are you feeling
well?

Alu: *[coming into the room with a piece of rag, overhears the last question.]* Is he unwell? What is the matter with him?

Makuri: He is not unwell. I merely asked him how he felt.

Alu: *[on her knees, begins to wipe the floor.]* Well, how does he feel?

Igwezu: *[without any kind of feeling.]* Glad to be home. Glad to be once
again with my own people . . . Is that not what every home-coming son should feel?

Makuri: *[after watching him for a moment.]* Have you seen the farm?

[Igwezu is silent.]

Son, you mustn't take it so hard. There is nothing that . . .
[Shakes his head in energetic despair and sees Alu *still wiping the
floor.]* Hurry up, woman! Is the man not to get any supper after
walking around by himself all day?

[Alu gasps.]

Igwezu: No, don't give yourself the trouble. I want no supper.

Makuri: But you've eaten nothing all day.

Igwezu: I have had my feast of welcome. I found it on the farm where
the beans and the corn had made an everlasting pottage with the
mud.

Beggar: *[coming forward.]* Master, it will thrive again.

Igwezu: *[He looks up at the* Beggar, *as if seeing him for the first time.]* Who
are you? And why do you call me master?

Beggar: I am a wanderer, a beggar by birth and fortunes. But you own
a farm. I have stood where your soil is good and cleaves to the
toes like the clay of bricks in the mixing; but it needs the fingers
of drought whose skin is parchment. I shall be your bondsman.
I shall give myself to you and work the land for your good. I feel
I can make it yield in my hands like an obedient child.

Igwezu: *[looks from* Alu *to* Makuri, *who only shrugs his shoulders.]* Where
do you come from?

Beggar: Bukanji.

Igwezu: *[relapsing into his former manner.]* Bukanji. Yes, I have heard
of it, I have heard of it . . .

[The Kadiye's *drum has begun again to sound off stage.]*

Makuri: The Kadiye! I had forgotten. Son, the Kadiye has been here.
I think I can hear him returning now. He wants you to shave him
tonight.

Igwezu: Does he?

Makuri: Yes. Now that the rains have ceased, his vow is come to an
end. He wanted me to do it, but I said, No, Kadiye; I am still

strong and healthy, but my fingers shake a little now and then, and your skin is tender.

Igwezu: Yes. Is it not strange that his skin is tender? Is it not strange that he is smooth and well-preserved?

Beggar: [eagerly.] Is he fat, master? When he spoke, I detected a certain bulk in his voice.

Igwezu: Ay, he is fat. He rolls himself like a fat and greasy porpoise.

Alu: Son, you must speak better of the holy man.

Makuri: [tut-tutting.] The city has done him no good. No good at all.

Beggar: Master, is it true what they say? Do you speak ill of the holy man because your heart is in the city?

Igwezu: Why? What does it matter to you?

Beggar: The bondsman must know the heart of the master; then he may serve him well.

[Igwezu continues to stare at the Beggar, puzzled.]

Beggar: Do you serve the Serpent, master? Do you believe with the old man—that the land may not be redeemed? That the rotting swamps may not be purified?

Igwezu: You make a strange slave with your questioning. What is all this to you?

Beggar: Even a slave may know the bounds of his master's kingdom.

Igwezu: You know that already.

Beggar: Perhaps. I know that the Serpent has his share, but not who sets the boundaries . . . Is it the priest, or is it the master?

Igwezu: What does it matter?

Beggar: I am a free bondsman. I give myself willingly. I gave without the asking. But I must know whom I serve, for then I will not stint my labour.

Igwezu: Serve whom you please. It does not matter to Igwezu.

Beggar: Does the priest live well? Is the Serpent well kept and nourished?

Igwezu: You may see for yourself. His thighs are like skinfuls of palm oil . . .

[The Beggar throws back his head and laughs. It is the first time he has done so, and the effect is immediate on Makuri and Alu, who stare at him in wonder. Igwezu looks up ordinarily.]

Igwezu: It is a careless bondsman who laughs before his master.

Beggar: How does the Serpent fare in times of dearth? Does he thrive on the poisonous crabs? Does he drink the ooze of the mire?

Makuri: [trembling with anger.] Beware. That borders upon sacrilege. That trespasses on the hospitality of this house.

Beggar: [with dignity.] I beg your forgiveness. It is for the master to question, not the slave. *[He feels his way to the far corner, and remains there, standing.]*

Igwezu: [thoughtfully.] Ay. So it is . . . So it is . . . And yet, I saw him
come into this house; but I turned and went away again, back to
the Serpent with whom I'd talked all afternoon.

Makuri: You did what? Who are you talking about?

Igwezu: The Kadiye. I saw him when he entered this house, but I went
away and continued my walk in the swamps.

Makuri: You did?

Igwezu: Yes, I did not trust myself.

Makuri: You did not trust yourself. Why? What has the Kadiye ever
done to you?

Igwezu: I do not know. At this moment, I do not know. So perhaps it
is as well that he comes. Perhaps he can explain. Perhaps he can
give meaning to what seems dark and sour . . . When I met with
harshness in the city, I did not complain. When I felt the nakedness of its hostility, I accepted it. When I saw its knife sever the
ties and the love of kinship, and turn brother against brother . . .

Alu: [quickly.] You met him then. You found your brother in the
city.

Igwezu: Did I?

Alu: Your silence has deceived no one, Igwezu. Do you think I did
not know all the time?

Igwezu: He is dead. You've said so yourself. You have said it often
enough.

Alu: Which death did he die—that is all I want to know. Surely a
mother may say that much, and be forgiven the sin of lying to
herself—even at the moment of the asking. And he is still my
son, Igwezu; he is still your own twin.

[Igwezu remains silent.]

Alu: I am too old to be pilgrim to his grave. I am too weak to seek
to bring him back to life . . . I only seek to know . . . Igwezu, did
you find my son?

[After a moment, Igwezu nods slowly.]

Alu: Let me hear it through your lips, and then I will know it is no
trick of my eyes. Does my son live?

Igwezu: [wearily.] He lives.

Alu: [nodding.] He lives. What does it matter that he breathes a
foreign air. Perhaps there is something in the place that makes
men forget. *[Going.]* What if he lives sufficient only to himself.
He lives. One cannot ask too much. *[Goes into the house.]*

Makuri: [ordinarily.] Was he well?

[Igwezu nods.]

*Makuri: [obviously uncertain how to proceed. He keeps his eyes on the
ground, from where he spies on Igwezu. Slowly, and with hesitation
. . .]* Did you . . . did you often . . . meet?

Igwezu: I lived under his roof—for a while.

Makuri: [shouting at the departed Alu.*]* Did you hear that? Did you hear that you stubborn old crow? . . . Was he . . . Did . . . er . . . ? You did say he was in good health?

Igwezu: Healthier than you or I. And a thousand times as wealthy.

Makuri: There! *[shouting out again.]* Did you hear? Did I not always say so? *[more confidently now.]* How did he make his money?

Igwezu: In timber. He felled it and floated it over the seas . . . He is wealthy, and he is big.

Makuri: Did he ever talk of his father? Does he remember his own home?

Igwezu: Awuchike is dead to you and to this house. Let us not raise his ghost.

Makuri: [stands bewildered for a moment. Then, with a sudden explosiveness . . .] What did he do, son? What happened in the city?

Igwezu: Nothing but what happens to a newcomer to the race. The city reared itself in the air, and with the strength of its legs of brass kicked the adventurer in the small of his back.

Makuri: And Awuchike? Was he on the horse that kicked?

*[*Igwezu *is silent.]*

Makuri: Did your own brother ride you down, Igwezu? . . . Son, talk to me. What took place between you two?

*[*Igwezu *is silent again, and then]*

Igwezu: The wound heals quicker if it is left unopened. What took place is not worth the memory . . . Does it not suffice that in the end I said to myself . . . I have a place, a home, and though it lies in the middle of the slough, I will go back to it. And I have a little plot of land which has rebelled against the waste that surrounds it, and yields a little fruit for the asking. I sowed this land before I went away. Now is the time for harvesting, and the cocoa-pods must be bursting with fullness . . . I came back with hope, with consolation in my heart. I came back with the assurance of one who has lived with his land and tilled it faithfully . . .

Makuri: It is the will of the heavens . . .

Igwezu: It was never in my mind . . . the thought that the farm could betray me so totally, that it could drive the final wedge into this growing loss of touch . . .

[The Kadiye's *drum has become more audible.]*

Beggar: Master, I think the Serpent approaches.

Igwezu: I can hear him, bondsman. I can hear him.

[The Kadiye's *party arrive at the door.* Makuri *runs to hold the matting aside, and the party enters as before.* Alu *comes out again and curtseys.]*

Wole Soyinka **1879**

Kadiye: Is he back? Ah, Igwezu, it is good to see you again. *[Igwezu rises unhurriedly. The* Kadiye *tries to bless him but* Igwezu *avoids this, as if by accident.]* I am glad to see you safe and well . . . *[Seats himself in the chair.]* Ah, what an affair that was. The child was crying loud enough to drown all the frogs in the swamp . . .

Makuri: *[leaning down to him. With fiendishness on his face—]* Did it happen, Kadiye? Did the child take his revenge?

Kadiye: Oh yes, he did. He drenched the healer with a sudden gush!

[Makuri dances delightedly, laughing in his ghoulish manner.]

Kadiye: And that wasn't all. The foolish mother! She heard the cries and tried to get to her son from where she has been locked.

Makuri: And pollute her own son!

Kadiye: Amazing, is it not? The mothers can never be trusted . . . And to think that she did succeed in the end!

Makuri: *[snapping his fingers over his head.]* The gods forbid it!

Kadiye: She did. I had to purify the boy and absolve him from the crime of contamination. That is the fourth circumcision where I have known it to happen.

Makuri: The best thing is to send the mother out of the house.

Kadiye: Do you think that hasn't been tried? It is harder to shift them than to get the child to stay still.

Makuri: Ay. That is true enough. All women are a blood-thirsty lot. They love to hear the child wailing and crying out in pain. Then they can hug themselves and say, Serve you right, you little brat. Now you'll know what pains I went through, giving birth to you.

Kadiye: Ah, that is the truth of it . . . Anyway, it is all over now . . . all over and done with . . . *[Hems with pomposity and turns to* Igwezu.*]* And how is the city, gentleman? Have you been making a lot of money, Igwezu?

Igwezu: None . . . where must I shave, Kadiye?

Kadiye: *[puzzled.]* Where?

Igwezu: Is it the head or the chin?

Makuri: *[gasps. Then tries to force a casualness in his tone.]* Pay no attention, Kadiye. It is only the humour of the townsmen.

Kadiye: A-ah . . . The chin, Igwezu. Shave off the beard.

Igwezu: *[begins to prepare the instruments.]* Did you make other vows, Kadiye? Were there other pleasures from which you abstained until the rains abated?

Kadiye: Oh, yes. Oh, yes indeed. I vowed that my body would remain unwashed.

Igwezu: Ah. Did you keep within doors?

Kadiye: No. I had my duties . . . People still die, you know. And mothers give birth to children.

Igwezu: And it rained throughout? Almost without a stop?

Kadiye: Yes, it did.

Igwezu: Then perhaps once or twice you were out in the rain . . . ?

Makuri: [quickly.] Igwezu . . . you . . . you . . . you were going to tell Kadiye about the big town.

Igwezu: Was I?

Kadiye: Ah, yes. Tell me about the place. Was business as good as they say?

Igwezu: For some people.

Kadiye: And you? Did your business thrive?

Igwezu: No more than my farming has done.

Kadiye: Come now, Igwezu. I am not trying to obtain the promise of an ox for sacrifice . . . You did make some money?

Igwezu: No.

Kadiye: I see he must be coaxed . . . Admit you've made enough to buy this village—men, livestock and all.

Igwezu: [slips the agbada over the Kadiye's head.] No, Kadiye. I made none at all.

Kadiye: A-ah, they are all modest . . . Did you make a little then?

Igwezu: No I made none at all.

Kadiye: [looks hard at him. He is obviously disturbed by Igwezu's manner. Speaks nervously.] Well, never mind, never mind. To some it comes quickly; to others a little more slowly. But your own turn will come soon, Igwezu; it will come before long.

Igwezu: I'm afraid I have had my turn already. I lost everything; my savings, even my standing as a man. I went into debt.

Kadiye: Impossible!

Igwezu: Shall I tell you what I offered as security? Would you like to know, Kadiye?

Kadiye: Not your pretty wife, I hope. *[guffawing.]* I notice you had to come without her.

Igwezu: No, holy one. It was not my wife. But what I offered had a lot in common with her. I put down the harvest from my farm.

Makuri: Ha?

Alu: Igwezu. My poor Igwezu.

Kadiye: [laughing.] Now what do you take us for? As if anyone in the city would lend money on a farm which he had never even seen. Are they such fools—these business men of yours?

Igwezu: No. They are not fools; my brother least of all. He is anything but a fool.

Alu: Awuchike!

Makuri: My own son? Your own flesh and blood?

[Alu remains staring at Igwezu for several moments. Then, shaking her head in complete and utter bewilderment, she turns round slowly and goes into the house, more slouched than ever before.]

Igwezu: [in the same calm relentlessness.] Wait, mother . . . I have not told you all. *[He begins to lather the Kadiye's face.]*

Alu: I know enough. *[She has stopped but does not turn round.]* But I no longer understand. I feel tired, son. I think I'll go to sleep.

Igwezu: Don't you want news of my wife? Have you no interest in the simple and unspoilt child whom you wooed on my behalf?

[Alu goes slowly out of the room.

Igwezu *begins to shave the* Kadiye. *There is silence.]*

Igwezu: [without stopping.] Father. Tell me, father, is my brother a better man than I?

Makuri: No, son. His heart is only more suited to the city.

Igwezu: And yet we are twins. And in spite of that, he looked at my wife, and she went to him of her own accord . . . Tell me, father, are women so easily swayed by wealth? Are all women the same?

Makuri: Alu was different. She turned their heads but she kept her own.

Igwezu: Thank you, father. Now where is the stranger who would be my bondsman?

Beggar: Here, master.

Igwezu: You sightless ones are known to be gifted with more than human wisdom. You detected from the Kadiye's voice that he was fat . . . Keep still, priest of the swamps; this razor is keen and my hand is unsettled . . . Have I still your attention, bondsman? You have listened to me. Is there anything in my voice which tells you what is lacking? Does something in my voice tell you why the bride of less than a season deserts her husband's side?

Beggar: I must seek that answer in the voice of the bride.

Igwezu: That was wisely spoken. You have all the makings of a true bondsman.

Makuri: You talk strangely, Igwezu. What is running in your head?

Igwezu: It is only a game of children, father. Only a game of riddles and you have answered yours. So has my bondsman. Now it is the turn of the Kadiye.

Kadiye: I am prepared.

Igwezu: With you, holy one, my questions must be roundabout. But you will unravel them, because you speak with the voice of gods . . . ?

Kadiye: As I said before, I am ready.

Igwezu: Who must appease the Serpent of the Swamps?

Kadiye: The Kadiye.

Igwezu: Who takes the gifts of the people, in order that the beast may be gorged and made sleepy-eyed with the feast of sacrifice?

Kadiye: The Kadiye.

Igwezu: [His speech is increasing in speed and intensity.] On whom does the land depend for the benevolence of the reptile? Tell me that, priest. Answer in one word.

Kadiye: Kadiye.

Igwezu: Can you see my mask, priest? Is it of this village?

Kadiye: Yes.

Igwezu: Was the wood grown in this village?

Kadiye: Yes.

Igwezu: Does it sing with the rest? Cry with the rest? Does it till the swamps with the rest of the tribe?

Kadiye: Yes.

Igwezu: And so that the Serpent might not vomit at the wrong season and drown the land, so that He might not swallow at the wrong moment and gulp down the unwary traveller, do I not offer my goats to the priest?

Kadiye: Yes.

Makuri: Igwezu, sometimes the guardians of the air are hard to please . . .

Igwezu: Be quite, father! . . . And did he offer them in turn to the Serpent?

Kadiye: He did.

Igwezu: Everything which he received, from the grain to the bull?

Kadiye: Everything.

Igwezu: The goat and the white cockerel which I gave before I left?

Kadiye: Every hair and feather of them.

Igwezu: And he made it clear—that the offering was from me? That I demanded the protection of the heavens on me and my house, on my father and my mother, on my wife, land and chattels?

Kadiye: All the prayers were repeated.

Igwezu: And ever since I began to till the soil, did I not give the soil his due? Did I not bring the first of the lentils to the shrine, and pour the first oil upon the altar?

Kadiye: Regularly.

Igwezu: And when the Kadiye blessed my marriage, and tied the heaven-made knot, did he not promise a long life? Did he not promise children? Did he not promise happiness?

[Igwezu has shaved off all except a last smear of lather. He remains standing with one hand around the Kadiye's jowl, the other retaining an indifferent hold on the razor, on the other side of his face.]

Kadiye: *[Does not reply this time.]*

Igwezu: *[slowly and disgustedly.]* Why are you so fat, Kadiye?

[The drummer stares, hesitates, and runs out. The servant moves nearer the door.]

Makuri: *[snapping his fingers round his head.]* May heaven forgive what has been uttered here tonight. May earth reject the folly spoken by my son.

Igwezu: You lie upon the land, Kadiye, and choke it in the folds of a serpent.

Makuri: Son, listen to me . . .

Igwezu: If I slew the fatted calf, Kadiye, do you think the land might breathe again? If I slew all the cattle in the land and sacrificed every measure of goodness, would it make any difference to our lives, Kadiye? Would it make any difference to our fates?

[The servant runs out also.]

Kadiye: *[in a choking voice.]* Makuri, speak to your son. . . .

Beggar: Master . . . master . . .

[Igwezu suddenly shaves off the final smear of lather with a rapid stroke which makes the Kadiye flinch. Releases him and throws the razor on the table.

Kadiye scrambles up at once, tearing the cloth from his neck. Makes for the door.]

Kadiye: *[panting.]* You shall pay for this . . . I swear I shall make you pay for this . . . Do you think that you can make an ass of the Kadiye? . . . Do you think that you can pour your sacrilege into my ears with impunity?

Igwezu: Go quickly, Kadiye. *[Sinks into the chair.]* And the next time that you wish to celebrate the stopping of the rains, do not choose a barber whose harvest rots beneath the mire.

Kadiye: You will pay, I swear . . . You will pay for this.

[Flings off the sheet and goes out.]

Makuri: Son, what have you done?

Igwezu: I know that the floods can come again. That the swamp will continue to laugh at our endeavours. I know that we can feed the Serpent of the Swamp and kiss the Kadiye's feet—but the vapours will still rise and corrupt the tassels of the corn.

Makuri: I must go after him or he'll stir up the village against us. *[Stops at the door.]* This is your home, Igwezu, and I would not drive you from it for all the world. But it might be best for you if you went back to the city until this is forgotten.

[Exit.]

[Pause.]

Beggar: *[softly.]* Master . . . master . . . slayer of serpents.

Igwezu: *[in a tired voice.]* I wonder what drove me on.

Beggar: What, master?

Igwezu: Do you think that my only strength was that of despair? Or was there something of a desire to prove myself?

[The Beggar remains silent.]

Igwezu: Your fat friend is gone. But will he stay away?

Beggar: I think that the old man was right. You should go back to the city.

Igwezu: Is it of any earthly use to change one slough for another?

Beggar: I will come and keep you company. If necessary, I will beg for you.

Igwezu: [*stares at him, slowly shaking his head.*] What manner of man are you? How have I deserved so much of you that you would beg for me?

Beggar: I made myself your bondsman. This means that I must share your hardships.

Igwezu: I am too tired to see it all. I think we all ought to go to bed. Have they given you a place to sleep?

Beggar: Will I return with you to the city?

Igwezu: No, friend. You like this soil. You love to scoop it up in your hands. You dream of cleaving ridges under the flood and making little balls of mud in which to wrap your seeds. Is that not so?

Beggar: Yes, master.

Igwezu: And you have faith, have you not? Do you not still believe in what you sow? That it will sprout and see the harvest sun?

Beggar: It must. In my wanderings, I think that I have grown a healer's hand.

Igwezu: Then stay. Stay here and take care of the farm. I must go away.

[*He crosses the room as if to go into the house.*

Hesitates at the door, then turns round and walks slowly away.]

       Tell my people I could not stop to say good-bye.

Beggar: You are not going now, master?

Igwezu: I must not be here when the people call for blood.

Beggar: But the water is high. You should wait until the floods subside.

Igwezu: No. I want to paddle as I go.

Beggar: Is it not night? Is it not dark outside?

Igwezu: It is.

Beggar: Then I shall come with you. I know the dark. Let me come with you over the swamp, as far as the river's edge.

Igwezu: Two blind men groping in the dark? No.

Beggar: And how would you cross the river? There is no ferryman to be found after dark.

Igwezu: [*still looking out of the window. Pauses. He walks away, picks up the old man's work in absent movements. He drops it and looks up.*] Only the children and the old stay here, bondsman. Only the innocent and the dotards. [*Walks slowly off.*]

Beggar: But you will return, master?

[*Igwezu checks briefly, but does not stop.*]

Beggar: The swallows find their nest again when the cold is over. Even the bats desert dark holes in the trees and flap wet leaves with wings of leather. There were wings everywhere as I wiped my feet against your threshold. I heard the cricket scratch himself beneath the armpit as the old man said to me . . .

[The door swings to. The Beggar *sighs, gestures a blessing and says.]*
I shall be here to give account.

[The oil lamps go out slowly and completely. The Beggar *remains on the same spot, the moonlight falling on him through the window.]*

THE END

Like ancient Greek dramatists, Nigerian playwright Wole Soyinka comes from a culture where drama has retained its roots in religious ritual. In Nigeria, he points out, much of the indigenous drama is an enactment of the attempt of humans to integrate themselves into their environment, to reach out to the spirits that share their living space.

"To master the immensity of the cosmos": Wole Soyinka

The concern of ritual theatre in this process of spatial definition which precedes, as we shall discover, the actual enactment must therefore be seen as an integral part of man's constant efforts to master the immensity of the cosmos with his minuscule self. The actual events which make up the enactment are themselves, in ritual theatre, a materialisation of this basic adventure of man's metaphysical self. . . .

Ritual theatre, let it be recalled, establishes the spatial medium not merely as a physical area for simulated events but as a manageable contraction of the cosmic envelope within which man—no matter how deeply buried such a consciousness has latterly become—fearfully exists. And this attempt to manage the immensity of his spatial awareness makes every manifestation in ritual theatre a paradigm for the cosmic human condition. There are transient parallels, brief visual moments of this experience in modern European theatre. The spectacle of a lone human figure under a spotlight on a darkened stage is, unlike a painting, a breathing, living, pulsating, threateningly fragile example of this paradigm. It is threatening because, unlike a similar parable on canvas, its fragility is experienced both at the level of its symbolism and in terms of sympathetic concern for the well-being of that immediate human medium. Let us say he is a tragic character: at the first sign of a check in the momentum of a tragic declamation, his audience becomes nervous for him, wondering—has he forgotten his line? has he blacked out? . . .

This ritual understanding is essential to a profound participation in the cathartic processes of the great tragedies. . . .

Ritual theatre, viewed from the spatial perspective, aims to reflect through physical and symbolic means the archetypal struggle of the mortal being against exterior forces. A tragic view of the theatre goes further and suggests that even the so-called realistic or literary drama can be interpreted as a mundane reflection of this essential struggle. Poetic drama especially may be regarded as a repository of this essential aspect of theatre; being largely metaphorical, it expands the immediate meaning and action of the protagonists into a world of nature forces and metaphysical conceptions. Or, to put it the other way round, powerful natural or cosmic influences are internalised within the protagonists and this implosive factor creates the titanic scale of their passions even when the basis of the conflict seems hardly to warrant it.

TOM STOPPARD

(b. 1937)

THE REAL INSPECTOR HOUND

CHARACTERS

Moon
Birdboot
Mrs. Drudge
Simon
Felicity
Cynthia
Magnus
Inspector Hound
BBC Voice

We are in a theatre, waiting for the play to begin. Also
waiting is Moon, *a critic. In front of* Moon *is an acting
area which represents, in as realistic an idiom as possible, the
drawing-room of Muldoon Manor. French windows at one
side. A telephone. The body of a man lies sprawled face
down on the floor in front of a large settee. This settee must
be of a size and design to allow it to be wheeled over the body,
hiding it completely. Silence. The room. The body.* Moon.

Moon *stares blankly ahead. He turns his head to one side then the other, then up,
then down—waiting. He picks up his programme and reads the front cover. He
turns over the page and reads. He turns over the page and reads. He turns over the
page and reads. He turns over the page and reads. He looks at the back cover and
reads. He puts it down, crosses his legs, and looks about. He stares front. Behind
him a man enters:* Birdboot. Birdboot, *with a box of Black Magic chocolates,
makes way down to join* Moon *and plumps himself down next to him, plumpish,
middle-aged* Birdboot *and younger, taller, less-relaxed* Moon.

Birdboot: (Conspiratorially.) Me and the lads have had a meeting in
the bar and decided it's first-class family entertainment but if
it goes on beyond half-past ten it's self-indulgent—pass it on
. . . *(And laughs jovially.)* I'm on my own tonight, don't mind
if I join you? *(Sits.)*
Moon: Hello, Birdboot.
Birdboot: Where's Higgs?
Moon: I'm standing in.
Moon and Birdboot: Where's Higgs?

Moon: Every time.

Birdboot: What?

Moon: It is as if we only existed one at a time, combining to achieve continuity. I keep space warm for Higgs. My presence defines his absence, his absence confirms my presence, his presence precludes mine. . . . When Higgs and I walk down this aisle together to claim our common seat, the oceans will fall into the sky and the trees will hang with fishes.

Birdboot: (*He has not been paying attention, looking around vaguely, now catches up.*) Where's Higgs?

Moon: The very sight of me with a complimentary ticket is enough. The streets are impassable tonight, the country is rising and the cry goes up from hill to hill—Where—is—Higgs? (*Small pause.*) Perhaps he's dead at last, or trapped in a lift somewhere, or succumbed to amnesia, wandering the land with his trouser cuffs stuffed with ticket-stubs. (Birdboot *regards him doubtfully for a moment.*)

Birdboot: Yes . . . Yes, well I didn't bring Myrtle tonight—not exactly her cup of tea, I thought, tonight.

Moon: Over her head, you mean?

Birdboot: Well, no—I mean it's a sort of a *thriller*, isn't it?

Moon: Is it?

Birdboot: That's what I heard. Who-killed-thing?—no-one-will-leave-the-room?

Moon: I suppose so. Underneath.

Birdboot: *Underneath?!?* It's a whodunnit, man!—Look at it! (*They look at it. The room. The body. Silence.*) Has it started yet?

Moon: Yes. (*Pause. They look at it.*)

Birdboot: Are you sure?

Moon: It's a pause.

Birdboot: You can't start with a *pause!* If you want my opinion there's total panic back there. (*Laughs and subsides.*) Where's Higgs tonight, then?

Moon: It will follow me to the grave and become my epitaph— Here lies Moon the second string: where's Higgs? . . . Sometimes I dream of revolution, a bloody *coup d'état* by the second rank—troupes of actors slaughtered by their understudies, magicians sawn in half by indefatigably smiling glamour girls, cricket teams wiped out by marauding bands of twelfth men —I dream of champions chopped down by rabbit-punching sparring partners while eternal bridesmaids turn and rape the bridegrooms over the sausage rolls and parliamentary private secretaries plant bombs in the Minister's Humber—comedians die on provincial stages, robbed of their feeds by mutely triumphant stooges— And march—an army of assistants and deputies, the seconds-in-command, the runners-up, the right-hand men—storming the palace gates wherein the second son has already mounted the throne having committed regicide with a croquet mallet—stand-ins of the world stand up!— (*Beat.*) Sometimes I dream of Higgs. (*Pause. Birdboot regards him doubtfully. He is at a loss, and grasps reality in the form of his box of chocolates.*)

Birdboot: (*Chewing.*) Have a chocolate!

  Moon: What kind?

Birdboot: (*Chewing.*) Black Magic.

  Moon: No thanks. (*Chewing stops dead. Of such tiny victories and defeats . . .*)

Birdboot: I'll give you a tip, then. Watch the girl.

  Moon: You think she did it?

Birdboot: No, no—the *girl,* watch her.

  Moon: What girl?

Birdboot: You won't know her. I'll give you a nudge.

  Moon: *You* know her, do you?

Birdboot: (*Suspiciously, bridling.*) What's *that* supposed to mean?

  Moon: I beg your pardon?

Birdboot: —for God's sake, Moon, what's the matter with you?— you could do yourself some good, spotting her first time out —she's new, from the provinces, going straight to the top. I don't want to put words into your mouth but a word from us and we could make her.

  Moon: I suppose you've made dozens of them, like that.

Birdboot: (*Instantly outraged.*) I'll have you know I'm a family man devoted to my homely but good-natured wife, and if you're suggesting—

  Moon: No, no—

Birdboot: —A man of my scrupulous morality—

  Moon: I'm sorry—

Birdboot: —falsely besmirched—

  Moon: Is that her? (*For* Mrs. Drudge *has entered.*)

Birdboot: —don't be absurd, wouldn't be seen dead with the old— ah. (Mrs. Drudge *is the char, middle-aged, turbanned. She heads straight for the radio, dusting on the trot.*)

  Moon: (*Reading his programme.*) Mrs. Drudge the Help.

  Radio: (*Without preamble, having been switched on by* Mrs. Drudge.) We interrupt our programme for a special police message. (Mrs. Drudge *stops to listen.*) The search still goes on for the escaped madman who is on the run in Essex.

Mrs. Drudge: (*Fear and dismay.*) Essex!

  Radio: County police led by Inspector Hound have received a report that the man has been seen in the desolate marshes around Muldoon Manor. (*Fearful gasp from* Mrs. Drudge.) The man is wearing a darkish suit with a lightish shirt. He is of medium height and build and youngish. Anyone seeing a man answering to this description and acting suspiciously, is advised to phone the nearest police station. *(A man answering this description has appeared behind* Mrs. Drudge. *He is acting suspiciously. He creeps in. He creeps out.* Mrs. Drudge *does not see him. He does not see the body.)* That is the end of the police message. *(*Mrs. Drudge *turns off the radio and resumes her cleaning. She does not see the body. Quite fortuitously, her view of the body is always blocked, and when it isn't she has her back to it. However, she is dusting and polishing her way towards it.)*

Birdboot: So that's what they say about me, is it?

Moon: What?

Birdboot: Oh, I know what goes on behind my back—sniggers— slanders—hole-in-corner innuendo— What have you heard?

Moon: Nothing.

Birdboot: *(Urbanely.)* Tittle tattle. Tittle, my dear fellow, tattle. I take no notice of it—the sly envy of scandal mongers—I can afford to ignore them, I'm a respectable married man—

Moon: Incidentally—

Birdboot: Water off a duck's back, I assure you.

Moon: Who was that lady I saw you with last night?

Birdboot: *(Unexpectedly stung into fury.)* How dare you! *(More quietly.)* How dare you. Don't you come here with your slimy insinuations! My wife Myrtle understands perfectly well that a man of my critical standing is obliged occasionally to mingle with the world of the footlights, simply by way of keeping *au fait* with the latest—

Moon: I'm sorry—

Birdboot: That a critic of my scrupulous integrity should be vilified and pilloried in the stocks of common gossip—

Moon: Ssssh—

Birdboot: I have nothing to hide!—why, if this should reach the ears of my beloved Myrtle—

Moon: Can I have a chocolate?

Birdboot: What? Oh— *(Mollified.)* Oh yes—my dear fellow—yes, let's have a chocolate— No point in—yes, good show. *(Pops chocolate into his mouth and chews.)* Which one do you fancy?— Cherry? Strawberry? Coffee cream? Turkish delight?

Moon: I'll have montelimar. *(Chewing stops.)*

Birdboot: Ah. Sorry. *(Just missed that one.)*

Birdboot: Gooseberry fondue?

Birdboot: No.

Moon: Pistachio fudge? Nectarine cluster? Hickory nut praline? Château Neuf du Pape '55 cracknell?

Birdboot: I'm afraid not. . . . Caramel?

Moon: Yes, all right.

Birdboot: Thanks very much. *(He gives* Moon *a chocolate. Pause.)* Incidentally, old chap, I'd be grateful if you didn't mention— I mean, you know how these misunderstandings get about. . . .

Moon: What?

Birdboot: The fact is, Myrtle simply doesn't *like* the theatre . . . *(He trails off hopelessly.* Mrs. Drudge, *whose discovery of the body has been imminent, now—by way of tidying the room—slides the couch over the corpse, hiding it completely. She resumes dusting and humming.)*

Moon: By the way, congratulations, Birdboot.

Birdboot: What?

Moon: At the Theatre Royal. Your entire review reproduced in neon!

Birdboot: *(Pleased.)* Oh . . . that old thing.

Moon: You've seen it, of course.

Birdboot: *(Vaguely.)* Well, I was passing. . . .

Moon: I definitely intend to take a second look when it has settled down.

Birdboot: As a matter of fact I have a few colour snapshots—I don't know whether you'd care to . . . ?

Moon: Please, please—love to, love to . . . *(Birdboot* hands over a few colour snapshots which *Moon* holds up to his eyes as he speaks.)* Yes . . . yes . . . lovely . . . awfully sound. *(Handing back the snaps morosely.)* All I ever got was "Unforgettable" on the posters for . . . What was it?

Birdboot: Oh—yes— I know . . . Was that you? I thought it was Higgs. *(The phone rings.)*

Mrs. Drudge: *(Into phone.)* Hello, the drawing-room of Lady Muldoon's country residence one morning in early spring? . . . He*llo!*— the draw—Who? Whom did you wish to speak to? I'm afraid there is no one of that name here, this is all very mysterious and I'm sure it's leading up to something, I hope nothing is amiss for we, that is Lady Muldoon and her houseguests, are here cut off from the world, including Magnus, the wheel-chair-ridden half-brother of her ladyship's husband Lord Albert Muldoon who ten years ago went out for a walk on the cliffs and was never seen again. Should a stranger enter our midst, which I very much doubt, I will tell him you called. Goodbye. *(She puts down the phone and catches sight of the previously seen suspicious character who has now entered again, more suspiciously than ever, through the French windows. He senses her stare, freezes, and straightens up.)*

Simon: Ah!—hello there! I'm Simon Gascoyne, I hope you don't mind, the door was open so I wandered in. I'm a friend of Lady Muldoon, the lady of the house, having made her acquaintance through a mutual friend, Felicity Cunningham, shortly after moving into this neighbourhood just the other day.

Mrs. Drudge: I'm Mrs. Drudge. I don't live in but I pop in on my bicycle when the weather allows to help in the running of charming though somewhat isolated Muldoon Manor. Judging by the time *(She glances at her watch.)* you did well to get here before high water cut us off for all practical purposes from the outside world.

Simon: I took the short cut over the cliffs and followed one of the old smugglers' paths through the treacherous swamps that surround this strangely inaccessible house.

Mrs. Drudge: Yes, many visitors have remarked on the topographical quirk in the local strata whereby there are no roads leading from the Manor, though there *are* ways of getting *to* it, weather allowing.

Simon: Yes, well I must say it's a lovely day so far.

Mrs. Drudge: Ah, but now that the cuckoo-beard is in bud there'll be fog before the sun hits Foster's Ridge.

Simon: I say, it's wonderful how you country people really know weather.

Mrs. Drudge: *(Suspiciously.)* Know whether what?

Simon: *(Glancing out of the window.)* Yes, it does seem to be coming on a bit foggy.

Mrs. Drudge: The fog is very treacherous around here—it rolls off the sea without warning, shrouding the cliffs in a deadly mantle of blind man's buff.

Simon: Yes, I've heard it said.

Mrs. Drudge: I've known whole week-ends when Muldoon Manor, as this lovely old house is called, might as well have been floating on the pack ice for all the good it would have done phoning the police. It was on such a week-end as this that Lord Muldoon who had lately brought his beautiful bride back to the home of his ancestors walked out of this house ten years ago, and his body was never found.

Simon: Yes indeed, poor Cynthia.

Mrs. Drudge: His name was Albert.

Simon: Yes indeed, poor Albert. But tell me, is Lady Muldoon about?

Mrs. Drudge: I believe she is playing tennis on the lawn with Felicity Cunningham.

Simon: *(Startled.)* Felicity Cunningham?

Mrs. Drudge: A mutual friend, I believe you said. A happy chance. I will tell them you are here.

Simon: Well, I can't really stay as a matter of fact—please don't disturb them—I really should be off.

Mrs. Drudge: They would be very disappointed. It is some time since we have had a four for pontoon bridge at the Manor, and I don't play cards myself.

Simon: There is another guest, then?

Mrs. Drudge: Major Magnus, the crippled half-brother of Lord Muldoon who turned up out of the blue from Canada just the other day, completes the house-party. *(Mrs. Drudge leaves on this.* Simon *is undecided.)*

Moon: (Ruminating quietly.) I think I must be waiting for Higgs to die.

Birdboot: What?

Moon: Half-afraid that I will vanish when he does. *(The phone rings.* Simon *picks it up.)*

Simon: Hello?

Moon: I wonder if it's the same for Puckeridge?

Birdboot and Simon: (Together.) Who?

Moon: Third string.

Birdboot: Your stand-in?

Moon: Does he wait for Higgs and I to write each other's obituary—does he dream—?

Simon: To whom did you wish to speak?

Birdboot: What's he like?

Moon: Bitter.

Simon: There is no one of that name here.

Birdboot: No—as a critic, what's Puckeridge like as a critic?

Moon: (Laughs poisonously.) Nobody knows—

Simon: You must have got the wrong number!

Moon: —There's always been me and Higgs. *(Simon replaces the phone and paces nervously. Pause.* Birdboot *consults his programme.)*

Birdboot: Simon Gascoyne. It's not him, of course.

Moon: What?

Birdboot: I said it's not him.

Moon: Who is it, then?

Birdboot: My guess is Magnus.

Moon: In disguise, you mean?

Birdboot: What?

Moon: You think he's Magnus in disguise?

Birdboot: I don't think you're concentrating, Moon.

Moon: I thought you said—

Birdboot: You keep chattering on about Higgs and Puckeridge—what's the matter with you?

Moon: (Thoughtfully.) I wonder if they talk about me . . . ? *(A strange impulse makes* Simon *turn on the radio.)*

Radio: Here is another police message. Essex County police are still searching in vain for the madman who is at large in the deadly marshes of the coastal region. Inspector Hound who is masterminding the operation is not available for comment but it is widely believed that he has a secret plan. . . . Meanwhile police and volunteers are combing the swamps with megaphones, shouting, "Don't be a madman, give yourself up." That is the end of the police message. *(Simon turns off the radio. He is clearly nervous.* Moon *and* Birdboot *are on separate tracks.)*

Birdboot: *(Knowingly.)* Oh yes . . .

    Moon: Yes, I should think my name is seldom off Puckeridge's lips . . . sad, really. I mean, it's no life at all, a stand-in's stand-in.

Birdboot: Yes . . . yes . . .

    Moon: Higgs never gives me a second thought. I can tell by the way he nods.

Birdboot: Revenge, of course.

    Moon: What?

Birdboot: Jealousy.

    Moon: Nonsense—there's nothing *personal* in it—

Birdboot: The paranoid grudge—

    Moon: *(Sharply first, then starting to career . . .)* It is merely that it is not enough to wax at another's wane, to be held in reserve, to be on hand, on call, to step in or not at all, the substitute— the near offer—the temporary-acting—for I am Moon, continuous Moon, in my own shoes, Moon in June, April, September and no member of the human race keeps warm my bit of space—yes, I can tell by the way he nods.

Birdboot: Quite mad, of course.

    Moon: What?

Birdboot: The answer lies out there in the swamps.

    Moon: Oh.

Birdboot: The skeleton in the closet is coming home to roost.

    Moon: Oh yes. *(He clears his throat . . . for both he and* Birdboot *have a "public" voice, a critic voice which they turn on for sustained pronouncements of opinion.)* Already in the opening stages we note the classic impact of the catalystic figure—the outsider —plunging through to the centre of an ordered world and setting up the disruptions—the shock waves—which unless I am much mistaken, will strip these comfortable people— these crustaceans in the rock pool of society—strip them of their shells and leave them exposed as the trembling raw meat which, at heart, is all of us. But there is more to it than that—

Birdboot: I agree—keep your eye on Magnus. *(A tennis ball bounces through the French windows, closely followed by* Felicity, *who is in her twenties. She wears a pretty tennis outfit, and carries a racket.)*

Felicity: *(Calling behind her.)* Out! *(It takes her a moment to notice*

Simon *who is standing shiftily to one side.* Moon *is stirred by a memory.*)

Moon: I say, Birdboot . . .

Birdboot: That's the one.

Felicity: (*Catching sight of* Simon.) You! (Felicity's *manner at the moment is one of great surprise but some pleasure.*)

Simon: (*Nervously.*) Er, yes—hello again.

Felicity: What are you doing here?

Simon: Well, I . . .

Moon: She's—

Birdboot: Sssh . . .

Simon: No doubt you're surprised to see me.

Felicity: Honestly, darling, you really are extraordinary.

Simon: Yes, well, here I am.

Felicity: You must have been desperate to see me—I mean, I'm *flattered,* but couldn't it wait till I got back?

Simon: (*Bravely.*) There is something you don't know.

Felicity: What is it?

Simon: Look, about the things I said—it may be that I got carried away a little—we both did—

Felicity: (*Stiffly.*) What are you trying to say?

Simon: I love another!

Felicity: I see.

Simon: I didn't make any promises—I merely—

Felicity: You don't have to say any more—

Simon: Oh, I didn't want to hurt you—

Felicity: Of all the nerve!

Simon: Well, I—

Felicity: You philandering coward—

Simon: Let me explain—

Felicity: This is hardly the time and place—you think you can barge in anywhere, whatever I happen to be doing—

Simon: But I want you to know that my admiration for you is sincere—I don't want you to think that I didn't mean those things I said—

Felicity: I'll kill you for this, Simon Gascoyne! (*She leaves in tears, passing* Mrs. Drudge *who has entered in time to overhear her last remark.*)

Moon: It was her.

Birdboot: I told you—straight to the top—

Moon: No, no—

Birdboot: Ssh. . . .

Simon: (*To* Mrs. Drudge.) Yes, what is it?

Mrs. Drudge: I have come to set up the card table, sir.

Simon: I don't think I can stay.

Mrs. Drudge: Oh, Lady Muldoon *will* be disappointed.

Simon: Does she know I'm here?

Mrs. Drudge: Oh yes, sir, I just told her and it put her in quite a tizzy.

Simon: Really? . . . Well, I suppose now that I've cleared the air . . . Quite a tizzy, you say . . . really . . . really . . . *(He and* Mrs. Drudge *start setting up for card game.* Mrs. Drudge *leaves when this is done.)*

Moon: Felicity!—she's the one.

Birdboot: Nonsense—red herring.

Moon: I mean, it was *her!*

Birdboot: *(Exasperated.)* *What* was?

Moon: That lady I saw you with last night!

Birdboot: *(Inhales with fury.)* Are you suggesting that a man of my scrupulous integrity would trade his pen for a mess of pottage?! Simply because in the course of my profession I happen to have struck up an acquaintance—to have, that is, a warm regard, if you like, for a fellow toiler in the vineyard of greasepaint—I find it simply intolerable to be pillified and viloried—

Moon: I never implied—

Birdboot: —to find myself the object of uninformed malice, the petty slanders of little men—

Moon: I'm sorry—

Birdboot: —to suggest that my good opinion in a journal of unimpeachable integrity is at the disposal of the first coquette who gives me what I want—

Moon: Sssssh—

Birdboot: A ladies' man! . . . Why, Myrtle and I have been together now for—Christ—who's *that?* *(Enter* Lady Cynthia Muldoon. *A beautiful woman in her thirties. She wears a cocktail dress, is formally coiffured. Her effect on* Birdboot *is also impressive. He half-rises and sinks back agape.)*

Cynthia: *(Entering.)* Simon! *(A dramatic freeze between her and* Simon.*)*

Moon: Lady Muldoon.

Birdboot: No, I mean—who *is* she?

Simon: *(Coming forward.)* Cynthia!

Cynthia: Don't say anything for a moment—just hold me. *(He seizes her and glues his lips to hers, as they say. While their lips are glued—)*

Birdboot: She's *beautiful*—a vision of eternal grace, a poem . . .

Moon: I think she's got her mouth open. *(Cynthia breaks away dramatically.)*

Cynthia: We can't go on meeting like this!

Simon: We have nothing to be ashamed of!

Cynthia: But darling, this is madness!

Simon: Yes?—I am mad with love for you!

Cynthia: Please—remember where we are!

Simon: Cynthia, I love you!

Cynthia: Don't—I love Albert!

Simon: He's dead! *(Shaking her.)* Do you understand me—Albert's dead!

Cynthia: No—I'll never give up hope! Let me go! We are not free!

Simon: I don't care, we were meant for each other—had we but met in time.

Cynthia: You're a cad, Simon! You will use me and cast me aside as you have cast aside so many others.

Simon: No, Cynthia!—you can make me a better person!

Cynthia: You're ruthless—so strong, so cruel— *(Ruthlessly he kisses her.)*

Moon: The son she never had, now projected in this handsome stranger and transformed into lover—youth, vigour, the animal, the athlete as aesthete—breaking down the barriers at the deepest level of desire.

Birdboot: By jove, I think you're right. Her mouth *is* open. *(Cynthia breaks away. Mrs. Drudge has entered.)*

Cynthia: Stop—can't you see you're making a fool of yourself!

Simon: I'll kill anyone who comes between us!

Cynthia: Yes, what is it, Mrs. Drudge?

Mrs. Drudge: Should I close the windows, my lady? The fog is beginning to roll off the sea like a deadly—

Cynthia: Yes, you'd better. It looks as if we're in for one of those days. Are the cards ready?

Mrs. Drudge: Yes, my lady.

Cynthia: Would you tell Miss Cunningham we are waiting.

Mrs. Drudge: Yes, my lady.

Cynthia: And fetch the Major down.

Mrs. Drudge: *(As she leaves.)* I think I hear him coming downstairs now. *(She does: the sound of a wheelchair approaching down several flights of stairs with landings in between. It arrives bearing Magnus at about 15 m.p.h., knocking Simon over violently.)*

Cynthia: Simon!

Magnus: *(Roaring.)* Never had a chance! Ran under the wheels!

Cynthia: Darling, are you all right?

Magnus: I have witnesses!

Cynthia: Oh, Simon—say something!

Simon: *(Sitting up suddenly.)* I say, I'm most frightfully sorry.

Magnus: *(Still shouting.)* How long have you been a pedestrian?

Simon: Ever since I could walk.

Cynthia: Can you walk now . . . ? *(Simon rises and walks.)* Thank God! Magnus, this is Simon Gascoyne.

Magnus: What's he doing here?

Cynthia: He just turned up.

Magnus: Really? How do you like it here?

  Simon: (*To* Cynthia.) I could stay forever. (Felicity *enters.*)

 Felicity: So— You're still here.

Cynthia: Of course he's still here. We're going to play cards.
There's no need to introduce you two, is there, for I recall
now that you, Simon, met me through Felicity, our mutual
friend.

 Felicity: Yes, Simon is an old friend, though not as old as you, Cynthia dear.

  Simon: Yes, I haven't seen Felicity since—

 Felicity: Last night.

Cynthia: Indeed? Well, you deal, Felicity. Simon, the sofa. Will
you partner Felicity, Magnus, against Simon and me?

Magnus: (*Aside.*) Will Simon and you always be partnered against
me, Cynthia?

Cynthia: What do you mean, Magnus?

Magnus: You are a damned attractive woman, Cynthia.

Cynthia: Please! Please! Remember Albert!

Magnus: Albert's dead, Cynthia—and you are still young. I'm
sure he would have wished that you and I—

Cynthia: No, Magnus, this is not to be!

Magnus: It's Gascoyne, isn't it? I'll kill him if he comes between
us.

Cynthia: (*Calling.*) Simon! (*The sofa is shoved towards the card table,
once more revealing the corpse, though not to the players.*)

Birdboot: Simon's going to get it.

Cynthia: Right! Who starts?

Magnus: I do. No bid. (*They start playing, putting down and picking
up cards.*)

Cynthia: Did I hear you say you saw Felicity last night, Simon?

  Simon: Did I?— Ah yes, yes quite—your turn, Felicity.

 Felicity: I've had my turn, haven't I, Simon?—now, it seems, it's
Cynthia's turn.

Cynthia: That's my trick, Felicity dear.

 Felicity: Hell hath no fury like a woman scorned, Simon.

  Simon: Yes, I've heard it said.

 Felicity: So I hope you have not been cheating, Simon.

  Simon: (*Standing up and throwing down his cards.*) No, Felicity, it's
just that I hold the cards!

Cynthia: Well done, Simon! (*Magnus deals.*)

 Felicity: Strange how Simon appeared in the neighbourhood
from nowhere. We know so little about him.

  Simon: It doesn't always pay to show your hand!

Cynthia: Right! Simon, it's your opening on the minor bid.
(*Simon* plays.)

Cynthia: Hm, let's see. . . . *(Plays.)*

Felicity: I hear there's a dangerous madman on the loose.

Cynthia: Simon?

Simon: Yes—yes—sorry. *(Plays.)*

Cynthia: I meld.

Felicity: Yes—personally, I think he's been hiding out in the deserted cottage on the cliffs. *(Plays.)*

Simon: Flush!

Cynthia: No! Simon—your luck's in tonight!

Felicity: We shall see—the night is not over yet, Simon Gascoyne! *(She exits.)*

Simon: *(To* Magnus.) So you're the crippled half-brother of Lord Muldoon who turned up out of the blue from Canada just the other day, are you? It's taken you a long time to get here. What did you do—walk? Oh, I say, I'm most frightfully sorry!

Magnus: Care for a spin round the rose garden, Cynthia?

Cynthia: No, Magnus, I must talk to Simon.

Simon: My round, I think, Major.

Magnus: You think so?

Simon: Yes, Major—I do.

Magnus: There's an old Canadian proverb handed down from the Blackfoot Indians, which says: He who laughs last laughs longest.

Simon: Yes, I've heard it said.

Cynthia: *(Calling.)* Simon!

Magnus: Well, I think I'll go and oil my gun. *(He exits.)*

Cynthia: I think Magnus suspects something. And Felicity . . . Simon, was there anything between you and Felicity?

Simon: No, no—it's over between her and me, Cynthia—it was a mere passing fleeting thing we had—but now that I have found you—

Cynthia: If I find that you have been untrue to me—if I find that you have falsely seduced me from my dear husband Albert—I will kill you, Simon Gascoyne! (Mrs. Drudge *has entered silently to witness this. On this tableau, pregnant with significance, the act ends, the body still undiscovered. Perfunctory applause.* Moon *and* Birdboot *seem to be completely preoccupied, becoming audible, as it were.)*

Moon: Camps it around the Old Vic in his opera cloak and passes me the tat.

Birdboot: Do you believe in love at first sight?

Moon: It's not that I think I'm a better critic—

Birdboot: I feel my whole life changing—

Moon: I am but it's not that.

Birdboot: Oh, the world will laugh at me, I know . . .

Moon: It is not that they are much in the way of shoes to step into . . .

Birdboot: . . . call me an infatuated old fool . . .

Moon: . . . They are not.

Birdboot: . . . condemn me . . .

Moon: He is standing in my light, that is all.

Birdboot: . . . betrayer of my class . . .

Moon: . . . an almost continuous eclipse, interrupted by the phenomenon of moonlight.

Birdboot: I don't care, I'm a goner.

Moon: And I dream . . .

Birdboot: The Blue Angel all over again.

Moon: . . . of the day his temperature climbs through the top of his head . . .

Birdboot: Ah, the sweet madness of love . . .

Moon: . . . of the spasm on the stairs . . .

Birdboot: Myrtle, farewell . . .

Moon: . . . dreaming of the stair he'll never reach—

Birdboot: —for I only live but once . . .

Moon: Sometimes I dream that I've killed him.

Birdboot: What?

Moon: What? *(They pull themselves together.)*

Birdboot: Yes . . . yes . . . A beautiful performance, a collector's piece. I shall say so.

Moon: A very promising debut. I'll put in a good word.

Birdboot: It would be as hypocritical of me to withhold praise on grounds of personal feelings, as to withhold censure.

Moon: You're right. Courageous.

Birdboot: Oh, I know what people will say— There goes Birdboot buttering up his latest—

Moon: Ignore them—

Birdboot: But I rise above that— The fact is I genuinely believe her performance to be one of the summits in the range of contemporary theatre.

Moon: Trim-buttocked, that's the word for her.

Birdboot: —the radiance, the inner sadness—

Moon: Does she actually come across with it?

Birdboot: The part as written is a mere cypher but she manages to make Cynthia a real person—

Moon: *Cynthia?*

Birdboot: And should she, as a result, care to meet me over a drink, simply by way of er—thanking me, as it were—

Moon: Well, you fickle old bastard!

Birdboot: *(Aggressively.)* Are you suggesting . . . ? *(He shudders to a halt and clears his throat.)* Well now—shaping up quite nicely, wouldn't you say?

Moon: Oh yes, yes. A nice trichotomy of forces. One must reserve judgement of course, until the confrontation, but I think it's pretty clear where we're heading.

Tom Stoppard   1901

Birdboot: I agree. It's Magnus a mile off. *(Small pause.)*

Moon: What's Magnus a mile off?

Birdboot: If we knew that we wouldn't be here.

Moon: *(Clears throat.)* Let me at once say that it has *élan* while at the same time avoiding *éclat*. Having said that, and I think it must be said, I am bound to ask—does this play know where it is going?

Birdboot: Well, it seems open and shut to me, Moon—Magnus is not what he pretends to be and he's got his next victim marked down—

Moon: Does it, I repeat, declare its affiliations? There are moments, and I would not begrudge it this, when the play, if we can call it that, and I think on balance we can, aligns itself uncompromisingly on the side of life. *Je suis,* it seems to be saying, *ergo sum.*[2] But is that enough? I think we are entitled to ask. For what in fact is this play concerned with? It is my belief that here we are concerned with what I have referred to elsewhere as the nature of identity. I think we are entitled to ask—and here one is irresistibly reminded of Voltaire's cry, *"Voilà"*—I think we are entitled to ask—*Where is God?*

Birdboot: *(Stunned.)* Who?

Moon: Go-od.

Birdboot: *(Peeping furtively into his programme.)* God?

Moon: I think we are entitled to ask. *(The phone rings. The set re-illumines to reveal* Cynthia, Felicity *and* Magnus *about to take coffee, which is being taken round by* Mrs. Drudge. Simon *is missing. The body lies in position.)*

Mrs. Drudge: *(Into phone.)* The same, later that evening . . . No, I'm sorry—there's no one of that name here. *(She replaces phone and goes round with coffee. To* Cynthia.*)* Black or white, my lady?

Cynthia: White please. *(*Mrs. Drudge *pours.)*

Mrs. Drudge: *(To* Felicity.*)* Black or white, miss?

Felicity: White please. *(*Mrs. Drudge *pours.)*

Mrs. Drudge: *(To* Magnus.*)* Black or white, Major?

Magnus: White please. *(Ditto.)*

Mrs. Drudge: *(To* Cynthia.*)* Sugar, my lady?

Cynthia: Yes please. *(Puts sugar in.)*

Mrs. Drudge: *(To* Felicity.*)* Sugar, miss?

Felicity: Yes please. *(Ditto.)*

Mrs. Drudge: *(To* Magnus.*)* Sugar, Major?

Magnus: Yes please. *(Ditto.* Mrs. Drudge *leaves, and reappears with a plate of biscuits.)*

---

2. *Je suis . . . ergo sum:* "I am" (French), "therefore I am" (Latin). Moon is echoing René Descartes' *Cogito, ergo sum,* "I think, therefore I am."

Mrs. Drudge: (*To* Cynthia.) Biscuit, my lady?

Cynthia: No thank you.

Birdboot: (*Writing elaborately in his notebook.*) The second act, however, fails to fulfill the promise . . .

Felicity: If you ask me, there's something funny going on. (Mrs. Drudge's *approach to* Felicity *makes* Felicity *jump to her feet in impatience. She goes to the radio while* Magnus *declines his biscuit, and* Mrs. Drudge *leaves.*)

Radio: We interrupt our programme for a special police message. The search for the dangerous madman who is on the loose in Essex has now narrowed to the immediate vicinity of Muldoon Manor. Police are hampered by the deadly swamps and the fog, but believe that the madman spent last night in a deserted cottage on the cliffs. The public is advised to stick together and make sure none of their number is missing. That is the end of the police message. (Felicity *turns off the radio nervously. Pause.*)

Cynthia: Where's Simon?

Felicity: Who?

Cynthia: Simon. Have you seen him?

Felicity: No.

Cynthia: Have you, Magnus?

Magnus: No.

Cynthia: Oh.

Felicity: Yes, there's something foreboding in the air, it is as if one of *us*—

Cynthia: Oh, Felicity, the house is locked up tight—no one can get in—and the police are practically on the doorstep.

Felicity: I don't know—it's just a feeling.

Cynthia: It's only the fog.

Magnus: Hound will never get through on a day like this—

Cynthia: (*Shouting at him.*) Fog!

Felicity: He means the Inspector.

Cynthia: Is he bringing a dog?

Felicity: Not that I know of.

Magnus: —never get through the swamps. Yes, I'm afraid the madman can show his hand in safety now. (*A mournful baying, hooting is heard in the distance, scary.*)

Cynthia: What's that?!

Felicity: (*Tensely.*) It sounded like a cry of a gigantic hound!

Magnus: Poor devil!

Cynthia: Ssssh! (*They listen. The sound is repeated, nearer.*)

Felicity: There it is again!

Cynthia: It's coming this way—it's right outside the house! (Mrs. Drudge *enters.*)

Mrs. Drudge: Inspector Hound! (*Enter* Inspector Hound. *On his feet*

*are his swamp boots. These are two inflatable—and inflated—pon-
toons with flat bottoms about two feet across. He carries a foghorn.)*

Hound: Lady Muldoon?

Cynthia: Yes.

Hound: I came as soon as I could. Where shall I put my foghorn
and my swamp boots?

Cynthia: Mrs. Drudge will take them out. Be prepared, as the
Force's motto has it, eh, Inspector? How very resourceful!

Hound: *(Divesting himself of boots and foghorn.)* It takes more than
a bit of weather to keep a policeman from his duty. *(Mrs.
Drudge leaves with chattels. A pause.)*

Cynthia: Oh—er, Inspector Hound—Felicity Cunningham,
Major Magnus Muldoon.

Hound: Good evening. *(He and* Cynthia *continue to look expectantly
at each other.)*

Cynthia and Hound: *(Together.)* Well? Sorry—

Cynthia and Hound: *(Together.)* Well?

Cynthia: No, do go on.

Hound: Thank you. Well, tell me about it in your own words—
take your time, begin at the beginning and don't leave anything out.

Cynthia: I beg your pardon?

Hound: Fear nothing. You are in safe hands now. I hope you
haven't touched anything.

Cynthia: I'm afraid I don't understand.

Hound: I'm Inspector Hound.

Cynthia: Yes.

Hound: Well, what's it all about?

Cynthia: I really have no idea.

Hound: How did it begin?

Cynthia: What?

Hound: The . . . thing.

Cynthia: What thing?

Hound: *(Rapidly losing confidence but exasperated.)* The trouble!

Cynthia: There hasn't *been* any trouble!

Hound: Didn't you phone the police?

Cynthia: No.

Felicity: I didn't.

Magnus: What for?

Hound: I see. *(Pause.)* This puts me in a very difficult position.
(A steady pause.) Well, I'll be getting along, then. *(He moves
towards the door.)*

Cynthia: I'm terribly sorry.

Hound: *(Stiffly.)* That's perfectly all right.

Cynthia: Thank you so much for coming.

Hound: Not at all. You never know, there might have been a seri-
ous matter.
Cynthia: Drink?
Hound: More serious than that, even.
Cynthia: *(Correcting.)* Drink before you go?
Hound: No thank you. *(Leaves.)*
Cynthia: *(Through the door.)* I do hope you find him.
Hound: *(Reappearing at once.)* Find who, Madam?—out with it!
Cynthia: I thought you were looking for a lunatic.
Hound: And what do you know about that?
Cynthia: It was on the radio.
Hound: Was it, indeed? Well, that's what I'm here about, really. I
didn't want to mention it because I didn't know how much
you knew. No point in causing unnecessary panic, even with a
murderer in our midst.
Felicity: Murderer, did you say?
Hound: Ah—so that was not on the radio?
Cynthia: Whom has he murdered, Inspector?
Hound: Perhaps no one—yet. Let us hope we are in time.
Magnus: You believe he is in our midst, Inspector?
Hound: I do. If anyone of you have recently encountered a
youngish good-looking fellow in a smart suit, white shirt, hat-
less, well-spoken—someone possibly claiming to have just
moved into the neighbourhood, someone who on the surface
seems as sane as you or I, then now is the time to speak!
Felicity: . . . I . . .
Hound: Don't interrupt!
Felicity: Inspector . . .
Hound: Very well.
Cynthia: No. Felicity!
Hound: Please, Lady Cynthia, we are all in this together. I must
ask you to put yourself completely in my hands.
Cynthia: I can't, Inspector. I love Albert.
Hound: I don't think you quite grasp my meaning.
Magnus: Is one of us in danger, Inspector?
Hound: Didn't it strike you as odd that on his escape the madman
made a beeline for Muldoon Manor? It is my guess that he
bears a deep-seated grudge against someone in this very
house! Lady Muldoon—where is your husband?
Cynthia: My husband?—you don't mean—?
Hound: I don't know—but I have a reason to believe that one of
you is the real McCoy!
Felicity: The real what?
Hound: William Herbert McCoy who as a young man, meeting
the madman in the street and being solicited for sixpence for

a cup of tea, replied, "Why don't you do a decent day's work, you shifty old bag of horse manure," in Canada all those many years ago. *(He starts to pace intensely.)* Our madman was a mere boy at the time but he never forgot that insult, and thenceforth carried in his heart the promise of revenge! *(At which point he finds himself standing on top of the corpse. He looks down carefully.)* Is there anything you have forgotten to tell me? *(They all see the corpse for the first time.)*

Felicity: So the madman has struck!

Cynthia: Oh—it's horrible—horrible—

Hound: Yes, just as I feared. Now you see the sort of man you are protecting.

Cynthia: I can't believe it!

Felicity: I'll have to tell him, Cynthia—Inspector, a stranger of that description has indeed appeared in our midst—Simon Gascoyne. Oh, he had charm, I'll give you that, and he took me in completely. I'm afraid I made a fool of myself over him, and so did Cynthia.

Hound: Where is he now?

Magnus: He must be around the house—he couldn't get away in these conditions.

Hound: You're right. Fear naught, Lady Muldoon—I shall apprehend the man who killed your husband.

Cynthia: My husband? I don't understand.

Hound: Everything points to Gascoyne.

Cynthia: But who's that? *(The corpse.)*

Hound: Your husband.

Cynthia: No, it's not.

Hound: Yes, it is.

Cynthia: I tell you it's not.

Hound: Are you sure?

Cynthia: For goodness sake!

Hound: Then who is it?

Cynthia: I don't know.

Hound: Anybody?

Felicity: I've never seen him before.

Magnus: Quite unlike anybody I've ever met.

Hound: I seem to have made a dreadful mistake. Lady Muldoon, I do apologize.

Cynthia: But what are we going to do?

Hound: *(Snatching the phone.)* I'll phone the police!

Cynthia: But you are the police!

Hound: Thank God I'm here—the lines have been cut!

Cynthia: You mean—?

Hound: Yes!—we're on our own, cut off from the world and in grave danger!

Felicity: You mean—?

Hound: Yes!—I think the killer will strike again!

Magnus: You mean—?

Hound: Yes! One of us ordinary mortals thrown together by fate and cut off by the elements, is the murderer! He must be found—search the house! *(All depart speedily in different directions leaving a momentarily empty stage.* Simon *strolls on.)*

Simon: *(Entering, calling.)* Anyone about?—funny . . . *(He notices the corpse and is surprised. He approaches it and turns it over. He stands up and looks about in alarm.)*

Birdboot: This is where Simon gets it. *(There is a shot.* Simon *falls dead.* Inspector Hound *runs on and crouches down by* Simon's *body.* Cynthia *appears at the French windows. She stops there and stares.)*

Cynthia: What happened, Inspector?! *(*Hound *turns to face her.)*

Hound: He's dead . . . Simon Gascoyne, I presume. Rough justice even for a killer—unless—unless— *(He looks thoughtfully at the sofa and the corpse.)* We assumed that the body could not have been lying there before Simon Gascoyne entered the house . . . but . . . *(He slides the sofa over the body.)* there's your answer. And now—who killed Simon Gascoyne? And why? *("Curtain," Freeze, Applause, Exeunt.)*

Moon: Why not?

Birdboot: Exactly. Good riddance.

Moon: Yes, getting away with murder must be quite easy provided that one's motive is sufficiently inscrutable.

Birdboot: Fickle young pup! He was deceiving her right, left and centre.

Moon: *(Thoughtfully.)* Of course, I'd still have Puckeridge behind *me* . . .

Birdboot: She needs someone steadier, more mature . . .

Moon: . . . And if I could, so could he . . .

Birdboot: Yes, I know of this rather nice hotel, very discreet, run by a man of the world. . . .

Moon: Uneasy lies the head that wears the crown.

Birdboot: Breakfast served in one's room and no questions asked.

Moon: Does Puckeridge dream of me?

Birdboot: *(Pause.)* Hello—what's happened?

Moon: What? Oh yes—what do you make of it, so far?

Birdboot: *(Clears throat.)* It is at this point that the play, for me, comes alive. The groundwork has been well and truly laid, and the author has taken the trouble to learn from the masters of the genre. He has created a real situation, and few will doubt his ability to resolve it with a startling dénouement. Certainly that is what it so far lacks, but it has a beginning, a middle and I have no doubt it will prove to have an end. For

Tom Stoppard   1907

this let us give thanks, and double thanks for a good clean show without a trace of smut. But perhaps even all this would be for nothing were it not for a performance which I consider to be one of the summits in the range of contemporary theatre. In what is possibly the finest Cynthia since the war—

Moon: If we examine this more closely, and I think close examination is the least tribute that this play deserves, I think we will find that within the austere framework of what is seen to be on one level a country-house week-end, and what a useful symbol that is, the author has given us—yes, I will go so far—he has given us the human condition—

Birdboot: More talent in her little finger—

Moon: An uncanny ear that might have belonged to a Van Gogh—

Birdboot: —a public scandal that the Queen has thus far neglected—

Moon: Faced as we are with such ubiquitous obliquity, it is hard, it is hard indeed, and therefore I will not attempt, to refrain from invoking the names of Kafka, Sartre, Shakespeare, St. Paul, Beckett, Birkett, Pinero, Pirandello, Dante and Dorothy L. Sayers.

Birdboot: A rattling good evening out. I was held.

(The phone starts to ring on the empty stage. Moon tries to ignore it.)

Moon: Harder still—Harder still if possible—Harder still if it is possible to be—Neither do I find it easy—Dante and Dorothy L. Sayers. Harder still—(For Birdboot has lost patience and is bearing down on the ringing phone. He is frankly irritated. Moon watches him go. He looks round and smiles weakly, expiating himself.)

Birdboot: (Into phone.) Hello. . . . (Explosion.) Oh, for God's sake, Myrtle—I've told you never to phone me at work! (He is naturally embarrassed, looking about with surreptitious fury.) What? Last night? Good God, woman, this is hardly the time to—I took her to dinner simply by way of keeping au fait with the world of the paint and the motley—yes, I promise—Yes, I do —Yes, I said yes—and you are mine too, Myrtle—darling—I can't—(Whispers.) I'm not alone— (Up.) No, she's not!—(He looks around furtively, licks his lips and mumbles.) All right! I love your little pink ears and you are my own fluffy bunny-boo—Now for God's sake—Good-bye, Myrtle—(Puts down phone. Birdboot mops his brow with his handkerchief. As he turns, a tennis ball bounces in through the French windows, followed by Felicity, as before, in tennis outfit. The lighting is as it was. Everything is as it was. It is, let us say, the same moment of time.)

Felicity: (*Calling.*) Out! (*She catches sight of* Birdboot *and is amazed.*) You!

Birdboot: Er, yes—hello again.

Felicity: What are you doing here?!

Birdboot: Well, I . . .

Felicity: Honestly, darling, you really are extraordinary—

Birdboot: Yes, well, here I am. (*He looks round sheepishly.*)

Felicity: You must have been desperate to see me—I mean, I'm flattered, but couldn't it wait till I got back?

Birdboot: No, no, you've got it all wrong—

Felicity: What is it?

Birdboot: And about last night—perhaps I gave you the wrong impression—got carried away a bit, perhaps—

Felicity: (*Stiffly.*) What are you trying to say?

Birdboot: I want to call it off.

Felicity: I see.

Birdboot: I didn't promise anything—and the fact is, I have my reputation—people do talk—

Felicity: You don't have to say any more—

Birdboot: And my wife, too—I don't know how she got to hear of it, but—

Felicity: Of all the nerve!

Birdboot: I'm sorry you had to find out like this—the fact is I didn't mean it this way—

Felicity: You philandering coward!

Birdboot: I'm sorry—but I want you to know that I meant those things I said—oh yes—shows brilliant promise—I shall say so—

Felicity: I'll kill you for this, Simon Gascoyne! (*She leaves in tears, passing* Mrs. Drudge *who has entered in time to overhear her last remark.*)

Birdboot: (*Wide-eyed.*) Good God . . .

Mrs. Drudge: I have come to set up the card table, sir.

Birdboot: (*Wildly.*) I can't stay for a game of *cards!*

Mrs. Drudge: Oh, Lady Cynthia *will* be disappointed.

(Birdboot, *on his way back, pauses and turns.*)

Birdboot: You mean . . . you mean, she wants to meet me . . . ?

Mrs. Drudge: Oh yes, sir, I just told her and it put her in quite a tizzy.

Birdboot: Really? Yes, well, a man of my influence is not to be sneezed at—I think I have some small name for the making of reputations—mmm, yes, quite a tizzy, you say? (Mrs. Drudge *is busied with the card table.* Birdboot *stands marooned and bemused for a moment. She exits.*)

Moon: (*From his seat.*) Birdboot!—(*A tense whisper.*) —Birdboot! (Birdboot *looks round vaguely.*) What the hell are you doing?

Birdboot: Nothing.

Moon: Stop making an ass of yourself. Come back.

Birdboot: Oh, I know what you're thinking—but the fact is I genuinely consider her performance to be one of the summits—*(Cynthia enters as before, Mrs. Drudge has gone.)*

Cynthia: Darling!

Birdboot: Ah, good evening—may I say that I genuinely consider—

Cynthia: Don't say anything for a moment—just hold me. *(She falls into his arms.)*

Birdboot: All right!—let us throw off the hollow pretenses of the gimcrack codes we live by! Dear lady, from the first moment I saw you, I felt my whole life changing—

Cynthia: *(Breaking free.)* We can't go on meeting like this!

Birdboot: I am not ashamed to proclaim nightly my love for you!—but fortunately that will not be necessary—I know of a very good hotel, discreet—run by a man of the world—

Cynthia: But darling, this is madness!

Birdboot: Yes! I am mad with love.

Cynthia: Please!—remember where we are!

Birdboot: I don't care! Let them think what they like, I love you!

Cynthia: Don't—I love Albert!

Birdboot: He's dead. *(Shaking her.)* Do you understand me—Albert's dead!

Cynthia: No—I'll never give up hope! Let me go! We are not free!

Birdboot: You mean Myrtle? She means nothing to me—nothing!—she's all cocoa and blue nylon fur slippers—not a spark of creative genius in her whole slumping knee-length-knickered body—

Cynthia: You're a cad, Simon! You will use me and cast me aside as you have cast aside so many others!

Birdboot: No, Cynthia—now that I have found you—

Cynthia: You're ruthless—so strong—so cruel— *(Birdboot seizes her in an embrace, during which Mrs. Drudge enters, and Moon's fevered voice is heard.)*

Moon: Have you taken leave of your tiny mind? *(Cynthia breaks free.)*

Cynthia: Stop—can't you see you're making a fool of yourself!

Moon: She's right.

Birdboot: *(To Moon.)* You keep out of this.

Cynthia: Yes, what is it, Mrs. Drudge?

Mrs. Drudge: Should I close the windows, my lady? The fog—

Cynthia: Yes, you'd better.

Moon: Look, they've got your number—

Birdboot: I'll leave in my own time, thank you very much.

Moon: It's the finish of you, I suppose you know that—

Birdboot: I don't need your twopenny Grub Street prognostica-
   tions—I have found something bigger and finer—
   Moon: (*Bemused, to himself.*) If only it were Higgs . . .
Cynthia: . . . And fetch the Major down.
Mrs. Drudge: I think I hear him coming downstairs now. (*She leaves.
   The sound of a wheelchair's approach as before.* Birdboot *pru-
   dently keeps out of the chair's former path but it enters from the next
   wing down and knocks him flying. A babble of anguish and
   protestation.*)
Cynthia: Simon—say something!
Birdboot: That reckless bastard. (*As he sits up.*)
Cynthia: Thank God!—
Magnus: What's *he* doing here?
Cynthia: He just turned up.
Magnus: Really? How do you like it here?
Birdboot: I couldn't take it night after night. (*Felicity enters.*)
Felicity: So—you're still here.
Cynthia: Of course he's still here. We're going to play cards.
   There is no need to introduce you two, is there, for I recall
   now that you, Simon, met me through Felicity, our mutual
   friend.
Felicity: Yes, Simon is an old friend . . .
Birdboot: Ah—yes—well I like to give young up-and-comers the
   benefit of my—er—of course, she lacks technique as yet—
Felicity: Last night.
Birdboot: I'm not talking about last night!
Cynthia: Indeed? Well, you deal, Felicity. Simon, the sofa. (*Cyn-
   thia and* Magnus *confer as in the earlier scene.*)
Birdboot: (*To* Moon.) Did you see that? Tried to kill me. I told you
   it was Magnus—not that it *is* Magnus.
   Moon: Who did it, you mean?
Birdboot: What?
   Moon: You think it's not Magnus who did it?
Birdboot: Get a grip on yourself, Moon—the facts are staring you
   in the face. He's after Cynthia for one thing.
Magnus: It's Gascoyne, isn't it?
Birdboot: Over my dead body!
Magnus: If he comes between us . . .
   Moon: (*Angrily.*) For God's sake sit down!
Cynthia: Simon!
Birdboot: She needs me, Moon. I've got to make up a four. (*Cyn-
   thia and* Birdboot *move the sofa as before, and they all sit at table.*)
Cynthia: Right! Who starts?
Magnus: I do. I'll dummy for a no-bid ruff and double holding on
   South's queen. (*While he moves cards.*)
Cynthia: Did I hear you say you saw Felicity last night, Simon?

Birdboot: Er—er—

Felicity: Pay twenty-ones or trump my contract. *(Discards.)* Cynthia's turn.

Cynthia: I'll trump your contract with five dummy no-trumps there *(Discards.)* and I'll move West's rook for the re-bid with a banker ruff on his second trick there. *(Discards.)* Simon?

Birdboot: Would you mind doing that again?

Cynthia: And I'll ruff your dummy with five no-bid trumps there *(Discards.)* and I support your re-bid with a banker for the solo ruff in the dummy trick there. *(Discards.)*

Birdboot: *(Standing up and throwing down his cards.)* And I call your bluff!

Cynthia: Well done, Simon! *(Magnus deals.)*

Felicity: Strange how Simon appeared in the neighbourhood from nowhere, we know so little about him.

Cynthia: Right Simon, it's your opening on the minor bid. Hmm. Let's see. I think I'll overbid the spade convention with two no trumps and King's gambit offered there— *(Discards.)* and West's dummy split double to Queen's Bishop 4 there!

Magnus: *(As he plays cards.)* Faites vos jeux. Rien ne va plus. Rouge et noir. Zéro.[1]

Cynthia: Simon?

Birdboot: *(Triumphant, leaping to his feet.)* And I call your bluff!

Cynthia: *(Imperturbably.)* I meld. *(Birdboot sits.)*

Felicity: I huff.

Magnus: I ruff.

Birdboot: I bluff.

Cynthia: Twist.

Felicity: Bust.

Magnus: Check.

Birdboot: Snap.

Cynthia: How's that?

Felicity: Not out.

Magnus: Double top.

Birdboot: Bingo! *(Climax.)*

Cynthia: No! Simon—your luck's in tonight.

Felicity: We shall see—the night is not over yet, Simon Gascoyne! *(She exits quickly.)*

Birdboot: *(Looking after* Felicity.*)* Red herring—smell it a mile off. *(To* Magnus.*)* Oh yes, she's as clean as a whistle, I've seen it a thousand times. And I've seen you before too, haven't I? Strange—there's something about you . . .

Magnus: Care for a spin round the rose garden, Cynthia?

————

1. Place your bets. Red and black. zero. (French)

Cynthia: No Magnus, I must talk to Simon.

Birdboot: There's nothing for you there, you know.

Magnus: You think so?

Birdboot: Oh yes, she knows which side her bread is buttered. I am a man not without a certain influence among those who would reap the limelight—she's not going to throw me over for a heavily disguised cripple.

Magnus: There's an old Canadian proverb—

Birdboot: Don't give me that—I tumbled to you right from the start—oh yes, you chaps are not as clever as you think. . . . Sooner or later you make your mistake. . . . Incidentally, where was it I saw you? . . . I've definitely. . . .

Cynthia: *(Calling.)* Simon!

Magnus: *(Leaving.)* Well, I think I'll go and oil my gun. *(Exit.)*

Birdboot: *(After* Magnus.*)* Double bluff!— *(To* Cynthia.*)* I've seen it a thousand times.

Cynthia: I think Magnus suspects something. And Felicity . . . Simon, was there anything between you and Felicity?

Birdboot: No, no—that's all over now. I merely flattered her a little over a drink, told her she'd go far, that sort of thing. Dear me, the fuss that's been made over a simple flirtation—

Cynthia: *(As* Mrs. Drudge *enters behind.)* If I find you have falsely seduced me from my dear husband Albert, I will kill you, Simon Gascoyne! *(The "Curtain" as before.* Mrs. Drudge *and* Cynthia *leave.* Birdboot *starts to follow them.)*

Moon: Birdboot! *(*Birdboot *stops.)*

Moon: For God's sake pull yourself together.

Birdboot: I can't help it.

Moon: What do you think you're doing? You're turning it into a complete farce!

Birdboot: I know, I know—but I can't live without her. *(He is making erratic neurotic journeys about the stage.)* I shall resign my position, of course. I don't care, I'm a goner, I tell you— *(He has arrived at the body. He looks at it in surprise, hesitates, bends and turns it over.)*

Moon: Birdboot, think of your family, your friends—your high standing in the world of letters—I say, what are you doing? *(*Birdboot *is staring at the body's face.)* Birdboot . . . leave it alone. Come and sit down—what's the matter with you?

Birdboot: *(Dead-voiced.)* It's Higgs.

Moon: What?

Birdboot: It's Higgs. *(Pause.)*

Moon: Don't be silly.

Birdboot: I tell you it's Higgs! *(*Moon *half-rises. Bewildered.)* I don't understand . . . He's dead.

Moon: Dead?

Birdboot: Who would want to . . .

Moon: He must have been lying there all the time. . . .

Birdboot: . . . kill Higgs?

Moon: But what's he doing here? I was standing in tonight. . . .

Birdboot: (*Turning.*) Moon? . . .

Moon: (*In wonder, quietly.*) So it's me and Puckeridge now.

Birdboot: Moon . . . ?

Moon: (*Faltering.*) But I swear I . . .

Birdboot: I've got it—

Birdboot: (*Quietly.*) My God . . . so that was it. . . . (*Up.*) Moon—
now I see—

Moon: —I swear I didn't—

Birdboot: Now—finally—I see it all— (*There is a shot and* Birdboot
falls dead.)

Moon: Birdboot! (*He runs on, to* Birdboot's *body.* Cynthia
appears at the French windows. She stops and stares. All as before.)

Cynthia: Oh my God—what happened, Inspector?

Moon: (*Almost to himself.*) He's dead. . . . (*He rises.*) That's a bit
rough, isn't it?—a bit extreme!— He may have had his faults
—I admit he was a fickle old . . . Who did this, and why?
(Moon *turns to face her. He stands up and makes swiftly for his
seat. Before he gets there he is stopped by the sound of voices.* Simon
and Hound *are occupying the critics' seats.* Moon *freezes.*)

Simon: To say that it is without pace, point, focus, interest,
drama, wit or originality is to say simply that it does not happen to be my cup of tea.

Hound: I'm sorry to be blunt but there is no getting away from it.
It lacks pace. A complete ragbag.

Simon: Hysteria is no substitute for *éclat*.

Hound: It lacks *élan*.

Simon: Some of the cast seem to have given up acting altogether.

Hound: I am not a prude but I fail to see any reason for the
shower of filth and sexual allusion foisted onto an unsuspected public in the guise of modernity at all costs. . . .
(*Behind* Moon, Felicity, Magnus *and* Mrs. Drudge *have made
their entrances, so that he turns to face their semicircle.*)

Magnus: (*Pointing to* Birdboot's *body.*) Well, Inspector, is this your
man?

Moon: (*Warily.*) . . . Yes. . . . Yes. . . .

Cynthia: It's Simon . . .

Moon: Yes . . . yes . . . poor. . . . (*Up.*) Is this some kind of a
joke?

Magnus: If it is, Inspector, it's in very poor taste.

(Moon *pulls himself together and becomes galvanic, a little wild, in grief for*
Birdboot.)

Moon: All right! I'm going to find out who did this! I want everyone to go to the positions they occupied when the shot was
fired— *(They move; hysterically.)* No one will leave the room!
(They move back.)

Magnus: I think we all had the opportunity to fire the shot,
Inspector—

Moon: *(Furious.)* I am not—

Magnus: —but which of us would want to?

Moon: Perhaps you, Major Magnus!

Magnus: Why should I want to kill him?

Moon: Because he was on to you—yes, he tumbled you right
from the start—and you shot him just when he was about to
reveal that you killed— *(Moon points, pauses and then crosses to*
Higgs' *body and falters.)* —killed— *(He turns* Higgs *over.)* . . .
this . . . chap.

Magnus: But what motive would there be for killing him? *(Pause.)*
Who *is* this chap? *(Pause.)* Inspector?

Moon: *(Rising.)* I don't know. Quite unlike anyone I've ever
met. *(Long pause.)* Well . . . now . . .

Mrs. Drudge: Inspector?

Moon: *(Eagerly.)* Yes? Yes, what is it, dear lady?

Mrs. Drudge: Happening to enter this room earlier in the day to close
the windows, I chanced to overhear a remark made by the
deceased Simon Gascoyne to her ladyship, viz., "I will kill anyone who comes between us."

Moon: Ah—yes—well, that's it, then. This . . . chap . . . *(Pointing to* Birdboot's *body.)* er . . . *(The moment of* Moon's *betrayal,
for which he is to pay with his life.)* . . . by *(Pause.)* Simon.

Cynthia: But he didn't come between us!

Magnus: And who, then, killed Simon?

Mrs. Drudge: Subsequent to that reported remark, I also happened to
be in earshot of a remark made by Lady Muldoon to the
deceased, to the effect, "I will kill you, Simon Gascoyne!" I
hope you don't mind my mentioning it.

Moon: Not at all. I'm glad you did. It is from these chance
remarks that we in the Force build up our complete picture
before moving in to make the arrest. It will not be long now, I
fancy, and I must warn you, Lady Muldoon, that anything you
say—

Cynthia: Yes!—I hated Simon Gascoyne, for he had me in his
thrall!— But I didn't kill him!

Mrs. Drudge: Prior to that, Inspector, I also chanced to overhear a
remark made by Miss Cunningham, no doubt in the heat of
the moment, but it stuck in my mind as these things do, viz., "I
will kill you for this, Simon Gascoyne!"

Moon: Ah! The final piece of the jigsaw! I think I am now in a position to reveal the mystery. This man *(The corpse.)* was, of course, McCoy, the Canadian who, as we heard, meeting Gascoyne in the street and being solicited for sixpence for a toffee apple, smacked him across the ear, with the cry, "How's that for a grudge to harbour, you sniffling little workshy!" all those many years ago. Gascoyne bided his time, but in due course tracked McCoy down to this house, having, on the way, met, in the neighbourhood, a simple ambitious girl from the provinces. He was charming, persuasive—told her, I have no doubt, that she would go straight to the top—and she, flattered by his sophistication, taken in by his promises to see her all right on the night, gave in to his simple desires. Perhaps she loved him. We shall never know. But in the very hour of her promised triumph, his eye fell on another—yes, I refer to Lady Cynthia Muldoon. From the moment he caught sight of her there was no other woman for him—he was in her spell, willing to sacrifice anything, even you, Felicity Cunningham. It was only today—unexpectedly finding him here—that you learned the truth. There was a bitter argument which ended with your promise to kill him—a promise that you carried out in this very room at your first opportunity! And I must warn you that anything you say—

Felicity: But it doesn't make sense!

Moon: Not at first glance, *perhaps.*

Magnus: Could not McCoy have been killed by the same person who killed Simon?

Felicity: But why should any of us want to kill a perfect stranger?

Magnus: Perhaps he was not a stranger to *one* of us.

Moon: *(Faltering.)* But Simon was the madman, wasn't he?

Magnus: We only have your word for that, Inspector. We only have your word for a lot of things. For instance—McCoy. Who is he? Is his name McCoy? Is there any truth in that fantastic and implausible tale of the insult inflicted in the Canadian streets? Or is there something else, something quite unknown to us, behind all this? Suppose for a moment that the madman, having killed this unknown stranger for private and inscrutable reasons of his own, was disturbed before he could dispose of the body, so having cut the telephone wires he decided to return to the scene of the crime, masquerading as—Police Inspector Hound!

Moon: But . . . I'm not mad . . . I'm almost sure I'm not mad . . .

Magnus: . . . only to discover that in the house was a man, Simon Gascoyne, who recognized the corpse as a man against whom you had held a deep-seated grudge—!

Moon: But I didn't kill—I'm almost sure I—

Magnus: I put it to you!—are you the real Inspector Hound?!

Moon: You know damn well I'm not! What's it all about?

Magnus: I thought as much.

Moon: I only dreamed . . . sometimes I dreamed—

Cynthia: So it was you!

Mrs. Drudge: The madman!

Felicity: The killer!

Cynthia: Oh, it's horrible, horrible.

Mrs. Drudge: The stranger in our midst!

Magnus: Yes, we had a shrewd suspicion he would turn up here—
and he walked into the trap!

Moon: What *trap?*

Magnus: I am not the real Magnus Muldoon— It was a mere subterfuge!—and *(Standing up and removing his moustaches.)* I
now reveal myself as—

Cynthia: You mean—?

Magnus: Yes! I am the real Inspector Hound!

Moon: *(Pause.)* Puckeridge!

Magnus: *(With pistol.)* Stand where you are, or I shoot!

Moon: *(Backing.)* Puckeridge! You killed Higgs—and Birdboot
tried to tell me—

Magnus: Stop in the name of the law! *(Moon turns to run. Magnus
fires. Moon drops to his knees.)* I have waited a long time for
this moment.

Cynthia: So you are the real Inspector Hound.

Magnus: Not only that!—I have been leading a double life—at
least!

Cynthia: You mean—?

Magnus: Yes!— It's been ten long years, but don't you know me?

Cynthia: You mean—?

Magnus: Yes!—it is I, Albert!—who lost his memory and joined
the Police Force, rising by merit to the rank of Inspector, his
past blotted out—until fate cast him back into the home he
left behind, back to the beautiful woman he had brought here
as his girlish bride—in short, my darling, my memory has
returned and your long wait is over!

Cynthia: Oh, Albert! *(They embrace.)*

Moon: *(With a trace of admiration.)* Puckeridge! . . . you cunning
bastard. *(He dies.)*

THE END

*Tom Stoppard has denied repeatedly that his plays are intended as vehicles
for the themes critics and scholars repeatedly find in them. In an interview*

with Louis Funke, he discussed his motives as a playwright and his reasons for avoiding the type of sociopolitical drama we might associate with Athol Fugard.

"Trying to make it explode at the end": Tom Stoppard

Funke: You have been compared in the reviews that I have been reading in regard to *The Real Inspector Hound* with Noel Coward. You know that that has been said? Do you feel that you reflect something of this time as Coward did of his time?

Stoppard: Coward reflected his time not out of any calculation. He had no ambition to do so, I'm sure. All he had was the beat of his personal drummer to march to, which is all that any of us has. With a bit of luck, it turns out that our particular drummer is shared by an awful lot of people. When that happens, a lot of people see one's play and say, "Yes, that is true." But there is no absolute truth. It is truth to them at a particular time in the way *Hay Fever* catches, I suppose, a certain spirit of its period. I wasn't around, but I imagine it does. I'm told it does, and it clearly does at this distance. I would not have thought that *The Inspector Hound* did that for 1968, myself. To me, it doesn't really radiate very much into the world outside the theatre, because its chief purpose and vindication, if anything, is pure structure.

Funke: Did you set out in any way to tease the critics?

Stoppard: Not in the least.

Funke: Not in the least?

Stoppard: Quite clearly, I was aware that I was parodying critics, but this simply because I had two critics on stage. It's rather more diverting to parody than do it straight. There's no particular interest in doing them straight. I was writing a comedy.

Funke: Well, you know that one critic—I don't remember which English critic it was—said that here again you were indicating that when you leave the ordered world and leap into the theatre, you leave all order behind, and you leap into chaos. This is a subtext that he read into it. This is not something that you had in mind, I presume.

Stoppard: No, but what I had in mind doesn't invalidate any subtext anybody reads into it. I am personally of the opinion that anything anybody reads into my work, or anybody else's, is absolutely valid since he is talking about his own reaction. Unless he is telling lies, it is valid. As far as I was concerned, I was trying to bring off a sort of puzzle structure made up of elements which I tried to make comic. In a way, looking back on it now, I suppose the basic situation might have lent something more explicit in the way of comment on life, but that wasn't what I was after. I was after constructing this magic box which unfolded and had insides which unfolded, and trying to make it explode at the end.

Funke: Do you consider that you, as a playwright, in your relationship to an audience, want to make that audience feel or think or do you want to teach them?

Stoppard: I just want them to have a good time and some people, as we discussed earlier, have a good time by watching a girl take off her clothes. I would not want the one group to be inflicted with the joys of the other. . . . If you are asking me a more intellectual question than the one I have answered, the answer would nevertheless be the same. Suppose that a playwright is facing the challenge of a society which can burn Vietnamese children. We're all facing that, and there's nothing a playwright can actually do about it in terms of writing plays in this particular sense. Don't misunderstand me. What I am saying is, as I said before, it is, to me, meaningless for a playwright to be asked what to ask himself, what challenge he ought to be facing or what he ought to be doing in his work, because if there is anything which I know about writing, it is that the instrument and the tuning fork are one and the same. He can't write to external griefs. He can only write about what moves him, and is the victim and beneficiary of his own mind. The challenge is negated. Somebody who rises self-consciously in a contrived way to the challenge of Viet Nam is going to write a bad play which removes the whole question from his career as a playwright. Then it is his career as a polemicist.

TINA HOWE

(b. 1937)

PAINTING CHURCHES

CHARACTERS

Fanny Sedgwick Church, a Bostonian from a fine old family,
  in her sixties
Gardner Church, her husband, an eminent New England
  poet from a finer family, in his seventies
Margaret Church (Mags), their daughter, a painter, in her
  early thirties

ACT I

Scene 1

Time: Several years ago.

Place: The living room of the Church's townhouse on
Beacon Hill one week before everything will be moved
to Cape Cod. Empty packing cartons line the room
and all the furniture has been tagged with brightly
colored markers. At first glance it looks like any
discreet Boston interior, but on closer scrutiny one
notices a certain flamboyance. Oddities from second-
hand stores are mixed in with the fine old furniture,
and exotic handmade curios vie with tasteful family
objets d'art. What makes the room remarkable,
though, is the play of light that pours through three
soaring arched windows. At one hour it's hard edged
and brilliant; the next, it's dappled and yielding. It
transforms whatever it touches, giving the room a
distinct feeling of unreality. It's several years ago, a
bright spring morning.

Fanny *is sitting on the sofa, wrapping a valuable old silver coffee service. She's
wearing a worn bathrobe and fashionable hat. As she works, she makes a list of everything on a yellow legal pad.* Gardner *can be heard typing in his study down the
hall.*

Fanny: [*She picks up a coffee pot.*] God, this is good-looking! I'd forgotten how handsome Mama's old silver was! It's probably
  worth a fortune. It certainly weighs enough! [*Calling out.*]

GARRRRRRRRRRRRRRRRDNERRRRRRRRRRR? . . . Well, it should bring us a pretty penny, that's for sure. *[Wraps it, places it in a carton, and then picks up the tray that goes with it. She holds it up like a mirror and adjusts her hat. Louder in another register.]* OH, GARRRRRRRRRRRRRRRRRDNERRRRR? . . .

[He continues typing.]

Fanny: *[She then reaches for a small box and opens it with reverence.]* I don't care how desperate things get, these will never go! One has to maintain some standards! *[She writes on her list.]* "Grandma's Paul Revere teaspoons, Cotuit!" . . . WASN'T IT THE AMERICAN WING OF THE METROPOLITAN MUSEUM OF ART THAT WANTED GRANDMA'S PAUL REVERE TEASPOONS SO BADLY? . . . *[She looks at her reflection in the tray again.]* This is a very good-looking hat, if I do say so. I was awfully smart to grab it up.

[Silence.]

DON'T YOU REMEMBER A DISTINGUISHED-LOOKING MAN COMING TO THE HOUSE AND OFFERING US FIFTY THOUSAND DOLLARS FOR GRANDMA'S PAUL REVERE TEASPOONS? . . . HE HAD ON THESE MARVELOUS SHOES! THEY WERE SO POINTED AT THE ENDS WE COULDN'T IMAGINE HOW HE EVER GOT THEM ON AND THEY WERE SHINED TO WITHIN AN INCH OF THEIR LIVES AND I REMEMBER HIM SAYING HE CAME FROM THE . . . AMERICAN WING OF THE METROPOLITAN MUSEUM OF ART! . . . HELLO? . . . GARDNER? . . . ARE YOU THERE!

[The typing stops.]

Fanny: YOO-HOOOOOOO . . . *[Like a foghorn.]* GARRRRRRRRRRRDNERRRRRRR? . . .
Gardner: *[Offstage; from his study.]* YES, DEAR . . . IS THAT YOU? . . .
Fanny: OF COURSE IT'S ME! WHO ELSE COULD IT POSSIBLY BE? . . . DARLING, PLEASE COME HERE FOR A MINUTE.

[The typing resumes.]

Fanny: FOR GOD'S SAKE, WILL YOU STOP THAT DREADFUL TYPING BEFORE YOU SEND ME STRAIGHT TO THE NUT HOUSE? . . . *[In a new register.]* GARRRRRRRRRRRRRRRD-NERRRRRR? . . .

[He stops.]

Gardner: *[Offstage.]* WHAT'S THAT? MAGS IS BACK FROM THE NUT HOUSE?

Fanny: I SAID . . . Lord, I hate this yelling. . . . PLEASE . . . COME . . . HERE!

[Brief silence.]

Gardner: [Offstage.] I'LL BE WITH YOU IN A MOMENT, I DIDN'T HEAR HER RING. [Starts singing.] "Nothing Could be Finer Than to be in Carolina."

Fanny: It's a wonder I'm not in a strait jacket already. Actually, it might be rather nice for a change . . . peaceful. DARLING . . . I WANT TO SHOW YOU MY NEW HAT!

[Silence.] Gardner enters, still singing. He's wearing mismatched tweeds and is holding a stack of papers which keep drifting to the floor.]

Gardner: Oh, don't you look nice! Very attractive, very attractive!

Fanny: But I'm still in my bathrobe.

Gardner: [Looking around the room, leaking more papers.] Well, where's Mags?

Fanny: Darling, you're dropping your papers all over the floor.

Gardner: [Spies the silver tray.] I remember this! Aunt Alice gave it to us, didn't she? [He picks it up.] Good Lord, it's heavy. What's it made of? Lead?!

Fanny: No, Aunt Alice did *not* give it to us. It was Mama's.

Gardner: Oh, yes . . .

[He starts to exit with it.]

Fanny: Could I have it back, please?

Gardner: [Hands it to her, dropping more papers.] Oh, sure thing. . . . Where's Mags? I thought you said she was here.

Fanny: I didn't say Mags was here, I asked *you* to come here.

Gardner: [Papers spilling.] Damned papers keep falling. . . .

Fanny: I wanted to show you my new hat. I bought it in honor of Mags' visit. Isn't it marvelous?

Gardner: [Picking up the papers as more drop.] Yes, yes, very nice . . .

Fanny: Gardner, you're not even looking at it!

Gardner: Very becoming . . .

Fanny: You don't think it's too bright, do you? I don't want to look like a traffic light. Guess how much it cost?

Gardner: [A whole sheaf of papers slides to the floor; he dives for them.] OH, SHIT!

Fanny: [Gets to them first.] It's all right, I've got them, I've got them. [She hands them to him.]

Gardner: You'd think they had wings on them. . . .

Fanny: Here you go . . . Gardner: . . . damned things won't hold still!

Fanny: Gar? . . .

Gardner: [Has become engrossed in one of the pages.] Mmmmm?

Fanny: HELLO?

Gardner: [*Startled.*] What's that?

Fanny: [*In a whisper.*] My hat. Guess how much it cost.

Gardner: Oh, yes. Let's see . . . ten dollars?

Fanny: Ten dollars . . . IS THAT ALL? . . .

Gardner: Twenty?

Fanny: GARDNER, THIS HAPPENS TO BE A DESIGNER HAT! DESIGNER HATS START AT FIFTY DOLLARS . . . SEVENTY-FIVE!

Gardner: [*Jumps.*] Was that the door bell?

Fanny: No, it wasn't the door bell. Though it's high time Mags were here. She was probably in a train wreck!

Gardner: [*Looking through his papers.*] I'm beginning to get fond of Wallace Stevens again.

Fanny: This damned move is going to kill me! Send me straight to my grave!

Gardner: [*Reading from a page.*]

"The mules that angels ride come slowly down

The blazing passes, from beyond the sun.

Descensions of their tinkling bells arrive.

These muleteers are dainty of their way . . ."

[*Pause.*] Don't you love that! "These muleteers are *dainty* of their way"!? . . .

Fanny: Gar, the hat. How much?

[*Gardner sighs.*]

Fanny: Darling? . . .

Gardner: Oh, yes. Let's see . . . fifty dollars? Seventy-five?

Fanny: It's French.

Gardner: Three hundred!

Fanny: [*Triumphant.*] No, eighty-five cents.

Gardner: Eighty-five cents! . . . I thought you said . . .

Fanny: That's right . . . eighty . . . five . . . *cents!*

Gardner: Well, you sure had me fooled!

Fanny: I found it at the thrift shop.

Gardner: I thought it cost at least fifty dollars or seventy-five. You know, designer hats are very expensive!

Fanny: It was on the mark-down table. [*She takes it off and shows him the label.*] See that? Lily Daché! When I saw that label, I nearly keeled over right into the fur coats!

Gardner: [*Handling it.*] Well, what do you know, that's the same label that's in my bathrobe.

Fanny: Darling, Lily Daché designed hats, not men's bathrobes!

Gardner: Yup . . . Lily Daché . . . same name . . .

Fanny: If you look again, I'm sure you'll see . . .

Gardner: . . . same script, same color, same size. I'll show you.

[He exits.]

    Fanny: Poor lamb can't keep anything straight anymore. *[Looks at herself in the tray again.]* God, this is a good-looking hat!

Gardner: [Returns with a nondescript plaid bathrobe. He points to the label.] See that? . . . What does it say?

    Fanny: [Refusing to look at it.] Lily Daché was a *hat* designer! She designed ladies' *hats!*

Gardner: What . . . does . . . it . . . say?

    Fanny: Gardner, you're being ridiculous.

Gardner: [Forcing it on her.] Read . . . the label!

    Fanny: Lily Daché did *not* design this bathrobe, I don't care what the label says!

Gardner: READ! *[Fanny reads it.]* ALL RIGHT, NOW WHAT DOES IT SAY? . . .

    Fanny: [Chagrined.] Lily Daché.

Gardner: I told you!

    Fanny: Wait a minute, let me look at that again. *[She does; then throws the robe at him in disgust.]* Gar, Lily Daché never designed a bathrobe in her life! Someone obviously ripped the label off one of her hats and then sewed it into the robe.

Gardner: [Puts it on over his jacket.] It's damned good-looking. I've always loved this robe. I think you gave it to me. . . . Well, I've got to get back to work.

[He abruptly exits.]

    Fanny: Where did you get that robe anyway? . . . I didn't give it to you, did I? . . .

[Silence. Gardner *resumes typing.]*

    Fanny: [Holding the tray up again and admiring herself.] You know, I think I *did* give it to him. I remember how excited I was when I found it at the thrift shop . . . fifty cents and never worn! *I* couldn't have sewn that label in to impress him, could I? . . . I can't be that far gone! . . . The poor lamb wouldn't even notice it, let alone understand its cachet. . . . Uuuuuuh, this damned tray is even heavier than the coffee pot. They must have been amazons in the old days! *[Writes on her pad.]* "Empire tray, Parke-Bernet Galleries," and good riddance! *[She wraps it and drops it into the carton with the coffee pot.]* Where *is* that wretched Mags? It would be just like her to get into a train wreck! She was supposed to be here hours ago. Well, if she doesn't show up soon, I'm going to drop dead of exhaustion. God, wouldn't that be wonderful? . . . Then they could just cart me off into storage with all the old chandeliers and china . . .

[The doorbell rings.]

Fanny: IT'S MAGS, IT'S MAGS! [A pause. Dashing out of the room, colliding into Gardner.] GOOD GOD, LOOK AT ME! I'M STILL IN MY BATHROBE!

Gardner: [Offstage.] COMING, COMING . . . I'VE GOT IT . . . COMING! [Dashing into the room, colliding into Fanny.] I'VE GOT IT . . . HOLD ON . . . COMING . . . COMING . . .

Fanny: [Offstage.] MAGS IS HERE! IT'S MAGS . . . SHE'S FINALLY HERE!

[Gardner exits to open the front door. Mags comes staggering in carrying a suitcase and an enormous duffel bag. She wears wonderfully distinctive clothes and has very much her own look. She's extremely out of breath and too wrought up to drop her heavy bags.]

Mags: I'm sorry. . . . I'm sorry I'm so late. . . . Everything went wrong! A passenger had a heart attack outside of New London and we had to stop. . . . It was terrifying! All these medics and policemen came swarming onto the train and the conductor kept running up and down the aisles telling everyone not to leave their seats under any circumstances. . . . Then the New London fire department came screeching down to the tracks, sirens blaring, lights whirling, and all these men in black rubber suits started pouring through the doors. . . . *That* took two hours. . . .

Fanny: DARLING . . . DARLING . . . WHERE ARE YOU? . . .

Mags: *Then,* I couldn't get a cab at the station. There just weren't any! I must have circled the block fifteen times. Finally I just stepped out into the traffic with my thumb out, but no one would pick me up . . . so I walked. . . .

Fanny: [Offstage.] Damned zipper's stuck. . . .

Gardner: You walked all the way from the South Station?

Mags: Well, actually, I ran. . . .

Gardner: You had poor Mum scared to death.

Mags: [Finally puts the bags down with a deep sigh.] I'm sorry. . . . I'm really sorry. It was a nightmare.

Fanny: [Reenters the room, her dress over her head. The zipper's stuck; she staggers around blindly.] Damned zipper! Gar, will you please help me with this?

Mags: I sprinted all the way up Beacon Hill.

Gardner: [Opening his arms wide.] Well, come here and let's get a look at you. [He hugs her.] Mags! . . .

Mags: [Squeezing him tight.] Oh, Daddy . . . Daddy!

Gardner: My Mags!

Mags: I never thought I'd get here! . . . Oh, you look wonderful!

Gardner: Well, you don't look so bad yourself!

Mags: I love your hair. It's gotten so . . . white!

Fanny: [Still lost in her dress, struggling with the zipper.] This is *so* typical . . . just as Mags arrives, my zipper has to break! [*Fanny grunts and struggles.*]

Mags: [*Waves at her.*] Hi, Mum. . . .

Fanny: Just a minute, dear, my zipper's . . .

Gardner: [*Picks up* Mags' *bags*] Well, sit down and take a load off your feet. . . .

Mags: I was so afraid I'd never make it. . . .

Gardner: [*Staggering under the weight of her bags.*] What have you got in here? Lead weights?

Mags: I can't believe you're finally letting me do you.

Fanny: [*Flings her arms around* Mags, *practically knocking her over.*] OH, DARLING . . . MY PRECIOUS MAGS, YOU'RE HERE AT LAST.	Gardner: [*Lurching around in circles.*] Now let's see . . . where should I put these? . . .

Fanny: I was sure your train had derailed and you were lying dead in some ditch!

Mags: [*Pulls away from* Fanny *to come to* Gardner's *rescue.*] Daddy, please, let me . . . these are much too heavy.

Fanny: [*Finally noticing* Mags.] GOOD LORD, WHAT HAVE YOU DONE TO YOUR HAIR?!

Mags: [*Struggling to take the bags from* Gardner.] Come on, give them to me . . . please? [*She sets them down by the sofa.*]

Fanny: [*As her dress starts to slide off one shoulder.*] Oh, not again! . . . Gar, would you give me a hand and see what's wrong with this zipper. One minute it's stuck, the next it's falling to pieces.

[Gardner *goes to her and starts fussing with it.*]

Mags: [*Pacing.*] I don't know, it's been crazy all week. Monday, I forgot to keep an appointment I'd made with a new model. . . . Tuesday, I overslept and stood up my advanced painting students. . . . Wednesday, the day of my meeting with Max Zoll, I forgot to put on my underpants. . . .

Fanny: GOD DAMNIT, GAR, CAN'T YOU DO ANYTHING ABOUT THIS ZIPPER?!

Mags: I mean, there I was, racing down Broome Street in this gauzy Tibetan skirt when I tripped and fell right at his feet . . . SPLATTT! My skirt goes flying over my head and there I am . . . everything staring him in the face . . .

Fanny: COME ON, GAR, USE A LITTLE MUSCLE!

Mags: [*Laughing.*] Oh, well, all that matters is that I finally got here. . . . I mean . . . there you are. . . .

Gardner: [*Struggling with the zipper.*] I can't see it, it's too small!

Fanny: [*Whirls away from* Gardner, *pulling her dress off altogether.*] OH, FORGET IT! JUST FORGET IT! . . . The trolley's probably missing half its teeth, just like someone else I know. *[To* Mags.*]* I grind my teeth in my sleep now, I've worn them all down to stubs. Look at that! *[She flings open her mouth and points.]* Nothing left but the gums!

Gardner: I never hear you grind your teeth. . . .

Fanny: That's because I'm snoring so loud. How could you hear anything through all that racket? It even wakes me up. It's no wonder poor Daddy has to sleep downstairs.

Mags: *[Looking around.]* Jeez, look at the place! So, you're finally doing it . . . selling the house and moving to Cotuit year round. I don't believe it. I just don't believe it!

Gardner: Well, how about a drink to celebrate Mags' arrival?

Mags: You've been here so long. Why move now?

Fanny: Gardner, what are you wearing that bathrobe for? . . .

Mags: You can't move. I won't let you!

Fanny: *[Softly to* Gardner.*]* Really, darling, you ought to pay more attention to your appearance.

Mags: You love this house. *I* love this house . . . this room . . . the light.

Gardner: So, Mags, how about a little . . . *[He drinks from an imaginary glass.]* to wet your whistle?

Fanny: We can't start drinking now, it isn't even noon yet!

Mags: I'm starving. I've got to get something to eat before I collapse!

[She exits towards the kitchen.]

Fanny: What *have* you done to your hair, dear? The color's so queer and all your nice curl is gone.

Gardner: It looks to me as if she dyed it.

Fanny: Yes, that's it. You're absolutely right! It's a completely different color. She dyed it bright red!

*[*Mags *can be heard thumping and thudding through the icebox.]*

Fanny: NOW, MAGS, I DON'T WANT YOU FILLING UP ON SNACKS. . . . I'VE MADE A PERFECTLY BEAUTIFUL LEG OF LAMB FOR LUNCH! . . . HELLO? . . . DO YOU HEAR ME? . . . *[To* Gardner.*]* No one in our family has *ever* had red hair, it's so common looking.

Gardner: I like it. It brings out her eyes.

Fanny: WHY ON EARTH DID YOU DYE YOUR HAIR *RED,* OF ALL COLORS?! . . .

Mags: *[Returns, eating Saltines out of the box.]* I didn't dye my hair, I just added some highlight.

Fanny: I suppose that's what your arty friends in New York do . . . dye their hair all the colors of the rainbow!

Gardner: Well, it's damned attractive if you ask me . . . damned attractive!

[Mags unzips her duffel bag and rummages around in it while eating the Saltines.]

Fanny: Darling, I told you not to bring a lot of stuff with you. We're trying to get rid of things.

Mags: [Pulls out a folding easel and starts setting it up.] AAAAAHHHHHH, here it is. Isn't it a beauty? I bought it just for you!

Fanny: Please don't get crumbs all over the floor. Crystal was just here yesterday. It was her last time before we move.

Mags: [At her easel.] God, I can hardly wait! I can't believe you're finally letting me do you.

Fanny: "Do" us? . . . What *are* you talking about?

Gardner: [Reaching for the Saltines.] Hey, Mags, could I have a couple of those?

Mags: [Tosses him the box.] Sure! *[To Fanny.]* Your portrait.

Gardner: Thanks. *[He starts munching on a handful.]*

Fanny: You're planning to paint our portrait now? While we're trying to move?

Gardner: [Sputtering Saltines.] Mmmmm, I'd forgotten just how delicious Saltines are!

Mags: It's a perfect opportunity. There'll be no distractions; you'll be completely at my mercy. Also, you promised.

Fanny: I did?

Mags: Yes, you did.

Fanny: Well, I must have been off my rocker.

Mags: No, you said, "You can paint us, you can dip us in concrete, you can do anything you want with us, just so long as you help us get out of here!"

Gardner: [Offering the box of Saltines to Fanny.] You really ought to try some of these, Fan, they're absolutely delicious!

Fanny: [Taking a few.] Why, thank you.

Mags: I figure we'll pack in the morning and you'll pose in the afternoons. It'll be a nice diversion.

Fanny: These *are* good!

Gardner: Here, dig in . . . take some more.

Mags: I have some wonderful news . . . amazing news! I wanted to wait 'til I got here to tell you.

[They eat their Saltines, passing the box back and forth as Mags speaks.]

Mags: You'll die! Just fall over into the packing cartons and die! Are you ready? . . . BRACE YOURSELVES. . . . OK, HERE GOES. . . . I'm being given a one woman show at one of the most important galleries in New York this fall. Me, Margaret Church, exhibited at Castelli's, 420 West Broadway. . . . Can you believe it?! . . . MY PORTRAITS HANGING IN THE SAME ROOMS THAT HAVE SHOWN RAUSCHENBERG, JOHNS, WARHOL, KELLY, LICHTENSTEIN, STELLA, SERRA, ALL THE HEAVIES. . . . It's incredible, beyond belief . . . I mean, at my age. . . . Do you know how good you have to be to get in there? It's a miracle . . . an honest-to-God, star-spangled miracle!

[Pause.]

Fanny: *[Mouth full.]* Oh, darling, that's wonderful. We're so happy for you!	*Gardner:* *[His mouth full.]* No one deserves it more, no one deserves it more!

Mags: Through some fluke, some of Castelli's people showed up at our last faculty show at Pratt and were knocked out. . . .

Fanny: *[Reaching for the box of Saltines.]* More, more . . .

Mags: They said they hadn't seen anyone handle light like me since the French Impressionists. They said I was this weird blend of Pierre Bonnard, Mary Cassatt and David Hockney. . . .

Gardner: *[Swallowing his own mouthful.]* I told you they were good.

Mags: Also, no one's doing portraits these days. They're considered passé. I'm so out of it, I'm in.

Gardner: Well, you're loaded with talent and always have been.

Fanny: She gets it all from Mama, you know. Her miniature of Henry James is still one of the main attractions at the Atheneum. Of course no woman of breeding could be a professional artist in her day. It simply wasn't done. But talk about talent . . . that woman had talent to burn!

Mags: I want to do one of you for the show.

Fanny: Oh, do Daddy, he's the famous one.

Mags: No, I want to do you both. I've always wanted to do you and now I've finally got a good excuse.

Fanny: It's high time somebody painted Daddy again! I'm sick to death of that dreadful portrait of him in the National Gallery they keep reproducing. He looks like an undertaker!

Gardner: Well, I think you should just do Mum. She's never looked handsomer.

Fanny: Oh, come on, I'm a perfect fright and you know it.

Mags: I want to do you both. Side by side. In this room. Something really classy. You look so great. Mum with her crazy hats and everything and you with that face. If I could just get you to hold still long enough and actually pose.

Gardner: *[Walking around, distracted.]* Where are those papers I just had? God damnit, Fanny. . . .

Mags: I have the feeling it's either now or never.

Gardner: I can't hold on to anything around here. *[He exits to his study.]*

Tina Howe   **1929**

Mags: I've always wanted to do you. It would be such a challenge.

Fanny: [*Pulling* Mags *next to her onto the sofa.*] I'm so glad you're finally here, Mags. I'm very worried about Daddy.

Mags: Mummy, please. I just got here.

Fanny: He's getting quite gaga.

Mags: Mummy! . . .

Fanny: You haven't seen him in almost a year. Two weeks ago he walked through the front door of the Codman's house, kissed Emily on the cheek and settled down in the maid's room, thinking he was home!

Mags: Oh, come on, you're exaggerating.

Fanny: He's as mad as a hatter and getting worse every day! It's this damned new book of his. He works on it around the clock. I've read some of it, and it doesn't make one word of sense, it's all at sixes and sevens. . . .

Gardner: [*Poking his head back in the room, spies some of his papers on a table and grabs them.*] Ahhh, here they are.

[*He exits.*]

Fanny: [*Voice lowered.*] Ever since this dry spell with his poetry, he's been frantic, absolutely . . . frantic!

Mags: I hate it when you do this.

Fanny: I'm just trying to get you to face the facts around here.

Mags: There's nothing wrong with him! He's just as sane as the next man. Even saner, if you ask me.

Fanny: You know what he's doing now? You couldn't guess in a million years! . . . He's writing criticism! Daddy! [*She laughs.*] Can you believe it? The man doesn't have one analytic bone in his body. His mind is a complete jumble and always has been!

[*There's a loud crash from* Gardner's *study.*]

Gardner: [*Offstage.*] SHIT!

Mags: He's abstracted. . . . That's the way he is.

Fanny: He doesn't spend any time with me anymore. He just holes up in that filthy study with Toots. God, I hate that bird! Though actually they're quite cunning together. Daddy's teaching him Grey's Elegy. You ought to see them in there, Toots perched on top of Daddy's head, spouting out verse after verse . . . Daddy, tap-tap-tapping away on his typewriter. They're quite a pair.

Gardner: [*Pokes his head back in.*] Have you seen that Stevens' poem I was reading before?

Fanny: [*Long suffering.*] NO, I HAVEN'T SEEN THAT STEVENS' POEM YOU WERE READING BEFORE! . . . Things are getting very tight around here, in case you haven't noticed. Daddy's last Pulitzer didn't even cover our real estate tax, and now that he's too doddery to give readings anymore, that income is gone. . . . [*Sud-*

denly handing Mags *the sugar bowl she'd been wrapping.]* Mags, *do*
take this sugar bowl. You can use it to serve tea to your students at
that wretched art school of yours. . . .

Mags: It's called Pratt! The Pratt Institute.

Fanny: Pratt, Splatt, whatever . . .

Mags: And I don't serve tea to my students, I teach them how to
paint.

Fanny: Well, I'm sure none of them has ever seen a sugar bowl as
handsome as this before.

Gardner: [Reappearing again.] You're sure you haven't seen it? . . .

Fanny: [Loud and angry.] YES, I'M SURE I HAVEN'T SEEN IT! I JUST
TOLD YOU I HAVEN'T SEEN IT!

Gardner: [Retreating.] Right you are, right you are.

[He exits.]

Fanny: God!

[Silence.]

Mags.: What do you have to yell at him like that for?

Fanny: Because the poor thing's as deaf as an adder!

[Mags sighs deeply; silence.]

Fanny: [Suddenly exuberant, leads her over to a lamp.] Come, I want to
show you something.

Mags: [Looking at it.] What is it?

Fanny: Something I made. *[Mags is about to turn it on.]* WAIT, DON'T
TURN IT ON YET! It's got to be dark to get the full effect. *[She
rushes to the windows and pulls down the shades.]*

Mags: What *are* you doing? . . .

Fanny: Hold your horses a minute. You'll see. . . . *[As the room gets
darker and darker.]* Poor me, you wouldn't believe the lengths I go
to to amuse myself these days. . . .

Mags: [Touching the lampshade.] What is this? It looks like a scene of
some sort.

Fanny: It's an invention I made . . . a kind of magic lantern.

Mags: Gee . . . it's amazing. . . .

Fanny: What I did was buy an old engraving of the Grand Canal. . . .

Mags: You *made* this?

Fanny: . . . and then color it in with crayons. Next, I got out my sewing scissors and cut out all the street lamps and windows . . . anything that light would shine through. Then I pasted it over a plain
lampshade, put the shade on this old horror of a lamp, turned on
the switch and . . . *[She turns it on.]* VOILÀ . . . VENICE TWIN-
KLING AT DUSK! It's quite effective, don't you think?

Mags: [Walking around it.] Jeez . . .

Fanny: And see, I poked out all the little lights on the gondolas with a straight pin.

Mags: Where on earth did you get the idea?

Fanny: Well you know, idle minds . . .

[Fanny spins the shade, making the lights whirl.]

Mags: It's really amazing. I mean, you could sell this in a store!

Gardner: [Enters.] HERE IT IS. IT WAS RIGHT ON TOP OF MY DESK THE WHOLE TIME. *[He crashes into a table.]* OOOOOWWWWW!

Fanny: LOOK OUT, LOOK OUT!

Mags: [Rushes over to him.] Oh, Daddy, are you all right?

Fanny: WATCH WHERE YOU'RE GOING, WATCH WHERE YOU'RE GOING!

Gardner: [Hopping up and down on one leg.] GOD DAMNIT! . . . I HIT MY SHIN.

Fanny: I was just showing Mags my lamp. . . .

Gardner: [Limping over to it.] Oh, yes, isn't that something? Mum is awfully clever with that kind of thing. . . . It was all her idea. Buying the engraving, coloring it in, cutting out all those little dots.

Fanny: Not "dots" . . . lights and windows, lights and windows!

Gardner: Right, right . . . lights and windows.

Fanny: Well, we'd better get some light back in here before someone breaks their neck. *[She zaps the shades back up.]*

Gardner: [Puts his arm around Mags.*]* Gee, it's good to have you back.

Mags: It's good to be back.

Gardner: And I like that new red hair of yours. It's very becoming.

Mags: But I told you, I hardly touched it. . . .

Gardner: Well, something's different. You've got a glow. So . . . how do you want us to pose for this grand portrait of yours? . . . *[He poses self-consciously.]*

Mags: Oh, Daddy, setting up a portrait takes a lot of time and thought. You've got to figure out the background, the lighting, what to wear, the sort of mood you want to . . .

Fanny: OOOOH, LET'S DRESS UP, LET'S DRESS UP! *[She grabs a packing blanket, drapes it around herself and links arms with* Gardner, *striking an elegant pose.]* This *is* going to be fun. She was absolutely right! Come on, Gar, look distinguished!

Mags: Mummy, please, it's not a game!

Fanny: [More and more excited.] You still have your tuxedo, don't you? And I'll wear my marvelous long black dress that makes me look like that fascinating woman in the Sargent painting! *[She strikes the famous profile pose.]*

Mags: MUMMY?! . . .

Fanny: I'm sorry, we'll behave, just tell us what to do.

[They settle down next to each other.]

Gardner: That's right, you're the boss.
   Fanny: Yes, you're the boss.
   Mags: But I'm not ready yet; I haven't set anything up.
   Fanny: Relax, darling, we just want to get the hang of it. . . .

[They stare straight ahead, trying to look like suitable subjects, but they can't hold still. They keep making faces, lifting an eyebrow, wriggling a nose, twitching a lip. Nothing big and grotesque, just flickering changes; a half-smile here, a self-important frown there. They steal glances at each other every so often.]

Gardner: How am I doing, Fan?
   Fanny: Brilliantly, absolutely brilliantly!
   Mags: But you're making faces.
   Fanny: *I'm* not making faces. *[Turning to* Gardner *and making a face.]* Are *you* making faces, Gar?
Gardner: *[Instantly making one.]* Certainly not! I'm the picture of restraint!

[Without meaning to, they get sillier and sillier. They start giggling, then laughing.]

   Mags: *[Can't help but join in.]* You two are impossible . . . completely impossible! I was crazy to think I could ever pull this off! *[Laughing away.]* Look at you . . . just . . . look at you!

BLACKOUT

Scene 2

Two days later, around five in the afternoon. Half of the Church household has been dragged into the living room for packing. Overflowing cartons are everywhere. They're filled with pots and pans, dishes and glasses, and the entire contents of two linen closets. Mags *has placed a stepladder under one of the windows. A pile of tablecloths and curtains is flung beneath it. Two side chairs are in readiness for the eventual pose.*

   Mags: *[Has just pulled a large crimson tablecloth out of a carton. She unfurls it with one shimmering toss.]* PERFECT . . . PERFECT! . . .
   Fanny: *[Seated on the sofa, clutches an old pair of galoshes to her chest.]* Look at these old horrors; half the rubber is rotted away and the fasteners are falling to pieces. . . . GARDNER? . . . OH, GARRRRRRRRRRDNERRRRR? . . .
   Mags: *[Rippling out the tablecloth with shorter snapping motions.]* Have you ever seen such a color? . . .
   Fanny: I'VE FOUND YOUR OLD SLEDDING GALOSHES IN WITH THE POTS AND PANS. DO YOU STILL WANT THEM?
   Mags: It's like something out of a Rubens! . . . *[She slings it over a chair and then sits on a footstool to finish the Sara Lee banana cake she*

Tina Howe   1933

started. As she eats, she looks at the tablecloth making happy grunting sounds.]

Fanny: *[Lovingly puts the galoshes on over her shoes and wiggles her feet.]* God, these bring back memories! There were real snow storms in the old days. Not these pathetic little two inch droppings we have now. After a particularly heavy one, Daddy and I used to go sledding on the Common. This was way before you were born. . . . God, it was a hundred years ago! . . . Daddy would stop writing early, put on these galoshes and come looking for me, jingling the fasteners like castanets. It was a kind of mating call, almost. . . . *[She jingles them.]* The Common was always deserted after a storm; we had the whole place to ourselves. It was so romantic. . . . We'd haul the sled up Beacon Street, stop under the State House, and aim it straight down to the Park Street Church, which was much further away in those days. . . . Then Daddy would lie down on the sled, I'd lower myself on top of him, we'd rock back and forth a few times to gain momentum and then . . . WHOOOOOOOOSSSSSSSHHHHH . . . down we'd plunge like a pair of eagles locked in a spasm of lovemaking. God, it was wonderful! . . . The city whizzing past us at ninety miles an hour . . . the cold . . . the darkness . . . Daddy's hair in my mouth . . . GAR . . . REMEMBER HOW WE USED TO GO SLEDDING IN THE OLD DAYS? . . . Sometimes he'd lie on top of me. That was fun. I liked that even more. *[In her foghorn voice.]* GARRRRRRRRRDNERRRRR? . . .

Mags: Didn't he say he was going out this afternoon?

Fanny: Why, so he did! I completely forgot. *[She takes off the galoshes.]* I'm getting just as bad as him. *[She drops them into a different carton—wistful.]* Gar's galoshes, Cotuit.

[A pause.]

Mags: *[Picks up the tablecloth again; holds it high over her head.]* Isn't this fabulous? . . . *[She then wraps* Fanny *in it.]* It's the perfect backdrop. Look what it does to your skin.

Fanny: Mags, what *are* you doing?

Mags: It makes you glow like a pomegranate. . . . *[She whips it off her.]* Now all I need is a hammer and nails. . . . *[She finds them.]* YES! *[She climbs up the stepladder and starts hammering a corner of the cloth into the moulding of one of the windows.]* This is going to look so great! . . . I've never seen such color!

Fanny: Darling, what is going on? . . .

Mags: Rembrandt, eat your heart out! You seventeenth-century Dutch has-been, you. *[She hammers more furiously.]*

Fanny: MARGARET, THIS IS NOT A CONSTRUCTION SITE. . . . PLEASE . . . STOP IT. . . . YOOHOOOOO . . . DO YOU HEAR ME? . . .

[Gardner *suddenly appears, dressed in a raincoat.*]

Gardner: YES, DEAR, HERE I AM. I JUST STEPPED OUT FOR A WALK DOWN CHESTNUT STREET. BEAUTIFUL AFTERNOON, ABSOLUTELY BEAUTIFUL!

Fanny: [*To* Mags.] YOU'RE GOING TO RUIN THE WALLS TO SAY NOTHING OF MAMA'S BEST TABLECLOTH. . . . MAGS, DO YOU HEAR ME? . . . YOOHOO! . . .

Gardner: WHY, THAT LOOKS VERY NICE, MAGS, very nice indeed. . . .

Fanny: DARLING, I MUST INSIST you stop that dreadful . . .

Mags: [*Steps down; stands back and looks at it.*] That's it. That's *IT!*

Fanny: [*To* Gardner, *worried.*] Where have *you* been? [*Mags kisses her fingers at the backdrop and settles back into her banana cake.*]

Gardner: [*To* Fanny.] You'll never guess who I ran into on Chestnut Street . . . Pate Baldwin!

[*He takes his coat off and drops it on the floor. He then sits in one of the posing chairs.*]

Mags: [*Mouth full of cake.*] Oh, Daddy, I'm nowhere near ready for you yet.

Fanny: [*Picks up his coat and hands it to him.*] Darling, coats do *not* go on the floor.

Gardner: [*Rises, but forgets where he's supposed to go.*] He was in terrible shape. I hardly recognized him. Well, it's the Parkinson's disease. . . .

Fanny: You mean, Hodgkin's disease. . . .

Gardner: Hodgkin's disease? . . .

Mags: [*Leaves her cake and returns to the tablecloth.*] Now to figure out exactly how to use this gorgeous light. . . .

Fanny: Yes, Pate has Hodgkin's disease, not Parkinson's disease. Sammy Bishop has Parkinson's disease. In the closet . . . your coat goes . . . in the closet!

Gardner: You're absolutely right! Pate has Hodgkin's disease. [*He stands motionless, the coat over his arm.*]

Fanny: . . . and Goat Davis has Addison's disease.

Gardner: I always get them confused.

Fanny: [*Pointing towards the closet.*] That way. . . . [*Gardner exits to the closet;* Fanny *calls after him.*] Grace Phelps has it too, I think. Or, it might be Hodgkin's, like Pate. I can't remember.

Gardner: [*Returns with a hanger.*] Doesn't the Goat have Parkinson's disease?

Fanny: No, that's Sammy Bishop.

Gardner: God, I haven't seen the Goat in ages! [*The coat still over his arm, he hands* Fanny *the hanger.*]

Fanny: He hasn't been well.

Gardner: Didn't Heppy . . . *die?*

Fanny: What are you giving me this for? . . . Oh, Heppy's been dead for years. She died on the same day as Luster Bright, don't you remember?

Gardner: I always liked her.

Fanny: *[Gives him back the hanger.]* Here, I don't want this.

Gardner: She was awfully attractive.

Fanny: Who?

Gardner: Heppy!

Fanny: Oh, yes, Heppy had real charm.

Mags: *[Keeps adjusting the tablecloth.]* Better . . . better . . .

Gardner: . . . which is something the Goat is short on, if you ask me. He has Hodgkin's disease, doesn't he? *[Puts his raincoat back on and sits down.]*

Fanny: Darling, what *are* you doing? I thought you wanted to hang up your coat!

Gardner: *[After a pause.]* OH, YES, THAT'S RIGHT! *[He goes back to the closet; a pause.]*

Fanny: Where were we?

Gardner: *[Returns with yet another hanger.]* Let's see. . . .

Fanny: *[Takes both hangers from him.]* FOR GOD'S SAKE, GAR, PAY ATTENTION!

Gardner: It was something about the Goat. . . .

Fanny: *[Takes the coat from* Gardner.*]* HERE, LET ME DO IT! . . . *[Under her breath to* Mags.*]* See what I mean about him? You don't know the half of it! *[She hangs it up in the closet.]* Not the half.

Mags: *[Still tinkering with the backdrop.]* Almost . . . almost . . .

Gardner: *[Sitting back down in one of the posing chairs.]* Oh, Fan, did I tell you, I ran into Pate Baldwin just now. I'm afraid he's not long for this world.

Fanny: *[Returning.]* Well, it's that Hodgkin's disease. . . . *[She sits on the posing chair next to him.]*

Gardner: God, I'd hate to see him go. He's one of the great editors of our times. I couldn't have done it without him. He gave me everything, everything!

Mags: *[Makes a final adjustment.]* Yes, that's it! *[She stands back and gazes at them.]* You look wonderful! . . .

Fanny: Isn't it getting to be . . . *[She taps at an imaginary watch on her wrist and drains an imaginary glass.]* cocktail time?!

Gardner: *[Looks at his watch.]* On the button, on the button! *[He rises.]*

Fanny: I'll have the usual, please. Do join us, Mags! Daddy bought some Dubonnet especially for you!

Mags: Hey. I was just getting some ideas.

Gardner: *[To* Mags, *as he exits for the bar.]* How about a little . . . *Dubonnet* to wet your whistle?

Fanny: Oh, Mags, it's like old times having you back with us like this!

Gardner: [Offstage.] THE USUAL FOR YOU, FAN?

Fanny: I wish we saw more of you. . . . PLEASE! . . . Isn't he darling? Have you ever known anyone more darling than Daddy? . . .

Gardner: [Offstage. Hums Jolson's "You Made Me Love You."] MAGS, HOW ABOUT YOU? . . . A LITTLE . . . DUBONNET? . . .

Fanny: Oh, do join us!   *Mags: [To* Gardner.*]* No, nothing, thanks.

Fanny: Well, what do you think of your aged parents picking up and moving to Cotuit year round? Pretty crazy, eh what? . . . Nothing but the gulls, oysters and us!

Gardner: [Returns with Fanny's *drink.]* Here you go. . . .

Fanny: Why thank you, Gar. *[To Mags.]* You sure you won't join us?

Gardner: [Lifts his glass towards Fanny *and* Mags.*]* Cheers!

*[*Gardner *and* Fanny *take that first life-saving gulp.]*

Fanny: Aaaaahhhhh!   *Gardner:* Hits the spot, hits the spot!

Mags: Well, I certainly can't do you like that!

Fanny: Why not? I think we look very . . . *comme il faut!*

[She slouches into a rummy pose; Gardner *joins her.]*

WAIT . . . I'VE GOT IT! I'VE GOT IT!

[She whispers excitedly to Gardner.*]*

Mags: Come on, let's not start this again!

Gardner: What's that? . . . Oh, yes . . . yes, yes . . . I know the one you mean. Yes, right, right . . . of course.

[A pause.]

Fanny: How's . . . this?! . . . *[Fanny grabs a large serving fork and they fly into an imitation of Grant Wood's* American Gothic.*]*

Mags: . . . and I wonder why it's taken me all these years to get you to pose for me. You just don't take me seriously! Poor old Mags and her ridiculous portraits . . .

Fanny: Oh, darling, your portraits aren't *ridiculous!* They may not be all that one *hopes* for, but they're certainly not . . .

Mags: Remember how you behaved at my first group show in Soho? . . . Oh, come on, you remember. It was a real circus! Think back. . . . It was about six years ago. . . . Daddy had just been awarded some presidential medal of achievement and you insisted he wear it around his neck on a bright red ribbon, and you wore this . . . *huge* feathered hat to match! I'll never forget it! It was the size of a giant pizza with twenty-inch red turkey feathers shooting straight up into the air. . . . Oh, come on, you remember, don't you? . . .

Fanny: [*Leaping to her feet.*] HOLD EVERYTHING! THIS IS IT! THIS IS REALLY IT! Forgive me for interrupting, Mags darling, it'll just take a minute.

[*She whispers excitedly to* Gardner.]

Mags: I had about eight portraits in the show, mostly of friends of mine, except for this old one I'd done of Mrs. Crowninshield.
Gardner: All right, all right . . . let's give it a whirl.

[*A pause; then they mime Michelangelo's* Pietà *with* Gardner *lying across* Fanny's *lap as the dead Christ.*]

Mags: [*Depressed.*] The *Pietà.* Terrific!
Fanny: [*Jabbing* Gardner *in the ribs.*] Hey, we're getting good at this.
Gardner: Of course it would help if we didn't have all these modern clothes on.
Mags: AS I WAS SAYING . . .
Fanny: Sorry, Mags . . . sorry . . .

[*Huffing and creaking with the physical exertion of it all, they return to their seats.*]

Mags: . . . As soon as you stepped foot in the gallery you spotted it and cried out, "MY GOD, WHAT'S MILLICENT CROWNINSHIELD DOING HERE?" Everyone looked up what with Daddy's clanking medal and your amazing hat which I was sure would take off and start flying around the room. A crowd gathered. . . . Through some utter fluke, you latched on to *the* most important critic in the city, I mean . . . Mr. Modern Art himself, and you hauled him over to the painting, trumpeting out for all to hear, "THAT'S MILLICENT CROWNINSHIELD! I GREW UP WITH HER. SHE LIVES RIGHT DOWN THE STREET FROM US IN BOSTON. BUT IT'S A VERY POOR LIKENESS, IF YOU ASK ME! HER NOSE ISN'T NEARLY THAT LARGE AND SHE DOESN'T HAVE SOMETHING QUEER GROWING OUT OF HER CHIN! THE CROWNINSHIELDS ARE REALLY QUITE GOOD-LOOKING, STUFFY, BUT GOOD-LOOKING NONETHELESS!"
Gardner: [*Suddenly jumps up, ablaze.*] WAIT, WAIT . . . IF IT'S MICHELANGELO YOU WANT . . . I'm sorry, Mags. . . . One more . . . just one more . . . please?
Mags: Sure, why not? Be my guest.
Gardner: Fanny, *prepare yourself!*

[*More whispering.*]

Fanny: But I think *you* should be God.
Gardner: Me? . . . Really?
Fanny: Yes, it's much more appropriate.
Gardner: Well, if you say so . . . [Fanny *and* Gardner *ease down to the floor with some difficulty and lie on their sides,* Fanny *as Adam,* Gardner *as*

God, their fingers inching closer and closer in the attitude of Michelan-
gelo's The Creation. *Finally they touch.]*

Mags: *[Cheers, whistles, applauds.]* THREE CHEERS . . . VERY GOOD
. . . NICELY DONE, NICELY DONE! . . . *[They hold the pose a moment*
more, flushed with pleasure; then rise, dust themselves off and grope back
to their chairs.] So, there we were. . . .

Fanny: Yes, *do* go on! . . .

Mags: . . . huddled around Millicent Crowninshield, when you
whipped into your pocketbook and suddenly announced, "HOLD
EVERYTHING! I'VE GOT A PHOTOGRAPH OF HER RIGHT
HERE, THEN YOU CAN SEE WHAT SHE REALLY LOOKS
LIKE!" . . . You then proceeded to crouch down to the floor and
dump everything out of your bag, and I mean . . . *everything!* . . .
leaking packets of sequins and gummed stars, sea shells, odd
pieces of fur, crochet hooks, a monarch butterfly embedded in
plastic, dental floss, antique glass buttons, small jingling bells, lace
. . . I thought I'd die! Just sink to the floor and quietly die! . . .
You couldn't find it, you see. I mean, you spent the rest of the
afternoon on your hands and knees crawling through this ocean
of junk, muttering, "It's *got* to be here somewhere; I know I had it
with me!" . . . Then Daddy pulled me into the thick of it all and
said, "By the way, have you met our daughter Mags yet? She's the
one who did all these pictures . . . paintings . . . portraits . . . whatever you call them." *[She drops to her hands and knees and begins*
crawling out of the room.] By this time, Mum had somehow crawled
out of the gallery and was lost on another floor. She began calling
for me . . . "YOO-HOO, MAGS . . . WHERE ARE YOU? . . . OH,
MAGS, DARLING . . . HELLO? . . . ARE YOU THERE? . . ." *[She*
reenters and faces them.] This was at my *first* show.

BLACKOUT

Scene 3

Twenty-four hours later. The impact of the impending move has struck with hurri-
cane force. Fanny *has lugged all their clothing into the room and dumped it in*
various cartons. There are coats, jackets, shoes, skirts, suits, hats, sweaters, dresses,
the works. She and Gardner *are seated on the sofa, going through it all.*

Fanny: *[Wearing a different hat and dress, holds up a ratty overcoat.]*
What about this gruesome old thing?

Gardner: *[Is wearing several sweaters and vests, a Hawaiian holiday shirt,*
and a variety of scarves and ties around his neck. He holds up a pair of
shoes.] God . . . remember these shoes? Pound gave them to me
when he came back from Italy. I remember it vividly.

Fanny: *Do* let me give it to the thrift shop! *[She stuffs the coat into the*
appropriate carton.]

Gardner: He bought them for me in Rome. Said he couldn't resist;

Tina Howe 1939

bought himself a pair too since we both wore the same size. God, I miss him! *[Pause.]* HEY, WHAT ARE YOU DOING WITH MY OVERCOAT?!

Fanny: Darling, it's threadbare!

Gardner: But that's my overcoat! *[He grabs it out of the carton.]* I've been wearing it every day for the past thirty-five years!

Fanny: That's just my point: It's had it.

Gardner: *[Puts it on over everything else.]* There's nothing wrong with this coat!

Fanny: I trust you remember that the cottage is an eighth the size of this place and you simply won't have room for half this stuff! *[She holds up a sports jacket.]* This dreary old jacket, for instance. You've had it since Hector was a pup!

Gardner: *[Grabs it and puts it on over his coat.]* Oh, no, you don't. . . .

Fanny: . . . and this God-awful hat . . .

Gardner: Let me see that.

[He stands next to her and they fall into a lovely tableau.]

Mags: *[Suddenly pops out from behind a wardrobe carton with a flash camera and takes a picture of them.]* PERFECT!

Fanny: *[Hands flying to her*   *Gardner:* *[Hands flying to his*
face.] GOOD GOD, WHAT   *heart.]* JESUS CHRIST,
WAS THAT? . . .   I'VE BEEN SHOT!

Mags: *[Walks to the center of the room, advancing the film.]* That was terrific. See if you can do it again.

Fanny: What *are* you doing?

Gardner: *[Feeling his chest.]* Is there blood?

Fanny: I see lace everywhere. . . .

Mags: It's all right, I was just taking a picture of you. I often use a Polaroid at this stage.

Fanny: *[Rubbing her eyes.]* Really, Mags, you might have given us some warning!

Mags: But that's the whole point: to catch you unawares!

Gardner: *[Rubbing his eyes.]* It's the damndest thing. . . . I see lace everywhere.

Fanny: Yes, so do I. . . .

Gardner: It's rather nice, actually. It looks as if you're wearing a veil.

Fanny: I *am* wearing a veil!

[The camera spits out the photograph.]

Mags: OH GOODY, HERE COMES THE PICTURE!

Fanny: *[Grabs the partially developed print out of her hands.]* Let me see, let me see. . . .

Gardner: Yes, let's have a look.

[They have another quiet moment together looking at the photograph.]

Mags: *[Tiptoes away from them and takes another picture.]* YES!

Fanny: NOT AGAIN! PLEASE,   Gardner: WHAT WAS THAT? . . .
DARLING!   WHAT HAPPENED? . . .

[They stagger towards each other.]

Mags: I'm sorry, I just couldn't resist. You looked so . . .

Fanny: WHAT ARE YOU TRYING TO DO . . . *BLIND* US?!

Gardner: Really, Mags, enough is enough. . . .

*[*Gardner *and* Fanny *keep stumbling about kiddingly.]*

Fanny: Are you still there, Gar?

Gardner: Right as rain, right as rain!

Mags: I'm sorry; I didn't mean to scare you. It's just a photograph can show you things you weren't aware of. Here, have a look. *[She gives them to* Fanny.] Well, I'm going out to the kitchen to get something to eat. Anybody want anything?

[She exits.]

Fanny: *[Looking at the photos, half-amused, half-horrified.]* Oh, Gardner, have you ever? . . .

Gardner: *[Looks at them and laughs.]* Good grief . . .

Mags: *[Offstage; from the kitchen.]* IS IT ALL RIGHT IF I TAKE THE REST OF THIS TAPIOCA FROM LAST NIGHT?

Fanny: IT'S ALL RIGHT WITH ME. How about you, Gar?

Gardner: Sure, go right ahead. I've never been that crazy about tapioca.

Fanny: What are you talking about, tapioca is one of your favorites.

Mags: *[Enters, slurping from a large bowl.]* Mmmmmmmmm . . .

Fanny: Really, Mags, I've never seen anyone eat as much as you.

Mags: *[Takes the photos back.]* It's strange. I only do this when I come home.

Fanny: What's the matter, don't I feed you enough?

Gardner: Gee, it's hot in here!

[Starts taking off his coat.]

Fanny: God knows, you didn't eat anything as a child! I've never seen such a fussy eater. Gar, what *are* you doing?

Gardner: Taking off some of these clothes. It's hotter than Tofit in here!

[Shedding clothes to the floor.]

Mags: *[Looking at her photos.]* Yes, I like you looking at each other like that. . . .

Fanny: *[To* Gardner*]* Please watch where you're dropping things; I'm trying to keep some order around here.

Gardner: [*Picks up what he dropped, dropping even more in the process.*] Right, right. . . .

Mags: Now all I've got to do is figure out what you should wear.

Fanny: Well, I'm going to wear my long black dress, and you'd be a fool not to do Daddy in his tuxedo. He looks so distinguished in it, just like a banker!

Mags: I haven't really decided yet.

Fanny: Just because you walk around looking like something the cat dragged in doesn't mean Daddy and I want to, do we, Gar?

[Gardner *is making a worse and worse tangle of his clothes.*]

Fanny: HELLO? . . .

Gardner: [*Looks up at* Fanny] Oh, yes, awfully attractive, awfully attractive!

Fanny: [*To* Mags] If you don't mind me saying so, I've never seen you looking so forlorn. You'll never catch a husband looking that way. Those peculiar clothes, that God-awful hair . . . really, Mags, it's very distressing!

Mags: I don't think my hair's so bad, not that it's terrific or anything . . .

Fanny: Well, I don't see other girls walking around like you. I mean, girls from your background. What would Lyman Wigglesworth think if he saw you in the street?

Mags: Lyman Wigglesworth?! . . . Uuuuuuughhhhhhh! [*She shudders.*]

Fanny: All right then, that brilliant Cabot boy . . . what *is* his name?

Gardner: Sammy.

Fanny: No, not Sammy. . . .

Gardner: Stephen . . . Stanley . . . Stuart . . . Sheldon . . . Sherlock . . . Sherlock! It's *Sherlock!*

Mags: Spence!

Fanny: SPENCE, THAT'S IT!   *Gardner:* THAT'S IT . . .
HIS NAME IS SPENCE!   SPENCE! SPENCE CABOT!

Fanny: Spence Cabot was first in his class at Harvard.

Mags: Mum, he has no facial hair.

Fanny: He has his own law firm on Arlington Street.

Mags: Spence Cabot has six fingers on his right hand!

Fanny: So, he isn't the best-looking thing in the world. Looks isn't everything. He can't help it if he has extra fingers. Have a little sympathy!

Mags: But the extra one has this weird nail on it that looks like a talon. . . . It's long and black and . . . [*She shudders.*]

Fanny: No one's perfect, darling. He has lovely handwriting and an absolutely saintly mother. Also, he's as rich as Croesus! He's a lot more promising than some of those creatures you've dragged home. What was the name of that dreadful Frenchman who smelled like sweaty socks? . . . Jean Duke of Scripto?

Mags: [*Laughing.*] Jean-Luc Zichot!

Fanny: . . . and that peculiar little Oriental fellow with all the teeth! Really, Mags, he could have been put on display at the circus!

Mags: Oh, yes, Tsu Chin. He was strange, but very sexy. . . .

Fanny: [*Shudders.*] He had such tiny . . . feet! Really, Mags, you've got to bear down. You're not getting any younger. Before you know it, all the nice young men will be taken and then where will you be? . . . All by yourself in that grim little apartment of yours with those peculiar clothes and that bright red hair . . .

Mags: MY HAIR IS NOT BRIGHT RED!

Fanny: I only want what's best for you, you know that. You seem to go out of your way to look wanting. I don't understand it. . . . Gar, what *are* you putting your coat on for? . . . You look like some derelict out on the street. We don't wear coats in the house. [*She helps him out of it.*] That's the way. . . . I'll just put this in the carton along with everything else. . . . [*She drops it into the carton, then pauses.*] Isn't it about time for . . . cocktails!

Gardner: What's that?

[Fanny *taps her wrist and mimes drinking.*]

Gardner: [*Looks at his watch.*] Right you are, right you are! [*Exits to the bar.*] THE USUAL? . . .

Fanny: Please!

Gardner: [*Offstage.*] HOW ABOUT SOMETHING FOR YOU, MAGS?

Mags: SURE, WHY NOT? . . . LET 'ER RIP!

Gardner: [*Offstage.*] WHAT'S THAT? . . .

Fanny: SHE SAID YES. SHE SAID YES.	*Mags:* I'LL HAVE SOME DUBONNET!

Gardner: [*Poking his head back in.*] How about a little Dubonnet?

Fanny: That's just what she said. . . . She'd like some . . . Dubonnet!

Gardner: [*Goes back to the bar and hums another Jolson tune.*] GEE, IT'S GREAT HAVING YOU BACK LIKE THIS, MAGS. . . . IT'S JUST GREAT! [*More singing.*]

Fanny: [*Leaning closer to* Mags.] You have such *potential*, darling! It breaks my heart to see how you've let yourself go. If Lyman Wigglesworth . . .

Mags: Amazing as it may seem, I don't *care* about Lyman Wigglesworth!

Fanny: From what I've heard, he's quite a lady killer!

Mags: But with whom? . . . Don't think I haven't heard about his fling with . . . Hopie Stonewall!

Fanny: [*Begins to laugh.*] Oh, God, let's not get started on Hopie Stonewall again . . . ten feet tall with spots on her neck. . . . [*To*

Gardner.] OH, DARLING, DO HURRY BACK! WE'RE TALKING
ABOUT PATHETIC HOPIE STONEWALL!

Mags: It's not so much her incredible height and spotted skin; it's
those tiny pointed teeth and the size eleven shoes!

Fanny: I love it when you're like this!

[Mags *starts clomping around the room making tiny pointed teeth nibbling
sounds.*]

Fanny: GARDNER . . . YOU'RE MISSING EVERYTHING! *[Still laughing.]* Why is it Boston girls are always so . . . tall?

Mags: Hopie Stonewall isn't a Boston girl; she's a giraffe. *[She
prances around the room with an imaginary dwarf-sized Lyman.]* She's
perfect for Lyman Wigglesworth!

Gardner: *[Returns with* Fanny's *drink, which he hands her.]* Now, where
were we? . . .

Fanny: *[Trying not to laugh.]* HOPIE STONEWALL! . . .

Gardner: Oh, yes, she's the very tall one, isn't she?

[Fanny *and* Mags *burst into gales.*]

Mags: The only hope for us . . . "Boston girls" is to get as far away
from our kind as possible.

Fanny: She always asks after you, darling. She's very fond of you, you
know.

Mags: Please, I don't want to hear!

Fanny: Your old friends are *always* asking after you.

Mags: It's not so much how creepy they all are, as how much they
remind me of myself!

Fanny: But you're not "creepy," darling . . . just . . . shabby!

Mags: I mean, give me a few more inches and some brown splotches
here and there, and Hopie and I could be sisters!

Fanny: *[In a whisper to* Gardner.] Don't you love it when Mags is like
this? I could listen to her forever!

Mags: I mean . . . look at me!

Gardner: *[Gasping.]* Don't stop, don't stop!

Mags: Awkward . . . plain . . . I don't know how to dress, I don't
know how to talk. When people find out Daddy's my father,
they're always amazed. . . . "Gardner Church is YOUR father?!
Aw, come on, you're kidding?!"

Fanny: *[In a whisper.]* Isn't she divine? . . .

Mags: Sometimes I don't even tell them. I pretend I grew up in the
Midwest somewhere . . . farming people . . . we work with our
hands.

Gardner: *[To* Mags.] Well, how about a little refill? . . .

Mags: No, no more, thanks.

[Pause.]

Fanny: What did you have to go and interrupt her for? She was just getting up a head of steam. . . .

Mags: *[Walking over to her easel.]* The great thing about being a portrait painter, you see, is it's the *other* guy that's exposed; you're safely hidden behind the canvas and easel. *[Standing behind it.]* You can be as plain as a pitchfork, as inarticulate as mud, but it doesn't matter because you're completely concealed: your body, your face, your intentions. Just as you make your most intimate move, throw open your soul . . . they stretch and yawn, remembering the dog has to be let out at five. . . . To be so invisible while so enthralled . . . it takes your breath away!

Gardner: Well put, Mags. Awfully well put!

Mags: That's why I've always wanted to paint you, to see if I'm up to it. It's quite a risk. Remember what I went through as a child with my great masterpiece? . . .

Fanny: You painted a masterpiece when you were a child? . . .

Mags: Well, it was a masterpiece to me.

Fanny: I had no idea you were precocious as a child. Gardner, do you remember Mags painting a masterpiece as a child?

Mags: I didn't paint it. It was something I made!

Fanny: Well, this is all news to me! Gar, *do* get me another drink! I haven't had this much fun in years! *[She hands him her glass and reaches for Mags'.]* Come on, darling, join me. . . .

Mags: No, no more, thanks. I don't really like the taste.

Fanny: Oh, come on, kick up your heels for once!

Mags: No, nothing . . . really.

Fanny: Please? Pretty please? . . . To keep me company?!

Mags: *[Hands Gardner her glass.]* Oh, all right, what the hell . . .

Fanny: That's a good girl! Gardner: *[Exiting.]* Coming right up, coming right up!

Fanny: *[Yelling after him.]* DON'T GIVE ME TOO MUCH NOW. THE LAST ONE WAS AWFULLY STRONG . . . AND HURRY BACK SO YOU DON'T MISS ANYTHING! . . . Daddy's so cunning, I don't know what I'd do without him. If anything should happen to him, I'd just . . .

Mags: Mummy, nothing's going to happen to him! . . .

Fanny: Well, wait 'til you're our age, it's no garden party. Now . . . where were we? . . .

Mags: My first masterpiece . . .

Fanny: Oh, yes, but *do* wait 'til Daddy gets back so he can hear it too. . . . YOO-HOO . . . GARRRRRRDNERRRRR? . . . ARE YOU COMING? . . . *[Silence.]* Go and check on him, will you?

Gardner: *[Enters with both drinks. He's very shaken.]* I couldn't find the ice.

Fanny: Well, *finally!*

Gardner: It just up and disappeared. . . . *[Hands* Fanny *her drink.]* There you go.

*[*Fanny *kisses her fingers and takes a hefty swig.]*

Gardner: Mags.

[He hands Mags *her drink.]*

   Mags: Thanks, Daddy.

Gardner: Sorry about the ice.

   Mags: No problem, no problem.

*[*Gardner *sits down; silence.]*

   Fanny: *[To* Mags.*]* Well, drink up, drink up! *[*Mags *downs it in one gulp.]* GOOD GIRL! . . . Now, what's all this about a masterpiece? . . .

   Mags: I did it during that winter you sent me away from the dinner table. I was about nine years old.

   Fanny: We sent you from the dinner table?

   Mags: I was banished for six months.

   Fanny: You *were?* . . . How extraordinary!

   Mags: Yes, it *was* rather extraordinary!

   Fanny: But why?

   Mags: Because I played with my food.

   Fanny: You did?

   Mags: I used to squirt it out between my front teeth.

   Fanny: Oh, I remember that! God, it used to drive me crazy, absolutely . . . crazy! *[Pause.]* "MARGARET, STOP THAT OOZING RIGHT THIS MINUTE, YOU ARE *NOT* A TUBE OF TOOTHPASTE!"

Gardner: Oh, yes . . .

   Fanny: It was perfectly disgusting!

Gardner: I remember. She used to lean over her plate and squirt it out in long runny ribbons. . . .

   Fanny: That's enough, dear.

Gardner: They were quite colorful, actually; decorative almost. She made the most intricate designs. They looked rather like small, moist Oriental rugs. . . .

   Fanny: *[To* Mags.*]* But why, darling? What on earth possessed you to do it?

   Mags: I couldn't swallow anything. My throat just closed up. I don't know, I must have been afraid of choking or something.

Gardner: I remember one in particular. We'd had chicken fricassee and spinach. . . . She made the most extraordinary . . .

   Fanny: *[To* Gardner.*]* WILL YOU PLEASE SHUT UP?! *[Pause.]* Mags, what *are* you talking about? You never choked in your entire life!

This is the most distressing conversation I've ever had. Don't you think it's distressing, Gar?

Gardner: Well, that's not quite the word I'd use.

Fanny: What word *would* you use, then?

Gardner: I don't know right off the bat, I'd have to think about it.

Fanny: THEN, THINK ABOUT IT!

[Silence.]

Mags: I guess I was afraid of making a mess. I don't know; you were awfully strict about table manners. I was always afraid of losing control. What if I started to choke and began spitting up over everything? . . .

Fanny: All right, dear, that's enough.

Mags: No, I was really terrified about making a mess; you always got so mad whenever I spilled. If I just got rid of everything in neat little curclicues beforehand, you see . . .

Fanny: I SAID: THAT'S ENOUGH!

[Silence.]

Mags: I thought it was quite ingenious, but you didn't see it that way. You finally sent me from the table with, "When you're ready to eat like a human being, you can come back and join us!" . . . So, it was off to my room with a tray. But I couldn't seem to eat there either. I mean, it was so strange settling down to dinner in my *bedroom*. . . . So I just flushed everything down the toilet and sat on my bed listening to you: clinkity, clink, clatter clatter, slurp, slurp . . . but that got pretty boring after a while, so I looked around for something to do. It was wintertime, because I noticed I'd left some crayons on top of my radiator and they'd melted down into these beautiful shimmering globs, like spilled jello, trembling and pulsing. . . . [overlapping]

Gardner: [Eyes closed.] "This luscious and impeccable fruit of life
Falls, it appears, of its own weight to earth. . . ."

Mags: Naturally, I wanted to try it myself, so I grabbed a red one and pressed it down against the hissing lid. It oozed and bubbled like raspberry jam!

Gardner: "When you were Eve, its acrid juice was sweet,
Untasted, in its heavenly, orchard air. . . ."

Mags: I mean, that radiator was really hot! It took incredible will power not to let go, but I held on, whispering, "Mags, if you let go of this crayon, you'll be run over by a truck on Newberry Street, so help you God!" . . . So I pressed down harder, my fingers steaming and blistering. . . .

Fanny: I had no idea about any of this, did you, Gar?

Mags: Once I'd melted one, I was hooked! I finished off my entire supply in one night, mixing color over color until my head swam! . . . The heat, the smell, the brilliance that sank and rose . . . I'd never felt such exhilaration! . . . Every week I spent my allowance on crayons. I must have cleared out every box of Crayolas in the city!

Gardner: [Gazing at Mags.] You know, I don't think I've ever seen you looking prettier! You're awfully attractive when you get going!

Fanny: Why, what a lovely thing to say.

Mags: AFTER THREE MONTHS THAT RADIATOR WAS . . . SPEC-TACULAR! I MEAN, IT LOOKED LIKE SOME COLOSSAL FRUIT CAKE, FIVE FEET TALL! . . .

Fanny: It sounds perfectly hideous.

Mags: It was a knockout; shimmering with pinks and blues, lavenders and maroons, turquoise and golds, oranges and creams. . . . For every color, I imagined a taste . . . YELLOW: lemon curls dipped in sugar . . . RED: glazed cherries laced with rum . . . GREEN: tiny peppermint leaves veined with chocolate . . . PUR-PLE: . . .

Fanny: That's quite enough!

Mags: And then the frosting . . . ahhhh, the frosting! A satiny mix of white and silver . . . I kept it hidden under blankets during the day. . . . My huge . . . [She starts laughing.] looming . . . teetering sweet . . .

Fanny: I ASKED YOU TO STOP! GARDNER, WILL YOU PLEASE GET HER TO STOP!

Gardner: See here, Mags, Mum asked you to . . .

Mags: I was so . . . hungry . . . losing weight every week. I looked like a scarecrow what with the bags under my eyes and bits of crayon wrapper leaking out of my clothes. It's a wonder you didn't notice. But finally you came to my rescue . . . if you could call what happened a rescue. It was more like a rout!

Fanny: Darling . . . Please!   Gardner: Now, look, young
                                                          lady . . .

Mags: The winter was almost over. . . . It was very late at night. . . . I must have been having a nightmare because suddenly you and Daddy were at my bed, shaking me. . . . I quickly glanced towards the radiator to see if it was covered. . . . It wasn't! It glittered and towered in the moonlight like some . . . gigantic Viennese pastry! You followed my gaze and saw it. Mummy screamed . . . "WHAT HAVE YOU GOT IN HERE? . . . MAGS, WHAT HAVE YOU BEEN DOING?" . . . She crept forward and touched it, and then jumped back. "IT'S FOOD!" she cried . . . "IT'S ALL THE FOOD SHE'S BEEN SPITTING OUT! OH, GARDNER, IT'S A MOUNTAIN OF ROTTING GARBAGE!"

Fanny: [Softly.] Yes . . . it's coming back . . . it's coming back. . . .

Mags: Daddy exited as usual; left the premises. He fainted, just keeled over onto the floor. . . .

Gardner: Gosh, I don't remember any of this. . . .

Mags: My heart stopped! I mean, I knew it was all over. My lovely creation didn't have a chance. Sure enough . . . out came the blow torch. Well, it couldn't have *really* been a blow torch, I mean, where would you have ever gotten a blow torch? . . . I just have this very strong memory of you standing over my bed, your hair streaming around your face, aiming this . . . flame thrower at my confection . . . my cake . . . my tart . . . my strudel. . . . "IT'S GOT TO BE DESTROYED IMMEDIATELY! THE THING'S ALIVE WITH VERMIN! . . . JUST LOOK AT IT! . . . IT'S PRACTICALLY CRAWLING ACROSS THE ROOM!" . . . Of course in a sense you were right. It *was* a monument of my cast-off dinners, only I hadn't built it with food. . . . I found my own materials. I was languishing with hunger, but oh, dear Mother . . . I FOUND MY OWN MATERIALS! . . .

Fanny: Darling . . . *please?!*

Mags: I tried to stop you, but you wouldn't listen. . . . OUT SHOT THE FLAME! . . . I remember these waves of wax rolling across the room and Daddy coming to, wondering what on earth was going on. . . . Well, what did you know about my abilities? . . . You see, I had . . . I mean, I *have* abilities. . . . *[Struggling to say it.]* I have abilities. I have . . . strong abilities. I have . . . very strong abilities. They are very strong . . . very, very strong. . . .

[She rises and runs out of the room overcome as Fanny *and* Gardner *watch, speechless.]*

THE CURTAIN FALLS

ACT II

Scene 1

Three days later. Miracles have been accomplished. Almost all of the Churches' furniture has been moved out, and the cartons of dishes and clothing are gone. All that remains are odds and ends. Mags' *tableau looms, impregnable.* Fanny *and* Gardner *are dressed in their formal evening clothes, frozen in their pose. They hold absolutely still.* Mags *stands at her easel, her hands covering her eyes.*

Fanny: All right, you can look now.

Mags: *[Removes her hands.]* Yes! . . . I told you you could trust me on the pose.

Fanny: Well, thank God you let us dress up. It makes all the difference. Now we really look like something.

Mags: *[Starts to sketch them.]* I'll say. . . .

Tina Howe   1949

[A silence as she sketches.]

Gardner: *[Recites Yeats's "The Song of Wandering Aengus" in a wonderfully resonant voice as they pose.]*

"I went out to the hazel wood,
Because a fire was in my head,
And cut and peeled a hazel wand,
And hooked a berry to a thread,
And when white moths were on the wing,
And moth-like stars were flickering out,
I dropped the berry in a stream
And caught a little silver trout.

When I had laid it on the floor
I went to blow the fire aflame,
But something rustled on the floor,
And someone called me by my name:

It had become a glimmering girl
With apple blossoms in her hair
Who called me by my name and ran
And faded through the brightening air.

Though I am old with wandering
Through hollow lands and hilly lands,
I will find out where she has gone,
And kiss her lips and take her hands;
And walk among long dappled grass,
And pluck till time and times are done,
The silver apples of the moon,
The golden apples of the sun."

Fanny: That's lovely, dear. Just lovely. Is it one of yours?

Gardner: No, no, it's Yeats. I'm using it in my book.

Fanny: Well, you recited it beautifully, but then you've always recited beautifully. That's how you wooed me, in case you've forgotten. . . . You must have memorized every love poem in the English language! There was no stopping you when you got going . . . your Shakespeare, Byron, and Shelley . . . you were shameless . . . *shameless!*

Gardner: *[Eyes closed.]* "I will find out where she has gone,
And kiss her lips and take her hands . . ."

Fanny: And then there was your own poetry to do battle with; your sonnets and quatrains. When you got going with them, there was nothing left of me! You could have had your pick of any girl in Boston! Why you chose me, I'll never understand. I had no looks to speak of and nothing much in the brains department. . . . Well, what did you know about women and the world? . . . What did any of us know? . . . *[Silence.]* GOD, MAGS, HOW LONG ARE WE SUPPOSED TO SIT LIKE THIS? . . . IT'S AGONY!

Mags: *[Working away.]* You're doing fine . . . just fine. . . .

Fanny: *[Breaking her pose.]* It's so . . . boring!

Mags: Come on, don't move. You can have a break soon.

Fanny: I had no idea it would be so boring!

Gardner: Gee, I'm enjoying it.

Fanny: You would! . . .

[A pause.]

Gardner: *[Begins reciting more Yeats, almost singing it.]*

"He stood among a crowd at Drumahair;
His heart hung all upon a silken dress,
And he had known at last some tenderness,
Before earth made of him her sleepy care;
But when a man poured fish into a pile,
It seemed they raised their little silver heads . . ."

Fanny: Gar . . . PLEASE! *[She lurches out of her seat.]* God, I can't take this anymore!

Mags: *[Keeps sketching* Gardner.*]* I know it's tedious at first, but it gets easier. . . .

Fanny: It's like a Chinese water torture! . . . *[Crosses to* Mags *and looks at* Gardner *posing.]* Oh, darling, you look marvelous, absolutely marvelous! Why don't you just do Daddy?

Mags: Because you look marvelous too. I want to do you both!

Fanny: Please! . . . I have one foot in the grave and you know it! Also, we're way behind in our packing. There's still one room left which everyone seems to have forgotten about!

Gardner: Which one is that?

Fanny: You know perfectly well which one it is!

Gardner: I do? . . .

Fanny: Yes, you do!

Gardner: Well, it's news to me.

Fanny: I'll give you a hint. It's in . . . *that* direction. *[She points.]*

Gardner: The dining room?

Fanny: No.

Gardner: The bedroom?

Fanny: No.

Gardner: Mags' room?

Fanny: No.

Gardner: The kitchen?

Fanny: Gar?! . . .

Gardner: The guest room?

Fanny: Your God-awful study!

Gardner: Oh, shit!

    Fanny: That's right, "Oh, shit!" It's books and papers up to the ceiling! If you ask me, we should just forget it's there and quietly tiptoe away. . . .

Gardner: My study! . . .

    Fanny: Let the new owners dispose of everything. . . .

Gardner: *[Gets out of his posing chair.]* Now, just one minute. . . .

    Fanny: You never look at half the stuff in there!

Gardner: I don't want you touching those books! They're mine!

    Fanny: Darling, we're moving to a cottage the size of a handkerchief! Where, pray tell, is there room for all your books?

Gardner: I don't know. We'll just have to make room!

    Mags: *[Sketching away.]* RATS!

    Fanny: I don't know what we're doing fooling around with Mags like this when there's still so much to do. . . .

Gardner: *[Sits back down, overwhelmed.]* My study! . . .

    Fanny: You can stay with her if you'd like, but one of us has got to tackle those books!

[She exits to his study.]

Gardner: I'm not up to this.

    Mags: Oh, good, you're staying!

Gardner: There's a lifetime of work in there. . . .

    Mags: Don't worry, I'll help. Mum and I will be able to pack everything up in no time.

Gardner: God. . . .

    Mags: It won't be so bad. . . .

Gardner: I'm just not up to it.

    Mags: We'll all pitch in. . . .

[Gardner sighs, speechless. A silence as Fanny comes staggering in with an armload of books which she drops to the floor with a crash.]

Gardner: WHAT WAS   *Mags:* GOOD GRIEF!
    THAT?! . . .

    Fanny: *[Sheepish.]* Sorry, sorry. . . .

[She exits for more.]

Gardner: I don't know if I can take this. . . .

    Mags: Moving is awful . . . I know. . . .

Gardner: *[Settling back into his pose.]* Ever since Mum began tearing the house apart, I've been having these dreams. . . . I'm a child again back at Sixteen Louisberg Square . . . and this stream of moving men is carrying furniture into our house . . . van after van of tables and chairs, sofas and love seats, desks and bureaus . . . rugs, bathtubs, mirrors, chiming clocks, pianos, iceboxes, china cabinets . . . but what's amazing is that all of it is familiar . . . *[Fanny comes in with another load which she drops on the floor. She exits for more.]* No matter how many items appear, I've seen every one of them before. Since my mother is standing in the midst of it direct-, ing traffic, I ask her where it's all coming from, but she doesn't hear me because of the racket . . . so finally I just scream out . . . "WHERE IS ALL THIS FURNITURE COMING FROM?" . . . Just as a moving man is carrying Toots into the room, she looks at me and says, "Why, from the land of Skye!" . . . The next thing I know, *people* are being carried in along with it. . . . *[Fanny enters with her next load; drops it and exits.]* People I've never seen before are sitting around our dining-room table. A group of foreigners is going through my books, chattering in a language I've never heard before. A man is playing a Chopin polonaise on Aunt Alice's piano. Several children are taking baths in our tubs from Cotuit. . . .

Mags: It sounds marvelous.
Gardner: Well, it isn't marvelous at all because all of these perfect strangers have taken over our things. . . .

[Fanny enters, hurls down another load and exits.]

Mags: How odd. . . .
Gardner: Well, it *is* odd, but then something even odder happens. . . .
Mags: *[Sketching away.]* Tell me, tell me!
Gardner: Well, our beds are carried in. They're all made up with sheets and everything, but instead of all these strange people in them, *we're* in them! . . .
Mags: What's so odd about that? . . .
Gardner: Well, you and Mum are brought in, both sleeping like angels . . . Mum snoring away to beat the band. . . .
Mags: Yes. . . .

[Fanny enters with another load; lets it fall.]

Gardner: But there's no one in mine. It's completely empty, never even been slept in! It's as if I were dead or had never even existed. . . . *[Fanny exits.]* "HEY . . . WAIT UP!" I yell to the moving men . . . "THAT'S MY BED YOU'VE GOT THERE!" But they don't stop; they don't even acknowledge me. . . . "HEY, COME BACK HERE . . . I WANT TO GET INTO MY BED!" I cry again and I start running after them . . . down the hall, through the dining room, past the library. . . . Finally I catch up to them and hurl myself right into the center of the pillow. Just as I'm about to land, the bed suddenly vanishes and I go crashing down to the floor like some insect that's been hit by a fly swatter!
Fanny: *[Staggers in with her final load; drops it with a crash and then col-*

lapses in her posing chair.] THAT'S IT FOR ME! I'M DEAD!
[Silence.] Come on, Mags, how about you doing a little work
around here.

Mags: That's all I've been doing! This is the first free moment
you've given me!

Fanny: You should see all the books in there . . . and papers! There
are enough loose papers to sink a ship!

Gardner: Why is it we're moving, again?

Fanny: Because life is getting too complicated here.

Gardner: *[Remembering.]* Oh, yes . . .

Fanny: And we can't afford it anymore.

Gardner: That's right, that's right. . . .

Fanny: We don't have the . . . *income* we used to!

Gardner: Oh, yes . . . *income!*

Fanny: *[Assuming her pose again.]* Of course, we have our savings and
various trust funds, but I wouldn't dream of touching those!

Gardner: No, no, you must never dip into capital!

Fanny: I told Daddy I'd be perfectly happy to buy a gun and put a
bullet through our heads so we could avoid all this, but he
wouldn't hear of it!

Mags: *[Sketching away.]* No, I shouldn't think so.

[Pause.]

Fanny: I've always admired people who kill themselves when they get
to our stage of life. Well, no one can touch my Uncle Edmond in
that department. . . .

Mags: I know, I know. . . .

Fanny: The day before his seventieth birthday he climbed to the top
of the Old North Church and hurled himself facedown into Salem
Street! They had to scrape him up with a spatula! God, he was a
remarkable man . . . state senator, president of Harvard. . . .

Gardner: *[Rises and wanders over to his books.]* Well, I guess I'm going to
have to do something about all of these. . . .

Fanny: Come on, Mags, help Daddy! Why don't you start bringing in
his papers. . . .

*[Gardner sits on the floor; picks up a book and soon is engrossed in it. Mags keeps
sketching, oblivious; silence.]*

Fanny: *[To* Mags.*]* Darling? . . . HELLO? . . . God, you two are
impossible! Just look at you . . . heads in the clouds! No one
would ever know we've got to be out of here in two days. If it
weren't for me, nothing would get done around here. . . . *[She
starts stacking* Gardner's *books into piles.]* There! That's all the
maroon ones!

Gardner: *[Looks up.]* What do you mean, *maroon* ones?! . . .

Fanny: All your books that are maroon are in *this* pile . . . and your books that are green in *that* pile! . . . I'm trying to bring some order into your life for once. This will make unpacking so much easier.

Gardner: But, my dear Fanny, it's not the color of a book that distinguishes it, but what's *inside* it!

Fanny: This will be a great help, you'll see. Now what about this awful striped thing? *[She picks up a slim, aged volume.]* Can't it go?

Gardner: No!

Fanny: But it's as queer as Dick's hat band! There are no others like it.

Gardner: Open it and read. Go on . . . open it!

Fanny: We'll get nowhere at this rate.

Gardner: I said . . . READ!

Fanny: Really, Gar, I . . .

Gardner: Read the dedication!

Fanny: *[Opens and reads.]* "To Gardner Church, you led the way. With gratitude and affection, Robert Frost."

[She closes it and hands it to him.]

Gardner: It was published the same year as my *Salem Gardens*.

Fanny: *[Picking up a very worn book.]* Well, what about this dreadful thing? It's filthy. *[She blows off a cloud of dust.]*

Gardner: Please . . . *please?!*

Fanny: *[Looking through it.]* It's all in French.

Gardner: *[Snatching it away from her.]* André Malraux gave me that! . . .

Fanny: I'm just trying to help.

Gardner: It's a first edition of Baudelaire's *Fleurs du Mal*.

Fanny: *[Giving it back.]* Well, pardon me for living!

Gardner: Why do you have to drag everything in here in the first place? . . .

Fanny: Because there's no room in your study. You ought to see the mess in there! . . . WAKE UP, MAGS, ARE YOU GOING TO PITCH IN OR NOT?! . . .

Gardner: I'm not up to this.

Fanny: Well, you'd better be unless you want to be left behind!

Mags: *[Stops her sketching.]* All right, all right . . . I just hope you'll give me some more time later this evening.

Fanny: *[To Mags.]* Since you're young and in the best shape, why don't you bring in the books and I'll cope with the papers. *[She exits to the study.]*

Gardner: Now just a minute. . . .

Fanny: *[Offstage.]* WE NEED A STEAM SHOVEL FOR THIS!

Mags: OK, what do you want me to do?

Gardner: Look, I don't want you messing around with my . . .

[Fanny enters with an armful of papers which she drops into an empty carton.]

Tina Howe 1955

Gardner: HEY, WHAT'S GOING ON HERE?! . . .
   Fanny: I'm packing up your papers. COME ON, MAGS, LET'S GET
      CRACKING!

[She exits for more papers.]

Gardner: *[Plucks several papers out of the carton.]* What is this? . . .
   Mags: *[Exits into his study.]* GOOD LORD, WHAT HAVE YOU DONE
      IN HERE?! . . .
Gardner: *[Reading.]* This is my manuscript.

*[*Fanny *enters with another batch which she tosses on top of the others.]*

Gardner: What *are* you doing?! . . .
   Fanny: Packing, darling . . . PACKING!

[She exits for more.]

Gardner: SEE HERE, YOU CAN'T MANHANDLE MY THINGS THIS
      WAY! *[*Mags *enters, staggering under a load of books which she sets
      down on the floor.]* I PACK MY MANUSCRIPT! I KNOW WHERE
      EVERYTHING IS!
   Fanny: *[Offstage.]* IF IT WERE UP TO YOU, WE'D NEVER GET OUT
      OF HERE! WE'RE UNDER A TIME LIMIT, GARDNER. KITTY'S
      PICKING US UP IN TWO DAYS . . . TWO . . . DAYS!

[She enters with a larger batch of papers and heads for the carton.]

Gardner: *[Grabbing* Fanny's *wrist.]* NOW, HOLD IT! . . . JUST . . . HOLD
      IT RIGHT THERE! . . .
   Fanny: OOOOOWWWWWWWW!
Gardner: *I* PACK MY THINGS! . . .
   Fanny: *[Lifting the papers high over her head.]* I'M IN CHARGE OF
      THIS MOVE, GARDNER! WE'VE GOT TO GET CRACKING!
Gardner: I said . . . GIVE IT TO ME!
   Mags: Come on, Mum, let him have it.

[They struggle.]

Gardner: *[Finally wrenches the pages from her.]* LET . . . ME . . . HAVE . . .
      IT! . . . THAT'S MORE LIKE IT! . . .
   Fanny: *[Soft and weepy.]* You see what he's like? . . . I try and help
      with his packing and what does he do? . . .
Gardner: *[Rescues the rest of his papers from the carton.]* YOU DON'T JUST
      THROW EVERYTHING INTO A BOX LIKE A PILE OF GARBAGE!
      THIS IS A BOOK, FANNY. SOMETHING I'VE BEEN WORKING ON
      FOR TWO YEARS! . . . *[Trying to assemble his papers, but only making
      things worse, dropping them all over the place.]* You show a little
      respect for my things. . . . You don't just throw them around
      every which way. . . . It's tricky trying to make sense of poetry; it's

much easier to write the stuff . . . that is, if you've still got it in you. . . .

Mags: Here, let me help. . . . *[Taking some of the papers.]*

Gardner: Criticism is tough sledding. You can't just dash off a few images here, a few rhymes there. . . .

Mags: Do you have these pages numbered in any way?

Fanny: *[Returning to her posing chair.]* HA!

Gardner: This is just the introduction.

Mags: I don't see any numbers on these.

Gardner: *[Exiting to his study.]* The important stuff is in my study. . . .

Fanny: *[To* Mags.] You don't know the half of it . . . *not the half!* . . .

Gardner: *[Offstage; thumping around.]* HAVE YOU SEEN THOSE YEATS POEMS I JUST HAD? . . .

Mags: *[Reading over several pages.]* What is this? . . . It doesn't make sense. It's just fragments . . . pieces of poems.

Fanny: That's it, honey! That's his book. His great critical study! Now that he can't write his own poetry, he's trying to explain other people's. The only problem is, he can't get beyond typing them out. The poor lamb doesn't have the stamina to get beyond the opening stanzas, let alone trying to make sense of them.

Gardner: *[Thundering back with more papers which keep falling.]* GOD DAMNIT, FANNY, WHAT DID YOU DO IN THERE? I CAN'T FIND ANYTHING!

Fanny: I just took the papers that were on your desk.

Gardner: Well, the entire beginning is gone.

[He exits.]

Fanny: I'M TRYING TO HELP YOU, DARLING!

Gardner: *[Returns with another armload.]* SEE THAT? . . . NO SIGN OF CHAPTER ONE OR TWO. . . . *[He flings it all down to the floor.]*

Fanny: Gardner . . . PLEASE?!

Gardner: *[Kicking through the mess.]* I TURN MY BACK FOR ONE MINUTE AND WHAT HAPPENS? . . . MY ENTIRE STUDY IS TORN APART!

[He exits.]

Mags: Oh, Daddy . . . don't . . . please . . . Daddy . . . *please?!*

Gardner: *[Returns with a new batch of papers which he tosses up into the air.]* THROWN OUT! . . . THE BEST PART IS THROWN OUT! . . . LOST. . . .

[He starts to exit again.]

Mags: *[Reads one of the fragments to steady herself.]*
"I have known the inexorable sadness of pencils,
Neat in their boxes, dolor of pad and paperweight,

Tina Howe   1957

All the misery of manila folders and mucilage . . ."
They're beautiful . . . just beautiful.

Gardner: [Stops.] Hey, what's that you've got there?

Fanny: It's your manuscript, darling. You see, it's right where you left it.

Gardner: [To Mags.*]* Read that again.

Mags: "I have known the inexorable sadness of pencils,
Neat in their boxes, dolor of pad and paperweight,
All the misery of manila folders and mucilage . . ."

Gardner: Well, well, what do you know. . . .

Fanny: [Hands him several random papers.] You see . . . no one lost anything. Everything's here, still intact.

Gardner: [Reads.] "I knew a woman, lovely in her bones,
When small birds sighed, she would sigh back at them;
Ah, when she moved, she moved more ways than one:
The shapes a bright container can contain! . . ."

Fanny: [Hands him another.] And . . .

Gardner: [Reads.] Ahh . . . Frost . . .

"Some say the world will end in fire,
Some say ice.
From what I've tasted of desire
I hold with those who favor fire."

Fanny: [Under her breath to Mags.*]* He can't give up the words. It's the best he can do. *[Handing him another.]* Here you go, here's more.

Gardner:

"Farm boys wild to couple
With anything with soft-wooded trees
With mounds of earth mounds
Of pinestraw will keep themselves off
Animals by legends of their own . . ."

Mags: [Eyes shut.] Oh, Daddy, I can't bear it . . . I . . .

Fanny: Of course no one will ever publish this.

Gardner: Oh, here's a marvelous one. Listen to this!

"There came a Wind like a Bugle—
It quivered through the Grass
And a Green Chill upon the heat
So ominous did pass
We barred the Windows and the Doors
As from an Emerald Ghost—
The Doom's electric Moccasin . . ."
SHIT, WHERE DID THE REST OF IT GO? . . .

Fanny: Well, don't ask *me.*

Gardner: It just stopped in mid-air!

Fanny: Then go look for the original.
Gardner: Good idea, good idea!

[He exits to his study.]

Fanny: [To Mags.*]* He's incontinent now, too. He wets his pants, in case you haven't noticed. *[She starts laughing.]* You're not laughing. Don't you think it's funny? Daddy needs diapers. . . . I don't know about you, but I could use a drink! GAR . . . WILL YOU GET ME A SPLASH WHILE YOU'RE OUT THERE? . . .

Mags: STOP IT!

Fanny: It means we can't go out anymore. I mean, what would people say? . . .

Mags: Stop it. Just stop it.

Fanny: My poet laureate can't hold it in! *[She laughs harder.]*

Mags: That's enough . . . STOP IT . . . Mummy . . . I beg of you . . . *please stop it!*

Gardner: [Enters with a book and indeed a large stain has blossomed on his trousers. He plucks it away from his leg.] Here we go . . . I found it. . . .

Fanny: [Pointing at it.] See that? See? . . . He just did it again! *[Goes off into a shower of laughter.]*

Mags: [Looks, turns away.] SHUT . . . UP! . . . *[Building to a howl.]* WILL YOU PLEASE JUST . . . SHUT . . . UP!

Fanny: [To Gardner.*]* Hey, what about that drink?

Gardner: Oh, yes . . . sorry, sorry . . .

[He heads towards the bar.]

Fanny: Never mind, I'll get it, I'll get it. *[She exits, convulsed; silence.]*

Gardner: Well, where were we? . . .

Mags: [Near tears.] Your poem.

Gardner: Oh, yes . . . the Dickinson. *[He shuts his eyes, reciting from memory, holding the book against his chest.]*

> "There came a Wind like a Bugle—
> It quivered through the Grass
> And a Green Chill upon the heat
> So ominous did pass
> We barred the Windows and the Doors
> As from an Emerald Ghost—"

[Opens the book and starts riffling through it.] Let's see now, where's the rest? . . . *[He finally finds it.]* Ahhh, here we go! . . .

Fanny: [Reenters, drink in hand.] I'm back! *[Takes one look at* Gardner *and bursts out laughing again.]*

Mags: I don't believe you! How can you laugh at him?! . . .

Fanny: I'm sorry, I wish I could stop, but there's really nothing else to do. Look at him . . . just . . . look at him . . . !

[This is all simultaneous as Mags gets angrier and angrier.]

> *Mags:* It's so cruel. . . . You're so . . . incredibly cruel to him. . . . I mean, YOUR DISDAIN REALLY TAKES MY BREATH AWAY! YOU'RE IN A CLASS BY YOURSELF WHEN IT COMES TO HUMILIATION! . . .

Gardner: *[Reading.]*

> "The Doom's electric Moccasin
> That very instant passed—
> On a strange Mob of panting Trees
> And Fences fled away
> And Rivers where the Houses ran
> Those looked that lived—that Day—
> The Bell within the steeple wild
> The flying tidings told—
> How much can come
> And much can go,
> And yet abide the World!"

[He shuts the book with a bang, pauses and looks around the room, confused.] Now, where was I? . . .

Fanny: Safe and sound in the middle of the living room with Mags and me.

Gardner: But I was looking for something, wasn't I? . . .

Fanny: Your manuscript.

Gardner: THAT'S RIGHT! MY MANUSCRIPT! My manuscript!

Fanny: And here it is all over the floor. See, you're standing on it.

Gardner: *[Picks up a few pages and looks at them.]* Why, so I am. . . .

Fanny: Now all we have to do is get it up off the floor and packed neatly into these cartons!

Gardner: Yes, yes, that's right. Into the cartons.

Fanny: *[Kicks a carton over to him.]* Here, you use this one and I'll start over here. . . . *[She starts dropping papers into a carton nearby.]* BOMBS AWAY! . . . Hey . . . this is fun! . . .

Gardner: *[Picks up his own pile, lifts it high over his head and flings it down into the carton.]* BOMBS AWAY . . . Hey . . . this *is* fun! . . .

Fanny: I told you! The whole thing is to figure out a system!

Gardner: I don't know what I'd do without you, Fan. I thought I'd lost everything.

Fanny: *[Makes dive-bomber noises and machine-gun explosions as she wheels more and more papers into the carton.]* TAKE THAT AND THAT AND THAT! . . .

Gardner: *[Joins in the fun, outdoing her with dips, dives and blastings of his own.]* BLAM BLAM BLAM BLAM! . . . ZZZZZZZZRAAAAAA FOOM! . . . BLATTY-DE-BLATTY-DE-BLATTY-DE-KABOOOOOOOOOM! . . . WHAAAAAAA . . . DA-DAT-DAT-DAT-DAT . . . WHEEEEEEEE AAAAAAAAAAAA . . . FOOOOOO . . .

[They get louder and louder as papers fly every which way.]

Fanny: *[Mimes getting hit with a bomb.]* AEEEEEEIIIIIIIIIIIII! YOU
   GOT ME RIGHT IN THE GIZZARD! *[She collapses on the floor and
   starts going through death throes, having an absolute ball.]*

Gardner: TAKE THAT AND THAT AND THAT AND THAT . . . *[A series of
   explosions follow.]*

Mags: *[Furious.]* This is how you help him? . . . THIS IS HOW YOU
   PACK HIS THINGS? . . .

Fanny: I keep him company. I get involved . . . which is a hell of a lot
   more than you do!

Mags: *[Wild with rage.]* BUT YOU'RE MAKING A MOCKERY OF
   HIM. . . . YOU TREAT HIM LIKE A CHILD OR SOME DIM-WIT-
   TED SERVING BOY. HE'S JUST AN AMUSEMENT TO YOU! . . .

Fanny: *[Fatigue has finally overtaken her. She's calm, almost serene.]* . . .
   and to you who see him once a year, if that . . . What is he to
   you? . . . I mean, what do you give him from yourself that costs
   you something? . . . Hmmmmmm? . . . *[Imitating her.]* "Oh, hi
   Daddy, it's great to see you again. How have you been? . . . Gee,
   I love your hair. It's gotten so . . . *white!*" . . . What color do you
   expect it to get when he's this age? . . . I mean, if you care so
   much how he looks, why don't you come and see him once in a
   while? . . . But oh, no . . . you have your paintings to do and your
   shows to put on. You just come and see us when the whim strikes.
   [Imitating her.] "Hey, you know what would be really great? . . .
   To do a portrait of you! I've always wanted to paint you, you're
   such great subjects!" . . . *Paint* us?! . . . What about opening
   your eyes and really *seeing* us? . . . Noticing what's going on
   around here for a change! It's all over for Daddy and me. This is
   it! "Finita la commedia!" . . . All I'm trying to do is exit with a little flourish; have some fun. . . . What's so terrible about
   that? . . . It can get pretty grim around here, in case you haven't
   noticed . . . Daddy, tap-tap-tapping out his nonsense all day; me
   traipsing around to the thrift shops trying to amuse myself . . . He
   never keeps me company anymore; never takes me out anywhere. . . . I'd put a bullet through my head in a minute, but then
   who'd look after him? . . . What do you think we're moving to the
   cottage for? . . . So I can watch him like a hawk and make sure he
   doesn't get lost. Do you think that's anything to look forward
   to? . . . Being Daddy's nursemaid out in the middle of nowhere?
   I'd much rather stay here in Boston with the few friends I have
   left, but you can't always do what you want in this world . . .
   "L'homme propose, Dieu dispose!" . . . If you want to paint us so
   badly, you ought to paint us as we really are. There's your picture! . . . *[She points to* Gardner *who's quietly playing with a paper
   glide.]* Daddy spread out on the floor with all his toys and me

hovering over him to make sure he doesn't hurt himself! *[She goes over to him.]* YOO-HOO . . . GAR? . . . HELLO? . . .

Gardner: *[Looks up at her.]* Oh, hi there, Fan. What's up?

    Fanny: How's the packing coming? . . .

Gardner: Packing? . . .

    Fanny: Yes, you were packing your manuscript, remember? *[She lifts up a page and lets it fall into a carton.]*

Gardner: Oh, yes. . . .

    Fanny: Here's your picture, Mags. Face over this way . . . turn your easel over here. . . . *[She lets a few more papers fall.]* Up, up . . . and away. . . .

BLACKOUT

Scene 2

The last day. All the books and boxes are gone. The room is completely empty except for Mags' backdrop. Late afternoon light dapples the walls; it changes from pale peach to deeper violet. The finished portrait sits on the easel, covered with a cloth. Mags *is taking down the backdrop.*

    Fanny: *[Offstage; to* Gardner.] DON'T FORGET TOOTS!

Gardner: *[Offstage; from another part of the house.]* WHAT'S THAT? . . .

    Fanny: *[Offstage:]* I SAID: DON'T FORGET TOOTS! HIS CAGE IS SITTING IN THE MIDDLE OF YOUR STUDY! *[Silence.]*

    Fanny: *[Offstage.]*   *Gardner:* *[Offstage.]* I'LL BE
HELLO? . . . ARE YOU   RIGHT WITH YOU: I'M
THERE? . . .   JUST GETTING TOOTS!

Gardner: *[Offstage.]* WHAT'S THAT? I CAN'T HEAR YOU?

    Fanny: *[Offstage.]* I'M GOING THROUGH THE ROOMS ONE MORE TIME TO MAKE SURE WE DIDN'T FORGET ANYTHING. . . . KITTY'S PICKING US UP IN FIFTEEN MINUTES, SO PLEASE BE READY. . . . SHE'S DROPPING MAGS OFF AT THE STATION AND THEN IT'S OUT TO ROUTE 3 AND THE CAPE HIGHWAY. . . .

Gardner: *[Enters, carrying* Toots *in his cage.]* Well, this is it. The big moment has finally come, eh what, Toots? *[He sees* Mags.] Oh, hi there, Mags, I didn't see you. . . .

    Mags: Oh, hi, Daddy, I'm just taking this down. . . . *[She does and walks over to* Toots.] Oh, Toots, I'll miss you. *[She makes little chattering noises into his cage.]*

Gardner: Come on, recite a little Grey's Elegy for Mags before we go.

    Mags: Yes, Mum said he was really good at it now.

Gardner: Well, the whole thing is to keep at it every day. *[Slowly to* Toots.]

        "The curfew tolls the knell of parting day,
          The lowing herd wind slowly o'er the lea . . ."

    Come on, show Mags your stuff!

[Slower.]

"The curfew tolls the knell of parting day,
The lowing herd wind slowly o'er the lea . . . ."

[Silence; Gardner *makes little chattering sounds.*]

Come on, Toots, old boy. . . .
Mags: How does it go?
Gardner: [*To* Mags.] "The curfew tolls the knell of parting day,
The lowing herd winds slowly o'er the lea . . . ."
Mags: [*Slowly to* Toots.] "The curfew tolls for you and me,
As quietly the herd winds down . . . ."
Gardner: No, no, it's, "The curfew tolls the knell of parting *day* . . . "*!
Mags: [*Repeating after him.*] "The curfew tolls the knell of parting
day . . . ."
Gardner: "The lowing herd wind slowly o'er the lea . . . ."
Mags: [*With a deep breath.*] "The curfew tolls at parting day,
The herd low slowly down the lea . . . no, *knell!*
They come winding down the *knell! . . . "*
Gardner: Listen, Mags . . . *listen!*

[A pause.]

Toots: [*Loud and clear with* Gardner'*s inflection.*]
"The curfew tolls the knell of parting day,
The lowing herd wind slowly o'er the lea,
The ploughman homeward plods his weary way,
And leaves the world to darkness and to me."
Mags: HE SAID IT. . . . HE SAID IT! . . . AND IN YOUR VOICE! . . .
OH, DADDY, THAT'S AMAZING!
Gardner: Well, Toots is very smart, which is more than I can say for a lot
of people I know. . . .
Mags: [*To* Toots.] Polly want a cracker? Polly want a cracker?
Gardner: You can teach a parakeet to say anything; all you need is
patience. . . .
Mags: But *poetry* . . . that's so hard. . . .
Fanny: [*Enters carrying a suitcase and* Gardner'*s typewriter in its case.
She's dressed in her traveling suit, wearing a hat to match.*] WELL,
THERE YOU ARE! I THOUGHT YOU'D DIED!
Mags: [*To* Fanny.] HE SAID IT! I FINALLY HEARD TOOTS RECITE
GREY'S ELEGY. [*She makes silly clucking sounds into the cage.*]
Fanny: Isn't it uncanny how much he sounds like Daddy? Sometimes
when I'm alone here with him, I've actually thought he *was* Daddy
and started talking to him. Oh, yes, Toots and I have had quite a
few meaty conversations together!

[Fanny *wolf-whistles into the cage; then draws back.* Gardner *covers the cage with
a traveling cloth. Silence.*]

Tina Howe   1963

Fanny: [*Looking around the room.*] God, the place looks so bare.

Mags: I still can't believe it . . . Cotuit, year round. I wonder if there'll be any phosphorus when you get there?

Fanny: What on earth are you talking about? [*She carries the discarded backdrop out into the hall.*]

Mags: Remember that summer when the ocean was full of phosphorus?

Gardner: [*Taking* Toots *out into the hall.*] Oh, yes. . . .

Mags: It was a great mystery where it came from or why it settled in Cotuit. But one evening when Daddy and I were taking a swim, suddenly it was there!

Gardner: [*Returns.*] I remember.

Mags: I don't know where Mum was. . . .

Fanny: [*Reentering.*] Probably doing the dishes!

Mags: [*To* Gardner.] As you dove into the water, this shower of silvery green sparks erupted all around you. It was incredible! I thought you were turning into a saint or something; but then you told me to jump in too and the same thing happened to me. . . .

Gardner: Oh, yes, I remember that . . . the water smelled all queer.

Mags: What *is* phosphorus, anyway?

Gardner: Chemicals, chemicals . . .

Fanny: No, it isn't. Phosphorus is a green liquid inside insects. Fireflies have it. When you see sparks in the water it means insects are swimming around. . . .

Gardner: Where on earth did you get that idea? . . .

Fanny: If you're bitten by one of them, it's fatal!

Mags: . . . and the next morning it was still there. . . .

Gardner: It was the damndest stuff to get off! We'd have to stay in the shower a good ten minutes. It comes from chemical waste, you see. . . .

Mags: Our bodies looked like mercury as we swam around. . . .

Gardner: It stained all the towels a strange yellow green.

Mags: I was in heaven, and so were you for that matter. You'd finished your day's poetry and would turn somersaults like some happy dolphin. . . .

Fanny: Damned dishes . . . why didn't I see any of this?! . . .

Mags: I remember one night in particular. . . . We sensed the phosphorus was about to desert us; blow off to another town. We were chasing each other under water. At one point I lost you, the brilliance was so intense . . . but finally your foot appeared . . . then your leg. I grabbed it! . . . I remember wishing the moment would hold forever; that we could just be fixed there, laughing and iridescent. . . . Then I began to get panicky because I knew it would pass; it was passing already. You were slipping from my grasp. The summer was almost over. I'd be going back to art school; you'd be going back to Boston. . . . Even as I was reaching for you, you were gone. We'd never be like that again.

[Silence.]

    Fanny: *[Spies* Mags's *portrait covered on the easel.]* What's that over there? Don't tell me we forgot something!

    Mags: It's your portrait. I finished it.

    Fanny: You finished it? How on earth did you manage that?

    Mags: I stayed up all night.

    Fanny: You did? . . . *I* didn't hear you, did you hear her, Gar? . . .

Gardner: Not a peep, not a peep!

    Mags: Well, I wanted to get it done before you left. You know, see what you thought. It's not bad, considering . . . I mean, I did it almost completely from memory. The light was terrible and I was trying to be quiet so I wouldn't wake you. It was hardly an ideal situation. . . . I mean, you weren't the most cooperative models. . . . *[She suddenly panics and snatches the painting off the easel. She hugs it to her chest and starts dancing around the room with it.]* Oh, God, you're going to hate it! You're going to hate it! How did I ever get into this? . . . Listen, you don't really want to see it . . . it's nothing . . . just a few dabs here and there. . . . It was awfully late when I finished it. The light was really impossible and my eyes were hurting like crazy. . . . Look, why don't we just go out to the sidewalk and wait for Kitty so she doesn't have to honk. . . .

Gardner: *[Snatches the painting out from under her.]* WOULD YOU JUST SHUT UP A MINUTE AND LET US SEE IT? . . .

    Mags: *[Laughing and crying.]* But it's nothing, Daddy . . . *really!* . . . I've done better with my eyes closed! It was so late I could hardly see anything and then I spilled a whole bottle of thinner into my palette. . . .

Gardner: *[Sets it down on the easel and stands back to look at it.]* THERE!

    Mags: *[Dancing around them in a panic.]* Listen, it's just a quick sketch. . . . It's still wet. . . . I didn't have enough time. . . . It takes at least forty hours to do a decent portrait. . . .

[Suddenly it's very quiet as Fanny *and* Gardner *stand back to look at it.]*

    Mags: *[More and more beside herself, keeps leaping around the room wrapping her arms around herself, making little whimpering sounds.]* Please don't . . . no . . . don't . . . oh, please! . . . Come on, don't look. . . . Oh, God, don't . . . please. . . .

[An eternity passes as Fanny *and* Gardner *gaze at it.]*

Gardner: Well . . .

    Fanny: Well . . . *[More silence.]*

Fanny: I think it's perfectly   *Gardner:* Awfully clever,
    dreadful!   awfully clever!

Fanny: What on earth did you do to my face? . . .

Gardner: I particularly like Mum!

Fanny: Since when do I have purple skin?! . . .

Mags: I told you it was nothing, just a silly . . .

Gardner: She looks like a million dollars!

Fanny: AND WILL YOU LOOK AT MY HAIR . . . IT'S BRIGHT ORANGE!

Gardner: *[Views it from another angle.]* It's really very good!

Fanny: *[Pointing.]* That doesn't look anything like me!

Gardner: . . . first rate!

Fanny: Since when do I have purple skin and bright orange hair?! . . .

Mags: *[Trying to snatch it off the easel.]* Listen, you don't have to worry about my feelings . . . really . . . I . . .

Gardner: *[Blocking her way.]* NOT SO FAST . . .

Fanny: . . . and look at how I'm sitting! I've never sat like that in my life!

Gardner: *[Moving closer to it.]* Yes, yes, it's awfully clever. . . .

Fanny: I HAVE NO FEET!

Gardner: The whole thing is quite remarkable!

Fanny: And what happened to my legs, pray tell? . . . They just vanish below the knees! . . . At least my dress is presentable. I've always loved that dress.

Gardner: It sparkles somehow. . . .

Fanny: *[To* Gardner.*]* Don't you think it's becoming?

Gardner: Yes, very becoming, awfully becoming . . .

Fanny: *[Examining it at closer range.]* Yes, she got the dress very well, how it shows off what's left of my figure. . . . My smile is nice too.

Gardner: Good and wide. . . .

Fanny: I love how the corners of my mouth turn up. . . .

Gardner: It's very clever. . . .

Fanny: They're almost quivering. . . .

Gardner: Good lighting effects!

Fanny: Actually, I look quite . . . *young,* don't you think?

Gardner: *[To* Mags.*]* You're awfully good with those highlights.

Fanny: *[Looking at it from different angles.]* And *you* look darling! . . .

Gardner: Well, I don't know about that. . . .

Fanny: No, you look absolutely darling. Good enough to eat!

Mags: *[In a whisper.]* They like it. . . . They like it!

[A silence as Fanny *and* Gardner *keep gazing at it.]*

Fanny: You know what it is? The wispy brush strokes make us look like a couple in a French Impressionist painting.

Gardner: Yes, I see what you mean. . . .

Fanny: . . . a Manet or Renoir . . .

Gardner: It's very evocative.

Fanny: There's something about the light. . . . *[They back up to survey it from a distance.]*

Fanny: You know those Renoir café scenes? . . .

Gardner: She doesn't lay on the paint with a trowel; it's just touches here and there. . . .

Mags: They *like* it! . . .

Fanny: You know the one with the couple dancing? . . . Not that we're dancing. There's just something similar in the mood . . . a kind of gaiety, almost. . . . The man has his back to you and he's swinging the woman around. . . . OH, GAR, YOU'VE SEEN IT A MILLION TIMES! IT'S HANGING IN THE MUSEUM OF FINE ARTS! . . . They're dancing like this. . . .

[She goes up to him and puts an arm on his shoulders.]

Mags: They like it. . . . They like it!

Fanny: She's got on this wonderful flowered dress with ruffles at the neck and he's holding her like this. . . . That's right . . . and she's got the most rhapsodic expression on her face. . . .

Gardner: [Getting into the spirit of it, takes Fanny *in his arms and slowly begins to dance around the room.]* Oh, yes . . . I know the one you mean. . . . They're in a sort of haze . . . and isn't there a little band playing off to one side? . . .

Fanny: Yes, that's it!

[Kitty's horn honks outside.]

Mags: [Is the only one who hears it.] There's Kitty! *[She's torn and keeps looking towards the door, but finally gives in to their stolen moment.]*

Fanny: . . . and there's a man in a dark suit playing the violin and someone's conducting, I think. . . . And aren't Japanese lanterns strung up? . . .

[They pick up speed, dipping and whirling around the room. Strains of a far-away Chopin waltz are heard.]

Gardner: Oh, yes! There are all these little lights twinkling in the trees. . . .

Fanny: . . . and doesn't the woman have a hat on? . . . A big red hat? . . .

Gardner: . . . and lights all over the dancers, too. Everything shimmers with this marvelous glow. Yes, yes . . . I can see it perfectly! The whole thing is absolutely extraordinary!

[The lights become dreamy and dappled as they dance around the room. Mags watches them, moved to tears as . . .]

SLOWLY THE CURTAIN FALLS

Tina Howe   *1967*

"Painting Churches" opened at the Lambs Theater, New York City, in November of 1983, with Marian Seldes attracting a good deal of attention for her portrayal of Fanny Gardner. In his review of the performance, Gerald Weales touches on the great difficulty of blending comedy with serious content, and points to the importance of one pivotal scene.

"The scene should be as horrifying as it is funny": Gerald Weales

Howe has more serious work at hand, however—work that never quite gets done. The play is concerned with both the physical and mental indignities of growing old and the conventional parental-child conflict. Gardner, who can no longer write poetry, has turned to criticism, but has been unable to do anything except type out the work of the poets that he intends to discuss. His professional decay has its counterpart in the collapse of the once beautiful marriage of the Churches which exists now only in the parody that the two of them play out under the commanding direction of Fanny. Howe (and Seldes) wants to suggest that Fanny's icy inanity is a survival pose, her way of sustaining Gardner, jollying him toward the grave that she longs to share.

If Mags's memory is correct—the six months she was banished from table and the melted-crayon masterpiece she constructed during her exile in the bedroom—Fanny has always been something of a martinet and the Gardner-Fanny team one that worked with greater charm when there are no intruders, not even children. Mags's memory of swimming in the phosphorus-covered water with her father is an exclude-mother recollection which suggests that this has been as much a triangle as it has a family. Yet, the central tension among the three figures is that the parents—the famous poet and the flamboyant mama—have so intimidated the child that even now, welcomed by the New York art world, she waits their approval most of all. And she gets in an oddly lyric, slightly wacky final scene in which they dance their way into a Renoir painting after looking at the portrait she has done of them.

At the end of the first act, as Mags's babbled demand for recognition brings the broad comedy to a close, the show becomes darker. There are still many laughs—and Seldes goes for them in earnest—but both Fanny and Gardner get angry or pathetic scenes which indicate that growing old is not a joke and the rebellious, loving daughter has her confrontations. Interesting scenes though these are, they seem to grow out of the playwright's skill, not out of the characters. Where the play goes wrong, I think, is in the hilarious scene in which the parents discover how tasty soda crackers are and vie for the box with total concentration while the daughter is trying to tell them that she is about to have her first one-woman show at the Castelli Gallery. The scene is as delicious as the soda crackers, and I and everyone around me laughed noisily; yet I suspect that the scene should be as horrifying as it is funny and the seeds for the later harsher tone planted here. . . .

Painting Churches keeps promising more than it delivers. Still, it is worth seeing because Tina Howe is clearly a talented playwright with an attractively oblique way of seeing, her play is acted with vigor, and the early scenes are triumphantly funny.

Tina Howe *1969*

SAM SHEPARD

(b. 1943)

FOOL FOR LOVE

CHARACTERS

May
Eddie
Martin
The Old Man

This play is to be performed relentlessly without a break.

Scene: Stark, low-rent motel room on the edge of the Mojave Desert. Faded green plaster walls. Dark brown linoleum floor. No rugs. Cast iron four poster single bed, slightly off center favoring stage right, set horizontally to audience. Bed covered with faded blue chenille bedspread. Metal table with well-worn yellow formica top. Two matching metal chairs in the 50s "S" shape design with yellow plastic seats and backs, also well-worn. Table set extreme down left (from actor's p.o.v.). Chairs set upstage and down right of table. Nothing on the table. Faded yellow exterior door in the center of the stage left wall. When this door is opened, a small orange porch light shines into room. Yellow bathroom door up right of the stage right wall. This door slightly ajar to begin with, revealing part of an old style porcelain sink, white towels, a general clutter of female belongings and allowing a yellow light to bleed onto stage. Large picture window dead center of upstage wall, framed by dirty, long, dark green plastic curtains. Yellow-orange light from a street lamp shines thru window.

Extreme down left, next to the table and chairs is a small extended platform on the same level as the stage. The floor is black and it's framed by black curtains. The only object on the platform is an old maple rocking chair facing upstage right. A pillow with no slipcover rests on the seat. An old horse blanket with holes is laced to the back of the rocker. The color of the blanket should be subdued—grays and blacks.

Lights fade to black on set. In the dark, Merle Haggard's tune, "Wake Up" from his "The Way I Am" album is heard. Lights begin to rise slowly on stage in the tempo of the song. Volume swells slightly with the lights until they arrive at their mark. The platform remains in darkness with only a slight spill from the stage lights. Three actors are revealed.

Characters

The Old Man *sits in the rocker facing up right so he's just slightly provile to the audience. A bottle of whiskey sits on the floor beside him. He picks up bottle and pours whiskey into a styrofoam cup and drinks. He has a scraggly red beard, wears an old stained "open-road" Stetson hat (the kind with the short brim), a sun-bleached, dark quilted jacket with the stuffing coming out at the elbows, black and white checkered slacks that are too short in the legs, beat up, dark Western boots, an old vest and a pale green shirt. He exists only in the minds of* May *and* Eddie, *even though they might talk to him directly and acknowledge his physical presence. The* Old Man *treats them as though they all existed in the same time and place.*

May *sits on edge of bed facing audience, feet on floor, legs apart, elbows on knees, hands hanging limp and crossed between her knees, head hanging forward, face staring at floor. She is absolutely still and maintains this attitude until she speaks. She wears a blue denim full skirt, baggy white t-shirt and bare feet with a silver ankle bracelet. She's in her early thirties.*

Eddie *sits in the upstage chair by the table, facing* May. *He wears muddy, broken-down cowboy boots with silver gaffer's tape wrapped around them at the toe and instep, well-worn, faded, dirty jeans that smell like horse sweat. Brown western shirt with snaps. A pair of spurs dangles from his belt. When he walks, he limps slightly and gives the impression he's rarely off a horse. There's a peculiar broken-down quality about his body in general, as though he's aged long before his time. He's in his late thirties.*

On the floor, between his feet, is a leather bucking strap like bronc riders use. He wears a bucking glove on his right hand and works resin into the glove from a small white bag. He stares at May *as he does this and ignores* The Old Man. *As the song nears the end of its fade, he leans over, sticks his gloved hand into the handle of the bucking strap and twists it so that it makes a weird stretching sound from the friction of the resin and leather. The song ends, lights up full. He pulls his hand out and removes gloves.*

> Eddie: *(seated, tossing glove on the table.)* *(short pause)* May, look. May? I'm not goin' anywhere. See? I'm right here. I'm not gone. Look *(She won't.)* I don't know why you won't just look at me. You know it's me. Who else do you think it is. *(Pause)* You want some water or somethin'? Huh? *(He gets up slowly, goes cautiously to her, strokes her head softly, she stays still.)* May? Come on. You can't just sit around here like this. How long you been sittin' here anyway? You want me to go outside and get you something? Some potato chips or

Sam Shepard 1971

something? *(She suddenly grabs his closest leg with both arms and holds tight burying her head between his knees.)* I'm not gonna' leave. Don't worry. I'm not gonna' leave. I'm stayin' right here. I already told ya' that. *(She squeezes tighter to his leg, he just stands there, strokes her head softly.)* May? Let go, okay? Honey? I'll put you back in bed. Okay? *(She grabs his other leg and holds on tight to both.)* Come on. I'll put you in bed and make you some hot tea or somethin'. You want some tea? *(She shakes her head violently, keeps holding on.)* With lemon? Some Ovaltine? May, you gotta' let go of me now, okay? *(Pause, then she pushes him away and returns to her original position.)* Now just lay back and try to relax. *(He starts to try to push her back gently on the bed as he pulls back the blankets. She erupts furiously, leaping off bed and lashing out at him with her fists. He backs off. She returns to bed and stares at him wild-eyed and angry, faces him squarely.)*

Eddie: *(after pause)* You want me to go? *(She shakes her head.)*
May: No!
Eddie: Well, what do you want then?
May: You smell.
Eddie: I smell.
May: You do.
Eddie: I been drivin' for days.
May: Your fingers smell.
Eddie: Horses.
May: Pussy.
Eddie: Come on, May.
May: They smell like metal.
Eddie: I'm not gonna' start this shit.
May: Rich pussy. Very clean.
Eddie: Yeah, sure.
May: You know it's true.
Eddie: I came to see if you were all right.
May: I don't need you!
Eddie: Okay. *(turns to go, collects his glove and bucking strap)* Fine.
May: Don't go!
Eddie: I'm goin'.

(He exits stage left door, slamming it behind him; the door booms.)

May: *(agonized scream)* Don't go!!!

(She grabs pillow, clutching it to her chest then throws herself face down on bed, moaning and moving from one end of bed to the other on her elbows and knees. Eddie is heard returning to stage left door outside. She leaps off bed clutching pillow, stands upstage right of bed, facing stage left door. Eddie enters stage left door,

banging it behind him. He's left the glove and bucking strap off stage. They stand there facing each other for a second. He makes a move toward her. May retreats to extreme upstage right corner of room clutching pillow to her chest. Eddie stays against left wall, facing her.)

    Eddie: What am I gonna' do? Huh? What am I supposed to do?

    May: You know.

    Eddie: What.

    May: You're gonna' erase me.

    Eddie: What're you talkin' about?

    May: You're either gonna' erase me or have me erased.

    Eddie: Why would I want that? Are you kidding?

    May: Because I'm in the way.

    Eddie: Don't be stupid.

    May: I'm smarter than you are and you know it. I can smell your thoughts before you even think 'em.

(Eddie moves along wall to upstage left corner. May holds her ground in opposite corner.)

    Eddie: May, I'm tryin' to take care of you. All right?

    May: No, you're not. You're just guilty. Gutless and guilty.

    Eddie: Great.

(He moves down left to table, sticking close to wall.) (Pause)

    May: (quietly, staying in corner) I'm gonna' kill her ya' know.

    Eddie: Who?

    May: Who.

    Eddie: Don't talk like that.

(May slowly begins to move down stage right as Eddie simultaneously moves up left. Both of them press the walls as they move)

    May: I am. I'm gonna' kill her and then I'm gonna' kill you. Systematically. With sharp knives. Two separate knives. One for her and one for you. *(She slams wall with her elbow. Wall resonates.)* So the blood doesn't mix. I'm gonna' torture her first though. Not you. I'm just gonna' let you have it. Probably in the midst of a kiss. Right when you think everything's been healed up. Right in the moment when you're sure you've got me buffaloed. That's when you'll die.

(She arrives exteme down right at the very limits of the set. Eddie in the extreme up left corner. Pause)

    Eddie: You know how many miles I went outa' my way just to come here and see you? You got any idea?

Sam Shepard   **1973**

 May: Nobody asked you to come.

 Eddie: Two thousand, four hundred and eighty.

 May: Yeah? Where were you, Katmandu or something?

 Eddie: Two thousand, four hundred and eighty miles.

 May: So what!

(He drops his head, stares at floor. Pause. She stares at him. He begins to move slowly down left, sticking close to wall as he speaks.)

 Eddie: I missed you. I did. I missed you more than anything I ever missed in my whole life. I kept thinkin' about you the whole time I was driving. Kept seeing you. Sometimes just a part of you.

 May: Which part?

 Eddie: Your neck.

 May: My neck?

 Eddie: Yeah.

 May: You missed my neck?

 Eddie: I missed all of you but your neck kept coming up for some reason. I kept crying about your neck.

 May: Crying?

 Eddie: *(He stops by stage left door. She stays down right.)* Yeah. Weeping. Like a little baby. Uncontrollable. It would just start up and stop and then start up all over again. For miles. I couldn't stop it. Cars would pass me on the road. People would stare at me. My face was all twisted up. I couldn't stop my face.

 May: Was this before or after your little fling with the Countess?

 Eddie: *(He bangs his head into wall. Wall booms.)* There wasn't any fling with any Countess!

 May: You're a liar.

 Eddie: I took her out to dinner once, okay?

 May: Ha!

(She moves upstage right wall.)

 Eddie: Twice.

 May: You were bumping her on a regular basis! Don't gimme that shit.

 Eddie: You can believe whatever you want.

 May: *(she stops by bathroom door, opposite* Eddie) I'll believe the truth! It's less confusing.

(Pause)

 Eddie: I'm takin' you back, May.

(She tosses pillow on bed and moves to upstage right corner.)

May: I'm not going back to that idiot trailer if that's what you think.

Eddie: I'm movin' it. I got a piece of ground up in Wyoming.

May: Wyoming? Are you crazy? I'm not moving to Wyoming. What's up there? Marlboro Men?

Eddie: You can't stay here.

May: Why not? I got a job. I'm a regular citizen here now.

Eddie: You got a job?

May: (*she moves back down to head of bed*) Yeah. What'd you think, I was helpless?

Eddie: No. I mean—it's been a long time since you had a job.

May: I'm a cook.

Eddie: A cook? You can't even flip an egg, can you?

May: I'm not talkin' to you anymore!

(*She turns away from him, runs into bathroom, slams door behind her. Eddie goes after her, tries door but she's locked it.*)

Eddie: (*at bathroom door*) May, I got everything worked out. I been thinkin' about this for weeks. I'm gonna' move the trailer. Build a little pipe corral to keep the horses. Have a big vegetable garden. Some chickens maybe.

May's Voice: (*unseen, behind bathroom door*) I hate chickens! I hate horses! I hate all that shit! You know that. You got me confused with somebody else. You keep comin' up here with this lame country dream life with chickens and vegetables and I can't stand any of it. It makes me puke to even think about it.

Eddie: (*Eddie has crossed stage left during this, stops at table.*) You'll get used to it.

May: (*enters from bathroom*) You're unbelievable!

(*She slams bathroom door, crosses upstage to window.*)

Eddie: I'm not lettin' go of you this time, May.

(*He sits in chair upstage of table.*)

May: You never had a hold of me to begin with. (*pause*) How many times have you done this to me?

Eddie: What.

May: Suckered me into some dumb little fantasy and then dropped me like a hot rock. How many times has that happened?

Eddie: It's no fantasy.

May: It's all a fantasy.

Eddie: And I never dropped you either.

May: No, you just disappeared!

Eddie: I'm here now aren't I?

Sam Shepard   1975

May: Well, praise Jesus God!

Eddie: I'm gonna take care of you, May. I am. I'm gonna' stick with you no matter what. I promise.

May: Get outa' here.

(Pause)

Eddie: What'd you have to go and run off for anyway.

May: Run off? Me?

Eddie: Yeah. Why couldn't you just stay put. You knew I was comin' back to get you.

May: (crossing down to head of bed) What do you think it's like sittin' in a tin trailer for weeks on end with the wind ripping through it? Waitin' around for the Butane to arrive. Hiking down to the laundromat in the rain. Do you think that's thrilling or somethin'?

Eddie: (still sitting) I bought you all those magazines.

May: What magazines?

Eddie: I bought you a whole stack of those fashion magazines before I left. I thought you liked those. Those French kind.

May: Yeah, I especially liked the one with the Countess on the cover. That was real cute.

(Pause)

Eddie: All right.

(He stands)

May: All right, what.

(He turns to go out stage left door.)

May: Where are you going?

Eddie: Just to get my stuff outa' the truck. I'll be right back.

May: What're you movin' in now or something?

Eddie: Well, I thought I'd spend the night if that's okay.

May: Are you kidding?

Eddie: (opens door) Then I'll just leave, I guess.

May: (she stands) Wait.

(He closes door. They stand there facing each other for a while. She crosses slowly to him. Stops. They both move closer. Stop. Pause as they look at each other. They embrace. Long, tender kiss. They are very soft with each other. She pulls away from him slightly. Smiles. She looks him straight in the eyes, then suddenly knees him in the groin with tremendous force. Eddie doubles over and drops like a rock. She stands over him. Pause.)

May: You can take it, right. You're a stuntman.

(She exits into bathroom, stage right, slams the door behind her. The door is amplified with microphones and a bass drum hidden in the frame so that each time an *actor slams it, the door booms loud and long. Same is true for the stage left door.* Eddie *remains on the floor holding his stomach in pain. Stage lights drop to half their intensity as a spot rises softly on* The Old Man. *He speaks directly to* Eddie.)

The Old Man: I thought you were supposed to be a fantasist, right? Isn't that basically the deal with you? You dream things up. Isn't that true?

Eddie: (stays on floor) I don't know.

The Old Man: You don't know. Well, if you don't know I don't know who the hell else does. I wanna' show you somethin'. Somethin' real, okay? Somethin' actual.

Eddie: Sure.

The Old Man: Take a look at that picture on the wall over there. *(He points at wall stage right. There is no picture but* Eddie *stares at the wall.)* Ya' see that? Take a good look at that. Ya' see it?

Eddie: (staring at wall) Yeah.

The Old Man: Ya' know who that is?

Eddie: I'm not sure.

The Old Man: Barbara Mandrell. That's who that is. Barbara Mandrell. You heard a' her?

Eddie: Sure.

The Old Man: Well, would you believe me if I told ya' I was married to her?

Eddie: (pause) No.

The Old Man: Well, see, now that's the difference right there. That's realism. I am actually married to Barbara Mandrell in my mind. Can you understand that?

Eddie: Sure.

The Old Man: Good. I'm glad we have an understanding.

(The Old Man *drinks from his cup. Spot slowly fades to black as stage lights come back up full. These light changes are cued to the opening and closing of doors.* May *enters from bathroom, closes door quietly. She is carrying a sleek red dress, panty hose, a pair of black high heels, a black shoulder purse and a hair brush. She crosses to foot of bed and throws the clothes on it. Hangs the purse on a bed post, sits on foot of bed her back to* Eddie *and starts brushing her hair.* Eddie *remains on floor. She finishes brushing her hair, throws brush on bed, then starts taking off her clothes and changing into the clothes she brought on stage. As she speaks to* Eddie *and changes into the new clothes, she gradually transforms from her former tough drabness into a very sexy woman. This occurs almost unnoticeably in the course of her speech.)*

May: (very cold, quick, almost monotone voice like she's writing him a letter) I don't understand my feelings. I really don't. I don't understand how I could hate you so much after so much time. How, no matter how much I'd like to not hate you, I hate you even more. It grows. I can't even see you now. All I see is a picture of you. You and her. I don't even

Sam Shepard   1977

know if the picture's real anymore. I don't even care. It's a made-up picture. It invades my head. The two of you. And this picture stings even more than if I'd actually seen you with her. It cuts me. It cuts me so deep I'll never get over it. And I can't get rid of this picture either. It just comes. Uninvited. Kinda' like a little torture. And I blame you more for this little torture than I do for what you did.

Eddie: (standing slowly) I'll go.

May: You better.

Eddie: Why?

May: You just better.

Eddie: I thought you wanted me to stay.

May: I got somebody coming to get me.

Eddie: (short pause, on his feet) Here?

May: Yeah, here. Where else?

Eddie: (makes a move toward her upstage) You been seeing somebody?

May: (she moves quickly down left, crosses right) When was the last time we were together, Eddie? Huh? Can you remember that far back?

Eddie: Who've you been seeing?

(He moves violently toward her.)

May: Don't you touch me! Don't you even think about it.

Eddie: How long have you been seeing him!

May: What difference does it make!

(Short pause. He stares at her, then turns suddenly and exits out the stage left door and slams it behind him. Door booms.)

May: Eddie! Where are you going? Eddie!

(Short pause. She looks after Eddie, then turns fast, moves upstage to window. She parts the Venetian blinds, looks out window, turns back into room. She rushes to upstage side of bed, gets down on hands and knees, pulls a suitcase out from under bed, throws it on top of bed, opens it. She rushes into bathroom, disappears, leaving door open. She comes back on with various items of clothing, throws stuff into suitcase, turns as if to go back into bathroom. Stops. She hears Eddie off left. She quickly shuts suitcase, slides it under bed again, rushes around to downstage side of bed. Sits on bed. Stands again. Rushes back into bathroom, returns with hairbrush, slams bathroom door. Starts brushing her hair as though that's what she's been doing all along. She sits on bed brushing her hair. Eddie enters stage left, slams door behind him, door booms. He stands there holding a ten gauge shotgun in one hand and a bottle of tequila in the other. He moves toward bed, tosses shotgun on bed beside her.)

May: (she stands, moves upstage, stops brushing her hair) Oh, wonderful. What're you gonna' do with that?

Eddie: Clean it.

(He opens the bottle.)

    Eddie: You got any glasses?
    May: In the bathroom.
    Eddie: What're they doin' in the bathroom?

(Eddie crosses toward bathroom door with bottle.)

    May: I keep everything in the bathroom. It's safer.
    Eddie: You want some a' this?
    May: I'm on the wagon.
    Eddie: Good. 'Bout time.

(He exits into bathroom. May moves back to bed, stares at shotgun.)

    May: Eddie, this is a very friendly person who's coming over here. He's not malicious in any way. *(pause)* Eddie?
Eddie's Voice: *(off right)* Where's the damn glasses?
    May: In the medicine cabinet!
Eddie's Voice: What the hell're they doin' in the medicine cabinet!

(Sound of medicine cabinet being opened and slammed shut off right)

    May: There's no germs in the medicine cabinet!
Eddie's Voice: Germs.
    May: Eddie, did you hear me?

(Eddie enters with a glass, pouring tequila into it slowly until it's full as he crosses to table down left.)

    May: Did you hear what I said, Eddie?
    Eddie: About what?
    May: About the man who's coming over here.
    Eddie: What man?
    May: Oh, brother.

(Eddie sets bottle of tequila on table then sits in upstage chair. Takes a long drink from glass. He ignores The Old Man.)

    Eddie: First off, it can't be very serious.
    May: Oh, really? And why is that?
    Eddie: Because you call him a "man."
    May: What am I supposed to call him?
    Eddie: A "guy" or something. If you called him a "guy", I'd be worried about it but since you call him a "man" you give yourself away. You're in a dumb situation with this guy by calling him a "man". You put yourself below him.
    May: What in the hell do you know about it.
    Eddie: This guy's gotta' be a twerp. He's gotta' be a punk chump in a two dollar suit or somethin'.

Sam Shepard   *1979*

May: Anybody who doesn't half kill themselves falling off horses or jumping on steers is a twerp in your book.

Eddie: That's right.

May: And what're you supposed to be, a "guy" or a "man"?

(Eddie *lowers his glass slowly. Stares at her. Pause. He smiles then speaks low and deliberately.*)

Eddie: I'll tell you what. We'll just wait for this "man" to come over here. The two of us. We'll just set right here and wait. Then I'll let you be the judge.

May: Why is everything a big contest with you? He's not competing with you. He doesn't even know you exist.

Eddie: You can introduce me.

May: I'm not introducing you. I am definitely not introducing you. He'd be very embarrassed to find me here with somebody else. Besides, I've only just met him.

Eddie: Embarrassed?

May: Yes! Embarrassed. He's a very gentle person.

Eddie: Is that right. Well, I'm a very gentle person myself. My feelings get easily damaged.

May: What feelings.

(Eddie *falls silent, takes a drink, then gets up slowly with glass, leaves bottle on table, crosses to bed, sits on bed, sets glass on floor, picks up shotgun and starts dismantling it.* May *watches him closely.*)

May: You can't keep messing me around like this. It's been going on too long. I can't take it anymore. I get sick everytime you come around. Then I get sick when you leave. You're like a disease to me. Besides, you got no right being jealous of me after all the bullshit I've been through with you.

(Pause. Eddie *keeps his attention on shotgun as he talks to her.*)

Eddie: We've got a pact.

May: Oh, God.

Eddie: We made a pact.

May: There's nothing between us now!

Eddie: Then what're you so excited about?

May: I'm not excited.

Eddie: You're beside yourself.

May: You're driving me crazy. You're driving me totally crazy!

Eddie: You know we're connected, May. We'll always be connected. That was decided a long time ago.

May: Nothing was decided! You made all that up.

Eddie: You know what happened.

May: You promised me that was finished. You can't start that
    up all over again. You promised me.

Eddie: A promise can't stop something like that. It happened.

May: Nothing happened! Nothing ever happened!

Eddie: Innocent to the last drop.

May: *(pause, controlled)* Eddie—will you please leave? Now.

Eddie: You're gonna' find out one way or the other.

May: I want you to leave.

Eddie: You didn't want me to leave before.

May: I want you to leave now. And it's not because of this
    man. It's just—

Eddie: What.

May: Stupid. You oughta' know that by now.

Eddie: You think so, huh?

May: It'll be the same thing over and over again. We'll be
    together for a little while and then you'll be gone.

Eddie: I'll be gone.

May: You will. You know it. You just want me now because
    I'm seeing somebody else. As soon as that's over, you'll be
    gone again.

Eddie: I didn't come here because you were seein' somebody
    else! I don't give a damn who you're seeing! You'll never
    replace me and you know it!

May: Get outa' here!

*(Long silence. Eddie lifts his glass and toasts her, then slowly drinks it dry. He
sets glass down softly on floor.)*

    Eddie: *(smiles at her)* All right.

*(He rises slowly, picks up the sections of his shotgun. He stands there looking down
at the shotgun pieces for a second. May moves slightly toward him.)*

    May: Eddie—

(His head jerks up and stares at her. She stops cold.)

    Eddie: You're a traitor.

(He exits left with shotgun. Slams door. Door booms. May runs toward door.)

    May: Eddie!!

*(She throws herself against stage left door. Her arms reach out and hug the walls.
She weeps and slowly begins to move along the stage left wall upstage to the corner,
embracing the wall as she moves and weeps. The Old Man begins to tell his story
as May moves slowly along the wall. He tells it directly to her as though she's a
child. May remains involved with her emotion of loss and keeps moving clear
around the room, hugging the walls during the course of the story until she arrives
in the extreme downstage right corner of the room. She sinks to her knees.)*

Sam Shepard   *1981*

(Slowly, in the course of May's *mourning, the spotlight softly rises on* The Old Man *and the stage lights decrease to half again.)*

The Old Man: Ya' know, one thing I'll never forget. I'll never forget this as long as I live—and I don't even know why I remember it exactly. We were drivin' through Southern Utah once, I think it was. Me, you and your mother—in that old Plymouth we had. You remember that Plymouth? Had a white plastic hood ornament on it. Replica of the Mayflower I think it was. Some kind a' ship. Anyway, we'd been drivin' all night and you were sound asleep in the front. And all of a sudden you woke up crying. Just bustin' a gut over somethin'. I don't know what it was. Nightmare or somethin'. Woke your Mom right up and she climbed over the seat in back there with you to try to get you settled down. But you wouldn't shut up for hell or high water. Just kept wailing away. So I stopped the Plymouth by the side of the road. Middle a' nowhere. I can't even remember where it was exactly. Pitch black. I picked you up outa' the back seat there and carried you into this field. Thought the cold air might quiet you down a little bit. But you just kept on howling away. Then, all of a sudden, I saw somethin' move out there. Somethin' bigger than both of us put together. And it started to move toward us kinda' slow.

(May begins to crawl slowly on her hands and knees from down right corner toward bed. When she reaches bed, she grabs pillow and embraces it, still on her knees. She rocks back and forth embracing pillow as Old Man *continues.)*

And then it started to get joined up by some other things just like it. Same shape and everything. It was so black out there I could hardly make out my own hand. But these things started to kinda' move in on us from all directions in a big circle. And I stopped dead still and turned back to the car to see if your mother was all right. But I couldn't see the car anymore. So I called out to her. I called her name loud and clear. And she answered me back from outa' the darkness. She yelled back to me. And just then these things started to "moo". They all started "mooing" away.

(He makes the sound of a cow.)

And it turns out, there we were, standin' smack in the middle of a goddamn herd of cattle. Well, you never heard a baby pipe down so fast in your life. You never made a peep after that. The whole rest of the trip.

(May stops rocking abruptly. Suddenly May *hears* Eddie *off left. Stage lights pop back up. Spot on* The Old Man *cuts to black. She leaps to her feet, completely drop-*

ping her grief, hesitates a second, then rushes to chair upstage of table and sits. She takes a drink straight from the bottle, slams bottle down on table, leans back in the chair and stares at the bottle as though she's been sitting like that the whole time since he left. Eddie *enters fast from stage left door carrying two steer ropes. He slams door. Door booms. He completely ignores* May. *She completely ignores him and keeps staring at the bottle. He crosses upstage of bed, throws one of the ropes on bed and starts building a loop in the other rope, feeding it with the left hand so that it makes a snake-like zipping sound as it passes through the honda. Now he begins to pay attention to* May *as he continues fooling with the rope. She remains staring at the bottle of tequila.)*

Eddie: Decided to jump off the wagon, huh?

(He spins the rope above his head in a flat hornloop, then ropes one of the bedposts, taking up the slack with a sharp snap of the right hand. He takes the loop off the bedpost, rebuilds it, swings and ropes another bedpost. He continues this right around the bed, roping every post and never missing. May *takes another drink and sets bottle down quietly.)*

May: (Still not looking at him) What're you doing?
Eddie: Little practice. Gotta' stay in practice these days. There's kids out there ropin' calves in six seconds dead. Can you believe that? Six and no change. Flyin' off the saddle on the right hand side like a bunch a' Spider Monkeys. I'm tellin' ya', they got it down to a science.

(He continues roping bedposts, making his way around the bed in a circle)

May: (Flatly, staring at bottle) I thought you were leaving. Didn't you say you were leaving?
Eddie: (as he ropes) Well, yeah, I was gonna'. But then it suddenly occurred to me in the middle of the parking lot out there that there probably isn't any man comin' over here at all. There probably isn't any "guy" or any "man" or anybody comin' over here. You just made all that up.
May: Why would I do that?
Eddie: Just to get even.

(She turns to him slowly in chair, takes a drink, stares at him, then sets bottle on table.)

May: I'll never get even with you.

(He laughs, crosses to table, takes a deep drink from bottle, cocks his head back, gargles, swallows, then does a back flip across stage and crashes into stage right wall.)

May: So, now we're gonna' get real mean and sloppy, is that it? Just like old times.
Eddie: Well, I haven't dropped the reins in quite a while ya' know. I've been real good. I have. No hooch. No slam-

mer. No women. No nothin'. I been a pretty boring kind
of a guy actually. I figure I owe it to myself. Once a once.

(He returns to roping the bedposts. She just stares at him from the chair.)

    May: Why are you doing this?
    Eddie: I already told ya'. I need the practice.
    May: I don't mean that.
    Eddie: Well, say what ya' mean then, honey.
    May: Why are you going through this whole thing again like
        you're trying to impress me or something. Like we just
        met. This is the same crap you laid on me in High School.
    Eddie: *(still roping)* Well, it's just a little testimony of my love,
        see baby. I mean if I stopped trying to impress you, that'd
        mean it was all over, wouldn't it?
    May: It *is* all over.
    Eddie: You're trying to impress me, too, aren't you?
    May: You know me inside and out. I got nothing new to show
        you.
    Eddie: You got this guy comin' over. This new guy. That's very
        impressive. I woulda' thought you'd be hung out to dry by
        now.
    May: Oh, thanks a lot.
    Eddie: What is he, a "younger man" or something?
    May: It's none of your damn business.
    Eddie: Have you balled him yet?

(She throws him a mean glare and just pins him with her eyes.)

    Eddie: Have you? I'm just curious. *(pause)* You don't have to
        tell me. I already know.
    May: You're just like a little kid, you know that? A jealous, lit-
        tle snot-nosed kid.

(Eddie laughs, spits, makes a 'snot-nosed-kid' face, keeps roping bedposts.)

    Eddie: I hope this guy comes over. I really hope he does. I
        wanna' see him walk through that door.
    May: What're you gonna' do?

(He stops roping, turns to her. He smiles.)

    Eddie: I'm gonna nail his ass to the floor. Directly.

(He suddenly ropes chair downstage, right next to May. *He takes up slack and
drags chair violently back toward bed. Pause. They stare at each other.* May *suddenly stands, goes to bedpost, grabs her purse, slings it on her shoulder and heads
for stage left door.)*

    May: I'm not sticking around for this.

(She exits stage left door leaving it open. Eddie runs off stage after her.)

> Eddie: Where're you goin'?
> May: *(off left)* Take your hands off a' me!
> Eddie: *(off left)* Wait a second, wait a second. Just a second, okay?

(May screams. Eddie carries her back on stage screaming and kicking. He sets her down, slams door shut. She walks away from him stage right, straightening her dress.)

> Eddie: Tell ya' what. I'll back off. I'll be real nice. I will. I promise. I'll be just like a little ole pussy cat, okay? You can introduce me to him as your brother or something. Well— maybe not your brother.
> May: Maybe not.
> Eddie: Your cousin. Okay? I'll be your cousin. I just wanna' meet him is all. Then I'll leave. Promise.
> May: Why do you want to meet him? He's just a friend.
> Eddie: Just to see where you stand these days. You can tell a lot about a person by the company they keep.
> May: Look. I'm going outside. I'm going to the pay phone across the street. I'm calling him up and I'm telling him to forget about the whole thing. Okay?
> Eddie: Good. I'll pack up your stuff while you're gone.
> May: I'm not going with you, Eddie!

(Suddenly headlights arc across the stage from upstage right, through the window. They slash across the audience, then dissolve off left. These should be two intense beams of piercing white light and not 'realistic' headlights.)

> May: Oh, great.

(She rushes upstage to window, looks out. Eddie laughs, takes a drink.)

> Eddie: Why don't ya' run on out there. Go ahead. Run on out. Throw yourself into his arms or somethin'. Blow kisses in the moonlight.

(Eddie laughs, moves to bed, pulls a pair of old spurs off his belt. Sits. Starts putting spurs on his boots. It's important these spurs look old and used, with small rowels—not cartoon "cowboy" spurs. May goes into bathroom leaving door open.)

> May: *(off right)* What're you doing?
> Eddie: Puttin' my hooks on. I wanna' look good for this "man". Give him the right impression. I'm yer cousin after all.
> May: *(entering from bathroom)* If you hurt him, Eddie—
> Eddie: I'm not gonna' hurt him. I'm a nice guy. Very sensitive, too. Very civilized.

Sam Shepard   1985

May: He's just a date, you know. Just an ordinary date.
Eddie: Yeah? Well, I'm gonna turn him into a fig.

(He starts laughing so hard at his own joke that he rolls off the bed and crashes to the floor. He goes into a fit of laughter, pounding his fists into the floor. May *makes a move toward the door, then stops and turns to* Eddie.*)*

May: Eddie! Do me a favor. Just this once, okay?
Eddie: (laughing hard) Anything you want, honey. Anything you want.

(He goes on laughing hysterically.)

May: (turning away from him) Shit.

(She goes to stage left door and throws it open. Pitch black outside with only the porch light glowing. She stands in the doorway, staring out. Pause as Eddie *slowly gains control of himself and stops laughing. He stares at* May.*)*

Eddie: (still on floor) What're you doing? *(Pause.* May *keeps looking out)* May?
May: (staring out open door) It's not him.
Eddie: It's not, huh?
May: No, it's not.
Eddie: Well, who is it then?
May: Somebody else.
Eddie: (slowly getting up and sitting on bed) Yeah. It's probably not ever gonna' be "him". What're you tryin' to make me jealous for? I know you've been livin' alone.
May: It's a big, huge, extra-long, black Mercedes Benz.
Eddie: (pause) Well, this is a motel, isn't it? People are allowed to park in front of a motel if they're stayin' here.
May: People who stay here don't drive a big, huge, extra-long, black Mercedes Benz.
Eddie: You don't, but somebody else might.
May: (still at door) This is not a black Mercedes Benz type of motel.
Eddie: Well, close the damn door then and get back inside.
May: Somebody's sitting out there in that car looking straight at me.
Eddie: (stands fast) What're they doing?
May: It's not a "they". It's a "she".

(Eddie drops to floor behind bed.)

Eddie: Well what's she doing, then?
May: Just sitting there. Staring at me.
Eddie: Get away from the door, May.

May: *(turning toward him slowly)* You don't know anybody with a black Mercedes Benz by any chance, do you?

Eddie: Get away from the door!

(Suddenly the white headlight beams slash across the stage through the open door. Eddie rushes to door, slams it shut and pushes May aside. Just as he slams the door the sound of a large caliber magnum pistol explodes off left, followed immediately by the sound of shattering glass then a car horn blares and continues on one relentless note.)

May: *(yelling over the sound of horn)* Who is that! Who in the hell is that out there!

Eddie: How should I know.

(Eddie flips the light switch off by stage left door. Stage lights go black. Bathroom light stays on.)

May: Eddie!

Eddie: Just get down will ya'! Get down on the floor!

(Eddie grabs her and tries to pull her down on the floor beside the bed. May struggles in the dark with him. Car horn keeps blaring. Headlights start popping back and forth from high beam to low beam, slashing across stage through the window now.)

May: Who is that? Did you bring her with you! You sonofabitch!

(She starts lashing out at Eddie, fighting with him as he tries to drag her down on the floor.)

Eddie: I didn't bring anybody with me! I don't know who she is! I don't know where she came from! Just get down on the floor will ya'!

May: She followed you here! Didn't she! You told her where you were going and she followed you.

Eddie: I didn't tell anybody where I was going. I didn't know where I was going 'til I got here.

May: You are gonna' pay for this! I swear to God. You are gonna' pay.

(Eddie finally pulls her down and rolls over on top of her so she can't get up. She slowly gives up struggling as he keeps her pinned to the floor. Car horn suddenly stops. Headlights snap off. Long pause. They listen in the dark.)

May: What do you think she's doing?

Eddie: How should I know.

May: Don't pretend you don't know her. That's the kind of a car a Countess drives. That's the kind of car I always pictured her in. *(She starts struggling again.)*

Sam Shepard   **1987**

Eddie: (holding her down) Just stay put.
　　May: I'm not gonna' lay here on my back with you on top of
　　　　me and get shot by some dumb rich twat. Now lemme up,
　　　　Eddie!

(Sound of tires burning rubber off left. Headlights arc back across the stage again
from left to right. A car drives off. Sound fades.)

Eddie: Just stay down!
　May: I'm down!

(Long pause in the dark. They listen.)

　May: How crazy is this chick anyway?
Eddie: She's pretty crazy.
　May: Have you balled her yet? (pause)

(Eddie gets up slowly, hunched over crosses upstage to window cautiously, parts
Venetian blinds and peeks outside.)

Eddie: (looking out) Shit, she's blown the windshield outa' my
　　　　truck. Goddamnit.
　May: (still on floor) Eddie?
Eddie: (still looking out window) What?
　May: Is she gone?
Eddie: I don't know. I can't see any headlights. (pause) I don't
　　　　believe it.
　May: (gets up, crosses to light switch.) Yeah, you shoulda'
　　　　thought of the consequences before you got in her pants.

(She switches the lights back on. Eddie whirls around toward her. He stands.)

Eddie: (moving toward her) Turn the lights off! Keep the lights
　　　　off!

(He rushes to light switch and turns lights back off. Stage goes back to darkness.
May shoves past him and turns the lights back on again. Stage lit.)

　May: This is my place!
Eddie: Look, she's gonna' come back here. I know she's gonna'
　　　　come back. We either have to get outa' here now or you
　　　　have to keep the fuckin' lights off.
　May: I thought you said you didn't know her!
Eddie: Get your stuff! We're gettin' outa' here.
　May: I'm not leaving! This is your mess, not mine.
Eddie: I came here to get you! Whatsa' matter with you! I came
　　　　all this way to get you! Do you think I'd do that if I didn't
　　　　love you! Huh? That bitch doesn't mean anything to me!
　　　　Nuthin'. I got no reason to be here but you.
　May: I'm not goin', Eddie.

(Pause. Eddie *stares at her.)*

(Spot rises on Old Man. *Stage lights stay the same.* Eddie *and* May *just stand there staring at each other through the duration of* The Old Man's *words. They are not 'frozen', they just stand there and face each other in a suspended moment of recognition.)*

The Old Man: Amazing thing is, neither one a' you look a bit familiar to
me. Can't figure that one out. I don't recognize myself in
either one a' you. Never did. 'Course your mothers both
put their stamp on ya'. That's plain to see. But my whole
side a' the issue is absent, in my opinion. Totally unrecogni-
zable. You could be anybody's. Probably are. I can't even
remember the original circumstances. Been so long. Probably a lot a' things I forgot. Good thing I got out when I did
though. Best thing I ever did.

(Spot fades on Old Man. *Stage lights come back up.* Eddie *picks up his rope and starts to coil it up.* May *watches him.)*

Eddie: I'm not leavin'. I don't care what you think anymore. I
don't care what you feel. None a' that matters. I'm not leavin'. I'm stayin' right here. I don't care if a hundred
"dates" walk through that door—I'll take every one of 'em
on. I don't care if you hate my guts. I don't care if you can't
stand the sight of me or the sound of me or the smell of me.
I'm never leavin'. You'll never get rid of me. You'll never
escape me either. I'll track you down no matter where you
go. I know exactly how your mind works. I've been right
every time. Every single time.

May: You've gotta' give this up, Eddie.

Eddie: I'm not giving it up!

(Pause)

May: (calm) Okay. Look. I don't understand what you've got
in your head anymore. I really don't. I don't get it. *Now,*
you desperately need me. *Now,* you can't live without me.
NOW, you'll do anything for me. Why should I believe it this
time?

Eddie: Because it's true.

May: It was supposed to have been true every time before.
Every other time. Now it's true again. You've been jerking
me off like this for fifteen years. Fifteen years I've been a
yo-yo for you. I've never been split. I've never been two
ways about you. I've either loved you or not loved you. And
now I just plain don't love you. Understand? Do you
understand that? I don't love you. I don't need you. I

Sam Shepard **1989**

don't want you. Do you get that? Now if you can still stay
then you're either crazy or pathetic.

(*She crosses down left to table, sits in upstage chair facing audience, takes slug of
tequila from bottle, slams it down on table. Headlights again come slashing across
the stage from up right, across audience then disappear off left.* Eddie *rushes to
light switch, flips it off. Stage goes black. Exterior lights shine through.*)

> Eddie: (*taking her by shoulder*) Get in the bathroom!
> May: (*pulls away*) I'm not going in the bathroom! I'm not
> gonna' hide in my own house! I'm gonna' go out there. I'm
> gonna' go out there and tear her damn head off! I'm gonna'
> wipe her out!

(*She moves toward stage left door.* Eddie *stops her. She screams. They struggle as*
May *yells at stage left door.*)

> May: (*yelling at door*) Come on in here! Come on in here and
> bring your dumb gun! You hear me? Bring all your
> weapons and your skinny silly self! I'll eat you alive!

(*Suddenly the stage left door bursts open and* Martin *crashes onstage in the darkness. He's in his mid-thirties, solidly built, wears a green plaid shirt, baggy work
pants with suspenders, heavy work boots.* May *and* Eddie *pull apart.* Martin
tackles Eddie *around the waist and the two of them go crashing into the stage right
bathroom door. The door booms.* May *rushes to light switch, flips it on. Lights
come back up on stage.* Martin *stands over* Eddie *who's crumpled up against the
wall on the floor.* Martin *is about to smash* Eddie *in the face with his fist.* May
stops him with her voice.)

> May: Martin, wait!

(*Pause.* Martin *turns and looks at* May. Eddie *is dazed, remains on floor.* May
goes to Martin *and pulls him away from* Eddie.)

> May: It's okay, Martin. It's uh—It's okay. We were just hav-
> ing a kind of an argument. Really. Just take it easy. All
> right?

(Martin *moves back away from* Eddie. Eddie *stays on floor. Pause.*)

> Martin: Oh. I heard you screaming when I drove up and then all
> the lights went off. I thought somebody was trying to—
> May: It's okay. This is my uh—cousin. Eddie.
> Martin: (*stares at* Eddie) Oh. I'm sorry.
> Eddie: (*grins at* Martin) She's lying.
> Martin: (*looks at* May) Oh.
> May: (*moving to table*) Everything's okay, Martin. You want a
> drink or something? Why don't you have a drink.
> Martin: Yeah. Sure.

> *Eddie:* (*stays on floor*) She's lying through her teeth.
>
> *May:* I gotta' get some glasses.

(May *exits quickly into bathroom, stepping over* Eddie. Martin *stares at* Eddie. Eddie *grins back. Pause.*)

> *Eddie:* She keeps the glasses in the bathroom. Isn't that weird?

(May *comes back on with two glasses. She goes to table, pours two drinks from bottle*)

> *May:* I was starting to think you weren't going to show up, Martin.
>
> *Martin:* Yeah, I'm sorry. I had to water the football field down at the High School. Forgot all about it.
>
> *Eddie:* Forgot all about what?
>
> *Martin:* I mean I forgot all about watering. I was halfway here when I remembered. Had to go back.
>
> *Eddie:* Oh, I thought you meant you forgot all about her.
>
> *Martin:* Oh, no.
>
> *Eddie:* How far was halfway?
>
> *Martin:* Excuse me?
>
> *Eddie:* How far were you when it was halfway here?
>
> *Martin:* Oh—uh—I don't know. I guess a couple miles or so.
>
> *Eddie:* Couple miles? That's all? Couple a' lousy little miles? You wanna' know how many miles I came? Huh?
>
> *May:* We've been drinking a little bit, Martin.
>
> *Eddie:* She hasn't touched a drop.

(*Pause*)

> *May:* (*offering drink to* Martin) Here.
>
> *Eddie:* Yeah, that's my tequila, Martin.
>
> *Martin:* Oh.
>
> *Eddie:* I don't care if you drink it. I just want you to know where it comes from.
>
> *Martin:* Thanks.
>
> *Eddie:* You don't have to thank me. Thank the Mexicans. They made it.
>
> *Martin:* Oh.
>
> *Eddie:* You should thank the entire Mexican nation in fact. We owe everything to Mexico down here. Do you realize that? You probably don't realize that do ya'. We're sittin' on Mexican ground right now. It's only by chance that you and me aren't Mexican ourselves. What kinda' people do you hail from anyway, Martin?
>
> *Martin:* Me? Uh—I don't know. I was adopted.
>
> *Eddie:* Oh. You must have a lota' problems then, huh?

Martin: Well—not really, no.

Eddie: No? You orphans are supposed to steal a lot aren't ya'? Shoplifting and stuff. You're also supposed to be the main group responsible for bumping off our Presidents.

Martin: Really? I never heard that.

Eddie: Well, you oughta' read the papers, Martin.

(Pause)

Martin: I'm really sorry I knocked you over. I mean, I thought she was in trouble or something.

Eddie: She is in trouble.

Martin: (looks at May) Oh.

Eddie: She's in big trouble.

Martin: What's the matter, May?

May: (moves to bed with drink, sits) Nothing.

Martin: How come you had the lights off?

May: We were uh—just about to go out.

Martin: You were?

May: Yeah—well, I mean, we were going to come back.

(Martin stands there between them. He looks at Eddie, then back to May. Pause.)

Eddie: (laughs) No, no, no. That's not what we were gonna' do. Your name's Martin, right?

Martin: Yeah, right.

Eddie: That's not what we were gonna' do, Marty.

Martin: Oh.

Eddie: Could you hand me that bottle, please?

Martin: (crossing to bottle at table) Sure.

Eddie: Thanks.

(Martin moves back to Eddie with bottle and hands it to him. Eddie drinks.)

Eddie: (after drink) We were actually having an argument about you. That's what we were doin'.

Martin: About me?

Eddie: Yeah. We were actually in the middle of a big huge argument about you. It got so heated up we had to turn the lights off.

Martin: What was it about?

Eddie: It was about whether or not you're actually a man or not. Ya' know? Whether you're a "man" or just a "guy".

(Pause. Martin looks at May. May smiles politely. Martin looks back to Eddie.)

Eddie: See, she says you're a man. That's what she calls you. A "man". Did you know that? That's what she calls you.

Martin: (looks back to May) No.

May: I never called you a man, Martin. Don't worry about it.

Martin: It's okay. I don't mind or anything.

Eddie: No, but see I uh—told her she was fulla' shit. I mean I told her that way before I even saw you. And now that I see you I can't exactly take it back. Ya' see what I mean, Martin?

(Pause, May *stands.)*

May: Martin, do you want to go to the movies?

Martin: Well, yeah—I mean, that's what I thought we were going to do.

May: So let's go to the movies.

(She crosses fast to bathroom, steps over Eddie, *goes into bathroom, slams door, door booms. Pause as* Martin *stares at bathroom door.* Eddie *stays on floor, grins at* Martin.*)*

Martin: She's not mad or anything is she?

Eddie: You got me, buddy.

Martin: I didn't mean to make her mad.

(Pause)

Eddie: What're you gonna' go see, Martin?

Martin: I can't decide.

Eddie: What d'ya' mean you can't decide? You're supposed to have all that worked out ahead of time aren't ya?

Martin: Yeah, but I'm not sure what she likes.

Eddie: What's that got to do with it? You're takin' her out to the movies, right?

Martin: Yeah.

Eddie: So you pick the movie, right? The guy picks the movie. The guy's always supposed to pick the movie.

Martin: Yeah, but I don't want to take her to see something she doesn't want to see.

Eddie: How do you know what she wants to see?

Martin: I don't. That's the reason I can't decide. I mean what if I take her to something she's already seen before?

Eddie: You miss the whole point, Martin. The reason you're taking her out to the movies isn't to see something she hasn't seen before.

Martin: Oh.

Eddie: The reason you're taking her out to the movies is because you just want to be with her. Right? You just wanna' be close to her. I mean you could take her just about anywhere.

Martin: I guess.

Eddie: I mean after a while you probably wouldn't have to take her out at all. You could just hang around here.

Martin: What would we do here?

Sam Shepard   1993

Eddie: Well, you could uh—tell each other stories.

Martin: Stories?

Eddie: Yeah.

Martin: I don't know any stories.

Eddie: Make 'em up.

Martin: That'd be lying wouldn't it?

Eddie: No, no. Lying's when you believe it's true. If you already know it's a lie, then it's not lying.

Martin: *(after pause)* Do you want some help getting up off the floor?

Eddie: I like it down here. Less tension. You notice how when you're standing up, there's a lot more tension?

Martin: Yeah. I've noticed that. A lot of times when I'm working, you know, I'm down on my hands and knees.

Eddie: What line a' work do you follow, Martin?

Martin: Yard work mostly. Maintenance.

Eddie: Oh, lawns and stuff?

Martin: Yeah.

Eddie: You do lawns on your hands and knees?

Martin: Well—edging. You know, trimming around the edges.

Eddie: Oh.

Martin: And weeding around the sprinkler heads. Stuff like that.

Eddie: I get ya'.

Martin: But I've always noticed how much more relaxed I get when I'm down low to the ground like that.

Eddie: Yeah. Well, you could get down on your hands and knees right now if you want to. I don't mind.

Martin: *(grins, gets embarrassed, looks at bathroom door)* Naw, I'll stand. Thanks.

Eddie: Suit yourself. You're just gonna' get more and more tense.

(Pause)

Martin: You're uh—May's cousin, huh?

Eddie: See now, right there. Askin' me that. Right there. That's a result of tension. See what I mean?

Martin: What?

Eddie: Askin' me if I'm her cousin. That's because you're tense you're askin' me that. You already know I'm not her cousin.

Martin: Well, how would I know that?

Eddie: Do I look like her cousin.

Martin: Well, she said that you were.

Eddie: *(grins)* She's lying.

(Pause)

Martin: Well—what are you then?

Eddie: *(laughs)* Now you're really gettin' tense, huh?

Martin: Look, maybe I should just go or something. I mean—

(Martin *makes a move to exit stage left.* Eddie *rushes to stage left door and beats* Martin *to it.* Martin *freezes then runs to window upstage, opens it and tries to escape.* Eddie *runs to him and catches him by the back of the pants, pulls him out of the window, slams him up against stage right wall then pulls him slowly down the wall as he speaks. They arrive at down right corner.*)

Eddie: No, no. Don't go, Martin. Don't go. You'll just get all blue and lonely out there in the black night. I know. I've wandered around lonely like that myself. Awful. Just eats away at ya'. *(He puts his arm around* Martin's *shoulder and leads him to table down left.)* Now just come on over here and sit down and we'll have us a little drink. Okay?

Martin: *(as he goes with* Eddie*)* Uh—do you think she's okay in there?

Eddie: Sure she's okay. She's always okay. She just likes to take her time. Just to torture you.

Martin: Well—we were supposed to go to the movies.

Eddie: She'll be out. Don't worry about it. She likes the movies.

(*They sit at table, down left.* Eddie *pulls out the down right chair and seats* Martin *in it, then he goes to the upstage chair and sits so that he's now partially facing* The Old Man. *Spot rises softly on* The Old Man *but* Martin *does not acknowledge his presence. Stage lights stay the same.* Martin *sets his glass on table.* Eddie *fills it up with the bottle.* The Old Man's *left arm slowly descends and reaches across the table holding out his empty styrofoam cup for a drink.* Eddie *looks* The Old Man *in the eye for a second then pours him a drink, too. All three of them drink.* Eddie *takes his from the bottle.*)

Martin: What exactly's the matter with her anyway?

Eddie: She's in a state a' shock.

(The Old Man *chuckles to himself. Drinks.*)

Martin: Shock? How come?

Eddie: Well, we haven't seen each other in a long time. I mean —me and her, we go back quite a ways, see. High School.

Martin: Oh. I didn't know that.

Eddie: Yeah. Lota' miles.

Martin: And you're not really cousins?

Eddie: No. Not really. No.

Martin: You're—her husband?

Eddie: No. She's my sister. *(He and* The Old Man *look at each other then he turns back to* Martin.*)* My half-sister.

(*Pause.* Eddie *and* Old Man *drink.*)

Martin: Your sister?

Eddie: Yeah.

Martin: Oh. So—you knew each other even before High School then, huh?

Eddie: No, see, I never even knew I had a sister until it was too late.

Martin: How do you mean?

Eddie: Well, by the time I found out we'd already—you know— fooled around.

(Old Man *shakes his head, drinks. Long pause.* Martin *just stares at* Eddie.)

Eddie: (grins) Whatsa' matter, Martin?

Martin: You fooled around?

Eddie: Yeah.

Martin: Well—um—that's illegal, isn't it?

Eddie: I suppose so.

The Old Man: (to Eddie) Who is this guy?

Martin: I mean—is that true? She's really your sister?

Eddie: Half. Only half.

Martin: Which half?

Eddie: Top half. In horses we call that the "topside".

The Old Man: Yeah, and the mare's what? The mare's uh—"distaff", isn't it? Isn't that the bottom half? "Distaff." Funny I should remember that.

Martin: And you fooled around in High School together?

Eddie: Yeah. Sure. Everybody fooled around in High School. Didn't you?

Martin: No. I never did.

Eddie: Maybe you should have, Martin.

Martin: Well, not with my sister.

Eddie: No, I wouldn't recommend that.

Martin: How could that happen? I mean—

Eddie: Well, see—(pause, he stares at Old Man)—our Daddy fell in love twice. That's basically how it happened. Once with my mother and once with her mother.

The Old Man: It was the same love. Just got split in two, that's all.

Martin: Well, how come you didn't know each other until High School, then?

Eddie: He had two separate lives. That's how come. Two completely separate lives. He'd live with me and my mother for a while and then he'd disappear and go live with her and her mother for a while.

The Old Man: Now don't be too hard on me, boy. It can happen to the best of us.

Martin: And you never knew what was going on?

Eddie: Nope. Neither did my mother.

The Old Man: She knew.

    Eddie: (*to* Martin) She never knew.

    Martin: She must've suspected something was going on.

    Eddie: Well, if she did she never let on to me. Maybe she was afraid of finding out. Or maybe she just loved him. I don't know. He'd disappear for months at a time and she never once asked him where he went. She was always glad to see him when he came back. The two of us used to go running out of the house to meet him as soon as we saw the Studebaker coming across the field.

The Old Man: (*to* Eddie) That was no Studebaker, that was a Plymouth. I never owned a goddamn Studebaker.

    Eddie: This went on for years. He kept disappearing and reappearing. For years that went on. Then, suddenly, one day it stopped. He stayed home for a while. Just stayed in the house. Never went outside. Just sat in his chair. Staring. Then he started going on these long walks. He'd walk all day. Then he'd walk all night. He'd walk out across the fields. In the dark. I used to watch him from my bedroom window. He'd disappear in the dark with his overcoat on.

    Martin: Where was he going?

    Eddie: Just walking.

The Old Man: I was making a decision.

(Eddie *gets* Martin *to his feet and takes him on a walk around the entire stage as he tells the story.* Martin *is reluctant but* Eddie *keeps pulling him along.*)

    Eddie: But one night I asked him if I could go with him. And he took me. We walked straight out across the fields together. In the dark. And I remember it was just plowed and our feet sank down in the powder and the dirt came up over the tops of my shoes and weighed me down. I wanted to stop and empty my shoes out but he wouldn't stop. He kept walking straight ahead and I was afraid of losing him in the dark so I just kept up as best I could. And we were completely silent the whole time. Never said a word to each other. We could barely see a foot in front of us, it was so dark. And these white owls kept swooping down out of nowhere, hunting for jackrabbits. Diving right past our heads, then disappearing. And we just kept walking silent like that for miles until we got to town. I could see the drive-in movie way off in the distance. That was the first thing I saw. Just square patches of color shifting. Then vague faces began to appear. And, as we got closer, I could recognize one of the faces. It was Spencer Tracy. Spencer Tracy moving his mouth. Speaking without words. Speaking to a woman in a red dress. Then we stopped at a liquor store and he made me wait outside in the parking lot while he bought a bottle. And there were all these Mexican migrant workers standing around a pick-up truck with red mud all over the tires. They were drinking beer and laughing and I remember being jealous of them and I didn't know why. And I remember seeing the old man through the glass door of the liquor store as he paid for the bottle. And I remember feeling sorry for him and I didn't know why. Then he came outside with the bottle wrapped in a brown paper sack and as soon as he came out, all the Mexican men stopped laughing. They just stared at us as we walked away.

(During the course of the story the lights shift down very slowly into blues and greens—moonlight.)

    Eddie: And we walked right through town. Past the donut shop, past the miniature golf course, past the Chevron station. And he opened the bottle up and offered it to me. Before he even took a drink, he offered it to me first. And I took it and drank it and handed it back to him. And we just kept passing it back and forth like that as we walked until we drank the whole thing dry. And we never said a word the whole time. Then, finally, we reached this little white house with a red awning, on the far side of town. I'll never forget the red awning because it flapped in the night breeze and the porch light made it glow. It was a hot, desert breeze and the air smelled like new cut alfalfa. We walked right up to the front porch and he rang the bell and I remember getting real nervous because I wasn't expecting to visit anybody. I thought we were just out for a walk. And then this woman comes to the door. This real pretty woman with red hair. And she throws herself into his arms. And he starts crying. He just breaks down right there in front of me. And she's kissing him all over the face and holding him real tight and he's just crying like a baby. And then through the doorway, behind them both, I see this girl. *(The bathroom door very slowly and silently swings open revealing* May, *standing in the door frame back-lit with yellow light in her red dress. She just watches* Eddie *as he keeps telling the story. He and* Martin *are unaware of her presence.)* She just appears. She's just standing there, staring at me and I'm staring back at her and we can't take our eyes off each other. It was like we knew each other from somewhere but we couldn't place where. But the second we saw each other, that very second, we knew we'd never stop being in love.

*(*May *slams bathroom door behind her.*

Door booms. Lights bang back up to their previous setting.)

> *May: (to* Eddie) Boy, you really are incredible! You're unbe-
> lievable! Martin comes over here. He doesn't know you
> from Adam and you start telling him a story like that. Are
> you crazy? None of it's true, Martin. He's had this weird,
> sick idea for years now and it's totally made up. He's nuts. I
> don't know where he got it from. He's completely nuts.
>
> *Eddie: (to* Martin) She's kinda embarrassed about the whole
> deal, see. You can't blame her really.
>
> *Martin:* I didn't even know you could hear us out here, May. I—
>
> *May:* I heard every word. I followed it very carefully. He's
> told me that story a thousand times and it always changes.
>
> *Eddie:* I never repeat myself.
>
> *May:* You do nothing but repeat yourself. That's all you do.
> You just go in a big circle.
>
> *Martin: (standing)* Well, maybe I should leave.
>
> *Eddie:* NO! You sit down.

(Silence. Martin *slowly sits again)*

> *Eddie: (quietly to* Martin, *leaning toward him)* Did you think that
> was a story, Martin? Did you think I made that whole thing
> up?
>
> *Martin:* No. I mean, at the time you were telling it, it seemed
> real.
>
> *Eddie:* But now you're doubting it because she says it's a lie?
>
> *Martin:* Well—
>
> *Eddie:* She suggests it's a lie to you and all of a sudden you
> change your mind? Is that it? You go from true to false like
> that, in a second?
>
> *Martin:* I don't know.
>
> *May:* Let's go to the movies, Martin.

(Martin stands again)

> *Eddie:* Sit down!

(Martin sits back down. Long pause.)

> *May:* Eddie—

(Pause)

> *Eddie:* What?
>
> *May:* We want to go to the movies. *(Pause.* Eddie *just stares at
> her.)* I want to go out to the movies with Martin. Right now.
>
> *Eddie:* Nobody's going to the movies. There's not a movie in
> this town that can match the story I'm gonna tell. I'm gonna
> finish this story.

May: Eddie—

Eddie: You wanna' hear the rest of the story, don't ya', Martin?

Martin: (Pause. He looks at May *then back to* Eddie) Sure.

May: Martin, let's go. Please.

Martin: I—

(Long pause. Eddie *and* Martin *stare at each other.)*

Eddie: You what?

Martin: I don't mind hearing the rest of it if you want to tell the rest of it.

The Old Man: (to himself) I'm dyin' to hear it myself.

*(*Eddie *leans back in his chair. Grins.)*

May: (to Eddie) What do you think this is going to do? Do you think this is going to change something?

Eddie: No.

May: Then what's the point?

Eddie: It's absolutely pointless.

May: Then why put everybody through this. Martin doesn't want to hear this bullshit. *I* don't want to hear it.

Eddie: I know *you* don't wanna' hear it.

May: Don't try to pass it off on me! You got it all turned around, Eddie. You got it all turned around. You don't even know which end is up anymore. Okay. Okay. I don't need either of you. I don't need any of it because I already know the rest of the story. I know the whole rest of the story, see. *(She speaks directly to* Eddie, *who remains sitting.)* I know it just exactly the way it happened. Without any little tricks added on to it.

*(*The Old Man *leans over to* Eddie, *confidentially.)*

The Old Man: What does she know?

Eddie: (to Old Man) She's lying.

(Lights begin to shift down again in the course of May's *story. She moves very slowly downstage then crosses toward* Old Man *as she tells it.)*

May: You want me to finish the story for you, Eddie? Huh? You want me to finish this story? *(Pause as* Martin *sits again)* See, my mother—the pretty red-haired woman in the little white house with the red awning, was desperately in love with the old man. Wasn't she, Eddie? You could tell that right away. You could see it in her eyes. She was obsessed with him to the point where she couldn't stand being without him for even a second. She kept hunting for him from town to town. Following little clues that he left behind, like a postcard maybe, or a motel on the back of a matchbook. *(To* Martin) He never left her a phone number or an address or anything as simple as that because my mother was his secret, see. She hounded him for years and he kept trying to keep her at a distance because the closer these two separate lives drew together, these two separate women, these two separate kids, the more nervous he got. The more filled with terror that the two lives would find out about each other and devour him whole. That his secret would take him by the throat. But finally she caught up with him. Just by a process of elimination she dogged him down. I remember the day we discovered the town. She was on fire. "This is it!" she kept saying; "this is the place!" Her whole body was trembling as we walked through the streets, looking for the house where he lived. She kept squeezing my hand to the point where I thought she'd crush the bones in my fingers. She was terrified she'd come across him by accident on the street because she knew she was trespassing. She knew she was crossing this forbidden zone but she couldn't help herself. We walked all day through that stupid hick town. All day long. We went through every neighborhood, peering through every open window, looking in at every dumb family, until finally we found him.

(Rest)

It was just exactly supper time and they were all sitting down at the table and they were having fried chicken. That's how close we were to the window. We could see what they were eating. We could hear their voices but we couldn't make out what they were saying. Eddie and his mother were talking but the old man never said a word. Did he, Eddie? Just sat there eating his chicken in silence.

The Old Man: (to Eddie) Boy, is she ever off the wall with this one. You gotta' do somethin' about this.

May: The funny thing was, that almost as soon as we'd found him—he disappeared. She was only with him about two weeks before he just vanished. Nobody saw him after that. Ever. And my mother—just turned herself inside out. I never could understand that. I kept watching her grieve, as though somebody'd died. She'd pull herself up into a ball and just stare at the floor. And I couldn't understand that because I was feeling the exact opposite feeling. I was in love, see. I'd come home after school, after being with Eddie, and I was filled with this joy and there she'd be—standing in the middle of the kitchen staring at the sink.

Her eyes looked like a funeral. And I didn't know what to say. I didn't even feel sorry for her. All I could think of was him.

The Old Man: (*to* Eddie) She's gettin' way outa' line, here.

>   *May:* And all he could think of was me. Isn't that right, Eddie. We couldn't take a breath without thinking of each other. We couldn't eat if we weren't together. We couldn't sleep. We got sick at night when we were apart. Violently sick. And my mother even took me to see a doctor. And Eddie's mother took him to see the same doctor but the doctor had no idea what was wrong with us. He thought it was the flu or something. And Eddie's mother had no idea what was wrong with him. But my mother—my mother knew exactly what was wrong. She knew it clear down to her bones. She recognized every symptom. And she begged me not to see him but I wouldn't listen. Then she begged Eddie not to see me but he wouldn't listen. Then she went to Eddie's mother and begged her. And Eddie's mother— (*Pause. She looks straight at* Eddie)— Eddie's mother blew her brains out. Didn't she, Eddie? Blew her brains right out.

The Old Man: (*Standing. He moves from the platform onto the stage, between* Eddie *and* May.) Now, wait a second! Wait a second. Just a goddamn second here. This story doesn't hold water. (*To* Eddie *who stays seated.*) You're not gonna' let her off the hook with that one are ya'? That's the dumbest version I ever heard in my whole life. She never blew her brains out. Nobody ever told me that. Where the hell did that come from? (*To* Eddie *who remains seated*) Stand up! Get on yer feet now goddamn it! I wanna' hear the male side a' this thing. You gotta' represent me now. Speak on my behalf. There's no one to speak for me now! Stand up!

(Eddie *stands slowly. Stares at* Old Man)

>   Now tell her. Tell her the way it happened. We've got a pact. Don't forget that.
>
>   *Eddie:* (*calmly to* Old Man) It was your shotgun. Same one we used to duck hunt with. Browning. She never fired a gun before in her life. That was the first time.

The Old Man: Nobody told me any a' that. I was left completely in the dark.

>   *Eddie:* You were gone.

The Old Man: Somebody could've found me! Somebody could've hunted me down. I wasn't that impossible to find.

>   *Eddie:* You were gone.

The Old Man: That's right, I was gone! I was gone. You're right. But I wasn't disconnected. There was nothing cut off in me. Everything went on just the same as though I'd never left. *(to May)* But *your* mother—your mother wouldn't give it up, would she?

(The Old Man moves toward May and speaks directly to her. May keeps her eyes on Eddie who very slowly turns toward her in the course of The Old Man's speech. Once their eyes meet they never leave each other's gaze.)

The Old Man: *(to May)* She drew me to her. She went out of her way to draw me in. She was a force. I told her I'd never come across for her. I told her that right from the very start. But she opened up to me. She wouldn't listen. She kept opening up her heart to me. How could I turn her down when she loved me like that? How could I turn away from her? We were completely whole.

(Eddie and May just stand there staring at each other. The Old Man moves back to Eddie. Speaks to him directly.)

The Old Man: *(to Eddie)* What're you doin'? Speak to her. Bring her around to our side. You gotta' make her see this thing in a clear light.

(Very slowly Eddie and May move toward each other.)

The Old Man: *(to Eddie)* Stay away from her! What the hell are you doin'! Keep away from her! You two can't come together! You gotta hold up my end a' this deal. I got nobody now! Nobody! You can't betray me! You gotta' represent me now! You're my son!

(Eddie and May come together center stage. They embrace. They kiss each other tenderly. Headlights suddenly arc across stage again from upright, cutting across the stage through window then disappearing off left. Sound of loud collision, shattering glass, an explosion. Bright orange and blue light of a gasoline fire suddenly illuminates upstage window. Then sounds of horses screaming wildly, hooves galloping on pavement, fading, then total silence. Light of gas fire continues now to end of play. Eddie and May never stop holding each other through all this. Long pause. No one moves. Then Martin stands and moves upstage to window, peers out through Venetian blinds. Pause.)

Martin: *(upstage at window, looking out into flames)* Is that your truck with the horse trailer out there?

Eddie: *(stays with May)* Yeah.

Martin: It's on fire.

Eddie: Yeah.

Martin: All the horses are loose.

Eddie: *(steps back away from May)* Yeah, I figured.

May: Eddie—

Eddie: *(to* May*)* I'm just gonna' go out and take a look. I gotta'
    at least take a look, don't I?

 May: What difference does it make?

Eddie: Well, I can't just let her get away with that. What am I
    supposed to do? *(moves toward stage left door)* I'll just be a
    second.

 May: Eddie—

Eddie: I'm only gonna' be a second. I'll just take a look at it and
    I'll come right back. Okay?

(Eddie exits stage left door. May stares at door, stays where she is. Martin stays upstage. Martin turns slowly from window upstage and looks at May. Pause. May moves to bed, pulls suitcase out from underneath, throws it on bed and opens it. She goes into bathroom and comes out with clothes. She packs the clothes in suitcase. Martin watches her for a while then moves slowly downstage to her as she continues.)

 Martin: May—

(May goes back into bathroom and comes back out with more clothes. She packs them.)

 Martin: Do you need some help or anything? I got a car. I could
    drive you somewhere if you want. *(Pause.* May *just keeps
    packing her clothes.)* Are you going to go with him?

(She stops. Straightens up. Stares at Martin. *Pause.)*

 May: He's gone.

Martin: He said he'd be back in a second.

 May: *(Pause)* He's gone.

(May exits with suitcase out stage left door. She leaves the door open behind her. Martin just stands there staring at open door for a while. The Old Man looks stage left at his rocking chair then a little above it, in blank space. Pause. Old Man starts moving slowly back to platform.)

The Old Man: *(pointing into space, stage left)* Ya' see that picture over
    there? Ya' see that? Ya' know who that is? That's the
    woman of my dreams. That's who that is. And she's mine.
    She's all mine. Forever.

(He reaches rocking chair, sits, but keeps staring at imaginary picture. He begins to rock very slowly in the chair. After Old Man *sits in rocker, Merle Haggard's "I'm the One who Loves You" starts playing as lights begin a very slow fade.* Martin *moves slowly upstage to window and stops. He stares out with his back to audience. The fire glows through window as stage lights fade.* Old Man *keeps rocking slowly. Stage lights keep fading slowly to black. Fire glows for a while in the dark then cuts to black. Song continues in dark and swells in volume.)*

END

Sam Shepard, perhaps because he writes plays set in the American West and makes free use of the mythology of the cowboy, is sometimes seen as a sort of primitive, writing plays that are unrelated to the great traditions of drama. Interviewed by Jonathan Cott for Rolling Stone, *however, Shepard showed a literary allegiance that few people would have expected.*

"Aeschylus, Sophocles . . . I studied up on those guys . . .": Sam Shepard

Interviewer: You seem to like Marlowe a lot. When did you first read him?

Shepard: I'll tell you—aside from assigned reading in high school, I didn't read any plays except for a couple of Brecht things when I was living in New York City. I avoided reading out of arrogance, really. But when I went to England in the early Seventies, I suddenly found myself having a kind of dry spell. It was difficult for me to write, so I started to read. And I read most of the Greek guys—Aeschylus, Sophocles. . . . I studied up on those guys, and I'm glad I did. I was just amazed by the simplicity of the ancient Greek plays, for instance—they were dead simple. Nothing complex or tricky . . . which surprised the hell out of me, because I'd assumed they were beyond me. But now I began to comprehend what they were talking about, and they turned out to be accessible.

Interviewer: They're a lot about the family romance, aren't they?

Shepard: They're all about destiny! That's the most powerful thing. Everything is foreseen, and we just play it out.

Interviewer: You don't think a person can shape his own destiny?

Shepard: Oh, maybe. But first you have to know what your destiny is.

Interviewer: When did you think you knew your own?

Shepard: I'm not so sure I do. I'm not saying I know my destiny; I'm saying that it exists. It exists, and it can become a duty to discover it. Or it can be shirked. But if you take it on as your duty, then it becomes a different thing from dismissing it altogether and just imagining that it'll work itself out anyway. I mean, it will. But it's more interesting to try to find it and know it.

Sam Shepard   2005

Interviewer: The words also pass by unnoticed because they're so well rooted in intense but simple colloquial speech.

Shepard: I think you have to start in that colloquial territory, and from there move on and arrive in poetic country . . . but not the other way around. I've noticed that even with the Greek guys, especially with Sophocles, there's a very simple, rawboned language. The choruses are poetic, but the speech of the characters themselves is terse, cut to the bone and pointed to the heart of the problem. It's like Merle Haggard tunes like "My Own Kind of Hat"—I do this, that and some other thing, but I wear my own kind of hat. . . . Real simple.

BETH HENLEY

(b. 1952)

CRIMES OF THE HEART

C H A R A C T E R S

Lenny MaGrath, thirty, the oldest sister
Chick Boyle, twenty-nine, the sister's first cousin
Doc Porter, thirty, Meg's old boyfriend
Meg MaGrath, twenty-seven, the middle sister
Babe Botrelle, twenty-four, the youngest sister
Barnette Lloyd, twenty-six, Babe's lawyer

The Setting: The setting of the entire play is the kitchen in the MaGrath sisters' house in Hazlehurst, Mississippi, a small Southern town. The old-fashioned kitchen is unusually spacious, but there is a lived-in, cluttered look about it. There are four different entrances and exits to the kitchen: the back door, the door leading to the dining room and the front of the house, a door leading to the downstairs bedroom, and a staircase leading to the upstairs room. There is a table near the center of the room, and a cot has been set up in one of the corners.

The Time: In the fall, five years after Hurricane Camille.

ACT ONE

The lights go up on the empty kitchen. It is late afternoon. Lenny MaGrath, *a thirty-year-old woman with a round figure and face, enters from the back door carrying a white suitcase, a saxophone case, and a brown paper sack. She sets the suitcase and the sax case down and takes the brown sack to the kitchen table. After glancing quickly at the door, she gets the cookie jar from the kitchen counter, a box of matches from the stove, and then brings both objects back to the kitchen table. Excitedly, she reaches into the brown sack and pulls out a package of birthday candles. She quickly opens the package and removes a candle. She tries to stick the candle onto a cookie—it falls off. She sticks the candle in again, but the cookie is too hard and it crumbles. Frantically, she gets a second cookie from the jar. She strikes a match, lights the candle, and begins dripping wax onto the cookie. Just as she is beginning to smile we hear* Chick's *voice from offstage.*

Chick's Voice: Lenny! Oh, Lenny! Lenny *quickly blows out the candle and stuffs the cookie and candle into her dress pocket.* Chick, *twenty-nine, enters from the back door. She is a brightly dressed matron with yellow hair and shiny red lips.*

    Chick: Hi! I saw your car pull up.

    Lenny: Hi.

    Chick: Well, did you see today's paper?

Lenny *nods.*

    Chick: It's just too awful! It's just way too awful! How I'm gonna continue holding my head up high in this community, I do not know. Did you remember to pick up those pantyhose for me?

    Lenny: They're in the sack.

    Chick: Well, thank goodness, at least I'm not gonna have to go into town wearing holes in my stockings. *She gets the package, tears it open, and proceeds to take off one pair of stockings and put on another throughout the following scene. There should be something slightly grotesque about this woman changing her stockings in the kitchen.*

    Lenny: Did Uncle Watson call?

    Chick: Yes, Daddy has called me twice already. He said Babe's ready to come home. We've got to get right over and pick her up before they change their simple minds.

    Lenny: *hesitantly:* Oh, I know, of course, it's just—

    Chick: What?

    Lenny: Well, I was hoping Meg would call.

    Chick: Meg?

    Lenny: Yes, I sent her a telegram: about Babe, and—

    Chick: A telegram?! Couldn't you just phone her up?

    Lenny: Well, no, 'cause her phone's . . . out of order.

    Chick: Out of order?

    Lenny: Disconnected. I don't know what.

    Chick: Well, that sounds like Meg. My, these are snug. Are you sure you bought my right size?

    Lenny: *looking at the box:* Size extra-petite.

    Chick: Well, they're skimping on the nylon material. *Struggling to pull up the stockings:* That's all there is to it. Skimping on the nylon. *She finishes one leg and starts the other.* Now, just what all did you say in this "telegram" to Meg?

    Lenny: I don't recall exactly. I, well, I just told her to come on home.

    Chick: To come on home! Why, Lenora Josephine, have you lost your only brain, or what?

    Lenny: *nervously, as she begins to pick up the mess of dirty stockings and plastic wrappings:* But Babe wants Meg home. She asked me to call her.

    Chick: I'm not talking about what Babe wants.

Lenny: Well, what then?

Chick: Listen, Lenora, I think it's pretty accurate to assume that after this morning's paper, Babe's gonna be incurring some mighty negative publicity around this town. And Meg's appearance isn't gonna help out a bit.

Lenny: What's wrong with Meg?

Chick: She had a loose reputation in high school.

Lenny: weakly: She was popular.

Chick: She was known all over Copiah County as cheap Christmas trash, and that was the least of it. There was that whole sordid affair with Doc Porter, leaving him a cripple.

Lenny: A cripple—he's got a limp. Just kind of, barely a limp.

Chick: Well, his mother was going to keep *me* out of the Ladies' Social League because of it.

Lenny: What?

Chick. That's right. I never told you, but I had to go plead with that mean old woman and convinced her that I was just as appalled with what Meg had done as she was, and that I was only a first cousin anyway and I could hardly be blamed for all the skeletons in the MaGraths' closet. It was humiliating. I tell you, she even brought up your mother's death. And that poor cat.

Lenny: Oh! Oh! Oh, please, Chick! I'm sorry. But you're in the Ladies' League now.

Chick: Yes. That's true, I am. But frankly, if Mrs. Porter hadn't developed that tumor in her bladder, I wouldn't be in the club today, much less a committee head. *As she brushes her hair:* Anyway, you be a sweet potato and wait right here for Meg to call, so's you can convince her not to come back home. It would make things a whole lot easier on everybody. Don't you think it really would?

Lenny: Probably.

Chick: Good, then suit yourself. How's my hair?

Lenny: Fine.

Chick: Not pooching out in the back, is it?

Lenny: No.

Chick: cleaning the hair from her brush: All right then, I'm on my way. I've got Annie May over there keeping an eye on Peekay and Buck Jr., but I don't trust her with them for long periods of time. *Dropping the ball of hair onto the floor:* Her mind is like a loose sieve. Honestly it is. *As she puts the brush back into her purse:* Oh! Oh! Oh! I almost forgot. Here's a present for you. Happy birthday to Lenny, from the Buck Boyles! *She takes a wrapped package from her bag and hands it to* Lenny.

Lenny: Why, thank you, Chick. It's so nice to have you remember my birthday every year like you do.

Chick: *modestly:* Oh, well, now, that's just the way I am, I suppose.
That's just the way I was brought up to be. Well, why don't you
go on and open up the present?

Lenny: All right. *She starts to unwrap the gift.*

Chick: It's a box of candy—assorted crèmes.

Lenny: Candy—that's always a nice gift.

Chick: And you have a sweet tooth, don't you?

Lenny: I guess.

Chick: Well, I'm glad you like it.

Lenny: I do.

Chick: Oh, speaking of which, remember that little polk-a-dot dress
you got Peekay for her fifth birthday last month?

Lenny: The red-and-white one?

Chick: Yes; well, the first time I put it in the washing machine, I mean
the very first time, it fell all to pieces. Those little polka dots just
dropped right off in the water.

Lenny: *crushed:* Oh, no. Well, I'll get something else for her, then—
a little toy.

Chick: Oh, no, no, no, no, no! We wouldn't hear of it! I just wanted
to let you know so you wouldn't go and waste any more of your
hard-earned money on that make of dress. Those inexpensive
brands just don't hold up. I'm sorry, but not in these modern
washing machines.

Doc Porter's Voice: Hello! Hello, Lenny!

Chick: *taking over:* Oh, look, it's Doc Porter! Come on in, Doc!
Please come right on in!

*Doc Porter enters through the back door. He is carrying a large sack of pecans.
Doc is an attractively worn man with a slight limp that adds rather than detracts
from his quiet seductive quality. He is thirty years old, but appears slightly older.*

Chick: Well, how are you doing? How in the world are you doing?

Doc: Just fine, Chick.

Chick: And how are you liking it now that you're back in Hazlehurst?

Doc: Oh, I'm finding it somewhat enjoyable.

Chick: Somewhat! Only somewhat! Will you listen to him! What a
silly, silly, silly man! Well, I'm on my way. I've got some people
waiting on me. *Whispering to* Doc: It's Babe. I'm on my way to
pick her up.

Doc: Oh.

Chick: Well, goodbye! Farewell and goodbye!

Lenny: 'Bye.

Chick exits.

Doc: Hello.

Lenny: Hi. I guess you heard about the thing with Babe.

Doc: Yeah.

Lenny: It was in the newspaper.

   Doc: Uh huh.

Lenny: What a mess.

   Doc: Yeah.

Lenny: Well, come on and sit down. I'll heat us up some coffee.

   Doc: That's okay. I can only stay a minute. I have to pick up Scott; he's at the dentist.

Lenny: Oh; well, I'll heat some up for myself. I'm kinda thirsty for a cup of hot coffee. *She puts the coffeepot on the burner.*

   Doc: Lenny—

Lenny: What?

   Doc: *not able to go on:* Ah . . .

Lenny: Yes?

   Doc: Here, some pecans for you. *He hands her the sack.*

Lenny: Why, thank you, Doc. I love pecans.

   Doc: My wife and Scott picked them up around the yard.

Lenny: Well, I can use them to make a pie. A pecan pie.

   Doc: Yeah. Look, Lenny, I've got some bad news for you.

Lenny: What?

   Doc: Well, you know, you've been keeping Billy Boy out on our farm; he's been grazing out there.

Lenny: Yes—

   Doc: Well, last night, Billy Boy died.

Lenny: He died?

   Doc: Yeah. I'm sorry to tell you when you've got all this on you, but I thought you'd want to know.

Lenny: Well, yeah. I do. He died?

   Doc: Uh huh. He was struck by lightning.

Lenny: Struck by lightning? In that storm yesterday?

   Doc: That's what we think.

Lenny: Gosh, struck by lightning. I've had Billy Boy so long. You know. Ever since I was ten years old.

   Doc: Yeah. He was a mighty old horse.

Lenny: *stung:* Mighty old.

   Doc: Almost twenty years old.

Lenny: That's right, twenty years. 'Cause; ah, I'm thirty years old today. Did you know that?

   Doc: No, Lenny, I didn't know. Happy birthday.

Lenny: Thanks. *She begins to cry.*

   Doc: Oh, come on now, Lenny. Come on. Hey, hey, now. You know I can't stand it when you MaGrath women start to cry. You know it just gets me.

Lenny: Oh ho! Sure! You mean when Meg cries! Meg's the one you could never stand to watch cry! Not me! I could fill up a pig's trough!

   Doc: Now, Lenny . . . stop it. Come on. Jesus!

Lenny: Okay! Okay! I don't know what's wrong with me. I don't mean to make a scene. I've been on this crying jag. *She blows her nose.* All this stuff with Babe, and Old Granddaddy's gotten worse in the hospital, and I can't get in touch with Meg.

Doc: You tried calling Meggy?

Lenny: Yes.

Doc: Is she coming home?

Lenny: Who knows. She hasn't called me. That's what I'm waiting here for—hoping she'll call.

Doc: She still living in California?

Lenny: Yes; in Hollywood.

Doc: Well, give me a call if she gets in. I'd like to see her.

Lenny: Oh, you would, huh?

Doc: Yeah, Lenny, sad to say, but I would.

Lenny: It is sad. It's very sad indeed.

They stare at each other, then look away. There is a moment of tense silence.

Doc: Hey, Jell-O Face, your coffee's boiling.

Lenny: going to check: Oh, it is? Thanks. *After she checks the pot:* Look, you'd better go on and pick Scott up. You don't want him to have to wait for you.

Doc: Yeah, you're right. Poor kid. It's his first time at the dentist.

Lenny: Poor thing.

Doc: Well, 'bye. I'm sorry to have to tell you about your horse.

Lenny: Oh, I know. Tell Joan thanks for picking up the pecans.

Doc: I will. *He starts to leave.*

Lenny: Oh, how's the baby?

Doc: She's fine. Real pretty. She, ah, holds your finger in her hand; like this.

Lenny: Oh, that's cute.

Doc: Yeah. 'Bye, Lenny.

Lenny: 'Bye.

Doc *exits.* Lenny *stares after him for a moment, then goes and sits back down at the kitchen table. She reaches into her pocket and pulls out a somewhat crumbled cookie and a wax candle. She lights the candle again, lets the wax drip onto the cookie, then sticks the candle on top of the cookie. She begins to sing the "Happy Birthday" song to herself. At the end of the song she pauses, silently makes a wish, and blows out the candle. She waits a moment, then relights the candle, and repeats her actions, only this time making a different wish at the end of the song. She starts to repeat the procedure for the third time, as the phone rings. She goes to answer it.*

Lenny: Hello . . . Oh, hello, Lucille, how's Zackery? . . . Oh, no! . . . Oh, I'm so sorry. Of course, it must be grueling for you . . . Yes, I understand. Your only brother . . . No, she's not here yet. Chick just went to pick her up . . . Oh, now, Lucille, she's still his wife, I'm sure she'll be interested . . . Well, you can just tell me the information and I'll relate it all to her . . . Uh hum, his liver's saved. Oh, that's good news! . . . Well, of course, when you look at it like that . . . Breathing stabilized . . . Damage to the spinal column, not yet determined . . . Okay . . . Yes, Lucille, I've got it all down . . . Uh huh, I'll give her that message. 'Bye, 'bye.

Lenny *drops the pencil and paper. She sighs deeply, wipes her cheeks with the back of her hand, and goes to the stove to pour herself a cup of coffee. After a few moments, the front door is heard slamming.* Lenny *starts. A whistle is heard, then* Meg's *voice.*

Meg's Voice: I'm home! *She whistles the family whistle.* Anybody home?
    Lenny: Meg? Meg!

Meg, *twenty-seven, enters from the dining room. She has sad, magic eyes and wears a hat. She carries a worn-out suitcase.*

    Meg: dropping her suitcase, running to hug Lenny: Lenny—
    Lenny: Well, Meg! Why, Meg! Oh, Meggy! Why didn't you call? Did you fly in? You didn't take a cab, did you? Why didn't you give us a call?
    Meg: overlapping: Oh, Lenny! Why, Lenny! Dear Lenny! *Then she looks at* Lenny's *face.* My God, we're getting so old! Oh, I called, for heaven's sake. Of course, I called!
    Lenny: Well, I never talked to you—
    Meg: Well, I know! I let the phone ring right off the hook!
    Lenny: Well, as a matter of fact, I was out most of the morning seeing to Babe—
    Meg: Now, just what's all this business about Babe? How could you send me such a telegram about Babe? And Zackery! You say somebody's shot Zackery?
    Lenny: Yes, they have.
    Meg: Well, good Lord! Is he dead?
    Lenny: No. But he's in the hospital. He was shot in his stomach.
    Meg: In his stomach! How awful! Do they know who shot him? Lenny *nods.* Well, who? Who was it? Who? Who?
    Lenny: Babe! They're all saying Babe shot him! They took her to jail! And they're saying she shot him! They're all saying it! It's horrible! It's awful!
    Meg: overlapping: Jail! Good Lord, jail! Well, who? Who's saying it? Who?
    Lenny: Everyone! The policemen, the sheriff, Zachery, even Babe's saying it! Even Babe herself!
    Meg: Well, for God's sake. For God's sake.
    Lenny: overlapping as she falls apart: It's horrible! It's horrible! It's just horrible!
    Meg: Now calm down, Lenny. Just calm down. Would you like a Coke? Here, I'll get you some Coke. *She gets a Coke from the*

refrigerator. She opens it and downs a large swig. Why? Why would she shoot him? Why? *She hands the Coke bottle to* Lenny.

Lenny: I talked to her this morning and I asked her that very question. I said, "Babe, why would you shoot Zackery? He was your own husband. Why would you shoot him?" And do you know what she said? Meg *shakes her head.* She said, "'Cause I didn't like his looks. I just didn't like his looks."

Meg: after a pause: Well, I don't like his looks.

Lenny: But you didn't shoot him! You wouldn't shoot a person 'cause you didn't like their looks! You wouldn't do that! Oh, I hate to say this—I do hate to say this—but I believe Babe is ill. I mean in-her-head ill.

Meg: Oh, now, Lenny, don't you say that! There're plenty of good sane reasons to shoot another person, and I'm sure that Babe had one. Now, what we've got to do is get her the best lawyer in town. Do you have any ideas on who's the best lawyer in town?

Lenny: Well, Zackery is, of course; but he's been shot!

Meg: Well, count him out! Just count him and his whole firm out!

Lenny: Anyway, you don't have to worry, she's already got her lawyer.

Meg: She does? Who?

Lenny: Barnette Lloyd. Annie Lloyd's boy. He just opened his office here in town. And Uncle Watson said we'd be doing Annie a favor by hiring him up.

Meg: Doing Annie a favor? Doing Annie a favor! Well, what about Babe? Have you thought about Babe? Do we want to do her a favor of thirty or forty years in jail? Have you thought about that?

Lenny: Now, don't snap at me! Just don't snap at me! I try to do what's right! All this responsibility keeps falling on my shoulders, and I try to do what's right!

Meg: Well, boo hoo, hoo, hoo! And how in the hell could you send me such a telegram about Babe!

Lenny: Well, if you had a phone, or if you didn't live way out there in Hollywood and not even come home for Christmas, maybe I wouldn't have to pay all that money to send you a telegram!

Meg: overlapping: BABE'S IN TERRIBLE TROUBLE—STOP! ZACKERY'S BEEN SHOT—STOP! COME HOME IMMEDIATELY—STOP! STOP! STOP!

Lenny: And what was that you said about how old we're getting? When you looked at my face, you said, "My God, we're getting so old!" But you didn't mean we—you meant me! Didn't you? I'm thirty years old today and my face is getting all pinched up and my hair is falling out in the comb.

Meg: Why, Lenny! It's your birthday, October 23. How could I forget. Happy birthday!

Lenny: Well, it's not. I'm thirty years old and Billy Boy died last night. He was struck by lightning. He was struck dead.

Meg: reaching for a cigarette: Struck dead. Oh, what a mess. What a mess. Are you really thirty? Then I must be twenty-seven and Babe is twenty-four. My God, we're getting so old.

They are silent for several moments as Meg *drags off her cigarette and* Lenny *drinks her Coke.*

Meg: What's the cot doing in the kitchen?

Lenny: Well, I rolled it out when Old Granddaddy got sick. So I could be close and hear him at night if he needed something.

Meg: glancing toward the door leading to the downstairs bedroom: Is Old Granddaddy here?

Lenny: Why, no. Old Granddaddy's at the hospital.

Meg: Again?

Lenny: Meg!

Meg: What?

Lenny: I wrote you all about it. He's been in the hospital over three months straight.

Meg: He has?

Lenny: Don't you remember? I wrote you about all those blood vessels popping in his brain?

Meg: Popping—

Lenny: And how he was so anxious to hear from you and to find out about your singing career. I wrote it all to you. How they have to feed him through those tubes now. Didn't you get my letters?

Meg: Oh, I don't know, Lenny. I guess I did. To tell you the truth, sometimes I kinda don't read your letters.

Lenny: What?

Meg: I'm sorry. I used to read them. It's just, since Christmas reading them gives me these slicing pains right here in my chest.

Lenny: I see. I see. Is that why you didn't use that money Old Granddaddy sent you to come home Christmas; because you hate us so much? We never did all that much to make you hate us. We didn't!

Meg: Oh, Lenny! Do you think I'd be getting slicing pains in my chest if I didn't care about you? If I hated you? Honestly, now, do you think I would?

Lenny: No.

Meg: Okay, then. Let's drop it. I'm sorry I didn't read your letters. Okay?

Lenny: Okay.

Meg: Anyway, we've got this whole thing with Babe to deal with. The first thing is to get her a good lawyer and get her out of jail.

Lenny: Well, she's out of jail.

Meg: She is?

Lenny: That young lawyer, he's gotten her out.

Meg: Oh, he has?

Lenny: Yes, on bail. Uncle Watson's put it up. Chick's bringing her back right now—she's driving her home.

Meg: Oh; well, that's a relief.

Lenny: Yes, and they're due home any minute now; so we can just wait right here for 'em.

Meg: Well, good. That's good. *As she leans against the counter:* So, Babe shot Zackery Botrelle, the richest and most powerful man in all of Hazlehurst, slap in the gut. It's hard to believe.

Lenny: It certainly is. Little Babe—shooting off a gun.

Meg: Little Babe.

Lenny: She was always the prettiest and most perfect of the three of us. Old Granddaddy used to call her his Dancing Sugar Plum. Why, remember how proud and happy he was the day she married Zackery.

Meg: Yes, I remember. It was his finest hour.

Lenny: He remarked how Babe was gonna skyrocket right to the heights of Hazlehurst society. And how Zackery was just the right man for her whether she knew it now or not.

Meg: Oh, Lordy, Lordy. And what does Old Granddaddy say now?

Lenny: Well, I haven't had the courage to tell him all about this as yet. I thought maybe tonight we could go to visit at the hospital, and you could talk to him and . . .

Meg: Yeah; well, we'll see. We'll see. Do we have anything to drink around here—to the tune of straight bourbon?

Lenny: No. There's no liquor.

Meg: Hell. *She gets a Coke from the refrigerator and opens it.*

Lenny: Then you *will* go with me to see him tonight?

Meg: Of course. *She goes to her purse and gets out a bottle of Empirin. She takes out a tablet and puts it on her tongue.* Brother, I know he's gonna go on about my singing career. Just like he always does.

Lenny: Well, how is your career going?

Meg: It's not.

Lenny: Why, aren't you still singing at that club down on Malibu beach?

Meg: No. Not since Christmas.

Lenny: Well, then, are you singing someplace new?

Meg: No, I'm not singing. I'm not singing at all.

Lenny: Oh. Well, what do you do then?

Meg: What I do is I pay cold-storage bills for a dog-food company. That's what I do.

Lenny: trying to be helpful: Gosh, don't you think it'd be a good idea to stay in the show business field?

Meg: Oh, maybe.

Lenny: Like Old Granddaddy says, "With your talent, all you need is exposure. Then you can make your own breaks!" Did you hear his suggestion about getting your foot put in one of those blocks of cement they've got out there? He thinks that's real important.

Meg: Yeah. I think I've heard that. And I'll probably hear it again when I go to visit him at the hospital tonight; so let's just drop it. Okay? *She notices the sack of pecans.* What's this? Pecans? Great, I love pecans! *She takes out two pecans and tries to open them by cracking them together.* Come on . . . Crack, you demons! Crack!

Lenny: We have a nutcracker!

Meg: trying with her teeth: Ah, where's the sport in a nutcracker? Where's the challenge?

Lenny: getting the nutcracker: It's over here in the utensil drawer.

As Lenny *gets the nutcracker,* Meg *opens the pecan by stepping on it with her shoe.*

Meg: There! Open! *She picks up the crumbled pecan and eats it.* Mmmm, delicious. Delicious. Where'd you get the fresh pecans?

Lenny: Oh . . . I don't know.

Meg: They sure are tasty.

Lenny: Doc Porter brought them over.

Meg: Doc. What's Doc doing here in town?

Lenny: Well, his father died a couple of months ago. Now he's back home seeing to his property.

Meg: Gosh, the last I heard of Doc, he was up in the East painting the walls of houses to earn a living. *Amused:* Heard he was living with some Yankee woman who made clay pots.

Lenny: Joan.

Meg: What?

Lenny: Her name's Joan. She came down here with him. That's one of her pots. Doc's married to her.

Meg: Married—

Lenny: Uh huh.

Meg: Doc married a Yankee?

Lenny: That's right; and they've got two kids.

Meg: Kids—

Lenny: A boy and a girl.

Meg: God. Then his kids must be half Yankee.

Lenny: I suppose.

Meg: God. That really gets me. I don't know why, but somehow that really gets me.

Lenny: I don't know why it should.

Meg: And what a stupid-looking pot! Who'd buy it, anyway?

Lenny: Wait—I think that's them. Yeah, that's Chick's car! Oh, there's Babe! Hello, Babe! They're home, Meg! They're home.

Meg *hides.*

Babe's Voice: Lenny! I'm home! I'm free!

Babe, *twenty-four, enters exuberantly. She has an angelic face and fierce, volatile eyes. She carries a pink pocketbook.*

 Babe: I'm home!

Meg *jumps out of hiding.*

 Babe: Oh, Meg— Look it's Meg! *Running to hug her:* Meg! When did you get home?
 Meg: Just now!
 Babe: Well, it's so good to see you! I'm so glad you're home! I'm so relieved.

Chick *enters.*

 Meg: Why, Chick; hello.
 Chick: Hello, Cousin Margaret. What brings you back to Hazlehurst?
 Meg: Oh, I came on home . . . *Turning to* Babe: I came on home to see about Babe.
 Babe: running to hug Meg: Oh, Meg—
 Meg: How are things with you, Babe?
 Chick: Well, they are dismal, if you want my opinion. She is refusing to cooperate with her lawyer, that nice-looking young Lloyd boy. She won't tell any of us why she committed this heinous crime, except to say that she didn't like Zackery's looks—
 Babe: Oh, look, Lenny brought my suitcase from home! And my saxophone! Thank you! *She runs over to the cot and gets out her saxophone.*
 Chick: Now, that young lawyer is coming over here this afternoon, and when he gets here he expects to get some concrete answers! That's what he expects! No more of this nonsense and stubbornness from you, Rebecca MaGrath, or they'll put you in jail and throw away the key!
 Babe: overlapping to Meg: Meg, come look at my new saxophone. I went to Jackson and bought it used. Feel it. It's so heavy.
 Meg: overlapping Chick: It's beautiful.

The room goes silent.

 Chick: Isn't that right, won't they throw away the key?
 Lenny: Well, honestly, I don't know about that—
 Chick: They will! And leave you there to rot. So, Rebecca, what are you going to tell Mr. Lloyd about shooting Zackery when he gets here? What are your reasons going to be?
 Babe: glaring: That I didn't like his looks! I just didn't like his

stinking looks! And I don't like yours much, either, Chick the Stick! So just leave me alone! I mean it! Leave me alone! Oooh! *She exits up the stairs.*

There is a long moment of silence.

Chick: Well, I was only trying to warn her that she's going to have to help herself. It's just that she doesn't understand how serious the situation is. Does she? She doesn't have the vaguest idea. Does she, now?

Lenny: Well, it's true, she does seem a little confused.

Chick: And that's putting it mildly, Lenny honey. That's putting it mighty mild. So, Margaret, how's your singing career going? We keep looking for your picture in the movie magazines.

Meg *moves to light a cigarete.*

Chick: You know, you shouldn't smoke. It causes cancer. Cancer of the lungs. They say each cigarette is just a little stick of cancer. A little death stick.

Meg: That's what I like about it, Chick—taking a drag off of death. *She takes a long, deep drag.* Mmm! Gives me a sense of controlling my own destiny. What power! What exhilaration! Want a drag?

Lenny: *trying to break the tension:* Ah, Zackery's liver's been saved! His sister called up and said his liver was saved. Isn't that good news?

Meg: Well, yes, that's fine news. Mighty fine news. Why, I've been told that the liver's a powerful important bodily organ. I believe it's used to absorb all of our excess bile.

Lenny: Yes—well—it's been saved.

The phone rings. Lenny *gets it.*

Meg: So! Did you hear all that good news about the liver, Little Chicken?

Chick: I heard it. And don't you call me Chicken! Meg *clucks like a chicken.* I've told you a hundred times if I've told you once not to call me Chicken. You cannot call me Chicken.

Lenny: . . . Oh, no! . . . Of course, we'll be right over! 'Bye! *She hangs up the phone.* That was Annie May—Peekay and Buck Jr. have eaten paint!

Chick: Oh, no! Are they all right? They're not sick? They're not sick, are they?

Lenny: I don't know. I don't know. Come on. We've got to run on next door.

Chick: *overlapping:* Oh, God! Oh, please! Please let them be all right! Don't let them die! Please, don't let them die!

Chick *runs off howling, with* Lenny *following after.* Megs *sits alone, finishing her cigarette. After a moment,* Babe's *voice is heard.*

Babe's Voice: Pst—Psst!

Meg *looks around.* Babe *comes tiptoeing down the stairs.*

    Babe: Has she gone?

    Meg: She's gone. Peekay and Buck Jr. just ate their paints.

    Babe: What idiots.

    Meg: Yeah.

    Babe: You know, Chick's hated us ever since we had to move here from Vicksburg to live with Old Grandmama and Old Granddaddy.

    Meg: She's an idiot.

    Babe: Yeah. Do you know what she told me this morning while I was still behind bars and couldn't get away?

    Meg: What?

    Babe: She told me how embarrassing it was for her all those years ago, you know, when Mama—

    Meg: Yeah, down in the cellar.

    Babe: She said our mama had shamed the entire family, and we were known notoriously all through Hazlehurst. *About to cry:* Then she went on to say how I would now be getting just as much bad publicity, and humiliating her and the family all over again.

    Meg: Ah, forget it, Babe. Just forget it.

    Babe: I told her, "Mama got national coverage! National!" And if Zackery wasn't a senator from Copiah County, I probably wouldn't even be getting statewide.

    Meg: Of course you wouldn't.

    Babe: after a pause: Gosh, sometimes I wonder . . .

    Meg: What?

    Babe: Why she did it. Why Mama hung herself.

    Meg: I don't know. She had a bad day. A real bad day. You know how it feels on a real bad day.

    Babe: And that old yellow cat. It was sad about that old cat.

    Meg: Yeah.

    Babe: I bet if Daddy hadn't of left us, they'd still be alive.

    Meg: Oh, I don't know.

    Babe: 'Cause it was after he left that she started spending whole days just sitting there and smoking on the back porch steps. She'd sling her ashes down onto the different bugs and ants that'd be passing by.

    Meg: Yeah. Well, I'm glad he left.

    Babe: That old yellow cat'd stay back there with her. I thought if she felt something for anyone it woulda been that old cat. Guess I musta been mistaken.

Meg: God, he was a bastard. Really, with his white teeth. Daddy was such a bastard.

Babe: Was he? I don't remember.

Meg *blows out a mouthful of smoke.*

Babe: after a moment, uneasily: I think I'm gonna make some lemonade. You want some?

Meg: Sure.

Babe *cuts lemons, dumps sugar, stirs ice cubes, etc., throughout the following exchange.*

Meg: Babe. Why won't you talk? Why won't you tell anyone about shooting Zackery?

Babe: Oooh—

Meg: Why not? You must have had a good reason. Didn't you?

Babe: I guess I did.

Meg: Well, what was it?

Babe: I . . . I can't say.

Meg: Why not? *Pause.* Babe, why not? You can tell me.

Babe: 'Cause . . . I'm sort of . . . protecting someone.

Meg: Protecting someone? Oh, Babe, then you really didn't shoot him! I knew you couldn't have done it! I knew it!

Babe: No, I shot him. I shot him all right. I meant to kill him. I was aiming for his heart, but I guess my hands were shaking and I— just got him in the stomach.

Meg: collapsing: I see.

Babe: stirring the lemonade: So I'm guilty. And I'm just gonna have to take my punishment and go on to jail.

Meg: Oh, Babe—

Babe: Don't worry, Meg, jail's gonna be a relief to me. I can learn to play my new saxophone. I won't have to live with Zackery anymore. And I won't have his snoopy old sister, Lucille, coming over and pushing me around. Jail will be a relief. Here's your lemonade.

Meg: Thanks.

Babe: It taste okay?

Meg: Perfect.

Babe: I like a lot of sugar in mine. I'm gonna add some more sugar.

Babe *goes to add more sugar to her lemonade as* Lenny *bursts through the back door in a state of excitement and confusion.*

Lenny: Well, it looks like the paint is primarily on their arms and faces, but Chick wants me to drive them all over to Dr. Winn's just to make sure. *She grabs her car keys from the counter, and as she does so, she notices the mess of lemons and sugar.* Oh, now, Babe, try not to make a mess here; and be careful with this sharp knife.

Beth Henley   2021

Honestly, all that sugar's gonna get you sick. Well, 'bye, 'bye. I'll be back as soon as I can.

Meg: 'Bye, Lenny.

Babe: 'Bye.

Lenny *exits.*

Babe: Boy, I don't know what's happening to Lenny.

Meg: What do you mean?

Babe: "Don't make a mess; don't make yourself sick; don't cut yourself with that sharp knife." She's turning into Old Grandmama.

Meg: You think so?

Babe: More and more. Do you know she's taken to wearing Old Grandmama's torn sunhat and her green garden gloves?

Meg: Those old lime-green ones?

Babe: Yeah; she works out in the garden wearing the lime-green gloves of a dead woman. Imagine wearing those gloves on your hands.

Meg: Poor Lenny. She needs some love in her life. All she does is work out at that brick yard and take care of Old Granddaddy.

Babe: Yeah. But she's so shy with men.

Meg: biting into an apple: Probably because of that *shrunken* ovary she has.

Babe: slinging ice cubes: Yeah, that *deformed* ovary.

Meg: Old Granddaddy's the one who's made her feel self-conscious about it. It's his fault. The old fool.

Babe: It's so sad.

Meg: God—you know what?

Babe: What?

Meg: I bet Lenny's never even slept with a man. Just think, thirty years old and never even had it once.

Babe: slyly: Oh, I don't know. Maybe she's . . . had it once.

Meg: She has?

Babe: Maybe. I think so.

Meg: When? When?

Babe: Well . . . maybe I shouldn't say—

Meg: Babe!

Babe: rapidly telling the story: All right, then. It was after Old Granddaddy went back to the hospital this second time. Lenny was really in a state of deep depression, I could tell that she was. Then one day she calls me up and asks me to come over and to bring along my Polaroid camera. Well, when I arrive she's waiting for me out there in the sun parlor wearing her powder-blue Sunday dress and this old curled-up wig. She confided that she was gonna try sending in her picture to one of those lonely-hearts clubs.

Meg: Oh, my God.

Babe: Lonely Hearts of the South. She'd seen their ad in a magazine.

Meg: Jesus.

Babe: Anyway, I take some snapshots and she sends them on in to the club, and about two weeks later she receives in the mail this whole load of pictures of available men, most of 'em fairly odd-looking. But of course she doesn't call any of 'em up 'cause she's real shy. But one of 'em, this Charlie Hill from Memphis, Tennessee, he calls her.

Meg: He does?

Babe: Yeah. And time goes on and she says he's real funny on the phone, so they decide to get together to meet.

Meg: Yeah?

Babe: Well, he drives down here to Hazlehurst 'bout three or four different times and has supper with her; then one weekend she goes up to Memphis to visit him, and I think that is where it happened.

Meg: What makes you think so?

Babe: Well, when I went to pick her up from the bus depot, she ran off the bus and threw her arms around me and started crying and sobbing as though she'd like to never stop. I asked her, I said, "Lenny, what's the matter?" And she said, "I've done it, Babe! Honey, I have done it!"

Meg: whispering: And you think she meant that she'd done *it?*

Babe: whispering back, slyly: I think so.

Meg: Well, goddamn!

They laugh.

Babe: But she didn't say anything else about it. She just went on to tell me about the boot factory where Charlie worked and what a nice city Memphis was.

Meg: So, what happened to this Charlie?

Babe: Well, he came to Hazlehurst just one more time. Lenny took him over to meet Old Granddaddy at the hospital, and after that they broke it off.

Meg: 'Cause of Old Granddaddy?

Babe: Well, she said it was on account of her missing ovary. That Charlie didn't want to marry her on account of it.

Meg: Ah, how mean. How hateful.

Babe: Oh, it was. He seemed like such a nice man, too—kinda chubby, with red hair and freckles, always telling these funny jokes.

Meg: Hmmm, that just doesn't seem right. Something about that doesn't seem exactly right. *She paces about the kitchen and comes across the box of candy* Lenny *got for her birthday.* Oh, God. "Happy birthday to Lenny, from the Buck Boyles."

Babe: Oh, no! Today's Lenny's birthday!

Meg: That's right.

Babe: I forgot all about it!

Meg: I know. I did, too.

Babe: Gosh, we'll have to order up a big cake for her. She always loves to make those wishes on her birthday cake.

Meg: Yeah, let's get her a big cake! A huge one! *Suddenly noticing the plastic wrapper on the candy box:* Oh, God, that Chick's so cheap!

Babe: What do you mean?

Meg: This plastic has poinsettias on it!

Babe: running to see: Oh, let me see—*She looks at the package with disgust.* Boy, oh, boy! I'm calling that bakery and ordering the very largest size cake they have! That jumbo deluxe!

Meg: Good!

Babe: Why, I imagine they can make one up to be about—*this* big. *She demonstrates.*

Meg: Oh, at least; at least that big. Why, maybe it'll even be *this* big. *She makes a very, very, very large-size cake.*

Babe: You think it could be *that* big?

Meg: Sure!

Babe: after a moment, getting the idea: Or, or what if it were *this* big? *She maps out a cake that covers the room.* What if we get the cake and it's *this* big? *She gulps down a fistful of cake.* Gulp! Gulp! Gulp! Tasty treat!

Meg: Hmmm—I'll have me some more! Give me some more of that birthday cake!

Suddenly there is a loud knock at the door.

Barnette's Voice: Hello . . . Hello! May I come in?

Babe: to Meg, *in a whisper, as she takes cover:* Who's that?

Meg: I don't know.

Barnette's Voice: He is still knocking. Hello! Hello, Mrs. Botrelle!

Babe: Oh, shoot! It's that lawyer. I don't want to see him.

Meg: Oh, Babe, come on. You've got to see him sometime.

Babe: No, I don't! *She starts up the stairs.* Just tell him I died. I'm going upstairs.

Meg: Oh, Babe! Will you come back here!

Babe: as she exits: You talk to him, please, Meg. Please! I just don't want to see him—

Meg: Babe—Babe! Oh, shit . . . Ah, come on in! Door's open!

Barnette Lloyd, *twenty-six, enters carrying a briefcase. He is a slender, intelligent young man with an almost fanatical intensity that he subdues by sheer will.*

Barnette: How do you do. I'm Barnette Lloyd.

Meg: Pleased to meet you. I'm Meg MaGrath, Babe's older sister.

Barnette: Yes, I know. You're the singer.

Meg: Well, yes . . .

Barnette: I came to hear you five different times when you were singing at that club in Biloxi. Greeny's I believe was the name of it.

Meg: Yes, Greeny's.

Barnette: You were very good. There was something sad and moving about how you sang those songs. It was like you had some sort of vision. Some special sort of vision.

Meg: Well, thank you. You're very kind. Now . . . about Babe's case—

Barnette: Yes?

Meg: We've just got to win it.

Barnette: I intend to.

Meg: Of course. But, ah . . . *She looks at him.* Ah, you know, you're very young.

Barnette: Yes. I am. I'm young.

Meg: It's just, I'm concerned, Mr. Lloyd—

Barnette: Barnette. Please.

Meg: Barnette; that, ah, just maybe we need someone with, well, with more experience. Someone totally familiar with all the ins and outs and the this and thats of the legal dealings and such. As that.

Barnette: Ah, you have reservations.

Meg: relieved: Reservations. Yes, I have . . . reservations.

Barnette: Well, possibly it would help you to know that I graduated first in my class from Ole Miss Law School. I also spent three different summers taking advanced courses in criminal law at Harvard Law School. I made Λ's in all the given courses. I was fascinated!

Meg: I'm sure.

Barnette: And even now, I've just completed one year working with Jackson's top criminal law firm, Manchester and Wayne. I was invaluable to them. Indispensable. They offered to double my percentage if I'd stay on; but I refused. I wanted to return to Hazlehurst and open my own office. The reason being, and this is a key point, that I have a personal vendetta to settle with one Zackery F. Botrelle.

Meg: A personal vendetta?

Barnette: Yes, ma'am. You are correct. Indeed, I do.

Meg: Hmmm. A personal vendetta . . . I think I like that. So you have some sort of a personal vendetta to settle with Zackery?

Barnette: Precisely. Just between the two of us, I not only intend to keep that sorry s.o.b. from ever being reelected to the state senate by exposing his shady, criminal dealings; but I also intend to decimate his personal credibility by exposing him as a bully, a brute, and a red-neck thug!

Meg: Well; I can see that you're—fanatical about this.

Barnette: Yes, I am. I'm sorry if I seem outspoken. But for some reason I feel I can talk to you . . . those songs you sang. Excuse me; I feel like a jackass.

Meg: It's all right. Relax. Relax, Barnette. Let me think this out a minute. *She takes out a cigarette. He lights it for her.* Now just exactly how do you intend to get Babe off? You know, keep her out of jail.

Barnette: It seems to me that we can get her off with a plea of self-defense, or possible we could go with innocent by reason of temporary insanity. But basically I intend to prove that Zackery Botrelle brutalized and tormented this poor woman to such an extent that she had no recourse but to defend herself in the only way she knew how!

Meg: I like that!

Barnette: Then, of course, I'm hoping this will break the ice and we'll be able to go on to prove that the man's a total criminal, as well as an abusive bully and contemptible slob!

Meg: That sounds good! To me that sounds very good!

Barnette: It's just our basic game plan.

Meg: But now, how are you going to prove all this about Babe being brutalized? We don't want anyone perjured. I mean to commit perjury.

Barnette: Perjury? According to my sources, there'll be no need for perjury.

Meg: You mean it's the truth?

Barnette: This is a small town, Miss MaGrath. The word gets out.

Meg: It's really the truth?

Barnette: opening his briefcase: Just look at this. It's a photostatic copy of Mrs. Botrelle's medical chart over the past four years. Take a good look at it, if you want your blood to boil!

Meg: looking over the chart: What! What! This is maddening. This is madness! Did he do this to her? I'll kill him; I will—I'll fry his blood! Did he do this?

Barnette: alarmed: To tell you the truth, I can't say for certain what was accidental and what was not. That's why I need to talk with Mrs. Botrelle. That's why it's very important that I see her!

Meg: her eyes are wild, as she shoves him toward the door: Well, look, I've got to see her first. I've got to talk to her first. What I'll do is I'll give you a call. Maybe you can come back over later on—

Barnette: Well, then, here's my card—

Meg: Okay. Goodbye.

Barnette: 'Bye!

Meg: Oh, wait! Wait! There's one problem with you.

Barnette: What?

Meg: What if you get so fanatically obsessed with this vendetta thing that you forget about Babe? You forget about her and sell her down the river just to get at Zackery. What about that?

Barnette: I—wouldn't do that.

    Meg: You wouldn't?

Barnette: No.

    Meg: Why not?

Barnette: Because I'm—I'm fond of her.

    Meg: What do you mean you're fond of her?

Barnette: Well, she . . . she sold me a pound cake at a bazaar once. And I'm fond of her.

    Meg: All right; I believe you. Goodbye.

Barnette: Goodbye. *He exits.*

    Meg: Babe! Babe, come down here! Babe!

Babe *comes hurrying down the stairs.*

    Babe: What? What is it? I called about the cake—

    Meg: What did Zackery do to you?

    Babe: They can't have it for today.

    Meg: Did he hurt you? Did he? Did he do that?

    Babe: Oh, Meg, please—

    Meg: Did he? Goddamnit, Babe—

    Babe: Yes, he did.

    Meg: Why? Why?

    Babe: I don't know! He started hating me, 'cause I couldn't laugh at his jokes. I just started finding it impossible to laugh at his jokes the way I used to. And then the sound of his voice got to where it tired me out awful bad to hear it. I'd fall asleep just listening to him at the dinner table. He'd say, "Hand me some of that gravy!" Or, "This roast beef is too damn bloody." And suddenly I'd be out cold like a light.

    Meg: Oh, Babe. Babe, this is very important. I want you to sit down here and tell me what all happened right before you shot Zachery. That's right, just sit down and tell me.

    Babe: after a pause: I told you, I can't tell you on account of I'm protecting someone.

    Meg: But, Babe, you've just got to talk to someone about all this. You just do.

    Babe: Why?

    Meg: Because it's a human need. To talk about our lives. It's an important human need.

    Babe: Oh. Well, I do feel like I want to talk to someone. I do.

    Meg: Then talk to me; please.

    Babe: making a decision: All right. *After thinking a minute:* I don't know where to start.

    Meg: Just start at the beginning. Just there at the beginning.

Babe: after a moment: Well, do you remember Willie Jay? Meg *shakes her head.* Cora's youngest boy?

Meg: Oh, yeah, that little kid we used to pay a nickel to, to run down to the drugstore and bring us back a cherry Coke.

Babe: Right. Well, Cora irons at my place on Wednesday now, and she just happened to mention that Willie Jay'd picked up this old stray dog and that he'd gotten real fond of him. But now they couldn't afford to feed him anymore. So she was gonna have to tell Willie Jay to set him loose in the woods.

Meg: trying to be patient: Uh huh.

Babe: Well, I said I liked dogs, and if he wanted to bring the dog over here, I'd take care of him. You see, I was alone by myself most of the time 'cause the senate was in session and Zackery was up in Jackson.

Meg: Uh huh. *She reaches for* Lenny's *box of birthday candy. She takes little nibbles out of each piece throughout the rest of the scene.*

Babe: So the next day, Willie Jay brings over this skinny old dog with these little crossed eyes. Will, I asked Willie Jay what his name was, and he said they called him Dog. Well, I liked the name, so I thought I'd keep it.

Meg: getting up: Uh huh. I'm listening. I'm just gonna get me a glass of cold water. Do you want one?

Babe: Okay.

Meg: So you kept the name—Dog.

Babe: Yeah. Anyway, when Willie Jay was leaving he gave Dog a hug and said, "Goodbye, Dog. You're a fine ole dog." Well, I felt something for him, so I told Willie Jay he could come back and visit with Dog any time he wanted, and his face just kinda lit right up.

Meg: offering the candy: Candy—

Babe: No, thanks. Anyhow, time goes on and Willie Jay keeps coming over and over. And we talk about Dog and how fat he's getting, and then, well, you know, things start up.

Meg: No, I don't know. What things start up?

Babe: Well, things start up. Like sex. Like that.

Meg: Babe, wait a minute—Willie Jay's a boy. A small boy, about this tall. He's about this tall!

Babe: No! Oh, no! He's taller now! He's fifteen now. When you knew him he was only about seven or eight.

Meg: But even so—fifteen. And he's a black boy; a colored boy; a Negro.

Babe: flustered: Well, I realize that, Meg. Why do you think I'm so worried about his getting public exposure? I don't want to ruin his reputation!

Meg: I'm amazed, Babe. I'm really completely amazed. I didn't even know you were a liberal.

Babe: Well, I'm not! I'm not a liberal! I'm a democratic! I was just lonely! I was so lonely. And he was good. Oh, he was so, so good. I'd never had it that good. We'd always go out into the garage and—

Meg: It's okay. I've got the picture; I've got the picture! Now, let's just get back to the story. To yesterday, when you shot Zackery.

Babe: All right, then. Let's see . . . Willie Jay was over. And it was after we'd—

Meg: Yeah! yeah.

Babe: And we were just standing around on the back porch playing with Dog. Well, suddenly Zackery comes from around the side of the house. And he startled me 'cause he's supposed to be away at the office, and there he is coming from round the side of the house. Anyway, he says to Willie Jay, "Hey, boy, what are you doing back here?" And I say, "He's not doing anything. You just go on home, Willie Jay! You just run right on home." Well, before he can move, Zackery comes up and knocks him once right across the face and then shoves him down the porch steps, causing him to skin up his elbow real bad on that hard concrete. Then he says, "Don't you ever come around here again, or I'll have them cut out your gizzard!" Well, Willie Jay starts crying— these tears come streaming down his face—then he gets up real quick and runs away, with Dog following off after him. After that, I don't remember much too clearly; let's see . . . I went on into the living room, and I went right up to the davenport and opened the drawer where we keep the burglar gun . . . I took it out. Then I—I brought it up to my ear. That's right. I put it right inside my ear. Why, I was gonna shoot off my own head! That's what I was gonna do. Then I heard the back door slamming and suddenly, for some reason, I thought about Mama . . . how she'd hung herself. And here I was about ready to shoot myself. Then I realized—that's right, I realized how I didn't want to kill myself! And she—she probably didn't want to kill herself. She wanted to kill him, and I wanted to kill him, too. I wanted to kill Zackery, not myself. 'Cause I—I wanted to live! So I waited for him to come on into the living room. Then I held out the gun, and I pulled the trigger, aiming for his heart but getting him in the stomach. *After a pause:* It's funny that I really did that.

Meg: It's a good thing that you did. It's a damn good thing that you did.

Babe: It was.

Meg: Please, Babe, talk to Barnette Lloyd. Just talk to him and see if he can help.

Babe: But how about Willie Jay?

Meg: *starting toward the phone:* Oh, he'll be all right. You just talk to that lawyer like you did to me. *Looking at the number on the card, she begins dialing.* See, 'cause he's gonna be on your side.

Babe: No! Stop, Meg, stop! Don't call him up! Please don't call him up! You can't! It's too awful. *She runs over and jerks the bottom half of the phone away from* Meg.

Meg *stands, holding the receiver.*

Meg: Babe!

Babe *slams her half of the phone into the refrigerator.*

Babe: I just can't tell some stranger all about my personal life. I just can't.

Meg: Well, hell, Babe; you're the one who said you wanted to live.

Babe: That's right. I did. *She takes the phone out of the refrigerator and hands it to* Meg. Here's the other part of the phone. *She moves to sit at the kitchen table.*

Meg *takes the phone back to the counter.*

Babe: *As she fishes a piece of lemon out of her glass and begins sucking on it:* Meg.

Meg: What?

Babe: I called the bakery. They're gonna have Lenny's cake ready first thing tomorrow morning. That's the earliest they can get it.

Meg: All right.

Babe: I told them to write on it, *Happy Birthday, Lenny—A Day Late.* That sound okay?

Meg: *at the phone:* It sounds nice.

Babe: I ordered up the very largest size cake they have. I told them chocolate cake with white icing and red trim. Think she'll like that?

Meg: *dialing the phone:* Yeah, I'm sure she will She'll like it.

Babe: I'm hoping.

CURTAIN

ACT TWO

The lights go up on the kitchen. It is evening of the same day. Meg's *suitcase has been moved upstairs.* Babe's *saxophone has been taken out of the case and put together.* Babe *and* Barnette *are sitting at the kitchen table.* Barnette *is writing and rechecking notes with explosive intensity.* Babe, *who has changed into a casual shift, sits eating a bowl of oatmeal, slowly.*

Barnette: *to himself:* Hmm huh! Yes! I see, I see! Well, we can work on that! And of course, this is mere conjecture! Difficult, if not impossible, to prove. Ha! Yes. Yes, indeed. Indeed—

Babe: Sure you don't want any oatmeal?

Barnette: What? Oh, no. No, thank you. Let's see; ah, where were we?

Babe: I just shot Zackery.

Barnette: looking at his notes: Right. Correct. You've just pulled the trigger.

Babe: Tell me, do you think Willie Jay can stay out of all this?

Barnette: Believe me, it is in our interest to keep him as far out of this as possible.

Babe: Good.

Barnette: throughout the following, Barnette *stays glued to* Babe's *every word:* All right, you've just shot one Zackery Botrelle, as a result of his continual physical and mental abuse—what happens now?

Babe: Well, after I shot him, I put the gun down on the piano bench, and then I went out into the kitchen and made up a pitcher of lemonade.

Barnette: Lemonade?

Babe: Yes, I was dying of thirst. My mouth was just as dry as a bone.

Barnette: So in order to quench this raging thirst that was choking you dry and preventing any possibility of you uttering intelligible sounds or phrases, you went out to the kitchen and made up a pitcher of lemonade?

Babe: Right. I made it just the way I like it, with lots of sugar and lots of lemon—about ten lemons in all. Then I added two trays of ice and stirred it up with my wooden stirring spoon.

Barnette: Then what?

Babe: Then I drank three glasses, one right after the other. They were large glasses—about this tall. Then suddenly my stomach kind of swole all up. I guess what caused it was all that sour lemon.

Barnette: Could be.

Babe: Then what I did was . . . I wiped my mouth off with the back of my hand, like this . . . *She demonstrates.*

Barnette: Hmmm.

Babe: I did it to clear off all those little beads of water that had settled there.

Barnette: I see.

Babe: Then I called out to Zackery. I said, "Zackery, I've made some lemonade. Can you use a glass?"

Barnette: Did he answer? Did you hear an answer?

Babe: No. He didn't answer.

Barnette: So what'd you do?

Babe: I poured him a glass anyway and took it out to him.

Barnette: You took it out to the living room?

Babe: I did. And there he was, lying on the rug. He was looking up at me trying to speak words. I said, "What? . . . Lemonade? . . . You don't want it? Would you like a Coke instead?" Then I got the idea—he was telling me to call on the phone for medical help. So I got on the phone and called up the hospital. I gave my name and address, and I told them my husband was shot and he was lying on the rug and there was plenty of blood. *She pauses a minute, as* Barnette *works frantically on his notes.* I guess that's gonna look kinda bad.

Barnette: What?

Babe: Me fixing that lemonade before I called the hospital.

Barnette: Well, not . . . necessarily.

Babe: I tell you, I think the reason I made up the lemonade, I mean besides the fact that my mouth was bone dry, was that I was afraid to call the authorities. I was afraid. I—I really think I was afraid they would see that I had tried to shoot Zackery, in fact, that I *had* shot him, and they would accuse me of possible murder and send me away to jail.

Barnette: Well, that's understandable.

Babe: I think so. I mean, in fact, that's what did happen. That's what is happening—'cause here I am just about ready to go right off to the Parchment Prison Farm. Yes, here I am just practically on the brink of utter doom. Why, I feel so all alone.

Barnette: Now, now, look— Why, there's no reason for you to get yourself so all upset and worried. Please don't. Please.

They look at each other for a moment.

Barnette: You just keep filling in as much detailed information as you can about those incidents on the medical reports. That's all you need to think about. Don't you worry, Mrs. Botrelle, we're going to have a solid defense.

Babe: Please don't call me Mrs. Botrelle.

Barnette: All right.

Babe: My name's Becky. People in the family call me Babe, but my real name's Becky.

Barnette *and* Babe *stare at each other for a long moment.*

Babe: Are you sure you didn't go to Hazlehurst High?

Barnette: No, I went away to a boarding school.

Babe: Gosh, you sure do look familiar. You sure do.

Barnette: Well, I—I doubt you'll remember, but I did meet you once.

Babe: You did? When?

Barnette: At the Christmas bazaar, year before last. You were selling cakes and cookies and . . . candy.

Babe: Oh, yes! You bought the orange pound cake!

Barnette: Right.

Babe: Of course, and then we talked for a while. We talked about the Christmas angel.

Barnette: You do remember.

Babe: I remember it very well. You were even thinner then than you are now.

Barnette: Well, I'm surprised. I'm certainly . . . surprised.

The phone rings.

Babe: as she goes to answer the phone: This is quite a coincidence! Don't you think it is? Why, it's almost a fluke. *She answers the phone.* Hello . . . Oh, hello, Lucille . . . Oh, he is? . . . Oh, he does? . . . Okay. Oh, Lucille, wait! Has Dog come back to the house? . . . Oh, I see . . . Okay. Okay. *After a brief pause:* Hello, Zackery? How are you doing? . . . Uh huh . . . uh huh . . . Oh, I'm sorry . . . Please don't scream . . . Uh huh . . . uh huh . . . You want what? . . . No, I can't come up there now . . . Well, for one thing, I don't even have the car. Lenny and Meg are up at the hospital right now, visiting with Old Granddaddy . . . What? . . . Oh, really? . . . Oh, really? . . . Well, I've got me a lawyer that's over here right now, and he's building me up a solid defense! . . . Wait just a minute, I'll see. *To* Barnette: He wants to talk to you. He says he's got some blackening evidence that's gonna convict me of attempting to murder him in the first degree!

Barnette: disgustedly: Oh, bluff! He's bluffing! Here, hand me the phone. *He takes the phone and becomes suddenly cool and suave.* Hello, this is Mr. Barnette Lloyd speaking. I'm Mrs. . . . ah, Becky's attorney . . . Why, certainly, Mr. Botrelle, I'd be more than glad to check out any pertinent information that you may have . . . Fine, then I'll be right on over. Goodbye. *He hangs up the phone.*

Babe: What did he say?

Barnette: He wants me to come see him at the hospital this evening. Says he's got some sort of evidence. Sounds highly suspect to me.

Babe: Oooh! Didn't you just hate his voice? Doesn't he have the most awful voice? I just hate—I can't bear to hear it!

Barnette: Well, now—now, wait. Wait just a minute.

Babe: What?

Barnette: I have a solution. From now on, I'll handle all communications between you two. You can simply refuse to speak with him.

Babe: All right—I will. I'll do that.

Barnette: starting to pack his briefcase: Well, I'd better get over there and see just what he's got up his sleeve.

Babe: after a pause: Barnette.

Barnette: Yes?

Babe: What's the personal vendetta about? You know, the one you have to settle with Zackery.

Barnette: Oh, it's—it's complicated. It's a very complicated matter.

Babe: I see.

Barnette: The major thing he did was to ruin my father's life. He took away his job, his home, his health, his respectability. I don't like to talk about it.

Babe: I'm sorry. I just wanted to say—I hope you win it. I hope you win your vendetta.

Barnette: Thank you.

Babe: I think it's an important thing that a person could win a life-long vendetta.

Barnette: Yes. Well, I'd better be going.

Babe: All right. Let me know what happens.

Barnette: I will. I'll get back to you right away.

Babe: Thanks.

Barnette: Goodbye, Becky.

Babe: Goodbye, Barnette.

Barnette *exits.* Babe *looks around the room for a moment, then goes over to her white suitcase and opens it up. She takes out her pink hair curlers and a brush. She begins brushing her hair.*

Babe: Goodbye, Becky. Goodbye, Barnette. Goodbye, Becky. Oooh.

Lenny *enters. She is fuming.* Babe *is rolling her hair throughout most of the following scene.*

Babe: Lenny, hi!

Lenny: Hi.

Babe: Where's Meg?

Lenny: Oh, she had to go by the store and pick some things up. I don't know what.

Babe: Well, how's Old Granddaddy?

Lenny: as she picks up Babe's *bowl of oatmeal:* He's fine. Wonderful! Never been better!

Babe: Lenny, what's wrong? What's the matter?

Lenny: It's Meg! I could just wring her neck! I could just wring it!

Babe: Why? Wha'd she do?

Lenny: She lied! She sat in that hospital room and shamelessly lied to Old Granddaddy. She went on and on telling such untrue stories and lies.

Babe: Well, what? What did she say?

Lenny: Well, for one thing, she said she was gonna have an RCA record coming out with her picture on the cover, eating pineapples under a palm tree.

Babe: Well, gosh, Lenny, maybe she is! Don't you think she really is?

Lenny: Babe, she sat here this very afternoon and told me how all that she's done this whole year is work as a clerk for a dog-food company.

Babe: Oh, shoot. I'm disappointed.

Lenny: And then she goes on to say that she'll be appearing on the Johnny Carson show in two weeks' time. Two weeks' time! Why, Old Granddaddy's got a TV set right in his room. Imagine what a letdown it's gonna be.

Babe: Why, mercy me.

Lenny: slamming the coffeepot on: Oh, and she told him the reason she didn't use the money he sent her to come home Christmas was that she was right in the middle of making a huge multimillion-dollar motion picture and was just under too much pressure.

Babe: My word!

Lenny: The movie's coming out this spring. It's called *Singing in a Shoe Factory*. But she only has a small leading role—not a large leading role.

Babe: laughing: For heaven's sake—

Lenny: I'm sizzling. Oh, I just can't help it! I'm sizzling!

Babe: Sometimes Meg does such strange things.

Lenny: slowly, as she picks up the opened box of birthday candy: Who ate this candy?

Babe: hesitantly: Meg.

Lenny: My one birthday present, and look what she does! Why, she's taken one little bite out of each piece and then just put it back in! Ooh! That's just like her! That is just like her!

Babe: Lenny, please—

Lenny: I can't help it! It gets me mad! It gets me upset! Why, Meg's always run wild—she started smoking and drinking when she was fourteen years old; she never made good grades—never made her own bed! But somehow she always seemed to get what she wanted. She's the one who got singing and dancing lessons, and a store-bought dress to wear to her senior prom. Why, do you remember how Meg always got to wear twelve jingle bells on her petticoats, while we were only allowed to wear three apiece? Why?! Why should Old Grandmama let her sew twelve golden jingle bells on her petticoats and us only three!

Babe: who has heard all this before: I don't know! Maybe she didn't jingle them as much!

Lenny: I can't help it! It gets me mad! I resent it. I do.

Babe: Oh, don't resent Meg. Things have been hard for Meg. After all, she was the one who found Mama.

Lenny: Oh, I know; she's the one who found Mama. But that's always been the excuse.

Babe: But I tell you, Lenny, after it happened, Meg started doing all sorts of these strange things.

Lenny: She did? Like what?

Babe: Like things I never even wanted to tell you about.

Lenny: What sort of things?

Babe: Well, for instance, back when we used to go over to the library, Meg would spend all her time reading and looking through this old black book called *Diseases of the Skin.* It was full of the most sickening pictures you've ever seen. Things like rotting-away noses and eyeballs drooping off down the sides of people's faces, and scabs and sores and eaten-away places all over all parts of people's bodies.

Lenny: trying to pour her coffee: Babe, please! That's enough.

Babe: Anyway, she'd spend hours and hours just forcing herself to look through this book. Why, it was the same way she'd force herself to look at the poster of crippled children stuck up in the window at Dixieland Drugs. You know, that one where they want you to give a dime. Meg would stand there and stare at their eyes and look at the braces on their little crippled-up legs—then she'd purposely go and spend her dime on a double-scoop ice cream cone and eat it all down. She'd say to me, "See, I can stand it. I can stand it. Just look how I'm gonna be able to stand it."

Lenny: That's awful.

Babe: She said she was afraid of being a weak person. I guess 'cause she cried in bed every night for such a long time.

Lenny: Goodness mercy. *After a pause:* Well, I suppose you'd have to be a pretty hard person to be able to do what she did to Doc Porter.

Babe: exasperated: Oh, shoot! It wasn't Meg's fault that hurricane wiped Biloxi away. I never understood why people were blaming all that on Meg—just because that roof fell in and crunched Doc's leg. It wasn't her fault.

Lenny: Well, it was Meg who refused to evacuate. Jim Craig and some of Doc's other friends were all down there, and they kept trying to get everyone to evacuate. But Meg refused. She wanted to stay on because she thought a hurricane would be—oh, I don't know—a lot of fun. Then everyone says she baited Doc into staying there with her. She said she'd marry him if he'd stay.

Babe: taken aback by this new information: Well, he has a mind of his own. He could have gone.

Lenny: But he didn't. 'Cause . . . 'cause he loved her. And then, after the roof caved in and they got Doc to the high school gym, Meg just left. She just left him here to leave for California—'cause of her career, she says. I think it was a shameful thing to do. It took almost a year for his leg to heal, and after that he gave up his medical career altogether. He said he was tired of hospitals. It's such a sad thing. Everyone always knew he was gonna be a doctor. We've called him Doc for years.

Babe: I don't know. I guess I don't have any room to talk; 'cause I just don't know. *Pause.* Gosh, you look so tired.

Lenny: I feel tired.

Babe: They say women need a lot of iron . . . so they won't feel tired.

Lenny: What's got iron in it? Liver?

Babe: Yeah, liver's got it. And vitamin pills.

After a moment, Meg enters. She carries a bottle of bourbon that is already minus a few slugs, and a newspaper. She is wearing black boots, a dark dress, and a hat. The room goes silent.

Meg: Hello.

Babe: fooling with her hair: Hi, Meg.

Lenny *quietly sips her coffee.*

Meg: handing the newspaper to Babe: Here's your paper.

Babe: Thanks. *She opens it.* Oh, here it is, right on the front page.

Meg *lights a cigarette.*

Babe: Where're the scissors, Lenny?

Lenny: Look in there in the ribbon drawer.

Babe: Okay. *She gets the scissors and glue out of the drawer and slowly begins cutting out the newspaper article.*

Meg: after a few moments, filled only with the snipping of scissors: All right—I lied! I lied! I couldn't help it . . . these stories just came pouring out of my mouth! When I saw how tired and sick Old Granddaddy'd gotten—they just flew out! All I wanted was to see him smiling and happy. I just wasn't going to sit there and look at him all miserable and sick and sad! I just wasn't!

Babe: Oh, Meg, he is sick, isn't he—

Meg: Why, he's gotten all white and milky—he's almost evaporated!

Lenny: gasping and turning to Meg: But still you shouldn't have lied! It just was wrong for you to tell such lies—

Meg: Well, I know that! Don't you think I know that? I hate myself when I lie for that old man. I do. I feel so weak. And then I have to go and do at least three or four things that I know he'd despise just to get even with that miserable, old, bossy man!

Lenny: Oh, Meg, please don't talk so about Old Granddaddy! It sounds so ungrateful. Why, he went out of his way to make a home for us, to treat us like we were his very own children. All he ever wanted was the best for us. That's all he ever wanted.

Meg: Well, I guess it was; but sometimes I wonder what we wanted.

Babe: taking the newspaper article and glue over to her suitcase: Well, one thing I wanted was a team of white horses to ride Mama's coffin to her grave. That's one thing I wanted.

Lenny *and* Meg *exchange looks.*

Babe: Lenny, did you remember to pack my photo album?

Beth Henley 2037

Lenny: It's down there at the bottom, under all that night stuff.

Babe: Oh, I found it.

Lenny: Really, Babe, I don't understand why you have to put in the articles that are about the unhappy things in your life. Why would you want to remember them?

Babe: pasting the article in: I don't know. I just like to keep an accurate record, I suppose. There. *She begins flipping through the book.* Look, here's a picture of me when I got married.

Meg: Let's see.

They all look at the photo album.

Lenny: My word, you look about twelve years old.

Babe: I was just eighteen.

Meg: You're smiling, Babe. Were you happy then?

Babe: laughing: Well, I was drunk on champagne punch. I remember that!

They turn the page.

Lenny: Oh, there's Meg singing at Greeny's!

Babe: Oooh, I wish you were still singing at Greeny's! I wish you were!

Lenny: You're so beautiful!

Babe: Yes, you are. You're beautiful.

Meg: Oh, stop! I'm not—

Lenny: Look, Meg's starting to cry.

Babe: Oh, Meg—

Meg: I'm not—

Babe: Quick, better turn the page; we don't want Meg crying—*She flips the pages.*

Lenny: Why, it's Daddy.

Meg: Where'd you get that picture, Babe? I thought she burned them all.

Babe: Ah, I just found it around.

Lenny: What does it say here? What's that inscription?

Babe: It says "Jimmy—clowning at the beach—1952."

Lenny: Well, will you look at that smile.

Meg: Jesus, those white teeth—turn the page, will you; we can't do any worse than this!

They turn the page. The room goes silent.

Babe: It's Mama and the cat.

Lenny: Oh, turn the page—

Babe: That old yellow cat. You know, I bet if she hadn't of hung that old cat along with her, she wouldn't have gotten all that national coverage.

Meg: after a moment, hopelessly: Why are we talking about this?

Lenny: Meg's right. It was so sad. It was awfully sad. I remember how we all three just sat up on that bed the day of the service all dressed up in our black velveteen suits crying the whole morning long.

Babe: We used up one whole big box of Kleenexes.

Meg: And then Old Granddaddy came in and said he was gonna take us out to breakfast. Remember, he told us not to cry anymore 'cause he was gonna take us out to get banana splits for breakfast.

Babe: That's right—banana splits for breakfast!

Meg: Why, Lenny was fourteen years old, and he thought that would make it all better—

Babe: Oh, I remember he said for us to eat all we wanted. I think I ate about five! He kept shoving them down us!

Meg: God, we were so sick!

Lenny: Oh, we were!

Meg: laughing: Lenny's face turned green—

Lenny: I was just as sick as a dog!

Babe: Old Grandmama was furious!

Lenny: Oh, she was!

Meg: The thing about Old Granddaddy is, he keeps trying to make us happy, and we end up getting stomachaches and turning green and throwing up in the flower arrangements.

Babe: Oh, that was me! I threw up in the flowers! Oh, no! How embarrassing!

Lenny: laughing: Oh, Babe—

Babe: hugging her sisters: Oh, Lenny! Oh, Meg!

Meg: Oh, Babe! Oh, Lenny! It's so good to be home!

Lenny: Hey, I have an idea—

Babe: What?

Lenny: Let's play cards!!

Babe: Oh, let's do!

Meg: All right!

Lenny: Oh, good! It'll be just like when we used to sit around the table playing hearts all night long.

Babe: I know! *Getting up:* I'll fix us up some popcorn and hot chocolate—

Meg: getting up: Here, let me get out that old black popcorn pot.

Lenny: getting up: Oh, yes! Now, let's see, I think I have a deck of cards around here somewhere.

Babe: Gosh, I hope I remember all the rules— Are hearts good or bad?

Meg: Bad, I think. Aren't they, Lenny?

Lenny: That's right. Hearts are bad, but the Black Sister is the worst of all—

Meg: Oh, that's right! And the Black Sister is the Queen of Spades.

Babe: figuring it out: And spades are the black cards that aren't the puppy dog feet?

Meg: thinking a moment: Right. And she counts a lot of points.

Babe: And points are bad?

Meg: Right. Here, I'll get some paper so we can keep score.

The phone rings.

Lenny: Oh, here they are!

Meg: I'll get it—

Lenny: Why, look at these cards! They're years old!

Babe: Oh, let me see!

Meg: Hello . . . No, this is Meg MaGrath . . . Doc. How are you? . . . Well, good . . . You're where? . . . Well, sure. Come on over . . . Sure I'm sure . . . Yeah, come right on over . . . All right. 'Bye. She hangs up. That was Doc Porter. He's down the street at Al's Grill. He's gonna come on over.

Lenny: He is?

Meg: He said he wanted to come see me.

Lenny: Oh. After a pause. Well, do you still want to play?

Meg: No, I don't think so.

Lenny: All right. She starts to shuffle the cards, as Meg brushes her hair. You know, it's really not much fun playing hearts with only two people.

Meg: I'm sorry; maybe after Doc leaves I'll join you.

Lenny: I know; maybe Doc'll want to play. Then we can have a game of bridge.

Meg: I don't think so. Doc never liked cards. Maybe we'll just go out somewhere.

Lenny: putting down the cards. Babe picks them up: Meg—

Meg: What?

Lenny: Well, Doc's married now.

Meg: I know. You told me.

Lenny: Oh. Well, as long as you know that. Pause. As long as you know that.

Meg: still primping: Yes, I know. She made the pot.

Babe: How many cards do I deal out?

Lenny: leaving the table: Excuse me.

Babe: All of 'em, or what?

Lenny: Ah, Meg, could I—could I ask you something?

Babe proceeds to deal out all the cards.

Meg: What?

Lenny: I just wanted to ask you—

Meg: What?

Unable to go on with what she really wants to say, Lenny runs and picks up the box of candy.

Lenny: Well, just why did you take one little bite out of each piece of candy in this box and then just put it back in?

Meg: Oh. Well, I was looking for the ones with nuts.

Lenny: The ones with nuts.

Meg: Yeah.

Lenny: But there are none with nuts. It's a box of assorted crèmes— all it has in it are crèmes!

Meg: Oh.

Lenny: Why couldn't you just read on the box? It says right here, *Assorted Crèmes,* not nuts! Besides, this was a birthday present to me! My one and only birthday present; my only one!

Meg: I'm sorry. I'll get you another box.

Lenny: I don't want another box. That's not the point!

Meg: What is the point?

Lenny: I don't know; it's—it's— You have no respect for other people's property! You just take whatever you want. You just take it! Why, remember how you had layers and layers of jingle bells sewed onto your petticoats while Babe and I only had three apiece?!

Meg: Oh, God! She's starting up about those stupid jingle bells!

Lenny: Well, it's an example! A specific example of how you always got what you wanted!

Meg: Oh, come on, Lenny, you're just upset because Doc called.

Lenny: Who said anything about Doc? Do you think I'm upset about Doc? Why, I've long since given up worrying about you and all your men.

Meg: turning in anger: Look, I know I've had too many men. Believe me, I've had way too many men. But it's not my fault you haven't had any—or maybe just that one from Memphis.

Lenny: stopping: What one from Memphis?

Meg: slowly: The one Babe told me about. From the—club.

Lenny: Babe!

Babe: Meg!

Lenny: How could you! I asked you not to tell anyone! I'm so ashamed! How could you? Who else have you told? Did you tell anyone else?

Babe: overlapping, to Meg: Why'd you have to open your big mouth?

Meg: overlapping: How am I supposed to know? You never said not to tell!

Babe: Can't you use your head just for once? *To* Lenny: No, I never told anyone else. Somehow it just slipped out to Meg. Really, it just flew out of my mouth—

Lenny: What do you two have—wings on your tongues?

Babe: I'm sorry, Lenny. Really sorry.

Lenny: I'll just never, never, never be able to trust you again—

Meg: furiously coming to Babe's *defense:* Oh, for heaven's sake,

Lenny, we were just worried about you! We wanted to find a way to make you happy!

Lenny: Happy! Happy! I'll never be happy!

Meg: Well, not if you keep living your life as Old Granddaddy's nursemaid—

Babe: Meg, shut up!

Meg: I can't help it! I just know that the reason you stopped seeing this man from Memphis was because of Old Granddaddy.

Lenny: What— Babe didn't tell you the rest of the story—

Meg: Oh, she said it was something about your shrunken ovary.

Babe: Meg!

Lenny: Babe!

Babe: I just mentioned it!

Meg: But I don't believe a word of that story!

Lenny: Oh, I don't care what you believe! It's so easy for you—you always have men falling in love with you! But I have this under-developed ovary and I can't have children and my hair is falling out in the comb—so what man can love me? What man's gonna love me?

Meg: A lot of men!

Babe: Yeah, a lot! A whole lot!

Meg: Old Granddaddy's the only one who seems to think otherwise.

Lenny: 'Cause he doesn't want to see me hurt! He doesn't want to see me rejected and humiliated.

Meg: Oh, come on now, Lenny, don't be so pathetic! God, you make me angry when you just stand there looking so pathetic! Just tell me, did you really ask the man from Memphis? Did you actually ask that man from Memphis all about it?

Lenny: *breaking apart:* No, I didn't. I didn't. Because I just didn't want him not to want me—

Meg: Lenny—

Lenny: *furious:* Don't talk to me anymore! Don't talk to me! I think I'm gonna vomit— I just hope all this doesn't cause me to vomit! *She exits up the stairs sobbing.*

Meg: See! See! She didn't even ask him about her stupid ovary! She just broke it all off 'cause of Old Granddaddy! What a jack-ass fool!

Babe: Oh, Meg, shut up! Why do you have to make Lenny cry? I just hate it when you make Lenny cry! *She runs up the stairs.* Lenny! Oh, Lenny—

Meg *gives a long sigh and goes to get a cigarette and a drink.*

Meg: I feel like hell. *She sits in despair, smoking and drinking bourbon. There is a knock at the back door. She starts. She brushes her hair out of her face and goes to answer the door. It is* Doc.

Doc: Hello, Meggy.

Meg: Well, Doc. Well, it's Doc.

Doc: after a pause: You're home, Meggy.

Meg: Yeah, I've come home. I've come on home to see about Babe.

Doc: And how's Babe?

Meg: Oh, fine. Well, fair. She's fair.

Doc *nods.*

Meg: Hey, do you want a drink?

Doc: Whatcha got?

Meg: Bourbon.

Doc: Oh, don't tell me Lenny's stocking bourbon.

Meg: Well, no. I've been to the store. *She gets him a glass and pours them each a drink. They click glasses.*

Meg: So, how's your wife?

Doc: She's fine.

Meg: I hear ya got two kids.

Doc: Yeah. Yeah, I got two kids.

Meg: A boy and a girl.

Doc: That's right, Meggy, a boy and a girl.

Meg: That's what you always said you wanted, wasn't it? A boy and a girl.

Doc: Is that what I said?

Meg: I don't know. I thought it's what you said.

They finish their drinks in silence.

Doc: Whose cot?

Meg: Lenny's. She's taken to sleeping in the kitchen.

Doc: Ah. Where is Lenny?

Meg: She's in the upstairs room. I made her cry. Babe's up there seeing to her.

Doc: How'd you make her cry?

Meg: I don't know. Eating her birthday candy; talking on about her boyfriend from Memphis. I don't know. I'm upset about it. She's got a lot on her. Why can't I keep my mouth shut?

Doc: I don't know, Meggy. Maybe it's because you don't want to.

Meg: Maybe.

They smile at each other. Meg *pours each of them another drink.*

Doc: Well, it's been a long time.

Meg: It has been a long time.

Doc: Let's see—when was the last time we saw each other?

Meg: I can't quite recall.

Doc: Wasn't it in Biloxi?

Meg: Ah, Biloxi. I believe so.

Doc: And wasn't there a—a hurricane going on at the time?

Meg: Was there?

Doc: Yes, there was; one hell of a hurricane. Camille, I believe they called it. Hurricane Camille.

Meg: Yes, now I remember. It was a beautiful hurricane.

Doc: We had a time down there. We had quite a time. Drinking vodka, eating oysters on the half shell, dancing all night long. And the wind was blowing.

Meg: Oh, God, was it blowing.

Doc: Goddamn, was it blowing.

Meg: There never has been such a wind blowing.

Doc: Oh, God, Meggy. Oh, God.

Meg: I know, Doc. It was my fault to leave you. I was crazy. I thought I was choking. I felt choked!

Doc: I felt like a fool.

Meg: No.

Doc: I just kept on wondering why.

Meg: I don't know why . . . 'Cause I didn't want to care. I don't know. I did care, though. I did.

Doc: after a pause: Ah, hell— *He pours them both another drink.* Are you still singing those sad songs?

Meg: No.

Doc: Why not?

Meg: I don't know, Doc. Things got worse for me. After a while, I just couldn't sing anymore. I tell you, I had one hell of a time over Christmas.

Doc: What do you mean?

Meg: I went nuts. I went insane. Ended up in L.A. County Hospital. Psychiatric ward.

Doc: Hell. Ah, hell, Meggy. What happened?

Meg: I don't really know. I couldn't sing anymore, so I lost my job. And I had a bad toothache. I had this incredibly painful toothache. For days I had it, but I wouldn't do anything about it. I just stayed inside my apartment. All I could do was sit around in chairs, chewing on my fingers. Then one afternoon I ran screaming out of the apartment with all my money and jewelry and valuables, and tried to stuff it all into one of those March of Dimes collection boxes. That was when they nabbed me. Sad story. Meg goes mad.

Doc *stares at her for a long moment. He pours them both another drink.*

Doc: after quite a pause: There's a moon out.

Meg: Is there?

Doc: Wanna go take a ride in my truck and look out at the moon?

Meg: I don't know, Doc. I don't wanna start up. It'll be too hard if we start up.

Doc: Who says we're gonna start up? We're just gonna look at the moon. For one night just you and me are gonna go for a ride in the country and look out at the moon.

Meg: One night?

Doc: Right.

Meg: Look out at the moon?

Doc: You got it.

Meg: Well . . . all right. *She gets up.*

Doc: Better take your coat. *He helps her into her coat.* And the bottle— *He takes the bottle.* Meg *picks up the glasses.* Forget the glasses—

Meg *shuts off the kitchen lights, leaving the kitchen with only a dim light over the kitchen sink.* Meg *and* Doc *leave. After a moment,* Babe *comes down the stairs in her slip.*

Babe: Meg—Meg? *She stands for a moment in the moonlight wearing only a slip. She sees her saxophone, then moves to pick it up. She plays a few shrieking notes. There is a loud knock on the back door.*

Barnette's Voice: Becky! Becky, is that you?

Babe *puts down the saxophone.*

Babe: Just a minute. I'm coming. *She puts a raincoat on over her slip and goes to answer the door.* Hello, Barnette. Come on in.

Barnette *comes in. He is troubled but is making a great effort to hide the fact.*

Barnette: Thank you.

Babe: What is it?

Barnette: I've, ah, I've just come from seeing Zackery at the hospital.

Babe: Oh?

Barnette: It seems . . . Well, it seems his sister, Lucille, was somewhat suspicious.

Babe: Suspicious?

Barnette: About you?

Babe: Me?

Barnette: She hired a private detective: he took these pictures.

He hands Babe *a small envelope containing several photographs.* Babe *opens the envelope and begins looking at the pictures in stunned silence.*

Barnette: They were taken about two weeks ago. It seems she wasn't going to show them to Botrelle straightaway. She, ah, wanted to wait till the time was right.

The phone rings one and a half times. Barnette *glances uneasily toward the phone.*

Barnette: Becky!

The phone stops ringing.

Babe: *looking up at* Barnette, *slowly:* These are pictures of Willie Jay
   and me . . . out in the garage.
Barnette: *looking away:* I know.
   Babe: You looked at these pictures?
Barnette: Yes—I—well . . . professionally, I looked at them.
   Babe: Oh, mercy. Oh, mercy! We can burn them, can't we? Quick,
   we can burn them—
Barnette: It won't do any good. They have the negatives.
   Babe: *Holding the pictures, as she bangs herself hopelessly into the stove,*
   table, cabinets, etc.: Oh, no; oh, no; oh, no! Oh, no—
Barnette: There—there, now—there—
Lenny's Voice: Babe? Are you all right? Babe—
   Babe: *hiding the pictures:* What? I'm all right. Go on back to bed.

Babe *hides the pictures as* Lenny *comes down the stairs. She is wearing a coat and*
wiping white night cream off of her face with a washrag.

   Lenny: What's the matter? What's going on down here?
   Babe: Nothing! *Then as she begins dancing ballet style around the*
   room: We're —we're just dancing. We were just dancing around
   down here. *Signaling to* Barnette *to dance.*
   Lenny: Well, you'd better get your shoes on, 'cause we've got—
   Babe: All right, I will! That's a good idea! *She goes to get her shoes.*
   Now, you go on back to bed. It's pretty late and—
   Lenny: Babe, will you listen a minute—
   Babe: *holding up her shoes:* I'm putting 'em on—
   Lenny: That was the hospital that just called. We've got to get over
   there. Old Granddaddy's had himself another stroke.
   Babe: Oh. All right. My shoes are on. *She stands.*

They all look at each other as the lights black out.

CURTAIN

ACT THREE

The lights go up on the empty kitchen. It is the following morning. After a few
moments, Babe enters from the back door. She is carrying her hair curlers in her
hands. She lies down on the cot. A few moments later, Lenny enters. She is tired
and weary. Chick's voice is heard.

Chick's Voice: Lenny! Oh, Lenny!

Lenny *turns to the door.* Chick *enters energetically.*

   Chick: Well . . . how is he?
   Lenny: He's stabilized; they say for now his functions are all
   stabilized.
   Chick: Well, is he still in the coma?

Lenny: Uh huh.

Chick: Hmmm. So do they think he's gonna be . . . passing on?

Lenny: He may be. He doesn't look so good. They said they'd phone us if there were any sudden changes.

Chick: Well, it seems to me we'd better get busy phoning on the phone ourselves. *Removing a list from her pocket:* Now, I've made out this list of all the people we need to notify about Old Grand-daddy's predicament. I'll phone half, if you'll phone half.

Lenny: But—what would we say?

Chick: Just tell them the facts: that Old Granddaddy's got himself in a coma, and it could be he doesn't have long for this world.

Lenny: I—I don't know. I don't feel like phoning.

Chick: Why, Lenora, I'm surprised; how can you be this way? I went to all the trouble of making up the list. And I offered to phone half of the people on it, even though I'm only one-fourth of the granddaughters. I mean, I just get tired of doing more than my fair share, when people like Meg can suddenly just disappear to where they can't even be reached in case of emergency!

Lenny: All right; give me the list. I'll phone half.

Chick: Well, don't do it just to suit me.

Lenny: *wearily tearing the list in half:* I'll phone these here.

Chick: *taking her half of the list:* Fine then. Suit yourself. Oh, wait— let me call Sally Bell. I need to talk to her, anyway.

Lenny: All right.

Chick: So you add Great-uncle Spark Dude to your list.

Lenny: Okay.

Chick: Fine. Well, I've got to get on back home and see to the kids. It is gonna be an uphill struggle till I can find someone to replace that good-for-nothing Annie May Jenkins. Well, you let me know if you hear any more.

Lenny: All right.

Chick: Goodbye, Rebecca. I said goodbye. Babe *blows her sax.* Chick *starts to exit in a flurry, then pauses to add:* And you really ought to try to get that phoning done before twelve noon. *She exits.*

Lenny: *after a long pause:* Babe, I feel bad. I feel real bad.

Babe: Why, Lenny?

Lenny: Because yesterday I—I wished it.

Babe: You wished what?

Lenny: I wished that Old Granddaddy would be put out of his pain. I wished it on one of my birthday candles. I did. And now he's in this coma, and they say he's feeling no pain.

Babe: Well, when did you have a cake yesterday? I don't remember you having any cake.

Lenny: Well, I didn't . . . have a cake. But I just blew out the candles, anyway.

Babe: Oh. Well, those birthday wishes don't count, unless you have a cake.

Lenny: They don't?

Babe: No. A lot of times they don't even count when you do have a cake. It just depends.

Lenny: Depends on what?

Babe: On how deep your wish is, I suppose.

Lenny: Still, I just wish I hadn't of wished it. Gosh, I wonder when Meg's coming home.

Babe: Should be soon.

Lenny: I just wish we wouldn't fight all the time. I don't like it when we do.

Babe: Me, neither.

Lenny: I guess it hurts my feelings, a little, the way Old Granddaddy's always put so much stock in Meg and all her singing talent. I think I've been, well, envious of her 'cause I can't seem to do too much.

Babe: Why, sure you can.

Lenny: I can?

Babe: Sure. You just have to put your mind to it, that's all. It's like how I went out and bought that saxophone, just hoping I'd be able to attend music school and start up my own career. I just went out and did it. Just on hope. Of course, now it looks like . . . Well, it just doesn't look like things are gonna work out for me. But I know they would for you.

Lenny: Well, they'll work out for you, too.

Babe: I doubt it.

Lenny: Listen, I heard up at the hospital that Zachery's already in fair condition. They say soon he'll probably be able to walk and everything.

Babe: Yeah. And life sure can be miserable.

Lenny: Well, I know, 'cause—day before yesterday, Billy Boy was struck down by lightning.

Babe: He was?

Lenny: *nearing sobs:* Yeah. He was struck dead.

Babe: *crushed:* Life sure can be miserable.

They sit together for several moments in morbid silence. Meg is heard singing a loud happy song. She suddenly enters through the dining room door. She is exuberant! Her hair is a mess, and the heel of one shoe has broken off. She is laughing radiantly and limping as she sings into the broken heel.

Meg: spotting her sisters: Good morning! Good morning! Oh, it's a wonderful morning! I tell you, I am surprised I feel this good. I should feel like hell. By all accounts, I should feel like utter hell! *She is looking for the glue.* Where's that glue? This damn heel has broken off my shoe. La, la, la, la, la! Ah, here it is! Now, let me just get these shoes off. Zip, zip, zip, zip, zip! Well, what's wrong with you two? My God, you look like doom!

Babe *and* Lenny *stare helplessly at* Meg.

Meg: Oh, I know, you're mad at me 'cause I stayed out all night long. Well, I did.

Lenny: No, we're—we're not mad at you. We're just . . . depressed. *She starts to sob.*

Meg: Oh, Lenny, listen to me, now; everything's all right with Doc. I mean, nothing happened. Well, actually a lot did happen, but it didn't come to anything. Not because of me, I'm afraid. *Smearing glue on her heel:* I mean, I was out there thinking, What will I say when he begs me to run away with him? Will I have pity on his wife and those two half-Yankee children? I mean, can I sacrifice their happiness for mine? Yes! Oh, yes! Yes, I can! But . . . he didn't ask me. He didn't even want to ask me. I could tell by this certain look in his eyes that he didn't even want to ask me. Why aren't I miserable! Why aren't I morbid! I should be humiliated! Devastated! Maybe these feelings are coming—I don't know. But for now it was . . . just such fun. I'm happy. I realized I could care about someone. I could want someone. And I sang! I sang all night long! I sang right up into the trees! But not for Old Granddaddy. None of it was to please Old Granddaddy!

Lenny *and* Babe *look at each other.*

Babe: Ah, Meg—
Meg: What—
Babe: Well, it's just— It's . . .
Lenny: It's about Old Granddaddy—
Meg: Oh, I know; I know. I told him all those stupid lies. Well, I'm gonna go right over there this morning and tell him the truth. I mean every horrible thing. I don't care if he wants to hear it or not. He's just gonna have to take me like I am. And if he can't take it, if it sends him into a coma, that's just too damn bad!

Babe *and* Lenny *look at each other.* Babe *cracks a smile.* Lenny *cracks a smile.*

Babe: You're too late— Ha, ha, ha!

They both break up laughing.

Lenny: Oh, stop! Please! Ha, ha, ha!
Meg: What is it? What's so funny?
Babe: still laughing: It's not— It's not funny!
Lenny: still laughing: No, it's not! It's not a bit funny!
Meg: Well, what is it, then? What?
Babe: trying to calm down: Well, it's just—it's just—

Meg: What?
Babe: Well, Old Granddaddy—he—he's in a coma!

Babe *and* Lenny *break up again.*

> *Meg:* He's what?
> *Babe: shrieking:* In a coma!
> *Meg:* My God! That's not funny!
> *Babe: calming down:* I know. I know. For some reason, it just struck us as funny.
> *Lenny:* I'm sorry. It's—it's not funny. It's sad. It's very sad. We've been up all night long.
> *Babe:* We're really tired.
> *Meg:* Well, my God. How is he? Is he gonna live?

Babe *and* Lenny *look at each other.*

> *Babe:* They don't think so!

They both break up again.

> *Lenny:* Oh, I don't know why we're laughing like this. We're just sick! We're just awful!
> *Babe:* We are—we're awful!
> *Lenny: as she collects herself:* Oh, good; now I feel bad. Now I feel like crying. I do; I feel like crying.
> *Babe:* Me, too. Me, too.
> *Meg:* Well, you've gotten me depressed!
> *Lenny:* I'm sorry. I'm sorry. It, ah, happened last night. He had another stroke.

They laugh again.

> *Meg:* I see.
> *Lenny:* But he's stabilized now. *She chokes up once more.*
> *Meg:* That's good. You two okay?

Babe *and* Lenny *nod.*

> *Meg:* You look like you need some rest.

Babe *and* Lenny *nod again.*

> *Meg: going on, about her heel:* I hope that'll stay. *She puts the top back on the glue. A realization:* Oh, of course, now I won't be able to tell him the truth about all those lies I told. I mean, finally I get my wits about me, and he conks out. It's just like him. Babe, can I wear your slippers till this glue dries?
> *Babe:* Sure.
> *Lenny: after a pause:* Things sure are gonna be different around here . . . when Old Granddaddy dies. Well, not for you two really, but for me.

Meg: It'll work out.

Babe: depressed: Yeah. It'll work out.

Lenny: I hope so. I'm just afraid of being here all by myself. All alone.

Meg: Well, you don't have to be alone. Maybe Babe'll move back in here.

Lenny *looks at* Babe *hopefully.*

Babe: No, I don't think I'll be living here.

Meg: realizing her mistake: Well, anyway, you're your own woman. Invite some people over. Have some parties. Go out with strange men.

Lenny: I don't know any strange men.

Meg: Well . . . you know that Charlie.

Lenny: shaking her head: Not anymore.

Meg: Why not?

Lenny: breaking down: I told him we should never see each other again.

Meg: Well, if you told him, you can just untell him.

Lenny: Oh, no, I couldn't. I'd feel like a fool.

Meg: Oh, that's not a good enough reason! All people in love feel like fools. Don't they, Babe?

Babe: Sure.

Meg: Look, why don't you give him a call right now? See how things stand.

Lenny: Oh, no! I'd be too scared—

Meg: But what harm could it possibly do? I mean, it's not gonna make things any worse than this never seeing him again, at all, forever.

Lenny: I suppose that's true—

Meg: Of course it is; so call him up! Take a chance, will you? Just take some sort of chance!

Lenny: You think I should?

Meg: Of course! You've got to try— You do!

Lenny *looks over at* Babe.

Babe: You do, Lenny— I think you do.

Lenny: Really? Really, really?

Meg: Yes! Yes!

Babe: You should!

Lenny: All right. I will! I will!

Meg: Oh, good!

Babe: Good!

Lenny: I'll call him right now, while I've got my confidence up!

Meg: Have you got the number?

Lenny: Uh huh. But, ah, I think I wanna call him upstairs. It'll be more private.

Meg: Ah, good idea.

Lenny: I'm just gonna go on and call him up and see what happens— *She has started up the stairs.* Wish me good luck!

Meg: Good luck!

Babe: Good luck, Lenny!

Lenny: Thanks.

Lenny *gets almost out of sight when the phone rings. She stops;* Meg *picks up the phone.*

Meg: Hello? *Then, in a whisper:* Oh, thank you very much . . . Yes, I will. 'Bye, 'bye.

Lenny: Who was it?

Meg: Wrong number. They wanted Weed's Body Shop.

Lenny: Oh. Well, I'll be right back down in a minute. *She exits.*

Meg: after a moment, whispering to Babe: That was the bakery; Lenny's cake is ready!

Babe: who has become increasingly depressed: Oh.

Meg: I think I'll sneak on down to the corner and pick it up. *She starts to leave.*

Babe: Meg—

Meg: What?

Babe: Nothing.

Meg: You okay?

Babe *shakes her head.*

Meg: What is it?

Babe: It's just—

Meg: What?

Babe *gets the envelope containing the photographs.*

Babe: Here. Take a look.

Meg: taking the envelope: What is it?

Babe: It's some evidence Zackery's collected against me. Looks like my goose is cooked.

Meg *opens the envelope and looks at the photographs.*

Meg: My God, it's—it's you and . . . is *that* Willie Jay?

Babe: Yah.

Meg: Well, he certainly *has* grown. You were right about that. My, oh, my.

Babe: Please don't tell Lenny. She'd hate me.

Meg: I won't. I won't tell Lenny. *Putting the pictures back into the envelope:* What are you gonna do?

Babe: What can I do?

There is a knock on the door. Babe *grabs the envelope and hides it.*

Meg: Who is it?
Barnette's Voice: It's Barnette Lloyd.
 Meg: Oh. Come on in, Barnette.

Barnette *enters. His eyes are ablaze with excitement.*

Barnette: as he paces around the room: Well, good morning! *Shaking*
 Meg's *hand:* Good morning, Miss MaGrath. *Touching* Babe *on
 the shoulder:* Becky. *Moving away:* What I meant to say is, How
 are you doing this morning?
 Meg: Ah—fine. Fine.
Barnette: Good. Good. I—I just had time to drop by for a minute.
 Meg: Oh.
Barnette: So, ah, how's your granddad doing?
 Meg: Well, not very, ah—ah, he's in this coma. *She breaks up
 laughing.*
Barnette: I see . . . I see. *To* Babe: Actually, the primary reason I came
 by was to pick up that—envelope. I left it here last night in all
 the confusion. *Pause.* You, ah, still do have it?

Babe *hands him the envelope.*

Barnette: Yes. *Taking the envelope:* That's the one. I'm sure it'll be
 much better off in my office safe. *He puts the envelope into his coat
 pocket.*
 Meg: I'm sure it will.
Barnette: Beg your pardon?
 Babe: It's all right. I showed her the pictures.
Barnette: Ah; I see.
 Meg: So what's going to happen now, Barnette? What are those
 pictures gonna mean?
Barnette: after pacing a moment: Hmmm. May I speak frankly and
 openly?
 Babe: Uh huh.
 Meg: Please do—
Barnette: Well, I tell you now, at first glance, I admit those pictures had
 me considerably perturbed and upset. Perturbed to the point
 that I spent most of last night going over certain suspect papers
 and reports that had fallen into my hands—rather recklessly.
 Babe: What papers do you mean?
Barnette: Papers that, pending word from three varied and unbiased
 experts, could prove graft, fraud, forgery, as well as a history of
 unethical behavior.
 Meg: You mean about Zackery?
Barnette: Exactly. You see, I now intend to make this matter just as
 sticky and gritty for one Z. Botrelle as it is for us. Why, with the

amount of scandal I'll dig up, Botrelle will be forced to settle this affair on our own terms!

Meg: Oh, Babe! Did you hear that?

Babe: Yes! Oh, yes! So you've won it! You've won your lifelong vendetta!

Barnette: Well . . . well, now of course it's problematic in that, well, in that we won't be able to expose him openly in the courts. That was the original game plan.

Babe: But why not? Why?

Barnette: Well, it's only that if, well, if a jury were to—to get, say, a glance at these, ah, photographs, well . . . well, possibly . . .

Babe: We could be sunk.

Barnette: In a sense. But! On the other hand, if a newspaper were to get a hold of our little item, Mr. Zackery Botrelle could find himself boiling in some awfully hot water. So what I'm looking for, very simply, is—a deal.

Babe: A deal?

Meg: Thank you, Barnette. It's a sunny day, Babe. *Realizing she is in the way:* Ooh, where's that broken shoe? *She grabs her boots and runs upstairs.*

Babe: So, you're having to give up your vendetta?

Barnette: Well, in a way. For the time. It, ah, seems to me you shouldn't always let your life be ruled by such things as, ah, personal vendettas. *Looking at* Babe *with meaning:* Other things can be important.

Babe: I don't know, I don't exactly know. How 'bout Willie Jay? Will he be all right?

Barnette: Yes, it's all been taken care of. He'll be leaving incognito on the midnight bus—heading north.

Babe: North.

Barnette: I'm sorry, it seemed the only . . . way.

Barnette *moves to her; she moves away.*

Babe: Look, you'd better be getting on back to your work.

Barnette: *awkwardly:* Right—'cause I—I've got those important calls out. *Full of hope for her:* They'll be pouring in directly. *He starts to leave, then says to her with love:* We'll talk.

Meg: *reappearing in her boots:* Oh, Barnette—

Barnette: Yes?

Meg: Could you give me a ride just down to the corner? I need to stop at Helen's Bakery.

Barnette: Be glad to.

Meg: Thanks. Listen, Babe, I'll be right back with the cake. We're gonna have the best celebration! Now, ah, if Lenny asks where I've gone, just say I'm . . . Just say, I've gone out back to, ah, pick up some pawpaws! Okay?

Babe: Okay.
Meg: Fine; I'll be back in a bit. Goodbye.
Babe: 'Bye.
Barnette: Goodbye, Becky.
Babe: Goodbye, Barnette. Take care.

Meg *and* Barnette *exit.* Babe *sits staring ahead, in a state of deep despair.*

Babe: Goodbye, Barnette. Goodbye, Becky. *She stops when* Lenny *comes down the stairs in a fluster.*
Lenny: Oh! Oh! Oh! I'm so ashamed! I'm such a coward! I'm such a yellow-bellied chicken! I'm so ashamed! Where's Meg?
Babe: suddenly bright: She's, ah—gone out back—to pick up some pawpaws.
Lenny: Oh. Well, at least I don't have to face her! I just couldn't do it! I couldn't make the call! My heart was pounding like a hammer. Pound! Pound! Pound! Why, I looked down and I could actually see my blouse moving back and forth! Oh, Babe, you look so disappointed. Are you?
Babe: despondently: Uh huh.
Lenny: Oh, no! I've disappointed Babe! I can't stand it! I've gone and disappointed my little sister, Babe! Oh, no! I feel like howling like a dog!
Chick's Voice: Oooh, Lenny! *She enters dramatically, dripping with sympathy.* Well, I just don't know what to say! I'm so sorry! I am so sorry for you! And for little Babe here, too. I mean, to have such a sister as that!
Lenny: What do you mean?
Chick: Oh, you don't need to pretend with me. I saw it all from over there in my own back yard; I saw Meg stumbling out of Doc Porter's pickup truck, not fifteen minutes ago. And her looking such a disgusting mess. You must be so ashamed! You must just want to die! Why, I always said that girl was nothing but cheap Christmas trash!
Lenny: Don't talk that way about Meg.
Chick: Oh, come on now, Lenny honey, I know exactly how you feel about Meg. Why, Meg's a low-class tramp and you need not have one more blessed thing to do with her and her disgusting behavior.
Lenny: I said, don't you ever talk that way about my sister Meg again.
Chick: Well, my goodness gracious, Lenora, don't be such a noodle —it's the truth!
Lenny: I don't care if it's the Ten Commandments. I don't want to hear it in my home. Not ever again.
Chick: In your home?! Why, I never in all my life— This is my grandfather's home! And you're just living here on his charity;

so don't you get high-falutin' with me, Miss Lenora Josephine MaGrath!

Lenny: Get out of here—

Chick: Don't you tell me to get out! What makes you think you can order me around? Why, I've had just about my fill of you trashy MaGraths and your trashy ways: hanging yourselves in cellars; carrying on with married men; shooting your own husbands!

Lenny: Get out!

Chick: to Babe: And don't you think she's not gonna end up at the state prison farm or in some—mental institution. Why, it's a clear-cut case of manslaughter with intent to kill!

Lenny: Out! Get out!

Chick: running on: That's what everyone's saying, deliberate intent to kill! And you'll pay for that! Do you hear me? You'll pay!

Lenny: picking up a broom and threatening Chick *with it:* And I'm telling you to get out!

Chick: You—you put that down this minute— Are you a raving lunatic?

Lenny: beating Chick *with the broom:* I said for you to get out! That means out! And never, never, never come back!

Chick: overlapping, as she runs around the room: Oh! Oh! Oh! You're crazy! You're crazy!

Lenny: chasing Chick *out the door:* Do you hear me, Chick the Stick! This is my home! This is my house! Get out! Out!

Chick: overlapping: Oh! Oh! Police! Police! You're crazy! Help! Help!

Lenny *chases* Chick *out of the house. They are both screaming. The phone rings.* Babe *goes and picks it up.*

Babe: Hello? . . . Oh, hello, Zackery! . . . Yes, he showed them to me! . . . You're what! . . . What do you mean? . . . What! . . . You can't put me out to Whitfield . . . 'Cause I'm not crazy . . . I'm not! I'm not! . . . She wasn't crazy, either . . . Don't you call my mother crazy! . . . No, you're not! You're not gonna. You're not! *She slams the phone down and stares wildly ahead.* He's not. He's not. *As she walks over to the ribbon drawer:* I'll do it. I will. And he won't . . . *She opens the drawer, pulls out the rope, becomes terrified, throws the rope back in the drawer, and slams it shut.*

Lenny *enters from the back door swinging the broom and laughing.*

Lenny: Oh, my! Oh, my! You should have seen us! Why, I chased Chick the Stick right up the mimosa tree. I did! I left her right up there screaming in the tree!

Babe: laughing; she is insanely delighted. Oh, you did!

Lenny: Yes, I did! And I feel so good! I do! I feel good! I feel good!

Babe: overlapping: Good! Good, Lenny! Good for you!

They dance around the kitchen.

Lenny: *stopping:* You know what—
Babe: What?
Lenny: I'm gonna call Charlie! I'm gonna call him up right now!
Babe: You are?
Lenny: Yeah, I feel like I can really do it!
Babe: You do?
Lenny: My courage is up; my heart's in it; the time is right! No more beating around the bush! Let's strike while the iron is hot!
Babe: Right! Right! No more beating around the bush! Strike while the iron is hot!

Lenny *goes to the phone.* Babe *rushes over to the ribbon drawer. She begins tearing through it.*

Lenny: *with the receiver in her hand:* I'm calling him up, Babe—I'm really gonna do it!
Babe: *still tearing through the drawer:* Good! Do it! Good!
Lenny: *as she dials:* Look. My hands aren't even shaking.
Babe: *pulling out a red rope:* Don't we have any stronger rope than this?
Lenny: I guess not. All the rope we've got's in that drawer. *About her hands:* Now they're shaking a little.

Babe *takes the rope and goes up the stairs.* Lenny *finishes dialing the number. She waits for an answer.*

Lenny: Hello? . . . Hello, Charlie. This is Lenny MaGrath . . . Well, I'm fine. I'm just fine. *An awkward pause:* I was, ah, just calling to see—how you're getting on . . . Well, good. Good . . . Yes, I know I said that. Now I wish I didn't say it . . . Well, the reason I said that before, about not seeing each other again, was 'cause of me, not you . . . Well, it's just I—I can't have any children. I— have this ovary problem . . . Why, Charlie, what a thing to say! . . . Well, they're not all little snot-nosed pigs! . . . You think they are! . . . Oh, Charlie, stop, stop! You're making me laugh . . . Yes, I guess I was. I can see now that I was . . . You are? . . . Well, I'm dying to see you, too . . . Well, I don't know when, Charlie . . . soon. How about, well, how about tonight? . . . You will? . . . Oh, you will! . . . All right, I'll be here. I'll be right here . . . Goodbye, then, Charlie. Goodbye for now. *She hangs up the phone in a daze.* Babe. Oh, Babe! He's coming. He's coming! Babe! Oh, Babe, where are you? Meg! Oh . . . out back—picking up paw-paws. *As she exits through the back door:* And those pawpaws are just ripe for picking up!

There is a moment of silence; then a loud, horrible thud is heard coming from upstairs. The telephone begins ringing immediately. It rings five times before

Babe *comes hurrying down the stairs with a broken piece of rope hanging around her neck. The phone continues to ring.*

> Babe: *to the phone:* Will you shut up! *She is jerking the rope from around her neck. She grabs a knife to cut it off.* Cheap! Miserable! I hate you! I hate you! *She throws the rope violently across the room. The phone stops ringing.* Thank God. *She looks at the stove, goes over to it, and turns the gas on. The sound of gas escaping is heard. She sniffs at it.* Come on. Come on . . . Hurry up . . . I beg of you— hurry up! *Finally, she feels the oven is ready; she takes a deep breath and opens the oven door to stick her head into it. She spots the rack and furiously jerks it out. Taking another breath, she sticks her head into the oven. She stands for several moments tapping her fingers furiously on top of the stove. She speaks from inside the oven:* Oh, please. Please. *After a few moments, she reaches for the box of matches with her head still in the oven. She tries to strike a match. It doesn't catch.* Oh, Mama, please! *She throws the match away and is getting a second one.* Mama . . . Mama . . . So that's why you done it! *In her excitement she starts to get up, bangs her head, and falls back in the oven.*

Meg *enters from the back door, carrying a birthday cake in a pink box.*

> Meg: Babe! *She throws the box down and runs to pull* Babe's *head out of the oven.* Oh, my God! What are you doing? What the hell are you doing?
> Babe: *dizzily:* Nothing. I don't know. Nothing.

Meg *turns off the gas and moves* Babe *to a chair near the open door.*

> Meg: Sit down. Sit down! Will you sit down!
> Babe: I'm okay. I'm okay.
> Meg: Put your head between your knees and breathe deep!
> Babe: Meg—
> Meg: Just do it! I'll get you some water. *She gets some water for* Babe. Here.
> Babe: Thanks.
> Meg: Are you okay?
> Babe: Uh huh.
> Meg: Are you sure?
> Babe: Yeah, I'm sure. I'm okay.
> Meg: *getting a damp rag and putting it over her own face:* Well, good. That's good.
> Babe: Meg—
> Meg: Yes?
> Babe: I know why she did it.
> Meg: What? Why who did what?
> Babe: *with joy:* Mama. I know why she hung that cat along with her.
> Meg: You do?

Babe: with enlightenment: It's 'cause she was afraid of dying all alone.

Meg: Was she?

Babe: She felt so unsure, you know, as to what was coming. It seems the best thing coming up would be a lot of angels and all of them singing. But I imagine they have high, scary voices and little gold pointed fingers that are as sharp as blades and you don't want to meet 'em all alone. You'd be afraid to meet 'em all alone. So it wasn't like what people were saying about her hating that cat. Fact is, she loved that cat. She needed him with her 'cause she felt so all alone.

Meg: Oh, Babe . . . Babe. Why, Babe? Why?

Babe: Why what?

Meg: Why did you stick your head into the oven?!

Babe: I don't know, Meg. I'm having a bad day. It's been a real bad day; those pictures, and Barnette giving up his vendetta; then Willie Jay heading north; and—and Zackery called me up. *Trembling with terror:* He says he's gonna have me classified insane and then send me on out to the Whitfield asylum.

Meg: What! Why, he could never do that!

Babe: Why not?

Meg: 'Cause you're not insane.

Babe: I'm not?

Meg: No! He's trying to bluff you. Don't you see it? Barnette's got him running scared.

Babe: Really?

Meg: Sure. He's scared to death—calling you insane. Ha! Why, you're just as perfectly sane as anyone walking the streets of Hazlehurst, Mississippi.

Babe: I am?

Meg: More so! A lot more so!

Babe: Good!

Meg: But, Babe, we've just got to learn how to get through these real bad days here. I mean, it's getting to be a thing in our family. *Slight pause as she looks at* Babe: Come on, now. Look, we've got Lenny's cake right here. I mean, don't you wanna be around to give her her cake, watch her blow out the candles?

Babe: realizing how much she wants to be here: Yeah, I do, I do. 'Cause she always loves to make her birthday wishes on those candles.

Meg: Well, then we'll give her her cake and maybe you won't be so miserable.

Babe: Okay.

Meg: Good. Go on and take it out of the box.

Babe: Okay. *She takes the cake out of the box. It is a magical moment.* Gosh, it's a pretty cake.

Meg: handing her some matches: Here now. You can go on and light
   up the candles.
Babe: All right. *She starts to light the candles.* I love to light up can-
   dles. And there are so many here. Thirty pink ones in all, plus
   one green one to grow on.
Meg: watching her light the candles: They're pretty.
Babe: They are. *She stops lighting the candles.* And I'm not like
   Mama. I'm not so all alone.
Meg: You're not.
Babe: as she goes back to lighting candles: Well, you'd better keep an
   eye out for Lenny. She's supposed to be surprised.
Meg: All right. Do you know where she's gone?
Babe: Well, she's not here inside—so she must have gone on
   outside.
Meg: Oh, well, then I'd better run and find her.
Babe: Okay; 'cause these candles are gonna melt down.

Meg *starts out the door.*

Meg: Wait—there she is coming. Lenny! Oh, Lenny! Come on!
   Hurry up!
Babe: overlapping and improvising as she finishes lighting candles: Oh,
   no! No! Well, yes— Yes! No, wait! Wait! Okay! Hurry up!

Lenny *enters.* Meg *covers* Lenny's *eyes with her hands.*

Lenny: terrified: What? What is it? What?
Meg and Babe: Surprise! Happy birthday! Happy birthday to Lenny!
Lenny: Oh, no! Oh, me! What a surprise! I could just cry! Oh, look:
   Happy birthday, Lenny—A Day Late! How cute! My! Will you
   look at all those candles—it's absolutely frightening.
Babe: a spontaneous thought: Oh, no, Lenny, it's good! 'Cause—
   'cause the more candles you have on your cake, the stronger your
   wish is.
Lenny: Really?
Babe: Sure!
Lenny: Mercy! Meg *and* Babe *start to sing.*
Lenny: interrupting the song: Oh, but wait! I—can't think of my
   wish! My body's gone all nervous inside.
Meg: For God's sake, Lenny— Come on!
Babe: The wax is all melting!
Lenny: My mind is just a blank, a total blank!
Meg: Will you please just—
Babe: overlapping: Lenny, hurry! Come on!
Lenny: Okay! Okay! Just go!

Meg *and* Babe *burst into the* "Happy Birthday" *song. As it ends,* Lenny *blows
out all the candles on the cake.* Meg *and* Babe *applaud loudly.*

Meg: Oh, you made it!

Babe: Hurray!

Lenny: Oh, me! Oh, me! I hope that wish comes true! I hope it does!

Babe: Why? What did you wish for?

Lenny: *as she removes the candles from the cake:* Why, I can't tell you that.

Babe: Oh, sure you can—

Lenny: Oh, no! Then it won't come true.

Babe: Why, that's just superstition! Of course it will, if you made it deep enough.

Meg: Really? I didn't know that.

Lenny: Well, Babe's the regular expert on birthday wishes.

Babe: It's just I get these feelings. Now, come on and tell us. What was it you wished for?

Meg: Yes, tell us. What was it?

Lenny: Well, I guess it wasn't really a specific wish. This—this vision just sort of came into my mind.

Babe: A vision? What was it of?

Lenny: I don't know exactly. It was something about the three of us smiling and laughing together.

Babe: Well, when was it? Was it far away or near?

Lenny: I'm not sure; but it wasn't forever; it wasn't for every minute. Just this one moment and we were all laughing.

Babe: Then, what were we laughing about?

Lenny: I don't know. Just nothing, I guess.

Meg: Well, that's a nice wish to make.

Lenny *and* Meg *look at each other a moment.*

Meg: Here, now, I'll get a knife so we can go ahead and cut the cake in celebration of Lenny being born!

Babe: Oh, yes! And give each one of us a rose. A whole rose apiece!

Lenny: *cutting the cake nervously:* Well, I'll try—I'll try!

Meg: *licking the icing off a candle:* Mmmm—this icing is delicious! Here, try some!

Babe: Mmmm! It's wonderful! Here, Lenny!

Lenny: *laughing joyously as she licks icing from her fingers and cuts huge pieces of cake that her sisters bite into ravenously:* Oh, how I do love having birthday cake for breakfast! How I do!

The sisters freeze for a moment laughing and catching cake. The lights change and frame them in a magical, golden, sparkling glimmer; saxophone music is heard. The lights dim to blackout, and the saxophone continues to play.

CURTAIN

When contemporary comedy runs aground, it is often because the characters are not well enough developed to take seriously: they seem to exist only for the sake of the humor that can be wrung out of them. Beth Henley's admirers see her as a playwright who has avoided this problem and brought credible comic characters to the stage, but not every critic shares this opinion, as we can see from the following reviews of Crimes of the Heart.

"Looking absurd reality in the eye and just plain outstaring it": John Simon

This is a loving and teasing look back at deep-southern, small-town life, at the effect of constricted living and confined thinking on three different yet not wholly unalike sisters amid Chekhovian boredom in honeysuckle country, and, above all, at the sorely tried but resilient affection and loyalty of these sisters for one another. However far misunderstandings, quarrels, exasperation may stretch their bond, they bounce back into embraces, Indian dances, leaps of joy, or, more simply, love.

For this is one of those rare plays about a family love that you can believe and participate in, because that love is never sappy or piously cloying, but, rather, irreverently prankish and often even acerb. Warmhearted Lenny is also an irritating fussbudget and martyr; Meg is selfish and irresponsible as well as sensible and ultimately generous; Babe, though blessed with the queer wisdom of the unreconstructed child, is also obtuse and infuriating. It is the ties of sympathy—or, if you will, the bloodline—among these three that form the play's crazy, convoluted, but finally exhilarating tracery: sisterly trajectories that diverge, waver, and explosively reunite. Laughter is squeezed from anguish as the logical consequence of looking absurd reality in the eye and just plain outstaring it. Babe's explanation of her mother's real and her own attempted suicide is the same: "a bad day"—nothing Freudian, only what happens when you do not gaze back at life unblinkingly enough.

The wonderful thing about the young author is that she understands a great deal about people and living.

"I also found myself . . . simply and flatly disbelieving": Walter Kerr

I found myself often grinning at what might have been gruesome, sometimes cocking my head sharply to catch a rueful inflection before it turned into a comic one, and always, always admiring the actresses involved. I also found myself, rather too often, and in spite of everything, disbelieving—simply and flatly disbelieving. Since this is scarcely the prevailing opinion, I'd best be specific. . . .

We do understand the ground-rules of matter-of-fact Southern grotesquerie, and we know that they're by no means altogether artificial. People do such things and, having done them, react in surprising ways. When Miss Dillon [as Babe], finally confiding some of the homelier details of the shooting to her siblings, reveals that immediately after pumping a bullet into her husband Zachery's stomach she went into the kitchen and made herself a pitcher of lemonade, we're still all right. As Miss Dillon says, she had a simply terrible thirst. Shock and a terrible thirst go very nicely together. It could have—no doubt *has*—happened. And the actress is personally persuasive.

Where my doubting psyche draws the line is a few seconds further along in Miss Dillon's narrative. Having refreshed herself with the lemonade, she bethought herself of her husband, lying conscious on the floor in the blood flowing from his open wound. "Zach," she called out, "I've made lemonade, do you want a glass?" I submit that we've now pressed the off-beat too far, that we've chased a notion past Carson McCullers country straight through Flannery O'Connor country and on into Joke country.

HANDBOOK OF LITERATURE
WRITING ABOUT LITERATURE
BIOGRAPHICAL SKETCHES
INDEXES

Handbook of Literature

NOTE: *Titles of works that are collected in* THE RIVERSIDE ANTHOLOGY *appear in italic type enclosed in quotation marks.*

Allegory: See *Figures of Speech.*

Allusion: an implicit reference to another work of art, a person, or an event. In making an allusion, the writer does not pause to explain the significance of the reference but assumes that the reader shares his or her experience and knowledge well enough to register the impact. Because the Bible is one of the most deeply read books in Western culture, allusions to it are particularly common. In T. S. Eliot's *"The Love Song of J. Alfred Prufrock,"* for instance, Prufrock says that he has seen his head "brought in upon a platter"—an allusion to the fate of John the Baptist. Allusions to Greek and Roman myths are almost as common as allusions to the Bible. Writers quite frequently and naturally allude to other writers whose work they admire: in *"Old Dominion,"* for example, Robert Hass alludes to the life, work, and suicide of Randall Jarrell. Such an allusion can present a momentary stumbling block to readers who know little about the person or thing alluded to, but the ultimate effect is to import into a work the emotional and intellectual force of other works and lives.

Antagonist: a character in a literary work who opposes or resists the action of the protagonist. The antagonist is not necessarily an evil or immoral character but merely one who directly or indirectly creates conflict for that character whose actions most directly affect the course of the work. Since Creon may be called the **protagonist** of Sophocles' *"Antigone,"* Antigone may be the antagonist although she possesses many heroic qualities and possibly the audience's sympathy as well.

Antithesis: See *Figures of Speech.*

Apostrophe: See *Figures of Speech.*

Blank Verse: unrhymed iambic pentameter. See *Sound of Poetry.*

Caesura: a pause inside a line of verse. In some cases such a pause occurs regularly at the midpoint, breaking the line in halves and becoming an element in the meter.

> And all the way,//to guide their chime,
> With falling oars//they kept the time.
> > (Marvell, *"Bermudas"*)

More often, caesuras appear irregularly, forced by the prose sense of the passage, and become one way that prose rhythm and verse rhythm are counterpointed. See also *Dipodic Meter, Enjambment, Dieresis.*

CHARACTERIZATION

Characterization is the creation from mere words of persons who appear so human and alive that we respond to them much as we respond to the people in our everyday lives. E. M. Forster, in "Aspects of the Novel," claims that we can know fictional characters more completely than we know real people, for unlike even our closest friends, fictional people have no secret places in their lives or minds. They are no more than a story or poem tells us they are, no matter how mysterious or complex the writer makes them seem.

Within this framework which literature imposes on characterization, Forster has developed a system for understanding the range of possible character types. He first labels characters "flat" or "round," noting at once that both qualities can exist in varying degrees, and then adds "dynamic" and "static" to these two. Flat characters lack complication because they possess only one dominant trait; they provide contrast for round ones and sometimes add humor. The concerned husband in Gilman's *"The Yellow Wallpaper"* is flat because he is never more than a concerned husband throughout the story. If the distinctive feature given to such a flat character were overly exaggerated, he would become a caricature, as the young man in Dorothy Parker's *"Here We Are"* nearly does. Round characters, according to Forster, are "capable of surprising in a convincing way." They are complex with several well-developed traits, and their personalities are surprisingly true to human nature. Hally, a round character in Athol Fugard's *"Master Harold . . . and the Boys,"* seems almost self-contradictory in his vast range of emotions and responses, and is therefore much more real to us than his two-dimensional father.

A dynamic character, like Mags in Tina Howe's *"Painting Churches,"* demonstrates an internal and substantial change in the course of the work. A static one, like Elisa's husband in John Steinbeck's *"The Chrysanthemums,"* is not internally affected by circumstances. We often assume that major characters will be both round and dynamic, but such consistency is not found in literature. Satan, in Milton's *"Paradise Lost,"* is round, but fails to change in the course of the poem. It can also be argued that the grandmother in Flannery O'Connor's *"A Good Man is Hard To Find"* is dynamic, but lacks the roundness expected in such a focal character.

Narration and point of view directly influence characterization, for they determine how a character is made known to the reader. In fiction and poetry, the author may tell us everything about a character through physical description and by entering the character's mind and reporting her thoughts. The author then may tell us about the character's past, explain her motivations, or report the opinions others have of her. The author may even give us a personal judgment of the character. But in drama the spoken words and actions of the characters alone reveal their personalities. The author can relate something about a character's inner life by using asides and soliloquies, which allow characters to express those inner emotions and thoughts intended for the audience alone. But in the play, characterization depends as much on the efforts of the director and actors as on the skill of the author.

COMEDY

In Shakespeare's comedy "A Midsummer Night's Dream," the character Puck gives what could be a standard formula for the comic plot:

Jack shall have Jill,
Nought will go ill,
The man shall have his mare again, and all shall be well.

Like tragedy, comedy begins with the introduction of disorder into an orderly society and ends with the restoration of a new order. It is oversimple to say that tragedy always ends in death and comedy in marriage, but the oversimplification points to a useful distinction: that the new order in tragedy involves a sense of loss, while the new order in comedy suggests a world grown brighter.

This is not to say, however, that the comic writer has a higher opinion of human nature than the tragic writer. Comedy sometimes has a cold, unsympathetic quality: it holds its characters up to scrutiny at arm's length, limiting the audience's emotional involvement with them. Often it ridicules inconsistencies and incongruities like Sir Andrew Aguecheek's combination of egotism and stupidity:

> *Sir Andrew:* ... Methinks sometimes I have no more wit than a Christian or an ordinary man has; but I am a great eater of beef, and I believe that does harm to my wit.
> *Sir Toby:* No question.
> *Sir Andrew:* And I thought that, I'd forswear it. I'll ride home tomorrow, Sir Toby.
> *Sir Toby:* *Pourquoi,* my dear knight?
> *Sir Andrew:* What is *"pourquoi"*? Do, or not do? I would I had bestow'd that time in the tongues that I have in fencing, dancing, and bear-baiting. O had I but follow'd the arts!
> *Sir Toby:* Then hadst thou had an excellent head of hair.
> (*Twelfth Night,* Act 1, scene 3, lines 82-96)

Comic characters tend to be simpler than tragic ones: we know all that there is to know about Sir Andrew from the few sentences above, and we can enjoy laughing at him partly because we do not see him as a fully rounded human being. When comic characters become more complex and realistic, we feel their plight and may cry rather than laugh. See, for example, *"Painting Churches,"* Act 2, scene 1, where our sudden understanding of Gardner and Fanny brings the play to the edge of tragedy.

The satiric, intellectual quality of a "high comedy" can be contrasted with "lower" types. The comic tendency to simplify characters can become caricature, and the use of the incongruous can become horseplay: at this point comedy has become farce. The audience can identify with a sympathetic character and become emotionally involved in his or her successful struggle: at this point we have sentimental comedy. A sentimental comedy can depend on a strong love interest; it then becomes romantic comedy, a type familiar to everyone who watches evening television. Many comedies, including *"Twelfth Night,"* are a blend of high comedy, farce, and sentimental or romantic comedy.

Conceit: See *Figures of Speech.*

Connotation: the set of implications and associations a word carries regardless of its denotation, or "objective" meaning. In the famous "To be or not to be" soliloquy of *"Hamlet,"* (Act 3, scene 1), the Prince wonders why anyone would "grunt and sweat under a weary life." An eighteenth century editor changed *grunt* to *groan,* because the original word could "hardly be born by modern ears." The alteration does not significantly affect denotation, but it eliminates the demeaning connotation of a word more often used of pigs or oxen than of well-bred gentlefolk. The connotation is, however, part of Shakespeare's meaning; the Prince feels like a coarse animal and his words express his emotional state. See *Diction*.

Couplet: See *Poetic Forms*.

CRITICISM: THE MAJOR APPROACHES

Literary criticism is the analysis and evaluation of a work of literature through a particular set of principles, as well as the justification of the principles used. The practice of criticism is commonly recognized as beginning with the Greeks in the third century B.C. While criticism continues to expand and take new forms yearly, all types find their roots in four basic approaches to literature. The clearest explanation of these approaches is given by M. H. Abrams in *"The Mirror and the Lamp,"* which locates each critical theory in one of these elements being stressed above the others: (1) the universe; (2) the artist or creator; (3) the work of literature produced; (4) the audience to whom the work is directed.

Oldest of the four is a focus on the universe through what is called the *mimetic theory of art*. Aristotle, the great ancient champion of this view, felt that the aim of art was to "delight and instruct" by showing us what the world is like. Until the eighteenth century, writers and critics who defended and evaluated literature did so in light of its verisimilitude, or affinity with what they saw as truth. Some, looking at Shakespeare's *"Measure for Measure,"* might have complained that his compression of an action of several days into a play of less than three hours violates Aristotle's dictum that the passage of time on stage should accurately imitate the passage of time offstage. Focus on the work's relation to the universe does not always, however, involve this sort of concern with accurate imitation of the natural world. Twentieth century ideological criticism, notably Marxist and feminist criticism, has focused on the world view expressed by the work. An ideological critic examining Shakespeare's play might be primarily concerned about the nature of justice in the play.

A focus on the author, found in expressive theory, tends to single out the artist as one gifted with a heightened ability to see the world; the emotions and perceptions of the artist, then, must prevail in art. The Romantic movement, best represented by the nineteenth century poets William Wordsworth and Samuel Taylor Coleridge, ushered in a period of self-expression which continues today. Yet criticism that emerged from an interest in the author has taken many different forms. Historical criticism took hold in the eighteenth century as critics began to wonder about the life of an artist and how it shaped his or her work. While a historical critic would study the cultural, social, and personal life of a writer like Shakespeare, a psychological critic would probe even deeper, attempting to study Shakespeare's unconscious. Freudian criticism, for example, may even look at the text of *"Measure for Measure,"* for signs of psychological tension or repression within Shakespeare.

When the work itself is the center of attention, the approach is called *objective criticism*. The nineteenth-century "art for art's sake" movement, supported by writers such as Walter Pater and Charles Baudelaire, appreciated art for its inherent worth, regardless of its moral or social value. Similarly, the New Critics of the twentieth century attempted to interpret and evaluate a piece of literature in complete isolation from external reality—especially biography and history. Objective criticism may include the examination of the work in light of the conventions appropriate to works of its kind (tragedy or comedy, for example), but has in recent years concentrated on the work's internal structure. A contemporary objective critic might focus attention, for instance, on conflicts in the diction of a character in the play.

M. H. Abrams claims, however, that the pragmatic approach with its focus on the audience is most significant to the Western world. Advocates of this approach sometimes attempt to analyze a work by re-creating the audience for which it was intended. The attitudes of his audience toward sexual conduct, legal procedures, and religious orders must have affected not only Shakespeare's methods in *"Measure for Measure"* (the types of humor, the allusions, etc.) but also the impact he strove to create. Recent reader-response critics pay less attention to the relations between writer and audience than to the interaction between the reader and the text. Their study concerns the manipulation of a reader's thoughts and emotions by a text that holds back information or floods the reader with particular images.

It is important to note, however, that no single form of criticism is the best method of analyzing every work of art. Most critics are relativists and use whatever type, or blend of types, that best enlightens the work. See also *Literary Movements*.

Deus ex machina: meaning "god out of the machine," a phrase that comes from a practice in some Greek drama of using stage machinery to lower onto the stage a god who could rescue the hero, untangle the plot, or set the world in order before the play closed. The term now refers to any contrivance by which an unexpected person or happening is introduced to solve the conflict and lead to a neat, positive ending. The deus ex machina is often regarded as a device by which an unskillful writer saves a plot that has somehow gotten out of control.

DICTION

Though, by definition, diction means no more than "the choice of words," this choice is so crucial that it deserves special scrutiny. Dictionaries ordinarily recognize at least four levels of diction: the formal, the informal, the colloquial, and the slang. Some writers operate almost exclusively within one of these levels. Milton's *"Paradise Lost,"* for example, is notably formal in its diction, full of words that belong in serious books and grave public discourse: Eve mentions to Adam at one point that "casual discourse" "intermits" the day's work. If the diction were informal, she might have said that conversation lightens the day's work; if colloquial, that a chance to talk breaks up the day; if slang, that it's always good to take a break and shoot the breeze.

Some poets, particularly those of the seventeenth and eighteenth centuries, choose to limit the range of words in their poems to achieve a "pure" or "poetic" diction limited largely to the formal and informal level. The Romantic poets sometimes adopt this pure diction (as in *"Tintern Abbey"*), but sometimes deliberately violate it: Wordsworth clearly enjoys violating the decorum of the drawing room by mentioning "leeches" in *"Resolution and Independence"* and "A stump of rotten wood" in "Simon Lee." Though the range of diction easily accepted in poetry today is much wider than it was a century or two ago, there are still words that raise the reader's eyebrows. When Sharon Olds, for instance, uses words like "pissing" and "cardiovascular," she is extending the diction of the poem further into vulgarity on one hand and medical terminology on the other than some poets would be inclined to do. When Richard Wilbur uses *esker, edile, euonymous,* and *mycelium* in *"All That Is,"* he is admitting words to the poem that W. S. Merwin would probably resist as unnatural in his own poems.

In fiction and drama, diction is obviously useful for characterization. In Toni Cade Bambara's *"The Lesson,"* the conflict between Miss Moore and the children echoes in the clash of their slang and her relatively formal speech. Shakespeare relishes the contrast between the diction of his "high" characters, well-bred and educated, and his "low" characters. See the graveyard scene (Act 5, scene 1) in *"Hamlet,"* where the Prince's eloquence is contrasted with the speech of a gravedigger who tells him, for instance, that "your water is a sore decayer of your whoreson dead body." See also *Connotation.*

Dieresis: though used in various senses, usually refers to the practice of ending words at the end of metrical feet, so that there is no conflict between the rhythm established by the slight pause between words and the rhythm established by the slight pause between metrical feet. Shakespeare's *"Sonnet 73"* observes strict dieresis in its first line.

That time/ of year/ thou mayst/ in me/ behold

but breaks the pattern with the second word of the second line

When yel/low leaves,/ or none,/ or few,/ do hang

Dieresis helps establish the poem's underlying meter, but if continued for long becomes monotonous. See *Sound of Poetry.*

Dipodic Meter: a meter in which feet with heavy stresses alternate with feet with light stresses. See, for example, Andrew Marvell's *"Bermudas":*

And all/the way,/to guide/their chime,
With fal/ling oars,/ they kept/ the time.

The effect here is nearly the same as if the basic foot were four syllables long ($\cup$ / $\cup$ $\cup$). The dipodic meter swings from strong stress to strong stress with very little interference from intervening syllables, giving the poem the rhythm of a song. Anapestic and dactylic passages also develop a rhythmic swing because there are two unstressed syllables for each beat. Without the dipodic effect (that is, the effect of two feet acting as one), iambic and trochaic meters are much less songlike. See *Sound of Poetry.*

Elegy: a formal poetic meditation on a serious theme. Renaissance love complaints, such as Thomas Wyatt's *"They Flee from Me,"* were called elegiac, but death is the subject of most modern elegies, including Louise Bogan's *"To My Brother"* and Dylan Thomas' *"Do not Go Gentle into that Good Night."* The **pastoral elegy** is characterized by the classical conventions of an invocation to a Muse, a procession of mourners, the pathetic fallacy, and an exaltation of immortality, while expressing grief over the loss of a friend. Alfred, Lord Tennyson, in *"In Memoriam"* and W. H. Auden, in *"In Memory of W. B. Yeats,"* use these conventions to create modern versions of the ancient form.

Enjambment: the running of one poetic line into another without a significant pause created by phrasing or punctuation. The first and second lines of Shakespeare's *"Sonnet 55"* are enjambed. The first line of *"Sonnet 138,"* on the other hand, is end-stopped. End-stopped lines help establish a poem's underlying meter, but an unvarying pattern of end-stopped lines, like unvarying dieresis, leads to monotony.

Exposition: the portion of a play, preceding the main action, devoted to establishing the situation, character, and conflict. In fiction, exposition is the injection of such material into the story before or between scenes by resort to the omniscient point of view.

Expressionism: See *Literary Movements.*

Fairy tale: a traditional story that contains elements of fantasy. The people in a fairy tale are often stock characters, the cruel stepmother or the greedy king, and their lack of individualization is reflected in the substitution of labels for personal names—"a princess" or "a poor man," for example. Generally one character appears human but possesses magical powers; sometimes what appears to be a human is actually a supernatural spirit in disguise. Although these characters can change forms or perform miracles, the fairy tale is often otherwise realistic. Finally innocence triumphs, often through reconciliation or ruthless vengeance, to lead the fairy tale to a happy ending. The Grimm brothers' *"Juniper Tree"* and Marguerite Yourcenar's oriental tale, *"How Wang-Fo Was Saved,"* although separated by time and culture, are both characteristic of the fairy tale.

Fantasy: a literary form involving a conscious departure from reality, in which the world imitated is, at least in part, an imaginary one. Often the principles of nature are invented or distorted so that animals can take on human traits, people can become animals or superhumans, and the subconscious mind can create monsters or new worlds. Fantasy can be found as an element in otherwise realistic literature, such as Gail Godwin's *"Dream Children,"* or it can permeate an entire story, like the Grimms' *"Juniper Tree."* Although some works of fantasy are distinctly philosophical, such as Jorge Luis Borges' *"The Aleph,"* fantasy can be written purely for entertainment.

FIGURES OF SPEECH

The special language of science uses words and expressions that, so far as possible, communicate one thing at a time without ambiguity or the danger of confusion. *Polytetrafluoroethylene* probably means the same thing in every sentence in which it appears. It is hard to imagine a circumstance where it could be used ironically and it is unlikely to find its way into a simile or metaphor. The language of literature and common life, however, is filled with words and expressions used figuratively, words that mean in a particular context something more than any dictionary definition would lead us to expect. The figures of speech that create these extra meanings are traditionally divided into TROPES (figures that change the meaning of a word) and RHETORICAL FIGURES (those that change the tone or emphasis of a statement without changing the meaning of individual words).

The Principal Tropes:

METAPHOR and SYMBOL are the most important tropes by far. They are discussed in a separate entry that should be read before preceding to the less important tropes listed below. The minor tropes can all be seen as offshoots of metaphor and can all be analyzed in terms of tenor, vehicle, and meaning (for a definition of which, see *Metaphor and Symbol*).

An IMPLIED METAPHOR is one in which either the vehicle or the tenor is not specifically named. When Hamlet asks, "What should such fellows as I do crawling between earth and heaven?" (*"Hamlet,"* Act 3, scene 1) the tenor (Hamlet) is specified, but the vehicle (an insect or other crawling creature) is merely implied.

A SIMILE is a type of metaphor which announces (usually by the use of "like" or "as") the comparison it is making between two essentially different things. In Amy Clampitt's *"Man Feeding Pigeons,"* the descending pigeons become "plump-contoured as the pomegranates and pears in a Della Robbia holiday wreath." Within a larger metaphor in her *"The Longing to be Saved,"* Maxine Kumin describes a burning barn with flames which "shoot like the tattered red cloth of dimestore devil suits." In each example, the two things being compared share at least one common element, shape in the first, and color and texture in the second.

The EPIC SIMILE is one in which the secondary image (vehicle) is substantially expanded until it becomes important in itself and ceases to be a mere illustration of the tenor. Homer uses such similes in the "Iliad" and the "Odyssey," and the epic poets who succeeded him followed his lead. In *"Paradise Lost"* (Book 9, lines 513–516), for example, Milton elaborately compares the movement of the serpent to that of a ship near the mouth of a river, guided by a skillful steersman who knows how to shift the sails with the varying winds.

A CONCEIT is a metaphor which draws an elaborate parallel between two things so remarkably different that great ingenuity (or wit) is required to find the connecting meaning. While a conceit can be a simple metaphor, it often encompasses an entire poem. The most common conceits are the Petrarchan, in which frequently a woman or love is compared to a ship or a rose, and the Metaphysical, which are more intellectual and abstract. John Donne's *"A Valediction: Forbidding Mourning"* contains one of the best-known Metaphysical conceits: a man and wife are compared to the arms of a compass.

PERSONIFICATION is a form of metaphor that compares animals, inanimate objects, or abstractions to humans. In *"Spring,"* for example, Edna St. Vincent Millay calls April "an idiot, babbling and strewing flowers." Often the personification is an implied metaphor, as when Alexander Pope writes in *"The Rape of the Lock"* that the "sun obliquely shoots his burning ray."

An ALLEGORY is an extended metaphor in which the essential meaning (the tenor) is found outside of the literary work. Allegory, like symbolism, uses characters, setting, and images to suggest meaning beyond themselves, but allegorical signs, unlike symbols, are so obviously used to present religious, moral, or political ideas that they retain little objective meaning. Allegorical characters are flat and unreal personifications of the abstract qualities they represent. Charles D'Orleans' *"The Castle of My Heart"* and John Donne's *"Holy Sonnet 14"* are based on a traditional allegory in which the soul is presented as a maiden in a castle defended by knights with names like Reason and Honor and besieged by others with names like Danger and Sorrow. A related allegory figures in Edgar Allan Poe's *"The Fall of the House of Usher."*

METONYMY is the replacement of the name of the thing discussed (the tenor) by the name of a commonly associated object (the vehicle). Orsino, in the opening scene of Shakespeare's *"Twelfth Night,"* looks forward to the time when Olivia will find one man who can simultaneously engage her "liver, brain, and heart." In the medical lore of Shakespeare's time the liver was associated with passions, as the brain and heart are still associated with intellect and emotion. Thus,

Orsino's statement means that Olivia will find a man who will satisfy her passions, intellect, and emotion.

SYNECDOCHE is a type of metonymy in which a part of a thing signifies the whole, and, occasionally, the whole signifies the parts. The "pair of ragged claws scuttling across the floors of silent seas" in T. S. Eliot's *"The Love Song of J. Alfred Prufrock"* signifies the whole crab.

The Principal Rhetorical Figures

The rhetorical figures affect the spirit in which a statement will be taken, and so are related to tone. **Irony** is generally taken to be the most important of these figures, and is treated in a separate entry.

ANTITHESIS involves a marked contrast in words or clauses, as well as in ideas, in order to emphasize both parts of the contrast. In William Blake's *"Auguries of Innocence,"* the antithesis is extended over four lines:

> Every Night & every Morn
> Some to Misery are Born
> Every Morn & every Night
> Some are Born to sweet delight

A successful antithesis provides a balance at both the level of structure and ideas so that the two sides directly play off one another.

An APOSTROPHE addresses an abstract quality or an absent or nonexistent person as if present and listening. Usually the apostrophe involves the expression of deep emotion; it can lend itself to humor and satire. Donne's *"Holy Sonnet 10"* seriously addresses death while his *"The Sun Rising"* is a witty appeal to the rising sun.

HYPERBOLE is conscious overstatement for dramatic or comic effect. Andrew Marvell uses hyperbole in *"To His Coy Mistress"* when the lover tells his mistress that had he time to woo at leisure his "love would grow/Vaster than empires, and more slow." When Mary, the storyteller in Ralph Ellison's *"Did You Ever Dream Lucky?"* says that her daughter's eyes "got round as silver dollars," she too is using hyperbole. In both these cases the hyperbole is also a simile.

OXYMORON, Greek for "pointedly foolish," is a linking of terms that seem to contradict each other. The Latin proverb *Festina lente* (hasten slowly) is a famous example of oxymoron. The expression "Dimity Convictions" in Emily Dickinson's *"What Soft—Cherubic Creatures"* is a more subtle example: Dimity is a sheer cotton fabric—pretty, but too insubstantial to be linked with convictions. Claudius uses oxymoron when he says that the period when he buried his brother and married his brother's widow was one of "defeated joy," filled "With mirth in funeral, and with dirge in marriage" (*Hamlet*, Act 2, scene 2, 10–12).

UNDERSTATEMENT (or LITOTES) is the opposite of hyperbole, a figure of speech which mutes the expression of an emotion, idea, or situation. The irony created by saying less than one means intensifies the effect. The detective stories of Dashiell Hammett are filled with understatement, as in the following lines from *"Fly Paper"*:

> The muzzle of a big black automatic was touching the glass in front of
> him. He had tapped the glass with it to catch our attention.
> > He had our attention.

Understatement is also common in poetry. Edna St. Vincent Millay's *"Love is Not All"* questions throughout whether the speaker would betray her lover "in difficult hour"; the understated conclusion is "I do not think I would."

See *Irony, Metaphor and Symbol.*

Foil: a person or sometimes an object that illuminates and clarifies the distinctive features of another character by sharply contrasting with him or her. The Prior in Robert Browning's *"Fra Lippo Lippi"* is a foil for Lippi as Professor Baglioni is for Rappaccini in Nathaniel Hawthorne's *"Rappaccini's Daughter,"* and both Horatio and Laertes are foils for Hamlet. The term originally meant a "leaf" of bright metal which, when placed under a gem or piece of jewelry, enhanced its brilliance.

Foreshadowing: the presentation of information early in a work which hints at events to follow. Foreshadowing can be the establishment of atmosphere, particular facts, or notable character traits. Edgar Allan Poe's "unredeemed dreariness" of "heart and thought" in the opening of *"The Fall of the House of Usher,"* like the appearance of the ghost in the first act of *"Hamlet,"* prepares the reader both emotionally and intellectually for what is to come.

Frame Story: a story, usually very simple, which creates a context in which a character can tell a second, more extensive story. See, for example, the opening and closing passages of Ralph Ellison's *"Did You Ever Dream Lucky?"*

Genre: a French word referring to a type or category of literature. While literary works are usually categorized by form and technique, sometimes the subject matter also helps define a work. Until the eighteenth century, most literature conformed to the specifications of a certain genre, so much that a writer was acknowledged nearly as much for his or her adherence to convention as for originality. Modern readers are probably more strongly affected than they realize by an awareness of genre conventions. We all acknowledge, for instance, that a detective novel follows different rules from those a science fiction novel follows, and we learn to read each according to its kind. The genres represented in this anthology include the epic, comedy, detective story, elegy, gothic, lyric, pastoral, tragedy, and tragicomedy. Classification by genre can be useful because, when we know the elements of a certain form, we have a frame of reference that allows us to appreciate both the author's skillful adherence to some aspects of the form and his or her skillful departure from other aspects.

Gothic: when first applied to literature in the eighteenth century, gothic meant "barbaric": that which defied classical order and dignity. The term was soon associated with dark castles, strange noises, ghosts, storms, horror, and the supernatural found in literature. The wildness and mystery of the gothic appealed to the nineteenth-century romantics and inspired works like Samuel Taylor Coleridge's *"Kubla Khan"* and John Keats' *"La Belle Dame Sans Merci."* In America, Edgar Allan Poe incorporated gothic elements in his poetry and stories, as in *"The Fall of the House of Usher."* More recently, a number of Southern writers have been recognized for their development of gothic elements. The distorted characters, violence, and obsession found in the works of William Faulkner and Flannery O'Connor have created a "Southern gothic" tradition to which Beth Henley and Leigh Allison Wilson at least partly belong.

Grotesque: first used consistently as a literary term in the eighteenth century, grotesque referred to the bizarre or unnatural, anything that opposed the balance and harmony sought by neoclassical art. Its meaning has been narrowed in this century as more writers have become concerned with the absurdity of humankind and the lack of order in the universe. In fiction and in theater, the grotesque is represented by spiritually or physically deformed characters who carry out abnormal behavior. Writers often use the grotesque for comic effect, as Samuel Beckett does in *"Krapp's Last Tape."* Flannery O'Connor, in contrast, uses it allegorically to demonstrate the spiritual condition of the world (see *"A Good Man is Hard to Find"*).

Hyperbole: See *Figures of Speech.*

IMAGERY

An image is a word or group of words which refer to any sensory experience. Notice the range of images in the following lines from Wilfred Owen's *"Dulce et Decorum Est":*

> If you could hear, at every jolt, the blood
> Come gargling from the froth-corrupted lungs,
> Obscene as cancer, bitter as the cud
> Of vile, incurable sores on innocent tongues,—

In these lines, visual, auditory, gustatory (taste), and tactile (feeling) images are most obvious. Also, with each jolt of the moving wagon, a kinaesthetic image, one which pertains to bodily movement, is created. The sound of the blood and the sight of sores on the tongues are both "literal" images, tied to objects that are present in the poem. Sometimes, however, the important images in a work are brought in as figures of speech, as in this simile from Alfred, Lord Tennyson's *"Tears, Idle Tears":*

> Ah, sad and strange as in dark summer dawns
> The earliest pipe of half-awakened birds
> To dying ears, when unto dying eyes
> The casement slowly grows a glimmering square;
> So sad, so strange, the days that are no more.

In some poems the images are so rich and have such psychological weight that they convey the "meaning" of the poem more completely than the prose sense of the sentences in which they occur. Some modern poems, such as Charles Baudelaire's *"Correspondences,"* employ **synaesthesia,** the description of one kind of sensation in terms of another: the description of "scents . . . /As mellow as oboes," for instance, crosses an olfactory image with an auditory one.

Although imagery is essential to poetry, it can be very important in fiction and drama as well. The opening images of Ernest Hemingway's *"A Clean Well-Lighted Place"* sets the scene for the reader in only a few lines.

> It was late and every one had left the cafe except an old man who sat in the
> shadow the leaves of the tree made against the electric light. In the day
> time the street was dusty, but at night the dew settled the dust and the old
> man liked to sit late because he was deaf and now at night it was quiet and
> he felt the difference.

Here the imagery is visual, tactile, and perhaps olfactory. We seem for a moment to sense the world as the deaf man senses it: seeing the interplay of shadow and light, feeling (and perhaps smelling) the dust during day and its absence by night.

Imagism: See *Literary Movements.*

Impressionism: See *Literary Movements.*

Initiation story: a story about the development of a young person from childhood or adolescence to maturity. The internal conflicts that the innocent individual has to face and resolve "initiate" him or her into the world of experience. James Joyce's *"Araby,"* Edna O'Brien's *"Sister Imelda,"* and William Faulkner's *"Barn Burning"* are initiation stories.

IRONY

Ancient histories tell us that when the Emperor Croesus of Lydia planned his campaign against the Emperor Cyrus of Persia, he took the precaution of asking the Oracle (a kind of fortune teller) at Delphi for a prediction of the outcome. The Oracle responded that if Croesus invaded, "a great empire would be destroyed." Croesus, hearing in this prophecy only what he wanted to hear, launched the invasion. The result, of course, was the fall of Lydia. This incident illustrates the characteristic grim humor of irony. It also shows its central principle: truth appears in a mask that disguises it. The mask may be verbal, created by an ambiguity in the meaning of an expression (as in the line "She lies not down to weep" in A. E. Housman's *"Is My Team Ploughing"*). It may be dramatic, created by the misunderstanding of a character who knows less than the audience (as in Act 3 of Beth Henley's *"Crimes of the Heart,"* where Meg does not know that Old Granddaddy is in a coma). It may be situational, created by juxtapositions that suggest grim humor (as in Charles Baudelaire's *"The Little Old Women,"* where we see that old people dwindle in stature until they can be buried in coffins made for children).

Crisp, clear examples of verbal, dramatic, and situational irony are relatively uncommon. Far more common are passages or whole works where the tone is ironic. An author or character says something as if with a wink or grimace to show the discrepancy between the words and the meaning. Hamlet, for instance, seems to praise Gertrude for remarrying immediately after his father's burial: "Thrift, thrift, Horatio! the funeral baked meats/Did coldly furnish forth the marriage tables" (*"Hamlet,"* Act 1, scene 2). Neither the audience nor Horatio needs to be told that Hamlet's supposed praise is a mask which both hides and reveals his actual outrage. Sometimes, however, the ironic tone is much harder to detect and interpret. Readers may disagree, for example, about the nature of the irony in Robert Frost's *"Provide, Provide."* Some will say that the poem is completely ironical, that Frost is presenting a world view with which he flatly disagrees. Some will say that he at least half agrees that "boughten friendship" is better than none. See also *Wit.*

LITERARY MOVEMENTS AND PERIODS

While some writers represented in this book consciously set out to create a literary movement, others, by virtue of birth and convention, were necessarily assigned to one. No writer escapes being associated with or influenced by the characteristics of some literary movement; knowing the background against which a particular writer has written may prove helpful in fully appreciating his or her work. The following is a discussion of major literary movements and periods.

The RENAISSANCE acquired its name from the French word meaning "rebirth," a word that captures the creative energy and optimism of a society expanding, geographically and culturally, beyond the limits of the medieval period. Harkening back to the humanism of classical times, Renaissance painting, sculpture, and literature often celebrated the beauty of humanity and the physical world. The English Renaissance flowered under Elizabeth I (1533–1603) and James I (1603–1625) and waned in the second half of the seventeenth century. It infused English literature with a range of allusion enriched by scholarship and travel and a poetic sensibility enlarged by European as well as classical influences. The breadth of Shakespeare's drama and Milton's epic poetry demonstrate the unlimited creativity of Renaissance writers.

The NEOCLASSICAL PERIOD arose as a reaction against the unrestrained energy and humanism of the Renaissance. During the eighteenth century, the neoclassicists stressed the imperfections and limitations of humanity. They imposed a new order and decorum on life and art. Art was valued for its exaltation of reason and its restraint of emotion and the imagination. Alexander Pope exemplified both these values in his *"Rape of the Lock,"* a mock-epic poem that ridiculed the pettiness of humanity in witty and flawless couplets. An essentially neoclassic sensibility sometimes appears in the twentieth century, as in W. H. Auden's *"The Unknown Citizen,"* with its ironic distance, restraint, and wit.

ROMANTICISM began as a movement when William Wordsworth and Samuel Taylor Coleridge published their *"Lyrical Ballads"* in 1798. Reacting against neoclassical order and restraint, the English Romantic poets enthusiastically embraced supernatural themes, the wildness of nature, imagination, and self-expression. In diction and poetic form, their verse often resembled impassioned prose or folk balladry. In England, William Blake, William Wordsworth, Samuel Taylor Coleridge, John Keats, and Percy Bysshe Shelley were the leading Romantic poets. In America, fiction was equally influenced by the movement. American romanticism tended toward symbolism and gothic elements while maintaining the imaginative qualities of the earlier romantics. The movement in America was led by Nathaniel Hawthorne, Herman Melville, Edgar Allan Poe, Walt Whitman, and Emily Dickinson.

The array of movements that followed romanticism are all "modern" in their decisive break from former literary traditions. While all can be roughly located in time, each presents a method of literary expression which continues to appear in literature to the present.

REALISM, first, is the attempt to reproduce the actual world in literature. It arose in the nineteenth century as a reaction against the sentimental, supernatural, and optimistic elements of romanticism. Realists generally choose the common or ordinary for subject matter, and they focus on the presentation of character instead of on plot. In drama, Henrik Ibsen and Anton Chekhov are responsible for the turn to realism on stage; Guy de Maupassant, Henry James, and Edith Wharton are forerunners of realism in fiction.

NATURALISM grew out of realism around the turn of this century. Although related to realism, naturalism moves beyond literary principles to scientific ones that govern both human nature and the order of the universe. Scientific determinism leaves characters defeated by both the natural world and their own animalistic nature, neither of which they can understand or control; social and economic determinism takes from them the power to direct their own destinies. Although Maupassant preferred to avoid being labeled, he is aligned with the naturalistic tradition.

SYMBOLISM began as a movement in France during the second half of the nineteenth century as a reaction against realism. The symbolists believed that the objective world was not the true reality, but rather a mere reflection of an Absolute one, with which the artist was closely attuned. Art revealed reality by re-creating the emotional response of the artist, but because emotional states cannot be shared directly, the symbolists believed a system of symbols was necessary to express what they experienced. They also relied on the musical and connotative qualities of words to evoke a response in the reader. Charles Baudelaire was the primary force behind symbolism, especially in his use of synaesthesia, the description of one kind of sensation in terms of another. The influence of the movement is apparent in the poetry of William Butler Yeats, the foremost English symbolist, and Louise Bogan.

IMAGISM was initiated in 1909 by American and English poets as a response to symbolism. To counteract the loosely-defined images of the Symbolists, the Imagists set out to give poetry a new concreteness. Influenced in part by Japanese haiku, the Imagists used precise language to create solid, sharply-defined representations of objects. Their ideal was a visual creation that would appeal to the intellect while its sound evoked emotion. Imagism continues to influence poets; its traits are seen, for example, in William Carlos Williams' *"The Red Wheelbarrow."*

MODERNISM, when defined specifically, refers to a direction in style and attitude taken by twentieth-century literature. "Modern" does not refer to a specific time period but rather to a conscious break with traditional forms. Rejecting objective truth as a source of meaning, the moderns believe that the individual creates meaning by perception, action, and imagination. Symbolism and personal mythmaking become the means of self-expression. Yet the glorification of the inner being leads the modern to alienation and a sense of loss and despair. William Butler Yeats, T. S. Eliot, James Joyce, Virginia Woolf, William Faulkner, and Samuel Beckett are among the many modern writers.

IMPRESSIONISM is a movement in literature in which things are portrayed as they would be perceived by a particular consciousness and point of view rather than as they objectively appear. Taking their method from the impressionistic painters of the nineteenth century, such as Renoir and Monet, the literary impressionists attempt to imitate, through words, the delicate brush strokes and varying patterns of light created in such art. The result is the reproduction of a fleeting impression upon the mind of how something momentarily looked or felt. Although impressionism is like expressionism in that it uses objects merely to portray the human consciousness, it differs in that it does not distort or abstract them. Virginia Woolf's *"Solid Objects,"* for example, is an impressionistic story.

EXPRESSIONISM, a term coined at the beginning of the twentieth century, describes art and literature that emphasize the internal emotions and experience of the artist. External objects merely transmit the artist's psyche and are not significant in themselves; therefore they are often substantially distorted. Expressionism in drama is characterized by symbolic and anti-realistic staging, and in fiction takes the form of stream of consciousness narration and dreamlike situations, as in Franz Kafka's *"Metamorphosis."* Federico García Lorca's *"Song of the Barren Orange Tree"* can be seen as expressionistic.

Finally, SURREALISM is a movement in art and literature which began during World War I in France. Influenced primarily by the psychology of Freud and poetry of Charles Baudelaire and Arthur Rimbaud, the surrealists believed that the illogical and uncontrolled thoughts and associations of the mind better represented objective truth than ideas controlled by convention and imposed rationality. Presenting a dreamlike world through free-form writing and leaving interpretation to the reader alone, the surrealists asserted their freedom from reason and moral purpose. Although the movement ended at the beginning of World War II, surrealism continued to influence contemporary writers. Robert Bly's *"Words Rising"* and Pablo Neruda's *"Love Sonnet VI"* both demonstrate surrealistic qualities.

Lyric: a relatively brief poem that expresses the personal emotions of a single speaker, usually love or sorrow, longing or tranquility. Many of the early and memorable lyrics in English, such as the anonymous *"Western Wind,"* were written to be sung, as popular song lyrics are today. Some later and more "literary" lyrics, such as Alfred, Lord Tennyson's *"Now Sleeps the Crimson Petal,"* are still at least nominally songs for music. Others, such as John Keats' *"When I Have Fears that I may Cease to Be"* and Elizabeth Bishop's *"One Art,"* were probably never intended to be sung but retain the tight metrical construction of a song lyric. In a somewhat looser sense, lyric is opposed to dramatic and epic as one of the three major genres of poetry: it is the genre of a single voice presenting a single mood or impression.

Melodrama: a term that literally means "a play with music" and that originally referred to a type of musical play popular in England in the nineteenth century. Today the term no longer implies that songs and music will be part of the performance. What is implied is a heavy-handed appeal to emotions: characters who are unrealistically good are pitted in a dire and apparently futile struggle against other characters who are unrealistically bad. When the audience's feelings of horror and pity have been sufficiently exercised, the plot usually turns (often via a deus ex machina) and the audience feels a rush of joy as the play comes to a happy ending. To call a play or story "melodramatic" is to condemn it because it manipulates the emotions of the audience and fails to satisfy their intelligence. But we should remember that the "correct" balance of emotional and intellectual appeal in a work has varied greatly from period to period and from culture to culture. Were it not preserved from the criticism by its antiquity, *Medea* might be called melodramatic: the literary establishment in ancient Greece seems to have been less put off by appeals to strong and predictable emotions than the majority of critics and literature professors in twentieth-century Britain and America.

METAPHOR AND SYMBOL

Ballroom dancing begins as a way for Sam and Willie to pass the rainy afternoon in Athol Fugard's play, *"Master Harold . . . and the Boys."* But as the play progresses, the dancing begins to accumulate meaning. Soon Sam has created for Willy a vision of the world free from personal, racial, and political "stumbles or bumps." Like the waltz of the professional dancers, Sam's ideal world is one in which people "learn to dance life like champions," with grace and in harmony. Before the play closes, ballroom dancing has come to represent "the way we want life to be." This representation of one thing by another is the essential characteristic of all the figures of speech.

Most figures of speech are variations on the metaphor, and if we understand how it works, we will understand the rest. Following the practice of the critic I. A. Richards, we can divide the metaphor into three parts: the "tenor" is the thing being described; the "vehicle" is the image the tenor is compared to; the "meaning" is the point of the comparison, the similarity between tenor and vehicle. In *"Master Harold"* the vehicle of the dance is applied to the tenor of human relations with the meaning that they should be graceful and harmonious. In the simplest metaphors, the nature of the comparison being made is perfectly clear. Alexander Pope tells us that at *"Timon's Villa"* "the building is a Town" and the "Pond is an

Ocean." The master of the house, on the other hand, is "A puny insect, shivering at a breeze." All here is so clear that we can construct a chart:

tenor		meaning		vehicle
building is	so remarkable in its	*size*	that we can compare it to	a *town*
pond is		*size*		an *ocean*
master is		*puniness*		an *insect*

More complex metaphors cannot be charted so easily. Dennis Brutus' *"Nightsong: City"* gives us the image of police cars that "cockroach through the tunnel streets" of a South African shantytown. Here we know the tenor and the vehicle, but what shall we say the meaning is? Is a police car like a cockroach because its appearance is black and buglike? Because it is a despised intruder in (or among) people's homes? Because it crawls through the streets that are dim, narrow, filthy and crooked like the tunnels insects find behind walls and under floors?

Such metaphors approach the rather hazy border that divides metaphor from symbol. The "vehicle" (the cockroach) is becoming so significant in its own right, so laden with meaning, that it points to several meanings in the tenor. We would probably not call it a symbol, however, because its presence in the poem depends on the presence of the police car; it has no independent existence, it is merely a rhetorical figure. A "fixed symbol" like the Lamb in Charles Wesley's hymn *"Gentle Jesus"* is almost indistinguishable from this sort of metaphor. The Lamb (vehicle) represents Jesus (tenor) because it, too, is perfectly innocent and mild and is offered up as a sacrifice (meanings).

The distinction between metaphor and symbol is easier to see when the symbol is "freer." Look at Louise Bogan's poem *"The Dragonfly"* and you will find an image that is tied neither to a particular tenor nor to a particular meaning. Bogan's dragonfly, far more definitely than Wesley's lamb, is a thing represented in its own right and not reduced to an illustration of some abstract meaning. Tenors and meanings may attach themselves to it, but it does not exist solely to carry them (it is no longer merely a vehicle). Yet Bogan writes about the dragonfly in a way that invites the meanings to attach themselves: the dragonfly, we might say, is like the human soul because it is nearly bodiless, because it is airborne and swift, because earth "repels" it. Or we might say that it is like the personality of certain people— restless, subject to an unending hunger. Or we might say that it is like the spirit of people who are "twice-born," who "split into the heat" of the mid-summer of their lives and attack life with a sudden energy before they fall "With the other husks of summer." Symbols like Bogan's dragonfly, the poison flower in Nathaniel Hawthorne's *"Rappaccini's Daughter,"* the serpent in Wole Soyinka's *"The Swamp Dwellers,"* and the dog in José Donoso's *"Paseo,"* become magnets that attract a range of tenors and meanings so wide and complex that we cannot list them definitively.

The metaphor, we can say, is an image (or action) intended primarily to represent an aspect of some other thing. The symbol is an image intended primarily to stand in its own right and to attract meanings to itself. The dancing in *"Master Harold"* might be called a metaphor by a reader who sees it as an illustration of the harmony that ought to exist in human relations; Sam makes it such a metaphor in a speech he gives near the play's end. Other readers, however, might say that the dancing is a symbol because it is an action that actually occurs on stage and that accumulates meanings wider, even, than those Sam proposes, meanings that have to do with dignity, art, and imagination. See also *Figures of Speech*.

Meter: the rhythmic pattern of a poem that has a regular rhythm. In some cases, this rhythmic pattern is established by including a fixed number of stresses in a line (see, for example, Gerard Manley Hopkins' *"The Windhover"* or the Old English poem *"The Seafarer"*). In some cases, the pattern depends on a fixed number of syllables per line (see, for example, Marianne Moore's *"The Fish"*). More often both stress and syllables are considered. See *Sound of Poetry*.

Metonymy: see *Figures of Speech*.

Modernism: see *Literary Movements*.

Naturalism: see *Literary Movements*.

Neoclassical Period: see *Literary Movements*.

Oxymoron: see *Figures of Speech*.

Pathetic Fallacy: a term coined by John Ruskin in 1856 to refer to the practice of ascribing human emotions to inanimate objects. Though Ruskin used the term pejoratively, it is now used neutrally, to indicate a form of personification created when the speaker's emotion is so powerful that he or she seems to see it echoed by the natural world. Federico García Lorca's *"Song of the Barren Orange Tree"* is a good illustration of the pathetic fallacy.

Persona: the voice (literally the mask) which an author of a work speaks through. The persona can be the actual author, a created voice or "implied author," or a character created by the author. The persona in Walt Whitman's *"Song of Myself,"* for example, may be Whitman himself in part, but takes on universal dimension in the course of the poem. The persona in Alice Walker's *"Everyday Use"* narrates the story while also revealing herself as a well-rounded character.

Personification: see *Figures of Speech*.

PLOT
E. M. Forster says in "The Art of the Novel" that "the king died and the queen died" is not a plot but merely a report of two incidents. "The king died, and then the queen died of grief," however, Forster will allow to be a plot. The distinction between a mere collection of incidents and a plot, then, is that within a plot one event causes another. A well-formed plot is self-contained "action," a chain of causes and effects: it begins with an event that needs no explanation; this event leads naturally to the next event, which leads to the next, and so the events tumble like carefully arranged dominoes until the last domino falls. The last domino, according to innumerable literary critics dating back to Aristotle, should *seem* like a last domino: that is, it should seem a fitting conclusion to the action the first event triggered and should leave the audience with the feeling that nothing else need follow. It is not surprising that plots very commonly end with the death or marriage of the protagonist: either event seems to satisfy the audience's curiosity about his or her fate.

Because drama depends heavily on plot, most of the terms we use to describe plot come from the writings of dramatic theorists, notably Gustav Freytag, whose "Techniques of the Drama" (1863) introduced the pyramid of rising and falling action that has become a standard tool for explaining the structure of plots.

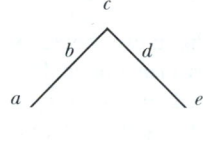

The introduction (*a*) involves the necessary business of establishing characters, setting, and situation. Once the protagonist becomes determined to pursue a goal, complication sets in, and we have a series of encounters between the protagonist and the forces that oppose the protagonist. The conflict increases in intensity during the phase of rising action (*b*) until it reaches the reversal of fortune at the climax (*c*). Here the conflict comes to a crisis and the protagonist begins a descent to destruction in tragedy or into calm contentment in comedy. This phase of falling action (*d*) is sometimes marked by events that add an element of suspense, but it leads finally to the denouement (*e*), called the catastrophe in tragedy, which reveals beyond doubt the fate of the protagonist.

The plot pattern of Freytag's pyramid is particularly accurate in describing the development of a classical tragedy like *"Antigone."* Most other works will vary the pattern somewhat. The phase of falling action in most short stories, for instance, is much shorter than the phase of rising action. Some writers present their story in an order that varies from the chronological order of the plot. Alice Munro's *"Circle of Prayer,"* for example, begins in the middle of things (*in medias res* is the classical term) with the protagonist throwing a jug across the room, then establishes by a flashback the circumstances that led up to the incident. Some writers present us with double plot: in Shakespeare's *"Twelfth Night"* the main plot that culminates with Viola's marriage to Orsino is interwoven with a subplot that culminates in the humiliation of Malvolio. See also *Deus ex Machina, Foreshadowing, Initiation Story.*

POETIC FORMS

Repetition and variation, two sources of artistic pleasure, pull us in opposite directions when we consider the issue of poetic form. As Robert Hass points out, a regular meter, a repeated rhyme, or a pattern of stanzas can appeal to "the hope of a shapeliness in things": we crave order, and the world outside the poem sometimes seems to have very little of it. On the other hand, an invariable order can produce monotony: a hundred lines of slavishly correct iambic pentameter couplets would rock a listener to sleep and probably drain the poet of any inspiration he or she had. The attempt to reconcile (or explore) the tension between repetition and variation has led some poets, among them Walt Whitman and W. S. Merwin, to favor free (that is, unmetered) verse and an "open form" that defines itself as the poem unfolds rather being fixed by tradition.

Those who have continued to work in the "closed forms," many of them legacies from the Middle Ages or the Renaissance, find ways to surprise the reader within the established pattern. See, for example, the discussion on Emily Dickinson's *"A Bird Came Down the Walk"* on pages 677–678. This sense of surprise, however, depends on a knowledge of what the standard forms are. A basic knowledge of the **Sound of Poetry** including meter and rhyme, is assumed in the following discussion of poetic forms that occur repeatedly in *The Riverside Anthology of Literature.*

The COUPLET is simply a pair of rhymed lines. When the couplet is a self-contained statement, it is easy to remember ("Red sky at morning,/Sailor take warning"). It lends itself to wit, as in the couplet Pope wrote for a royal dog's collar: "I am his majesty's dog at Kew./Pray tell me, Sir, whose dog are you?" Though a couplet can be a self-contained poem, it more often is the basic unit of a longer poem, as in Alexander Pope's *"Essay on Criticism,"* which is written in iambic pentameter ("heroic") couplets.

A TERCET or TRIPLET is a three-line stanza, either rhyming in every line, as in Robert Frost's *"Provide, Provide"* or rhyming *aba* as part of a terza rima poem like his *"Acquainted with the Night."* In TERZA RIMA, the unrhymed line from one stanza provides the rhyme for the next stanza, so that the rhymes link the stanzas into a chain: *aba bcb cdc*, etc.

The QUATRAIN is simply a four-line unit of poetry, usually with at least one rhyme (on the second and fourth line: *abcb*) to give it definition. See, for example, the anonymous lyric *"Western Wind."* The quatrain can be more elaborately rhymed (*abab, abba,* etc.), and it is a common stanza form in traditional ballads, popular songs, and hymns. Particularly frequent users of the ballad form are William Blake, William Wordsworth, Samuel Taylor Coleridge, Emily Dickinson, and A. E. Housman.

The RHYME ROYAL is a seven-line stanza in iambic pentameter which rhymes *ababbcc*. An alexandrine (hexameter) often comprises the final line. Thomas Wyatt's *"They Flee from Me"* and Wordsworth's *"Resolution and Independence"* both use the rhyme royal.

The SONNET, like the ballad, was originally written to be sung. In its basic form it is fourteen lines long, most commonly written in iambic pentameter, and rhymed on one of two patterns. The English or Shakespearian pattern is *abab cdcd efef gg;* the Italian or Petrarchan pattern is *abba abba cde cde.* The number of variations on the sonnet form is enormous, however: see, for example, Niccolo degli Albizzi's *"Prolonged Sonnet"* and Gerard Manley Hopkins' "curtal" sonnet, *"Pied Beauty."*

In reading sonnets on the English pattern it is worth noting that the three quatrains often allow the poet to develop a series of three related images or ideas. The closing couplet lends itself to (or sometimes seems to demand) a neat resolution to the tensions introduced by the quatrains. The Italian sonnet breaks naturally between the first eight lines (the octave) and the last six (the sestet). Even poets who are not following the Italian form precisely may be attracted to its tradition of introducing a problem or tension in the octave and commenting on it in the sestet. See, for instance, William Wordsworth's *"The World Is Too Much with Us."* Among the most important sonneteers in English are Shakespeare, John Donne, Milton, William Wordsworth, John Keats, Christina Rossetti, D. G. Rossetti, Edwin Arlington Robinson, Robert Frost, Edna St. Vincent Millay, and Countee Cullen. Of poets represented in *The Riverside Anthology* in translation, the Chilean Pablo Neruda and the Austrian Rainer Maria Rilke are masters of the sonnet form.

The VILLANELLE is a nineteen-line poem using only two rhymes: *aba aba aba aba abba.* The first line is repeated verbatim as lines 6, 12, and 18. The third line is repeated as line 9, 15, and 19. This abstract description does little to clarify the form and nothing to show the emotional effect it can have when masterfully done. See Elizabeth Bishop's *"One Art"* and Dylan Thomas' *"Do Not Go Gentle into that Good Night."*

POINT OF VIEW
One of the most important tools of the storyteller is the ability to choose the point of view from which events will be described. In their pure form, the principal

points of view can be seen as vertices of a triangle. At one corner is the omniscient point of view, in which the author freely uses all that he or she knows about the world of the story, moving into and out of the minds of characters at will and also making observations that no character in the story is capable of making. This method is commonly used in tales like the Grimms' *"The Juniper Tree."* At another corner of the triangle is the dramatic point of view, so named because it is the natural perspective of the dramatic performance. The writer limits his or her observations to what the senses of an objective observer can take in; the actions and spoken words of the characters are recorded, therefore, but not their thoughts. The purely dramatic point of view is very rare in fiction, but Ernest Hemingway's *"A Clean Well-Lighted Place"* breaks with its objectivity only twice, trivially in the first paragraph, and significantly when the older waiter has a "conversation with himself" (an interior monologue). At the third corner of the triangle is the limited point of view, which restricts itself to the observations of a single character in the story. First person stories are generally limited in this way (see Elizabeth Tallent's *"No One's a Mystery"*); third-person stories may be (see Arthur Conan Doyle's *"The Speckled Band"*).

It is unusual for a modern short story or novel to use any of the three points of view purely. The most comon perspective for fiction is, in fact, a hybrid called the limited omniscient point of view. This mixed method allows the writer to descend into the consciousness of characters so that the reader can see the world through their eyes, but it also allows her to escape from their limited horizons to make an observation on her own behalf or to move the story along with simple exposition. A fairly common pattern is that used in Doris Lessing's *"To Room Nineteen"*: the story begins with omniscient narration and restricts itself increasingly to the consciousness of the protagonist after the circumstances and tone have been established.

The descent from omniscience into the consciousness of a character is like the movement from the perspective of the general looking at the map of the battle to that of the soldier at the front. The soldier's view is in some ways more realistic, since he sees the face of battle; but it can be less reliable since he sees only a part of the field and may conclude that the battle is being won even at the moment that, just out of sight, the enemy is surrounding him. One of the pleasures of reading fiction is looking at the world through the eyes of a naive or unreliable narrator like Sylvia in Toni Cade Bambara's *"The Lesson"* and watching her understanding of what she sees gradually increase.

Protagonist: in a play or story, the principal actor or character, whose pursuit of a goal provides the work with its plot. The protagonist is not necessarily a hero, because the leading figure in a work often is not endowed with heroic qualities. Creon best represents the protagonist in Sophocles' *"Antigone,"* although Antigone may obtain the audience's greater sympathy. See also *Antagonist.*

Quatrain: See *Poetic Forms.*

Renaissance: See *Literary Movements.*

Rhyme: a term often synonymous with true rhyme (see *Sound of Poetry*). Variations on true rhyme include double-rhyme (plaster/master) and triple rhyme (admonish you/astonish you). Poets since Emily Dickinson have often substituted assonance (wave/sail) or consonance (wave/sieve) for true rhyme, a practice called half-rhyme, near rhyme, or slant-rhyme. Some, like Marianne Moore, have also rhymed on an unstressed syllable, a practice called light rhyme (full/eagle).

Romanticism: See *Literary Movements.*

Rhyme Royal: See *Poetic Forms.*

SETTING AND SCENE
Setting does for fiction (a story, play, or narrative poem) what the background does for a painting. Both establish a fixed context of detail against which the characters are portrayed and the action takes place. On the physical level, setting includes both general and specific geography, the state of Mississippi as well as the back porch of a house; likewise, both the era and the time of day or night are the temporal elements of setting. But the setting in a literary work, in addition, provides the cultural and psychological locale which illuminate the background and mental life of the characters.

Eudora Welty's *"Livvie"* begins with five long paragraphs which seem to do little more than describe the setting. The opening lines, however, also establish an overwhelming sense of isolation.

> Solomon carried Livvie twenty-one miles away from her home when he married her. He carried her away up on the Old Natchez Trace into the deep country to live in his house. She was sixteen—an only girl, then. Once people said he thought nobody would ever come along there.

Soon we also learn that Solomon is an old, dying man who scarcely allows Livvie to leave his side. Yet as the paragraphs continue to describe the house, the tall scrolled rocker, the jelly glass with pretty hen feathers in it, the snow-white curtains, the pickled peaches, fig preserves, and blackberry jam, we begin to see the place as Livvie sees it despite her constant loneliness. "It was a nice house," repeated through the description, become the words of Livvie's perception. By the time we hear of Livvie's attraction to angels and fear of ghosts, the setting has introduced us to a delightful and imaginative young girl, without giving any direct description of her. The parallel between the physical setting and the character's psychology has created the illusion of a concrete world and of a real person as well.

The setting in a dramatic work is of equal importance. As in fiction, dramatic settings should parallel the psychological conditions of the characters. Sam Shepard's *"Fool for Love,"* for example, is set entirely in a "stark, low-rent motel room on the edge of the Mojave Desert." The drab and sordid details of the room, green plaster walls meeting a brown linoleum floor, a cast iron bed and metal chairs with yellow plastic seats, combined with the faint sound of a Merle Haggard tune, establish the atmosphere before any words are spoken.

Fiction and drama are alike in that each establishes scene as well as setting. In drama, a scene is a division of an act, but its purpose can be defined in various ways. The break between scenes may complete an action, signify an emotional break, emphasize the entrance or speech of an important character, or work as a transition. It may or may not involve a change in location, but it does require a clearing of the stage, producing a break in the action and a lapse in time. A new scene, then, creates a new setting. Defining the dramatic scene as a period of continuous action, we will find its counterpart in fiction. The short story writer creates characters and then places them in a particular situation in which action occurs. Scene change is again noted through a change in setting, a transition normally achieved by exposition. In some stories, such as Herman Melville's *"Bartleby the Scrivener,"* the progression of scenes builds intensity (see *Plot*). In others, such as

Alice Munro's *"Circle of Prayer,"* the repetition of a particular scene adds both depth and unity. Tina Howe's *"Painting Churches"* demonstrates the interaction of setting and scene, for while the location of the scenes is always the same room, the details of the setting (furniture, boxes, litter, walls sometimes with paintings, sometimes bare) change scene-by-scene to indicate the passage of time and to suggest the progress of the characters from one emotional order, through a period of chaos, to a new emotional order.

SHORT STORY

We have all grown so familiar with the short story that we tend to think of it as a form that is somehow natural or spontaneous. In fact, though storytelling is part of human nature, the literary short story is an invented or developed form, not much more natural than the sonnet or the villanelle, though considerably harder to define. Among the more important "inventors" of the form were Nathaniel Hawthorne, Edgar Allan Poe, and Guy de Maupassant, and if we look at what these writers set out to do, we will gain a sense of how much the short story differs from the story that happens to be short.

Hawthorne's fiction, long or short, borrows from the fable a tendency to moralize, but adds to this an exploration of psychological truths that defy neat moral application. *"Rappaccini's Daughter,"* for instance, is based on an old fable intended to decorate a priest's sermon and to teach a lesson: "The envenomed beauty is Luxury and Gluttony, which feed men with delicacies, that are poison to the soul." Hawthorne's story explores in a much more complex way the human desires for knowledge, love, and power. No longer is the story subordinate to its "theme" or "message" or "point," but *pointedness* is still there. It does not teach a lesson, but it expresses an attitude toward life.

When, in 1842, Poe reviewed Hawthorne's "Twice-Told Tales," he established an explicit definition of the short story: it should occupy no more than two hours reading time and it should encompass "a certain unique or single effect." Poe insisted that the short story was not a pared down novel, any more than a lyric poem was a shortened epic. Because the story was short enough to be taken in at a sitting, the reader could keep it all in mind, could see how each part related to each other part, and could be kept in an unbroken mood of excitement, dread, anticipation, horror, or sorrow. Everything should work toward the effect, description and dialogue no less than action. Charles Baudelaire, who read both Poe's literary works and his critical writing with interest, took Poe's views on the short story to their logical conclusion when he developed such prose poems as *"Knock Down the Poor!"*

Although it seems implicit in Poe's definition of the short story, a third characteristic of the genre did not manifest itself fully until Maupassant's enormously popular stories began to exert their influence in the 1880s and 1890s. This characteristic is an absolute economy of style that strips away every detail or word not essential to the story's "unique or single effect."

If we combine Hawthorne's interest in exploring psychological and moral truth with Poe's interest in a "poetic" unity and Maupassant's insistence on a lean, economical style, we have a fairly good definition of the central qualities of the short story. Ernest Hemingway's *"A Clean Well-Lighted Place,"* Anton Chekhov's *"The Lady with the Pet Dog"* and Nadine Gordimer's *"The Catch"* display these qualities to great advantage and are close to the heart of the genre. This is not to say that being near the heart is essential to success. Such stories as E. M. Forster's *"The Eternal*

Moment" and Toni Cade Bambara's *"The Lesson"* move in the direction of the novel, where unity of effect is often traded for variety and a reflection of the bustle of life. Virginia Woolf's *"Solid Objects"* and Gabriel García Márquez's *"A Very Old Man with Enormous Wings"* have turned away from the moral intentness that Hawthorne brought to the genre. Margaret Atwood's *"Rape Fantasies"* and Alice Adams's *"Return Trips"* use a narrative technique that Maupassant would surely find uneconomical.

Nonetheless, the central qualities of the short story are so firmly established that even writers who choose to avoid them seem to be defining their art by that act. See also *Plot, Fairy Tale.*

Simile: See *Figures of Speech.*

Sonnet: See *Poetic Forms.*

THE SOUND OF POETRY

When the poet W. H. Auden was an undergraduate at Oxford University he heard Professor J. R. R. Tolkien read a passage of Old English poetry. The passage was complete nonsense to Auden, who had not studied Old English, but the sound enchanted him. An encounter like Auden's with the music of a poem as a thing separate from the meaning is a good starting point when we study the sound in poetry. Consider the first two stanzas of Lewis Carroll's "Jabberwocky":

> 'Twas brillig, and the slithy* toves
>   Did gyre* and gimble in the wabe
> All mimsy were the borogoves,
>   And the mome raths outgrabe.

> "Beware the Jabberwock, my son!
>   The jaws that bite, the claws that catch!
> Beware the Jubjub bird, and shun
>   The frumious Bandersnatch."

There is very little to understand here, but a great deal to listen to, and thousands of people who have no idea what the words "brillig" and "slithy" and "gimble" mean remember them because they fit so well into the structure of vowel and consonant sounds that stitch the poem together. Assonance, the repetition of vowel sounds, runs through this entire quatrain: listen to the short "i" in

> br*i*ll*i*g g*i*mble m*i*msy.

Even more extensive is the use of repeated consonant sounds:

> *b*rilli*g* gim*b*le mi*m*sey *b*orogoves *m*ome outgra*b*e.

These connections are more obvious in some cases than others. Alliteration, the repetition of the first consonant sound in a word, can be particularly conspicuous ("claws that catch"). True rhyme, which requires an exact match in the vowel of a

---

* *Slithy* is pronounced with a long *i*, as in *slimy; gyre* in *gyroscope.*

stressed syllable and any subsequent consonant (*toves*/borogoves, *wabe*/outgrabe), is, of course, the most obvious sound echo of all. We expect it most often at the end of verses, but internal rhyme ("The *jaws* that bite, the *claws* that catch!") is not uncommon.

In addition to echoing each other in a way that unites the poem, the sounds of vowels and consonants combine in ways that are sweet (euphonious) or harsh (cacophonous) to our ears. Euphony and cacophony exist in the ear of the listener; they are subjective. It is hard to say how much they depend on meaning rather than pure sound: if *murmur* sounds pleasant and *murder* sounds harsh, the difference must depend more on definition than phonetics. Nonetheless, a Bandersnatch sounds like an ugly creature, even if we have never seen one. It seems that certain consonants and clusters of consonants (*ck, g, gr, k, scr, sk, st, str, tch*) sound harsh, especially when they are crowded together without the leavening of long, open vowels. Open vowels and such liquid consonants as *m, n, l,* and *r* tend to be more pleasing. When John Milton wants the corrupt clergymen of "Lycidas" to sound cacophonous, he says that their songs "Grate on their scrannel pipes of wretched straw." When Robert Herrick wants to make his Julia's voice sound euphonious, he says that it is capable of "Melting melodious notes to lutes of amber."

Euphony and cacophony may be indirectly related to onomatopoeia, the use of words that imitate sounds or that match the sound with the sense. *Snap* and *scratch,* for instance, seem to originate in the imitation of abrupt, harsh sounds. *Snatch,* as in "Bandersnatch," is not itself onomatopoeic, but its final syllable is made up of sounds that recollect some of the grating noises of the world. In the final lines of Alfred, Lord Tennyson's *"Come Down O Maid"* we get onomatopoeia linked with euphony: "the moaning of doves," and the "murmuring of innumerable bees."

The aspect of a poem's sound most laboriously studied in literature classes is its rhythm. What makes the study so laborious and frustrating is that the rhythm can be very complex, and the system we use to analyze it is complicated without being complete. Linguists can identify at least half a dozen factors that determine the rhythm of ordinary prose. When we add to these factors the special demands of the poetic line, we have a very complex situation, indeed. To simplify the situation, we limit our attention to the regular beat of syllables per line or to accents (stresses*) per line, or both.

Our two stanzas from "Jabberwocky" contain a fairly fixed number of syllables: 8,8,8,6 in the first stanza, 8,8,8,7 in the second. (The third and fourth stanzas, by the way, are 8,8,9,6 and 8,8,8,6: that the slight irregularities are not *heard* as errors indicates that the fingers and the ear experience rhythm differently.) Which of these syllables are stressed? Since stress is related to (not quite synonymous with) volume, we could approach this question by reading the poem into a tape recorder, then watching the needle on the volume indicator as we play it back.

----

* *Stress* sometimes refers to the emphasis created by the sense of the sentence; *accent* sometimes refers to the emphasis inherent in the pronunciation of a word (indicated in dictionaries). Here *accent* and *stress* will be used interchangeably since in practice they become intertwined.

Here is my reading of the first stanza, with volume levels noted above each syllable:

```
 25   30 10  15  10  25 20 25
'Twas bril lig, and the slith y toves
   15   60   25   40  20 25 25   50
   Did gyre and gim ble in the wabe:
45  50 20  20   15 60 15  20
All mim sy were the bo ro goves,
    20  20   60    50  35   40
    And the mome raths out grabe.
```

Others would undoubtedly read the poem with a different stress, depending partly on their notions of the "meaning" of some words. I read *brillig* as a relatively insignificant word, equal to *morning*. If I read it as a more important word like *ghastly* or *horrid*, it would get more stress.

The traditional method of scansion is to divide the line into feet, a process that can be made simpler by some toe-tapping: the foot is presumably so named because if we were to dance or march to the rhythm of the verse, our foot would strike the ground one time for each of these units. We would expect our foot to hit on a stressed syllable, of course, and some theorists argue therefore that every foot must contain a stress. Traditionally we mark the more heavily stressed syllables in each foot with an accent mark (/) and less stressed with a droop. (⌣).

```
     /      /   ⌣   /  ⌣  /   ⌣  /
'Twas bril/lig, and/the slith/y toves
   ⌣    /   ⌣   /  ⌣  /  ⌣  /
   Did gyre/and gim/ble in/the wabe:
  /   /   ⌣   ⌣   ⌣  /   ⌣  /
All mim/sy were/the bo/rogoves,
```

Notice that the traditional method corresponds much more closely to our actual reading in line 2 than in any other. Traditional scansion is a very imperfect way of recording the actual rhythm of the line as we read it; it usually records a compromise between actual rhythm and a more regular rhythm toward which the line tends. The fourth line is so irregular that it makes traditional scansion difficult. We might try

```
    ⌣    ⌣   /    /   ⌣   /
    And the/mome/raths/outgrabe.
```

which corresponds well to what we hear, or

```
    ⌣    ⌣   /    /   ⌣   /
    And the/mome raths/outgrabe.
```

which fits the conventions more neatly. At this point, the rules of scansion become as cumbersome as the instructions on a tax form. We all grow up with an instinct for the rhythms of the language; if the sheet music becomes too confusing to us, we can lay it aside and play by ear.

Each foot available in the traditional method has a name: iamb (⌣/), trochee (/⌣), anapest (⌣⌣/), dactyl (/⌣⌣), spondee (//), pyrrhic (⌣⌣). The stanza above could therefore be described as

```
    spondee/iamb/iamb/iamb
     iamb/iamb/iamb/iamb
    spondee/pyrrhic/iamb/iamb
     pyrrhic/spondee/iamb
```

Or, scanned by other readers, it might be

<table>
<tr><td>iamb/iamb/iamb/iamb
iamb/iamb/iamb/iamb
iamb/iamb/iamb/iamb
pyrrhic/trochee/spondee</td><td>OR</td><td>iamb/pyrrhic/iamb/iamb
iamb/iamb/pyrrhic/iamb
iamb/pyrrhic/iamb/iamb
pyrrhic/spondee/iamb</td></tr>
</table>

Notice that the last reading reduces the number of stresses in the lines and makes them swing along like a chant (see *Dipodic Meter*). The whole poem could be described as one in which each stanza consists of three lines of iambic tetrameter (*tetra* is Greek for four) followed by one of iambic trimeter. Some lines, of course, vary from this pattern, but the pattern itself is quite clear. Regularly metered poetic lines can thus be described by a binomial system where the first word designates the predominant foot (iambic, trochaic, anapestic, dactylic) and the second gives the number of feet, using Greek prefixes: monometer, dimeter, trimeter, tetrameter, pentameter, hexameter, heptameter. See related entries on *Meter, Poetic Forms, Rhyme* and *Syncopation*.

Stream of consciousness: a technique in which the writer assumes the point of view of a character so completely that every passing thought or impression of the character is recorded.

Substitution: the replacement of one metrical foot (an iamb, for example) by another (a trochee, for example). This variation in stress is produced when the natural speech rhythm of a verse passage conflicts with the rhythm created by the underlying meter. The first two lines of William Wordsworth's sonnet "*Composed Upon Westminster Bridge*" illustrate such a substitution.

Earth hath/not anything/to show/more fair:
Dull would/he be/of soul/that could/pass by

The prose sense of the passage here demands that stress be placed on *Earth* and *Dull* even though a mechanically iambic reading of the lines would leave them unstressed. One effect of such a substitution is to vary the rhythm and avoid monotony. Another effect is to highlight the rhetorical emphasis that caused the substitution. The attentive reader conscious of the underlying iambic rhythm registers the displaced stress with special force and so thinks harder about Wordsworth's meaning and feeling. The stress on *Earth* then seems so strong as to suggest an antithesis (*Earth* has nothing to show more fair; *heaven* might). The special stress on *Dull* seems to add to its force (*very* dull). See *Sound of Poetry*.

Surrealism: see *Literary Movements*.

Symbolism: see *Literary Movements*.

Synecdoche: see *Figures of Speech*.

Tercet: see *Poetic Forms*.

Theater of the Absurd: a term applied to the works of several dramatists of the 1950s who expounded the absurdity of both humanity and the universe. Influenced by the farcical comedy of the Renaissance, by Surrealism, and by the philosophy of French writer Albert Camus, dramatists such as Harold Pinter and Samuel Beckett presented human beings as ridiculous creatures attempting to make sense of an irrational world. To emphasize their existential beliefs, the dramatists created plays that defy many of the conventions that give drama its apparent order, so that both their content and their form reflect a loss of direction and purpose.

Theme: the central idea of a literary work. ·Generally we think of this theme as a general statement about the human condition expressable in a sentence. One might state the theme of Edwin Arlington Robinson's *"Richard Cory"* as "Even the most apparently fortunate person may be on the brink of despair." Too often, naive readers assume that every literary work exists solely for the purpose of illustrating a theme. In fact, good literary works often succeed with themes so faint or ambiguous that readers cannot agree on what they are, and many writers say that the theme cannot be completely stated except as it is embodied in the work. Nonetheless, most literary works derive partly from the writer's desire to deal with general truths, and the attempt to state the theme (even when it is impossible to do so definitively) can help us see what large issues lie beneath the surface of the poem, play, or story. See *Tone.*

TONE

Literature textbooks usually define tone as the author's implied attitude toward the audience and the subject. This literary definition has its roots in a more general meaning of the word, the meaning that a mother has in mind when she says to her daughter, "Don't take that tone with me, young lady!" The tone of a statement cannot be settled by *what* was said; the question is, *in what spirit* were the words spoken?

The tone of a remark made in conversation is relatively easy to establish because we can hear the speaker's inflections and see her gestures and facial expressions. The tone of a remark made by a character in a play or story will very often be clarified by the context or by the author's comment. Henrik Ibsen's *"Hedda Gabler,"* for example, is sprinkled with stage directions to help establish the spirit in which the characters speak:

> *Hedda:* (Concealing a scornful smile): So, my darling little Thea, you've
>   actually reformed him.

Substitute another stage direction ("vehemently but in a low voice"), and the tone is completely changed.

The author's tone is much more difficult to detect than a character's. Even when we know that Hedda's attitude toward Thea is scornful, how can we know what Ibsen's attitude toward Hedda is? By what general rules can we determine whether the author is being sympathetic or unsympathetic, approving or disapproving, humorous or serious?

Sometimes the author establishes a tone by speaking directly to the audience. "This is a story, I suppose, about a failure in intelligence," Doris Lessing writes at the beginning of *"To Room Nineteen"* and so establishes the tone of cold disapproval that characterizes the opening pages of the story. When the author chooses not to address the audience directly, he or she may delegate to one of the characters the role of making judgments that establish the tone. In *"Medea,"* for instance, Jason makes a long and clever speech justifying his actions in abandoning his wife so that he may marry the king's daughter. So effective is the speech that it might sway the audience, might give the impression that Euripides' sympathies are with Jason and that he approves of his actions. The chorus, however, immediately speaks:

> *Chorus:* Jason, though you have made this speech of yours look well,
> Still, I think, even though others do not agree,
> You have betrayed your wife and are acting badly.

The judgment of the chorus leaves little doubt about Euripides' tone of disapproval. The narrator in a story like José Donoso's *"Paseo"* functions almost as a chorus. We should be careful, though, not to assume that the chorus-figure in a story reflects the attitudes of the writer precisely. Toni Cade Bambara begins *"The Lesson"* with a sentence that separates her somewhat from the narrator of the story: "Back in the days when everyone was old and stupid or young and foolish and me and Sugar was the only ones just right, this lady . . . " We see immediately that hiding behind the point of view of the young narrator will be the mature perspective of a grown woman: the tone will be humorous, the author's attitude toward her protagonist will be a combination of admiration and condescension.

When the writer does not establish the tone by direct comment and does not establish a character clearly intended to register his or her values, we can only apprehend the tone by looking very carefully at the style and substance of what is said. Alfred, Lord Tennyson's *"Ulysses,"* for example, establishes its highly serious tone by **diction** that is uniformly elevated and by the use of blank verse, a form long used for contemplative and heroic poems. Robert Frost's *"Departmental,"* on the other hand, establishes its humorous tone partly by a combination of high and low diction and partly by a number of outrageous rhymes (any/antennae; Formic McCormic; Jerry/Janizary; atwiddle/middle). See also *Irony.*

TRAGEDY

The first tragedies were religious dramas performed before the citizens of ancient Greek city-states, assembled to consider the largest questions of the human struggle with destiny. The most notable of the Greek tragedies were performed in Athens in the fifth century B.C. and reflected an attitude that helped define Greek culture and gave the Athenian citizen an elevated view of human dignity. Aristotle, defining tragedy about 350 B.C., emphasized its highly serious tone and its plot, which carries a person of extraordinary virtue from a state of happiness to a state of misery. This downfall is caused by what Aristotle calls *hamartia*, an error or frailty— very often the error of pride. Error leads the hero to *anagnorsis* (recognition of the dark truth of his or her life) and *peripeteia* (reversal of good fortune). Though this is hardly the outline of a cheerful plot, Aristotle found the effect of tragedy to be finally uplifting. The audience gains a renewed sense of human dignity by the nobility with which the protagonist faces the truth, and experiences a feeling of *catharsis* (purging of the emotions of fear and pity that the play creates).

Exactly what Aristotle meant by *catharsis* is hard to say, but the purgation may come from the shape of the play. The audience begins by seeing the precarious order of the individual and community life shattered by dangerous emotions and injustice. In the end, the audience sees order restored: the suffering of the protagonist has led to new knowledge that helps create this new order.

Aristotle's description of tragedy applies most clearly to the plays of Sophocles, who was confident about the justice of the gods and the possibility of redemptive knowledge leading to a new order. Euripides and most other tragedians, ancient and modern, have been less confident. A useful supplement to Aristotle's definition—useful in examining both ancient and modern drama—is Friedrich Hegel's notion that tragedy comes from the conflict of two almost equally powerful principles of life. Certainly no single definition will adequately cover all the works that have been called tragic. Shakespeare's tragedies, for instance, mix scenes of high seriousness (like *"Hamlet,"* Act 3, scene 3, where the prince contemplates killing Claudius) with scenes of comic relief (like *"Hamlet,"* Act 5, scene 1, where the prince trades wisecracks with the gravediggers). Shakespearian tragedy also places less emphasis than classical tragedy on unity of plot (certainly it ignores the classical "unities" that required the play to represent a single day, a single setting, and a single chain of causes and effects). It places more emphasis, however, on the realistic representation of the central characters.

Modern tragedies sometimes (as in Arthur Miller's *"Death of a Salesman"*) preserve the unity of plot, the high seriousness, the *anagnorsis* (discovery), *peripeteia* (reversal), and *catharsis* (purging) of Greek tragedy. In a democratic society, however, as Miller points out in "Tragedy and the Common Man," the protagonist will naturally be born without royal status, and his or her fall will produce domestic tragedy without the political upheaval we see in Greek or Shakespearian tragedy. Many other modern plays, like Anton Chekhov's *"The Three Sisters,"* blend a note of tragedy into compositions that defy the neat traditional distinction between tragedy and comedy. See also *Tragicomedy* and *Melodrama*.

Tragicomedy: a term which is, in its narrow sense, used to characterize a play that seems for most of its length to be a **tragedy**, but that by a sudden reversal of fortune achieves the happy ending appropriate to **comedy**. Shakespeare's *"Measure for Measure"* would fit this narrow definition very well if the audience were not informed until the final act that the Duke is in Vienna, disguised as a Friar, ready to save the day. Were this information withheld, the audience would have reason to fear that Angelo might actually have his way with Isabella and that Claudio might actually be executed; this fear would be suddenly lifted by the apparently miraculous appearance of the Duke. Clearly this sort of tragicomedy is related to **melodrama.** In a broader sense, tragicomedy is applied to plays which balance tragic and comic elements so closely that neither clearly predominates. In this sense, *"Measure for Measure,"* *"The Three Sisters,"* and *"Painting Churches"* might all be classed tragicomedies.

Understatement: see *Figures of Speech*.

Villanelle: see *Poetic Forms*.

Voice: see *Persona*.

Well-made Play: a type of play, popular in France during the nineteenth century, with a prescribed orderly structure. The plot had to make use of a secret, revealed at the climax to produce a reversal and a favorable ending. The suspense, then, was commonly created by a misplaced document, a mistaken identity, or precise, timely entrances and exits. Finally, a battle of wits had to lead the protagonist to success so that a neat, logical resolution could end the play. Sometimes these characteristics were incorporated into each act as well as into the overall play. Henrik Ibsen directed several well-made plays before he began writing his own drama. His plays contain elements of the formula, but do not adhere to it slavishly. Today the term refers to the neatly-constructed plays which loosely carry out the tradition.

Wit: a quality that has been defined very differently in different periods of literary history, largely because most writers want to claim they have it. In the early seventeenth century, poets like John Donne cultivated a species of "Metaphysical" wit that involved unlikely and even far-fetched comparisons. Thus, in *"The Good-Morrow"* a lover's eyes are compared to the earth's hemispheres. The comparison ingeniously brings together two otherwise unrelated ideas: that the curve of the eyes echoes the curve of the earth, and that a person looking into the eyes of his lover is seeing everything that counts in the world. If we were to define wit narrowly, we would probably say that it is the writer's ability to bring together such ideas and to have the comparison both surprise us and please us by its appropriateness.

Later in the seventeenth and throughout the eighteenth century, poets like Alexander Pope rejected the Metaphysical conception of wit because they believed it violently joined together ideas and images that were separate in nature. They attempted to replace the older concept with something more consistent with the neoclassical ideal of precise observation of men and manners:

> True wit is nature to advantage dress'd,
> What oft was thought, but ne'er so well express'd.
> (Pope, "Essay on Criticism")

The modern conception of wit includes elements of both the Metaphysical and the neoclassical, and almost always involves humor as well. Dorothy Parker was one of the great wits of the twentieth century because she combined verbal dexterity, a quick sense of humor, and an intelligent skepticism that undercuts sentiment with withering irony. W. H. Auden, Edna St. Vincent Millay, Robert Frost, and Richard Wilbur are among the wittier poets of the twentieth century. Samuel Beckett, Harold Pinter, and Tom Stoppard are notable for the wit of their plays, and Jorge Luis Borges, Gabriel García Márquez, and Flannery O'Connor for the wit of their stories.

Writing About Literature

A textbook's general principles on writing about literature are not likely to help you much when you sit down to write a paper of your own. It is as hard to learn to write from general instructions as it is to learn to draw a still life or shoot a hook shot from general instructions. On the other hand, a series of example essays thrown together without guiding principles can be as useless as a drawer full of odd socks. The plan of this chapter is, therefore, to alternate between general observations ("the hook shot has five parts") and demonstration ("now watch me do it").

A word of warning about this method is in order before we proceed. The hook shot has one clear and undisputable goal, and its method of execution varies only slightly from one competent basketball player to another. The essay about literature may have a number of goals: some teachers may value originality more than careful research, others vice-versa; some may insist that the work be discussed without direct reference to your reaction as a reader, others may prefer that your personal reactions be taken into consideration. And the writing methods of one individual will naturally vary from those of another. The advice given in this chapter should, therefore, be read cautiously, as a basis for further discussion between yourself and your teacher.

In the course of this chapter you will be looking at two drafts and two completed essays based on the following prose-poem by Charles Baudelaire.

Knock Down the Poor!

I had provided myself with the popular books of the day (this was sixteen or seventeen years ago), and for two weeks I had never left my room. I am speaking now of those books that treat of the art of making nations happy, wise and rich in twenty-four hours. I had therefore digested—swallowed, I should say—all the lucubrations of all the authorities on the happiness of society—those who advise the poor to become slaves, and those who persuade them that they are all dethroned kings. So it is not astonishing if I was in a state of mind bordering on stupidity or madness. Only it seemed to me that deep in my mind, I was conscious of an obscure germ of an idea, superior to all the old wives' formulas whose dictionary I had just been perusing. But it was only the idea of an idea, something infinitely vague. And I went out with a great thirst, for a passionate taste for bad books engenders a proportionate desire for the open air and for refreshments.

As I was about to enter a tavern, a beggar held out his hat to me, and gave me one of those unforgettable glances which might overturn thrones if spirit could move matter, and if the eyes of a mesmerist could ripen grapes. At the same time I heard a voice whispering in my ear, a voice I recognized: it was that of a good Angel, or of a good Demon, who is always following me about. Since Socrates had his good Demon, why should I not have my good Angel, and why should I not have the honour, like Socrates, of obtaining my certificate of folly, signed by the subtle Lelut and by the sage Baillarger? There is this difference between Socrates' Demon and mine: his did not appear except to defend, warn or hinder him, whereas mine deigns to counsel, suggest, or persuade. Poor Socrates had only a prohibitive Demon; mine is a great master of affirmations, mine is a Demon of action, a Demon of combat. And his voice was now whispering to me: "He alone is the equal of another who proves it, and he alone is worthy of liberty who knows how to obtain it."

Immediately, I sprang at the beggar. With a single blow of my fist, I closed one of his eyes, which became, in a second, as big as a ball. In breaking two of his teeth I split a nail; but being of a delicate constitution from birth, and not used to boxing, I didn't feel strong enough to knock the old man senseless; so I seized the collar of his coat with one hand, grasped his throat with the other, and began vigorously to beat his head against a wall. I must confess that I had first glanced around carefully, and had made certain that in this lonely suburb I should find myself, for a short while, at least, out of immediate danger from the police.

Next, having knocked down this feeble man of sixty with a kick in the back sufficiently vicious to have broken his shoulder blades, I picked up a big branch of a tree which lay on the ground, and beat him with the persistent energy of a cook pounding a tough steak.

All of a sudden—O miracle! O happiness of the philosopher proving the excellence of his theory!—I saw this ancient carcass turn, stand up with an energy I should never have suspected in a machine so badly out of order, and with a glance of hatred which seemed to me of good omen, the decrepit ruffian hurled himself upon me, blackened both my eyes, broke four of my teeth, and with the same tree-branch, beat me to a pulp. Thus by an energetic treatment, I had restored to him his pride and his life.

Then I motioned to him to make him understand that I considered the discussion ended, and getting up, I said to him, with all the satisfaction of a Sophist of the Porch: "Sir, you are my equal! Will you do me the honour of sharing my purse, and will you remember, if you are really philanthropic, that you must apply to all the members of your profession, when they seek alms from you, the theory it has been my misfortune to practice on your back?"

He swore to me that he had understood my theory, and that he would carry out my advice.

STEP 1: FIND A GOOD PROBLEM

Most of us read a literary work, like it or dislike it, and have no particular desire to complicate either our like or dislike by too much analysis. This is a valid response. Many things that are significant about a work of art require no analysis: they are self-evident to every competent reader. If we have read *"Twelfth Night"* no one needs to tell us that a great deal of the pleasure of the play comes from the use of disguises. If we have read *"Sister Imelda,"* no one needs to tell us that the bittersweetness of growing up is a central theme in the story. Important as these self-evident truths might be, they are not likely to be bases for good essays. A student writing on the thesis " 'Knock Down the Poor!' describes an action most people find offensive" might seem to be on safe ground. In fact, he or she is in great peril of spending several boring hours producing a paper that will bore the teacher. An essay about literature needs to demonstrate something about the work that *needs* demonstration.

A good way to find a topic to write about is to concentrate on what you do not understand about a work rather than what you do understand. Find a difficulty or ambiguity you could not resolve on the basis of your first reading. Sometimes your teacher will assign topics that point toward such a problem ("What is the tone in Baudelaire's 'Knock Down the Poor!'?"), but it is up to you to discover why this problem *is* problematic and interesting: to put your lack of understanding to good use. Discussion inside class or out can be a great help: sometimes an hour spent talking with a friend about a literary work will uncover a number of interesting problems. Usually, though, the serious search for a problem will lead us to another sort of conversation, one we have with ourselves on paper.

It is an unhappy fact that for most writers every finished page is preceded by other pages that go into the wastebasket or the desk drawer. The mind is a leaky bucket, and if we try to sort out a paper without committing anything to writing, our thoughts trickle out about as fast as they trickle in, leaving us very nearly where we started. Some writers solve this problem by doing several drafts, each written *as if* it were the last, each collecting thoughts that can be carefully scrutinized because they have been gotten out of the leaky bucket and onto the page. Others write their early drafts very informally, sometimes as journal entries or "free writings" meant for their eyes only. Such private jottings may be written without much attention to form or coherence. Here are mine on "Knock Down the Poor!"

Example 1: Freewriting to Discover a Problem

What interests me most about this story is the tone. In some ways it seems like Baudelaire intends just to shock us—sort of a man-bites-dog story to get our attention. The idea that he can seriously boast about beating a beggar is hardly credible, unless what he is boasting about is his ability to boast about it—a sort of intellectual or moral one-upsmanship. This would be consistent with the talk in the first paragraph about the "popular books" about poverty. He may be simply showing that he is above fashion.

The wording here is far less formal, less correct, than it will be in the final paper.

But is this all, and is it serious? Sometimes Baudelaire is clearly just being funny. The bit about the passion for reading bad books making him thirsty,

A sentence fragment—unacceptable in a final paper, natural here.

for instance. I don't think this a good joke, but I think I can see that Baudelaire does, or (since the whole tone is so murky), that his protagonist is making a joke that he (the protagonist) thinks is funny, though Baudelaire may find it feeble. How closely does Baudelaire identify with the protagonist? How can we tell?

Speculation about the author's intent must be more cautious in a critical paper. In a free-writing, they are often useful.

Better humor, I think, when Baudelaire/protagonist admits that he looks around for the police before beating the beggar, or when he admits that he is too feeble to do a good job of beating him. And, of course, the whole thing is a sort of shaggy-dog story. We can't believe that such a thing would happen.

Another fragment.

Nonetheless, I think there is something serious here, and beneath all its outrageousness, the point is worth making. Sticking out at us as moral is the good Angel's statement that "He alone is the equal of another who can prove it, and he alone is worthy of liberty who knows how to obtain it." Maybe. Actually, the statement stands just to one side of what the story says to me. Dorothy H. once told me (accusing, in a friendly way) that when I went out of my way to spare people's feelings, I was actually being condescending and avoiding dealing with them as equals and friends. Her view was that real friends could give it to each other with both barrels, criticism, affection, anger, feeling always the implied compliment of not holding back. Baudelaire may be serious about applying his story to the problem of the poor, but I feel it moving out to other things.

An entirely personal and idiosyncratic reaction. Useful here, forbidden in final paper.

Lots of things I don't know about in this story. Socrates' Demon. Is Baulelaire using Demon and Angel interchangeably. I think the Greek word is probably Daemon, and means something neutral like spirit. Where, if anywhere, was this story published in B's lifetime? Who are Lelut and Baillarger? Psychologists?

The question with the question mark carelessly omitted will turn out to be very important.

As a finished paper, this effort would rate a flat "F." It is ungrammatical, incoherent, and given to private observations that have little to do with the work. But in the half-hour I spent writing it, I found the germs of the essays that will follow.

STEP 2: WRITE A DRAFT THAT HAS THE FORM AND SUBSTANCE OF A FINAL PRODUCT

Just what the proper "form and substance" will be depends on your teacher's expectations, some of which will be made explicit by the assignment. Many of these expectations, however, may be so obvious to your teacher that he or she will not mention them explicitly. They are the usually unstated conventions of writing about literature.

Bear in mind when you sit down to write a serious draft that your teacher will eventually read the final product by the standards of a well-established profession. Because your teacher knows you as an individual, he or she might *personally* be very interested in every aspect of your response to Baudelaire's story, including your feelings about Baudelaire's condemnation of the middle class, your thoughts on violence and human equality, and even personal anecdotes the story brings to mind. In fact, your teacher may enjoy your free-form journal entries on a story more than your more formal critical writing. But as a *professional* teaching a literature class, he or she must evaluate you on your ability to respond to the work *as literature* rather than as a springboard for non-literary thoughts.

The teacher, therefore, reads your essay as a representative of a larger professional audience that knows nothing about you personally and that is interested in your essay only insofar as it casts light on the work discussed. The members of this professional audience are assumed to have these characteristics:

- They are careful readers familiar with the work; therefore, they will not be interested in mere summary. ("Charles Baudelaire's 'Knock Down the Poor!' is the story of a man who spends two weeks alone in his room reading books that teach the poor how to be happy with their role in life. After he has read these books, he goes out for fresh air and a drink. On his way into a bar, he sees a beggar. . . . ")

- They are skeptical, and they will not accept your generalizations without adequate evidence.

- They expect a writer to be reasonably well-informed. This does not mean that you have to do exhaustive research before you can hazard an opinion. It does mean, however, that you would do well to look at a few sources before you undertake an essay, even though the assignment does not call for research. In preparing to write my own draft, I did what research I could within the confines of *The Riverside Anthology*. The short biography of Baudelaire on page 2118 mentioned that his "dandyism" was "partly outrageous display, partly strict aesthetic discipline." The passage from his journal on page 861 showed how much "debasement of the human heart" he found in his bourgeois fellow-citizens. His poems collected on pages 854–861 gave me a sense of the tone of his other writings.

- They demand objectivity. Most professionals in literature are suspicious of discussions that place too much emphasis on the emotions a work inspires rather than the work itself ("The reader's heart is touched when . . ."). They are equally suspicious of analyses that assume too much insight into the intentions of the author ("What Baudelaire is trying to do here is . . ."). The creature on the laboratory bench, so to speak, is the literary work, not the heart of the reader or the mind of the author.

- They expect an essay that follows certain rules of behavior. The action in a literary work should be reported in present tense ("The protagonist *beats* the beggar"). Quotations from the story, poem, or play should be worked into the essay without being intrusive or overlong. Contractions and colloquialisms should be avoided. Standard terms of literary analysis ("theme," "tone") should be used where they are appropriate. The writer should refer to himself or herself ("I think," "my own feeling") sparingly, if at all.

Frankly, this is not an audience most of us feel comfortable writing for, and one of the problems of writing an effective essay about literature is to avoid losing heart when we face it. One way to keep your courage and your direction is to think of yourself as part of the audience and try to keep yourself interested.

Example 2: A First Draft on "Knock Down the Poor!"

The Theme of "Knock Down the Poor!"

The theme of Charles Baudelaire's "Knock Down the Poor!" seems on first reading to be precisely what the protagonist's demon announces it to be mid-way through the prose poem: "He alone is the equal of another who proves it, and he alone is worthy of liberty who knows how to obtain it." Careful readers, however, will find reason to doubt that the theme can be so easily located or neatly expressed.

"Knock Down the Poor!," like many of Baude-laire's other poems, involves a good deal of theatrical-ity. Offended by what he perceives to be the hypocrisies of bourgeois life, Baudelaire puts himself in a pose that will offend bourgeois sensibilities. The prose poem begins with an irritant, the "popular books" that middle-class Frenchmen used to salve their consciences. Disgust with books "that advise the poor to become willing slaves" or that encourage them to live in a fantasy world is really at the heart of the story. The first-person protagonist—Baudelaire's pose in this work—outraged by this hypocrisy, dramatizes the real attitude of the bourgeois toward the poor when he beats the old beggar mercilessly in order to teach him self-reliance (after carefully checking to make sure that the police were out of sight). The theme of the story, then, is not really that the poor must earn equality and liberty, but rather that the middle-class insistence that they do so is really an excuse for the worst sort of inhumanity. The demon is a demon and what he says is naturally the opposite of the truth.

We cannot rest comfortably here, however, because the story's plot turns at the end in a direction inconsistent with the hypothesis that the protagonist is mimicking the behavior of the middle class: the bourgeois people Baudelaire so despises would hardly divide their wealth evenly with the poor, and hardly

It is standard practice to mention the name of the author and work early in the essay.

A thesis of sorts, but see comments below.

The use of short quotations from the poem keeps the essay "in contact" with it, and so adds credibility to the argument. By integrating these quotations into my own sentences, I avoid an awkward interruption of the essay. If the poem were longer, I would need to give page or line numbers.

The end (at last) of a bad sentence.

Yet another sentence that is far too convoluted.

be happy to have the poor drub them more soundly than they have been drubbed. At this point, the protagonist appears to be behaving like a saint, taking very seriously the equality of rich and poor, young and old. Now it seems that the demon is a good angel after all, since his advice leads to the happy conclusion.

It is unclear who "they" are.

There are perhaps two ways out of the quandary created by the ambiguity of the story. One is to say that we should apply the demon's words equally to the protagonist and to the beggar. The protagonist (the typical bourgeois) must prove that he is equal to the beggar by treating him as an equal, show that he is worthy of liberty by breaking away from the conventional but unacceptable attitudes of society. The other way is to say that any action that strips away the layers of hypocrisy, even an act of frank violence and brutality, will get us closer to the understanding that all of us are brothers.

The conclusion proposes a solution to the problem, as it should; but see comments below.

STEP 3: EVALUATE THE FIRST DRAFT HONESTLY

When we try to evaluate our own writing, both pride and humility stand in the way. Sometimes we convince ourselves that a bad passage is good; sometimes we raise niggling objections to something that any objective observer would find perfectly acceptable. Nothing is more helpful at this point than friends willing to give frank opinions, and most successful writers learn to cherish such friends. The essayist E. B. White used to call his wife, the editor Katharine Sergeant White, his "B.F. and M.S.C." Anyone familiar with marriage and writing will catch his meaning: Best Friend and Most Severe Critic.

Not everyone has the advantage of being married to a brilliant editor, of course, and even the comments of the best editor must be held at arm's length. The essay is ours: only we know its intentions, only we will be responsible for its final form. Eventually, with or without the help of friends, we must arrive at our own evaluation of the essay's strengths and weaknesses. Writing this evaluation out as a "revision agenda" sometimes increases objectivity and helps the memory. Like a free-writing, a revision agenda need not conform to the standard rules of usage.

Example 3: A Revision Agenda

STRENGTHS OF THE FIRST DRAFT

1. Saying that the theme is stated by the demon, but that we don't know how to *understand* the demon, is good. I had missed the ambiguity of the demon's statement entirely when I first read the poem, and I think many other readers must miss it.

2. I like the turn the paper takes in the third paragraph. The poem forces us to do a double-take when the protagonist behaves so well at the end, and it is a pleasure to recreate that double-take by "solving" the problem of theme, then saying, "We cannot rest comfortably here . . . ." I like the way the word "saint" works here, too, since the shock of calling this mugger a saint is consistent with the shock of the story.

3. The stuff in the second paragraph about self-dramatization and offending the bourgeoisie is pretty useful because it helps solve the problem of tone. If B. is posing, and even clowning, he is doing so with a serious intent. We don't have to choose between a serious reading and a comic reading. The tone is both serious and comic.

4. I *feel* after completing this draft that I understand the poem better than I did before I began to write. I *think* that some other readers would understand the poem better if they read this paper.

WEAKNESSES

1. The thesis and title are both vague and weak, even deceptive. It doesn't tell the reader much to say that the "careful reader" will be skeptical about an easy interpretation. "Careful readers" are always skeptical about this. What direction should their skepticism take? I need to be more up front.

2. The organization of the paper is not clear. If I am saying that there are two ways to read the story, each shedding light on the theme, then I should have a neat self-contained discussion of each one. The theatricality discussion, much as I like it, muddies the water.

3. The conclusion is not crisp. I say, in effect, "Look, the theme *is* just what the demon says, but we've got to *apply* it right." Then I turn right around and say that, if you prefer, the theme is no such thing, that the theme has something (rather vague) to do with violence as an antidote to hypocrisy. Stand firm, Hunt, stop moving your feet.

4. I confuse things unnecessarily by talking about whether the demon is lying or telling the truth. This is a red herring. Eventually, I will have to say that the demon is telling the truth. The real question is whether it is a demonic truth or an angelic truth.

5. Several of the sentences are murky and overlong, just the sort of pseudo-academic prose I love to hate.

STEP 4: REWRITE THE PAPER

The standard advice at this point is to *revise* the paper, but too often we think of revision as a conservative process that leaves the essay essentially intact. Relatively few first drafts deserve such gentle treatment. Most need to be dismantled and rebuilt, sometimes more than once. Of the twenty sentences in the rewritten paper below only four are taken essentially unchanged from the rough draft.

Example 4: A Rewritten Paper

Ambiguity in the Theme of Baudelaire's "Knock Down the Poor!"

The "good Angel, or good Demon" in Charles Baudelaire's "Knock Down the Poor!" seems to announce the theme of the prose poem at its midpoint: "He alone is the equal of another who proves it, and he alone is worthy of liberty who knows how to obtain it." The poem's tone is generally hard to establish, however; it hovers between humor and serious social criticism. With the general tone so uncertain, the reader naturally has difficulty deciding how to interpret a statement that may come either from hell or from heaven. One way to work out the riddle and find the theme is to read the poem first on the assumption that the demon is tempting the protagonist to sin, then on the assumption that he is an angel instructing him in virtue.

The hypothesis that the demon is a tempter has a good deal of evidence on its side. Offended by what he perceives to be the hypocrisies of bourgeois life, Baudelaire often holds a distorting mirror up to his readers, one that exaggerates our faults to the same degree that most of us are inclined to exaggerate our virtues. "Knock Down the Poor!" begins with satiric comments on the "popular books" that deceive the poor and salve the consciences of the middle class. After the protagonist has "swallowed down" the notions contained in these books, he finds "the obscure germ of an idea" grander than the "old wives' formulas" these books contain. The idea becomes concrete when he beats the old beggar mercilessly in order to teach him self-reliance. He is acting out in an exaggerated way the unspoken attitude of the middle class: "Let's knock down the poor if they can't take care of themselves, and if there are no police watching." The theme of the story, then, is not that the poor must rise to the equality and liberty of the middle class, since the inhumanity of middle-class people puts them far below the level of beggars. The demon <u>is</u> a demon, speaking the most degraded thoughts of the ungenerous bourgeoisie.

We cannot rest comfortably here, however, because the story's plot turns at the end in a direction inconsistent with the hypothesis that the protagonist and his demon are mimicking the attitudes of the middle class. The people Baudelaire so despises would never divide their wealth with beggars, and never be happy to have the poor drub them more soundly than

Marginal annotations:

A statement that the theme *seems* perfectly clear.

A statement of the problem.

A thesis that the problem can be solved by reading the poem two ways.

Straightforward step to first way of reading poem. Clear topic sentence for the paragraph.

Generalization about Baudelaire's technique, followed by evidence of that technique at work in poem.

Analysis closely tied to text of poem by quotations and echoes of Baudelaire's wording.

Statement of what the theme is *not*.

Sentence to round off investigation of first hypothesis.

Move to second hypothesis.

Generalization and evidence.

they have drubbed the poor. At this point, the protagonist is behaving like a saint, taking very seriously the equality of rich and poor, young and old. Now it seems that the demon is a good angel after all, since his advice leads to saintly behavior and a happy conclusion.

Again, a rounding off.

The best way to resolve the ambiguity of the story is probably to assume that, like many oracular statements, the demon's statement is true in an unexpected way. His words apply to the protagonist at least as much as to the beggar. The protagonist (representing the bourgeoisie) must prove that he is equal to the beggar by treating him as an equal, show that he is worthy of liberty by breaking away from conventional and hypocritical attitudes toward the poor. The poem's theme <u>is</u> that equality and liberty must be earned by merit, but the bourgeoisie are the ones who most need to earn them.

Statement of result of investigation.

Clear statement of what the theme really is.

STEP 5: EVALUATE THE REWRITTEN ESSAY OBJECTIVELY

Essays often seem to be finished on the second draft because we want to be rid of them and because we have invested so much intellectual energy in them that we have an irrational faith in their quality. Once again, though, we should evaluate the essay objectively before we let it go. There is a fair chance that the essay would improve significantly if taken through another draft or two. Even if we decide not to change it, the re-evaluation may give us ideas worth pursuing.

Example 5: Evaluation of the Second Draft

STRENGTHS

1. The essay is more clearly organized than before. I think any reader could now see my thesis—that the theme can be found by giving the poem both a demonic and an angelic reading. I am clear (maybe clearly wrong, but clear) about what I believe the theme to be: that the solid citizen must earn equality and freedom.

2. The individual paragraphs are organized as miniature essays, each proving a point.

3. The bits of quotation establish enough contact with the poem to keep the reader from thinking that I am drifting into freewheeling speculation, but the quotations don't get in the way of the argument.

4. Focusing on the *purpose* of the demon's statement—to damn or to save —seems more useful than focusing on its *truth*. I've got my red herring out.

WEAKNESSES

1. I think I've sold the poem short. Reconciling the angelic and demonic aspects of the poem pointing out the irony of the demon's statement is clever, but it is shallow. The more I think about it, the less sure I am that the ambiguity is really there. I'm sure that Baudelaire does resent the hypocrisy of the middle class, but there must be more to it than this. Baudelaire *has* to use a demon to speak angelic truth, for reasons I've not yet fathomed.

2. I've not come to grips with the grotesque humor in the poem, the thing that first attracted me to it.

3. I know too little about Baudelaire's politics to be at all sure what his attitude toward the poor actually was. In a poem where the tone is so uncertain, I've no rock to stand on.

The essay is not yet entirely satisfactory, but I feel it has gone about as far as it can within the limits of a 500-word non-research paper. An additional revision of the essay within these limits would improve it slightly, but I now feel the need to do more research.

WRITING A RESEARCH PAPER

There is a tendency to talk about the research papers as if they were all cast from the same mold and served the same purpose. In fact, essays that involve research can be expressions of essentially independent opinion, reinforced slightly by a reference to one or two sources, or they can be works of exhaustive scholarship in which almost every sentence is justified by the citation of an authority. Most will fall somewhere between. If you are assigned a research paper, you should check with your teacher to see where on the spectrum he or she expects the paper to lie. (The sample paper below is somewhere near the midpoint.)

A few general observations about writing a research paper are worth making:

■ Go into the research with a notion of what you are looking for, what you *think* your essay will prove and what sort of evidence is necessary for the proof. It may well be that your tentative thesis will be overthrown by the research, but unless you have some idea of what you intend to prove, you may find yourself wallowing in data that has no particular significance. Sometimes it is wise to write a very brief "pilot paper" giving your hypothesis and general line of reasoning before you become too deeply involved in the research.

■ Take time to be methodical in your search for sources. Working carefully through the card catalogue, computer catalogue, and periodical indices* before you begin reading at random will save you time in the long run. So, too, will compiling a set of notecards with the bibliographic information needed for the "works cited" page: the few

---

* Those most useful for research in literature are the *PMLA* and the *Humanities* indices.

minutes spent jotting down this information every time you locate a potentially useful source can save you hours of frustration as the paper develops.

■ Make notes in a convenient form. Otherwise, the physical problem of trying to shuffle several books will distract you when you write. So, too, will the confusion created by having more than one note on a page or having notes on the back of a page. The time-honored method of using one side of a $4'' \times 6''$ notecard for each note and carefully recording the source and page number remains the most efficient.

■ Be prepared to discard most of the information you uncover. Attempts to use every scrap of research almost always produce papers that are disorganized. It should be clear to the reader that you are selecting information judiciously. Beware, on the other hand, of *physically* discarding note cards or bibliography cards too soon. The information that seems irrelevant at one point may later become important.

■ Pay attention to the credibility of the source as well as the usefulness of the information. Primary sources (works by the author you are discussing) generally have more weight than secondary sources (works by critics and commentators). Works by commentators with undeniable expertise (the scholars other scholars quote) have more weight than works by commentators who are relatively unknown. When you introduce a quotation or paraphrase from a source, be sure that the reader can tell immediately whether the source is primary or secondary.

■ Remember that the proper citation of sources serves three practical purposes. It (a) gives your reader a guide to other sources he or she may want to read; (b) gives your sources credit for the intellectual debt you owe them, and (c) gives you the chance to reinforce your points by showing that other commentators agree with you. Sources that give historical background, biographical data, and other "general information" need not be cited because the reader can find it in any number of places and you are not indebted to or relying on the work of a particular thinker.

Sample Research Paper

"Knock Down the Poor!" as Satanic Comedy

Charles Baudelaire's "Knock Down the Poor!" is built on a paradox: by beating a beggar nearly to death, the protagonist gives him back "his pride and his life" (Prose and Poetry 83). This paradox[1] makes it very hard to determine the theme of the prose poem. Some critics find it a political statement about the resilience of the poor and the possibility of an honest relation between social classes. Others see it as an example of Baudelaire's dwelling on the perversity of human nature. Both views are correct; they can be reconciled by seeing the poem as a satanic comedy in which the urge to evil, followed to its conclusion, leads the protagonist to good.

Politically, the poem is related to the wave of utopian socialism that swept France from 1840 to 1848 and helped cause the overthrow of the monarchy in the Revolution of 1848. Baudelaire makes this connection clear by placing the poem's action "sixteen or seventeen years" before the date of the poem's composition and intended publication in 1865 (Hyslop 98). The socialists and their opponents flooded France with tracts, many of them silly (". . . the art of making nations happy, wise, and rich in twenty-four

Citations in the essay give the minimum information necessary to identify who is being quoted, from what work, and from which pages. Since full information appears on the "works cited" page, titles are sometimes given in abbreviated form.

I insert the explanatory footnote because the bit of information it gives, while it reinforces my point, is not essential and would interrupt the paragraph needlessly.

The opening paragraph previews the main lines of development.

"Satanic comedy" is not a standard literary term, but one I've had to coin to cover the occasion. Therefore, it needs immediate definition.

I cite Hyslop here not because he gives the year that Baudelaire attempted publication (a fact that would fall under the "general knowledge" rule) but because he told me how to understand this fact (as a reference to the Revolution of 1848).

Short quotations from the work discussed keep the essay in contact with the poem.

hours''), some of them dishonest and self-serving (Prose and Poetry 81). Though the protagonist of the poem dismisses his interest in the tracts as "a passionate taste for bad books," Baudelaire himself was strongly influenced by one of the socialist writers: Pierre Joseph Proudhon (Hyslop 99–125). Proudhon was not a middle-class liberal attempting to salve his conscience by expressing liberal views. He was a radical from the working class who believed laborers were superior to the money-hungry bourgeoisie, and that if the economic system did not repress them they would be able to escape from poverty ("Proudhon" 744–5). F. W. J. Hemmings argues that "Knock Down the Poor!" illustrates a theme from Proudhon: that it is better for the poor to secure justice for themselves than to rely on the help of "utopian dreamers whose remedies, if applied, would prove more devitalizing than the social evils they are proposing to abolish" (Hemmings 95).[2] Lois Hyslop agrees that Baudelaire's message in the poem is political, and that the protagonist is "the beggar's benefactor" acting "out of his intention to restore the man's dignity and self-pride" (123).

Such interpretations of the poem make the protagonist seem a thoroughly well-meaning political

The quotation about "passionate taste" so clearly comes from the same portion of the poem as the description of the tracts that no citation is necessary.

I cite a whole section of Hyslop's article because the whole section proves the Baudelaire/ Proudhon connection.

Unsigned encyclopedia articles are poor sources for many purposes. The information they contain is either opinion, in which case we would like to know whose, or it is "general knowledge" requiring no citation. Here, however, the background information is useful, and I want to show the reader the basis of my very sweeping generalizations about Proudhon's philosophy.

The politically optimistic interpretations of the poem strike me as so intuitively unlikely (though finally reasonably convincing) that I want to show two reputable examples. Otherwise, the reader may think that this line of interpretation is largely a figment of my imagination.

philosopher. But well-meaning philosophers do not ordinarily take up tree limbs and thrash old men nearly to death. To get at the motive for the beating we need to look at a second level of the poem: the demonic. The voice that advises the protagonist is that "of a good angel, or of a good demon" (82). Demons have a peculiar role in Baudelaire's view of morality and psychology. In "The Evil Glazier," for example, Baudelaire's protagonist, about to torment a poor man for no good reason, says "I have more than once been the victim of these crises and of these impulses that appear to be the action of malicious Demons that possess us and, unknown to ourselves, make us accomplish their most absurd desires" (Prose and Poetry 11). In "Beatrice" the poet is surrounded by a cloud of demons who accuse him of being a bad actor mouthing the lines they write (Fleurs 132–33). In "Knock Down the Poor!", Baudelaire pauses to make a caustic comment about Lelut and Baillanger, psychologists who had declared Socrates insane because he mentions demons who controlled human actions:[3] Baudelaire believed that even the sanest of men could be controlled by evil impulses (in effect, demons) far stronger than their sanity. Critics like George Ross Ridge see "Knock Down the Poor!" as an example of

I allow my skepticism about the adequacy of the political interpretations to show, but decide not to refute them: only to say that though they are right on one level, there *must* be more.

Primary sources (in this case, Baudelaire's own poems) are generally more convincing than secondary sources. The route to these poems was via a concordance that allowed me to locate every reference to demons in "The Flowers of Evil."

Once again, a concordance helped. In this case, it allowed me to find out what Socrates said about demons in Plato's dialogues. The information is not important enough to mention in the text, but I add it as an explanatory footnote.

I draw my conclusion about Baudelaire's fascination from accumulated reading of the poems and several secondary sources. No particular source gives it to me directly, so I cite nothing and stand on my own authority. If I were writing a more scholarly paper, I would look for an authority to confirm my opinion.

Baudelaire's emphasis on this demonic side of human psychology: "As sadist, satanist, artist, aesthete, the hero of the prose poem is always the imp of the perverse. His acts are gratuitous, unmotivated; hence, they are pure evil" (20). The distressing implication of the poem is that all humans, even those who read and write Utopian tracts, share the perversity of the protagonist. Those who do not cudgel the poor honestly in the street repress them with a system of hypocritical, degrading charity.

I like the obvious conflict between the Ridge quotation and the earlier Hyslop quotation.

The political and the demonic readings of the poem seem at first to be irreconcilable. One makes the protagonist seem a saint motivated by a good angel;[4] one makes him seem a villain motivated by a demon. The only possible way to a reconciliation is to accept the idea that the prompting voice may be that of a good demon. This view makes the protagonist into a comic figure, a man who surrenders to an evil impulse and ends up, surprisingly, doing something better than all the people who set out to do good.

Having outlined the two apparently opposite views, I re-announce my plan for reconciliation. Notice that I am reminding the reader of the thesis.

The idea that a poem about beating a beggar should be humorous is shocking, but Baudelaire is often shocking, and the evidence of humor is every-where. Sometimes this humor shows in sarcasm: in the parody of the political tracts and the statement

I go to perhaps excessive lengths to show the humorous side of the poem because I have found very little commentary on it, and I am afraid that some readers don't see it—are perhaps reluctant to see it.

that reading them makes a person thirsty, for
instance. Sometimes it shows in a grotesque turn of
phrase, as when the protagonist beats the old beggar
"with the persistent energy of a cook pounding a
tough steak" (82). There are a series of passages in
which the protagonist humorously undercuts his own
dignity: when he mentions that his high-minded
philosophical experiment needed to be conducted "out
of immediate danger from the police" for example, and
when he observes that he was so inept as a mugger
that he broke a fingernail in the process of smashing
two of the man's teeth (82). The denouement of the
poem is almost certain to produce an uneasy smile.
When the beggar turns on the protagonist, the violence
that has made us cringe is doubled—two black eyes
for one, four broken teeth for two—very much in the
manner of the violent pantomimes popular in Baudelaire's time. And, like the violence in the pantomimes,
it never really hurts: the protagonist, though "beat to
a pulp" (83), is delighted to have his hypothesis
verified.

     Of course, the poem could have these humor-
ous elements without being comic in the sense of
achieving a happy ending, but "Knock Down the
Poor!" ends happily on both the political level and the
"demonic" level of Baudelaire's view of human

The mention of the
pantomimes prepares the
reader for the next
paragraph. It also helps
the reader see the
comedy in the poem by
comparing it to a more
generally accepted genre
that links violence and
laughter. I suppose that
the present day
equivalent of these cruel
and funny pantomimes are
some Saturday morning
cartoons and a number of
comic strips.

nature. The political happy ending is obvious: the beggar rises out of his misery to a new independence. The demonic happy ending is harder to articulate and can perhaps be best seen by analogy to an English pantomime Baudelaire loved and wrote about in his essay "The Essence of Laughter."

In the pantomime, Pierrot is a notorious pickpocket, eager to steal absolutely anything. In one scene he meets a woman who is trying to wash her doorstep. Not only does he steal her money, but he also tries to stuff everything else he finds into his pockets: "the mop, the broom, and the pail—even the water" (125). Pierrot persists in a wanton and lawless life until he is condemned to the guillotine. His head is chopped off, rolling noisily across the stage and displaying "the bleeding circle of the neck, the severed vertebrae," and other gory details added courtesy of a local butcher shop:

> But, suddenly, the decapitated trunk, revived
>
> by the force of the creature's irresistible
>
> thievish monomania, got to its feet, and
>
> triumphantly made off with its head, which
>
> like a ham or a bottle of wine, and far more
>
> sagaciously than St. Denis, it stuffed into its
>
> pocket. (126)

The humor here is certainly laced with cruelty, and

Here is a primary source of a particularly valuable kind. A critical essay by an author whose creative writing is being evaluated often casts a fascinating indirect light. It may make a useful observation about literature in general and at the same time open a window on the author's attitude toward his or her own work.

I include the gory details so that the reader will connect them with the violence in the poem.

Quotations longer than two lines are usually indented and typed without quotation marks.

Baudelaire believed that laughter was "one of the more obvious marks of the satanic in man" (Essence 115). He also believed, however, that there were higher and lower forms of laughter. We sometimes laugh because we feel superior to some unfortunate person who deserves our sympathy, but we sometimes laugh because a person's behavior makes us feel "the superiority of Man to Nature" (130). Pierrot goes to the guillotine as a miserable clown, but he rises from the guillotine as a man whose vices, even, are stronger than death.

This paraphrase of a very complex argument from Baudelaire's essay does not do it full justice. To develop it in greater detail, however, would have taken us too far from "Knock Down the Poor!" I paraphrase briefly, with as little distortion as possible.

What the pantomime does with physical humor, "Knock Down the Poor!" does with psychological or moral humor. Just as Pierrot persists in his crime so thoroughly that it eventually saves him from death, Baudelaire's protagonist persists in his demonic behavior until it proves a kind of salvation not only for the beggar, but for himself. Baudelaire, never optimistic about the sanctioned roads to political improvement or to individual grace (Murray 95–96), suspected that the unsanctioned roads might lead to the same destination: ". . . with tears a man may wash away man's sufferings, and with laughter sometimes soften men's hearts and draw them to him. For the phenomena that engendered the Fall can become the means to salvation" (Essence 113).

From my first exposure to this prose poem, I have wanted to insist that the issue is not the beggar's financial or political welfare, but the protagonist's spiritual welfare. My sources have now shifted my thinking somewhat, so I concede that Baudelaire is talking spiritually and politically at the same time.

Baudelaire believed in excess as fervently as some philosophers believe in moderation. "Knock Down the Poor!" is a comedy of excess in which a degenerate man, "sadist, satanist, artist, aesthete," becomes useful to the poor precisely because he avoids the hypocrisy of seeming to be charitable. Instead he follows the prompting of his authentic demon, however cruel that demon might be, until he achieves at the end an unexpected saintliness.

I state Baudelaire's position as strongly as possible in order to tie down the argument of the essay. As a personal matter, I don't agree with Baudelaire. I could get on my soapbox and declare that charity can be real, that people can care for each other in ways that have nothing to do with dominance and submission, and that the angelic forces of the personality are often strong enough to hold the demons at bay. But my job in this paper is to clarify Baudelaire's work, not to preach.

NOTES

[1] The original title of the poem was, in fact, "Le Paradoxe l'aumone" ("The Paradox of Charity") (Oeuvres I: 1349).

Explanatory footnotes include citations on the same principles as the main text of the essay.

[2] Supporting Hemmings' position is the fact that the manuscript version of the poem ended with the sentence "Qu'en dis-tu, Citoyen Proudhon?" ("What do you say about it, Citizen Proudhon?").

[3] In the Phaedo, Socrates says that every person has a demon. He also says, in a passage that might have interested Baudelaire, that a person trying to control his passion is like a charioteer trying to rein in two horses—one good and one evil.

The information may be of interest to those concerned about Socrates' reputation. It is, however, so peripheral to the essay that I give only a casual citation, not noting edition or page number.

[4] Monroe says that the "bon Ange" may be a composite of Proudhon and Charles-Augustin Sainte-Beuve, Baudelaire's literary mentor (184).

WORKS CITED

Baudelaire, Charles. "The Essence of Laughter."
  Trans. Gerard Hopkins. The Essence of
  Laughter and other Essays, Journals, and
  Letters. Ed. Peter Quennell. New York:
  Meridian, 1956.

---.Les Fleurs du Mal. Trans. Richard Howard.
  Boston: Godine, 1982.

---.Oeuvres Completes. Ed. Charles Pichois. Paris:
  Gallimard, 1975.

---.Prose and Poetry. Trans. Arthur Symons. New
  York: Albert and Charles Boni, 1926.

Drost, Wolfgang. "Baudelaire between Marx, Sade, and
  Satan." Baudelaire, Mallarme, Valery: New
  Essays in Honour of Lloyd Austin. Cambridge
  U P, 1982.

Hemmings, F. W. J. Baudelaire the Damned. New
  York: Scribner's, 1982.

Hyslop, Lois Boe. Baudelaire: Man of His Time. New
  Haven: Yale U P, 1980.

Monroe, Jonathan. "Baudelaire's Poor: The Petite
  Poems en Prose and the Social Reincarnation
  of the Lyric." Stanford French Review 9
  (1985): 169–88.

The rather unusual form of the first entry reflects the importance of noting the translator of a literary work. Had translation not been an issue, I could have gone from Baudelaire's name directly to the book's title.

Publishers' names are shortened when familiar enough for the reader to easily identify.

Note that three hyphens are used to avoid repeating the author's name.

Cite the full name of those publishers less familiar to the reader.

"U P" is a standard abbreviation for University Press.

"9" is the volume number for the periodical.

Murry, John Middleton. "Baudelaire." Baudelaire: A

    Collection of Critical Essays. Ed. Henri Peyne.

    Englewood Cliffs: Prentice, 1962.

"Proudhon, Pierre Joseph." Encyclopedia Britannica.

    1986 ed.

Ridge, George Ross. "Images of Original Sin in

    Baudelaire's Prose Poems." Kentucky Foreign

    Language Quarterly 7.1 (1960): 19–21.

Unsigned articles are alphabetized by last name.

"7.1" means "volume 7, issue number 1," a citation form necessary when each issue is separately paginated.

Biographical Sketches

Chinua Achebe (1932–) was born in Ogidi, Nigeria, and has been a professor of English at the University of Nigeria, Nsukku, since 1975, receiving the title of Professor Emeritus in 1985. Although he is a native of Africa and has lived most of his life there, Achebe has taught at several universities in the United States and actually does most of his writing in English. Achebe's concern for preserving African culture in the midst of European influence is revealed in his writing, which is often permeated with Ibo proverbs. His many works include *Things Fall Apart* (1958), *Arrow of God* (1969), *Beware Soul-Brother and Other Poems* (1971), and *African Short Stories* (1985), as well as several essays and children's books.

Alice Adams (1926–) grew up in Fredericksburg, Virginia, and was educated at Radcliffe College. She worked as a secretary and bookkeeper, but then turned her full attention to writing. Among her works, of which many are autobiographical, are the novels *Careless Love* (1966), *Families and Survivors* (1974), and *Superior Women* (1984), and the short story collections *Beautiful Girl* (1979), *To See You Again* (1982), and *Return Trips* (1985). Adams' stories frequently appear in *The New Yorker* and the *Atlantic Monthly*. In 1982 Adams won the O. Henry Award for Continuing Achievement as a short story writer.

Niccolo degli Albizzi (Fourteenth century) was a member of the noble Florentine family of Albizzi which produced several writers of poetry. "Prolonged Sonnet: When the Troops were Returning from Milan" is the only known poem by Niccolo.

Jean Anouilh (1910–1987) has been one of the most popular French playwrights since the 1930s. He is the author of over forty plays, many of which focus on historical figures. Anouilh characterizes his plays as either "rosy" or "black," corresponding to comedy or tragedy. He also attempts to create characters with strong inner vision, a vision which can blind them to the outer reality. *Antigone* (1944), *Joan of Arc* (1956), and *Becket; or, The Honour of God* (1959) are among his many works.

Margaret Atwood (1939–) has been a cashier and a filmscript writer, an editor with one of Canada's largest presses, and a professor of English literature. Born in Ottawa, Ontario, Atwood began writing as a child. Recently relating her love for domestic life to her literary career, Atwood claimed that "if Shakespeare could have kids and avoid suicide" then so could she. The fiction she produces ranges from serious probing into the psychological effects of modern culture to light and humorous stories. Her nonfiction works include

Survival: A Thematic Guide to Canadian Literature (1972) and *Second Words: Selected Critical Prose* (1982); *Surfacing* (1972), *Bodily Harm* (1982), and *The Handmaid's Tale* (1986) are among her novels; *Power Politics* (1971), a collection of poems, produced a wave of critical controversy; *Bluebeard's Egg and Other Stories* (1986) is her most recent collection of stories.

W(ystan) H(ugh) Auden (1907–1973) was born in England and educated at Oxford. He was the principal British poet of his generation, using a vocabulary conspicuous for its technical formality and colloquial tone. Like many of his peers he learned wit and irony from T.S. Eliot and metrical techniques from Gerard Manly Hopkins and Wilfred Owen. Of his later volumes, *Nones* (1951) shows the manner in which he combined wit and deep, if unsentimental, feeling. He was at first influenced by Marxism and wrote poems concerned with England's social ills, but later he cultivated a more religious view of personal responsibility and conventional values. As opposed to T.S. Eliot, who moved from America to England in search of tradition, Auden moved to America in search of variety. There he taught before returning to England to live at Oxford. Among his works are *About the House* (1967), *City Without Walls* (1970), and a collection of prose writings, *The Dyer's Hand and Other Essays* (1968). His poetry is collected in *W.H. Auden: Collected Poems* (1976).

Toni Cade Bambara (1939–) was born in New York City and was educated there as well as in Paris. While most interested in linguistics and dance, Bambara worked as a social investigator and a psychiatric department recreation director before becoming a professor of English. She has taught and lectured at several colleges and universities across the country. Bambara's writing reflects her diversified life (she calls herself a Pan-Africanist-socialist-feminist); she writes about the experiences of black women in order to "tap Black potential" and "join the chorus of voices that argue that exploitation and misery are neither inevitable nor necessary." Her works include a novel *The Black Woman* (1970), and collections of stories, *Gorilla, My Love* (1972) and *The Sea Birds are Still Alive* (1977).

Charles Baudelaire (1821–1867) was born in Paris, were he spent most of his life. When Baudelaire was six his father died, and a year later his mother married General (later Ambassador) Aupick. Baudelaire's relations with his parents prefigured his bitter relationship with the bourgeois Parisian critics and public. At eighteen Baudelaire was expelled from college on disciplinary grounds. He lived a life of dandyism (which was partly outrageous display, partly strict aesthetic discipline), until the Aupicks restricted the income from his inheritance. In 1845 Baudelaire published his first art criticism and poetry, followed two years later by a novel *La Fanfarlo* (1847). Attacks on his writing peaked with the publication of *Les Fleurs du mal* in 1857, when he received a 300-franc fine for immorality. Despite the setback, he continued working on his *Petits Poemes en prose* (1868), *Les Paradis artificiels* (1860), and a revised edition of *Les Fleurs du mal* (1861). Inventor of the term "modernism", Baudelaire struggled to define a place for the artist in a world he saw as corrupt and materialistic. His work is known for its images of evil and ugliness, yet Baudelaire was also a worshipper of beauty and called imagination the "queen of faculties."

Samuel Beckett (1906–   ), a native of Dublin, Ireland, has written most of his important works in French. He began a career teaching both French and English, but abandoned academics when he decided that it was absurd to teach what he felt he could not know himself, the nature of language. This peculiar attitude toward language permeates his works, which emphasize silence as much as sound, voices speaking in isolation, and expression without definite meaning. After World War II Beckett began writing seriously and has become a leading figure of the "Theatre of the Absurd," producing plays such as *Waiting For Godot* (1952), *Endgame* (1957), *Krapp's Last Tape* (1958), and *Happy Days* (1961). While Beckett has been criticized for too often portraying humanity as depraved and grotesque, Harold Pinter claims that Beckett "brings forth a body of beauty" through his writing. Beckett considers himself primarily a novelist; his novels include *Molloy* (1951), *Malone Dies* (1951), *The Unnamable* (1953), and *How It Is* (1961). In 1969 he won the Nobel Prize for Literature.

Gustavo Adolfo Bécquer (1836–1870), poet and author of prose legends during the late Romantic period, is considered one of the first modern Spanish poets. Between 1861 and 1868 he wrote regularly for the newspaper *El Contemporaneo*. As a lyric poet, Becquer emphasized atmosphere in his works, creating dream-like imagery which reflected his pantheistic love of nature. His literary production is composed of his *Rimas* (1871), *Romantic Legends of Spain* (1871), and the literary essays, *Letters from my Cell* (1871), all which appeared individually in *El Contemporaneo* and were collected shortly after his death.

John Berger (1926–   ), an essayist, translator, poet, novelist, playwright, and painter, is probably best known for his Marxist art criticism. Berger feels that if twentieth-century art is to be great it must reflect the impact of socialism as a profound influence in this century. His theories of art, politics, and perception are found in collections such as *Permanent Red: Essays in Seeing* (1960), *The Moment of Cubism, and Other Essays* (1969), *A Seventh Man: Migrant Workers in Europe* (1975), and *The Sense of Sight* (1985). He has also written several novels, including *A Painter of Our Time* (1958), *Corker's Freedom* (1972), and *G* (1972).

John Berryman (1914–1972) taught at Brown, Harvard, Princeton, and the University of Minnesota, but was most accomplished as a poet, acquiring both the Pulitzer Prize (1965) and the National Book Award (1969) during his lifetime. Aligned with the confessional poets of the sixties, Berryman wrote extremely personal verse, reacting against the academic poetry common at the time. He is best known for his "Dream Songs" which chronicle the epic-like life of his fictional Henry Pussycat. Berryman's poetry is collected in *The Dispossessed* (1948), *Homage to Mistress Bradstreet* (1956), *The Dream Songs* (1969), and *Henry's Fate and Other Poems, 1967–1972* (1977).

Elizabeth Bishop (1911–1979) was born in Worcester, Massachusetts. Her father died in the year of her birth, and her mother succumbed to mental illness a short time later. Raised by her grandparents in their Nova Scotian village, she attended boarding school in Boston before enrolling at Vassar College. In her senior year she met poet Marianne Moore. Under Moore's influence she abandoned her plans to study medicine and decided to devote her life to writing. The poems of Moore and Bishop have in common a wry intelligence and are formal without being bound by traditional forms. Both write from a detached perspective, closely observing the characteristics of animate and inanimate objects. Many of Bishop's poems evoke her experiences in Key West and in Brazil, where she spent long periods. Bishop's relatively modest poetic production has been disproportionately influential. Seen in the context of postwar women's poetry, that influence is at least partly due to the contrast Bishop's objectivity and concentration on the external world provide to the emotional and subjective poetry of Sylvia Plath and Anne Sexton. Bishop's books of poetry are *North and South* (1946); the Pulitzer Prize-winning *Poems* (1955); *A Question of Travel* (1965); *The Complete Poems* (1965), which received the National Book Award; and *Geography III* (1976). She also translated poems from the Portuguese. Her *Collected Prose* appeared in 1984.

William Blake (1757–1827) was born in London and lived virtually his entire life there. The radical upheavals of the French, American, and Industrial Revolutions are echoed in his poetry. Apprenticed at an early age, he earned his living as a highly skilled engraver and illustrator. With Catherine Boucher, whom he married when he was 24, Blake produced his own books of poems by hand. The first of these, *Songs of Innocence* (1789) and *Songs of Experience* (1794), contain his best-known poems and were admired by Wordsworth and Coleridge. It is in his longer books, including *The Marriage of Heaven and Hell* (1790), *Milton* (1803–08), and *Jerusalem* (1804–20), that Blake strove for a visionary overview of human existence, past and future. His readings of the Bible, alchemical literature, Plato, and Swedenborg, together with the misery he witnessed on the streets of London, made him sympathetic to revolution. His idiosyncratic genius, though scarcely recognized during his own life, prefigured Romanticism and influenced poets right up to the present.

Robert Bly (1926–) was born in Madison, Minnesota, of Norwegian descent. He served in the army during World War II, then entered St. Olaf College. After a year he transferred to Harvard, where he earned his degree in 1950. He lived in New York for several years, but soon returned to rural Minnesota where he and his wife brought up their three children. In the tradition of William Blake, Bly's poetry addresses the harsh political realities of his day (he founded Writers Against the Vietnam War) from an intensely spiritual perspective. Like Blake, Bly has sought to remain independent of institutions, making his living by giving readings and leading workshops around the country. Bly's beliefs about poetry—for example, the use of simple syntax so as to approach a visionary world by the most direct means—have influenced many contemporaries, including James Wright, Donald Hall, and Galway Kinnell. He has also been influential as an editor, and as translator of Garcia Lorca, Neruda, Rilke, the Sufi poet Kabir and the Norwegian poet Thomas Transtromer. Bly's first of many books of poems was *Silence in the Snowy Fields* (1962); his most recent was *Loving a Woman in Two Worlds* (1987).

Louise Bogan (1897–1970), born in Livermore Falls, Maine, is considered one of the chief American exponents of the English Metaphysical poets. After travelling to Vienna in the early 20s on a Guggenheim Fellowship, she published her first collection, *Body of This Death* (1923). From 1931 until a year before her death Bogan was poetry critic for *The New Yorker*. She was honored with a chair of poetry at the Library of Congress in 1945–46 and shared the prestigious Bollingen Prize with Leonie Adams for *Selected Criticism: Poetry and Prose* in 1955. In an effort to bring the contradictions in life to bold relief, Bogan is true to the Metaphysicals, employing psychological analysis of love, religion, and all matters emotional. She did not have a large readership during her lifetime, but her work as poet, critic, translator, and philosopher of art is receiving increasing attention. Among her works are *Dark Summer* (1929), *The Sleeping Fury* (1937), *Poems and New Poems* (1941), *The Blue Estuaries: Poems 1923–1968* (1968), and *A Poet's Alphabet: Reflections on the Literary Art and Vocation* (posthumously in 1970).

Jorge Luis Borges (1899–1986) never received a Nobel prize but was nominated nineteen times. Born in Buenos Aires, Argentina, Borges became one of the pioneers of *Ultraisme*, a Spanish avant-garde literary movement based on Surrealism and Imagism. Even though the movement drifted too far from conventional literature for even Borges, his mature writing maintained its anti-realistic flavor. Borges is also known for his "literature about literature," found in his essays and sketches which present literary history and human experience simultaneously. His collections of short prose pieces and short stories include *Fictions* (1944), *Labyrinths* (1962), *The Aleph and Other Stories* (1970), and *Doctor Brodie's Report* (1972). His critical views on fiction, poetry, and translation are found in *Borges on Writing* (1973).

Gwendolyn Brooks (1917–) began her professional career in 1941 when she attended a workshop for new poets. By 1950 she had won the Pulitzer Prize for *Annie Allen*, written in 1949. A native of Chicago, Brooks was made poet laureate of Illinois in 1969. Her poetry is both social and personal, but her later poems, especially, reflect her belief that she should be writing for and about black people. In order to support other black writers, Brooks conducted a workshop for a group of Chicago teenagers, the Blackstone Rangers, through which she encouraged young people to portray the endurance of blacks despite constant battles against racism. Her use of street language and jazz rhythms also distinguishes her work. *A Street in Bronzeville* (1945), *The Bean-Eaters* (1960), *Beckonings* (1975), and *To Disembark* (1981), are among her poetic works. Brooks writes of her own life in *Report from Part One* (1972).

Olga Broumas (1949–) was born in Greece and educated at the University of Pennsylvania. Since 1982 she has been on the faculty of Freehand, a learning community for women writers and photographers which she originally founded in Provincetown, Massachusetts. As a feminist lesbian, Broumas writes poetry to explore the relationships possible among women. Her works are collected in *Caritas* (1976), *Soie Sauvage* (1979), *Pastoral Jazz* (1983), *Black Holes, Black Stockings* (1985), and several other volumes, all written in her second language, English. She has translated the poems of Greek Nobel Laureate Odysseas Elytis in *What I Love and Other Poems* (1986). Broumas won the Yale Younger Poets Award in 1977.

Robert Browning (1812–1889) was for many years known primarily as "Elizabeth Barrett's husband." Even today readers retain a fascination in their love affair, which was carried on largely in poems and letters until they eloped in 1846. Browning wrote most of his poetry while living in Italy with Elizabeth, whose fame as a poet was already established. Only after her death and Browning's return to England was he able to build his reputation, particularly with the publication of *The Ring and the Book* in 1868. Browning was most successful in refining the dramatic monologue; his are famous for their psychological depth and ironic objectivity. Striving to portray the "intensest life," Browning created some of the most vivid characters in English literature. By 1881 he had become so popular that a literary society had been formed in his honor. His other works include *Men and Women* (1855) and *Dramatis Personae* (1864).

Dennis Brutus (1924–), born in Zimbabwe of South African parents, has not been allowed into South Africa for over twenty years. Considered too outspoken in his fight against apartheid while teaching in South Africa, Brutus was constantly in political trouble and was finally arrested and sentenced to eighteen months hard labor. After being banned from South Africa, he joined the staff of the English department at Northwestern University. His works include *Sirens, Knuckles, Boots* (1963), *Letters to Martha and Other Poems from a South African Prison* (1968), *Poems from Algiers* (1973), *Thoughts Abroad* (1970), and *A Simple Lust* (1973).

Anton Chekhov (1860–1904), the Russian physician, short story writer, and playwright, was born in Taganrog, Russia, and educated at the University of Moscow. Preferring his literary life to his medical one, Chekhov had his first story published in 1880 and went on to write over six hundred more stories and sketches by 1887. His acute sensitivity to the psychological and social lives people live is best reflected in stories such as "Ward No. 6" (1892), "Peasants" (1897), "Gooseberries" (1898), and "The Lady with the Pet Dog" (1899). Chekhov's attempt to bring realism to the stage revolutionized the theater; to this day he continues to serve as a major influence on playwrights who strive to present life as it is experienced. Among his plays are *The Seagull* (1896), *The Three Sisters* (1901), and *The Cherry Orchard* (1903).

Amy Clampitt (1923–   ) was born and raised in New Providence, Iowa, of Quaker heritage. After graduating from Grinnell College in Iowa, she moved to New York City where she has lived most of her life. A librarian by career, she never published a poem until 1978, when her work began appearing regularly in *The New Yorker*. Since that time she has published three volumes and has established herself as one of America's major poets. In a style given to literary allusions, Clampitt places nearly as much emphasis upon the aural qualities of the work as on the subject matter itself. Through a montage of vivid sounds, she explores themes of history, political strife, and the social position of women. Her published works include: *The Kingfisher* (1983), *What the Light Was Like* (1985), and *Archaic Figure* (1987).

Lucille Clifton (1936–   ) grew up in New York and was educated at Howard University. When her first book of poems, *Good Times* (1969), was published, she was thirty-three years old and had six children under ten years of age. Since that time she has become a lecturer and professor, has been named poet laureate of Maryland, and has been nominated for the Pulitzer Prize. Clifton's poems, brief like those of Emily Dickinson, typically remake the sounds of black spirituals and blues. Clifton purposely keeps her poems simple, claiming she is not interested if anyone knows whether or not she is "familiar with big words" for she is primarily "interested in trying to render big ideas in a simple way." Her works include *Good News about the Earth* (1972), *An Ordinary Woman* (1974), and *Two-Headed Woman* (1980), as well as a memoir, *Generation* (1976).

Samuel Taylor Coleridge (1772–1834), through his collaboration with Wordsworth in the birth of the Romantic Movement and his own poetic and critical production, established himself as one of the towering figures of English literature. Born in rural Devonshire, Coleridge was sent to school in London and went on to Cambridge University. His brilliant mind was understimulated, and he left without a degree in 1794. A year later and married, he met Wordsworth, and thus began the poetic collaboration which resulted in the *Lyrical Ballads* (1798). During a year in Germany Coleridge studied Kant and other German philosophers. Their ideas helped shape his own philosophic, religious, and aesthetic thought, which is articulated mainly in the *Biographia Literaria* and *The Friend*, a periodical Coleridge founded in 1809. Opposed to the prevailing rationalism, he saw the mind as active and creative, the imagination as a participant in perception. In 1799 Coleridge fell deeply in love with Wordsworth's sister-in-law and at the same time suffered the first of many physical ailments. The next ten years were a nightmare of ill health and drug addiction (opium being the standard cure). In 1810 Coleridge and Wordsworth had a falling out which was not resolved for many years. Coleridge's later years were happier; his early radicalism, like Wordsworth's, turned to a philosophic conservatism, and he returned to the Anglican Church. He had the good fortune of being recognized in his own lifetime for his enormous creative accomplishments.

William Cowper (1731–1800), called to the bar in 1754, was unable to endure the examination because of mental depression. Stricken with acute melancholia, Cowper became obsessed with religion and damnation and had to be institutionalized as a young man. His poetry, collected in *Memoir* (c. 1767) and *Olney Hymns* (1799) generally reflects his sense of isolation and helplessness, yet many of Cowper's poems are light and witty, expressing both a love for nature and a sense of tranquility.

Countee Cullen (1903–1946) was adopted by a Methodist minister and raised in Harlem. By the time he was twenty years old, *Nation, Harper's,* and *Poetry* had published his poems. *Color* (1925), his first collection of poems, was published while he was a student at New York University. Cullen's early poetry brought him immediate fame as the youngest of the black writers who inspired the Harlem Renaissance. However, his next work, *Copper Sun* (1927), disappointed black nationalists with its display of love poems, and with the writing of *The Black Christ* in 1929, Cullen stopped writing poetry. After receiving his master's degree from Harvard, he taught high school in New York City for the rest of his life. His other literary work includes a novel, *One Way to Heaven* (1932), and a version of Euripides' *Medea* (1935).

E(dward) E(stlin) Cummings (1894–1962), from Cambridge, Massachusetts, earned his degree from Harvard where he studied both painting and poetry. During World War I he served as an ambulance driver in France and was mistakenly committed to a French prison camp for three months. His account of this experience, recorded through the prose narrative *The Enormous Room* (1922), attracted international attention. *Tulips and Chimneys* (1923), his first book of poetry, was soon followed by *&* (1925), *XLI Poems* (1925), and *is 5* (1926), all of which demonstrate faith in the loving and carefree individual and denounce the "unman" who possesses intellect without emotion. Cummings is known for his experimental typography, technical skill, and inventive language. His *Complete Poems, 1910–1962* was published in 1980.

Joy Davidman (1915–1960) was a high school English teacher in New York City and a communist when her first book, *Letter to a Comrade* (1938) was published. It was this work which won Davidman both the Yale Younger Poets Award (1938) and the Loines Award for Poetry (1939). In 1955 she moved to England and became acquainted with C. S. Lewis, whose books were in part responsible for her conversion to Christianity. The two were married in 1957. Davidman also wrote two novels, *Anya* (1940) and *Weeping Bay* (1950).

Emily Dickinson (1830–1886) lived her entire life in her parents' home in Amherst, Massachusetts. As a young girl she was said to be charming and bright, and a promising student at Mount Holyoke Female Seminary. But with each passing year Dickinson grew more and more withdrawn until finally she would not leave the house at all. Twentieth-century scholarship has attributed her isolation to her passion for a young minister she saw two or three times in 1854. After he moved to California, Dickinson became acutely withdrawn, refused to wear anything but white, and began writing poetry which focused on love and renunciation, referring to herself as a "queen of Calvary." The precise metaphors and images of her poems anticipate the Imagist movement of the twentieth century. Although only seven poems were published during Dickinson's lifetime, nearly 2000 poems were found after her death; many were drastically edited and then published in 1890. In 1955 Thomas Johnson restored Dickinson's poems to their original form and published them in *The Poems of Emily Dickinson*.

John Donne (1572–1631) led a life which brought him the wealth and prestige of the Court, the hunger of absolute poverty, and eventually in 1615, priesthood in the Anglican Church, where he was known for his deeply moving sermons. By the time of his death he had become Dean of St. Paul's Cathedral in London. Donne's status among the English metaphysical movement of the 17th century is unchallenged. Relying less on form than on subtlety of thought, the metaphysical poets analyzed love and religion from a psychological standpoint, laying bare the contradictions of life. Donne's first collection, *Songs and Sonnets*, was published in 1634, three years after his death; it was not until 1912, with the publication of a scholarly edition of his *Holy Sonnets*, that his work achieved the recognition it deserves.

Jose Donoso (1924–   ), beginning his career as a shepherd in Patagonia, is now regarded as one of the most significant writers of recent Latin American fiction. Born in Santiago, Chile, Donoso remained unknown as a writer for several years. Even after his first book, *Summertime and Other Stories* (1955), was published, he found himself peddling his first novel, *Coronation* (1957), on the streets of Santiago. Donoso is known for the experimental nature of his works which range from realistic stories of self-disintegration and madness to those which employ supernatural transformations and mythical monsters. Besides two collections of short stories, *The Charleston* (1960) and *The Major Stories of Jose Donoso* (1966), he has written novels, *The Obscene Bird of the Night* (1973) and *A House in the Country* (1984), and literary criticism, *The Boom in Spanish American Literature: A Personal History* (1977).

Arthur Conan Doyle (1859–1930) was a Scottish physician and writer born in Edinburgh. Known for his diverse accomplishments, Doyle is credited with bringing the sport of skiing to Switzerland and was knighted for his participation in the Boer War. While he would have preferred to be remembered for his scholarly work or historical novels, it was the creation of Sherlock Holmes that established his literary immortality. Holmes first appeared in "A Study in Scarlet" (1887) and later in four novels and over fifty short stories. Doyle's work made detective fiction a literary genre of prestige. His works include *A Study in Scarlet* (1887), *The Adventures of Sherlock Holmes* (1881), *The Hound of the Baskervilles* (1902), and the historical novel, *The White Company* (1890).

Alan Dugan (1923–   ) became an acclaimed writer with the publication of his first book, *Poems* (1961), which won the Yale Series of Younger Poets award, the Pulitzer Prize, and the National Book Award. Although born in Brooklyn, he was educated in Mexico City. Dugan's poetry is often satirical and unsentimental, written in straightforward, honest, unpoetic language: he has defined it as "words wrung out of intense experience." Other works include *Poems 2* (1963), *Poems 3* (1967), *Poems 4* (1974), which also won a Pulitzer Prize, and *New and Collected Poems* (1983).

Richard Eberhart (1904–   ), originally from Austin, Minnesota, studied at Cambridge and Harvard before becoming the tutor to the son of the king of Siam. After four years in the navy, he joined the Butcher Polish Company in Boston, and since 1956 he has taught at many universities and colleges in the United States. Eberhart is considered one of the major lyric poets of this century. His belief in poetic inspiration, that the poet is "out of his mind" when creating, is closely tied to the visionary nature of his poems: his vivid sensory images are linked to something abstract and dark beyond what he presents for the reader to see. Eberhart's ideas are further emphasized by rough, forced sound and meter. His works include *A Bravery of Earth* (1930), *Thirty One Sonnets* (1967), *Collected Poems, 1930–1986* (1986), and *Poems to Poets* (1976).

T(homas) S(tearns) Eliot (1888–1965) dominated the world of English language poetry and criticism between the two world wars. He was born into an influential New England family which had been transplanted to St. Louis. Eliot was never comfortable with either heritage and lived the greater part of his life in England. After graduating from Harvard, he spent a year in France, where he wrote and furthered his exposure to the French Symbolists. He returned to Harvard where he studied philosophy. There he developed an interest in Buddhism, and the Buddhist notions of Nirvana. Later he became an Anglican, advocating a return to Christian values and beliefs. His early work, especially "The Love Song of J. Alfred Prufrock" and "The Waste Land," profoundly influenced a whole generation of poets. He was also active in bringing French Symbolism into English poetry and reviving interest in the Metaphysical poets. He was enormously influential as a critic and editor for the publishing house of Faber and Fader. His last major work, completed in 1943, was *Four Quartets,* in which he strove to structure a poem on musical principals. He also wrote plays for the stage, *Murder in the Cathedral* and *The Cocktail Party* among them. In 1948 he received the Nobel Prize for Literature.

Ralph Ellison (1914–) was born in Oklahoma City, Oklahoma, and studied music and composition at Tuskegee Institute. The influence of music, especially jazz, is strongly reflected in both Ellison's method of writing and in the works themselves. Studying T.S. Eliot's poetry provoked Ellison's interest in literature; Richard Wright, who always inspired Ellison with his commitment to racial justice, personally encouraged him to pursue a literary career. Ellison is known for his novel *Invisible Man* (1952), which chronicles the life of a man who is both a black and an artist and who faces in both roles the problem, as Ellison says, "of becoming a man, of becoming visible." He also has produced two collections of essays, *Shadow and Act* (1964) and *Going to the Territory* (1986), which continue to explore the problem of black identity within the American culture.

Euripides (484 B.C.–406 B.C.), one of the most reknowned tragedians of ancient Greece, was born on the island of Salamis and became an Athenian citizen. He was said to be very wealthy, yet took no part in public affairs, preferring instead to sit alone in a cave overlooking the sea. His passion for ideas and his pessimistic view of the universe limited Euripides' popularity in his lifetime, during which he won only four prizes at the annual Dionysian drama festival While Euripides adhered to the formal dramatic structure and drew his plots from ancient legends, he commonly gave his characters contemporary ideas, attitudes, and problems. His heros are not idealized but are instead created as flawed people. Likewise, the supernatural aspects of his plays do not glorify Greek gods but merely imply a divine force uninvolved in human affairs. Among his nineteen surviving plays are *Alcestis, Bacchae, Medea, Ion* and *Hippolytus.*

William Faulkner (1887–1962), bank clerk, cadet pilot, postmaster, carpenter, coal-shoveler, and finally full-time writer, was born in New Albany, Mississippi. From his experiences in the South, Faulkner created his mythical Yoknapatawpha County, the setting for most of his novels. With the writing of *Sartoris* (1929) Faulkner began the legend of the heroic Col. John Sartoris and his troubled descendents, constantly in conflict with the crafty, savage, landless Snopeses. Faulkner's style is dense and varied, often effectively experimenting with point of view and stream of consciousness. One of the great novelists of this century, he received the Nobel Prize in 1949. His major works include: *The Sound and the Fury* (1929), *As I Lay Dying* (1930), *Light in August* (1932), *Absalom, Absalom!* (1936), *The Hamlet* (1940), *Go Down, Moses* (1942), *The Town* (1957), and *The Mansion* (1959).

Gustave Flaubert (1821–1880) was born in Rouen, France, and briefly studied law in Paris before being forced by epilepsy to return home. The remainder of his life was consistently uneventful, lived too near the bourgeois society he despised. Ironically, it was this mundane setting that was the focus of Flaubert's masterpiece, *Madame Bovary* (1856), a novel condemned in France as pornographic yet praised internationally by other writers. Flaubert is generally considered the initiator of the Realist school of French literature. While his aim in fiction was to create beauty, he insisted on dispassionately recording the lives and minds of his characters. As an escape from the bourgeois reality, he turned to the past, studying the mystical lives of the saints as a means of evoking the romanic interest of his youth. Other works include the novels *Salammbo* (1862), *The Sentimental Education* (1869), *Bouvard and Pecuchet* (1881), and his *Three Tales* (1877).

E. M. Forster (1879–1970) lived much of his life away from his native England, and his travels became the basis for many of his novels and stories. His years in Italy produced two of his early novels, *Where Angels Fear to Tread* (1905) and *A Room With a View* (1908); India, where he became the secretary of the Maharajah of Dewas, provided Forster with much of the material for his masterpiece, *A Passage to India* (1924). His works most often study people striving for love and friendship against personal, social, and cultural barriers. Sensing that the average English person possessed an "undeveloped heart," Forster believed that if people would "only connect," they would find a sort of salvation. He also wrote the novels *Howard's End* (1910) and *Maurice* (1913, published posthumously in 1971), as well as the libretto for the opera *Billy Budd.* Other important works include *Abinger Harvest—A Miscellany* (1936) and *Two Cheers for Democracy* (1951), two collections of essays. *Aspects of the Novel* (1927), Forster's theory of fiction, was originally a series of lectures given at Cambridge University.

Robert Frost (1874–1963) was born in San Francisco but as a young boy moved to New England, the homeland of the Frost family. While growing up, Frost held many craftsman jobs—in a mill, a shoe factory, and on a farm—and all influenced his later writing. Although he studied at Harvard with the intention of teaching Latin, Frost bought a poultry farm and settled there to write poetry. His reputation was established a few years later with the publication of *North of Boston* (1914). He went on to win four Pulitzer Prizes. His poetry is characterized by colloquial, restrained verse that implies messages rather than openly expressing them. Also politically active, Frost served as a good-will ambassador for the State Department to South America, Israel, Greece, and Russia. His works include *A Boy's Will* (1913), *New Hampshire* (1923), *A Further Range* (1936), *A Witness Tree* (1942), and *In the Clearing* (1962).

Gloria Fuertes (1920–) has lived in Madrid, Spain, most of her life, working as a secretary. She has written stories and children's books, including her recent *A Crazy Book, a Little Bit about Everything: First Book* (1984), which is a collection of poems depicting everyday happenings through the eyes of a child. Fuertes primarily enjoys writing poetry, as well as reading her poems in the bars and coffeehouses of Madrid. She also actively supports other women poets by organizing readings for them. *Off the Map* (1984) is her most recent collection of poetry.

Athol Fugard (1932–) was born in Cape Province, South Africa, of an English-speaking father and an Afrikaner mother. His first major success came with *The Blood Knot*, which he wrote, directed, and starred in. That was the first time a white and black actor had shared a South African stage, and it introduced what would be the central theme of Fugard's work: the inhumanity of man to man, brutally visible in the apartheid of his native land, but present universally. With his later plays, including *Boesman and Lena* (1969), *A Lesson from Aloes* (1978), *Master Harold . . . and the Boys* (1982), and *The Road to Mecca* (1985), Fugard has gained an international reputation. He has taught at Yale University, but lives mainly in South Africa, where he continues "to witness, as truthfully as I could, the nameless and destitute . . . of this one little corner of the world."

Tess Gallagher (1943–) was born into a family of loggers in Washington and now teaches English at Syracuse University in New York. Gallagher writes about family conflicts, departures and returns, and self-exploration. Her poems are collected in *Stepping Outside* (1974), *Instructions to the Double* (1976), *Under Stars* (1978), *Portable Kisses* (1978), and *The Lover of Horses* (1986). She has recently written a collection of essays on poetry, *A Concert of Tenses* (1986).

Mavis Gallant (1922–) at 28 left her home of Montreal, Quebec, to live and write in Paris. Virtually ignored by her country until the late 1970s, Gallant meanwhile produced internationally known stories and novels. In 1983, however, she accepted a position of writer-in-residence at the University of Toronto. The Toronto Tarragon Theatre welcomed her home by mounting the first production of her first play, *What is to be Done?* (1983). Her sensitivity to the unique qualities of individuals, created in part by her diverse background, is reflected in Gallant's literary exploration of differences in culture, personality, and expectations among people of varying origins. Gallant's works include two novels, *Green Water, Green Sky* (1959) and *A Fairly Good Time* (1970); and several collections of stories, *The Other Paris* (1956), *My Heart is Broken* (1964), *The Pegnitz Junction* (1973), *The End of the World* (1974), *From the Fifteenth District: Stories* (1979), *Home Truths* (1981), and *Overhead in a Balloon* (1987).

Charlotte Perkins Gilman (1860–1935), a lecturer and author from Hartford, Connecticut, is probably best known for her promotion of feminism. Her first major work, *Women and Economics* (1898), is an appeal for the financial independence of women. Her more startling theories are found in *Concerning Children* (1900), which proposes that children should be cared for collectively by women best suited for child-rearing; and *Man-Made World* (1911), in which she claims women are socially and intellectually superior to men. Gilman also

co-founded the Women's Peace Party in 1915. Her success, however, came only after she fought off incipient insanity and left her husband and child. Her last work, *The Living of Charlotte Perkins Gilman* (1935), concludes with a letter to her survivors, written shortly before she took her own life. Gilman also wrote several short stories, collected in *The Charlotte Perkins Gilman Reader* (1980).

Allen Ginsberg (1926–) was born in Newark, New Jersey, and became a leader of the Beat Movement and the San Francisco Renaissance. Claiming Whitman, Melville, and Williams as writers whose works most shaped his own, Ginsberg writes poetry which ranges from the comic to the religious to the outrageous. His political concerns, reflected in much of his poetry, have often won him notoriety. One of the most influential poets of this century, Ginsberg has compiled such collections as *Howl and Other Poems* (1956), *T.V. Baby Poems* (1967), *Mostly Sitting Haiku* (1979), *Scenes Along the Road* (1985), and *White Shroud* (1986).

Louise Glück (1943–) was born in New York City and raised on Long Island. Her first book was published in 1973. Glück draws on nature and animals to define that which is uniquely human; at the same time she affirms our interdependence with the world around us. In a similar way her poetry probes the issues around gender relations. In what ways are men and women unknowable to each other, and in what ways do we require others to help us know ourselves? These concerns, and her frequent forays into the territory of her familial past, make Glück typical of the poets of her generation (Sharon Olds, for example). Glück now lives in Vermont and teaches at nearby Williams College in western Massachusetts. Her books of poetry include *Firstborn* (1973), *The House on Marshland* (1975), *Descending Figure* (1980), and *The Triumph of Achilles* (1985).

Gail Godwin (1937–), a journalist and a travel consultant before becoming a lecturer in literature and creative writing, was born in Birmingham, Alabama. She was first introduced to writing as a child: her mother wrote love stories for women's magazines to support the family. Godwin's fiction addresses conventional female roles, particularly those she grew up with in the South. Often cutting through the conservative feminine myth, she leads her characters to self-discovery. Among her works of fiction are *The Perfectionists* (1970), *Glass People* (1972), *The Odd Woman* (1974), *Violet Clay* (1978), *A Mother and Two Daughters* (1982), *The Finishing School* (1985), and *A Southern Family* (1987) all novels. Her short fiction collections include *Dream Children* (1976) and *Mr. Bedford and the Muses* (1983). Godwin has also written four librettos and several critical essays.

Nadine Gordimer (1923–) has seen three of her works banned in South Africa because of their sensitivity to racial injustice. Although she has lived all her life in South Africa, many of Gordimer's stories were first published in American literary magazines, for her liberal politics and harsh critique of apartheid made them unpublishable in her own country. However, Gordimer's sensitivity to the emotional lives of her characters and her objective portrayal of the customs and beliefs of black and white Africans give her works artistic depth as well as political intent. Among her major works are *The Soft Voice of the Serpent, and Other Stories* (1952), *The Lying Days* (1953), *Six Feet of the Country* (1956), *Friday's Footprint, and Other Stories* (1960), *The Conservationist* (1975), *Burgher's Daughter* (1979), *A Soldier's Embrace* (1980), *Something Out There* (1983), and *A Sport of Nature* (1987).

George Gordon, Lord Byron (1788–1824) published his first book of poetry when he was only eighteen years old. His journeys to Greece and Turkey served as the basis for *Childe Harold's Pilgrimage* (1812) and the notorious *Don Juan* (1824), which glorify both Byron's travels and his love affairs. Although widely condemned on moral grounds, Byron's poetry was immensely popular in England during his lifetime. His works include *Manfred: A Dramatic Poem* (1817), *Beppo: A Venetian Story* (1818), and *The Vision of Judgment* (1822).

Jacob (1785–1863) and **Wilhelm** (1786–1859) **Grimm** were both born in Hanau, Germany, studied law and science, and became intensely interested in folklore. From the folk poetry and stories they collected, the brothers recorded over 200 fairy tales of Germany, carefully preserving the imagination, beliefs, and personality of the people. From their work emerged the science of folklore. Their most famous work is *Kinder-und Hausmarchen* (1812–1822), generally known as *Grimms' Fairy Tales* in English (translated by Margaret Hunt, 1944). In addition, Jacob wrote many studies of philology and grammar while Wilhelm continued to research folklore and literary history. Among other works translated into English is *The German Legends of the Brothers Grimm* (1981).

Dashiell Hammett (1894–1961), considered the father of hard-boiled detective fiction, actually worked as an investigator for the Pinkerton National Detective Agency. His style demonstrates a turning away from genteel investigators who stalk clever crooks to realistic, callous detectives and commonplace criminals. Hammett's Sam Spade remains the classic of an often imitated type, the tough-talking, unflappable and illusion-free private eye. Hammett's literary production decreased after World War II when he began to devote himself almost entirely to left-wing politics and was briefly jailed for his support of communists. Among his many novels and short stories are *Red Harvest* (1929), *The Dain Curse* (1929), *The Maltese Falcon* (1930), *The Glass Key* (1931), *Creeps By Night* (1931), and *The Thin Man* (1934).

Thomas Hardy (1840–1928) was an architect in London when he first became interested in literature. At thirty he began to write novels and had completed sixteen of them before he turned exclusively to writing poetry, some twenty-five years later. Despite his late start as a poet, Hardy produced eight volumes and is now considered among the greatest twentieth-century poets. Like Wordsworth and Browning, Hardy attempted to meld poetic language with that of common speech but enjoyed experimenting with poetic forms, rhythm, and sound. Among his best-known novels

are *Tess of the D'Urbervilles* (1891) and *Jude the Obscure* (1895); his poetry collections include *Wessex Poems* (1898) and *Winter Words* (1928).

Robert Hass (1941–) has spent most of his life in the San Francisco Bay area. He was born and raised in San Francisco, and attended St. Mary's College in Oakland (where he now teaches) and Stanford University. His writing is dominated by a strong sense of place; the history, politics, and natural surroundings of northern California are frequent themes. In 1973 his first book, *Field Guide,* won the Yale Series of Younger Poets Award. *Praise,* his second book, appeared in 1979. Hass has also distinguished himself as gifted prose-stylist and translator. His essays and reviews, collected under the title *Twentieth Century Pleasures: Prose on Poetry* (1984) received the National Book Critics Award for Criticism. He was co-translator of Czeslaw Milosz' *The Separate Notebooks* (1984) and *Unattainable Earth* (1986).

Nathaniel Hawthorne (1804–1864) was born in Salem, Massachusetts, and continued to live in the state throughout his life. He worked as an editor while beginning his writing career, and in 1837 his *Twice-Told Tales* was published. Although Hawthorne's affinity with New England's Puritan traditions was inconsistent with Transcendentalist optimism, he did join for a time in the utopian experiment at Brook Farm, and his *Blithedale Romance* (1852) grew out of his experience of living there. Hawthorne consistently wrote in the romance tradition, although the realistic period was already well established when he began writing. His best-known novel is *The Scarlet Letter* (1850); he also wrote *The House of Seven Gables* (1851), *The Marble Faun* (1860), and the stories collected in *Mosses from an Old Manse* (1846).

Anthony Hecht (1923–) was born in New York City and served in the U.S. Army in World War II. He has taught at several universities, most recently the University of Rochester. His poetry includes *Hard Hours* (1967), *Millions of Strage Shadows* (1977), *The Venetian Vespers* (1979), and *Obbligati: Essays in Criticism* (1986). Besides writing poetry, Hecht is a translator, collaborating with Helen Bacon on Aeschylus' *Seven Against Thebes.*

Ernest Hemingway (1899–1961), born in Oak Park, Illinois, began his writing career as a journalist. During World War I, he drove an ambulance in Italy and was seriously wounded in combat. After the war he lived in Paris and wrote many of his stories and novels; his *A Moveable Feast* (1964) describes the literary and artistic subculture he found there. During the Spanish Civil War, Hemingway returned to journalism as a war correspondent in Spain. Known for prose stripped of excess adjectives and rhetorical coloring, Hemingway writes with simplicity, allowing the direct experiences of his characters to communicate emotion. His extensive travelling and interest in bullfighting, fishing, and hunting are reflected in many of his works, which include *The Sun Also Rises* (1926), *A Farewell to Arms* (1929), *Death In The Afternoon* (1932), *For Whom The Bell Tolls* (1940), and *In Our Time* (1924). In 1954 Hemingway was awarded the Nobel Prize for Literature.

Beth Henley (1952–) was born in Jackson, Mississippi, and began acting and playwriting as a student at Southern Methodist University in Texas. Before she was thirty years old she had seen her award-winning *Crimes of the Heart* (1979) performed on Broadway. Often compared to other Southern writers such as Flannery O'Connor and Tennessee Williams, Henley is known for her blend of off-beat humor and compassion. As she explains, her relationship with the South involves "looking at these people and liking them for who they are" and for their ability to "do outrageous things like throw steaks out your plate glass window." She has also written *Am I Blue* (1973), *The Miss Firecracker Contest* (1980), *The Wake of Jamey Foster* (1982), and *The Moon Watcher* (1983). Henley won the 1981 Pulitzer Prize for drama.

Robert Herrick (1591–1674) was a priest in the Church of England who became a part of the "sons of Ben," the group of poets who frequented London taverns with Ben Jonson and imitated his poetic style. Herrick's poetry reflects the influence of classical literature, English folklore, and various religious writings. Often light and witty, sometimes serious and melancholy, Herrick's works always portray insight into the range of human emotions. *Hesperides* (1648), a collection of almost 1,400 poems, was the only book he published during his lifetime.

Gerard Manley Hopkins (1844–1889) was a writer, painter, and composer of experimental music as a young man. While at Oxford he left the Anglican church and was accepted into the Roman Catholic by Cardinal Newman. He became a Jesuit priest in 1868 and was ordained in 1877. Also a professor of classics, Hopkins was asked to chair the department of Greek and Latin in Dublin in 1884; he spent his last years there in the failing health and depression reflected in his "terrible sonnets." Although his friends admired his writing, only three poems were actually published during Hopkins' lifetime. In 1918, when a friend published his works, Hopkins gained immediate recognition. Brilliant imagery and "sprung rhythm" (a term he coined for meter based on stresses regardless of syllabic count) most consistently characterize his poetry. Hopkins' poems are collected in *The Poems of Gerard Manley Hopkins*, published in 1967.

Alfred Edward Housman (1859–1936), after failing his finals at Oxford, became a clerk in the Patent Office in London. Extremely capable in interpreting the classics, Housman began publishing his studies of classical authors and was eventually appointed professor of Latin at Cambridge. In 1896 he published *Shropshire Lad,* a nostalgic collection of ballads about an imaginary Shropshire. Although little noticed at the time, by World War I the collection was immensely popular. Likewise, Housman's *Last Poems* of 1922 was well received. The tragedy of doomed youth is a common theme in Housman's poetry, which is often admired for its lyric beauty and classic perfection. Housman is also remembered for his lecture "The Name and Nature of Poetry," an important and controversial comment on poetic invention.

Tina Howe (1937–) was born into an elite family of New York City eccentrics: her grandfather was a Pulitzer Prize-winning biographer, her father a reknowned broadcaster, and her mother a transplanted Bostonian aristocrat. Howe attended Sarah Lawrence College and then left for Paris where she lived among, and was inspired by, a group of bohemian writers. Writing, she says, was her "way of turning somersaults, of wreaking havoc"—things she felt compelled to do. Howe's plays are known for their commonplace settings, those places, she says, in which "supposedly nothing ever happened." Her blend of reality and fantasy—the absurd appearing within very credible plots—is finally a means into the psychic and emotional lives of her characters. Among her works are *Birth and After Birth* (1973), *Museum* (1976), *The Art of Dining* (1979), *Painting Churches* (1982), and *Coastal Disturbances* (1986).

Langston Hughes (1902–1967) was the leading interpreter of the black experience in the United States. Born in Joplin, Missouri, he attained in his work a cultivated artlessness by combining verse form with spirituals and blues. He attempted dialect poetry under the influence of Paul Lawrence Dunbar and experimented with free verse influenced by Carl Sandberg, Vachel Lindsey, and Amy Lowell. He earned his baccalaureate from Lincoln University in 1929, a year which also marked the publication of his first novel, *Not Without Laughter* (1930). Other works include: *Shakespeare in Harlem* (1941), *Fields of Wonder* (1947), *Montage of a Dream Deferred* (1951), and *Ask Your Mama* (1961).

Zora Neale Hurston (1903–1960) grew up in the all-black community of Eatonville, Florida, the town which became the primary source for her literary and scholarly work. Both a fiction writer and a folklorist, Hurston began her career at Howard University. Her fiction commonly reshapes folk material by synthesizing it with art, thus showing readers lives and places that are both realistic and legendary. She was active in the Harlem Renaissance in the 1920s, during which she wrote a play with Langston Hughes, *Mule Bones: A Comedy of Negro Life in Three Acts* (1931). An important source of black mythology and what Alice Walker calls "racial health," Hurston wrote a novel *Their Eyes Were Watching God* (1937); short stories, *The Eatonville Anthology* (1927); folklore, *Mules and Men* (1935); and an autobiography, *Dust Tracks on a Road* (1942).

Henrik Ibsen (1828–1906), left his native Norway in 1865 because he found its theatrical tradition old-fashioned and constraining. His plays, however, brought Norwegian theater to the forefront of modern literature. Also a poet and theatrical advisor, Ibsen is best known for breaking away from the romantic tradition in drama in order to portray life realistically. His early social dramas, *A Doll's House* (1879), *Ghosts* (1881), and *Hedda Gabler* (1890), gained worldwide attention by shocking audiences with topics previously unmentionable in public: the problem of venereal disease, controversial roles for women in a male-dominated world, and the hypocrisy of modern society. These studies of how people function within society and his exploration of the unconscious have earned Ibsen the title of "father of modern drama." Also by Ibsen are *Peer Gynt* (1867), *The Pillars of Society* (1877), and *The Master Builder* (1897).

Henry James (1843–1916), was born in New York City and educated in Europe. In 1876 he moved permanently to England; thereafter the clash between European sophistication and American innocence became a dominant theme in his works. Primarily a novelist and short story writer, James focused his energies on creating psychological realism by studying the process of the individual mind. His dense style is complicated by his use of the limited point of view, in which the reader shares the partial perception and gradually increasing awareness of the focal character. Also notable are his critical prefaces, collected in *The Art of Fiction* (1884), in which he explains his theories of literature at length. Among his over 70 short stories and several novels are *The American* (1877), *Daisy Miller* (1879), *The Portrait of a Lady* (1881), *The Bostonians* (1886), *The Wings of the Dove* (1902), *The Ambassadors* (1903), and *The Golden Bowl* (1904). *The Complete Tales of Henry James* was published in 1964.

Randall Jarrell (1914–1965) is recognized as one of the most powerful and eloquent spokespersons on war in the history of American literature. Jarrell's childhood was divided between the South and California. He studied psychology and English at Vanderbilt University, then spent two years as a professor at Kenyon College. During World War II he enlisted in the Army Air Corps, serving as a control tower operator for B-29 crews. Two of his collections—*Little Friend, Little Friend* (1945) and *Losses* (1948)—demonstrate the war's profound effect on him. After the war he returned to the life of professor, poet, and critic; in 1965 he was struck and killed by an automobile. His last book of poetry, *The Lost World,* was published a year later. Other works include *Blood From a Stranger* (1942), and his only published novel, *Pictures From an Institution* (1954).

James Joyce (1882–1941), the most influential Irish novelist of the twentieth century, left the country as a young expatriate in 1904, rejecting his Irish Catholic heritage. In Paris he began writing seriously, working on "Epiphanies," a collection of sketches which depicted sudden flashes of personal insight. The rest of his literary career was marked by preference for Irish subject matter while he developed a highly artistic, stream-of-consciousness style. *Ulysses* (1922), Joyce's first experimental novel, proved decidedly controversial for its convoluted language and open sexuality. The book was banned in the United States until 1933. *Dubliners* (1916), *A Portrait of the Artist as a Young Man* (1916), and *Finnegan's Wake* (1939), are his other best-known works.

Franz Kafka (1883–1924) was born into a middle-class Jewish family in Prague, Czechoslovakia. He received a law degree in 1906 and spent most of his life working for an insurance company, publishing very little. Yet because his unpublished manuscripts were not destroyed after his death as he requested, Kafka has now gained worldwide fame as one of the greatest writers of visionary fiction in the twentieth century. His fiction is marked by anxiety, like that he experienced in life from his frustrated love affairs, his struggle against tuberculosis, and his guilt over not living up to his father's expectations. Among his works translated into English are *The Trial* (1925), *The Castle* (1926), and *Amerika* (1927), all novels; *Metamorphosis and Other Stories* (1915) and *The Country Doctor* (1919), both short story collections.

John Keats (1795–1821) was born in London, the eldest son of a stable keeper. Following his early schooling he was apprenticed to a surgeon and licensed by the Society of Apothecaries in 1816; however, his intense literary interests led him to abandon medicine to write poetry. He greatly admired Wordsworth, and together with Byron and Shelley he helped establish the Romantic revolution as a tradition. Their work reveled in emotion, the purest expression of experience, and had a profound effect upon early Victorian poets such as Tennyson, Robert Browning, and Elizabeth Barrett Browning. In an effort to capture the essence of his subject, Keats constantly refined his small but extraordinary body of work. He died at age 26, of tuberculosis.

Garrison Keillor (1942–), was until June 1987 the host of American Public Radio's "A Prairie Home Companion," a music and comedy show for which Keillor told stories of the mythical Lake Wobegon, the "little town that time forgot, where all the women are strong, all the men are good-looking, and all the children are above average." Keillor's short stories have been published in *The New Yorker* and *The Atlantic* and are gathered in three collections: *Happy to be Here* (1982), *Lake Wobegon Days* (1985), and *Leaving Home* (1987). Although originally from Minnesota, Keillor and his wife, Ulla, recently moved to New York, where he is working on his first novel.

Walter Kerr (1913–) began his career as a movie and drama critic at an early age and has become one of the most important critics of this century. He has written for both *Commonweal* and the *New York Times,* among several other publications, and in 1978 won the Pulitzer Prize for drama criticism. As a conservative critic, Kerr has been denounced for agreeing too closely with the Broadway audiences. He explains that the theater should please people, so the best plays are naturally the popular ones. Kerr has written several books, including *How Not to Write a Play* (1955), *Harold Pinter* (1967), and *Journey to the Center of the Theater* (1979), as well as several plays.

Galway Kinnell (1927–) is the director of creative writing at the University of New York at Binghamton and the 1982 Pulitzer Prize winner for poetry. Kinnell's poems have always reflected a Christian sensibility, and have become increasingly experimental in both form and tone. For Kinnell, poetry is both myth and prayer; his has been described as producing rhythm like a "shaman's chant." His works include *What a Kingdom It Was* (1960), *The Book of Nightmares* (1971), *Mortal Acts,*

Mortal Words (1980), *Selected Poems* (1982), and *The Past* (1985). Kinnell also translates French poetry, including a collection of Francois Villon's poems published in 1977.

Hugh Kingsmill (1889–1949) was chiefly a biographer, writing the lives of Matthew Arnold (1928), Charles Dickens (1935), and D. H. Lawrence (1938), but during his lifetime he was most popular for his prose and poetic parodies. Captured by Germans during World War I, Kingsmill produced his first novel, *The Will to Live* (1919) while confined in a prison camp. He also wrote literary criticism, found in the essays of *The Progress of a Biographer* (1949) and interjected in his fictional fantasy *The Return of William Shakespeare* (1929); both are included in *The Best of Hugh Kingsmill* (1970).

Maxine Kumin (1925–   ) lives on a farm in New Hampshire where she breeds horses and writes. Born in Philadelphia and educated at Radcliffe, Kumin also teaches occasionally, at universities such as Princeton, Tufts, and the University of Massachusetts. Kumin's poems are characterized by their focus on the ordinary and the common-place; she claims that such things as pine groves, barnyard animals, and watering troughs are the salvation of sanity in the world. She has written over twenty children's books, essays, and fiction as well as several volumes of poetry. Her works include *Halfway* (1961), *Up Country* (1972) which won the 1973 Pulitzer Prize, the novel *Through Dooms of Love* (1965), and *To Make a Prairie: Essays on Poets, Poetry, and Country Living* (1979)

Doris Lessing (1919–   ) is a British writer who was born in Kermanshan, Iran, and grew up on a farm in Rhodesia. Many of her works focus on African life, including the novels *The Grass is Singing* (1950) and *Children of Violence* (1964-5), and the stories collected in *The Sun Between their Feet* (1973) and *Stories* (1978). While concerned with racial exploitation, Lessing extends her concern with oppression to the human condition all people experience. Likewise, her feminist stance reaches beyond women to the problem all individuals face in coping with a fragmented society. *The Golden Notebook* (1962), for example, portrays a woman writer attempting to deal emotionally and artistically with the materialistic modern world. A diversified writer, Lessing has written a science fiction sequence which includes *Shikasta* (1979), *The Sirian Experiments* (1981), and *Documents Relating to the Sentimental Agents in the Volyen Empire* (1983). *The Diaries of Jane Somers* (1984) and *The Good Terrorist* (1985) are among her most recent works.

Denise Levertov (1923–   ), from Essex, England, served as a nurse in World War II. She moved to the United States in 1948 and has taught in several universities. Her poetry reflects the influence of William Carlos Williams while presenting a distinctly female voice. Collections of her poetry include *The Double Image* (1946), *The Jacob's Ladder* (1961), *Oblique Prayers* (1984), and *Stay Alive and Footprints* (1987).

Federico García Lorca (1899–1936) ranks with Pablo Neruda and Antonio Machado as one of this century's greatest poets writing in Spanish. Born

into a prominent Andalusian farming family, García Lorca was educated in Granada and in Madrid, where he lived for fifteen years. He was very popular in his own lifetime, as much for his powerful plays as for his poetry. As a poet he is not unconventional—it is his authenticity which transcends his time. His poems seem effortlessly to extend the folk and gypsy traditions in which they are rooted. García Lorca drew sparingly on the avant-garde movements of his day; he probably marked them more strongly than they did him. He spent the Depression year 1929-30 teaching at Columbia University in New York City. The alienation he felt and his antipathy to urban conditions he witnessed is captured in *The Poet in New York*. In the next years he travelled throughout Latin America and in his native Spain, reading his poetry and having his plays performed. Fighting on the Loyalist side in the Spanish Civil War, he was captured and killed in Granada by Franco's Falangists. He was buried in an unmarked grave near Fuente Vaqueros, the village of his birth.

Robert Lowell (1917–1977) was born into a famous New England family whose ancestors included the poets Amy Lowell and James Russell Lowell. He attended Harvard, but graduated from Kenyon College, where he studied under John Crowe Ransom. During World War II he first tried, unsuccessfully, to enlist; when he was finally drafted he was so opposed to war that he served six months in prison. His concern with moral and spiritual decline made up much of what was to become his Pulitzer Prize-winning book of poems, *Lord Weary's Castle* (1946). *Life Studies* (1960) and *For the Union Dead* (1969) marked the pinnacle of his career. The first gave full expression to self-revelation, beginning the "confessional" movement of poetry; the second was a departure, starting a wide concern for human suffering which culminated in *History* (1973), and *Day by Day* published shortly before his death.

Sandra McPherson (1943–   ) began her writing career as a technical writer for the Honeywell Corporation. Soon after the publication of her first poem, however, she became a faculty member at the University of Iowa's Writers' Workshop and now teaches at Pacific Northwest College of Art. McPherson's stark, unembellished poems have been compared to those of Sylvia Plath, as both poets typically define their lives in terms of contemporary metaphors. Joyce Carol Oates described McPherson's work as "beautifully rendered poems with the lucidity of parables." McPherson's books include *Elegies for the Hot Season* (1970), *Radiation* (1973), *Patron Happiness* (1983), and *Floralia* (1985). She contributes frequently to various periodicals, including *The New Yorker*, *Poetry*, *Harper's*, and *New Republic*.

Archibald MacLeish (1892–1982) was born in Chicago and graduated both from Yale and from Harvard Law School. He also fought in World War I, was a librarian for the Library of Congress, and served as the Assistant Secretary of State. He wrote over a dozen books of poetry as well as radio and television plays. Both his *Conquistador* (1933) and *Collected Poems: 1917–1952* (1952) were awarded Pulitzer Prizes for poetry; his *J.B.: A Play in Verse* (1958) won the Pulitzer Prize for drama. Other volumes of poetry include *Songs for a Summer's Day* (1915), *Songs for Eve* (1954), and *New and Collected Poems: 1917–1984* (1985). MacLeish has also written several other plays, prose works, and librettos.

Gabriel García Márquez (1928–) was born in Aracataca, Colombia. He studied law until civil war closed the university and then became a journalist, film critic, and fiction writer. His journalism tends toward revolutionary socialism, for which he writes rather controversial arguments. But his foremost contribution to the renaissance of Spanish-language literature is *One Hundred Years of Solitude* (1970), a comic and poignant novel about the magical town of Macondo. García Márquez is known for "magic realism," by which possible events are depicted as wonders, and the impossible as commonplace. In 1982 he won the Nobel Prize for Literature. His other works include *Leaf Storm and Other Stories* (1955), *No One Writes to the Colonel and Other Stories* (1961), *In Evil Hour* (1962), *The Autumn of the Patriarch* (1976), and *Chronicle of a Death Foretold* (1982).

Andrew Marvell (1621–1678) wrote most of his poetry while tutoring the daughter of Sir Thomas Fairfax, the Lord-General of the Parliamentary forces. In 1657 he was appointed to assist Milton and soon became a member of Parliament: his influence is said to have saved Milton from prison. Although often satirizing contemporary politics, Marvell's poems were seldom taken seriously, and their intellectual depth and insight were frequently overlooked during his lifetime. Many of his poems are casual and witty, and their emphasis on the enjoyment of country life anticipates the work of Wordsworth. Marvell's *Miscellaneous Poems* were published in 1681 and his *Poems on Affairs of State* in 1689. A recent collection of his works, *Poems and Letters*, was produced in 1971.

Guy de Maupassant (1850–1893) was born in Normandy, France, and fought in the Franco-Prussian War before beginning his literary career. His distant relative, Gustave Flaubert, then took him in for seven years, during which time Maupassant learned to write and destroyed nearly everything he wrote. His work was first published in 1880, and he produced nearly 300 stories in the next ten years. His work is characterized by realism and a turn away from the sentimental fiction of his time—indeed, he demanded "a more complete, striking, and convincing vision of life than the reality itself." Although sympathetic in his portrayal of characters, Maupassant consistently presents bleak and futile existence. His stories are collected in *Complete Stories* (1903); his novels include *A Life* (1883), *Handsome Friend* (1885), and *Pierre et Jean* (1888).

Herman Melville (1819–1891), born in New York City, was forced by poverty to go to sea as a cabin boy in 1839. His adventures there ranged from whaling to living with cannibals, and many were recounted in the early novels *Typee* (1846), *Omoo* (1847), *Mardi* (1849), *Redburn* (1849), and *White-Jacket* (1850). Melville was attracted to Hawthorne's method of weaving philosophy into fiction, a practice that most influenced the writing of his masterpiece, *Moby-Dick* (1851). Although his reputation declined when *Moby-Dick* proved too difficult for popular interest, Melville was rediscovered in the 1920s and is now acknowledged as one of America's finest writers. Considered "legends of wild and gloomy power," Melville's short stories are collected in *Piazza Tales* (1856). *Billy Budd* (1921), which Melville wrote late in life, was published several years after his death.

W.S. Merwin (1927–) was raised in Union City, New Jersey, and Scranton, Pennsylvania. After graduating from Princeton University he made the first of many trips abroad. On the Spanish island of Mallorca he continued his study of Romance languages and completed his first book of poems. *A Mask for Janus*, which received the Yale Series of Younger Poets award in 1954, displays a marked classical influence. From this initial formalism Merwin developed a spare and elusive style, restrained yet urgent, shot through with imagery of darkness and water. His true subject has been described as "the nature of loneliness or separation, the burden of consciousness." Merwin has received most of the significant prizes and fellowships available to contemporary poets, including a Pulitzer Prize for *The Carrier of Ladders* (1970). The most recent of his fourteen volumes of poetry is *Opening the Hand* (1984). He has also published three books of prose and some twenty books of translation from many languages.

Edna St. Vincent Millay (1892–1950) had already made herself known as an actress, poet, and playwright when she graduated from Vassar in 1917. She then moved to Greenwich Village where she continued to write poetry and involve herself in politics. Part of the crusade to save Sacco and Vanzetti, the alleged anarchists executed in 1927, Millay began using her poetry to speak out politically, and continued doing so through World War II. Her poetry is also notable for its engaging persona, a reckless and romantic New Woman who promoted both sexual and emotional liberation. Millay's works include *Renascence and Other Poems* (1917), *A Few Figs from Thistles* (1920), *The Harp-Weaver* (1923), for which she won the Pulitzer Prize, and *Collected Poems* (1956).

Arthur Miller (1915–) was born in New York City and educated at the University of Michigan. He first found employment in a box factory, a job which actually prompted his literary career by giving his mind limitless hours in which to create. By 1944 Miller had a play, *The Man Who Had All the Luck*, performed on Broadway. His *Death of a Salesman* (1949) won the Pulitzer Prize for drama. Miller's works typically involve an individual's struggle for personal dignity within a society which offers nothing but betrayal. Miller's interests, however, were not limited to literature. In 1956 (the same year he married Marilyn Monroe), Miller appeared before the House Un-American Activities Committee to answer questions about his participation in Communist-sponsored activities. Though he answered all questions about his own activities, he was cited for contempt because he refused to implicate others. *All My Sons* (1947), *The Crucible*

(1953), *A View from the Bridge* (1965), and *The American Clock* (1980) are among his many plays. Miller is also known for his critical writings, collected in *The Theatre Essays of Arthur Miller* (1978). In 1987 he published his autobiography, *Timebends*.

John Milton (1608–1674) received a classical education at Cambridge, but instead of taking holy orders as expected, he isolated himself in his parents' country home for months of extensive reading. After completing his education by traveling to Italy, Milton returned home and began writing political and social tracts. He became Cromwell's Latin secretary during the civil war between the king and Parliament, answering correspondence and writing Puritan propaganda. When he was 43 Milton lost his eyesight. He was arrested when the monarchy was restored in 1660; his income and his role in public life subsequently declined. In the final fourteen years of his life, however, he produced his epic poems *Paradise Lost* (1667) and *Paradise Regained* (1671), and the tragedy *Samson Agonistes* (1671).

Yukio Mishima (1925–1970) was the pseudonym of Kimitake Hiraoka, the Japanese singer, actor, and swordsman remembered most for his literary works. Born and educated in Tokyo, Mishima was highly concerned with restoring Japan to the samurai tradition free from materialistic Western influence. In 1968 he formed a society of over 80 university men devoted to furthering the samurai cause. Two years later he took his own life in a ritual suicide. Yasunari Kawabata, the Japanese Nobel Prize winner, finds Mishima's writing "far superior" to his own work and believes that such genius "comes along perhaps once every 300 years." Mishima's works translated into English include *Confessions of a Mask* (1949), *Temple of the Golden Pavilion* (1959), *The Sailor Who Fell From Grace With The Sea* (1965), *Death in Midsummer* (1966), and *The Sea of Fertility* (1975).

Eugenio Montale (1896–1981) was awarded the Nobel Prize for Poetry in 1975. In the half century since the publication of his first book, *Cuttlefish Bones* (1925), Montale had established himself by the scope of his career, his stylistic inventiveness, and the profundity of his concerns as second to none among modern Italian poets. He was born in Genoa, and many of his poems describe the Ligurian landscape where he grew up. After serving as an infantry officer in World War I, he lived for twenty years in Florence as director of the Vieusseux Library. In 1948 he joined the Milanese newspaper *Il Corriere della Sera*, for which he wrote hundreds of articles on music and literature. Following the death of his wife in 1962 Montale's work took on a character that allows it to stand with the poetry of Dante and Hardy as one of the supreme poetic responses to the death of a beloved. Translations of his work into English include *Selected Poems* (1965); *New Poems* (1976); *The Storm and Other Things* (1978); *The Second Life of Art: Selected Essays* (1982); and *Otherwise: Last and First Poems* (1984).

Marianne Moore (1887–1972) was born in St. Louis, Missouri, but spent most of her life elsewhere. She attended the Metzger Institute and then Bryn Mawr College. Over the years Moore taught typing and bookkeeping at the Carlisle Indian School, worked at the New York Public Library, and, from 1925 to 1929, edited *The Dial*, a leading review of its time. She never married; in her early adult years, she lived with her mother in a Brooklyn apartment where Elizabeth Bishop and others would visit to drink tea and converse. Moore's generation included the major American modernist poets—Eliot, Ezra Pound, William Carlos Williams, and Wallace Stevens—all of whom she knew. Through her keen perceptions, wit, and idiosyncratic line-breaks, she carved out a significant niche for her work. Often taking as subjects animals and inanimate objects, Moore's poems proceed from the "personalities" that she perceives in them to forge dry and ironic comparisons with mankind. Her books include: *Poems, Selected Poems, Observations,* and *A Marianne Moore Reader.*

Alice Munro (1931–) is a Canadian writer from Wingham, Ontario. Having grown up on a fox farm in a rural community, Munro focuses her work on small-town living, and particularly on the lives of women. Her women, although quite ordinary and often self-conscious and awkward in society, possess emotional lives of surprising depth. Munro writes short stories almost exclusively, claiming that the genre allows her to present "intense, but not connected, moments of experience." Two of her collections have won the Governor General's Award. Among her books are *Dance of the Happy Shades* (1968), *Lives of Girls and Women* (1971), *Something I've Been Meaning to Tell You* (1974), *The Moons of Jupiter* (1983), *The Beggar Maid* (1984), and *The Progress of Love* (1986).

Pablo Neruda (1904–1973) is regarded as one of this century's greatest poets. He was also a political activist and diplomat, serving his country of Chile as a consular official in many countries from 1924 to 1938. He joined the Communist Party in 1939 and travelled in the USSR, China and Eastern Europe. He was a fiercely elemental poet, coupling meditations on political oppression with intense personal lyrics on the possibilities of romantic love. His influence on European and American, as well as Latin American, poets has been enormous. His best known works include *Twenty Love Poems and a Song of Despair* (1924), *Residence on Earth* (three series, 1925–45), *Spain in the Heart* (1937), and *The Captain's Verses* (1953).

Joyce Carol Oates (1938–) was born in Lockport, New York, and had written thousands of pages of prose by the time she went to high school. She graduated from Syracuse University as valedictorian, and is now a professor of English at Princeton University. Always a prolific writer, Oates has written over 100 stories and nearly 40 books, as well as critical essays. Fascinated by psychological and social disorder, she often examines in her fiction the moral implications of madness and violence. Her works include *By the North Gate* (1963), *Upon the Sweeping Flood* (1966), *Childwold* (1976), *Marya: A Life* (1985), and *Raven's Wing* (1986). *New Heaven, New Earth* (1974) and *Last Days: Stories* (1984) are two of her best-known critical books. Oates also writes poetry, collected in *Invisible Woman: New and Selected Poems* (1982).

Edna O'Brien (1936–   ) was educated at a convent as a child and then attended Pharmaceutical College of Ireland where she studied chemistry. She began writing when she left Ireland for London as a young woman. Attending a lecture on the fiction of Hemingway, O'Brien found herself compelled by a precise, uncluttered, yet lyrical and moving style which dramatically influenced her own writing. O'Brien's reputation was then established through the rise of the feminist movement, for feminists were attracted to her portrayal of sensitive, yet often victimized, women. Finally, however, O'Brien writes of her relationship to Ireland and to her strictly religious past, for she claims that fiction must be autobiographical: no one can "fabricate emotion," she states, and emotion is what matters most in art. O'Brien's fiction includes *The Country Girls* (1960), *August is a Wicked Month* (1965), *I Hardly Knew You* (1977), *A Rose in the Heart* (1979), and a play about Virginia Woolf, *Virginia* (1981). Her selected short stories are gathered in *A Fanatic Heart* (1984). *James and Nora: A Portrait of Joyce's Marriage* (1981) and *Mother Ireland* (1976) are among her non-fiction works. O'Brien has also written several plays for the stage, screen, and television.

Flannery O'Connor (1925–1964) was born in Milledgeville, Georgia, and lived most of her life there on a farm with her mother and pet peacocks. She has been characterized as a Southern writer of gothic humor, but it is her Roman Catholicism which most fervently figures in her works. She once stated that her writing concerns "the conflict between an attraction for the Holy and the disbelief in it" and that since everything is "ultimately saved or lost," she must bring her characters to an awareness of their spiritual depravity. Although sick with lupus most of her life, O'Connor devoted as much time as possible to writing, traveling, and lecturing. She wrote two novels, *Wise Blood* (1952) and *The Violent Bear it Away* (1960), as well as short fiction, collected in *The Complete Short Stories* (1971). O'Connor's essays and speeches, which focus on writing and its relationship to Christianity, are found in *Mystery and Manners: Occasional Prose* (1969).

Frank O'Hara (1926–1966) enjoyed music, art, and drama as well as poetry throughout his lifetime. For most of his life, he worked as the curator at the Museum of Modern Art in New York City and also as an editorial associate for *Art News*. His poetry is known for endowing the very common with mythic proportions and for its blend of exuberance and melancholy. O'Hara's poems are collected in *A City Winter and Other Poems* (1952), *Second Avenue* (1960), and *The Collected Poems of Frank O'Hara* (1974).

Sharon Olds (1942–   ) was born in San Francisco and educated at Stanford University. After further study at Columbia University she settled in New York, where she teaches writing at universities and at Goldwater Hospital on Roosevelt Island. Olds' poetry is in many ways "confessional" along the lines of Sylvia Plath or Anne Sexton. In their

preoccupation with sexuality, and with family and male-female relationships, these poets examine the political in the personal. Olds has published three books of poems to date: *Satan Says,* for which she was given the inaugural San Francisco Poetry Center Award in 1980; *The Dead and the Living,* which received the National Book Critics Circle Award and was the Lamont Poetry Selection for 1983; and *The Gold Cell* (1987).

Wilfred Owen (1893–1918) was born in Shropshire, England, and educated in Liverpool. He worked temporarily as a teacher of English in Bordeaux, where he met a minor Symbolist poet who inspired him to write. In 1915 he joined the English army and fought in World War I. Trench-fever and a concussion, however, forced Owen to be hospitalized in Edinburgh for several months; during this time he wrote all of his major poetry. He finally returned to the war in 1918 and was killed one week before the Armistice. His poetry is marked by technical accuracy, especially in meter and sound. Writing mainly about his war experiences, Owen expressed his hatred for war and the horrors of combat, as well as his pity for all those involved in it. His poems were collected and published in 1920.

Dorothy Parker (1893–1967) is still remembered for saying that Katharine Hepburn, in a play, "ran the whole gamut of emotions, from A to B" and is still quoted for witty lines like "Men seldom make passes/At girls who wear glasses." Known best for her lively sense of humor, Parker was actually a serious editor and writer, producing best-selling books and reputable essays. After being fired from *Vanity Fair* for writing cutting theater reviews, Parker reviewed books for *The New Yorker* in her column "Constant Reader." *The New Yorker* then published her stories, poems, and articles continuously for over thirty years. In addition, Parker's political voice attracted the attention of the House Un-American Activities Committee, which became concerned in 1951 about her association with communist organizations. Her works are found in *Collected Stories* (1942), *Collected Poetry* (1944), *The Best of Dorothy Parker* (1952), and *A Month of Saturdays* (1971).

Walter Pater (1839–1894) was a tutor of classics at Oxford who believed that great poetry must combine romanticism and classicism. His writing, similarly, tended to blend poetry and prose, for he considered prose writing an art equal to poetry which must be calculated with equal precision of language and rhythm. Pater's followers exalt him most for turning away from traditional Victorianism, at least in theory, and embracing a form of Epicureanism which stressed the enjoyment of life and art. His works include *Studies in the History of the Renaissance* (1873), *Marius the Epicurean* (1885), and *Appreciations* (1889).

Francesco Petrarch (1304–1374) began writing love poetry as a young man, presumably inspired by a woman, "Laura," whom he met in 1327 and praised in his poems. Always popular in Italy, Petrarch was named poet laureate in 1341. He was also the most popular Italian poet in the English Renaissance; his many sonnets were both translated and imitated by English poets. In addition to perfecting the Italian sonnet form, Petrarch is known for reviving the study of ancient Greek and Latin literature in Italy. His collected works were published in 1554 and 1581.

Harold Pinter (1930–   ), born in London, is one of the pre-eminent living dramatists of the British stage. His first play was produced in 1957, and in 1960 he achieved significant success on both sides of the Atlantic with *The Caretaker*. Other plays include *The Birthday Party, No Man's Land, The Homecoming, Betrayal, The Dumb-waiter*, and *Landscape and Silence*. There are often only two or three characters in a Pinter play, and they are usually desperate in one way or another. The dialogue is stripped down and punctuated by the famous Pinter pauses. Pinter has proved himself a true master of the dramatic form by adapting other works for the screen—*The Last Tycoon, The Go-Between*, and *The French Lieutenant's Woman* among them.

Sylvia Plath (1932–1963), daughter of a Polish immigrant, was raised in rural New England. She won a scholarship to Smith College where, at the end of her junior year, she suffered the emotional breakdown chronicled in her novel *The Bell Jar*. After graduating from Smith Plath went to Cambridge University on a Fulbright. While in England she met and married the English poet Ted Hughes, with whom she had a son and a daughter. Plath taught briefly at Smith, but her writing suffered. She and Hughes returned to England. Her emotional problems grew worse with time, leading to several suicide attempts. Before long the strains on their marriage forced Plath and Hughes to separate. In 1963 she took her own life. Her writing, which typifies what has come to be called "confessional" poetry, embodies the frantic, white-knuckled grip on sanity that her troubled emotional history would suggest. Her best known works include *Ariel, Uncollected Poems, The Bell Jar* (all published posthumously in 1965), *Crossing the Water* (1971), and *Winter Trees* (1972).

Edgar Allan Poe (1809–1849) was born in Boston and educated in both Europe and the United States. He began writing early, publishing *Tamerlane, and Other Poems* in 1827. Admitted to and then expelled within a year from West Point Military Academy, Poe returned to writing and editing to make a living. Introduced to Europe through the translations of Charles Baudelaire, Poe became a major influence on the symbolist movement. He was also internationally acclaimed as a romantic writer of poetry, fiction, and essays about art. Walt Whitman described Poe and his writing as an image in the midst of a midnight storm, "enjoying all the terror, the murk, and the dislocation of which he was the centre and the victim." Poe's works are collected in *Poems by Edgar Allan Poe* (1831), *The Raven and Other Poems* (1945), *Tales of the Grotesque* (1940), and *The Prose Romances of Edgar A. Poe* (1843), among others.

Elena Poniatowska (1933–   ), although born in Paris and educated in the United States, is a Latin American writer of Polish descent who writes exclusively in Spanish. Journalism, especially in the form of interviews or aggressive political commentaries, dominates Poniatowska's writing. She considers the writing of short stories, therefore, "a sort of self-indulgence," through which she joins all Latin American writers in creating what she calls a literature "of the barefoot . . . of those who eat dirt . . . of those who take up arms . . . of rage." In the stories of *De Noche Vienes* (1979), Poniatowska presents the oppressive dependency of women who are often cut off from the world beyond their own. Her books translated into English are *Massacre in Mexico* (1971) and *Dear Diego* (1986).

Alexander Pope (1688–1744), a small and sickly man born near London, became one of England's finest poets and satirists. His curvature of the spine and tuberculosis, which stopped his growth when he was only four feet six inches tall, forced Pope to put his energy into reading and writing. He was largely self-taught, owing not only to his poor health but also to his Catholicism, which precluded a university education. His devotion to the classics eventually produced translations of both the *Iliad* and the *Odyssey*, works so successful they brought him financial independence. Sometimes criticized for writing poetry that is overly artificial, Pope is a master of irony and wit. His works include *An Essay on Criticism* (1711), *The Rape of the Lock* (1714), *The Dunciad* (1728), and *An Essay on Man* (1733–34).

Katherine Anne Porter (1890–1980), born in Indian Creek, Texas, was primarily a fiction writer, but she also worked for a Chicago newspaper, played bit-parts in movies, and studied Aztec art in Mexico. Her fiction reflects her concern for situation and character over a sharply defined plot. Although considered a Southern writer, Porter locates her fiction in experiences from her numerous and varied travels; *Ship of Fools* (1962), for example, is drawn from a cruise from Mexico to Europe. Porter's works include *Flowering Judas and Other Stories* (1930), *Noon Wine* (1937), *Pale Horse, Pale Rider: Three Short Novels* (1939), *The Collected Essays and Occasional Writings of Katherine Anne Porter* (1970), and *The Never Ending Wrong* (1977). Her *Collected Stories* (1967) won the Pulitzer Prize and the National Book Award the year it was published.

Ezra Pound (1885–1972), originally from Hailey, Idaho, spent his life in Venice, London, Paris, and finally, Rapallo, Italy. He is known as the founder of the Imagist school of poetry which stressed the use of free rhythms, concreteness, and precise language and imagery. In addition, Pound frequently advised other writers, most notably James Joyce and T. S. Eliot. While in Italy, Pound became preoccupied with economics and began to support Mussolini's social program. During World War II he was arrested and sent to a U.S. Disciplinary Training Center, then to a mental institution in Washington, before being released and allowed to return to Italy. Pound's best-known poetry is his collection of Cantos which he began in 1917. In his later years he wrote his much-admired *Pisan Cantos* (1948).

Kathleen Raine (1908–) is a British poet, critic, and translator. Her poetry most often encompasses Scottish landscapes that express the sacredness and vitality of the natural world. Raine is linked to the romantic tradition not only by her affinity with nature but also by her use of archaic language. She claims, in fact, to be most influenced by Blake, who has been the focus of many of her critical works, including *Blake and England* (1960), *Blake and the New Age* (1979) and *William Blake* (1970). Raine's poetry is found in *Collected Poems* (1981), and she has written an autobiographical trilogy, *Farewell Happy Fields* (1973), *The Land Unknown* (1975), and *The Lion's Mouth* (1977).

Carter Revard (1931–), an Osage Indian, was born in Pawhuska, Oklahoma, and studied as a Rhodes Scholar at Oxford University. After receiving his Ph.D. from Yale University, Revard began teaching and is now a professor of literature and linguistics at Washington University. His research and writing include scholarly works such as *How to Make a New Utopian Dictionary of English* (1973) and *Decipherment of the four-letter word in a Medieval Manuscript* (1977), but he also writes poetry, collected in *My Right Hand Don't Leave Me No More* (1970), *Ponca War Dancers* (1978), *The Remembered Earth* (1978), and *Nonymosity* (1980).

Adrienne Rich (1929–) was born into a prosperous Jewish family in Baltimore. When she was a senior at Radcliffe College her first book of poems, *A Change of World* (1951), was selected by W.H. Auden for the Yale Series of Younger Poets. She studied at Oxford, then married and had three sons. She called her marriage and motherhood a "radicalizing" experience; so, too, was the Vietnam War, which she actively resisted. Most of her adult life, especially after the death of her estranged husband in 1970, has centered around a commitment to advancing feminism. Her eloquent articulation of woman's place in history and society has made her a leading voice in contemporary poetry. Her numerous volumes of poetry, including *Snapshots of a Daughter-in-Law* (1962), *The Dream of a Common Language* (1978), *Diving into the Wreck* (1973), and *A Wild Patience Has Taken Me This Far* (1981), have won many prizes. She has also published *Of Woman Born* (1976), a study of the institution of motherhood, and *On Lies, Secrets, and Silence* (1979), a collection of essays. Rich now teaches at Stanford University.

Rainer Maria Rilke (1875–1926) was born in Prague of German-speaking parents. Educated in Prague, Munich, and Berlin, he was never fully at home in any one place. He spent most of his life criss-crossing the European continent. His first major trip was to Russia (1899–1900), where he met Tolstoy and other writers and returned a changed man. His first recognition came in 1902 with the publication of *The Book of Images*. During the next twelve years, spent on and off in Paris, Rilke produced some of his greatest work. Serving as secretary to the sculptor Rodin, he learned a sharpness of concentration on the things of the external world which culminated in the *New Poems* (1907–08). He wrote a monograph on Rodin, and an autobiographical novel, *The Notebooks of Malte*

Laurids Brigge, in 1910. That same year he began work on the *Duino Elegies*, his overwhelming statement on transformation and transcendance. In 1922, in the small town of Muzot in Switzerland, Rilke in a single month was able both to finish the Elegies and write the 29 *Sonnets to Orpheus*. He lived and wrote mainly in Switzerland until his premature death from pneumonia.

Edwin Arlington Robinson (1869–1935) was led to writing poetry by his passionate interest in English blank verse. Born in Maine a descendant of the Puritan Anne Bradstreet, Robinson wrote poems that focus on New England living. His first collection of poems portrays types of people found in his hometown; the psychological depth of these poems is comparable to that of Robert Browning's dramatic monologues. Throughout his life Robinson was a popular poet, winning three Pulitzer Prizes. Robinson's collections include *The Torrent and the Night Before* (1896), *The Children of the Night* (1897), *The Man who Died Twice* (1924).

Theodore Roethke (1908–1963) considered himself a "mad poet" yet enjoyed the poetic vision with which the condition endowed him. Born in Saginaw, Michigan, Roethke grew up near his father's 25-acre greenhouse complex, a place which later acquired symbolic meaning in his poetry. He first worked as a professor of English and tennis coach at Lafayette College, and finally settled at the University of Washington, which appointed him poet-in-residence just one year before he died. Roethke was accomplished as a poet, winning both the Pulitzer Prize (1954) and the National Book Award (1958 and 1965). In his poetry he expressed a concern for details and for the poet's ability to see the world with precision. His reverence for and fear of the physical world was always blended with humor and irony. Roethke's works include *Open House* (1941), *Praise to the End!* (1951), *Sequence, Sometimes Metaphysical* (1963), and *The Collected Poems* (1966).

Christina Rossetti (1830–1894), too sickly to work as a governess, lived as an invalid, spending her time reading and writing. She was briefly engaged to James Collinson, a member of the Pre-Raphaelite Brotherhood founded by her brother, painter-poet Dante Gabriel Rossetti, but her devotion to the Anglican church prohibited their marriage when he converted to Catholicism. Her lyric poetry typically expresses frustration and parting in relationships, rarely happiness and fulfillment. Although Rossetti was intensely religious throughout her life, her poetry contains the erotic as well as the spiritual. The poems range in form from ballads to fantasies to religious sonnets and in tone from melancholy to playful. Her works include *The Goblin Market and Other Poems* (1862), *The Prince's Progress and Other Poems* (1866), and *A Pageant and Other Poems* (1881).

Lucius Annaeus Seneca (c.4 BC–AD 65) was a Roman Stoic philosopher, a tragic poet, and a rhetorician. He became Nero's tutor and later advisor, but when he withdrew from the court in 62 he was accused of conspiracy and forced to commit suicide. Seneca's tragedies are marked by exaggerated rhetoric and gory details reported through narrative speeches rather than acted on stage; they were intended for reading rather than for performance. All nine of his tragedies, including *Phaedra, Medea, Oedipus,* and *Hercules* (dates unknown), were translated into English and frequently imitated by dramatists of the English Renaissance and Restoration. Seneca also wrote several satires and philosophical treatises.

William Shakespeare (1554–1616) is indisputably among the most timeless writers in any language. Surprisingly little is known of his life. Church and legal registers show that he married in 1582, had two sons and a daughter, and owned a large house in Stratford. It is known that between 1585 and 1592 he left Stratford for London to begin his career as a playwright and actor. However, no dates of his professional career are recorded, nor is it certain in what order he composed his plays and poems. In fact, were it not for his actors, who recalled the text of his plays largely from memory for the historic *First Folio* (the first collection of Shakespeare's work, published in 1623), many of the plays themselves might never have survived. Shakespeare was tremendously prolific; his approximately 35 plays, as well as the 150 sonnets, were written in a span of 25 years. Working largely within story lines borrowed from Roman, English, French, and Italian sources, he proved himself master of a range of genres, including tragedy, comedy, romance and historical drama. Moreover, he created some of the most complex and three-dimensional characters in the history of the theater, skillfully interweaving them in single, double and sometimes triple plots. His sonnets are counted by many as some of the most beautiful and stirring love poems ever written.

Percy Bysshe Shelley (1792–1822) was expelled from Oxford for writing an anti-religious pamphlet, "The Necessity of Atheism." The rest of his short life was equally tumultous: he left his wife for Mary Godwin, left huge debts in England to settle in Italy, saw two of his young children die, and then drowned in a sailing accident. Shelley began writing gothic romances, but soon devoted himself to poetry and criticism, publishing most of his greatest poetic works—*Prometheus Unbound* and "*Ode to the West Wind*"—in 1819, and his *Defense of Poetry* in 1821. His works are collected in a ten-volume series, the *Complete Works* (1930).

Sam Shepard (1943–) is one of the outstanding American dramatists of his generation. Born in Fort Sheridan, Illinois, he grew up in the car culture of 1950s Southern California. Before establishing himself as a playwright Shepard worked in horse stables, as a rock musician, and as an actor. In 1967 *La Turista* won an Obie (Off-Broadway) Award. Twelve years later *Buried Child* became the first Off-Broadway play to receive the Pulitzer Prize. Set in the West, and centering around one troubled family's efforts to regenerate lives grown as barren as the land they inhabit, *Buried Child* typifies Shepard's concern with the deterioration of American values and dreams. Prolific and experimental, Shepard's dozens of plays include *Curse of the Starving Class* (1978), *True West* (1980), and *A Lie of the Mind* (1985). An accomplished actor and director, Shepard has

appeared in *Days of Heaven* (1978), *Country* (1984), *Crimes of the Heart* (1986), and the film version of his own play *Fool for Love* (1985).

Leslie Marmon Silko (1948–), a Native American author and educator from Laguna, New Mexico, studied law before devoting herself to writing. Her experiences growing up on the Laguna Pueblo Indian reservation and her knowledge of Indian ritual both figure into her fiction: many of her stories are re-creations of the stories and legends of her people. Concerned primarily with relationships, Silko believes unity with nature is as vital as unity among individuals; she works to create "the interior landscapes of the characters" yet landscapes always tied to "the tundra and the river." Her diverse works include a novel, *Ceremony* (1977); short stories, *Storyteller* (1981); and *Laguna Woman: Poems* (1974).

John Simon (1925–) was born in Yugoslavia and educated at Harvard. He has been a professor of humanities and English, an editor, and a critic; he is currently a theater and film critic for *New York* magazine. Simon is known for his consistently harsh criticism: he has been accused of believing not more than a half-dozen good films have ever been made. He responds that positive reviews are always passionate and subjective, thus we should not expect less from negative ones. His criticism is gathered in *Acid Test* (1963), *Private Screenings: Views of the Cinema of the Sixties* (1967), *Movies into Film* (1971), and *Singularities: Essays on the Theatre: 1964–1974* (1976), among several others.

Isaac Bashevis Singer (1904–) was born in Radzymin, Poland, and emigrated to the United States in 1935 Working as a journalist for a Yiddish-language newspaper, Singer wrote all of his early fiction in Yiddish. Since 1950, however, he has been writing English translations along with his Yiddish originals. As the son of a rabbi and a teacher of Hebrew, Singer has maintained a dedication for the Jewish orthodoxy and traditions; his writing persists in exploring the relationship of the natural to the supernatural and that of history to fiction. Among his works are *The Family Moskat* (1950), *Gimpel the Fool and Other Stories* (1957), *The Spinoza of Market Street and Other Stories* (1961), and *Old Love and Other Stories* (1979). Singer won the Nobel Prize for Literature in 1978.

Christopher Smart (1722–1771) was a Cambridge classics scholar who went to London to write poetry and reviews in 1749. By 1756 he displayed marked symptoms of insanity, most particularly a compulsion to fervently praying in the city streets. While institutionalized, Smart wrote a number of striking poems, collected in *Poems on Several Occasions* (1752) and *A Song to David* (1763). His poems are marked by religious imagery, mathematically precise structure, and use of repetition for dramatic effect. Insane most of his life and never able to pay his debts, Smart died in prison.

Sophocles (496–406 B.C.) wrote over 120 plays, but only seven have survived. Born in Colonus, near Athens, Sophocles studied under Aeschylus, the master of Greek tragedy whom he later defeated in the annual dramatic festival of Dionysis. He then went on to win over twenty more prizes, a record unmatched by any other tragedian. His protagonists are admirably strong-willed, but their pride and lack of self-knowledge often leads them to tragedy. Unlike Eurpides, Sophocles did not question the justice of the gods: his tragedies imply a divine order to which men must learn to conform. Sophocles also maintained an active public life, holding several official positions and possibly establishing a society for music and literature. His best known plays include *Ajax, Antigone, Trachiniae, Oedipus Tyrannus, Electra,* and *Philoctetes.*

Wole Soyinka (1934–) calls himself "a very political animal" both in his lifestyle and art. A controversial social critic, Soyinka has had to flee Nigeria on several occasions for criticizing government policies and has been jailed twice. At the same time, he is Nigeria's leading playwright. He was educated at Leeds University in England and has written fifteen plays along with two novels and three volumes of poetry. His first published play, *Swamp Dwellers,* was staged at a London drama festival in 1958. In 1986 he won the Nobel Prize for Literature. Wanting to write for and about Africa, Soyinka often reveals his compassion and concern for his countrymen by depicting them as victims of natural disasters and social turmoil. His plays include *Lion and the Jewel* (1957), *The Invention* (1959), and *Death and the King's Horseman* (1975); he has also written an autobiography, *The Man Died* (1973).

John Steinbeck (1902–1968), having grown up in California's Salinas Valley where he worked as a fruit-picker and hod-carrier, wrote often about the difficulty of living in rural California. His best known work, the Pulitzer Prize winning *The Grapes of Wrath* (1939), is about a family from the Dust Bowl which emigrates west and struggles against agricultural exploitation there. Steinbeck consistently sympathized with and wrote about the oppressed in his stories and novels, which are often realistic and sociological. Yet he is also known for a mystical, romantic style blended into his realistic fiction. Other works include *Of Mice and Men* (1937), *The Long Valley* (1938), *Cannery Row* (1945), and *East of Eden* (1952). In 1962 he published *Travels With Charley: In Search of America* and won the Nobel Prize for Literature.

Wallace Stevens (1879–1955) was born in Reading, Pennsylvania, studied under the philosopher George Santayana at Harvard, then went on to earn a law degree at New York University. Except for a few years of private law practice, Stevens worked for the rest of his life at the Hartford Accident and Indemnity Company. The facts of his biography are relatively simple; the complexity of his poetry grows out of a rich inner life. Indeed, it is appropriate that Stevens as a worshipper of the mind and imagination, travelled far less than his poems would suggest. From his first book, *Harmonium* (1923), he established himself as a poet less interested in "the thing itself" (William Carlos Williams) than in "the essential poem at the center of things." His striking imagery generally serves to give weight to such free-floating concepts as time, being, meaning, and poetry itself. As one of the key figures in modernist literature, he profoundly affected the writing of poetry in this country. In 1954 his *Collected Poems,* which included his five previous volumes, was awarded the Pulitzer Prize. Many of the thoughts embodied in his poetry are elucidated in *The Necessary Angel* (1951), a collection of essays. Two volumes were published posthumously: *Opus Posthumous* (1957), plays and poetry not included in earlier books; and *The Palm at the End of the Mind: Selected Poems* (1972).

Tom Stoppard (1937–) was born in Czechoslovakia two years before Hitler's armies invaded that country. Stoppard's family moved first to Singapore, where his father died, and later to India. In 1945 his mother married an Englishman; they moved to England, where Stoppard attended several boarding schools. Stoppard's first serious exposure to the stage came as a journalist and drama critic. As a playwright, he first received attention in 1967 with the London production of his play *Rosenkrantz and Guildenstern are Dead,* which won a Tony Award for Best Play in New York the following year. In its treatment of two characters' agonizing search for identity, *Rosenkrantz and Guildenstern are Dead* showed that, although Stoppard's concerns are philosophical, his treatment is farcical. Like Pinter, Stoppard works in the tradition of Samuel Beckett's absurdist, existential gallows humor. However, where Pinter emphasizes the darker aspects of human existence, Stoppard is best known for his comic skills—for the "humor" rather than the "gallows." With later productions of *The Real Inspector Hound* (1969) and *Jumpers* (1972), Stoppard established himself as one of the leading writers for the British stage. His other plays include *Travesties* (1974), *Night and Day* (1978), and *The Real Thing* (1982), for which he won another Tony in 1984.

May Swenson (1919–) grew up in Logan, Utah, but eventually settled in New York City where she became an editor at New Directions, an avant-garde publishing house. In 1966 she retired in order to write poetry exclusively, but she continues to give lectures and readings at universities all over the country. Elizabeth Bishop characterized Swenson's poetry as direct and optimistic: the poet "looks, and sees, and rejoices in what she sees." Swenson's works include *Another Animal* (1954), *To Mix with Time: New and Selected Poems* (1963), *Iconographs* (1970), and *New and Selected Things Taking Place* (1978).

Elizabeth Tallent (1954–) was born in Washington D.C. but grew up in the Southwest, the location for many of her stories. While in college she first aspired to be an archeologist, but instead established her career as a writer. Publishing stories in *The New Yorker, Esquire,* and *Harper's,* Tallent has won a number of prestigious literary awards. The voice she creates in her stories remains remarkably consistent, as if the same young woman is appearing in each. She writes of modern alienation and the difficulty of people truly knowing one another, often illuminating painful relationships between men and women. In addition to her collection of short stories, *In Constant Flight* (1983), Tallent has written one novel, *Museum Pieces*

(1985), and a critical study, *Married Men and Magic Tricks: John Updike's Erotic Heroes* (1982).

Alfred, Lord Tennyson (1809–1892), who succeeded Wordsworth as the English poet laureate, left his university studies at Cambridge without receiving a degree. Though he devoted himself to poetry from childhood, he received discouraging criticism for his early *Poems, Chiefly Lyrical* (1830). The death of his close Cambridge friend Arthur Hallam inspired Tennyson to write his extended elegy *In Memoriam* (1850), through which he gained the favor of Queen Victoria, was named Lord Tennyson, and became the most popular poet of his time. Although Tennyson's poetry typically focuses on the past and classical mythology, the poet was equally concerned with the present condition of the world, often raising philosophical and technological questions. *Maud, and Other Poems* (1855) and *Idylls of the King* (1859) are among his major works.

Dylan Thomas (1914–1953) was born in Swansea, Wales. Despite his father's exhortations, he shunned all formal education, embarking instead on his life's career as a writer, first of poems, later of plays, short stories, and film scripts. By the age of twenty he had published his first collection, *18 Poems,* to modest acclaim. The core of his vision lies in his fascination with the doubleness of nature. The theme of life springing from death, of "womb in tomb," led Thomas to a philosophy that is decidedly Christian, exulting in life and its endless rejuvenation. Among his works are *Under Milk Wood* (1954), a radio play; *Adventures in the Skin Trade,* an autobiography; and *The Poems of Dylan Thomas* (1974).

Walter James Turner (1889–1946) was born in Melbourne, England, and studied music in Munich and Vienna. After serving with the Royal Garrison Artillery during World War I, Turner became a music critic for the *New Statesman.* Also interested in literature, he wrote drama reviews for the *London Mercury* and then became the literary editor for the *Spectator.* In addition, he produced several volumes of poetry, including *The Hunter* (1916), *The Seven Days of the Sun* (1925), and *Fables, Parables, and Plots* (1943); three novels, *The Man Who Ate the Popomack* (1922), *The Aesthetes* (1927), and *The Duchess of Popocatapetl* (1939); and several books on musical theory.

Francois Villon (1431–1463 and after?) was a French poet whose life was marked by constant turmoil. Repeatedly in and out of jail for theft and brawling, Villon narrowly escaped execution in 1463, and then vanished. Today he is considered one of France's greatest medieval poets. He is credited with reviving the ancient French *ballade* and with perfecting the satirical *testament* popular in his time. His works include *Le Lais* (1456), a collection of witty poems in which he bequeaths sundry items to various characters of the city: tavern signs, blows to the head, deserted houses, and an assortment of compliments. *Le Testament* (1462), his masterpiece, is a portrait of life in France at the close of the Middle Ages.

Alice Walker (1944–) is the daughter of sharecroppers from Eatonton, Georgia. She began writing while at Sarah Lawrence College and published her first book of poetry, *Once,* in 1968. She was active in the Civil Rights movement in Mississippi and worked for the welfare department in New York City; her writing reflects her commitment to social and racial change. Although physical and sexual violence within the black community figures consistently in Walker's fiction, she uses violence to emphasize her hope for spiritual survival, freedom, and the power of community, claiming that "the human spirit can be so much more incredible and beautiful than most people ever dream." Walker's works include two collections of stories, *In Love and Trouble* (1973) and *You Can't Keep a Good Woman Down,* and three novels, *The Third Life of Grange Copeland* (1970), *Meridian* (1976), and the Pulitzer Prize winning *The Color Purple* (1982). Her essays are collected in *In Search of Our Mothers' Gardens* (1983).

Isaac Watts (1674–1748) was forced to give up active ministry by poor health and so turned to writing poetry, hymns, and theological works. He is remembered most for his hymns, which are still popular today in many churches. Watts also wrote poetry, experimenting with the Pindaric ode and blank verse. His collections of poems include *Horae Lyricae* (1706), *Hymns and Spiritual Songs* (1707), and *The Psalms of David Imitated* (1719).

Gerald Weales (1925–) is a professor of English at the University of Pennsylvania and the drama critic for *Commonweal.* In addition, he writes juvenile literature, including *Miss Grimsbee is a Witch* (1957), literary criticism, including *Tennessee Williams* (1965) and *Religion in Modern English Drama* (1961), and edits editions of plays, including Miller's *Death of a Salesman* (1967).

Eudora Welty (1909–) has spent most of her life in Jackson, Mississippi. Temporarily a publicity agent for the WPA during the Depression and staffer on the *New York Times Book Review,* Welty has primarily been a writer of fiction, poetry, and literary criticism. She is known as one of the premier American regionalists, for most of her work captures the atmosphere, language, and lifestyle of the South. Her novels include *Delta Wedding* (1946), *The Ponder Heart* (1954), *Losing Battles* (1970), and *The Optimist's Daughter* (1969), which won the Pulitzer Prize in 1972. More recently Welty wrote an exploration of short fiction, *The Eye of the Story* (1978); had her stories collected in *Collected Stories* (1980); and finished an autobiographical account of her literary career, *One Writer's Beginnings* (1984).

Charles Wesley (1707–1788) studied at Oxford and was ordained in 1835. Shortly thereafter he went to Georgia with his brother John, the founder of the Methodist faith. After three years of efforts to convert Indians, the two evangelists returned to England and travelled throughout the country spreading Methodism. Although considered a better preacher than his brother, Wesley is remembered most for his hymns, which present biblical messages through striking figures of speech.

During his lifetime Wesley wrote over 6000 hymns; many have remained popular in protestant churches all over the world. Wesley's *Journal* was published in 1849.

Edith Wharton (1862–1937), although originally from New York City, spent most of her life with the American expatriate community in France. During World War I, she wrote propaganda for the Allied cause and was honored for her work with Belgian orphans. Along with her close friend Henry James, Wharton provided readers with both social history and psychological realism in her works. She was awarded the Pulitzer Prize in 1921. Wharton's first collection of stories, *The Greater Inclination* (1899), was followed by ten others; her novels include *The House of Mirth* (1905), *Ethan Frome* (1911), *The Age of Innocence* (1920), and *The Children* (1928). *The Writing of Fiction,* her analysis of short story and novel writing, was published in 1925.

George Whetstone (1550–1587), an English poet, was best known for his elegies and prose tales. His rhymed-verse play, *Promos and Cassandra* (1587), comes from the same source as Shakespeare's *Measure for Measure*, Cinthio's *Hecatommithi*. Whetstone's plays are considered early versions of the English romantic comedy.

Walt Whitman (1819–1892), one of nine children of a house-builder, grew up on Long Island and later in Brooklyn. Largely self-educated, Whitman worked as a printer, journalist, and teacher. In 1855, after he received some admiring remarks from Ralph Waldo Emerson, Whitman published *Leaves of Grass*. This first version contained just twelve poems; eventually the book expanded to 122 poems. During the Civil War Whitman served as a battlefield nurse near Washington, D.C. He later worked for the Bureau of Indian Affairs and was discharged when his superior read *Leaves of Grass*. After he suffered a stroke, Whitman went to live with his brother in New Jersey. There he continued to write and receive visitors from abroad, where his reputation was greater than in the United States. He broke many conventional barriers, both in the loose, expansive form of his poetry and in his subjects: the spiritual love of man for man, the union of man and nature, the goodness of the body, and the visionary role of the poet. He is heir to the Romanticism of Blake and Wordsworth, yet his poetry is distinctly American. William Carlos Williams, Frank O'Hara, Allen Ginsburg and the Beat poets, as well as numerous foreign poets such as Pablo Neruda, have kept the "Whitman tradition" alive.

Richard Wilbur (1921–), a native of New York City, earned a B.A from Amherst College and an M.A. from Harvard. He has held teaching positons at Harvard, Wellesley College in Massachusetts, and Wesleyan University in Connecticut. Of the postwar poets, Wilbur is considered to be among the most ordered and refined. Calling upon traditional forms to thrust his sometimes extraordinary perceptions into bold relief, he writes poetry that at times recalls Robert Frost and Robert Lowell. His books of poetry include *The Beautiful Changes* (1947), *Ceremony* (1950), *Things of This World* (Pulitzer Prize and National Book Award,

1956), *The Bestiary* (1955), *Advice to a Prophet* (1961), *The Poems of Richard Wilbur* (1963), *Walking to Sleep* (1969), and *The Mind-Reader* (1976). He is also known for his excellent translations of Moliere's plays.

William Carlos Williams (1883–1963) spent almost his entire life as a physician in Rutherford, New Jersey. Yet from the voices of his patients he heard "inarticulate poems" which compelled him to write—snatching minutes between patients to scribble down lines, phrases, and whole poems. As part of the Imagist movement, Williams became a revolutionary poet, breaking all poetic conventions to produce uncluttered lines of colloquial language. Randall Jarrell characterizes Williams' work as "stubborn or invincible joyousness" free from "optimistic blindness." Williams also wrote short stories, most of which come directly from his medical experiences, as well as several novels. His numerous works include *The Complete Collected Poems of William Carlos Williams, 1906–1938* (1938), *Paterson* (complete, 1963), *Pictures from Brueghel and Other Poems* (1962), all poetry; *The Farmers' Daughters: Collected Stories* (1961); and *The Autobiography of William Carlos Williams* (1967).

Leigh Allison Wilson (1957–), now a professor of fiction writing at the State University of New York College in Oswego, is from Rogersville, Tennessee, and writes colorful tales of the South. When accused of excessive eccentricity in her characters and plots, Wilson answered that she is drawn to absurdity because it is what surrounds her. She also describes her vision of fiction as a comic one which allows her to "approach things without despairing of them." Wilson's short stories are collected in *From the Bottom Up* (1983).

Virginia Woolf (1882–1941) broke all the rules of convention when she and her sister Vanessa, as young, unmarried women, moved into their own London flat. The two were later part of the Bloomsbury Group, a literary circle that included E. M. Forster, John Maynard Keynes, and Leonard Woolf. After they were married, Virginia and Leonard founded the Hogarth Press and began publishing Virginia's own work, giving her the freedom to experiment with prose writing. Woolf is known for the stream of consciousness style found in most of her novels, which include *The Voyage Out* (1915), *Mrs. Dalloway* (1925), *To the Lighthouse* (1927), and *The Waves* (1931). She also wrote short stories, collected in *A Haunted House and Other Stories* (1953) and *The Collected Short Fiction of Virginia Woolf* (1986), and both feminist essays and literary criticism, collected in *A Room of One's Own* (1929), *The Common Reader* (1925), *The Death of the Moth and Other Essays* (1942), and many other books.

William Wordsworth (1770–1850) was born in England's Lake District and spent much of his life in "drinking in" nature and the rural life. Later, after studying at Cambridge and experiencing firsthand the French Revolution, Wordsworth returned to live in the Lake District with his sister Dorothy. There he collaborated closely with Coleridge on the *Lyrical Ballads* (1798), prefaced (in the 1800 edition) with a call for a poetry "in the real language of men." Wordsworth's poetic production was prodigious and lasted until the end of his life. However, with the exception of *The Excursion* (1814), *Poems in Two Volumes* (1807) marked the apex of his creative powers. *The Prelude*, though revised until his death and published posthumously, was largely complete in 1805. Written to chart "the growth of the poet's mind", *The Prelude* is full of biographical insights. Later in life Wordsworth did marry, but it was his partnerships with his sister Dorothy and friend Coleridge which allowed him to reach the imaginative heights he did. In his later life Wordsworth reaped many of the rewards of recognition, including being appointed poet laureate in 1843.

Richard Wright (1908–1960) was born on a plantation near Natchez, Mississippi, but moved north as a young man. In New York City he became involved with the Communist Party and began concentrating on writing poetry and short stories from a Marxist perspective. His first collection, *Uncle Tom's Children,* portrayed the racial conflict through the harsh voice of an insider and earned him immediate literary prominence. Although he spent the last several years of his life in Paris, Wright continued to write about the racial problem in the United States in such novels as *The Outsider* (1953), *Savage Holiday* (1954), and *The Long Dream* (1958). He is acclaimed equally for the sociological and literary value of his works, through which he speaks for all black people. His autobiography, *Black Boy* (1945), is possibly his most important work, followed by his first novel, *Native Son* (1940).

Thomas Wyatt (1503–1542), originally from Yorkshire, served Henry VIII as a courtier and diplomat in France, Italy, Spain, and the Netherlands. Spending time in Italy possibly cultivated Wyatt's interest in Petrarch, whose poetry he translated and imitated when he began writing verse. Wyatt is best known for his songs and sonnets, which are marked by irregular meter and a subjective, often passionate, tone. His love poems are said to prefigure those of Donne. Wyatt's works include *Certayne Psalms . . . drawen into Eng-*

lyshe meter (1549) and *Songes and Sonnettes,* published in *Tottel's Miscellany* in 1557.

William Butler Yeats (1865–1939) was born in Dublin into a family of English ancestry, and at a time when Ireland was essentially a colony of England he grew up in both countries. Yeats briefly appeared to be following in the footstops of his father, a painter. In 1889, after deciding to pursue a literary career, Yeats met Maud Gonne, whose beauty and nationalist passions were a lifelong influence. Ten years later, already a respected poet, Yeats founded the Irish National Theater and subsequently wrote and produced many plays. In Yeats' own view he was different from his contemporaries by virtue of his deep, though unorthodox, religious beliefs. Like Blake, whose work he edited, Yeats fused esoteric spiritual ideas with a highly individualized vision to create complexly symbolic poetry. Yeats was politically active as well, first as a leader of the Irish cultural renaissance, later as a senator when the Irish Free State was formed. His numerous books of poetry, his mastery of Irish folk. Pre-Raphaelite, and modernist styles, include *The Wanderings of Oisin and Other Poems* (1889), *In the Seven Woods* (1903), *The Green Helmet and Other Poems* (1910), *Responsibilities* (1914), *The Wild Swans at Coole* (1919), *The Tower* (1928), and *The Winding Stair* (1933).

Marguerite Yourcenar (1913–   ) is a French author and a classicist who was born in Brussels and now lives in Maine. Best known for her historical novels, *Memoirs of Hadrian* (1951) and *The Abyss* (1968), Yourcenar has also specialized in retelling tales, first through prose poems in *Fires* (1936) which modernized the legends of ancient Greece, and then through her short-story rendition of *Oriental Tales* (1938). Her works always reflect her fascination with ancient myths and themes; her adaptations of Greek drama show sensitivity to the demands of the modern stage. Yourcenar was admitted to the French Academy as the first female member since its founding in 1635. A translator, literary critic, and biographer, she has also published *Mishima, or the Vision of the Void* (1981) and a collection of essays, *The Dark Brain of Piranesi* (1984).

ACKNOWLEDGMENTS (continued from p. iv)

Press. Story reprinted by permission of Margaret Atwood and McClelland and Stewart from *Dancing Girls* published by McClelland Stewart, © 1977. Excerpts from "What's So Funny?" Notes on Canadian Humour" and "An End to Audience?" From *Second Words: Selected Critical Prose,* copyright © 1982, O. W. Toad Limited (Toronto: House of Anansi Press). Reprinted by permission.

Toni Cade Bambara. "The Lesson" from *Gorilla, My Love* by Toni Cade Bambara. Copyright © 1972 by Toni Cade Bambara. Reprinted by permission of Random House, Inc. Extract from Janet Sternberg, *The Writer on Her Work,* by permission of W. W. Norton, Co.

John Berger. "An Independent Woman" from *Pig Earth* by John Berger. Copyright © 1979 by John Berger. Reprinted by permission of Pantheon Books, a Division of Random House.

Jorge Louis Borges. From *The Aleph and Other Stories* 1933–1969 by Jorge Luis Borges, ed. and tr. by Norman Thomas di Giovanni in collaboration with the author. English translations copyright © 1968, 1969, 1970 by Emecé Editores, S.A., and Norman Thomas di Giovanni; copyright © 1970 by Jorge Luis Borges, Adolfo Bioy-Casares and Norman Thomas di Giovanni. Reprinted by permission of the publisher, E. P. Dutton, a division of NAL Penguin, Inc.

Anton Chekhov. "Lady with the Pet Dog" from *The Portable Chekhov,* tr. and ed. by Avrahm Yarmolinsky. Copyright 1947, 1968 by The Viking Press, Inc. Copyright renewed © 1975 by Avrahm Yarmolinsky. Reprinted by permission of Viking Penguin Inc.

L. S. Dembo. Extract from *Contemporary Literature,* Summer 1970, XI, 3, reprinted by permission of the University of Wisconsin Press.

Jose Donoso. "Paseo" reprinted by permission of Carmen Balcells Agencia Literaria, Barcelona. © José Donoso, 1971.

Ralph Ellison. "Did You Ever Dream Lucky" reprinted by permission of William Morris Agency, Inc., on behalf of the author. Copyright © 1954 by Ralph Ellison.

William Faulkner. "Barn Burning" copyright 1939 and renewed 1967 by Estelle Faulkner and Jill Faulkner Summers. Reprinted from *Collected Stories of William Faulkner* by permission of Random House, Inc.

Gustav Flaubert. Reprinted from Gustav Flaubert: "The Legend of Saint Julian the Hospitaler," translated by Michel Grimaud in *Saint/Oedipus: Psychocritical Approaches to Flaubert's Art* by William J. Berg, Michel Grimaud and George Moskos. Copyright © 1982 by Cornell University Press. Used by permission of the publisher.

E. M. Forster. Excerpt from *Aspects of the Novel* by E. M. Forster, Copyright 1927 by Harcourt Brace Jovanovich, Inc.; renewed 1955 by E. M. Forster. Reprinted by permission of Harcourt Brace Jovanovich, Inc., and Edward Arnold. Story from *The Eternal Moment and Other Stories* by E. M. Forster copyright 1928 by Harcourt Brace Jovanovich, Inc.; renewed 1956 by E. M. Forster. (British title *The Collected Tales* of E. M. Forster.) Reprinted by permission of Harcourt Brace Jovanovich, Inc., and Sidgwick and Jackson.

Mavis Gallant. "The Remission" from *The Fifteenth District* reprinted by permission of Georges Borchardt, Inc., the author, and Macmillan of Canada, a Division of Canada Publishing Corporation. Copyright © 1973, 1974, 1975, 1976, 1977, 1978, 1979 by Mavis Gallant.

Gabriel García Marquez. "A Very Old Man with Enormous Wings" from *Collected Stories* by Gabriel García Marquez copyright © 1971 by Gabriel García Marquez. Reprinted by permission of Harper & Row, Publishers, Inc. Extract from "Gabriel García Marquez," from *Writers at Work,* Sixth Series, ed., George Plimpton. Copyright © 1984 by The Paris Review, Inc. All rights reserved. Reprinted by permission of Viking Penguin, Inc.

Gail Godwin. "Dream Children" copyright © 1976 by Gail Godwin. Reprinted from *Dream Children* by Gail Godwin, by permission of Alfred A. Knopf Inc. Extract from Janet Sternberg, *The Writer on Her Work,* by permission of W. W. Norton, Co.

Nadine Gordimer. From *Selected Stories* by Nadine Gordimer. Copyright 1952, © 1956, 1957, 1959, 1960, 1964, 1965, 1968, 1969, 1971, 1975 by Nadine Gordimer. Reprinted by permission of Viking Penguin, Inc. Extract from "Nadine Gordimer" *Writers at Work*, Sixth Series, Ed., George Plimpton. Copyright © 1984 by The Paris Review Inc. All rights reserved. Reprinted by permission of Viking Penguin Inc. and The Paris Review.

Jacob Ludwig Karl Grimm & Wilhelm Karl Grimm. Selection from *The Complete Grimm's Fairy Tales* by Jacob Ludwig Karl Grimm and Wilhelm Karl Grimm, translated by Margaret Hunt and James Stern. Copyright 1944 by Pantheon Books, Inc., and renewed 1972 by Random House, Inc. Reprinted by permission of the publisher.

Dashiell Hammett. "Fly Paper" from *The Big Knockover; Selected Stories and Short Stories* by Dashiell Hammett edited by Lillian Hellman. Copyright © 1966 by Lillian Hellman. Reprinted by permission of Random House, Inc.

Ernest Hemingway. "A Clean Well-Lighted Place from *Winner Take Nothing.* Copyright 1933 Charles Scribner's Sons: copyright renewed © 1961 by Mary Hemingway. Reprinted with permission of Charles Scribner's Sons.

Zora Neale Hurston. "Spunk" reprinted by permission of Turtle Island Foundation.

James Joyce. "Araby" from *Dubliners* by James Joyce. Copyright 1916 by B. W. Huebsch, Inc. Definitive text copyright © 1967 by the Estate of James Joyce. Reprinted by permission of Viking Penguin Inc.

Franz Kafka. "The Metamorphosis" from *The Penal Colony* by Franz Kafka, trans. Willa and Edwin Muir copyright © 1948, 1976 by Schocken Books Inc. Reprinted by permission of Schocken Books Inc.

Garrison Keillor. Selection reprinted by permission of Garrison Keillor. Copyright © 1981 by Garrison Keillor. First published in *Atlantic* Magazine. From *Happy to Be Here*, Penguin Books (1983).

Doris Lessing. "To Room Nineteen" from *A Man and Two Women* by Doris Lessing copyright © 1958, 1962, 1963 by Doris Lessing. Reprinted by permission of Simon & Schuster, Inc. and Jonathan Clowes, Ltd.

Guy de Maupassant. "The String" from *The Portable Maupassant*, selected and edited by Lewis Galantiere. Copyright 1947, renewal © 1974 by the Viking Press, Inc. Reprinted by permission of Viking Penguin Inc.

Yukio Mishima. "Swaddling Clothes" from *Death in Midsummer*. Copyright © 1966 by New Directions Publishing Corporation. Reprinted by permission of New Directions Publishing Corporation.

Alice Munro. Selection from *The Progress of Love* by Alice Munro. Copyright © 1986 by Alice Munro. Reprinted by permission of Alfred A. Knopf, Inc., and the Canadian Publishers, McClelland and Stewart, Toronto.

Joyce Carol Oates. Extract from "The Short Story," *Southern Humanities Review* 5: 3, Summer 1971, reprinted by permission. Story reprinted from *The Wheel of Love* by Joyce Carol Oates, by permission of the publisher, Vanguard Press, Inc. Copyright © 1970, 1969, 1968, 1967, 1966, 1965 by Joyce Carol Oates.

Edna O'Brien. "Sister Imelda" from *A Fanatic Heart: Selected Stories of Edna O'Brien*. Copyright © 1984 by Edna O'Brien. Originally appeared in *The New Yorker*. Reprinted by permission of Farrar, Straus & Giroux, Inc.

Flannery O'Connor. "A Good Man Is Hard to Find" copyright 1953 by Flannery O'Connor; renewed 1981 by Regina O'Connor. Reprinted from *A Good Man Is Hard to Find and Other Stories* by Flannery O'Connor by permission of Harcourt Brace Jovanovich, Inc. Excerpts from *Mystery and Manners* by Flannery O'Connor. Copyright ©1957, 1961, 1963, 1964, 1966, 1967, 1969 by Flannery O'Connor. Reprinted by permission of Farrar, Straus & Giroux, Inc.

Dorothy Parker. "Here We Are" copyright 1931, renewed © 1959 by Dorothy Parker. From *The Portable Dorothy Parker*. Reprinted by permission of Viking Penguin Inc.

Elena Poniatowska. "A Little Fairy Tale" translated by Magda Bogin reprinted from *The Massachusetts Review* © 1987 The Massachusetts Review, Inc. Used by permission.

Katherine Anne Porter. "The Jilting of Granny Weatherall" copyright 1930, 1958 by Katherine Anne Porter. Reprinted from her volume *Flowering Judas and Other Stories* by permission of Harcourt Brace Jovanovich, Inc.

Philip Shabecoff. Excerpt from "You've Heard of Yukio Mishima . . ." copyright © 1970 by The New York Times Company. Reprinted by permission.

Leslie Marmon Silko. "Lullaby" copyright © 1981 by Leslie Marmon Silko. Reprinted from *Storyteller* by Leslie Marmon Silko, published by Seaver Books, New York, 1981.

Issac Bashevis Singer. "Gimpel the Fool" by Isaac Bashevis Singer, translated by Saul Bellow, from *A Treasury of Yiddish Stories* edited by Irving Rowe and Eliezer Greenberg. Copyright 1953, 1954, by The Viking Press, Inc. Copyright renewed © 1981 by Isaac Bashevis Singer. Reprinted by permission of Viking Penguin Inc.

John Steinbeck. "The Chrysanthemums" from *The Long Valley* by John Steinbeck. Copyright 1937, renewed 1965 by John Steinbeck. Reprinted by permission of Viking Penguin Inc.

Elizabeth Tallent. "No One's a Mystery" reprinted by permission of the author.

Alice Walker. "Everyday Use" copyright © 1973 by Alice Walker. Reprinted from her volume *In Love & Trouble* by permission of Harcourt Brace Jovanovich.

Eudora Welty. "Livvie" copyright 1941, 1970 by Eudora Welty. Reprinted from her volume *The Wide Net* by permission of Harcourt Brace Jovanovich Inc. Extracts copyright © 1965 by Eudora Welty. Reprinted from *The Eye of the Storm* by Eudora Welty, by permission of Random House, Inc.

Edith Wharton. "Roman Fever" from *Roman Fever and Other Stories*. Copyright 1934 Liberty Magazine: copyright renewed © 1962 William R. Tyler. Reprinted with permission of Charles Scribner's Sons, a division of Macmillan, Inc.

William C. Williams. "Jack Beicke." William Carlos Williams, *The Doctor Stories*. Copyright © 1962 by William Carlos Williams. Reprinted by permission of New Directions Publishing Corporation.

Leigh Allison Wilson. Story © 1983 by Leigh Allison Wilson. Reprinted by permission of Harold Matson Company, Inc.

Virginia Woolf. "Solid Objects" from *The Complete Short Fiction of Virginia Woolf*, copyright © 1985 by Quentin Bell and Angelica Garnett. Excerpts from "Modern Fiction" in *The Common Reader* First Series by Virginia Woolf, copyright 1925 by Harcourt Brace Jovanovich,

Inc.; renewed 1953 by Leonard Woolf. Extract from *The Collected Essays of Virginia Woolf,* Vol. IV, copyright © 1950 by Harcourt Brace Jovanovich, Inc.; renewed 1958 by Leonard Woolf. All reprinted by permission of Harcourt Brace Jovanovich, Inc., and The Hogarth Press.

Richard Wright. "The Library Card" Chapter XIII (pp. 214–222) in *Black Boy* by Richard Wright. Copyright 1937, 1942, 1944, 1945 by Richard Wright. Reprinted by permission of Harper & Row, Publishers, Inc.

Marguerite Yourcenar. "How Wang-Fo Was Saved" from *Oriental Tales* by Marguerite Yourcenar. English translation copyright © 1983, 1984 by Alberto Manguel. Reprinted by permission of Farrar, Straus & Giroux, Inc. Extract from *With Open Eyes* by Marguerite Yourcenar. Translator's Preface and English translation copyright © 1984 by Beacon Press. Reprinted by permission of Beacon Press.

POETRY

W. H. Auden. "A. E. Housman" copyright 1940 and renewed 1968 by W. H. Auden. Reprinted from *The English Auden: Poems, Essays and Dramatic Writings 1927–1939* edited by Edward Mendelson. Poems from *W. H. Auden: Collected Poems,* edited by Edward Mendelson. Copyright © 1976 by Edward Mendelson, William Meredith and Monroe K. Spears, Executors of the Estate of W. H. Auden. Excerpts from *Forewords and Afterwords* by W. H. Auden. Copyright 1952 by W. H. Auden. All reprinted by permission of Random House, Inc. and Faber & Faber Ltd. Excerpt from the Introduction to *The Oxford Book of Light Verse,* 1938, reprinted by permission of The Oxford University Press.

Charles Baudelaire. Poems from *Les Fleurs du Mal* by Charles Baudelaire, translated by Richard Howard. Copyright © 1982 by Richard Howard. Reprinted by permission of David Godine, Publisher. "The Albatross" (translation) in Marthiel and Jackson Matthews, eds., *The Flowers of Evil,* reprinted by permission of Richard Wilbur.

John Berryman. "Dream Song #4" "Dream Song #14" from *77 Dream Songs* by John Berryman. Copyright © 1959, 1962, 1963, 1964 by John Berryman. Reprinted by permission of Farrar, Straus, & Giroux, Inc.

Elizabeth Bishop. "In the Waiting Room," "Questions of Travel," "Filling Station," "The Prodigal," "Crusoe in England," "The Armadillo," "One Art" from *The Complete Poems 1927–1979* by Elizabeth Bishop. Copyright © 1979, 1983 by Alice Helen Methfessel. Excerpt from *The Collected Prose by Elizabeth Bishop.* Copyright © 1984 by Alice Helen Methfessel. All reprinted by permission of Farrar, Straus & Giroux, Inc.

Robert Bly. " The Indigo Bunting" and "In Rainy September" from *Loving a Woman in Two Worlds,* 1985 by Robert Bly. Copyright © 1985 by Robert Bly. "Pablo Neruda" and "Words Rising" from *Man in the Black Coat Turns* by Robert Bly. Copyright © 1981 by Robert Bly. All reprinted by permission of Doubleday, a division of Bantam, Doubleday, Dell Publishing Group, Inc. "For My Son Noah, Ten Years Old" and "My Father's Wedding" by Robert Bly from the book *The Man in the Black Coat Turns.* Copyright © 1981 by Robert Bly. Reprinted by permission of Doubleday Publishing Group.

Louise Bogan. "Medusa," "To My Brother," "Zone," "The Dragonfly" from *The Blue Estuaries* by Louise Bogan. Copyright © 1968 by Louise Bogan. "Evening in the Sanitarium," "Come Break with Time," and "The Dream" from *Collected Poems 1923–1953* by Louise Bogan. Copyright 1954 by Louise Bogan. Copyright renewed © 1982 by Maidie Alexander Scannell. All reprinted by permission of Farrar, Straus & Giroux, Inc. Extracts from *A Poet's Alphabet* reprinted by permission of Ruth Limmer, Literary Executor, Estate of Louise Bogan. First publication in *The New Yorker.* "Castle of My Heart" from *Journey Around My Room* reprinted by permission of Ruth Limmer, Literary Executor, Estate of Louise Bogan. "Engine," first publication in *The New Yorker,* by permission of Ruth Limmer, Literary Executor, Estate of Louise Bogan.

Bertolt Brecht. Poem reprinted from *Bertolt Brecht Poems 1913–1956* by permission of Michael Hamburger and the publisher, Methuen, Inc., (New York & London) by arrangement with Suhrkamp Verlag. All rights reserved.

Gwendolyn Brooks. "Riot" and an extract from *Report from Past One* reprinted by permission of Broadside Press. "The Blackstone Rangers" from *In the Mecca* reprinted by permission of Gwendolyn Brooks and the David Company, Chicago. Four poems from *Blacks* reprinted by permission of the author.

Olga Broumas. "Cinderella" from *Beginning with O* reprinted by permission of Yale University Press. Copyright © 1977 by The Yale University Press.

Dennis Brutus. "Nightsong: City" from *Sirens, Knuckles, Boots,* Mbari Press/Northwestern University, 1963. Reprinted by permission of the author.

Amy Clampitt. "Ano Prinius" copyright © 1986 and "Man Feeding Pigeons" copyright © (1987) from *Archaic Figure* by Amy Clampitt. Five poems from *The Kingfisher* by Amy Clampitt. Copyright © 1983 by Amy Clampitt. All reprinted by permission of Alfred A. Knopf, Inc. Interview excerpt courtesy of Laura Fairchild. First appeared in *The American Poetry Review.*

Lucille Clifton. Five poems reprinted from *Two-Headed Woman* by Lucille Clifton (Amherst: University of Massachusetts Press, 1980), copyright © 1980 by The University of Massachusetts Press. Poem from *Good News About the Earth* and two poems from *An Ordinary*

Woman reprinted by permission of Curtis Brown, Ltd. Copyright © 1972 and © 1974 by Lucille Clifton. Extract from "We Are the Grapevine" reprinted by permission of the author.

Countee Cullen. From *On These I Stand* by Countee Cullen. "Yet Do I Marvel," "Epitaph for a Poet," "To John Keats, Poet at Springtime" copyright 1925 by Harper & Row, Publishers, Inc. Renewed 1953 by Ida M. Cullen. "Black Majesty" copyright 1929 by Harper & Row, Publishers, Inc. Renewed 1957 by Ida M. Cullen. "Only the Polished Skeleton" copyright 1935 by Harper & Row, Publishers, Inc. Renewed 1963 by Ida M. Cullen. "Incident" copyright 1925 by Harper & Row, Publishers, Inc. Renewed 1953 by Ida M. Cullen. "From the Dark Tower" copyright 1927 by Harper & Row, Publishers, Inc. Renewed 1955 by Ida M. Cullen. All preprinted by permission of Harper & Row, Publishers, Inc.

E. E. Cummings. Two poems reprinted from *ViVa* by E. E. Cummings by permission of Liveright Publishing Corporation. Copyright 1931, © 1959 by E. E. Cummings. Copyright © 1979, 1973 by the Trustees for the E. E. Cummings Trust. Copyright © 1979, 1973 by George James Firmage. Poem reprinted from NO THANKS by E. E. Cummings, by permission of Liveright Publishing Corporation. Copyright 1935 by E. E. Cummings. Copyright © 1968 by Marion Moorehouse Cummings. Copyright © 1973, 1978 by The Trustees for the E. E. Cummings Trust. Copyright © 1973, 1978 by George James Firmage. Four poems reprinted from TULIPS & CHIMNEYS by E. E. Cummings by permission of Liveright Publishing Corporation. Copyright 1923, 1925 and renewed 1951, 1953 by E. E. Cummings. Copyright © 1973, 1976 by The Trustees for the E. E. Cummings Estate. Copyright © 1973, 1976 by George James Firmage.

Joy Davidman. "Snow in Madrid" from *Letter to a Comrade* reprinted by permission of Yale University Press.

Emily Dickinson. Poems reprinted by permission of the publishers and the Trustees of Amherst College from *The Poems of Emily Dickinson* edited by Thomas H. Johnson, Cambridge, Mass.: The Belknap Press of Harvard University Press Copyright 1951, © 1955, 1979, 1983 by The President and Fellows of Harvard College and Little, Brown and Company.

Alan Dugan. "Love Song I and Thou" copyright © 1961, 1962, 1968, 1972, 1973, 1974, 1983 by Alan Dugan. From *New and Collected Poems: 1961–1983* by Alan Dugan, published by The Ecco Press in 1983. Reprinted by permission.

Richard Eberhart. Two poems from *Collected Poems 1930–1976* by Richard Eberhart. Copyright © 1960, 1976 by Richard Eberhart. Reprinted by permission of Oxford University Press.

T. S. Eliot. Selections from *Collected Poems 1909–1962* by T. S. Eliot, copyright 1936 by Harcourt Brace Jovanovich, Inc.: copyright © 1963, 1964 by T. S. Eliot. Extracts from "Tradition and the Individual Talent" copyright 1950 by Harcourt Brace Jovanovich, Inc.; renewed 1978 by Esme Valerie Eliot. Extract from "In Memoriam" copyright 1936 by Harcourt Brace Jovanovich, Inc.; renewed 1964 by T. S. Eliot. Extract from "Andrew Marvell" copyright 1950 by Harcourt Brace Jovanovich, Inc.; renewed 1978 by Esme Valerie Eliot. All reprinted by permission of Harcourt Brace Jovanovich, Inc., and Faber & Faber Ltd.

Laura Fairchild. Extract from *The American Poetry Review*, July/August 1987 issue, reprinted by permission of the author.

Robert Frost. Selections from *The Poetry of Robert Frost* edited by Edward Connery Latham. Copyright © 1969 by Holt, Rinehart and Winston, Inc. Copyright © 1962 by Robert Frost. Copyright © 1975 by Lesley Frost Ballantine. Extract from *Robert Frost: Poetry and Prose* edited by Edward Connery Latham and Lawrence Thompson. Copyright © 1972 by Holt, Rinehart and Winston, Inc. All reprinted by permission of Henry Holt and Company, Inc.

Gloria Fuertes. Selection copyright © by Gloria Fuertes: Translation Copyright © by Philip Levine and Ada Long. Reprinted from *Off the Map: Selected Poems* by permission of Wesleyan University Press.

Tess Gallagher. Selection from *Willingly* reprinted by permission of Graywolf Press.

Federico García Lorca. Selections from Federico García Lorca, *Selected Poems*. Copyright 1952 by New Directions Publishing Corporation. Reprinted by permission of New Directions Publishing Corporation. "New York: Office and Denunciation" translated by Betty J. Craige reprinted by permission of the University Press of Kentucky. Excerpt from "Play and Theory of the Duende" by permission of Mercedes Casanova Literary Agency, Barcelona and the estate of Federico García Lorca.

Allan Ginsberg. "A Supermarket in California" from *Collected Poems 1947–1980* by Allen Ginsberg. Copyright © 1955 by Allen Ginsberg. Reprinted by permission of Harper & Row, Publishers, Inc.

Dana Gioia. Excerpt from "Studying with Miss Bishop" reprinted by permission; © 1986 by Dana Gioia. Originally in *The New Yorker*.

Louise Glück. "For My Mother" "The Apple Trees" "Still Life" copyright © 1971, 1972, 1973, 1974, 1975 by Louise Glück. From *The House on Marshland* by Louise Glück, published by The Ecco Press in 1975. "Metamorphosis" "The Triumph of Achilles'" "Horse" "Night Song" from "Marathon" copyright © 1985 by Louise Glück. From *The Triumph of Achilles* by Louise Glück, published by The Ecco Press in 1985. All reprinted by permission.

Excerpt from "The Dreamer and the Watcher," *Singular Voices,* reprinted by permission of Stephen Berg and Louise glück.

Patricia Hampl. "The Moment" reprinted by permission; © 1985 Patricia Hampl. Originally in *The New Yorker.*

Robert Hass. "Heroic Smile," "Meditation at Lagunitas," "Santa Lucia," "Old Dominion," and "Weed" copyright © 1974, 1975, 1976, 1977, 1978, 1979 by Robert Hass. From *Praise* by Robert Hass published by The Ecco Press in 1979. "Robert Hass on Poetry and Repetition" and "Robert Hass on Poetry and Image" copyright © 1984 by Robert Hass. From *Twentieth Century Pleasures* by Robert Hass, published by The Ecco Press in 1984. All reprinted by permission. "Palo Alto: The Marshes" from *Field Guide* by Robert Hass reprinted by permission of Yale University Press. Copyright © 1973.

Anthony E. Hecht. "More Light! More Light!" from *The Hard Hours.* Copyright © 1967 Anthony E. Hecht. Reprinted with permission of Atheneum Publishers.

A. E. Housman. Excerpts from *Selected Prose* by A. E. Housman (1961) reprinted by permission of Cambridge University Press. Copyright 1961 by Cambridge University Press. Selections from *The Collected Poems of A. E. Housman.* Copyright © 1965 by Holt, Rinehart and Winston, Inc. Reprinted by permission of Henry Holt and Company, Inc.

Langston Hughes. Selections from *Selected Poems of Langston Hughes.* Copyright © 1959 by Langston Hughes. "Harlem Sweeties" copyright 1962 by Alfred A. Knopf, Inc. and renewed 1970 by Arna Bontemps and George Houston Bass. Reprinted from *Shakespeare in Harlem* by Langston Hughes. Lines from "Negro Dancers" and from "The Cat and the Saxaphone" from *The Weary Blues* copyright 1926 by Alfred A. Knopf, Inc. and renewed 1954 by Langston Hughes. All reprinted by permission of the publisher. Two poems from *Montage of a Dream Deferred* copyright 1951 by Langston Hughes. Copyright renewed 1979 by George Houston Bass. Reprinted by permission of Harold Ober Associates Inc. Extract from "The Negro Artist and the Racial Mountain" by Langston Hughes, *The Nation,* June 23, 1926. Copyright The Nation Company Inc., 1926. Used by permission.

Randall Jarrell. Excerpt from *A Sad Heart at the Supermarket* by Randall Jarrell. Copyright © 1962 by Randall Jarrell. "Death of the Ball Turret Gunner" and "The Snow Leopard" from *The Complete Poems* by Randall Jarrell. Copyright © 1969 by Mrs. Randall Jarrell. Excerpts from *Kipling, Auden & Co.* by Randall Jarrell. Copyright © 1980 by Mrs. Randall Jarrell. "In Montecito" and "Field and Forest" reprinted from *The Lost World* by Randall Jarrell. Copyright © Randall Jarrell 1962, 1963, 1965. "In Montecito" originally appeared in *The New Yorker.* "'Nestus Gurley" & "The Woman at the Washington Zoo" from *The Woman at the Washington Zoo.* Copyright © 1960 Randall Jarrell. Reprinted with permission of Atheneum Publishers.

Hugh Kingsmill. "What, Still Alive" copyright Hugh Kingsmill. Reproduced by permission of Curtis Brown Ltd., London.

Galway Kinnell. Selection fom *Flower Herding on Mount Monadnock* by Galway Kinnell. Copyright © 1964 by Galway Kinnell. Reprinted by permission of Houghton Mifflin Company.

Maxine Kumin. "The Envelope," "In April, In Princeton," and "The Longing to Be Saved" from *Our Ground Time Here Will Be Brief* by Maxine Kumin. All copyright © 1978 by Maxine Kumin. "Making Jam Without You" copyright © 1970 by Maxine Kumin and "Morning Swim" copyright © 1965 by Maxine Kumin from *Our Ground Time Here Will Be Brief* by Maxine Kumin. "At a Private Showing in 1982" from *The Long Approach* by Maxine Kumin. Copyright © 1982 by Maxine Kumin. Originally published in *The New Yorker.* Extract from "A Way of Staying Sane" from *Singular Voices* reprinted by permission of Stephen Berg and Maxine Kumin.

Denise Levertov. "Life at War" Denise Levertov, *Poems 1960–1967.* Copyright © 1966 by Denise Levertov Goodman. First published in "Poetry." Reprinted by permission of New Directions Publishing Corporation.

Joseph McCulloch. Excerpt from *Under Bow Bells: Conversations with Joseph McCulloch* reprinted by permission of Sheldon Press.

Robert Lowell. "The Eel" and "Little Testament" from *Imitations* by Robert Lowell copyright © 1958, 1959, 1960, 1961 by Robert Lowell. "To the Reader," "The Sleeper in the Valley" from *Imitations* by Robert Lowell. Copyright © 1958, 1959, 1961 by Robert Lowell. "For the Union Dead," "The Neo-Classical Urn," "Night Sweat" from *For the Union Dead* by Robert Lowell. Copyright © 1956, 1960, 1961, 1962, 1963, 1964 by Robert Lowell. "Epilogue" from *Day by Day* by Robert Lowell. Copyright © 1975, 1976, 1977 by Robert Lowell. "Waiting in Blue" from *Life Studies* by Robert Lowell. Copyright © 1956, 1959 by Robert Lowell. "Will Not Come Back" (Volverán) from *Selected Poems* by Robert Lowell. Copyright © 1976 by Robert Lowell. All reprinted by permission of Farrar, Straus and Giroux, Inc. "The Drunken Fisherman" from *Lord Weary's Castle* copyright 1946, 1978 by Robert Lowell. Reprinted by permission of Harcourt Brace Jovanovich.

Archibald MacLeish. "You, Andrew Marvell" from *New and Collected Poems 1917–1976* by Archibald MacLeish. Copyright © 1976 by Archibald MacLeish. Reprinted by permission of Houghton Mifflin Company.

Sandra McPherson. "7,22,66" copyright © 1979, 1980, 1981, 1982 by Sandra McPherson. From *Patron Happiness* by Sandra McPherson published by The Ecco Press in 1982. Reprinted by permission.

W. S. Merwin. Extracts from *Regions of Memory* reprinted by permission of the University of Illinois Press. © 1986. "For the Anniversary of My Death" & "The Last One" from *The Lice*. Copyright © 1967 by W. S. Merwin. "The Judgment of Paris" & "The Different Stars" from *The Carrier of Ladders*. Copyright © 1970 W. S. Merwin. "Grandmother Watching at Her Window" from *The First Four Books of Poems*. Copyright © 1975 W. S. Merwin. "Noah's Raven" from *The Moving Target*. Copyright © 1963 W. S. Merwin. All reprinted with permission of Atheneum Publishers. "History" reprinted by permission; © 1986 W. S. Merwin. Originally in *The New Yorker*. "Emigré" reprinted by permission; © 1982 W. S. Merwin. Originally in *Grand Street*.

Edna St. Vincent Millay. "The King of the Rainy Country" translation from the French by Edna St. Vincent Millay, of Charles Baudelaire's *Les Fleurs Du Mal*. *Flowers of Evil*, Harper & Row. Copyright © 1936, 1963 by Edna St. Vincent Millay and Norma Millay Ellis. "Spring," "Recuerdo," "An Ancient Gesture," "Modern Declaration," "From a Train Window," "The Oak Leaves," "Childhood Is the Kingdom Where Nobody Dies," and "Love is not all: it is not meat nor drink" by Edna St. Vincent Millay. From *Collected Poems*, Harper & Row. Copyright © 1921, 1922, 1931, 1939, 1948, 1950, 1954, 1958, 1967, 1982 by Edna St. Vincent Millay and Norma Millay Ellis. All reprinted by permission.

Eugenio Montale. No. 5 from Xenia II and "La belle dame sans merci" Eugenio Montale, *New Poems*. Copyright © 1970, 1972 by Eugenio Montale and G. Singh. "The Sunflower" and "The Wall" Eugenio Montale, *Selected Poems*. Copyright ©1965 by New Directions Publishing Corporation. Translated by Maurice English. All reprinted by permission of New Directions Publishing Corporation. Extracts from *The Second Life of Art* by Eugenio Montale copyright © 1977, 1978, 1979, 1980, 1981, 1982 by Eugenio Montale. Published by The Ecco Press in 1982. Reprinted by permission.

Marianne Moore. Selections reprinted from *Collected Poems* by Marianne Moore. Copyright 1935 by Marianne Moore, renewed 1963 by Marianne Moore and T. S. Eliot. Selection from *Collected Poems* copyright 1941, and renewed 1969, by Marianne Moore. Selection from *Collected Poems* copyright 1944 and renewed 1972, by Marianne Moore. All reprinted with permission of Macmillan Publishing Company.

Pablo Neruda. "Love" "Sweetness Always" from *Extravagaria* by Pablo Neruda, tr. by Alastair Reid. English translation copyright © 1969, 1970, 1972, 1974 by Alastair Reid. Sonnet VI reprinted from *100 Love Sonnets, Cien Sonetos de Amor* by Pablo Neruda, translated by Stephen Tapscott, by permission of the University of Texas Press, copyright © Pablo Neruda 1959, © 1986 by the University of Texas Press. Selections from *Five Decades: Poems 1925–1970* reprinted by permission of Grove Press, Inc. Copyright © 1974 by Grove Press, Inc. "Here I Love You," translated by W. S. Merwin, reprinted by permission of Jonathan Cope, Ltd. and W. S. Merwin.

John O'Hara. "Steps" copyright © 1964 by Frank O'Hara. Reprinted by permission of City Lights Books. "Why I Am Not a Painter" copyright © 1958 by Maureen Granville-Smith, Administratrix of the Estate of Frank O'Hara. Reprinted from *The Collected Poems of Frank O'Hara* by permission of Alfred A. Knopf, Inc.

Sharon Olds. Poems from *The Dead and the Living* by Sharon Olds copyright © 1983 by Sharon Olds. Poem from *The Gold Cell* by Sharon Olds copyright © 1987 by Sharon Olds. All reprinted by permission of Alfred A. Knopf Inc. "Bathing the New Born" © 1984 Sharon Olds. "The Race" © 1985 Sharon Olds. Both originally in *The New Yorker*. Both reprinted by permission.

Wilfred Owen. Selections from Wilfred Owen, *Collected Poems*. Copyright © 1963 by Chatto & Windus. Reprinted by permission of New Directions Publishing Corporation, Chatto & Windus, and the author's estate.

Dorothy Parker. "Thought for a Sunshiny Morning" copyright 1928, renewed © 1956 by Dorothy Parker. "The Flaw in Paganism" copyright 1931, renewed © 1956 by Dorothy Parker. From *The Portable Dorothy Parker*. Published by permission of Viking Penguin. Copyright © the Estate of Dorothy Parker/The National Association for the Advancement of Colored People. Reprinted by permission of Marie Brown Associates.

David Paul. Excerpt from *Poison and Vision: Poems and Prose of Baudelaire, Mallarme and Rimbaud* edited and translated by David Paul. Copyright © 1974 by David Paul. Reprinted by permission of Random House, Inc.

Sylvia Plath. "Medallion" copyright © 1962 by Sylvia Plath. Reprinted from *The Colossus and Other Poems* by Sylvia Plath, by permission of Alfred A. Knopf, Inc. From *Ariel* by Sylvia Plath "Tulips" copyright © 1962 by Ted Hughes. "The Arrival of the Bee Box" copyright © 1963 by Ted Hughes. From *The Collected Poems of Sylvia Plath* edited by Ted Hughes. "Daddy," "Lady Lazarus," "Cut" copyright © 1963 by Ted Hughes. "Black Rook in Rainy Weather" copyright © 1960 by the Estate of Sylvia Plath. All reprinted by permission of Harper & Row, Publishers, Inc., and Blwyn Hughes.

Cyrena N. Pondrum. Extract from *Contemporary Literature* X, 3, (Winter/Summer 1969) reprinted by permission of the University of Wisconsin Press.

Ezra Pound. "The Seafarer" and "Mr. Housman's Message" Ezra Pound, *Personae*. Copyright 1926 by Ezra Pound. Reprinted by permission of New Directions Publishing Corporation.

Katherine Raine. "Statues" reprinted by permission; © 1965 The New Yorker Magazine Inc.

Carter Revard. "Discovery of the New World" reprinted by permission of the author.

Rainer Maria Rilke. Poems from The *Selected Poetry of Rainer Maria Rilke*. Edited and translated by Stephen Mitchell. Copyright © 1982 by Stephen Mitchell. Reprinted by permission of Random House, Inc. Extract reprinted from LETTERS TO A YOUNG POET by Ranier Maria Rilke, translated by M. D. Herter Morton, by permission of W. W. Norton. Copyright 1934 by W. W. Norton & Company, Inc. Copyright renewed 1962 by M. D. Herter Norton. Revised Edition copyright 1954 by W. W. Norton & Company, Inc.

Adrienne Rich. "Gabriel" is reprinted from POEMS SELECTED AND NEW, 1950–1974 by Adrienne Rich, by permission of W. W. Norton & Company, Inc. Copyright © 1975, 1973, 1971, 1969, 1966 by W. W. Norton & Company, Inc. Copyright © 1967, 1963, 1962, 1961, 1960, 1959, 1958, 1957, 1956, 1955, 1954, 1953, 1952, 1951 by Adrienne Rich. Poems reprinted from THE FACT OF A DOORFRAME Poems Selected and New, 1950–1984 by Adrienne Rich, by permission of W. W. Norton & Company, Inc. Copyright © 1984 by Adrienne Rich. Copyright © 1975, 1978 by W. W. Norton & Company, Inc. Copyright © 1981 by Adrienne Rich. Extract reprinted from "When We Dead Awaken: Writing as a Re-vision" from ON LIES, SECRETS, AND SILENCE, Selected Prose, 1966–1978 by Adrienne Rich by permission of W. W. Norton & Company and the author. Copyright © 1979 by W. W. Norton & Company, Inc. "Love in the Museum" reprinted by permission; © 1954, 1952 The New Yorker Magazine Inc.

Edwin Arlington Robinson. "The Sheaves" copyright 1925 by Edwin Arlington Robinson, renewed 1953 by Ruth Nivison and Barbara R. Holt. "Mr. Flood's Party" copyright 1921 by Edwin Arlington Robinson, renewed 1949 by Ruth Nivison. "The Mill" copyright 1920 by Edwin Arlington Robinson, renewed 1948 by Ruth Nivison. "Eros Turannos" copyright 1916 by Edwin Arlington Robinson, renewed 1944 by Ruth Nivison. All reprinted with permission of Macmillan Publishing Company from *Collected Poems* by Edwin Arlington Robinson.

Theodore Roethke. "Big Wind" copyright 1947 by United Chapters of Phi Beta Kappa; "My Papa's Waltz" copyright 1942 by Hearst Magazines, Inc.; "I Knew a Woman" copyright 1954 by Theodore Roethke; "Frau Bauman, Frau Schmidt and Frau Schwartz" copyright 1952 by Theodore Roethke; "Root Cellar" copyright 1943 by Modern Poetry Assn., Inc.; and "Child on Top of a Greenhouse" copyright by Editorial Publications, Inc. All from *The Collected Poems of Theodore Roethke*. Reprinted by permission of Doubleday Publishing Company. Excerpts from Ralph J. Mills, Ed., *On the Poet and His Craft—Selected Prose of Theodore Roethke* reprinted by permission of the University of Washington Press.

Gary Snyder. "Hitch Haiku" Gary Synder, *The Back Country*. Copyright © 1968 by Gary Snyder. Reprinted by permission of New Directions Publishing Corporation.

Wole Soyinka. "Telephone Conversation" by Wole Soyinka copyright 1960 by Wole Soyinka. Reprinted by permission of Brandt & Brandt Literary Agents, Inc.

William Stafford. "Traveling Through the Dark" from *Stories that Could Be True* by William Stafford. Copyright © 1960 by William Stafford. Reprinted by permission of Harper & Row, Publishers, Inc.

Stern. Extract from *December* Magazine, Vol. III, no 2 (Winter 1961) used by permission.

Wallace Stevens. "Page from a Tale" copyright 1950 by Wallace Stevens. Excerpt from "Final Soliloquy of the Interior Paramour" copyright 1951 by Wallace Stevens. "Study of Two Pears," "Disillusionment of Ten O'Clock," "Anecdote of the Jar," "Sunday Morning," "The Emperor of Ice Cream" copyright 1954 by Wallace Stevens. All from *The Collected Poems of Wallace Stevens*. Reprinted by permission of Alfred A. Knopf, Inc.

May Swenson. "Question" by May Swenson is reprinted by permission of the author from the collection *Another Animal*. Copyright © 1954 renewed 1982 by May Swenson. "How Everything Happens—Based on a Study of the Wave" by May Swenson is reprinted by permission of the author, copyright © 1969 by May Swenson.

Dylan Thomas. Selections from Dylan Thomas, *The Poems of Dylan Thomas*. Copyright 1939, 1943 by New Directions Publishing Corporation, 1945 by The Trustees for the Copyrights of Dylan Thomas, 1952 by Dylan Thomas. "Poem in October" first published in "Poetry." All reprinted by permission of New Directions Publishing Corporation and David Higham Associates Ltd.

Walter James Turner. "Hymn to Her Unknown" from *Songs and Incantations* reprinted by permission of J M Dent & Sons Ltd Publishers.

Richard Wilbur. Selections excerpted and reprinted from "Sumptuous Destination" and "Poetry and Happiness" in his volume *Responses*. Copyright © 1960, 1967 by Richard Wilbur. "A Late Aubade" copyright © 1968 by Richard Wilbur. Reprinted from his volume *Walking to Sleep*. "The Undead" copyright © 1961 by Richard Wilbur. Reprinted from his volume *Advice to a Prophet and Other Poems*. First published in *The New Yorker*. "Cottage Street" copyright © 1972 by Richard Wilbur. Reprinted from his volume *The Mind Reader*. "The Death of a Toad" and "Still, Citizen Sparrow" from *Ceremony and Other Poems*, copyright 1950, 1978 by Richard Wilbur. "Praise in Summer" from *The Beautiful Changes and Other*

Poems copyright 1947, 1975 by Richard Wilbur. "After the Last Bulletins" from *Things of This World* by Richard Wilbur copyright 1953 by The New Yorker Magazine, Inc.; renewed 1981 by Richard Wilbur. First published in *The New Yorker*. All reprinted by permission of Harcourt Brace Jovanovich, Inc. "All that Is" by Richard Wilbur reprinted by permission: © 1985 Richard Wilbur. Originally in *The New Yorker*. Extract from *The Paris Review* no. 72, Winter 1973, reprinted by permission.

William C. Williams. Ten poems by William Carlos Williams from *Collected Poems Volume I: 1909–1939*. Copyright 1938 by New Directions Publishing Corporation. Extracts from William Carlos Williams, *Selected Essays*. Copyright 1954 by William Carlos Williams. Extract from William Carlos Williams, *The Autobiography of William Carlos Williams*. Copyright 1951 by William Carlos Williams. All reprinted by permission of New Directions Publishing Corporation.

W. B. Yeats. "The Scholars," "The Cat and the Moon," "The Wild Swans at Coole" copyright 1919 by Macmillan Publishing Company, renewed 1947 by Bertha Georgie Yeats. "Leda and the Swan," "Sailing to Byzantium" "Among School Children" copyright 1928 by Macmillan Publishing Company, renewed 1956 by Georgie Yeats. "Crazy Jane Talks with the Bishop" copyright 1935 by Macmillan Publishing Company, renewed 1961 by Bertha Georgie Yeats. All reprinted by permission of Macmillan Publishing Company and A. P. Watt Ltd. from *Collected Poems* by W B. Yeats. "The Lake Isle of Innisfree" and "The Folly of Being Comforted" from *The Collected Poems of W. B. Yeats* reprinted by permission of A. P. Watt Ltd. on behalf of Michael B. Yeats and Macmillan London Ltd. Extracts from the Introduction to *The Oxford Book of Modern Verse* (1936) reprinted by permission of Oxford University Press.

DRAMA

Jean Anouilh. Excerpt from "Medea" from *Seven Plays* by Jean Anouilh, trans. by Luce and Arthur Klein. Copyright © 1957 by Arthur Klein. Copyright renewed © 1985 by Luce and Arthur Klein. Reprinted by permission of Hill and Wang, a division of Farrar, Straus and Giroux, Inc. Excerpt from *Antigone* by Jean Anouilh, adapted and translated by Lewis Galantiere. Copyright 1946 by Random House, Inc., and renewed 1974 by Lewis Galantiere. Reprinted by permission of Random House, Inc.

Samuel Beckett. "Krapp's Last Tape" reprinted by permission of Grove Press, Inc., Copyright © 1957 by Samuel Beckett. Copyright © 1958, 1959, 1960 by Grove Press, Inc. and Faber & Faber, Ltd. CAUTION: This play is fully protected, in whole, in part, or in any form under the copyright laws of the United States of America, the British Empire including the Dominion of Canada, and all other countries of the Copyright Union and is subject to royalty. All rights, including professional, amateur, motion picture, radio, television, recitation, public reading, and any method of photographic reproduction are strictly reserved. For amateur rights and stock rights, apply to Samuel French, Inc., 25 West 45th St., New York, NY 10036. For all other rights, apply to Grove Press, Inc., 196 West Houston St., New York, N Y 10014.

Jonathan Cott. Extract from interview with Sam Shepard. Reprinted by permission of Jonathan Cott. First appeared in *Rolling Stone* magazine.

Anton Chekhov. "The Three Sisters" translated by Randall Jarrell reprinted by permission of Mary Jarrell. All rights reserved. Performance permission for film, theater, radio and television are solely controlled by Mary Jarrell. Extract from the Introduction to the play used by permission of Mary Jarrell.

Euripedes. "Medea," translated by Rex Warner reprinted by permission of The Bodley Head. Extract from "Medea," translated by Frank Justus Miller, *The Complete Roman Drama*, Vol. II, copyright 1942, reprinted by permission of Random House, Inc.

Athol Fugard. Play from *"Master Harold"* . . . *and the Boys* by Athol Fugard. Copyright © 1982 by Athol Fugard. Extract from *Notebooks 1960–1977* by Athol Fugard. Copyright © 1983 by Athol Fugard. Both reprinted by permission of Alfred A. Knopf, Inc. CAUTION: Professionals and amateurs are hereby notified that this play being fully protected under the copyright laws of the United States of America, the British Commonwealth, including the Dominion of Canada and all other countries which are members of the Berne and University Copyright Conventions, is subject to royalty. All rights including but not limited to professional, amateur publication, motion picture, recitation, public readings, radio and television broadcasting, and the right of translation into foreign languages, are expressly reserved to the Author. All inquiries concerning rights should be addressed to The William Morris Agency, 1350 Avenue of the Americas, New York, N Y 10019. Originally produced on Broadway by The Shubert Organization, Freydberg/Block Productions, Dasha, Epstein, Emanuel Azenberg and David Geffen. Orginally produced in 1972 by The Yale Repertory Theatre, New Haven, Ct.

Lewis Funke. Excerpt from *Playwrights Talk About Writing: Twelve Interviews with Lewis Funke*. Reprinted by permission of Lewis Funke.

Beth Henley. *Crimes of the Heart* by Beth Henley. Copyright © 1981, 1982 by Beth Henley. All rights reserved. Reprinted by permission of Viking Penguin Inc. CAUTION: Professionals and amateurs are hereby notified that this play being fully protected under the copyright laws of the United States of America, the British Commonwealth, including the

Tina Howe. "Painting Churches" reprinted by permission of Flora Roberts, Inc. CAUTION: Professionals and amateurs are hereby warned that *Painting Churches* is subject to a royalty. It is fully protected under the copyright laws of the United States of America, the British Commonwealth, including Canada and all other countries of the Copyright Union. All rights, including professional, amateur, motion pictures, recitation, lecturing, public reading, radio broadcasting, television, and the rights of translation into foreign languages are strictly reserved. All inquiries regarding stock or amateur rights should be addressed to Samuel French, Inc., at 45 West 25th St., New York, NY 10010. All other inquiries regarding rights should be addressed to the author's agent, Flora Roberts, Inc., at 157 West 57th St., New York, NY 10019

Henrik Ibsen. "Hedda Gabler" translated by Jens Arup from *The Oxford Ibsen* edited by J. W. McFarlane, vol 7 (1966) reprinted by permission of Oxford University Press.

Walter Kerr. Extract from "Offbeat—but a Beat Too Far" copyright © 1981 by The New York Times Company. Reprinted by permission.

Arthur Miller. Extracts from "The Nature of Tragedy" and "Tragedy and the Common Man," *The Theater Essays of Arthur Miller* by Arthur Miller. Copyright © 1978 by Arthur Miller. All rights reserved. Reprinted by permission of Viking Penguin Inc. *Death of a Salesman* by Arthur Miller. Copyright © 1949 by Arthur Miller. Copyright renewed © 1977 by Arthur Miller. Reprinted by permission of Viking Penguin Inc. CAUTION: This play in its printed form is designed for the reading public only. All dramatic rights in it are fully protected by copyright, and no public performance—professional or amateur—may be given without the written permission of the author and payment of royalty. As the courts have also ruled that the public reading of a play constitutes a public performance, no such may be given except under the conditions stated above. Communication should be addressed to the author's representative, International Creative Management, Inc., 40 West 57th St., New York, N Y 10019.

Harold Pinter. "The Dumb Waiter" copyright © 1960 by Harold Pinter. Reprinted by permission of Grove Press, Inc., and Metheun & Co. Ltd. CAUTION: This play is fully protected by copyright. All enquiries concerning performance rights both professional and amateur, readings, or any other use of this material should be directed to the author's sole agents: ACTAC (Theatrical & Cinematic) Ltd., c/o Judy Daish Associates, 83 Eastbourne Mews, London W26LQ. Extract from "Harold Pinter" *Writer at Work*, Third Series, ed. George Plimpton. Copyright © 1967 by The Paris Review Inc. All rights reserved. Reprinted by permission of Viking Penguin Inc.

William Shakespeare. Plays and verse from *The Riverside Shakespeare*, edited by G. Blakemore Evans. Copyright © 1974 by Houghton Mifflin Company. Used by permission.

Sam Shepard. "Fool for Love" copyright © 1983 by Sam Shepard. Reprinted by permission of City Lights Books.

John Simon. Extract from "Living Beings, Cardboard Symbols" *New York* Magazine, Vol. 14 #45, November 16, 1981. Used by permission.

Sophocles: "Antigone" from David Grene and Richmond Lattimore, *Greek Tragedies*, Vol. I, Elizabeth Wyckoff, Trans. Reprinted by permission of The University of Chicago Press.

Wole Soyinka. "The Swamp Dwellers" reprinted from *Collected Plays 1* by Wole Soyinka by permission of Oxford University Press. © Wole Soyinka 1964. Excerpt from *Myth, Literature and the African World* copyright 1976 by Cambridge University Press. Reproduced with the permission of the publisher.

Tom Stoppard. "The Real Inspector Hound" copyright © 1968 by Tom Stoppard. Reprinted by permission of Grove Press, Inc., and Faber & Faber Ltd. CAUTION: This play is fully protected, in whole, in part or in any form under the copyright laws of the United States of America, the British Empire including the Dominion of Canada, and all other countries of the Copyright Union, and are subject to royalty. All rights, including professional, amateur, motion picture, radio, television, recitation, public reading, and any method of photographic reproduction, are strictly reserved. All inquiries concerning all performances in the United States should be addressed to the author's agent: Samuel French, Inc., 25 West 45th St., New York, N Y 10036.

Gerald Weales. Extract from *Commonweal* January 13, 1984 reprinted by permission.

Marianne Moore. Extract from "A Bold Virtuoso" in *The Complete Prose of Marianne Moore,* edited by Patricia Willis. Copyright 1955 by Marianne Moore, renewed © 1983 by Lawrence E. Brinn and Louise Crane, Executors of the Estate of Marianne Moore. Reprinted by permission of Viking Penguin Inc.

Index of Authors and Titles

Index to First Lines of Poetry

Dark swallows will doubtless come back killing, 691
Death be not proud, though some have called thee, 698
Dejection has its catacombs, 856
Did it once issue from the carver's hand, 1047
Does man love Art? Man visits Art, but squirms, 1105
Do not go gentle into that good night, 1097
Downstairs I laugh, I sport and jest with all, 872
Dreamwork, the mnemonic flicker, 1121
Drink and dance and laugh and lie, 727

Earth has not anything to show more fair, 760
Even as children they were late sleepers, 1117
Every year without knowing it I have passed the day, 1146
Exposed on the cliffs of the heart. Look, how tiny, 923

Far back when I went zig-zagging, 1156
Father has his arm around Tereze, 676
Fear no more the heat o' the sun, 685
Filling her compact & delicious body, 849
First having read the book of myths, 1160
Five years have passed; five summers, with the length, 754
For a long time I have stayed looking at my long legs, 1036
For God's sake, hold your tongue and let me love, 693
For I will consider my cat Jeoffry, 749
Framed in her phoenix fire-screen, Edna Ward, 1177
Frame within frame, the evolving conversation, 1126
From my mother's sleep I fell into the State, 1078
From the window I saw the horses, 1038

Gather ye rosebuds while ye may, 725
Gentle Jesus, meek and mild, 748
Glory be to God for dappled things—, 878
Gone the three ancient ladies, 1061

Had we but world enough, and time, 721
happen you will rise, 1180
Hatred and vengeance, my eternal portion, 752
Have you dug the spill, 1021
He disappeared in the dead of winter, 1049
He sat in a wheeled chair, waiting for dark, 974
Her body is not so white as, 938
Here I love you, 1036
He saw her from the bottom of the stairs, 909
He was found by the Bureau of Statistics to be, 1048
His pads furring the scarp's rime, 1078
His vision, from the constantly passing bars, 927
Horse is Lorca's word, fierce as wind, 1191
How do they do it, the ones who make love, 1195
How funny you are today New York, 851
How wisely nature did decree, 717
Hush, my dear, lie still and slumber, 747

I, having loved ever since I was a child a few things, 970
I, too, dislike it; these are things that are important, 945
I, too, sing America, 1020
i am going blind, 1181
I am not a painter, I am a poet, 853
I am poor brother Lippo, by your leave! 821
I believe in you my soul, the other I am must not abase itself to you, 841
I caught this morning morning's minion, king—, 877
I could never have come to the present without you, 1148
I died for Beauty—but was scarce, 864
I doubt not God is good, well-meaning, kind, 1027
If I die, 1004
If you could see, fair brother, how dead beat, 976
I go to the door often, 1143
I had come to the house, in a cave of trees, 998
I have been one acquainted with the night, 914

I have done it again, 1174
I have eaten, 940
I have wrapped my dreams in a silken cloth, 1029
I knew a woman, lovely in her bones, 1061
I like a look of Agony, 862
I lived in a house, 929
I love with a fearful love to remember the, 1194
I meet a traveler from an antique land, 1031
I met the Bishop on the road, 900
In a bistro on the Boulevard St. Michel, 840
In a fashionable suburb of Santa Barbara, 1082
In a hard intellectual light, 753
In despair at not being able to rival the creations of God, 838
Infatuation, sadism, lust, avarice, 854
in Just (spring), 984
In Little Rock the people bear, 1100
In murky corners of old cities where, 858
In rainy September, when leaves grow down to the dark, 1142
In the hard brightness of that winter day, 935
In the mustardseed sun, 1095
In the story of Patroclus, 1203
Into a bistro on the Boulevard St. Michel, 840
Into my empty head there come, 1131
In Worcester, Massachusetts, 1068
In Xanadu did Kubla Kahn, 774
I open my journal, write a few, 1141
I ordered this, this clean wood box, 1170
I placed a jar in Tennessee, 933
I rub my head and find a turtle shell, 1112
I said to my baby, 1023
I saw on the slant hill a putrid lamb, 753
I saw the vision of armies, 976
i sing of Olaf glad and big, 986
'Is my team ploughing,' 887
'Issues from the hand of God, the simple soul,' 960
It costs me never a stab nor squirm, 892
I think I could turn and live awhile with the animals . . . , 843
I thought, as I wiped my eyes on the corner of my apron, 971
it is all blood and breaking, 1179

It is an ancient Mariner, 776
It is true, Martin Heidegger, as you have written, 1134
It little profits that an idle king, 812
It was better when we were, 1200
It was my thirtieth year to heaven, 1091
It was not Death, for I stoop up, 865
It was the form of the thing, the unmanaged, 1128
I've known rivers, 1019
I walk through the long schoolroom questioning, 898
I wander thro' each charter'd street, 741
I was angry with my friend, 741
I will arise and go now, and go to Innisfree, 893
I wonder, by my troth, what thou and I, 696
I wonder do you feel today, 835
I would not if I could undo my past, 874

joan, 1180
John Cabot, out of Wilma, once a Wycliffe, 1104

Let the boy try along this bayonet-blade, 973
Let us go then, you and I, 955
Life, friends, is boring. We must not say so, 850
Life is not sweet. One day it will be sweet, 873
Little Lamb, who made thee? 738
Long afterwards, 1149
Look up into the light of the lantern, 1204
Lord, who createdst man in wealth and store, 989
Lost in the forest, I broke off a dark twig, 1042
Love is not all: it is not meat nor drink, 967
Loveliest of trees, the cherry now, 884

Mark but this flea, and mark in this, 697
May I, for my own self, song's truth reckon, 882
Methought I saw my late espouséd saint, 706
Miniver Cheevy, child of scorn, 903
Morning glories, 671
munching a plum on, 940
My father used to say, 946

They are moving the trees in Princeton, 1134

They flee from me, that sometime did me seek, 689

They more than we are what we are, 928

they will blow from your mouth one morning, 1180

This is the time of year, 1066

This is the weather the cuckoo likes, 692

This loving attention to the details, 1136

This thing the night flashes, 994

Those blessed structures, plot and rhyme—, 1113

Thou art indeed just, Lord, if I contend, 879

Thou still unravished bride of quietness, 800

To be sure the cantonal seagulls, 995

Today, lonely for my father, I saw, 1139

To lie in shadow on the lawn, 991

To see a World in a Grain of Sand, 742

To what purpose, April, do you return again?, 967

Transport was what we'd come in search of, 1127

Traveling through the dark I found a deer, 679

Turning and turning in the widening gyre, 896

Twenty-eight young men bathe by the shore, 842

Twilight approaches, with its last brief spot-lit, 1118

Tyger! Tyger! burning bright, 740

Uplifted and waved till immobilized, 951

wade, 947

Wallowing in this bloody sty, 1107

Water is practical, 1044

We are the hollow men, 961

We cannot know his legendary head, 926

We have struck the regions wherein we are keel or reef, 1002

Well they'd made up their minds to be everywhere, 1146

We real cool. We, 1100

Western wind, when will thou blow, 689

We were very tired, we were very merry—, 966

What, still alive at twenty-two, 891

What a thrill—, 1171

What does the horse give you, 1204

What happens to a dream deferred? 1023

What passing-bells for these who die as cattle?, 972

What shall I say, because talk I must?, 941

What Soft—Cherubic Creatures—, 864

What thoughts I have of you tonight, Walt, 850

Whenever Richard Cory went down town, 903

When first my way to fair I took, 890

When I am dead, my dearest, 871

When I consider how my light is spent, 705

When I got to the airport I rushed up to the desk, 1196

When I have fears that I may cease to be, 795

When I heard the learn'd astronomer, 846

When I look at my elder sister now, 1193

When in disgrace with fortune and men's eyes, 674

When Mother divorced you, we were glad. She took it and, 1194

When my grave is broke up again, 692

When my love swears that she is made of truth, 684

When my mother died I was very young, 738

When nothing is happening, 990

When the barn catches fire, 1133

When the swordsman fell in Kurosawa's *Seven Samurai*, 1186

When we two parted, 690

When you look down from the airplane you see lines, 1081

Where long the shadows of the wind had rolled, 908

Where the remote Bermudas ride, 723

Where were the greenhouses going, 1059

Which doesn't belong in this group of three?—, 704

While you walk the water's edge, 1123

Whose woods these are I think I know, 914

Why, if this interval of being can be spent serenely, 923

Why does the sea moan evermore?, 874